A2 ALTITUDE CORRECTION TABLES 10°–90°—SUN, STARS, PLANETS

OCT.—MAR. SUN APR.—SEPT.

App. Alt.	Lower Limb	Upper Limb	App. Alt.	Lower Limb	Upper Limb
9 33	+10.8	−21.5	9 39	+10.6	−21.2
9 45	+10.9	−21.4	9 50	+10.7	−21.1
9 56	+11.0	−21.3	10 02	+10.8	−21.0
10 08	+11.1	−21.2	10 14	+10.9	−20.9
10 20	+11.2	−21.1	10 27	+11.0	−20.8
10 33	+11.3	−21.0	10 40	+11.1	−20.7
10 46	+11.4	−20.9	10 53	+11.2	−20.6
11 00	+11.5	−20.8	11 07	+11.3	−20.5
11 15	+11.6	−20.7	11 22	+11.4	−20.4
11 30	+11.7	−20.6	11 37	+11.5	−20.3
11 45	+11.8	−20.5	11 53	+11.6	−20.2
12 01	+11.9	−20.4	12 10	+11.7	−20.1
12 18	+12.0	−20.3	12 27	+11.8	−20.0
12 36	+12.1	−20.2	12 45	+11.9	−19.9
12 54	+12.2	−20.1	13 04	+12.0	−19.8
13 14	+12.3	−20.0	13 24	+12.1	−19.7
13 34	+12.4	−19.9	13 44	+12.2	−19.6
13 55	+12.5	−19.8	14 06	+12.3	−19.5
14 17	+12.6	−19.7	14 29	+12.4	−19.4
14 41	+12.7	−19.6	14 53	+12.5	−19.3
15 05	+12.8	−19.5	15 18	+12.6	−19.2
15 31	+12.9	−19.4	15 45	+12.7	−19.1
15 59	+13.0	−19.3	16 13	+12.8	−19.0
16 27	+13.1	−19.2	16 43	+12.9	−18.9
16 58	+13.2	−19.1	17 14	+13.0	−18.8
17 30	+13.3	−19.0	17 47	+13.1	−18.7
18 05	+13.4	−18.9	18 23	+13.2	−18.6
18 41	+13.5	−18.8	19 00	+13.3	−18.5
19 20	+13.6	−18.7	19 41	+13.4	−18.4
20 02	+13.7	−18.6	20 24	+13.5	−18.3
20 46	+13.8	−18.5	21 10	+13.6	−18.2
21 34	+13.9	−18.4	21 59	+13.7	−18.1
22 25	+14.0	−18.3	22 52	+13.8	−18.0
23 20	+14.1	−18.2	23 49	+13.9	−17.9
24 20	+14.2	−18.1	24 51	+14.0	−17.8
25 24	+14.3	−18.0	25 58	+14.1	−17.7
26 34	+14.4	−17.9	27 11	+14.2	−17.6
27 50	+14.5	−17.8	28 31	+14.3	−17.5
29 13	+14.6	−17.7	29 58	+14.4	−17.4
30 44	+14.7	−17.6	31 33	+14.5	−17.3
32 24	+14.8	−17.5	33 18	+14.6	−17.2
34 15	+14.9	−17.4	35 15	+14.7	−17.1
36 17	+15.0	−17.3	37 24	+14.8	−17.0
38 34	+15.1	−17.2	39 48	+14.9	−16.9
41 06	+15.2	−17.1	42 28	+15.0	−16.8
43 56	+15.3	−17.0	45 29	+15.1	−16.7
47 07	+15.4	−16.9	48 52	+15.2	−16.6
50 43	+15.5	−16.8	52 41	+15.3	−16.5
54 46	+15.6	−16.7	56 59	+15.4	−16.4
59 21	+15.7	−16.6	61 50	+15.5	−16.3
64 28	+15.8	−16.5	67 15	+15.6	−16.2
70 10	+15.9	−16.4	73 14	+15.7	−16.1
76 24	+16.0	−16.3	79 42	+15.8	−16.0
83 05	+16.1	−16.2	86 31	+15.9	−15.9
90 00			90 00		

STARS AND PLANETS

App Alt.	Corrn
9 55	−5.3
10 07	−5.2
10 20	−5.1
10 32	−5.0
10 46	−4.9
10 59	−4.8
11 14	−4.7
11 29	−4.6
11 44	−4.5
12 00	−4.4
12 17	−4.3
12 35	−4.2
12 53	−4.1
13 12	−4.0
13 32	−3.9
13 53	−3.8
14 16	−3.7
14 39	−3.6
15 03	−3.5
15 29	−3.4
15 56	−3.3
16 25	−3.2
16 55	−3.1
17 27	−3.0
18 01	−2.9
18 37	−2.8
19 16	−2.7
19 56	−2.6
20 40	−2.5
21 27	−2.4
22 17	−2.3
23 11	−2.2
24 09	−2.1
25 12	−2.0
26 20	−1.9
27 34	−1.8
28 54	−1.7
30 22	−1.6
31 58	−1.5
33 43	−1.4
35 38	−1.3
37 45	−1.2
40 06	−1.1
42 42	−1.0
45 34	−0.9
48 45	−0.8
52 16	−0.7
56 09	−0.6
60 26	−0.5
65 06	−0.4
70 09	−0.3
75 32	−0.2
81 12	−0.1
87 03	0.0
90 00	

App. Alt. — Additional Corrn

2014

VENUS

Jan. 1–Jan. 9
Jan. 13–Jan. 31

App. Alt.	Corrn
26	+0.5
46	+0.4
60	+0.3
73	+0.2
84	+0.1

Jan. 10–Jan. 12

App. Alt.	Corrn
24	+0.6
41	+0.5
54	+0.4
65	+0.3
76	+0.2
85	+0.1

Feb. 1–Feb. 16

App. Alt.	Corrn
29	+0.4
51	+0.3
68	+0.2
83	+0.1

Feb. 17–Mar. 10

App. Alt.	Corrn
34	+0.3
60	+0.2
80	+0.1

Mar. 11–Apr. 30

App. Alt.	Corrn
41	+0.2
76	+0.1

May 1–Dec. 31

App. Alt.	Corrn
60	+0.1

MARS

Jan. 1–Feb. 9
June 30–Dec. 31

App. Alt.	Corrn
60	+0.1

Feb. 10–June 29

App. Alt.	Corrn
41	+0.2
76	+0.1

DIP

Ht. of Eye (m)	Corrn	Ht. of Eye (ft)	Ht. of Eye (m)	Corrn
2.4	−2.8	8.0	1.0	−1.8
2.6	−2.8	8.6	1.5	−2.2
2.8	−2.9	9.2	2.0	−2.5
3.0	−3.0	9.8	2.5	−2.8
3.2	−3.1	10.5	3.0	−3.0
3.4	−3.2	11.2		See table ←
3.6	−3.3	11.9		
3.8	−3.4	12.6	m	
4.0	−3.5	13.3	20	−7.9
4.3	−3.6	14.1	22	−8.3
4.5	−3.7	14.9	24	−8.6
4.7	−3.8	15.7	26	−9.0
5.0	−3.9	16.5	28	−9.3
5.2	−4.0	17.4		
5.5	−4.1	18.3		
5.8	−4.2	19.1	30	−9.6
6.1	−4.3	20.1	32	−10.0
6.3	−4.4	21.0	34	−10.3
6.6	−4.5	22.0	36	−10.6
6.9	−4.6	22.9	38	−10.8
7.2	−4.7	23.9		
7.5	−4.8	24.9	40	−11.1
7.9	−4.9	26.0	42	−11.4
8.2	−5.0	27.1	44	−11.7
8.5	−5.1	28.1	46	−11.9
8.8	−5.2	29.2	48	−12.2
9.2	−5.3	30.4		
9.5	−5.4	31.5	ft	
9.9	−5.5	32.7	2	−1.4
10.3	−5.6	33.9	4	−1.9
10.6	−5.7	35.1	6	−2.4
11.0	−5.8	36.3	8	−2.7
11.4	−5.9	37.6	10	−3.1
11.8	−6.0	38.9		See table ←
12.2	−6.1	40.1	ft	
12.6	−6.2	41.5	70	−8.1
13.0	−6.3	42.8	75	−8.4
13.4	−6.4	44.2	80	−8.7
13.8	−6.5	45.5	85	−8.9
14.2	−6.6	46.9	90	−9.2
14.7	−6.7	48.4	95	−9.5
15.1	−6.8	49.8	100	−9.7
15.5	−6.9	51.3	105	−9.9
16.0	−7.0	52.8	110	−10.2
16.5	−7.1	54.3	115	−10.4
16.9	−7.2	55.8	120	−10.6
17.4	−7.3	57.4	125	−10.8
17.9	−7.4	58.9		
18.4	−7.5	60.5		
18.8	−7.6	62.1	130	−11.1
19.3	−7.7	63.8	135	−11.3
19.8	−7.8	65.4	140	−11.5
20.4	−7.9	67.1	145	−11.7
20.9	−8.0	68.8	150	−11.9
21.4	−8.1	70.5	155	−12.1

App. Alt. = Apparent altitude = Sextant altitude corrected for index error and dip.

ALTITUDE CORRECTION TABLES 0°-10°—SUN,STARS,PLANETS A3

App. Alt.	OCT.—MAR. SUN Lower Limb	OCT.—MAR. SUN Upper Limb	APR.—SEPT. SUN Lower Limb	APR.—SEPT. SUN Upper Limb	STARS PLANETS
° ′	′	′	′	′	′
0 00	− 17·5	− 49·8	− 17·8	− 49·6	− 33·8
0 03	16·9	49·2	17·2	49·0	33·2
0 06	16·3	48·6	16·6	48·4	32·6
0 09	15·7	48·0	16·0	47·8	32·0
0 12	15·2	47·5	15·4	47·2	31·5
0 15	14·6	46·9	14·8	46·6	30·9
0 18	− 14·1	− 46·4	− 14·3	− 46·1	− 30·4
0 21	13·5	45·8	13·8	45·6	29·8
0 24	13·0	45·3	13·3	45·1	29·3
0 27	12·5	44·8	12·8	44·6	28·8
0 30	12·0	44·3	12·3	44·1	28·3
0 33	11·6	43·9	11·8	43·6	27·9
0 36	− 11·1	− 43·4	− 11·3	− 43·1	− 27·4
0 39	10·6	42·9	10·9	42·7	26·9
0 42	10·2	42·5	10·5	42·3	26·5
0 45	9·8	42·1	10·0	41·8	26·1
0 48	9·4	41·7	9·6	41·4	25·7
0 51	9·0	41·3	9·2	41·0	25·3
0 54	− 8·6	− 40·9	− 8·8	− 40·6	− 24·9
0 57	8·2	40·5	8·4	40·2	24·5
1 00	7·8	40·1	8·0	39·8	24·1
1 03	7·4	39·7	7·7	39·5	23·7
1 06	7·1	39·4	7·3	39·1	23·4
1 09	6·7	39·0	7·0	38·8	23·0
1 12	− 6·4	− 38·7	− 6·6	− 38·4	− 22·7
1 15	6·0	38·3	6·3	38·1	22·3
1 18	5·7	38·0	6·0	37·8	22·0
1 21	5·4	37·7	5·7	37·5	21·7
1 24	5·1	37·4	5·3	37·1	21·4
1 27	4·8	37·1	5·0	36·8	21·1
1 30	− 4·5	− 36·8	− 4·7	− 36·5	− 20·8
1 35	4·0	36·3	4·3	36·1	20·3
1 40	3·6	35·9	3·8	35·6	19·9
1 45	3·1	35·4	3·4	35·2	19·4
1 50	2·7	35·0	2·9	34·7	19·0
1 55	2·3	34·6	2·5	34·3	18·6
2 00	− 1·9	− 34·2	− 2·1	− 33·9	− 18·2
2 05	1·5	33·8	1·7	33·5	17·8
2 10	1·1	33·4	1·4	33·2	17·4
2 15	0·8	33·1	1·0	32·8	17·1
2 20	0·4	32·7	0·7	32·5	16·7
2 25	− 0·1	32·4	− 0·3	32·1	16·4
2 30	+ 0·2	− 32·1	0·0	− 31·8	− 16·1
2 35	0·5	31·8	+ 0·3	31·5	15·8
2 40	0·8	31·5	0·6	31·2	15·4
2 45	1·1	31·2	0·9	30·9	15·2
2 50	1·4	30·9	1·2	30·6	14·9
2 55	1·7	30·6	1·4	30·4	14·6
3 00	+ 2·0	− 30·3	+ 1·7	− 30·1	− 14·3
3 05	2·2	30·1	2·0	29·8	14·1
3 10	2·5	29·8	2·2	29·6	13·8
3 15	2·7	29·6	2·5	29·3	13·6
3 20	2·9	29·4	2·7	29·1	13·4
3 25	3·2	29·1	2·9	28·9	13·1
3 30	+ 3·4	− 28·9	+ 3·1	− 28·7	− 12·9

App. Alt.	OCT.—MAR. SUN Lower Limb	OCT.—MAR. SUN Upper Limb	APR.—SEPT. SUN Lower Limb	APR.—SEPT. SUN Upper Limb	STARS PLANETS
° ′	′	′	′	′	′
3 30	+ 3·4	− 28·9	+ 3·1	− 28·7	− 12·9
3 35	3·6	28·7	3·3	28·5	12·7
3 40	3·8	28·5	3·6	28·2	12·5
3 45	4·0	28·3	3·8	28·0	12·3
3 50	4·2	28·1	4·0	27·8	12·1
3 55	4·4	27·9	4·1	27·7	11·9
4 00	+ 4·6	− 27·7	+ 4·3	− 27·5	− 11·7
4 05	4·8	27·5	4·5	27·3	11·5
4 10	4·9	27·4	4·7	27·1	11·4
4 15	5·1	27·2	4·9	26·9	11·2
4 20	5·3	27·0	5·0	26·8	11·0
4 25	5·4	26·9	5·2	26·6	10·9
4 30	+ 5·6	− 26·7	+ 5·3	− 26·5	− 10·7
4 35	5·7	26·6	5·5	26·3	10·6
4 40	5·9	26·4	5·6	26·2	10·4
4 45	6·0	26·3	5·8	26·0	10·3
4 50	6·2	26·1	5·9	25·9	10·1
4 55	6·3	26·0	6·1	25·7	10·0
5 00	+ 6·4	− 25·9	+ 6·2	− 25·6	− 9·8
5 05	6·6	25·7	6·3	25·5	9·7
5 10	6·7	25·6	6·5	25·3	9·6
5 15	6·8	25·5	6·6	25·2	9·5
5 20	7·0	25·3	6·7	25·1	9·3
5 25	7·1	25·2	6·8	25·0	9·2
5 30	+ 7·2	− 25·1	+ 6·9	− 24·9	− 9·1
5 35	7·3	25·0	7·1	24·7	9·0
5 40	7·4	24·9	7·2	24·6	8·9
5 45	7·5	24·8	7·3	24·5	8·8
5 50	7·6	24·7	7·4	24·4	8·7
5 55	7·7	24·6	7·5	24·3	8·6
6 00	+ 7·8	− 24·5	+ 7·6	− 24·2	− 8·5
6 10	8·0	24·3	7·8	24·0	8·3
6 20	8·2	24·1	8·0	23·8	8·1
6 30	8·4	23·9	8·2	23·6	7·9
6 40	8·6	23·7	8·3	23·5	7·7
6 50	8·7	23·6	8·5	23·3	7·6
7 00	+ 8·9	− 23·4	+ 8·7	− 23·1	− 7·4
7 10	9·1	23·2	8·8	23·0	7·2
7 20	9·2	23·1	9·0	22·8	7·1
7 30	9·3	23·0	9·1	22·7	6·9
7 40	9·5	22·8	9·2	22·6	6·8
7 50	9·6	22·7	9·4	22·4	6·7
8 00	+ 9·7	− 22·6	+ 9·5	− 22·3	− 6·6
8 10	9·9	22·4	9·6	22·2	6·4
8 20	10·0	22·3	9·7	22·1	6·3
8 30	10·1	22·2	9·9	21·9	6·2
8 40	10·2	22·1	10·0	21·8	6·1
8 50	10·3	22·0	10·1	21·7	6·0
9 00	+ 10·4	− 21·9	+ 10·2	− 21·6	− 5·9
9 10	10·5	21·8	10·3	21·5	5·8
9 20	10·6	21·7	10·4	21·4	5·7
9 30	10·7	21·6	10·5	21·3	5·6
9 40	10·8	21·5	10·6	21·2	5·5
9 50	10·9	21·4	10·6	21·2	5·4
10 00	+ 11·0	− 21·3	+ 10·7	− 21·1	− 5·3

Additional corrections for temperature and pressure are given on the following page.

For bubble sextant observations ignore dip and use the star corrections for Sun, planets and stars.

A4 ALTITUDE CORRECTION TABLES—ADDITIONAL CORRECTIONS

ADDITIONAL REFRACTION CORRECTIONS FOR NON-STANDARD CONDITIONS

App. Alt.	A	B	C	D	E	F	G	H	J	K	L	M	N	P	App. Alt.
° ′	′	′	′	′	′	′	′	′	′	′	′	′	′	′	° ′
00 00	−7·3	−5·9	−4·6	−3·4	−2·2	−1·1	0·0	+1·0	+2·0	+3·0	+4·0	+4·9	+5·9	+6·9	00 00
00 30	5·5	4·5	3·5	2·6	1·7	0·8	0·0	0·8	1·6	2·3	3·1	3·8	4·5	5·3	00 30
01 00	4·4	3·5	2·8	2·0	1·3	0·7	0·0	0·6	1·2	1·8	2·4	3·0	3·6	4·2	01 00
01 30	3·5	2·9	2·2	1·7	1·1	0·5	0·0	0·5	1·0	1·5	2·0	2·5	2·9	3·4	01 30
02 00	2·9	2·4	1·9	1·4	0·9	0·4	0·0	0·4	0·8	1·3	1·7	2·0	2·4	2·8	02 00
02 30	−2·5	−2·0	−1·6	−1·2	−0·8	−0·4	0·0	+0·4	+0·7	+1·1	+1·4	+1·7	+2·1	+2·4	02 30
03 00	2·1	1·7	1·4	1·0	0·7	0·3	0·0	0·3	0·6	0·9	1·2	1·5	1·8	2·1	03 00
03 30	1·9	1·5	1·2	0·9	0·6	0·3	0·0	0·3	0·5	0·8	1·1	1·3	1·6	1·8	03 30
04 00	1·6	1·3	1·1	0·8	0·5	0·3	0·0	0·2	0·5	0·7	0·9	1·2	1·4	1·6	04 00
04 30	1·5	1·2	0·9	0·7	0·5	0·2	0·0	0·2	0·4	0·6	0·8	1·0	1·3	1·5	04 30
05 00	−1·3	−1·1	−0·9	−0·6	−0·4	−0·2	0·0	+0·2	+0·4	+0·6	+0·8	+0·9	+1·1	+1·3	05 00
06	1·1	0·9	0·7	0·5	0·3	0·2	0·0	0·2	0·3	0·5	0·6	0·8	0·9	1·1	06
07	1·0	0·8	0·6	0·5	0·3	0·1	0·0	0·1	0·3	0·4	0·5	0·7	0·8	0·9	07
08	0·8	0·7	0·5	0·4	0·3	0·1	0·0	0·1	0·2	0·4	0·5	0·6	0·7	0·8	08
09	0·7	0·6	0·5	0·4	0·2	0·1	0·0	0·1	0·2	0·3	0·4	0·5	0·6	0·7	09
10 00	−0·7	−0·5	−0·4	−0·3	−0·2	−0·1	0·0	+0·1	+0·2	+0·3	+0·4	+0·5	+0·6	+0·7	10 00
12	0·6	0·5	0·4	0·3	0·2	0·1	0·0	0·1	0·2	0·2	0·3	0·4	0·5	0·5	12
14	0·5	0·4	0·3	0·2	0·1	0·1	0·0	0·1	0·1	0·2	0·3	0·3	0·4	0·5	14
16	0·4	0·3	0·3	0·2	0·1	0·1	0·0	0·1	0·1	0·2	0·2	0·3	0·3	0·4	16
18	0·4	0·3	0·2	0·2	0·1	−0·1	0·0	+0·1	0·1	0·2	0·2	0·3	0·3	0·4	18
20 00	−0·3	−0·3	−0·2	−0·2	−0·1	0·0	0·0	0·0	+0·1	+0·1	+0·2	+0·2	+0·3	+0·3	20 00
25	0·3	0·2	0·2	0·1	0·1	0·0	0·0	0·0	0·1	0·1	0·1	0·2	0·2	0·2	25
30	0·2	0·2	0·1	0·1	0·1	0·0	0·0	0·0	+0·1	0·1	0·1	0·1	0·2	0·2	30
35	0·2	0·1	0·1	0·1	−0·1	0·0	0·0	0·0	0·0	0·1	0·1	0·1	0·1	0·2	35
40	0·1	0·1	0·1	−0·1	0·0	0·0	0·0	0·0	0·0	+0·1	0·1	0·1	0·1	0·1	40
50 00	−0·1	−0·1	−0·1	0·0	0·0	0·0	0·0	0·0	0·0	0·0	+0·1	+0·1	+0·1	+0·1	50 00

The graph is entered with arguments temperature and pressure to find a zone letter; using as arguments this zone letter and apparent altitude (sextant altitude corrected for index error and dip), a correction is taken from the table. This correction is to be applied to the sextant altitude in addition to the corrections for standard conditions (for the Sun, stars and planets from page A2-A3 and for the Moon from pages xxxiv and xxxv).

2014
Nautical Almanac
COMMERCIAL EDITION

PUBLISHED BY:

Paradise Cay Publications, Inc.
Post Office Box 29
Arcata, CA 95518-0029
Tel: 1-707-822-9063
Fax: 1-707-822-9163
www.paracay.com

ISBN: 978-1-937196-96-7

Printed and distributed with permission by Paradise Cay Publications, Inc.

NOTE

Every care is taken to prevent errors in the production of this publication. As a final precaution it is recommended that the sequence of pages in this copy be examined on receipt. If faulty, it should be returned for replacement.

PREFACE

The first three sections of this book are a complete and accurate duplication from *The Nautical Almanac* produced jointly by Her Majesty's Nautical Almanac Office, United Kingdom Hydrographic Office, Admiralty Way, Taunton, Somerset, TA1 2DN, United Kingdom and the Nautical Almanac Office of the US Naval Observatory.

We gratefully acknowledge the United Kingdom Hydrographic Office and the United States Naval Observatory for permission to use the material contained in the almanac sections of this publication.

The 2014 Nautical Almanac
Commercial Edition

CALENDAR, 2014

RELIGIOUS CALENDARS

Epiphany	Jan. 6	Low Sunday	Apr. 27
Septuagesima Sunday	Feb. 16	Rogation Sunday	May 25
Quinquagesima Sunday	Mar. 2	Ascension Day—Holy Thursday	May 29
Ash Wednesday	Mar. 5	Whit Sunday—Pentecost	June 8
Quadragesima Sunday	Mar. 9	Trinity Sunday	June 15
Palm Sunday	Apr. 13	Corpus Christi	June 19
Good Friday	Apr. 18	First Sunday in Advent	Nov. 30
Easter Day	Apr. 20	Christmas Day (Thursday)	Dec. 25
First Day of Passover (Pesach)	Apr. 15	Day of Atonement (Yom Kippur)	Oct. 4
Feast of Weeks (Shavuot)	June 4	First day of Tabernacles (Succoth)	Oct. 9
Jewish New Year 5775 (Rosh Hashanah)	Sept. 25		
Ramadân, First day of (tabular)	June 29	Islamic New Year (1436)	Oct. 25

The Jewish and Islamic dates above are tabular dates, which begin at sunset on the previous evening and end at sunset on the date tabulated. In practice, the dates of Islamic fasts and festivals are determined by an actual sighting of the appropriate new moon.

CIVIL CALENDAR—UNITED KINGDOM

Accession of Queen Elizabeth II	Feb. 6	Birthday of Prince Philip, Duke of	
St David (Wales)	Mar. 1	Edinburgh	June 10
Commonwealth Day	Mar. 10	The Queen's Official Birthday†	June 14
St Patrick (Ireland)	Mar. 17	Remembrance Sunday	Nov. 9
Birthday of Queen Elizabeth II	Apr. 21	Birthday of the Prince of Wales	Nov. 14
St George (England)	Apr. 23	St Andrew (Scotland)	Nov. 30
Coronation Day	June 2		

PUBLIC HOLIDAYS

England and Wales—Jan. 1†, Apr. 18, Apr. 21, May 5†, May 26, Aug. 25, Dec. 25, Dec. 26

Northern Ireland—Jan. 1†, Mar. 17, Apr. 18, Apr. 21, May 5†, May 26, July 14†, Aug. 25, Dec. 25, Dec. 26

Scotland—Jan. 1, Jan. 2, Apr. 18, May 5, May 26†, Aug. 4, Dec. 25, Dec. 26†

CIVIL CALENDAR—UNITED STATES OF AMERICA

New Year's Day	Jan. 1	Labor Day	Sept. 1
Martin Luther King's Birthday	Jan. 20	Columbus Day	Oct. 13
Washington's Birthday	Feb. 17	General Election Day	Nov. 4
Memorial Day	May 26	Veterans Day	Nov. 11
Independence Day	July 4	Thanksgiving Day	Nov. 27

†Dates subject to confirmation

PHASES OF THE MOON

New Moon				First Quarter				Full Moon				Last Quarter			
	d	h	m		d	h	m		d	h	m		d	h	m
Jan.	1	11	14	Jan.	8	03	39	Jan.	16	04	52	Jan.	24	05	19
Jan.	30	21	39	Feb.	6	19	22	Feb.	14	23	53	Feb.	22	17	15
Mar.	1	08	00	Mar.	8	13	27	Mar.	16	17	08	Mar.	24	01	46
Mar.	30	18	45	Apr.	7	08	31	Apr.	15	07	42	Apr.	22	07	52
Apr.	29	06	14	May	7	03	15	May	14	19	16	May	21	12	59
May	28	18	40	June	5	20	39	June	13	04	11	June	19	18	39
June	27	08	08	July	5	11	59	July	12	11	25	July	19	02	08
July	26	22	42	Aug.	4	00	50	Aug.	10	18	09	Aug.	17	12	26
Aug.	25	14	13	Sept.	2	11	11	Sept.	9	01	38	Sept.	16	02	05
Sept.	24	06	14	Oct.	1	19	33	Oct.	8	10	51	Oct.	15	19	12
Oct.	23	21	57	Oct.	31	02	48	Nov.	6	22	23	Nov.	14	15	16
Nov.	22	12	32	Nov.	29	10	06	Dec.	6	12	27	Dec.	14	12	51
Dec.	22	01	36	Dec.	28	18	31								

DAYS OF THE WEEK AND DAYS OF THE YEAR

	JAN.	FEB.	MAR.	APR.	MAY	JUNE	JULY	AUG.	SEPT.	OCT.	NOV.	DEC.
Day	Wk Yr	Wk Yr	Wk Yr	Wk Yr	Wk Yr	Wk Yr	Wk Yr	Wk Yr	Wk Yr	Wk Yr	Wk Yr	Wk Yr
1	W. 1	Sa. 32	Sa. 60	Tu. 91	Th. 121	Su. 152	Tu. 182	F. 213	M. 244	W. 274	Sa. 305	M. 335
2	Th. 2	Su. 33	Su. 61	W. 92	F. 122	M. 153	W. 183	Sa. 214	Tu. 245	Th. 275	Su. 306	Tu. 336
3	F. 3	M. 34	M. 62	Th. 93	Sa. 123	Tu. 154	Th. 184	Su. 215	W. 246	F. 276	M. 307	W. 337
4	Sa. 4	Tu. 35	Tu. 63	F. 94	Su. 124	W. 155	F. 185	M. 216	Th. 247	Sa. 277	Tu. 308	Th. 338
5	Su. 5	W. 36	W. 64	Sa. 95	M. 125	Th. 156	Sa. 186	Tu. 217	F. 248	Su. 278	W. 309	F. 339
6	M. 6	Th. 37	Th. 65	Su. 96	Tu. 126	F. 157	Su. 187	W. 218	Sa. 249	M. 279	Th. 310	Sa. 340
7	Tu. 7	F. 38	F. 66	M. 97	W. 127	Sa. 158	M. 188	Th. 219	Su. 250	Tu. 280	F. 311	Su. 341
8	W. 8	Sa. 39	Sa. 67	Tu. 98	Th. 128	Su. 159	Tu. 189	F. 220	M. 251	W. 281	Sa. 312	M. 342
9	Th. 9	Su. 40	Su. 68	W. 99	F. 129	M. 160	W. 190	Sa. 221	Tu. 252	Th. 282	Su. 313	Tu. 343
10	F. 10	M. 41	M. 69	Th. 100	Sa. 130	Tu. 161	Th. 191	Su. 222	W. 253	F. 283	M. 314	W. 344
11	Sa. 11	Tu. 42	Tu. 70	F. 101	Su. 131	W. 162	F. 192	M. 223	Th. 254	Sa. 284	Tu. 315	Th. 345
12	Su. 12	W. 43	W. 71	Sa. 102	M. 132	Th. 163	Sa. 193	Tu. 224	F. 255	Su. 285	W. 316	F. 346
13	M. 13	Th. 44	Th. 72	Su. 103	Tu. 133	F. 164	Su. 194	W. 225	Sa. 256	M. 286	Th. 317	Sa. 347
14	Tu. 14	F. 45	F. 73	M. 104	W. 134	Sa. 165	M. 195	Th. 226	Su. 257	Tu. 287	F. 318	Su. 348
15	W. 15	Sa. 46	Sa. 74	Tu. 105	Th. 135	Su. 166	Tu. 196	F. 227	M. 258	W. 288	Sa. 319	M. 349
16	Th. 16	Su. 47	Su. 75	W. 106	F. 136	M. 167	W. 197	Sa. 228	Tu. 259	Th. 289	Su. 320	Tu. 350
17	F. 17	M. 48	M. 76	Th. 107	Sa. 137	Tu. 168	Th. 198	Su. 229	W. 260	F. 290	M. 321	W. 351
18	Sa. 18	Tu. 49	Tu. 77	F. 108	Su. 138	W. 169	F. 199	M. 230	Th. 261	Sa. 291	Tu. 322	Th. 352
19	Su. 19	W. 50	W. 78	Sa. 109	M. 139	Th. 170	Sa. 200	Tu. 231	F. 262	Su. 292	W. 323	F. 353
20	M. 20	Th. 51	Th. 79	Su. 110	Tu. 140	F. 171	Su. 201	W. 232	Sa. 263	M. 293	Th. 324	Sa. 354
21	Tu. 21	F. 52	F. 80	M. 111	W. 141	Sa. 172	M. 202	Th. 233	Su. 264	Tu. 294	F. 325	Su. 355
22	W. 22	Sa. 53	Sa. 81	Tu. 112	Th. 142	Su. 173	Tu. 203	F. 234	M. 265	W. 295	Sa. 326	M. 356
23	Th. 23	Su. 54	Su. 82	W. 113	F. 143	M. 174	W. 204	Sa. 235	Tu. 266	Th. 296	Su. 327	Tu. 357
24	F. 24	M. 55	M. 83	Th. 114	Sa. 144	Tu. 175	Th. 205	Su. 236	W. 267	F. 297	M. 328	W. 358
25	Sa. 25	Tu. 56	Tu. 84	F. 115	Su. 145	W. 176	F. 206	M. 237	Th. 268	Sa. 298	Tu. 329	Th. 359
26	Su. 26	W. 57	W. 85	Sa. 116	M. 146	Th. 177	Sa. 207	Tu. 238	F. 269	Su. 299	W. 330	F. 360
27	M. 27	Th. 58	Th. 86	Su. 117	Tu. 147	F. 178	Su. 208	W. 239	Sa. 270	M. 300	Th. 331	Sa. 361
28	Tu. 28	F. 59	F. 87	M. 118	W. 148	Sa. 179	M. 209	Th. 240	Su. 271	Tu. 301	F. 332	Su. 362
29	W. 29		Sa. 88	Tu. 119	Th. 149	Su. 180	Tu. 210	F. 241	M. 272	W. 302	Sa. 333	M. 363
30	Th. 30		Su. 89	W. 120	F. 150	M. 181	W. 211	Sa. 242	Tu. 273	Th. 303	Su. 334	Tu. 364
31	F. 31		M. 90		Sa. 151		Th. 212	Su. 243		F. 304		W. 365

ECLIPSES

There are two eclipses of the Sun and two of the Moon.

1. *A total eclipse of the Moon*, April 15. The umbral eclipse begins at $05^h\ 58^m$ and ends at $09^h\ 33^m$. Totality lasts from $07^h\ 06^m$ to $08^h\ 25^m$. It is visible from the Americas, the eastern and central Pacific Ocean region, New Zealand, eastern Australia and the eastern tip of Russia.

2. *An annular eclipse of the Sun*, April 29. See map on page 6. The eclipse begins at $03^h\ 53^m$ and ends at $08^h\ 14^m$; the annular phase begins at $05^h\ 58^m$ and ends at $06^h\ 09^m$. This is a rare non-central eclipse generating a short duration of annularity at sunset.

3. *A total eclipse of the Moon*, October 08. The umbral eclipse begins at $09^h\ 14^m$ and ends at $12^h\ 35^m$. Totality lasts from $10^h\ 25^m$ to $11^h\ 25^m$. It is visible from North America and westernmost parts of South America, the Pacific Ocean, Australasia and the eastern half of Asia.

4. *A partial eclipse of the Sun*, October 23. See map on page 7. The eclipse begins at $19^h\ 38^m$ and ends at $23^h\ 52^m$. The time of greatest eclipse is $21^h\ 45^m$, when 0.81 of the Sun's diameter is obscured.

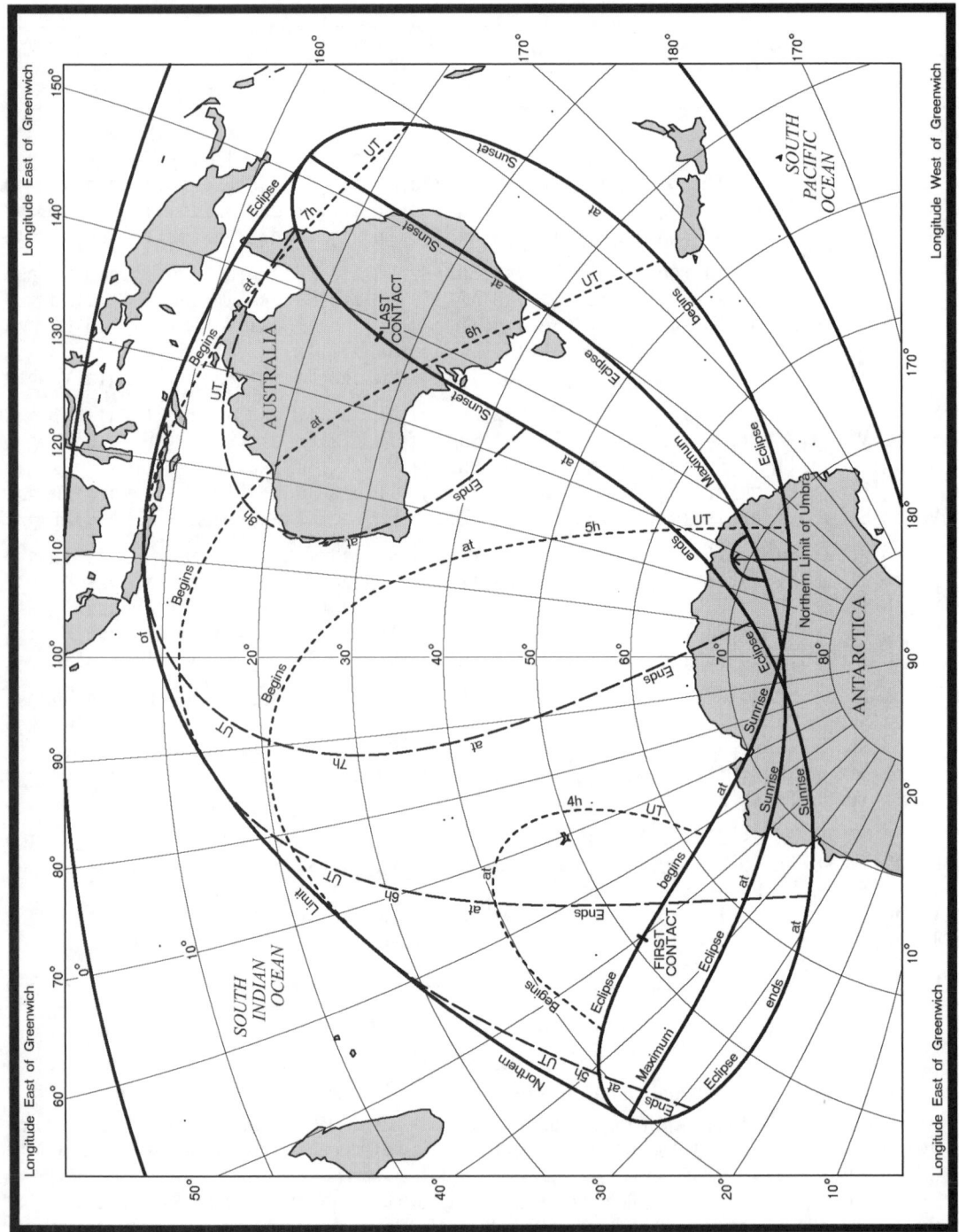

SOLAR ECLIPSE DIAGRAMS

The principal features shown on the above diagrams are: the paths of
total and annular eclipses; the northern and southern limits of partial
eclipse; the sunrise and sunset curves; dashed lines which show the
times of beginning and end of partial eclipse at hourly intervals.

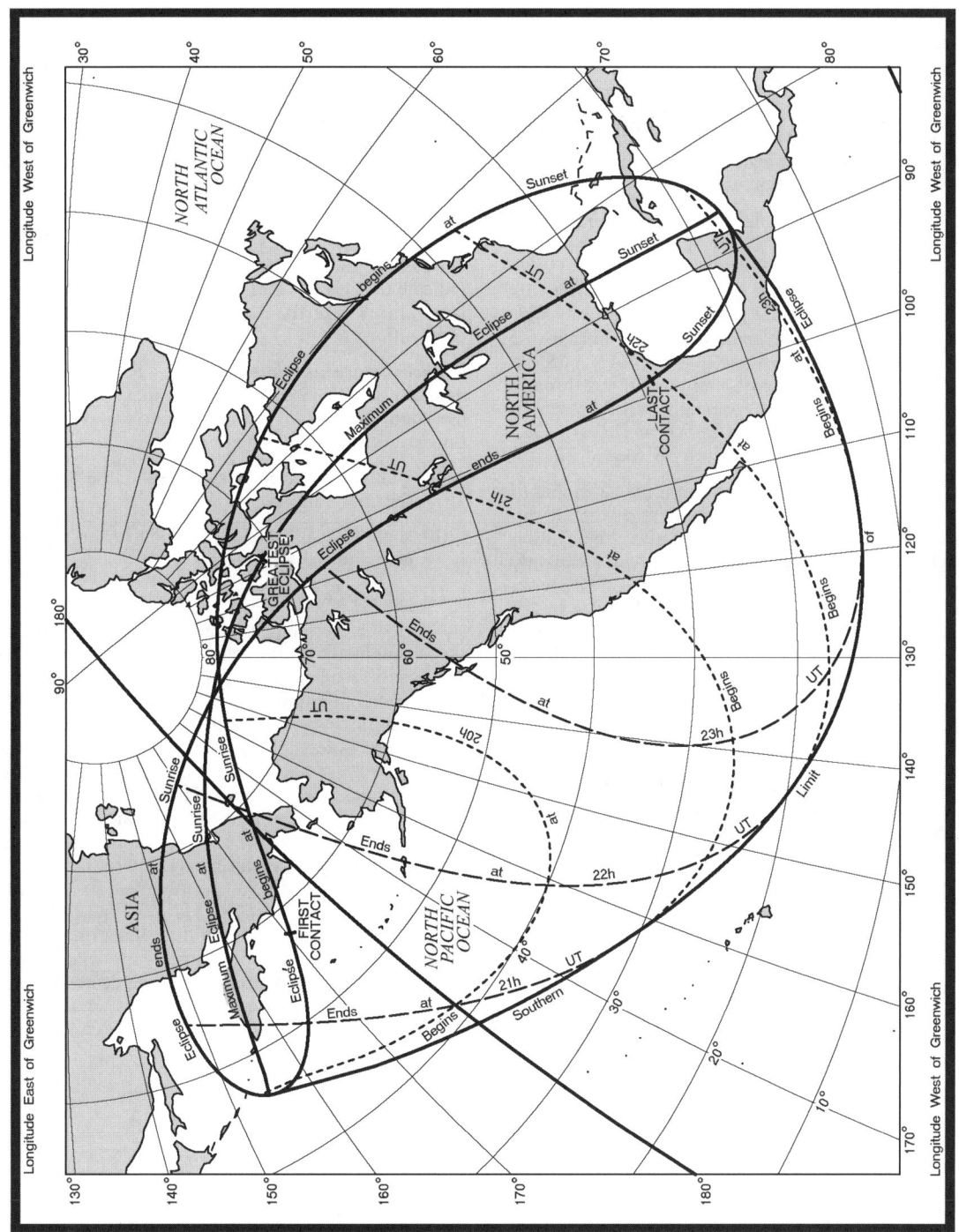

SOLAR ECLIPSE DIAGRAMS

Further details of the paths and times of central eclipse are given in
The Astronomical Almanac.

VISIBILITY OF PLANETS

VENUS is a brilliant object in the evening sky until the end of the first week of Jan. when it becomes too close to the Sun for observation. It reappears in the third week of Jan. as a morning star and can be seen in the morning sky until mid-September when it again becomes too close to the Sun for observation; from early Dec. until the end of the year it is visible in the evening sky. Venus is in conjunction with Jupiter on August 18.

MARS rises around midnight at the beginning of the year in Virgo (passing 5° N. of *Spica* on Jan. 28 and Mar. 31). It is at opposition on Apr. 8, when it is visible throughout the night as a bright, reddish object. Its eastern elongation gradually decreases and from mid-July until the end of the year it is visible only in the evening sky. It remains in Virgo (passing 1°.4 N. of *Spica* on July 12) until mid-August, and then moves through Libra, Scorpius, Ophiuchus (passing 3° N. of *Antares* on Sept. 27), Sagittarius and into Capricornus in early Dec. Mars is in conjunction with Saturn on August 27.

JUPITER can be seen in Gemini from the beginning of the year. It is at opposition on January 5 when it can be seen throughout the night. Its eastward elongation then gradually decreases and from early Apr. it can only be seen in the evening sky (passing 6° S. of *Pollux* on June 21) and moves into Cancer in early July. In the second week of July it becomes too close to the Sun for observation until early Aug. when it reappears in the morning sky. It passes into Leo in mid-Oct. and from mid-Nov. can be seen for more than half the night. Jupiter is in conjunction with Venus on August 18.

SATURN rises well after midnight at the beginning of the year in Libra and remains in this constellation throughout the year. It is at opposition on May 10 when it can be seen throughout the night and from early August until the start of November it is visible only in the evening sky. It then becomes too close to the Sun for observation until in early December it reappears, and it can be seen in the morning sky for the rest of the year. Saturn is in conjunction with Mars on August 27.

MERCURY can only be seen low in the east before sunrise, or low in the west after sunset (about the time of beginning or end of civil twilight). It is visible in the mornings between the following approximate dates: Feb. 22 (+2·5) to Apr. 18 (−1·2), June 29 (+3·0) to Aug. 1 (−1·5) and Oct. 23 (+1·7) to Nov. 22 (−0·9); the planet is brighter at the end of each period. It is visible in the evenings between the following approximate dates: Jan. 13 (−1·0) to Feb. 9 (+1·5), May 4 (−1·5) to June 10 (+3·1), Aug. 18 (−1·0) to Oct. 11 (+2·4) and Dec. 25 (−0·8) to Dec. 31 (−0·8); the planet is brighter at the beginning of each period. The figures in parentheses are the magnitudes.

PLANET DIAGRAM

General Description. The diagram on the opposite page shows, in graphical form for any date during the year, the local mean time of meridian passage of the Sun, of the five planets Mercury, Venus, Mars, Jupiter, and Saturn, and of each 30° of SHA; intermediate lines corresponding to particular stars, may be drawn in by the user if desired. It is intended to provide a general picture of the availability of planets and stars for observation.

On each side of the line marking the time of meridian passage of the Sun a band, 45^m wide, is shaded to indicate that planets and most stars crossing the meridian within 45^m of the Sun are too close to the Sun for observation.

Method of use and interpretation. For any date the diagram provides immediately the local mean times of meridian passage of the Sun, planets and stars, and thus the following information:

(a) whether a planet or star is too close to the Sun for observation;

(b) some indication of its position in the sky, especially during twilight;

(c) the proximity of other planets.

When the meridian passage of an outer planet occurs at midnight the body is in opposition to the Sun and is visible all night; a planet may then be observable during both morning and evening twilights. As the time of meridian passage decreases, the body eventually ceases to be observable in the morning, but its altitude above the eastern horizon at sunset gradually increases; this continues until the body is on the meridian during evening twilight. From then onwards the body is observable above the western horizon and its altitude at sunset gradually decreases; eventually the body becomes too close to the Sun for observation. When the body again becomes visible it is seen low in the east during morning twilight; its altitude at sunrise increases until meridian passage occurs during morning twilight. Then, as the time of meridian passage decreases to 0^h, the body is observable in the west during morning twilight with a gradually decreasing altitude, until it once again reaches opposition.

DO NOT CONFUSE

Venus with Jupiter in mid-August and with Mercury in late December on both occasions Venus is the brighter object.

Mars with Saturn in mid-August to early September when Mars is the brighter object.

LOCAL MEAN TIME OF MERIDIAN PASSAGE

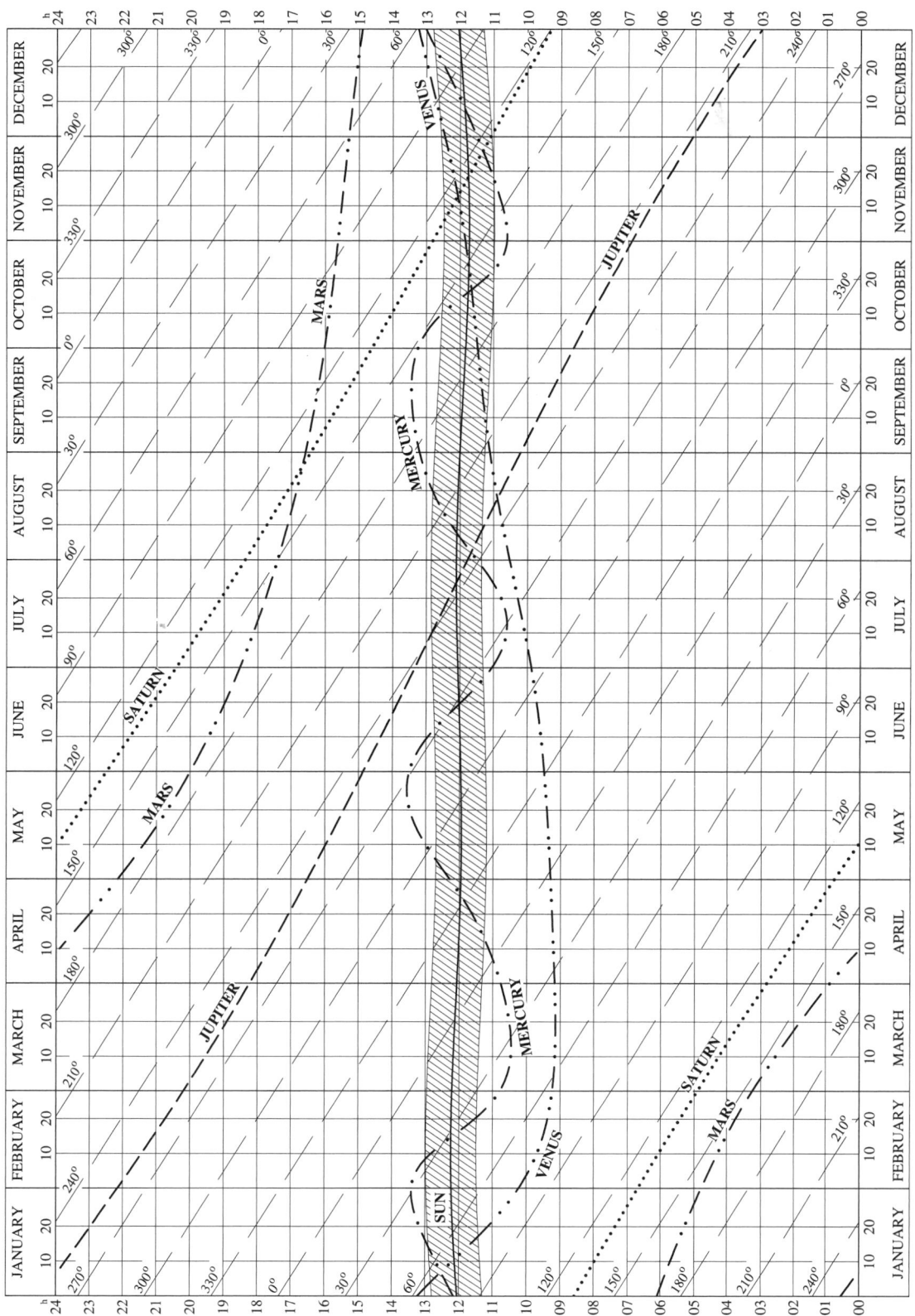

UT	ARIES GHA	VENUS −4.3 GHA	VENUS Dec	MARS +0.8 GHA	MARS Dec	JUPITER −2.7 GHA	JUPITER Dec	SATURN +0.6 GHA	SATURN Dec	STARS Name	SHA	Dec
1 00	100 34.3	162 10.0	S18 13.1	269 00.9	S 2 36.2	353 04.4	N22 35.1	232 03.1	S15 44.5	Acamar	315 17.8	S40 15.2
01	115 36.7	177 13.7	12.6	284 02.3	36.6	8 07.2	35.2	247 05.4	44.5	Achernar	335 26.4	S57 10.3
02	130 39.2	192 17.3	12.2	299 03.7	37.1	23 10.1	35.2	262 07.6	44.6	Acrux	173 08.6	S63 10.4
03	145 41.7	207 21.0	.. 11.7	314 05.2	.. 37.5	38 12.9	.. 35.3	277 09.9	.. 44.6	Adhara	255 11.8	S28 59.7
04	160 44.1	222 24.6	11.3	329 06.6	37.9	53 15.7	35.3	292 12.1	44.7	Aldebaran	290 48.6	N16 32.1
05	175 46.6	237 28.3	10.8	344 08.0	38.3	68 18.5	35.3	307 14.3	44.8			
W 06	190 49.0	252 31.9	S18 10.4	359 09.5	S 2 38.7	83 21.4	N22 35.4	322 16.6	S15 44.8	Alioth	166 20.5	N55 52.7
E 07	205 51.5	267 35.6	10.0	14 10.9	39.1	98 24.2	35.4	337 18.8	44.9	Alkaid	152 58.8	N49 14.4
D 08	220 54.0	282 39.3	09.5	29 12.3	39.5	113 27.0	35.5	352 21.0	44.9	Al Na'ir	27 43.6	S46 53.6
N 09	235 56.4	297 42.9	.. 09.1	44 13.8	.. 39.9	128 29.8	.. 35.5	7 23.3	.. 45.0	Alnilam	275 45.6	S 1 11.8
E 10	250 58.9	312 46.6	08.6	59 15.2	40.3	143 32.7	35.6	22 25.5	45.0	Alphard	217 55.4	S 8 43.3
S 11	266 01.4	327 50.3	08.2	74 16.6	40.7	158 35.5	35.6	37 27.7	45.1			
D 12	281 03.8	342 54.0	S18 07.7	89 18.1	S 2 41.1	173 38.3	N22 35.7	52 30.0	S15 45.1	Alphecca	126 11.0	N26 40.0
A 13	296 06.3	357 57.7	07.3	104 19.5	41.5	188 41.1	35.7	67 32.2	45.2	Alpheratz	357 43.1	N29 10.3
Y 14	311 08.8	13 01.4	06.9	119 20.9	41.9	203 44.0	35.8	82 34.5	45.2	Altair	62 08.2	N 8 54.5
15	326 11.2	28 05.0	.. 06.4	134 22.4	.. 42.3	218 46.8	.. 35.8	97 36.7	.. 45.3	Ankaa	353 15.4	S42 14.0
16	341 13.7	43 08.7	06.0	149 23.8	42.7	233 49.6	35.9	112 38.9	45.3	Antares	112 26.1	S26 27.6
17	356 16.2	58 12.4	05.5	164 25.3	43.1	248 52.4	35.9	127 41.2	45.4			
18	11 18.6	73 16.1	S18 05.1	179 26.7	S 2 43.5	263 55.3	N22 35.9	142 43.4	S15 45.5	Arcturus	145 55.5	N19 06.5
19	26 21.1	88 19.8	04.7	194 28.1	43.9	278 58.1	36.0	157 45.6	45.5	Atria	107 28.0	S69 02.8
20	41 23.5	103 23.6	04.2	209 29.6	44.3	294 00.9	36.0	172 47.9	45.6	Avior	234 17.2	S59 33.3
21	56 26.0	118 27.3	.. 03.8	224 31.0	.. 44.7	309 03.7	.. 36.1	187 50.1	.. 45.6	Bellatrix	278 31.3	N 6 21.5
22	71 28.5	133 31.0	03.3	239 32.4	45.1	324 06.6	36.1	202 52.4	45.7	Betelgeuse	271 00.5	N 7 24.4
23	86 30.9	148 34.7	02.9	254 33.9	45.5	339 09.4	36.2	217 54.6	45.7			
2 00	101 33.4	163 38.4	S18 02.5	269 35.3	S 2 45.9	354 12.2	N22 36.2	232 56.8	S15 45.8	Canopus	263 55.4	S52 42.4
01	116 35.9	178 42.2	02.0	284 36.8	46.3	9 15.0	36.3	247 59.1	45.8	Capella	280 33.4	N46 00.6
02	131 38.3	193 45.9	01.6	299 38.2	46.8	24 17.9	36.3	263 01.3	45.9	Deneb	49 31.6	N45 20.1
03	146 40.8	208 49.6	.. 01.2	314 39.6	.. 47.2	39 20.7	.. 36.4	278 03.5	.. 45.9	Denebola	182 33.2	N14 29.4
04	161 43.3	223 53.4	00.7	329 41.1	47.6	54 23.5	36.4	293 05.8	46.0	Diphda	348 55.5	S17 54.7
05	176 45.7	238 57.1	18 00.3	344 42.5	48.0	69 26.3	36.4	308 08.0	46.0			
T 06	191 48.2	254 00.8	S17 59.9	359 44.0	S 2 48.4	84 29.2	N22 36.5	323 10.3	S15 46.1	Dubhe	193 51.0	N61 40.1
H 07	206 50.7	269 04.6	59.4	14 45.4	48.8	99 32.0	36.5	338 12.5	46.2	Elnath	278 11.7	N28 37.0
U 08	221 53.1	284 08.3	59.0	29 46.8	49.2	114 34.8	36.6	353 14.7	46.2	Eltanin	90 46.5	N51 29.3
R 09	236 55.6	299 12.1	.. 58.6	44 48.3	.. 49.6	129 37.6	.. 36.6	8 17.0	.. 46.3	Enif	33 47.0	N 9 56.5
S 10	251 58.0	314 15.9	58.1	59 49.7	50.0	144 40.5	36.7	23 19.2	46.3	Fomalhaut	15 23.8	S29 32.9
D 11	267 00.5	329 19.6	57.7	74 51.2	50.4	159 43.3	36.7	38 21.5	46.4			
A 12	282 03.0	344 23.4	S17 57.3	89 52.6	S 2 50.8	174 46.1	N22 36.8	53 23.7	S15 46.4	Gacrux	172 00.3	S57 11.3
Y 13	297 05.4	359 27.2	56.8	104 54.1	51.2	189 49.0	36.8	68 25.9	46.5	Gienah	175 51.8	S17 37.2
14	312 07.9	14 30.9	56.4	119 55.5	51.6	204 51.8	36.9	83 28.2	46.5	Hadar	148 47.5	S60 26.1
15	327 10.4	29 34.7	.. 56.0	134 56.9	.. 52.0	219 54.6	.. 36.9	98 30.4	.. 46.6	Hamal	328 00.1	N23 31.8
16	342 12.8	44 38.5	55.6	149 58.4	52.4	234 57.4	37.0	113 32.7	46.6	Kaus Aust.	83 43.7	S34 22.5
17	357 15.3	59 42.3	55.1	164 59.8	52.8	250 00.3	37.0	128 34.9	46.7			
18	12 17.8	74 46.0	S17 54.7	180 01.3	S 2 53.2	265 03.1	N22 37.0	143 37.1	S15 46.7	Kochab	137 20.9	N74 05.6
19	27 20.2	89 49.8	54.3	195 02.7	53.6	280 05.9	37.1	158 39.4	46.8	Markab	13 38.1	N15 17.0
20	42 22.7	104 53.6	53.9	210 04.2	54.0	295 08.7	37.1	173 41.6	46.8	Menkar	314 14.4	N 4 08.6
21	57 25.2	119 57.4	.. 53.4	225 05.6	.. 54.4	310 11.6	.. 37.2	188 43.9	.. 46.9	Menkent	148 07.2	S36 26.1
22	72 27.6	135 01.2	53.0	240 07.1	54.8	325 14.4	37.2	203 46.1	46.9	Miaplacidus	221 38.7	S69 46.5
23	87 30.1	150 05.0	52.6	255 08.5	55.1	340 17.2	37.3	218 48.3	47.0			
3 00	102 32.5	165 08.8	S17 52.2	270 10.0	S 2 55.5	355 20.0	N22 37.3	233 50.6	S15 47.0	Mirfak	308 39.4	N49 54.7
01	117 35.0	180 12.6	51.7	285 11.4	55.9	10 22.9	37.4	248 52.8	47.1	Nunki	75 58.2	S26 16.6
02	132 37.5	195 16.4	51.3	300 12.8	56.3	25 25.7	37.4	263 55.1	47.2	Peacock	53 19.2	S56 41.3
03	147 39.9	210 20.3	.. 50.9	315 14.3	.. 56.7	40 28.5	.. 37.5	278 57.3	.. 47.2	Pollux	243 26.9	N27 59.3
04	162 42.4	225 24.1	50.5	330 15.7	57.1	55 31.3	37.5	293 59.6	47.3	Procyon	244 59.0	N 5 11.1
05	177 44.9	240 27.9	50.0	345 17.2	57.5	70 34.2	37.5	309 01.8	47.3			
F 06	192 47.3	255 31.7	S17 49.6	0 18.6	S 2 57.9	85 37.0	N22 37.6	324 04.0	S15 47.4	Rasalhague	96 06.4	N12 33.1
R 07	207 49.8	270 35.5	49.2	15 20.1	58.3	100 39.8	37.6	339 06.3	47.4	Regulus	207 42.9	N11 53.7
I 08	222 52.3	285 39.4	48.8	30 21.5	58.7	115 42.7	37.7	354 08.5	47.5	Rigel	281 11.4	S 8 11.4
D 09	237 54.7	300 43.2	.. 48.4	45 23.0	.. 59.1	130 45.5	.. 37.7	9 10.8	.. 47.5	Rigil Kent.	139 51.4	S60 53.2
A 10	252 57.2	315 47.0	48.0	60 24.4	59.5	145 48.3	37.8	24 13.0	47.6	Sabik	102 12.4	S15 44.3
Y 11	267 59.7	330 50.9	47.5	75 25.9	2 59.9	160 51.1	37.8	39 15.2	47.6			
12	283 02.1	345 54.7	S17 47.1	90 27.3	S 3 00.3	175 54.0	N22 37.9	54 17.5	S15 47.7	Schedar	349 40.0	N56 37.2
13	298 04.6	0 58.6	46.7	105 28.8	00.7	190 56.8	37.9	69 19.7	47.7	Shaula	96 21.8	S37 06.6
14	313 07.0	16 02.4	46.3	120 30.3	01.1	205 59.6	38.0	84 22.0	47.8	Sirius	258 33.0	S16 44.4
15	328 09.5	31 06.3	.. 45.9	135 31.7	.. 01.5	221 02.4	.. 38.0	99 24.2	.. 47.8	Spica	158 30.9	S11 14.0
16	343 12.0	46 10.1	45.5	150 33.2	01.9	236 05.3	38.0	114 26.5	47.9	Suhail	222 51.7	S43 29.4
17	358 14.4	61 14.0	45.0	165 34.6	02.3	251 08.1	38.1	129 28.7	47.9			
18	13 16.9	76 17.8	S17 44.6	180 36.1	S 3 02.7	266 10.9	N22 38.1	144 30.9	S15 48.0	Vega	80 39.1	N38 48.0
19	28 19.4	91 21.7	44.2	195 37.5	03.1	281 13.8	38.2	159 33.2	48.0	Zuben'ubi	137 05.2	S16 05.9
20	43 21.8	106 25.6	43.8	210 39.0	03.5	296 16.6	38.2	174 35.4	48.1		SHA	Mer. Pass.
21	58 24.3	121 29.4	.. 43.4	225 40.4	.. 03.9	311 19.4	.. 38.3	189 37.7	.. 48.1	Venus	62 05.0	13 02
22	73 26.8	136 33.3	43.0	240 41.9	04.3	326 22.2	38.3	204 39.9	48.2	Mars	168 01.9	6 01
23	88 29.2	151 37.2	42.6	255 43.3	04.6	341 25.1	38.4	219 42.2	48.2	Jupiter	252 38.8	0 23
Mer. Pass. 17 11.0		v 3.8	d 0.4	v 1.4	d 0.4	v 2.8	d 0.0	v 2.2	d 0.1	Saturn	131 23.4	8 27

UT	SUN GHA	SUN Dec	MOON GHA	v	Dec	d	HP
d h	° ′	° ′	° ′	′	° ′	′	′
1 00	179 10.2	S23 01.3	186 33.9	3.3	S19 05.1	2.9	61.3
01	194 09.9	01.1	200 56.2	3.2	19 02.2	3.0	61.3
02	209 09.6	00.9	215 18.4	3.3	18 59.2	3.2	61.3
03	224 09.3	.. 00.7	229 40.7	3.4	18 56.0	3.3	61.3
04	239 09.0	00.5	244 03.1	3.3	18 52.7	3.5	61.3
05	254 08.8	00.3	258 25.4	3.3	18 49.2	3.6	61.4
06	269 08.5	S23 00.1	272 47.7	3.4	S18 45.6	3.8	61.4
W 07	284 08.2	22 59.9	287 10.1	3.4	18 41.8	3.9	61.4
E 08	299 07.9	59.7	301 32.5	3.4	18 37.9	4.0	61.4
D 09	314 07.6	.. 59.5	315 54.9	3.4	18 33.9	4.2	61.4
N 10	329 07.3	59.2	330 17.3	3.4	18 29.7	4.4	61.4
E 11	344 07.0	59.0	344 39.7	3.5	18 25.3	4.4	61.4
S 12	359 06.7	S22 58.8	359 02.2	3.5	S18 20.9	4.6	61.4
D 13	14 06.4	58.6	13 24.7	3.6	18 16.3	4.8	61.4
A 14	29 06.1	58.4	27 47.3	3.5	18 11.5	4.9	61.4
Y 15	44 05.8	.. 58.2	42 09.8	3.6	18 06.6	5.0	61.4
16	59 05.5	58.0	56 32.4	3.6	18 01.6	5.2	61.4
17	74 05.2	57.8	70 55.0	3.7	17 56.4	5.2	61.4
18	89 04.9	S22 57.6	85 17.7	3.7	S17 51.2	5.5	61.4
19	104 04.6	57.3	99 40.4	3.8	17 45.7	5.5	61.4
20	119 04.3	57.1	114 03.2	3.7	17 40.2	5.7	61.4
21	134 04.0	.. 56.9	128 25.9	3.9	17 34.5	5.8	61.4
22	149 03.7	56.7	142 48.8	3.8	17 28.7	6.0	61.4
23	164 03.4	56.5	157 11.6	4.0	17 22.7	6.1	61.4
2 00	179 03.2	S22 56.2	171 34.6	3.9	S17 16.6	6.2	61.4
01	194 02.9	56.0	185 57.5	4.0	17 10.4	6.3	61.4
02	209 02.6	55.8	200 20.5	4.1	17 04.1	6.5	61.4
03	224 02.3	.. 55.6	214 43.6	4.1	16 57.6	6.6	61.4
04	239 02.0	55.4	229 06.7	4.2	16 51.0	6.7	61.4
05	254 01.7	55.1	243 29.9	4.2	16 44.3	6.8	61.4
06	269 01.4	S22 54.9	257 53.1	4.3	S16 37.5	7.0	61.4
T 07	284 01.1	54.7	272 16.4	4.3	16 30.5	7.0	61.4
H 08	299 00.8	54.5	286 39.7	4.4	16 23.5	7.2	61.4
U 09	314 00.5	.. 54.2	301 03.1	4.4	16 16.3	7.3	61.4
R 10	329 00.2	54.0	315 26.5	4.6	16 09.0	7.5	61.4
S 11	343 59.9	53.8	329 50.1	4.5	16 01.5	7.5	61.4
D 12	358 59.6	S22 53.6	344 13.6	4.6	S15 54.0	7.7	61.4
A 13	13 59.3	53.3	358 37.2	4.7	15 46.3	7.7	61.4
Y 14	28 59.1	53.1	13 00.9	4.8	15 38.6	7.9	61.3
15	43 58.8	.. 52.9	27 24.7	4.8	15 30.7	8.0	61.3
16	58 58.5	52.6	41 48.5	4.9	15 22.7	8.1	61.3
17	73 58.2	52.4	56 12.4	4.9	15 14.6	8.2	61.3
18	88 57.9	S22 52.2	70 36.3	5.1	S15 06.4	8.2	61.3
19	103 57.6	51.9	85 00.4	5.0	14 58.2	8.4	61.3
20	118 57.3	51.7	99 24.4	5.2	14 49.8	8.6	61.3
21	133 57.0	.. 51.5	113 48.6	5.2	14 41.2	8.6	61.3
22	148 56.7	51.2	128 12.8	5.3	14 32.6	8.7	61.3
23	163 56.4	51.0	142 37.1	5.4	14 23.9	8.8	61.2
3 00	178 56.1	S22 50.8	157 01.5	5.4	S14 15.1	8.8	61.2
01	193 55.9	50.5	171 25.9	5.5	14 06.3	9.0	61.2
02	208 55.6	50.3	185 50.4	5.6	13 57.3	9.1	61.2
03	223 55.3	.. 50.0	200 15.0	5.6	13 48.2	9.2	61.2
04	238 55.0	49.8	214 39.6	5.8	13 39.0	9.2	61.2
05	253 54.7	49.6	229 04.4	5.8	13 29.8	9.4	61.1
06	268 54.4	S22 49.3	243 29.2	5.8	S13 20.4	9.4	61.1
F 07	283 54.1	49.1	257 54.0	6.0	13 11.0	9.5	61.1
R 08	298 53.8	48.8	272 19.0	6.0	13 01.5	9.6	61.1
I 09	313 53.5	.. 48.6	286 44.0	6.1	12 51.9	9.7	61.1
D 10	328 53.3	48.3	301 09.1	6.1	12 42.2	9.8	61.0
A 11	343 53.0	48.1	315 34.2	6.3	12 32.4	9.8	61.0
Y 12	358 52.7	S22 47.8	329 59.5	6.3	S12 22.6	9.9	61.0
13	13 52.4	47.6	344 24.8	6.4	12 12.7	10.0	61.0
14	28 52.1	47.3	358 50.2	6.5	12 02.7	10.1	61.0
15	43 51.8	.. 47.1	13 15.7	6.5	11 52.6	10.1	60.9
16	58 51.5	46.8	27 41.2	6.6	11 42.5	10.2	60.9
17	73 51.2	46.6	42 06.8	6.7	11 32.3	10.3	60.9
18	88 51.0	S22 46.3	56 32.5	6.8	S11 22.0	10.3	60.9
19	103 50.7	46.1	70 58.3	6.9	11 11.7	10.4	60.8
20	118 50.4	45.8	85 24.2	6.9	11 01.3	10.5	60.8
21	133 50.1	.. 45.6	99 50.1	7.0	10 50.8	10.5	60.8
22	148 49.8	45.3	114 16.1	7.1	10 40.3	10.6	60.8
23	163 49.5	45.1	128 42.2	7.1	S10 29.7	10.6	60.7
	SD 16.3	d 0.2	SD 16.7		16.7		16.6

Twilight / Moonrise

Lat.	Naut.	Civil	Sunrise	Moonrise 1	2	3	4
°	h m	h m	h m	h m	h m	h m	h m
N 72	08 23	10 39	■	■	11 14	10 54	10 41
N 70	08 04	09 48	■	10 32	10 33	10 31	10 29
68	07 49	09 16	■	09 46	10 04	10 13	10 19
66	07 37	08 52	10 26	09 15	09 43	09 59	10 10
64	07 26	08 34	09 48	08 53	09 25	09 47	10 03
62	07 17	08 18	09 22	08 34	09 11	09 37	09 56
60	07 09	08 05	09 02	08 19	08 59	09 28	09 51
N 58	07 02	07 54	08 45	08 06	08 48	09 21	09 46
56	06 55	07 44	08 31	07 55	08 39	09 14	09 42
54	06 50	07 35	08 19	07 45	08 31	09 08	09 38
52	06 44	07 27	08 08	07 37	08 24	09 02	09 34
50	06 39	07 20	07 58	07 29	08 17	08 57	09 31
45	06 28	07 05	07 38	07 12	08 03	08 47	09 24
N 40	06 18	06 52	07 22	06 58	07 51	08 38	09 18
35	06 09	06 40	07 08	06 47	07 41	08 30	09 13
30	06 00	06 30	06 56	06 36	07 32	08 23	09 09
20	05 44	06 11	06 35	06 19	07 17	08 11	09 01
N 10	05 28	05 55	06 17	06 03	07 04	08 01	08 54
0	05 12	05 38	06 00	05 49	06 51	07 51	08 48
S 10	04 53	05 20	05 43	05 35	06 39	07 41	08 41
20	04 31	05 00	05 25	05 19	06 25	07 31	08 34
30	04 03	04 36	05 03	05 02	06 10	07 19	08 27
35	03 44	04 21	04 50	04 52	06 01	07 12	08 22
40	03 22	04 03	04 36	04 40	05 51	07 04	08 17
45	02 52	03 41	04 18	04 26	05 39	06 55	08 11
S 50	02 09	03 12	03 56	04 09	05 25	06 44	08 04
52	01 43	02 58	03 46	04 01	05 18	06 39	08 00
54	01 03	02 41	03 34	03 53	05 10	06 33	07 57
56	////	02 19	03 20	03 43	05 02	06 27	07 53
58	////	01 52	03 04	03 31	04 52	06 19	07 48
S 60	////	01 09	02 44	03 18	04 41	06 11	07 43

Sunset / Twilight / Moonset

Lat.	Sunset	Civil	Naut.	Moonset 1	2	3	4
°	h m	h m	h m	h m	h m	h m	h m
N 72	■	13 29	15 46	■	15 12	17 36	19 45
N 70	■	14 21	16 04	13 44	15 52	17 57	19 55
68	■	14 53	16 19	14 30	16 20	18 13	20 03
66	13 42	15 16	16 32	14 59	16 41	18 26	20 10
64	14 20	15 35	16 42	15 22	16 57	18 37	20 16
62	14 46	15 50	16 51	15 40	17 11	18 46	20 21
60	15 07	16 03	16 59	15 54	17 22	18 54	20 25
N 58	15 23	16 14	17 06	16 07	17 32	19 01	20 29
56	15 37	16 24	17 13	16 18	17 41	19 07	20 33
54	15 50	16 33	17 19	16 27	17 48	19 12	20 36
52	16 00	16 41	17 24	16 36	17 55	19 17	20 38
50	16 10	16 48	17 29	16 43	18 01	19 22	20 41
45	16 30	17 03	17 41	17 00	18 15	19 31	20 46
N 40	16 46	17 17	17 52	17 13	18 25	19 39	20 51
35	17 00	17 28	18 00	17 24	18 35	19 45	20 55
30	17 12	17 38	18 08	17 34	18 43	19 51	20 58
20	17 33	17 57	18 24	17 51	18 57	20 01	21 04
N 10	17 51	18 13	18 40	18 05	19 09	20 10	21 09
0	18 08	18 30	18 56	18 19	19 20	20 18	21 14
S 10	18 25	18 48	19 15	18 32	19 31	20 27	21 18
20	18 43	19 08	19 37	18 47	19 43	20 35	21 23
30	19 05	19 32	20 05	19 03	19 57	20 45	21 29
35	19 17	19 47	20 23	19 13	20 04	20 50	21 32
40	19 32	20 05	20 46	19 23	20 13	20 57	21 35
45	19 50	20 27	21 15	19 36	20 23	21 04	21 40
S 50	20 11	20 55	21 58	19 51	20 36	21 13	21 44
52	20 22	21 10	22 24	19 59	20 41	21 17	21 47
54	20 34	21 27	23 02	20 07	20 48	21 21	21 49
56	20 47	21 48	////	20 15	20 55	21 26	21 52
58	21 03	22 15	////	20 25	21 03	21 31	21 55
S 60	21 23	22 57	////	20 37	21 11	21 37	21 58

	SUN			MOON			
Day	Eqn. of Time 00ʰ	12ʰ	Mer. Pass.	Mer. Pass. Upper	Lower	Age	Phase
d	m s	m s	h m	h m	h m	d	%
1	03 18	03 33	12 04	12 04	24 35	00	0
2	03 47	04 01	12 04	13 06	00 35	01	2
3	04 15	04 29	12 04	14 05	01 36	02	6 ●

UT (d h)	ARIES GHA	VENUS −4.3 GHA	Dec	MARS +0.8 GHA	Dec	JUPITER −2.7 GHA	Dec	SATURN +0.6 GHA	Dec	STARS Name	SHA	Dec
4 00	103 31.7	166 41.0	S17 42.2	270 44.8	S 3 05.0	356 27.9	N22 38.4	234 44.4	S15 48.3	Acamar	315 17.8	S40 15.2
01	118 34.1	181 44.9	.41.7	285 46.3	05.4	11 30.7	38.5	249 46.6	48.4	Achernar	335 26.4	S57 10.3
02	133 36.6	196 48.8	41.3	300 47.7	05.8	26 33.5	38.5	264 48.9	48.4	Acrux	173 08.6	S63 10.4
03	148 39.1	211 52.7 ..	40.9	315 49.2 ..	06.2	41 36.4 ..	38.5	279 51.1 ..	48.5	Adhara	255 11.8	S28 59.7
04	163 41.5	226 56.6	40.5	330 50.6	06.6	56 39.2	38.6	294 53.4	48.5	Aldebaran	290 48.6	N16 32.1
05	178 44.0	242 00.5	40.1	345 52.1	07.0	71 42.0	38.6	309 55.6	48.6			
06	193 46.5	257 04.4	S17 39.7	0 53.5	S 3 07.4	86 44.8	N22 38.7	324 57.9	S15 48.6	Alioth	166 20.4	N55 52.7
S 07	208 48.9	272 08.3	39.3	15 55.0	07.8	101 47.7	38.7	340 00.1	48.7	Alkaid	152 58.8	N49 14.3
A 08	223 51.4	287 12.2	38.9	30 56.5	08.2	116 50.5	38.8	355 02.4	48.7	Al Na'ir	27 43.6	S46 53.6
T 09	238 53.9	302 16.1 ..	38.5	45 57.9 ..	08.6	131 53.3 ..	38.8	10 04.6 ..	48.8	Alnilam	275 45.6	S 1 11.8
U 10	253 56.3	317 20.0	38.1	60 59.4	09.0	146 56.2	38.9	25 06.8	48.8	Alphard	217 55.4	S 8 43.3
R 11	268 58.8	332 23.9	37.7	76 00.8	09.3	161 59.0	38.9	40 09.1	48.9			
D 12	284 01.3	347 27.8	S17 37.3	91 02.3	S 3 09.7	177 01.8	N22 38.9	55 11.3	S15 48.9	Alphecca	126 10.9	N26 40.0
A 13	299 03.7	2 31.7	36.9	106 03.8	10.1	192 04.6	39.0	70 13.6	49.0	Alpheratz	357 43.1	N29 10.3
Y 14	314 06.2	17 35.6	36.5	121 05.2	10.5	207 07.5	39.0	85 15.8	49.0	Altair	62 08.2	N 8 54.5
15	329 08.6	32 39.5 ..	36.1	136 06.7 ..	10.9	222 10.3 ..	39.1	100 18.1 ..	49.1	Ankaa	353 15.4	S42 14.0
16	344 11.1	47 43.5	35.7	151 08.1	11.3	237 13.1	39.1	115 20.3	49.1	Antares	112 26.1	S26 27.6
17	359 13.6	62 47.4	35.3	166 09.6	11.7	252 16.0	39.2	130 22.6	49.2			
18	14 16.0	77 51.3	S17 34.9	181 11.1	S 3 12.1	267 18.8	N22 39.2	145 24.8	S15 49.2	Arcturus	145 55.5	N19 06.5
19	29 18.5	92 55.2	34.5	196 12.5	12.5	282 21.6	39.3	160 27.1	49.3	Atria	107 28.0	S69 02.8
20	44 21.0	107 59.2	34.1	211 14.0	12.9	297 24.4	39.3	175 29.3	49.3	Avior	234 17.2	S59 33.4
21	59 23.4	123 03.1 ..	33.7	226 15.5 ..	13.2	312 27.3 ..	39.4	190 31.5 ..	49.4	Bellatrix	278 31.3	N 6 21.5
22	74 25.9	138 07.0	33.3	241 16.9	13.6	327 30.1	39.4	205 33.8	49.4	Betelgeuse	271 00.5	N 7 24.4
23	89 28.4	153 11.0	32.9	256 18.4	14.0	342 32.9	39.4	220 36.0	49.5			
5 00	104 30.8	168 14.9	S17 32.5	271 19.8	S 3 14.4	357 35.7	N22 39.5	235 38.3	S15 49.5	Canopus	263 55.4	S52 42.4
01	119 33.3	183 18.9	32.1	286 21.3	14.8	12 38.6	39.5	250 40.5	49.6	Capella	280 33.4	N46 00.6
02	134 35.8	198 22.8	31.7	301 22.8	15.2	27 41.4	39.6	265 42.8	49.6	Deneb	49 31.6	N45 20.1
03	149 38.2	213 26.8 ..	31.3	316 24.2 ..	15.6	42 44.2 ..	39.6	280 45.0 ..	49.7	Denebola	182 33.2	N14 29.4
04	164 40.7	228 30.7	30.9	331 25.7	16.0	57 47.1	39.7	295 47.3	49.7	Diphda	348 55.5	S17 54.7
05	179 43.1	243 34.7	30.5	346 27.2	16.4	72 49.9	39.7	310 49.5	49.8			
06	194 45.6	258 38.6	S17 30.1	1 28.6	S 3 16.7	87 52.7	N22 39.8	325 51.8	S15 49.8	Dubhe	193 51.0	N61 40.1
07	209 48.1	273 42.6	29.7	16 30.1	17.1	102 55.5	39.8	340 54.0	49.9	Elnath	278 11.7	N28 37.0
08	224 50.5	288 46.6	29.3	31 31.6	17.5	117 58.4	39.8	355 56.3	49.9	Eltanin	90 46.5	N51 29.3
S 09	239 53.0	303 50.5 ..	29.0	46 33.1 ..	17.9	133 01.2 ..	39.9	10 58.5 ..	50.0	Enif	33 47.0	N 9 56.5
U 10	254 55.5	318 54.5	28.6	61 34.5	18.3	148 04.0	39.9	26 00.8	50.0	Fomalhaut	15 23.8	S29 32.9
N 11	269 57.9	333 58.5	28.2	76 36.0	18.7	163 06.8	40.0	41 03.0	50.1			
D 12	285 00.4	349 02.4	S17 27.8	91 37.5	S 3 19.1	178 09.7	N22 40.0	56 05.3	S15 50.1	Gacrux	172 00.3	S57 11.3
A 13	300 02.9	4 06.4	27.4	106 38.9	19.4	193 12.5	40.1	71 07.5	50.2	Gienah	175 51.8	S17 37.2
Y 14	315 05.3	19 10.4	27.0	121 40.4	19.8	208 15.3	40.1	86 09.7	50.2	Hadar	148 47.4	S60 26.1
15	330 07.8	34 14.4 ..	26.6	136 41.9 ..	20.2	223 18.2 ..	40.2	101 12.0 ..	50.3	Hamal	328 00.2	N23 31.8
16	345 10.2	49 18.3	26.2	151 43.3	20.6	238 21.0	40.2	116 14.2	50.3	Kaus Aust.	83 43.7	S34 22.5
17	0 12.7	64 22.3	25.9	166 44.8	21.0	253 23.8	40.3	131 16.5	50.4			
18	15 15.2	79 26.3	S17 25.5	181 46.3	S 3 21.4	268 26.6	N22 40.3	146 18.7	S15 50.4	Kochab	137 20.8	N74 05.6
19	30 17.6	94 30.3	25.1	196 47.8	21.8	283 29.5	40.3	161 21.0	50.5	Markab	13 38.1	N15 17.0
20	45 20.1	109 34.3	24.7	211 49.2	22.1	298 32.3	40.4	176 23.2	50.5	Menkar	314 14.4	N 4 08.6
21	60 22.6	124 38.3 ..	24.3	226 50.7 ..	22.5	313 35.1 ..	40.4	191 25.5 ..	50.6	Menkent	148 07.2	S36 26.1
22	75 25.0	139 42.3	23.9	241 52.2	22.9	328 38.0	40.5	206 27.7	50.6	Miaplacidus	221 38.6	S69 46.5
23	90 27.5	154 46.3	23.6	256 53.6	23.3	343 40.8	40.5	221 30.0	50.7			
6 00	105 30.0	169 50.3	S17 23.2	271 55.1	S 3 23.7	358 43.6	N22 40.6	236 32.2	S15 50.7	Mirfak	308 39.4	N49 54.7
01	120 32.4	184 54.3	22.8	286 56.6	24.1	13 46.4	40.6	251 34.5	50.8	Nunki	75 58.2	S26 16.6
02	135 34.9	199 58.3	22.4	301 58.1	24.4	28 49.3	40.7	266 36.7	50.8	Peacock	53 19.2	S56 41.3
03	150 37.4	215 02.3 ..	22.0	316 59.5 ..	24.8	43 52.1 ..	40.7	281 39.0 ..	50.9	Pollux	243 26.9	N27 59.3
04	165 39.8	230 06.3	21.7	332 01.0	25.2	58 54.9	40.7	296 41.2	50.9	Procyon	244 59.0	N 5 11.1
05	180 42.3	245 10.3	21.3	347 02.5	25.6	73 57.7	40.8	311 43.5	51.0			
06	195 44.7	260 14.3	S17 20.9	2 04.0	S 3 26.0	89 00.6	N22 40.8	326 45.7	S15 51.0	Rasalhague	96 06.4	N12 33.1
07	210 47.2	275 18.3	20.5	17 05.4	26.4	104 03.4	40.9	341 48.0	51.1	Regulus	207 42.9	N11 53.7
08	225 49.7	290 22.3	20.2	32 06.9	26.7	119 06.2	40.9	356 50.2	51.1	Rigel	281 11.4	S 8 11.4
M 09	240 52.1	305 26.3 ..	19.8	47 08.4 ..	27.1	134 09.1 ..	41.0	11 52.5 ..	51.2	Rigil Kent.	139 51.4	S60 53.2
O 10	255 54.6	320 30.4	19.4	62 09.9	27.5	149 11.9	41.0	26 54.7	51.2	Sabik	102 12.4	S15 44.3
N 11	270 57.1	335 34.4	19.0	77 11.4	27.9	164 14.7	41.1	41 57.0	51.3			
D 12	285 59.5	350 38.4	S17 18.7	92 12.8	S 3 28.3	179 17.5	N22 41.1	56 59.2	S15 51.3	Schedar	349 40.0	N56 37.2
A 13	301 02.0	5 42.4	18.3	107 14.3	28.6	194 20.4	41.1	72 01.5	51.4	Shaula	96 21.8	S37 06.6
Y 14	316 04.5	20 46.5	17.9	122 15.8	29.0	209 23.2	41.2	87 03.7	51.4	Sirius	258 33.0	S16 44.4
15	331 06.9	35 50.5 ..	17.5	137 17.3 ..	29.4	224 26.0 ..	41.2	102 06.0 ..	51.5	Spica	158 30.9	S11 14.0
16	346 09.4	50 54.5	17.2	152 18.8	29.8	239 28.8	41.3	117 08.2	51.5	Suhail	222 51.7	S43 29.4
17	1 11.9	65 58.5	16.8	167 20.2	30.2	254 31.7	41.3	132 10.5	51.6			
18	16 14.3	81 02.6	S17 16.4	182 21.7	S 3 30.6	269 34.5	N22 41.4	147 12.7	S15 51.6	Vega	80 39.1	N38 47.9
19	31 16.8	96 06.6	16.1	197 23.2	30.9	284 37.3	41.4	162 15.0	51.7	Zuben'ubi	137 05.1	S16 05.9
20	46 19.2	111 10.7	15.7	212 24.7	31.3	299 40.2	41.5	177 17.2	51.7			
21	61 21.7	126 14.7 ..	15.3	227 26.2 ..	31.7	314 43.0 ..	41.5	192 19.5 ..	51.8		SHA	Mer. Pass.
22	76 24.2	141 18.7	15.0	242 27.6	32.1	329 45.8	41.5	207 21.7	51.8	Venus	63 44.1	12 44
23	91 26.6	156 22.8	14.6	257 29.1	32.4	344 48.6	41.6	222 24.0	51.9	Mars	166 49.0	5 54
Mer. Pass. 16 59.2		v 4.0	d 0.4	v 1.5	d 0.4	v 2.8	d 0.0	v 2.2	d 0.1	Jupiter	253 04.9	0 10
										Saturn	131 07.5	8 16

UT	SUN GHA	SUN Dec	MOON GHA	v	MOON Dec	d	HP
d h	° ′	° ′	° ′	′	° ′	′	′
4 00	178 49.2	S22 44.8	143 08.3	7.2	S10 19.1	10.7	60.7
01	193 49.0	44.5	157 34.5	7.3	10 08.4	10.8	60.7
02	208 48.7	44.3	172 00.8	7.4	9 57.6	10.8	60.7
03	223 48.4 ..	44.0	186 27.2	7.5	9 46.8	10.8	60.6
04	238 48.1	43.8	200 53.7	7.5	9 36.0	10.9	60.6
05	253 47.8	43.5	215 20.2	7.6	9 25.1	11.0	60.6
06	268 47.5	S22 43.2	229 46.8	7.7	S 9 14.1	11.0	60.5
07	283 47.2	43.0	244 13.5	7.7	9 03.1	11.1	60.5
S 08	298 47.0	42.7	258 40.2	7.9	8 52.0	11.1	60.5
A 09	313 46.7 ..	42.5	273 07.1	7.9	8 40.9	11.1	60.4
T 10	328 46.4	42.2	287 34.0	7.9	8 29.8	11.2	60.4
U 11	343 46.1	41.9	302 00.9	8.1	8 18.6	11.2	60.4
R 12	358 45.8	S22 41.7	316 28.0	8.1	S 8 07.4	11.3	60.4
D 13	13 45.5	41.4	330 55.1	8.2	7 56.1	11.3	60.3
A 14	28 45.3	41.1	345 22.3	8.2	7 44.8	11.3	60.3
Y 15	43 45.0 ..	40.9	359 49.5	8.4	7 33.5	11.4	60.3
16	58 44.7	40.6	14 16.9	8.4	7 22.1	11.4	60.2
17	73 44.4	40.3	28 44.3	8.4	7 10.7	11.4	60.2
18	88 44.1	S22 40.0	43 11.7	8.6	S 6 59.3	11.5	60.2
19	103 43.8	39.8	57 39.3	8.6	6 47.8	11.4	60.1
20	118 43.6	39.5	72 06.9	8.7	6 36.4	11.6	60.1
21	133 43.3 ..	39.2	86 34.6	8.7	6 24.8	11.5	60.1
22	148 43.0	39.0	101 02.3	8.8	6 13.3	11.6	60.0
23	163 42.7	38.7	115 30.1	8.9	6 01.7	11.5	60.0
5 00	178 42.4	S22 38.4	129 58.0	8.9	S 5 50.2	11.6	60.0
01	193 42.2	38.1	144 25.9	9.0	5 38.6	11.7	59.9
02	208 41.9	37.9	158 53.9	9.1	5 26.9	11.6	59.9
03	223 41.6 ..	37.6	173 22.0	9.2	5 15.3	11.7	59.9
04	238 41.3	37.3	187 50.2	9.2	5 03.6	11.6	59.8
05	253 41.0	37.0	202 18.4	9.2	4 52.0	11.7	59.8
06	268 40.8	S22 36.7	216 46.6	9.4	S 4 40.3	11.7	59.7
07	283 40.5	36.5	231 15.0	9.3	4 28.6	11.7	59.7
S 08	298 40.2	36.2	245 43.3	9.5	4 16.9	11.8	59.7
U 09	313 39.9 ..	35.9	260 11.8	9.5	4 05.1	11.7	59.6
N 10	328 39.6	35.6	274 40.3	9.6	3 53.4	11.7	59.6
D 11	343 39.4	35.3	289 08.9	9.6	3 41.7	11.8	59.6
A 12	358 39.1	S22 35.0	303 37.5	9.7	S 3 29.9	11.7	59.5
Y 13	13 38.8	34.8	318 06.2	9.7	3 18.2	11.7	59.5
14	28 38.5	34.5	332 34.9	9.8	3 06.5	11.8	59.5
15	43 38.2 ..	34.2	347 03.7	9.9	2 54.7	11.8	59.4
16	58 38.0	33.9	1 32.6	9.9	2 42.9	11.7	59.4
17	73 37.7	33.6	16 01.5	10.0	2 31.2	11.8	59.3
18	88 37.4	S22 33.3	30 30.5	10.0	S 2 19.4	11.7	59.3
19	103 37.1	33.0	44 59.5	10.1	2 07.7	11.8	59.3
20	118 36.9	32.7	59 28.6	10.1	1 56.0	11.8	59.2
21	133 36.6 ..	32.4	73 57.7	10.2	1 44.2	11.7	59.2
22	148 36.3	32.1	88 26.9	10.2	1 32.5	11.7	59.2
23	163 36.0	31.9	102 56.1	10.3	1 20.8	11.8	59.1
6 00	178 35.8	S22 31.6	117 25.4	10.3	S 1 09.0	11.7	59.1
01	193 35.5	31.3	131 54.7	10.4	0 57.3	11.7	59.0
02	208 35.2	31.0	146 24.1	10.4	0 45.6	11.6	59.0
03	223 34.9 ..	30.7	160 53.5	10.5	0 34.0	11.7	59.0
04	238 34.6	30.4	175 23.0	10.5	0 22.3	11.7	58.9
05	253 34.4	30.1	189 52.5	10.6	S 0 10.6	11.6	58.9
06	268 34.1	S22 29.8	204 22.1	10.6	N 0 01.0	11.6	58.9
07	283 33.8	29.5	218 51.7	10.6	0 12.6	11.7	58.8
08	298 33.5	29.2	233 21.3	10.7	0 24.3	11.5	58.8
M 09	313 33.3 ..	28.9	247 51.0	10.8	0 35.8	11.6	58.7
O 10	328 33.0	28.6	262 20.8	10.8	0 47.4	11.6	58.7
N 11	343 32.7	28.3	276 50.6	10.8	0 59.0	11.5	58.7
D 12	358 32.5	S22 28.0	291 20.4	10.8	N 1 10.5	11.5	58.6
A 13	13 32.2	27.7	305 50.2	11.0	1 22.0	11.5	58.6
Y 14	28 31.9	27.4	320 20.2	10.9	1 33.5	11.4	58.5
15	43 31.6 ..	27.1	334 50.1	11.0	1 44.9	11.5	58.5
16	58 31.4	26.7	349 20.1	11.0	1 56.4	11.4	58.5
17	73 31.1	26.4	3 50.1	11.0	2 07.8	11.4	58.4
18	88 30.8	S22 26.1	18 20.1	11.1	N 2 19.2	11.3	58.4
19	103 30.5	25.8	32 50.2	11.1	2 30.5	11.4	58.3
20	118 30.3	25.5	47 20.3	11.2	2 41.9	11.2	58.3
21	133 30.0 ..	25.2	61 50.5	11.2	2 53.1	11.3	58.3
22	148 29.7	24.9	76 20.7	11.2	3 04.4	11.2	58.2
23	163 29.5	24.6	90 50.9	11.3	N 3 15.6	11.2	58.2
	SD 16.3 d 0.3		SD 16.4	16.2			16.0

Lat.	Twilight Naut.	Twilight Civil	Sunrise	Moonrise 4	Moonrise 5	Moonrise 6	Moonrise 7
°	h m	h m	h m	h m	h m	h m	h m
N 72	08 19	10 30	■■■	10 41	10 31	10 23	10 14
N 70	08 01	09 43	■■■	10 29	10 26	10 24	10 21
68	07 47	09 12	11 29	10 19	10 22	10 24	10 27
66	07 35	08 49	10 20	10 10	10 18	10 25	10 32
64	07 25	08 31	09 45	10 03	10 15	10 26	10 36
62	07 16	08 17	09 19	09 56	10 12	10 26	10 40
60	07 08	08 04	09 00	09 51	10 10	10 27	10 43
N 58	07 01	07 53	08 43	09 46	10 08	10 27	10 46
56	06 55	07 43	08 30	09 42	10 06	10 27	10 48
54	06 49	07 35	08 18	09 38	10 04	10 28	10 51
52	06 44	07 27	08 07	09 34	10 02	10 28	10 53
50	06 39	07 20	07 58	09 31	10 01	10 28	10 55
45	06 28	07 05	07 38	09 24	09 58	10 29	10 59
N 40	06 18	06 52	07 22	09 18	09 55	10 29	11 03
35	06 09	06 41	07 09	09 13	09 53	10 30	11 06
30	06 01	06 30	06 57	09 09	09 51	10 30	11 08
20	05 45	06 12	06 36	09 01	09 47	10 31	11 13
N 10	05 30	05 56	06 18	08 54	09 44	10 32	11 17
0	05 13	05 39	06 02	08 48	09 41	10 32	11 22
S 10	04 55	05 22	05 45	08 41	09 38	10 33	11 26
20	04 33	05 02	05 26	08 34	09 35	10 34	11 30
30	04 05	04 38	05 05	08 27	09 32	10 35	11 35
35	03 47	04 23	04 53	08 22	09 30	10 35	11 38
40	03 25	04 06	04 38	08 17	09 28	10 36	11 41
45	02 56	03 44	04 21	08 11	09 25	10 36	11 45
S 50	02 14	03 16	04 00	08 04	09 22	10 37	11 50
52	01 49	03 02	03 49	08 00	09 20	10 37	11 52
54	01 13	02 45	03 38	07 57	09 19	10 38	11 54
56	////	02 25	03 24	07 53	09 17	10 38	11 57
58	////	01 58	03 09	07 48	09 15	10 39	12 00
S 60	////	01 19	02 50	07 43	09 13	10 39	12 03

Lat.	Sunset	Twilight Civil	Twilight Naut.	Moonset 4	Moonset 5	Moonset 6	Moonset 7
°	h m	h m	h m	h m	h m	h m	h m
N 72	■■■	13 42	15 52	19 45	21 44	23 38	25 29
N 70	■■■	14 29	16 10	19 55	21 47	23 33	25 17
68	12 42	14 59	16 24	20 03	21 49	23 29	25 07
66	13 51	15 22	16 36	20 10	21 50	23 26	24 59
64	14 27	15 40	16 46	20 16	21 52	23 24	24 52
62	14 52	15 55	16 55	20 21	21 53	23 21	24 46
60	15 11	16 07	17 03	20 25	21 54	23 19	24 41
N 58	15 28	16 18	17 10	20 29	21 55	23 17	24 37
56	15 41	16 28	17 16	20 33	21 56	23 16	24 33
54	15 53	16 36	17 22	20 36	21 57	23 14	24 29
52	16 04	16 44	17 27	20 38	21 57	23 13	24 26
50	16 13	16 51	17 32	20 41	21 58	23 12	24 23
45	16 33	17 06	17 43	20 46	21 59	23 09	24 17
N 40	16 49	17 19	17 53	20 51	22 00	23 07	24 12
35	17 02	17 30	18 02	20 55	22 01	23 05	24 07
30	17 14	17 40	18 10	20 58	22 02	23 04	24 03
20	17 35	17 58	18 26	21 04	22 03	23 01	23 56
N 10	17 52	18 15	18 41	21 09	22 05	22 58	23 50
0	18 09	18 32	18 58	21 14	22 06	22 56	23 45
S 10	18 26	18 49	19 16	21 18	22 07	22 54	23 39
20	18 44	19 09	19 38	21 23	22 08	22 51	23 33
30	19 05	19 32	20 05	21 29	22 09	22 48	23 26
35	19 18	19 47	20 23	21 32	22 10	22 46	23 22
40	19 32	20 05	20 45	21 35	22 11	22 45	23 18
45	19 49	20 26	21 14	21 40	22 12	22 42	23 13
S 50	20 11	20 54	21 56	21 44	22 13	22 40	23 07
52	20 21	21 08	22 20	21 47	22 13	22 39	23 04
54	20 32	21 25	22 56	21 49	22 14	22 37	23 01
56	20 46	21 45	////	21 52	22 15	22 36	22 57
58	21 01	22 11	////	21 55	22 15	22 34	22 54
S 60	21 20	22 49	////	21 58	22 16	22 33	22 49

Day	SUN Eqn. of Time 00h	SUN Eqn. of Time 12h	SUN Mer. Pass.	MOON Mer. Pass. Upper	MOON Mer. Pass. Lower	Age	Phase
d	m s	m s	h m	h m	h m	d %	
4	04 42	04 56	12 05	15 01	02 33	03 14	
5	05 10	05 23	12 05	15 54	03 28	04 23	
6	05 36	05 50	12 06	16 44	04 19	05 33	

UT	ARIES	VENUS −4.3		MARS +0.7		JUPITER −2.7		SATURN +0.6		STARS		
	GHA	GHA	Dec	GHA	Dec	GHA	Dec	GHA	Dec	Name	SHA	Dec
d h	° ′	° ′	° ′	° ′	° ′	° ′	° ′	° ′	° ′		° ′	° ′
7 00	106 29.1	171 26.8	S17 14.2	272 30.6	S 3 32.8	359 51.5	N22 41.6	237 26.3	S15 51.9	Acamar	315 17.9	S40 15.2
01	121 31.6	186 30.9	13.9	287 32.1	33.2	14 54.3	41.7	252 28.5	52.0	Achernar	335 26.5	S57 10.3
02	136 34.0	201 34.9	13.5	302 33.6	33.6	29 57.1	41.7	267 30.8	52.0	Acrux	173 08.6	S63 10.4
03	151 36.5	216 39.0	. . 13.1	317 35.1	. . 34.0	45 00.0	. . 41.8	282 33.0	. . 52.1	Adhara	255 11.8	S28 59.7
04	166 39.0	231 43.0	12.8	332 36.5	34.3	60 02.8	41.8	297 35.3	52.1	Aldebaran	290 48.6	N16 32.1
05	181 41.4	246 47.1	12.4	347 38.0	34.7	75 05.6	41.9	312 37.5	52.2			
06	196 43.9	261 51.1	S17 12.1	2 39.5	S 3 35.1	90 08.4	N22 41.9	327 39.8	S15 52.2	Alioth	166 20.4	N55 52.7
07	211 46.3	276 55.2	11.7	17 41.0	35.5	105 11.3	41.9	342 42.0	52.3	Alkaid	152 58.7	N49 14.3
T 08	226 48.8	291 59.2	11.3	32 42.5	35.9	120 14.1	42.0	357 44.3	52.3	Al Na'ir	27 43.6	S46 53.6
U 09	241 51.3	307 03.3	. . 11.0	47 44.0	. . 36.2	135 16.9	. . 42.0	12 46.5	. . 52.3	Alnilam	275 45.6	S 1 11.8
E 10	256 53.7	322 07.4	10.6	62 45.5	36.6	150 19.7	42.1	27 48.8	52.4	Alphard	217 55.4	S 8 43.3
S 11	271 56.2	337 11.4	10.3	77 47.0	37.0	165 22.6	42.1	42 51.0	52.4			
D 12	286 58.7	352 15.5	S17 09.9	92 48.4	S 3 37.4	180 25.4	N22 42.2	57 53.3	S15 52.5	Alphecca	126 10.9	N26 40.0
A 13	302 01.1	7 19.6	09.5	107 49.9	37.7	195 28.2	42.2	72 55.5	52.5	Alpheratz	357 43.1	N29 10.3
Y 14	317 03.6	22 23.6	09.2	122 51.4	38.1	210 31.1	42.2	87 57.8	52.6	Altair	62 08.2	N 8 54.5
15	332 06.1	37 27.7	. . 08.8	137 52.9	. . 38.5	225 33.9	. . 42.3	103 00.1	. . 52.6	Ankaa	353 15.4	S42 14.0
16	347 08.5	52 31.8	08.5	152 54.4	38.9	240 36.7	42.3	118 02.3	52.7	Antares	112 26.0	S26 27.6
17	2 11.0	67 35.8	08.1	167 55.9	39.2	255 39.5	42.4	133 04.6	52.7			
18	17 13.5	82 39.9	S17 07.8	182 57.4	S 3 39.6	270 42.4	N22 42.4	148 06.8	S15 52.8	Arcturus	145 55.5	N19 06.5
19	32 15.9	97 44.0	07.4	197 58.9	40.0	285 45.2	42.5	163 09.1	52.8	Atria	107 27.9	S69 02.8
20	47 18.4	112 48.1	07.1	213 00.4	40.4	300 48.0	42.5	178 11.3	52.9	Avior	234 17.2	S59 33.4
21	62 20.8	127 52.1	. . 06.7	228 01.9	. . 40.7	315 50.8	. . 42.6	193 13.6	. . 52.9	Bellatrix	278 31.3	N 6 21.5
22	77 23.3	142 56.2	06.4	243 03.3	41.1	330 53.7	42.6	208 15.8	53.0	Betelgeuse	271 00.5	N 7 24.4
23	92 25.8	158 00.3	06.0	258 04.8	41.5	345 56.5	42.6	223 18.1	53.0			
8 00	107 28.2	173 04.4	S17 05.7	273 06.3	S 3 41.9	0 59.3	N22 42.7	238 20.3	S15 53.1	Canopus	263 55.4	S52 42.4
01	122 30.7	188 08.4	05.3	288 07.8	42.2	16 02.1	42.7	253 22.6	53.1	Capella	280 33.4	N46 00.6
02	137 33.2	203 12.5	05.0	303 09.3	42.6	31 05.0	42.8	268 24.9	53.2	Deneb	49 31.6	N45 20.1
03	152 35.6	218 16.6	. . 04.6	318 10.8	. . 43.0	46 07.8	. . 42.8	283 27.1	. . 53.2	Denebola	182 33.1	N14 29.4
04	167 38.1	233 20.7	04.3	333 12.3	43.4	61 10.6	42.9	298 29.4	53.3	Diphda	348 55.5	S17 54.7
05	182 40.6	248 24.8	03.9	348 13.8	43.7	76 13.5	42.9	313 31.6	53.3			
06	197 43.0	263 28.9	S17 03.6	3 15.3	S 3 44.1	91 16.3	N22 42.9	328 33.9	S15 53.4	Dubhe	193 51.0	N61 40.1
W 07	212 45.5	278 33.0	03.2	18 16.8	44.5	106 19.1	43.0	343 36.1	53.4	Elnath	278 11.7	N28 37.0
E 08	227 48.0	293 37.1	02.9	33 18.3	44.8	121 21.9	43.0	358 38.4	53.5	Eltanin	90 46.5	N51 29.3
D 09	242 50.4	308 41.2	. . 02.6	48 19.8	. . 45.2	136 24.8	. . 43.1	13 40.6	. . 53.5	Enif	33 47.0	N 9 56.5
N 10	257 52.9	323 45.2	02.2	63 21.3	45.6	151 27.6	43.1	28 42.9	53.5	Fomalhaut	15 23.8	S29 32.9
E 11	272 55.3	338 49.3	01.9	78 22.8	46.0	166 30.4	43.2	43 45.2	53.6			
S 12	287 57.8	353 53.4	S17 01.5	93 24.3	S 3 46.3	181 33.2	N22 43.2	58 47.4	S15 53.6	Gacrux	172 00.2	S57 11.3
.D 13	303 00.3	8 57.5	01.2	108 25.8	46.7	196 36.1	43.3	73 49.7	53.7	Gienah	175 51.8	S17 37.2
A 14	318 02.7	24 01.6	00.8	123 27.3	47.1	211 38.9	43.3	88 51.9	53.7	Hadar	148 47.4	S60 26.1
Y 15	333 05.2	39 05.7	. . 00.5	138 28.8	. . 47.4	226 41.7	. . 43.3	103 54.2	. . 53.8	Hamal	328 00.2	N23 31.8
16	348 07.7	54 09.8	17 00.2	153 30.3	47.8	241 44.5	43.4	118 56.4	53.8	Kaus Aust.	83 43.7	S34 22.5
17	3 10.1	69 13.9	16 59.8	168 31.8	48.2	256 47.4	43.4	133 58.7	53.9			
18	18 12.6	84 18.0	S16 59.5	183 33.3	S 3 48.6	271 50.2	N22 43.5	149 01.0	S15 53.9	Kochab	137 20.7	N74 05.6
19	33 15.1	99 22.1	59.2	198 34.8	48.9	286 53.0	43.5	164 03.2	54.0	Markab	13 38.1	N15 17.0
20	48 17.5	114 26.2	58.8	213 36.3	49.3	301 55.9	43.6	179 05.5	54.0	Menkar	314 14.5	N 4 08.6
21	63 20.0	129 30.3	. . 58.5	228 37.8	. . 49.7	316 58.7	. . 43.6	194 07.7	. . 54.1	Menkent	148 07.2	S36 26.1
22	78 22.4	144 34.4	58.2	243 39.3	50.0	332 01.5	43.6	209 10.0	54.1	Miaplacidus	221 38.6	S69 46.5
23	93 24.9	159 38.5	57.8	258 40.8	50.4	347 04.3	43.7	224 12.2	54.2			
9 00	108 27.4	174 42.6	S16 57.5	273 42.3	S 3 50.8	2 07.2	N22 43.7	239 14.5	S15 54.2	Mirfak	308 39.4	N49 54.7
01	123 29.8	189 46.8	57.2	288 43.8	51.1	17 10.0	43.8	254 16.8	54.3	Nunki	75 58.2	S26 16.6
02	138 32.3	204 50.9	56.8	303 45.3	51.5	32 12.8	43.8	269 19.0	54.3	Peacock	53 19.2	S56 41.3
03	153 34.8	219 55.0	. . 56.5	318 46.8	. . 51.9	47 15.6	. . 43.9	284 21.3	. . 54.3	Pollux	243 26.9	N27 59.3
04	168 37.2	234 59.1	56.2	333 48.3	52.2	62 18.5	43.9	299 23.5	54.4	Procyon	244 59.0	N 5 11.1
05	183 39.7	250 03.2	55.8	348 49.8	52.6	77 21.3	43.9	314 25.8	54.4			
06	198 42.2	265 07.3	S16 55.5	3 51.3	S 3 53.0	92 24.1	N22 44.0	329 28.0	S15 54.5	Rasalhague	96 06.4	N12 33.1
07	213 44.6	280 11.4	55.2	18 52.8	53.4	107 26.9	44.0	344 30.3	54.5	Regulus	207 42.9	N11 53.7
T 08	228 47.1	295 15.5	54.9	33 54.3	53.7	122 29.8	44.1	359 32.6	54.6	Rigel	281 11.4	S 8 11.4
H 09	243 49.6	310 19.6	. . 54.5	48 55.8	. . 54.1	137 32.6	. . 44.1	14 34.8	. . 54.6	Rigil Kent.	139 51.3	S60 53.2
U 10	258 52.0	325 23.7	54.2	63 57.3	54.5	152 35.4	44.2	29 37.1	54.7	Sabik	102 12.4	S15 44.3
R 11	273 54.5	340 27.9	53.9	78 58.8	54.8	167 38.2	44.2	44 39.3	54.7			
S 12	288 56.9	355 32.0	S16 53.6	94 00.3	S 3 55.2	182 41.1	N22 44.3	59 41.6	S15 54.8	Schedar	349 40.0	N56 37.1
D 13	303 59.4	10 36.1	53.2	109 01.8	55.6	197 43.9	44.3	74 43.9	54.8	Shaula	96 21.7	S37 06.6
A 14	319 01.9	25 40.2	52.9	124 03.3	55.9	212 46.7	44.3	89 46.1	54.9	Sirius	258 33.0	S16 44.4
Y 15	334 04.3	40 44.3	. . 52.6	139 04.9	. . 56.3	227 49.5	. . 44.4	104 48.4	. . 54.9	Spica	158 30.8	S11 14.0
16	349 06.8	55 48.4	52.3	154 06.4	56.7	242 52.4	44.4	119 50.6	54.9	Suhail	222 51.7	S43 29.4
17	4 09.3	70 52.6	51.9	169 07.9	57.0	257 55.2	44.5	134 52.9	55.0			
18	19 11.7	85 56.7	S16 51.6	184 09.4	S 3 57.4	272 58.0	N22 44.5	149 55.2	S15 55.0	Vega	80 39.1	N38 47.9
19	34 14.2	101 00.8	51.3	199 10.9	57.7	288 00.9	44.6	164 57.4	55.1	Zuben'ubi	137 05.1	S16 05.9
20	49 16.7	116 04.9	51.0	214 12.4	58.1	303 03.7	44.6	179 59.7	55.1		SHA	Mer.Pass.
21	64 19.1	131 09.0	. . 50.7	229 13.9	. . 58.5	318 06.5	. . 44.6	195 01.9	. . 55.2		° ′	h m
22	79 21.6	146 13.1	50.4	244 15.4	58.8	333 09.3	44.7	210 04.2	55.2	Venus	65 36.1	12 24
23	94 24.1	161 17.3	50.0	259 16.9	59.2	348 12.2	44.7	225 06.5	55.3	Mars	165 38.1	5 47
	h m									Jupiter	253 31.1	23 52
Mer.Pass. 16 47.4		v 4.1	d 0.3	v 1.5	d 0.4	v 2.8	d 0.0	v 2.3	d 0.0	Saturn	130 52.1	8 05

UT	SUN GHA	SUN Dec	MOON GHA	v	MOON Dec	d	HP
d h	° ′	° ′	° ′	′	° ′	′	′
7 00	178 29.2	S22 24.3	105 21.2	11.2	N 3 26.8	11.2	58.2
01	193 28.9	24.0	119 51.4	11.4	3 38.0	11.1	58.1
02	208 28.6	23.6	134 21.8	11.3	3 49.1	11.1	58.1
03	223 28.4	23.3	148 52.1	11.4	4 00.2	11.1	58.0
04	238 28.1	23.0	163 22.5	11.4	4 11.3	11.0	58.0
05	253 27.8	22.7	177 52.9	11.4	4 22.3	11.0	58.0
06	268 27.6	S22 22.4	192 23.3	11.5	N 4 33.3	11.0	57.9
07	283 27.3	22.1	206 53.8	11.4	4 44.3	10.9	57.9
T 08	298 27.0	21.7	221 24.2	11.6	4 55.2	10.8	57.9
U 09	313 26.7	21.4	235 54.8	11.5	5 06.0	10.9	57.8
E 10	328 26.5	21.1	250 25.3	11.5	5 16.9	10.8	57.8
S 11	343 26.2	20.8	264 55.8	11.6	5 27.7	10.7	57.7
D 12	358 25.9	S22 20.5	279 26.4	11.6	N 5 38.4	10.7	57.7
A 13	13 25.7	20.1	293 57.0	11.6	5 49.1	10.7	57.7
Y 14	28 25.4	19.8	308 27.6	11.7	5 59.8	10.6	57.6
15	43 25.1	19.5	322 58.3	11.6	6 10.4	10.5	57.6
16	58 24.9	19.2	337 28.9	11.7	6 20.9	10.6	57.6
17	73 24.6	18.8	351 59.6	11.7	6 31.5	10.4	57.5
18	88 24.3	S22 18.5	6 30.3	11.7	N 6 41.9	10.5	57.5
19	103 24.1	18.2	21 01.0	11.8	6 52.4	10.3	57.4
20	118 23.8	17.9	35 31.8	11.7	7 02.7	10.4	57.4
21	133 23.5	17.5	50 02.5	11.8	7 13.1	10.3	57.4
22	148 23.3	17.2	64 33.3	11.8	7 23.4	10.2	57.3
23	163 23.0	16.9	79 04.1	11.8	7 33.6	10.2	57.3
8 00	178 22.7	S22 16.5	93 34.9	11.8	N 7 43.8	10.1	57.3
01	193 22.5	16.2	108 05.7	11.8	7 53.9	10.1	57.2
02	208 22.2	15.9	122 36.5	11.9	8 04.0	10.0	57.2
03	223 21.9	15.5	137 07.4	11.8	8 14.0	10.0	57.2
04	238 21.7	15.2	151 38.2	11.9	8 24.0	9.9	57.1
05	253 21.4	14.9	166 09.1	11.9	8 33.9	9.8	57.1
06	268 21.1	S22 14.5	180 40.0	11.9	N 8 43.7	9.8	57.0
W 07	283 20.9	14.2	195 10.9	11.9	8 53.5	9.8	57.0
E 08	298 20.6	13.9	209 41.8	11.9	9 03.3	9.7	57.0
D 09	313 20.4	13.5	224 12.7	11.9	9 13.0	9.6	56.9
N 10	328 20.1	13.2	238 43.6	11.9	9 22.6	9.6	56.9
E 11	343 19.8	12.8	253 14.5	12.0	9 32.2	9.5	56.9
S 12	358 19.6	S22 12.5	267 45.5	11.9	N 9 41.7	9.5	56.8
D 13	13 19.3	12.2	282 16.4	12.0	9 51.2	9.4	56.8
A 14	28 19.0	11.8	296 47.4	11.9	10 00.6	9.3	56.8
Y 15	43 18.8	11.5	311 18.3	12.0	10 09.9	9.3	56.7
16	58 18.5	11.1	325 49.3	12.0	10 19.2	9.2	56.7
17	73 18.2	10.8	340 20.3	11.9	10 28.4	9.1	56.7
18	88 18.0	S22 10.4	354 51.2	12.0	N10 37.5	9.1	56.6
19	103 17.7	10.1	9 22.2	12.0	10 46.6	9.1	56.6
20	118 17.5	09.8	23 53.2	12.0	10 55.7	8.9	56.6
21	133 17.2	09.4	38 24.2	12.0	11 04.6	8.9	56.5
22	148 16.9	09.1	52 55.2	12.0	11 13.5	8.9	56.5
23	163 16.7	08.7	67 26.2	12.0	11 22.4	8.7	56.5
9 00	178 16.4	S22 08.4	81 57.2	12.0	N11 31.1	8.7	56.4
01	193 16.2	08.0	96 28.2	12.0	11 39.8	8.7	56.4
02	208 15.9	07.7	110 59.2	12.0	11 48.5	8.5	56.4
03	223 15.6	07.3	125 30.2	12.0	11 57.0	8.5	56.4
04	238 15.4	07.0	140 01.2	12.0	12 05.5	8.5	56.3
05	253 15.1	06.6	154 32.2	12.0	12 14.0	8.3	56.3
06	268 14.9	S22 06.3	169 03.2	12.0	N12 22.3	8.3	56.3
07	283 14.6	05.9	183 34.2	12.0	12 30.6	8.3	56.2
T 08	298 14.3	05.5	198 05.2	12.0	12 38.9	8.1	56.2
H 09	313 14.1	05.2	212 36.2	12.0	12 47.0	8.1	56.2
U 10	328 13.8	04.8	227 07.2	12.0	12 55.1	8.0	56.1
R 11	343 13.6	04.5	241 38.2	12.0	13 03.1	8.0	56.1
S 12	358 13.3	S22 04.1	256 09.2	12.0	N13 11.1	7.9	56.1
D 13	13 13.1	03.8	270 40.2	11.9	13 19.0	7.8	56.1
A 14	28 12.8	03.4	285 11.1	12.0	13 26.8	7.7	56.0
Y 15	43 12.5	03.0	299 42.1	12.0	13 34.5	7.6	56.0
16	58 12.3	02.7	314 13.1	12.0	13 42.1	7.6	56.0
17	73 12.0	02.3	328 44.1	12.0	13 49.7	7.5	55.9
18	88 11.8	S22 01.9	343 15.1	11.9	N13 57.2	7.5	55.9
19	103 11.5	01.6	357 46.0	12.0	14 04.7	7.3	55.9
20	118 11.3	01.2	12 17.0	12.0	14 12.0	7.3	55.9
21	133 11.0	00.9	26 48.0	11.9	14 19.3	7.2	55.8
22	148 10.8	00.5	41 18.9	12.0	14 26.5	7.1	55.8
23	163 10.5	00.1	55 49.9	11.9	N14 33.6	7.1	55.8
	SD 16.3	d 0.3	SD 15.7		15.5		15.3

Lat.	Twilight Naut.	Twilight Civil	Sunrise	Moonrise 7	Moonrise 8	Moonrise 9	Moonrise 10
°	h m	h m	h m	h m	h m	h m	h m
N 72	08 15	10 19	■■	10 14	10 05	09 54	09 39
N 70	07 58	09 36	■■	10 21	10 19	10 17	10 16
68	07 44	09 08	11 09	10 27	10 30	10 35	10 42
66	07 32	08 46	10 13	10 32	10 40	10 49	11 02
64	07 23	08 29	09 40	10 36	10 48	11 01	11 19
62	07 14	08 14	09 16	10 40	10 54	11 11	11 32
60	07 07	08 02	08 57	10 43	11 00	11 20	11 44
N 58	07 00	07 51	08 41	10 46	11 06	11 28	11 54
56	06 54	07 42	08 28	10 48	11 10	11 35	12 02
54	06 48	07 34	08 16	10 51	11 15	11 41	12 10
52	06 43	07 26	08 06	10 53	11 19	11 46	12 17
50	06 38	07 19	07 57	10 55	11 22	11 51	12 23
45	06 28	07 04	07 38	10 59	11 30	12 02	12 37
N 40	06 18	06 52	07 22	11 03	11 36	12 11	12 48
35	06 09	06 41	07 09	11 06	11 42	12 19	12 58
30	06 01	06 31	06 57	11 08	11 47	12 26	13 06
20	05 46	06 13	06 37	11 13	11 55	12 37	13 21
N 10	05 31	05 57	06 19	11 17	12 03	12 48	13 34
0	05 15	05 41	06 03	11 22	12 10	12 58	13 46
S 10	04 57	05 24	05 46	11 26	12 17	13 08	13 58
20	04 35	05 04	05 28	11 30	12 25	13 18	14 11
30	04 08	04 41	05 08	11 35	12 33	13 30	14 26
35	03 50	04 26	04 55	11 38	12 39	13 38	14 35
40	03 28	04 09	04 41	11 41	12 44	13 46	14 44
45	03 00	03 48	04 24	11 45	12 51	13 55	14 56
S 50	02 19	03 20	04 03	11 50	12 59	14 07	15 10
52	01 56	03 06	03 53	11 52	13 03	14 12	15 17
54	01 22	02 50	03 42	11 54	13 07	14 18	15 24
56	////	02 31	03 29	11 57	13 12	14 24	15 33
58	////	02 05	03 14	12 00	13 17	14 32	15 42
S 60	////	01 30	02 55	12 03	13 23	14 40	15 53

Lat.	Sunset	Twilight Civil	Twilight Naut.	Moonset 7	Moonset 8	Moonset 9	Moonset 10
°	h m	h m	h m	h m	h m	h m	h m
N 72	■■	13 55	15 59	25 29	01 29	03 20	05 15
N 70		14 38	16 16	25 17	01 17	02 58	04 39
68	13 05	15 06	16 30	25 07	01 07	02 42	04 14
66	14 01	15 28	16 41	24 59	00 59	02 28	03 54
64	14 34	15 45	16 51	24 52	00 52	02 17	03 39
62	14 58	16 00	17 00	24 46	00 46	02 08	03 26
60	15 17	16 12	17 07	24 41	00 41	02 00	03 15
N 58	15 33	16 22	17 14	24 37	00 37	01 53	03 05
56	15 46	16 32	17 20	24 33	00 33	01 47	02 57
54	15 57	16 40	17 26	24 29	00 29	01 41	02 50
52	16 08	16 48	17 31	24 26	00 26	01 36	02 43
50	16 17	16 54	17 35	24 23	00 23	01 32	02 37
45	16 36	17 09	17 46	24 17	00 17	01 22	02 25
N 40	16 52	17 22	17 56	24 12	00 12	01 14	02 14
35	17 05	17 33	18 04	24 07	00 07	01 07	02 05
30	17 17	17 43	18 12	24 03	00 03	01 01	01 57
20	17 37	18 00	18 28	23 56	24 51	00 51	01 44
N 10	17 54	18 17	18 43	23 50	24 41	00 41	01 32
0	18 10	18 33	18 59	23 45	24 33	00 33	01 21
S 10	18 27	18 50	19 17	23 39	24 24	00 24	01 10
20	18 45	19 09	19 38	23 33	24 15	00 15	00 58
30	19 06	19 33	20 05	23 26	24 05	00 05	00 45
35	19 18	19 47	20 23	23 22	23 59	24 37	00 37
40	19 32	20 04	20 44	23 18	23 52	24 28	00 28
45	19 49	20 25	21 13	23 13	23 44	24 18	00 18
S 50	20 09	20 52	21 53	23 07	23 35	24 05	00 05
52	20 19	21 06	22 16	23 04	23 30	23 59	24 32
54	20 31	21 22	22 48	23 01	23 26	23 53	24 25
56	20 44	21 41	////	22 57	23 20	23 46	24 16
58	20 59	22 06	////	22 54	23 14	23 38	24 06
S 60	21 17	22 41	////	22 49	23 08	23 29	23 55

	SUN			MOON			
Day	Eqn. of Time 00h	Eqn. of Time 12h	Mer. Pass.	Mer. Pass. Upper	Mer. Pass. Lower	Age	Phase
d	m s	m s	h m	h m	h m	d	%
7	06 03	06 16	12 06	17 33	05 09	06	43
8	06 29	06 41	12 07	18 21	05 57	07	54
9	06 54	07 06	12 07	19 09	06 45	08	64

UT (d h)	ARIES GHA	VENUS −4.4 GHA	VENUS Dec	MARS +0.7 GHA	MARS Dec	JUPITER −2.7 GHA	JUPITER Dec	SATURN +0.6 GHA	SATURN Dec
10 00	109 26.5	176 21.4	S16 49.7	274 18.4	S 3 59.6	3 15.0	N22 44.8	240 08.7	S15 55.3
01	124 29.0	191 25.5	49.4	289 20.0	3 59.9	18 17.8	44.8	255 11.0	55.4
02	139 31.4	206 29.6	49.1	304 21.5	4 00.3	33 20.6	44.9	270 13.2	55.4
03	154 33.9	221 33.7	.. 48.8	319 23.0	.. 00.7	48 23.5	.. 44.9	285 15.5	.. 55.5
04	169 36.4	236 37.9	48.5	334 24.5	01.0	63 26.3	44.9	300 17.8	55.5
05	184 38.8	251 42.0	48.2	349 26.0	01.4	78 29.1	45.0	315 20.0	55.5
06	199 41.3	266 46.1	S16 47.8	4 27.5	S 4 01.7	93 31.9	N22 45.0	330 22.3	S15 55.6
07	214 43.8	281 50.2	47.5	19 29.0	02.1	108 34.8	45.1	345 24.6	55.6
08	229 46.2	296 54.4	47.2	34 30.6	02.5	123 37.6	45.1	0 26.8	55.7
F 09	244 48.7	311 58.5	.. 46.9	49 32.1	.. 02.8	138 40.4	.. 45.2	15 29.1	.. 55.7
R 10	259 51.2	327 02.6	46.6	64 33.6	03.2	153 43.2	45.2	30 31.3	55.8
I 11	274 53.6	342 06.7	46.3	79 35.1	03.6	168 46.1	45.2	45 33.6	55.8
D 12	289 56.1	357 10.8	S16 46.0	94 36.6	S 4 03.9	183 48.9	N22 45.3	60 35.9	S15 55.9
A 13	304 58.5	12 15.0	45.7	109 38.1	04.3	198 51.7	45.3	75 38.1	55.9
Y 14	320 01.0	27 19.1	45.4	124 39.7	04.6	213 54.5	45.4	90 40.4	56.0
15	335 03.5	42 23.2	.. 45.1	139 41.2	.. 05.0	228 57.4	.. 45.4	105 42.7	.. 56.0
16	350 05.9	57 27.3	44.8	154 42.7	05.4	244 00.2	45.4	120 44.9	56.0
17	5 08.4	72 31.5	44.5	169 44.2	05.7	259 03.0	45.5	135 47.2	56.1
18	20 10.9	87 35.6	S16 44.2	184 45.7	S 4 06.1	274 05.8	N22 45.5	150 49.4	S15 56.1
19	35 13.3	102 39.7	43.8	199 47.3	06.4	289 08.6	45.6	165 51.7	56.2
20	50 15.8	117 43.8	43.5	214 48.8	06.8	304 11.5	45.6	180 54.0	56.2
21	65 18.3	132 47.9	.. 43.2	229 50.3	.. 07.2	319 14.3	.. 45.7	195 56.2	.. 56.3
22	80 20.7	147 52.1	42.9	244 51.8	07.5	334 17.1	45.7	210 58.5	56.3
23	95 23.2	162 56.2	42.6	259 53.3	07.9	349 19.9	45.7	226 00.8	56.4
11 00	110 25.7	178 00.3	S16 42.3	274 54.9	S 4 08.2	4 22.8	N22 45.8	241 03.0	S15 56.4
01	125 28.1	193 04.4	42.0	289 56.4	08.6	19 25.6	45.8	256 05.3	56.5
02	140 30.6	208 08.6	41.7	304 57.9	09.0	34 28.4	45.9	271 07.6	56.5
03	155 33.0	223 12.7	.. 41.4	319 59.4	.. 09.3	49 31.2	.. 45.9	286 09.8	.. 56.5
04	170 35.5	238 16.8	41.2	335 00.9	09.7	64 34.1	46.0	301 12.1	56.6
05	185 38.0	253 20.9	40.9	350 02.5	10.0	79 36.9	46.0	316 14.3	56.6
06	200 40.4	268 25.0	S16 40.6	5 04.0	S 4 10.4	94 39.7	N22 46.0	331 16.6	S15 56.7
07	215 42.9	283 29.2	40.3	20 05.5	10.7	109 42.5	46.1	346 18.9	56.7
S 08	230 45.4	298 33.3	40.0	35 07.0	11.1	124 45.4	46.1	1 21.1	56.8
A 09	245 47.8	313 37.4	.. 39.7	50 08.6	.. 11.5	139 48.2	.. 46.2	16 23.4	.. 56.8
T 10	260 50.3	328 41.5	39.4	65 10.1	11.8	154 51.0	46.2	31 25.7	56.9
U 11	275 52.8	343 45.7	39.1	80 11.6	12.2	169 53.8	46.3	46 27.9	56.9
R 12	290 55.2	358 49.8	S16 38.8	95 13.2	S 4 12.5	184 56.7	N22 46.3	61 30.2	S15 57.0
D 13	305 57.7	13 53.9	38.5	110 14.7	12.9	199 59.5	46.3	76 32.5	57.0
A 14	321 00.2	28 58.0	38.2	125 16.2	13.2	215 02.3	46.4	91 34.7	57.0
Y 15	336 02.6	44 02.1	.. 37.9	140 17.7	.. 13.6	230 05.1	.. 46.4	106 37.0	.. 57.1
16	351 05.1	59 06.3	37.6	155 19.3	14.0	245 07.9	46.5	121 39.3	57.1
17	6 07.5	74 10.4	37.4	170 20.8	14.3	260 10.8	46.5	136 41.5	57.2
18	21 10.0	89 14.5	S16 37.1	185 22.3	S 4 14.7	275 13.6	N22 46.5	151 43.8	S15 57.2
19	36 12.5	104 18.6	36.8	200 23.9	15.0	290 16.4	46.6	166 46.1	57.3
20	51 14.9	119 22.7	36.5	215 25.4	15.4	305 19.2	46.6	181 48.3	57.3
21	66 17.4	134 26.9	.. 36.2	230 26.9	.. 15.7	320 22.1	.. 46.7	196 50.6	.. 57.3
22	81 19.9	149 31.0	35.9	245 28.4	16.1	335 24.9	46.7	211 52.9	57.4
23	96 22.3	164 35.1	35.6	260 30.0	16.4	350 27.7	46.8	226 55.1	57.4
12 00	111 24.8	179 39.2	S16 35.3	275 31.5	S 4 16.8	5 30.5	N22 46.8	241 57.4	S15 57.5
01	126 27.3	194 43.3	35.1	290 33.0	17.1	20 33.3	46.8	256 59.7	57.5
02	141 29.7	209 47.4	34.8	305 34.6	17.5	35 36.2	46.9	272 01.9	57.6
03	156 32.2	224 51.5	.. 34.5	320 36.1	.. 17.9	50 39.0	.. 46.9	287 04.2	.. 57.6
04	171 34.7	239 55.7	34.2	335 37.6	18.2	65 41.8	47.0	302 06.5	57.6
05	186 37.1	254 59.8	33.9	350 39.2	18.6	80 44.6	47.0	317 08.7	57.7
06	201 39.6	270 03.9	S16 33.7	5 40.7	S 4 18.9	95 47.5	N22 47.0	332 11.0	S15 57.7
07	216 42.0	285 08.0	33.4	20 42.2	19.3	110 50.3	47.1	347 13.3	57.8
08	231 44.5	300 12.1	33.1	35 43.8	19.6	125 53.1	47.1	2 15.5	57.8
S 09	246 47.0	315 16.2	.. 32.8	50 45.3	.. 20.0	140 55.9	.. 47.2	17 17.8	.. 57.9
U 10	261 49.4	330 20.3	32.6	65 46.9	20.3	155 58.7	47.2	32 20.1	57.9
N 11	276 51.9	345 24.4	32.3	80 48.4	20.7	171 01.6	47.3	47 22.3	58.0
D 12	291 54.4	0 28.6	S16 32.0	95 49.9	S 4 21.0	186 04.4	N22 47.3	62 24.6	S15 58.0
A 13	306 56.8	15 32.7	31.7	110 51.5	21.4	201 07.2	47.3	77 26.9	58.0
Y 14	321 59.3	30 36.8	31.5	125 53.0	21.7	216 10.0	47.4	92 29.2	58.1
15	337 01.8	45 40.9	.. 31.2	140 54.5	.. 22.1	231 12.8	.. 47.4	107 31.4	.. 58.1
16	352 04.2	60 45.0	30.9	155 56.1	22.4	246 15.7	47.5	122 33.7	58.2
17	7 06.7	75 49.1	30.7	170 57.6	22.8	261 18.5	47.5	137 36.0	58.2
18	22 09.2	90 53.2	S16 30.4	185 59.2	S 4 23.1	276 21.3	N22 47.5	152 38.2	S15 58.3
19	37 11.6	105 57.3	30.1	201 00.7	23.5	291 24.1	47.6	167 40.5	58.3
20	52 14.1	121 01.4	29.8	216 02.2	23.8	306 27.0	47.6	182 42.8	58.3
21	67 16.5	136 05.5	.. 29.6	231 03.8	.. 24.2	321 29.8	.. 47.7	197 45.0	.. 58.4
22	82 19.0	151 09.6	29.3	246 05.3	24.5	336 32.6	47.7	212 47.3	58.4
23	97 21.5	166 13.7	29.0	261 06.9	24.9	351 35.4	47.8	227 49.6	58.5
Mer. Pass.	16 35.6	v 4.1	d 0.3	v 1.5	d 0.4	v 2.8	d 0.0	v 2.3	d 0.0

STARS

Name	SHA	Dec
Acamar	315 17.9	S40 15.2
Achernar	335 26.5	S57 10.3
Acrux	173 08.5	S63 10.4
Adhara	255 11.8	S28 59.7
Aldebaran	290 48.6	N16 32.1
Alioth	166 20.4	N55 52.7
Alkaid	152 58.7	N49 14.3
Al Na'ir	27 43.6	S46 53.6
Alnilam	275 45.6	S 1 11.8
Alphard	217 55.4	S 8 43.4
Alphecca	126 10.9	N26 40.0
Alpheratz	357 43.1	N29 10.3
Altair	62 08.2	N 8 54.5
Ankaa	353 15.4	S42 14.0
Antares	112 26.0	S26 27.6
Arcturus	145 55.5	N19 06.5
Atria	107 27.9	S69 02.8
Avior	234 17.1	S59 33.4
Bellatrix	278 31.3	N 6 21.5
Betelgeuse	271 00.5	N 7 24.3
Canopus	263 55.4	S52 42.5
Capella	280 33.4	N46 00.6
Deneb	49 31.6	N45 20.1
Denebola	182 33.1	N14 29.4
Diphda	348 55.5	S17 54.7
Dubhe	193 50.9	N61 40.1
Elnath	278 11.7	N28 37.0
Eltanin	90 46.5	N51 29.3
Enif	33 47.0	N 9 56.5
Fomalhaut	15 23.8	S29 32.9
Gacrux	172 00.2	S57 11.3
Gienah	175 51.8	S17 37.2
Hadar	148 47.3	S60 26.1
Hamal	328 00.2	N23 31.8
Kaus Aust.	83 43.7	S34 22.5
Kochab	137 20.7	N74 05.6
Markab	13 38.1	N15 17.0
Menkar	314 14.5	N 4 08.6
Menkent	148 07.1	S36 26.1
Miaplacidus	221 38.6	S69 46.5
Mirfak	308 39.4	N49 54.7
Nunki	75 58.2	S26 16.6
Peacock	53 19.2	S56 41.3
Pollux	243 26.9	N27 59.3
Procyon	244 59.0	N 5 11.1
Rasalhague	96 06.4	N12 33.1
Regulus	207 42.8	N11 53.7
Rigel	281 11.4	S 8 11.4
Rigil Kent.	139 51.3	S60 53.2
Sabik	102 12.4	S15 44.4
Schedar	349 40.0	N56 37.1
Shaula	96 21.7	S37 06.6
Sirius	258 33.0	S16 44.4
Spica	158 30.8	S11 14.0
Suhail	222 51.7	S43 29.5
Vega	80 39.1	N38 47.9
Zuben'ubi	137 05.1	S16 05.9

	SHA	Mer. Pass.
Venus	67 34.7	12 05
Mars	164 29.2	5 40
Jupiter	253 57.1	23 38
Saturn	130 37.4	7 55

UT	SUN GHA	SUN Dec	MOON GHA	v	MOON Dec	d	HP
d h	° ′	° ′	° ′	′	° ′	′	′
10 00	178 10.2	S21 59.8	70 20.8	12.0	N14 40.7	7.0	55.7
01	193 10.0	59.4	84 51.8	11.9	14 47.7	6.9	55.7
02	208 09.7	59.0	99 22.7	11.9	14 54.6	6.8	55.7
03	223 09.5	.. 58.7	113 53.6	12.0	15 01.4	6.7	55.7
04	238 09.2	58.3	128 24.6	11.9	15 08.1	6.7	55.6
05	253 09.0	57.9	142 55.5	11.9	15 14.8	6.6	55.6
06	268 08.7	S21 57.5	157 26.4	11.9	N15 21.4	6.5	55.6
07	283 08.5	57.2	171 57.3	11.9	15 27.9	6.4	55.6
08	298 08.2	56.8	186 28.2	11.9	15 34.3	6.4	55.5
F 09	313 08.0	.. 56.4	200 59.1	11.9	15 40.7	6.2	55.5
R 10	328 07.7	56.0	215 30.0	11.9	15 46.9	6.2	55.5
I 11	343 07.5	55.7	230 00.9	11.9	15 53.1	6.1	55.5
D 12	358 07.2	S21 55.3	244 31.8	11.8	N15 59.2	6.1	55.4
A 13	13 07.0	54.9	259 02.6	11.9	16 05.3	5.9	55.4
Y 14	28 06.7	54.5	273 33.5	11.9	16 11.2	5.9	55.4
15	43 06.5	.. 54.2	288 04.4	11.8	16 17.1	5.7	55.4
16	58 06.2	53.8	302 35.2	11.9	16 22.8	5.7	55.3
17	73 06.0	53.4	317 06.1	11.8	16 28.5	5.6	55.3
18	88 05.7	S21 53.0	331 36.9	11.8	N16 34.1	5.6	55.3
19	103 05.5	52.6	346 07.7	11.8	16 39.7	5.4	55.3
20	118 05.2	52.3	0 38.5	11.9	16 45.1	5.4	55.2
21	133 05.0	.. 51.9	15 09.4	11.8	16 50.5	5.3	55.2
22	148 04.7	51.5	29 40.2	11.8	16 55.8	5.1	55.2
23	163 04.5	51.1	44 11.0	11.8	17 00.9	5.2	55.2
11 00	178 04.2	S21 50.7	58 41.8	11.8	N17 06.1	5.0	55.2
01	193 04.0	50.3	73 12.6	11.8	17 11.1	4.9	55.1
02	208 03.7	50.0	87 43.4	11.7	17 16.0	4.9	55.1
03	223 03.5	.. 49.6	102 14.1	11.8	17 20.9	4.7	55.1
04	238 03.2	49.2	116 44.9	11.8	17 25.6	4.7	55.1
05	253 03.0	48.8	131 15.7	11.7	17 30.3	4.6	55.1
06	268 02.7	S21 48.4	145 46.4	11.8	N17 34.9	4.5	55.0
07	283 02.5	48.0	160 17.2	11.7	17 39.4	4.4	55.0
S 08	298 02.2	47.6	174 47.9	11.8	17 43.8	4.3	55.0
A 09	313 02.0	.. 47.2	189 18.7	11.7	17 48.1	4.3	55.0
T 10	328 01.7	46.8	203 49.4	11.8	17 52.4	4.1	55.0
U 11	343 01.5	46.4	218 20.2	11.7	17 56.5	4.1	54.9
R 12	358 01.3	S21 46.1	232 50.9	11.7	N18 00.6	4.0	54.9
D 13	13 01.0	45.7	247 21.6	11.7	18 04.6	3.9	54.9
A 14	28 00.8	45.3	261 52.3	11.7	18 08.5	3.8	54.9
Y 15	43 00.5	.. 44.9	276 23.0	11.7	18 12.3	3.7	54.9
16	58 00.3	44.5	290 53.7	11.8	18 16.0	3.6	54.8
17	73 00.0	44.1	305 24.5	11.7	18 19.6	3.5	54.8
18	87 59.8	S21 43.7	319 55.2	11.7	N18 23.1	3.5	54.8
19	102 59.5	43.3	334 25.9	11.6	18 26.6	3.3	54.8
20	117 59.3	42.9	348 56.5	11.7	18 29.9	3.3	54.8
21	132 59.1	.. 42.5	3 27.2	11.7	18 33.2	3.2	54.8
22	147 58.8	42.1	17 57.9	11.7	18 36.4	3.0	54.7
23	162 58.6	41.7	32 28.6	11.7	18 39.4	3.0	54.7
12 00	177 58.3	S21 41.3	46 59.3	11.7	N18 42.4	2.9	54.7
01	192 58.1	40.9	61 30.0	11.7	18 45.3	2.8	54.7
02	207 57.9	40.5	76 00.7	11.6	18 48.1	2.8	54.7
03	222 57.6	.. 40.1	90 31.3	11.7	18 50.9	2.6	54.7
04	237 57.4	39.7	105 02.0	11.7	18 53.5	2.5	54.6
05	252 57.1	39.2	119 32.7	11.7	18 56.0	2.5	54.6
06	267 56.9	S21 38.8	134 03.4	11.7	N18 58.5	2.3	54.6
07	282 56.7	38.4	148 34.1	11.6	19 00.8	2.3	54.6
08	297 56.4	38.0	163 04.7	11.7	19 03.1	2.2	54.6
S 09	312 56.2	.. 37.6	177 35.4	11.7	19 05.3	2.1	54.6
U 10	327 55.9	37.2	192 06.1	11.7	19 07.4	2.0	54.5
N 11	342 55.7	36.8	206 36.8	11.6	19 09.4	1.9	54.5
D 12	357 55.5	S21 36.4	221 07.4	11.7	N19 11.3	1.8	54.5
A 13	12 55.2	36.0	235 38.1	11.7	19 13.1	1.7	54.5
Y 14	27 55.0	35.6	250 08.8	11.7	19 14.8	1.6	54.5
15	42 54.7	.. 35.1	264 39.5	11.7	19 16.4	1.5	54.5
16	57 54.5	34.7	279 10.2	11.7	19 17.9	1.5	54.5
17	72 54.3	34.3	293 40.9	11.7	19 19.4	1.3	54.4
18	87 54.0	S21 33.9	308 11.6	11.7	N19 20.7	1.3	54.4
19	102 53.8	33.5	322 42.3	11.7	19 22.0	1.1	54.4
20	117 53.6	33.1	337 13.0	11.7	19 23.1	1.1	54.4
21	132 53.3	.. 32.6	351 43.7	11.7	19 24.2	1.0	54.4
22	147 53.1	32.2	6 14.4	11.7	19 25.2	0.9	54.4
23	162 52.8	31.8	20 45.1	11.7	N19 26.1	0.8	54.4
SD	16.3	d 0.4	SD 15.1		15.0		14.9

Moonrise

Lat.	Twilight Naut.	Twilight Civil	Sunrise	Moonrise 10	11	12	13
°	h m	h m	h m	h m	h m	h m	h m
N 72	08 09	10 08	■■■	09 39	09 06	▭	▭
N 70	07 53	09 29	■■■	10 16	10 18	10 26	10 59
68	07 40	09 02	10 53	10 42	10 55	11 19	12 00
66	07 29	08 41	10 05	11 02	11 22	11 51	12 34
64	07 20	08 25	09 34	11 19	11 42	12 15	13 00
62	07 12	08 11	09 12	11 32	11 59	12 34	13 19
60	07 05	07 59	08 53	11 44	12 13	12 50	13 35
N 58	06 58	07 49	08 38	11 54	12 25	13 03	13 49
56	06 52	07 40	08 25	12 02	12 35	13 14	14 01
54	06 47	07 32	08 14	12 10	12 44	13 24	14 11
52	06 42	07 25	08 04	12 17	12 52	13 33	14 20
50	06 37	07 18	07 55	12 23	13 00	13 41	14 28
45	06 27	07 04	07 37	12 37	13 15	13 58	14 45
N 40	06 18	06 51	07 21	12 48	13 28	14 12	15 00
35	06 09	06 41	07 08	12 58	13 39	14 24	15 12
30	06 01	06 31	06 57	13 06	13 49	14 34	15 22
20	05 47	06 14	06 37	13 21	14 06	14 52	15 40
N 10	05 32	05 58	06 20	13 34	14 20	15 08	15 56
0	05 16	05 42	06 04	13 46	14 34	15 22	16 11
S 10	04 58	05 25	05 48	13 58	14 48	15 37	16 26
20	04 37	05 06	05 30	14 11	15 02	15 53	16 41
30	04 10	04 43	05 10	14 26	15 19	16 11	17 00
35	03 53	04 29	04 58	14 35	15 29	16 21	17 10
40	03 32	04 12	04 44	14 44	15 41	16 33	17 22
45	03 04	03 52	04 28	14 56	15 54	16 48	17 36
S 50	02 25	03 25	04 07	15 10	16 10	17 05	17 54
52	02 03	03 12	03 58	15 17	16 18	17 13	18 02
54	01 32	02 56	03 47	15 24	16 26	17 22	18 11
56	00 31	02 37	03 34	15 33	16 36	17 33	18 22
58	////	02 13	03 19	15 42	16 47	17 44	18 33
S 60	////	01 41	03 02	15 53	16 59	17 58	18 47

Moonset

Lat.	Sunset	Twilight Civil	Twilight Naut.	Moonset 10	11	12	13
°	h m	h m	h m	h m	h m	h m	h m
N 72	■■■	14 09	16 07	05 15	07 29	▭	▭
N 70	■■■	14 48	16 23	04 39	06 18	07 50	08 58
68	13 24	15 14	16 36	04 14	05 41	06 58	07 57
66	14 12	15 35	16 47	03 54	05 15	06 26	07 22
64	14 42	15 51	16 57	03 39	04 55	06 02	06 57
62	15 05	16 05	17 05	03 26	04 38	05 43	06 38
60	15 23	16 17	17 12	03 15	04 25	05 28	06 21
N 58	15 38	16 27	17 18	03 05	04 13	05 15	06 08
56	15 51	16 36	17 24	02 57	04 03	05 03	05 56
54	16 02	16 44	17 29	02 50	03 54	04 53	05 46
52	16 12	16 52	17 34	02 43	03 46	04 45	05 37
50	16 21	16 58	17 39	02 37	03 39	04 37	05 29
45	16 40	17 13	17 49	02 25	03 24	04 20	05 11
N 40	16 55	17 25	17 58	02 14	03 12	04 06	04 57
35	17 08	17 35	18 07	02 05	03 01	03 55	04 45
30	17 19	17 45	18 15	01 57	02 52	03 44	04 35
20	17 38	18 02	18 29	01 44	02 36	03 27	04 16
N 10	17 56	18 18	18 44	01 32	02 22	03 12	04 01
0	18 12	18 34	19 00	01 21	02 09	02 57	03 46
S 10	18 28	18 51	19 17	01 10	01 56	02 43	03 31
20	18 45	19 09	19 38	00 58	01 42	02 28	03 15
30	19 05	19 32	20 05	00 45	01 26	02 10	02 57
35	19 17	19 46	20 22	00 37	01 17	02 00	02 47
40	19 31	20 03	20 43	00 28	01 07	01 49	02 34
45	19 47	20 24	21 10	00 18	00 54	01 35	02 20
S 50	20 08	20 50	21 49	00 05	00 39	01 18	02 03
52	20 17	21 03	22 11	24 32	00 32	01 11	01 54
54	20 28	21 19	22 41	24 16	00 16	01 02	01 45
56	20 41	21 37	23 35	24 06	00 06	00 52	01 35
58	20 55	22 01	////	24 06	00 06	00 41	01 23
S 60	21 13	22 32	////	23 55	24 28	00 28	01 09

	SUN		MOON			
Day	Eqn. of Time 00h	Eqn. of Time 12h	Mer. Pass.	Mer. Pass. Upper	Lower	Age	Phase
d	m s	m s	h m	h m	h m	d	%
10	07 19	07 31	12 08	19 57	07 33	09	73
11	07 43	07 54	12 08	20 46	08 22	10	81
12	08 06	08 18	12 08	21 34	09 10	11	88

UT	ARIES GHA	VENUS −4.3 GHA	Dec	MARS +0.6 GHA	Dec	JUPITER −2.7 GHA	Dec	SATURN +0.6 GHA	Dec
13 00	112 23.9	181 17.8	S16 28.8	276 08.4	S 4 25.2	6 38.2	N22 47.8	242 51.8	S15 58.5
01	127 26.4	196 21.9	28.5	291 10.0	25.6	21 41.1	47.8	257 54.1	58.6
02	142 28.9	211 26.0	28.3	306 11.5	25.9	36 43.9	47.9	272 56.4	58.6
03	157 31.3	226 30.1	.. 28.0	321 13.0	.. 26.3	51 46.7	.. 47.9	287 58.7	.. 58.6
04	172 33.8	241 34.2	27.7	336 14.6	26.6	66 49.5	48.0	303 00.9	58.7
05	187 36.3	256 38.3	27.5	351 16.1	27.0	81 52.3	48.0	318 03.2	58.7
M 06	202 38.7	271 42.4	S16 27.2	6 17.7	S 4 27.3	96 55.2	N22 48.0	333 05.5	S15 58.8
O 07	217 41.2	286 46.5	26.9	21 19.2	27.6	111 58.0	48.1	348 07.7	58.8
N 08	232 43.6	301 50.6	26.7	36 20.8	28.0	127 00.8	48.1	3 10.0	58.9
D 09	247 46.1	316 54.7	.. 26.4	51 22.3	.. 28.3	142 03.6	.. 48.2	18 12.3	.. 58.9
A 10	262 48.6	331 58.7	26.2	66 23.9	28.7	157 06.4	48.2	33 14.6	58.9
Y 11	277 51.0	347 02.8	25.9	81 25.4	29.0	172 09.3	48.2	48 16.8	59.0
12	292 53.5	2 06.9	S16 25.7	96 27.0	S 4 29.4	187 12.1	N22 48.3	63 19.1	S15 59.0
13	307 56.0	17 11.0	25.4	111 28.5	29.7	202 14.9	48.3	78 21.4	59.1
14	322 58.4	32 15.1	25.1	126 30.1	30.1	217 17.7	48.4	93 23.6	59.1
15	338 00.9	47 19.2	.. 24.9	141 31.6	.. 30.4	232 20.5	.. 48.4	108 25.9	.. 59.2
16	353 03.4	62 23.3	24.6	156 33.2	30.8	247 23.4	48.5	123 28.2	59.2
17	8 05.8	77 27.3	24.4	171 34.7	31.1	262 26.2	48.5	138 30.5	59.2
18	23 08.3	92 31.4	S16 24.1	186 36.3	S 4 31.4	277 29.0	N22 48.5	153 32.7	S15 59.3
19	38 10.8	107 35.5	23.9	201 37.8	31.8	292 31.8	48.6	168 35.0	59.3
20	53 13.2	122 39.6	23.6	216 39.4	32.1	307 34.6	48.6	183 37.3	59.4
21	68 15.7	137 43.7	.. 23.4	231 40.9	.. 32.5	322 37.4	.. 48.7	198 39.6	.. 59.4
22	83 18.1	152 47.7	23.1	246 42.5	32.8	337 40.3	48.7	213 41.8	59.4
23	98 20.6	167 51.8	22.9	261 44.0	33.2	352 43.1	48.7	228 44.1	59.5
14 00	113 23.1	182 55.9	S16 22.7	276 45.6	S 4 33.5	7 45.9	N22 48.8	243 46.4	S15 59.5
01	128 25.5	197 59.9	22.4	291 47.1	33.9	22 48.7	48.8	258 48.6	59.6
02	143 28.0	213 04.0	22.2	306 48.7	34.2	37 51.5	48.9	273 50.9	59.6
03	158 30.5	228 08.1	.. 21.9	321 50.2	.. 34.5	52 54.4	.. 48.9	288 53.2	.. 59.7
04	173 32.9	243 12.1	21.7	336 51.8	34.9	67 57.2	48.9	303 55.5	59.7
05	188 35.4	258 16.2	21.4	351 53.3	35.2	83 00.0	49.0	318 57.7	59.7
T 06	203 37.9	273 20.3	S16 21.2	6 54.9	S 4 35.6	98 02.8	N22 49.0	334 00.0	S15 59.8
U 07	218 40.3	288 24.3	21.0	21 56.4	35.9	113 05.6	49.1	349 02.3	59.8
E 08	233 42.8	303 28.4	20.7	36 58.0	36.2	128 08.4	49.1	4 04.6	59.9
S 09	248 45.3	318 32.5	.. 20.5	51 59.6	.. 36.6	143 11.3	.. 49.1	19 06.8	15 59.9
D 10	263 47.7	333 36.5	20.2	67 01.1	36.9	158 14.1	49.2	34 09.1	16 00.0
A 11	278 50.2	348 40.6	20.0	82 02.7	37.3	173 16.9	49.2	49 11.4	00.0
Y 12	293 52.6	3 44.6	S16 19.8	97 04.2	S 4 37.6	188 19.7	N22 49.3	64 13.7	S16 00.0
13	308 55.1	18 48.7	19.5	112 05.8	38.0	203 22.5	49.3	79 15.9	00.1
14	323 57.6	33 52.7	19.3	127 07.4	38.3	218 25.4	49.3	94 18.2	00.1
15	339 00.0	48 56.8	.. 19.1	142 08.9	.. 38.6	233 28.2	.. 49.4	109 20.5	.. 00.2
16	354 02.5	64 00.8	18.8	157 10.5	39.0	248 31.0	49.4	124 22.8	00.2
17	9 05.0	79 04.9	18.6	172 12.0	39.3	263 33.8	49.5	139 25.0	00.2
18	24 07.4	94 08.9	S16 18.4	187 13.6	S 4 39.6	278 36.6	N22 49.5	154 27.3	S16 00.3
19	39 09.9	109 12.9	18.1	202 15.2	40.0	293 39.4	49.6	169 29.6	00.3
20	54 12.4	124 17.0	17.9	217 16.7	40.3	308 42.3	49.6	184 31.9	00.4
21	69 14.8	139 21.0	.. 17.7	232 18.3	.. 40.7	323 45.1	.. 49.6	199 34.1	.. 00.4
22	84 17.3	154 25.1	17.5	247 19.8	41.0	338 47.9	49.7	214 36.4	00.4
23	99 19.8	169 29.1	17.2	262 21.4	41.3	353 50.7	49.7	229 38.7	00.5
15 00	114 22.2	184 33.1	S16 17.0	277 23.0	S 4 41.7	8 53.5	N22 49.8	244 41.0	S16 00.5
01	129 24.7	199 37.2	16.8	292 24.5	42.0	23 56.3	49.8	259 43.2	00.6
02	144 27.1	214 41.2	16.5	307 26.1	42.4	38 59.2	49.8	274 45.5	00.6
03	159 29.6	229 45.2	.. 16.3	322 27.7	.. 42.7	54 02.0	.. 49.9	289 47.8	.. 00.7
04	174 32.1	244 49.2	16.1	337 29.2	43.0	69 04.8	49.9	304 50.1	00.7
05	189 34.5	259 53.3	15.9	352 30.8	43.4	84 07.6	50.0	319 52.4	00.7
W 06	204 37.0	274 57.3	S16 15.7	7 32.4	S 4 43.7	99 10.4	N22 50.0	334 54.6	S16 00.8
E 07	219 39.5	290 01.3	15.4	22 33.9	44.0	114 13.2	50.0	349 56.9	00.8
D 08	234 41.9	305 05.3	15.2	37 35.5	44.4	129 16.0	50.1	4 59.2	00.9
N 09	249 44.4	320 09.3	.. 15.0	52 37.1	.. 44.7	144 18.9	.. 50.1	20 01.5	.. 00.9
E 10	264 46.9	335 13.3	14.8	67 38.6	45.0	159 21.7	50.2	35 03.7	00.9
S 11	279 49.3	350 17.4	14.6	82 40.2	45.4	174 24.5	50.2	50 06.0	01.0
D 12	294 51.8	5 21.4	S16 14.4	97 41.8	S 4 45.7	189 27.3	N22 50.2	65 08.3	S16 01.0
A 13	309 54.2	20 25.4	14.1	112 43.3	46.0	204 30.1	50.3	80 10.6	01.1
Y 14	324 56.7	35 29.4	13.9	127 44.9	46.4	219 32.9	50.3	95 12.9	01.1
15	339 59.2	50 33.4	.. 13.7	142 46.5	.. 46.7	234 35.7	.. 50.4	110 15.1	.. 01.1
16	355 01.6	65 37.4	13.5	157 48.1	47.0	249 38.6	50.4	125 17.4	01.2
17	10 04.1	80 41.4	13.3	172 49.6	47.4	264 41.4	50.4	140 19.7	01.2
18	25 06.6	95 45.4	S16 13.1	187 51.2	S 4 47.7	279 44.2	N22 50.5	155 22.0	S16 01.3
19	40 09.0	110 49.4	12.9	202 52.8	48.0	294 47.0	50.5	170 24.2	01.3
20	55 11.5	125 53.4	12.7	217 54.4	48.4	309 49.8	50.6	185 26.5	01.3
21	70 14.0	140 57.4	.. 12.4	232 55.9	.. 48.7	324 52.6	.. 50.6	200 28.8	.. 01.4
22	85 16.4	156 01.3	12.2	247 57.5	49.0	339 55.4	50.6	215 31.1	01.4
23	100 18.9	171 05.3	12.0	262 59.1	49.4	354 58.3	50.7	230 33.4	01.5
Mer. Pass.	h m 16 23.8	v 4.1	d 0.2	v 1.6	d 0.3	v 2.8	d 0.0	v 2.3	d 0.0

STARS

Name	SHA	Dec
Acamar	315 17.9	S40 15.2
Achernar	335 26.5	S57 10.3
Acrux	173 08.5	S63 10.4
Adhara	255 11.8	S28 59.7
Aldebaran	290 48.6	N16 32.1
Alioth	166 20.3	N55 52.7
Alkaid	152 58.7	N49 14.3
Al Na'ir	27 43.6	S46 53.6
Alnilam	275 45.6	S 1 11.8
Alphard	217 55.4	S 8 43.4
Alphecca	126 10.9	N26 40.0
Alpheratz	357 43.1	N29 10.2
Altair	62 08.2	N 8 54.5
Ankaa	353 15.5	S42 14.0
Antares	112 26.0	S26 27.6
Arcturus	145 55.4	N19 06.4
Atria	107 27.8	S69 02.8
Avior	234 17.1	S59 33.4
Bellatrix	278 31.3	N 6 21.5
Betelgeuse	271 00.5	N 7 24.3
Canopus	263 55.4	S52 42.5
Capella	280 33.4	N46 00.6
Deneb	49 31.6	N45 20.0
Denebola	182 33.1	N14 29.4
Diphda	348 55.6	S17 54.7
Dubhe	193 50.9	N61 40.1
Elnath	278 11.7	N28 37.0
Eltanin	90 46.4	N51 29.3
Enif	33 47.0	N 9 56.5
Fomalhaut	15 23.8	S29 32.9
Gacrux	172 00.2	S57 11.3
Gienah	175 51.7	S17 37.2
Hadar	148 47.3	S60 26.1
Hamal	328 00.2	N23 31.8
Kaus Aust.	83 43.6	S34 22.5
Kochab	137 20.6	N74 05.6
Markab	13 38.1	N15 17.0
Menkar	314 14.5	N 4 08.6
Menkent	148 07.1	S36 26.1
Miaplacidus	221 38.6	S69 46.5
Mirfak	308 39.4	N49 54.7
Nunki	75 58.2	S26 16.6
Peacock	53 19.2	S56 41.3
Pollux	243 26.9	N27 59.3
Procyon	244 59.0	N 5 11.1
Rasalhague	96 06.4	N12 33.1
Regulus	207 42.8	N11 53.7
Rigel	281 11.4	S 8 11.4
Rigil Kent.	139 51.2	S60 53.2
Sabik	102 12.3	S15 44.4
Schedar	349 40.1	N56 37.1
Shaula	96 21.7	S37 06.6
Sirius	258 33.0	S16 44.4
Spica	158 30.8	S11 14.1
Suhail	222 51.7	S43 29.5
Vega	80 39.1	N38 47.9
Zuben'ubi	137 05.1	S16 05.9

	SHA	Mer. Pass.
	o '	h m
Venus	69 32.8	11 45
Mars	163 22.5	5 32
Jupiter	254 22.8	23 25
Saturn	130 23.3	7 44

UT	SUN GHA	SUN Dec	MOON GHA	v	Dec	d	HP
d h	° ′	° ′	° ′	′	° ′	′	′
13 00	177 52.6	S21 31.4	35 15.8	11.8	N19 26.9	0.7	54.4
01	192 52.4	31.0	49 46.6	11.7	19 27.6	0.6	54.3
02	207 52.1	30.6	64 17.3	11.8	19 28.2	0.5	54.3
03	222 51.9	.. 30.1	78 48.1	11.7	19 28.7	0.5	54.3
04	237 51.7	29.7	93 18.8	11.8	19 29.2	0.3	54.3
05	252 51.4	29.3	107 49.6	11.8	19 29.5	0.2	54.3
06	267 51.2	S21 28.9	122 20.4	11.7	N19 29.7	0.2	54.3
M 07	282 51.0	28.4	136 51.1	11.8	19 29.9	0.1	54.3
O 08	297 50.7	28.0	151 21.9	11.8	19 30.0	0.1	54.3
N 09	312 50.5	.. 27.6	165 52.7	11.8	19 29.9	0.1	54.3
D 10	327 50.3	27.2	180 23.5	11.8	19 29.8	0.2	54.2
A 11	342 50.0	26.7	194 54.3	11.9	19 29.6	0.3	54.2
Y 12	357 49.8	S21 26.3	209 25.2	11.8	N19 29.3	0.4	54.2
13	12 49.6	25.9	223 56.0	11.9	19 28.9	0.5	54.2
14	27 49.3	25.4	238 26.9	11.8	19 28.4	0.5	54.2
15	42 49.1	.. 25.0	252 57.7	11.9	19 27.9	0.7	54.2
16	57 48.9	24.6	267 28.6	11.9	19 27.2	0.8	54.2
17	72 48.7	24.1	281 59.5	11.9	19 26.4	0.8	54.2
18	87 48.4	S21 23.7	296 30.4	11.9	N19 25.6	0.9	54.2
19	102 48.2	23.3	311 01.3	11.9	19 24.7	1.1	54.2
20	117 48.0	22.8	325 32.2	12.0	19 23.6	1.1	54.2
21	132 47.7	.. 22.4	340 03.2	11.9	19 22.5	1.2	54.1
22	147 47.5	22.0	354 34.1	12.0	19 21.3	1.3	54.1
23	162 47.3	21.5	9 05.1	12.0	19 20.0	1.4	54.1
14 00	177 47.0	S21 21.1	23 36.1	12.0	N19 18.6	1.4	54.1
01	192 46.8	20.7	38 07.1	12.0	19 17.2	1.6	54.1
02	207 46.6	20.2	52 38.1	12.1	19 15.6	1.6	54.1
03	222 46.4	.. 19.8	67 09.2	12.0	19 14.0	1.8	54.1
04	237 46.1	19.3	81 40.2	12.1	19 12.2	1.8	54.1
05	252 45.9	18.9	96 11.3	12.1	19 10.4	1.9	54.1
06	267 45.7	S21 18.5	110 42.4	12.1	N19 08.5	2.0	54.1
T 07	282 45.5	18.0	125 13.5	12.1	19 06.5	2.1	54.1
U 08	297 45.2	17.6	139 44.6	12.1	19 04.4	2.2	54.1
E 09	312 45.0	.. 17.1	154 15.7	12.2	19 02.2	2.3	54.1
S 10	327 44.8	16.7	168 46.9	12.2	18 59.9	2.3	54.1
D 11	342 44.5	16.2	183 18.1	12.2	18 57.6	2.5	54.1
A 12	357 44.3	S21 15.8	197 49.3	12.2	N18 55.1	2.5	54.0
Y 13	12 44.1	15.4	212 20.5	12.3	18 52.6	2.6	54.0
14	27 43.9	14.9	226 51.8	12.2	18 50.0	2.7	54.0
15	42 43.6	.. 14.5	241 23.0	12.3	18 47.3	2.8	54.0
16	57 43.4	14.0	255 54.3	12.3	18 44.5	2.8	54.0
17	72 43.2	13.6	270 25.6	12.4	18 41.7	3.0	54.0
18	87 43.0	S21 13.1	284 57.0	12.3	N18 38.7	3.0	54.0
19	102 42.8	12.7	299 28.3	12.4	18 35.7	3.2	54.0
20	117 42.5	12.2	313 59.7	12.4	18 32.5	3.2	54.0
21	132 42.3	.. 11.8	328 31.1	12.4	18 29.3	3.2	54.0
22	147 42.1	11.3	343 02.5	12.5	18 26.1	3.4	54.0
23	162 41.9	10.9	357 34.0	12.4	18 22.7	3.5	54.0
15 00	177 41.6	S21 10.4	12 05.4	12.5	N18 19.2	3.5	54.0
01	192 41.4	09.9	26 36.9	12.5	18 15.7	3.6	54.0
02	207 41.2	09.5	41 08.4	12.6	18 12.1	3.7	54.0
03	222 41.0	.. 09.0	55 40.0	12.6	18 08.4	3.8	54.0
04	237 40.8	08.6	70 11.6	12.5	18 04.6	3.9	54.0
05	252 40.5	08.1	84 43.1	12.7	18 00.7	3.9	54.0
06	267 40.3	S21 07.7	99 14.8	12.6	N17 56.8	4.0	54.0
W 07	282 40.1	07.2	113 46.4	12.7	17 52.8	4.1	54.0
E 08	297 39.9	06.7	128 18.1	12.7	17 48.7	4.2	54.0
D 09	312 39.7	.. 06.3	142 49.8	12.7	17 44.5	4.3	54.0
N 10	327 39.4	05.8	157 21.5	12.7	17 40.2	4.3	54.0
E 11	342 39.2	05.4	171 53.2	12.8	17 35.9	4.5	54.0
S 12	357 39.0	S21 04.9	186 25.0	12.8	N17 31.4	4.5	54.0
D 13	12 38.8	04.4	200 56.8	12.8	17 26.9	4.5	53.9
A 14	27 38.6	04.0	215 28.6	12.9	17 22.4	4.7	53.9
Y 15	42 38.3	.. 03.5	230 00.5	12.9	17 17.7	4.7	53.9
16	57 38.1	03.0	244 32.4	12.9	17 13.0	4.8	53.9
17	72 37.9	02.6	259 04.3	12.9	17 08.2	4.9	53.9
18	87 37.7	S21 02.1	273 36.2	13.0	N17 03.3	5.0	53.9
19	102 37.5	01.6	288 08.2	13.0	16 58.3	5.0	53.9
20	117 37.3	01.2	302 40.2	13.0	16 53.3	5.1	53.9
21	132 37.0	.. 00.7	317 12.2	13.0	16 48.2	5.2	53.9
22	147 36.8	21 00.2	331 44.2	13.1	16 43.0	5.2	53.9
23	162 36.6	S20 59.8	346 16.3	13.1	N16 37.8	5.3	53.9
	SD 16.3	d 0.4	SD 14.8		14.7		14.7

Twilight / Moonrise

Lat.	Naut.	Civil	Sunrise	13	14	15	16
°	h m	h m	h m	h m	h m	h m	h m
N 72	08 03	09 56	████	☐	☐	12 37	14 41
N 70	07 48	09 21	████	10 59	12 11	13 42	15 16
68	07 36	08 56	10 38	12 00	13 01	14 18	15 41
66	07 25	08 36	09 56	12 34	13 33	14 43	16 00
64	07 16	08 21	09 28	13 00	13 56	15 02	16 15
62	07 09	08 07	09 07	13 19	14 15	15 18	16 28
60	07 02	07 56	08 49	13 35	14 30	15 32	16 39
N 58	06 56	07 46	08 35	13 49	14 43	15 43	16 48
56	06 50	07 38	08 22	14 01	14 54	15 53	16 56
54	06 45	07 30	08 12	14 11	15 04	16 02	17 03
52	06 40	07 23	08 02	14 20	15 12	16 09	17 10
50	06 36	07 16	07 53	14 28	15 20	16 16	17 16
45	06 26	07 02	07 35	14 45	15 37	16 31	17 28
N 40	06 17	06 51	07 20	15 00	15 50	16 44	17 39
35	06 09	06 40	07 08	15 12	16 02	16 54	17 47
30	06 01	06 31	06 57	15 22	16 12	17 03	17 55
20	05 47	06 14	06 38	15 40	16 29	17 19	18 09
N 10	05 33	05 59	06 21	15 56	16 44	17 33	18 20
0	05 17	05 43	06 05	16 11	16 59	17 45	18 31
S 10	05 00	05 27	05 50	16 26	17 13	17 58	18 42
20	04 40	05 08	05 32	16 41	17 28	18 12	18 54
30	04 13	04 46	05 13	17 00	17 45	18 28	19 07
35	03 57	04 32	05 01	17 10	17 55	18 37	19 15
40	03 36	04 16	04 48	17 22	18 07	18 47	19 23
45	03 09	03 56	04 32	17 36	18 20	18 59	19 34
S 50	02 31	03 30	04 12	17 54	18 37	19 14	19 46
52	02 10	03 17	04 02	18 02	18 44	19 21	19 51
54	01 43	03 02	03 52	18 11	18 53	19 28	19 58
56	00 56	02 44	03 40	18 22	19 03	19 37	20 05
58	////	02 22	03 25	18 33	19 14	19 46	20 12
S 60	////	01 52	03 09	18 47	19 26	19 57	20 21

Sunset / Twilight / Moonset

Lat.	Sunset	Civil	Naut.	13	14	15	16
°	h m	h m	h m	h m	h m	h m	h m
N 72	████	14 23	16 16	☐	☐	10 38	10 10
N 70	████	14 58	16 31	08 58	09 26	09 33	09 34
68	13 41	15 23	16 43	07 57	08 35	08 56	09 08
66	14 23	15 42	16 53	07 22	08 03	08 31	08 49
64	14 51	15 58	17 02	06 57	07 40	08 11	08 33
62	15 12	16 11	17 10	06 38	07 21	07 54	08 19
60	15 29	16 22	17 17	06 22	07 06	07 41	08 08
N 58	15 44	16 32	17 23	06 08	06 53	07 29	07 58
56	15 56	16 41	17 28	05 56	06 41	07 19	07 50
54	16 07	16 49	17 33	05 46	06 31	07 10	07 42
52	16 16	16 56	17 38	05 37	06 23	07 02	07 35
50	16 25	17 02	17 43	05 29	06 15	06 55	07 29
45	16 43	17 16	17 52	05 11	05 58	06 39	07 16
N 40	16 58	17 28	18 01	04 57	05 44	06 26	07 05
35	17 11	17 38	18 09	04 45	05 32	06 15	06 55
30	17 22	17 47	18 17	04 35	05 22	06 06	06 47
20	17 40	18 04	18 31	04 16	05 04	05 49	06 32
N 10	17 57	18 20	18 46	04 01	04 49	05 35	06 20
0	18 13	18 35	19 01	03 46	04 34	05 21	06 08
S 10	18 28	18 51	19 18	03 31	04 19	05 08	05 56
20	18 45	19 10	19 38	03 15	04 04	04 53	05 43
30	19 05	19 32	20 04	02 57	03 46	04 37	05 28
35	19 17	19 46	20 21	02 47	03 36	04 27	05 20
40	19 30	20 02	20 41	02 34	03 24	04 16	05 10
45	19 46	20 22	21 08	02 20	03 09	04 03	04 58
S 50	20 06	20 47	21 45	02 03	02 52	03 47	04 44
52	20 15	21 00	22 06	01 54	02 44	03 39	04 38
54	20 26	21 15	22 33	01 45	02 35	03 31	04 31
56	20 37	21 33	23 16	01 35	02 25	03 21	04 23
58	20 51	21 54	////	01 23	02 13	03 10	04 13
S 60	21 08	22 23	////	01 09	02 00	02 58	04 03

Day	SUN Eqn. of Time 00h	SUN Eqn. of Time 12h	Mer. Pass.	MOON Mer. Pass. Upper	MOON Mer. Pass. Lower	Age	Phase
d	m s	m s	h m	h m	h m	d	%
13	08 29	08 40	12 09	22 22	09 58	12	94
14	08 51	09 02	12 09	23 10	10 46	13	97
15	09 13	09 24	12 09	23 57	11 34	14	99

2014 JANUARY 16, 17, 18 (THURS., FRI., SAT.)

UT	ARIES GHA	VENUS −4.2 GHA	Dec	MARS +0.6 GHA	Dec	JUPITER −2.7 GHA	Dec	SATURN +0.6 GHA	Dec	STARS Name	SHA	Dec
16 00	115 21.4	186 09.3	S16 11.8	278 00.6	S 4 49.7	10 01.1	N22 50.7	245 35.6	S16 01.5	Acamar	315 17.9	S40 15.2
01	130 23.8	201 13.3	11.6	293 02.2	50.0	25 03.9	50.7	260 37.9	01.5	Achernar	335 26.5	S57 10.3
02	145 26.3	216 17.3	11.4	308 03.8	50.4	40 06.7	50.8	275 40.2	01.6	Acrux	173 08.4	S63 10.4
03	160 28.7	231 21.2	.. 11.2	323 05.4	.. 50.7	55 09.5	.. 50.8	290 42.5	.. 01.6	Adhara	255 11.8	S28 59.8
04	175 31.2	246 25.2	11.0	338 07.0	51.0	70 12.3	50.9	305 44.8	01.7	Aldebaran	290 48.6	N16 32.1
05	190 33.7	261 29.2	10.8	353 08.5	51.4	85 15.1	50.9	320 47.0	01.7			
T 06	205 36.1	276 33.2	S16 10.6	8 10.1	S 4 51.7	100 18.0	N22 50.9	335 49.3	S16 01.7	Alioth	166 20.3	N55 52.7
H 07	220 38.6	291 37.1	10.4	23 11.7	52.0	115 20.8	51.0	350 51.6	01.8	Alkaid	152 58.6	N49 14.3
U 08	235 41.1	306 41.1	10.2	38 13.3	52.4	130 23.6	51.0	5 53.9	01.8	Al Na'ir	27 43.6	S46 53.6
R 09	250 43.5	321 45.1	.. 10.0	53 14.8	.. 52.7	145 26.4	.. 51.1	20 56.2	.. 01.9	Alnilam	275 45.6	S 1 11.8
S 10	265 46.0	336 49.0	09.8	68 16.4	53.0	160 29.2	51.1	35 58.5	01.9	Alphard	217 55.4	S 8 43.4
D 11	280 48.5	351 53.0	09.6	83 18.0	53.3	175 32.0	51.1	51 00.7	01.9			
A 12	295 50.9	6 56.9	S16 09.4	98 19.6	S 4 53.7	190 34.8	N22 51.2	66 03.0	S16 02.0	Alphecca	126 10.8	N26 40.0
Y 13	310 53.4	22 00.9	09.2	113 21.2	54.0	205 37.6	51.2	81 05.3	02.0	Alpheratz	357 43.2	N29 10.2
14	325 55.9	37 04.8	09.0	128 22.8	54.3	220 40.4	51.3	96 07.6	02.1	Altair	62 08.2	N 8 54.5
15	340 58.3	52 08.8	.. 08.8	143 24.3	.. 54.7	235 43.3	.. 51.3	111 09.9	.. 02.1	Ankaa	353 15.5	S42 14.0
16	356 00.8	67 12.7	08.6	158 25.9	55.0	250 46.1	51.3	126 12.1	02.1	Antares	112 26.0	S26 27.6
17	11 03.2	82 16.7	08.5	173 27.5	55.3	265 48.9	51.4	141 14.4	02.2			
18	26 05.7	97 20.6	S16 08.3	188 29.1	S 4 55.6	280 51.7	N22 51.4	156 16.7	S16 02.2	Arcturus	145 55.4	N19 06.4
19	41 08.2	112 24.5	08.1	203 30.7	56.0	295 54.5	51.5	171 19.0	02.3	Atria	107 27.8	S69 02.8
20	56 10.6	127 28.5	07.9	218 32.3	56.3	310 57.3	51.5	186 21.3	02.3	Avior	234 17.1	S59 33.4
21	71 13.1	142 32.4	.. 07.7	233 33.8	.. 56.6	326 00.1	.. 51.5	201 23.6	.. 02.3	Bellatrix	278 31.3	N 6 21.5
22	86 15.6	157 36.3	07.5	248 35.4	57.0	341 02.9	51.6	216 25.8	02.4	Betelgeuse	271 00.5	N 7 24.3
23	101 18.0	172 40.3	07.3	263 37.0	57.3	356 05.8	51.6	231 28.1	02.4			
17 00	116 20.5	187 44.2	S16 07.1	278 38.6	S 4 57.6	11 08.6	N22 51.7	246 30.4	S16 02.4	Canopus	263 55.4	S52 42.5
01	131 23.0	202 48.1	07.0	293 40.2	57.9	26 11.4	51.7	261 32.7	02.5	Capella	280 33.4	N46 00.6
02	146 25.4	217 52.0	06.8	308 41.8	58.3	41 14.2	51.7	276 35.0	02.5	Deneb	49 31.6	N45 20.0
03	161 27.9	232 55.9	.. 06.6	323 43.4	.. 58.6	56 17.0	.. 51.8	291 37.3	.. 02.6	Denebola	182 33.1	N14 29.4
04	176 30.4	247 59.8	06.4	338 44.9	58.9	71 19.8	51.8	306 39.5	02.6	Diphda	348 55.6	S17 54.7
05	191 32.8	263 03.8	06.2	353 46.5	59.2	86 22.6	51.8	321 41.8	02.6			
F 06	206 35.3	278 07.7	S16 06.0	8 48.1	S 4 59.6	101 25.4	N22 51.9	336 44.1	S16 02.7	Dubhe	193 50.8	N61 40.1
R 07	221 37.7	293 11.6	05.9	23 49.7	4 59.9	116 28.2	51.9	351 46.4	02.7	Elnath	278 11.7	N28 37.0
I 08	236 40.2	308 15.5	05.7	38 51.3	5 00.2	131 31.0	52.0	6 48.7	02.8	Eltanin	90 46.4	N51 29.2
D 09	251 42.7	323 19.4	.. 05.5	53 52.9	.. 00.5	146 33.9	.. 52.0	21 51.0	.. 02.8	Enif	33 47.0	N 9 56.5
A 10	266 45.1	338 23.3	05.3	68 54.5	00.9	161 36.7	52.0	36 53.2	02.8	Fomalhaut	15 23.8	S29 32.9
Y 11	281 47.6	353 27.2	05.2	83 56.1	01.2	176 39.5	52.1	51 55.5	02.9			
12	296 50.1	8 31.0	S16 05.0	98 57.7	S 5 01.5	191 42.3	N22 52.1	66 57.8	S16 02.9	Gacrux	172 00.1	S57 11.3
13	311 52.5	23 34.9	04.8	113 59.3	01.8	206 45.1	52.2	82 00.1	03.0	Gienah	175 51.7	S17 37.2
14	326 55.0	38 38.8	04.6	129 00.9	02.2	221 47.9	52.2	97 02.4	03.0	Hadar	148 47.2	S60 26.1
15	341 57.5	53 42.7	.. 04.5	144 02.4	.. 02.5	236 50.7	.. 52.2	112 04.7	.. 03.0	Hamal	328 00.2	N23 31.8
16	356 59.9	68 46.6	04.3	159 04.0	02.8	251 53.5	52.3	127 06.9	03.1	Kaus Aust.	83 43.6	S34 22.5
17	12 02.4	83 50.5	04.1	174 05.6	03.1	266 56.3	52.3	142 09.2	03.1			
18	27 04.8	98 54.3	S16 03.9	189 07.2	S 5 03.4	281 59.1	N22 52.3	157 11.5	S16 03.1	Kochab	137 20.6	N74 05.6
19	42 07.3	113 58.2	03.8	204 08.8	03.8	297 01.9	52.4	172 13.8	03.2	Markab	13 38.1	N15 17.0
20	57 09.8	129 02.1	03.6	219 10.4	04.1	312 04.7	52.4	187 16.1	03.2	Menkar	314 14.5	N 4 08.6
21	72 12.2	144 05.9	.. 03.4	234 12.0	.. 04.4	327 07.6	.. 52.5	202 18.4	.. 03.3	Menkent	148 07.1	S36 26.1
22	87 14.7	159 09.8	03.3	249 13.6	04.7	342 10.4	52.5	217 20.7	03.3	Miaplacidus	221 38.6	S69 46.6
23	102 17.2	174 13.7	03.1	264 15.2	05.1	357 13.2	52.5	232 22.9	03.3			
18 00	117 19.6	189 17.5	S16 02.9	279 16.8	S 5 05.4	12 16.0	N22 52.6	247 25.2	S16 03.4	Mirfak	308 39.4	N49 54.7
01	132 22.1	204 21.4	02.8	294 18.4	05.7	27 18.8	52.6	262 27.5	03.4	Nunki	75 58.2	S26 16.6
02	147 24.6	219 25.2	02.6	309 20.0	06.0	42 21.6	52.7	277 29.8	03.4	Peacock	53 19.2	S56 41.3
03	162 27.0	234 29.1	.. 02.5	324 21.6	.. 06.3	57 24.4	.. 52.7	292 32.1	.. 03.5	Pollux	243 26.8	N27 59.3
04	177 29.5	249 32.9	02.3	339 23.2	06.7	72 27.2	52.7	307 34.4	03.5	Procyon	244 58.9	N 5 11.1
05	192 32.0	264 36.7	02.1	354 24.8	07.0	87 30.0	52.8	322 36.7	03.6			
S 06	207 34.4	279 40.6	S16 02.0	9 26.4	S 5 07.3	102 32.8	N22 52.8	337 39.0	S16 03.6	Rasalhague	96 06.3	N12 33.1
A 07	222 36.9	294 44.4	01.8	24 28.0	07.6	117 35.6	52.8	352 41.2	03.6	Regulus	207 42.8	N11 53.7
T 08	237 39.3	309 48.2	01.7	39 29.6	07.9	132 38.4	52.9	7 43.5	03.7	Rigel	281 11.4	S 8 11.4
U 09	252 41.8	324 52.1	.. 01.5	54 31.2	.. 08.3	147 41.2	.. 52.9	22 45.8	.. 03.7	Rigil Kent.	139 51.2	S60 53.2
R 10	267 44.3	339 55.9	01.3	69 32.8	08.6	162 44.0	53.0	37 48.1	03.8	Sabik	102 12.3	S15 44.4
D 11	282 46.7	354 59.7	01.2	84 34.4	08.9	177 46.9	53.0	52 50.4	03.8			
A 12	297 49.2	10 03.5	S16 01.0	99 36.0	S 5 09.2	192 49.7	N22 53.0	67 52.7	S16 03.8	Schedar	349 40.1	N56 37.1
Y 13	312 51.7	25 07.4	00.9	114 37.6	09.5	207 52.5	53.1	82 55.0	03.9	Shaula	96 21.7	S37 06.6
14	327 54.1	40 11.2	00.7	129 39.2	09.8	222 55.3	53.1	97 57.3	03.9	Sirius	258 33.0	S16 44.4
15	342 56.6	55 15.0	.. 00.6	144 40.8	.. 10.2	237 58.1	.. 53.2	112 59.5	.. 03.9	Spica	158 30.8	S11 14.1
16	357 59.1	70 18.8	00.4	159 42.5	10.5	253 00.9	53.2	128 01.8	04.0	Suhail	222 51.6	S43 29.5
17	13 01.5	85 22.6	00.3	174 44.1	10.8	268 03.7	53.2	143 04.1	04.0			
18	28 04.0	100 26.4	S16 00.1	189 45.7	S 5 11.1	283 06.5	N22 53.3	158 06.4	S16 04.0	Vega	80 39.1	N38 47.9
19	43 06.5	115 30.2	16 00.0	204 47.3	11.4	298 09.3	53.3	173 08.7	04.1	Zuben'ubi	137 05.0	S16 05.9
20	58 08.9	130 34.0	15 59.8	219 48.9	11.7	313 12.1	53.3	188 11.0	04.1			
21	73 11.4	145 37.8	.. 59.7	234 50.5	.. 12.1	328 14.9	.. 53.4	203 13.3	.. 04.2			
22	88 13.8	160 41.5	59.5	249 52.1	12.4	343 17.7	53.4	218 15.6	04.2			
23	103 16.3	175 45.3	59.4	264 53.7	12.7	358 20.5	53.5	233 17.9	04.2			
Mer. Pass.	16 12.0 h m	v 3.9	d 0.2	v 1.6	d 0.3	v 2.8	d 0.0	v 2.3	d 0.0			

	SHA	Mer. Pass.
	° ′	h m
Venus	71 23.7	11 26
Mars	162 18.1	5 25
Jupiter	254 48.1	23 11
Saturn	130 09.9	7 33

UT	SUN GHA	SUN Dec	MOON GHA	v	MOON Dec	d	HP
d h	° ′	° ′	° ′	′	° ′	′	′
16 00	177 36.4	S20 59.3	0 48.4	13.1	N16 32.5	5.4	53.9
01	192 36.2	58.8	15 20.5	13.2	16 27.1	5.5	53.9
02	207 36.0	58.3	29 52.7	13.2	16 21.6	5.6	53.9
03	222 35.8	.. 57.9	44 24.9	13.2	16 16.0	5.6	53.9
04	237 35.5	57.4	58 57.1	13.2	16 10.4	5.7	53.9
05	252 35.3	56.9	73 29.3	13.3	16 04.7	5.7	53.9
06	267 35.1	S20 56.4	88 01.6	13.3	N15 59.0	5.8	53.9
T 07	282 34.9	56.0	102 33.9	13.3	15 53.2	5.9	53.9
H 08	297 34.7	55.5	117 06.2	13.4	15 47.3	6.0	53.9
U 09	312 34.5	.. 55.0	131 38.6	13.4	15 41.3	6.0	53.9
R 10	327 34.3	54.5	146 11.0	13.4	15 35.3	6.1	53.9
S 11	342 34.1	54.1	160 43.4	13.4	15 29.2	6.2	53.9
D 12	357 33.8	S20 53.6	175 15.8	13.5	N15 23.0	6.2	53.9
A 13	12 33.6	53.1	189 48.3	13.5	15 16.8	6.3	53.9
Y 14	27 33.4	52.6	204 20.8	13.5	15 10.5	6.4	53.9
15	42 33.2	.. 52.1	218 53.3	13.6	15 04.1	6.4	54.0
16	57 33.0	51.7	233 25.9	13.6	14 57.7	6.5	54.0
17	72 32.8	51.2	247 58.5	13.6	14 51.2	6.6	54.0
18	87 32.6	S20 50.7	262 31.1	13.6	N14 44.6	6.6	54.0
19	102 32.4	50.2	277 03.7	13.7	14 38.0	6.7	54.0
20	117 32.2	49.7	291 36.4	13.7	14 31.3	6.7	54.0
21	132 32.0	.. 49.2	306 09.1	13.7	14 24.6	6.8	54.0
22	147 31.8	48.8	320 41.8	13.8	14 17.8	6.9	54.0
23	162 31.5	48.3	335 14.6	13.7	14 10.9	7.0	54.0
17 00	177 31.3	S20 47.8	349 47.3	13.8	N14 03.9	7.0	54.0
01	192 31.1	47.3	4 20.1	13.9	13 56.9	7.0	54.0
02	207 30.9	46.8	18 53.0	13.8	13 49.9	7.1	54.0
03	222 30.7	.. 46.3	33 25.8	13.9	13 42.8	7.2	54.0
04	237 30.5	45.8	47 58.7	13.9	13 35.6	7.2	54.0
05	252 30.3	45.3	62 31.6	14.0	13 28.4	7.3	54.0
06	267 30.1	S20 44.8	77 04.6	13.9	N13 21.1	7.4	54.0
07	282 29.9	44.3	91 37.5	14.0	13 13.7	7.4	54.0
F 08	297 29.7	43.9	106 10.5	14.0	13 06.3	7.4	54.0
R 09	312 29.5	.. 43.4	120 43.5	14.1	12 58.9	7.5	54.0
I 10	327 29.3	42.9	135 16.6	14.1	12 51.4	7.6	54.0
D 11	342 29.1	42.4	149 49.7	14.0	12 43.8	7.6	54.0
A 12	357 28.9	S20 41.9	164 22.7	14.2	N12 36.2	7.7	54.0
Y 13	12 28.7	41.4	178 55.9	14.1	12 28.5	7.7	54.0
14	27 28.5	40.9	193 29.0	14.2	12 20.8	7.8	54.0
15	42 28.3	.. 40.4	208 02.2	14.2	12 13.0	7.9	54.0
16	57 28.1	39.9	222 35.4	14.2	12 05.1	7.9	54.0
17	72 27.9	39.4	237 08.6	14.2	11 57.2	7.9	54.1
18	87 27.7	S20 38.9	251 41.8	14.3	N11 49.3	8.0	54.1
19	102 27.4	38.4	266 15.1	14.3	11 41.3	8.0	54.1
20	117 27.2	37.9	280 48.4	14.3	11 33.3	8.1	54.1
21	132 27.0	.. 37.4	295 21.7	14.3	11 25.2	8.2	54.1
22	147 26.8	36.9	309 55.0	14.3	11 17.0	8.2	54.1
23	162 26.6	36.4	324 28.3	14.4	11 08.8	8.2	54.1
18 00	177 26.4	S20 35.9	339 01.7	14.4	N11 00.6	8.3	54.1
01	192 26.2	35.4	353 35.1	14.4	10 52.3	8.3	54.1
02	207 26.0	34.9	8 08.5	14.5	10 44.0	8.4	54.1
03	222 25.8	.. 34.4	22 42.0	14.4	10 35.6	8.4	54.1
04	237 25.6	33.9	37 15.4	14.5	10 27.2	8.5	54.1
05	252 25.4	33.3	51 48.9	14.5	10 18.7	8.5	54.1
06	267 25.2	S20 32.8	66 22.4	14.5	N10 10.2	8.6	54.1
07	282 25.1	32.3	80 55.9	14.5	10 01.6	8.6	54.1
S 08	297 24.9	31.8	95 29.4	14.6	9 53.0	8.6	54.2
A 09	312 24.7	.. 31.3	110 03.0	14.6	9 44.4	8.7	54.2
T 10	327 24.5	30.8	124 36.6	14.5	9 35.7	8.7	54.2
U 11	342 24.3	30.3	139 10.1	14.6	9 27.0	8.8	54.2
R 12	357 24.1	S20 29.8	153 43.7	14.7	N 9 18.2	8.8	54.2
D 13	12 23.9	29.3	168 17.4	14.6	9 09.4	8.8	54.2
A 14	27 23.7	28.7	182 51.0	14.6	9 00.6	8.9	54.2
Y 15	42 23.5	.. 28.2	197 24.6	14.7	8 51.7	8.9	54.2
16	57 23.3	27.7	211 58.3	14.7	8 42.8	9.0	54.2
17	72 23.1	27.2	226 32.0	14.7	8 33.8	9.0	54.2
18	87 22.9	S20 26.7	241 05.7	14.7	N 8 24.8	9.0	54.2
19	102 22.7	26.2	255 39.4	14.7	8 15.8	9.1	54.3
20	117 22.5	25.7	270 13.1	14.8	8 06.7	9.1	54.3
21	132 22.3	.. 25.1	284 46.9	14.7	7 57.6	9.2	54.3
22	147 22.1	24.6	299 20.6	14.8	7 48.4	9.2	54.3
23	162 21.9	24.1	313 54.4	14.7	N 7 39.2	9.2	54.3
	SD 16.3	d 0.5	SD 14.7		14.7		14.8

Lat.	Twilight Naut.	Twilight Civil	Sunrise	Moonrise 16	17	18	19
°	h m	h m	h m	h m	h m	h m	h m
N 72	07 56	09 43	■■■	14 41	16 28	18 09	19 48
N 70	07 42	09 12	11 42	15 16	16 50	18 22	19 54
68	07 30	08 49	10 24	15 41	17 07	18 33	19 59
66	07 21	08 30	09 47	16 00	17 20	18 41	20 03
64	07 12	08 16	09 21	16 15	17 31	18 48	20 07
62	07 05	08 03	09 01	16 28	17 40	18 55	20 10
60	06 59	07 52	08 45	16 39	17 48	19 00	20 12
N 58	06 53	07 43	08 31	16 48	17 55	19 05	20 15
56	06 48	07 35	08 19	16 56	18 02	19 09	20 17
54	06 43	07 27	08 09	17 03	18 07	19 12	20 19
52	06 38	07 21	07 59	17 10	18 12	19 16	20 20
50	06 34	07 14	07 51	17 16	18 17	19 19	20 22
45	06 25	07 01	07 34	17 28	18 26	19 26	20 25
N 40	06 16	06 50	07 19	17 39	18 35	19 31	20 28
35	06 09	06 40	07 07	17 47	18 41	19 36	20 30
30	06 01	06 31	06 56	17 55	18 48	19 40	20 33
20	05 47	06 14	06 38	18 09	18 58	19 47	20 36
N 10	05 33	05 59	06 22	18 20	19 07	19 54	20 40
0	05 19	05 44	06 06	18 31	19 16	19 59	20 43
S 10	05 02	05 28	05 51	18 42	19 24	20 05	20 46
20	04 42	05 10	05 34	18 54	19 34	20 12	20 49
30	04 16	04 49	05 15	19 07	19 44	20 19	20 53
35	04 00	04 35	05 04	19 15	19 50	20 23	20 55
40	03 40	04 19	04 51	19 23	19 57	20 28	20 57
45	03 14	04 00	04 35	19 34	20 05	20 33	21 00
S 50	02 38	03 35	04 16	19 46	20 14	20 39	21 03
52	02 18	03 23	04 07	19 51	20 18	20 42	21 05
54	01 53	03 08	03 57	19 58	20 23	20 46	21 06
56	01 15	02 51	03 45	20 05	20 28	20 49	21 08
58	////	02 30	03 32	20 12	20 34	20 53	21 10
S 60	////	02 03	03 16	20 21	20 41	20 58	21 13

Lat.	Sunset	Twilight Civil	Twilight Naut.	Moonset 16	17	18	19
°	h m	h m	h m	h m	h m	h m	h m
N 72	■■■	14 38	16 25	10 10	09 56	09 46	09 37
N 70	12 38	15 09	16 39	09 34	09 33	09 31	09 29
68	13 57	15 32	16 51	09 08	09 15	09 19	09 22
66	14 34	15 50	17 00	08 49	09 01	09 10	09 17
64	15 00	16 05	17 08	08 33	08 49	09 01	09 12
62	15 20	16 18	17 16	08 19	08 39	08 54	09 07
60	15 36	16 28	17 22	08 08	08 30	08 48	09 04
N 58	15 50	16 38	17 28	07 58	08 22	08 43	09 00
56	16 02	16 46	17 33	07 50	08 16	08 38	08 58
54	16 12	16 53	17 38	07 42	08 10	08 33	08 55
52	16 21	17 00	17 42	07 35	08 04	08 29	08 53
50	16 29	17 06	17 46	07 29	07 59	08 26	08 50
45	16 47	17 20	17 56	07 16	07 48	08 18	08 46
N 40	17 01	17 31	18 04	07 05	07 39	08 11	08 42
35	17 13	17 41	18 12	06 55	07 32	08 06	08 38
30	17 24	17 50	18 19	06 47	07 25	08 01	08 35
20	17 42	18 06	18 33	06 32	07 13	07 52	08 30
N 10	17 59	18 21	18 47	06 20	07 03	07 44	08 25
0	18 14	18 36	19 02	06 08	06 53	07 37	08 20
S 10	18 29	18 52	19 18	05 56	06 43	07 30	08 16
20	18 46	19 09	19 38	05 43	06 33	07 22	08 11
30	19 05	19 31	20 03	05 28	06 20	07 13	08 05
35	19 16	19 44	20 20	05 20	06 13	07 08	08 02
40	19 29	20 00	20 39	05 10	06 05	07 02	07 58
45	19 44	20 19	21 05	04 58	05 56	06 55	07 54
S 50	20 03	20 44	21 40	04 44	05 45	06 46	07 49
52	20 12	20 56	22 00	04 38	05 39	06 43	07 47
54	20 22	21 10	22 25	04 31	05 34	06 38	07 44
56	20 34	21 27	23 01	04 23	05 27	06 34	07 41
58	20 47	21 48	////	04 13	05 20	06 28	07 38
S 60	21 02	22 14	////	04 03	05 12	06 22	07 34

Day	SUN Eqn. of Time 00h	SUN Eqn. of Time 12h	SUN Mer. Pass.	MOON Mer. Pass. Upper	MOON Mer. Pass. Lower	Age	Phase
d	m s	m s	h m	h m	h m	d	%
16	09 34	09 44	12 10	24 42	12 20	15 100	
17	09 54	10 04	12 10	00 42	13 04	16 98	◯
18	10 14	10 23	12 10	01 26	13 48	17 95	

UT	ARIES	VENUS −4.4		MARS +0.5		JUPITER −2.7		SATURN +0.6		STARS		
	GHA	GHA	Dec	GHA	Dec	GHA	Dec	GHA	Dec	Name	SHA	Dec
d h	° ′	° ′	° ′	° ′	° ′	° ′	° ′	° ′	° ′		° ′	° ′
19 00	118 18.8	190 49.1	S15 59.2	279 55.3	S 5 13.0	13 23.3	N22 53.5	248 20.1	S16 04.3	Acamar	315 17.9	S40 15.2
01	133 21.2	205 52.9	59.1	294 56.9	13.3	28 26.1	53.5	263 22.4	04.3	Achernar	335 26.6	S57 10.3
02	148 23.7	220 56.7	59.0	309 58.5	13.6	43 28.9	53.6	278 24.7	04.3	Acrux	173 08.4	S63 10.4
03	163 26.2	236 00.4	.. 58.8	325 00.2	.. 13.9	58 31.7	.. 53.6	293 27.0	.. 04.4	Adhara	255 11.8	S28 59.8
04	178 28.6	251 04.2	58.7	340 01.8	14.3	73 34.5	53.6	308 29.3	04.4	Aldebaran	290 48.6	N16 32.1
05	193 31.1	266 08.0	58.5	355 03.4	14.6	88 37.3	53.7	323 31.6	04.5			
06	208 33.6	281 11.7	S15 58.4	10 05.0	S 5 14.9	103 40.1	N22 53.7	338 33.9	S16 04.5	Alioth	166 20.2	N55 52.7
07	223 36.0	296 15.5	58.2	25 06.6	15.2	118 42.9	53.8	353 36.2	04.5	Alkaid	152 58.6	N49 14.3
08	238 38.5	311 19.2	58.1	40 08.2	15.5	133 45.7	53.8	8 38.5	04.6	Al Na'ir	27 43.6	S46 53.6
S 09	253 40.9	326 23.0	.. 58.0	55 09.8	.. 15.8	148 48.6	.. 53.8	23 40.8	.. 04.6	Alnilam	275 45.6	S 1 11.8
U 10	268 43.4	341 26.7	57.8	70 11.5	16.1	163 51.4	53.9	38 43.1	04.6	Alphard	217 55.3	S 8 43.4
N 11	283 45.9	356 30.5	57.7	85 13.1	16.5	178 54.2	53.9	53 45.3	04.7			
D 12	298 48.3	11 34.2	S15 57.6	100 14.7	S 5 16.8	193 57.0	N22 53.9	68 47.6	S16 04.7	Alphecca	126 10.8	N26 40.0
A 13	313 50.8	26 37.9	57.4	115 16.3	17.1	208 59.8	54.0	83 49.9	04.7	Alpheratz	357 43.2	N29 10.2
Y 14	328 53.3	41 41.7	57.3	130 17.9	17.4	224 02.6	54.0	98 52.2	04.8	Altair	62 08.1	N 8 54.5
15	343 55.7	56 45.4	.. 57.2	145 19.5	.. 17.7	239 05.4	.. 54.1	113 54.5	.. 04.8	Ankaa	353 15.5	S42 14.0
16	358 58.2	71 49.1	57.0	160 21.2	18.0	254 08.2	54.1	128 56.8	04.9	Antares	112 25.9	S26 27.6
17	14 00.7	86 52.8	56.9	175 22.8	18.3	269 11.0	54.1	143 59.1	04.9			
18	29 03.1	101 56.5	S15 56.8	190 24.4	S 5 18.6	284 13.8	N22 54.2	159 01.4	S16 04.9	Arcturus	145 55.4	N19 06.4
19	44 05.6	117 00.3	56.6	205 26.0	18.9	299 16.6	54.2	174 03.7	05.0	Atria	107 27.8	S69 02.8
20	59 08.1	132 04.0	56.5	220 27.6	19.3	314 19.4	54.2	189 06.0	05.0	Avior	234 17.1	S59 33.4
21	74 10.5	147 07.7	.. 56.4	235 29.3	.. 19.6	329 22.2	.. 54.3	204 08.3	.. 05.0	Bellatrix	278 31.3	N 6 21.5
22	89 13.0	162 11.4	56.3	250 30.9	19.9	344 25.0	54.3	219 10.6	05.1	Betelgeuse	271 00.5	N 7 24.3
23	104 15.4	177 15.1	56.1	265 32.5	20.2	359 27.8	54.4	234 12.8	05.1			
20 00	119 17.9	192 18.8	S15 56.0	280 34.1	S 5 20.5	14 30.6	N22 54.4	249 15.1	S16 05.1	Canopus	263 55.4	S52 42.5
01	134 20.4	207 22.5	55.9	295 35.7	20.8	29 33.4	54.4	264 17.4	05.2	Capella	280 33.4	N46 00.6
02	149 22.8	222 26.2	55.8	310 37.4	21.1	44 36.2	54.5	279 19.7	05.2	Deneb	49 31.6	N45 20.0
03	164 25.3	237 29.8	.. 55.6	325 39.0	.. 21.4	59 39.0	.. 54.5	294 22.0	.. 05.3	Denebola	182 33.1	N14 29.4
04	179 27.8	252 33.5	55.5	340 40.6	21.7	74 41.8	54.5	309 24.3	05.3	Diphda	348 55.6	S17 54.7
05	194 30.2	267 37.2	55.4	355 42.2	22.0	89 44.6	54.6	324 26.6	05.3			
06	209 32.7	282 40.9	S15 55.3	10 43.9	S 5 22.3	104 47.4	N22 54.6	339 28.9	S16 05.4	Dubhe	193 50.8	N61 40.1
07	224 35.2	297 44.5	55.2	25 45.5	22.6	119 50.2	54.6	354 31.2	05.4	Elnath	278 11.8	N28 37.0
08	239 37.6	312 48.2	55.0	40 47.1	23.0	134 53.0	54.7	9 33.5	05.4	Eltanin	90 46.4	N51 29.2
M 09	254 40.1	327 51.9	.. 54.9	55 48.7	.. 23.3	149 55.8	.. 54.7	24 35.8	.. 05.5	Enif	33 47.0	N 9 56.5
O 10	269 42.6	342 55.5	54.8	70 50.4	23.6	164 58.6	54.8	39 38.1	05.5	Fomalhaut	15 23.8	S29 32.9
N 11	284 45.0	357 59.2	54.7	85 52.0	23.9	180 01.4	54.8	54 40.4	05.5			
D 12	299 47.5	13 02.8	S15 54.6	100 53.6	S 5 24.2	195 04.2	N22 54.8	69 42.7	S16 05.6	Gacrux	172 00.1	S57 11.3
A 13	314 49.9	28 06.5	54.5	115 55.3	24.5	210 07.0	54.9	84 45.0	05.6	Gienah	175 51.7	S17 37.2
Y 14	329 52.4	43 10.1	54.4	130 56.9	24.8	225 09.8	54.9	99 47.3	05.6	Hadar	148 47.2	S60 26.1
15	344 54.9	58 13.8	.. 54.2	145 58.5	.. 25.1	240 12.6	.. 54.9	114 49.6	.. 05.7	Hamal	328 00.2	N23 31.8
16	359 57.3	73 17.4	54.1	161 00.1	25.4	255 15.4	55.0	129 51.8	05.7	Kaus Aust.	83 43.6	S34 22.4
17	14 59.8	88 21.0	54.0	176 01.8	25.7	270 18.2	55.0	144 54.1	05.8			
18	30 02.3	103 24.7	S15 53.9	191 03.4	S 5 26.0	285 21.0	N22 55.0	159 56.4	S16 05.8	Kochab	137 20.5	N74 05.6
19	45 04.7	118 28.3	53.8	206 05.0	26.3	300 23.8	55.1	174 58.7	05.8	Markab	13 38.1	N15 17.0
20	60 07.2	133 31.9	53.7	221 06.7	26.6	315 26.6	55.1	190 01.0	05.9	Menkar	314 14.5	N 4 08.6
21	75 09.7	148 35.5	.. 53.6	236 08.3	.. 26.9	330 29.4	.. 55.2	205 03.3	.. 05.9	Menkent	148 07.0	S36 26.2
22	90 12.1	163 39.2	53.5	251 09.9	27.2	345 32.1	55.2	220 05.6	05.9	Miaplacidus	221 38.5	S69 46.6
23	105 14.6	178 42.8	53.4	266 11.6	27.5	0 34.9	55.2	235 07.9	06.0			
21 00	120 17.0	193 46.4	S15 53.3	281 13.2	S 5 27.8	15 37.7	N22 55.3	250 10.2	S16 06.0	Mirfak	308 39.5	N49 54.7
01	135 19.5	208 50.0	53.2	296 14.8	28.1	30 40.5	55.3	265 12.5	06.0	Nunki	75 58.1	S26 16.6
02	150 22.0	223 53.6	53.1	311 16.5	28.4	45 43.3	55.3	280 14.8	06.1	Peacock	53 19.2	S56 41.3
03	165 24.4	238 57.2	.. 53.0	326 18.1	.. 28.7	60 46.1	.. 55.4	295 17.1	.. 06.1	Pollux	243 26.8	N27 59.3
04	180 26.9	254 00.8	52.9	341 19.8	29.0	75 48.9	55.4	310 19.4	06.1	Procyon	244 58.9	N 5 11.1
05	195 29.4	269 04.3	52.8	356 21.4	29.3	90 51.7	55.4	325 21.7	06.2			
06	210 31.8	284 07.9	S15 52.7	11 23.0	S 5 29.6	105 54.5	N22 55.5	340 24.0	S16 06.2	Rasalhague	96 06.3	N12 33.1
07	225 34.3	299 11.5	52.6	26 24.7	29.9	120 57.3	55.5	355 26.3	06.2	Regulus	207 42.8	N11 53.6
08	240 36.8	314 15.1	52.5	41 26.3	30.2	136 00.1	55.6	10 28.6	06.3	Rigel	281 11.4	S 8 11.4
T 09	255 39.2	329 18.6	.. 52.4	56 28.0	.. 30.5	151 02.9	.. 55.6	25 30.9	.. 06.3	Rigil Kent.	139 51.2	S60 53.2
U 10	270 41.7	344 22.2	52.3	71 29.6	30.8	166 05.7	55.6	40 33.2	06.3	Sabik	102 12.3	S15 44.4
E 11	285 44.2	359 25.8	52.2	86 31.2	31.1	181 08.5	55.7	55 35.5	06.4			
S 12	300 46.6	14 29.3	S15 52.1	101 32.9	S 5 31.4	196 11.3	N22 55.7	70 37.8	S16 06.4	Schedar	349 40.1	N56 37.1
D 13	315 49.1	29 32.9	52.0	116 34.5	31.7	211 14.1	55.7	85 40.1	06.4	Shaula	96 21.7	S37 06.6
A 14	330 51.5	44 36.4	51.9	131 36.2	32.0	226 16.9	55.8	100 42.4	06.5	Sirius	258 33.0	S16 44.4
Y 15	345 54.0	59 40.0	.. 51.8	146 37.8	.. 32.3	241 19.7	.. 55.8	115 44.7	.. 06.5	Spica	158 30.7	S11 14.1
16	0 56.5	74 43.5	51.7	161 39.4	32.6	256 22.5	55.8	130 47.0	06.6	Suhail	222 51.6	S43 29.5
17	15 58.9	89 47.1	51.6	176 41.1	32.9	271 25.3	55.9	145 49.3	06.6			
18	31 01.4	104 50.6	S15 51.5	191 42.7	S 5 33.2	286 28.1	N22 55.9	160 51.6	S16 06.6	Vega	80 39.1	N38 47.9
19	46 03.9	119 54.1	51.4	206 44.4	33.5	301 30.8	56.0	175 53.9	06.7	Zuben'ubi	137 05.0	S16 05.9
20	61 06.3	134 57.7	51.3	221 46.0	33.8	316 33.6	56.0	190 56.2	06.7		SHA	Mer. Pass.
21	76 08.8	150 01.2	.. 51.3	236 47.7	.. 34.1	331 36.4	.. 56.0	205 58.5	.. 06.7		° ′	h m
22	91 11.3	165 04.7	51.2	251 49.3	34.4	346 39.2	56.1	221 00.8	06.8	Venus	73 00.9	11 08
23	106 13.7	180 08.2	51.1	266 51.0	34.7	1 42.0	56.1	236 03.1	06.8	Mars	161 16.2	5 17
	h m									Jupiter	255 12.7	22 58
Mer. Pass. 16 00.2		v 3.6	d 0.1	v 1.6	d 0.3	v 2.8	d 0.0	v 2.3	d 0.0	Saturn	129 57.2	7 22

UT	SUN GHA	SUN Dec	MOON GHA	v	MOON Dec	d	HP
d h	° ′	° ′	° ′	′	° ′	′	′
19 00	177 21.7	S20 23.6	328 28.1	14.8	N 7 30.0	9.2	54.3
01	192 21.5	23.1	343 01.9	14.8	7 20.8	9.3	54.3
02	207 21.3	22.5	357 35.7	14.8	7 11.5	9.3	54.3
03	222 21.2	.. 22.0	12 09.5	14.8	7 02.2	9.4	54.3
04	237 21.0	21.5	26 43.3	14.9	6 52.8	9.3	54.4
05	252 20.8	21.0	41 17.2	14.8	6 43.5	9.5	54.4
S 06	267 20.6	S20 20.4	55 51.0	14.8	N 6 34.0	9.4	54.4
U 07	282 20.4	19.9	70 24.8	14.9	6 24.6	9.5	54.4
N 08	297 20.2	19.4	84 58.7	14.8	6 15.1	9.5	54.4
D 09	312 20.0	.. 18.9	99 32.5	14.9	6 05.6	9.5	54.4
A 10	327 19.8	18.3	114 06.4	14.8	5 56.1	9.5	54.4
Y 11	342 19.6	17.8	128 40.2	14.9	5 46.6	9.6	54.4
12	357 19.4	S20 17.3	143 14.1	14.9	N 5 37.0	9.6	54.5
13	12 19.3	16.8	157 48.0	14.9	5 27.4	9.7	54.5
14	27 19.1	16.2	172 21.9	14.8	5 17.7	9.6	54.5
15	42 18.9	.. 15.7	186 55.7	14.9	5 08.1	9.7	54.5
16	57 18.7	15.2	201 29.6	14.9	4 58.4	9.7	54.5
17	72 18.5	14.6	216 03.5	14.9	4 48.7	9.7	54.5
18	87 18.3	S20 14.1	230 37.4	14.9	N 4 39.0	9.8	54.5
19	102 18.1	13.6	245 11.3	14.8	4 29.2	9.8	54.6
20	117 17.9	13.0	259 45.1	14.9	4 19.4	9.8	54.6
21	132 17.8	.. 12.5	274 19.0	14.9	4 09.6	9.8	54.6
22	147 17.6	12.0	288 52.9	14.9	3 59.8	9.8	54.6
23	162 17.4	11.4	303 26.8	14.9	3 50.0	9.9	54.6
20 00	177 17.2	S20 10.9	318 00.7	14.8	N 3 40.1	9.9	54.6
01	192 17.0	10.4	332 34.5	14.9	3 30.2	9.9	54.6
02	207 16.8	09.8	347 08.4	14.9	3 20.3	9.9	54.7
03	222 16.6	.. 09.3	1 42.3	14.8	3 10.4	9.9	54.7
04	237 16.5	08.7	16 16.1	14.9	3 00.5	10.0	54.7
05	252 16.3	08.2	30 50.0	14.9	2 50.5	9.9	54.7
M 06	267 16.1	S20 07.7	45 23.9	14.8	N 2 40.6	10.0	54.7
O 07	282 15.9	07.1	59 57.7	14.8	2 30.6	10.0	54.7
N 08	297 15.7	06.6	74 31.5	14.9	2 20.6	10.0	54.8
D 09	312 15.5	.. 06.0	89 05.4	14.8	2 10.6	10.1	54.8
A 10	327 15.4	05.5	103 39.2	14.8	2 00.5	10.0	54.8
Y 11	342 15.2	05.0	118 13.0	14.8	1 50.5	10.0	54.8
12	357 15.0	S20 04.4	132 46.8	14.8	N 1 40.5	10.1	54.8
13	12 14.8	03.9	147 20.6	14.7	1 30.4	10.1	54.8
14	27 14.6	03.3	161 54.3	14.8	1 20.3	10.1	54.9
15	42 14.5	.. 02.8	176 28.1	14.8	1 10.2	10.1	54.9
16	57 14.3	02.2	191 01.9	14.7	1 00.1	10.1	54.9
17	72 14.1	01.7	205 35.6	14.7	0 50.0	10.1	54.9
18	87 13.9	S20 01.1	220 09.3	14.7	N 0 39.9	10.1	54.9
19	102 13.7	00.6	234 43.0	14.7	0 29.8	10.2	55.0
20	117 13.6	20 00.0	249 16.7	14.7	0 19.6	10.1	55.0
21	132 13.4	19 59.5	263 50.4	14.6	N 0 09.5	10.1	55.0
22	147 13.2	58.9	278 24.0	14.7	S 0 00.7	10.1	55.0
23	162 13.0	58.4	292 57.7	14.6	0 10.8	10.2	55.0
21 00	177 12.8	S19 57.8	307 31.3	14.6	S 0 21.0	10.1	55.1
01	192 12.7	57.3	322 04.9	14.6	0 31.1	10.2	55.1
02	207 12.5	56.7	336 38.5	14.5	0 41.3	10.2	55.1
03	222 12.3	.. 56.2	351 12.0	14.5	0 51.5	10.2	55.1
04	237 12.1	55.6	5 45.5	14.6	1 01.7	10.1	55.1
05	252 12.0	55.1	20 19.1	14.4	1 11.8	10.2	55.2
T 06	267 11.8	S19 54.5	34 52.5	14.5	S 1 22.0	10.2	55.2
U 07	282 11.6	54.0	49 26.0	14.4	1 32.2	10.2	55.2
E 08	297 11.4	53.4	63 59.4	14.5	1 42.4	10.2	55.2
S 09	312 11.3	.. 52.8	78 32.9	14.3	1 52.6	10.2	55.3
D 10	327 11.1	52.3	93 06.2	14.4	2 02.8	10.1	55.3
A 11	342 10.9	51.7	107 39.6	14.3	2 12.9	10.2	55.3
Y 12	357 10.7	S19 51.2	122 12.9	14.3	S 2 23.1	10.2	55.3
13	12 10.6	50.6	136 46.2	14.3	2 33.3	10.1	55.3
14	27 10.4	50.0	151 19.5	14.2	2 43.4	10.2	55.4
15	42 10.2	.. 49.5	165 52.7	14.3	2 53.6	10.2	55.4
16	57 10.0	48.9	180 26.0	14.1	3 03.8	10.1	55.4
17	72 09.9	48.4	194 59.1	14.2	3 13.9	10.2	55.4
18	87 09.7	S19 47.8	209 32.3	14.1	S 3 24.1	10.1	55.4
19	102 09.5	47.2	224 05.4	14.1	3 34.2	10.2	55.5
20	117 09.4	46.7	238 38.5	14.0	3 44.4	10.1	55.5
21	132 09.2	.. 46.1	253 11.5	14.0	3 54.5	10.1	55.5
22	147 09.0	45.5	267 44.5	14.0	4 04.6	10.1	55.5
23	162 08.8	45.0	282 17.5	13.9	S 4 14.7	10.1	55.6
SD	16.3	d 0.5	SD 14.8		14.9		15.1

Lat.	Twilight Naut.	Twilight Civil	Sunrise	Moonrise 19	20	21	22
°	h m	h m	h m	h m	h m	h m	h m
N 72	07 48	09 31	■■	19 48	21 26	23 05	24 50
N 70	07 35	09 02	11 05	19 54	21 26	22 59	24 36
68	07 24	08 41	10 10	19 59	21 26	22 54	24 25
66	07 16	08 24	09 37	20 03	21 26	22 50	24 16
64	07 08	08 10	09 14	20 07	21 26	22 46	24 09
62	07 01	07 58	08 55	20 10	21 26	22 43	24 02
60	06 55	07 48	08 39	20 12	21 26	22 40	23 57
N 58	06 50	07 39	08 26	20 15	21 26	22 38	23 52
56	06 45	07 31	08 15	20 17	21 26	22 36	23 47
54	06 40	07 24	08 05	20 19	21 26	22 34	23 44
52	06 36	07 18	07 56	20 20	21 26	22 32	23 40
50	06 32	07 12	07 48	20 22	21 26	22 31	23 37
45	06 23	06 59	07 32	20 25	21 26	22 27	23 30
N 40	06 15	06 48	07 18	20 28	21 26	22 24	23 24
35	06 08	06 39	07 06	20 30	21 26	22 22	23 19
30	06 01	06 30	06 56	20 33	21 26	22 20	23 15
20	05 47	06 14	06 38	20 36	21 26	22 16	23 08
N 10	05 34	06 00	06 22	20 40	21 26	22 13	23 01
0	05 20	05 45	06 07	20 43	21 26	22 10	22 55
S 10	05 04	05 30	05 52	20 46	21 26	22 07	22 49
20	04 44	05 13	05 36	20 49	21 26	22 04	22 43
30	04 19	04 51	05 18	20 53	21 26	22 00	22 36
35	04 04	04 38	05 07	20 55	21 26	21 58	22 32
40	03 44	04 23	04 54	20 57	21 26	21 56	22 27
45	03 19	04 04	04 39	21 00	21 26	21 53	22 22
S 50	02 45	03 40	04 21	21 03	21 26	21 50	22 15
52	02 27	03 29	04 12	21 05	21 27	21 49	22 12
54	02 03	03 15	04 03	21 06	21 27	21 47	22 09
56	01 30	02 59	03 51	21 08	21 27	21 45	22 06
58	////	02 39	03 39	21 10	21 27	21 43	22 02
S 60	////	02 14	03 24	21 13	21 27	21 41	21 57

Lat.	Sunset	Twilight Civil	Twilight Naut.	Moonset 19	20	21	22
°	h m	h m	h m	h m	h m	h m	h m
N 72	■■	14 52	16 35	09 37	09 29	09 21	09 13
N 70	13 18	15 21	16 48	09 29	09 26	09 24	09 21
68	14 13	15 42	16 58	09 22	09 24	09 26	09 28
66	14 45	15 59	17 07	09 16	09 22	09 28	09 34
64	15 09	16 13	17 15	09 12	09 21	09 30	09 39
62	15 28	16 24	17 22	09 07	09 19	09 31	09 43
60	15 43	16 34	17 28	09 04	09 18	09 32	09 47
N 58	15 56	16 43	17 33	09 00	09 17	09 33	09 51
56	16 08	16 51	17 38	08 58	09 16	09 34	09 54
54	16 17	16 58	17 42	08 55	09 15	09 35	09 56
52	16 26	17 05	17 47	08 53	09 14	09 36	09 59
50	16 34	17 10	17 50	08 50	09 14	09 37	10 01
45	16 51	17 23	17 59	08 46	09 12	09 38	10 06
N 40	17 05	17 34	18 07	08 42	09 11	09 40	10 10
35	17 16	17 44	18 15	08 38	09 09	09 41	10 13
30	17 27	17 52	18 21	08 35	09 08	09 42	10 17
20	17 44	18 08	18 35	08 30	09 07	09 44	10 22
N 10	18 00	18 22	18 48	08 25	09 05	09 45	10 27
0	18 15	18 37	19 02	08 20	09 03	09 47	10 31
S 10	18 29	18 52	19 18	08 16	09 02	09 48	10 36
20	18 45	19 09	19 37	08 11	09 00	09 50	10 41
30	19 04	19 30	20 02	08 05	08 58	09 52	10 46
35	19 15	19 43	20 18	08 02	08 57	09 53	10 49
40	19 27	19 58	20 37	07 58	08 56	09 54	10 53
45	19 42	20 17	21 01	07 54	08 54	09 55	10 57
S 50	20 00	20 40	21 35	07 49	08 51	09 57	11 02
52	20 09	20 52	21 53	07 47	08 51	09 57	11 04
54	20 18	21 06	22 16	07 44	08 51	09 58	11 07
56	20 29	21 21	22 48	07 41	08 50	09 59	11 10
58	20 42	21 41	////	07 38	08 48	10 00	11 13
S 60	20 57	22 05	////	07 34	08 47	10 01	11 16

Day	SUN Eqn. of Time 00h	12h	Mer. Pass.	MOON Mer. Pass. Upper	Lower	Age	Phase
d	m s	m s	h m	h m	h m	d	%
19	10 33	10 42	12 11	02 10	14 31	18	90
20	10 51	11 00	12 11	02 53	15 15	19	84
21	11 08	11 17	12 11	03 36	15 58	20	76

24 2014 JANUARY 22, 23, 24 (WED., THURS., FRI.)

UT	ARIES	VENUS −4.5		MARS +0.4		JUPITER −2.7		SATURN +0.6		STARS		
	GHA	GHA	Dec	GHA	Dec	GHA	Dec	GHA	Dec	Name	SHA	Dec
d h	° ′	° ′	° ′	° ′	° ′	° ′	° ′	° ′	° ′		° ′	° ′
22 00	121 16.2	195 11.7	S15 51.0	281 52.6	S 5 35.0	16 44.8	N22 56.1	251 05.4	S16 06.8	Acamar	315 17.9	S40 15.2
01	136 18.6	210 15.2	50.9	296 54.3	35.3	31 47.6	56.2	266 07.7	06.9	Achernar	335 26.6	S57 10.3
02	151 21.1	225 18.7	50.8	311 55.9	35.6	46 50.4	56.2	281 10.0	06.9	Acrux	173 08.4	S63 10.4
03	166 23.6	240 22.2 ..	50.8	326 57.6 ..	35.9	61 53.2 ..	56.2	296 12.3 ..	06.9	Adhara	255 11.8	S28 59.8
04	181 26.0	255 25.7	50.7	341 59.2	36.2	76 56.0	56.3	311 14.6	07.0	Aldebaran	290 48.6	N16 32.1
05	196 28.5	270 29.2	50.6	357 00.9	36.5	91 58.8	56.3	326 16.9	07.0			
06	211 31.0	285 32.7	S15 50.5	12 02.5	S 5 36.8	107 01.6	N22 56.3	341 19.2	S16 07.0	Alioth	166 20.2	N55 52.7
W 07	226 33.4	300 36.2	50.4	27 04.2	37.1	122 04.4	56.4	356 21.5	07.1	Alkaid	152 58.6	N49 14.3
E 08	241 35.9	315 39.7	50.3	42 05.8	37.4	137 07.2	56.4	11 23.8	07.1	Al Na'ir	27 43.7	S46 53.6
D 09	256 38.4	330 43.2 ..	50.3	57 07.5 ..	37.7	152 09.9 ..	56.5	26 26.1 ..	07.1	Alnilam	275 45.7	S 1 11.8
N 10	271 40.8	345 46.6	50.2	72 09.1	38.0	167 12.7	56.5	41 28.4	07.2	Alphard	217 55.3	S 8 43.4
E 11	286 43.3	0 50.1	50.1	87 10.8	38.3	182 15.5	56.5	56 30.7	07.2			
S 12	301 45.8	15 53.6	S15 50.0	102 12.4	S 5 38.6	197 18.3	N22 56.6	71 33.0	S16 07.2	Alphecca	126 10.8	N26 39.9
D 13	316 48.2	30 57.0	50.0	117 14.1	38.9	212 21.1	56.6	86 35.3	07.3	Alpheratz	357 43.2	N29 10.2
A 14	331 50.7	46 00.5	49.9	132 15.7	39.2	227 23.9	56.6	101 37.6	07.3	Altair	62 08.1	N 8 54.5
Y 15	346 53.1	61 03.9 ..	49.8	147 17.4 ..	39.5	242 26.7 ..	56.7	116 39.9 ..	07.3	Ankaa	353 15.5	S42 14.0
16	1 55.6	76 07.4	49.7	162 19.1	39.7	257 29.5	56.7	131 42.2	07.4	Antares	112 25.9	S26 27.6
17	16 58.1	91 10.8	49.7	177 20.7	40.0	272 32.3	56.7	146 44.5	07.4			
18	32 00.5	106 14.2	S15 49.6	192 22.4	S 5 40.3	287 35.1	N22 56.8	161 46.8	S16 07.4	Arcturus	145 55.4	N19 06.4
19	47 03.0	121 17.7	49.5	207 24.0	40.6	302 37.8	56.8	176 49.1	07.5	Atria	107 27.7	S69 02.8
20	62 05.5	136 21.1	49.5	222 25.7	40.9	317 40.6	56.8	191 51.4	07.5	Avior	234 17.1	S59 33.5
21	77 07.9	151 24.5 ..	49.4	237 27.3 ..	41.2	332 43.4 ..	56.9	206 53.7 ..	07.5	Bellatrix	278 31.3	N 6 21.5
22	92 10.4	166 27.9	49.3	252 29.0	41.5	347 46.2	56.9	221 56.0	07.6	Betelgeuse	271 00.5	N 7 24.3
23	107 12.9	181 31.4	49.3	267 30.7	41.8	2 49.0	56.9	236 58.3	07.6			
23 00	122 15.3	196 34.8	S15 49.2	282 32.3	S 5 42.1	17 51.8	N22 57.0	252 00.6	S16 07.6	Canopus	263 55.4	S52 42.5
01	137 17.8	211 38.2	49.1	297 34.0	42.4	32 54.6	57.0	267 02.9	07.7	Capella	280 33.4	N46 00.6
02	152 20.3	226 41.6	49.1	312 35.7	42.7	47 57.4	57.0	282 05.2	07.7	Deneb	49 31.6	N45 20.0
03	167 22.7	241 45.0 ..	49.0	327 37.3 ..	42.9	63 00.2 ..	57.1	297 07.5 ..	07.7	Denebola	182 33.0	N14 29.4
04	182 25.2	256 48.4	48.9	342 39.0	43.2	78 02.9	57.1	312 09.8	07.8	Diphda	348 55.6	S17 54.7
05	197 27.6	271 51.8	48.9	357 40.6	43.5	93 05.7	57.2	327 12.1	07.8			
06	212 30.1	286 55.2	S15 48.8	12 42.3	S 5 43.8	108 08.5	N22 57.2	342 14.4	S16 07.8	Dubhe	193 50.8	N61 40.1
T 07	227 32.6	301 58.5	48.8	27 44.0	44.1	123 11.3	57.2	357 16.7	07.9	Elnath	278 11.8	N28 37.0
H 08	242 35.0	317 01.9	48.7	42 45.6	44.4	138 14.1	57.3	12 19.1	07.9	Eltanin	90 46.4	N51 29.2
U 09	257 37.5	332 05.3 ..	48.6	57 47.3 ..	44.7	153 16.9 ..	57.3	27 21.4 ..	07.9	Enif	33 47.0	N 9 56.5
R 10	272 40.0	347 08.7	48.6	72 49.0	45.0	168 19.7	57.3	42 23.7	08.0	Fomalhaut	15 23.8	S29 32.9
S 11	287 42.4	2 12.0	48.5	87 50.6	45.3	183 22.4	57.4	57 26.0	08.0			
D 12	302 44.9	17 15.4	S15 48.5	102 52.3	S 5 45.5	198 25.2	N22 57.4	72 28.3	S16 08.0	Gacrux	172 00.1	S57 11.3
A 13	317 47.4	32 18.7	48.4	117 54.0	45.8	213 28.0	57.4	87 30.6	08.0	Gienah	175 51.7	S17 37.2
Y 14	332 49.8	47 22.1	48.4	132 55.6	46.1	228 30.8	57.5	102 32.9	08.1	Hadar	148 47.2	S60 26.1
15	347 52.3	62 25.4 ..	48.3	147 57.3 ..	46.4	243 33.6 ..	57.5	117 35.2 ..	08.1	Hamal	328 00.2	N23 31.8
16	2 54.7	77 28.8	48.2	162 59.0	46.7	258 36.4	57.5	132 37.5	08.1	Kaus Aust.	83 43.6	S34 22.4
17	17 57.2	92 32.1	48.2	178 00.7	47.0	273 39.2	57.6	147 39.8	08.2			
18	32 59.7	107 35.5	S15 48.1	193 02.3	S 5 47.3	288 41.9	N22 57.6	162 42.1	S16 08.2	Kochab	137 20.4	N74 05.6
19	48 02.1	122 38.8	48.1	208 04.0	47.6	303 44.7	57.6	177 44.4	08.2	Markab	13 38.1	N15 17.0
20	63 04.6	137 42.1	48.0	223 05.7	47.8	318 47.5	57.7	192 46.7	08.3	Menkar	314 14.5	N 4 08.6
21	78 07.1	152 45.4 ..	48.0	238 07.3 ..	48.1	333 50.3 ..	57.7	207 49.0 ..	08.3	Menkent	148 07.0	S36 26.2
22	93 09.5	167 48.7	47.9	253 09.0	48.4	348 53.1	57.7	222 51.3	08.3	Miaplacidus	221 38.5	S69 46.6
23	108 12.0	182 52.1	47.9	268 10.7	48.7	3 55.9	57.8	237 53.6	08.4			
24 00	123 14.5	197 55.4	S15 47.8	283 12.4	S 5 49.0	18 58.7	N22 57.8	252 55.9	S16 08.4	Mirfak	308 39.5	N49 54.7
01	138 16.9	212 58.7	47.8	298 14.0	49.3	34 01.4	57.8	267 58.3	08.4	Nunki	75 58.1	S26 16.6
02	153 19.4	228 02.0	47.7	313 15.7	49.5	49 04.2	57.9	283 00.6	08.5	Peacock	53 19.2	S56 41.3
03	168 21.9	243 05.3 ..	47.7	328 17.4 ..	49.8	64 07.0 ..	57.9	298 02.9 ..	08.5	Pollux	243 26.8	N27 59.3
04	183 24.3	258 08.6	47.7	343 19.1	50.1	79 09.8	57.9	313 05.2	08.5	Procyon	244 58.9	N 5 11.1
05	198 26.8	273 11.8	47.6	358 20.7	50.4	94 12.6	58.0	328 07.5	08.6			
06	213 29.2	288 15.1	S15 47.6	13 22.4	S 5 50.7	109 15.4	N22 58.0	343 09.8	S16 08.6	Rasalhague	96 06.3	N12 33.1
07	228 31.7	303 18.4	47.5	28 24.1	51.0	124 18.1	58.0	358 12.1	08.6	Regulus	207 42.8	N11 53.6
08	243 34.2	318 21.7	47.5	43 25.8	51.2	139 20.9	58.1	13 14.4	08.7	Rigel	281 11.4	S 8 11.4
F 09	258 36.6	333 24.9 ..	47.4	58 27.5 ..	51.5	154 23.7 ..	58.1	28 16.7 ..	08.7	Rigil Kent.	139 51.1	S60 53.2
R 10	273 39.1	348 28.2	47.4	73 29.1	51.8	169 26.5	58.1	43 19.0	08.7	Sabik	102 12.3	S15 44.4
I 11	288 41.6	3 31.5	47.4	88 30.8	52.1	184 29.3	58.2	58 21.3	08.7			
D 12	303 44.0	18 34.7	S15 47.3	103 32.5	S 5 52.4	199 32.0	N22 58.2	73 23.6	S16 08.8	Schedar	349 40.1	N56 37.1
A 13	318 46.5	33 38.0	47.3	118 34.2	52.6	214 34.8	58.2	88 26.0	08.8	Shaula	96 21.6	S37 06.6
Y 14	333 49.0	48 41.2	47.2	133 35.9	52.9	229 37.6	58.3	103 28.3	08.8	Sirius	258 33.0	S16 44.4
15	348 51.4	63 44.5 ..	47.2	148 37.6 ..	53.2	244 40.4 ..	58.3	118 30.6 ..	08.9	Spica	158 30.7	S11 14.1
16	3 53.9	78 47.7	47.2	163 39.2	53.5	259 43.2	58.3	133 32.9	08.9	Suhail	222 51.6	S43 29.5
17	18 56.4	93 50.9	47.1	178 40.9	53.8	274 45.9	58.4	148 35.2	08.9			
18	33 58.8	108 54.2	S15 47.1	193 42.6	S 5 54.1	289 48.7	N22 58.4	163 37.5	S16 09.0	Vega	80 39.1	N38 47.9
19	49 01.3	123 57.4	47.1	208 44.3	54.3	304 51.5	58.4	178 39.8	09.0	Zuben'ubi	137 05.0	S16 05.9
20	64 03.7	139 00.6	47.0	223 46.0	54.6	319 54.3	58.5	193 42.1	09.0		SHA	Mer.Pass.
21	79 06.2	154 03.8 ..	47.0	238 47.7 ..	54.9	334 57.1 ..	58.5	208 44.4 ..	09.1		° ′	h m
22	94 08.7	169 07.0	47.0	253 49.4	55.2	349 59.8	58.5	223 46.7	09.1	Venus	74 19.4	10 51
23	109 11.1	184 10.3	46.9	268 51.0	55.4	5 02.6	58.6	238 49.0	09.1	Mars	160 17.0	5 09
	h m									Jupiter	255 36.5	22 44
Mer. Pass. 15 48.4		v 3.4	d 0.1	v 1.7	d 0.3	v 2.8	d 0.0	v 2.3	d 0.0	Saturn	129 45.3	7 11

UT	SUN GHA	SUN Dec	MOON GHA	v	Dec	d	HP
d h	° ′	° ′	° ′	′	° ′	′	′
22 00	177 08.7	S19 44.4	296 50.4	13.9	S 4 24.8	10.1	55.6
01	192 08.5	43.8	311 23.3	13.9	4 34.9	10.1	55.6
02	207 08.3	43.3	325 56.2	13.8	4 45.0	10.0	55.6
03	222 08.2	.. 42.7	340 29.0	13.8	4 55.0	10.1	55.7
04	237 08.0	42.1	355 01.8	13.7	5 05.1	10.0	55.7
05	252 07.8	41.6	9 34.5	13.7	5 15.1	10.0	55.7
W 06	267 07.7	S19 41.0	24 07.2	13.6	S 5 25.1	10.0	55.8
E 07	282 07.5	40.4	38 39.8	13.6	5 35.1	10.0	55.8
D 08	297 07.3	39.8	53 12.4	13.6	5 45.1	10.0	55.8
N 09	312 07.2	.. 39.3	67 45.0	13.5	5 55.1	9.9	55.8
E 10	327 07.0	38.7	82 17.5	13.5	6 05.0	9.9	55.9
S 11	342 06.8	38.1	96 50.0	13.4	6 14.9	10.0	55.9
D 12	357 06.7	S19 37.5	111 22.4	13.4	S 6 24.9	9.9	55.9
A 13	12 06.5	37.0	125 54.8	13.3	6 34.8	9.8	55.9
Y 14	27 06.3	36.4	140 27.1	13.3	6 44.6	9.9	56.0
15	42 06.2	.. 35.8	154 59.4	13.2	6 54.5	9.8	56.0
16	57 06.0	35.2	169 31.6	13.2	7 04.3	9.8	56.0
17	72 05.8	34.7	184 03.8	13.1	7 14.1	9.8	56.1
18	87 05.7	S19 34.1	198 35.9	13.1	S 7 23.9	9.7	56.1
19	102 05.5	33.5	213 08.0	13.0	7 33.6	9.8	56.1
20	117 05.4	32.9	227 40.0	12.9	7 43.4	9.7	56.1
21	132 05.2	.. 32.3	242 11.9	13.0	7 53.1	9.7	56.2
22	147 05.0	31.8	256 43.9	12.8	8 02.8	9.6	56.2
23	162 04.9	31.2	271 15.7	12.8	8 12.4	9.6	56.2
23 00	177 04.7	S19 30.6	285 47.5	12.8	S 8 22.0	9.6	56.3
01	192 04.5	30.0	300 19.3	12.6	8 31.6	9.6	56.3
02	207 04.4	29.4	314 50.9	12.7	8 41.2	9.5	56.3
03	222 04.2	.. 28.8	329 22.6	12.5	8 50.7	9.5	56.4
04	237 04.1	28.3	343 54.1	12.5	9 00.2	9.5	56.4
05	252 03.9	27.7	358 25.6	12.5	9 09.7	9.4	56.4
T 06	267 03.7	S19 27.1	12 57.1	12.4	S 9 19.1	9.4	56.4
H 07	282 03.6	26.5	27 28.5	12.3	9 28.5	9.3	56.5
U 08	297 03.4	25.9	41 59.8	12.2	9 37.8	9.4	56.5
R 09	312 03.3	.. 25.3	56 31.0	12.2	9 47.2	9.2	56.5
S 10	327 03.1	24.7	71 02.2	12.2	9 56.4	9.3	56.6
D 11	342 02.9	24.1	85 33.4	12.0	10 05.7	9.2	56.6
A 12	357 02.8	S19 23.6	100 04.4	12.0	S10 14.9	9.2	56.6
Y 13	12 02.6	23.0	114 35.4	12.0	10 24.1	9.1	56.7
14	27 02.5	22.4	129 06.4	11.8	10 33.2	9.1	56.7
15	42 02.3	.. 21.8	143 37.2	11.8	10 42.3	9.0	56.7
16	57 02.2	21.2	158 08.0	11.8	10 51.3	9.0	56.8
17	72 02.0	20.6	172 38.8	11.6	11 00.3	9.0	56.8
18	87 01.8	S19 20.0	187 09.4	11.6	S11 09.3	8.9	56.8
19	102 01.7	19.4	201 40.0	11.6	11 18.2	8.8	56.9
20	117 01.5	18.8	216 10.6	11.4	11 27.0	8.9	56.9
21	132 01.4	.. 18.2	230 41.0	11.4	11 35.9	8.7	56.9
22	147 01.2	17.6	245 11.4	11.3	11 44.6	8.7	57.0
23	162 01.1	17.0	259 41.7	11.2	11 53.3	8.7	57.0
24 00	177 00.9	S19 16.4	274 11.9	11.2	S12 02.0	8.6	57.0
01	192 00.8	15.8	288 42.1	11.1	12 10.6	8.6	57.1
02	207 00.6	15.2	303 12.2	11.0	12 19.2	8.5	57.1
03	222 00.5	.. 14.6	317 42.2	10.9	12 27.7	8.4	57.1
04	237 00.3	14.0	332 12.1	10.9	12 36.1	8.4	57.2
05	252 00.1	13.4	346 42.0	10.8	12 44.5	8.4	57.2
F 06	267 00.0	S19 12.8	1 11.8	10.7	S12 52.9	8.3	57.2
R 07	281 59.8	12.2	15 41.5	10.6	13 01.2	8.2	57.3
I 08	296 59.7	11.6	30 11.1	10.6	13 09.4	8.2	57.3
D 09	311 59.5	.. 11.0	44 40.7	10.5	13 17.6	8.1	57.4
A 10	326 59.4	10.4	59 10.2	10.4	13 25.7	8.0	57.4
Y 11	341 59.2	09.8	73 39.6	10.3	13 33.7	8.0	57.4
12	356 59.1	S19 09.2	88 08.9	10.2	S13 41.7	7.9	57.5
13	11 58.9	08.6	102 38.1	10.2	13 49.6	7.9	57.5
14	26 58.8	08.0	117 07.3	10.1	13 57.5	7.7	57.5
15	41 58.6	.. 07.4	131 36.4	10.0	14 05.2	7.8	57.6
16	56 58.5	06.8	146 05.4	9.9	14 13.0	7.6	57.6
17	71 58.3	06.2	160 34.3	9.8	14 20.6	7.6	57.6
18	86 58.2	S19 05.6	175 03.1	9.8	S14 28.2	7.5	57.7
19	101 58.0	05.0	189 31.9	9.6	14 35.7	7.5	57.7
20	116 57.9	04.4	204 00.5	9.6	14 43.2	7.3	57.8
21	131 57.8	.. 03.7	218 29.1	9.5	14 50.5	7.3	57.8
22	146 57.6	03.1	232 57.6	9.5	14 57.8	7.3	57.8
23	161 57.5	02.5	247 26.1	9.3	S15 05.1	7.1	57.9
SD	16.3	d 0.6	SD 15.2		15.4		15.7

Lat.	Twilight Naut.	Twilight Civil	Sunrise	Moonrise 22	23	24	25
°	h m	h m	h m	h m	h m	h m	h m
N 72	07 39	09 18	■	24 50	00 50	02 42	04 47
N 70	07 28	08 52	10 41	24 36	00 36	02 18	04 06
68	07 18	08 33	09 57	24 25	00 25	02 00	03 37
66	07 10	08 17	09 27	24 16	00 16	01 45	03 16
64	07 03	08 04	09 06	24 09	00 09	01 33	02 59
62	06 57	07 53	08 48	24 02	00 02	01 23	02 46
60	06 51	07 43	08 34	23 57	25 15	01 15	02 34
N 58	06 46	07 35	08 21	23 52	25 07	01 07	02 24
56	06 41	07 28	08 11	23 47	25 01	01 01	02 15
54	06 37	07 21	08 01	23 44	24 55	00 55	02 07
52	06 33	07 15	07 53	23 40	24 50	00 50	02 00
50	06 30	07 09	07 45	23 37	24 45	00 45	01 54
45	06 21	06 57	07 29	23 30	24 35	00 35	01 41
N 40	06 14	06 47	07 16	23 24	24 26	00 26	01 30
35	06 07	06 37	07 05	23 19	24 19	00 19	01 20
30	06 00	06 29	06 55	23 15	24 13	00 13	01 12
20	05 47	06 14	06 37	23 08	24 02	00 02	00 58
N 10	05 35	06 00	06 22	23 01	23 52	24 46	00 46
0	05 21	05 46	06 08	22 55	23 43	24 34	00 34
S 10	05 05	05 31	05 54	22 49	23 34	24 23	00 23
20	04 47	05 15	05 38	22 43	23 25	24 11	00 11
30	04 23	04 54	05 20	22 36	23 14	23 57	24 45
35	04 07	04 42	05 10	22 32	23 08	23 49	24 35
40	03 49	04 27	04 58	22 27	23 01	23 40	24 24
45	03 25	04 09	04 44	22 22	22 53	23 29	24 12
S 50	02 52	03 46	04 26	22 15	22 44	23 17	23 57
52	02 35	03 35	04 18	22 12	22 39	23 11	23 50
54	02 13	03 22	04 08	22 09	22 34	23 04	23 42
56	01 44	03 07	03 58	22 06	22 29	22 57	23 33
58	00 54	02 48	03 46	22 02	22 23	22 49	23 23
S 60	////	02 25	03 32	21 57	22 16	22 40	23 11

Lat.	Sunset	Twilight Civil	Twilight Naut.	Moonset 22	23	24	25
°	h m	h m	h m	h m	h m	h m	h m
N 72	■	15 07	16 46	09 13	09 04	08 52	08 34
N 70	13 43	15 32	16 57	09 21	09 19	09 17	09 17
68	14 28	15 52	17 07	09 28	09 31	09 37	09 46
66	14 57	16 07	17 15	09 34	09 42	09 52	10 07
64	15 19	16 20	17 22	09 39	09 50	10 05	10 25
62	15 36	16 31	17 28	09 43	09 58	10 16	10 39
60	15 51	16 41	17 33	09 47	10 04	10 25	10 52
N 58	16 03	16 49	17 38	09 51	10 10	10 33	11 02
56	16 14	16 57	17 43	09 54	10 15	10 40	11 11
54	16 23	17 03	17 47	09 56	10 19	10 47	11 20
52	16 32	17 09	17 51	09 59	10 24	10 52	11 27
50	16 39	17 15	17 55	10 01	10 27	10 58	11 34
45	16 55	17 27	18 03	10 06	10 36	11 09	11 48
N 40	17 08	17 37	18 10	10 10	10 44	11 18	12 00
35	17 19	17 47	18 17	10 13	10 48	11 27	12 10
30	17 29	17 55	18 24	10 17	10 53	11 34	12 19
20	17 46	18 10	18 36	10 22	11 02	11 46	12 34
N 10	18 01	18 23	18 49	10 27	11 10	11 57	12 47
0	18 15	18 37	19 03	10 31	11 18	12 07	13 00
S 10	18 30	18 52	19 18	10 36	11 25	12 17	13 12
20	18 45	19 09	19 37	10 41	11 33	12 28	13 26
30	19 03	19 29	20 01	10 46	11 42	12 41	13 41
35	19 13	19 41	20 16	10 49	11 48	12 48	13 50
40	19 25	19 56	20 34	10 53	11 54	12 56	14 00
45	19 39	20 14	20 58	10 57	12 01	13 06	14 12
S 50	19 57	20 36	21 30	11 02	12 09	13 18	14 27
52	20 05	20 48	21 47	11 04	12 13	13 23	14 34
54	20 14	21 00	22 08	11 07	12 17	13 29	14 41
56	20 25	21 15	22 35	11 10	12 22	13 36	14 50
58	20 36	21 33	23 21	11 13	12 27	13 43	14 59
S 60	20 50	21 55	////	11 16	12 33	13 52	15 10

Day	Eqn. of Time 00h	Eqn. of Time 12h	SUN Mer. Pass.	MOON Mer. Pass. Upper	Mer. Pass. Lower	Age	Phase %
d	m s	m s	h m	h m	h m	d	%
22	11 25	11 33	12 12	16 43	04 20	21	67
23	11 41	11 49	12 12	17 30	05 06	22	58
24	11 56	12 03	12 12	18 21	05 55	23	47

2014 JANUARY 25, 26, 27 (SAT., SUN., MON.)

UT	ARIES GHA	VENUS −4.6 GHA	Dec	MARS +0.4 GHA	Dec	JUPITER −2.6 GHA	Dec	SATURN +0.5 GHA	Dec	STARS Name	SHA	Dec
d h	° ′	° ′	° ′	° ′	° ′	° ′	° ′	° ′	° ′		° ′	° ′
25 00	124 13.6	199 13.5	S15 46.9	283 52.7	S 5 55.7	20 05.4	N22 58.6	253 51.4	S16 09.2	Acamar	315 18.0	S40 15.2
01	139 16.1	214 16.7	46.9	298 54.4	56.0	35 08.2	58.6	268 53.7	09.2	Achernar	335 26.6	S57 10.3
02	154 18.5	229 19.9	46.9	313 56.1	56.3	50 11.0	58.7	283 56.0	09.2	Acrux	173 08.3	S63 10.4
03	169 21.0	244 23.0 ..	46.8	328 57.8 ..	56.6	65 13.7 ..	58.7	298 58.3 ..	09.2	Adhara	255 11.8	S28 59.8
04	184 23.5	259 26.2	46.8	343 59.5	56.8	80 16.5	58.7	314 00.6	09.3	Aldebaran	290 48.7	N16 32.1
05	199 25.9	274 29.4	46.8	359 01.2	57.1	95 19.3	58.8	329 02.9	09.3			
06	214 28.4	289 32.6	S15 46.8	14 02.9	S 5 57.4	110 22.1	N22 58.8	344 05.2	S16 09.3	Alioth	166 20.2	N55 52.7
07	229 30.8	304 35.8	46.7	29 04.6	57.7	125 24.9	58.8	359 07.5	09.4	Alkaid	152 58.5	N49 14.3
S 08	244 33.3	319 38.9	46.7	44 06.3	57.9	140 27.6	58.9	14 09.9	09.4	Al Na'ir	27 43.7	S46 53.6
A 09	259 35.8	334 42.1 ..	46.7	59 08.0 ..	58.2	155 30.4 ..	58.9	29 12.2 ..	09.4	Alnilam	275 45.7	S 1 11.8
T 10	274 38.2	349 45.2	46.7	74 09.7	58.5	170 33.2	58.9	44 14.5	09.5	Alphard	217 55.3	S 8 43.4
U 11	289 40.7	4 48.4	46.6	89 11.4	58.8	185 36.0	59.0	59 16.8	09.5			
R 12	304 43.2	19 51.5	S15 46.6	104 13.0	S 5 59.0	200 38.7	N22 59.0	74 19.1	S16 09.5	Alphecca	126 10.8	N26 39.9
D 13	319 45.6	34 54.7	46.6	119 14.7	59.3	215 41.5	59.0	89 21.4	09.5	Alpheratz	357 43.2	N29 10.2
A 14	334 48.1	49 57.8	46.6	134 16.4	59.6	230 44.3	59.1	104 23.7	09.6	Altair	62 08.1	N 8 54.4
Y 15	349 50.6	65 01.0 ..	46.6	149 18.1	5 59.9	245 47.1 ..	59.1	119 26.0 ..	09.6	Ankaa	353 15.5	S42 14.0
16	4 53.0	80 04.1	46.5	164 19.8	6 00.1	260 49.8	59.1	134 28.4	09.6	Antares	112 25.9	S26 27.6
17	19 55.5	95 07.2	46.5	179 21.5	00.4	275 52.6	59.2	149 30.7	09.7			
18	34 58.0	110 10.3	S15 46.5	194 23.2	S 6 00.7	290 55.4	N22 59.2	164 33.0	S16 09.7	Arcturus	145 55.3	N19 06.4
19	50 00.4	125 13.5	46.5	209 24.9	01.0	305 58.2	59.2	179 35.3	09.7	Atria	107 27.7	S69 02.8
20	65 02.9	140 16.6	46.5	224 26.6	01.2	321 00.9	59.3	194 37.6	09.8	Avior	234 17.1	S59 33.5
21	80 05.3	155 19.7 ..	46.5	239 28.3 ..	01.5	336 03.7 ..	59.3	209 39.9 ..	09.8	Bellatrix	278 31.3	N 6 21.5
22	95 07.8	170 22.8	46.4	254 30.0	01.8	351 06.5	59.3	224 42.2	09.8	Betelgeuse	271 00.5	N 7 24.3
23	110 10.3	185 25.9	46.4	269 31.7	02.0	6 09.3	59.4	239 44.5	09.8			
26 00	125 12.7	200 29.0	S15 46.4	284 33.4	S 6 02.3	21 12.0	N22 59.4	254 46.9	S16 09.9	Canopus	263 55.5	S52 42.5
01	140 15.2	215 32.1	46.4	299 35.2	02.6	36 14.8	59.4	269 49.2	09.9	Capella	280 33.4	N46 00.6
02	155 17.7	230 35.2	46.4	314 36.9	02.9	51 17.6	59.5	284 51.5	09.9	Deneb	49 31.6	N45 20.0
03	170 20.1	245 38.2 ..	46.4	329 38.6 ..	03.1	66 20.4 ..	59.5	299 53.8 ..	10.0	Denebola	182 33.0	N14 29.4
04	185 22.6	260 41.3	46.4	344 40.3	03.4	81 23.1	59.5	314 56.1	10.0	Diphda	348 55.6	S17 54.7
05	200 25.1	275 44.4	46.4	359 42.0	03.7	96 25.9	59.6	329 58.4	10.0			
06	215 27.5	290 47.5	S15 46.3	14 43.7	S 6 03.9	111 28.7	N22 59.6	345 00.8	S16 10.1	Dubhe	193 50.7	N61 40.2
07	230 30.0	305 50.5	46.3	29 45.4	04.2	126 31.5	59.6	0 03.1	10.1	Elnath	278 11.8	N28 37.0
08	245 32.5	320 53.6	46.3	44 47.1	04.5	141 34.2	59.7	15 05.4	10.1	Eltanin	90 46.4	N51 29.2
S 09	260 34.9	335 56.6 ..	46.3	59 48.8 ..	04.7	156 37.0 ..	59.7	30 07.7 ..	10.1	Enif	33 47.0	N 9 56.5
U 10	275 37.4	350 59.7	46.3	74 50.5	05.0	171 39.8	59.7	45 10.0	10.2	Fomalhaut	15 23.8	S29 32.9
N 11	290 39.8	6 02.7	46.3	89 52.2	05.3	186 42.5	59.8	60 12.3	10.2			
D 12	305 42.3	21 05.8	S15 46.3	104 53.9	S 6 05.6	201 45.3	N22 59.8	75 14.6	S16 10.2	Gacrux	172 00.0	S57 11.4
A 13	320 44.8	36 08.8	46.3	119 55.6	05.8	216 48.1	59.8	90 17.0	10.3	Gienah	175 51.6	S17 37.2
Y 14	335 47.2	51 11.8	46.3	134 57.4	06.1	231 50.9	59.9	105 19.3	10.3	Hadar	148 47.1	S60 26.2
15	350 49.7	66 14.9 ..	46.3	149 59.1 ..	06.4	246 53.6 ..	59.9	120 21.6 ..	10.3	Hamal	328 00.2	N23 31.8
16	5 52.2	81 17.9	46.3	165 00.8	06.6	261 56.4	22 59.9	135 23.9	10.3	Kaus Aust.	83 43.6	S34 22.4
17	20 54.6	96 20.9	46.3	180 02.5	06.9	276 59.2	23 00.0	150 26.2	10.4			
18	35 57.1	111 23.9	S15 46.3	195 04.2	S 6 07.2	292 01.9	N23 00.0	165 28.5	S16 10.4	Kochab	137 20.4	N74 05.6
19	50 59.6	126 26.9	46.3	210 05.9	07.4	307 04.7	00.0	180 30.9	10.4	Markab	13 38.1	N15 17.0
20	66 02.0	141 29.9	46.3	225 07.6	07.7	322 07.5	00.1	195 33.2	10.5	Menkar	314 14.5	N 4 08.5
21	81 04.5	156 32.9 ..	46.3	240 09.4 ..	08.0	337 10.2 ..	00.1	210 35.5 ..	10.5	Menkent	148 07.0	S36 26.2
22	96 07.0	171 35.9	46.3	255 11.1	08.2	352 13.0	00.1	225 37.8	10.5	Miaplacidus	221 38.5	S69 46.6
23	111 09.4	186 38.9	46.3	270 12.8	08.5	7 15.8	00.2	240 40.1	10.6			
27 00	126 11.9	201 41.9	S15 46.3	285 14.5	S 6 08.7	22 18.6	N23 00.2	255 42.5	S16 10.6	Mirfak	308 39.5	N49 54.7
01	141 14.3	216 44.9	46.3	300 16.2	09.0	37 21.3	00.2	270 44.8	10.6	Nunki	75 58.1	S26 16.6
02	156 16.8	231 47.9	46.3	315 17.9	09.3	52 24.1	00.2	285 47.1	10.6	Peacock	53 19.2	S56 41.2
03	171 19.3	246 50.8 ..	46.3	330 19.7 ..	09.5	67 26.9 ..	00.3	300 49.4 ..	10.7	Pollux	243 26.8	N27 59.3
04	186 21.7	261 53.8	46.3	345 21.4	09.8	82 29.6	00.3	315 51.7	10.7	Procyon	244 58.9	N 5 11.0
05	201 24.2	276 56.8	46.3	0 23.1	10.1	97 32.4	00.3	330 54.0	10.7			
06	216 26.7	291 59.7	S15 46.3	15 24.8	S 6 10.3	112 35.2	N23 00.4	345 56.4	S16 10.8	Rasalhague	96 06.3	N12 33.0
07	231 29.1	307 02.7	46.3	30 26.6	10.6	127 37.9	00.4	0 58.7	10.8	Regulus	207 42.8	N11 53.6
08	246 31.6	322 05.6	46.4	45 28.3	10.9	142 40.7	00.4	16 01.0	10.8	Rigel	281 11.4	S 8 11.4
M 09	261 34.1	337 08.6 ..	46.4	60 30.0 ..	11.1	157 43.5 ..	00.5	31 03.3 ..	10.8	Rigil Kent.	139 51.1	S60 53.2
O 10	276 36.5	352 11.5	46.4	75 31.7	11.4	172 46.2	00.5	46 05.6	10.9	Sabik	102 12.3	S15 44.4
N 11	291 39.0	7 14.5	46.4	90 33.4	11.6	187 49.0	00.5	61 08.0	10.9			
D 12	306 41.5	22 17.4	S15 46.4	105 35.2	S 6 11.9	202 51.8	N23 00.6	76 10.3	S16 10.9	Schedar	349 40.1	N56 37.1
A 13	321 43.9	37 20.3	46.4	120 36.9	12.2	217 54.5	00.6	91 12.6	10.9	Shaula	96 21.6	S37 06.6
Y 14	336 46.4	52 23.2	46.4	135 38.6	12.4	232 57.3	00.6	106 14.9	11.0	Sirius	258 33.0	S16 44.4
15	351 48.8	67 26.2 ..	46.4	150 40.4 ..	12.7	248 00.1 ..	00.7	121 17.2 ..	11.0	Spica	158 30.7	S11 14.1
16	6 51.3	82 29.1	46.4	165 42.1	12.9	263 02.8	00.7	136 19.6	11.0	Suhail	222 51.6	S43 29.5
17	21 53.8	97 32.0	46.5	180 43.8	13.2	278 05.6	00.7	151 21.9	11.1			
18	36 56.2	112 34.9	S15 46.5	195 45.5	S 6 13.5	293 08.4	N23 00.8	166 24.2	S16 11.1	Vega	80 39.0	N38 47.8
19	51 58.7	127 37.8	46.5	210 47.3	13.7	308 11.1	00.8	181 26.5	11.1	Zuben'ubi	137 05.0	S16 05.9
20	67 01.2	142 40.7	46.5	225 49.0	14.0	323 13.9	00.8	196 28.8	11.1		SHA	Mer. Pass.
21	82 03.6	157 43.6 ..	46.5	240 50.7 ..	14.2	338 16.6 ..	00.8	211 31.2 ..	11.2		° ′	h m
22	97 06.1	172 46.5	46.5	255 52.5	14.5	353 19.4	00.9	226 33.5	11.2	Venus	75 16.2	10 36
23	112 08.6	187 49.3	46.6	270 54.2	14.8	8 22.2	00.9	241 35.8	11.2	Mars	159 20.7	5 01
	h m									Jupiter	255 59.3	22 31
Mer. Pass. 15 36.6		v 3.0	d 0.0	v 1.7	d 0.3	v 2.8	d 0.0	v 2.3	d 0.0	Saturn	129 34.1	7 00

UT	SUN GHA	SUN Dec	MOON GHA	MOON v	MOON Dec	MOON d	MOON HP
d h	° ′	° ′	° ′	′	° ′	′	′
25 00	176 57.3	S19 01.9	261 54.4	9.3	S15 12.2	7.1	57.9
01	191 57.2	01.3	276 22.7	9.1	15 19.3	7.0	57.9
02	206 57.0	00.7	290 50.8	9.1	15 26.3	6.9	58.0
03	221 56.9	19 00.1	305 18.9	9.0	15 33.2	6.8	58.0
04	236 56.7	18 59.5	319 46.9	9.0	15 40.0	6.8	58.1
05	251 56.6	58.8	334 14.9	8.8	15 46.8	6.7	58.1
S 06	266 56.4	S18 58.2	348 42.7	8.8	S15 53.5	6.6	58.1
A 07	281 56.3	57.6	3 10.5	8.6	16 00.1	6.5	58.2
T 08	296 56.2	57.0	17 38.1	8.6	16 06.6	6.4	58.2
U 09	311 56.0 ..	56.4	32 05.7	8.5	16 13.0	6.3	58.2
R 10	326 55.9	55.8	46 33.2	8.4	16 19.3	6.3	58.3
D 11	341 55.7	55.1	61 00.6	8.4	16 25.6	6.1	58.3
A 12	356 55.6	S18 54.5	75 28.0	8.2	S16 31.7	6.1	58.4
Y 13	11 55.4	53.9	89 55.2	8.2	16 37.8	6.0	58.4
14	26 55.3	53.3	104 22.4	8.0	16 43.8	5.9	58.4
15	41 55.2 ..	52.7	118 49.4	8.0	16 49.7	5.7	58.5
16	56 55.0	52.0	133 16.4	7.9	16 55.4	5.7	58.5
17	71 54.9	51.4	147 43.3	7.9	17 01.1	5.6	58.6
18	86 54.7	S18 50.8	162 10.2	7.7	S17 06.7	5.6	58.6
19	101 54.6	50.2	176 36.9	7.7	17 12.3	5.4	58.6
20	116 54.5	49.5	191 03.6	7.5	17 17.7	5.3	58.7
21	131 54.3 ..	48.9	205 30.1	7.5	17 23.0	5.2	58.7
22	146 54.2	48.3	219 56.6	7.5	17 28.2	5.1	58.7
23	161 54.0	47.7	234 23.1	7.3	17 33.3	5.0	58.8
26 00	176 53.9	S18 47.0	248 49.4	7.2	S17 38.3	4.9	58.8
01	191 53.8	46.4	263 15.6	7.2	17 43.2	4.8	58.9
02	206 53.6	45.8	277 41.8	7.1	17 48.0	4.7	58.9
03	221 53.5 ..	45.2	292 07.9	7.0	17 52.7	4.6	58.9
04	236 53.4	44.5	306 33.9	6.9	17 57.3	4.5	59.0
05	251 53.2	43.9	320 59.8	6.8	18 01.8	4.3	59.0
S 06	266 53.1	S18 43.3	335 25.6	6.8	S18 06.1	4.3	59.0
U 07	281 53.0	42.6	349 51.4	6.7	18 10.4	4.2	59.1
N 08	296 52.8	42.0	4 17.1	6.6	18 14.6	4.0	59.1
D 09	311 52.7 ..	41.4	18 42.7	6.5	18 18.6	3.9	59.2
A 10	326 52.5	40.7	33 08.2	6.5	18 22.5	3.8	59.2
Y 11	341 52.4	40.1	47 33.7	6.3	18 26.3	3.7	59.2
12	356 52.3	S18 39.5	61 59.0	6.3	S18 30.0	3.6	59.3
13	11 52.1	38.8	76 24.3	6.3	18 33.6	3.5	59.3
14	26 52.0	38.2	90 49.6	6.1	18 37.1	3.4	59.3
15	41 51.9 ..	37.6	105 14.7	6.1	18 40.5	3.2	59.4
16	56 51.7	36.9	119 39.8	6.0	18 43.7	3.1	59.4
17	71 51.6	36.3	134 04.8	5.9	18 46.8	3.0	59.5
18	86 51.5	S18 35.7	148 29.7	5.9	S18 49.8	2.9	59.5
19	101 51.3	35.0	162 54.6	5.8	18 52.7	2.7	59.5
20	116 51.2	34.4	177 19.4	5.7	18 55.4	2.6	59.6
21	131 51.1 ..	33.7	191 44.1	5.7	18 58.0	2.5	59.6
22	146 51.0	33.1	206 08.8	5.6	19 00.5	2.4	59.6
23	161 50.8	32.5	220 33.4	5.5	19 02.9	2.3	59.7
27 00	176 50.7	S18 31.8	234 57.9	5.5	S19 05.2	2.1	59.7
01	191 50.6	31.2	249 22.4	5.4	19 07.3	2.0	59.7
02	206 50.4	30.5	263 46.8	5.3	19 09.3	1.9	59.8
03	221 50.3 ..	29.9	278 11.1	5.3	19 11.2	1.7	59.8
04	236 50.2	29.3	292 35.4	5.2	19 12.9	1.6	59.8
05	251 50.1	28.6	306 59.6	5.2	19 14.5	1.5	59.9
M 06	266 49.9	S18 28.0	321 23.8	5.1	S19 16.0	1.3	59.9
O 07	281 49.8	27.3	335 47.9	5.0	19 17.3	1.3	60.0
N 08	296 49.7	26.7	350 11.9	5.0	19 18.6	1.0	60.0
D 09	311 49.5 ..	26.0	4 35.9	4.9	19 19.6	1.0	60.0
A 10	326 49.4	25.4	18 59.8	4.9	19 20.6	0.8	60.1
Y 11	341 49.3	24.7	33 23.7	4.8	19 21.4	0.7	60.1
12	356 49.2	S18 24.1	47 47.5	4.8	S19 22.1	0.5	60.1
13	11 49.0	23.4	62 11.3	4.7	19 22.6	0.5	60.2
14	26 48.9	22.8	76 35.0	4.7	19 23.1	0.2	60.2
15	41 48.8 ..	22.1	90 58.7	4.6	19 23.3	0.2	60.2
16	56 48.7	21.5	105 22.3	4.6	19 23.5	0.0	60.2
17	71 48.5	20.8	119 45.9	4.6	19 23.5	0.2	60.3
18	86 48.4	S18 20.2	134 09.5	4.5	S19 23.3	0.2	60.3
19	101 48.3	19.5	148 33.0	4.5	19 23.1	0.4	60.3
20	116 48.2	18.9	162 56.5	4.4	19 22.7	0.6	60.4
21	131 48.0 ..	18.2	177 19.9	4.4	19 22.1	0.7	60.4
22	146 47.9	17.6	191 43.3	4.3	19 21.4	0.8	60.4
23	161 47.8	16.9	206 06.6	4.4	S19 20.6	1.0	60.5
	SD 16.3	d 0.6	SD 15.9		16.1		16.4

Lat.	Twilight Naut.	Twilight Civil	Sunrise	Moonrise 25	Moonrise 26	Moonrise 27	Moonrise 28
°	h m	h m	h m	h m	h m	h m	h m
N 72	07 30	09 05	11 40	04 47	▬▬	▬▬	▬▬
N 70	07 20	08 42	10 21	04 06	05 58	07 43	08 34
68	07 11	08 24	09 43	03 37	05 14	06 40	07 37
66	07 04	08 10	09 17	03 16	04 45	06 04	07 03
64	06 57	07 57	08 57	02 59	04 23	05 39	06 38
62	06 51	07 47	08 41	02 46	04 06	05 19	06 19
60	06 46	07 38	08 27	02 34	03 51	05 03	06 03
N 58	06 42	07 30	08 16	02 24	03 39	04 49	05 49
56	06 38	07 23	08 06	02 15	03 28	04 37	05 38
54	06 34	07 17	07 57	02 07	03 19	04 27	05 27
52	06 30	07 11	07 49	02 00	03 11	04 18	05 18
50	06 27	07 06	07 42	01 54	03 03	04 09	05 10
45	06 19	06 55	07 26	01 41	02 47	03 52	04 53
N 40	06 12	06 45	07 14	01 30	02 34	03 38	04 38
35	06 05	06 36	07 03	01 20	02 23	03 26	04 26
30	05 59	06 28	06 53	01 12	02 13	03 15	04 16
20	05 47	06 14	06 37	00 58	01 57	02 57	03 58
N 10	05 35	06 00	06 23	00 46	01 42	02 41	03 42
0	05 22	05 47	06 09	00 34	01 29	02 27	03 27
S 10	05 07	05 33	05 55	00 23	01 15	02 12	03 12
20	04 49	05 17	05 40	00 11	01 01	01 56	02 57
30	04 26	04 57	05 23	24 45	00 45	01 39	02 39
35	04 11	04 45	05 13	24 35	00 35	01 28	02 28
40	03 53	04 31	05 02	24 24	00 24	01 16	02 16
45	03 30	04 14	04 48	24 12	00 12	01 02	02 02
S 50	02 59	03 52	04 31	23 57	24 46	00 46	01 45
52	02 43	03 41	04 23	23 49	24 38	00 38	01 37
54	02 23	03 29	04 14	23 42	24 29	00 29	01 28
56	01 58	03 15	04 04	23 33	24 19	00 19	01 18
58	01 19	02 57	03 53	23 23	24 07	00 07	01 06
S 60	////	02 36	03 40	23 11	23 54	24 52	00 52

Lat.	Sunset	Twilight Civil	Twilight Naut.	Moonset 25	Moonset 26	Moonset 27	Moonset 28
°	h m	h m	h m	h m	h m	h m	h m
N 72	12 46	15 21	16 56	08 34	▬▬	▬▬	▬▬
N 70	14 05	15 44	17 07	09 17	09 19	09 37	10 54
68	14 43	16 02	17 15	09 46	10 03	10 40	11 50
66	15 09	16 16	17 23	10 07	10 33	11 16	12 24
64	15 29	16 28	17 29	10 25	10 55	11 41	12 49
62	15 45	16 39	17 34	10 39	11 13	12 01	13 08
60	15 58	16 48	17 39	10 52	11 28	12 18	13 24
N 58	16 10	16 55	17 44	11 02	11 41	12 32	13 37
56	16 20	17 02	17 48	11 11	11 52	12 43	13 49
54	16 29	17 09	17 52	11 20	12 01	12 54	13 59
52	16 37	17 14	17 56	11 27	12 10	13 03	14 08
50	16 44	17 19	17 59	11 34	12 18	13 11	14 16
45	16 59	17 31	18 07	11 48	12 34	13 29	14 33
N 40	17 12	17 41	18 14	12 00	12 48	13 43	14 47
35	17 22	17 49	18 20	12 10	12 59	13 56	14 59
30	17 32	17 57	18 26	12 19	13 09	14 06	15 09
20	17 48	18 11	18 38	12 34	13 27	14 24	15 27
N 10	18 03	18 25	18 50	12 47	13 42	14 40	15 42
0	18 16	18 38	19 03	13 00	13 56	14 55	15 56
S 10	18 30	18 52	19 18	13 12	14 10	15 10	16 11
20	18 44	19 08	19 36	13 26	14 25	15 26	16 26
30	19 01	19 28	19 59	13 41	14 43	15 44	16 43
35	19 11	19 39	20 13	13 50	14 53	15 54	16 53
40	19 23	19 53	20 31	14 00	15 04	16 07	17 05
45	19 36	20 10	20 54	14 12	15 18	16 21	17 18
S 50	19 53	20 32	21 24	14 27	15 34	16 38	17 35
52	20 01	20 43	21 40	14 34	15 42	16 46	17 43
54	20 10	20 55	21 59	14 41	15 51	16 55	17 51
56	20 19	21 09	22 24	14 50	16 01	17 06	18 01
58	20 31	21 25	23 00	14 59	16 12	17 17	18 12
S 60	20 44	21 46	////	15 10	16 25	17 31	18 24

	SUN			MOON			
Day	Eqn. of Time 00ʰ	Eqn. of Time 12ʰ	Mer. Pass.	Mer. Pass. Upper	Mer. Pass. Lower	Age	Phase
d	m s	m s	h m	h m	h m	d	%
25	12 10	12 17	12 12	06 47	19 14	24	36
26	12 24	12 31	12 13	07 42	20 11	25	26
27	12 37	12 43	12 13	08 41	21 11	26	17

UT	ARIES GHA	VENUS −4.7 GHA	Dec	MARS +0.3 GHA	Dec	JUPITER −2.6 GHA	Dec	SATURN +0.5 GHA	Dec	STARS Name	SHA	Dec
d h	° ′	° ′	° ′	° ′	° ′	° ′	° ′	° ′	° ′		° ′	° ′
28 00	127 11.0	202 52.2	S15 46.6	285 55.9	S 6 15.0	23 24.9	N23 00.9	256 38.1	S16 11.3	Acamar	315 18.0	S40 15.3
01	142 13.5	217 55.1	46.6	300 57.7	15.3	38 27.7	01.0	271 40.5	11.3	Achernar	335 26.6	S57 10.2
02	157 15.9	232 58.0	46.6	315 59.4	15.5	53 30.5	01.0	286 42.8	11.3	Acrux	173 08.3	S63 10.5
03	172 18.4	248 00.8	.. 46.6	331 01.1	.. 15.8	68 33.2	.. 01.0	301 45.1	.. 11.3	Adhara	255 11.8	S28 59.8
04	187 20.9	263 03.7	46.7	346 02.9	16.1	83 36.0	01.1	316 47.4	11.4	Aldebaran	290 48.7	N16 32.1
05	202 23.3	278 06.5	46.7	1 04.6	16.3	98 38.7	01.1	331 49.7	11.4			
06	217 25.8	293 09.4	S15 46.7	16 06.3	S 6 16.6	113 41.5	N23 01.1	346 52.1	S16 11.4	Alioth	166 20.1	N55 52.7
T 07	232 28.3	308 12.2	46.7	31 08.1	16.8	128 44.3	01.2	1 54.4	11.4	Alkaid	152 58.5	N49 14.3
U 08	247 30.7	323 15.1	46.7	46 09.8	17.1	143 47.0	01.2	16 56.7	11.5	Al Na'ir	27 43.7	S46 53.6
E 09	262 33.2	338 17.9	.. 46.8	61 11.6	.. 17.3	158 49.8	.. 01.2	31 59.0	.. 11.5	Alnilam	275 45.7	S 1 11.9
S 10	277 35.7	353 20.7	46.8	76 13.3	17.6	173 52.6	01.3	47 01.4	11.5	Alphard	217 55.3	S 8 43.4
11	292 38.1	8 23.6	46.8	91 15.0	17.8	188 55.3	01.3	62 03.7	11.6			
D 12	307 40.6	23 26.4	S15 46.8	106 16.8	S 6 18.1	203 58.1	N23 01.3	77 06.0	S16 11.6	Alphecca	126 10.7	N26 39.9
A 13	322 43.1	38 29.2	46.9	121 18.5	18.4	219 00.8	01.3	92 08.3	11.6	Alpheratz	357 43.2	N29 10.2
Y 14	337 45.5	53 32.0	46.9	136 20.3	18.6	234 03.6	01.4	107 10.6	11.6	Altair	62 08.1	N 8 54.4
15	352 48.0	68 34.8	.. 46.9	151 22.0	.. 18.9	249 06.4	.. 01.4	122 13.0	.. 11.7	Ankaa	353 15.5	S42 14.0
16	7 50.4	83 37.6	47.0	166 23.7	19.1	264 09.1	01.4	137 15.3	11.7	Antares	112 25.9	S26 27.6
17	22 52.9	98 40.4	47.0	181 25.5	19.4	279 11.9	01.5	152 17.6	11.7			
18	37 55.4	113 43.2	S15 47.0	196 27.2	S 6 19.6	294 14.6	N23 01.5	167 19.9	S16 11.7	Arcturus	145 55.3	N19 06.4
19	52 57.8	128 46.0	47.0	211 29.0	19.9	309 17.4	01.5	182 22.3	11.8	Atria	107 27.6	S69 02.8
20	68 00.3	143 48.8	47.1	226 30.7	20.1	324 20.2	01.6	197 24.6	11.8	Avior	234 17.1	S59 33.5
21	83 02.8	158 51.6	.. 47.1	241 32.5	.. 20.4	339 22.9	.. 01.6	212 26.9	.. 11.8	Bellatrix	278 31.3	N 6 21.5
22	98 05.2	173 54.4	47.1	256 34.2	20.6	354 25.7	01.6	227 29.2	11.9	Betelgeuse	271 00.5	N 7 24.3
23	113 07.7	188 57.1	47.2	271 36.0	20.9	9 28.4	01.6	242 31.6	11.9			
29 00	128 10.2	203 59.9	S15 47.2	286 37.7	S 6 21.1	24 31.2	N23 01.7	257 33.9	S16 11.9	Canopus	263 55.5	S52 42.6
01	143 12.6	219 02.7	47.2	301 39.5	21.4	39 33.9	01.7	272 36.2	11.9	Capella	280 33.4	N46 00.7
02	158 15.1	234 05.4	47.3	316 41.2	21.6	54 36.7	01.7	287 38.5	12.0	Deneb	49 31.6	N45 20.0
03	173 17.6	249 08.2	.. 47.3	331 43.0	.. 21.9	69 39.5	.. 01.8	302 40.9	.. 12.0	Denebola	182 33.0	N14 29.4
04	188 20.0	264 10.9	47.3	346 44.7	22.1	84 42.2	01.8	317 43.2	12.0	Diphda	348 55.6	S17 54.7
05	203 22.5	279 13.7	47.4	1 46.5	22.4	99 45.0	01.8	332 45.5	12.0			
06	218 24.9	294 16.4	S15 47.4	16 48.2	S 6 22.6	114 47.7	N23 01.9	347 47.9	S16 12.1	Dubhe	193 50.7	N61 40.2
W 07	233 27.4	309 19.2	47.4	31 50.0	22.9	129 50.5	01.9	2 50.2	12.1	Elnath	278 11.8	N28 37.0
E 08	248 29.9	324 21.9	47.5	46 51.7	23.1	144 53.2	01.9	17 52.5	12.1	Eltanin	90 46.3	N51 29.2
D 09	263 32.3	339 24.6	.. 47.5	61 53.5	.. 23.4	159 56.0	.. 02.0	32 54.8	.. 12.1	Enif	33 47.0	N 9 56.5
N 10	278 34.8	354 27.3	47.6	76 55.2	23.6	174 58.7	02.0	47 57.2	12.2	Fomalhaut	15 23.8	S29 32.9
E 11	293 37.3	9 30.0	47.6	91 57.0	23.9	190 01.5	02.0	62 59.5	12.2			
S 12	308 39.7	24 32.8	S15 47.7	106 58.8	S 6 24.1	205 04.3	N23 02.0	78 01.8	S16 12.2	Gacrux	172 00.0	S57 11.4
D 13	323 42.2	39 35.5	47.7	122 00.5	24.4	220 07.0	02.1	93 04.1	12.3	Gienah	175 51.6	S17 37.3
A 14	338 44.7	54 38.2	47.7	137 02.3	24.6	235 09.8	02.1	108 06.5	12.3	Hadar	148 47.1	S60 26.2
Y 15	353 47.1	69 40.9	.. 47.8	152 04.0	.. 24.9	250 12.5	.. 02.1	123 08.8	.. 12.3	Hamal	328 00.2	N23 31.7
16	8 49.6	84 43.6	47.8	167 05.8	25.1	265 15.3	02.2	138 11.1	12.3	Kaus Aust.	83 43.6	S34 22.4
17	23 52.1	99 46.3	47.8	182 07.5	25.4	280 18.0	02.2	153 13.5	12.4			
18	38 54.5	114 48.9	S15 47.9	197 09.3	S 6 25.6	295 20.8	N23 02.2	168 15.8	S16 12.4	Kochab	137 20.3	N74 05.6
19	53 57.0	129 51.6	47.9	212 11.1	25.9	310 23.5	02.3	183 18.1	12.4	Markab	13 38.1	N15 16.9
20	68 59.4	144 54.3	48.0	227 12.8	26.1	325 26.3	02.3	198 20.4	12.4	Menkar	314 14.5	N 4 08.5
21	84 01.9	159 57.0	.. 48.0	242 14.6	.. 26.3	340 29.0	.. 02.3	213 22.8	.. 12.5	Menkent	148 06.9	S36 26.2
22	99 04.4	174 59.6	48.1	257 16.4	26.6	355 31.8	02.3	228 25.1	12.5	Miaplacidus	221 38.5	S69 46.6
23	114 06.8	190 02.3	48.1	272 18.1	26.8	10 34.5	02.4	243 27.4	12.5			
30 00	129 09.3	205 05.0	S15 48.2	287 19.9	S 6 27.1	25 37.3	N23 02.4	258 29.8	S16 12.5	Mirfak	308 39.5	N49 54.7
01	144 11.8	220 07.6	48.2	302 21.7	27.3	40 40.0	02.4	273 32.1	12.6	Nunki	75 58.1	S26 16.6
02	159 14.2	235 10.3	48.3	317 23.4	27.6	55 42.8	02.5	288 34.4	12.6	Peacock	53 19.2	S56 41.2
03	174 16.7	250 12.9	.. 48.3	332 25.2	.. 27.8	70 45.5	.. 02.5	303 36.7	.. 12.6	Pollux	243 26.8	N27 59.3
04	189 19.2	265 15.6	48.3	347 27.0	28.1	85 48.3	02.5	318 39.1	12.6	Procyon	244 58.9	N 5 11.0
05	204 21.6	280 18.2	48.4	2 28.7	28.3	100 51.0	02.5	333 41.4	12.7			
06	219 24.1	295 20.8	S15 48.4	17 30.5	S 6 28.5	115 53.8	N23 02.6	348 43.7	S16 12.7	Rasalhague	96 06.3	N12 33.0
T 07	234 26.6	310 23.5	48.5	32 32.3	28.8	130 56.5	02.6	3 46.1	12.7	Regulus	207 42.7	N11 53.6
H 08	249 29.0	325 26.1	48.5	47 34.0	29.0	145 59.3	02.6	18 48.4	12.7	Rigel	281 11.4	S 8 11.4
U 09	264 31.5	340 28.7	.. 48.6	62 35.8	.. 29.3	161 02.0	.. 02.7	33 50.7	.. 12.8	Rigil Kent.	139 51.0	S60 53.2
R 10	279 33.9	355 31.3	48.6	77 37.6	29.5	176 04.8	02.7	48 53.1	12.8	Sabik	102 12.2	S15 44.4
11	294 36.4	10 33.9	48.7	92 39.3	29.8	191 07.5	02.7	63 55.4	12.8			
S 12	309 38.9	25 36.5	S15 48.8	107 41.1	S 6 30.0	206 10.3	N23 02.8	78 57.7	S16 12.8	Schedar	349 40.2	N56 37.1
D 13	324 41.3	40 39.1	48.8	122 42.9	30.2	221 13.0	02.8	94 00.1	12.9	Shaula	96 21.6	S37 06.6
A 14	339 43.8	55 41.7	48.9	137 44.7	30.5	236 15.8	02.8	109 02.4	12.9	Sirius	258 33.0	S16 44.5
Y 15	354 46.3	70 44.3	.. 48.9	152 46.4	.. 30.7	251 18.5	.. 02.8	124 04.7	.. 12.9	Spica	158 30.7	S11 14.1
16	9 48.7	85 46.9	49.0	167 48.2	31.0	266 21.3	02.9	139 07.0	12.9	Suhail	222 51.6	S43 29.6
17	24 51.2	100 49.5	49.0	182 50.0	31.2	281 24.0	02.9	154 09.4	13.0			
18	39 53.7	115 52.1	S15 49.1	197 51.8	S 6 31.4	296 26.8	N23 02.9	169 11.7	S16 13.0	Vega	80 39.0	N38 47.8
19	54 56.1	130 54.6	49.1	212 53.5	31.7	311 29.5	03.0	184 14.0	13.0	Zuben'ubi	137 04.9	S16 05.9
20	69 58.6	145 57.2	49.2	227 55.3	31.9	326 32.3	03.0	199 16.4	13.0		SHA	Mer. Pass.
21	85 01.0	160 59.8	.. 49.2	242 57.1	.. 32.1	341 35.0	.. 03.0	214 18.7	.. 13.1		° ′	h m
22	100 03.5	176 02.3	49.3	257 58.9	32.4	356 37.8	03.0	229 21.0	13.1	Venus	75 49.7	10 22
23	115 06.0	191 04.9	49.4	273 00.7	32.6	11 40.5	03.1	244 23.4	13.1	Mars	158 27.6	4 53
Mer. Pass.	h m 15 24.8	v 2.7 d 0.0		v 1.8 d 0.2		v 2.8 d 0.0		v 2.3 d 0.0		Jupiter	256 21.0	22 18
										Saturn	129 23.7	6 49

UT	SUN GHA	SUN Dec	MOON GHA	v	Dec	d	HP
d h	o '	o '	o '	'	o '	'	'
28 00	176 47.7	S18 16.3	220 30.0	4.3	S19 19.6	1.1	60.5
01	191 47.6	15.6	234 53.3	4.2	19 18.5	1.2	60.5
02	206 47.4	15.0	249 16.5	4.3	19 17.3	1.4	60.5
03	221 47.3 ..	14.3	263 39.8	4.2	19 15.9	1.6	60.6
04	236 47.2	13.6	278 03.0	4.1	19 14.3	1.6	60.6
05	251 47.1	13.0	292 26.1	4.2	19 12.7	1.8	60.6
06	266 47.0	S18 12.3	306 49.3	4.1	S19 10.9	2.0	60.7
07	281 46.8	11.7	321 12.4	4.1	19 08.9	2.1	60.7
T 08	296 46.7	11.0	335 35.5	4.1	19 06.8	2.2	60.7
U 09	311 46.6 ..	10.4	349 58.6	4.1	19 04.6	2.4	60.7
E 10	326 46.5	09.7	4 21.7	4.0	19 02.2	2.5	60.8
S 11	341 46.4	09.0	18 44.7	4.1	18 59.7	2.7	60.8
D 12	356 46.3	S18 08.4	33 07.8	4.0	S18 57.0	2.8	60.8
A 13	11 46.1	07.7	47 30.8	4.0	18 54.2	2.9	60.8
Y 14	26 46.0	07.0	61 53.8	4.0	18 51.3	3.1	60.9
15	41 45.9 ..	06.4	76 16.8	4.0	18 48.2	3.2	60.9
16	56 45.8	05.7	90 39.8	4.0	18 45.0	3.4	60.9
17	71 45.7	05.1	105 02.8	4.0	18 41.6	3.5	60.9
18	86 45.6	S18 04.4	119 25.8	4.0	S18 38.1	3.6	61.0
19	101 45.4	03.7	133 48.8	4.0	18 34.5	3.8	61.0
20	116 45.3	03.1	148 11.8	4.0	18 30.7	3.9	61.0
21	131 45.2 ..	02.4	162 34.8	3.9	18 26.8	4.1	61.0
22	146 45.1	01.7	176 57.7	4.0	18 22.7	4.2	61.0
23	161 45.0	01.1	191 20.7	4.0	18 18.5	4.3	61.1
29 00	176 44.9	S18 00.4	205 43.7	4.0	S18 14.2	4.5	61.1
01	191 44.8	17 59.7	220 06.7	4.0	18 09.7	4.6	61.1
02	206 44.6	59.0	234 29.7	4.0	18 05.1	4.7	61.1
03	221 44.5 ..	58.4	248 52.7	4.1	18 00.4	4.9	61.1
04	236 44.4	57.7	263 15.8	4.0	17 55.5	5.0	61.1
05	251 44.3	57.0	277 38.8	4.1	17 50.5	5.1	61.2
06	266 44.2	S17 56.4	292 01.9	4.0	S17 45.4	5.3	61.2
W 07	281 44.1	55.7	306 24.9	4.1	17 40.1	5.4	61.2
E 08	296 44.0	55.0	320 48.0	4.1	17 34.7	5.6	61.2
D 09	311 43.9 ..	54.3	335 11.1	4.1	17 29.1	5.7	61.2
N 10	326 43.8	53.7	349 34.2	4.2	17 23.4	5.8	61.2
E 11	341 43.6	53.0	3 57.4	4.2	17 17.6	5.9	61.3
S 12	356 43.5	S17 52.3	18 20.6	4.2	S17 11.7	6.1	61.3
D 13	11 43.4	51.6	32 43.8	4.2	17 05.6	6.2	61.3
A 14	26 43.3	51.0	47 07.0	4.2	16 59.4	6.3	61.3
Y 15	41 43.2 ..	50.3	61 30.2	4.3	16 53.1	6.5	61.3
16	56 43.1	49.6	75 53.5	4.3	16 46.6	6.5	61.3
17	71 43.0	48.9	90 16.8	4.3	16 40.1	6.7	61.3
18	86 42.9	S17 48.3	104 40.1	4.4	S16 33.4	6.9	61.3
19	101 42.8	47.6	119 03.5	4.4	16 26.5	6.9	61.3
20	116 42.7	46.9	133 26.9	4.4	16 19.6	7.1	61.4
21	131 42.6 ..	46.2	147 50.3	4.5	16 12.5	7.2	61.4
22	146 42.5	45.5	162 13.8	4.5	16 05.3	7.3	61.4
23	161 42.4	44.9	176 37.3	4.6	15 58.0	7.4	61.4
30 00	176 42.3	S17 44.2	191 00.9	4.5	S15 50.6	7.5	61.4
01	191 42.1	43.5	205 24.4	4.7	15 43.1	7.7	61.4
02	206 42.0	42.8	219 48.1	4.6	15 35.4	7.8	61.4
03	221 41.9 ..	42.1	234 11.7	4.7	15 27.6	7.8	61.4
04	236 41.8	41.4	248 35.4	4.8	15 19.8	8.0	61.4
05	251 41.7	40.8	262 59.2	4.8	15 11.8	8.1	61.4
06	266 41.6	S17 40.1	277 23.0	4.8	S15 03.7	8.3	61.4
07	281 41.5	39.4	291 46.8	4.9	14 55.4	8.3	61.4
T 08	296 41.4	38.7	306 10.7	5.0	14 47.1	8.4	61.4
H 09	311 41.3 ..	38.0	320 34.7	4.9	14 38.7	8.6	61.4
U 10	326 41.2	37.3	334 58.6	5.1	14 30.1	8.6	61.4
R 11	341 41.1	36.6	349 22.7	5.1	14 21.5	8.7	61.4
S 12	356 41.0	S17 36.0	3 46.8	5.1	S14 12.8	8.9	61.4
D 13	11 40.9	35.3	18 10.9	5.2	14 03.9	8.9	61.4
A 14	26 40.8	34.6	32 35.1	5.2	13 55.0	9.1	61.4
Y 15	41 40.7 ..	33.9	46 59.3	5.3	13 45.9	9.1	61.4
16	56 40.6	33.2	61 23.6	5.4	13 36.8	9.2	61.4
17	71 40.5	32.5	75 48.0	5.3	13 27.6	9.4	61.4
18	86 40.4	S17 31.8	90 12.3	5.5	S13 18.2	9.4	61.4
19	101 40.3	31.1	104 36.8	5.5	13 08.8	9.5	61.4
20	116 40.2	30.4	119 01.3	5.6	12 59.3	9.6	61.4
21	131 40.1 ..	29.7	133 25.9	5.6	12 49.7	9.7	61.4
22	146 40.0	29.0	147 50.5	5.7	12 40.0	9.8	61.4
23	161 39.9	28.4	162 15.2	5.7	S12 30.2	9.8	61.4
	SD 16.3	d 0.7	SD 16.6		16.7		16.7

Lat.	Twilight Naut.	Twilight Civil	Sunrise	Moonrise 28	Moonrise 29	Moonrise 30	Moonrise 31
o	h m	h m	h m	h m	h m	h m	h m
N 72	07 20	08 52	10 56	■■■	09 50	09 16	09 01
N 70	07 11	08 31	10 03	08 34	08 43	08 44	08 43
68	07 03	08 15	09 30	07 37	08 07	08 21	08 29
66	06 57	08 02	09 07	07 03	07 40	08 03	08 17
64	06 51	07 50	08 49	06 38	07 20	07 48	08 08
62	06 46	07 41	08 34	06 19	07 04	07 36	07 59
60	06 41	07 33	08 21	06 03	06 50	07 25	07 52
N 58	06 37	07 25	08 10	05 49	06 38	07 16	07 45
56	06 33	07 19	08 01	05 38	06 28	07 08	07 40
54	06 30	07 13	07 52	05 27	06 18	07 00	07 35
52	06 27	07 08	07 45	05 18	06 10	06 54	07 30
50	06 24	07 03	07 38	05 10	06 03	06 48	07 26
45	06 16	06 52	07 23	04 53	05 47	06 35	07 17
N 40	06 09	06 42	07 11	04 38	05 34	06 24	07 09
35	06 04	06 34	07 01	04 26	05 23	06 15	07 02
30	05 58	06 27	06 52	04 16	05 14	06 07	06 57
20	05 47	06 13	06 36	03 58	04 57	05 54	06 46
N 10	05 35	06 01	06 23	03 42	04 42	05 41	06 38
0	05 23	05 48	06 10	03 27	04 29	05 30	06 29
S 10	05 08	05 34	05 56	03 12	04 15	05 19	06 21
20	04 51	05 19	05 42	02 57	04 01	05 06	06 12
30	04 29	05 00	05 26	02 39	03 44	04 52	06 02
35	04 15	04 48	05 16	02 28	03 34	04 44	05 56
40	03 58	04 35	05 05	02 16	03 23	04 35	05 49
45	03 36	04 18	04 52	02 02	03 10	04 24	05 41
S 50	03 07	03 58	04 36	01 45	02 54	04 11	05 32
52	02 52	03 47	04 29	01 37	02 47	04 05	05 27
54	02 33	03 36	04 20	01 28	02 39	03 58	05 23
56	02 10	03 22	04 11	01 18	02 29	03 51	05 17
58	01 38	03 07	04 00	01 06	02 19	03 42	05 11
S 60	////	02 47	03 48	00 52	02 06	03 32	05 04

Lat.	Sunset	Twilight Civil	Twilight Naut.	Moonset 28	Moonset 29	Moonset 30	Moonset 31
o	h m	h m	h m	h m	h m	h m	h m
N 72	13 32	15 36	17 08	■■■	11 48	14 30	16 47
N 70	14 25	15 56	17 17	10 54	12 54	15 00	17 03
68	14 57	16 12	17 24	11 50	13 30	15 22	17 15
66	15 20	16 26	17 31	12 24	13 55	15 39	17 26
64	15 38	16 37	17 36	12 49	14 15	15 53	17 34
62	15 53	16 46	17 41	13 08	14 31	16 05	17 42
60	16 06	16 54	17 46	13 24	14 44	16 14	17 48
N 58	16 17	17 02	17 50	13 37	14 56	16 23	17 53
56	16 26	17 08	17 53	13 49	15 06	16 31	17 58
54	16 35	17 14	17 57	13 59	15 15	16 37	18 03
52	16 42	17 19	18 00	14 08	15 22	16 43	18 06
50	16 49	17 24	18 03	14 16	15 29	16 49	18 10
45	17 03	17 35	18 10	14 33	15 44	17 00	18 18
N 40	17 15	17 44	18 17	14 47	15 57	17 10	18 24
35	17 26	17 52	18 23	14 59	16 07	17 18	18 30
30	17 34	18 00	18 28	15 09	16 16	17 25	18 34
20	17 50	18 13	18 40	15 27	16 32	17 38	18 43
N 10	18 04	18 26	18 51	15 42	16 45	17 48	18 50
0	18 17	18 38	19 04	15 56	16 58	17 58	18 57
S 10	18 30	18 52	19 18	16 11	17 11	18 08	19 03
20	18 44	19 07	19 35	16 26	17 24	18 19	19 10
30	19 00	19 26	19 57	16 43	17 39	18 31	19 18
35	19 09	19 37	20 11	16 53	17 48	18 38	19 22
40	19 20	19 51	20 28	17 05	17 58	18 45	19 28
45	19 33	20 07	20 49	17 18	18 10	18 54	19 33
S 50	19 49	20 27	21 18	17 35	18 24	19 05	19 41
52	19 56	20 37	21 33	17 43	18 30	19 10	19 44
54	20 05	20 49	21 50	17 51	18 38	19 16	19 47
56	20 14	21 02	22 13	18 01	18 46	19 22	19 51
58	20 24	21 17	22 43	18 12	18 55	19 28	19 55
S 60	20 37	21 36	23 42	18 24	19 05	19 36	20 00

	SUN			MOON			
Day	Eqn. of Time 00h	Eqn. of Time 12h	Mer. Pass.	Mer. Pass. Upper	Mer. Pass. Lower	Age	Phase
d	m s	m s	h m	h m	h m	d	%
28	12 49	12 55	12 13	09 42	22 13	27	9
29	13 00	13 06	12 13	10 44	23 14	28	3
30	13 11	13 16	12 13	11 44	24 14	29	0

UT	ARIES GHA	VENUS −4.8 GHA	VENUS Dec	MARS +0.2 GHA	MARS Dec	JUPITER −2.6 GHA	JUPITER Dec	SATURN +0.5 GHA	SATURN Dec	Star Name	SHA	Star Dec
d h	° ′	° ′	° ′	° ′	° ′	° ′	° ′	° ′	° ′		° ′	° ′
31 00	130 08.4	206 07.4	S15 49.4	288 02.4	S 6 32.9	26 43.3	N23 03.1	259 25.7	S16 13.1	Acamar	315 18.0	S40 15.3
01	145 10.9	221 10.0	49.5	303 04.2	33.1	41 46.0	03.1	274 28.0	13.2	Achernar	335 26.7	S57 10.2
02	160 13.4	236 12.5	49.5	318 06.0	33.3	56 48.7	03.2	289 30.4	13.2	Acrux	173 08.2	S63 10.5
03	175 15.8	251 15.1 ..	49.6	333 07.8 ..	33.6	71 51.5 ..	03.2	304 32.7 ..	13.2	Adhara	255 11.8	S28 59.8
04	190 18.3	266 17.6	49.7	348 09.6	33.8	86 54.2	03.2	319 35.0	13.2	Aldebaran	290 48.7	N16 32.1
05	205 20.8	281 20.1	49.7	3 11.4	34.0	101 57.0	03.2	334 37.4	13.3			
06	220 23.2	296 22.7	S15 49.8	18 13.1	S 6 34.3	116 59.7	N23 03.3	349 39.7	S16 13.3	Alioth	166 20.1	N55 52.7
F 07	235 25.7	311 25.2	49.8	33 14.9	34.5	132 02.5	03.3	4 42.0	13.3	Alkaid	152 58.5	N49 14.3
R 08	250 28.2	326 27.7	49.9	48 16.7	34.7	147 05.2	03.3	19 44.4	13.3	Al Na'ir	27 43.6	S46 53.6
I 09	265 30.6	341 30.2 ..	50.0	63 18.5 ..	35.0	162 08.0 ..	03.4	34 46.7 ..	13.4	Alnilam	275 45.7	S 1 11.9
D 10	280 33.1	356 32.7	50.0	78 20.3	35.2	177 10.7	03.4	49 49.0	13.4	Alphard	217 55.3	S 8 43.4
A 11	295 35.5	11 35.2	50.1	93 22.1	35.5	192 13.4	03.4	64 51.4	13.4			
Y 12	310 38.0	26 37.7	S15 50.2	108 23.9	S 6 35.7	207 16.2	N23 03.4	79 53.7	S16 13.4	Alphecca	126 10.7	N26 39.9
13	325 40.5	41 40.2	50.2	123 25.7	35.9	222 18.9	03.5	94 56.1	13.5	Alpheratz	357 43.2	N29 10.2
14	340 42.9	56 42.7	50.3	138 27.5	36.2	237 21.7	03.5	109 58.4	13.5	Altair	62 08.1	N 8 54.4
15	355 45.4	71 45.2 ..	50.3	153 29.2 ..	36.4	252 24.4 ..	03.5	125 00.7 ..	13.5	Ankaa	353 15.5	S42 14.0
16	10 47.9	86 47.7	50.4	168 31.0	36.6	267 27.2	03.6	140 03.1	13.5	Antares	112 25.8	S26 27.6
17	25 50.3	101 50.2	50.5	183 32.8	36.9	282 29.9	03.6	155 05.4	13.5			
18	40 52.8	116 52.6	S15 50.5	198 34.6	S 6 37.1	297 32.6	N23 03.6	170 07.7	S16 13.6	Arcturus	145 55.3	N19 06.4
19	55 55.3	131 55.1	50.6	213 36.4	37.3	312 35.4	03.6	185 10.1	13.6	Atria	107 27.5	S69 02.8
20	70 57.7	146 57.6	50.7	228 38.2	37.5	327 38.1	03.7	200 12.4	13.6	Avior	234 17.1	S59 33.5
21	86 00.2	162 00.0 ..	50.7	243 40.0 ..	37.8	342 40.9 ..	03.7	215 14.7 ..	13.6	Bellatrix	278 31.3	N 6 21.5
22	101 02.7	177 02.5	50.8	258 41.8	38.0	357 43.6	03.7	230 17.1	13.7	Betelgeuse	271 00.5	N 7 24.3
23	116 05.1	192 04.9	50.9	273 43.6	38.2	12 46.3	03.8	245 19.4	13.7			
1 00	131 07.6	207 07.4	S15 51.0	288 45.4	S 6 38.5	27 49.1	N23 03.8	260 21.8	S16 13.7	Canopus	263 55.5	S52 42.6
01	146 10.0	222 09.8	51.0	303 47.2	38.7	42 51.8	03.8	275 24.1	13.7	Capella	280 33.4	N46 00.7
02	161 12.5	237 12.2	51.1	318 49.0	38.9	57 54.6	03.8	290 26.4	13.8	Deneb	49 31.6	N45 20.0
03	176 15.0	252 14.7 ..	51.2	333 50.8 ..	39.2	72 57.3 ..	03.9	305 28.8 ..	13.8	Denebola	182 33.0	N14 29.4
04	191 17.4	267 17.1	51.2	348 52.6	39.4	88 00.0	03.9	320 31.1	13.8	Diphda	348 55.6	S17 54.7
05	206 19.9	282 19.5	51.3	3 54.4	39.6	103 02.8	03.9	335 33.4	13.8			
06	221 22.4	297 21.9	S15 51.4	18 56.2	S 6 39.8	118 05.5	N23 04.0	350 35.8	S16 13.9	Dubhe	193 50.7	N61 40.2
S 07	236 24.8	312 24.4	51.5	33 58.0	40.1	133 08.2	04.0	5 38.1	13.9	Elnath	278 11.8	N28 37.0
A 08	251 27.3	327 26.8	51.5	48 59.8	40.3	148 11.0	04.0	20 40.5	13.9	Eltanin	90 46.3	N51 29.2
T 09	266 29.8	342 29.2 ..	51.6	64 01.6 ..	40.5	163 13.7 ..	04.0	35 42.8 ..	13.9	Enif	33 47.0	N 9 56.5
U 10	281 32.2	357 31.6	51.7	79 03.4	40.8	178 16.5	04.1	50 45.1	13.9	Fomalhaut	15 23.8	S29 32.9
R 11	296 34.7	12 34.0	51.7	94 05.2	41.0	193 19.2	04.1	65 47.5	14.0			
D 12	311 37.1	27 36.4	S15 51.8	109 07.0	S 6 41.2	208 21.9	N23 04.1	80 49.8	S16 14.0	Gacrux	172 00.0	S57 11.4
A 13	326 39.6	42 38.8	51.9	124 08.8	41.4	223 24.7	04.1	95 52.1	14.0	Gienah	175 51.6	S17 37.3
Y 14	341 42.1	57 41.1	52.0	139 10.6	41.7	238 27.4	04.2	110 54.5	14.0	Hadar	148 47.0	S60 26.2
15	356 44.5	72 43.5 ..	52.0	154 12.5 ..	41.9	253 30.1 ..	04.2	125 56.8 ..	14.1	Hamal	328 00.3	N23 31.7
16	11 47.0	87 45.9	52.1	169 14.3	42.1	268 32.9	04.2	140 59.2	14.1	Kaus Aust.	83 43.5	S34 22.4
17	26 49.5	102 48.3	52.2	184 16.1	42.3	283 35.6	04.3	156 01.5	14.1			
18	41 51.9	117 50.6	S15 52.3	199 17.9	S 6 42.6	298 38.3	N23 04.3	171 03.8	S16 14.1	Kochab	137 20.2	N74 05.6
19	56 54.4	132 53.0	52.3	214 19.7	42.8	313 41.1	04.3	186 06.2	14.1	Markab	13 38.1	N15 16.9
20	71 56.9	147 55.4	52.4	229 21.5	43.0	328 43.8	04.3	201 08.5	14.2	Menkar	314 14.5	N 4 08.5
21	86 59.3	162 57.7 ..	52.5	244 23.3 ..	43.2	343 46.5 ..	04.4	216 10.9 ..	14.2	Menkent	148 06.9	S36 26.2
22	102 01.8	178 00.1	52.6	259 25.1	43.5	358 49.3	04.4	231 13.2	14.2	Miaplacidus	221 38.5	S69 46.6
23	117 04.3	193 02.4	52.7	274 26.9	43.7	13 52.0	04.4	246 15.5	14.2			
2 00	132 06.7	208 04.8	S15 52.7	289 28.8	S 6 43.9	28 54.7	N23 04.5	261 17.9	S16 14.3	Mirfak	308 39.5	N49 54.7
01	147 09.2	223 07.1	52.8	304 30.6	44.1	43 57.5	04.5	276 20.2	14.3	Nunki	75 58.1	S26 16.6
02	162 11.6	238 09.4	52.9	319 32.4	44.4	59 00.2	04.5	291 22.6	14.3	Peacock	53 19.2	S56 41.2
03	177 14.1	253 11.8 ..	53.0	334 34.2 ..	44.6	74 02.9 ..	04.5	306 24.9 ..	14.3	Pollux	243 26.8	N27 59.3
04	192 16.6	268 14.1	53.1	349 36.0	44.8	89 05.7	04.6	321 27.3	14.4	Procyon	244 58.9	N 5 11.0
05	207 19.0	283 16.4	53.1	4 37.8	45.0	104 08.4	04.6	336 29.6	14.4			
06	222 21.5	298 18.7	S15 53.2	19 39.7	S 6 45.2	119 11.1	N23 04.6	351 31.9	S16 14.4	Rasalhague	96 06.3	N12 33.0
07	237 24.0	313 21.0	53.3	34 41.5	45.5	134 13.9	04.6	6 34.3	14.4	Regulus	207 42.7	N11 53.6
S 08	252 26.4	328 23.3	53.4	49 43.3	45.7	149 16.6	04.7	21 36.6	14.4	Rigel	281 11.4	S 8 11.4
U 09	267 28.9	343 25.6 ..	53.5	64 45.1 ..	45.9	164 19.3 ..	04.7	36 39.0 ..	14.5	Rigil Kent.	139 51.0	S60 53.3
N 10	282 31.4	358 27.9	53.6	79 46.9	46.1	179 22.0	04.7	51 41.3	14.5	Sabik	102 12.2	S15 44.4
D 11	297 33.8	13 30.2	53.6	94 48.8	46.3	194 24.8	04.7	66 43.7	14.5			
A 12	312 36.3	28 32.5	S15 53.7	109 50.6	S 6 46.6	209 27.5	N23 04.8	81 46.0	S16 14.5	Schedar	349 40.2	N56 37.1
Y 13	327 38.8	43 34.8	53.8	124 52.4	46.8	224 30.2	04.8	96 48.3	14.5	Shaula	96 21.6	S37 06.6
14	342 41.2	58 37.1	53.9	139 54.2	47.0	239 33.0	04.8	111 50.7	14.6	Sirius	258 33.0	S16 44.5
15	357 43.7	73 39.4 ..	54.0	154 56.1 ..	47.2	254 35.7 ..	04.9	126 53.0 ..	14.6	Spica	158 30.6	S11 14.1
16	12 46.1	88 41.6	54.1	169 57.9	47.4	269 38.4	04.9	141 55.4	14.6	Suhail	222 51.6	S43 29.6
17	27 48.6	103 43.9	54.1	184 59.7	47.7	284 41.1	04.9	156 57.7	14.6			
18	42 51.1	118 46.2	S15 54.2	200 01.6	S 6 47.9	299 43.9	N23 04.9	172 00.1	S16 14.7	Vega	80 39.0	N38 47.8
19	57 53.5	133 48.4	54.3	215 03.4	48.1	314 46.6	05.0	187 02.4	14.7	Zuben'ubi	137 04.9	S16 05.9
20	72 56.0	148 50.7	54.4	230 05.2	48.3	329 49.3	05.0	202 04.7	14.7		SHA	Mer. Pass.
21	87 58.5	163 52.9 ..	54.5	245 07.0 ..	48.5	344 52.1 ..	05.0	217 07.1 ..	14.7		° ′	h m
22	103 00.9	178 55.2	54.6	260 08.9	48.7	359 54.8	05.0	232 09.4	14.7	Venus	75 59.8	10 10
23	118 03.4	193 57.4	54.7	275 10.7	49.0	14 57.5	05.1	247 11.8	14.8	Mars	157 37.8	4 44
Mer. Pass.	h m 15 13.0	v 2.4	d 0.1	v 1.8	d 0.2	v 2.7	d 0.0	v 2.3	d 0.0	Jupiter Saturn	256 41.5 129 14.2	22 05 6 38

UT	SUN GHA	SUN Dec	MOON GHA	v	Dec	d	HP
31 FRIDAY	° '	° '	° '	'	° '	'	'
00	176 39.8	S17 27.7	176 39.9	5.8	S12 20.4	10.0	61.3
01	191 39.7	27.0	191 04.7	5.8	12 10.4	10.0	61.3
02	206 39.6	26.3	205 29.5	5.9	12 00.4	10.1	61.3
03	221 39.5	.. 25.6	219 54.4	6.0	11 50.3	10.2	61.3
04	236 39.5	24.9	234 19.4	6.0	11 40.1	10.2	61.3
05	251 39.4	24.2	248 44.4	6.1	11 29.9	10.4	61.3
06	266 39.3	S17 23.5	263 09.5	6.2	S11 19.5	10.4	61.3
07	281 39.2	22.8	277 34.7	6.2	11 09.1	10.5	61.3
08	296 39.1	22.1	291 59.9	6.2	10 58.6	10.5	61.3
09	311 39.0	.. 21.4	306 25.1	6.4	10 48.1	10.6	61.3
10	326 38.9	20.7	320 50.5	6.4	10 37.5	10.7	61.2
11	341 38.8	20.0	335 15.9	6.4	10 26.8	10.8	61.2
12	356 38.7	S17 19.3	349 41.3	6.5	S10 16.0	10.8	61.2
13	11 38.6	18.6	4 06.8	6.6	10 05.2	10.9	61.2
14	26 38.5	17.9	18 32.4	6.6	9 54.3	10.9	61.2
15	41 38.4	.. 17.2	32 58.0	6.7	9 43.4	11.0	61.2
16	56 38.3	16.5	47 23.7	6.8	9 32.4	11.1	61.1
17	71 38.3	15.8	61 49.5	6.8	9 21.3	11.1	61.1
18	86 38.2	S17 15.1	76 15.3	6.9	S 9 10.2	11.1	61.1
19	101 38.1	14.4	90 41.2	6.9	8 59.1	11.2	61.1
20	116 38.0	13.7	105 07.1	7.0	8 47.9	11.3	61.1
21	131 37.9	.. 12.9	119 33.1	7.1	8 36.6	11.3	61.0
22	146 37.8	12.2	133 59.2	7.1	8 25.3	11.4	61.0
23	161 37.7	11.5	148 25.3	7.2	8 13.9	11.4	61.0
1 SATURDAY							
00	176 37.6	S17 10.8	162 51.5	7.2	S 8 02.5	11.4	61.0
01	191 37.5	10.1	177 17.7	7.3	7 51.1	11.5	61.0
02	206 37.5	09.4	191 44.0	7.4	7 39.6	11.6	60.9
03	221 37.4	.. 08.7	206 10.4	7.4	7 28.0	11.5	60.9
04	236 37.3	08.0	220 36.8	7.5	7 16.5	11.7	60.9
05	251 37.2	07.3	235 03.3	7.5	7 04.8	11.6	60.9
06	266 37.1	S17 06.6	249 29.8	7.6	S 6 53.2	11.7	60.8
07	281 37.0	05.9	263 56.4	7.7	6 41.5	11.7	60.8
08	296 36.9	05.2	278 23.1	7.7	6 29.8	11.7	60.8
09	311 36.9	.. 04.4	292 49.8	7.8	6 18.1	11.8	60.8
10	326 36.8	03.7	307 16.6	7.9	6 06.3	11.8	60.7
11	341 36.7	03.0	321 43.5	7.9	5 54.5	11.9	60.7
12	356 36.6	S17 02.3	336 10.4	7.9	S 5 42.6	11.8	60.7
13	11 36.5	01.6	350 37.3	8.0	5 30.8	11.9	60.7
14	26 36.4	00.9	5 04.3	8.1	5 18.9	11.9	60.6
15	41 36.4	17 00.2	19 31.4	8.2	5 07.0	11.9	60.6
16	56 36.3	16 59.4	33 58.6	8.1	4 55.1	11.9	60.6
17	71 36.2	58.7	48 25.7	8.3	4 43.2	12.0	60.6
18	86 36.1	S16 58.0	62 53.0	8.3	S 4 31.2	12.0	60.5
19	101 36.0	57.3	77 20.3	8.3	4 19.2	11.9	60.5
20	116 36.0	56.6	91 47.6	8.5	4 07.3	12.0	60.5
21	131 35.9	.. 55.9	106 15.1	8.4	3 55.3	12.0	60.4
22	146 35.8	55.1	120 42.5	8.5	3 43.3	12.1	60.4
23	161 35.7	54.4	135 10.0	8.6	3 31.2	12.0	60.4
2 SUNDAY							
00	176 35.6	S16 53.7	149 37.6	8.6	S 3 19.2	12.0	60.3
01	191 35.6	53.0	164 05.2	8.7	3 07.2	12.1	60.3
02	206 35.5	52.3	178 32.9	8.8	2 55.1	12.0	60.3
03	221 35.4	.. 51.5	193 00.7	8.7	2 43.1	12.0	60.2
04	236 35.3	50.8	207 28.4	8.9	2 31.1	12.1	60.2
05	251 35.2	50.1	221 56.3	8.9	2 19.0	12.0	60.2
06	266 35.2	S16 49.4	236 24.2	8.9	S 2 07.0	12.1	60.1
07	281 35.1	48.6	250 52.1	9.0	1 54.9	12.0	60.1
08	296 35.0	47.9	265 20.1	9.0	1 42.9	12.0	60.1
09	311 34.9	.. 47.2	279 48.1	9.1	1 30.9	12.0	60.0
10	326 34.9	46.5	294 16.2	9.1	1 18.9	12.1	60.0
11	341 34.8	45.7	308 44.3	9.2	1 06.8	12.0	60.0
12	356 34.7	S16 45.0	323 12.5	9.2	S 0 54.8	12.0	59.9
13	11 34.6	44.3	337 40.7	9.3	0 42.8	12.0	59.9
14	26 34.6	43.6	352 09.0	9.3	0 30.8	11.9	59.9
15	41 34.5	.. 42.8	6 37.3	9.4	0 18.9	12.0	59.8
16	56 34.4	42.1	21 05.7	9.4	S 0 06.9	11.9	59.8
17	71 34.3	41.4	35 34.1	9.5	N 0 05.0	12.0	59.7
18	86 34.3	S16 40.7	50 02.6	9.5	N 0 17.0	11.9	59.7
19	101 34.2	39.9	64 31.1	9.5	0 28.9	11.9	59.7
20	116 34.1	39.2	78 59.6	9.6	0 40.8	11.8	59.6
21	131 34.0	.. 38.5	93 28.2	9.6	0 52.6	11.9	59.6
22	146 34.0	37.7	107 56.8	9.7	1 04.5	11.8	59.6
23	161 33.9	37.0	122 25.5	9.7	N 1 16.3	11.8	59.5
	SD 16.3	d 0.7	SD 16.7		16.5		16.3

Moonrise / Twilight / Sunrise

Lat.	Twilight Naut.	Twilight Civil	Sunrise	31	1	2	3
°	h m	h m	h m	h m	h m	h m	h m
N 72	07 10	08 39	10 28	09 01	08 51	08 42	08 33
N 70	07 02	08 20	09 46	08 43	08 41	08 39	08 37
68	06 55	08 05	09 18	08 29	08 34	08 37	08 41
66	06 49	07 53	08 56	08 17	08 28	08 36	08 43
64	06 44	07 43	08 40	08 08	08 22	08 34	08 46
62	06 40	07 34	08 26	07 59	08 18	08 33	08 48
60	06 36	07 27	08 14	07 52	08 14	08 32	08 50
N 58	06 32	07 20	08 04	07 45	08 10	08 31	08 51
56	06 29	07 14	07 55	07 40	08 07	08 30	08 53
54	06 26	07 08	07 47	07 35	08 04	08 30	08 54
52	06 23	07 03	07 40	07 30	08 01	08 29	08 55
50	06 20	06 59	07 34	07 26	07 59	08 28	08 57
45	06 14	06 49	07 20	07 17	07 53	08 27	08 59
N 40	06 08	06 40	07 09	07 09	07 49	08 26	09 01
35	06 02	06 32	06 59	07 02	07 45	08 25	09 03
30	05 57	06 25	06 50	06 57	07 42	08 24	09 04
20	05 46	06 13	06 36	06 46	07 36	08 23	09 07
N 10	05 35	06 01	06 22	06 38	07 31	08 21	09 10
0	05 23	05 48	06 10	06 29	07 26	08 20	09 12
S 10	05 10	05 35	05 58	06 21	07 21	08 19	09 14
20	04 53	05 21	05 44	06 12	07 16	08 18	09 17
30	04 32	05 03	05 28	06 02	07 10	08 16	09 20
35	04 18	04 52	05 19	05 56	07 07	08 15	09 22
40	04 02	04 39	05 09	05 49	07 03	08 14	09 24
45	03 41	04 23	04 57	05 41	06 58	08 13	09 26
S 50	03 14	04 03	04 41	05 32	06 53	08 12	09 29
52	03 00	03 54	04 34	05 27	06 50	08 12	09 30
54	02 43	03 43	04 27	05 23	06 48	08 11	09 31
56	02 22	03 30	04 18	05 17	06 45	08 10	09 33
58	01 54	03 16	04 08	05 11	06 41	08 09	09 35
S 60	01 10	02 58	03 56	05 04	06 37	08 09	09 37

Moonset / Twilight / Sunset

Lat.	Sunset	Twilight Civil	Twilight Naut.	31	1	2	3
°	h m	h m	h m	h m	h m	h m	h m
N 72	14 01	15 50	17 19	16 47	18 54	20 54	22 50
N 70	14 43	16 08	17 27	17 03	19 01	20 53	22 42
68	15 11	16 23	17 33	17 15	19 06	20 53	22 35
66	15 32	16 35	17 39	17 26	19 11	20 52	22 29
64	15 48	16 45	17 44	17 34	19 14	20 51	22 25
62	16 02	16 54	17 48	17 42	19 18	20 51	22 21
60	16 14	17 01	17 52	17 48	19 20	20 50	22 17
N 58	16 24	17 08	17 56	17 53	19 23	20 50	22 14
56	16 33	17 14	17 59	17 58	19 25	20 50	22 11
54	16 41	17 19	18 02	18 03	19 27	20 49	22 08
52	16 48	17 24	18 05	18 06	19 29	20 49	22 06
50	16 54	17 29	18 08	18 10	19 31	20 49	22 04
45	17 08	17 39	18 14	18 18	19 34	20 48	22 00
N 40	17 19	17 48	18 20	18 24	19 37	20 48	21 56
35	17 29	17 55	18 25	18 30	19 40	20 47	21 53
30	17 37	18 02	18 31	18 34	19 42	20 47	21 50
20	17 52	18 15	18 41	18 43	19 46	20 46	21 45
N 10	18 05	18 27	18 52	18 50	19 49	20 46	21 40
0	18 17	18 39	19 04	18 56	19 52	20 45	21 36
S 10	18 29	18 52	19 17	19 03	19 55	20 44	21 32
20	18 43	19 06	19 34	19 10	19 58	20 44	21 28
30	18 58	19 24	19 55	19 18	20 02	20 43	21 23
35	19 07	19 35	20 08	19 22	20 04	20 42	21 20
40	19 18	19 47	20 24	19 28	20 06	20 42	21 17
45	19 30	20 03	20 44	19 33	20 09	20 41	21 13
S 50	19 45	20 22	21 12	19 41	20 13	20 41	21 09
52	19 52	20 32	21 25	19 44	20 13	20 40	21 07
54	19 59	20 43	21 42	19 47	20 15	20 40	21 04
56	20 08	20 55	22 02	19 51	20 16	20 40	21 02
58	20 18	21 09	22 29	19 55	20 18	20 39	20 59
S 60	20 29	21 26	23 09	20 00	20 20	20 39	20 56

SUN / MOON

Day	SUN Eqn. of Time 00ʰ	SUN Eqn. of Time 12ʰ	SUN Mer. Pass.	MOON Mer. Pass. Upper	MOON Mer. Pass. Lower	Age	Phase
d	m s	m s	h m	h m	h m	d	%
31	13 20	13 25	12 13	12 43	00 14	01	1
1	13 29	13 33	12 14	13 39	01 11	02	4
2	13 37	13 41	12 14	14 33	02 06	03	10

UT	ARIES GHA	VENUS −4.8 GHA	Dec	MARS +0.2 GHA	Dec	JUPITER −2.6 GHA	Dec	SATURN +0.5 GHA	Dec	STARS Name	SHA	Dec
3 00	133 05.9	208 59.7	S15 54.7	290 12.5	S 6 49.2	30 00.2	N23 05.1	262 14.1	S16 14.8	Acamar	315 18.0	S40 15.3
01	148 08.3	224 01.9	54.8	305 14.4	49.4	45 03.0	05.1	277 16.5	14.8	Achernar	335 26.7	S57 10.2
02	163 10.8	239 04.1	54.9	320 16.2	49.6	60 05.7	05.1	292 18.8	14.8	Acrux	173 08.2	S63 10.5
03	178 13.2	254 06.4 ..	55.0	335 18.0 ..	49.8	75 08.4 ..	05.2	307 21.2 ..	14.8	Adhara	255 11.8	S28 59.8
04	193 15.7	269 08.6	55.1	350 19.9	50.0	90 11.1	05.2	322 23.5	14.9	Aldebaran	290 48.7	N16 32.1
05	208 18.2	284 10.8	55.2	5 21.7	50.2	105 13.9	05.2	337 25.9	14.9			
06	223 20.6	299 13.0	S15 55.3	20 23.5	S 6 50.5	120 16.6	N23 05.3	352 28.2	S16 14.9	Alioth	166 20.1	N55 52.7
07	238 23.1	314 15.2	55.4	35 25.4	50.7	135 19.3	05.3	7 30.5	14.9	Alkaid	152 58.4	N49 14.3
08	253 25.6	329 17.4	55.5	50 27.2	50.9	150 22.0	05.3	22 32.9	15.0	Al Na'ir	27 43.7	S46 53.6
M 09	268 28.0	344 19.6 ..	55.6	65 29.1 ..	51.1	165 24.8 ..	05.3	37 35.2 ..	15.0	Alnilam	275 45.7	S 1 11.9
O 10	283 30.5	359 21.8	55.6	80 30.9	51.3	180 27.5	05.4	52 37.6	15.0	Alphard	217 55.3	S 8 43.4
N 11	298 33.0	14 24.0	55.7	95 32.7	51.5	195 30.2	05.4	67 39.9	15.0			
D 12	313 35.4	29 26.2	S15 55.8	110 34.6	S 6 51.7	210 32.9	N23 05.4	82 42.3	S16 15.0	Alphecca	126 10.7	N26 39.7
A 13	328 37.9	44 28.4	55.9	125 36.4	51.9	225 35.6	05.4	97 44.6	15.1	Alpheratz	357 43.2	N29 10.2
Y 14	343 40.4	59 30.6	56.0	140 38.3	52.2	240 38.4	05.5	112 47.0	15.1	Altair	62 08.1	N 8 54.4
15	358 42.8	74 32.7 ..	56.1	155 40.1 ..	52.4	255 41.1 ..	05.5	127 49.3 ..	15.1	Ankaa	353 15.5	S42 14.0
16	13 45.3	89 34.9	56.2	170 42.0	52.6	270 43.8	05.5	142 51.7	15.1	Antares	112 25.8	S26 27.6
17	28 47.7	104 37.1	56.3	185 43.8	52.8	285 46.5	05.5	157 54.0	15.1			
18	43 50.2	119 39.2	S15 56.4	200 45.6	S 6 53.0	300 49.3	N23 05.6	172 56.4	S16 15.2	Arcturus	145 55.3	N19 06.4
19	58 52.7	134 41.4	56.5	215 47.5	53.2	315 52.0	05.6	187 58.7	15.2	Atria	107 27.5	S69 02.8
20	73 55.1	149 43.6	56.6	230 49.3	53.4	330 54.7	05.6	203 01.1	15.2	Avior	234 17.1	S59 33.5
21	88 57.6	164 45.7 ..	56.7	245 51.2 ..	53.6	345 57.4 ..	05.6	218 03.4 ..	15.2	Bellatrix	278 31.3	N 6 21.5
22	104 00.1	179 47.9	56.8	260 53.0	53.8	1 00.1	05.7	233 05.8	15.2	Betelgeuse	271 00.6	N 7 24.3
23	119 02.5	194 50.0	56.9	275 54.9	54.0	16 02.9	05.7	248 08.1	15.3			
4 00	134 05.0	209 52.1	S15 56.9	290 56.7	S 6 54.3	31 05.6	N23 05.7	263 10.5	S16 15.3	Canopus	263 55.5	S52 42.6
01	149 07.5	224 54.3	57.0	305 58.6	54.5	46 08.3	05.7	278 12.8	15.3	Capella	280 33.5	N46 00.7
02	164 09.9	239 56.4	57.1	321 00.4	54.7	61 11.0	05.8	293 15.1	15.3	Deneb	49 31.6	N45 19.9
03	179 12.4	254 58.5 ..	57.2	336 02.3 ..	54.9	76 13.7 ..	05.8	308 17.5 ..	15.3	Denebola	182 33.0	N14 29.4
04	194 14.8	270 00.6	57.3	351 04.1	55.1	91 16.4	05.8	323 19.8	15.4	Diphda	348 55.6	S17 54.7
05	209 17.3	285 02.8	57.4	6 06.0	55.3	106 19.2	05.8	338 22.2	15.4			
06	224 19.8	300 04.9	S15 57.5	21 07.8	S 6 55.5	121 21.9	N23 05.9	353 24.5	S16 15.4	Dubhe	193 50.7	N61 40.2
07	239 22.2	315 07.0	57.6	36 09.7	55.7	136 24.6	05.9	8 26.9	15.4	Elnath	278 11.8	N28 37.0
T 08	254 24.7	330 09.1	57.7	51 11.6	55.9	151 27.3	05.9	23 29.2	15.4	Eltanin	90 46.3	N51 29.2
U 09	269 27.2	345 11.2 ..	57.8	66 13.4 ..	56.1	166 30.0 ..	06.0	38 31.6 ..	15.5	Enif	33 47.0	N 9 56.5
E 10	284 29.6	0 13.3	57.9	81 15.3	56.3	181 32.8	06.0	53 33.9	15.5	Fomalhaut	15 23.8	S29 32.9
S 11	299 32.1	15 15.4	58.0	96 17.1	56.5	196 35.5	06.0	68 36.3	15.5			
D 12	314 34.6	30 17.5	S15 58.1	111 19.0	S 6 56.7	211 38.2	N23 06.0	83 38.7	S16 15.5	Gacrux	171 59.9	S57 11.4
A 13	329 37.0	45 19.6	58.2	126 20.9	56.9	226 40.9	06.1	98 41.0	15.5	Gienah	175 51.6	S17 37.3
Y 14	344 39.5	60 21.6	58.3	141 22.7	57.1	241 43.6	06.1	113 43.4	15.6	Hadar	148 47.0	S60 26.2
15	359 42.0	75 23.7 ..	58.4	156 24.6 ..	57.3	256 46.3 ..	06.1	128 45.7 ..	15.6	Hamal	328 00.3	N23 31.7
16	14 44.4	90 25.8	58.5	171 26.4	57.5	271 49.0	06.1	143 48.1	15.6	Kaus Aust.	83 43.5	S34 22.4
17	29 46.9	105 27.9	58.6	186 28.3	57.8	286 51.8	06.2	158 50.4	15.6			
18	44 49.3	120 29.9	S15 58.7	201 30.2	S 6 58.0	301 54.5	N23 06.2	173 52.8	S16 15.6	Kochab	137 20.2	N74 05.6
19	59 51.8	135 32.0	58.8	216 32.0	58.2	316 57.2	06.2	188 55.1	15.7	Markab	13 38.1	N15 16.9
20	74 54.3	150 34.0	58.9	231 33.9	58.4	331 59.9	06.2	203 57.5	15.7	Menkar	314 14.5	N 4 08.5
21	89 56.7	165 36.1 ..	59.0	246 35.8 ..	58.6	347 02.6 ..	06.3	218 59.8 ..	15.7	Menkent	148 06.9	S36 26.2
22	104 59.2	180 38.1	59.1	261 37.6	58.8	2 05.3	06.3	234 02.2	15.7	Miaplacidus	221 38.5	S69 46.7
23	120 01.7	195 40.2	59.2	276 39.5	59.0	17 08.0	06.3	249 04.5	15.7			
5 00	135 04.1	210 42.2	S15 59.3	291 41.4	S 6 59.2	32 10.7	N23 06.3	264 06.9	S16 15.8	Mirfak	308 39.6	N49 54.7
01	150 06.6	225 44.3	59.4	306 43.2	59.4	47 13.5	06.4	279 09.2	15.8	Nunki	75 58.1	S26 16.6
02	165 09.1	240 46.3	59.5	321 45.1	59.6	62 16.2	06.4	294 11.6	15.8	Peacock	53 19.2	S56 41.2
03	180 11.5	255 48.3 ..	59.6	336 47.0	6 59.8	77 18.9 ..	06.4	309 13.9 ..	15.8	Pollux	243 26.8	N27 59.3
04	195 14.0	270 50.4	59.7	351 48.8	7 00.0	92 21.6	06.4	324 16.3	15.8	Procyon	244 58.9	N 5 11.0
05	210 16.5	285 52.4	59.8	6 50.7	00.2	107 24.3	06.5	339 18.6	15.8			
06	225 18.9	300 54.4	S15 59.9	21 52.6	S 7 00.4	122 27.0	N23 06.5	354 21.0	S16 15.9	Rasalhague	96 06.2	N12 33.0
W 07	240 21.4	315 56.4	16 00.0	36 54.5	00.6	137 29.7	06.5	9 23.3	15.9	Regulus	207 42.7	N11 53.6
E 08	255 23.8	330 58.4	00.1	51 56.3	00.8	152 32.4	06.5	24 25.7	15.9	Rigel	281 11.4	S 8 11.4
D 09	270 26.3	346 00.4 ..	00.2	66 58.2 ..	01.0	167 35.1 ..	06.5	39 28.1 ..	15.9	Rigil Kent.	139 50.9	S60 53.3
N 10	285 28.8	1 02.4	00.3	82 00.1	01.2	182 37.9	06.6	54 30.4	15.9	Sabik	102 12.2	S15 44.4
E 11	300 31.2	16 04.4	00.4	97 02.0	01.4	197 40.6	06.6	69 32.8	16.0			
S 12	315 33.7	31 06.4	S16 00.5	112 03.8	S 7 01.6	212 43.3	N23 06.6	84 35.1	S16 16.0	Schedar	349 40.2	N56 37.1
D 13	330 36.2	46 08.4	00.6	127 05.7	01.7	227 46.0	06.6	99 37.5	16.0	Shaula	96 21.5	S37 06.6
A 14	345 38.6	61 10.4	00.7	142 07.6	01.9	242 48.7	06.7	114 39.8	16.0	Sirius	258 33.0	S16 44.5
Y 15	0 41.1	76 12.4 ..	00.9	157 09.5 ..	02.1	257 51.4 ..	06.7	129 42.2 ..	16.0	Spica	158 30.6	S11 14.1
16	15 43.6	91 14.3	01.0	172 11.4	02.3	272 54.1	06.7	144 44.5	16.1	Suhail	222 51.6	S43 29.6
17	30 46.0	106 16.3	01.1	187 13.2	02.5	287 56.8	06.7	159 46.9	16.1			
18	45 48.5	121 18.3	S16 01.2	202 15.1	S 7 02.7	302 59.5	N23 06.8	174 49.3	S16 16.1	Vega	80 39.0	N38 47.8
19	60 50.9	136 20.2	01.3	217 17.0	02.9	318 02.2	06.8	189 51.6	16.1	Zuben'ubi	137 04.9	S16 05.9
20	75 53.4	151 22.2	01.4	232 18.9	03.1	333 04.9	06.8	204 54.0	16.1		SHA	Mer.Pass.
21	90 55.9	166 24.2 ..	01.5	247 20.8 ..	03.3	348 07.6 ..	06.8	219 56.3 ..	16.1	Venus	75 47.1	h m 9 59
22	105 58.3	181 26.1	01.6	262 22.7	03.5	3 10.3	06.9	234 58.7	16.2	Mars	156 51.7	4 36
23	121 00.8	196 28.1	01.7	277 24.5	03.7	18 13.0	06.9	250 01.0	16.2	Jupiter	257 00.6	21 52
Mer.Pass.	h m 15 01.2	v 2.1	d 0.1	v 1.9	d 0.2	v 2.7	d 0.0	v 2.4	d 0.0	Saturn	129 05.5	6 26

UT	SUN GHA	SUN Dec	MOON GHA	v	MOON Dec	d	HP
d h	° ′	° ′	° ′	′	° ′	′	′
3 00	176 33.8	S16 36.3	136 54.2	9.7	N 1 28.1	11.8	59.5
01	191 33.8	35.5	151 22.9	9.8	1 39.9	11.8	59.4
02	206 33.7	34.8	165 51.7	9.9	1 51.7	11.7	59.4
03	221 33.6 ..	34.1	180 20.6	9.8	2 03.4	11.7	59.4
04	236 33.6	33.3	194 49.4	9.9	2 15.1	11.6	59.3
05	251 33.5	32.6	209 18.3	10.0	2 26.7	11.7	59.3
M 06	266 33.4	S16 31.9	223 47.3	9.9	N 2 38.4	11.6	59.2
O 07	281 33.4	31.1	238 16.2	10.1	2 50.0	11.6	59.2
N 08	296 33.3	30.4	252 45.3	10.0	3 01.6	11.5	59.2
D 09	311 33.2 ..	29.7	267 14.3	10.1	3 13.1	11.5	59.1
A 10	326 33.1	28.9	281 43.4	10.1	3 24.6	11.5	59.1
Y 11	341 33.1	28.2	296 12.5	10.2	3 36.1	11.4	59.0
12	356 33.0	S16 27.4	310 41.7	10.1	N 3 47.5	11.4	59.0
13	11 33.0	26.7	325 10.8	10.3	3 58.9	11.3	59.0
14	26 32.9	26.0	339 40.1	10.2	4 10.2	11.4	58.9
15	41 32.8 ..	25.2	354 09.3	10.3	4 21.6	11.2	58.9
16	56 32.8	24.5	8 38.6	10.3	4 32.8	11.3	58.8
17	71 32.7	23.7	23 07.9	10.3	4 44.1	11.1	58.8
18	86 32.6	S16 23.0	37 37.2	10.4	N 4 55.2	11.2	58.8
19	101 32.6	22.3	52 06.6	10.4	5 06.4	11.1	58.7
20	116 32.5	21.5	66 36.0	10.5	5 17.5	11.0	58.7
21	131 32.4 ..	20.8	81 05.5	10.4	5 28.5	11.0	58.6
22	146 32.4	20.0	95 34.9	10.5	5 39.5	11.0	58.6
23	161 32.3	19.3	110 04.4	10.5	5 50.5	10.9	58.6
4 00	176 32.2	S16 18.6	124 33.9	10.6	N 6 01.4	10.9	58.5
01	191 32.2	17.8	139 03.5	10.5	6 12.3	10.8	58.5
02	206 32.1	17.1	153 33.0	10.6	6 23.1	10.8	58.4
03	221 32.1 ..	16.3	168 02.6	10.6	6 33.9	10.7	58.4
04	236 32.0	15.6	182 32.2	10.7	6 44.6	10.6	58.4
05	251 31.9	14.8	197 01.9	10.6	6 55.2	10.6	58.3
T 06	266 31.9	S16 14.1	211 31.5	10.7	N 7 05.8	10.6	58.3
U 07	281 31.8	13.3	226 01.2	10.7	7 16.4	10.5	58.2
E 08	296 31.8	12.6	240 30.9	10.8	7 26.9	10.4	58.2
S 09	311 31.7 ..	11.8	255 00.7	10.7	7 37.3	10.4	58.1
D 10	326 31.6	11.1	269 30.4	10.8	7 47.7	10.3	58.1
A 11	341 31.6	10.3	284 00.2	10.8	7 58.0	10.3	58.1
Y 12	356 31.5	S16 09.6	298 30.0	10.8	N 8 08.3	10.2	58.0
13	11 31.5	08.8	312 59.8	10.8	8 18.5	10.1	58.0
14	26 31.4	08.1	327 29.6	10.9	8 28.6	10.1	57.9
15	41 31.4 ..	07.3	341 59.5	10.9	8 38.7	10.0	57.9
16	56 31.3	06.6	356 29.4	10.9	8 48.7	10.0	57.9
17	71 31.2	05.8	10 59.3	10.9	8 58.7	9.9	57.8
18	86 31.2	S16 05.1	25 29.2	10.9	N 9 08.6	9.8	57.8
19	101 31.1	04.3	39 59.1	11.0	9 18.4	9.8	57.7
20	116 31.1	03.6	54 29.1	10.9	9 28.2	9.7	57.7
21	131 31.0 ..	02.8	68 59.0	11.0	9 37.9	9.7	57.7
22	146 31.0	02.1	83 29.0	11.0	9 47.6	9.6	57.6
23	161 30.9	01.3	97 59.0	11.0	9 57.2	9.5	57.6
5 00	176 30.9	S16 00.6	112 29.0	11.0	N10 06.7	9.4	57.5
01	191 30.8	15 59.8	126 59.0	11.1	10 16.1	9.4	57.5
02	206 30.8	59.0	141 29.1	11.0	10 25.5	9.3	57.5
03	221 30.7 ..	58.3	155 59.1	11.1	10 34.8	9.3	57.4
04	236 30.7	57.5	170 29.2	11.1	10 44.1	9.1	57.4
05	251 30.6	56.8	184 59.3	11.0	10 53.2	9.1	57.3
W 06	266 30.6	S15 56.0	199 29.3	11.2	N11 02.3	9.1	57.3
E 07	281 30.5	55.3	213 59.5	11.1	11 11.4	8.9	57.3
D 08	296 30.5	54.5	228 29.6	11.1	11 20.3	8.9	57.2
N 09	311 30.4 ..	53.7	242 59.7	11.1	11 29.2	8.9	57.2
E 10	326 30.4	53.0	257 29.8	11.2	11 38.1	8.7	57.1
S 11	341 30.3	52.2	272 00.0	11.2	11 46.8	8.7	57.1
D 12	356 30.3	S15 51.5	286 30.2	11.1	N11 55.5	8.6	57.1
A 13	11 30.2	50.7	301 00.3	11.2	12 04.1	8.5	57.0
Y 14	26 30.2	49.9	315 30.5	11.2	12 12.6	8.5	57.0
15	41 30.1 ..	49.2	330 00.7	11.2	12 21.1	8.3	57.0
16	56 30.1	48.4	344 30.9	11.2	12 29.4	8.4	56.9
17	71 30.0	47.6	359 01.1	11.2	12 37.8	8.2	56.9
18	86 30.0	S15 46.9	13 31.3	11.3	N12 46.0	8.1	56.8
19	101 29.9	46.1	28 01.6	11.2	12 54.1	8.1	56.8
20	116 29.9	45.3	42 31.8	11.2	13 02.2	8.0	56.8
21	131 29.8 ..	44.6	57 02.0	11.3	13 10.2	7.9	56.7
22	146 29.8	43.8	71 32.3	11.3	13 18.1	7.9	56.7
23	161 29.7	43.0	86 02.6	11.2	N13 26.0	7.7	56.7
	SD 16.3	d 0.7	SD 16.1		15.8	15.6	

Lat.	Twilight Naut.	Twilight Civil	Sunrise	Moonrise 3	4	5	6
°	h m	h m	h m	h m	h m	h m	h m
N 72	06 59	08 25	10 04	08 33	08 25	08 16	08 04
N 70	06 52	08 09	09 29	08 37	08 35	08 34	08 34
68	06 47	07 55	09 05	08 41	08 44	08 49	08 56
66	06 42	07 45	08 46	08 43	08 51	09 01	09 13
64	06 37	07 35	08 30	08 46	08 58	09 11	09 27
62	06 34	07 27	08 18	08 48	09 03	09 20	09 39
60	06 30	07 20	08 07	08 50	09 08	09 27	09 50
N 58	06 27	07 14	07 57	08 51	09 12	09 34	09 59
56	06 24	07 09	07 49	08 53	09 15	09 40	10 07
54	06 21	07 04	07 42	08 54	09 19	09 45	10 14
52	06 19	06 59	07 35	08 55	09 22	09 50	10 20
50	06 16	06 55	07 29	08 57	09 25	09 54	10 26
45	06 10	06 45	07 16	08 59	09 31	10 03	10 38
N 40	06 05	06 37	07 06	09 01	09 36	10 11	10 48
35	06 00	06 30	06 57	09 03	09 40	10 18	10 57
30	05 55	06 24	06 49	09 04	09 44	10 24	11 05
20	05 45	06 12	06 34	09 07	09 51	10 34	11 18
N 10	05 35	06 00	06 10	09 10	09 57	10 43	11 30
0	05 24	05 49	06 10	09 12	10 03	10 52	11 41
S 10	05 11	05 37	05 59	09 14	10 08	11 01	11 53
20	04 55	05 23	05 46	09 17	10 15	11 10	12 05
30	04 35	05 05	05 31	09 20	10 22	11 21	12 18
35	04 22	04 55	05 22	09 22	10 26	11 27	12 26
40	04 07	04 43	05 13	09 24	10 30	11 34	12 36
45	03 47	04 28	05 01	09 26	10 36	11 43	12 46
S 50	03 21	04 09	04 47	09 29	10 42	11 53	12 59
52	03 08	04 00	04 40	09 30	10 45	11 57	13 06
54	02 52	03 50	04 33	09 31	10 49	12 03	13 12
56	02 33	03 38	04 24	09 33	10 53	12 08	13 20
58	02 09	03 25	04 15	09 35	10 57	12 15	13 28
S 60	01 34	03 09	04 04	09 37	11 01	12 22	13 38

Lat.	Sunset	Twilight Civil	Twilight Naut.	Moonset 3	4	5	6
°	h m	h m	h m	h m	h m	h m	h m
N 72	14 25	16 04	17 31	22 50	24 44	00 44	02 39
N 70	15 00	16 20	17 37	22 42	24 27	00 27	02 11
68	15 24	16 34	17 43	22 35	24 14	00 14	01 49
66	15 43	16 44	17 47	22 29	24 03	00 03	01 33
64	15 58	16 54	17 52	22 25	23 54	25 19	01 19
62	16 11	17 01	17 55	22 21	23 47	25 08	01 08
60	16 22	17 08	17 59	22 17	23 40	24 58	00 58
N 58	16 31	17 14	18 02	22 14	23 34	24 50	00 50
56	16 39	17 20	18 05	22 11	23 29	24 43	00 43
54	16 47	17 25	18 07	22 08	23 24	24 36	00 36
52	16 53	17 30	18 10	22 06	23 20	24 30	00 30
50	16 59	17 34	18 12	22 04	23 16	24 25	00 25
45	17 12	17 43	18 18	22 00	23 08	24 14	00 14
N 40	17 23	17 51	18 23	21 56	23 01	24 04	00 04
35	17 32	17 58	18 28	21 53	22 55	23 56	24 54
30	17 40	18 05	18 33	21 50	22 50	23 49	24 45
20	17 54	18 16	18 43	21 45	22 41	23 37	24 30
N 10	18 06	18 28	18 53	21 40	22 34	23 26	24 17
0	18 17	18 39	19 04	21 36	22 26	23 16	24 05
S 10	18 29	18 51	19 17	21 32	22 19	23 06	23 53
20	18 42	19 05	19 32	21 28	22 11	22 55	23 40
30	18 56	19 22	19 52	21 23	22 03	22 43	23 25
35	19 05	19 32	20 05	21 20	21 58	22 36	23 16
40	19 15	19 44	20 20	21 17	21 52	22 28	23 07
45	19 26	19 59	20 40	21 13	21 45	22 19	22 55
S 50	19 40	20 17	21 05	21 09	21 37	22 08	22 41
52	19 47	20 26	21 18	21 07	21 34	22 03	22 35
54	19 54	20 36	21 33	21 04	21 30	21 57	22 28
56	20 02	20 47	21 51	21 02	21 25	21 51	22 20
58	20 11	21 01	22 15	20 59	21 20	21 44	22 11
S 60	20 22	21 17	22 48	20 56	21 15	21 36	22 01

Day	SUN Eqn. of Time 00h	SUN Eqn. of Time 12h	SUN Mer. Pass.	MOON Mer. Pass. Upper	MOON Mer. Pass. Lower	Age	Phase
d	m s	m s	h m	h m	h m	d	%
3	13 45	13 48	12 14	15 24	02 59	04	18
4	13 51	13 54	12 14	16 15	03 49	05	27
5	13 56	13 59	12 14	17 04	04 39	06	37

UT	ARIES	VENUS −4.8		MARS +0.1		JUPITER −2.6		SATURN +0.5		STARS		
	GHA	GHA	Dec	GHA	Dec	GHA	Dec	GHA	Dec	Name	SHA	Dec
d h	° ′	° ′	° ′	° ′	° ′	° ′	° ′	° ′	° ′		° ′	° ′
6 00	136 03.3	211 30.0	S16 01.8	292 26.4	S 7 03.9	33 15.7	N23 06.9	265 03.4	S16 16.2	Acamar	315 18.0	S40 15.3
01	151 05.7	226 31.9	01.9	307 28.3	04.1	48 18.5	06.9	280 05.8	16.2	Achernar	335 26.7	S57 10.2
02	166 08.2	241 33.9	02.0	322 30.2	04.3	63 21.2	07.0	295 08.1	16.2	Acrux	173 08.2	S63 10.5
03	181 10.7	256 35.8 . .	02.1	337 32.1 . .	04.5	78 23.9 . .	07.0	310 10.5 . .	16.3	Adhara	255 11.8	S28 59.8
04	196 13.1	271 37.7	02.2	352 34.0	04.7	93 26.6	07.0	325 12.8	16.3	Aldebaran	290 48.7	N16 32.1
05	211 15.6	286 39.7	02.3	7 35.9	04.9	108 29.3	07.0	340 15.2	16.3			
06	226 18.1	301 41.6	S16 02.4	22 37.8	S 7 05.0	123 32.0	N23 07.1	355 17.5	S16 16.3	Alioth	166 20.0	N55 52.7
T 07	241 20.5	316 43.5	02.6	37 39.7	05.2	138 34.7	07.1	10 19.9	16.3	Alkaid	152 58.4	N49 14.3
H 08	256 23.0	331 45.4	02.7	52 41.6	05.4	153 37.4	07.1	25 22.3	16.3	Al Na'ir	27 43.7	S46 53.5
U 09	271 25.4	346 47.3 . .	02.8	67 43.4 . .	05.6	168 40.1 . .	07.1	40 24.6 . .	16.4	Alnilam	275 45.7	S 1 11.9
R 10	286 27.9	1 49.2	02.9	82 45.3	05.8	183 42.8	07.2	55 27.0	16.4	Alphard	217 55.3	S 8 43.5
S 11	301 30.4	16 51.1	03.0	97 47.2	06.0	198 45.5	07.2	70 29.3	16.4			
D 12	316 32.8	31 53.0	S16 03.1	112 49.1	S 7 06.2	213 48.2	N23 07.2	85 31.7	S16 16.4	Alphecca	126 10.7	N26 39.9
A 13	331 35.3	46 54.9	03.2	127 51.0	06.4	228 50.9	07.2	100 34.0	16.4	Alpheratz	357 43.2	N29 10.2
Y 14	346 37.8	61 56.8	03.3	142 52.9	06.6	243 53.6	07.2	115 36.4	16.4	Altair	62 08.1	N 8 54.4
15	1 40.2	76 58.7 . .	03.4	157 54.8 . .	06.8	258 56.3 . .	07.3	130 38.8 . .	16.5	Ankaa	353 15.6	S42 14.0
16	16 42.7	92 00.6	03.5	172 56.7	06.9	273 59.0	07.3	145 41.1	16.5	Antares	112 25.8	S26 27.6
17	31 45.2	107 02.5	03.6	187 58.6	07.1	289 01.7	07.3	160 43.5	16.5			
18	46 47.6	122 04.3	S16 03.7	203 00.5	S 7 07.3	304 04.4	N23 07.3	175 45.8	S16 16.5	Arcturus	145 55.2	N19 06.4
19	61 50.1	137 06.2	03.9	218 02.4	07.5	319 07.1	07.4	190 48.2	16.5	Atria	107 27.4	S69 02.8
20	76 52.5	152 08.1	04.0	233 04.3	07.7	334 09.8	07.4	205 50.6	16.6	Avior	234 17.1	S59 33.6
21	91 55.0	167 09.9 . .	04.1	248 06.2 . .	07.9	349 12.5 . .	07.4	220 52.9 . .	16.6	Bellatrix	278 31.3	N 6 21.5
22	106 57.5	182 11.8	04.2	263 08.1	08.1	4 15.2	07.4	235 55.3	16.6	Betelgeuse	271 00.6	N 7 24.3
23	121 59.9	197 13.7	04.3	278 10.0	08.3	19 17.9	07.5	250 57.7	16.6			
7 00	137 02.4	212 15.5	S16 04.4	293 12.0	S 7 08.4	34 20.6	N23 07.5	266 00.0	S16 16.6	Canopus	263 55.5	S52 42.6
01	152 04.9	227 17.4	04.5	308 13.9	08.6	49 23.3	07.5	281 02.4	16.6	Capella	280 33.5	N46 00.7
02	167 07.3	242 19.2	04.6	323 15.8	08.8	64 26.0	07.5	296 04.7	16.7	Deneb	49 31.6	N45 19.9
03	182 09.8	257 21.0 . .	04.7	338 17.7 . .	09.0	79 28.7 . .	07.6	311 07.1 . .	16.7	Denebola	182 32.9	N14 29.4
04	197 12.3	272 22.9	04.8	353 19.6	09.2	94 31.4	07.6	326 09.5	16.7	Diphda	348 55.6	S17 54.7
05	212 14.7	287 24.7	05.0	8 21.5	09.4	109 34.1	07.6	341 11.8	16.7			
06	227 17.2	302 26.5	S16 05.1	23 23.4	S 7 09.5	124 36.8	N23 07.6	356 14.2	S16 16.7	Dubhe	193 50.6	N61 40.2
07	242 19.7	317 28.4	05.2	38 25.3	09.7	139 39.5	07.6	11 16.5	16.7	Elnath	278 11.8	N28 37.0
F 08	257 22.1	332 30.2	05.3	53 27.2	09.9	154 42.1	07.7	26 18.9	16.8	Eltanin	90 46.3	N51 29.1
R 09	272 24.6	347 32.0 . .	05.4	68 29.1 . .	10.1	169 44.8 . .	07.7	41 21.3 . .	16.8	Enif	33 47.0	N 9 56.5
I 10	287 27.0	2 33.8	05.5	83 31.1	10.3	184 47.5	07.7	56 23.6	16.8	Fomalhaut	15 23.8	S29 32.9
D 11	302 29.5	17 35.6	05.6	98 33.0	10.5	199 50.2	07.7	71 26.0	16.8			
A 12	317 32.0	32 37.4	S16 05.7	113 34.9	S 7 10.6	214 52.9	N23 07.8	86 28.4	S16 16.8	Gacrux	171 59.9	S57 11.4
Y 13	332 34.4	47 39.2	05.8	128 36.8	10.8	229 55.6	07.8	101 30.7	16.8	Gienah	175 51.6	S17 37.3
14	347 36.9	62 41.0	06.0	143 38.7	11.0	244 58.3	07.8	116 33.1	16.9	Hadar	148 46.9	S60 26.2
15	2 39.4	77 42.8 . .	06.1	158 40.6 . .	11.2	260 01.0 . .	07.8	131 35.4 . .	16.9	Hamal	328 00.3	N23 31.7
16	17 41.8	92 44.6	06.2	173 42.6	11.4	275 03.7	07.9	146 37.8	16.9	Kaus Aust.	83 43.5	S34 22.4
17	32 44.3	107 46.4	06.3	188 44.5	11.6	290 06.4	07.9	161 40.2	16.9			
18	47 46.8	122 48.2	S16 06.4	203 46.4	S 7 11.7	305 09.1	N23 07.9	176 42.5	S16 16.9	Kochab	137 20.1	N74 05.6
19	62 49.2	137 50.0	06.5	218 48.3	11.9	320 11.8	07.9	191 44.9	16.9	Markab	13 38.1	N15 16.9
20	77 51.7	152 51.7	06.6	233 50.2	12.1	335 14.5	07.9	206 47.3	17.0	Menkar	314 14.6	N 4 08.5
21	92 54.2	167 53.5 . .	06.7	248 52.2 . .	12.3	350 17.2 . .	08.0	221 49.6 . .	17.0	Menkent	148 06.9	S36 26.2
22	107 56.6	182 55.3	06.9	263 54.1	12.4	5 19.8	08.0	236 52.0	17.0	Miaplacidus	221 38.5	S69 46.7
23	122 59.1	197 57.1	07.0	278 56.0	12.6	20 22.5	08.0	251 54.4	17.0			
8 00	138 01.5	212 58.8	S16 07.1	293 57.9	S 7 12.8	35 25.2	N23 08.0	266 56.7	S16 17.0	Mirfak	308 39.6	N49 54.7
01	153 04.0	228 00.6	07.2	308 59.9	13.0	50 27.9	08.1	281 59.1	17.0	Nunki	75 58.0	S26 16.6
02	168 06.5	243 02.3	07.3	324 01.8	13.2	65 30.6	08.1	297 01.5	17.0	Peacock	53 19.1	S56 41.2
03	183 08.9	258 04.1 . .	07.4	339 03.7 . .	13.3	80 33.3 . .	08.1	312 03.8 . .	17.1	Pollux	243 26.8	N27 59.3
04	198 11.4	273 05.8	07.5	354 05.6	13.5	95 36.0	08.1	327 06.2	17.1	Procyon	244 58.9	N 5 11.0
05	213 13.9	288 07.6	07.6	9 07.6	13.7	110 38.7	08.1	342 08.6	17.1			
06	228 16.3	303 09.3	S16 07.8	24 09.5	S 7 13.9	125 41.4	N23 08.2	357 10.9	S16 17.1	Rasalhague	96 06.2	N12 33.0
07	243 18.8	318 11.0	07.9	39 11.4	14.0	140 44.0	08.2	12 13.3	17.1	Regulus	207 42.7	N11 53.6
S 08	258 21.3	333 12.8	08.0	54 13.4	14.2	155 46.7	08.2	27 15.7	17.1	Rigel	281 11.4	S 8 11.4
A 09	273 23.7	348 14.5 . .	08.1	69 15.3 . .	14.4	170 49.4 . .	08.2	42 18.0 . .	17.2	Rigil Kent.	139 50.9	S60 53.3
T 10	288 26.2	3 16.2	08.2	84 17.2	14.6	185 52.1	08.3	57 20.4	17.2	Sabik	102 12.2	S15 44.4
U 11	303 28.7	18 17.9	08.3	99 19.2	14.7	200 54.8	08.3	72 22.8	17.2			
R 12	318 31.1	33 19.7	S16 08.4	114 21.1	S 7 14.9	215 57.5	N23 08.3	87 25.1	S16 17.2	Schedar	349 40.2	N56 37.1
D 13	333 33.6	48 21.4	08.5	129 23.0	15.1	231 00.2	08.3	102 27.5	17.2	Shaula	96 21.5	S37 06.6
A 14	348 36.0	63 23.1	08.7	144 25.0	15.3	246 02.9	08.3	117 29.9	17.2	Sirius	258 33.0	S16 44.5
Y 15	3 38.5	78 24.8 . .	08.8	159 26.9 . .	15.4	261 05.5 . .	08.4	132 32.2 . .	17.2	Spica	158 30.6	S11 14.1
16	18 41.0	93 26.5	08.9	174 28.8	15.6	276 08.2	08.4	147 34.6	17.3	Suhail	222 51.6	S43 29.6
17	33 43.4	108 28.2	09.0	189 30.8	15.8	291 10.9	08.4	162 37.0	17.3			
18	48 45.9	123 29.9	S16 09.1	204 32.7	S 7 16.0	306 13.6	N23 08.4	177 39.3	S16 17.3	Vega	80 39.0	N38 47.8
19	63 48.4	138 31.6	09.2	219 34.7	16.1	321 16.3	08.5	192 41.7	17.3	Zuben'ubi	137 04.9	S16 05.9
20	78 50.8	153 33.3	09.3	234 36.6	16.3	336 19.0	08.5	207 44.1	17.3			
21	93 53.3	168 34.9 . .	09.5	249 38.5 . .	16.5	351 21.6 . .	08.5	222 46.4 . .	17.3		SHA	Mer. Pass.
22	108 55.8	183 36.6	09.6	264 40.5	16.6	6 24.3	08.5	237 48.8	17.4		° ′	h m
23	123 58.2	198 38.3	09.7	279 42.4	16.8	21 27.0	08.5	252 51.2	17.4	Venus	75 13.1	9 50
	h m									Mars	156 09.5	4 27
Mer. Pass. 14 49.4		v 1.8	d 0.1	v 1.9	d 0.2	v 2.7	d 0.0	v 2.4	d 0.0	Jupiter	257 18.2	21 39
										Saturn	128 57.6	6 15

UT	SUN GHA	SUN Dec	MOON GHA	v	MOON Dec	d	HP
d h	° ′	° ′	° ′	′	° ′	′	′
6 00	176 29.7	S15 42.3	100 32.8	11.3	N13 33.7	7.7	56.6
01	191 29.7	41.5	115 03.1	11.3	13 41.4	7.6	56.6
02	206 29.6	40.7	129 33.4	11.3	13 49.0	7.5	56.6
03	221 29.6	.. 40.0	144 03.7	11.3	13 56.5	7.5	56.5
04	236 29.5	39.2	158 34.0	11.3	14 04.0	7.4	56.5
05	251 29.5	38.4	173 04.3	11.3	14 11.4	7.2	56.4
06	266 29.4	S15 37.7	187 34.6	11.3	N14 18.6	7.2	56.4
T 07	281 29.4	36.9	202 04.9	11.3	14 25.8	7.2	56.4
H 08	296 29.3	36.1	216 35.2	11.3	14 33.0	7.0	56.3
U 09	311 29.3	.. 35.4	231 05.5	11.4	14 40.0	7.0	56.3
R 10	326 29.3	34.6	245 35.9	11.3	14 47.0	6.8	56.3
S 11	341 29.2	33.8	260 06.2	11.3	14 53.8	6.8	56.2
D 12	356 29.2	S15 33.0	274 36.5	11.4	N15 00.6	6.7	56.2
A 13	11 29.1	32.3	289 06.9	11.3	15 07.3	6.7	56.2
Y 14	26 29.1	31.5	303 37.2	11.4	15 14.0	6.5	56.1
15	41 29.1	.. 30.7	318 07.6	11.4	15 20.5	6.5	56.1
16	56 29.0	30.0	332 38.0	11.3	15 27.0	6.3	56.1
17	71 29.0	29.2	347 08.3	11.4	15 33.3	6.3	56.0
18	86 28.9	S15 28.4	1 38.7	11.4	N15 39.6	6.2	56.0
19	101 28.9	27.6	16 09.1	11.4	15 45.8	6.1	56.0
20	116 28.9	26.9	30 39.5	11.3	15 51.9	6.1	55.9
21	131 28.8	.. 26.1	45 09.8	11.4	15 58.0	5.9	55.9
22	146 28.8	25.3	59 40.2	11.4	16 03.9	5.9	55.9
23	161 28.8	24.5	74 10.6	11.4	16 09.8	5.7	55.8
7 00	176 28.7	S15 23.7	88 41.0	11.4	N16 15.5	5.7	55.8
01	191 28.7	23.0	103 11.4	11.4	16 21.2	5.6	55.8
02	206 28.7	22.2	117 41.8	11.4	16 26.8	5.5	55.8
03	221 28.6	.. 21.4	132 12.2	11.4	16 32.3	5.5	55.7
04	236 28.6	20.6	146 42.6	11.4	16 37.8	5.3	55.7
05	251 28.6	19.8	161 13.0	11.5	16 43.1	5.3	55.7
06	266 28.5	S15 19.1	175 43.5	11.4	N16 48.4	5.1	55.6
F 07	281 28.5	18.3	190 13.9	11.4	16 53.5	5.1	55.6
R 08	296 28.4	17.5	204 44.3	11.4	16 58.6	5.0	55.6
I 09	311 28.4	.. 16.7	219 14.7	11.5	17 03.6	4.9	55.5
D 10	326 28.4	15.9	233 45.2	11.4	17 08.5	4.8	55.5
A 11	341 28.4	15.2	248 15.6	11.5	17 13.3	4.7	55.5
Y 12	356 28.3	S15 14.4	262 46.1	11.4	N17 18.0	4.6	55.5
13	11 28.3	13.6	277 16.5	11.5	17 22.6	4.6	55.4
14	26 28.3	12.8	291 47.0	11.4	17 27.2	4.4	55.4
15	41 28.2	.. 12.0	306 17.4	11.5	17 31.6	4.4	55.4
16	56 28.2	11.2	320 47.9	11.4	17 36.0	4.2	55.4
17	71 28.2	10.5	335 18.3	11.5	17 40.2	4.2	55.3
18	86 28.1	S15 09.7	349 48.8	11.5	N17 44.4	4.1	55.3
19	101 28.1	08.9	4 19.3	11.5	17 48.5	4.0	55.3
20	116 28.1	08.1	18 49.8	11.5	17 52.5	3.9	55.3
21	131 28.0	.. 07.3	33 20.3	11.4	17 56.4	3.8	55.2
22	146 28.0	06.5	47 50.7	11.5	18 00.2	3.8	55.2
23	161 28.0	05.7	62 21.2	11.5	18 04.0	3.6	55.2
8 00	176 28.0	S15 04.9	76 51.7	11.5	N18 07.6	3.6	55.1
01	191 27.9	04.2	91 22.2	11.5	18 11.2	3.4	55.1
02	206 27.9	03.4	105 52.7	11.6	18 14.6	3.4	55.1
03	221 27.9	.. 02.6	120 23.3	11.5	18 18.0	3.3	55.1
04	236 27.9	01.8	134 53.8	11.5	18 21.3	3.1	55.1
05	251 27.8	01.0	149 24.3	11.5	18 24.4	3.1	55.0
06	266 27.8	S15 00.2	163 54.8	11.6	N18 27.5	3.0	55.0
S 07	281 27.8	14 59.4	178 25.4	11.5	18 30.5	2.9	55.0
A 08	296 27.8	58.6	192 55.9	11.6	18 33.4	2.9	55.0
T 09	311 27.7	.. 57.8	207 26.5	11.5	18 36.3	2.7	54.9
U 10	326 27.7	57.0	221 57.0	11.6	18 39.0	2.6	54.9
R 11	341 27.7	56.2	236 27.6	11.6	18 41.6	2.6	54.9
D 12	356 27.7	S14 55.4	250 58.2	11.6	N18 44.2	2.4	54.9
A 13	11 27.6	54.7	265 28.8	11.6	18 46.6	2.4	54.9
Y 14	26 27.6	53.9	279 59.4	11.5	18 49.0	2.2	54.8
15	41 27.6	.. 53.1	294 29.9	11.7	18 51.2	2.2	54.8
16	56 27.6	52.3	309 00.6	11.6	18 53.4	2.1	54.8
17	71 27.5	51.5	323 31.2	11.6	18 55.5	2.0	54.8
18	86 27.5	S14 50.7	338 01.8	11.6	N18 57.5	1.9	54.8
19	101 27.5	49.9	352 32.4	11.7	18 59.4	1.8	54.7
20	116 27.5	49.1	7 03.1	11.6	19 01.2	1.7	54.7
21	131 27.5	.. 48.3	21 33.7	11.7	19 02.9	1.7	54.7
22	146 27.4	47.5	36 04.4	11.6	19 04.6	1.5	54.7
23	161 27.4	46.7	50 35.0	11.7	N19 06.1	1.4	54.7
SD	16.2	d 0.8	SD 15.3		15.1		15.0

Lat.	Twilight Naut.	Twilight Civil	Sunrise	Moonrise 6	7	8	9
°	h m	h m	h m	h m	h m	h m	h m
N 72	06 47	08 12	09 43	08 04	07 46	▭	▭
N 70	06 42	07 57	09 14	08 34	08 35	08 43	09 06
68	06 38	07 45	08 52	08 56	09 07	09 27	10 01
66	06 34	07 36	08 35	09 13	09 31	09 57	10 35
64	06 30	07 27	08 21	09 27	09 49	10 19	10 59
62	06 27	07 20	08 09	09 39	10 04	10 37	11 18
60	06 24	07 14	07 59	09 50	10 17	10 51	11 34
N 58	06 21	07 08	07 51	09 59	10 28	11 04	11 47
56	06 19	07 03	07 43	10 07	10 38	11 15	11 59
54	06 16	06 58	07 36	10 14	10 46	11 25	12 09
52	06 14	06 54	07 30	10 20	10 54	11 33	12 18
50	06 12	06 50	07 25	10 26	11 01	11 41	12 26
45	06 07	06 42	07 13	10 38	11 16	11 57	12 42
N 40	06 02	06 34	07 03	10 48	11 28	12 11	12 57
35	05 58	06 28	06 54	10 57	11 38	12 22	13 09
30	05 53	06 22	06 46	11 05	11 48	12 32	13 19
20	05 44	06 11	06 33	11 18	12 03	12 50	13 37
N 10	05 35	06 00	06 22	11 30	12 17	13 05	13 53
0	05 24	05 49	06 11	11 41	12 30	13 19	14 08
S 10	05 12	05 38	06 00	11 53	12 43	13 33	14 22
20	04 57	05 24	05 48	12 05	12 57	13 49	14 38
30	04 38	05 08	05 34	12 18	13 14	14 06	14 56
35	04 26	04 58	05 26	12 26	13 23	14 16	15 06
40	04 11	04 47	05 16	12 36	13 34	14 28	15 18
45	03 52	04 33	05 05	12 46	13 46	14 42	15 33
S 50	03 28	04 15	04 52	12 59	14 02	14 59	15 50
52	03 16	04 07	04 46	13 06	14 09	15 07	15 58
54	03 02	03 57	04 39	13 12	14 17	15 16	16 07
56	02 44	03 46	04 31	13 20	14 26	15 25	16 17
58	02 23	03 34	04 23	13 28	14 36	15 37	16 29
S 60	01 53	03 19	04 13	13 38	14 48	15 50	16 43

Lat.	Sunset	Twilight Civil	Twilight Naut.	Moonset 6	7	8	9
°	h m	h m	h m	h m	h m	h m	h m
N 72	14 46	16 18	17 43	02 39	04 40	▭	▭
N 70	15 16	16 33	17 48	02 11	03 51	05 25	06 43
68	15 37	16 44	17 52	01 49	03 20	04 41	05 48
66	15 54	16 54	17 56	01 33	02 57	04 12	05 15
64	16 08	17 02	17 59	01 19	02 39	03 50	04 50
62	16 20	17 09	18 02	01 08	02 24	03 33	04 31
60	16 30	17 15	18 05	00 58	02 12	03 18	04 15
N 58	16 38	17 21	18 08	00 50	02 01	03 06	04 02
56	16 46	17 26	18 10	00 43	01 52	02 55	03 51
54	16 53	17 31	18 13	00 36	01 44	02 45	03 41
52	16 59	17 35	18 15	00 30	01 36	02 37	03 32
50	17 04	17 39	18 18	00 25	01 30	02 29	03 24
45	17 16	17 47	18 22	00 14	01 15	02 13	03 07
N 40	17 26	17 54	18 26	00 04	01 04	02 00	02 53
35	17 35	18 01	18 31	24 54	00 54	01 49	02 41
30	17 42	18 07	18 35	24 45	00 45	01 39	02 30
20	17 55	18 18	18 44	24 30	00 30	01 22	02 13
N 10	18 07	18 28	18 54	24 17	00 17	01 08	01 57
0	18 18	18 39	19 04	24 05	00 05	00 54	01 43
S 10	18 29	18 50	19 16	23 53	24 40	00 40	01 28
20	18 40	19 03	19 31	23 40	24 26	00 26	01 12
30	18 54	19 19	19 50	23 25	24 09	00 09	00 55
35	19 02	19 29	20 02	23 16	23 59	24 44	00 44
40	19 11	19 41	20 16	23 07	23 48	24 32	00 32
45	19 22	19 54	20 35	22 55	23 35	24 18	00 18
S 50	19 35	20 12	20 58	22 41	23 19	24 01	00 01
52	19 41	20 20	21 10	22 35	23 11	23 53	24 41
54	19 48	20 29	21 24	22 28	23 03	23 44	24 32
56	19 55	20 40	21 41	22 20	22 54	23 34	24 22
58	20 04	20 52	22 02	22 11	22 43	23 23	24 10
S 60	20 14	21 07	22 30	22 01	22 31	23 09	23 56

Day	SUN Eqn. of Time 00h	12h	Mer. Pass.	MOON Mer. Pass. Upper	Lower	Age	Phase
d	m s	m s	h m	h m	h m	d	%
6	14 01	14 03	12 14	17 53	05 29	07	47
7	14 05	14 07	12 14	18 42	06 18	08	57
8	14 08	14 09	12 14	19 31	07 07	09	66

UT	ARIES	VENUS −4.9		MARS +0.0		JUPITER −2.6		SATURN +0.5		STARS		
	GHA	GHA	Dec	GHA	Dec	GHA	Dec	GHA	Dec	Name	SHA	Dec
d h	° ′	° ′	° ′	° ′	° ′	° ′	° ′	° ′	° ′		° ′	° ′
9 00	139 00.7	213 40.0	S16 09.8	294 44.4	S 7 17.0	36 29.7	N23 08.6	267 53.5	S16 17.4	Acamar	315 18.0	S40 15.3
01	154 03.1	228 41.6	09.9	309 46.3	17.2	51 32.4	08.6	282 55.9	17.4	Achernar	335 26.7	S57 10.2
02	169 05.6	243 43.3	10.0	324 48.3	17.3	66 35.1	08.6	297 58.3	17.4	Acrux	173 08.1	S63 10.5
03	184 08.1	258 45.0	.. 10.1	339 50.2	.. 17.5	81 37.7	.. 08.6	313 00.6	.. 17.4	Adhara	255 11.8	S28 59.8
04	199 10.5	273 46.6	10.3	354 52.2	17.7	96 40.4	08.6	328 03.0	17.4	Aldebaran	290 48.7	N16 32.1
05	214 13.0	288 48.3	10.4	9 54.1	17.8	111 43.1	08.7	343 05.4	17.5			
06	229 15.5	303 49.9	S16 10.5	24 56.1	S 7 18.0	126 45.8	N23 08.7	358 07.8	S16 17.5	Alioth	166 20.0	N55 52.7
07	244 17.9	318 51.6	10.6	39 58.0	18.2	141 48.5	08.7	13 10.1	17.5	Alkaid	152 58.4	N49 14.3
08	259 20.4	333 53.2	10.7	55 00.0	18.3	156 51.1	08.7	28 12.5	17.5	Al Na'ir	27 43.6	S46 53.5
S 09	274 22.9	348 54.9	.. 10.8	70 01.9	.. 18.5	171 53.8	.. 08.8	43 14.9	.. 17.5	Alnilam	275 45.7	S 1 11.9
U 10	289 25.3	3 56.5	10.9	85 03.9	18.7	186 56.5	08.8	58 17.2	17.5	Alphard	217 55.3	S 8 43.5
N 11	304 27.8	18 58.1	11.1	100 05.8	18.8	201 59.2	08.8	73 19.6	17.5			
D 12	319 30.3	33 59.8	S16 11.2	115 07.8	S 7 19.0	217 01.9	N23 08.8	88 22.0	S16 17.6	Alphecca	126 10.6	N26 39.9
A 13	334 32.7	49 01.4	11.3	130 09.7	19.2	232 04.5	08.8	103 24.4	17.6	Alpheratz	357 43.2	N29 10.2
Y 14	349 35.2	64 03.0	11.4	145 11.7	19.3	247 07.2	08.9	118 26.7	17.6	Altair	62 08.1	N 8 54.4
15	4 37.6	79 04.6	.. 11.5	160 13.7	.. 19.5	262 09.9	.. 08.9	133 29.1	.. 17.6	Ankaa	353 15.6	S42 13.9
16	19 40.1	94 06.3	11.6	175 15.6	19.7	277 12.6	08.9	148 31.5	17.6	Antares	112 25.8	S26 27.6
17	34 42.6	109 07.9	11.7	190 17.6	19.8	292 15.2	08.9	163 33.8	17.6			
18	49 45.0	124 09.5	S16 11.9	205 19.5	S 7 20.0	307 17.9	N23 08.9	178 36.2	S16 17.6	Arcturus	145 55.2	N19 06.4
19	64 47.5	139 11.1	12.0	220 21.5	20.2	322 20.6	09.0	193 38.6	17.7	Atria	107 27.4	S69 02.8
20	79 50.0	154 12.7	12.1	235 23.5	20.3	337 23.3	09.0	208 41.0	17.7	Avior	234 17.1	S59 33.6
21	94 52.4	169 14.3	.. 12.2	250 25.4	.. 20.5	352 26.0	.. 09.0	223 43.3	.. 17.7	Bellatrix	278 31.3	N 6 21.5
22	109 54.9	184 15.9	12.3	265 27.4	20.6	7 28.6	09.0	238 45.7	17.7	Betelgeuse	271 00.6	N 7 24.3
23	124 57.4	199 17.5	12.4	280 29.3	20.8	22 31.3	09.1	253 48.1	17.7			
10 00	139 59.8	214 19.1	S16 12.5	295 31.3	S 7 21.0	37 34.0	N23 09.1	268 50.4	S16 17.7	Canopus	263 55.5	S52 42.6
01	155 02.3	229 20.6	12.7	310 33.3	21.1	52 36.7	09.1	283 52.8	17.7	Capella	280 33.5	N46 00.7
02	170 04.8	244 22.2	12.8	325 35.2	21.3	67 39.3	09.1	298 55.2	17.8	Deneb	49 31.6	N45 19.9
03	185 07.2	259 23.8	.. 12.9	340 37.2	.. 21.5	82 42.0	.. 09.1	313 57.6	.. 17.8	Denebola	182 32.9	N14 29.4
04	200 09.7	274 25.4	13.0	355 39.2	21.6	97 44.7	09.2	328 59.9	17.8	Diphda	348 55.6	S17 54.7
05	215 12.1	289 26.9	13.1	10 41.1	21.8	112 47.3	09.2	344 02.3	17.8			
06	230 14.6	304 28.5	S16 13.2	25 43.1	S 7 21.9	127 50.0	N23 09.2	359 04.7	S16 17.8	Dubhe	193 50.6	N61 40.2
07	245 17.1	319 30.1	13.3	40 45.1	22.1	142 52.7	09.2	14 07.1	17.8	Elnath	278 11.8	N28 37.0
08	260 19.5	334 31.6	13.4	55 47.1	22.3	157 55.4	09.2	29 09.4	17.8	Eltanin	90 46.3	N51 29.1
M 09	275 22.0	349 33.2	.. 13.6	70 49.0	.. 22.4	172 58.0	.. 09.3	44 11.8	.. 17.9	Enif	33 47.0	N 9 56.4
O 10	290 24.5	4 34.7	13.7	85 51.0	22.6	188 00.7	09.3	59 14.2	17.9	Fomalhaut	15 23.8	S29 32.9
N 11	305 26.9	19 36.3	13.8	100 53.0	22.7	203 03.4	09.3	74 16.6	17.9			
D 12	320 29.4	34 37.8	S16 13.9	115 55.0	S 7 22.9	218 06.0	N23 09.3	89 18.9	S16 17.9	Gacrux	171 59.9	S57 11.4
A 13	335 31.9	49 39.4	14.0	130 56.9	23.1	233 08.7	09.3	104 21.3	17.9	Gienah	175 51.5	S17 37.3
Y 14	350 34.3	64 40.9	14.1	145 58.9	23.2	248 11.4	09.4	119 23.7	17.9	Hadar	148 46.9	S60 26.2
15	5 36.8	79 42.5	.. 14.2	161 00.9	.. 23.4	263 14.1	.. 09.4	134 26.1	.. 17.9	Hamal	328 00.3	N23 31.7
16	20 39.3	94 44.0	14.4	176 02.9	23.5	278 16.7	09.4	149 28.4	17.9	Kaus Aust.	83 43.5	S34 22.4
17	35 41.7	109 45.5	14.5	191 04.8	23.7	293 19.4	09.4	164 30.8	18.0			
18	50 44.2	124 47.0	S16 14.6	206 06.8	S 7 23.8	308 22.1	N23 09.4	179 33.2	S16 18.0	Kochab	137 20.0	N74 05.6
19	65 46.6	139 48.6	14.7	221 08.8	24.0	323 24.7	09.5	194 35.6	18.0	Markab	13 38.1	N15 16.9
20	80 49.1	154 50.1	14.8	236 10.8	24.2	338 27.4	09.5	209 37.9	18.0	Menkar	314 14.6	N 4 08.5
21	95 51.6	169 51.6	.. 14.9	251 12.8	.. 24.3	353 30.1	.. 09.5	224 40.3	.. 18.0	Menkent	148 06.8	S36 26.2
22	110 54.0	184 53.1	15.0	266 14.8	24.5	8 32.7	09.5	239 42.7	18.0	Miaplacidus	221 38.5	S69 46.7
23	125 56.5	199 54.6	15.2	281 16.7	24.6	23 35.4	09.5	254 45.1	18.0			
11 00	140 59.0	214 56.1	S16 15.3	296 18.7	S 7 24.8	38 38.1	N23 09.6	269 47.5	S16 18.0	Mirfak	308 39.6	N49 54.7
01	156 01.4	229 57.6	15.4	311 20.7	24.9	53 40.7	09.6	284 49.8	18.1	Nunki	75 58.0	S26 16.6
02	171 03.9	244 59.1	15.5	326 22.7	25.1	68 43.4	09.6	299 52.2	18.1	Peacock	53 19.1	S56 41.2
03	186 06.4	260 00.6	.. 15.6	341 24.7	.. 25.2	83 46.1	.. 09.6	314 54.6	.. 18.1	Pollux	243 26.8	N27 59.3
04	201 08.8	275 02.1	15.7	356 26.7	25.4	98 48.7	09.6	329 57.0	18.1	Procyon	244 58.9	N 5 11.0
05	216 11.3	290 03.6	15.8	11 28.7	25.5	113 51.4	09.7	344 59.3	18.1			
06	231 13.7	305 05.1	S16 15.9	26 30.7	S 7 25.7	128 54.1	N23 09.7	0 01.7	S16 18.1	Rasalhague	96 06.2	N12 33.0
07	246 16.2	320 06.6	16.1	41 32.6	25.8	143 56.7	09.7	15 04.1	18.1	Regulus	207 42.7	N11 53.6
08	261 18.7	335 08.0	16.2	56 34.6	26.0	158 59.4	09.7	30 06.5	18.1	Rigel	281 11.4	S 8 11.4
T 09	276 21.1	350 09.5	.. 16.3	71 36.6	.. 26.1	174 02.1	.. 09.7	45 08.9	.. 18.2	Rigil Kent.	139 50.8	S60 53.3
U 10	291 23.6	5 11.0	16.4	86 38.6	26.3	189 04.7	09.8	60 11.2	18.2	Sabik	102 12.1	S15 44.4
E 11	306 26.1	20 12.4	16.5	101 40.6	26.4	204 07.4	09.8	75 13.6	18.2			
S 12	321 28.5	35 13.9	S16 16.6	116 42.6	S 7 26.6	219 10.1	N23 09.8	90 16.0	S16 18.2	Schedar	349 40.2	N56 37.1
D 13	336 31.0	50 15.4	16.7	131 44.6	26.7	234 12.7	09.8	105 18.4	18.2	Shaula	96 21.5	S37 06.6
A 14	351 33.5	65 16.8	16.8	146 46.6	26.9	249 15.4	09.8	120 20.8	18.2	Sirius	258 33.0	S16 44.5
Y 15	6 35.9	80 18.3	.. 17.0	161 48.6	.. 27.0	264 18.0	.. 09.9	135 23.1	.. 18.2	Spica	158 30.6	S11 14.1
16	21 38.4	95 19.7	17.1	176 50.6	27.2	279 20.7	09.9	150 25.5	18.2	Suhail	222 51.6	S43 29.6
17	36 40.9	110 21.2	17.2	191 52.6	27.3	294 23.4	09.9	165 27.9	18.3			
18	51 43.3	125 22.6	S16 17.3	206 54.6	S 7 27.5	309 26.0	N23 09.9	180 30.3	S16 18.3	Vega	80 38.9	N38 47.8
19	66 45.8	140 24.1	17.4	221 56.6	27.6	324 28.7	09.9	195 32.7	18.3	Zuben'ubi	137 04.8	S16 06.0
20	81 48.2	155 25.5	17.5	236 58.6	27.8	339 31.3	10.0	210 35.0	18.3		SHA	Mer.Pass.
21	96 50.7	170 26.9	.. 17.6	252 00.6	.. 27.9	354 34.0	.. 10.0	225 37.4	.. 18.3		° ′	h m
22	111 53.2	185 28.4	17.7	267 02.6	28.1	9 36.7	10.0	240 39.8	18.3	Venus	74 19.2	9 42
23	126 55.6	200 29.8	17.8	282 04.6	28.2	24 39.3	10.0	255 42.2	18.3	Mars	155 31.5	4 17
	h m									Jupiter	257 34.2	21 26
Mer. Pass. 14 37.6		v 1.5	d 0.1	v 2.0	d 0.2	v 2.7	d 0.0	v 2.4	d 0.0	Saturn	128 50.6	6 04

UT	SUN GHA	SUN Dec	MOON GHA	v	Dec	d	HP
d h	° ′	° ′	° ′	′	° ′	′	′
9 00	176 27.4	S14 45.9	65 05.7	11.7	N19 07.5	1.4	54.6
01	191 27.4	45.1	79 36.4	11.7	19 08.9	1.2	54.6
02	206 27.4	44.3	94 07.1	11.7	19 10.1	1.2	54.6
03	221 27.3	.. 43.5	108 37.8	11.7	19 11.3	1.1	54.6
04	236 27.3	42.7	123 08.5	11.7	19 12.4	1.0	54.6
05	251 27.3	41.9	137 39.2	11.8	19 13.4	0.9	54.5
06	266 27.3	S14 41.1	152 10.0	11.7	N19 14.3	0.8	54.5
S 07	281 27.3	40.3	166 40.7	11.8	19 15.1	0.7	54.5
U 08	296 27.3	39.5	181 11.5	11.8	19 15.8	0.6	54.5
N 09	311 27.2	.. 38.7	195 42.3	11.7	19 16.4	0.5	54.5
D 10	326 27.2	37.9	210 13.0	11.8	19 16.9	0.5	54.5
A 11	341 27.2	37.1	224 43.8	11.8	19 17.4	0.3	54.5
Y 12	356 27.2	S14 36.3	239 14.6	11.9	N19 17.7	0.3	54.4
13	11 27.2	35.5	253 45.5	11.8	19 18.0	0.1	54.4
14	26 27.2	34.7	268 16.3	11.9	19 18.1	0.1	54.4
15	41 27.2	.. 33.9	282 47.2	11.8	19 18.2	0.0	54.4
16	56 27.1	33.0	297 18.0	11.9	19 18.2	0.1	54.4
17	71 27.1	32.2	311 48.9	11.9	19 18.1	0.2	54.4
18	86 27.1	S14 31.4	326 19.8	11.9	N19 17.9	0.3	54.4
19	101 27.1	30.6	340 50.7	11.9	19 17.6	0.4	54.3
20	116 27.1	29.8	355 21.6	12.0	19 17.2	0.4	54.3
21	131 27.1	.. 29.0	9 52.6	11.9	19 16.8	0.6	54.3
22	146 27.1	28.2	24 23.5	12.0	19 16.2	0.6	54.3
23	161 27.1	27.4	38 54.5	12.0	19 15.6	0.8	54.3
10 00	176 27.0	S14 26.6	53 25.5	12.0	N19 14.8	0.8	54.3
01	191 27.0	25.8	67 56.5	12.0	19 14.0	0.9	54.3
02	206 27.0	25.0	82 27.5	12.0	19 13.1	1.0	54.3
03	221 27.0	.. 24.2	96 58.5	12.0	19 12.1	1.1	54.2
04	236 27.0	23.3	111 29.5	12.1	19 11.0	1.2	54.2
05	251 27.0	22.5	126 00.6	12.1	19 09.8	1.2	54.2
06	266 27.0	S14 21.7	140 31.7	12.1	N19 08.6	1.4	54.2
M 07	281 27.0	20.9	155 02.8	12.1	19 07.2	1.4	54.2
O 08	296 27.0	20.1	169 33.9	12.1	19 05.8	1.5	54.2
N 09	311 27.0	.. 19.3	184 05.0	12.2	19 04.3	1.7	54.2
D 10	326 26.9	18.5	198 36.2	12.2	19 02.6	1.7	54.2
A 11	341 26.9	17.7	213 07.4	12.2	19 00.9	1.8	54.2
Y 12	356 26.9	S14 16.8	227 38.6	12.2	N18 59.1	1.8	54.2
13	11 26.9	16.0	242 09.8	12.2	18 57.3	2.0	54.1
14	26 26.9	15.2	256 41.0	12.2	18 55.3	2.1	54.1
15	41 26.9	.. 14.4	271 12.2	12.3	18 53.2	2.1	54.1
16	56 26.9	13.6	285 43.5	12.3	18 51.1	2.2	54.1
17	71 26.9	12.8	300 14.8	12.3	18 48.9	2.3	54.1
18	86 26.9	S14 12.0	314 46.1	12.3	N18 46.6	2.4	54.1
19	101 26.9	11.1	329 17.4	12.4	18 44.2	2.5	54.1
20	116 26.9	10.3	343 48.8	12.3	18 41.7	2.6	54.1
21	131 26.9	.. 09.5	358 20.1	12.4	18 39.1	2.6	54.1
22	146 26.9	08.7	12 51.5	12.4	18 36.5	2.7	54.1
23	161 26.9	07.9	27 22.9	12.5	18 33.8	2.8	54.1
11 00	176 26.9	S14 07.0	41 54.4	12.4	N18 31.0	2.9	54.1
01	191 26.9	06.2	56 25.8	12.5	18 28.1	3.0	54.1
02	206 26.9	05.4	70 57.3	12.5	18 25.1	3.1	54.1
03	221 26.9	.. 04.6	85 28.8	12.5	18 22.0	3.1	54.0
04	236 26.9	03.8	100 00.3	12.6	18 18.9	3.3	54.0
05	251 26.9	02.9	114 31.9	12.5	18 15.6	3.3	54.0
06	266 26.9	S14 02.1	129 03.4	12.6	N18 12.3	3.4	54.0
07	281 26.9	01.3	143 35.0	12.6	18 08.9	3.4	54.0
T 08	296 26.9	14 00.5	158 06.6	12.6	18 05.5	3.6	54.0
U 09	311 26.9	13 59.7	172 38.2	12.7	18 01.9	3.8	54.0
E 10	326 26.9	58.8	187 09.9	12.7	17 58.3	3.8	54.0
S 11	341 26.9	58.0	201 41.6	12.7	17 54.5	3.8	54.0
D 12	356 26.9	S13 57.2	216 13.3	12.7	N17 50.7	3.8	54.0
A 13	11 26.9	56.4	230 45.0	12.7	17 46.9	4.0	54.0
Y 14	26 26.9	55.5	245 16.7	12.8	17 42.9	4.0	54.0
15	41 26.9	.. 54.7	259 48.5	12.8	17 38.9	4.1	54.0
16	56 26.9	53.9	274 20.3	12.8	17 34.8	4.2	54.0
17	71 26.9	53.1	288 52.1	12.9	17 30.6	4.3	54.0
18	86 26.9	S13 52.2	303 24.0	12.8	N17 26.3	4.4	54.0
19	101 26.9	51.4	317 55.8	12.9	17 21.9	4.4	54.0
20	116 26.9	50.6	332 27.7	12.9	17 17.5	4.5	54.0
21	131 26.9	.. 49.8	346 59.6	12.9	17 13.0	4.6	54.0
22	146 26.9	48.9	1 31.5	13.0	17 08.4	4.6	54.0
23	161 26.9	48.1	16 03.5	13.0	N17 03.8	4.7	54.0
	SD 16.2	d 0.8	SD 14.8		14.8		14.7

Lat.	Twilight Naut.	Twilight Civil	Sunrise	Moonrise 9	Moonrise 10	Moonrise 11	Moonrise 12
°	h m	h m	h m	h m	h m	h m	h m
N 72	06 36	07 58	09 24	▭	▭	09 58	12 18
N 70	06 32	07 45	08 59	09 06	10 03	11 27	12 58
68	06 28	07 35	08 39	10 01	10 55	12 06	13 26
66	06 25	07 26	08 24	10 35	11 27	12 33	13 47
64	06 22	07 19	08 11	10 59	11 51	12 53	14 03
62	06 20	07 12	08 01	11 18	12 10	13 10	14 17
60	06 17	07 07	07 52	11 34	12 25	13 24	14 29
N 58	06 15	07 02	07 44	11 47	12 38	13 36	14 39
56	06 13	06 57	07 37	11 59	12 49	13 46	14 47
54	06 11	06 53	07 30	12 09	12 59	13 55	14 55
52	06 09	06 49	07 25	12 18	13 08	14 03	15 02
50	06 08	06 46	07 20	12 26	13 16	14 10	15 08
45	06 03	06 38	07 08	12 43	13 33	14 26	15 22
N 40	05 59	06 31	06 59	12 57	13 46	14 39	15 33
35	05 55	06 25	06 51	13 09	13 58	14 49	15 42
30	05 51	06 20	06 44	13 19	14 08	14 59	15 50
20	05 43	06 09	06 32	13 37	14 26	15 15	16 05
N 10	05 34	05 59	06 21	13 53	14 41	15 29	16 17
0	05 25	05 49	06 11	14 08	14 55	15 42	16 29
S 10	05 13	05 39	06 00	14 22	15 10	15 56	16 40
20	04 59	05 26	05 49	14 38	15 25	16 10	16 52
30	04 41	05 11	05 36	14 56	15 42	16 26	17 06
35	04 29	05 02	05 29	15 06	15 53	16 35	17 15
40	04 15	04 51	05 20	15 18	16 04	16 46	17 24
45	03 58	04 38	05 10	15 33	16 18	16 59	17 35
S 50	03 35	04 21	04 57	15 50	16 35	17 14	17 48
52	03 24	04 13	04 52	15 58	16 43	17 21	17 54
54	03 10	04 04	04 45	16 07	16 51	17 29	18 01
56	02 55	03 54	04 38	16 17	17 01	17 38	18 08
58	02 35	03 43	04 30	16 29	17 12	17 48	18 16
S 60	02 10	03 29	04 21	16 43	17 25	17 59	18 26

Lat.	Sunset	Twilight Civil	Twilight Naut.	Moonset 9	Moonset 10	Moonset 11	Moonset 12
°	h m	h m	h m	h m	h m	h m	h m
N 72	15 06	16 32	17 55	▭	▭	09 09	08 26
N 70	15 31	16 45	17 59	06 43	07 26	07 40	07 45
68	15 50	16 55	18 02	05 48	06 34	07 01	07 16
66	16 06	17 03	18 05	05 15	06 01	06 33	06 55
64	16 18	17 11	18 07	04 50	05 38	06 12	06 38
62	16 29	17 17	18 10	04 31	05 19	05 55	06 24
60	16 38	17 23	18 12	04 15	05 03	05 41	06 11
N 58	16 46	17 28	18 14	04 02	04 50	05 29	06 01
56	16 53	17 32	18 16	03 51	04 39	05 19	05 52
54	16 59	17 36	18 18	03 41	04 29	05 09	05 44
52	17 04	17 40	18 20	03 32	04 20	05 01	05 37
50	17 10	17 43	18 22	03 24	04 12	04 54	05 30
45	17 21	17 51	18 26	03 07	03 55	04 38	05 16
N 40	17 30	17 58	18 30	02 53	03 41	04 25	05 04
35	17 38	18 04	18 34	02 41	03 29	04 14	04 54
30	17 45	18 09	18 38	02 30	03 19	04 04	04 46
20	17 57	18 19	18 46	02 13	03 01	03 47	04 31
N 10	18 07	18 29	18 54	01 57	02 45	03 32	04 17
0	18 18	18 39	19 04	01 43	02 31	03 18	04 05
S 10	18 28	18 50	19 15	01 28	02 16	03 04	03 52
20	18 39	19 02	19 29	01 12	02 01	02 50	03 39
30	18 52	19 17	19 47	00 55	01 43	02 33	03 24
35	18 59	19 26	19 58	00 44	01 32	02 23	03 15
40	19 08	19 37	20 12	00 32	01 20	02 11	03 04
45	19 18	19 50	20 29	00 18	01 06	01 58	02 52
S 50	19 30	20 06	20 52	00 01	00 49	01 41	02 38
52	19 36	20 14	21 03	24 41	00 41	01 34	02 31
54	19 42	20 22	21 16	24 32	00 32	01 25	02 23
56	19 49	20 32	21 31	24 22	00 22	01 15	02 15
58	19 57	20 44	21 50	24 10	00 10	01 04	02 05
S 60	20 06	20 57	22 14	23 56	24 52	00 52	01 54

Day	SUN Eqn. of Time 00ʰ	SUN Eqn. of Time 12ʰ	SUN Mer. Pass.	MOON Mer. Pass. Upper	MOON Mer. Pass. Lower	Age	Phase
d	m s	m s	h m	h m	h m	d	%
9	14 10	14 11	12 14	20 19	07 55	10	75
10	14 12	14 12	12 14	21 07	08 43	11	83
11	14 12	14 13	12 14	21 54	09 30	12	89

UT	ARIES GHA	VENUS −4.9 GHA	Dec	MARS −0.1 GHA	Dec	JUPITER −2.5 GHA	Dec	SATURN +0.5 GHA	Dec	Name	SHA	Dec
12 WEDNESDAY												
00	141 58.1	215 31.2	S16 18.0	297 06.6	S 7 28.4	39 42.0	N23 10.0	270 44.6	S16 18.3	Acamar	315 18.1	S40 15.3
01	157 00.6	230 32.7	18.1	312 08.6	28.5	54 44.6	10.1	285 46.9	18.4	Achernar	335 26.8	S57 10.2
02	172 03.0	245 34.1	18.2	327 10.7	28.7	69 47.3	10.1	300 49.3	18.4	Acrux	173 08.1	S63 10.5
03	187 05.5	260 35.5	.. 18.3	342 12.7	.. 28.8	84 50.0	.. 10.1	315 51.7	.. 18.4	Adhara	255 11.8	S28 59.9
04	202 08.0	275 36.9	18.4	357 14.7	29.0	99 52.6	10.1	330 54.1	18.4	Aldebaran	290 48.7	N16 32.1
05	217 10.4	290 38.3	18.5	12 16.7	29.1	114 55.3	10.1	345 56.5	18.4			
06	232 12.9	305 39.7	S16 18.6	27 18.7	S 7 29.2	129 57.9	N23 10.2	0 58.9	S16 18.4	Alioth	166 20.0	N55 52.7
07	247 15.4	320 41.1	18.7	42 20.7	29.4	145 00.6	10.2	16 01.2	18.4	Alkaid	152 58.4	N49 14.3
08	262 17.8	335 42.5	18.8	57 22.7	29.5	160 03.2	10.2	31 03.6	18.4	Al Na'ir	27 43.6	S46 53.5
09	277 20.3	350 43.9	.. 18.9	72 24.7	.. 29.7	175 05.9	.. 10.2	46 06.0	.. 18.4	Alnilam	275 45.7	S 1 11.9
10	292 22.7	5 45.3	19.1	87 26.8	29.8	190 08.6	10.2	61 08.4	18.5	Alphard	217 55.3	S 8 43.5
11	307 25.2	20 46.7	19.2	102 28.8	30.0	205 11.2	10.3	76 10.8	18.5			
12	322 27.7	35 48.1	S16 19.3	117 30.8	S 7 30.1	220 13.9	N23 10.3	91 13.2	S16 18.5	Alphecca	126 10.6	N26 39.9
13	337 30.1	50 49.5	19.4	132 32.8	30.2	235 16.5	10.3	106 15.5	18.5	Alpheratz	357 43.2	N29 10.2
14	352 32.6	65 50.8	19.5	147 34.8	30.4	250 19.2	10.3	121 17.9	18.5	Altair	62 08.1	N 8 54.4
15	7 35.1	80 52.2	.. 19.6	162 36.8	.. 30.5	265 21.8	.. 10.3	136 20.3	.. 18.5	Ankaa	353 15.6	S42 13.9
16	22 37.5	95 53.6	19.7	177 38.9	30.7	280 24.5	10.4	151 22.7	18.5	Antares	112 25.7	S26 27.6
17	37 40.0	110 55.0	19.8	192 40.9	30.8	295 27.1	10.4	166 25.1	18.5			
18	52 42.5	125 56.3	S16 19.9	207 42.9	S 7 31.0	310 29.8	N23 10.4	181 27.5	S16 18.5	Arcturus	145 55.2	N19 06.4
19	67 44.9	140 57.7	20.0	222 44.9	31.1	325 32.4	10.4	196 29.8	18.6	Atria	107 27.3	S69 02.8
20	82 47.4	155 59.0	20.2	237 47.0	31.2	340 35.1	10.4	211 32.2	18.6	Avior	234 17.1	S59 33.6
21	97 49.8	171 00.4	.. 20.3	252 49.0	.. 31.4	355 37.7	.. 10.4	226 34.6	.. 18.6	Bellatrix	278 31.3	N 6 21.5
22	112 52.3	186 01.8	20.4	267 51.0	31.5	10 40.4	10.5	241 37.0	18.6	Betelgeuse	271 00.6	N 7 24.3
23	127 54.8	201 03.1	20.5	282 53.0	31.6	25 43.0	10.5	256 39.4	18.6			
13 THURSDAY												
00	142 57.2	216 04.5	S16 20.6	297 55.1	S 7 31.8	40 45.7	N23 10.5	271 41.8	S16 18.6	Canopus	263 55.5	S52 42.6
01	157 59.7	231 05.8	20.7	312 57.1	31.9	55 48.3	10.5	286 44.2	18.6	Capella	280 33.5	N46 00.7
02	173 02.2	246 07.1	20.8	327 59.1	32.1	70 51.0	10.5	301 46.5	18.6	Deneb	49 31.6	N45 19.9
03	188 04.6	261 08.5	.. 20.9	343 01.2	.. 32.2	85 53.7	.. 10.6	316 48.9	.. 18.6	Denebola	182 32.9	N14 29.4
04	203 07.1	276 09.8	21.0	358 03.2	32.3	100 56.3	10.6	331 51.3	18.6	Diphda	348 55.6	S17 54.7
05	218 09.6	291 11.1	21.1	13 05.2	32.5	115 58.9	10.6	346 53.7	18.7			
06	233 12.0	306 12.5	S16 21.2	28 07.2	S 7 32.6	131 01.6	N23 10.6	1 56.1	S16 18.7	Dubhe	193 50.6	N61 40.2
07	248 14.5	321 13.8	21.3	43 09.3	32.7	146 04.2	10.6	16 58.5	18.7	Elnath	278 11.8	N28 37.0
08	263 17.0	336 15.1	21.4	58 11.3	32.9	161 06.9	10.7	32 00.9	18.7	Eltanin	90 46.2	N51 29.1
09	278 19.4	351 16.4	.. 21.5	73 13.4	.. 33.0	176 09.5	.. 10.7	47 03.3	.. 18.7	Enif	33 47.0	N 9 56.4
10	293 21.9	6 17.8	21.7	88 15.4	33.1	191 12.2	10.7	62 05.6	18.7	Fomalhaut	15 23.8	S29 32.9
11	308 24.3	21 19.1	21.8	103 17.4	33.3	206 14.8	10.7	77 08.0	18.7			
12	323 26.8	36 20.4	S16 21.9	118 19.5	S 7 33.4	221 17.5	N23 10.7	92 10.4	S16 18.7	Gacrux	171 59.8	S57 11.4
13	338 29.3	51 21.7	22.0	133 21.5	33.5	236 20.1	10.7	107 12.8	18.7	Gienah	175 51.5	S17 37.3
14	353 31.7	66 23.0	22.1	148 23.5	33.7	251 22.8	10.8	122 15.2	18.8	Hadar	148 46.9	S60 26.2
15	8 34.2	81 24.3	.. 22.2	163 25.6	.. 33.8	266 25.4	.. 10.8	137 17.6	.. 18.8	Hamal	328 00.3	N23 31.7
16	23 36.7	96 25.6	22.3	178 27.6	33.9	281 28.1	10.8	152 20.0	18.8	Kaus Aust.	83 43.4	S34 22.4
17	38 39.1	111 26.9	22.4	193 29.7	34.1	296 30.7	10.8	167 22.4	18.8			
18	53 41.6	126 28.2	S16 22.5	208 31.7	S 7 34.2	311 33.4	N23 10.8	182 24.7	S16 18.8	Kochab	137 20.0	N74 05.6
19	68 44.1	141 29.5	22.6	223 33.8	34.3	326 36.0	10.9	197 27.1	18.8	Markab	13 38.1	N15 16.9
20	83 46.5	156 30.8	22.7	238 35.8	34.5	341 38.6	10.9	212 29.5	18.8	Menkar	314 14.6	N 4 08.5
21	98 49.0	171 32.0	.. 22.8	253 37.9	.. 34.6	356 41.3	.. 10.9	227 31.9	.. 18.8	Menkent	148 06.8	S36 26.2
22	113 51.5	186 33.3	22.9	268 39.9	34.7	11 43.9	10.9	242 34.3	18.8	Miaplacidus	221 38.5	S69 46.7
23	128 53.9	201 34.6	23.0	283 42.0	34.9	26 46.6	10.9	257 36.7	18.8			
14 FRIDAY												
00	143 56.4	216 35.9	S16 23.1	298 44.0	S 7 35.0	41 49.2	N23 10.9	272 39.1	S16 18.8	Mirfak	308 39.6	N49 54.7
01	158 58.8	231 37.1	23.2	313 46.1	35.1	56 51.9	11.0	287 41.5	18.9	Nunki	75 58.0	S26 16.6
02	174 01.3	246 38.4	23.3	328 48.1	35.3	71 54.5	11.0	302 43.9	18.9	Peacock	53 19.1	S56 41.2
03	189 03.8	261 39.7	.. 23.4	343 50.2	.. 35.4	86 57.1	.. 11.0	317 46.3	.. 18.9	Pollux	243 26.8	N27 59.3
04	204 06.2	276 40.9	23.5	358 52.2	35.5	101 59.8	11.0	332 48.6	18.9	Procyon	244 58.9	N 5 11.0
05	219 08.7	291 42.2	23.6	13 54.3	35.6	117 02.4	11.0	347 51.0	18.9			
06	234 11.2	306 43.4	S16 23.7	28 56.3	S 7 35.8	132 05.1	N23 11.0	2 53.4	S16 18.9	Rasalhague	96 06.2	N12 33.0
07	249 13.6	321 44.7	23.8	43 58.4	35.9	147 07.7	11.1	17 55.8	18.9	Regulus	207 42.7	N11 53.6
08	264 16.1	336 45.9	23.9	59 00.4	36.0	162 10.4	11.1	32 58.2	18.9	Rigel	281 11.4	S 8 11.4
09	279 18.6	351 47.2	.. 24.0	74 02.5	.. 36.1	177 13.0	.. 11.1	48 00.6	.. 18.9	Rigil Kent.	139 50.8	S60 53.3
10	294 21.0	6 48.4	24.1	89 04.6	36.3	192 15.6	11.1	63 03.0	18.9	Sabik	102 12.1	S15 44.4
11	309 23.5	21 49.7	24.2	104 06.6	36.4	207 18.3	11.1	78 05.4	18.9			
12	324 25.9	36 50.9	S16 24.3	119 08.7	S 7 36.5	222 20.9	N23 11.2	93 07.8	S16 19.0	Schedar	349 40.3	N56 37.1
13	339 28.4	51 52.1	24.4	134 10.7	36.7	237 23.5	11.2	108 10.2	19.0	Shaula	96 21.5	S37 06.6
14	354 30.9	66 53.4	24.5	149 12.8	36.8	252 26.2	11.2	123 12.6	19.0	Sirius	258 33.0	S16 44.5
15	9 33.3	81 54.6	.. 24.6	164 14.9	.. 36.9	267 28.8	.. 11.2	138 14.9	.. 19.0	Spica	158 30.6	S11 14.2
16	24 35.8	96 55.8	24.7	179 16.9	37.0	282 31.5	11.2	153 17.3	19.0	Suhail	222 51.6	S43 29.6
17	39 38.3	111 57.0	24.8	194 19.0	37.2	297 34.1	11.2	168 19.7	19.0			
18	54 40.7	126 58.3	S16 24.9	209 21.1	S 7 37.3	312 36.7	N23 11.3	183 22.1	S16 19.0	Vega	80 38.9	N38 47.8
19	69 43.2	141 59.5	25.0	224 23.1	37.4	327 39.4	11.3	198 24.5	19.0	Zuben'ubi	137 04.8	S16 06.0
20	84 45.7	157 00.7	25.1	239 25.2	37.5	342 42.0	11.3	213 26.9	19.0			
21	99 48.1	172 01.9	.. 25.2	254 27.3	.. 37.6	357 44.6	.. 11.3	228 29.3	.. 19.0			
22	114 50.6	187 03.1	25.3	269 29.3	37.8	12 47.3	11.3	243 31.7	19.0			
23	129 53.1	202 04.3	25.4	284 31.4	37.9	27 49.9	11.3	258 34.1	19.1			

	SHA	Mer. Pass.
	° ′	h m
Venus	73 07.2	9 35
Mars	154 57.8	4 08
Jupiter	257 48.5	21 13
Saturn	128 44.5	5 52

Mer. Pass. 14 25.8	v 1.3 d 0.1	v 2.0 d 0.1	v 2.6 d 0.0	v 2.4 d 0.0	

UT	SUN		MOON					Lat.	Twilight		Sunrise	Moonrise			
	GHA	Dec	GHA	v	Dec	d	HP		Naut.	Civil		12	13	14	15
d h	° ′	° ′	° ′	′	° ′	′	′	°	h m	h m	h m	h m	h m	h m	h m
12 00	176 26.9	S13 47.3	30 35.5	13.0	N16 59.1	4.9	54.0	N 72	06 23	07 44	09 06	12 18	14 06	15 48	17 27
01	191 26.9	46.4	45 07.5	13.0	16 54.2	4.8	54.0	N 70	06 21	07 33	08 44	12 58	14 31	16 04	17 36
02	206 26.9	45.6	59 39.5	13.1	16 49.4	5.0	54.0	68	06 18	07 24	08 27	13 26	14 50	16 16	17 43
03	221 26.9	.. 44.8	74 11.6	13.1	16 44.4	5.0	54.0	66	06 16	07 17	08 13	13 47	15 06	16 26	17 48
04	236 26.9	44.0	88 43.7	13.1	16 39.4	5.1	54.0	64	06 14	07 10	08 02	14 03	15 18	16 35	17 53
05	251 26.9	43.1	103 15.8	13.1	16 34.3	5.2	54.0	62	06 12	07 04	07 52	14 17	15 28	16 42	17 57
06	266 26.9	S13 42.3	117 47.9	13.2	N16 29.1	5.3	54.0	60	06 11	06 59	07 44	14 29	15 37	16 48	18 01
W 07	281 27.0	41.5	132 20.1	13.1	16 23.8	5.3	54.0	N 58	06 09	06 55	07 37	14 39	15 45	16 54	18 04
E 08	296 27.0	40.6	146 52.2	13.3	16 18.5	5.4	54.0	56	06 07	06 51	07 30	14 47	15 52	16 59	18 07
D 09	311 27.0	.. 39.8	161 24.5	13.2	16 13.1	5.4	54.0	54	06 06	06 47	07 24	14 55	15 58	17 03	18 09
N 10	326 27.0	39.0	175 56.7	13.2	16 07.7	5.6	54.0	52	06 04	06 44	07 19	15 02	16 04	17 07	18 12
E 11	341 27.0	38.1	190 28.9	13.3	16 02.1	5.6	54.0	50	06 03	06 41	07 14	15 08	16 09	17 11	18 14
S 12	356 27.0	S13 37.3	205 01.2	13.3	N15 56.5	5.7	54.0	45	05 59	06 34	07 04	15 22	16 19	17 18	18 18
D 13	11 27.0	36.5	219 33.5	13.3	15 50.8	5.7	54.0	N 40	05 56	06 28	06 56	15 33	16 28	17 25	18 22
A 14	26 27.0	35.6	234 05.8	13.4	15 45.1	5.8	54.0	35	05 53	06 22	06 48	15 42	16 36	17 30	18 25
Y 15	41 27.0	.. 34.8	248 38.2	13.4	15 39.3	5.9	54.0	30	05 49	06 17	06 42	15 50	16 43	17 35	18 28
16	56 27.0	34.0	263 10.6	13.4	15 33.4	6.0	54.0	20	05 42	06 08	06 30	16 05	16 54	17 44	18 33
17	71 27.0	33.1	277 43.0	13.4	15 27.4	6.0	54.0	N 10	05 34	05 59	06 17	16 17	17 04	17 51	18 37
18	86 27.1	S13 32.3	292 15.4	13.4	N15 21.4	6.1	54.0	0	05 25	05 50	06 11	16 29	17 14	17 58	18 41
19	101 27.1	31.5	306 47.8	13.5	15 15.3	6.1	54.0	S 10	05 14	05 39	06 01	16 40	17 23	18 05	18 46
20	116 27.1	30.6	321 20.3	13.5	15 09.2	6.2	54.0	20	05 01	05 28	05 51	16 52	17 33	18 12	18 50
21	131 27.1	.. 29.8	335 52.8	13.5	15 03.0	6.3	54.0	30	04 44	05 14	05 39	17 06	17 44	18 20	18 55
22	146 27.1	28.9	350 25.3	13.6	14 56.7	6.4	54.0	35	04 33	05 05	05 32	17 15	17 51	18 25	18 58
23	161 27.1	28.1	4 57.9	13.6	14 50.3	6.4	54.0	40	04 20	04 55	05 24	17 24	17 58	18 30	19 01
13 00	176 27.1	S13 27.3	19 30.5	13.5	N14 43.9	6.5	54.0	45	04 03	04 42	05 14	17 35	18 07	18 37	19 05
01	191 27.1	26.4	34 03.0	13.7	14 37.4	6.5	54.0	S 50	03 42	04 27	05 03	17 48	18 18	18 44	19 09
02	206 27.2	25.6	48 35.7	13.6	14 30.9	6.7	54.0	52	03 31	04 20	04 57	17 54	18 22	18 48	19 11
03	221 27.2	.. 24.8	63 08.3	13.7	14 24.2	6.6	54.0	54	03 19	04 11	04 52	18 01	18 28	18 51	19 13
04	236 27.2	23.9	77 41.0	13.7	14 17.6	6.8	54.0	56	03 05	04 02	04 45	18 08	18 33	18 56	19 16
05	251 27.2	23.1	92 13.7	13.7	14 10.8	6.8	54.0	58	02 47	03 51	04 38	18 16	18 40	19 00	19 18
06	266 27.2	S13 22.2	106 46.4	13.7	N14 04.0	6.8	54.0	S 60	02 25	03 39	04 29	18 26	18 47	19 05	19 21

UT	SUN		MOON					Lat.	Sunset	Twilight		Moonset			
										Civil	Naut.	12	13	14	15
07	281 27.2	21.4	121 19.1	13.7	13 57.2	7.0	54.0	°	h m	h m	h m	h m	h m	h m	h m
T 08	296 27.2	20.6	135 51.8	13.8	13 50.2	6.9	54.0	N 72	15 24	16 46	18 07	08 26	08 12	08 02	07 53
H 09	311 27.3	.. 19.7	150 24.6	13.8	13 43.3	7.1	54.0	N 70	15 46	16 57	18 10	07 45	07 45	07 45	07 43
U 10	326 27.3	18.9	164 57.4	13.9	13 36.2	7.1	54.1	68	16 03	17 06	18 12	07 16	07 25	07 31	07 35
R 11	341 27.3	18.0	179 30.3	13.8	13 29.1	7.2	54.1	66	16 17	17 13	18 14	06 55	07 09	07 20	07 28
S 12	356 27.3	S13 17.2	194 03.1	13.9	N13 21.9	7.2	54.1	64	16 28	17 19	18 16	06 38	06 56	07 10	07 22
D 13	11 27.3	16.3	208 36.0	13.9	13 14.7	7.3	54.1	62	16 37	17 25	18 17	06 24	06 45	07 02	07 17
A 14	26 27.3	15.5	223 08.9	13.9	13 07.4	7.3	54.1	60	16 46	17 30	18 19	06 11	06 36	06 55	07 12
Y 15	41 27.4	.. 14.7	237 41.8	13.9	13 00.1	7.4	54.1	N 58	16 53	17 34	18 21	06 01	06 27	06 49	07 08
16	56 27.4	13.8	252 14.7	14.0	12 52.7	7.5	54.1	56	16 59	17 38	18 22	05 52	06 20	06 43	07 04
17	71 27.4	13.0	266 47.7	13.9	12 45.2	7.5	54.1	54	17 05	17 42	18 23	05 44	06 13	06 39	07 01
18	86 27.4	S13 12.1	281 20.6	14.0	N12 37.7	7.5	54.1	52	17 10	17 45	18 25	05 37	06 07	06 34	06 58
19	101 27.4	11.3	295 53.6	14.0	12 30.2	7.6	54.1	50	17 15	17 48	18 26	05 30	06 02	06 30	06 56
20	116 27.5	10.4	310 26.6	14.1	12 22.6	7.7	54.1	45	17 25	17 55	18 30	05 16	05 50	06 21	06 50
21	131 27.5	.. 09.6	324 59.7	14.0	12 14.9	7.7	54.1	N 40	17 33	18 01	18 33	05 04	05 41	06 14	06 45
22	146 27.5	08.7	339 32.7	14.1	12 07.2	7.8	54.1	35	17 41	18 07	18 36	04 54	05 32	06 07	06 41
23	161 27.5	07.9	354 05.8	14.1	11 59.4	7.9	54.1	30	17 47	18 12	18 40	04 46	05 25	06 02	06 37
14 00	176 27.5	S13 07.0	8 38.9	14.1	N11 51.5	7.8	54.1	20	17 58	18 21	18 47	04 31	05 12	05 52	06 30
01	191 27.6	06.2	23 12.0	14.2	11 43.7	8.0	54.1	N 10	18 08	18 30	18 55	04 17	05 01	05 43	06 24
02	206 27.6	05.4	37 45.2	14.1	11 35.7	8.0	54.2	0	18 18	18 39	19 03	04 05	04 50	05 35	06 19
03	221 27.6	.. 04.5	52 18.3	14.2	11 27.7	8.0	54.2	S 10	18 27	18 49	19 14	03 52	04 40	05 27	06 13
04	236 27.6	03.7	66 51.5	14.2	11 19.7	8.1	54.2	20	18 37	19 00	19 27	03 39	04 29	05 18	06 07
05	251 27.7	02.8	81 24.7	14.2	11 11.6	8.1	54.2	30	18 49	19 14	19 44	03 24	04 16	05 08	06 01
06	266 27.7	S13 02.0	95 57.9	14.2	N11 03.5	8.2	54.2	35	18 56	19 23	19 55	03 15	04 08	05 02	05 57
07	281 27.7	01.1	110 31.1	14.2	10 55.3	8.3	54.2	40	19 04	19 33	20 08	03 04	03 59	04 55	05 52
08	296 27.7	13 00.3	125 04.3	14.3	10 47.0	8.3	54.2	45	19 13	19 45	20 24	02 52	03 49	04 48	05 47
F 09	311 27.7	12 59.4	139 37.6	14.3	10 38.7	8.3	54.2	S 50	19 25	20 00	20 45	02 38	03 37	04 38	05 41
R 10	326 27.8	58.6	154 10.9	14.3	10 30.4	8.4	54.2	52	19 30	20 07	20 55	02 31	03 31	04 34	05 38
I 11	341 27.8	57.7	168 44.2	14.3	10 22.0	8.4	54.2	54	19 36	20 15	21 07	02 23	03 25	04 29	05 35
D 12	356 27.8	S12 56.9	183 17.5	14.3	N10 13.6	8.5	54.2	56	19 42	20 25	21 21	02 15	03 18	04 24	05 31
A 13	11 27.8	56.0	197 50.8	14.3	10 05.1	8.5	54.2	58	19 49	20 35	21 38	02 05	03 10	04 18	05 27
Y 14	26 27.9	55.2	212 24.1	14.4	9 56.6	8.5	54.3	S 60	19 57	20 47	21 59	01 54	03 01	04 11	05 23
15	41 27.9	.. 54.3	226 57.5	14.4	9 48.1	8.7	54.3								
16	56 27.9	53.4	241 30.9	14.4	9 39.4	8.6	54.3								
17	71 27.9	52.6	256 04.3	14.4	9 30.8	8.7	54.3								

UT	SUN		MOON					Day	SUN			MOON			
									Eqn. of Time		Mer.	Mer. Pass.		Age	Phase
									00h	12h	Pass.	Upper	Lower		
18	86 28.0	S12 51.7	270 37.7	14.4	N 9 22.1	8.7	54.3	d	m s	m s	h m	h m	h m	d	%
19	101 28.0	50.9	285 11.1	14.4	9 13.4	8.8	54.3	12	14 12	14 12	12 14	22 40	10 17	13	94
20	116 28.0	50.0	299 44.5	14.4	9 04.6	8.8	54.3	13	14 12	14 11	12 14	23 24	11 02	14	98
21	131 28.1	.. 49.2	314 17.9	14.5	8 55.8	8.9	54.3	14	14 10	14 09	12 14	24 08	11 46	15	100
22	146 28.1	48.3	328 51.4	14.4	8 46.9	8.9	54.3								
23	161 28.1	47.5	343 24.8	14.5	N 8 38.0	8.9	54.3								
	SD 16.2	d 0.8	SD 14.7		14.7		14.8								⃝	

UT	ARIES GHA	VENUS −4.9 GHA	VENUS Dec	MARS −0.1 GHA	MARS Dec	JUPITER −2.5 GHA	JUPITER Dec	SATURN +0.5 GHA	SATURN Dec	STARS Name	SHA	Dec
d h	° ′	° ′	° ′	° ′	° ′	° ′	° ′	° ′	° ′		° ′	° ′
15 00	144 55.5	217 05.5	S16 25.5	299 33.5	S 7 38.0	42 52.5	N23 11.4	273 36.5	S16 19.1	Acamar	315 18.1	S40 15.3
01	159 58.0	232 06.7	25.6	314 35.6	38.1	57 55.2	11.4	288 38.9	19.1	Achernar	335 26.8	S57 10.2
02	175 00.4	247 07.9	25.7	329 37.6	38.2	72 57.8	11.4	303 41.3	19.1	Acrux	173 08.1	S63 10.6
03	190 02.9	262 09.1 ..	25.8	344 39.7 ..	38.4	88 00.5 ..	11.4	318 43.7 ..	19.1	Adhara	255 11.9	S28 59.9
04	205 05.4	277 10.3	25.9	359 41.8	38.5	103 03.1	11.4	333 46.1	19.1	Aldebaran	290 48.7	N16 32.1
05	220 07.8	292 11.5	26.0	14 43.9	38.6	118 05.7	11.4	348 48.5	19.1			
S 06	235 10.3	307 12.7	S16 26.1	29 45.9	S 7 38.7	133 08.3	N23 11.5	3 50.9	S16 19.1	Alioth	166 20.0	N55 52.7
A 07	250 12.8	322 13.8	26.2	44 48.0	38.8	148 11.0	11.5	18 53.3	19.1	Alkaid	152 58.3	N49 14.3
T 08	265 15.2	337 15.0	26.3	59 50.1	39.0	163 13.6	11.5	33 55.6	19.1	Al Na'ir	27 43.6	S46 53.5
U 09	280 17.7	352 16.2 ..	26.4	74 52.2 ..	39.1	178 16.2 ..	11.5	48 58.0 ..	19.1	Alnilam	275 45.7	S 1 11.9
R 10	295 20.2	7 17.4	26.5	89 54.3	39.2	193 18.9	11.5	64 00.4	19.1	Alphard	217 55.3	S 8 43.5
D 11	310 22.6	22 18.5	26.6	104 56.3	39.3	208 21.5	11.6	79 02.8	19.2			
A 12	325 25.1	37 19.7	S16 26.7	119 58.4	S 7 39.4	223 24.1	N23 11.6	94 05.2	S16 19.2	Alphecca	126 10.6	N26 39.9
Y 13	340 27.6	52 20.9	26.8	135 00.5	39.6	238 26.8	11.6	109 07.6	19.2	Alpheratz	357 43.2	N29 10.2
14	355 30.0	67 22.0	26.9	150 02.6	39.7	253 29.4	11.6	124 10.0	19.2	Altair	62 08.0	N 8 54.4
15	10 32.5	82 23.2 ..	27.0	165 04.7 ..	39.8	268 32.0 ..	11.6	139 12.4 ..	19.2	Ankaa	353 15.6	S42 13.9
16	25 34.9	97 24.3	27.1	180 06.8	39.9	283 34.7	11.6	154 14.8	19.2	Antares	112 25.7	S26 27.6
17	40 37.4	112 25.5	27.2	195 08.9	40.0	298 37.3	11.7	169 17.2	19.2			
18	55 39.9	127 26.6	S16 27.3	210 10.9	S 7 40.1	313 39.9	N23 11.7	184 19.6	S16 19.2	Arcturus	145 55.2	N19 06.4
19	70 42.3	142 27.8	27.4	225 13.0	40.2	328 42.5	11.7	199 22.0	19.2	Atria	107 27.3	S69 02.8
20	85 44.8	157 28.9	27.5	240 15.1	40.4	343 45.2	11.7	214 24.4	19.2	Avior	234 17.2	S59 33.6
21	100 47.3	172 30.1 ..	27.5	255 17.2 ..	40.5	358 47.8 ..	11.7	229 26.8 ..	19.2	Bellatrix	278 31.3	N 6 21.5
22	115 49.7	187 31.2	27.6	270 19.3	40.6	13 50.4	11.7	244 29.2	19.2	Betelgeuse	271 00.6	N 7 24.3
23	130 52.2	202 32.3	27.7	285 21.4	40.7	28 53.1	11.8	259 31.6	19.2			
16 00	145 54.7	217 33.5	S16 27.8	300 23.5	S 7 40.8	43 55.7	N23 11.8	274 34.0	S16 19.3	Canopus	263 55.6	S52 42.6
01	160 57.1	232 34.6	27.9	315 25.6	40.9	58 58.3	11.8	289 36.4	19.3	Capella	280 33.5	N46 00.7
02	175 59.6	247 35.7	28.0	330 27.7	41.0	74 00.9	11.8	304 38.8	19.3	Deneb	49 31.5	N45 19.9
03	191 02.0	262 36.8 ..	28.1	345 29.8 ..	41.2	89 03.6 ..	11.8	319 41.2 ..	19.3	Denebola	182 32.9	N14 29.4
04	206 04.5	277 38.0	28.2	0 31.9	41.3	104 06.2	11.8	334 43.6	19.3	Diphda	348 55.6	S17 54.7
05	221 07.0	292 39.1	28.3	15 34.0	41.4	119 08.8	11.8	349 46.0	19.3			
S 06	236 09.4	307 40.2	S16 28.4	30 36.1	S 7 41.5	134 11.4	N23 11.9	4 48.4	S16 19.3	Dubhe	193 50.6	N61 40.2
U 07	251 11.9	322 41.3	28.5	45 38.2	41.6	149 14.1	11.9	19 50.8	19.3	Elnath	278 11.8	N28 37.0
N 08	266 14.4	337 42.4	28.5	60 40.3	41.7	164 16.7	11.9	34 53.2	19.3	Eltanin	90 46.2	N51 29.1
D 09	281 16.8	352 43.5 ..	28.6	75 42.4 ..	41.8	179 19.3 ..	11.9	49 55.6 ..	19.3	Enif	33 47.0	N 9 56.4
A 10	296 19.3	7 44.6	28.7	90 44.5	41.9	194 21.9	11.9	64 58.0	19.3	Fomalhaut	15 23.8	S29 32.9
Y 11	311 21.8	22 45.7	28.8	105 46.6	42.0	209 24.5	11.9	80 00.4	19.3			
12	326 24.2	37 46.8	S16 28.9	120 48.7	S 7 42.1	224 27.2	N23 12.0	95 02.8	S16 19.3	Gacrux	171 59.8	S57 11.5
13	341 26.7	52 47.9	29.0	135 50.8	42.2	239 29.8	12.0	110 05.2	19.3	Gienah	175 51.5	S17 37.3
14	356 29.2	67 49.0	29.1	150 52.9	42.4	254 32.4	12.0	125 07.6	19.4	Hadar	148 46.8	S60 26.2
15	11 31.6	82 50.1 ..	29.2	165 55.0 ..	42.5	269 35.0 ..	12.0	140 10.0 ..	19.4	Hamal	328 00.3	N23 31.7
16	26 34.1	97 51.2	29.3	180 57.2	42.6	284 37.7	12.0	155 12.4	19.4	Kaus Aust.	83 43.4	S34 22.4
17	41 36.5	112 52.3	29.3	195 59.3	42.7	299 40.3	12.0	170 14.8	19.4			
18	56 39.0	127 53.3	S16 29.4	211 01.4	S 7 42.8	314 42.9	N23 12.1	185 17.2	S16 19.4	Kochab	137 19.9	N74 05.6
19	71 41.5	142 54.4	29.5	226 03.5	42.9	329 45.5	12.1	200 19.6	19.4	Markab	13 38.1	N15 16.9
20	86 43.9	157 55.5	29.6	241 05.6	43.0	344 48.1	12.1	215 22.0	19.4	Menkar	314 14.6	N 4 08.5
21	101 46.4	172 56.6 ..	29.7	256 07.7 ..	43.1	359 50.8 ..	12.1	230 24.4 ..	19.4	Menkent	148 06.8	S36 26.2
22	116 48.9	187 57.6	29.8	271 09.8	43.2	14 53.4	12.1	245 26.8	19.4	Miaplacidus	221 38.5	S69 46.7
23	131 51.3	202 58.7	29.9	286 12.0	43.3	29 56.0	12.1	260 29.2	19.4			
17 00	146 53.8	217 59.8	S16 29.9	301 14.1	S 7 43.4	44 58.6	N23 12.2	275 31.6	S16 19.4	Mirfak	308 39.6	N49 54.7
01	161 56.3	233 00.8	30.0	316 16.2	43.5	60 01.2	12.2	290 34.0	19.4	Nunki	75 58.0	S26 16.6
02	176 58.7	248 01.9	30.1	331 18.3	43.6	75 03.8	12.2	305 36.4	19.4	Peacock	53 19.1	S56 41.2
03	192 01.2	263 03.0 ..	30.2	346 20.4 ..	43.7	90 06.5 ..	12.2	320 38.8 ..	19.4	Pollux	243 26.8	N27 59.3
04	207 03.6	278 04.0	30.3	1 22.6	43.8	105 09.1	12.2	335 41.2	19.4	Procyon	244 58.9	N 5 11.0
05	222 06.1	293 05.1	30.4	16 24.7	43.9	120 11.7	12.2	350 43.6	19.4			
M 06	237 08.6	308 06.1	S16 30.4	31 26.8	S 7 44.0	135 14.3	N23 12.2	5 46.0	S16 19.5	Rasalhague	96 06.2	N12 33.0
O 07	252 11.0	323 07.2	30.5	46 28.9	44.1	150 16.9	12.3	20 48.4	19.5	Regulus	207 42.7	N11 53.6
N 08	267 13.5	338 08.2	30.6	61 31.1	44.2	165 19.5	12.3	35 50.8	19.5	Rigel	281 11.5	S 8 11.4
D 09	282 16.0	353 09.2 ..	30.7	76 33.2 ..	44.3	180 22.2 ..	12.3	50 53.2 ..	19.5	Rigil Kent.	139 50.8	S60 53.3
A 10	297 18.4	8 10.3	30.8	91 35.3	44.4	195 24.8	12.3	65 55.6	19.5	Sabik	102 12.1	S15 44.4
Y 11	312 20.9	23 11.3	30.9	106 37.4	44.5	210 27.4	12.3	80 58.1	19.5			
12	327 23.4	38 12.3	S16 30.9	121 39.6	S 7 44.6	225 30.0	N23 12.3	96 00.5	S16 19.5	Schedar	349 40.3	N56 37.1
13	342 25.8	53 13.4	31.0	136 41.7	44.7	240 32.6	12.4	111 02.9	19.5	Shaula	96 21.4	S37 06.6
14	357 28.3	68 14.4	31.1	151 43.8	44.8	255 35.2	12.4	126 05.3	19.5	Sirius	258 33.0	S16 44.5
15	12 30.8	83 15.4 ..	31.2	166 46.0 ..	44.9	270 37.8 ..	12.4	141 07.7 ..	19.5	Spica	158 30.5	S11 14.2
16	27 33.2	98 16.4	31.3	181 48.1	45.0	285 40.4	12.4	156 10.1	19.5	Suhail	222 51.6	S43 29.7
17	42 35.7	113 17.5	31.3	196 50.2	45.1	300 43.1	12.4	171 12.5	19.5			
18	57 38.1	128 18.5	S16 31.4	211 52.4	S 7 45.2	315 45.7	N23 12.4	186 14.9	S16 19.5	Vega	80 38.9	N38 47.8
19	72 40.6	143 19.5	31.5	226 54.5	45.3	330 48.3	12.4	201 17.3	19.5	Zuben'ubi	137 04.8	S16 06.0
20	87 43.1	158 20.5	31.6	241 56.7	45.4	345 50.9	12.5	216 19.7	19.5		SHA	Mer. Pass.
21	102 45.5	173 21.5 ..	31.6	256 58.8 ..	45.5	0 53.5 ..	12.5	231 22.1 ..	19.5		° ′	h m
22	117 48.0	188 22.5	31.7	272 00.9	45.6	15 56.1	12.5	246 24.5	19.5	Venus	71 38.8	9 29
23	132 50.5	203 23.5	31.8	287 03.1	45.7	30 58.7	12.5	261 26.9	19.5	Mars	154 28.8	3 58
	h m									Jupiter	258 01.0	21 01
Mer. Pass. 14 14.0		v 1.1	d 0.1	v 2.1	d 0.1	v 2.6	d 0.0	v 2.4	d 0.0	Saturn	128 39.3	5 41

UT	SUN GHA	SUN Dec	MOON GHA	v	Dec	d	HP
d h	° ′	° ′	° ′	′	° ′	′	′
15 00	176 28.1	S12 46.6	357 58.3	14.5	N 8 29.1	9.0	54.3
01	191 28.2	45.8	12 31.8	14.5	8 20.1	9.0	54.4
02	206 28.2	44.9	27 05.3	14.5	8 11.1	9.0	54.4
03	221 28.2	.. 44.0	41 38.8	14.5	8 02.1	9.1	54.4
04	236 28.3	43.2	56 12.3	14.6	7 53.0	9.1	54.4
05	251 28.3	42.3	70 45.9	14.5	7 43.9	9.2	54.4
06	266 28.3	S12 41.5	85 19.4	14.5	N 7 34.7	9.2	54.4
07	281 28.3	40.6	99 52.9	14.6	7 25.5	9.2	54.4
08	296 28.4	39.8	114 26.5	14.6	7 16.3	9.3	54.4
09	311 28.4	.. 38.9	129 00.1	14.5	7 07.0	9.3	54.4
10	326 28.4	38.0	143 33.6	14.6	6 57.7	9.3	54.5
11	341 28.5	37.2	158 07.2	14.6	6 48.4	9.4	54.5
12	356 28.5	S12 36.3	172 40.8	14.6	N 6 39.0	9.4	54.5
13	11 28.5	35.5	187 14.4	14.6	6 29.6	9.4	54.5
14	26 28.6	34.6	201 48.0	14.6	6 20.2	9.4	54.5
15	41 28.6	.. 33.7	216 21.6	14.6	6 10.8	9.5	54.5
16	56 28.6	32.9	230 55.2	14.6	6 01.3	9.5	54.5
17	71 28.7	32.0	245 28.8	14.6	5 51.8	9.6	54.5
18	86 28.7	S12 31.2	260 02.4	14.6	N 5 42.2	9.5	54.6
19	101 28.7	30.3	274 36.0	14.6	5 32.7	9.6	54.6
20	116 28.8	29.4	289 09.6	14.6	5 23.1	9.7	54.6
21	131 28.8	.. 28.6	303 43.2	14.7	5 13.4	9.6	54.6
22	146 28.8	27.7	318 16.9	14.6	5 03.8	9.7	54.6
23	161 28.9	26.8	332 50.5	14.6	4 54.1	9.7	54.6
16 00	176 28.9	S12 26.0	347 24.1	14.6	N 4 44.4	9.7	54.6
01	191 29.0	25.1	1 57.7	14.7	4 34.7	9.7	54.6
02	206 29.0	24.2	16 31.4	14.6	4 25.0	9.8	54.7
03	221 29.0	.. 23.4	31 05.0	14.6	4 15.2	9.8	54.7
04	236 29.1	22.5	45 38.6	14.6	4 05.4	9.8	54.7
05	251 29.1	21.6	60 12.2	14.7	3 55.6	9.8	54.7
06	266 29.1	S12 20.8	74 45.9	14.6	N 3 45.8	9.9	54.7
07	281 29.2	19.9	89 19.5	14.6	3 35.9	9.8	54.7
08	296 29.2	19.1	103 53.1	14.6	3 26.1	9.9	54.7
09	311 29.3	.. 18.2	118 26.7	14.6	3 16.2	9.9	54.8
10	326 29.3	17.3	133 00.3	14.6	3 06.3	10.0	54.8
11	341 29.3	16.4	147 33.9	14.6	2 56.3	9.9	54.8
12	356 29.4	S12 15.6	162 07.5	14.6	N 2 46.4	10.0	54.8
13	11 29.4	14.7	176 41.1	14.6	2 36.4	9.9	54.8
14	26 29.5	13.8	191 14.7	14.5	2 26.5	10.0	54.8
15	41 29.5	.. 13.0	205 48.2	14.6	2 16.5	10.0	54.8
16	56 29.5	12.1	220 21.8	14.6	2 06.5	10.0	54.9
17	71 29.6	11.2	234 55.4	14.5	1 56.5	10.1	54.9
18	86 29.6	S12 10.4	249 28.9	14.6	N 1 46.4	10.0	54.9
19	101 29.7	09.5	264 02.5	14.5	1 36.4	10.1	54.9
20	116 29.7	08.6	278 36.0	14.6	1 26.3	10.0	54.9
21	131 29.7	.. 07.8	293 09.5	14.5	1 16.3	10.1	54.9
22	146 29.8	06.9	307 43.0	14.5	1 06.2	10.1	55.0
23	161 29.8	06.0	322 16.5	14.5	0 56.1	10.1	55.0
17 00	176 29.9	S12 05.1	336 50.0	14.5	N 0 46.0	10.1	55.0
01	191 29.9	04.3	351 23.5	14.4	0 35.9	10.1	55.0
02	206 30.0	03.4	5 56.9	14.5	0 25.8	10.1	55.0
03	221 30.0	.. 02.5	20 30.4	14.4	0 15.7	10.1	55.0
04	236 30.1	01.6	35 03.8	14.4	N 0 05.6	10.1	55.0
05	251 30.1	12 00.8	49 37.2	14.4	S 0 04.5	10.2	55.1
06	266 30.1	S11 59.9	64 10.6	14.4	S 0 14.7	10.1	55.1
07	281 30.2	59.0	78 44.0	14.4	0 24.8	10.1	55.1
08	296 30.2	58.1	93 17.4	14.3	0 34.9	10.2	55.1
09	311 30.3	.. 57.3	107 50.7	14.3	0 45.1	10.1	55.1
10	326 30.3	56.4	122 24.0	14.3	0 55.2	10.1	55.1
11	341 30.4	55.5	136 57.3	14.3	1 05.3	10.2	55.2
12	356 30.4	S11 54.6	151 30.6	14.3	S 1 15.5	10.1	55.2
13	11 30.5	53.8	166 03.9	14.3	1 25.6	10.2	55.2
14	26 30.5	52.9	180 37.2	14.2	1 35.8	10.1	55.2
15	41 30.6	.. 52.0	195 10.4	14.2	1 45.9	10.2	55.2
16	56 30.6	51.1	209 43.6	14.2	1 56.1	10.1	55.3
17	71 30.7	50.3	224 16.8	14.1	2 06.2	10.1	55.3
18	86 30.7	S11 49.4	238 49.9	14.2	S 2 16.3	10.1	55.3
19	101 30.8	48.5	253 23.1	14.1	2 26.4	10.2	55.3
20	116 30.8	47.6	267 56.2	14.1	2 36.6	10.1	55.3
21	131 30.9	.. 46.7	282 29.3	14.0	2 46.7	10.1	55.4
22	146 30.9	45.9	297 02.3	14.0	2 56.8	10.1	55.4
23	161 31.0	45.0	311 35.3	14.1	S 3 06.9	10.1	55.4
	SD 16.2	d 0.9	SD 14.8		14.9		15.0

UT day labels: 15 SATURDAY, 16 SUNDAY, 17 MONDAY

Twilight / Moonrise

Lat.	Naut.	Civil	Sunrise	Moonrise 15	16	17	18
°	h m	h m	h m	h m	h m	h m	h m
N 72	06 11	07 30	08 48	17 27	19 06	20 45	22 27
N 70	06 09	07 21	08 29	17 36	19 08	20 41	22 16
68	06 08	07 13	08 14	17 43	19 10	20 37	22 07
66	06 07	07 07	08 02	17 48	19 11	20 35	22 00
64	06 06	07 01	07 52	17 53	19 12	20 32	21 54
62	06 04	06 56	07 43	17 57	19 13	20 30	21 49
60	06 03	06 52	07 36	18 01	19 14	20 29	21 44
N 58	06 02	06 48	07 29	18 04	19 15	20 27	21 40
56	06 01	06 45	07 23	18 07	19 16	20 26	21 37
54	06 00	06 41	07 18	18 09	19 16	20 24	21 34
52	05 59	06 38	07 13	18 12	19 17	20 23	21 31
50	05 58	06 36	07 09	18 14	19 18	20 22	21 28
45	05 55	06 30	07 00	18 18	19 19	20 20	21 23
N 40	05 52	06 24	06 52	18 22	19 20	20 18	21 18
35	05 50	06 19	06 45	18 25	19 21	20 17	21 14
30	05 47	06 15	06 39	18 28	19 21	20 15	21 10
20	05 40	06 06	06 29	18 33	19 23	20 13	21 04
N 10	05 33	05 58	06 19	18 37	19 24	20 11	20 59
0	05 25	05 49	06 11	18 41	19 25	20 09	20 54
S 10	05 15	05 40	06 02	18 46	19 26	20 07	20 49
20	05 03	05 29	05 52	18 50	19 27	20 05	20 44
30	04 47	05 16	05 41	18 55	19 29	20 03	20 38
35	04 36	05 08	05 35	18 58	19 29	20 01	20 35
40	04 24	04 59	05 27	19 01	19 30	20 00	20 31
45	04 09	04 47	05 18	19 05	19 31	19 58	20 26
S 50	03 49	04 33	05 08	19 09	19 33	19 56	20 21
52	03 39	04 26	05 03	19 11	19 33	19 55	20 19
54	03 28	04 18	04 58	19 13	19 34	19 55	20 16
56	03 14	04 09	04 52	19 16	19 35	19 53	20 13
58	02 59	04 00	04 45	19 18	19 35	19 52	20 10
S 60	02 39	03 48	04 37	19 21	19 36	19 51	20 07

Twilight / Moonset

Lat.	Sunset	Civil	Naut.	Moonset 15	16	17	18
°	h m	h m	h m	h m	h m	h m	h m
N 72	15 41	17 00	18 20	07 53	07 46	07 38	07 31
N 70	16 00	17 09	18 21	07 43	07 41	07 39	07 37
68	16 15	17 16	18 22	07 35	07 38	07 40	07 43
66	16 27	17 23	18 23	07 28	07 34	07 41	07 47
64	16 37	17 28	18 24	07 22	07 32	07 41	07 51
62	16 46	17 33	18 25	07 17	07 29	07 41	07 54
60	16 53	17 37	18 26	07 12	07 27	07 42	07 57
N 58	17 00	17 41	18 27	07 08	07 25	07 42	07 59
56	17 06	17 44	18 28	07 04	07 24	07 42	08 02
54	17 11	17 48	18 29	07 01	07 22	07 43	08 04
52	17 16	17 51	18 30	06 58	07 21	07 43	08 06
50	17 20	17 53	18 31	06 56	07 20	07 43	08 07
45	17 29	17 59	18 34	06 50	07 17	07 44	08 11
N 40	17 37	18 05	18 36	06 45	07 15	07 44	08 14
35	17 43	18 09	18 39	06 41	07 13	07 44	08 17
30	17 49	18 14	18 42	06 37	07 11	07 45	08 19
20	18 00	18 22	18 48	06 30	07 08	07 45	08 23
N 10	18 09	18 30	18 55	06 24	07 05	07 46	08 27
0	18 17	18 39	19 03	06 19	07 02	07 46	08 30
S 10	18 26	18 48	19 13	06 13	07 00	07 46	08 34
20	18 36	18 58	19 25	06 07	06 57	07 47	08 37
30	18 47	19 11	19 41	06 01	06 54	07 47	08 42
35	18 53	19 19	19 51	05 57	06 52	07 48	08 44
40	19 00	19 29	20 03	05 52	06 50	07 48	08 47
45	19 09	19 40	20 18	05 47	06 47	07 48	08 50
S 50	19 19	19 54	20 38	05 41	06 44	07 48	08 54
52	19 24	20 01	20 47	05 38	06 43	07 49	08 55
54	19 29	20 08	20 58	05 35	06 41	07 49	08 57
56	19 35	20 17	21 11	05 31	06 40	07 49	08 59
58	19 42	20 26	21 27	05 27	06 38	07 49	09 02
S 60	19 49	20 38	21 45	05 23	06 36	07 50	09 04

SUN / MOON

Day	Eqn. of Time 00h	12h	Mer. Pass.	Mer. Pass. Upper	Lower	Age	Phase
d	m s	m s	h m	h m	h m	d	%
15	14 08	14 06	12 14	00 08	12 30	16	100
16	14 04	14 03	12 14	00 52	13 14	17	98
17	14 01	13 58	12 14	01 35	13 57	18	94

UT	ARIES	VENUS −4.8		MARS −0.2		JUPITER −2.5		SATURN +0.5		STARS		
	GHA	GHA	Dec	GHA	Dec	GHA	Dec	GHA	Dec	Name	SHA	Dec
d h	° ′	° ′	° ′	° ′	° ′	° ′	° ′	° ′	° ′		° ′	° ′
18 00	147 52.9	218 24.5	S16 31.9	302 05.2	S 7 45.8	46 01.3	N23 12.5	276 29.3	S16 19.6	Acamar	315 18.1	S40 15.2
01	162 55.4	233 25.5	32.0	317 07.4	45.9	61 03.9	12.5	291 31.7	19.6	Achernar	335 26.8	S57 10.2
02	177 57.9	248 26.5	32.0	332 09.5	46.0	76 06.6	12.5	306 34.1	19.6	Acrux	173 08.1	S63 10.6
03	193 00.3	263 27.5	. . 32.1	347 11.7	. . 46.1	91 09.2	. . 12.6	321 36.5	. . 19.6	Adhara	255 11.9	S28 59.9
04	208 02.8	278 28.5	32.2	2 13.8	46.2	106 11.8	12.6	336 39.0	19.6	Aldebaran	290 48.7	N16 32.1
05	223 05.2	293 29.5	32.3	17 15.9	46.3	121 14.4	12.6	351 41.4	19.6			
06	238 07.7	308 30.5	S16 32.3	32 18.1	S 7 46.4	136 17.0	N23 12.6	6 43.8	S16 19.6	Alioth	166 19.9	N55 52.7
07	253 10.2	323 31.5	32.4	47 20.2	46.5	151 19.6	12.6	21 46.2	19.6	Alkaid	152 58.3	N49 14.3
T 08	268 12.6	338 32.4	32.5	62 22.4	46.6	166 22.2	12.6	36 48.6	19.6	Al Na'ir	27 43.6	S46 53.5
U 09	283 15.1	353 33.4	. . 32.5	77 24.5	. . 46.7	181 24.8	. . 12.7	51 51.0	. . 19.6	Alnilam	275 45.7	S 1 11.9
E 10	298 17.6	8 34.4	32.6	92 26.7	46.7	196 27.4	12.7	66 53.4	19.6	Alphard	217 55.3	S 8 43.5
S 11	313 20.0	23 35.4	32.7	107 28.9	46.8	211 30.0	12.7	81 55.8	19.6			
D 12	328 22.5	38 36.3	S16 32.8	122 31.0	S 7 46.9	226 32.6	N23 12.7	96 58.2	S16 19.6	Alphecca	126 10.6	N26 39.9
A 13	343 25.0	53 37.3	32.8	137 33.2	47.0	241 35.2	12.7	112 00.6	19.6	Alpheratz	357 43.3	N29 10.2
Y 14	358 27.4	68 38.3	32.9	152 35.3	47.1	256 37.8	12.7	127 03.0	19.6	Altair	62 08.0	N 8 54.4
15	13 29.9	83 39.2	. . 33.0	167 37.5	. . 47.2	271 40.4	. . 12.7	142 05.4	. . 19.6	Ankaa	353 15.6	S42 13.9
16	28 32.4	98 40.2	33.1	182 39.6	47.3	286 43.0	12.8	157 07.9	19.6	Antares	112 25.7	S26 27.6
17	43 34.8	113 41.1	33.1	197 41.8	47.4	301 45.6	12.8	172 10.3	19.6			
18	58 37.3	128 42.1	S16 33.2	212 44.0	S 7 47.5	316 48.2	N23 12.8	187 12.7	S16 19.6	Arcturus	145 55.2	N19 06.4
19	73 39.7	143 43.0	33.3	227 46.1	47.6	331 50.8	12.8	202 15.1	19.6	Atria	107 27.2	S69 02.8
20	88 42.2	158 44.0	33.3	242 48.3	47.6	346 53.5	12.8	217 17.5	19.6	Avior	234 17.2	S59 33.6
21	103 44.7	173 44.9	. . 33.4	257 50.4	. . 47.7	1 56.1	. . 12.8	232 19.9	. . 19.7	Bellatrix	278 31.4	N 6 21.5
22	118 47.1	188 45.9	33.5	272 52.6	47.8	16 58.7	12.8	247 22.3	19.7	Betelgeuse	271 00.6	N 7 24.3
23	133 49.6	203 46.8	33.5	287 54.8	47.9	32 01.3	12.9	262 24.7	19.7			
19 00	148 52.1	218 47.8	S16 33.6	302 56.9	S 7 48.0	47 03.9	N23 12.9	277 27.1	S16 19.7	Canopus	263 55.6	S52 42.6
01	163 54.5	233 48.7	33.7	317 59.1	48.1	62 06.5	12.9	292 29.6	19.7	Capella	280 33.5	N46 00.7
02	178 57.0	248 49.6	33.7	333 01.3	48.2	77 09.1	12.9	307 32.0	19.7	Deneb	49 31.5	N45 19.9
03	193 59.5	263 50.6	. . 33.8	348 03.4	. . 48.2	92 11.7	. . 12.9	322 34.4	. . 19.7	Denebola	182 32.9	N14 29.4
04	209 01.9	278 51.5	33.9	3 05.6	48.3	107 14.3	12.9	337 36.8	19.7	Diphda	348 55.7	S17 54.7
05	224 04.4	293 52.4	33.9	18 07.8	48.4	122 16.9	12.9	352 39.2	19.7			
06	239 06.9	308 53.3	S16 34.0	33 10.0	S 7 48.5	137 19.5	N23 13.0	7 41.6	S16 19.7	Dubhe	193 50.6	N61 40.2
W 07	254 09.3	323 54.3	34.1	48 12.1	48.6	152 22.1	13.0	22 44.0	19.7	Elnath	278 11.8	N28 37.0
E 08	269 11.8	338 55.2	34.1	63 14.3	48.7	167 24.7	13.0	37 46.4	19.7	Eltanin	90 46.2	N51 29.1
D 09	284 14.2	353 56.1	. . 34.2	78 16.5	. . 48.8	182 27.3	. . 13.0	52 48.8	. . 19.7	Enif	33 47.0	N 9 56.4
N 10	299 16.7	8 57.0	34.3	93 18.7	48.8	197 29.9	13.0	67 51.3	19.7	Fomalhaut	15 23.8	S29 32.9
E 11	314 19.2	23 57.9	34.3	108 20.8	48.9	212 32.4	13.0	82 53.7	19.7			
S 12	329 21.6	38 58.8	S16 34.4	123 23.0	S 7 49.0	227 35.0	N23 13.0	97 56.1	S16 19.7	Gacrux	171 59.8	S57 11.5
D 13	344 24.1	53 59.7	34.4	138 25.2	49.1	242 37.6	13.1	112 58.5	19.7	Gienah	175 51.5	S17 37.3
A 14	359 26.6	69 00.6	34.5	153 27.4	49.2	257 40.2	13.1	128 00.9	19.7	Hadar	148 46.8	S60 26.2
Y 15	14 29.0	84 01.5	. . 34.6	168 29.6	. . 49.2	272 42.8	. . 13.1	143 03.3	. . 19.7	Hamal	328 00.3	N23 31.7
16	29 31.5	99 02.4	34.6	183 31.8	49.3	287 45.4	13.1	158 05.7	19.7	Kaus Aust.	83 43.4	S34 22.4
17	44 34.0	114 03.3	34.7	198 33.9	49.4	302 48.0	13.1	173 08.2	19.7			
18	59 36.4	129 04.2	S16 34.8	213 36.1	S 7 49.5	317 50.6	N23 13.1	188 10.6	S16 19.7	Kochab	137 19.9	N74 05.6
19	74 38.9	144 05.1	34.8	228 38.3	49.6	332 53.2	13.1	203 13.0	19.7	Markab	13 38.1	N15 16.9
20	89 41.3	159 06.0	34.9	243 40.5	49.6	347 55.8	13.1	218 15.4	19.7	Menkar	314 14.6	N 4 08.5
21	104 43.8	174 06.9	. . 34.9	258 42.7	. . 49.7	2 58.4	. . 13.2	233 17.8	. . 19.7	Menkent	148 06.8	S36 26.2
22	119 46.3	189 07.8	35.0	273 44.9	49.8	18 01.0	13.2	248 20.2	19.7	Miaplacidus	221 38.5	S69 46.8
23	134 48.7	204 08.7	35.0	288 47.1	49.9	33 03.6	13.2	263 22.6	19.7			
20 00	149 51.2	219 09.5	S16 35.1	303 49.3	S 7 50.0	48 06.2	N23 13.2	278 25.1	S16 19.8	Mirfak	308 39.7	N49 54.7
01	164 53.7	234 10.4	35.2	318 51.4	50.0	63 08.8	13.2	293 27.5	19.8	Nunki	75 58.0	S26 16.5
02	179 56.1	249 11.3	35.2	333 53.6	50.1	78 11.4	13.2	308 29.9	19.8	Peacock	53 19.1	S56 41.1
03	194 58.6	264 12.2	. . 35.3	348 55.8	. . 50.2	93 14.0	. . 13.2	323 32.3	. . 19.8	Pollux	243 26.8	N27 59.3
04	210 01.1	279 13.0	35.3	3 58.0	50.3	108 16.5	13.3	338 34.7	19.8	Procyon	244 59.0	N 5 11.0
05	225 03.5	294 13.9	35.4	19 00.2	50.3	123 19.1	13.3	353 37.1	19.8			
06	240 06.0	309 14.8	S16 35.4	34 02.4	S 7 50.4	138 21.7	N23 13.3	8 39.6	S16 19.8	Rasalhague	96 06.1	N12 33.0
07	255 08.5	324 15.6	35.5	49 04.6	50.5	153 24.3	13.3	23 42.0	19.8	Regulus	207 42.7	N11 53.6
T 08	270 10.9	339 16.5	35.6	64 06.8	50.6	168 26.9	13.3	38 44.4	19.8	Rigel	281 11.5	S 8 11.4
H 09	285 13.4	354 17.3	. . 35.6	79 09.0	. . 50.6	183 29.5	. . 13.3	53 46.8	. . 19.8	Rigil Kent.	139 50.7	S60 53.3
U 10	300 15.8	9 18.2	35.7	94 11.2	50.7	198 32.1	13.3	68 49.2	19.8	Sabik	102 12.1	S15 44.4
R 11	315 18.3	24 19.1	35.7	109 13.4	50.8	213 34.7	13.3	83 51.6	19.8			
S 12	330 20.8	39 19.9	S16 35.8	124 15.6	S 7 50.9	228 37.3	N23 13.4	98 54.1	S16 19.8	Schedar	349 40.3	N56 37.0
D 13	345 23.2	54 20.7	35.8	139 17.8	50.9	243 39.8	13.4	113 56.5	19.8	Shaula	96 21.4	S37 06.6
A 14	0 25.7	69 21.6	35.9	154 20.0	51.0	258 42.4	13.4	128 58.9	19.8	Sirius	258 33.1	S16 44.5
Y 15	15 28.2	84 22.4	. . 35.9	169 22.3	. . 51.1	273 45.0	. . 13.4	144 01.3	. . 19.8	Spica	158 30.5	S11 14.2
16	30 30.6	99 23.3	36.0	184 24.5	51.1	288 47.6	13.4	159 03.7	19.8	Suhail	222 51.6	S43 29.7
17	45 33.1	114 24.1	36.0	199 26.7	51.2	303 50.2	13.4	174 06.1	19.8			
18	60 35.6	129 25.0	S16 36.1	214 28.9	S 7 51.3	318 52.8	N23 13.4	189 08.6	S16 19.8	Vega	80 38.9	N38 47.7
19	75 38.0	144 25.8	36.1	229 31.1	51.4	333 55.4	13.5	204 11.0	19.8	Zuben'ubi	137 04.8	S16 06.0
20	90 40.5	159 26.6	36.2	244 33.3	51.4	348 58.0	13.5	219 13.4	19.8		SHA	Mer. Pass.
21	105 42.9	174 27.4	. . 36.2	259 35.5	. . 51.5	4 00.5	. . 13.5	234 15.8	. . 19.8		° ′	h m
22	120 45.4	189 28.3	36.3	274 37.7	51.6	19 03.1	13.5	249 18.2	19.8	Venus	69 55.7	9 24
23	135 47.9	204 29.1	36.3	289 40.0	51.6	34 05.7	13.5	264 20.7	19.8	Mars	154 04.9	3 48
	h m									Jupiter	258 11.8	20 48
Mer. Pass. 14 02.2		v 0.9	d 0.1	v 2.2	d 0.1	v 2.6	d 0.0	v 2.4	d 0.0	Saturn	128 35.1	5 29

SUN / MOON

UT	SUN GHA	SUN Dec	MOON GHA	v	MOON Dec	d	HP
d h	° ′	° ′	° ′	′	° ′	′	′
18 00	176 31.0	S11 44.1	326 08.4	13.9	S 3 17.0	10.1	55.4
01	191 31.1	43.2	340 41.3	14.0	3 27.1	10.1	55.4
02	206 31.1	42.3	355 14.3	13.9	3 37.2	10.0	55.4
03	221 31.2	.. 41.5	9 47.2	13.9	3 47.2	10.1	55.5
04	236 31.2	40.6	24 20.1	13.9	3 57.3	10.1	55.5
05	251 31.3	39.7	38 53.0	13.8	4 07.3	10.1	55.5
06	266 31.3	S11 38.8	53 25.8	13.8	S 4 17.4	10.0	55.5
07	281 31.4	37.9	67 58.6	13.7	4 27.4	10.0	55.5
08	296 31.4	37.0	82 31.3	13.8	4 37.4	10.0	55.6
09	311 31.5	.. 36.2	97 04.1	13.7	4 47.4	9.9	55.6
10	326 31.5	35.3	111 36.8	13.6	4 57.3	10.0	55.6
11	341 31.6	34.4	126 09.4	13.7	5 07.3	9.9	55.6
12	356 31.6	S11 33.5	140 42.1	13.6	S 5 17.2	10.0	55.6
13	11 31.7	32.6	155 14.7	13.5	5 27.2	9.9	55.7
14	26 31.7	31.7	169 47.2	13.6	5 37.1	9.9	55.7
15	41 31.8	.. 30.9	184 19.8	13.4	5 47.0	9.8	55.7
16	56 31.9	30.0	198 52.2	13.5	5 56.8	9.8	55.7
17	71 31.9	29.1	213 24.7	13.4	6 06.7	9.8	55.7
18	86 32.0	S11 28.2	227 57.1	13.4	S 6 16.5	9.8	55.8
19	101 32.0	27.3	242 29.5	13.3	6 26.3	9.8	55.8
20	116 32.1	26.4	257 01.8	13.3	6 36.1	9.7	55.8
21	131 32.1	.. 25.5	271 34.1	13.3	6 45.8	9.7	55.8
22	146 32.2	24.7	286 06.4	13.2	6 55.6	9.7	55.8
23	161 32.2	23.8	300 38.6	13.1	7 05.3	9.6	55.9
19 00	176 32.3	S11 22.9	315 10.7	13.2	S 7 14.9	9.7	55.9
01	191 32.4	22.0	329 42.9	13.0	7 24.6	9.6	55.9
02	206 32.4	21.1	344 14.9	13.1	7 34.2	9.6	55.9
03	221 32.5	.. 20.2	358 47.0	13.0	7 43.8	9.6	56.0
04	236 32.5	19.3	13 19.0	12.9	7 53.4	9.5	56.0
05	251 32.6	18.4	27 50.9	12.9	8 02.9	9.5	56.0
06	266 32.7	S11 17.5	42 22.8	12.9	S 8 12.4	9.5	56.0
07	281 32.7	16.7	56 54.7	12.8	8 21.9	9.4	56.0
08	296 32.8	15.8	71 26.5	12.7	8 31.3	9.4	56.1
09	311 32.8	.. 14.9	85 58.2	12.8	8 40.7	9.4	56.1
10	326 32.9	14.0	100 30.0	12.6	8 50.1	9.3	56.1
11	341 33.0	13.1	115 01.6	12.6	8 59.4	9.3	56.1
12	356 33.0	S11 12.2	129 33.2	12.6	S 9 08.7	9.3	56.2
13	11 33.1	11.3	144 04.8	12.5	9 18.0	9.2	56.2
14	26 33.1	10.4	158 36.3	12.5	9 27.2	9.2	56.2
15	41 33.2	.. 09.5	173 07.8	12.4	9 36.4	9.1	56.2
16	56 33.3	08.6	187 39.2	12.4	9 45.5	9.1	56.3
17	71 33.3	07.7	202 10.6	12.3	9 54.6	9.1	56.3
18	86 33.4	S11 06.8	216 41.9	12.2	S10 03.7	9.0	56.3
19	101 33.5	06.0	231 13.1	12.2	10 12.7	9.0	56.3
20	116 33.5	05.1	245 44.3	12.2	10 21.7	9.0	56.3
21	131 33.6	.. 04.2	260 15.5	12.1	10 30.7	8.8	56.4
22	146 33.6	03.3	274 46.6	12.0	10 39.5	8.9	56.4
23	161 33.7	02.4	289 17.6	12.0	10 48.4	8.8	56.4
20 00	176 33.8	S11 01.5	303 48.6	11.9	S10 57.2	8.8	56.4
01	191 33.8	11 00.6	318 19.5	11.9	11 06.0	8.7	56.5
02	206 33.9	10 59.7	332 50.4	11.8	11 14.7	8.6	56.5
03	221 34.0	.. 58.8	347 21.2	11.7	11 23.3	8.6	56.5
04	236 34.0	57.9	1 51.9	11.7	11 31.9	8.6	56.5
05	251 34.1	57.0	16 22.6	11.7	11 40.5	8.5	56.6
06	266 34.2	S10 56.1	30 53.3	11.6	S11 49.0	8.4	56.6
07	281 34.2	55.2	45 23.9	11.5	11 57.4	8.4	56.6
08	296 34.3	54.3	59 54.4	11.4	12 05.8	8.4	56.6
09	311 34.4	.. 53.4	74 24.8	11.4	12 14.2	8.3	56.7
10	326 34.4	52.5	88 55.2	11.4	12 22.5	8.2	56.7
11	341 34.5	51.6	103 25.6	11.2	12 30.7	8.2	56.7
12	356 34.6	S10 50.7	117 55.8	11.3	S12 38.9	8.1	56.7
13	11 34.6	49.8	132 26.1	11.1	12 47.0	8.1	56.8
14	26 34.7	48.9	146 56.2	11.1	12 55.1	8.0	56.8
15	41 34.8	.. 48.0	161 26.3	11.0	13 03.1	7.9	56.8
16	56 34.8	47.1	175 56.3	11.0	13 11.0	7.9	56.9
17	71 34.9	46.2	190 26.3	10.9	13 18.9	7.8	56.9
18	86 35.0	S10 45.3	204 56.2	10.8	S13 26.7	7.7	56.9
19	101 35.0	44.4	219 26.0	10.8	13 34.4	7.7	56.9
20	116 35.1	43.5	233 55.8	10.7	13 42.1	7.7	57.0
21	131 35.2	.. 42.6	248 25.5	10.6	13 49.8	7.5	57.0
22	146 35.3	41.7	262 55.1	10.6	13 57.3	7.5	57.0
23	161 35.3	40.8	277 24.7	10.5	S14 04.8	7.4	57.0
	SD 16.2	d 0.9	SD 15.2		15.3		15.5

(Left margin day labels: **18** TUESDAY; **19** WEDNESDAY; **20** THURSDAY)

Twilight / Sunrise / Moonrise

Lat.	Twilight Naut.	Twilight Civil	Sunrise	Moonrise 18	19	20	21
°	h m	h m	h m	h m	h m	h m	h m
N 72	05 57	07 16	08 31	22 27	24 14	00 14	02 10
N 70	05 57	07 08	08 15	22 16	23 55	25 37	01 37
68	05 57	07 02	08 02	22 07	23 39	25 14	01 14
66	05 57	06 57	07 51	22 00	23 27	24 56	00 56
64	05 57	06 52	07 42	21 54	23 17	24 41	00 41
62	05 56	06 48	07 34	21 49	23 09	24 29	00 29
60	05 56	06 44	07 27	21 44	23 01	24 18	00 18
N 58	05 55	06 41	07 21	21 40	22 55	24 10	00 10
56	05 55	06 38	07 16	21 37	22 49	24 02	00 02
54	05 54	06 35	07 12	21 34	22 44	23 55	25 05
52	05 53	06 33	07 07	21 31	22 39	23 48	24 57
50	05 53	06 30	07 03	21 28	22 35	23 43	24 50
45	05 51	06 25	06 55	21 23	22 26	23 31	24 35
N 40	05 49	06 20	06 48	21 18	22 19	23 20	24 23
35	05 46	06 16	06 42	21 14	22 12	23 12	24 13
30	05 44	06 12	06 36	21 10	22 07	23 04	24 03
20	05 39	06 04	06 27	21 04	21 57	22 52	23 48
N 10	05 32	05 57	06 18	20 59	21 49	22 40	23 34
0	05 25	05 49	06 10	20 54	21 41	22 30	23 22
S 10	05 16	05 41	06 02	20 49	21 33	22 19	23 09
20	05 04	05 31	05 54	20 44	21 25	22 08	22 56
30	04 49	05 19	05 43	20 38	21 15	21 56	22 41
35	04 40	05 11	05 37	20 35	21 10	21 49	22 32
40	04 28	05 02	05 31	20 31	21 04	21 40	22 22
45	04 14	04 52	05 23	20 26	20 57	21 31	22 10
S 50	03 55	04 38	05 13	20 21	20 48	21 19	21 56
52	03 46	04 32	05 09	20 19	20 45	21 14	21 49
54	03 36	04 25	05 04	20 16	20 40	21 08	21 42
56	03 24	04 17	04 58	20 13	20 36	21 02	21 34
58	03 09	04 08	04 52	20 10	20 30	20 54	21 25
S 60	02 52	03 58	04 45	20 07	20 25	20 46	21 14

Sunset / Twilight / Moonset

Lat.	Sunset	Twilight Civil	Twilight Naut.	Moonset 18	19	20	21
°	h m	h m	h m	h m	h m	h m	h m
N 72	15 58	17 13	18 32	07 31	07 23	07 13	07 01
N 70	16 14	17 21	18 32	07 37	07 36	07 34	07 34
68	16 27	17 27	18 32	07 43	07 46	07 51	07 59
66	16 38	17 32	18 32	07 47	07 54	08 04	08 18
64	16 47	17 37	18 32	07 51	08 02	08 15	08 33
62	16 55	17 41	18 33	07 54	08 08	08 24	08 46
60	17 01	17 45	18 33	07 57	08 13	08 33	08 57
N 58	17 07	17 48	18 33	07 59	08 18	08 40	09 06
56	17 12	17 51	18 34	08 02	08 22	08 46	09 15
54	17 17	17 53	18 34	08 04	08 26	08 52	09 22
52	17 21	17 56	18 35	08 06	08 30	08 57	09 29
50	17 25	17 58	18 36	08 07	08 33	09 02	09 35
45	17 33	18 03	18 38	08 11	08 40	09 12	09 48
N 40	17 40	18 08	18 39	08 14	08 46	09 20	09 59
35	17 46	18 12	18 42	08 17	08 51	09 28	10 08
30	17 52	18 16	18 44	08 19	08 55	09 34	10 16
20	18 01	18 23	18 49	08 23	09 03	09 45	10 30
N 10	18 09	18 31	18 55	08 27	09 10	09 55	10 43
0	18 17	18 38	19 03	08 30	09 16	10 04	10 54
S 10	18 25	18 47	19 12	08 34	09 23	10 13	11 06
20	18 34	18 56	19 23	08 37	09 29	10 23	11 18
30	18 44	19 08	19 38	08 42	09 37	10 34	11 33
35	18 50	19 16	19 47	08 44	09 42	10 41	11 41
40	18 56	19 24	19 58	08 47	09 47	10 48	11 50
45	19 04	19 35	20 13	08 50	09 53	10 57	12 01
S 50	19 13	19 48	20 31	08 54	10 00	11 07	12 15
52	19 18	19 54	20 40	08 55	10 03	11 12	12 21
54	19 22	20 01	20 50	08 57	10 07	11 17	12 28
56	19 28	20 09	21 02	08 59	10 11	11 23	12 36
58	19 34	20 18	21 16	09 02	10 15	11 30	12 44
S 60	19 40	20 28	21 32	09 04	10 21	11 38	12 54

SUN and MOON

Day	SUN Eqn. of Time 00h	SUN Eqn. of Time 12h	Mer. Pass.	MOON Mer. Pass. Upper	MOON Mer. Pass. Lower	Age	Phase
d	m s	m s	h m	h m	h m	d	%
18	13 56	13 54	12 14	02 20	14 42	19	89
19	13 51	13 48	12 14	03 05	15 28	20	82
20	13 45	13 42	12 14	03 52	16 17	21	73

UT	ARIES	VENUS −4.8		MARS −0.3		JUPITER −2.5		SATURN +0.5		STARS		
	GHA	GHA	Dec	GHA	Dec	GHA	Dec	GHA	Dec	Name	SHA	Dec
d h	° ′	° ′	° ′	° ′	° ′	° ′	° ′	° ′	° ′		° ′	° ′
21 00	150 50.3	219 29.9	S16 36.4	304 42.2	S 7 51.7	49 08.3	N23 13.5	279 23.1	S16 19.8	Acamar	315 18.1	S40 15.2
01	165 52.8	234 30.7	36.4	319 44.4	51.8	64 10.9	13.5	294 25.5	19.8	Achernar	335 26.8	S57 10.2
02	180 55.3	249 31.6	36.5	334 46.6	51.8	79 13.5	13.5	309 27.9	19.8	Acrux	173 08.0	S63 10.6
03	195 57.7	264 32.4 ..	36.5	349 48.8 ..	51.9	94 16.0 ..	13.6	324 30.3 ..	19.8	Adhara	255 11.9	S28 59.9
04	211 00.2	279 33.2	36.5	4 51.1	52.0	109 18.6	13.6	339 32.8	19.8	Aldebaran	290 48.8	N16 32.1
05	226 02.7	294 34.0	36.6	19 53.3	52.0	124 21.2	13.6	354 35.2	19.8			
06	241 05.1	309 34.8	S16 36.6	34 55.5	S 7 52.1	139 23.8	N23 13.6	9 37.6	S16 19.8	Alioth	166 19.9	N55 52.7
07	256 07.6	324 35.6	36.7	49 57.7	52.2	154 26.4	13.6	24 40.0	19.8	Alkaid	152 58.3	N49 14.3
08	271 10.1	339 36.4	36.7	64 59.9	52.2	169 28.9	13.6	39 42.4	19.8	Al Na'ir	27 43.6	S46 53.5
F 09	286 12.5	354 37.2 ..	36.8	80 02.2 ..	52.3	184 31.5 ..	13.6	54 44.9 ..	19.8	Alnilam	275 45.7	S 1 11.9
R 10	301 15.0	9 38.0	36.8	95 04.4	52.4	199 34.1	13.6	69 47.3	19.8	Alphard	217 55.3	S 8 43.5
I 11	316 17.4	24 38.8	36.8	110 06.6	52.4	214 36.7	13.7	84 49.7	19.8			
D 12	331 19.9	39 39.6	S16 36.9	125 08.9	S 7 52.5	229 39.3	N23 13.7	99 52.1	S16 19.8	Alphecca	126 10.6	N26 39.9
A 13	346 22.4	54 40.4	36.9	140 11.1	52.6	244 41.8	13.7	114 54.6	19.8	Alpheratz	357 43.3	N29 10.1
Y 14	1 24.8	69 41.2	37.0	155 13.3	52.6	259 44.4	13.7	129 57.0	19.8	Altair	62 08.0	N 8 54.4
15	16 27.3	84 42.0 ..	37.0	170 15.6 ..	52.7	274 47.0 ..	13.7	144 59.4 ..	19.8	Ankaa	353 15.6	S42 13.9
16	31 29.8	99 42.8	37.0	185 17.8	52.8	289 49.6	13.7	160 01.8	19.8	Antares	112 25.7	S26 27.6
17	46 32.2	114 43.6	37.1	200 20.0	52.8	304 52.2	13.7	175 04.2	19.8			
18	61 34.7	129 44.3	S16 37.1	215 22.3	S 7 52.9	319 54.7	N23 13.7	190 06.7	S16 19.8	Arcturus	145 55.1	N19 06.4
19	76 37.2	144 45.1	37.2	230 24.5	52.9	334 57.3	13.8	205 09.1	19.8	Atria	107 27.1	S69 02.8
20	91 39.6	159 45.9	37.2	245 26.7	53.0	349 59.9	13.8	220 11.5	19.8	Avior	234 17.2	S59 33.6
21	106 42.1	174 46.7 ..	37.2	260 29.0 ..	53.1	5 02.5 ..	13.8	235 13.9 ..	19.8	Bellatrix	278 31.4	N 6 21.5
22	121 44.6	189 47.4	37.3	275 31.2	53.1	20 05.0	13.8	250 16.4	19.8	Betelgeuse	271 00.6	N 7 24.3
23	136 47.0	204 48.2	37.3	290 33.5	53.2	35 07.6	13.8	265 18.8	19.8			
22 00	151 49.5	219 49.0	S16 37.3	305 35.7	S 7 53.2	50 10.2	N23 13.8	280 21.2	S16 19.8	Canopus	263 55.6	S52 42.6
01	166 51.9	234 49.7	37.4	320 37.9	53.3	65 12.8	13.8	295 23.6	19.8	Capella	280 33.6	N46 00.7
02	181 54.4	249 50.5	37.4	335 40.2	53.4	80 15.3	13.8	310 26.1	19.9	Deneb	49 31.5	N45 19.9
03	196 56.9	264 51.3 ..	37.5	350 42.4 ..	53.4	95 17.9 ..	13.8	325 28.5 ..	19.9	Denebola	182 32.9	N14 29.4
04	211 59.3	279 52.0	37.5	5 44.7	53.5	110 20.5	13.9	340 30.9	19.9	Diphda	348 55.7	S17 54.7
05	227 01.8	294 52.8	37.5	20 46.9	53.5	125 23.1	13.9	355 33.3	19.9			
06	242 04.3	309 53.5	S16 37.5	35 49.2	S 7 53.6	140 25.6	N23 13.9	10 35.8	S16 19.9	Dubhe	193 50.5	N61 40.2
S 07	257 06.7	324 54.3	37.6	50 51.4	53.6	155 28.2	13.9	25 38.2	19.9	Elnath	278 11.9	N28 37.0
A 08	272 09.2	339 55.0	37.6	65 53.7	53.7	170 30.8	13.9	40 40.6	19.9	Eltanin	90 46.1	N51 29.1
T 09	287 11.7	354 55.8 ..	37.6	80 55.9 ..	53.8	185 33.4 ..	13.9	55 43.0 ..	19.9	Enif	33 46.9	N 9 56.4
U 10	302 14.1	9 56.5	37.7	95 58.2	53.8	200 35.9	13.9	70 45.5	19.9	Fomalhaut	15 23.8	S29 32.9
R 11	317 16.6	24 57.3	37.7	111 00.4	53.9	215 38.5	13.9	85 47.9	19.9			
D 12	332 19.1	39 58.0	S16 37.7	126 02.7	S 7 53.9	230 41.1	N23 14.0	100 50.3	S16 19.9	Gacrux	171 59.8	S57 11.5
A 13	347 21.5	54 58.8	37.8	141 05.0	54.0	245 43.6	14.0	115 52.7	19.9	Gienah	175 51.5	S17 37.3
Y 14	2 24.0	69 59.5	37.8	156 07.2	54.0	260 46.2	14.0	130 55.2	19.9	Hadar	148 46.8	S60 26.2
15	17 26.4	85 00.2 ..	37.8	171 09.5 ..	54.1	275 48.8 ..	14.0	145 57.6 ..	19.9	Hamal	328 00.3	N23 31.7
16	32 28.9	100 01.0	37.8	186 11.7	54.1	290 51.3	14.0	161 00.0	19.9	Kaus Aust.	83 43.4	S34 22.4
17	47 31.4	115 01.7	37.9	201 14.0	54.2	305 53.9	14.0	176 02.4	19.9			
18	62 33.8	130 02.4	S16 37.9	216 16.3	S 7 54.2	320 56.5	N23 14.0	191 04.9	S16 19.9	Kochab	137 19.8	N74 05.6
19	77 36.3	145 03.1	37.9	231 18.5	54.3	335 59.1	14.0	206 07.3	19.9	Markab	13 38.1	N15 16.9
20	92 38.8	160 03.9	38.0	246 20.8	54.3	351 01.6	14.0	221 09.7	19.9	Menkar	314 14.6	N 4 08.5
21	107 41.2	175 04.6 ..	38.0	261 23.1 ..	54.4	6 04.2 ..	14.1	236 12.1 ..	19.9	Menkent	148 06.8	S36 26.3
22	122 43.7	190 05.3	38.0	276 25.3	54.4	21 06.8	14.1	251 14.6	19.9	Miaplacidus	221 38.6	S69 46.8
23	137 46.2	205 06.0	38.0	291 27.6	54.5	36 09.3	14.1	266 17.0	19.9			
23 00	152 48.6	220 06.7	S16 38.1	306 29.9	S 7 54.5	51 11.9	N23 14.1	281 19.4	S16 19.9	Mirfak	308 39.7	N49 54.7
01	167 51.1	235 07.5	38.1	321 32.1	54.6	66 14.5	14.1	296 21.9	19.9	Nunki	75 58.0	S26 16.5
02	182 53.5	250 08.2	38.1	336 34.4	54.6	81 17.0	14.1	311 24.3	19.9	Peacock	53 19.0	S56 41.1
03	197 56.0	265 08.9 ..	38.1	351 36.7 ..	54.7	96 19.6 ..	14.1	326 26.7 ..	19.9	Pollux	243 26.8	N27 59.3
04	212 58.5	280 09.6	38.1	6 39.0	54.7	111 22.2	14.1	341 29.1	19.9	Procyon	244 59.0	N 5 11.0
05	228 00.9	295 10.3	38.2	21 41.2	54.8	126 24.7	14.1	356 31.6	19.9			
06	243 03.4	310 11.0	S16 38.2	36 43.5	S 7 54.8	141 27.3	N23 14.2	11 34.0	S16 19.9	Rasalhague	96 06.1	N12 33.0
07	258 05.9	325 11.7	38.2	51 45.8	54.9	156 29.8	14.2	26 36.4	19.9	Regulus	207 42.7	N11 53.6
08	273 08.3	340 12.4	38.2	66 48.1	54.9	171 32.4	14.2	41 38.9	19.9	Rigel	281 11.5	S 8 11.5
S 09	288 10.8	355 13.1 ..	38.2	81 50.3 ..	55.0	186 35.0 ..	14.2	56 41.3 ..	19.9	Rigil Kent.	139 50.7	S60 53.3
U 10	303 13.3	10 13.8	38.3	96 52.6	55.0	201 37.5	14.2	71 43.7	19.9	Sabik	102 12.1	S15 44.4
N 11	318 15.7	25 14.5	38.3	111 54.9	55.1	216 40.1	14.2	86 46.2	19.9			
D 12	333 18.2	40 15.2	S16 38.3	126 57.2	S 7 55.1	231 42.7	N23 14.2	101 48.6	S16 19.9	Schedar	349 40.3	N56 37.0
A 13	348 20.7	55 15.9	38.3	141 59.5	55.2	246 45.2	14.2	116 51.0	19.9	Shaula	96 21.4	S37 06.6
Y 14	3 23.1	70 16.5	38.3	157 01.8	55.2	261 47.8	14.2	131 53.4	19.9	Sirius	258 33.1	S16 44.5
15	18 25.6	85 17.2 ..	38.3	172 04.0 ..	55.3	276 50.3 ..	14.3	146 55.9 ..	19.9	Spica	158 30.5	S11 14.2
16	33 28.0	100 17.9	38.4	187 06.3	55.3	291 52.9	14.3	161 58.3	19.9	Suhail	222 51.6	S43 29.7
17	48 30.5	115 18.6	38.4	202 08.6	55.3	306 55.5	14.3	177 00.7	19.9			
18	63 33.0	130 19.3	S16 38.4	217 10.9	S 7 55.4	321 58.0	N23 14.3	192 03.2	S16 19.8	Vega	80 38.9	N38 47.7
19	78 35.4	145 19.9	38.4	232 13.2	55.4	337 00.6	14.3	207 05.6	19.8	Zuben'ubi	137 04.7	S16 06.0
20	93 37.9	160 20.6	38.4	247 15.5	55.5	352 03.1	14.3	222 08.0	19.8		SHA	Mer. Pass.
21	108 40.4	175 21.3 ..	38.4	262 17.8 ..	55.5	7 05.7 ..	14.3	237 10.5 ..	19.8		° ′	h m
22	123 42.8	190 22.0	38.4	277 20.1	55.5	22 08.3	14.3	252 12.9	19.8	Venus	67 59.5	9 20
23	138 45.3	205 22.6	38.4	292 22.4	55.6	37 10.8	14.3	267 15.3	19.8	Mars	153 46.2	3 37
	h m									Jupiter	258 20.7	20 36
Mer. Pass. 13 50.4		v 0.7	d 0.0	v 2.3	d 0.1	v 2.6	d 0.0	v 2.4	d 0.0	Saturn	128 31.7	5 18

UT	SUN GHA	SUN Dec	MOON GHA	MOON v	MOON Dec	MOON d	MOON HP
d h	° ′	° ′	° ′	′	° ′	′	′
21 00	176 35.4	S10 39.9	291 54.2	10.5	S14 12.2	7.4	57.1
01	191 35.5	39.0	306 23.7	10.4	14 19.6	7.3	57.1
02	206 35.5	38.1	320 53.1	10.3	14 26.9	7.2	57.1
03	221 35.6	.. 37.2	335 22.4	10.2	14 34.1	7.1	57.2
04	236 35.7	36.3	349 51.6	10.2	14 41.2	7.1	57.2
05	251 35.8	35.4	4 20.8	10.1	14 48.3	7.0	57.2
06	266 35.8	S10 34.5	18 49.9	10.1	S14 55.3	6.9	57.2
07	281 35.9	33.6	33 19.0	9.9	15 02.2	6.9	57.3
08	296 36.0	32.7	47 47.9	9.9	15 09.1	6.7	57.3
F 09	311 36.0	.. 31.8	62 16.8	9.9	15 15.8	6.7	57.3
R 10	326 36.1	30.9	76 45.7	9.8	15 22.5	6.7	57.3
I 11	341 36.2	30.0	91 14.5	9.7	15 29.2	6.5	57.4
D 12	356 36.3	S10 29.1	105 43.2	9.6	S15 35.7	6.4	57.4
A 13	11 36.3	28.2	120 11.8	9.6	15 42.1	6.4	57.4
Y 14	26 36.4	27.2	134 40.4	9.5	15 48.5	6.3	57.5
15	41 36.5	.. 26.3	149 08.9	9.4	15 54.8	6.2	57.5
16	56 36.6	25.4	163 37.3	9.4	16 01.0	6.2	57.5
17	71 36.6	24.5	178 05.7	9.3	16 07.2	6.0	57.5
18	86 36.7	S10 23.6	192 34.0	9.2	S16 13.2	6.0	57.6
19	101 36.8	22.7	207 02.2	9.2	16 19.2	5.8	57.6
20	116 36.9	21.8	221 30.4	9.1	16 25.0	5.8	57.6
21	131 37.0	.. 20.9	235 58.5	9.0	16 30.8	5.7	57.7
22	146 37.0	20.0	250 26.5	9.0	16 36.5	5.6	57.7
23	161 37.1	19.1	264 54.5	8.9	16 42.1	5.5	57.7
22 00	176 37.2	S10 18.2	279 22.4	8.8	S16 47.6	5.5	57.8
01	191 37.3	17.3	293 50.2	8.8	16 53.1	5.3	57.8
02	206 37.3	16.3	308 18.0	8.7	16 58.4	5.2	57.8
03	221 37.4	.. 15.4	322 45.7	8.6	17 03.6	5.2	57.8
04	236 37.5	14.5	337 13.3	8.5	17 08.8	5.0	57.9
05	251 37.6	13.6	351 40.8	8.5	17 13.8	5.0	57.9
06	266 37.7	S10 12.7	6 08.3	8.4	S17 18.8	4.9	57.9
07	281 37.7	11.8	20 35.7	8.4	17 23.7	4.7	58.0
S 08	296 37.8	10.9	35 03.1	8.3	17 28.4	4.7	58.0
A 09	311 37.9	.. 10.0	49 30.4	8.2	17 33.1	4.6	58.0
T 10	326 38.0	09.1	63 57.6	8.2	17 37.7	4.4	58.0
U 11	341 38.1	08.1	78 24.8	8.1	17 42.1	4.4	58.1
R 12	356 38.1	S10 07.2	92 51.9	8.0	S17 46.5	4.3	58.1
D 13	11 38.2	06.3	107 18.9	8.0	17 50.8	4.1	58.1
A 14	26 38.3	05.4	121 45.9	7.9	17 54.9	4.1	58.2
Y 15	41 38.4	.. 04.5	136 12.8	7.8	17 59.0	3.9	58.2
16	56 38.5	03.6	150 39.6	7.8	18 02.9	3.9	58.2
17	71 38.5	02.7	165 06.4	7.7	18 06.8	3.7	58.3
18	86 38.6	S10 01.8	179 33.1	7.6	S18 10.5	3.7	58.3
19	101 38.7	10 00.8	193 59.7	7.6	18 14.2	3.5	58.3
20	116 38.8	9 59.9	208 26.3	7.5	18 17.7	3.4	58.4
21	131 38.9	.. 59.0	222 52.8	7.5	18 21.1	3.3	58.4
22	146 39.0	58.1	237 19.3	7.4	18 24.4	3.2	58.4
23	161 39.0	57.2	251 45.7	7.4	18 27.6	3.1	58.4
23 00	176 39.1	S 9 56.3	266 12.1	7.2	S18 30.7	3.0	58.5
01	191 39.2	55.3	280 38.3	7.3	18 33.7	2.9	58.5
02	206 39.3	54.4	295 04.6	7.1	18 36.6	2.7	58.5
03	221 39.4	.. 53.5	309 30.7	7.1	18 39.3	2.7	58.6
04	236 39.5	52.6	323 56.8	7.1	18 42.0	2.5	58.6
05	251 39.5	51.7	338 22.9	7.0	18 44.5	2.4	58.6
06	266 39.6	S 9 50.8	352 48.9	6.9	S18 46.9	2.3	58.7
07	281 39.7	49.8	7 14.8	6.9	18 49.2	2.2	58.7
08	296 39.8	48.9	21 40.7	6.9	18 51.4	2.1	58.7
S 09	311 39.9	.. 48.0	36 06.6	6.7	18 53.5	1.9	58.7
U 10	326 40.0	47.1	50 32.3	6.8	18 55.4	1.9	58.8
N 11	341 40.1	46.2	64 58.1	6.6	18 57.3	1.7	58.8
D 12	356 40.1	S 9 45.3	79 23.7	6.7	S18 59.0	1.6	58.8
A 13	11 40.2	44.3	93 49.4	6.5	19 00.6	1.4	58.9
Y 14	26 40.3	43.4	108 14.9	6.6	19 02.0	1.4	58.9
15	41 40.4	.. 42.5	122 40.5	6.5	19 03.4	1.2	58.9
16	56 40.5	41.6	137 06.0	6.4	19 04.6	1.1	59.0
17	71 40.6	40.7	151 31.4	6.4	19 05.7	1.0	59.0
18	86 40.7	S 9 39.7	165 56.8	6.3	S19 06.7	0.9	59.0
19	101 40.8	38.8	180 22.1	6.3	19 07.6	0.7	59.0
20	116 40.8	37.9	194 47.4	6.2	19 08.3	0.6	59.1
21	131 40.9	.. 37.0	209 12.6	6.3	19 08.9	0.5	59.1
22	146 41.0	36.1	223 37.9	6.1	19 09.4	0.4	59.1
23	161 41.1	35.1	238 03.0	6.1	S19 09.8	0.2	59.2
	SD 16.2	d 0.9	SD 15.6		15.8		16.0

Lat.	Twilight Naut.	Twilight Civil	Sunrise	Moonrise 21	Moonrise 22	Moonrise 23	Moonrise 24
°	h m	h m	h m	h m	h m	h m	h m
N 72	05 44	07 02	08 15	02 10	04 27	■■■■	■■■■
N 70	05 45	06 56	08 01	01 37	03 24	05 07	06 22
68	05 46	06 51	07 49	01 14	02 48	04 16	05 23
66	05 47	06 46	07 40	00 56	02 23	03 44	04 49
64	05 48	06 43	07 32	00 41	02 04	03 20	04 24
62	05 48	06 39	07 25	00 29	01 48	03 01	04 05
60	05 48	06 36	07 19	00 18	01 35	02 46	03 49
N 58	05 48	06 34	07 14	00 10	01 23	02 33	03 35
56	05 48	06 31	07 09	00 02	01 13	02 22	03 23
54	05 48	06 29	07 05	25 05	01 05	02 12	03 13
52	05 48	06 27	07 01	24 57	00 57	02 03	03 04
50	05 47	06 25	06 58	24 50	00 50	01 55	02 56
45	05 46	06 20	06 50	24 35	00 35	01 38	02 39
N 40	05 45	06 16	06 44	24 23	00 23	01 25	02 24
35	05 43	06 13	06 38	24 13	00 13	01 13	02 12
30	05 41	06 09	06 33	24 03	00 03	01 03	02 02
20	05 37	06 03	06 25	23 48	24 46	00 46	01 44
N 10	05 31	05 56	06 17	23 34	24 31	00 31	01 28
0	05 25	05 49	06 10	23 22	24 16	00 16	01 14
S 10	05 16	05 41	06 03	23 09	24 02	00 02	00 59
20	05 06	05 32	05 55	22 56	23 47	24 43	00 43
30	04 52	05 21	05 46	22 41	23 30	24 26	00 26
35	04 43	05 14	05 40	22 32	23 20	24 15	00 15
40	04 32	05 06	05 34	22 22	23 09	24 03	00 03
45	04 19	04 56	05 27	22 10	22 56	23 49	24 51
S 50	04 02	04 44	05 18	21 56	22 40	23 32	24 35
52	03 53	04 38	05 14	21 49	22 32	23 24	24 27
54	03 44	04 32	05 10	21 42	22 24	23 15	24 18
56	03 33	04 25	05 05	21 34	22 14	23 05	24 08
58	03 20	04 16	05 00	21 25	22 03	22 54	23 57
S 60	03 04	04 07	04 53	21 14	21 51	22 41	23 45

Lat.	Sunset	Twilight Civil	Twilight Naut.	Moonset 21	Moonset 22	Moonset 23	Moonset 24
°	h m	h m	h m	h m	h m	h m	h m
N 72	16 14	17 27	18 46	07 01	06 33	■■■■	■■■■
N 70	16 28	17 33	18 44	07 34	07 37	07 49	08 35
68	16 39	17 38	18 42	07 59	08 13	08 40	09 33
66	16 49	17 42	18 42	08 18	08 38	09 13	10 07
64	16 56	17 46	18 41	08 33	08 58	09 36	10 32
62	17 03	17 49	18 40	08 46	09 15	09 55	10 51
60	17 09	17 52	18 40	08 57	09 28	10 11	11 07
N 58	17 14	17 54	18 40	09 06	09 40	10 24	11 21
56	17 19	17 57	18 40	09 15	09 50	10 36	11 33
54	17 23	17 59	18 40	09 22	09 59	10 46	11 43
52	17 27	18 01	18 40	09 29	10 07	10 55	11 52
50	17 30	18 03	18 41	09 35	10 15	11 03	12 00
45	17 38	18 07	18 41	09 48	10 30	11 20	12 17
N 40	17 44	18 11	18 43	09 59	10 43	11 34	12 31
35	17 49	18 15	18 44	10 08	10 54	11 45	12 43
30	17 54	18 18	18 46	10 16	11 03	11 56	12 54
20	18 02	18 25	18 50	10 30	11 20	12 13	13 11
N 10	18 10	18 31	18 56	10 43	11 34	12 29	13 27
0	18 17	18 38	19 02	10 54	11 48	12 43	13 42
S 10	18 24	18 45	19 11	11 06	12 01	12 58	13 56
20	18 32	18 54	19 21	11 18	12 15	13 13	14 11
30	18 41	19 05	19 34	11 33	12 32	13 31	14 29
35	18 46	19 12	19 43	11 41	12 41	13 41	14 39
40	18 52	19 20	19 54	11 50	12 52	13 53	14 51
45	18 59	19 30	20 07	12 01	13 05	14 07	15 05
S 50	19 07	19 42	20 24	12 15	13 21	14 24	15 22
52	19 11	19 47	20 32	12 21	13 28	14 32	15 30
54	19 16	19 54	20 41	12 28	13 36	14 41	15 38
56	19 20	20 01	20 52	12 36	13 46	14 51	15 48
58	19 26	20 09	21 05	12 44	13 56	15 02	15 59
S 60	19 32	20 18	21 20	12 54	14 08	15 15	16 12

Day	SUN Eqn. of Time 00h	SUN Eqn. of Time 12h	SUN Mer. Pass.	MOON Mer. Pass. Upper	MOON Mer. Pass. Lower	Age	Phase
d	m s	m s	h m	h m	h m	d	%
21	13 39	13 35	12 14	04 42	17 08	22	63
22	13 31	13 28	12 13	05 35	18 02	23	53
23	13 24	13 20	12 13	06 30	18 58	24	41

UT	ARIES	VENUS −4.8		MARS −0.4		JUPITER −2.5		SATURN +0.4		STARS		
	GHA	GHA	Dec	GHA	Dec	GHA	Dec	GHA	Dec	Name	SHA	Dec
d h	° ′	° ′	° ′	° ′	° ′	° ′	° ′	° ′	° ′		° ′	° ′
24 00	153 47.8	220 23.3	S16 38.5	307 24.7	S 7 55.6	52 13.4	N23 14.4	282 17.8	S16 19.8	Acamar	315 18.1	S40 15.2
01	168 50.2	235 24.0	38.5	322 27.0	55.7	67 15.9	14.4	297 20.2	19.8	Achernar	335 26.9	S57 10.2
02	183 52.7	250 24.6	38.5	337 29.3	55.7	82 18.5	14.4	312 22.6	19.8	Acrux	173 08.0	S63 10.6
03	198 55.2	265 25.3 ..	38.5	352 31.6 ..	55.8	97 21.0 ..	14.4	327 25.1 ..	19.8	Adhara	255 11.9	S28 59.9
04	213 57.6	280 25.9	38.5	7 33.9	55.8	112 23.6	14.4	342 27.5	19.8	Aldebaran	290 48.8	N16 32.1
05	229 00.1	295 26.6	38.5	22 36.2	55.8	127 26.2	14.4	357 29.9	19.8			
06	244 02.5	310 27.2	S16 38.5	37 38.5	S 7 55.9	142 28.7	N23 14.4	12 32.4	S16 19.8	Alioth	166 19.9	N55 52.7
07	259 05.0	325 27.9	38.5	52 40.8	55.9	157 31.3	14.4	27 34.8	19.8	Alkaid	152 58.3	N49 14.3
08	274 07.5	340 28.5	38.5	67 43.1	55.9	172 33.8	14.4	42 37.2	19.8	Al Na'ir	27 43.6	S46 53.5
M 09	289 09.9	355 29.2 ..	38.5	82 45.4 ..	56.0	187 36.4 ..	14.4	57 39.7 ..	19.8	Alnilam	275 45.7	S 1 11.9
O 10	304 12.4	10 29.8	38.5	97 47.7	56.0	202 38.9	14.5	72 42.1	19.8	Alphard	217 55.3	S 8 43.5
N 11	319 14.9	25 30.5	38.5	112 50.0	56.1	217 41.5	14.5	87 44.5	19.8			
D 12	334 17.3	40 31.1	S16 38.5	127 52.3	S 7 56.1	232 44.0	N23 14.5	102 47.0	S16 19.8	Alphecca	126 10.5	N26 39.9
A 13	349 19.8	55 31.8	38.6	142 54.6	56.1	247 46.6	14.5	117 49.4	19.8	Alpheratz	357 43.3	N29 10.1
Y 14	4 22.3	70 32.4	38.6	157 56.9	56.2	262 49.1	14.5	132 51.8	19.8	Altair	62 08.0	N 8 54.4
15	19 24.7	85 33.0 ..	38.6	172 59.2 ..	56.2	277 51.7 ..	14.5	147 54.3 ..	19.8	Ankaa	353 15.6	S42 13.9
16	34 27.2	100 33.7	38.6	188 01.6	56.2	292 54.2	14.5	162 56.7	19.8	Antares	112 25.6	S26 27.6
17	49 29.7	115 34.3	38.6	203 03.9	56.3	307 56.8	14.5	177 59.1	19.8			
18	64 32.1	130 34.9	S16 38.6	218 06.2	S 7 56.3	322 59.3	N23 14.5	193 01.6	S16 19.8	Arcturus	145 55.1	N19 06.4
19	79 34.6	145 35.6	38.6	233 08.5	56.3	338 01.9	14.5	208 04.0	19.8	Atria	107 27.1	S69 02.8
20	94 37.0	160 36.2	38.6	248 10.8	56.4	353 04.4	14.6	223 06.5	19.8	Avior	234 17.2	S59 33.7
21	109 39.5	175 36.8 ..	38.6	263 13.2 ..	56.4	8 07.0 ..	14.6	238 08.9 ..	19.8	Bellatrix	278 31.4	N 6 21.5
22	124 42.0	190 37.4	38.6	278 15.5	56.4	23 09.5	14.6	253 11.3	19.8	Betelgeuse	271 00.6	N 7 24.3
23	139 44.4	205 38.1	38.6	293 17.8	56.5	38 12.1	14.6	268 13.8	19.8			
25 00	154 46.9	220 38.7	S16 38.6	308 20.1	S 7 56.5	53 14.6	N23 14.6	283 16.2	S16 19.8	Canopus	263 55.6	S52 42.7
01	169 49.4	235 39.3	38.6	323 22.4	56.5	68 17.2	14.6	298 18.6	19.8	Capella	280 33.6	N46 00.7
02	184 51.8	250 39.9	38.5	338 24.8	56.6	83 19.7	14.6	313 21.1	19.8	Deneb	49 31.5	N45 19.8
03	199 54.3	265 40.5 ..	38.5	353 27.1 ..	56.6	98 22.3 ..	14.6	328 23.5 ..	19.8	Denebola	182 32.9	N14 29.3
04	214 56.8	280 41.1	38.5	8 29.4	56.6	113 24.8	14.6	343 26.0	19.8	Diphda	348 55.7	S17 54.7
05	229 59.2	295 41.7	38.5	23 31.8	56.6	128 27.4	14.6	358 28.4	19.8			
06	245 01.7	310 42.3	S16 38.5	38 34.1	S 7 56.7	143 29.9	N23 14.7	13 30.8	S16 19.8	Dubhe	193 50.5	N61 40.3
07	260 04.1	325 42.9	38.5	53 36.4	56.7	158 32.5	14.7	28 33.3	19.8	Elnath	278 11.9	N28 37.0
T 08	275 06.6	340 43.5	38.5	68 38.8	56.7	173 35.0	14.7	43 35.7	19.8	Eltanin	90 46.1	N51 29.1
U 09	290 09.1	355 44.1 ..	38.5	83 41.1 ..	56.8	188 37.6 ..	14.7	58 38.1 ..	19.8	Enif	33 46.9	N 9 56.4
E 10	305 11.5	10 44.7	38.5	98 43.4	56.8	203 40.1	14.7	73 40.6	19.8	Fomalhaut	15 23.8	S29 32.9
S 11	320 14.0	25 45.3	38.5	113 45.8	56.8	218 42.7	14.7	88 43.0	19.8			
D 12	335 16.5	40 45.9	S16 38.5	128 48.1	S 7 56.8	233 45.2	N23 14.7	103 45.5	S16 19.8	Gacrux	171 59.8	S57 11.5
A 13	350 18.9	55 46.5	38.5	143 50.4	56.9	248 47.7	14.7	118 47.9	19.8	Gienah	175 51.5	S17 37.4
Y 14	5 21.4	70 47.1	38.5	158 52.8	56.9	263 50.3	14.7	133 50.3	19.8	Hadar	148 46.7	S60 26.3
15	20 23.9	85 47.7 ..	38.4	173 55.1 ..	56.9	278 52.8 ..	14.7	148 52.8 ..	19.8	Hamal	328 00.4	N23 31.7
16	35 26.3	100 48.3	38.4	188 57.5	56.9	293 55.4	14.8	163 55.2	19.8	Kaus Aust.	83 43.3	S34 22.4
17	50 28.8	115 48.9	38.4	203 59.8	57.0	308 57.9	14.8	178 57.7	19.8			
18	65 31.3	130 49.5	S16 38.4	219 02.1	S 7 57.0	324 00.5	N23 14.8	194 00.1	S16 19.8	Kochab	137 19.7	N74 05.6
19	80 33.7	145 50.0	38.4	234 04.5	57.0	339 03.0	14.8	209 02.5	19.8	Markab	13 38.1	N15 16.9
20	95 36.2	160 50.6	38.4	249 06.8	57.0	354 05.5	14.8	224 05.0	19.8	Menkar	314 14.6	N 4 08.5
21	110 38.6	175 51.2 ..	38.4	264 09.2 ..	57.1	9 08.1 ..	14.8	239 07.4 ..	19.7	Menkent	148 06.7	S36 26.3
22	125 41.1	190 51.8	38.4	279 11.5	57.1	24 10.6	14.8	254 09.9	19.7	Miaplacidus	221 38.6	S69 46.8
23	140 43.6	205 52.4	38.3	294 13.9	57.1	39 13.2	14.8	269 12.3	19.7			
26 00	155 46.0	220 52.9	S16 38.3	309 16.2	S 7 57.1	54 15.7	N23 14.8	284 14.7	S16 19.7	Mirfak	308 39.7	N49 54.7
01	170 48.5	235 53.5	38.3	324 18.6	57.1	69 18.2	14.8	299 17.2	19.7	Nunki	75 57.9	S26 16.5
02	185 51.0	250 54.1	38.3	339 20.9	57.2	84 20.8	14.8	314 19.6	19.7	Peacock	53 19.0	S56 41.1
03	200 53.4	265 54.6 ..	38.3	354 23.3 ..	57.2	99 23.3 ..	14.9	329 22.1 ..	19.7	Pollux	243 26.9	N27 59.3
04	215 55.9	280 55.2	38.2	9 25.7	57.2	114 25.9	14.9	344 24.5	19.7	Procyon	244 59.0	N 5 11.0
05	230 58.4	295 55.8	38.2	24 28.0	57.2	129 28.4	14.9	359 27.0	19.7			
06	246 00.8	310 56.3	S16 38.2	39 30.4	S 7 57.2	144 30.9	N23 14.9	14 29.4	S16 19.7	Rasalhague	96 06.1	N12 33.0
W 07	261 03.3	325 56.9	38.2	54 32.7	57.3	159 33.5	14.9	29 31.8	19.7	Regulus	207 42.7	N11 53.6
E 08	276 05.8	340 57.4	38.2	69 35.1	57.3	174 36.0	14.9	44 34.3	19.7	Rigel	281 11.5	S 8 11.5
D 09	291 08.2	355 58.0 ..	38.1	84 37.5 ..	57.3	189 38.5 ..	14.9	59 36.7 ..	19.7	Rigil Kent.	139 50.7	S60 53.3
N 10	306 10.7	10 58.6	38.1	99 39.8	57.3	204 41.1	14.9	74 39.2	19.7	Sabik	102 12.0	S15 44.4
E 11	321 13.1	25 59.1	38.1	114 42.2	57.3	219 43.6	14.9	89 41.6	19.7			
S 12	336 15.6	40 59.7	S16 38.1	129 44.5	S 7 57.3	234 46.2	N23 14.9	104 44.1	S16 19.7	Schedar	349 40.3	N56 37.0
D 13	351 18.1	56 00.2	38.0	144 46.9	57.4	249 48.7	14.9	119 46.5	19.7	Shaula	96 21.4	S37 06.6
A 14	6 20.5	71 00.7	38.0	159 49.3	57.4	264 51.2	15.0	134 48.9	19.7	Sirius	258 33.1	S16 44.5
Y 15	21 23.0	86 01.3 ..	38.0	174 51.7 ..	57.4	279 53.8 ..	15.0	149 51.4 ..	19.7	Spica	158 30.5	S11 14.2
16	36 25.5	101 01.8	38.0	189 54.0	57.4	294 56.3	15.0	164 53.8	19.7	Suhail	222 51.6	S43 29.7
17	51 27.9	116 02.4	37.9	204 56.4	57.4	309 58.8	15.0	179 56.3	19.7			
18	66 30.4	131 02.9	S16 37.9	219 58.8	S 7 57.4	325 01.4	N23 15.0	194 58.7	S16 19.7	Vega	80 38.8	N38 47.7
19	81 32.9	146 03.5	37.9	235 01.1	57.5	340 03.9	15.0	210 01.2	19.7	Zuben'ubi	137 04.7	S16 06.0
20	96 35.3	161 04.0	37.9	250 03.5	57.5	355 06.4	15.0	225 03.6	19.7		SHA	Mer.Pass.
21	111 37.8	176 04.5 ..	37.8	265 05.9 ..	57.5	10 09.0 ..	15.0	240 06.1 ..	19.7		° ′	h m
22	126 40.2	191 05.1	37.8	280 08.3	57.5	25 11.5	15.0	255 08.5	19.7	Venus	65 51.8	9 17
23	141 42.7	206 05.6	37.8	295 10.6	57.5	40 14.0	15.0	270 10.9	19.7	Mars	153 33.2	3 26
	h m									Jupiter	258 27.7	20 24
Mer.Pass. 13 38.6	v 0.6	d 0.0	v 2.3	d 0.0	v 2.5	d 0.0	v 2.4	d 0.0	Saturn	128 29.3	5 06

UT	SUN GHA	SUN Dec	MOON GHA	v	MOON Dec	d	HP
d h	° ′	° ′	° ′	′	° ′	′	′
24 00	176 41.2	S 9 34.2	252 28.1	6.1	S19 10.0	0.1	59.2
01	191 41.3	33.3	266 53.2	6.1	19 10.1	0.0	59.2
02	206 41.4	32.4	281 18.3	6.0	19 10.1	0.1	59.3
03	221 41.5	.. 31.4	295 43.3	6.0	19 10.0	0.3	59.3
04	236 41.6	30.5	310 08.3	5.9	19 09.7	0.4	59.3
05	251 41.7	29.6	324 33.2	5.9	19 09.3	0.5	59.3
06	266 41.7	S 9 28.7	338 58.1	5.9	S19 08.8	0.6	59.4
M 07	281 41.8	27.7	353 23.0	5.8	19 08.2	0.8	59.4
O 08	296 41.9	26.8	7 47.8	5.8	19 07.4	0.9	59.4
N 09	311 42.0	.. 25.9	22 12.6	5.8	19 06.5	1.0	59.5
D 10	326 42.1	25.0	36 37.4	5.7	19 05.5	1.2	59.5
A 11	341 42.2	24.1	51 02.1	5.7	19 04.3	1.3	59.5
Y 12	356 42.3	S 9 23.1	65 26.8	5.7	S19 03.0	1.4	59.5
13	11 42.4	22.2	79 51.5	5.7	19 01.6	1.5	59.6
14	26 42.5	21.3	94 16.2	5.6	19 00.1	1.7	59.6
15	41 42.6	.. 20.4	108 40.8	5.6	18 58.4	1.8	59.6
16	56 42.7	19.4	123 05.4	5.6	18 56.6	1.9	59.6
17	71 42.8	18.5	137 30.0	5.6	18 54.7	2.1	59.7
18	86 42.9	S 9 17.6	151 54.6	5.6	S18 52.6	2.2	59.7
19	101 43.0	16.6	166 19.2	5.5	18 50.4	2.3	59.7
20	116 43.1	15.7	180 43.7	5.5	18 48.1	2.5	59.8
21	131 43.1	.. 14.8	195 08.2	5.5	18 45.6	2.6	59.8
22	146 43.2	13.9	209 32.7	5.5	18 43.0	2.7	59.8
23	161 43.3	12.9	223 57.2	5.4	18 40.3	2.8	59.8
25 00	176 43.4	S 9 12.0	238 21.6	5.5	S18 37.5	3.0	59.9
01	191 43.5	11.1	252 46.1	5.4	18 34.5	3.1	59.9
02	206 43.6	10.2	267 10.5	5.5	18 31.4	3.2	59.9
03	221 43.7	.. 09.2	281 35.0	5.4	18 28.2	3.4	59.9
04	236 43.8	08.3	295 59.4	5.4	18 24.8	3.5	60.0
05	251 43.9	07.4	310 23.8	5.4	18 21.3	3.6	60.0
06	266 44.0	S 9 06.4	324 48.2	5.4	S18 17.7	3.8	60.0
T 07	281 44.1	05.5	339 12.6	5.4	18 13.9	3.8	60.0
U 08	296 44.2	04.6	353 37.0	5.4	18 10.1	4.0	60.1
E 09	311 44.3	.. 03.6	8 01.4	5.4	18 06.1	4.2	60.1
S 10	326 44.4	02.7	22 25.8	5.4	18 01.9	4.2	60.1
D 11	341 44.5	01.8	36 50.2	5.3	17 57.7	4.4	60.1
A 12	356 44.6	S 9 00.9	51 14.5	5.4	S17 53.3	4.5	60.1
Y 13	11 44.7	8 59.9	65 38.9	5.4	17 48.8	4.7	60.2
14	26 44.8	59.0	80 03.3	5.4	17 44.1	4.7	60.2
15	41 44.9	.. 58.1	94 27.7	5.4	17 39.4	4.9	60.2
16	56 45.0	57.1	108 52.1	5.4	17 34.5	5.0	60.2
17	71 45.1	56.2	123 16.5	5.4	17 29.5	5.2	60.3
18	86 45.2	S 8 55.3	137 40.9	5.4	S17 24.3	5.2	60.3
19	101 45.3	54.3	152 05.3	5.4	17 19.1	5.4	60.3
20	116 45.4	53.4	166 29.7	5.4	17 13.7	5.5	60.3
21	131 45.5	.. 52.5	180 54.1	5.5	17 08.2	5.7	60.3
22	146 45.6	51.5	195 18.6	5.4	17 02.5	5.7	60.4
23	161 45.7	50.6	209 43.0	5.5	16 56.8	5.9	60.4
26 00	176 45.8	S 8 49.7	224 07.5	5.4	S16 50.9	6.0	60.4
01	191 45.9	48.7	238 31.9	5.5	16 44.9	6.1	60.4
02	206 46.0	47.8	252 56.4	5.5	16 38.8	6.3	60.4
03	221 46.1	.. 46.9	267 20.9	5.6	16 32.5	6.3	60.5
04	236 46.2	45.9	281 45.5	5.5	16 26.2	6.5	60.5
05	251 46.3	45.0	296 10.0	5.5	16 19.7	6.6	60.5
06	266 46.4	S 8 44.1	310 34.5	5.6	S16 13.1	6.7	60.5
W 07	281 46.5	43.1	324 59.1	5.6	16 06.4	6.8	60.5
E 08	296 46.6	42.2	339 23.7	5.6	15 59.6	6.9	60.5
D 09	311 46.7	.. 41.3	353 48.3	5.7	15 52.7	7.1	60.6
N 10	326 46.8	40.3	8 13.0	5.6	15 45.6	7.1	60.6
E 11	341 46.9	39.4	22 37.6	5.7	15 38.5	7.3	60.6
S 12	356 47.0	S 8 38.5	37 02.3	5.7	S15 31.2	7.4	60.6
D 13	11 47.1	37.5	51 27.0	5.7	15 23.8	7.5	60.6
A 14	26 47.3	36.6	65 51.7	5.8	15 16.3	7.6	60.6
Y 15	41 47.4	.. 35.6	80 16.5	5.7	15 08.7	7.7	60.6
16	56 47.5	34.7	94 41.2	5.9	15 01.0	7.8	60.7
17	71 47.6	33.8	109 06.1	5.8	14 53.2	7.9	60.7
18	86 47.7	S 8 32.8	123 30.9	5.9	S14 45.3	8.0	60.7
19	101 47.8	31.9	137 55.7	5.9	14 37.3	8.2	60.7
20	116 47.9	31.0	152 20.6	6.0	14 29.1	8.2	60.7
21	131 48.0	.. 30.0	166 45.6	5.9	14 20.9	8.3	60.7
22	146 48.1	29.1	181 10.5	6.0	14 12.6	8.5	60.7
23	161 48.2	28.1	195 35.5	6.0	S14 04.1	8.5	60.7
	SD 16.2	d 0.9	SD 16.2		16.4		16.5

Twilight / Moonrise

Lat.	Naut.	Civil	Sunrise	Moonrise 24	25	26	27
°	h m	h m	h m	h m	h m	h m	h m
N 72	05 30	06 48	07 58	■■■■	■■■■	07 35	07 18
N 70	05 33	06 43	07 46	06 22	06 47	06 53	06 55
68	05 35	06 39	07 37	05 23	06 04	06 25	06 36
66	05 37	06 36	07 28	04 49	05 34	06 03	06 22
64	05 38	06 33	07 22	04 24	05 12	05 46	06 09
62	05 39	06 30	07 16	04 05	04 55	05 32	05 59
60	05 40	06 28	07 10	03 49	04 40	05 19	05 50
N 58	05 41	06 26	07 06	03 35	04 27	05 09	05 42
56	05 41	06 24	07 02	03 23	04 16	05 00	05 35
54	05 41	06 22	06 58	03 13	04 07	04 52	05 29
52	05 42	06 21	06 55	03 04	03 58	04 44	05 23
50	05 42	06 19	06 52	02 56	03 50	04 38	05 18
45	05 41	06 15	06 45	02 39	03 34	04 23	05 07
N 40	05 41	06 12	06 40	02 24	03 20	04 12	04 58
35	05 40	06 09	06 35	02 12	03 09	04 02	04 50
30	05 38	06 06	06 30	02 02	02 59	03 53	04 43
20	05 35	06 01	06 23	01 44	02 42	03 38	04 31
N 10	05 30	05 55	06 16	01 28	02 27	03 24	04 20
0	05 24	05 49	06 10	01 14	02 12	03 12	04 10
S 10	05 17	05 42	06 03	00 59	01 58	02 59	04 00
20	05 07	05 34	05 56	00 43	01 43	02 46	03 50
30	04 55	05 23	05 48	00 26	01 26	02 31	03 38
35	04 46	05 17	05 43	00 15	01 16	02 22	03 31
40	04 36	05 10	05 38	00 03	01 05	02 12	03 23
45	04 24	05 01	05 31	24 51	00 51	02 00	03 13
S 50	04 08	04 50	05 24	24 35	00 35	01 45	03 02
52	04 00	04 44	05 20	24 27	00 27	01 38	02 56
54	03 51	04 38	05 16	24 18	00 18	01 31	02 51
56	03 41	04 32	05 12	24 08	00 08	01 22	02 44
58	03 29	04 24	05 07	23 57	25 13	01 13	02 37
S 60	03 15	04 16	05 01	23 45	25 02	01 02	02 28

Twilight / Moonset

Lat.	Sunset	Civil	Naut.	Moonset 24	25	26	27
°	h m	h m	h m	h m	h m	h m	h m
N 72	16 29	17 41	18 59	■■■■	■■■■	11 30	13 49
N 70	16 41	17 45	18 56	08 35	10 13	12 11	14 11
68	16 51	17 49	18 53	09 33	10 56	12 38	14 28
66	16 59	17 52	18 51	10 07	11 25	12 59	14 42
64	17 06	17 55	18 50	10 32	11 46	13 16	14 53
62	17 12	17 57	18 48	10 51	12 04	13 29	15 02
60	17 17	17 59	18 47	11 07	12 18	13 41	15 10
N 58	17 21	18 01	18 47	11 21	12 31	13 51	15 18
56	17 25	18 03	18 46	11 33	12 41	14 00	15 24
54	17 29	18 05	18 46	11 43	12 51	14 07	15 29
52	17 32	18 06	18 45	11 52	12 59	14 14	15 34
50	17 35	18 08	18 45	12 00	13 06	14 20	15 39
45	17 42	18 11	18 45	12 17	13 22	14 34	15 49
N 40	17 47	18 14	18 46	12 31	13 35	14 45	15 57
35	17 52	18 17	18 47	12 43	13 47	14 54	16 04
30	17 56	18 20	18 48	12 54	13 56	15 02	16 10
20	18 03	18 26	18 51	13 11	14 13	15 16	16 20
N 10	18 10	18 31	18 56	13 27	14 27	15 28	16 29
0	18 16	18 37	19 02	13 42	14 41	15 40	16 38
S 10	18 23	18 44	19 09	13 56	14 54	15 51	16 46
20	18 30	18 52	19 18	14 11	15 08	16 03	16 55
30	18 38	19 02	19 31	14 29	15 25	16 17	17 05
35	18 42	19 08	19 39	14 39	15 34	16 24	17 11
40	18 48	19 16	19 49	14 51	15 45	16 33	17 17
45	18 54	19 24	20 01	15 05	15 57	16 44	17 25
S 50	19 01	19 35	20 17	15 22	16 12	16 56	17 34
52	19 05	19 40	20 24	15 30	16 20	17 02	17 38
54	19 09	19 46	20 33	15 38	16 27	17 08	17 43
56	19 13	19 53	20 43	15 48	16 36	17 15	17 48
58	19 18	20 00	20 54	15 59	16 46	17 23	17 53
S 60	19 23	20 08	21 08	16 12	16 58	17 32	18 00

SUN / MOON

Day	SUN Eqn. of Time 00h	12h	Mer. Pass.	MOON Mer. Pass. Upper	Lower	Age	Phase
d	m s	m s	h m	h m	h m	d	%
24	13 15	13 11	12 13	07 28	19 57	25	31
25	13 06	13 02	12 13	08 27	20 56	26	20
26	12 57	12 52	12 13	09 26	21 55	27	12

UT	ARIES GHA	VENUS −4.8 GHA	Dec	MARS −0.5 GHA	Dec	JUPITER −2.4 GHA	Dec	SATURN +0.4 GHA	Dec	STARS Name	SHA	Dec
d h	° ′	° ′	° ′	° ′	° ′	° ′	° ′	° ′	° ′		° ′	° ′
27 00	156 45.2	221 06.1	S16 37.7	310 13.0	S 7 57.5	55 16.6	N23 15.0	285 13.4	S16 19.6	Acamar	315 18.1	S40 15.2
01	171 47.6	236 06.6	37.7	325 15.4	57.5	70 19.1	15.0	300 15.8	19.6	Achernar	335 26.9	S57 10.2
02	186 50.1	251 07.2	37.7	340 17.8	57.5	85 21.6	15.1	315 18.3	19.6	Acrux	173 08.0	S63 10.6
03	201 52.6	266 07.7 ..	37.6	355 20.2 ..	57.5	100 24.1 ..	15.1	330 20.7 ..	19.6	Adhara	255 11.9	S28 59.9
04	216 55.0	281 08.2	37.6	10 22.6	57.6	115 26.7	15.1	345 23.2	19.6	Aldebaran	290 48.8	N16 32.1
05	231 57.5	296 08.7	37.6	25 24.9	57.6	130 29.2	15.1	0 25.6	19.6			
06	247 00.0	311 09.3	S16 37.5	40 27.3	S 7 57.6	145 31.7	N23 15.1	15 28.1	S16 19.6	Alioth	166 19.9	N55 52.7
07	262 02.4	326 09.8	37.5	55 29.7	57.6	160 34.3	15.1	30 30.5	19.6	Alkaid	152 58.2	N49 14.3
T 08	277 04.9	341 10.3	37.5	70 32.1	57.6	175 36.8	15.1	45 33.0	19.6	Al Na'ir	27 43.6	S46 53.5
H 09	292 07.4	356 10.8 ..	37.4	85 34.5 ..	57.6	190 39.3 ..	15.1	60 35.4 ..	19.6	Alnilam	275 45.8	S 1 11.9
U 10	307 09.8	11 11.3	37.4	100 36.9	57.6	205 41.8	15.1	75 37.9	19.6	Alphard	217 55.3	S 8 43.5
R 11	322 12.3	26 11.8	37.4	115 39.3	57.6	220 44.4	15.1	90 40.3	19.6			
S 12	337 14.7	41 12.3	S16 37.3	130 41.7	S 7 57.6	235 46.9	N23 15.1	105 42.8	S16 19.6	Alphecca	126 10.5	N26 39.9
D 13	352 17.2	56 12.8	37.3	145 44.1	57.6	250 49.4	15.1	120 45.2	19.6	Alpheratz	357 43.3	N29 10.1
A 14	7 19.7	71 13.3	37.2	160 46.5	57.6	265 51.9	15.2	135 47.6	19.6	Altair	62 08.0	N 8 54.4
Y 15	22 22.1	86 13.8 ..	37.2	175 48.9 ..	57.6	280 54.5 ..	15.2	150 50.1 ..	19.6	Ankaa	353 15.6	S42 13.9
16	37 24.6	101 14.3	37.2	190 51.3	57.6	295 57.0	15.2	165 52.5	19.6	Antares	112 25.6	S26 27.6
17	52 27.1	116 14.8	37.1	205 53.7	57.7	310 59.5	15.2	180 55.0	19.6			
18	67 29.5	131 15.3	S16 37.1	220 56.1	S 7 57.7	326 02.0	N23 15.2	195 57.4	S16 19.6	Arcturus	145 55.1	N19 06.4
19	82 32.0	146 15.8	37.0	235 58.5	57.7	341 04.6	15.2	210 59.9	19.6	Atria	107 27.0	S69 02.8
20	97 34.5	161 16.3	37.0	251 00.9	57.7	356 07.1	15.2	226 02.3	19.6	Avior	234 17.2	S59 33.7
21	112 36.9	176 16.8 ..	36.9	266 03.3 ..	57.7	11 09.6 ..	15.2	241 04.8 ..	19.5	Bellatrix	278 31.4	N 6 21.5
22	127 39.4	191 17.3	36.9	281 05.7	57.7	26 12.1	15.2	256 07.2	19.5	Betelgeuse	271 00.6	N 7 24.3
23	142 41.9	206 17.8	36.9	296 08.1	57.7	41 14.7	15.2	271 09.7	19.5			
28 00	157 44.3	221 18.3	S16 36.8	311 10.5	S 7 57.7	56 17.2	N23 15.2	286 12.1	S16 19.5	Canopus	263 55.7	S52 42.7
01	172 46.8	236 18.8	36.8	326 12.9	57.7	71 19.7	15.2	301 14.6	19.5	Capella	280 33.6	N46 00.7
02	187 49.2	251 19.3	36.7	341 15.3	57.7	86 22.2	15.2	316 17.0	19.5	Deneb	49 31.5	N45 19.8
03	202 51.7	266 19.7 ..	36.7	356 17.7 ..	57.7	101 24.7 ..	15.3	331 19.5 ..	19.5	Denebola	182 32.8	N14 29.3
04	217 54.2	281 20.2	36.6	11 20.2	57.7	116 27.3	15.3	346 21.9	19.5	Diphda	348 55.7	S17 54.7
05	232 56.6	296 20.7	36.6	26 22.6	57.7	131 29.8	15.3	1 24.4	19.5			
06	247 59.1	311 21.2	S16 36.5	41 25.0	S 7 57.7	146 32.3	N23 15.3	16 26.8	S16 19.5	Dubhe	193 50.5	N61 40.3
07	263 01.6	326 21.7	36.5	56 27.4	57.7	161 34.8	15.3	31 29.3	19.5	Elnath	278 11.9	N28 37.0
08	278 04.0	341 22.1	36.4	71 29.8	57.7	176 37.3	15.3	46 31.7	19.5	Eltanin	90 46.1	N51 29.1
F 09	293 06.5	356 22.6 ..	36.4	86 32.2 ..	57.7	191 39.9 ..	15.3	61 34.2 ..	19.5	Enif	33 46.9	N 9 56.4
R 10	308 09.0	11 23.1	36.3	101 34.7	57.7	206 42.4	15.3	76 36.7	19.5	Fomalhaut	15 23.8	S29 32.8
I 11	323 11.4	26 23.5	36.3	116 37.1	57.7	221 44.9	15.3	91 39.1	19.5			
D 12	338 13.9	41 24.0	S16 36.2	131 39.5	S 7 57.7	236 47.4	N23 15.3	106 41.6	S16 19.5	Gacrux	171 59.7	S57 11.5
A 13	353 16.3	56 24.5	36.1	146 41.9	57.7	251 49.9	15.3	121 44.0	19.5	Gienah	175 51.5	S17 37.4
Y 14	8 18.8	71 24.9	36.1	161 44.4	57.7	266 52.5	15.3	136 46.5	19.5	Hadar	148 46.7	S60 26.3
15	23 21.3	86 25.4 ..	36.0	176 46.8 ..	57.7	281 55.0 ..	15.3	151 48.9 ..	19.4	Hamal	328 00.4	N23 31.7
16	38 23.7	101 25.9	36.0	191 49.2	57.7	296 57.5	15.4	166 51.4	19.4	Kaus Aust.	83 43.3	S34 22.4
17	53 26.2	116 26.3	35.9	206 51.6	57.7	312 00.0	15.4	181 53.8	19.4			
18	68 28.7	131 26.8	S16 35.9	221 54.1	S 7 57.6	327 02.5	N23 15.4	196 56.3	S16 19.4	Kochab	137 19.7	N74 05.6
19	83 31.1	146 27.2	35.8	236 56.5	57.6	342 05.0	15.4	211 58.7	19.4	Markab	13 38.1	N15 16.9
20	98 33.6	161 27.7	35.7	251 58.9	57.6	357 07.5	15.4	227 01.2	19.4	Menkar	314 14.6	N 4 08.5
21	113 36.1	176 28.2 ..	35.7	267 01.4 ..	57.6	12 10.1 ..	15.4	242 03.6 ..	19.4	Menkent	148 06.7	S36 26.3
22	128 38.5	191 28.6	35.6	282 03.8	57.6	27 12.6	15.4	257 06.1	19.4	Miaplacidus	221 38.6	S69 46.8
23	143 41.0	206 29.1	35.6	297 06.2	57.6	42 15.1	15.4	272 08.5	19.4			
1 00	158 43.5	221 29.5	S16 35.5	312 08.7	S 7 57.6	57 17.6	N23 15.4	287 11.0	S16 19.4	Mirfak	308 39.7	N49 54.7
01	173 45.9	236 29.9	35.4	327 11.1	57.6	72 20.1	15.4	302 13.5	19.4	Nunki	75 57.9	S26 16.5
02	188 48.4	251 30.4	35.4	342 13.6	57.6	87 22.6	15.4	317 15.9	19.4	Peacock	53 19.0	S56 41.1
03	203 50.8	266 30.8 ..	35.3	357 16.0 ..	57.6	102 25.1 ..	15.4	332 18.4 ..	19.4	Pollux	243 26.9	N27 59.3
04	218 53.3	281 31.3	35.3	12 18.4	57.6	117 27.6	15.4	347 20.8	19.4	Procyon	244 59.0	N 5 11.0
05	233 55.8	296 31.7	35.2	27 20.9	57.6	132 30.2	15.4	2 23.3	19.4			
06	248 58.2	311 32.2	S16 35.1	42 23.3	S 7 57.5	147 32.7	N23 15.4	17 25.7	S16 19.4	Rasalhague	96 06.1	N12 33.0
07	264 00.7	326 32.6	35.1	57 25.8	57.5	162 35.2	15.5	32 28.2	19.3	Regulus	207 42.7	N11 53.6
S 08	279 03.2	341 33.0	35.0	72 28.2	57.5	177 37.7	15.5	47 30.6	19.3	Rigel	281 11.5	S 8 11.5
A 09	294 05.6	356 33.5 ..	34.9	87 30.7 ..	57.5	192 40.2 ..	15.5	62 33.1 ..	19.3	Rigil Kent.	139 50.6	S60 53.3
T 10	309 08.1	11 33.9	34.9	102 33.1	57.5	207 42.7	15.5	77 35.6	19.3	Sabik	102 12.0	S15 44.4
U 11	324 10.6	26 34.3	34.8	117 35.6	57.5	222 45.2	15.5	92 38.0	19.3			
R 12	339 13.0	41 34.8	S16 34.7	132 38.0	S 7 57.5	237 47.7	N23 15.5	107 40.5	S16 19.3	Schedar	349 40.3	N56 37.0
D 13	354 15.5	56 35.2	34.6	147 40.5	57.5	252 50.2	15.5	122 42.9	19.3	Shaula	96 21.3	S37 06.6
A 14	9 18.0	71 35.6	34.6	162 42.9	57.5	267 52.7	15.5	137 45.4	19.3	Sirius	258 33.1	S16 44.5
Y 15	24 20.4	86 36.0 ..	34.5	177 45.4 ..	57.4	282 55.3 ..	15.5	152 47.8 ..	19.3	Spica	158 30.5	S11 14.2
16	39 22.9	101 36.5	34.4	192 47.8	57.4	297 57.8	15.5	167 50.3	19.3	Suhail	222 51.6	S43 29.7
17	54 25.3	116 36.9	34.4	207 50.3	57.4	313 00.3	15.5	182 52.7	19.3			
18	69 27.8	131 37.3	S16 34.3	222 52.8	S 7 57.4	328 02.8	N23 15.5	197 55.2	S16 19.3	Vega	80 38.8	N38 47.7
19	84 30.3	146 37.7	34.2	237 55.2	57.4	343 05.3	15.5	212 57.7	19.3	Zuben'ubi	137 04.7	S16 06.0
20	99 32.7	161 38.1	34.1	252 57.7	57.4	358 07.8	15.5	228 00.1	19.3		SHA	Mer.Pass.
21	114 35.2	176 38.6 ..	34.1	268 00.2 ..	57.3	13 10.3 ..	15.5	243 02.6 ..	19.2		° ′	h m
22	129 37.7	191 39.0	34.0	283 02.6	57.3	28 12.8	15.6	258 05.0	19.2	Venus	63 14.0	9 14
23	144 40.1	206 39.4	33.9	298 05.1	57.3	43 15.3	15.6	273 07.5	19.2	Mars	153 26.2	3 15
	h m									Jupiter	258 32.9	20 11
Mer.Pass. 13 26.8		v 0.5	d 0.1	v 2.4	d 0.0	v 2.5	d 0.0	v 2.5	d 0.0	Saturn	128 27.8	4 54

UT	SUN GHA	SUN Dec	MOON GHA	MOON v	MOON Dec	MOON d	MOON HP
d h	° ′	° ′	° ′	′	° ′	′	′
27 00	176 48.3	S 8 27.2	210 00.5	6.1	S13 55.6	8.6	60.7
01	191 48.4	26.3	224 25.6	6.0	13 47.0	8.8	60.7
02	206 48.5	25.3	238 50.6	6.1	13 38.2	8.8	60.8
03	221 48.6	.. 24.4	253 15.7	6.2	13 29.4	8.9	60.8
04	236 48.7	23.4	267 40.9	6.2	13 20.5	9.0	60.8
05	251 48.9	22.5	282 06.1	6.2	13 11.5	9.1	60.8
06	266 49.0	S 8 21.6	296 31.3	6.2	S13 02.4	9.2	60.8
07	281 49.1	20.6	310 56.5	6.3	12 53.2	9.3	60.8
T 08	296 49.2	19.7	325 21.8	6.3	12 43.9	9.4	60.8
H 09	311 49.3	.. 18.7	339 47.1	6.4	12 34.5	9.4	60.8
U 10	326 49.4	17.8	354 12.5	6.4	12 25.1	9.6	60.8
R 11	341 49.5	16.9	8 37.9	6.4	12 15.5	9.6	60.8
S 12	356 49.6	S 8 15.9	23 03.3	6.5	S12 05.9	9.7	60.8
D 13	11 49.7	15.0	37 28.8	6.5	11 56.2	9.8	60.8
A 14	26 49.8	14.0	51 54.3	6.6	11 46.4	9.9	60.8
Y 15	41 50.0	.. 13.1	66 19.9	6.5	11 36.5	9.9	60.8
16	56 50.1	12.1	80 45.4	6.7	11 26.6	10.1	60.8
17	71 50.2	11.2	95 11.1	6.6	11 16.5	10.1	60.8
18	86 50.3	S 8 10.3	109 36.7	6.7	S11 06.4	10.2	60.8
19	101 50.4	09.3	124 02.4	6.8	10 56.2	10.2	60.8
20	116 50.5	08.4	138 28.2	6.8	10 46.0	10.4	60.8
21	131 50.6	.. 07.4	152 54.0	6.8	10 35.6	10.4	60.8
22	146 50.7	06.5	167 19.8	6.9	10 25.2	10.4	60.8
23	161 50.8	05.5	181 45.7	6.9	10 14.8	10.6	60.8
28 00	176 51.0	S 8 04.6	196 11.6	6.9	S10 04.2	10.6	60.8
01	191 51.1	03.7	210 37.5	7.0	9 53.6	10.6	60.8
02	206 51.2	02.7	225 03.5	7.0	9 43.0	10.8	60.8
03	221 51.3	.. 01.8	239 29.5	7.1	9 32.2	10.8	60.8
04	236 51.4	8 00.8	253 55.6	7.1	9 21.4	10.8	60.8
05	251 51.5	7 59.9	268 21.7	7.2	9 10.6	10.9	60.8
06	266 51.6	S 7 58.9	282 47.9	7.1	S 8 59.7	11.0	60.8
07	281 51.8	58.0	297 14.0	7.3	8 48.7	11.0	60.8
08	296 51.9	57.0	311 40.3	7.3	8 37.7	11.1	60.8
F 09	311 52.0	.. 56.1	326 06.6	7.3	8 26.6	11.1	60.8
R 10	326 52.1	55.2	340 32.9	7.3	8 15.5	11.2	60.8
I 11	341 52.2	54.2	354 59.2	7.4	8 04.3	11.2	60.8
D 12	356 52.3	S 7 53.3	9 25.6	7.5	S 7 53.1	11.3	60.8
A 13	11 52.4	52.3	23 52.1	7.4	7 41.8	11.4	60.8
Y 14	26 52.6	51.4	38 18.5	7.6	7 30.4	11.3	60.8
15	41 52.7	.. 50.4	52 45.1	7.5	7 19.1	11.4	60.7
16	56 52.8	49.5	67 11.6	7.6	7 07.7	11.5	60.7
17	71 52.9	48.5	81 38.2	7.7	6 56.2	11.5	60.7
18	86 53.0	S 7 47.6	96 04.9	7.7	S 6 44.7	11.6	60.7
19	101 53.1	46.6	110 31.6	7.7	6 33.1	11.5	60.7
20	116 53.3	45.7	124 58.3	7.7	6 21.6	11.6	60.7
21	131 53.4	.. 44.7	139 25.0	7.9	6 10.0	11.7	60.7
22	146 53.5	43.8	153 51.9	7.8	5 58.3	11.7	60.7
23	161 53.6	42.8	168 18.7	7.9	5 46.6	11.7	60.7
1 00	176 53.7	S 7 41.9	182 45.6	7.9	S 5 34.9	11.7	60.6
01	191 53.8	40.9	197 12.5	8.0	5 23.2	11.8	60.6
02	206 54.0	40.0	211 39.5	8.0	5 11.4	11.8	60.6
03	221 54.1	.. 39.0	226 06.5	8.0	4 59.6	11.8	60.6
04	236 54.2	38.1	240 33.5	8.1	4 47.8	11.9	60.6
05	251 54.3	37.1	255 00.6	8.1	4 35.9	11.8	60.6
06	266 54.4	S 7 36.2	269 27.7	8.2	S 4 24.1	11.9	60.5
07	281 54.6	35.2	283 54.9	8.2	4 12.2	11.9	60.5
S 08	296 54.7	34.3	298 22.1	8.2	4 00.3	12.0	60.5
A 09	311 54.8	.. 33.3	312 49.3	8.3	3 48.3	11.9	60.5
T 10	326 54.9	32.4	327 16.6	8.3	3 36.4	12.0	60.5
U 11	341 55.0	31.4	341 43.9	8.3	3 24.4	12.0	60.5
R 12	356 55.2	S 7 30.5	356 11.2	8.4	S 3 12.5	12.0	60.4
D 13	11 55.3	29.5	10 38.6	8.4	3 00.5	12.0	60.4
A 14	26 55.4	28.6	25 06.0	8.5	2 48.5	12.0	60.4
Y 15	41 55.5	.. 27.6	39 33.5	8.5	2 36.5	12.0	60.4
16	56 55.7	26.7	54 01.0	8.5	2 24.5	12.1	60.4
17	71 55.8	25.7	68 28.5	8.5	2 12.4	12.0	60.3
18	86 55.9	S 7 24.8	82 56.0	8.6	S 2 00.4	12.0	60.3
19	101 56.0	23.8	97 23.6	8.7	1 48.4	12.0	60.3
20	116 56.1	22.9	111 51.3	8.6	1 36.4	12.1	60.3
21	131 56.3	.. 21.9	126 18.9	8.7	1 24.3	12.0	60.2
22	146 56.4	21.0	140 46.6	8.7	1 12.3	12.0	60.2
23	161 56.5	20.0	155 14.3	8.8	S 1 00.3	12.0	60.2
	SD 16.2	d 0.9	SD 16.6		16.6		16.5

Twilight / Sunrise / Moonrise

Lat.	Naut.	Civil	Sunrise	27	28	1	2
°	h m	h m	h m	h m	h m	h m	h m
N 72	05 15	06 33	07 43	07 18	07 08	06 59	06 51
N 70	05 20	06 30	07 32	06 55	06 54	06 53	06 52
68	05 23	06 27	07 24	06 36	06 43	06 48	06 52
66	05 26	06 25	07 17	06 22	06 34	06 44	06 52
64	05 28	06 23	07 11	06 09	06 26	06 40	06 53
62	05 30	06 21	07 06	05 59	06 20	06 37	06 53
60	05 32	06 20	07 02	05 50	06 14	06 35	06 53
N 58	05 33	06 18	06 58	05 42	06 09	06 32	06 53
56	05 34	06 17	06 54	05 35	06 04	06 30	06 54
54	05 35	06 16	06 51	05 29	06 00	06 28	06 54
52	05 35	06 14	06 48	05 23	05 57	06 26	06 54
50	05 36	06 13	06 46	05 18	05 53	06 25	06 54
45	05 37	06 10	06 40	05 07	05 46	06 21	06 55
N 40	05 37	06 08	06 35	04 58	05 40	06 18	06 55
35	05 36	06 06	06 31	04 50	05 34	06 16	06 55
30	05 35	06 03	06 27	04 43	05 30	06 13	06 55
20	05 33	05 59	06 21	04 31	05 21	06 10	06 56
N 10	05 29	05 54	06 15	04 20	05 14	06 06	06 56
0	05 24	05 48	06 09	04 10	05 08	06 03	06 57
S 10	05 18	05 42	06 03	04 00	05 01	06 00	06 57
20	05 09	05 35	05 57	03 50	04 54	05 56	06 58
30	04 57	05 26	05 50	03 38	04 45	05 52	06 58
35	04 49	05 20	05 46	03 31	04 41	05 50	06 59
40	04 40	05 13	05 41	03 23	04 35	05 48	06 59
45	04 29	05 05	05 35	03 13	04 29	05 45	06 59
S 50	04 14	04 55	05 29	03 02	04 21	05 41	07 00
52	04 07	04 50	05 26	02 56	04 18	05 40	07 00
54	03 59	04 45	05 22	02 51	04 14	05 38	07 01
56	03 50	04 39	05 18	02 44	04 10	05 36	07 01
58	03 39	04 32	05 14	02 37	04 05	05 34	07 01
S 60	03 26	04 24	05 09	02 28	03 59	05 31	07 02

Sunset / Twilight / Moonset

Lat.	Sunset	Civil	Naut.	27	28	1	2
°	h m	h m	h m	h m	h m	h m	h m
N 72	16 44	17 54	19 12	13 49	15 58	18 01	20 01
N 70	16 54	17 57	19 08	14 11	16 09	18 05	19 56
68	17 03	17 59	19 04	14 28	16 18	18 07	19 53
66	17 09	18 01	19 01	14 42	16 26	18 09	19 50
64	17 15	18 03	18 58	14 53	16 32	18 11	19 47
62	17 20	18 05	18 56	15 02	16 38	18 12	19 45
60	17 24	18 07	18 55	15 10	16 42	18 14	19 43
N 58	17 28	18 08	18 53	15 16	16 46	18 15	19 42
56	17 32	18 09	18 52	15 24	16 50	18 16	19 40
54	17 35	18 10	18 51	15 29	16 53	18 17	19 39
52	17 38	18 12	18 51	15 34	16 56	18 18	19 38
50	17 40	18 13	18 50	15 39	16 59	18 19	19 37
45	17 46	18 15	18 49	15 49	17 05	18 20	19 34
N 40	17 51	18 18	18 49	15 57	17 10	18 22	19 32
35	17 55	18 20	18 49	16 04	17 14	18 23	19 31
30	17 58	18 22	18 50	16 10	17 17	18 24	19 29
20	18 05	18 27	18 52	16 20	17 24	18 26	19 26
N 10	18 10	18 32	18 56	16 29	17 29	18 27	19 24
0	18 16	18 37	19 01	16 38	17 34	18 29	19 22
S 10	18 21	18 43	19 07	16 46	17 39	18 30	19 20
20	18 27	18 50	19 16	16 55	17 44	18 31	19 17
30	18 34	18 59	19 27	17 05	17 50	18 33	19 14
35	18 39	19 04	19 35	17 11	17 54	18 34	19 13
40	18 43	19 11	19 44	17 17	17 58	18 35	19 11
45	18 49	19 19	19 55	17 25	18 02	18 36	19 09
S 50	18 55	19 29	20 10	17 34	18 07	18 38	19 07
52	18 58	19 33	20 16	17 38	18 10	18 38	19 06
54	19 02	19 39	20 24	17 43	18 12	18 39	19 04
56	19 05	19 44	20 33	17 48	18 15	18 40	19 03
58	19 09	19 51	20 44	17 53	18 18	18 40	19 02
S 60	19 14	19 59	20 56	18 00	18 22	18 41	19 00

SUN / MOON

Day	Eqn. of Time 00ʰ	Eqn. of Time 12ʰ	Mer. Pass.	Mer. Pass. Upper	Mer. Pass. Lower	Age	Phase
d	m s	m s	h m	h m	h m	d	%
27	12 47	12 42	12 13	10 24	22 53	28	5
28	12 36	12 31	12 13	11 21	23 49	29	1
1	12 25	12 20	12 12	12 16	24 43	00	0

UT (d h)	ARIES GHA	VENUS −4.7 GHA	Dec	MARS −0.5 GHA	Dec	JUPITER −2.4 GHA	Dec	SATURN +0.4 GHA	Dec	STARS Name	SHA	Dec
2 00	159 42.6	221 39.8	S16 33.8	313 07.5	S 7 57.3	58 17.8	N23 15.6	288 10.0	S16 19.2	Acamar	315 18.2	S40 15.2
01	174 45.1	236 40.2	33.8	328 10.0	57.3	73 20.3	15.6	303 12.4	19.2	Achernar	335 26.9	S57 10.2
02	189 47.5	251 40.6	33.7	343 12.5	57.3	88 22.8	15.6	318 14.9	19.2	Acrux	173 08.0	S63 10.6
03	204 50.0	266 41.0 ..	33.6	358 15.0 ..	57.2	103 25.3 ..	15.6	333 17.3 ..	19.2	Adhara	255 11.9	S28 59.9
04	219 52.4	281 41.4	33.5	13 17.4	57.2	118 27.8	15.6	348 19.8	19.2	Aldebaran	290 48.8	N16 32.1
05	234 54.9	296 41.8	33.4	28 19.9	57.2	133 30.3	15.6	3 22.3	19.2			
06	249 57.4	311 42.2	S16 33.3	43 22.4	S 7 57.2	148 32.8	N23 15.6	18 24.7	S16 19.2	Alioth	166 19.8	N55 52.7
07	264 59.8	326 42.6	33.3	58 24.9	57.2	163 35.3	15.6	33 27.2	19.2	Alkaid	152 58.2	N49 14.3
08	280 02.3	341 43.0	33.2	73 27.3	57.1	178 37.8	15.6	48 29.6	19.2	Al Na'ir	27 43.6	S46 53.4
S 09	295 04.8	356 43.4 ..	33.1	88 29.8 ..	57.1	193 40.3 ..	15.6	63 32.1 ..	19.2	Alnilam	275 45.8	S 1 11.9
U 10	310 07.2	11 43.8	33.0	103 32.3	57.1	208 42.8	15.6	78 34.6	19.1	Alphard	217 55.3	S 8 43.5
N 11	325 09.7	26 44.2	32.9	118 34.8	57.1	223 45.3	15.6	93 37.0	19.1			
D 12	340 12.2	41 44.6	S16 32.8	133 37.3	S 7 57.1	238 47.8	N23 15.6	108 39.5	S16 19.1	Alphecca	126 10.5	N26 39.9
A 13	355 14.6	56 45.0	32.8	148 39.7	57.0	253 50.3	15.6	123 41.9	19.1	Alpheratz	357 43.3	N29 10.1
Y 14	10 17.1	71 45.4	32.7	163 42.2	57.0	268 52.8	15.7	138 44.4	19.1	Altair	62 08.0	N 8 54.4
15	25 19.6	86 45.8 ..	32.6	178 44.7 ..	57.0	283 55.3 ..	15.7	153 46.9 ..	19.1	Ankaa	353 15.6	S42 13.9
16	40 22.0	101 46.2	32.5	193 47.2	57.0	298 57.8	15.7	168 49.3	19.1	Antares	112 25.6	S26 27.6
17	55 24.5	116 46.5	32.4	208 49.7	56.9	314 00.3	15.7	183 51.8	19.1			
18	70 26.9	131 46.9	S16 32.3	223 52.2	S 7 56.9	329 02.8	N23 15.7	198 54.2	S16 19.1	Arcturus	145 55.1	N19 06.4
19	85 29.4	146 47.3	32.2	238 54.7	56.9	344 05.3	15.7	213 56.7	19.1	Atria	107 27.0	S69 02.8
20	100 31.9	161 47.7	32.1	253 57.2	56.9	359 07.8	15.7	228 59.2	19.1	Avior	234 17.2	S59 33.7
21	115 34.3	176 48.1 ..	32.0	268 59.6 ..	56.8	14 10.3 ..	15.7	244 01.6 ..	19.1	Bellatrix	278 31.4	N 6 21.5
22	130 36.8	191 48.4	31.9	284 02.1	56.8	29 12.8	15.7	259 04.1	19.0	Betelgeuse	271 00.6	N 7 24.3
23	145 39.3	206 48.8	31.9	299 04.6	56.8	44 15.3	15.7	274 06.6	19.0			
3 00	160 41.7	221 49.2	S16 31.8	314 07.1	S 7 56.8	59 17.8	N23 15.7	289 09.0	S16 19.0	Canopus	263 55.7	S52 42.7
01	175 44.2	236 49.6	31.7	329 09.6	56.7	74 20.3	15.7	304 11.5	19.0	Capella	280 33.6	N46 00.7
02	190 46.7	251 49.9	31.6	344 12.1	56.7	89 22.8	15.7	319 13.9	19.0	Deneb	49 31.5	N45 19.8
03	205 49.1	266 50.3 ..	31.5	359 14.6 ..	56.7	104 25.3 ..	15.7	334 16.4 ..	19.0	Denebola	182 32.8	N14 29.3
04	220 51.6	281 50.7	31.4	14 17.1	56.6	119 27.8	15.7	349 18.9	19.0	Diphda	348 55.7	S17 54.7
05	235 54.0	296 51.1	31.3	29 19.6	56.6	134 30.3	15.7	4 21.3	19.0			
06	250 56.5	311 51.4	S16 31.2	44 22.1	S 7 56.6	149 32.7	N23 15.7	19 23.8	S16 19.0	Dubhe	193 50.5	N61 40.3
07	265 59.0	326 51.8	31.1	59 24.6	56.5	164 35.2	15.7	34 26.3	19.0	Elnath	278 11.9	N28 37.0
08	281 01.4	341 52.1	31.0	74 27.1	56.5	179 37.7	15.8	49 28.7	19.0	Eltanin	90 46.1	N51 29.1
M 09	296 03.9	356 52.5 ..	30.9	89 29.7 ..	56.5	194 40.2 ..	15.8	64 31.2 ..	19.0	Enif	33 46.9	N 9 56.4
O 10	311 06.4	11 52.9	30.8	104 32.2	56.5	209 42.7	15.8	79 33.7	18.9	Fomalhaut	15 23.8	S29 32.8
N 11	326 08.8	26 53.2	30.7	119 34.7	56.4	224 45.2	15.8	94 36.1	18.9			
D 12	341 11.3	41 53.6	S16 30.6	134 37.2	S 7 56.4	239 47.7	N23 15.8	109 38.6	S16 18.9	Gacrux	171 59.7	S57 11.5
A 13	356 13.8	56 53.9	30.5	149 39.7	56.4	254 50.2	15.8	124 41.1	18.9	Gienah	175 51.5	S17 37.4
Y 14	11 16.2	71 54.3	30.4	164 42.2	56.3	269 52.7	15.8	139 43.5	18.9	Hadar	148 46.7	S60 26.3
15	26 18.7	86 54.7 ..	30.3	179 44.7 ..	56.3	284 55.2 ..	15.8	154 46.0 ..	18.9	Hamal	328 00.4	N23 31.7
16	41 21.2	101 55.0	30.2	194 47.2	56.3	299 57.7	15.8	169 48.5	18.9	Kaus Aust.	83 43.3	S34 22.4
17	56 23.6	116 55.4	30.1	209 49.8	56.2	315 00.1	15.8	184 50.9	18.9			
18	71 26.1	131 55.7	S16 29.9	224 52.3	S 7 56.2	330 02.6	N23 15.8	199 53.4	S16 18.9	Kochab	137 19.6	N74 05.6
19	86 28.5	146 56.1	29.8	239 54.8	56.2	345 05.1	15.8	214 55.9	18.9	Markab	13 38.1	N15 16.9
20	101 31.0	161 56.4	29.7	254 57.3	56.1	0 07.6	15.8	229 58.3	18.9	Menkar	314 14.6	N 4 08.5
21	116 33.5	176 56.7 ..	29.6	269 59.9 ..	56.1	15 10.1 ..	15.8	245 00.8 ..	18.8	Menkent	148 06.7	S36 26.3
22	131 35.9	191 57.1	29.5	285 02.4	56.0	30 12.6	15.8	260 03.3	18.8	Miaplacidus	221 38.6	S69 46.8
23	146 38.4	206 57.4	29.4	300 04.9	56.0	45 15.1	15.8	275 05.7	18.8			
4 00	161 40.9	221 57.8	S16 29.3	315 07.4	S 7 56.0	60 17.6	N23 15.8	290 08.2	S16 18.8	Mirfak	308 39.7	N49 54.7
01	176 43.3	236 58.1	29.2	330 10.0	55.9	75 20.0	15.8	305 10.7	18.8	Nunki	75 57.9	S26 16.5
02	191 45.8	251 58.4	29.1	345 12.5	55.9	90 22.5	15.8	320 13.1	18.8	Peacock	53 19.0	S56 41.1
03	206 48.3	266 58.8 ..	29.0	0 15.0 ..	55.9	105 25.0 ..	15.9	335 15.6 ..	18.8	Pollux	243 26.9	N27 59.3
04	221 50.7	281 59.1	28.8	15 17.5	55.8	120 27.5	15.9	350 18.1	18.8	Procyon	244 59.0	N 5 11.0
05	236 53.2	296 59.5	28.7	30 20.1	55.8	135 30.0	15.9	5 20.5	18.8			
06	251 55.6	311 59.8	S16 28.6	45 22.6	S 7 55.7	150 32.5	N23 15.9	20 23.0	S16 18.8	Rasalhague	96 06.1	N12 33.0
07	266 58.1	327 00.1	28.5	60 25.1	55.7	165 34.9	15.9	35 25.5	18.7	Regulus	207 42.7	N11 53.6
08	282 00.6	342 00.4	28.4	75 27.7	55.7	180 37.4	15.9	50 27.9	18.7	Rigel	281 11.5	S 8 11.5
T 09	297 03.0	357 00.8 ..	28.3	90 30.2 ..	55.6	195 39.9 ..	15.9	65 30.4 ..	18.7	Rigil Kent.	139 50.6	S60 53.3
U 10	312 05.5	12 01.1	28.1	105 32.8	55.6	210 42.4	15.9	80 32.9	18.7	Sabik	102 12.0	S15 44.4
E 11	327 08.0	27 01.4	28.0	120 35.3	55.5	225 44.9	15.9	95 35.3	18.7			
S 12	342 10.4	42 01.8	S16 27.9	135 37.8	S 7 55.5	240 47.4	N23 15.9	110 37.8	S16 18.7	Schedar	349 40.4	N56 37.0
D 13	357 12.9	57 02.1	27.8	150 40.4	55.4	255 49.8	15.9	125 40.3	18.7	Shaula	96 21.3	S37 06.6
A 14	12 15.4	72 02.4	27.7	165 42.9	55.4	270 52.3	15.9	140 42.8	18.7	Sirius	258 33.1	S16 44.5
Y 15	27 17.8	87 02.7 ..	27.5	180 45.5 ..	55.4	285 54.8 ..	15.9	155 45.2 ..	18.7	Spica	158 30.5	S11 14.2
16	42 20.3	102 03.0	27.4	195 48.0	55.3	300 57.3	15.9	170 47.7	18.7	Suhail	222 51.6	S43 29.7
17	57 22.8	117 03.4	27.3	210 50.6	55.3	315 59.8	15.9	185 50.2	18.6			
18	72 25.2	132 03.7	S16 27.2	225 53.1	S 7 55.2	331 02.2	N23 15.9	200 52.6	S16 18.6	Vega	80 38.8	N38 47.7
19	87 27.7	147 04.0	27.1	240 55.7	55.2	346 04.7	15.9	215 55.1	18.6	Zuben'ubi	137 04.7	S16 06.0
20	102 30.1	162 04.3	26.9	255 58.2	55.1	1 07.2	15.9	230 57.6	18.6			
21	117 32.6	177 04.6 ..	26.8	271 00.8 ..	55.1	16 09.7 ..	15.9	246 00.1 ..	18.6		SHA	Mer.Pass.
22	132 35.1	192 04.9	26.7	286 03.3	55.0	31 12.2	15.9	261 02.5	18.6	Venus	61 07.5	9 12
23	147 37.5	207 05.2	26.5	301 05.9	55.0	46 14.6	15.9	276 05.0	18.6	Mars	153 25.4	3 03
	h m									Jupiter	258 36.1	19 59
Mer. Pass. 13 15.0	v 0.4 d 0.1			v 2.5 d 0.0		v 2.5 d 0.0		v 2.5 d 0.0		Saturn	128 27.3	4 43

UT	SUN GHA	SUN Dec	MOON GHA	v	MOON Dec	d	HP
d h	° '	° '	° '	'	° '	'	'
2 00	176 56.6	S 7 19.1	169 42.1	8.8	S 0 48.3	12.0	60.2
01	191 56.8	18.1	184 09.9	8.8	0 36.3	12.0	60.1
02	206 56.9	17.2	198 37.7	8.9	0 24.3	12.0	60.1
03	221 57.0	.. 16.2	213 05.6	8.9	0 12.3	12.0	60.1
04	236 57.1	15.2	227 33.5	8.9	S 0 00.3	12.0	60.1
05	251 57.3	14.3	242 01.4	8.9	N 0 11.7	12.0	60.0
S 06	266 57.4	S 7 13.3	256 29.3	9.0	N 0 23.7	11.9	60.0
U 07	281 57.5	12.4	270 57.3	9.0	0 35.6	11.9	60.0
N 08	296 57.6	11.4	285 25.3	9.1	0 47.5	12.0	60.0
D 09	311 57.8	.. 10.5	299 53.4	9.0	0 59.5	11.9	59.9
A 10	326 57.9	09.5	314 21.4	9.1	1 11.4	11.8	59.9
Y 11	341 58.0	08.6	328 49.5	9.2	1 23.2	11.9	59.9
12	356 58.1	S 7 07.6	343 17.7	9.1	N 1 35.1	11.8	59.8
13	11 58.3	06.7	357 45.8	9.2	1 46.9	11.9	59.8
14	26 58.4	05.7	12 14.0	9.2	1 58.8	11.8	59.8
15	41 58.5	.. 04.7	26 42.2	9.3	2 10.6	11.7	59.8
16	56 58.6	03.8	41 10.5	9.2	2 22.3	11.8	59.7
17	71 58.8	02.8	55 38.7	9.3	2 34.1	11.7	59.7
18	86 58.9	S 7 01.9	70 07.0	9.3	N 2 45.8	11.7	59.7
19	101 59.0	00.9	84 35.3	9.4	2 57.5	11.6	59.6
20	116 59.1	7 00.0	99 03.7	9.3	3 09.1	11.6	59.6
21	131 59.3	6 59.0	113 32.0	9.4	3 20.7	11.6	59.6
22	146 59.4	58.0	128 00.4	9.4	3 32.3	11.6	59.5
23	161 59.5	57.1	142 28.8	9.5	3 43.9	11.5	59.5
3 00	176 59.7	S 6 56.1	156 57.3	9.4	N 3 55.4	11.5	59.5
01	191 59.8	55.2	171 25.7	9.5	4 06.9	11.4	59.4
02	206 59.9	54.2	185 54.2	9.5	4 18.3	11.4	59.4
03	222 00.0	.. 53.3	200 22.7	9.6	4 29.7	11.4	59.4
04	237 00.2	52.3	214 51.3	9.5	4 41.1	11.3	59.3
05	252 00.3	51.3	229 19.8	9.6	4 52.4	11.3	59.3
M 06	267 00.4	S 6 50.4	243 48.4	9.6	N 5 03.7	11.2	59.3
O 07	282 00.6	49.4	258 17.0	9.6	5 14.9	11.2	59.2
N 08	297 00.7	48.5	272 45.6	9.7	5 26.1	11.1	59.2
D 09	312 00.8	.. 47.5	287 14.3	9.6	5 37.2	11.1	59.2
A 10	327 01.0	46.6	301 42.9	9.7	5 48.3	11.1	59.1
Y 11	342 01.1	45.6	316 11.6	9.7	5 59.4	11.0	59.1
12	357 01.2	S 6 44.6	330 40.3	9.7	N 6 10.4	11.0	59.1
13	12 01.3	43.7	345 09.0	9.7	6 21.4	10.9	59.0
14	27 01.5	42.7	359 37.7	9.8	6 32.3	10.8	59.0
15	42 01.6	.. 41.8	14 06.5	9.8	6 43.1	10.8	59.0
16	57 01.7	40.8	28 35.3	9.8	6 53.9	10.8	58.9
17	72 01.9	39.8	43 04.1	9.8	7 04.7	10.6	58.9
18	87 02.0	S 6 38.9	57 32.9	9.8	N 7 15.3	10.7	58.8
19	102 02.1	37.9	72 01.7	9.9	7 26.0	10.6	58.8
20	117 02.3	37.0	86 30.6	9.8	7 36.6	10.5	58.8
21	132 02.4	.. 36.0	100 59.4	9.9	7 47.1	10.4	58.7
22	147 02.5	35.0	115 28.3	9.9	7 57.5	10.4	58.7
23	162 02.7	34.1	129 57.2	9.9	8 07.9	10.4	58.7
4 00	177 02.8	S 6 33.1	144 26.1	9.9	N 8 18.3	10.3	58.6
01	192 02.9	32.1	158 55.0	10.0	8 28.6	10.2	58.6
02	207 03.1	31.2	173 24.0	9.9	8 38.8	10.2	58.5
03	222 03.2	.. 30.2	187 52.9	10.0	8 49.0	10.1	58.5
04	237 03.3	29.3	202 21.9	10.0	8 59.1	10.0	58.5
05	252 03.5	28.3	216 50.9	10.0	9 09.1	9.9	58.4
T 06	267 03.6	S 6 27.3	231 19.9	10.0	N 9 19.0	9.9	58.4
U 07	282 03.7	26.4	245 48.9	10.0	9 28.9	9.9	58.4
E 08	297 03.9	25.4	260 17.9	10.1	9 38.8	9.7	58.3
S 09	312 04.0	.. 24.5	274 47.0	10.0	9 48.5	9.7	58.3
D 10	327 04.1	23.5	289 16.0	10.1	9 58.2	9.7	58.2
A 11	342 04.3	22.5	303 45.1	10.1	10 07.9	9.5	58.2
Y 12	357 04.4	S 6 21.6	318 14.2	10.1	N 10 17.4	9.5	58.2
13	12 04.6	20.6	332 43.3	10.1	10 26.9	9.4	58.1
14	27 04.7	19.6	347 12.4	10.1	10 36.3	9.4	58.1
15	42 04.8	.. 18.7	1 41.5	10.2	10 45.7	9.2	58.1
16	57 05.0	17.7	16 10.7	10.1	10 54.9	9.2	58.0
17	72 05.1	16.7	30 39.8	10.2	11 04.1	9.2	58.0
18	87 05.2	S 6 15.8	45 09.0	10.1	N 11 13.3	9.0	57.9
19	102 05.4	14.8	59 38.1	10.2	11 22.3	9.0	57.9
20	117 05.5	13.9	74 07.3	10.2	11 31.3	8.9	57.9
21	132 05.7	.. 12.9	88 36.5	10.2	11 40.2	8.8	57.8
22	147 05.8	11.9	103 05.7	10.2	11 49.0	8.8	57.8
23	162 05.9	11.0	117 34.9	10.3	N 11 57.8	8.6	57.7
	SD 16.2	d 1.0	SD 16.3		16.1		15.8

Lat.	Twilight Naut.	Twilight Civil	Sunrise	Moonrise 2	3	4	5
°	h m	h m	h m	h m	h m	h m	h m
N 72	05 00	06 18	07 27	06 51	06 43	06 35	06 26
N 70	05 06	06 17	07 18	06 52	06 50	06 49	06 49
68	05 11	06 16	07 12	06 52	06 56	07 01	07 07
66	05 15	06 14	07 06	06 52	07 01	07 10	07 22
64	05 18	06 13	07 01	06 53	07 05	07 18	07 34
62	05 21	06 12	06 57	06 53	07 08	07 25	07 44
60	05 23	06 11	06 53	06 53	07 12	07 31	07 53
N 58	05 25	06 10	06 50	06 53	07 14	07 36	08 01
56	05 27	06 10	06 47	06 54	07 17	07 41	08 08
54	05 28	06 09	06 44	06 54	07 19	07 45	08 14
52	05 29	06 08	06 42	06 54	07 21	07 49	08 19
50	05 30	06 07	06 40	06 54	07 23	07 53	08 25
45	05 31	06 05	06 35	06 55	07 27	08 00	08 35
N 40	05 32	06 04	06 31	06 55	07 31	08 07	08 45
35	05 32	06 02	06 27	06 55	07 34	08 12	08 52
30	05 32	06 00	06 24	06 55	07 36	08 17	08 59
20	05 31	05 56	06 18	06 56	07 41	08 26	09 11
N 10	05 28	05 52	06 13	06 56	07 45	08 34	09 22
0	05 24	05 48	06 09	06 57	07 49	08 41	09 32
S 10	05 18	05 43	06 04	06 57	07 53	08 48	09 42
20	05 10	05 36	05 58	06 58	07 57	08 56	09 53
30	04 59	05 28	05 52	06 58	08 02	09 05	10 05
35	04 53	05 23	05 49	06 59	08 05	09 10	10 12
40	04 44	05 17	05 44	06 59	08 08	09 16	10 20
45	04 34	05 10	05 40	06 59	08 12	09 23	10 30
S 50	04 20	05 00	05 34	07 00	08 17	09 31	10 41
52	04 13	04 56	05 31	07 00	08 19	09 35	10 47
54	04 06	04 51	05 28	07 01	08 21	09 39	10 53
56	03 58	04 46	05 25	07 01	08 24	09 44	10 59
58	03 48	04 40	05 21	07 01	08 27	09 49	11 07
S 60	03 36	04 33	05 17	07 02	08 30	09 55	11 15

Lat.	Sunset	Twilight Civil	Twilight Naut.	Moonset 2	3	4	5
°	h m	h m	h m	h m	h m	h m	h m
N 72	16 59	18 08	19 26	20 01	21 58	23 54	25 53
N 70	17 07	18 09	19 20	19 56	21 46	23 32	25 16
68	17 14	18 10	19 15	19 53	21 36	23 15	24 50
66	17 20	18 11	19 11	19 50	21 28	23 02	24 31
64	17 24	18 12	19 07	19 47	21 21	22 51	24 15
62	17 28	18 13	19 04	19 45	21 15	22 41	24 02
60	17 32	18 14	19 02	19 43	21 10	22 33	23 51
N 58	17 35	18 15	19 00	19 42	21 06	22 26	23 42
56	17 38	18 15	18 58	19 40	21 02	22 20	23 33
54	17 41	18 16	18 57	19 39	20 58	22 14	23 26
52	17 43	18 17	18 56	19 38	20 55	22 09	23 19
50	17 45	18 18	18 55	19 37	20 52	22 05	23 13
45	17 50	18 19	18 53	19 34	20 46	21 55	23 00
N 40	17 54	18 21	18 52	19 32	20 41	21 47	22 50
35	17 57	18 23	18 52	19 31	20 36	21 40	22 41
30	18 00	18 24	18 52	19 29	20 32	21 34	22 33
20	18 06	18 28	18 53	19 26	20 25	21 23	22 19
N 10	18 11	18 32	18 56	19 24	20 19	21 14	22 07
0	18 15	18 36	19 00	19 22	20 14	21 05	21 56
S 10	18 20	18 41	19 06	19 20	20 08	20 57	21 45
20	18 25	18 47	19 13	19 17	20 02	20 47	21 33
30	18 31	18 55	19 24	19 14	19 55	20 37	21 19
35	18 35	19 00	19 31	19 13	19 52	20 31	21 12
40	18 39	19 06	19 41	19 11	19 47	20 24	21 03
45	18 43	19 13	19 49	19 09	19 42	20 16	20 52
S 50	18 49	19 22	20 02	19 07	19 36	20 07	20 40
52	18 52	19 26	20 09	19 06	19 33	20 02	20 34
54	18 55	19 31	20 16	19 04	19 30	19 57	20 28
56	18 58	19 36	20 24	19 03	19 27	19 52	20 20
58	19 01	19 42	20 34	19 02	19 23	19 46	20 12
S 60	19 05	19 49	20 45	19 00	19 19	19 39	20 03

Day	SUN Eqn. of Time 00h	SUN Eqn. of Time 12h	SUN Mer. Pass.	MOON Mer. Pass. Upper	MOON Mer. Pass. Lower	Age	Phase
d	m s	m s	h m	h m	h m	d	%
2	12 14	12 08	12 12	13 09	00 43	01	2
3	12 02	11 55	12 12	14 02	01 36	02	6
4	11 49	11 43	12 12	14 53	02 27	03	13

UT	ARIES GHA	VENUS −4.7 GHA	Dec	MARS −0.6 GHA	Dec	JUPITER −2.4 GHA	Dec	SATURN +0.4 GHA	Dec	STARS Name	SHA	Dec
5 00	162 40.0	222 05.5	S16 26.4	316 08.4	S 7 54.9	61 17.1	N23 15.9	291 07.5	S16 18.6	Acamar	315 18.2	S40 15.2
01	177 42.5	237 05.9	26.3	331 11.0	54.9	76 19.6	16.0	306 09.9	18.6	Achernar	335 26.9	S57 10.1
02	192 44.9	252 06.2	26.2	346 13.6	54.8	91 22.1	16.0	321 12.4	18.6	Acrux	173 07.9	S63 10.7
03	207 47.4	267 06.5 ..	26.0	1 16.1 ..	54.8	106 24.5 ..	16.0	336 14.9 ..	18.5	Adhara	255 11.9	S28 59.9
04	222 49.9	282 06.8	25.9	16 18.7	54.8	121 27.0	16.0	351 17.4	18.5	Aldebaran	290 48.8	N16 32.1
05	237 52.3	297 07.1	25.8	31 21.2	54.7	136 29.5	16.0	6 19.8	18.5			
W 06	252 54.8	312 07.4	S16 25.6	46 23.8	S 7 54.7	151 32.0	N23 16.0	21 22.3	S16 18.5	Alioth	166 19.8	N55 52.7
E 07	267 57.3	327 07.7	25.5	61 26.4	54.6	166 34.4	16.0	36 24.8	18.5	Alkaid	152 58.2	N49 14.3
D 08	282 59.7	342 08.0	25.4	76 28.9	54.6	181 36.9	16.0	51 27.2	18.5	Al Na'ir	27 43.6	S46 53.4
N 09	298 02.2	357 08.3 ..	25.2	91 31.5 ..	54.5	196 39.4 ..	16.0	66 29.7 ..	18.5	Alnilam	275 45.8	S 1 11.9
E 10	313 04.6	12 08.6	25.1	106 34.1	54.4	211 41.9	16.0	81 32.2	18.5	Alphard	217 55.3	S 8 43.5
S 11	328 07.1	27 08.9	25.0	121 36.7	54.4	226 44.3	16.0	96 34.7	18.5			
D 12	343 09.6	42 09.1	S16 24.8	136 39.2	S 7 54.3	241 46.8	N23 16.0	111 37.1	S16 18.4	Alphecca	126 10.5	N26 39.9
A 13	358 12.0	57 09.4	24.7	151 41.8	54.3	256 49.3	16.0	126 39.6	18.4	Alpheratz	357 43.3	N29 10.1
Y 14	13 14.5	72 09.7	24.5	166 44.4	54.2	271 51.7	16.0	141 42.1	18.4	Altair	62 08.0	N 8 54.4
15	28 17.0	87 10.0 ..	24.4	181 46.9 ..	54.2	286 54.2 ..	16.0	156 44.6 ..	18.4	Ankaa	353 15.6	S42 13.9
16	43 19.4	102 10.3	24.3	196 49.5	54.1	301 56.7	16.0	171 47.0	18.4	Antares	112 25.6	S26 27.6
17	58 21.9	117 10.6	24.1	211 52.1	54.1	316 59.2	16.0	186 49.5	18.4			
18	73 24.4	132 10.9	S16 24.0	226 54.7	S 7 54.0	332 01.6	N23 16.0	201 52.0	S16 18.4	Arcturus	145 55.1	N19 06.4
19	88 26.8	147 11.2	23.8	241 57.3	54.0	347 04.1	16.0	216 54.5	18.4	Atria	107 26.9	S69 02.8
20	103 29.3	162 11.4	23.7	256 59.8	53.9	2 06.6	16.0	231 56.9	18.4	Avior	234 17.3	S59 33.7
21	118 31.7	177 11.7 ..	23.6	272 02.4 ..	53.9	17 09.0 ..	16.0	246 59.4 ..	18.3	Bellatrix	278 31.4	N 6 21.5
22	133 34.2	192 12.0	23.4	287 05.0	53.8	32 11.5	16.0	262 01.9	18.3	Betelgeuse	271 00.7	N 7 24.3
23	148 36.7	207 12.3	23.3	302 07.6	53.7	47 14.0	16.0	277 04.4	18.3			
6 00	163 39.1	222 12.6	S16 23.1	317 10.2	S 7 53.7	62 16.4	N23 16.0	292 06.8	S16 18.3	Canopus	263 55.7	S52 42.7
01	178 41.6	237 12.8	23.0	332 12.8	53.6	77 18.9	16.0	307 09.3	18.3	Capella	280 33.6	N46 00.7
02	193 44.1	252 13.1	22.8	347 15.4	53.6	92 21.4	16.0	322 11.8	18.3	Deneb	49 31.5	N45 19.8
03	208 46.5	267 13.4 ..	22.7	2 18.0 ..	53.5	107 23.8 ..	16.0	337 14.3 ..	18.3	Denebola	182 32.8	N14 29.4
04	223 49.0	282 13.7	22.5	17 20.5	53.5	122 26.3	16.1	352 16.8	18.3	Diphda	348 55.7	S17 54.7
05	238 51.5	297 13.9	22.4	32 23.1	53.4	137 28.8	16.1	7 19.2	18.2			
T 06	253 53.9	312 14.2	S16 22.2	47 25.7	S 7 53.3	152 31.2	N23 16.1	22 21.7	S16 18.2	Dubhe	193 50.5	N61 40.3
H 07	268 56.4	327 14.5	22.1	62 28.3	53.3	167 33.7	16.1	37 24.2	18.2	Elnath	278 11.9	N28 37.0
U 08	283 58.9	342 14.7	21.9	77 30.9	53.2	182 36.2	16.1	52 26.7	18.2	Eltanin	90 46.0	N51 29.1
R 09	299 01.3	357 15.0 ..	21.8	92 33.5 ..	53.1	197 38.6 ..	16.1	67 29.1 ..	18.2	Enif	33 46.9	N 9 56.4
S 10	314 03.8	12 15.3	21.6	107 36.1	53.1	212 41.1	16.1	82 31.6	18.2	Fomalhaut	15 23.8	S29 32.8
D 11	329 06.2	27 15.5	21.5	122 38.7	53.0	227 43.6	16.1	97 34.1	18.2			
A 12	344 08.7	42 15.8	S16 21.3	137 41.3	S 7 53.0	242 46.0	N23 16.1	112 36.6	S16 18.2	Gacrux	171 59.7	S57 11.6
Y 13	359 11.2	57 16.1	21.2	152 43.9	52.9	257 48.5	16.1	127 39.1	18.2	Gienah	175 51.4	S17 37.4
14	14 13.6	72 16.3	21.0	167 46.5	52.8	272 51.0	16.1	142 41.5	18.1	Hadar	148 46.6	S60 26.3
15	29 16.1	87 16.6 ..	20.9	182 49.1 ..	52.8	287 53.4 ..	16.1	157 44.0 ..	18.1	Hamal	328 00.4	N23 31.7
16	44 18.6	102 16.8	20.7	197 51.7	52.7	302 55.9	16.1	172 46.5	18.1	Kaus Aust.	83 43.3	S34 22.4
17	59 21.0	117 17.1	20.5	212 54.4	52.6	317 58.3	16.1	187 49.0	18.1			
18	74 23.5	132 17.4	S16 20.4	227 57.0	S 7 52.6	333 00.8	N23 16.1	202 51.4	S16 18.1	Kochab	137 19.6	N74 05.6
19	89 26.0	147 17.6	20.2	242 59.6	52.5	348 03.3	16.1	217 53.9	18.1	Markab	13 38.1	N15 16.9
20	104 28.4	162 17.9	20.1	258 02.2	52.5	3 05.7	16.1	232 56.4	18.1	Menkar	314 14.7	N 4 08.5
21	119 30.9	177 18.1 ..	19.9	273 04.8 ..	52.4	18 08.2 ..	16.1	247 58.9 ..	18.1	Menkent	148 06.7	S36 26.3
22	134 33.3	192 18.4	19.7	288 07.4	52.3	33 10.6	16.1	263 01.4	18.0	Miaplacidus	221 38.6	S69 46.8
23	149 35.8	207 18.6	19.6	303 10.0	52.3	48 13.1	16.1	278 03.8	18.0			
7 00	164 38.3	222 18.9	S16 19.4	318 12.7	S 7 52.2	63 15.6	N23 16.1	293 06.3	S16 18.0	Mirfak	308 39.8	N49 54.7
01	179 40.7	237 19.1	19.2	333 15.3	52.1	78 18.0	16.0	308 08.8	18.0	Nunki	75 57.9	S26 16.5
02	194 43.2	252 19.4	19.1	348 17.9	52.0	93 20.5	16.1	323 11.3	18.0	Peacock	53 18.9	S56 41.1
03	209 45.7	267 19.6 ..	18.9	3 20.5 ..	52.0	108 22.9 ..	16.1	338 13.8 ..	18.0	Pollux	243 26.9	N27 59.3
04	224 48.1	282 19.8	18.7	18 23.1	51.9	123 25.4	16.1	353 16.2	18.0	Procyon	244 59.0	N 5 11.0
05	239 50.6	297 20.1	18.6	33 25.8	51.8	138 27.9	16.1	8 18.7	18.0			
F 06	254 53.1	312 20.3	S16 18.4	48 28.4	S 7 51.8	153 30.3	N23 16.1	23 21.2	S16 17.9	Rasalhague	96 06.0	N12 33.0
R 07	269 55.5	327 20.6	18.2	63 31.0	51.7	168 32.8	16.1	38 23.7	17.9	Regulus	207 42.7	N11 53.6
I 08	284 58.0	342 20.8	18.1	78 33.6	51.6	183 35.2	16.1	53 26.2	17.9	Rigel	281 11.5	S 8 11.5
D 09	300 00.5	357 21.0 ..	17.9	93 36.3 ..	51.6	198 37.7 ..	16.1	68 28.7 ..	17.9	Rigil Kent.	139 50.6	S60 53.4
A 10	315 02.9	12 21.3	17.7	108 38.9	51.5	213 40.1	16.1	83 31.1	17.9	Sabik	102 12.0	S15 44.4
Y 11	330 05.4	27 21.5	17.6	123 41.5	51.4	228 42.6	16.1	98 33.6	17.9			
12	345 07.8	42 21.8	S16 17.4	138 44.2	S 7 51.3	243 45.0	N23 16.1	113 36.1	S16 17.9	Schedar	349 40.4	N56 37.0
13	0 10.3	57 22.0	17.2	153 46.8	51.3	258 47.5	16.1	128 38.6	17.8	Shaula	96 21.3	S37 06.6
14	15 12.8	72 22.2	17.0	168 49.4	51.2	273 49.9	16.2	143 41.1	17.8	Sirius	258 33.1	S16 44.5
15	30 15.2	87 22.5 ..	16.9	183 52.1 ..	51.1	288 52.4 ..	16.2	158 43.6 ..	17.8	Spica	158 30.4	S11 14.2
16	45 17.7	102 22.7	16.7	198 54.7	51.1	303 54.9	16.2	173 46.0	17.8	Suhail	222 51.6	S43 29.7
17	60 20.2	117 22.9	16.5	213 57.3	51.0	318 57.3	16.2	188 48.5	17.8			
18	75 22.6	132 23.1	S16 16.3	229 00.0	S 7 50.9	333 59.8	N23 16.2	203 51.0	S16 17.8	Vega	80 38.8	N38 47.7
19	90 25.1	147 23.4	16.2	244 02.6	50.8	349 02.2	16.2	218 53.5	17.8	Zuben'ubi	137 04.7	S16 06.0
20	105 27.6	162 23.6	16.0	259 05.3	50.8	4 04.7	16.2	233 56.0	17.8			
21	120 30.0	177 23.8 ..	15.8	274 07.9 ..	50.7	19 07.1 ..	16.2	248 58.5 ..	17.7			
22	135 32.5	192 24.0	15.6	289 10.6	50.6	34 09.6	16.2	264 00.9	17.7			
23	150 35.0	207 24.3	15.4	304 13.2	50.5	49 12.0	16.2	279 03.4	17.7			

	h m										SHA	Mer. Pass.
Mer. Pass.	13 03.2	v 0.3	d 0.2	v 2.6	d 0.1	v 2.5	d 0.0	v 2.5	d 0.0	Venus	58 33.4	9 11
										Mars	153 31.0	2 51
										Jupiter	258 37.3	19 48
										Saturn	128 27.7	4 31

UT	SUN GHA	SUN Dec	MOON GHA	v	MOON Dec	d	HP
d h	° ′	° ′	° ′	′	° ′	′	′
5 00	177 06.1	S 6 10.0	132 04.2	10.2	N12 06.4	8.6	57.7
01	192 06.2	09.0	146 33.4	10.3	12 15.0	8.5	57.7
02	207 06.3	08.1	161 02.7	10.2	12 23.5	8.5	57.6
03	222 06.5	.. 07.1	175 31.9	10.3	12 32.0	8.3	57.6
04	237 06.6	06.1	190 01.2	10.3	12 40.3	8.3	57.6
05	252 06.8	05.2	204 30.5	10.3	12 48.6	8.2	57.5
06	267 06.9	S 6 04.2	218 59.8	10.3	N12 56.8	8.1	57.5
W 07	282 07.0	03.2	233 29.1	10.3	13 04.9	8.0	57.4
E 08	297 07.2	02.3	247 58.4	10.3	13 12.9	8.0	57.4
D 09	312 07.3	.. 01.3	262 27.7	10.3	13 20.9	7.8	57.4
N 10	327 07.5	6 00.3	276 57.0	10.4	13 28.7	7.8	57.3
E 11	342 07.6	5 59.4	291 26.4	10.4	13 36.5	7.7	57.3
S 12	357 07.7	S 5 58.4	305 55.8	10.3	N13 44.2	7.6	57.2
D 13	12 07.9	57.4	320 25.1	10.4	13 51.8	7.5	57.2
A 14	27 08.0	56.5	334 54.5	10.4	13 59.3	7.5	57.2
Y 15	42 08.2	.. 55.5	349 23.9	10.4	14 06.8	7.3	57.1
16	57 08.3	54.5	3 53.3	10.4	14 14.1	7.3	57.1
17	72 08.4	53.6	18 22.7	10.4	14 21.4	7.2	57.1
18	87 08.6	S 5 52.6	32 52.1	10.4	N14 28.6	7.0	57.0
19	102 08.7	51.6	47 21.5	10.5	14 35.6	7.1	57.0
20	117 08.9	50.7	61 51.0	10.4	14 42.7	6.9	57.0
21	132 09.0	.. 49.7	76 20.4	10.5	14 49.6	6.8	56.9
22	147 09.2	48.7	90 49.9	10.4	14 56.4	6.7	56.9
23	162 09.3	47.8	105 19.3	10.5	15 03.1	6.7	56.8
6 00	177 09.4	S 5 46.8	119 48.8	10.5	N15 09.8	6.6	56.8
01	192 09.6	45.8	134 18.3	10.5	15 16.4	6.4	56.8
02	207 09.7	44.9	148 47.8	10.5	15 22.8	6.4	56.7
03	222 09.9	.. 43.9	163 17.3	10.5	15 29.2	6.3	56.7
04	237 10.0	42.9	177 46.8	10.6	15 35.5	6.2	56.7
05	252 10.2	41.9	192 16.4	10.5	15 41.7	6.1	56.6
06	267 10.3	S 5 41.0	206 45.9	10.5	N15 47.8	6.1	56.6
T 07	282 10.4	40.0	221 15.4	10.6	15 53.9	5.9	56.6
H 08	297 10.6	39.0	235 45.0	10.6	15 59.8	5.8	56.5
U 09	312 10.7	.. 38.1	250 14.6	10.6	16 05.6	5.8	56.5
R 10	327 10.9	37.1	264 44.2	10.6	16 11.4	5.7	56.4
S 11	342 11.0	36.1	279 13.8	10.6	16 17.1	5.5	56.4
D 12	357 11.2	S 5 35.2	293 43.4	10.6	N16 22.6	5.5	56.4
A 13	12 11.3	34.2	308 13.0	10.6	16 28.1	5.4	56.3
Y 14	27 11.5	33.2	322 42.6	10.6	16 33.5	5.3	56.3
15	42 11.6	.. 32.3	337 12.2	10.7	16 38.8	5.2	56.3
16	57 11.8	31.3	351 41.9	10.7	16 44.0	5.1	56.2
17	72 11.9	30.3	6 11.6	10.6	16 49.1	5.0	56.2
18	87 12.0	S 5 29.3	20 41.2	10.7	N16 54.1	4.9	56.2
19	102 12.2	28.4	35 10.9	10.7	16 59.0	4.8	56.1
20	117 12.3	27.4	49 40.6	10.7	17 03.8	4.7	56.1
21	132 12.5	.. 26.4	64 10.3	10.8	17 08.5	4.7	56.1
22	147 12.6	25.5	78 40.1	10.7	17 13.2	4.5	56.0
23	162 12.8	24.5	93 09.8	10.7	17 17.7	4.5	56.0
7 00	177 12.9	S 5 23.5	107 39.5	10.8	N17 22.2	4.3	56.0
01	192 13.1	22.5	122 09.3	10.8	17 26.5	4.3	55.9
02	207 13.2	21.6	136 39.1	10.8	17 30.8	4.2	55.9
03	222 13.4	.. 20.6	151 08.9	10.8	17 35.0	4.0	55.9
04	237 13.5	19.6	165 38.7	10.8	17 39.0	4.0	55.9
05	252 13.7	18.7	180 08.5	10.8	17 43.0	3.9	55.8
06	267 13.8	S 5 17.7	194 38.3	10.8	N17 46.9	3.8	55.8
F 07	282 14.0	16.7	209 08.1	10.9	17 50.7	3.7	55.8
R 08	297 14.1	15.7	223 38.0	10.9	17 54.4	3.6	55.7
I 09	312 14.3	.. 14.8	238 07.9	10.9	17 58.0	3.5	55.7
D 10	327 14.4	13.8	252 37.8	10.9	18 01.5	3.4	55.7
A 11	342 14.6	12.8	267 07.7	10.9	18 04.9	3.3	55.6
Y 12	357 14.7	S 5 11.8	281 37.6	10.9	N18 08.2	3.2	55.6
13	12 14.9	10.9	296 07.5	10.9	18 11.4	3.2	55.6
14	27 15.0	09.9	310 37.4	11.0	18 14.6	3.0	55.6
15	42 15.2	.. 08.9	325 07.4	11.0	18 17.6	2.9	55.5
16	57 15.3	08.0	339 37.4	11.0	18 20.5	2.9	55.5
17	72 15.5	07.0	354 07.4	11.0	18 23.4	2.7	55.5
18	87 15.6	S 5 06.0	8 37.4	11.0	N18 26.1	2.7	55.4
19	102 15.8	05.0	23 07.4	11.0	18 28.8	2.5	55.4
20	117 15.9	04.1	37 37.4	11.1	18 31.3	2.5	55.4
21	132 16.1	.. 03.1	52 07.5	11.1	18 33.8	2.4	55.4
22	147 16.2	02.1	66 37.6	11.1	18 36.2	2.2	55.3
23	162 16.4	01.1	81 07.7	11.1	N18 38.4	2.2	55.3
	SD 16.1	d 1.0	SD 15.6		15.4		15.2

Lat.	Twilight Naut.	Twilight Civil	Sunrise	Moonrise 5	Moonrise 6	Moonrise 7	Moonrise 8
°	h m	h m	h m	h m	h m	h m	h m
N 72	04 45	06 04	07 11	06 26	06 14	05 47	▭
N 70	04 53	06 04	07 04	06 49	06 51	06 58	07 15
68	04 59	06 03	06 59	07 07	07 18	07 35	08 04
66	05 04	06 03	06 54	07 22	07 38	08 01	08 35
64	05 08	06 03	06 51	07 34	07 54	08 21	08 58
62	05 12	06 03	06 47	07 44	08 08	08 38	09 16
60	05 15	06 03	06 44	07 53	08 19	08 52	09 32
N 58	05 17	06 02	06 42	08 01	08 29	09 04	09 44
56	05 19	06 02	06 39	08 08	08 38	09 14	09 56
54	05 21	06 02	06 37	08 14	08 46	09 23	10 06
52	05 22	06 01	06 35	08 19	08 53	09 31	10 14
50	05 24	06 01	06 33	08 25	08 59	09 38	10 22
45	05 26	06 00	06 29	08 35	09 13	09 54	10 39
N 40	05 28	05 59	06 26	08 45	09 24	10 07	10 53
35	05 29	05 58	06 23	08 52	09 34	10 18	11 04
30	05 29	05 57	06 21	08 59	09 43	10 28	11 14
20	05 28	05 54	06 16	09 11	09 57	10 44	11 32
N 10	05 26	05 51	06 12	09 22	10 10	10 59	11 47
0	05 23	05 47	06 08	09 32	10 22	11 12	12 02
S 10	05 18	05 43	06 04	09 42	10 35	11 26	12 16
20	05 11	05 37	05 59	09 53	10 48	11 41	12 32
30	05 02	05 30	05 54	10 05	11 03	11 58	12 49
35	04 55	05 26	05 51	10 12	11 11	12 07	13 00
40	04 48	05 20	05 48	10 20	11 21	12 19	13 11
45	04 38	05 14	05 44	10 30	11 33	12 32	13 25
S 50	04 26	05 06	05 39	10 41	11 47	12 48	13 42
52	04 20	05 02	05 37	10 47	11 54	12 56	13 50
54	04 13	04 58	05 34	10 53	12 02	13 04	13 59
56	04 05	04 53	05 31	10 59	12 10	13 14	14 09
58	03 57	04 47	05 28	11 07	12 19	13 24	14 21
S 60	03 46	04 41	05 25	11 15	12 30	13 37	14 34

Lat.	Sunset	Twilight Civil	Twilight Naut.	Moonset 5	Moonset 6	Moonset 7	Moonset 8
°	h m	h m	h m	h m	h m	h m	h m
N 72	17 14	18 21	19 41	25 53	01 53	04 04	▭
N 70	17 20	18 21	19 33	25 16	01 16	02 54	04 20
68	17 25	18 21	19 26	24 50	00 50	02 18	03 32
66	17 30	18 21	19 21	24 31	00 31	01 52	03 01
64	17 33	18 21	19 16	24 15	00 15	01 32	02 38
62	17 37	18 21	19 13	24 02	00 02	01 16	02 20
60	17 40	18 21	19 10	23 51	25 02	01 02	02 05
N 58	17 42	18 21	19 07	23 42	24 51	00 51	01 52
56	17 44	18 22	19 05	23 33	24 41	00 41	01 41
54	17 47	18 22	19 03	23 26	24 32	00 32	01 31
52	17 48	18 22	19 01	23 19	24 24	00 24	01 22
50	17 50	18 22	19 00	23 13	24 17	00 17	01 14
45	17 54	18 23	18 57	23 00	24 02	00 02	00 58
N 40	17 57	18 24	18 56	22 50	23 49	24 44	00 44
35	18 00	18 25	18 55	22 41	23 39	24 33	00 33
30	18 02	18 26	18 54	22 33	23 29	24 23	00 23
20	18 07	18 29	18 54	22 19	23 13	24 05	00 05
N 10	18 11	18 32	18 56	22 07	22 59	23 50	24 40
0	18 15	18 35	18 59	21 56	22 46	23 36	24 25
S 10	18 18	18 40	19 04	21 45	22 33	23 22	24 11
20	18 23	18 45	19 11	21 33	22 20	23 07	23 55
30	18 28	18 52	19 20	21 19	22 04	22 50	23 38
35	18 31	18 56	19 26	21 12	21 54	22 40	23 27
40	18 34	19 01	19 34	21 03	21 44	22 28	23 15
45	18 38	19 08	19 43	20 52	21 32	22 15	23 01
S 50	18 43	19 16	19 55	20 40	21 17	21 58	22 44
52	18 45	19 19	20 01	20 34	21 10	21 50	22 36
54	18 47	19 24	20 08	20 28	21 02	21 42	22 27
56	18 50	19 28	20 15	20 20	20 53	21 32	22 17
58	18 53	19 33	20 24	20 12	20 44	21 21	22 06
S 60	18 56	19 39	20 34	20 03	20 32	21 08	21 52

Day	SUN Eqn. of Time 00h	SUN Eqn. of Time 12h	SUN Mer. Pass.	MOON Mer. Pass. Upper	MOON Mer. Pass. Lower	Age	Phase
d	m s	m s	h m	h m	h m	d	%
5	11 36	11 29	12 11	15 44	03 19	04	21
6	11 23	11 16	12 11	16 34	04 09	05	30
7	11 09	11 01	12 11	17 24	04 59	06	40

UT	ARIES GHA	VENUS −4.7 GHA	Dec	MARS −0.7 GHA	Dec	JUPITER −2.4 GHA	Dec	SATURN +0.4 GHA	Dec	STARS Name	SHA	Dec
d h	° ′	° ′	° ′	° ′	° ′	° ′	° ′	° ′	° ′		° ′	° ′
8 00	165 37.4	222 24.5	S16 15.3	319 15.9	S 7 50.4	64 14.5	N23 16.2	294 05.9	S16 17.7	Acamar	315 18.2	S40 15.2
01	180 39.9	237 24.7	15.1	334 18.5	50.4	79 16.9	16.2	309 08.4	17.7	Achernar	335 26.9	S57 10.1
02	195 42.3	252 24.9	14.9	349 21.2	50.3	94 19.4	16.2	324 10.9	17.7	Acrux	173 07.9	S63 10.7
03	210 44.8	267 25.1	. . 14.7	4 23.8	. . 50.2	109 21.8	. . 16.2	339 13.4	. . 17.7	Adhara	255 11.9	S28 59.9
04	225 47.3	282 25.4	14.5	19 26.5	50.1	124 24.3	16.2	354 15.9	17.6	Aldebaran	290 48.8	N16 32.1
05	240 49.7	297 25.6	14.3	34 29.1	50.1	139 26.7	16.2	9 18.3	17.6			
06	255 52.2	312 25.8	S16 14.2	49 31.8	S 7 50.0	154 29.2	N23 16.2	24 20.8	S16 17.6	Alioth	166 19.8	N55 52.8
07	270 54.7	327 26.0	14.0	64 34.4	49.9	169 31.6	16.2	39 23.3	17.6	Alkaid	152 58.2	N49 14.3
S 08	285 57.1	342 26.2	13.8	79 37.1	49.8	184 34.1	16.2	54 25.8	17.6	Al Na'ir	27 43.6	S46 53.4
A 09	300 59.6	357 26.4	. . 13.6	94 39.7	. . 49.7	199 36.5	. . 16.2	69 28.3	. . 17.6	Alnilam	275 45.8	S 1 11.9
T 10	316 02.1	12 26.6	13.4	109 42.4	49.6	214 38.9	16.2	84 30.8	17.6	Alphard	217 55.3	S 8 43.5
U 11	331 04.5	27 26.8	13.2	124 45.1	49.6	229 41.4	16.2	99 33.3	17.6			
R 12	346 07.0	42 27.0	S16 13.0	139 47.7	S 7 49.5	244 43.8	N23 16.2	114 35.7	S16 17.5	Alphecca	126 10.4	N26 39.9
D 13	1 09.5	57 27.2	12.8	154 50.4	49.4	259 46.3	16.2	129 38.2	17.5	Alpheratz	357 43.3	N29 10.1
A 14	16 11.9	72 27.4	12.6	169 53.1	49.3	274 48.7	16.2	144 40.7	17.5	Altair	62 07.9	N 8 54.4
Y 15	31 14.4	87 27.7	. . 12.4	184 55.7	. . 49.2	289 51.2	. . 16.2	159 43.2	. . 17.5	Ankaa	353 15.6	S42 13.9
16	46 16.8	102 27.9	12.3	199 58.4	49.2	304 53.6	16.2	174 45.7	17.5	Antares	112 25.5	S26 27.6
17	61 19.3	117 28.1	12.1	215 01.1	49.1	319 56.1	16.2	189 48.2	17.5			
18	76 21.8	132 28.3	S16 11.9	230 03.7	S 7 49.0	334 58.5	N23 16.2	204 50.7	S16 17.5	Arcturus	145 55.0	N19 06.4
19	91 24.2	147 28.5	11.7	245 06.4	48.9	350 00.9	16.2	219 53.2	17.4	Atria	107 26.8	S69 02.8
20	106 26.7	162 28.7	11.5	260 09.1	48.8	5 03.4	16.2	234 55.6	17.4	Avior	234 17.3	S59 33.7
21	121 29.2	177 28.9	. . 11.3	275 11.8	. . 48.7	20 05.8	. . 16.2	249 58.1	. . 17.4	Bellatrix	278 31.4	N 6 21.5
22	136 31.6	192 29.1	11.1	290 14.4	48.6	35 08.3	16.2	265 00.6	17.4	Betelgeuse	271 00.7	N 7 24.3
23	151 34.1	207 29.2	10.9	305 17.1	48.6	50 10.7	16.2	280 03.1	17.4			
9 00	166 36.6	222 29.4	S16 10.7	320 19.8	S 7 48.5	65 13.2	N23 16.2	295 05.6	S16 17.4	Canopus	263 55.7	S52 42.7
01	181 39.0	237 29.6	10.5	335 22.5	48.4	80 15.6	16.2	310 08.1	17.4	Capella	280 33.7	N46 00.7
02	196 41.5	252 29.8	10.3	350 25.2	48.3	95 18.0	16.2	325 10.6	17.3	Deneb	49 31.4	N45 19.8
03	211 43.9	267 30.0	. . 10.1	5 27.8	. . 48.2	110 20.5	. . 16.2	340 13.1	. . 17.3	Denebola	182 32.8	N14 29.4
04	226 46.4	282 30.2	09.9	20 30.5	48.1	125 22.9	16.2	355 15.6	17.3	Diphda	348 55.7	S17 54.7
05	241 48.9	297 30.4	09.7	35 33.2	48.0	140 25.4	16.2	10 18.0	17.3			
06	256 51.3	312 30.6	S16 09.5	50 35.9	S 7 47.9	155 27.8	N23 16.2	25 20.5	S16 17.3	Dubhe	193 50.5	N61 40.3
07	271 53.8	327 30.8	09.3	65 38.6	47.8	170 30.2	16.2	40 23.0	17.3	Elnath	278 11.9	N28 37.0
S 08	286 56.3	342 31.0	09.0	80 41.3	47.8	185 32.7	16.2	55 25.5	17.2	Eltanin	90 46.0	N51 29.1
U 09	301 58.7	357 31.1	. . 08.8	95 44.0	. . 47.7	200 35.1	. . 16.2	70 28.0	. . 17.2	Enif	33 46.9	N 9 56.4
N 10	317 01.2	12 31.3	08.6	110 46.7	47.6	215 37.5	16.2	85 30.5	17.2	Fomalhaut	15 23.8	S29 32.8
D 11	332 03.7	27 31.5	08.4	125 49.3	47.5	230 40.0	16.2	100 33.0	17.2			
A 12	347 06.1	42 31.7	S16 08.2	140 52.0	S 7 47.4	245 42.4	N23 16.2	115 35.5	S16 17.2	Gacrux	171 59.7	S57 11.6
Y 13	2 08.6	57 31.9	08.0	155 54.7	47.3	260 44.9	16.2	130 38.0	17.2	Gienah	175 51.4	S17 37.4
14	17 11.1	72 32.0	07.8	170 57.4	47.2	275 47.3	16.2	145 40.5	17.2	Hadar	148 46.6	S60 26.3
15	32 13.5	87 32.2	. . 07.6	186 00.1	. . 47.1	290 49.7	. . 16.2	160 43.0	. . 17.1	Hamal	328 00.4	N23 31.7
16	47 16.0	102 32.4	07.4	201 02.8	47.0	305 52.2	16.2	175 45.4	17.1	Kaus Aust.	83 43.2	S34 22.4
17	62 18.4	117 32.6	07.2	216 05.5	46.9	320 54.6	16.2	190 47.9	17.1			
18	77 20.9	132 32.8	S16 06.9	231 08.2	S 7 46.8	335 57.0	N23 16.2	205 50.4	S16 17.1	Kochab	137 19.5	N74 05.6
19	92 23.4	147 32.9	06.7	246 10.9	46.7	350 59.5	16.2	220 52.9	17.1	Markab	13 38.1	N15 16.9
20	107 25.8	162 33.1	06.5	261 13.6	46.6	6 01.9	16.2	235 55.4	17.1	Menkar	314 14.7	N 4 08.5
21	122 28.3	177 33.3	. . 06.3	276 16.3	. . 46.5	21 04.3	. . 16.2	250 57.9	. . 17.1	Menkent	148 06.6	S36 26.3
22	137 30.8	192 33.4	06.1	291 19.0	46.4	36 06.8	16.2	266 00.4	17.0	Miaplacidus	221 38.7	S69 46.9
23	152 33.2	207 33.6	05.9	306 21.8	46.3	51 09.2	16.2	281 02.9	17.0			
10 00	167 35.7	222 33.8	S16 05.6	321 24.5	S 7 46.2	66 11.6	N23 16.3	296 05.4	S16 17.0	Mirfak	308 39.8	N49 54.7
01	182 38.2	237 33.9	05.4	336 27.2	46.2	81 14.1	16.2	311 07.9	17.0	Nunki	75 57.8	S26 16.5
02	197 40.6	252 34.1	05.2	351 29.9	46.1	96 16.5	16.2	326 10.4	17.0	Peacock	53 18.9	S56 41.1
03	212 43.1	267 34.3	. . 05.0	6 32.6	. . 46.0	111 18.9	. . 16.2	341 12.9	. . 17.0	Pollux	243 26.9	N27 59.3
04	227 45.6	282 34.4	04.8	21 35.3	45.9	126 21.4	16.2	356 15.4	16.9	Procyon	244 59.0	N 5 11.0
05	242 48.0	297 34.6	04.5	36 38.0	45.8	141 23.8	16.2	11 17.9	16.9			
06	257 50.5	312 34.8	S16 04.3	51 40.8	S 7 45.7	156 26.2	N23 16.3	26 20.3	S16 16.9	Rasalhague	96 06.0	N12 33.0
07	272 52.9	327 34.9	04.1	66 43.5	45.6	171 28.7	16.3	41 22.8	16.9	Regulus	207 42.7	N11 53.6
08	287 55.4	342 35.1	03.9	81 46.2	45.5	186 31.1	16.3	56 25.3	16.9	Rigel	281 11.6	S 8 11.5
M 09	302 57.9	357 35.3	. . 03.6	96 48.9	. . 45.4	201 33.5	. . 16.3	71 27.8	. . 16.9	Rigil Kent.	139 50.5	S60 53.4
O 10	318 00.3	12 35.4	03.4	111 51.6	45.3	216 35.9	16.3	86 30.3	16.8	Sabik	102 11.9	S15 44.4
N 11	333 02.8	27 35.6	03.2	126 54.4	45.3	231 38.4	16.3	101 32.8	16.8			
D 12	348 05.3	42 35.7	S16 03.0	141 57.1	S 7 45.1	246 40.8	N23 16.3	116 35.3	S16 16.8	Schedar	349 40.4	N56 37.0
A 13	3 07.7	57 35.9	02.7	156 59.8	44.9	261 43.2	16.3	131 37.8	16.8	Shaula	96 21.2	S37 06.6
Y 14	18 10.2	72 36.0	02.5	172 02.5	44.8	276 45.6	16.3	146 40.3	16.8	Sirius	258 33.1	S16 44.5
15	33 12.7	87 36.2	. . 02.3	187 05.3	. . 44.7	291 48.1	. . 16.3	161 42.8	. . 16.8	Spica	158 30.4	S11 14.2
16	48 15.1	102 36.3	02.0	202 08.0	44.6	306 50.5	16.3	176 45.3	16.7	Suhail	222 51.6	S43 29.8
17	63 17.6	117 36.5	01.8	217 10.7	44.5	321 52.9	16.3	191 47.8	16.7			
18	78 20.0	132 36.6	S16 01.6	232 13.5	S 7 44.4	336 55.4	N23 16.3	206 50.3	S16 16.7	Vega	80 38.7	N38 47.7
19	93 22.5	147 36.8	01.3	247 16.2	44.3	351 57.8	16.3	221 52.8	16.7	Zuben'ubi	137 04.6	S16 06.0
20	108 25.0	162 36.9	01.1	262 18.9	44.2	7 00.2	16.3	236 55.3	16.7			
21	123 27.4	177 37.1	. . 00.9	277 21.7	. . 44.1	22 02.6	. . 16.3	251 57.8	. . 16.7		SHA	Mer.Pass.
22	138 29.9	192 37.2	00.6	292 24.4	44.0	37 05.1	16.3	267 00.3	16.7		° ′	h m
23	153 32.4	207 37.4	00.4	307 27.1	43.9	52 07.5	16.3	282 02.8	16.6	Venus	55 52.9	9 10
	h m									Mars	153 43.2	2 38
Mer. Pass. 12 51.5		v 0.2	d 0.2	v 2.7	d 0.1	v 2.4	d 0.0	v 2.5	d 0.0	Jupiter	258 36.6	19 36
										Saturn	128 29.0	4 19

SUN / MOON

UT (d h)	SUN GHA	SUN Dec	MOON GHA	v	MOON Dec	d	HP
8 00	177 16.5	S 5 00.2	95 37.8	11.1	N18 40.6	2.1	55.3
01	192 16.7	4 59.2	110 07.9	11.1	18 42.7	2.0	55.3
02	207 16.8	58.2	124 38.0	11.2	18 44.7	1.9	55.2
03	222 17.0	.. 57.2	139 08.2	11.2	18 46.6	1.8	55.2
04	237 17.1	56.3	153 38.4	11.2	18 48.4	1.7	55.2
05	252 17.3	55.3	168 08.6	11.2	18 50.1	1.6	55.2
06	267 17.4	S 4 54.3	182 38.8	11.2	N18 51.7	1.5	55.1
07	282 17.6	53.3	197 09.0	11.3	18 53.2	1.5	55.1
08	297 17.7	52.4	211 39.3	11.3	18 54.7	1.3	55.1
09	312 17.9	.. 51.4	226 09.6	11.3	18 56.0	1.2	55.1
10	327 18.0	50.4	240 39.9	11.3	18 57.2	1.2	55.0
11	342 18.2	49.4	255 10.2	11.3	18 58.4	1.0	55.0
12	357 18.4	S 4 48.5	269 40.5	11.4	N18 59.4	1.0	55.0
13	12 18.5	47.5	284 10.9	11.3	19 00.4	0.9	55.0
14	27 18.7	46.5	298 41.2	11.4	19 01.3	0.7	54.9
15	42 18.8	.. 45.5	313 11.6	11.5	19 02.0	0.7	54.9
16	57 19.0	44.6	327 42.1	11.4	19 02.7	0.6	54.9
17	72 19.1	43.6	342 12.5	11.4	19 03.3	0.5	54.9
18	87 19.3	S 4 42.6	356 42.9	11.5	N19 03.8	0.4	54.9
19	102 19.4	41.6	11 13.4	11.5	19 04.2	0.3	54.8
20	117 19.6	40.7	25 43.9	11.6	19 04.5	0.2	54.8
21	132 19.7	.. 39.7	40 14.5	11.5	19 04.7	0.2	54.8
22	147 19.9	38.7	54 45.0	11.6	19 04.9	0.0	54.8
23	162 20.0	37.7	69 15.6	11.6	19 04.9	0.1	54.8
9 00	177 20.2	S 4 36.8	83 46.2	11.6	N19 04.8	0.1	54.7
01	192 20.4	35.8	98 16.8	11.6	19 04.7	0.2	54.7
02	207 20.5	34.8	112 47.4	11.7	19 04.5	0.4	54.7
03	222 20.7	.. 33.8	127 18.1	11.6	19 04.1	0.4	54.7
04	237 20.8	32.8	141 48.7	11.7	19 03.7	0.5	54.7
05	252 21.0	31.9	156 19.4	11.8	19 03.2	0.6	54.6
06	267 21.1	S 4 30.9	170 50.2	11.7	N19 02.6	0.7	54.6
07	282 21.3	29.9	185 20.9	11.8	19 01.9	0.8	54.6
08	297 21.5	28.9	199 51.7	11.8	19 01.1	0.8	54.6
09	312 21.6	.. 28.0	214 22.5	11.8	19 00.3	1.0	54.6
10	327 21.8	27.0	228 53.3	11.9	18 59.3	1.0	54.6
11	342 21.9	26.0	243 24.2	11.9	18 58.3	1.2	54.5
12	357 22.1	S 4 25.0	257 55.1	11.8	N18 57.1	1.2	54.5
13	12 22.2	24.0	272 25.9	12.0	18 55.9	1.3	54.5
14	27 22.4	23.1	286 56.9	11.9	18 54.6	1.4	54.5
15	42 22.6	.. 22.1	301 27.8	12.0	18 53.2	1.5	54.5
16	57 22.7	21.1	315 58.8	12.0	18 51.7	1.6	54.5
17	72 22.9	20.1	330 29.8	12.0	18 50.1	1.6	54.4
18	87 23.0	S 4 19.2	345 00.8	12.1	N18 48.5	1.8	54.4
19	102 23.2	18.2	359 31.9	12.0	18 46.7	1.8	54.4
20	117 23.4	17.2	14 02.9	12.1	18 44.9	1.9	54.4
21	132 23.5	.. 16.2	28 34.0	12.2	18 43.0	2.0	54.4
22	147 23.7	15.2	43 05.2	12.1	18 41.0	2.1	54.4
23	162 23.8	14.3	57 36.3	12.2	18 38.9	2.2	54.4
10 00	177 24.0	S 4 13.3	72 07.5	12.2	N18 36.7	2.3	54.4
01	192 24.1	12.3	86 38.7	12.2	18 34.4	2.3	54.3
02	207 24.3	11.3	101 09.9	12.3	18 32.1	2.4	54.3
03	222 24.5	.. 10.3	115 41.2	12.3	18 29.7	2.6	54.3
04	237 24.6	09.4	130 12.5	12.3	18 27.1	2.6	54.3
05	252 24.8	08.4	144 43.8	12.3	18 24.5	2.6	54.3
06	267 24.9	S 4 07.4	159 15.1	12.4	N18 21.9	2.8	54.3
07	282 25.1	06.4	173 46.5	12.4	18 19.1	2.9	54.3
08	297 25.3	05.4	188 17.9	12.4	18 16.2	2.9	54.3
09	312 25.4	.. 04.5	202 49.3	12.4	18 13.3	3.0	54.3
10	327 25.6	03.5	217 20.7	12.5	18 10.3	3.1	54.2
11	342 25.8	02.5	231 52.2	12.5	18 07.2	3.2	54.2
12	357 25.9	S 4 01.5	246 23.7	12.5	N18 04.0	3.2	54.2
13	12 26.1	4 00.5	260 55.2	12.6	18 00.8	3.4	54.2
14	27 26.2	3 59.6	275 26.8	12.5	17 57.4	3.4	54.2
15	42 26.4	.. 58.6	289 58.3	12.6	17 54.0	3.5	54.2
16	57 26.6	57.6	304 29.9	12.7	17 50.5	3.6	54.2
17	72 26.7	56.6	319 01.6	12.6	17 46.9	3.6	54.2
18	87 26.9	S 3 55.6	333 33.2	12.7	N17 43.3	3.8	54.2
19	102 27.0	54.7	348 04.9	12.7	17 39.5	3.8	54.2
20	117 27.2	53.7	2 36.6	12.8	17 35.7	3.9	54.2
21	132 27.4	.. 52.7	17 08.4	12.7	17 31.8	4.0	54.2
22	147 27.5	51.7	31 40.1	12.8	17 27.8	4.0	54.2
23	162 27.7	50.7	46 11.9	12.8	N17 23.8	4.1	54.2
SD	16.1	d 1.0	15.0		14.9		14.8

(Rows 8 00–23 = SATURDAY; 9 00–23 = SUNDAY; 10 00–23 = MONDAY)

Twilight / Sunrise / Moonrise

Lat.	Naut.	Civil	Sunrise	Moonrise 8	9	10	11
N 72	04 29	05 49	06 56	▭	▭	▭	09 53
N 70	04 38	05 50	06 51	07 15	07 59	09 13	10 41
68	04 46	05 51	06 46	08 04	08 50	09 55	11 11
66	04 52	05 52	06 43	08 35	09 22	10 23	11 34
64	04 58	05 53	06 40	08 58	09 46	10 44	11 52
62	05 02	05 53	06 37	09 16	10 04	11 02	12 06
60	05 06	05 54	06 35	09 32	10 20	11 16	12 19
N 58	05 09	05 54	06 33	09 44	10 33	11 28	12 29
56	05 11	05 54	06 31	09 56	10 44	11 39	12 38
54	05 14	05 55	06 30	10 06	10 54	11 48	12 46
52	05 16	05 55	06 28	10 14	11 03	11 56	12 54
50	05 17	05 55	06 27	10 22	11 11	12 04	13 00
45	05 21	05 55	06 24	10 39	11 27	12 20	13 14
N 40	05 23	05 54	06 21	10 53	11 41	12 33	13 26
35	05 25	05 54	06 19	11 04	11 53	12 44	13 36
30	05 26	05 53	06 17	11 14	12 03	12 53	13 44
20	05 26	05 52	06 14	11 32	12 21	13 10	13 59
N 10	05 25	05 49	06 10	11 47	12 36	13 24	14 12
0	05 22	05 47	06 07	12 02	12 50	13 38	14 24
S 10	05 18	05 43	06 04	12 16	13 05	13 51	14 36
20	05 13	05 38	06 00	12 32	13 20	14 06	14 49
30	05 06	05 32	05 56	12 49	13 38	14 22	15 04
35	04 58	05 28	05 54	13 00	13 48	14 32	15 13
40	04 51	05 24	05 51	13 11	14 00	14 43	15 22
45	04 43	05 18	05 48	13 25	14 13	14 56	15 34
S 50	04 32	05 11	05 44	13 42	14 30	15 12	15 47
52	04 26	05 08	05 42	13 50	14 38	15 19	15 54
54	04 20	05 04	05 40	13 59	14 47	15 27	16 01
56	04 13	05 00	05 38	14 09	14 57	15 36	16 09
58	04 05	04 55	05 35	14 21	15 08	15 47	16 18
S 60	03 56	04 49	05 32	14 34	15 21	15 58	16 28

Sunset / Twilight / Moonset

Lat.	Sunset	Civil	Naut.	Moonset 8	9	10	11
N 72	17 28	18 35	19 56	▭	▭	▭	06 41
N 70	17 32	18 33	19 46	04 20	05 18	05 43	05 52
68	17 36	18 32	19 38	03 32	04 27	05 01	05 21
66	17 40	18 31	19 31	03 01	03 55	04 33	04 58
64	17 42	18 30	19 25	02 38	03 31	04 11	04 40
62	17 45	18 29	19 21	02 20	03 12	03 53	04 25
60	17 47	18 29	19 17	02 05	02 57	03 39	04 12
N 58	17 49	18 28	19 14	01 52	02 44	03 27	04 01
56	17 51	18 28	19 11	01 41	02 32	03 16	03 52
54	17 52	18 28	19 09	01 31	02 22	03 06	03 43
52	17 54	18 27	19 07	01 22	02 14	02 58	03 36
50	17 55	18 27	19 05	01 14	02 06	02 50	03 29
45	17 58	18 27	19 01	00 58	01 49	02 34	03 14
N 40	18 00	18 27	18 59	00 44	01 35	02 21	03 02
35	18 02	18 28	18 57	00 33	01 23	02 09	02 52
30	18 04	18 28	18 56	00 23	01 13	02 00	02 43
20	18 08	18 30	18 55	00 05	00 55	01 42	02 27
N 10	18 11	18 32	18 56	24 40	00 40	01 27	02 13
0	18 14	18 35	18 59	24 25	00 25	01 13	02 00
S 10	18 17	18 38	19 02	24 11	00 11	00 59	01 48
20	18 20	18 42	19 08	23 55	24 44	00 44	01 34
30	18 24	18 48	19 16	23 38	24 27	00 27	01 18
35	18 27	18 52	19 22	23 27	24 17	00 17	01 09
40	18 32	18 57	19 29	23 15	24 06	00 06	00 58
45	18 34	19 02	19 37	23 01	23 52	24 45	00 45
S 50	18 36	19 09	19 48	22 44	23 35	24 30	00 30
52	18 38	19 12	19 53	22 36	23 27	24 23	00 23
54	18 40	19 16	19 59	22 27	23 19	24 15	00 15
56	18 42	19 20	20 06	22 17	23 09	24 06	00 06
58	18 45	19 25	20 14	22 06	22 58	23 56	25 00
S 60	18 47	19 30	20 23	21 52	22 45	23 45	24 50

SUN / MOON — Equation of Time, Mer. Pass., Age, Phase

Day	Eqn. of Time 00h	Eqn. of Time 12h	Mer. Pass.	Mer. Pass. Upper	Mer. Pass. Lower	Age	Phase
8	10 54	10 47	12 11	18 14	05 49	07	50
9	10 39	10 32	12 11	19 02	06 38	08	59
10	10 24	10 17	12 10	19 49	07 26	09	68

UT	ARIES GHA	VENUS −4.6 GHA	Dec	MARS −0.8 GHA	Dec	JUPITER −2.3 GHA	Dec	SATURN +0.4 GHA	Dec	STARS Name	SHA	Dec
d h	° ′	° ′	° ′	° ′	° ′	° ′	° ′	° ′	° ′		° ′	° ′
11 00	168 34.8	222 37.5	S16 00.2	322 29.9	S 7 43.8	67 09.9	N23 16.3	297 05.3	S16 16.6	Acamar	315 18.2	S40 15.2
01	183 37.3	237 37.7	15 59.9	337 32.6	43.7	82 12.3	16.3	312 07.8	16.6	Achernar	335 26.9	S57 10.1
02	198 39.8	252 37.8	59.7	352 35.4	43.6	97 14.7	16.3	327 10.3	16.6	Acrux	173 07.9	S63 10.7
03	213 42.2	267 38.0 ..	59.4	7 38.1 ..	43.5	112 17.2 ..	16.3	342 12.8 ..	16.6	Adhara	255 12.0	S28 59.9
04	228 44.7	282 38.1	59.2	22 40.9	43.4	127 19.6	16.3	357 15.3	16.6	Aldebaran	290 48.8	N16 32.1
05	243 47.2	297 38.2	59.0	37 43.6	43.3	142 22.0	16.3	12 17.8	16.5			
06	258 49.6	312 38.4	S15 58.7	52 46.3	S 7 43.1	157 24.4	N23 16.3	27 20.3	S16 16.5	Alioth	166 19.8	N55 52.8
07	273 52.1	327 38.5	58.5	67 49.1	43.0	172 26.9	16.3	42 22.8	16.5	Alkaid	152 58.1	N49 14.3
08	288 54.5	342 38.7	58.2	82 51.8	42.9	187 29.3	16.3	57 25.3	16.5	Al Na'ir	27 43.6	S46 53.4
09	303 57.0	357 38.8 ..	58.0	97 54.6 ..	42.8	202 31.7 ..	16.3	72 27.8 ..	16.5	Alnilam	275 45.8	S 1 11.9
10	318 59.5	12 38.9	57.7	112 57.4	42.7	217 34.1	16.3	87 30.3	16.5	Alphard	217 55.3	S 8 43.5
11	334 01.9	27 39.1	57.5	128 00.1	42.6	232 36.5	16.3	102 32.8	16.4			
12	349 04.4	42 39.2	S15 57.2	143 02.9	S 7 42.5	247 39.0	N23 16.3	117 35.3	S16 16.4	Alphecca	126 10.4	N26 39.9
13	4 06.9	57 39.3	57.0	158 05.6	42.4	262 41.4	16.3	132 37.8	16.4	Alpheratz	357 43.3	N29 10.1
14	19 09.3	72 39.5	56.8	173 08.4	42.3	277 43.8	16.3	147 40.3	16.4	Altair	62 07.9	N 8 54.4
15	34 11.8	87 39.6 ..	56.5	188 11.1 ..	42.1	292 46.2 ..	16.3	162 42.8 ..	16.4	Ankaa	353 15.6	S42 13.8
16	49 14.3	102 39.7	56.3	203 13.9	42.0	307 48.6	16.3	177 45.3	16.3	Antares	112 25.5	S26 27.6
17	64 16.7	117 39.8	56.0	218 16.7	41.9	322 51.0	16.3	192 47.8	16.3			
18	79 19.2	132 40.0	S15 55.7	233 19.4	S 7 41.8	337 53.5	N23 16.3	207 50.3	S16 16.3	Arcturus	145 55.0	N19 06.4
19	94 21.7	147 40.1	55.5	248 22.2	41.7	352 55.9	16.3	222 52.8	16.3	Atria	107 26.8	S69 02.8
20	109 24.1	162 40.2	55.2	263 25.0	41.6	7 58.3	16.3	237 55.3	16.3	Avior	234 17.3	S59 33.7
21	124 26.6	177 40.4 ..	55.0	278 27.7 ..	41.5	23 00.7 ..	16.3	252 57.8 ..	16.3	Bellatrix	278 31.4	N 6 21.5
22	139 29.0	192 40.5	54.7	293 30.5	41.3	38 03.1	16.3	268 00.3	16.2	Betelgeuse	271 00.7	N 7 24.3
23	154 31.5	207 40.6	54.5	308 33.3	41.2	53 05.5	16.3	283 02.8	16.2			
12 00	169 34.0	222 40.7	S15 54.2	323 36.0	S 7 41.1	68 08.0	N23 16.3	298 05.3	S16 16.2	Canopus	263 55.8	S52 42.7
01	184 36.4	237 40.8	54.0	338 38.8	41.0	83 10.4	16.3	313 07.8	16.2	Capella	280 33.7	N46 00.7
02	199 38.9	252 41.0	53.7	353 41.6	40.9	98 12.8	16.3	328 10.3	16.2	Deneb	49 31.4	N45 19.8
03	214 41.4	267 41.1 ..	53.4	8 44.4 ..	40.7	113 15.2 ..	16.3	343 12.8 ..	16.2	Denebola	182 32.8	N14 29.4
04	229 43.8	282 41.2	53.2	23 47.1	40.6	128 17.6	16.3	358 15.3	16.1	Diphda	348 55.7	S17 54.7
05	244 46.3	297 41.3	52.9	38 49.9	40.5	143 20.0	16.3	13 17.8	16.1			
06	259 48.8	312 41.4	S15 52.7	53 52.7	S 7 40.4	158 22.4	N23 16.2	28 20.3	S16 16.1	Dubhe	193 50.5	N61 40.3
07	274 51.2	327 41.6	52.4	68 55.5	40.3	173 24.8	16.2	43 22.8	16.1	Elnath	278 11.9	N28 37.0
08	289 53.7	342 41.7	52.1	83 58.2	40.2	188 27.3	16.2	58 25.3	16.1	Eltanin	90 46.0	N51 29.1
09	304 56.1	357 41.8 ..	51.9	99 01.0 ..	40.0	203 29.7 ..	16.2	73 27.8 ..	16.1	Enif	33 46.9	N 9 56.4
10	319 58.6	12 41.9	51.6	114 03.8	39.9	218 32.1	16.2	88 30.3	16.0	Fomalhaut	15 23.8	S29 32.8
11	335 01.1	27 42.0	51.3	129 06.6	39.8	233 34.5	16.2	103 32.8	16.0			
12	350 03.5	42 42.1	S15 51.1	144 09.4	S 7 39.7	248 36.9	N23 16.2	118 35.3	S16 16.0	Gacrux	171 59.7	S57 11.6
13	5 06.0	57 42.2	50.8	159 12.2	39.5	263 39.3	16.2	133 37.8	16.0	Gienah	175 51.4	S17 37.4
14	20 08.5	72 42.3	50.5	174 15.0	39.4	278 41.7	16.2	148 40.3	16.0	Hadar	148 46.6	S60 26.3
15	35 10.9	87 42.4 ..	50.3	189 17.7 ..	39.3	293 44.1 ..	16.2	163 42.8 ..	15.9	Hamal	328 00.4	N23 31.7
16	50 13.4	102 42.6	50.0	204 20.5	39.2	308 46.5	16.2	178 45.3	15.9	Kaus Aust.	83 43.2	S34 22.4
17	65 15.9	117 42.7	49.7	219 23.3	39.1	323 49.0	16.2	193 47.8	15.9			
18	80 18.3	132 42.8	S15 49.5	234 26.1	S 7 38.9	338 51.4	N23 16.2	208 50.3	S16 15.9	Kochab	137 19.5	N74 05.6
19	95 20.8	147 42.9	49.2	249 28.9	38.8	353 53.8	16.2	223 52.8	15.9	Markab	13 38.1	N15 16.9
20	110 23.3	162 43.0	48.9	264 31.7	38.7	8 56.2	16.2	238 55.3	15.9	Menkar	314 14.7	N 4 08.5
21	125 25.7	177 43.1 ..	48.7	279 34.5 ..	38.6	23 58.6 ..	16.2	253 57.8 ..	15.8	Menkent	148 06.6	S36 26.3
22	140 28.2	192 43.2	48.4	294 37.3	38.4	39 01.0	16.2	269 00.3	15.8	Miaplacidus	221 38.7	S69 46.9
23	155 30.6	207 43.3	48.1	309 40.1	38.3	54 03.4	16.2	284 02.9	15.8			
13 00	170 33.1	222 43.4	S15 47.8	324 42.9	S 7 38.2	69 05.8	N23 16.2	299 05.4	S16 15.8	Mirfak	308 39.8	N49 54.7
01	185 35.6	237 43.5	47.6	339 45.7	38.0	84 08.2	16.2	314 07.9	15.8	Nunki	75 57.8	S26 16.5
02	200 38.0	252 43.6	47.3	354 48.5	37.9	99 10.6	16.2	329 10.4	15.7	Peacock	53 18.9	S56 41.1
03	215 40.5	267 43.7 ..	47.0	9 51.3 ..	37.8	114 13.0 ..	16.2	344 12.9 ..	15.7	Pollux	243 26.9	N27 59.3
04	230 43.0	282 43.8	46.7	24 54.1	37.7	129 15.4	16.2	359 15.4	15.7	Procyon	244 59.0	N 5 11.0
05	245 45.4	297 43.9	46.4	39 56.9	37.5	144 17.8	16.2	14 17.9	15.7			
06	260 47.9	312 44.0	S15 46.2	54 59.8	S 7 37.4	159 20.2	N23 16.2	29 20.4	S16 15.7	Rasalhague	96 06.0	N12 33.0
07	275 50.4	327 44.1	45.9	70 02.6	37.3	174 22.6	16.2	44 22.9	15.6	Regulus	207 42.7	N11 53.6
08	290 52.8	342 44.2	45.6	85 05.4	37.1	189 25.0	16.2	59 25.4	15.6	Rigel	281 11.6	S 8 11.5
09	305 55.3	357 44.3 ..	45.3	100 08.2 ..	37.0	204 27.4 ..	16.2	74 27.9 ..	15.6	Rigil Kent.	139 50.5	S60 53.4
10	320 57.8	12 44.4	45.0	115 11.0	36.9	219 29.8	16.2	89 30.4	15.6	Sabik	102 11.9	S15 44.4
11	336 00.2	27 44.4	44.7	130 13.8	36.8	234 32.2	16.2	104 32.9	15.6			
12	351 02.7	42 44.5	S15 44.5	145 16.6	S 7 36.6	249 34.6	N23 16.2	119 35.4	S16 15.6	Schedar	349 40.4	N56 37.0
13	6 05.1	57 44.6	44.2	160 19.5	36.5	264 37.0	16.2	134 38.0	15.5	Shaula	96 21.2	S37 06.6
14	21 07.6	72 44.7	43.9	175 22.3	36.4	279 39.4	16.2	149 40.5	15.5	Sirius	258 33.1	S16 44.5
15	36 10.1	87 44.8 ..	43.6	190 25.1 ..	36.2	294 41.8 ..	16.2	164 43.0 ..	15.5	Spica	158 30.4	S11 14.2
16	51 12.5	102 44.9	43.3	205 27.9	36.1	309 44.2	16.2	179 45.5	15.5	Suhail	222 51.7	S43 29.8
17	66 15.0	117 45.0	43.0	220 30.7	36.0	324 46.6	16.2	194 48.0	15.5			
18	81 17.5	132 45.1	S15 42.7	235 33.6	S 7 35.8	339 49.0	N23 16.2	209 50.5	S16 15.4	Vega	80 38.7	N38 47.7
19	96 19.9	147 45.1	42.4	250 36.4	35.7	354 51.4	16.2	224 53.0	15.4	Zuben'ubi	137 04.6	S16 06.0
20	111 22.4	162 45.2	42.1	265 39.2	35.6	9 53.8	16.2	239 55.5	15.4		SHA	Mer.Pass.
21	126 24.9	177 45.3 ..	41.9	280 42.1 ..	35.4	24 56.2 ..	16.2	254 58.0 ..	15.4		° ′	h m
22	141 27.3	192 45.4	41.6	295 44.9	35.3	39 58.6	16.2	270 00.5	15.4	Venus	53 06.8	9 09
23	156 29.8	207 45.5	41.3	310 47.7	35.1	55 01.0	16.2	285 03.0	15.3	Mars	154 02.1	2 25
	h m									Jupiter	258 34.0	19 24
Mer. Pass. 12 39.7		v 0.1	d 0.3	v 2.8	d 0.1	v 2.4	d 0.0	v 2.5	d 0.0	Saturn	128 31.3	4 07

UT	SUN GHA	SUN Dec	MOON GHA	v	MOON Dec	d	HP
d h	° ′	° ′	° ′	′	° ′	′	′
11 00	177 27.9	S 3 49.8	60 43.7	12.9	N17 19.7	4.2	54.1
01	192 28.0	48.8	75 15.6	12.9	17 15.5	4.3	54.1
02	207 28.2	47.8	89 47.5	12.9	17 11.2	4.4	54.1
03	222 28.3	.. 46.8	104 19.4	12.9	17 06.8	4.4	54.1
04	237 28.5	45.8	118 51.3	12.9	17 02.4	4.5	54.1
05	252 28.7	44.9	133 23.2	13.0	16 57.9	4.6	54.1
06	267 28.8	S 3 43.9	147 55.2	13.0	N16 53.3	4.7	54.1
07	282 29.0	42.9	162 27.2	13.1	16 48.6	4.7	54.1
08	297 29.2	41.9	176 59.3	13.0	16 43.9	4.8	54.1
09	312 29.3	.. 40.9	191 31.3	13.1	16 39.1	4.9	54.1
10	327 29.5	39.9	206 03.4	13.1	16 34.2	5.0	54.1
11	342 29.7	39.0	220 35.5	13.2	16 29.2	5.0	54.1
12	357 29.8	S 3 38.0	235 07.7	13.1	N16 24.2	5.1	54.1
13	12 30.0	37.0	249 39.8	13.2	16 19.1	5.2	54.1
14	27 30.2	36.0	264 12.0	13.2	16 13.9	5.2	54.1
15	42 30.3	.. 35.0	278 44.2	13.3	16 08.7	5.3	54.1
16	57 30.5	34.1	293 16.5	13.3	16 03.4	5.4	54.1
17	72 30.7	33.1	307 48.8	13.2	15 58.0	5.4	54.1
18	87 30.8	S 3 32.1	322 21.0	13.4	N15 52.6	5.6	54.1
19	102 31.0	31.1	336 53.4	13.3	15 47.0	5.6	54.1
20	117 31.1	30.1	351 25.7	13.4	15 41.4	5.6	54.1
21	132 31.3	.. 29.1	5 58.1	13.4	15 35.8	5.8	54.1
22	147 31.5	28.2	20 30.5	13.4	15 30.0	5.8	54.1
23	162 31.6	27.2	35 02.9	13.4	15 24.2	5.8	54.1
12 00	177 31.8	S 3 26.2	49 35.3	13.5	N15 18.4	6.0	54.1
01	192 32.0	25.2	64 07.8	13.5	15 12.4	6.0	54.1
02	207 32.1	24.2	78 40.3	13.5	15 06.4	6.0	54.1
03	222 32.3	.. 23.2	93 12.8	13.6	15 00.4	6.2	54.1
04	237 32.5	22.3	107 45.4	13.5	14 54.2	6.2	54.1
05	252 32.6	21.3	122 17.9	13.6	14 48.0	6.2	54.1
06	267 32.8	S 3 20.3	136 50.5	13.6	N14 41.8	6.4	54.1
07	282 33.0	19.3	151 23.1	13.6	14 35.4	6.4	54.1
08	297 33.2	18.3	165 55.7	13.7	14 29.0	6.4	54.1
09	312 33.3	.. 17.3	180 28.4	13.7	14 22.6	6.5	54.1
10	327 33.5	16.4	195 01.1	13.7	14 16.1	6.6	54.1
11	342 33.7	15.4	209 33.8	13.7	14 09.5	6.7	54.1
12	357 33.8	S 3 14.4	224 06.5	13.7	N14 02.8	6.7	54.1
13	12 34.0	13.4	238 39.2	13.8	13 56.1	6.7	54.1
14	27 34.2	12.4	253 12.0	13.8	13 49.4	6.9	54.1
15	42 34.3	.. 11.4	267 44.8	13.8	13 42.5	6.9	54.1
16	57 34.5	10.5	282 17.6	13.8	13 35.6	6.9	54.1
17	72 34.7	09.5	296 50.4	13.9	13 28.7	7.0	54.1
18	87 34.8	S 3 08.5	311 23.3	13.8	N13 21.7	7.1	54.2
19	102 35.0	07.5	325 56.1	13.9	13 14.6	7.1	54.2
20	117 35.2	06.5	340 29.0	13.9	13 07.5	7.2	54.2
21	132 35.3	.. 05.5	355 01.9	14.0	13 00.3	7.2	54.2
22	147 35.5	04.6	9 34.9	13.9	12 53.1	7.3	54.2
23	162 35.7	03.6	24 07.8	14.0	12 45.8	7.4	54.2
13 00	177 35.8	S 3 02.6	38 40.8	14.0	N12 38.4	7.4	54.2
01	192 36.0	01.6	53 13.8	14.0	12 31.0	7.5	54.2
02	207 36.2	3 00.6	67 46.8	14.0	12 23.5	7.5	54.2
03	222 36.4	2 59.6	82 19.8	14.0	12 16.0	7.6	54.2
04	237 36.5	58.6	96 52.8	14.1	12 08.4	7.6	54.2
05	252 36.7	57.7	111 25.9	14.1	12 00.8	7.7	54.2
06	267 36.9	S 2 56.7	125 59.0	14.0	N11 53.1	7.8	54.2
07	282 37.0	55.7	140 32.0	14.2	11 45.3	7.8	54.2
08	297 37.2	54.7	155 05.2	14.1	11 37.5	7.8	54.2
09	312 37.4	.. 53.7	169 38.3	14.1	11 29.7	7.9	54.3
10	327 37.6	52.7	184 11.4	14.2	11 21.8	7.9	54.3
11	342 37.7	51.8	198 44.6	14.1	11 13.9	8.0	54.3
12	357 37.9	S 2 50.8	213 17.7	14.2	N11 05.9	8.1	54.3
13	12 38.1	49.8	227 50.9	14.2	10 57.8	8.1	54.3
14	27 38.2	48.8	242 24.1	14.2	10 49.7	8.1	54.3
15	42 38.4	.. 47.8	256 57.3	14.2	10 41.6	8.2	54.3
16	57 38.6	46.8	271 30.5	14.3	10 33.4	8.3	54.3
17	72 38.7	45.8	286 03.8	14.2	10 25.1	8.3	54.3
18	87 38.9	S 2 44.9	300 37.0	14.3	N10 16.8	8.3	54.3
19	102 39.1	43.9	315 10.3	14.3	10 08.5	8.4	54.4
20	117 39.3	42.9	329 43.6	14.2	10 00.1	8.5	54.4
21	132 39.4	.. 41.9	344 16.8	14.3	9 51.6	8.4	54.4
22	147 39.6	40.9	358 50.1	14.3	9 43.2	8.6	54.4
23	162 39.8	39.9	13 23.4	14.3	N 9 34.6	8.5	54.4
	SD 16.1	d 1.0	SD 14.7		14.7		14.8

The left side rows are labelled **TUESDAY** (11), **WEDNESDAY** (12), **THURSDAY** (13).

Twilight / Moonrise

Lat.	Twilight Naut.	Twilight Civil	Sunrise	Moonrise 11	12	13	14
°	h m	h m	h m	h m	h m	h m	h m
N 72	04 12	05 33	06 40	09 53	11 43	13 25	15 05
N 70	04 24	05 36	06 37	10 41	12 12	13 44	15 16
68	04 33	05 39	06 34	11 11	12 34	13 58	15 24
66	04 40	05 41	06 32	11 34	12 51	14 10	15 31
64	04 47	05 42	06 30	11 52	13 04	14 20	15 38
62	04 52	05 44	06 28	12 06	13 16	14 28	15 43
60	04 56	05 45	06 26	12 19	13 26	14 35	15 47
N 58	05 00	05 46	06 25	12 29	13 34	14 42	15 51
56	05 03	05 47	06 24	12 38	13 42	14 47	15 55
54	05 06	05 47	06 23	12 46	13 48	14 52	15 58
52	05 09	05 48	06 21	12 54	13 54	14 57	16 01
50	05 11	05 48	06 21	13 00	14 00	15 01	16 03
45	05 15	05 49	06 18	13 14	14 11	15 10	16 09
N 40	05 18	05 50	06 17	13 26	14 21	15 17	16 14
35	05 21	05 50	06 15	13 36	14 29	15 23	16 18
30	05 22	05 50	06 14	13 44	14 36	15 29	16 21
20	05 24	05 49	06 11	13 59	14 49	15 38	16 28
N 10	05 23	05 48	06 09	14 12	15 00	15 46	16 33
0	05 22	05 46	06 06	14 24	15 10	15 54	16 38
S 10	05 19	05 43	06 04	14 36	15 20	16 02	16 43
20	05 14	05 39	06 01	14 49	15 31	16 10	16 49
30	05 06	05 34	05 58	15 04	15 43	16 20	16 55
35	05 01	05 31	05 56	15 13	15 50	16 25	16 58
40	04 55	05 27	05 54	15 22	15 58	16 31	17 02
45	04 47	05 22	05 52	15 34	16 08	16 38	17 07
S 50	04 37	05 16	05 49	15 47	16 19	16 47	17 12
52	04 32	05 13	05 47	15 54	16 24	16 51	17 15
54	04 27	05 10	05 46	16 01	16 30	16 55	17 18
56	04 20	05 06	05 44	16 09	16 36	17 00	17 21
58	04 13	05 02	05 42	16 18	16 43	17 05	17 24
S 60	04 05	04 57	05 40	16 28	16 51	17 11	17 28

Moonset

Lat.	Sunset	Twilight Civil	Twilight Naut.	Moonset 11	12	13	14
°	h m	h m	h m	h m	h m	h m	h m
N 72	17 42	18 49	20 11	06 41	06 26	06 16	06 08
N 70	17 45	18 46	19 59	05 52	05 55	05 56	05 55
68	17 47	18 43	19 49	05 21	05 33	05 40	05 45
66	17 50	18 41	19 41	04 58	05 15	05 28	05 37
64	17 51	18 39	19 35	04 40	05 01	05 17	05 30
62	17 53	18 37	19 29	04 25	04 49	05 08	05 23
60	17 55	18 36	19 25	04 12	04 39	05 00	05 18
N 58	17 56	18 35	19 21	04 01	04 30	04 53	05 13
56	17 57	18 34	19 17	03 52	04 22	04 47	05 09
54	17 58	18 33	19 15	03 43	04 15	04 41	05 05
52	17 59	18 33	19 12	03 36	04 08	04 36	05 02
50	18 00	18 32	19 10	03 29	04 02	04 32	04 59
45	18 02	18 31	19 05	03 14	03 50	04 22	04 52
N 40	18 03	18 30	19 02	03 02	03 40	04 14	04 46
35	18 05	18 30	19 00	02 52	03 31	04 07	04 41
30	18 06	18 30	18 58	02 43	03 23	04 01	04 36
20	18 09	18 31	18 56	02 27	03 09	03 50	04 29
N 10	18 11	18 32	18 56	02 13	02 58	03 40	04 22
0	18 13	18 34	18 58	02 00	02 46	03 31	04 15
S 10	18 15	18 36	19 01	01 48	02 35	03 22	04 09
20	18 18	18 40	19 07	01 34	02 23	03 13	04 02
30	18 21	18 45	19 13	01 18	02 09	03 01	03 54
35	18 23	18 48	19 18	01 09	02 01	02 55	03 49
40	18 25	18 52	19 24	00 58	01 52	02 48	03 44
45	18 27	18 56	19 31	00 45	01 41	02 39	03 38
S 50	18 30	19 02	19 41	00 30	01 28	02 29	03 31
52	18 31	19 05	19 46	00 23	01 22	02 24	03 27
54	18 33	19 08	19 51	00 15	01 16	02 19	03 24
56	18 34	19 12	19 57	00 06	01 08	02 13	03 19
58	18 36	19 16	20 04	25 00	01 00	02 06	03 15
S 60	18 38	19 20	20 12	24 50	00 50	01 59	03 10

SUN and MOON

Day	SUN Eqn. of Time 00h	12h	Mer. Pass.	MOON Mer. Pass. Upper	Lower	Age	Phase
d	m s	m s	h m	h m	h m	d	%
11	10 09	10 01	12 10	20 35	08 12	10	77
12	09 53	09 45	12 10	21 20	08 58	11	84
13	09 37	09 29	12 09	22 05	09 43	12	90

UT	ARIES GHA	VENUS −4.6 GHA	Dec	MARS −0.9 GHA	Dec	JUPITER −2.3 GHA	Dec	SATURN +0.4 GHA	Dec	STARS Name	SHA	Dec
d h	° ′	° ′	° ′	° ′	° ′	° ′	° ′	° ′	° ′		° ′	° ′
14 00	171 32.2	222 45.5	S15 41.0	325 50.5	S 7 35.0	70 03.4	N23 16.2	300 05.6	S16 15.3	Acamar	315 18.2	S40 15.2
01	186 34.7	237 45.6	40.7	340 53.4	34.9	85 05.8	16.2	315 08.1	15.3	Achernar	335 27.0	S57 10.1
02	201 37.2	252 45.7	40.4	355 56.2	34.7	100 08.2	16.2	330 10.6	15.3	Acrux	173 07.9	S63 10.7
03	216 39.6	267 45.8 ..	40.1	10 59.0 ..	34.6	115 10.6 ..	16.2	345 13.1 ..	15.3	Adhara	255 12.0	S28 59.9
04	231 42.1	282 45.9	39.8	26 01.9	34.5	130 13.0	16.2	0 15.6	15.2	Aldebaran	290 48.9	N16 32.1
05	246 44.6	297 45.9	39.5	41 04.7	34.3	145 15.4	16.2	15 18.1	15.2			
06	261 47.0	312 46.0	S15 39.2	56 07.6	S 7 34.2	160 17.8	N23 16.2	30 20.6	S16 15.2	Alioth	166 19.8	N55 52.8
07	276 49.5	327 46.1	38.9	71 10.4	34.0	175 20.2	16.2	45 23.1	15.2	Alkaid	152 58.1	N49 14.3
08	291 52.0	342 46.2	38.6	86 13.2	33.9	190 22.6	16.2	60 25.6	15.2	Al Na'ir	27 43.5	S46 53.4
F 09	306 54.4	357 46.2 ..	38.3	101 16.1 ..	33.8	205 25.0 ..	16.2	75 28.2 ..	15.1	Alnilam	275 45.8	S 1 11.9
R 10	321 56.9	12 46.3	38.0	116 18.9	33.6	220 27.4	16.2	90 30.7	15.1	Alphard	217 55.3	S 8 43.5
I 11	336 59.4	27 46.4	37.7	131 21.8	33.5	235 29.8	16.2	105 33.2	15.1			
D 12	352 01.8	42 46.4	S15 37.4	146 24.6	S 7 33.3	250 32.2	N23 16.2	120 35.7	S16 15.1	Alphecca	126 10.4	N26 39.9
A 13	7 04.3	57 46.5	37.1	161 27.5	33.2	265 34.6	16.2	135 38.2	15.1	Alpheratz	357 43.3	N29 10.1
Y 14	22 06.7	72 46.6	36.8	176 30.3	33.1	280 37.0	16.2	150 40.7	15.0	Altair	62 07.9	N 8 54.4
15	37 09.2	87 46.7 ..	36.4	191 33.2 ..	32.9	295 39.4 ..	16.2	165 43.2 ..	15.0	Ankaa	353 15.6	S42 13.8
16	52 11.7	102 46.7	36.1	206 36.0	32.8	310 41.7	16.2	180 45.7	15.0	Antares	112 25.5	S26 27.6
17	67 14.1	117 46.8	35.8	221 38.9	32.6	325 44.1	16.2	195 48.2	15.0			
18	82 16.6	132 46.9	S15 35.5	236 41.7	S 7 32.5	340 46.5	N23 16.2	210 50.8	S16 15.0	Arcturus	145 55.0	N19 06.4
19	97 19.1	147 46.9	35.2	251 44.6	32.3	355 48.9	16.2	225 53.3	14.9	Atria	107 26.7	S69 02.8
20	112 21.5	162 47.0	34.9	266 47.5	32.2	10 51.3	16.2	240 55.8	14.9	Avior	234 17.3	S59 33.7
21	127 24.0	177 47.0 ..	34.6	281 50.3 ..	32.0	25 53.7 ..	16.2	255 58.3 ..	14.9	Bellatrix	278 31.5	N 6 21.5
22	142 26.5	192 47.1	34.3	296 53.2	31.9	40 56.1	16.1	271 00.8	14.9	Betelgeuse	271 00.7	N 7 24.3
23	157 28.9	207 47.2	34.0	311 56.0	31.8	55 58.5	16.1	286 03.3	14.9			
15 00	172 31.4	222 47.2	S15 33.6	326 58.9	S 7 31.6	71 00.9	N23 16.1	301 05.8	S16 14.8	Canopus	263 55.8	S52 42.7
01	187 33.8	237 47.3	33.3	342 01.8	31.5	86 03.3	16.1	316 08.4	14.8	Capella	280 33.7	N46 00.7
02	202 36.3	252 47.4	33.0	357 04.6	31.3	101 05.6	16.1	331 10.9	14.8	Deneb	49 31.4	N45 19.8
03	217 38.8	267 47.4 ..	32.7	12 07.5 ..	31.2	116 08.0 ..	16.1	346 13.4 ..	14.8	Denebola	182 32.8	N14 29.4
04	232 41.2	282 47.5	32.4	27 10.4	31.0	131 10.4	16.1	1 15.9	14.8	Diphda	348 55.7	S17 54.7
05	247 43.7	297 47.5	32.1	42 13.2	30.9	146 12.8	16.1	16 18.4	14.7			
06	262 46.2	312 47.6	S15 31.7	57 16.1	S 7 30.7	161 15.2	N23 16.1	31 20.9	S16 14.7	Dubhe	193 50.5	N61 40.3
07	277 48.6	327 47.6	31.4	72 19.0	30.6	176 17.6	16.1	46 23.4	14.7	Elnath	278 12.0	N28 37.0
S 08	292 51.1	342 47.7	31.1	87 21.9	30.4	191 20.0	16.1	61 26.0	14.7	Eltanin	90 45.9	N51 29.1
A 09	307 53.6	357 47.7 ..	30.8	102 24.7 ..	30.3	206 22.3 ..	16.1	76 28.5 ..	14.7	Enif	33 46.9	N 9 56.4
T 10	322 56.0	12 47.8	30.5	117 27.6	30.1	221 24.7	16.1	91 31.0	14.6	Fomalhaut	15 23.8	S29 32.8
U 11	337 58.5	27 47.9	30.1	132 30.5	30.0	236 27.1	16.1	106 33.5	14.6			
R 12	353 01.0	42 47.9	S15 29.8	147 33.4	S 7 29.8	251 29.5	N23 16.1	121 36.0	S16 14.6	Gacrux	171 59.7	S57 11.6
D 13	8 03.4	57 48.0	29.5	162 36.2	29.7	266 31.9	16.1	136 38.5	14.6	Gienah	175 51.4	S17 37.4
A 14	23 05.9	72 48.0	29.2	177 39.1	29.5	281 34.3	16.1	151 41.1	14.6	Hadar	148 46.5	S60 26.3
Y 15	38 08.3	87 48.1 ..	28.8	192 42.0 ..	29.4	296 36.6 ..	16.1	166 43.6 ..	14.5	Hamal	328 00.4	N23 31.7
16	53 10.8	102 48.1	28.5	207 44.9	29.2	311 39.0	16.1	181 46.1	14.5	Kaus Aust.	83 43.2	S34 22.4
17	68 13.3	117 48.2	28.2	222 47.8	29.1	326 41.4	16.1	196 48.6	14.5			
18	83 15.7	132 48.2	S15 27.9	237 50.7	S 7 28.9	341 43.8	N23 16.1	211 51.1	S16 14.5	Kochab	137 19.4	N74 05.6
19	98 18.2	147 48.2	27.5	252 53.5	28.8	356 46.2	16.1	226 53.6	14.5	Markab	13 38.1	N15 16.9
20	113 20.7	162 48.3	27.2	267 56.4	28.6	11 48.6	16.1	241 56.2	14.4	Menkar	314 14.7	N 4 08.5
21	128 23.1	177 48.3 ..	26.9	282 59.3 ..	28.4	26 50.9 ..	16.1	256 58.7 ..	14.4	Menkent	148 06.6	S36 26.3
22	143 25.6	192 48.4	26.5	298 02.2	28.3	41 53.3	16.1	272 01.2	14.4	Miaplacidus	221 38.7	S69 46.9
23	158 28.1	207 48.4	26.2	313 05.1	28.1	56 55.7	16.1	287 03.7	14.4			
16 00	173 30.5	222 48.5	S15 25.9	328 08.0	S 7 28.0	71 58.1	N23 16.1	302 06.2	S16 14.3	Mirfak	308 39.8	N49 54.7
01	188 33.0	237 48.5	25.5	343 10.9	27.8	87 00.5	16.1	317 08.8	14.3	Nunki	75 57.8	S26 16.5
02	203 35.4	252 48.6	25.2	358 13.8	27.7	102 02.8	16.1	332 11.3	14.3	Peacock	53 18.8	S56 41.0
03	218 37.9	267 48.6 ..	24.9	13 16.7 ..	27.5	117 05.2 ..	16.1	347 13.8 ..	14.3	Pollux	243 26.9	N27 59.3
04	233 40.4	282 48.6	24.5	28 19.6	27.4	132 07.6	16.1	2 16.3	14.3	Procyon	244 59.0	N 5 11.0
05	248 42.8	297 48.7	24.2	43 22.5	27.2	147 10.0	16.1	17 18.8	14.2			
06	263 45.3	312 48.7	S15 23.8	58 25.4	S 7 27.0	162 12.4	N23 16.1	32 21.3	S16 14.2	Rasalhague	96 06.0	N12 33.0
07	278 47.8	327 48.8	23.5	73 28.3	26.9	177 14.7	16.1	47 23.9	14.2	Regulus	207 42.7	N11 53.6
08	293 50.2	342 48.8	23.2	88 31.2	26.7	192 17.1	16.0	62 26.4	14.2	Rigel	281 11.6	S 8 11.5
S 09	308 52.7	357 48.8 ..	22.8	103 34.1 ..	26.6	207 19.5 ..	16.0	77 28.9 ..	14.2	Rigil Kent.	139 50.5	S60 53.4
U 10	323 55.2	12 48.9	22.5	118 37.0	26.4	222 21.9	16.0	92 31.4	14.1	Sabik	102 11.9	S15 44.4
N 11	338 57.6	27 48.9	22.1	133 39.9	26.2	237 24.2	16.0	107 33.9	14.1			
D 12	354 00.1	42 48.9	S15 21.8	148 42.8	S 7 26.1	252 26.6	N23 16.0	122 36.5	S16 14.1	Schedar	349 40.4	N56 36.9
A 13	9 02.6	57 49.0	21.4	163 45.7	25.9	267 29.0	16.0	137 39.0	14.1	Shaula	96 21.2	S37 06.6
Y 14	24 05.0	72 49.0	21.1	178 48.6	25.8	282 31.4	16.0	152 41.5	14.0	Sirius	258 33.2	S16 44.5
15	39 07.5	87 49.0 ..	20.8	193 51.5 ..	25.6	297 33.7 ..	16.0	167 44.0 ..	14.0	Spica	158 30.4	S11 14.2
16	54 09.9	102 49.1	20.4	208 54.5	25.4	312 36.1	16.0	182 46.5	14.0	Suhail	222 51.7	S43 29.8
17	69 12.4	117 49.1	20.1	223 57.4	25.3	327 38.5	16.0	197 49.1	14.0			
18	84 14.9	132 49.1	S15 19.7	239 00.3	S 7 25.1	342 40.9	N23 16.0	212 51.6	S16 14.0	Vega	80 38.7	N38 47.7
19	99 17.3	147 49.2	19.4	254 03.2	24.9	357 43.2	16.0	227 54.1	13.9	Zuben'ubi	137 04.6	S16 06.0
20	114 19.8	162 49.2	19.0	269 06.1	24.8	12 45.6	16.0	242 56.6	13.9		SHA	Mer. Pass.
21	129 22.3	177 49.2 ..	18.7	284 09.0 ..	24.6	27 48.0 ..	16.0	257 59.2 ..	13.9		° ′	h m
22	144 24.7	192 49.2	18.3	299 12.0	24.5	42 50.4	16.0	273 01.7	13.9	Venus	50 15.8	9 09
23	159 27.2	207 49.3	18.0	314 14.9	24.3	57 52.7	16.0	288 04.2	13.8	Mars	154 27.5	2 12
	h m									Jupiter	258 29.5	19 13
Mer. Pass. 12 27.9		v 0.1	d 0.3	v 2.9	d 0.2	v 2.4	d 0.0	v 2.5	d 0.0	Saturn	128 34.5	3 55

UT	SUN GHA	SUN Dec	MOON GHA	v	Dec	d	HP
d h	° ′	° ′	° ′	′	° ′	′	′
14 00	177 40.0	S 2 38.9	27 56.7	14.4	N 9 26.1	8.6	54.4
01	192 40.1	38.0	42 30.1	14.3	9 17.5	8.7	54.4
02	207 40.3	37.0	57 03.4	14.3	9 08.8	8.7	54.4
03	222 40.5	.. 36.0	71 36.7	14.4	9 00.1	8.7	54.4
04	237 40.6	35.0	86 10.1	14.4	8 51.4	8.8	54.5
05	252 40.8	34.0	100 43.5	14.3	8 42.6	8.9	54.5
06	267 41.0	S 2 33.0	115 16.8	14.4	N 8 33.7	8.8	54.5
07	282 41.2	32.0	129 50.2	14.4	8 24.9	8.9	54.5
08	297 41.3	31.1	144 23.6	14.4	8 16.0	9.0	54.5
F 09	312 41.5	.. 30.1	158 57.0	14.4	8 07.0	9.0	54.5
R 10	327 41.7	29.1	173 30.4	14.4	7 58.0	9.0	54.5
I 11	342 41.9	28.1	188 03.8	14.4	7 49.0	9.0	54.5
D 12	357 42.0	S 2 27.1	202 37.2	14.4	N 7 40.0	9.1	54.6
A 13	12 42.2	26.1	217 10.6	14.4	7 30.9	9.2	54.6
Y 14	27 42.4	25.1	231 44.0	14.4	7 21.7	9.1	54.6
15	42 42.6	.. 24.2	246 17.4	14.4	7 12.6	9.2	54.6
16	57 42.7	23.2	260 50.8	14.4	7 03.4	9.3	54.6
17	72 42.9	22.2	275 24.2	14.5	6 54.1	9.3	54.6
18	87 43.1	S 2 21.2	289 57.7	14.4	N 6 44.8	9.3	54.6
19	102 43.3	20.2	304 31.1	14.4	6 35.5	9.3	54.6
20	117 43.4	19.2	319 04.5	14.5	6 26.2	9.4	54.7
21	132 43.6	.. 18.2	333 38.0	14.4	6 16.8	9.4	54.7
22	147 43.8	17.3	348 11.4	14.4	6 07.4	9.4	54.7
23	162 44.0	16.3	2 44.8	14.4	5 58.0	9.5	54.7
15 00	177 44.1	S 2 15.3	17 18.2	14.5	N 5 48.5	9.5	54.7
01	192 44.3	14.3	31 51.7	14.4	5 39.0	9.5	54.7
02	207 44.5	13.3	46 25.1	14.4	5 29.5	9.6	54.8
03	222 44.7	.. 12.3	60 58.5	14.4	5 19.9	9.6	54.8
04	237 44.8	11.3	75 31.9	14.4	5 10.3	9.6	54.8
05	252 45.0	10.3	90 05.3	14.5	5 00.7	9.6	54.8
06	267 45.2	S 2 09.4	104 38.8	14.4	N 4 51.1	9.7	54.8
S 07	282 45.4	08.4	119 12.2	14.4	4 41.4	9.7	54.8
A 08	297 45.5	07.4	133 45.6	14.4	4 31.7	9.7	54.8
T 09	312 45.7	.. 06.4	148 19.0	14.4	4 22.0	9.7	54.9
U 10	327 45.9	05.4	162 52.4	14.4	4 12.3	9.8	54.9
R 11	342 46.1	04.4	177 25.8	14.3	4 02.5	9.8	54.9
D 12	357 46.2	S 2 03.4	191 59.1	14.4	N 3 52.7	9.8	54.9
A 13	12 46.4	02.5	206 32.5	14.4	3 42.9	9.8	54.9
Y 14	27 46.6	01.5	221 05.9	14.3	3 33.1	9.9	54.9
15	42 46.8	2 00.5	235 39.2	14.4	3 23.2	9.9	55.0
16	57 46.9	1 59.5	250 12.6	14.3	3 13.3	9.9	55.0
17	72 47.1	58.5	264 45.9	14.3	3 03.4	9.9	55.0
18	87 47.3	S 1 57.5	279 19.2	14.4	N 2 53.5	9.9	55.0
19	102 47.5	56.5	293 52.6	14.3	2 43.6	10.0	55.0
20	117 47.7	55.5	308 25.9	14.3	2 33.6	9.9	55.0
21	132 47.8	.. 54.6	322 59.2	14.2	2 23.7	10.0	55.1
22	147 48.0	53.6	337 32.4	14.3	2 13.7	10.0	55.1
23	162 48.2	52.6	352 05.7	14.3	2 03.7	10.0	55.1
16 00	177 48.4	S 1 51.6	6 39.0	14.2	N 1 53.7	10.1	55.1
01	192 48.5	50.6	21 12.2	14.2	1 43.6	10.0	55.1
02	207 48.7	49.6	35 45.4	14.3	1 33.6	10.1	55.1
03	222 48.9	.. 48.6	50 18.7	14.2	1 23.5	10.0	55.1
04	237 49.1	47.6	64 51.9	14.1	1 13.5	10.1	55.2
05	252 49.3	46.7	79 25.0	14.2	1 03.4	10.1	55.2
06	267 49.4	S 1 45.7	93 58.2	14.2	N 0 53.3	10.1	55.2
07	282 49.6	44.7	108 31.4	14.1	0 43.2	10.1	55.2
08	297 49.8	43.7	123 04.5	14.1	0 33.1	10.2	55.3
S 09	312 50.0	.. 42.7	137 37.6	14.1	0 22.9	10.1	55.3
U 10	327 50.1	41.7	152 10.7	14.1	0 12.8	10.1	55.3
N 11	342 50.3	40.7	166 43.8	14.0	N 0 02.7	10.2	55.3
D 12	357 50.5	S 1 39.7	181 16.8	14.1	S 0 07.5	10.1	55.3
A 13	12 50.7	38.8	195 49.9	14.0	0 17.6	10.2	55.3
Y 14	27 50.9	37.8	210 22.9	14.0	0 27.8	10.1	55.4
15	42 51.0	.. 36.8	224 55.9	14.0	0 37.9	10.2	55.4
16	57 51.2	35.8	239 28.9	13.9	0 48.1	10.2	55.4
17	72 51.4	34.8	254 01.8	14.0	0 58.3	10.1	55.4
18	87 51.6	S 1 33.8	268 34.8	13.9	S 1 08.4	10.2	55.4
19	102 51.8	32.8	283 07.7	13.8	1 18.6	10.2	55.5
20	117 51.9	31.8	297 40.5	13.9	1 28.8	10.2	55.5
21	132 52.1	.. 30.9	312 13.4	13.8	1 39.0	10.1	55.5
22	147 52.3	29.9	326 46.2	13.8	1 49.1	10.2	55.5
23	162 52.5	28.9	341 19.0	13.8	S 1 59.3	10.2	55.5
SD	16.1	d 1.0	SD 14.9		15.0		15.1

Lat.	Twilight Naut.	Twilight Civil	Sunrise	Moonrise 14	15	16	17
°	h m	h m	h m	h m	h m	h m	h m
N 72	03 54	05 18	06 25	15 05	16 43	18 23	20 04
N 70	04 08	05 22	06 23	15 16	16 48	18 21	19 56
68	04 19	05 26	06 21	15 24	16 51	18 19	19 49
66	04 28	05 29	06 20	15 31	16 54	18 18	19 44
64	04 36	05 32	06 19	15 38	16 57	18 17	19 39
62	04 42	05 34	06 18	15 43	16 59	18 16	19 35
60	04 47	05 36	06 17	15 47	17 01	18 15	19 31
N 58	04 51	05 38	06 16	15 51	17 02	18 14	19 28
56	04 55	05 39	06 16	15 55	17 04	18 14	19 25
54	04 59	05 40	06 15	15 58	17 05	18 13	19 23
52	05 02	05 41	06 15	16 01	17 06	18 13	19 21
50	05 04	05 42	06 14	16 03	17 07	18 12	19 19
45	05 10	05 44	06 13	16 09	17 10	18 11	19 14
N 40	05 13	05 45	06 12	16 14	17 12	18 10	19 10
35	05 16	05 46	06 11	16 18	17 13	18 10	19 07
30	05 19	05 46	06 10	16 21	17 15	18 09	19 05
20	05 21	05 47	06 09	16 28	17 18	18 08	19 00
N 10	05 22	05 46	06 07	16 33	17 20	18 07	18 56
0	05 21	05 45	06 06	16 38	17 22	18 06	18 52
S 10	05 19	05 43	06 04	16 43	17 24	18 05	18 48
20	05 15	05 40	06 02	16 49	17 27	18 05	18 44
30	05 08	05 36	06 00	16 55	17 29	18 04	18 39
35	05 04	05 34	05 59	16 58	17 31	18 03	18 36
40	04 58	05 30	05 57	17 02	17 32	18 02	18 33
45	04 51	05 26	05 56	17 07	17 34	18 02	18 30
S 50	04 42	05 21	05 54	17 12	17 37	18 01	18 26
52	04 38	05 19	05 53	17 15	17 38	18 01	18 24
54	04 33	05 16	05 51	17 18	17 39	18 00	18 22
56	04 28	05 13	05 50	17 21	17 40	18 00	18 20
58	04 21	05 09	05 49	17 24	17 42	17 59	18 17
S 60	04 14	05 05	05 47	17 28	17 43	17 59	18 14

Lat.	Sunset	Twilight Civil	Twilight Naut.	Moonset 14	15	16	17
°	h m	h m	h m	h m	h m	h m	h m
N 72	17 56	19 03	20 28	06 08	06 01	05 54	05 47
N 70	17 57	18 58	20 13	05 55	05 54	05 53	05 51
68	17 58	18 54	20 02	05 45	05 49	05 52	05 55
66	17 59	18 51	19 52	05 37	05 44	05 51	05 58
64	18 00	18 48	19 45	05 30	05 40	05 50	06 00
62	18 01	18 45	19 38	05 23	05 37	05 50	06 03
60	18 02	18 43	19 33	05 18	05 34	05 49	06 05
N 58	18 03	18 42	19 28	05 13	05 32	05 49	06 06
56	18 03	18 40	19 24	05 09	05 29	05 48	06 08
54	18 04	18 39	19 20	05 05	05 27	05 48	06 09
52	18 04	18 38	19 17	05 02	05 25	05 48	06 11
50	18 05	18 37	19 15	04 59	05 23	05 47	06 12
45	18 06	18 35	19 09	04 52	05 20	05 47	06 14
N 40	18 07	18 34	19 05	04 46	05 16	05 46	06 17
35	18 07	18 33	19 02	04 41	05 14	05 46	06 18
30	18 08	18 32	19 00	04 36	05 11	05 45	06 20
20	18 10	18 32	18 57	04 29	05 07	05 45	06 23
N 10	18 11	18 32	18 56	04 22	05 03	05 44	06 26
0	18 12	18 33	18 57	04 15	04 59	05 43	06 28
S 10	18 14	18 35	18 59	04 09	04 56	05 43	06 30
20	18 15	18 37	19 03	04 02	04 52	05 42	06 33
30	18 17	18 41	19 09	03 54	04 47	05 41	06 36
35	18 18	18 44	19 13	03 49	04 45	05 40	06 37
40	18 20	18 47	19 19	03 44	04 42	05 40	06 39
45	18 21	18 51	19 25	03 38	04 38	05 39	06 41
S 50	18 23	18 56	19 34	03 31	04 34	05 38	06 44
52	18 24	18 58	19 38	03 27	04 32	05 38	06 45
54	18 25	19 01	19 43	03 24	04 30	05 38	06 46
56	18 26	19 04	19 49	03 19	04 28	05 37	06 48
58	18 28	19 07	19 55	03 15	04 25	05 37	06 49
S 60	18 29	19 11	20 02	03 10	04 22	05 36	06 51

Day	SUN Eqn. of Time 00h	SUN Eqn. of Time 12h	SUN Mer. Pass.	MOON Mer. Pass. Upper	MOON Mer. Pass. Lower	Age	Phase
d	m s	m s	h m	h m	h m	d	%
14	09 21	09 12	12 09	10 27	22 49	13	95
15	09 04	08 55	12 09	23 33	11 11	14	98
16	08 47	08 38	12 09	24 17	11 55	15	100

UT	ARIES GHA	VENUS −4.6 GHA	Dec	MARS −1.0 GHA	Dec	JUPITER −2.3 GHA	Dec	SATURN +0.3 GHA	Dec	STARS Name	SHA	Dec
d h	° ′	° ′	° ′	° ′	° ′	° ′	° ′	° ′	° ′		° ′	° ′
17 00	174 29.7	222 49.3	S15 17.6	329 17.8	S 7 24.1	72 55.1	N23 16.0	303 06.7	S16 13.8	Acamar	315 18.2	S40 15.2
01	189 32.1	237 49.3	17.3	344 20.7	24.0	87 57.5	16.0	318 09.2	13.8	Achernar	335 27.0	S57 10.1
02	204 34.6	252 49.3	16.9	359 23.7	23.8	102 59.8	16.0	333 11.8	13.8	Acrux	173 07.9	S63 10.7
03	219 37.1	267 49.4 ..	16.5	14 26.6 ..	23.6	118 02.2 ..	16.0	348 14.3 ..	13.8	Adhara	255 12.0	S28 59.9
04	234 39.5	282 49.4	16.2	29 29.5	23.5	133 04.6	16.0	3 16.8	13.7	Aldebaran	290 48.9	N16 32.1
05	249 42.0	297 49.4	15.8	44 32.4	23.3	148 07.0	16.0	18 19.3	13.7			
06	264 44.4	312 49.4	S15 15.5	59 35.4	S 7 23.1	163 09.3	N23 16.0	33 21.9	S16 13.7	Alioth	166 19.8	N55 52.8
07	279 46.9	327 49.4	15.1	74 38.3	23.0	178 11.7	16.0	48 24.4	13.7	Alkaid	152 58.1	N49 14.4
08	294 49.4	342 49.5	14.7	89 41.2	22.8	193 14.1	16.0	63 26.9	13.6	Al Na'ir	27 43.5	S46 53.4
M 09	309 51.8	357 49.5 ..	14.4	104 44.2 ..	22.6	208 16.4 ..	16.0	78 29.4 ..	13.6	Alnilam	275 45.8	S 1 11.9
O 10	324 54.3	12 49.5	14.0	119 47.1	22.5	223 18.8	16.0	93 32.0	13.6	Alphard	217 55.3	S 8 43.5
N 11	339 56.8	27 49.5	13.7	134 50.0	22.3	238 21.2	15.9	108 34.5	13.6			
D 12	354 59.2	42 49.5	S15 13.3	149 53.0	S 7 22.1	253 23.5	N23 15.9	123 37.0	S16 13.6	Alphecca	126 10.4	N26 39.9
A 13	10 01.7	57 49.6	12.9	164 55.9	21.9	268 25.9	15.9	138 39.5	13.5	Alpheratz	357 43.3	N29 10.1
Y 14	25 04.2	72 49.6	12.6	179 58.9	21.8	283 28.3	15.9	153 42.1	13.5	Altair	62 07.9	N 8 54.4
15	40 06.6	87 49.6 ..	12.2	195 01.8 ..	21.6	298 30.6 ..	15.9	168 44.6 ..	13.5	Ankaa	353 15.6	S42 13.8
16	55 09.1	102 49.6	11.8	210 04.7	21.4	313 33.0	15.9	183 47.1	13.5	Antares	112 25.5	S26 27.6
17	70 11.5	117 49.6	11.5	225 07.7	21.3	328 35.4	15.9	198 49.6	13.4			
18	85 14.0	132 49.6	S15 11.1	240 10.6	S 7 21.1	343 37.7	N23 15.9	213 52.2	S16 13.4	Arcturus	145 55.0	N19 06.4
19	100 16.5	147 49.6	10.7	255 13.6	20.9	358 40.1	15.9	228 54.7	13.4	Atria	107 26.7	S69 02.8
20	115 18.9	162 49.7	10.4	270 16.5	20.7	13 42.5	15.9	243 57.2	13.4	Avior	234 17.4	S59 33.7
21	130 21.4	177 49.7 ..	10.0	285 19.5 ..	20.6	28 44.8 ..	15.9	258 59.7 ..	13.3	Bellatrix	278 31.5	N 6 21.5
22	145 23.9	192 49.7	09.6	300 22.4	20.4	43 47.2	15.9	274 02.3	13.3	Betelgeuse	271 00.7	N 7 24.3
23	160 26.3	207 49.7	09.3	315 25.4	20.2	58 49.5	15.9	289 04.8	13.3			
18 00	175 28.8	222 49.7	S15 08.9	330 28.3	S 7 20.0	73 51.9	N23 15.9	304 07.3	S16 13.3	Canopus	263 55.8	S52 42.7
01	190 31.3	237 49.7	08.5	345 31.3	19.9	88 54.3	15.9	319 09.8	13.3	Capella	280 33.7	N46 00.7
02	205 33.7	252 49.7	08.1	0 34.2	19.7	103 56.6	15.9	334 12.4	13.2	Deneb	49 31.4	N45 19.8
03	220 36.2	267 49.7 ..	07.8	15 37.2 ..	19.5	118 59.0 ..	15.9	349 14.9 ..	13.2	Denebola	182 32.8	N14 29.4
04	235 38.7	282 49.7	07.4	30 40.2	19.3	134 01.4	15.9	4 17.4	13.2	Diphda	348 55.7	S17 54.6
05	250 41.1	297 49.7	07.0	45 43.1	19.2	149 03.7	15.9	19 19.9	13.2			
06	265 43.6	312 49.7	S15 06.6	60 46.1	S 7 19.0	164 06.1	N23 15.9	34 22.5	S16 13.1	Dubhe	193 50.5	N61 40.3
07	280 46.0	327 49.7	06.2	75 49.0	18.8	179 08.4	15.9	49 25.0	13.1	Elnath	278 12.0	N28 37.0
08	295 48.5	342 49.8	05.9	90 52.0	18.6	194 10.8	15.9	64 27.5	13.1	Eltanin	90 45.9	N51 29.1
T 09	310 51.0	357 49.8 ..	05.5	105 55.0 ..	18.5	209 13.2 ..	15.8	79 30.1 ..	13.1	Enif	33 46.9	N 9 56.4
U 10	325 53.4	12 49.8	05.1	120 57.9	18.3	224 15.5	15.8	94 32.6	13.0	Fomalhaut	15 23.8	S29 32.8
E 11	340 55.9	27 49.8	04.7	136 00.9	18.1	239 17.9	15.8	109 35.1	13.0			
S 12	355 58.4	42 49.8	S15 04.3	151 03.9	S 7 17.9	254 20.2	N23 15.8	124 37.6	S16 13.0	Gacrux	171 59.7	S57 11.6
D 13	11 00.8	57 49.8	04.0	166 06.8	17.7	269 22.6	15.8	139 40.2	13.0	Gienah	175 51.4	S17 37.4
A 14	26 03.3	72 49.8	03.6	181 09.8	17.6	284 25.0	15.8	154 42.7	12.9	Hadar	148 46.5	S60 26.4
Y 15	41 05.8	87 49.8 ..	03.2	196 12.8 ..	17.4	299 27.3 ..	15.8	169 45.2 ..	12.9	Hamal	328 00.4	N23 31.7
16	56 08.2	102 49.8	02.8	211 15.8	17.2	314 29.7	15.8	184 47.8	12.9	Kaus Aust.	83 43.2	S34 22.4
17	71 10.7	117 49.8	02.4	226 18.7	17.0	329 32.0	15.8	199 50.3	12.9			
18	86 13.1	132 49.8	S15 02.0	241 21.7	S 7 16.8	344 34.4	N23 15.8	214 52.8	S16 13.0	Kochab	137 19.4	N74 05.6
19	101 15.6	147 49.8	01.6	256 24.7	16.7	359 36.7	15.8	229 55.3	12.8	Markab	13 38.1	N15 16.9
20	116 18.1	162 49.8	01.2	271 27.7	16.5	14 39.1	15.8	244 57.9	12.8	Menkar	314 14.7	N 4 08.5
21	131 20.5	177 49.7 ..	00.9	286 30.6 ..	16.3	29 41.5 ..	15.8	260 00.4 ..	12.8	Menkent	148 06.6	S36 26.3
22	146 23.0	192 49.7	00.5	301 33.6	16.1	44 43.8	15.8	275 02.9	12.8	Miaplacidus	221 38.8	S69 46.9
23	161 25.5	207 49.7	15 00.1	316 36.6	15.9	59 46.2	15.8	290 05.5	12.7			
19 00	176 27.9	222 49.7	S14 59.7	331 39.6	S 7 15.7	74 48.5	N23 15.8	305 08.0	S16 12.7	Mirfak	308 39.8	N49 54.7
01	191 30.4	237 49.7	59.3	346 42.6	15.6	89 50.9	15.8	320 10.5	12.7	Nunki	75 57.8	S26 16.5
02	206 32.9	252 49.7	58.9	1 45.6	15.4	104 53.2	15.8	335 13.1	12.7	Peacock	53 18.8	S56 41.0
03	221 35.3	267 49.7 ..	58.5	16 48.5 ..	15.2	119 55.6 ..	15.8	350 15.6 ..	12.6	Pollux	243 26.9	N27 59.3
04	236 37.8	282 49.7	58.1	31 51.5	15.0	134 57.9	15.8	5 18.1	12.6	Procyon	244 59.0	N 5 11.0
05	251 40.3	297 49.7	57.7	46 54.5	14.8	150 00.3	15.7	20 20.6	12.6			
06	266 42.7	312 49.7	S14 57.3	61 57.5	S 7 14.6	165 02.6	N23 15.7	35 23.2	S16 12.6	Rasalhague	96 05.9	N12 33.0
W 07	281 45.2	327 49.7	56.9	77 00.5	14.4	180 05.0	15.7	50 25.7	12.5	Regulus	207 42.7	N11 53.6
E 08	296 47.6	342 49.7	56.5	92 03.5	14.3	195 07.3	15.7	65 28.2	12.5	Rigel	281 11.6	S 8 11.5
D 09	311 50.1	357 49.7 ..	56.1	107 06.5 ..	14.1	210 09.7 ..	15.7	80 30.8 ..	12.5	Rigil Kent.	139 50.4	S60 53.4
N 10	326 52.6	12 49.7	55.7	122 09.5	13.9	225 12.0	15.7	95 33.3	12.5	Sabik	102 11.9	S15 44.4
E 11	341 55.0	27 49.6	55.3	137 12.5	13.7	240 14.4	15.7	110 35.8	12.4			
S 12	356 57.5	42 49.6	S14 54.9	152 15.5	S 7 13.5	255 16.7	N23 15.7	125 38.4	S16 12.4	Schedar	349 40.4	N56 36.9
D 13	12 00.0	57 49.6	54.5	167 18.5	13.3	270 19.1	15.7	140 40.9	12.4	Shaula	96 21.2	S37 06.6
A 14	27 02.4	72 49.6	54.1	182 21.5	13.1	285 21.4	15.7	155 43.4	12.4	Sirius	258 33.2	S16 44.5
Y 15	42 04.9	87 49.6 ..	53.7	197 24.5 ..	12.9	300 23.8 ..	15.7	170 46.0 ..	12.3	Spica	158 30.4	S11 14.2
16	57 07.4	102 49.6	53.3	212 27.5	12.8	315 26.1	15.7	185 48.5	12.3	Suhail	222 51.7	S43 29.8
17	72 09.8	117 49.6	52.9	227 30.5	12.6	330 28.5	15.7	200 51.0	12.3			
18	87 12.3	132 49.5	S14 52.5	242 33.5	S 7 12.4	345 30.8	N23 15.7	215 53.6	S16 12.3	Vega	80 38.7	N38 47.7
19	102 14.7	147 49.5	52.1	257 36.5	12.2	0 33.2	15.7	230 56.1	12.2	Zuben'ubi	137 04.6	S16 06.0
20	117 17.2	162 49.5	51.7	272 39.5	12.0	15 35.5	15.7	245 58.6	12.2		SHA	Mer. Pass.
21	132 19.7	177 49.5	51.3	287 42.5 ..	11.8	30 37.9 ..	15.7	261 01.2 ..	12.2		° ′	h m
22	147 22.1	192 49.5	50.8	302 45.5	11.6	45 40.2	15.6	276 03.7	12.2	Venus	47 20.9	9 09
23	162 24.6	207 49.4	50.4	317 48.5	11.4	60 42.6	15.6	291 06.2	12.1	Mars	154 59.5	1 58
	h m									Jupiter	258 23.1	19 02
Mer. Pass. 12 16.1		v 0.0	d 0.4	v 3.0	d 0.2	v 2.4	d 0.0	v 2.5	d 0.0	Saturn	128 38.5	3 43

UT	SUN GHA	SUN Dec	MOON GHA	v	MOON Dec	d	HP
d h	° ′	° ′	° ′	′	° ′	′	′
17 00	177 52.7	S 1 27.9	355 51.8	13.8	S 2 09.5	10.1	55.6
01	192 52.8	26.9	10 24.6	13.7	2 19.6	10.2	55.6
02	207 53.0	25.9	24 57.3	13.7	2 29.8	10.2	55.6
03	222 53.2	.. 24.9	39 30.0	13.6	2 40.0	10.1	55.6
04	237 53.4	23.9	54 02.6	13.7	2 50.1	10.1	55.6
05	252 53.6	22.9	68 35.3	13.6	3 00.2	10.2	55.6
06	267 53.7	S 1 22.0	83 07.9	13.6	S 3 10.4	10.1	55.7
07	282 53.9	21.0	97 40.5	13.5	3 20.5	10.1	55.7
M 08	297 54.1	20.0	112 13.0	13.5	3 30.6	10.2	55.7
O 09	312 54.3	.. 19.0	126 45.5	13.5	3 40.8	10.1	55.7
N 10	327 54.5	18.0	141 18.0	13.5	3 50.9	10.0	55.7
D 11	342 54.6	17.0	155 50.5	13.4	4 00.9	10.1	55.8
A 12	357 54.8	S 1 16.0	170 22.9	13.4	S 4 11.0	10.1	55.8
Y 13	12 55.0	15.0	184 55.3	13.3	4 21.1	10.1	55.8
14	27 55.2	14.1	199 27.6	13.4	4 31.1	10.1	55.8
15	42 55.4	.. 13.1	214 00.0	13.2	4 41.2	10.0	55.8
16	57 55.5	12.1	228 32.2	13.3	4 51.2	10.0	55.9
17	72 55.7	11.1	243 04.5	13.2	5 01.2	10.0	55.9
18	87 55.9	S 1 10.1	257 36.7	13.2	S 5 11.2	10.0	55.9
19	102 56.1	09.1	272 08.9	13.1	5 21.2	9.9	55.9
20	117 56.3	08.1	286 41.0	13.1	5 31.1	10.0	55.9
21	132 56.4	.. 07.1	301 13.1	13.1	5 41.1	9.9	56.0
22	147 56.6	06.2	315 45.2	13.0	5 51.0	9.9	56.0
23	162 56.8	05.2	330 17.2	13.0	6 00.9	9.9	56.0
18 00	177 57.0	S 1 04.2	344 49.2	12.9	S 6 10.8	9.8	56.0
01	192 57.2	03.2	359 21.1	12.9	6 20.6	9.9	56.0
02	207 57.4	02.2	13 53.0	12.9	6 30.5	9.8	56.1
03	222 57.5	.. 01.2	28 24.9	12.8	6 40.3	9.7	56.1
04	237 57.7	1 00.2	42 56.7	12.8	6 50.0	9.8	56.1
05	252 57.9	0 59.2	57 28.5	12.7	6 59.8	9.7	56.1
06	267 58.1	S 0 58.2	72 00.2	12.7	S 7 09.5	9.7	56.1
T 07	282 58.3	57.3	86 31.9	12.7	7 19.2	9.7	56.2
U 08	297 58.4	56.3	101 03.6	12.6	7 28.9	9.6	56.2
E 09	312 58.6	.. 55.3	115 35.2	12.6	7 38.5	9.6	56.2
S 10	327 58.8	54.3	130 06.8	12.5	7 48.1	9.6	56.2
D 11	342 59.0	53.3	144 38.3	12.5	7 57.7	9.6	56.2
A 12	357 59.2	S 0 52.3	159 09.8	12.4	S 8 07.3	9.5	56.3
Y 13	12 59.4	51.3	173 41.2	12.4	8 16.8	9.5	56.3
14	27 59.5	50.3	188 12.6	12.3	8 26.3	9.4	56.3
15	42 59.7	.. 49.4	202 43.9	12.3	8 35.7	9.4	56.3
16	57 59.9	48.4	217 15.2	12.3	8 45.1	9.4	56.4
17	73 00.1	47.4	231 46.5	12.2	8 54.5	9.3	56.4
18	88 00.3	S 0 46.4	246 17.7	12.1	S 9 03.8	9.3	56.4
19	103 00.5	45.4	260 48.8	12.1	9 13.1	9.3	56.4
20	118 00.6	44.4	275 19.9	12.1	9 22.4	9.2	56.4
21	133 00.8	.. 43.4	289 51.0	12.0	9 31.6	9.2	56.5
22	148 01.0	42.4	304 22.0	11.9	9 40.8	9.1	56.5
23	163 01.2	41.4	318 52.9	11.9	9 49.9	9.1	56.5
19 00	178 01.4	S 0 40.5	333 23.8	11.9	S 9 59.0	9.1	56.5
01	193 01.6	39.5	347 54.7	11.8	10 08.1	9.0	56.5
02	208 01.7	38.5	2 25.5	11.7	10 17.1	8.9	56.6
03	223 01.9	.. 37.5	16 56.2	11.7	10 26.0	9.0	56.6
04	238 02.1	36.5	31 26.9	11.7	10 35.0	8.8	56.6
05	253 02.3	35.5	45 57.6	11.6	10 43.8	8.8	56.6
06	268 02.5	S 0 34.5	60 28.2	11.5	S10 52.6	8.8	56.7
W 07	283 02.7	33.5	74 58.7	11.5	11 01.4	8.7	56.7
E 08	298 02.8	32.6	89 29.2	11.4	11 10.1	8.7	56.7
D 09	313 03.0	.. 31.6	103 59.6	11.4	11 18.8	8.6	56.7
N 10	328 03.2	30.6	118 30.0	11.4	11 27.4	8.6	56.7
E 11	343 03.4	29.6	133 00.4	11.2	11 36.0	8.5	56.7
S 12	358 03.6	S 0 28.6	147 30.6	11.3	S11 44.5	8.4	56.8
D 13	13 03.8	27.6	162 00.9	11.1	11 52.9	8.4	56.8
A 14	28 03.9	26.6	176 31.0	11.2	12 01.3	8.4	56.8
Y 15	43 04.1	.. 25.6	191 01.2	11.0	12 09.7	8.2	56.8
16	58 04.3	24.6	205 31.2	11.0	12 17.9	8.3	56.8
17	73 04.5	23.7	220 01.2	11.0	12 26.2	8.1	56.9
18	88 04.7	S 0 22.7	234 31.2	10.9	S12 34.3	8.1	56.9
19	103 04.9	21.7	249 01.1	10.8	12 42.4	8.1	56.9
20	118 05.1	20.7	263 30.9	10.8	12 50.5	8.0	56.9
21	133 05.2	.. 19.7	278 00.7	10.7	12 58.5	7.9	56.9
22	148 05.4	18.7	292 30.4	10.7	13 06.4	7.8	57.0
23	163 05.6	17.7	307 00.1	10.6	S13 14.2	7.8	57.0
	SD 16.1	d 1.0	SD 15.2		15.3		15.5

Lat.	Twilight Naut.	Twilight Civil	Sunrise	Moonrise 17	18	19	20
°	h m	h m	h m	h m	h m	h m	h m
N 72	03 35	05 02	06 09	20 04	21 50	23 43	25 48
N 70	03 52	05 08	06 09	19 56	21 34	23 16	25 01
68	04 05	05 13	06 09	19 49	21 21	22 56	24 30
66	04 15	05 18	06 09	19 44	21 11	22 40	24 08
64	04 24	05 21	06 08	19 39	21 02	22 27	23 50
62	04 31	05 24	06 08	19 35	20 55	22 16	23 36
60	04 37	05 27	06 08	19 31	20 49	22 07	23 23
N 58	04 43	05 29	06 08	19 28	20 43	21 58	23 13
56	04 47	05 31	06 08	19 25	20 38	21 51	23 04
54	04 51	05 33	06 08	19 23	20 34	21 45	22 56
52	04 55	05 34	06 08	19 21	20 30	21 39	22 48
50	04 58	05 35	06 08	19 19	20 26	21 34	22 42
45	05 04	05 38	06 07	19 14	20 18	21 23	22 28
N 40	05 09	05 40	06 07	19 10	20 12	21 14	22 16
35	05 12	05 42	06 07	19 07	20 06	21 06	22 07
30	05 15	05 43	06 07	19 05	20 01	20 59	21 58
20	05 18	05 44	06 06	19 00	19 53	20 47	21 43
N 10	05 20	05 44	06 05	18 56	19 45	20 37	21 31
0	05 20	05 44	06 05	18 52	19 38	20 27	21 19
S 10	05 19	05 43	06 04	18 48	19 32	20 18	21 07
20	05 16	05 41	06 03	18 44	19 24	20 08	20 54
30	05 10	05 38	06 02	18 39	19 16	19 56	20 40
35	05 06	05 36	06 01	18 36	19 12	19 50	20 32
40	05 02	05 33	06 01	18 33	19 06	19 42	20 22
45	04 56	05 30	06 00	18 30	19 00	19 33	20 11
S 50	04 48	05 26	05 58	18 26	18 53	19 23	19 58
52	04 44	05 24	05 58	18 24	18 49	19 18	19 52
54	04 39	05 22	05 57	18 22	18 46	19 13	19 45
56	04 34	05 19	05 56	18 20	18 42	19 07	19 37
58	04 29	05 16	05 56	18 17	18 37	19 00	19 29
S 60	04 22	05 13	05 55	18 14	18 32	18 53	19 19

Lat.	Sunset	Twilight Civil	Twilight Naut.	Moonset 17	18	19	20
°	h m	h m	h m	h m	h m	h m	h m
N 72	18 09	19 17	20 45	05 47	05 39	05 31	05 21
N 70	18 09	19 11	20 28	05 51	05 50	05 49	05 49
68	18 09	19 05	20 14	05 55	05 58	06 03	06 10
66	18 09	19 01	20 03	05 58	06 05	06 15	06 27
64	18 09	18 57	19 54	06 00	06 11	06 24	06 41
62	18 09	18 54	19 47	06 03	06 16	06 33	06 53
60	18 09	18 51	19 41	06 05	06 21	06 40	07 03
N 58	18 09	18 49	19 35	06 06	06 25	06 46	07 12
56	18 09	18 46	19 31	06 08	06 29	06 52	07 19
54	18 09	18 45	19 26	06 09	06 32	06 57	07 26
52	18 09	18 43	19 23	06 11	06 35	07 02	07 32
50	18 09	18 42	19 20	06 12	06 37	07 06	07 38
45	18 10	18 39	19 13	06 14	06 43	07 15	07 50
N 40	18 10	18 37	19 08	06 17	06 48	07 22	08 00
35	18 10	18 35	19 05	06 18	06 52	07 29	08 09
30	18 10	18 34	19 02	06 20	06 56	07 35	08 16
20	18 10	18 32	18 58	06 23	07 03	07 45	08 29
N 10	18 11	18 32	18 56	06 26	07 08	07 53	08 41
0	18 11	18 32	18 56	06 28	07 14	08 02	08 52
S 10	18 12	18 33	18 57	06 30	07 19	08 10	09 02
20	18 13	18 35	19 00	06 33	07 25	08 19	09 14
30	18 14	18 37	19 05	06 36	07 32	08 29	09 27
35	18 14	18 39	19 09	06 37	07 35	08 35	09 35
40	18 15	18 42	19 14	06 39	07 40	08 41	09 44
45	18 16	18 45	19 20	06 41	07 45	08 49	09 54
S 50	18 17	18 49	19 27	06 44	07 51	08 58	10 06
52	18 17	18 51	19 31	06 45	07 53	09 03	10 12
54	18 18	18 53	19 35	06 46	07 56	09 07	10 18
56	18 19	18 56	19 40	06 48	08 00	09 13	10 26
58	18 19	18 58	19 46	06 49	08 04	09 19	10 34
S 60	18 20	19 02	19 52	06 51	08 08	09 25	10 43

Day	SUN Eqn. of Time 00h	12h	SUN Mer. Pass.	MOON Mer. Pass. Upper	Lower	Age	Phase
d	m s	m s	h m	h m	h m	d	%
17	08 30	08 21	12 08	00 17	12 40	16	99
18	08 12	08 04	12 08	01 03	13 26	17	97
19	07 55	07 46	12 08	01 50	14 14	18	92

UT	ARIES	VENUS −4.5		MARS −1.1		JUPITER −2.3		SATURN +0.3		STARS		
	GHA	GHA	Dec	GHA	Dec	GHA	Dec	GHA	Dec	Name	SHA	Dec
d h	° ′	° ′	° ′	° ′	° ′	° ′	° ′	° ′	° ′		° ′	° ′
20 00	177 27.1	222 49.4	S14 50.0	332 51.5	S 7 11.2	75 44.9	N23 15.6	306 08.8	S16 12.1	Acamar	315 18.3	S40 15.2
01	192 29.5	237 49.4	49.6	347 54.5	11.0	90 47.3	15.6	321 11.3	12.1	Achernar	335 27.0	S57 10.1
02	207 32.0	252 49.4	49.2	2 57.6	10.8	105 49.6	15.6	336 13.8	12.1	Acrux	173 07.9	S63 10.7
03	222 34.5	267 49.4 ..	48.8	18 00.6 ..	10.6	120 52.0 ..	15.6	351 16.4 ..	12.0	Adhara	255 12.0	S28 59.9
04	237 36.9	282 49.3	48.4	33 03.6	10.4	135 54.3	15.6	6 18.9	12.0	Aldebaran	290 48.9	N16 32.1
05	252 39.4	297 49.3	47.9	48 06.6	10.3	150 56.6	15.6	21 21.4	12.0			
06	267 41.9	312 49.3	S14 47.5	63 09.6	S 7 10.1	165 59.0	N23 15.6	36 24.0	S16 12.0	Alioth	166 19.8	N55 52.8
07	282 44.3	327 49.3	47.1	78 12.6	09.9	181 01.3	15.6	51 26.5	11.9	Alkaid	152 58.1	N49 14.4
T 08	297 46.8	342 49.2	46.7	93 15.7	09.7	196 03.7	15.6	66 29.0	11.9	Al Na'ir	27 43.5	S46 53.4
H 09	312 49.2	357 49.2 ..	46.3	108 18.7 ..	09.5	211 06.0 ..	15.6	81 31.6 ..	11.9	Alnilam	275 45.9	S 1 11.9
U 10	327 51.7	12 49.2	45.9	123 21.7	09.3	226 08.4	15.6	96 34.1	11.9	Alphard	217 55.3	S 8 43.5
R 11	342 54.2	27 49.2	45.4	138 24.7	09.1	241 10.7	15.6	111 36.7	11.8			
S 12	357 56.6	42 49.1	S14 45.0	153 27.8	S 7 08.9	256 13.1	N23 15.6	126 39.2	S16 11.8	Alphecca	126 10.4	N26 39.9
D 13	12 59.1	57 49.1	44.6	168 30.8	08.7	271 15.4	15.6	141 41.7	11.8	Alpheratz	357 43.3	N29 10.1
A 14	28 01.6	72 49.1	44.2	183 33.8	08.5	286 17.7	15.6	156 44.3	11.8	Altair	62 07.9	N 8 54.4
Y 15	43 04.0	87 49.1 ..	43.7	198 36.9 ..	08.3	301 20.1 ..	15.5	171 46.8 ..	11.7	Ankaa	353 15.6	S42 13.8
16	58 06.5	102 49.0	43.3	213 39.9	08.1	316 22.4	15.5	186 49.3	11.7	Antares	112 25.5	S26 27.6
17	73 09.0	117 49.0	42.9	228 42.9	07.9	331 24.8	15.5	201 51.9	11.7			
18	88 11.4	132 49.0	S14 42.5	243 45.9	S 7 07.7	346 27.1	N23 15.5	216 54.4	S16 11.7	Arcturus	145 55.0	N19 06.4
19	103 13.9	147 48.9	42.0	258 49.0	07.5	1 29.4	15.5	231 57.0	11.6	Atria	107 26.6	S69 02.8
20	118 16.4	162 48.9	41.6	273 52.0	07.3	16 31.8	15.5	246 59.5	11.6	Avior	234 17.4	S59 33.8
21	133 18.8	177 48.9 ..	41.2	288 55.1 ..	07.1	31 34.1 ..	15.5	262 02.0 ..	11.6	Bellatrix	278 31.5	N 6 21.5
22	148 21.3	192 48.8	40.7	303 58.1	06.9	46 36.5	15.5	277 04.6	11.6	Betelgeuse	271 00.7	N 7 24.3
23	163 23.7	207 48.8	40.3	319 01.1	06.7	61 38.8	15.5	292 07.1	11.5			
21 00	178 26.2	222 48.8	S14 39.9	334 04.2	S 7 06.5	76 41.1	N23 15.5	307 09.6	S16 11.5	Canopus	263 55.9	S52 42.7
01	193 28.7	237 48.7	39.5	349 07.2	06.3	91 43.5	15.5	322 12.2	11.5	Capella	280 33.7	N46 00.7
02	208 31.1	252 48.7	39.0	4 10.3	06.1	106 45.8	15.5	337 14.7	11.5	Deneb	49 31.4	N45 19.8
03	223 33.6	267 48.7 ..	38.6	19 13.3 ..	05.9	121 48.1 ..	15.5	352 17.3 ..	11.4	Denebola	182 32.8	N14 29.4
04	238 36.1	282 48.6	38.1	34 16.3	05.7	136 50.5	15.5	7 19.8	11.4	Diphda	348 55.7	S17 54.6
05	253 38.5	297 48.6	37.7	49 19.4	05.5	151 52.8	15.5	22 22.3	11.4			
06	268 41.0	312 48.6	S14 37.3	64 22.4	S 7 05.3	166 55.2	N23 15.4	37 24.9	S16 11.4	Dubhe	193 50.5	N61 40.4
07	283 43.5	327 48.5	36.8	79 25.5	05.1	181 57.5	15.4	52 27.4	11.3	Elnath	278 12.0	N28 37.0
08	298 45.9	342 48.5	36.4	94 28.5	04.9	196 59.8	15.4	67 30.0	11.3	Eltanin	90 45.9	N51 29.1
F 09	313 48.4	357 48.5 ..	36.0	109 31.6 ..	04.7	212 02.2 ..	15.4	82 32.5 ..	11.3	Enif	33 46.9	N 9 56.4
R 10	328 50.8	12 48.4	35.5	124 34.6	04.5	227 04.5	15.4	97 35.0	11.2	Fomalhaut	15 23.8	S29 32.8
I 11	343 53.3	27 48.4	35.1	139 37.7	04.2	242 06.8	15.4	112 37.6	11.2			
D 12	358 55.8	42 48.3	S14 34.6	154 40.7	S 7 04.0	257 09.2	N23 15.4	127 40.1	S16 11.2	Gacrux	171 59.6	S57 11.6
A 13	13 58.2	57 48.3	34.2	169 43.8	03.8	272 11.5	15.4	142 42.7	11.2	Gienah	175 51.4	S17 37.4
Y 14	29 00.7	72 48.3	33.8	184 46.9	03.6	287 13.8	15.4	157 45.2	11.1	Hadar	148 46.5	S60 26.4
15	44 03.2	87 48.2 ..	33.3	199 49.9 ..	03.4	302 16.2 ..	15.4	172 47.7 ..	11.1	Hamal	328 00.4	N23 31.7
16	59 05.6	102 48.2	32.9	214 53.0	03.2	317 18.5	15.4	187 50.3	11.1	Kaus Aust.	83 43.2	S34 22.4
17	74 08.1	117 48.1	32.4	229 56.0	03.0	332 20.8	15.4	202 52.8	11.1			
18	89 10.6	132 48.1	S14 32.0	244 59.1	S 7 02.8	347 23.2	N23 15.4	217 55.4	S16 11.0	Kochab	137 19.3	N74 05.6
19	104 13.0	147 48.0	31.5	260 02.2	02.6	2 25.5	15.4	232 57.9	11.0	Markab	13 38.1	N15 16.9
20	119 15.5	162 48.0	31.1	275 05.2	02.4	17 27.8	15.3	248 00.4	11.0	Menkar	314 14.7	N 4 08.5
21	134 18.0	177 48.0 ..	30.6	290 08.3 ..	02.2	32 30.1 ..	15.3	263 03.0 ..	11.0	Menkent	148 06.6	S36 26.4
22	149 20.4	192 47.9	30.2	305 11.4	02.0	47 32.5	15.3	278 05.5	10.9	Miaplacidus	221 38.8	S69 46.9
23	164 22.9	207 47.9	29.7	320 14.4	01.8	62 34.8	15.3	293 08.1	10.9			
22 00	179 25.3	222 47.8	S14 29.3	335 17.5	S 7 01.5	77 37.1	N23 15.3	308 10.6	S16 10.9	Mirfak	308 39.9	N49 54.7
01	194 27.8	237 47.8	28.8	350 20.6	01.3	92 39.5	15.3	323 13.2	10.9	Nunki	75 57.7	S26 16.5
02	209 30.3	252 47.7	28.4	5 23.6	01.1	107 41.8	15.3	338 15.7	10.8	Peacock	53 18.8	S56 41.0
03	224 32.7	267 47.7 ..	27.9	20 26.7 ..	00.9	122 44.1 ..	15.3	353 18.2 ..	10.8	Pollux	243 26.9	N27 59.3
04	239 35.2	282 47.6	27.5	35 29.8	00.7	137 46.5	15.3	8 20.8	10.8	Procyon	244 59.1	N 5 11.0
05	254 37.7	297 47.6	27.0	50 32.9	00.5	152 48.8	15.3	23 23.3	10.7			
06	269 40.1	312 47.5	S14 26.6	65 35.9	S 7 00.3	167 51.1	N23 15.3	38 25.9	S16 10.7	Rasalhague	96 05.9	N12 33.0
07	284 42.6	327 47.5	26.1	80 39.0	7 00.1	182 53.4	15.3	53 28.4	10.7	Regulus	207 42.7	N11 53.6
S 08	299 45.1	342 47.4	25.6	95 42.1	6 59.9	197 55.8	15.3	68 31.0	10.7	Rigel	281 11.6	S 8 11.5
A 09	314 47.5	357 47.4 ..	25.2	110 45.2 ..	59.6	212 58.1 ..	15.3	83 33.5 ..	10.6	Rigil Kent.	139 50.4	S60 53.4
T 10	329 50.0	12 47.3	24.7	125 48.2	59.4	228 00.4	15.2	98 36.0	10.6	Sabik	102 11.9	S15 44.4
U 11	344 52.5	27 47.3	24.3	140 51.3	59.2	243 02.7	15.2	113 38.6	10.6			
R 12	359 54.9	42 47.2	S14 23.8	155 54.4	S 6 59.0	258 05.1	N23 15.2	128 41.1	S16 10.6	Schedar	349 40.4	N56 36.9
D 13	14 57.4	57 47.2	23.3	170 57.5	58.8	273 07.4	15.2	143 43.7	10.5	Shaula	96 21.1	S37 06.6
A 14	29 59.8	72 47.1	22.9	186 00.6	58.6	288 09.7	15.2	158 46.2	10.5	Sirius	258 33.2	S16 44.5
Y 15	45 02.3	87 47.1 ..	22.4	201 03.7 ..	58.4	303 12.0 ..	15.2	173 48.8 ..	10.5	Spica	158 30.4	S11 14.2
16	60 04.8	102 47.0	22.0	216 06.7	58.1	318 14.4	15.2	188 51.3	10.4	Suhail	222 51.7	S43 29.8
17	75 07.2	117 47.0	21.5	231 09.8	57.9	333 16.7	15.2	203 53.9	10.4			
18	90 09.7	132 46.9	S14 21.0	246 12.9	S 6 57.7	348 19.0	N23 15.2	218 56.4	S16 10.4	Vega	80 38.7	N38 47.7
19	105 12.2	147 46.9	20.6	261 16.0	57.5	3 21.3	15.2	233 58.9	10.4	Zuben'ubi	137 04.6	S16 06.0
20	120 14.6	162 46.8	20.1	276 19.1	57.3	18 23.7	15.2	249 01.5	10.3		SHA	Mer. Pass.
21	135 17.1	177 46.8 ..	19.6	291 22.2 ..	57.1	33 26.0 ..	15.2	264 04.0 ..	10.3		° ′	h m
22	150 19.6	192 46.7	19.2	306 25.3	56.8	48 28.3	15.2	279 06.6	10.3	Venus	44 22.6	9 09
23	165 22.0	207 46.6	18.7	321 28.4	56.6	63 30.6	15.1	294 09.1	10.3	Mars	155 38.0	1 43
	h m									Jupiter	258 14.9	18 50
Mer. Pass. 12 04.3		v 0.0	d 0.4	v 3.1	d 0.2	v 2.3	d 0.0	v 2.5	d 0.0	Saturn	128 43.4	3 31

UT	SUN GHA	SUN Dec	MOON GHA	v	Dec	d	HP
d h	° ′	° ′	° ′	′	° ′	′	′
20 00	178 05.8	S 0 16.7	321 29.7	10.5	S13 22.0	7.7	57.0
01	193 06.0	15.8	335 59.2	10.5	13 29.7	7.7	57.0
02	208 06.2	14.8	350 28.7	10.5	13 37.4	7.6	57.1
03	223 06.3	.. 13.8	4 58.2	10.4	13 45.0	7.5	57.1
04	238 06.5	12.8	19 27.6	10.3	13 52.5	7.5	57.1
05	253 06.7	11.8	33 56.9	10.3	14 00.0	7.3	57.1
06	268 06.9	S 0 10.8	48 26.2	10.2	S14 07.3	7.4	57.1
07	283 07.1	09.8	62 55.4	10.1	14 14.7	7.2	57.2
08	298 07.3	08.8	77 24.5	10.1	14 21.9	7.2	57.2
09	313 07.5	.. 07.9	91 53.6	10.1	14 29.1	7.0	57.2
10	328 07.6	06.9	106 22.7	10.0	14 36.1	7.1	57.2
11	343 07.8	05.9	120 51.7	9.9	14 43.2	6.9	57.2
12	358 08.0	S 0 04.9	135 20.6	9.9	S14 50.1	6.9	57.3
13	13 08.2	03.9	149 49.5	9.8	14 57.0	6.7	57.3
14	28 08.4	02.9	164 18.3	9.7	15 03.7	6.7	57.3
15	43 08.6	.. 01.9	178 47.0	9.7	15 10.4	6.7	57.3
16	58 08.8	S 00.9	193 15.7	9.7	15 17.1	6.5	57.3
17	73 08.9	N 00.1	207 44.4	9.6	15 23.6	6.5	57.4
18	88 09.1	N 0 01.0	222 13.0	9.5	S15 30.1	6.4	57.4
19	103 09.3	02.0	236 41.5	9.5	15 36.5	6.3	57.4
20	118 09.5	03.0	251 10.0	9.4	15 42.8	6.2	57.4
21	133 09.7	.. 04.0	265 38.4	9.3	15 49.0	6.1	57.4
22	148 09.9	05.0	280 06.7	9.3	15 55.1	6.1	57.5
23	163 10.1	06.0	294 35.0	9.3	16 01.2	5.9	57.5
21 00	178 10.2	N 0 07.0	309 03.3	9.2	S16 07.1	5.9	57.5
01	193 10.4	08.0	323 31.5	9.1	16 13.0	5.8	57.5
02	208 10.6	08.9	337 59.6	9.1	16 18.8	5.7	57.5
03	223 10.8	.. 09.9	352 27.7	9.0	16 24.5	5.6	57.6
04	238 11.0	10.9	6 55.7	9.0	16 30.1	5.5	57.6
05	253 11.2	11.9	21 23.7	8.9	16 35.6	5.4	57.6
06	268 11.4	N 0 12.9	35 51.6	8.8	S16 41.0	5.3	57.6
07	283 11.5	13.9	50 19.4	8.8	16 46.3	5.3	57.7
08	298 11.7	14.9	64 47.2	8.8	16 51.6	5.1	57.7
09	313 11.9	.. 15.9	79 15.0	8.7	16 56.7	5.0	57.7
10	328 12.1	16.8	93 42.7	8.6	17 01.7	5.0	57.7
11	343 12.3	17.8	108 10.3	8.6	17 06.7	4.9	57.7
12	358 12.5	N 0 18.8	122 37.9	8.5	S17 11.6	4.7	57.8
13	13 12.7	19.8	137 05.4	8.5	17 16.3	4.7	57.8
14	28 12.9	20.8	151 32.9	8.4	17 21.0	4.5	57.8
15	43 13.0	.. 21.8	166 00.3	8.4	17 25.5	4.5	57.8
16	58 13.2	22.8	180 27.7	8.3	17 30.0	4.4	57.8
17	73 13.4	23.7	194 55.0	8.3	17 34.4	4.2	57.9
18	88 13.6	N 0 24.7	209 22.3	8.2	S17 38.6	4.2	57.9
19	103 13.8	25.7	223 49.5	8.2	17 42.8	4.0	57.9
20	118 14.0	26.7	238 16.7	8.2	17 46.8	4.0	57.9
21	133 14.2	.. 27.7	252 43.9	8.0	17 50.8	3.8	57.9
22	148 14.3	28.7	267 10.9	8.1	17 54.6	3.8	58.0
23	163 14.5	29.7	281 38.0	8.0	17 58.4	3.6	58.0
22 00	178 14.7	N 0 30.7	296 05.0	7.9	S18 02.0	3.6	58.0
01	193 14.9	31.6	310 31.9	7.9	18 05.6	3.4	58.0
02	208 15.1	32.6	324 58.8	7.8	18 09.0	3.3	58.0
03	223 15.3	.. 33.6	339 25.6	7.8	18 12.3	3.2	58.1
04	238 15.5	34.6	353 52.4	7.8	18 15.5	3.1	58.1
05	253 15.7	35.6	8 19.2	7.7	18 18.6	3.0	58.1
06	268 15.8	N 0 36.6	22 45.9	7.7	S18 21.6	2.9	58.1
07	283 16.0	37.6	37 12.6	7.6	18 24.5	2.8	58.1
08	298 16.2	38.6	51 39.2	7.6	18 27.3	2.7	58.2
09	313 16.4	.. 39.5	66 05.8	7.5	18 30.0	2.5	58.2
10	328 16.6	40.5	80 32.3	7.5	18 32.5	2.5	58.2
11	343 16.8	41.5	94 58.8	7.5	18 35.0	2.3	58.2
12	358 17.0	N 0 42.5	109 25.3	7.4	S18 37.3	2.2	58.2
13	13 17.2	43.5	123 51.7	7.4	18 39.5	2.1	58.3
14	28 17.3	44.5	138 18.1	7.3	18 41.6	2.0	58.3
15	43 17.5	.. 45.5	152 44.4	7.3	18 43.6	1.9	58.3
16	58 17.7	46.4	167 10.7	7.3	18 45.5	1.8	58.3
17	73 17.9	47.4	181 37.0	7.2	18 47.3	1.6	58.3
18	88 18.1	N 0 48.4	196 03.2	7.2	S18 48.9	1.5	58.4
19	103 18.3	49.4	210 29.4	7.2	18 50.4	1.5	58.4
20	118 18.5	50.4	224 55.6	7.1	18 51.9	1.3	58.4
21	133 18.7	.. 51.4	239 21.7	7.1	18 53.2	1.1	58.4
22	148 18.8	52.4	253 47.8	7.1	18 54.3	1.1	58.4
23	163 19.0	53.3	268 13.9	7.1	S18 55.4	0.9	58.5
	SD 16.1	d 1.0	SD 15.6		15.7		15.9

Lat.	Twilight Naut.	Twilight Civil	Sunrise	Moonrise 20	Moonrise 21	Moonrise 22	Moonrise 23
°	h m	h m	h m	h m	h m	h m	h m
N 72	03 15	04 46	05 54	25 48	01 48	■■	■■
N 70	03 35	04 54	05 55	25 01	01 01	02 44	04 08
68	03 50	05 00	05 56	24 30	00 30	02 00	03 13
66	04 02	05 06	05 57	24 08	00 08	01 30	02 40
64	04 12	05 10	05 58	23 50	25 08	01 08	02 16
62	04 21	05 14	05 59	23 36	24 51	00 51	01 56
60	04 28	05 18	05 59	23 23	24 36	00 36	01 41
N 58	04 34	05 20	06 00	23 13	24 24	00 24	01 27
56	04 39	05 23	06 00	23 04	24 13	00 13	01 16
54	04 43	05 25	06 00	22 56	24 03	00 03	01 06
52	04 47	05 27	06 01	22 48	23 55	24 57	00 57
50	04 51	05 29	06 01	22 42	23 47	24 49	00 49
45	04 58	05 32	06 02	22 28	23 31	24 32	00 32
N 40	05 04	05 35	06 02	22 16	23 18	24 18	00 18
35	05 08	05 37	06 02	22 07	23 07	24 06	00 06
30	05 11	05 39	06 03	21 58	22 57	23 56	24 52
20	05 16	05 41	06 03	21 43	22 40	23 38	24 34
N 10	05 18	05 43	06 04	21 31	22 26	23 22	24 19
0	05 19	05 43	06 04	21 19	22 12	23 08	24 05
S 10	05 19	05 43	06 04	21 07	21 59	22 54	23 51
20	05 16	05 42	06 04	20 54	21 44	22 38	23 36
30	05 12	05 40	06 04	20 40	21 28	22 21	23 18
35	05 09	05 39	06 04	20 32	21 18	22 10	23 08
40	05 05	05 37	06 04	20 22	21 07	21 59	22 56
45	05 00	05 34	06 03	20 11	20 55	21 45	22 43
S 50	04 53	05 31	06 03	19 58	20 39	21 28	22 26
52	04 49	05 29	06 03	19 52	20 32	21 20	22 18
54	04 46	05 27	06 03	19 45	20 24	21 12	22 10
56	04 41	05 25	06 03	19 37	20 15	21 02	22 00
58	04 36	05 23	06 02	19 29	20 05	20 51	21 49
S 60	04 30	05 20	06 02	19 19	19 53	20 38	21 36

Lat.	Sunset	Twilight Civil	Twilight Naut.	Moonset 20	Moonset 21	Moonset 22	Moonset 23
°	h m	h m	h m	h m	h m	h m	h m
N 72	18 23	19 32	21 04	05 21	05 04	■■	■■
N 70	18 21	19 23	20 43	05 49	05 52	06 02	06 34
68	18 20	19 16	20 27	06 10	06 23	06 46	07 30
66	18 19	19 11	20 15	06 27	06 46	07 16	08 03
64	18 18	19 06	20 05	06 41	07 05	07 38	08 27
62	18 17	19 02	19 56	06 53	07 20	07 56	08 46
60	18 17	18 58	19 49	07 03	07 32	08 11	09 02
N 58	18 16	18 55	19 43	07 12	07 43	08 24	09 15
56	18 16	18 53	19 37	07 19	07 53	08 35	09 27
54	18 15	18 50	19 33	07 26	08 01	08 44	09 37
52	18 15	18 48	19 28	07 32	08 09	08 53	09 46
50	18 14	18 47	19 25	07 38	08 16	09 01	09 54
45	18 13	18 43	19 17	07 50	08 30	09 17	10 11
N 40	18 13	18 40	19 12	08 00	08 42	09 31	10 25
35	18 12	18 38	19 07	08 09	08 53	09 42	10 37
30	18 12	18 36	19 04	08 16	09 02	09 52	10 47
20	18 11	18 33	18 59	08 29	09 18	10 10	11 05
N 10	18 11	18 32	18 56	08 41	09 31	10 25	11 21
0	18 10	18 31	18 55	08 52	09 44	10 39	11 35
S 10	18 10	18 31	18 55	09 02	09 57	10 53	11 50
20	18 10	18 32	18 58	09 14	10 11	11 08	12 05
30	18 10	18 34	19 02	09 27	10 26	11 25	12 23
35	18 10	18 35	19 05	09 35	10 35	11 35	12 33
40	18 10	18 37	19 09	09 44	10 46	11 47	12 45
45	18 11	18 39	19 14	09 54	10 58	12 00	12 58
S 50	18 10	18 42	19 20	10 06	11 13	12 17	13 15
52	18 10	18 44	19 24	10 12	11 20	12 24	13 23
54	18 10	18 46	19 27	10 18	11 28	12 33	13 32
56	18 11	18 48	19 32	10 26	11 36	12 43	13 42
58	18 11	18 50	19 36	10 34	11 46	12 54	13 53
S 60	18 11	18 52	19 42	10 43	11 58	13 07	14 06

Day	SUN Eqn. of Time 00h	SUN Eqn. of Time 12h	SUN Mer. Pass.	MOON Mer. Pass. Upper	MOON Mer. Pass. Lower	Age	Phase
d	m s	m s	h m	h m	h m	d %	
20	07 37	07 28	12 07	02 39	15 05	19 86	
21	07 19	07 10	12 07	03 31	15 58	20 77	
22	07 01	06 53	12 07	04 25	16 53	21 67	

2014 MARCH 23, 24, 25 (SUN., MON., TUES.)

UT	ARIES	VENUS −4.5		MARS −1.1		JUPITER −2.3		SATURN +0.3		STARS		
	GHA	GHA	Dec	GHA	Dec	GHA	Dec	GHA	Dec	Name	SHA	Dec
d h	° ′	° ′	° ′	° ′	° ′	° ′	° ′	° ′	° ′		° ′	° ′
23 00	180 24.5	222 46.6	S14 18.2	336 31.5	S 6 56.4	78 32.9	N23 15.1	309 11.7	S16 10.2	Acamar	315 18.3	S40 15.2
01	195 26.9	237 46.5	17.7	351 34.6	56.2	93 35.3	15.1	324 14.2	10.2	Achernar	335 27.0	S57 10.1
02	210 29.4	252 46.5	17.3	6 37.7	56.0	108 37.6	15.1	339 16.8	10.2	Acrux	173 07.9	S63 10.8
03	225 31.9	267 46.4	.. 16.8	21 40.8	.. 55.7	123 39.9	.. 15.1	354 19.3	.. 10.1	Adhara	255 12.0	S28 59.9
04	240 34.3	282 46.3	16.3	36 43.9	55.5	138 42.2	15.1	9 21.9	10.1	Aldebaran	290 48.9	N16 32.1
05	255 36.8	297 46.3	15.9	51 47.0	55.3	153 44.5	15.1	24 24.4	10.1			
06	270 39.3	312 46.2	S14 15.4	66 50.1	S 6 55.1	168 46.9	N23 15.1	39 26.9	S16 10.1	Alioth	166 19.7	N55 52.8
07	285 41.7	327 46.2	14.9	81 53.2	54.9	183 49.2	15.1	54 29.5	10.0	Alkaid	152 58.1	N49 14.4
S 08	300 44.2	342 46.1	14.4	96 56.3	54.6	198 51.5	15.1	69 32.0	10.0	Al Na'ir	27 43.5	S46 53.4
U 09	315 46.7	357 46.0	.. 13.9	111 59.4	.. 54.4	213 53.8	.. 15.1	84 34.6	.. 10.0	Alnilam	275 45.9	S 1 11.9
N 10	330 49.1	12 46.0	13.5	127 02.5	54.2	228 56.1	15.1	99 37.1	09.9	Alphard	217 55.3	S 8 43.5
D 11	345 51.6	27 45.9	13.0	142 05.6	54.0	243 58.5	15.0	114 39.7	09.9			
A 12	0 54.1	42 45.9	S14 12.5	157 08.7	S 6 53.8	259 00.8	N23 15.0	129 42.2	S16 09.9	Alphecca	126 10.3	N26 39.9
Y 13	15 56.5	57 45.8	12.0	172 11.8	53.5	274 03.1	15.0	144 44.8	09.9	Alpheratz	357 43.3	N29 10.1
14	30 59.0	72 45.7	11.5	187 14.9	53.3	289 05.4	15.0	159 47.3	09.8	Altair	62 07.8	N 8 54.4
15	46 01.4	87 45.7	.. 11.1	202 18.1	.. 53.1	304 07.7	.. 15.0	174 49.9	.. 09.8	Ankaa	353 15.6	S42 13.8
16	61 03.9	102 45.6	10.6	217 21.2	52.9	319 10.0	15.0	189 52.4	09.8	Antares	112 25.4	S26 27.6
17	76 06.4	117 45.5	10.1	232 24.3	52.6	334 12.4	15.0	204 55.0	09.8			
18	91 08.8	132 45.5	S14 09.6	247 27.4	S 6 52.4	349 14.7	N23 15.0	219 57.5	S16 09.7	Arcturus	145 55.0	N19 06.4
19	106 11.3	147 45.4	09.1	262 30.5	52.2	4 17.0	15.0	235 00.1	09.7	Atria	107 26.6	S69 02.8
20	121 13.8	162 45.3	08.6	277 33.6	52.0	19 19.3	15.0	250 02.6	09.7	Avior	234 17.4	S59 33.8
21	136 16.2	177 45.3	.. 08.2	292 36.8	.. 51.7	34 21.6	.. 15.0	265 05.2	.. 09.6	Bellatrix	278 31.5	N 6 21.5
22	151 18.7	192 45.2	07.7	307 39.9	51.5	49 23.9	15.0	280 07.7	09.6	Betelgeuse	271 00.7	N 7 24.3
23	166 21.2	207 45.1	07.2	322 43.0	51.3	64 26.2	14.9	295 10.3	09.6			
24 00	181 23.6	222 45.1	S14 06.7	337 46.1	S 6 51.1	79 28.6	N23 14.9	310 12.8	S16 09.5	Canopus	263 55.9	S52 42.7
01	196 26.1	237 45.0	06.2	352 49.2	50.8	94 30.9	14.9	325 15.4	09.5	Capella	280 33.8	N46 00.7
02	211 28.6	252 44.9	05.7	7 52.4	50.6	109 33.2	14.9	340 17.9	09.5	Deneb	49 31.3	N45 19.8
03	226 31.0	267 44.9	.. 05.2	22 55.5	.. 50.4	124 35.5	.. 14.9	355 20.5	.. 09.5	Denebola	182 32.8	N14 29.4
04	241 33.5	282 44.8	04.7	37 58.6	50.2	139 37.8	14.9	10 23.0	09.4	Diphda	348 55.7	S17 54.6
05	256 35.9	297 44.7	04.2	53 01.7	49.9	154 40.1	14.9	25 25.6	09.4			
06	271 38.4	312 44.7	S14 03.7	68 04.9	S 6 49.7	169 42.4	N23 14.9	40 28.1	S16 09.4	Dubhe	193 50.5	N61 40.4
07	286 40.9	327 44.6	03.2	83 08.0	49.5	184 44.7	14.9	55 30.7	09.4	Elnath	278 12.0	N28 37.0
08	301 43.3	342 44.5	02.7	98 11.1	49.2	199 47.1	14.9	70 33.2	09.3	Eltanin	90 45.9	N51 29.1
M 09	316 45.8	357 44.4	.. 02.2	113 14.3	.. 49.0	214 49.4	.. 14.9	85 35.8	.. 09.3	Enif	33 46.8	N 9 56.4
O 10	331 48.3	12 44.4	01.7	128 17.4	48.8	229 51.7	14.8	100 38.3	09.3	Fomalhaut	15 23.8	S29 32.8
N 11	346 50.7	27 44.3	01.3	143 20.5	48.6	244 54.0	14.8	115 40.9	09.2			
D 12	1 53.2	42 44.2	S14 00.8	158 23.7	S 6 48.3	259 56.3	N23 14.8	130 43.4	S16 09.2	Gacrux	171 59.6	S57 11.7
A 13	16 55.7	57 44.1	14 00.3	173 26.8	48.1	274 58.6	14.8	145 46.0	09.2	Gienah	175 51.4	S17 37.4
Y 14	31 58.1	72 44.1	13 59.8	188 29.9	47.9	290 00.9	14.8	160 48.5	09.2	Hadar	148 46.5	S60 26.4
15	47 00.6	87 44.0	.. 59.3	203 33.1	.. 47.6	305 03.2	.. 14.8	175 51.1	.. 09.1	Hamal	328 00.4	N23 31.7
16	62 03.1	102 43.9	58.7	218 36.2	47.4	320 05.5	14.8	190 53.6	09.1	Kaus Aust.	83 43.1	S34 22.4
17	77 05.5	117 43.8	58.2	233 39.4	47.2	335 07.8	14.8	205 56.2	09.1			
18	92 08.0	132 43.8	S13 57.7	248 42.5	S 6 46.9	350 10.1	N23 14.8	220 58.7	S16 09.0	Kochab	137 19.3	N74 05.7
19	107 10.4	147 43.7	57.2	263 45.7	46.7	5 12.4	14.8	236 01.3	09.0	Markab	13 38.1	N15 16.9
20	122 12.9	162 43.6	56.7	278 48.8	46.5	20 14.8	14.8	251 03.9	09.0	Menkar	314 14.7	N 4 08.5
21	137 15.4	177 43.5	.. 56.2	293 51.9	.. 46.2	35 17.1	.. 14.7	266 06.4	.. 08.9	Menkent	148 06.6	S36 26.4
22	152 17.8	192 43.5	55.7	308 55.1	46.0	50 19.4	14.7	281 09.0	08.9	Miaplacidus	221 38.8	S69 46.9
23	167 20.3	207 43.4	55.2	323 58.2	45.8	65 21.7	14.7	296 11.5	08.9			
25 00	182 22.8	222 43.3	S13 54.7	339 01.4	S 6 45.5	80 24.0	N23 14.7	311 14.1	S16 08.9	Mirfak	308 39.9	N49 54.7
01	197 25.2	237 43.2	54.2	354 04.5	45.3	95 26.3	14.7	326 16.6	08.8	Nunki	75 57.7	S26 16.5
02	212 27.7	252 43.2	53.7	9 07.7	45.1	110 28.6	14.7	341 19.2	08.8	Peacock	53 22.5	S56 41.0
03	227 30.2	267 43.1	.. 53.2	24 10.8	.. 44.8	125 30.9	.. 14.7	356 21.7	.. 08.8	Pollux	243 27.0	N27 59.3
04	242 32.6	282 43.0	52.7	39 14.0	44.6	140 33.2	14.7	11 24.3	08.7	Procyon	244 59.1	N 5 11.0
05	257 35.1	297 42.9	52.1	54 17.1	44.4	155 35.5	14.7	26 26.8	08.7			
06	272 37.5	312 42.8	S13 51.6	69 20.3	S 6 44.1	170 37.8	N23 14.7	41 29.4	S16 08.7	Rasalhague	96 05.9	N12 33.0
07	287 40.0	327 42.8	51.1	84 23.5	43.9	185 40.1	14.7	56 31.9	08.7	Regulus	207 42.7	N11 53.6
T 08	302 42.5	342 42.7	50.6	99 26.6	43.7	200 42.4	14.6	71 34.5	08.6	Rigel	281 11.6	S 8 11.5
U 09	317 44.9	357 42.6	.. 50.1	114 29.8	.. 43.4	215 44.7	.. 14.6	86 37.1	.. 08.6	Rigil Kent.	139 50.4	S60 53.4
E 10	332 47.4	12 42.5	49.6	129 32.9	43.2	230 47.0	14.6	101 39.6	08.6	Sabik	102 11.8	S15 44.4
S 11	347 49.9	27 42.4	49.1	144 36.1	42.9	245 49.3	14.6	116 42.2	08.5			
D 12	2 52.3	42 42.3	S13 48.5	159 39.3	S 6 42.7	260 51.6	N23 14.6	131 44.7	S16 08.5	Schedar	349 40.4	N56 36.9
A 13	17 54.8	57 42.3	48.0	174 42.4	42.5	275 53.9	14.6	146 47.3	08.5	Shaula	96 21.1	S37 06.6
Y 14	32 57.3	72 42.2	47.5	189 45.6	42.2	290 56.2	14.6	161 49.8	08.4	Sirius	258 33.2	S16 44.5
15	47 59.7	87 42.1	.. 47.0	204 48.7	.. 42.0	305 58.5	.. 14.6	176 52.4	.. 08.4	Spica	158 30.4	S11 14.2
16	63 02.2	102 42.0	46.5	219 51.9	41.8	321 00.8	14.6	191 55.0	08.4	Suhail	222 51.7	S43 29.8
17	78 04.7	117 41.9	45.9	234 55.1	41.5	336 03.1	14.6	206 57.5	08.4			
18	93 07.1	132 41.8	S13 45.4	249 58.2	S 6 41.3	351 05.4	N23 14.5	222 00.1	S16 08.3	Vega	80 38.6	N38 47.7
19	108 09.6	147 41.8	44.9	265 01.4	41.0	6 07.7	14.5	237 02.6	08.3	Zuben'ubi	137 04.6	S16 06.0
20	123 12.0	162 41.7	44.4	280 04.6	40.8	21 10.0	14.5	252 05.2	08.3		SHA	Mer. Pass.
21	138 14.5	177 41.6	.. 43.8	295 07.8	.. 40.6	36 12.3	.. 14.5	267 07.7	.. 08.2		° ′	h m
22	153 17.0	192 41.5	43.3	310 10.9	40.3	51 14.6	14.5	282 10.3	08.2	Venus	41 21.4	9 09
23	168 19.4	207 41.4	42.8	325 14.1	40.1	66 16.9	14.5	297 12.8	08.2	Mars	156 22.5	1 29
Mer. Pass.	h m 11 52.5	v −0.1	d 0.5	v 3.1	d 0.2	v 2.3	d 0.0	v 2.6	d 0.0	Jupiter	258 04.9	18 39
										Saturn	128 49.2	3 19

UT	SUN GHA	Dec	MOON GHA	v	Dec	d	HP
	° ′	° ′	° ′	′	° ′	′	′
23 00	178 19.2	N 0 54.3	282 40.0	7.0	S18 56.3	0.9	58.5
01	193 19.4	55.3	297 06.0	6.9	18 57.2	0.7	58.5
02	208 19.6	56.3	311 31.9	7.0	18 57.9	0.6	58.5
03	223 19.8	.. 57.3	325 57.9	6.9	18 58.5	0.5	58.5
04	238 20.0	58.3	340 23.8	6.9	18 59.0	0.3	58.6
05	253 20.2	0 59.3	354 49.7	6.9	18 59.3	0.2	58.6
06	268 20.3	N 1 00.2	9 15.6	6.8	S18 59.5	0.2	58.6
07	283 20.5	01.2	23 41.4	6.9	18 59.7	0.1	58.6
S 08	298 20.7	02.2	38 07.3	6.8	18 59.6	0.1	58.6
U 09	313 20.9	.. 03.2	52 33.1	6.7	18 59.5	0.2	58.7
N 10	328 21.1	04.2	66 58.8	6.8	18 59.3	0.4	58.7
D 11	343 21.3	05.2	81 24.6	6.7	18 58.9	0.5	58.7
A 12	358 21.5	N 1 06.2	95 50.3	6.8	S18 58.4	0.6	58.7
Y 13	13 21.7	07.1	110 16.1	6.7	18 57.8	0.7	58.7
14	28 21.8	08.1	124 41.8	6.6	18 57.1	0.9	58.8
15	43 22.0	.. 09.1	139 07.4	6.7	18 56.2	0.9	58.8
16	58 22.2	10.1	153 33.1	6.7	18 55.3	1.1	58.8
17	73 22.4	11.1	167 58.8	6.6	18 54.2	1.3	58.8
18	88 22.6	N 1 12.1	182 24.4	6.6	S18 52.9	1.3	58.8
19	103 22.8	13.1	196 50.0	6.6	18 51.6	1.5	58.9
20	118 23.0	14.0	211 15.6	6.6	18 50.1	1.5	58.9
21	133 23.2	.. 15.0	225 41.2	6.6	18 48.6	1.7	58.9
22	148 23.4	16.0	240 06.8	6.6	18 46.9	1.9	58.9
23	163 23.5	17.0	254 32.4	6.5	18 45.0	1.9	58.9
24 00	178 23.7	N 1 18.0	268 57.9	6.6	S18 43.1	2.1	58.9
01	193 23.9	19.0	283 23.5	6.6	18 41.0	2.2	59.0
02	208 24.1	20.0	297 49.1	6.5	18 38.8	2.3	59.0
03	223 24.3	.. 20.9	312 14.6	6.5	18 36.5	2.4	59.0
04	238 24.5	21.9	326 40.1	6.6	18 34.1	2.6	59.0
05	253 24.7	22.9	341 05.7	6.5	18 31.5	2.6	59.0
06	268 24.9	N 1 23.9	355 31.2	6.5	S18 28.9	2.8	59.1
07	283 25.0	24.9	9 56.7	6.6	18 26.1	3.0	59.1
08	298 25.2	25.9	24 22.3	6.6	18 23.1	3.0	59.1
M 09	313 25.4	.. 26.8	38 47.8	6.5	18 20.1	3.2	59.1
O 10	328 25.6	27.8	53 13.3	6.5	18 16.9	3.2	59.1
N 11	343 25.8	28.8	67 38.8	6.5	18 13.7	3.4	59.1
D 12	358 26.0	N 1 29.8	82 04.3	6.6	S18 10.3	3.6	59.2
A 13	13 26.2	30.8	96 29.9	6.5	18 06.7	3.6	59.2
Y 14	28 26.4	31.8	110 55.4	6.5	18 03.1	3.7	59.2
15	43 26.6	.. 32.7	125 20.9	6.6	17 59.4	3.9	59.2
16	58 26.7	33.7	139 46.5	6.5	17 55.5	4.0	59.2
17	73 26.9	34.7	154 12.0	6.6	17 51.5	4.1	59.2
18	88 27.1	N 1 35.7	168 37.6	6.5	S17 47.4	4.3	59.3
19	103 27.3	36.7	183 03.1	6.6	17 43.1	4.3	59.3
20	118 27.5	37.7	197 28.7	6.6	17 38.8	4.5	59.3
21	133 27.7	.. 38.6	211 54.3	6.6	17 34.3	4.5	59.3
22	148 27.9	39.6	226 19.9	6.6	17 29.8	4.7	59.3
23	163 28.1	40.6	240 45.5	6.6	17 25.1	4.9	59.3
25 00	178 28.2	N 1 41.6	255 11.1	6.6	S17 20.2	4.9	59.4
01	193 28.4	42.6	269 36.7	6.6	17 15.3	5.0	59.4
02	208 28.6	43.6	284 02.3	6.7	17 10.3	5.2	59.4
03	223 28.8	.. 44.5	298 28.0	6.6	17 05.1	5.2	59.4
04	238 29.0	45.5	312 53.6	6.7	16 59.9	5.4	59.4
05	253 29.2	46.5	327 19.3	6.7	16 54.5	5.5	59.4
06	268 29.4	N 1 47.5	341 45.0	6.7	S16 49.0	5.6	59.5
07	283 29.6	48.5	356 10.7	6.7	16 43.4	5.7	59.5
T 08	298 29.8	49.5	10 36.4	6.7	16 37.7	5.9	59.5
U 09	313 29.9	.. 50.4	25 02.1	6.8	16 31.8	5.9	59.5
E 10	328 30.1	51.4	39 27.9	6.8	16 25.9	6.1	59.5
S 11	343 30.3	52.4	53 53.7	6.8	16 19.8	6.1	59.5
D 12	358 30.5	N 1 53.4	68 19.5	6.8	S16 13.7	6.3	59.5
A 13	13 30.7	54.4	82 45.3	6.8	16 07.4	6.4	59.6
Y 14	28 30.9	55.4	97 11.1	6.9	16 01.0	6.4	59.6
15	43 31.1	.. 56.3	111 37.0	6.9	15 54.6	6.6	59.6
16	58 31.3	57.3	126 02.8	6.9	15 48.0	6.7	59.6
17	73 31.5	58.3	140 28.7	6.9	15 41.3	6.8	59.6
18	88 31.6	N 1 59.3	154 54.6	7.0	S15 34.5	6.9	59.6
19	103 31.8	2 00.3	169 20.6	7.0	15 27.6	7.0	59.6
20	118 32.0	01.3	183 46.6	6.9	15 20.6	7.1	59.6
21	133 32.2	.. 02.2	198 12.5	7.1	15 13.5	7.2	59.7
22	148 32.4	03.2	212 38.6	7.0	15 06.3	7.3	59.7
23	163 32.6	04.2	227 04.6	7.1	S14 59.0	7.4	59.7
	SD 16.1	d 1.0	SD 16.0		16.1		16.2

Lat.	Twilight Naut.	Civil	Sunrise	Moonrise 23	24	25	26
°	h m	h m	h m	h m	h m	h m	h m
N 72	02 54	04 29	05 38	■■	■■	05 53	05 33
N 70	03 17	04 39	05 41	04 08	04 48	05 01	05 04
68	03 35	04 47	05 44	03 13	04 01	04 28	04 43
66	03 49	04 54	05 46	02 40	03 31	04 04	04 26
64	04 00	04 59	05 47	02 16	03 08	03 45	04 11
62	04 10	05 04	05 49	01 56	02 50	03 30	04 00
60	04 18	05 08	05 50	01 41	02 34	03 17	03 49
N 58	04 24	05 12	05 51	01 27	02 22	03 06	03 41
56	04 30	05 15	05 52	01 16	02 10	02 56	03 33
54	04 35	05 18	05 53	01 06	02 01	02 47	03 26
52	04 40	05 20	05 54	00 57	01 52	02 39	03 20
50	04 44	05 22	05 54	00 49	01 44	02 32	03 14
45	04 52	05 27	05 56	00 32	01 27	02 17	03 02
N 40	04 59	05 30	05 57	00 18	01 14	02 05	02 51
35	05 04	05 33	05 58	00 06	01 02	01 54	02 43
30	05 07	05 35	05 59	24 52	00 52	01 45	02 35
20	05 13	05 39	06 01	24 34	00 34	01 29	02 22
N 10	05 17	05 41	06 02	24 19	00 19	01 15	02 10
0	05 18	05 42	06 03	24 05	00 05	01 02	01 59
S 10	05 19	05 43	06 04	23 51	24 49	00 49	01 48
20	05 17	05 43	06 05	23 36	24 35	00 35	01 36
30	05 14	05 42	06 06	23 18	24 19	00 19	01 23
35	05 12	05 41	06 06	23 08	24 10	00 10	01 15
40	05 08	05 40	06 07	22 56	23 59	25 06	01 06
45	05 04	05 38	06 07	22 43	23 47	24 56	00 56
S 50	04 58	05 36	06 08	22 26	23 32	24 43	00 43
52	04 55	05 34	06 08	22 18	23 25	24 38	00 38
54	04 52	05 33	06 08	22 10	23 17	24 31	00 31
56	04 48	05 32	06 09	22 00	23 08	24 24	00 24
58	04 43	05 30	06 09	21 49	22 58	24 16	00 16
S 60	04 38	05 28	06 09	21 36	22 46	24 06	00 06

Lat.	Sunset	Twilight Civil	Naut.	Moonset 23	24	25	26
°	h m	h m	h m	h m	h m	h m	h m
N 72	18 37	19 47	21 25	■■	■■	08 50	11 08
N 70	18 34	19 36	21 00	06 34	07 54	09 41	11 35
68	18 31	19 28	20 41	07 30	08 40	10 13	11 56
66	18 29	19 21	20 27	08 03	09 11	10 36	12 12
64	18 27	19 15	20 15	08 27	09 33	10 55	12 25
62	18 25	19 10	20 05	08 46	09 51	11 10	12 36
60	18 24	19 06	19 57	09 02	10 06	11 22	12 46
N 58	18 23	19 02	19 50	09 15	10 19	11 33	12 54
56	18 22	18 59	19 44	09 27	10 30	11 42	13 01
54	18 21	18 56	19 39	09 37	10 39	11 51	13 08
52	18 20	18 54	19 34	09 46	10 48	11 58	13 13
50	18 19	18 51	19 30	09 54	10 56	12 05	13 19
45	18 17	18 47	19 21	10 11	11 12	12 19	13 30
N 40	18 16	18 43	19 15	10 25	11 25	12 31	13 39
35	18 15	18 40	19 10	10 37	11 37	12 41	13 47
30	18 14	18 38	19 06	10 47	11 47	12 49	13 54
20	18 12	18 34	19 00	11 05	12 04	13 04	14 06
N 10	18 11	18 32	18 56	11 21	12 19	13 17	14 16
0	18 10	18 30	18 54	11 35	12 32	13 29	14 26
S 10	18 08	18 29	18 54	11 50	12 46	13 42	14 35
20	18 07	18 29	18 55	12 05	13 01	13 54	14 45
30	18 06	18 30	18 58	12 23	13 17	14 09	14 57
35	18 06	18 31	19 00	12 33	13 27	14 17	15 04
40	18 05	18 32	19 04	12 45	13 38	14 27	15 11
45	18 05	18 34	19 08	12 58	13 51	14 38	15 20
S 50	18 04	18 36	19 14	13 15	14 07	14 52	15 30
52	18 03	18 37	19 16	13 23	14 14	14 58	15 35
54	18 03	18 38	19 20	13 32	14 22	15 05	15 40
56	18 03	18 40	19 23	13 42	14 32	15 13	15 46
58	18 02	18 41	19 27	13 53	14 42	15 21	15 53
S 60	18 02	18 43	19 32	14 06	14 54	15 31	16 00

	SUN			MOON			
Day	Eqn. of Time 00ʰ	12ʰ	Mer. Pass.	Mer. Pass. Upper	Lower	Age	Phase
d	m s	m s	h m	h m	h m	d	%
23	06 44	06 34	12 07	05 22	17 50	22	57
24	06 25	06 16	12 06	06 19	18 47	23	45
25	06 07	05 58	12 06	07 16	19 44	24	34

UT	ARIES	VENUS −4.5		MARS −1.2		JUPITER −2.2		SATURN +0.3		STARS		
	GHA	GHA	Dec	GHA	Dec	GHA	Dec	GHA	Dec	Name	SHA	Dec
d h	° ′	° ′	° ′	° ′	° ′	° ′	° ′	° ′	° ′		° ′	° ′
26 00	183 21.9	222 41.3	S13 42.3	340 17.3	S 6 39.8	81 19.2	N23 14.5	312 15.4	S16 08.1	Acamar	315 18.3	S40 15.2
01	198 24.4	237 41.2	41.7	355 20.4	39.6	96 21.5	14.5	327 18.0	08.1	Achernar	335 27.0	S57 10.0
02	213 26.8	252 41.1	41.2	10 23.6	39.3	111 23.8	14.5	342 20.5	08.1	Acrux	173 07.9	S63 10.8
03	228 29.3	267 41.1 ..	40.7	25 26.8 ..	39.1	126 26.1 ..	14.5	357 23.1 ..	08.1	Adhara	255 12.0	S28 59.9
04	243 31.8	282 41.0	40.1	40 30.0	38.9	141 28.4	14.4	12 25.6	08.0	Aldebaran	290 48.9	N16 32.1
05	258 34.2	297 40.9	39.6	55 33.2	38.6	156 30.7	14.4	27 28.2	08.0			
06	273 36.7	312 40.8	S13 39.1	70 36.3	S 6 38.4	171 33.0	N23 14.4	42 30.8	S16 08.0	Alioth	166 19.7	N55 52.8
W 07	288 39.2	327 40.7	38.5	85 39.5	38.1	186 35.3	14.4	57 33.3	07.9	Alkaid	152 58.1	N49 14.4
E 08	303 41.6	342 40.6	38.0	100 42.7	37.9	201 37.6	14.4	72 35.9	07.9	Al Na'ir	27 43.5	S46 53.3
D 09	318 44.1	357 40.5 ..	37.5	115 45.9 ..	37.6	216 39.9 ..	14.4	87 38.4 ..	07.9	Alnilam	275 45.9	S 1 11.9
N 10	333 46.5	12 40.4	36.9	130 49.1	37.4	231 42.2	14.4	102 41.0	07.8	Alphard	217 55.3	S 8 43.5
E 11	348 49.0	27 40.3	36.4	145 52.2	37.2	246 44.4	14.4	117 43.5	07.8			
S 12	3 51.5	42 40.2	S13 35.9	160 55.4	S 6 36.9	261 46.7	N23 14.4	132 46.1	S16 07.8	Alphecca	126 10.3	N26 39.9
D 13	18 53.9	57 40.2	35.3	175 58.6	36.7	276 49.0	14.4	147 48.7	07.8	Alpheratz	357 43.3	N29 10.1
A 14	33 56.4	72 40.1	34.8	191 01.8	36.4	291 51.3	14.3	162 51.2	07.7	Altair	62 07.8	N 8 54.4
Y 15	48 58.9	87 40.0 ..	34.3	206 05.0 ..	36.2	306 53.6 ..	14.3	177 53.8 ..	07.7	Ankaa	353 15.6	S42 13.8
16	64 01.3	102 39.9	33.7	221 08.2	35.9	321 55.9	14.3	192 56.3	07.7	Antares	112 25.4	S26 27.7
17	79 03.8	117 39.8	33.2	236 11.4	35.7	336 58.2	14.3	207 58.9	07.6			
18	94 06.3	132 39.7	S13 32.6	251 14.6	S 6 35.4	352 00.5	N23 14.3	223 01.5	S16 07.6	Arcturus	145 55.0	N19 06.4
19	109 08.7	147 39.6	32.1	266 17.8	35.2	7 02.8	14.3	238 04.0	07.6	Atria	107 26.5	S69 02.8
20	124 11.2	162 39.5	31.5	281 21.0	34.9	22 05.1	14.3	253 06.6	07.5	Avior	234 17.4	S59 33.8
21	139 13.6	177 39.4 ..	31.0	296 24.1 ..	34.7	37 07.4 ..	14.3	268 09.1 ..	07.5	Bellatrix	278 31.5	N 6 21.5
22	154 16.1	192 39.3	30.5	311 27.3	34.4	52 09.7	14.3	283 11.7	07.5	Betelgeuse	271 00.8	N 7 24.3
23	169 18.6	207 39.2	29.9	326 30.5	34.2	67 11.9	14.2	298 14.3	07.4			
27 00	184 21.0	222 39.1	S13 29.4	341 33.7	S 6 33.9	82 14.2	N23 14.2	313 16.8	S16 07.4	Canopus	263 55.9	S52 42.7
01	199 23.5	237 39.0	28.8	356 36.9	33.7	97 16.5	14.2	328 19.4	07.4	Capella	280 33.8	N46 00.7
02	214 26.0	252 38.9	28.3	11 40.1	33.5	112 18.8	14.2	343 22.0	07.4	Deneb	49 31.3	N45 19.8
03	229 28.4	267 38.8 ..	27.7	26 43.3 ..	33.2	127 21.1 ..	14.2	358 24.5 ..	07.3	Denebola	182 32.8	N14 29.4
04	244 30.9	282 38.7	27.2	41 46.5	33.0	142 23.4	14.2	13 27.1	07.3	Diphda	348 55.7	S17 54.6
05	259 33.4	297 38.6	26.6	56 49.7	32.7	157 25.7	14.2	28 29.6	07.3			
06	274 35.8	312 38.5	S13 26.1	71 52.9	S 6 32.5	172 28.0	N23 14.2	43 32.2	S16 07.2	Dubhe	193 50.5	N61 40.4
07	289 38.3	327 38.4	25.5	86 56.2	32.2	187 30.2	14.2	58 34.8	07.2	Elnath	278 12.0	N28 37.0
T 08	304 40.8	342 38.3	25.0	101 59.4	32.0	202 32.5	14.1	73 37.3	07.2	Eltanin	90 45.8	N51 29.1
H 09	319 43.2	357 38.2 ..	24.4	117 02.6 ..	31.7	217 34.8 ..	14.1	88 39.9 ..	07.1	Enif	33 46.8	N 9 56.4
U 10	334 45.7	12 38.1	23.9	132 05.8	31.4	232 37.1	14.1	103 42.5	07.1	Fomalhaut	15 23.7	S29 32.8
R 11	349 48.1	27 38.0	23.3	147 09.0	31.2	247 39.4	14.1	118 45.0	07.1			
S 12	4 50.6	42 37.9	S13 22.8	162 12.2	S 6 30.9	262 41.7	N23 14.1	133 47.6	S16 07.0	Gacrux	171 59.6	S57 11.7
D 13	19 53.1	57 37.8	22.2	177 15.4	30.7	277 44.0	14.1	148 50.1	07.0	Gienah	175 51.4	S17 37.4
A 14	34 55.5	72 37.7	21.6	192 18.6	30.4	292 46.2	14.1	163 52.7	07.0	Hadar	148 46.4	S60 26.4
Y 15	49 58.0	87 37.6 ..	21.1	207 21.8 ..	30.2	307 48.5 ..	14.1	178 55.3 ..	06.9	Hamal	328 00.4	N23 31.7
16	65 00.5	102 37.5	20.5	222 25.0	29.9	322 50.8	14.1	193 57.8	06.9	Kaus Aust.	83 43.1	S34 22.4
17	80 02.9	117 37.4	20.0	237 28.3	29.7	337 53.1	14.0	209 00.4	06.9			
18	95 05.4	132 37.3	S13 19.4	252 31.5	S 6 29.4	352 55.4	N23 14.0	224 03.0	S16 06.9	Kochab	137 19.2	N74 05.7
19	110 07.9	147 37.2	18.8	267 34.7	29.2	7 57.7	14.0	239 05.5	06.8	Markab	13 38.1	N15 16.9
20	125 10.3	162 37.1	18.3	282 37.9	28.9	22 59.9	14.0	254 08.1	06.8	Menkar	314 14.7	N 4 08.5
21	140 12.8	177 37.0 ..	17.7	297 41.1 ..	28.7	38 02.2 ..	14.0	269 10.7 ..	06.8	Menkent	148 06.5	S36 26.4
22	155 15.3	192 36.9	17.2	312 44.3	28.4	53 04.5	14.0	284 13.2	06.7	Miaplacidus	221 38.9	S69 46.9
23	170 17.7	207 36.8	16.6	327 47.6	28.2	68 06.8	14.0	299 15.8	06.7			
28 00	185 20.2	222 36.7	S13 16.0	342 50.8	S 6 27.9	83 09.1	N23 14.0	314 18.3	S16 06.7	Mirfak	308 39.9	N49 54.7
01	200 22.6	237 36.6	15.5	357 54.0	27.7	98 11.4	14.0	329 20.9	06.6	Nunki	75 57.7	S26 16.5
02	215 25.1	252 36.5	14.9	12 57.2	27.4	113 13.6	13.9	344 23.5	06.6	Peacock	53 18.7	S56 41.0
03	230 27.6	267 36.4 ..	14.3	28 00.4 ..	27.1	128 15.9 ..	13.9	359 26.0 ..	06.6	Pollux	243 27.0	N27 59.3
04	245 30.0	282 36.3	13.8	43 03.7	26.9	143 18.2	13.9	14 28.6	06.5	Procyon	244 59.1	N 5 11.0
05	260 32.5	297 36.2	13.2	58 06.9	26.6	158 20.5	13.9	29 31.2	06.5			
06	275 35.0	312 36.1	S13 12.6	73 10.1	S 6 26.4	173 22.8	N23 13.9	44 33.7	S16 06.5	Rasalhague	96 05.9	N12 33.0
07	290 37.4	327 36.0	12.1	88 13.3	26.1	188 25.0	13.9	59 36.3	06.4	Regulus	207 42.7	N11 53.6
08	305 39.9	342 35.9	11.5	103 16.6	25.9	203 27.3	13.9	74 38.9	06.4	Rigel	281 11.6	S 8 11.5
F 09	320 42.4	357 35.8 ..	10.9	118 19.8 ..	25.6	218 29.6 ..	13.9	89 41.4 ..	06.4	Rigil Kent.	139 50.3	S60 53.4
R 10	335 44.8	12 35.7	10.3	133 23.0	25.3	233 31.9	13.9	104 44.0	06.3	Sabik	102 11.8	S15 44.4
I 11	350 47.3	27 35.6	09.8	148 26.3	25.1	248 34.1	13.8	119 46.6	06.3			
D 12	5 49.7	42 35.5	S13 09.2	163 29.5	S 6 24.8	263 36.4	N23 13.8	134 49.1	S16 06.3	Schedar	349 40.4	N56 36.9
A 13	20 52.2	57 35.4	08.6	178 32.7	24.6	278 38.7	13.8	149 51.7	06.2	Shaula	96 21.1	S37 06.6
Y 14	35 54.7	72 35.2	08.0	193 36.0	24.3	293 41.0	13.8	164 54.3	06.2	Sirius	258 33.2	S16 44.5
15	50 57.1	87 35.1 ..	07.5	208 39.2 ..	24.1	308 43.3 ..	13.8	179 56.8 ..	06.2	Spica	158 30.4	S11 14.2
16	65 59.6	102 35.0	06.9	223 42.4	23.8	323 45.5	13.8	194 59.4	06.1	Suhail	222 51.7	S43 29.8
17	81 02.1	117 34.9	06.3	238 45.7	23.5	338 47.8	13.8	210 02.0	06.1			
18	96 04.5	132 34.8	S13 05.7	253 48.9	S 6 23.3	353 50.1	N23 13.8	225 04.5	S16 06.1	Vega	80 38.6	N38 47.7
19	111 07.0	147 34.7	05.2	268 52.1	23.0	8 52.4	13.7	240 07.1	06.1	Zuben'ubi	137 04.5	S16 06.0
20	126 09.5	162 34.6	04.6	283 55.4	22.8	23 54.6	13.7	255 09.7	06.0			
21	141 11.9	177 34.5 ..	04.0	298 58.6 ..	22.5	38 56.9 ..	13.7	270 12.2 ..	06.0			
22	156 14.4	192 34.4	03.4	314 01.9	22.2	53 59.2	13.7	285 14.8	06.0			
23	171 16.9	207 34.3	02.8	329 05.1	22.0	69 01.4	13.7	300 17.4	05.9			

	SHA	Mer. Pass.
	° ′	h m
Venus	38 18.1	9 09
Mars	157 12.7	1 13
Jupiter	257 53.2	18 28
Saturn	128 55.8	3 06

	h m								
Mer. Pass.	11 40.7	v −0.1	d 0.6	v 3.2	d 0.3	v 2.3	d 0.0	v 2.6	d 0.0

UT	SUN GHA	SUN Dec	MOON GHA	v	MOON Dec	d	HP
d h	° ′	° ′	° ′	′	° ′	′	′
26 00	178 32.8	N 2 05.2	241 30.7	7.1	S14 51.6	7.5	59.7
01	193 33.0	06.2	255 56.8	7.1	14 44.1	7.6	59.7
02	208 33.1	07.1	270 22.9	7.1	14 36.5	7.7	59.7
03	223 33.3	.. 08.1	284 49.0	7.2	14 28.8	7.8	59.7
04	238 33.5	09.1	299 15.2	7.2	14 21.0	7.9	59.7
05	253 33.7	10.1	313 41.4	7.2	14 13.1	8.0	59.8
06	268 33.9	N 2 11.1	328 07.6	7.3	S14 05.1	8.0	59.8
W 07	283 34.1	12.0	342 33.9	7.2	13 57.1	8.2	59.8
E 08	298 34.3	13.0	357 00.1	7.3	13 48.9	8.3	59.8
D 09	313 34.5	.. 14.0	11 26.4	7.4	13 40.6	8.3	59.8
N 10	328 34.7	15.0	25 52.8	7.3	13 32.3	8.5	59.8
E 11	343 34.8	16.0	40 19.1	7.4	13 23.8	8.5	59.8
S 12	358 35.0	N 2 17.0	54 45.5	7.5	S13 15.3	8.6	59.8
D 13	13 35.2	17.9	69 12.0	7.4	13 06.7	8.7	59.8
A 14	28 35.4	18.9	83 38.4	7.5	12 58.0	8.8	59.8
Y 15	43 35.6	.. 19.9	98 04.9	7.5	12 49.2	8.9	59.8
16	58 35.8	20.9	112 31.4	7.6	12 40.3	8.9	59.9
17	73 36.0	21.9	126 58.0	7.5	12 31.4	9.1	59.9
18	88 36.2	N 2 22.8	141 24.5	7.6	S12 22.3	9.1	59.9
19	103 36.4	23.8	155 51.1	7.7	12 13.2	9.2	59.9
20	118 36.5	24.8	170 17.8	7.6	12 04.0	9.2	59.9
21	133 36.7	.. 25.8	184 44.4	7.7	11 54.8	9.4	59.9
22	148 36.9	26.8	199 11.1	7.7	11 45.4	9.4	59.9
23	163 37.1	27.7	213 37.8	7.8	11 36.0	9.5	59.9
27 00	178 37.3	N 2 28.7	228 04.6	7.8	S11 26.5	9.6	59.9
01	193 37.5	29.7	242 31.4	7.8	11 16.9	9.7	59.9
02	208 37.7	30.7	256 58.2	7.8	11 07.2	9.7	59.9
03	223 37.9	.. 31.7	271 25.0	7.9	10 57.5	9.8	59.9
04	238 38.0	32.6	285 51.9	7.9	10 47.7	9.9	59.9
05	253 38.2	33.6	300 18.8	8.0	10 37.8	9.9	59.9
06	268 38.4	N 2 34.6	314 45.8	7.9	S10 27.9	10.0	59.9
T 07	283 38.6	35.6	329 12.7	8.1	10 17.9	10.1	59.9
H 08	298 38.8	36.6	343 39.8	8.0	10 07.8	10.1	59.9
U 09	313 39.0	.. 37.5	358 06.8	8.0	9 57.7	10.2	59.9
R 10	328 39.2	38.5	12 33.8	8.1	9 47.5	10.3	59.9
S 11	343 39.4	39.5	27 00.9	8.2	9 37.2	10.3	60.0
D 12	358 39.6	N 2 40.5	41 28.1	8.1	S 9 26.9	10.4	60.0
A 13	13 39.7	41.4	55 55.2	8.2	9 16.5	10.4	60.0
Y 14	28 39.9	42.4	70 22.4	8.2	9 06.1	10.5	60.0
15	43 40.1	.. 43.4	84 49.6	8.3	8 55.6	10.6	60.0
16	58 40.3	44.4	99 16.9	8.2	8 45.0	10.6	60.0
17	73 40.5	45.4	113 44.1	8.3	8 34.4	10.6	60.0
18	88 40.7	N 2 46.3	128 11.4	8.4	S 8 23.8	10.8	60.0
19	103 40.9	47.3	142 38.8	8.3	8 13.0	10.7	60.0
20	118 41.1	48.3	157 06.1	8.4	8 02.3	10.8	60.0
21	133 41.2	.. 49.3	171 33.5	8.4	7 51.5	10.9	60.0
22	148 41.4	50.2	186 00.9	8.5	7 40.6	10.9	60.0
23	163 41.6	51.2	200 28.4	8.5	7 29.7	11.0	60.0
28 00	178 41.8	N 2 52.2	214 55.9	8.5	S 7 18.7	11.0	60.0
01	193 42.0	53.2	229 23.4	8.5	7 07.7	11.0	60.0
02	208 42.2	54.2	243 50.9	8.6	6 56.7	11.1	60.0
03	223 42.4	.. 55.1	258 18.5	8.6	6 45.6	11.2	59.9
04	238 42.6	56.1	272 46.1	8.6	6 34.4	11.1	59.9
05	253 42.7	57.1	287 13.7	8.6	6 23.3	11.2	59.9
06	268 42.9	N 2 58.1	301 41.3	8.7	S 6 12.1	11.3	59.9
07	283 43.1	2 59.0	316 09.0	8.7	6 00.8	11.3	59.9
08	298 43.3	3 00.0	330 36.7	8.7	5 49.5	11.3	59.9
F 09	313 43.5	.. 01.0	345 04.4	8.8	5 38.2	11.3	59.9
R 10	328 43.7	02.0	359 32.2	8.7	5 26.9	11.4	59.9
I 11	343 43.9	02.9	13 59.9	8.8	5 15.5	11.4	59.9
D 12	358 44.1	N 3 03.9	28 27.7	8.9	S 5 04.1	11.5	59.9
A 13	13 44.3	04.9	42 55.6	8.8	4 52.6	11.5	59.9
Y 14	28 44.4	05.9	57 23.4	8.9	4 41.1	11.4	59.9
15	43 44.6	.. 06.9	71 51.3	8.9	4 29.7	11.6	59.9
16	58 44.8	07.8	86 19.2	8.9	4 18.1	11.5	59.9
17	73 45.0	08.8	100 47.1	9.0	4 06.6	11.6	59.9
18	88 45.2	N 3 09.8	115 15.1	8.9	S 3 55.0	11.6	59.9
19	103 45.4	10.8	129 43.0	9.0	3 43.4	11.6	59.9
20	118 45.6	11.7	144 11.0	9.0	3 31.8	11.6	59.8
21	133 45.8	.. 12.7	158 39.0	9.1	3 20.2	11.6	59.8
22	148 45.9	13.7	173 07.1	9.0	3 08.6	11.7	59.8
23	163 46.1	14.7	187 35.1	9.1	S 2 56.9	11.7	59.8
	SD 16.1	d 1.0	SD 16.3		16.3		16.3

Lat.	Twilight Naut.	Twilight Civil	Sunrise	Moonrise 26	27	28	29
°	h m	h m	h m	h m	h m	h m	h m
N 72	02 30	04 12	05 23	05 33	05 22	05 14	05 06
N 70	02 58	04 24	05 27	05 04	05 05	05 05	05 04
68	03 19	04 34	05 31	04 43	04 51	04 57	05 02
66	03 35	04 42	05 34	04 26	04 40	04 51	05 00
64	03 48	04 48	05 37	04 11	04 31	04 46	04 58
62	03 58	04 54	05 39	04 00	04 22	04 41	04 57
60	04 07	04 59	05 41	03 49	04 15	04 37	04 56
N 58	04 15	05 03	05 43	03 41	04 09	04 33	04 55
56	04 22	05 07	05 44	03 33	04 03	04 30	04 54
54	04 27	05 10	05 46	03 26	03 59	04 27	04 53
52	04 32	05 13	05 47	03 20	03 54	04 24	04 52
50	04 37	05 16	05 48	03 14	03 50	04 22	04 52
45	04 46	05 21	05 50	03 02	03 41	04 17	04 50
N 40	04 53	05 25	05 52	02 51	03 33	04 12	04 49
35	04 59	05 29	05 54	02 43	03 27	04 08	04 48
30	05 04	05 32	05 56	02 35	03 21	04 05	04 47
20	05 10	05 36	05 58	02 22	03 12	03 59	04 45
N 10	05 15	05 39	06 00	02 10	03 03	03 54	04 44
0	05 17	05 41	06 02	01 59	02 55	03 49	04 42
S 10	05 19	05 43	06 04	01 48	02 47	03 44	04 41
20	05 18	05 44	06 06	01 36	02 38	03 39	04 40
30	05 16	05 44	06 08	01 23	02 28	03 33	04 38
35	05 14	05 43	06 09	01 15	02 22	03 30	04 37
40	05 11	05 43	06 10	01 06	02 16	03 26	04 36
45	05 08	05 42	06 11	00 56	02 08	03 22	04 35
S 50	05 03	05 40	06 13	00 43	01 59	03 16	04 34
52	05 00	05 40	06 13	00 38	01 55	03 14	04 32
54	04 57	05 39	06 14	00 31	01 50	03 11	04 32
56	04 54	05 38	06 15	00 24	01 45	03 08	04 31
58	04 50	05 37	06 16	00 16	01 39	03 05	04 31
S 60	04 46	05 35	06 17	00 06	01 32	03 01	04 30

Lat.	Sunset	Twilight Civil	Naut.	Moonset 26	27	28	29
°	h m	h m	h m	h m	h m	h m	h m
N 72	18 51	20 02	21 48	11 08	13 14	15 16	17 14
N 70	18 46	19 50	21 18	11 35	13 30	15 22	17 13
68	18 42	19 40	20 56	11 56	13 42	15 28	17 13
66	18 39	19 31	20 39	12 12	13 52	15 32	17 12
64	18 36	19 25	20 26	12 25	14 00	15 36	17 12
62	18 33	19 19	20 15	12 36	14 07	15 40	17 11
60	18 31	19 14	20 06	12 46	14 13	15 42	17 11
N 58	18 29	19 09	19 58	12 54	14 19	15 45	17 11
56	18 28	19 05	19 51	13 01	14 24	15 47	17 11
54	18 26	19 02	19 45	13 08	14 28	15 49	17 10
52	18 25	18 59	19 40	13 13	14 32	15 51	17 10
50	18 24	18 56	19 35	13 19	14 35	15 53	17 10
45	18 21	18 51	19 26	13 30	14 43	15 56	17 10
N 40	18 19	18 46	19 18	13 39	14 49	15 59	17 09
35	18 17	18 43	19 12	13 47	14 54	16 02	17 09
30	18 16	18 40	19 07	13 54	14 59	16 04	17 09
20	18 13	18 35	19 01	14 06	15 07	16 08	17 08
N 10	18 11	18 32	18 56	14 16	15 14	16 11	17 08
0	18 09	18 29	18 53	14 26	15 21	16 15	17 07
S 10	18 07	18 28	18 52	14 35	15 27	16 18	17 07
20	18 05	18 27	18 52	14 45	15 34	16 21	17 06
30	18 03	18 27	18 54	14 57	15 42	16 25	17 06
35	18 02	18 27	18 56	15 04	15 46	16 27	17 06
40	18 00	18 27	18 58	15 11	15 51	16 29	17 05
45	17 59	18 28	19 02	15 20	15 57	16 32	17 05
S 50	17 57	18 29	19 07	15 30	16 04	16 35	17 04
52	17 57	18 30	19 09	15 35	16 07	16 36	17 04
54	17 56	18 31	19 12	15 40	16 11	16 38	17 04
56	17 55	18 32	19 15	15 46	16 15	16 40	17 03
58	17 54	18 33	19 19	15 53	16 19	16 42	17 03
S 60	17 53	18 34	19 23	16 00	16 24	16 44	17 03

Day	SUN Eqn. of Time 00h	12h	Mer. Pass.	MOON Mer. Pass. Upper	Lower	Age	Phase
d	m s	m s	h m	h m	h m	d	%
26	05 49	05 40	12 06	08 12	20 40	25	23
27	05 31	05 22	12 05	09 08	21 35	26	14
28	05 13	05 04	12 05	10 02	22 29	27	7

UT	ARIES GHA	VENUS −4.4 GHA	Dec	MARS −1.3 GHA	Dec	JUPITER −2.2 GHA	Dec	SATURN +0.3 GHA	Dec	STARS Name	SHA	Dec
29 00	186 19.3	222 34.2	S13 02.2	344 08.3	S 6 21.7	84 03.7	N23 13.7	315 20.0	S16 05.9	Acamar	315 18.3	S40 15.2
01	201 21.8	237 34.0	01.7	359 11.6	21.4	99 06.0	13.7	330 22.5	05.9	Achernar	335 27.0	S57 10.0
02	216 24.2	252 33.9	01.1	14 14.8	21.2	114 08.3	13.7	345 25.1	05.8	Acrux	173 07.9	S63 10.8
03	231 26.7	267 33.8	13 00.5	29 18.1	.. 20.9	129 10.5	.. 13.6	0 27.7	.. 05.8	Adhara	255 12.1	S28 59.9
04	246 29.2	282 33.7	12 59.9	44 21.3	20.7	144 12.8	13.6	15 30.2	05.8	Aldebaran	290 48.9	N16 32.1
05	261 31.6	297 33.6	59.3	59 24.6	20.4	159 15.1	13.6	30 32.8	05.7			
S 06	276 34.1	312 33.5	S12 58.7	74 27.8	S 6 20.1	174 17.4	N23 13.6	45 35.4	S16 05.7	Alioth	166 19.7	N55 52.8
A 07	291 36.6	327 33.4	58.1	89 31.1	19.9	189 19.6	13.6	60 37.9	05.7	Alkaid	152 58.1	N49 14.4
T 08	306 39.0	342 33.3	57.6	104 34.3	19.6	204 21.9	13.6	75 40.5	05.6	Al Na'ir	27 43.5	S46 53.3
U 09	321 41.5	357 33.2	.. 57.0	119 37.6	.. 19.3	219 24.2	.. 13.6	90 43.1	.. 05.6	Alnilam	275 45.9	S 1 11.9
R 10	336 44.0	12 33.0	56.4	134 40.8	19.1	234 26.4	13.6	105 45.6	05.6	Alphard	217 55.3	S 8 43.5
11	351 46.4	27 32.9	55.8	149 44.1	18.8	249 28.7	13.5	120 48.2	05.5			
D 12	6 48.9	42 32.8	S12 55.2	164 47.3	S 6 18.6	264 31.0	N23 13.5	135 50.8	S16 05.5	Alphecca	126 10.3	N26 39.9
A 13	21 51.3	57 32.7	54.6	179 50.6	18.3	279 33.2	13.5	150 53.4	05.5	Alpheratz	357 43.3	N29 10.1
Y 14	36 53.8	72 32.6	54.0	194 53.8	18.0	294 35.5	13.5	165 55.9	05.4	Altair	62 07.8	N 8 54.4
15	51 56.3	87 32.5	.. 53.4	209 57.1	.. 17.8	309 37.8	.. 13.5	180 58.5	.. 05.4	Ankaa	353 15.6	S42 13.8
16	66 58.7	102 32.4	52.8	225 00.3	17.5	324 40.1	13.5	196 01.1	05.4	Antares	112 25.4	S26 27.7
17	82 01.2	117 32.2	52.2	240 03.6	17.2	339 42.3	13.5	211 03.6	05.3			
18	97 03.7	132 32.1	S12 51.6	255 06.9	S 6 17.0	354 44.6	N23 13.5	226 06.2	S16 05.3	Arcturus	145 54.9	N19 06.4
19	112 06.1	147 32.0	51.0	270 10.1	16.7	9 46.9	13.4	241 08.8	05.3	Atria	107 26.5	S69 02.8
20	127 08.6	162 31.9	50.4	285 13.4	16.4	24 49.1	13.4	256 11.4	05.2	Avior	234 17.5	S59 33.8
21	142 11.1	177 31.8	.. 49.8	300 16.6	.. 16.2	39 51.4	.. 13.4	271 13.9	.. 05.2	Bellatrix	278 31.5	N 6 21.5
22	157 13.5	192 31.7	49.2	315 19.9	15.9	54 53.7	13.4	286 16.5	05.2	Betelgeuse	271 00.8	N 7 24.3
23	172 16.0	207 31.5	48.6	330 23.2	15.6	69 55.9	13.4	301 19.1	05.1			
30 00	187 18.5	222 31.4	S12 48.0	345 26.4	S 6 15.4	84 58.2	N23 13.4	316 21.6	S16 05.1	Canopus	263 55.9	S52 42.7
01	202 20.9	237 31.3	47.4	0 29.7	15.1	100 00.5	13.4	331 24.2	05.1	Capella	280 33.8	N46 00.7
02	217 23.4	252 31.2	46.8	15 33.0	14.8	115 02.7	13.4	346 26.8	05.0	Deneb	49 31.3	N45 19.7
03	232 25.8	267 31.1	.. 46.2	30 36.2	.. 14.6	130 05.0	.. 13.3	1 29.4	.. 05.0	Denebola	182 32.8	N14 29.4
04	247 28.3	282 31.0	45.6	45 39.5	14.3	145 07.2	13.3	16 31.9	05.0	Diphda	348 55.7	S17 54.6
05	262 30.8	297 30.8	45.0	60 42.8	14.0	160 09.5	13.3	31 34.5	04.9			
S 06	277 33.2	312 30.7	S12 44.4	75 46.0	S 6 13.8	175 11.8	N23 13.3	46 37.1	S16 04.9	Dubhe	193 50.5	N61 40.4
U 07	292 35.7	327 30.6	43.8	90 49.3	13.5	190 14.0	13.3	61 39.7	04.9	Elnath	278 12.0	N28 37.0
N 08	307 38.2	342 30.5	43.2	105 52.6	13.2	205 16.3	13.3	76 42.2	04.8	Eltanin	90 45.8	N51 29.1
D 09	322 40.6	357 30.4	.. 42.6	120 55.8	.. 13.0	220 18.6	.. 13.3	91 44.8	.. 04.8	Enif	33 46.8	N 9 56.4
A 10	337 43.1	12 30.2	42.0	135 59.1	12.7	235 20.8	13.2	106 47.4	04.8	Fomalhaut	15 23.7	S29 32.8
Y 11	352 45.6	27 30.1	41.4	151 02.4	12.4	250 23.1	13.2	121 49.9	04.7			
12	7 48.0	42 30.0	S12 40.8	166 05.6	S 6 12.2	265 25.3	N23 13.2	136 52.5	S16 04.7	Gacrux	171 59.6	S57 11.7
13	22 50.5	57 29.9	40.2	181 08.9	11.9	280 27.6	13.2	151 55.1	04.7	Gienah	175 51.4	S17 37.4
14	37 52.9	72 29.8	39.5	196 12.2	11.6	295 29.9	13.2	166 57.7	04.6	Hadar	148 46.4	S60 26.4
15	52 55.4	87 29.7	.. 38.9	211 15.5	.. 11.3	310 32.1	.. 13.2	182 00.2	.. 04.6	Hamal	328 00.4	N23 31.7
16	67 57.9	102 29.5	38.3	226 18.7	11.1	325 34.4	13.2	197 02.8	04.6	Kaus Aust.	83 43.1	S34 22.4
17	83 00.3	117 29.4	37.7	241 22.0	10.8	340 36.7	13.2	212 05.4	04.5			
18	98 02.8	132 29.3	S12 37.1	256 25.3	S 6 10.5	355 38.9	N23 13.1	227 08.0	S16 04.5	Kochab	137 19.2	N74 05.7
19	113 05.3	147 29.2	36.5	271 28.6	10.3	10 41.2	13.1	242 10.5	04.5	Markab	13 38.1	N15 16.8
20	128 07.7	162 29.0	35.9	286 31.9	10.0	25 43.4	13.1	257 13.1	04.4	Menkar	314 14.7	N 4 08.5
21	143 10.2	177 28.9	.. 35.2	301 35.1	.. 09.7	40 45.7	.. 13.1	272 15.7	.. 04.4	Menkent	148 06.5	S36 26.4
22	158 12.7	192 28.8	34.6	316 38.4	09.5	55 47.9	13.1	287 18.3	04.4	Miaplacidus	221 38.9	S69 47.0
23	173 15.1	207 28.7	34.0	331 41.7	09.2	70 50.2	13.1	302 20.8	04.3			
31 00	188 17.6	222 28.6	S12 33.4	346 45.0	S 6 08.9	85 52.5	N23 13.1	317 23.4	S16 04.3	Mirfak	308 39.9	N49 54.7
01	203 20.1	237 28.4	32.8	1 48.3	08.6	100 54.7	13.0	332 26.0	04.3	Nunki	75 57.7	S26 16.5
02	218 22.5	252 28.3	32.1	16 51.5	08.4	115 57.0	13.0	347 28.6	04.2	Peacock	53 18.7	S56 41.0
03	233 25.0	267 28.2	.. 31.5	31 54.8	.. 08.1	130 59.2	.. 13.0	2 31.1	.. 04.2	Pollux	243 27.0	N27 59.3
04	248 27.4	282 28.1	30.9	46 58.1	07.8	146 01.5	13.0	17 33.7	04.2	Procyon	244 59.1	N 5 11.0
05	263 29.9	297 27.9	30.3	62 01.4	07.5	161 03.7	13.0	32 36.3	04.1			
M 06	278 32.4	312 27.8	S12 29.7	77 04.7	S 6 07.3	176 06.0	N23 13.0	47 38.9	S16 04.1	Rasalhague	96 05.9	N12 33.0
O 07	293 34.8	327 27.7	29.0	92 08.0	07.0	191 08.3	13.0	62 41.4	04.0	Regulus	207 42.7	N11 53.6
N 08	308 37.3	342 27.6	28.4	107 11.3	06.7	206 10.5	12.9	77 44.0	04.0	Rigel	281 11.7	S 8 11.5
D 09	323 39.8	357 27.4	.. 27.8	122 14.5	.. 06.5	221 12.8	.. 12.9	92 46.6	.. 04.0	Rigil Kent.	139 50.3	S60 53.5
A 10	338 42.2	12 27.3	27.2	137 17.8	06.2	236 15.0	12.9	107 49.2	03.9	Sabik	102 11.8	S15 44.4
Y 11	353 44.7	27 27.2	26.5	152 21.1	05.9	251 17.3	12.9	122 51.8	03.9			
12	8 47.2	42 27.1	S12 25.9	167 24.4	S 6 05.6	266 19.5	N23 12.9	137 54.3	S16 03.9	Schedar	349 40.4	N56 36.9
13	23 49.6	57 26.9	25.3	182 27.7	05.4	281 21.8	12.9	152 56.9	03.8	Shaula	96 21.1	S37 06.6
14	38 52.1	72 26.8	24.6	197 31.0	05.1	296 24.0	12.9	167 59.5	03.8	Sirius	258 33.2	S16 44.5
15	53 54.6	87 26.7	.. 24.0	212 34.3	.. 04.8	311 26.3	.. 12.8	183 02.1	.. 03.8	Spica	158 30.4	S11 14.2
16	68 57.0	102 26.6	23.4	227 37.6	04.5	326 28.5	12.8	198 04.6	03.7	Suhail	222 51.7	S43 29.8
17	83 59.5	117 26.4	22.8	242 40.9	04.3	341 30.8	12.8	213 07.2	03.7			
18	99 01.9	132 26.3	S12 22.1	257 44.2	S 6 04.0	356 33.0	N23 12.8	228 09.8	S16 03.7	Vega	80 38.6	N38 47.7
19	114 04.4	147 26.2	21.5	272 47.5	03.7	11 35.3	12.8	243 12.4	03.6	Zuben'ubi	137 04.5	S16 06.0
20	129 06.9	162 26.1	20.9	287 50.8	03.4	26 37.6	12.8	258 15.0	03.6		SHA	Mer.Pass.
21	144 09.3	177 25.9	.. 20.2	302 54.1	.. 03.2	41 39.8	.. 12.8	273 17.5	.. 03.6	Venus	35 13.0	9 10
22	159 11.8	192 25.8	19.6	317 57.4	02.9	56 42.1	12.7	288 20.1	03.5	Mars	158 08.0	0 58
23	174 14.3	207 25.7	19.0	333 00.7	02.6	71 44.3	12.7	303 22.7	03.5	Jupiter	257 39.7	18 17
Mer.Pass. 11 28.9		v −0.1	d 0.6	v 3.3	d 0.3	v 2.3	d 0.0	v 2.6	d 0.0	Saturn	129 03.2	2 54

UT	SUN GHA	SUN Dec	MOON GHA	v	MOON Dec	d	HP
d h	° ′	° ′	° ′	′	° ′	′	′
29 00	178 46.3	N 3 15.6	202 03.2	9.1	S 2 45.2	11.7	59.8
01	193 46.5	16.6	216 31.3	9.1	2 33.5	11.7	59.8
02	208 46.7	17.6	230 59.4	9.1	2 21.8	11.7	59.8
03	223 46.9 ..	18.6	245 27.5	9.2	2 10.1	11.7	59.8
04	238 47.1	19.5	259 55.7	9.2	1 58.4	11.7	59.8
05	253 47.3	20.5	274 23.9	9.2	1 46.7	11.7	59.8
06	268 47.4	N 3 21.5	288 52.1	9.2	S 1 35.0	11.8	59.7
S 07	283 47.6	22.5	303 20.3	9.2	1 23.2	11.7	59.7
A 08	298 47.8	23.4	317 48.5	9.3	1 11.5	11.8	59.7
T 09	313 48.0 ..	24.4	332 16.8	9.3	0 59.7	11.7	59.7
U 10	328 48.2	25.4	346 45.1	9.2	0 48.0	11.8	59.7
R 11	343 48.4	26.3	1 13.3	9.4	0 36.2	11.7	59.7
D 12	358 48.6	N 3 27.3	15 41.7	9.3	S 0 24.5	11.7	59.7
A 13	13 48.8	28.3	30 10.0	9.3	0 12.8	11.8	59.7
Y 14	28 48.9	29.3	44 38.3	9.4	S 0 01.0	11.7	59.6
15	43 49.1 ..	30.2	59 06.7	9.3	N 0 10.7	11.7	59.6
16	58 49.3	31.2	73 35.0	9.4	0 22.4	11.7	59.6
17	73 49.5	32.2	88 03.4	9.4	0 34.1	11.7	59.6
18	88 49.7	N 3 33.2	102 31.8	9.4	N 0 45.8	11.7	59.6
19	103 49.9	34.1	117 00.2	9.5	0 57.5	11.7	59.6
20	118 50.1	35.1	131 28.7	9.4	1 09.2	11.7	59.5
21	133 50.3 ..	36.1	145 57.1	9.5	1 20.9	11.7	59.5
22	148 50.4	37.1	160 25.6	9.4	1 32.6	11.6	59.5
23	163 50.6	38.0	174 54.0	9.5	1 44.2	11.6	59.5
30 00	178 50.8	N 3 39.0	189 22.5	9.5	N 1 55.8	11.6	59.5
01	193 51.0	40.0	203 51.0	9.5	2 07.4	11.6	59.5
02	208 51.2	40.9	218 19.5	9.5	2 19.0	11.6	59.4
03	223 51.4 ..	41.9	232 48.0	9.5	2 30.6	11.5	59.4
04	238 51.6	42.9	247 16.5	9.6	2 42.1	11.5	59.4
05	253 51.7	43.9	261 45.1	9.5	2 53.6	11.5	59.4
06	268 51.9	N 3 44.8	276 13.6	9.6	N 3 05.1	11.5	59.4
07	283 52.1	45.8	290 42.2	9.5	3 16.6	11.4	59.3
S 08	298 52.3	46.8	305 10.7	9.6	3 28.0	11.4	59.3
U 09	313 52.5 ..	47.7	319 39.3	9.6	3 39.4	11.4	59.3
N 10	328 52.7	48.7	334 07.9	9.6	3 50.8	11.3	59.3
D 11	343 52.9	49.7	348 36.5	9.6	4 02.1	11.3	59.2
A 12	358 53.1	N 3 50.7	3 05.1	9.6	N 4 13.5	11.3	59.2
Y 13	13 53.2	51.6	17 33.7	9.6	4 24.8	11.2	59.2
14	28 53.4	52.6	32 02.3	9.7	4 36.0	11.3	59.2
15	43 53.6 ..	53.6	46 31.0	9.6	4 47.3	11.1	59.2
16	58 53.8	54.5	60 59.6	9.7	4 58.4	11.2	59.1
17	73 54.0	55.5	75 28.3	9.6	5 09.6	11.1	59.1
18	88 54.2	N 3 56.5	89 56.9	9.7	N 5 20.7	11.1	59.1
19	103 54.4	57.4	104 25.6	9.6	5 31.8	11.0	59.1
20	118 54.5	58.4	118 54.2	9.7	5 42.8	11.0	59.0
21	133 54.7 ..	59.4	133 22.9	9.7	5 53.8	10.9	59.0
22	148 54.9	4 00.4	147 51.6	9.7	6 04.7	10.9	59.0
23	163 55.1	01.3	162 20.3	9.6	6 15.6	10.9	59.0
31 00	178 55.3	N 4 02.3	176 48.9	9.7	N 6 26.5	10.8	58.9
01	193 55.5	03.3	191 17.6	9.7	6 37.3	10.7	58.9
02	208 55.7	04.2	205 46.3	9.7	6 48.0	10.7	58.9
03	223 55.8 ..	05.2	220 15.0	9.7	6 58.7	10.7	58.9
04	238 56.0	06.2	234 43.7	9.8	7 09.4	10.6	58.8
05	253 56.2	07.1	249 12.5	9.7	7 20.0	10.5	58.8
06	268 56.4	N 4 08.1	263 41.2	9.7	N 7 30.5	10.5	58.8
07	283 56.6	09.1	278 09.9	9.7	7 41.0	10.5	58.8
08	298 56.8	10.0	292 38.6	9.7	7 51.5	10.4	58.7
M 09	313 57.0 ..	11.0	307 07.3	9.8	8 01.9	10.3	58.7
O 10	328 57.1	12.0	321 36.1	9.7	8 12.2	10.3	58.7
N 11	343 57.3	13.0	336 04.8	9.7	8 22.5	10.2	58.6
D 12	358 57.5	N 4 13.9	350 33.5	9.8	N 8 32.7	10.2	58.6
A 13	13 57.7	14.9	5 02.3	9.7	8 42.9	10.1	58.6
Y 14	28 57.9	15.9	19 31.0	9.8	8 53.0	10.0	58.6
15	43 58.1 ..	16.8	33 59.8	9.7	9 03.0	10.0	58.5
16	58 58.3	17.8	48 28.5	9.8	9 13.0	9.9	58.5
17	73 58.4	18.8	62 57.3	9.7	9 22.9	9.9	58.5
18	88 58.6	N 4 19.7	77 26.0	9.8	N 9 32.8	9.8	58.4
19	103 58.8	20.7	91 54.8	9.7	9 42.6	9.7	58.4
20	118 59.0	21.7	106 23.5	9.8	9 52.3	9.7	58.4
21	133 59.2 ..	22.6	120 52.3	9.8	10 02.0	9.6	58.4
22	148 59.4	23.6	135 21.1	9.7	10 11.6	9.5	58.3
23	163 59.6	24.6	149 49.8	9.8	N10 21.1	9.4	58.3
	SD 16.0	d 1.0	SD 16.3		16.1		16.0

Lat.	Twilight Naut.	Twilight Civil	Sunrise	Moonrise 29	30	31	1
°	h m	h m	h m	h m	h m	h m	h m
N 72	02 02	03 54	05 07	05 06	04 59	04 52	04 44
N 70	02 37	04 09	05 13	05 04	05 03	05 02	05 02
68	03 02	04 20	05 18	05 02	05 06	05 11	05 17
66	03 20	04 29	05 22	05 00	05 08	05 18	05 28
64	03 35	04 37	05 26	04 58	05 11	05 24	05 38
62	03 47	04 44	05 29	04 57	05 13	05 29	05 47
60	03 57	04 49	05 32	04 56	05 14	05 33	05 54
N 58	04 05	04 54	05 34	04 55	05 16	05 37	06 01
56	04 13	04 59	05 36	04 54	05 17	05 41	06 07
54	04 19	05 02	05 38	04 53	05 18	05 44	06 12
52	04 25	05 06	05 40	04 52	05 20	05 47	06 17
50	04 30	05 09	05 41	04 52	05 21	05 50	06 21
45	04 40	05 15	05 45	04 50	05 23	05 56	06 30
N 40	04 48	05 20	05 48	04 49	05 25	06 01	06 38
35	04 55	05 25	05 50	04 48	05 26	06 05	06 45
30	05 00	05 28	05 52	04 47	05 28	06 09	06 51
20	05 08	05 33	05 56	04 45	05 30	06 15	07 01
N 10	05 13	05 37	05 59	04 44	05 33	06 21	07 10
0	05 16	05 40	06 01	04 42	05 35	06 27	07 19
S 10	05 18	05 43	06 04	04 41	05 37	06 32	07 27
20	05 19	05 44	06 06	04 40	05 39	06 38	07 36
30	05 18	05 45	06 09	04 38	05 42	06 45	07 47
35	05 16	05 46	06 11	04 37	05 44	06 49	07 53
40	05 14	05 46	06 13	04 36	05 46	06 54	08 00
45	05 12	05 46	06 15	04 35	05 48	06 59	08 09
S 50	05 08	05 45	06 17	04 34	05 50	07 06	08 18
52	05 05	05 45	06 18	04 33	05 51	07 09	08 23
54	05 03	05 44	06 20	04 32	05 53	07 12	08 28
56	05 00	05 44	06 21	04 31	05 54	07 15	08 34
58	04 57	05 43	06 22	04 31	05 56	07 19	08 40
S 60	04 54	05 42	06 24	04 30	05 58	07 24	08 47

Lat.	Sunset	Twilight Civil	Twilight Naut.	Moonset 29	30	31	1
°	h m	h m	h m	h m	h m	h m	h m
N 72	19 05	20 19	22 16	17 14	19 10	21 07	23 05
N 70	18 58	20 04	21 37	17 13	19 02	20 50	22 36
68	18 53	19 52	21 12	17 13	18 56	20 37	22 16
66	18 48	19 42	20 52	17 12	18 50	20 27	21 59
64	18 45	19 34	20 37	17 12	18 46	20 18	21 46
62	18 41	19 27	20 25	17 11	18 42	20 10	21 35
60	18 39	19 21	20 14	17 11	18 38	20 04	21 25
N 58	18 36	19 16	20 06	17 11	18 35	19 58	21 17
56	18 34	19 12	19 58	17 11	18 33	19 53	21 09
54	18 32	19 08	19 51	17 10	18 30	19 48	21 03
52	18 30	19 04	19 46	17 10	18 28	19 44	20 57
50	18 28	19 01	19 40	17 10	18 26	19 40	20 52
45	18 25	18 55	19 30	17 10	18 22	19 32	20 40
N 40	18 22	18 49	19 22	17 09	18 18	19 26	20 31
35	18 20	18 45	19 15	17 09	18 15	19 20	20 23
30	18 17	18 41	19 10	17 09	18 12	19 15	20 16
20	18 14	18 36	19 02	17 08	18 08	19 06	20 04
N 10	18 11	18 32	18 56	17 08	18 04	18 59	19 53
0	18 08	18 28	18 53	17 07	18 00	18 51	19 43
S 10	18 05	18 26	18 50	17 07	17 56	18 44	19 33
20	18 02	18 24	18 50	17 06	17 52	18 37	19 23
30	17 59	18 23	18 51	17 06	17 47	18 28	19 11
35	17 57	18 23	18 52	17 06	17 44	18 23	19 04
40	17 56	18 22	18 54	17 05	17 41	18 18	18 56
45	17 53	18 23	18 57	17 05	17 37	18 11	18 47
S 50	17 51	18 23	19 00	17 04	17 33	18 03	18 36
52	17 50	18 23	19 02	17 04	17 31	18 00	18 30
54	17 48	18 23	19 04	17 04	17 29	17 56	18 25
56	17 47	18 24	19 07	17 03	17 27	17 51	18 19
58	17 45	18 24	19 10	17 03	17 24	17 46	18 12
S 60	17 44	18 25	19 13	17 03	17 21	17 41	18 04

Day	SUN Eqn. of Time 00h	12h	SUN Mer. Pass.	MOON Mer. Pass. Upper	Lower	Age	Phase
d	m s	m s	h m	h m	h m	d	%
29	04 55	04 46	12 05	10 55	23 21	28	2
30	04 37	04 28	12 04	11 47	24 13	29	0
31	04 19	04 10	12 04	12 39	00 13	01	1

2014 APRIL 1, 2, 3 (TUES., WED., THURS.)

UT	ARIES GHA	VENUS −4.4 GHA	Dec	MARS −1.4 GHA	Dec	JUPITER −2.2 GHA	Dec	SATURN +0.3 GHA	Dec	STARS Name	SHA	Dec
d h	° ′	° ′	° ′	° ′	° ′	° ′	° ′	° ′	° ′		° ′	° ′
1 00	189 16.7	222 25.6	S12 18.3	348 04.0	S 6 02.3	86 46.6	N23 12.7	318 25.3	S16 03.5	Acamar	315 18.3	S40 15.1
01	204 19.2	237 25.4	17.7	3 07.3	02.1	101 48.8	12.7	333 27.9	03.4	Achernar	335 27.0	S57 10.0
02	219 21.7	252 25.3	17.0	18 10.6	01.8	116 51.1	12.7	348 30.4	03.4	Acrux	173 07.9	S63 10.8
03	234 24.1	267 25.2	.. 16.4	33 13.9	.. 01.5	131 53.3	.. 12.7	3 33.0	.. 03.4	Adhara	255 12.1	S28 59.9
04	249 26.6	282 25.0	15.8	48 17.2	01.2	146 55.6	12.7	18 35.6	03.3	Aldebaran	290 48.9	N16 32.1
05	264 29.0	297 24.9	15.1	63 20.5	00.9	161 57.8	12.6	33 38.2	03.3			
06	279 31.5	312 24.8	S12 14.5	78 23.8	S 6 00.7	177 00.0	N23 12.6	48 40.8	S16 03.2	Alioth	166 19.7	N55 52.9
07	294 34.0	327 24.7	13.8	93 27.1	00.4	192 02.3	12.6	63 43.3	03.2	Alkaid	152 58.1	N49 14.4
T 08	309 36.4	342 24.5	13.2	108 30.4	6 00.1	207 04.5	12.6	78 45.9	03.2	Al Na'ir	27 43.4	S46 53.3
U 09	324 38.9	357 24.4	.. 12.6	123 33.7	5 59.8	222 06.8	.. 12.6	93 48.5	.. 03.1	Alnilam	275 45.9	S 1 11.9
E 10	339 41.4	12 24.3	11.9	138 37.0	59.6	237 09.0	12.6	108 51.1	03.1	Alphard	217 55.4	S 8 43.5
S 11	354 43.8	27 24.1	11.3	153 40.3	59.3	252 11.3	12.6	123 53.7	03.1			
D 12	9 46.3	42 24.0	S12 10.6	168 43.6	S 5 59.0	267 13.5	N23 12.5	138 56.2	S16 03.0	Alphecca	126 10.3	N26 39.9
A 13	24 48.8	57 23.9	10.0	183 46.9	58.7	282 15.8	12.5	153 58.8	03.0	Alpheratz	357 43.3	N29 10.0
Y 14	39 51.2	72 23.7	09.3	198 50.2	58.4	297 18.0	12.5	169 01.4	03.0	Altair	62 07.8	N 8 54.4
15	54 53.7	87 23.6	.. 08.7	213 53.5	.. 58.2	312 20.3	.. 12.5	184 04.0	.. 02.9	Ankaa	353 15.6	S42 13.8
16	69 56.2	102 23.5	08.0	228 56.8	57.9	327 22.5	12.5	199 06.6	02.9	Antares	112 25.4	S26 27.7
17	84 58.6	117 23.4	07.4	244 00.2	57.6	342 24.8	12.5	214 09.1	02.9			
18	100 01.1	132 23.2	S12 06.7	259 03.5	S 5 57.3	357 27.0	N23 12.5	229 11.7	S16 02.8	Arcturus	145 54.9	N19 06.4
19	115 03.5	147 23.1	06.1	274 06.8	57.0	12 29.2	12.4	244 14.3	02.8	Atria	107 26.4	S69 02.8
20	130 06.0	162 23.0	05.4	289 10.1	56.8	27 31.5	12.4	259 16.9	02.8	Avior	234 17.5	S59 33.8
21	145 08.5	177 22.8	.. 04.8	304 13.4	.. 56.5	42 33.7	.. 12.4	274 19.5	.. 02.7	Bellatrix	278 31.5	N 6 21.5
22	160 10.9	192 22.7	04.1	319 16.7	56.2	57 36.0	12.4	289 22.0	02.7	Betelgeuse	271 00.8	N 7 24.3
23	175 13.4	207 22.6	03.5	334 20.0	55.9	72 38.2	12.4	304 24.6	02.6			
2 00	190 15.9	222 22.4	S12 02.8	349 23.4	S 5 55.6	87 40.5	N23 12.4	319 27.2	S16 02.6	Canopus	263 56.0	S52 42.7
01	205 18.3	237 22.3	02.2	4 26.7	55.4	102 42.7	12.3	334 29.8	02.6	Capella	280 33.8	N46 00.7
02	220 20.8	252 22.2	01.5	19 30.0	55.1	117 44.9	12.3	349 32.4	02.5	Deneb	49 31.3	N45 19.7
03	235 23.3	267 22.0	.. 00.9	34 33.3	.. 54.8	132 47.2	.. 12.3	4 35.0	.. 02.5	Denebola	182 32.8	N14 29.4
04	250 25.7	282 21.9	12 00.2	49 36.6	54.5	147 49.4	12.3	19 37.5	02.5	Diphda	348 55.7	S17 54.6
05	265 28.2	297 21.8	11 59.5	64 39.9	54.2	162 51.7	12.3	34 40.1	02.4			
06	280 30.6	312 21.6	S11 58.9	79 43.3	S 5 54.0	177 53.9	N23 12.3	49 42.7	S16 02.4	Dubhe	193 50.5	N61 40.4
W 07	295 33.1	327 21.5	58.2	94 46.6	53.7	192 56.2	12.3	64 45.3	02.4	Elnath	278 12.1	N28 37.0
E 08	310 35.6	342 21.4	57.6	109 49.9	53.4	207 58.4	12.2	79 47.9	02.3	Eltanin	90 45.8	N51 29.1
D 09	325 38.0	357 21.2	.. 56.9	124 53.2	.. 53.1	223 00.6	.. 12.2	94 50.5	.. 02.3	Enif	33 46.8	N 9 56.4
N 10	340 40.5	12 21.1	56.2	139 56.5	52.8	238 02.9	12.2	109 53.0	02.3	Fomalhaut	15 23.7	S29 32.7
E 11	355 43.0	27 21.0	55.6	154 59.9	52.6	253 05.1	12.2	124 55.6	02.2			
S 12	10 45.4	42 20.8	S11 54.9	170 03.2	S 5 52.3	268 07.4	N23 12.2	139 58.2	S16 02.2	Gacrux	171 59.6	S57 11.7
D 13	25 47.9	57 20.7	54.3	185 06.5	52.0	283 09.6	12.2	155 00.8	02.1	Gienah	175 51.4	S17 37.4
A 14	40 50.4	72 20.6	53.6	200 09.8	51.7	298 11.8	12.1	170 03.4	02.1	Hadar	148 46.4	S60 26.4
Y 15	55 52.8	87 20.4	.. 52.9	215 13.2	.. 51.4	313 14.1	.. 12.1	185 06.0	.. 02.1	Hamal	328 00.4	N23 31.6
16	70 55.3	102 20.3	52.3	230 16.5	51.1	328 16.3	12.1	200 08.6	02.0	Kaus Aust.	83 43.0	S34 22.4
17	85 57.8	117 20.2	51.6	245 19.8	50.9	343 18.5	12.1	215 11.1	02.0			
18	101 00.2	132 20.0	S11 50.9	260 23.1	S 5 50.6	358 20.8	N23 12.1	230 13.7	S16 02.0	Kochab	137 19.2	N74 05.7
19	116 02.7	147 19.9	50.3	275 26.5	50.3	13 23.0	12.1	245 16.3	01.9	Markab	13 38.1	N15 16.8
20	131 05.1	162 19.7	49.6	290 29.8	50.0	28 25.3	12.1	260 18.9	01.9	Menkar	314 14.7	N 4 08.5
21	146 07.6	177 19.6	.. 48.9	305 33.1	.. 49.7	43 27.5	.. 12.0	275 21.5	.. 01.9	Menkent	148 06.5	S36 26.4
22	161 10.1	192 19.5	48.3	320 36.5	49.4	58 29.7	12.0	290 24.1	01.8	Miaplacidus	221 38.9	S69 47.0
23	176 12.5	207 19.3	47.6	335 39.8	49.2	73 32.0	12.0	305 26.6	01.8			
3 00	191 15.0	222 19.2	S11 46.9	350 43.1	S 5 48.9	88 34.2	N23 12.0	320 29.2	S16 01.7	Mirfak	308 39.9	N49 54.6
01	206 17.5	237 19.1	46.3	5 46.4	48.6	103 36.4	12.0	335 31.8	01.7	Nunki	75 57.7	S26 16.5
02	221 19.9	252 18.9	45.6	20 49.8	48.3	118 38.7	12.0	350 34.4	01.7	Peacock	53 18.7	S56 41.0
03	236 22.4	267 18.8	.. 44.9	35 53.1	.. 48.0	133 40.9	.. 11.9	5 37.0	.. 01.6	Pollux	243 27.0	N27 59.3
04	251 24.9	282 18.7	44.2	50 56.4	47.7	148 43.1	11.9	20 39.6	01.6	Procyon	244 59.1	N 5 11.0
05	266 27.3	297 18.5	43.6	65 59.8	47.5	163 45.4	11.9	35 42.2	01.6			
06	281 29.8	312 18.4	S11 42.9	81 03.1	S 5 47.2	178 47.6	N23 11.9	50 44.8	S16 01.5	Rasalhague	96 05.8	N12 33.0
07	296 32.3	327 18.2	42.2	96 06.4	46.9	193 49.8	11.9	65 47.3	01.5	Regulus	207 42.7	N11 53.6
T 08	311 34.7	342 18.1	41.5	111 09.8	46.6	208 52.1	11.9	80 49.9	01.5	Rigel	281 11.7	S 8 11.5
H 09	326 37.2	357 18.0	.. 40.9	126 13.1	.. 46.3	223 54.3	.. 11.8	95 52.5	.. 01.4	Rigil Kent.	139 50.3	S60 53.5
U 10	341 39.6	12 17.8	40.2	141 16.4	46.0	238 56.5	11.8	110 55.1	01.4	Sabik	102 11.8	S15 44.4
R 11	356 42.1	27 17.7	39.5	156 19.8	45.7	253 58.8	11.8	125 57.7	01.3			
S 12	11 44.6	42 17.5	S11 38.8	171 23.1	S 5 45.5	269 01.0	N23 11.8	141 00.3	S16 01.3	Schedar	349 40.4	N56 36.9
D 13	26 47.0	57 17.4	38.1	186 26.5	45.2	284 03.2	11.8	156 02.9	01.3	Shaula	96 21.0	S37 06.6
A 14	41 49.5	72 17.3	37.5	201 29.8	44.9	299 05.5	11.8	171 05.4	01.2	Sirius	258 33.3	S16 44.5
Y 15	56 52.0	87 17.1	.. 36.8	216 33.1	.. 44.6	314 07.7	.. 11.7	186 08.0	.. 01.2	Spica	158 30.3	S11 14.2
16	71 54.4	102 17.0	36.1	231 36.5	44.3	329 09.9	11.7	201 10.6	01.2	Suhail	222 51.8	S43 29.8
17	86 56.9	117 16.9	35.4	246 39.8	44.0	344 12.1	11.7	216 13.2	01.1			
18	101 59.4	132 16.7	S11 34.7	261 43.1	S 5 43.7	359 14.4	N23 11.7	231 15.8	S16 01.1	Vega	80 38.6	N38 47.7
19	117 01.8	147 16.6	34.0	276 46.5	43.5	14 16.6	11.7	246 18.4	01.1	Zuben'ubi	137 04.5	S16 06.1
20	132 04.3	162 16.4	33.4	291 49.8	43.2	29 18.8	11.7	261 21.0	01.0			
21	147 06.7	177 16.3	.. 32.7	306 53.2	.. 42.9	44 21.1	.. 11.6	276 23.6	.. 01.0			
22	162 09.2	192 16.2	32.0	321 56.5	42.6	59 23.3	11.6	291 26.2	00.9			
23	177 11.7	207 16.0	31.3	336 59.9	42.3	74 25.5	11.6	306 28.7	00.9			

	SHA	Mer.Pass.
	° ′	h m
Venus	32 06.6	9 11
Mars	159 07.5	0 42
Jupiter	257 24.6	18 07
Saturn	129 11.4	2 42

	ARIES	VENUS	MARS	JUPITER	SATURN
Mer. Pass.	11h 17.1m	v −0.1 d 0.7	v 3.3 d 0.3	v 2.2 d 0.0	v 2.6 d 0.0

UT	SUN GHA	SUN Dec	MOON GHA	v	MOON Dec	d	HP
d h	° ′	° ′	° ′	′	° ′	′	′
1 00	178 59.7	N 4 25.5	164 18.6	9.8	N10 30.5	9.4	58.3
01	193 59.9	26.5	178 47.4	9.7	10 39.9	9.4	58.2
02	209 00.1	27.5	193 16.1	9.8	10 49.3	9.2	58.2
03	224 00.3	.. 28.4	207 44.9	9.8	10 58.5	9.2	58.2
04	239 00.5	29.4	222 13.7	9.8	11 07.7	9.1	58.1
05	254 00.7	30.4	236 42.5	9.7	11 16.8	9.0	58.1
06	269 00.9	N 4 31.3	251 11.2	9.8	N11 25.8	9.0	58.1
07	284 01.0	32.3	265 40.0	9.8	11 34.8	8.8	58.1
08	299 01.2	33.2	280 08.8	9.8	11 43.6	8.8	58.0
09	314 01.4	.. 34.2	294 37.6	9.8	11 52.4	8.8	58.0
10	329 01.6	35.2	309 06.4	9.8	12 01.2	8.6	58.0
11	344 01.8	36.1	323 35.2	9.8	12 09.8	8.6	57.9
12	359 02.0	N 4 37.1	338 04.0	9.8	N12 18.4	8.5	57.9
13	14 02.1	38.1	352 32.8	9.7	12 26.9	8.4	57.9
14	29 02.3	39.0	7 01.5	9.8	12 35.3	8.3	57.8
15	44 02.5	.. 40.0	21 30.3	9.9	12 43.6	8.3	57.8
16	59 02.7	41.0	35 59.2	9.8	12 51.9	8.1	57.8
17	74 02.9	41.9	50 28.0	9.8	13 00.0	8.1	57.7
18	89 03.1	N 4 42.9	64 56.8	9.8	N13 08.1	8.0	57.7
19	104 03.3	43.9	79 25.6	9.8	13 16.1	8.0	57.7
20	119 03.4	44.8	93 54.4	9.8	13 24.1	7.8	57.6
21	134 03.6	.. 45.8	108 23.2	9.8	13 31.9	7.7	57.6
22	149 03.8	46.7	122 52.0	9.8	13 39.6	7.7	57.6
23	164 04.0	47.7	137 20.8	9.9	13 47.3	7.6	57.5
2 00	179 04.2	N 4 48.7	151 49.7	9.8	N13 54.9	7.5	57.5
01	194 04.4	49.6	166 18.5	9.8	14 02.4	7.4	57.5
02	209 04.5	50.6	180 47.3	9.9	14 09.8	7.3	57.4
03	224 04.7	.. 51.6	195 16.2	9.8	14 17.1	7.3	57.4
04	239 04.9	52.5	209 45.0	9.9	14 24.4	7.1	57.4
05	254 05.1	53.5	224 13.9	9.8	14 31.5	7.1	57.3
06	269 05.3	N 4 54.4	238 42.7	9.9	N14 38.6	7.0	57.3
07	284 05.5	55.4	253 11.6	9.8	14 45.6	6.8	57.3
08	299 05.6	56.4	267 40.4	9.9	14 52.4	6.8	57.2
09	314 05.8	.. 57.3	282 09.3	9.9	14 59.2	6.7	57.2
10	329 06.0	58.3	296 38.2	9.9	15 05.9	6.6	57.2
11	344 06.2	4 59.2	311 07.1	9.9	15 12.5	6.6	57.1
12	359 06.4	N 5 00.2	325 36.0	9.8	N15 19.1	6.4	57.1
13	14 06.6	01.2	340 04.8	9.9	15 25.5	6.3	57.1
14	29 06.7	02.1	354 33.7	10.0	15 31.8	6.3	57.1
15	44 06.9	.. 03.1	9 02.7	9.9	15 38.1	6.1	57.0
16	59 07.1	04.0	23 31.6	9.9	15 44.2	6.1	57.0
17	74 07.3	05.0	38 00.5	9.9	15 50.3	6.0	57.0
18	89 07.5	N 5 06.0	52 29.4	10.0	N15 56.3	5.8	56.9
19	104 07.7	06.9	66 58.4	9.9	16 02.1	5.8	56.9
20	119 07.8	07.9	81 27.3	9.9	16 07.9	5.7	56.9
21	134 08.0	.. 08.8	95 56.2	10.0	16 13.6	5.6	56.8
22	149 08.2	09.8	110 25.2	10.0	16 19.2	5.5	56.8
23	164 08.4	10.8	124 54.2	10.0	16 24.7	5.4	56.8
3 00	179 08.6	N 5 11.7	139 23.2	10.0	N16 30.1	5.3	56.7
01	194 08.8	12.7	153 52.2	10.0	16 35.4	5.2	56.7
02	209 08.9	13.6	168 21.2	10.0	16 40.6	5.1	56.7
03	224 09.1	.. 14.6	182 50.2	10.0	16 45.7	5.0	56.6
04	239 09.3	15.6	197 19.2	10.0	16 50.7	4.9	56.6
05	254 09.5	16.5	211 48.2	10.1	16 55.6	4.9	56.6
06	269 09.7	N 5 17.5	226 17.3	10.0	N17 00.5	4.7	56.5
07	284 09.9	18.4	240 46.3	10.1	17 05.2	4.6	56.5
08	299 10.0	19.4	255 15.4	10.1	17 09.8	4.5	56.5
09	314 10.2	.. 20.3	269 44.5	10.1	17 14.3	4.5	56.4
10	329 10.4	21.3	284 13.6	10.1	17 18.8	4.3	56.4
11	344 10.6	22.3	298 42.7	10.1	17 23.1	4.3	56.4
12	359 10.8	N 5 23.2	313 11.8	10.1	N17 27.4	4.1	56.3
13	14 11.0	24.2	327 40.9	10.2	17 31.5	4.0	56.3
14	29 11.1	25.1	342 10.1	10.2	17 35.5	4.0	56.3
15	44 11.3	.. 26.1	356 39.3	10.1	17 39.5	3.8	56.3
16	59 11.5	27.0	11 08.4	10.2	17 43.3	3.8	56.2
17	74 11.7	28.0	25 37.6	10.2	17 47.1	3.6	56.2
18	89 11.9	N 5 29.0	40 06.8	10.3	N17 50.7	3.6	56.2
19	104 12.0	29.9	54 36.1	10.2	17 54.3	3.5	56.1
20	119 12.2	30.9	69 05.3	10.3	17 57.8	3.3	56.1
21	134 12.4	.. 31.8	83 34.6	10.3	18 01.1	3.3	56.1
22	149 12.6	32.8	98 03.9	10.3	18 04.4	3.1	56.0
23	164 12.8	33.7	112 33.2	10.3	N18 07.5	3.1	56.0
	SD 16.0	d 1.0	SD 15.8		15.6		15.4

Tuesday / Wednesday / Thursday labels mark the day blocks.

Twilight, Sunrise, Moonrise

Lat.	Naut.	Civil	Sunrise	Moonrise 1	2	3	4
°	h m	h m	h m	h m	h m	h m	h m
N 72	01 26	03 36	04 51	04 44	04 35	04 20	▭
N 70	02 14	03 53	04 59	05 02	05 04	05 09	05 21
68	02 43	04 06	05 06	05 17	05 26	05 40	06 04
66	03 05	04 17	05 11	05 28	05 43	06 03	06 32
64	03 21	04 26	05 15	05 38	05 57	06 21	06 54
62	03 35	04 33	05 19	05 47	06 09	06 36	07 12
60	03 46	04 40	05 23	05 54	06 19	06 49	07 26
N 58	03 56	04 45	05 26	06 01	06 28	07 00	07 39
56	04 04	04 50	05 28	06 07	06 36	07 10	07 50
54	04 11	04 55	05 31	06 12	06 43	07 18	07 59
52	04 17	04 59	05 33	06 17	06 49	07 26	08 08
50	04 23	05 02	05 35	06 21	06 55	07 33	08 15
45	04 34	05 10	05 39	06 30	07 07	07 47	08 32
N 40	04 43	05 15	05 43	06 38	07 17	08 00	08 45
35	04 50	05 20	05 46	06 45	07 26	08 10	08 56
30	04 56	05 24	05 48	06 51	07 34	08 19	09 06
20	05 05	05 31	05 53	07 01	07 47	08 35	09 23
N 10	05 11	05 36	05 57	07 10	07 59	08 49	09 38
0	05 15	05 40	06 00	07 19	08 10	09 02	09 52
S 10	05 18	05 43	06 04	07 27	08 21	09 15	10 07
20	05 20	05 45	06 07	07 36	08 33	09 29	10 22
30	05 20	05 47	06 11	07 47	08 47	09 45	10 39
35	05 19	05 48	06 13	07 53	08 55	09 54	10 49
40	05 17	05 49	06 16	08 00	09 04	10 05	11 01
45	05 15	05 49	06 19	08 09	09 15	10 17	11 14
S 50	05 12	05 50	06 22	08 18	09 28	10 32	11 31
52	05 11	05 50	06 23	08 23	09 34	10 40	11 39
54	05 09	05 50	06 25	08 28	09 41	10 48	11 47
56	05 07	05 50	06 27	08 34	09 48	10 57	11 57
58	05 04	05 50	06 29	08 40	09 57	11 07	12 09
S 60	05 01	05 50	06 31	08 47	10 06	11 19	12 21

Sunset, Twilight, Moonset

Lat.	Sunset	Civil	Naut.	Moonset 1	2	3	4
°	h m	h m	h m	h m	h m	h m	h m
N 72	19 19	20 36	22 54	23 05	25 07	01 07	▭
N 70	19 11	20 18	22 00	22 36	24 19	00 19	01 53
68	19 04	20 04	21 29	22 16	23 48	25 11	01 11
66	18 58	19 53	21 06	21 59	23 26	24 42	00 42
64	18 54	19 44	20 49	21 46	23 08	24 21	00 21
62	18 49	19 36	20 35	21 35	22 53	24 03	00 03
60	18 46	19 29	20 23	21 25	22 41	23 49	24 47
N 58	18 43	19 23	20 14	21 17	22 30	23 37	24 34
56	18 40	19 18	20 05	21 09	22 21	23 26	24 23
54	18 38	19 14	19 58	21 03	22 13	23 17	24 13
52	18 35	19 10	19 51	20 57	22 06	23 08	24 04
50	18 33	19 06	19 46	20 52	21 59	23 01	23 56
45	18 29	18 59	19 34	20 40	21 45	22 45	23 39
N 40	18 25	18 52	19 25	20 31	21 33	22 32	23 26
35	18 22	18 47	19 18	20 23	21 24	22 21	23 14
30	18 19	18 43	19 12	20 16	21 15	22 11	23 04
20	18 15	18 37	19 03	20 04	21 00	21 54	22 46
N 10	18 11	18 32	18 56	19 53	20 47	21 40	22 31
0	18 07	18 28	18 52	19 43	20 35	21 26	22 17
S 10	18 03	18 24	18 49	19 33	20 23	21 12	22 02
20	18 00	18 22	18 47	19 23	20 10	20 58	21 47
30	17 56	18 19	18 47	19 11	19 55	20 41	21 29
35	17 53	18 17	18 48	19 04	19 46	20 32	21 19
40	17 51	18 18	18 49	18 56	19 37	20 20	21 07
45	17 48	18 17	18 51	18 47	19 25	20 07	20 54
S 50	17 44	18 17	18 54	18 36	19 11	19 52	20 37
52	17 43	18 16	18 55	18 30	19 05	19 44	20 29
54	17 41	18 16	18 57	18 25	18 58	19 36	20 20
56	17 39	18 16	19 00	18 19	18 50	19 27	20 10
58	17 37	18 16	19 02	18 12	18 41	19 16	19 59
S 60	17 35	18 16	19 04	18 04	18 31	19 04	19 46

SUN / MOON

Day	Eqn. of Time 00h	Eqn. of Time 12h	Mer. Pass.	Moon Mer. Pass. Upper	Lower	Age	Phase
d	m s	m s	h m	h m	h m	d	%
1	04 01	03 53	12 04	13 31	01 05	02	4
2	03 44	03 35	12 04	14 23	01 57	03	9
3	03 26	03 17	12 03	15 14	02 48	04	16

2014 APRIL 4, 5, 6 (FRI., SAT., SUN.)

UT	ARIES	VENUS −4.4		MARS −1.4		JUPITER −2.2		SATURN +0.2		STARS		
	GHA	GHA	Dec	GHA	Dec	GHA	Dec	GHA	Dec	Name	SHA	Dec
d h	° ′	° ′	° ′	° ′	° ′	° ′	° ′	° ′	° ′		° ′	° ′
4 00	192 14.1	222 15.9	S11 30.6	352 03.2	S 5 42.0	89 27.7	N23 11.6	321 31.3	S16 00.9	Acamar	315 18.3	S40 15.1
01	207 16.6	237 15.7	29.9	7 06.5	41.7	104 30.0	11.6	336 33.9	00.8	Achernar	335 27.0	S57 10.0
02	222 19.1	252 15.6	29.2	22 09.9	41.5	119 32.2	11.6	351 36.5	00.8	Acrux	173 07.9	S63 10.8
03	237 21.5	267 15.5 ..	28.5	37 13.2 ..	41.2	134 34.4 ..	11.5	6 39.1 ..	00.8	Adhara	255 12.1	S28 59.9
04	252 24.0	282 15.3	27.9	52 16.6	40.9	149 36.7	11.5	21 41.7	00.7	Aldebaran	290 48.9	N16 32.1
05	267 26.5	297 15.2	27.2	67 19.9	40.6	164 38.9	11.5	36 44.3	00.7			
F 06	282 28.9	312 15.0	S11 26.5	82 23.3	S 5 40.3	179 41.1	N23 11.5	51 46.9	S16 00.6	Alioth	166 19.7	N55 52.9
R 07	297 31.4	327 14.9	25.8	97 26.6	40.0	194 43.3	11.5	66 49.5	00.6	Alkaid	152 58.0	N49 14.4
I 08	312 33.9	342 14.7	25.1	112 30.0	39.7	209 45.6	11.5	81 52.0	00.6	Al Na'ir	27 43.4	S46 53.3
D 09	327 36.3	357 14.6 ..	24.4	127 33.3 ..	39.4	224 47.8 ..	11.4	96 54.6 ..	00.5	Alnilam	275 45.9	S 1 11.9
A 10	342 38.8	12 14.5	23.7	142 36.7	39.2	239 50.0	11.4	111 57.2	00.5	Alphard	217 55.4	S 8 43.5
Y 11	357 41.2	27 14.3	23.0	157 40.0	38.9	254 52.2	11.4	126 59.8	00.5			
12	12 43.7	42 14.2	S11 22.3	172 43.3	S 5 38.6	269 54.5	N23 11.4	142 02.4	S16 00.4	Alphecca	126 10.3	N26 39.9
13	27 46.2	57 14.0	21.6	187 46.7	38.3	284 56.7	11.4	157 05.0	00.4	Alpheratz	357 43.2	N29 10.0
14	42 48.6	72 13.9	20.9	202 50.0	38.0	299 58.9	11.4	172 07.6	00.3	Altair	62 07.8	N 8 54.4
15	57 51.1	87 13.7 ..	20.2	217 53.4 ..	37.7	315 01.1 ..	11.3	187 10.2 ..	00.3	Ankaa	353 15.6	S42 13.7
16	72 53.6	102 13.6	19.5	232 56.7	37.4	330 03.3	11.3	202 12.8	00.3	Antares	112 25.3	S26 27.7
17	87 56.0	117 13.5	18.8	248 00.1	37.1	345 05.6	11.3	217 15.4	00.2			
18	102 58.5	132 13.3	S11 18.1	263 03.4	S 5 36.9	0 07.8	N23 11.3	232 18.0	S16 00.2	Arcturus	145 54.9	N19 06.4
19	118 01.0	147 13.2	17.4	278 06.8	36.6	15 10.0	11.3	247 20.5	00.2	Atria	107 26.4	S69 02.8
20	133 03.4	162 13.0	16.7	293 10.2	36.3	30 12.2	11.3	262 23.1	00.1	Avior	234 17.5	S59 33.8
21	148 05.9	177 12.9 ..	16.0	308 13.5 ..	36.0	45 14.5 ..	11.2	277 25.7 ..	00.1	Bellatrix	278 31.6	N 6 21.5
22	163 08.4	192 12.7	15.3	323 16.9	35.7	60 16.7	11.2	292 28.3	00.0	Betelgeuse	271 00.8	N 7 24.3
23	178 10.8	207 12.6	14.6	338 20.2	35.4	75 18.9	11.2	307 30.9	00.0			
5 00	193 13.3	222 12.5	S11 13.9	353 23.6	S 5 35.1	90 21.1	N23 11.2	322 33.5	S16 00.0	Canopus	263 56.0	S52 42.7
01	208 15.7	237 12.3	13.2	8 26.9	34.8	105 23.3	11.2	337 36.1	15 59.9	Capella	280 33.8	N46 00.7
02	223 18.2	252 12.2	12.5	23 30.3	34.5	120 25.6	11.2	352 38.7	59.9	Deneb	49 31.2	N45 19.7
03	238 20.7	267 12.0 ..	11.8	38 33.6 ..	34.3	135 27.8 ..	11.1	7 41.3 ..	59.9	Denebola	182 32.8	N14 29.4
04	253 23.1	282 11.9	11.1	53 37.0	34.0	150 30.0	11.1	22 43.9	59.8	Diphda	348 55.7	S17 54.6
05	268 25.6	297 11.7	10.4	68 40.3	33.7	165 32.2	11.1	37 46.5	59.8			
S 06	283 28.1	312 11.6	S11 09.7	83 43.7	S 5 33.4	180 34.4	N23 11.1	52 49.1	S15 59.7	Dubhe	193 50.6	N61 40.4
A 07	298 30.5	327 11.4	09.0	98 47.1	33.1	195 36.7	11.1	67 51.7	59.7	Elnath	278 12.1	N28 37.0
T 08	313 33.0	342 11.3	08.2	113 50.4	32.8	210 38.9	11.0	82 54.3	59.7	Eltanin	90 45.7	N51 29.1
U 09	328 35.5	357 11.2 ..	07.5	128 53.8 ..	32.5	225 41.1 ..	11.0	97 56.8 ..	59.6	Enif	33 46.8	N 9 56.4
R 10	343 37.9	12 11.0	06.8	143 57.1	32.2	240 43.3	11.0	112 59.4	59.6	Fomalhaut	15 23.7	S29 32.7
11	358 40.4	27 10.9	06.1	159 00.5	31.9	255 45.5	11.0	128 02.0	59.6			
D 12	13 42.8	42 10.7	S11 05.4	174 03.8	S 5 31.6	270 47.7	N23 11.0	143 04.6	S15 59.5	Gacrux	171 59.6	S57 11.7
A 13	28 45.3	57 10.6	04.7	189 07.2	31.4	285 50.0	11.0	158 07.2	59.5	Gienah	175 51.4	S17 37.5
Y 14	43 47.8	72 10.4	04.0	204 10.6	31.1	300 52.2	10.9	173 09.8	59.4	Hadar	148 46.4	S60 26.4
15	58 50.2	87 10.3 ..	03.3	219 13.9 ..	30.8	315 54.4 ..	10.9	188 12.4 ..	59.4	Hamal	328 03.4	N23 31.6
16	73 52.7	102 10.1	02.5	234 17.3	30.5	330 56.6	10.9	203 15.0	59.4	Kaus Aust.	83 43.0	S34 22.4
17	88 55.2	117 10.0	01.8	249 20.6	30.2	345 58.8	10.9	218 17.6	59.3			
18	103 57.6	132 09.8	S11 01.1	264 24.0	S 5 29.9	1 01.0	N23 10.9	233 20.2	S15 59.3	Kochab	137 19.1	N74 05.7
19	119 00.1	147 09.7	11 00.4	279 27.4	29.6	16 03.3	10.9	248 22.8	59.3	Markab	13 38.0	N15 16.8
20	134 02.6	162 09.6	10 59.7	294 30.7	29.3	31 05.5	10.8	263 25.4	59.2	Menkar	314 14.7	N 4 08.5
21	149 05.0	177 09.4 ..	59.0	309 34.1 ..	29.0	46 07.7 ..	10.8	278 28.0 ..	59.2	Menkent	148 06.5	S36 26.4
22	164 07.5	192 09.3	58.2	324 37.5	28.7	61 09.9	10.8	293 30.6	59.1	Miaplacidus	221 39.0	S69 47.0
23	179 10.0	207 09.1	57.5	339 40.8	28.5	76 12.1	10.8	308 33.2	59.1			
6 00	194 12.4	222 09.0	S10 56.8	354 44.2	S 5 28.2	91 14.3	N23 10.8	323 35.8	S15 59.1	Mirfak	308 39.9	N49 54.6
01	209 14.9	237 08.8	56.1	9 47.6	27.9	106 16.5	10.7	338 38.4	59.0	Nunki	75 57.6	S26 16.5
02	224 17.3	252 08.7	55.4	24 50.9	27.6	121 18.7	10.7	353 41.0	59.0	Peacock	53 18.6	S56 41.0
03	239 19.8	267 08.5 ..	54.6	39 54.3 ..	27.3	136 21.0 ..	10.7	8 43.5 ..	58.9	Pollux	243 27.0	N27 59.3
04	254 22.3	282 08.4	53.9	54 57.6	27.0	151 23.2	10.7	23 46.1	58.9	Procyon	244 59.1	N 5 11.0
05	269 24.7	297 08.2	53.2	70 01.0	26.7	166 25.4	10.7	38 48.7	58.9			
S 06	284 27.2	312 08.1	S10 52.5	85 04.4	S 5 26.4	181 27.6	N23 10.7	53 51.3	S15 58.8	Rasalhague	96 05.8	N12 33.0
U 07	299 29.7	327 07.9	51.7	100 07.7	26.1	196 29.8	10.6	68 53.9	58.8	Regulus	207 42.7	N11 53.6
N 08	314 32.1	342 07.8	51.0	115 11.1	25.8	211 32.0	10.6	83 56.5	58.8	Rigel	281 11.7	S 8 11.5
D 09	329 34.6	357 07.6 ..	50.3	130 14.5 ..	25.6	226 34.2 ..	10.6	98 59.1 ..	58.7	Rigil Kent.	139 50.3	S60 53.5
A 10	344 37.1	12 07.5	49.6	145 17.8	25.3	241 36.4	10.6	114 01.7	58.7	Sabik	102 11.7	S15 44.4
Y 11	359 39.5	27 07.3	48.8	160 21.2	25.0	256 38.6	10.6	129 04.3	58.6			
12	14 42.0	42 07.2	S10 48.1	175 24.6	S 5 24.7	271 40.9	N23 10.5	144 06.9	S15 58.6	Schedar	349 40.4	N56 36.9
13	29 44.5	57 07.0	47.4	190 27.9	24.4	286 43.1	10.5	159 09.5	58.6	Shaula	96 21.0	S37 06.6
14	44 46.9	72 06.9	46.7	205 31.3	24.1	301 45.3	10.5	174 12.1	58.5	Sirius	258 33.3	S16 44.5
15	59 49.4	87 06.7 ..	45.9	220 34.7 ..	23.8	316 47.5 ..	10.5	189 14.7 ..	58.5	Spica	158 30.3	S11 14.2
16	74 51.8	102 06.6	45.2	235 38.1	23.5	331 49.7	10.5	204 17.3	58.4	Suhail	222 51.8	S43 29.8
17	89 54.3	117 06.4	44.5	250 41.4	23.2	346 51.9	10.4	219 19.9	58.4			
18	104 56.8	132 06.3	S10 43.7	265 44.8	S 5 22.9	1 54.1	N23 10.4	234 22.5	S15 58.4	Vega	80 38.5	N38 47.7
19	119 59.2	147 06.2	43.0	280 48.2	22.6	16 56.3	10.4	249 25.1	58.3	Zuben'ubi	137 04.5	S16 06.1
20	135 01.7	162 06.0	42.3	295 51.5	22.4	31 58.5	10.4	264 27.7	58.3		SHA	Mer.Pass.
21	150 04.2	177 05.9 ..	41.5	310 54.9 ..	22.1	47 00.7 ..	10.4	279 30.3 ..	58.2		° ′	h m
22	165 06.6	192 05.7	40.8	325 58.3	21.8	62 02.9	10.4	294 32.9	58.2	Venus	28 59.2	9 11
23	180 09.1	207 05.6	40.1	341 01.6	21.5	77 05.1	10.3	309 35.5	58.2	Mars	160 10.3	0 26
	h m									Jupiter	257 07.8	17 56
Mer.Pass. 11 05.3	v −0.1 d 0.7		v 3.4 d 0.3		v 2.2 d 0.0		v 2.6 d 0.0			Saturn	129 20.2	2 29

UT	SUN GHA	SUN Dec	MOON GHA	v	MOON Dec	d	HP
d h	° ′	° ′	° ′	′	° ′	′	′
4 00	179 13.0	N 5 34.7	127 02.5	10.3	N18 10.6	3.0	56.0
01	194 13.1	35.6	141 31.8	10.4	18 13.6	2.8	56.0
02	209 13.3	36.6	156 01.2	10.3	18 16.4	2.8	55.9
03	224 13.5	.. 37.6	170 30.5	10.4	18 19.2	2.7	55.9
04	239 13.7	38.5	184 59.9	10.4	18 21.9	2.6	55.9
05	254 13.9	39.5	199 29.3	10.5	18 24.5	2.4	55.8
06	269 14.0	N 5 40.4	213 58.8	10.4	N18 26.9	2.4	55.8
07	284 14.2	41.4	228 28.2	10.5	18 29.3	2.3	55.8
08	299 14.4	42.3	242 57.7	10.5	18 31.6	2.2	55.7
F 09	314 14.6	.. 43.3	257 27.2	10.5	18 33.8	2.1	55.7
R 10	329 14.8	44.2	271 56.7	10.5	18 35.9	1.9	55.7
I 11	344 14.9	45.2	286 26.2	10.6	18 37.8	1.9	55.7
D 12	359 15.1	N 5 46.1	300 55.8	10.6	N18 39.7	1.8	55.6
A 13	14 15.3	47.1	315 25.4	10.6	18 41.5	1.7	55.6
Y 14	29 15.5	48.0	329 55.0	10.6	18 43.2	1.6	55.6
15	44 15.7	.. 49.0	344 24.6	10.7	18 44.8	1.5	55.6
16	59 15.8	49.9	358 54.3	10.7	18 46.3	1.4	55.5
17	74 16.0	50.9	13 24.0	10.7	18 47.7	1.3	55.5
18	89 16.2	N 5 51.8	27 53.7	10.7	N18 49.0	1.2	55.5
19	104 16.4	52.8	42 23.4	10.7	18 50.2	1.2	55.5
20	119 16.6	53.7	56 53.1	10.8	18 51.4	1.0	55.4
21	134 16.7	.. 54.7	71 22.9	10.8	18 52.4	0.9	55.4
22	149 16.9	55.7	85 52.7	10.9	18 53.3	0.8	55.4
23	164 17.1	56.6	100 22.6	10.8	18 54.1	0.8	55.4
5 00	179 17.3	N 5 57.6	114 52.4	10.9	N18 54.9	0.6	55.3
01	194 17.5	58.5	129 22.3	10.9	18 55.5	0.5	55.3
02	209 17.6	5 59.5	143 52.2	11.0	18 56.0	0.5	55.3
03	224 17.8	6 00.4	158 22.2	10.9	18 56.5	0.3	55.3
04	239 18.0	01.4	172 52.1	11.0	18 56.8	0.3	55.2
05	254 18.2	02.3	187 22.1	11.1	18 57.1	0.1	55.2
06	269 18.4	N 6 03.3	201 52.2	11.0	N18 57.2	0.1	55.2
07	284 18.5	04.2	216 22.2	11.1	18 57.3	0.0	55.2
08	299 18.7	05.2	230 52.3	11.1	18 57.3	0.2	55.1
S 09	314 18.9	.. 06.1	245 22.4	11.1	18 57.2	0.3	55.1
A 10	329 19.1	07.0	259 52.5	11.2	18 56.9	0.3	55.1
T 11	344 19.3	08.0	274 22.7	11.2	18 56.6	0.4	55.1
U 12	359 19.4	N 6 08.9	288 52.9	11.3	N18 56.2	0.5	55.0
R 13	14 19.6	09.9	303 23.2	11.2	18 55.7	0.5	55.0
D 14	29 19.8	10.8	317 53.4	11.3	18 55.2	0.7	55.0
A 15	44 20.0	.. 11.8	332 23.7	11.3	18 54.5	0.8	55.0
Y 16	59 20.2	12.7	346 54.0	11.4	18 53.7	0.8	55.0
17	74 20.3	13.7	1 24.4	11.4	18 52.9	1.0	54.9
18	89 20.5	N 6 14.6	15 54.8	11.4	N18 51.9	1.0	54.9
19	104 20.7	15.6	30 25.2	11.4	18 50.9	1.2	54.9
20	119 20.9	16.5	44 55.6	11.5	18 49.7	1.2	54.9
21	134 21.0	.. 17.5	59 26.1	11.5	18 48.5	1.3	54.9
22	149 21.2	18.4	73 56.6	11.6	18 47.2	1.4	54.8
23	164 21.4	19.4	88 27.2	11.6	18 45.8	1.5	54.8
6 00	179 21.6	N 6 20.3	102 57.8	11.6	N18 44.3	1.6	54.8
01	194 21.8	21.3	117 28.4	11.6	18 42.7	1.6	54.8
02	209 21.9	22.2	131 59.0	11.7	18 41.1	1.8	54.8
03	224 22.1	.. 23.2	146 29.7	11.7	18 39.3	1.8	54.7
04	239 22.3	24.1	161 00.4	11.8	18 37.5	2.0	54.7
05	254 22.5	25.0	175 31.2	11.7	18 35.5	2.0	54.7
06	269 22.6	N 6 26.0	190 01.9	11.9	N18 33.5	2.1	54.7
07	284 22.8	26.9	204 32.8	11.8	18 31.4	2.2	54.7
08	299 23.0	27.9	219 03.6	11.9	18 29.2	2.3	54.7
S 09	314 23.2	.. 28.8	233 34.5	11.9	18 26.9	2.3	54.6
U 10	329 23.4	29.8	248 05.4	11.9	18 24.6	2.5	54.6
N 11	344 23.5	30.7	262 36.3	12.0	18 22.1	2.5	54.6
D 12	359 23.7	N 6 31.7	277 07.3	12.0	N18 19.6	2.6	54.6
A 13	14 23.9	32.6	291 38.3	12.1	18 17.0	2.7	54.6
Y 14	29 24.1	33.5	306 09.4	12.1	18 14.3	2.8	54.6
15	44 24.2	.. 34.5	320 40.5	12.1	18 11.5	2.9	54.5
16	59 24.4	35.4	335 11.6	12.1	18 08.6	2.9	54.5
17	74 24.6	36.4	349 42.7	12.2	18 05.7	3.1	54.5
18	89 24.8	N 6 37.3	4 13.9	12.3	N18 02.6	3.1	54.5
19	104 24.9	38.3	18 45.2	12.2	17 59.5	3.2	54.5
20	119 25.1	39.2	33 16.4	12.3	17 56.3	3.2	54.5
21	134 25.3	.. 40.1	47 47.7	12.3	17 53.1	3.4	54.5
22	149 25.5	41.1	62 19.0	12.4	17 49.7	3.4	54.5
23	164 25.7	42.0	76 50.4	12.4	N17 46.3	3.6	54.4
	SD 16.0	d 0.9	SD 15.2		15.0		14.9

Lat.	Naut.	Civil	Sunrise	Moonrise 4	5	6	7
°	h m	h m	h m	h m	h m	h m	h m
N 72	00 17	03 16	04 35	▭	▭	▭	07 22
N 70	01 47	03 36	04 45	05 21	05 53	06 57	08 20
68	02 23	03 52	04 53	06 04	06 43	07 41	08 54
66	02 48	04 04	04 59	06 32	07 15	08 11	09 19
64	03 07	04 14	05 05	06 54	07 38	08 33	09 38
62	03 23	04 23	05 10	07 12	07 57	08 51	09 53
60	03 35	04 30	05 14	07 26	08 12	09 06	10 06
N 58	03 46	04 37	05 17	07 39	08 25	09 18	10 17
56	03 55	04 42	05 21	07 50	08 36	09 29	10 27
54	04 03	04 47	05 23	07 59	08 46	09 39	10 36
52	04 09	04 52	05 26	08 08	08 55	09 47	10 43
50	04 16	04 55	05 29	08 15	09 03	09 55	10 50
45	04 28	05 04	05 34	08 32	09 19	10 11	11 05
N 40	04 38	05 11	05 38	08 45	09 33	10 24	11 17
35	04 46	05 16	05 42	08 56	09 45	10 35	11 27
30	04 52	05 21	05 45	09 06	09 55	10 45	11 36
20	05 02	05 28	05 50	09 23	10 13	11 02	11 52
N 10	05 09	05 34	05 55	09 38	10 28	11 17	12 06
0	05 15	05 39	05 59	09 52	10 42	11 31	12 18
S 10	05 18	05 43	06 04	10 07	10 57	11 45	12 31
20	05 20	05 46	06 08	10 22	11 12	12 00	12 44
30	05 21	05 49	06 13	10 39	11 30	12 17	13 00
35	05 21	05 50	06 16	10 49	11 40	12 26	13 09
40	05 20	05 52	06 19	11 01	11 52	12 38	13 19
45	05 19	05 53	06 22	11 14	12 06	12 51	13 31
S 50	05 17	05 54	06 27	11 31	12 22	13 07	13 45
52	05 16	05 55	06 29	11 39	12 30	13 15	13 52
54	05 14	05 55	06 31	11 47	12 39	13 23	14 00
56	05 13	05 56	06 33	11 57	12 49	13 32	14 08
58	05 11	05 56	06 36	12 09	13 01	13 43	14 17
S 60	05 08	05 57	06 38	12 21	13 14	13 55	14 28

Lat.	Sunset	Civil	Naut.	Moonset 4	5	6	7
°	h m	h m	h m	h m	h m	h m	h m
N 72	19 33	20 54	////	▭	▭	▭	04 58
N 70	19 23	20 33	22 28	01 53	03 05	03 44	03 59
68	19 15	20 17	21 48	01 11	02 15	02 59	03 25
66	19 08	20 04	21 21	00 42	01 44	02 29	03 00
64	19 03	19 54	21 01	00 21	01 20	02 07	02 40
62	18 58	19 45	20 46	00 03	01 02	01 49	02 24
60	18 53	19 37	20 33	24 47	00 47	01 34	02 11
N 58	18 49	19 31	20 22	24 34	00 34	01 21	01 59
56	18 46	19 25	20 13	24 23	00 23	01 10	01 49
54	18 43	19 20	20 05	24 13	00 13	00 52	01 41
52	18 40	19 15	19 57	24 04	00 04	00 52	01 33
50	18 38	19 11	19 51	23 56	24 44	00 44	01 26
45	18 33	19 03	19 38	23 39	24 28	00 28	01 10
N 40	18 28	18 56	19 28	23 26	24 14	00 14	00 58
35	18 24	18 50	19 20	23 14	24 03	00 03	00 47
30	18 21	18 45	19 14	23 04	23 53	24 38	00 38
20	18 15	18 38	19 04	22 46	23 35	24 21	00 21
N 10	18 10	18 32	18 56	22 31	23 20	24 07	00 07
0	18 06	18 27	18 51	22 17	23 06	23 54	24 41
S 10	18 02	18 23	18 47	22 02	22 52	23 41	24 29
20	17 57	18 19	18 45	21 47	22 37	23 26	24 16
30	17 52	18 16	18 44	21 29	22 19	23 10	24 01
35	17 49	18 14	18 44	21 19	22 09	23 00	23 53
40	17 46	18 13	18 44	21 07	21 57	22 49	23 43
45	17 42	18 12	18 46	20 54	21 43	22 36	23 32
S 50	17 38	18 10	18 48	20 37	21 27	22 21	23 18
52	17 36	18 10	18 49	20 29	21 19	22 13	23 11
54	17 34	18 09	18 50	20 20	21 10	22 05	23 04
56	17 31	18 09	18 51	20 10	21 00	21 56	22 56
58	17 29	18 08	18 53	19 59	20 49	21 45	22 47
S 60	17 26	18 07	18 55	19 46	20 36	21 33	22 37

	SUN		MOON			
Day	Eqn. of Time 00h	12h	Mer. Pass.	Mer. Pass. Upper	Lower	Age	Phase
d	m s	m s	h m	h m	h m	d	%
4	03 09	03 00	12 03	16 05	03 39	05	24
5	02 51	02 43	12 03	16 54	04 30	06	33
6	02 34	02 26	12 02	17 43	05 19	07	42

UT	ARIES GHA	VENUS −4.3 GHA	Dec	MARS −1.5 GHA	Dec	JUPITER −2.2 GHA	Dec	SATURN +0.2 GHA	Dec	STARS Name	SHA	Dec
7 00	195 11.6	222 05.4	S10 39.3	356 05.0	S 5 21.2	92 07.4	N23 10.3	324 38.1	S15 58.1	Acamar	315 18.3	S40 15.1
01	210 14.0	237 05.3	38.6	11 08.4	20.9	107 09.6	10.3	339 40.7	58.1	Achernar	335 27.0	S57 10.0
02	225 16.5	252 05.1	37.8	26 11.8	20.6	122 11.8	10.3	354 43.3	58.1	Acrux	173 07.9	S63 10.8
03	240 19.0	267 05.0	.. 37.1	41 15.1	.. 20.3	137 14.0	.. 10.3	9 45.9	.. 58.0	Adhara	255 12.1	S28 59.9
04	255 21.4	282 04.8	36.4	56 18.5	20.0	152 16.2	10.2	24 48.5	58.0	Aldebaran	290 48.9	N16 32.1
05	270 23.9	297 04.7	35.6	71 21.9	19.7	167 18.4	10.2	39 51.1	57.9			
06	285 26.3	312 04.5	S10 34.9	86 25.2	S 5 19.4	182 20.6	N23 10.2	54 53.7	S15 57.9	Alioth	166 19.7	N55 52.9
07	300 28.8	327 04.4	34.1	101 28.6	19.1	197 22.8	10.2	69 56.3	57.9	Alkaid	152 58.0	N49 14.4
M 08	315 31.3	342 04.2	33.4	116 32.0	18.9	212 25.0	10.2	84 58.9	57.8	Al Na'ir	27 43.4	S46 53.3
O 09	330 33.7	357 04.1	.. 32.7	131 35.4	.. 18.6	227 27.2	.. 10.1	100 01.5	.. 57.8	Alnilam	275 45.9	S 1 11.9
N 10	345 36.2	12 03.9	31.9	146 38.7	18.3	242 29.4	10.1	115 04.1	57.7	Alphard	217 55.4	S 8 43.6
D 11	0 38.7	27 03.7	31.2	161 42.1	18.0	257 31.6	10.1	130 06.7	57.7			
A 12	15 41.1	42 03.6	S10 30.4	176 45.5	S 5 17.7	272 33.8	N23 10.1	145 09.3	S15 57.7	Alphecca	126 10.3	N26 39.9
Y 13	30 43.6	57 03.4	29.7	191 48.9	17.4	287 36.0	10.1	160 11.9	57.6	Alpheratz	357 43.2	N29 10.0
14	45 46.1	72 03.3	28.9	206 52.2	17.1	302 38.2	10.0	175 14.5	57.6	Altair	62 07.7	N 8 54.4
15	60 48.5	87 03.1	.. 28.2	221 55.6	.. 16.8	317 40.4	.. 10.0	190 17.1	.. 57.5	Ankaa	353 15.6	S42 13.7
16	75 51.0	102 03.0	27.5	236 59.0	16.5	332 42.6	10.0	205 19.7	57.5	Antares	112 25.3	S26 27.7
17	90 53.4	117 02.8	26.7	252 02.4	16.2	347 44.8	10.0	220 22.3	57.5			
18	105 55.9	132 02.7	S10 26.0	267 05.7	S 5 15.9	2 47.0	N23 10.0	235 24.9	S15 57.4	Arcturus	145 54.9	N19 06.4
19	120 58.4	147 02.5	25.2	282 09.1	15.6	17 49.2	09.9	250 27.5	57.4	Atria	107 26.3	S69 02.8
20	136 00.8	162 02.4	24.5	297 12.5	15.4	32 51.4	09.9	265 30.1	57.3	Avior	234 17.6	S59 33.8
21	151 03.3	177 02.2	.. 23.7	312 15.9	.. 15.1	47 53.6	.. 09.9	280 32.7	.. 57.3	Bellatrix	278 31.6	N 6 21.5
22	166 05.8	192 02.1	23.0	327 19.3	14.8	62 55.8	09.9	295 35.3	57.3	Betelgeuse	271 00.8	N 7 24.3
23	181 08.2	207 01.9	22.2	342 22.6	14.5	77 58.0	09.9	310 37.9	57.2			
8 00	196 10.7	222 01.8	S10 21.5	357 26.0	S 5 14.2	93 00.2	N23 09.9	325 40.5	S15 57.2	Canopus	263 56.0	S52 42.7
01	211 13.2	237 01.6	20.7	12 29.4	13.9	108 02.4	09.8	340 43.1	57.1	Capella	280 33.8	N46 00.7
02	226 15.6	252 01.5	19.9	27 32.8	13.6	123 04.6	09.8	355 45.7	57.1	Deneb	49 31.2	N45 19.7
03	241 18.1	267 01.3	.. 19.2	42 36.1	.. 13.3	138 06.8	.. 09.8	10 48.3	.. 57.1	Denebola	182 32.8	N14 29.4
04	256 20.6	282 01.2	18.4	57 39.5	13.0	153 09.0	09.8	25 50.9	57.0	Diphda	348 55.7	S17 54.6
05	271 23.0	297 01.0	17.7	72 42.9	12.7	168 11.2	09.8	40 53.5	57.0			
06	286 25.5	312 00.9	S10 16.9	87 46.3	S 5 12.4	183 13.4	N23 09.7	55 56.1	S15 57.0	Dubhe	193 50.6	N61 40.4
07	301 27.9	327 00.7	16.2	102 49.7	12.1	198 15.6	09.7	70 58.7	56.9	Elnath	278 12.1	N28 37.0
T 08	316 30.4	342 00.6	15.4	117 53.0	11.9	213 17.8	09.7	86 01.3	56.9	Eltanin	90 45.7	N51 29.1
U 09	331 32.9	357 00.4	.. 14.7	132 56.4	.. 11.6	228 20.0	.. 09.7	101 03.9	.. 56.8	Enif	33 46.8	N 9 56.4
E 10	346 35.3	12 00.2	13.9	147 59.8	11.3	243 22.2	09.7	116 06.5	56.8	Fomalhaut	15 23.7	S29 32.7
S 11	1 37.8	27 00.1	13.1	163 03.2	11.0	258 24.4	09.6	131 09.1	56.8			
D 12	16 40.3	41 59.9	S10 12.4	178 06.6	S 5 10.7	273 26.6	N23 09.6	146 11.7	S15 56.7	Gacrux	171 59.6	S57 11.7
A 13	31 42.7	56 59.8	11.6	193 09.9	10.4	288 28.8	09.6	161 14.3	56.7	Gienah	175 51.4	S17 37.5
Y 14	46 45.2	71 59.6	10.9	208 13.3	10.1	303 31.0	09.6	176 16.9	56.6	Hadar	148 46.4	S60 26.5
15	61 47.7	86 59.5	.. 10.1	223 16.7	.. 09.8	318 33.2	.. 09.6	191 19.5	.. 56.6	Hamal	328 00.4	N23 31.6
16	76 50.1	101 59.3	09.3	238 20.1	09.5	333 35.4	09.5	206 22.1	56.6	Kaus Aust.	83 43.0	S34 22.4
17	91 52.6	116 59.2	08.6	253 23.5	09.2	348 37.6	09.5	221 24.7	56.5			
18	106 55.1	131 59.0	S10 07.8	268 26.8	S 5 08.9	3 39.7	N23 09.5	236 27.3	S15 56.5	Kochab	137 19.1	N74 05.7
19	121 57.5	146 58.9	07.0	283 30.2	08.6	18 41.9	09.5	251 29.9	56.4	Markab	13 38.0	N15 16.8
20	137 00.0	161 58.7	06.3	298 33.6	08.4	33 44.1	09.4	266 32.5	56.4	Menkar	314 14.7	N 4 08.5
21	152 02.4	176 58.6	.. 05.5	313 37.0	.. 08.1	48 46.3	.. 09.4	281 35.1	.. 56.4	Menkent	148 06.5	S36 26.4
22	167 04.9	191 58.4	04.8	328 40.4	07.8	63 48.5	09.4	296 37.7	56.3	Miaplacidus	221 39.0	S69 47.0
23	182 07.4	206 58.2	04.0	343 43.7	07.5	78 50.7	09.4	311 40.3	56.3			
9 00	197 09.8	221 58.1	S10 03.2	358 47.1	S 5 07.2	93 52.9	N23 09.4	326 42.9	S15 56.2	Mirfak	308 39.9	N49 54.4
01	212 12.3	236 57.9	02.5	13 50.5	06.9	108 55.1	09.3	341 45.6	56.2	Nunki	75 57.6	S26 16.5
02	227 14.8	251 57.8	01.7	28 53.9	06.6	123 57.3	09.3	356 48.2	56.1	Peacock	53 18.6	S56 41.0
03	242 17.2	266 57.6	.. 00.9	43 57.3	.. 06.3	138 59.5	.. 09.3	11 50.8	.. 56.1	Pollux	243 27.0	N27 59.3
04	257 19.7	281 57.5	10 00.1	59 00.7	06.0	154 01.7	09.3	26 53.4	56.1	Procyon	244 59.1	N 5 11.0
05	272 22.2	296 57.3	9 59.4	74 04.0	05.7	169 03.9	09.3	41 56.0	56.0			
06	287 24.6	311 57.2	S 9 58.6	89 07.4	S 5 05.4	184 06.0	N23 09.2	56 58.6	S15 56.0	Rasalhague	96 05.8	N12 33.0
W 07	302 27.1	326 57.0	57.8	104 10.8	05.1	199 08.2	09.2	72 01.2	55.9	Regulus	207 42.7	N11 53.6
E 08	317 29.5	341 56.9	57.1	119 14.2	04.9	214 10.4	09.2	87 03.8	55.9	Rigel	281 11.7	S 8 11.4
D 09	332 32.0	356 56.7	.. 56.3	134 17.6	.. 04.6	229 12.6	.. 09.2	102 06.4	.. 55.9	Rigil Kent.	139 50.3	S60 53.5
N 10	347 34.5	11 56.5	55.5	149 20.9	04.3	244 14.8	09.2	117 09.0	55.8	Sabik	102 11.7	S15 44.4
E 11	2 36.9	26 56.4	54.7	164 24.3	04.0	259 17.0	09.1	132 11.6	55.8			
S 12	17 39.4	41 56.2	S 9 54.0	179 27.7	S 5 03.7	274 19.2	N23 09.1	147 14.2	S15 55.7	Schedar	349 40.4	N56 36.8
D 13	32 41.9	56 56.1	53.2	194 31.1	03.4	289 21.4	09.1	162 16.8	55.7	Shaula	96 21.0	S37 06.6
A 14	47 44.3	71 55.9	52.4	209 34.5	03.1	304 23.6	09.1	177 19.4	55.7	Sirius	258 33.3	S16 44.5
Y 15	62 46.8	86 55.8	.. 51.6	224 37.9	.. 02.8	319 25.8	.. 09.1	192 22.0	.. 55.6	Spica	158 30.3	S11 14.3
16	77 49.3	101 55.6	50.9	239 41.2	02.5	334 27.9	09.0	207 24.6	55.6	Suhail	222 51.8	S43 29.9
17	92 51.7	116 55.5	50.1	254 44.6	02.2	349 30.1	09.0	222 27.2	55.5			
18	107 54.2	131 55.3	S 9 49.3	269 48.0	S 5 01.9	4 32.3	N23 09.0	237 29.8	S15 55.5	Vega	80 38.5	N38 47.7
19	122 56.7	146 55.1	48.5	284 51.4	01.7	19 34.5	09.0	252 32.4	55.5	Zuben'ubi	137 04.5	S16 06.1
20	137 59.1	161 55.0	47.7	299 54.8	01.4	34 36.7	09.0	267 35.1	55.4		SHA	Mer.Pass.
21	153 01.6	176 54.8	.. 47.0	314 58.2	.. 01.1	49 38.9	.. 08.9	282 37.7	.. 55.4		° ′	h m
22	168 04.0	191 54.7	46.2	330 01.6	00.8	64 41.1	08.9	297 40.3	55.3	Venus	25 51.1	9 12
23	183 06.5	206 54.5	45.4	345 04.9	00.5	79 43.2	08.9	312 42.9	55.3	Mars	161 15.3	0 10
	h m									Jupiter	256 49.5	17 45
Mer. Pass. 10 53.5		v −0.2	d 0.8	v 3.4	d 0.3	v 2.2	d 0.0	v 2.6	d 0.0	Saturn	129 29.8	2 17

©Copyright United Kingdom Hydrographic Office 2013

UT	SUN GHA	SUN Dec	MOON GHA	v	Dec	d	HP
d h	° ′	° ′	° ′	′	° ′	′	′
7 00	179 25.8	N 6 43.0	91 21.8	12.4	N17 42.7	3.6	54.4
01	194 26.0	43.9	105 53.2	12.5	17 39.1	3.6	54.4
02	209 26.2	44.8	120 24.7	12.5	17 35.5	3.8	54.4
03	224 26.4	.. 45.8	134 56.2	12.5	17 31.7	3.8	54.4
04	239 26.5	46.7	149 27.7	12.6	17 27.9	4.0	54.4
05	254 26.7	47.7	163 59.3	12.6	17 23.9	3.9	54.4
06	269 26.9	N 6 48.6	178 30.9	12.6	N17 20.0	4.1	54.4
07	284 27.1	49.5	193 02.5	12.7	17 15.9	4.2	54.4
08	299 27.2	50.5	207 34.2	12.7	17 11.7	4.2	54.4
M 09	314 27.4	.. 51.4	222 05.9	12.7	17 07.5	4.3	54.3
O 10	329 27.6	52.4	236 37.6	12.8	17 03.2	4.4	54.3
N 11	344 27.8	53.3	251 09.4	12.8	16 58.8	4.4	54.3
D 12	359 27.9	N 6 54.2	265 41.2	12.8	N16 54.4	4.5	54.3
A 13	14 28.1	55.2	280 13.0	12.9	16 49.9	4.6	54.3
Y 14	29 28.3	56.1	294 44.9	12.9	16 45.3	4.7	54.3
15	44 28.5	.. 57.1	309 16.8	12.9	16 40.6	4.7	54.3
16	59 28.6	58.0	323 48.7	13.0	16 35.9	4.9	54.3
17	74 28.8	58.9	338 20.7	13.0	16 31.0	4.9	54.3
18	89 29.0	N 6 59.9	352 52.7	13.0	N16 26.1	4.9	54.3
19	104 29.2	7 00.8	7 24.7	13.0	16 21.2	5.1	54.3
20	119 29.3	01.8	21 56.7	13.1	16 16.1	5.1	54.3
21	134 29.5	.. 02.7	36 28.8	13.2	16 11.0	5.1	54.3
22	149 29.7	03.6	51 01.0	13.1	16 05.9	5.3	54.3
23	164 29.9	04.6	65 33.1	13.2	16 00.6	5.3	54.2
8 00	179 30.0	N 7 05.5	80 05.3	13.2	N15 55.3	5.4	54.2
01	194 30.2	06.4	94 37.5	13.3	15 49.9	5.4	54.2
02	209 30.4	07.4	109 09.8	13.3	15 44.5	5.6	54.2
03	224 30.6	.. 08.3	123 42.1	13.3	15 38.9	5.6	54.2
04	239 30.7	09.2	138 14.4	13.3	15 33.3	5.6	54.2
05	254 30.9	10.2	152 46.7	13.4	15 27.7	5.7	54.2
06	269 31.1	N 7 11.1	167 19.1	13.4	N15 22.0	5.8	54.2
T 07	284 31.2	12.0	181 51.5	13.4	15 16.2	5.9	54.2
U 08	299 31.4	13.0	196 23.9	13.5	15 10.3	5.9	54.2
E 09	314 31.6	.. 13.9	210 56.4	13.5	15 04.4	6.0	54.2
S 10	329 31.8	14.9	225 28.9	13.5	14 58.4	6.1	54.2
D 11	344 31.9	15.8	240 01.4	13.6	14 52.3	6.1	54.2
A 12	359 32.1	N 7 16.7	254 34.0	13.5	N14 46.2	6.2	54.2
Y 13	14 32.3	17.7	269 06.5	13.6	14 40.0	6.2	54.2
14	29 32.5	18.6	283 39.1	13.7	14 33.8	6.4	54.2
15	44 32.6	.. 19.5	298 11.8	13.6	14 27.4	6.3	54.2
16	59 32.8	20.5	312 44.4	13.7	14 21.1	6.5	54.2
17	74 33.0	21.4	327 17.1	13.7	14 14.6	6.5	54.2
18	89 33.1	N 7 22.3	341 49.8	13.8	N14 08.1	6.5	54.2
19	104 33.3	23.3	356 22.6	13.7	14 01.6	6.6	54.2
20	119 33.5	24.2	10 55.3	13.8	13 55.0	6.7	54.2
21	134 33.7	.. 25.1	25 28.1	13.8	13 48.3	6.8	54.2
22	149 33.8	26.0	40 00.9	13.9	13 41.5	6.8	54.2
23	164 34.0	27.0	54 33.8	13.8	13 34.7	6.8	54.2
9 00	179 34.2	N 7 27.9	69 06.6	13.9	N13 27.9	7.0	54.2
01	194 34.3	28.8	83 39.5	13.9	13 20.9	6.9	54.2
02	209 34.5	29.8	98 12.4	13.9	13 14.0	7.1	54.2
03	224 34.7	.. 30.7	112 45.3	14.0	13 06.9	7.1	54.2
04	239 34.9	31.6	127 18.3	14.0	12 59.8	7.1	54.2
05	254 35.0	32.6	141 51.3	14.0	12 52.7	7.2	54.2
06	269 35.2	N 7 33.5	156 24.3	14.0	N12 45.5	7.3	54.2
W 07	284 35.4	34.4	170 57.3	14.0	12 38.2	7.3	54.2
E 08	299 35.5	35.4	185 30.3	14.1	12 30.9	7.4	54.3
D 09	314 35.7	.. 36.3	200 03.4	14.1	12 23.5	7.4	54.3
N 10	329 35.9	37.2	214 36.5	14.1	12 16.1	7.5	54.3
E 11	344 36.1	38.1	229 09.6	14.1	12 08.6	7.5	54.3
S 12	359 36.2	N 7 39.1	243 42.7	14.2	N12 01.1	7.6	54.3
D 13	14 36.4	40.0	258 15.9	14.1	11 53.5	7.7	54.3
A 14	29 36.6	40.9	272 49.0	14.2	11 45.8	7.6	54.3
Y 15	44 36.7	.. 41.9	287 22.2	14.2	11 38.2	7.8	54.3
16	59 36.9	42.8	301 55.4	14.2	11 30.4	7.8	54.3
17	74 37.1	43.7	316 28.6	14.2	11 22.6	7.8	54.3
18	89 37.2	N 7 44.6	331 01.8	14.3	N11 14.8	7.9	54.3
19	104 37.4	45.6	345 35.1	14.2	11 06.9	8.0	54.3
20	119 37.6	46.5	0 08.3	14.3	10 58.9	8.0	54.3
21	134 37.8	.. 47.4	14 41.6	14.3	10 50.9	8.0	54.3
22	149 37.9	48.3	29 14.9	14.3	10 42.9	8.1	54.3
23	164 38.1	49.3	43 48.2	14.3	N10 34.8	8.2	54.4
	SD 16.0	d 0.9	SD 14.8		14.8		14.8

Twilight / Sunrise / Moonrise

Lat.	Naut.	Civil	Sunrise	7	8	9	10
°	h m	h m	h m	h m	h m	h m	h m
N 72	////	02 56	04 19	07 22	09 16	10 59	12 39
N 70	01 11	03 19	04 31	08 20	09 50	11 21	12 52
68	02 01	03 37	04 40	08 54	10 14	11 38	13 03
66	02 31	03 51	04 48	09 19	10 33	11 51	13 12
64	02 53	04 03	04 54	09 38	10 48	12 03	13 19
62	03 10	04 12	05 00	09 53	11 01	12 12	13 26
60	03 24	04 21	05 05	10 06	11 12	12 20	13 31
N 58	03 36	04 28	05 09	10 17	11 21	12 27	13 36
56	03 46	04 34	05 13	10 27	11 29	12 34	13 40
54	03 54	04 39	05 16	10 36	11 36	12 39	13 44
52	04 02	04 44	05 19	10 43	11 43	12 44	13 48
50	04 08	04 49	05 22	10 50	11 49	12 49	13 51
45	04 22	04 58	05 28	11 05	12 01	12 59	13 58
N 40	04 33	05 06	05 33	11 17	12 12	13 07	14 03
35	04 42	05 12	05 38	11 27	12 20	13 14	14 08
30	04 49	05 17	05 41	11 36	12 28	13 20	14 13
20	05 00	05 26	05 48	11 52	12 41	13 31	14 20
N 10	05 08	05 32	05 53	12 06	12 53	13 40	14 27
0	05 14	05 38	05 59	12 18	13 04	13 49	14 33
S 10	05 18	05 42	06 04	12 31	13 15	13 57	14 39
20	05 21	05 47	06 09	12 44	13 27	14 07	14 45
30	05 23	05 51	06 15	13 00	13 40	14 17	14 53
35	05 23	05 53	06 18	13 09	13 47	14 23	14 57
40	05 23	05 55	06 22	13 19	13 56	14 30	15 02
45	05 23	05 57	06 26	13 31	14 06	14 38	15 07
S 50	05 21	05 59	06 31	13 45	14 19	14 48	15 14
52	05 21	06 00	06 34	13 52	14 24	14 52	15 17
54	05 20	06 01	06 36	14 00	14 30	14 57	15 21
56	05 19	06 02	06 39	14 08	14 37	15 02	15 24
58	05 17	06 03	06 42	14 17	14 45	15 08	15 28
S 60	05 16	06 04	06 46	14 28	14 54	15 15	15 33

Twilight / Moonset

Lat.	Sunset	Civil	Naut.	7	8	9	10
°	h m	h m	h m	h m	h m	h m	h m
N 72	19 48	21 13	////	04 58	04 40	04 30	04 22
N 70	19 36	20 49	23 08	03 59	04 05	04 07	04 07
68	19 26	20 30	22 10	03 25	03 40	03 49	03 55
66	19 18	20 16	21 37	03 00	03 20	03 34	03 45
64	19 11	20 04	21 15	02 40	03 04	03 22	03 36
62	19 06	19 54	20 57	02 24	02 51	03 12	03 29
60	19 01	19 45	20 42	02 11	02 40	03 03	03 23
N 58	18 56	19 38	20 30	01 59	02 30	02 56	03 17
56	18 52	19 31	20 20	01 49	02 22	02 49	03 12
54	18 49	19 26	20 11	01 41	02 14	02 43	03 08
52	18 46	19 21	20 04	01 33	02 07	02 37	03 04
50	18 43	19 16	19 57	01 26	02 01	02 32	03 00
45	18 36	19 07	19 43	01 10	01 48	02 21	02 52
N 40	18 31	18 59	19 32	00 58	01 37	02 12	02 45
35	18 27	18 52	19 23	00 47	01 28	02 05	02 39
30	18 23	18 47	19 16	00 38	01 19	01 58	02 34
20	18 16	18 38	19 05	00 21	01 05	01 46	02 25
N 10	18 10	18 32	18 56	00 07	00 52	01 36	02 17
0	18 05	18 26	18 50	24 41	00 41	01 26	02 10
S 10	18 00	18 21	18 46	24 29	00 29	01 16	02 03
20	17 55	18 17	18 42	24 16	00 16	01 05	01 55
30	17 49	18 13	18 40	24 01	00 01	00 53	01 45
35	17 45	18 11	18 40	23 53	24 46	00 46	01 40
40	17 41	18 08	18 40	23 43	24 38	00 38	01 34
45	17 37	18 06	18 40	23 32	24 29	00 29	01 27
S 50	17 32	18 04	18 41	23 18	24 17	00 17	01 18
52	17 29	18 03	18 42	23 11	24 12	00 12	01 14
54	17 27	18 02	18 43	23 04	24 06	00 06	01 10
56	17 24	18 01	18 44	22 56	24 00	00 00	01 05
58	17 21	18 00	18 45	22 47	23 52	25 00	01 00
S 60	17 17	17 59	18 47	22 37	23 44	24 54	00 54

Day	SUN Eqn. of Time 00h	SUN Eqn. of Time 12h	SUN Mer. Pass.	MOON Mer. Pass. Upper	MOON Mer. Pass. Lower	Age	Phase
d	m s	m s	h m	h m	h m	d	%
7	02 17	02 09	12 02	18 29	06 06	08	52
8	02 00	01 52	12 02	19 15	06 52	09	61
9	01 44	01 35	12 02	19 59	07 37	10	70

UT	ARIES GHA	VENUS −4.3 GHA	Dec	MARS −1.5 GHA	Dec	JUPITER −2.1 GHA	Dec	SATURN +0.2 GHA	Dec	STARS Name	SHA	Dec
10 00	198 09.0	221 54.4	S 9 44.6	0 08.3	S 5 00.2	94 45.4	N23 08.9	327 45.5	S15 55.3	Acamar	315 18.3	S40 15.1
01	213 11.4	236 54.2	43.8	15 11.7	4 59.9	109 47.6	08.8	342 48.1	55.2	Achernar	335 27.0	S57 10.0
02	228 13.9	251 54.0	43.1	30 15.1	59.6	124 49.8	08.8	357 50.7	55.2	Acrux	173 07.9	S63 10.9
03	243 16.4	266 53.9	.. 42.3	45 18.5	.. 59.3	139 52.0	.. 08.8	12 53.3	.. 55.1	Adhara	255 12.1	S28 59.9
04	258 18.8	281 53.7	41.5	60 21.9	59.0	154 54.2	08.8	27 55.9	55.1	Aldebaran	290 49.0	N16 32.1
05	273 21.3	296 53.6	40.7	75 25.2	58.8	169 56.4	08.8	42 58.5	55.1			
T 06	288 23.8	311 53.4	S 9 39.9	90 28.6	S 4 58.5	184 58.5	N23 08.7	58 01.1	S15 55.0	Alioth	166 19.7	N55 52.9
H 07	303 26.2	326 53.3	39.1	105 32.0	58.2	200 00.7	08.7	73 03.7	55.0	Alkaid	152 58.0	N49 14.5
U 08	318 28.7	341 53.1	38.3	120 35.4	57.9	215 02.9	08.7	88 06.3	54.9	Al Na'ir	27 43.4	S46 53.3
R 09	333 31.1	356 52.9	.. 37.6	135 38.8	.. 57.6	230 05.1	.. 08.7	103 09.0	.. 54.9	Alnilam	275 46.0	S 1 11.9
S 10	348 33.6	11 52.8	36.8	150 42.2	57.3	245 07.3	08.7	118 11.6	54.8	Alphard	217 55.4	S 8 43.6
D 11	3 36.1	26 52.6	36.0	165 45.6	57.0	260 09.4	08.6	133 14.2	54.8			
A 12	18 38.5	41 52.5	S 9 35.2	180 48.9	S 4 56.7	275 11.6	N23 08.6	148 16.8	S15 54.8	Alphecca	126 10.2	N26 39.9
Y 13	33 41.0	56 52.3	34.4	195 52.3	56.4	290 13.8	08.6	163 19.4	54.7	Alpheratz	357 43.2	N29 10.0
14	48 43.5	71 52.2	33.6	210 55.7	56.1	305 16.0	08.6	178 22.0	54.7	Altair	62 07.7	N 8 54.4
15	63 45.9	86 52.0	.. 32.8	225 59.1	.. 55.9	320 18.2	.. 08.5	193 24.6	.. 54.6	Ankaa	353 15.6	S42 13.7
16	78 48.4	101 51.8	32.0	241 02.5	55.6	335 20.4	08.5	208 27.2	54.6	Antares	112 25.3	S26 27.7
17	93 50.9	116 51.7	31.2	256 05.9	55.3	350 22.5	08.5	223 29.8	54.6			
18	108 53.3	131 51.5	S 9 30.4	271 09.3	S 4 55.0	5 24.7	N23 08.5	238 32.4	S15 54.5	Arcturus	145 54.9	N19 06.4
19	123 55.8	146 51.4	29.6	286 12.6	54.7	20 26.9	08.5	253 35.0	54.5	Atria	107 26.3	S69 02.8
20	138 58.3	161 51.2	28.9	301 16.0	54.4	35 29.1	08.4	268 37.6	54.4	Avior	234 17.6	S59 33.8
21	154 00.7	176 51.1	.. 28.1	316 19.4	.. 54.1	50 31.3	.. 08.4	283 40.3	.. 54.4	Bellatrix	278 31.6	N 6 21.5
22	169 03.2	191 50.9	27.3	331 22.8	53.8	65 33.4	08.4	298 42.9	54.4	Betelgeuse	271 00.8	N 7 24.3
23	184 05.6	206 50.7	26.5	346 26.2	53.5	80 35.6	08.4	313 45.5	54.3			
11 00	199 08.1	221 50.6	S 9 25.7	1 29.6	S 4 53.3	95 37.8	N23 08.3	328 48.1	S15 54.3	Canopus	263 56.0	S52 42.7
01	214 10.6	236 50.4	24.9	16 32.9	53.0	110 40.0	08.3	343 50.7	54.2	Capella	280 33.9	N46 00.7
02	229 13.0	251 50.3	24.1	31 36.3	52.7	125 42.1	08.3	358 53.3	54.2	Deneb	49 31.2	N45 19.7
03	244 15.5	266 50.1	.. 23.3	46 39.7	.. 52.4	140 44.3	.. 08.3	13 55.9	.. 54.1	Denebola	182 32.8	N14 29.4
04	259 18.0	281 49.9	22.5	61 43.1	52.1	155 46.5	08.3	28 58.5	54.1	Diphda	348 55.7	S17 54.6
05	274 20.4	296 49.8	21.7	76 46.5	51.8	170 48.7	08.2	44 01.1	54.1			
06	289 22.9	311 49.6	S 9 20.9	91 49.9	S 4 51.5	185 50.9	N23 08.2	59 03.7	S15 54.0	Dubhe	193 50.6	N61 40.4
07	304 25.4	326 49.5	20.1	106 53.3	51.2	200 53.0	08.2	74 06.4	54.0	Elnath	278 12.1	N28 37.0
F 08	319 27.8	341 49.3	19.3	121 56.6	50.9	215 55.2	08.2	89 09.0	53.9	Eltanin	90 45.7	N51 29.1
R 09	334 30.3	356 49.1	.. 18.5	137 00.0	.. 50.7	230 57.4	.. 08.1	104 11.6	.. 53.9	Enif	33 46.7	N 9 56.4
I 10	349 32.8	11 49.0	17.7	152 03.4	50.4	245 59.6	08.1	119 14.2	53.9	Fomalhaut	15 23.7	S29 32.7
D 11	4 35.2	26 48.8	16.9	167 06.8	50.1	261 01.7	08.1	134 16.8	53.8			
A 12	19 37.7	41 48.7	S 9 16.1	182 10.2	S 4 49.8	276 03.9	N23 08.1	149 19.4	S15 53.8	Gacrux	171 59.6	S57 11.7
Y 13	34 40.1	56 48.5	15.3	197 13.6	49.5	291 06.1	08.1	164 22.0	53.7	Gienah	175 51.4	S17 37.5
14	49 42.6	71 48.4	14.5	212 17.0	49.2	306 08.3	08.0	179 24.6	53.7	Hadar	148 46.4	S60 26.5
15	64 45.1	86 48.2	.. 13.6	227 20.3	.. 48.9	321 10.4	.. 08.0	194 27.2	.. 53.6	Hamal	328 00.4	N23 31.6
16	79 47.5	101 48.0	12.8	242 23.7	48.6	336 12.6	08.0	209 29.9	53.6	Kaus Aust.	83 43.0	S34 22.4
17	94 50.0	116 47.9	12.0	257 27.1	48.4	351 14.8	08.0	224 32.5	53.6			
18	109 52.5	131 47.7	S 9 11.2	272 30.5	S 4 48.1	6 17.0	N23 07.9	239 35.1	S15 53.5	Kochab	137 19.1	N74 05.7
19	124 54.9	146 47.6	10.4	287 33.9	47.8	21 19.1	07.9	254 37.7	53.5	Markab	13 38.0	N15 16.8
20	139 57.4	161 47.4	09.6	302 37.3	47.5	36 21.3	07.9	269 40.3	53.4	Menkar	314 14.8	N 4 08.5
21	154 59.9	176 47.2	.. 08.8	317 40.7	.. 47.2	51 23.5	.. 07.9	284 42.9	.. 53.4	Menkent	148 06.5	S36 26.4
22	170 02.3	191 47.1	08.0	332 44.0	46.9	66 25.7	07.9	299 45.5	53.4	Miaplacidus	221 39.0	S69 47.0
23	185 04.8	206 46.9	07.2	347 47.4	46.6	81 27.8	07.8	314 48.1	53.3			
12 00	200 07.2	221 46.8	S 9 06.4	2 50.8	S 4 46.3	96 30.0	N23 07.8	329 50.8	S15 53.3	Mirfak	308 39.9	N49 54.6
01	215 09.7	236 46.6	05.6	17 54.2	46.1	111 32.2	07.8	344 53.4	53.2	Nunki	75 57.6	S26 16.5
02	230 12.2	251 46.4	04.7	32 57.6	45.8	126 34.3	07.8	359 56.0	53.2	Peacock	53 18.5	S56 41.0
03	245 14.6	266 46.3	.. 03.9	48 01.0	.. 45.5	141 36.5	.. 07.7	14 58.6	.. 53.1	Pollux	243 27.0	N27 59.3
04	260 17.1	281 46.1	03.1	63 04.3	45.2	156 38.7	07.7	30 01.2	53.1	Procyon	244 59.1	N 5 11.0
05	275 19.6	296 46.0	02.3	78 07.7	44.9	171 40.9	07.7	45 03.8	53.1			
06	290 22.0	311 45.8	S 9 01.5	93 11.1	S 4 44.6	186 43.0	N23 07.7	60 06.4	S15 53.0	Rasalhague	96 05.8	N12 33.0
07	305 24.5	326 45.6	9 00.7	108 14.5	44.3	201 45.2	07.6	75 09.0	53.0	Regulus	207 42.7	N11 53.6
S 08	320 27.0	341 45.5	8 59.9	123 17.9	44.1	216 47.4	07.6	90 11.7	52.9	Rigel	281 11.7	S 8 11.4
A 09	335 29.4	356 45.3	.. 59.0	138 21.3	.. 43.8	231 49.5	.. 07.6	105 14.3	.. 52.9	Rigil Kent.	139 50.2	S60 53.5
T 10	350 31.9	11 45.1	58.2	153 24.6	43.5	246 51.7	07.6	120 16.9	52.8	Sabik	102 11.7	S15 44.4
U 11	5 34.4	26 45.0	57.4	168 28.0	43.2	261 53.9	07.6	135 19.5	52.8			
R 12	20 36.8	41 44.8	S 8 56.6	183 31.4	S 4 42.9	276 56.0	N23 07.5	150 22.1	S15 52.8	Schedar	349 40.3	N56 36.8
D 13	35 39.3	56 44.7	55.8	198 34.8	42.6	291 58.2	07.5	165 24.7	52.7	Shaula	96 21.0	S37 06.6
A 14	50 41.7	71 44.5	55.0	213 38.2	42.3	307 00.4	07.5	180 27.3	52.7	Sirius	258 33.3	S16 44.5
Y 15	65 44.2	86 44.3	.. 54.1	228 41.6	.. 42.1	322 02.5	.. 07.5	195 30.0	.. 52.6	Spica	158 30.3	S11 14.3
16	80 46.7	101 44.2	53.3	243 44.9	41.8	337 04.7	07.4	210 32.6	52.6	Suhail	222 51.8	S43 29.9
17	95 49.1	116 44.0	52.5	258 48.3	41.5	352 06.9	07.4	225 35.2	52.6			
18	110 51.6	131 43.9	S 8 51.7	273 51.7	S 4 41.2	7 09.0	N23 07.4	240 37.8	S15 52.5	Vega	80 38.5	N38 47.7
19	125 54.1	146 43.7	50.8	288 55.1	40.9	22 11.2	07.4	255 40.4	52.5	Zuben'ubi	137 04.5	S16 06.1
20	140 56.5	161 43.5	50.0	303 58.5	40.6	37 13.4	07.3	270 43.0	52.4		SHA	Mer.Pass.
21	155 59.0	176 43.4	.. 49.2	319 01.9	.. 40.3	52 15.5	.. 07.3	285 45.6	.. 52.4		° '	h m
22	171 01.5	191 43.2	48.4	334 05.2	40.1	67 17.7	07.3	300 48.3	52.3	Venus	22 42.5	9 13
23	186 03.9	206 43.1	47.6	349 08.6	39.8	82 19.9	07.3	315 50.9	52.3	Mars	162 21.5	23 49
Mer.Pass.	10 41.7	v −0.2	d 0.8	v 3.4	d 0.3	v 2.2	d 0.0	v 2.6	d 0.0	Jupiter	256 29.7	17 35
										Saturn	129 40.0	2 04

UT	SUN GHA	SUN Dec	MOON GHA	v	MOON Dec	d	HP
10 00	179 38.3	N 7 50.2	58 21.5	14.4	N10 26.6	8.1	54.4
01	194 38.4	51.1	72 54.9	14.3	10 18.5	8.3	54.4
02	209 38.6	52.0	87 28.2	14.4	10 10.2	8.3	54.4
03	224 38.8	.. 53.0	102 01.6	14.4	10 01.9	8.3	54.4
04	239 38.9	53.9	116 35.0	14.3	9 53.6	8.4	54.4
05	254 39.1	54.8	131 08.3	14.4	9 45.2	8.4	54.4
T 06	269 39.3	N 7 55.7	145 41.7	14.4	N 9 36.8	8.4	54.4
07	284 39.4	56.7	160 15.1	14.4	9 28.4	8.6	54.4
H 08	299 39.6	57.6	174 48.5	14.5	9 19.8	8.5	54.4
U 09	314 39.8	.. 58.5	189 22.0	14.4	9 11.3	8.6	54.5
R 10	329 39.9	7 59.4	203 55.4	14.4	9 02.7	8.6	54.5
S 11	344 40.1	8 00.4	218 28.8	14.5	8 54.1	8.7	54.5
D 12	359 40.3	N 8 01.3	233 02.3	14.4	N 8 45.4	8.7	54.5
A 13	14 40.5	02.2	247 35.7	14.5	8 36.7	8.8	54.5
Y 14	29 40.6	03.1	262 09.2	14.5	8 27.9	8.8	54.5
15	44 40.8	.. 04.1	276 42.7	14.4	8 19.1	8.8	54.5
16	59 41.0	05.0	291 16.1	14.5	8 10.3	8.9	54.5
17	74 41.1	05.9	305 49.6	14.5	8 01.4	8.9	54.6
18	89 41.3	N 8 06.8	320 23.1	14.5	N 7 52.5	9.0	54.6
19	104 41.5	07.7	334 56.6	14.5	7 43.5	9.0	54.6
20	119 41.6	08.7	349 30.1	14.5	7 34.5	9.0	54.6
21	134 41.8	.. 09.6	4 03.6	14.5	7 25.5	9.1	54.6
22	149 42.0	10.5	18 37.1	14.4	7 16.4	9.1	54.6
23	164 42.1	11.4	33 10.5	14.5	7 07.3	9.1	54.6
11 00	179 42.3	N 8 12.4	47 44.0	14.5	N 6 58.2	9.2	54.7
01	194 42.5	13.3	62 17.5	14.5	6 49.0	9.2	54.7
02	209 42.6	14.2	76 51.0	14.5	6 39.8	9.3	54.7
03	224 42.8	.. 15.1	91 24.5	14.5	6 30.5	9.2	54.7
04	239 43.0	16.0	105 58.0	14.5	6 21.3	9.4	54.7
05	254 43.1	16.9	120 31.5	14.5	6 11.9	9.3	54.7
06	269 43.3	N 8 17.9	135 05.0	14.5	N 6 02.6	9.4	54.8
07	284 43.4	18.8	149 38.5	14.5	5 53.2	9.4	54.8
08	299 43.6	19.7	164 12.0	14.4	5 43.8	9.4	54.8
F 09	314 43.8	.. 20.6	178 45.4	14.5	5 34.4	9.5	54.8
R 10	329 43.9	21.5	193 18.9	14.5	5 24.9	9.5	54.8
I 11	344 44.1	22.5	207 52.4	14.4	5 15.4	9.5	54.8
D 12	359 44.3	N 8 23.4	222 25.8	14.5	N 5 05.9	9.6	54.9
A 13	14 44.4	24.3	236 59.3	14.4	4 56.3	9.6	54.9
Y 14	29 44.6	25.2	251 32.7	14.5	4 46.7	9.6	54.9
15	44 44.8	.. 26.1	266 06.2	14.4	4 37.1	9.6	54.9
16	59 44.9	27.0	280 39.6	14.4	4 27.5	9.7	54.9
17	74 45.1	28.0	295 13.0	14.4	4 17.8	9.7	54.9
18	89 45.3	N 8 28.9	309 46.4	14.4	N 4 08.1	9.7	55.0
19	104 45.4	29.8	324 19.8	14.4	3 58.4	9.7	55.0
20	119 45.6	30.7	338 53.2	14.4	3 48.7	9.8	55.0
21	134 45.8	.. 31.6	353 26.6	14.4	3 38.9	9.8	55.0
22	149 45.9	32.5	8 00.0	14.3	3 29.1	9.8	55.0
23	164 46.1	33.4	22 33.3	14.4	3 19.3	9.8	55.1
12 00	179 46.2	N 8 34.4	37 06.7	14.3	N 3 09.5	9.9	55.1
01	194 46.4	35.3	51 40.0	14.3	2 59.6	9.9	55.1
02	209 46.6	36.2	66 13.3	14.3	2 49.8	9.9	55.1
03	224 46.7	.. 37.1	80 46.6	14.3	2 39.9	10.0	55.1
04	239 46.9	38.0	95 19.9	14.3	2 29.9	9.9	55.2
05	254 47.1	38.9	109 53.2	14.2	2 20.0	9.9	55.2
S 06	269 47.2	N 8 39.8	124 26.4	14.2	N 2 10.1	10.0	55.2
07	284 47.4	40.8	138 59.6	14.2	2 00.1	10.0	55.2
A 08	299 47.5	41.7	153 32.8	14.2	1 50.1	10.0	55.2
T 09	314 47.7	.. 42.6	168 06.0	14.2	1 40.1	10.0	55.3
U 10	329 47.9	43.5	182 39.2	14.2	1 30.1	10.0	55.3
R 11	344 48.0	44.4	197 12.4	14.1	1 20.1	10.1	55.3
D 12	359 48.2	N 8 45.3	211 45.5	14.1	N 1 10.0	10.0	55.3
A 13	14 48.4	46.2	226 18.6	14.1	1 00.0	10.1	55.4
Y 14	29 48.5	47.1	240 51.7	14.0	0 49.9	10.1	55.4
15	44 48.7	.. 48.0	255 24.7	14.1	0 39.8	10.1	55.4
16	59 48.8	49.0	269 57.8	14.0	0 29.7	10.1	55.4
17	74 49.0	49.9	284 30.8	14.0	0 19.6	10.1	55.4
18	89 49.2	N 8 50.8	299 03.8	14.0	N 0 09.5	10.2	55.5
19	104 49.3	51.7	313 36.8	13.9	S 0 00.7	10.1	55.5
20	119 49.5	52.6	328 09.7	13.9	0 10.8	10.1	55.5
21	134 49.6	.. 53.5	342 42.6	13.9	0 20.9	10.2	55.5
22	149 49.8	54.4	357 15.5	13.9	0 31.1	10.1	55.5
23	164 50.0	55.3	11 48.4	13.8	S 0 41.2	10.2	55.6
SD	16.0	d 0.9	SD 14.8		14.9		15.1

Lat.	Twilight Naut.	Twilight Civil	Sunrise	Moonrise 10	11	12	13
N 72	////	02 33	04 03	12 39	14 17	15 55	17 36
N 70	////	03 01	04 16	12 52	14 23	15 56	17 30
68	01 34	03 22	04 27	13 03	14 29	15 56	17 26
66	02 12	03 38	04 36	13 12	14 33	15 57	17 22
64	02 37	03 51	04 44	13 19	14 37	15 57	17 19
62	02 57	04 02	04 50	13 26	14 41	15 57	17 16
60	03 12	04 11	04 56	13 31	14 43	15 57	17 13
N 58	03 25	04 19	05 01	13 36	14 46	15 58	17 11
56	03 36	04 26	05 05	13 40	14 48	15 58	17 09
54	03 46	04 32	05 09	13 44	14 50	15 58	17 07
52	03 54	04 37	05 13	13 48	14 52	15 58	17 06
50	04 01	04 42	05 16	13 51	14 54	15 58	17 04
45	04 16	04 53	05 23	13 58	14 58	15 59	17 01
N 40	04 28	05 01	05 29	14 03	15 01	15 59	16 59
35	04 37	05 08	05 34	14 08	15 03	15 59	16 57
30	04 45	05 14	05 38	14 13	15 06	15 59	16 55
20	04 57	05 23	05 45	14 20	15 10	16 00	16 51
N 10	05 06	05 31	05 52	14 27	15 13	16 00	16 48
0	05 13	05 37	05 58	14 33	15 16	16 01	16 46
S 10	05 18	05 42	06 04	14 39	15 20	16 01	16 43
20	05 22	05 48	06 10	14 45	15 23	16 01	16 40
30	05 25	05 52	06 17	14 53	15 27	16 02	16 37
35	05 26	05 55	06 20	14 57	15 30	16 02	16 35
40	05 26	05 58	06 25	15 02	15 32	16 02	16 33
45	05 26	06 00	06 30	15 07	15 35	16 03	16 31
S 50	05 26	06 03	06 36	15 14	15 39	16 03	16 28
52	05 26	06 05	06 39	15 17	15 41	16 03	16 27
54	05 25	06 06	06 42	15 21	15 42	16 04	16 25
56	05 24	06 07	06 45	15 24	15 44	16 04	16 24
58	05 24	06 09	06 49	15 28	15 47	16 04	16 22
S 60	05 22	06 11	06 53	15 33	15 49	16 04	16 20

Lat.	Sunset	Twilight Civil	Twilight Naut.	Moonset 10	11	12	13
N 72	20 03	21 35	////	04 22	04 15	04 08	04 01
N 70	19 49	21 06	////	04 07	04 06	04 05	04 04
68	19 38	20 44	22 37	03 55	03 59	04 02	04 05
66	19 28	20 27	21 56	03 45	03 53	04 00	04 07
64	19 14	20 14	21 29	03 36	03 48	03 58	04 08
62	19 14	20 03	21 08	03 29	03 43	03 57	04 09
60	19 08	19 53	20 52	03 23	03 40	03 55	04 10
N 58	19 03	19 45	20 39	03 17	03 36	03 54	04 11
56	18 58	19 38	20 28	03 12	03 33	03 53	04 12
54	18 54	19 32	20 18	03 08	03 30	03 52	04 13
52	18 51	19 26	20 10	03 04	03 28	03 51	04 13
50	18 47	19 21	20 02	03 00	03 25	03 50	04 14
45	18 40	19 11	19 47	02 52	03 20	03 48	04 15
N 40	18 34	19 02	19 35	02 45	03 16	03 46	04 16
35	18 29	18 55	19 25	02 39	03 12	03 45	04 17
30	18 25	18 49	19 18	02 34	03 09	03 44	04 18
20	18 17	18 39	19 06	02 25	03 04	03 41	04 21
N 10	18 10	18 32	18 56	02 17	02 59	03 39	04 21
0	18 04	18 25	18 50	02 10	02 54	03 38	04 22
S 10	17 58	18 20	18 44	02 03	02 49	03 36	04 23
20	17 52	18 14	18 40	01 55	02 44	03 34	04 24
30	17 45	18 09	18 37	01 45	02 38	03 31	04 26
35	17 41	18 07	18 36	01 40	02 35	03 30	04 27
40	17 37	18 04	18 35	01 34	02 31	03 29	04 28
45	17 32	18 01	18 35	01 27	02 26	03 27	04 29
S 50	17 25	17 58	18 35	01 18	02 21	03 25	04 30
52	17 23	17 57	18 36	01 14	02 18	03 24	04 30
54	17 20	17 55	18 36	01 10	02 16	03 23	04 31
56	17 16	17 54	18 37	01 05	02 13	03 21	04 32
58	17 12	17 52	18 37	01 00	02 09	03 20	04 32
S 60	17 08	17 51	18 38	00 54	02 05	03 18	04 33

Day	SUN Eqn. of Time 00h	SUN Eqn. of Time 12h	SUN Mer. Pass.	MOON Mer. Pass. Upper	MOON Mer. Pass. Lower	Age	Phase
10	01 27	01 19	12 01	20 43	08 21	11	78
11	01 11	01 03	12 01	21 27	09 05	12	86
12	00 55	00 48	12 01	22 11	09 49	13	92

UT	ARIES	VENUS −4.3		MARS −1.4		JUPITER −2.1		SATURN +0.2		STARS		
	GHA	GHA	Dec	GHA	Dec	GHA	Dec	GHA	Dec	Name	SHA	Dec
d h	° ′	° ′	° ′	° ′	° ′	° ′	° ′	° ′	° ′		° ′	° ′
13 00	201 06.4	221 42.9	S 8 46.7	4 12.0	S 4 39.5	97 22.0	N23 07.3	330 53.5	S15 52.3	Acamar	315 18.3	S40 15.1
01	216 08.8	236 42.7	45.9	19 15.4	39.2	112 24.2	07.2	345 56.1	52.2	Achernar	335 27.0	S57 09.9
02	231 11.3	251 42.6	45.1	34 18.8	38.9	127 26.4	07.2	0 58.7	52.2	Acrux	173 07.9	S63 10.9
03	246 13.8	266 42.4	.. 44.3	49 22.1	.. 38.6	142 28.5	.. 07.2	16 01.3	.. 52.1	Adhara	255 12.1	S28 59.9
04	261 16.2	281 42.2	43.4	64 25.5	38.4	157 30.7	07.2	31 03.9	52.1	Aldebaran	290 49.0	N16 32.1
05	276 18.7	296 42.1	42.6	79 28.9	38.1	172 32.9	07.1	46 06.6	52.0			
06	291 21.2	311 41.9	S 8 41.8	94 32.3	S 4 37.8	187 35.0	N23 07.1	61 09.2	S15 52.0	Alioth	166 19.7	N55 52.9
07	306 23.6	326 41.8	40.9	109 35.7	37.5	202 37.2	07.1	76 11.8	52.0	Alkaid	152 58.0	N49 14.5
08	321 26.1	341 41.6	40.1	124 39.1	37.2	217 39.4	07.1	91 14.4	51.9	Al Na'ir	27 43.4	S46 53.3
S 09	336 28.6	356 41.4	.. 39.3	139 42.4	.. 36.9	232 41.5	.. 07.0	106 17.0	.. 51.9	Alnilam	275 46.0	S 1 11.9
U 10	351 31.0	11 41.3	38.4	154 45.8	36.7	247 43.7	07.0	121 19.6	51.8	Alphard	217 55.4	S 8 43.6
N 11	6 33.5	26 41.1	37.6	169 49.2	36.4	262 45.8	07.0	136 22.3	51.8			
D 12	21 36.0	41 40.9	S 8 36.8	184 52.6	S 4 36.1	277 48.0	N23 07.0	151 24.9	S15 51.7	Alphecca	126 10.2	N26 39.9
A 13	36 38.4	56 40.8	36.0	199 56.0	35.8	292 50.2	06.9	166 27.5	51.7	Alpheratz	357 43.2	N29 10.0
Y 14	51 40.9	71 40.6	35.1	214 59.3	35.5	307 52.3	06.9	181 30.1	51.7	Altair	62 07.7	N 8 54.4
15	66 43.3	86 40.5	.. 34.3	230 02.7	.. 35.3	322 54.5	.. 06.9	196 32.7	.. 51.6	Ankaa	353 15.6	S42 13.7
16	81 45.8	101 40.3	33.5	245 06.1	35.0	337 56.7	06.9	211 35.3	51.6	Antares	112 25.3	S26 27.7
17	96 48.3	116 40.1	32.6	260 09.5	34.7	352 58.8	06.8	226 38.0	51.5			
18	111 50.7	131 40.0	S 8 31.8	275 12.9	S 4 34.4	8 01.0	N23 06.8	241 40.6	S15 51.5	Arcturus	145 54.9	N19 06.4
19	126 53.2	146 39.8	30.9	290 16.2	34.1	23 03.1	06.8	256 43.2	51.4	Atria	107 26.2	S69 02.8
20	141 55.7	161 39.6	30.1	305 19.6	33.8	38 05.3	06.8	271 45.8	51.4	Avior	234 17.6	S59 33.8
21	156 58.1	176 39.5	.. 29.3	320 23.0	.. 33.6	53 07.5	.. 06.7	286 48.4	.. 51.4	Bellatrix	278 31.6	N 6 21.5
22	172 00.6	191 39.3	28.4	335 26.4	33.3	68 09.6	06.7	301 51.0	51.3	Betelgeuse	271 00.8	N 7 24.3
23	187 03.1	206 39.2	27.6	350 29.7	33.0	83 11.8	06.7	316 53.7	51.3			
14 00	202 05.5	221 39.0	S 8 26.8	5 33.1	S 4 32.7	98 13.9	N23 06.7	331 56.3	S15 51.2	Canopus	263 56.1	S52 42.7
01	217 08.0	236 38.8	25.9	20 36.5	32.4	113 16.1	06.6	346 58.9	51.2	Capella	280 33.9	N46 00.6
02	232 10.4	251 38.7	25.1	35 39.9	32.2	128 18.2	06.6	2 01.5	51.1	Deneb	49 31.2	N45 19.7
03	247 12.9	266 38.5	.. 24.2	50 43.3	.. 31.9	143 20.4	.. 06.6	17 04.1	.. 51.1	Denebola	182 32.8	N14 29.4
04	262 15.4	281 38.3	23.4	65 46.6	31.6	158 22.6	06.6	32 06.7	51.1	Diphda	348 55.7	S17 54.6
05	277 17.8	296 38.2	22.6	80 50.0	31.3	173 24.7	06.6	47 09.4	51.0			
06	292 20.3	311 38.0	S 8 21.7	95 53.4	S 4 31.0	188 26.9	N23 06.5	62 12.0	S15 51.0	Dubhe	193 50.6	N61 40.5
07	307 22.8	326 37.9	20.9	110 56.8	30.8	203 29.0	06.5	77 14.6	50.9	Elnath	278 12.1	N28 37.0
08	322 25.2	341 37.7	20.0	126 00.1	30.5	218 31.2	06.5	92 17.2	50.9	Eltanin	90 45.7	N51 29.1
M 09	337 27.7	356 37.5	.. 19.2	141 03.5	.. 30.2	233 33.3	.. 06.5	107 19.8	.. 50.8	Enif	33 46.7	N 9 56.4
O 10	352 30.2	11 37.4	18.3	156 06.9	29.9	248 35.5	06.4	122 22.5	50.8	Fomalhaut	15 23.7	S29 32.7
N 11	7 32.6	26 37.2	17.5	171 10.3	29.6	263 37.7	06.4	137 25.1	50.8			
D 12	22 35.1	41 37.0	S 8 16.6	186 13.6	S 4 29.4	278 39.8	N23 06.4	152 27.7	S15 50.7	Gacrux	171 59.6	S57 11.8
A 13	37 37.6	56 36.9	15.8	201 17.0	29.1	293 42.0	06.4	167 30.3	50.7	Gienah	175 51.4	S17 37.5
Y 14	52 40.0	71 36.7	15.0	216 20.4	28.8	308 44.1	06.3	182 32.9	50.6	Hadar	148 46.4	S60 26.5
15	67 42.5	86 36.5	.. 14.1	231 23.8	.. 28.5	323 46.3	.. 06.3	197 35.5	.. 50.6	Hamal	328 00.4	N23 31.6
16	82 44.9	101 36.4	13.3	246 27.1	28.3	338 48.4	06.3	212 38.2	50.5	Kaus Aust.	83 42.9	S34 22.4
17	97 47.4	116 36.2	12.4	261 30.5	28.0	353 50.6	06.3	227 40.8	50.5			
18	112 49.9	131 36.0	S 8 11.6	276 33.9	S 4 27.7	8 52.7	N23 06.2	242 43.4	S15 50.5	Kochab	137 19.1	N74 05.8
19	127 52.3	146 35.9	10.7	291 37.3	27.4	23 54.9	06.2	257 46.0	50.4	Markab	13 38.0	N15 16.8
20	142 54.8	161 35.7	09.9	306 40.6	27.1	38 57.1	06.2	272 48.6	50.4	Menkar	314 14.8	N 4 08.5
21	157 57.3	176 35.6	.. 09.0	321 44.0	.. 26.9	53 59.2	.. 06.2	287 51.3	.. 50.3	Menkent	148 06.5	S36 26.4
22	172 59.7	191 35.4	08.2	336 47.4	26.6	69 01.4	06.1	302 53.9	50.3	Miaplacidus	221 39.1	S69 47.0
23	188 02.2	206 35.2	07.3	351 50.7	26.3	84 03.5	06.1	317 56.5	50.2			
15 00	203 04.7	221 35.1	S 8 06.5	6 54.1	S 4 26.0	99 05.7	N23 06.1	332 59.1	S15 50.2	Mirfak	308 39.9	N49 54.6
01	218 07.1	236 34.9	05.6	21 57.5	25.8	114 07.8	06.1	348 01.7	50.1	Nunki	75 57.6	S26 16.5
02	233 09.6	251 34.7	04.8	37 00.9	25.5	129 10.0	06.0	3 04.4	50.1	Peacock	53 18.5	S56 41.0
03	248 12.1	266 34.6	.. 03.9	52 04.2	.. 25.2	144 12.1	.. 06.0	18 07.0	.. 50.1	Pollux	243 27.1	N27 59.3
04	263 14.5	281 34.4	03.1	67 07.6	24.9	159 14.3	06.0	33 09.6	50.0	Procyon	244 59.2	N 5 11.0
05	278 17.0	296 34.2	02.2	82 11.0	24.7	174 16.4	05.9	48 12.2	50.0			
06	293 19.4	311 34.1	S 8 01.3	97 14.3	S 4 24.4	189 18.6	N23 05.9	63 14.8	S15 49.9	Rasalhague	96 05.8	N12 33.0
07	308 21.9	326 33.9	8 00.5	112 17.7	24.1	204 20.7	05.9	78 17.5	49.9	Regulus	207 42.7	N11 53.6
08	323 24.4	341 33.7	7 59.6	127 21.1	23.8	219 22.9	05.9	93 20.1	49.8	Rigel	281 11.7	S 8 11.4
T 09	338 26.8	356 33.6	.. 58.8	142 24.4	.. 23.6	234 25.0	.. 05.8	108 22.7	.. 49.8	Rigil Kent.	139 50.2	S60 53.5
U 10	353 29.3	11 33.4	57.9	157 27.8	23.3	249 27.2	05.8	123 25.3	49.8	Sabik	102 11.7	S15 44.4
E 11	8 31.8	26 33.3	57.1	172 31.2	23.0	264 29.3	05.8	138 27.9	49.7			
S 12	23 34.2	41 33.1	S 7 56.2	187 34.6	S 4 22.7	279 31.5	N23 05.8	153 30.6	S15 49.7	Schedar	349 40.3	N56 36.8
D 13	38 36.7	56 32.9	55.3	202 37.9	22.5	294 33.6	05.7	168 33.2	49.6	Shaula	96 20.9	S37 06.6
A 14	53 39.2	71 32.8	54.5	217 41.3	22.2	309 35.8	05.7	183 35.8	49.6	Sirius	258 33.5	S16 44.5
Y 15	68 41.6	86 32.6	.. 53.6	232 44.7	.. 21.9	324 37.9	.. 05.7	198 38.4	.. 49.5	Spica	158 30.3	S11 14.3
16	83 44.1	101 32.4	52.8	247 48.0	21.6	339 40.1	05.7	213 41.1	49.5	Suhail	222 51.8	S43 29.9
17	98 46.5	116 32.3	51.9	262 51.4	21.4	354 42.2	05.6	228 43.7	49.4			
18	113 49.0	131 32.1	S 7 51.0	277 54.8	S 4 21.1	9 44.4	N23 05.6	243 46.3	S15 49.4	Vega	80 38.5	N38 47.7
19	128 51.5	146 31.9	50.2	292 58.1	20.8	24 46.5	05.6	258 48.9	49.4	Zuben'ubi	137 04.5	S16 06.1
20	143 53.9	161 31.8	49.3	308 01.5	20.5	39 48.7	05.6	273 51.5	49.3		SHA	Mer.Pass.
21	158 56.4	176 31.6	.. 48.5	323 04.9	.. 20.3	54 50.8	.. 05.5	288 54.2	.. 49.3		° ′	h m
22	173 58.9	191 31.4	47.6	338 08.2	20.0	69 53.0	05.5	303 56.8	49.2	Venus	19 33.5	9 13
23	189 01.3	206 31.3	46.7	353 11.6	19.7	84 55.1	05.5	318 59.4	49.2	Mars	163 27.6	23 32
	h m									Jupiter	256 08.4	17 25
Mer.Pass. 10 29.9		v −0.2	d 0.8	v 3.4	d 0.3	v 2.2	d 0.0	v 2.6	d 0.0	Saturn	129 50.8	1 52

UT	SUN GHA	SUN Dec	MOON GHA	v	Dec	d	HP
d h	° ′	° ′	° ′	′	° ′	′	′
13 00	179 50.1	N 8 56.2	26 21.2	13.8	S 0 51.4	10.2	55.6
01	194 50.3	57.1	40 54.0	13.8	1 01.6	10.2	55.6
02	209 50.5	58.0	55 26.8	13.7	1 11.8	10.1	55.6
03	224 50.6	.. 59.0	69 59.5	13.7	1 21.9	10.2	55.7
04	239 50.8	8 59.9	84 32.2	13.7	1 32.1	10.2	55.7
05	254 50.9	9 00.8	99 04.9	13.6	1 42.3	10.2	55.7
S 06	269 51.1	N 9 01.7	113 37.5	13.7	S 1 52.5	10.2	55.7
U 07	284 51.2	02.6	128 10.2	13.5	2 02.7	10.1	55.8
N 08	299 51.4	03.5	142 42.7	13.6	2 12.8	10.2	55.8
D 09	314 51.6	.. 04.4	157 15.3	13.5	2 23.0	10.2	55.8
A 10	329 51.7	05.3	171 47.8	13.5	2 33.2	10.2	55.8
Y 11	344 51.9	06.2	186 20.3	13.4	2 43.4	10.2	55.9
12	359 52.0	N 9 07.1	200 52.7	13.4	S 2 53.6	10.1	55.9
13	14 52.2	08.0	215 25.1	13.4	3 03.7	10.2	55.9
14	29 52.4	08.9	229 57.5	13.3	3 13.9	10.2	55.9
15	44 52.5	.. 09.8	244 29.8	13.3	3 24.1	10.1	55.9
16	59 52.7	10.7	259 02.1	13.3	3 34.2	10.2	56.0
17	74 52.8	11.6	273 34.4	13.2	3 44.4	10.1	56.0
18	89 53.0	N 9 12.5	288 06.6	13.2	S 3 54.5	10.1	56.0
19	104 53.2	13.4	302 38.8	13.1	4 04.6	10.2	56.0
20	119 53.3	14.3	317 10.9	13.1	4 14.8	10.1	56.1
21	134 53.5	.. 15.2	331 43.0	13.0	4 24.9	10.1	56.1
22	149 53.6	16.1	346 15.0	13.1	4 35.0	10.1	56.1
23	164 53.8	17.1	0 47.1	12.9	4 45.1	10.0	56.1
14 00	179 53.9	N 9 18.0	15 19.0	12.9	S 4 55.1	10.1	56.2
01	194 54.1	18.9	29 50.9	12.9	5 05.2	10.0	56.2
02	209 54.3	19.8	44 22.8	12.9	5 15.2	10.1	56.2
03	224 54.4	.. 20.7	58 54.7	12.8	5 25.3	10.0	56.2
04	239 54.6	21.6	73 26.5	12.7	5 35.3	10.0	56.3
05	254 54.7	22.5	87 58.2	12.7	5 45.3	10.0	56.3
06	269 54.9	N 9 23.4	102 29.9	12.7	S 5 55.3	9.9	56.3
07	284 55.0	24.3	117 01.6	12.6	6 05.2	10.0	56.3
M 08	299 55.2	25.2	131 33.2	12.5	6 15.2	9.9	56.4
O 09	314 55.3	.. 26.1	146 04.7	12.5	6 25.1	9.9	56.4
N 10	329 55.5	27.0	160 36.2	12.5	6 35.0	9.8	56.4
D 11	344 55.7	27.9	175 07.7	12.4	6 44.8	9.9	56.4
A 12	359 55.8	N 9 28.8	189 39.1	12.4	S 6 54.7	9.8	56.5
Y 13	14 56.0	29.7	204 10.5	12.3	7 04.5	9.8	56.5
14	29 56.1	30.6	218 41.8	12.3	7 14.3	9.8	56.5
15	44 56.3	.. 31.5	233 13.1	12.2	7 24.1	9.7	56.5
16	59 56.4	32.3	247 44.3	12.1	7 33.8	9.7	56.6
17	74 56.6	33.2	262 15.4	12.1	7 43.5	9.7	56.6
18	89 56.7	N 9 34.1	276 46.5	12.1	S 7 53.2	9.7	56.6
19	104 56.9	35.0	291 17.6	12.0	8 02.9	9.6	56.6
20	119 57.0	35.9	305 48.6	12.0	8 12.5	9.6	56.7
21	134 57.2	.. 36.8	320 19.6	11.9	8 22.1	9.5	56.7
22	149 57.4	37.7	334 50.5	11.8	8 31.6	9.6	56.7
23	164 57.5	38.6	349 21.3	11.8	8 41.2	9.5	56.7
15 00	179 57.7	N 9 39.5	3 52.1	11.7	S 8 50.7	9.4	56.8
01	194 57.8	40.4	18 22.8	11.7	9 00.1	9.4	56.8
02	209 58.0	41.3	32 53.5	11.6	9 09.5	9.4	56.8
03	224 58.1	.. 42.2	47 24.1	11.6	9 18.9	9.3	56.8
04	239 58.3	43.1	61 54.7	11.5	9 28.2	9.3	56.8
05	254 58.4	44.0	76 25.2	11.5	9 37.5	9.3	56.9
06	269 58.6	N 9 44.9	90 55.7	11.4	S 9 46.8	9.2	56.9
07	284 58.7	45.8	105 26.1	11.3	9 56.0	9.2	56.9
T 08	299 58.9	46.7	119 56.4	11.3	10 05.2	9.1	56.9
U 09	314 59.0	.. 47.6	134 26.7	11.2	10 14.3	9.1	57.0
E 10	329 59.2	48.5	148 56.9	11.2	10 23.4	9.0	57.0
S 11	344 59.3	49.4	163 27.1	11.1	10 32.4	9.0	57.0
D 12	359 59.5	N 9 50.2	177 57.2	11.1	S10 41.4	9.0	57.0
A 13	14 59.6	51.1	192 27.3	10.9	10 50.4	8.8	57.1
Y 14	29 59.8	52.0	206 57.2	11.0	10 59.2	8.8	57.1
15	44 59.9	.. 52.9	221 27.2	10.9	11 08.1	8.8	57.1
16	60 00.1	53.8	235 57.1	10.8	11 16.9	8.7	57.1
17	75 00.3	54.7	250 26.9	10.7	11 25.6	8.7	57.2
18	90 00.4	N 9 55.6	264 56.6	10.7	S11 34.3	8.6	57.2
19	105 00.6	56.5	279 26.3	10.7	11 42.9	8.6	57.2
20	120 00.7	57.4	293 56.0	10.5	11 51.5	8.5	57.2
21	135 00.9	.. 58.3	308 25.5	10.5	12 00.0	8.5	57.3
22	150 01.0	9 59.1	322 55.0	10.5	12 08.5	8.4	57.3
23	165 01.2	N10 00.0	337 24.5	10.4	S12 16.9	8.3	57.3
SD	16.0	d 0.9	SD 15.2		15.4		15.5

Twilight / Sunrise / Moonrise

Lat.	Twilight Naut.	Twilight Civil	Sunrise	Moonrise 13	14	15	16
°	h m	h m	h m	h m	h m	h m	h m
N 72	////	02 08	03 46	17 36	19 21	21 13	23 15
N 70	////	02 42	04 01	17 30	19 08	20 50	22 36
68	00 58	03 06	04 14	17 26	18 58	20 33	22 10
66	01 50	03 24	04 24	17 22	18 50	20 19	21 50
64	02 21	03 39	04 33	17 19	18 42	20 08	21 34
62	02 43	03 51	04 40	17 16	18 36	19 58	21 20
60	03 01	04 01	04 47	17 13	18 31	19 50	21 09
N 58	03 15	04 10	04 52	17 11	18 26	19 43	21 00
56	03 27	04 17	04 57	17 09	18 22	19 37	20 51
54	03 37	04 24	05 02	17 07	18 19	19 31	20 44
52	03 46	04 30	05 06	17 06	18 15	19 26	20 37
50	03 54	04 36	05 10	17 04	18 12	19 21	20 31
45	04 10	04 47	05 17	17 01	18 06	19 11	20 18
N 40	04 23	04 56	05 24	16 59	18 00	19 03	20 07
35	04 33	05 04	05 30	16 57	17 56	18 56	19 58
30	04 41	05 10	05 35	16 55	17 51	18 50	19 50
20	04 54	05 21	05 43	16 51	17 44	18 39	19 36
N 10	05 04	05 29	05 50	16 48	17 38	18 30	19 24
0	05 12	05 36	05 57	16 46	17 33	18 21	19 13
S 10	05 18	05 42	06 04	16 43	17 27	18 13	19 02
20	05 23	05 48	06 11	16 40	17 21	18 04	18 50
30	05 26	05 54	06 18	16 37	17 14	17 53	18 37
35	05 28	05 57	06 23	16 35	17 10	17 48	18 29
40	05 29	06 00	06 28	16 33	17 06	17 41	18 20
45	05 30	06 04	06 34	16 31	17 00	17 33	18 10
S 50	05 30	06 08	06 41	16 28	16 54	17 24	17 58
52	05 30	06 09	06 44	16 27	16 52	17 20	17 52
54	05 30	06 11	06 47	16 25	16 49	17 15	17 46
56	05 30	06 13	06 51	16 24	16 45	17 10	17 39
58	05 30	06 15	06 55	16 22	16 41	17 04	17 31
S 60	05 29	06 17	07 00	16 20	16 37	16 57	17 22

Sunset / Twilight / Moonset

Lat.	Sunset	Twilight Civil	Twilight Naut.	Moonset 13	14	15	16
°	h m	h m	h m	h m	h m	h m	h m
N 72	20 19	22 00	////	04 01	03 55	03 47	03 38
N 70	20 02	21 24	////	04 04	04 02	04 02	04 02
68	19 49	20 59	23 19	04 05	04 09	04 13	04 20
66	19 39	20 40	22 17	04 07	04 14	04 23	04 35
64	19 30	20 24	21 44	04 08	04 19	04 31	04 47
62	19 22	20 12	21 21	04 09	04 23	04 39	04 58
60	19 15	20 02	21 03	04 10	04 27	04 45	05 07
N 58	19 10	19 53	20 48	04 11	04 30	04 50	05 14
56	19 04	19 45	20 36	04 12	04 32	04 55	05 21
54	19 00	19 38	20 25	04 13	04 35	04 59	05 28
52	18 56	19 32	20 16	04 13	04 37	05 03	05 33
50	18 52	19 26	20 08	04 14	04 39	05 07	05 38
45	18 44	19 15	19 52	04 15	04 44	05 15	05 49
N 40	18 37	19 05	19 39	04 16	04 48	05 21	05 58
35	18 32	18 58	19 28	04 17	04 51	05 27	06 06
30	18 27	18 51	19 20	04 18	04 54	05 32	06 13
20	18 18	18 40	19 07	04 20	04 59	05 41	06 25
N 10	18 10	18 32	18 57	04 21	05 04	05 48	06 36
0	18 04	18 25	18 49	04 22	05 08	05 56	06 46
S 10	17 57	18 18	18 43	04 23	05 12	06 03	06 56
20	17 50	18 12	18 38	04 24	05 17	06 11	07 06
30	17 42	18 06	18 34	04 26	05 22	06 19	07 18
35	17 37	18 03	18 32	04 27	05 25	06 24	07 25
40	17 32	18 00	18 31	04 28	05 28	06 30	07 34
45	17 26	17 56	18 30	04 29	05 32	06 37	07 43
S 50	17 19	17 52	18 29	04 30	05 37	06 45	07 54
52	17 16	17 50	18 29	04 30	05 39	06 49	08 00
54	17 13	17 48	18 29	04 31	05 41	06 53	08 05
56	17 09	17 46	18 29	04 32	05 44	06 57	08 12
58	17 04	17 44	18 30	04 32	05 47	07 03	08 19
S 60	16 59	17 42	18 30	04 33	05 50	07 08	08 27

SUN and MOON

Day	SUN Eqn. of Time 00h	SUN Eqn. of Time 12h	Mer. Pass.	MOON Mer. Pass. Upper	MOON Mer. Pass. Lower	Age	Phase
d	m s	m s	h m	h m	h m	d	%
13	00 40	00 32	12 01	22 57	10 34	14	96
14	00 25	00 17	12 00	23 44	11 20	15	99
15	00 10	00 02	12 00	24 34	12 08	16	100

UT	ARIES GHA	VENUS −4.3 GHA	VENUS Dec	MARS −1.4 GHA	MARS Dec	JUPITER −2.1 GHA	JUPITER Dec	SATURN +0.2 GHA	SATURN Dec
16 00	204 03.8	221 31.1	S 7 45.9	8 14.9	S 4 19.5	99 57.2	N23 05.5	334 02.0	S15 49.1
01	219 06.3	236 30.9	45.0	23 18.3	19.2	114 59.4	05.4	349 04.7	49.1
02	234 08.7	251 30.8	44.1	38 21.7	18.9	130 01.5	05.4	4 07.3	49.1
03	249 11.2	266 30.6	.. 43.3	53 25.0	.. 18.6	145 03.7	.. 05.4	19 09.9	.. 49.0
04	264 13.7	281 30.4	42.4	68 28.4	18.4	160 05.8	05.4	34 12.5	49.0
05	279 16.1	296 30.3	41.5	83 31.8	18.1	175 08.0	05.3	49 15.1	48.9
W 06	294 18.6	311 30.1	S 7 40.7	98 35.1	S 4 17.8	190 10.1	N23 05.3	64 17.8	S15 48.9
E 07	309 21.0	326 29.9	39.8	113 38.5	17.6	205 12.3	05.3	79 20.4	48.8
D 08	324 23.5	341 29.8	38.9	128 41.9	17.3	220 14.4	05.2	94 23.0	48.8
N 09	339 26.0	356 29.6	.. 38.1	143 45.2	.. 17.0	235 16.6	.. 05.2	109 25.6	.. 48.7
E 10	354 28.4	11 29.4	37.2	158 48.6	16.8	250 18.7	05.2	124 28.3	48.7
S 11	9 30.9	26 29.3	36.3	173 51.9	16.5	265 20.8	05.2	139 30.9	48.7
D 12	24 33.4	41 29.1	S 7 35.4	188 55.3	S 4 16.2	280 23.0	N23 05.1	154 33.5	S15 48.6
A 13	39 35.8	56 28.9	34.6	203 58.7	15.9	295 25.1	05.1	169 36.1	48.6
Y 14	54 38.3	71 28.8	33.7	219 02.0	15.7	310 27.3	05.1	184 38.8	48.5
15	69 40.8	86 28.6	.. 32.8	234 05.4	.. 15.4	325 29.4	.. 05.1	199 41.4	.. 48.5
16	84 43.2	101 28.4	32.0	249 08.7	15.1	340 31.6	05.0	214 44.0	48.4
17	99 45.7	116 28.3	31.1	264 12.1	14.9	355 33.7	05.0	229 46.6	48.4
18	114 48.1	131 28.1	S 7 30.2	279 15.4	S 4 14.6	10 35.8	N23 05.0	244 49.2	S15 48.3
19	129 50.6	146 27.9	29.3	294 18.8	14.3	25 38.0	05.0	259 51.9	48.3
20	144 53.1	161 27.8	28.5	309 22.2	14.1	40 40.1	04.9	274 54.5	48.3
21	159 55.5	176 27.6	.. 27.6	324 25.5	.. 13.8	55 42.3	.. 04.9	289 57.1	.. 48.2
22	174 58.0	191 27.4	26.7	339 28.9	13.5	70 44.4	04.9	304 59.7	48.2
23	190 00.5	206 27.3	25.8	354 32.2	13.3	85 46.5	04.8	320 02.4	48.1
17 00	205 02.9	221 27.1	S 7 25.0	9 35.6	S 4 13.0	100 48.7	N23 04.8	335 05.0	S15 48.1
01	220 05.4	236 26.9	24.1	24 38.9	12.7	115 50.8	04.8	350 07.6	48.0
02	235 07.9	251 26.8	23.2	39 42.3	12.5	130 53.0	04.8	5 10.2	48.0
03	250 10.3	266 26.6	.. 22.3	54 45.6	.. 12.2	145 55.1	.. 04.7	20 12.9	.. 47.9
04	265 12.8	281 26.4	21.4	69 49.0	11.9	160 57.2	04.7	35 15.5	47.9
05	280 15.3	296 26.3	20.6	84 52.4	11.7	175 59.4	04.7	50 18.1	47.9
T 06	295 17.7	311 26.1	S 7 19.7	99 55.7	S 4 11.4	191 01.5	N23 04.7	65 20.7	S15 47.8
H 07	310 20.2	326 25.9	18.8	114 59.1	11.1	206 03.7	04.6	80 23.4	47.8
U 08	325 22.6	341 25.8	17.9	130 02.4	10.9	221 05.8	04.6	95 26.0	47.7
R 09	340 25.1	356 25.6	.. 17.0	145 05.8	.. 10.6	236 07.9	.. 04.6	110 28.6	.. 47.7
S 10	355 27.6	11 25.4	16.2	160 09.1	10.3	251 10.1	04.6	125 31.2	47.6
D 11	10 30.0	26 25.3	15.3	175 12.5	10.1	266 12.2	04.5	140 33.9	47.6
A 12	25 32.5	41 25.1	S 7 14.4	190 15.8	S 4 09.8	281 14.3	N23 04.5	155 36.5	S15 47.5
Y 13	40 35.0	56 24.9	13.5	205 19.2	09.6	296 16.5	04.5	170 39.1	47.5
14	55 37.4	71 24.8	12.6	220 22.5	09.3	311 18.6	04.4	185 41.7	47.5
15	70 39.9	86 24.6	.. 11.7	235 25.9	.. 09.0	326 20.7	.. 04.4	200 44.4	.. 47.4
16	85 42.4	101 24.4	10.8	250 29.2	08.8	341 22.9	04.4	215 47.0	47.4
17	100 44.8	116 24.3	10.0	265 32.6	08.5	356 25.0	04.4	230 49.6	47.3
18	115 47.3	131 24.1	S 7 09.1	280 35.9	S 4 08.2	11 27.2	N23 04.3	245 52.3	S15 47.3
19	130 49.8	146 23.9	08.2	295 39.2	08.0	26 29.3	04.3	260 54.9	47.2
20	145 52.2	161 23.8	07.3	310 42.6	07.7	41 31.4	04.3	275 57.5	47.2
21	160 54.7	176 23.6	.. 06.4	325 45.9	.. 07.5	56 33.6	.. 04.2	291 00.1	.. 47.1
22	175 57.1	191 23.4	05.5	340 49.3	07.2	71 35.7	04.2	306 02.8	47.1
23	190 59.6	206 23.3	04.6	355 52.6	06.9	86 37.8	04.2	321 05.4	47.1
18 00	206 02.1	221 23.1	S 7 03.7	10 56.0	S 4 06.7	101 40.0	N23 04.2	336 08.0	S15 47.0
01	221 04.5	236 22.9	02.9	25 59.3	06.4	116 42.1	04.1	351 10.6	47.0
02	236 07.0	251 22.8	02.0	41 02.7	06.2	131 44.2	04.1	6 13.3	46.9
03	251 09.5	266 22.6	.. 01.1	56 06.0	.. 05.9	146 46.4	.. 04.1	21 15.9	.. 46.9
04	266 11.9	281 22.4	7 00.2	71 09.4	05.6	161 48.5	04.1	36 18.5	46.8
05	281 14.4	296 22.3	6 59.3	86 12.7	05.4	176 50.6	04.0	51 21.1	46.8
F 06	296 16.9	311 22.1	S 6 58.4	101 16.0	S 4 05.1	191 52.8	N23 04.0	66 23.8	S15 46.7
R 07	311 19.3	326 21.9	57.5	116 19.4	04.9	206 54.9	04.0	81 26.4	46.7
I 08	326 21.8	341 21.8	56.6	131 22.7	04.6	221 57.0	03.9	96 29.0	46.7
D 09	341 24.3	356 21.6	.. 55.7	146 26.1	.. 04.3	236 59.2	.. 03.9	111 31.7	.. 46.6
A 10	356 26.7	11 21.4	54.8	161 29.4	04.1	252 01.3	03.9	126 34.3	46.6
Y 11	11 29.2	26 21.3	53.9	176 32.7	03.8	267 03.4	03.9	141 36.9	46.5
12	26 31.6	41 21.1	S 6 53.0	191 36.1	S 4 03.6	282 05.5	N23 03.8	156 39.5	S15 46.5
13	41 34.1	56 20.9	52.1	206 39.4	03.3	297 07.7	03.8	171 42.2	46.4
14	56 36.6	71 20.7	51.2	221 42.7	03.1	312 09.8	03.8	186 44.8	46.4
15	71 39.0	86 20.6	.. 50.3	236 46.1	.. 02.8	327 11.9	.. 03.7	201 47.4	.. 46.3
16	86 41.5	101 20.4	49.5	251 49.4	02.5	342 14.1	03.7	216 50.1	46.3
17	101 44.0	116 20.2	48.6	266 52.8	02.3	357 16.2	03.7	231 52.7	46.2
18	116 46.4	131 20.1	S 6 47.7	281 56.1	S 4 02.0	12 18.3	N23 03.7	246 55.3	S15 46.2
19	131 48.9	146 19.9	46.8	296 59.4	01.8	27 20.5	03.6	261 57.9	46.2
20	146 51.4	161 19.7	45.9	312 02.8	01.5	42 22.6	03.6	277 00.6	46.1
21	161 53.8	176 19.6	.. 45.0	327 06.1	.. 01.3	57 24.7	.. 03.6	292 03.2	.. 46.1
22	176 56.3	191 19.4	44.1	342 09.4	01.0	72 26.8	03.5	307 05.8	46.0
23	191 58.7	206 19.2	43.2	357 12.8	00.8	87 29.0	03.5	322 08.5	46.0
Mer. Pass.	h m 10 18.1	v −0.2	d 0.9	v 3.3	d 0.3	v 2.1	d 0.0	v 2.6	d 0.0

STARS

Name	SHA	Dec
Acamar	315 18.3	S40 15.1
Achernar	335 27.0	S57 09.9
Acrux	173 07.9	S63 10.9
Adhara	255 12.2	S28 59.9
Aldebaran	290 49.0	N16 32.1
Alioth	166 19.7	N55 52.9
Alkaid	152 58.0	N49 14.5
Al Na'ir	27 43.3	S46 53.3
Alnilam	275 46.0	S 1 11.9
Alphard	217 55.4	S 8 43.6
Alphecca	126 10.2	N26 39.9
Alpheratz	357 43.2	N29 10.0
Altair	62 07.7	N 8 54.4
Ankaa	353 15.6	S42 13.7
Antares	112 25.3	S26 27.7
Arcturus	145 54.9	N19 06.4
Atria	107 26.2	S69 02.8
Avior	234 17.7	S59 33.8
Bellatrix	278 31.6	N 6 21.5
Betelgeuse	271 00.9	N 7 24.3
Canopus	263 56.1	S52 42.7
Capella	280 33.9	N46 00.6
Deneb	49 31.1	N45 19.7
Denebola	182 32.8	N14 29.4
Diphda	348 55.7	S17 54.6
Dubhe	193 50.6	N61 40.5
Elnath	278 12.1	N28 37.0
Eltanin	90 45.6	N51 29.1
Enif	33 46.7	N 9 56.4
Fomalhaut	15 23.7	S29 32.7
Gacrux	171 59.6	S57 11.8
Gienah	175 51.4	S17 37.5
Hadar	148 46.3	S60 26.5
Hamal	328 00.4	N23 31.6
Kaus Aust.	83 42.9	S34 22.4
Kochab	137 19.1	N74 05.8
Markab	13 38.0	N15 16.8
Menkar	314 14.8	N 4 08.5
Menkent	148 06.5	S36 26.4
Miaplacidus	221 39.1	S69 47.0
Mirfak	308 39.9	N49 54.6
Nunki	75 57.5	S26 16.5
Peacock	53 18.5	S56 41.0
Pollux	243 27.1	N27 59.3
Procyon	244 59.2	N 5 11.0
Rasalhague	96 05.7	N12 33.0
Regulus	207 42.8	N11 53.6
Rigel	281 11.7	S 8 11.4
Rigil Kent.	139 50.2	S60 53.5
Sabik	102 11.7	S15 44.4
Schedar	349 40.3	N56 36.8
Shaula	96 20.9	S37 06.6
Sirius	258 33.3	S16 44.5
Spica	158 30.3	S11 14.3
Suhail	222 51.9	S43 29.9
Vega	80 38.4	N38 47.7
Zuben'ubi	137 04.5	S16 06.1

	SHA	Mer. Pass.
	° ′	h m
Venus	16 24.2	9 14
Mars	164 32.6	23 16
Jupiter	255 45.7	17 14
Saturn	130 02.1	1 39

SUN and MOON

UT	SUN GHA	SUN Dec	MOON GHA	v	MOON Dec	d	HP
d h	° ′	° ′	° ′	′	° ′	′	′
16 00	180 01.3	N10 00.9	351 53.9	10.3	S12 25.2	8.3	57.3
01	195 01.5	01.8	6 23.2	10.3	12 33.5	8.2	57.3
02	210 01.6	02.7	20 52.5	10.2	12 41.7	8.2	57.4
03	225 01.8 ..	03.6	35 21.7	10.1	12 49.9	8.1	57.4
04	240 01.9	04.5	49 50.8	10.1	12 58.0	8.0	57.4
05	255 02.0	05.4	64 19.9	10.1	13 06.0	8.0	57.4
W 06	270 02.2	N10 06.3	78 49.0	9.9	S13 14.0	7.9	57.5
E 07	285 02.3	07.1	93 17.9	9.9	13 21.9	7.8	57.5
D 08	300 02.5	08.0	107 46.8	9.9	13 29.7	7.8	57.5
N 09	315 02.6 ..	08.9	122 15.7	9.7	13 37.5	7.6	57.5
E 10	330 02.8	09.8	136 44.4	9.8	13 45.1	7.7	57.6
S 11	345 02.9	10.7	151 13.2	9.6	13 52.8	7.5	57.6
D 12	0 03.1	N10 11.6	165 41.8	9.6	S14 00.3	7.5	57.6
A 13	15 03.2	12.5	180 10.4	9.6	14 07.8	7.4	57.6
Y 14	30 03.4	13.3	194 39.0	9.4	14 15.2	7.3	57.6
15	45 03.5 ..	14.2	209 07.4	9.4	14 22.5	7.3	57.7
16	60 03.7	15.1	223 35.8	9.4	14 29.8	7.1	57.7
17	75 03.8	16.0	238 04.2	9.3	14 36.9	7.1	57.7
18	90 04.0	N10 16.9	252 32.5	9.2	S14 44.0	7.1	57.7
19	105 04.1	17.8	267 00.7	9.2	14 51.1	6.9	57.7
20	120 04.3	18.6	281 28.9	9.1	14 58.0	6.8	57.8
21	135 04.4 ..	19.5	295 57.0	9.1	15 04.8	6.8	57.8
22	150 04.6	20.4	310 25.1	8.9	15 11.6	6.7	57.8
23	165 04.7	21.3	324 53.0	9.0	15 18.3	6.6	57.8
17 00	180 04.9	N10 22.2	339 21.0	8.9	S15 24.9	6.5	57.8
01	195 05.0	23.0	353 48.9	8.8	15 31.4	6.5	57.9
02	210 05.1	23.9	8 16.7	8.7	15 37.9	6.3	57.9
03	225 05.3 ..	24.8	22 44.4	8.7	15 44.2	6.3	57.9
04	240 05.4	25.7	37 12.1	8.7	15 50.5	6.2	57.9
05	255 05.6	26.6	51 39.8	8.6	15 56.7	6.1	57.9
06	270 05.7	N10 27.4	66 07.4	8.5	S16 02.8	5.9	58.0
T 07	285 05.9	28.3	80 34.9	8.5	16 08.7	5.9	58.0
H 08	300 06.0	29.2	95 02.4	8.4	16 14.6	5.9	58.0
U 09	315 06.2 ..	30.1	109 29.8	8.3	16 20.5	5.7	58.0
R 10	330 06.3	31.0	123 57.1	8.3	16 26.2	5.6	58.0
S 11	345 06.4	31.8	138 24.4	8.3	16 31.8	5.5	58.1
D 12	0 06.6	N10 32.7	152 51.7	8.2	S16 37.3	5.5	58.1
A 13	15 06.7	33.6	167 18.9	8.1	16 42.8	5.3	58.1
Y 14	30 06.9	34.5	181 46.0	8.1	16 48.1	5.2	58.1
15	45 07.0 ..	35.4	196 13.1	8.1	16 53.3	5.2	58.1
16	60 07.2	36.2	210 40.2	7.9	16 58.5	5.0	58.2
17	75 07.3	37.1	225 07.1	8.0	17 03.5	5.0	58.2
18	90 07.4	N10 38.0	239 34.1	7.9	S17 08.5	4.8	58.2
19	105 07.6	38.9	254 01.0	7.8	17 13.3	4.7	58.2
20	120 07.7	39.7	268 27.8	7.8	17 18.0	4.7	58.2
21	135 07.9 ..	40.6	282 54.6	7.7	17 22.7	4.5	58.2
22	150 08.0	41.5	297 21.3	7.7	17 27.2	4.4	58.3
23	165 08.2	42.4	311 48.0	7.6	17 31.6	4.4	58.3
18 00	180 08.3	N10 43.2	326 14.6	7.6	S17 36.0	4.2	58.3
01	195 08.4	44.1	340 41.2	7.6	17 40.2	4.1	58.3
02	210 08.6	45.0	355 07.8	7.5	17 44.3	4.0	58.3
03	225 08.7 ..	45.9	9 34.3	7.4	17 48.3	3.9	58.3
04	240 08.9	46.7	24 00.7	7.5	17 52.2	3.8	58.4
05	255 09.0	47.6	38 27.2	7.3	17 56.0	3.7	58.4
06	270 09.1	N10 48.5	52 53.5	7.4	S17 59.7	3.5	58.4
F 07	285 09.3	49.3	67 19.9	7.2	18 03.2	3.5	58.4
R 08	300 09.4	50.2	81 46.1	7.3	18 06.7	3.3	58.4
I 09	315 09.6 ..	51.1	96 12.4	7.2	18 10.0	3.3	58.4
D 10	330 09.7	52.0	110 38.6	7.2	18 13.3	3.1	58.5
A 11	345 09.9	52.8	125 04.8	7.1	18 16.4	3.0	58.5
Y 12	0 10.0	N10 53.7	139 30.9	7.1	S18 19.4	2.9	58.5
13	15 10.1	54.6	153 57.0	7.0	18 22.3	2.8	58.5
14	30 10.3	55.4	168 23.0	7.1	18 25.1	2.7	58.5
15	45 10.4 ..	56.3	182 49.1	7.0	18 27.8	2.5	58.5
16	60 10.5	57.2	197 15.1	6.9	18 30.3	2.5	58.5
17	75 10.7	58.1	211 41.0	6.9	18 32.8	2.3	58.6
18	90 10.8	N10 58.9	226 06.9	6.9	S18 35.1	2.2	58.6
19	105 11.0	10 59.8	240 32.8	6.9	18 37.3	2.1	58.6
20	120 11.1	11 00.7	254 58.7	6.8	18 39.4	1.9	58.6
21	135 11.2 ..	01.5	269 24.5	6.8	18 41.3	1.9	58.6
22	150 11.4	02.4	283 50.3	6.8	18 43.2	1.7	58.6
23	165 11.5	03.3	298 16.1	6.7	S18 44.9	1.7	58.6
	SD 16.0	d 0.9	SD 15.7		15.8		15.9

Twilight / Sunrise / Moonrise

Lat.	Naut.	Civil	Sunrise	Moonrise 16	17	18	19
°	h m	h m	h m	h m	h m	h m	h m
N 72	////	01 39	03 28	23 15	25 51	01 51	■■
N 70	////	02 21	03 47	22 36	24 23	00 23	01 57
68	////	02 49	04 01	22 10	23 44	25 04	01 04
66	01 25	03 10	04 13	21 50	23 16	24 32	00 32
64	02 03	03 27	04 22	21 34	22 56	24 08	00 08
62	02 29	03 40	04 31	21 20	22 39	23 49	24 47
60	02 48	03 51	04 38	21 09	22 25	23 34	24 32
N 58	03 04	04 01	04 44	21 00	22 13	23 21	24 19
56	03 17	04 09	04 50	20 51	22 03	23 09	24 07
54	03 28	04 17	04 55	20 44	21 54	22 59	23 57
52	03 38	04 23	04 59	20 37	21 46	22 51	23 49
50	03 47	04 29	05 03	20 31	21 39	22 43	23 41
45	04 04	04 41	05 12	20 18	21 23	22 26	23 24
N 40	04 18	04 51	05 20	20 07	21 10	22 12	23 10
35	04 29	05 00	05 26	19 58	21 00	22 00	22 58
30	04 38	05 07	05 31	19 50	20 50	21 50	22 48
20	04 52	05 18	05 41	19 36	20 34	21 33	22 30
N 10	05 02	05 27	05 49	19 24	20 21	21 17	22 15
0	05 11	05 35	05 56	19 13	20 07	21 03	22 00
S 10	05 18	05 42	06 04	19 02	19 54	20 49	21 46
20	05 23	05 49	06 11	18 50	19 40	20 34	21 31
30	05 28	05 56	06 20	18 37	19 24	20 16	21 13
35	05 30	06 00	06 25	18 29	19 15	20 06	21 03
40	05 32	06 03	06 31	18 20	19 05	19 55	20 51
45	05 33	06 07	06 37	18 10	18 52	19 41	20 38
S 50	05 35	06 12	06 45	17 58	18 38	19 25	20 21
52	05 35	06 14	06 49	17 52	18 31	19 17	20 13
54	05 35	06 16	06 53	17 46	18 23	19 09	20 04
56	05 36	06 19	06 57	17 39	18 14	18 59	19 54
58	05 36	06 21	07 02	17 31	18 05	18 48	19 43
S 60	05 36	06 24	07 07	17 22	17 54	18 36	19 30

Sunset / Twilight / Moonset

Lat.	Sunset	Civil	Naut.	Moonset 16	17	18	19
°	h m	h m	h m	h m	h m	h m	h m
N 72	20 35	22 31	////	03 38	03 24	02 42	■■
N 70	20 16	21 44	////	04 02	04 04	04 11	04 35
68	20 01	21 14	////	04 20	04 31	04 50	05 27
66	19 49	20 52	22 43	04 35	04 52	05 18	06 00
64	19 39	20 35	22 01	04 47	05 08	05 39	06 24
62	19 30	20 22	21 34	04 58	05 22	05 56	06 42
60	19 23	20 10	21 14	05 07	05 34	06 10	06 58
N 58	19 16	20 00	20 57	05 14	05 44	06 22	07 11
56	19 11	19 51	20 44	05 21	05 53	06 33	07 23
54	19 05	19 44	20 33	05 28	06 01	06 42	07 33
52	19 01	19 37	20 23	05 33	06 08	06 51	07 42
50	18 57	19 31	20 14	05 38	06 15	06 58	07 50
45	18 48	19 19	19 56	05 49	06 29	07 14	08 07
N 40	18 40	19 09	19 42	05 58	06 40	07 27	08 21
35	18 34	19 00	19 31	06 06	06 50	07 38	08 32
30	18 28	18 53	19 22	06 13	06 58	07 48	08 43
20	18 19	18 41	19 08	06 25	07 13	08 05	09 01
N 10	18 11	18 32	18 57	06 36	07 26	08 20	09 16
0	18 03	18 24	18 48	06 46	07 38	08 34	09 30
S 10	17 55	18 17	18 41	06 56	07 51	08 47	09 45
20	17 47	18 10	18 36	07 06	08 04	09 02	10 00
30	17 39	18 03	18 31	07 18	08 19	09 19	10 18
35	17 33	17 59	18 29	07 25	08 27	09 29	10 28
40	17 28	17 55	18 27	07 34	08 37	09 40	10 40
45	17 21	17 51	18 25	07 43	08 49	09 53	10 54
S 50	17 13	17 46	18 24	07 54	09 03	10 09	11 10
52	17 10	17 44	18 23	08 00	09 10	10 17	11 18
54	17 06	17 42	18 23	08 05	09 17	10 25	11 27
56	17 01	17 39	18 22	08 12	09 25	10 35	11 37
58	16 56	17 37	18 22	08 19	09 34	10 45	11 48
S 60	16 51	17 34	18 22	08 27	09 45	10 58	12 01

SUN and MOON (daily data)

Day	SUN Eqn. of Time 00h	SUN Eqn. of Time 12h	SUN Mer. Pass.	MOON Mer. Pass. Upper	MOON Mer. Pass. Lower	Age	Phase
d	m s	m s	h m	h m	h m	d	%
16	00 05	00 12	12 00	00 34	12 59	17	98
17	00 19	00 26	12 00	01 26	13 53	18	95
18	00 33	00 40	11 59	02 20	14 48	19	88

UT	ARIES	VENUS −4.2		MARS −1.4		JUPITER −2.1		SATURN +0.2		STARS		
	GHA	GHA	Dec	GHA	Dec	GHA	Dec	GHA	Dec	Name	SHA	Dec
d h	° ′	° ′	° ′	° ′	° ′	° ′	° ′	° ′	° ′		° ′	° ′
19 00	207 01.2	221 19.1	S 6 42.3	12 16.1	S 4 00.5	102 31.1	N23 03.5	337 11.1	S15 45.9	Acamar	315 18.4	S40 15.1
01	222 03.7	236 18.9	41.4	27 19.4	00.2	117 33.2	03.5	352 13.7	45.9	Achernar	335 27.0	S57 09.9
02	237 06.1	251 18.7	40.5	42 22.8	4 00.0	132 35.4	03.4	7 16.3	45.8	Acrux	173 07.9	S63 10.9
03	252 08.6	266 18.6	. . 39.6	57 26.1	3 59.7	147 37.5	. . 03.4	22 19.0	. . 45.8	Adhara	255 12.2	S28 59.9
04	267 11.1	281 18.4	38.6	72 29.4	59.5	162 39.6	03.4	37 21.6	45.7	Aldebaran	290 49.0	N16 32.1
05	282 13.5	296 18.2	37.7	87 32.8	59.2	177 41.7	03.3	52 24.2	45.7			
06	297 16.0	311 18.0	S 6 36.8	102 36.1	S 3 59.0	192 43.9	N23 03.3	67 26.9	S15 45.7	Alioth	166 19.7	N55 52.9
07	312 18.5	326 17.9	35.9	117 39.4	58.7	207 46.0	03.3	82 29.5	45.6	Alkaid	152 58.0	N49 14.5
S 08	327 20.9	341 17.7	35.0	132 42.7	58.5	222 48.1	03.3	97 32.1	45.6	Al Na'ir	27 43.3	S46 53.2
A 09	342 23.4	356 17.5	. . 34.1	147 46.1	. . 58.2	237 50.2	. . 03.2	112 34.7	. . 45.5	Alnilam	275 46.0	S 1 11.9
T 10	357 25.9	11 17.4	33.2	162 49.4	58.0	252 52.4	03.2	127 37.4	45.5	Alphard	217 55.4	S 8 43.6
U 11	12 28.3	26 17.2	32.3	177 52.7	57.7	267 54.5	03.2	142 40.0	45.4			
R 12	27 30.8	41 17.0	S 6 31.4	192 56.0	S 3 57.5	282 56.6	N23 03.1	157 42.6	S15 45.4	Alphecca	126 10.2	N26 40.0
D 13	42 33.2	56 16.9	30.5	207 59.4	57.2	297 58.7	03.1	172 45.3	45.3	Alpheratz	357 43.2	N29 10.0
A 14	57 35.7	71 16.7	29.6	223 02.7	57.0	313 00.9	03.1	187 47.9	45.3	Altair	62 07.6	N 8 54.4
Y 15	72 38.2	86 16.5	. . 28.7	238 06.0	. . 56.7	328 03.0	. . 03.1	202 50.5	. . 45.2	Ankaa	353 15.6	S42 13.7
16	87 40.6	101 16.4	27.8	253 09.3	56.5	343 05.1	03.0	217 53.2	45.2	Antares	112 25.3	S26 27.7
17	102 43.1	116 16.2	26.9	268 12.7	56.2	358 07.2	03.0	232 55.8	45.2			
18	117 45.6	131 16.0	S 6 26.0	283 16.0	S 3 56.0	13 09.4	N23 03.0	247 58.4	S15 45.1	Arcturus	145 54.9	N19 06.4
19	132 48.0	146 15.8	25.0	298 19.3	55.7	28 11.5	02.9	263 01.0	45.1	Atria	107 26.1	S69 02.9
20	147 50.5	161 15.7	24.1	313 22.6	55.5	43 13.6	02.9	278 03.7	45.0	Avior	234 17.7	S59 33.8
21	162 53.0	176 15.5	. . 23.2	328 25.9	. . 55.2	58 15.7	. . 02.9	293 06.3	. . 45.0	Bellatrix	278 31.6	N 6 21.5
22	177 55.4	191 15.3	22.3	343 29.3	55.0	73 17.8	02.8	308 08.9	44.9	Betelgeuse	271 00.9	N 7 24.3
23	192 57.9	206 15.2	21.4	358 32.6	54.7	88 20.0	02.8	323 11.6	44.9			
20 00	208 00.4	221 15.0	S 6 20.5	13 35.9	S 3 54.5	103 22.1	N23 02.8	338 14.2	S15 44.8	Canopus	263 56.1	S52 42.7
01	223 02.8	236 14.8	19.6	28 39.2	54.2	118 24.2	02.8	353 16.8	44.8	Capella	280 33.9	N46 00.6
02	238 05.3	251 14.7	18.7	43 42.5	54.0	133 26.3	02.7	8 19.5	44.7	Deneb	49 31.1	N45 19.7
03	253 07.7	266 14.5	. . 17.7	58 45.9	. . 53.7	148 28.5	. . 02.7	23 22.1	. . 44.7	Denebola	182 32.8	N14 29.4
04	268 10.2	281 14.3	16.8	73 49.2	53.5	163 30.6	02.7	38 24.7	44.7	Diphda	348 55.6	S17 54.6
05	283 12.7	296 14.1	15.9	88 52.5	53.2	178 32.7	02.6	53 27.4	44.6			
06	298 15.1	311 14.0	S 6 15.0	103 55.8	S 3 53.0	193 34.8	N23 02.6	68 30.0	S15 44.6	Dubhe	193 50.6	N61 40.5
07	313 17.6	326 13.8	14.1	118 59.1	52.8	208 36.9	02.6	83 32.6	44.5	Elnath	278 12.1	N28 37.0
08	328 20.1	341 13.6	13.2	134 02.4	52.5	223 39.1	02.6	98 35.3	44.5	Eltanin	90 45.6	N51 29.1
S 09	343 22.5	356 13.5	. . 12.3	149 05.7	. . 52.3	238 41.2	. . 02.5	113 37.9	. . 44.4	Enif	33 46.7	N 9 56.4
U 10	358 25.0	11 13.3	11.3	164 09.1	52.0	253 43.3	02.5	128 40.5	44.4	Fomalhaut	15 23.6	S29 32.7
N 11	13 27.5	26 13.1	10.4	179 12.4	51.8	268 45.4	02.5	143 43.1	44.3			
D 12	28 29.9	41 13.0	S 6 09.5	194 15.7	S 3 51.5	283 47.5	N23 02.4	158 45.8	S15 44.3	Gacrux	171 59.6	S57 11.8
A 13	43 32.4	56 12.8	08.6	209 19.0	51.3	298 49.7	02.4	173 48.4	44.2	Gienah	175 51.4	S17 37.5
Y 14	58 34.9	71 12.6	07.7	224 22.3	51.0	313 51.8	02.4	188 51.0	44.2	Hadar	148 46.3	S60 26.5
15	73 37.3	86 12.4	. . 06.7	239 25.6	. . 50.8	328 53.9	. . 02.3	203 53.7	. . 44.2	Hamal	328 00.4	N23 31.6
16	88 39.8	101 12.3	05.8	254 28.9	50.6	343 56.0	02.3	218 56.3	44.1	Kaus Aust.	83 42.9	S34 22.4
17	103 42.2	116 12.1	04.9	269 32.2	50.3	358 58.1	02.3	233 58.9	44.1			
18	118 44.7	131 11.9	S 6 04.0	284 35.5	S 3 50.1	14 00.2	N23 02.3	249 01.6	S15 44.0	Kochab	137 19.0	N74 05.8
19	133 47.2	146 11.8	03.1	299 38.8	49.8	29 02.4	02.2	264 04.2	44.0	Markab	13 38.0	N15 16.9
20	148 49.6	161 11.6	02.1	314 42.1	49.6	44 04.5	02.2	279 06.8	43.9	Menkar	314 14.8	N 4 08.5
21	163 52.1	176 11.4	. . 01.2	329 45.5	. . 49.4	59 06.6	. . 02.2	294 09.5	. . 43.9	Menkent	148 06.5	S36 26.4
22	178 54.6	191 11.2	6 00.3	344 48.8	49.1	74 08.7	02.1	309 12.1	43.8	Miaplacidus	221 39.2	S69 47.0
23	193 57.0	206 11.1	5 59.4	359 52.1	48.9	89 10.8	02.1	324 14.7	43.8			
21 00	208 59.5	221 10.9	S 5 58.5	14 55.4	S 3 48.6	104 12.9	N23 02.1	339 17.4	S15 43.7	Mirfak	308 39.9	N49 54.6
01	224 02.0	236 10.7	57.5	29 58.7	48.4	119 15.1	02.0	354 20.0	43.7	Nunki	75 57.5	S26 16.5
02	239 04.4	251 10.6	56.6	45 02.0	48.2	134 17.2	02.0	9 22.6	43.6	Peacock	53 18.4	S56 40.9
03	254 06.9	266 10.4	. . 55.7	60 05.3	. . 47.9	149 19.3	. . 02.0	24 25.3	. . 43.6	Pollux	243 27.1	N27 59.3
04	269 09.3	281 10.2	54.8	75 08.6	47.7	164 21.4	02.0	39 27.9	43.6	Procyon	244 59.2	N 5 11.0
05	284 11.8	296 10.0	53.8	90 11.9	47.4	179 23.5	01.9	54 30.5	43.5			
06	299 14.3	311 09.9	S 5 52.9	105 15.2	S 3 47.2	194 25.6	N23 01.9	69 33.2	S15 43.5	Rasalhague	96 05.7	N12 33.0
07	314 16.7	326 09.7	52.0	120 18.5	47.0	209 27.7	01.9	84 35.8	43.4	Regulus	207 42.8	N11 53.6
08	329 19.2	341 09.5	51.1	135 21.8	46.7	224 29.9	01.8	99 38.4	43.4	Rigel	281 11.7	S 8 11.4
M 09	344 21.7	356 09.4	. . 50.1	150 25.1	. . 46.5	239 32.0	. . 01.8	114 41.1	. . 43.3	Rigil Kent.	139 50.2	S60 53.6
O 10	359 24.1	11 09.2	49.2	165 28.4	46.2	254 34.1	01.8	129 43.7	43.3	Sabik	102 11.6	S15 44.4
N 11	14 26.6	26 09.0	48.3	180 31.7	46.0	269 36.2	01.7	144 46.3	43.2			
D 12	29 29.1	41 08.8	S 5 47.3	195 35.0	S 3 45.8	284 38.3	N23 01.7	159 49.0	S15 43.2	Schedar	349 40.3	N56 36.8
A 13	44 31.5	56 08.7	46.4	210 38.3	45.5	299 40.4	01.7	174 51.6	43.1	Shaula	96 20.9	S37 06.6
Y 14	59 34.0	71 08.5	45.5	225 41.5	45.3	314 42.5	01.6	189 54.2	43.1	Sirius	258 33.3	S16 44.5
15	74 36.5	86 08.3	. . 44.6	240 44.8	. . 45.1	329 44.6	. . 01.6	204 56.9	. . 43.0	Spica	158 30.3	S11 14.3
16	89 38.9	101 08.2	43.6	255 48.1	44.8	344 46.8	01.6	219 59.5	43.0	Suhail	222 51.9	S43 29.9
17	104 41.4	116 08.0	42.7	270 51.4	44.6	359 48.9	01.6	235 02.1	43.0			
18	119 43.8	131 07.8	S 5 41.8	285 54.7	S 3 44.4	14 51.0	N23 01.5	250 04.8	S15 42.9	Vega	80 38.4	N38 47.7
19	134 46.3	146 07.6	40.8	300 58.0	44.1	29 53.1	01.5	265 07.4	42.9	Zuben'ubi	137 04.4	S16 06.1
20	149 48.8	161 07.5	39.9	316 01.3	43.9	44 55.2	01.5	280 10.0	42.8		SHA	Mer.Pass.
21	164 51.2	176 07.3	. . 39.0	331 04.6	. . 43.7	59 57.3	. . 01.4	295 12.7	. . 42.8		° ′	h m
22	179 53.7	191 07.1	38.0	346 07.9	43.4	74 59.4	01.4	310 15.3	42.7	Venus	13 14.6	9 15
23	194 56.2	206 07.0	37.1	1 11.2	43.2	90 01.5	01.4	325 17.9	42.7	Mars	165 35.6	23 01
	h m									Jupiter	255 21.7	17 04
Mer.Pass. 10 06.3		v −0.2	d 0.9	v 3.3	d 0.2	v 2.1	d 0.0	v 2.6	d 0.0	Saturn	130 13.8	1 27

UT	SUN GHA	Dec	MOON GHA	v	Dec	d	HP
d h	° ′	° ′	° ′	′	° ′	′	′
19 00	180 11.7	N11 04.1	312 41.8	6.8	S18 46.6	1.5	58.7
01	195 11.8	05.0	327 07.6	6.7	18 48.1	1.3	58.7
02	210 11.9	05.9	341 33.3	6.6	18 49.4	1.3	58.7
03	225 12.1 ..	06.7	355 58.9	6.7	18 50.7	1.1	58.7
04	240 12.2	07.6	10 24.6	6.6	18 51.8	1.1	58.7
05	255 12.3	08.5	24 50.2	6.6	18 52.9	0.9	58.7
06	270 12.5	N11 09.3	39 15.8	6.6	S18 53.8	0.7	58.7
S 07	285 12.6	10.2	53 41.4	6.6	18 54.5	0.7	58.7
A 08	300 12.7	11.1	68 07.0	6.6	18 55.2	0.5	58.8
T 09	315 12.9 ..	11.9	82 32.6	6.5	18 55.7	0.4	58.8
U 10	330 13.0	12.8	96 58.1	6.5	18 56.1	0.3	58.8
R 11	345 13.2	13.6	111 23.6	6.5	18 56.4	0.2	58.8
D 12	0 13.3	N11 14.5	125 49.1	6.5	S18 56.6	0.1	58.8
A 13	15 13.4	15.4	140 14.6	6.5	18 56.7	0.1	58.8
Y 14	30 13.6	16.2	154 40.1	6.5	18 56.6	0.2	58.8
15	45 13.7 ..	17.1	169 05.6	6.5	18 56.4	0.3	58.8
16	60 13.8	18.0	183 31.1	6.4	18 56.1	0.5	58.9
17	75 14.0	18.8	197 56.5	6.5	18 55.6	0.5	58.9
18	90 14.1	N11 19.7	212 22.0	6.4	S18 55.1	0.7	58.9
19	105 14.2	20.5	226 47.4	6.5	18 54.4	0.8	58.9
20	120 14.4	21.4	241 12.9	6.4	18 53.6	1.0	58.9
21	135 14.5 ..	22.3	255 38.3	6.4	18 52.6	1.0	58.9
22	150 14.6	23.1	270 03.7	6.4	18 51.6	1.2	58.9
23	165 14.8	24.0	284 29.1	6.5	18 50.4	1.3	58.9
20 00	180 14.9	N11 24.8	298 54.6	6.4	S18 49.1	1.4	58.9
01	195 15.0	25.7	313 20.0	6.4	18 47.7	1.5	58.9
02	210 15.2	26.6	327 45.4	6.5	18 46.2	1.7	59.0
03	225 15.3 ..	27.4	342 10.9	6.4	18 44.5	1.8	59.0
04	240 15.4	28.3	356 36.3	6.4	18 42.7	1.9	59.0
05	255 15.6	29.1	11 01.7	6.5	18 40.8	2.0	59.0
06	270 15.7	N11 30.0	25 27.2	6.4	S18 38.8	2.2	59.0
S 07	285 15.8	30.8	39 52.6	6.5	18 36.6	2.2	59.0
U 08	300 16.0	31.7	54 18.1	6.4	18 34.4	2.4	59.0
N 09	315 16.1 ..	32.6	68 43.5	6.5	18 32.0	2.5	59.0
D 10	330 16.2	33.4	83 09.0	6.5	18 29.5	2.7	59.0
A 11	345 16.3	34.3	97 34.5	6.5	18 26.8	2.7	59.0
Y 12	0 16.5	N11 35.1	112 00.0	6.5	S18 24.1	2.9	59.0
13	15 16.6	36.0	126 25.5	6.5	18 21.2	3.0	59.1
14	30 16.7	36.8	140 51.0	6.5	18 18.2	3.1	59.1
15	45 16.9 ..	37.7	155 16.5	6.6	18 15.1	3.2	59.1
16	60 17.0	38.5	169 42.1	6.5	18 11.9	3.4	59.1
17	75 17.1	39.4	184 07.6	6.6	18 08.5	3.4	59.1
18	90 17.3	N11 40.3	198 33.2	6.6	S18 05.1	3.6	59.1
19	105 17.4	41.1	212 58.8	6.6	18 01.5	3.7	59.1
20	120 17.5	42.0	227 24.4	6.6	17 57.8	3.8	59.1
21	135 17.6 ..	42.9	241 50.0	6.7	17 54.0	4.0	59.1
22	150 17.8	43.7	256 15.7	6.7	17 50.0	4.0	59.1
23	165 17.9	44.5	270 41.4	6.7	17 46.0	4.2	59.1
21 00	180 18.0	N11 45.4	285 07.1	6.7	S17 41.8	4.2	59.1
01	195 18.2	46.2	299 32.8	6.7	17 37.6	4.4	59.1
02	210 18.3	47.1	313 58.5	6.8	17 33.2	4.5	59.2
03	225 18.4 ..	47.9	328 24.3	6.7	17 28.7	4.7	59.2
04	240 18.5	48.8	342 50.0	6.9	17 24.0	4.7	59.2
05	255 18.7	49.6	357 15.9	6.8	17 19.3	4.8	59.2
06	270 18.8	N11 50.5	11 41.7	6.9	S17 14.5	5.0	59.2
M 07	285 18.9	51.3	26 07.6	6.8	17 09.5	5.1	59.2
O 08	300 19.1	52.2	40 33.4	7.0	17 04.4	5.1	59.2
N 09	315 19.2 ..	53.0	54 59.4	6.9	16 59.3	5.3	59.2
D 10	330 19.3	53.9	69 25.3	7.0	16 54.0	5.4	59.2
A 11	345 19.4	54.7	83 51.3	7.0	16 48.6	5.5	59.2
Y 12	0 19.6	N11 55.6	98 17.3	7.0	S16 43.1	5.6	59.2
13	15 19.7	56.4	112 43.3	7.1	16 37.5	5.7	59.2
14	30 19.8	57.3	127 09.4	7.1	16 31.8	5.8	59.2
15	45 19.9 ..	58.1	141 35.5	7.1	16 26.0	6.0	59.2
16	60 20.1	58.9	156 01.6	7.2	16 20.0	6.0	59.2
17	75 20.2	11 59.8	170 27.8	7.2	16 14.0	6.1	59.2
18	90 20.3	N12 00.6	184 54.0	7.2	S16 07.9	6.3	59.2
19	105 20.4	01.5	199 20.2	7.2	16 01.6	6.3	59.2
20	120 20.6	02.3	213 46.4	7.3	15 55.3	6.4	59.2
21	135 20.7 ..	03.2	228 12.7	7.4	15 48.9	6.6	59.2
22	150 20.8	04.0	242 39.1	7.3	15 42.3	6.6	59.3
23	165 20.9	04.9	257 05.4	7.4	S15 35.7	6.7	59.3
	SD 15.9	d 0.9	SD 16.0		16.1		16.1

Lat.	Twilight Naut.	Civil	Sunrise	Moonrise 19	20	21	22
°	h m	h m	h m	h m	h m	h m	h m
N 72	////	00 58	03 10	■■■	■■■	04 15	03 49
N 70	////	01 58	03 31	01 57	02 51	03 10	03 15
68	////	02 32	03 48	01 04	02 01	02 33	02 51
66	00 50	02 56	04 01	00 32	01 29	02 08	02 32
64	01 43	03 14	04 12	00 08	01 06	01 47	02 16
62	02 14	03 29	04 21	24 47	00 47	01 31	02 03
60	02 36	03 41	04 29	24 32	00 32	01 17	01 52
N 58	02 53	03 52	04 36	24 19	00 19	01 06	01 43
56	03 08	04 01	04 42	24 07	00 07	00 55	01 34
54	03 20	04 09	04 48	23 57	24 46	00 46	01 27
52	03 30	04 16	04 53	23 49	24 38	00 38	01 20
50	03 39	04 23	04 57	23 41	24 31	00 31	01 14
45	03 58	04 36	05 07	23 24	24 15	00 15	01 01
N 40	04 13	04 47	05 15	23 10	24 03	00 03	00 50
35	04 24	04 56	05 22	22 58	23 52	24 41	00 41
30	04 34	05 03	05 28	22 48	23 42	24 32	00 32
20	04 49	05 16	05 38	22 30	23 26	24 18	00 18
N 10	05 01	05 26	05 47	22 15	23 11	24 06	00 06
0	05 10	05 34	05 56	22 00	22 58	23 54	24 49
S 10	05 18	05 42	06 04	21 46	22 44	23 43	24 40
20	05 24	05 50	06 12	21 31	22 30	23 30	24 31
30	05 30	05 58	06 22	21 13	22 13	23 16	24 19
35	05 32	06 02	06 28	21 03	22 04	23 08	24 13
40	05 35	06 06	06 34	20 51	21 53	22 58	24 06
45	05 37	06 11	06 41	20 38	21 40	22 47	23 57
S 50	05 39	06 17	06 50	20 21	21 24	22 34	23 47
52	05 40	06 19	06 54	20 13	21 17	22 27	23 42
54	05 40	06 22	06 58	20 04	21 09	22 20	23 37
56	05 41	06 24	07 03	19 54	20 59	22 13	23 31
58	05 42	06 28	07 08	19 43	20 49	22 04	23 24
S 60	05 42	06 31	07 14	19 30	20 37	21 54	23 17

Lat.	Sunset	Twilight Civil	Naut.	Moonset 19	20	21	22
°	h m	h m	h m	h m	h m	h m	h m
N 72	20 52	23 20	////	■■■	■■■	06 17	08 40
N 70	20 30	22 07	////	04 35	05 40	07 21	09 13
68	20 13	21 31	////	05 27	06 30	07 57	09 36
66	19 59	21 06	23 25	06 00	07 02	08 22	09 55
64	19 48	20 47	22 21	06 24	07 25	08 42	10 09
62	19 38	20 31	21 49	06 42	07 44	08 58	10 22
60	19 30	20 18	21 25	06 58	07 59	09 11	10 32
N 58	19 23	20 08	21 07	07 11	08 12	09 23	10 41
56	19 17	19 58	20 52	07 23	08 23	09 33	10 49
54	19 11	19 50	20 40	07 33	08 33	09 41	10 56
52	19 06	19 43	20 29	07 42	08 42	09 49	11 02
50	19 01	19 36	20 20	07 50	08 49	09 56	11 08
45	18 52	19 23	20 01	08 07	09 06	10 11	11 20
N 40	18 43	19 12	19 46	08 21	09 20	10 23	11 30
35	18 36	19 03	19 34	08 32	09 31	10 34	11 39
30	18 30	18 55	19 24	08 43	09 41	10 43	11 46
20	18 20	18 42	19 09	09 01	09 59	10 59	11 59
N 10	18 11	18 32	18 57	09 16	10 14	11 12	12 10
0	18 02	18 23	18 48	09 30	10 28	11 25	12 21
S 10	17 54	18 15	18 40	09 45	10 42	11 38	12 31
20	17 45	18 08	18 34	10 00	10 57	11 51	12 42
30	17 35	18 00	18 28	10 18	11 14	12 06	12 55
35	17 30	17 56	18 25	10 28	11 24	12 15	13 02
40	17 23	17 51	18 23	10 40	11 35	12 25	13 10
45	17 16	17 46	18 20	10 54	11 48	12 37	13 20
S 50	17 07	17 40	18 18	11 10	12 05	12 51	13 31
52	17 03	17 38	18 17	11 18	12 12	12 58	13 36
54	16 59	17 35	18 16	11 27	12 20	13 05	13 42
56	16 54	17 32	18 16	11 37	12 30	13 13	13 49
58	16 49	17 29	18 15	11 48	12 41	13 23	13 56
S 60	16 42	17 26	18 14	12 01	12 53	13 33	14 04

Day	SUN Eqn. of Time 00ʰ	12ʰ	Mer. Pass.	MOON Mer. Pass. Upper	Lower	Age	Phase
d	m s	m s	h m	h m	h m	d %	
19	00 46	00 53	11 59	03 17	15 45	20 80	
20	00 59	01 06	11 59	04 14	16 43	21 70	
21	01 12	01 18	11 59	05 11	17 40	22 60	

UT	ARIES	VENUS −4.2		MARS −1.3		JUPITER −2.1		SATURN +0.1		STARS		
	GHA	GHA	Dec	GHA	Dec	GHA	Dec	GHA	Dec	Name	SHA	Dec
d h	° ′	° ′	° ′	° ′	° ′	° ′	° ′	° ′	° ′		° ′	° ′
22 00	209 58.6	221 06.8	S 5 36.2	16 14.4	S 3 43.0	105 03.6	N23 01.3	340 20.6	S15 42.6	Acamar	315 18.4	S40 15.1
01	225 01.1	236 06.6	35.2	31 17.7	42.7	120 05.8	01.3	355 23.2	42.6	Achernar	335 27.0	S57 09.9
02	240 03.6	251 06.4	34.3	46 21.0	42.5	135 07.9	01.3	10 25.9	42.5	Acrux	173 07.9	S63 10.9
03	255 06.0	266 06.3 . .	33.4	61 24.3 . .	42.3	150 10.0 . .	01.2	25 28.5 . .	42.5	Adhara	255 12.2	S28 59.9
04	270 08.5	281 06.1	32.4	76 27.6	42.0	165 12.1	01.2	40 31.1	42.4	Aldebaran	290 49.0	N16 32.1
05	285 11.0	296 05.9	31.5	91 30.9	41.8	180 14.2	01.2	55 33.8	42.4			
06	300 13.4	311 05.8	S 5 30.6	106 34.2	S 3 41.6	195 16.3	N23 01.1	70 36.4	S15 42.4	Alioth	166 19.7	N55 53.0
07	315 15.9	326 05.6	29.6	121 37.4	41.4	210 18.4	01.1	85 39.0	42.3	Alkaid	152 58.0	N49 14.5
T 08	330 18.3	341 05.4	28.7	136 40.7	41.1	225 20.5	01.1	100 41.7	42.3	Al Na'ir	27 43.3	S46 53.2
U 09	345 20.8	356 05.2 . .	27.7	151 44.0 . .	40.9	240 22.6 . .	01.1	115 44.3 . .	42.2	Alnilam	275 46.0	S 1 11.9
E 10	0 23.3	11 05.1	26.8	166 47.3	40.7	255 24.7	01.0	130 46.9	42.2	Alphard	217 55.4	S 8 43.6
S 11	15 25.7	26 04.9	25.9	181 50.6	40.4	270 26.8	01.0	145 49.6	42.1			
D 12	30 28.2	41 04.7	S 5 24.9	196 53.8	S 3 40.2	285 28.9	N23 01.0	160 52.2	S15 42.1	Alphecca	126 10.2	N26 40.0
A 13	45 30.7	56 04.6	24.0	211 57.1	40.0	300 31.1	00.9	175 54.8	42.0	Alpheratz	357 43.2	N29 10.0
Y 14	60 33.1	71 04.4	23.0	227 00.4	39.8	315 33.2	00.9	190 57.5	42.0	Altair	62 07.6	N 8 54.4
15	75 35.6	86 04.2 . .	22.1	242 03.7 . .	39.5	330 35.3 . .	00.9	206 00.1 . .	41.9	Ankaa	353 15.6	S42 13.6
16	90 38.1	101 04.0	21.2	257 06.9	39.3	345 37.4	00.8	221 02.7	41.9	Antares	112 25.2	S26 27.7
17	105 40.5	116 03.9	20.2	272 10.2	39.1	0 39.5	00.8	236 05.4	41.8			
18	120 43.0	131 03.7	S 5 19.3	287 13.5	S 3 38.9	15 41.6	N23 00.8	251 08.0	S15 41.8	Arcturus	145 54.9	N19 06.4
19	135 45.4	146 03.5	18.3	302 16.8	38.6	30 43.7	00.7	266 10.7	41.7	Atria	107 26.1	S69 02.9
20	150 47.9	161 03.3	17.4	317 20.0	38.4	45 45.8	00.7	281 13.3	41.7	Avior	234 17.7	S59 33.8
21	165 50.4	176 03.2 . .	16.5	332 23.3 . .	38.2	60 47.9 . .	00.7	296 15.9 . .	41.7	Bellatrix	278 31.6	N 6 21.5
22	180 52.8	191 03.0	15.5	347 26.6	38.0	75 50.0	00.6	311 18.6	41.6	Betelgeuse	271 00.9	N 7 24.3
23	195 55.3	206 02.8	14.6	2 29.8	37.7	90 52.1	00.6	326 21.2	41.6			
23 00	210 57.8	221 02.7	S 5 13.6	17 33.1	S 3 37.5	105 54.2	N23 00.6	341 23.8	S15 41.5	Canopus	263 56.1	S52 42.7
01	226 00.2	236 02.5	12.7	32 36.4	37.3	120 56.3	00.5	356 26.5	41.5	Capella	280 33.9	N46 00.6
02	241 02.7	251 02.3	11.7	47 39.6	37.1	135 58.4	00.5	11 29.1	41.4	Deneb	49 31.1	N45 19.7
03	256 05.2	266 02.1 . .	10.8	62 42.9 . .	36.8	151 00.5 . .	00.5	26 31.7 . .	41.4	Denebola	182 32.8	N14 29.4
04	271 07.6	281 02.0	09.8	77 46.2	36.6	166 02.6	00.4	41 34.4	41.3	Diphda	348 55.6	S17 54.5
05	286 10.1	296 01.8	08.9	92 49.4	36.4	181 04.7	00.4	56 37.0	41.3			
06	301 12.6	311 01.6	S 5 08.0	107 52.7	S 3 36.2	196 06.8	N23 00.4	71 39.7	S15 41.2	Dubhe	193 50.7	N61 40.5
W 07	316 15.0	326 01.4	07.0	122 56.0	36.0	211 08.9	00.3	86 42.3	41.2	Elnath	278 12.1	N28 37.0
E 08	331 17.5	341 01.3	06.1	137 59.2	35.7	226 11.0	00.3	101 44.9	41.1	Eltanin	90 45.6	N51 29.1
D 09	346 19.9	356 01.1 . .	05.1	153 02.5 . .	35.5	241 13.1 . .	00.3	116 47.6 . .	41.1	Enif	33 46.7	N 9 56.4
N 10	1 22.4	11 00.9	04.2	168 05.8	35.3	256 15.2	00.3	131 50.2	41.0	Fomalhaut	15 23.6	S29 32.7
E 11	16 24.9	26 00.7	03.2	183 09.0	35.1	271 17.3	00.2	146 52.8	41.0			
S 12	31 27.3	41 00.6	S 5 02.3	198 12.3	S 3 34.9	286 19.4	N23 00.2	161 55.5	S15 41.0	Gacrux	171 59.6	S57 11.8
D 13	46 29.8	56 00.4	01.3	213 15.5	34.6	301 21.5	00.2	176 58.1	40.9	Gienah	175 51.4	S17 37.5
A 14	61 32.3	71 00.2	5 00.4	228 18.8	34.4	316 23.7	00.1	192 00.8	40.9	Hadar	148 46.3	S60 26.5
Y 15	76 34.7	86 00.1	4 59.4	243 22.0 . .	34.2	331 25.8 . .	00.1	207 03.4 . .	40.8	Hamal	328 00.4	N23 31.6
16	91 37.2	100 59.9	58.5	258 25.3	34.0	346 27.9	00.1	222 06.0	40.8	Kaus Aust.	83 42.9	S34 22.4
17	106 39.7	115 59.7	57.5	273 28.6	33.8	1 30.0	00.0	237 08.7	40.7			
18	121 42.1	130 59.5	S 4 56.6	288 31.8	S 3 33.5	16 32.1	N23 00.0	252 11.3	S15 40.7	Kochab	137 19.0	N74 05.8
19	136 44.6	145 59.4	55.6	303 35.1	33.3	31 34.2	23 00.0	267 13.9	40.6	Markab	13 38.0	N15 16.9
20	151 47.1	160 59.2	54.7	318 38.3	33.1	46 36.3	22 59.9	282 16.6	40.6	Menkar	314 14.8	N 4 08.5
21	166 49.5	175 59.0 . .	53.7	333 41.6 . .	32.9	61 38.4 . .	59.9	297 19.2 . .	40.5	Menkent	148 06.4	S36 26.5
22	181 52.0	190 58.8	52.8	348 44.8	32.7	76 40.4	59.9	312 21.9	40.5	Miaplacidus	221 39.2	S69 47.0
23	196 54.4	205 58.7	51.8	3 48.1	32.5	91 42.5	59.8	327 24.5	40.4			
24 00	211 56.9	220 58.5	S 4 50.9	18 51.3	S 3 32.3	106 44.6	N22 59.8	342 27.1	S15 40.4	Mirfak	308 39.9	N49 54.6
01	226 59.4	235 58.3	49.9	33 54.6	32.0	121 46.7	59.8	357 29.8	40.3	Nunki	75 57.5	S26 16.5
02	242 01.8	250 58.1	48.9	48 57.8	31.8	136 48.8	59.7	12 32.4	40.3	Peacock	53 18.4	S56 40.9
03	257 04.3	265 58.0 . .	48.0	64 01.1 . .	31.6	151 50.9 . .	59.7	27 35.1 . .	40.2	Pollux	243 27.1	N27 59.3
04	272 06.8	280 57.8	47.0	79 04.3	31.4	166 53.0	59.7	42 37.7	40.2	Procyon	244 59.2	N 5 11.0
05	287 09.2	295 57.6	46.1	94 07.6	31.2	181 55.1	59.6	57 40.3	40.2			
06	302 11.7	310 57.4	S 4 45.1	109 10.8	S 3 31.0	196 57.2	N22 59.6	72 43.0	S15 40.1	Rasalhague	96 05.7	N12 33.0
07	317 14.2	325 57.3	44.2	124 14.0	30.8	211 59.3	59.6	87 45.6	40.1	Regulus	207 42.8	N11 53.6
T 08	332 16.6	340 57.1	43.2	139 17.3	30.6	227 01.4	59.5	102 48.2	40.0	Rigel	281 11.7	S 8 11.4
H 09	347 19.1	355 56.9 . .	42.3	154 20.5 . .	30.3	242 03.5 . .	59.5	117 50.9 . .	40.0	Rigil Kent.	139 50.2	S60 53.6
U 10	2 21.5	10 56.8	41.3	169 23.8	30.1	257 05.6	59.5	132 53.5	39.9	Sabik	102 11.6	S15 44.4
R 11	17 24.0	25 56.6	40.3	184 27.0	29.9	272 07.7	59.4	147 56.2	39.9			
S 12	32 26.5	40 56.4	S 4 39.4	199 30.3	S 3 29.7	287 09.8	N22 59.4	162 58.8	S15 39.8	Schedar	349 40.3	N56 36.8
D 13	47 28.9	55 56.2	38.4	214 33.5	29.5	302 11.9	59.4	178 01.4	39.8	Shaula	96 20.9	S37 06.6
A 14	62 31.4	70 56.1	37.5	229 36.7	29.3	317 14.0	59.3	193 04.1	39.7	Sirius	258 33.5	S16 44.5
Y 15	77 33.9	85 55.9 . .	36.5	244 40.0 . .	29.1	332 16.1 . .	59.3	208 06.7 . .	39.7	Spica	158 30.3	S11 14.3
16	92 36.3	100 55.7	35.5	259 43.2	28.9	347 18.2	59.3	223 09.4	39.6	Suhail	222 51.9	S43 29.9
17	107 38.8	115 55.5	34.6	274 46.4	28.7	2 20.3	59.2	238 12.0	39.6			
18	122 41.3	130 55.4	S 4 33.6	289 49.7	S 3 28.5	17 22.4	N22 59.2	253 14.6	S15 39.5	Vega	80 38.4	N38 47.7
19	137 43.7	145 55.2	32.7	304 52.9	28.2	32 24.5	59.2	268 17.3	39.5	Zuben'ubi	137 04.4	S16 06.1
20	152 46.2	160 55.0	31.7	319 56.1	28.0	47 26.6	59.1	283 19.9	39.4		SHA	Mer. Pass.
21	167 48.7	175 54.8 . .	30.7	334 59.4 . .	27.8	62 28.7 . .	59.1	298 22.6 . .	39.4		° ′	h m
22	182 51.1	190 54.7	29.8	350 02.6	27.6	77 30.8	59.1	313 25.2	39.4	Venus	10 04.9	9 16
23	197 53.6	205 54.5	28.8	5 05.8	27.4	92 32.9	59.0	328 27.8	39.3	Mars	166 35.3	22 45
	h m									Jupiter	254 56.4	16 54
Mer. Pass. 9 54.5		v −0.2 d 0.9		v 3.3 d 0.2		v 2.1 d 0.0		v 2.6 d 0.0		Saturn	130 26.1	1 14

UT	SUN GHA	SUN Dec	MOON GHA	v	MOON Dec	d	HP
d h	° ′	° ′	° ′	′	° ′	′	′
22 00	180 21.1	N12 05.7	271 31.8	7.5	S15 29.0	6.9	59.3
01	195 21.2	06.5	285 58.3	7.4	15 22.1	6.9	59.3
02	210 21.3	07.4	300 24.7	7.5	15 15.2	7.0	59.3
03	225 21.4 ..	08.2	314 51.2	7.6	15 08.2	7.2	59.3
04	240 21.5	09.1	329 17.8	7.6	15 01.0	7.2	59.3
05	255 21.7	09.9	343 44.4	7.6	14 53.8	7.3	59.3
06	270 21.8	N12 10.8	358 11.0	7.6	S14 46.5	7.4	59.3
07	285 21.9	11.6	12 37.6	7.7	14 39.1	7.5	59.3
08	300 22.0	12.4	27 04.3	7.8	14 31.6	7.6	59.3
09	315 22.2 ..	13.3	41 31.1	7.7	14 24.0	7.7	59.3
10	330 22.3	14.1	55 57.8	7.8	14 16.3	7.7	59.3
11	345 22.4	15.0	70 24.6	7.9	14 08.6	7.9	59.3
12	0 22.5	N12 15.8	84 51.5	7.9	S14 00.7	7.9	59.3
13	15 22.6	16.6	99 18.4	7.9	13 52.8	8.0	59.3
14	30 22.8	17.5	113 45.3	8.0	13 44.8	8.2	59.3
15	45 22.9 ..	18.3	128 12.3	8.0	13 36.6	8.2	59.3
16	60 23.0	19.1	142 39.3	8.0	13 28.4	8.2	59.3
17	75 23.1	20.0	157 06.3	8.1	13 20.2	8.4	59.3
18	90 23.2	N12 20.8	171 33.4	8.1	S13 11.8	8.4	59.3
19	105 23.4	21.7	186 00.5	8.1	13 03.4	8.6	59.3
20	120 23.5	22.5	200 27.6	8.2	12 54.8	8.6	59.3
21	135 23.6 ..	23.3	214 54.8	8.3	12 46.2	8.6	59.3
22	150 23.7	24.2	229 22.1	8.2	12 37.6	8.8	59.3
23	165 23.8	25.0	243 49.3	8.4	12 28.8	8.8	59.3
23 00	180 24.0	N12 25.8	258 16.7	8.3	S12 20.0	8.9	59.3
01	195 24.1	26.7	272 44.0	8.4	12 11.1	9.0	59.3
02	210 24.2	27.5	287 11.4	8.4	12 02.1	9.1	59.3
03	225 24.3 ..	28.3	301 38.8	8.5	11 53.0	9.1	59.3
04	240 24.4	29.2	316 06.3	8.5	11 43.9	9.2	59.3
05	255 24.6	30.0	330 33.8	8.5	11 34.7	9.3	59.3
06	270 24.7	N12 30.8	345 01.3	8.6	S11 25.4	9.3	59.3
07	285 24.8	31.7	359 28.9	8.6	11 16.1	9.4	59.3
08	300 24.9	32.5	13 56.5	8.7	11 06.7	9.5	59.3
09	315 25.0 ..	33.3	28 24.2	8.7	10 57.2	9.5	59.3
10	330 25.1	34.2	42 51.9	8.7	10 47.7	9.6	59.3
11	345 25.3	35.0	57 19.6	8.8	10 38.1	9.7	59.3
12	0 25.4	N12 35.8	71 47.4	8.8	S10 28.4	9.7	59.3
13	15 25.5	36.7	86 15.2	8.8	10 18.7	9.8	59.3
14	30 25.6	37.5	100 43.0	8.9	10 08.9	9.9	59.3
15	45 25.7 ..	38.3	115 10.9	8.9	9 59.0	9.9	59.3
16	60 25.8	39.2	129 38.8	9.0	9 49.1	9.9	59.3
17	75 25.9	40.0	144 06.8	9.0	9 39.2	10.1	59.3
18	90 26.1	N12 40.8	158 34.8	9.0	S 9 29.1	10.1	59.3
19	105 26.2	41.6	173 02.8	9.0	9 19.0	10.1	59.3
20	120 26.3	42.5	187 30.8	9.1	9 08.9	10.2	59.3
21	135 26.4 ..	43.3	201 58.9	9.2	8 58.7	10.2	59.3
22	150 26.5	44.1	216 27.1	9.1	8 48.5	10.3	59.3
23	165 26.6	44.9	230 55.2	9.2	8 38.2	10.3	59.3
24 00	180 26.8	N12 45.8	245 23.4	9.2	S 8 27.9	10.4	59.3
01	195 26.9	46.6	259 51.6	9.3	8 17.5	10.5	59.3
02	210 27.0	47.4	274 19.9	9.3	8 07.0	10.5	59.3
03	225 27.1 ..	48.2	288 48.2	9.3	7 56.5	10.5	59.2
04	240 27.2	49.1	303 16.5	9.4	7 46.0	10.6	59.2
05	255 27.3	49.9	317 44.9	9.3	7 35.4	10.6	59.2
06	270 27.4	N12 50.7	332 13.2	9.5	S 7 24.8	10.6	59.2
07	285 27.5	51.5	346 41.7	9.4	7 14.2	10.7	59.2
08	300 27.7	52.4	1 10.1	9.5	7 03.5	10.8	59.2
09	315 27.8 ..	53.2	15 38.6	9.5	6 52.7	10.8	59.2
10	330 27.9	54.0	30 07.1	9.5	6 41.9	10.8	59.2
11	345 28.0	54.8	44 35.6	9.6	6 31.1	10.8	59.2
12	0 28.1	N12 55.7	59 04.2	9.6	S 6 20.3	10.9	59.2
13	15 28.2	56.5	73 32.8	9.6	6 09.4	10.9	59.2
14	30 28.3	57.3	88 01.4	9.6	5 58.5	11.0	59.2
15	45 28.4 ..	58.1	102 30.0	9.7	5 47.5	11.0	59.2
16	60 28.5	58.9	116 58.7	9.7	5 36.5	11.0	59.2
17	75 28.7	12 59.8	131 27.4	9.7	5 25.5	11.1	59.2
18	90 28.8	N13 00.6	145 56.1	9.8	S 5 14.4	11.0	59.2
19	105 28.9	01.4	160 24.9	9.8	5 03.4	11.1	59.2
20	120 29.0	02.2	174 53.7	9.8	4 52.3	11.2	59.2
21	135 29.1 ..	03.0	189 22.5	9.8	4 41.1	11.1	59.1
22	150 29.2	03.9	203 51.3	9.8	4 30.0	11.2	59.1
23	165 29.3	04.7	218 20.1	9.9	S 4 18.8	11.2	59.1
	SD 15.9	d 0.8	SD 16.2		16.2		16.1

Days of week (left margin): TUESDAY (22), WEDNESDAY (23), THURSDAY (24)

Twilight / Sunrise / Moonrise

Lat.	Naut.	Civil	Sunrise	22	23	24	25
°	h m	h m	h m	h m	h m	h m	h m
N 72	////	////	02 51	03 49	03 37	03 29	03 21
N 70	////	01 31	03 16	03 15	03 17	03 17	03 16
68	////	02 13	03 34	02 51	03 01	03 07	03 12
66	////	02 41	03 49	02 32	02 48	02 59	03 09
64	01 19	03 01	04 02	02 16	02 37	02 53	03 06
62	01 57	03 18	04 12	02 03	02 28	02 47	03 03
60	02 23	03 32	04 21	01 52	02 20	02 42	03 01
N 58	02 42	03 43	04 28	01 43	02 13	02 37	02 59
56	02 58	03 53	04 35	01 34	02 06	02 33	02 57
54	03 11	04 02	04 41	01 27	02 01	02 30	02 56
52	03 22	04 10	04 47	01 20	01 56	02 26	02 54
50	03 32	04 16	04 52	01 14	01 51	02 23	02 53
45	03 52	04 31	05 02	01 01	01 41	02 17	02 50
N 40	04 08	04 42	05 11	00 50	01 33	02 11	02 47
35	04 20	04 52	05 18	00 41	01 25	02 07	02 45
30	04 31	05 00	05 25	00 32	01 19	02 02	02 43
20	04 47	05 13	05 36	00 18	01 08	01 55	02 40
N 10	04 59	05 24	05 46	00 06	00 58	01 49	02 37
0	05 09	05 34	05 55	24 49	00 49	01 43	02 35
S 10	05 18	05 42	06 04	24 40	00 40	01 37	02 32
20	05 25	05 51	06 13	24 31	00 31	01 30	02 29
30	05 31	05 59	06 24	24 19	00 19	01 23	02 26
35	05 34	06 04	06 30	24 13	00 13	01 19	02 24
40	05 37	06 09	06 37	24 06	00 06	01 14	02 22
45	05 40	06 15	06 45	23 57	25 08	01 08	02 20
S 50	05 43	06 21	06 54	23 47	25 02	01 02	02 17
52	05 44	06 24	06 59	23 42	24 59	00 59	02 15
54	05 45	06 27	07 04	23 37	24 55	00 55	02 14
56	05 46	06 30	07 09	23 31	24 51	00 51	02 12
58	05 48	06 34	07 15	23 24	24 47	00 47	02 11
S 60	05 49	06 38	07 22	23 17	24 42	00 42	02 08

Sunset / Twilight / Moonset

Lat.	Sunset	Civil	Naut.	22	23	24	25
°	h m	h m	h m	h m	h m	h m	h m
N 72	21 10	////	////	08 40	10 46	12 45	14 40
N 70	20 45	22 35	////	09 13	11 05	12 55	14 43
68	20 25	21 49	////	09 36	11 19	13 02	14 44
66	20 10	21 20	////	09 55	11 31	13 09	14 46
64	19 57	20 58	22 45	10 09	11 41	13 14	14 47
62	19 47	20 41	22 04	10 22	11 49	13 19	14 48
60	19 38	20 27	21 38	10 32	11 57	13 23	14 49
N 58	19 30	20 15	21 17	10 41	12 03	13 26	14 50
56	19 23	20 05	21 01	10 49	12 09	13 29	14 50
54	19 17	19 56	20 48	10 56	12 13	13 32	14 51
52	19 11	19 48	20 36	11 02	12 18	13 35	14 52
50	19 06	19 41	20 26	11 08	12 22	13 37	14 52
45	18 55	19 27	20 05	11 20	12 31	13 42	14 53
N 40	18 46	19 15	19 50	11 30	12 38	13 46	14 54
35	18 39	19 05	19 37	11 39	12 44	13 50	14 55
30	18 32	18 57	19 27	11 46	12 50	13 53	14 56
20	18 21	18 43	19 10	11 59	12 59	13 58	14 57
N 10	18 11	18 32	18 58	12 10	13 07	14 03	14 58
0	18 02	18 23	18 47	12 21	13 15	14 08	14 59
S 10	17 53	18 14	18 39	12 31	13 22	14 12	15 00
20	17 43	18 06	18 32	12 42	13 30	14 16	15 01
30	17 32	17 57	18 25	12 55	13 40	14 22	15 02
35	17 26	17 52	18 22	13 02	13 45	14 25	15 03
40	17 19	17 47	18 19	13 10	13 51	14 28	15 03
45	17 11	17 41	18 16	13 20	13 57	14 32	15 04
S 50	17 02	17 35	18 13	13 31	14 06	14 36	15 05
52	16 57	17 32	18 12	13 36	14 09	14 38	15 05
54	16 52	17 29	18 10	13 42	14 13	14 41	15 06
56	16 47	17 26	18 09	13 49	14 18	14 43	15 06
58	16 41	17 22	18 08	13 56	14 23	14 46	15 07
S 60	16 34	17 18	18 07	14 04	14 29	14 49	15 08

SUN / MOON

Day	Eqn. of Time 00h	Eqn. of Time 12h	Mer. Pass.	Mer. Pass. Upper	Mer. Pass. Lower	Age	Phase
d	m s	m s	h m	h m	h m	d	%
22	01 24	01 30	11 59	06 08	18 35	23	48
23	01 36	01 41	11 58	07 02	19 29	24	37
24	01 47	01 52	11 58	07 55	20 21	25	26

UT (d h)	ARIES GHA	VENUS −4.2 GHA	Dec	MARS −1.3 GHA	Dec	JUPITER −2.0 GHA	Dec	SATURN +0.1 GHA	Dec	STARS Name	SHA	Dec
25 00	212 56.0	220 54.3	S 4 27.9	20 09.1	S 3 27.2	107 34.9	N22 59.0	343 30.5	S15 39.3	Acamar	315 18.4	S40 15.0
01	227 58.5	235 54.1	26.9	35 12.3	27.0	122 37.0	59.0	358 33.1	39.2	Achernar	335 27.0	S57 09.9
02	243 01.0	250 54.0	25.9	50 15.5	26.8	137 39.1	58.9	13 35.8	39.2	Acrux	173 07.9	S63 10.9
03	258 03.4	265 53.8	.. 25.0	65 18.7	.. 26.6	152 41.2	.. 58.9	28 38.4	.. 39.1	Adhara	255 12.2	S28 59.9
04	273 05.9	280 53.6	24.0	80 22.0	26.4	167 43.3	58.9	43 41.0	39.1	Aldebaran	290 49.0	N16 32.1
05	288 08.4	295 53.4	23.0	95 25.2	26.2	182 45.4	58.8	58 43.7	39.0			
06	303 10.8	310 53.3	S 4 22.1	110 28.4	S 3 26.0	197 47.5	N22 58.8	73 46.3	S15 39.0	Alioth	166 19.7	N55 53.0
07	318 13.3	325 53.1	21.1	125 31.6	25.8	212 49.6	58.8	88 49.0	38.9	Alkaid	152 58.0	N49 14.5
08	333 15.8	340 52.9	20.1	140 34.9	25.6	227 51.7	58.7	103 51.6	38.9	Al Na'ir	27 43.3	S46 53.2
F 09	348 18.2	355 52.7	.. 19.2	155 38.1	.. 25.4	242 53.8	.. 58.7	118 54.2	.. 38.8	Alnilam	275 46.0	S 1 11.9
R 10	3 20.7	10 52.6	18.2	170 41.3	25.2	257 55.9	58.7	133 56.9	38.8	Alphard	217 55.4	S 8 43.6
I 11	18 23.2	25 52.4	17.2	185 44.5	25.0	272 58.0	58.6	148 59.5	38.7			
D 12	33 25.6	40 52.2	S 4 16.3	200 47.7	S 3 24.8	288 00.0	N22 58.6	164 02.2	S15 38.7	Alphecca	126 10.2	N26 40.0
A 13	48 28.1	55 52.0	15.3	215 51.0	24.6	303 02.1	58.5	179 04.8	38.6	Alpheratz	357 43.2	N29 10.0
Y 14	63 30.5	70 51.9	14.3	230 54.2	24.4	318 04.2	58.5	194 07.4	38.6	Altair	62 07.6	N 8 54.4
15	78 33.0	85 51.7	.. 13.4	245 57.4	.. 24.2	333 06.3	.. 58.5	209 10.1	.. 38.5	Ankaa	353 15.5	S42 13.6
16	93 35.5	100 51.5	12.4	261 00.6	24.0	348 08.4	58.4	224 12.7	38.5	Antares	112 25.2	S26 27.7
17	108 37.9	115 51.3	11.4	276 03.8	23.8	3 10.5	58.4	239 15.4	38.5			
18	123 40.4	130 51.2	S 4 10.5	291 07.0	S 3 23.6	18 12.6	N22 58.4	254 18.0	S15 38.4	Arcturus	145 54.9	N19 06.4
19	138 42.9	145 51.0	09.5	306 10.2	23.4	33 14.7	58.3	269 20.6	38.4	Atria	107 26.0	S69 02.9
20	153 45.3	160 50.8	08.5	321 13.4	23.2	48 16.8	58.3	284 23.3	38.3	Avior	234 17.7	S59 33.8
21	168 47.8	175 50.6	.. 07.6	336 16.7	.. 23.0	63 18.8	.. 58.3	299 25.9	.. 38.3	Bellatrix	278 31.6	N 6 21.5
22	183 50.3	190 50.5	06.6	351 19.9	22.8	78 20.9	58.2	314 28.6	38.2	Betelgeuse	271 00.9	N 7 24.3
23	198 52.7	205 50.3	05.6	6 23.1	22.6	93 23.0	58.2	329 31.2	38.2			
26 00	213 55.2	220 50.1	S 4 04.6	21 26.3	S 3 22.4	108 25.1	N22 58.2	344 33.9	S15 38.1	Canopus	263 56.2	S52 42.7
01	228 57.6	235 49.9	03.7	36 29.5	22.2	123 27.2	58.1	359 36.5	38.1	Capella	280 33.9	N46 00.6
02	244 00.1	250 49.8	02.7	51 32.7	22.0	138 29.3	58.1	14 39.1	38.0	Deneb	49 31.1	N45 19.7
03	259 02.6	265 49.6	.. 01.7	66 35.9	.. 21.8	153 31.4	.. 58.1	29 41.8	.. 38.0	Denebola	182 32.8	N14 29.4
04	274 05.0	280 49.4	4 00.8	81 39.1	21.6	168 33.5	58.0	44 44.4	37.9	Diphda	348 55.6	S17 54.5
05	289 07.5	295 49.2	3 59.8	96 42.3	21.4	183 35.5	58.0	59 47.1	37.9			
06	304 10.0	310 49.1	S 3 58.8	111 45.5	S 3 21.2	198 37.6	N22 58.0	74 49.7	S15 37.8	Dubhe	193 50.7	N61 40.5
07	319 12.4	325 48.9	57.8	126 48.7	21.1	213 39.7	57.9	89 52.3	37.8	Elnath	278 12.1	N28 37.0
S 08	334 14.9	340 48.7	56.9	141 51.9	20.9	228 41.8	57.9	104 55.0	37.7	Eltanin	90 45.5	N51 29.1
A 09	349 17.4	355 48.5	.. 55.9	156 55.1	.. 20.7	243 43.9	.. 57.9	119 57.6	.. 37.7	Enif	33 46.6	N 9 56.4
T 10	4 19.8	10 48.3	54.9	171 58.3	20.5	258 46.0	57.8	135 00.3	37.6	Fomalhaut	15 23.6	S29 32.7
U 11	19 22.3	25 48.2	53.9	187 01.5	20.3	273 48.1	57.8	150 02.9	37.6			
R 12	34 24.8	40 48.0	S 3 53.0	202 04.7	S 3 20.1	288 50.1	N22 57.7	165 05.6	S15 37.5	Gacrux	171 59.6	S57 11.8
D 13	49 27.2	55 47.8	52.0	217 07.9	19.9	303 52.2	57.7	180 08.2	37.5	Gienah	175 51.4	S17 37.5
A 14	64 29.7	70 47.6	51.0	232 11.1	19.7	318 54.3	57.7	195 10.8	37.5	Hadar	148 46.3	S60 26.5
Y 15	79 32.1	85 47.5	.. 50.0	247 14.3	.. 19.5	333 56.4	.. 57.6	210 13.5	.. 37.4	Hamal	328 00.4	N23 31.6
16	94 34.6	100 47.3	49.1	262 17.5	19.3	348 58.5	57.6	225 16.1	37.4	Kaus Aust.	83 42.8	S34 22.4
17	109 37.1	115 47.1	48.1	277 20.6	19.2	4 00.6	57.6	240 18.8	37.3			
18	124 39.5	130 46.9	S 3 47.1	292 23.8	S 3 19.0	19 02.6	N22 57.5	255 21.4	S15 37.3	Kochab	137 19.0	N74 05.8
19	139 42.0	145 46.8	46.1	307 27.0	18.8	34 04.7	57.5	270 24.1	37.2	Markab	13 37.9	N15 16.9
20	154 44.5	160 46.6	45.1	322 30.2	18.6	49 06.8	57.5	285 26.7	37.2	Menkar	314 14.8	N 4 08.5
21	169 46.9	175 46.4	.. 44.2	337 33.4	.. 18.4	64 08.9	.. 57.4	300 29.3	.. 37.1	Menkent	148 06.4	S36 26.5
22	184 49.4	190 46.2	43.2	352 36.6	18.2	79 11.0	57.4	315 32.0	37.1	Miaplacidus	221 39.3	S69 47.0
23	199 51.9	205 46.1	42.2	7 39.8	18.0	94 13.1	57.4	330 34.6	37.0			
27 00	214 54.3	220 45.9	S 3 41.2	22 43.0	S 3 17.9	109 15.1	N22 57.3	345 37.3	S15 37.0	Mirfak	308 40.0	N49 54.6
01	229 56.8	235 45.7	40.2	37 46.1	17.7	124 17.2	57.3	0 39.9	36.9	Nunki	75 57.5	S26 16.5
02	244 59.2	250 45.5	39.3	52 49.3	17.5	139 19.3	57.3	15 42.6	36.9	Peacock	53 18.4	S56 40.9
03	260 01.7	265 45.3	.. 38.3	67 52.5	.. 17.3	154 21.4	.. 57.2	30 45.2	.. 36.8	Pollux	243 27.1	N27 59.3
04	275 04.2	280 45.2	37.3	82 55.7	17.1	169 23.5	57.2	45 47.8	36.8	Procyon	244 59.2	N 5 11.0
05	290 06.6	295 45.0	36.3	97 58.9	16.9	184 25.5	57.1	60 50.5	36.7			
06	305 09.1	310 44.8	S 3 35.3	113 02.0	S 3 16.7	199 27.6	N22 57.1	75 53.1	S15 36.7	Rasalhague	96 05.7	N12 33.0
07	320 11.6	325 44.6	34.4	128 05.2	16.6	214 29.7	57.1	90 55.8	36.6	Regulus	207 42.8	N11 53.7
08	335 14.0	340 44.5	33.4	143 08.4	16.4	229 31.8	57.0	105 58.4	36.6	Rigel	281 11.7	S 8 11.4
S 09	350 16.5	355 44.3	.. 32.4	158 11.6	.. 16.2	244 33.9	.. 57.0	121 01.1	.. 36.5	Rigil Kent.	139 50.2	S60 53.6
U 10	5 19.0	10 44.1	31.4	173 14.7	16.0	259 35.9	57.0	136 03.7	36.5	Sabik	102 11.6	S15 44.4
N 11	20 21.4	25 43.9	30.4	188 17.9	15.8	274 38.0	56.9	151 06.3	36.5			
D 12	35 23.9	40 43.8	S 3 29.4	203 21.1	S 3 15.7	289 40.1	N22 56.9	166 09.0	S15 36.4	Schedar	349 40.3	N56 36.8
A 13	50 26.4	55 43.6	28.5	218 24.3	15.5	304 42.2	56.9	181 11.6	36.4	Shaula	96 20.8	S37 06.6
Y 14	65 28.8	70 43.4	27.5	233 27.4	15.3	319 44.3	56.8	196 14.3	36.3	Sirius	258 33.4	S16 44.5
15	80 31.3	85 43.2	.. 26.5	248 30.6	.. 15.1	334 46.3	.. 56.8	211 16.9	.. 36.3	Spica	158 30.3	S11 14.3
16	95 33.7	100 43.0	25.5	263 33.8	14.9	349 48.4	56.7	226 19.6	36.2	Suhail	222 51.9	S43 29.9
17	110 36.2	115 42.9	24.5	278 36.9	14.8	4 50.5	56.7	241 22.2	36.2			
18	125 38.7	130 42.7	S 3 23.5	293 40.1	S 3 14.6	19 52.6	N22 56.7	256 24.9	S15 36.1	Vega	80 38.4	N38 47.7
19	140 41.1	145 42.5	22.5	308 43.3	14.4	34 54.7	56.6	271 27.5	36.1	Zuben'ubi	137 04.4	S16 06.1
20	155 43.6	160 42.3	21.6	323 46.4	14.2	49 56.7	56.6	286 30.1	36.0			
21	170 46.1	175 42.2	.. 20.6	338 49.6	.. 14.1	64 58.8	.. 56.6	301 32.8	.. 36.0		SHA	Mer. Pass.
22	185 48.5	190 42.0	19.6	353 52.7	13.9	80 00.9	56.5	316 35.4	35.9	Venus	6 54.9	9 17
23	200 51.0	205 41.8	18.6	8 55.9	13.7	95 03.0	56.5	331 38.1	35.9	Mars	167 31.1	22 29
										Jupiter	254 29.9	16 44
Mer. Pass. 9 42.7		v −0.2	d 1.0	v 3.2	d 0.2	v 2.1	d 0.0	v 2.6	d 0.0	Saturn	130 38.7	1 02

SUN / MOON

UT	SUN GHA	SUN Dec	MOON GHA	v	MOON Dec	d	HP
d h	° ′	° ′	° ′	′	° ′	′	′
25 00	180 29.4	N13 05.5	232 49.0	9.9	S 4 07.6	11.2	59.1
01	195 29.5	06.3	247 17.9	9.9	3 56.4	11.3	59.1
02	210 29.6	07.1	261 46.8	9.9	3 45.1	11.2	59.1
03	225 29.7 ..	07.9	276 15.7	10.0	3 33.9	11.3	59.1
04	240 29.8	08.8	290 44.7	10.0	3 22.6	11.3	59.1
05	255 30.0	09.6	305 13.7	10.0	3 11.3	11.3	59.1
06	270 30.1	N13 10.4	319 42.7	10.0	S 3 00.0	11.4	59.1
07	285 30.2	11.2	334 11.7	10.0	2 48.6	11.3	59.1
08	300 30.3	12.0	348 40.7	10.1	2 37.3	11.3	59.1
F 09	315 30.4 ..	12.8	3 09.8	10.0	2 26.0	11.4	59.0
R 10	330 30.5	13.7	17 38.8	10.1	2 14.6	11.4	59.0
I 11	345 30.6	14.5	32 07.9	10.1	2 03.2	11.4	59.0
D 12	0 30.7	N13 15.3	46 37.0	10.1	S 1 51.8	11.4	59.0
A 13	15 30.8	16.1	61 06.1	10.2	1 40.4	11.4	59.0
Y 14	30 30.9	16.9	75 35.3	10.1	1 29.0	11.4	59.0
15	45 31.0 ..	17.7	90 04.4	10.2	1 17.6	11.4	59.0
16	60 31.1	18.5	104 33.6	10.1	1 06.2	11.4	59.0
17	75 31.2	19.3	119 02.7	10.2	0 54.8	11.4	59.0
18	90 31.3	N13 20.1	133 31.9	10.2	S 0 43.4	11.4	59.0
19	105 31.4	21.0	148 01.1	10.2	0 32.0	11.4	58.9
20	120 31.5	21.8	162 30.3	10.3	0 20.6	11.4	58.9
21	135 31.6 ..	22.6	176 59.6	10.2	S 0 09.2	11.4	58.9
22	150 31.7	23.4	191 28.8	10.2	N 0 02.2	11.4	58.9
23	165 31.9	24.2	205 58.0	10.3	0 13.6	11.4	58.9
26 00	180 32.0	N13 25.0	220 27.3	10.3	N 0 25.0	11.4	58.9
01	195 32.1	25.8	234 56.6	10.2	0 36.4	11.4	58.9
02	210 32.2	26.6	249 25.8	10.3	0 47.8	11.4	58.9
03	225 32.3 ..	27.4	263 55.1	10.3	0 59.2	11.3	58.9
04	240 32.4	28.2	278 24.4	10.3	1 10.5	11.4	58.8
05	255 32.5	29.0	292 53.7	10.3	1 21.9	11.3	58.8
06	270 32.6	N13 29.8	307 23.0	10.3	N 1 33.2	11.4	58.8
S 07	285 32.7	30.7	321 52.3	10.4	1 44.6	11.3	58.8
A 08	300 32.8	31.5	336 21.7	10.3	1 55.9	11.3	58.8
T 09	315 32.9 ..	32.3	350 51.0	10.3	2 07.2	11.3	58.8
U 10	330 33.0	33.1	5 20.3	10.3	2 18.5	11.3	58.8
R 11	345 33.1	33.9	19 49.6	10.4	2 29.7	11.3	58.7
D 12	0 33.2	N13 34.7	34 19.0	10.3	N 2 41.0	11.2	58.7
A 13	15 33.3	35.5	48 48.3	10.4	2 52.2	11.2	58.7
Y 14	30 33.4	36.3	63 17.7	10.3	3 03.4	11.2	58.7
15	45 33.5 ..	37.1	77 47.0	10.4	3 14.6	11.2	58.7
16	60 33.6	37.9	92 16.4	10.3	3 25.8	11.1	58.7
17	75 33.7	38.7	106 45.7	10.4	3 36.9	11.1	58.6
18	90 33.8	N13 39.5	121 15.1	10.3	N 3 48.0	11.1	58.6
19	105 33.9	40.3	135 44.4	10.4	3 59.1	11.1	58.6
20	120 34.0	41.1	150 13.8	10.4	4 10.2	11.0	58.6
21	135 34.1 ..	41.9	164 43.2	10.3	4 21.2	11.0	58.6
22	150 34.2	42.7	179 12.5	10.4	4 32.2	11.0	58.6
23	165 34.3	43.5	193 41.9	10.3	4 43.2	10.9	58.6
27 00	180 34.4	N13 44.3	208 11.2	10.4	N 4 54.1	11.0	58.5
01	195 34.5	45.1	222 40.6	10.3	5 05.1	10.8	58.5
02	210 34.6	45.9	237 09.9	10.4	5 15.9	10.9	58.5
03	225 34.7 ..	46.7	251 39.3	10.3	5 26.8	10.8	58.5
04	240 34.8	47.5	266 08.6	10.4	5 37.6	10.8	58.5
05	255 34.9	48.3	280 38.0	10.3	5 48.4	10.7	58.5
06	270 35.0	N13 49.1	295 07.3	10.4	N 5 59.1	10.7	58.4
07	285 35.0	49.9	309 36.7	10.3	6 09.8	10.6	58.4
08	300 35.1	50.7	324 06.0	10.3	6 20.4	10.6	58.4
S 09	315 35.2 ..	51.5	338 35.3	10.4	6 31.0	10.6	58.4
U 10	330 35.3	52.3	353 04.7	10.3	6 41.6	10.5	58.4
N 11	345 35.4	53.1	7 34.0	10.3	6 52.1	10.5	58.3
D 12	0 35.5	N13 53.9	22 03.3	10.3	N 7 02.6	10.5	58.3
A 13	15 35.6	54.6	36 32.6	10.3	7 13.1	10.3	58.3
Y 14	30 35.7	55.4	51 01.9	10.3	7 23.4	10.4	58.3
15	45 35.8 ..	56.2	65 31.2	10.3	7 33.8	10.3	58.3
16	60 35.9	57.0	80 00.5	10.3	7 44.1	10.2	58.3
17	75 36.0	57.8	94 29.8	10.3	7 54.3	10.2	58.2
18	90 36.1	N13 58.6	108 59.1	10.3	N 8 04.5	10.2	58.2
19	105 36.2	13 59.4	123 28.4	10.2	8 14.7	10.1	58.2
20	120 36.3	14 00.2	137 57.6	10.3	8 24.8	10.0	58.2
21	135 36.4 ..	01.0	152 26.9	10.3	8 34.8	10.0	58.2
22	150 36.5	01.8	166 56.2	10.2	8 44.8	9.9	58.1
23	165 36.6	02.6	181 25.4	10.2	N 8 54.7	9.9	58.1
	SD 15.9	d 0.8	SD 16.1		16.0		15.9

Twilight / Sunrise / Moonrise

Lat.	Naut.	Civil	Sunrise	Moonrise 25	26	27	28
°	h m	h m	h m	h m	h m	h m	h m
N 72	////	////	02 31	03 21	03 14	03 07	03 00
N 70	////	00 54	03 00	03 16	03 15	03 14	03 14
68	////	01 52	03 21	03 12	03 16	03 20	03 26
66	////	02 25	03 38	03 09	03 17	03 26	03 35
64	00 47	02 48	03 51	03 06	03 18	03 30	03 43
62	01 39	03 07	04 02	03 03	03 18	03 34	03 50
60	02 09	03 22	04 12	03 01	03 19	03 37	03 57
N 58	02 31	03 34	04 21	02 59	03 19	03 40	04 02
56	02 48	03 45	04 28	02 57	03 20	03 43	04 07
54	03 02	03 55	04 35	02 56	03 20	03 45	04 11
52	03 15	04 03	04 40	02 54	03 21	03 47	04 15
50	03 25	04 10	04 46	02 53	03 21	03 49	04 19
45	03 47	04 26	04 57	02 50	03 22	03 53	04 26
N 40	04 03	04 38	05 07	02 47	03 22	03 57	04 33
35	04 16	04 48	05 15	02 45	03 23	04 00	04 39
30	04 27	04 57	05 22	02 43	03 23	04 03	04 44
20	04 44	05 11	05 34	02 40	03 24	04 08	04 52
N 10	04 58	05 23	05 45	02 37	03 25	04 12	05 00
0	05 08	05 33	05 54	02 35	03 26	04 17	05 07
S 10	05 18	05 43	06 04	02 32	03 27	04 21	05 15
20	05 26	05 52	06 14	02 29	03 27	04 25	05 23
30	05 33	06 01	06 26	02 26	03 28	04 30	05 32
35	05 36	06 06	06 32	02 24	03 29	04 33	05 37
40	05 40	06 12	06 40	02 22	03 30	04 37	05 43
45	05 44	06 18	06 48	02 20	03 31	04 41	05 50
S 50	05 47	06 25	06 59	02 17	03 31	04 46	05 58
52	05 49	06 28	07 04	02 15	03 32	04 48	06 02
54	05 50	06 32	07 09	02 14	03 32	04 50	06 06
56	05 52	06 36	07 15	02 12	03 33	04 53	06 11
58	05 53	06 40	07 21	02 11	03 34	04 56	06 17
S 60	05 55	06 44	07 29	02 08	03 34	04 59	06 23

Sunset / Twilight / Moonset

Lat.	Sunset	Civil	Naut.	Moonset 25	26	27	28
°	h m	h m	h m	h m	h m	h m	h m
N 72	21 30	////	////	14 40	16 34	18 28	20 23
N 70	21 00	23 19	////	14 43	16 29	18 15	20 01
68	20 38	22 10	////	14 44	16 25	18 05	19 44
66	20 21	21 35	////	14 46	16 22	17 57	19 30
64	20 07	21 10	23 24	14 47	16 19	17 50	19 19
62	19 55	20 51	22 22	14 48	16 16	17 44	19 09
60	19 45	20 36	21 51	14 49	16 14	17 39	19 01
N 58	19 37	20 23	21 28	14 50	16 12	17 34	18 54
56	19 29	20 12	21 10	14 50	16 11	17 30	18 47
54	19 22	20 03	20 55	14 51	16 09	17 26	18 42
52	19 16	19 54	20 43	14 52	16 08	17 23	18 37
50	19 11	19 47	20 32	14 52	16 07	17 20	18 32
45	18 59	19 31	20 10	14 53	16 04	17 14	18 22
N 40	18 49	19 18	19 53	14 54	16 02	17 08	18 14
35	18 41	19 08	19 40	14 55	16 00	17 04	18 07
30	18 34	18 59	19 29	14 56	15 58	17 00	18 01
20	18 22	18 45	19 11	14 57	15 55	16 53	17 50
N 10	18 11	18 33	18 58	14 58	15 52	16 47	17 41
0	18 01	18 22	18 47	14 59	15 50	16 41	17 32
S 10	17 51	18 13	18 38	15 00	15 48	16 35	17 23
20	17 41	18 04	18 30	15 01	15 45	16 29	17 14
30	17 30	17 54	18 22	15 02	15 42	16 22	17 03
35	17 23	17 49	18 19	15 03	15 40	16 18	16 57
40	17 15	17 43	18 15	15 03	15 38	16 13	16 50
45	17 07	17 37	18 11	15 04	15 36	16 08	16 42
S 50	16 56	17 30	18 08	15 05	15 33	16 02	16 33
52	16 51	17 26	18 06	15 05	15 32	15 59	16 28
54	16 46	17 23	18 05	15 06	15 31	15 56	16 23
56	16 40	17 19	18 03	15 06	15 29	15 52	16 18
58	16 33	17 15	18 01	15 07	15 27	15 48	16 12
S 60	16 26	17 10	17 59	15 08	15 25	15 44	16 05

SUN / MOON

Day	Eqn. of Time 00h	12h	Mer. Pass.	Mer. Pass. Upper	Lower	Age	Phase
d	m s	m s	h m	h m	h m	d	%
25	01 57	02 03	11 58	08 47	21 12	26	17
26	02 08	02 13	11 58	09 38	22 03	27	9
27	02 17	02 22	11 58	10 29	22 54	28	4

UT	ARIES GHA	VENUS −4.2 GHA	Dec	MARS −1.2 GHA	Dec	JUPITER −2.0 GHA	Dec	SATURN +0.1 GHA	Dec	STARS Name	SHA	Dec
28 00	215 53.5	220 41.6	S 3 17.6	23 59.1	S 3 13.5	110 05.0	N22 56.5	346 40.7	S15 35.8	Acamar	315 18.4	S40 15.0
01	230 55.9	235 41.4	16.6	39 02.2	13.4	125 07.1	56.4	1 43.4	35.8	Achernar	335 27.0	S57 09.9
02	245 58.4	250 41.3	15.6	54 05.4	13.2	140 09.2	56.4	16 46.0	35.7	Acrux	173 07.9	S63 10.9
03	261 00.8	265 41.1	.. 14.7	69 08.5	.. 13.0	155 11.3	.. 56.3	31 48.6	.. 35.7	Adhara	255 12.2	S28 59.9
04	276 03.3	280 40.9	13.7	84 11.7	12.8	170 13.3	56.3	46 51.3	35.6	Aldebaran	290 49.0	N16 32.1
05	291 05.8	295 40.7	12.7	99 14.8	12.7	185 15.4	56.3	61 53.9	35.6			
06	306 08.2	310 40.6	S 3 11.7	114 18.0	S 3 12.5	200 17.5	N22 56.2	76 56.6	S15 35.5	Alioth	166 19.8	N55 53.0
07	321 10.7	325 40.4	10.7	129 21.2	12.3	215 19.6	56.2	91 59.2	35.5	Alkaid	152 58.0	N49 14.5
M 08	336 13.2	340 40.2	09.7	144 24.3	12.2	230 21.6	56.2	107 01.9	35.4	Al Na'ir	27 43.2	S46 53.2
O 09	351 15.6	355 40.0	.. 08.7	159 27.5	.. 12.0	245 23.7	.. 56.1	122 04.5	.. 35.4	Alnilam	275 46.0	S 1 11.9
N 10	6 18.1	10 39.8	07.7	174 30.6	11.8	260 25.8	56.1	137 07.2	35.3	Alphard	217 55.4	S 8 43.5
D 11	21 20.6	25 39.7	06.7	189 33.7	11.6	275 27.9	56.1	152 09.8	35.3			
A 12	36 23.0	40 39.5	S 3 05.7	204 36.9	S 3 11.5	290 29.9	N22 56.0	167 12.4	S15 35.3	Alphecca	126 10.2	N26 40.0
Y 13	51 25.5	55 39.3	04.7	219 40.0	11.3	305 32.0	56.0	182 15.1	35.2	Alpheratz	357 43.1	N29 10.0
14	66 28.0	70 39.1	03.8	234 43.2	11.1	320 34.1	55.9	197 17.7	35.2	Altair	62 07.6	N 8 54.4
15	81 30.4	85 39.0	.. 02.8	249 46.3	.. 11.0	335 36.2	.. 55.9	212 20.4	.. 35.1	Ankaa	353 15.5	S42 13.6
16	96 32.9	100 38.8	01.8	264 49.5	10.8	350 38.2	55.9	227 23.0	35.1	Antares	112 25.2	S26 27.7
17	111 35.3	115 38.6	3 00.8	279 52.6	10.6	5 40.3	55.8	242 25.7	35.0			
18	126 37.8	130 38.4	S 2 59.8	294 55.8	S 3 10.5	20 42.4	N22 55.8	257 28.3	S15 35.0	Arcturus	145 54.9	N19 06.5
19	141 40.3	145 38.2	58.8	309 58.9	10.3	35 44.5	55.8	272 31.0	34.9	Atria	107 26.0	S69 02.9
20	156 42.7	160 38.1	57.8	325 02.0	10.1	50 46.5	55.7	287 33.6	34.9	Avior	234 17.8	S59 33.8
21	171 45.2	175 37.9	.. 56.8	340 05.2	.. 10.0	65 48.6	.. 55.7	302 36.3	.. 34.8	Bellatrix	278 31.6	N 6 21.5
22	186 47.7	190 37.7	55.8	355 08.3	09.8	80 50.7	55.6	317 38.9	34.8	Betelgeuse	271 00.9	N 7 24.3
23	201 50.1	205 37.5	54.8	10 11.4	09.6	95 52.7	55.6	332 41.5	34.7			
29 00	216 52.6	220 37.3	S 2 53.8	25 14.6	S 3 09.5	110 54.8	N22 55.6	347 44.2	S15 34.7	Canopus	263 56.2	S52 42.7
01	231 55.1	235 37.2	52.8	40 17.7	09.3	125 56.9	55.5	2 46.8	34.6	Capella	280 33.9	N46 00.6
02	246 57.5	250 37.0	51.8	55 20.8	09.2	140 59.0	55.5	17 49.5	34.6	Deneb	49 31.0	N45 19.8
03	262 00.0	265 36.8	.. 50.8	70 24.0	.. 09.0	156 01.0	.. 55.5	32 52.1	.. 34.5	Denebola	182 32.8	N14 29.4
04	277 02.5	280 36.6	49.8	85 27.1	08.8	171 03.1	55.4	47 54.8	34.5	Diphda	348 55.6	S17 54.5
05	292 04.9	295 36.4	48.8	100 30.2	08.7	186 05.2	55.4	62 57.4	34.4			
06	307 07.4	310 36.3	S 2 47.8	115 33.4	S 3 08.5	201 07.2	N22 55.3	78 00.1	S15 34.4	Dubhe	193 50.7	N61 40.5
07	322 09.8	325 36.1	46.8	130 36.5	08.3	216 09.3	55.3	93 02.7	34.3	Elnath	278 12.2	N28 37.0
T 08	337 12.3	340 35.9	45.8	145 39.6	08.2	231 11.4	55.3	108 05.4	34.3	Eltanin	90 45.5	N51 29.1
U 09	352 14.8	355 35.7	.. 44.8	160 42.7	.. 08.0	246 13.4	.. 55.2	123 08.0	.. 34.2	Enif	33 46.6	N 9 56.4
E 10	7 17.2	10 35.6	43.9	175 45.9	07.9	261 15.5	55.2	138 10.6	34.2	Fomalhaut	15 23.6	S29 32.6
S 11	22 19.7	25 35.4	42.9	190 49.0	07.7	276 17.6	55.2	153 13.3	34.1			
D 12	37 22.2	40 35.2	S 2 41.9	205 52.1	S 3 07.6	291 19.7	N22 55.1	168 15.9	S15 34.1	Gacrux	171 59.6	S57 11.8
A 13	52 24.6	55 35.0	40.9	220 55.2	07.4	306 21.7	55.1	183 18.6	34.0	Gienah	175 51.4	S17 37.5
Y 14	67 27.1	70 34.8	39.9	235 58.3	07.2	321 23.8	55.0	198 21.2	34.0	Hadar	148 46.3	S60 26.6
15	82 29.6	85 34.7	.. 38.9	251 01.5	.. 07.1	336 25.9	.. 55.0	213 23.9	.. 34.0	Hamal	328 00.4	N23 31.6
16	97 32.0	100 34.5	37.9	266 04.6	06.9	351 27.9	55.0	228 26.5	33.9	Kaus Aust.	83 42.8	S34 22.4
17	112 34.5	115 34.3	36.9	281 07.7	06.8	6 30.0	54.9	243 29.2	33.9			
18	127 36.9	130 34.1	S 2 35.9	296 10.8	S 3 06.6	21 32.1	N22 54.9	258 31.8	S15 33.8	Kochab	137 19.0	N74 05.8
19	142 39.4	145 33.9	34.9	311 13.9	06.5	36 34.1	54.8	273 34.5	33.8	Markab	13 37.9	N15 16.9
20	157 41.9	160 33.8	33.9	326 17.0	06.3	51 36.2	54.8	288 37.1	33.7	Menkar	314 14.8	N 4 08.5
21	172 44.3	175 33.6	.. 32.9	341 20.1	.. 06.2	66 38.3	.. 54.8	303 39.8	.. 33.7	Menkent	148 06.4	S36 26.5
22	187 46.8	190 33.4	31.9	356 23.3	06.0	81 40.3	54.7	318 42.4	33.6	Miaplacidus	221 39.3	S69 47.0
23	202 49.3	205 33.2	30.9	11 26.4	05.8	96 42.4	54.7	333 45.0	33.6			
30 00	217 51.7	220 33.0	S 2 29.8	26 29.5	S 3 05.7	111 44.5	N22 54.7	348 47.7	S15 33.5	Mirfak	308 40.0	N49 54.6
01	232 54.2	235 32.9	28.8	41 32.6	05.5	126 46.5	54.6	3 50.3	33.5	Nunki	75 57.4	S26 16.5
02	247 56.7	250 32.7	27.8	56 35.7	05.4	141 48.6	54.6	18 53.0	33.4	Peacock	53 18.3	S56 40.9
03	262 59.1	265 32.5	.. 26.8	71 38.8	.. 05.2	156 50.7	.. 54.5	33 55.6	.. 33.4	Pollux	243 27.1	N27 59.3
04	278 01.6	280 32.3	25.8	86 41.9	05.1	171 52.7	54.5	48 58.3	33.3	Procyon	244 59.2	N 5 11.0
05	293 04.1	295 32.1	24.8	101 45.0	04.9	186 54.8	54.5	64 00.9	33.3			
06	308 06.5	310 32.0	S 2 23.8	116 48.1	S 3 04.8	201 56.9	N22 54.4	79 03.6	S15 33.2	Rasalhague	96 05.7	N12 33.0
W 07	323 09.0	325 31.8	22.8	131 51.2	04.6	216 58.9	54.4	94 06.2	33.2	Regulus	207 42.8	N11 53.7
E 08	338 11.4	340 31.6	21.8	146 54.3	04.5	232 01.0	54.3	109 08.9	33.1	Rigel	281 11.8	S 8 11.4
D 09	353 13.9	355 31.4	.. 20.8	161 57.4	.. 04.3	247 03.0	.. 54.3	124 11.5	.. 33.1	Rigil Kent.	139 50.2	S60 53.6
N 10	8 16.4	10 31.2	19.8	177 00.5	04.2	262 05.1	54.3	139 14.2	33.0	Sabik	102 11.6	S15 44.4
E 11	23 18.8	25 31.0	18.8	192 03.6	04.0	277 07.2	54.2	154 16.8	33.0			
S 12	38 21.3	40 30.9	S 2 17.8	207 06.7	S 3 03.9	292 09.2	N22 54.2	169 19.5	S15 32.9	Schedar	349 40.3	N56 36.8
D 13	53 23.8	55 30.7	16.8	222 09.8	03.8	307 11.3	54.2	184 22.1	32.9	Shaula	96 20.8	S37 06.6
A 14	68 26.2	70 30.5	15.8	237 12.9	03.6	322 13.4	54.1	199 24.8	32.8	Sirius	258 33.4	S16 44.5
Y 15	83 28.7	85 30.3	.. 14.8	252 16.0	.. 03.5	337 15.4	.. 54.1	214 27.4	.. 32.8	Spica	158 30.3	S11 14.3
16	98 31.2	100 30.1	13.8	267 19.0	03.3	352 17.5	54.0	229 30.0	32.7	Suhail	222 51.9	S43 29.9
17	113 33.6	115 30.0	12.8	282 22.1	03.2	7 19.6	54.0	244 32.7	32.7			
18	128 36.1	130 29.8	S 2 11.8	297 25.2	S 3 03.0	22 21.6	N22 54.0	259 35.3	S15 32.6	Vega	80 38.3	N38 47.7
19	143 38.6	145 29.6	10.8	312 28.3	02.9	37 23.7	53.9	274 38.0	32.6	Zuben'ubi	137 04.4	S16 06.1
20	158 41.0	160 29.4	09.7	327 31.4	02.7	52 25.7	53.9	289 40.6	32.5		SHA	Mer. Pass.
21	173 43.5	175 29.2	.. 08.7	342 34.5	.. 02.6	67 27.8	.. 53.8	304 43.3	.. 32.5	Venus	3 44.7	9 18
22	188 45.9	190 29.1	07.7	357 37.6	02.5	82 29.9	53.8	319 45.9	32.5	Mars	168 22.0	22 14
23	203 48.4	205 28.9	06.7	12 40.6	02.3	97 31.9	53.8	334 48.6	32.4	Jupiter	254 02.2	16 34
Mer. Pass. h m 9 30.9		v −0.2	d 1.0	v 3.1	d 0.2	v 2.1	d 0.0	v 2.6	d 0.0	Saturn	130 51.6	0 49

UT	SUN GHA	SUN Dec	MOON GHA	v	MOON Dec	d	HP
d h	° ′	° ′	° ′	′	° ′	′	′
28 00	180 36.7	N14 03.4	195 54.6	10.3	N 9 04.6	9.8	58.1
01	195 36.7	04.1	210 23.9	10.2	9 14.4	9.8	58.1
02	210 36.8	04.9	224 53.1	10.2	9 24.2	9.7	58.0
03	225 36.9	.. 05.7	239 22.3	10.2	9 33.9	9.6	58.0
04	240 37.0	06.5	253 51.5	10.2	9 43.5	9.6	58.0
05	255 37.1	07.3	268 20.7	10.2	9 53.1	9.5	58.0
06	270 37.2	N14 08.1	282 49.9	10.2	N10 02.6	9.5	58.0
07	285 37.3	08.9	297 19.1	10.2	10 12.1	9.4	57.9
08	300 37.4	09.7	311 48.3	10.1	10 21.5	9.3	57.9
M 09	315 37.5	.. 10.4	326 17.4	10.2	10 30.8	9.3	57.9
O 10	330 37.6	11.2	340 46.6	10.1	10 40.1	9.2	57.9
N 11	345 37.7	12.0	355 15.7	10.2	10 49.3	9.1	57.9
D 12	0 37.8	N14 12.8	9 44.9	10.1	N10 58.4	9.1	57.8
A 13	15 37.8	13.6	24 14.0	10.1	11 07.5	9.0	57.8
Y 14	30 37.9	14.4	38 43.1	10.1	11 16.5	9.0	57.8
15	45 38.0	.. 15.2	53 12.2	10.1	11 25.5	8.8	57.8
16	60 38.1	15.9	67 41.3	10.1	11 34.3	8.8	57.7
17	75 38.2	16.7	82 10.4	10.1	11 43.1	8.7	57.7
18	90 38.3	N14 17.5	96 39.5	10.1	N11 51.8	8.7	57.7
19	105 38.4	18.3	111 08.6	10.0	12 00.5	8.6	57.7
20	120 38.5	19.1	125 37.6	10.1	12 09.1	8.5	57.6
21	135 38.5	.. 19.8	140 06.7	10.0	12 17.6	8.4	57.6
22	150 38.6	20.6	154 35.7	10.1	12 26.0	8.4	57.6
23	165 38.7	21.4	169 04.8	10.0	12 34.4	8.2	57.6
29 00	180 38.8	N14 22.2	183 33.8	10.0	N12 42.6	8.2	57.5
01	195 38.9	23.0	198 02.8	10.0	12 50.8	8.2	57.5
02	210 39.0	23.7	212 31.8	10.0	12 59.0	8.0	57.5
03	225 39.1	.. 24.5	227 00.8	10.0	13 07.0	8.0	57.5
04	240 39.2	25.3	241 29.8	10.0	13 15.0	7.9	57.5
05	255 39.2	26.1	255 58.8	10.0	N13 22.9	7.8	57.4
06	270 39.3	N14 26.9					
07	285 39.4	27.6					
T 08	300 39.5	28.4	An annular eclipse of				
U 09	315 39.6	.. 29.2	the Sun occurs on this				
E 10	330 39.7	30.0	date. See page 5.				
S 11	345 39.8	30.7					
D 12	0 39.8	N14 31.5	357 21.5	10.0	N14 15.8	7.2	57.3
A 13	15 39.9	32.3	11 50.5	9.9	14 23.0	7.2	57.2
Y 14	30 40.0	33.1	26 19.4	9.9	14 30.2	7.0	57.2
15	45 40.1	.. 33.8	40 48.3	9.9	14 37.2	7.0	57.2
16	60 40.2	34.6	55 17.2	10.0	14 44.2	6.9	57.2
17	75 40.3	35.4	69 46.2	9.9	14 51.1	6.8	57.1
18	90 40.3	N14 36.2	84 15.1	9.9	N14 57.9	6.7	57.1
19	105 40.4	36.9	98 44.0	9.9	15 04.6	6.6	57.1
20	120 40.5	37.7	113 12.9	9.9	15 11.2	6.6	57.0
21	135 40.6	.. 38.5	127 41.7	9.9	15 17.8	6.4	57.0
22	150 40.7	39.2	142 10.6	9.9	15 24.2	6.4	57.0
23	165 40.8	40.0	156 39.5	9.9	15 30.6	6.2	57.0
30 00	180 40.8	N14 40.8	171 08.4	9.9	N15 36.8	6.2	56.9
01	195 40.9	41.6	185 37.3	9.9	15 43.0	6.1	56.9
02	210 41.0	42.3	200 06.2	9.8	15 49.1	6.0	56.9
03	225 41.1	.. 43.1	214 35.0	9.9	15 55.1	5.9	56.8
04	240 41.2	43.9	229 03.9	9.9	16 01.0	5.8	56.8
05	255 41.2	44.6	243 32.8	9.9	16 06.8	5.7	56.8
06	270 41.3	N14 45.4	258 01.7	9.8	N16 12.5	5.6	56.8
W 07	285 41.4	46.2	272 30.5	9.9	16 18.1	5.6	56.8
E 08	300 41.5	46.9	286 59.4	9.9	16 23.7	5.4	56.7
D 09	315 41.6	.. 47.7	301 28.3	9.9	16 29.1	5.3	56.7
N 10	330 41.6	48.5	315 57.2	9.8	16 34.4	5.3	56.7
E 11	345 41.7	49.2	330 26.0	9.9	16 39.7	5.1	56.7
S 12	0 41.8	N14 50.0	344 54.9	9.9	N16 44.8	5.1	56.6
D 13	15 41.9	50.8	359 23.8	9.9	16 49.9	4.9	56.6
A 14	30 42.0	51.5	13 52.7	9.9	16 54.8	4.9	56.6
Y 15	45 42.0	.. 52.3	28 21.6	9.9	16 59.7	4.8	56.6
16	60 42.1	53.0	42 50.5	9.9	17 04.5	4.6	56.5
17	75 42.2	53.8	57 19.4	9.9	17 09.1	4.6	56.5
18	90 42.3	N14 54.6	71 48.3	9.9	N17 13.7	4.5	56.5
19	105 42.4	55.3	86 17.2	9.9	17 18.2	4.4	56.5
20	120 42.4	56.1	100 46.1	9.9	17 22.6	4.2	56.4
21	135 42.5	.. 56.9	115 15.0	9.9	17 26.8	4.2	56.4
22	150 42.6	57.6	129 43.9	10.0	17 31.0	4.1	56.4
23	165 42.7	58.4	144 12.9	9.9	N17 35.1	4.0	56.3
	SD 15.9 d 0.8		SD 15.8		15.6		15.4

Twilight / Sunrise / Moonrise

Lat.	Naut.	Civil	Sunrise	Moonrise 28	29	30	1
°	h m	h m	h m	h m	h m	h m	h m
N 72	////	////	02 09	03 00	02 51	02 40	02 15
N 70	////	////	02 43	03 14	03 15	03 18	03 26
68	////	01 28	03 07	03 26	03 33	03 44	04 03
66	////	02 08	03 26	03 35	03 48	04 05	04 34
64	////	02 35	03 41	03 43	04 00	04 21	04 50
62	01 17	02 55	03 53	03 50	04 10	04 35	05 07
60	01 54	03 12	04 04	03 57	04 19	04 47	05 21
N 58	02 19	03 26	04 13	04 02	04 27	04 57	05 33
56	02 38	03 37	04 21	04 07	04 34	05 06	05 43
54	02 54	03 47	04 28	04 11	04 40	05 13	05 52
52	03 07	03 56	04 35	04 15	04 46	05 20	06 00
50	03 18	04 04	04 40	04 19	04 51	05 27	06 07
45	03 41	04 21	04 53	04 26	05 02	05 41	06 23
N 40	03 58	04 34	05 03	04 33	05 11	05 52	06 36
35	04 12	04 45	05 12	04 39	05 19	06 02	06 47
30	04 24	04 54	05 19	04 44	05 26	06 10	06 57
20	04 42	05 09	05 32	04 52	05 38	06 25	07 13
N 10	04 56	05 22	05 43	05 00	05 49	06 38	07 28
0	05 08	05 33	05 54	05 07	05 59	06 50	07 42
S 10	05 18	05 43	06 04	05 15	06 09	07 02	07 55
20	05 26	05 53	06 15	05 23	06 20	07 16	08 10
30	05 35	06 03	06 28	05 32	06 32	07 31	08 27
35	05 39	06 09	06 35	05 37	06 39	07 39	08 37
40	05 43	06 15	06 43	05 43	06 47	07 49	08 48
45	05 47	06 22	06 52	05 50	06 57	08 01	09 01
S 50	05 51	06 29	07 03	05 58	07 09	08 16	09 17
52	05 53	06 33	07 09	06 02	07 14	08 22	09 25
54	05 55	06 37	07 14	06 06	07 20	08 30	09 34
56	05 57	06 41	07 21	06 11	07 27	08 38	09 43
58	05 59	06 46	07 28	06 17	07 34	08 48	09 54
S 60	06 01	06 51	07 36	06 23	07 43	08 59	10 06

Sunset / Twilight / Moonset

Lat.	Sunset	Civil	Naut.	Moonset 28	29	30	1
°	h m	h m	h m	h m	h m	h m	h m
N 72	21 52	////	////	20 23	22 22	24 35	00 35
N 70	21 16	////	////	20 01	21 45	22 47	24 49
68	20 51	22 35	////	19 44	21 19	22 21	24 01
66	20 32	21 51	////	19 30	20 59	22 01	23 30
64	20 16	21 23	////	19 19	20 43	21 45	23 08
62	20 03	21 02	22 44	19 09	20 30	21 31	22 49
60	19 53	20 45	22 05	19 01	20 19	21 20	22 34
N 58	19 43	20 31	21 39	18 54	20 10	21 20	22 22
56	19 35	20 19	21 19	18 47	20 01	21 09	22 10
54	19 28	20 09	21 03	18 42	19 54	21 01	22 01
52	19 21	20 00	20 50	18 37	19 47	20 53	21 52
50	19 15	19 52	20 38	18 32	19 41	20 46	21 44
45	19 03	19 35	20 15	18 22	19 28	20 30	21 28
N 40	18 58	19 22	19 57	18 14	19 17	20 18	21 14
35	18 44	19 11	19 43	18 07	19 08	20 07	21 03
30	18 36	19 01	19 31	18 01	19 00	19 58	20 53
20	18 23	18 46	19 13	17 50	18 47	19 42	20 35
N 10	18 11	18 33	18 59	17 41	18 35	19 28	20 20
0	18 01	18 22	18 47	17 32	18 23	19 15	20 06
S 10	17 50	18 12	18 37	17 23	18 12	19 02	19 52
20	17 39	18 02	18 28	17 14	18 00	18 48	19 37
30	17 27	17 51	18 20	17 03	17 46	18 32	19 20
35	17 20	17 46	18 16	16 57	17 39	18 23	19 10
40	17 11	17 40	18 11	16 50	17 30	18 12	18 58
45	17 02	17 33	18 07	16 42	17 19	18 00	18 45
S 50	16 51	17 25	18 03	16 33	17 07	17 45	18 28
52	16 45	17 21	18 01	16 28	17 01	17 38	18 20
54	16 40	17 17	17 59	16 23	16 54	17 30	18 12
56	16 33	17 13	17 57	16 18	16 47	17 21	18 02
58	16 26	17 08	17 55	16 12	16 39	17 12	17 51
S 60	16 18	17 03	17 52	16 05	16 30	17 01	17 38

SUN / MOON

Day	SUN Eqn. of Time 00h	SUN Eqn. of Time 12h	SUN Mer. Pass.	MOON Mer. Pass. Upper	MOON Mer. Pass. Lower	Age	Phase
d	m s	m s	h m	h m	h m	d	%
28	02 26	02 31	11 57	11 20	23 45	29	1
29	02 35	02 39	11 57	12 11	24 37	00	0
30	02 43	02 47	11 57	13 02	00 37	01	2	●

UT	ARIES	VENUS −4.1		MARS −1.1		JUPITER −2.0		SATURN +0.1		STARS		
	GHA	GHA	Dec	GHA	Dec	GHA	Dec	GHA	Dec	Name	SHA	Dec
d h	° ′	° ′	° ′	° ′	° ′	° ′	° ′	° ′	° ′		° ′	° ′
1 00	218 50.9	220 28.7	S 2 05.7	27 43.7	S 3 02.2	112 34.0	N22 53.7	349 51.2	S15 32.4	Acamar	315 18.4	S40 15.0
01	233 53.3	235 28.5	04.7	42 46.8	02.0	127 36.0	53.7	4 53.9	32.3	Achernar	335 27.0	S57 09.8
02	248 55.8	250 28.3	03.7	57 49.9	01.9	142 38.1	53.6	19 56.5	32.3	Acrux	173 07.9	S63 11.0
03	263 58.3	265 28.2 . .	02.7	72 53.0 . .	01.8	157 40.2 . .	53.6	34 59.2 . .	32.2	Adhara	255 12.2	S28 59.9
04	279 00.7	280 28.0	01.7	87 56.0	01.7	172 42.2	53.6	50 01.8	32.2	Aldebaran	290 49.0	N16 32.1
05	294 03.2	295 27.8	2 00.7	102 59.1	01.5	187 44.3	53.5	65 04.5	32.1			
06	309 05.7	310 27.6	S 1 59.7	118 02.2	S 3 01.3	202 46.3	N22 53.5	80 07.1	S15 32.1	Alioth	166 19.8	N55 53.0
07	324 08.1	325 27.4	58.6	133 05.3	01.2	217 48.4	53.4	95 09.8	32.0	Alkaid	152 58.0	N49 14.6
T 08	339 10.6	340 27.2	57.6	148 08.3	01.1	232 50.5	53.4	110 12.4	32.0	Al Na'ir	27 43.2	S46 53.2
H 09	354 13.1	355 27.1 . .	56.6	163 11.4 . .	00.9	247 52.5 . .	53.4	125 15.1 . .	31.9	Alnilam	275 46.0	S 1 11.9
U 10	9 15.5	10 26.9	55.6	178 14.5	00.8	262 54.6	53.3	140 17.7	31.9	Alphard	217 55.5	S 8 43.5
R 11	24 18.0	25 26.7	54.6	193 17.5	00.7	277 56.6	53.3	155 20.4	31.8			
S 12	39 20.4	40 26.5	S 1 53.6	208 20.6	S 3 00.5	292 58.7	N22 53.2	170 23.0	S15 31.8	Alphecca	126 10.2	N26 40.0
D 13	54 22.9	55 26.3	52.6	223 23.7	00.4	308 00.8	53.2	185 25.6	31.7	Alpheratz	357 43.1	N29 10.0
A 14	69 25.4	70 26.1	51.6	238 26.7	00.3	323 02.8	53.2	200 28.3	31.7	Altair	62 07.6	N 8 54.4
Y 15	84 27.8	85 26.0 . .	50.6	253 29.8 . .	00.1	338 04.9 . .	53.1	215 30.9 . .	31.6	Ankaa	353 15.5	S42 13.6
16	99 30.3	100 25.8	49.5	268 32.9	3 00.0	353 06.9	53.1	230 33.6	31.6	Antares	112 25.2	S26 27.7
17	114 32.8	115 25.6	48.5	283 35.9	2 59.9	8 09.0	53.0	245 36.2	31.5			
18	129 35.2	130 25.4	S 1 47.5	298 39.0	S 2 59.7	23 11.0	N22 53.0	260 38.9	S15 31.5	Arcturus	145 54.9	N19 06.5
19	144 37.7	145 25.2	46.5	313 42.0	59.6	38 13.1	53.0	275 41.5	31.4	Atria	107 26.0	S69 02.9
20	159 40.2	160 25.1	45.5	328 45.1	59.5	53 15.2	52.9	290 44.2	31.4	Avior	234 17.8	S59 33.8
21	174 42.6	175 24.9 . .	44.5	343 48.1 . .	59.3	68 17.2 . .	52.9	305 46.8 . .	31.3	Bellatrix	278 31.6	N 6 21.5
22	189 45.1	190 24.7	43.5	358 51.2	59.2	83 19.3	52.8	320 49.5	31.3	Betelgeuse	271 00.9	N 7 24.3
23	204 47.5	205 24.5	42.4	13 54.3	59.1	98 21.3	52.8	335 52.1	31.2			
2 00	219 50.0	220 24.3	S 1 41.4	28 57.3	S 2 58.9	113 23.4	N22 52.8	350 54.8	S15 31.2	Canopus	263 56.2	S52 42.6
01	234 52.5	235 24.1	40.4	44 00.4	58.8	128 25.4	52.7	5 57.4	31.1	Capella	280 33.9	N46 00.6
02	249 54.9	250 24.0	39.4	59 03.4	58.7	143 27.5	52.7	21 00.1	31.1	Deneb	49 31.0	N45 19.8
03	264 57.4	265 23.8 . .	38.4	74 06.5 . .	58.6	158 29.6 . .	52.6	36 02.7 . .	31.0	Denebola	182 32.9	N14 29.4
04	279 59.9	280 23.6	37.4	89 09.5	58.4	173 31.6	52.6	51 05.4	31.0	Diphda	348 55.6	S17 54.5
05	295 02.3	295 23.4	36.4	104 12.6	58.3	188 33.7	52.6	66 08.0	30.9			
06	310 04.8	310 23.2	S 1 35.3	119 15.6	S 2 58.2	203 35.7	N22 52.5	81 10.7	S15 30.9	Dubhe	193 50.7	N61 40.5
07	325 07.3	325 23.0	34.3	134 18.6	58.1	218 37.8	52.5	96 13.3	30.9	Elnath	278 12.2	N28 37.0
F 08	340 09.7	340 22.9	33.3	149 21.7	57.9	233 39.8	52.4	111 16.0	30.8	Eltanin	90 45.5	N51 29.2
R 09	355 12.2	355 22.7 . .	32.3	164 24.7 . .	57.8	248 41.9 . .	52.4	126 18.6 . .	30.8	Enif	33 46.6	N 9 56.4
I 10	10 14.7	10 22.5	31.3	179 27.8	57.7	263 43.9	52.4	141 21.3	30.7	Fomalhaut	15 23.6	S29 32.6
D 11	25 17.1	25 22.3	30.3	194 30.8	57.6	278 46.0	52.3	156 23.9	30.7			
A 12	40 19.6	40 22.1	S 1 29.2	209 33.8	S 2 57.4	293 48.0	N22 52.3	171 26.6	S15 30.6	Gacrux	171 59.6	S57 11.8
Y 13	55 22.0	55 21.9	28.2	224 36.9	57.3	308 50.1	52.2	186 29.2	30.6	Gienah	175 51.4	S17 37.5
14	70 24.5	70 21.8	27.2	239 39.9	57.2	323 52.1	52.2	201 31.9	30.5	Hadar	148 46.3	S60 26.6
15	85 27.0	85 21.6 . .	26.2	254 43.0 . .	57.1	338 54.2 . .	52.2	216 34.5 . .	30.5	Hamal	328 00.4	N23 31.6
16	100 29.4	100 21.4	25.2	269 46.0	56.9	353 56.3	52.1	231 37.2	30.4	Kaus Aust.	83 42.8	S34 22.4
17	115 31.9	115 21.2	24.1	284 49.0	56.8	8 58.3	52.1	246 39.8	30.4			
18	130 34.4	130 21.0	S 1 23.1	299 52.1	S 2 56.7	24 00.4	N22 52.0	261 42.5	S15 30.3	Kochab	137 19.0	N74 05.8
19	145 36.8	145 20.8	22.1	314 55.1	56.6	39 02.4	52.0	276 45.1	30.3	Markab	13 37.9	N15 16.9
20	160 39.3	160 20.6	21.1	329 58.1	56.5	54 04.5	51.9	291 47.8	30.2	Menkar	314 14.8	N 4 08.5
21	175 41.8	175 20.5 . .	20.1	345 01.1 . .	56.3	69 06.5 . .	51.9	306 50.4 . .	30.2	Menkent	148 06.4	S36 26.5
22	190 44.2	190 20.3	19.0	0 04.2	56.2	84 08.6	51.9	321 53.1	30.1	Miaplacidus	221 39.3	S69 47.0
23	205 46.7	205 20.1	18.0	15 07.2	56.1	99 10.6	51.8	336 55.7	30.1			
3 00	220 49.2	220 19.9	S 1 17.0	30 10.2	S 2 56.0	114 12.7	N22 51.8	351 58.4	S15 30.0	Mirfak	308 39.9	N49 54.6
01	235 51.6	235 19.7	16.0	45 13.2	55.9	129 14.7	51.7	7 01.0	30.0	Nunki	75 57.4	S26 16.5
02	250 54.1	250 19.5	15.0	60 16.3	55.8	144 16.8	51.7	22 03.7	29.9	Peacock	53 18.3	S56 40.9
03	265 56.5	265 19.4 . .	13.9	75 19.3 . .	55.6	159 18.8 . .	51.7	37 06.3 . .	29.9	Pollux	243 27.1	N27 59.3
04	280 59.0	280 19.2	12.9	90 22.3	55.5	174 20.9	51.6	52 09.0	29.8	Procyon	244 59.2	N 5 11.0
05	296 01.5	295 19.0	11.9	105 25.3	55.4	189 22.9	51.6	67 11.6	29.8			
06	311 03.9	310 18.8	S 1 10.9	120 28.3	S 2 55.3	204 25.0	N22 51.5	82 14.3	S15 29.7	Rasalhague	96 05.6	N12 33.0
07	326 06.4	325 18.6	09.9	135 31.4	55.2	219 27.0	51.5	97 16.9	29.7	Regulus	207 42.8	N11 53.7
S 08	341 08.9	340 18.4	08.8	150 34.4	55.1	234 29.1	51.5	112 19.5	29.6	Rigel	281 11.8	S 8 11.4
A 09	356 11.3	355 18.2 . .	07.8	165 37.4 . .	55.0	249 31.1 . .	51.4	127 22.2 . .	29.6	Rigil Kent.	139 50.2	S60 53.6
T 10	11 13.8	10 18.1	06.8	180 40.4	54.9	264 33.2	51.4	142 24.8	29.5	Sabik	102 11.6	S15 44.4
U 11	26 16.3	25 17.9	05.8	195 43.4	54.7	279 35.2	51.3	157 27.5	29.5			
R 12	41 18.7	40 17.7	S 1 04.7	210 46.4	S 2 54.6	294 37.3	N22 51.3	172 30.1	S15 29.4	Schedar	349 40.2	N56 36.8
D 13	56 21.2	55 17.5	03.7	225 49.4	54.5	309 39.3	51.2	187 32.8	29.4	Shaula	96 20.8	S37 06.6
A 14	71 23.7	70 17.3	02.7	240 52.4	54.4	324 41.4	51.2	202 35.4	29.3	Sirius	258 33.4	S16 44.5
Y 15	86 26.1	85 17.1 . .	01.7	255 55.4 . .	54.3	339 43.4 . .	51.2	217 38.1 . .	29.3	Spica	158 30.3	S11 14.3
16	101 28.6	100 16.9	1 00.6	270 58.4	54.2	354 45.5	51.1	232 40.7	29.2	Suhail	222 51.9	S43 29.9
17	116 31.0	115 16.8	0 59.6	286 01.4	54.1	9 47.5	51.1	247 43.4	29.2			
18	131 33.5	130 16.6	S 0 58.5	301 04.4	S 2 54.0	24 49.6	N22 51.0	262 46.0	S15 29.2	Vega	80 38.3	N38 47.8
19	146 36.0	145 16.4	57.6	316 07.4	53.9	39 51.6	51.0	277 48.7	29.1	Zuben'ubi	137 04.4	S16 06.1
20	161 38.4	160 16.2	56.5	331 10.4	53.8	54 53.6	51.0	292 51.3	29.1		SHA	Mer. Pass.
21	176 40.9	175 16.0 . .	55.5	346 13.4 . .	53.7	69 55.7 . .	50.9	307 54.0 . .	29.0		° ′	h m
22	191 43.4	190 15.8	54.5	1 16.4	53.5	84 57.7	50.9	322 56.6	29.0	Venus	0 34.3	9 18
23	206 45.8	205 15.6	53.5	16 19.4	53.4	99 59.8	50.8	337 59.3	28.9	Mars	169 07.3	22 00
	h m									Jupiter	253 33.4	16 24
Mer. Pass.	9 19.1	v −0.2	d 1.0	v 3.0	d 0.1	v 2.1	d 0.0	v 2.6	d 0.0	Saturn	131 04.8	0 36

UT	SUN GHA	SUN Dec	MOON GHA	MOON v	MOON Dec	d	HP
d h	° ′	° ′	° ′	′	° ′	′	′
1 00	180 42.7	N14 59.1	158 41.8	9.9	N17 39.1	3.9	56.3
01	195 42.8	14 59.9	173 10.7	10.0	17 43.0	3.8	56.3
02	210 42.9	15 00.7	187 39.7	10.0	17 46.8	3.7	56.3
03	225 43.0 ..	01.4	202 08.7	10.0	17 50.5	3.6	56.2
04	240 43.0	02.2	216 37.7	9.9	17 54.1	3.5	56.2
05	255 43.1	02.9	231 06.6	10.0	17 57.6	3.4	56.2
T 06	270 43.2	N15 03.7	245 35.6	10.0	N18 01.0	3.2	56.2
H 07	285 43.3	04.4	260 04.6	10.1	18 04.2	3.2	56.1
U 08	300 43.3	05.2	274 33.7	10.0	18 07.4	3.1	56.1
R 09	315 43.4 ..	06.0	289 02.7	10.1	18 10.5	3.0	56.1
S 10	330 43.5	06.7	303 31.8	10.0	18 13.5	2.9	56.1
D 11	345 43.6	07.5	318 00.8	10.1	18 16.4	2.8	56.0
A 12	0 43.6	N15 08.2	332 29.9	10.1	N18 19.2	2.7	56.0
Y 13	15 43.7	09.0	346 59.0	10.1	18 21.9	2.7	56.0
14	30 43.8	09.7	1 28.1	10.1	18 24.6	2.5	56.0
15	45 43.9 ..	10.5	15 57.2	10.2	18 27.1	2.4	55.9
16	60 43.9	11.2	30 26.4	10.1	18 29.5	2.3	55.9
17	75 44.0	12.0	44 55.5	10.2	18 31.8	2.2	55.9
18	90 44.1	N15 12.7	59 24.7	10.2	N18 34.0	2.1	55.9
19	105 44.1	13.5	73 53.9	10.2	18 36.1	2.0	55.8
20	120 44.2	14.2	88 23.1	10.2	18 38.1	1.9	55.8
21	135 44.3 ..	15.0	102 52.3	10.3	18 40.0	1.8	55.8
22	150 44.4	15.7	117 21.6	10.2	18 41.8	1.7	55.8
23	165 44.4	16.5	131 50.8	10.3	18 43.5	1.6	55.7
2 00	180 44.5	N15 17.2	146 20.1	10.3	N18 45.1	1.5	55.7
01	195 44.6	18.0	160 49.4	10.4	18 46.6	1.4	55.7
02	210 44.6	18.7	175 18.8	10.3	18 48.0	1.4	55.7
03	225 44.7 ..	19.5	189 48.1	10.4	18 49.4	1.2	55.6
04	240 44.8	20.2	204 17.5	10.4	18 50.6	1.1	55.6
05	255 44.9	21.0	218 46.9	10.4	18 51.7	1.0	55.6
06	270 44.9	N15 21.7	233 16.3	10.5	N18 52.7	0.9	55.6
F 07	285 45.0	22.5	247 45.8	10.4	18 53.6	0.9	55.5
R 08	300 45.1	23.2	262 15.2	10.5	18 54.5	0.7	55.5
I 09	315 45.1 ..	24.0	276 44.7	10.6	18 55.2	0.6	55.5
D 10	330 45.2	24.7	291 14.3	10.5	18 55.8	0.5	55.5
A 11	345 45.3	25.5	305 43.8	10.6	18 56.3	0.5	55.5
Y 12	0 45.3	N15 26.2	320 13.4	10.6	N18 56.8	0.3	55.4
13	15 45.4	26.9	334 43.0	10.6	18 57.1	0.3	55.4
14	30 45.5	27.7	349 12.6	10.7	18 57.4	0.1	55.4
15	45 45.5 ..	28.4	3 42.3	10.7	18 57.5	0.1	55.4
16	60 45.6	29.2	18 12.0	10.7	18 57.6	0.1	55.3
17	75 45.7	29.9	32 41.7	10.8	18 57.5	0.1	55.3
18	90 45.7	N15 30.7	47 11.5	10.7	N18 57.4	0.3	55.3
19	105 45.8	31.4	61 41.2	10.8	18 57.1	0.3	55.3
20	120 45.9	32.1	76 11.0	10.9	18 56.8	0.4	55.3
21	135 45.9 ..	32.9	90 40.9	10.9	18 56.4	0.5	55.2
22	150 46.0	33.6	105 10.8	10.9	18 55.9	0.7	55.2
23	165 46.1	34.4	119 40.7	10.9	18 55.2	0.7	55.2
3 00	180 46.1	N15 35.1	134 10.6	11.0	N18 54.5	0.8	55.2
01	195 46.2	35.8	148 40.6	11.0	18 53.7	0.9	55.1
02	210 46.3	36.6	163 10.6	11.0	18 52.8	1.0	55.1
03	225 46.3 ..	37.3	177 40.6	11.1	18 51.8	1.0	55.1
04	240 46.4	38.0	192 10.7	11.1	18 50.8	1.2	55.1
05	255 46.5	38.8	206 40.8	11.1	18 49.6	1.3	55.1
06	270 46.5	N15 39.5	221 10.9	11.2	N18 48.3	1.3	55.0
S 07	285 46.6	40.2	235 41.1	11.2	18 47.0	1.5	55.0
A 08	300 46.6	41.0	250 11.3	11.2	18 45.5	1.5	55.0
T 09	315 46.7 ..	41.7	264 41.5	11.3	18 44.0	1.7	55.0
U 10	330 46.8	42.5	279 11.8	11.3	18 42.3	1.7	55.0
R 11	345 46.8	43.2	293 42.1	11.3	18 40.6	1.8	54.9
D 12	0 46.9	N15 43.9	308 12.4	11.4	N18 38.8	1.9	54.9
A 13	15 47.0	44.7	322 42.8	11.4	18 36.9	2.0	54.9
Y 14	30 47.0	45.4	337 13.2	11.5	18 34.9	2.1	54.9
15	45 47.1 ..	46.1	351 43.7	11.5	18 32.8	2.1	54.9
16	60 47.1	46.8	6 14.2	11.5	18 30.7	2.3	54.9
17	75 47.2	47.6	20 44.7	11.5	18 28.4	2.3	54.8
18	90 47.3	N15 48.3	35 15.2	11.7	N18 26.1	2.4	54.8
19	105 47.3	49.0	49 45.9	11.6	18 23.7	2.6	54.8
20	120 47.4	49.8	64 16.5	11.7	18 21.1	2.6	54.8
21	135 47.4 ..	50.5	78 47.2	11.7	18 18.5	2.6	54.8
22	150 47.5	51.2	93 17.9	11.7	18 15.9	2.8	54.8
23	165 47.6	52.0	107 48.6	11.8	N18 13.1	2.9	54.7
	SD 15.9	d 0.7	SD 15.3		15.1		15.0

Lat.	Twilight Naut.	Twilight Civil	Sunrise	Moonrise 1	Moonrise 2	Moonrise 3	Moonrise 4
°	h m	h m	h m	h m	h m	h m	h m
N 72	////	////	01 45	02 15	▭	▭	04 31
N 70	////	////	02 26	03 26	03 48	04 38	05 56
68	////	00 57	02 53	04 03	04 36	05 26	06 34
66	////	01 50	03 14	04 30	05 06	05 57	07 01
64	////	02 21	03 31	04 50	05 29	06 20	07 22
62	00 50	02 44	03 44	05 07	05 48	06 39	07 38
60	01 38	03 02	03 56	05 21	06 03	06 54	07 52
N 58	02 06	03 17	04 06	05 33	06 16	07 07	08 04
56	02 28	03 29	04 14	05 43	06 27	07 18	08 14
54	02 45	03 40	04 22	05 52	06 37	07 27	08 23
52	02 59	03 50	04 29	06 00	06 45	07 36	08 31
50	03 11	03 58	04 35	06 07	06 53	07 44	08 39
45	03 35	04 16	04 48	06 23	07 10	08 00	08 54
N 40	03 54	04 30	04 59	06 36	07 24	08 14	09 07
35	04 09	04 41	05 08	06 47	07 35	08 26	09 18
30	04 21	04 51	05 16	06 57	07 45	08 36	09 27
20	04 40	05 07	05 30	07 13	08 03	08 53	09 43
N 10	04 55	05 21	05 42	07 28	08 18	09 08	09 58
0	05 07	05 32	05 54	07 42	08 33	09 22	10 11
S 10	05 18	05 43	06 05	07 55	08 47	09 37	10 24
20	05 27	05 53	06 16	08 10	09 02	09 52	10 38
30	05 36	06 05	06 29	08 27	09 20	10 09	10 54
35	05 41	06 11	06 37	08 37	09 30	10 19	11 04
40	05 45	06 17	06 46	08 48	09 42	10 31	11 14
45	05 50	06 25	06 56	09 01	09 56	10 44	11 27
S 50	05 55	06 34	07 08	09 17	10 13	11 01	11 42
52	05 57	06 37	07 13	09 25	10 21	11 09	11 49
54	06 00	06 42	07 20	09 34	10 30	11 17	11 57
56	06 02	06 46	07 27	09 43	10 40	11 27	12 06
58	06 05	06 51	07 34	09 54	10 51	11 38	12 16
S 60	06 07	06 57	07 43	10 06	11 04	11 51	12 28

Lat.	Sunset	Twilight Civil	Twilight Naut.	Moonset 1	Moonset 2	Moonset 3	Moonset 4
°	h m	h m	h m	h m	h m	h m	h m
N 72	22 17	////	////	00 35	▭	▭	03 32
N 70	21 33	////	////	24 49	00 49	01 43	02 07
68	21 04	23 11	////	24 01	00 01	00 55	01 28
66	20 43	22 10	////	23 30	24 24	00 24	01 00
64	20 26	21 37	////	23 08	24 00	00 00	00 40
62	20 12	21 13	23 16	22 49	23 42	24 23	00 23
60	20 00	20 54	22 21	22 34	23 27	24 09	00 09
N 58	19 50	20 39	21 51	22 22	23 14	23 56	24 31
56	19 41	20 26	21 29	22 10	23 03	23 46	24 21
54	19 33	20 15	21 11	22 01	22 53	23 37	24 13
52	19 26	20 06	20 57	21 52	22 44	23 28	24 06
50	19 20	19 57	20 44	21 44	22 36	23 21	23 59
45	19 07	19 39	20 20	21 28	22 19	23 05	23 45
N 40	18 56	19 25	20 01	21 14	22 06	22 52	23 33
35	18 46	19 13	19 46	21 03	21 54	22 41	23 23
30	18 38	19 03	19 34	20 53	21 44	22 31	23 15
20	18 24	18 47	19 14	20 35	21 26	22 14	22 59
N 10	18 12	18 34	18 59	20 20	21 11	22 00	22 46
0	18 00	18 22	18 47	20 06	20 57	21 46	22 34
S 10	17 49	18 11	18 36	19 52	20 42	21 32	22 21
20	17 37	18 00	18 27	19 37	20 27	21 17	22 08
30	17 24	17 49	18 17	19 20	20 09	21 00	21 53
35	17 16	17 43	18 13	19 10	19 59	20 50	21 43
40	17 08	17 36	18 08	18 58	19 47	20 39	21 33
45	16 58	17 28	18 03	18 45	19 33	20 26	21 21
S 50	16 45	17 20	17 58	18 28	19 16	20 09	21 06
52	16 40	17 16	17 56	18 20	19 08	20 02	20 59
54	16 34	17 11	17 54	18 12	19 00	19 53	20 51
56	16 27	17 07	17 51	18 02	18 50	19 44	20 43
58	16 19	17 02	17 48	17 51	18 38	19 33	20 33
S 60	16 10	16 56	17 46	17 38	18 25	19 20	20 22

	SUN Eqn. of Time 00h	SUN Eqn. of Time 12h	SUN Mer. Pass.	MOON Mer. Pass. Upper	MOON Mer. Pass. Lower	Age	Phase
Day	m s	m s	h m	h m	h m	d	%
1	02 51	02 54	11 57	13 54	01 28	02	6
2	02 58	03 01	11 57	14 45	02 19	03	11
3	03 04	03 07	11 57	15 34	03 10	04	18

UT	ARIES GHA	VENUS −4.1 GHA	Dec	MARS −1.1 GHA	Dec	JUPITER −2.0 GHA	Dec	SATURN +0.1 GHA	Dec	Name	SHA	Dec
d h	° ′	° ′	° ′	° ′	° ′	° ′	° ′	° ′	° ′		° ′	° ′
4 00	221 48.3	220 15.5	S 0 52.4	31 22.4	S 2 53.3	115 01.8	N22 50.8	353 01.9	S15 28.9	Acamar	315 18.4	S40 15.0
01	236 50.8	235 15.3	51.4	46 25.4	53.2	130 03.9	50.7	8 04.6	28.8	Achernar	335 27.0	S57 09.8
02	251 53.2	250 15.1	50.4	61 28.4	53.1	145 05.9	50.7	23 07.2	28.8	Acrux	173 07.9	S63 11.0
03	266 55.7	265 14.9 ..	49.4	76 31.4 ..	53.0	160 08.0 ..	50.7	38 09.9 ..	28.7	Adhara	255 12.2	S28 59.9
04	281 58.1	280 14.7	48.3	91 34.4	52.9	175 10.0	50.6	53 12.5	28.7	Aldebaran	290 49.0	N16 32.1
05	297 00.6	295 14.5	47.3	106 37.4	52.8	190 12.1	50.6	68 15.2	28.6			
06	312 03.1	310 14.3	S 0 46.3	121 40.4	S 2 52.7	205 14.1	N22 50.5	83 17.8	S15 28.6	Alioth	166 19.8	N55 53.0
07	327 05.5	325 14.2	45.3	136 43.4	52.6	220 16.2	50.5	98 20.5	28.5	Alkaid	152 58.0	N49 14.6
08	342 08.0	340 14.0	44.2	151 46.4	52.5	235 18.2	50.4	113 23.1	28.5	Al Na'ir	27 43.2	S46 53.2
S 09	357 10.5	355 13.8 ..	43.2	166 49.3 ..	52.4	250 20.2 ..	50.4	128 25.8 ..	28.4	Alnilam	275 46.0	S 1 11.9
U 10	12 12.9	10 13.6	42.2	181 52.3	52.3	265 22.3	50.4	143 28.4	28.4	Alphard	217 55.5	S 8 43.5
N 11	27 15.4	25 13.4	41.1	196 55.3	52.2	280 24.3	50.3	158 31.1	28.3			
D 12	42 17.9	40 13.2	S 0 40.1	211 58.3	S 2 52.1	295 26.4	N22 50.3	173 33.7	S15 28.3	Alphecca	126 10.2	N26 40.0
A 13	57 20.3	55 13.0	39.1	227 01.3	52.0	310 28.4	50.2	188 36.4	28.2	Alpheratz	357 43.1	N29 10.0
Y 14	72 22.8	70 12.8	38.1	242 04.2	51.9	325 30.5	50.2	203 39.1	28.2	Altair	62 07.5	N 8 54.4
15	87 25.3	85 12.7 ..	37.0	257 07.2 ..	51.8	340 32.5 ..	50.1	218 41.7 ..	28.1	Ankaa	353 15.5	S42 13.6
16	102 27.7	100 12.5	36.0	272 10.2	51.7	355 34.5	50.1	233 44.4	28.1	Antares	112 25.2	S26 27.7
17	117 30.2	115 12.3	35.0	287 13.2	51.6	10 36.6	50.1	248 47.0	28.0			
18	132 32.6	130 12.1	S 0 33.9	302 16.1	S 2 51.5	25 38.6	N22 50.0	263 49.7	S15 28.0	Arcturus	145 54.9	N19 06.5
19	147 35.1	145 11.9	32.9	317 19.1	51.4	40 40.7	50.0	278 52.3	27.9	Atria	107 25.9	S69 02.9
20	162 37.6	160 11.7	31.9	332 22.1	51.3	55 42.7	49.9	293 55.0	27.9	Avior	234 17.8	S59 33.8
21	177 40.0	175 11.5 ..	30.9	347 25.0 ..	51.2	70 44.8 ..	49.9	308 57.6 ..	27.8	Bellatrix	278 31.6	N 6 21.5
22	192 42.5	190 11.3	29.8	2 28.0	51.2	85 46.8	49.8	324 00.3	27.8	Betelgeuse	271 00.9	N 7 24.3
23	207 45.0	205 11.1	28.8	17 31.0	51.1	100 48.8	49.8	339 02.9	27.7			
5 00	222 47.4	220 11.0	S 0 27.8	32 33.9	S 2 51.0	115 50.9	N22 49.8	354 05.6	S15 27.7	Canopus	263 56.2	S52 42.6
01	237 49.9	235 10.8	26.7	47 36.9	50.9	130 52.9	49.7	9 08.2	27.6	Capella	280 33.9	N46 00.6
02	252 52.4	250 10.6	25.7	62 39.9	50.8	145 55.0	49.7	24 10.9	27.6	Deneb	49 31.0	N45 19.8
03	267 54.8	265 10.4 ..	24.7	77 42.8 ..	50.7	160 57.0 ..	49.6	39 13.5 ..	27.5	Denebola	182 32.9	N14 29.4
04	282 57.3	280 10.2	23.6	92 45.8	50.6	175 59.1	49.6	54 16.2	27.5	Diphda	348 55.6	S17 54.5
05	297 59.8	295 10.0	22.6	107 48.8	50.5	191 01.1	49.5	69 18.8	27.4			
06	313 02.2	310 09.8	S 0 21.6	122 51.7	S 2 50.4	206 03.1	N22 49.5	84 21.5	S15 27.4	Dubhe	193 50.8	N61 40.5
07	328 04.7	325 09.6	20.5	137 54.7	50.3	221 05.2	49.5	99 24.1	27.4	Elnath	278 12.2	N28 37.0
08	343 07.1	340 09.4	19.5	152 57.6	50.2	236 07.2	49.4	114 26.8	27.3	Eltanin	90 45.5	N51 29.2
M 09	358 09.6	355 09.3 ..	18.5	168 00.6 ..	50.2	251 09.3 ..	49.4	129 29.4 ..	27.3	Enif	33 46.6	N 9 56.4
O 10	13 12.1	10 09.1	17.5	183 03.5	50.1	266 11.3	49.3	144 32.1	27.2	Fomalhaut	15 23.5	S29 32.6
N 11	28 14.5	25 08.9	16.4	198 06.5	50.0	281 13.3	49.3	159 34.7	27.2			
D 12	43 17.0	40 08.7	S 0 15.4	213 09.4	S 2 49.9	296 15.4	N22 49.2	174 37.4	S15 27.1	Gacrux	171 59.7	S57 11.9
A 13	58 19.5	55 08.5	14.4	228 12.4	49.8	311 17.4	49.2	189 40.0	27.1	Gienah	175 51.4	S17 37.5
Y 14	73 21.9	70 08.3	13.3	243 15.3	49.7	326 19.4	49.2	204 42.7	27.0	Hadar	148 46.3	S60 26.6
15	88 24.4	85 08.1 ..	12.3	258 18.3 ..	49.6	341 21.5 ..	49.1	219 45.3 ..	27.0	Hamal	328 00.4	N23 31.6
16	103 26.9	100 07.9	11.3	273 21.2	49.6	356 23.5	49.1	234 48.0	26.9	Kaus Aust.	83 42.8	S34 22.4
17	118 29.3	115 07.7	10.2	288 24.2	49.5	11 25.6	49.0	249 50.6	26.9			
18	133 31.8	130 07.6	S 0 09.2	303 27.1	S 2 49.4	26 27.6	N22 49.0	264 53.3	S15 26.8	Kochab	137 19.0	N74 05.9
19	148 34.2	145 07.4	08.1	318 30.1	49.3	41 29.6	48.9	279 55.9	26.8	Markab	13 37.9	N15 16.9
20	163 36.7	160 07.2	07.1	333 33.0	49.2	56 31.7	48.9	294 58.6	26.7	Menkar	314 14.7	N 4 08.5
21	178 39.2	175 07.0 ..	06.1	348 35.9 ..	49.1	71 33.7 ..	48.8	310 01.2 ..	26.7	Menkent	148 06.4	S36 26.5
22	193 41.6	190 06.8	05.0	3 38.9	49.1	86 35.8	48.8	325 03.9	26.6	Miaplacidus	221 39.4	S69 47.0
23	208 44.1	205 06.6	04.0	18 41.8	49.0	101 37.8	48.8	340 06.5	26.6			
6 00	223 46.6	220 06.4	S 0 03.0	33 44.7	S 2 48.9	116 39.8	N22 48.7	355 09.2	S15 26.5	Mirfak	308 39.9	N49 54.5
01	238 49.0	235 06.2	01.9	48 47.7	48.8	131 41.9	48.7	10 11.8	26.5	Nunki	75 57.4	S26 16.5
02	253 51.5	250 06.0	S 00.9	63 50.6	48.7	146 43.9	48.6	25 14.5	26.4	Peacock	53 18.3	S56 40.9
03	268 54.0	265 05.8	N 00.1	78 53.5 ..	48.7	161 45.9 ..	48.6	40 17.1 ..	26.4	Pollux	243 27.2	N27 59.3
04	283 56.4	280 05.6	01.2	93 56.5	48.6	176 48.0	48.5	55 19.8	26.3	Procyon	244 59.2	N 5 11.0
05	298 58.9	295 05.5	02.2	108 59.4	48.5	191 50.0	48.5	70 22.4	26.3			
06	314 01.4	310 05.3	N 0 03.2	124 02.3	S 2 48.4	206 52.0	N22 48.4	85 25.1	S15 26.2	Rasalhague	96 05.6	N12 33.0
07	329 03.8	325 05.1	04.3	139 05.3	48.3	221 54.1	48.4	100 27.7	26.2	Regulus	207 42.8	N11 53.7
T 08	344 06.3	340 04.9	05.3	154 08.2	48.3	236 56.1	48.4	115 30.4	26.1	Rigel	281 11.8	S 8 11.4
U 09	359 08.7	355 04.7 ..	06.3	169 11.1 ..	48.2	251 58.2 ..	48.3	130 33.0 ..	26.1	Rigil Kent.	139 50.1	S60 53.6
E 10	14 11.2	10 04.5	07.4	184 14.0	48.1	267 00.2	48.3	145 35.7	26.0	Sabik	102 11.6	S15 44.4
S 11	29 13.7	25 04.3	08.4	199 16.9	48.0	282 02.2	48.2	160 38.3	26.0			
D 12	44 16.1	40 04.1	N 0 09.5	214 19.9	S 2 48.0	297 04.3	N22 48.2	175 41.0	S15 25.9	Schedar	349 40.2	N56 36.8
A 13	59 18.6	55 03.9	10.5	229 22.8	47.9	312 06.3	48.1	190 43.6	25.9	Shaula	96 20.8	S37 06.6
Y 14	74 21.1	70 03.7	11.5	244 25.7	47.8	327 08.3	48.1	205 46.3	25.8	Sirius	258 33.4	S16 44.5
15	89 23.5	85 03.5 ..	12.6	259 28.6 ..	47.7	342 10.4 ..	48.0	220 48.9 ..	25.8	Spica	158 30.3	S11 14.3
16	104 26.0	100 03.3	13.6	274 31.5	47.7	357 12.4	48.0	235 51.6	25.7	Suhail	222 52.0	S43 29.9
17	119 28.5	115 03.2	14.6	289 34.4	47.6	12 14.4	48.0	250 54.3	25.7			
18	134 30.9	130 03.0	N 0 15.7	304 37.4	S 2 47.5	27 16.5	N22 47.9	265 56.9	S15 25.6	Vega	80 38.3	N38 47.8
19	149 33.4	145 02.8	16.7	319 40.3	47.5	42 18.5	47.9	280 59.6	25.6	Zuben'ubi	137 04.4	S16 06.1
20	164 35.9	160 02.6	17.8	334 43.2	47.4	57 20.5	47.8	296 02.2	25.5		SHA	Mer.Pass.
21	179 38.3	175 02.4 ..	18.8	349 46.1 ..	47.3	72 22.6 ..	47.8	311 04.9 ..	25.5		° ′	h m
22	194 40.8	190 02.2	19.8	4 49.0	47.3	87 24.6	47.7	326 07.5	25.5	Venus	357 23.5	9 19
23	209 43.2	205 02.0	20.9	19 51.9	47.2	102 26.6	47.7	341 10.2	25.4	Mars	169 46.5	21 45
Mer.Pass.	h m 9 07.3	v −0.2	d 1.0	v 2.9	d 0.1	v 2.0	d 0.0	v 2.7	d 0.0	Jupiter Saturn	253 03.5 131 18.1	16 14 0 24

UT	SUN GHA	SUN Dec	MOON GHA	v	MOON Dec	d	HP
d h	° ′	° ′	° ′	′	° ′	′	′
4 00	180 47.6	N15 52.7	122 19.4	11.9	N18 10.2	2.9	54.7
01	195 47.7	53.4	136 50.3	11.8	18 07.3	3.0	54.7
02	210 47.7	54.1	151 21.1	11.9	18 04.3	3.1	54.7
03	225 47.8 ..	54.9	165 52.0	12.0	18 01.2	3.2	54.7
04	240 47.9	55.6	180 23.0	12.0	17 58.0	3.3	54.7
05	255 47.9	56.3	194 54.0	12.0	17 54.7	3.4	54.6
S 06	270 48.0	N15 57.0	209 25.0	12.1	N17 51.3	3.4	54.6
U 07	285 48.0	57.8	223 56.1	12.1	17 47.9	3.5	54.6
N 08	300 48.1	58.5	238 27.2	12.1	17 44.4	3.6	54.6
D 09	315 48.2 ..	59.2	252 58.3	12.2	17 40.8	3.7	54.6
A 10	330 48.2	15 59.9	267 29.5	12.2	17 37.1	3.7	54.6
Y 11	345 48.3	16 00.7	282 00.7	12.3	17 33.4	3.9	54.6
12	0 48.3	N16 01.4	296 32.0	12.3	N17 29.5	3.9	54.5
13	15 48.4	02.1	311 03.3	12.3	17 25.6	4.0	54.5
14	30 48.4	02.8	325 34.6	12.4	17 21.6	4.1	54.5
15	45 48.5 ..	03.5	340 06.0	12.4	17 17.5	4.1	54.5
16	60 48.5	04.3	354 37.4	12.5	17 13.4	4.2	54.5
17	75 48.6	05.0	9 08.9	12.5	17 09.2	4.3	54.5
18	90 48.7	N16 05.7	23 40.4	12.5	N17 04.9	4.4	54.5
19	105 48.7	06.4	38 11.9	12.6	17 00.5	4.5	54.5
20	120 48.8	07.1	52 43.5	12.6	16 56.0	4.5	54.4
21	135 48.8 ..	07.9	67 15.1	12.6	16 51.5	4.6	54.4
22	150 48.9	08.6	81 46.7	12.7	16 46.9	4.7	54.4
23	165 48.9	09.3	96 18.4	12.8	16 42.2	4.7	54.4
5 00	180 49.0	N16 10.0	110 50.2	12.7	N16 37.5	4.9	54.4
01	195 49.0	10.7	125 21.9	12.8	16 32.6	4.9	54.4
02	210 49.1	11.4	139 53.7	12.9	16 27.7	4.9	54.4
03	225 49.2 ..	12.2	154 25.6	12.9	16 22.8	5.1	54.4
04	240 49.2	12.9	168 57.5	12.9	16 17.7	5.1	54.4
05	255 49.3	13.6	183 29.4	13.0	16 12.6	5.2	54.4
06	270 49.3	N16 14.3	198 01.4	13.0	N16 07.4	5.2	54.4
07	285 49.4	15.0	212 33.4	13.0	16 02.2	5.4	54.3
M 08	300 49.4	15.7	227 05.4	13.1	15 56.8	5.4	54.3
O 09	315 49.5 ..	16.4	241 37.5	13.1	15 51.4	5.4	54.3
N 10	330 49.5	17.2	256 09.6	13.1	15 46.0	5.5	54.3
D 11	345 49.6	17.9	270 41.7	13.2	15 40.5	5.6	54.3
A 12	0 49.6	N16 18.6	285 13.9	13.2	N15 34.9	5.7	54.3
Y 13	15 49.7	19.3	299 46.1	13.3	15 29.2	5.7	54.3
14	30 49.7	20.0	314 18.4	13.3	15 23.5	5.8	54.3
15	45 49.8 ..	20.7	328 50.7	13.3	15 17.7	5.9	54.3
16	60 49.8	21.4	343 23.0	13.4	15 11.8	5.9	54.3
17	75 49.9	22.1	357 55.4	13.4	15 05.9	6.0	54.3
18	90 49.9	N16 22.8	12 27.8	13.4	N14 59.9	6.1	54.3
19	105 50.0	23.5	27 00.2	13.5	14 53.8	6.1	54.3
20	120 50.0	24.2	41 32.7	13.5	14 47.7	6.2	54.3
21	135 50.1 ..	25.0	56 05.2	13.5	14 41.5	6.2	54.3
22	150 50.1	25.7	70 37.7	13.6	14 35.3	6.4	54.3
23	165 50.2	26.4	85 10.3	13.6	14 28.9	6.3	54.3
6 00	180 50.2	N16 27.1	99 42.9	13.6	N14 22.6	6.5	54.2
01	195 50.3	27.8	114 15.5	13.7	14 16.1	6.5	54.2
02	210 50.3	28.5	128 48.2	13.7	14 09.6	6.5	54.2
03	225 50.4 ..	29.2	143 20.9	13.7	14 03.1	6.6	54.2
04	240 50.4	29.9	157 53.6	13.8	13 56.5	6.7	54.2
05	255 50.5	30.6	172 26.4	13.8	13 49.8	6.7	54.2
06	270 50.5	N16 31.3	186 59.2	13.8	N13 43.1	6.8	54.2
07	285 50.6	32.0	201 32.0	13.9	13 36.3	6.9	54.2
T 08	300 50.6	32.7	216 04.9	13.9	13 29.4	6.9	54.2
U 09	315 50.6 ..	33.4	230 37.8	13.9	13 22.5	6.9	54.2
E 10	330 50.7	34.1	245 10.7	13.9	13 15.6	7.1	54.2
S 11	345 50.7	34.8	259 43.6	14.0	13 08.5	7.0	54.2
D 12	0 50.8	N16 35.5	274 16.6	14.0	N13 01.5	7.2	54.2
A 13	15 50.8	36.2	288 49.6	14.1	12 54.3	7.2	54.2
Y 14	30 50.9	36.9	303 22.7	14.0	12 47.1	7.2	54.2
15	45 50.9 ..	37.6	317 55.7	14.1	12 39.9	7.3	54.2
16	60 51.0	38.3	332 28.8	14.1	12 32.6	7.3	54.2
17	75 51.0	39.0	347 01.9	14.1	12 25.3	7.4	54.2
18	90 51.1	N16 39.7	1 35.0	14.2	N12 17.9	7.5	54.2
19	105 51.1	40.4	16 08.2	14.2	12 10.4	7.5	54.2
20	120 51.1	41.1	30 41.4	14.2	12 02.9	7.6	54.2
21	135 51.2 ..	41.8	45 14.6	14.3	11 55.3	7.6	54.2
22	150 51.2	42.5	59 47.9	14.2	11 47.7	7.6	54.3
23	165 51.3	43.2	74 21.1	14.3	N11 40.1	7.7	54.3
	SD 15.9	d 0.7	SD 14.9		14.8		14.8

Lat.	Twilight Naut.	Twilight Civil	Sunrise	Moonrise 4	5	6	7
°	h m	h m	h m	h m	h m	h m	h m
N 72	////	////	01 15	04 31	06 42	08 29	10 10
N 70	////	////	02 07	05 56	07 24	08 56	10 26
68	////	////	02 39	06 34	07 53	09 15	10 40
66	////	01 29	03 02	07 01	08 14	09 31	10 50
64	////	02 07	03 20	07 22	08 31	09 44	10 59
62	////	02 32	03 35	07 38	08 45	09 55	11 07
60	01 19	02 52	03 48	07 52	08 56	10 04	11 14
N 58	01 53	03 08	03 58	08 04	09 06	10 12	11 19
56	02 17	03 22	04 08	08 14	09 15	10 19	11 25
54	02 36	03 33	04 16	08 23	09 23	10 25	11 29
52	02 51	03 44	04 23	08 31	09 30	10 31	11 33
50	03 04	03 52	04 30	08 39	09 36	10 36	11 37
45	03 30	04 11	04 44	08 54	09 50	10 47	11 45
N 40	03 50	04 26	04 55	09 07	10 01	10 56	11 52
35	04 05	04 38	05 05	09 18	10 11	11 04	11 58
30	04 18	04 48	05 14	09 27	10 19	11 11	12 03
20	04 38	05 05	05 29	09 43	10 33	11 23	12 12
N 10	04 54	05 19	05 41	09 58	10 46	11 33	12 20
0	05 07	05 32	05 53	10 11	10 58	11 43	12 27
S 10	05 18	05 43	06 05	10 24	11 09	11 52	12 34
20	05 28	05 54	06 17	10 38	11 22	12 03	12 42
30	05 38	06 06	06 31	10 54	11 36	12 14	12 51
35	05 43	06 13	06 39	11 04	11 44	12 21	12 56
40	05 48	06 20	06 49	11 14	11 54	12 29	13 01
45	05 53	06 28	06 59	11 27	12 05	12 38	13 08
S 50	05 59	06 38	07 12	11 42	12 18	12 48	13 16
52	06 02	06 42	07 18	11 49	12 24	12 53	13 19
54	06 04	06 47	07 25	11 57	12 31	12 59	13 23
56	06 07	06 52	07 32	12 06	12 38	13 05	13 28
58	06 10	06 57	07 41	12 16	12 47	13 12	13 33
S 60	06 13	07 03	07 50	12 28	12 56	13 19	13 38

Lat.	Sunset	Twilight Civil	Twilight Naut.	Moonset 4	5	6	7
°	h m	h m	h m	h m	h m	h m	h m
N 72	22 49	////	////	03 32	02 58	02 46	02 38
N 70	21 51	////	////	02 07	02 16	02 19	02 20
68	21 18	////	////	01 28	01 47	01 58	02 05
66	20 54	22 31	////	01 00	01 25	01 42	01 53
64	20 35	21 51	////	00 40	01 08	01 28	01 43
62	20 20	21 24	////	00 23	00 53	01 17	01 35
60	20 07	21 04	22 40	00 09	00 41	01 07	01 28
N 58	19 57	20 47	22 04	24 31	00 31	00 58	01 21
56	19 47	20 33	21 39	24 21	00 21	00 51	01 15
54	19 39	20 21	21 20	24 13	00 13	00 44	01 10
52	19 31	20 11	21 04	24 06	00 06	00 38	01 06
50	19 25	20 02	20 51	23 59	24 32	00 32	01 01
45	19 10	19 43	20 24	23 45	24 20	00 20	00 52
N 40	18 59	19 28	20 05	23 33	24 11	00 11	00 44
35	18 49	19 16	19 49	23 23	24 02	00 02	00 38
30	18 40	19 05	19 36	23 15	23 55	24 32	00 32
20	18 25	18 48	19 16	22 59	23 42	24 22	00 22
N 10	18 12	18 34	19 00	22 46	23 30	24 13	00 13
0	18 00	18 22	18 47	22 34	23 20	24 04	00 04
S 10	17 48	18 10	18 35	22 21	23 09	23 56	24 42
20	17 36	17 59	18 25	22 08	22 57	23 46	24 35
30	17 22	17 47	18 15	21 52	22 44	23 36	24 24
35	17 14	17 40	18 10	21 43	22 36	23 30	24 24
40	17 04	17 33	18 05	21 33	22 28	23 23	24 19
45	16 53	17 25	18 00	21 21	22 17	23 15	24 13
S 50	16 40	17 15	17 54	21 06	22 05	23 05	24 07
52	16 34	17 11	17 51	20 59	21 59	23 01	24 04
54	16 28	17 06	17 48	20 51	21 53	22 56	24 00
56	16 20	17 01	17 46	20 43	21 45	22 50	23 56
58	16 12	16 55	17 43	20 33	21 37	22 44	23 52
S 60	16 02	16 49	17 39	20 22	21 28	22 37	23 47

Day	SUN Eqn. of Time 00h	12h	Mer. Pass.	MOON Mer. Pass. Upper	Lower	Age	Phase
d	m s	m s	h m	h m	h m	d	%
4	03 10	03 13	11 57	16 22	04 58	05	26
5	03 16	03 18	11 57	17 09	04 46	06	35
6	03 21	03 23	11 57	17 53	05 31	07	44

UT	ARIES	VENUS −4.1		MARS −1.0		JUPITER −2.0		SATURN +0.1		STARS		
	GHA	GHA	Dec	GHA	Dec	GHA	Dec	GHA	Dec	Name	SHA	Dec
d h	° ′	° ′	° ′	° ′	° ′	° ′	° ′	° ′	° ′		° ′	° ′
7 00	224 45.7	220 01.8	N 0 21.9	34 54.8	S 2 47.1	117 28.7	N22 47.6	356 12.8	S15 25.4	Acamar	315 18.3	S40 15.0
01	239 48.2	235 01.6	23.0	49 57.7	47.0	132 30.7	47.6	11 15.5	25.3	Achernar	335 27.0	S57 09.8
02	254 50.6	250 01.4	24.0	65 00.6	47.0	147 32.7	47.6	26 18.1	25.3	Acrux	173 07.9	S63 11.0
03	269 53.1	265 01.2	.. 25.0	80 03.5	.. 46.9	162 34.8	.. 47.5	41 20.8	.. 25.2	Adhara	255 12.3	S28 59.9
04	284 55.6	280 01.0	26.1	95 06.4	46.8	177 36.8	47.5	56 23.4	25.2	Aldebaran	290 49.0	N16 32.1
05	299 58.0	295 00.8	27.1	110 09.3	46.8	192 38.8	47.4	71 26.1	25.1			
06	315 00.5	310 00.6	N 0 28.2	125 12.2	S 2 46.7	207 40.8	N22 47.4	86 28.7	S15 25.1	Alioth	166 19.8	N55 53.0
W 07	330 03.0	325 00.4	29.2	140 15.1	46.7	222 42.9	47.3	101 31.4	25.0	Alkaid	152 58.0	N49 14.6
E 08	345 05.4	340 00.3	30.2	155 18.0	46.6	237 44.9	47.3	116 34.0	25.0	Al Na'ir	27 43.1	S46 53.2
D 09	0 07.9	355 00.1	.. 31.3	170 20.9	.. 46.5	252 46.9	.. 47.2	131 36.7	.. 24.9	Alnilam	275 46.0	S 1 11.9
N 10	15 10.3	9 59.9	32.3	185 23.8	46.5	267 49.0	47.2	146 39.3	24.9	Alphard	217 55.5	S 8 43.5
E 11	30 12.8	24 59.7	33.4	200 26.7	46.4	282 51.0	47.1	161 42.0	24.8			
S 12	45 15.3	39 59.5	N 0 34.4	215 29.6	S 2 46.3	297 53.0	N22 47.1	176 44.6	S15 24.8	Alphecca	126 10.2	N26 40.0
D 13	60 17.7	54 59.3	35.4	230 32.5	46.3	312 55.1	47.1	191 47.3	24.7	Alpheratz	357 43.1	N29 10.0
A 14	75 20.2	69 59.1	36.5	245 35.3	46.2	327 57.1	47.0	206 49.9	24.7	Altair	62 07.5	N 8 54.4
Y 15	90 22.7	84 58.9	.. 37.5	260 38.2	.. 46.2	342 59.1	.. 47.0	221 52.6	.. 24.6	Ankaa	353 15.5	S42 13.6
16	105 25.1	99 58.7	38.6	275 41.1	46.1	358 01.1	46.9	236 55.2	24.6	Antares	112 25.2	S26 27.7
17	120 27.6	114 58.5	39.6	290 44.0	46.0	13 03.2	46.9	251 57.9	24.5			
18	135 30.1	129 58.3	N 0 40.6	305 46.9	S 2 46.0	28 05.2	N22 46.8	267 00.5	S15 24.5	Arcturus	145 54.9	N19 06.5
19	150 32.5	144 58.1	41.7	320 49.8	45.9	43 07.2	46.8	282 03.2	24.4	Atria	107 25.9	S69 02.9
20	165 35.0	159 57.9	42.7	335 52.6	45.9	58 09.3	46.7	297 05.8	24.4	Avior	234 17.9	S59 33.8
21	180 37.5	174 57.7	.. 43.8	350 55.5	.. 45.8	73 11.3	.. 46.7	312 08.5	.. 24.3	Bellatrix	278 31.6	N 6 21.5
22	195 39.9	189 57.5	44.8	5 58.4	45.8	88 13.3	46.6	327 11.2	24.3	Betelgeuse	271 00.9	N 7 24.3
23	210 42.4	204 57.3	45.9	21 01.3	45.7	103 15.3	46.6	342 13.8	24.2			
8 00	225 44.8	219 57.1	N 0 46.9	36 04.1	S 2 45.6	118 17.4	N22 46.6	357 16.5	S15 24.2	Canopus	263 56.2	S52 42.6
01	240 47.3	234 56.9	47.9	51 07.0	45.6	133 19.4	46.5	12 19.1	24.1	Capella	280 34.0	N46 00.6
02	255 49.8	249 56.7	49.0	66 09.9	45.5	148 21.4	46.5	27 21.8	24.1	Deneb	49 30.9	N45 19.8
03	270 52.2	264 56.5	.. 50.0	81 12.8	.. 45.5	163 23.5	.. 46.4	42 24.4	.. 24.0	Denebola	182 32.9	N14 29.4
04	285 54.7	279 56.4	51.1	96 15.6	45.4	178 25.5	46.4	57 27.1	24.0	Diphda	348 55.6	S17 54.5
05	300 57.2	294 56.2	52.1	111 18.5	45.4	193 27.5	46.3	72 29.7	23.9			
06	315 59.6	309 56.0	N 0 53.2	126 21.4	S 2 45.3	208 29.5	N22 46.3	87 32.4	S15 23.9	Dubhe	193 50.8	N61 40.5
T 07	331 02.1	324 55.8	54.2	141 24.2	45.3	223 31.6	46.2	102 35.0	23.8	Elnath	278 12.2	N28 37.0
H 08	346 04.6	339 55.6	55.2	156 27.1	45.2	238 33.6	46.2	117 37.7	23.8	Eltanin	90 45.5	N51 29.2
U 09	1 07.0	354 55.4	.. 56.3	171 30.0	.. 45.2	253 35.6	.. 46.1	132 40.3	.. 23.8	Enif	33 46.6	N 9 56.4
R 10	16 09.5	9 55.2	57.3	186 32.8	45.1	268 37.6	46.1	147 43.0	23.7	Fomalhaut	15 23.5	S29 32.6
S 11	31 12.0	24 55.0	58.4	201 35.7	45.1	283 39.7	46.0	162 45.6	23.7			
D 12	46 14.4	39 54.8	N 0 59.4	216 38.5	S 2 45.0	298 41.7	N22 46.0	177 48.3	S15 23.6	Gacrux	171 59.7	S57 11.9
A 13	61 16.9	54 54.6	1 00.5	231 41.4	45.0	313 43.7	45.9	192 50.9	23.6	Gienah	175 51.4	S17 37.5
Y 14	76 19.3	69 54.4	01.5	246 44.2	44.9	328 45.7	45.9	207 53.6	23.5	Hadar	148 46.3	S60 26.6
15	91 21.8	84 54.2	.. 02.5	261 47.1	.. 44.9	343 47.8	.. 45.9	222 56.2	.. 23.5	Hamal	328 00.4	N23 31.6
16	106 24.3	99 54.0	03.6	276 50.0	44.8	358 49.8	45.8	237 58.9	23.4	Kaus Aust.	83 42.7	S34 22.4
17	121 26.7	114 53.8	04.6	291 52.8	44.8	13 51.8	45.8	253 01.5	23.4			
18	136 29.2	129 53.6	N 1 05.7	306 55.7	S 2 44.7	28 53.8	N22 45.7	268 04.2	S15 23.3	Kochab	137 19.0	N74 05.9
19	151 31.7	144 53.4	06.7	321 58.5	44.7	43 55.9	45.7	283 06.8	23.3	Markab	13 37.9	N15 16.9
20	166 34.1	159 53.2	07.8	337 01.4	44.6	58 57.9	45.6	298 09.5	23.2	Menkar	314 14.7	N 4 08.6
21	181 36.6	174 53.0	.. 08.8	352 04.2	.. 44.6	73 59.9	.. 45.6	313 12.1	.. 23.2	Menkent	148 06.4	S36 26.5
22	196 39.1	189 52.8	09.9	7 07.0	44.5	89 01.9	45.5	328 14.8	23.1	Miaplacidus	221 39.4	S69 47.0
23	211 41.5	204 52.6	10.9	22 09.9	44.5	104 04.0	45.5	343 17.5	23.1			
9 00	226 44.0	219 52.4	N 1 12.0	37 12.7	S 2 44.5	119 06.0	N22 45.4	358 20.1	S15 23.0	Mirfak	308 39.9	N49 54.5
01	241 46.4	234 52.2	13.0	52 15.6	44.4	134 08.0	45.4	13 22.8	23.0	Nunki	75 57.4	S26 16.5
02	256 48.9	249 52.0	14.0	67 18.4	44.4	149 10.0	45.3	28 25.4	22.9	Peacock	53 18.2	S56 40.9
03	271 51.4	264 51.8	.. 15.1	82 21.3	.. 44.3	164 12.1	.. 45.3	43 28.1	.. 22.9	Pollux	243 27.2	N27 59.3
04	286 53.8	279 51.6	16.1	97 24.1	44.3	179 14.1	45.2	58 30.7	22.8	Procyon	244 59.2	N 5 11.0
05	301 56.3	294 51.4	17.2	112 26.9	44.3	194 16.1	45.2	73 33.4	22.8			
06	316 58.8	309 51.2	N 1 18.2	127 29.8	S 2 44.2	209 18.1	N22 45.2	88 36.0	S15 22.7	Rasalhague	96 05.6	N12 33.0
07	332 01.2	324 51.0	19.3	142 32.6	44.2	224 20.2	45.1	103 38.7	22.7	Regulus	207 42.8	N11 53.7
08	347 03.7	339 50.8	20.3	157 35.4	44.1	239 22.2	45.1	118 41.3	22.6	Rigel	281 11.8	S 8 11.4
F 09	2 06.2	354 50.6	.. 21.4	172 38.3	.. 44.1	254 24.2	.. 45.0	133 44.0	.. 22.6	Rigil Kent.	139 50.1	S60 53.6
R 10	17 08.6	9 50.4	22.4	187 41.1	44.1	269 26.2	45.0	148 46.6	22.5	Sabik	102 11.5	S15 44.4
I 11	32 11.1	24 50.2	23.5	202 43.9	44.0	284 28.2	44.9	163 49.3	22.5			
D 12	47 13.6	39 50.0	N 1 24.5	217 46.8	S 2 44.0	299 30.3	N22 44.9	178 51.9	S15 22.4	Schedar	349 40.2	N56 36.7
A 13	62 16.0	54 49.8	25.6	232 49.6	43.9	314 32.3	44.8	193 54.6	22.4	Shaula	96 20.7	S37 06.6
Y 14	77 18.5	69 49.6	26.6	247 52.4	43.9	329 34.3	44.8	208 57.2	22.3	Sirius	258 33.4	S16 44.5
15	92 20.9	84 49.4	.. 27.6	262 55.2	.. 43.9	344 36.3	.. 44.7	223 59.9	.. 22.3	Spica	158 30.3	S11 14.3
16	107 23.4	99 49.2	28.7	277 58.1	43.8	359 38.3	44.7	239 02.5	22.2	Suhail	222 52.0	S43 29.9
17	122 25.9	114 49.0	29.7	293 00.9	43.8	14 40.4	44.6	254 05.2	22.2			
18	137 28.3	129 48.8	N 1 30.8	308 03.7	S 2 43.8	29 42.4	N22 44.6	269 07.8	S15 22.1	Vega	80 38.3	N38 47.8
19	152 30.8	144 48.6	31.8	323 06.5	43.7	44 44.4	44.5	284 10.5	22.1	Zuben'ubi	137 04.4	S16 06.1
20	167 33.3	159 48.4	32.9	338 09.3	43.7	59 46.4	44.5	299 13.1	22.1			
21	182 35.7	174 48.2	.. 33.9	353 12.1	.. 43.7	74 48.4	.. 44.4	314 15.8	.. 22.0		SHA	Mer. Pass.
22	197 38.2	189 48.0	35.0	8 15.0	43.6	89 50.5	44.4	329 18.5	22.0		° ′	h m
23	212 40.7	204 47.8	36.0	23 17.8	43.6	104 52.5	44.3	344 21.1	21.9	Venus	354 12.3	9 23
	h m									Mars	170 19.3	21 32
Mer. Pass. 8 55.5		v −0.2	d 1.0	v 2.9	d 0.0	v 2.0	d 0.0	v 2.7	d 0.0	Jupiter	252 32.5	16 05
										Saturn	131 31.6	0 11

SUN and MOON

UT	SUN GHA	SUN Dec	MOON GHA	v	MOON Dec	d	HP
d h	° ′	° ′	° ′	′	° ′	′	′
7 00	180 51.3	N16 43.9	88 54.4	14.3	N11 32.4	7.8	54.3
01	195 51.4	44.5	103 27.7	14.3	11 24.6	7.8	54.3
02	210 51.4	45.2	118 01.0	14.4	11 16.8	7.9	54.3
03	225 51.4 ..	45.9	132 34.4	14.3	11 08.9	7.9	54.3
04	240 51.5	46.6	147 07.8	14.3	11 01.0	7.9	54.3
05	255 51.5	47.3	161 41.1	14.5	10 53.1	8.0	54.3
06	270 51.6	N16 48.0	176 14.6	14.5	N10 45.1	8.1	54.3
07	285 51.6	48.7	190 48.0	14.4	10 37.0	8.0	54.3
08	300 51.6	49.4	205 21.4	14.5	10 29.0	8.2	54.3
09	315 51.7 ..	50.1	219 54.9	14.5	10 20.8	8.2	54.3
10	330 51.7	50.8	234 28.4	14.5	10 12.6	8.2	54.3
11	345 51.8	51.5	249 01.9	14.5	10 04.4	8.3	54.3
12	0 51.8	N16 52.1	263 35.4	14.5	N 9 56.1	8.3	54.3
13	15 51.8	52.8	278 08.9	14.6	9 47.8	8.3	54.3
14	30 51.9	53.5	292 42.5	14.5	9 39.5	8.5	54.3
15	45 51.9 ..	54.2	307 16.0	14.6	9 31.0	8.4	54.4
16	60 52.0	54.9	321 49.6	14.6	9 22.6	8.5	54.4
17	75 52.0	55.6	336 23.2	14.6	9 14.1	8.5	54.4
18	90 52.0	N16 56.3	350 56.8	14.6	N 9 05.6	8.6	54.4
19	105 52.1	56.9	5 30.4	14.7	8 57.0	8.6	54.4
20	120 52.1	57.6	20 04.1	14.6	8 48.4	8.6	54.4
21	135 52.2 ..	58.3	34 37.7	14.7	8 39.8	8.7	54.4
22	150 52.2	59.0	49 11.4	14.6	8 31.1	8.8	54.4
23	165 52.2	16 59.7	63 45.0	14.7	8 22.3	8.7	54.4
8 00	180 52.3	N17 00.4	78 18.7	14.7	N 8 13.6	8.8	54.4
01	195 52.3	01.0	92 52.4	14.6	8 04.8	8.9	54.5
02	210 52.3	01.7	107 26.0	14.7	7 55.9	8.9	54.5
03	225 52.4 ..	02.4	121 59.7	14.7	7 47.0	8.9	54.5
04	240 52.4	03.1	136 33.4	14.7	7 38.1	8.9	54.5
05	255 52.4	03.8	151 07.1	14.8	7 29.2	9.0	54.5
06	270 52.5	N17 04.4	165 40.9	14.7	N 7 20.2	9.0	54.5
07	285 52.5	05.1	180 14.6	14.7	7 11.2	9.1	54.5
08	300 52.6	05.8	194 48.3	14.7	7 02.1	9.1	54.5
09	315 52.6 ..	06.5	209 22.0	14.7	6 53.0	9.1	54.6
10	330 52.6	07.1	223 55.7	14.8	6 43.9	9.2	54.6
11	345 52.7	07.8	238 29.5	14.7	6 34.7	9.2	54.6
12	0 52.7	N17 08.5	253 03.2	14.7	N 6 25.5	9.2	54.6
13	15 52.7	09.2	267 36.9	14.7	6 16.3	9.3	54.6
14	30 52.8	09.9	282 10.6	14.8	6 07.0	9.2	54.6
15	45 52.8 ..	10.5	296 44.4	14.7	5 57.8	9.4	54.6
16	60 52.8	11.2	311 18.1	14.7	5 48.4	9.3	54.7
17	75 52.9	11.9	325 51.8	14.7	5 39.1	9.4	54.7
18	90 52.9	N17 12.5	340 25.5	14.8	N 5 29.7	9.4	54.7
19	105 52.9	13.2	354 59.3	14.7	5 20.3	9.4	54.7
20	120 53.0	13.9	9 33.0	14.7	5 10.9	9.5	54.7
21	135 53.0 ..	14.6	24 06.7	14.7	5 01.4	9.5	54.7
22	150 53.0	15.2	38 40.4	14.7	4 51.9	9.5	54.8
23	165 53.1	15.9	53 14.1	14.7	4 42.4	9.5	54.8
9 00	180 53.1	N17 16.6	67 47.8	14.7	N 4 32.9	9.6	54.8
01	195 53.1	17.2	82 21.5	14.6	4 23.3	9.6	54.8
02	210 53.1	17.9	96 55.1	14.7	4 13.7	9.6	54.8
03	225 53.2 ..	18.6	111 28.8	14.7	4 04.1	9.7	54.9
04	240 53.2	19.3	126 02.5	14.6	3 54.4	9.6	54.9
05	255 53.2	19.9	140 36.1	14.6	3 44.8	9.7	54.9
06	270 53.3	N17 20.6	155 09.7	14.7	N 3 35.1	9.7	54.9
07	285 53.3	21.3	169 43.4	14.6	3 25.4	9.8	54.9
08	300 53.3	21.9	184 17.0	14.6	3 15.6	9.7	55.0
09	315 53.4 ..	22.6	198 50.6	14.5	3 05.9	9.8	55.0
10	330 53.4	23.2	213 24.1	14.6	2 56.1	9.8	55.0
11	345 53.4	23.9	227 57.7	14.5	2 46.3	9.8	55.1
12	0 53.4	N17 24.6	242 31.2	14.6	N 2 36.5	9.9	55.0
13	15 53.5	25.2	257 04.8	14.5	2 26.6	9.8	55.1
14	30 53.5	25.9	271 38.3	14.5	2 16.8	9.9	55.1
15	45 53.5 ..	26.6	286 11.8	14.5	2 06.9	9.9	55.1
16	60 53.6	27.2	300 45.3	14.4	1 57.0	9.9	55.1
17	75 53.6	27.9	315 18.7	14.5	1 47.1	9.9	55.1
18	90 53.6	N17 28.6	329 52.2	14.4	N 1 37.2	10.0	55.2
19	105 53.6	29.2	344 25.6	14.4	1 27.2	9.9	55.2
20	120 53.7	29.9	358 59.0	14.4	1 17.3	10.0	55.2
21	135 53.7 ..	30.5	13 32.4	14.3	1 07.3	10.0	55.2
22	150 53.7	31.2	28 05.7	14.3	0 57.3	10.0	55.3
23	165 53.7	31.8	42 39.0	14.3	N 0 47.3	10.0	55.3
	SD 15.9 d 0.7		SD 14.8		14.9		15.0

Day labels: 7 = WEDNESDAY, 8 = THURSDAY, 9 = FRIDAY

Twilight, Sunrise and Moonrise

Lat.	Naut.	Civil	Sunrise	Moonrise 7	8	9	10
°	h m	h m	h m	h m	h m	h m	h m
N 72	////	////	00 28	10 10	11 47	13 24	15 03
N 70	////	////	01 47	10 26	11 57	13 28	15 00
68	////	////	02 24	10 40	12 04	13 30	14 58
66	////	01 05	02 50	10 50	12 11	13 32	14 56
64	////	01 51	03 10	10 59	12 16	13 34	14 54
62	////	02 21	03 26	11 07	12 21	13 36	14 53
60	00 57	02 42	03 40	11 14	12 25	13 37	14 52
N 58	01 40	03 00	03 51	11 19	12 28	13 39	14 51
56	02 07	03 14	04 01	11 25	12 31	13 40	14 50
54	02 27	03 27	04 10	11 29	12 34	13 41	14 49
52	02 44	03 37	04 18	11 33	12 37	13 42	14 48
50	02 58	03 47	04 25	11 37	12 39	13 42	14 47
45	03 25	04 07	04 40	11 45	12 44	13 44	14 46
N 40	03 45	04 22	04 52	11 52	12 48	13 46	14 44
35	04 02	04 35	05 02	11 58	12 52	13 47	14 43
30	04 15	04 46	05 12	12 03	12 55	13 48	14 42
20	04 36	05 04	05 27	12 12	13 01	13 50	14 41
N 10	04 53	05 18	05 41	12 20	13 06	13 52	14 39
0	05 06	05 31	05 53	12 27	13 10	13 54	14 38
S 10	05 18	05 43	06 05	12 34	13 15	13 55	14 37
20	05 29	05 55	06 18	12 42	13 20	13 57	14 35
30	05 40	06 08	06 33	12 51	13 25	13 59	14 34
35	05 45	06 15	06 42	12 56	13 28	14 00	14 33
40	05 50	06 23	06 52	13 01	13 32	14 02	14 32
45	05 56	06 32	07 03	13 08	13 36	14 03	14 31
S 50	06 03	06 42	07 17	13 16	13 41	14 05	14 29
52	06 06	06 46	07 23	13 19	13 43	14 06	14 29
54	06 09	06 51	07 30	13 23	13 46	14 07	14 28
56	06 12	06 57	07 38	13 28	13 48	14 08	14 27
58	06 15	07 03	07 47	13 33	13 51	14 09	14 26
S 60	06 19	07 10	07 57	13 38	13 55	14 10	14 25

Sunset, Twilight and Moonset

Lat.	Sunset	Civil	Naut.	Moonset 7	8	9	10
°	h m	h m	h m	h m	h m	h m	h m
N 72	23 26	☐	☐	02 38	02 30	02 24	02 17
N 70	22 12	////	////	02 20	02 19	02 18	02 17
68	21 33	////	////	02 05	02 10	02 13	02 16
66	21 06	22 58	////	01 53	02 02	02 10	02 16
64	20 45	22 06	////	01 43	01 56	02 06	02 16
62	20 29	21 36	////	01 35	01 50	02 03	02 16
60	20 15	21 13	23 04	01 28	01 45	02 01	02 16
N 58	20 03	20 55	22 17	01 21	01 41	01 59	02 16
56	19 53	20 40	21 49	01 15	01 37	01 57	02 16
54	19 44	20 28	21 28	01 10	01 33	01 55	02 16
52	19 36	20 17	21 11	01 06	01 30	01 53	02 16
50	19 29	20 07	20 57	01 01	01 27	01 52	02 16
45	19 14	19 47	20 29	00 52	01 21	01 49	02 16
N 40	19 02	19 32	20 08	00 44	01 16	01 46	02 15
35	18 51	19 19	19 52	00 38	01 11	01 43	02 15
30	18 42	19 08	19 38	00 32	01 07	01 41	02 15
20	18 26	18 49	19 17	00 22	01 00	01 37	02 15
N 10	18 13	18 35	19 00	00 13	00 54	01 34	02 15
0	18 00	18 22	18 47	00 04	00 48	01 31	02 15
S 10	17 48	18 09	18 35	24 42	00 42	01 28	02 15
20	17 34	17 57	18 24	24 35	00 35	01 25	02 14
30	17 19	17 44	18 13	24 28	00 28	01 21	02 14
35	17 11	17 37	18 08	24 24	00 24	01 18	02 14
40	17 01	17 30	18 02	24 19	00 19	01 16	02 14
45	16 50	17 21	17 56	24 13	00 13	01 13	02 14
S 50	16 36	17 11	17 49	24 07	00 07	01 09	02 13
52	16 29	17 06	17 47	24 04	00 04	01 08	02 13
54	16 22	17 01	17 44	24 00	00 00	01 06	02 13
56	16 14	16 55	17 40	23 56	25 04	01 04	02 13
58	16 05	16 49	17 37	23 52	25 02	01 02	02 13
S 60	15 55	16 43	17 33	23 47	24 59	00 59	02 13

SUN and MOON data

Day	Eqn. of Time 00h	12h	Mer. Pass.	Mer. Pass. Upper	Lower	Age	Phase
d	m s	m s	h m	h m	h m	d	%
7	03 25	03 27	11 57	18 37	06 15	08	54
8	03 29	03 31	11 56	19 21	06 59	09	63
9	03 32	03 34	11 56	20 04	07 42	10	72

UT	ARIES GHA	VENUS −4.1 GHA	Dec	MARS −0.9 GHA	Dec	JUPITER −2.0 GHA	Dec	SATURN +0.1 GHA	Dec	STARS Name	SHA	Dec
10 00	227 43.1	219 47.6	N 1 37.1	38 20.6	S 2 43.6	119 54.5	N22 44.3	359 23.8	S15 21.9	Acamar	315 18.3	S40 15.0
01	242 45.6	234 47.4	38.1	53 23.4	43.6	134 56.5	44.2	14 26.4	21.8	Achernar	335 27.0	S57 09.8
02	257 48.0	249 47.2	39.2	68 26.2	43.5	149 58.5	44.2	29 29.1	21.8	Acrux	173 08.0	S63 11.0
03	272 50.5	264 47.0	.. 40.2	83 29.0	.. 43.5	165 00.6	.. 44.2	44 31.7	.. 21.7	Adhara	255 12.3	S28 59.9
04	287 53.0	279 46.8	41.3	98 31.8	43.5	180 02.6	44.1	59 34.4	21.7	Aldebaran	290 49.0	N16 32.1
05	302 55.4	294 46.6	42.3	113 34.6	43.4	195 04.6	44.1	74 37.0	21.6			
06	317 57.9	309 46.4	N 1 43.4	128 37.4	S 2 43.4	210 06.6	N22 44.0	89 39.7	S15 21.6	Alioth	166 19.8	N55 53.0
S 07	333 00.4	324 46.2	44.4	143 40.2	43.4	225 08.6	44.0	104 42.3	21.5	Alkaid	152 58.0	N49 14.6
A 08	348 02.8	339 46.0	45.5	158 43.0	43.4	240 10.6	43.9	119 45.0	21.5	Al Na'ir	27 43.1	S46 53.2
T 09	3 05.3	354 45.8	.. 46.5	173 45.8	.. 43.3	255 12.7	.. 43.9	134 47.6	.. 21.4	Alnilam	275 46.0	S 1 11.8
U 10	18 07.8	9 45.6	47.6	188 48.6	43.3	270 14.7	43.8	149 50.3	21.4	Alphard	217 55.5	S 8 43.5
R 11	33 10.2	24 45.4	48.6	203 51.4	43.3	285 16.7	43.8	164 52.9	21.3			
D 12	48 12.7	39 45.2	N 1 49.7	218 54.2	S 2 43.3	300 18.7	N22 43.7	179 55.6	S15 21.3	Alphecca	126 10.1	N26 40.0
A 13	63 15.2	54 45.0	50.7	233 57.0	43.2	315 20.7	43.7	194 58.2	21.2	Alpheratz	357 43.1	N29 10.0
Y 14	78 17.6	69 44.8	51.8	248 59.8	43.2	330 22.8	43.6	210 00.9	21.2	Altair	62 07.5	N 8 54.4
15	93 20.1	84 44.6	.. 52.8	264 02.6	.. 43.2	345 24.8	.. 43.6	225 03.5	.. 21.1	Ankaa	353 15.5	S42 13.6
16	108 22.5	99 44.3	53.9	279 05.4	43.2	0 26.8	43.5	240 06.2	21.1	Antares	112 25.1	S26 27.7
17	123 25.0	114 44.1	54.9	294 08.2	43.1	15 28.8	43.5	255 08.8	21.0			
18	138 27.5	129 43.9	N 1 56.0	309 11.0	S 2 43.1	30 30.8	N22 43.4	270 11.5	S15 21.0	Arcturus	145 54.9	N19 06.5
19	153 29.9	144 43.7	57.0	324 13.8	43.1	45 32.8	43.4	285 14.2	20.9	Atria	107 25.9	S69 02.9
20	168 32.4	159 43.5	58.1	339 16.6	43.1	60 34.8	43.3	300 16.8	20.9	Avior	234 17.9	S59 33.8
21	183 34.9	174 43.3	1 59.1	354 19.3	43.1	75 36.9	.. 43.3	315 19.5	.. 20.8	Bellatrix	278 31.6	N 6 21.5
22	198 37.3	189 43.1	2 00.2	9 22.1	43.0	90 38.9	43.2	330 22.1	20.8	Betelgeuse	271 00.9	N 7 24.3
23	213 39.8	204 42.9	01.2	24 24.9	43.0	105 40.9	43.2	345 24.8	20.7			
11 00	228 42.3	219 42.7	N 2 02.3	39 27.7	S 2 43.0	120 42.9	N22 43.1	0 27.4	S15 20.7	Canopus	263 56.3	S52 42.6
01	243 44.7	234 42.5	03.3	54 30.5	43.0	135 44.9	43.1	15 30.1	20.6	Capella	280 34.0	N46 00.6
02	258 47.2	249 42.3	04.4	69 33.2	43.0	150 46.9	43.0	30 32.7	20.6	Deneb	49 30.9	N45 19.8
03	273 49.7	264 42.1	.. 05.4	84 36.0	.. 43.0	165 49.0	.. 43.0	45 35.4	.. 20.6	Denebola	182 32.9	N14 29.4
04	288 52.1	279 41.9	06.5	99 38.8	42.9	180 51.0	42.9	60 38.0	20.5	Diphda	348 55.6	S17 54.5
05	303 54.6	294 41.7	07.5	114 41.6	42.9	195 53.0	42.9	75 40.7	20.5			
06	318 57.0	309 41.5	N 2 08.6	129 44.4	S 2 42.9	210 55.0	N22 42.8	90 43.3	S15 20.4	Dubhe	193 50.8	N61 40.5
07	333 59.5	324 41.3	09.6	144 47.1	42.9	225 57.0	42.8	105 46.0	20.4	Elnath	278 12.2	N28 37.0
08	349 02.0	339 41.1	10.7	159 49.9	42.9	240 59.0	42.7	120 48.6	20.3	Eltanin	90 45.4	N51 29.2
S 09	4 04.4	354 40.9	.. 11.7	174 52.7	.. 42.9	256 01.0	.. 42.7	135 51.3	.. 20.3	Enif	33 46.5	N 9 56.5
U 10	19 06.9	9 40.7	12.8	189 55.4	42.8	271 03.1	42.6	150 53.9	20.2	Fomalhaut	15 23.5	S29 32.6
N 11	34 09.4	24 40.4	13.8	204 58.2	42.8	286 05.1	42.6	165 56.6	20.2			
D 12	49 11.8	39 40.2	N 2 14.9	220 01.0	S 2 42.8	301 07.1	N22 42.5	180 59.2	S15 20.1	Gacrux	171 59.7	S57 11.9
A 13	64 14.3	54 40.0	15.9	235 03.7	42.8	316 09.1	42.5	196 01.9	20.1	Gienah	175 51.4	S17 37.5
Y 14	79 16.8	69 39.8	17.0	250 06.5	42.8	331 11.1	42.4	211 04.5	20.0	Hadar	148 46.3	S60 26.6
15	94 19.2	84 39.6	.. 18.0	265 09.3	.. 42.8	346 13.1	.. 42.4	226 07.2	.. 20.0	Hamal	328 00.4	N23 31.6
16	109 21.7	99 39.4	19.1	280 12.0	42.8	1 15.1	42.3	241 09.8	19.9	Kaus Aust.	83 42.7	S34 22.4
17	124 24.1	114 39.2	20.1	295 14.8	42.8	16 17.1	42.3	256 12.5	19.9			
18	139 26.6	129 39.0	N 2 21.2	310 17.5	S 2 42.8	31 19.2	N22 42.2	271 15.2	S15 19.8	Kochab	137 19.0	N74 05.9
19	154 29.1	144 38.8	22.2	325 20.3	42.8	46 21.2	42.2	286 17.8	19.8	Markab	13 37.8	N15 16.9
20	169 31.5	159 38.6	23.3	340 23.0	42.7	61 23.2	42.1	301 20.5	19.7	Menkar	314 14.7	N 4 08.6
21	184 34.0	174 38.4	.. 24.3	355 25.8	42.7	76 25.2	.. 42.1	316 23.1	.. 19.7	Menkent	148 06.4	S36 26.5
22	199 36.5	189 38.2	25.4	10 28.5	42.7	91 27.2	42.0	331 25.8	19.6	Miaplacidus	221 39.5	S69 47.0
23	214 38.9	204 38.0	26.4	25 31.3	42.7	106 29.2	42.0	346 28.4	19.6			
12 00	229 41.4	219 37.7	N 2 27.5	40 34.1	S 2 42.7	121 31.2	N22 41.9	1 31.1	S15 19.5	Mirfak	308 39.9	N49 54.5
01	244 43.9	234 37.5	28.6	55 36.8	42.7	136 33.2	41.9	16 33.7	19.5	Nunki	75 57.3	S26 16.5
02	259 46.3	249 37.3	29.6	70 39.5	42.7	151 35.2	41.8	31 36.4	19.4	Peacock	53 18.2	S56 40.9
03	274 48.8	264 37.1	.. 30.7	85 42.3	.. 42.7	166 37.2	.. 41.8	46 39.0	.. 19.4	Pollux	243 27.2	N27 59.3
04	289 51.3	279 36.9	31.7	100 45.0	42.7	181 39.3	41.7	61 41.7	19.3	Procyon	244 59.3	N 5 11.0
05	304 53.7	294 36.7	32.8	115 47.8	42.7	196 41.3	41.7	76 44.3	19.3			
06	319 56.2	309 36.5	N 2 33.8	130 50.5	S 2 42.7	211 43.3	N22 41.6	91 47.0	S15 19.2	Rasalhague	96 05.6	N12 33.0
07	334 58.6	324 36.3	34.9	145 53.3	42.7	226 45.3	41.6	106 49.6	19.2	Regulus	207 42.8	N11 53.7
M 08	350 01.1	339 36.1	35.9	160 56.0	42.7	241 47.3	41.5	121 52.3	19.2	Rigel	281 11.8	S 8 11.4
O 09	5 03.6	354 35.9	.. 37.0	175 58.7	.. 42.7	256 49.3	.. 41.5	136 54.9	.. 19.1	Rigil Kent.	139 50.1	S60 53.6
N 10	20 06.0	9 35.6	38.0	191 01.5	42.7	271 51.3	41.4	151 57.6	19.1	Sabik	102 11.5	S15 44.4
11	35 08.5	24 35.4	39.1	206 04.2	42.7	286 53.3	41.4	167 00.2	19.0			
D 12	50 11.0	39 35.2	N 2 40.1	221 07.0	S 2 42.7	301 55.3	N22 41.3	182 02.9	S15 19.0	Schedar	349 40.2	N56 36.7
A 13	65 13.4	54 35.0	41.2	236 09.7	42.7	316 57.3	41.3	197 05.5	18.9	Shaula	96 20.7	S37 06.6
Y 14	80 15.9	69 34.8	42.2	251 12.4	42.7	331 59.4	41.2	212 08.2	18.9	Sirius	258 33.4	S16 44.5
15	95 18.4	84 34.6	.. 43.3	266 15.1	.. 42.7	347 01.4	.. 41.2	227 10.8	.. 18.8	Spica	158 30.3	S11 14.3
16	110 20.8	99 34.4	44.3	281 17.9	42.7	2 03.4	41.1	242 13.5	18.8	Suhail	222 52.0	S43 29.9
17	125 23.3	114 34.2	45.4	296 20.6	42.7	17 05.4	41.1	257 16.2	18.7			
18	140 25.8	129 34.0	N 2 46.5	311 23.3	S 2 42.7	32 07.4	N22 41.0	272 18.8	S15 18.7	Vega	80 38.2	N38 47.8
19	155 28.2	144 33.7	47.5	326 26.1	42.7	47 09.4	41.0	287 21.5	18.6	Zuben'ubi	137 04.4	S16 06.1
20	170 30.7	159 33.5	48.6	341 28.8	42.7	62 11.4	40.9	302 24.1	18.6		SHA	Mer. Pass.
21	185 33.1	174 33.3	.. 49.6	356 31.5	42.7	77 13.4	.. 40.9	317 26.8	.. 18.5			
22	200 35.6	189 33.1	50.7	11 34.2	42.7	92 15.4	40.8	332 29.4	18.5	Venus	351 00.5	9 21
23	215 38.1	204 32.9	51.7	26 36.9	42.7	107 17.4	40.8	347 32.1	18.4	Mars	170 45.4	21 18
Mer. Pass. 8 43.7		v −0.2	d 1.1	v 2.8	d 0.0	v 2.0	d 0.0	v 2.7	d 0.0	Jupiter	252 00.7	15 55
										Saturn	131 45.2	23 54

UT	SUN GHA	SUN Dec	MOON GHA	v	MOON Dec	d	HP
d h	° ′	° ′	° ′	′	° ′	′	′
10 00	180 53.8	N17 32.5	57 12.3	14.3	N 0 37.3	10.0	55.3
01	195 53.8	33.2	71 45.6	14.3	0 27.3	10.0	55.3
02	210 53.8	33.8	86 18.9	14.2	0 17.3	10.1	55.3
03	225 53.8	.. 34.5	100 52.1	14.2	N 0 07.2	10.0	55.3
04	240 53.9	35.1	115 25.3	14.2	S 0 02.8	10.1	55.4
05	255 53.9	35.8	129 58.5	14.1	0 12.9	10.1	55.4
S 06	270 53.9	N17 36.4	144 31.6	14.1	S 0 23.0	10.0	55.4
A 07	285 53.9	37.1	159 04.7	14.1	0 33.1	10.0	55.5
T 08	300 54.0	37.8	173 37.8	14.0	0 43.1	10.1	55.5
U 09	315 54.0	.. 38.4	188 10.8	14.1	0 53.2	10.1	55.5
R 10	330 54.0	39.1	202 43.9	13.9	1 03.3	10.2	55.5
D 11	345 54.0	39.7	217 16.8	14.0	1 13.5	10.1	55.6
A 12	0 54.0	N17 40.4	231 49.8	13.9	S 1 23.6	10.1	55.6
Y 13	15 54.1	41.0	246 22.7	13.9	1 33.7	10.1	55.6
14	30 54.1	41.7	260 55.6	13.8	1 43.8	10.1	55.7
15	45 54.1	.. 42.3	275 28.4	13.8	1 53.9	10.2	55.7
16	60 54.1	43.0	290 01.2	13.8	2 04.1	10.1	55.7
17	75 54.2	43.6	304 34.0	13.8	2 14.2	10.1	55.7
18	90 54.2	N17 44.3	319 06.8	13.6	S 2 24.3	10.1	55.8
19	105 54.2	44.9	333 39.4	13.7	2 34.4	10.2	55.8
20	120 54.2	45.6	348 12.1	13.6	2 44.6	10.1	55.8
21	135 54.2	.. 46.2	2 44.7	13.6	2 54.7	10.1	55.8
22	150 54.3	46.9	17 17.3	13.5	3 04.8	10.1	55.9
23	165 54.3	47.5	31 49.8	13.5	3 14.9	10.2	55.9
11 00	180 54.3	N17 48.1	46 22.3	13.5	S 3 25.1	10.1	55.9
01	195 54.3	48.8	60 54.8	13.4	3 35.2	10.1	56.0
02	210 54.3	49.4	75 27.2	13.3	3 45.3	10.1	56.0
03	225 54.4	.. 50.1	89 59.5	13.3	3 55.4	10.1	56.0
04	240 54.4	50.7	104 31.8	13.3	4 05.5	10.1	56.0
05	255 54.4	51.4	119 04.1	13.2	4 15.6	10.0	56.1
S 06	270 54.4	N17 52.0	133 36.3	13.2	S 4 25.6	10.1	56.1
U 07	285 54.4	52.6	148 08.5	13.1	4 35.7	10.1	56.1
N 08	300 54.5	53.3	162 40.6	13.1	4 45.8	10.0	56.2
D 09	315 54.5	.. 53.9	177 12.7	13.0	4 55.8	10.1	56.2
A 10	330 54.5	54.6	191 44.7	13.0	5 05.9	10.0	56.2
Y 11	345 54.5	55.2	206 16.7	12.9	5 15.9	10.0	56.2
12	0 54.5	N17 55.8	220 48.6	12.9	S 5 25.9	10.0	56.3
13	15 54.6	56.5	235 20.5	12.8	5 35.9	10.0	56.3
14	30 54.6	57.1	249 52.3	12.8	5 45.9	9.9	56.3
15	45 54.6	.. 57.8	264 24.1	12.7	5 55.8	10.0	56.4
16	60 54.6	58.4	278 55.8	12.7	6 05.8	9.9	56.4
17	75 54.6	59.0	293 27.5	12.6	6 15.7	9.9	56.4
18	90 54.6	N17 59.7	307 59.1	12.6	S 6 25.6	9.9	56.5
19	105 54.6	18 00.3	322 30.7	12.5	6 35.5	9.9	56.5
20	120 54.6	00.9	337 02.2	12.4	6 45.4	9.9	56.5
21	135 54.7	.. 01.6	351 33.6	12.4	6 55.3	9.8	56.5
22	150 54.7	02.2	6 05.0	12.3	7 05.1	9.8	56.6
23	165 54.7	02.8	20 36.3	12.3	7 14.9	9.8	56.6
12 00	180 54.7	N18 03.5	35 07.6	12.2	S 7 24.7	9.7	56.6
01	195 54.7	04.1	49 38.8	12.2	7 34.4	9.7	56.7
02	210 54.7	04.7	64 10.0	12.1	7 44.2	9.7	56.7
03	225 54.7	.. 05.4	78 41.1	12.0	7 53.9	9.6	56.7
04	240 54.8	06.0	93 12.1	12.0	8 03.5	9.7	56.8
05	255 54.8	06.6	107 43.1	11.9	8 13.2	9.6	56.8
M 06	270 54.8	N18 07.3	122 14.0	11.8	S 8 22.8	9.6	56.8
O 07	285 54.8	07.9	136 44.8	11.8	8 32.4	9.6	56.8
N 08	300 54.8	08.5	151 15.6	11.7	8 42.0	9.5	56.9
D 09	315 54.8	.. 09.2	165 46.3	11.7	8 51.5	9.5	56.9
A 10	330 54.8	09.8	180 17.0	11.6	9 01.0	9.4	56.9
Y 11	345 54.8	10.4	194 47.6	11.5	9 10.4	9.4	57.0
12	0 54.8	N18 11.0	209 18.1	11.4	S 9 19.8	9.4	57.0
13	15 54.9	11.7	223 48.5	11.4	9 29.2	9.4	57.0
14	30 54.9	12.3	238 18.9	11.4	9 38.6	9.3	57.1
15	45 54.9	.. 12.9	252 49.3	11.2	9 47.9	9.3	57.1
16	60 54.9	13.5	267 19.5	11.2	9 57.2	9.2	57.1
17	75 54.9	14.2	281 49.7	11.2	10 06.4	9.2	57.2
18	90 54.9	N18 14.8	296 19.9	11.0	S10 15.6	9.1	57.2
19	105 54.9	15.4	310 49.9	11.0	10 24.7	9.1	57.2
20	120 54.9	16.0	325 19.9	10.9	10 33.8	9.1	57.2
21	135 54.9	.. 16.6	339 49.8	10.9	10 42.9	9.0	57.3
22	150 54.9	17.3	354 19.7	10.8	10 51.9	8.9	57.3
23	165 55.0	17.9	8 49.5	10.7	S11 00.8	8.9	57.3
	SD 15.9	d 0.6	SD 15.1		15.3		15.5

Lat.	Twilight Naut.	Twilight Civil	Sunrise	Moonrise 10	11	12	13
°	h m	h m	h m	h m	h m	h m	h m
N 72	☐	☐	☐	15 03	16 46	18 35	20 33
N 70	////	////	01 24	15 00	16 36	18 17	20 02
68	////	////	02 09	14 58	16 29	18 03	19 40
66	////	00 27	02 39	14 56	16 22	17 51	19 23
64	////	01 35	03 00	14 54	16 17	17 42	19 09
62	////	02 08	03 18	14 53	16 12	17 34	18 57
60	00 23	02 33	03 32	14 52	16 08	17 27	18 47
N 58	01 25	02 51	03 45	14 51	16 05	17 21	18 39
56	01 56	03 07	03 55	14 50	16 02	17 16	18 31
54	02 18	03 20	04 04	14 49	15 59	17 11	18 24
52	02 36	03 32	04 13	14 48	15 56	17 07	18 18
50	02 51	03 42	04 20	14 47	15 54	17 03	18 13
45	03 20	04 02	04 36	14 46	15 49	16 54	18 01
N 40	03 41	04 19	04 49	14 44	15 45	16 47	17 51
35	03 58	04 32	05 00	14 43	15 41	16 41	17 43
30	04 12	04 43	05 09	14 42	15 38	16 36	17 36
20	04 35	05 02	05 26	14 41	15 33	16 27	17 23
N 10	04 52	05 18	05 40	14 39	15 28	16 19	17 13
0	05 06	05 31	05 53	14 38	15 24	16 12	17 02
S 10	05 18	05 44	06 06	14 37	15 19	16 04	16 52
20	05 30	05 56	06 20	14 35	15 15	15 56	16 42
30	05 41	06 10	06 35	14 34	15 09	15 48	16 30
35	05 47	06 17	06 44	14 33	15 06	15 43	16 23
40	05 53	06 26	06 54	14 32	15 03	15 37	16 15
45	05 59	06 35	07 06	14 31	14 59	15 30	16 05
S 50	06 07	06 46	07 21	14 29	14 55	15 22	15 54
52	06 10	06 51	07 28	14 29	14 52	15 19	15 49
54	06 13	06 56	07 35	14 28	14 50	15 15	15 44
56	06 16	07 02	07 44	14 27	14 48	15 11	15 37
58	06 20	07 08	07 53	14 26	14 45	15 06	15 31
S 60	06 24	07 16	08 04	14 25	14 42	15 00	15 23

Lat.	Sunset	Twilight Civil	Twilight Naut.	Moonset 10	11	12	13
°	h m	h m	h m	h m	h m	h m	h m
N 72	☐	☐	☐	02 17	02 10	02 03	01 54
N 70	22 36	////	////	02 17	02 15	02 14	02 14
68	21 48	////	////	02 16	02 20	02 23	02 29
66	21 17	////	////	02 16	02 23	02 31	02 41
64	20 55	22 23	////	02 16	02 26	02 38	02 52
62	20 37	21 48	////	02 16	02 29	02 43	03 01
60	20 22	21 23	////	02 16	02 32	02 48	03 08
N 58	20 10	21 03	22 33	02 16	02 34	02 53	03 15
56	19 59	20 47	22 00	02 16	02 36	02 57	03 21
54	19 49	20 34	21 37	02 16	02 37	03 00	03 27
52	19 41	20 22	21 18	02 16	02 39	03 04	03 32
50	19 33	20 12	21 03	02 16	02 40	03 07	03 36
45	19 18	19 51	20 34	02 16	02 43	03 13	03 46
N 40	19 04	19 35	20 12	02 15	02 46	03 18	03 54
35	18 53	19 21	19 55	02 15	02 48	03 23	04 01
30	18 44	19 10	19 41	02 15	02 50	03 27	04 07
20	18 27	18 51	19 19	02 15	02 54	03 34	04 17
N 10	18 13	18 35	19 01	02 15	02 57	03 40	04 27
0	18 00	18 22	18 47	02 15	03 00	03 46	04 36
S 10	17 47	18 09	18 34	02 15	03 02	03 52	04 44
20	17 33	17 56	18 23	02 14	03 05	03 58	04 54
30	17 17	17 42	18 11	02 14	03 09	04 06	05 04
35	17 08	17 35	18 05	02 14	03 11	04 10	05 11
40	16 58	17 27	17 59	02 14	03 13	04 14	05 18
45	16 46	17 17	17 53	02 14	03 16	04 20	05 26
S 50	16 31	17 06	17 46	02 13	03 19	04 26	05 36
52	16 24	17 02	17 42	02 13	03 20	04 30	05 40
54	16 17	16 56	17 39	02 13	03 22	04 33	05 46
56	16 08	16 50	17 36	02 13	03 24	04 37	05 51
58	15 59	16 44	17 32	02 13	03 26	04 41	05 58
S 60	15 48	16 36	17 28	02 13	03 28	04 45	06 05

Day	SUN Eqn. of Time 00h	SUN Eqn. of Time 12h	SUN Mer. Pass.	MOON Mer. Pass. Upper	MOON Mer. Pass. Lower	Age	Phase
d	m s	m s	h m	h m	h m	d	%
10	03 35	03 36	11 56	20 49	08 26	11	80
11	03 37	03 38	11 56	21 35	09 12	12	88
12	03 39	03 39	11 56	22 23	09 59	13	94

UT	ARIES GHA	VENUS −4.1 GHA	Dec	MARS −0.9 GHA	Dec	JUPITER −1.9 GHA	Dec	SATURN +0.1 GHA	Dec	STARS Name	SHA	Dec
d h	° ′	° ′	° ′	° ′	° ′	° ′	° ′	° ′	° ′		° ′	° ′
13 00	230 40.5	219 32.7	N 2 52.8	41 39.7	S 2 42.7	122 19.4	N22 40.7	2 34.7	S15 18.4	Acamar	315 18.3	S40 15.0
01	245 43.0	234 32.5	53.8	56 42.4	42.7	137 21.4	40.7	17 37.4	18.3	Achernar	335 26.9	S57 09.8
02	260 45.5	249 32.3	54.9	71 45.1	42.8	152 23.4	40.6	32 40.0	18.3	Acrux	173 08.0	S63 11.0
03	275 47.9	264 32.0	.. 55.9	86 47.8	.. 42.8	167 25.4	.. 40.6	47 42.7	.. 18.2	Adhara	255 12.3	S28 59.9
04	290 50.4	279 31.8	57.0	101 50.5	42.8	182 27.5	40.5	62 45.3	18.2	Aldebaran	290 49.0	N16 32.1
05	305 52.9	294 31.6	58.0	116 53.2	42.8	197 29.5	40.5	77 48.0	18.1			
06	320 55.3	309 31.4	N 2 59.1	131 56.0	S 2 42.8	212 31.5	N22 40.4	92 50.6	S15 18.1	Alioth	166 19.8	N55 53.0
07	335 57.8	324 31.2	3 00.1	146 58.7	42.8	227 33.5	40.4	107 53.3	18.0	Alkaid	152 58.0	N49 14.6
T 08	351 00.2	339 31.0	01.2	162 01.4	42.8	242 35.5	40.3	122 55.9	18.0	Al Na'ir	27 43.1	S46 53.2
U 09	6 02.7	354 30.8	.. 02.3	177 04.1	.. 42.8	257 37.5	.. 40.3	137 58.6	.. 18.0	Alnilam	275 46.0	S 1 11.8
E 10	21 05.2	9 30.5	03.3	192 06.8	42.8	272 39.5	40.2	153 01.2	17.9	Alphard	217 55.5	S 8 43.5
S 11	36 07.6	24 30.3	04.4	207 09.5	42.8	287 41.5	40.2	168 03.9	17.9			
D 12	51 10.1	39 30.1	N 3 05.4	222 12.2	S 2 42.9	302 43.5	N22 40.1	183 06.5	S15 17.8	Alphecca	126 10.1	N26 40.0
A 13	66 12.6	54 29.9	06.5	237 14.9	42.9	317 45.5	40.1	198 09.2	17.8	Alpheratz	357 43.0	N29 10.0
Y 14	81 15.0	69 29.7	07.5	252 17.6	42.9	332 47.5	40.0	213 11.8	17.7	Altair	62 07.5	N 8 54.4
15	96 17.5	84 29.5	.. 08.6	267 20.3	.. 42.9	347 49.5	.. 40.0	228 14.5	.. 17.7	Ankaa	353 15.4	S42 13.5
16	111 20.0	99 29.3	09.6	282 23.0	42.9	2 51.5	39.9	243 17.2	17.7	Antares	112 25.1	S26 27.7
17	126 22.4	114 29.0	10.7	297 25.7	42.9	17 53.5	39.9	258 19.8	17.6			
18	141 24.9	129 28.8	N 3 11.7	312 28.4	S 2 42.9	32 55.5	N22 39.8	273 22.5	S15 17.5	Arcturus	145 54.9	N19 06.5
19	156 27.4	144 28.6	12.8	327 31.1	43.0	47 57.5	39.8	288 25.1	17.5	Atria	107 25.8	S69 02.9
20	171 29.8	159 28.4	13.9	342 33.8	43.0	62 59.5	39.7	303 27.8	17.4	Avior	234 17.9	S59 33.8
21	186 32.3	174 28.2	.. 14.9	357 36.5	.. 43.0	78 01.5	.. 39.7	318 30.4	.. 17.4	Bellatrix	278 31.7	N 6 21.5
22	201 34.7	189 28.0	16.0	12 39.2	43.0	93 03.5	39.6	333 33.1	17.3	Betelgeuse	271 00.9	N 7 24.3
23	216 37.2	204 27.7	17.0	27 41.8	43.0	108 05.5	39.6	348 35.7	17.3			
14 00	231 39.7	219 27.5	N 3 18.1	42 44.5	S 2 43.1	123 07.5	N22 39.5	3 38.4	S15 17.2	Canopus	263 56.3	S52 42.6
01	246 42.1	234 27.3	19.1	57 47.2	43.1	138 09.5	39.5	18 41.0	17.2	Capella	280 34.0	N46 00.6
02	261 44.6	249 27.1	20.2	72 49.9	43.1	153 11.5	39.4	33 43.7	17.1	Deneb	49 30.9	N45 19.8
03	276 47.1	264 26.9	.. 21.2	87 52.6	.. 43.1	168 13.5	.. 39.3	48 46.3	.. 17.1	Denebola	182 32.9	N14 29.4
04	291 49.5	279 26.7	22.3	102 55.3	43.1	183 15.6	39.3	63 49.0	17.0	Diphda	348 55.5	S17 54.5
05	306 52.0	294 26.4	23.3	117 58.0	43.2	198 17.6	39.2	78 51.6	17.0			
06	321 54.5	309 26.2	N 3 24.4	133 00.6	S 2 43.2	213 19.6	N22 39.2	93 54.3	S15 16.9	Dubhe	193 50.8	N61 40.6
W 07	336 56.9	324 26.0	25.5	148 03.3	43.2	228 21.6	39.1	108 56.9	16.9	Elnath	278 12.2	N28 37.0
E 08	351 59.4	339 25.8	26.5	163 06.0	43.2	243 23.6	39.1	123 59.6	16.9	Eltanin	90 45.4	N51 29.2
D 09	7 01.9	354 25.6	.. 27.6	178 08.7	.. 43.2	258 25.6	.. 39.0	139 02.2	.. 16.8	Enif	33 46.5	N 9 56.5
N 10	22 04.3	9 25.3	28.6	193 11.3	43.3	273 27.6	39.0	154 04.9	16.8	Fomalhaut	15 23.5	S29 32.6
E 11	37 06.8	24 25.1	29.7	208 14.0	43.3	288 29.6	38.9	169 07.5	16.7			
S 12	52 09.2	39 24.9	N 3 30.7	223 16.7	S 2 43.3	303 31.6	N22 38.9	184 10.2	S15 16.7	Gacrux	171 59.7	S57 11.9
D 13	67 11.7	54 24.7	31.8	238 19.4	43.3	318 33.6	38.8	199 12.8	16.6	Gienah	175 51.4	S17 37.5
A 14	82 14.2	69 24.5	32.8	253 22.0	43.4	333 35.6	38.8	214 15.5	16.6	Hadar	148 46.3	S60 26.6
Y 15	97 16.6	84 24.2	.. 33.9	268 24.7	.. 43.4	348 37.6	.. 38.7	229 18.1	.. 16.5	Hamal	328 00.4	N23 31.6
16	112 19.1	99 24.0	34.9	283 27.4	43.4	3 39.6	38.7	244 20.8	16.5	Kaus Aust.	83 42.7	S34 22.4
17	127 21.6	114 23.8	36.0	298 30.0	43.5	18 41.6	38.6	259 23.4	16.4			
18	142 24.0	129 23.6	N 3 37.1	313 32.7	S 2 43.5	33 43.6	N22 38.6	274 26.1	S15 16.4	Kochab	137 19.0	N74 05.9
19	157 26.5	144 23.4	38.1	328 35.4	43.5	48 45.6	38.5	289 28.7	16.3	Markab	13 37.8	N15 16.9
20	172 29.0	159 23.1	39.2	343 38.0	43.5	63 47.6	38.5	304 31.4	16.3	Menkar	314 14.7	N 4 08.6
21	187 31.4	174 22.9	.. 40.2	358 40.7	.. 43.6	78 49.6	.. 38.4	319 34.1	.. 16.2	Menkent	148 06.4	S36 26.5
22	202 33.9	189 22.7	41.3	13 43.3	43.6	93 51.6	38.4	334 36.7	16.2	Miaplacidus	221 39.5	S69 47.0
23	217 36.3	204 22.5	42.3	28 46.0	43.6	108 53.6	38.3	349 39.4	16.1			
15 00	232 38.8	219 22.3	N 3 43.4	43 48.7	S 2 43.7	123 55.6	N22 38.2	4 42.0	S15 16.1	Mirfak	308 39.9	N49 54.5
01	247 41.3	234 22.0	44.4	58 51.3	43.7	138 57.6	38.2	19 44.7	16.0	Nunki	75 57.3	S26 16.5
02	262 43.7	249 21.8	45.5	73 54.0	43.7	153 59.6	38.1	34 47.3	16.0	Peacock	53 18.2	S56 40.9
03	277 46.2	264 21.6	.. 46.5	88 56.6	.. 43.8	169 01.6	.. 38.1	49 50.0	.. 15.9	Pollux	243 27.2	N27 59.3
04	292 48.7	279 21.4	47.6	103 59.3	43.8	184 03.6	38.0	64 52.6	15.9	Procyon	244 59.3	N 5 11.0
05	307 51.1	294 21.1	48.7	119 01.9	43.8	199 05.6	38.0	79 55.3	15.9			
06	322 53.6	309 20.9	N 3 49.7	134 04.6	S 2 43.9	214 07.6	N22 37.9	94 57.9	S15 15.8	Rasalhague	96 05.6	N12 33.1
T 07	337 56.1	324 20.7	50.8	149 07.2	43.9	229 09.5	37.9	110 00.6	15.8	Regulus	207 42.8	N11 53.7
H 08	352 58.5	339 20.5	51.8	164 09.9	43.9	244 11.5	37.8	125 03.2	15.7	Rigel	281 11.8	S 8 11.4
U 09	8 01.0	354 20.3	.. 52.9	179 12.5	.. 44.0	259 13.5	.. 37.8	140 05.9	.. 15.7	Rigil Kent.	139 50.1	S60 53.7
R 10	23 03.5	9 20.0	53.9	194 15.2	44.0	274 15.5	37.7	155 08.5	15.6	Sabik	102 11.5	S15 44.4
S 11	38 05.9	24 19.8	55.0	209 17.8	44.0	289 17.5	37.7	170 11.2	15.6			
D 12	53 08.4	39 19.6	N 3 56.0	224 20.4	S 2 44.1	304 19.5	N22 37.6	185 13.8	S15 15.5	Schedar	349 40.1	N56 36.7
A 13	68 10.8	54 19.4	57.1	239 23.1	44.1	319 21.5	37.6	200 16.5	15.5	Shaula	96 20.7	S37 06.6
Y 14	83 13.3	69 19.1	58.2	254 25.7	44.1	334 23.5	37.5	215 19.1	15.4	Sirius	258 33.4	S16 44.5
15	98 15.8	84 18.9	3 59.2	269 28.4	.. 44.2	349 25.5	.. 37.4	230 21.8	.. 15.4	Spica	158 30.3	S11 14.3
16	113 18.2	99 18.7	4 00.3	284 31.0	44.2	4 27.5	37.4	245 24.4	15.3	Suhail	222 52.0	S43 29.9
17	128 20.7	114 18.5	01.3	299 33.6	44.3	19 29.5	37.3	260 27.1	15.3			
18	143 23.2	129 18.2	N 4 02.4	314 36.3	S 2 44.3	34 31.5	N22 37.3	275 29.7	S15 15.2	Vega	80 38.2	N38 47.8
19	158 25.6	144 18.0	03.4	329 38.9	44.3	49 33.5	37.2	290 32.4	15.2	Zuben'ubi	137 04.4	S16 06.1
20	173 28.1	159 17.8	04.5	344 41.5	44.4	64 35.5	37.2	305 35.0	15.1			
21	188 30.6	174 17.6	.. 05.5	359 44.2	.. 44.4	79 37.5	.. 37.1	320 37.7	.. 15.1		SHA	Mer. Pass.
22	203 33.0	189 17.3	06.6	14 46.8	44.5	94 39.5	37.1	335 40.3	15.0	Venus	347 47.8	9 22
23	218 35.5	204 17.1	07.6	29 49.4	44.5	109 41.5	37.0	350 43.0	15.0	Mars	171 04.9	21 05
Mer. Pass.	h m 8 32.0	v −0.2	d 1.1	v 2.7	d 0.0	v 2.0	d 0.1	v 2.7	d 0.0	Jupiter	251 27.9	15 45
										Saturn	131 58.7	23 41

UT	SUN GHA	SUN Dec	MOON GHA	v	MOON Dec	d	HP
13 00	180 55.0	N18 18.5	23 19.2	10.6	S11 09.7	8.9	57.4
01	195 55.0	19.1	37 48.8	10.6	11 18.6	8.8	57.4
02	210 55.0	19.7	52 18.4	10.5	11 27.4	8.8	57.4
03	225 55.0 ..	20.4	66 47.9	10.4	11 36.2	8.7	57.5
04	240 55.0	21.0	81 17.3	10.4	11 44.9	8.6	57.5
05	255 55.0	21.6	95 46.7	10.3	11 53.5	8.6	57.5
06	270 55.0	N18 22.2	110 16.0	10.2	S12 02.1	8.6	57.6
07	285 55.0	22.8	124 45.2	10.1	12 10.7	8.5	57.6
08	300 55.0	23.5	139 14.3	10.1	12 19.2	8.4	57.6
09	315 55.0 ..	24.1	153 43.4	10.0	12 27.6	8.4	57.6
10	330 55.0	24.7	168 12.4	9.9	12 36.0	8.3	57.7
11	345 55.0	25.3	182 41.3	9.9	12 44.3	8.2	57.7
12	0 55.0	N18 25.9	197 10.2	9.8	S12 52.5	8.2	57.7
13	15 55.0	26.5	211 39.0	9.7	13 00.7	8.1	57.8
14	30 55.0	27.1	226 07.7	9.6	13 08.8	8.1	57.8
15	45 55.1 ..	27.7	240 36.3	9.6	13 16.9	8.0	57.8
16	60 55.1	28.4	255 04.9	9.5	13 24.9	7.9	57.8
17	75 55.1	29.0	269 33.4	9.4	13 32.8	7.9	57.9
18	90 55.1	N18 29.6	284 01.8	9.3	S13 40.7	7.7	57.9
19	105 55.1	30.2	298 30.1	9.3	13 48.4	7.8	57.9
20	120 55.1	30.8	312 58.4	9.2	13 56.2	7.6	58.0
21	135 55.1 ..	31.4	327 26.6	9.1	14 03.8	7.6	58.0
22	150 55.1	32.0	341 54.7	9.1	14 11.4	7.5	58.0
23	165 55.1	32.6	356 22.8	9.0	14 18.9	7.4	58.1
14 00	180 55.1	N18 33.2	10 50.8	8.9	S14 26.3	7.3	58.1
01	195 55.1	33.8	25 18.7	8.8	14 33.6	7.3	58.1
02	210 55.0	34.4	39 46.5	8.8	14 40.9	7.2	58.1
03	225 55.1 ..	35.1	54 14.3	8.7	14 48.1	7.1	58.2
04	240 55.1	35.7	68 42.0	8.6	14 55.2	7.1	58.2
05	255 55.1	36.3	83 09.6	8.5	15 02.3	6.9	58.2
06	270 55.1	N18 36.9	97 37.1	8.5	S15 09.2	6.9	58.2
07	285 55.1	37.5	112 04.6	8.4	15 16.1	6.8	58.3
08	300 55.1	38.1	126 32.0	8.4	15 22.9	6.6	58.3
09	315 55.1 ..	38.7	140 59.4	8.2	15 29.5	6.7	58.3
10	330 55.1	39.3	155 26.6	8.2	15 36.2	6.5	58.4
11	345 55.1	39.9	169 53.8	8.1	15 42.7	6.4	58.4
12	0 55.1	N18 40.5	184 20.9	8.1	S15 49.1	6.4	58.4
13	15 55.1	41.1	198 48.0	8.0	15 55.5	6.2	58.5
14	30 55.1	41.7	213 15.0	7.9	16 01.7	6.2	58.5
15	45 55.1 ..	42.3	227 41.9	7.8	16 07.9	6.1	58.5
16	60 55.1	42.9	242 08.7	7.8	16 14.0	5.9	58.5
17	75 55.1	43.5	256 35.5	7.7	16 19.9	5.9	58.5
18	90 55.1	N18 44.1	271 02.2	7.7	S16 25.8	5.8	58.6
19	105 55.1	44.7	285 28.9	7.6	16 31.6	5.7	58.6
20	120 55.1	45.3	299 55.5	7.5	16 37.3	5.6	58.6
21	135 55.1 ..	45.9	314 22.0	7.4	16 42.9	5.5	58.6
22	150 55.1	46.5	328 48.4	7.4	16 48.4	5.4	58.7
23	165 55.1	47.1	343 14.8	7.3	16 53.8	5.3	58.7
15 00	180 55.1	N18 47.6	357 41.1	7.3	S16 59.1	5.2	58.7
01	195 55.0	48.2	12 07.4	7.2	17 04.3	5.0	58.7
02	210 55.0	48.8	26 33.6	7.1	17 09.3	5.0	58.8
03	225 55.0 ..	49.4	40 59.7	7.1	17 14.3	4.9	58.8
04	240 55.0	50.0	55 25.8	7.0	17 19.2	4.8	58.8
05	255 55.0	50.6	69 51.8	7.0	17 24.0	4.6	58.8
06	270 55.0	N18 51.2	84 17.8	6.9	S17 28.6	4.6	58.9
07	285 55.0	51.8	98 43.7	6.8	17 33.2	4.5	58.9
08	300 55.0	52.4	113 09.5	6.8	17 37.7	4.3	58.9
09	315 55.0 ..	53.0	127 35.3	6.7	17 42.0	4.2	58.9
10	330 55.0	53.6	142 01.0	6.7	17 46.2	4.1	58.9
11	345 55.0	54.1	156 26.7	6.6	17 50.3	4.1	59.0
12	0 55.0	N18 54.7	170 52.3	6.6	S17 54.4	3.8	59.0
13	15 55.0	55.3	185 17.9	6.5	17 58.2	3.8	59.0
14	30 55.0	55.9	199 43.4	6.5	18 02.0	3.7	59.0
15	45 55.0 ..	56.5	214 08.9	6.4	18 05.7	3.5	59.0
16	60 55.0	57.1	228 34.3	6.4	18 09.2	3.5	59.1
17	75 55.0	57.7	242 59.7	6.3	18 12.7	3.3	59.1
18	90 54.9	N18 58.2	257 25.0	6.3	S18 16.0	3.2	59.1
19	105 54.9	58.8	271 50.3	6.2	18 19.2	3.1	59.1
20	120 54.9	18 59.4	286 15.5	6.2	18 22.3	3.0	59.1
21	135 54.9	19 00.0	300 40.7	6.1	18 25.3	2.8	59.2
22	150 54.9	00.6	315 05.8	6.1	18 28.1	2.7	59.2
23	165 54.9	01.2	329 30.9	6.1	S18 30.8	2.6	59.2
	SD 15.9 d 0.6		SD 15.7		15.9		16.1

Day-of-week labels: TUESDAY (13), WEDNESDAY (14), THURSDAY (15)

Twilight / Moonrise

Lat.	Naut.	Civil	Sunrise	Moonrise 13	14	15	16
N 72	☐	☐	☐	20 33	22 48	■■	■■
N 70	////	////	00 55	20 02	21 52	23 37	24 52
68	////	////	01 53	19 40	21 18	22 48	23 57
66	////	////	02 27	19 23	20 54	22 17	23 24
64	////	01 16	02 51	19 09	20 35	21 54	23 00
62	////	01 56	03 10	18 57	20 19	21 36	22 41
60	////	02 23	03 25	18 47	20 07	21 21	22 25
N 58	01 08	02 43	03 38	18 39	19 56	21 08	22 12
56	01 45	03 00	03 49	18 31	19 46	20 57	22 00
54	02 10	03 14	03 59	18 24	19 37	20 47	21 50
52	02 29	03 26	04 08	18 18	19 30	20 38	21 41
50	02 45	03 37	04 16	18 13	19 23	20 31	21 33
45	03 15	03 58	04 32	18 01	19 08	20 14	21 16
N 40	03 38	04 15	04 46	17 51	18 56	20 01	21 02
35	03 55	04 29	04 57	17 43	18 46	19 49	20 50
30	04 10	04 41	05 07	17 36	18 37	19 39	20 39
20	04 33	05 01	05 24	17 23	18 22	19 22	20 22
N 10	04 51	05 17	05 39	17 13	18 09	19 07	20 06
0	05 06	05 31	05 53	17 02	17 56	18 53	19 52
S 10	05 19	05 44	06 06	16 52	17 44	18 39	19 37
20	05 31	05 58	06 21	16 42	17 31	18 24	19 22
30	05 43	06 12	06 37	16 30	17 16	18 07	19 04
35	05 49	06 20	06 47	16 23	17 07	17 58	18 54
40	05 55	06 28	06 57	16 15	16 57	17 46	18 42
45	06 02	06 38	07 10	16 05	16 46	17 33	18 28
S 50	06 10	06 50	07 25	15 54	16 32	17 17	18 11
52	06 13	06 55	07 32	15 49	16 26	17 10	18 03
54	06 17	07 00	07 40	15 44	16 19	17 02	17 55
56	06 21	07 07	07 49	15 37	16 11	16 52	17 45
58	06 25	07 14	07 59	15 31	16 02	16 42	17 33
S 60	06 30	07 22	08 11	15 23	15 51	16 30	17 20

Twilight / Moonset

Lat.	Sunset	Civil	Naut.	Moonset 13	14	15	16
N 72	☐	☐	☐	01 54	01 43	01 21	■■
N 70	23 10	////	////	02 14	02 14	02 18	02 33
68	22 04	////	////	02 29	02 37	02 53	03 22
66	21 29	////	////	02 41	02 56	03 18	03 53
64	21 04	22 43	////	02 52	03 10	03 37	04 16
62	20 45	22 00	////	03 01	03 23	03 53	04 35
60	20 29	21 32	////	03 08	03 33	04 06	04 50
N 58	20 16	21 11	22 50	03 15	03 43	04 18	05 03
56	20 05	20 54	22 11	03 21	03 51	04 28	05 14
54	19 55	20 40	21 45	03 27	03 58	04 36	05 24
52	19 46	20 28	21 26	03 32	04 05	04 44	05 33
50	19 38	20 17	21 09	03 36	04 10	04 52	05 41
45	19 21	19 55	20 39	03 46	04 23	05 07	05 58
N 40	19 07	19 38	20 16	03 54	04 34	05 19	06 12
35	18 56	19 24	19 58	04 01	04 43	05 30	06 23
30	18 46	19 12	19 43	04 07	04 51	05 39	06 34
20	18 28	18 52	19 20	04 17	05 04	05 56	06 51
N 10	18 14	18 36	19 02	04 27	05 16	06 10	07 06
0	18 00	18 22	18 47	04 36	05 28	06 23	07 21
S 10	17 46	18 08	18 34	04 44	05 39	06 36	07 35
20	17 32	17 55	18 22	04 54	05 51	06 51	07 50
30	17 15	17 41	18 10	05 04	06 05	07 07	08 08
35	17 06	17 33	18 03	05 11	06 13	07 16	08 18
40	16 55	17 24	17 57	05 18	06 22	07 27	08 30
45	16 42	17 14	17 50	05 26	06 33	07 40	08 44
S 50	16 27	17 03	17 42	05 36	06 46	07 55	09 00
52	16 20	16 57	17 39	05 40	06 52	08 02	09 08
54	16 12	16 52	17 35	05 46	06 59	08 10	09 17
56	16 03	16 45	17 31	05 51	07 06	08 19	09 27
58	15 53	16 38	17 27	05 58	07 15	08 30	09 38
S 60	15 41	16 30	17 22	06 05	07 25	08 42	09 51

SUN / MOON

Day	Eqn. of Time 00h	12h	Mer. Pass.	MOON Mer. Pass. Upper	Lower	Age	Phase
d	m s	m s	h m	h m	h m	d	%
13	03 40	03 40	11 56	23 15	10 49	14	98
14	03 40	03 40	11 56	24 10	11 42	15	100
15	03 40	03 40	11 56	00 10	12 38	16	99

UT	ARIES GHA	VENUS −4.0 GHA	Dec	MARS −0.8 GHA	Dec	JUPITER −1.9 GHA	Dec	SATURN +0.1 GHA	Dec	Name	SHA	Dec
16 00	233 38.0	219 16.9	N 4 08.7	44 52.1	S 2 44.6	124 43.5	N22 37.0	5 45.6	S15 15.0	Acamar	315 18.3	S40 14.9
01	248 40.4	234 16.7	09.8	59 54.7	44.6	139 45.5	36.9	20 48.3	14.9	Achernar	335 26.9	S57 09.8
02	263 42.9	249 16.4	10.8	74 57.3	44.6	154 47.5	36.9	35 50.9	14.9	Acrux	173 08.0	S63 11.0
03	278 45.3	264 16.2 ..	11.9	89 59.9 ..	44.7	169 49.5 ..	36.8	50 53.6 ..	14.8	Adhara	255 12.3	S28 59.9
04	293 47.8	279 16.0	12.9	105 02.5	44.7	184 51.5	36.7	65 56.2	14.8	Aldebaran	290 49.0	N16 32.1
05	308 50.3	294 15.7	14.0	120 05.2	44.8	199 53.5	36.7	80 58.9	14.7			
06	323 52.7	309 15.5	N 4 15.0	135 07.8	S 2 44.8	214 55.5	N22 36.6	96 01.5	S15 14.7	Alioth	166 19.8	N55 53.1
07	338 55.2	324 15.3	16.1	150 10.4	44.9	229 57.4	36.6	111 04.2	14.6	Alkaid	152 58.0	N49 14.6
08	353 57.7	339 15.1	17.1	165 13.0	44.9	244 59.4	36.5	126 06.8	14.6	Al Na'ir	27 43.1	S46 53.2
F 09	9 00.1	354 14.8 ..	18.2	180 15.6 ..	45.0	260 01.4 ..	36.5	141 09.5 ..	14.5	Alnilam	275 46.0	S 1 11.8
R 10	24 02.6	9 14.6	19.3	195 18.2	45.0	275 03.4	36.4	156 12.1	14.5	Alphard	217 55.5	S 8 43.5
I 11	39 05.1	24 14.4	20.3	210 20.9	45.1	290 05.4	36.4	171 14.8	14.4			
D 12	54 07.5	39 14.1	N 4 21.4	225 23.5	S 2 45.1	305 07.4	N22 36.3	186 17.4	S15 14.4	Alphecca	126 10.1	N26 40.1
A 13	69 10.0	54 13.9	22.4	240 26.1	45.2	320 09.4	36.3	201 20.1	14.3	Alpheratz	357 43.0	N29 10.0
Y 14	84 12.5	69 13.7	23.5	255 28.7	45.2	335 11.4	36.2	216 22.7	14.3	Altair	62 07.5	N 8 54.5
15	99 14.9	84 13.5 ..	24.5	270 31.3 ..	45.3	350 13.4 ..	36.1	231 25.4 ..	14.2	Ankaa	353 15.4	S42 13.5
16	114 17.4	99 13.2	25.6	285 33.9	45.3	5 15.4	36.1	246 28.1	14.2	Antares	112 25.1	S26 27.7
17	129 19.8	114 13.0	26.6	300 36.5	45.4	20 17.4	36.0	261 30.7	14.2			
18	144 22.3	129 12.8	N 4 27.7	315 39.1	S 2 45.4	35 19.4	N22 36.0	276 33.4	S15 14.1	Arcturus	145 54.9	N19 06.5
19	159 24.8	144 12.5	28.7	330 41.7	45.5	50 21.4	35.9	291 36.0	14.1	Atria	107 25.8	S69 03.0
20	174 27.2	159 12.3	29.8	345 44.3	45.5	65 23.4	35.9	306 38.7	14.0	Avior	234 17.9	S59 33.8
21	189 29.7	174 12.1 ..	30.9	0 46.9 ..	45.6	80 25.3 ..	35.8	321 41.3 ..	14.0	Bellatrix	278 31.6	N 6 21.5
22	204 32.2	189 11.8	31.9	15 49.5	45.6	95 27.3	35.8	336 44.0	13.9	Betelgeuse	271 00.9	N 7 24.3
23	219 34.6	204 11.6	33.0	30 52.1	45.7	110 29.3	35.7	351 46.6	13.9			
17 00	234 37.1	219 11.4	N 4 34.0	45 54.7	S 2 45.7	125 31.3	N22 35.7	6 49.3	S15 13.8	Canopus	263 56.3	S52 42.6
01	249 39.6	234 11.2	35.1	60 57.3	45.8	140 33.3	35.6	21 51.9	13.8	Capella	280 34.0	N46 00.6
02	264 42.0	249 10.9	36.1	75 59.9	45.9	155 35.3	35.5	36 54.6	13.7	Deneb	49 30.9	N45 19.8
03	279 44.5	264 10.7 ..	37.2	91 02.5 ..	45.9	170 37.3 ..	35.5	51 57.2 ..	13.7	Denebola	182 32.9	N14 29.4
04	294 46.9	279 10.5	38.2	106 05.1	46.0	185 39.3	35.4	66 59.9	13.6	Diphda	348 55.5	S17 54.5
05	309 49.4	294 10.2	39.3	121 07.7	46.0	200 41.3	35.4	82 02.5	13.6			
06	324 51.9	309 10.0	N 4 40.3	136 10.3	S 2 46.1	215 43.3	N22 35.3	97 05.2	S15 13.5	Dubhe	193 50.9	N61 40.6
07	339 54.3	324 09.8	41.4	151 12.8	46.1	230 45.3	35.3	112 07.8	13.5	Elnath	278 12.2	N28 37.0
S 08	354 56.8	339 09.5	42.5	166 15.4	46.2	245 47.2	35.2	127 10.5	13.4	Eltanin	90 45.4	N51 29.2
A 09	9 59.3	354 09.3 ..	43.5	181 18.0 ..	46.3	260 49.2 ..	35.2	142 13.1 ..	13.4	Enif	33 46.5	N 9 56.5
T 10	25 01.7	9 09.1	44.6	196 20.6	46.3	275 51.2	35.1	157 15.8	13.4	Fomalhaut	15 23.4	S29 32.6
U 11	40 04.2	24 08.8	45.6	211 23.2	46.4	290 53.2	35.1	172 18.4	13.3			
R 12	55 06.7	39 08.6	N 4 46.7	226 25.8	S 2 46.4	305 55.2	N22 35.0	187 21.1	S15 13.3	Gacrux	171 59.7	S57 11.9
D 13	70 09.1	54 08.4	47.7	241 28.3	46.5	320 57.2	34.9	202 23.7	13.2	Gienah	175 51.4	S17 37.5
A 14	85 11.6	69 08.1	48.8	256 30.9	46.6	335 59.2	34.9	217 26.4	13.2	Hadar	148 46.3	S60 26.6
Y 15	100 14.1	84 07.9 ..	49.8	271 33.5 ..	46.6	351 01.2 ..	34.8	232 29.0 ..	13.1	Hamal	328 00.3	N23 31.6
16	115 16.5	99 07.6	50.9	286 36.1	46.7	6 03.2	34.8	247 31.7	13.1	Kaus Aust.	83 42.7	S34 22.4
17	130 19.0	114 07.4	51.9	301 38.7	46.8	21 05.2	34.7	262 34.3	13.0			
18	145 21.4	129 07.2	N 4 53.0	316 41.2	S 2 46.8	36 07.1	N22 34.7	277 37.0	S15 13.0	Kochab	137 19.1	N74 05.9
19	160 23.9	144 06.9	54.0	331 43.8	46.9	51 09.1	34.6	292 39.6	12.9	Markab	13 37.8	N15 16.9
20	175 26.4	159 06.7	55.1	346 46.4	47.0	66 11.1	34.5	307 42.3	12.9	Menkar	314 14.7	N 4 08.0
21	190 28.8	174 06.5 ..	56.2	1 48.9 ..	47.0	81 13.1 ..	34.5	322 44.9 ..	12.8	Menkent	148 06.4	S36 26.5
22	205 31.3	189 06.2	57.2	16 51.5	47.1	96 15.1	34.4	337 47.6	12.8	Miaplacidus	221 39.6	S69 47.1
23	220 33.8	204 06.0	58.3	31 54.1	47.2	111 17.1	34.4	352 50.2	12.7			
18 00	235 36.2	219 05.8	N 4 59.3	46 56.6	S 2 47.2	126 19.1	N22 34.3	7 52.9	S15 12.7	Mirfak	308 39.9	N49 54.5
01	250 38.7	234 05.5	5 00.4	61 59.2	47.3	141 21.1	34.3	22 55.5	12.7	Nunki	75 57.3	S26 16.5
02	265 41.2	249 05.3	01.4	77 01.8	47.4	156 23.0	34.2	37 58.2	12.6	Peacock	53 18.1	S56 40.9
03	280 43.6	264 05.0 ..	02.5	92 04.3 ..	47.4	171 25.0 ..	34.2	53 00.8 ..	12.6	Pollux	243 27.2	N27 59.3
04	295 46.1	279 04.8	03.5	107 06.9	47.5	186 27.0	34.1	68 03.5	12.5	Procyon	244 59.3	N 5 11.0
05	310 48.6	294 04.6	04.6	122 09.4	47.6	201 29.0	34.0	83 06.1	12.5			
06	325 51.0	309 04.3	N 5 05.6	137 12.0	S 2 47.6	216 31.0	N22 34.0	98 08.8	S15 12.4	Rasalhague	96 05.6	N12 33.1
07	340 53.5	324 04.1	06.7	152 14.6	47.7	231 33.0	33.9	113 11.4	12.4	Regulus	207 42.9	N11 53.7
08	355 55.9	339 03.9	07.7	167 17.1	47.8	246 35.0	33.9	128 14.1	12.3	Rigel	281 11.8	S 8 11.4
S 09	10 58.4	354 03.6 ..	08.8	182 19.7 ..	47.8	261 36.9 ..	33.8	143 16.7 ..	12.3	Rigil Kent.	139 50.1	S60 53.7
U 10	26 00.9	9 03.4	09.9	197 22.2	47.9	276 38.9	33.8	158 19.4	12.2	Sabik	102 11.5	S15 44.4
N 11	41 03.3	24 03.1	10.9	212 24.8	48.0	291 40.9	33.7	173 22.0	12.2			
D 12	56 05.8	39 02.9	N 5 12.0	227 27.3	S 2 48.1	306 42.9	N22 33.7	188 24.7	S15 12.1	Schedar	349 40.1	N56 36.7
A 13	71 08.3	54 02.7	13.0	242 29.9	48.1	321 44.9	33.6	203 27.3	12.1	Shaula	96 20.7	S37 06.6
Y 14	86 10.7	69 02.4	14.1	257 32.4	48.2	336 46.9	33.5	218 30.0	12.0	Sirius	258 33.4	S16 44.5
15	101 13.2	84 02.2 ..	15.1	272 35.0 ..	48.3	351 48.9 ..	33.5	233 32.6 ..	12.0	Spica	158 30.3	S11 14.3
16	116 15.7	99 01.9	16.2	287 37.5	48.4	6 50.8	33.4	248 35.3	12.0	Suhail	222 52.0	S43 29.9
17	131 18.1	114 01.7	17.2	302 40.1	48.4	21 52.8	33.4	263 37.9	11.9			
18	146 20.6	129 01.5	N 5 18.3	317 42.6	S 2 48.5	36 54.8	N22 33.3	278 40.6	S15 11.9	Vega	80 38.2	N38 47.8
19	161 23.1	144 01.2	19.3	332 45.1	48.6	51 56.8	33.3	293 43.2	11.8	Zuben'ubi	137 04.4	S16 06.1
20	176 25.5	159 01.0	20.4	347 47.7	48.7	66 58.8	33.2	308 45.9	11.8		SHA	Mer. Pass.
21	191 28.0	174 00.7 ..	21.4	2 50.2 ..	48.7	82 00.8 ..	33.1	323 48.5 ..	11.7		° ′	h m
22	206 30.4	189 00.5	22.5	17 52.8	48.8	97 02.8	33.1	338 51.2	11.7	Venus	344 34.3	9 23
23	221 32.9	204 00.3	23.5	32 55.3	48.9	112 04.7	33.0	353 53.8	11.6	Mars	171 17.6	20 53
	h m									Jupiter	250 54.2	15 36
Mer. Pass.	8 20.2	v −0.2	d 1.1	v 2.6	d 0.1	v 2.0	d 0.1	v 2.7	d 0.0	Saturn	132 12.2	23 29

UT	SUN GHA	SUN Dec	MOON GHA	v	MOON Dec	d	HP
d h	° ′	° ′	° ′	′	° ′	′	′
16 00	180 54.9	N19 01.7	343 56.0	6.0	S18 33.4	2.5	59.2
01	195 54.9	02.3	358 21.0	6.0	18 35.9	2.4	59.2
02	210 54.9	02.9	12 46.0	6.0	18 38.3	2.2	59.2
03	225 54.9	.. 03.5	27 11.0	5.9	18 40.5	2.1	59.3
04	240 54.9	04.1	41 35.9	5.8	18 42.6	2.0	59.3
05	255 54.8	04.6	56 00.7	5.9	18 44.6	1.9	59.3
06	270 54.8	N19 05.2	70 25.6	5.8	S18 46.5	1.7	59.3
07	285 54.8	05.8	84 50.4	5.8	18 48.2	1.7	59.3
08	300 54.8	06.4	99 15.2	5.7	18 49.9	1.5	59.3
F 09	315 54.8	.. 06.9	113 39.9	5.7	18 51.4	1.3	59.4
R 10	330 54.8	07.5	128 04.6	5.7	18 52.7	1.3	59.4
I 11	345 54.8	08.1	142 29.3	5.7	18 54.0	1.1	59.4
D 12	0 54.8	N19 08.7	156 54.0	5.7	S18 55.1	1.0	59.4
A 13	15 54.7	09.2	171 18.7	5.6	18 56.1	0.8	59.4
Y 14	30 54.7	09.8	185 43.3	5.6	18 56.9	0.8	59.4
15	45 54.7	.. 10.4	200 07.9	5.6	18 57.7	0.6	59.4
16	60 54.7	11.0	214 32.5	5.5	18 58.3	0.4	59.5
17	75 54.7	11.5	228 57.0	5.6	18 58.7	0.4	59.5
18	90 54.7	N19 12.1	243 21.6	5.5	S18 59.1	0.2	59.5
19	105 54.7	12.7	257 46.1	5.5	18 59.3	0.1	59.5
20	120 54.6	13.2	272 10.6	5.5	18 59.4	0.0	59.5
21	135 54.6	.. 13.8	286 35.1	5.5	18 59.4	0.0	59.5
22	150 54.6	14.4	300 59.6	5.5	18 59.2	0.3	59.5
23	165 54.6	14.9	315 24.1	5.5	18 58.9	0.4	59.5
17 00	180 54.6	N19 15.5	329 48.6	5.5	S18 58.5	0.6	59.5
01	195 54.6	16.1	344 13.1	5.4	18 57.9	0.6	59.6
02	210 54.6	16.6	358 37.5	5.5	18 57.3	0.8	59.6
03	225 54.5	.. 17.2	13 02.0	5.4	18 56.5	1.0	59.6
04	240 54.5	17.8	27 26.4	5.5	18 55.5	1.0	59.6
05	255 54.5	18.3	41 50.9	5.4	18 54.5	1.2	59.6
06	270 54.5	N19 18.9	56 15.3	5.5	S18 53.3	1.4	59.6
S 07	285 54.5	19.5	70 39.8	5.4	18 51.9	1.4	59.6
A 08	300 54.4	20.0	85 04.2	5.5	18 50.5	1.6	59.6
T 09	315 54.4	.. 20.6	99 28.7	5.5	18 48.9	1.7	59.6
U 10	330 54.4	21.2	113 53.2	5.4	18 47.2	1.9	59.6
R 11	345 54.4	21.7	128 17.6	5.5	18 45.3	1.9	59.6
D 12	0 54.4	N19 22.3	142 42.1	5.5	S18 43.4	2.1	59.7
A 13	15 54.4	22.8	157 06.6	5.5	18 41.3	2.2	59.7
Y 14	30 54.3	23.4	171 31.1	5.5	18 39.1	2.4	59.7
15	45 54.3	.. 24.0	185 55.6	5.5	18 36.7	2.5	59.7
16	60 54.3	24.5	200 20.1	5.6	18 34.2	2.6	59.7
17	75 54.3	25.1	214 44.7	5.5	18 31.6	2.7	59.7
18	90 54.3	N19 25.6	229 09.2	5.6	S18 28.9	2.9	59.7
19	105 54.2	26.2	243 33.8	5.6	18 26.0	2.9	59.7
20	120 54.2	26.7	257 58.4	5.6	18 23.1	3.1	59.7
21	135 54.2	.. 27.3	272 23.0	5.6	18 20.0	3.3	59.7
22	150 54.2	27.8	286 47.6	5.6	18 16.7	3.3	59.7
23	165 54.2	28.4	301 12.2	5.7	18 13.4	3.5	59.7
18 00	180 54.1	N19 29.0	315 36.9	5.7	S18 09.9	3.6	59.7
01	195 54.1	29.5	330 01.6	5.7	18 06.3	3.7	59.7
02	210 54.1	30.1	344 26.3	5.8	18 02.6	3.9	59.7
03	225 54.1	.. 30.6	358 51.1	5.7	17 58.7	3.9	59.7
04	240 54.0	31.2	13 15.8	5.8	17 54.8	4.1	59.7
05	255 54.0	31.7	27 40.6	5.9	17 50.7	4.2	59.7
06	270 54.0	N19 32.3	42 05.5	5.8	S17 46.5	4.4	59.7
07	285 54.0	32.8	56 30.3	5.9	17 42.1	4.4	59.7
08	300 53.9	33.4	70 55.2	6.0	17 37.7	4.6	59.7
S 09	315 53.9	.. 33.9	85 20.2	5.9	17 33.1	4.6	59.7
U 10	330 53.9	34.5	99 45.1	6.0	17 28.5	4.8	59.7
N 11	345 53.9	35.0	114 10.1	6.0	17 23.7	4.9	59.7
D 12	0 53.9	N19 35.6	128 35.1	6.1	S17 18.8	5.1	59.7
A 13	15 53.8	36.1	143 00.2	6.1	17 13.7	5.1	59.7
Y 14	30 53.8	36.6	157 25.3	6.1	17 08.6	5.3	59.7
15	45 53.8	.. 37.2	171 50.4	6.2	17 03.3	5.3	59.7
16	60 53.8	37.7	186 15.6	6.3	16 58.0	5.5	59.7
17	75 53.7	38.3	200 40.8	6.3	16 52.5	5.6	59.7
18	90 53.7	N19 38.8	215 06.1	6.3	S16 46.9	5.7	59.7
19	105 53.7	39.4	229 31.4	6.3	16 41.2	5.8	59.7
20	120 53.7	39.9	243 56.7	6.4	16 35.4	6.0	59.7
21	135 53.6	.. 40.5	258 22.1	6.5	16 29.4	6.0	59.7
22	150 53.6	41.0	272 47.6	6.4	16 23.4	6.1	59.7
23	165 53.6	41.5	287 13.0	6.5	S16 17.3	6.3	59.7
	SD 15.8	d 0.6	SD 16.2	16.3	16.3		

Lat.	Twilight Naut.	Twilight Civil	Sunrise	Moonrise 16	17	18	19
°	h m	h m	h m	h m	h m	h m	h m
N 72	□	□	□	■	■	■	02 09
N 70	□	□	□	24 52	00 52	01 20	01 28
68	////	////	01 36	23 57	24 39	00 39	01 00
66	////	////	02 15	23 24	24 10	00 10	00 39
64	////	00 53	02 41	23 00	23 48	24 22	00 22
62	////	01 43	03 02	22 41	23 31	24 08	00 08
60	////	02 13	03 18	22 25	23 16	23 56	24 25
N 58	00 48	02 35	03 32	22 12	23 04	23 45	24 17
56	01 33	02 53	03 44	22 00	22 53	23 36	24 10
54	02 01	03 08	03 54	21 50	22 44	23 28	24 04
52	02 22	03 21	04 03	21 41	22 35	23 21	23 59
50	02 39	03 32	04 12	21 33	22 28	23 14	23 55
45	03 11	03 55	04 29	21 16	22 11	23 00	23 42
N 40	03 34	04 12	04 43	21 02	21 58	22 48	23 33
35	03 53	04 27	04 55	20 50	21 47	22 38	23 25
30	04 08	04 39	05 06	20 39	21 37	22 30	23 18
20	04 31	05 00	05 23	20 22	21 20	22 15	23 06
N 10	04 50	05 16	05 39	20 06	21 05	22 01	22 55
0	05 05	05 31	05 53	19 52	20 51	21 49	22 46
S 10	05 19	05 45	06 07	19 37	20 37	21 37	22 36
20	05 32	05 59	06 22	19 22	20 22	21 23	22 25
30	05 44	06 13	06 39	19 04	20 05	21 08	22 13
35	05 51	06 22	06 49	18 54	19 55	20 59	22 06
40	05 58	06 31	07 00	18 42	19 44	20 49	21 57
45	06 05	06 41	07 13	18 28	19 30	20 38	21 48
S 50	06 14	06 53	07 29	18 11	19 14	20 23	21 37
52	06 17	06 59	07 37	18 03	19 06	20 16	21 31
54	06 21	07 05	07 45	17 55	18 58	20 09	21 25
56	06 25	07 11	07 54	17 45	18 48	20 01	21 19
58	06 30	07 19	08 05	17 33	18 37	19 51	21 12
S 60	06 35	07 27	08 17	17 20	18 25	19 40	21 03

Lat.	Sunset	Twilight Civil	Twilight Naut.	Moonset 16	17	18	19
°	h m	h m	h m	h m	h m	h m	h m
N 72	□	□	□	■	■	■	06 09
N 70	22 22	□	□	02 33	03 21	04 56	06 49
68	22 22	////	////	03 22	04 15	05 37	07 16
66	21 41	////	////	03 53	04 48	06 05	07 37
64	21 14	23 08	////	04 16	05 13	06 27	07 53
62	20 53	22 13	////	04 35	05 32	06 44	08 07
60	20 36	21 42	////	04 50	05 47	06 58	08 18
N 58	20 22	21 19	23 13	05 03	06 01	07 10	08 28
56	20 10	21 01	22 23	05 14	06 12	07 21	08 37
54	20 00	20 46	21 54	05 24	06 22	07 30	08 44
52	19 50	20 33	21 33	05 33	06 31	07 38	08 51
50	19 42	20 22	21 16	05 41	06 39	07 46	08 57
45	19 24	19 59	20 43	05 58	06 56	08 01	09 11
N 40	19 10	19 41	20 19	06 12	07 10	08 14	09 21
35	18 58	19 26	20 01	06 23	07 22	08 25	09 31
30	18 48	19 14	19 46	06 34	07 32	08 35	09 39
20	18 30	18 53	19 22	06 51	07 50	08 51	09 53
N 10	18 14	18 37	19 03	07 06	08 05	09 05	10 05
0	18 00	18 22	18 47	07 20	08 20	09 19	10 16
S 10	17 46	18 08	18 34	07 35	08 34	09 32	10 27
20	17 31	17 54	18 21	07 50	08 49	09 46	10 39
30	17 14	17 39	18 08	08 08	09 07	10 02	10 53
35	17 04	17 31	18 01	08 18	09 17	10 12	11 01
40	16 52	17 22	17 55	08 30	09 29	10 23	11 10
45	16 39	17 11	17 47	08 44	09 42	10 35	11 20
S 50	16 23	16 59	17 39	09 00	09 59	10 50	11 32
52	16 16	16 53	17 35	09 08	10 07	10 57	11 37
54	16 07	16 47	17 31	09 17	10 15	11 04	11 45
56	15 58	16 41	17 27	09 27	10 25	11 13	11 52
58	15 47	16 33	17 22	09 38	10 36	11 23	11 59
S 60	15 35	16 25	17 17	09 51	10 49	11 34	12 08

Day	SUN Eqn. of Time 00h	SUN Eqn. of Time 12h	SUN Mer. Pass.	MOON Mer. Pass. Upper	MOON Mer. Pass. Lower	Age	Phase
d	m s	m s	h m	h m	h m	d	%
16	03 40	03 39	11 56	01 07	13 36	17	96
17	03 38	03 38	11 56	02 06	14 35	18	90
18	03 37	03 35	11 56	03 05	15 34	19	83

UT	ARIES	VENUS −4.0		MARS −0.7		JUPITER −1.9		SATURN +0.1		STARS		
	GHA	GHA	Dec	GHA	Dec	GHA	Dec	GHA	Dec	Name	SHA	Dec
d h	° ′	° ′	° ′	° ′	° ′	° ′	° ′	° ′	° ′		° ′	° ′
19 00	236 35.4	219 00.0 N 5 24.6		47 57.8 S 2 49.0		127 06.7 N22 33.0		8 56.5 S15 11.6		Acamar	315 18.3	S40 14.9
01	251 37.8	233 59.8	25.6	63 00.4	49.1	142 08.7	32.9	23 59.1	11.5	Achernar	335 26.9	S57 09.7
02	266 40.3	248 59.5	26.7	78 02.9	49.1	157 10.7	32.9	39 01.8	11.5	Acrux	173 08.0	S63 11.0
03	281 42.8	263 59.3 . .	27.7	93 05.4 . .	49.2	172 12.7 . .	32.8	54 04.4 . .	11.4	Adhara	255 12.3	S28 59.9
04	296 45.2	278 59.0	28.8	108 08.0	49.3	187 14.7	32.7	69 07.0	11.4	Aldebaran	290 49.0	N16 32.1
05	311 47.7	293 58.8	29.8	123 10.5	49.4	202 16.6	32.7	84 09.7	11.3			
06	326 50.2	308 58.5 N 5 30.9		138 13.0 S 2 49.5		217 18.6 N22 32.6		99 12.3 S15 11.3		Alioth	166 19.8	N55 53.1
07	341 52.6	323 58.3	32.0	153 15.6	49.5	232 20.6	32.6	114 15.0	11.3	Alkaid	152 58.1	N49 14.6
08	356 55.1	338 58.1	33.0	168 18.1	49.6	247 22.6	32.5	129 17.6	11.2	Al Na'ir	27 43.0	S46 53.1
M 09	11 57.6	353 57.8 . .	34.1	183 20.6 . .	49.7	262 24.6 . .	32.5	144 20.3 . .	11.2	Alnilam	275 46.0	S 1 11.8
O 10	27 00.0	8 57.6	35.1	198 23.1	49.8	277 26.6	32.4	159 22.9	11.1	Alphard	217 55.5	S 8 43.5
N 11	42 02.5	23 57.3	36.2	213 25.7	49.9	292 28.5	32.3	174 25.6	11.1			
D 12	57 04.9	38 57.1 N 5 37.2		228 28.2 S 2 50.0		307 30.5 N22 32.3		189 28.2 S15 11.0		Alphecca	126 10.1	N26 40.1
A 13	72 07.4	53 56.8	38.3	243 30.7	50.0	322 32.5	32.2	204 30.9	11.0	Alpheratz	357 43.0	N29 10.0
Y 14	87 09.9	68 56.6	39.3	258 33.2	50.1	337 34.5	32.2	219 33.5	10.9	Altair	62 07.4	N 8 54.5
15	102 12.3	83 56.3 . .	40.4	273 35.7 . .	50.2	352 36.5 . .	32.1	234 36.2 . .	10.9	Ankaa	353 15.4	S42 13.5
16	117 14.8	98 56.1	41.4	288 38.2	50.3	7 38.4	32.1	249 38.8	10.8	Antares	112 25.1	S26 27.7
17	132 17.3	113 55.8	42.5	303 40.8	50.4	22 40.4	32.0	264 41.5	10.8			
18	147 19.7	128 55.6 N 5 43.5		318 43.3 S 2 50.5		37 42.4 N22 31.9		279 44.1 S15 10.7		Arcturus	145 54.9	N19 06.5
19	162 22.2	143 55.4	44.6	333 45.8	50.6	52 44.4	31.9	294 46.8	10.7	Atria	107 25.8	S69 03.0
20	177 24.7	158 55.1	45.6	348 48.3	50.7	67 46.4	31.8	309 49.4	10.7	Avior	234 18.0	S59 33.8
21	192 27.1	173 54.9 . .	46.7	3 50.8 . .	50.7	82 48.4 . .	31.8	324 52.1 . .	10.6	Bellatrix	278 31.6	N 6 21.5
22	207 29.6	188 54.6	47.7	18 53.3	50.8	97 50.3	31.7	339 54.7	10.6	Betelgeuse	271 00.9	N 7 24.3
23	222 32.0	203 54.4	48.8	33 55.8	50.9	112 52.3	31.7	354 57.4	10.5			
20 00	237 34.5	218 54.1 N 5 49.8		48 58.3 S 2 51.0		127 54.3 N22 31.6		10 00.0 S15 10.5		Canopus	263 56.3	S52 42.6
01	252 37.0	233 53.9	50.9	64 00.8	51.1	142 56.3	31.5	25 02.7	10.4	Capella	280 34.0	N46 00.6
02	267 39.4	248 53.6	51.9	79 03.3	51.2	157 58.3	31.5	40 05.3	10.4	Deneb	49 30.8	N45 19.8
03	282 41.9	263 53.4 . .	53.0	94 05.8 . .	51.3	173 00.2 . .	31.4	55 08.0 . .	10.3	Denebola	182 32.9	N14 29.5
04	297 44.4	278 53.1	54.0	109 08.3	51.4	188 02.2	31.4	70 10.6	10.3	Diphda	348 55.5	S17 54.4
05	312 46.8	293 52.9	55.1	124 10.8	51.5	203 04.2	31.3	85 13.3	10.2			
06	327 49.3	308 52.6 N 5 56.1		139 13.3 S 2 51.6		218 06.2 N22 31.2		100 15.9 S15 10.2		Dubhe	193 50.9	N61 40.6
07	342 51.8	323 52.4	57.2	154 15.8	51.7	233 08.2	31.2	115 18.6	10.1	Elnath	278 12.2	N28 37.0
08	357 54.2	338 52.1	58.2	169 18.3	51.8	248 10.1	31.1	130 21.2	10.1	Eltanin	90 45.4	N51 29.2
T 09	12 56.7	353 51.9 . .	5 59.3	184 20.8 . .	51.9	263 12.1 . .	31.1	145 23.9 . .	10.1	Enif	33 46.5	N 9 56.5
U 10	27 59.2	8 51.6	6 00.3	199 23.3	52.0	278 14.1	31.0	160 26.5	10.0	Fomalhaut	15 23.4	S29 32.6
E 11	43 01.6	23 51.4	01.4	214 25.8	52.0	293 16.1	31.0	175 29.2	10.0			
S 12	58 04.1	38 51.1 N 6 02.4		229 28.3 S 2 52.1		308 18.1 N22 30.9		190 31.8 S15 09.9		Gacrux	171 59.7	S57 11.9
D 13	73 06.5	53 50.9	03.5	244 30.8	52.2	323 20.0	30.8	205 34.5	09.9	Gienah	175 51.4	S17 37.5
A 14	88 09.0	68 50.6	04.5	259 33.3	52.3	338 22.0	30.8	220 37.1	09.8	Hadar	148 46.3	S60 26.6
Y 15	103 11.5	83 50.4 . .	05.6	274 35.8 . .	52.4	353 24.0 . .	30.7	235 39.7 . .	09.8	Hamal	328 00.3	N23 31.6
16	118 13.9	98 50.1	06.6	289 38.2	52.5	8 26.0	30.7	250 42.4	09.7	Kaus Aust.	83 42.7	S34 22.4
17	133 16.4	113 49.9	07.7	304 40.7	52.6	23 27.9	30.6	265 45.0	09.7			
18	148 18.9	128 49.6 N 6 08.7		319 43.2 S 2 52.7		38 29.9 N22 30.5		280 47.7 S15 09.6		Kochab	137 19.1	N74 05.9
19	163 21.3	143 49.3	09.8	334 45.7	52.8	53 31.9	30.5	295 50.3	09.6	Markab	13 37.8	N15 16.9
20	178 23.8	158 49.1	10.8	349 48.2	52.9	68 33.9	30.4	310 53.0	09.6	Menkar	314 14.7	N 4 08.6
21	193 26.3	173 48.8 . .	11.9	4 50.7 . .	53.0	83 35.9 . .	30.4	325 55.6 . .	09.5	Menkent	148 06.4	S36 26.5
22	208 28.7	188 48.6	12.9	19 53.1	53.1	98 37.8	30.3	340 58.3	09.5	Miaplacidus	221 39.6	S69 47.1
23	223 31.2	203 48.3	14.0	34 55.6	53.2	113 39.8	30.2	356 00.9	09.4			
21 00	238 33.7	218 48.1 N 6 15.0		49 58.1 S 2 53.3		128 41.8 N22 30.2		11 03.6 S15 09.4		Mirfak	308 39.9	N49 54.5
01	253 36.1	233 47.8	16.1	65 00.6	53.4	143 43.8	30.1	26 06.2	09.3	Nunki	75 57.3	S26 16.5
02	268 38.6	248 47.6	17.1	80 03.0	53.5	158 45.7	30.1	41 08.9	09.3	Peacock	53 18.1	S56 40.9
03	283 41.0	263 47.3 . .	18.1	95 05.5 . .	53.6	173 47.7 . .	30.0	56 11.5 . .	09.2	Pollux	243 27.2	N27 59.3
04	298 43.5	278 47.1	19.2	110 08.0	53.7	188 49.7	30.0	71 14.2	09.2	Procyon	244 59.3	N 5 11.0
05	313 46.0	293 46.8	20.2	125 10.5	53.9	203 51.7	29.9	86 16.8	09.1			
06	328 48.4	308 46.5 N 6 21.3		140 12.9 S 2 54.0		218 53.6 N22 29.8		101 19.5 S15 09.1		Rasalhague	96 05.6	N12 33.1
W 07	343 50.9	323 46.3	22.3	155 15.4	54.1	233 55.6	29.8	116 22.1	09.1	Regulus	207 42.9	N11 53.7
E 08	358 53.4	338 46.0	23.4	170 17.9	54.2	248 57.6	29.7	131 24.8	09.0	Rigel	281 11.8	S 8 11.4
D 09	13 55.8	353 45.8 . .	24.4	185 20.3 . .	54.3	263 59.6 . .	29.7	146 27.4 . .	09.0	Rigil Kent.	139 50.1	S60 53.7
N 10	28 58.3	8 45.5	25.5	200 22.8	54.4	279 01.5	29.6	161 30.1	08.9	Sabik	102 11.5	S15 44.4
E 11	44 00.8	23 45.3	26.5	215 25.2	54.5	294 03.5	29.5	176 32.7	08.9			
S 12	59 03.2	38 45.0 N 6 27.6		230 27.7 S 2 54.6		309 05.5 N22 29.5		191 35.3 S15 08.8		Schedar	349 40.1	N56 36.7
D 13	74 05.7	53 44.7	28.6	245 30.2	54.7	324 07.5	29.4	206 38.0	08.8	Shaula	96 20.7	S37 06.6
A 14	89 08.1	68 44.5	29.7	260 32.6	54.8	339 09.4	29.4	221 40.6	08.7	Sirius	258 33.4	S16 44.5
Y 15	104 10.6	83 44.2 . .	30.7	275 35.1 . .	54.9	354 11.4 . .	29.3	236 43.3 . .	08.7	Spica	158 30.3	S11 14.3
16	119 13.1	98 44.0	31.8	290 37.5	55.0	9 13.4	29.2	251 45.9	08.6	Suhail	222 52.0	S43 29.9
17	134 15.5	113 43.7	32.8	305 40.0	55.1	24 15.4	29.2	266 48.6	08.6			
18	149 18.0	128 43.5 N 6 33.8		320 42.5 S 2 55.3		39 17.3 N22 29.1		281 51.2 S15 08.6		Vega	80 38.2	N38 47.8
19	164 20.5	143 43.2	34.9	335 44.9	55.4	54 19.3	29.1	296 53.9	08.5	Zuben'ubi	137 04.4	S16 06.1
20	179 22.9	158 42.9	35.9	350 47.4	55.5	69 21.3	29.0	311 56.5	08.5		SHA	Mer.Pass.
21	194 25.4	173 42.7 . .	37.0	5 49.8 . .	55.6	84 23.3 . .	28.9	326 59.2 . .	08.4		° ′	h m
22	209 27.9	188 42.4	38.0	20 52.3	55.7	99 25.2	28.9	342 01.8	08.4	Venus	341 19.6	9 25
23	224 30.3	203 42.2	39.1	35 54.7	55.8	114 27.2	28.8	357 04.5	08.3	Mars	171 23.8	20 41
	h m									Jupiter	250 19.8	15 26
Mer. Pass. 8 08.4		v −0.3 d 1.0		v 2.5 d 0.1		v 2.0 d 0.1		v 2.6 d 0.0		Saturn	132 25.5	23 16

UT	SUN GHA	SUN Dec	MOON GHA	v	Dec	d	HP
d h	° ′	° ′	° ′	′	° ′	′	′
19 00	180 53.5	N19 42.1	301 38.5	6.6	S16 11.0	6.3	59.7
01	195 53.5	42.6	316 04.1	6.6	16 04.7	6.5	59.7
02	210 53.5	43.1	330 29.7	6.7	15 58.2	6.5	59.7
03	225 53.5	.. 43.7	344 55.4	6.7	15 51.7	6.7	59.7
04	240 53.4	44.2	359 21.1	6.7	15 45.0	6.7	59.7
05	255 53.4	44.8	13 46.8	6.8	15 38.3	6.9	59.7
06	270 53.4	N19 45.3	28 12.6	6.9	S15 31.4	6.9	59.7
M 07	285 53.3	45.8	42 38.5	6.9	15 24.5	7.1	59.7
O 08	300 53.3	46.4	57 04.4	6.9	15 17.4	7.1	59.7
N 09	315 53.3	.. 46.9	71 30.3	7.0	15 10.3	7.3	59.7
D 10	330 53.3	47.4	85 56.3	7.1	15 03.0	7.3	59.7
A 11	345 53.2	48.0	100 22.4	7.1	14 55.7	7.5	59.7
Y 12	0 53.2	N19 48.5	114 48.5	7.1	S14 48.2	7.5	59.7
13	15 53.2	49.0	129 14.6	7.2	14 40.7	7.6	59.7
14	30 53.1	49.6	143 40.8	7.3	14 33.1	7.7	59.6
15	45 53.1	.. 50.1	158 07.1	7.3	14 25.4	7.8	59.6
16	60 53.1	50.6	172 33.4	7.3	14 17.6	7.9	59.6
17	75 53.0	51.2	186 59.7	7.4	14 09.7	8.0	59.6
18	90 53.0	N19 51.7	201 26.1	7.5	S14 01.7	8.1	59.6
19	105 53.0	52.2	215 52.6	7.5	13 53.6	8.1	59.6
20	120 52.9	52.7	230 19.1	7.6	13 45.5	8.2	59.6
21	135 52.9	.. 53.3	244 45.7	7.6	13 37.3	8.3	59.6
22	150 52.9	53.8	259 12.3	7.7	13 29.0	8.4	59.6
23	165 52.8	54.3	273 39.0	7.7	13 20.6	8.5	59.6
20 00	180 52.8	N19 54.9	288 05.7	7.8	S13 12.1	8.6	59.6
01	195 52.8	55.4	302 32.5	7.8	13 03.5	8.6	59.6
02	210 52.7	55.9	316 59.3	7.9	12 54.9	8.7	59.6
03	225 52.7	.. 56.4	331 26.2	7.9	12 46.2	8.8	59.5
04	240 52.7	56.9	345 53.1	8.0	12 37.4	8.9	59.5
05	255 52.6	57.5	0 20.1	8.1	12 28.5	8.9	59.5
06	270 52.6	N19 58.0	14 47.2	8.1	S12 19.6	9.0	59.5
T 07	285 52.6	58.5	29 14.3	8.1	12 10.6	9.1	59.5
U 08	300 52.5	59.0	43 41.4	8.2	12 01.5	9.2	59.5
E 09	315 52.5	19 59.6	58 08.6	8.3	11 52.3	9.2	59.5
S 10	330 52.5	20 00.1	72 35.9	8.3	11 43.1	9.3	59.5
D 11	345 52.4	00.6	87 03.2	8.3	11 33.8	9.3	59.5
A 12	0 52.4	N20 01.1	101 30.5	8.5	S11 24.5	9.5	59.5
Y 13	15 52.4	01.6	115 58.0	8.4	11 15.0	9.5	59.4
14	30 52.3	02.2	130 25.4	8.5	11 05.5	9.5	59.4
15	45 52.3	.. 02.7	144 52.9	8.6	10 56.0	9.6	59.4
16	60 52.2	03.2	159 20.5	8.6	10 46.4	9.7	59.4
17	75 52.2	03.7	173 48.1	8.7	10 36.7	9.7	59.4
18	90 52.2	N20 04.2	188 15.8	8.7	S10 27.0	9.8	59.4
19	105 52.1	04.7	202 43.5	8.8	10 17.2	9.9	59.4
20	120 52.1	05.2	217 11.3	8.8	10 07.3	9.9	59.4
21	135 52.0	.. 05.8	231 39.1	8.9	9 57.4	9.9	59.4
22	150 52.0	06.3	246 07.0	8.9	9 47.5	10.1	59.3
23	165 52.0	06.8	260 34.9	9.0	9 37.4	10.0	59.3
21 00	180 51.9	N20 07.3	275 02.9	9.0	S 9 27.4	10.1	59.3
01	195 51.9	07.8	289 30.9	9.1	9 17.3	10.2	59.3
02	210 51.9	08.3	303 59.0	9.1	9 07.1	10.2	59.3
03	225 51.8	.. 08.8	318 27.1	9.1	8 56.9	10.3	59.3
04	240 51.8	09.3	332 55.2	9.2	8 46.6	10.3	59.3
05	255 51.7	09.8	347 23.4	9.3	8 36.3	10.4	59.3
06	270 51.7	N20 10.3	1 51.7	9.3	S 8 25.9	10.4	59.2
W 07	285 51.7	10.9	16 20.0	9.3	8 15.5	10.4	59.2
E 08	300 51.6	11.4	30 48.3	9.4	8 05.1	10.5	59.2
D 09	315 51.6	.. 11.9	45 16.7	9.5	7 54.6	10.6	59.2
N 10	330 51.5	12.4	59 45.2	9.5	7 44.0	10.6	59.2
E 11	345 51.5	12.9	74 13.7	9.5	7 33.5	10.6	59.2
S 12	0 51.4	N20 13.4	88 42.2	9.5	S 7 22.9	10.7	59.2
D 13	15 51.4	13.9	103 10.7	9.7	7 12.2	10.7	59.2
A 14	30 51.4	14.4	117 39.4	9.6	7 01.5	10.7	59.1
Y 15	45 51.3	.. 14.9	132 08.0	9.7	6 50.8	10.7	59.1
16	60 51.3	15.4	146 36.7	9.7	6 40.1	10.8	59.1
17	75 51.2	15.9	161 05.4	9.8	6 29.3	10.9	59.1
18	90 51.2	N20 16.4	175 34.2	9.8	S 6 18.4	10.8	59.1
19	105 51.1	16.9	190 03.0	9.9	6 07.6	10.9	59.1
20	120 51.1	17.4	204 31.9	9.9	5 56.7	10.9	59.1
21	135 51.1	.. 17.9	219 00.8	9.9	5 45.8	10.9	59.0
22	150 51.0	18.4	233 29.7	10.0	5 34.9	11.0	59.0
23	165 51.0	18.9	247 58.7	10.0	S 5 23.9	11.0	59.0
	SD 15.8	d 0.5	SD 16.3		16.2		16.1

Twilight / Moonrise

Lat.	Naut.	Civil	Sunrise	Moonrise 19	20	21	22
°	h m	h m	h m	h m	h m	h m	h m
N 72	□	□	□	02 09	01 55	01 45	01 37
N 70	□	□	□	01 28	01 31	01 31	01 30
68	////	////	01 17	01 00	01 12	01 19	01 24
66	////	////	02 03	00 39	00 57	01 10	01 19
64	////	00 16	02 32	00 22	00 45	01 02	01 15
62	////	01 30	02 54	00 08	00 34	00 55	01 12
60	////	02 03	03 11	24 25	00 25	00 49	01 09
N 58	00 14	02 28	03 26	24 17	00 17	00 44	01 06
56	01 21	02 47	03 39	24 07	00 10	00 39	01 03
54	01 52	03 02	03 50	24 04	00 04	00 35	01 01
52	02 15	03 16	03 59	23 59	24 31	00 31	00 59
50	02 33	03 27	04 08	23 53	24 27	00 27	00 57
45	03 06	03 51	04 26	23 42	24 20	00 20	00 53
N 40	03 31	04 10	04 41	23 33	24 13	00 13	00 50
35	03 50	04 25	04 53	23 25	24 08	00 08	00 47
30	04 06	04 37	05 04	23 18	24 03	00 03	00 44
20	04 28	04 58	05 22	23 06	23 54	24 40	00 40
N 10	04 49	05 16	05 38	22 55	23 47	24 36	00 36
0	05 05	05 31	05 53	22 46	23 40	24 32	00 32
S 10	05 20	05 45	06 08	22 36	23 33	24 28	00 28
20	05 33	06 00	06 23	22 25	23 25	24 24	00 24
30	05 46	06 15	06 41	22 13	23 17	24 20	00 20
35	05 53	06 24	06 51	22 06	23 12	24 17	00 17
40	06 00	06 33	07 03	21 57	23 06	24 14	00 14
45	06 08	06 44	07 16	21 48	22 59	24 11	00 11
S 50	06 17	06 57	07 33	21 37	22 52	24 06	00 06
52	06 21	07 03	07 41	21 31	22 48	24 05	00 05
54	06 25	07 09	07 50	21 25	22 44	24 02	00 02
56	06 30	07 16	08 00	21 19	22 39	24 00	00 00
58	06 34	07 24	08 11	21 12	22 35	23 58	25 20
S 60	06 40	07 33	08 24	21 03	22 29	23 55	25 20

Sunset / Twilight / Moonset

Lat.	Sunset	Civil	Naut.	Moonset 19	20	21	22
°	h m	h m	h m	h m	h m	h m	h m
N 72	□	□	□	06 09	08 20	10 22	12 17
N 70	□	□	□	06 49	08 43	10 34	12 21
68	22 42	////	////	07 16	09 00	10 44	12 25
66	21 54	////	////	07 37	09 14	10 52	12 28
64	21 24	////	////	07 53	09 25	10 58	12 31
62	21 01	22 28	////	08 07	09 35	11 04	12 33
60	20 43	21 52	////	08 18	09 43	11 09	12 35
N 58	20 28	21 27	////	08 28	09 50	11 14	12 36
56	20 16	21 08	22 36	08 37	09 57	11 18	12 38
54	20 04	20 52	22 03	08 44	10 02	11 21	12 39
52	19 55	20 38	21 40	08 51	10 07	11 24	12 41
50	19 46	20 27	21 22	08 57	10 12	11 27	12 42
45	19 28	20 03	20 48	09 11	10 22	11 33	12 44
N 40	19 13	19 44	20 23	09 21	10 30	11 38	12 46
35	19 00	19 29	20 04	09 31	10 37	11 43	12 48
30	18 49	19 16	19 48	09 39	10 43	11 47	12 49
20	18 31	18 55	19 23	09 53	10 54	11 53	12 52
N 10	18 15	18 37	19 04	10 05	11 03	11 59	12 54
0	18 00	18 22	18 48	10 16	11 12	12 05	12 56
S 10	17 45	18 08	18 33	10 27	11 20	12 10	12 58
20	17 30	17 53	18 20	10 39	11 29	12 16	13 00
30	17 12	17 38	18 07	10 53	11 39	12 22	13 03
35	17 02	17 29	18 00	11 01	11 45	12 26	13 04
40	16 50	17 19	17 52	11 10	11 52	12 30	13 06
45	16 36	17 09	17 45	11 20	12 00	12 35	13 07
S 50	16 19	16 56	17 36	11 32	12 09	12 41	13 09
52	16 12	16 50	17 32	11 38	12 13	12 43	13 10
54	16 03	16 43	17 28	11 45	12 18	12 46	13 11
56	15 53	16 36	17 23	11 52	12 23	12 49	13 13
58	15 42	16 29	17 18	11 59	12 29	12 53	13 14
S 60	15 29	16 13	17 13	12 08	12 35	12 57	13 15

Day	SUN Eqn. of Time 00h	12h	SUN Mer. Pass.	MOON Mer. Pass. Upper	Lower	Age	Phase
d	m s	m s	h m	h m	h m	d	%
19	03 34	03 33	11 56	04 03	16 31	20	73
20	03 31	03 30	11 57	04 59	17 26	21	62
21	03 28	03 26	11 57	05 52	18 18	22	51

UT	ARIES GHA	VENUS −4.0 GHA	Dec	MARS −0.7 GHA	Dec	JUPITER −1.9 GHA	Dec	SATURN +0.1 GHA	Dec	STARS Name	SHA	Dec
22 00	239 32.8	218 41.9	N 6 40.1	50 57.2	S 2 55.9	129 29.2	N22 28.8	12 07.1	S15 08.3	Acamar	315 18.3	S40 14.9
01	254 35.3	233 41.6	41.2	65 59.6	56.0	144 31.2	28.7	27 09.8	08.2	Achernar	335 26.9	S57 09.7
02	269 37.7	248 41.4	42.2	81 02.0	56.2	159 33.1	28.6	42 12.4	08.2	Acrux	173 08.0	S63 11.0
03	284 40.2	263 41.1 ..	43.3	96 04.5 ..	56.3	174 35.1 ..	28.6	57 15.1 ..	08.1	Adhara	255 12.3	S28 59.9
04	299 42.6	278 40.8	44.3	111 06.9	56.4	189 37.1	28.5	72 17.7	08.1	Aldebaran	290 49.0	N16 32.1
05	314 45.1	293 40.6	45.3	126 09.4	56.5	204 39.1	28.5	87 20.3	08.1			
06	329 47.6	308 40.3	N 6 46.4	141 11.8	S 2 56.6	219 41.0	N22 28.4	102 23.0	S15 08.0	Alioth	166 19.9	N55 53.1
T 07	344 50.0	323 40.1	47.4	156 14.2	56.7	234 43.0	28.3	117 25.6	08.0	Alkaid	152 58.1	N49 14.6
H 08	359 52.5	338 39.8	48.5	171 16.7	56.9	249 45.0	28.3	132 28.3	07.9	Al Na'ir	27 43.0	S46 53.1
U 09	14 55.0	353 39.5 ..	49.5	186 19.1 ..	57.0	264 46.9 ..	28.2	147 30.9 ..	07.9	Alnilam	275 46.0	S 1 11.8
R 10	29 57.4	8 39.3	50.6	201 21.6	57.1	279 48.9	28.2	162 33.6	07.8	Alphard	217 55.5	S 8 43.5
S 11	44 59.9	23 39.0	51.6	216 24.0	57.2	294 50.9	28.1	177 36.2	07.8			
D 12	60 02.4	38 38.7	N 6 52.7	231 26.4	S 2 57.3	309 52.9	N22 28.0	192 38.9	S15 07.7	Alphecca	126 10.1	N26 40.1
A 13	75 04.8	53 38.5	53.7	246 28.8	57.4	324 54.8	28.0	207 41.5	07.7	Alpheratz	357 43.0	N29 10.0
Y 14	90 07.3	68 38.2	54.7	261 31.3	57.6	339 56.8	27.9	222 44.2	07.6	Altair	62 07.4	N 8 54.5
15	105 09.8	83 37.9 ..	55.8	276 33.7 ..	57.7	354 58.8 ..	27.9	237 46.8 ..	07.6	Ankaa	353 15.4	S42 13.5
16	120 12.2	98 37.7	56.8	291 36.1	57.8	10 00.7	27.8	252 49.5	07.6	Antares	112 25.1	S26 27.7
17	135 14.7	113 37.4	57.9	306 38.6	57.9	25 02.7	27.7	267 52.1	07.5			
18	150 17.1	128 37.1	N 6 58.9	321 41.0	S 2 58.0	40 04.7	N22 27.7	282 54.7	S15 07.5	Arcturus	145 54.9	N19 06.5
19	165 19.6	143 36.9	7 00.0	336 43.4	58.2	55 06.7	27.6	297 57.4	07.4	Atria	107 25.7	S69 03.0
20	180 22.1	158 36.6	01.0	351 45.8	58.3	70 08.6	27.6	313 00.0	07.4	Avior	234 18.0	S59 33.8
21	195 24.5	173 36.3 ..	02.0	6 48.2 ..	58.4	85 10.6 ..	27.5	328 02.7 ..	07.3	Bellatrix	278 31.6	N 6 21.5
22	210 27.0	188 36.1	03.1	21 50.7	58.5	100 12.6	27.4	343 05.3	07.3	Betelgeuse	271 00.9	N 7 24.3
23	225 29.5	203 35.8	04.1	36 53.1	58.7	115 14.5	27.4	358 08.0	07.2			
23 00	240 31.9	218 35.5	N 7 05.2	51 55.5	S 2 58.8	130 16.5	N22 27.3	13 10.6	S15 07.2	Canopus	263 56.3	S52 42.6
01	255 34.4	233 35.3	06.2	66 57.9	58.9	145 18.5	27.2	28 13.3	07.2	Capella	280 34.0	N46 00.6
02	270 36.9	248 35.0	07.3	82 00.3	59.0	160 20.4	27.2	43 15.9	07.1	Deneb	49 30.8	N45 19.8
03	285 39.3	263 34.7 ..	08.3	97 02.7 ..	59.2	175 22.4 ..	27.1	58 18.6 ..	07.1	Denebola	182 32.9	N14 29.5
04	300 41.8	278 34.5	09.3	112 05.2	59.3	190 24.4	27.1	73 21.2	07.0	Diphda	348 55.5	S17 54.4
05	315 44.2	293 34.2	10.4	127 07.6	59.4	205 26.4	27.0	88 23.8	07.0			
06	330 46.7	308 33.9	N 7 11.4	142 10.0	S 2 59.5	220 28.3	N22 26.9	103 26.5	S15 06.9	Dubhe	193 50.9	N61 40.6
07	345 49.2	323 33.7	12.5	157 12.4	59.7	235 30.3	26.9	118 29.1	06.9	Elnath	278 12.2	N28 37.0
F 08	0 51.6	338 33.4	13.5	172 14.8	59.8	250 32.3	26.8	133 31.8	06.8	Eltanin	90 45.4	N51 29.3
R 09	15 54.1	353 33.1 ..	14.5	187 17.2	2 59.9	265 34.2 ..	26.8	148 34.4 ..	06.8	Enif	33 46.4	N 9 56.5
I 10	30 56.6	8 32.9	15.6	202 19.6	3 00.1	280 36.2	26.7	163 37.1	06.8	Fomalhaut	15 23.4	S29 32.6
D 11	45 59.0	23 32.6	16.6	217 22.0	00.2	295 38.2	26.6	178 39.7	06.7			
A 12	61 01.5	38 32.3	N 7 17.7	232 24.4	S 3 00.3	310 40.1	N22 26.6	193 42.4	S15 06.7	Gacrux	171 59.7	S57 11.9
Y 13	76 04.0	53 32.0	18.7	247 26.8	00.5	325 42.1	26.5	208 45.0	06.6	Gienah	175 51.4	S17 37.5
14	91 06.4	68 31.8	19.7	262 29.2	00.6	340 44.1	26.5	223 47.7	06.6	Hadar	148 46.3	S60 26.7
15	106 08.9	83 31.5 ..	20.8	277 31.6 ..	00.7	355 46.0 ..	26.4	238 50.3 ..	06.5	Hamal	328 00.3	N23 31.6
16	121 11.4	98 31.2	21.8	292 34.0	00.8	10 48.0	26.3	253 52.9	06.5	Kaus Aust.	83 42.6	S34 22.4
17	136 13.8	113 31.0	22.9	307 36.4	01.0	25 50.0	26.3	268 55.6	06.4			
18	151 16.3	128 30.7	N 7 23.9	322 38.8	S 3 01.1	40 51.9	N22 26.2	283 58.2	S15 06.4	Kochab	137 19.1	N74 06.0
19	166 18.7	143 30.4	24.9	337 41.2	01.2	55 53.9	26.1	299 00.9	06.3	Markab	13 37.8	N15 16.9
20	181 21.2	158 30.1	26.0	352 43.6	01.4	70 55.9	26.1	314 03.5	06.3	Menkar	314 14.7	N 4 08.6
21	196 23.7	173 29.9 ..	27.0	7 46.0 ..	01.5	85 57.8 ..	26.0	329 06.2 ..	06.3	Menkent	148 06.4	S36 26.5
22	211 26.1	188 29.6	28.1	22 48.4	01.7	100 59.8	26.0	344 08.8	06.2	Miaplacidus	221 39.7	S69 47.0
23	226 28.6	203 29.3	29.1	37 50.8	01.8	116 01.8	25.9	359 11.5	06.2			
24 00	241 31.1	218 29.0	N 7 30.1	52 53.2	S 3 01.9	131 03.7	N22 25.8	14 14.1	S15 06.1	Mirfak	308 39.9	N49 54.5
01	256 33.5	233 28.8	31.2	67 55.5	02.1	146 05.7	25.8	29 16.7	06.1	Nunki	75 57.3	S26 16.5
02	271 36.0	248 28.5	32.2	82 57.9	02.2	161 07.7	25.7	44 19.4	06.0	Peacock	53 18.0	S56 40.9
03	286 38.5	263 28.2 ..	33.2	98 00.3 ..	02.3	176 09.6 ..	25.6	59 22.0 ..	06.0	Pollux	243 27.2	N27 59.3
04	301 40.9	278 27.9	34.3	113 02.7	02.5	191 11.6	25.6	74 24.7	05.9	Procyon	244 59.3	N 5 11.0
05	316 43.4	293 27.7	35.3	128 05.1	02.6	206 13.6	25.5	89 27.3	05.9			
06	331 45.9	308 27.4	N 7 36.4	143 07.5	S 3 02.7	221 15.5	N22 25.5	104 30.0	S15 05.9	Rasalhague	96 05.5	N12 33.1
07	346 48.3	323 27.1	37.4	158 09.8	02.9	236 17.5	25.4	119 32.6	05.8	Regulus	207 42.9	N11 53.7
S 08	1 50.8	338 26.8	38.4	173 12.2	03.0	251 19.5	25.3	134 35.3	05.8	Rigel	281 11.8	S 8 11.4
A 09	16 53.2	353 26.6 ..	39.5	188 14.6 ..	03.2	266 21.4 ..	25.3	149 37.9 ..	05.7	Rigil Kent.	139 50.1	S60 53.7
T 10	31 55.7	8 26.3	40.5	203 17.0	03.3	281 23.4	25.2	164 40.5	05.7	Sabik	102 11.5	S15 44.4
U 11	46 58.2	23 26.0	41.5	218 19.4	03.4	296 25.4	25.1	179 43.2	05.6			
R 12	62 00.6	38 25.7	N 7 42.6	233 21.7	S 3 03.6	311 27.3	N22 25.1	194 45.8	S15 05.6	Schedar	349 40.0	N56 36.7
D 13	77 03.1	53 25.4	43.6	248 24.1	03.7	326 29.3	25.0	209 48.5	05.6	Shaula	96 20.7	S37 06.6
A 14	92 05.6	68 25.2	44.7	263 26.5	03.9	341 31.3	25.0	224 51.1	05.5	Sirius	258 33.4	S16 44.5
Y 15	107 08.0	83 24.9 ..	45.7	278 28.8 ..	04.0	356 33.2 ..	24.9	239 53.8 ..	05.5	Spica	158 30.3	S11 14.3
16	122 10.5	98 24.6	46.7	293 31.2	04.2	11 35.2	24.8	254 56.4	05.4	Suhail	222 52.1	S43 29.9
17	137 13.0	113 24.3	47.8	308 33.6	04.3	26 37.2	24.8	269 59.0	05.4			
18	152 15.4	128 24.1	N 7 48.8	323 35.9	S 3 04.4	41 39.1	N22 24.7	285 01.7	S15 05.3	Vega	80 38.2	N38 47.8
19	167 17.9	143 23.8	49.8	338 38.3	04.6	56 41.1	24.6	300 04.3	05.3	Zuben'ubi	137 04.4	S16 06.1
20	182 20.3	158 23.5	50.9	353 40.7	04.7	71 43.1	24.6	315 07.0	05.2		SHA	Mer.Pass.
21	197 22.8	173 23.2 ..	51.9	8 43.0 ..	04.9	86 45.0 ..	24.5	330 09.6 ..	05.2		° '	h m
22	212 25.3	188 22.9	52.9	23 45.4	05.0	101 47.0	24.5	345 12.3	05.2	Venus	338 03.6	9 26
23	227 27.7	203 22.7	54.0	38 47.8	05.2	116 48.9	24.4	0 14.9	05.1	Mars	171 23.6	20 29
	h m									Jupiter	249 44.6	15 17
Mer.Pass.	7 56.6	v −0.3	d 1.0	v 2.4	d 0.1	v 2.0	d 0.1	v 2.6	d 0.0	Saturn	132 38.7	23 03

SUN and MOON

UT	SUN GHA	SUN Dec	MOON GHA	v	MOON Dec	d	HP
22 00	180 50.9	N20 19.4	262 27.7	10.0	S 5 12.9	11.0	59.0
01	195 50.9	19.9	276 56.7	10.1	5 01.9	11.0	59.0
02	210 50.8	20.4	291 25.8	10.1	4 50.9	11.1	59.0
03	225 50.8 ..	20.9	305 54.9	10.2	4 39.8	11.1	58.9
04	240 50.7	21.4	320 24.0	10.2	4 28.7	11.1	58.9
05	255 50.7	21.9	334 53.2	10.2	4 17.6	11.1	58.9
T 06	270 50.6	N20 22.4	349 22.4	10.3	S 4 06.5	11.1	58.9
H 07	285 50.6	22.9	3 51.7	10.3	3 55.4	11.2	58.9
U 08	300 50.5	23.3	18 21.0	10.3	3 44.2	11.1	58.9
R 09	315 50.5 ..	23.8	32 50.3	10.3	3 33.1	11.2	58.9
S 10	330 50.5	24.3	47 19.6	10.4	3 21.9	11.2	58.8
D 11	345 50.4	24.8	61 49.0	10.4	3 10.7	11.2	58.8
A 12	0 50.4	N20 25.3	76 18.4	10.4	S 2 59.5	11.2	58.8
Y 13	15 50.3	25.8	90 47.8	10.4	2 48.3	11.2	58.8
14	30 50.3	26.3	105 17.2	10.5	2 37.1	11.3	58.8
15	45 50.2 ..	26.8	119 46.7	10.5	2 25.8	11.2	58.8
16	60 50.2	27.3	134 16.2	10.6	2 14.6	11.2	58.7
17	75 50.1	27.7	148 45.8	10.5	2 03.4	11.3	58.7
18	90 50.1	N20 28.2	163 15.3	10.6	S 1 52.1	11.2	58.7
19	105 50.0	28.7	177 44.9	10.6	1 40.9	11.3	58.7
20	120 50.0	29.2	192 14.5	10.6	1 29.6	11.3	58.7
21	135 49.9 ..	29.7	206 44.1	10.7	1 18.3	11.2	58.7
22	150 49.9	30.2	221 13.8	10.7	1 07.1	11.3	58.6
23	165 49.8	30.7	235 43.5	10.7	0 55.8	11.2	58.6
23 00	180 49.8	N20 31.1	250 13.2	10.7	S 0 44.6	11.3	58.6
01	195 49.7	31.6	264 42.9	10.7	0 33.3	11.3	58.6
02	210 49.7	32.1	279 12.6	10.8	0 22.0	11.2	58.6
03	225 49.6 ..	32.6	293 42.4	10.7	S 0 10.8	11.3	58.6
04	240 49.6	33.1	308 12.1	10.8	N 0 00.5	11.2	58.5
05	255 49.5	33.5	322 41.9	10.8	0 11.7	11.2	58.5
F 06	270 49.5	N20 34.0	337 11.7	10.8	N 0 22.9	11.3	58.5
R 07	285 49.4	34.5	351 41.5	10.9	0 34.2	11.2	58.5
I 08	300 49.4	35.0	6 11.4	10.8	0 45.4	11.2	58.5
D 09	315 49.3 ..	35.5	20 41.2	10.9	0 56.6	11.2	58.4
A 10	330 49.2	35.9	35 11.1	10.9	1 07.8	11.2	58.4
Y 11	345 49.2	36.4	49 41.0	10.9	1 19.0	11.1	58.4
12	0 49.1	N20 36.9	64 10.9	10.9	N 1 30.1	11.2	58.4
13	15 49.1	37.4	78 40.8	10.9	1 41.3	11.1	58.4
14	30 49.0	37.8	93 10.7	10.9	1 52.4	11.2	58.4
15	45 49.0 ..	38.3	107 40.6	11.0	2 03.6	11.1	58.3
16	60 48.9	38.8	122 10.6	10.9	2 14.7	11.1	58.3
17	75 48.9	39.3	136 40.5	11.0	2 25.8	11.0	58.3
18	90 48.8	N20 39.7	151 10.5	11.0	N 2 36.8	11.1	58.3
19	105 48.8	40.2	165 40.5	10.9	2 47.9	11.0	58.3
20	120 48.7	40.7	180 10.4	11.0	2 58.9	11.0	58.2
21	135 48.6 ..	41.1	194 40.4	11.0	3 09.9	11.0	58.2
22	150 48.6	41.6	209 10.4	11.0	3 20.9	11.0	58.2
23	165 48.5	42.1	223 40.4	11.0	3 31.9	10.9	58.2
24 00	180 48.5	N20 42.5	238 10.4	11.0	N 3 42.8	10.9	58.2
01	195 48.4	43.0	252 40.4	11.0	3 53.7	10.9	58.2
02	210 48.4	43.5	267 10.4	11.1	4 04.6	10.8	58.1
03	225 48.3 ..	43.9	281 40.5	11.0	4 15.4	10.9	58.1
04	240 48.3	44.4	296 10.5	11.0	4 26.3	10.8	58.1
05	255 48.2	44.9	310 40.5	11.0	4 37.1	10.7	58.1
S 06	270 48.1	N20 45.3	325 10.5	11.1	N 4 47.8	10.8	58.1
A 07	285 48.1	45.8	339 40.6	11.0	4 58.6	10.7	58.0
T 08	300 48.0	46.3	354 10.6	11.0	5 09.3	10.6	58.0
U 09	315 48.0 ..	46.7	8 40.6	11.1	5 19.9	10.7	58.0
R 10	330 47.9	47.2	23 10.7	11.0	5 30.6	10.6	58.0
D 11	345 47.8	47.6	37 40.7	11.0	5 41.2	10.5	58.0
A 12	0 47.8	N20 48.1	52 10.7	11.1	N 5 51.7	10.6	57.9
Y 13	15 47.7	48.6	66 40.8	11.0	6 02.3	10.4	57.9
14	30 47.7	49.0	81 10.8	11.0	6 12.7	10.5	57.9
15	45 47.6 ..	49.5	95 40.8	11.0	6 23.2	10.4	57.9
16	60 47.6	49.9	110 10.8	11.0	6 33.6	10.4	57.9
17	75 47.5	50.4	124 40.8	11.1	6 44.0	10.3	57.9
18	90 47.4	N20 50.9	139 10.9	11.0	N 6 54.3	10.3	57.8
19	105 47.4	51.3	153 40.9	11.0	7 04.6	10.2	57.8
20	120 47.3	51.8	168 10.9	11.0	7 14.8	10.2	57.8
21	135 47.2 ..	52.2	182 40.9	11.0	7 25.0	10.2	57.8
22	150 47.2	52.7	197 10.9	11.0	7 35.2	10.1	57.8
23	165 47.1	53.1	211 40.9	10.9	N 7 45.3	10.0	57.7
	SD 15.8	d 0.5	SD 16.0		15.9		15.8

Twilight, Sunrise and Moonrise

Lat.	Naut.	Civil	Sunrise	Moonrise 22	23	24	25
N 72	▭	▭	▭	01 37	01 30	01 23	01 15
N 70	▭	▭	▭	01 30	01 29	01 28	01 27
68	////	////	00 55	01 24	01 28	01 32	01 37
66	////	////	01 50	01 19	01 28	01 36	01 44
64	////	////	02 23	01 15	01 27	01 39	01 51
62	////	01 15	02 47	01 12	01 27	01 41	01 57
60	////	01 54	03 05	01 09	01 26	01 44	02 02
N 58	////	02 20	03 21	01 06	01 26	01 46	02 07
56	01 08	02 41	03 34	01 03	01 26	01 48	02 11
54	01 44	02 57	03 45	01 01	01 26	01 50	02 14
52	02 08	03 11	03 55	00 59	01 25	01 51	02 18
50	02 27	03 23	04 04	00 57	01 25	01 53	02 21
45	03 03	03 48	04 23	00 53	01 25	01 56	02 27
N 40	03 28	04 07	04 38	00 50	01 24	01 58	02 33
35	03 48	04 23	04 51	00 47	01 24	02 01	02 38
30	04 04	04 36	05 02	00 44	01 24	02 03	02 42
20	04 29	04 58	05 21	00 40	01 23	02 06	02 49
N 10	04 49	05 15	05 38	00 36	01 23	02 09	02 56
0	05 05	05 31	05 53	00 32	01 22	02 12	03 02
S 10	05 20	05 46	06 08	00 28	01 22	02 15	03 08
20	05 34	06 01	06 24	00 24	01 22	02 19	03 15
30	05 48	06 17	06 43	00 20	01 21	02 22	03 22
35	05 55	06 26	06 53	00 17	01 21	02 24	03 27
40	06 02	06 36	07 05	00 14	01 21	02 27	03 32
45	06 11	06 47	07 20	00 11	01 21	02 30	03 38
S 50	06 20	07 00	07 37	00 06	01 20	02 33	03 45
52	06 24	07 06	07 45	00 05	01 20	02 35	03 48
54	06 29	07 13	07 54	00 02	01 20	02 37	03 52
56	06 33	07 20	08 04	00 00	01 20	02 39	03 56
58	06 39	07 29	08 16	25 20	01 20	02 41	04 00
S 60	06 44	07 38	08 30	25 20	01 20	02 43	04 05

Sunset, Twilight and Moonset

Lat.	Sunset	Civil	Naut.	Moonset 22	23	24	25
N 72	▭	▭	▭	12 17	14 09	16 00	17 52
N 70	▭	▭	▭	12 21	14 07	15 51	17 34
68	23 07	////	////	12 25	14 05	15 43	17 20
66	22 07	////	////	12 28	14 03	15 36	17 08
64	21 33	////	////	12 31	14 01	15 31	16 59
62	21 09	22 43	////	12 33	14 00	15 26	16 50
60	20 50	22 02	////	12 35	13 59	15 22	16 43
N 58	20 34	21 35	////	12 36	13 58	15 18	16 37
56	20 21	21 14	22 50	12 38	13 57	15 15	16 32
54	20 09	20 58	22 12	12 39	13 56	15 12	16 27
52	19 59	20 43	21 47	12 41	13 56	15 10	16 22
50	19 50	20 31	21 28	12 42	13 55	15 07	16 18
45	19 31	20 06	20 52	12 44	13 54	15 02	16 10
N 40	19 15	19 47	20 26	12 46	13 53	14 58	16 03
35	19 03	19 31	20 06	12 48	13 51	14 54	15 56
30	18 51	19 18	19 50	12 49	13 51	14 51	15 51
20	18 32	18 56	19 25	12 52	13 49	14 45	15 42
N 10	18 16	18 38	19 05	12 54	13 48	14 41	15 33
0	18 00	18 22	18 48	12 56	13 46	14 36	15 26
S 10	17 45	18 08	18 33	12 58	13 45	14 31	15 18
20	17 29	17 53	18 20	13 00	13 43	14 26	15 10
30	17 11	17 36	18 06	13 03	13 42	14 21	15 01
35	17 00	17 27	17 58	13 04	13 41	14 18	14 55
40	16 48	17 17	17 51	13 06	13 40	14 14	14 49
45	16 34	17 06	17 42	13 07	13 39	14 10	14 42
S 50	16 16	16 53	17 33	13 09	13 37	14 05	14 34
52	16 08	16 47	17 29	13 10	13 36	14 02	14 30
54	15 59	16 41	17 24	13 11	13 36	14 00	14 26
56	15 49	16 33	17 20	13 13	13 35	13 57	14 21
58	15 37	16 24	17 14	13 14	13 34	13 54	14 16
S 60	15 23	16 15	17 09	13 15	13 33	13 51	14 10

SUN / MOON

Day	SUN Eqn. of Time 00h	12h	Mer. Pass.	MOON Mer. Pass. Upper	Lower	Age	Phase
d	m s	m s	h m	h m	h m	d	%
22	03 24	03 22	11 57	06 44	19 09	23	39
23	03 19	03 17	11 57	07 34	19 59	24	29
24	03 14	03 11	11 57	08 24	20 49	25	19

UT	ARIES	VENUS −4.0		MARS −0.6		JUPITER −1.9		SATURN +0.1		STARS		
	GHA	GHA	Dec	GHA	Dec	GHA	Dec	GHA	Dec	Name	SHA	Dec
d h	° ′	° ′	° ′	° ′	° ′	° ′	° ′	° ′	° ′		° ′	° ′
25 00	242 30.2	218 22.4	N 7 55.0	53 50.1	S 3 05.3	131 50.9	N22 24.3	15 17.5	S15 05.1	Acamar	315 18.3	S40 14.9
01	257 32.7	233 22.1	56.0	68 52.5	05.5	146 52.9	24.3	30 20.2	05.0	Achernar	335 26.9	S57 09.7
02	272 35.1	248 21.8	57.1	83 54.8	05.6	161 54.8	24.2	45 22.8	05.0	Acrux	173 08.0	S63 11.0
03	287 37.6	263 21.5	.. 58.1	98 57.2	.. 05.8	176 56.8	.. 24.1	60 25.5	.. 04.9	Adhara	255 12.3	S28 59.8
04	302 40.1	278 21.2	7 59.1	113 59.6	05.9	191 58.8	24.1	75 28.1	04.9	Aldebaran	290 49.0	N16 32.1
05	317 42.5	293 21.0	8 00.2	129 01.9	06.1	207 00.7	24.0	90 30.8	04.8			
06	332 45.0	308 20.7	N 8 01.2	144 04.3	S 3 06.2	222 02.7	N22 23.9	105 33.4	S15 04.8	Alioth	166 19.9	N55 53.1
07	347 47.5	323 20.4	02.2	159 06.6	06.4	237 04.7	23.9	120 36.0	04.8	Alkaid	152 58.1	N49 14.7
08	2 49.9	338 20.1	03.3	174 09.0	06.5	252 06.6	23.8	135 38.7	04.7	Al Na'ir	27 43.0	S46 53.1
S 09	17 52.4	353 19.8	.. 04.3	189 11.3	.. 06.7	267 08.6	.. 23.8	150 41.3	.. 04.7	Alnilam	275 46.0	S 1 11.8
U 10	32 54.8	8 19.5	05.3	204 13.7	06.8	282 10.5	23.7	165 44.0	04.6	Alphard	217 55.5	S 8 43.5
N 11	47 57.3	23 19.3	06.4	219 16.0	07.0	297 12.5	23.6	180 46.6	04.6			
D 12	62 59.8	38 19.0	N 8 07.4	234 18.3	S 3 07.1	312 14.5	N22 23.6	195 49.3	S15 04.5	Alphecca	126 10.1	N26 40.1
A 13	78 02.2	53 18.7	08.4	249 20.7	07.3	327 16.4	23.5	210 51.9	04.5	Alpheratz	357 43.0	N29 10.0
Y 14	93 04.7	68 18.4	09.5	264 23.0	07.4	342 18.4	23.4	225 54.5	04.5	Altair	62 07.4	N 8 54.5
15	108 07.2	83 18.1	.. 10.5	279 25.4	.. 07.6	357 20.3	.. 23.4	240 57.2	.. 04.4	Ankaa	353 15.4	S42 13.5
16	123 09.6	98 17.8	11.5	294 27.7	07.7	12 22.3	23.3	255 59.8	04.4	Antares	112 25.1	S26 27.7
17	138 12.1	113 17.5	12.6	309 30.1	07.9	27 24.3	23.2	271 02.5	04.3			
18	153 14.6	128 17.3	N 8 13.6	324 32.4	S 3 08.0	42 26.2	N22 23.2	286 05.1	S15 04.3	Arcturus	145 54.9	N19 06.5
19	168 17.0	143 17.0	14.6	339 34.7	08.2	57 28.2	23.1	301 07.8	04.2	Atria	107 25.7	S69 03.0
20	183 19.5	158 16.7	15.6	354 37.1	08.4	72 30.2	23.1	316 10.4	04.2	Avior	234 18.0	S59 33.8
21	198 21.9	173 16.4	.. 16.7	9 39.4	.. 08.5	87 32.1	.. 23.0	331 13.0	.. 04.1	Bellatrix	278 31.6	N 6 21.5
22	213 24.4	188 16.1	17.7	24 41.7	08.7	102 34.1	22.9	346 15.7	04.1	Betelgeuse	271 00.9	N 7 24.3
23	228 26.9	203 15.8	18.7	39 44.1	08.8	117 36.0	22.9	1 18.3	04.1			
26 00	243 29.3	218 15.5	N 8 19.8	54 46.4	S 3 09.0	132 38.0	N22 22.8	16 21.0	S15 04.0	Canopus	263 56.3	S52 42.6
01	258 31.8	233 15.2	20.8	69 48.7	09.1	147 40.0	22.7	31 23.6	04.0	Capella	280 34.0	N46 00.5
02	273 34.3	248 14.9	21.8	84 51.1	09.3	162 41.9	22.7	46 26.3	03.9	Deneb	49 30.8	N45 19.8
03	288 36.7	263 14.7	.. 22.8	99 53.4	.. 09.5	177 43.9	.. 22.6	61 28.9	.. 03.9	Denebola	182 32.9	N14 29.5
04	303 39.2	278 14.4	23.9	114 55.7	09.6	192 45.8	22.5	76 31.5	03.8	Diphda	348 55.5	S17 54.4
05	318 41.7	293 14.1	24.9	129 58.0	09.8	207 47.8	22.5	91 34.2	03.8			
06	333 44.1	308 13.8	N 8 25.9	145 00.4	S 3 09.9	222 49.8	N22 22.4	106 36.8	S15 03.8	Dubhe	193 50.9	N61 40.6
07	348 46.6	323 13.5	27.0	160 02.7	10.1	237 51.7	22.3	121 39.5	03.7	Elnath	278 12.2	N28 37.0
08	3 49.1	338 13.2	28.0	175 05.0	10.3	252 53.7	22.3	136 42.1	03.7	Eltanin	90 45.3	N51 29.3
M 09	18 51.5	353 12.9	.. 29.0	190 07.3	.. 10.4	267 55.6	.. 22.2	151 44.7	.. 03.6	Enif	33 46.4	N 9 56.5
O 10	33 54.0	8 12.6	30.0	205 09.7	10.6	282 57.6	22.2	166 47.4	03.6	Fomalhaut	15 23.4	S29 32.5
N 11	48 56.4	23 12.3	31.1	220 12.0	10.7	297 59.6	22.1	181 50.0	03.5			
D 12	63 58.9	38 12.0	N 8 32.1	235 14.3	S 3 10.9	313 01.5	N22 22.0	196 52.7	S15 03.5	Gacrux	171 59.8	S57 11.9
A 13	79 01.4	53 11.7	33.1	250 16.6	11.1	328 03.5	22.0	211 55.3	03.5	Gienah	175 51.5	S17 37.5
Y 14	94 03.8	68 11.4	34.2	265 18.9	11.2	343 05.4	21.9	226 57.9	03.4	Hadar	148 46.3	S60 26.7
15	109 06.3	83 11.2	.. 35.2	280 21.2	.. 11.4	358 07.4	.. 21.8	242 00.6	.. 03.4	Hamal	328 00.3	N23 31.6
16	124 08.8	98 10.9	36.2	295 23.5	11.6	13 09.3	21.8	257 03.2	03.3	Kaus Aust.	83 42.6	S34 22.4
17	139 11.2	113 10.6	37.2	310 25.9	11.7	28 11.3	21.7	272 05.9	03.3			
18	154 13.7	128 10.3	N 8 38.3	325 28.2	S 3 11.9	43 13.3	N22 21.6	287 08.5	S15 03.2	Kochab	137 19.1	N74 06.0
19	169 16.2	143 10.0	39.3	340 30.5	12.1	58 15.2	21.6	302 11.2	03.2	Markab	13 37.7	N15 16.9
20	184 18.6	158 09.7	40.3	355 32.8	12.2	73 17.2	21.5	317 13.8	03.2	Menkar	314 14.7	N 4 08.6
21	199 21.1	173 09.4	.. 41.3	10 35.1	.. 12.4	88 19.1	.. 21.4	332 16.4	.. 03.1	Menkent	148 06.4	S36 26.5
22	214 23.6	188 09.1	42.4	25 37.4	12.6	103 21.1	21.4	347 19.1	03.1	Miaplacidus	221 39.7	S69 47.0
23	229 26.0	203 08.8	43.4	40 39.7	12.7	118 23.1	21.3	2 21.7	03.0			
27 00	244 28.5	218 08.5	N 8 44.4	55 42.0	S 3 12.9	133 25.0	N22 21.2	17 24.4	S15 03.0	Mirfak	308 39.9	N49 54.5
01	259 30.9	233 08.2	45.4	70 44.3	13.1	148 27.0	21.2	32 27.0	02.9	Nunki	75 57.2	S26 16.5
02	274 33.4	248 07.9	46.5	85 46.6	13.2	163 28.9	21.1	47 29.6	02.9	Peacock	53 18.0	S56 40.9
03	289 35.9	263 07.6	.. 47.5	100 48.9	.. 13.4	178 30.9	.. 21.0	62 32.3	.. 02.9	Pollux	243 27.2	N27 59.3
04	304 38.3	278 07.3	48.5	115 51.2	13.6	193 32.8	21.0	77 34.9	02.8	Procyon	244 59.3	N 5 11.0
05	319 40.8	293 07.0	49.5	130 53.5	13.7	208 34.8	20.9	92 37.6	02.8			
06	334 43.3	308 06.7	N 8 50.5	145 55.8	S 3 13.9	223 36.7	N22 20.9	107 40.2	S15 02.7	Rasalhague	96 05.5	N12 33.1
07	349 45.7	323 06.4	51.6	160 58.1	14.1	238 38.7	20.8	122 42.8	02.7	Regulus	207 42.9	N11 53.7
08	4 48.2	338 06.1	52.6	176 00.4	14.3	253 40.7	20.7	137 45.5	02.6	Rigel	281 11.8	S 8 11.4
T 09	19 50.7	353 05.8	.. 53.6	191 02.7	.. 14.4	268 42.6	.. 20.7	152 48.1	.. 02.6	Rigil Kent.	139 50.1	S60 53.7
U 10	34 53.1	8 05.5	54.6	206 05.0	14.6	283 44.6	20.6	167 50.8	02.6	Sabik	102 11.5	S15 44.4
E 11	49 55.6	23 05.2	55.7	221 07.3	14.8	298 46.5	20.5	182 53.4	02.5			
S 12	64 58.1	38 04.9	N 8 56.7	236 09.5	S 3 15.0	313 48.5	N22 20.5	197 56.0	S15 02.5	Schedar	349 40.0	N56 36.7
D 13	80 00.5	53 04.6	57.7	251 11.8	15.1	328 50.4	20.4	212 58.7	02.4	Shaula	96 20.6	S37 06.6
A 14	95 03.0	68 04.3	58.7	266 14.1	15.3	343 52.4	20.3	228 01.3	02.4	Sirius	258 33.4	S16 44.5
Y 15	110 05.4	83 04.0	8 59.7	281 16.4	.. 15.5	358 54.4	.. 20.3	243 04.0	.. 02.3	Spica	158 30.3	S11 14.3
16	125 07.9	98 03.7	9 00.8	296 18.7	15.7	13 56.3	20.2	258 06.6	02.3	Suhail	222 52.1	S43 29.9
17	140 10.4	113 03.4	01.8	311 21.0	15.8	28 58.3	20.1	273 09.2	02.3			
18	155 12.8	128 03.1	N 9 02.8	326 23.3	S 3 16.0	44 00.2	N22 20.1	288 11.9	S15 02.2	Vega	80 38.2	N38 47.9
19	170 15.3	143 02.8	03.8	341 25.5	16.2	59 02.2	20.0	303 14.5	02.2	Zuben'ubi	137 04.4	S16 06.1
20	185 17.8	158 02.5	04.8	356 27.8	16.4	74 04.1	19.9	318 17.1	02.1		SHA	Mer. Pass.
21	200 20.2	173 02.2	.. 05.9	11 30.1	.. 16.5	89 06.1	.. 19.9	333 19.8	.. 02.1		° ′	h m
22	215 22.7	188 01.9	06.9	26 32.4	16.7	104 08.0	19.8	348 22.4	02.0	Venus	334 46.2	9 27
23	230 25.2	203 01.6	07.9	41 34.7	16.9	119 10.0	19.7	3 25.1	02.0	Mars	171 17.1	20 18
	h m									Jupiter	249 08.7	15 07
Mer. Pass. 7 44.8		v −0.3	d 1.0	v 2.3	d 0.2	v 2.0	d 0.1	v 2.6	d 0.0	Saturn	132 51.6	22 51

SUN / MOON / Twilight / Moonrise

UT	SUN GHA	SUN Dec	MOON GHA	v	MOON Dec	d	HP
d h	° ′	° ′	° ′	′	° ′	′	′
25 00	180 47.1	N20 53.6	226 10.8	11.0	N 7 55.3	10.0	57.7
01	195 47.0	54.0	240 40.8	11.0	8 05.3	10.0	57.7
02	210 46.9	54.5	255 10.8	11.0	8 15.3	9.9	57.7
03	225 46.9 ..	54.9	269 40.8	10.9	8 25.2	9.9	57.7
04	240 46.8	55.4	284 10.7	11.0	8 35.1	9.8	57.6
05	255 46.8	55.8	298 40.7	10.9	8 44.9	9.7	57.6
06	270 46.7	N20 56.3	313 10.6	10.9	N 8 54.6	9.7	57.6
07	285 46.6	56.7	327 40.5	10.9	9 04.3	9.7	57.6
08	300 46.6	57.2	342 10.4	11.0	9 14.0	9.6	57.6
S 09	315 46.5 ..	57.6	356 40.4	10.9	9 23.6	9.5	57.5
U 10	330 46.4	58.1	11 10.3	10.9	9 33.1	9.5	57.5
N 11	345 46.4	58.5	25 40.2	10.8	9 42.6	9.4	57.5
D 12	0 46.3	N20 59.0	40 10.0	10.9	N 9 52.0	9.4	57.5
A 13	15 46.2	59.4	54 39.9	10.9	10 01.4	9.3	57.5
Y 14	30 46.2	20 59.9	69 09.8	10.8	10 10.7	9.3	57.4
15	45 46.1	21 00.3	83 39.6	10.8	10 20.0	9.2	57.4
16	60 46.0	00.7	98 09.4	10.9	10 29.2	9.1	57.4
17	75 46.0	01.2	112 39.3	10.8	10 38.3	9.1	57.4
18	90 45.9	N21 01.6	127 09.1	10.8	N10 47.4	9.0	57.4
19	105 45.9	02.1	141 38.9	10.8	10 56.4	8.9	57.3
20	120 45.8	02.5	156 08.7	10.8	11 05.3	8.9	57.3
21	135 45.7 ..	02.9	170 38.5	10.7	11 14.2	8.8	57.3
22	150 45.7	03.4	185 08.2	10.8	11 23.0	8.7	57.3
23	165 45.6	03.8	199 38.0	10.7	11 31.7	8.7	57.3
26 00	180 45.5	N21 04.3	214 07.7	10.7	N11 40.4	8.6	57.2
01	195 45.5	04.7	228 37.5	10.7	11 49.0	8.6	57.2
02	210 45.4	05.1	243 07.2	10.7	11 57.6	8.5	57.2
03	225 45.3 ..	05.6	257 36.9	10.7	12 06.1	8.4	57.2
04	240 45.2	06.0	272 06.6	10.6	12 14.5	8.3	57.1
05	255 45.2	06.4	286 36.2	10.7	12 22.8	8.3	57.1
06	270 45.1	N21 06.9	301 05.9	10.7	N12 31.1	8.2	57.1
07	285 45.0	07.3	315 35.6	10.6	12 39.3	8.1	57.1
08	300 45.0	07.7	330 05.2	10.6	12 47.4	8.1	57.1
M 09	315 44.9 ..	08.2	344 34.8	10.6	12 55.5	7.9	57.0
O 10	330 44.8	08.6	359 04.4	10.6	13 03.4	7.9	57.0
N 11	345 44.8	09.0	13 34.0	10.6	13 11.3	7.9	57.0
D 12	0 44.7	N21 09.5	28 03.6	10.6	N13 19.2	7.7	57.0
A 13	15 44.6	09.9	42 33.2	10.5	13 26.9	7.7	57.0
Y 14	30 44.6	10.3	57 02.7	10.6	13 34.6	7.6	56.9
15	45 44.5 ..	10.8	71 32.3	10.5	13 42.2	7.5	56.9
16	60 44.4	11.2	86 01.8	10.5	13 49.7	7.5	56.9
17	75 44.3	11.6	100 31.3	10.5	13 57.2	7.3	56.9
18	90 44.3	N21 12.0	115 00.8	10.5	N14 04.5	7.3	56.9
19	105 44.2	12.5	129 30.3	10.5	14 11.8	7.2	56.8
20	120 44.1	12.9	143 59.8	10.5	14 19.0	7.2	56.8
21	135 44.1 ..	13.3	158 29.3	10.4	14 26.2	7.0	56.8
22	150 44.0	13.7	172 58.7	10.4	14 33.2	7.0	56.8
23	165 43.9	14.2	187 28.2	10.4	14 40.2	6.8	56.8
27 00	180 43.8	N21 14.6	201 57.6	10.4	N14 47.0	6.8	56.7
01	195 43.8	15.0	216 27.0	10.5	14 53.8	6.8	56.7
02	210 43.7	15.4	230 56.5	10.3	15 00.6	6.6	56.7
03	225 43.6 ..	15.8	245 25.8	10.4	15 07.2	6.5	56.7
04	240 43.6	16.3	259 55.2	10.4	15 13.7	6.5	56.6
05	255 43.5	16.7	274 24.6	10.4	15 20.2	6.4	56.6
06	270 43.4	N21 17.1	288 54.0	10.3	N15 26.6	6.3	56.6
07	285 43.3	17.5	303 23.3	10.4	15 32.9	6.2	56.6
T 08	300 43.3	17.9	317 52.7	10.3	15 39.1	6.1	56.6
U 09	315 43.2 ..	18.4	332 22.0	10.3	15 45.2	6.0	56.5
E 10	330 43.1	18.8	346 51.3	10.4	15 51.2	6.0	56.5
S 11	345 43.0	19.2	1 20.7	10.3	15 57.2	5.8	56.5
D 12	0 43.0	N21 19.6	15 50.0	10.3	N16 03.0	5.8	56.5
A 13	15 42.9	20.0	30 19.3	10.3	16 08.8	5.6	56.5
Y 14	30 42.8	20.4	44 48.6	10.2	16 14.4	5.6	56.4
15	45 42.7 ..	20.8	59 17.8	10.3	16 20.0	5.5	56.4
16	60 42.7	21.3	73 47.1	10.3	16 25.5	5.4	56.4
17	75 42.6	21.7	88 16.4	10.2	16 30.9	5.3	56.4
18	90 42.5	N21 22.1	102 45.6	10.3	N16 36.2	5.3	56.3
19	105 42.4	22.5	117 14.9	10.3	16 41.5	5.1	56.3
20	120 42.4	22.9	131 44.2	10.2	16 46.6	5.0	56.3
21	135 42.3 ..	23.3	146 13.4	10.2	16 51.6	5.0	56.3
22	150 42.2	23.7	160 42.6	10.3	16 56.6	4.8	56.3
23	165 42.1	24.1	175 11.9	10.2	N17 01.4	4.8	56.2
	SD 15.8	d 0.4	SD 15.7		15.5		15.4

Twilight / Moonrise

Lat.	Naut.	Civil	Sunrise	Moonrise 25	26	27	28
°	h m	h m	h m	h m	h m	h m	h m
N 72	▭	▭	▭	01 15	01 07	00 57	00 40
N 70	▭	▭	▭	01 27	01 27	01 29	01 34
68	////	////	00 19	01 37	01 43	01 52	02 06
66	////	////	01 38	01 44	01 55	02 10	02 31
64	////	////	02 14	01 51	02 06	02 25	02 50
62	////	00 59	02 40	01 57	02 15	02 37	03 05
60	////	01 45	03 00	02 02	02 23	02 48	03 18
N 58	////	02 13	03 16	02 07	02 30	02 57	03 29
56	00 53	02 35	03 30	02 11	02 36	03 05	03 39
54	01 35	02 52	03 41	02 14	02 41	03 12	03 48
52	02 02	03 07	03 52	02 18	02 46	03 19	03 56
50	02 22	03 20	04 01	02 21	02 51	03 25	04 03
45	02 59	03 45	04 21	02 27	03 01	03 37	04 18
N 40	03 25	04 05	04 36	02 33	03 09	03 48	04 30
35	03 46	04 21	04 50	02 38	03 16	03 57	04 41
30	04 02	04 34	05 01	02 42	03 22	04 05	04 50
20	04 28	04 57	05 21	02 49	03 33	04 19	05 06
N 10	04 49	05 15	05 38	02 56	03 43	04 31	05 20
0	05 05	05 31	05 53	03 02	03 52	04 42	05 33
S 10	05 21	05 47	06 09	03 08	04 01	04 54	05 46
20	05 35	06 02	06 25	03 15	04 11	05 06	06 01
30	05 49	06 18	06 44	03 22	04 22	05 20	06 17
35	05 57	06 28	06 55	03 27	04 28	05 28	06 26
40	06 05	06 38	07 08	03 32	04 36	05 38	06 37
45	06 13	06 50	07 22	03 38	04 44	05 49	06 50
S 50	06 23	07 03	07 40	03 45	04 55	06 02	07 06
52	06 27	07 10	07 49	03 48	05 00	06 08	07 13
54	06 32	07 17	07 58	03 52	05 05	06 15	07 21
56	06 37	07 24	08 09	03 56	05 11	06 23	07 30
58	06 43	07 33	08 21	04 00	05 18	06 32	07 41
S 60	06 49	07 43	08 36	04 05	05 25	06 42	07 53

Twilight / Moonset

Lat.	Sunset	Civil	Naut.	Moonset 25	26	27	28
°	h m	h m	h m	h m	h m	h m	h m
N 72	▭	▭	▭	17 52	19 47	21 51	▭
N 70	▭	▭	▭	17 34	19 17	20 58	22 30
68	▭	▭	▭	17 20	18 55	20 26	21 46
66	22 20	////	////	17 08	18 38	20 02	21 17
64	21 42	////	////	16 59	18 24	19 44	20 55
62	21 16	23 01	////	16 50	18 12	19 28	20 37
60	20 56	22 12	////	16 43	18 02	19 16	20 22
N 58	20 39	21 43	////	16 37	17 53	19 05	20 10
56	20 26	21 21	23 06	16 32	17 46	18 55	19 59
54	20 14	21 03	22 21	16 27	17 39	18 47	19 50
52	20 03	20 48	21 54	16 22	17 33	18 40	19 41
50	19 54	20 35	21 33	16 18	17 27	18 33	19 34
45	19 34	20 10	20 56	16 10	17 15	18 18	19 18
N 40	19 18	19 50	20 29	16 03	17 06	18 07	19 04
35	19 05	19 34	20 09	15 56	16 57	17 56	18 53
30	18 53	19 20	19 52	15 51	16 50	17 48	18 43
20	18 33	18 57	19 26	15 42	16 37	17 32	18 26
N 10	18 16	18 39	19 06	15 33	16 26	17 19	18 11
0	18 01	18 23	18 49	15 26	16 16	17 07	17 58
S 10	17 45	18 07	18 33	15 18	16 06	16 54	17 44
20	17 28	17 52	18 19	15 10	15 55	16 41	17 29
30	17 10	17 35	18 05	15 01	15 42	16 26	17 12
35	16 59	17 26	17 57	14 55	15 35	16 17	17 02
40	16 46	17 16	17 49	14 49	15 27	16 07	16 51
45	16 31	17 04	17 40	14 42	15 17	15 55	16 38
S 50	16 13	16 50	17 31	14 34	15 06	15 41	16 22
52	16 05	16 44	17 26	14 30	15 00	15 35	16 14
54	15 55	16 37	17 22	14 26	14 54	15 27	16 06
56	15 44	16 29	17 16	14 21	14 48	15 19	15 57
58	15 32	16 21	17 11	14 16	14 41	15 10	15 46
S 60	15 18	16 11	17 05	14 10	14 32	15 00	15 34

SUN / MOON

Day	Eqn. of Time 00h	Eqn. of Time 12h	Mer. Pass.	Mer. Pass. Upper	Mer. Pass. Lower	Age	Phase
d	m s	m s	h m	h m	h m	d	%
25	03 08	03 05	11 57	09 14	21 39	26	11
26	03 02	02 59	11 57	10 04	22 29	27	6
27	02 56	02 52	11 57	10 54	23 20	28	2

UT	ARIES	VENUS −4.0		MARS −0.6		JUPITER −1.9		SATURN +0.2		STARS		
	GHA	GHA	Dec	GHA	Dec	GHA	Dec	GHA	Dec	Name	SHA	Dec
d h	° ′	° ′	° ′	° ′	° ′	° ′	° ′	° ′	° ′		° ′	° ′
28 00	245 27.6	218 01.3 N 9 08.9		56 36.9 S 3 17.1		134 11.9 N22 19.7		18 27.7 S15 02.0		Acamar	315 18.3	S40 14.9
01	260 30.1	233 01.0	09.9	71 39.2	17.3	149 13.9	19.6	33 30.3	01.9	Achernar	335 26.8	S57 09.7
02	275 32.5	248 00.7	11.0	86 41.5	17.4	164 15.9	19.5	48 33.0	01.9	Acrux	173 08.1	S63 11.1
03	290 35.0	263 00.4 ..	12.0	101 43.7 ..	17.6	179 17.8 ..	19.5	63 35.6 ..	01.8	Adhara	255 12.3	S28 59.8
04	305 37.5	278 00.1	13.0	116 46.0	17.8	194 19.8	19.4	78 38.3	01.8	Aldebaran	290 49.0	N16 32.1
05	320 39.9	292 59.8	14.0	131 48.3	18.0	209 21.7	19.3	93 40.9	01.7			
06	335 42.4	307 59.5 N 9 15.0		146 50.6 S 3 18.2		224 23.7 N22 19.3		108 43.5 S15 01.7		Alioth	166 19.9	N55 53.1
W 07	350 44.9	322 59.2	16.0	161 52.8	18.3	239 25.6	19.2	123 46.2	01.7	Alkaid	152 58.1	N49 14.7
E 08	5 47.3	337 58.8	17.1	176 55.1	18.5	254 27.6	19.1	138 48.8	01.6	Al Na'ir	27 42.9	S46 53.1
D 09	20 49.8	352 58.5 ..	18.1	191 57.4 ..	18.7	269 29.5 ..	19.1	153 51.5 ..	01.6	Alnilam	275 46.0	S 1 11.8
N 10	35 52.3	7 58.2	19.1	206 59.6	18.9	284 31.5	19.0	168 54.1	01.5	Alphard	217 55.6	S 8 43.5
E 11	50 54.7	22 57.9	20.1	222 01.9	19.1	299 33.4	18.9	183 56.7	01.5			
S 12	65 57.2	37 57.6 N 9 21.1		237 04.1 S 3 19.3		314 35.4 N22 18.9		198 59.4 S15 01.4		Alphecca	126 10.1	N26 40.1
D 13	80 59.7	52 57.3	22.1	252 06.4	19.4	329 37.3	18.8	214 02.0	01.4	Alpheratz	357 42.9	N29 10.0
A 14	96 02.1	67 57.0	23.2	267 08.7	19.6	344 39.3	18.7	229 04.6	01.4	Altair	62 07.4	N 8 54.5
Y 15	111 04.6	82 56.7 ..	24.2	282 10.9 ..	19.8	359 41.2 ..	18.7	244 07.3 ..	01.3	Ankaa	353 15.3	S42 13.5
16	126 07.0	97 56.4	25.2	297 13.2	20.0	14 43.2	18.6	259 09.9	01.3	Antares	112 25.1	S26 27.7
17	141 09.5	112 56.1	26.2	312 15.4	20.2	29 45.1	18.5	274 12.6	01.2			
18	156 12.0	127 55.8 N 9 27.2		327 17.7 S 3 20.4		44 47.1 N22 18.5		289 15.2 S15 01.2		Arcturus	145 54.9	N19 06.5
19	171 14.4	142 55.4	28.2	342 19.9	20.6	59 49.1	18.4	304 17.8	01.2	Atria	107 25.7	S69 03.0
20	186 16.9	157 55.1	29.2	357 22.2	20.7	74 51.0	18.3	319 20.5	01.1	Avior	234 18.0	S59 33.8
21	201 19.4	172 54.8 ..	30.2	12 24.4 ..	20.9	89 53.0 ..	18.3	334 23.1 ..	01.1	Bellatrix	278 31.6	N 6 21.5
22	216 21.8	187 54.5	31.3	27 26.7	21.1	104 54.9	18.2	349 25.7	01.0	Betelgeuse	271 00.9	N 7 24.3
23	231 24.3	202 54.2	32.3	42 28.9	21.3	119 56.9	18.1	4 28.4	01.0			
29 00	246 26.8	217 53.9 N 9 33.3		57 31.2 S 3 21.5		134 58.8 N22 18.1		19 31.0 S15 00.9		Canopus	263 56.3	S52 42.5
01	261 29.2	232 53.6	34.3	72 33.4	21.7	150 00.8	18.0	34 33.7	00.9	Capella	280 34.0	N46 00.5
02	276 31.7	247 53.3	35.3	87 35.7	21.9	165 02.7	17.9	49 36.3	00.9	Deneb	49 30.8	N45 19.8
03	291 34.2	262 53.0 ..	36.3	102 37.9 ..	22.1	180 04.7 ..	17.9	64 38.9 ..	00.8	Denebola	182 32.9	N14 29.5
04	306 36.6	277 52.6	37.3	117 40.2	22.3	195 06.6	17.8	79 41.6	00.8	Diphda	348 55.4	S17 54.4
05	321 39.1	292 52.3	38.3	132 42.4	22.5	210 08.6	17.7	94 44.2	00.7			
06	336 41.5	307 52.0 N 9 39.4		147 44.7 S 3 22.6		225 10.5 N22 17.7		109 46.8 S15 00.7		Dubhe	193 51.0	N61 40.6
T 07	351 44.0	322 51.7	40.4	162 46.9	22.8	240 12.5	17.6	124 49.5	00.7	Elnath	278 12.2	N28 37.0
H 08	6 46.5	337 51.4	41.4	177 49.1	23.0	255 14.4	17.5	139 52.1	00.6	Eltanin	90 45.3	N51 29.3
U 09	21 48.9	352 51.1 ..	42.4	192 51.4 ..	23.2	270 16.4 ..	17.5	154 54.7 ..	00.6	Enif	33 46.4	N 9 56.5
R 10	36 51.4	7 50.8	43.4	207 53.6	23.4	285 18.3	17.4	169 57.4	00.6	Fomalhaut	15 23.3	S29 32.5
S 11	51 53.9	22 50.4	44.4	222 55.8	23.6	300 20.3	17.3	185 00.0	00.5			
D 12	66 56.3	37 50.1 N 9 45.4		237 58.1 S 3 23.8		315 22.2 N22 17.3		200 02.7 S15 00.4		Gacrux	171 59.8	S57 11.9
A 13	81 58.8	52 49.8	46.4	253 00.3	24.0	330 24.2	17.2	215 05.3	00.4	Gienah	175 51.5	S17 37.5
Y 14	97 01.3	67 49.5	47.4	268 02.5	24.2	345 26.1	17.1	230 07.9	00.4	Hadar	148 46.3	S60 26.7
15	112 03.7	82 49.2 ..	48.4	283 04.8 ..	24.4	0 28.1 ..	17.0	245 10.6 ..	00.3	Hamal	328 00.3	N23 31.6
16	127 06.2	97 48.9	49.5	298 07.0	24.6	15 30.0	17.0	260 13.2	00.3	Kaus Aust.	83 42.6	S34 22.4
17	142 08.7	112 48.5	50.5	313 09.2	24.8	30 32.0	16.9	275 15.8	00.2			
18	157 11.1	127 48.2 N 9 51.5		328 11.5 S 3 25.0		45 33.9 N22 16.8		290 18.5 S15 00.2		Kochab	137 19.1	N74 06.0
19	172 13.6	142 47.9	52.5	343 13.7	25.2	60 35.9	16.8	305 21.1	00.2	Markab	13 37.7	N15 16.9
20	187 16.0	157 47.6	53.5	358 15.9	25.4	75 37.8	16.7	320 23.7	00.1	Menkar	314 14.7	N 4 08.6
21	202 18.5	172 47.3 ..	54.5	13 18.1 ..	25.6	90 39.8 ..	16.7	335 26.4 ..	00.1	Menkent	148 06.4	S36 26.5
22	217 21.0	187 46.9	55.5	28 20.4	25.8	105 41.7	16.6	350 29.0	00.0	Miaplacidus	221 39.7	S69 47.0
23	232 23.4	202 46.6	56.5	43 22.6	26.0	120 43.7	16.5	5 31.7	00.0			
30 00	247 25.9	217 46.3 N 9 57.5		58 24.8 S 3 26.2		135 45.6 N22 16.4		20 34.3 S15 00.0		Mirfak	308 39.9	N49 54.5
01	262 28.4	232 46.0	58.5	73 27.0	26.4	150 47.6	16.4	35 36.9 14 59.9		Nunki	75 57.2	S26 16.5
02	277 30.8	247 45.7	9 59.5	88 29.2	26.6	165 49.5	16.3	50 39.6	59.9	Peacock	53 18.0	S56 40.9
03	292 33.3	262 45.3	10 00.5	103 31.5 ..	26.8	180 51.5 ..	16.2	65 42.2 ..	59.8	Pollux	243 27.2	N27 59.3
04	307 35.8	277 45.0	01.5	118 33.7	27.0	195 53.4	16.2	80 44.8	59.8	Procyon	244 59.3	N 5 11.0
05	322 38.2	292 44.7	02.5	133 35.9	27.2	210 55.3	16.1	95 47.5	59.7			
06	337 40.7	307 44.4 N10 03.5		148 38.1 S 3 27.4		225 57.3 N22 16.0		110 50.1 S14 59.7		Rasalhague	96 05.5	N12 33.1
07	352 43.1	322 44.0	04.5	163 40.3	27.6	240 59.2	16.0	125 52.7	59.7	Regulus	207 42.9	N11 53.7
08	7 45.6	337 43.7	05.5	178 42.5	27.8	256 01.2	15.9	140 55.4	59.6	Rigel	281 11.8	S 8 11.4
F 09	22 48.1	352 43.4 ..	06.5	193 44.7 ..	28.0	271 03.1 ..	15.8	155 58.0 ..	59.6	Rigil Kent.	139 50.1	S60 53.7
R 10	37 50.5	7 43.1	07.5	208 47.0	28.2	286 05.1	15.7	171 00.6	59.5	Sabik	102 11.4	S15 44.4
I 11	52 53.0	22 42.8	08.6	223 49.2	28.4	301 07.0	15.7	186 03.3	59.5			
D 12	67 55.5	37 42.4 N10 09.6		238 51.4 S 3 28.6		316 09.0 N22 15.6		201 05.9 S14 59.5		Schedar	349 40.0	N56 36.7
A 13	82 57.9	52 42.1	10.6	253 53.6	28.8	331 10.9	15.5	216 08.5	59.4	Shaula	96 20.6	S37 06.6
Y 14	98 00.4	67 41.8	11.6	268 55.8	29.0	346 12.9	15.5	231 11.2	59.4	Sirius	258 33.4	S16 44.5
15	113 02.9	82 41.5 ..	12.6	283 58.0 ..	29.2	1 14.8 ..	15.4	246 13.8 ..	59.3	Spica	158 30.3	S11 14.3
16	128 05.3	97 41.1	13.6	299 00.2	29.4	16 16.8	15.3	261 16.4	59.3	Suhail	222 52.1	S43 29.9
17	143 07.8	112 40.8	14.6	314 02.4	29.6	31 18.7	15.3	276 19.1	59.3			
18	158 10.3	127 40.5 N10 15.6		329 04.6 S 3 29.8		46 20.7 N22 15.2		291 21.7 S14 59.2		Vega	80 38.1	N38 47.9
19	173 12.7	142 40.1	16.6	344 06.8	30.0	61 22.6	15.1	306 24.4	59.2	Zuben'ubi	137 04.4	S16 06.1
20	188 15.2	157 39.8	17.6	359 09.0	30.2	76 24.6	15.1	321 27.0	59.1		SHA	Mer.Pass.
21	203 17.6	172 39.5 ..	18.6	14 11.2 ..	30.5	91 26.5 ..	15.0	336 29.6 ..	59.1		° ′	h m
22	218 20.1	187 39.2	19.6	29 13.4	30.7	106 28.4	14.9	351 32.3	59.1	Venus	331 27.1	9 29
23	233 22.6	202 38.8	20.6	44 15.6	30.9	121 30.4	14.8	6 34.9	59.0	Mars	171 04.4	20 07
	h m									Jupiter	248 32.1	14 58
Mer.Pass. 7 33.0		v −0.3 d 1.0		v 2.2 d 0.2		v 1.9 d 0.1		v 2.6 d 0.0		Saturn	133 04.3	22 38

SUN and MOON

UT	SUN GHA	SUN Dec	MOON GHA	v	MOON Dec	d	HP
d h	° ′	° ′	° ′	′	° ′	′	′
28 00	180 42.1	N21 24.5	189 41.1	10.2	N17 06.2	4.7	56.2
01	195 42.0	24.9	204 10.3	10.3	17 10.9	4.5	56.2
02	210 41.9	25.3	218 39.6	10.2	17 15.4	4.5	56.2
03	225 41.8	.. 25.8	233 08.8	10.2	17 19.9	4.4	56.2
04	240 41.7	26.2	247 38.0	10.2	17 24.3	4.3	56.1
05	255 41.7	26.6	262 07.2	10.2	17 28.6	4.2	56.1
W 06	270 41.6	N21 27.0	276 36.4	10.2	N17 32.8	4.1	56.1
E 07	285 41.5	27.4	291 05.6	10.3	17 36.9	4.0	56.1
D 08	300 41.4	27.8	305 34.9	10.2	17 40.9	3.9	56.1
N 09	315 41.4	.. 28.2	320 04.1	10.2	17 44.8	3.8	56.0
E 10	330 41.3	28.6	334 33.3	10.2	17 48.6	3.7	56.0
S 11	345 41.2	29.0	349 02.5	10.2	17 52.3	3.6	56.0
D 12	0 41.1	N21 29.4	3 31.7	10.2	N17 55.9	3.6	56.0
A 13	15 41.0	29.8	18 00.9	10.3	17 59.5	3.4	55.9
Y 14	30 41.0	30.2	32 30.2	10.2	18 02.9	3.3	55.9
15	45 40.9	.. 30.6	46 59.4	10.2	18 06.2	3.3	55.9
16	60 40.8	31.0	61 28.6	10.3	18 09.5	3.1	55.9
17	75 40.7	31.4	75 57.9	10.2	18 12.6	3.0	55.9
18	90 40.6	N21 31.8	90 27.1	10.2	N18 15.6	3.0	55.8
19	105 40.6	32.2	104 56.3	10.3	18 18.6	2.8	55.8
20	120 40.5	32.5	119 25.6	10.3	18 21.4	2.8	55.8
21	135 40.4	.. 32.9	133 54.9	10.2	18 24.2	2.6	55.8
22	150 40.3	33.3	148 24.1	10.3	18 26.8	2.6	55.7
23	165 40.2	33.7	162 53.4	10.3	18 29.4	2.4	55.7
29 00	180 40.2	N21 34.1	177 22.7	10.3	N18 31.8	2.4	55.7
01	195 40.1	34.5	191 52.0	10.3	18 34.2	2.2	55.7
02	210 40.0	34.9	206 21.3	10.3	18 36.4	2.2	55.7
03	225 39.9	.. 35.3	220 50.6	10.3	18 38.6	2.0	55.7
04	240 39.8	35.7	235 19.9	10.3	18 40.6	2.0	55.6
05	255 39.7	36.1	249 49.2	10.4	18 42.6	1.9	55.6
T 06	270 39.7	N21 36.5	264 18.6	10.4	N18 44.5	1.7	55.6
H 07	285 39.6	36.8	278 48.0	10.3	18 46.2	1.7	55.6
U 08	300 39.5	37.2	293 17.3	10.4	18 47.9	1.6	55.6
R 09	315 39.4	.. 37.6	307 46.7	10.4	18 49.5	1.4	55.5
S 10	330 39.3	38.0	322 16.1	10.4	18 50.9	1.4	55.5
D 11	345 39.2	38.4	336 45.5	10.5	18 52.3	1.3	55.5
A 12	0 39.2	N21 38.8	351 15.0	10.4	N18 53.6	1.2	55.5
Y 13	15 39.1	39.2	5 44.4	10.5	18 54.8	1.0	55.5
14	30 39.0	39.5	20 13.9	10.5	18 55.8	1.0	55.4
15	45 38.9	.. 39.9	34 43.4	10.5	18 56.8	0.9	55.4
16	60 38.8	40.3	49 12.9	10.5	18 57.7	0.8	55.4
17	75 38.7	40.7	63 42.4	10.5	18 58.5	0.7	55.4
18	90 38.6	N21 41.1	78 11.9	10.6	N18 59.2	0.6	55.4
19	105 38.6	41.4	92 41.5	10.6	18 59.8	0.5	55.3
20	120 38.5	41.8	107 11.1	10.6	19 00.3	0.4	55.3
21	135 38.4	.. 42.2	121 40.7	10.6	19 00.7	0.3	55.3
22	150 38.3	42.6	136 10.3	10.6	19 01.0	0.2	55.3
23	165 38.2	43.0	150 39.9	10.7	19 01.2	0.1	55.3
30 00	180 38.1	N21 43.3	165 09.6	10.7	N19 01.3	0.0	55.2
01	195 38.0	43.7	179 39.3	10.7	19 01.3	0.1	55.2
02	210 38.0	44.1	194 09.0	10.7	19 01.2	0.2	55.2
03	225 37.9	.. 44.5	208 38.7	10.8	19 01.0	0.2	55.2
04	240 37.8	44.8	223 08.5	10.8	19 00.8	0.4	55.2
05	255 37.7	45.2	237 38.3	10.8	19 00.4	0.5	55.2
F 06	270 37.6	N21 45.6	252 08.1	10.8	N18 59.9	0.5	55.1
R 07	285 37.5	45.9	266 37.9	10.9	18 59.4	0.7	55.1
I 08	300 37.4	46.3	281 07.8	10.9	18 58.7	0.7	55.1
D 09	315 37.3	.. 46.7	295 37.7	10.9	18 58.0	0.9	55.1
A 10	330 37.3	47.1	310 07.6	11.0	18 57.1	0.9	55.1
Y 11	345 37.2	47.4	324 37.6	10.9	18 56.2	1.0	55.0
12	0 37.1	N21 47.8	339 07.5	11.1	N18 55.2	1.1	55.0
13	15 37.0	48.2	353 37.6	11.0	18 54.1	1.3	55.0
14	30 36.9	48.5	8 07.6	11.1	18 52.8	1.3	55.0
15	45 36.8	.. 48.9	22 37.7	11.1	18 51.5	1.4	55.0
16	60 36.7	49.3	37 07.8	11.1	18 50.1	1.5	55.0
17	75 36.6	49.6	51 37.9	11.2	18 48.6	1.5	54.9
18	90 36.5	N21 50.0	66 08.1	11.2	N18 47.1	1.7	54.9
19	105 36.5	50.3	80 38.3	11.2	18 45.4	1.8	54.9
20	120 36.4	50.7	95 08.5	11.3	18 43.6	1.8	54.9
21	135 36.3	.. 51.1	109 38.7	11.3	18 41.8	2.0	54.9
22	150 36.2	51.4	124 09.0	11.4	18 39.8	2.0	54.9
23	165 36.1	51.8	138 39.4	11.3	N18 37.8	2.1	54.8
	SD 15.8	d 0.4	SD 15.2		15.1		15.0

Twilight, Sunrise and Moonrise

Lat.	Twilight Naut.	Twilight Civil	Sunrise	Moonrise 28	Moonrise 29	Moonrise 30	Moonrise 31
°	h m	h m	h m	h m	h m	h m	h m
N 72	□	□	□	00 40	□	□	□
N 70	□	□	□	01 34	01 47	02 23	03 31
68	□	□	□	02 06	02 32	03 14	04 15
66	////	////	01 26	02 31	03 01	03 46	04 45
64	////	////	02 06	02 50	03 24	04 09	05 07
62	////	00 40	02 33	03 05	03 42	04 28	05 24
60	////	01 35	02 54	03 18	03 56	04 43	05 39
N 58	////	02 07	03 11	03 29	04 09	04 57	05 51
56	00 36	02 30	03 26	03 39	04 20	05 08	06 02
54	01 27	02 48	03 38	03 48	04 30	05 18	06 12
52	01 56	03 03	03 49	03 56	04 38	05 27	06 20
50	02 17	03 16	03 58	04 03	04 46	05 34	06 28
45	02 56	03 43	04 19	04 18	05 02	05 51	06 44
N 40	03 23	04 03	04 35	04 30	05 16	06 05	06 57
35	03 44	04 19	04 48	04 41	05 27	06 17	07 08
30	04 01	04 33	05 00	04 50	05 37	06 27	07 18
20	04 28	04 56	05 20	05 06	05 55	06 45	07 35
N 10	04 48	05 15	05 38	05 20	06 10	07 00	07 50
0	05 06	05 32	05 54	05 33	06 24	07 14	08 04
S 10	05 21	05 47	06 10	05 46	06 38	07 29	08 17
20	05 36	06 03	06 27	06 01	06 53	07 44	08 32
30	05 51	06 20	06 46	06 17	07 11	08 02	08 49
35	05 58	06 30	06 57	06 26	07 21	08 12	08 59
40	06 07	06 40	07 10	06 37	07 33	08 24	09 10
45	06 16	06 52	07 25	06 50	07 47	08 38	09 23
S 50	06 26	07 07	07 44	07 06	08 03	08 55	09 39
52	06 30	07 13	07 53	07 13	08 11	09 03	09 47
54	06 35	07 20	08 02	07 21	08 20	09 12	09 55
56	06 41	07 28	08 13	07 30	08 30	09 22	10 04
58	06 46	07 37	08 26	07 41	08 41	09 33	10 15
S 60	06 53	07 47	08 41	07 53	08 55	09 46	10 27

Sunset, Twilight and Moonset

Lat.	Sunset	Twilight Civil	Twilight Naut.	Moonset 28	Moonset 29	Moonset 30	Moonset 31
°	h m	h m	h m	h m	h m	h m	h m
N 72	□	□	□	22 30	23 40	24 15	00 15
N 70	□	□	□	21 46	22 49	23 30	23 54
68	□	□	□	21 17	22 17	23 01	23 30
66	22 33	////	////	20 55	21 54	22 38	23 11
64	21 51	////	////	20 37	21 35	22 21	22 55
62	21 23	23 23	////	20 22	21 19	22 06	22 42
60	21 02	22 22	////	20 10	21 06	21 53	22 31
N 58	20 45	21 50	////	19 59	20 55	21 42	22 21
56	20 30	21 27	23 26	19 50	20 45	21 33	22 12
54	20 18	21 08	22 30	19 41	20 36	21 24	22 05
52	20 07	20 53	22 01	19 34	20 28	21 16	21 58
50	19 57	20 39	21 39	19 26	20 20	21 08	21 50
45	19 37	20 13	21 00	19 18	20 12	21 00	21 42
N 40	19 20	19 52	20 32	19 04	19 58	20 46	21 30
35	19 07	19 36	20 11	18 53	19 46	20 35	21 19
30	18 55	19 22	19 54	18 43	19 36	20 25	21 10
20	18 35	18 59	19 27	18 26	19 18	20 08	20 54
N 10	18 17	18 40	19 07	18 11	19 03	19 52	20 40
0	18 01	18 23	18 49	17 58	18 48	19 38	20 27
S 10	17 45	18 08	18 34	17 44	18 34	19 24	20 14
20	17 28	17 52	18 19	17 29	18 19	19 09	19 59
30	17 09	17 35	18 04	17 12	18 01	18 51	19 43
35	16 57	17 25	17 56	17 02	17 51	18 41	19 34
40	16 44	17 14	17 48	16 51	17 39	18 30	19 23
45	16 29	17 00	17 39	16 38	17 25	18 16	19 10
S 50	16 11	16 48	17 29	16 22	17 08	17 59	18 54
52	16 02	16 41	17 24	16 14	17 00	17 51	18 47
54	15 52	16 34	17 19	16 06	16 51	17 42	18 39
56	15 41	16 26	17 14	15 57	16 41	17 32	18 30
58	15 28	16 17	17 08	15 46	16 30	17 21	18 19
S 60	15 13	16 02	17 02	15 34	16 16	17 08	18 08

SUN and MOON — Equation of Time, Meridian Passage, Age, Phase

Day	Eqn. of Time 00h	Eqn. of Time 12h	Mer. Pass.	Mer. Pass. Upper	Mer. Pass. Lower	Age	Phase
d	m s	m s	h m	h m	h m	d	%
28	02 48	02 45	11 57	11 45	24 11	29	0
29	02 41	02 37	11 57	12 36	00 11	01	1
30	02 33	02 29	11 58	13 26	01 01	02	3

UT	ARIES GHA	VENUS −4.0 GHA	Dec	MARS −0.5 GHA	Dec	JUPITER −1.9 GHA	Dec	SATURN +0.2 GHA	Dec	STARS Name	SHA	Dec
31 00	248 25.0	217 38.5	N10 21.6	59 17.8	S 3 31.1	136 32.3	N22 14.8	21 37.5	S14 59.0	Acamar	315 18.3	S40 14.9
01	263 27.5	232 38.2	22.6	74 20.0	31.3	151 34.3	14.7	36 40.2	58.9	Achernar	335 26.8	S57 09.7
02	278 30.0	247 37.8	23.6	89 22.2	31.5	166 36.2	14.6	51 42.8	58.9	Acrux	173 08.1	S63 11.1
03	293 32.4	262 37.5 ..	24.6	104 24.3 ..	31.7	181 38.2 ..	14.6	66 45.4 ..	58.9	Adhara	255 12.3	S28 59.8
04	308 34.9	277 37.2	25.6	119 26.5	31.9	196 40.1	14.5	81 48.1	58.8	Aldebaran	290 49.0	N16 32.1
05	323 37.4	292 36.9	26.5	134 28.7	32.1	211 42.1	14.4	96 50.7	58.8			
S 06	338 39.8	307 36.5	N10 27.5	149 30.9	S 3 32.3	226 44.0	N22 14.4	111 53.3	S14 58.7	Alioth	166 19.9	N55 53.1
A 07	353 42.3	322 36.2	28.5	164 33.1	32.6	241 46.0	14.3	126 56.0	58.7	Alkaid	152 58.1	N49 14.7
T 08	8 44.8	337 35.9	29.5	179 35.3	32.8	256 47.9	14.2	141 58.6	58.6	Al Na'ir	27 42.9	S46 53.1
U 09	23 47.2	352 35.5 ..	30.5	194 37.5 ..	33.0	271 49.8 ..	14.2	157 01.2 ..	58.6	Alnilam	275 46.0	S 1 11.8
R 10	38 49.7	7 35.2	31.5	209 39.7	33.2	286 51.8	14.1	172 03.9	58.6	Alphard	217 55.6	S 8 43.5
D 11	53 52.1	22 34.9	32.5	224 41.8	33.4	301 53.7	14.0	187 06.5	58.5			
A 12	68 54.6	37 34.5	N10 33.5	239 44.0	S 3 33.6	316 55.7	N22 13.9	202 09.1	S14 58.5	Alphecca	126 10.1	N26 40.1
Y 13	83 57.1	52 34.2	34.5	254 46.2	33.8	331 57.6	13.9	217 11.8	58.4	Alpheratz	357 42.9	N29 10.0
14	98 59.5	67 33.9	35.5	269 48.4	34.1	346 59.6	13.8	232 14.4	58.4	Altair	62 07.4	N 8 54.5
15	114 02.0	82 33.5 ..	36.5	284 50.6 ..	34.3	2 01.5 ..	13.7	247 17.0 ..	58.4	Ankaa	353 15.3	S42 13.5
16	129 04.5	97 33.2	37.5	299 52.7	34.5	17 03.5	13.7	262 19.6	58.3	Antares	112 25.1	S26 27.7
17	144 06.9	112 32.9	38.5	314 54.9	34.7	32 05.4	13.6	277 22.3	58.3			
18	159 09.4	127 32.5	N10 39.5	329 57.1	S 3 34.9	47 07.3	N22 13.5	292 24.9	S14 58.2	Arcturus	145 54.9	N19 06.5
19	174 11.9	142 32.2	40.5	344 59.3	35.1	62 09.3	13.5	307 27.5	58.2	Atria	107 25.7	S69 03.0
20	189 14.3	157 31.9	41.5	0 01.4	35.4	77 11.2	13.4	322 30.2	58.2	Avior	234 18.1	S59 33.8
21	204 16.8	172 31.5 ..	42.5	15 03.6 ..	35.6	92 13.2 ..	13.3	337 32.8 ..	58.1	Bellatrix	278 31.6	N 6 21.5
22	219 19.3	187 31.2	43.5	30 05.8	35.8	107 15.1	13.2	352 35.4	58.1	Betelgeuse	271 00.9	N 7 24.3
23	234 21.7	202 30.8	44.4	45 07.9	36.0	122 17.1	13.2	7 38.1	58.0			
1 00	249 24.2	217 30.5	N10 45.4	60 10.1	S 3 36.2	137 19.0	N22 13.1	22 40.7	S14 58.0	Canopus	263 56.4	S52 42.5
01	264 26.6	232 30.2	46.4	75 12.3	36.5	152 20.9	13.0	37 43.3	58.0	Capella	280 33.9	N46 00.5
02	279 29.1	247 29.8	47.4	90 14.4	36.7	167 22.9	13.0	52 46.0	57.9	Deneb	49 30.7	N45 19.9
03	294 31.6	262 29.5 ..	48.4	105 16.6 ..	36.9	182 24.8 ..	12.9	67 48.6 ..	57.9	Denebola	182 32.9	N14 29.5
04	309 34.0	277 29.1	49.4	120 18.8	37.1	197 26.8	12.8	82 51.2	57.8	Diphda	348 55.4	S17 54.4
05	324 36.5	292 28.8	50.4	135 20.9	37.3	212 28.7	12.7	97 53.9	57.8			
S 06	339 39.0	307 28.5	N10 51.4	150 23.1	S 3 37.6	227 30.7	N22 12.7	112 56.5	S14 57.8	Dubhe	193 51.0	N61 40.6
U 07	354 41.4	322 28.1	52.4	165 25.2	37.8	242 32.6	12.6	127 59.1	57.7	Elnath	278 12.2	N28 37.0
N 08	9 43.9	337 27.8	53.4	180 27.4	38.0	257 34.5	12.5	143 01.8	57.7	Eltanin	90 45.3	N51 29.3
D 09	24 46.4	352 27.4 ..	54.3	195 29.6 ..	38.2	272 36.5 ..	12.5	158 04.4 ..	57.6	Enif	33 46.4	N 9 56.5
A 10	39 48.8	7 27.1	55.3	210 31.7	38.4	287 38.4	12.4	173 07.0	57.6	Fomalhaut	15 23.3	S29 32.5
Y 11	54 51.3	22 26.8	56.3	225 33.9	38.7	302 40.4	12.3	188 09.7	57.6			
12	69 53.7	37 26.4	N10 57.3	240 36.0	S 3 38.9	317 42.3	N22 12.3	203 12.3	S14 57.5	Gacrux	171 59.8	S57 11.9
13	84 56.2	52 26.1	58.3	255 38.2	39.1	332 44.2	12.2	218 14.9	57.5	Gienah	175 51.5	S17 37.5
14	99 58.7	67 25.7	10 59.3	270 40.3	39.3	347 46.2	12.1	233 17.5	57.4	Hadar	148 46.3	S60 26.7
15	115 01.1	82 25.4	11 00.3	285 42.5 ..	39.6	2 48.1 ..	12.0	248 20.2 ..	57.4	Hamal	328 00.3	N23 31.6
16	130 03.6	97 25.1	01.3	300 44.6	39.8	17 50.1	12.0	263 22.8	57.4	Kaus Aust.	83 42.6	S34 22.4
17	145 06.1	112 24.7	02.2	315 46.8	40.0	32 52.0	11.9	278 25.4	57.3			
18	160 08.5	127 24.4	N11 03.2	330 48.9	S 3 40.2	47 54.0	N22 11.8	293 28.1	S14 57.3	Kochab	137 19.2	N74 06.0
19	175 11.0	142 24.0	04.2	345 51.1	40.5	62 55.9	11.8	308 30.7	57.3	Markab	13 37.7	N15 16.9
20	190 13.5	157 23.7	05.2	0 53.2	40.7	77 57.8	11.7	323 33.3	57.2	Menkar	314 14.7	N 4 08.4
21	205 15.9	172 23.3 ..	06.2	15 55.4 ..	40.9	92 59.8 ..	11.6	338 36.0 ..	57.2	Menkent	148 06.4	S36 26.5
22	220 18.4	187 23.0	07.2	30 57.5	41.2	108 01.7	11.5	353 38.6	57.1	Miaplacidus	221 39.8	S69 47.0
23	235 20.9	202 22.6	08.1	45 59.7	41.4	123 03.7	11.5	8 41.2	57.1			
2 00	250 23.3	217 22.3	N11 09.1	61 01.8	S 3 41.6	138 05.6	N22 11.4	23 43.8	S14 57.1	Mirfak	308 39.8	N49 54.5
01	265 25.8	232 21.9	10.1	76 03.9	41.8	153 07.5	11.3	38 46.5	57.0	Nunki	75 57.2	S26 16.5
02	280 28.2	247 21.6	11.1	91 06.1	42.1	168 09.5	11.3	53 49.1	57.0	Peacock	53 17.9	S56 40.9
03	295 30.7	262 21.2 ..	12.1	106 08.2 ..	42.3	183 11.4 ..	11.2	68 51.7 ..	56.9	Pollux	243 27.2	N27 59.3
04	310 33.2	277 20.9	13.1	121 10.4	42.5	198 13.4	11.1	83 54.4	56.9	Procyon	244 59.3	N 5 11.0
05	325 35.6	292 20.6	14.0	136 12.5	42.8	213 15.3	11.0	98 57.0	56.9			
M 06	340 38.1	307 20.2	N11 15.0	151 14.6	S 3 43.0	228 17.2	N22 11.0	113 59.6	S14 56.8	Rasalhague	96 05.5	N12 33.1
O 07	355 40.6	322 19.9	16.0	166 16.8	43.2	243 19.2	10.9	129 02.3	56.8	Regulus	207 42.9	N11 53.7
N 08	10 43.0	337 19.5	17.0	181 18.9	43.5	258 21.1	10.8	144 04.9	56.7	Rigel	281 11.8	S 8 11.3
D 09	25 45.5	352 19.2 ..	18.0	196 21.0 ..	43.7	273 23.1 ..	10.8	159 07.5 ..	56.7	Rigil Kent.	139 50.1	S60 53.7
A 10	40 48.0	7 18.8	18.9	211 23.2	43.9	288 25.0	10.7	174 10.1	56.7	Sabik	102 11.4	S15 44.4
Y 11	55 50.4	22 18.5	19.9	226 25.3	44.2	303 26.9	10.6	189 12.8	56.6			
12	70 52.9	37 18.1	N11 20.9	241 27.4	S 3 44.4	318 28.9	N22 10.5	204 15.4	S14 56.6	Schedar	349 39.9	N56 36.7
13	85 55.4	52 17.8	21.9	256 29.6	44.6	333 30.8	10.5	219 18.0	56.5	Shaula	96 20.6	S37 06.6
14	100 57.8	67 17.4	22.9	271 31.7	44.9	348 32.8	10.4	234 20.7	56.5	Sirius	258 33.4	S16 44.4
15	116 00.3	82 17.0 ..	23.8	286 33.8 ..	45.1	3 34.7 ..	10.3	249 23.3 ..	56.5	Spica	158 30.3	S11 14.3
16	131 02.7	97 16.7	24.8	301 35.9	45.3	18 36.6	10.2	264 25.9	56.4	Suhail	222 52.1	S43 29.9
17	146 05.2	112 16.3	25.8	316 38.1	45.6	33 38.6	10.2	279 28.5	56.4			
18	161 07.7	127 16.0	N11 26.8	331 40.2	S 3 45.8	48 40.5	N22 10.1	294 31.2	S14 56.4	Vega	80 38.1	N38 47.9
19	176 10.1	142 15.6	27.7	346 42.3	46.0	63 42.4	10.0	309 33.8	56.3	Zuben'ubi	137 04.4	S16 06.1
20	191 12.6	157 15.3	28.7	1 44.4	46.3	78 44.4	10.0	324 36.4	56.3		SHA	Mer. Pass.
21	206 15.1	172 14.9 ..	29.7	16 46.5 ..	46.5	93 46.3 ..	09.9	339 39.1 ..	56.2		° '	h m
22	221 17.5	187 14.6	30.7	31 48.7	46.8	108 48.3	09.8	354 41.7	56.2	Venus	328 06.3	9 30
23	236 20.0	202 14.2	31.6	46 50.8	47.0	123 50.2	09.7	9 44.3	56.2	Mars	170 45.9	19 56
	h m									Jupiter	247 54.8	14 49
Mer. Pass.	7 21.2	v −0.3	d 1.0	v 2.2	d 0.2	v 1.9	d 0.1	v 2.6	d 0.0	Saturn	133 16.5	22 25

UT	SUN GHA	SUN Dec	MOON GHA	v	MOON Dec	d	HP
d h	° ′	° ′	° ′	′	° ′	′	′
31 00	180 36.0	N21 52.2	153 09.7	11.4	N18 35.7	2.2	54.8
01	195 35.9	52.5	167 40.1	11.5	18 33.5	2.3	54.8
02	210 35.8	52.9	182 10.6	11.4	18 31.2	2.4	54.8
03	225 35.7	.. 53.2	196 41.0	11.5	18 28.8	2.5	54.8
04	240 35.6	53.6	211 11.5	11.6	18 26.3	2.6	54.8
05	255 35.6	54.0	225 42.1	11.5	18 23.7	2.6	54.7
06	270 35.5	N21 54.3	240 12.6	11.7	N18 21.1	2.7	54.7
S 07	285 35.4	54.7	254 43.3	11.6	18 18.4	2.9	54.7
A 08	300 35.3	55.0	269 13.9	11.7	18 15.5	2.9	54.7
T 09	315 35.2	.. 55.4	283 44.6	11.7	18 12.6	3.0	54.7
U 10	330 35.1	55.7	298 15.3	11.8	18 09.6	3.0	54.7
R 11	345 35.0	56.1	312 46.1	11.8	18 06.6	3.2	54.7
D 12	0 34.9	N21 56.4	327 16.9	11.8	N18 03.4	3.2	54.6
A 13	15 34.8	56.8	341 47.7	11.9	18 00.2	3.4	54.6
Y 14	30 34.7	57.1	356 18.6	11.9	17 56.8	3.4	54.6
15	45 34.6	.. 57.5	10 49.5	11.9	17 53.4	3.5	54.6
16	60 34.5	57.8	25 20.4	12.0	17 49.9	3.5	54.6
17	75 34.4	58.2	39 51.4	12.0	17 46.4	3.7	54.6
18	90 34.3	N21 58.5	54 22.4	12.1	N17 42.7	3.7	54.6
19	105 34.3	58.9	68 53.5	12.1	17 39.0	3.9	54.5
20	120 34.2	59.2	83 24.6	12.2	17 35.1	3.9	54.5
21	135 34.1	.. 59.6	97 55.8	12.1	17 31.2	3.9	54.5
22	150 34.0	21 59.9	112 26.9	12.3	17 27.3	4.1	54.5
23	165 33.9	22 00.3	126 58.2	12.2	17 23.2	4.1	54.5
1 00	180 33.8	N22 00.6	141 29.4	12.3	N17 19.1	4.2	54.5
01	195 33.7	01.0	156 00.7	12.4	17 14.9	4.3	54.5
02	210 33.6	01.3	170 32.1	12.4	17 10.6	4.4	54.5
03	225 33.5	.. 01.6	185 03.5	12.4	17 06.2	4.4	54.4
04	240 33.4	02.0	199 34.9	12.5	17 01.8	4.5	54.4
05	255 33.3	02.3	214 06.4	12.5	16 57.3	4.6	54.4
06	270 33.2	N22 02.7	228 37.9	12.5	N16 52.7	4.7	54.4
S 07	285 33.1	03.0	243 09.4	12.6	16 48.0	4.8	54.4
U 08	300 33.0	03.3	257 41.0	12.6	16 43.2	4.8	54.4
N 09	315 32.9	.. 03.7	272 12.6	12.7	16 38.4	4.9	54.4
D 10	330 32.8	04.0	286 44.3	12.7	16 33.5	4.9	54.4
A 11	345 32.7	04.4	301 16.0	12.8	16 28.6	5.1	54.4
Y 12	0 32.6	N22 04.7	315 47.8	12.7	N16 23.5	5.1	54.4
13	15 32.5	05.0	330 19.5	12.9	16 18.4	5.1	54.3
14	30 32.4	05.4	344 51.4	12.8	16 13.3	5.3	54.3
15	45 32.3	.. 05.7	359 23.2	12.9	16 08.0	5.3	54.3
16	60 32.2	06.0	13 55.1	13.0	16 02.7	5.4	54.3
17	75 32.1	06.4	28 27.1	13.0	15 57.3	5.5	54.3
18	90 32.0	N22 06.7	42 59.1	13.0	N15 51.8	5.5	54.3
19	105 31.9	07.0	57 31.1	13.1	15 46.3	5.6	54.3
20	120 31.9	07.4	72 03.2	13.1	15 40.7	5.6	54.3
21	135 31.8	.. 07.7	86 35.3	13.1	15 35.1	5.8	54.3
22	150 31.7	08.0	101 07.4	13.2	15 29.3	5.8	54.3
23	165 31.6	08.3	115 39.6	13.2	15 23.5	5.8	54.3
2 00	180 31.5	N22 08.7	130 11.8	13.3	N15 17.7	5.9	54.3
01	195 31.4	09.0	144 44.1	13.3	15 11.8	6.0	54.2
02	210 31.3	09.3	159 16.4	13.3	15 05.8	6.1	54.2
03	225 31.2	.. 09.7	173 48.7	13.4	14 59.7	6.1	54.2
04	240 31.1	10.0	188 21.1	13.4	14 53.6	6.2	54.2
05	255 31.0	10.3	202 53.5	13.5	14 47.4	6.2	54.2
06	270 30.9	N22 10.6	217 26.0	13.5	N14 41.2	6.3	54.2
M 07	285 30.8	11.0	231 58.5	13.5	14 34.9	6.4	54.2
O 08	300 30.7	11.3	246 31.0	13.6	14 28.5	6.4	54.2
N 09	315 30.6	.. 11.6	261 03.6	13.6	14 22.1	6.5	54.2
D 10	330 30.5	11.9	275 36.2	13.6	14 15.6	6.6	54.2
A 11	345 30.4	12.2	290 08.8	13.7	14 09.0	6.6	54.2
Y 12	0 30.3	N22 12.6	304 41.5	13.7	N14 02.4	6.7	54.2
13	15 30.2	12.9	319 14.2	13.7	13 55.7	6.7	54.2
14	30 30.1	13.2	333 46.9	13.8	13 49.0	6.8	54.2
15	45 30.0	.. 13.5	348 19.7	13.8	13 42.2	6.8	54.2
16	60 29.9	13.8	2 52.5	13.9	13 35.4	6.9	54.2
17	75 29.8	14.2	17 25.4	13.9	13 28.5	7.0	54.2
18	90 29.7	N22 14.5	31 58.3	13.9	N13 21.5	7.0	54.2
19	105 29.6	14.8	46 31.2	13.9	13 14.5	7.0	54.2
20	120 29.4	15.1	61 04.1	14.0	13 07.5	7.2	54.2
21	135 29.3	.. 15.4	75 37.1	14.0	13 00.3	7.1	54.2
22	150 29.2	15.7	90 10.1	14.1	12 53.2	7.3	54.2
23	165 29.1	16.0	104 43.2	14.1	N12 45.9	7.2	54.2
	SD 15.8	d 0.3	SD 14.9		14.8		14.8

Twilight / Sunrise / Moonrise

Lat.	Naut.	Civil	Sunrise	Moonrise 31	1	2	3
°	h m	h m	h m	h m	h m	h m	h m
N 72	□	□	□	□	04 04	05 57	07 40
N 70	□	□	□	03 31	04 58	06 29	08 01
68	□	□	□	04 15	05 31	06 53	08 17
66	////	////	01 13	04 45	05 55	07 11	08 29
64	////	////	01 58	05 07	06 13	07 25	08 40
62	////	////	02 27	05 24	06 29	07 38	08 49
60	////	01 27	02 50	05 39	06 41	07 48	08 57
N 58	////	02 00	03 07	05 51	06 52	07 57	09 04
56	////	02 25	03 22	06 02	07 02	08 05	09 10
54	01 19	02 44	03 35	06 12	07 10	08 12	09 15
52	01 50	03 00	03 46	06 20	07 18	08 18	09 20
50	02 13	03 13	03 56	06 28	07 25	08 24	09 24
45	02 53	03 40	04 17	06 44	07 39	08 36	09 34
N 40	03 21	04 01	04 33	06 57	07 51	08 46	09 42
35	03 42	04 18	04 47	07 08	08 01	08 55	09 48
30	04 00	04 32	04 59	07 18	08 10	09 02	09 54
20	04 27	04 56	05 20	07 35	08 25	09 15	10 04
N 10	04 48	05 15	05 38	07 50	08 39	09 27	10 13
0	05 06	05 32	05 54	08 04	08 51	09 37	10 22
S 10	05 22	05 48	06 11	08 17	09 04	09 48	10 30
20	05 37	06 04	06 28	08 32	09 17	09 59	10 39
30	05 52	06 22	06 48	08 49	09 32	10 12	10 49
35	06 00	06 31	06 59	08 59	09 41	10 20	10 55
40	06 09	06 42	07 12	09 10	09 51	10 28	11 01
45	06 18	06 55	07 28	09 23	10 03	10 38	11 09
S 50	06 29	07 09	07 47	09 39	10 17	10 50	11 18
52	06 33	07 16	07 56	09 47	10 24	10 55	11 23
54	06 38	07 24	08 06	09 55	10 31	11 01	11 27
56	06 44	07 32	08 18	10 04	10 39	11 08	11 32
58	06 50	07 41	08 31	10 15	10 49	11 16	11 38
S 60	06 56	07 52	08 46	10 27	10 59	11 24	11 45

Sunset / Twilight / Moonset

Lat.	Sunset	Civil	Naut.	Moonset 31	1	2	3
°	h m	h m	h m	h m	h m	h m	h m
N 72	□	□	□	□	01 23	01 06	00 56
N 70	□	□	□	23 54	24 08	00 08	00 34
68	22 47	////	////	23 30	23 50	24 03	00 17
66	22 00	////	////	23 11	23 34	23 51	00 03
64	21 30	////	////	22 55	23 21	23 42	23 58
62	21 07	22 32	////	22 42	23 11	23 33	23 52
N 58	20 49	21 57	////	22 31	23 01	23 26	23 47
56	20 34	21 32	////	22 21	22 53	23 19	23 42
54	20 21	21 13	22 39	22 12	22 45	23 13	23 38
52	20 10	20 57	22 07	22 05	22 39	23 08	23 34
50	20 00	20 43	21 44	21 58	22 33	23 03	23 30
45	19 39	20 16	21 03	21 42	22 20	22 53	23 23
N 40	19 23	19 55	20 35	21 30	22 09	22 44	23 16
35	19 09	19 38	20 14	21 19	22 00	22 37	23 11
30	18 56	19 23	19 56	21 10	21 52	22 30	23 06
20	18 36	19 00	19 29	20 54	21 38	22 19	22 57
N 10	18 18	18 41	19 08	20 40	21 25	22 08	22 50
0	18 01	18 24	18 50	20 27	21 14	21 59	22 43
S 10	17 45	18 08	18 34	20 14	21 02	21 49	22 36
20	17 28	17 51	18 19	19 59	20 50	21 39	22 28
30	17 08	17 34	18 03	19 43	20 35	21 27	22 19
35	16 56	17 24	17 55	19 34	20 27	21 21	22 14
40	16 43	17 13	17 47	19 23	20 17	21 13	22 09
45	16 28	17 01	17 37	19 10	20 06	21 04	22 02
S 50	16 08	16 46	17 27	18 54	19 53	20 53	21 54
52	15 59	16 39	17 22	18 47	19 46	20 48	21 50
54	15 49	16 32	17 17	18 39	19 39	20 42	21 46
56	15 38	16 23	17 11	18 30	19 31	20 36	21 41
58	15 25	16 14	17 05	18 19	19 23	20 29	21 36
S 60	15 09	16 04	16 59	18 08	19 12	20 21	21 30

SUN / MOON

Day	Eqn. of Time 00h	Eqn. of Time 12h	Mer. Pass.	Mer. Pass. Upper	Mer. Pass. Lower	Age	Phase
d	m s	m s	h m	h m	h m	d	%
31	02 24	02 20	11 58	14 15	01 51	03	7
1	02 15	02 11	11 58	15 03	02 39	04	13
2	02 06	02 01	11 58	15 48	03 26	05	20

UT	ARIES GHA	VENUS −3.9 GHA	VENUS Dec	MARS −0.4 GHA	MARS Dec	JUPITER −1.9 GHA	JUPITER Dec	SATURN +0.2 GHA	SATURN Dec	STARS Name	SHA	Dec
3 00	251 22.5	217 13.9	N11 32.6	61 52.9	S 3 47.2	138 52.1	N22 09.7	24 46.9	S14 56.1	Acamar	315 18.3	S40 14.8
01	266 24.9	232 13.5	33.6	76 55.0	47.5	153 54.1	09.6	39 49.6	56.1	Achernar	335 26.8	S57 09.7
02	281 27.4	247 13.1	34.6	91 57.1	47.7	168 56.0	09.5	54 52.2	56.0	Acrux	173 08.1	S63 11.1
03	296 29.9	262 12.8 ..	35.5	106 59.2 ..	47.9	183 57.9 ..	09.5	69 54.8 ..	56.0	Adhara	255 12.3	S28 59.8
04	311 32.3	277 12.4	36.5	122 01.4	48.2	198 59.9	09.4	84 57.4	56.0	Aldebaran	290 49.0	N16 32.1
05	326 34.8	292 12.1	37.5	137 03.5	48.4	214 01.8	09.3	100 00.1	55.9			
T 06	341 37.2	307 11.7	N11 38.5	152 05.6	S 3 48.7	229 03.8	N22 09.2	115 02.7	S14 55.9	Alioth	166 19.9	N55 53.1
U 07	356 39.7	322 11.4	39.4	167 07.7	48.9	244 05.7	09.2	130 05.3	55.9	Alkaid	152 58.1	N49 14.7
E 08	11 42.2	337 11.0	40.4	182 09.8	49.1	259 07.6	09.1	145 08.0	55.8	Al Na'ir	27 42.9	S46 53.1
S 09	26 44.6	352 10.6 ..	41.4	197 11.9 ..	49.4	274 09.6 ..	09.0	160 10.6 ..	55.8	Alnilam	275 46.0	S 1 11.8
D 10	41 47.1	7 10.3	42.3	212 14.0	49.6	289 11.5	08.9	175 13.2	55.7	Alphard	217 55.6	S 8 43.5
A 11	56 49.6	22 09.9	43.3	227 16.1	49.9	304 13.4	08.9	190 15.8	55.7			
Y 12	71 52.0	37 09.6	N11 44.3	242 18.2	S 3 50.1	319 15.4	N22 08.8	205 18.5	S14 55.7	Alphecca	126 10.1	N26 40.1
13	86 54.5	52 09.2	45.3	257 20.3	50.4	334 17.3	08.7	220 21.1	55.6	Alpheratz	357 42.9	N29 10.1
14	101 57.0	67 08.8	46.2	272 22.4	50.6	349 19.3	08.7	235 23.7	55.6	Altair	62 07.3	N 8 54.5
15	116 59.4	82 08.5 ..	47.2	287 24.5 ..	50.8	4 21.2 ..	08.6	250 26.3 ..	55.5	Ankaa	353 15.3	S42 13.4
16	132 01.9	97 08.1	48.2	302 26.6	51.1	19 23.1	08.5	265 29.0	55.5	Antares	112 25.1	S26 27.7
17	147 04.3	112 07.8	49.1	317 28.7	51.3	34 25.1	08.4	280 31.6	55.5			
18	162 06.8	127 07.4	N11 50.1	332 30.8	S 3 51.6	49 27.0	N22 08.3	295 34.2	S14 55.4	Arcturus	145 54.9	N19 06.5
19	177 09.3	142 07.0	51.1	347 32.9	51.8	64 28.9	08.3	310 36.8	55.4	Atria	107 25.7	S69 03.0
20	192 11.7	157 06.7	52.0	2 35.0	52.1	79 30.9	08.2	325 39.5	55.4	Avior	234 18.1	S59 33.8
21	207 14.2	172 06.3 ..	53.0	17 37.1 ..	52.3	94 32.8 ..	08.1	340 42.1 ..	55.3	Bellatrix	278 31.6	N 6 21.5
22	222 16.7	187 05.9	54.0	32 39.2	52.6	109 34.7	08.1	355 44.7	55.3	Betelgeuse	271 00.9	N 7 24.3
23	237 19.1	202 05.6	54.9	47 41.3	52.8	124 36.7	08.0	10 47.4	55.2			
4 00	252 21.6	217 05.2	N11 55.9	62 43.4	S 3 53.1	139 38.6	N22 07.9	25 50.0	S14 55.2	Canopus	263 56.4	S52 42.5
01	267 24.1	232 04.8	56.9	77 45.5	53.3	154 40.5	07.8	40 52.6	55.2	Capella	280 33.9	N46 00.5
02	282 26.5	247 04.5	57.8	92 47.6	53.6	169 42.5	07.8	55 55.2	55.1	Deneb	49 30.7	N45 19.9
03	297 29.0	262 04.1 ..	58.8	107 49.7 ..	53.8	184 44.4 ..	07.7	70 57.9 ..	55.1	Denebola	182 32.9	N14 29.5
04	312 31.5	277 03.7	11 59.8	122 51.7	54.1	199 46.4	07.6	86 00.5	55.1	Diphda	348 55.4	S17 54.4
05	327 33.9	292 03.4	12 00.7	137 53.8	54.3	214 48.3	07.5	101 03.1	55.0			
W 06	342 36.4	307 03.0	N12 01.7	152 55.9	S 3 54.6	229 50.2	N22 07.5	116 05.7	S14 55.0	Dubhe	193 51.0	N61 40.6
E 07	357 38.8	322 02.6	02.7	167 58.0	54.8	244 52.2	07.4	131 08.4	54.9	Elnath	278 12.2	N28 37.0
D 08	12 41.3	337 02.3	03.6	183 00.1	55.1	259 54.1	07.3	146 11.0	54.9	Eltanin	90 45.3	N51 29.3
N 09	27 43.8	352 01.9 ..	04.6	198 02.2 ..	55.3	274 56.0 ..	07.3	161 13.6 ..	54.9	Enif	33 46.4	N 9 56.5
E 10	42 46.2	7 01.5	05.5	213 04.2	55.6	289 58.0	07.2	176 16.2	54.8	Fomalhaut	15 23.3	S29 32.5
S 11	57 48.7	22 01.2	06.5	228 06.3	55.8	304 59.9	07.1	191 18.9	54.8			
D 12	72 51.2	37 00.8	N12 07.5	243 08.4	S 3 56.1	320 01.8	N22 07.0	206 21.5	S14 54.8	Gacrux	171 59.8	S57 11.9
A 13	87 53.6	52 00.4	08.4	258 10.5	56.3	335 03.8	07.0	221 24.1	54.7	Gienah	175 51.5	S17 37.5
Y 14	102 56.1	67 00.1	09.4	273 12.6	56.6	350 05.7	06.9	236 26.7	54.7	Hadar	148 46.3	S60 26.7
15	117 58.6	81 59.7 ..	10.3	288 14.6 ..	56.8	5 07.6 ..	06.8	251 29.4 ..	54.6	Hamal	328 00.2	N23 31.6
16	133 01.0	96 59.3	11.3	303 16.7	57.1	20 09.6	06.7	266 32.0	54.6	Kaus Aust.	83 42.6	S34 22.4
17	148 03.5	111 58.9	12.3	318 18.8	57.3	35 11.5	06.7	281 34.6	54.6			
18	163 06.0	126 58.6	N12 13.2	333 20.9	S 3 57.6	50 13.4	N22 06.6	296 37.2	S14 54.5	Kochab	137 19.2	N74 06.0
19	178 08.4	141 58.2	14.2	348 22.9	57.8	65 15.4	06.5	311 39.8	54.5	Markab	13 37.7	N15 16.9
20	193 10.9	156 57.8	15.1	3 25.0	58.1	80 17.3	06.4	326 42.5	54.5	Menkar	314 14.6	N 4 08.6
21	208 13.3	171 57.4 ..	16.1	18 27.1 ..	58.3	95 19.2 ..	06.4	341 45.1 ..	54.4	Menkent	148 06.4	S36 26.5
22	223 15.8	186 57.1	17.0	33 29.1	58.6	110 21.2	06.3	356 47.7	54.4	Miaplacidus	221 39.8	S69 47.0
23	238 18.3	201 56.7	18.0	48 31.2	58.9	125 23.1	06.2	11 50.3	54.3			
5 00	253 20.7	216 56.3	N12 19.0	63 33.3	S 3 59.1	140 25.0	N22 06.1	26 53.0	S14 54.3	Mirfak	308 39.8	N49 54.5
01	268 23.2	231 56.0	19.9	78 35.3	59.4	155 27.0	06.1	41 55.6	54.3	Nunki	75 57.2	S26 16.5
02	283 25.7	246 55.6	20.9	93 37.4	59.6	170 28.9	06.0	56 58.2	54.2	Peacock	53 17.9	S56 40.9
03	298 28.1	261 55.2 ..	21.8	108 39.5	3 59.9	185 30.8 ..	05.9	72 00.8 ..	54.2	Pollux	243 27.2	N27 59.3
04	313 30.6	276 54.8	22.8	123 41.5	4 00.1	200 32.8	05.8	87 03.5	54.2	Procyon	244 59.3	N 5 11.1
05	328 33.1	291 54.4	23.7	138 43.6	00.4	215 34.7	05.8	102 06.1	54.1			
T 06	343 35.5	306 54.1	N12 24.7	153 45.7	S 4 00.7	230 36.6	N22 05.7	117 08.7	S14 54.1	Rasalhague	96 05.5	N12 33.1
H 07	358 38.0	321 53.7	25.6	168 47.7	00.9	245 38.6	05.6	132 11.3	54.0	Regulus	207 42.9	N11 53.7
U 08	13 40.4	336 53.3	26.6	183 49.8	01.2	260 40.5	05.5	147 13.9	54.0	Rigel	281 11.8	S 8 11.3
R 09	28 42.9	351 52.9 ..	27.5	198 51.8 ..	01.4	275 42.4 ..	05.5	162 16.6 ..	54.0	Rigil Kent.	139 50.2	S60 53.7
S 10	43 45.4	6 52.6	28.5	213 53.9	01.7	290 44.4	05.4	177 19.2	53.9	Sabik	102 11.4	S15 44.4
D 11	58 47.8	21 52.2	29.5	228 55.9	02.0	305 46.3	05.3	192 21.8	53.9			
A 12	73 50.3	36 51.8	N12 30.4	243 58.0	S 4 02.2	320 48.2	N22 05.2	207 24.4	S14 53.9	Schedar	349 39.9	N56 36.7
Y 13	88 52.8	51 51.4	31.4	259 00.1	02.5	335 50.1	05.2	222 27.1	53.8	Shaula	96 20.6	S37 06.6
14	103 55.2	66 51.0	32.3	274 02.1	02.7	350 52.1	05.1	237 29.7	53.8	Sirius	258 33.4	S16 44.4
15	118 57.7	81 50.7 ..	33.3	289 04.2 ..	03.0	5 54.0 ..	05.0	252 32.3 ..	53.7	Spica	158 30.3	S11 14.3
16	134 00.2	96 50.3	34.2	304 06.2	03.3	20 55.9	04.9	267 34.9	53.7	Suhail	222 52.1	S43 29.8
17	149 02.6	111 49.9	35.2	319 08.3	03.5	35 57.9	04.9	282 37.5	53.7			
18	164 05.1	126 49.5	N12 36.1	334 10.3	S 4 03.8	50 59.8	N22 04.8	297 40.2	S14 53.6	Vega	80 38.1	N38 47.9
19	179 07.6	141 49.1	37.1	349 12.4	04.1	66 01.7	04.7	312 42.8	53.6	Zuben'ubi	137 04.4	S16 06.1
20	194 10.0	156 48.7	38.0	4 14.4	04.3	81 03.7	04.6	327 45.4	53.6		SHA	Mer. Pass.
21	209 12.5	171 48.4 ..	38.9	19 16.4 ..	04.6	96 05.6 ..	04.6	342 48.0 ..	53.5		° '	h m
22	224 14.9	186 48.0	39.9	34 18.5	04.9	111 07.5	04.5	357 50.7	53.5	Venus	324 43.6	9 32
23	239 17.4	201 47.6	40.8	49 20.5	05.1	126 09.5	04.4	12 53.3	53.5	Mars	170 21.8	19 46
Mer. Pass.	h m 7 09.4	v −0.4	d 1.0	v 2.1	d 0.3	v 1.9	d 0.1	v 2.6	d 0.0	Jupiter	247 17.0	14 40
										Saturn	133 28.4	22 13

SUN and MOON

UT	SUN GHA	SUN Dec	MOON GHA	v	MOON Dec	d	HP
3 00	180 29.0	N22 16.4	119 16.3	14.1	N12 38.7	7.4	54.2
01	195 28.9	16.7	133 49.4	14.1	12 31.3	7.4	54.1
02	210 28.8	17.0	148 22.5	14.2	12 23.9	7.4	54.1
03	225 28.7 ..	17.3	162 55.7	14.2	12 16.5	7.5	54.1
04	240 28.6	17.6	177 28.9	14.2	12 09.0	7.5	54.1
05	255 28.5	17.9	192 02.1	14.3	12 01.5	7.6	54.1
06	270 28.4	N22 18.2	206 35.4	14.3	N11 53.9	7.7	54.1
07	285 28.3	18.5	221 08.7	14.3	11 46.2	7.6	54.1
08	300 28.2	18.8	235 42.0	14.4	11 38.6	7.8	54.1
09	315 28.1 ..	19.1	250 15.4	14.3	11 30.8	7.8	54.2
10	330 28.0	19.4	264 48.7	14.4	11 23.0	7.8	54.2
11	345 27.9	19.7	279 22.1	14.5	11 15.2	7.9	54.2
12	0 27.8	N22 20.1	293 55.6	14.4	N11 07.3	7.9	54.2
13	15 27.7	20.4	308 29.0	14.5	10 59.4	8.0	54.2
14	30 27.6	20.7	323 02.5	14.5	10 51.4	8.0	54.2
15	45 27.5 ..	21.0	337 36.0	14.5	10 43.4	8.0	54.2
16	60 27.4	21.3	352 09.5	14.6	10 35.4	8.1	54.2
17	75 27.3	21.6	6 43.1	14.6	10 27.3	8.2	54.2
18	90 27.2	N22 21.9	21 16.7	14.6	N10 19.1	8.2	54.2
19	105 27.1	22.2	35 50.3	14.6	10 10.9	8.2	54.2
20	120 27.0	22.5	50 23.9	14.6	10 02.7	8.3	54.2
21	135 26.9 ..	22.8	64 57.5	14.7	9 54.4	8.3	54.2
22	150 26.7	23.1	79 31.2	14.7	9 46.1	8.4	54.2
23	165 26.6	23.4	94 04.9	14.7	9 37.7	8.4	54.2
4 00	180 26.5	N22 23.6	108 38.6	14.7	N 9 29.3	8.4	54.2
01	195 26.4	23.9	123 12.3	14.8	9 20.9	8.5	54.2
02	210 26.3	24.2	137 46.1	14.7	9 12.4	8.5	54.2
03	225 26.2 ..	24.5	152 19.8	14.8	9 03.9	8.6	54.2
04	240 26.1	24.8	166 53.6	14.8	8 55.3	8.6	54.2
05	255 26.0	25.1	181 27.4	14.8	8 46.7	8.6	54.2
06	270 25.9	N22 25.4	196 01.2	14.8	N 8 38.1	8.7	54.2
07	285 25.8	25.7	210 35.0	14.9	8 29.4	8.7	54.2
08	300 25.7	26.0	225 08.9	14.8	8 20.7	8.7	54.3
09	315 25.6 ..	26.3	239 42.7	14.9	8 12.0	8.8	54.3
10	330 25.5	26.6	254 16.6	14.9	8 03.2	8.8	54.3
11	345 25.4	26.9	268 50.5	14.9	7 54.4	8.9	54.3
12	0 25.3	N22 27.1	283 24.4	14.9	N 7 45.5	8.8	54.3
13	15 25.1	27.4	297 58.3	14.9	7 36.7	9.0	54.3
14	30 25.0	27.7	312 32.2	14.9	7 27.7	8.9	54.3
15	45 24.9 ..	28.0	327 06.1	15.0	7 18.8	9.0	54.3
16	60 24.8	28.3	341 40.1	14.9	7 09.8	9.0	54.3
17	75 24.7	28.6	356 14.0	15.0	7 00.8	9.1	54.3
18	90 24.6	N22 28.9	10 48.0	15.0	N 6 51.7	9.0	54.3
19	105 24.5	29.1	25 22.0	14.9	6 42.7	9.1	54.4
20	120 24.4	29.4	39 55.9	15.0	6 33.6	9.2	54.4
21	135 24.3 ..	29.7	54 29.9	15.0	6 24.4	9.1	54.4
22	150 24.2	30.0	69 03.9	15.0	6 15.3	9.2	54.4
23	165 24.1	30.3	83 37.9	15.0	6 06.1	9.3	54.4
5 00	180 23.9	N22 30.5	98 11.9	15.0	N 5 56.8	9.2	54.4
01	195 23.8	30.8	112 45.9	15.0	5 47.6	9.3	54.4
02	210 23.7	31.1	127 19.9	15.0	5 38.3	9.3	54.4
03	225 23.6 ..	31.4	141 53.9	15.0	5 29.0	9.4	54.5
04	240 23.5	31.7	156 27.9	15.0	5 19.6	9.3	54.5
05	255 23.4	31.9	171 01.9	15.0	5 10.3	9.4	54.5
06	270 23.3	N22 32.2	185 35.9	15.0	N 5 00.9	9.4	54.5
07	285 23.2	32.5	200 09.9	15.0	4 51.5	9.5	54.5
08	300 23.1	32.8	214 43.9	15.0	4 42.0	9.4	54.5
09	315 23.0 ..	33.0	229 17.9	15.0	4 32.6	9.5	54.5
10	330 22.8	33.3	243 51.9	15.0	4 23.1	9.5	54.6
11	345 22.7	33.6	258 25.9	15.0	4 13.6	9.5	54.6
12	0 22.6	N22 33.9	272 59.9	15.0	N 4 04.1	9.6	54.6
13	15 22.5	34.1	287 33.9	15.0	3 54.5	9.6	54.6
14	30 22.4	34.4	302 07.9	14.9	3 44.9	9.6	54.6
15	45 22.3 ..	34.7	316 41.8	15.0	3 35.3	9.6	54.6
16	60 22.2	34.9	331 15.8	15.0	3 25.7	9.6	54.7
17	75 22.1	35.2	345 49.8	14.9	3 16.1	9.7	54.7
18	90 22.0	N22 35.5	0 23.7	15.0	N 3 06.4	9.7	54.7
19	105 21.8	35.7	14 57.7	14.9	2 56.7	9.7	54.7
20	120 21.7	36.0	29 31.6	14.9	2 47.0	9.7	54.7
21	135 21.6 ..	36.3	44 05.5	14.9	2 37.3	9.7	54.7
22	150 21.5	36.5	58 39.4	14.9	2 27.6	9.7	54.8
23	165 21.4	36.8	73 13.3	14.9	N 2 17.9	9.8	54.8
SD	15.8	d 0.3	14.8		14.8		14.9

Days: **3** = TUESDAY; **4** = WEDNESDAY; **5** = THURSDAY

Twilight, Sunrise and Moonrise

Lat.	Naut.	Civil	Sunrise	Moonrise 3	4	5	6
N 72	□	□	□	07 40	09 18	10 55	12 31
N 70	□	□	□	08 01	09 31	11 01	12 31
68	□	□	□	08 17	09 41	11 05	12 31
66	////	////	01 00	08 29	09 49	11 10	12 31
64	////	////	01 51	08 40	09 56	11 13	12 31
62	////	////	02 22	08 49	10 02	11 16	12 31
60	////	01 18	02 45	08 57	10 07	11 19	12 31
N 58	////	01 55	03 04	09 04	10 12	11 21	12 31
56	////	02 21	03 19	09 10	10 16	11 23	12 31
54	01 11	02 40	03 32	09 15	10 19	11 25	12 31
52	01 45	02 57	03 44	09 20	10 23	11 26	12 31
50	02 09	03 11	03 54	09 24	10 26	11 28	12 31
45	02 51	03 39	04 15	09 34	10 32	11 31	12 31
N 40	03 19	04 00	04 32	09 42	10 38	11 34	12 31
35	03 41	04 17	04 46	09 48	10 42	11 36	12 31
30	03 59	04 32	04 59	09 54	10 46	11 38	12 31
20	04 27	04 55	05 20	10 04	10 53	11 42	12 31
N 10	04 48	05 15	05 38	10 13	10 59	11 45	12 31
0	05 06	05 32	05 55	10 22	11 05	11 48	12 31
S 10	05 22	05 49	06 11	10 30	11 11	11 51	12 31
20	05 38	06 05	06 29	10 39	11 17	11 54	12 31
30	05 53	06 23	06 49	10 49	11 24	11 58	12 31
35	06 02	06 33	07 01	10 55	11 28	12 00	12 31
40	06 10	06 44	07 14	11 01	11 33	12 02	12 32
45	06 20	06 57	07 30	11 09	11 38	12 05	12 32
S 50	06 31	07 12	07 50	11 18	11 44	12 08	12 32
52	06 36	07 19	07 59	11 23	11 47	12 10	12 32
54	06 41	07 27	08 09	11 27	11 50	12 11	12 32
56	06 47	07 35	08 21	11 32	11 54	12 13	12 32
58	06 53	07 45	08 35	11 38	11 57	12 15	12 32
S 60	07 00	07 55	08 51	11 45	12 02	12 17	12 32

Sunset, Twilight and Moonset

Lat.	Sunset	Civil	Naut.	Moonset 3	4	5	6
N 72	□	□	□	00 56	00 48	00 41	00 34
N 70	□	□	□	00 34	00 34	00 33	00 31
68	□	□	□	00 17	00 22	00 26	00 29
66	23 01	////	////	00 03	00 13	00 20	00 27
64	22 07	////	////	24 05	00 05	00 16	00 26
62	21 36	////	////	23 58	24 12	00 12	00 24
60	21 12	22 41	////	23 52	24 08	00 08	00 23
N 58	20 54	22 03	////	23 47	24 05	00 05	00 22
56	20 38	21 37	////	23 42	24 02	00 02	00 21
54	20 25	21 17	22 48	23 38	24 00	00 00	00 20
52	20 13	21 01	22 13	23 34	23 57	24 19	00 19
50	20 03	20 46	21 49	23 30	23 55	24 19	00 19
45	19 42	20 19	21 07	23 23	23 50	24 17	00 17
N 40	19 25	19 57	20 38	23 16	23 47	24 16	00 16
35	19 10	19 40	20 16	23 11	23 43	24 15	00 15
30	18 58	19 25	19 58	23 06	23 40	24 14	00 14
20	18 37	19 01	19 30	22 57	23 35	24 12	00 12
N 10	18 19	18 42	19 09	22 50	23 30	24 10	00 10
0	18 02	18 24	18 50	22 43	23 26	24 09	00 09
S 10	17 45	18 08	18 34	22 36	23 21	24 07	00 07
20	17 28	17 51	18 19	22 28	23 17	24 06	00 06
30	17 07	17 33	18 03	22 19	23 11	24 04	00 04
35	16 56	17 23	17 55	22 14	23 08	24 02	00 02
40	16 42	17 12	17 46	22 09	23 05	24 01	00 01
45	16 26	17 00	17 36	22 02	23 00	24 00	00 00
S 50	16 07	16 44	17 25	21 54	22 55	23 58	25 02
52	15 57	16 37	17 21	21 50	22 53	23 57	25 02
54	15 47	16 30	17 15	21 46	22 51	23 56	25 03
56	15 35	16 21	17 10	21 41	22 48	23 55	25 04
58	15 22	16 12	17 03	21 36	22 45	23 54	25 05
S 60	15 05	16 01	16 57	21 30	22 41	23 53	25 06

SUN and MOON

Day	Eqn. of Time 00h	Eqn. of Time 12h	Mer. Pass.	Mer. Pass. Upper	Mer. Pass. Lower	Age	Phase
	m s	m s	h m	h m	h m	d	%
3	01 56	01 51	11 58	16 32	04 10	06	28
4	01 46	01 41	11 58	17 16	04 54	07	37
5	01 36	01 31	11 58	17 58	05 37	08	47

2014 JUNE 6, 7, 8 (FRI., SAT., SUN.)

UT	ARIES GHA	VENUS −3.9 GHA	VENUS Dec	MARS −0.4 GHA	MARS Dec	JUPITER −1.9 GHA	JUPITER Dec	SATURN +0.2 GHA	SATURN Dec	STARS Name	SHA	Dec
d h	° ′	° ′	° ′	° ′	° ′	° ′	° ′	° ′	° ′		° ′	° ′
6 00	254 19.9	216 47.2	N12 41.8	64 22.6	S 4 05.4	141 11.4	N22 04.3	27 55.9	S14 53.4	Acamar	315 18.3	S40 14.8
01	269 22.3	231 46.8	42.7	79 24.6	05.7	156 13.3	04.3	42 58.5	53.4	Achernar	335 26.8	S57 09.6
02	284 24.8	246 46.4	43.7	94 26.7	05.9	171 15.2	04.2	58 01.1	53.3	Acrux	173 08.1	S63 11.1
03	299 27.3	261 46.1	.. 44.6	109 28.7	.. 06.2	186 17.2	.. 04.1	73 03.8	.. 53.3	Adhara	255 12.3	S28 59.8
04	314 29.7	276 45.7	45.6	124 30.7	06.4	201 19.1	04.0	88 06.4	53.3	Aldebaran	290 49.0	N16 32.1
05	329 32.2	291 45.3	46.5	139 32.8	06.7	216 21.0	04.0	103 09.0	53.2			
06	344 34.7	306 44.9	N12 47.5	154 34.8	S 4 07.0	231 23.0	N22 03.9	118 11.6	S14 53.2	Alioth	166 19.9	N55 53.1
07	359 37.1	321 44.5	48.4	169 36.9	07.3	246 24.9	03.8	133 14.2	53.2	Alkaid	152 58.1	N49 14.7
08	14 39.6	336 44.1	49.3	184 38.9	07.5	261 26.8	03.7	148 16.9	53.1	Al Na'ir	27 42.8	S46 53.1
F 09	29 42.1	351 43.7	.. 50.3	199 40.9	.. 07.8	276 28.8	.. 03.7	163 19.5	.. 53.1	Alnilam	275 46.0	S 1 11.8
R 10	44 44.5	6 43.3	51.2	214 43.0	08.1	291 30.7	03.6	178 22.1	53.1	Alphard	217 55.6	S 8 43.5
I 11	59 47.0	21 43.0	52.2	229 45.0	08.3	306 32.6	03.5	193 24.7	53.0			
D 12	74 49.4	36 42.6	N12 53.1	244 47.0	S 4 08.6	321 34.5	N22 03.4	208 27.3	S14 53.0	Alphecca	126 10.1	N26 40.1
A 13	89 51.9	51 42.2	54.0	259 49.0	08.9	336 36.5	03.4	223 30.0	52.9	Alpheratz	357 42.9	N29 10.1
Y 14	104 54.4	66 41.8	55.0	274 51.1	09.1	351 38.4	03.3	238 32.6	52.9	Altair	62 07.3	N 8 54.5
15	119 56.8	81 41.4	.. 55.9	289 53.1	.. 09.4	6 40.3	.. 03.2	253 35.2	.. 52.9	Ankaa	353 15.3	S42 13.4
16	134 59.3	96 41.0	56.9	304 55.1	09.7	21 42.3	03.1	268 37.8	52.8	Antares	112 25.1	S26 27.7
17	150 01.8	111 40.6	57.8	319 57.2	10.0	36 44.2	03.0	283 40.4	52.8			
18	165 04.2	126 40.2	N12 58.7	334 59.2	S 4 10.2	51 46.1	N22 03.0	298 43.1	S14 52.8	Arcturus	145 54.9	N19 06.6
19	180 06.7	141 39.8	12 59.7	350 01.2	10.5	66 48.0	02.9	313 45.7	52.7	Atria	107 25.7	S69 03.0
20	195 09.2	156 39.4	13 00.6	5 03.2	10.8	81 50.0	02.8	328 48.3	52.7	Avior	234 18.1	S59 33.8
21	210 11.6	171 39.0	.. 01.6	20 05.3	.. 11.0	96 51.9	.. 02.7	343 50.9	.. 52.7	Bellatrix	278 31.6	N 6 21.5
22	225 14.1	186 38.6	02.5	35 07.3	11.3	111 53.8	02.7	358 53.5	52.6	Betelgeuse	271 00.9	N 7 24.4
23	240 16.5	201 38.2	03.4	50 09.3	11.6	126 55.8	02.6	13 56.2	52.6			
7 00	255 19.0	216 37.9	N13 04.4	65 11.3	S 4 11.9	141 57.7	N22 02.5	28 58.8	S14 52.6	Canopus	263 56.4	S52 42.5
01	270 21.5	231 37.5	05.3	80 13.3	12.1	156 59.6	02.4	44 01.4	52.5	Capella	280 33.9	N46 00.5
02	285 23.9	246 37.1	06.2	95 15.3	12.4	172 01.5	02.4	59 04.0	52.5	Deneb	49 30.7	N45 19.9
03	300 26.4	261 36.7	.. 07.2	110 17.4	.. 12.7	187 03.5	.. 02.3	74 06.6	.. 52.4	Denebola	182 32.9	N14 29.5
04	315 28.9	276 36.3	08.1	125 19.4	13.0	202 05.4	02.2	89 09.3	52.4	Diphda	348 55.4	S17 54.4
05	330 31.3	291 35.9	09.0	140 21.4	13.2	217 07.3	02.1	104 11.9	52.4			
06	345 33.8	306 35.5	N13 10.0	155 23.4	S 4 13.5	232 09.3	N22 02.0	119 14.5	S14 52.3	Dubhe	193 51.0	N61 40.6
07	0 36.3	321 35.1	10.9	170 25.4	13.8	247 11.2	02.0	134 17.1	52.3	Elnath	278 12.2	N28 36.9
S 08	15 38.7	336 34.7	11.8	185 27.4	14.1	262 13.1	01.9	149 19.7	52.3	Eltanin	90 45.3	N51 29.3
A 09	30 41.2	351 34.3	.. 12.8	200 29.4	.. 14.3	277 15.0	.. 01.8	164 22.3	.. 52.2	Enif	33 46.3	N 9 56.5
T 10	45 43.7	6 33.9	13.7	215 31.5	14.6	292 17.0	01.7	179 25.0	52.2	Fomalhaut	15 23.3	S29 32.5
U 11	60 46.1	21 33.5	14.6	230 33.5	14.9	307 18.9	01.7	194 27.6	52.2			
R 12	75 48.6	36 33.1	N13 15.6	245 35.5	S 4 15.2	322 20.8	N22 01.6	209 30.2	S14 52.1	Gacrux	171 59.8	S57 11.9
D 13	90 51.0	51 32.7	16.5	260 37.5	15.5	337 22.8	01.5	224 32.8	52.1	Gienah	175 51.5	S17 37.5
A 14	105 53.5	66 32.3	17.4	275 39.5	15.7	352 24.7	01.4	239 35.4	52.1	Hadar	148 46.3	S60 26.7
Y 15	120 56.0	81 31.9	.. 18.4	290 41.5	.. 16.0	7 26.6	.. 01.4	254 38.0	.. 52.0	Hamal	328 00.2	N23 31.6
16	135 58.4	96 31.5	19.3	305 43.5	16.3	22 28.5	01.3	269 40.7	52.0	Kaus Aust.	83 42.5	S34 22.4
17	151 00.9	111 31.1	20.2	320 45.5	16.6	37 30.5	01.2	284 43.3	52.0			
18	166 03.4	126 30.7	N13 21.1	335 47.5	S 4 16.9	52 32.4	N22 01.1	299 45.9	S14 51.9	Kochab	137 19.2	N74 06.0
19	181 05.8	141 30.3	22.1	350 49.5	17.1	67 34.3	01.0	314 48.5	51.9	Markab	13 37.6	N15 16.9
20	196 08.3	156 29.9	23.0	5 51.5	17.4	82 36.2	01.0	329 51.1	51.8	Menkar	314 14.6	N 4 08.6
21	211 10.8	171 29.5	.. 23.9	20 53.5	.. 17.7	97 38.2	.. 00.9	344 53.8	.. 51.8	Menkent	148 06.4	S36 26.5
22	226 13.2	186 29.1	24.8	35 55.5	18.0	112 40.1	00.8	359 56.4	51.8	Miaplacidus	221 39.9	S69 47.0
23	241 15.7	201 28.7	25.8	50 57.5	18.3	127 42.0	00.7	14 59.0	51.7			
8 00	256 18.1	216 28.3	N13 26.7	65 59.5	S 4 18.5	142 43.9	N22 00.7	30 01.6	S14 51.7	Mirfak	308 39.8	N49 54.5
01	271 20.6	231 27.8	27.6	81 01.5	18.8	157 45.9	00.6	45 04.2	51.7	Nunki	75 57.2	S26 16.5
02	286 23.1	246 27.4	28.5	96 03.5	19.1	172 47.8	00.5	60 06.8	51.6	Peacock	53 17.9	S56 40.9
03	301 25.5	261 27.0	.. 29.5	111 05.5	.. 19.4	187 49.7	.. 00.4	75 09.4	.. 51.6	Pollux	243 27.2	N27 59.3
04	316 28.0	276 26.6	30.4	126 07.5	19.7	202 51.6	00.3	90 12.1	51.6	Procyon	244 59.3	N 5 11.1
05	331 30.5	291 26.2	31.3	141 09.5	20.0	217 53.6	00.3	105 14.7	51.5			
06	346 32.9	306 25.8	N13 32.2	156 11.4	S 4 20.2	232 55.5	N22 00.2	120 17.3	S14 51.5	Rasalhague	96 05.5	N12 33.1
07	1 35.4	321 25.4	33.2	171 13.4	20.5	247 57.4	00.1	135 19.9	51.5	Regulus	207 42.9	N11 53.7
08	16 37.9	336 25.0	34.1	186 15.4	20.8	262 59.3	00.0	150 22.5	51.4	Rigel	281 11.8	S 8 11.3
S 09	31 40.3	351 24.6	.. 35.0	201 17.4	.. 21.1	278 01.3	22 00.0	165 25.1	.. 51.4	Rigil Kent.	139 50.2	S60 53.8
U 10	46 42.8	6 24.2	35.9	216 19.4	21.4	293 03.2	21 59.9	180 27.8	51.4	Sabik	102 11.4	S15 44.4
N 11	61 45.3	21 23.8	36.8	231 21.4	21.7	308 05.1	59.8	195 30.4	51.3			
D 12	76 47.7	36 23.4	N13 37.8	246 23.4	S 4 22.0	323 07.0	N21 59.7	210 33.0	S14 51.3	Schedar	349 39.9	N56 36.7
A 13	91 50.2	51 23.0	38.7	261 25.3	22.2	338 09.0	59.6	225 35.6	51.3	Shaula	96 20.6	S37 06.6
Y 14	106 52.6	66 22.5	39.6	276 27.3	22.5	353 10.9	59.6	240 38.2	51.2	Sirius	258 33.5	S16 44.4
15	121 55.1	81 22.1	.. 40.5	291 29.3	.. 22.8	8 12.8	.. 59.5	255 40.8	.. 51.2	Spica	158 30.3	S11 14.2
16	136 57.6	96 21.7	41.4	306 31.3	23.1	23 14.7	59.4	270 43.4	51.2	Suhail	222 52.1	S43 29.8
17	152 00.0	111 21.3	42.3	321 33.3	23.4	38 16.7	59.3	285 46.1	51.1			
18	167 02.5	126 20.9	N13 43.3	336 35.3	S 4 23.7	53 18.6	N21 59.3	300 48.7	S14 51.1	Vega	80 38.1	N38 47.9
19	182 05.0	141 20.5	44.2	351 37.2	24.0	68 20.5	59.2	315 51.3	51.1	Zuben'ubi	137 04.4	S16 06.1
20	197 07.4	156 20.1	45.1	6 39.2	24.3	83 22.4	59.1	330 53.9	51.0		SHA	Mer.Pass.
21	212 09.9	171 19.7	.. 46.0	21 41.2	.. 24.6	98 24.4	.. 59.0	345 56.5	.. 51.0		° ′	h m
22	227 12.4	186 19.2	46.9	36 43.2	24.8	113 26.3	58.9	0 59.1	51.0	Venus	321 18.8	9 34
23	242 14.7	201 18.8	47.8	51 45.1	25.1	128 28.2	58.9	16 01.7	50.9	Mars	169 52.3	19 37
	h m									Jupiter	246 38.7	14 30
Mer.Pass.	6 57.6	v −0.4	d 0.9	v 2.0	d 0.3	v 1.9	d 0.1	v 2.6	d 0.0	Saturn	133 39.8	22 00

UT	SUN GHA	SUN Dec	MOON GHA	v	MOON Dec	d	HP
6 00	180 21.3	N22 37.1	87 47.2	14.9	N 2 08.1	9.8	54.8
01	195 21.2	37.3	102 21.1	14.8	1 58.3	9.8	54.8
02	210 21.1	37.6	116 54.9	14.8	1 48.5	9.8	54.8
03	225 20.9 ..	37.8	131 28.7	14.9	1 38.7	9.8	54.9
04	240 20.8	38.1	146 02.6	14.8	1 28.9	9.8	54.9
05	255 20.7	38.4	160 36.4	14.7	1 19.1	9.9	54.9
06	270 20.6	N22 38.6	175 10.1	14.8	N 1 09.2	9.9	54.9
07	285 20.5	38.9	189 43.9	14.7	0 59.3	9.9	54.9
F 08	300 20.4	39.1	204 17.6	14.8	0 49.5	9.9	55.0
R 09	315 20.3 ..	39.4	218 51.4	14.7	0 39.6	9.9	55.0
I 10	330 20.1	39.6	233 25.1	14.6	0 29.7	9.9	55.0
D 11	345 20.0	39.9	247 58.7	14.7	0 19.8	9.9	55.0
A 12	0 19.9	N22 40.2	262 32.4	14.6	N 0 09.9	10.0	55.1
Y 13	15 19.8	40.4	277 06.0	14.6	S 0 00.1	9.8	55.1
14	30 19.7	40.7	291 39.6	14.6	0 10.0	9.9	55.1
15	45 19.6 ..	40.9	306 13.2	14.6	0 19.9	10.0	55.1
16	60 19.5	41.2	320 46.8	14.5	0 29.9	10.0	55.1
17	75 19.3	41.4	335 20.3	14.5	0 39.9	9.9	55.2
18	90 19.2	N22 41.7	349 53.8	14.5	S 0 49.8	10.0	55.2
19	105 19.1	41.9	4 27.3	14.4	0 59.8	10.0	55.2
20	120 19.0	42.2	19 00.7	14.4	1 09.8	9.9	55.2
21	135 18.9 ..	42.4	33 34.1	14.4	1 19.7	10.0	55.3
22	150 18.8	42.7	48 07.5	14.3	1 29.7	10.0	55.3
23	165 18.7	42.9	62 40.8	14.4	1 39.7	10.0	55.3
7 00	180 18.5	N22 43.2	77 14.2	14.2	S 1 49.7	10.0	55.3
01	195 18.4	43.4	91 47.4	14.3	1 59.7	10.0	55.4
02	210 18.3	43.7	106 20.7	14.2	2 09.7	10.0	55.4
03	225 18.2 ..	43.9	120 53.9	14.2	2 19.7	10.0	55.4
04	240 18.1	44.1	135 27.1	14.1	2 29.7	9.9	55.5
05	255 18.0	44.4	150 00.2	14.1	2 39.6	10.0	55.5
06	270 17.8	N22 44.6	164 33.3	14.1	S 2 49.6	10.0	55.5
S 07	285 17.7	44.9	179 06.4	14.0	2 59.6	10.0	55.5
A 08	300 17.6	45.1	193 39.4	14.0	3 09.6	10.0	55.6
T 09	315 17.5 ..	45.3	208 12.4	13.9	3 19.6	10.0	55.6
U 10	330 17.4	45.6	222 45.3	13.9	3 29.6	9.9	55.6
R 11	345 17.3	45.8	237 18.2	13.8	3 39.5	10.0	55.6
D 12	0 17.1	N22 46.1	251 51.0	13.9	S 3 49.5	10.0	55.7
A 13	15 17.0	46.3	266 23.9	13.7	3 59.5	9.9	55.7
Y 14	30 16.9	46.5	280 56.6	13.7	4 09.4	10.0	55.7
15	45 16.8 ..	46.8	295 29.3	13.7	4 19.4	9.9	55.8
16	60 16.7	47.0	310 02.0	13.6	4 29.3	9.9	55.8
17	75 16.6	47.2	324 34.6	13.6	4 39.2	10.0	55.8
18	90 16.4	N22 47.5	339 07.2	13.6	S 4 49.2	9.9	55.9
19	105 16.3	47.7	353 39.8	13.4	4 59.1	9.9	55.9
20	120 16.2	47.9	8 12.2	13.5	5 09.0	9.8	55.9
21	135 16.1 ..	48.2	22 44.7	13.3	5 18.8	9.9	55.9
22	150 16.0	48.4	37 17.0	13.4	5 28.7	9.9	56.0
23	165 15.9	48.6	51 49.4	13.3	5 38.6	9.8	56.0
8 00	180 15.7	N22 48.9	66 21.7	13.2	S 5 48.4	9.9	56.0
01	195 15.6	49.1	80 53.9	13.1	5 58.3	9.8	56.1
02	210 15.5	49.3	95 26.0	13.3	6 08.1	9.8	56.1
03	225 15.4 ..	49.6	109 58.2	13.0	6 17.9	9.8	56.1
04	240 15.3	49.8	124 30.2	13.0	6 27.7	9.7	56.2
05	255 15.1	50.0	139 02.2	13.0	6 37.4	9.8	56.2
06	270 15.0	N22 50.2	153 34.2	12.9	S 6 47.2	9.7	56.2
07	285 14.9	50.5	168 06.1	12.8	6 56.9	9.7	56.3
S 08	300 14.8	50.7	182 37.9	12.8	7 06.6	9.7	56.3
U 09	315 14.7 ..	50.9	197 09.7	12.7	7 16.3	9.6	56.3
N 10	330 14.5	51.1	211 41.4	12.6	7 25.9	9.6	56.4
D 11	345 14.4	51.4	226 13.0	12.6	7 35.6	9.6	56.4
A 12	0 14.3	N22 51.6	240 44.6	12.5	S 7 45.2	9.6	56.4
Y 13	15 14.2	51.8	255 16.1	12.5	7 54.8	9.5	56.5
14	30 14.1	52.0	269 47.6	12.4	8 04.3	9.6	56.5
15	45 13.9 ..	52.2	284 19.0	12.3	8 13.9	9.5	56.5
16	60 13.8	52.5	298 50.3	12.3	8 23.4	9.5	56.6
17	75 13.7	52.7	313 21.6	12.2	8 32.9	9.4	56.6
18	90 13.6	N22 52.9	327 52.8	12.1	S 8 42.3	9.4	56.6
19	105 13.5	53.1	342 23.9	12.1	8 51.7	9.4	56.7
20	120 13.3	53.3	356 55.0	12.0	9 01.1	9.4	56.7
21	135 13.2 ..	53.5	11 26.0	11.9	9 10.5	9.3	56.7
22	150 13.1	53.8	25 56.9	11.9	9 19.8	9.3	56.8
23	165 13.0	54.0	40 27.8	11.8	S 9 29.1	9.2	56.8
	SD 15.8	d 0.2	SD 15.0		15.2		15.4

Moonrise

Lat.	Twilight Naut.	Twilight Civil	Sunrise	Moonrise 6	7	8	9
N 72	▨	▨	▨	12 31	14 10	15 54	17 46
N 70	▨	▨	▨	12 31	14 04	15 41	17 23
68	▨	▨	▨	12 31	13 59	15 30	17 05
66	////	////	00 45	12 31	13 55	15 21	16 51
64	////	////	01 45	12 31	13 51	15 14	16 39
62	////	////	02 18	12 31	13 48	15 07	16 29
60	////	01 10	02 42	12 31	13 45	15 02	16 21
N 58	////	01 50	03 01	12 31	13 43	14 57	16 13
56	////	02 17	03 17	12 31	13 41	14 53	16 07
54	01 04	02 38	03 30	12 31	13 39	14 49	16 01
52	01 41	02 54	03 42	12 31	13 37	14 46	15 56
50	02 06	03 09	03 52	12 31	13 36	14 42	15 51
45	02 49	03 37	04 14	12 31	13 32	14 36	15 41
N 40	03 18	03 59	04 31	12 31	13 29	14 30	15 33
35	03 40	04 16	04 46	12 31	13 27	14 25	15 25
30	03 58	04 31	04 58	12 31	13 25	14 21	15 19
20	04 26	04 55	05 20	12 31	13 21	14 14	15 08
N 10	04 48	05 15	05 38	12 31	13 18	14 07	14 59
0	05 07	05 33	05 55	12 31	13 15	14 01	14 50
S 10	05 23	05 49	06 12	12 31	13 12	13 55	14 41
20	05 39	06 06	06 30	12 31	13 09	13 49	14 32
30	05 55	06 24	06 51	12 31	13 06	13 42	14 22
35	06 03	06 35	07 03	12 31	13 04	13 38	14 15
40	06 12	06 46	07 16	12 32	13 02	13 34	14 09
45	06 22	06 59	07 32	12 32	12 59	13 28	14 01
S 50	06 33	07 14	07 52	12 32	12 56	13 22	13 51
52	06 38	07 21	08 02	12 32	12 55	13 19	13 47
54	06 43	07 29	08 12	12 32	12 53	13 16	13 42
56	06 49	07 38	08 24	12 32	12 51	13 12	13 37
58	06 56	07 48	08 38	12 32	12 49	13 09	13 31
S 60	07 03	07 59	08 55	12 32	12 47	13 04	13 24

Moonset

Lat.	Sunset	Twilight Civil	Twilight Naut.	Moonset 6	7	8	9
N 72	▨	▨	▨	00 34	00 27	00 20	00 12
N 70	▨	▨	▨	00 31	00 30	00 28	00 27
68	▨	▨	▨	00 29	00 32	00 35	00 39
66	23 17	////	////	00 27	00 34	00 41	00 49
64	22 15	////	////	00 26	00 35	00 46	00 58
62	21 41	////	////	00 24	00 37	00 50	01 05
60	21 17	22 50	////	00 23	00 38	00 54	01 12
N 58	20 57	22 11	////	00 22	00 39	00 57	01 17
56	20 42	21 42	////	00 21	00 40	01 00	01 22
54	20 28	21 21	22 56	00 20	00 41	01 03	01 27
52	20 16	21 04	22 18	00 19	00 42	01 05	01 31
50	20 06	20 49	21 53	00 19	00 42	01 07	01 34
45	19 44	20 21	21 10	00 17	00 44	01 12	01 42
N 40	19 27	19 59	20 40	00 16	00 45	01 16	01 49
35	19 12	19 41	20 18	00 15	00 46	01 19	01 55
30	18 59	19 27	20 00	00 14	00 47	01 23	02 00
20	18 38	19 02	19 31	00 12	00 49	01 28	02 09
N 10	18 20	18 43	19 09	00 10	00 51	01 33	02 17
0	18 03	18 25	18 51	00 09	00 52	01 37	02 24
S 10	17 46	18 08	18 35	00 07	00 54	01 42	02 32
20	17 28	17 52	18 19	00 06	00 55	01 46	02 40
30	17 07	17 33	18 03	00 04	00 57	01 52	02 49
35	16 55	17 23	17 55	00 02	00 58	01 55	02 54
40	16 41	17 12	17 46	00 01	00 59	01 58	03 00
45	16 25	16 59	17 36	00 00	01 01	02 02	03 07
S 50	16 05	16 43	17 24	25 02	01 02	02 07	03 15
52	15 56	16 36	17 19	25 02	01 02	02 10	03 19
54	15 45	16 28	17 14	25 03	01 03	02 12	03 23
56	15 33	16 20	17 08	25 04	01 04	02 15	03 28
58	15 19	16 10	17 02	25 05	01 05	02 18	03 33
S 60	15 03	15 59	16 55	25 06	01 06	02 21	03 39

Day	SUN Eqn. of Time 00h	12h	SUN Mer. Pass.	MOON Mer. Pass. Upper	Lower	Age	Phase
	m s	m s	h m	h m	h m	d	%
6	01 25	01 20	11 59	18 42	06 20	09	56
7	01 14	01 09	11 59	19 26	07 04	10	66
8	01 03	00 57	11 59	20 13	07 49	11	75

UT	ARIES	VENUS −3.9		MARS −0.3		JUPITER −1.9		SATURN +0.2		STARS		
	GHA	GHA	Dec	GHA	Dec	GHA	Dec	GHA	Dec	Name	SHA	Dec
d h	° ′	° ′	° ′	° ′	° ′	° ′	° ′	° ′	° ′		° ′	° ′
9 00	257 17.3	216 18.4	N13 48.7	66 47.1	S 4 25.4	143 30.1	N21 58.8	31 04.4	S14 50.9	Acamar	315 18.2	S40 14.8
01	272 19.8	231 18.0	49.7	81 49.1	25.7	158 32.1	58.7	46 07.0	50.8	Achernar	335 26.7	S57 09.6
02	287 22.2	246 17.6	50.6	96 51.1	26.0	173 34.0	58.6	61 09.6	50.8	Acrux	173 08.2	S63 11.1
03	302 24.7	261 17.2	. . 51.5	111 53.0	. . 26.3	188 35.9	. . 58.5	76 12.2	. . 50.8	Adhara	255 12.3	S28 59.8
04	317 27.1	276 16.7	52.4	126 55.0	26.6	203 37.8	58.5	91 14.8	50.7	Aldebaran	290 48.9	N16 32.1
05	332 29.6	291 16.3	53.3	141 57.0	26.9	218 39.8	58.4	106 17.4	50.7			
06	347 32.1	306 15.9	N13 54.2	156 58.9	S 4 27.2	233 41.7	N21 58.3	121 20.0	S14 50.7	Alioth	166 20.0	N55 53.1
07	2 34.5	321 15.5	55.1	172 00.9	27.5	248 43.6	58.2	136 22.7	50.6	Alkaid	152 58.1	N49 14.7
08	17 37.0	336 15.1	56.0	187 02.9	27.8	263 45.5	58.1	151 25.3	50.6	Al Na'ir	27 42.8	S46 53.1
M 09	32 39.5	351 14.6	. . 56.9	202 04.8	. . 28.1	278 47.5	. . 58.1	166 27.9	. . 50.6	Alnilam	275 46.0	S 1 11.8
O 10	47 41.9	6 14.2	57.9	217 06.8	28.3	293 49.4	58.0	181 30.5	50.5	Alphard	217 55.6	S 8 43.5
N 11	62 44.4	21 13.8	58.8	232 08.8	28.6	308 51.3	57.9	196 33.1	50.5			
D 12	77 46.9	36 13.4	N13 59.7	247 10.7	S 4 28.9	323 53.2	N21 57.8	211 35.7	S14 50.5	Alphecca	126 10.1	N26 40.1
A 13	92 49.3	51 13.0	14 00.6	262 12.7	29.2	338 55.1	57.8	226 38.3	50.4	Alpheratz	357 42.8	N29 10.1
Y 14	107 51.8	66 12.5	01.5	277 14.6	29.5	353 57.1	57.7	241 40.9	50.4	Altair	62 07.3	N 8 54.5
15	122 54.2	81 12.1	. . 02.4	292 16.6	. . 29.8	8 59.0	. . 57.6	256 43.6	. . 50.4	Ankaa	353 15.2	S42 13.4
16	137 56.7	96 11.7	03.3	307 18.6	30.1	24 00.9	57.5	271 46.2	50.3	Antares	112 25.0	S26 27.7
17	152 59.2	111 11.3	04.2	322 20.5	30.4	39 02.8	57.4	286 48.8	50.3			
18	168 01.6	126 10.9	N14 05.1	337 22.5	S 4 30.7	54 04.8	N21 57.4	301 51.4	S14 50.3	Arcturus	145 54.9	N19 06.6
19	183 04.1	141 10.4	06.0	352 24.4	31.0	69 06.7	57.3	316 54.0	50.2	Atria	107 25.6	S69 03.1
20	198 06.6	156 10.0	06.9	7 26.4	31.3	84 08.6	57.2	331 56.6	50.2	Avior	234 18.1	S59 33.7
21	213 09.0	171 09.6	. . 07.8	22 28.3	. . 31.6	99 10.5	. . 57.1	346 59.2	. . 50.2	Bellatrix	278 31.6	N 6 21.5
22	228 11.5	186 09.2	08.7	37 30.3	31.9	114 12.4	57.0	2 01.8	50.1	Betelgeuse	271 00.9	N 7 24.4
23	243 14.0	201 08.7	09.6	52 32.2	32.2	129 14.4	57.0	17 04.5	50.1			
10 00	258 16.4	216 08.3	N14 10.5	67 34.2	S 4 32.5	144 16.3	N21 56.9	32 07.1	S14 50.1	Canopus	263 56.4	S52 42.5
01	273 18.9	231 07.9	11.4	82 36.1	32.8	159 18.2	56.8	47 09.7	50.0	Capella	280 33.9	N46 00.5
02	288 21.4	246 07.4	12.3	97 38.1	33.1	174 20.1	56.7	62 12.3	50.0	Deneb	49 30.7	N45 19.9
03	303 23.8	261 07.0	. . 13.2	112 40.0	. . 33.4	189 22.1	. . 56.6	77 14.9	. . 50.0	Denebola	182 33.0	N14 29.5
04	318 26.3	276 06.6	14.1	127 42.0	33.7	204 24.0	56.6	92 17.5	49.9	Diphda	348 55.4	S17 54.4
05	333 28.7	291 06.2	15.0	142 43.9	34.0	219 25.9	56.5	107 20.1	49.9			
06	348 31.2	306 05.7	N14 15.9	157 45.9	S 4 34.3	234 27.8	N21 56.4	122 22.7	S14 49.9	Dubhe	193 51.1	N61 40.6
07	3 33.7	321 05.3	16.8	172 47.8	34.6	249 29.7	56.3	137 25.3	49.8	Elnath	278 12.2	N28 36.9
T 08	18 36.1	336 04.9	17.7	187 49.8	34.9	264 31.7	56.2	152 28.0	49.8	Eltanin	90 45.3	N51 29.4
U 09	33 38.6	351 04.4	. . 18.6	202 51.7	. . 35.2	279 33.6	. . 56.2	167 30.6	. . 49.8	Enif	33 46.3	N 9 56.5
E 10	48 41.1	6 04.0	19.5	217 53.6	35.5	294 35.5	56.1	182 33.2	49.7	Fomalhaut	15 23.2	S29 32.5
S 11	63 43.5	21 03.6	20.4	232 55.6	35.8	309 37.4	56.0	197 35.8	49.7			
D 12	78 46.0	36 03.2	N14 21.3	247 57.5	S 4 36.1	324 39.3	N21 55.9	212 38.4	S14 49.7	Gacrux	171 59.8	S57 11.9
A 13	93 48.5	51 02.7	22.2	262 59.5	36.4	339 41.3	55.8	227 41.0	49.6	Gienah	175 51.5	S17 37.5
Y 14	108 50.9	66 02.3	23.1	278 01.4	36.7	354 43.2	55.8	242 43.6	49.6	Hadar	148 46.4	S60 26.7
15	123 53.4	81 01.9	. . 24.0	293 03.3	. . 37.0	9 45.1	. . 55.7	257 46.2	. . 49.6	Hamal	328 00.2	N23 31.6
16	138 55.9	96 01.4	24.9	308 05.3	37.3	24 47.0	55.6	272 48.8	49.5	Kaus Aust.	83 42.5	S34 22.4
17	153 58.3	111 01.0	25.8	323 07.2	37.6	39 49.0	55.5	287 51.4	49.5			
18	169 00.8	126 00.6	N14 26.7	338 09.1	S 4 37.9	54 50.9	N21 55.4	302 54.0	S14 49.5	Kochab	137 19.3	N74 06.0
19	184 03.2	141 00.1	27.6	353 11.1	38.2	69 52.8	55.4	317 56.7	49.5	Markab	13 37.6	N15 17.0
20	199 05.7	155 59.7	28.5	8 13.0	38.5	84 54.7	55.3	332 59.3	49.4	Menkar	314 14.6	N 4 08.6
21	214 08.2	170 59.2	. . 29.3	23 14.9	. . 38.8	99 56.6	. . 55.2	348 01.9	. . 49.4	Menkent	148 06.5	S36 26.6
22	229 10.6	185 58.8	30.2	38 16.9	39.2	114 58.6	55.1	3 04.5	49.4	Miaplacidus	221 39.9	S69 47.0
23	244 13.1	200 58.4	31.1	53 18.8	39.5	130 00.5	55.0	18 07.1	49.3			
11 00	259 15.6	215 57.9	N14 32.0	68 20.7	S 4 39.8	145 02.4	N21 54.9	33 09.7	S14 49.3	Mirfak	308 39.8	N49 54.5
01	274 18.0	230 57.5	32.9	83 22.7	40.1	160 04.3	54.9	48 12.3	49.3	Nunki	75 57.1	S26 16.5
02	289 20.5	245 57.1	33.8	98 24.6	40.4	175 06.2	54.8	63 14.9	49.2	Peacock	53 17.8	S56 40.9
03	304 23.0	260 56.6	. . 34.7	113 26.5	. . 40.7	190 08.2	. . 54.7	78 17.5	. . 49.2	Pollux	243 27.2	N27 59.3
04	319 25.4	275 56.2	35.6	128 28.4	41.0	205 10.1	54.6	93 20.1	49.2	Procyon	244 59.3	N 5 11.1
05	334 27.9	290 55.7	36.5	143 30.4	41.3	220 12.0	54.5	108 22.7	49.1			
06	349 30.4	305 55.3	N14 37.3	158 32.3	S 4 41.6	235 13.9	N21 54.5	123 25.4	S14 49.1	Rasalhague	96 05.5	N12 33.1
W 07	4 32.8	320 54.9	38.2	173 34.2	41.9	250 15.8	54.4	138 28.0	49.1	Regulus	207 42.9	N11 53.7
E 08	19 35.3	335 54.4	39.1	188 36.1	42.2	265 17.7	54.3	153 30.6	49.0	Rigel	281 11.8	S 8 11.3
D 09	34 37.7	350 54.0	. . 40.0	203 38.1	. . 42.5	280 19.7	. . 54.2	168 33.2	. . 49.0	Rigil Kent.	139 50.2	S60 53.8
N 10	49 40.2	5 53.5	40.9	218 40.0	42.8	295 21.6	54.1	183 35.8	49.0	Sabik	102 11.4	S15 44.4
E 11	64 42.7	20 53.1	41.8	233 41.9	43.2	310 23.5	54.1	198 38.4	48.9			
S 12	79 45.1	35 52.7	N14 42.6	248 43.8	S 4 43.5	325 25.4	N21 54.0	213 41.0	S14 48.9	Schedar	349 39.8	N56 36.7
D 13	94 47.6	50 52.2	43.5	263 45.7	43.8	340 27.3	53.9	228 43.6	48.9	Shaula	96 20.6	S37 06.6
A 14	109 50.1	65 51.8	44.4	278 47.7	44.1	355 29.3	53.8	243 46.2	48.8	Sirius	258 33.5	S16 44.4
Y 15	124 52.5	80 51.3	. . 45.3	293 49.6	. . 44.4	10 31.2	. . 53.7	258 48.8	. . 48.8	Spica	158 30.4	S11 14.2
16	139 55.0	95 50.9	46.2	308 51.5	44.7	25 33.1	53.6	273 51.4	48.8	Suhail	222 52.2	S43 29.8
17	154 57.5	110 50.4	47.1	323 53.4	45.0	40 35.0	53.6	288 54.0	48.7			
18	169 59.9	125 50.0	N14 47.9	338 55.3	S 4 45.3	55 36.9	N21 53.5	303 56.6	S14 48.7	Vega	80 38.1	N38 47.9
19	185 02.4	140 49.5	48.8	353 57.3	45.6	70 38.9	53.4	318 59.2	48.7	Zuben'ubi	137 04.4	S16 06.1
20	200 04.8	155 49.1	49.7	8 59.1	46.0	85 40.8	53.3	334 01.9	48.6		SHA	Mer.Pass.
21	215 07.3	170 48.7	. . 50.6	24 01.0	. . 46.3	100 42.7	. . 53.2	349 04.5	. . 48.6		° ′	h m
22	230 09.8	185 48.2	51.4	39 03.0	46.6	115 44.6	53.2	4 07.1	48.6	Venus	317 51.9	9 36
23	245 12.2	200 47.8	52.3	54 04.9	46.9	130 46.5	53.1	19 09.7	48.6	Mars	169 17.8	19 27
	h m									Jupiter	245 59.9	14 21
Mer.Pass. 6 45.8		v −0.4	d 0.9	v 1.9	d 0.3	v 1.9	d 0.1	v 2.6	d 0.0	Saturn	133 50.6	21 48

UT	SUN GHA	SUN Dec	MOON GHA	v	Dec	d	HP
9 00	180 12.9	N22 54.2	54 58.6	11.7	S 9 38.3	9.3	56.8
01	195 12.7	54.4	69 29.3	11.7	9 47.6	9.1	56.9
02	210 12.6	54.6	84 00.0	11.6	9 56.7	9.2	56.9
03	225 12.5 ..	54.8	98 30.6	11.5	10 05.9	9.1	56.9
04	240 12.4	55.0	113 01.1	11.4	10 15.0	9.1	57.0
05	255 12.3	55.2	127 31.5	11.4	10 24.1	9.0	57.0
M 06	270 12.1	N22 55.4	142 01.9	11.2	S10 33.1	9.0	57.1
O 07	285 12.0	55.6	156 32.1	11.3	10 42.1	8.9	57.1
N 08	300 11.9	55.9	171 02.4	11.1	10 51.0	8.9	57.1
D 09	315 11.8 ..	56.1	185 32.5	11.1	10 59.9	8.8	57.2
A 10	330 11.7	56.3	200 02.6	11.0	11 08.7	8.9	57.2
Y 11	345 11.5	56.5	214 32.6	10.9	11 17.6	8.7	57.2
12	0 11.4	N22 56.7	229 02.5	10.8	S11 26.3	8.7	57.3
13	15 11.3	56.9	243 32.3	10.8	11 35.0	8.7	57.3
14	30 11.2	57.1	258 02.1	10.6	11 43.7	8.6	57.3
15	45 11.0 ..	57.3	272 31.7	10.6	11 52.3	8.5	57.4
16	60 10.9	57.5	287 01.3	10.6	12 00.8	8.6	57.4
17	75 10.8	57.7	301 30.9	10.4	12 09.4	8.4	57.4
18	90 10.7	N22 57.9	316 00.3	10.4	S12 17.8	8.4	57.5
19	105 10.5	58.1	330 29.7	10.2	12 26.2	8.3	57.5
20	120 10.4	58.3	344 58.9	10.2	12 34.5	8.3	57.6
21	135 10.3 ..	58.5	359 28.1	10.2	12 42.8	8.3	57.6
22	150 10.2	58.7	13 57.3	10.0	12 51.1	8.1	57.6
23	165 10.1	58.9	28 26.3	10.0	12 59.2	8.1	57.7
10 00	180 09.9	N22 59.1	42 55.3	9.8	S13 07.3	8.1	57.7
01	195 09.8	59.3	57 24.1	9.8	13 15.4	8.0	57.7
02	210 09.7	59.5	71 52.9	9.8	13 23.4	7.9	57.8
03	225 09.6 ..	59.7	86 21.7	9.6	13 31.3	7.8	57.8
04	240 09.4	22 59.9	100 50.3	9.5	13 39.1	7.8	57.8
05	255 09.3	23 00.1	115 18.8	9.5	13 46.9	7.7	57.9
T 06	270 09.2	N23 00.2	129 47.3	9.4	S13 54.6	7.7	57.9
U 07	285 09.1	00.4	144 15.7	9.3	14 02.3	7.6	58.0
E 08	300 08.9	00.6	158 44.0	9.2	14 09.9	7.5	58.0
S 09	315 08.8 ..	00.8	173 12.2	9.1	14 17.4	7.4	58.0
D 10	330 08.7	01.0	187 40.3	9.1	14 24.8	7.4	58.1
A 11	345 08.6	01.2	202 08.4	9.0	14 32.2	7.3	58.1
Y 12	0 08.4	N23 01.4	216 36.4	8.8	S14 39.5	7.2	58.1
13	15 08.3	01.6	231 04.2	8.8	14 46.7	7.2	58.2
14	30 08.2	01.8	245 32.0	8.8	14 53.9	7.0	58.2
15	45 08.1 ..	01.9	259 59.8	8.6	15 00.9	7.0	58.2
16	60 08.0	02.1	274 27.4	8.5	15 07.9	6.9	58.3
17	75 07.8	02.3	288 54.9	8.5	15 14.8	6.9	58.3
18	90 07.7	N23 02.5	303 22.4	8.4	S15 21.7	6.7	58.4
19	105 07.6	02.7	317 49.8	8.3	15 28.4	6.7	58.4
20	120 07.5	02.9	332 17.1	8.2	15 35.1	6.6	58.4
21	135 07.3 ..	03.0	346 44.3	8.2	15 41.7	6.4	58.5
22	150 07.2	03.2	1 11.5	8.0	15 48.1	6.5	58.5
23	165 07.1	03.4	15 38.5	8.0	15 54.6	6.3	58.5
11 00	180 07.0	N23 03.6	30 05.5	7.9	S16 00.9	6.2	58.6
01	195 06.8	03.8	44 32.4	7.8	16 07.1	6.1	58.6
02	210 06.7	03.9	58 59.2	7.7	16 13.2	6.1	58.6
03	225 06.6 ..	04.1	73 25.9	7.7	16 19.3	5.9	58.7
04	240 06.4	04.3	87 52.6	7.5	16 25.2	5.9	58.7
05	255 06.3	04.4	102 19.1	7.5	16 31.1	5.8	58.7
W 06	270 06.2	N23 04.6	116 45.6	7.4	S16 36.9	5.6	58.8
E 07	285 06.1	04.8	131 12.0	7.4	16 42.5	5.6	58.8
D 08	300 05.9	05.0	145 38.4	7.2	16 48.1	5.5	58.8
N 09	315 05.8 ..	05.2	160 04.6	7.2	16 53.6	5.3	58.9
E 10	330 05.7	05.3	174 30.8	7.1	16 58.9	5.3	58.9
S 11	345 05.6	05.5	188 56.9	7.0	17 04.2	5.2	58.9
D 12	0 05.4	N23 05.7	203 22.9	7.0	S17 09.4	5.0	59.0
A 13	15 05.3	05.8	217 48.9	6.8	17 14.4	5.0	59.0
Y 14	30 05.2	06.0	232 14.7	6.8	17 19.4	4.9	59.0
15	45 05.1 ..	06.2	246 40.5	6.8	17 24.3	4.7	59.1
16	60 04.9	06.4	261 06.3	6.6	17 29.0	4.7	59.1
17	75 04.8	06.5	275 31.9	6.6	17 33.7	4.5	59.1
18	90 04.7	N23 06.7	289 57.5	6.5	S17 38.2	4.4	59.2
19	105 04.6	06.9	304 23.0	6.4	17 42.6	4.4	59.2
20	120 04.4	07.0	318 48.4	6.4	17 47.0	4.2	59.2
21	135 04.3 ..	07.2	333 13.8	6.3	17 51.2	4.1	59.3
22	150 04.2	07.4	347 39.1	6.2	17 55.3	3.9	59.3
23	165 04.0	07.5	2 04.3	6.2	S17 59.2	3.9	59.3
SD	15.8	d 0.2	SD 15.6		15.8		16.1

Twilight / Moonrise

Lat.	Naut.	Civil	Sunrise	Moonrise 9	10	11	12
N 72	□	□	□	17 46	19 50	■■	■■
N 70	□	□	□	17 23	19 10	21 00	22 37
68	□	□	□	17 05	18 43	20 19	21 42
66	////	////	00 29	16 51	18 22	19 51	21 08
64	////	////	01 40	16 39	18 06	19 30	20 44
62	////	////	02 14	16 29	17 52	19 12	20 25
60	////	01 03	02 39	16 21	17 40	18 58	20 09
N 58	////	01 46	02 59	16 13	17 31	18 46	19 56
56	////	02 14	03 15	16 07	17 22	18 36	19 44
54	00 57	02 35	03 29	16 01	17 14	18 26	19 34
52	01 37	02 53	03 41	15 56	17 07	18 18	19 25
50	02 03	03 07	03 51	15 51	17 01	18 11	19 17
45	02 47	03 36	04 13	15 41	16 48	17 55	19 00
N 40	03 17	03 58	04 31	15 33	16 37	17 42	18 46
35	03 40	04 16	04 46	15 25	16 28	17 31	18 34
30	03 58	04 31	04 58	15 19	16 20	17 22	18 24
20	04 26	04 55	05 20	15 08	16 06	17 05	18 06
N 10	04 49	05 16	05 39	14 59	15 53	16 51	17 51
0	05 07	05 33	05 56	14 50	15 42	16 38	17 36
S 10	05 24	05 50	06 13	14 41	15 31	16 24	17 22
20	05 40	06 07	06 31	14 32	15 19	16 10	17 07
30	05 56	06 26	06 52	14 22	15 05	15 54	16 49
35	06 04	06 36	07 04	14 15	14 57	15 45	16 39
40	06 13	06 47	07 18	14 09	14 48	15 34	16 27
45	06 24	07 01	07 34	14 01	14 38	15 22	16 14
S 50	06 35	07 16	07 55	13 51	14 26	15 07	15 57
52	06 40	07 24	08 04	13 47	14 20	15 00	15 49
54	06 46	07 32	08 15	13 42	14 13	14 52	15 40
56	06 52	07 40	08 27	13 37	14 06	14 43	15 31
58	06 58	07 50	08 42	13 31	13 58	14 34	15 20
S 60	07 05	08 02	08 58	13 24	13 49	14 22	15 07

Moonset

Lat.	Sunset	Civil	Naut.	Moonset 9	10	11	12
N 72	□	□	□	00 12	{00 02 / 23 47}	■■	■■
N 70	□	□	□	00 27	00 27	00 29	00 36
68	□	□	□	00 39	00 46	00 57	01 17
66	23 37	////	////	00 49	01 01	01 18	01 46
64	22 21	////	////	00 58	01 14	01 35	02 08
62	21 46	////	////	01 05	01 24	01 50	02 25
60	21 20	22 58	////	01 12	01 33	02 02	02 40
N 58	21 01	22 14	////	01 17	01 41	02 12	02 52
56	20 44	21 46	////	01 22	01 49	02 21	03 03
54	20 31	21 24	23 04	01 27	01 55	02 29	03 12
52	20 19	21 07	22 23	01 31	02 01	02 37	03 21
50	20 08	20 52	21 56	01 34	02 06	02 43	03 28
45	19 46	20 23	21 12	01 42	02 17	02 57	03 45
N 40	19 28	20 01	20 42	01 49	02 27	03 09	03 58
35	19 13	19 43	20 20	01 55	02 34	03 19	04 09
30	19 01	19 28	20 01	02 00	02 41	03 28	04 19
20	18 39	19 04	19 33	02 09	02 54	03 43	04 36
N 10	18 20	18 43	19 10	02 17	03 04	03 56	04 51
0	18 03	18 26	18 52	02 24	03 15	04 08	05 05
S 10	17 46	18 09	18 35	02 32	03 25	04 21	05 19
20	17 28	17 52	18 19	02 40	03 35	04 34	05 34
30	17 07	17 33	18 03	02 49	03 48	04 49	05 51
35	16 55	17 23	17 54	02 54	03 55	04 58	06 01
40	16 41	17 11	17 45	03 00	04 03	05 08	06 13
45	16 24	16 58	17 35	03 07	04 13	05 20	06 26
S 50	16 04	16 42	17 24	03 15	04 24	05 34	06 42
52	15 55	16 35	17 19	03 19	04 30	05 41	06 50
54	15 44	16 27	17 13	03 23	04 35	05 48	06 58
56	15 31	16 18	17 07	03 28	04 42	05 57	07 08
58	15 17	16 08	17 01	03 33	04 50	06 06	07 19
S 60	15 00	15 57	16 53	03 39	04 58	06 17	07 31

Day	SUN Eqn. of Time 00h	12h	Mer. Pass.	MOON Mer. Pass. Upper	Lower	Age	Phase
	m s	m s	h m	h m	h m	d	%
9	00 52	00 46	11 59	21 02	08 37	12	84
10	00 40	00 34	11 59	21 55	09 28	13	91
11	00 28	00 22	12 00	22 51	10 23	14	96

UT	ARIES GHA	VENUS −3.9 GHA	Dec	MARS −0.3 GHA	Dec	JUPITER −1.8 GHA	Dec	SATURN +0.3 GHA	Dec	STARS Name	SHA	Dec
12 00	260 14.7	215 47.3	N14 53.2	69 06.8	S 4 47.2	145 48.4	N21 53.0	34 12.3	S14 48.5	Acamar	315 18.2	S40 14.8
01	275 17.2	230 46.9	54.1	84 08.7	47.5	160 50.4	52.9	49 14.9	48.5	Achernar	335 26.7	S57 09.6
02	290 19.6	245 46.4	55.0	99 10.6	47.8	175 52.3	52.8	64 17.5	48.5	Acrux	173 08.2	S63 11.1
03	305 22.1	260 46.0	.. 55.8	114 12.5	.. 48.2	190 54.2	.. 52.7	79 20.1	.. 48.4	Adhara	255 12.3	S28 59.8
04	320 24.6	275 45.5	56.7	129 14.4	48.5	205 56.1	52.7	94 22.7	48.4	Aldebaran	290 48.9	N16 32.1
05	335 27.0	290 45.1	57.6	144 16.3	48.8	220 58.0	52.6	109 25.3	48.4			
06	350 29.5	305 44.6	N14 58.4	159 18.2	S 4 49.1	235 59.9	N21 52.5	124 27.9	S14 48.3	Alioth	166 20.0	N55 53.1
T 07	5 32.0	320 44.2	14 59.3	174 20.1	49.4	251 01.9	52.4	139 30.5	48.3	Alkaid	152 58.2	N49 14.7
H 08	20 34.4	335 43.7	15 00.2	189 22.0	49.7	266 03.8	52.3	154 33.1	48.3	Al Na'ir	27 42.8	S46 53.1
U 09	35 36.9	350 43.3	.. 01.1	204 23.9	.. 50.1	281 05.7	.. 52.3	169 35.7	.. 48.2	Alnilam	275 46.0	S 1 11.8
R 10	50 39.3	5 42.8	01.9	219 25.8	50.4	296 07.6	52.2	184 38.3	48.2	Alphard	217 55.6	S 8 43.5
S 11	65 41.8	20 42.4	02.8	234 27.7	50.7	311 09.5	52.1	199 40.9	48.2			
D 12	80 44.3	35 41.9	N15 03.7	249 29.6	S 4 51.0	326 11.5	N21 52.0	214 43.5	S14 48.1	Alphecca	126 10.1	N26 40.2
A 13	95 46.7	50 41.4	04.5	264 31.5	51.3	341 13.4	51.9	229 46.1	48.1	Alpheratz	357 42.8	N29 10.1
Y 14	110 49.2	65 41.0	05.4	279 33.4	51.6	356 15.3	51.8	244 48.8	48.1	Altair	62 07.3	N 8 54.6
15	125 51.7	80 40.5	.. 06.3	294 35.3	.. 52.0	11 17.2	.. 51.8	259 51.4	.. 48.1	Ankaa	353 15.2	S42 13.4
16	140 54.1	95 40.1	07.2	309 37.2	52.3	26 19.1	51.7	274 54.0	48.0	Antares	112 25.0	S26 27.7
17	155 56.6	110 39.6	08.0	324 39.1	52.6	41 21.0	51.6	289 56.6	48.0			
18	170 59.1	125 39.2	N15 08.9	339 41.0	S 4 52.9	56 23.0	N21 51.5	304 59.2	S14 48.0	Arcturus	145 54.9	N19 06.6
19	186 01.5	140 38.7	09.8	354 42.8	53.2	71 24.9	51.4	320 01.8	47.9	Atria	107 25.6	S69 03.1
20	201 04.0	155 38.3	10.6	9 44.7	53.6	86 26.8	51.3	335 04.4	47.9	Avior	234 18.2	S59 33.7
21	216 06.5	170 37.8	.. 11.5	24 46.6	.. 53.9	101 28.7	.. 51.3	350 07.0	.. 47.9	Bellatrix	278 31.6	N 6 21.5
22	231 08.9	185 37.3	12.3	39 48.5	54.2	116 30.6	51.2	5 09.6	47.8	Betelgeuse	271 00.9	N 7 24.4
23	246 11.4	200 36.9	13.2	54 50.4	54.5	131 32.5	51.1	20 12.2	47.8			
13 00	261 13.8	215 36.4	N15 14.1	69 52.3	S 4 54.8	146 34.4	N21 51.0	35 14.8	S14 47.8	Canopus	263 56.4	S52 42.5
01	276 16.3	230 36.0	14.9	84 54.2	55.2	161 36.4	50.9	50 17.4	47.7	Capella	280 33.9	N46 00.5
02	291 18.8	245 35.5	15.8	99 56.1	55.5	176 38.3	50.9	65 20.0	47.7	Deneb	49 30.6	N45 19.9
03	306 21.2	260 35.0	.. 16.7	114 57.9	.. 55.8	191 40.2	.. 50.8	80 22.6	.. 47.7	Denebola	182 33.0	N14 29.5
04	321 23.7	275 34.6	17.5	129 59.8	56.1	206 42.1	50.8	95 25.2	47.7	Diphda	348 55.3	S17 54.4
05	336 26.2	290 34.1	18.4	145 01.7	56.5	221 44.0	50.6	110 27.8	47.6			
06	351 28.6	305 33.7	N15 19.2	160 03.6	S 4 56.8	236 45.9	N21 50.5	125 30.4	S14 47.6	Dubhe	193 51.1	N61 40.6
F 07	6 31.1	320 33.2	20.1	175 05.5	57.1	251 47.9	50.4	140 33.0	47.6	Elnath	278 12.1	N28 36.9
R 08	21 33.6	335 32.7	21.0	190 07.4	57.4	266 49.8	50.4	155 35.6	47.5	Eltanin	90 45.3	N51 29.4
I 09	36 36.0	350 32.3	.. 21.8	205 09.2	.. 57.8	281 51.7	.. 50.3	170 38.2	.. 47.5	Enif	33 46.3	N 9 56.6
D 10	51 38.5	5 31.8	22.7	220 11.1	58.1	296 53.6	50.2	185 40.8	47.5	Fomalhaut	15 23.2	S29 32.5
A 11	66 41.0	20 31.3	23.5	235 13.0	58.4	311 55.5	50.1	200 43.4	47.4			
Y 12	81 43.4	35 30.9	N15 24.4	250 14.9	S 4 58.7	326 57.4	N21 50.0	215 46.0	S14 47.4	Gacrux	171 59.9	S57 11.9
13	96 45.9	50 30.4	25.2	265 16.7	59.1	341 59.4	49.9	230 48.6	47.4	Gienah	175 51.5	S17 37.5
14	111 48.3	65 29.9	26.1	280 18.6	59.4	357 01.3	49.9	245 51.2	47.4	Hadar	148 46.4	S60 26.7
15	126 50.8	80 29.5	.. 27.0	295 20.5	4 59.7	12 03.2	.. 49.8	260 53.8	.. 47.3	Hamal	328 00.2	N23 31.6
16	141 53.3	95 29.0	27.8	310 22.4	5 00.0	27 05.1	49.7	275 56.4	47.3	Kaus Aust.	83 42.5	S34 22.4
17	156 55.7	110 28.5	28.7	325 24.2	00.4	42 07.0	49.6	290 59.0	47.3			
18	171 58.2	125 28.1	N15 29.5	340 26.1	S 5 00.7	57 08.9	N21 49.5	306 01.6	S14 47.2	Kochab	137 19.3	N74 06.1
19	187 00.7	140 27.6	30.4	355 28.0	01.0	72 10.8	49.4	321 04.2	47.2	Markab	13 37.6	N15 17.0
20	202 03.1	155 27.1	31.2	10 29.8	01.3	87 12.8	49.4	336 06.8	47.2	Menkar	314 14.6	N 4 08.6
21	217 05.6	170 26.7	.. 32.1	25 31.7	.. 01.7	102 14.7	.. 49.3	351 09.4	.. 47.1	Menkent	148 06.5	S36 26.6
22	232 08.1	185 26.2	32.9	40 33.6	02.0	117 16.6	49.2	6 12.0	47.1	Miaplacidus	221 39.9	S69 47.0
23	247 10.5	200 25.7	33.8	55 35.4	02.3	132 18.5	49.1	21 14.6	47.1			
14 00	262 13.0	215 25.3	N15 34.6	70 37.3	S 5 02.7	147 20.4	N21 49.0	36 17.2	S14 47.1	Mirfak	308 39.8	N49 54.5
01	277 15.5	230 24.8	35.5	85 39.2	03.0	162 22.3	48.9	51 19.8	47.0	Nunki	75 57.1	S26 16.5
02	292 17.9	245 24.3	36.3	100 41.0	03.3	177 24.2	48.8	66 22.4	47.0	Peacock	53 17.8	S56 40.9
03	307 20.4	260 23.8	.. 37.2	115 42.9	.. 03.6	192 26.2	.. 48.8	81 25.0	.. 47.0	Pollux	243 27.2	N27 59.3
04	322 22.8	275 23.4	38.0	130 44.8	04.0	207 28.1	48.7	96 27.6	46.9	Procyon	244 59.3	N 5 11.1
05	337 25.3	290 22.9	38.9	145 46.6	04.3	222 30.0	48.6	111 30.2	46.9			
06	352 27.8	305 22.4	N15 39.7	160 48.5	S 5 04.6	237 31.9	N21 48.5	126 32.8	S14 46.9	Rasalhague	96 05.5	N12 33.2
S 07	−7 30.2	320 21.9	40.6	175 50.4	05.0	252 33.8	48.4	141 35.4	46.8	Regulus	207 42.9	N11 53.7
A 08	22 32.7	335 21.5	41.4	190 52.2	05.3	267 35.7	48.3	156 38.0	46.8	Rigel	281 11.7	S 8 11.3
T 09	37 35.2	350 21.0	.. 42.2	205 54.1	.. 05.6	282 37.6	.. 48.3	171 40.6	.. 46.8	Rigil Kent.	139 50.2	S60 53.8
U 10	52 37.6	5 20.5	43.1	220 55.9	06.0	297 39.5	48.2	186 43.2	46.8	Sabik	102 11.4	S15 44.4
R 11	67 40.1	20 20.0	43.9	235 57.8	06.3	312 41.5	48.1	201 45.8	46.7			
D 12	82 42.6	35 19.6	N15 44.8	250 59.6	S 5 06.6	327 43.4	N21 48.0	216 48.4	S14 46.7	Schedar	349 39.8	N56 36.7
A 13	97 45.0	50 19.1	45.6	266 01.5	07.0	342 45.3	47.9	231 51.0	46.7	Shaula	96 20.6	S37 06.6
Y 14	112 47.5	65 18.6	46.5	281 03.4	07.3	357 47.2	47.8	246 53.6	46.6	Sirius	258 33.5	S16 44.4
15	127 50.0	80 18.1	.. 47.3	296 05.2	.. 07.6	12 49.1	.. 47.8	261 56.2	.. 46.6	Spica	158 30.4	S11 14.2
16	142 52.4	95 17.7	48.1	311 07.1	08.0	27 51.0	47.7	276 58.8	46.6	Suhail	222 52.2	S43 29.8
17	157 54.9	110 17.2	49.0	326 08.9	08.3	42 52.9	47.6	292 01.4	46.6			
18	172 57.3	125 16.7	N15 49.8	341 10.8	S 5 08.6	57 54.9	N21 47.5	307 04.0	S14 46.5	Vega	80 38.1	N38 48.0
19	187 59.8	140 16.2	50.7	356 12.6	09.0	72 56.8	47.4	322 06.6	46.5	Zuben'ubi	137 04.4	S16 06.1
20	203 02.3	155 15.7	51.5	11 14.5	09.3	87 58.7	47.3	337 09.2	46.5		SHA	Mer. Pass.
21	218 04.7	170 15.3	.. 52.3	26 16.3	.. 09.6	103 00.6	.. 47.2	352 11.8	.. 46.4	Venus	314 22.6	9 38
22	233 07.2	185 14.8	53.2	41 18.2	10.0	118 02.5	47.2	7 14.4	46.4	Mars	168 38.4	19 18
23	248 09.7	200 14.3	54.0	56 20.0	10.3	133 04.4	47.1	22 17.0	46.4	Jupiter	245 20.6	14 12
Mer. Pass.	h m 6 34.0	v −0.5	d 0.9	v 1.9	d 0.3	v 1.9	d 0.1	v 2.6	d 0.0	Saturn	134 00.9	21 35

SUN / MOON

UT	SUN GHA	SUN Dec	MOON GHA	v	MOON Dec	d	HP
d h	° ′	° ′	° ′	′	° ′	′	′
12 00	180 03.9	N23 07.7	16 29.5	6.1	S18 03.1	3.8	59.3
01	195 03.8	07.8	30 54.6	6.0	18 06.9	3.6	59.4
02	210 03.7	08.0	45 19.6	6.0	18 10.5	3.5	59.4
03	225 03.5	.. 08.2	59 44.6	5.9	18 14.0	3.4	59.4
04	240 03.4	08.3	74 09.5	5.8	18 17.4	3.3	59.5
05	255 03.3	08.5	88 34.3	5.8	18 20.7	3.2	59.5
06	270 03.2	N23 08.6	102 59.1	5.7	S18 23.9	3.0	59.5
07	285 03.0	08.8	117 23.8	5.7	18 26.9	2.9	59.6
T 08	300 02.9	08.9	131 48.5	5.6	18 29.8	2.8	59.6
H 09	315 02.8	.. 09.1	146 13.1	5.6	18 32.6	2.7	59.6
U 10	330 02.6	09.3	160 37.7	5.4	18 35.3	2.5	59.6
R 11	345 02.5	09.4	175 02.1	5.5	18 37.8	2.5	59.7
S 12	0 02.4	N23 09.6	189 26.6	5.4	S18 40.3	2.3	59.7
D 13	15 02.3	09.7	203 51.0	5.3	18 42.6	2.1	59.7
A 14	30 02.1	09.9	218 15.3	5.3	18 44.7	2.1	59.7
Y 15	45 02.0	.. 10.0	232 39.6	5.3	18 46.8	1.9	59.8
16	60 01.9	10.2	247 03.9	5.2	18 48.7	1.8	59.8
17	75 01.7	10.3	261 28.1	5.1	18 50.5	1.7	59.8
18	90 01.6	N23 10.5	275 52.2	5.1	S18 52.2	1.5	59.8
19	105 01.5	10.6	290 16.3	5.1	18 53.7	1.4	59.9
20	120 01.4	10.8	304 40.4	5.0	18 55.1	1.3	59.9
21	135 01.2	.. 10.9	319 04.4	5.0	18 56.4	1.1	59.9
22	150 01.1	11.1	333 28.4	4.9	18 57.5	1.1	59.9
23	165 01.0	11.2	347 52.3	4.9	18 58.6	0.8	60.0
13 00	180 00.8	N23 11.4	2 16.2	4.9	S18 59.4	0.8	60.0
01	195 00.7	11.5	16 40.1	4.9	19 00.2	0.6	60.0
02	210 00.6	11.7	31 04.0	4.8	19 00.8	0.5	60.0
03	225 00.5	.. 11.8	45 27.8	4.7	19 01.3	0.3	60.0
04	240 00.3	11.9	59 51.5	4.8	19 01.6	0.3	60.1
05	255 00.2	12.1	74 15.3	4.7	19 01.9	0.0	60.1
06	270 00.1	N23 12.2	88 39.0	4.7	S19 01.9	0.0	60.1
07	284 59.9	12.4	103 02.7	4.7	19 01.9	0.2	60.1
F 08	299 59.8	12.5	117 26.4	4.6	19 01.7	0.3	60.1
R 09	314 59.7	.. 12.6	131 50.0	4.7	19 01.4	0.5	60.2
I 10	329 59.5	12.8	146 13.7	4.6	19 00.9	0.6	60.2
D 11	344 59.4	12.9	160 37.3	4.6	19 00.3	0.7	60.2
A 12	359 59.3	N23 13.1	175 00.9	4.5	S18 59.6	0.8	60.2
Y 13	14 59.2	13.2	189 24.4	4.6	18 58.8	1.0	60.2
14	29 59.0	13.3	203 48.0	4.6	18 57.8	1.2	60.3
15	44 58.9	.. 13.5	218 11.6	4.5	18 56.6	1.2	60.3
16	59 58.8	13.6	232 35.1	4.5	18 55.4	1.4	60.3
17	74 58.6	13.7	246 58.6	4.6	18 54.0	1.6	60.3
18	89 58.5	N23 13.9	261 22.2	4.5	S18 52.4	1.6	60.3
19	104 58.4	14.0	275 45.7	4.5	18 50.8	1.9	60.3
20	119 58.2	14.1	290 09.2	4.5	18 48.9	1.9	60.3
21	134 58.1	.. 14.3	304 32.7	4.5	18 47.0	2.1	60.4
22	149 58.0	14.4	318 56.2	4.5	18 44.9	2.2	60.4
23	164 57.8	14.5	333 19.7	4.5	18 42.7	2.3	60.4
14 00	179 57.7	N23 14.6	347 43.2	4.5	S18 40.4	2.5	60.4
01	194 57.6	14.8	2 06.7	4.6	18 37.9	2.6	60.4
02	209 57.5	14.9	16 30.3	4.5	18 35.3	2.8	60.4
03	224 57.3	.. 15.0	30 53.8	4.5	18 32.5	2.9	60.4
04	239 57.2	15.1	45 17.3	4.6	18 29.6	3.0	60.4
05	254 57.1	15.3	59 40.9	4.5	18 26.6	3.1	60.5
06	269 56.9	N23 15.4	74 04.4	4.6	S18 23.5	3.3	60.5
07	284 56.8	15.5	88 28.0	4.6	18 20.2	3.4	60.5
S 08	299 56.7	15.6	102 51.6	4.6	18 16.8	3.6	60.5
A 09	314 56.5	.. 15.8	117 15.2	4.6	18 13.2	3.7	60.5
T 10	329 56.4	15.9	131 38.8	4.7	18 09.5	3.8	60.5
U 11	344 56.3	16.0	146 02.5	4.6	18 05.7	3.9	60.5
R 12	359 56.1	N23 16.1	160 26.1	4.7	S18 01.8	4.1	60.5
D 13	14 56.0	16.2	174 49.8	4.7	17 57.7	4.2	60.5
A 14	29 55.9	16.4	189 13.5	4.7	17 53.5	4.3	60.5
Y 15	44 55.8	.. 16.5	203 37.2	4.8	17 49.2	4.4	60.5
16	59 55.6	16.6	218 01.0	4.8	17 44.8	4.6	60.5
17	74 55.5	16.7	232 24.8	4.8	17 40.2	4.7	60.5
18	89 55.4	N23 16.8	246 48.6	4.8	S17 35.5	4.9	60.5
19	104 55.2	16.9	261 12.4	4.9	17 30.6	4.9	60.5
20	119 55.1	17.1	275 36.3	4.9	17 25.7	5.1	60.6
21	134 55.0	.. 17.2	290 00.2	5.0	17 20.6	5.2	60.6
22	149 54.8	17.3	304 24.2	4.9	17 15.4	5.3	60.6
23	164 54.7	17.4	318 48.1	5.0	S17 10.1	5.4	60.6
SD	15.8	d 0.1	SD 16.3		16.4		16.5

Twilight / Sunrise / Moonrise

Lat.	Naut.	Civil	Sunrise	12	13	14	15
°	h m	h m	h m	h m	h m	h m	h m
N 72	▭	▭	▭	■	■	■	00 37
N 70	▭	▭	▭	22 37	23 27	23 41	23 45
68	▭	▭	▭	21 42	22 37	23 07	23 23
66	▭	▭	▭	21 08	22 06	22 43	23 05
64	////	////	01 35	20 44	21 42	22 23	22 51
62	////	////	02 12	20 25	21 24	22 07	22 39
60	////	00 57	02 37	20 09	21 08	21 54	22 29
N 58	////	01 43	02 57	19 56	20 55	21 43	22 20
56	////	02 12	03 14	19 44	20 44	21 33	22 12
54	00 52	02 34	03 28	19 34	20 34	21 24	22 05
52	01 35	02 51	03 40	19 25	20 25	21 16	21 58
50	02 02	03 06	03 50	19 17	20 17	21 09	21 53
45	02 46	03 36	04 13	19 00	20 00	20 54	21 40
N 40	03 16	03 58	04 31	18 46	19 46	20 41	21 30
35	03 39	04 16	04 45	18 34	19 34	20 30	21 21
30	03 58	04 31	04 58	18 24	19 24	20 21	21 13
20	04 26	04 56	05 20	18 06	19 06	20 05	21 00
N 10	04 49	05 16	05 39	17 51	18 51	19 51	20 48
0	05 08	05 34	05 56	17 36	18 37	19 37	20 37
S 10	05 25	05 51	06 14	17 22	18 22	19 24	20 26
20	05 41	06 08	06 32	17 07	18 07	19 10	20 14
30	05 57	06 27	06 53	16 49	17 49	18 54	20 00
35	06 05	06 37	07 05	16 39	17 39	18 44	19 52
40	06 15	06 49	07 19	16 27	17 27	18 33	19 43
45	06 25	07 02	07 36	16 14	17 14	18 21	19 33
S 50	06 37	07 18	07 56	15 57	16 57	18 05	19 20
52	06 42	07 25	08 06	15 49	16 49	17 58	19 14
54	06 47	07 33	08 17	15 40	16 40	17 50	19 07
56	06 53	07 42	08 30	15 31	16 30	17 41	19 00
58	07 00	07 53	08 44	15 20	16 19	17 31	18 52
S 60	07 07	08 04	09 01	15 07	16 06	17 19	18 42

Sunset / Twilight / Moonset

Lat.	Sunset	Civil	Naut.	12	13	14	15
°	h m	h m	h m	h m	h m	h m	h m
N 72	▭	▭	▭	■	■	■	03 17
N 70	▭	▭	▭	00 36	01 03	02 20	04 12
68	▭	▭	▭	01 17	01 58	03 09	04 45
66	▭	▭	▭	01 46	02 31	03 40	05 09
64	22 26	////	////	02 08	02 56	04 04	05 28
62	21 49	////	////	02 25	03 15	04 22	05 43
60	21 23	23 05	////	02 40	03 31	04 37	05 56
N 58	21 03	22 18	////	02 52	03 44	04 50	06 07
56	20 47	21 49	////	03 03	03 56	05 01	06 17
54	20 33	21 27	23 10	03 12	04 06	05 11	06 25
52	20 21	21 09	22 26	03 21	04 15	05 20	06 33
50	20 11	20 54	21 59	03 28	04 23	05 28	06 40
45	19 48	20 25	21 14	03 45	04 40	05 44	06 54
N 40	19 30	20 02	20 44	03 58	04 55	05 58	07 06
35	19 15	19 44	20 21	04 09	05 06	06 09	07 16
30	19 02	19 29	20 03	04 19	05 17	06 19	07 25
20	18 40	19 05	19 34	04 36	05 35	06 37	07 40
N 10	18 21	18 44	19 11	04 51	05 50	06 52	07 54
0	18 04	18 26	18 52	05 05	06 05	07 06	08 06
S 10	17 46	18 09	18 36	05 19	06 19	07 20	08 18
20	17 28	17 52	18 19	05 34	06 35	07 34	08 31
30	17 07	17 33	18 03	05 51	06 53	07 51	08 46
35	16 55	17 23	17 55	06 01	07 03	08 01	08 54
40	16 41	17 11	17 45	06 13	07 15	08 12	09 04
45	16 24	16 58	17 35	06 26	07 29	08 26	09 16
S 50	16 04	16 42	17 23	06 42	07 46	08 42	09 29
52	15 54	16 35	17 18	06 50	07 54	08 49	09 36
54	15 43	16 26	17 13	06 58	08 02	08 57	09 43
56	15 30	16 17	17 06	07 08	08 12	09 07	09 50
58	15 16	16 07	17 00	07 19	08 24	09 17	09 59
S 60	14 59	15 56	16 52	07 31	08 37	09 29	10 09

SUN and MOON

Day	Eqn. of Time 00h	Eqn. of Time 12h	Mer. Pass.	Mer. Pass. Upper	Mer. Pass. Lower	Age	Phase
d	m s	m s	h m	h m	h m	d	%
12	00 16	00 10	12 00	23 51	11 21	15	99
13	00 04	00 03	12 00	24 51	12 21	16	100
14	00 09	00 15	12 00	00 51	13 22	17	97

UT	ARIES GHA	VENUS −3.9 GHA	Dec	MARS −0.2 GHA	Dec	JUPITER −1.8 GHA	Dec	SATURN +0.3 GHA	Dec	STARS Name	SHA	Dec
15 00	263 12.1	215 13.8	N15 54.8	71 21.8	S 5 10.6	148 06.3	N21 47.0	37 19.6	S14 46.3	Acamar	315 18.2	S40 14.8
01	278 14.6	230 13.3	55.7	86 23.7	11.0	163 08.2	46.9	52 22.2	46.3	Achernar	335 26.7	S57 09.6
02	293 17.1	245 12.8	56.5	101 25.5	11.3	178 10.2	46.8	67 24.8	46.3	Acrux	173 08.2	S63 11.1
03	308 19.5	260 12.4	.. 57.3	116 27.4	.. 11.6	193 12.1	.. 46.7	82 27.4	.. 46.3	Adhara	255 12.3	S28 59.8
04	323 22.0	275 11.9	58.2	131 29.2	12.0	208 14.0	46.6	97 30.0	46.2	Aldebaran	290 48.9	N16 32.1
05	338 24.4	290 11.4	59.0	146 31.1	12.3	223 15.9	46.6	112 32.6	46.2			
06	353 26.9	305 10.9	N15 59.8	161 32.9	S 5 12.7	238 17.8	N21 46.5	127 35.2	S14 46.2	Alioth	166 20.0	N55 53.1
07	8 29.4	320 10.4	16 00.7	176 34.7	13.0	253 19.7	46.4	142 37.8	46.1	Alkaid	152 58.2	N49 14.7
08	23 31.8	335 09.9	01.5	191 36.6	13.3	268 21.6	46.3	157 40.4	46.1	Al Na'ir	27 42.7	S46 53.1
S 09	38 34.3	350 09.4	.. 02.3	206 38.4	.. 13.7	283 23.5	.. 46.2	172 43.0	.. 46.1	Alnilam	275 46.0	S 1 11.8
U 10	53 36.8	5 09.0	03.2	221 40.3	14.0	298 25.4	46.1	187 45.6	46.1	Alphard	217 55.6	S 8 43.5
N 11	68 39.2	20 08.5	04.0	236 42.1	14.4	313 27.4	46.1	202 48.2	46.0			
D 12	83 41.7	35 08.0	N16 04.8	251 43.9	S 5 14.7	328 29.3	N21 46.0	217 50.8	S14 46.0	Alphecca	126 10.1	N26 40.2
A 13	98 44.2	50 07.5	05.6	266 45.8	15.0	343 31.2	45.9	232 53.4	46.0	Alpheratz	357 42.8	N29 10.1
Y 14	113 46.6	65 07.0	06.5	281 47.6	15.4	358 33.1	45.8	247 56.0	46.0	Altair	62 07.3	N 8 54.6
15	128 49.1	80 06.5	.. 07.3	296 49.4	.. 15.7	13 35.0	.. 45.7	262 58.6	.. 45.9	Ankaa	353 15.2	S42 13.4
16	143 51.6	95 06.0	08.1	311 51.3	16.1	28 36.9	45.6	278 01.2	45.9	Antares	112 25.0	S26 27.7
17	158 54.0	110 05.5	08.9	326 53.1	16.4	43 38.8	45.5	293 03.7	45.9			
18	173 56.5	125 05.0	N16 09.8	341 54.9	S 5 16.7	58 40.7	N21 45.5	308 06.3	S14 45.8	Arcturus	145 54.9	N19 06.6
19	188 58.9	140 04.6	10.6	356 56.8	17.1	73 42.6	45.4	323 08.9	45.8	Atria	107 25.6	S69 03.1
20	204 01.4	155 04.1	11.4	11 58.6	17.4	88 44.6	45.3	338 11.5	45.8	Avior	234 18.2	S59 33.7
21	219 03.9	170 03.6	.. 12.2	27 00.4	.. 17.8	103 46.5	.. 45.2	353 14.1	.. 45.8	Bellatrix	278 31.6	N 6 21.5
22	234 06.3	185 03.1	13.1	42 02.2	18.1	118 48.4	45.1	8 16.7	45.7	Betelgeuse	271 00.9	N 7 24.4
23	249 08.8	200 02.6	13.9	57 04.1	18.4	133 50.3	45.0	23 19.3	45.7			
16 00	264 11.3	215 02.1	N16 14.7	72 05.9	S 5 18.8	148 52.2	N21 44.9	38 21.9	S14 45.7	Canopus	263 56.4	S52 42.5
01	279 13.7	230 01.6	15.5	87 07.7	19.1	163 54.1	44.9	53 24.5	45.6	Capella	280 33.9	N46 00.5
02	294 16.2	245 01.1	16.3	102 09.5	19.5	178 56.0	44.8	68 27.1	45.6	Deneb	49 30.6	N45 19.9
03	309 18.7	260 00.6	.. 17.2	117 11.4	.. 19.8	193 57.9	.. 44.7	83 29.7	.. 45.6	Denebola	182 33.0	N14 29.5
04	324 21.1	275 00.1	18.0	132 13.2	20.2	208 59.8	44.6	98 32.3	45.6	Diphda	348 55.3	S17 54.3
05	339 23.6	289 59.6	18.8	147 15.0	20.5	224 01.8	44.5	113 34.9	45.5			
06	354 26.1	304 59.1	N16 19.6	162 16.8	S 5 20.9	239 03.7	N21 44.4	128 37.5	S14 45.5	Dubhe	193 51.1	N61 40.6
07	9 28.5	319 58.6	20.4	177 18.7	21.2	254 05.6	44.3	143 40.1	45.5	Elnath	278 12.1	N28 36.9
08	24 31.0	334 58.1	21.2	192 20.5	21.5	269 07.5	44.2	158 42.7	45.4	Eltanin	90 45.3	N51 29.4
M 09	39 33.4	349 57.6	.. 22.1	207 22.3	.. 21.9	284 09.4	.. 44.2	173 45.3	.. 45.4	Enif	33 46.3	N 9 56.6
O 10	54 35.9	4 57.1	22.9	222 24.1	22.2	299 11.3	44.1	188 47.9	45.4	Fomalhaut	15 23.2	S29 32.5
N 11	69 38.4	19 56.6	23.7	237 25.9	22.6	314 13.2	44.0	203 50.4	45.4			
D 12	84 40.8	34 56.1	N16 24.5	252 27.7	S 5 22.9	329 15.1	N21 43.9	218 53.0	S14 45.3	Gacrux	171 59.9	S57 11.9
A 13	99 43.3	49 55.6	25.3	267 29.6	23.3	344 17.0	43.8	233 55.6	45.3	Gienah	175 51.5	S17 37.5
Y 14	114 45.8	64 55.1	26.1	282 31.4	23.6	359 18.9	43.7	248 58.2	45.3	Hadar	148 46.4	S60 26.7
15	129 48.2	79 54.6	.. 26.9	297 33.2	.. 24.0	14 20.9	.. 43.6	264 00.8	.. 45.3	Hamal	328 00.2	N23 31.7
16	144 50.7	94 54.1	27.7	312 35.0	24.3	29 22.8	43.6	279 03.4	45.2	Kaus Aust.	83 42.5	S34 22.4
17	159 53.2	109 53.6	28.6	327 36.8	24.7	44 24.7	43.5	294 06.0	45.2			
18	174 55.6	124 53.1	N16 29.4	342 38.6	S 5 25.0	59 26.6	N21 43.4	309 08.6	S14 45.2	Kochab	137 19.3	N74 06.1
19	189 58.1	139 52.6	30.2	357 40.4	25.4	74 28.5	43.3	324 11.2	45.1	Markab	13 37.6	N15 17.0
20	205 00.6	154 52.1	31.0	12 42.2	25.7	89 30.4	43.2	339 13.8	45.1	Menkar	314 14.6	N 4 08.6
21	220 03.0	169 51.6	.. 31.8	27 44.1	.. 26.1	104 32.3	.. 43.1	354 16.4	.. 45.1	Menkent	148 06.5	S36 26.6
22	235 05.5	184 51.1	32.6	42 45.9	26.4	119 34.2	43.0	9 19.0	45.1	Miaplacidus	221 40.0	S69 47.0
23	250 07.9	199 50.6	33.4	57 47.7	26.7	134 36.1	42.9	24 21.6	45.0			
17 00	265 10.4	214 50.1	N16 34.2	72 49.5	S 5 27.1	149 38.0	N21 42.9	39 24.2	S14 45.0	Mirfak	308 39.7	N49 54.5
01	280 12.9	229 49.6	35.0	87 51.3	27.4	164 39.9	42.8	54 26.7	45.0	Nunki	75 57.1	S26 16.5
02	295 15.3	244 49.1	35.8	102 53.1	27.8	179 41.9	42.7	69 29.3	45.0	Peacock	53 17.8	S56 40.9
03	310 17.8	259 48.6	.. 36.6	117 54.9	.. 28.1	194 43.8	.. 42.6	84 31.9	.. 44.9	Pollux	243 27.2	N27 59.3
04	325 20.3	274 48.1	37.4	132 56.7	28.5	209 45.7	42.5	99 34.5	44.9	Procyon	244 59.3	N 5 11.1
05	340 22.7	289 47.6	38.2	147 58.5	28.9	224 47.6	42.4	114 37.1	44.9			
06	355 25.2	304 47.0	N16 39.0	163 00.3	S 5 29.2	239 49.5	N21 42.3	129 39.7	S14 44.8	Rasalhague	96 05.5	N12 33.2
07	10 27.7	319 46.5	39.8	178 02.1	29.6	254 51.4	42.3	144 42.3	44.8	Regulus	207 42.9	N11 53.7
08	25 30.1	334 46.0	40.6	193 03.9	29.9	269 53.3	42.2	159 44.9	44.8	Rigel	281 11.7	S 8 11.3
T 09	40 32.6	349 45.5	.. 41.4	208 05.7	.. 30.3	284 55.2	.. 42.1	174 47.5	.. 44.8	Rigil Kent.	139 50.2	S60 53.8
U 10	55 35.0	4 45.0	42.2	223 07.5	30.6	299 57.1	42.0	189 50.1	44.7	Sabik	102 11.4	S15 44.4
E 11	70 37.5	19 44.5	43.0	238 09.3	31.0	314 59.0	41.9	204 52.7	44.7			
S 12	85 40.0	34 44.0	N16 43.8	253 11.1	S 5 31.3	330 00.9	N21 41.8	219 55.2	S14 44.7	Schedar	349 39.8	N56 36.7
D 13	100 42.4	49 43.5	44.6	268 12.9	31.7	345 02.8	41.7	234 57.8	44.7	Shaula	96 20.5	S37 06.7
A 14	115 44.9	64 43.0	45.4	283 14.7	32.0	0 04.8	41.6	250 00.4	44.6	Sirius	258 33.4	S16 44.4
Y 15	130 47.4	79 42.4	.. 46.2	298 16.5	.. 32.4	15 06.7	.. 41.6	265 03.0	.. 44.6	Spica	158 30.4	S11 14.2
16	145 49.8	94 41.9	47.0	313 18.3	32.7	30 08.6	41.5	280 05.6	44.6	Suhail	222 52.2	S43 29.8
17	160 52.3	109 41.4	47.8	328 20.1	33.1	45 10.5	41.4	295 08.2	44.6			
18	175 54.8	124 40.9	N16 48.6	343 21.9	S 5 33.4	60 12.4	N21 41.3	310 10.8	S14 44.5	Vega	80 38.1	N38 48.0
19	190 57.2	139 40.4	49.4	358 23.6	33.8	75 14.3	41.2	325 13.4	44.5	Zuben'ubi	137 04.4	S16 06.1
20	205 59.7	154 39.9	50.2	13 25.4	34.1	90 16.2	41.1	340 16.0	44.5			
21	221 02.2	169 39.4	.. 51.0	28 27.2	.. 34.5	105 18.1	.. 41.0	355 18.6	.. 44.5		SHA	Mer. Pass.
22	236 04.6	184 38.8	51.8	43 29.0	34.9	120 20.0	40.9	10 21.1	44.4	Venus	310 50.8	9 40
23	251 07.1	199 38.3	52.6	58 30.8	35.2	135 21.9	40.9	25 23.7	44.4	Mars	167 54.6	19 09
	h m									Jupiter	244 40.9	14 03
Mer. Pass. 6 22.2	v −0.5 d 0.8	v 1.8 d 0.3		v 1.9 d 0.1		v 2.6 d 0.0				Saturn	134 10.6	21 23

UT	SUN GHA	SUN Dec	MOON GHA	v	MOON Dec	d	HP
d h	° ′	° ′	° ′	′	° ′	′	′
15 00	179 54.6	N23 17.5	333 12.1	5.1	S17 04.7	5.6	60.6
01	194 54.4	17.6	347 36.2	5.1	16 59.1	5.7	60.6
02	209 54.3	17.7	2 00.3	5.1	16 53.4	5.8	60.6
03	224 54.2	. . 17.8	16 24.4	5.2	16 47.6	5.9	60.6
04	239 54.0	17.9	30 48.6	5.2	16 41.7	6.0	60.6
05	254 53.9	18.1	45 12.8	5.3	16 35.7	6.2	60.6
06	269 53.8	N23 18.2	59 37.1	5.3	S16 29.5	6.3	60.6
07	284 53.6	18.3	74 01.4	5.3	16 23.2	6.3	60.6
08	299 53.5	18.4	88 25.7	5.4	16 16.9	6.5	60.6
S 09	314 53.4	. . 18.5	102 50.1	5.5	16 10.4	6.6	60.6
U 10	329 53.2	18.6	117 14.6	5.4	16 03.8	6.7	60.6
N 11	344 53.1	18.7	131 39.0	5.6	15 57.1	6.9	60.6
D 12	359 53.0	N23 18.8	146 03.6	5.6	S15 50.2	6.9	60.5
A 13	14 52.8	18.9	160 28.2	5.6	15 43.3	7.0	60.5
Y 14	29 52.7	19.0	174 52.8	5.7	15 36.3	7.2	60.5
15	44 52.6	. . 19.1	189 17.5	5.7	15 29.1	7.2	60.5
16	59 52.4	19.2	203 42.2	5.8	15 21.9	7.4	60.5
17	74 52.3	19.3	218 07.0	5.9	15 14.5	7.4	60.5
18	89 52.2	N23 19.4	232 31.9	5.9	S15 07.1	7.6	60.5
19	104 52.0	19.5	246 56.8	5.9	14 59.5	7.6	60.5
20	119 51.9	19.6	261 21.7	6.1	14 51.9	7.8	60.5
21	134 51.8	. . 19.7	275 46.8	6.0	14 44.1	7.8	60.5
22	149 51.6	19.8	290 11.8	6.2	14 36.3	8.0	60.5
23	164 51.5	19.9	304 37.0	6.1	14 28.3	8.0	60.5
16 00	179 51.4	N23 20.0	319 02.1	6.3	S14 20.3	8.1	60.5
01	194 51.2	20.1	333 27.4	6.3	14 12.2	8.3	60.5
02	209 51.1	20.2	347 52.7	6.3	14 03.9	8.3	60.5
03	224 51.0	. . 20.2	2 18.0	6.5	13 55.6	8.4	60.4
04	239 50.8	20.3	16 43.5	6.4	13 47.2	8.5	60.4
05	254 50.7	20.4	31 08.9	6.6	13 38.7	8.6	60.4
06	269 50.6	N23 20.5	45 34.5	6.6	S13 30.1	8.7	60.4
07	284 50.4	20.6	60 00.1	6.6	13 21.4	8.7	60.4
08	299 50.3	20.7	74 25.7	6.7	13 12.7	8.9	60.4
M 09	314 50.2	. . 20.8	88 51.4	6.8	13 03.8	8.9	60.4
O 10	329 50.0	20.9	103 17.2	6.9	12 54.9	9.0	60.4
N 11	344 49.9	21.0	117 43.1	6.9	12 45.9	9.1	60.4
D 12	359 49.8	N23 21.0	132 09.0	6.9	S12 36.8	9.1	60.3
A 13	14 49.6	21.1	146 34.9	7.0	12 27.7	9.2	60.3
Y 14	29 49.5	21.2	161 00.9	7.1	12 18.5	9.4	60.3
15	44 49.4	. . 21.3	175 27.0	7.2	12 09.1	9.3	60.3
16	59 49.2	21.4	189 53.2	7.2	11 59.8	9.5	60.3
17	74 49.1	21.5	204 19.4	7.3	11 50.3	9.5	60.3
18	89 49.0	N23 21.6	218 45.7	7.3	S11 40.8	9.6	60.3
19	104 48.8	21.6	233 12.0	7.4	11 31.2	9.7	60.2
20	119 48.7	21.7	247 38.4	7.4	11 21.5	9.7	60.2
21	134 48.6	. . 21.8	262 04.8	7.6	11 11.8	9.8	60.2
22	149 48.4	21.9	276 31.4	7.5	11 02.0	9.9	60.2
23	164 48.3	21.9	290 57.9	7.7	10 52.1	9.9	60.2
17 00	179 48.2	N23 22.0	305 24.6	7.7	S10 42.2	10.0	60.2
01	194 48.0	22.1	319 51.3	7.8	10 32.2	10.1	60.1
02	209 47.9	22.2	334 18.1	7.8	10 22.1	10.1	60.1
03	224 47.8	. . 22.2	348 44.9	7.9	10 12.0	10.1	60.1
04	239 47.6	22.3	3 11.8	7.9	10 01.9	10.2	60.1
05	254 47.5	22.4	17 38.7	8.0	9 51.7	10.3	60.1
06	269 47.3	N23 22.5	32 05.7	8.1	S 9 41.4	10.3	60.1
07	284 47.2	22.5	46 32.8	8.1	9 31.1	10.4	60.0
08	299 47.1	22.6	60 59.9	8.2	9 20.7	10.5	60.0
T 09	314 46.9	. . 22.7	75 27.1	8.2	9 10.2	10.4	60.0
U 10	329 46.8	22.7	89 54.3	8.3	8 59.8	10.6	60.0
E 11	344 46.7	22.8	104 21.6	8.4	8 49.2	10.5	60.0
S 12	359 46.5	N23 22.9	118 49.0	8.4	S 8 38.7	10.7	59.9
D 13	14 46.4	22.9	133 16.4	8.5	8 28.0	10.6	59.9
A 14	29 46.3	23.0	147 43.9	8.6	8 17.4	10.7	59.9
Y 15	44 46.1	. . 23.1	162 11.5	8.5	8 06.7	10.8	59.9
16	59 46.0	23.1	176 39.0	8.7	7 55.9	10.8	59.9
17	74 45.9	23.2	191 06.7	8.7	7 45.1	10.8	59.8
18	89 45.7	N23 23.3	205 34.4	8.8	S 7 34.3	10.9	59.8
19	104 45.6	23.3	220 02.2	8.8	7 23.4	10.9	59.8
20	119 45.5	23.4	234 30.0	8.9	7 12.5	10.9	59.8
21	134 45.3	. . 23.5	248 57.9	8.9	7 01.6	11.0	59.8
22	149 45.2	23.5	263 25.8	9.0	6 50.6	11.0	59.7
23	164 45.1	23.6	277 53.8	9.0	S 6 39.6	11.0	59.7
	SD 15.8	d 0.1	SD 16.5		16.4		16.3

Lat.	Twilight Naut.	Twilight Civil	Sunrise	Moonrise 15	Moonrise 16	Moonrise 17	Moonrise 18
°	h m	h m	h m	h m	h m	h m	h m
N 72	▢	▢	▢	00 37	00 15	{ 00 03 / 23 55 }	23 47
N 70	▢	▢	▢	23 45	23 46	23 45	23 44
68	▢	▢	▢	23 23	23 32	23 38	23 42
66	▢	▢	▢	23 05	23 20	23 31	23 40
64	////	////	01 33	22 51	23 11	23 26	23 38
62	////	////	02 10	22 39	23 02	23 21	23 37
60	////	00 52	02 36	22 29	22 55	23 17	23 35
N 58	////	01 41	02 56	22 20	22 49	23 13	23 34
56	////	02 11	03 13	22 12	22 43	23 10	23 33
54	00 48	02 33	03 27	22 05	22 38	23 07	23 32
52	01 33	02 51	03 39	21 58	22 34	23 04	23 31
50	02 00	03 06	03 50	21 53	22 29	23 01	23 30
45	02 46	03 35	04 13	21 40	22 20	22 56	23 29
N 40	03 16	03 58	04 31	21 30	22 13	22 52	23 27
35	03 39	04 16	04 46	21 21	22 06	22 48	23 26
30	03 58	04 31	04 59	21 13	22 01	22 44	23 25
20	04 27	04 56	05 21	21 00	21 51	22 38	23 23
N 10	04 49	05 16	05 39	20 48	21 42	22 33	23 21
0	05 08	05 34	05 57	20 37	21 34	22 28	23 20
S 10	05 25	05 52	06 14	20 26	21 25	22 23	23 18
20	05 41	06 09	06 33	20 14	21 17	22 18	23 17
30	05 58	06 28	06 54	20 00	21 06	22 12	23 15
35	06 07	06 38	07 06	19 52	21 01	22 08	23 14
40	06 16	06 50	07 20	19 43	20 54	22 04	23 13
45	06 26	07 03	07 37	19 33	20 46	22 00	23 11
S 50	06 38	07 19	07 58	19 20	20 37	21 54	23 10
52	06 43	07 27	08 08	19 14	20 33	21 52	23 09
54	06 49	07 35	08 19	19 07	20 28	21 49	23 08
56	06 55	07 44	08 31	19 00	20 23	21 46	23 07
58	07 02	07 54	08 46	18 52	20 17	21 42	23 06
S 60	07 09	08 06	09 04	18 42	20 10	21 38	23 05

Lat.	Sunset	Twilight Civil	Twilight Naut.	Moonset 15	Moonset 16	Moonset 17	Moonset 18
°	h m	h m	h m	h m	h m	h m	h m
N 72	▢	▢	▢	03 17	05 42	07 51	09 51
N 70	▢	▢	▢	04 12	06 11	08 07	09 58
68	▢	▢	▢	04 45	06 32	08 19	10 04
66	▢	▢	▢	05 09	06 48	08 29	10 09
64	22 30	////	////	05 28	07 02	08 38	10 13
62	21 52	////	////	05 43	07 13	08 45	10 16
60	21 26	23 10	////	05 56	07 23	08 51	10 19
N 58	21 05	22 21	////	06 07	07 31	08 57	10 22
56	20 49	21 51	////	06 17	07 38	09 02	10 24
54	20 34	21 29	23 15	06 25	07 45	09 06	10 26
52	20 22	21 11	22 29	06 33	07 51	09 10	10 28
50	20 11	20 56	22 01	06 40	07 56	09 13	10 30
45	19 49	20 26	21 16	06 54	08 07	09 21	10 34
N 40	19 31	20 04	20 45	07 06	08 16	09 27	10 37
35	19 16	19 46	20 22	07 16	08 25	09 33	10 40
30	19 03	19 30	20 04	07 25	08 32	09 38	10 42
20	18 41	19 05	19 35	07 40	08 44	09 46	10 46
N 10	18 22	18 45	19 12	07 54	08 54	09 53	10 50
0	18 04	18 27	18 53	08 06	09 04	10 00	10 53
S 10	17 47	18 10	18 36	08 18	09 14	10 06	10 56
20	17 28	17 52	18 20	08 31	09 24	10 13	11 00
30	17 07	17 34	18 04	08 46	09 36	10 21	11 03
35	16 55	17 23	17 55	08 54	09 42	10 26	11 06
40	16 41	17 11	17 45	09 04	09 50	10 31	11 08
45	16 24	16 58	17 37	09 16	09 59	10 37	11 11
S 50	16 03	16 42	17 23	09 29	10 09	10 44	11 14
52	15 54	16 34	17 18	09 36	10 14	10 47	11 16
54	15 42	16 26	17 12	09 43	10 20	10 51	11 17
56	15 30	16 17	17 06	09 51	10 26	10 54	11 19
58	15 15	16 07	17 00	09 59	10 32	10 59	11 21
S 60	14 58	15 55	16 52	10 09	10 40	11 04	11 24

	SUN			MOON			
Day	Eqn. of Time 00ʰ	Eqn. of Time 12ʰ	Mer. Pass.	Mer. Pass. Upper	Mer. Pass. Lower	Age	Phase
d	m s	m s	h m	h m	h m	d	%
15	00 21	00 28	12 00	01 52	14 21	18	92
16	00 34	00 41	12 01	02 50	15 19	19	85
17	00 47	00 54	12 01	03 47	16 14	20	75

UT	ARIES GHA	VENUS −3.9 GHA	VENUS Dec	MARS −0.2 GHA	MARS Dec	JUPITER −1.8 GHA	JUPITER Dec	SATURN +0.3 GHA	SATURN Dec	STARS Name	SHA	Dec
18 00	266 09.5	214 37.8	N16 53.3	73 32.6	S 5 35.6	150 23.8	N21 40.8	40 26.3	S14 44.4	Acamar	315 18.2	S40 14.8
01	281 12.0	229 37.3	54.1	88 34.4	35.9	165 25.7	40.7	55 28.9	44.3	Achernar	335 26.6	S57 09.6
02	296 14.5	244 36.8	54.9	103 36.2	36.3	180 27.6	40.6	70 31.5	44.3	Acrux	173 08.2	S63 11.1
03	311 16.9	259 36.2	.. 55.7	118 37.9	.. 36.6	195 29.6	.. 40.5	85 34.1	.. 44.3	Adhara	255 12.3	S28 59.8
04	326 19.4	274 35.7	56.5	133 39.7	37.0	210 31.5	40.4	100 36.7	44.3	Aldebaran	290 48.9	N16 32.1
05	341 21.9	289 35.2	57.3	148 41.5	37.4	225 33.4	40.3	115 39.3	44.2			
W 06	356 24.3	304 34.7	N16 58.1	163 43.3	S 5 37.7	240 35.3	N21 40.2	130 41.8	S14 44.2	Alioth	166 20.0	N55 53.1
E 07	11 26.8	319 34.2	58.9	178 45.1	38.1	255 37.2	40.1	145 44.4	44.2	Alkaid	152 58.2	N49 14.7
D 08	26 29.3	334 33.6	16 59.6	193 46.9	38.4	270 39.1	40.1	160 47.0	44.2	Al Na'ir	27 42.7	S46 53.1
N 09	41 31.7	349 33.1	17 00.4	208 48.6	.. 38.8	285 41.0	.. 40.0	175 49.6	.. 44.1	Alnilam	275 46.0	S 1 11.8
E 10	56 34.2	4 32.6	01.2	223 50.4	39.1	300 42.9	39.9	190 52.2	44.1	Alphard	217 55.6	S 8 43.5
S 11	71 36.7	19 32.1	02.0	238 52.2	39.5	315 44.8	39.8	205 54.8	44.1			
D 12	86 39.1	34 31.6	N17 02.8	253 54.0	S 5 39.9	330 46.7	N21 39.7	220 57.4	S14 44.1	Alphecca	126 10.1	N26 40.2
A 13	101 41.6	49 31.0	03.6	268 55.8	40.2	345 48.6	39.6	236 00.0	44.0	Alpheratz	357 42.8	N29 10.1
Y 14	116 44.0	64 30.5	04.3	283 57.5	40.6	0 50.5	39.5	251 02.5	44.0	Altair	62 07.3	N 8 54.6
15	131 46.5	79 30.0	.. 05.1	298 59.3	.. 40.9	15 52.4	.. 39.4	266 05.1	.. 44.0	Ankaa	353 15.1	S42 13.4
16	146 49.0	94 29.5	05.9	314 01.1	41.3	30 54.3	39.3	281 07.7	44.0	Antares	112 25.0	S26 27.7
17	161 51.4	109 28.9	06.7	329 02.9	41.7	45 56.2	39.3	296 10.3	43.9			
18	176 53.9	124 28.4	N17 07.4	344 04.6	S 5 42.0	60 58.2	N21 39.2	311 12.9	S14 43.9	Arcturus	145 54.9	N19 06.6
19	191 56.4	139 27.9	08.2	359 06.4	42.4	76 00.1	39.1	326 15.5	43.9	Atria	107 25.6	S69 03.1
20	206 58.8	154 27.3	09.0	14 08.2	42.7	91 02.0	39.0	341 18.1	43.9	Avior	234 18.2	S59 33.7
21	222 01.3	169 26.8	.. 09.8	29 09.9	.. 43.1	106 03.9	.. 38.9	356 20.7	.. 43.8	Bellatrix	278 31.6	N 6 21.6
22	237 03.8	184 26.3	10.6	44 11.7	43.5	121 05.8	38.8	11 23.2	43.8	Betelgeuse	271 00.9	N 7 24.4
23	252 06.2	199 25.8	11.3	59 13.5	43.8	136 07.7	38.7	26 25.8	43.8			
19 00	267 08.7	214 25.2	N17 12.1	74 15.2	S 5 44.2	151 09.6	N21 38.6	41 28.4	S14 43.8	Canopus	263 56.4	S52 42.4
01	282 11.1	229 24.7	12.9	89 17.0	44.6	166 11.5	38.5	56 31.0	43.7	Capella	280 33.9	N46 00.5
02	297 13.6	244 24.2	13.6	104 18.8	44.9	181 13.4	38.5	71 33.6	43.7	Deneb	49 30.6	N45 19.9
03	312 16.1	259 23.6	.. 14.4	119 20.5	.. 45.3	196 15.3	.. 38.4	86 36.2	.. 43.7	Denebola	182 33.0	N14 29.5
04	327 18.5	274 23.1	15.2	134 22.3	45.6	211 17.2	38.3	101 38.7	43.7	Diphda	348 55.3	S17 54.3
05	342 21.0	289 22.6	16.0	149 24.1	46.0	226 19.1	38.2	116 41.3	43.6			
T 06	357 23.5	304 22.0	N17 16.7	164 25.8	S 5 46.4	241 21.0	N21 38.1	131 43.9	S14 43.6	Dubhe	193 51.1	N61 40.6
H 07	12 25.9	319 21.5	17.5	179 27.6	46.7	256 22.9	38.0	146 46.5	43.6	Elnath	278 12.1	N28 36.9
U 08	27 28.4	334 21.0	18.3	194 29.4	47.1	271 24.8	37.9	161 49.1	43.6	Eltanin	90 45.3	N51 29.4
R 09	42 30.9	349 20.4	.. 19.0	209 31.1	.. 47.5	286 26.7	.. 37.8	176 51.7	.. 43.5	Enif	33 46.2	N 9 56.6
S 10	57 33.3	4 19.9	19.8	224 32.9	47.8	301 28.6	37.7	191 54.3	43.5	Fomalhaut	15 23.2	S29 32.5
D 11	72 35.8	19 19.4	20.6	239 34.6	48.2	316 30.5	37.7	206 56.8	43.5			
A 12	87 38.3	34 18.8	N17 21.3	254 36.4	S 5 48.6	331 32.4	N21 37.6	221 59.4	S14 43.5	Gacrux	171 59.9	S57 12.0
Y 13	102 40.7	49 18.3	22.1	269 38.2	48.9	346 34.4	37.5	237 02.0	43.4	Gienah	175 51.5	S17 37.5
14	117 43.2	64 17.8	22.9	284 39.9	49.3	1 36.3	37.4	252 04.6	43.4	Hadar	148 46.4	S60 26.7
15	132 45.6	79 17.2	.. 23.6	299 41.7	.. 49.7	16 38.2	.. 37.3	267 07.2	.. 43.4	Hamal	328 00.1	N23 31.7
16	147 48.1	94 16.7	24.4	314 43.4	50.0	31 40.1	37.2	282 09.8	43.4	Kaus Aust.	83 42.5	S34 22.4
17	162 50.6	109 16.2	25.1	329 45.2	50.4	46 42.0	37.1	297 12.3	43.3			
18	177 53.0	124 15.6	N17 25.9	344 46.9	S 5 50.8	61 43.9	N21 37.0	312 14.9	S14 43.3	Kochab	137 19.4	N74 06.1
19	192 55.5	139 15.1	26.7	359 48.7	51.1	76 45.8	36.9	327 17.5	43.3	Markab	13 37.5	N15 17.0
20	207 58.0	154 14.5	27.4	14 50.4	51.5	91 47.7	36.8	342 20.1	43.3	Menkar	314 14.6	N 4 08.6
21	223 00.4	169 14.0	.. 28.2	29 52.2	.. 51.9	106 49.6	.. 36.8	357 22.7	.. 43.2	Menkent	148 06.5	S36 26.6
22	238 02.9	184 13.5	28.9	44 53.9	52.2	121 51.5	36.7	12 25.3	43.2	Miaplacidus	221 40.0	S69 47.0
23	253 05.4	199 12.9	29.7	59 55.7	52.6	136 53.4	36.6	27 27.8	43.2			
20 00	268 07.8	214 12.4	N17 30.5	74 57.4	S 5 53.0	151 55.3	N21 36.5	42 30.4	S14 43.2	Mirfak	308 39.7	N49 54.4
01	283 10.3	229 11.8	31.2	89 59.2	53.3	166 57.2	36.4	57 33.0	43.1	Nunki	75 57.1	S26 16.5
02	298 12.8	244 11.3	32.0	105 00.9	53.7	181 59.1	36.3	72 35.6	43.1	Peacock	53 17.7	S56 40.9
03	313 15.2	259 10.8	.. 32.7	120 02.7	.. 54.1	197 01.0	.. 36.2	87 38.2	.. 43.1	Pollux	243 27.2	N27 59.3
04	328 17.7	274 10.2	33.5	135 04.4	54.5	212 02.9	36.1	102 40.8	43.1	Procyon	244 59.3	N 5 11.1
05	343 20.1	289 09.7	34.2	150 06.2	54.8	227 04.8	36.0	117 43.3	43.1			
F 06	358 22.6	304 09.1	N17 35.0	165 07.9	S 5 55.2	242 06.7	N21 35.9	132 45.9	S14 43.0	Rasalhague	96 05.5	N12 33.2
R 07	13 25.1	319 08.6	35.7	180 09.7	55.6	257 08.6	35.9	147 48.5	43.0	Regulus	207 42.9	N11 53.7
I 08	28 27.5	334 08.0	36.5	195 11.4	55.9	272 10.5	35.8	162 51.1	43.0	Rigel	281 11.7	S 8 11.3
D 09	43 30.0	349 07.5	.. 37.2	210 13.2	.. 56.3	287 12.4	.. 35.7	177 53.7	.. 43.0	Rigil Kent.	139 50.2	S60 53.8
A 10	58 32.5	4 06.9	38.0	225 14.9	56.7	302 14.3	35.6	192 56.2	42.9	Sabik	102 11.4	S15 44.4
Y 11	73 34.9	19 06.4	38.7	240 16.6	57.0	317 16.2	35.5	207 58.8	42.9			
12	88 37.4	34 05.8	N17 39.5	255 18.4	S 5 57.4	332 18.1	N21 35.4	223 01.4	S14 42.9	Schedar	349 39.7	N56 36.7
13	103 39.9	49 05.3	40.2	270 20.1	57.8	347 20.1	35.3	238 04.0	42.9	Shaula	96 20.5	S37 06.7
14	118 42.3	64 04.8	41.0	285 21.9	58.2	2 22.0	35.2	253 06.6	42.8	Sirius	258 33.4	S16 44.4
15	133 44.8	79 04.2	.. 41.7	300 23.6	.. 58.5	17 23.9	.. 35.1	268 09.1	.. 42.8	Spica	158 30.4	S11 14.2
16	148 47.2	94 03.7	42.5	315 25.3	58.9	32 25.8	35.0	283 11.7	42.8	Suhail	222 52.5	S43 29.8
17	163 49.7	109 03.1	43.2	330 27.1	59.3	47 27.7	35.0	298 14.3	42.8			
18	178 52.2	124 02.6	N17 44.0	345 28.8	S 5 59.7	62 29.6	N21 34.9	313 16.9	S14 42.7	Vega	80 38.0	N38 48.0
19	193 54.6	139 02.0	44.7	0 30.5	6 00.0	77 31.5	34.8	328 19.5	42.7	Zuben'ubi	137 04.4	S16 06.1
20	208 57.1	154 01.5	45.4	15 32.3	00.4	92 33.4	34.7	343 22.0	42.7			
21	223 59.6	169 00.9	.. 46.2	30 34.0	.. 00.8	107 35.3	.. 34.6	358 24.6	.. 42.7			
22	239 02.0	184 00.3	46.9	45 35.7	01.2	122 37.2	34.5	13 27.2	42.7			
23	254 04.5	198 59.8	47.7	60 37.5	01.5	137 39.1	34.4	28 29.8	42.6			

		SHA	Mer. Pass.
		° ′	h m
Venus		307 16.5	9 43
Mars		167 06.6	19 01
Jupiter		244 00.9	13 54
Saturn		134 19.7	21 10

	ARIES	VENUS	MARS	JUPITER	SATURN
Mer. Pass.	6ʰ 10.4ᵐ	v −0.5 d 0.8	v 1.8 d 0.4	v 1.9 d 0.1	v 2.6 d 0.0

UT	SUN GHA	SUN Dec	MOON GHA	v	MOON Dec	d	HP
d h	° ′	° ′	° ′	′	° ′	′	′
18 00	179 44.9	N23 23.6	292 21.8	9.1	S 6 28.6	11.1	59.7
01	194 44.8	23.7	306 49.9	9.1	6 17.5	11.0	59.7
02	209 44.6	23.8	321 18.0	9.2	6 06.5	11.2	59.6
03	224 44.5 ..	23.8	335 46.2	9.3	5 55.3	11.1	59.6
04	239 44.4	23.9	350 14.5	9.3	5 44.2	11.2	59.6
05	254 44.2	23.9	4 42.8	9.3	5 33.0	11.2	59.6
W 06	269 44.1	N23 24.0	19 11.1	9.4	S 5 21.8	11.2	59.5
E 07	284 44.0	24.0	33 39.5	9.5	5 10.6	11.2	59.5
D 08	299 43.8	24.1	48 08.0	9.4	4 59.4	11.3	59.5
N 09	314 43.7 ..	24.1	62 36.4	9.6	4 48.1	11.2	59.5
E 10	329 43.6	24.2	77 05.0	9.6	4 36.9	11.3	59.5
S 11	344 43.4	24.3	91 33.6	9.6	4 25.6	11.3	59.4
D 12	359 43.3	N23 24.3	106 02.2	9.7	S 4 14.3	11.3	59.4
A 13	14 43.2	24.4	120 30.9	9.7	4 03.0	11.4	59.4
Y 14	29 43.0	24.4	134 59.6	9.8	3 51.6	11.3	59.4
15	44 42.9 ..	24.5	149 28.4	9.8	3 40.3	11.4	59.3
16	59 42.7	24.5	163 57.2	9.8	3 28.9	11.3	59.3
17	74 42.6	24.5	178 26.0	9.9	3 17.6	11.4	59.3
18	89 42.5	N23 24.6	192 54.9	10.0	S 3 06.2	11.4	59.3
19	104 42.3	24.6	207 23.9	9.9	2 54.8	11.4	59.2
20	119 42.2	24.7	221 52.8	10.1	2 43.4	11.4	59.2
21	134 42.1 ..	24.7	236 21.9	10.0	2 32.0	11.3	59.2
22	149 41.9	24.8	250 50.9	10.1	2 20.7	11.4	59.2
23	164 41.8	24.8	265 20.0	10.1	2 09.3	11.4	59.1
19 00	179 41.7	N23 24.9	279 49.1	10.2	S 1 57.9	11.4	59.1
01	194 41.5	24.9	294 18.3	10.2	1 46.5	11.5	59.1
02	209 41.4	24.9	308 47.5	10.3	1 35.0	11.3	59.0
03	224 41.3 ..	25.0	323 16.8	10.3	1 23.7	11.4	59.0
04	239 41.1	25.0	337 46.1	10.3	1 12.3	11.4	59.0
05	254 41.0	25.1	352 15.4	10.3	1 00.9	11.4	59.0
T 06	269 40.8	N23 25.1	6 44.7	10.4	S 0 49.5	11.4	58.9
H 07	284 40.7	25.1	21 14.1	10.4	0 38.1	11.4	58.9
U 08	299 40.6	25.2	35 43.5	10.5	0 26.7	11.4	58.9
R 09	314 40.4 ..	25.2	50 13.0	10.5	0 15.3	11.3	58.9
S 10	329 40.3	25.2	64 42.5	10.5	S 0 04.0	11.4	58.8
D 11	344 40.2	25.3	79 12.0	10.5	N 0 07.4	11.3	58.8
A 12	359 40.0	N23 25.3	93 41.5	10.6	N 0 18.7	11.3	58.8
Y 13	14 39.9	25.4	108 11.1	10.6	0 30.0	11.3	58.8
14	29 39.8	25.4	122 40.7	10.6	0 41.3	11.3	58.7
15	44 39.6 ..	25.4	137 10.3	10.7	0 52.6	11.3	58.7
16	59 39.5	25.4	151 40.0	10.6	1 03.9	11.3	58.7
17	74 39.3	25.5	166 09.6	10.7	1 15.2	11.2	58.7
18	89 39.2	N23 25.5	180 39.3	10.8	N 1 26.4	11.3	58.6
19	104 39.1	25.5	195 09.1	10.7	1 37.7	11.2	58.6
20	119 38.9	25.6	209 38.8	10.8	1 48.9	11.2	58.6
21	134 38.8 ..	25.6	224 08.6	10.8	2 00.1	11.1	58.5
22	149 38.7	25.6	238 38.4	10.8	2 11.2	11.2	58.5
23	164 38.5	25.6	253 08.2	10.9	2 22.4	11.1	58.5
20 00	179 38.4	N23 25.7	267 38.1	10.8	N 2 33.5	11.1	58.5
01	194 38.3	25.7	282 07.9	10.9	2 44.6	11.1	58.4
02	209 38.1	25.7	296 37.8	10.9	2 55.7	11.0	58.4
03	224 38.0 ..	25.7	311 07.7	10.9	3 06.7	11.1	58.4
04	239 37.8	25.8	325 37.6	11.0	3 17.8	11.0	58.4
05	254 37.7	25.8	340 07.6	10.9	3 28.8	10.9	58.3
F 06	269 37.6	N23 25.8	354 37.5	11.0	N 3 39.7	11.0	58.3
R 07	284 37.4	25.8	9 07.5	11.0	3 50.7	10.9	58.3
I 08	299 37.3	25.8	23 37.5	11.0	4 01.6	10.8	58.2
D 09	314 37.2 ..	25.9	38 07.5	11.0	4 12.4	10.9	58.2
A 10	329 37.0	25.9	52 37.5	11.0	4 23.3	10.8	58.2
Y 11	344 36.9	25.9	67 07.5	11.1	4 34.1	10.8	58.2
12	359 36.8	N23 25.9	81 37.6	11.0	N 4 44.9	10.7	58.1
13	14 36.6	25.9	96 07.6	11.1	4 55.6	10.7	58.1
14	29 36.5	25.9	110 37.7	11.1	5 06.3	10.7	58.1
15	44 36.3 ..	26.0	125 07.8	11.1	5 17.0	10.6	58.1
16	59 36.2	26.0	139 37.9	11.1	5 27.6	10.6	58.0
17	74 36.1	26.0	154 08.0	11.1	5 38.2	10.6	58.0
18	89 35.9	N23 26.0	168 38.1	11.1	N 5 48.8	10.5	58.0
19	104 35.8	26.0	183 08.2	11.1	5 59.3	10.4	57.9
20	119 35.7	26.0	197 38.3	11.2	6 09.7	10.5	57.9
21	134 35.5 ..	26.0	212 08.5	11.1	6 20.2	10.4	57.9
22	149 35.4	26.0	226 38.6	11.2	6 30.6	10.3	57.9
23	164 35.3	26.0	241 08.8	11.1	N 6 40.9	10.3	57.8
	SD 15.8	d 0.0	SD 16.2		16.0		15.8

Twilight / Sunrise / Moonrise

Lat.	Twilight Naut.	Twilight Civil	Sunrise	Moonrise 18	19	20	21
°	h m	h m	h m	h m	h m	h m	h m
N 72	□	□	□	23 47	23 40	23 33	23 25
N 70	□	□	□	23 44	23 43	23 42	23 42
68	□	□	□	23 42	23 46	23 50	23 55
66	□	□	□	23 40	23 48	23 56	24 06
64	////	////	01 31	23 38	23 50	24 02	00 02
62	////	////	02 09	23 37	23 51	24 06	00 06
60	////	00 50	02 36	23 35	23 53	24 11	00 11
N 58	////	01 40	02 56	23 34	23 54	24 14	00 14
56	////	02 10	03 13	23 33	23 55	24 18	00 18
54	00 45	02 33	03 27	23 32	23 56	24 21	00 21
52	01 32	02 51	03 39	23 31	23 57	24 23	00 23
50	02 00	03 06	03 50	23 30	23 58	24 26	00 26
45	02 44	03 35	04 13	23 29	24 00	00 00	00 31
N 40	03 16	03 58	04 31	23 27	24 02	00 02	00 36
35	03 39	04 16	04 46	23 26	24 03	00 03	00 40
30	03 58	04 32	04 59	23 25	24 04	00 04	00 43
20	04 27	04 56	05 21	23 23	24 07	00 07	00 49
N 10	04 50	05 17	05 40	23 21	24 09	00 09	00 55
0	05 09	05 35	05 58	23 20	24 10	00 10	01 00
S 10	05 26	05 52	06 15	23 18	24 12	00 12	01 05
20	05 42	06 10	06 34	23 17	24 14	00 14	01 11
30	05 59	06 29	06 55	23 15	24 17	00 17	01 17
35	06 07	06 39	07 07	23 14	24 18	00 18	01 21
40	06 17	06 51	07 21	23 13	24 20	00 20	01 25
45	06 27	07 04	07 38	23 11	24 21	00 21	01 30
S 50	06 39	07 21	07 59	23 10	24 24	00 24	01 36
52	06 44	07 28	08 09	23 09	24 25	00 25	01 38
54	06 50	07 36	08 20	23 08	24 26	00 26	01 41
56	06 56	07 45	08 33	23 07	24 27	00 27	01 45
58	07 03	07 56	08 48	23 06	24 28	00 28	01 48
S 60	07 10	08 07	09 05	23 05	24 30	00 30	01 53

Sunset / Twilight / Moonset

Lat.	Sunset	Twilight Civil	Twilight Naut.	Moonset 18	19	20	21
°	h m	h m	h m	h m	h m	h m	h m
N 72	□	□	□	09 51	11 46	13 38	15 29
N 70	□	□	□	09 58	11 46	13 31	15 14
68	□	□	□	10 04	11 46	13 25	15 02
66	□	□	□	10 09	11 46	13 20	14 52
64	22 32	////	////	10 13	11 46	13 16	14 44
62	21 54	////	////	10 16	11 45	13 12	14 37
60	21 27	23 14	////	10 19	11 45	13 09	14 31
N 58	21 07	22 23	////	10 22	11 45	13 06	14 25
56	20 50	21 53	////	10 24	11 45	13 04	14 21
54	20 36	21 30	23 18	10 26	11 45	13 02	14 16
52	20 23	21 12	22 31	10 28	11 45	13 00	14 13
50	20 12	20 57	22 03	10 30	11 45	12 58	14 09
45	19 50	20 30	21 17	10 34	11 45	12 54	14 02
N 40	19 32	20 05	20 46	10 37	11 45	12 51	13 55
35	19 17	19 46	20 23	10 40	11 45	12 48	13 50
30	19 04	19 31	20 05	10 42	11 45	12 46	13 45
20	18 42	19 06	19 35	10 46	11 44	12 41	13 37
N 10	18 23	18 46	19 13	10 50	11 44	12 38	13 30
0	18 05	18 28	18 54	10 53	11 44	12 34	13 24
S 10	17 48	18 10	18 37	10 56	11 44	12 31	13 17
20	17 29	17 53	18 21	11 00	11 44	12 27	13 10
30	17 08	17 34	18 04	11 03	11 43	12 22	13 02
35	16 55	17 24	17 55	11 06	11 43	12 20	12 57
40	16 41	17 12	17 46	11 08	11 43	12 17	12 52
45	16 24	16 58	17 35	11 11	11 43	12 14	12 46
S 50	16 04	16 42	17 24	11 14	11 42	12 10	12 38
52	15 54	16 35	17 18	11 16	11 42	12 08	12 35
54	15 43	16 26	17 13	11 18	11 42	12 06	12 31
56	15 30	16 17	17 07	11 19	11 42	12 04	12 27
58	15 15	16 07	17 00	11 21	11 42	12 02	12 23
S 60	14 58	15 55	16 52	11 24	11 42	11 59	12 18

SUN / MOON

Day	SUN Eqn. of Time 00h	12h	Mer. Pass.	MOON Mer. Pass. Upper	Lower	Age	Phase
d	m s	m s	h m	h m	h m	d	%
18	01 00	01 07	12 01	04 40	17 06	21	64
19	01 13	01 20	12 01	05 32	17 57	22	53
20	01 26	01 33	12 02	06 22	18 47	23	42

UT	ARIES	VENUS −3.9		MARS −0.1		JUPITER −1.8		SATURN +0.3		STARS		
	GHA	GHA	Dec	GHA	Dec	GHA	Dec	GHA	Dec	Name	SHA	Dec
d h	° ′	° ′	° ′	° ′	° ′	° ′	° ′	° ′	° ′		° ′	° ′
21 00	269 07.0	213 59.2	N17 48.4	75 39.2	S 6 01.9	152 41.0	N21 34.3	43 32.4	S14 42.6	Acamar	315 18.2	S40 14.7
01	284 09.4	228 58.7	49.2	90 40.9	02.3	167 42.9	34.2	58 34.9	42.6	Achernar	335 26.6	S57 09.6
02	299 11.9	243 58.1	49.9	105 42.7	02.7	182 44.8	34.1	73 37.5	42.6	Acrux	173 08.3	S63 11.1
03	314 14.4	258 57.6 · ·	50.6	120 44.4 · ·	03.0	197 46.7 · ·	34.0	88 40.1 · ·	42.5	Adhara	255 12.3	S28 59.7
04	329 16.8	273 57.0	51.4	135 46.1	03.4	212 48.6	34.0	103 42.7	42.5	Aldebaran	290 48.9	N16 32.1
05	344 19.3	288 56.5	52.1	150 47.8	03.8	227 50.5	33.9	118 45.3	42.5			
06	359 21.7	303 55.9	N17 53.6	165 49.6	S 6 04.2	242 52.4	N21 33.8	133 47.8	S14 42.4	Alioth	166 20.1	N55 53.1
S 07	14 24.2	318 55.4	53.6	180 51.3	04.5	257 54.3	33.7	148 50.4	42.4	Alkaid	152 58.2	N49 14.7
A 08	29 26.7	333 54.8	54.3	195 53.0	04.9	272 56.2	33.6	163 53.0	42.4	Al Na'ir	27 42.7	S46 53.1
T 09	44 29.1	348 54.2 · ·	55.0	210 54.7 · ·	05.3	287 58.1 · ·	33.5	178 55.6 · ·	42.4	Alnilam	275 46.0	S 1 11.8
U 10	59 31.6	3 53.7	55.8	225 56.5	05.7	303 00.0	33.4	193 58.2	42.4	Alphard	217 55.6	S 8 43.5
R 11	74 34.1	18 53.1	56.5	240 58.2	06.0	318 01.9	33.3	209 00.7	42.4			
D 12	89 36.5	33 52.6	N17 57.2	255 59.9	S 6 06.4	333 03.8	N21 33.2	224 03.3	S14 42.3	Alphecca	126 10.1	N26 40.2
A 13	104 39.0	48 52.0	58.0	271 01.6	06.8	348 05.7	33.1	239 05.9	42.3	Alpheratz	357 42.7	N29 10.1
Y 14	119 41.5	63 51.4	58.7	286 03.4	07.2	3 07.6	33.0	254 08.5	42.3	Altair	62 07.2	N 8 54.6
15	134 43.9	78 50.9	17 59.4	301 05.1 · ·	07.6	18 09.5 · ·	32.9	269 11.0 · ·	42.3	Ankaa	353 15.1	S42 13.4
16	149 46.4	93 50.3	18 00.2	316 06.8	07.9	33 11.4	32.9	284 13.6	42.2	Antares	112 25.0	S26 27.7
17	164 48.9	108 49.8	00.9	331 08.5	08.3	48 13.3	32.8	299 16.2	42.2			
18	179 51.3	123 49.2	N18 01.6	346 10.2	S 6 08.7	63 15.2	N21 32.7	314 18.8	S14 42.2	Arcturus	145 54.9	N19 06.6
19	194 53.8	138 48.6	02.3	1 11.9	09.1	78 17.1	32.6	329 21.3	42.2	Atria	107 25.6	S69 03.1
20	209 56.2	153 48.1	03.1	16 13.7	09.5	93 19.0	32.5	344 23.9	42.2	Avior	234 18.2	S59 33.7
21	224 58.7	168 47.5 · ·	03.8	31 15.4 · ·	09.8	108 20.9 · ·	32.4	359 26.5 · ·	42.1	Bellatrix	278 31.6	N 6 21.6
22	240 01.2	183 47.0	04.5	46 17.1	10.2	123 22.8	32.3	14 29.1	42.1	Betelgeuse	271 00.9	N 7 24.4
23	255 03.6	198 46.4	05.2	61 18.8	10.6	138 24.7	32.2	29 31.7	42.1			
22 00	270 06.1	213 45.8	N18 06.0	76 20.5	S 6 11.0	153 26.6	N21 32.1	44 34.2	S14 42.1	Canopus	263 56.4	S52 42.4
01	285 08.6	228 45.3	06.7	91 22.2	11.4	168 28.5	32.0	59 36.8	42.0	Capella	280 33.9	N46 00.5
02	300 11.0	243 44.7	07.4	106 23.9	11.7	183 30.4	31.9	74 39.4	42.0	Deneb	49 30.6	N45 19.9
03	315 13.5	258 44.1 · ·	08.1	121 25.6 · ·	12.1	198 32.3 · ·	31.8	89 42.0 · ·	42.0	Denebola	182 33.0	N14 29.5
04	330 16.0	273 43.6	08.8	136 27.4	12.5	213 34.2	31.7	104 44.5	42.0	Diphda	348 55.3	S17 54.3
05	345 18.4	288 43.0	09.6	151 29.1	12.9	228 36.1	31.7	119 47.1	42.0			
06	0 20.9	303 42.4	N18 10.3	166 30.8	S 6 13.3	243 38.0	N21 31.6	134 49.7	S14 41.9	Dubhe	193 51.2	N61 40.6
07	15 23.3	318 41.9	11.0	181 32.5	13.7	258 39.9	31.5	149 52.3	41.9	Elnath	278 12.1	N28 36.9
08	30 25.8	333 41.3	11.7	196 34.2	14.0	273 41.8	31.4	164 54.8	41.9	Eltanin	90 45.3	N51 29.4
S 09	45 28.3	348 40.7 · ·	12.4	211 35.9 · ·	14.4	288 43.7 · ·	31.3	179 57.4 · ·	41.9	Enif	33 46.2	N 9 56.6
U 10	60 30.7	3 40.1	13.1	226 37.6	14.8	303 45.6	31.2	195 00.0	41.8	Fomalhaut	15 23.1	S29 32.5
N 11	75 33.2	18 39.6	13.8	241 39.3	15.2	318 47.5	31.1	210 02.6	41.8			
D 12	90 35.7	33 39.0	N18 14.6	256 41.0	S 6 15.6	333 49.4	N21 31.0	225 05.1	S14 41.8	Gacrux	171 59.9	S57 12.0
A 13	105 38.1	48 38.4	15.3	271 42.7	16.0	348 51.3	30.9	240 07.7	41.8	Gienah	175 51.5	S17 37.5
Y 14	120 40.6	63 37.9	16.0	286 44.4	16.3	3 53.2	30.8	255 10.3	41.8	Hadar	148 46.4	S60 26.7
15	135 43.1	78 37.3 · ·	16.7	301 46.1 · ·	16.7	18 55.1 · ·	30.7	270 12.9 · ·	41.7	Hamal	328 00.1	N23 31.7
16	150 45.5	93 36.7	17.4	316 47.8	17.1	33 57.0	30.6	285 15.4	41.7	Kaus Aust.	83 42.5	S34 22.4
17	165 48.0	108 36.1	18.1	331 49.5	17.5	48 58.9	30.5	300 18.0	41.7			
18	180 50.5	123 35.6	N18 18.8	346 51.2	S 6 17.9	64 00.8	N21 30.5	315 20.6	S14 41.7	Kochab	137 19.4	N74 06.1
19	195 52.9	138 35.0	19.5	1 52.9	18.3	79 02.7	30.4	330 23.1	41.7	Markab	13 37.5	N15 17.0
20	210 55.4	153 34.4	20.2	16 54.6	18.6	94 04.6	30.3	345 25.7	41.6	Menkar	314 14.6	N 4 08.7
21	225 57.8	168 33.8 · ·	20.9	31 56.3 · ·	19.0	109 06.5 · ·	30.2	0 28.3 · ·	41.6	Menkent	148 06.5	S36 26.6
22	241 00.3	183 33.3	21.7	46 58.0	19.4	124 08.4	30.1	15 30.9	41.6	Miaplacidus	221 40.0	S69 47.0
23	256 02.8	198 32.7	22.4	61 59.7	19.8	139 10.3	30.0	30 33.4	41.6			
23 00	271 05.2	213 32.1	N18 23.1	77 01.4	S 6 20.2	154 12.2	N21 29.9	45 36.0	S14 41.5	Mirfak	308 39.7	N49 54.4
01	286 07.7	228 31.5	23.8	92 03.1	20.6	169 14.1	29.8	60 38.6	41.5	Nunki	75 57.1	S26 16.5
02	301 10.2	243 31.0	24.5	107 04.8	21.0	184 16.0	29.7	75 41.2	41.5	Peacock	53 17.7	S56 40.9
03	316 12.6	258 30.4 · ·	25.2	122 06.5 · ·	21.4	199 17.9 · ·	29.6	90 43.7 · ·	41.5	Pollux	243 27.2	N27 59.3
04	331 15.1	273 29.8	25.9	137 08.2	21.7	214 19.8	29.5	105 46.3	41.5	Procyon	244 59.3	N 5 11.1
05	346 17.6	288 29.2	26.6	152 09.9	22.1	229 21.7	29.4	120 48.9	41.4			
06	1 20.0	303 28.6	N18 27.3	167 11.6	S 6 22.5	244 23.6	N21 29.3	135 51.4	S14 41.4	Rasalhague	96 05.5	N12 33.2
07	16 22.5	318 28.1	28.0	182 13.2	22.9	259 25.5	29.2	150 54.0	41.4	Regulus	207 43.0	N11 53.7
08	31 25.0	333 27.5	28.7	197 14.9	23.3	274 27.4	29.1	165 56.6	41.4	Rigel	281 11.7	S 8 11.3
M 09	46 27.4	348 26.9 · ·	29.4	212 16.6 · ·	23.7	289 29.3 · ·	29.1	180 59.2 · ·	41.4	Rigil Kent.	139 50.2	S60 53.8
O 10	61 29.9	3 26.3	30.1	227 18.3	24.1	304 31.2	29.0	196 01.7	41.3	Sabik	102 11.4	S15 44.4
N 11	76 32.3	18 25.7	30.8	242 20.0	24.5	319 33.1	28.9	211 04.3	41.3			
D 12	91 34.8	33 25.2	N18 31.5	257 21.7	S 6 24.9	334 35.0	N21 28.8	226 06.9	S14 41.3	Schedar	349 39.7	N56 36.7
A 13	106 37.3	48 24.6	32.1	272 23.4	25.2	349 36.9	28.7	241 09.4	41.3	Shaula	96 20.5	S37 06.7
Y 14	121 39.7	63 24.0	32.8	287 25.0	25.6	4 38.8	28.6	256 12.0	41.3	Sirius	258 33.4	S16 44.4
15	136 42.2	78 23.4 · ·	33.5	302 26.7 · ·	26.0	19 40.7 · ·	28.5	271 14.6 · ·	41.2	Spica	158 30.4	S11 14.2
16	151 44.7	93 22.8	34.2	317 28.4	26.4	34 42.6	28.4	286 17.2	41.2	Suhail	222 52.2	S43 29.8
17	166 47.1	108 22.2	34.9	332 30.1	26.8	49 44.5	28.3	301 19.7	41.2			
18	181 49.6	123 21.7	N18 35.6	347 31.8	S 6 27.2	64 46.4	N21 28.2	316 22.3	S14 41.2	Vega	80 38.0	N38 48.0
19	196 52.1	138 21.1	36.3	2 33.5	27.6	79 48.3	28.1	331 24.9	41.2	Zuben'ubi	137 04.4	S16 06.1
20	211 54.5	153 20.5	37.0	17 35.1	28.0	94 50.2	28.0	346 27.4	41.1		SHA	Mer. Pass.
21	226 57.0	168 19.9 · ·	37.7	32 36.8 · ·	28.4	109 52.1 · ·	27.9	1 30.0 · ·	41.1		° ′	h m
22	241 59.4	183 19.3	38.4	47 38.5	28.8	124 54.0	27.8	16 32.6	41.1	Venus	303 39.7	9 45
23	257 01.9	198 18.7	39.0	62 40.2	29.2	139 55.9	27.7	31 35.1	41.1	Mars	166 14.4	18 52
	h m									Jupiter	243 20.5	13 44
Mer. Pass.	5 58.6	v −0.6	d 0.7	v 1.7	d 0.4	v 1.9	d 0.1	v 2.6	d 0.0	Saturn	134 28.1	20 58

UT	SUN GHA	SUN Dec	MOON GHA	v	Dec	d	HP
d h	° ′	° ′	° ′	′	° ′	′	′
21 00	179 35.1	N23 26.1	255 38.9	11.2	N 6 51.2	10.3	57.8
01	194 35.0	26.1	270 09.1	11.2	7 01.5	10.2	57.8
02	209 34.8	26.1	284 39.3	11.1	7 11.7	10.1	57.8
03	224 34.7	.. 26.1	299 09.4	11.2	7 21.8	10.2	57.7
04	239 34.6	26.1	313 39.6	11.2	7 32.0	10.0	57.7
05	254 34.4	26.1	328 09.8	11.2	7 42.0	10.0	57.7
06	269 34.3	N23 26.1	342 40.0	11.2	N 7 52.0	10.0	57.7
S 07	284 34.2	26.1	357 10.2	11.1	8 02.0	9.9	57.6
A 08	299 34.0	26.1	11 40.3	11.2	8 11.9	9.9	57.6
T 09	314 33.9	.. 26.1	26 10.5	11.2	8 21.8	9.8	57.6
U 10	329 33.8	26.1	40 40.7	11.2	8 31.6	9.8	57.5
R 11	344 33.6	26.1	55 10.9	11.2	8 41.4	9.7	57.5
D 12	359 33.5	N23 26.1	69 41.1	11.2	N 8 51.1	9.6	57.5
A 13	14 33.3	26.1	84 11.3	11.2	9 00.7	9.6	57.5
Y 14	29 33.2	26.1	98 41.5	11.1	9 10.3	9.6	57.4
15	44 33.1	.. 26.1	113 11.6	11.2	9 19.9	9.5	57.4
16	59 32.9	26.1	127 41.8	11.2	9 29.4	9.4	57.4
17	74 32.8	26.1	142 12.0	11.2	9 38.8	9.4	57.4
18	89 32.7	N23 26.1	156 42.2	11.2	N 9 48.2	9.3	57.3
19	104 32.5	26.1	171 12.4	11.1	9 57.5	9.2	57.3
20	119 32.4	26.1	185 42.5	11.2	10 06.7	9.2	57.3
21	134 32.3	.. 26.1	200 12.7	11.2	10 15.9	9.2	57.3
22	149 32.1	26.1	214 42.9	11.1	10 25.1	9.0	57.2
23	164 32.0	26.0	229 13.0	11.2	10 34.1	9.1	57.2
22 00	179 31.8	N23 26.0	243 43.2	11.1	N10 43.2	8.9	57.2
01	194 31.7	26.0	258 13.3	11.2	10 52.1	8.9	57.2
02	209 31.6	26.0	272 43.5	11.1	11 01.0	8.8	57.1
03	224 31.4	.. 26.0	287 13.6	11.2	11 09.8	8.8	57.1
04	239 31.3	26.0	301 43.8	11.1	11 18.6	8.7	57.1
05	254 31.2	26.0	316 13.9	11.1	11 27.3	8.6	57.1
06	269 31.0	N23 26.0	330 44.0	11.1	N11 35.9	8.5	57.0
07	284 30.9	26.0	345 14.1	11.1	11 44.4	8.5	57.0
S 08	299 30.8	25.9	359 44.2	11.1	11 52.9	8.5	57.0
U 09	314 30.6	.. 25.9	14 14.3	11.1	12 01.4	8.3	57.0
N 10	329 30.5	25.9	28 44.4	11.1	12 09.7	8.3	56.9
D 11	344 30.3	25.9	43 14.5	11.1	12 18.0	8.2	56.9
A 12	359 30.2	N23 25.9	57 44.6	11.0	N12 26.2	8.1	56.9
Y 13	14 30.1	25.8	72 14.6	11.1	12 34.3	8.1	56.9
14	29 29.9	25.8	86 44.7	11.0	12 42.4	8.0	56.8
15	44 29.8	.. 25.8	101 14.7	11.1	12 50.4	8.0	56.8
16	59 29.7	25.8	115 44.8	11.0	12 58.4	7.8	56.8
17	74 29.5	25.8	130 14.8	11.0	13 06.2	7.8	56.8
18	89 29.4	N23 25.7	144 44.8	11.0	N13 14.0	7.7	56.7
19	104 29.3	25.7	159 14.8	11.0	13 21.7	7.6	56.7
20	119 29.1	25.7	173 44.8	11.0	13 29.3	7.6	56.7
21	134 29.0	.. 25.7	188 14.8	11.0	13 36.9	7.5	56.7
22	149 28.8	25.7	202 44.8	11.0	13 44.4	7.4	56.6
23	164 28.7	25.6	217 14.8	11.0	13 51.8	7.3	56.6
23 00	179 28.6	N23 25.6	231 44.8	10.9	N13 59.1	7.3	56.6
01	194 28.4	25.6	246 14.7	11.0	14 06.4	7.1	56.6
02	209 28.3	25.5	260 44.7	10.9	14 13.5	7.1	56.5
03	224 28.2	.. 25.5	275 14.6	10.9	14 20.6	7.1	56.5
04	239 28.0	25.5	289 44.5	10.9	14 27.7	6.9	56.5
05	254 27.9	25.5	304 14.4	10.9	14 34.6	6.9	56.5
06	269 27.8	N23 25.4	318 44.3	10.9	N14 41.5	6.7	56.5
07	284 27.6	25.4	333 14.2	10.9	14 48.2	6.7	56.4
08	299 27.5	25.4	347 44.1	10.9	14 54.9	6.6	56.4
M 09	314 27.4	.. 25.3	2 14.0	10.9	15 01.5	6.6	56.4
O 10	329 27.2	25.3	16 43.9	10.8	15 08.1	6.4	56.4
N 11	344 27.1	25.3	31 13.7	10.9	15 14.5	6.4	56.3
D 12	359 26.9	N23 25.2	45 43.6	10.8	N15 20.9	6.3	56.3
A 13	14 26.8	25.2	60 13.4	10.9	15 27.2	6.2	56.3
Y 14	29 26.7	25.2	74 43.3	10.8	15 33.4	6.1	56.3
15	44 26.5	.. 25.1	89 13.1	10.8	15 39.5	6.0	56.3
16	59 26.4	25.1	103 42.9	10.8	15 45.5	6.0	56.2
17	74 26.3	25.0	118 12.7	10.8	15 51.5	5.8	56.2
18	89 26.1	N23 25.0	132 42.5	10.8	N15 57.3	5.8	56.2
19	104 26.0	25.0	147 12.3	10.8	16 03.1	5.7	56.2
20	119 25.9	24.9	161 42.1	10.7	16 08.8	5.6	56.1
21	134 25.7	.. 24.9	176 11.8	10.8	16 14.4	5.5	56.1
22	149 25.6	24.8	190 41.6	10.7	16 19.9	5.5	56.1
23	164 25.5	24.8	205 11.3	10.8	N16 25.4	5.3	56.1
	SD 15.8	d 0.0	SD 15.7		15.5		15.3

Lat.	Twilight Naut.	Twilight Civil	Sunrise	Moonrise 21	Moonrise 22	Moonrise 23	Moonrise 24
°	h m	h m	h m	h m	h m	h m	h m
N 72	☐	☐	☐	23 25	23 16	23 02	22 13
N 70	☐	☐	☐	23 42	23 42	23 45	23 54
68	☐	☐	☐	23 55	24 02	00 02	00 14
66	☐	☐	☐	24 06	00 06	00 19	00 36
64	////	////	01 31	00 02	00 15	00 32	00 54
62	////	////	02 10	00 06	00 23	00 43	01 08
60	////	00 49	02 36	00 11	00 30	00 53	01 20
N 58	////	01 41	02 57	00 14	00 36	01 01	01 31
56	////	02 11	03 13	00 18	00 42	01 09	01 40
54	00 45	02 33	03 28	00 21	00 46	01 15	01 48
52	01 33	02 51	03 40	00 23	00 51	01 21	01 56
50	02 00	03 06	03 51	00 26	00 55	01 27	02 02
45	02 46	03 36	04 13	00 31	01 04	01 38	02 17
N 40	03 17	03 59	04 31	00 36	01 11	01 48	02 28
35	03 40	04 17	04 47	00 40	01 17	01 57	02 39
30	03 59	04 32	05 00	00 43	01 23	02 04	02 47
20	04 28	04 57	05 22	00 49	01 33	02 17	03 03
N 10	04 51	05 18	05 41	00 55	01 41	02 28	03 16
0	05 10	05 36	05 58	01 00	01 49	02 39	03 29
S 10	05 27	05 53	06 16	01 05	01 57	02 49	03 41
20	05 43	06 10	06 34	01 11	02 06	03 01	03 55
30	05 59	06 29	06 56	01 17	02 16	03 14	04 11
35	06 08	06 40	07 08	01 21	02 22	03 22	04 20
40	06 17	06 52	07 22	01 25	02 29	03 30	04 30
45	06 28	07 05	07 39	01 30	02 36	03 41	04 42
S 50	06 40	07 21	08 00	01 36	02 46	03 53	04 57
52	06 45	07 29	08 10	01 38	02 50	03 59	05 04
54	06 51	07 37	08 21	01 41	02 55	04 05	05 12
56	06 57	07 46	08 34	01 45	03 00	04 12	05 21
58	07 04	07 56	08 48	01 48	03 06	04 21	05 30
S 60	07 11	08 08	09 06	01 53	03 13	04 30	05 42

Lat.	Sunset	Twilight Civil	Twilight Naut.	Moonset 21	Moonset 22	Moonset 23	Moonset 24
°	h m	h m	h m	h m	h m	h m	h m
N 72	☐	☐	☐	15 29	17 21	19 19	21 53
N 70	☐	☐	☐	15 14	16 56	18 36	20 12
68	☐	☐	☐	15 02	16 37	18 08	19 32
66	☐	☐	☐	14 52	16 21	17 47	19 05
64	22 32	////	////	14 44	16 09	17 30	18 44
62	21 54	////	////	14 37	15 58	17 16	18 27
60	21 28	23 14	////	14 31	15 49	17 04	18 13
N 58	21 07	22 23	////	14 25	15 42	16 54	18 01
56	20 51	21 53	////	14 21	15 35	16 45	17 50
54	20 36	21 31	23 18	14 16	15 29	16 37	17 41
52	20 24	21 13	22 31	14 13	15 23	16 30	17 33
50	20 13	20 58	22 03	14 09	15 18	16 24	17 26
45	19 51	20 28	21 18	14 02	15 07	16 10	17 10
N 40	19 32	20 05	20 47	13 55	14 58	15 59	16 57
35	19 17	19 47	20 24	13 50	14 51	15 50	16 46
30	19 04	19 32	20 05	13 45	14 44	15 41	16 37
20	18 42	19 07	19 36	13 37	14 33	15 27	16 21
N 10	18 23	18 46	19 13	13 30	14 22	15 14	16 06
0	18 06	18 28	18 54	13 24	14 13	15 03	15 53
S 10	17 48	18 11	18 37	13 17	14 04	14 51	15 40
20	17 30	17 54	18 21	13 10	13 53	14 39	15 25
30	17 08	17 35	18 05	13 02	13 42	14 24	15 09
35	16 56	17 24	17 56	12 57	13 35	14 16	14 59
40	16 42	17 12	17 46	12 52	13 28	14 07	14 49
45	16 25	16 59	17 36	12 46	13 19	13 56	14 36
S 50	16 04	16 43	17 24	12 38	13 09	13 42	14 20
52	15 54	16 35	17 19	12 35	13 04	13 36	14 13
54	15 43	16 27	17 13	12 31	12 59	13 29	14 05
56	15 30	16 18	17 07	12 27	12 53	13 22	13 56
58	15 16	16 08	17 00	12 23	12 46	13 13	13 46
S 60	14 58	15 56	16 53	12 18	12 39	13 04	13 35

	SUN			MOON			
Day	Eqn. of Time 00h	Eqn. of Time 12h	Mer. Pass.	Mer. Pass. Upper	Mer. Pass. Lower	Age	Phase
d	m s	m s	h m	h m	h m	d	%
21	01 39	01 46	12 02	07 12	19 36	24	32
22	01 52	01 59	12 02	08 01	20 26	25	22
23	02 05	02 12	12 02	08 51	21 16	26	14

UT	ARIES GHA	VENUS −3.9 GHA	Dec	MARS −0.1 GHA	Dec	JUPITER −1.8 GHA	Dec	SATURN +0.3 GHA	Dec	STARS Name	SHA	Dec
d h	° ′	° ′	° ′	° ′	° ′	° ′	° ′	° ′	° ′		° ′	° ′
24 00	272 04.4	213 18.1	N18 39.7	77 41.9	S 6 29.5	154 57.8	N21 27.6	46 37.7	S14 41.1	Acamar	315 18.1	S40 14.7
01	287 06.8	228 17.5	40.4	92 43.5	29.9	169 59.7	27.6	61 40.3	41.0	Achernar	335 26.6	S57 09.6
02	302 09.3	243 17.0	41.1	107 45.2	30.3	185 01.6	27.5	76 42.9	41.0	Acrux	173 08.5	S63 11.1
03	317 11.8	258 16.4 ..	41.8	122 46.9 ..	30.7	200 03.5 ..	27.4	91 45.4 ..	41.0	Adhara	255 12.3	S28 59.7
04	332 14.2	273 15.8	42.5	137 48.6	31.1	215 05.4	27.3	106 48.0	41.0	Aldebaran	290 48.9	N16 32.1
05	347 16.7	288 15.2	43.2	152 50.2	31.5	230 07.3	27.2	121 50.6	41.0			
06	2 19.2	303 14.6	N18 43.8	167 51.9	S 6 31.9	245 09.2	N21 27.1	136 53.1	S14 40.9	Alioth	166 20.1	N55 53.2
07	17 21.6	318 14.0	44.5	182 53.6	32.3	260 11.1	27.0	151 55.7	40.9	Alkaid	152 58.2	N49 14.7
T 08	32 24.1	333 13.4	45.2	197 55.2	32.7	275 13.0	26.9	166 58.3	40.9	Al Na'ir	27 42.7	S46 53.1
U 09	47 26.6	348 12.8 ..	45.9	212 56.9 ..	33.1	290 14.9 ..	26.8	182 00.8 ..	40.9	Alnilam	275 46.0	S 1 11.8
E 10	62 29.0	3 12.2	46.5	227 58.6	33.5	305 16.8	26.7	197 03.4	40.9	Alphard	217 55.6	S 8 43.5
S 11	77 31.5	18 11.6	47.2	243 00.3	33.9	320 18.7	26.6	212 06.0	40.8			
D 12	92 33.9	33 11.0	N18 47.9	258 01.9	S 6 34.3	335 20.6	N21 26.5	227 08.5	S14 40.8	Alphecca	126 10.1	N26 40.2
A 13	107 36.4	48 10.4	48.6	273 03.6	34.7	350 22.5	26.4	242 11.1	40.8	Alpheratz	357 42.7	N29 10.1
Y 14	122 38.9	63 09.8	49.3	288 05.3	35.1	5 24.4	26.3	257 13.7	40.8	Altair	62 07.2	N 8 54.6
15	137 41.3	78 09.3 ..	49.9	303 06.9 ..	35.5	20 26.3 ..	26.2	272 16.2 ..	40.7	Ankaa	353 15.1	S42 13.4
16	152 43.8	93 08.7	50.6	318 08.6	35.9	35 28.2	26.1	287 18.8	40.7	Antares	112 25.0	S26 27.7
17	167 46.3	108 08.1	51.3	333 10.3	36.3	50 30.1	26.0	302 21.4	40.7			
18	182 48.7	123 07.5	N18 51.9	348 11.9	S 6 36.7	65 32.0	N21 25.9	317 23.9	S14 40.7	Arcturus	145 54.9	N19 06.6
19	197 51.2	138 06.9	52.6	3 13.6	37.0	80 33.9	25.9	332 26.5	40.7	Atria	107 25.6	S69 03.1
20	212 53.7	153 06.3	53.3	18 15.2	37.4	95 35.8	25.8	347 29.1	40.7	Avior	234 18.2	S59 33.7
21	227 56.1	168 05.7 ..	54.0	33 16.9 ..	37.8	110 37.7 ..	25.7	2 31.6 ..	40.6	Bellatrix	278 31.6	N 6 21.6
22	242 58.6	183 05.1	54.6	48 18.6	38.2	125 39.6	25.6	17 34.2	40.6	Betelgeuse	271 00.9	N 7 24.4
23	258 01.1	198 04.5	55.3	63 20.2	38.6	140 41.5	25.5	32 36.8	40.6			
25 00	273 03.5	213 03.9	N18 56.0	78 21.9	S 6 39.0	155 43.4	N21 25.4	47 39.3	S14 40.6	Canopus	263 56.4	S52 42.4
01	288 06.0	228 03.3	56.6	93 23.5	39.4	170 45.3	25.3	62 41.9	40.6	Capella	280 33.9	N46 00.5
02	303 08.4	243 02.7	57.3	108 25.2	39.8	185 47.2	25.2	77 44.5	40.5	Deneb	49 30.6	N45 20.0
03	318 10.9	258 02.1 ..	58.0	123 26.9 ..	40.2	200 49.1 ..	25.1	92 47.0 ..	40.5	Denebola	182 33.0	N14 29.5
04	333 13.4	273 01.5	58.6	138 28.5	40.6	215 51.0	25.0	107 49.6	40.5	Diphda	348 55.2	S17 54.3
05	348 15.8	288 00.9	59.3	153 30.2	41.0	230 52.9	24.9	122 52.2	40.5			
06	3 18.3	303 00.3	N18 59.9	168 31.8	S 6 41.4	245 54.8	N21 24.8	137 54.7	S14 40.5	Dubhe	193 51.2	N61 40.6
W 07	18 20.8	317 59.7	19 00.6	183 33.5	41.8	260 56.7	24.7	152 57.3	40.5	Elnath	278 12.1	N28 36.9
E 08	33 23.2	332 59.1	01.3	198 35.1	42.2	275 58.6	24.6	167 59.9	40.4	Eltanin	90 45.3	N51 29.4
D 09	48 25.7	347 58.4 ..	01.9	213 36.8 ..	42.6	291 00.5 ..	24.5	183 02.4 ..	40.4	Enif	33 46.2	N 9 56.6
N 10	63 28.2	2 57.8	02.6	228 38.4	43.0	306 02.4	24.4	198 05.0	40.4	Fomalhaut	15 23.1	S29 32.5
E 11	78 30.6	17 57.2	03.2	243 40.1	43.4	321 04.2	24.3	213 07.6	40.4			
S 12	93 33.1	32 56.6	N19 03.9	258 41.7	S 6 43.8	336 06.1	N21 24.2	228 10.1	S14 40.4	Gacrux	171 59.9	S57 12.0
D 13	108 35.6	47 56.0	04.6	273 43.4	44.2	351 08.0	24.1	243 12.7	40.3	Gienah	175 51.5	S17 37.5
A 14	123 38.0	62 55.4	05.2	288 45.0	44.6	6 09.9	24.0	258 15.2	40.3	Hadar	148 46.4	S60 26.7
Y 15	138 40.5	77 54.8 ..	05.9	303 46.7 ..	45.0	21 11.8 ..	23.9	273 17.8 ..	40.3	Hamal	328 00.1	N23 31.7
16	153 42.9	92 54.2	06.5	318 48.3	45.4	36 13.7	23.8	288 20.4	40.3	Kaus Aust.	83 42.5	S34 22.4
17	168 45.4	107 53.6	07.2	333 50.0	45.8	51 15.6	23.8	303 22.9	40.3			
18	183 47.9	122 53.0	N19 07.8	348 51.6	S 6 46.2	66 17.5	N21 23.7	318 25.5	S14 40.3	Kochab	137 19.5	N74 06.1
19	198 50.3	137 52.4	08.5	3 53.3	46.6	81 19.4	23.6	333 28.1	40.2	Markab	13 37.5	N15 17.0
20	213 52.8	152 51.8	09.1	18 54.9	47.0	96 21.3	23.5	348 30.6	40.2	Menkar	314 14.5	N 4 08.7
21	228 55.3	167 51.2 ..	09.8	33 56.6 ..	47.4	111 23.2 ..	23.4	3 33.2 ..	40.2	Menkent	148 06.5	S36 26.6
22	243 57.7	182 50.6	10.4	48 58.2	47.8	126 25.1	23.3	18 35.8	40.2	Miaplacidus	221 40.1	S69 47.0
23	259 00.2	197 49.9	11.1	63 59.9	48.3	141 27.0	23.2	33 38.3	40.2			
26 00	274 02.7	212 49.3	N19 11.7	79 01.5	S 6 48.7	156 28.9	N21 23.1	48 40.9	S14 40.1	Mirfak	308 39.7	N49 54.4
01	289 05.1	227 48.7	12.4	94 03.1	49.1	171 30.8	23.0	63 43.4	40.1	Nunki	75 57.1	S26 16.5
02	304 07.6	242 48.1	13.0	109 04.8	49.5	186 32.7	22.9	78 46.0	40.1	Peacock	53 17.7	S56 40.9
03	319 10.1	257 47.5 ..	13.7	124 06.4 ..	49.9	201 34.6 ..	22.8	93 48.6 ..	40.1	Pollux	243 27.2	N27 59.3
04	334 12.5	272 46.9	14.3	139 08.1	50.3	216 36.5	22.7	108 51.1	40.1	Procyon	244 59.3	N 5 11.1
05	349 15.0	287 46.3	15.0	154 09.7	50.7	231 38.4	22.6	123 53.7	40.1			
06	4 17.4	302 45.7	N19 15.6	169 11.3	S 6 51.1	246 40.3	N21 22.5	138 56.3	S14 40.0	Rasalhague	96 05.5	N12 33.2
T 07	19 19.9	317 45.0	16.2	184 13.0	51.5	261 42.2	22.4	153 58.8	40.0	Regulus	207 43.0	N11 53.7
H 08	34 22.4	332 44.4	16.9	199 14.6	51.9	276 44.1	22.3	169 01.4	40.0	Rigel	281 11.7	S 8 11.3
U 09	49 24.8	347 43.8 ..	17.5	214 16.3 ..	52.3	291 46.0 ..	22.2	184 03.9 ..	40.0	Rigil Kent.	139 50.2	S60 53.8
R 10	64 27.3	2 43.2	18.2	229 17.9	52.7	306 47.9	22.1	199 06.5	40.0	Sabik	102 11.4	S15 44.4
S 11	79 29.8	17 42.6	18.8	244 19.5	53.1	321 49.8	22.0	214 09.1	39.9			
D 12	94 32.2	32 42.0	N19 19.4	259 21.2	S 6 53.5	336 51.7	N21 21.9	229 11.6	S14 39.9	Schedar	349 39.7	N56 36.7
A 13	109 34.7	47 41.3	20.1	274 22.8	53.9	351 53.5	21.8	244 14.2	39.9	Shaula	96 20.5	S37 06.7
Y 14	124 37.2	62 40.7	20.7	289 24.4	54.3	6 55.4	21.7	259 16.7	39.9	Sirius	258 33.4	S16 44.4
15	139 39.6	77 40.1 ..	21.3	304 26.1 ..	54.7	21 57.3 ..	21.6	274 19.3 ..	39.9	Spica	158 30.4	S11 14.2
16	154 42.1	92 39.5	22.0	319 27.7	55.1	36 59.2	21.5	289 21.9	39.9	Suhail	222 52.2	S43 29.8
17	169 44.5	107 38.9	22.6	334 29.3	55.5	52 01.1	21.4	304 24.4	39.8			
18	184 47.0	122 38.2	N19 23.2	349 30.9	S 6 56.0	67 03.0	N21 21.3	319 27.0	S14 39.8	Vega	80 38.0	N38 48.0
19	199 49.5	137 37.6	23.9	4 32.6	56.4	82 04.9	21.2	334 29.5	39.8	Zuben'ubi	137 04.4	S16 06.1
20	214 51.9	152 37.0	24.5	19 34.2	56.8	97 06.8	21.2	349 32.1	39.8			
21	229 54.4	167 36.4 ..	25.1	34 35.8 ..	57.2	112 08.7 ..	21.1	4 34.7 ..	39.8		SHA	Mer. Pass.
22	244 56.9	182 35.8	25.8	49 37.5	57.6	127 10.6	21.0	19 37.2	39.8	Venus	300 00.4	h m 9 48
23	259 59.5	197 35.1	26.4	64 39.1	58.0	142 12.5	20.9	34 39.8	39.7	Mars	165 18.4	18 44
Mer. Pass.	h m 5 46.8	v −0.6	d 0.7	v 1.7	d 0.4	v 1.9	d 0.1	v 2.6	d 0.0	Jupiter Saturn	242 39.9 134 35.8	13 35 20 46

SUN and MOON

UT	SUN GHA	SUN Dec	MOON GHA	v	MOON Dec	d	HP
24 00	179 25.3	N23 24.7	219 41.1	10.7	N16 30.7	5.3	56.1
01	194 25.2	24.7	234 10.8	10.8	16 36.0	5.1	56.0
02	209 25.1	24.7	248 40.6	10.7	16 41.1	5.1	56.0
03	224 24.9 ..	24.6	263 10.3	10.7	16 46.2	5.0	56.0
04	239 24.8	24.6	277 40.0	10.7	16 51.2	4.9	56.0
05	254 24.6	24.5	292 09.7	10.7	16 56.1	4.8	55.9
T 06	269 24.5	N23 24.5	306 39.4	10.7	N17 00.9	4.7	55.9
U 07	284 24.4	24.4	321 09.1	10.7	17 05.6	4.6	55.9
E 08	299 24.2	24.4	335 38.8	10.7	17 10.2	4.6	55.9
S 09	314 24.1 ..	24.3	350 08.5	10.7	17 14.8	4.4	55.9
D 10	329 24.0	24.3	4 38.2	10.7	17 19.2	4.4	55.8
A 11	344 23.8	24.2	19 07.9	10.7	17 23.6	4.2	55.8
Y 12	359 23.7	N23 24.2	33 37.6	10.6	N17 27.8	4.2	55.8
13	14 23.6	24.1	48 07.2	10.6	17 32.0	4.1	55.8
14	29 23.4	24.1	62 36.9	10.7	17 36.1	3.9	55.8
15	44 23.3 ..	24.0	77 06.6	10.7	17 40.0	3.9	55.7
16	59 23.2	24.0	91 36.3	10.6	17 43.9	3.8	55.7
17	74 23.0	23.9	106 05.9	10.7	17 47.7	3.7	55.7
18	89 22.9	N23 23.8	120 35.6	10.6	N17 51.4	3.7	55.7
19	104 22.8	23.8	135 05.2	10.7	17 55.1	3.5	55.7
20	119 22.6	23.7	149 34.9	10.7	17 58.6	3.4	55.6
21	134 22.5 ..	23.7	164 04.6	10.6	18 02.0	3.3	55.6
22	149 22.4	23.6	178 34.2	10.7	18 05.3	3.3	55.6
23	164 22.2	23.5	193 03.9	10.6	18 08.6	3.1	55.6
25 00	179 22.1	N23 23.5	207 33.5	10.7	N18 11.7	3.1	55.6
01	194 22.0	23.4	222 03.2	10.7	18 14.8	2.9	55.5
02	209 21.8	23.4	236 32.9	10.6	18 17.7	2.9	55.5
03	224 21.7 ..	23.3	251 02.5	10.7	18 20.6	2.7	55.5
04	239 21.6	23.2	265 32.2	10.7	18 23.3	2.7	55.5
05	254 21.4	23.2	280 01.9	10.7	18 26.0	2.6	55.5
W 06	269 21.3	N23 23.1	294 31.6	10.6	N18 28.6	2.4	55.4
E 07	284 21.2	23.0	309 01.2	10.7	18 31.0	2.4	55.4
D 08	299 21.0	23.0	323 30.9	10.7	18 33.4	2.3	55.4
N 09	314 20.9 ..	22.9	338 00.6	10.7	18 35.7	2.2	55.4
E 10	329 20.7	22.8	352 30.3	10.7	18 37.9	2.1	55.4
S 11	344 20.6	22.8	7 00.0	10.7	18 40.0	2.0	55.4
D 12	359 20.5	N23 22.7	21 29.7	10.7	N18 42.0	1.9	55.3
A 13	14 20.3	22.6	35 59.4	10.8	18 43.9	1.8	55.3
Y 14	29 20.2	22.6	50 29.2	10.7	18 45.7	1.7	55.3
15	44 20.1 ..	22.5	64 58.9	10.7	18 47.4	1.7	55.3
16	59 19.9	22.4	79 28.6	10.7	18 49.1	1.5	55.3
17	74 19.8	22.3	93 58.4	10.7	18 50.6	1.4	55.2
18	89 19.7	N23 22.3	108 28.1	10.8	N18 52.0	1.3	55.2
19	104 19.5	22.2	122 57.9	10.8	18 53.3	1.3	55.2
20	119 19.4	22.1	137 27.7	10.8	18 54.6	1.1	55.2
21	134 19.3 ..	22.0	151 57.5	10.8	18 55.7	1.1	55.2
22	149 19.1	22.0	166 27.3	10.8	18 56.8	0.9	55.2
23	164 19.0	21.9	180 57.1	10.8	18 57.7	0.9	55.1
26 00	179 18.9	N23 21.8	195 26.9	10.9	N18 58.6	0.7	55.1
01	194 18.7	21.7	209 56.8	10.8	18 59.3	0.7	55.1
02	209 18.6	21.7	224 26.6	10.9	19 00.0	0.6	55.1
03	224 18.5 ..	21.6	238 56.5	10.9	19 00.6	0.4	55.1
04	239 18.4	21.5	253 26.4	10.9	19 01.0	0.4	55.1
05	254 18.2	21.4	267 56.3	10.9	19 01.4	0.3	55.0
T 06	269 18.1	N23 21.3	282 26.2	11.0	N19 01.7	0.2	55.0
H 07	284 18.0	21.3	296 56.2	10.9	19 01.9	0.0	55.0
U 08	299 17.8	21.2	311 26.1	11.0	19 02.0	0.0	55.0
R 09	314 17.7 ..	21.1	325 56.1	10.9	19 02.0	0.1	55.0
S 10	329 17.6	21.0	340 26.1	11.0	19 01.9	0.2	55.0
D 11	344 17.4	20.9	354 56.1	11.0	19 01.7	0.3	54.9
A 12	359 17.3	N23 20.8	9 26.1	11.1	N19 01.4	0.3	54.9
Y 13	14 17.2	20.7	23 56.2	11.0	19 01.1	0.5	54.9
14	29 17.0	20.7	38 26.2	11.1	19 00.6	0.6	54.9
15	44 16.9 ..	20.6	52 56.3	11.1	19 00.0	0.6	54.9
16	59 16.8	20.5	67 26.4	11.2	18 59.4	0.8	54.9
17	74 16.6	20.4	81 56.6	11.1	18 58.6	0.8	54.9
18	89 16.5	N23 20.3	96 26.7	11.2	N18 57.8	0.9	54.8
19	104 16.4	20.2	110 56.9	11.2	18 56.9	1.1	54.8
20	119 16.2	20.1	125 27.1	11.2	18 55.8	1.1	54.8
21	134 16.1 ..	20.0	139 57.3	11.3	18 54.7	1.2	54.8
22	149 16.0	19.9	154 27.6	11.2	18 53.5	1.3	54.8
23	164 15.8	19.8	168 57.8	11.3	N18 52.2	1.4	54.8
SD	15.8	d 0.1	SD 15.2		15.1		15.0

Twilight, Sunrise and Moonrise

Lat.	Twilight Naut.	Civil	Sunrise	Moonrise 24	25	26	27
N 72	☐	☐	☐	22 13	☐	☐	☐
N 70	☐	☐	☐	23 54	24 19	00 19	01 14
68	☐	☐	☐	00 14	00 35	01 09	02 03
66	☐	☐	☐	00 36	01 02	01 41	02 34
64	////	////	01 33	00 54	01 24	02 04	02 57
62	////	////	02 11	01 08	01 41	02 23	03 15
60	////	00 52	02 37	01 20	01 55	02 38	03 30
N 58	////	01 42	02 58	01 31	02 07	02 51	03 43
56	////	02 12	03 14	01 40	02 18	03 02	03 54
54	00 48	02 34	03 29	01 48	02 27	03 12	04 04
52	01 34	02 52	03 41	01 56	02 35	03 21	04 12
50	02 02	03 07	03 52	02 02	02 43	03 29	04 20
45	02 47	03 37	04 14	02 17	02 59	03 46	04 37
N 40	03 18	03 59	04 32	02 28	03 12	04 00	04 49
35	03 41	04 18	04 47	02 39	03 23	04 11	05 02
30	04 00	04 33	05 00	02 47	03 33	04 22	05 12
20	04 29	04 58	05 22	03 03	03 50	04 39	05 29
N 10	04 51	05 18	05 41	03 16	04 05	04 55	05 44
0	05 10	05 36	05 59	03 29	04 19	05 09	05 58
S 10	05 27	05 54	06 16	03 41	04 33	05 23	06 12
20	05 43	06 11	06 35	03 55	04 48	05 39	06 28
30	06 00	06 30	06 56	04 11	05 05	05 57	06 45
35	06 09	06 40	07 08	04 20	05 15	06 07	06 55
40	06 18	06 52	07 23	04 30	05 26	06 19	07 06
45	06 28	07 06	07 39	04 42	05 40	06 33	07 20
S 50	06 40	07 22	08 00	04 57	05 56	06 50	07 37
52	06 45	07 29	08 10	05 04	06 04	06 58	07 44
54	06 51	07 37	08 21	05 12	06 13	07 07	07 53
56	06 57	07 46	08 34	05 21	06 22	07 17	08 03
58	07 04	07 57	08 48	05 30	06 34	07 28	08 14
S 60	07 11	08 08	09 06	05 42	06 46	07 41	08 26

Sunset, Twilight and Moonset

Lat.	Sunset	Twilight Civil	Naut.	Moonset 24	25	26	27
N 72	☐	☐	☐	21 53	☐	☐	23 54
N 70	☐	☐	☐	20 12	21 32	22 19	22 39
68	☐	☐	☐	19 32	20 42	21 31	22 01
66	☐	☐	☐	19 05	20 10	21 00	21 34
64	22 32	////	////	18 44	19 47	20 37	21 14
62	21 54	////	////	18 27	19 28	20 18	20 57
60	21 28	23 12	////	18 13	19 13	20 03	20 43
N 58	21 07	22 23	////	18 01	19 00	19 50	20 31
56	20 51	21 53	////	17 50	18 49	19 39	20 21
54	20 36	21 31	23 17	17 41	18 39	19 29	20 12
52	20 24	21 13	22 31	17 33	18 30	19 20	20 03
50	20 13	20 58	22 03	17 26	18 22	19 12	19 56
45	19 51	20 28	21 21	17 10	18 06	18 56	19 40
N 40	19 33	20 06	20 47	16 57	17 52	18 42	19 27
35	19 18	19 48	20 24	16 46	17 40	18 30	19 16
30	19 05	19 32	20 06	16 37	17 30	18 20	19 06
20	18 43	19 07	19 37	16 21	17 13	18 03	18 50
N 10	18 24	18 47	19 14	16 06	16 57	17 47	18 35
0	18 06	18 29	18 55	15 53	16 43	17 33	18 22
S 10	17 49	18 12	18 38	15 40	16 29	17 19	18 08
20	17 30	17 54	18 22	15 25	16 14	17 03	17 53
30	17 09	17 36	18 05	15 09	15 56	16 45	17 36
35	16 57	17 25	17 57	14 59	15 46	16 35	17 27
40	16 43	17 13	17 47	14 49	15 34	16 23	17 15
45	16 26	17 00	17 37	14 36	15 20	16 09	17 02
S 50	16 05	16 44	17 25	14 20	15 04	15 52	16 46
52	15 55	16 36	17 20	14 13	14 56	15 44	16 38
54	15 44	16 28	17 14	14 05	14 47	15 35	16 30
56	15 32	16 19	17 08	13 56	14 37	15 25	16 20
58	15 17	16 09	17 01	13 46	14 26	15 14	16 09
S 60	14 59	15 57	16 54	13 35	14 13	15 01	15 57

SUN and MOON

Day	SUN Eqn. of Time 00h	12h	Mer. Pass.	MOON Mer. Pass. Upper	Lower	Age	Phase
	m s	m s	h m	h m	h m	d	%
24	02 18	02 25	12 02	09 41	22 06	27	8
25	02 31	02 38	12 03	10 31	22 56	28	3
26	02 44	02 51	12 03	11 21	23 46	29	1

UT	ARIES GHA	VENUS −3.9 GHA	Dec	MARS +0.0 GHA	Dec	JUPITER −1.8 GHA	Dec	SATURN +0.4 GHA	Dec	STARS Name	SHA	Dec
27 00	275 01.8	212 34.5	N19 27.0	79 40.7	S 6 58.4	157 14.4	N21 20.8	49 42.3	S14 39.7	Acamar	315 18.1	S40 14.7
01	290 04.3	227 33.9	27.6	94 42.3	58.8	172 16.3	20.7	64 44.9	39.7	Achernar	335 26.5	S57 09.6
02	305 06.7	242 33.3	28.3	109 44.0	59.2	187 18.2	20.6	79 47.5	39.7	Acrux	173 08.3	S63 11.1
03	320 09.2	257 32.6 ..	28.9	124 45.6	6 59.6	202 20.1 ..	20.5	94 50.0 ..	39.7	Adhara	255 12.3	S28 59.7
04	335 11.7	272 32.0	29.5	139 47.2	7 00.0	217 22.0	20.4	109 52.6	39.7	Aldebaran	290 48.9	N16 32.1
05	350 14.1	287 31.4	30.1	154 48.8	00.4	232 23.9	20.3	124 55.1	39.6			
06	5 16.6	302 30.8	N19 30.8	169 50.4	S 7 00.9	247 25.8	N21 20.2	139 57.7	S14 39.6	Alioth	166 20.1	N55 53.2
07	20 19.0	317 30.1	31.4	184 52.1	01.3	262 27.7	20.1	155 00.2	39.6	Alkaid	152 58.2	N49 14.7
08	35 21.5	332 29.5	32.0	199 53.7	01.7	277 29.6	20.0	170 02.8	39.6	Al Na'ir	27 42.6	S46 53.1
F 09	50 24.0	347 28.9 ..	32.6	214 55.3 ..	02.1	292 31.5 ..	19.9	185 05.4 ..	39.6	Alnilam	275 46.0	S 1 11.7
R 10	65 26.4	2 28.3	33.2	229 56.9	02.5	307 33.3	19.8	200 07.9	39.6	Alphard	217 55.6	S 8 43.5
I 11	80 28.9	17 27.6	33.9	244 58.5	02.9	322 35.2	19.7	215 10.5	39.5			
D 12	95 31.4	32 27.0	N19 34.5	260 00.2	S 7 03.3	337 37.1	N21 19.6	230 13.0	S14 39.5	Alphecca	126 10.1	N26 40.2
A 13	110 33.8	47 26.4	35.1	275 01.8	03.7	352 39.0	19.5	245 15.6	39.5	Alpheratz	357 42.7	N29 10.1
Y 14	125 36.3	62 25.7	35.7	290 03.4	04.1	7 40.9	19.4	260 18.1	39.5	Altair	62 07.2	N 8 54.6
15	140 38.8	77 25.1 ..	36.3	305 05.0 ..	04.6	22 42.8 ..	19.3	275 20.7 ..	39.5	Ankaa	353 15.1	S42 13.4
16	155 41.2	92 24.5	36.9	320 06.6	05.0	37 44.7	19.2	290 23.3	39.5	Antares	112 25.0	S26 27.7
17	170 43.7	107 23.9	37.6	335 08.2	05.4	52 46.6	19.1	305 25.8	39.4			
18	185 46.2	122 23.2	N19 38.2	350 09.9	S 7 05.8	67 48.5	N21 19.0	320 28.4	S14 39.4	Arcturus	145 54.9	N19 06.6
19	200 48.6	137 22.6	38.8	5 11.5	06.2	82 50.4	18.9	335 30.9	39.4	Atria	107 25.6	S69 03.1
20	215 51.1	152 22.0	39.4	20 13.1	06.6	97 52.3	18.8	350 33.5	39.4	Avior	234 18.2	S59 33.7
21	230 53.5	167 21.3 ..	40.0	35 14.7 ..	07.0	112 54.2 ..	18.7	5 36.0 ..	39.4	Bellatrix	278 31.6	N 6 21.6
22	245 56.0	182 20.7	40.6	50 16.3	07.4	127 56.1	18.6	20 38.6	39.4	Betelgeuse	271 00.9	N 7 24.4
23	260 58.5	197 20.1	41.2	65 17.9	07.9	142 58.0	18.5	35 41.2	39.4			
28 00	276 00.9	212 19.4	N19 41.8	80 19.5	S 7 08.3	157 59.9	N21 18.4	50 43.7	S14 39.3	Canopus	263 56.4	S52 42.4
01	291 03.4	227 18.8	42.4	95 21.1	08.7	173 01.8	18.3	65 46.3	39.3	Capella	280 33.8	N46 00.5
02	306 05.9	242 18.2	43.0	110 22.7	09.1	188 03.7	18.2	80 48.8	39.3	Deneb	49 30.5	N45 20.0
03	321 08.3	257 17.5 ..	43.6	125 24.3 ..	09.5	203 05.5 ..	18.1	95 51.4 ..	39.3	Denebola	182 33.0	N14 29.5
04	336 10.8	272 16.9	44.2	140 25.9	09.9	218 07.4	18.0	110 53.9	39.3	Diphda	348 55.2	S17 54.3
05	351 13.3	287 16.3	44.9	155 27.6	10.3	233 09.3	17.9	125 56.5	39.3			
06	6 15.7	302 15.6	N19 45.5	170 29.2	S 7 10.8	248 11.2	N21 17.8	140 59.0	S14 39.2	Dubhe	193 51.2	N61 40.6
07	21 18.2	317 15.0	46.1	185 30.8	11.2	263 13.1	17.7	156 01.6	39.2	Elnath	278 12.1	N28 36.9
S 08	36 20.7	332 14.3	46.7	200 32.4	11.6	278 15.0	17.6	171 04.1	39.2	Eltanin	90 45.3	N51 29.5
A 09	51 23.1	347 13.7 ..	47.3	215 34.0 ..	12.0	293 16.9 ..	17.5	186 06.7 ..	39.2	Enif	33 46.2	N 9 56.6
T 10	66 25.6	2 13.1	47.9	230 35.6	12.4	308 18.8	17.4	201 09.3	39.2	Fomalhaut	15 23.1	S29 32.5
U 11	81 28.0	17 12.4	48.5	245 37.2	12.8	323 20.7	17.3	216 11.8	39.2			
R 12	96 30.5	32 11.8	N19 49.1	260 38.8	S 7 13.3	338 22.6	N21 17.2	231 14.4	S14 39.2	Gacrux	171 59.9	S57 12.0
D 13	111 33.0	47 11.1	49.6	275 40.4	13.7	353 24.5	17.1	246 16.9	39.1	Gienah	175 51.5	S17 37.5
A 14	126 35.4	62 10.5	50.2	290 42.0	14.1	8 26.4	17.0	261 19.5	39.1	Hadar	148 46.4	S60 26.8
Y 15	141 37.9	77 09.9 ..	50.8	305 43.6 ..	14.5	23 28.3 ..	16.9	276 22.0 ..	39.1	Hamal	328 00.1	N23 31.7
16	156 40.4	92 09.2	51.4	320 45.2	14.9	38 30.2	16.9	291 24.6	39.1	Kaus Aust.	83 42.5	S34 22.4
17	171 42.8	107 08.6	52.0	335 46.8	15.3	53 32.1	16.8	306 27.1	39.1			
18	186 45.3	122 07.9	N19 52.6	350 48.4	S 7 15.8	68 34.0	N21 16.7	321 29.7	S14 39.1	Kochab	137 19.5	N74 06.1
19	201 47.8	137 07.3	53.2	5 50.0	16.2	83 35.8	16.6	336 32.2	39.0	Markab	13 37.5	N15 17.0
20	216 50.2	152 06.7	53.8	20 51.6	16.6	98 37.7	16.5	351 34.8	39.0	Menkar	314 14.5	N 4 08.7
21	231 52.7	167 06.0 ..	54.4	35 53.1 ..	17.0	113 39.6 ..	16.4	6 37.3 ..	39.0	Menkent	148 06.5	S36 26.6
22	246 55.2	182 05.4	55.0	50 54.7	17.4	128 41.5	16.3	21 39.9	39.0	Miaplacidus	221 40.1	S69 47.0
23	261 57.6	197 04.7	55.6	65 56.3	17.8	143 43.4	16.2	36 42.4	39.0			
29 00	277 00.1	212 04.1	N19 56.1	80 57.9	S 7 18.3	158 45.3	N21 16.1	51 45.0	S14 39.0	Mirfak	308 39.6	N49 54.4
01	292 02.5	227 03.4	56.7	95 59.5	18.7	173 47.2	16.0	66 47.5	39.0	Nunki	75 57.1	S26 16.5
02	307 05.0	242 02.8	57.3	111 01.1	19.1	188 49.1	15.9	81 50.1	38.9	Peacock	53 17.7	S56 40.9
03	322 07.5	257 02.1 ..	57.9	126 02.7 ..	19.5	203 51.0 ..	15.8	96 52.7 ..	38.9	Pollux	243 27.2	N27 59.3
04	337 09.9	272 01.5	58.5	141 04.3	19.9	218 52.9	15.7	111 55.2	38.9	Procyon	244 59.3	N 5 11.1
05	352 12.4	287 00.8	59.1	156 05.9	20.4	233 54.8	15.6	126 57.8	38.9			
06	7 14.9	302 00.2	N19 59.7	171 07.5	S 7 20.8	248 56.7	N21 15.5	142 00.3	S14 38.9	Rasalhague	96 05.4	N12 33.2
07	22 17.3	316 59.6	20 00.2	186 09.1	21.2	263 58.6	15.4	157 02.9	38.9	Regulus	207 43.0	N11 53.7
08	37 19.8	331 58.9	00.8	201 10.6	21.6	279 00.5	15.3	172 05.4	38.9	Rigel	281 11.7	S 8 11.3
S 09	52 22.3	346 58.3 ..	01.4	216 12.2 ..	22.0	294 02.3 ..	15.2	187 08.0 ..	38.8	Rigil Kent.	139 50.3	S60 53.8
U 10	67 24.7	1 57.6	02.0	231 13.8	22.5	309 04.2	15.1	202 10.5	38.8	Sabik	102 11.4	S15 44.4
N 11	82 27.2	16 57.0	02.5	246 15.4	22.9	324 06.1	15.0	217 13.1	38.8			
D 12	97 29.6	31 56.3	N20 03.1	261 17.0	S 7 23.3	339 08.0	N21 14.9	232 15.6	S14 38.8	Schedar	349 39.6	N56 36.7
A 13	112 32.1	46 55.7	03.7	276 18.6	23.7	354 09.9	14.8	247 18.2	38.8	Shaula	96 20.5	S37 06.7
Y 14	127 34.6	61 55.0	04.3	291 20.2	24.1	9 11.8	14.7	262 20.7	38.8	Sirius	258 33.4	S16 44.4
15	142 37.0	76 54.4 ..	04.8	306 21.7 ..	24.6	24 13.7 ..	14.6	277 23.3 ..	38.8	Spica	158 30.4	S11 14.2
16	157 39.5	91 53.7	05.4	321 23.3	25.0	39 15.6	14.5	292 25.8	38.7	Suhail	222 52.2	S43 29.8
17	172 42.0	106 53.0	06.0	336 24.9	25.4	54 17.5	14.4	307 28.4	38.7			
18	187 44.4	121 52.4	N20 06.6	351 26.5	S 7 25.8	69 19.4	N21 14.3	322 30.9	S14 38.7	Vega	80 38.0	N38 48.0
19	202 46.9	136 51.7	07.1	6 28.1	26.3	84 21.3	14.2	337 33.5	38.7	Zuben'ubi	137 04.4	S16 06.1
20	217 49.4	151 51.1	07.7	21 29.6	26.7	99 23.2	14.1	352 36.0	38.7			
21	232 51.8	166 50.4 ..	08.3	36 31.2 ..	27.1	114 25.1 ..	14.0	7 38.6 ..	38.7		SHA	Mer.Pass.
22	247 54.3	181 49.8	08.8	51 32.8	27.5	129 26.9	13.9	22 41.1	38.7	Venus	296 18.5	9 51
23	262 56.8	196 49.1	09.4	66 34.4	27.9	144 28.8	13.8	37 43.6	38.6	Mars	164 18.6	18 37
										Jupiter	241 58.9	13 26
Mer.Pass.	5 35.0	v −0.6	d 0.6	v 1.6	d 0.4	v 1.9	d 0.1	v 2.6	d 0.0	Saturn	134 42.8	20 34

UT	SUN GHA	SUN Dec	MOON GHA	v	MOON Dec	d	HP
27 00	179 15.7	N23 19.7	183 28.1	11.4	N18 50.8	1.5	54.7
01	194 15.6	19.6	197 58.5	11.3	18 49.3	1.5	54.7
02	209 15.4	19.5	212 28.8	11.4	18 47.8	1.7	54.7
03	224 15.3 ..	19.4	226 59.2	11.4	18 46.1	1.7	54.7
04	239 15.2	19.3	241 29.6	11.4	18 44.4	1.9	54.7
05	254 15.1	19.2	256 00.0	11.5	18 42.5	1.9	54.7
06	269 14.9	N23 19.1	270 30.5	11.5	N18 40.6	2.0	54.7
07	284 14.8	19.0	285 01.0	11.5	18 38.6	2.1	54.7
F 08	299 14.7	18.9	299 31.5	11.6	18 36.5	2.2	54.7
R 09	314 14.5 ..	18.8	314 02.1	11.6	18 34.3	2.3	54.6
I 10	329 14.4	18.7	328 32.6	11.6	18 32.0	2.4	54.6
D 11	344 14.3	18.6	343 03.2	11.7	18 29.6	2.5	54.6
A 12	359 14.1	N23 18.5	357 33.9	11.7	N18 27.1	2.5	54.6
Y 13	14 14.0	18.4	12 04.6	11.7	18 24.6	2.6	54.6
14	29 13.9	18.3	26 35.3	11.7	18 22.0	2.7	54.6
15	44 13.7 ..	18.2	41 06.0	11.8	18 19.3	2.8	54.5
16	59 13.6	18.1	55 36.8	11.7	18 16.5	2.9	54.5
17	74 13.5	18.0	70 07.5	11.9	18 13.6	3.0	54.5
18	89 13.4	N23 17.9	84 38.4	11.8	N18 10.6	3.1	54.5
19	104 13.2	17.8	99 09.2	11.9	18 07.5	3.1	54.5
20	119 13.1	17.7	113 40.1	12.0	18 04.4	3.2	54.5
21	134 13.0 ..	17.6	128 11.1	11.9	18 01.2	3.3	54.5
22	149 12.8	17.5	142 42.0	12.0	17 57.9	3.4	54.5
23	164 12.7	17.4	157 13.0	12.1	17 54.5	3.5	54.4
28 00	179 12.6	N23 17.2	171 44.1	12.0	N17 51.0	3.6	54.4
01	194 12.4	17.1	186 15.1	12.1	17 47.4	3.6	54.4
02	209 12.3	17.0	200 46.2	12.2	17 43.8	3.7	54.4
03	224 12.2 ..	16.9	215 17.4	12.1	17 40.1	3.8	54.4
04	239 12.1	16.8	229 48.5	12.2	17 36.3	3.9	54.4
05	254 11.9	16.7	244 19.7	12.3	17 32.4	3.9	54.4
06	269 11.8	N23 16.6	258 51.0	12.2	N17 28.5	4.1	54.4
S 07	284 11.7	16.4	273 22.2	12.4	17 24.4	4.1	54.4
A 08	299 11.5	16.3	287 53.6	12.3	17 20.3	4.2	54.3
T 09	314 11.4 ..	16.2	302 24.9	12.4	17 16.1	4.3	54.3
U 10	329 11.3	16.1	316 56.3	12.4	17 11.8	4.3	54.3
R 11	344 11.2	16.0	331 27.7	12.5	17 07.5	4.4	54.3
D 12	359 11.0	N23 15.8	345 59.2	12.5	N17 03.1	4.5	54.3
A 13	14 10.9	15.7	0 30.7	12.5	16 58.6	4.6	54.3
Y 14	29 10.8	15.6	15 02.2	12.6	16 54.0	4.7	54.3
15	44 10.6 ..	15.5	29 33.8	12.6	16 49.3	4.7	54.3
16	59 10.5	15.3	44 05.4	12.6	16 44.6	4.8	54.3
17	74 10.4	15.2	58 37.0	12.7	16 39.8	4.8	54.3
18	89 10.3	N23 15.1	73 08.7	12.8	N16 35.0	5.0	54.3
19	104 10.1	15.0	87 40.5	12.7	16 30.0	5.0	54.2
20	119 10.0	14.8	102 12.2	12.8	16 25.0	5.1	54.2
21	134 09.9 ..	14.7	116 44.0	12.8	16 19.9	5.2	54.2
22	149 09.7	14.6	131 15.8	12.9	16 14.7	5.2	54.2
23	164 09.6	14.5	145 47.7	12.9	16 09.5	5.3	54.2
29 00	179 09.5	N23 14.3	160 19.6	13.0	N16 04.2	5.4	54.2
01	194 09.4	14.2	174 51.6	13.0	15 58.8	5.4	54.2
02	209 09.2	14.1	189 23.6	13.0	15 53.4	5.5	54.2
03	224 09.1 ..	13.9	203 55.6	13.1	15 47.9	5.6	54.2
04	239 09.0	13.8	218 27.7	13.1	15 42.3	5.7	54.2
05	254 08.9	13.7	232 59.8	13.1	15 36.6	5.7	54.2
06	269 08.7	N23 13.5	247 31.9	13.2	N15 30.9	5.7	54.2
07	284 08.6	13.4	262 04.1	13.2	15 25.2	5.9	54.1
08	299 08.5	13.3	276 36.3	13.2	15 19.3	5.9	54.1
S 09	314 08.3 ..	13.1	291 08.5	13.3	15 13.4	6.0	54.1
U 10	329 08.2	13.0	305 40.8	13.3	15 07.4	6.0	54.1
N 11	344 08.1	12.9	320 13.1	13.4	15 01.4	6.1	54.1
D 12	359 08.0	N23 12.7	334 45.5	13.4	N14 55.3	6.2	54.1
A 13	14 07.8	12.6	349 17.9	13.4	14 49.1	6.2	54.1
Y 14	29 07.7	12.5	3 50.3	13.5	14 42.9	6.3	54.1
15	44 07.6 ..	12.3	18 22.8	13.5	14 36.6	6.4	54.1
16	59 07.5	12.2	32 55.3	13.6	14 30.2	6.4	54.1
17	74 07.3	12.0	47 27.9	13.6	14 23.8	6.5	54.1
18	89 07.2	N23 11.9	62 00.5	13.6	N14 17.3	6.5	54.1
19	104 07.1	11.8	76 33.1	13.6	14 10.8	6.6	54.1
20	119 07.0	11.6	91 05.7	13.7	14 04.2	6.7	54.1
21	134 06.8 ..	11.5	105 38.4	13.8	13 57.5	6.7	54.1
22	149 06.7	11.3	120 11.2	13.7	13 50.8	6.8	54.1
23	164 06.6	11.2	134 43.9	13.8	N13 44.0	6.8	54.1
SD	15.8	d 0.1	14.9		14.8		14.7

Twilight / Sunrise / Moonrise

Lat.	Twilight Naut.	Twilight Civil	Sunrise	Moonrise 27	28	29	30
N 72	□	□	□		01 21	03 26	05 13
N 70	□	□	□	01 14	02 36	04 06	05 38
68	□	□	□	02 03	03 13	04 33	05 56
66	□	□	□	02 34	03 39	04 53	06 11
64	////	////	01 36	02 57	04 00	05 10	06 24
62	////	////	02 13	03 15	04 16	05 23	06 34
60	////	00 57	02 39	03 30	04 30	05 35	06 43
N 58	////	01 45	02 59	03 43	04 41	05 44	06 51
56	////	02 14	03 16	03 54	04 51	05 53	06 57
54	00 52	02 36	03 30	04 04	05 00	06 01	07 03
52	01 36	02 54	03 42	04 12	05 08	06 08	07 09
50	02 04	03 09	03 53	04 20	05 15	06 14	07 14
45	02 49	03 38	04 16	04 37	05 31	06 27	07 24
N 40	03 19	04 01	04 33	04 50	05 43	06 38	07 33
35	03 42	04 19	04 48	05 02	05 54	06 47	07 41
30	04 01	04 34	05 01	05 12	06 03	06 55	07 47
20	04 30	04 59	05 23	05 29	06 19	07 09	07 59
N 10	04 52	05 19	05 42	05 44	06 33	07 22	08 09
0	05 11	05 37	06 00	05 58	06 46	07 33	08 18
S 10	05 28	05 54	06 17	06 12	07 00	07 45	08 28
20	05 44	06 11	06 35	06 28	07 14	07 57	08 37
30	06 00	06 30	06 56	06 45	07 30	08 11	08 49
35	06 09	06 41	07 09	06 55	07 39	08 19	08 55
40	06 18	06 52	07 23	07 06	07 49	08 28	09 03
45	06 28	07 06	07 39	07 20	08 02	08 39	09 11
S 50	06 40	07 22	08 00	07 37	08 17	08 52	09 22
52	06 45	07 29	08 10	07 44	08 24	08 58	09 26
54	06 51	07 37	08 21	07 53	08 32	09 04	09 32
56	06 57	07 46	08 33	08 03	08 40	09 12	09 38
58	07 04	07 56	08 48	08 14	08 50	09 20	09 44
S 60	07 11	08 08	09 05	08 26	09 02	09 29	09 51

Sunset / Twilight / Moonset

Lat.	Sunset	Twilight Civil	Twilight Naut.	Moonset 27	28	29	30
N 72	□	□	□	23 54	23 26	23 14	23 06
N 70	□	□	□	22 39	22 46	22 48	22 49
68	□	□	□	22 01	22 18	22 29	22 35
66	□	□	□	21 34	21 57	22 13	22 22
64	22 29	////	////	21 14	21 40	22 00	22 14
62	21 53	////	////	20 57	21 26	21 49	22 06
60	21 27	23 08	////	20 43	21 14	21 39	21 59
N 58	21 07	22 21	////	20 31	21 04	21 31	21 53
56	20 50	21 52	////	20 21	20 55	21 24	21 48
54	20 36	21 30	23 13	20 12	20 47	21 17	21 43
52	20 24	21 12	22 29	20 03	20 40	21 11	21 38
50	20 13	20 58	22 02	19 56	20 34	21 06	21 34
45	19 51	20 28	21 18	19 40	20 20	20 54	21 25
N 40	19 33	20 06	20 47	19 27	20 08	20 45	21 18
35	19 18	19 48	20 24	19 16	19 58	20 36	21 12
30	19 05	19 34	20 06	19 07	19 50	20 29	21 06
20	18 43	19 08	19 37	18 50	19 35	20 17	20 56
N 10	18 24	18 47	19 14	18 35	19 22	20 06	20 48
0	18 07	18 29	18 56	18 22	19 09	19 55	20 39
S 10	17 50	18 12	18 39	18 08	18 57	19 45	20 31
20	17 31	17 55	18 23	17 53	18 44	19 33	20 23
30	17 10	17 36	18 06	17 36	18 28	19 21	20 13
35	16 58	17 26	17 58	17 27	18 19	19 13	20 07
40	16 44	17 14	17 48	17 15	18 09	19 05	20 00
45	16 27	17 01	17 38	17 02	17 57	18 55	19 52
S 50	16 07	16 45	17 26	16 46	17 43	18 42	19 43
52	15 57	16 38	17 21	16 38	17 36	18 37	19 39
54	15 46	16 30	17 16	16 30	17 29	18 30	19 34
56	15 33	16 20	17 10	16 20	17 20	18 24	19 29
58	15 19	16 10	17 03	16 09	17 11	18 16	19 23
S 60	15 01	15 59	16 55	15 57	17 00	18 07	19 16

SUN / MOON

Day	Eqn. of Time 00h	12h	Mer. Pass.	MOON Mer. Pass. Upper	Lower	Age	Phase
d	m s	m s	h m	h m	h m	d	%
27	02 57	03 03	12 03	12 10	24 34	00	0
28	03 09	03 16	12 03	12 58	00 34	01	1
29	03 22	03 28	12 03	13 44	01 21	02	5

2014 JUNE 30, JULY 1, 2 (MON., TUES., WED.)

UT	ARIES GHA	VENUS −3.9 GHA	Dec	MARS +0.0 GHA	Dec	JUPITER −1.8 GHA	Dec	SATURN +0.4 GHA	Dec	STARS Name	SHA	Dec
30 00	277 59.2	211 48.5	N20 10.0	81 35.9	S 7 28.4	159 30.7	N21 13.7	52 46.2	S14 38.6	Acamar	315 18.1	S40 14.7
01	293 01.7	226 47.8	10.5	96 37.5	28.8	174 32.6	13.6	67 48.7	38.6	Achernar	335 26.5	S57 09.5
02	308 04.1	241 47.2	11.1	111 39.1	29.2	189 34.5	13.5	82 51.3	38.6	Acrux	173 08.3	S63 11.1
03	323 06.6	256 46.5	.. 11.7	126 40.7	.. 29.6	204 36.4	.. 13.4	97 53.8	.. 38.6	Adhara	255 12.3	S28 59.7
04	338 09.1	271 45.8	12.2	141 42.2	30.1	219 38.3	13.3	112 56.4	38.6	Aldebaran	290 48.8	N16 32.1
05	353 11.5	286 45.2	12.8	156 43.8	30.5	234 40.2	13.2	127 58.9	38.6			
06	8 14.0	301 44.5	N20 13.3	171 45.4	S 7 30.9	249 42.1	N21 13.1	143 01.5	S14 38.6	Alioth	166 20.1	N55 53.2
07	23 16.5	316 43.9	13.9	186 47.0	31.3	264 44.0	13.0	158 04.0	38.5	Alkaid	152 58.2	N49 14.8
08	38 18.9	331 43.2	14.5	201 48.5	31.8	279 45.9	12.9	173 06.6	38.5	Al Na'ir	27 42.6	S46 53.1
M 09	53 21.4	346 42.5	.. 15.0	216 50.1	.. 32.2	294 47.8	.. 12.8	188 09.1	.. 38.5	Alnilam	275 46.0	S 1 11.7
O 10	68 23.9	1 41.9	15.6	231 51.7	32.6	309 49.6	12.7	203 11.7	38.5	Alphard	217 55.6	S 8 43.5
N 11	83 26.3	16 41.2	16.1	246 53.2	33.0	324 51.5	12.6	218 14.2	38.5			
D 12	98 28.8	31 40.6	N20 16.7	261 54.8	S 7 33.5	339 53.4	N21 12.5	233 16.8	S14 38.5	Alphecca	126 10.1	N26 40.2
A 13	113 31.3	46 39.9	17.2	276 56.4	33.9	354 55.3	12.4	248 19.3	38.5	Alpheratz	357 42.7	N29 10.1
Y 14	128 33.7	61 39.2	17.8	291 57.9	34.3	9 57.2	12.3	263 21.9	38.4	Altair	62 07.2	N 8 54.6
15	143 36.2	76 38.6	.. 18.3	306 59.5	.. 34.7	24 59.1	.. 12.2	278 24.4	.. 38.4	Ankaa	353 15.0	S42 13.4
16	158 38.6	91 37.9	18.9	322 01.1	35.2	40 01.0	12.1	293 26.9	38.4	Antares	112 25.0	S26 27.7
17	173 41.1	106 37.2	19.4	337 02.6	35.6	55 02.9	12.0	308 29.5	38.4			
18	188 43.6	121 36.6	N20 20.0	352 04.2	S 7 36.0	70 04.8	N21 11.9	323 32.0	S14 38.4	Arcturus	145 54.9	N19 06.6
19	203 46.0	136 35.9	20.5	7 05.8	36.5	85 06.7	11.8	338 34.6	38.4	Atria	107 25.6	S69 03.1
20	218 48.5	151 35.3	21.1	22 07.3	36.9	100 08.6	11.7	353 37.1	38.4	Avior	234 18.2	S59 33.7
21	233 51.0	166 34.6	.. 21.6	37 08.9	.. 37.3	115 10.5	.. 11.6	8 39.7	.. 38.4	Bellatrix	278 31.6	N 6 21.6
22	248 53.4	181 33.9	22.2	52 10.5	37.7	130 12.3	11.5	23 42.2	38.3	Betelgeuse	271 00.8	N 7 24.4
23	263 55.9	196 33.3	22.7	67 12.0	38.2	145 14.2	11.4	38 44.8	38.3			
1 00	278 58.4	211 32.6	N20 23.3	82 13.6	S 7 38.6	160 16.1	N21 11.3	53 47.3	S14 38.3	Canopus	263 56.4	S52 42.4
01	294 00.8	226 31.9	23.8	97 15.1	39.0	175 18.0	11.2	68 49.9	38.3	Capella	280 33.8	N46 00.5
02	309 03.3	241 31.3	24.4	112 16.7	39.4	190 19.9	11.1	83 52.4	38.3	Deneb	49 30.5	N45 20.0
03	324 05.7	256 30.6	.. 24.9	127 18.3	.. 39.9	205 21.8	.. 11.0	98 54.9	.. 38.3	Denebola	182 33.0	N14 29.5
04	339 08.2	271 29.9	25.4	142 19.8	40.3	220 23.7	10.9	113 57.5	38.3	Diphda	348 55.2	S17 54.3
05	354 10.7	286 29.3	26.0	157 21.4	40.7	235 25.6	10.8	129 00.0	38.3			
06	9 13.1	301 28.6	N20 26.5	172 22.9	S 7 41.2	250 27.5	N21 10.7	144 02.6	S14 38.2	Dubhe	193 51.2	N61 40.6
07	24 15.6	316 27.9	27.1	187 24.5	41.6	265 29.4	10.6	159 05.1	38.2	Elnath	278 12.1	N28 36.9
T 08	39 18.1	331 27.2	27.6	202 26.0	42.0	280 31.3	10.5	174 07.7	38.2	Eltanin	90 45.3	N51 29.5
U 09	54 20.5	346 26.6	.. 28.1	217 27.6	.. 42.4	295 33.2	.. 10.4	189 10.2	.. 38.2	Enif	33 46.2	N 9 56.6
E 10	69 23.0	1 25.9	28.7	232 29.2	42.9	310 35.0	10.3	204 12.7	38.2	Fomalhaut	15 23.1	S29 32.4
S 11	84 25.5	16 25.2	29.2	247 30.7	43.3	325 36.9	10.2	219 15.3	38.2			
D 12	99 27.9	31 24.6	N20 29.7	262 32.3	S 7 43.7	340 38.8	N21 10.1	234 17.8	S14 38.2	Gacrux	172 00.0	S57 12.0
A 13	114 30.4	46 23.9	30.3	277 33.8	44.2	355 40.7	09.9	249 20.4	38.2	Gienah	175 51.6	S17 37.5
Y 14	129 32.9	61 23.2	30.8	292 35.4	44.6	10 42.6	09.8	264 22.9	38.2	Hadar	148 46.5	S60 26.8
15	144 35.3	76 22.5	.. 31.3	307 36.9	.. 45.0	25 44.5	.. 09.7	279 25.5	.. 38.1	Hamal	328 00.0	N23 31.7
16	159 37.8	91 21.9	31.9	322 38.5	45.5	40 46.4	09.6	294 28.0	38.1	Kaus Aust.	83 42.4	S34 22.4
17	174 40.2	106 21.2	32.4	337 40.0	45.9	55 48.3	09.5	309 30.5	38.1			
18	189 42.7	121 20.5	N20 32.9	352 41.6	S 7 46.3	70 50.2	N21 09.4	324 33.1	S14 38.1	Kochab	137 19.6	N74 06.1
19	204 45.2	136 19.8	33.4	7 43.1	46.8	85 52.1	09.3	339 35.6	38.1	Markab	13 37.4	N15 17.0
20	219 47.6	151 19.2	34.0	22 44.7	47.2	100 53.9	09.2	354 38.2	38.1	Menkar	314 14.5	N 4 08.7
21	234 50.1	166 18.5	.. 34.5	37 46.2	.. 47.7	115 55.8	.. 09.1	9 40.7	.. 38.1	Menkent	148 06.5	S36 26.6
22	249 52.6	181 17.8	35.0	52 47.8	48.1	130 57.7	09.0	24 43.2	38.1	Miaplacidus	221 40.1	S69 47.0
23	264 55.0	196 17.1	35.5	67 49.3	48.5	145 59.6	08.9	39 45.8	38.1			
2 00	279 57.5	211 16.5	N20 36.1	82 50.8	S 7 48.9	161 01.5	N21 08.8	54 48.3	S14 38.0	Mirfak	308 39.6	N49 54.4
01	295 00.0	226 15.8	36.6	97 52.4	49.3	176 03.4	08.7	69 50.9	38.0	Nunki	75 57.0	S26 16.5
02	310 02.4	241 15.1	37.1	112 53.9	49.8	191 05.3	08.6	84 53.4	38.0	Peacock	53 17.6	S56 40.9
03	325 04.9	256 14.4	.. 37.6	127 55.5	.. 50.2	206 07.2	.. 08.5	99 56.0	.. 38.0	Pollux	243 27.2	N27 59.3
04	340 07.4	271 13.8	38.1	142 57.0	50.6	221 09.1	08.4	114 58.5	38.0	Procyon	244 59.3	N 5 11.1
05	355 09.8	286 13.1	38.7	157 58.6	51.1	236 11.0	08.3	130 01.0	38.0			
06	10 12.3	301 12.4	N20 39.2	173 00.1	S 7 51.5	251 12.9	N21 08.2	145 03.6	S14 38.0	Rasalhague	96 05.4	N12 33.2
W 07	25 14.7	316 11.7	39.7	188 01.6	51.9	266 14.7	08.1	160 06.1	38.0	Regulus	207 43.0	N11 53.7
E 08	40 17.2	331 11.0	40.2	203 03.2	52.4	281 16.6	08.0	175 08.7	37.9	Rigel	281 11.7	S 8 11.2
D 09	55 19.7	346 10.4	.. 40.7	218 04.7	.. 52.8	296 18.5	.. 07.9	190 11.2	.. 37.9	Rigil Kent.	139 50.3	S60 53.8
N 10	70 22.1	1 09.7	41.2	233 06.3	53.3	311 20.4	07.8	205 13.7	37.9	Sabik	102 11.4	S15 44.4
E 11	85 24.6	16 09.0	41.7	248 07.8	53.7	326 22.3	07.7	220 16.3	37.9			
S 12	100 27.1	31 08.3	N20 42.3	263 09.3	S 7 54.1	341 24.2	N21 07.6	235 18.8	S14 37.9	Schedar	349 39.6	N56 36.8
D 13	115 29.5	46 07.6	42.8	278 10.9	54.6	356 26.1	07.5	250 21.3	37.9	Shaula	96 20.5	S37 06.7
A 14	130 32.0	61 07.0	43.3	293 12.4	55.0	11 28.0	07.4	265 23.9	37.9	Sirius	258 33.4	S16 44.4
Y 15	145 34.5	76 06.3	.. 43.8	308 13.9	.. 55.4	26 29.9	.. 07.3	280 26.4	.. 37.9	Spica	158 30.4	S11 14.2
16	160 36.9	91 05.6	44.3	323 15.5	55.9	41 31.8	07.2	295 29.0	37.9	Suhail	222 52.2	S43 29.8
17	175 39.4	106 04.9	44.8	338 17.0	56.3	56 33.6	07.1	310 31.5	37.9			
18	190 41.8	121 04.2	N20 45.3	353 18.5	S 7 56.7	71 35.5	N21 07.0	325 34.0	S14 37.8	Vega	80 38.0	N38 48.0
19	205 44.3	136 03.5	45.8	8 20.1	57.2	86 37.4	06.9	340 36.6	37.8	Zuben'ubi	137 04.4	S16 06.1
20	220 46.8	151 02.8	46.3	23 21.6	57.6	101 39.3	06.8	355 39.1	37.8			
21	235 49.2	166 02.2	.. 46.8	38 23.1	.. 58.0	116 41.2	.. 06.7	10 41.7	.. 37.8		SHA	Mer.Pass.
22	250 51.7	181 01.5	47.3	53 24.7	58.5	131 43.1	06.6	25 44.2	37.8	Venus	292 34.2	9 54
23	265 54.2	196 00.8	47.8	68 26.2	58.9	146 45.0	06.5	40 46.7	37.8	Mars	163 15.2	18 29
	h m									Jupiter	241 17.8	13 17
Mer.Pass. 5 23.2	v −0.7 d 0.5	v 1.6	d 0.4	v 1.9	d 0.1	v 2.5	d 0.0			Saturn	134 49.0	20 21

SUN and MOON

UT	SUN GHA	SUN Dec	MOON GHA	v	MOON Dec	d	HP
30 d h	° ′	° ′	° ′	′	° ′	′	′
00	179 06.5	N23 11.0	149 16.7	13.9	N13 37.2	6.9	54.1
01	194 06.3	10.9	163 49.6	13.8	13 30.3	6.9	54.1
02	209 06.2	10.7	178 22.4	13.9	13 23.4	7.0	54.0
03	224 06.1 ..	10.6	192 55.3	14.0	13 16.4	7.1	54.0
04	239 06.0	10.4	207 28.3	13.9	13 09.3	7.1	54.0
05	254 05.8	10.3	222 01.2	14.0	13 02.2	7.1	54.0
06	269 05.7	N23 10.1	236 34.2	14.1	N12 55.1	7.3	54.0
07	284 05.6	10.0	251 07.3	14.0	12 47.8	7.2	54.0
08	299 05.5	09.8	265 40.3	14.1	12 40.6	7.3	54.0
09	314 05.3 ..	09.7	280 13.4	14.2	12 33.3	7.4	54.0
10	329 05.2	09.5	294 46.6	14.1	12 25.9	7.4	54.0
11	344 05.1	09.4	309 19.7	14.2	12 18.5	7.5	54.0
12	359 05.0	N23 09.2	323 52.9	14.3	N12 11.0	7.5	54.0
13	14 04.8	09.1	338 26.2	14.2	12 03.5	7.6	54.0
14	29 04.7	08.9	352 59.4	14.3	11 55.9	7.6	54.0
15	44 04.6 ..	08.8	7 32.7	14.4	11 48.3	7.7	54.0
16	59 04.5	08.6	22 06.1	14.3	11 40.6	7.7	54.0
17	74 04.3	08.4	36 39.4	14.4	11 32.9	7.8	54.0
18	89 04.2	N23 08.3	51 12.8	14.4	N11 25.1	7.8	54.0
19	104 04.1	08.1	65 46.2	14.4	11 17.3	7.9	54.0
20	119 04.0	08.0	80 19.6	14.5	11 09.4	7.9	54.0
21	134 03.9 ..	07.8	94 53.1	14.5	11 01.5	7.9	54.0
22	149 03.7	07.6	109 26.6	14.5	10 53.6	8.0	54.0
23	164 03.6	07.5	124 00.1	14.6	10 45.6	8.0	54.0
1 00	179 03.5	N23 07.3	138 33.7	14.6	N10 37.6	8.1	54.0
01	194 03.4	07.1	153 07.3	14.6	10 29.5	8.1	54.0
02	209 03.2	07.0	167 40.9	14.6	10 21.4	8.2	54.0
03	224 03.1 ..	06.8	182 14.5	14.7	10 13.2	8.2	54.0
04	239 03.0	06.7	196 48.2	14.6	10 05.0	8.3	54.0
05	254 02.9	06.5	211 21.8	14.7	9 56.7	8.2	54.0
06	269 02.8	N23 06.3	225 55.5	14.8	N 9 48.5	8.4	54.0
07	284 02.6	06.2	240 29.3	14.7	9 40.1	8.3	54.0
08	299 02.5	06.0	255 03.0	14.8	9 31.8	8.4	54.0
09	314 02.4 ..	05.8	269 36.8	14.8	9 23.4	8.5	54.0
10	329 02.3	05.6	284 10.6	14.8	9 14.9	8.5	54.0
11	344 02.1	05.5	298 44.4	14.8	9 06.4	8.5	54.0
12	359 02.0	N23 05.3	313 18.2	14.9	N 8 57.9	8.6	54.0
13	14 01.9	05.1	327 52.1	14.9	8 49.3	8.5	54.1
14	29 01.8	05.0	342 26.0	14.9	8 40.8	8.7	54.1
15	44 01.7 ..	04.8	356 59.9	14.9	8 32.1	8.6	54.1
16	59 01.5	04.6	11 33.8	14.9	8 23.5	8.7	54.1
17	74 01.4	04.4	26 07.7	15.0	8 14.8	8.8	54.1
18	89 01.3	N23 04.3	40 41.7	15.0	N 8 06.0	8.7	54.1
19	104 01.2	04.1	55 15.7	15.0	7 57.3	8.8	54.1
20	119 01.1	03.9	69 49.7	15.0	7 48.5	8.9	54.1
21	134 00.9 ..	03.7	84 23.7	15.0	7 39.6	8.8	54.1
22	149 00.8	03.6	98 57.7	15.0	7 30.8	8.9	54.1
23	164 00.7	03.4	113 31.7	15.1	7 21.9	9.0	54.1
2 00	179 00.6	N23 03.2	128 05.8	15.1	N 7 12.9	8.9	54.1
01	194 00.5	03.0	142 39.9	15.0	7 04.0	9.0	54.1
02	209 00.3	02.9	157 13.9	15.1	6 55.0	9.0	54.1
03	224 00.2 ..	02.7	171 48.0	15.1	6 46.0	9.1	54.1
04	239 00.1	02.5	186 22.1	15.1	6 36.9	9.0	54.1
05	254 00.0	02.3	200 56.2	15.2	6 27.9	9.1	54.1
06	268 59.9	N23 02.1	215 30.4	15.1	N 6 18.8	9.2	54.2
07	283 59.7	01.9	230 04.5	15.2	6 09.6	9.1	54.2
08	298 59.6	01.7	244 38.7	15.1	6 00.5	9.2	54.2
09	313 59.5 ..	01.5	259 12.8	15.2	5 51.3	9.2	54.2
10	328 59.4	01.4	273 47.0	15.2	5 42.1	9.3	54.2
11	343 59.3	01.2	288 21.2	15.1	5 32.8	9.2	54.2
12	358 59.2	N23 01.0	302 55.3	15.2	N 5 23.6	9.3	54.2
13	13 59.0	00.8	317 29.5	15.2	5 14.3	9.3	54.2
14	28 58.9	00.6	332 03.7	15.2	5 05.0	9.3	54.2
15	43 58.8 ..	00.4	346 37.9	15.2	4 55.7	9.4	54.2
16	58 58.7	00.2	1 12.1	15.2	4 46.3	9.4	54.3
17	73 58.6	23 00.0	15 46.3	15.2	4 36.9	9.4	54.3
18	88 58.4	N22 59.8	30 20.5	15.2	N 4 27.5	9.4	54.3
19	103 58.3	59.6	44 54.7	15.2	4 18.1	9.4	54.3
20	118 58.2	59.5	59 28.9	15.2	4 08.7	9.5	54.3
21	133 58.1 ..	59.3	74 03.1	15.3	3 59.2	9.4	54.3
22	148 58.0	59.1	88 37.4	15.2	3 49.8	9.5	54.3
23	163 57.9	58.9	103 11.6	15.2	N 3 40.3	9.6	54.3
	SD 15.8	d 0.2	SD 14.7	14.7			14.8

Twilight and Moonrise

Lat.	Naut.	Civil	Sunrise	30	1	2	3
°	h m	h m	h m	h m	h m	h m	h m
N 72	▭	▭	▭	05 13	06 52	08 29	10 04
N 70	▭	▭	▭	05 38	07 08	08 37	10 07
68	▭	▭	▭	05 56	07 20	08 44	10 09
66	////	////	00 19	06 11	07 31	08 50	10 10
64	////	////	01 41	06 24	07 39	08 55	10 12
62	////	////	02 17	06 34	07 46	08 59	10 13
60	////	01 03	02 42	06 43	07 53	09 03	10 14
N 58	////	01 48	03 02	06 51	07 58	09 06	10 15
56	////	02 17	03 18	06 57	08 03	09 09	10 16
54	00 58	02 38	03 32	07 03	08 07	09 12	10 17
52	01 40	02 56	03 44	07 09	08 11	09 14	10 18
50	02 06	03 11	03 55	07 14	08 15	09 16	10 18
45	02 51	03 40	04 17	07 24	08 23	09 21	10 20
N 40	03 21	04 02	04 35	07 33	08 29	09 25	10 21
35	03 43	04 20	04 50	07 41	08 34	09 28	10 22
30	04 02	04 35	05 02	07 47	08 39	09 31	10 23
20	04 31	05 00	05 24	07 59	08 48	09 36	10 25
N 10	04 53	05 20	05 43	08 09	08 55	09 41	10 26
0	05 12	05 38	06 00	08 18	09 02	09 45	10 27
S 10	05 28	05 55	06 17	08 28	09 09	09 49	10 29
20	05 44	06 12	06 36	08 37	09 16	09 53	10 30
30	06 00	06 30	06 57	08 49	09 24	09 58	10 32
35	06 09	06 41	07 09	08 55	09 29	10 01	10 33
40	06 18	06 52	07 23	09 03	09 35	10 05	10 34
45	06 28	07 05	07 39	09 11	09 41	10 08	10 35
S 50	06 40	07 21	08 00	09 22	09 48	10 13	10 36
52	06 45	07 29	08 09	09 26	09 52	10 15	10 37
54	06 51	07 37	08 20	09 32	09 56	10 17	10 38
56	06 57	07 45	08 32	09 38	10 00	10 20	10 39
58	07 03	07 55	08 47	09 44	10 04	10 23	10 40
S 60	07 10	08 07	09 04	09 51	10 10	10 26	10 41

Sunset, Twilight and Moonset

Lat.	Sunset	Civil	Naut.	30	1	2	3
°	h m	h m	h m	h m	h m	h m	h m
N 72	▭	▭	▭	23 06	22 58	22 52	22 45
N 70	▭	▭	▭	22 49	22 48	22 47	22 45
68	▭	▭	▭	22 35	22 39	22 43	22 46
66	23 40	////	////	22 24	22 32	22 39	22 46
64	22 25	////	////	22 14	22 26	22 36	22 46
62	21 50	////	////	22 06	22 21	22 34	22 46
60	21 25	23 03	////	21 59	22 16	22 32	22 46
N 58	21 05	22 18	////	21 53	22 12	22 30	22 46
56	20 49	21 50	////	21 48	22 09	22 28	22 47
54	20 35	21 29	23 08	21 43	22 05	22 26	22 47
52	20 23	21 11	22 27	21 38	22 02	22 25	22 47
50	20 13	20 57	22 01	21 34	22 00	22 24	22 47
45	19 50	20 28	21 17	21 25	21 54	22 21	22 47
N 40	19 33	20 05	20 47	21 18	21 49	22 18	22 47
35	19 18	19 48	20 24	21 12	21 45	22 16	22 47
30	19 05	19 33	20 06	21 06	21 41	22 14	22 47
20	18 43	19 08	19 37	20 56	21 34	22 11	22 48
N 10	18 25	18 48	19 15	20 48	21 28	22 08	22 48
0	18 08	18 30	18 56	20 39	21 23	22 05	22 48
S 10	17 50	18 13	18 39	20 31	21 17	22 03	22 48
20	17 33	17 56	18 24	20 23	21 11	22 00	22 48
30	17 11	17 38	18 07	20 13	21 04	21 56	22 48
35	16 59	17 27	17 59	20 07	21 00	21 54	22 48
40	16 45	17 16	17 50	20 00	20 56	21 52	22 48
45	16 29	17 02	17 39	19 52	20 51	21 49	22 48
S 50	16 08	16 47	17 28	19 43	20 44	21 46	22 48
52	15 59	16 39	17 23	19 39	20 41	21 45	22 49
54	15 48	16 31	17 17	19 34	20 38	21 43	22 49
56	15 35	16 22	17 11	19 29	20 35	21 41	22 49
58	15 21	16 12	17 05	19 23	20 31	21 39	22 49
S 60	15 04	16 01	16 57	19 16	20 26	21 37	22 49

SUN and MOON

Day	Eqn. of Time 00h	Eqn. of Time 12h	Mer. Pass.	Mer. Pass. Upper	Mer. Pass. Lower	Age	Phase
d	m s	m s	h m	h m	h m	d	%
30	03 34	03 40	12 04	14 29	02 07	03	9
1	03 46	03 52	12 04	15 12	02 51	04	15
2	03 57	04 03	12 04	15 55	03 34	05	23

UT	ARIES	VENUS −3.9		MARS +0.1		JUPITER −1.8		SATURN +0.4		STARS		
d h	GHA	GHA	Dec	GHA	Dec	GHA	Dec	GHA	Dec	Name	SHA	Dec
3 00	280 56.6	211 00.1	N20 48.3	83 27.7	S 7 59.3	161 46.9	N21 06.4	55 49.3	S14 37.8	Acamar	315 18.1	S40 14.7
01	295 59.1	225 59.4	48.8	98 29.3	7 59.8	176 48.8	06.3	70 51.8	37.8	Achernar	335 26.5	S57 09.5
02	311 01.6	240 58.7	49.3	113 30.8	8 00.2	191 50.7	06.2	85 54.3	37.8	Acrux	173 08.4	S63 11.1
03	326 04.0	255 58.0	.. 49.8	128 32.3	.. 00.7	206 52.5	.. 06.1	100 56.9	.. 37.8	Adhara	255 12.3	S28 59.7
04	341 06.5	270 57.3	50.3	143 33.8	01.1	221 54.4	06.0	115 59.4	37.7	Aldebaran	290 48.8	N16 32.1
05	356 09.0	285 56.7	50.8	158 35.4	01.5	236 56.3	05.9	131 02.0	37.7			
T 06	11 11.4	300 56.0	N20 51.3	173 36.9	S 8 02.0	251 58.2	N21 05.8	146 04.5	S14 37.7	Alioth	166 20.1	N55 53.2
H 07	26 13.9	315 55.3	51.8	188 38.4	02.4	267 00.1	05.7	161 07.0	37.7	Alkaid	152 58.3	N49 14.8
U 08	41 16.3	330 54.6	52.3	203 39.9	02.8	282 02.0	05.6	176 09.6	37.7	Al Na'ir	27 42.6	S46 53.1
R 09	56 18.8	345 53.9	.. 52.8	218 41.5	.. 03.3	297 03.9	.. 05.5	191 12.1	.. 37.7	Alnilam	275 45.9	S 1 11.7
S 10	71 21.3	0 53.2	53.3	233 43.0	03.7	312 05.8	05.3	206 14.6	37.7	Alphard	217 55.6	S 8 43.5
D 11	86 23.7	15 52.5	53.8	248 44.5	04.2	327 07.7	05.2	221 17.2	37.7			
A 12	101 26.2	30 51.8	N20 54.2	263 46.0	S 8 04.6	342 09.5	N21 05.1	236 19.7	S14 37.7	Alphecca	126 10.2	N26 40.2
Y 13	116 28.7	45 51.1	54.7	278 47.6	05.0	357 11.4	05.0	251 22.2	37.7	Alpheratz	357 42.6	N29 10.1
14	131 31.1	60 50.4	55.2	293 49.1	05.5	12 13.3	04.9	266 24.8	37.6	Altair	62 07.2	N 8 54.6
15	146 33.6	75 49.7	.. 55.7	308 50.6	.. 05.9	27 15.2	.. 04.8	281 27.3	.. 37.6	Ankaa	353 15.0	S42 13.4
16	161 36.1	90 49.1	56.2	323 52.1	06.4	42 17.1	04.7	296 29.8	37.6	Antares	112 25.0	S26 27.7
17	176 38.5	105 48.4	56.7	338 53.6	06.8	57 19.0	04.6	311 32.4	37.6			
18	191 41.0	120 47.7	N20 57.2	353 55.2	S 8 07.2	72 20.9	N21 04.5	326 34.9	S14 37.6	Arcturus	145 55.0	N19 06.6
19	206 43.5	135 47.0	57.6	8 56.7	07.7	87 22.8	04.4	341 37.4	37.6	Atria	107 25.6	S69 03.2
20	221 45.9	150 46.3	58.1	23 58.2	08.1	102 24.7	04.3	356 40.0	37.6	Avior	234 18.3	S59 33.6
21	236 48.4	165 45.6	.. 58.6	38 59.7	.. 08.6	117 26.5	.. 04.2	11 42.5	.. 37.6	Bellatrix	278 31.5	N 6 21.6
22	251 50.8	180 44.9	59.1	54 01.2	09.0	132 28.4	04.1	26 45.0	37.6	Betelgeuse	271 00.8	N 7 24.4
23	266 53.3	195 44.2	20 59.6	69 02.7	09.4	147 30.3	04.0	41 47.6	37.6			
4 00	281 55.8	210 43.5	N21 00.0	84 04.3	S 8 09.9	162 32.2	N21 03.9	56 50.1	S14 37.5	Canopus	263 56.4	S52 42.4
01	296 58.2	225 42.8	00.5	99 05.8	10.3	177 34.1	03.8	71 52.6	37.5	Capella	280 33.8	N46 00.5
02	312 00.7	240 42.1	01.0	114 07.3	10.8	192 36.0	03.7	86 55.2	37.5	Deneb	49 30.5	N45 20.0
03	327 03.2	255 41.4	.. 01.5	129 08.8	.. 11.2	207 37.9	.. 03.6	101 57.7	.. 37.5	Denebola	182 33.0	N14 29.5
04	342 05.6	270 40.7	01.9	144 10.3	11.6	222 39.8	03.5	117 00.2	37.5	Diphda	348 55.2	S17 54.3
05	357 08.1	285 40.0	02.4	159 11.8	12.1	237 41.7	03.4	132 02.8	37.5			
F 06	12 10.6	300 39.3	N21 02.9	174 13.3	S 8 12.5	252 43.6	N21 03.3	147 05.3	S14 37.5	Dubhe	193 51.3	N61 40.5
R 07	27 13.0	315 38.6	03.4	189 14.8	13.0	267 45.4	03.2	162 07.8	37.5	Elnath	278 12.1	N28 36.9
I 08	42 15.5	330 37.9	03.8	204 16.3	13.4	282 47.3	03.1	177 10.4	37.5	Eltanin	90 45.3	N51 29.5
D 09	57 17.9	345 37.2	.. 04.3	219 17.9	.. 13.9	297 49.2	.. 03.0	192 12.9	.. 37.5	Enif	33 46.1	N 9 56.6
A 10	72 20.4	0 36.5	04.8	234 19.4	14.3	312 51.1	02.9	207 15.4	37.5	Fomalhaut	15 23.0	S29 32.4
Y 11	87 22.9	15 35.8	05.2	249 20.9	14.7	327 53.0	02.8	222 18.0	37.5			
12	102 25.3	30 35.1	N21 05.7	264 22.4	S 8 15.2	342 54.9	N21 02.7	237 20.5	S14 37.4	Gacrux	172 00.0	S57 12.0
13	117 27.8	45 34.4	06.2	279 23.9	15.6	357 56.8	02.6	252 23.0	37.4	Gienah	175 51.6	S17 37.5
14	132 30.3	60 33.7	06.6	294 25.4	16.1	12 58.7	02.4	267 25.6	37.4	Hadar	148 46.5	S60 26.8
15	147 32.7	75 33.0	.. 07.1	309 26.9	.. 16.5	28 00.5	.. 02.3	282 28.1	.. 37.4	Hamal	328 00.0	N23 31.7
16	162 35.2	90 32.3	07.5	324 28.4	17.0	43 02.4	02.2	297 30.6	37.4	Kaus Aust.	83 42.4	S34 22.4
17	177 37.7	105 31.6	08.0	339 29.9	17.4	58 04.3	02.1	312 33.2	37.4			
18	192 40.1	120 30.9	N21 08.5	354 31.4	S 8 17.8	73 06.2	N21 02.0	327 35.7	S14 37.4	Kochab	137 19.6	N74 06.1
19	207 42.6	135 30.2	08.9	9 32.9	18.3	88 08.1	01.9	342 38.2	37.4	Markab	13 37.4	N15 17.0
20	222 45.1	150 29.5	09.4	24 34.4	18.7	103 10.0	01.8	357 40.7	37.4	Menkar	314 14.5	N 4 08.7
21	237 47.5	165 28.8	.. 09.8	39 35.9	.. 19.2	118 11.9	.. 01.7	12 43.3	.. 37.4	Menkent	148 06.5	S36 26.6
22	252 50.0	180 28.1	10.3	54 37.4	19.6	133 13.8	01.6	27 45.8	37.4	Miaplacidus	221 40.1	S69 46.9
23	267 52.4	195 27.3	10.8	69 38.9	20.1	148 15.7	01.5	42 48.3	37.4			
5 00	282 54.9	210 26.6	N21 11.2	84 40.4	S 8 20.5	163 17.5	N21 01.4	57 50.9	S14 37.3	Mirfak	308 39.6	N49 54.4
01	297 57.4	225 25.9	11.7	99 41.9	21.0	178 19.4	01.3	72 53.4	37.3	Nunki	75 57.0	S26 16.5
02	312 59.8	240 25.2	12.1	114 43.4	21.4	193 21.3	01.2	87 55.9	37.3	Peacock	53 17.6	S56 41.0
03	328 02.3	255 24.5	.. 12.6	129 44.9	.. 21.8	208 23.2	.. 01.1	102 58.5	.. 37.3	Pollux	243 27.2	N27 59.3
04	343 04.8	270 23.8	13.0	144 46.4	22.3	223 25.1	01.0	118 01.0	37.3	Procyon	244 59.3	N 5 11.1
05	358 07.2	285 23.1	13.5	159 47.9	22.7	238 27.0	00.9	133 03.5	37.3			
S 06	13 09.7	300 22.4	N21 13.9	174 49.4	S 8 23.2	253 28.9	N21 00.8	148 06.0	S14 37.3	Rasalhague	96 05.4	N12 33.2
A 07	28 12.2	315 21.7	14.4	189 50.9	23.6	268 30.8	00.7	163 08.6	37.3	Regulus	207 43.0	N11 53.7
T 08	43 14.6	330 21.0	14.8	204 52.4	24.1	283 32.7	00.6	178 11.1	37.3	Rigel	281 11.7	S 8 11.2
U 09	58 17.1	345 20.3	.. 15.3	219 53.9	.. 24.5	298 34.5	.. 00.5	193 13.6	.. 37.3	Rigil Kent.	139 50.3	S60 53.8
R 10	73 19.6	0 19.6	15.7	234 55.4	25.0	313 36.4	00.4	208 16.2	37.3	Sabik	102 11.4	S15 44.4
D 11	88 22.0	15 18.8	16.1	249 56.9	25.4	328 38.3	00.3	223 18.7	37.3			
A 12	103 24.5	30 18.1	N21 16.6	264 58.4	S 8 25.9	343 40.2	N21 00.1	238 21.2	S14 37.3	Schedar	349 39.5	N56 36.8
Y 13	118 26.9	45 17.4	17.0	279 59.9	26.3	358 42.1	21 00.0	253 23.7	37.2	Shaula	96 20.5	S37 06.7
14	133 29.4	60 16.7	17.5	295 01.4	26.8	13 44.0	20 59.9	268 26.3	37.2	Sirius	258 33.4	S16 44.3
15	148 31.9	75 16.0	.. 17.9	310 02.8	.. 27.2	28 45.9	.. 59.8	283 28.8	.. 37.2	Spica	158 30.4	S11 14.2
16	163 34.3	90 15.3	18.3	325 04.3	27.6	43 47.8	59.7	298 31.3	37.2	Suhail	222 52.2	S43 29.8
17	178 36.8	105 14.6	18.8	340 05.8	28.1	58 49.6	59.6	313 33.8	37.2			
18	193 39.3	120 13.9	N21 19.2	355 07.3	S 8 28.5	73 51.5	N20 59.5	328 36.4	S14 37.2	Vega	80 38.0	N38 48.1
19	208 41.7	135 13.1	19.7	10 08.8	29.0	88 53.4	59.4	343 38.9	37.2	Zuben'ubi	137 04.4	S16 06.1
20	223 44.2	150 12.4	20.1	25 10.3	29.4	103 55.3	59.3	358 41.4	37.2		SHA	Mer.Pass.
21	238 46.7	165 11.7	.. 20.5	40 11.8	.. 29.9	118 57.2	.. 59.2	13 44.0	.. 37.2	Venus	288 47.7	9 58
22	253 49.1	180 11.0	21.0	55 13.3	30.3	133 59.1	59.1	28 46.5	37.2	Mars	162 08.5	18 22
23	268 51.6	195 10.3	21.4	70 14.7	30.8	149 01.0	59.0	43 49.0	37.2	Jupiter	240 36.4	13 08
Mer.Pass.	5 11.4	v −0.7	d 0.5	v 1.5	d 0.4	v 1.9	d 0.1	v 2.5	d 0.0	Saturn	134 54.3	20 09

UT	SUN GHA	SUN Dec	MOON GHA	v	MOON Dec	d	HP
d h	° ′	° ′	° ′	′	° ′	′	′
3 00	178 57.7	N22 58.7	117 45.8	15.2	N 3 30.7	9.5	54.3
01	193 57.6	58.5	132 20.0	15.2	3 21.2	9.5	54.4
02	208 57.5	58.3	146 54.2	15.2	3 11.7	9.6	54.4
03	223 57.4	.. 58.1	161 28.4	15.2	3 02.1	9.6	54.4
04	238 57.3	57.9	176 02.6	15.2	2 52.5	9.6	54.4
05	253 57.2	57.7	190 36.8	15.2	2 42.9	9.6	54.4
06	268 57.0	N22 57.5	205 11.0	15.2	N 2 33.3	9.6	54.4
07	283 56.9	57.3	219 45.2	15.1	2 23.7	9.6	54.4
08	298 56.8	57.1	234 19.3	15.2	2 14.0	9.6	54.5
09	313 56.7	.. 56.9	248 53.5	15.2	2 04.4	9.7	54.5
10	328 56.6	56.7	263 27.7	15.1	1 54.7	9.7	54.5
11	343 56.5	56.5	278 01.8	15.2	1 45.0	9.7	54.5
12	358 56.4	N22 56.3	292 36.0	15.1	N 1 35.3	9.7	54.5
13	13 56.2	56.1	307 10.1	15.1	1 25.6	9.7	54.5
14	28 56.1	55.9	321 44.2	15.1	1 15.9	9.7	54.6
15	43 56.0	.. 55.6	336 18.3	15.1	1 06.2	9.7	54.6
16	58 55.9	55.4	350 52.4	15.1	0 56.5	9.8	54.6
17	73 55.8	55.2	5 26.5	15.0	0 46.7	9.7	54.6
18	88 55.7	N22 55.0	20 00.5	15.1	N 0 37.0	9.8	54.6
19	103 55.6	54.8	34 34.6	15.0	0 27.2	9.8	54.6
20	118 55.4	54.6	49 08.6	15.0	0 17.4	9.7	54.7
21	133 55.3	.. 54.4	63 42.6	15.0	N 0 07.7	9.8	54.7
22	148 55.2	54.2	78 16.6	15.0	S 0 02.1	9.8	54.7
23	163 55.1	54.0	92 50.6	15.0	0 11.9	9.8	54.7
4 00	178 55.0	N22 53.8	107 24.6	14.9	S 0 21.7	9.8	54.7
01	193 54.9	53.5	121 58.5	14.9	0 31.5	9.8	54.8
02	208 54.8	53.3	136 32.4	14.9	0 41.3	9.8	54.8
03	223 54.6	.. 53.1	151 06.3	14.9	0 51.1	9.9	54.8
04	238 54.5	52.9	165 40.2	14.9	1 00.9	9.9	54.8
05	253 54.4	52.7	180 14.1	14.8	1 10.8	9.8	54.8
06	268 54.3	N22 52.5	194 47.9	14.8	S 1 20.6	9.8	54.9
07	283 54.2	52.2	209 21.7	14.8	1 30.4	9.8	54.9
08	298 54.1	52.0	223 55.5	14.7	1 40.2	9.8	54.9
09	313 54.0	.. 51.8	238 29.2	14.8	1 50.0	9.8	54.9
10	328 53.9	51.6	253 03.0	14.7	1 59.8	9.9	54.9
11	343 53.8	51.4	267 36.7	14.6	2 09.7	9.8	55.0
12	358 53.6	N22 51.1	282 10.3	14.7	S 2 19.5	9.8	55.0
13	13 53.5	50.9	296 44.0	14.6	2 29.3	9.8	55.0
14	28 53.4	50.7	311 17.6	14.6	2 39.1	9.8	55.0
15	43 53.3	.. 50.5	325 51.2	14.5	2 48.9	9.8	55.1
16	58 53.2	50.2	340 24.7	14.5	2 58.7	9.8	55.1
17	73 53.1	50.0	354 58.2	14.5	3 08.5	9.8	55.1
18	88 53.0	N22 49.8	9 31.7	14.4	S 3 18.3	9.8	55.1
19	103 52.9	49.6	24 05.1	14.4	3 28.1	9.8	55.2
20	118 52.8	49.3	38 38.5	14.4	3 37.9	9.8	55.2
21	133 52.6	.. 49.1	53 11.9	14.4	3 47.6	9.8	55.2
22	148 52.5	48.9	67 45.3	14.3	3 57.4	9.8	55.2
23	163 52.4	48.7	82 18.6	14.2	4 07.2	9.7	55.3
5 00	178 52.3	N22 48.4	96 51.8	14.2	S 4 16.9	9.8	55.3
01	193 52.2	48.2	111 25.0	14.2	4 26.7	9.7	55.3
02	208 52.1	48.0	125 58.2	14.1	4 36.4	9.7	55.3
03	223 52.0	.. 47.7	140 31.3	14.1	4 46.1	9.7	55.4
04	238 51.9	47.5	155 04.4	14.1	4 55.8	9.7	55.4
05	253 51.8	47.3	169 37.5	14.0	5 05.5	9.7	55.4
06	268 51.7	N22 47.0	184 10.5	14.0	S 5 15.2	9.7	55.5
07	283 51.6	46.8	198 43.5	13.9	5 24.9	9.6	55.5
08	298 51.4	46.6	213 16.4	13.9	5 34.5	9.7	55.5
09	313 51.3	.. 46.3	227 49.3	13.8	5 44.2	9.6	55.5
10	328 51.2	46.1	242 22.1	13.8	5 53.8	9.6	55.6
11	343 51.1	45.9	256 54.9	13.7	6 03.4	9.6	55.6
12	358 51.0	N22 45.6	271 27.6	13.7	S 6 13.0	9.6	55.6
13	13 50.9	45.4	286 00.3	13.6	6 22.6	9.5	55.6
14	28 50.8	45.1	300 32.9	13.6	6 32.1	9.6	55.7
15	43 50.7	.. 44.9	315 05.5	13.5	6 41.7	9.5	55.7
16	58 50.6	44.7	329 38.0	13.5	6 51.2	9.5	55.7
17	73 50.5	44.4	344 10.5	13.4	7 00.7	9.4	55.8
18	88 50.4	N22 44.2	358 42.9	13.4	S 7 10.1	9.5	55.8
19	103 50.3	43.9	13 15.3	13.3	7 19.6	9.4	55.8
20	118 50.2	43.7	27 47.6	13.3	7 29.0	9.4	55.8
21	133 50.0	.. 43.5	42 19.9	13.2	7 38.4	9.4	55.9
22	148 49.9	43.2	56 52.1	13.2	7 47.8	9.4	55.9
23	163 49.8	43.0	71 24.3	13.0	S 7 57.2	9.3	55.9
	SD 15.8	d 0.2	SD 14.9		15.0		15.2

Day rows: Thursday (3), Friday (4), Saturday (5).

Moonrise

Lat.	Twilight Naut.	Twilight Civil	Sunrise	Moonrise 3	4	5	6
°	h m	h m	h m	h m	h m	h m	h m
N 72	▢	▢	▢	10 04	11 40	13 19	15 04
N 70	▢	▢	▢	10 07	11 37	13 09	14 46
68	▢	▢	▢	10 09	11 34	13 02	14 32
66	////	////	00 41	10 10	11 32	12 55	14 21
64	////	////	01 47	10 12	11 30	12 49	14 11
62	////	////	02 21	10 13	11 28	12 45	14 03
60	////	01 11	02 46	10 14	11 27	12 41	13 56
N 58	////	01 53	03 05	10 15	11 25	12 37	13 50
56	////	02 20	03 21	10 16	11 24	12 34	13 45
54	01 05	02 41	03 35	10 17	11 23	12 31	13 40
52	01 44	02 59	03 47	10 18	11 22	12 28	13 36
50	02 10	03 13	03 57	10 18	11 21	12 26	13 32
45	02 53	03 42	04 19	10 20	11 20	12 21	13 23
N 40	03 23	04 04	04 36	10 21	11 18	12 16	13 16
35	03 45	04 21	04 51	10 22	11 17	12 13	13 10
30	04 03	04 36	05 04	10 23	11 16	12 09	13 05
20	04 32	05 01	05 25	10 25	11 14	12 04	12 56
N 10	04 54	05 21	05 44	10 26	11 12	11 59	12 48
0	05 12	05 38	06 01	10 27	11 10	11 54	12 41
S 10	05 29	05 55	06 18	10 29	11 09	11 50	12 33
20	05 45	06 12	06 36	10 30	11 07	11 45	12 25
30	06 00	06 30	06 56	10 32	11 05	11 40	12 17
35	06 09	06 40	07 08	10 33	11 04	11 37	12 12
40	06 18	06 52	07 22	10 34	11 03	11 33	12 06
45	06 28	07 05	07 39	10 35	11 01	11 29	11 59
S 50	06 39	07 21	07 59	10 36	11 00	11 24	11 51
52	06 44	07 28	08 08	10 37	10 59	11 22	11 48
54	06 50	07 36	08 19	10 38	10 58	11 20	11 44
56	06 56	07 44	08 31	10 39	10 57	11 17	11 39
58	07 02	07 54	08 45	10 40	10 56	11 14	11 34
S 60	07 09	08 05	09 02	10 41	10 55	11 11	11 29

Moonset

Lat.	Sunset	Twilight Civil	Twilight Naut.	Moonset 3	4	5	6
°	h m	h m	h m	h m	h m	h m	h m
N 72	▢	▢	▢	22 45	22 38	22 31	22 23
N 70	▢	▢	▢	22 45	22 44	22 43	22 42
68	▢	▢	▢	22 46	22 49	22 52	22 57
66	23 23	////	////	22 46	22 52	23 00	23 10
64	22 20	////	////	22 46	22 56	23 07	23 20
62	21 47	////	////	22 46	22 59	23 13	23 29
60	21 22	22 56	////	22 46	23 01	23 18	23 37
N 58	21 03	22 15	////	22 46	23 03	23 22	23 44
56	20 47	21 47	////	22 47	23 06	23 26	23 50
54	20 34	21 27	23 02	22 47	23 07	23 30	23 55
52	20 22	21 10	22 24	22 47	23 09	23 33	24 00
50	20 11	20 55	21 58	22 47	23 11	23 36	24 03
45	19 50	20 27	21 15	22 47	23 14	23 42	24 14
N 40	19 32	20 05	20 46	22 47	23 17	23 48	24 22
35	19 18	19 47	20 23	22 47	23 19	23 53	24 29
30	19 05	19 32	20 05	22 47	23 22	23 57	24 35
20	18 44	19 08	19 37	22 48	23 25	24 04	00 04
N 10	18 25	18 48	19 15	22 48	23 28	24 10	00 10
0	18 08	18 31	18 57	22 48	23 31	24 16	00 16
S 10	17 51	18 14	18 40	22 48	23 34	24 22	00 22
20	17 33	17 57	18 24	22 48	23 38	24 29	00 29
30	17 12	17 39	18 08	22 48	23 41	24 36	00 36
35	17 00	17 28	18 00	22 48	23 43	24 40	00 40
40	16 47	17 17	17 51	22 48	23 45	24 45	00 45
45	16 30	17 04	17 41	22 48	23 49	24 50	00 50
S 50	16 10	16 49	17 30	22 48	23 52	24 57	00 57
52	16 01	16 41	17 25	22 49	23 54	25 00	01 00
54	15 50	16 33	17 19	22 49	23 55	25 04	01 04
56	15 38	16 25	17 13	22 49	23 57	25 07	01 07
58	15 24	16 15	17 07	22 49	23 59	25 12	01 12
S 60	15 07	16 04	17 00	22 49	24 02	00 02	01 16

Day	SUN Eqn. of Time 00h	SUN Eqn. of Time 12h	SUN Mer. Pass.	MOON Mer. Pass. Upper	MOON Mer. Pass. Lower	Age	Phase
d	m s	m s	h m	h m	h m	d	%
3	04 09	04 14	12 04	16 38	04 16	06	31
4	04 20	04 25	12 04	17 21	04 59	07	40
5	04 31	04 36	12 05	18 05	05 43	08	50

2014 JULY 6, 7, 8 (SUN., MON., TUES.)

UT	ARIES GHA	VENUS −3.9 GHA	VENUS Dec	MARS +0.1 GHA	MARS Dec	JUPITER −1.8 GHA	JUPITER Dec	SATURN +0.4 GHA	SATURN Dec	STARS Name	SHA	Dec
6 00	283 54.0	210 09.6	N21 21.8	85 16.2	S 8 31.2	164 02.9	N20 58.9	58 51.5	S14 37.2	Acamar	315 18.1	S40 14.7
01	298 56.5	225 08.8	22.2	100 17.7	31.7	179 04.7	58.8	73 54.1	37.2	Achernar	335 26.4	S57 09.5
02	313 59.0	240 08.1	22.7	115 19.2	32.1	194 06.6	58.7	88 56.6	37.2	Acrux	173 08.4	S63 11.1
03	329 01.4	255 07.4 ..	23.1	130 20.7 ..	32.6	209 08.5 ..	58.6	103 59.1 ..	37.1	Adhara	255 12.3	S28 59.7
04	344 03.9	270 06.7	23.5	145 22.2	33.0	224 10.4	58.5	119 01.6	37.1	Aldebaran	290 48.8	N16 32.1
05	359 06.4	285 06.0	24.0	160 23.6	33.5	239 12.3	58.4	134 04.2	37.1			
06	14 08.8	300 05.3	N21 24.4	175 25.1	S 8 33.9	254 14.2	N20 58.2	149 06.7	S14 37.1	Alioth	166 20.2	N55 53.2
07	29 11.3	315 04.5	24.8	190 26.6	34.4	269 16.1	58.1	164 09.2	37.1	Alkaid	152 58.3	N49 14.8
08	44 13.8	330 03.8	25.2	205 28.1	34.8	284 18.0	58.0	179 11.7	37.1	Al Na'ir	27 42.6	S46 53.1
09	59 16.2	345 03.1 ..	25.7	220 29.6 ..	35.3	299 19.9 ..	57.9	194 14.3 ..	37.1	Alnilam	275 45.9	S 1 11.7
10	74 18.7	0 02.4	26.1	235 31.0	35.7	314 21.7	57.8	209 16.8	37.1	Alphard	217 55.6	S 8 43.5
11	89 21.2	15 01.7	26.5	250 32.5	36.2	329 23.6	57.7	224 19.3	37.1			
12	104 23.6	30 00.9	N21 26.9	265 34.0	S 8 36.6	344 25.5	N20 57.6	239 21.8	S14 37.1	Alphecca	126 10.2	N26 40.2
13	119 26.1	45 00.2	27.3	280 35.5	37.1	359 27.4	57.5	254 24.3	37.1	Alpheratz	357 42.6	N29 10.1
14	134 28.5	59 59.5	27.7	295 37.0	37.5	14 29.3	57.4	269 26.9	37.1	Altair	62 07.2	N 8 54.6
15	149 31.0	74 58.8 ..	28.2	310 38.4 ..	38.0	29 31.2 ..	57.3	284 29.4 ..	37.1	Ankaa	353 15.0	S42 13.3
16	164 33.5	89 58.1	28.6	325 39.9	38.4	44 33.1	57.2	299 31.9	37.1	Antares	112 25.0	S26 27.7
17	179 35.9	104 57.3	29.0	340 41.4	38.9	59 35.0	57.1	314 34.4	37.1			
18	194 38.4	119 56.6	N21 29.4	355 42.9	S 8 39.3	74 36.8	N20 57.0	329 37.0	S14 37.1	Arcturus	145 55.0	N19 06.6
19	209 40.9	134 55.9	29.8	10 44.3	39.8	89 38.7	56.9	344 39.5	37.0	Atria	107 25.6	S69 03.2
20	224 43.3	149 55.2	30.2	25 45.8	40.2	104 40.6	56.8	359 42.0	37.0	Avior	234 18.3	S59 33.6
21	239 45.8	164 54.4 ..	30.6	40 47.3 ..	40.7	119 42.5 ..	56.7	14 44.5 ..	37.0	Bellatrix	278 31.5	N 6 21.6
22	254 48.3	179 53.7	31.0	55 48.8	41.1	134 44.4	56.6	29 47.1	37.0	Betelgeuse	271 00.8	N 7 24.4
23	269 50.7	194 53.0	31.5	70 50.2	41.6	149 46.3	56.4	44 49.6	37.0			
7 00	284 53.2	209 52.3	N21 31.9	85 51.7	S 8 42.0	164 48.2	N20 56.3	59 52.1	S14 37.0	Canopus	263 56.4	S52 42.3
01	299 55.6	224 51.5	32.3	100 53.2	42.5	179 50.0	56.2	74 54.6	37.0	Capella	280 33.8	N46 00.5
02	314 58.1	239 50.8	32.7	115 54.6	42.9	194 51.9	56.1	89 57.1	37.0	Deneb	49 30.5	N45 20.0
03	330 00.6	254 50.1 ..	33.1	130 56.1 ..	43.4	209 53.8 ..	56.0	104 59.7 ..	37.0	Denebola	182 33.0	N14 29.5
04	345 03.0	269 49.4	33.5	145 57.6	43.9	224 55.7	55.9	120 02.2	37.0	Diphda	348 55.2	S17 54.3
05	0 05.5	284 48.6	33.9	160 59.0	44.3	239 57.6	55.8	135 04.7	37.0			
06	15 08.0	299 47.9	N21 34.3	176 00.5	S 8 44.8	254 59.5	N20 55.7	150 07.2	S14 37.0	Dubhe	193 51.3	N61 40.5
07	30 10.4	314 47.2	34.7	191 02.0	45.2	270 01.4	55.6	165 09.7	37.0	Elnath	278 12.0	N28 36.9
08	45 12.9	329 46.5	35.1	206 03.4	45.7	285 03.3	55.5	180 12.3	37.0	Eltanin	90 45.3	N51 29.5
09	60 15.4	344 45.7 ..	35.5	221 04.9 ..	46.1	300 05.1 ..	55.4	195 14.8 ..	37.0	Enif	33 46.1	N 9 56.6
10	75 17.8	359 45.0	35.9	236 06.4	46.6	315 07.0	55.3	210 17.3	37.0	Fomalhaut	15 23.0	S29 32.4
11	90 20.3	14 44.3	36.3	251 07.8	47.0	330 08.9	55.2	225 19.8	37.0			
12	105 22.8	29 43.5	N21 36.7	266 09.3	S 8 47.5	345 10.8	N20 55.1	240 22.4	S14 37.0	Gacrux	172 00.0	S57 11.9
13	120 25.2	44 42.8	37.1	281 10.8	47.9	0 12.7	55.0	255 24.9	36.9	Gienah	175 51.6	S17 37.5
14	135 27.7	59 42.1	37.5	296 12.2	48.4	15 14.6	54.8	270 27.4	36.9	Hadar	148 46.5	S60 26.8
15	150 30.1	74 41.4 ..	37.9	311 13.7 ..	48.8	30 16.5 ..	54.7	285 29.9 ..	36.9	Hamal	328 00.0	N23 31.7
16	165 32.6	89 40.6	38.2	326 15.1	49.3	45 18.4	54.6	300 32.4	36.9	Kaus Aust.	83 42.4	S34 22.4
17	180 35.1	104 39.9	38.6	341 16.6	49.8	60 20.2	54.5	315 34.9	36.9			
18	195 37.5	119 39.2	N21 39.0	356 18.1	S 8 50.2	75 22.1	N20 54.4	330 37.5	S14 36.9	Kochab	137 19.7	N74 06.1
19	210 40.0	134 38.4	39.4	11 19.5	50.7	90 24.0	54.3	345 40.0	36.9	Markab	13 37.4	N15 17.1
20	225 42.5	149 37.7	39.8	26 21.0	51.1	105 25.9	54.2	0 42.5	36.9	Menkar	314 14.5	N 4 08.7
21	240 44.9	164 37.0 ..	40.2	41 22.4 ..	51.6	120 27.8 ..	54.1	15 45.0 ..	36.9	Menkent	148 06.5	S36 26.6
22	255 47.4	179 36.2	40.6	56 23.9	52.0	135 29.7	54.0	30 47.5	36.9	Miaplacidus	221 40.2	S69 46.9
23	270 49.9	194 35.5	41.0	71 25.4	52.5	150 31.6	53.9	45 50.1	36.9			
8 00	285 52.3	209 34.8	N21 41.3	86 26.8	S 8 52.9	165 33.5	N20 53.8	60 52.6	S14 36.9	Mirfak	308 39.5	N49 54.4
01	300 54.8	224 34.0	41.7	101 28.3	53.4	180 35.3	53.7	75 55.1	36.9	Nunki	75 57.0	S26 16.5
02	315 57.3	239 33.3	42.1	116 29.7	53.9	195 37.2	53.6	90 57.6	36.9	Peacock	53 17.6	S56 41.0
03	330 59.7	254 32.6 ..	42.5	131 31.2 ..	54.3	210 39.1 ..	53.5	106 00.1 ..	36.9	Pollux	243 27.2	N27 59.3
04	346 02.2	269 31.8	42.9	146 32.6	54.8	225 41.0	53.3	121 02.6	36.9	Procyon	244 59.3	N 5 11.1
05	1 04.6	284 31.1	43.2	161 34.1	55.2	240 42.9	53.2	136 05.2	36.9			
06	16 07.1	299 30.3	N21 43.6	176 35.5	S 8 55.7	255 44.8	N20 53.1	151 07.7	S14 36.9	Rasalhague	96 05.4	N12 33.2
07	31 09.6	314 29.6	44.0	191 37.0	56.1	270 46.7	53.0	166 10.2	36.9	Regulus	207 43.0	N11 53.7
08	46 12.0	329 28.9	44.4	206 38.4	56.6	285 48.5	52.9	181 12.7	36.9	Rigel	281 11.7	S 8 11.2
09	61 14.5	344 28.1 ..	44.7	221 39.9 ..	57.0	300 50.4 ..	52.8	196 15.2 ..	36.9	Rigil Kent.	139 50.3	S60 53.8
10	76 17.0	359 27.4	45.1	236 41.3	57.5	315 52.3	52.7	211 17.8	36.9	Sabik	102 11.4	S15 44.4
11	91 19.4	14 26.7	45.5	251 42.8	58.0	330 54.2	52.6	226 20.3	36.9			
12	106 21.9	29 25.9	N21 45.9	266 44.2	S 8 58.4	345 56.1	N20 52.5	241 22.8	S14 36.8	Schedar	349 39.5	N56 36.8
13	121 24.4	44 25.2	46.2	281 45.7	58.9	0 58.0	52.4	256 25.3	36.8	Shaula	96 20.5	S37 06.7
14	136 26.8	59 24.4	46.6	296 47.1	59.3	15 59.9	52.3	271 27.8	36.8	Sirius	258 33.4	S16 44.3
15	151 29.3	74 23.7 ..	47.0	311 48.6	8 59.8	31 01.8 ..	52.2	286 30.3 ..	36.8	Spica	158 30.4	S11 14.2
16	166 31.8	89 23.0	47.3	326 50.0	9 00.3	46 03.6	52.1	301 32.8	36.8	Suhail	222 52.2	S43 29.7
17	181 34.2	104 22.2	47.7	341 51.5	00.7	61 05.5	51.9	316 35.4	36.8			
18	196 36.7	119 21.5	N21 48.1	356 52.9	S 9 01.2	76 07.4	N20 51.8	331 37.9	S14 36.8	Vega	80 38.0	N38 48.1
19	211 39.2	134 20.8	48.4	11 54.4	01.6	91 09.3	51.7	346 40.4	36.8	Zuben'ubi	137 04.4	S16 06.1
20	226 41.6	149 20.0	48.8	26 55.8	02.1	106 11.2	51.6	1 42.9	36.8			
21	241 44.1	164 19.3 ..	49.1	41 57.3 ..	02.5	121 13.1 ..	51.5	16 45.4 ..	36.8			
22	256 46.5	179 18.5	49.5	56 58.7	03.0	136 15.0	51.4	31 47.9	36.8	Venus	284 59.1	10 01
23	271 49.0	194 17.8	49.9	72 00.2	03.5	151 16.8	51.3	46 50.5	36.8	Mars	160 58.5	18 15

	ARIES	VENUS		MARS		JUPITER		SATURN		STARS	SHA	Mer. Pass.
Mer. Pass.	h m 4 59.6	v −0.7	d 0.4	v 1.5	d 0.5	v 1.9	d 0.1	v 2.5	d 0.0	Jupiter	239 55.0	12 59
										Saturn	134 58.9	19 57

UT	SUN GHA	SUN Dec	MOON GHA	v	MOON Dec	d	HP
d h	° ′	° ′	° ′	′	° ′	′	′
6 00	178 49.7	N22 42.7	85 56.3	13.1	S 8 06.5	9.3	56.0
01	193 49.6	42.5	100 28.4	12.9	8 15.8	9.3	56.0
02	208 49.5	42.2	115 00.3	13.0	8 25.1	9.2	56.0
03	223 49.4 ..	42.0	129 32.3	12.8	8 34.3	9.3	56.1
04	238 49.3	41.7	144 04.1	12.8	8 43.6	9.1	56.1
05	253 49.2	41.5	158 35.9	12.7	8 52.7	9.2	56.1
S 06	268 49.1	N22 41.2	173 07.6	12.7	S 9 01.9	9.1	56.2
07	283 49.0	41.0	187 39.3	12.6	9 11.0	9.1	56.2
U 08	298 48.9	40.7	202 10.9	12.5	9 20.1	9.1	56.2
N 09	313 48.8 ..	40.5	216 42.4	12.5	9 29.2	9.0	56.3
D 10	328 48.7	40.2	231 13.9	12.4	9 38.2	9.0	56.3
A 11	343 48.6	40.0	245 45.3	12.3	9 47.2	9.0	56.3
Y 12	358 48.5	N22 39.7	260 16.6	12.3	S 9 56.2	8.9	56.4
13	13 48.4	39.5	274 47.9	12.2	10 05.1	8.9	56.4
14	28 48.3	39.2	289 19.1	12.1	10 14.0	8.8	56.4
15	43 48.2 ..	38.9	303 50.2	12.1	10 22.8	8.8	56.5
16	58 48.1	38.7	318 21.3	12.0	10 31.6	8.8	56.5
17	73 48.0	38.4	332 52.3	11.9	10 40.4	8.7	56.5
18	88 47.9	N22 38.2	347 23.2	11.8	S10 49.1	8.7	56.6
19	103 47.7	37.9	1 54.0	11.8	10 57.8	8.6	56.6
20	118 47.6	37.7	16 24.8	11.7	11 06.4	8.6	56.7
21	133 47.5 ..	37.4	30 55.5	11.7	11 15.0	8.6	56.7
22	148 47.4	37.1	45 26.2	11.5	11 23.6	8.5	56.7
23	163 47.3	36.9	59 56.7	11.5	11 32.1	8.4	56.8
7 00	178 47.2	N22 36.6	74 27.2	11.4	S11 40.5	8.4	56.8
01	193 47.1	36.3	88 57.6	11.3	11 48.9	8.4	56.8
02	208 47.0	36.1	103 27.9	11.3	11 57.3	8.3	56.9
03	223 46.9 ..	35.8	117 58.2	11.2	12 05.6	8.3	56.9
04	238 46.8	35.5	132 28.4	11.1	12 13.9	8.2	57.0
05	253 46.7	35.3	146 58.5	11.0	12 22.1	8.1	57.0
06	268 46.6	N22 35.0	161 28.5	10.9	S12 30.2	8.1	57.0
07	283 46.5	34.7	175 58.4	10.9	12 38.3	8.1	57.1
M 08	298 46.4	34.5	190 28.3	10.8	12 46.4	8.0	57.1
O 09	313 46.3 ..	34.2	204 58.1	10.7	12 54.4	7.9	57.1
N 10	328 46.2	33.9	219 27.8	10.6	13 02.3	7.9	57.2
D 11	343 46.1	33.7	233 57.4	10.5	13 10.2	7.8	57.2
A 12	358 46.0	N22 33.4	248 26.9	10.5	S13 18.0	7.8	57.3
Y 13	13 45.9	33.1	262 56.4	10.4	13 25.8	7.7	57.3
14	28 45.8	32.9	277 25.8	10.3	13 33.5	7.6	57.3
15	43 45.7 ..	32.6	291 55.1	10.2	13 41.1	7.6	57.4
16	58 45.6	32.3	306 24.3	10.1	13 48.7	7.5	57.4
17	73 45.5	32.0	320 53.4	10.1	13 56.2	7.4	57.4
18	88 45.4	N22 31.8	335 22.5	10.0	S14 03.6	7.4	57.5
19	103 45.3	31.5	349 51.5	9.8	14 11.0	7.3	57.5
20	118 45.2	31.2	4 20.3	9.8	14 18.3	7.3	57.6
21	133 45.1 ..	30.9	18 49.1	9.7	14 25.6	7.1	57.6
22	148 45.0	30.7	33 17.8	9.7	14 32.7	7.1	57.6
23	163 44.9	30.4	47 46.5	9.5	14 39.8	7.1	57.7
8 00	178 44.8	N22 30.1	62 15.0	9.5	S14 46.9	6.9	57.7
01	193 44.7	29.8	76 43.5	9.3	14 53.8	6.9	57.8
02	208 44.6	29.5	91 11.8	9.3	15 00.7	6.8	57.8
03	223 44.6 ..	29.3	105 40.1	9.2	15 07.5	6.8	57.8
04	238 44.5	29.0	120 08.3	9.2	15 14.3	6.6	57.9
05	253 44.4	28.7	134 36.5	9.0	15 20.9	6.6	57.9
06	268 44.3	N22 28.4	149 04.5	8.9	S15 27.5	6.5	58.0
07	283 44.2	28.1	163 32.4	8.9	15 34.0	6.4	58.0
T 08	298 44.1	27.8	178 00.3	8.8	15 40.4	6.4	58.0
U 09	313 44.0 ..	27.6	192 28.1	8.6	15 46.8	6.2	58.1
E 10	328 43.9	27.3	206 55.7	8.6	15 53.0	6.2	58.1
S 11	343 43.8	27.0	221 23.3	8.6	15 59.2	6.1	58.2
D 12	358 43.7	N22 26.7	235 50.9	8.4	S16 05.3	6.0	58.2
A 13	13 43.6	26.4	250 18.3	8.3	16 11.3	5.9	58.2
Y 14	28 43.5	26.1	264 45.6	8.3	16 17.2	5.8	58.3
15	43 43.4 ..	25.8	279 12.9	8.2	16 23.0	5.8	58.3
16	58 43.3	25.6	293 40.1	8.0	16 28.8	5.6	58.4
17	73 43.2	25.3	308 07.1	8.0	16 34.4	5.6	58.4
18	88 43.1	N22 25.0	322 34.1	8.0	S16 40.0	5.4	58.4
19	103 43.0	24.7	337 01.1	7.8	16 45.4	5.4	58.5
20	118 42.9	24.4	351 27.9	7.7	16 50.8	5.3	58.5
21	133 42.8 ..	24.1	5 54.6	7.7	16 56.1	5.2	58.6
22	148 42.7	23.8	20 21.3	7.6	17 01.3	5.1	58.6
23	163 42.6	23.5	34 47.9	7.5	S17 06.4	4.9	58.6
	SD 15.8	d 0.3	SD 15.4		15.6		15.9

Twilight / Sunrise / Moonrise

Lat.	Twilight Naut.	Twilight Civil	Sunrise	Moonrise 6	Moonrise 7	Moonrise 8	Moonrise 9
°	h m	h m	h m	h m	h m	h m	h m
N 72	▭	▭	▭	15 04	16 58	19 10	▬
N 70	▭	▭	▭	14 46	16 28	18 15	20 00
68	▭	▭	▭	14 32	16 06	17 42	19 13
66	////	////	00 57	14 21	15 49	17 18	18 42
64	////	////	01 54	14 11	15 35	17 00	18 19
62	////	////	02 26	14 03	15 24	16 44	18 01
60	////	01 19	02 50	13 56	15 14	16 32	17 46
N 58	////	01 58	03 09	13 50	15 05	16 21	17 33
56	////	02 25	03 24	13 45	14 58	16 11	17 22
54	01 13	02 45	03 38	13 40	14 51	16 03	17 12
52	01 49	03 02	03 49	13 36	14 45	15 55	17 04
50	02 14	03 16	03 59	13 32	14 40	15 48	16 56
45	02 56	03 44	04 21	13 23	14 28	15 34	16 39
N 40	03 25	04 06	04 38	13 16	14 18	15 22	16 26
35	03 47	04 23	04 53	13 10	14 10	15 12	16 14
30	04 05	04 38	05 05	13 05	14 03	15 03	16 04
20	04 33	05 02	05 26	12 56	13 51	14 48	15 47
N 10	04 55	05 21	05 44	12 48	13 40	14 35	15 32
0	05 13	05 39	06 01	12 41	13 30	14 22	15 19
S 10	05 29	05 55	06 18	12 33	13 20	14 10	15 05
20	05 45	06 12	06 36	12 25	13 09	13 57	14 50
30	06 00	06 30	06 56	12 17	12 57	13 42	14 33
35	06 09	06 40	07 08	12 12	12 50	13 34	14 23
40	06 18	06 51	07 22	12 06	12 42	13 24	14 12
45	06 27	07 04	07 38	11 59	12 33	13 12	13 59
S 50	06 38	07 19	07 57	11 51	12 22	12 59	13 43
52	06 43	07 26	08 07	11 48	12 17	12 52	13 36
54	06 49	07 34	08 17	11 44	12 11	12 45	13 28
56	06 54	07 43	08 29	11 39	12 05	12 37	13 18
58	07 01	07 52	08 43	11 34	11 58	12 29	13 08
S 60	07 08	08 03	08 59	11 29	11 51	12 18	12 56

Sunset / Twilight / Moonset

Lat.	Sunset	Twilight Civil	Twilight Naut.	Moonset 6	Moonset 7	Moonset 8	Moonset 9
°	h m	h m	h m	h m	h m	h m	h m
N 72	▭	▭	▭	22 23	22 12	21 51	▬
N 70	▭	▭	▭	22 42	22 43	22 46	23 00
68	▭	▭	▭	22 57	23 06	23 20	23 48
66	23 08	////	////	23 10	23 24	23 45	24 19
64	22 14	////	////	23 20	23 38	24 04	00 04
62	21 43	////	////	23 29	23 50	24 20	00 20
60	21 19	22 48	////	23 37	24 01	00 01	00 33
N 58	21 00	22 10	////	23 44	24 10	00 10	00 44
56	20 45	21 44	////	23 50	24 18	00 18	00 54
54	20 32	21 24	22 55	23 55	24 25	00 25	01 03
52	20 20	21 07	22 22	24 00	00 00	00 32	01 11
50	20 10	20 53	21 55	24 04	00 04	00 38	01 18
45	19 49	20 25	21 13	24 14	00 14	00 50	01 33
N 40	19 31	20 04	20 45	24 22	00 22	01 01	01 45
35	19 17	19 46	20 23	24 29	00 29	01 10	01 56
30	19 05	19 32	20 05	24 35	00 35	01 18	02 05
20	18 44	19 08	19 37	00 04	00 46	01 31	02 22
N 10	18 25	18 48	19 15	00 10	00 55	01 43	02 36
0	18 09	18 31	18 57	00 16	01 04	01 54	02 49
S 10	17 52	18 15	18 41	00 22	01 13	02 06	03 02
20	17 34	17 58	18 25	00 29	01 22	02 18	03 16
30	17 14	17 40	18 10	00 36	01 33	02 31	03 32
35	17 02	17 30	18 01	00 40	01 39	02 39	03 42
40	16 48	17 19	17 53	00 45	01 46	02 49	03 52
45	16 32	17 06	17 43	00 50	01 54	02 59	04 05
S 50	16 13	16 51	17 32	00 57	02 04	03 12	04 20
52	16 03	16 44	17 27	01 00	02 09	03 18	04 27
54	15 53	16 36	17 22	01 04	02 14	03 25	04 35
56	15 41	16 27	17 16	01 07	02 19	03 32	04 44
58	15 27	16 18	17 10	01 12	02 26	03 41	04 55
S 60	15 11	16 07	17 03	01 16	02 33	03 50	05 06

SUN / MOON

Day	SUN Eqn. of Time 00h	SUN Eqn. of Time 12h	SUN Mer. Pass.	MOON Mer. Pass. Upper	MOON Mer. Pass. Lower	Age	Phase
d	m s	m s	h m	h m	h m	d %	
6	04 41	04 46	12 05	18 52	06 28	09 60	◖
7	04 51	04 56	12 05	19 42	07 17	10 70	
8	05 00	05 05	12 05	20 35	08 08	11 79	

UT	ARIES GHA	VENUS −3.8 GHA	Dec	MARS +0.2 GHA	Dec	JUPITER −1.8 GHA	Dec	SATURN +0.4 GHA	Dec	STARS Name	SHA	Dec
9 00	286 51.5	209 17.0	N21 50.2	87 01.6	S 9 03.9	166 18.7	N20 51.2	61 53.0	S14 36.8	Acamar	315 18.0	S40 14.7
01	301 53.9	224 16.3	50.6	102 03.0	04.4	181 20.6	51.1	76 55.5	36.8	Achernar	335 26.4	S57 09.5
02	316 56.4	239 15.6	50.9	117 04.5	04.8	196 22.5	51.0	91 58.0	36.8	Acrux	173 08.4	S63 11.1
03	331 58.9	254 14.8 ..	51.3	132 05.9 ..	05.3	211 24.4 ..	50.9	107 00.5 ..	36.8	Adhara	255 12.3	S28 59.7
04	347 01.3	269 14.1	51.7	147 07.4	05.8	226 26.3	50.8	122 03.0	36.8	Aldebaran	290 48.8	N16 32.1
05	2 03.8	284 13.3	52.0	162 08.8	06.2	241 28.2	50.7	137 05.5	36.8			
06	17 06.2	299 12.6	N21 52.4	177 10.2	S 9 06.7	256 30.1	N20 50.5	152 08.0	S14 36.8	Alioth	166 20.2	N55 53.2
W 07	32 08.7	314 11.8	52.7	192 11.7	07.1	271 31.9	50.5	167 10.6	36.8	Alkaid	152 58.3	N49 14.8
E 08	47 11.2	329 11.1	53.1	207 13.1	07.6	286 33.8	50.3	182 13.1	36.8	Al Na'ir	27 42.5	S46 53.1
D 09	62 13.6	344 10.3 ..	53.4	222 14.6 ..	08.1	301 35.7 ..	50.2	197 15.6 ..	36.8	Alnilam	275 45.9	S 1 11.7
N 10	77 16.1	359 09.6	53.8	237 16.0	08.5	316 37.6	50.1	212 18.1	36.8	Alphard	217 55.6	S 8 43.5
E 11	92 18.6	14 08.9	54.1	252 17.4	09.0	331 39.5	50.0	227 20.6	36.8			
S 12	107 21.0	29 08.1	N21 54.5	267 18.9	S 9 09.4	346 41.4	N20 49.9	242 23.1	S14 36.8	Alphecca	126 10.2	N26 40.2
D 13	122 23.5	44 07.4	54.8	282 20.3	09.9	1 43.3	49.8	257 25.6	36.8	Alpheratz	357 42.6	N29 10.2
A 14	137 26.0	59 06.6	55.1	297 21.7	10.4	16 45.1	49.7	272 28.1	36.8	Altair	62 07.2	N 8 54.6
Y 15	152 28.4	74 05.9 ..	55.5	312 23.2 ..	10.8	31 47.0 ..	49.6	287 30.7 ..	36.8	Ankaa	353 15.0	S42 13.3
16	167 30.9	89 05.1	55.8	327 24.6	11.3	46 48.9	49.5	302 33.2	36.8	Antares	112 25.0	S26 27.7
17	182 33.4	104 04.4	56.2	342 26.0	11.7	61 50.8	49.3	317 35.7	36.8			
18	197 35.8	119 03.6	N21 56.5	357 27.5	S 9 12.2	76 52.7	N20 49.2	332 38.2	S14 36.8	Arcturus	145 55.0	N19 06.6
19	212 38.3	134 02.9	56.8	12 28.9	12.7	91 54.6	49.1	347 40.7	36.7	Atria	107 25.6	S69 03.2
20	227 40.7	149 02.1	57.2	27 30.3	13.1	106 56.5	49.0	2 43.2	36.7	Avior	234 18.3	S59 33.6
21	242 43.2	164 01.4 ..	57.5	42 31.8 ..	13.6	121 58.3 ..	48.9	17 45.7 ..	36.7	Bellatrix	278 31.5	N 6 21.6
22	257 45.7	179 00.6	57.9	57 33.2	14.1	137 00.2	48.8	32 48.2	36.7	Betelgeuse	271 00.8	N 7 24.4
23	272 48.1	193 59.9	58.2	72 34.6	14.5	152 02.1	48.7	47 50.7	36.7			
10 00	287 50.6	208 59.1	N21 58.5	87 36.1	S 9 15.0	167 04.0	N20 48.6	62 53.3	S14 36.7	Canopus	263 56.4	S52 42.3
01	302 53.1	223 58.4	58.9	102 37.5	15.4	182 05.9	48.5	77 55.8	36.7	Capella	280 33.8	N46 00.5
02	317 55.5	238 57.6	59.2	117 38.9	15.9	197 07.8	48.4	92 58.3	36.7	Deneb	49 30.5	N45 20.0
03	332 58.0	253 56.9 ..	59.5	132 40.3 ..	16.4	212 09.7 ..	48.3	108 00.8 ..	36.7	Denebola	182 33.0	N14 29.5
04	348 00.5	268 56.1	21 59.9	147 41.8	16.8	227 11.5	48.1	123 03.3	36.7	Diphda	348 55.1	S17 54.3
05	3 02.9	283 55.4	22 00.2	162 43.2	17.3	242 13.4	48.0	138 05.8	36.7			
06	18 05.4	298 54.6	N22 00.5	177 44.6	S 9 17.8	257 15.3	N20 47.9	153 08.3	S14 36.7	Dubhe	193 51.3	N61 40.5
T 07	33 07.9	313 53.9	00.8	192 46.0	18.2	272 17.2	47.8	168 10.8	36.7	Elnath	278 12.0	N28 36.9
H 08	48 10.3	328 53.1	01.2	207 47.5	18.7	287 19.1	47.7	183 13.3	36.7	Eltanin	90 45.3	N51 29.5
U 09	63 12.8	343 52.4 ..	01.5	222 48.9 ..	19.1	302 21.0 ..	47.6	198 15.8 ..	36.7	Enif	33 46.1	N 9 56.7
R 10	78 15.2	358 51.6	01.8	237 50.3	19.6	317 22.9	47.5	213 18.4	36.7	Fomalhaut	15 23.0	S29 32.4
S 11	93 17.7	13 50.9	02.1	252 51.7	20.1	332 24.7	47.4	228 20.9	36.7			
D 12	108 20.2	28 50.1	N22 02.5	267 53.2	S 9 20.5	347 26.6	N20 47.3	243 23.4	S14 36.7	Gacrux	172 00.0	S57 11.9
A 13	123 22.6	43 49.3	02.8	282 54.6	21.0	2 28.5	47.2	258 25.9	36.7	Gienah	175 51.6	S17 37.4
Y 14	138 25.1	58 48.6	03.1	297 56.0	21.5	17 30.4	47.1	273 28.4	36.7	Hadar	148 46.5	S60 26.8
15	153 27.6	73 47.8 ..	03.4	312 57.4 ..	21.9	32 32.3 ..	46.9	288 30.9 ..	36.7	Hamal	328 00.0	N23 31.7
16	168 30.0	88 47.1	03.7	327 58.8	22.4	47 34.2	46.8	303 33.4	36.7	Kaus Aust.	83 42.4	S34 22.4
17	183 32.5	103 46.3	04.0	343 00.3	22.9	62 36.1	46.7	318 35.9	36.7			
18	198 35.0	118 45.6	N22 04.4	358 01.7	S 9 23.3	77 38.0	N20 46.6	333 38.4	S14 36.7	Kochab	137 19.7	N74 06.1
19	213 37.4	133 44.8	04.7	13 03.1	23.8	92 39.8	46.5	348 40.9	36.7	Markab	13 37.4	N15 17.1
20	228 39.9	148 44.1	05.0	28 04.5	24.3	107 41.7	46.4	3 43.4	36.7	Menkar	314 14.4	N 4 08.7
21	243 42.4	163 43.3 ..	05.3	43 05.9 ..	24.7	122 43.6 ..	46.3	18 45.9 ..	36.7	Menkent	148 06.5	S36 26.6
22	258 44.8	178 42.5	05.6	58 07.4	25.2	137 45.5	46.2	33 48.4	36.7	Miaplacidus	221 40.2	S69 46.9
23	273 47.3	193 41.8	05.9	73 08.8	25.6	152 47.4	46.1	48 51.0	36.7			
11 00	288 49.7	208 41.0	N22 06.2	88 10.2	S 9 26.1	167 49.3	N20 46.0	63 53.5	S14 36.7	Mirfak	308 39.5	N49 54.4
01	303 52.2	223 40.3	06.5	103 11.6	26.6	182 51.2	45.8	78 56.0	36.7	Nunki	75 57.0	S26 16.5
02	318 54.7	238 39.5	06.8	118 13.0	27.0	197 53.0	45.7	93 58.5	36.7	Peacock	53 17.6	S56 41.0
03	333 57.1	253 38.7 ..	07.2	133 14.4 ..	27.5	212 54.9 ..	45.6	109 01.0 ..	36.7	Pollux	243 27.2	N27 59.3
04	348 59.6	268 38.0	07.5	148 15.8	28.0	227 56.8	45.5	124 03.5	36.7	Procyon	244 59.3	N 5 11.1
05	4 02.1	283 37.2	07.8	163 17.3	28.4	242 58.7	45.4	139 06.0	36.7			
06	19 04.5	298 36.5	N22 08.1	178 18.7	S 9 28.9	258 00.6	N20 45.3	154 08.5	S14 36.7	Rasalhague	96 05.4	N12 33.2
07	34 07.0	313 35.7	08.4	193 20.1	29.4	273 02.5	45.2	169 11.0	36.7	Regulus	207 43.0	N11 53.7
F 08	49 09.5	328 34.9	08.7	208 21.5	29.8	288 04.4	45.1	184 13.5	36.7	Rigel	281 11.6	S 8 11.2
R 09	64 11.9	343 34.2 ..	09.0	223 22.9 ..	30.3	303 06.2 ..	45.0	199 16.0 ..	36.7	Rigil Kent.	139 50.3	S60 53.8
I 10	79 14.4	358 33.4	09.3	238 24.3	30.8	318 08.1	44.9	214 18.5	36.7	Sabik	102 11.4	S15 44.4
D 11	94 16.9	13 32.7	09.6	253 25.7	31.2	333 10.0	44.7	229 21.0	36.7			
A 12	109 19.3	28 31.9	N22 09.9	268 27.1	S 9 31.7	348 11.9	N20 44.6	244 23.5	S14 36.7	Schedar	349 39.5	N56 36.8
Y 13	124 21.8	43 31.1	10.2	283 28.5	32.2	3 13.8	44.5	259 26.0	36.7	Shaula	96 20.5	S37 06.7
14	139 24.2	58 30.4	10.5	298 29.9	32.6	18 15.7	44.4	274 28.5	36.7	Sirius	258 33.4	S16 44.3
15	154 26.7	73 29.6 ..	10.7	313 31.4 ..	33.1	33 17.6 ..	44.3	289 31.0 ..	36.7	Spica	158 30.4	S11 14.2
16	169 29.2	88 28.9	11.0	328 32.8	33.6	48 19.4	44.2	304 33.5	36.7	Suhail	222 52.2	S43 29.7
17	184 31.6	103 28.1	11.3	343 34.2	34.0	63 21.3	44.1	319 36.0	36.7			
18	199 34.1	118 27.3	N22 11.6	358 35.6	S 9 34.5	78 23.2	N20 44.0	334 38.5	S14 36.7	Vega	80 38.0	N38 48.1
19	214 36.6	133 26.6	11.9	13 37.0	35.0	93 25.1	43.9	349 41.1	36.7	Zuben'ubi	137 04.4	S16 06.1
20	229 39.0	148 25.8	12.2	28 38.4	35.4	108 27.0	43.8	4 43.6	36.7		SHA	Mer.Pass.
21	244 41.5	163 25.0 ..	12.5	43 39.8 ..	35.9	123 28.9 ..	43.6	19 46.1 ..	36.7		° '	h m
22	259 44.0	178 24.3	12.8	58 41.2	36.4	138 30.8	43.5	34 48.6	36.7	Venus	281 08.5	10 05
23	274 46.3	193 23.5	13.1	73 42.6	36.8	153 32.6	43.4	49 51.1	36.7	Mars	159 45.5	18 08
	h m									Jupiter	239 13.4	12 50
Mer.Pass. 4 47.8	v −0.8	d 0.3	v 1.4	d 0.5	v 1.9	d 0.1	v 2.5	d 0.0	Saturn	135 02.7	19 45

UT	SUN GHA	SUN Dec	MOON GHA	MOON v	MOON Dec	MOON d	MOON HP
d h	° ′	° ′	° ′	′	° ′	′	′
9 00	178 42.6	N22 23.2	49 14.4	7.4	S17 11.3	4.9	58.7
01	193 42.5	22.9	63 40.8	7.3	17 16.2	4.8	58.7
02	208 42.4	22.6	78 07.1	7.3	17 21.0	4.7	58.8
03	223 42.3 ..	22.3	92 33.4	7.3	17 25.7	4.6	58.8
04	238 42.2	22.0	106 59.5	7.1	17 30.3	4.5	58.8
05	253 42.1	21.7	121 25.6	7.0	17 34.8	4.3	58.9
06	268 42.0	N22 21.4	135 51.6	7.0	S17 39.1	4.3	58.9
W 07	283 41.9	21.1	150 17.6	6.8	17 43.4	4.2	58.9
E 08	298 41.8	20.8	164 43.4	6.8	17 47.6	4.0	59.0
D 09	313 41.7 ..	20.5	179 09.2	6.7	17 51.6	4.0	59.0
N 10	328 41.6	20.2	193 34.9	6.6	17 55.6	3.8	59.1
E 11	343 41.5	19.9	208 00.5	6.5	17 59.4	3.7	59.1
S 12	358 41.4	N22 19.6	222 26.0	6.5	S18 03.1	3.6	59.1
D 13	13 41.4	19.3	236 51.5	6.4	18 06.7	3.5	59.2
A 14	28 41.3	19.0	251 16.9	6.3	18 10.2	3.4	59.2
Y 15	43 41.2 ..	18.7	265 42.2	6.2	18 13.6	3.3	59.3
16	58 41.1	18.4	280 07.4	6.2	18 16.9	3.1	59.3
17	73 41.0	18.1	294 32.6	6.1	18 20.0	3.1	59.3
18	88 40.9	N22 17.8	308 57.7	6.0	S18 23.1	2.9	59.4
19	103 40.8	17.5	323 22.7	6.0	18 26.0	2.8	59.4
20	118 40.7	17.2	337 47.7	5.8	18 28.8	2.7	59.4
21	133 40.6 ..	16.9	352 12.5	5.9	18 31.5	2.6	59.5
22	148 40.5	16.6	6 37.4	5.7	18 34.1	2.4	59.5
23	163 40.5	16.3	21 02.1	5.7	18 36.5	2.3	59.5
10 00	178 40.4	N22 15.9	35 26.8	5.6	S18 38.8	2.2	59.6
01	193 40.3	15.6	49 51.4	5.6	18 41.0	2.1	59.6
02	208 40.2	15.3	64 16.0	5.5	18 43.1	1.9	59.7
03	223 40.1 ..	15.0	78 40.5	5.4	18 45.0	1.9	59.7
04	238 40.0	14.7	93 04.9	5.4	18 46.9	1.7	59.7
05	253 39.9	14.4	107 29.3	5.3	18 48.6	1.5	59.8
06	268 39.8	N22 14.1	121 53.6	5.2	S18 50.1	1.5	59.8
T 07	283 39.8	13.7	136 17.8	5.2	18 51.6	1.3	59.8
H 08	298 39.7	13.4	150 42.0	5.2	18 52.9	1.2	59.9
U 09	313 39.6 ..	13.1	165 06.2	5.1	18 54.1	1.0	59.9
R 10	328 39.5	12.8	179 30.3	5.0	18 55.1	1.0	59.9
S 11	343 39.4	12.5	193 54.3	5.0	18 56.1	0.8	60.0
D 12	358 39.3	N22 12.1	208 18.3	5.0	S18 56.9	0.6	60.0
A 13	13 39.2	11.8	222 42.3	4.8	18 57.5	0.6	60.0
Y 14	28 39.1	11.5	237 06.1	4.9	18 58.1	0.4	60.1
15	43 39.1 ..	11.2	251 30.0	4.8	18 58.5	0.2	60.1
16	58 39.0	10.9	265 53.8	4.7	18 58.7	0.2	60.1
17	73 38.9	10.6	280 17.5	4.8	18 58.9	0.0	60.2
18	88 38.8	N22 10.2	294 41.3	4.6	S18 58.9	0.2	60.2
19	103 38.7	09.9	309 04.9	4.7	18 58.7	0.2	60.2
20	118 38.6	09.6	323 28.6	4.6	18 58.5	0.4	60.3
21	133 38.5 ..	09.3	337 52.2	4.5	18 58.1	0.6	60.3
22	148 38.5	08.9	352 15.7	4.5	18 57.5	0.6	60.3
23	163 38.4	08.6	6 39.2	4.5	18 56.9	0.8	60.3
11 00	178 38.3	N22 08.3	21 02.7	4.5	S18 56.1	1.0	60.4
01	193 38.2	08.0	35 26.2	4.4	18 55.1	1.1	60.4
02	208 38.1	07.6	49 49.6	4.4	18 54.0	1.2	60.4
03	223 38.0 ..	07.3	64 13.0	4.4	18 52.8	1.3	60.4
04	238 38.0	07.0	78 36.4	4.4	18 51.5	1.5	60.5
05	253 37.9	06.6	92 59.8	4.3	18 50.0	1.7	60.5
06	268 37.8	N22 06.3	107 23.1	4.3	S18 48.3	1.7	60.5
F 07	283 37.7	06.0	121 46.4	4.3	18 46.6	1.9	60.6
R 08	298 37.6	05.6	136 09.7	4.2	18 44.7	2.1	60.6
I 09	313 37.5 ..	05.3	150 32.9	4.3	18 42.6	2.1	60.6
D 10	328 37.5	05.0	164 56.2	4.2	18 40.5	2.4	60.6
A 11	343 37.4	04.6	179 19.4	4.3	18 38.1	2.4	60.6
Y 12	358 37.3	N22 04.3	193 42.7	4.2	S18 35.7	2.6	60.7
13	13 37.2	04.0	208 05.9	4.2	18 33.1	2.7	60.7
14	28 37.1	03.6	222 29.1	4.1	18 30.4	2.9	60.7
15	43 37.1 ..	03.3	236 52.2	4.2	18 27.5	3.0	60.7
16	58 37.0	03.0	251 15.4	4.2	18 24.5	3.1	60.8
17	73 36.9	02.6	265 38.6	4.2	18 21.4	3.3	60.8
18	88 36.8	N22 02.3	280 01.8	4.2	S18 18.1	3.4	60.8
19	103 36.7	01.9	294 25.0	4.1	18 14.7	3.5	60.8
20	118 36.6	01.6	308 48.1	4.2	18 11.2	3.7	60.8
21	133 36.6 ..	01.3	323 11.3	4.2	18 07.5	3.8	60.9
22	148 36.5	00.9	337 34.5	4.2	18 03.7	4.0	60.9
23	163 36.4	00.6	351 57.7	4.1	S17 59.7	4.0	60.9
	SD 15.8	d 0.3	SD 16.1		16.3		16.5

Lat.	Twilight Naut.	Twilight Civil	Sunrise	Moonrise 9	Moonrise 10	Moonrise 11	Moonrise 12
°	h m	h m	h m	h m	h m	h m	h m
N 72	☐	☐	☐	■	■	■	22 37
N 70	☐	☐	☐	20 00	21 19	21 49	21 58
68	☐	☐	☐	19 13	20 24	21 07	21 30
66	////	////	01 12	18 42	19 51	20 39	21 09
64	////	////	02 01	18 19	19 26	20 17	20 52
62	////	////	02 32	18 01	19 07	19 59	20 38
60	////	01 29	02 54	17 46	18 51	19 45	20 26
N 58	////	02 04	03 13	17 33	18 38	19 32	20 16
56	////	02 29	03 28	17 22	18 26	19 22	20 07
54	01 21	02 49	03 41	17 12	18 16	19 12	19 58
52	01 54	03 05	03 52	17 04	18 07	19 04	19 51
50	02 18	03 19	04 02	16 56	17 59	18 56	19 45
45	02 59	03 47	04 23	16 39	17 42	18 40	19 31
N 40	03 27	04 08	04 40	16 26	17 28	18 26	19 19
35	03 49	04 25	04 54	16 14	17 16	18 15	19 09
30	04 07	04 39	05 06	16 04	17 06	18 05	19 01
20	04 34	05 03	05 27	15 47	16 48	17 48	18 46
N 10	04 55	05 22	05 45	15 32	16 32	17 33	18 32
0	05 13	05 39	06 02	15 19	16 18	17 19	18 20
S 10	05 29	05 56	06 18	15 05	16 03	17 05	18 08
20	05 45	06 12	06 36	14 50	15 48	16 50	17 55
30	06 00	06 30	06 56	14 33	15 30	16 33	17 40
35	06 08	06 39	07 07	14 23	15 20	16 23	17 31
40	06 17	06 50	07 21	14 12	15 08	16 12	17 21
45	06 26	07 03	07 36	13 59	14 54	15 58	17 09
S 50	06 37	07 18	07 56	13 43	14 38	15 42	16 55
52	06 42	07 25	08 05	13 36	14 30	15 34	16 48
54	06 47	07 32	08 15	13 28	14 21	15 26	16 41
56	06 52	07 41	08 26	13 18	14 11	15 16	16 32
58	06 59	07 50	08 40	13 08	14 00	15 05	16 23
S 60	07 05	08 01	08 56	12 56	13 47	14 53	16 12

Lat.	Sunset	Twilight Civil	Twilight Naut.	Moonset 9	Moonset 10	Moonset 11	Moonset 12
°	h m	h m	h m	h m	h m	h m	h m
N 72	☐	☐	☐	■	■	■	01 25
N 70	☐	☐	☐	23 00	23 47	25 25	01 25
68	☐	☐	☐	23 48	24 42	00 42	02 07
66	22 55	////	////	24 19	00 19	01 15	02 35
64	22 07	////	////	00 04	00 42	01 39	02 56
62	21 38	////	////	00 20	01 01	01 58	03 13
60	21 15	22 40	////	00 33	01 16	02 14	03 27
N 58	20 57	22 05	////	00 44	01 29	02 27	03 39
56	20 42	21 40	////	00 54	01 40	02 39	03 50
54	20 29	21 21	22 47	01 03	01 50	02 49	03 59
52	20 18	21 05	22 15	01 11	01 59	02 58	04 07
50	20 08	20 51	21 52	01 18	02 07	03 06	04 15
45	19 47	20 24	21 11	01 33	02 24	03 23	04 31
N 40	19 30	20 03	20 43	01 45	02 37	03 37	04 44
35	19 16	19 46	20 21	01 56	02 49	03 49	04 55
30	19 04	19 31	20 04	02 05	02 59	03 59	05 04
20	18 43	19 08	19 37	02 22	03 17	04 17	05 21
N 10	18 26	18 48	19 15	02 36	03 32	04 32	05 35
0	18 09	18 31	18 57	02 49	03 46	04 47	05 48
S 10	17 53	18 15	18 41	03 02	04 01	05 01	06 01
20	17 35	17 59	18 26	03 16	04 16	05 16	06 15
30	17 15	17 41	18 11	03 32	04 34	05 34	06 32
35	17 04	17 31	18 03	03 42	04 44	05 44	06 41
40	16 50	17 21	17 54	03 52	04 55	05 56	06 51
45	16 35	17 08	17 45	04 05	05 09	06 09	07 04
S 50	16 15	16 53	17 34	04 20	05 26	06 26	07 19
52	16 06	16 46	17 29	04 27	05 34	06 34	07 26
54	15 56	16 39	17 24	04 35	05 42	06 43	07 34
56	15 45	16 30	17 19	04 44	05 52	06 52	07 42
58	15 31	16 21	17 13	04 55	06 03	07 03	07 52
S 60	15 16	16 11	17 06	05 06	06 16	07 16	08 03

	SUN			MOON			
Day	Eqn. of Time 00ʰ	Eqn. of Time 12ʰ	Mer. Pass.	Mer. Pass. Upper	Mer. Pass. Lower	Age	Phase
d	m s	m s	h m	h m	h m	d	%
9	05 10	05 14	12 05	21 32	09 04	12	88
10	05 18	05 23	12 05	22 32	10 02	13	94
11	05 27	05 31	12 06	23 34	11 03	14	98

UT	ARIES	VENUS −3.8		MARS +0.2		JUPITER −1.8		SATURN +0.4		STARS		
d h	GHA	GHA	Dec	GHA	Dec	GHA	Dec	GHA	Dec	Name	SHA	Dec
12 00	289 48.9	208 22.7	N22 13.3	88 44.0	S 9 37.3	168 34.5	N20 43.3	64 53.6	S14 36.7	Acamar	315 18.0	S40 14.7
01	304 51.4	223 22.0	13.6	103 45.4	37.8	183 36.4	43.2	79 56.1	36.7	Achernar	335 26.4	S57 09.5
02	319 53.8	238 21.2	13.9	118 46.8	38.3	198 38.3	43.1	94 58.6	36.7	Acrux	173 08.4	S63 11.1
03	334 56.3	253 20.4 ..	14.2	133 48.2 ..	38.7	213 40.2 ..	43.0	110 01.1 ..	36.7	Adhara	255 12.3	S28 59.7
04	349 58.7	268 19.7	14.5	148 49.6	39.2	228 42.1	42.9	125 03.6	36.7	Aldebaran	290 48.8	N16 32.1
05	5 01.2	283 18.9	14.7	163 51.0	39.7	243 43.9	42.8	140 06.1	36.7			
S 06	20 03.7	298 18.1	N22 15.0	178 52.4	S 9 40.1	258 45.8	N20 42.6	155 08.6	S14 36.7	Alioth	166 20.2	N55 53.2
A 07	35 06.1	313 17.4	15.3	193 53.8	40.6	273 47.7	42.5	170 11.1	36.7	Alkaid	152 58.3	N49 14.8
T 08	50 08.6	328 16.6	15.6	208 55.2	41.1	288 49.6	42.4	185 13.6	36.7	Al Na'ir	27 42.5	S46 53.1
U 09	65 11.1	343 15.8 ..	15.8	223 56.6 ..	41.5	303 51.5 ..	42.3	200 16.1 ..	36.7	Alnilam	275 45.9	S 1 11.7
R 10	80 13.5	358 15.1	16.1	238 58.0	42.0	318 53.4	42.2	215 18.6	36.7	Alphard	217 55.6	S 8 43.4
D 11	95 16.0	13 14.3	16.4	253 59.4	42.5	333 55.3	42.1	230 21.1	36.7			
A 12	110 18.5	28 13.5	N22 16.7	269 00.8	S 9 42.9	348 57.1	N20 42.0	245 23.6	S14 36.7	Alphecca	126 10.2	N26 40.2
Y 13	125 20.9	43 12.8	16.9	284 02.2	43.4	3 59.0	41.9	260 26.1	36.7	Alpheratz	357 42.6	N29 10.2
14	140 23.4	58 12.0	17.2	299 03.6	43.9	19 00.9	41.8	275 28.6	36.7	Altair	62 07.2	N 8 54.7
15	155 25.8	73 11.2 ..	17.5	314 05.0 ..	44.4	34 02.8 ..	41.6	290 31.1 ..	36.7	Ankaa	353 14.9	S42 13.3
16	170 28.3	88 10.5	17.7	329 06.4	44.8	49 04.7	41.5	305 33.6	36.7	Antares	112 25.0	S26 27.7
17	185 30.8	103 09.7	18.0	344 07.8	45.3	64 06.6	41.4	320 36.1	36.7			
18	200 33.2	118 08.9	N22 18.3	359 09.1	S 9 45.8	79 08.5	N20 41.3	335 38.6	S14 36.7	Arcturus	145 55.0	N19 06.6
19	215 35.7	133 08.1	18.5	14 10.5	46.2	94 10.3	41.2	350 41.1	36.7	Atria	107 25.7	S69 03.2
20	230 38.2	148 07.4	18.8	29 11.9	46.7	109 12.2	41.1	5 43.6	36.7	Avior	234 18.3	S59 33.6
21	245 40.6	163 06.6 ..	19.1	44 13.3 ..	47.2	124 14.1 ..	41.0	20 46.1 ..	36.7	Bellatrix	278 31.5	N 6 21.6
22	260 43.1	178 05.8	19.3	59 14.7	47.6	139 16.0	40.9	35 48.6	36.7	Betelgeuse	271 00.8	N 7 24.4
23	275 45.6	193 05.1	19.6	74 16.1	48.1	154 17.9	40.8	50 51.1	36.7			
13 00	290 48.0	208 04.3	N22 19.8	89 17.5	S 9 48.6	169 19.8	N20 40.6	65 53.6	S14 36.7	Canopus	263 56.3	S52 42.3
01	305 50.5	223 03.5	20.1	104 18.9	49.1	184 21.7	40.5	80 56.1	36.7	Capella	280 33.7	N46 00.5
02	320 53.0	238 02.7	20.3	119 20.3	49.5	199 23.5	40.4	95 58.6	36.7	Deneb	49 30.5	N45 20.1
03	335 55.4	253 02.0 ..	20.6	134 21.7 ..	50.0	214 25.4 ..	40.3	111 01.1 ..	36.7	Denebola	182 33.0	N14 29.5
04	350 57.9	268 01.2	20.9	149 23.0	50.5	229 27.3	40.2	126 03.6	36.7	Diphda	348 55.1	S17 54.3
05	6 00.3	283 00.4	21.1	164 24.4	50.9	244 29.2	40.1	141 06.1	36.7			
S 06	21 02.8	297 59.6	N22 21.4	179 25.8	S 9 51.4	259 31.1	N20 40.0	156 08.6	S14 36.7	Dubhe	193 51.3	N61 40.5
U 07	36 05.3	312 58.9	21.6	194 27.2	51.9	274 33.0	39.9	171 11.1	36.7	Elnath	278 12.0	N28 36.9
N 08	51 07.7	327 58.1	21.9	209 28.6	52.4	289 34.9	39.7	186 13.6	36.7	Eltanin	90 45.3	N51 29.5
D 09	66 10.2	342 57.3 ..	22.1	224 30.0 ..	52.8	304 36.7 ..	39.6	201 16.1 ..	36.7	Enif	33 46.1	N 9 56.7
A 10	81 12.7	357 56.5	22.4	239 31.4	53.3	319 38.6	39.5	216 18.6	36.7	Fomalhaut	15 23.0	S29 32.4
Y 11	96 15.1	12 55.8	22.6	254 32.7	53.8	334 40.5	39.4	231 21.1	36.7			
12	111 17.6	27 55.0	N22 22.9	269 34.1	S 9 54.2	349 42.4	N20 39.3	246 23.5	S14 36.7	Gacrux	172 00.1	S57 11.9
13	126 20.1	42 54.2	23.1	284 35.5	54.7	4 44.3	39.2	261 26.0	36.7	Gienah	175 51.6	S17 37.4
14	141 22.5	57 53.4	23.3	299 36.9	55.2	19 46.2	39.1	276 28.5	36.7	Hadar	148 46.5	S60 26.8
15	156 25.0	72 52.7 ..	23.6	314 38.3 ..	55.7	34 48.0 ..	39.0	291 31.0 ..	36.7	Hamal	327 59.9	N23 31.7
16	171 27.5	87 51.9	23.8	329 39.6	56.1	49 49.9	38.9	306 33.5	36.7	Kaus Aust.	83 42.4	S34 22.4
17	186 29.9	102 51.1	24.1	344 41.0	56.6	64 51.8	38.7	321 36.0	36.7			
18	201 32.4	117 50.3	N22 24.3	359 42.4	S 9 57.1	79 53.7	N20 38.6	336 38.5	S14 36.7	Kochab	137 19.8	N74 06.1
19	216 34.8	132 49.6	24.5	14 43.8	57.6	94 55.6	38.5	351 41.0	36.7	Markab	13 37.4	N15 17.1
20	231 37.3	147 48.8	24.8	29 45.2	58.0	109 57.5	38.4	6 43.5	36.7	Menkar	314 14.4	N 4 08.7
21	246 39.8	162 48.0 ..	25.0	44 46.5 ..	58.5	124 59.4 ..	38.3	21 46.0 ..	36.7	Menkent	148 06.5	S36 26.6
22	261 42.2	177 47.2	25.2	59 47.9	59.0	140 01.2	38.2	36 48.5	36.8	Miaplacidus	221 40.2	S69 46.9
23	276 44.7	192 46.4	25.5	74 49.3	59.4	155 03.1	38.1	51 51.0	36.8			
14 00	291 47.2	207 45.7	N22 25.7	89 50.7	S 9 59.9	170 05.0	N20 38.0	66 53.5	S14 36.8	Mirfak	308 39.5	N49 54.4
01	306 49.6	222 44.9	25.9	104 52.1	10 00.4	185 06.9	37.8	81 56.0	36.8	Nunki	75 57.0	S26 16.5
02	321 52.1	237 44.1	26.2	119 53.4	00.9	200 08.8	37.7	96 58.5	36.8	Peacock	53 17.5	S56 41.0
03	336 54.6	252 43.3 ..	26.4	134 54.8 ..	01.3	215 10.7 ..	37.6	112 01.0 ..	36.8	Pollux	243 27.2	N27 59.3
04	351 57.0	267 42.5	26.6	149 56.2	01.8	230 12.6	37.5	127 03.5	36.8	Procyon	244 59.3	N 5 11.1
05	6 59.5	282 41.8	26.9	164 57.6	02.3	245 14.4	37.4	142 06.0	36.8			
M 06	22 02.0	297 41.0	N22 27.1	179 58.9	S10 02.8	260 16.3	N20 37.3	157 08.5	S14 36.8	Rasalhague	96 05.4	N12 33.2
O 07	37 04.4	312 40.2	27.3	195 00.3	03.2	275 18.2	37.2	172 11.0	36.8	Regulus	207 43.0	N11 53.7
N 08	52 06.9	327 39.4	27.5	210 01.7	03.7	290 20.1	37.1	187 13.4	36.8	Rigel	281 11.6	S 8 11.2
D 09	67 09.3	342 38.6 ..	27.8	225 03.0 ..	04.2	305 22.0 ..	36.9	202 15.9 ..	36.8	Rigil Kent.	139 50.4	S60 53.8
A 10	82 11.8	357 37.9	28.0	240 04.4	04.7	320 23.9	36.8	217 18.4	36.8	Sabik	102 11.4	S15 44.4
Y 11	97 14.3	12 37.1	28.2	255 05.8	05.1	335 25.8	36.7	232 20.9	36.8			
12	112 16.7	27 36.3	N22 28.4	270 07.2	S10 05.6	350 27.6	N20 36.6	247 23.4	S14 36.8	Schedar	349 39.4	N56 36.8
13	127 19.2	42 35.5	28.6	285 08.5	06.1	5 29.5	36.5	262 25.9	36.8	Shaula	96 20.5	S37 06.7
14	142 21.7	57 34.7	28.9	300 09.9	06.6	20 31.4	36.4	277 28.4	36.8	Sirius	258 33.4	S16 44.3
15	157 24.1	72 33.9 ..	29.1	315 11.3 ..	07.0	35 33.3 ..	36.3	292 30.9 ..	36.8	Spica	158 30.4	S11 14.2
16	172 26.6	87 33.2	29.3	330 12.6	07.5	50 35.2	36.2	307 33.4	36.8	Suhail	222 52.2	S43 29.7
17	187 29.1	102 32.4	29.5	345 14.0	08.0	65 37.1	36.0	322 35.9	36.8			
18	202 31.5	117 31.6	N22 29.7	0 15.4	S10 08.5	80 38.9	N20 35.9	337 38.4	S14 36.8	Vega	80 38.0	N38 48.1
19	217 34.0	132 30.8	29.9	15 16.7	08.9	95 40.8	35.8	352 40.9	36.8	Zuben'ubi	137 04.4	S16 06.1
20	232 36.4	147 30.0	30.1	30 18.1	09.4	110 42.7	35.7	7 43.4	36.8		SHA	Mer. Pass.
21	247 38.9	162 29.2 ..	30.3	45 19.5 ..	09.9	125 44.6 ..	35.6	22 45.8 ..	36.8		° ′	h m
22	262 41.4	177 28.5	30.6	60 20.8	10.4	140 46.5	35.5	37 48.3	36.8	Venus	277 16.3	10 08
23	277 43.8	192 27.7	30.8	75 22.2	10.8	155 48.4	35.4	52 50.8	36.8	Mars	158 29.5	18 01
	h m									Jupiter	238 31.7	12 41
Mer. Pass.	4 36.0	v −0.8	d 0.2	v 1.4	d 0.5	v 1.9	d 0.1	v 2.5	d 0.0	Saturn	135 05.6	19 33

UT	SUN GHA	SUN Dec	MOON GHA	v	MOON Dec	d	HP
d h	° ′	° ′	° ′	′	° ′	′	′
12 00	178 36.3	N22 00.2	6 20.8	4.2	S17 55.7	4.3	60.9
01	193 36.3	21 59.9	20 44.0	4.2	17 51.4	4.3	60.9
02	208 36.2	59.6	35 07.2	4.2	17 47.1	4.5	61.0
03	223 36.1 ..	59.2	49 30.4	4.3	17 42.6	4.6	61.0
04	238 36.0	58.9	63 53.7	4.2	17 38.0	4.7	61.0
05	253 35.9	58.5	78 16.9	4.3	17 33.3	4.9	61.0
06	268 35.9	N21 58.2	92 40.2	4.2	S17 28.4	5.0	61.0
S 07	283 35.8	57.8	107 03.4	4.3	17 23.4	5.1	61.0
A 08	298 35.7	57.5	121 26.7	4.3	17 18.3	5.3	61.0
T 09	313 35.6 ..	57.1	135 50.0	4.3	17 13.0	5.4	61.1
U 10	328 35.5	56.8	150 13.3	4.4	17 07.6	5.5	61.1
R 11	343 35.5	56.4	164 36.7	4.4	17 02.1	5.6	61.1
D 12	358 35.4	N21 56.1	179 00.1	4.4	S16 56.5	5.8	61.1
A 13	13 35.3	55.7	193 23.5	4.4	16 50.7	5.9	61.1
Y 14	28 35.2	55.4	207 46.9	4.4	16 44.8	6.0	61.1
15	43 35.2 ..	55.0	222 10.3	4.5	16 38.8	6.2	61.1
16	58 35.1	54.7	236 33.8	4.5	16 32.6	6.2	61.1
17	73 35.0	54.3	250 57.3	4.6	16 26.4	6.4	61.1
18	88 34.9	N21 54.0	265 20.9	4.6	S16 20.0	6.5	61.1
19	103 34.9	53.6	279 44.5	4.6	16 13.5	6.6	61.2
20	118 34.8	53.3	294 08.1	4.6	16 06.9	6.8	61.2
21	133 34.7 ..	52.9	308 31.7	4.7	16 00.1	6.8	61.2
22	148 34.6	52.5	322 55.4	4.7	15 53.3	7.0	61.2
23	163 34.6	52.1	337 19.1	4.8	15 46.3	7.1	61.2
13 00	178 34.5	N21 51.8	351 42.9	4.8	S15 39.2	7.2	61.2
01	193 34.4	51.5	6 06.7	4.8	15 32.0	7.3	61.2
02	208 34.3	51.1	20 30.5	4.9	15 24.7	7.4	61.2
03	223 34.3 ..	50.7	34 54.4	4.9	15 17.3	7.5	61.2
04	238 34.2	50.4	49 18.3	5.0	15 09.8	7.7	61.2
05	253 34.1	50.0	63 42.3	5.0	15 02.1	7.7	61.2
06	268 34.0	N21 49.7	78 06.3	5.1	S14 54.4	7.9	61.2
07	283 34.0	49.3	92 30.4	5.1	14 46.5	7.9	61.2
S 08	298 33.9	48.9	106 54.5	5.1	14 38.6	8.1	61.2
U 09	313 33.8 ..	48.6	121 18.6	5.2	14 30.5	8.2	61.2
N 10	328 33.7	48.2	135 42.8	5.3	14 22.3	8.3	61.2
D 11	343 33.7	47.8	150 07.1	5.3	14 14.0	8.3	61.2
A 12	358 33.6	N21 47.5	164 31.4	5.3	S14 05.7	8.5	61.2
Y 13	13 33.5	47.1	178 55.7	5.4	13 57.2	8.6	61.2
14	28 33.5	46.7	193 20.1	5.5	13 48.6	8.6	61.2
15	43 33.4 ..	46.4	207 44.6	5.5	13 40.0	8.8	61.2
16	58 33.4	46.0	222 09.1	5.5	13 31.2	8.8	61.2
17	73 33.2	45.6	236 33.6	5.6	13 22.4	9.0	61.2
18	88 33.2	N21 45.3	250 58.2	5.7	S13 13.4	9.0	61.2
19	103 33.1	44.9	265 22.9	5.7	13 04.4	9.1	61.2
20	118 33.0	44.5	279 47.6	5.8	12 55.3	9.2	61.2
21	133 33.0 ..	44.2	294 12.4	5.8	12 46.1	9.3	61.2
22	148 32.9	43.8	308 37.2	5.9	12 36.8	9.4	61.2
23	163 32.8	43.4	323 02.1	6.0	12 27.4	9.5	61.1
14 00	178 32.8	N21 43.0	337 27.1	6.0	S12 17.9	9.5	61.1
01	193 32.7	42.7	351 52.1	6.0	12 08.4	9.6	61.1
02	208 32.6	42.3	6 17.1	6.1	11 58.8	9.7	61.1
03	223 32.5 ..	41.9	20 42.2	6.2	11 49.1	9.8	61.1
04	238 32.5	41.5	35 07.4	6.2	11 39.3	9.9	61.1
05	253 32.4	41.2	49 32.6	6.3	11 29.4	9.9	61.1
06	268 32.3	N21 40.8	63 57.9	6.4	S11 19.5	10.0	61.1
07	283 32.3	40.4	78 23.3	6.4	11 09.5	10.1	61.1
08	298 32.2	40.0	92 48.7	6.5	10 59.4	10.1	61.1
M 09	313 32.1 ..	39.6	107 14.2	6.5	10 49.3	10.2	61.0
O 10	328 32.1	39.3	121 39.7	6.6	10 39.1	10.3	61.0
N 11	343 32.0	38.9	136 05.3	6.6	10 28.8	10.4	61.0
D 12	358 31.9	N21 38.5	150 30.9	6.7	S10 18.4	10.4	61.0
A 13	13 31.9	38.1	164 56.6	6.8	10 08.0	10.4	61.0
Y 14	28 31.8	37.7	179 22.4	6.8	9 57.6	10.6	61.0
15	43 31.7 ..	37.3	193 48.2	6.9	9 47.0	10.6	61.0
16	58 31.7	37.0	208 14.1	7.0	9 36.4	10.6	60.9
17	73 31.6	36.6	222 40.1	7.0	9 25.8	10.7	60.9
18	88 31.5	N21 36.2	237 06.1	7.0	S 9 15.1	10.8	60.9
19	103 31.5	35.8	251 32.1	7.2	9 04.3	10.8	60.9
20	118 31.4	35.4	265 58.3	7.1	8 53.5	10.8	60.9
21	133 31.3 ..	35.0	280 24.4	7.3	8 42.7	10.9	60.9
22	148 31.3	34.6	294 50.7	7.3	8 31.8	11.0	60.8
23	163 31.2	34.3	309 17.0	7.4	S 8 20.8	11.0	60.8
	SD 15.8	d 0.4	SD 16.6		16.7		16.6

Lat.	Twilight Naut.	Twilight Civil	Sunrise	Moonrise 12	Moonrise 13	Moonrise 14	Moonrise 15
°	h m	h m	h m	h m	h m	h m	h m
N 72	▢	▢	▢	22 37	22 23	22 13	22 05
N 70	▢	▢	▢	21 58	22 00	22 00	22 00
68	▢	▢	▢	21 30	21 42	21 50	21 55
66	////	////	01 26	21 09	21 28	21 41	21 51
64	////	////	02 09	20 52	21 16	21 34	21 48
62	////	00 30	02 38	20 38	21 06	21 27	21 45
60	////	01 38	03 00	20 26	20 57	21 22	21 42
N 58	////	02 11	03 17	20 16	20 49	21 17	21 40
56	00 28	02 35	03 32	20 07	20 43	21 12	21 38
54	01 30	02 54	03 44	19 58	20 37	21 08	21 36
52	02 01	03 09	03 55	19 51	20 31	21 05	21 35
50	02 23	03 23	04 05	19 45	20 26	21 02	21 33
45	03 02	03 49	04 26	19 31	20 15	20 54	21 30
N 40	03 30	04 10	04 42	19 19	20 06	20 49	21 27
35	03 51	04 27	04 56	19 09	19 59	20 43	21 25
30	04 08	04 41	05 08	19 01	19 52	20 39	21 22
20	04 35	05 04	05 28	18 46	19 40	20 31	21 19
N 10	04 56	05 23	05 46	18 32	19 30	20 24	21 15
0	05 14	05 40	06 02	18 20	19 20	20 17	21 12
S 10	05 30	05 56	06 18	18 08	19 10	20 11	21 09
20	05 44	06 12	06 35	17 55	19 00	20 04	21 06
30	05 59	06 29	06 55	17 40	18 48	19 56	21 03
35	06 07	06 39	07 06	17 31	18 41	19 51	21 00
40	06 16	06 49	07 19	17 21	18 33	19 46	20 58
45	06 25	07 02	07 35	17 09	18 24	19 40	20 55
S 50	06 35	07 16	07 53	16 55	18 13	19 33	20 52
52	06 40	07 23	08 02	16 48	18 08	19 29	20 50
54	06 46	07 30	08 12	16 41	18 02	19 26	20 49
56	06 50	07 38	08 23	16 32	17 56	19 22	20 47
58	06 56	07 47	08 36	16 23	17 49	19 17	20 45
S 60	07 03	07 57	08 51	16 12	17 40	19 12	20 43

Lat.	Sunset	Twilight Civil	Twilight Naut.	Moonset 12	Moonset 13	Moonset 14	Moonset 15
°	h m	h m	h m	h m	h m	h m	h m
N 72	▢	▢	▢	■■	02 46	05 04	07 12
N 70	▢	▢	▢	01 25	03 24	05 26	07 23
68	▢	▢	▢	02 07	03 51	05 42	07 32
66	22 42	////	////	02 35	04 11	05 55	07 39
64	22 00	////	////	02 56	04 28	06 06	07 45
62	21 32	23 32	////	03 13	04 41	06 15	07 50
60	21 11	22 31	////	03 27	04 52	06 23	07 54
N 58	20 53	21 59	////	03 39	05 02	06 30	07 58
56	20 39	21 35	23 35	03 50	05 10	06 36	08 02
54	20 26	21 17	22 39	03 59	05 18	06 41	08 05
52	20 15	21 01	22 09	04 07	05 25	06 46	08 08
50	20 06	20 48	21 47	04 15	05 31	06 50	08 11
45	19 45	20 21	21 08	04 31	05 44	07 00	08 16
N 40	19 29	20 01	20 41	04 44	05 55	07 08	08 20
35	19 15	19 44	20 20	04 55	06 04	07 15	08 24
30	19 03	19 30	20 03	05 04	06 12	07 20	08 28
20	18 43	19 07	19 36	05 21	06 26	07 31	08 34
N 10	18 26	18 48	19 15	05 35	06 38	07 39	08 39
0	18 09	18 32	18 58	05 48	06 49	07 48	08 44
S 10	17 53	18 16	18 42	06 01	07 00	07 56	08 49
20	17 36	18 00	18 27	06 15	07 12	08 04	08 54
30	17 17	17 43	18 12	06 32	07 25	08 14	08 59
35	17 05	17 33	18 04	06 41	07 33	08 20	09 03
40	16 52	17 22	17 56	06 51	07 41	08 26	09 06
45	16 37	17 10	17 47	07 04	07 52	08 33	09 10
S 50	16 18	16 56	17 37	07 19	08 04	08 42	09 16
52	16 10	16 49	17 32	07 26	08 10	08 46	09 18
54	16 00	16 42	17 27	07 34	08 16	08 51	09 20
56	15 48	16 34	17 22	07 42	08 23	08 55	09 23
58	15 36	16 25	17 16	07 52	08 30	09 01	09 26
S 60	15 20	16 15	17 09	08 03	08 39	09 07	09 30

	SUN			MOON			
Day	Eqn. of Time 00h	Eqn. of Time 12h	Mer. Pass.	Mer. Pass. Upper	Mer. Pass. Lower	Age	Phase
d	m s	m s	h m	h m	h m	d	%
12	05 35	05 38	12 06	24 35	12 04	15	100
13	05 42	05 45	12 06	00 35	13 04	16	98
14	05 49	05 52	12 06	01 34	14 03	17	94

UT	ARIES	VENUS −3.8		MARS +0.2		JUPITER −1.8		SATURN +0.5		STARS		
	GHA	GHA	Dec	GHA	Dec	GHA	Dec	GHA	Dec	Name	SHA	Dec
d h	° ′	° ′	° ′	° ′	° ′	° ′	° ′	° ′	° ′		° ′	° ′
15 00	292 46.3	207 26.9	N22 31.0	90 23.6	S10 11.3	170 50.3	N20 35.2	67 53.3	S14 36.8	Acamar	315 18.0	S40 14.6
01	307 48.8	222 26.1	31.2	105 24.9	11.8	185 52.1	35.1	82 55.8	36.8	Achernar	335 26.3	S57 09.5
02	322 51.2	237 25.3	31.4	120 26.3	12.3	200 54.0	35.0	97 58.3	36.8	Acrux	173 08.5	S63 11.1
03	337 53.7	252 24.5 ..	31.6	135 27.6 ..	12.7	215 55.9 ..	34.9	113 00.8 ..	36.8	Adhara	255 12.3	S28 59.6
04	352 56.2	267 23.7	31.8	150 29.0	13.2	230 57.8	34.8	128 03.3	36.8	Aldebaran	290 48.7	N16 32.1
05	7 58.6	282 23.0	32.0	165 30.4	13.7	245 59.7	34.7	143 05.8	36.8			
06	23 01.1	297 22.2	N22 32.2	180 31.7	S10 14.2	261 01.6	N20 34.6	158 08.3	S14 36.9	Alioth	166 20.2	N55 53.2
T 07	38 03.6	312 21.4	32.4	195 33.1	14.7	276 03.5	34.5	173 10.8	36.9	Alkaid	152 58.3	N49 14.8
U 08	53 06.0	327 20.6	32.6	210 34.4	15.1	291 05.3	34.3	188 13.2	36.9	Al Na'ir	27 42.5	S46 53.1
E 09	68 08.5	342 19.8 ..	32.8	225 35.8 ..	15.6	306 07.2 ..	34.2	203 15.7 ..	36.9	Alnilam	275 45.9	S 1 11.7
S 10	83 10.9	357 19.0	33.0	240 37.2	16.1	321 09.1	34.1	218 18.2	36.9	Alphard	217 55.6	S 8 43.4
D 11	98 13.4	12 18.2	33.2	255 38.5	16.6	336 11.0	34.1	233 20.7	36.9			
A 12	113 15.9	27 17.5	N22 33.4	270 39.9	S10 17.0	351 12.9	N20 33.9	248 23.2	S14 36.9	Alphecca	126 10.2	N26 40.3
Y 13	128 18.3	42 16.7	33.6	285 41.2	17.5	6 14.8	33.8	263 25.7	36.9	Alpheratz	357 42.5	N29 10.2
14	143 20.8	57 15.9	33.7	300 42.6	18.0	21 16.6	33.7	278 28.2	36.9	Altair	62 07.2	N 8 54.7
15	158 23.3	72 15.1 ..	33.9	315 43.9 ..	18.5	36 18.5 ..	33.5	293 30.7 ..	36.9	Ankaa	353 14.9	S42 13.3
16	173 25.7	87 14.3	34.1	330 45.3	18.9	51 20.4	33.4	308 33.2	36.9	Antares	112 25.0	S26 27.7
17	188 28.2	102 13.5	34.3	345 46.7	19.4	66 22.3	33.3	323 35.6	36.9			
18	203 30.7	117 12.7	N22 34.5	0 48.0	S10 19.9	81 24.2	N20 33.2	338 38.1	S14 36.9	Arcturus	145 55.0	N19 06.6
19	218 33.1	132 11.9	34.7	15 49.4	20.4	96 26.1	33.1	353 40.6	36.9	Atria	107 25.7	S69 03.2
20	233 35.6	147 11.1	34.9	30 50.7	20.9	111 28.0	33.0	8 43.1	36.9	Avior	234 18.3	S59 33.6
21	248 38.1	162 10.4 ..	35.1	45 52.1 ..	21.3	126 29.8 ..	32.9	23 45.6 ..	36.9	Bellatrix	278 31.5	N 6 21.6
22	263 40.5	177 09.6	35.2	60 53.4	21.8	141 31.7	32.7	38 48.1	36.9	Betelgeuse	271 00.8	N 7 24.4
23	278 43.0	192 08.8	35.4	75 54.8	22.3	156 33.6	32.6	53 50.6	36.9			
16 00	293 45.4	207 08.0	N22 35.6	90 56.1	S10 22.8	171 35.5	N20 32.5	68 53.1	S14 36.9	Canopus	263 56.3	S52 42.3
01	308 47.9	222 07.2	35.8	105 57.5	23.3	186 37.4	32.4	83 55.5	36.9	Capella	280 33.7	N46 00.5
02	323 50.4	237 06.4	36.0	120 58.8	23.7	201 39.3	32.3	98 58.0	36.9	Deneb	49 30.5	N45 20.1
03	338 52.8	252 05.6 ..	36.1	136 00.2 ..	24.2	216 41.1 ..	32.2	114 00.5 ..	36.9	Denebola	182 33.1	N14 29.5
04	353 55.3	267 04.8	36.3	151 01.5	24.7	231 43.0	32.1	129 03.0	37.0	Diphda	348 55.1	S17 54.2
05	8 57.8	282 04.0	36.5	166 02.9	25.2	246 44.9	32.0	144 05.5	37.0			
06	24 00.2	297 03.2	N22 36.7	181 04.2	S10 25.6	261 46.8	N20 31.8	159 08.0	S14 37.0	Dubhe	193 51.3	N61 40.5
W 07	39 02.7	312 02.4	36.8	196 05.6	26.1	276 48.7	31.7	174 10.5	37.0	Elnath	278 12.0	N28 36.9
E 08	54 05.2	327 01.6	37.0	211 06.9	26.6	291 50.6	31.6	189 12.9	37.0	Eltanin	90 45.3	N51 29.5
D 09	69 07.6	342 00.9 ..	37.2	226 08.3 ..	27.1	306 52.5 ..	31.5	204 15.4 ..	37.0	Enif	33 46.1	N 9 56.7
N 10	84 10.1	357 00.1	37.3	241 09.6	27.6	321 54.3	31.4	219 17.9	37.0	Fomalhaut	15 22.9	S29 32.4
E 11	99 12.5	11 59.3	37.5	256 10.9	28.0	336 56.2	31.3	234 20.4	37.0			
S 12	114 15.0	26 58.5	N22 37.7	271 12.3	S10 28.5	351 58.1	N20 31.2	249 22.9	S14 37.0	Gacrux	172 00.1	S57 11.9
D 13	129 17.5	41 57.7	37.8	286 13.6	29.0	7 00.0	31.0	264 25.4	37.0	Gienah	175 51.6	S17 37.4
A 14	144 19.9	56 56.9	38.0	301 15.0	29.5	22 01.9	30.9	279 27.8	37.0	Hadar	148 46.6	S60 26.8
Y 15	159 22.4	71 56.1 ..	38.2	316 16.3 ..	30.0	37 03.8 ..	30.8	294 30.3 ..	37.0	Hamal	327 59.9	N23 31.7
16	174 24.9	86 55.3	38.3	331 17.7	30.4	52 05.7	30.7	309 32.8	37.0	Kaus Aust.	83 42.4	S34 22.4
17	189 27.3	101 54.5	38.5	346 19.0	30.9	67 07.5	30.6	324 35.3	37.0			
18	204 29.8	116 53.7	N22 38.7	1 20.3	S10 31.4	82 09.4	N20 30.5	339 37.8	S14 37.0	Kochab	137 19.8	N74 06.1
19	219 32.3	131 52.9	38.8	16 21.7	31.9	97 11.3	30.3	354 40.3	37.0	Markab	13 37.3	N15 17.1
20	234 34.7	146 52.1	39.0	31 23.0	32.4	112 13.2	30.2	9 42.8	37.0	Menkar	314 14.4	N 4 08.7
21	249 37.2	161 51.3 ..	39.1	46 24.4 ..	32.8	127 15.1 ..	30.1	24 45.2 ..	37.0	Menkent	148 06.6	S36 26.6
22	264 39.7	176 50.5	39.3	61 25.7	33.3	142 17.0	30.0	39 47.7	37.0	Miaplacidus	221 40.2	S69 46.9
23	279 42.1	191 49.7	39.4	76 27.0	33.8	157 18.8	29.9	54 50.2	37.1			
17 00	294 44.6	206 48.9	N22 39.6	91 28.4	S10 34.3	172 20.7	N20 29.8	69 52.7	S14 37.1	Mirfak	308 39.4	N49 54.4
01	309 47.0	221 48.1	39.7	106 29.7	34.8	187 22.6	29.7	84 55.2	37.1	Nunki	75 57.0	S26 16.5
02	324 49.5	236 47.3	39.9	121 31.1	35.2	202 24.5	29.5	99 57.7	37.1	Peacock	53 17.5	S56 41.0
03	339 52.0	251 46.5 ..	40.0	136 32.4 ..	35.7	217 26.4 ..	29.4	115 00.1 ..	37.1	Pollux	243 27.2	N27 59.3
04	354 54.4	266 45.7	40.2	151 33.7	36.2	232 28.3	29.3	130 02.6	37.1	Procyon	244 59.3	N 5 11.1
05	9 56.9	281 45.0	40.3	166 35.1	36.7	247 30.2	29.2	145 05.1	37.1			
06	24 59.4	296 44.2	N22 40.5	181 36.4	S10 37.2	262 32.0	N20 29.1	160 07.6	S14 37.1	Rasalhague	96 05.4	N12 33.3
T 07	40 01.8	311 43.4	40.6	196 37.7	37.6	277 33.9	29.0	175 10.1	37.1	Regulus	207 43.0	N11 53.7
H 08	55 04.3	326 42.6	40.8	211 39.1	38.1	292 35.8	28.9	190 12.5	37.1	Rigel	281 11.6	S 8 11.2
U 09	70 06.8	341 41.8 ..	40.9	226 40.4 ..	38.6	307 37.7 ..	28.7	205 15.0 ..	37.1	Rigil Kent.	139 50.4	S60 53.8
R 10	85 09.2	356 41.0	41.1	241 41.7	39.1	322 39.6	28.6	220 17.5	37.1	Sabik	102 11.4	S15 44.4
S 11	100 11.7	11 40.2	41.2	256 43.1	39.6	337 41.5	28.5	235 20.0	37.1			
D 12	115 14.2	26 39.4	N22 41.4	271 44.4	S10 40.1	352 43.3	N20 28.4	250 22.5	S14 37.1	Schedar	349 39.4	N56 36.8
A 13	130 16.6	41 38.6	41.5	286 45.7	40.5	7 45.2	28.3	265 24.9	37.1	Shaula	96 20.5	S37 06.7
Y 14	145 19.1	56 37.8	41.6	301 47.1	41.0	22 47.1	28.2	280 27.4	37.1	Sirius	258 33.6	S16 44.3
15	160 21.5	71 37.0 ..	41.8	316 48.4 ..	41.5	37 49.0 ..	28.0	295 29.9 ..	37.2	Spica	158 30.4	S11 14.2
16	175 24.0	86 36.2	41.9	331 49.7	42.0	52 50.9	27.9	310 32.4	37.2	Suhail	222 52.2	S43 29.7
17	190 26.5	101 35.4	42.0	346 51.1	42.5	67 52.8	27.8	325 34.9	37.2			
18	205 28.9	116 34.6	N22 42.2	1 52.4	S10 42.9	82 54.7	N20 27.7	340 37.3	S14 37.2	Vega	80 38.0	N38 48.1
19	220 31.4	131 33.8	42.3	16 53.7	43.4	97 56.5	27.6	355 39.8	37.2	Zuben'ubi	137 04.4	S16 06.1
20	235 33.9	146 33.0	42.4	31 55.0	43.9	112 58.4	27.5	10 42.3	37.2		SHA	Mer. Pass.
21	250 36.3	161 32.2 ..	42.6	46 56.4 ..	44.4	128 00.3 ..	27.4	25 44.8 ..	37.2		° ′	h m
22	265 38.8	176 31.4	42.7	61 57.7	44.9	143 02.2	27.2	40 47.3	37.2	Venus	273 22.5	10 12
23	280 41.3	191 30.6	42.8	76 59.0	45.4	158 04.1	27.1	55 49.7	37.2	Mars	157 10.7	17 55
	h m									Jupiter	237 50.1	12 32
Mer. Pass. 4 24.2		v −0.8	d 0.2	v 1.3	d 0.5	v 1.9	d 0.1	v 2.5	d 0.0	Saturn	135 07.6	19 21

UT	SUN GHA	SUN Dec	MOON GHA	v	MOON Dec	d	HP
d h	° ′	° ′	° ′	′	° ′	′	′
15 00	178 31.1	N21 33.9	323 43.4	7.4	S 8 09.8	11.0	60.8
01	193 31.1	33.5	338 09.8	7.5	7 58.8	11.1	60.8
02	208 31.0	33.1	352 36.3	7.5	7 47.7	11.2	60.8
03	223 30.9 ..	32.7	7 02.8	7.6	7 36.5	11.1	60.7
04	238 30.9	32.3	21 29.4	7.7	7 25.4	11.2	60.7
05	253 30.8	31.9	35 56.1	7.7	7 14.2	11.3	60.7
06	268 30.8	N21 31.5	50 22.8	7.7	S 7 02.9	11.3	60.7
07	283 30.7	31.1	64 49.5	7.9	6 51.6	11.3	60.6
T 08	298 30.6	30.7	79 16.4	7.9	6 40.3	11.3	60.6
U 09	313 30.6 ..	30.3	93 43.3	7.9	6 29.0	11.4	60.6
E 10	328 30.5	29.9	108 10.2	8.0	6 17.6	11.4	60.6
S 11	343 30.4	29.5	122 37.2	8.0	6 06.2	11.5	60.6
D 12	358 30.4	N21 29.1	137 04.2	8.2	S 5 54.7	11.5	60.5
A 13	13 30.3	28.8	151 31.4	8.1	5 43.2	11.4	60.5
Y 14	28 30.3	28.4	165 58.5	8.2	5 31.8	11.6	60.5
15	43 30.2 ..	28.0	180 25.7	8.3	5 20.2	11.5	60.5
16	58 30.1	27.6	194 53.0	8.3	5 08.7	11.6	60.4
17	73 30.1	27.2	209 20.3	8.4	4 57.1	11.6	60.4
18	88 30.0	N21 26.8	223 47.7	8.5	S 4 45.5	11.6	60.4
19	103 30.0	26.4	238 15.2	8.4	4 33.9	11.6	60.3
20	118 29.9	26.0	252 42.6	8.6	4 22.3	11.6	60.3
21	133 29.8 ..	25.6	267 10.2	8.6	4 10.7	11.6	60.3
22	148 29.8	25.1	281 37.8	8.6	3 59.1	11.7	60.3
23	163 29.7	24.7	296 05.4	8.7	3 47.4	11.7	60.2
16 00	178 29.7	N21 24.3	310 33.1	8.7	S 3 35.7	11.7	60.2
01	193 29.6	23.9	325 00.8	8.8	3 24.0	11.6	60.2
02	208 29.5	23.5	339 28.6	8.9	3 12.4	11.7	60.2
03	223 29.5 ..	23.1	353 56.5	8.8	3 00.7	11.7	60.1
04	238 29.4	22.7	8 24.3	9.0	2 49.0	11.8	60.1
05	253 29.4	22.3	22 52.3	9.0	2 37.2	11.7	60.1
06	268 29.3	N21 21.9	37 20.3	9.0	S 2 25.5	11.7	60.0
W 07	283 29.2	21.5	51 48.3	9.1	2 13.8	11.7	60.0
E 08	298 29.2	21.1	66 16.4	9.1	2 02.1	11.7	60.0
D 09	313 29.1 ..	20.7	80 44.5	9.1	1 50.4	11.7	59.9
N 10	328 29.1	20.3	95 12.6	9.2	1 38.7	11.7	59.9
E 11	343 29.0	19.8	109 40.8	9.3	1 27.0	11.7	59.9
S 12	358 29.0	N21 19.4	124 09.1	9.3	S 1 15.3	11.7	59.9
D 13	13 28.9	19.0	138 37.4	9.3	1 03.6	11.7	59.8
A 14	28 28.8	18.6	153 05.7	9.4	0 51.9	11.7	59.8
Y 15	43 28.8 ..	18.2	167 34.1	9.4	0 40.2	11.7	59.8
16	58 28.7	17.8	182 02.5	9.5	0 28.5	11.6	59.7
17	73 28.7	17.4	196 31.0	9.5	0 16.9	11.7	59.7
18	88 28.6	N21 17.0	210 59.5	9.5	S 0 05.2	11.6	59.7
19	103 28.6	16.5	225 28.0	9.6	N 0 06.4	11.6	59.6
20	118 28.5	16.1	239 56.6	9.6	0 18.0	11.6	59.6
21	133 28.5 ..	15.7	254 25.2	9.7	0 29.6	11.6	59.6
22	148 28.4	15.3	268 53.9	9.7	0 41.2	11.6	59.5
23	163 28.3	14.9	283 22.6	9.7	0 52.8	11.5	59.5
17 00	178 28.3	N21 14.4	297 51.3	9.8	N 1 04.3	11.6	59.5
01	193 28.2	14.0	312 20.1	9.8	1 15.9	11.5	59.4
02	208 28.2	13.6	326 48.9	9.8	1 27.4	11.5	59.4
03	223 28.1 ..	13.2	341 17.7	9.9	1 38.9	11.4	59.4
04	238 28.1	12.8	355 46.6	9.9	1 50.3	11.5	59.3
05	253 28.0	12.3	10 15.5	9.9	2 01.8	11.4	59.3
06	268 28.0	N21 11.9	24 44.4	9.9	N 2 13.2	11.4	59.3
07	283 27.9	11.5	39 13.3	10.0	2 24.6	11.3	59.2
T 08	298 27.9	11.1	53 42.3	10.1	2 35.9	11.4	59.2
H 09	313 27.8 ..	10.6	68 11.4	10.0	2 47.3	11.3	59.2
U 10	328 27.8	10.2	82 40.4	10.1	2 58.6	11.2	59.1
R 11	343 27.7	09.8	97 09.5	10.1	3 09.8	11.3	59.1
S 12	358 27.7	N21 09.4	111 38.6	10.2	N 3 21.1	11.2	59.0
D 13	13 27.6	08.9	126 07.8	10.1	3 32.3	11.2	59.0
A 14	28 27.5	08.5	140 36.9	10.2	3 43.5	11.1	59.0
Y 15	43 27.5 ..	08.1	155 06.1	10.2	3 54.6	11.1	58.9
16	58 27.4	07.6	169 35.3	10.3	4 05.7	11.1	58.9
17	73 27.4	07.2	184 04.6	10.3	4 16.8	11.0	58.9
18	88 27.3	N21 06.8	198 33.9	10.3	N 4 27.8	11.0	58.8
19	103 27.3	06.4	213 03.2	10.3	4 38.8	11.0	58.8
20	118 27.2	05.9	227 32.5	10.3	4 49.8	10.9	58.8
21	133 27.2 ..	05.5	242 01.8	10.4	5 00.7	10.9	58.7
22	148 27.1	05.1	256 31.2	10.4	5 11.5	10.9	58.7
23	163 27.1	04.6	271 00.6	10.4	N 5 22.4	10.7	58.7
	SD 15.8	d 0.4	SD 16.5		16.3		16.1

Twilight / Sunrise / Moonrise

Lat.	Twilight Naut.	Twilight Civil	Sunrise	Moonrise 15	16	17	18
°	h m	h m	h m	h m	h m	h m	h m
N 72	▭	▭	▭	22 05	21 58	21 51	21 44
N 70	▭	▭	▭	22 00	21 59	21 58	21 57
68	▭	▭	▭	21 55	21 59	22 04	22 09
66	////	////	01 39	21 51	22 00	22 08	22 18
64	////	////	02 18	21 48	22 00	22 12	22 26
62	////	00 56	02 45	21 45	22 01	22 16	22 32
60	////	01 48	03 05	21 42	22 01	22 19	22 38
N 58	////	02 18	03 22	21 40	22 01	22 22	22 44
56	00 52	02 40	03 36	21 38	22 01	22 24	22 48
54	01 39	02 58	03 48	21 36	22 02	22 27	22 52
52	02 07	03 14	03 59	21 35	22 02	22 29	22 56
50	02 28	03 26	04 08	21 33	22 02	22 31	23 00
45	03 06	03 53	04 28	21 30	22 03	22 35	23 07
N 40	03 33	04 13	04 44	21 27	22 03	22 38	23 14
35	03 53	04 29	04 58	21 25	22 03	22 41	23 19
30	04 10	04 43	05 10	21 22	22 04	22 44	23 24
20	04 37	05 05	05 29	21 19	22 04	22 48	23 32
N 10	04 57	05 24	05 47	21 15	22 05	22 53	23 40
0	05 14	05 40	06 02	21 12	22 05	22 56	23 47
S 10	05 30	05 56	06 18	21 09	22 06	23 00	23 54
20	05 44	06 11	06 35	21 06	22 06	23 05	24 01
30	05 59	06 28	06 54	21 03	22 07	23 09	24 10
35	06 06	06 38	07 05	21 00	22 07	23 12	24 15
40	06 14	06 48	07 18	20 58	22 08	23 16	24 21
45	06 23	07 00	07 33	20 55	22 08	23 19	24 28
S 50	06 33	07 14	07 51	20 52	22 09	23 24	24 36
52	06 38	07 20	07 59	20 50	22 09	23 26	24 40
54	06 43	07 27	08 09	20 49	22 10	23 28	24 44
56	06 48	07 35	08 20	20 47	22 10	23 31	24 48
58	06 53	07 44	08 32	20 45	22 11	23 33	24 53
S 60	06 59	07 54	08 47	20 43	22 11	23 37	24 59

Sunset / Twilight / Moonset

Lat.	Sunset	Twilight Civil	Twilight Naut.	Moonset 15	16	17	18
°	h m	h m	h m	h m	h m	h m	h m
N 72	▭	▭	▭	07 12	09 13	11 09	13 03
N 70	▭	▭	▭	07 23	09 16	11 05	12 51
68	▭	▭	▭	07 32	09 18	11 01	12 41
66	22 29	////	////	07 39	09 20	10 58	12 33
64	21 52	////	////	07 45	09 22	10 56	12 27
62	21 26	23 10	////	07 50	09 23	10 54	12 21
60	21 05	22 22	////	07 54	09 24	10 52	12 16
N 58	20 49	21 52	////	07 58	09 25	10 50	12 12
56	20 35	21 30	23 15	08 02	09 26	10 48	12 08
54	20 23	21 12	22 31	08 05	09 27	10 47	12 04
52	20 12	20 58	22 03	08 08	09 28	10 46	12 01
50	20 03	20 45	21 43	08 10	09 29	10 45	11 58
45	19 43	20 19	21 05	08 16	09 30	10 42	11 52
N 40	19 27	19 59	20 39	08 20	09 31	10 40	11 47
35	19 14	19 43	20 18	08 24	09 33	10 39	11 43
30	19 02	19 29	20 01	08 28	09 33	10 37	11 39
20	18 43	19 07	19 35	08 34	09 35	10 34	11 32
N 10	18 25	18 48	19 15	08 39	09 36	10 32	11 26
0	18 10	18 32	18 58	08 44	09 38	10 30	11 20
S 10	17 54	18 16	18 42	08 49	09 39	10 27	11 15
20	17 37	18 01	18 28	08 54	09 40	10 25	11 09
30	17 18	17 44	18 14	08 59	09 42	10 22	11 02
35	17 07	17 35	18 06	09 03	09 43	10 21	10 59
40	16 55	17 24	17 58	09 06	09 43	10 19	10 54
45	16 40	17 13	17 49	09 10	09 44	10 17	10 49
S 50	16 22	16 59	17 39	09 16	09 46	10 14	10 43
52	16 13	16 52	17 35	09 18	09 46	10 13	10 40
54	16 03	16 45	17 30	09 20	09 47	10 12	10 37
56	15 53	16 37	17 25	09 23	09 48	10 11	10 34
58	15 40	16 29	17 19	09 26	09 48	10 09	10 30
S 60	15 26	16 19	17 13	09 30	09 49	10 08	10 26

SUN / MOON

Day	SUN Eqn. of Time 00h	SUN Eqn. of Time 12h	SUN Mer. Pass.	MOON Mer. Pass. Upper	MOON Mer. Pass. Lower	Age	Phase
d	m s	m s	h m	h m	h m	d	%
15	05 55	05 58	12 06	02 31	14 58	18	87
16	06 01	06 04	12 06	03 25	15 52	19	78
17	06 07	06 09	12 06	04 17	16 43	20	67

UT	ARIES GHA	VENUS −3.8 GHA	VENUS Dec	MARS +0.3 GHA	MARS Dec	JUPITER −1.8 GHA	JUPITER Dec	SATURN +0.5 GHA	SATURN Dec	STARS Name	SHA	Dec
	° ′	° ′	° ′	° ′	° ′	° ′	° ′	° ′	° ′		° ′	° ′
18 00	295 43.7	206 29.8	N22 43.0	92 00.3	S10 45.8	173 06.0	N20 27.0	70 52.2	S14 37.2	Acamar	315 18.0	S40 14.6
01	310 46.2	221 29.0	43.1	107 01.7	46.3	188 07.9	26.9	85 54.7	37.2	Achernar	335 26.3	S57 09.5
02	325 48.6	236 28.2	43.2	122 03.0	46.8	203 09.7	26.8	100 57.2	37.2	Acrux	173 08.5	S63 11.1
03	340 51.1	251 27.4 ..	43.3	137 04.3 ..	47.3	218 11.6 ..	26.7	115 59.7 ..	37.2	Adhara	255 12.3	S28 59.6
04	355 53.6	266 26.6	43.5	152 05.6	47.8	233 13.5	26.5	131 02.1	37.2	Aldebaran	290 48.7	N16 32.1
05	10 56.0	281 25.8	43.6	167 07.0	48.3	248 15.4	26.4	146 04.6	37.3			
06	25 58.5	296 25.0	N22 43.7	182 08.3	S10 48.7	263 17.3	N20 26.3	161 07.1	S14 37.3	Alioth	166 20.2	N55 53.2
07	41 01.0	311 24.2	43.8	197 09.6	49.2	278 19.2	26.2	176 09.6	37.3	Alkaid	152 58.4	N49 14.8
08	56 03.4	326 23.4	43.9	212 10.9	49.7	293 21.0	26.1	191 12.0	37.3	Al Na'ir	27 42.5	S46 53.1
F 09	71 05.9	341 22.6 ..	44.1	227 12.3 ..	50.2	308 22.9 ..	26.0	206 14.5 ..	37.3	Alnilam	275 45.9	S 1 11.7
R 10	86 08.4	356 21.8	44.2	242 13.6	50.7	323 24.8	25.8	221 17.0	37.3	Alphard	217 55.6	S 8 43.4
I 11	101 10.8	11 21.0	44.3	257 14.9	51.2	338 26.7	25.7	236 19.5	37.3			
D 12	116 13.3	26 20.2	N22 44.4	272 16.2	S10 51.6	353 28.6	N20 25.6	251 22.0	S14 37.3	Alphecca	126 10.2	N26 40.3
A 13	131 15.8	41 19.3	44.5	287 17.5	52.1	8 30.5	25.5	266 24.4	37.3	Alpheratz	357 42.5	N29 10.2
Y 14	146 18.2	56 18.5	44.6	302 18.9	52.6	23 32.4	25.4	281 26.9	37.3	Altair	62 07.1	N 8 54.7
15	161 20.7	71 17.7 ..	44.7	317 20.2 ..	53.1	38 34.2 ..	25.3	296 29.4 ..	37.3	Ankaa	353 14.9	S42 13.3
16	176 23.1	86 16.9	44.8	332 21.5	53.6	53 36.1	25.2	311 31.9	37.3	Antares	112 25.0	S26 27.7
17	191 25.6	101 16.1	44.9	347 22.8	54.1	68 38.0	25.0	326 34.3	37.3			
18	206 28.1	116 15.3	N22 45.1	2 24.1	S10 54.5	83 39.9	N20 24.9	341 36.8	S14 37.4	Arcturus	145 55.0	N19 06.6
19	221 30.5	131 14.5	45.2	17 25.4	55.0	98 41.8	24.8	356 39.3	37.4	Atria	107 25.7	S69 03.2
20	236 33.0	146 13.7	45.3	32 26.8	55.5	113 43.7	24.7	11 41.8	37.4	Avior	234 18.3	S59 33.6
21	251 35.5	161 12.9 ..	45.4	47 28.1 ..	56.0	128 45.5 ..	24.6	26 44.2 ..	37.4	Bellatrix	278 31.5	N 6 21.6
22	266 37.9	176 12.1	45.5	62 29.4	56.5	143 47.4	24.5	41 46.7	37.4	Betelgeuse	271 00.8	N 7 24.4
23	281 40.4	191 11.3	45.6	77 30.7	57.0	158 49.3	24.3	56 49.2	37.4			
19 00	296 42.9	206 10.5	N22 45.7	92 32.0	S10 57.4	173 51.2	N20 24.2	71 51.7	S14 37.4	Canopus	263 56.3	S52 42.3
01	311 45.3	221 09.7	45.8	107 33.3	57.9	188 53.1	24.1	86 54.1	37.4	Capella	280 33.7	N46 00.4
02	326 47.8	236 08.9	45.9	122 34.6	58.4	203 55.0	24.0	101 56.6	37.4	Deneb	49 30.4	N45 20.1
03	341 50.2	251 08.1 ..	46.0	137 35.9 ..	58.9	218 56.9 ..	23.9	116 59.1 ..	37.4	Denebola	182 33.1	N14 29.5
04	356 52.7	266 07.3	46.1	152 37.3	59.4	233 58.7	23.8	132 01.6	37.4	Diphda	348 55.1	S17 54.2
05	11 55.2	281 06.5	46.2	167 38.6	10 59.9	249 00.6	23.6	147 04.0	37.4			
06	26 57.6	296 05.7	N22 46.3	182 39.9	S11 00.4	264 02.5	N20 23.5	162 06.5	S14 37.5	Dubhe	193 51.3	N61 40.5
07	42 00.1	311 04.9	46.3	197 41.2	00.8	279 04.4	23.4	177 09.0	37.5	Elnath	278 12.0	N28 36.9
S 08	57 02.6	326 04.1	46.4	212 42.5	01.3	294 06.3	23.3	192 11.5	37.5	Eltanin	90 45.3	N51 29.6
A 09	72 05.0	341 03.3 ..	46.5	227 43.8 ..	01.8	309 08.2 ..	23.2	207 13.9 ..	37.5	Enif	33 46.1	N 9 56.7
T 10	87 07.5	356 02.4	46.6	242 45.1	02.3	324 10.0	23.1	222 16.4	37.5	Fomalhaut	15 22.9	S29 32.4
U 11	102 10.0	11 01.6	46.7	257 46.4	02.8	339 11.9	22.9	237 18.9	37.5			
R 12	117 12.4	26 00.8	N22 46.8	272 47.7	S11 03.3	354 13.8	N20 22.8	252 21.4	S14 37.5	Gacrux	172 00.1	S57 11.9
D 13	132 14.9	41 00.0	46.9	287 49.0	03.8	9 15.7	22.7	267 23.8	37.5	Gienah	175 51.6	S17 37.4
A 14	147 17.4	55 59.2	47.0	302 50.3	04.2	24 17.6	22.6	282 26.3	37.5	Hadar	148 46.6	S60 26.8
Y 15	162 19.8	70 58.4 ..	47.0	317 51.7 ..	04.7	39 19.5 ..	22.5	297 28.8 ..	37.5	Hamal	327 59.9	N23 31.7
16	177 22.3	85 57.6	47.1	332 53.0	05.2	54 21.4	22.4	312 31.2	37.5	Kaus Aust.	83 42.4	S34 22.4
17	192 24.7	100 56.8	47.2	347 54.3	05.7	69 23.2	22.2	327 33.7	37.5			
18	207 27.2	115 56.0	N22 47.3	2 55.6	S11 06.2	84 25.1	N20 22.1	342 36.2	S14 37.6	Kochab	137 19.9	N74 06.1
19	222 29.7	130 55.2	47.4	17 56.9	06.7	99 27.0	22.0	357 38.7	37.6	Markab	13 37.3	N15 17.1
20	237 32.1	145 54.4	47.5	32 58.2	07.2	114 28.9	21.9	12 41.1	37.6	Menkar	314 14.4	N 4 08.7
21	252 34.6	160 53.6 ..	47.5	47 59.5 ..	07.6	129 30.8 ..	21.8	27 43.6 ..	37.6	Menkent	148 06.6	S36 26.6
22	267 37.1	175 52.8	47.6	63 00.8	08.1	144 32.7	21.7	42 46.1	37.6	Miaplacidus	221 40.2	S69 46.9
23	282 39.5	190 52.0	47.7	78 02.1	08.6	159 34.6	21.5	57 48.5	37.6			
20 00	297 42.0	205 51.1	N22 47.8	93 03.4	S11 09.1	174 36.4	N20 21.4	72 51.0	S14 37.6	Mirfak	308 39.4	N49 54.4
01	312 44.5	220 50.3	47.8	108 04.7	09.6	189 38.3	21.3	87 53.5	37.6	Nunki	75 57.0	S26 16.5
02	327 46.9	235 49.5	47.9	123 06.0	10.1	204 40.2	21.2	102 56.0	37.6	Peacock	53 17.5	S56 41.0
03	342 49.4	250 48.7 ..	48.0	138 07.3 ..	10.6	219 42.1 ..	21.1	117 58.4 ..	37.6	Pollux	243 27.2	N27 59.3
04	357 51.9	265 47.9	48.0	153 08.6	11.0	234 44.0	20.9	133 00.9	37.7	Procyon	244 59.3	N 5 11.1
05	12 54.3	280 47.1	48.1	168 09.9	11.5	249 45.9	20.8	148 03.4	37.7			
06	27 56.8	295 46.3	N22 48.2	183 11.2	S11 12.0	264 47.7	N20 20.7	163 05.8	S14 37.7	Rasalhague	96 05.5	N12 33.3
07	42 59.2	310 45.5	48.2	198 12.5	12.5	279 49.6	20.6	178 08.3	37.7	Regulus	207 43.0	N11 53.7
08	58 01.7	325 44.7	48.3	213 13.8	13.0	294 51.5	20.5	193 10.8	37.7	Rigel	281 11.6	S 8 11.2
S 09	73 04.2	340 43.9 ..	48.4	228 15.1 ..	13.5	309 53.4 ..	20.4	208 13.2 ..	37.7	Rigil Kent.	139 50.4	S60 53.8
U 10	88 06.6	355 43.1	48.4	243 16.4	14.0	324 55.3	20.2	223 15.7	37.7	Sabik	102 11.4	S15 44.4
N 11	103 09.1	10 42.2	48.5	258 17.7	14.5	339 57.2	20.1	238 18.2	37.7			
D 12	118 11.6	25 41.4	N22 48.5	273 19.0	S11 14.9	354 59.1	N20 20.0	253 20.7	S14 37.7	Schedar	349 39.4	N56 36.8
A 13	133 14.0	40 40.6	48.6	288 20.2	15.4	10 00.9	19.9	268 23.1	37.7	Shaula	96 20.5	S37 06.7
Y 14	148 16.5	55 39.8	48.7	303 21.5	15.9	25 02.8	19.8	283 25.6	37.8	Sirius	258 33.6	S16 44.3
15	163 19.0	70 39.0 ..	48.7	318 22.8 ..	16.4	40 04.7 ..	19.7	298 28.1 ..	37.8	Spica	158 30.5	S11 14.2
16	178 21.4	85 38.2	48.8	333 24.1	16.9	55 06.6	19.5	313 30.5	37.8	Suhail	222 52.3	S43 29.7
17	193 23.9	100 37.4	48.8	348 25.4	17.4	70 08.5	19.4	328 33.0	37.8			
18	208 26.3	115 36.6	N22 48.9	3 26.7	S11 17.9	85 10.4	N20 19.3	343 35.5	S14 37.8	Vega	80 38.0	N38 48.1
19	223 28.8	130 35.8	48.9	18 28.0	18.4	100 12.3	19.2	358 37.9	37.8	Zuben'ubi	137 04.4	S16 06.1
20	238 31.3	145 34.9	49.0	33 29.3	18.8	115 14.1	19.1	13 40.4	37.8		SHA	Mer.Pass.
21	253 33.7	160 34.1 ..	49.0	48 30.6 ..	19.3	130 16.0 ..	18.9	28 42.9 ..	37.8		° ′	h m
22	268 36.2	175 33.3	49.1	63 31.9	19.8	145 17.9	18.8	43 45.3	37.8	Venus	269 27.6	10 16
23	283 38.7	190 32.5	49.1	78 33.2	20.3	160 19.8	18.7	58 47.8	37.8	Mars	155 49.2	17 48
	h m									Jupiter	237 08.3	12 23
Mer.Pass.	4 12.5	v −0.8	d 0.1	v 1.3	d 0.5	v 1.9	d 0.1	v 2.5	d 0.0	Saturn	135 08.8	19 09

SUN and MOON

UT (d h)	SUN GHA	SUN Dec	MOON GHA	v	Dec	d	HP
18 00	178 27.0	N21 04.2	285 30.0	10.4	N 5 33.1	10.8	58.6
01	193 27.0	03.8	299 59.4	10.5	5 43.9	10.7	58.6
02	208 27.0	03.3	314 28.9	10.4	5 54.6	10.6	58.5
03	223 26.9 · ·	02.9	328 58.3	10.5	6 05.2	10.6	58.5
04	238 26.9	02.4	343 27.8	10.5	6 15.8	10.6	58.5
05	253 26.8	02.0	357 57.3	10.5	6 26.4	10.5	58.5
06	268 26.8	N21 01.6	12 26.8	10.6	N 6 36.9	10.5	58.4
07	283 26.7	01.1	26 56.4	10.5	6 47.4	10.4	58.4
08	298 26.7	00.7	41 25.9	10.6	6 57.8	10.3	58.3
F 09	313 26.6	21 00.2	55 55.5	10.6	7 08.1	10.3	58.3
R 10	328 26.6	20 59.8	70 25.1	10.6	7 18.4	10.3	58.3
I 11	343 26.5	59.4	84 54.7	10.6	7 28.7	10.2	58.2
D 12	358 26.5	N20 58.9	99 24.3	10.7	N 7 38.9	10.1	58.2
A 13	13 26.4	58.5	113 54.0	10.6	7 49.0	10.1	58.2
Y 14	28 26.4	58.0	128 23.6	10.7	7 59.1	10.1	58.1
15	43 26.3 · ·	57.6	142 53.3	10.6	8 09.2	9.9	58.1
16	58 26.3	57.2	157 22.9	10.7	8 19.1	10.0	58.0
17	73 26.2	56.7	171 52.6	10.7	8 29.1	9.8	58.0
18	88 26.2	N20 56.3	186 22.3	10.7	N 8 38.9	9.8	58.0
19	103 26.2	55.8	200 52.0	10.7	8 48.7	9.8	58.0
20	118 26.1	55.4	215 21.7	10.8	8 58.5	9.7	57.9
21	133 26.1 · ·	54.9	229 51.5	10.7	9 08.2	9.6	57.9
22	148 26.0	54.5	244 21.2	10.8	9 17.8	9.6	57.9
23	163 26.0	54.1	258 51.0	10.7	9 27.4	9.5	57.8
19 00	178 25.9	N20 53.6	273 20.7	10.8	N 9 36.9	9.4	57.8
01	193 25.9	53.1	287 50.5	10.8	9 46.3	9.4	57.8
02	208 25.9	52.7	302 20.3	10.7	9 55.7	9.3	57.7
03	223 25.8 · ·	52.2	316 50.0	10.8	10 05.0	9.3	57.7
04	238 25.8	51.8	331 19.8	10.8	10 14.3	9.1	57.7
05	253 25.7	51.3	345 49.6	10.8	10 23.4	9.2	57.6
06	268 25.7	N20 50.9	0 19.4	10.8	N10 32.6	9.0	57.6
S 07	283 25.6	50.4	14 49.2	10.9	10 41.6	9.0	57.5
A 08	298 25.6	50.0	29 19.1	10.8	10 50.6	8.9	57.5
T 09	313 25.6 · ·	49.5	43 48.9	10.8	10 59.5	8.9	57.5
U 10	328 25.5	49.0	58 18.7	10.8	11 08.4	8.8	57.4
R 11	343 25.5	48.6	72 48.5	10.9	11 17.2	8.7	57.4
D 12	358 25.4	N20 48.1	87 18.4	10.8	N11 25.9	8.6	57.4
A 13	13 25.4	47.7	101 48.2	10.8	11 34.5	8.6	57.3
Y 14	28 25.4	47.2	116 18.0	10.9	11 43.1	8.5	57.3
15	43 25.3 · ·	46.8	130 47.9	10.8	11 51.6	8.4	57.3
16	58 25.3	46.3	145 17.7	10.9	12 00.0	8.4	57.2
17	73 25.2	45.8	159 47.6	10.8	12 08.4	8.2	57.2
18	88 25.2	N20 45.4	174 17.4	10.9	N12 16.6	8.3	57.2
19	103 25.2	44.9	188 47.3	10.9	12 24.9	8.1	57.2
20	118 25.1	44.5	203 17.2	10.9	12 33.0	8.0	57.1
21	133 25.1 · ·	44.0	217 47.0	10.9	12 41.0	8.0	57.1
22	148 25.0	43.5	232 16.9	10.9	12 49.0	7.9	57.1
23	163 25.0	43.1	246 46.8	10.8	12 56.9	7.9	57.0
20 00	178 25.0	N20 42.6	261 16.6	10.9	N13 04.8	7.7	57.0
01	193 24.9	42.1	275 46.5	10.9	13 12.5	7.7	57.0
02	208 24.9	41.7	290 16.4	10.8	13 20.2	7.6	56.9
03	223 24.8 · ·	41.2	304 46.2	10.9	13 27.8	7.5	56.9
04	238 24.8	40.7	319 16.1	10.9	13 35.3	7.5	56.9
05	253 24.8	40.3	333 46.0	10.8	13 42.8	7.4	56.8
06	268 24.7	N20 39.8	348 15.8	10.9	N13 50.2	7.3	56.8
07	283 24.7	39.3	2 45.7	10.9	13 57.5	7.2	56.8
08	298 24.7	38.9	17 15.6	10.8	14 04.7	7.1	56.7
S 09	313 24.6 · ·	38.4	31 45.4	10.9	14 11.8	7.0	56.7
U 10	328 24.6	37.9	46 15.3	10.9	14 18.8	7.0	56.7
N 11	343 24.6	37.5	60 45.2	10.8	14 25.8	6.9	56.6
D 12	358 24.5	N20 37.0	75 15.0	10.9	N14 32.7	6.8	56.6
A 13	13 24.5	36.5	89 44.9	10.9	14 39.5	6.7	56.6
Y 14	28 24.5	36.0	104 14.8	10.8	14 46.2	6.7	56.5
15	43 24.4 · ·	35.6	118 44.6	10.9	14 52.9	6.5	56.5
16	58 24.4	35.1	133 14.5	10.9	14 59.4	6.5	56.5
17	73 24.3	34.6	147 44.4	10.8	15 05.9	6.4	56.5
18	88 24.3	N20 34.2	162 14.2	10.9	N15 12.3	6.3	56.4
19	103 24.3	33.7	176 44.1	10.9	15 18.6	6.2	56.4
20	118 24.2	33.2	191 14.0	10.8	15 24.8	6.1	56.4
21	133 24.2 · ·	32.7	205 43.8	10.9	15 30.9	6.1	56.4
22	148 24.2	32.2	220 13.7	10.9	15 37.0	5.9	56.3
23	163 24.1	31.8	234 43.6	10.8	N15 42.9	5.9	56.3
	SD 15.8	d 0.5	SD 15.9		15.6		15.4

Twilight, Sunrise, Moonrise

Lat.	Naut.	Civil	Sunrise	Moonrise 18	19	20	21
N 72	□	□	□	21 44	21 36	21 25	21 05
N 70	□	□	□	21 57	21 58	22 01	22 08
68	////	////	00 45	22 09	22 16	22 26	22 43
66	////	////	01 52	22 18	22 30	22 46	23 08
64	////	////	02 27	22 26	22 41	23 02	23 28
62	////	01 15	02 52	22 32	22 51	23 15	23 44
60	////	01 58	03 11	22 38	23 00	23 26	23 58
N 58	////	02 25	03 27	22 44	23 08	23 36	24 10
56	01 08	02 47	03 41	22 48	23 14	23 44	24 20
54	01 48	03 04	03 53	22 52	23 20	23 52	24 29
52	02 14	03 18	04 03	22 56	23 26	23 59	24 37
50	02 34	03 31	04 12	23 00	23 31	24 05	00 05
45	03 10	03 56	04 31	23 07	23 41	24 18	00 18
N 40	03 36	04 15	04 47	23 14	23 50	24 30	00 30
35	03 56	04 31	05 00	23 19	23 58	24 39	00 39
30	04 12	04 45	05 11	23 24	24 05	00 05	00 47
20	04 38	05 07	05 31	23 32	24 17	00 17	01 02
N 10	04 58	05 25	05 47	23 40	24 27	00 27	01 15
0	05 15	05 41	06 03	23 47	24 37	00 37	01 26
S 10	05 30	05 56	06 18	23 54	24 46	00 46	01 38
20	05 44	06 11	06 34	24 01	00 01	00 57	01 51
30	05 58	06 27	06 53	24 10	00 10	01 09	02 06
35	06 05	06 36	07 04	24 15	00 15	01 16	02 15
40	06 13	06 46	07 16	24 21	00 21	01 24	02 24
45	06 21ᵐ	06 58	07 30	24 28	00 28	01 33	02 36
S 50	06 31	07 11	07 48	24 36	00 36	01 45	02 50
52	06 35	07 17	07 56	24 40	00 40	01 50	02 57
54	06 40	07 24	08 06	24 44	00 44	01 56	03 04
56	06 45	07 32	08 16	24 48	00 48	02 02	03 12
58	06 50	07 40	08 28	24 53	00 53	02 10	03 21
S 60	06 56	07 50	08 42	24 59	00 59	02 18	03 32

Sunset, Twilight, Moonset

Lat.	Sunset	Civil	Naut.	Moonset 18	19	20	21
N 72	□	□	□	13 03	14 55	16 50	18 54
N 70	□	□	□	12 51	14 34	16 15	17 52
68	23 18	////	////	12 41	14 18	15 51	17 17
66	22 17	////	////	12 33	14 05	15 32	16 52
64	21 43	////	////	12 27	13 54	15 17	16 33
62	21 19	22 53	////	12 21	13 45	15 04	16 17
60	21 00	22 12	////	12 16	13 37	14 53	16 04
N 58	20 44	21 45	////	12 12	13 30	14 44	15 53
56	20 31	21 25	23 00	12 08	13 24	14 36	15 43
54	20 19	21 08	22 22	12 04	13 18	14 29	15 34
52	20 09	20 53	21 57	12 01	13 13	14 22	15 19
50	20 00	20 41	21 38	11 58	13 09	14 16	15 19
45	19 41	20 16	21 02	11 52	12 59	14 04	15 04
N 40	19 25	19 57	20 36	11 47	12 51	13 53	14 52
35	19 12	19 41	20 16	11 43	12 44	13 44	14 42
30	19 01	19 28	20 00	11 39	12 38	13 37	14 33
20	18 42	19 06	19 34	11 32	12 28	13 23	14 17
N 10	18 25	18 48	19 14	11 26	12 19	13 11	14 03
0	18 10	18 32	18 58	11 20	12 11	13 01	13 50
S 10	17 55	18 17	18 43	11 15	12 02	12 50	13 38
20	17 38	18 02	18 29	11 09	11 53	12 38	13 24
30	17 20	17 46	18 15	11 02	11 43	12 25	13 08
35	17 09	17 37	18 08	10 59	11 37	12 17	12 59
40	16 57	17 27	18 00	10 54	11 30	12 08	12 49
45	16 43	17 15	17 52	10 49	11 22	11 58	12 37
S 50	16 25	17 02	17 42	10 43	11 13	11 46	12 22
52	16 17	16 56	17 38	10 40	11 09	11 40	12 15
54	16 07	16 49	17 33	10 37	11 04	11 34	12 08
56	15 57	16 41	17 28	10 34	10 59	11 27	11 59
58	15 45	16 33	17 23	10 30	10 53	11 19	11 50
S 60	15 31	16 23	17 17	10 26	10 47	11 10	11 39

SUN and MOON

Day	SUN Eqn. of Time 00ʰ	12ʰ	Mer. Pass.	MOON Mer. Pass. Upper	Lower	Age	Phase
	m s	m s	h m	h m	h m	d	%
18	06 12	06 14	12 06	05 08	17 34	21	57
19	06 16	06 18	12 06	05 59	18 24	22	46
20	06 20	06 22	12 06	06 49	19 14	23	35

UT	ARIES GHA	VENUS −3.8 GHA	Dec	MARS +0.3 GHA	Dec	JUPITER −1.8 GHA	Dec	SATURN +0.5 GHA	Dec	Name	SHA	Dec
21 00	298 41.1	205 31.7	N22 49.2	93 34.4	S11 20.8	175 21.7	N20 18.6	73 50.3	S14 37.9	Acamar	315 17.9	S40 14.6
01	313 43.6	220 30.9	49.2	108 35.7	21.3	190 23.6	18.5	88 52.7	37.9	Achernar	335 26.3	S57 09.5
02	328 46.1	235 30.1	49.3	123 37.0	21.8	205 25.4	18.4	103 55.2	37.9	Acrux	173 08.5	S63 11.1
03	343 48.5	250 29.3 ..	49.3	138 38.3 ..	22.3	220 27.3 ..	18.2	118 57.7 ..	37.9	Adhara	255 12.3	S28 59.6
04	358 51.0	265 28.5	49.4	153 39.6	22.8	235 29.2	18.1	134 00.1	37.9	Aldebaran	290 48.7	N16 32.1
05	13 53.5	280 27.6	49.4	168 40.9	23.2	250 31.1	18.0	149 02.6	37.9			
06	28 55.9	295 26.8	N22 49.4	183 42.2	S11 23.7	265 33.0	N20 17.9	164 05.1	S14 37.9	Alioth	166 20.3	N55 53.1
07	43 58.4	310 26.0	49.5	198 43.5	24.2	280 34.9	17.8	179 07.5	37.9	Alkaid	152 58.4	N49 14.8
08	59 00.8	325 25.2	49.5	213 44.7	24.7	295 36.8	17.6	194 10.0	37.9	Al Na'ir	27 42.4	S46 53.1
M 09	74 03.3	340 24.4 ..	49.6	228 46.0 ..	25.2	310 38.6 ..	17.5	209 12.5 ..	38.0	Alnilam	275 45.9	S 1 11.7
O 10	89 05.8	355 23.6	49.6	243 47.3	25.7	325 40.5	17.4	224 14.9	38.0	Alphard	217 55.6	S 8 43.4
N 11	104 08.2	10 22.8	49.6	258 48.6	26.2	340 42.4	17.3	239 17.4	38.0			
D 12	119 10.7	25 22.0	N22 49.7	273 49.9	S11 26.7	355 44.3	N20 17.2	254 19.9	S14 38.0	Alphecca	126 10.2	N26 40.3
A 13	134 13.2	40 21.1	49.7	288 51.2	27.2	10 46.2	17.1	269 22.3	38.0	Alpheratz	357 42.5	N29 10.2
Y 14	149 15.6	55 20.3	49.7	303 52.4	27.6	25 48.1	16.9	284 24.8	38.0	Altair	62 07.1	N 8 54.7
15	164 18.1	70 19.5 ..	49.7	318 53.7 ..	28.1	40 50.0 ..	16.8	299 27.2 ..	38.0	Ankaa	353 14.8	S42 13.3
16	179 20.6	85 18.7	49.8	333 55.0	28.6	55 51.8	16.7	314 29.7	38.0	Antares	112 25.1	S26 27.7
17	194 23.0	100 17.9	49.8	348 56.3	29.1	70 53.7	16.6	329 32.2	38.0			
18	209 25.5	115 17.1	N22 49.8	3 57.6	S11 29.6	85 55.6	N20 16.5	344 34.6	S14 38.1	Arcturus	145 55.0	N19 06.6
19	224 28.0	130 16.3	49.9	18 58.8	30.1	100 57.5	16.3	359 37.1	38.1	Atria	107 25.7	S69 03.2
20	239 30.4	145 15.4	49.9	34 00.1	30.6	115 59.4	16.2	14 39.6	38.1	Avior	234 18.3	S59 33.6
21	254 32.9	160 14.6 ..	49.9	49 01.4 ..	31.1	131 01.3 ..	16.1	29 42.0 ..	38.1	Bellatrix	278 31.4	N 6 21.6
22	269 35.3	175 13.8	49.9	64 02.7	31.6	146 03.1	16.0	44 44.5	38.1	Betelgeuse	271 00.8	N 7 24.4
23	284 37.8	190 13.0	49.9	79 04.0	32.0	161 05.0	15.9	59 47.0	38.1			
22 00	299 40.3	205 12.2	N22 50.0	94 05.2	S11 32.5	176 06.9	N20 15.8	74 49.4	S14 38.1	Canopus	263 56.3	S52 42.3
01	314 42.7	220 11.4	50.0	109 06.5	33.0	191 08.8	15.6	89 51.9	38.1	Capella	280 33.7	N46 00.4
02	329 45.2	235 10.6	50.0	124 07.8	33.5	206 10.7	15.5	104 54.3	38.1	Deneb	49 30.4	N45 20.1
03	344 47.7	250 09.7 ..	50.0	139 09.1 ..	34.0	221 12.6 ..	15.4	119 56.8 ..	38.2	Denebola	182 33.1	N14 29.5
04	359 50.1	265 08.9	50.0	154 10.3	34.5	236 14.5	15.3	134 59.3	38.2	Diphda	348 55.0	S17 54.2
05	14 52.6	280 08.1	50.0	169 11.6	35.0	251 16.3	15.2	150 01.7	38.2			
06	29 55.1	295 07.3	N22 50.1	184 12.9	S11 35.5	266 18.2	N20 15.0	165 04.2	S14 38.2	Dubhe	193 51.4	N61 40.5
07	44 57.5	310 06.5	50.1	199 14.1	36.0	281 20.1	14.9	180 06.7	38.2	Elnath	278 11.9	N28 36.9
T 08	60 00.0	325 05.7	50.1	214 15.4	36.5	296 22.0	14.8	195 09.1	38.2	Eltanin	90 45.3	N51 29.6
U 09	75 02.5	340 04.9 ..	50.1	229 16.7 ..	36.9	311 23.9 ..	14.7	210 11.6 ..	38.2	Enif	33 46.1	N 9 56.7
E 10	90 04.9	355 04.0	50.1	244 18.0	37.4	326 25.8	14.6	225 14.0	38.2	Fomalhaut	15 22.9	S29 32.4
S 11	105 07.4	10 03.2	50.1	259 19.2	37.9	341 27.7	14.4	240 16.5	38.3			
D 12	120 09.8	25 02.4	N22 50.1	274 20.5	S11 38.4	356 29.5	N20 14.3	255 19.0	S14 38.3	Gacrux	172 00.1	S57 11.9
A 13	135 12.3	40 01.6	50.1	289 21.8	38.9	11 31.4	14.2	270 21.4	38.3	Gienah	175 51.6	S17 37.4
Y 14	150 14.8	55 00.8	50.1	304 23.0	39.4	26 33.3	14.1	285 23.9	38.3	Hadar	148 46.6	S60 26.8
15	165 17.2	70 00.0 ..	50.1	319 24.3 ..	39.9	41 35.2 ..	14.0	300 26.3 ..	38.3	Hamal	327 59.9	N23 31.7
16	180 19.7	84 59.1	50.1	334 25.6	40.4	56 37.1	13.8	315 28.8	38.3	Kaus Aust.	83 42.4	S34 22.4
17	195 22.2	99 58.3	50.1	349 26.9	40.9	71 39.0	13.7	330 31.3	38.3			
18	210 24.6	114 57.5	N22 50.1	4 28.1	S11 41.4	86 40.9	N20 13.6	345 33.7	S14 38.3	Kochab	137 19.9	N74 06.1
19	225 27.1	129 56.7	50.1	19 29.4	41.9	101 42.7	13.5	0 36.2	38.4	Markab	13 37.3	N15 17.1
20	240 29.6	144 55.9	50.1	34 30.7	42.3	116 44.6	13.4	15 38.6	38.4	Menkar	314 14.3	N 4 08.7
21	255 32.0	159 55.1 ..	50.1	49 31.9 ..	42.8	131 46.5 ..	13.3	30 41.1 ..	38.4	Menkent	148 06.6	S36 26.6
22	270 34.5	174 54.3	50.1	64 33.2	43.3	146 48.4	13.1	45 43.6	38.4	Miaplacidus	221 40.3	S69 46.9
23	285 36.9	189 53.4	50.1	79 34.4	43.8	161 50.3	13.0	60 46.0	38.4			
23 00	300 39.4	204 52.6	N22 50.1	94 35.7	S11 44.3	176 52.2	N20 12.9	75 48.5	S14 38.4	Mirfak	308 39.4	N49 54.4
01	315 41.9	219 51.8	50.1	109 37.0	44.8	191 54.1	12.8	90 50.9	38.4	Nunki	75 57.0	S26 16.5
02	330 44.3	234 51.0	50.1	124 38.2	45.3	206 55.9	12.7	105 53.4	38.4	Peacock	53 17.5	S56 41.0
03	345 46.8	249 50.2 ..	50.1	139 39.5 ..	45.8	221 57.8 ..	12.5	120 55.8 ..	38.5	Pollux	243 27.2	N27 59.3
04	0 49.3	264 49.4	50.0	154 40.8	46.3	236 59.7	12.4	135 58.3	38.5	Procyon	244 59.3	N 5 11.1
05	15 51.7	279 48.5	50.0	169 42.0	46.8	252 01.6	12.3	151 00.8	38.5			
06	30 54.2	294 47.7	N22 50.0	184 43.3	S11 47.3	267 03.5	N20 12.2	166 03.2	S14 38.5	Rasalhague	96 05.5	N12 33.3
W 07	45 56.7	309 46.9	50.0	199 44.6	47.8	282 05.4	12.1	181 05.7	38.5	Regulus	207 43.0	N11 53.7
E 08	60 59.1	324 46.1	50.0	214 45.8	48.2	297 07.3	11.9	196 08.1	38.5	Rigel	281 11.6	S 8 11.2
D 09	76 01.6	339 45.3 ..	50.0	229 47.1 ..	48.7	312 09.1 ..	11.8	211 10.6 ..	38.5	Rigil Kent.	139 50.4	S60 53.8
N 10	91 04.1	354 44.5	50.0	244 48.3	49.2	327 11.0	11.7	226 13.1	38.6	Sabik	102 11.4	S15 44.4
E 11	106 06.5	9 43.6	49.9	259 49.6	49.7	342 12.9	11.6	241 15.5	38.6			
S 12	121 09.0	24 42.8	N22 49.9	274 50.8	S11 50.2	357 14.8	N20 11.5	256 18.0	S14 38.6	Schedar	349 39.3	N56 36.8
D 13	136 11.4	39 42.0	49.9	289 52.1	50.7	12 16.7	11.3	271 20.4	38.6	Shaula	96 20.5	S37 06.7
A 14	151 13.9	54 41.2	49.9	304 53.4	51.2	27 18.6	11.2	286 22.9	38.6	Sirius	258 33.4	S16 44.3
Y 15	166 16.4	69 40.4 ..	49.8	319 54.6 ..	51.7	42 20.4 ..	11.1	301 25.3 ..	38.6	Spica	158 30.5	S11 14.2
16	181 18.8	84 39.6	49.8	334 55.9	52.2	57 22.3	11.0	316 27.8	38.6	Suhail	222 52.3	S43 29.7
17	196 21.3	99 38.7	49.8	349 57.1	52.7	72 24.2	10.9	331 30.2	38.6			
18	211 23.8	114 37.9	N22 49.8	4 58.4	S11 53.2	87 26.1	N20 10.7	346 32.7	S14 38.7	Vega	80 38.0	N38 48.2
19	226 26.2	129 37.1	49.7	19 59.6	53.7	102 28.0	10.6	1 35.2	38.7	Zuben'ubi	137 04.5	S16 06.1
20	241 28.7	144 36.3	49.7	35 00.9	54.2	117 29.9	10.5	16 37.6	38.7			
21	256 31.2	159 35.5 ..	49.7	50 02.2 ..	54.6	132 31.8 ..	10.4	31 40.1 ..	38.7		SHA	Mer. Pass.
22	271 33.6	174 34.6	49.6	65 03.4	55.1	147 33.6	10.3	46 42.5	38.7	Venus	265 31.9	10 20
23	286 36.1	189 33.8	49.6	80 04.7	55.6	162 35.5	10.1	61 45.0	38.7	Mars	154 25.0	17 42
Mer. Pass.	4 00.7	v −0.8	d 0.0	v 1.3	d 0.5	v 1.9	d 0.1	v 2.5	d 0.0	Jupiter	236 26.6	12 14
										Saturn	135 09.1	18 58

UT	SUN GHA	SUN Dec	MOON GHA	v	Dec	d	HP
d h	° ′	° ′	° ′	′	° ′	′	′
21 00	178 24.1	N20 31.3	249 13.4	10.9	N15 48.8	5.8	56.3
01	193 24.1	30.8	263 43.3	10.9	15 54.6	5.7	56.2
02	208 24.1	30.3	278 13.1	10.9	16 00.3	5.6	56.2
03	223 24.0	.. 29.9	292 43.0	10.9	16 05.9	5.5	56.2
04	238 24.0	29.4	307 12.9	10.8	16 11.4	5.5	56.2
05	253 24.0	28.9	321 42.7	10.9	16 16.9	5.3	56.1
M 06	268 23.9	N20 28.4	336 12.6	10.8	N16 22.2	5.3	56.1
O 07	283 23.9	27.9	350 42.4	10.9	16 27.5	5.2	56.1
N 08	298 23.9	27.4	5 12.3	10.8	16 32.7	5.1	56.1
D 09	313 23.8	.. 27.0	19 42.1	10.9	16 37.8	5.0	56.0
A 10	328 23.8	26.5	34 12.0	10.9	16 42.8	4.9	56.0
Y 11	343 23.8	26.0	48 41.9	10.8	16 47.7	4.8	56.0
12	358 23.7	N20 25.5	63 11.7	10.9	N16 52.5	4.7	55.9
13	13 23.7	25.0	77 41.6	10.8	16 57.2	4.7	55.9
14	28 23.7	24.5	92 11.4	10.9	17 01.9	4.5	55.9
15	43 23.7	.. 24.0	106 41.3	10.9	17 06.4	4.5	55.9
16	58 23.6	23.6	121 11.2	10.8	17 10.9	4.3	55.8
17	73 23.6	23.1	135 41.0	10.9	17 15.2	4.3	55.8
18	88 23.6	N20 22.6	150 10.9	10.9	N17 19.5	4.2	55.8
19	103 23.5	22.1	164 40.8	10.8	17 23.7	4.1	55.8
20	118 23.5	21.6	179 10.6	10.9	17 27.8	4.0	55.7
21	133 23.5	.. 21.1	193 40.5	10.9	17 31.8	3.9	55.7
22	148 23.5	20.6	208 10.4	10.8	17 35.7	3.8	55.7
23	163 23.4	20.1	222 40.2	10.9	17 39.5	3.8	55.7
22 00	178 23.4	N20 19.6	237 10.1	10.9	N17 43.3	3.6	55.6
01	193 23.4	19.1	251 40.0	10.9	17 46.9	3.5	55.6
02	208 23.4	18.6	266 09.9	10.9	17 50.4	3.5	55.6
03	223 23.3	.. 18.1	280 39.8	10.9	17 53.9	3.4	55.6
04	238 23.3	17.7	295 09.7	10.9	17 57.3	3.2	55.5
05	253 23.3	17.2	309 39.6	10.9	18 00.5	3.2	55.5
T 06	268 23.3	N20 16.7	324 09.5	10.9	N18 03.7	3.1	55.5
U 07	283 23.2	16.2	338 39.4	10.9	18 06.8	3.0	55.5
E 08	298 23.2	15.7	353 09.3	10.9	18 09.8	2.9	55.5
S 09	313 23.2	.. 15.2	7 39.2	10.9	18 12.7	2.8	55.4
D 10	328 23.2	14.7	22 09.1	11.0	18 15.5	2.7	55.4
A 11	343 23.1	14.2	36 39.1	10.9	18 18.2	2.6	55.4
Y 12	358 23.1	N20 13.7	51 09.0	10.9	N18 20.8	2.5	55.4
13	13 23.1	13.2	65 38.9	11.0	18 23.3	2.4	55.4
14	28 23.1	12.7	80 08.9	11.0	18 25.7	2.4	55.3
15	43 23.0	.. 12.2	94 38.9	10.9	18 28.1	2.2	55.3
16	58 23.0	11.7	109 08.8	11.0	18 30.3	2.1	55.3
17	73 23.0	11.2	123 38.8	11.0	18 32.4	2.1	55.3
18	88 23.0	N20 10.7	138 08.8	11.0	N18 34.5	2.0	55.2
19	103 22.9	10.2	152 38.8	11.0	18 36.5	1.8	55.2
20	118 22.9	09.6	167 08.8	11.0	18 38.3	1.8	55.2
21	133 22.9	.. 09.1	181 38.8	11.0	18 40.1	1.7	55.2
22	148 22.9	08.6	196 08.8	11.0	18 41.8	1.6	55.2
23	163 22.9	08.1	210 38.8	11.1	18 43.4	1.4	55.1
23 00	178 22.8	N20 07.6	225 08.9	11.0	N18 44.8	1.4	55.1
01	193 22.8	07.1	239 38.9	11.1	18 46.2	1.3	55.1
02	208 22.8	06.6	254 09.0	11.1	18 47.5	1.3	55.1
03	223 22.8	.. 06.1	268 39.1	11.1	18 48.8	1.1	55.1
04	238 22.8	05.6	283 09.2	11.1	18 49.9	1.0	55.0
05	253 22.7	05.0	297 39.3	11.1	18 50.9	0.9	55.0
W 06	268 22.7	N20 04.6	312 09.4	11.1	N18 51.8	0.9	55.0
E 07	283 22.7	04.1	326 39.5	11.2	18 52.7	0.9	55.0
D 08	298 22.7	03.5	341 09.7	11.1	18 53.4	0.7	55.0
N 09	313 22.7	.. 03.0	355 39.8	11.2	18 54.1	0.7	54.9
E 10	328 22.6	02.5	10 10.0	11.2	18 54.6	0.5	54.9
S 11	343 22.6	02.0	24 40.2	11.2	18 55.1	0.3	54.9
D 12	358 22.6	N20 01.5	39 10.4	11.2	N18 55.4	0.3	54.9
A 13	13 22.6	01.0	53 40.6	11.2	18 55.7	0.2	54.9
Y 14	28 22.6	00.5	68 10.8	11.3	18 55.9	0.1	54.9
15	43 22.6	20 00.0	82 41.1	11.3	18 56.0	0.0	54.8
16	58 22.5	19 59.4	97 11.4	11.2	18 56.0	0.1	54.8
17	73 22.5	58.9	111 41.6	11.3	18 55.9	0.2	54.8
18	88 22.5	N19 58.4	126 11.9	11.4	N18 55.7	0.2	54.8
19	103 22.5	57.9	140 42.3	11.3	18 55.5	0.4	54.8
20	118 22.5	57.4	155 12.6	11.4	18 55.1	0.5	54.8
21	133 22.5	.. 56.8	169 43.0	11.4	18 54.6	0.5	54.8
22	148 22.4	56.3	184 13.4	11.4	18 54.1	0.7	54.7
23	163 22.4	55.8	198 43.8	11.4	N18 53.4	0.7	54.7
	SD 15.8	d 0.5	SD 15.2		15.1		15.0

Lat.	Twilight Naut.	Twilight Civil	Sunrise	Moonrise 21	Moonrise 22	Moonrise 23	Moonrise 24
°	h m	h m	h m	h m	h m	h m	h m
N 72	☐	☐	☐	21 05	☐	☐	☐
N 70	☐	☐	☐	22 08	22 26	23 09	24 21
68	////	////	01 13	22 43	23 12	23 58	25 02
66	////	////	02 05	23 08	23 42	24 29	00 29
64	////	////	02 36	23 28	24 05	00 05	00 52
62	////	01 30	02 59	23 44	24 23	00 23	01 11
60	////	02 07	03 18	23 58	24 38	00 38	01 26
N 58	////	02 33	03 33	24 10	00 10	00 50	01 39
56	01 23	02 53	03 46	24 20	00 20	01 01	01 50
54	01 57	03 09	03 57	24 29	00 29	01 11	02 00
52	02 20	03 23	04 07	24 37	00 37	01 20	02 08
50	02 39	03 35	04 16	00 05	00 44	01 27	02 16
45	03 14	03 59	04 44	00 18	00 59	01 44	02 33
N 40	03 39	04 18	04 49	00 30	01 12	01 58	02 47
35	03 59	04 33	05 02	00 39	01 23	02 09	02 58
30	04 14	04 46	05 13	00 47	01 32	02 19	03 08
20	04 39	05 08	05 32	01 02	01 49	02 37	03 26
N 10	04 59	05 25	05 48	01 15	02 03	02 52	03 41
0	05 15	05 41	06 03	01 26	02 16	03 06	03 55
S 10	05 30	05 55	06 18	01 38	02 30	03 20	04 09
20	05 43	06 10	06 34	01 51	02 44	03 36	04 25
30	05 57	06 26	06 52	02 06	03 01	03 53	04 42
35	06 04	06 35	07 02	02 15	03 11	04 03	04 52
40	06 11	06 44	07 14	02 24	03 22	04 15	05 04
45	06 19	06 55	07 28	02 36	03 35	04 29	05 18
S 50	06 28	07 08	07 45	02 50	03 51	04 46	05 34
52	06 32	07 14	07 53	02 57	03 58	04 54	05 42
54	06 37	07 21	08 02	03 04	04 06	05 02	05 51
56	06 41	07 28	08 12	03 12	04 16	05 12	06 01
58	06 46	07 36	08 23	03 21	04 26	05 24	06 12
S 60	06 52	07 45	08 36	03 32	04 39	05 37	06 25

Lat.	Sunset	Twilight Civil	Twilight Naut.	Moonset 21	Moonset 22	Moonset 23	Moonset 24
°	h m	h m	h m	h m	h m	h m	h m
N 72	☐	☐	☐	18 54	☐	☐	☐
N 70	☐	☐	☐	17 52	19 18	20 17	20 46
68	22 53	////	////	17 17	18 32	19 28	20 05
66	22 05	////	////	16 52	18 02	18 57	19 36
64	21 34	////	////	16 33	17 39	18 34	19 15
62	21 12	22 38	////	16 17	17 21	18 15	18 58
60	20 54	22 03	////	16 04	17 07	18 00	18 43
N 58	20 39	21 38	////	15 53	16 54	17 47	18 31
56	20 26	21 18	22 46	15 43	16 43	17 36	18 20
54	20 15	21 02	22 14	15 34	16 34	17 26	18 11
52	20 05	20 49	21 51	15 26	16 25	17 17	18 02
50	19 56	20 37	21 32	15 19	16 17	17 09	17 55
45	19 38	20 13	20 58	15 04	16 01	16 53	17 39
N 40	19 23	19 54	20 33	14 52	15 48	16 39	17 26
35	19 11	19 39	20 14	14 42	15 36	16 27	17 14
30	19 00	19 26	19 58	14 33	15 26	16 17	17 04
20	18 41	19 05	19 33	14 17	15 09	15 59	16 47
N 10	18 25	18 47	19 14	14 03	14 54	15 44	16 33
0	18 10	18 32	18 58	13 50	14 40	15 30	16 19
S 10	17 55	18 18	18 43	13 38	14 26	15 15	16 05
20	17 40	18 03	18 30	13 24	14 11	15 00	15 50
30	17 22	17 47	18 16	13 08	13 54	14 42	15 32
35	17 11	17 39	18 09	12 59	13 44	14 32	15 22
40	16 59	17 29	18 02	12 49	13 33	14 20	15 11
45	16 46	17 18	17 54	12 37	13 20	14 07	14 57
S 50	16 29	17 05	17 45	12 22	13 03	13 50	14 41
52	16 21	16 59	17 41	12 15	12 56	13 42	14 33
54	16 12	16 53	17 37	12 08	12 47	13 33	14 25
56	16 02	16 46	17 32	11 59	12 38	13 23	14 15
58	15 50	16 38	17 27	11 50	12 27	13 12	14 04
S 60	15 37	16 29	17 22	11 39	12 14	12 58	13 51

Day	SUN Eqn. of Time 00h	SUN Eqn. of Time 12h	Mer. Pass.	MOON Mer. Pass. Upper	MOON Mer. Pass. Lower	Age	Phase
d	m s	m s	h m	h m	h m	d	%
21	06 23	06 25	12 06	07 38	20 03	24	26
22	06 26	06 28	12 06	08 28	20 53	25	18
23	06 29	06 30	12 06	09 18	21 43	26	11

2014 JULY 24, 25, 26 (THURS., FRI., SAT.)

UT	ARIES GHA	VENUS −3.8 GHA	Dec	MARS +0.3 GHA	Dec	JUPITER −1.8 GHA	Dec	SATURN +0.5 GHA	Dec	STARS Name	SHA	Dec
24 00	301 38.6	204 33.0	N22 49.6	95 05.9	S11 56.1	177 37.4	N20 10.0	76 47.4	S14 38.7	Acamar	315 17.9	S40 14.6
01	316 41.0	219 32.2	49.5	110 07.2	56.6	192 39.3	09.9	91 49.9	38.8	Achernar	335 26.2	S57 09.5
02	331 43.5	234 31.4	49.5	125 08.4	57.1	207 41.2	09.8	106 52.3	38.8	Acrux	173 08.5	S63 11.1
03	346 45.9	249 30.6 ..	49.5	140 09.7 ..	57.6	222 43.1 ..	09.7	121 54.8 ..	38.8	Adhara	255 12.3	S28 59.6
04	1 48.4	264 29.7	49.4	155 10.9	58.1	237 45.0	09.5	136 57.3	38.8	Aldebaran	290 48.7	N16 32.1
05	16 50.9	279 28.9	49.4	170 12.2	58.6	252 46.8	09.4	151 59.7	38.8			
06	31 53.3	294 28.1	N22 49.3	185 13.4	S11 59.1	267 48.7	N20 09.3	167 02.2	S14 38.8	Alioth	166 20.3	N55 53.1
07	46 55.8	309 27.3	49.3	200 14.7	11 59.6	282 50.6	09.2	182 04.6	38.8	Alkaid	152 58.4	N49 14.8
T 08	61 58.3	324 26.5	49.2	215 15.9	12 00.1	297 52.5	09.1	197 07.1	38.9	Al Na'ir	27 42.4	S46 53.1
H 09	77 00.7	339 25.7 ..	49.2	230 17.2 ..	00.6	312 54.4 ..	08.9	212 09.5 ..	38.9	Alnilam	275 45.8	S 1 11.7
U 10	92 03.2	354 24.8	49.2	245 18.4	01.0	327 56.3	08.8	227 12.0	38.9	Alphard	217 55.6	S 8 43.4
R 11	107 05.7	9 24.0	49.1	260 19.7	01.5	342 58.2	08.7	242 14.4	38.9			
S 12	122 08.1	24 23.2	N22 49.1	275 20.9	S12 02.0	358 00.0	N20 08.6	257 16.9	S14 38.9	Alphecca	126 10.2	N26 40.3
D 13	137 10.6	39 22.4	49.0	290 22.1	02.5	13 01.9	08.5	272 19.3	38.9	Alpheratz	357 42.5	N29 10.2
A 14	152 13.1	54 21.6	49.0	305 23.4	03.0	28 03.8	08.3	287 21.8	38.9	Altair	62 07.1	N 8 54.7
Y 15	167 15.5	69 20.7 ..	48.9	320 24.6 ..	03.5	43 05.7 ..	08.2	302 24.2 ..	39.0	Ankaa	353 14.8	S42 13.3
16	182 18.0	84 19.9	48.9	335 25.9	04.0	58 07.6	08.1	317 26.7	39.0	Antares	112 25.1	S26 27.7
17	197 20.4	99 19.1	48.8	350 27.1	04.5	73 09.5	08.0	332 29.1	39.0			
18	212 22.9	114 18.3	N22 48.7	5 28.4	S12 05.0	88 11.4	N20 07.9	347 31.6	S14 39.0	Arcturus	145 55.0	N19 06.6
19	227 25.4	129 17.5	48.7	20 29.6	05.5	103 13.3	07.7	2 34.0	39.0	Atria	107 25.7	S69 03.2
20	242 27.8	144 16.7	48.6	35 30.9	06.0	118 15.1	07.6	17 36.5	39.0	Avior	234 18.3	S59 33.5
21	257 30.3	159 15.8 ..	48.6	50 32.1 ..	06.5	133 17.0 ..	07.5	32 38.9 ..	39.1	Bellatrix	278 31.4	N 6 21.6
22	272 32.8	174 15.0	48.5	65 33.3	07.0	148 18.9	07.4	47 41.4	39.1	Betelgeuse	271 00.7	N 7 24.4
23	287 35.2	189 14.2	48.4	80 34.6	07.5	163 20.8	07.3	62 43.8	39.1			
25 00	302 37.7	204 13.4	N22 48.4	95 35.8	S12 08.0	178 22.7	N20 07.1	77 46.3	S14 39.1	Canopus	263 56.3	S52 42.2
01	317 40.2	219 12.6	48.3	110 37.1	08.5	193 24.6	07.0	92 48.7	39.1	Capella	280 33.6	N46 00.4
02	332 42.6	234 11.7	48.3	125 38.3	08.9	208 26.5	06.9	107 51.2	39.1	Deneb	49 30.4	N45 20.1
03	347 45.1	249 10.9 ..	48.2	140 39.5 ..	09.4	223 28.4 ..	06.8	122 53.6 ..	39.1	Denebola	182 33.1	N14 29.5
04	2 47.6	264 10.1	48.1	155 40.8	09.9	238 30.2	06.7	137 56.1	39.2	Diphda	348 55.0	S17 54.2
05	17 50.0	279 09.3	48.1	170 42.0	10.4	253 32.1	06.5	152 58.5	39.2			
06	32 52.5	294 08.5	N22 48.0	185 43.3	S12 10.9	268 34.0	N20 06.4	168 01.0	S14 39.2	Dubhe	193 51.4	N61 40.5
07	47 54.9	309 07.6	47.9	200 44.5	11.4	283 35.9	06.3	183 03.4	39.2	Elnath	278 11.9	N28 36.9
F 08	62 57.4	324 06.8	47.8	215 45.7	11.9	298 37.8	06.2	198 05.9	39.2	Eltanin	90 45.3	N51 29.6
R 09	77 59.9	339 06.0 ..	47.8	230 47.0 ..	12.4	313 39.7 ..	06.0	213 08.3 ..	39.2	Enif	33 46.0	N 9 56.7
I 10	93 02.3	354 05.2	47.7	245 48.2	12.9	328 41.6	05.9	228 10.8	39.3	Fomalhaut	15 22.9	S29 32.4
D 11	108 04.8	9 04.4	47.6	260 49.4	13.4	343 43.4	05.8	243 13.2	39.3			
A 12	123 07.3	24 03.6	N22 47.5	275 50.7	S12 13.9	358 45.3	N20 05.7	258 15.7	S14 39.3	Gacrux	172 00.1	S57 11.9
Y 13	138 09.7	39 02.7	47.5	290 51.9	14.4	13 47.2	05.6	273 18.1	39.3	Gienah	175 51.6	S17 37.4
14	153 12.2	54 01.9	47.4	305 53.1	14.9	28 49.1	05.4	288 20.6	39.3	Hadar	148 46.6	S60 26.8
15	168 14.7	69 01.1 ..	47.3	320 54.4 ..	15.4	43 51.0 ..	05.3	303 23.0 ..	39.3	Hamal	327 59.9	N23 31.7
16	183 17.1	84 00.3	47.2	335 55.6	15.9	58 52.9	05.2	318 25.5	39.4	Kaus Aust.	83 42.4	S34 22.4
17	198 19.6	98 59.5	47.2	350 56.8	16.4	73 54.8	05.1	333 27.9	39.4			
18	213 22.0	113 58.6	N22 47.1	5 58.1	S12 16.9	88 56.6	N20 04.9	348 30.4	S14 39.4	Kochab	137 20.0	N74 06.1
19	228 24.5	128 57.8	47.0	20 59.3	17.4	103 58.5	04.8	3 32.8	39.4	Markab	13 37.3	N15 17.1
20	243 27.0	143 57.0	46.9	36 00.5	17.8	119 00.4	04.7	18 35.3	39.4	Menkar	314 14.3	N 4 08.7
21	258 29.4	158 56.2 ..	46.8	51 01.8 ..	18.3	134 02.3 ..	04.6	33 37.7 ..	39.4	Menkent	148 06.6	S36 26.6
22	273 31.9	173 55.4	46.7	66 03.0	18.8	149 04.2	04.5	48 40.2	39.4	Miaplacidus	221 40.3	S69 46.8
23	288 34.4	188 54.5	46.6	81 04.2	19.3	164 06.1	04.3	63 42.6	39.5			
26 00	303 36.8	203 53.7	N22 46.5	96 05.4	S12 19.8	179 08.0	N20 04.2	78 45.1	S14 39.5	Mirfak	308 39.3	N49 54.4
01	318 39.3	218 52.9	46.5	111 06.7	20.3	194 09.9	04.1	93 47.5	39.5	Nunki	75 57.0	S26 16.5
02	333 41.8	233 52.1	46.4	126 07.9	20.8	209 11.7	04.0	108 50.0	39.5	Peacock	53 17.5	S56 41.0
03	348 44.2	248 51.3 ..	46.3	141 09.1 ..	21.3	224 13.6 ..	03.9	123 52.4 ..	39.5	Pollux	243 27.2	N27 59.3
04	3 46.7	263 50.5	46.2	156 10.4	21.8	239 15.5	03.7	138 54.8	39.5	Procyon	244 59.3	N 5 11.1
05	18 49.2	278 49.6	46.1	171 11.6	22.3	254 17.4	03.6	153 57.3	39.6			
06	33 51.6	293 48.8	N22 46.0	186 12.8	S12 22.8	269 19.3	N20 03.5	168 59.7	S14 39.6	Rasalhague	96 05.5	N12 33.3
07	48 54.1	308 48.0	45.9	201 14.0	23.3	284 21.2	03.4	184 02.2	39.6	Regulus	207 43.0	N11 53.7
S 08	63 56.5	323 47.2	45.8	216 15.3	23.8	299 23.1	03.2	199 04.6	39.6	Rigel	281 11.6	S 8 11.2
A 09	78 59.0	338 46.4 ..	45.7	231 16.5 ..	24.3	314 24.9 ..	03.1	214 07.1 ..	39.6	Rigil Kent.	139 50.5	S60 53.8
T 10	94 01.5	353 45.5	45.6	246 17.7	24.8	329 26.8	03.0	229 09.5	39.6	Sabik	102 11.4	S15 44.4
U 11	109 03.9	8 44.7	45.5	261 18.9	25.3	344 28.7	02.9	244 12.0	39.7			
R 12	124 06.4	23 43.9	N22 45.4	276 20.1	S12 25.8	359 30.6	N20 02.8	259 14.4	S14 39.7	Schedar	349 39.3	N56 36.8
D 13	139 08.9	38 43.1	45.3	291 21.4	26.3	14 32.5	02.6	274 16.9	39.7	Shaula	96 20.5	S37 06.7
A 14	154 11.3	53 42.3	45.2	306 22.6	26.8	29 34.4	02.5	289 19.3	39.7	Sirius	258 33.4	S16 44.3
Y 15	169 13.8	68 41.4 ..	45.1	321 23.8 ..	27.3	44 36.3 ..	02.4	304 21.7 ..	39.7	Spica	158 30.5	S11 14.2
16	184 16.3	83 40.6	45.0	336 25.0	27.7	59 38.2	02.3	319 24.2	39.8	Suhail	222 52.3	S43 29.7
17	199 18.7	98 39.8	44.8	351 26.3	28.2	74 40.0	02.1	334 26.6	39.8			
18	214 21.2	113 39.0	N22 44.7	6 27.5	S12 28.7	89 41.9	N20 02.0	349 29.1	S14 39.8	Vega	80 38.0	N38 48.2
19	229 23.7	128 38.2	44.6	21 28.7	29.2	104 43.8	01.9	4 31.5	39.8	Zuben'ubi	137 04.5	S16 06.1
20	244 26.1	143 37.4	44.5	36 29.9	29.7	119 45.7	01.8	19 34.0	39.8		SHA	Mer. Pass.
21	259 28.6	158 36.5 ..	44.4	51 31.1 ..	30.2	134 47.6 ..	01.7	34 36.4 ..	39.8		° ′	h m
22	274 31.0	173 35.7	44.3	66 32.3	30.7	149 49.5	01.5	49 38.8	39.9	Venus	261 35.7	10 24
23	289 33.5	188 34.9	44.2	81 33.6	31.2	164 51.4	01.4	64 41.3	39.9	Mars	152 58.1	17 36
Mer. Pass.	h m 3 48.9	v −0.8	d 0.1	v 1.2	d 0.5	v 1.9	d 0.1	v 2.4	d 0.0	Jupiter	235 45.0	12 05
										Saturn	135 08.6	18 46

UT	SUN GHA	SUN Dec	MOON GHA	v	Dec	d	HP
d h	° '	° '	° '	'	° '	'	'
24 00	178 22.4	N19 55.3	213 14.2	11.4	N18 52.7	0.8	54.7
01	193 22.4	54.8	227 44.6	11.5	18 51.9	0.9	54.7
02	208 22.4	54.2	242 15.1	11.5	18 51.0	1.0	54.7
03	223 22.4 ..	53.7	256 45.6	11.5	18 50.0	1.1	54.7
04	238 22.4	53.2	271 16.1	11.5	18 48.9	1.2	54.6
05	253 22.3	52.7	285 46.6	11.5	18 47.7	1.3	54.6
T 06	268 22.3	N19 52.1	300 17.1	11.6	N18 46.4	1.3	54.6
H 07	283 22.3	51.6	314 47.7	11.6	18 45.1	1.5	54.6
U 08	298 22.3	51.1	329 18.3	11.6	18 43.6	1.5	54.6
R 09	313 22.3 ..	50.6	343 48.9	11.7	18 42.1	1.6	54.6
S 10	328 22.3	50.0	358 19.6	11.7	18 40.5	1.8	54.6
D 11	343 22.3	49.5	12 50.3	11.6	18 38.7	1.8	54.5
A 12	358 22.3	N19 49.0	27 20.9	11.8	N18 36.9	1.8	54.5
Y 13	13 22.2	48.5	41 51.7	11.7	18 35.1	2.0	54.5
14	28 22.2	47.9	56 22.4	11.8	18 33.1	2.1	54.5
15	43 22.2 ..	47.4	70 53.2	11.8	18 31.0	2.1	54.5
16	58 22.2	46.9	85 24.0	11.8	18 28.9	2.3	54.5
17	73 22.2	46.3	99 54.8	11.9	18 26.6	2.3	54.5
18	88 22.2	N19 45.8	114 25.7	11.8	N18 24.3	2.4	54.5
19	103 22.2	45.3	128 56.5	11.9	18 21.9	2.5	54.4
20	118 22.2	44.7	143 27.4	12.0	18 19.4	2.6	54.4
21	133 22.2 ..	44.2	157 58.4	11.9	18 16.8	2.6	54.4
22	148 22.1	43.7	172 29.3	12.0	18 14.2	2.8	54.4
23	163 22.1	43.1	187 00.3	12.0	18 11.4	2.8	54.4
25 00	178 22.1	N19 42.6	201 31.3	12.1	N18 08.6	2.9	54.4
01	193 22.1	42.1	216 02.4	12.1	18 05.7	3.0	54.4
02	208 22.1	41.5	230 33.5	12.1	18 02.7	3.1	54.4
03	223 22.1 ..	41.0	245 04.6	12.1	17 59.6	3.2	54.3
04	238 22.1	40.5	259 35.7	12.2	17 56.4	3.2	54.3
05	253 22.1	39.9	274 06.9	12.2	17 53.2	3.4	54.3
06	268 22.1	N19 39.4	288 38.1	12.2	N17 49.8	3.4	54.3
07	283 22.1	38.9	303 09.3	12.2	17 46.4	3.5	54.3
F 08	298 22.1	38.3	317 40.5	12.3	17 42.9	3.5	54.3
R 09	313 22.1 ..	37.8	332 11.8	12.3	17 39.4	3.7	54.3
I 10	328 22.1	37.2	346 43.1	12.4	17 35.7	3.7	54.3
D 11	343 22.0	36.7	1 14.5	12.4	17 32.0	3.8	54.3
A 12	358 22.0	N19 36.2	15 45.9	12.4	N17 28.2	3.9	54.2
Y 13	13 22.0	35.6	30 17.3	12.4	17 24.3	4.0	54.2
14	28 22.0	35.1	44 48.7	12.5	17 20.3	4.0	54.2
15	43 22.0 ..	34.5	59 20.2	12.5	17 16.3	4.1	54.2
16	58 22.0	34.0	73 51.7	12.6	17 12.2	4.2	54.2
17	73 22.0	33.4	88 23.3	12.5	17 08.0	4.3	54.2
18	88 22.0	N19 32.9	102 54.8	12.6	N17 03.7	4.4	54.2
19	103 22.0	32.4	117 26.4	12.7	16 59.3	4.4	54.2
20	118 22.0	31.8	131 58.1	12.6	16 54.9	4.5	54.2
21	133 22.0 ..	31.3	146 29.7	12.7	16 50.4	4.6	54.2
22	148 22.0	30.7	161 01.4	12.8	16 45.8	4.6	54.2
23	163 22.0	30.2	175 33.2	12.8	16 41.2	4.7	54.1
26 00	178 22.0	N19 29.6	190 05.0	12.8	N16 36.5	4.8	54.1
01	193 22.0	29.1	204 36.8	12.8	16 31.7	4.9	54.1
02	208 22.0	28.5	219 08.6	12.9	16 26.8	5.0	54.1
03	223 22.0 ..	28.0	233 40.5	12.9	16 21.8	5.0	54.1
04	238 22.0	27.4	248 12.4	12.9	16 16.8	5.1	54.1
05	253 22.0	26.9	262 44.3	13.0	16 11.7	5.1	54.1
06	268 22.0	N19 26.3	277 16.3	13.0	N16 06.6	5.2	54.1
S 07	283 22.0	25.8	291 48.3	13.0	16 01.4	5.3	54.1
A 08	298 22.0	25.2	306 20.3	13.1	15 56.1	5.4	54.1
T 09	313 22.0 ..	24.7	320 52.4	13.1	15 50.7	5.4	54.1
U 10	328 22.0	24.1	335 24.5	13.1	15 45.3	5.6	54.1
R 11	343 22.0	23.5	349 56.7	13.1	15 39.7	5.5	54.1
D 12	358 22.0	N19 23.0	4 28.8	13.3	N15 34.2	5.7	54.1
A 13	13 22.0	22.4	19 01.1	13.2	15 28.5	5.7	54.1
Y 14	28 22.0	21.9	33 33.3	13.3	15 22.8	5.7	54.0
15	43 22.0 ..	21.3	48 05.6	13.3	15 17.1	5.9	54.0
16	58 22.0	20.8	62 37.9	13.3	15 11.2	5.9	54.0
17	73 22.0	20.2	77 10.2	13.4	15 05.3	5.9	54.0
18	88 22.0	N19 19.7	91 42.6	13.4	N14 59.4	6.1	54.0
19	103 22.0	19.1	106 15.0	13.5	14 53.3	6.1	54.0
20	118 22.0	18.5	120 47.5	13.5	14 47.2	6.1	54.0
21	133 22.0 ..	18.0	135 20.0	13.5	14 41.1	6.3	54.0
22	148 22.0	17.4	149 52.5	13.5	14 34.8	6.2	54.0
23	163 22.0	16.9	164 25.0	13.6	N14 28.6	6.4	54.0
SD	15.8	d 0.5	SD	14.9		14.8	14.7

Lat.	Twilight Naut.	Twilight Civil	Sunrise	Moonrise 24	25	26	27
°	h m	h m	h m	h m	h m	h m	h m
N 72	▢	▢	▢			01 01	02 49
N 70	▢	▢		24 21	00 21	01 48	03 18
68	////	////	01 34	25 02	01 02	02 18	03 40
66	////	////	02 17	00 29	01 30	02 41	03 57
64	////	00 43	02 46	00 52	01 51	02 58	04 11
62	////	01 45	03 07	01 11	02 08	03 13	04 22
60	////	02 17	03 24	01 26	02 22	03 25	04 32
N 58	00 39	02 41	03 39	01 39	02 34	03 35	04 40
56	01 35	02 59	03 51	01 50	02 45	03 45	04 48
54	02 05	03 15	04 02	02 00	02 54	03 53	04 54
52	02 28	03 28	04 11	02 08	03 02	04 00	05 00
50	02 45	03 39	04 20	02 16	03 10	04 07	05 06
45	03 18	04 03	04 37	02 33	03 25	04 21	05 17
N 40	03 42	04 21	04 52	02 47	03 38	04 32	05 27
35	04 01	04 36	05 04	02 58	03 49	04 42	05 35
30	04 17	04 48	05 15	03 08	03 59	04 51	05 42
20	04 41	05 09	05 33	03 26	04 15	05 05	05 55
N 10	05 00	05 26	05 48	03 41	04 30	05 18	06 06
0	05 16	05 41	06 03	03 55	04 43	05 30	06 16
S 10	05 29	05 55	06 17	04 09	04 57	05 42	06 26
20	05 42	06 09	06 33	04 25	05 11	05 55	06 37
30	05 55	06 24	06 50	04 42	05 28	06 10	06 49
35	06 02	06 33	07 00	04 52	05 37	06 19	06 56
40	06 09	06 42	07 11	05 04	05 48	06 28	07 04
45	06 17	06 53	07 25	05 18	06 01	06 40	07 14
S 50	06 25	07 05	07 41	05 34	06 17	06 53	07 25
52	06 29	07 11	07 49	05 42	06 24	07 00	07 30
54	06 33	07 17	07 57	05 51	06 32	07 07	07 36
56	06 37	07 24	08 07	06 01	06 41	07 15	07 42
58	06 42	07 31	08 18	06 12	06 51	07 23	07 50
S 60	06 47	07 40	08 30	06 25	07 03	07 34	07 58

Lat.	Sunset	Twilight Civil	Twilight Naut.	Moonset 24	25	26	27
°	h m	h m	h m	h m	h m	h m	h m
N 72	▢	▢	▢		21 45	21 32	21 23
N 70	▢	▢	▢	20 46	20 57	21 01	21 03
68	22 33	////	////	20 05	20 26	20 39	20 47
66	21 53	////	////	19 36	20 03	20 21	20 34
64	21 25	23 19	////	19 15	19 45	20 07	20 23
62	21 04	22 24	////	18 58	19 30	19 55	20 14
60	20 47	21 53	////	18 43	19 18	19 45	20 06
N 58	20 33	21 30	23 24	18 31	19 07	19 36	19 59
56	20 21	21 12	22 34	18 20	18 57	19 28	19 53
54	20 10	20 57	22 05	18 11	18 49	19 21	19 48
52	20 01	20 44	21 44	18 02	18 41	19 14	19 43
50	19 53	20 33	21 26	17 55	18 34	19 08	19 38
45	19 35	20 10	20 54	17 39	18 20	18 56	19 28
N 40	19 21	19 52	20 30	17 26	18 08	18 46	19 20
35	19 09	19 37	20 11	17 14	17 57	18 37	19 13
30	18 58	19 24	19 56	17 04	17 48	18 29	19 07
20	18 40	19 04	19 32	16 47	17 33	18 16	18 56
N 10	18 24	18 47	19 13	16 33	17 19	18 04	18 46
0	18 10	18 32	18 58	16 19	17 06	17 53	18 37
S 10	17 56	18 18	18 44	16 05	16 53	17 41	18 28
20	17 41	18 04	18 31	15 50	16 40	17 29	18 19
30	17 23	17 49	18 18	15 32	16 24	17 16	18 08
35	17 13	17 41	18 11	15 22	16 15	17 08	18 01
40	17 02	17 31	18 04	15 11	16 04	16 58	17 54
45	16 49	17 21	17 57	14 57	15 52	16 48	17 45
S 50	16 32	17 08	17 48	14 41	15 36	16 35	17 35
52	16 25	17 03	17 44	14 33	15 29	16 29	17 30
54	16 16	16 57	17 40	14 25	15 21	16 22	17 25
56	16 07	16 50	17 36	14 15	15 13	16 14	17 19
58	15 56	16 42	17 32	14 04	15 03	16 06	17 12
S 60	15 43	16 34	17 26	13 51	14 51	15 56	17 05

	SUN			MOON			
Day	Eqn. of Time 00h	12h	Mer. Pass.	Mer. Pass. Upper	Lower	Age	Phase
d	m s	m s	h m	h m	h m	d	%
24	06 30	06 31	12 07	10 07	22 31	27	6
25	06 31	06 31	12 07	10 55	23 18	28	2
26	06 32	06 32	12 07	11 42	24 04	29	0 ●

UT	ARIES	VENUS −3.8		MARS +0.4		JUPITER −1.8		SATURN +0.5		STARS		
	GHA	GHA	Dec	GHA	Dec	GHA	Dec	GHA	Dec	Name	SHA	Dec
d h	° ′	° ′	° ′	° ′	° ′	° ′	° ′	° ′	° ′		° ′	° ′
27 00	304 36.0	203 34.1	N22 44.1	96 34.8	S12 31.7	179 53.2	N20 01.3	79 43.7	S14 39.9	Acamar	315 17.9	S40 14.6
01	319 38.4	218 33.3	43.9	111 36.0	32.2	194 55.1	01.2	94 46.2	39.9	Achernar	335 26.2	S57 09.5
02	334 40.9	233 32.4	43.8	126 37.2	32.7	209 57.0	01.0	109 48.6	39.9	Acrux	173 08.6	S63 11.1
03	349 43.4	248 31.6 . .	43.7	141 38.4 . .	33.2	224 58.9 . .	00.9	124 51.1 . .	39.9	Adhara	255 12.3	S28 59.6
04	4 45.8	263 30.8	43.6	156 39.6	33.7	240 00.8	00.8	139 53.5	40.0	Aldebaran	290 48.7	N16 32.1
05	19 48.3	278 30.0	43.4	171 40.9	34.2	255 02.7	00.7	154 55.9	40.0			
06	34 50.8	293 29.2	N22 43.3	186 42.1	S12 34.7	270 04.6	N20 00.6	169 58.4	S14 40.0	Alioth	166 20.3	N55 53.1
07	49 53.2	308 28.3	43.2	201 43.3	35.2	285 06.5	00.4	185 00.8	40.0	Alkaid	152 58.4	N49 14.8
08	64 55.7	323 27.5	43.1	216 44.5	35.7	300 08.3	00.3	200 03.3	40.0	Al Na'ir	27 42.4	S46 53.1
S 09	79 58.1	338 26.7 . .	43.0	231 45.7 . .	36.2	315 10.2 . .	00.2	215 05.7 . .	40.0	Alnilam	275 45.8	S 1 11.7
U 10	95 00.6	353 25.9	42.8	246 46.9	36.7	330 12.1	20 00.1	230 08.1	40.1	Alphard	217 55.6	S 8 43.4
N 11	110 03.1	8 25.1	42.7	261 48.1	37.2	345 14.0	19 59.9	245 10.6	40.1			
D 12	125 05.5	23 24.3	N22 42.6	276 49.3	S12 37.7	0 15.9	N19 59.8	260 13.0	S14 40.1	Alphecca	126 10.2	N26 40.3
A 13	140 08.0	38 23.4	42.4	291 50.6	38.2	15 17.8	59.7	275 15.5	40.1	Alpheratz	357 42.4	N29 10.2
Y 14	155 10.5	53 22.6	42.3	306 51.8	38.7	30 19.7	59.6	290 17.9	40.1	Altair	62 07.1	N 8 54.7
15	170 12.9	68 21.8 . .	42.2	321 53.0 . .	39.2	45 21.6 . .	59.4	305 20.3 . .	40.2	Ankaa	353 14.8	S42 13.3
16	185 15.4	83 21.0	42.0	336 54.2	39.7	60 23.4	59.3	320 22.8	40.2	Antares	112 25.1	S26 27.7
17	200 17.9	98 20.2	41.9	351 55.4	40.1	75 25.3	59.2	335 25.2	40.2			
18	215 20.3	113 19.3	N22 41.8	6 56.6	S12 40.6	90 27.2	N19 59.1	350 27.7	S14 40.2	Arcturus	145 55.0	N19 06.6
19	230 22.8	128 18.5	41.6	21 57.8	41.1	105 29.1	59.0	5 30.1	40.2	Atria	107 25.8	S69 03.2
20	245 25.3	143 17.7	41.5	36 59.0	41.6	120 31.0	58.8	20 32.5	40.3	Avior	234 18.3	S59 33.5
21	260 27.7	158 16.9 . .	41.3	52 00.2 . .	42.1	135 32.9 . .	58.7	35 35.0 . .	40.3	Bellatrix	278 31.4	N 6 21.6
22	275 30.2	173 16.1	41.2	67 01.4	42.6	150 34.8	58.6	50 37.4	40.3	Betelgeuse	271 00.7	N 7 24.4
23	290 32.6	188 15.3	41.0	82 02.6	43.1	165 36.7	58.5	65 39.9	40.3			
28 00	305 35.1	203 14.4	N22 40.9	97 03.8	S12 43.6	180 38.5	N19 58.3	80 42.3	S14 40.3	Canopus	263 56.3	S52 42.2
01	320 37.6	218 13.6	40.8	112 05.0	44.1	195 40.4	58.2	95 44.7	40.3	Capella	280 33.6	N46 00.4
02	335 40.0	233 12.8	40.6	127 06.3	44.6	210 42.3	58.1	110 47.2	40.4	Deneb	49 30.4	N45 20.1
03	350 42.5	248 12.0 . .	40.5	142 07.5 . .	45.1	225 44.2 . .	58.0	125 49.6 . .	40.4	Denebola	182 33.1	N14 29.5
04	5 45.0	263 11.2	40.3	157 08.7	45.6	240 46.1	57.9	140 52.1	40.4	Diphda	348 55.0	S17 54.2
05	20 47.4	278 10.4	40.2	172 09.9	46.1	255 48.0	57.7	155 54.5	40.4			
06	35 49.9	293 09.5	N22 40.0	187 11.1	S12 46.6	270 49.9	N19 57.6	170 56.9	S14 40.4	Dubhe	193 51.4	N61 40.5
07	50 52.4	308 08.7	39.9	202 12.3	47.1	285 51.8	57.5	185 59.4	40.5	Elnath	278 11.9	N28 36.9
08	65 54.8	323 07.9	39.7	217 13.5	47.6	300 53.6	57.4	201 01.8	40.5	Eltanin	90 45.3	N51 29.6
M 09	80 57.3	338 07.1 . .	39.6	232 14.7 . .	48.1	315 55.5 . .	57.2	216 04.2 . .	40.5	Enif	33 46.0	N 9 56.7
O 10	95 59.8	353 06.3	39.4	247 15.9	48.6	330 57.4	57.1	231 06.7	40.5	Fomalhaut	15 22.9	S29 32.4
N 11	111 02.2	8 05.4	39.2	262 17.1	49.1	345 59.3	57.0	246 09.1	40.5			
D 12	126 04.7	23 04.6	N22 39.1	277 18.3	S12 49.6	1 01.2	N19 56.9	261 11.5	S14 40.6	Gacrux	172 00.2	S57 11.9
A 13	141 07.1	38 03.8	38.9	292 19.5	50.1	16 03.1	56.7	276 14.0	40.6	Gienah	175 51.6	S17 37.4
Y 14	156 09.6	53 03.0	38.8	307 20.7	50.6	31 05.0	56.6	291 16.4	40.6	Hadar	148 46.7	S60 26.8
15	171 12.1	68 02.2 . .	38.6	322 21.9 . .	51.1	46 06.9 . .	56.5	306 18.9 . .	40.6	Hamal	327 59.8	N23 31.8
16	186 14.5	83 01.4	38.4	337 23.1	51.6	61 08.7	56.4	321 21.3	40.6	Kaus Aust.	83 42.4	S34 22.5
17	201 17.0	98 00.5	38.3	352 24.3	52.1	76 10.6	56.3	336 23.7	40.7			
18	216 19.5	112 59.7	N22 38.1	7 25.5	S12 52.6	91 12.5	N19 56.1	351 26.2	S14 40.7	Kochab	137 20.0	N74 06.1
19	231 21.9	127 58.9	37.9	22 26.6	53.1	106 14.4	56.0	6 28.6	40.7	Markab	13 37.3	N15 17.1
20	246 24.4	142 58.1	37.8	37 27.8	53.6	121 16.3	55.9	21 31.0	40.7	Menkar	314 14.3	N 4 08.4
21	261 26.9	157 57.3 . .	37.6	52 29.0 . .	54.1	136 18.2 . .	55.8	36 33.5 . .	40.7	Menkent	148 06.6	S36 26.6
22	276 29.3	172 56.5	37.4	67 30.2	54.6	151 20.1	55.6	51 35.9	40.7	Miaplacidus	221 40.3	S69 46.8
23	291 31.8	187 55.6	37.3	82 31.4	55.1	166 22.0	55.5	66 38.3	40.8			
29 00	306 34.2	202 54.8	N22 37.1	97 32.6	S12 55.6	181 23.9	N19 55.4	81 40.8	S14 40.8	Mirfak	308 39.3	N49 54.4
01	321 36.7	217 54.0	36.9	112 33.8	56.0	196 25.7	55.3	96 43.2	40.8	Nunki	75 57.0	S26 16.5
02	336 39.2	232 53.2	36.8	127 35.0	56.5	211 27.6	55.1	111 45.6	40.8	Peacock	53 17.5	S56 41.0
03	351 41.6	247 52.4 . .	36.6	142 36.2 . .	57.0	226 29.5 . .	55.0	126 48.1 . .	40.8	Pollux	243 27.2	N27 59.3
04	6 44.1	262 51.6	36.4	157 37.4	57.5	241 31.4	54.9	141 50.5	40.9	Procyon	244 59.2	N 5 11.1
05	21 46.6	277 50.7	36.2	172 38.6	58.0	256 33.3	54.8	156 52.9	40.9			
06	36 49.0	292 49.9	N22 36.0	187 39.8	S12 58.5	271 35.2	N19 54.6	171 55.4	S14 40.9	Rasalhague	96 05.5	N12 33.3
07	51 51.5	307 49.1	35.9	202 41.0	59.0	286 37.1	54.5	186 57.8	40.9	Regulus	207 43.0	N11 53.7
08	66 54.0	322 48.3	35.7	217 42.2	12 59.5	301 39.0	54.4	202 00.2	40.9	Rigel	281 11.5	S 8 11.2
T 09	81 56.4	337 47.5 . .	35.5	232 43.3	13 00.0	316 40.8 . .	54.3	217 02.7 . .	41.0	Rigil Kent.	139 50.5	S60 53.8
U 10	96 58.9	352 46.7	35.3	247 44.5	00.5	331 42.7	54.1	232 05.1	41.0	Sabik	102 11.4	S15 44.4
E 11	112 01.4	7 45.9	35.1	262 45.7	01.0	346 44.6	54.0	247 07.5	41.0			
S 12	127 03.8	22 45.0	N22 35.0	277 46.9	S13 01.5	1 46.5	N19 53.9	262 10.0	S14 41.0	Schedar	349 39.3	N56 36.8
D 13	142 06.3	37 44.2	34.8	292 48.1	02.0	16 48.4	53.8	277 12.4	41.1	Shaula	96 20.5	S37 06.7
A 14	157 08.7	52 43.4	34.6	307 49.3	02.5	31 50.3	53.7	292 14.8	41.1	Sirius	258 33.5	S16 44.3
Y 15	172 11.2	67 42.6 . .	34.4	322 50.5 . .	03.0	46 52.2 . .	53.5	307 17.3 . .	41.1	Spica	158 30.5	S11 14.2
16	187 13.7	82 41.8	34.2	337 51.7	03.5	61 54.1	53.4	322 19.7	41.1	Suhail	222 52.3	S43 29.7
17	202 16.1	97 41.0	34.0	352 52.8	04.0	76 56.0	53.3	337 22.1	41.1			
18	217 18.6	112 40.1	N22 33.8	7 54.0	S13 04.5	91 57.8	N19 53.2	352 24.6	S14 41.2	Vega	80 38.0	N38 48.2
19	232 21.1	127 39.3	33.6	22 55.2	05.0	106 59.7	53.0	7 27.0	41.2	Zuben'ubi	137 04.5	S16 06.0
20	247 23.5	142 38.5	33.4	37 56.4	05.5	122 01.6	52.9	22 29.4	41.2		SHA	Mer.Pass.
21	262 26.0	157 37.7 . .	33.2	52 57.6 . .	06.0	137 03.5 . .	52.8	37 31.9 . .	41.2		° ′	h m
22	277 28.5	172 36.9	33.0	67 58.8	06.5	152 05.4	52.7	52 34.3	41.2	Venus	257 39.3	10 28
23	292 30.9	187 36.1	32.8	82 59.9	07.0	167 07.3	52.5	67 36.7	41.3	Mars	151 28.7	17 30
	h m									Jupiter	235 03.4	11 56
Mer.Pass. 3 37.1		v −0.8	d 0.2	v 1.2	d 0.5	v 1.9	d 0.1	v 2.4	d 0.0	Saturn	135 07.2	18 34

SUN / MOON

UT	SUN GHA	SUN Dec	MOON GHA	v	MOON Dec	d	HP
d h	° ′	° ′	° ′	′	° ′	′	′
27 00	178 22.0	N19 16.3	178 57.6	13.6	N14 22.2	6.4	54.0
01	193 22.0	15.7	193 30.2	13.7	14 15.8	6.5	54.0
02	208 22.0	15.2	208 02.9	13.6	14 09.3	6.5	54.0
03	223 22.0	.. 14.6	222 35.5	13.7	14 02.8	6.6	54.0
04	238 22.0	14.0	237 08.2	13.8	13 56.2	6.6	54.0
05	253 22.0	13.5	251 41.0	13.8	13 49.6	6.7	54.0
06	268 22.0	N19 12.9	266 13.8	13.8	N13 42.9	6.8	54.0
07	283 22.0	12.3	280 46.6	13.8	13 36.1	6.8	54.0
08	298 22.0	11.8	295 19.4	13.9	13 29.3	6.9	54.0
S 09	313 22.0	.. 11.2	309 52.3	13.9	13 22.4	6.9	54.0
U 10	328 22.1	10.6	324 25.2	13.9	13 15.5	7.0	54.0
N 11	343 22.1	10.1	338 58.1	14.0	13 08.5	7.0	54.0
D 12	358 22.1	N19 09.5	353 31.1	14.0	N13 01.5	7.1	54.0
A 13	13 22.1	08.9	8 04.1	14.0	12 54.4	7.2	53.9
Y 14	28 22.1	08.4	22 37.1	14.1	12 47.2	7.2	53.9
15	43 22.1	.. 07.8	37 10.2	14.1	12 40.0	7.2	53.9
16	58 22.1	07.2	51 43.3	14.1	12 32.8	7.3	53.9
17	73 22.1	06.7	66 16.4	14.2	12 25.5	7.4	53.9
18	88 22.1	N19 06.1	80 49.6	14.1	N12 18.1	7.4	53.9
19	103 22.1	05.5	95 22.7	14.2	12 10.7	7.4	53.9
20	118 22.1	04.9	109 55.9	14.3	12 03.3	7.5	53.9
21	133 22.1	.. 04.4	124 29.2	14.3	11 55.8	7.6	53.9
22	148 22.1	03.8	139 02.5	14.3	11 48.2	7.6	53.9
23	163 22.2	03.2	153 35.8	14.3	11 40.6	7.7	53.9
28 00	178 22.2	N19 02.7	168 09.1	14.3	N11 32.9	7.7	53.9
01	193 22.2	02.1	182 42.4	14.4	11 25.2	7.7	53.9
02	208 22.2	01.5	197 15.8	14.4	11 17.5	7.8	53.9
03	223 22.2	.. 00.9	211 49.2	14.5	11 09.7	7.9	53.9
04	238 22.2	19 00.4	226 22.7	14.4	11 01.8	7.8	53.9
05	253 22.2	18 59.8	240 56.1	14.5	10 54.0	8.0	53.9
06	268 22.2	N18 59.2	255 29.6	14.5	N10 46.0	7.9	53.9
07	283 22.2	58.6	270 03.1	14.6	10 38.1	8.1	53.9
08	298 22.3	58.0	284 36.7	14.5	10 30.0	8.0	53.9
M 09	313 22.3	.. 57.5	299 10.2	14.6	10 22.0	8.1	53.9
O 10	328 22.3	56.9	313 43.8	14.6	10 13.9	8.2	53.9
N 11	343 22.3	56.3	328 17.4	14.7	10 05.7	8.2	53.9
D 12	358 22.3	N18 55.7	342 51.1	14.7	N 9 57.5	8.2	53.9
A 13	13 22.3	55.1	357 24.8	14.6	9 49.3	8.3	53.9
Y 14	28 22.3	54.6	11 58.4	14.8	9 41.0	8.3	53.9
15	43 22.3	.. 54.0	26 32.2	14.7	9 32.7	8.3	53.9
16	58 22.4	53.4	41 05.9	14.7	9 24.4	8.4	53.9
17	73 22.4	52.8	55 39.6	14.8	9 16.0	8.4	53.9
18	88 22.4	N18 52.2	70 13.4	14.8	N 9 07.6	8.5	54.0
19	103 22.4	51.6	84 47.2	14.8	8 59.1	8.5	54.0
20	118 22.4	51.0	99 21.0	14.9	8 50.6	8.5	54.0
21	133 22.4	.. 50.5	113 54.9	14.8	8 42.1	8.6	54.0
22	148 22.4	49.9	128 28.7	14.9	8 33.5	8.6	54.0
23	163 22.5	49.3	143 02.6	14.9	8 24.9	8.6	54.0
29 00	178 22.5	N18 48.7	157 36.5	14.9	N 8 16.3	8.7	54.0
01	193 22.5	48.1	172 10.4	15.0	8 07.6	8.7	54.0
02	208 22.5	47.5	186 44.4	14.9	7 58.9	8.8	54.0
03	223 22.5	.. 46.9	201 18.3	15.0	7 50.1	8.7	54.0
04	238 22.5	46.3	215 52.3	15.0	7 41.4	8.8	54.0
05	253 22.6	45.8	230 26.3	15.0	7 32.6	8.9	54.0
06	268 22.6	N18 45.2	245 00.3	15.0	N 7 23.7	8.8	54.0
07	283 22.6	44.6	259 34.3	15.1	7 14.9	8.9	54.0
08	298 22.6	44.0	274 08.4	15.0	7 06.0	9.0	54.0
T 09	313 22.6	.. 43.4	288 42.4	15.1	6 57.0	8.9	54.0
U 10	328 22.7	42.8	303 16.5	15.1	6 48.1	9.0	54.0
E 11	343 22.7	42.2	317 50.6	15.1	6 39.1	9.0	54.0
S 12	358 22.7	N18 41.6	332 24.7	15.1	N 6 30.1	9.0	54.0
D 13	13 22.7	41.0	346 58.8	15.1	6 21.1	9.1	54.0
A 14	28 22.7	40.4	1 32.9	15.1	6 12.0	9.1	54.0
Y 15	43 22.8	.. 39.8	16 07.0	15.2	6 02.9	9.1	54.0
16	58 22.8	39.2	30 41.2	15.1	5 53.8	9.2	54.0
17	73 22.8	38.6	45 15.3	15.2	5 44.6	9.1	54.1
18	88 22.8	N18 38.0	59 49.5	15.1	N 5 35.5	9.2	54.1
19	103 22.8	37.4	74 23.6	15.2	5 26.3	9.2	54.1
20	118 22.9	36.8	88 57.8	15.2	5 17.1	9.3	54.1
21	133 22.9	.. 36.2	103 32.0	15.2	5 07.8	9.2	54.1
22	148 22.9	35.6	118 06.2	15.2	4 58.6	9.3	54.1
23	163 22.9	35.0	132 40.4	15.2	N 4 49.3	9.3	54.1
	SD 15.8	d 0.6	SD 14.7		14.7		14.7

Twilight / Moonrise

Lat.	Twilight Naut.	Twilight Civil	Sunrise	Moonrise 27	Moonrise 28	Moonrise 29	Moonrise 30
°	h m	h m	h m	h m	h m	h m	h m
N 72	▭	▭	▭	02 49	04 30	06 08	07 43
N 70	////	////	00 33	03 18	04 49	06 19	07 47
68	////	////	01 53	03 40	05 04	06 28	07 51
66	////	////	02 29	03 57	05 16	06 35	07 55
64	////	01 12	02 55	04 11	05 25	06 41	07 57
62	////	01 58	03 15	04 22	05 34	06 46	08 00
60	////	02 27	03 31	04 32	05 41	06 51	08 02
N 58	01 05	02 49	03 45	04 40	05 47	06 55	08 04
56	01 47	03 06	03 56	04 48	05 53	06 59	08 05
54	02 14	03 21	04 06	04 54	05 58	07 02	08 07
52	02 35	03 33	04 15	05 00	06 02	07 05	08 08
50	02 51	03 44	04 24	05 06	06 06	07 08	08 09
45	03 23	04 06	04 41	05 17	06 15	07 14	08 11
N 40	03 46	04 24	04 55	05 27	06 23	07 18	08 14
35	04 04	04 38	05 06	05 35	06 29	07 23	08 16
30	04 19	04 50	05 17	05 42	06 34	07 26	08 18
20	04 42	05 10	05 34	05 55	06 44	07 33	08 21
N 10	05 01	05 27	05 50	06 06	06 52	07 38	08 23
0	05 16	05 41	06 03	06 16	07 00	07 43	08 26
S 10	05 29	05 55	06 17	06 26	07 08	07 49	08 28
20	05 42	06 08	06 32	06 37	07 16	07 54	08 31
30	05 54	06 23	06 48	06 49	07 26	08 00	08 34
35	06 00	06 31	06 58	06 56	07 31	08 04	08 36
40	06 07	06 40	07 09	07 04	07 37	08 08	08 37
45	06 14	06 50	07 22	07 14	07 44	08 13	08 40
S 50	06 22	07 02	07 37	07 25	07 53	08 18	08 42
52	06 26	07 07	07 45	07 30	07 57	08 21	08 44
54	06 29	07 13	07 53	07 36	08 01	08 24	08 45
56	06 33	07 19	08 02	07 42	08 06	08 27	08 46
58	06 38	07 26	08 12	07 50	08 11	08 30	08 48
S 60	06 42	07 34	08 24	07 58	08 17	08 34	08 50

Sunset / Twilight / Moonset

Lat.	Sunset	Twilight Civil	Twilight Naut.	Moonset 27	Moonset 28	Moonset 29	Moonset 30
°	h m	h m	h m	h m	h m	h m	h m
N 72	▭	▭	▭	21 23	21 15	21 09	21 03
N 70	23 22	////	////	21 03	21 03	21 02	21 01
68	22 16	////	////	20 47	20 52	20 56	20 59
66	21 41	////	////	20 34	20 44	20 51	20 58
64	21 16	22 54	////	20 23	20 36	20 47	20 57
62	20 56	22 11	////	20 14	20 30	20 44	20 56
60	20 40	21 44	////	20 06	20 25	20 41	20 56
N 58	20 27	21 22	23 01	19 59	20 20	20 38	20 55
56	20 15	21 05	22 22	19 53	20 16	20 36	20 54
54	20 05	20 51	21 56	19 48	20 12	20 33	20 54
52	19 57	20 39	21 37	19 43	20 08	20 31	20 53
50	19 49	20 28	21 20	19 38	20 05	20 29	20 53
45	19 32	20 06	20 49	19 28	19 58	20 25	20 52
N 40	19 18	19 49	20 26	19 20	19 52	20 22	20 51
35	19 06	19 34	20 08	19 13	19 47	20 19	20 50
30	18 56	19 22	19 54	19 07	19 42	20 16	20 50
20	18 39	19 02	19 30	18 56	19 35	20 12	20 48
N 10	18 24	18 46	19 12	18 46	19 28	20 08	20 47
0	18 10	18 32	18 57	18 37	19 21	20 04	20 46
S 10	17 56	18 18	18 44	18 28	19 15	20 00	20 45
20	17 42	18 05	18 32	18 19	19 08	19 56	20 44
30	17 25	17 50	18 19	18 08	18 59	19 51	20 43
35	17 16	17 43	18 13	18 01	18 55	19 48	20 42
40	17 05	17 34	18 07	17 53	18 49	19 45	20 41
45	16 52	17 24	17 59	17 45	18 43	19 42	20 40
S 50	16 36	17 12	17 51	17 35	18 36	19 37	20 39
52	16 29	17 07	17 48	17 30	18 32	19 35	20 39
54	16 21	17 01	17 44	17 25	18 29	19 33	20 38
56	16 12	16 54	17 40	17 19	18 24	19 31	20 37
58	16 02	16 47	17 36	17 12	18 20	19 28	20 37
S 60	15 50	16 39	17 31	17 05	18 14	19 25	20 36

SUN / MOON

Day	SUN Eqn. of Time 00h	SUN Eqn. of Time 12h	SUN Mer. Pass.	MOON Mer. Pass. Upper	MOON Mer. Pass. Lower	Age	Phase
d	m s	m s	h m	h m	h m	d	%
27	06 32	06 32	12 07	12 27	00 04	01	0
28	06 31	06 31	12 07	13 11	00 49	02	2
29	06 30	06 29	12 06	13 54	01 32	03	6

UT	ARIES GHA	VENUS −3.8 GHA	Dec	MARS +0.4 GHA	Dec	JUPITER −1.8 GHA	Dec	SATURN +0.5 GHA	Dec	Star Name	SHA	Dec
d h	° ′	° ′	° ′	° ′	° ′	° ′	° ′	° ′	° ′		° ′	° ′
30 00	307 33.4	202 35.3	N22 32.6	98 01.1	S13 07.5	182 09.2	N19 52.4	82 39.1	S14 41.3	Acamar	315 17.8	S40 14.6
01	322 35.9	217 34.4	32.4	113 02.3	08.0	197 11.1	52.3	97 41.6	41.3	Achernar	335 26.2	S57 09.5
02	337 38.3	232 33.6	32.2	128 03.5	08.5	212 13.0	52.2	112 44.0	41.3	Acrux	173 08.6	S63 11.0
03	352 40.8	247 32.8 ..	32.0	143 04.7 ..	09.0	227 14.8 ..	52.0	127 46.4 ..	41.3	Adhara	255 12.2	S28 59.6
04	7 43.2	262 32.0	31.8	158 05.9	09.5	242 16.7	51.9	142 48.9	41.4	Aldebaran	290 48.6	N16 32.1
05	22 45.7	277 31.2	31.6	173 07.0	10.0	257 18.6	51.8	157 51.3	41.4			
W 06	37 48.2	292 30.4	N22 31.4	188 08.2	S13 10.5	272 20.5	N19 51.7	172 53.7	S14 41.4	Alioth	166 20.3	N55 53.1
E 07	52 50.6	307 29.6	31.2	203 09.4	11.0	287 22.4	51.5	187 56.2	41.4	Alkaid	152 58.4	N49 14.8
D 08	67 53.1	322 28.7	31.0	218 10.6	11.5	302 24.3	51.4	202 58.6	41.4	Al Na'ir	27 42.4	S46 53.1
N 09	82 55.6	337 27.9 ..	30.8	233 11.7 ..	12.0	317 26.2 ..	51.3	218 01.0 ..	41.5	Alnilam	275 45.8	S 1 11.7
E 10	97 58.0	352 27.1	30.6	248 12.9	12.5	332 28.1	51.2	233 03.4	41.5	Alphard	217 55.6	S 8 43.4
S 11	113 00.5	7 26.3	30.4	263 14.1	13.0	347 30.0	51.0	248 05.9	41.5			
D 12	128 03.0	22 25.5	N22 30.2	278 15.3	S13 13.5	2 31.8	N19 50.9	263 08.3	S14 41.5	Alphecca	126 10.2	N26 40.3
A 13	143 05.4	37 24.7	30.0	293 16.5	14.0	17 33.7	50.8	278 10.7	41.6	Alpheratz	357 42.4	N29 10.2
Y 14	158 07.9	52 23.9	29.7	308 17.6	14.5	32 35.6	50.7	293 13.2	41.6	Altair	62 07.1	N 8 54.7
15	173 10.3	67 23.0 ..	29.5	323 18.8 ..	15.0	47 37.5 ..	50.5	308 15.6 ..	41.6	Ankaa	353 14.8	S42 13.3
16	188 12.8	82 22.2	29.3	338 20.0	15.5	62 39.4	50.4	323 18.0	41.6	Antares	112 25.1	S26 27.7
17	203 15.3	97 21.4	29.1	353 21.2	16.0	77 41.3	50.3	338 20.4	41.6			
18	218 17.7	112 20.6	N22 28.9	8 22.3	S13 16.5	92 43.2	N19 50.2	353 22.9	S14 41.7	Arcturus	145 55.0	N19 06.6
19	233 20.2	127 19.8	28.6	23 23.5	17.0	107 45.1	50.0	8 25.3	41.7	Atria	107 25.8	S69 03.2
20	248 22.7	142 19.0	28.4	38 24.7	17.5	122 47.0	49.9	23 27.7	41.7	Avior	234 18.3	S59 33.5
21	263 25.1	157 18.2 ..	28.2	53 25.8 ..	18.0	137 48.8 ..	49.8	38 30.1 ..	41.7	Bellatrix	278 31.4	N 6 21.6
22	278 27.6	172 17.4	28.0	68 27.0	18.4	152 50.7	49.7	53 32.6	41.8	Betelgeuse	271 00.7	N 7 24.4
23	293 30.1	187 16.5	27.8	83 28.2	18.9	167 52.6	49.5	68 35.0	41.8			
31 00	308 32.5	202 15.7	N22 27.5	98 29.4	S13 19.4	182 54.5	N19 49.4	83 37.4	S14 41.8	Canopus	263 56.3	S52 42.2
01	323 35.0	217 14.9	27.3	113 30.5	19.9	197 56.4	49.3	98 39.9	41.8	Capella	280 33.6	N46 00.4
02	338 37.5	232 14.1	27.1	128 31.7	20.4	212 58.3	49.2	113 42.3	41.8	Deneb	49 30.4	N45 20.2
03	353 39.9	247 13.3 ..	26.8	143 32.9 ..	20.9	228 00.2 ..	49.1	128 44.7 ..	41.9	Denebola	182 33.1	N14 29.5
04	8 42.4	262 12.5	26.6	158 34.0	21.4	243 02.1	48.9	143 47.1	41.9	Diphda	348 55.0	S17 54.2
05	23 44.8	277 11.7	26.4	173 35.2	21.9	258 04.0	48.8	158 49.6	41.9			
T 06	38 47.3	292 10.9	N22 26.1	188 36.4	S13 22.4	273 05.8	N19 48.7	173 52.0	S14 41.9	Dubhe	193 51.4	N61 40.5
H 07	53 49.8	307 10.0	25.9	203 37.5	22.9	288 07.7	48.6	188 54.4	42.0	Elnath	278 11.9	N28 36.9
U 08	68 52.2	322 09.2	25.7	218 38.7	23.4	303 09.6	48.4	203 56.8	42.0	Eltanin	90 45.4	N51 29.6
R 09	83 54.7	337 08.4 ..	25.4	233 39.9 ..	23.9	318 11.5 ..	48.3	218 59.3 ..	42.0	Enif	33 46.0	N 9 56.7
S 10	98 57.2	352 07.6	25.2	248 41.0	24.4	333 13.4	48.2	234 01.7	42.0	Fomalhaut	15 22.9	S29 32.4
11	113 59.6	7 06.8	25.0	263 42.2	24.9	348 15.3	48.1	249 04.1	42.0			
D 12	129 02.1	22 06.0	N22 24.7	278 43.4	S13 25.4	3 17.2	N19 47.9	264 06.5	S14 42.1	Gacrux	172 00.2	S57 11.9
A 13	144 04.6	37 05.2	24.5	293 44.5	25.9	18 19.1	47.8	279 09.0	42.1	Gienah	175 51.6	S17 37.4
Y 14	159 07.0	52 04.4	24.2	308 45.7	26.4	33 21.0	47.7	294 11.4	42.1	Hadar	148 46.7	S60 26.8
15	174 09.5	67 03.6 ..	24.0	323 46.9 ..	26.9	48 22.9 ..	47.5	309 13.8 ..	42.1	Hamal	327 59.8	N23 31.8
16	189 11.9	82 02.8	23.8	338 48.0	27.4	63 24.7	47.4	324 16.2	42.2	Kaus Aust.	83 42.4	S34 22.5
17	204 14.4	97 01.9	23.5	353 49.2	27.9	78 26.6	47.3	339 18.7	42.2			
18	219 16.9	112 01.1	N22 23.3	8 50.4	S13 28.4	93 28.5	N19 47.2	354 21.1	S14 42.2	Kochab	137 20.1	N74 06.1
19	234 19.3	127 00.3	23.0	23 51.5	28.9	108 30.4	47.0	9 23.5	42.2	Markab	13 37.3	N15 17.1
20	249 21.8	141 59.5	22.8	38 52.7	29.4	123 32.3	46.9	24 25.9	42.3	Menkar	314 14.3	N 4 08.8
21	264 24.3	156 58.7 ..	22.5	53 53.8 ..	29.9	138 34.2 ..	46.8	39 28.3 ..	42.3	Menkent	148 06.6	S36 26.6
22	279 26.7	171 57.9	22.3	68 55.0	30.4	153 36.1	46.7	54 30.8	42.3	Miaplacidus	221 40.3	S69 46.8
23	294 29.2	186 57.1	22.0	83 56.2	30.9	168 38.0	46.5	69 33.2	42.3			
1 00	309 31.7	201 56.3	N22 21.8	98 57.3	S13 31.4	183 39.9	N19 46.4	84 35.6	S14 42.3	Mirfak	308 39.3	N49 54.4
01	324 34.1	216 55.5	21.5	113 58.5	31.9	198 41.8	46.3	99 38.0	42.4	Nunki	75 57.0	S26 16.5
02	339 36.6	231 54.7	21.3	128 59.6	32.4	213 43.6	46.2	114 40.5	42.4	Peacock	53 17.5	S56 41.0
03	354 39.1	246 53.8 ..	21.0	144 00.8 ..	32.9	228 45.5 ..	46.0	129 42.9 ..	42.4	Pollux	243 27.2	N27 59.3
04	9 41.5	261 53.0	20.7	159 01.9	33.4	243 47.4	45.9	144 45.3	42.4	Procyon	244 59.2	N 5 11.1
05	24 44.0	276 52.2	20.5	174 03.1	33.9	258 49.3	45.8	159 47.7	42.5			
06	39 46.4	291 51.4	N22 20.2	189 04.3	S13 34.4	273 51.2	N19 45.7	174 50.1	S14 42.5	Rasalhague	96 05.5	N12 33.3
07	54 48.9	306 50.6	20.0	204 05.4	34.9	288 53.1	45.5	189 52.6	42.5	Regulus	207 43.0	N11 53.7
F 08	69 51.4	321 49.8	19.7	219 06.6	35.4	303 55.0	45.4	204 55.0	42.5	Rigel	281 11.5	S 8 11.2
R 09	84 53.8	336 49.0 ..	19.4	234 07.7 ..	35.9	318 56.9 ..	45.3	219 57.4 ..	42.6	Rigil Kent.	139 50.5	S60 53.8
I 10	99 56.3	351 48.2	19.2	249 08.9	36.4	333 58.8	45.2	234 59.8	42.6	Sabik	102 11.4	S15 44.4
11	114 58.8	6 47.4	18.9	264 10.0	36.9	349 00.7	45.0	250 02.2	42.6			
D 12	130 01.2	21 46.6	N22 18.6	279 11.2	S13 37.4	4 02.6	N19 44.9	265 04.7	S14 42.6	Schedar	349 39.2	N56 36.9
A 13	145 03.7	36 45.8	18.4	294 12.3	37.9	19 04.4	44.8	280 07.1	42.6	Shaula	96 20.5	S37 06.7
Y 14	160 06.2	51 45.0	18.1	309 13.5	38.4	34 06.3	44.7	295 09.5	42.7	Sirius	258 33.3	S16 44.3
15	175 08.6	66 44.2 ..	17.8	324 14.7 ..	38.9	49 08.2 ..	44.5	310 11.9 ..	42.7	Spica	158 30.5	S11 14.2
16	190 11.1	81 43.3	17.6	339 15.8	39.4	64 10.1	44.4	325 14.3	42.7	Suhail	222 52.3	S43 29.6
17	205 13.6	96 42.5	17.3	354 17.0	39.9	79 12.0	44.3	340 16.8	42.7			
18	220 16.0	111 41.7	N22 17.0	9 18.1	S13 40.4	94 13.9	N19 44.2	355 19.2	S14 42.8	Vega	80 38.0	N38 48.2
19	235 18.5	126 40.9	16.7	24 19.3	40.9	109 15.8	44.0	10 21.6	42.8	Zuben'ubi	137 04.5	S16 06.0
20	250 20.9	141 40.1	16.5	39 20.4	41.4	124 17.7	43.9	25 24.0	42.8		SHA	Mer.Pass.
21	265 23.4	156 39.3 ..	16.2	54 21.6 ..	41.9	139 19.6 ..	43.8	40 26.4 ..	42.8		° ′	h m
22	280 25.9	171 38.5	15.9	69 22.7	42.4	154 21.5	43.7	55 28.9	42.9	Venus	253 43.2	10 32
23	295 28.3	186 37.7	15.6	84 23.9	42.9	169 23.4	43.5	70 31.3	42.9	Mars	149 56.8	17 25
										Jupiter	234 22.0	11 47
Mer. Pass.	h m 3 25.3	v −0.8	d 0.2	v 1.2	d 0.5	v 1.9	d 0.1	v 2.4	d 0.0	Saturn	135 04.9	18 23

UT	SUN GHA	Dec	MOON GHA	v	Dec	d	HP
d h	° '	° '	° '	'	° '	'	'
30 00	178 22.9	N18 34.4	147 14.6	15.2	N 4 40.0	9.3	54.1
01	193 23.0	33.8	161 48.8	15.3	4 30.7	9.4	54.1
02	208 23.0	33.2	176 23.1	15.2	4 21.3	9.3	54.1
03	223 23.0 ..	32.6	190 57.3	15.2	4 12.0	9.4	54.1
04	238 23.0	32.0	205 31.5	15.3	4 02.6	9.4	54.1
05	253 23.1	31.4	220 05.8	15.2	3 53.2	9.4	54.1
06	268 23.1	N18 30.8	234 40.0	15.2	N 3 43.8	9.4	54.2
W 07	283 23.1	30.2	249 14.2	15.3	3 34.4	9.5	54.2
E 08	298 23.1	29.6	263 48.5	15.2	3 24.9	9.5	54.2
D 09	313 23.2 ..	29.0	278 22.7	15.3	3 15.4	9.4	54.2
N 10	328 23.2	28.4	292 57.0	15.2	3 06.0	9.5	54.2
E 11	343 23.2	27.8	307 31.2	15.3	2 56.5	9.5	54.2
S 12	358 23.2	N18 27.2	322 05.5	15.2	N 2 47.0	9.6	54.2
D 13	13 23.3	26.6	336 39.7	15.3	2 37.4	9.5	54.2
A 14	28 23.3	26.0	351 14.0	15.2	2 27.9	9.6	54.2
Y 15	43 23.3 ..	25.4	5 48.2	15.2	2 18.3	9.5	54.2
16	58 23.3	24.8	20 22.4	15.3	2 08.8	9.6	54.3
17	73 23.4	24.2	34 56.7	15.2	1 59.2	9.6	54.3
18	88 23.4	N18 23.5	49 30.9	15.2	N 1 49.6	9.6	54.3
19	103 23.4	22.9	64 05.1	15.3	1 40.0	9.6	54.3
20	118 23.5	22.3	78 39.4	15.2	1 30.4	9.6	54.3
21	133 23.5	21.7	93 13.6	15.2	1 20.8	9.6	54.3
22	148 23.5	21.1	107 47.8	15.2	1 11.2	9.6	54.3
23	163 23.5	20.5	122 22.0	15.2	1 01.6	9.7	54.3
31 00	178 23.6	N18 19.9	136 56.2	15.2	N 0 51.9	9.6	54.4
01	193 23.6	19.3	151 30.4	15.1	0 42.3	9.7	54.4
02	208 23.6	18.6	166 04.5	15.1	0 32.6	9.6	54.4
03	223 23.7 ..	18.0	180 38.7	15.1	0 23.0	9.7	54.4
04	238 23.7	17.4	195 12.8	15.2	0 13.3	9.7	54.4
05	253 23.7	16.8	209 47.0	15.1	N 0 03.6	9.6	54.4
06	268 23.7	N18 16.2	224 21.1	15.1	S 0 06.0	9.7	54.4
T 07	283 23.8	15.6	238 55.2	15.1	0 15.7	9.7	54.5
H 08	298 23.8	15.0	253 29.3	15.1	0 25.4	9.7	54.5
U 09	313 23.8 ..	14.3	268 03.4	15.1	0 35.1	9.7	54.5
R 10	328 23.9	13.7	282 37.5	15.0	0 44.8	9.6	54.5
S 11	343 23.9	13.1	297 11.5	15.1	0 54.4	9.7	54.5
D 12	358 23.9	N18 12.5	311 45.6	15.0	S 1 04.1	9.7	54.5
A 13	13 24.0	11.9	326 19.6	15.0	1 13.8	9.7	54.5
Y 14	28 24.0	11.2	340 53.6	15.0	1 23.5	9.7	54.6
15	43 24.0 ..	10.6	355 27.6	15.0	1 33.2	9.7	54.6
16	58 24.1	10.0	10 01.6	14.9	1 42.9	9.6	54.6
17	73 24.1	09.4	24 35.5	14.9	1 52.5	9.7	54.6
18	88 24.1	N18 08.8	39 09.4	14.9	S 2 02.2	9.7	54.6
19	103 24.2	08.1	53 43.3	14.9	2 11.9	9.7	54.6
20	118 24.2	07.5	68 17.2	14.9	2 21.6	9.6	54.7
21	133 24.2 ..	06.9	82 51.1	14.8	2 31.2	9.7	54.7
22	148 24.3	06.3	97 24.9	14.8	2 40.9	9.6	54.7
23	163 24.3	05.6	111 58.7	14.8	2 50.5	9.7	54.7
1 00	178 24.3	N18 05.0	126 32.5	14.8	S 3 00.2	9.6	54.7
01	193 24.4	04.4	141 06.3	14.7	3 09.8	9.7	54.8
02	208 24.4	03.8	155 40.0	14.7	3 19.5	9.6	54.8
03	223 24.4 ..	03.1	170 13.7	14.7	3 29.1	9.6	54.8
04	238 24.5	02.5	184 47.4	14.7	3 38.7	9.6	54.8
05	253 24.5	01.9	199 21.1	14.6	3 48.3	9.6	54.8
06	268 24.6	N18 01.2	213 54.7	14.6	S 3 57.9	9.6	54.9
F 07	283 24.6	00.6	228 28.3	14.5	4 07.5	9.6	54.9
R 08	298 24.6	18 00.0	243 01.8	14.6	4 17.1	9.5	54.9
I 09	313 24.7	17 59.4	257 35.4	14.5	4 26.6	9.6	54.9
D 10	328 24.7	58.7	272 08.9	14.4	4 36.2	9.5	54.9
A 11	343 24.7	58.1	286 42.3	14.5	4 45.7	9.5	55.0
Y 12	358 24.8	N17 57.5	301 15.8	14.4	S 4 55.2	9.5	55.0
13	13 24.8	56.8	315 49.2	14.3	5 04.7	9.5	55.0
14	28 24.9	56.2	330 22.5	14.4	5 14.2	9.5	55.0
15	43 24.9 ..	55.6	344 55.9	14.3	5 23.7	9.4	55.0
16	58 24.9	54.9	359 29.2	14.2	5 33.2	9.4	55.1
17	73 25.0	54.3	14 02.4	14.2	5 42.6	9.4	55.1
18	88 25.0	N17 53.7	28 35.6	14.2	S 5 52.0	9.5	55.1
19	103 25.0	53.0	43 08.8	14.1	6 01.5	9.3	55.1
20	118 25.1	52.4	57 41.9	14.1	6 10.8	9.4	55.2
21	133 25.1 ..	51.8	72 15.0	14.1	6 20.2	9.4	55.2
22	148 25.2	51.1	86 48.1	14.0	6 29.6	9.3	55.2
23	163 25.2	50.5	101 21.1	14.0	S 6 38.9	9.3	55.2
	SD 15.8	d 0.6	SD 14.8		14.9		15.0

Lat.	Twilight Naut.	Civil	Sunrise	Moonrise 30	31	1	2
°	h m	h m	h m	h m	h m	h m	h m
N 72	☐	☐	☐	07 43	09 17	10 54	12 33
N 70	////	////	01 16	07 47	09 16	10 47	12 19
68	////	////	02 09	07 51	09 15	10 41	12 08
66	////	////	02 41	07 55	09 15	10 36	11 59
64	////	01 33	03 05	07 57	09 14	10 32	11 51
62	////	02 11	03 23	08 00	09 14	10 29	11 45
60	////	02 36	03 38	08 02	09 13	10 26	11 39
N 58	01 24	02 56	03 51	08 04	09 13	10 23	11 34
56	01 59	03 13	04 02	08 05	09 12	10 20	11 30
54	02 23	03 27	04 11	08 07	09 12	10 18	11 26
52	02 42	03 38	04 20	08 08	09 12	10 16	11 22
50	02 57	03 49	04 28	08 09	09 12	10 15	11 19
45	03 27	04 10	04 44	08 12	09 11	10 11	11 12
N 40	03 49	04 27	04 57	08 14	09 11	10 08	11 06
35	04 07	04 41	05 09	08 16	09 10	10 05	11 01
30	04 21	04 52	05 18	08 18	09 10	10 03	10 57
20	04 44	05 11	05 35	08 21	09 09	09 58	10 49
N 10	05 01	05 27	05 49	08 23	09 09	09 55	10 42
0	05 16	05 41	06 03	08 26	09 08	09 52	10 36
S 10	05 29	05 54	06 16	08 28	09 08	09 48	10 30
20	05 41	06 07	06 30	08 31	09 08	09 45	10 23
30	05 52	06 21	06 46	08 34	09 07	09 41	10 16
35	05 58	06 29	06 55	08 36	09 07	09 38	10 12
40	06 04	06 37	07 06	08 37	09 06	09 36	10 07
45	06 11	06 47	07 18	08 40	09 06	09 33	10 02
S 50	06 19	06 58	07 33	08 42	09 06	09 29	09 55
52	06 22	07 03	07 40	08 44	09 05	09 28	09 52
54	06 25	07 08	07 48	08 45	09 05	09 26	09 49
56	06 29	07 14	07 56	08 46	09 05	09 24	09 45
58	06 33	07 21	08 06	08 48	09 05	09 22	09 41
S 60	06 37	07 29	08 17	08 50	09 05	09 20	09 36

Lat.	Sunset	Twilight Civil	Naut.	Moonset 30	31	1	2
°	h m	h m	h m	h m	h m	h m	h m
N 72	☐	☐	☐	21 03	20 56	20 50	20 43
N 70	22 48	////	////	21 01	21 00	20 59	20 58
68	21 59	////	////	20 59	21 03	21 06	21 11
66	21 29	////	////	20 58	21 05	21 12	21 20
64	21 06	22 35	////	20 57	21 07	21 18	21 30
62	20 48	21 59	////	20 56	21 09	21 22	21 37
60	20 33	21 34	////	20 56	21 10	21 26	21 44
N 58	20 21	21 14	22 44	20 55	21 12	21 30	21 50
56	20 10	20 58	22 11	20 54	21 13	21 33	21 55
54	20 00	20 45	21 48	20 54	21 14	21 36	21 59
52	19 52	20 33	21 29	20 53	21 15	21 38	22 03
50	19 44	20 23	21 14	20 53	21 16	21 41	22 07
45	19 28	20 02	20 45	20 52	21 18	21 46	22 15
N 40	19 15	19 45	20 23	20 51	21 20	21 50	22 22
35	19 04	19 32	20 05	20 50	21 22	21 54	22 28
30	18 54	19 22	19 51	20 50	21 23	21 57	22 34
20	18 38	19 01	19 29	20 48	21 25	22 03	22 43
N 10	18 23	18 45	19 11	20 47	21 27	22 08	22 51
0	18 10	18 32	18 57	20 46	21 29	22 13	22 58
S 10	17 57	18 19	18 44	20 45	21 31	22 18	23 06
20	17 43	18 06	18 32	20 44	21 33	22 23	23 14
30	17 27	17 52	18 21	20 43	21 35	22 28	23 23
35	17 18	17 45	18 15	20 42	21 37	22 32	23 28
40	17 07	17 34	18 09	20 41	21 38	22 36	23 34
45	16 55	17 27	18 02	20 40	21 40	22 40	23 41
S 50	16 40	17 16	17 55	20 39	21 42	22 45	23 50
52	16 33	17 11	17 52	20 39	21 43	22 48	23 54
54	16 26	17 05	17 48	20 38	21 44	22 50	23 58
56	16 17	16 59	17 45	20 37	21 45	22 53	24 03
58	16 07	16 52	17 41	20 37	21 46	22 57	24 08
S 60	15 56	16 45	17 36	20 36	21 48	23 00	24 14

Day	SUN Eqn. of Time 00h	12h	Mer. Pass.	MOON Mer. Pass. Upper	Lower	Age	Phase
d	m s	m s	h m	h m	h m	d	%
30	06 28	06 27	12 06	14 36	02 15	04	11
31	06 26	06 24	12 06	15 19	02 57	05	18
1	06 23	06 21	12 06	16 02	03 40	06	26

UT	ARIES GHA	VENUS −3.8 GHA	Dec	MARS +0.4 GHA	Dec	JUPITER −1.8 GHA	Dec	SATURN +0.5 GHA	Dec	STARS Name	SHA	Dec
d h	° ′	° ′	° ′	° ′	° ′	° ′	° ′	° ′	° ′		° ′	° ′
2 00	310 30.8	201 36.9	N22 15.3	99 25.0	S13 43.4	184 25.2	N19 43.4	85 33.7	S14 42.9	Acamar	315 17.8	S40 14.6
01	325 33.3	216 36.1	15.1	114 26.2	43.9	199 27.1	43.3	100 36.1	42.9	Achernar	335 26.1	S57 09.5
02	340 35.7	231 35.3	14.8	129 27.3	44.4	214 29.0	43.2	115 38.5	43.0	Acrux	173 08.6	S63 11.0
03	355 38.2	246 34.5 ..	14.5	144 28.4 ..	44.9	229 30.9 ..	43.0	130 41.0 ..	43.0	Adhara	255 12.2	S28 59.6
04	10 40.7	261 33.7	14.2	159 29.6	45.4	244 32.8	42.9	145 43.4	43.0	Aldebaran	290 48.6	N16 32.1
05	25 43.1	276 32.9	13.9	174 30.7	45.9	259 34.7	42.8	160 45.8	43.0			
06	40 45.6	291 32.1	N22 13.6	189 31.9	S13 46.4	274 36.6	N19 42.6	175 48.2	S14 43.1	Alioth	166 20.3	N55 53.1
07	55 48.0	306 31.3	13.4	204 33.0	46.9	289 38.5	42.5	190 50.6	43.1	Alkaid	152 58.4	N49 14.8
S 08	70 50.5	321 30.4	13.1	219 34.2	47.4	304 40.4	42.4	205 53.0	43.1	Al Na'ir	27 42.4	S46 53.1
A 09	85 53.0	336 29.6 ..	12.8	234 35.3 ..	47.9	319 42.3 ..	42.3	220 55.5 ..	43.1	Alnilam	275 45.8	S 1 11.7
T 10	100 55.4	351 28.8	12.5	249 36.5	48.4	334 44.2	42.1	235 57.9	43.2	Alphard	217 55.6	S 8 43.4
U 11	115 57.9	6 28.0	12.2	264 37.6	48.9	349 46.0	42.0	251 00.3	43.2			
R 12	131 00.4	21 27.2	N22 11.9	279 38.7	S13 49.3	4 47.9	N19 41.9	266 02.7	S14 43.2	Alphecca	126 10.3	N26 40.3
D 13	146 02.8	36 26.4	11.6	294 39.9	49.8	19 49.8	41.8	281 05.1	43.2	Alpheratz	357 42.4	N29 10.3
A 14	161 05.3	51 25.6	11.3	309 41.0	50.3	34 51.7	41.6	296 07.5	43.3	Altair	62 07.1	N 8 54.7
Y 15	176 07.8	66 24.8 ..	11.0	324 42.2 ..	50.8	49 53.6 ..	41.5	311 10.0 ..	43.3	Ankaa	353 14.7	S42 13.3
16	191 10.2	81 24.0	10.7	339 43.3	51.3	64 55.5	41.4	326 12.4	43.3	Antares	112 25.1	S26 27.7
17	206 12.7	96 23.2	10.4	354 44.5	51.8	79 57.4	41.3	341 14.8	43.3			
18	221 15.2	111 22.4	N22 10.1	9 45.6	S13 52.3	94 59.3	N19 41.1	356 17.2	S14 43.4	Arcturus	145 55.1	N19 06.6
19	236 17.6	126 21.6	09.8	24 46.7	52.8	110 01.2	41.0	11 19.6	43.4	Atria	107 25.8	S69 03.2
20	251 20.1	141 20.8	09.5	39 47.9	53.3	125 03.1	40.9	26 22.0	43.4	Avior	234 18.3	S59 33.5
21	266 22.5	156 20.0 ..	09.2	54 49.0 ..	53.8	140 05.0 ..	40.8	41 24.4 ..	43.4	Bellatrix	278 31.4	N 6 21.6
22	281 25.0	171 19.2	08.9	69 50.2	54.3	155 06.9	40.6	56 26.9	43.5	Betelgeuse	271 00.7	N 7 24.4
23	296 27.5	186 18.4	08.6	84 51.3	54.8	170 08.7	40.5	71 29.3	43.5			
3 00	311 29.9	201 17.6	N22 08.3	99 52.4	S13 55.3	185 10.6	N19 40.4	86 31.7	S14 43.5	Canopus	263 56.2	S52 42.2
01	326 32.4	216 16.8	08.0	114 53.6	55.8	200 12.5	40.2	101 34.1	43.5	Capella	280 33.6	N46 00.4
02	341 34.9	231 16.0	07.7	129 54.7	56.3	215 14.4	40.1	116 36.5	43.6	Deneb	49 30.4	N45 20.2
03	356 37.3	246 15.2 ..	07.4	144 55.8 ..	56.8	230 16.3 ..	40.0	131 38.9 ..	43.6	Denebola	182 33.1	N14 29.5
04	11 39.8	261 14.4	07.0	159 57.0	57.3	245 18.2	39.9	146 41.3	43.6	Diphda	348 55.0	S17 54.2
05	26 42.3	276 13.6	06.7	174 58.1	57.8	260 20.1	39.7	161 43.8	43.6			
06	41 44.7	291 12.8	N22 06.4	189 59.2	S13 58.3	275 22.0	N19 39.6	176 46.2	S14 43.7	Dubhe	193 51.4	N61 40.5
07	56 47.2	306 12.0	06.1	205 00.4	58.8	290 23.9	39.5	191 48.6	43.7	Elnath	278 11.9	N28 36.9
S 08	71 49.7	321 11.2	05.8	220 01.5	59.3	305 25.8	39.4	206 51.0	43.7	Eltanin	90 45.4	N51 29.6
U 09	86 52.1	336 10.4 ..	05.5	235 02.6	13 59.8	320 27.7 ..	39.2	221 53.4 ..	43.7	Enif	33 46.0	N 9 56.7
N 10	101 54.6	351 09.6	05.2	250 03.8	14 00.3	335 29.6	39.1	236 55.8	43.8	Fomalhaut	15 22.8	S29 32.4
D 11	116 57.0	6 08.8	04.8	265 04.9	00.8	350 31.5	39.0	251 58.2	43.8			
A 12	131 59.5	21 08.0	N22 04.5	280 06.0	S14 01.3	5 33.3	N19 38.9	267 00.6	S14 43.8	Gacrux	172 00.2	S57 11.9
Y 13	147 02.0	36 07.2	04.2	295 07.2	01.8	20 35.2	38.7	282 03.1	43.8	Gienah	175 51.7	S17 37.4
14	162 04.4	51 06.4	03.9	310 08.3	02.3	35 37.1	38.6	297 05.5	43.9	Hadar	148 46.7	S60 26.8
15	177 06.9	66 05.6 ..	03.5	325 09.4 ..	02.8	50 39.0 ..	38.5	312 07.9 ..	43.9	Hamal	327 59.8	N23 31.8
16	192 09.4	81 04.8	03.2	340 10.6	03.3	65 40.9	38.3	327 10.3	43.9	Kaus Aust.	83 42.4	S34 22.5
17	207 11.8	96 04.0	02.9	355 11.7	03.8	80 42.8	38.2	342 12.7	44.0			
18	222 14.3	111 03.2	N22 02.6	10 12.8	S14 04.3	95 44.7	N19 38.1	357 15.1	S14 44.0	Kochab	137 20.1	N74 06.1
19	237 16.8	126 02.4	02.2	25 13.9	04.8	110 46.6	38.0	12 17.5	44.0	Markab	13 37.2	N15 17.2
20	252 19.2	141 01.6	01.9	40 15.1	05.3	125 48.5	37.8	27 19.9	44.0	Menkar	314 14.3	N 4 08.8
21	267 21.7	156 00.8 ..	01.6	55 16.2 ..	05.8	140 50.4 ..	37.7	42 22.3 ..	44.1	Menkent	148 06.6	S36 26.6
22	282 24.1	171 00.0	01.3	70 17.3	06.3	155 52.3	37.6	57 24.8	44.1	Miaplacidus	221 40.3	S69 46.8
23	297 26.6	185 59.2	00.9	85 18.5	06.8	170 54.2	37.5	72 27.2	44.1			
4 00	312 29.1	200 58.4	N22 00.6	100 19.6	S14 07.3	185 56.1	N19 37.3	87 29.6	S14 44.1	Mirfak	308 39.3	N49 54.5
01	327 31.5	215 57.6	22 00.2	115 20.7	07.8	200 57.9	37.2	102 32.0	44.2	Nunki	75 57.0	S26 16.5
02	342 34.0	230 56.8	21 59.9	130 21.8	08.3	215 59.8	37.1	117 34.4	44.2	Peacock	53 17.5	S56 41.0
03	357 36.5	245 56.0 ..	59.6	145 23.0 ..	08.8	231 01.7 ..	36.9	132 36.8 ..	44.2	Pollux	243 27.1	N27 59.3
04	12 38.9	260 55.2	59.2	160 24.1	09.3	246 03.6	36.8	147 39.2	44.2	Procyon	244 59.2	N 5 11.1
05	27 41.4	275 54.4	58.9	175 25.2	09.8	261 05.5	36.7	162 41.6	44.3			
06	42 43.9	290 53.6	N21 58.6	190 26.3	S14 10.3	276 07.4	N19 36.6	177 44.0	S14 44.3	Rasalhague	96 05.5	N12 33.3
07	57 46.3	305 52.8	58.2	205 27.5	10.8	291 09.3	36.4	192 46.4	44.3	Regulus	207 43.0	N11 53.7
08	72 48.8	320 52.0	57.9	220 28.6	11.3	306 11.2	36.3	207 48.9	44.4	Rigel	281 11.5	S 8 11.2
M 09	87 51.3	335 51.2 ..	57.5	235 29.7 ..	11.8	321 13.1 ..	36.2	222 51.3 ..	44.4	Rigil Kent.	139 50.5	S60 53.8
O 10	102 53.7	350 50.4	57.2	250 30.8	12.3	336 15.0	36.1	237 53.7	44.4	Sabik	102 11.4	S15 44.4
N 11	117 56.2	5 49.6	56.8	265 31.9	12.8	351 16.9	35.9	252 56.1	44.4			
D 12	132 58.6	20 48.8	N21 56.5	280 33.1	S14 13.3	6 18.8	N19 35.8	267 58.5	S14 44.5	Schedar	349 39.2	N56 36.9
A 13	148 01.1	35 48.1	56.1	295 34.2	13.8	21 20.7	35.7	283 00.9	44.5	Shaula	96 20.5	S37 06.7
Y 14	163 03.6	50 47.3	55.8	310 35.3	14.3	36 22.6	35.5	298 03.3	44.5	Sirius	258 33.3	S16 44.2
15	178 06.0	65 46.5 ..	55.4	325 36.4 ..	14.8	51 24.4 ..	35.4	313 05.7 ..	44.5	Spica	158 30.5	S11 14.2
16	193 08.5	80 45.7	55.1	340 37.5	15.3	66 26.3	35.3	328 08.1	44.6	Suhail	222 52.3	S43 29.6
17	208 11.0	95 44.9	54.7	355 38.7	15.8	81 28.2	35.2	343 10.5	44.6			
18	223 13.4	110 44.1	N21 54.4	10 39.8	S14 16.3	96 30.1	N19 35.0	358 12.9	S14 44.6	Vega	80 38.0	N38 48.2
19	238 15.9	125 43.3	54.0	25 40.9	16.8	111 32.0	34.9	13 15.3	44.7	Zuben'ubi	137 04.5	S16 06.0
20	253 18.4	140 42.5	53.7	40 42.0	17.3	126 33.9	34.8	28 17.8	44.7			
21	268 20.8	155 41.7 ..	53.3	55 43.1 ..	17.8	141 35.8 ..	34.7	43 20.2 ..	44.7			
22	283 23.3	170 40.9	53.0	70 44.2	18.2	156 37.7	34.5	58 22.6	44.7			
23	298 25.8	185 40.1	52.6	85 45.4	18.7	171 39.6	34.4	73 25.0	44.8			
	h m											
Mer.Pass.	3 13.5	v −0.8	d 0.3	v 1.1	d 0.5	v 1.9	d 0.1	v 2.4	d 0.0			

	SHA	Mer. Pass.
	° ′	h m
Venus	249 47.7	10 35
Mars	148 22.5	17 19
Jupiter	233 40.7	11 38
Saturn	135 01.7	18 11

SUN / MOON

UT (d h)	SUN GHA	SUN Dec	MOON GHA	v	MOON Dec	d	HP
2 00	178 25.3	N17 49.8	115 54.1	13.9	S 6 48.2	9.3	55.2
01	193 25.3	49.2	130 27.0	13.9	6 57.5	9.2	55.3
02	208 25.4	48.6	144 59.9	13.8	7 06.7	9.3	55.3
03	223 25.4	.. 47.9	159 32.7	13.8	7 16.0	9.2	55.3
04	238 25.4	47.3	174 05.5	13.8	7 25.2	9.2	55.3
05	253 25.5	46.7	188 38.3	13.7	7 34.4	9.1	55.4
S 06	268 25.5	N17 46.0	203 11.0	13.6	S 7 43.5	9.2	55.4
A 07	283 25.6	45.4	217 43.6	13.6	7 52.7	9.1	55.4
T 08	298 25.6	44.7	232 16.2	13.6	8 01.8	9.1	55.4
U 09	313 25.7	.. 44.1	246 48.8	13.5	8 10.9	9.0	55.5
R 10	328 25.7	43.4	261 21.3	13.5	8 19.9	9.0	55.5
D 11	343 25.8	42.8	275 53.8	13.4	8 28.9	9.0	55.5
A 12	358 25.8	N17 42.2	290 26.2	13.3	S 8 37.9	9.0	55.6
Y 13	13 25.8	41.5	304 58.5	13.3	8 46.9	8.9	55.6
14	28 25.9	40.9	319 30.8	13.3	8 55.8	8.9	55.6
15	43 25.9	.. 40.2	334 03.1	13.2	9 04.7	8.9	55.6
16	58 26.0	39.6	348 35.3	13.1	9 13.6	8.8	55.7
17	73 26.0	38.9	3 07.4	13.1	9 22.4	8.8	55.7
18	88 26.1	N17 38.3	17 39.5	13.1	S 9 31.2	8.7	55.7
19	103 26.1	37.6	32 11.6	12.9	9 39.9	8.8	55.7
20	118 26.2	37.0	46 43.5	12.9	9 48.7	8.7	55.8
21	133 26.2	.. 36.3	61 15.4	12.9	9 57.4	8.6	55.8
22	148 26.3	35.7	75 47.3	12.8	10 06.0	8.6	55.8
23	163 26.3	35.0	90 19.1	12.8	10 14.6	8.6	55.9
3 00	178 26.4	N17 34.4	104 50.9	12.6	S10 23.2	8.5	55.9
01	193 26.4	33.7	119 22.5	12.7	10 31.7	8.5	55.9
02	208 26.5	33.1	133 54.2	12.5	10 40.2	8.4	56.0
03	223 26.5	.. 32.4	148 25.7	12.5	10 48.6	8.5	56.0
04	238 26.6	31.8	162 57.2	12.5	10 57.1	8.3	56.0
05	253 26.6	31.1	177 28.7	12.3	11 05.4	8.3	56.0
S 06	268 26.7	N17 30.5	192 00.0	12.3	S11 13.7	8.3	56.1
U 07	283 26.7	29.8	206 31.3	12.3	11 22.0	8.2	56.1
N 08	298 26.8	29.2	221 02.6	12.2	11 30.2	8.2	56.1
D 09	313 26.8	.. 28.5	235 33.8	12.1	11 38.4	8.1	56.2
A 10	328 26.9	27.9	250 04.9	12.0	11 46.5	8.1	56.2
Y 11	343 26.9	27.2	264 35.9	12.0	11 54.6	8.1	56.2
12	358 27.0	N17 26.6	279 06.9	11.9	S12 02.7	8.0	56.3
13	13 27.0	25.9	293 37.8	11.9	12 10.7	7.9	56.3
14	28 27.1	25.3	308 08.7	11.8	12 18.6	7.9	56.3
15	43 27.1	.. 24.6	322 39.5	11.7	12 26.5	7.8	56.4
16	58 27.2	23.9	337 10.2	11.6	12 34.3	7.8	56.4
17	73 27.2	23.3	351 40.8	11.6	12 42.1	7.7	56.4
18	88 27.3	N17 22.6	6 11.4	11.5	S12 49.8	7.7	56.5
19	103 27.3	22.0	20 41.9	11.5	12 57.5	7.6	56.5
20	118 27.4	21.3	35 12.4	11.3	13 05.1	7.5	56.5
21	133 27.4	.. 20.6	49 42.7	11.3	13 12.6	7.5	56.6
22	148 27.5	20.0	64 13.0	11.2	13 20.1	7.5	56.6
23	163 27.5	19.3	78 43.2	11.2	13 27.6	7.4	56.6
4 00	178 27.6	N17 18.7	93 13.4	11.0	S13 35.0	7.3	56.7
01	193 27.7	18.0	107 43.4	11.0	13 42.3	7.2	56.7
02	208 27.7	17.3	122 13.4	11.0	13 49.5	7.2	56.7
03	223 27.8	.. 16.7	136 43.4	10.8	13 56.7	7.2	56.8
04	238 27.8	16.0	151 13.2	10.8	14 03.9	7.0	56.8
05	253 27.9	15.3	165 43.0	10.7	14 10.9	7.0	56.8
M 06	268 27.9	N17 14.7	180 12.7	10.6	S14 17.9	7.0	56.9
O 07	283 28.0	14.0	194 42.3	10.6	14 24.9	6.8	56.9
N 08	298 28.1	13.4	209 11.9	10.5	14 31.7	6.8	56.9
D 09	313 28.1	.. 12.7	223 41.4	10.4	14 38.5	6.7	57.0
A 10	328 28.2	12.0	238 10.8	10.3	14 45.3	6.6	57.0
Y 11	343 28.2	11.4	252 40.1	10.2	14 51.9	6.6	57.1
12	358 28.3	N17 10.7	267 09.3	10.2	S14 58.5	6.5	57.1
13	13 28.3	10.0	281 38.5	10.1	15 05.0	6.5	57.1
14	28 28.4	09.4	296 07.6	10.0	15 11.5	6.4	57.2
15	43 28.5	.. 08.7	310 36.6	9.9	15 17.9	6.3	57.2
16	58 28.5	08.0	325 05.5	9.9	15 24.2	6.2	57.2
17	73 28.6	07.4	339 34.4	9.8	15 30.4	6.1	57.3
18	88 28.6	N17 06.7	354 03.2	9.7	S15 36.5	6.1	57.3
19	103 28.7	06.0	8 31.9	9.6	15 42.6	6.0	57.4
20	118 28.8	05.3	23 00.5	9.6	15 48.6	5.9	57.4
21	133 28.8	.. 04.7	37 29.1	9.4	15 54.5	5.8	57.4
22	148 28.9	04.0	51 57.5	9.4	16 00.3	5.8	57.5
23	163 28.9	03.3	66 25.9	9.3	S16 06.1	5.7	57.5
	SD 15.8	d 0.7	SD 15.1		15.3		15.6

Moonrise

Lat.	Twilight Naut.	Twilight Civil	Sunrise	Moonrise 2	3	4	5
N 72	▭	▭	▭	12 33	14 20	16 16	18 44
N 70	////	////	01 42	12 19	13 56	15 37	17 20
68	////	////	02 25	12 08	13 38	15 11	16 41
66	////	00 52	02 53	11 59	13 24	14 50	16 14
64	////	01 50	03 14	11 51	13 12	14 34	15 53
62	////	02 23	03 31	11 45	13 02	14 21	15 37
60	00 47	02 46	03 45	11 39	12 54	14 09	15 23
N 58	01 40	03 04	03 57	11 34	12 47	14 00	15 11
56	02 09	03 20	04 07	11 30	12 40	13 51	15 01
54	02 31	03 33	04 17	11 26	12 34	13 43	14 52
52	02 49	03 44	04 25	11 22	12 29	13 37	14 44
50	03 03	03 54	04 32	11 19	12 24	13 31	14 37
45	03 32	04 14	04 47	11 12	12 14	13 17	14 21
N 40	03 53	04 30	05 00	11 06	12 06	13 07	14 08
35	04 10	04 43	05 11	11 01	11 58	12 57	13 58
30	04 23	04 54	05 20	10 57	11 52	12 49	13 48
20	04 45	05 13	05 36	10 49	11 41	12 36	13 32
N 10	05 02	05 28	05 50	10 42	11 32	12 24	13 18
0	05 16	05 41	06 03	10 36	11 23	12 12	13 05
S 10	05 28	05 53	06 15	10 30	11 14	12 01	12 52
20	05 39	06 06	06 29	10 23	11 05	11 49	12 38
30	05 50	06 19	06 44	10 16	10 54	11 36	12 22
35	05 56	06 26	06 53	10 12	10 48	11 28	12 13
40	06 02	06 34	07 03	10 07	10 41	11 19	12 03
45	06 08	06 43	07 15	10 02	10 33	11 09	11 51
S 50	06 15	06 54	07 29	09 55	10 23	10 56	11 36
52	06 18	06 58	07 35	09 52	10 19	10 51	11 29
54	06 21	07 04	07 42	09 49	10 14	10 44	11 21
56	06 24	07 09	07 51	09 45	10 09	10 37	11 13
58	06 28	07 15	08 00	09 41	10 03	10 29	11 03
S 60	06 32	07 22	08 10	09 36	09 56	10 20	10 52

Moonset

Lat.	Sunset	Twilight Civil	Twilight Naut.	Moonset 2	3	4	5
N 72	▭	▭	▭	20 43	20 34	20 22	19 45
N 70	22 24	////	////	20 58	20 59	21 01	21 10
68	21 44	////	////	21 11	21 18	21 29	21 49
66	21 17	23 10	////	21 21	21 33	21 50	22 17
64	20 56	22 17	////	21 30	21 45	22 07	22 38
62	20 39	21 47	////	21 37	21 56	22 21	22 55
60	20 26	21 24	23 16	21 44	22 05	22 32	23 09
N 58	20 14	21 06	22 28	21 50	22 13	22 43	23 21
56	20 04	20 51	22 00	21 55	22 20	22 52	23 31
54	19 55	20 38	21 39	21 59	22 27	23 00	23 41
52	19 47	20 27	21 22	22 03	22 32	23 07	23 49
50	19 40	20 18	21 07	22 07	22 38	23 13	23 56
45	19 24	19 58	20 40	22 15	22 49	23 27	24 12
N 40	19 12	19 42	20 19	22 22	22 58	23 39	24 25
35	19 01	19 29	20 02	22 28	23 06	23 48	24 37
30	18 52	19 18	19 49	22 34	23 13	23 57	24 46
20	18 36	18 59	19 27	22 43	23 25	24 12	00 12
N 10	18 22	18 44	19 10	22 51	23 36	24 25	00 25
0	18 10	18 31	18 54	22 58	23 46	24 37	00 37
S 10	17 57	18 19	18 44	23 06	23 56	24 49	00 49
20	17 44	18 07	18 33	23 14	24 07	00 07	01 02
30	17 29	17 54	18 22	23 23	24 19	00 19	01 17
35	17 20	17 47	18 11	23 28	24 26	00 26	01 26
40	17 10	17 39	18 11	23 34	24 35	00 35	01 36
45	16 58	17 30	18 05	23 41	24 44	00 44	01 48
S 50	16 44	17 19	17 58	23 50	24 56	00 56	02 02
52	16 38	17 15	17 55	23 54	25 01	01 01	02 08
54	16 31	17 10	17 52	23 58	25 07	01 07	02 16
56	16 22	17 04	17 49	24 03	00 03	01 14	02 24
58	16 13	16 58	17 46	24 08	00 08	01 21	02 33
S 60	16 03	16 51	17 42	24 14	00 14	01 29	02 44

SUN / MOON

Day	SUN Eqn. of Time 00h	12h	SUN Mer. Pass.	MOON Mer. Pass. Upper	Lower	Age	Phase
	m s	m s	h m	h m	h m	d	%
2	06 19	06 17	12 06	16 47	04 24	07	35
3	06 15	06 12	12 06	17 34	05 10	08	45
4	06 10	06 07	12 06	18 25	05 59	09	55

UT	ARIES	VENUS −3.8		MARS +0.5		JUPITER −1.8		SATURN +0.5		STARS		
	GHA	GHA	Dec	GHA	Dec	GHA	Dec	GHA	Dec	Name	SHA	Dec
d h	° ′	° ′	° ′	° ′	° ′	° ′	° ′	° ′	° ′		° ′	° ′
5 00	313 28.2	200 39.3	N21 52.2	100 46.5	S14 19.2	186 41.5	N19 34.3	88 27.4	S14 44.8	Acamar	315 17.8	S40 14.6
01	328 30.7	215 38.5	51.9	115 47.6	19.7	201 43.4	34.1	103 29.8	44.8	Achernar	335 26.1	S57 09.5
02	343 33.1	230 37.7	51.5	130 48.7	20.2	216 45.3	34.0	118 32.2	44.8	Acrux	173 08.6	S63 11.0
03	358 35.6	245 36.9 ..	51.2	145 49.8 ..	20.7	231 47.2 ..	33.9	133 34.6 ..	44.9	Adhara	255 12.2	S28 59.6
04	13 38.1	260 36.1	50.8	160 50.9	21.2	246 49.1	33.8	148 37.0	44.9	Aldebaran	290 48.6	N16 32.1
05	28 40.5	275 35.4	50.4	175 52.1	21.7	261 51.0	33.6	163 39.4	44.9			
06	43 43.0	290 34.6	N21 50.1	190 53.2	S14 22.2	276 52.9	N19 33.5	178 41.8	S14 45.0	Alioth	166 20.4	N55 53.1
07	58 45.5	305 33.8	49.7	205 54.3	22.7	291 54.7	33.4	193 44.2	45.0	Alkaid	152 58.5	N49 14.8
T 08	73 47.9	320 33.0	49.3	220 55.4	23.2	306 56.6	33.2	208 46.6	45.0	Al Na'ir	27 42.3	S46 53.1
U 09	88 50.4	335 32.2 ..	48.9	235 56.5 ..	23.7	321 58.5 ..	33.1	223 49.0 ..	45.0	Alnilam	275 45.8	S 1 11.7
E 10	103 52.9	350 31.4	48.6	250 57.6	24.2	337 00.4	33.0	238 51.4	45.1	Alphard	217 55.6	S 8 43.4
S 11	118 55.3	5 30.6	48.2	265 58.7	24.7	352 02.3	32.9	253 53.8	45.1			
D 12	133 57.8	20 29.8	N21 47.8	280 59.8	S14 25.2	7 04.2	N19 32.7	268 56.2	S14 45.1	Alphecca	126 10.3	N26 40.3
A 13	149 00.2	35 29.0	47.5	296 00.9	25.7	22 06.1	32.6	283 58.6	45.2	Alpheratz	357 42.4	N29 10.3
Y 14	164 02.7	50 28.2	47.1	311 02.0	26.2	37 08.0	32.5	299 01.1	45.2	Altair	62 07.1	N 8 54.7
15	179 05.2	65 27.5 ..	46.7	326 03.2 ..	26.7	52 09.9 ..	32.4	314 03.5 ..	45.2	Ankaa	353 14.7	S42 13.3
16	194 07.6	80 26.7	46.3	341 04.3	27.2	67 11.8	32.2	329 05.9	45.2	Antares	112 25.1	S26 27.7
17	209 10.1	95 25.9	45.9	356 05.4	27.7	82 13.7	32.1	344 08.3	45.3			
18	224 12.6	110 25.1	N21 45.6	11 06.5	S14 28.2	97 15.6	N19 32.0	359 10.7	S14 45.3	Arcturus	145 55.1	N19 06.6
19	239 15.0	125 24.3	45.2	26 07.6	28.7	112 17.5	31.8	14 13.1	45.3	Atria	107 25.8	S69 03.3
20	254 17.5	140 23.5	44.8	41 08.7	29.2	127 19.4	31.7	29 15.5	45.4	Avior	234 18.3	S59 33.5
21	269 20.0	155 22.7 ..	44.4	56 09.8 ..	29.7	142 21.3 ..	31.6	44 17.9 ..	45.4	Bellatrix	278 31.4	N 6 21.6
22	284 22.4	170 21.9	44.0	71 10.9	30.2	157 23.2	31.5	59 20.3	45.4	Betelgeuse	271 00.7	N 7 24.4
23	299 24.9	185 21.1	43.7	86 12.0	30.7	172 25.1	31.3	74 22.7	45.4			
6 00	314 27.4	200 20.4	N21 43.3	101 13.1	S14 31.2	187 27.0	N19 31.2	89 25.1	S14 45.5	Canopus	263 56.2	S52 42.2
01	329 29.8	215 19.6	42.9	116 14.2	31.7	202 28.8	31.1	104 27.5	45.5	Capella	280 33.5	N46 00.4
02	344 32.3	230 18.8	42.5	131 15.3	32.2	217 30.7	30.9	119 29.9	45.5	Deneb	49 30.4	N45 20.2
03	359 34.7	245 18.0 ..	42.1	146 16.4 ..	32.7	232 32.6 ..	30.8	134 32.3 ..	45.6	Denebola	182 33.1	N14 29.5
04	14 37.2	260 17.2	41.7	161 17.5	33.2	247 34.5	30.7	149 34.7	45.6	Diphda	348 54.9	S17 54.2
05	29 39.7	275 16.4	41.3	176 18.6	33.7	262 36.4	30.6	164 37.1	45.6			
06	44 42.1	290 15.6	N21 40.9	191 19.7	S14 34.2	277 38.3	N19 30.4	179 39.5	S14 45.6	Dubhe	193 51.4	N61 40.4
07	59 44.6	305 14.8	40.5	206 20.8	34.7	292 40.2	30.3	194 41.9	45.7	Elnath	278 11.8	N28 36.9
W 08	74 47.1	320 14.1	40.1	221 21.9	35.2	307 42.1	30.2	209 44.3	45.7	Eltanin	90 45.4	N51 29.6
E 09	89 49.5	335 13.3 ..	39.7	236 23.0 ..	35.7	322 44.0 ..	30.0	224 46.7 ..	45.7	Enif	33 46.0	N 9 56.8
D 10	104 52.0	350 12.5	39.3	251 24.1	36.2	337 45.9	29.9	239 49.1	45.8	Fomalhaut	15 22.8	S29 32.4
N 11	119 54.5	5 11.7	38.9	266 25.2	36.7	352 47.8	29.8	254 51.5	45.8			
E 12	134 56.9	20 10.9	N21 38.5	281 26.3	S14 37.2	7 49.7	N19 29.7	269 53.9	S14 45.8	Gacrux	172 00.2	S57 11.9
S 13	149 59.4	35 10.1	38.1	296 27.4	37.7	22 51.6	29.5	284 56.3	45.8	Gienah	175 51.7	S17 37.4
D 14	165 01.9	50 09.4	37.7	311 28.5	38.2	37 53.5	29.4	299 58.7	45.9	Hadar	148 46.8	S60 26.8
A 15	180 04.3	65 08.6 ..	37.3	326 29.6 ..	38.6	52 55.4 ..	29.3	315 01.1 ..	45.9	Hamal	327 59.8	N23 31.8
Y 16	195 06.8	80 07.8	36.9	341 30.7	39.1	67 57.3	29.1	330 03.5	45.9	Kaus Aust.	83 42.4	S34 22.5
17	210 09.2	95 07.0	36.5	356 31.8	39.6	82 59.2	29.0	345 05.9	46.0			
18	225 11.7	110 06.2	N21 36.1	11 32.9	S14 40.1	98 01.1	N19 28.9	0 08.3	S14 46.0	Kochab	137 20.2	N74 06.1
19	240 14.2	125 05.4	35.7	26 34.0	40.6	113 03.0	28.8	15 10.7	46.0	Markab	13 37.2	N15 17.2
20	255 16.6	140 04.7	35.3	41 35.1	41.1	128 04.9	28.6	30 13.1	46.1	Menkar	314 14.2	N 4 08.8
21	270 19.1	155 03.9 ..	34.9	56 36.2 ..	41.6	143 06.8 ..	28.5	45 15.5 ..	46.1	Menkent	148 06.6	S36 26.5
22	285 21.6	170 03.1	34.5	71 37.3	42.1	158 08.6	28.4	60 17.9	46.1	Miaplacidus	221 40.3	S69 46.8
23	300 24.0	185 02.3	34.1	86 38.4	42.6	173 10.5	28.2	75 20.3	46.1			
7 00	315 26.5	200 01.5	N21 33.7	101 39.5	S14 43.1	188 12.4	N19 28.1	90 22.7	S14 46.2	Mirfak	308 39.2	N49 54.5
01	330 29.0	215 00.7	33.2	116 40.6	43.6	203 14.3	28.0	105 25.1	46.2	Nunki	75 57.0	S26 16.5
02	345 31.4	230 00.0	32.8	131 41.7	44.1	218 16.2	27.9	120 27.5	46.2	Peacock	53 17.5	S56 41.0
03	0 33.9	244 59.2 ..	32.4	146 42.8 ..	44.6	233 18.1 ..	27.7	135 29.9 ..	46.3	Pollux	243 27.1	N27 59.3
04	15 36.4	259 58.4	32.0	161 43.9	45.1	248 20.0	27.6	150 32.3	46.3	Procyon	244 59.2	N 5 11.1
05	30 38.8	274 57.6	31.6	176 45.0	45.6	263 21.9	27.5	165 34.7	46.3			
06	45 41.3	289 56.8	N21 31.2	191 46.0	S14 46.1	278 23.8	N19 27.3	180 37.1	S14 46.4	Rasalhague	96 05.5	N12 33.3
07	60 43.7	304 56.1	30.7	206 47.1	46.6	293 25.7	27.2	195 39.5	46.4	Regulus	207 43.0	N11 53.7
T 08	75 46.2	319 55.3	30.3	221 48.2	47.1	308 27.6	27.1	210 41.9	46.4	Rigel	281 11.5	S 8 11.1
H 09	90 48.7	334 54.5 ..	29.9	236 49.3 ..	47.6	323 29.5 ..	27.0	225 44.3 ..	46.4	Rigil Kent.	139 50.6	S60 53.8
U 10	105 51.1	349 53.7	29.5	251 50.4	48.1	338 31.4	26.8	240 46.7	46.5	Sabik	102 11.4	S15 44.4
R 11	120 53.6	4 52.9	29.0	266 51.5	48.6	353 33.3	26.7	255 49.1	46.5			
S 12	135 56.1	19 52.2	N21 28.6	281 52.6	S14 49.1	8 35.2	N19 26.6	270 51.5	S14 46.5	Schedar	349 39.2	N56 36.9
D 13	150 58.5	34 51.4	28.2	296 53.7	49.6	23 37.1	26.4	285 53.9	46.6	Shaula	96 20.5	S37 06.7
A 14	166 01.0	49 50.6	27.8	311 54.8	50.1	38 39.0	26.3	300 56.3	46.6	Sirius	258 33.5	S16 44.2
Y 15	181 03.5	64 49.8 ..	27.3	326 55.9 ..	50.6	53 40.9 ..	26.2	315 58.7 ..	46.6	Spica	158 30.5	S11 14.2
16	196 05.9	79 49.0	26.9	341 56.9	51.1	68 42.8	26.1	331 01.0	46.7	Suhail	222 52.3	S43 29.6
17	211 08.4	94 48.3	26.5	356 58.0	51.6	83 44.7	25.9	346 03.4	46.7			
18	226 10.8	109 47.5	N21 26.0	11 59.1	S14 52.1	98 46.6	N19 25.8	1 05.8	S14 46.7	Vega	80 38.1	N38 48.2
19	241 13.3	124 46.7	25.6	27 00.2	52.6	113 48.5	25.7	16 08.2	46.7	Zuben'ubi	137 04.5	S16 06.0
20	256 15.8	139 45.9	25.2	42 01.3	53.1	128 50.4	25.5	31 10.6	46.8		SHA	Mer. Pass.
21	271 18.2	154 45.2 ..	24.7	57 02.4 ..	53.5	143 52.3 ..	25.4	46 13.0 ..	46.8		° ′	h m
22	286 20.7	169 44.4	24.3	72 03.5	54.0	158 54.2	25.3	61 15.4	46.8	Venus	245 53.0	10 39
23	301 23.2	184 43.6	23.9	87 04.5	54.5	173 56.1	25.2	76 17.8	46.9	Mars	146 45.8	17 14
	h m									Jupiter	232 59.6	11 29
Mer. Pass. 3 01.7		v −0.8	d 0.4	v 1.1	d 0.5	v 1.9	d 0.1	v 2.4	d 0.0	Saturn	134 57.7	17 59

SUN and MOON

UT (d h)	SUN GHA	Dec	MOON GHA	v	Dec	d	HP
5 00	178 29.0	N17 02.7	80 54.2	9.2	S16 11.8	5.5	57.5
01	193 29.1	02.0	95 22.4	9.2	16 17.3	5.5	57.6
02	208 29.1	01.3	109 50.6	9.1	16 22.8	5.5	57.6
03	223 29.2	.. 00.6	124 18.7	9.0	16 28.3	5.3	57.7
04	238 29.3	17 00.0	138 46.7	8.9	16 33.6	5.2	57.7
05	253 29.3	16 59.3	153 14.6	8.8	16 38.8	5.2	57.7
T 06	268 29.4	N16 58.6	167 42.4	8.8	S16 44.0	5.0	57.8
U 07	283 29.4	57.9	182 10.2	8.6	16 49.0	5.0	57.8
E 08	298 29.5	57.3	196 37.8	8.6	16 54.0	4.9	57.9
S 09	313 29.6	.. 56.6	211 05.4	8.6	16 58.9	4.8	57.9
D 10	328 29.6	55.9	225 33.0	8.4	17 03.7	4.7	57.9
A 11	343 29.7	55.2	240 00.4	8.4	17 08.4	4.6	58.0
Y 12	358 29.8	N16 54.5	254 27.8	8.2	S17 13.0	4.5	58.0
13	13 29.8	53.9	268 55.0	8.3	17 17.5	4.4	58.1
14	28 29.9	53.2	283 22.3	8.1	17 21.9	4.3	58.1
15	43 30.0	.. 52.5	297 49.4	8.0	17 26.2	4.2	58.1
16	58 30.0	51.8	312 16.4	8.0	17 30.4	4.1	58.2
17	73 30.1	51.1	326 43.4	7.9	17 34.5	4.1	58.2
18	88 30.2	N16 50.5	341 10.3	7.8	S17 38.6	3.9	58.2
19	103 30.2	49.8	355 37.1	7.8	17 42.5	3.8	58.3
20	118 30.3	49.1	10 03.9	7.6	17 46.3	3.7	58.3
21	133 30.4	.. 48.4	24 30.5	7.6	17 50.0	3.6	58.4
22	148 30.4	47.7	38 57.1	7.6	17 53.6	3.5	58.4
23	163 30.5	47.0	53 23.7	7.4	17 57.1	3.4	58.4
6 00	178 30.6	N16 46.4	67 50.1	7.4	S18 00.5	3.3	58.5
01	193 30.6	45.7	82 16.5	7.3	18 03.8	3.2	58.5
02	208 30.7	45.0	96 42.8	7.2	18 07.0	3.1	58.6
03	223 30.8	.. 44.3	111 09.0	7.2	18 10.1	2.9	58.6
04	238 30.8	43.6	125 35.2	7.1	18 13.0	2.9	58.6
05	253 30.9	42.9	140 01.3	7.0	18 15.9	2.7	58.7
W 06	268 31.0	N16 42.3	154 27.3	6.9	S18 18.6	2.7	58.7
E 07	283 31.0	41.6	168 53.2	6.9	18 21.3	2.5	58.8
D 08	298 31.1	40.9	183 19.1	6.8	18 23.8	2.4	58.8
N 09	313 31.2	.. 40.2	197 44.9	6.7	18 26.2	2.3	58.8
E 10	328 31.3	39.5	212 10.6	6.7	18 28.5	2.2	58.9
S 11	343 31.3	38.8	226 36.3	6.6	18 30.7	2.1	58.9
D 12	358 31.4	N16 38.1	241 01.9	6.6	S18 32.8	1.9	59.0
A 13	13 31.5	37.4	255 27.5	6.4	18 34.7	1.8	59.0
Y 14	28 31.5	36.7	269 52.9	6.4	18 36.5	1.8	59.0
15	43 31.6	.. 36.0	284 18.3	6.4	18 38.3	1.6	59.1
16	58 31.7	35.4	298 43.7	6.3	18 39.9	1.4	59.1
17	73 31.8	34.7	313 09.0	6.2	18 41.3	1.4	59.2
18	88 31.8	N16 34.0	327 34.2	6.1	S18 42.7	1.2	59.2
19	103 31.9	33.3	341 59.3	6.1	18 43.9	1.1	59.2
20	118 32.0	32.6	356 24.4	6.1	18 45.0	1.0	59.3
21	133 32.0	.. 31.9	10 49.5	6.0	18 46.0	0.9	59.3
22	148 32.1	31.2	25 14.5	5.9	18 46.9	0.8	59.3
23	163 32.2	30.5	39 39.4	5.9	18 47.7	0.6	59.4
7 00	178 32.3	N16 29.8	54 04.3	5.8	S18 48.3	0.5	59.4
01	193 32.3	29.1	68 29.1	5.8	18 48.8	0.3	59.5
02	208 32.4	28.4	82 53.9	5.7	18 49.1	0.3	59.5
03	223 32.5	.. 27.7	97 18.6	5.6	18 49.4	0.1	59.5
04	238 32.6	27.0	111 43.2	5.6	18 49.5	0.0	59.6
05	253 32.6	26.3	126 07.8	5.6	18 49.5	0.1	59.6
T 06	268 32.7	N16 25.6	140 32.4	5.5	S18 49.4	0.3	59.6
H 07	283 32.8	24.9	154 56.9	5.5	18 49.1	0.4	59.7
U 08	298 32.9	24.2	169 21.4	5.4	18 48.7	0.5	59.7
R 09	313 32.9	.. 23.5	183 45.8	5.4	18 48.2	0.5	59.8
S 10	328 33.0	22.8	198 10.2	5.3	18 47.6	0.8	59.8
D 11	343 33.1	22.1	212 34.5	5.3	18 46.8	0.9	59.8
A 12	358 33.2	N16 21.4	226 58.8	5.2	S18 45.9	1.1	59.9
Y 13	13 33.3	20.7	241 23.0	5.3	18 44.8	1.1	59.9
14	28 33.3	20.0	255 47.3	5.1	18 43.7	1.3	59.9
15	43 33.4	.. 19.3	270 11.4	5.2	18 42.4	1.5	60.0
16	58 33.5	18.6	284 35.6	5.1	18 40.9	1.5	60.0
17	73 33.6	17.9	298 59.7	5.0	18 39.4	1.7	60.0
18	88 33.6	N16 17.2	313 23.7	5.1	S18 37.7	1.8	60.1
19	103 33.7	16.5	327 47.8	5.0	18 35.9	2.0	60.1
20	118 33.8	15.8	342 11.8	4.9	18 33.9	2.1	60.1
21	133 33.9	.. 15.1	356 35.7	5.0	18 31.8	2.2	60.2
22	148 34.0	14.4	10 59.7	4.9	18 29.6	2.3	60.2
23	163 34.0	13.7	25 23.6	4.9	S18 27.3	2.5	60.2
	SD 15.8	d 0.7	SD 15.8		16.1		16.3

Twilight, Sunrise and Moonrise

Lat.	Twilight Naut.	Civil	Sunrise	Moonrise 5	6	7	8
N 72	////	////	00 56	18 44	■■■■	■■■■	21 01
N 70	////	////	02 04	17 20	18 52	19 46	20 05
68	////	////	02 39	16 41	18 01	18 58	19 30
66	////	01 23	03 04	16 14	17 29	18 27	19 06
64	////	02 06	03 23	15 53	17 05	18 04	18 46
62	////	02 34	03 39	15 37	16 47	17 45	18 30
60	01 14	02 55	03 52	15 23	16 31	17 30	18 17
N 58	01 54	03 12	04 03	15 11	16 18	17 17	18 06
56	02 20	03 27	04 13	15 01	16 07	17 06	17 56
54	02 40	03 39	04 22	14 52	15 57	16 56	17 47
52	02 56	03 49	04 29	14 44	15 48	16 47	17 39
50	03 09	03 58	04 36	14 37	15 40	16 39	17 32
45	03 36	04 18	04 51	14 21	15 24	16 23	17 16
N 40	03 56	04 33	05 03	14 08	15 10	16 09	17 04
35	04 12	04 46	05 13	13 58	14 58	15 57	16 53
30	04 26	04 56	05 22	13 48	14 48	15 47	16 44
20	04 46	05 14	05 37	13 32	14 30	15 29	16 28
N 10	05 02	05 28	05 50	13 18	14 15	15 14	16 13
0	05 16	05 41	06 02	13 05	14 01	15 00	16 00
S 10	05 27	05 53	06 15	12 52	13 47	14 46	15 47
20	05 38	06 04	06 27	12 38	13 32	14 30	15 33
30	05 48	06 17	06 42	12 22	13 15	14 13	15 17
35	05 53	06 24	06 50	12 13	13 05	14 03	15 07
40	05 59	06 31	07 00	12 03	12 53	13 51	14 56
45	06 04	06 39	07 11	11 51	12 40	13 38	14 44
S 50	06 10	06 49	07 24	11 36	12 23	13 21	14 28
52	06 13	06 54	07 30	11 29	12 16	13 13	14 21
54	06 16	06 58	07 37	11 21	12 07	13 05	14 13
56	06 19	07 04	07 45	11 13	11 58	12 55	14 04
58	06 22	07 10	07 53	11 03	11 47	12 44	13 54
S 60	06 26	07 16	08 03	10 52	11 34	12 31	13 42

Sunset, Twilight and Moonset

Lat.	Sunset	Twilight Civil	Naut.	Moonset 5	6	7	8
N 72	23 02	////	////	19 45	■■■■	■■■■	23 38
N 70	22 03	////	////	21 10	21 36	22 47	24 34
68	21 29	////	////	21 49	22 27	23 34	25 08
66	21 05	22 42	////	22 17	22 59	24 05	00 05
64	20 46	22 02	////	22 38	23 23	24 28	00 28
62	20 31	21 35	////	22 55	23 42	24 46	00 46
60	20 18	21 14	22 51	23 09	23 57	25 01	01 01
N 58	20 07	20 57	22 14	23 21	24 11	00 11	01 14
56	19 57	20 44	21 49	23 31	24 22	00 22	01 25
54	19 49	20 32	21 30	23 41	24 32	00 32	01 35
52	19 41	20 21	21 14	23 49	24 41	00 41	01 43
50	19 35	20 12	21 01	23 56	24 49	00 49	01 51
45	19 20	19 53	20 34	24 12	00 12	01 06	02 08
N 40	19 08	19 38	20 15	24 25	00 25	01 19	02 21
35	18 58	19 26	19 59	24 37	00 37	01 31	02 33
30	18 49	19 15	19 46	24 46	00 46	01 42	02 43
20	18 34	18 58	19 25	00 12	01 03	01 59	03 00
N 10	18 21	18 43	19 09	00 25	01 18	02 15	03 15
0	18 09	18 31	18 56	00 37	01 31	02 29	03 29
S 10	17 57	18 19	18 45	00 49	01 45	02 43	03 42
20	17 45	18 08	18 34	01 02	02 00	02 59	03 57
30	17 30	17 55	18 24	01 17	02 17	03 16	04 14
35	17 22	17 49	18 19	01 26	02 26	03 26	04 24
40	17 13	17 41	18 14	01 36	02 38	03 38	04 35
45	17 02	17 33	18 08	01 48	02 51	03 52	04 48
S 50	16 49	17 23	18 02	02 02	03 07	04 08	05 04
52	16 42	17 19	17 59	02 08	03 14	04 16	05 11
54	16 36	17 14	17 57	02 16	03 23	04 25	05 20
56	16 28	17 09	17 54	02 24	03 32	04 35	05 29
58	16 19	17 03	17 51	02 33	03 43	04 46	05 39
S 60	16 10	16 57	17 47	02 44	03 55	04 59	05 51

SUN and MOON

Day	SUN Eqn. of Time 00h	12h	Mer. Pass.	MOON Mer. Pass. Upper	Lower	Age	Phase
d	m s	m s	h m	h m	h m	d	%
5	06 04	06 01	12 06	19 18	06 51	10	65
6	05 58	05 55	12 06	20 15	07 46	11	76
7	05 51	05 47	12 06	21 14	08 44	12	85

UT	ARIES GHA	VENUS −3.8 GHA	Dec	MARS +0.5 GHA	Dec	JUPITER −1.8 GHA	Dec	SATURN +0.6 GHA	Dec	Name	SHA	Dec
8 00	316 25.6	199 42.8	N21 23.4	102 05.6	S14 55.0	188 57.9	N19 25.0	91 20.2	S14 46.9	Acamar	315 17.8	S40 14.6
01	331 28.1	214 42.1	23.0	117 06.7	55.5	203 59.8	24.9	106 22.6	46.9	Achernar	335 26.1	S57 09.5
02	346 30.6	229 41.3	22.5	132 07.8	56.0	219 01.7	24.8	121 25.0	47.0	Acrux	173 08.7	S63 11.0
03	1 33.0	244 40.5	.. 22.1	147 08.9	.. 56.5	234 03.6	.. 24.6	136 27.4	.. 47.0	Adhara	255 12.2	S28 59.6
04	16 35.5	259 39.7	21.7	162 09.9	57.0	249 05.5	24.5	151 29.8	47.0	Aldebaran	290 48.6	N16 32.1
05	31 38.0	274 39.0	21.2	177 11.0	57.5	264 07.4	24.4	166 32.2	47.1			
06	46 40.4	289 38.2	N21 20.8	192 12.1	S14 58.0	279 09.3	N19 24.2	181 34.6	S14 47.1	Alioth	166 20.4	N55 53.1
07	61 42.9	304 37.4	20.3	207 13.2	58.5	294 11.2	24.1	196 37.0	47.1	Alkaid	152 58.5	N49 14.8
08	76 45.3	319 36.6	19.9	222 14.3	59.0	309 13.1	24.0	211 39.4	47.1	Al Na'ir	27 42.3	S46 53.1
F 09	91 47.8	334 35.9	.. 19.4	237 15.3	14 59.5	324 15.0	.. 23.9	226 41.8	.. 47.2	Alnilam	275 45.8	S 1 11.7
R 10	106 50.3	349 35.1	19.0	252 16.4	15 00.0	339 16.9	23.7	241 44.1	47.2	Alphard	217 55.6	S 8 43.4
I 11	121 52.7	4 34.3	18.5	267 17.5	00.5	354 18.8	23.6	256 46.5	47.2			
D 12	136 55.2	19 33.5	N21 18.1	282 18.6	S15 01.0	9 20.7	N19 23.5	271 48.9	S14 47.3	Alphecca	126 10.3	N26 40.3
A 13	151 57.7	34 32.8	17.6	297 19.7	01.5	24 22.6	23.3	286 51.3	47.3	Alpheratz	357 42.4	N29 10.3
Y 14	167 00.1	49 32.0	17.2	312 20.7	02.0	39 24.5	23.2	301 53.7	47.3	Altair	62 07.1	N 8 54.7
15	182 02.6	64 31.2	.. 16.7	327 21.8	.. 02.5	54 26.4	.. 23.1	316 56.1	.. 47.4	Ankaa	353 14.7	S42 13.3
16	197 05.1	79 30.5	16.3	342 22.9	03.0	69 28.3	23.0	331 58.5	47.4	Antares	112 25.1	S26 27.7
17	212 07.5	94 29.7	15.8	357 24.0	03.5	84 30.2	22.8	347 00.9	47.4			
18	227 10.0	109 28.9	N21 15.3	12 25.0	S15 04.0	99 32.1	N19 22.7	2 03.3	S14 47.5	Arcturus	145 55.1	N19 06.6
19	242 12.5	124 28.1	14.9	27 26.1	04.5	114 34.0	22.6	17 05.7	47.5	Atria	107 25.9	S69 03.3
20	257 14.9	139 27.4	14.4	42 27.2	04.9	129 35.9	22.4	32 08.1	47.5	Avior	234 18.2	S59 33.5
21	272 17.4	154 26.6	.. 14.0	57 28.3	.. 05.4	144 37.8	.. 22.3	47 10.5	.. 47.6	Bellatrix	278 31.3	N 6 21.6
22	287 19.8	169 25.8	13.5	72 29.3	05.9	159 39.7	22.2	62 12.8	47.6	Betelgeuse	271 00.7	N 7 24.4
23	302 22.3	184 25.1	13.0	87 30.4	06.4	174 41.6	22.0	77 15.2	47.6			
9 00	317 24.8	199 24.3	N21 12.6	102 31.5	S15 06.9	189 43.5	N19 21.9	92 17.6	S14 47.7	Canopus	263 56.2	S52 42.2
01	332 27.2	214 23.5	12.1	117 32.6	07.4	204 45.4	21.8	107 20.0	47.7	Capella	280 33.5	N46 00.4
02	347 29.7	229 22.8	11.6	132 33.6	07.9	219 47.3	21.7	122 22.4	47.7	Deneb	49 30.4	N45 20.2
03	2 32.2	244 22.0	.. 11.2	147 34.7	.. 08.4	234 49.2	.. 21.5	137 24.8	.. 47.8	Denebola	182 33.1	N14 29.5
04	17 34.6	259 21.2	10.7	162 35.8	08.9	249 51.1	21.4	152 27.2	47.8	Diphda	348 54.9	S17 54.2
05	32 37.1	274 20.5	10.2	177 36.8	09.4	264 53.0	21.3	167 29.6	47.8			
06	47 39.6	289 19.7	N21 09.8	192 37.9	S15 09.9	279 54.9	N19 21.1	182 32.0	S14 47.8	Dubhe	193 51.4	N61 40.4
S 07	62 42.0	304 18.9	09.3	207 39.0	10.4	294 56.8	21.0	197 34.4	47.9	Elnath	278 11.8	N28 36.9
A 08	77 44.5	319 18.1	08.8	222 40.1	10.9	309 58.7	20.9	212 36.7	47.9	Eltanin	90 45.4	N51 29.6
T 09	92 47.0	334 17.4	.. 08.3	237 41.1	.. 11.4	325 00.6	.. 20.8	227 39.1	.. 47.9	Enif	33 46.0	N 9 56.8
U 10	107 49.4	349 16.6	07.9	252 42.2	11.9	340 02.5	20.6	242 41.5	48.0	Fomalhaut	15 22.8	S29 32.4
R 11	122 51.9	4 15.8	07.4	267 43.3	12.4	355 04.4	20.5	257 43.9	48.0			
D 12	137 54.3	19 15.1	N21 06.9	282 44.3	S15 12.9	10 06.3	N19 20.4	272 46.3	S14 48.0	Gacrux	172 00.2	S57 11.9
A 13	152 56.8	34 14.3	06.4	297 45.4	13.4	25 08.2	20.2	287 48.7	48.1	Gienah	175 51.7	S17 37.4
Y 14	167 59.3	49 13.6	05.9	312 46.5	13.9	40 10.1	20.1	302 51.1	48.1	Hadar	148 46.8	S60 26.8
15	183 01.7	64 12.8	.. 05.5	327 47.5	.. 14.4	55 12.0	.. 20.0	317 53.5	.. 48.1	Hamal	327 59.7	N23 31.8
16	198 04.2	79 12.0	05.0	342 48.6	14.8	70 13.9	19.8	332 55.9	48.2	Kaus Aust.	83 42.4	S34 22.5
17	213 06.7	94 11.3	04.5	357 49.7	15.3	85 15.8	19.7	347 58.2	48.2			
18	228 09.1	109 10.5	N21 04.0	12 50.7	S15 15.8	100 17.7	N19 19.6	3 00.6	S14 48.2	Kochab	137 20.3	N74 06.1
19	243 11.6	124 09.7	03.5	27 51.8	16.3	115 19.6	19.5	18 03.0	48.3	Markab	13 37.2	N15 17.2
20	258 14.1	139 09.0	03.1	42 52.9	16.8	130 21.5	19.3	33 05.4	48.3	Menkar	314 14.2	N 4 08.8
21	273 16.5	154 08.2	.. 02.6	57 53.9	.. 17.3	145 23.4	.. 19.2	48 07.8	.. 48.3	Menkent	148 06.7	S36 26.5
22	288 19.0	169 07.4	02.1	72 55.0	17.8	160 25.3	19.1	63 10.2	48.4	Miaplacidus	221 40.3	S69 46.8
23	303 21.5	184 06.7	01.6	87 56.0	18.3	175 27.2	18.9	78 12.6	48.4			
10 00	318 23.9	199 05.9	N21 01.1	102 57.1	S15 18.8	190 29.1	N19 18.8	93 15.0	S14 48.4	Mirfak	308 39.2	N49 54.5
01	333 26.4	214 05.2	00.6	117 58.2	19.3	205 31.0	18.7	108 17.3	48.5	Nunki	75 57.0	S26 16.5
02	348 28.8	229 04.4	21 00.0	132 59.2	19.8	220 32.9	18.5	123 19.7	48.5	Peacock	53 17.4	S56 41.1
03	3 31.3	244 03.6	20 59.6	148 00.3	.. 20.3	235 34.8	.. 18.4	138 22.1	.. 48.5	Pollux	243 27.1	N27 59.3
04	18 33.8	259 02.9	59.1	163 01.4	20.8	250 36.7	18.3	153 24.5	48.6	Procyon	244 59.2	N 5 11.1
05	33 36.2	274 02.1	58.6	178 02.4	21.3	265 38.5	18.2	168 26.9	48.6			
06	48 38.7	289 01.3	N20 58.1	193 03.5	S15 21.8	280 40.4	N19 18.0	183 29.3	S14 48.6	Rasalhague	96 05.5	N12 33.3
07	63 41.2	304 00.6	57.6	208 04.5	22.3	295 42.3	17.9	198 31.7	48.7	Regulus	207 43.0	N11 53.7
08	78 43.6	318 59.8	57.1	223 05.6	22.8	310 44.2	17.8	213 34.0	48.7	Rigel	281 11.5	S 8 11.1
S 09	93 46.1	333 59.1	.. 56.6	238 06.7	.. 23.2	325 46.1	.. 17.6	228 36.4	.. 48.7	Rigil Kent.	139 50.6	S60 53.8
U 10	108 48.6	348 58.3	56.1	253 07.7	23.7	340 48.0	17.5	243 38.8	48.8	Sabik	102 11.4	S15 44.4
N 11	123 51.0	3 57.5	55.6	268 08.8	24.2	355 49.9	17.4	258 41.2	48.8			
D 12	138 53.5	18 56.8	N20 55.1	283 09.8	S15 24.7	10 51.8	N19 17.2	273 43.6	S14 48.8	Schedar	349 39.1	N56 36.9
A 13	153 55.9	33 56.0	54.6	298 10.9	25.2	25 53.7	17.1	288 46.0	48.9	Shaula	96 20.5	S37 06.7
Y 14	168 58.4	48 55.3	54.1	313 11.9	25.7	40 55.6	17.0	303 48.4	48.9	Sirius	258 33.3	S16 44.2
15	184 00.9	63 54.5	.. 53.6	328 13.0	.. 26.2	55 57.5	.. 16.8	318 50.7	.. 48.9	Spica	158 30.5	S11 14.2
16	199 03.3	78 53.8	53.1	343 14.1	26.7	70 59.4	16.7	333 53.1	49.0	Suhail	222 52.2	S43 29.6
17	214 05.8	93 53.0	52.6	358 15.1	27.2	86 01.3	16.6	348 55.5	49.0			
18	229 08.3	108 52.2	N20 52.1	13 16.2	S15 27.7	101 03.2	N19 16.5	3 57.9	S14 49.0	Vega	80 38.1	N38 48.2
19	244 10.7	123 51.5	51.6	28 17.2	28.2	116 05.1	16.3	19 00.3	49.1	Zuben'ubi	137 04.5	S16 06.0
20	259 13.2	138 50.7	51.1	43 18.3	28.7	131 07.0	16.2	34 02.7	49.1			
21	274 15.7	153 50.0	.. 50.6	58 19.3	.. 29.2	146 08.9	.. 16.1	49 05.0	.. 49.1			
22	289 18.1	168 49.2	50.0	73 20.4	29.7	161 10.8	15.9	64 07.4	49.2			
23	304 20.6	183 48.5	49.5	88 21.4	30.1	176 12.7	15.8	79 09.8	49.2			
Mer.Pass.	h m 2 49.9	v −0.8	d 0.5	v 1.1	d 0.5	v 1.9	d 0.1	v 2.4	d 0.0			

	SHA	Mer.Pass.
	° ′	h m
Venus	241 59.5	10 43
Mars	145 06.7	17 09
Jupiter	232 18.7	11 20
Saturn	134 52.9	17 48

UT	SUN GHA	SUN Dec	MOON GHA	v	Dec	d	HP
d h	° ′	° ′	° ′	′	° ′	′	′
8 00	178 34.1	N16 13.0	39 47.5	4.8	S18 24.8	2.6	60.3
01	193 34.2	12.3	54 11.3	4.9	18 22.2	2.8	60.3
02	208 34.3	11.6	68 35.2	4.8	18 19.4	2.9	60.3
03	223 34.4	.. 10.9	82 59.0	4.8	18 16.5	3.0	60.4
04	238 34.5	10.2	97 22.8	4.8	18 13.5	3.1	60.4
05	253 34.5	09.4	111 46.6	4.7	18 10.4	3.3	60.4
06	268 34.6	N16 08.7	126 10.3	4.8	S18 07.1	3.4	60.5
07	283 34.7	08.0	140 34.1	4.7	18 03.7	3.6	60.5
08	298 34.8	07.3	154 57.8	4.7	18 00.1	3.6	60.5
F 09	313 34.9	.. 06.6	169 21.5	4.7	17 56.5	3.9	60.6
R 10	328 34.9	05.9	183 45.2	4.7	17 52.6	3.9	60.6
I 11	343 35.0	05.2	198 08.9	4.7	17 48.7	4.1	60.6
D 12	358 35.1	N16 04.5	212 32.6	4.6	S17 44.6	4.2	60.7
A 13	13 35.2	03.8	226 56.2	4.7	17 40.4	4.3	60.7
Y 14	28 35.3	03.1	241 19.9	4.6	17 36.1	4.5	60.7
15	43 35.4	.. 02.3	255 43.5	4.7	17 31.6	4.5	60.7
16	58 35.5	01.6	270 07.2	4.6	17 27.1	4.8	60.7
17	73 35.5	00.9	284 30.8	4.7	17 22.3	4.8	60.8
18	88 35.6	N16 00.2	298 54.5	4.6	S17 17.5	5.0	60.8
19	103 35.7	15 59.5	313 18.1	4.7	17 12.5	5.1	60.8
20	118 35.8	58.8	327 41.8	4.6	17 07.4	5.2	60.8
21	133 35.9	.. 58.1	342 05.4	4.7	17 02.2	5.4	60.9
22	148 36.0	57.3	356 29.1	4.6	16 56.8	5.5	60.9
23	163 36.1	56.6	10 52.7	4.7	16 51.3	5.6	60.9
9 00	178 36.1	N15 55.9	25 16.4	4.7	S16 45.7	5.7	60.9
01	193 36.2	55.2	39 40.1	4.7	16 40.0	5.9	61.0
02	208 36.3	54.5	54 03.8	4.7	16 34.1	6.0	61.0
03	223 36.4	.. 53.8	68 27.5	4.7	16 28.1	6.1	61.0
04	238 36.5	53.0	82 51.2	4.7	16 22.0	6.2	61.0
05	253 36.6	52.3	97 14.9	4.7	16 15.8	6.3	61.1
06	268 36.7	N15 51.6	111 38.6	4.7	S16 09.5	6.5	61.1
S 07	283 36.8	50.9	126 02.3	4.8	16 03.0	6.6	61.1
A 08	298 36.8	50.2	140 26.1	4.8	15 56.4	6.7	61.1
T 09	313 36.9	.. 49.4	154 49.9	4.8	15 49.7	6.8	61.1
U 10	328 37.0	48.7	169 13.7	4.8	15 42.9	7.0	61.1
R 11	343 37.1	48.0	183 37.5	4.8	15 35.9	7.1	61.2
D 12	358 37.2	N15 47.3	198 01.3	4.9	S15 28.8	7.1	61.2
A 13	13 37.3	46.5	212 25.2	4.8	15 21.7	7.3	61.2
Y 14	28 37.4	45.8	226 49.0	4.9	15 14.4	7.4	61.2
15	43 37.5	.. 45.1	241 12.9	5.0	15 07.0	7.6	61.2
16	58 37.6	44.4	255 36.9	4.9	14 59.4	7.6	61.2
17	73 37.7	43.7	270 00.8	5.0	14 51.8	7.7	61.3
18	88 37.7	N15 42.9	284 24.8	5.0	S14 44.1	7.9	61.3
19	103 37.8	42.2	298 48.8	5.0	14 36.2	7.9	61.3
20	118 37.9	41.5	313 12.8	5.1	14 28.3	8.1	61.3
21	133 38.0	.. 40.8	327 36.9	5.1	14 20.2	8.2	61.3
22	148 38.1	40.0	342 01.0	5.1	14 12.0	8.2	61.3
23	163 38.2	39.3	356 25.1	5.1	14 03.8	8.4	61.3
10 00	178 38.3	N15 38.6	10 49.2	5.2	S13 55.4	8.5	61.3
01	193 38.4	37.8	25 13.4	5.2	13 46.9	8.6	61.4
02	208 38.5	37.1	39 37.6	5.3	13 38.3	8.7	61.4
03	223 38.6	.. 36.4	54 01.9	5.3	13 29.6	8.8	61.4
04	238 38.7	35.7	68 26.2	5.3	13 20.8	8.8	61.4
05	253 38.8	34.9	82 50.5	5.4	13 12.0	9.0	61.4
06	268 38.9	N15 34.2	97 14.9	5.4	S13 03.0	9.1	61.4
07	283 39.0	33.5	111 39.3	5.4	12 53.9	9.1	61.4
S 08	298 39.0	32.7	126 03.7	5.5	12 44.8	9.3	61.4
U 09	313 39.1	.. 32.0	140 28.2	5.5	12 35.5	9.3	61.4
N 10	328 39.2	31.3	154 52.7	5.5	12 26.2	9.5	61.4
D 11	343 39.3	30.5	169 17.2	5.6	12 16.7	9.5	61.4
A 12	358 39.4	N15 29.8	183 41.8	5.6	S12 07.2	9.6	61.4
Y 13	13 39.5	29.1	198 06.4	5.7	11 57.6	9.7	61.4
14	28 39.6	28.3	212 31.1	5.7	11 47.9	9.8	61.4
15	43 39.7	.. 27.6	226 55.8	5.8	11 38.1	9.8	61.4
16	58 39.8	26.9	241 20.6	5.8	11 28.3	10.0	61.4
17	73 39.9	26.1	255 45.4	5.8	11 18.3	10.0	61.4
18	88 40.0	N15 25.4	270 10.2	5.9	S11 08.3	10.1	61.4
19	103 40.1	24.7	284 35.1	5.9	10 58.2	10.1	61.4
20	118 40.2	23.9	299 00.0	6.0	10 48.1	10.3	61.4
21	133 40.3	.. 23.2	313 25.0	6.0	10 37.8	10.3	61.4
22	148 40.4	22.5	327 50.0	6.1	10 27.5	10.4	61.4
23	163 40.5	21.7	342 15.1	6.1	S10 17.1	10.5	61.4
SD	15.8	d 0.7	SD 16.5		16.7		16.7

Twilight / Moonrise

Lat.	Naut.	Civil	Sunrise	Moonrise 8	9	10	11
°	h m	h m	h m	h m	h m	h m	h m
N 72	////	////	01 34	21 01	20 41	20 31	20 23
N 70	////	////	02 22	20 05	20 11	20 13	20 13
68	////	00 25	02 53	19 30	19 48	19 59	20 06
66	////	01 45	03 15	19 06	19 31	19 47	20 00
64	////	02 20	03 33	18 46	19 16	19 38	19 54
62	00 23	02 45	03 47	18 30	19 04	19 29	19 49
60	01 34	03 04	03 59	18 17	18 54	19 22	19 45
N 58	02 06	03 20	04 10	18 06	18 44	19 16	19 42
56	02 30	03 33	04 19	17 56	18 36	19 10	19 39
54	02 48	03 45	04 27	17 47	18 29	19 05	19 36
52	03 03	03 55	04 34	17 39	18 23	19 00	19 33
50	03 16	04 03	04 41	17 32	18 17	18 56	19 30
45	03 41	04 22	04 54	17 16	18 05	18 47	19 25
N 40	04 00	04 36	05 06	17 04	17 54	18 39	19 21
35	04 15	04 48	05 15	16 53	17 45	18 33	19 17
30	04 28	04 58	05 24	16 44	17 37	18 27	19 14
20	04 48	05 15	05 38	16 28	17 24	18 17	19 08
N 10	05 03	05 29	05 51	16 13	17 12	18 08	19 02
0	05 16	05 41	06 02	16 00	17 01	18 00	18 58
S 10	05 27	05 52	06 14	15 47	16 50	17 52	18 53
20	05 36	06 03	06 26	15 33	16 38	17 43	18 47
30	05 46	06 16	06 39	15 17	16 24	17 33	18 42
35	05 51	06 21	06 47	15 07	16 16	17 27	18 38
40	05 56	06 28	06 56	14 56	16 07	17 20	18 34
45	06 01	06 36	07 06	14 44	15 56	17 13	18 30
S 50	06 06	06 45	07 19	14 28	15 43	17 03	18 24
52	06 08	06 49	07 25	14 21	15 37	16 59	18 22
54	06 11	06 53	07 31	14 13	15 31	16 54	18 19
56	06 13	06 58	07 38	14 04	15 23	16 49	18 16
58	06 16	07 03	07 46	13 54	15 15	16 43	18 13
S 60	06 19	07 09	07 55	13 42	15 05	16 36	18 09

Twilight / Moonset

Lat.	Sunset	Civil	Naut.	Moonset 8	9	10	11
°	h m	h m	h m	h m	h m	h m	h m
N 72	22 28	////	////	23 38	26 05	02 05	04 19
N 70	21 44	////	////	24 34	00 34	02 34	04 35
68	21 15	23 23	////	25 08	01 08	02 55	04 47
66	20 53	22 20	////	00 05	01 32	03 12	04 57
64	20 36	21 47	////	00 28	01 51	03 26	05 06
62	20 22	21 23	23 28	00 46	02 06	03 37	05 13
60	20 10	21 04	22 32	01 01	02 19	03 47	05 19
N 58	20 00	20 49	22 01	01 14	02 30	03 55	05 25
56	19 51	20 36	21 39	01 25	02 40	04 03	05 30
54	19 43	20 25	21 21	01 35	02 48	04 09	05 34
52	19 36	20 15	21 06	01 43	02 56	04 15	05 38
50	19 29	20 06	20 54	01 51	03 03	04 20	05 41
45	19 16	19 48	20 29	02 08	03 17	04 32	05 49
N 40	19 05	19 34	20 10	02 21	03 29	04 41	05 55
35	18 55	19 22	19 55	02 33	03 39	04 49	06 01
30	18 47	19 12	19 43	02 43	03 48	04 57	06 06
20	18 33	18 56	19 23	03 00	04 03	05 09	06 14
N 10	18 20	18 42	19 08	03 15	04 17	05 19	06 21
0	18 09	18 30	18 55	03 29	04 29	05 29	06 28
S 10	17 58	18 19	18 45	03 42	04 41	05 39	06 34
20	17 46	18 09	18 35	03 57	04 54	05 49	06 41
30	17 32	17 57	18 25	04 14	05 09	06 01	06 49
35	17 24	17 51	18 21	04 24	05 18	06 08	06 54
40	17 15	17 44	18 16	04 35	05 28	06 15	06 59
45	17 05	17 36	18 11	04 48	05 39	06 24	07 04
S 50	16 53	17 27	18 06	05 04	05 53	06 35	07 11
52	16 47	17 23	18 03	05 11	05 59	06 40	07 15
54	16 41	17 18	18 01	05 20	06 06	06 45	07 18
56	16 34	17 14	17 58	05 29	06 14	06 51	07 22
58	16 26	17 09	17 56	05 39	06 23	06 58	07 26
S 60	16 17	17 03	17 53	05 51	06 33	07 05	07 31

Day	SUN Eqn. of Time 00h	12h	Mer. Pass.	MOON Mer. Pass. Upper	Lower	Age	Phase
d	m s	m s	h m	h m	h m	d	%
8	05 44	05 40	12 06	22 15	09 44	13	92
9	05 36	05 31	12 06	23 15	10 45	14	97
10	05 27	05 22	12 05	24 14	11 45	15	100

UT	ARIES GHA	VENUS −3.8 GHA	Dec	MARS +0.5 GHA	Dec	JUPITER −1.8 GHA	Dec	SATURN +0.6 GHA	Dec	STARS Name	SHA	Dec
11 00	319 23.1	198 47.7	N20 49.0	103 22.5	S15 30.6	191 14.6	N19 15.7	94 12.2	S14 49.2	Acamar	315 17.7	S40 14.6
01	334 25.5	213 46.9	48.5	118 23.5	31.1	206 16.5	15.5	109 14.6	49.3	Achernar	335 26.0	S57 09.5
02	349 28.0	228 46.2	48.0	133 24.6	31.6	221 18.4	15.4	124 17.0	49.3	Acrux	173 08.7	S63 11.0
03	4 30.4	243 45.4	.. 47.5	148 25.6	.. 32.1	236 20.3	.. 15.3	139 19.3	.. 49.3	Adhara	255 12.2	S28 59.5
04	19 32.9	258 44.7	46.9	163 26.7	32.6	251 22.2	15.2	154 21.7	49.4	Aldebaran	290 48.6	N16 32.2
05	34 35.4	273 43.9	46.4	178 27.7	33.1	266 24.1	15.0	169 24.1	49.4			
M 06	49 37.8	288 43.2	N20 45.9	193 28.8	S15 33.6	281 26.1	N19 14.9	184 26.5	S14 49.4	Alioth	166 20.4	N55 53.1
O 07	64 40.3	303 42.4	45.4	208 29.8	34.1	296 28.0	14.8	199 28.9	49.5	Alkaid	152 58.5	N49 14.8
N 08	79 42.8	318 41.7	44.9	223 30.9	34.6	311 29.9	14.6	214 31.3	49.5	Al Na'ir	27 42.3	S46 53.1
D 09	94 45.2	333 40.9	.. 44.3	238 31.9	.. 35.1	326 31.8	.. 14.5	229 33.6	.. 49.6	Alnilam	275 45.7	S 1 11.6
A 10	109 47.7	348 40.2	43.8	253 33.0	35.6	341 33.7	14.4	244 36.0	49.6	Alphard	217 55.6	S 8 43.4
Y 11	124 50.2	3 39.4	43.3	268 34.0	36.1	356 35.6	14.2	259 38.4	49.6			
12	139 52.6	18 38.7	N20 42.8	283 35.1	S15 36.6	11 37.5	N19 14.1	274 40.8	S14 49.7	Alphecca	126 10.3	N26 40.3
13	154 55.1	33 37.9	42.2	298 36.1	37.0	26 39.4	14.0	289 43.2	49.7	Alpheratz	357 42.3	N29 10.3
14	169 57.6	48 37.2	41.7	313 37.2	37.5	41 41.3	13.8	304 45.5	49.7	Altair	62 07.1	N 8 54.7
15	185 00.0	63 36.4	.. 41.2	328 38.2	.. 38.0	56 43.2	.. 13.7	319 47.9	.. 49.8	Ankaa	353 14.7	S42 13.3
16	200 02.5	78 35.7	40.6	343 39.3	38.5	71 45.1	13.6	334 50.3	49.8	Antares	112 25.1	S26 27.7
17	215 04.9	93 34.9	40.1	358 40.3	39.0	86 47.0	13.5	349 52.7	49.8			
18	230 07.4	108 34.2	N20 39.6	13 41.3	S15 39.5	101 48.9	N19 13.3	4 55.1	S14 49.9	Arcturus	145 55.1	N19 06.6
19	245 09.9	123 33.4	39.0	28 42.4	40.0	116 50.8	13.2	19 57.4	49.9	Atria	107 25.9	S69 03.3
20	260 12.3	138 32.7	38.5	43 43.4	40.5	131 52.7	13.1	34 59.8	49.9	Avior	234 18.2	S59 33.4
21	275 14.8	153 31.9	.. 38.0	58 44.5	.. 41.0	146 54.6	.. 12.9	50 02.2	.. 50.0	Bellatrix	278 31.3	N 6 21.7
22	290 17.3	168 31.2	37.4	73 45.5	41.5	161 56.5	12.8	65 04.6	50.0	Betelgeuse	271 00.6	N 7 24.5
23	305 19.7	183 30.4	36.9	88 46.6	42.0	176 58.4	12.7	80 07.0	50.0			
12 00	320 22.2	198 29.7	N20 36.3	103 47.6	S15 42.5	192 00.3	N19 12.5	95 09.3	S14 50.1	Canopus	263 56.2	S52 42.2
01	335 24.7	213 28.9	35.8	118 48.6	42.9	207 02.2	12.4	110 11.7	50.1	Capella	280 33.5	N46 00.4
02	350 27.1	228 28.2	35.3	133 49.7	43.4	222 04.1	12.3	125 14.1	50.1	Deneb	49 30.4	N45 20.2
03	5 29.6	243 27.4	.. 34.7	148 50.7	.. 43.9	237 06.0	.. 12.1	140 16.5	.. 50.2	Denebola	182 33.1	N14 29.5
04	20 32.0	258 26.7	34.2	163 51.8	44.4	252 07.9	12.0	155 18.9	50.2	Diphda	348 54.9	S17 54.2
05	35 34.5	273 25.9	33.6	178 52.8	44.9	267 09.8	11.9	170 21.2	50.2			
T 06	50 37.0	288 25.2	N20 33.1	193 53.8	S15 45.4	282 11.7	N19 11.8	185 23.6	S14 50.3	Dubhe	193 51.4	N61 40.4
U 07	65 39.4	303 24.4	32.5	208 54.9	45.9	297 13.6	11.6	200 26.0	50.3	Elnath	278 11.8	N28 36.9
E 08	80 41.9	318 23.7	32.0	223 55.9	46.4	312 15.5	11.5	215 28.4	50.4	Eltanin	90 45.4	N51 29.7
S 09	95 44.4	333 22.9	.. 31.4	238 57.0	.. 46.9	327 17.4	.. 11.4	230 30.7	.. 50.4	Enif	33 46.0	N 9 56.8
D 10	110 46.8	348 22.2	30.9	253 58.0	47.4	342 19.3	11.2	245 33.1	50.4	Fomalhaut	15 22.8	S29 32.4
A 11	125 49.3	3 21.4	30.3	268 59.0	47.9	357 21.2	11.1	260 35.5	50.5			
Y 12	140 51.8	18 20.7	N20 29.8	284 00.1	S15 48.3	12 23.1	N19 11.0	275 37.9	S14 50.5	Gacrux	172 00.3	S57 11.9
13	155 54.2	33 20.0	29.2	299 01.1	48.8	27 25.0	10.8	290 40.3	50.5	Gienah	175 51.7	S17 37.4
14	170 56.7	48 19.2	28.7	314 02.1	49.3	42 26.9	10.7	305 42.6	50.6	Hadar	148 46.8	S60 26.8
15	185 59.2	63 18.5	.. 28.1	329 03.2	.. 49.8	57 28.8	.. 10.6	320 45.0	.. 50.6	Hamal	327 59.7	N23 31.8
16	201 01.6	78 17.7	27.6	344 04.2	50.3	72 30.7	10.4	335 47.4	50.6	Kaus Aust.	83 42.4	S34 22.5
17	216 04.1	93 17.0	27.0	359 05.2	50.8	87 32.6	10.3	350 49.8	50.7			
18	231 06.5	108 16.2	N20 26.4	14 06.3	S15 51.3	102 34.5	N19 10.2	5 52.1	S14 50.7	Kochab	137 20.3	N74 06.1
19	246 09.0	123 15.5	25.9	29 07.3	51.8	117 36.4	10.0	20 54.5	50.7	Markab	13 37.2	N15 17.2
20	261 11.5	138 14.8	25.3	44 08.3	52.3	132 38.3	09.9	35 56.9	50.8	Menkar	314 14.2	N 4 08.8
21	276 13.9	153 14.0	.. 24.8	59 09.4	.. 52.8	147 40.2	.. 09.8	50 59.3	.. 50.8	Menkent	148 06.7	S36 26.5
22	291 16.4	168 13.3	24.2	74 10.4	53.3	162 42.1	09.7	66 01.6	50.9	Miaplacidus	221 40.3	S69 46.8
23	306 18.9	183 12.5	23.6	89 11.4	53.7	177 44.0	09.5	81 04.0	50.9			
13 00	321 21.3	198 11.8	N20 23.1	104 12.5	S15 54.2	192 45.9	N19 09.4	96 06.4	S14 50.9	Mirfak	308 39.2	N49 54.5
01	336 23.8	213 11.1	22.5	119 13.5	54.7	207 47.8	09.3	111 08.8	51.0	Nunki	75 57.0	S26 16.5
02	351 26.3	228 10.3	21.9	134 14.5	55.2	222 49.7	09.1	126 11.1	51.0	Peacock	53 17.4	S56 41.1
03	6 28.7	243 09.6	.. 21.4	149 15.6	.. 55.7	237 51.6	.. 09.0	141 13.5	.. 51.0	Pollux	243 27.1	N27 59.3
04	21 31.2	258 08.8	20.8	164 16.6	56.2	252 53.5	08.9	156 15.9	51.1	Procyon	244 59.2	N 5 11.1
05	36 33.6	273 08.1	20.2	179 17.6	56.7	267 55.4	08.7	171 18.3	51.1			
W 06	51 36.1	288 07.4	N20 19.6	194 18.7	S15 57.2	282 57.3	N19 08.6	186 20.6	S14 51.1	Rasalhague	96 05.5	N12 33.3
E 07	66 38.6	303 06.6	19.1	209 19.7	57.7	297 59.2	08.5	201 23.0	51.2	Regulus	207 43.0	N11 53.7
D 08	81 41.0	318 05.9	18.5	224 20.7	58.1	313 01.1	08.3	216 25.4	51.2	Rigel	281 11.4	S 8 11.1
N 09	96 43.5	333 05.1	.. 17.9	239 21.7	.. 58.6	328 03.1	.. 08.2	231 27.8	.. 51.3	Rigil Kent.	139 50.6	S60 53.8
E 10	111 46.0	348 04.4	17.4	254 22.8	59.1	343 05.0	08.1	246 30.1	51.3	Sabik	102 11.4	S15 44.4
S 11	126 48.4	3 03.7	16.8	269 23.8	15 59.6	358 06.9	07.9	261 32.5	51.3			
D 12	141 50.9	18 02.9	N20 16.2	284 24.8	S16 00.1	13 08.8	N19 07.8	276 34.9	S14 51.4	Schedar	349 39.1	N56 36.9
A 13	156 53.4	33 02.2	15.6	299 25.8	00.6	28 10.7	07.7	291 37.3	51.4	Shaula	96 20.6	S37 06.7
Y 14	171 55.8	48 01.5	15.0	314 26.9	01.1	43 12.6	07.5	306 39.6	51.4	Sirius	258 33.3	S16 44.2
15	186 58.3	63 00.7	.. 14.5	329 27.9	.. 01.6	58 14.5	.. 07.4	321 42.0	.. 51.5	Spica	158 30.5	S11 14.2
16	202 00.8	78 00.0	13.9	344 28.9	02.1	73 16.4	07.3	336 44.4	51.5	Suhail	222 52.2	S43 29.6
17	217 03.2	92 59.3	13.3	359 29.9	02.6	88 18.3	07.2	351 46.7	51.5			
18	232 05.7	107 58.5	N20 12.7	14 31.0	S16 03.0	103 20.2	N19 07.0	6 49.1	S14 51.6	Vega	80 38.1	N38 48.2
19	247 08.1	122 57.8	12.1	29 32.0	03.5	118 22.1	06.9	21 51.5	51.6	Zuben'ubi	137 04.5	S16 06.0
20	262 10.6	137 57.1	11.5	44 33.0	04.0	133 24.0	06.8	36 53.9	51.7		SHA	Mer.Pass.
21	277 13.1	152 56.3	.. 11.0	59 34.0	.. 04.5	148 25.9	.. 06.6	51 56.2	.. 51.7		° '	h m
22	292 15.5	167 55.6	10.4	74 35.1	05.0	163 27.8	06.5	66 58.6	51.7	Venus	238 07.5	10 47
23	307 18.0	182 54.9	09.8	89 36.1	05.5	178 29.7	06.4	82 01.0	51.8	Mars	143 25.4	17 04
Mer.Pass.	h m 2 38.1	v −0.7	d 0.6	v 1.0	d 0.5	v 1.9	d 0.1	v 2.4	d 0.0	Jupiter	231 38.1	11 11
										Saturn	134 47.1	17 37

UT	SUN GHA	SUN Dec	MOON GHA	v	Dec	d	HP
d h	° ′	° ′	° ′	′	° ′	′	′
11 00	178 40.6	N15 21.0	356 40.2	6.2	S10 06.6	10.5	61.4
01	193 40.7	20.2	11 05.4	6.2	9 56.1	10.6	61.4
02	208 40.8	19.5	25 30.6	6.2	9 45.5	10.6	61.4
03	223 40.9	.. 18.8	39 55.8	6.3	9 34.9	10.8	61.4
04	238 41.0	18.0	54 21.1	6.3	9 24.1	10.7	61.4
05	253 41.1	17.3	68 46.4	6.4	9 13.4	10.9	61.4
06	268 41.2	N15 16.5	83 11.8	6.4	S 9 02.5	10.9	61.4
07	283 41.3	15.8	97 37.2	6.5	8 51.6	11.0	61.4
08	298 41.4	15.1	112 02.7	6.5	8 40.6	11.0	61.4
M 09	313 41.5	.. 14.3	126 28.2	6.6	8 29.6	11.1	61.4
O 10	328 41.6	13.6	140 53.8	6.6	8 18.5	11.1	61.4
N 11	343 41.7	12.8	155 19.4	6.7	8 07.4	11.2	61.4
D 12	358 41.8	N15 12.1	169 45.1	6.7	S 7 56.2	11.2	61.3
A 13	13 41.9	11.4	184 10.8	6.8	7 45.0	11.3	61.3
Y 14	28 42.0	10.6	198 36.6	6.8	7 33.7	11.3	61.3
15	43 42.1	.. 09.9	213 02.4	6.8	7 22.4	11.3	61.3
16	58 42.2	09.1	227 28.2	6.9	7 11.1	11.4	61.3
17	73 42.3	08.4	241 54.1	7.0	6 59.7	11.5	61.3
18	88 42.4	N15 07.6	256 20.1	7.0	S 6 48.2	11.5	61.3
19	103 42.5	06.9	270 46.1	7.0	6 36.7	11.5	61.3
20	118 42.6	06.1	285 12.1	7.1	6 25.2	11.6	61.2
21	133 42.7	.. 05.4	299 38.2	7.1	6 13.6	11.6	61.2
22	148 42.8	04.6	314 04.3	7.2	6 02.0	11.6	61.2
23	163 42.9	03.9	328 30.5	7.2	5 50.4	11.6	61.2
12 00	178 43.0	N15 03.2	342 56.7	7.3	S 5 38.8	11.7	61.2
01	193 43.2	02.4	357 23.0	7.3	5 27.1	11.8	61.2
02	208 43.3	01.7	11 49.3	7.4	5 15.3	11.7	61.1
03	223 43.4	.. 00.9	26 15.7	7.4	5 03.6	11.8	61.1
04	238 43.5	15 00.2	40 42.1	7.4	4 51.8	11.8	61.1
05	253 43.6	14 59.4	55 08.5	7.5	4 40.0	11.8	61.1
06	268 43.7	N14 58.7	69 35.0	7.6	S 4 28.2	11.8	61.1
07	283 43.8	57.9	84 01.6	7.6	4 16.4	11.9	61.0
T 08	298 43.9	57.2	98 28.2	7.6	4 04.5	11.8	61.0
U 09	313 44.0	.. 56.4	112 54.8	7.7	3 52.7	11.9	61.0
E 10	328 44.1	55.7	127 21.5	7.7	3 40.8	11.9	61.0
S 11	343 44.2	54.9	141 48.2	7.7	3 28.9	11.9	61.0
D 12	358 44.3	N14 54.1	156 14.9	7.9	S 3 17.0	12.0	60.9
A 13	13 44.4	53.4	170 41.8	7.8	3 05.0	11.9	60.9
Y 14	28 44.5	52.6	185 08.6	7.9	2 53.1	12.0	60.9
15	43 44.6	.. 51.9	199 35.5	7.9	2 41.1	11.9	60.9
16	58 44.8	51.1	214 02.4	8.0	2 29.2	12.0	60.8
17	73 44.9	50.4	228 29.4	8.0	2 17.2	11.9	60.8
18	88 45.0	N14 49.6	242 56.4	8.1	S 2 05.3	12.0	60.8
19	103 45.1	48.9	257 23.5	8.1	1 53.3	11.9	60.8
20	118 45.2	48.1	271 50.6	8.1	1 41.4	12.0	60.7
21	133 45.3	.. 47.4	286 17.7	8.2	1 29.4	12.0	60.7
22	148 45.4	46.6	300 44.9	8.2	1 17.4	11.9	60.7
23	163 45.5	45.8	315 12.1	8.3	1 05.5	12.0	60.6
13 00	178 45.6	N14 45.1	329 39.4	8.3	S 0 53.5	11.9	60.6
01	193 45.7	44.3	344 06.7	8.3	0 41.6	12.0	60.6
02	208 45.9	43.6	358 34.0	8.4	0 29.6	11.9	60.6
03	223 46.0	.. 42.8	13 01.4	8.4	0 17.7	11.9	60.5
04	238 46.1	42.0	27 28.8	8.4	S 0 05.8	11.9	60.5
05	253 46.2	41.3	41 56.2	8.5	N 0 06.1	11.9	60.5
06	268 46.3	N14 40.5	56 23.7	8.5	N 0 18.0	11.9	60.4
W 07	283 46.4	39.8	70 51.2	8.6	0 29.9	11.8	60.4
E 08	298 46.5	39.0	85 18.8	8.6	0 41.7	11.9	60.4
D 09	313 46.6	.. 38.2	99 46.4	8.6	0 53.6	11.8	60.3
N 10	328 46.7	37.5	114 14.0	8.7	1 05.4	11.8	60.3
E 11	343 46.9	36.7	128 41.7	8.7	1 17.2	11.8	60.3
S 12	358 47.0	N14 36.0	143 09.4	8.7	N 1 29.0	11.7	60.3
D 13	13 47.1	35.2	157 37.1	8.8	1 40.7	11.7	60.2
A 14	28 47.2	34.4	172 04.9	8.8	1 52.4	11.8	60.2
Y 15	43 47.3	.. 33.7	186 32.7	8.8	2 04.2	11.6	60.2
16	58 47.4	32.9	201 00.5	8.8	2 15.8	11.7	60.1
17	73 47.5	32.1	215 28.3	8.9	2 27.5	11.6	60.1
18	88 47.7	N14 31.4	229 56.2	9.0	N 2 39.1	11.6	60.1
19	103 47.8	30.6	244 24.2	8.9	2 50.7	11.6	60.0
20	118 47.9	29.8	258 52.1	9.0	3 02.3	11.5	60.0
21	133 48.0	.. 29.1	273 20.1	9.0	3 13.8	11.5	59.9
22	148 48.1	28.3	287 48.1	9.0	3 25.3	11.4	59.9
23	163 48.2	27.5	302 16.1	9.1	N 3 36.7	11.5	59.9
	SD 15.8	d 0.8	SD 16.7	16.6	16.4		

Twilight / Moonrise

Lat.	Naut.	Civil	Sunrise	Moonrise 11	12	13	14
°	h m	h m	h m	h m	h m	h m	h m
N 72	////	////	02 01	20 23	20 16	20 09	20 02
N 70	////	////	02 40	20 13	20 13	20 13	20 13
68	////	01 15	03 06	20 06	20 11	20 16	20 21
66	////	02 04	03 26	20 00	20 10	20 19	20 29
64	////	02 34	03 42	19 54	20 08	20 21	20 35
62	01 07	02 56	03 55	19 49	20 07	20 23	20 40
60	01 51	03 13	04 07	19 45	20 06	20 25	20 45
N 58	02 18	03 28	04 16	19 42	20 05	20 27	20 49
56	02 39	03 40	04 25	19 39	20 04	20 28	20 53
54	02 56	03 51	04 32	19 36	20 03	20 29	20 56
52	03 10	04 00	04 39	19 33	20 02	20 31	20 59
50	03 22	04 08	04 45	19 30	20 02	20 32	21 02
45	03 45	04 26	04 58	19 25	20 00	20 34	21 08
N 40	04 04	04 39	05 09	19 21	19 59	20 36	21 13
35	04 18	04 51	05 18	19 17	19 58	20 38	21 17
30	04 30	05 00	05 25	19 14	19 57	20 39	21 21
20	04 49	05 16	05 39	19 08	19 54	20 42	21 28
N 10	05 03	05 29	05 51	19 02	19 54	20 45	21 34
0	05 15	05 40	06 02	18 58	19 53	20 47	21 39
S 10	05 26	05 51	06 12	18 53	19 52	20 49	21 45
20	05 35	06 01	06 24	18 47	19 50	20 52	21 51
30	05 44	06 12	06 37	18 42	19 49	20 55	21 58
35	05 48	06 18	06 44	18 38	19 48	20 56	22 02
40	05 52	06 24	06 52	18 34	19 47	20 58	22 07
45	05 57	06 31	07 02	18 30	19 46	21 01	22 12
S 50	06 01	06 40	07 14	18 24	19 45	21 03	22 19
52	06 03	06 43	07 19	18 22	19 44	21 05	22 22
54	06 06	06 47	07 25	18 19	19 44	21 06	22 25
56	06 08	06 52	07 32	18 16	19 43	21 07	22 29
58	06 10	06 57	07 39	18 13	19 42	21 09	22 33
S 60	06 13	07 02	07 48	18 09	19 41	21 11	22 38

Sunset / Twilight / Moonset

Lat.	Sunset	Civil	Naut.	Moonset 11	12	13	14
°	h m	h m	h m	h m	h m	h m	h m
N 72	22 02	////	////	04 19	06 26	08 27	10 25
N 70	21 26	////	////	04 35	06 32	08 26	10 17
68	21 01	22 46	////	04 47	06 38	08 26	10 10
66	20 41	22 01	////	04 57	06 42	08 25	10 05
64	20 26	21 33	////	05 06	06 46	08 24	10 00
62	20 13	21 11	22 55	05 13	06 49	08 24	09 56
60	20 02	20 54	22 15	05 19	06 52	08 24	09 52
N 58	19 52	20 40	21 49	05 25	06 55	08 23	09 49
56	19 44	20 28	21 28	05 30	06 57	08 23	09 46
54	19 37	20 18	21 12	05 34	06 59	08 23	09 44
52	19 30	20 09	20 59	05 38	07 01	08 22	09 41
50	19 24	20 01	20 47	05 41	07 03	08 22	09 39
45	19 11	19 44	20 24	05 49	07 06	08 22	09 35
N 40	19 01	19 30	20 06	05 55	07 09	08 21	09 31
35	18 52	19 19	19 51	06 01	07 12	08 21	09 28
30	18 44	19 09	19 40	06 06	07 14	08 20	09 25
20	18 31	18 54	19 21	06 14	07 18	08 20	09 20
N 10	18 19	18 41	19 06	06 21	07 21	08 19	09 16
0	18 08	18 30	18 55	06 28	07 24	08 19	09 12
S 10	17 58	18 19	18 45	06 34	07 27	08 18	09 08
20	17 47	18 09	18 35	06 41	07 30	08 17	09 04
30	17 34	17 59	18 27	06 49	07 34	08 17	08 59
35	17 27	17 53	18 23	06 54	07 36	08 16	08 56
40	17 18	17 46	18 18	06 59	07 38	08 16	08 53
45	17 08	17 39	18 14	07 04	07 41	08 15	08 49
S 50	16 57	17 31	18 09	07 11	07 44	08 15	08 45
52	16 52	17 27	18 07	07 15	07 46	08 14	08 43
54	16 46	17 23	18 05	07 18	07 47	08 14	08 40
56	16 39	17 19	18 03	07 22	07 49	08 14	08 38
58	16 32	17 14	18 01	07 26	07 51	08 13	08 35
S 60	16 23	17 09	17 59	07 31	07 53	08 13	08 32

SUN / MOON

Day	Eqn. of Time 00h	12h	Mer. Pass.	Mer. Pass. Upper	Lower	Age	Phase
d	m s	m s	h m	h m	h m	d	%
11	05 18	05 13	12 05	00 14	12 43	16	99
12	05 08	05 03	12 05	01 11	13 39	17	95
13	04 58	04 52	12 05	02 06	14 33	18	89

UT	ARIES	VENUS −3.8		MARS +0.5		JUPITER −1.8		SATURN +0.6		STARS		
	GHA	GHA	Dec	GHA	Dec	GHA	Dec	GHA	Dec	Name	SHA	Dec
d h	° ′	° ′	° ′	° ′	° ′	° ′	° ′	° ′	° ′		° ′	° ′
14 00	322 20.5	197 54.1	N20 09.2	104 37.1	S16 06.0	193 31.6	N19 06.2	97 03.3	S14 51.8	Acamar	315 17.7	S40 14.6
01	337 22.9	212 53.4	08.6	119 38.1	06.5	208 33.5	06.1	112 05.7	51.8	Achernar	335 26.0	S57 09.5
02	352 25.4	227 52.7	08.0	134 39.1	06.9	223 35.4	06.0	127 08.1	51.9	Acrux	173 08.7	S63 11.0
03	7 27.9	242 51.9 · ·	07.4	149 40.2 · ·	07.4	238 37.3 · ·	05.8	142 10.5 · ·	51.9	Adhara	255 12.2	S28 59.5
04	22 30.3	257 51.2	06.8	164 41.2	07.9	253 39.2	05.7	157 12.8	52.0	Aldebaran	290 48.5	N16 32.2
05	37 32.8	272 50.5	06.2	179 42.2	08.4	268 41.1	05.6	172 15.2	52.0			
06	52 35.2	287 49.7	N20 05.6	194 43.2	S16 08.9	283 43.0	N19 05.4	187 17.6	S14 52.0	Alioth	166 20.4	N55 53.1
07	67 37.7	302 49.0	05.0	209 44.2	09.4	298 44.9	05.3	202 19.9	52.1	Alkaid	152 58.5	N49 14.7
T 08	82 40.2	317 48.3	04.4	224 45.3	09.9	313 46.8	05.2	217 22.3	52.1	Al Na'ir	27 42.3	S46 53.1
H 09	97 42.6	332 47.5 · ·	03.8	239 46.3 · ·	10.4	328 48.8 · ·	05.0	232 24.7 · ·	52.1	Alnilam	275 45.7	S 1 11.6
U 10	112 45.1	347 46.8	03.2	254 47.3	10.9	343 50.7	04.9	247 27.1	52.2	Alphard	217 55.6	S 8 43.4
R 11	127 47.6	2 46.1	02.6	269 48.3	11.3	358 52.6	04.8	262 29.4	52.2			
S 12	142 50.0	17 45.4	N20 02.0	284 49.3	S16 11.8	13 54.5	N19 04.7	277 31.8	S14 52.3	Alphecca	126 10.3	N26 40.3
D 13	157 52.5	32 44.6	01.4	299 50.3	12.3	28 56.4	04.5	292 34.2	52.3	Alpheratz	357 42.3	N29 10.3
A 14	172 55.0	47 43.9	00.8	314 51.3	12.8	43 58.3	04.4	307 36.5	52.3	Altair	62 07.1	N 8 54.7
Y 15	187 57.4	62 43.2	20 00.2	329 52.4 · ·	13.3	59 00.2 · ·	04.3	322 38.9 · ·	52.4	Ankaa	353 14.6	S42 13.3
16	202 59.9	77 42.5	19 59.6	344 53.4	13.8	74 02.1	04.1	337 41.3	52.4	Antares	112 25.1	S26 27.7
17	218 02.4	92 41.7	59.0	359 54.4	14.3	89 04.0	04.0	352 43.6	52.4			
18	233 04.8	107 41.0	N19 58.4	14 55.4	S16 14.8	104 05.9	N19 03.9	7 46.0	S14 52.5	Arcturus	145 55.1	N19 06.6
19	248 07.3	122 40.3	57.8	29 56.4	15.2	119 07.8	03.7	22 48.4	52.5	Atria	107 25.9	S69 03.3
20	263 09.7	137 39.5	57.2	44 57.4	15.7	134 09.7	03.6	37 50.7	52.6	Avior	234 18.2	S59 33.4
21	278 12.2	152 38.8 · ·	56.6	59 58.4 · ·	16.2	149 11.6 · ·	03.5	52 53.1 · ·	52.6	Bellatrix	278 31.3	N 6 21.7
22	293 14.7	167 38.1	56.0	74 59.5	16.7	164 13.5	03.3	67 55.5	52.6	Betelgeuse	271 00.6	N 7 24.5
23	308 17.1	182 37.4	55.4	90 00.5	17.2	179 15.4	03.2	82 57.9	52.7			
15 00	323 19.6	197 36.6	N19 54.7	105 01.5	S16 17.7	194 17.3	N19 03.1	98 00.2	S14 52.7	Canopus	263 56.2	S52 42.1
01	338 22.1	212 35.9	54.1	120 02.5	18.2	209 19.2	02.9	113 02.6	52.7	Capella	280 33.4	N46 00.4
02	353 24.5	227 35.2	53.5	135 03.5	18.6	224 21.1	02.8	128 05.0	52.8	Deneb	49 30.4	N45 20.2
03	8 27.0	242 34.5 · ·	52.9	150 04.5 · ·	19.1	239 23.0 · ·	02.7	143 07.3 · ·	52.8	Denebola	182 33.1	N14 29.5
04	23 29.5	257 33.8	52.3	165 05.5	19.6	254 25.0	02.5	158 09.7	52.8	Diphda	348 54.9	S17 54.2
05	38 31.9	272 33.0	51.7	180 06.5	20.1	269 26.9	02.4	173 12.1	52.9			
06	53 34.4	287 32.3	N19 51.0	195 07.5	S16 20.6	284 28.8	N19 02.3	188 14.4	S14 52.9	Dubhe	193 51.4	N61 40.4
07	68 36.9	302 31.6	50.4	210 08.5	21.1	299 30.7	02.1	203 16.8	53.0	Elnath	278 11.8	N28 36.9
08	83 39.3	317 30.9	49.8	225 09.5	21.6	314 32.6	02.0	218 19.2	53.0	Eltanin	90 45.4	N51 29.7
F 09	98 41.8	332 30.1 · ·	49.2	240 10.6 · ·	22.0	329 34.5 · ·	01.9	233 21.5 · ·	53.1	Enif	33 46.0	N 9 56.8
R 10	113 44.2	347 29.4	48.6	255 11.6	22.5	344 36.4	01.7	248 23.9	53.1	Fomalhaut	15 22.8	S29 32.4
I 11	128 46.7	2 28.7	47.9	270 12.6	23.0	359 38.3	01.6	263 26.3	53.1			
D 12	143 49.2	17 28.0	N19 47.3	285 13.6	S16 23.5	14 40.2	N19 01.5	278 28.6	S14 53.2	Gacrux	172 00.3	S57 11.9
A 13	158 51.6	32 27.3	46.7	300 14.6	24.0	29 42.1	01.3	293 31.0	53.2	Gienah	175 51.7	S17 37.4
Y 14	173 54.1	47 26.5	46.0	315 15.6	24.5	44 44.0	01.2	308 33.4	53.2	Hadar	148 46.8	S60 26.8
15	188 56.6	62 25.8 · ·	45.4	330 16.6 · ·	25.0	59 45.9 · ·	01.1	323 35.7 · ·	53.3	Hamal	327 59.7	N23 31.8
16	203 59.0	77 25.1	44.8	345 17.6	25.4	74 47.8	00.9	338 38.1	53.3	Kaus Aust.	83 42.5	S34 22.5
17	219 01.5	92 24.4	44.2	0 18.6	25.9	89 49.7	00.8	353 40.4	53.4			
18	234 04.0	107 23.7	N19 43.5	15 19.6	S16 26.4	104 51.6	N19 00.7	8 42.8	S14 53.4	Kochab	137 20.4	N74 06.1
19	249 06.4	122 23.0	42.9	30 20.6	26.9	119 53.5	00.6	23 45.2	53.4	Markab	13 37.2	N15 17.2
20	264 08.9	137 22.2	42.3	45 21.6	27.4	134 55.5	00.4	38 47.5	53.5	Menkar	314 14.2	N 4 08.8
21	279 11.3	152 21.5 · ·	41.6	60 22.6 · ·	27.9	149 57.4 · ·	00.3	53 49.9 · ·	53.5	Menkent	148 06.7	S36 26.5
22	294 13.8	167 20.8	41.0	75 23.6	28.4	164 59.3	00.2	68 52.3	53.6	Miaplacidus	221 40.3	S69 46.7
23	309 16.3	182 20.1	40.4	90 24.6	28.8	180 01.2	19 00.0	83 54.6	53.6			
16 00	324 18.7	197 19.4	N19 39.7	105 25.6	S16 29.3	195 03.1	N18 59.9	98 57.0	S14 53.6	Mirfak	308 39.1	N49 54.5
01	339 21.2	212 18.7	39.1	120 26.6	29.8	210 05.0	59.8	113 59.4	53.7	Nunki	75 57.0	S26 16.5
02	354 23.7	227 17.9	38.4	135 27.6	30.3	225 06.9	59.6	129 01.7	53.7	Peacock	53 17.5	S56 41.1
03	9 26.1	242 17.2 · ·	37.8	150 28.6 · ·	30.8	240 08.8 · ·	59.5	144 04.1 · ·	53.8	Pollux	243 27.1	N27 59.3
04	24 28.6	257 16.5	37.2	165 29.6	31.3	255 10.7	59.4	159 06.5	53.8	Procyon	244 59.2	N 5 11.1
05	39 31.1	272 15.8	36.5	180 30.6	31.8	270 12.6	59.2	174 08.8	53.8			
06	54 33.5	287 15.1	N19 35.9	195 31.6	S16 32.2	285 14.5	N18 59.1	189 11.2	S14 53.9	Rasalhague	96 05.5	N12 33.3
07	69 36.0	302 14.4	35.2	210 32.6	32.7	300 16.4	59.0	204 13.5	53.9	Regulus	207 43.0	N11 53.7
S 08	84 38.5	317 13.7	34.6	225 33.6	33.2	315 18.3	58.8	219 15.9	53.9	Rigel	281 11.4	S 8 11.1
A 09	99 40.9	332 12.9 · ·	33.9	240 34.6 · ·	33.7	330 20.2 · ·	58.7	234 18.3 · ·	54.0	Rigil Kent.	139 50.7	S60 53.8
T 10	114 43.4	347 12.2	33.3	255 35.6	34.2	345 22.2	58.6	249 20.6	54.0	Sabik	102 11.4	S15 44.4
U 11	129 45.8	2 11.5	32.6	270 36.6	34.7	0 24.1	58.4	264 23.0	54.1			
R 12	144 48.3	17 10.8	N19 32.0	285 37.6	S16 35.1	15 26.0	N18 58.3	279 25.4	S14 54.1	Schedar	349 39.1	N56 36.9
D 13	159 50.8	32 10.1	31.3	300 38.6	35.6	30 27.9	58.2	294 27.7	54.1	Shaula	96 20.6	S37 06.7
A 14	174 53.2	47 09.4	30.7	315 39.6	36.1	45 29.8	58.0	309 30.1	54.2	Sirius	258 33.5	S16 44.2
Y 15	189 55.7	62 08.7 · ·	30.0	330 40.6 · ·	36.6	60 31.7 · ·	57.9	324 32.4 · ·	54.2	Spica	158 30.5	S11 14.2
16	204 58.2	77 08.0	29.4	345 41.6	37.1	75 33.6	57.8	339 34.8	54.3	Suhail	222 52.2	S43 29.6
17	220 00.6	92 07.3	28.7	0 42.5	37.6	90 35.5	57.6	354 37.2	54.3			
18	235 03.1	107 06.5	N19 28.1	15 43.5	S16 38.0	105 37.4	N18 57.5	9 39.5	S14 54.3	Vega	80 38.1	N38 48.2
19	250 05.6	122 05.8	27.4	30 44.5	38.5	120 39.3	57.4	24 41.9	54.4	Zuben'ubi	137 04.5	S16 06.0
20	265 08.0	137 05.1	26.8	45 45.5	39.0	135 41.2	57.2	39 44.2	54.4		SHA	Mer.Pass.
21	280 10.5	152 04.4 · ·	26.1	60 46.5 · ·	39.5	150 43.1 · ·	57.1	54 46.6 · ·	54.5		° ′	h m
22	295 13.0	167 03.7	25.5	75 47.5	40.0	165 45.0	57.0	69 49.0	54.5	Venus	234 17.0	10 50
23	310 15.4	182 03.0	24.8	90 48.5	40.5	180 47.0	56.8	84 51.3	54.5	Mars	141 41.9	16 59
	h m									Jupiter	230 57.7	11 01
Mer.Pass. 2 26.3		v −0.7	d 0.6	v 1.0	d 0.5	v 1.9	d 0.1	v 2.4	d 0.0	Saturn	134 40.6	17 25

SUN and MOON

UT	SUN GHA	SUN Dec	MOON GHA	v	MOON Dec	d	HP
d h	° ′	° ′	° ′	′	° ′	′	′
14 00	178 48.4	N14 26.8	316 44.2	9.1	N 3 48.2	11.4	59.8
01	193 48.5	26.0	331 12.3	9.1	3 59.6	11.3	59.8
02	208 48.6	25.2	345 40.4	9.2	4 10.9	11.3	59.8
03	223 48.7	.. 24.5	0 08.6	9.2	4 22.2	11.3	59.7
04	238 48.8	23.7	14 36.8	9.2	4 33.5	11.2	59.7
05	253 48.9	22.9	29 05.0	9.2	4 44.7	11.2	59.7
06	268 49.1	N14 22.2	43 33.2	9.3	N 4 55.9	11.1	59.6
07	283 49.2	21.4	58 01.5	9.3	5 07.0	11.1	59.6
T 08	298 49.3	20.6	72 29.8	9.3	5 18.1	11.1	59.5
H 09	313 49.4	.. 19.8	86 58.1	9.3	5 29.2	11.0	59.5
U 10	328 49.5	19.1	101 26.4	9.4	5 40.2	10.9	59.5
R 11	343 49.6	18.3	115 54.8	9.3	5 51.1	10.9	59.4
S 12	358 49.8	N14 17.5	130 23.1	9.4	N 6 02.0	10.9	59.4
D 13	13 49.9	16.8	144 51.5	9.5	6 12.9	10.8	59.4
A 14	28 50.0	16.0	159 20.0	9.4	6 23.7	10.7	59.3
Y 15	43 50.1	.. 15.2	173 48.4	9.5	6 34.4	10.7	59.3
16	58 50.2	14.4	188 16.9	9.5	6 45.1	10.6	59.2
17	73 50.4	13.7	202 45.4	9.5	6 55.7	10.6	59.2
18	88 50.5	N14 12.9	217 13.9	9.5	N 7 06.3	10.6	59.2
19	103 50.6	12.1	231 42.4	9.6	7 16.9	10.4	59.1
20	118 50.7	11.3	246 11.0	9.6	7 27.3	10.4	59.1
21	133 50.8	.. 10.6	260 39.6	9.6	7 37.7	10.4	59.0
22	148 51.0	09.8	275 08.2	9.6	7 48.1	10.3	59.0
23	163 51.1	09.0	289 36.8	9.6	7 58.4	10.2	59.0
15 00	178 51.2	N14 08.2	304 05.4	9.7	N 8 08.6	10.2	58.9
01	193 51.3	07.5	318 34.1	9.6	8 18.8	10.1	58.9
02	208 51.4	06.7	333 02.7	9.7	8 28.9	10.1	58.9
03	223 51.6	.. 05.9	347 31.4	9.7	8 39.0	10.0	58.8
04	238 51.7	05.1	2 00.1	9.8	8 49.0	9.9	58.8
05	253 51.8	04.3	16 28.9	9.7	8 58.9	9.8	58.7
06	268 51.9	N14 03.6	30 57.6	9.8	N 9 08.7	9.8	58.7
07	283 52.1	02.8	45 26.4	9.7	9 18.5	9.8	58.7
F 08	298 52.2	02.0	59 55.1	9.8	9 28.3	9.6	58.6
R 09	313 52.3	.. 01.2	74 23.9	9.8	9 37.9	9.6	58.6
I 10	328 52.4	14 00.4	88 52.7	9.9	9 47.5	9.5	58.5
D 11	343 52.6	13 59.7	103 21.6	9.8	9 57.0	9.5	58.5
A 12	358 52.7	N13 58.9	117 50.4	9.8	N10 06.5	9.4	58.5
Y 13	13 52.8	58.1	132 19.2	9.9	10 15.9	9.3	58.4
14	28 52.9	57.3	146 48.1	9.9	10 25.2	9.2	58.4
15	43 53.1	.. 56.5	161 17.0	9.9	10 34.4	9.2	58.3
16	58 53.2	55.7	175 45.9	9.9	10 43.6	9.1	58.3
17	73 53.3	55.0	190 14.8	9.9	10 52.7	9.0	58.3
18	88 53.4	N13 54.2	204 43.7	9.9	N11 01.7	8.9	58.2
19	103 53.6	53.4	219 12.6	10.0	11 10.6	8.9	58.2
20	118 53.7	52.6	233 41.6	9.9	11 19.5	8.8	58.1
21	133 53.8	.. 51.8	248 10.5	10.0	11 28.3	8.7	58.1
22	148 53.9	51.0	262 39.5	10.0	11 37.0	8.6	58.1
23	163 54.1	50.3	277 08.5	10.0	11 45.6	8.6	58.0
16 00	178 54.2	N13 49.5	291 37.5	10.0	N11 54.2	8.5	58.0
01	193 54.3	48.7	306 06.5	10.0	12 02.7	8.4	57.9
02	208 54.4	47.9	320 35.5	10.1	12 11.1	8.3	57.9
03	223 54.6	.. 47.1	335 04.6	10.0	12 19.4	8.3	57.9
04	238 54.7	46.3	349 33.6	10.1	12 27.7	8.1	57.8
05	253 54.8	45.5	4 02.7	10.0	12 35.8	8.1	57.8
06	268 55.0	N13 44.7	18 31.7	10.1	N12 43.9	8.0	57.7
07	283 55.1	44.0	33 00.8	10.1	12 51.9	8.0	57.7
S 08	298 55.2	43.2	47 29.9	10.1	12 59.9	7.8	57.7
A 09	313 55.3	.. 42.4	61 59.0	10.1	13 07.7	7.8	57.6
T 10	328 55.5	41.6	76 28.1	10.1	13 15.5	7.7	57.6
U 11	343 55.6	40.8	90 57.2	10.1	13 23.2	7.6	57.5
R 12	358 55.7	N13 40.0	105 26.3	10.2	N13 30.8	7.5	57.5
D 13	13 55.9	39.2	119 55.5	10.1	13 38.3	7.4	57.5
A 14	28 56.0	38.4	134 24.6	10.2	13 45.7	7.3	57.4
Y 15	43 56.1	.. 37.6	148 53.8	10.2	13 53.0	7.3	57.4
16	58 56.2	36.8	163 23.0	10.1	14 00.3	7.2	57.4
17	73 56.4	36.0	177 52.1	10.2	14 07.5	7.1	57.3
18	88 56.5	N13 35.2	192 21.3	10.2	N14 14.6	7.0	57.3
19	103 56.6	34.5	206 50.5	10.2	14 21.6	6.9	57.2
20	118 56.8	33.7	221 19.7	10.3	14 28.5	6.8	57.2
21	133 56.9	.. 32.9	235 49.0	10.2	14 35.3	6.7	57.2
22	148 57.0	32.1	250 18.2	10.2	14 42.0	6.7	57.1
23	163 57.2	31.3	264 47.4	10.3	N14 48.7	6.5	57.1
SD	15.8	d 0.8	SD 16.2		15.9		15.7

Twilight, Sunrise and Moonrise

Lat.	Naut.	Civil	Sunrise	Moonrise 14	15	16	17
°	h m	h m	h m	h m	h m	h m	h m
N 72	////	////	02 23	20 02	19 55	19 47	19 35
N 70	////	////	02 56	20 13	20 14	20 16	20 22
68	////	01 42	03 19	20 21	20 28	20 38	20 53
66	////	02 20	03 37	20 29	20 40	20 55	21 16
64	////	02 46	03 51	20 35	20 50	21 09	21 34
62	01 31	03 06	04 04	20 40	20 59	21 21	21 49
60	02 05	03 22	04 14	20 45	21 06	21 31	22 02
N 58	02 29	03 36	04 23	20 49	21 13	21 40	22 12
56	02 48	03 47	04 31	20 53	21 19	21 48	22 22
54	03 04	03 57	04 38	20 56	21 24	21 55	22 30
52	03 16	04 06	04 44	20 59	21 29	22 01	22 38
50	03 28	04 13	04 49	21 02	21 33	22 07	22 45
45	03 50	04 29	05 01	21 08	21 42	22 19	22 59
N 40	04 07	04 42	05 11	21 13	21 50	22 29	23 11
35	04 21	04 53	05 20	21 17	21 57	22 38	23 22
30	04 32	05 02	05 27	21 21	22 03	22 46	23 31
20	04 50	05 17	05 40	21 28	22 13	22 59	23 46
N 10	05 04	05 29	05 51	21 34	22 22	23 11	24 00
0	05 15	05 40	06 01	21 39	22 31	23 22	24 13
S 10	05 25	05 50	06 11	21 45	22 40	23 33	24 26
20	05 33	05 59	06 22	21 51	22 49	23 45	24 40
30	05 41	06 09	06 34	21 58	23 00	23 59	24 55
35	05 45	06 15	06 41	22 02	23 06	24 07	00 07
40	05 49	06 20	06 48	22 07	23 13	24 16	00 16
45	05 52	06 27	06 57	22 12	23 21	24 27	00 27
S 50	05 57	06 35	07 08	22 19	23 31	24 40	00 40
52	05 58	06 38	07 13	22 22	23 36	24 46	00 46
54	06 00	06 42	07 19	22 25	23 41	24 52	00 52
56	06 02	06 46	07 25	22 29	23 47	25 00	01 00
58	06 04	06 50	07 32	22 33	23 53	25 08	01 08
S 60	06 06	06 55	07 40	22 38	24 00	00 00	01 18

Sunset, Twilight and Moonset

Lat.	Sunset	Civil	Naut.	Moonset 14	15	16	17
°	h m	h m	h m	h m	h m	h m	h m
N 72	21 40	////	////	10 25	12 21	14 17	16 15
N 70	21 09	23 34	////	10 17	12 04	13 49	15 28
68	20 47	22 20	////	10 10	11 51	13 28	14 58
66	20 29	21 44	////	10 05	11 40	13 11	14 36
64	20 15	21 19	23 38	10 00	11 31	12 58	14 18
62	20 04	21 00	22 32	09 56	11 24	12 47	14 04
60	19 53	20 44	22 00	09 52	11 17	12 37	13 52
N 58	19 45	20 31	21 36	09 49	11 11	12 29	13 41
56	19 37	20 20	21 18	09 46	11 06	12 22	13 32
54	19 30	20 11	21 03	09 44	11 02	12 15	13 24
52	19 24	20 02	20 51	09 41	10 57	12 09	13 17
50	19 19	19 54	20 40	09 39	10 54	12 04	13 10
45	19 07	19 39	20 18	09 35	10 45	11 53	12 56
N 40	18 57	19 26	20 01	09 31	10 39	11 43	12 45
35	18 49	19 15	19 47	09 28	10 33	11 35	12 35
30	18 41	19 06	19 36	09 25	10 28	11 28	12 26
20	18 29	18 52	19 19	09 20	10 19	11 16	12 11
N 10	18 18	18 40	19 05	09 16	10 11	11 05	11 59
0	18 08	18 29	18 54	09 12	10 04	10 55	11 46
S 10	17 58	18 20	18 44	09 08	09 57	10 46	11 34
20	17 47	18 10	18 36	09 04	09 49	10 35	11 22
30	17 36	18 00	18 28	08 59	09 40	10 23	11 07
35	17 29	17 55	18 25	08 56	09 35	10 16	10 58
40	17 21	17 49	18 21	08 53	09 30	10 08	10 49
45	17 12	17 43	18 17	08 49	09 23	09 59	10 37
S 50	17 01	17 35	18 13	08 45	09 15	09 48	10 24
52	16 56	17 32	18 12	08 43	09 11	09 43	10 17
54	16 51	17 28	18 10	08 40	09 07	09 37	10 10
56	16 45	17 24	18 08	08 38	09 03	09 31	10 02
58	16 38	17 20	18 06	08 35	08 58	09 24	09 53
S 60	16 30	17 15	18 04	08 32	08 53	09 16	09 43

Day	SUN Eqn. of Time 00h	12h	Mer. Pass.	MOON Mer. Pass. Upper	Lower	Age	Phase
d	m s	m s	h m	h m	h m	d	%
14	04 47	04 41	12 05	02 59	15 26	19	81
15	04 35	04 30	12 04	03 52	16 18	20	71
16	04 24	04 17	12 04	04 43	17 09	21	61

UT	ARIES GHA	VENUS −3.8 GHA	Dec	MARS +0.6 GHA	Dec	JUPITER −1.8 GHA	Dec	SATURN +0.6 GHA	Dec	STARS Name	SHA	Dec
17 00	325 17.9	197 02.3	N19 24.1	105 49.5	S16 40.9	195 48.9	N18 56.7	99 53.7	S14 54.6	Acamar	315 17.7	S40 14.6
01	340 20.3	212 01.6	23.5	120 50.5	41.4	210 50.8	56.6	114 56.0	54.6	Achernar	335 26.0	S57 09.5
02	355 22.8	227 00.9	22.8	135 51.5	41.9	225 52.7	56.4	129 58.4	54.7	Acrux	173 08.7	S63 11.0
03	10 25.3	242 00.2 ..	22.1	150 52.5 ..	42.4	240 54.6 ..	56.3	145 00.8 ..	54.7	Adhara	255 12.2	S28 59.5
04	25 27.7	256 59.5	21.5	165 53.4	42.9	255 56.5	56.2	160 03.1	54.7	Aldebaran	290 48.5	N16 32.2
05	40 30.2	271 58.8	20.8	180 54.4	43.4	270 58.4	56.0	175 05.5	54.8			
06	55 32.7	286 58.1	N19 20.1	195 55.4	S16 43.8	286 00.3	N18 55.9	190 07.8	S14 54.8	Alioth	166 20.4	N55 53.1
07	70 35.1	301 57.4	19.5	210 56.4	44.3	301 02.2	55.8	205 10.2	54.9	Alkaid	152 58.5	N49 14.7
S 08	85 37.6	316 56.7	18.8	225 57.4	44.8	316 04.1	55.6	220 12.6	54.9	Al Na'ir	27 42.3	S46 53.2
U 09	100 40.1	331 56.0 ..	18.1	240 58.4 ..	45.3	331 06.0 ..	55.5	235 14.9 ..	54.9	Alnilam	275 45.7	S 1 11.6
N 10	115 42.5	346 55.3	17.5	255 59.4	45.8	346 08.0	55.4	250 17.3	55.0	Alphard	217 55.6	S 8 43.4
D 11	130 45.0	1 54.5	16.8	271 00.3	46.2	1 09.9	55.2	265 19.6	55.0			
A 12	145 47.4	16 53.8	N19 16.1	286 01.3	S16 46.7	16 11.8	N18 55.1	280 22.0	S14 55.1	Alphecca	126 10.3	N26 40.3
Y 13	160 49.9	31 53.1	15.5	301 02.3	47.2	31 13.7	55.0	295 24.4	55.1	Alpheratz	357 42.3	N29 10.3
14	175 52.4	46 52.4	14.8	316 03.3	47.7	46 15.6	54.8	310 26.7	55.2	Altair	62 07.1	N 8 54.8
15	190 54.8	61 51.7 ..	14.1	331 04.3 ..	48.2	61 17.5 ..	54.7	325 29.1 ..	55.2	Ankaa	353 14.6	S42 13.3
16	205 57.3	76 51.0	13.4	346 05.3	48.7	76 19.4	54.6	340 31.4	55.2	Antares	112 25.1	S26 27.7
17	220 59.8	91 50.3	12.7	1 06.2	49.1	91 21.3	54.4	355 33.8	55.3			
18	236 02.2	106 49.6	N19 12.1	16 07.2	S16 49.6	106 23.2	N18 54.3	10 36.1	S14 55.3	Arcturus	145 55.1	N19 06.6
19	251 04.7	121 48.9	11.4	31 08.2	50.1	121 25.1	54.2	25 38.5	55.4	Atria	107 26.0	S69 03.3
20	266 07.2	136 48.2	10.7	46 09.2	50.6	136 27.0	54.0	40 40.9	55.4	Avior	234 18.2	S59 33.4
21	281 09.6	151 47.5 ..	10.0	61 10.2 ..	51.1	151 29.0 ..	53.9	55 43.2 ..	55.4	Bellatrix	278 31.3	N 6 21.7
22	296 12.1	166 46.8	09.3	76 11.2	51.5	166 30.9	53.8	70 45.6	55.5	Betelgeuse	271 00.6	N 7 24.5
23	311 14.6	181 46.1	08.7	91 12.1	52.0	181 32.8	53.6	85 47.9	55.5			
18 00	326 17.0	196 45.4	N19 08.0	106 13.1	S16 52.5	196 34.7	N18 53.5	100 50.3	S14 55.6	Canopus	263 56.1	S52 42.1
01	341 19.5	211 44.7	07.3	121 14.1	53.0	211 36.6	53.4	115 52.6	55.6	Capella	280 33.4	N46 00.4
02	356 21.9	226 44.0	06.6	136 15.1	53.5	226 38.5	53.2	130 55.0	55.6	Deneb	49 30.4	N45 20.3
03	11 24.4	241 43.4 ..	05.9	151 16.1 ..	53.9	241 40.4 ..	53.1	145 57.3 ..	55.7	Denebola	182 33.1	N14 29.5
04	26 26.9	256 42.7	05.2	166 17.0	54.4	256 42.3	53.0	160 59.7	55.7	Diphda	348 54.9	S17 54.2
05	41 29.3	271 42.0	04.5	181 18.0	54.9	271 44.2	52.8	176 02.1	55.8			
06	56 31.8	286 41.3	N19 03.9	196 19.0	S16 55.4	286 46.1	N18 52.7	191 04.4	S14 55.8	Dubhe	193 51.5	N61 40.4
07	71 34.3	301 40.6	03.2	211 20.0	55.9	301 48.1	52.6	206 06.8	55.8	Elnath	278 11.7	N28 36.9
08	86 36.7	316 39.9	02.5	226 20.9	56.3	316 50.0	52.4	221 09.1	55.9	Eltanin	90 45.5	N51 29.7
M 09	101 39.2	331 39.2 ..	01.8	241 21.9 ..	56.8	331 51.9 ..	52.3	236 11.5 ..	55.9	Enif	33 46.0	N 9 56.8
O 10	116 41.7	346 38.5	01.1	256 22.9	57.3	346 53.8	52.2	251 13.8	56.0	Fomalhaut	15 22.8	S29 32.4
N 11	131 44.1	1 37.8	19 00.4	271 23.9	57.8	1 55.7	52.0	266 16.2	56.0			
D 12	146 46.6	16 37.1	N18 59.7	286 24.8	S16 58.3	16 57.6	N18 51.9	281 18.5	S14 56.1	Gacrux	172 00.3	S57 11.9
A 13	161 49.1	31 36.4	59.0	301 25.8	58.7	31 59.5	51.8	296 20.9	56.1	Gienah	175 51.7	S17 37.4
Y 14	176 51.5	46 35.7	58.3	316 26.8	59.2	47 01.4	51.6	311 23.3	56.1	Hadar	148 46.8	S60 26.7
15	191 54.0	61 35.0 ..	57.6	331 27.8	16 59.7	62 03.3 ..	51.5	326 25.6 ..	56.2	Hamal	327 59.7	N23 31.8
16	206 56.4	76 34.3	56.9	346 28.7	17 00.2	77 05.3	51.4	341 28.0	56.2	Kaus Aust.	83 42.5	S34 22.5
17	221 58.9	91 33.6	56.2	1 29.7	00.7	92 07.2	51.2	356 30.3	56.3			
18	237 01.4	106 32.9	N18 55.5	16 30.7	S17 01.1	107 09.1	N18 51.1	11 32.7	S14 56.3	Kochab	137 20.4	N74 06.1
19	252 03.8	121 32.2	54.8	31 31.6	01.6	122 11.0	51.0	26 35.0	56.3	Markab	13 37.2	N15 17.2
20	267 06.3	136 31.6	54.1	46 32.6	02.1	137 12.9	50.8	41 37.4	56.4	Menkar	314 14.1	N 4 08.8
21	282 08.8	151 30.9 ..	53.4	61 33.6 ..	02.6	152 14.8 ..	50.7	56 39.7 ..	56.4	Menkent	148 06.7	S36 26.5
22	297 11.2	166 30.2	52.7	76 34.6	03.1	167 16.7	50.6	71 42.1	56.5	Miaplacidus	221 40.3	S69 46.7
23	312 13.7	181 29.5	52.0	91 35.5	03.5	182 18.6	50.4	86 44.4	56.5			
19 00	327 16.2	196 28.8	N18 51.3	106 36.5	S17 04.0	197 20.5	N18 50.3	101 46.8	S14 56.6	Mirfak	308 39.1	N49 54.5
01	342 18.6	211 28.1	50.6	121 37.5	04.5	212 22.5	50.2	116 49.1	56.6	Nunki	75 57.0	S26 16.5
02	357 21.1	226 27.4	49.9	136 38.4	05.0	227 24.4	50.0	131 51.5	56.6	Peacock	53 17.5	S56 41.1
03	12 23.5	241 26.7 ..	49.2	151 39.4 ..	05.4	242 26.3 ..	49.9	146 53.8 ..	56.7	Pollux	243 27.1	N27 59.3
04	27 26.0	256 26.0	48.5	166 40.4	05.9	257 28.2	49.8	161 56.2	56.7	Procyon	244 59.2	N 5 11.1
05	42 28.5	271 25.4	47.7	181 41.3	06.4	272 30.1	49.6	176 58.6	56.8			
06	57 30.9	286 24.7	N18 47.0	196 42.3	S17 06.9	287 32.0	N18 49.5	192 00.9	S14 56.8	Rasalhague	96 05.5	N12 33.3
07	72 33.4	301 24.0	46.3	211 43.3	07.4	302 33.9	49.4	207 03.3	56.9	Regulus	207 43.0	N11 53.5
T 08	87 35.9	316 23.3	45.6	226 44.2	07.8	317 35.8	49.2	222 05.6	56.9	Rigel	281 11.4	S 8 11.1
U 09	102 38.3	331 22.6 ..	44.9	241 45.2 ..	08.3	332 37.8 ..	49.1	237 08.0 ..	56.9	Rigil Kent.	139 50.7	S60 53.8
E 10	117 40.8	346 21.9	44.2	256 46.2	08.8	347 39.7	49.0	252 10.3	57.0	Sabik	102 11.5	S15 44.4
S 11	132 43.3	1 21.2	43.5	271 47.1	09.3	2 41.6	48.8	267 12.7	57.0			
D 12	147 45.7	16 20.6	N18 42.7	286 48.1	S17 09.7	17 43.5	N18 48.7	282 15.0	S14 57.1	Schedar	349 39.1	N56 36.9
A 13	162 48.2	31 19.9	42.0	301 49.1	10.2	32 45.4	48.6	297 17.4	57.1	Shaula	96 20.6	S37 06.7
Y 14	177 50.7	46 19.2	41.3	316 50.0	10.7	47 47.3	48.4	312 19.7	57.1	Sirius	258 33.2	S16 44.2
15	192 53.1	61 18.5 ..	40.6	331 51.0 ..	11.2	62 49.2 ..	48.3	327 22.1 ..	57.2	Spica	158 30.5	S11 14.2
16	207 55.6	76 17.8	39.9	346 52.0	11.7	77 51.1	48.2	342 24.4	57.2	Suhail	222 52.2	S43 29.6
17	222 58.0	91 17.1	39.1	1 52.9	12.1	92 53.1	48.0	357 26.8	57.3			
18	238 00.5	106 16.5	N18 38.4	16 53.9	S17 12.6	107 55.0	N18 47.9	12 29.1	S14 57.3	Vega	80 38.1	N38 48.3
19	253 03.0	121 15.8	37.7	31 54.8	13.1	122 56.9	47.8	27 31.5	57.4	Zuben'ubi	137 04.6	S16 06.0
20	268 05.4	136 15.1	37.0	46 55.8	13.6	137 58.8	47.6	42 33.8	57.4		SHA	Mer. Pass.
21	283 07.9	151 14.4 ..	36.2	61 56.8 ..	14.0	153 00.7 ..	47.5	57 36.2 ..	57.4		° ′	h m
22	298 10.4	166 13.7	35.5	76 57.7	14.5	168 02.6	47.4	72 38.5	57.5	Venus	230 28.4	10 53
23	313 12.8	181 13.1	34.8	91 58.7	15.0	183 04.5	47.2	87 40.9	57.5	Mars	139 56.1	16 54
Mer. Pass.	h m 2 14.5	v −0.7	d 0.7	v 1.0	d 0.5	v 1.9	d 0.1	v 2.4	d 0.0	Jupiter Saturn	230 17.7 134 33.3	10 52 17 14

UT	SUN GHA	SUN Dec	MOON GHA	v	Dec	d	HP
d h	° ′	° ′	° ′	′	° ′	′	′
17 00	178 57.3	N13 30.5	279 16.7	10.2	N14 55.2	6.5	57.1
01	193 57.4	29.7	293 45.9	10.3	15 01.7	6.4	57.0
02	208 57.6	28.9	308 15.2	10.3	15 08.1	6.3	57.0
03	223 57.7	.. 28.1	322 44.5	10.3	15 14.4	6.2	56.9
04	238 57.8	27.3	337 13.8	10.3	15 20.6	6.1	56.9
05	253 58.0	26.5	351 43.1	10.3	15 26.7	6.1	56.9
06	268 58.1	N13 25.7	6 12.4	10.3	N15 32.8	5.9	56.8
07	283 58.2	24.9	20 41.7	10.3	15 38.7	5.8	56.8
08	298 58.4	24.1	35 11.0	10.4	15 44.5	5.8	56.8
S 09	313 58.5	.. 23.3	49 40.4	10.3	15 50.3	5.7	56.7
U 10	328 58.6	22.5	64 09.7	10.4	15 56.0	5.5	56.7
N 11	343 58.8	21.7	78 39.1	10.3	16 01.5	5.5	56.7
D 12	358 58.9	N13 20.9	93 08.4	10.4	N16 07.0	5.4	56.6
A 13	13 59.0	20.1	107 37.8	10.4	16 12.4	5.3	56.6
Y 14	28 59.2	19.3	122 07.2	10.4	16 17.7	5.2	56.6
15	43 59.3	.. 18.5	136 36.6	10.4	16 22.9	5.2	56.5
16	58 59.4	17.7	151 06.0	10.4	16 28.1	5.0	56.5
17	73 59.6	16.9	165 35.4	10.5	16 33.1	4.9	56.5
18	88 59.7	N13 16.1	180 04.9	10.4	N16 38.0	4.8	56.4
19	103 59.8	15.3	194 34.3	10.5	16 42.8	4.8	56.4
20	119 00.0	14.5	209 03.8	10.4	16 47.6	4.6	56.4
21	134 00.1	.. 13.7	223 33.2	10.5	16 52.2	4.6	56.3
22	149 00.3	12.9	238 02.7	10.5	16 56.8	4.5	56.3
23	164 00.4	12.1	252 32.2	10.5	17 01.3	4.3	56.3
18 00	179 00.5	N13 11.3	267 01.7	10.5	N17 05.6	4.3	56.2
01	194 00.7	10.5	281 31.2	10.5	17 09.9	4.2	56.2
02	209 00.8	09.7	296 00.7	10.5	17 14.1	4.1	56.2
03	224 00.9	.. 08.9	310 30.2	10.6	17 18.2	4.0	56.1
04	239 01.1	08.1	324 59.8	10.6	17 22.2	3.9	56.1
05	254 01.2	07.2	339 29.4	10.5	17 26.1	3.8	56.1
06	269 01.4	N13 06.4	353 58.9	10.6	N17 29.9	3.7	56.0
07	284 01.5	05.6	8 28.5	10.6	17 33.6	3.6	56.0
08	299 01.6	04.8	22 58.1	10.6	17 37.2	3.6	56.0
M 09	314 01.8	.. 04.0	37 27.7	10.6	17 40.8	3.4	55.9
O 10	329 01.9	03.2	51 57.3	10.7	17 44.2	3.3	55.9
N 11	344 02.0	02.4	66 27.0	10.6	17 47.5	3.3	55.9
D 12	359 02.2	N13 01.6	80 56.6	10.7	N17 50.8	3.1	55.9
A 13	14 02.3	00.8	95 26.3	10.7	17 53.9	3.1	55.8
Y 14	29 02.5	13 00.0	109 56.0	10.7	17 57.0	2.9	55.8
15	44 02.6	12 59.2	124 25.7	10.7	17 59.9	2.9	55.8
16	59 02.7	58.4	138 55.4	10.7	18 02.8	2.8	55.7
17	74 02.9	57.5	153 25.1	10.8	18 05.6	2.7	55.7
18	89 03.0	N12 56.7	167 54.9	10.7	N18 08.3	2.5	55.7
19	104 03.2	55.9	182 24.6	10.8	18 10.8	2.5	55.7
20	119 03.3	55.1	196 54.4	10.8	18 13.3	2.4	55.6
21	134 03.5	.. 54.3	211 24.2	10.8	18 15.7	2.3	55.6
22	149 03.6	53.5	225 54.0	10.8	18 18.0	2.2	55.6
23	164 03.7	52.7	240 23.8	10.8	18 20.2	2.1	55.5
19 00	179 03.9	N12 51.9	254 53.6	10.9	N18 22.3	2.0	55.5
01	194 04.0	51.1	269 23.5	10.9	18 24.3	2.0	55.5
02	209 04.2	50.2	283 53.4	10.8	18 26.3	1.8	55.5
03	224 04.3	.. 49.4	298 23.2	11.0	18 28.1	1.7	55.4
04	239 04.4	48.6	312 53.2	10.9	18 29.8	1.6	55.4
05	254 04.6	47.8	327 23.1	10.9	18 31.4	1.6	55.4
06	269 04.7	N12 47.0	341 53.0	11.0	N18 33.0	1.4	55.4
07	284 04.9	46.2	356 23.0	11.0	18 34.4	1.4	55.3
08	299 05.0	45.3	10 53.0	11.0	18 35.8	1.3	55.3
T 09	314 05.2	.. 44.5	25 23.0	11.0	18 37.1	1.1	55.3
U 10	329 05.3	43.7	39 53.0	11.0	18 38.2	1.1	55.3
E 11	344 05.5	42.9	54 23.0	11.1	18 39.3	1.0	55.2
S 12	359 05.6	N12 42.1	68 53.1	11.1	N18 40.3	0.9	55.2
D 13	14 05.7	41.3	83 23.2	11.1	18 41.2	0.8	55.2
A 14	29 05.9	40.4	97 53.3	11.1	18 42.0	0.7	55.2
Y 15	44 06.0	.. 39.6	112 23.4	11.1	18 42.7	0.6	55.1
16	59 06.2	38.8	126 53.5	11.2	18 43.3	0.5	55.1
17	74 06.3	38.0	141 23.7	11.2	18 43.8	0.4	55.1
18	89 06.5	N12 37.2	155 53.9	11.2	N18 44.2	0.4	55.1
19	104 06.6	36.4	170 24.1	11.2	18 44.6	0.2	55.1
20	119 06.8	35.5	184 54.3	11.3	18 44.8	0.1	55.0
21	134 06.9	.. 34.7	199 24.6	11.2	18 44.9	0.1	55.0
22	149 07.1	33.9	213 54.8	11.3	18 45.0	0.0	55.0
23	164 07.2	33.1	228 25.1	11.3	N18 45.0	0.2	55.0
	SD 15.8	d 0.8	SD 15.4		15.2		15.0

Lat.	Twilight Naut.	Twilight Civil	Sunrise	Moonrise 17	18	19	20
°	h m	h m	h m	h m	h m	h m	h m
N 72	////	////	02 43	19 35	□	□	□
N 70	////	01 12	03 11	20 22	20 37	21 11	22 13
68	////	02 04	03 31	20 53	21 18	21 58	22 55
66	////	02 36	03 47	21 16	21 46	22 28	23 24
64	01 03	02 58	04 01	21 34	22 07	22 51	23 46
62	01 50	03 16	04 12	21 49	22 24	23 09	24 03
60	02 19	03 31	04 21	22 02	22 39	23 24	24 18
N 58	02 40	03 43	04 29	22 12	22 51	23 37	24 30
56	02 57	03 54	04 36	22 22	23 02	23 48	24 41
54	03 11	04 03	04 43	22 30	23 11	23 58	24 50
52	03 23	04 11	04 49	22 38	23 19	24 06	00 06
50	03 33	04 18	04 54	22 45	23 27	24 14	00 14
45	03 54	04 33	05 05	22 59	23 43	24 31	00 31
N 40	04 11	04 45	05 14	23 11	23 56	24 44	00 44
35	04 24	04 55	05 22	23 22	24 07	00 07	00 56
30	04 34	05 04	05 29	23 31	24 17	00 17	01 06
20	04 51	05 18	05 41	23 46	24 34	00 34	01 23
N 10	05 04	05 29	05 51	24 00	00 00	00 49	01 38
0	05 15	05 39	06 00	24 13	00 13	01 03	01 52
S 10	05 23	05 48	06 10	24 26	00 26	01 17	02 07
20	05 31	05 57	06 20	24 40	00 40	01 32	02 22
30	05 38	06 06	06 31	24 55	00 55	01 49	02 39
35	05 42	06 11	06 37	00 07	01 05	01 59	02 49
40	05 45	06 17	06 44	00 16	01 15	02 10	03 01
45	05 48	06 22	06 53	00 27	01 28	02 24	03 15
S 50	05 51	06 29	07 03	00 40	01 43	02 40	03 31
52	05 53	06 32	07 07	00 46	01 50	02 48	03 39
54	05 54	06 36	07 12	00 52	01 58	02 57	03 48
56	05 56	06 39	07 18	01 00	02 07	03 06	03 58
58	05 57	06 43	07 24	01 08	02 17	03 17	04 09
S 60	05 58	06 47	07 31	01 18	02 28	03 30	04 22

Lat.	Sunset	Twilight Civil	Twilight Naut.	Moonset 17	18	19	20
°	h m	h m	h m	h m	h m	h m	h m
N 72	21 19	////	////	16 15	□	□	□
N 70	20 53	22 45	////	15 28	16 59	18 08	18 47
68	20 33	21 58	////	14 58	16 18	17 21	18 05
66	20 18	21 28	////	14 36	15 50	16 51	17 36
64	20 05	21 06	22 55	14 18	15 29	16 28	17 14
62	19 54	20 49	22 13	14 04	15 12	16 10	16 56
60	19 45	20 35	21 45	13 52	14 58	15 55	16 42
N 58	19 37	20 23	21 25	13 41	14 46	15 42	16 29
56	19 30	20 12	21 08	13 32	14 36	15 31	16 18
54	19 24	20 03	20 55	13 24	14 26	15 21	16 09
52	19 18	19 55	20 43	13 17	14 18	15 13	16 01
50	19 13	19 48	20 33	13 10	14 11	15 05	15 53
45	19 02	19 33	20 12	12 56	13 55	14 49	15 37
N 40	18 53	19 21	19 56	12 45	13 42	14 35	15 23
35	18 45	19 12	19 43	12 35	13 31	14 24	15 12
30	18 38	19 03	19 33	12 26	13 21	14 13	15 02
20	18 27	18 49	19 16	12 11	13 05	13 56	14 45
N 10	18 17	18 38	19 03	11 59	12 51	13 41	14 30
0	18 07	18 28	18 53	11 46	12 37	13 27	14 16
S 10	17 58	18 19	18 44	11 34	12 24	13 13	14 02
20	17 48	18 11	18 37	11 22	12 09	12 58	13 47
30	17 37	18 02	18 30	11 07	11 53	12 40	13 30
35	17 31	17 57	18 27	10 58	11 43	12 30	13 20
40	17 24	17 52	18 23	10 49	11 32	12 19	13 08
45	17 16	17 46	18 20	10 37	11 19	12 05	12 54
S 50	17 06	17 39	18 17	10 24	11 04	11 48	12 38
52	17 01	17 36	18 16	10 17	10 56	11 41	12 30
54	16 56	17 33	18 14	10 10	10 48	11 32	12 21
56	16 50	17 29	18 13	10 02	10 39	11 22	12 12
58	16 44	17 26	18 12	09 53	10 29	11 11	12 01
S 60	16 37	17 21	18 10	09 43	10 17	10 58	11 48

Day	SUN Eqn. of Time 00h	SUN Eqn. of Time 12h	SUN Mer. Pass.	MOON Mer. Pass. Upper	MOON Mer. Pass. Lower	Age	Phase
d	m s	m s	h m	h m	h m	d	%
17	04 11	04 05	12 04	05 34	18 00	22	50
18	03 58	03 52	12 04	06 25	18 50	23	40
19	03 45	03 38	12 04	07 15	19 40	24	31

UT	ARIES GHA	VENUS −3.8 GHA	VENUS Dec	MARS +0.6 GHA	MARS Dec	JUPITER −1.8 GHA	JUPITER Dec	SATURN +0.6 GHA	SATURN Dec	STARS Name	SHA	Dec
20 00	328 15.3	196 12.4	N18 34.1	106 59.6	S17 15.5	198 06.4	N18 47.1	102 43.2	S14 57.6	Acamar	315 17.7	S40 14.6
01	343 17.8	211 11.7	33.3	122 00.6	15.9	213 08.4	47.0	117 45.6	57.6	Achernar	335 25.9	S57 09.5
02	358 20.2	226 11.0	32.6	137 01.6	16.4	228 10.3	46.8	132 47.9	57.7	Acrux	173 08.7	S63 11.0
03	13 22.7	241 10.3	.. 31.9	152 02.5	.. 16.9	243 12.2	.. 46.7	147 50.3	.. 57.7	Adhara	255 12.1	S28 59.5
04	28 25.2	256 09.7	31.1	167 03.5	17.4	258 14.1	46.6	162 52.6	57.7	Aldebaran	290 48.5	N16 32.2
05	43 27.6	271 09.0	30.4	182 04.4	17.8	273 16.0	46.4	177 55.0	57.8			
06	58 30.1	286 08.3	N18 29.7	197 05.4	S17 18.3	288 17.9	N18 46.3	192 57.3	S14 57.8	Alioth	166 20.4	N55 53.1
W 07	73 32.5	301 07.6	28.9	212 06.3	18.8	303 19.8	46.2	207 59.6	57.9	Alkaid	152 58.6	N49 14.7
E 08	88 35.0	316 07.0	28.2	227 07.3	19.3	318 21.7	46.0	223 02.0	57.9	Al Na'ir	27 42.3	S46 53.2
D 09	103 37.5	331 06.3	.. 27.5	242 08.3	.. 19.7	333 23.7	.. 45.9	238 04.3	.. 58.0	Alnilam	275 45.7	S 1 11.6
N 10	118 39.9	346 05.6	26.7	257 09.2	20.2	348 25.6	45.8	253 06.7	58.0	Alphard	217 55.6	S 8 43.4
E 11	133 42.4	1 04.9	26.0	272 10.2	20.7	3 27.5	45.6	268 09.0	58.1			
S 12	148 44.9	16 04.3	N18 25.2	287 11.1	S17 21.2	18 29.4	N18 45.5	283 11.4	S14 58.1	Alphecca	126 10.3	N26 40.3
D 13	163 47.3	31 03.6	24.5	302 12.1	21.6	33 31.3	45.4	298 13.7	58.1	Alpheratz	357 42.3	N29 10.3
A 14	178 49.8	46 02.9	23.8	317 13.0	22.1	48 33.2	45.2	313 16.1	58.2	Altair	62 07.1	N 8 54.8
Y 15	193 52.3	61 02.2	.. 23.0	332 14.0	.. 22.6	63 35.1	.. 45.1	328 18.4	.. 58.2	Ankaa	353 14.6	S42 13.3
16	208 54.7	76 01.6	22.3	347 14.9	23.1	78 37.1	45.0	343 20.8	58.3	Antares	112 25.2	S26 27.7
17	223 57.2	91 00.9	21.5	2 15.9	23.5	93 39.0	44.8	358 23.1	58.3			
18	238 59.7	106 00.2	N18 20.8	17 16.8	S17 24.0	108 40.9	N18 44.7	13 25.5	S14 58.4	Arcturus	145 55.1	N19 06.6
19	254 02.1	120 59.5	20.0	32 17.8	24.5	123 42.8	44.6	28 27.8	58.4	Atria	107 26.0	S69 03.3
20	269 04.6	135 58.9	19.3	47 18.7	25.0	138 44.7	44.4	43 30.2	58.4	Avior	234 18.2	S59 33.4
21	284 07.0	150 58.2	.. 18.5	62 19.7	.. 25.4	153 46.6	.. 44.3	58 32.5	.. 58.5	Bellatrix	278 31.3	N 6 21.7
22	299 09.5	165 57.5	17.8	77 20.6	25.9	168 48.5	44.2	73 34.8	58.5	Betelgeuse	271 00.6	N 7 24.5
23	314 12.0	180 56.9	17.0	92 21.6	26.4	183 50.5	44.0	88 37.2	58.6			
21 00	329 14.4	195 56.2	N18 16.3	107 22.5	S17 26.9	198 52.4	N18 43.9	103 39.5	S14 58.6	Canopus	263 56.1	S52 42.1
01	344 16.9	210 55.5	15.5	122 23.5	27.3	213 54.3	43.8	118 41.9	58.7	Capella	280 33.4	N46 00.4
02	359 19.4	225 54.8	14.8	137 24.4	27.8	228 56.2	43.6	133 44.2	58.7	Deneb	49 30.4	N45 20.3
03	14 21.8	240 54.2	.. 14.0	152 25.4	.. 28.3	243 58.1	.. 43.5	148 46.6	.. 58.8	Denebola	182 33.1	N14 29.5
04	29 24.3	255 53.5	13.3	167 26.3	28.7	259 00.0	43.4	163 48.9	58.8	Diphda	348 54.8	S17 54.2
05	44 26.8	270 52.8	12.5	182 27.3	29.2	274 02.0	43.2	178 51.3	58.8			
06	59 29.2	285 52.2	N18 11.8	197 28.2	S17 29.7	289 03.9	N18 43.1	193 53.6	S14 58.9	Dubhe	193 51.5	N61 40.4
T 07	74 31.7	300 51.5	11.0	212 29.2	30.2	304 05.8	43.0	208 56.0	58.9	Elnath	278 11.7	N28 36.9
H 08	89 34.1	315 50.8	10.3	227 30.1	30.6	319 07.7	42.8	223 58.3	59.0	Eltanin	90 45.5	N51 29.7
U 09	104 36.6	330 50.2	.. 09.5	242 31.0	.. 31.1	334 09.6	.. 42.7	239 00.6	.. 59.0	Enif	33 46.0	N 9 56.8
R 10	119 39.1	345 49.5	08.7	257 32.0	31.6	349 11.5	42.6	254 03.0	59.1	Fomalhaut	15 22.8	S29 32.4
S 11	134 41.5	0 48.8	08.0	272 32.9	32.1	4 13.4	42.4	269 05.3	59.1			
D 12	149 44.0	15 48.2	N18 07.2	287 33.9	S17 32.5	19 15.4	N18 42.3	284 07.7	S14 59.2	Gacrux	172 00.3	S57 11.8
A 13	164 46.5	30 47.5	06.4	302 34.8	33.0	34 17.3	42.2	299 10.0	59.2	Gienah	175 51.7	S17 37.4
Y 14	179 48.9	45 46.8	05.7	317 35.8	33.5	49 19.2	42.0	314 12.4	59.2	Hadar	148 46.9	S60 26.7
15	194 51.4	60 46.2	.. 04.9	332 36.7	.. 33.9	64 21.1	.. 41.9	329 14.7	.. 59.3	Hamal	327 59.6	N23 31.8
16	209 53.9	75 45.5	04.2	347 37.7	34.4	79 23.0	41.8	344 17.0	59.3	Kaus Aust.	83 42.5	S34 22.5
17	224 56.3	90 44.9	03.4	2 38.6	34.9	94 24.9	41.6	359 19.4	59.4			
18	239 58.8	105 44.2	N18 02.6	17 39.5	S17 35.4	109 26.9	N18 41.5	14 21.7	S14 59.4	Kochab	137 20.5	N74 06.1
19	255 01.3	120 43.5	01.9	32 40.5	35.8	124 28.8	41.4	29 24.1	59.5	Markab	13 37.2	N15 17.2
20	270 03.7	135 42.9	01.1	47 41.4	36.3	139 30.7	41.2	44 26.4	59.5	Menkar	314 14.1	N 4 08.8
21	285 06.2	150 42.2	18 00.3	62 42.4	.. 36.8	154 32.6	.. 41.1	59 28.8	.. 59.6	Menkent	148 06.7	S36 26.5
22	300 08.6	165 41.5	17 59.5	77 43.3	37.2	169 34.5	40.9	74 31.1	59.6	Miaplacidus	221 40.3	S69 46.7
23	315 11.1	180 40.9	58.8	92 44.2	37.7	184 36.4	40.8	89 33.4	59.6			
22 00	330 13.6	195 40.2	N17 58.0	107 45.2	S17 38.2	199 38.4	N18 40.7	104 35.8	S14 59.7	Mirfak	308 39.1	N49 54.5
01	345 16.0	210 39.6	57.2	122 46.1	38.7	214 40.3	40.5	119 38.1	59.7	Nunki	75 57.0	S26 16.5
02	0 18.5	225 38.9	56.5	137 47.0	39.1	229 42.2	40.4	134 40.5	59.8	Peacock	53 17.5	S56 41.1
03	15 21.0	240 38.2	.. 55.7	152 48.0	.. 39.6	244 44.1	.. 40.3	149 42.8	.. 59.8	Pollux	243 27.1	N27 59.3
04	30 23.4	255 37.6	54.9	167 48.9	40.1	259 46.0	40.1	164 45.1	59.9	Procyon	244 59.1	N 5 11.1
05	45 25.9	270 36.9	54.1	182 49.9	40.5	274 47.9	40.0	179 47.5	14 59.9			
06	60 28.4	285 36.3	N17 53.4	197 50.8	S17 41.0	289 49.9	N18 39.9	194 49.8	S15 00.0	Rasalhague	96 05.5	N12 33.3
07	75 30.8	300 35.6	52.6	212 51.7	41.5	304 51.8	39.7	209 52.2	00.0	Regulus	207 43.0	N11 53.7
08	90 33.3	315 34.9	51.8	227 52.7	42.0	319 53.7	39.6	224 54.5	00.0	Rigel	281 11.4	S 8 11.1
F 09	105 35.8	330 34.3	.. 51.0	242 53.6	.. 42.4	334 55.6	.. 39.5	239 56.8	.. 00.1	Rigil Kent.	139 50.7	S60 53.8
R 10	120 38.2	345 33.6	50.2	257 54.5	42.9	349 57.5	39.3	254 59.2	00.1	Sabik	102 11.5	S15 44.4
I 11	135 40.7	0 33.0	49.5	272 55.5	43.4	4 59.4	39.2	270 01.5	00.2			
D 12	150 43.1	15 32.3	N17 48.7	287 56.4	S17 43.8	20 01.4	N18 39.1	285 03.9	S15 00.2	Schedar	349 39.0	N56 36.9
A 13	165 45.6	30 31.7	47.9	302 57.3	44.3	35 03.3	38.9	300 06.2	00.3	Shaula	96 20.6	S37 06.7
Y 14	180 48.1	45 31.0	47.1	317 58.3	44.8	50 05.2	38.8	315 08.5	00.3	Sirius	258 33.2	S16 44.2
15	195 50.5	60 30.4	.. 46.3	332 59.2	.. 45.2	65 07.1	.. 38.7	330 10.9	.. 00.4	Spica	158 30.5	S11 14.2
16	210 53.0	75 29.7	45.5	348 00.1	45.7	80 09.0	38.5	345 13.2	00.4	Suhail	222 52.2	S43 29.5
17	225 55.5	90 29.1	44.7	3 01.1	46.2	95 10.9	38.4	0 15.6	00.5			
18	240 57.9	105 28.4	N17 44.0	18 02.0	S17 46.6	110 12.9	N18 38.3	15 17.9	S15 00.5	Vega	80 38.1	N38 48.3
19	256 00.4	120 27.7	43.2	33 02.9	47.1	125 14.8	38.1	30 20.2	00.5	Zuben'ubi	137 04.6	S16 06.0
20	271 02.9	135 27.1	42.4	48 03.9	47.6	140 16.7	38.0	45 22.6	00.6			
21	286 05.3	150 26.4	.. 41.6	63 04.8	.. 48.0	155 18.6	.. 37.9	60 24.9	.. 00.6		SHA	Mer.Pass.
22	301 07.8	165 25.8	40.8	78 05.7	48.5	170 20.5	37.7	75 27.3	00.7	Venus	226 41.8	h m 10 57
23	316 10.2	180 25.1	40.0	93 06.6	49.0	185 22.5	37.6	90 29.6	00.7	Mars	138 08.1	16 49
Mer.Pass.	h m 2 02.7	v −0.7	d 0.8	v 0.9	d 0.5	v 1.9	d 0.1	v 2.3	d 0.0	Jupiter	229 37.9	10 43
										Saturn	134 25.1	17 03

UT	SUN GHA	SUN Dec	MOON GHA	v	MOON Dec	d	HP
d h	° ′	° ′	° ′	′	° ′	′	′
20 00	179 07.4	N12 32.2	242 55.4	11.4	N18 44.8	0.2	54.9
01	194 07.5	31.4	257 25.8	11.4	18 44.6	0.3	54.9
02	209 07.6	30.6	271 56.2	11.3	18 44.3	0.4	54.9
03	224 07.9	.. 29.8	286 26.5	11.5	18 43.9	0.5	54.9
04	239 07.9	29.0	300 57.0	11.4	18 43.4	0.6	54.9
05	254 08.1	28.1	315 27.4	11.5	18 42.8	0.6	54.8
06	269 08.2	N12 27.3	329 57.9	11.5	N18 42.2	0.8	54.8
W 07	284 08.4	26.5	344 28.4	11.5	18 41.4	0.8	54.8
E 08	299 08.5	25.7	358 58.9	11.5	18 40.6	1.0	54.8
D 09	314 08.7	.. 24.8	13 29.4	11.6	18 39.6	1.0	54.8
N 10	329 08.8	24.0	28 00.0	11.6	18 38.6	1.1	54.7
E 11	344 09.0	23.2	42 30.6	11.6	18 37.5	1.2	54.7
S 12	359 09.1	N12 22.4	57 01.2	11.6	N18 36.3	1.3	54.7
D 13	14 09.3	21.5	71 31.8	11.7	18 35.0	1.4	54.7
A 14	29 09.4	20.7	86 02.5	11.7	18 33.6	1.5	54.7
Y 15	44 09.6	.. 19.9	100 33.2	11.7	18 32.1	1.5	54.7
16	59 09.7	19.1	115 03.9	11.8	18 30.6	1.7	54.6
17	74 09.9	18.2	129 34.7	11.8	18 28.9	1.7	54.6
18	89 10.0	N12 17.4	144 05.5	11.8	N18 27.2	1.8	54.6
19	104 10.2	16.6	158 36.3	11.8	18 25.4	1.9	54.6
20	119 10.3	15.7	173 07.1	11.9	18 23.5	2.0	54.6
21	134 10.5	.. 14.9	187 38.0	11.9	18 21.5	2.1	54.6
22	149 10.6	14.1	202 08.9	11.9	18 19.4	2.1	54.5
23	164 10.8	13.3	216 39.8	11.9	18 17.3	2.3	54.5
21 00	179 10.9	N12 12.4	231 10.7	12.0	N18 15.0	2.3	54.5
01	194 11.1	11.6	245 41.7	12.0	18 12.7	2.4	54.5
02	209 11.2	10.8	260 12.7	12.1	18 10.3	2.5	54.5
03	224 11.4	.. 09.9	274 43.8	12.0	18 07.8	2.6	54.5
04	239 11.5	09.1	289 14.8	12.1	18 05.2	2.6	54.4
05	254 11.7	08.3	303 45.9	12.1	18 02.6	2.8	54.4
06	269 11.9	N12 07.4	318 17.0	12.2	N17 59.8	2.8	54.4
T 07	284 12.0	06.6	332 48.2	12.2	17 57.0	2.9	54.4
H 08	299 12.2	05.8	347 19.4	12.2	17 54.1	3.0	54.4
U 09	314 12.3	.. 05.0	1 50.6	12.2	17 51.1	3.1	54.4
R 10	329 12.5	04.1	16 21.8	12.3	17 48.0	3.1	54.4
S 11	344 12.6	03.3	30 53.1	12.3	17 44.9	3.3	54.4
D 12	359 12.8	N12 02.5	45 24.4	12.4	N17 41.6	3.3	54.3
A 13	14 12.9	01.6	59 55.8	12.3	17 38.3	3.4	54.3
Y 14	29 13.1	12 00.8	74 27.1	12.4	17 34.9	3.5	54.3
15	44 13.2	11 59.9	88 58.5	12.5	17 31.4	3.5	54.3
16	59 13.4	59.1	103 30.0	12.4	17 27.9	3.6	54.3
17	74 13.5	58.3	118 01.4	12.5	17 24.3	3.8	54.3
18	89 13.7	N11 57.4	132 32.9	12.6	N17 20.5	3.7	54.3
19	104 13.9	56.6	147 04.5	12.5	17 16.8	3.9	54.3
20	119 14.0	55.8	161 36.0	12.6	17 12.9	3.9	54.2
21	134 14.2	.. 54.9	176 07.6	12.6	17 09.0	4.1	54.2
22	149 14.3	54.1	190 39.2	12.7	17 04.9	4.1	54.2
23	164 14.5	53.3	205 10.9	12.7	17 00.8	4.1	54.2
22 00	179 14.6	N11 52.4	219 42.6	12.7	N16 56.7	4.3	54.2
01	194 14.8	51.6	234 14.3	12.7	16 52.4	4.3	54.2
02	209 15.0	50.7	248 46.0	12.8	16 48.1	4.4	54.2
03	224 15.1	.. 49.9	263 17.8	12.8	16 43.7	4.5	54.2
04	239 15.3	49.1	277 49.6	12.9	16 39.2	4.5	54.2
05	254 15.4	48.2	292 21.5	12.8	16 34.7	4.6	54.2
06	269 15.6	N11 47.4	306 53.3	12.9	N16 30.1	4.7	54.1
F 07	284 15.7	46.6	321 25.2	13.0	16 25.4	4.8	54.1
R 08	299 15.9	45.7	335 57.2	12.9	16 20.6	4.8	54.1
I 09	314 16.1	.. 44.9	350 29.1	13.1	16 15.8	4.9	54.1
D 10	329 16.2	44.0	5 01.2	13.0	16 10.9	5.0	54.1
A 11	344 16.4	43.2	19 33.2	13.1	16 05.9	5.0	54.1
Y 12	359 16.5	N11 42.3	34 05.3	13.1	N16 00.9	5.1	54.1
13	14 16.7	41.5	48 37.4	13.1	15 55.8	5.2	54.1
14	29 16.8	40.7	63 09.5	13.1	15 50.6	5.3	54.1
15	44 17.0	.. 39.8	77 41.6	13.2	15 45.3	5.3	54.1
16	59 17.2	39.0	92 13.8	13.3	15 40.0	5.4	54.1
17	74 17.3	38.1	106 46.1	13.2	15 34.6	5.4	54.1
18	89 17.5	N11 37.3	121 18.3	13.3	N15 29.2	5.5	54.1
19	104 17.6	36.4	135 50.6	13.3	15 23.7	5.6	54.0
20	119 17.8	35.6	150 22.9	13.4	15 18.1	5.7	54.0
21	134 18.0	.. 34.8	164 55.3	13.4	15 12.4	5.7	54.0
22	149 18.1	33.9	179 27.7	13.4	15 06.7	5.8	54.0
23	164 18.3	33.1	194 00.1	13.4	N15 00.9	5.8	54.0
	SD 15.8	d 0.8	SD 14.9		14.8		14.7

Lat.	Naut.	Civil	Sunrise	Moonrise 20	21	22	23
°	h m	h m	h m	h m	h m	h m	h m
N 72	////	////	03 02	▭	22 40	24 30	00 30
N 70	////	01 44	03 25	22 13	23 34	25 03	01 03
68	////	02 23	03 43	22 55	24 07	00 07	01 27
66	////	02 50	03 58	23 24	24 31	00 31	01 45
64	01 31	03 10	04 10	23 46	24 50	00 50	02 00
62	02 06	03 26	04 20	24 03	00 03	01 05	02 13
60	02 31	03 39	04 28	24 18	00 18	01 18	02 23
N 58	02 50	03 51	04 36	24 30	00 30	01 29	02 32
56	03 06	04 00	04 42	24 41	00 41	01 38	02 40
54	03 19	04 09	04 48	24 50	00 50	01 47	02 47
52	03 30	04 16	04 54	00 06	00 58	01 54	02 54
50	03 39	04 23	04 58	00 14	01 06	02 01	02 59
45	03 59	04 37	05 09	00 31	01 22	02 16	03 12
N 40	04 14	04 49	05 17	00 44	01 35	02 28	03 22
35	04 26	04 58	05 24	00 56	01 46	02 38	03 31
30	04 36	05 06	05 31	01 06	01 56	02 47	03 38
20	04 52	05 19	05 42	01 23	02 13	03 02	03 52
N 10	05 04	05 30	05 51	01 38	02 27	03 16	04 03
0	05 14	05 39	06 00	01 52	02 41	03 28	04 14
S 10	05 22	05 47	06 08	02 07	02 55	03 41	04 25
20	05 29	05 55	06 18	02 22	03 09	03 54	04 36
30	05 35	06 03	06 28	02 39	03 26	04 09	04 49
35	05 38	06 08	06 34	02 49	03 36	04 18	04 57
40	05 41	06 13	06 40	03 01	03 47	04 28	05 05
45	05 44	06 18	06 48	03 15	04 00	04 40	05 15
S 50	05 46	06 24	06 57	03 31	04 16	04 54	05 28
52	05 47	06 26	07 01	03 39	04 23	05 01	05 33
54	05 48	06 29	07 06	03 48	04 31	05 08	05 39
56	05 49	06 32	07 11	03 58	04 41	05 16	05 46
58	05 50	06 36	07 17	04 09	04 52	05 26	05 54
S 60	05 51	06 40	07 23	04 22	05 03	05 36	06 03

Lat.	Sunset	Civil	Naut.	Moonset 20	21	22	23
°	h m	h m	h m	h m	h m	h m	h m
N 72	21 00	23 36	////	▭	20 00	19 46	19 37
N 70	20 37	22 15	////	18 47	19 04	19 12	19 15
68	20 20	21 34	////	18 05	18 31	18 47	18 57
66	20 06	21 13	23 40	17 36	18 07	18 28	18 43
64	19 54	20 53	22 29	17 14	17 48	18 12	18 31
62	19 45	20 38	21 55	16 56	17 32	17 59	18 21
60	19 36	20 25	21 32	16 42	17 19	17 48	18 12
N 58	19 29	20 14	21 14	16 29	17 08	17 39	18 05
56	19 23	20 04	20 58	16 18	16 58	17 30	17 58
54	19 17	19 56	20 46	16 09	16 49	17 23	17 52
52	19 12	19 49	20 35	16 01	16 41	17 16	17 46
50	19 07	19 42	20 25	15 53	16 34	17 10	17 41
45	18 57	19 28	20 06	15 37	16 19	16 57	17 31
N 40	18 49	19 17	19 51	15 23	16 07	16 46	17 22
35	18 41	19 08	19 39	15 12	15 56	16 37	17 14
30	18 35	19 00	19 29	15 02	15 47	16 29	17 07
20	18 24	18 47	19 14	14 45	15 31	16 15	16 56
N 10	18 15	18 37	19 02	14 30	15 17	16 02	16 45
0	18 06	18 28	18 52	14 16	15 04	15 50	16 36
S 10	17 58	18 19	18 44	14 02	14 51	15 39	16 26
20	17 49	18 11	18 37	13 47	14 37	15 26	16 15
30	17 39	18 03	18 31	13 30	14 20	15 12	16 03
35	17 33	17 59	18 28	13 20	14 11	15 03	15 57
40	17 27	17 54	18 26	13 08	14 00	14 54	15 49
45	17 19	17 49	18 23	12 54	13 47	14 42	15 39
S 50	17 10	17 43	18 21	12 38	13 32	14 29	15 28
52	17 06	17 41	18 20	12 30	13 24	14 22	15 23
54	17 01	17 38	18 19	12 21	13 16	14 15	15 17
56	16 56	17 35	18 18	12 12	13 07	14 07	15 11
58	16 51	17 31	18 17	12 01	12 57	13 58	15 03
S 60	16 44	17 28	18 16	11 48	12 45	13 48	14 55

	SUN			MOON			
Day	Eqn. of Time 00ʰ	12ʰ	Mer. Pass.	Mer. Pass. Upper	Lower	Age	Phase
d	m s	m s	h m	h m	h m	d	%
20	03 31	03 24	12 03	08 04	20 28	25	22
21	03 17	03 09	12 03	08 52	21 16	26	15
22	03 02	02 54	12 03	09 39	22 02	27	9

UT	ARIES	VENUS −3.9		MARS +0.6		JUPITER −1.8		SATURN +0.6		STARS		
d h	GHA	GHA	Dec	GHA	Dec	GHA	Dec	GHA	Dec	Name	SHA	Dec
23 00	331 12.7	195 24.5	N17 39.2	108 07.6	S17 49.5	200 24.4	N18 37.5	105 31.9	S15 00.8	Acamar	315 17.6	S40 14.6
01	346 15.2	210 23.8	38.4	123 08.5	49.9	215 26.3	37.3	120 34.3	00.8	Achernar	335 25.9	S57 09.5
02	1 17.6	225 23.2	37.6	138 09.4	50.4	230 28.2	37.2	135 36.6	00.9	Acrux	173 08.8	S63 11.0
03	16 20.1	240 22.5 ..	36.8	153 10.4 ..	50.9	245 30.1 ..	37.1	150 38.9 ..	00.9	Adhara	255 12.1	S28 59.5
04	31 22.6	255 21.9	36.0	168 11.3	51.3	260 32.1	36.9	165 41.3	01.0	Aldebaran	290 48.5	N16 32.2
05	46 25.0	270 21.2	35.2	183 12.2	51.8	275 34.0	36.8	180 43.6	01.0			
06	61 27.5	285 20.6	N17 34.4	198 13.1	S17 52.3	290 35.9	N18 36.7	195 46.0	S15 01.0	Alioth	166 20.5	N55 53.1
07	76 30.0	300 19.9	33.6	213 14.1	52.7	305 37.8	36.5	210 48.3	01.1	Alkaid	152 58.6	N49 14.7
S 08	91 32.4	315 19.3	32.8	228 15.0	53.2	320 39.7	36.4	225 50.6	01.1	Al Na'ir	27 42.3	S46 53.2
A 09	106 34.9	330 18.6 ..	32.0	243 15.9 ..	53.7	335 41.6 ..	36.2	240 53.0 ..	01.2	Alnilam	275 45.7	S 1 11.6
T 10	121 37.4	345 18.0	31.2	258 16.8	54.1	350 43.6	36.1	255 55.3	01.2	Alphard	217 55.6	S 8 43.4
U 11	136 39.8	0 17.4	30.4	273 17.8	54.6	5 45.5	36.0	270 57.6	01.3			
R 12	151 42.3	15 16.7	N17 29.6	288 18.7	S17 55.1	20 47.4	N18 35.8	286 00.0	S15 01.3	Alphecca	126 10.4	N26 40.3
D 13	166 44.7	30 16.1	28.8	303 19.6	55.5	35 49.3	35.7	301 02.3	01.4	Alpheratz	357 42.3	N29 10.3
A 14	181 47.2	45 15.4	28.0	318 20.5	56.0	50 51.2	35.6	316 04.6	01.4	Altair	62 07.1	N 8 54.8
Y 15	196 49.7	60 14.8 ..	27.2	333 21.4 ..	56.5	65 53.2 ..	35.4	331 07.0 ..	01.5	Ankaa	353 14.6	S42 13.3
16	211 52.1	75 14.1	26.4	348 22.4	56.9	80 55.1	35.3	346 09.3	01.5	Antares	112 25.2	S26 27.7
17	226 54.6	90 13.5	25.6	3 23.3	57.4	95 57.0	35.2	1 11.7	01.6			
18	241 57.1	105 12.8	N17 24.8	18 24.2	S17 57.9	110 58.9	N18 35.0	16 14.0	S15 01.6	Arcturus	145 55.1	N19 06.6
19	256 59.5	120 12.2	24.0	33 25.1	58.3	126 00.8	34.9	31 16.3	01.7	Atria	107 26.0	S69 03.3
20	272 02.0	135 11.6	23.2	48 26.0	58.8	141 02.8	34.8	46 18.7	01.7	Avior	234 18.2	S59 33.4
21	287 04.5	150 10.9 ..	22.3	63 27.0 ..	59.3	156 04.7 ..	34.6	61 21.0 ..	01.7	Bellatrix	278 31.2	N 6 21.7
22	302 06.9	165 10.3	21.5	78 27.9	17 59.7	171 06.6	34.5	76 23.3	01.8	Betelgeuse	271 00.6	N 7 24.5
23	317 09.4	180 09.6	20.7	93 28.8	18 00.2	186 08.5	34.4	91 25.7	01.8			
24 00	332 11.9	195 09.0	N17 19.9	108 29.7	S18 00.6	201 10.4	N18 34.2	106 28.0	S15 01.9	Canopus	263 56.1	S52 42.1
01	347 14.3	210 08.3	19.1	123 30.6	01.1	216 12.4	34.1	121 30.3	01.9	Capella	280 33.4	N46 00.4
02	2 16.8	225 07.7	18.3	138 31.6	01.6	231 14.3	34.0	136 32.7	02.0	Deneb	49 30.4	N45 20.3
03	17 19.2	240 07.1 ..	17.5	153 32.5 ..	02.0	246 16.2 ..	33.8	151 35.0 ..	02.0	Denebola	182 33.1	N14 29.5
04	32 21.7	255 06.4	16.6	168 33.4	02.5	261 18.1	33.7	166 37.3	02.1	Diphda	348 54.8	S17 54.2
05	47 24.2	270 05.8	15.8	183 34.3	03.0	276 20.0	33.6	181 39.7	02.1			
06	62 26.6	285 05.1	N17 15.0	198 35.2	S18 03.4	291 22.0	N18 33.4	196 42.0	S15 02.2	Dubhe	193 51.5	N61 40.4
07	77 29.1	300 04.5	14.2	213 36.1	03.9	306 23.9	33.3	211 44.3	02.2	Elnath	278 11.7	N28 36.9
S 08	92 31.6	315 03.9	13.4	228 37.1	04.4	321 25.8	33.2	226 46.7	02.3	Eltanin	90 45.5	N51 29.7
U 09	107 34.0	330 03.2 ..	12.5	243 38.0 ..	04.8	336 27.7 ..	33.0	241 49.0 ..	02.3	Enif	33 46.0	N 9 56.8
N 10	122 36.5	345 02.6	11.7	258 38.9	05.3	351 29.6	32.9	256 51.3	02.4	Fomalhaut	15 22.7	S29 32.4
11	137 39.0	0 02.0	10.9	273 39.8	05.8	6 31.6	32.8	271 53.7	02.4			
D 12	152 41.4	15 01.3	N17 10.1	288 40.7	S18 06.2	21 33.5	N18 32.6	286 56.0	S15 02.4	Gacrux	172 00.3	S57 11.8
A 13	167 43.9	30 00.7	09.2	303 41.6	06.7	36 35.4	32.5	301 58.3	02.5	Gienah	175 51.7	S17 37.4
Y 14	182 46.3	45 00.1	08.4	318 42.5	07.1	51 37.3	32.3	317 00.7	02.5	Hadar	148 46.9	S60 26.7
15	197 48.8	59 59.4 ..	07.6	333 43.4 ..	07.6	66 39.3 ..	32.2	332 03.0 ..	02.6	Hamal	327 59.6	N23 31.8
16	212 51.3	74 58.8	06.8	348 44.4	08.1	81 41.2	32.1	347 05.3	02.6	Kaus Aust.	83 42.5	S34 22.5
17	227 53.7	89 58.1	05.9	3 45.3	08.5	96 43.1	31.9	2 07.7	02.7			
18	242 56.2	104 57.5	N17 05.1	18 46.2	S18 09.0	111 45.0	N18 31.8	17 10.0	S15 02.7	Kochab	137 20.6	N74 06.1
19	257 58.7	119 56.9	04.3	33 47.1	09.5	126 46.9	31.7	32 12.3	02.8	Markab	13 37.2	N15 17.2
20	273 01.1	134 56.2	03.5	48 48.0	09.9	141 48.9	31.5	47 14.7	02.8	Menkar	314 14.1	N 4 08.8
21	288 03.6	149 55.6 ..	02.6	63 48.9 ..	10.4	156 50.8 ..	31.4	62 17.0 ..	02.9	Menkent	148 06.7	S36 26.5
22	303 06.1	164 55.0	01.8	78 49.8	10.8	171 52.7	31.3	77 19.3	02.9	Miaplacidus	221 40.3	S69 46.7
23	318 08.5	179 54.4	01.0	93 50.7	11.3	186 54.6	31.1	92 21.6	03.0			
25 00	333 11.0	194 53.7	N17 00.1	108 51.6	S18 11.8	201 56.5	N18 31.0	107 24.0	S15 03.0	Mirfak	308 39.0	N49 54.5
01	348 13.5	209 53.1	16 59.3	123 52.5	12.2	216 58.5	30.9	122 26.3	03.1	Nunki	75 57.0	S26 16.5
02	3 15.9	224 52.5	58.4	138 53.4	12.7	232 00.4	30.7	137 28.6	03.1	Peacock	53 17.5	S56 41.1
03	18 18.4	239 51.8 ..	57.6	153 54.4 ..	13.2	247 02.3 ..	30.6	152 31.0 ..	03.2	Pollux	243 27.0	N27 59.3
04	33 20.8	254 51.2	56.8	168 55.3	13.6	262 04.2	30.5	167 33.3	03.2	Procyon	244 59.1	N 5 11.1
05	48 23.3	269 50.6	55.9	183 56.2	14.1	277 06.2	30.3	182 35.6	03.3			
06	63 25.8	284 49.9	N16 55.1	198 57.1	S18 14.5	292 08.1	N18 30.2	197 38.0	S15 03.3	Rasalhague	96 05.5	N12 33.3
07	78 28.2	299 49.3	54.3	213 58.0	15.0	307 10.0	30.1	212 40.3	03.3	Regulus	207 43.0	N11 53.7
08	93 30.7	314 48.7	53.4	228 58.9	15.5	322 11.9	29.9	227 42.6	03.4	Rigel	281 11.4	S 8 11.1
M 09	108 33.2	329 48.1 ..	52.6	243 59.8 ..	15.9	337 13.9 ..	29.8	242 45.0 ..	03.4	Rigil Kent.	139 50.7	S60 53.8
O 10	123 35.6	344 47.4	51.7	259 00.7	16.4	352 15.8	29.7	257 47.3	03.5	Sabik	102 11.5	S15 44.4
N 11	138 38.1	359 46.8	50.9	274 01.6	16.8	7 17.7	29.5	272 49.6	03.5			
D 12	153 40.6	14 46.2	N16 50.0	289 02.5	S18 17.3	22 19.6	N18 29.4	287 51.9	S15 03.6	Schedar	349 39.0	N56 37.0
A 13	168 43.0	29 45.6	49.2	304 03.4	17.8	37 21.5	29.2	302 54.3	03.6	Shaula	96 20.6	S37 06.7
Y 14	183 45.5	44 44.9	48.4	319 04.3	18.2	52 23.5	29.1	317 56.6	03.7	Sirius	258 33.2	S16 44.2
15	198 48.0	59 44.3 ..	47.5	334 05.2 ..	18.7	67 25.4 ..	29.0	332 58.9 ..	03.7	Spica	158 30.6	S11 14.2
16	213 50.4	74 43.7	46.7	349 06.1	19.1	82 27.3	28.8	348 01.3	03.8	Suhail	222 52.2	S43 29.5
17	228 52.9	89 43.1	45.8	4 07.0	19.6	97 29.2	28.7	3 03.6	03.8			
18	243 55.3	104 42.4	N16 45.0	19 07.9	S18 20.1	112 31.2	N18 28.6	18 05.9	S15 03.9	Vega	80 38.1	N38 48.3
19	258 57.8	119 41.8	44.1	34 08.8	20.5	127 33.1	28.4	33 08.2	03.9	Zuben'ubi	137 04.6	S16 06.0
20	274 00.3	134 41.2	43.3	49 09.7	21.0	142 35.0	28.3	48 10.6	04.0			
21	289 02.7	149 40.6 ..	42.4	64 10.6 ..	21.4	157 36.9 ..	28.2	63 12.9 ..	04.0		SHA	Mer.Pass.
22	304 05.2	164 39.9	41.6	79 11.5	21.9	172 38.9	28.0	78 15.2	04.1	Venus	222 57.1	11 00
23	319 07.8	179 39.3	40.7	94 12.4	22.4	187 40.8	27.9	93 17.5	04.1	Mars	136 17.9	16 45
	h m									Jupiter	228 58.6	10 34
Mer.Pass.	1 50.9	v −0.6	d 0.8	v 0.9	d 0.5	v 1.9	d 0.1	v 2.3	d 0.0	Saturn	134 16.1	16 52

UT	SUN GHA	SUN Dec	MOON GHA	v	Dec	d	HP
d h	° '	° '	° '	'	° '	'	'
23 00	179 18.5	N11 32.2	208 32.5 13.5		N14 55.1	6.0	54.0
01	194 18.6	31.4	223 05.0 13.5		14 49.1	5.9	54.0
02	209 18.8	30.5	237 37.5 13.5		14 43.2	6.1	54.0
03	224 18.9	.. 29.7	252 10.0 13.6		14 37.1	6.1	54.0
04	239 19.1	28.8	266 42.6 13.6		14 31.0	6.1	54.0
05	254 19.3	28.0	281 15.2 13.6		14 24.9	6.3	54.0
06	269 19.4	N11 27.1	295 47.8 13.7		N14 18.6	6.3	54.0
07	284 19.6	26.3	310 20.5 13.7		14 12.3	6.3	54.0
S 08	299 19.7	25.5	324 53.2 13.7		14 06.0	6.4	54.0
A 09	314 19.9	.. 24.6	339 25.9 13.8		13 59.6	6.5	54.0
T 10	329 20.1	23.8	353 58.7 13.7		13 53.1	6.5	54.0
U 11	344 20.2	22.9	8 31.4 13.9		13 46.6	6.6	54.0
R 12	359 20.4	N11 22.1	23 04.3 13.8		N13 40.0	6.7	54.0
D 13	14 20.6	21.2	37 37.1 13.9		13 33.3	6.7	54.0
A 14	29 20.7	20.4	52 10.0 13.9		13 26.6	6.7	54.0
Y 15	44 20.9	.. 19.5	66 42.9 13.9		13 19.9	6.8	54.0
16	59 21.1	18.7	81 15.8 13.9		13 13.1	6.9	54.0
17	74 21.2	17.8	95 48.7 14.0		13 06.2	6.9	54.0
18	89 21.4	N11 17.0	110 21.7 14.0		N12 59.3	7.0	54.0
19	104 21.5	16.1	124 54.7 14.1		12 52.3	7.0	53.9
20	119 21.7	15.3	139 27.8 14.0		12 45.3	7.1	53.9
21	134 21.9	.. 14.4	154 00.8 14.1		12 38.2	7.2	53.9
22	149 22.0	13.5	168 33.9 14.1		12 31.0	7.2	53.9
23	164 22.2	12.7	183 07.0 14.2		12 23.8	7.2	53.9
24 00	179 22.4	N11 11.8	197 40.2 14.2		N12 16.6	7.3	53.9
01	194 22.5	11.0	212 13.4 14.2		12 09.3	7.4	53.9
02	209 22.7	10.1	226 46.6 14.2		12 01.9	7.4	53.9
03	224 22.9	.. 09.3	241 19.8 14.2		11 54.5	7.4	53.9
04	239 23.0	08.4	255 53.0 14.3		11 47.1	7.5	53.9
05	254 23.2	07.6	270 26.3 14.3		11 39.6	7.6	53.9
06	269 23.4	N11 06.7	284 59.6 14.3		N11 32.0	7.6	53.9
07	284 23.5	05.9	299 32.9 14.4		11 24.4	7.6	53.9
08	299 23.7	05.0	314 06.3 14.4		11 16.8	7.7	53.9
S 09	314 23.9	.. 04.2	328 39.7 14.4		11 09.1	7.8	53.9
U 10	329 24.0	03.3	343 13.1 14.4		11 01.3	7.7	53.9
N 11	344 24.2	02.4	357 46.5 14.4		10 53.6	7.9	53.9
D 12	359 24.4	N11 01.6	12 19.9 14.5		N10 45.7	7.9	53.9
A 13	14 24.5	11 00.7	26 53.4 14.5		10 37.8	7.9	53.9
Y 14	29 24.7	10 59.9	41 26.9 14.5		10 29.9	7.9	53.9
15	44 24.9	.. 59.0	56 00.4 14.5		10 22.0	8.0	53.9
16	59 25.0	58.2	70 33.9 14.6		10 14.0	8.1	53.9
17	74 25.2	57.3	85 07.5 14.6		10 05.9	8.1	53.9
18	89 25.4	N10 56.4	99 41.1 14.6		N 9 57.8	8.1	54.0
19	104 25.6	55.6	114 14.7 14.6		9 49.7	8.2	54.0
20	119 25.7	54.7	128 48.3 14.6		9 41.5	8.2	54.0
21	134 25.9	.. 53.9	143 21.9 14.7		9 33.3	8.3	54.0
22	149 26.1	53.0	157 55.6 14.7		9 25.0	8.3	54.0
23	164 26.2	52.1	172 29.3 14.7		9 16.7	8.3	54.0
25 00	179 26.4	N10 51.3	187 03.0 14.7		N 9 08.4	8.4	54.0
01	194 26.6	50.4	201 36.7 14.7		9 00.0	8.4	54.0
02	209 26.7	49.6	216 10.4 14.8		8 51.6	8.5	54.0
03	224 26.9	.. 48.7	230 44.2 14.8		8 43.1	8.4	54.0
04	239 27.1	47.8	245 18.0 14.8		8 34.7	8.6	54.0
05	254 27.2	47.0	259 51.8 14.8		8 26.1	8.5	54.0
06	269 27.4	N10 46.1	274 25.6 14.8		N 8 17.6	8.6	54.0
07	284 27.6	45.3	288 59.4 14.8		8 09.0	8.7	54.0
08	299 27.8	44.4	303 33.2 14.9		8 00.3	8.6	54.0
M 09	314 27.9	.. 43.5	318 07.1 14.9		7 51.7	8.7	54.0
O 10	329 28.1	42.7	332 41.0 14.8		7 43.0	8.7	54.0
N 11	344 28.3	41.8	347 14.8 14.9		7 34.3	8.8	54.0
D 12	359 28.4	N10 40.9	1 48.7 15.0		N 7 25.5	8.8	54.0
A 13	14 28.6	40.1	16 22.7 14.9		7 16.7	8.8	54.0
Y 14	29 28.8	39.2	30 56.6 14.9		7 07.9	8.9	54.0
15	44 29.0	.. 38.3	45 30.5 15.0		6 59.0	8.9	54.0
16	59 29.1	37.5	60 04.5 14.9		6 50.1	8.9	54.0
17	74 29.3	36.6	74 38.4 15.0		6 41.2	8.9	54.0
18	89 29.5	N10 35.8	89 12.4 15.0		N 6 32.3	9.0	54.0
19	104 29.7	34.9	103 46.4 15.0		6 23.3	9.0	54.0
20	119 29.8	34.0	118 20.4 15.0		6 14.3	9.1	54.0
21	134 30.0	.. 33.2	132 54.4 15.0		6 05.3	9.1	54.1
22	149 30.2	32.3	147 28.4 15.0		5 56.2	9.0	54.1
23	164 30.4	31.4	162 02.4 15.1		N 5 47.2	9.1	54.1
	SD 15.8	d 0.9	SD 14.7	14.7		14.7	

Lat.	Twilight Naut.	Twilight Civil	Sunrise	Moonrise 23	24	25	26
°	h m	h m	h m	h m	h m	h m	h m
N 72	////	01 13	03 19	00 30	02 11	03 49	05 24
N 70	////	02 08	03 39	01 03	02 33	04 02	05 31
68	////	02 40	03 55	01 27	02 49	04 13	05 37
66	01 03	03 03	04 08	01 45	03 03	04 22	05 41
64	01 52	03 21	04 19	02 00	03 14	04 29	05 45
62	02 21	03 36	04 28	02 13	03 23	04 35	05 48
60	02 43	03 48	04 35	02 23	03 31	04 41	05 51
N 58	03 00	03 58	04 42	02 32	03 38	04 46	05 54
56	03 14	04 07	04 48	02 40	03 44	04 50	05 56
54	03 26	04 15	04 54	02 47	03 50	04 54	05 58
52	03 36	04 22	04 58	02 54	03 55	04 57	06 00
50	03 45	04 28	05 03	02 59	03 59	05 00	06 02
45	04 03	04 41	05 12	03 12	04 09	05 07	06 06
N 40	04 18	04 52	05 20	03 22	04 17	05 13	06 09
35	04 29	05 00	05 27	03 31	04 24	05 18	06 12
30	04 38	05 08	05 32	03 38	04 30	05 22	06 14
20	04 53	05 20	05 42	03 52	04 41	05 30	06 18
N 10	05 05	05 30	05 51	04 03	04 50	05 36	06 22
0	05 14	05 38	05 59	04 14	04 59	05 42	06 25
S 10	05 21	05 46	06 07	04 25	05 07	05 48	06 28
20	05 27	05 53	06 15	04 36	05 16	05 55	06 32
30	05 32	06 00	06 25	04 49	05 27	06 02	06 36
35	05 35	06 04	06 30	04 57	05 33	06 06	06 38
40	05 37	06 08	06 36	05 05	05 39	06 11	06 41
45	05 39	06 13	06 43	05 15	05 47	06 17	06 44
S 50	05 41	06 18	06 51	05 28	05 57	06 23	06 48
52	05 41	06 20	06 55	05 33	06 01	06 26	06 50
54	05 42	06 23	06 59	05 39	06 06	06 30	06 51
56	05 42	06 26	07 04	05 46	06 11	06 33	06 53
58	05 43	06 28	07 09	05 54	06 17	06 37	06 56
S 60	05 43	06 32	07 15	06 03	06 24	06 42	06 58

Lat.	Sunset	Twilight Civil	Twilight Naut.	Moonset 23	24	25	26
°	h m	h m	h m	h m	h m	h m	h m
N 72	20 42	22 40	////	19 37	19 30	19 24	19 18
N 70	20 22	21 51	////	19 15	19 16	19 15	19 15
68	20 07	21 20	////	18 57	19 04	19 08	19 12
66	19 54	20 58	22 51	18 43	18 54	19 02	19 10
64	19 44	20 41	22 07	18 31	18 45	18 57	19 08
62	19 35	20 27	21 40	18 21	18 38	18 53	19 06
60	19 28	20 15	21 19	18 12	18 32	18 49	19 04
N 58	19 21	20 05	21 02	18 05	18 26	18 45	19 03
56	19 15	19 56	20 49	17 58	18 21	18 42	19 02
54	19 10	19 48	20 37	17 52	18 17	18 39	19 01
52	19 05	19 42	20 27	17 46	18 13	18 37	19 00
50	19 01	19 35	20 18	17 41	18 09	18 35	18 59
45	18 52	19 23	20 00	17 31	18 01	18 30	18 57
N 40	18 44	19 12	19 46	17 22	17 55	18 25	18 55
35	18 38	19 04	19 35	17 14	17 49	18 22	18 53
30	18 32	18 57	19 26	17 07	17 44	18 18	18 52
20	18 22	18 45	19 11	16 56	17 35	18 13	18 50
N 10	18 14	18 35	19 00	16 45	17 27	18 08	18 48
0	18 06	18 27	18 51	16 36	17 20	18 03	18 46
S 10	17 58	18 19	18 44	16 26	17 12	17 58	18 44
20	17 50	18 12	18 38	16 15	17 04	17 53	18 41
30	17 41	18 05	18 33	16 03	16 55	17 47	18 39
35	17 35	18 01	18 31	15 57	16 50	17 44	18 38
40	17 29	17 57	18 29	15 49	16 44	17 40	18 36
45	17 23	17 53	18 27	15 39	16 37	17 35	18 34
S 50	17 14	17 47	18 25	15 28	16 29	17 30	18 32
52	17 11	17 45	18 24	15 23	16 25	17 27	18 31
54	17 06	17 43	18 24	15 17	16 20	17 25	18 30
56	17 02	17 40	18 23	15 11	16 16	17 22	18 28
58	16 57	17 37	18 23	15 03	16 10	17 18	18 27
S 60	16 51	17 34	18 23	14 55	16 04	17 15	18 25

	SUN			MOON			
Day	Eqn. of Time 00h	Eqn. of Time 12h	Mer. Pass.	Mer. Pass. Upper	Mer. Pass. Lower	Age	Phase
d	m s	m s	h m	h m	h m	d	%
23	02 47	02 39	12 03	10 25	22 47	28	4
24	02 31	02 23	12 02	11 09	23 31	29	1
25	02 15	02 07	12 02	11 53	24 14	30	0

UT	ARIES GHA	VENUS −3.9 GHA	Dec	MARS +0.6 GHA	Dec	JUPITER −1.8 GHA	Dec	SATURN +0.6 GHA	Dec	STARS Name	SHA	Dec
26 TUESDAY												
00	334 10.1	194 38.7	N16 39.9	109 13.3	S18 22.8	202 42.7	N18 27.8	108 19.9	S15 04.2	Acamar	315 17.6	S40 14.6
01	349 12.6	209 38.1	39.0	124 14.2	23.3	217 44.6	27.6	123 22.2	04.2	Achernar	335 25.9	S57 09.5
02	4 15.1	224 37.5	38.1	139 15.1	23.7	232 46.6	27.5	138 24.5	04.3	Acrux	173 08.8	S63 11.0
03	19 17.5	239 36.8 ..	37.3	154 16.0 ..	24.2	247 48.5 ..	27.4	153 26.9 ..	04.3	Adhara	255 12.1	S28 59.5
04	34 20.0	254 36.2	36.4	169 16.9	24.7	262 50.4	27.2	168 29.2	04.3	Aldebaran	290 48.4	N16 32.2
05	49 22.4	269 35.6	35.6	184 17.8	25.1	277 52.3	27.1	183 31.5	04.4			
06	64 24.9	284 35.0	N16 34.7	199 18.7	S18 25.6	292 54.3	N18 27.0	198 33.8	S15 04.5	Alioth	166 20.5	N55 53.1
07	79 27.4	299 34.4	33.8	214 19.6	26.0	307 56.2	26.8	213 36.2	04.5	Alkaid	152 58.6	N49 14.7
08	94 29.8	314 33.7	33.0	229 20.5	26.5	322 58.1	26.7	228 38.5	04.6	Al Na'ir	27 42.3	S46 53.2
09	109 32.3	329 33.1 ..	32.1	244 21.4 ..	26.9	338 00.0 ..	26.6	243 40.8 ..	04.6	Alnilam	275 45.6	S 1 11.6
10	124 34.8	344 32.5	31.3	259 22.2	27.4	353 02.0	26.4	258 43.1	04.7	Alphard	217 55.6	S 8 43.4
11	139 37.2	359 31.9	30.4	274 23.1	27.9	8 03.9	26.3	273 45.5	04.7			
12	154 39.7	14 31.3	N16 29.5	289 24.0	S18 28.3	23 05.8	N18 26.1	288 47.8	S15 04.8	Alphecca	126 10.4	N26 40.3
13	169 42.2	29 30.7	28.7	304 24.9	28.8	38 07.7	26.0	303 50.1	04.8	Alpheratz	357 42.3	N29 10.4
14	184 44.6	44 30.0	27.8	319 25.8	29.2	53 09.7	25.9	318 52.4	04.8	Altair	62 07.2	N 8 54.8
15	199 47.1	59 29.4 ..	26.9	334 26.7 ..	29.7	68 11.6 ..	25.7	333 54.8 ..	04.9	Ankaa	353 14.6	S42 13.3
16	214 49.6	74 28.8	26.1	349 27.6	30.1	83 13.5	25.6	348 57.1	04.9	Antares	112 25.2	S26 27.7
17	229 52.0	89 28.2	25.2	4 28.5	30.6	98 15.4	25.5	3 59.4	05.0			
18	244 54.5	104 27.6	N16 24.3	19 29.4	S18 31.1	113 17.4	N18 25.3	19 01.7	S15 05.0	Arcturus	145 55.1	N19 06.6
19	259 56.9	119 27.0	23.5	34 30.3	31.5	128 19.3	25.2	34 04.1	05.1	Atria	107 26.1	S69 03.3
20	274 59.4	134 26.4	22.6	49 31.2	32.0	143 21.2	25.1	49 06.4	05.1	Avior	234 18.2	S59 33.4
21	290 01.9	149 25.7 ..	21.7	64 32.1 ..	32.4	158 23.1 ..	24.9	64 08.7 ..	05.2	Bellatrix	278 31.2	N 6 21.7
22	305 04.3	164 25.1	20.9	79 32.9	32.9	173 25.1	24.8	79 11.0	05.2	Betelgeuse	271 00.5	N 7 24.5
23	320 06.8	179 24.5	20.0	94 33.8	33.3	188 27.0	24.7	94 13.4	05.3			
27 WEDNESDAY												
00	335 09.3	194 23.9	N16 19.1	109 34.7	S18 33.8	203 28.9	N18 24.5	109 15.7	S15 05.3	Canopus	263 56.1	S52 42.1
01	350 11.7	209 23.3	18.2	124 35.6	34.2	218 30.8	24.4	124 18.0	05.4	Capella	280 33.3	N46 00.4
02	5 14.2	224 22.7	17.4	139 36.5	34.7	233 32.8	24.3	139 20.3	05.4	Deneb	49 30.4	N45 20.3
03	20 16.7	239 22.1 ..	16.5	154 37.4 ..	35.2	248 34.7 ..	24.1	154 22.7 ..	05.5	Denebola	182 33.1	N14 29.5
04	35 19.1	254 21.5	15.6	169 38.3	35.6	263 36.6	24.0	169 25.0	05.5	Diphda	348 54.8	S17 54.2
05	50 21.6	269 20.9	14.7	184 39.1	36.1	278 38.5	23.9	184 27.3	05.6			
06	65 24.0	284 20.2	N16 13.9	199 40.0	S18 36.5	293 40.5	N18 23.7	199 29.6	S15 05.6	Dubhe	193 51.5	N61 40.3
07	80 26.5	299 19.6	13.0	214 40.9	37.0	308 42.4	23.6	214 31.9	05.7	Elnath	278 11.7	N28 36.9
08	95 29.0	314 19.0	12.1	229 41.8	37.4	323 44.3	23.5	229 34.3	05.7	Eltanin	90 45.5	N51 29.7
09	110 31.4	329 18.4 ..	11.2	244 42.7 ..	37.9	338 46.2 ..	23.3	244 36.6 ..	05.8	Enif	33 46.0	N 9 56.8
10	125 33.9	344 17.8	10.3	259 43.6	38.3	353 48.2	23.2	259 38.9	05.8	Fomalhaut	15 22.7	S29 32.4
11	140 36.4	359 17.2	09.5	274 44.5	38.8	8 50.1	23.0	274 41.2	05.9			
12	155 38.8	14 16.6	N16 08.6	289 45.3	S18 39.2	23 52.0	N18 22.9	289 43.6	S15 05.9	Gacrux	172 00.3	S57 11.8
13	170 41.3	29 16.0	07.7	304 46.2	39.7	38 54.0	22.8	304 45.9	06.0	Gienah	175 51.7	S17 37.4
14	185 43.8	44 15.4	06.8	319 47.1	40.1	53 55.9	22.6	319 48.2	06.0	Hadar	148 46.9	S60 26.7
15	200 46.2	59 14.8 ..	05.9	334 48.0 ..	40.6	68 57.8 ..	22.5	334 50.5 ..	06.1	Hamal	327 59.6	N23 31.8
16	215 48.7	74 14.2	05.0	349 48.9	41.1	83 59.7	22.4	349 52.8	06.1	Kaus Aust.	83 42.5	S34 22.5
17	230 51.2	89 13.6	04.1	4 49.7	41.5	99 01.7	22.2	4 55.2	06.2			
18	245 53.6	104 13.0	N16 03.3	19 50.6	S18 42.0	114 03.6	N18 22.1	19 57.5	S15 06.2	Kochab	137 20.6	N74 06.1
19	260 56.1	119 12.4	02.4	34 51.5	42.4	129 05.5	22.0	34 59.8	06.3	Markab	13 37.2	N15 17.2
20	275 58.5	134 11.8	01.5	49 52.4	42.9	144 07.5	21.8	50 02.1	06.3	Menkar	314 14.1	N 4 08.8
21	291 01.0	149 11.2	16 00.6	64 53.3 ..	43.3	159 09.4 ..	21.7	65 04.4 ..	06.4	Menkent	148 06.7	S36 26.5
22	306 03.5	164 10.6	15 59.7	79 54.1	43.8	174 11.3	21.6	80 06.8	06.4	Miaplacidus	221 40.3	S69 46.7
23	321 05.9	179 10.0	58.8	94 55.0	44.2	189 13.2	21.4	95 09.1	06.5			
28 THURSDAY												
00	336 08.4	194 09.4	N15 57.9	109 55.9	S18 44.7	204 15.2	N18 21.3	110 11.4	S15 06.5	Mirfak	308 39.0	N49 54.5
01	351 10.9	209 08.8	57.0	124 56.8	45.1	219 17.1	21.2	125 13.7	06.6	Nunki	75 57.1	S26 16.5
02	6 13.3	224 08.2	56.1	139 57.6	45.6	234 19.0	21.0	140 16.0	06.6	Peacock	53 17.5	S56 41.1
03	21 15.8	239 07.6 ..	55.2	154 58.5 ..	46.0	249 20.9 ..	20.9	155 18.4 ..	06.7	Pollux	243 27.0	N27 59.3
04	36 18.3	254 07.0	54.3	169 59.4	46.5	264 22.9	20.8	170 20.7	06.7	Procyon	244 59.1	N 5 11.1
05	51 20.7	269 06.4	53.4	185 00.3	46.9	279 24.8	20.6	185 23.0	06.8			
06	66 23.2	284 05.8	N15 52.5	200 01.2	S18 47.4	294 26.7	N18 20.5	200 25.3	S15 06.8	Rasalhague	96 05.6	N12 33.3
07	81 25.6	299 05.2	51.6	215 02.0	47.8	309 28.7	20.3	215 27.6	06.9	Regulus	207 43.0	N11 52.9
08	96 28.1	314 04.6	50.7	230 02.9	48.3	324 30.6	20.2	230 30.0	06.9	Rigel	281 11.3	S 8 11.1
09	111 30.6	329 04.0 ..	49.8	245 03.8 ..	48.7	339 32.5 ..	20.1	245 32.3 ..	07.0	Rigil Kent.	139 50.8	S60 53.8
10	126 33.0	344 03.4	48.9	260 04.6	49.2	354 34.5	19.9	260 34.6	07.0	Sabik	102 11.5	S15 44.4
11	141 35.5	359 02.8	48.0	275 05.5	49.6	9 36.4	19.8	275 36.9	07.1			
12	156 38.0	14 02.2	N15 47.1	290 06.4	S18 50.1	24 38.3	N18 19.7	290 39.2	S15 07.1	Schedar	349 39.0	N56 37.0
13	171 40.4	29 01.6	46.2	305 07.3	50.5	39 40.2	19.5	305 41.6	07.2	Shaula	96 20.6	S37 06.7
14	186 42.9	44 01.0	45.3	320 08.1	51.0	54 42.2	19.4	320 43.9	07.2	Sirius	258 33.2	S16 44.2
15	201 45.4	59 00.4 ..	44.4	335 09.0 ..	51.4	69 44.1 ..	19.3	335 46.2 ..	07.3	Spica	158 30.6	S11 14.2
16	216 47.8	73 59.8	43.5	350 09.9	51.9	84 46.0	19.1	350 48.5	07.3	Suhail	222 52.2	S43 29.5
17	231 50.3	88 59.2	42.6	5 10.8	52.3	99 48.0	19.0	5 50.8	07.4			
18	246 52.8	103 58.6	N15 41.7	20 11.6	S18 52.8	114 49.9	N18 18.9	20 53.1	S15 07.4	Vega	80 38.1	N38 48.3
19	261 55.2	118 58.0	40.8	35 12.5	53.2	129 51.8	18.7	35 55.5	07.5	Zuben'ubi	137 04.6	S16 06.0
20	276 57.7	133 57.4	39.9	50 13.4	53.7	144 53.7	18.6	50 57.8	07.5		SHA	Mer.Pass.
21	292 00.1	148 56.8 ..	39.0	65 14.2 ..	54.1	159 55.7 ..	18.5	66 00.1 ..	07.6	Venus	219 14.6	11 03
22	307 02.6	163 56.2	38.1	80 15.1	54.6	174 57.6	18.3	81 02.4	07.6	Mars	134 25.5	16 41
23	322 05.1	178 55.6	37.2	95 16.0	55.0	189 59.5	18.2	96 04.7	07.7	Jupiter	228 19.6	10 25
Mer.Pass. 1 39.1		v −0.6 d 0.9		v 0.9 d 0.5		v 1.9 d 0.1		v 2.3 d 0.0		Saturn	134 06.4	16 40

SUN and MOON

UT	SUN GHA	SUN Dec	MOON GHA	v	MOON Dec	d	HP
d h	° ′	° ′	° ′	′	° ′	′	′
26 00	179 30.5	N10 30.6	176 36.5	15.0	N 5 38.1	9.2	54.1
01	194 30.7	29.7	191 10.5	15.1	5 28.9	9.1	54.1
02	209 30.9	28.8	205 44.6	15.0	5 19.8	9.2	54.1
03	224 31.0	.. 28.0	220 18.6	15.1	5 10.6	9.2	54.1
04	239 31.2	27.1	234 52.7	15.1	5 01.4	9.2	54.1
05	254 31.4	26.2	249 26.8	15.0	4 52.2	9.3	54.1
06	269 31.6	N10 25.3	264 00.8	15.1	N 4 42.9	9.2	54.1
07	284 31.7	24.5	278 34.9	15.1	4 33.7	9.3	54.1
08	299 31.9	23.6	293 09.0	15.1	4 24.4	9.3	54.1
09	314 32.1	.. 22.7	307 43.1	15.1	4 15.1	9.3	54.1
10	329 32.3	21.9	322 17.2	15.1	4 05.8	9.4	54.1
11	344 32.5	21.0	336 51.3	15.1	3 56.4	9.3	54.2
12	359 32.6	N10 20.1	351 25.4	15.1	N 3 47.1	9.4	54.2
13	14 32.8	19.3	5 59.5	15.1	3 37.7	9.4	54.2
14	29 33.0	18.4	20 33.6	15.1	3 28.3	9.4	54.2
15	44 33.2	.. 17.5	35 07.7	15.1	3 18.9	9.4	54.2
16	59 33.3	16.6	49 41.8	15.1	3 09.5	9.5	54.2
17	74 33.5	15.8	64 15.9	15.1	3 00.0	9.4	54.2
18	89 33.7	N10 14.9	78 50.0	15.1	N 2 50.6	9.5	54.2
19	104 33.9	14.0	93 24.1	15.2	2 41.1	9.5	54.2
20	119 34.0	13.2	107 58.3	15.1	2 31.6	9.5	54.2
21	134 34.2	.. 12.3	122 32.4	15.1	2 22.1	9.5	54.2
22	149 34.4	11.4	137 06.5	15.1	2 12.6	9.5	54.3
23	164 34.6	10.5	151 40.6	15.1	2 03.1	9.6	54.3
27 00	179 34.8	N10 09.7	166 14.7	15.0	N 1 53.5	9.5	54.3
01	194 34.9	08.8	180 48.7	15.1	1 44.0	9.6	54.3
02	209 35.1	07.9	195 22.8	15.1	1 34.4	9.6	54.3
03	224 35.3	.. 07.0	209 56.9	15.1	1 24.9	9.6	54.3
04	239 35.5	06.2	224 31.0	15.0	1 15.3	9.6	54.3
05	254 35.6	05.3	239 05.0	15.1	1 05.7	9.6	54.3
06	269 35.8	N10 04.4	253 39.1	15.1	N 0 56.1	9.6	54.3
07	284 36.0	03.5	268 13.2	15.0	0 46.5	9.6	54.3
08	299 36.2	02.7	282 47.2	15.0	0 36.9	9.6	54.4
09	314 36.4	.. 01.8	297 21.2	15.1	0 27.3	9.6	54.4
10	329 36.5	00.9	311 55.3	15.0	0 17.7	9.6	54.4
11	344 36.7	10 00.0	326 29.3	15.0	N 0 08.1	9.6	54.4
12	359 36.9	N 9 59.2	341 03.3	15.0	S 0 01.5	9.6	54.4
13	14 37.1	58.3	355 37.3	15.0	0 11.1	9.7	54.4
14	29 37.3	57.4	10 11.3	15.0	0 20.8	9.6	54.4
15	44 37.4	.. 56.5	24 45.3	14.9	0 30.4	9.6	54.4
16	59 37.6	55.6	39 19.2	15.0	0 40.0	9.7	54.5
17	74 37.8	54.8	53 53.2	14.9	0 49.7	9.6	54.5
18	89 38.0	N 9 53.9	68 27.1	14.9	S 0 59.3	9.6	54.5
19	104 38.2	53.0	83 01.0	14.9	1 08.9	9.7	54.5
20	119 38.4	52.1	97 34.9	14.9	1 18.6	9.6	54.5
21	134 38.5	.. 51.2	112 08.8	14.9	1 28.2	9.6	54.5
22	149 38.7	50.4	126 42.7	14.8	1 37.8	9.6	54.5
23	164 38.9	49.5	141 16.5	14.9	1 47.4	9.6	54.5
28 00	179 39.1	N 9 48.6	155 50.4	14.8	S 1 57.0	9.7	54.6
01	194 39.3	47.7	170 24.2	14.8	2 06.7	9.6	54.6
02	209 39.4	46.8	184 58.0	14.8	2 16.3	9.6	54.6
03	224 39.6	.. 46.0	199 31.8	14.7	2 25.9	9.6	54.6
04	239 39.8	45.1	214 05.5	14.8	2 35.5	9.6	54.6
05	254 40.0	44.2	228 39.3	14.7	2 45.1	9.5	54.6
06	269 40.2	N 9 43.3	243 13.0	14.7	S 2 54.6	9.6	54.6
07	284 40.4	42.4	257 46.7	14.7	3 04.2	9.6	54.7
08	299 40.5	41.6	272 20.4	14.6	3 13.8	9.5	54.7
09	314 40.7	.. 40.7	286 54.0	14.7	3 23.3	9.6	54.7
10	329 40.9	39.8	301 27.7	14.6	3 32.9	9.5	54.7
11	344 41.1	38.9	316 01.3	14.5	3 42.4	9.6	54.7
12	359 41.3	N 9 38.0	330 34.8	14.6	S 3 52.0	9.5	54.7
13	14 41.5	37.1	345 08.4	14.5	4 01.5	9.5	54.8
14	29 41.6	36.3	359 41.9	14.5	4 11.0	9.5	54.8
15	44 41.8	.. 35.4	14 15.4	14.5	4 20.5	9.4	54.8
16	59 42.0	34.5	28 48.9	14.5	4 29.9	9.5	54.8
17	74 42.2	33.6	43 22.4	14.4	4 39.4	9.4	54.8
18	89 42.4	N 9 32.7	57 55.8	14.4	S 4 48.8	9.5	54.8
19	104 42.6	31.8	72 29.2	14.3	4 58.3	9.4	54.8
20	119 42.8	30.9	87 02.5	14.4	5 07.7	9.3	54.9
21	134 42.9	.. 30.1	101 35.9	14.3	5 17.1	9.4	54.9
22	149 43.1	29.2	116 09.2	14.3	5 26.4	9.4	54.9
23	164 43.3	28.3	130 42.5	14.2	S 5 35.8	9.3	54.9
SD	15.9	d 0.9	SD 14.8	14.8	14.9		

Note: Tuesday = August 26; Wednesday = August 27; Thursday = August 28.

Twilight / Sunrise / Moonrise

Lat.	Twilight Naut.	Twilight Civil	Sunrise	Moonrise 26	27	28	29
°	h m	h m	h m	h m	h m	h m	h m
N 72	////	01 48	03 35	05 24	06 59	08 34	10 12
N 70	////	02 29	03 53	05 31	07 00	08 29	10 01
68	////	02 56	04 07	05 37	07 00	08 25	09 51
66	01 33	03 16	04 18	05 41	07 01	08 22	09 44
64	02 10	03 32	04 28	05 45	07 02	08 19	09 38
62	02 35	03 45	04 36	05 48	07 02	08 17	09 32
60	02 54	03 56	04 43	05 51	07 03	08 15	09 27
N 58	03 09	04 05	04 49	05 54	07 03	08 13	09 23
56	03 22	04 14	04 54	05 56	07 03	08 11	09 20
54	03 33	04 21	04 59	05 58	07 04	08 10	09 16
52	03 42	04 27	05 03	06 00	07 04	08 08	09 13
50	03 51	04 33	05 07	06 02	07 04	08 07	09 11
45	04 08	04 45	05 16	06 06	07 05	08 04	09 05
N 40	04 21	04 55	05 23	06 09	07 05	08 02	09 00
35	04 32	05 03	05 29	06 12	07 06	08 00	08 56
30	04 41	05 10	05 34	06 14	07 06	07 59	08 52
20	04 54	05 21	05 43	06 18	07 07	07 56	08 46
N 10	05 05	05 30	05 51	06 22	07 07	07 53	08 40
0	05 13	05 37	05 58	06 25	07 08	07 51	08 35
S 10	05 19	05 44	06 05	06 28	07 08	07 48	08 30
20	05 25	05 51	06 13	06 32	07 09	07 46	08 24
30	05 29	05 57	06 21	06 36	07 10	07 43	08 18
35	05 31	06 00	06 26	06 38	07 10	07 42	08 14
40	05 33	06 04	06 31	06 41	07 10	07 40	08 10
45	05 34	06 08	06 38	06 44	07 11	07 38	08 06
S 50	05 35	06 12	06 45	06 48	07 12	07 35	08 00
52	05 35	06 14	06 48	06 50	07 12	07 34	07 58
54	05 35	06 16	06 52	06 51	07 12	07 33	07 55
56	05 35	06 18	06 56	06 53	07 13	07 32	07 52
58	05 35	06 21	07 01	06 56	07 13	07 30	07 49
S 60	05 35	06 23	07 06	06 58	07 13	07 29	07 45

Sunset / Twilight / Moonset

Lat.	Sunset	Twilight Civil	Twilight Naut.	Moonset 26	27	28	29
°	h m	h m	h m	h m	h m	h m	h m
N 72	20 24	22 07	////	19 18	19 13	19 07	19 00
N 70	20 07	21 29	////	19 15	19 14	19 14	19 13
68	19 54	21 03	23 32	19 12	19 16	19 19	19 24
66	19 43	20 44	22 22	19 10	19 17	19 24	19 33
64	19 33	20 28	21 49	19 08	19 18	19 28	19 40
62	19 26	20 16	21 25	19 06	19 19	19 32	19 47
60	19 19	20 05	21 07	19 04	19 19	19 35	19 52
N 58	19 13	19 56	20 52	19 03	19 20	19 38	19 57
56	19 08	19 48	20 39	19 02	19 21	19 40	20 01
54	19 03	19 41	20 28	19 01	19 22	19 43	20 05
52	18 59	19 35	20 19	19 00	19 22	19 45	20 09
50	18 55	19 29	20 11	18 59	19 22	19 46	20 12
45	18 46	19 17	19 54	18 57	19 23	19 51	20 19
N 40	18 40	19 08	19 41	18 55	19 24	19 54	20 25
35	18 34	19 00	19 31	18 53	19 25	19 57	20 31
30	18 28	18 53	19 22	18 52	19 25	19 59	20 35
20	18 20	18 42	19 08	18 50	19 27	20 04	20 43
N 10	18 12	18 33	18 58	18 48	19 27	20 08	20 50
0	18 05	18 26	18 50	18 46	19 28	20 12	20 56
S 10	17 58	18 19	18 44	18 44	19 29	20 16	21 03
20	17 51	18 13	18 39	18 41	19 30	20 20	21 10
30	17 42	18 06	18 34	18 39	19 31	20 24	21 18
35	17 38	18 03	18 33	18 38	19 32	20 27	21 23
40	17 32	18 00	18 31	18 36	19 33	20 30	21 28
45	17 26	17 56	18 30	18 34	19 33	20 33	21 34
S 50	17 19	17 52	18 29	18 32	19 34	20 37	21 41
52	17 15	17 50	18 29	18 31	19 35	20 39	21 45
54	17 11	17 48	18 29	18 30	19 35	20 41	21 48
56	17 08	17 46	18 29	18 28	19 36	20 44	21 52
58	17 03	17 43	18 29	18 27	19 36	20 46	21 57
S 60	16 58	17 41	18 29	18 25	19 37	20 49	22 02

SUN and MOON

Day	SUN Eqn. of Time 00h	12h	SUN Mer. Pass.	MOON Mer. Pass. Upper	Lower	Age	Phase
d	m s	m s	h m	h m	h m	d	%
26	01 58	01 50	12 02	12 35	00 14	01	1
27	01 41	01 33	12 02	13 18	00 57	02	3
28	01 24	01 15	12 01	14 01	01 40	03	8

UT	ARIES	VENUS −3.9		MARS +0.6		JUPITER −1.8		SATURN +0.6		STARS		
	GHA	GHA	Dec	GHA	Dec	GHA	Dec	GHA	Dec	Name	SHA	Dec
d h	° ′	° ′	° ′	° ′	° ′	° ′	° ′	° ′	° ′		° ′	° ′
29 00	337 07.5	193 55.1	N15 36.3	110 16.8	S18 55.5	205 01.5	N18 18.0	111 07.0	S15 07.7	Acamar	315 17.6	S40 14.6
01	352 10.0	208 54.5	35.4	125 17.7	55.9	220 03.4	17.9	126 09.4	07.8	Achernar	335 25.9	S57 09.5
02	7 12.5	223 53.9	34.4	140 18.6	56.4	235 05.3	17.8	141 11.7	07.9	Acrux	173 08.8	S63 10.9
03	22 14.9	238 53.3 ..	33.5	155 19.4 ..	56.8	250 07.3 ..	17.6	156 14.0 ..	07.9	Adhara	255 12.1	S28 59.5
04	37 17.4	253 52.7	32.6	170 20.3	57.3	265 09.2	17.5	171 16.3	08.0	Aldebaran	290 48.4	N16 32.2
05	52 19.9	268 52.1	31.7	185 21.2	57.7	280 11.1	17.4	186 18.6	08.0			
06	67 22.3	283 51.5	N15 30.8	200 22.0	S18 58.2	295 13.1	N18 17.2	201 20.9	S15 08.1	Alioth	166 20.5	N55 53.0
07	82 24.8	298 50.9	29.9	215 22.9	58.6	310 15.0	17.1	216 23.3	08.1	Alkaid	152 58.6	N49 14.7
08	97 27.2	313 50.3	29.0	230 23.8	59.0	325 16.9	17.0	231 25.6	08.2	Al Na'ir	27 42.3	S46 53.2
F 09	112 29.7	328 49.7 ..	28.0	245 24.6 ..	59.5	340 18.8 ..	16.8	246 27.9 ..	08.2	Alnilam	275 45.6	S 1 11.6
R 10	127 32.2	343 49.2	27.1	260 25.5	18 59.9	355 20.8	16.7	261 30.2	08.3	Alphard	217 55.6	S 8 43.4
I 11	142 34.6	358 48.6	26.2	275 26.4	19 00.4	10 22.7	16.6	276 32.5	08.3			
D 12	157 37.1	13 48.0	N15 25.3	290 27.2	S19 00.8	25 24.6	N18 16.4	291 34.8	S15 08.4	Alphecca	126 10.4	N26 40.3
A 13	172 39.6	28 47.4	24.4	305 28.1	01.3	40 26.6	16.3	306 37.2	08.4	Alpheratz	357 42.3	N29 10.4
Y 14	187 42.0	43 46.8	23.4	320 28.9	01.7	55 28.5	16.2	321 39.5	08.5	Altair	62 07.2	N 8 54.8
15	202 44.5	58 46.2 ..	22.5	335 29.8 ..	02.2	70 30.4 ..	16.0	336 41.8 ..	08.5	Ankaa	353 14.6	S42 13.4
16	217 47.0	73 45.6	21.6	350 30.7	02.6	85 32.4	15.9	351 44.1	08.6	Antares	112 25.2	S26 27.7
17	232 49.4	88 45.1	20.7	5 31.5	03.1	100 34.3	15.8	6 46.4	08.6			
18	247 51.9	103 44.5	N15 19.7	20 32.4	S19 03.5	115 36.2	N18 15.6	21 48.7	S15 08.7	Arcturus	145 55.2	N19 06.6
19	262 54.4	118 43.9	18.8	35 33.2	04.0	130 38.2	15.5	36 51.0	08.7	Atria	107 26.1	S69 03.3
20	277 56.8	133 43.3	17.9	50 34.1	04.4	145 40.1	15.3	51 53.4	08.8	Avior	234 18.2	S59 33.4
21	292 59.3	148 42.7 ..	17.0	65 35.0 ..	04.8	160 42.0 ..	15.2	66 55.7 ..	08.8	Bellatrix	278 31.2	N 6 21.7
22	308 01.7	163 42.1	16.0	80 35.8	05.3	175 44.0	15.1	81 58.0	08.9	Betelgeuse	271 00.5	N 7 24.5
23	323 04.2	178 41.6	15.1	95 36.7	05.7	190 45.9	14.9	97 00.3	08.9			
30 00	338 06.7	193 41.0	N15 14.2	110 37.5	S19 06.2	205 47.8	N18 14.8	112 02.6	S15 09.0	Canopus	263 56.0	S52 42.1
01	353 09.1	208 40.4	13.2	125 38.4	06.6	220 49.8	14.7	127 04.9	09.0	Capella	280 33.3	N46 00.4
02	8 11.6	223 39.8	12.3	140 39.3	07.1	235 51.7	14.5	142 07.2	09.1	Deneb	49 30.5	N45 20.3
03	23 14.1	238 39.2 ..	11.4	155 40.1 ..	07.5	250 53.6 ..	14.4	157 09.5 ..	09.1	Denebola	182 33.1	N14 29.5
04	38 16.5	253 38.7	10.5	170 41.0	07.9	265 55.6	14.3	172 11.9	09.2	Diphda	348 54.8	S17 54.2
05	53 19.0	268 38.1	09.5	185 41.8	08.4	280 57.5	14.1	187 14.2	09.2			
06	68 21.5	283 37.5	N15 08.6	200 42.7	S19 08.8	295 59.4	N18 14.0	202 16.5	S15 09.3	Dubhe	193 51.5	N61 40.3
07	83 23.9	298 36.9	07.7	215 43.5	09.3	311 01.4	13.9	217 18.8	09.3	Elnath	278 11.7	N28 36.9
S 08	98 26.4	313 36.3	06.7	230 44.4	09.7	326 03.3	13.7	232 21.1	09.4	Eltanin	90 45.5	N51 29.7
A 09	113 28.9	328 35.8 ..	05.8	245 45.2 ..	10.2	341 05.2 ..	13.6	247 23.4 ..	09.5	Enif	33 46.0	N 9 56.8
T 10	128 31.3	343 35.2	04.8	260 46.1	10.6	356 07.2	13.5	262 25.7	09.5	Fomalhaut	15 22.7	S29 32.4
U 11	143 33.8	358 34.6	03.9	275 46.9	11.1	11 09.1	13.3	277 28.0	09.6			
R 12	158 36.2	13 34.0	N15 03.0	290 47.8	S19 11.5	26 11.0	N18 13.2	292 30.4	S15 09.6	Gacrux	172 00.4	S57 11.8
D 13	173 38.7	28 33.5	02.0	305 48.7	11.9	41 13.0	13.1	307 32.7	09.7	Gienah	175 51.7	S17 37.4
A 14	188 41.2	43 32.9	01.1	320 49.5	12.4	56 14.9	12.9	322 35.0	09.7	Hadar	148 47.0	S60 26.7
Y 15	203 43.6	58 32.3	15 00.2	335 50.4 ..	12.8	71 16.8 ..	12.8	337 37.3 ..	09.8	Hamal	327 59.6	N23 31.8
16	218 46.1	73 31.7	14 59.2	350 51.2	13.3	86 18.8	12.6	352 39.6	09.8	Kaus Aust.	83 42.5	S34 22.5
17	233 48.6	88 31.2	58.3	5 52.1	13.7	101 20.7	12.5	7 41.9	09.9			
18	248 51.0	103 30.6	N14 57.3	20 52.9	S19 14.1	116 22.6	N18 12.4	22 44.2	S15 09.9	Kochab	137 20.7	N74 06.1
19	263 53.5	118 30.0	56.4	35 53.8	14.6	131 24.6	12.2	37 46.5	10.0	Markab	13 37.2	N15 17.2
20	278 56.0	133 29.4	55.4	50 54.6	15.0	146 26.5	12.1	52 48.8	10.0	Menkar	314 14.1	N 4 08.8
21	293 58.4	148 28.9 ..	54.5	65 55.5 ..	15.5	161 28.4 ..	12.0	67 51.2 ..	10.1	Menkent	148 06.8	S36 26.5
22	309 00.9	163 28.3	53.6	80 56.3	15.9	176 30.4	11.8	82 53.5	10.1	Miaplacidus	221 40.2	S69 46.7
23	324 03.3	178 27.7	52.6	95 57.2	16.3	191 32.3	11.7	97 55.8	10.2			
31 00	339 05.8	193 27.1	N14 51.7	110 58.0	S19 16.8	206 34.2	N18 11.6	112 58.1	S15 10.2	Mirfak	308 39.0	N49 54.5
01	354 08.3	208 26.6	50.7	125 58.8	17.2	221 36.2	11.4	128 00.4	10.3	Nunki	75 57.1	S26 16.5
02	9 10.7	223 26.0	49.8	140 59.7	17.7	236 38.1	11.3	143 02.7	10.3	Peacock	53 17.5	S56 41.1
03	24 13.2	238 25.4 ..	48.8	156 00.5 ..	18.1	251 40.0 ..	11.2	158 05.0 ..	10.4	Pollux	243 27.0	N27 59.3
04	39 15.7	253 24.9	47.9	171 01.4	18.5	266 42.0	11.0	173 07.3	10.4	Procyon	244 59.1	N 5 11.1
05	54 18.1	268 24.3	46.9	186 02.2	19.0	281 43.9	10.9	188 09.6	10.5			
06	69 20.6	283 23.7	N14 46.0	201 03.1	S19 19.4	296 45.8	N18 10.8	203 11.9	S15 10.6	Rasalhague	96 05.6	N12 33.3
07	84 23.1	298 23.2	45.0	216 03.9	19.9	311 47.8	10.6	218 14.2	10.6	Regulus	207 43.0	N11 53.7
08	99 25.5	313 22.6	44.1	231 04.8	20.3	326 49.7	10.5	233 16.6	10.7	Rigel	281 11.3	S 8 11.1
S 09	114 28.0	328 22.0 ..	43.1	246 05.6 ..	20.7	341 51.7 ..	10.3	248 18.9 ..	10.7	Rigil Kent.	139 50.8	S60 53.8
U 10	129 30.5	343 21.4	42.2	261 06.5	21.2	356 53.6	10.2	263 21.2	10.8	Sabik	102 11.5	S15 44.4
N 11	144 32.9	358 20.9	41.2	276 07.3	21.6	11 55.5	10.1	278 23.5	10.8			
D 12	159 35.4	13 20.3	N14 40.3	291 08.1	S19 22.1	26 57.5	N18 09.9	293 25.8	S15 10.9	Schedar	349 39.0	N56 37.0
A 13	174 37.8	28 19.7	39.3	306 09.0	22.5	41 59.4	09.8	308 28.1	10.9	Shaula	96 20.6	S37 06.7
Y 14	189 40.3	43 19.2	38.3	321 09.8	22.9	57 01.3	09.7	323 30.4	11.0	Sirius	258 33.2	S16 44.2
15	204 42.8	58 18.6 ..	37.4	336 10.7 ..	23.4	72 03.3 ..	09.5	338 32.7 ..	11.0	Spica	158 30.6	S11 14.2
16	219 45.2	73 18.0	36.4	351 11.5	23.8	87 05.2	09.4	353 35.0	11.1	Suhail	222 52.2	S43 29.5
17	234 47.7	88 17.5	35.5	6 12.4	24.2	102 07.1	09.3	8 37.3	11.1			
18	249 50.2	103 16.9	N14 34.5	21 13.2	S19 24.7	117 09.1	N18 09.1	23 39.6	S15 11.2	Vega	80 38.2	N38 48.3
19	264 52.6	118 16.4	33.5	36 14.0	25.1	132 11.0	09.0	38 41.9	11.2	Zuben'ubi	137 04.6	S16 06.0
20	279 55.1	133 15.8	32.6	51 14.9	25.6	147 13.0	08.9	53 44.3	11.3			
21	294 57.6	148 15.2 ..	31.6	66 15.7 ..	26.0	162 14.9 ..	08.7	68 46.6 ..	11.3		SHA	Mer.Pass.
22	310 00.0	163 14.7	30.7	81 16.6	26.4	177 16.8	08.6	83 48.9	11.4		° ′	h m
23	325 02.5	178 14.1	29.7	96 17.4	26.9	192 18.8	08.5	98 51.2	11.5	Venus	215 34.3	11 06
	h m									Mars	132 30.9	16 37
Mer. Pass.	1 27.3	v −0.6	d 0.9	v 0.9	d 0.4	v 1.9	d 0.1	v 2.3	d 0.1	Jupiter	227 41.1	10 15
										Saturn	133 55.9	16 29

UT	SUN GHA	SUN Dec	MOON GHA	v	MOON Dec	d	HP
d h	° ′	° ′	° ′	′	° ′	′	′
29 00	179 43.5	N 9 27.4	145 15.7	14.2	S 5 45.1	9.4	54.9
01	194 43.7	26.5	159 48.9	14.2	5 54.5	9.3	55.0
02	209 43.9	25.6	174 22.1	14.1	6 03.8	9.2	55.0
03	224 44.1	.. 24.7	188 55.2	14.1	6 13.0	9.3	55.0
04	239 44.2	23.8	203 28.3	14.1	6 22.3	9.2	55.0
05	254 44.4	23.0	218 01.4	14.0	6 31.5	9.2	55.0
06	269 44.6	N 9 22.1	232 34.4	14.0	S 6 40.7	9.2	55.0
07	284 44.8	21.2	247 07.4	14.0	6 49.9	9.2	55.1
08	299 45.0	20.3	261 40.4	13.9	6 59.1	9.1	55.1
F 09	314 45.2	.. 19.4	276 13.3	13.9	7 08.2	9.1	55.1
R 10	329 45.4	18.5	290 46.2	13.9	7 17.3	9.1	55.1
I 11	344 45.6	17.6	305 19.1	13.8	7 26.4	9.1	55.1
D 12	359 45.7	N 9 16.7	319 51.9	13.8	S 7 35.5	9.0	55.2
A 13	14 45.9	15.8	334 24.7	13.7	7 44.5	9.0	55.2
Y 14	29 46.1	15.0	348 57.4	13.7	7 53.5	9.0	55.2
15	44 46.3	.. 14.1	3 30.1	13.6	8 02.5	8.9	55.2
16	59 46.5	13.2	18 02.7	13.7	8 11.4	8.9	55.2
17	74 46.7	12.3	32 35.4	13.5	8 20.3	8.9	55.3
18	89 46.9	N 9 11.4	47 07.9	13.6	S 8 29.2	8.8	55.3
19	104 47.1	10.5	61 40.5	13.4	8 38.0	8.9	55.3
20	119 47.3	09.6	76 12.9	13.5	8 46.9	8.7	55.3
21	134 47.4	.. 08.7	90 45.4	13.4	8 55.6	8.8	55.3
22	149 47.6	07.8	105 17.8	13.3	9 04.4	8.7	55.4
23	164 47.8	06.9	119 50.1	13.3	9 13.1	8.7	55.4
30 00	179 48.0	N 9 06.0	134 22.4	13.3	S 9 21.8	8.6	55.4
01	194 48.2	05.1	148 54.7	13.2	9 30.4	8.6	55.4
02	209 48.4	04.2	163 26.9	13.1	9 39.0	8.5	55.4
03	224 48.6	.. 03.4	177 59.0	13.2	9 47.5	8.6	55.5
04	239 48.8	02.5	192 31.2	13.0	9 56.1	8.4	55.5
05	254 49.0	01.6	207 03.2	13.0	10 04.5	8.5	55.5
06	269 49.2	N 9 00.7	221 35.2	13.0	S10 13.0	8.4	55.5
07	284 49.3	8 59.8	236 07.2	12.9	10 21.4	8.3	55.6
S 08	299 49.5	58.9	250 39.1	12.9	10 29.7	8.4	55.6
A 09	314 49.7	.. 58.0	265 11.0	12.8	10 38.1	8.2	55.6
T 10	329 49.9	57.1	279 42.8	12.8	10 46.3	8.3	55.6
U 11	344 50.1	56.2	294 14.6	12.7	10 54.6	8.1	55.7
R 12	359 50.3	N 8 55.3	308 46.3	12.7	S11 02.7	8.2	55.7
D 13	14 50.5	54.4	323 18.0	12.6	11 10.9	8.1	55.7
A 14	29 50.7	53.5	337 49.6	12.5	11 19.0	8.0	55.7
Y 15	44 50.9	.. 52.6	352 21.1	12.5	11 27.0	8.0	55.7
16	59 51.1	51.7	6 52.6	12.5	11 35.0	8.0	55.8
17	74 51.3	50.8	21 24.1	12.4	11 43.0	7.9	55.8
18	89 51.5	N 8 49.9	35 55.5	12.3	S11 50.9	7.8	55.8
19	104 51.6	49.0	50 26.8	12.3	11 58.7	7.8	55.8
20	119 51.8	48.1	64 58.1	12.2	12 06.5	7.7	55.9
21	134 52.0	.. 47.2	79 29.3	12.2	12 14.2	7.7	55.9
22	149 52.2	46.3	94 00.5	12.1	12 21.9	7.7	55.9
23	164 52.4	45.4	108 31.6	12.1	12 29.6	7.5	55.9
31 00	179 52.6	N 8 44.5	123 02.7	12.0	S12 37.1	7.6	56.0
01	194 52.8	43.6	137 33.7	11.9	12 44.7	7.4	56.0
02	209 53.0	42.7	152 04.6	11.9	12 52.1	7.5	56.0
03	224 53.2	.. 41.8	166 35.5	11.8	12 59.6	7.3	56.0
04	239 53.4	40.9	181 06.3	11.8	13 06.9	7.3	56.1
05	254 53.6	40.0	195 37.1	11.7	13 14.2	7.3	56.1
06	269 53.8	N 8 39.1	210 07.8	11.6	S13 21.5	7.1	56.1
07	284 54.0	38.2	224 38.4	11.6	13 28.6	7.2	56.2
08	299 54.2	37.3	239 09.0	11.5	13 35.8	7.0	56.2
S 09	314 54.4	.. 36.4	253 39.5	11.5	13 42.8	7.0	56.2
U 10	329 54.5	35.5	268 10.0	11.4	13 49.8	7.0	56.2
N 11	344 54.7	34.6	282 40.4	11.3	13 56.8	6.8	56.3
D 12	359 54.9	N 8 33.7	297 10.7	11.3	S14 03.6	6.8	56.3
A 13	14 55.1	32.8	311 41.0	11.2	14 10.4	6.8	56.3
Y 14	29 55.3	31.9	326 11.2	11.2	14 17.2	6.6	56.3
15	44 55.5	.. 31.0	340 41.4	11.0	14 23.8	6.7	56.4
16	59 55.7	30.1	355 11.4	11.1	14 30.5	6.5	56.4
17	74 55.9	29.2	9 41.5	10.9	14 37.0	6.5	56.4
18	89 56.1	N 8 28.3	24 11.4	10.9	S14 43.5	6.4	56.5
19	104 56.3	27.4	38 41.3	10.9	14 49.9	6.3	56.5
20	119 56.5	26.5	53 11.2	10.7	14 56.2	6.3	56.5
21	134 56.7	.. 25.6	67 40.9	10.7	15 02.5	6.1	56.5
22	149 56.9	24.7	82 10.6	10.7	15 08.6	6.2	56.6
23	164 57.1	23.8	96 40.3	10.6	S15 14.8	6.0	56.6
	SD 15.9	d 0.9	SD 15.0		15.2		15.3

Lat.	Twilight Naut.	Twilight Civil	Sunrise	Moonrise 29	Moonrise 30	Moonrise 31	Moonrise 1
°	h m	h m	h m	h m	h m	h m	h m
N 72	////	02 15	03 51	10 12	11 54	13 43	15 44
N 70	////	02 47	04 06	10 01	11 35	13 12	14 50
68	01 08	03 10	04 18	09 51	11 19	12 49	14 18
66	01 56	03 28	04 28	09 44	11 07	12 31	13 54
64	02 25	03 42	04 36	09 38	10 57	12 17	13 35
62	02 47	03 54	04 44	09 32	10 48	12 05	13 20
60	03 04	04 04	04 50	09 27	10 41	11 55	13 07
N 58	03 18	04 13	04 55	09 23	10 35	11 46	12 57
56	03 30	04 20	05 00	09 20	10 29	11 38	12 47
54	03 40	04 27	05 04	09 16	10 24	11 32	12 39
52	03 48	04 33	05 08	09 13	10 19	11 25	12 31
50	03 56	04 38	05 12	09 11	10 15	11 20	12 24
45	04 12	04 49	05 19	09 05	10 06	11 08	12 10
N 40	04 24	04 58	05 26	09 00	09 58	10 58	11 58
35	04 34	05 05	05 31	08 56	09 52	10 50	11 48
30	04 42	05 11	05 36	08 52	09 46	10 42	11 39
20	04 55	05 21	05 44	08 46	09 37	10 29	11 24
N 10	05 05	05 30	05 51	08 40	09 28	10 18	11 11
0	05 12	05 36	05 57	08 35	09 20	10 08	10 58
S 10	05 18	05 42	06 04	08 30	09 12	09 58	10 46
20	05 22	05 48	06 10	08 24	09 04	09 47	10 33
30	05 26	05 54	06 18	08 18	08 55	09 34	10 18
35	05 27	05 57	06 22	08 14	08 49	09 27	10 10
40	05 28	06 00	06 27	08 10	08 43	09 19	10 00
45	05 29	06 03	06 32	08 06	08 36	09 10	09 48
S 50	05 29	06 06	06 39	08 00	08 28	08 58	09 35
52	05 29	06 08	06 42	07 58	08 24	08 53	09 28
54	05 29	06 09	06 45	07 55	08 19	08 47	09 21
56	05 28	06 11	06 49	07 52	08 14	08 41	09 13
58	05 28	06 13	06 53	07 49	08 09	08 34	09 04
S 60	05 27	06 15	06 57	07 45	08 03	08 26	08 54

Lat.	Sunset	Twilight Civil	Twilight Naut.	Moonset 29	Moonset 30	Moonset 31	Moonset 1
°	h m	h m	h m	h m	h m	h m	h m
N 72	20 07	21 40	////	19 00	18 53	18 44	18 29
N 70	19 52	21 09	////	19 13	19 14	19 17	19 23
68	19 41	20 47	22 43	19 24	19 30	19 40	19 57
66	19 31	20 30	22 00	19 33	19 44	19 59	20 21
64	19 23	20 16	21 32	19 40	19 55	20 14	20 40
62	19 16	20 05	21 11	19 47	20 04	20 26	20 55
60	19 10	19 55	20 55	19 52	20 12	20 37	21 09
N 58	19 05	19 47	20 41	19 57	20 19	20 46	21 20
56	19 00	19 40	20 30	20 01	20 26	20 54	21 30
54	18 56	19 33	20 20	20 05	20 31	21 02	21 38
52	18 52	19 27	20 11	20 09	20 36	21 08	21 46
50	18 49	19 22	20 04	20 12	20 41	21 14	21 53
45	18 41	19 12	19 48	20 19	20 51	21 27	22 08
N 40	18 35	19 03	19 36	20 25	20 59	21 38	22 21
35	18 30	18 56	19 26	20 31	21 07	21 47	22 31
30	18 25	18 49	19 18	20 35	21 13	21 55	22 41
20	18 17	18 39	19 06	20 43	21 24	22 08	22 56
N 10	18 10	18 32	18 56	20 50	21 34	22 21	23 10
0	18 04	18 25	18 49	20 56	21 43	22 32	23 23
S 10	17 58	18 19	18 44	21 03	21 52	22 43	23 37
20	17 51	18 13	18 39	21 10	22 02	22 55	23 51
30	17 44	18 08	18 36	21 18	22 13	23 09	24 07
35	17 40	18 05	18 35	21 23	22 19	23 17	24 16
40	17 35	18 02	18 34	21 28	22 27	23 27	24 26
45	17 30	17 59	18 33	21 34	22 35	23 37	24 39
S 50	17 23	17 56	18 33	21 41	22 46	23 50	24 54
52	17 20	17 54	18 33	21 45	22 51	23 57	25 01
54	17 17	17 53	18 34	21 48	22 56	24 03	00 03
56	17 13	17 51	18 34	21 52	23 02	24 11	00 11
58	17 09	17 49	18 35	21 57	23 08	24 19	00 19
S 60	17 05	17 47	18 36	22 02	23 16	24 29	00 29

	SUN Eqn. of Time 00h	SUN Eqn. of Time 12h	SUN Mer. Pass.	MOON Mer. Pass. Upper	MOON Mer. Pass. Lower	Age	Phase
Day	m s	m s	h m	h m	h m	d	%
29	01 06	00 57	12 01	14 46	02 23	04 14	
30	00 48	00 39	12 01	15 32	03 08	05 21	
31	00 30	00 21	12 00	16 20	03 55	06 30	

UT	ARIES GHA	VENUS −3.9 GHA	Dec	MARS +0.7 GHA	Dec	JUPITER −1.8 GHA	Dec	SATURN +0.6 GHA	Dec	STARS Name	SHA	Dec
1 MONDAY												
00	340 05.0	193 13.5	N14 28.7	111 18.2	S19 27.3	207 20.7	N18 08.3	113 53.5	S15 11.5	Acamar	315 17.6	S40 14.6
01	355 07.4	208 13.0	27.8	126 19.1	27.7	222 22.6	08.2	128 55.8	11.6	Achernar	335 25.8	S57 09.5
02	10 09.9	223 12.4	26.8	141 19.9	28.2	237 24.6	08.0	143 58.1	11.6	Acrux	173 08.8	S63 10.9
03	25 12.3	238 11.9	.. 25.8	156 20.7	.. 28.6	252 26.5	.. 07.9	159 00.4	.. 11.7	Adhara	255 12.1	S28 59.5
04	40 14.8	253 11.3	24.9	171 21.6	29.0	267 28.4	07.8	174 02.7	11.7	Aldebaran	290 48.4	N16 32.2
05	55 17.3	268 10.7	23.9	186 22.4	29.5	282 30.4	07.6	189 05.0	11.8			
06	70 19.7	283 10.2	N14 22.9	201 23.3	S19 29.9	297 32.3	N18 07.5	204 07.3	S15 11.8	Alioth	166 20.5	N55 53.0
07	85 22.2	298 09.6	22.0	216 24.1	30.4	312 34.3	07.4	219 09.6	11.9	Alkaid	152 58.6	N49 14.7
08	100 24.7	313 09.1	21.0	231 24.9	30.8	327 36.2	07.2	234 11.9	11.9	Al Na'ir	27 42.3	S46 53.2
M 09	115 27.1	328 08.5	.. 20.0	246 25.8	.. 31.2	342 38.1	.. 07.1	249 14.2	.. 12.0	Alnilam	275 45.6	S 1 11.6
O 10	130 29.6	343 07.9	19.1	261 26.6	31.7	357 40.1	07.0	264 16.5	12.0	Alphard	217 55.6	S 8 43.3
N 11	145 32.1	358 07.4	18.1	276 27.4	32.1	12 42.0	06.8	279 18.8	12.1			
D 12	160 34.5	13 06.8	N14 17.1	291 28.3	S19 32.5	27 44.0	N18 06.7	294 21.1	S15 12.2	Alphecca	126 10.4	N26 40.3
A 13	175 37.0	28 06.3	16.1	306 29.1	33.0	42 45.9	06.6	309 23.4	12.2	Alpheratz	357 42.3	N29 10.4
Y 14	190 39.4	43 05.7	15.2	321 29.9	33.4	57 47.8	06.4	324 25.8	12.3	Altair	62 07.2	N 8 54.8
15	205 41.9	58 05.2	.. 14.2	336 30.8	.. 33.8	72 49.8	.. 06.3	339 28.1	.. 12.3	Ankaa	353 14.5	S42 13.4
16	220 44.4	73 04.6	13.2	351 31.6	34.3	87 51.7	06.2	354 30.4	12.4	Antares	112 25.2	S26 27.7
17	235 46.8	88 04.0	12.2	6 32.4	34.7	102 53.6	06.0	9 32.7	12.4			
18	250 49.3	103 03.5	N14 11.3	21 33.2	S19 35.1	117 55.6	N18 05.9	24 35.0	S15 12.5	Arcturus	145 55.2	N19 06.6
19	265 51.8	118 02.9	10.3	36 34.1	35.6	132 57.5	05.8	39 37.3	12.5	Atria	107 26.2	S69 03.3
20	280 54.2	133 02.4	09.3	51 34.9	36.0	147 59.5	05.6	54 39.6	12.6	Avior	234 18.1	S59 33.3
21	295 56.7	148 01.8	.. 08.3	66 35.7	.. 36.4	163 01.4	.. 05.5	69 41.9	.. 12.6	Bellatrix	278 31.2	N 6 21.7
22	310 59.2	163 01.3	07.4	81 36.6	36.9	178 03.3	05.3	84 44.2	12.7	Betelgeuse	271 00.5	N 7 24.5
23	326 01.6	178 00.7	06.4	96 37.4	37.3	193 05.3	05.2	99 46.5	12.7			
2 TUESDAY												
00	341 04.1	193 00.2	N14 05.4	111 38.2	S19 37.7	208 07.2	N18 05.1	114 48.8	S15 12.8	Canopus	263 56.0	S52 42.1
01	356 06.6	207 59.6	04.4	126 39.1	38.1	223 09.2	04.9	129 51.1	12.9	Capella	280 33.3	N46 00.4
02	11 09.0	222 59.1	03.4	141 39.9	38.6	238 11.1	04.8	144 53.4	12.9	Deneb	49 30.5	N45 20.3
03	26 11.5	237 58.5	.. 02.5	156 40.7	.. 39.0	253 13.0	.. 04.7	159 55.7	.. 13.0	Denebola	182 33.1	N14 29.5
04	41 13.9	252 58.0	01.5	171 41.5	39.4	268 15.0	04.5	174 58.0	13.0	Diphda	348 54.8	S17 54.2
05	56 16.4	267 57.4	14 00.5	186 42.4	39.9	283 16.9	04.4	190 00.3	13.1			
06	71 18.9	282 56.9	N13 59.5	201 43.2	S19 40.3	298 18.9	N18 04.3	205 02.6	S15 13.1	Dubhe	193 51.5	N61 40.3
07	86 21.3	297 56.3	58.5	216 44.0	40.7	313 20.8	04.1	220 04.9	13.2	Elnath	278 11.6	N28 36.9
08	101 23.8	312 55.8	57.5	231 44.8	41.2	328 22.7	04.0	235 07.2	13.2	Eltanin	90 45.6	N51 29.7
T 09	116 26.3	327 55.2	.. 56.6	246 45.7	.. 41.6	343 24.7	.. 03.9	250 09.5	.. 13.3	Enif	33 46.0	N 9 56.8
U 10	131 28.7	342 54.7	55.6	261 46.5	42.0	358 26.6	03.7	265 11.8	13.3	Fomalhaut	15 22.7	S29 32.4
E 11	146 31.2	357 54.1	54.6	276 47.3	42.5	13 28.6	03.6	280 14.1	13.4			
S 12	161 33.7	12 53.6	N13 53.6	291 48.1	S19 42.9	28 30.5	N18 03.5	295 16.4	S15 13.5	Gacrux	172 00.4	S57 11.8
D 13	176 36.1	27 53.0	52.6	306 49.0	43.3	43 32.4	03.3	310 18.7	13.5	Gienah	175 51.7	S17 37.4
A 14	191 38.6	42 52.5	51.6	321 49.8	43.7	58 34.4	03.2	325 21.0	13.6	Hadar	148 47.0	S60 26.7
Y 15	206 41.1	57 51.9	.. 50.6	336 50.6	.. 44.2	73 36.3	.. 03.1	340 23.3	.. 13.6	Hamal	327 59.6	N23 31.9
16	221 43.5	72 51.4	49.6	351 51.4	44.6	88 38.3	02.9	355 25.6	13.7	Kaus Aust.	83 42.5	S34 22.5
17	236 46.0	87 50.8	48.6	6 52.2	45.0	103 40.2	02.8	10 27.9	13.7			
18	251 48.4	102 50.3	N13 47.6	21 53.1	S19 45.5	118 42.1	N18 02.6	25 30.2	S15 13.8	Kochab	137 20.7	N74 06.1
19	266 50.9	117 49.8	46.7	36 53.9	45.9	133 44.1	02.5	40 32.5	13.8	Markab	13 37.1	N15 17.3
20	281 53.4	132 49.2	45.7	51 54.7	46.3	148 46.0	02.4	55 34.8	13.9	Menkar	314 14.0	N 4 08.8
21	296 55.8	147 48.7	.. 44.7	66 55.5	.. 46.7	163 48.0	.. 02.2	70 37.1	.. 13.9	Menkent	148 06.8	S36 26.5
22	311 58.3	162 48.1	43.7	81 56.4	47.2	178 49.9	02.1	85 39.4	14.0	Miaplacidus	221 40.2	S69 46.6
23	327 00.8	177 47.6	42.7	96 57.2	47.6	193 51.9	02.0	100 41.7	14.1			
3 WEDNESDAY												
00	342 03.2	192 47.0	N13 41.7	111 58.0	S19 48.0	208 53.8	N18 01.8	115 44.0	S15 14.1	Mirfak	308 38.9	N49 54.5
01	357 05.7	207 46.5	40.7	126 58.8	48.5	223 55.7	01.7	130 46.3	14.2	Nunki	75 57.1	S26 16.5
02	12 08.2	222 45.9	39.7	141 59.6	48.9	238 57.7	01.6	145 48.6	14.2	Peacock	53 17.5	S56 41.1
03	27 10.6	237 45.4	.. 38.7	157 00.4	.. 49.3	253 59.6	.. 01.4	160 50.9	.. 14.3	Pollux	243 27.0	N27 59.2
04	42 13.1	252 44.9	37.7	172 01.3	49.7	269 01.6	01.3	175 53.2	14.3	Procyon	244 59.1	N 5 11.1
05	57 15.5	267 44.3	36.7	187 02.1	50.2	284 03.5	01.2	190 55.5	14.4			
06	72 18.0	282 43.8	N13 35.7	202 02.9	S19 50.6	299 05.4	N18 01.0	205 57.8	S15 14.4	Rasalhague	96 05.6	N12 33.3
W 07	87 20.5	297 43.2	34.7	217 03.7	51.0	314 07.4	00.9	221 00.1	14.5	Regulus	207 43.0	N11 53.7
E 08	102 22.9	312 42.7	33.7	232 04.5	51.4	329 09.3	00.8	236 02.4	14.6	Rigel	281 11.3	S 8 11.1
D 09	117 25.4	327 42.2	.. 32.7	247 05.3	.. 51.9	344 11.3	.. 00.6	251 04.7	.. 14.6	Rigil Kent.	139 50.8	S60 53.8
N 10	132 27.9	342 41.6	31.7	262 06.2	52.3	359 13.2	00.5	266 07.0	14.7	Sabik	102 11.5	S15 44.4
E 11	147 30.3	357 41.1	30.7	277 07.0	52.7	14 15.2	00.3	281 09.3	14.7			
S 12	162 32.8	12 40.5	N13 29.7	292 07.8	S19 53.1	29 17.1	N18 00.2	296 11.6	S15 14.8	Schedar	349 39.0	N56 37.0
D 13	177 35.3	27 40.0	28.7	307 08.6	53.6	44 19.0	18 00.1	311 13.9	14.8	Shaula	96 20.7	S37 06.7
A 14	192 37.7	42 39.5	27.7	322 09.4	54.0	59 21.0	17 59.9	326 16.2	14.9	Sirius	258 33.1	S16 44.2
Y 15	207 40.2	57 38.9	.. 26.7	337 10.2	.. 54.4	74 22.9	.. 59.8	341 18.5	.. 14.9	Spica	158 30.6	S11 14.2
16	222 42.7	72 38.4	25.6	352 11.0	54.8	89 24.9	59.7	356 20.8	15.0	Suhail	222 52.2	S43 29.5
17	237 45.1	87 37.9	24.6	7 11.8	55.3	104 26.8	59.5	11 23.1	15.1			
18	252 47.6	102 37.3	N13 23.6	22 12.7	S19 55.7	119 28.8	N17 59.4	26 25.4	S15 15.1	Vega	80 38.2	N38 48.3
19	267 50.0	117 36.8	22.6	37 13.5	56.1	134 30.7	59.3	41 27.7	15.2	Zuben'ubi	137 04.6	S16 06.0
20	282 52.5	132 36.3	21.6	52 14.3	56.5	149 32.7	59.1	56 30.0	15.2		SHA	Mer.Pass.
21	297 55.0	147 35.7	.. 20.6	67 15.1	.. 57.0	164 34.6	.. 59.0	71 32.3	.. 15.3		° ′	h m
22	312 57.4	162 35.2	19.6	82 15.9	57.4	179 36.5	58.9	86 34.6	15.3	Venus	211 56.1	11 08
23	327 59.9	177 34.7	18.6	97 16.7	57.8	194 38.5	58.7	101 36.9	15.4	Mars	130 34.1	16 33
Mer.Pass. 1 15.5 (h m)		*v* −0.5 *d* 1.0		*v* 0.8 *d* 0.4		*v* 1.9 *d* 0.1		*v* 2.3 *d* 0.1		Jupiter	227 03.1	10 06
										Saturn	133 44.7	16 18

SUN and MOON

UT	SUN GHA	SUN Dec	MOON GHA	v	MOON Dec	d	HP
1 00	179 57.3	N 8 22.9	111 09.9	10.5	S15 20.8	6.0	56.6
01	194 57.5	22.0	125 39.4	10.4	15 26.8	5.9	56.7
02	209 57.7	21.1	140 08.8	10.4	15 32.7	5.8	56.7
03	224 57.9	.. 20.2	154 38.2	10.3	15 38.5	5.7	56.7
04	239 58.1	19.3	169 07.5	10.3	15 44.2	5.7	56.8
05	254 58.3	18.4	183 36.8	10.2	15 49.9	5.5	56.8
06	269 58.5	N 8 17.5	198 06.0	10.1	S15 55.4	5.5	56.8
07	284 58.7	16.5	212 35.1	10.1	16 00.9	5.5	56.8
08	299 58.9	15.6	227 04.2	10.0	16 06.4	5.3	56.9
M 09	314 59.1	.. 14.7	241 33.2	9.9	16 11.7	5.3	56.9
O 10	329 59.3	13.8	256 02.1	9.9	16 17.0	5.1	56.9
N 11	344 59.5	12.9	270 31.0	9.8	16 22.1	5.1	57.0
D 12	359 59.7	N 8 12.0	284 59.8	9.7	S16 27.2	5.0	57.0
A 13	14 59.9	11.1	299 28.5	9.7	16 32.2	5.0	57.0
Y 14	30 00.1	10.2	313 57.2	9.6	16 37.2	4.8	57.1
15	45 00.3	.. 09.3	328 25.8	9.5	16 42.0	4.7	57.1
16	60 00.5	08.4	342 54.3	9.5	16 46.7	4.7	57.1
17	75 00.7	07.5	357 22.8	9.4	16 51.4	4.6	57.2
18	90 00.9	N 8 06.6	11 51.2	9.3	S16 56.0	4.5	57.2
19	105 01.1	05.7	26 19.5	9.3	17 00.5	4.4	57.2
20	120 01.3	04.7	40 47.8	9.2	17 04.9	4.3	57.3
21	135 01.5	.. 03.8	55 16.0	9.2	17 09.2	4.2	57.3
22	150 01.7	02.9	69 44.2	9.0	17 13.4	4.1	57.3
23	165 01.9	02.0	84 12.2	9.1	17 17.5	4.0	57.4
2 00	180 02.1	N 8 01.1	98 40.3	8.9	S17 21.5	4.0	57.4
01	195 02.3	8 00.2	113 08.2	8.9	17 25.5	3.8	57.4
02	210 02.5	7 59.3	127 36.1	8.8	17 29.3	3.7	57.5
03	225 02.7	.. 58.4	142 03.9	8.8	17 33.0	3.7	57.5
04	240 02.9	57.5	156 31.7	8.7	17 36.7	3.5	57.5
05	255 03.1	56.6	170 59.4	8.6	17 40.2	3.5	57.6
06	270 03.3	N 7 55.6	185 27.0	8.6	S17 43.7	3.3	57.6
07	285 03.5	54.7	199 54.6	8.5	17 47.0	3.3	57.6
T 08	300 03.7	53.8	214 22.1	8.5	17 50.3	3.1	57.7
U 09	315 03.9	.. 52.9	228 49.6	8.4	17 53.4	3.1	57.7
E 10	330 04.1	52.0	243 17.0	8.3	17 56.5	2.9	57.7
S 11	345 04.3	51.1	257 44.3	8.3	17 59.4	2.9	57.8
D 12	0 04.5	N 7 50.2	272 11.6	8.2	S18 02.3	2.7	57.8
A 13	15 04.7	49.3	286 38.8	8.1	18 05.0	2.7	57.8
Y 14	30 04.9	48.3	301 05.9	8.1	18 07.7	2.5	57.9
15	45 05.1	.. 47.4	315 33.0	8.1	18 10.2	2.4	57.9
16	60 05.3	46.5	330 00.1	7.9	18 12.6	2.4	57.9
17	75 05.5	45.6	344 27.0	7.9	18 15.0	2.2	58.0
18	90 05.7	N 7 44.7	358 53.9	7.9	S18 17.2	2.1	58.0
19	105 05.9	43.8	13 20.8	7.8	18 19.3	2.0	58.0
20	120 06.1	42.9	27 47.6	7.8	18 21.3	1.9	58.1
21	135 06.3	.. 41.9	42 14.4	7.6	18 23.2	1.8	58.1
22	150 06.5	41.0	56 41.0	7.7	18 25.0	1.7	58.1
23	165 06.7	40.1	71 07.7	7.6	18 26.7	1.5	58.2
3 00	180 06.9	N 7 39.2	85 34.3	7.5	S18 28.2	1.5	58.2
01	195 07.1	38.3	100 00.8	7.4	18 29.7	1.3	58.2
02	210 07.3	37.4	114 27.2	7.5	18 31.0	1.3	58.3
03	225 07.5	.. 36.5	128 53.7	7.3	18 32.3	1.1	58.3
04	240 07.7	35.5	143 20.0	7.3	18 33.4	1.0	58.3
05	255 07.9	34.6	157 46.3	7.3	18 34.4	0.9	58.4
06	270 08.1	N 7 33.7	172 12.6	7.2	S18 35.3	0.8	58.4
W 07	285 08.3	32.8	186 38.8	7.2	18 36.1	0.6	58.5
E 08	300 08.5	31.9	201 05.0	7.1	18 36.7	0.6	58.5
D 09	315 08.7	.. 31.0	215 31.1	7.1	18 37.3	0.4	58.5
N 10	330 08.9	30.0	229 57.2	7.0	18 37.7	0.3	58.6
E 11	345 09.1	29.1	244 23.2	7.0	18 38.0	0.1	58.6
S 12	0 09.3	N 7 28.2	258 49.2	6.9	S18 38.2	0.1	58.6
D 13	15 09.5	27.3	273 15.1	6.9	18 38.3	0.0	58.7
A 14	30 09.7	26.4	287 41.0	6.8	18 38.3	0.2	58.7
Y 15	45 09.9	.. 25.5	302 06.8	6.8	18 38.1	0.2	58.7
16	60 10.2	24.5	316 32.6	6.7	18 37.9	0.4	58.8
17	75 10.4	23.6	330 58.3	6.8	18 37.5	0.5	58.8
18	90 10.6	N 7 22.7	345 24.1	6.6	S18 37.0	0.7	58.8
19	105 10.8	21.8	359 49.7	6.7	18 36.3	0.7	58.9
20	120 11.0	20.9	14 15.4	6.5	18 35.6	0.9	58.9
21	135 11.2	.. 19.9	28 40.9	6.6	18 34.7	1.0	58.9
22	150 11.4	19.0	43 06.5	6.5	18 33.7	1.1	59.0
23	165 11.6	18.1	57 32.0	6.5	S18 32.6	1.2	59.0
SD	15.9	d 0.9	SD 15.5		15.7		16.0

Twilight / Moonrise

Lat.	Twilight Naut.	Twilight Civil	Sunrise	Moonrise 1	2	3	4
N 72	////	02 37	04 06	15 44	■	■	19 29
N 70	////	03 04	04 19	14 50	16 24	17 33	18 06
68	01 39	03 24	04 29	14 18	15 40	16 45	17 27
66	02 15	03 40	04 38	13 54	15 10	16 14	16 59
64	02 40	03 52	04 45	13 35	14 48	15 50	16 38
62	02 59	04 03	04 51	13 20	14 31	15 32	16 21
60	03 14	04 12	04 57	13 07	14 16	15 17	16 07
N 58	03 27	04 20	05 02	12 57	14 03	15 04	15 55
56	03 37	04 27	05 06	12 47	13 53	14 53	15 45
54	03 46	04 33	05 10	12 39	13 43	14 43	15 35
52	03 55	04 38	05 13	12 31	13 35	14 34	15 27
50	04 02	04 43	05 16	12 24	13 27	14 26	15 20
45	04 16	04 53	05 23	12 10	13 11	14 09	15 04
N 40	04 28	05 01	05 29	11 58	12 58	13 56	14 51
35	04 37	05 07	05 33	11 48	12 46	13 44	14 40
30	04 44	05 13	05 37	11 39	12 37	13 34	14 30
20	04 56	05 22	05 45	11 24	12 20	13 16	14 13
N 10	05 05	05 30	05 51	11 11	12 05	13 01	13 58
0	05 11	05 36	05 56	10 58	11 51	12 47	13 45
S 10	05 16	05 41	06 02	10 46	11 38	12 33	13 31
20	05 20	05 46	06 08	10 33	11 23	12 18	13 16
30	05 23	05 50	06 14	10 18	11 07	12 01	13 00
35	05 23	05 53	06 18	10 10	10 57	11 50	12 50
40	05 24	05 55	06 22	10 00	10 46	11 39	12 39
45	05 24	05 58	06 27	09 48	10 33	11 25	12 26
S 50	05 23	06 00	06 33	09 35	10 18	11 09	12 10
52	05 22	06 01	06 35	09 28	10 10	11 01	12 02
54	05 22	06 03	06 38	09 21	10 02	10 53	11 54
56	05 21	06 04	06 41	09 13	09 53	10 43	11 45
58	05 20	06 05	06 45	09 04	09 43	10 32	11 34
S 60	05 19	06 07	06 49	08 54	09 31	10 20	11 22

Sunset / Moonset

Lat.	Sunset	Twilight Civil	Twilight Naut.	Moonset 1	2	3	4
N 72	19 50	21 16	////	18 29	■	■	20 35
N 70	19 38	20 51	23 17	19 23	19 41	20 29	21 58
68	19 28	20 32	22 13	19 57	20 26	21 18	22 36
66	19 19	20 17	21 40	20 21	20 56	21 49	23 03
64	19 12	20 04	21 16	20 40	21 18	22 12	23 24
62	19 06	19 54	20 58	20 55	21 36	22 30	23 41
60	19 00	19 45	20 43	21 09	21 51	22 46	23 54
N 58	18 56	19 38	20 31	21 20	22 03	22 59	24 06
56	18 52	19 31	20 20	21 30	22 14	23 10	24 17
54	18 49	19 26	20 11	21 38	22 24	23 19	24 26
52	18 45	19 20	20 03	21 46	22 32	23 28	24 34
50	18 42	19 16	19 56	21 53	22 40	23 36	24 41
45	18 36	19 06	19 42	22 08	22 57	23 53	24 56
N 40	18 30	18 58	19 31	22 21	23 10	24 06	00 06
35	18 26	18 51	19 22	22 31	23 22	24 18	00 18
30	18 22	18 46	19 14	22 41	23 32	24 28	00 28
20	18 15	18 37	19 03	22 56	23 49	24 45	00 45
N 10	18 09	18 30	18 54	23 10	24 04	00 04	01 00
0	18 03	18 24	18 48	23 23	24 18	00 18	01 14
S 10	17 58	18 19	18 43	23 37	24 32	00 32	01 28
20	17 52	18 14	18 40	23 51	24 47	00 47	01 43
30	17 46	18 10	18 37	24 07	00 07	01 04	02 01
35	17 42	18 07	18 37	24 16	00 16	01 14	02 10
40	17 38	18 05	18 36	24 26	00 26	01 25	02 22
45	17 33	18 03	18 37	24 39	00 39	01 39	02 35
S 50	17 28	18 00	18 38	24 54	00 54	01 55	02 51
52	17 25	17 59	18 38	25 01	01 01	02 03	02 59
54	17 22	17 58	18 39	00 01	01 09	02 11	03 07
56	17 19	17 57	18 40	00 11	01 18	02 21	03 17
58	17 16	17 55	18 41	00 19	01 28	02 32	03 28
S 60	17 12	17 54	18 42	00 29	01 40	02 44	03 40

SUN / MOON

Day	Eqn. of Time 00h	Eqn. of Time 12h	Mer. Pass.	Mer. Pass. Upper	Mer. Pass. Lower	Age	Phase
d	m s	m s	h m	h m	h m	d	%
1	00 11	00 02	12 00	17 11	04 45	07	40
2	00 08	00 17	12 00	18 05	05 37	08	50
3	00 27	00 37	11 59	19 01	06 32	09	61

UT (d h)	ARIES GHA	VENUS −3.9 GHA	Dec	MARS +0.7 GHA	Dec	JUPITER −1.8 GHA	Dec	SATURN +0.6 GHA	Dec	Star Name	SHA	Dec
4 00	343 02.4	192 34.1	N13 17.6	112 17.5	S19 58.2	209 40.4	N17 58.6	116 39.2	S15 15.4	Acamar	315 17.5	S40 14.6
01	358 04.8	207 33.6	16.6	127 18.3	58.7	224 42.4	58.5	131 41.5	15.5	Achernar	335 25.8	S57 09.5
02	13 07.3	222 33.1	15.5	142 19.1	59.1	239 44.3	58.3	146 43.8	15.6	Acrux	173 08.8	S63 10.9
03	28 09.8	237 32.5 ..	14.5	157 19.9 ..	59.5	254 46.3 ..	58.2	161 46.1 ..	15.6	Adhara	255 12.0	S28 59.5
04	43 12.2	252 32.0	13.5	172 20.8	19 59.9	269 48.2	58.1	176 48.4	15.7	Aldebaran	290 48.4	N16 32.2
05	58 14.7	267 31.5	12.5	187 21.6	20 00.3	284 50.2	57.9	191 50.7	15.7			
06	73 17.2	282 30.9	N13 11.5	202 22.4	S20 00.8	299 52.1	N17 57.8	206 53.0	S15 15.8	Alioth	166 20.5	N55 53.0
07	88 19.6	297 30.4	10.5	217 23.2	01.2	314 54.0	57.6	221 55.3	15.8	Alkaid	152 58.6	N49 14.7
T 08	103 22.1	312 29.9	09.4	232 24.0	01.6	329 56.0	57.5	236 57.5	15.9	Al Na'ir	27 42.3	S46 53.2
H 09	118 24.5	327 29.3 ..	08.4	247 24.8 ..	02.0	344 57.9 ..	57.4	251 59.8 ..	15.9	Alnilam	275 45.6	S 1 11.6
U 10	133 27.0	342 28.8	07.4	262 25.6	02.5	359 59.9	57.2	267 02.1	16.0	Alphard	217 55.5	S 8 43.3
R 11	148 29.5	357 28.3	06.4	277 26.4	02.9	15 01.8	57.1	282 04.4	16.1			
S 12	163 31.9	12 27.7	N13 05.4	292 27.2	S20 03.3	30 03.8	N17 57.0	297 06.7	S15 16.1	Alphecca	126 10.4	N26 40.3
D 13	178 34.4	27 27.2	04.4	307 28.0	03.7	45 05.7	56.8	312 09.0	16.2	Alpheratz	357 42.2	N29 10.4
A 14	193 36.9	42 26.7	03.3	322 28.8	04.1	60 07.7	56.7	327 11.3	16.2	Altair	62 07.2	N 8 54.8
Y 15	208 39.3	57 26.2 ..	02.3	337 29.6 ..	04.6	75 09.6 ..	56.6	342 13.6 ..	16.3	Ankaa	353 14.5	S42 13.4
16	223 41.8	72 25.6	01.3	352 30.4	05.0	90 11.6	56.4	357 15.9	16.3	Antares	112 25.2	S26 27.7
17	238 44.3	87 25.1	13 00.3	7 31.2	05.4	105 13.5	56.3	12 18.2	16.4			
18	253 46.7	102 24.6	N12 59.2	22 32.0	S20 05.8	120 15.4	N17 56.2	27 20.5	S15 16.5	Arcturus	145 55.2	N19 06.6
19	268 49.2	117 24.1	58.2	37 32.8	06.2	135 17.4	56.0	42 22.8	16.5	Atria	107 26.2	S69 03.3
20	283 51.7	132 23.5	57.2	52 33.6	06.6	150 19.3	55.9	57 25.1	16.6	Avior	234 18.1	S59 33.3
21	298 54.1	147 23.0 ..	56.2	67 34.4 ..	07.1	165 21.3 ..	55.8	72 27.4 ..	16.6	Bellatrix	278 31.1	N 6 21.7
22	313 56.6	162 22.5	55.1	82 35.2	07.5	180 23.2	55.6	87 29.7	16.7	Betelgeuse	271 00.5	N 7 24.5
23	328 59.0	177 21.9	54.1	97 36.0	07.9	195 25.2	55.5	102 32.0	16.7			
5 00	344 01.5	192 21.4	N12 53.1	112 36.8	S20 08.3	210 27.1	N17 55.4	117 34.3	S15 16.8	Canopus	263 56.0	S52 42.1
01	359 04.0	207 20.9	52.1	127 37.6	08.7	225 29.1	55.2	132 36.5	16.8	Capella	280 33.2	N46 00.4
02	14 06.4	222 20.4	51.0	142 38.4	09.2	240 31.0	55.1	147 38.8	16.9	Deneb	49 30.5	N45 20.3
03	29 08.9	237 19.9 ..	50.0	157 39.2 ..	09.6	255 33.0 ..	55.0	162 41.1 ..	17.0	Denebola	182 33.1	N14 29.5
04	44 11.4	252 19.3	49.0	172 40.0	10.0	270 34.9	54.8	177 43.4	17.0	Diphda	348 54.8	S17 54.2
05	59 13.8	267 18.8	47.9	187 40.8	10.4	285 36.9	54.7	192 45.7	17.1			
06	74 16.3	282 18.3	N12 46.9	202 41.6	S20 10.8	300 38.8	N17 54.5	207 48.0	S15 17.1	Dubhe	193 51.4	N61 40.3
07	89 18.8	297 17.8	45.9	217 42.4	11.2	315 40.8	54.4	222 50.3	17.2	Elnath	278 11.6	N28 36.9
F 08	104 21.2	312 17.2	44.8	232 43.2	11.7	330 42.7	54.3	237 52.6	17.2	Eltanin	90 45.6	N51 29.7
R 09	119 23.7	327 16.7 ..	43.8	247 44.0 ..	12.1	345 44.7 ..	54.1	252 54.9 ..	17.3	Enif	33 46.0	N 9 56.8
I 10	134 26.1	342 16.2	42.8	262 44.8	12.5	0 46.6	54.0	267 57.2	17.4	Fomalhaut	15 22.7	S29 32.5
D 11	149 28.6	357 15.7	41.7	277 45.6	12.9	15 48.5	53.9	282 59.5	17.4			
A 12	164 31.1	12 15.2	N12 40.7	292 46.4	S20 13.3	30 50.5	N17 53.7	298 01.8	S15 17.5	Gacrux	172 00.4	S57 11.8
Y 13	179 33.5	27 14.6	39.7	307 47.2	13.7	45 52.4	53.6	313 04.1	17.5	Gienah	175 51.7	S17 37.3
14	194 36.0	42 14.1	38.6	322 48.0	14.2	60 54.4	53.5	328 06.3	17.6	Hadar	148 47.0	S60 26.7
15	209 38.5	57 13.6 ..	37.6	337 48.8 ..	14.6	75 56.3 ..	53.3	343 08.6 ..	17.6	Hamal	327 59.5	N23 31.9
16	224 40.9	72 13.1	36.6	352 49.6	15.0	90 58.3	53.2	358 10.9	17.7	Kaus Aust.	83 42.5	S34 22.5
17	239 43.4	87 12.6	35.5	7 50.4	15.4	106 00.2	53.1	13 13.2	17.8			
18	254 45.9	102 12.0	N12 34.5	22 51.2	S20 15.8	121 02.2	N17 52.9	28 15.5	S15 17.8	Kochab	137 20.8	N74 06.1
19	269 48.3	117 11.5	33.5	37 51.9	16.2	136 04.1	52.8	43 17.8	17.9	Markab	13 37.1	N15 17.3
20	284 50.8	132 11.0	32.4	52 52.7	16.6	151 06.1	52.7	58 20.1	17.9	Menkar	314 14.0	N 4 08.8
21	299 53.3	147 10.5 ..	31.4	67 53.5 ..	17.1	166 08.0 ..	52.5	73 22.4 ..	18.0	Menkent	148 06.8	S36 26.5
22	314 55.7	162 10.0	30.3	82 54.3	17.5	181 10.0	52.4	88 24.7	18.0	Miaplacidus	221 40.2	S69 46.6
23	329 58.2	177 09.5	29.3	97 55.1	17.9	196 11.9	52.3	103 27.0	18.1			
6 00	345 00.6	192 08.9	N12 28.2	112 55.9	S20 18.3	211 13.9	N17 52.1	118 29.3	S15 18.2	Mirfak	308 38.9	N49 54.5
01	0 03.1	207 08.4	27.2	127 56.7	18.7	226 15.8	52.0	133 31.5	18.2	Nunki	75 57.1	S26 16.5
02	15 05.6	222 07.9	26.2	142 57.5	19.1	241 17.8	51.9	148 33.8	18.3	Peacock	53 17.5	S56 41.1
03	30 08.0	237 07.4 ..	25.1	157 58.3 ..	19.5	256 19.7 ..	51.7	163 36.1 ..	18.3	Pollux	243 27.0	N27 59.2
04	45 10.5	252 06.9	24.1	172 59.1	20.0	271 21.7	51.6	178 38.4	18.4	Procyon	244 59.1	N 5 11.1
05	60 13.0	267 06.4	23.0	187 59.9	20.4	286 23.6	51.4	193 40.7	18.4			
06	75 15.4	282 05.9	N12 22.0	203 00.6	S20 20.8	301 25.6	N17 51.3	208 43.0	S15 18.5	Rasalhague	96 05.6	N12 33.3
07	90 17.9	297 05.3	20.9	218 01.4	21.2	316 27.5	51.2	223 45.3	18.6	Regulus	207 42.9	N11 53.7
S 08	105 20.4	312 04.8	19.9	233 02.2	21.6	331 29.5	51.0	238 47.6	18.6	Rigel	281 11.3	S 8 11.1
A 09	120 22.8	327 04.3 ..	18.8	248 03.0 ..	22.0	346 31.4 ..	50.9	253 49.9 ..	18.7	Rigil Kent.	139 50.8	S60 53.8
T 10	135 25.3	342 03.8	17.8	263 03.8	22.4	1 33.4	50.8	268 52.2	18.7	Sabik	102 11.5	S15 44.4
U 11	150 27.8	357 03.3	16.7	278 04.6	22.8	16 35.3	50.6	283 54.4	18.8			
R 12	165 30.2	12 02.8	N12 15.7	293 05.4	S20 23.2	31 37.3	N17 50.5	298 56.7	S15 18.8	Schedar	349 38.9	N56 37.0
D 13	180 32.7	27 02.3	14.6	308 06.1	23.7	46 39.2	50.4	313 59.0	18.9	Shaula	96 20.7	S37 06.7
A 14	195 35.1	42 01.8	13.6	323 06.9	24.1	61 41.2	50.2	329 01.3	19.0	Sirius	258 33.1	S16 44.2
Y 15	210 37.6	57 01.3 ..	12.5	338 07.7 ..	24.5	76 43.1 ..	50.1	344 03.6 ..	19.0	Spica	158 30.6	S11 14.2
16	225 40.1	72 00.7	11.5	353 08.5	24.9	91 45.1	50.0	359 05.9	19.1	Suhail	222 52.2	S43 29.5
17	240 42.5	87 00.2	10.4	8 09.3	25.3	106 47.0	49.8	14 08.2	19.1			
18	255 45.0	101 59.7	N12 09.4	23 10.1	S20 25.7	121 49.0	N17 49.7	29 10.5	S15 19.2	Vega	80 38.2	N38 48.3
19	270 47.5	116 59.2	08.3	38 10.9	26.1	136 50.9	49.6	44 12.7	19.2	Zuben'ubi	137 04.6	S16 06.0
20	285 49.9	131 58.7	07.3	53 11.6	26.5	151 52.9	49.4	59 15.0	19.3			
21	300 52.4	146 58.2 ..	06.2	68 12.4 ..	26.9	166 54.8 ..	49.3	74 17.3 ..	19.4			
22	315 54.9	161 57.7	05.2	83 13.2	27.3	181 56.8	49.2	89 19.6	19.4			
23	330 57.3	176 57.2	04.1	98 14.0	27.7	196 58.7	49.0	104 21.9	19.5			

	h m										SHA	Mer.Pass.
Mer. Pass.	1 03.7	v −0.5	d 1.0	v 0.8	d 0.4	v 1.9	d 0.1	v 2.3	d 0.1	Venus	208 19.9	11 11
										Mars	128 35.3	16 29
										Jupiter	226 25.6	9 57
										Saturn	133 32.7	16 07

UT	SUN GHA	SUN Dec	MOON GHA	v	MOON Dec	d	HP
d h	° ′	° ′	° ′	′	° ′	′	′
4 00	180 11.8	N 7 17.2	71 57.5	6.4	S18 31.4	1.4	59.0
01	195 12.0	16.3	86 22.9	6.4	18 30.0	1.4	59.1
02	210 12.2	15.3	100 48.3	6.4	18 28.6	1.6	59.1
03	225 12.4	.. 14.4	115 13.7	6.4	18 27.0	1.8	59.1
04	240 12.6	13.5	129 39.1	6.3	18 25.2	1.8	59.2
05	255 12.8	12.6	144 04.4	6.3	18 23.4	2.0	59.2
06	270 13.0	N 7 11.7	158 29.7	6.2	S18 21.4	2.1	59.2
07	285 13.2	10.7	172 54.9	6.2	18 19.3	2.2	59.3
T 08	300 13.5	09.8	187 20.1	6.2	18 17.1	2.3	59.3
H 09	315 13.7	.. 08.9	201 45.3	6.2	18 14.8	2.5	59.3
U 10	330 13.9	08.0	216 10.5	6.1	18 12.3	2.5	59.4
R 11	345 14.1	07.0	230 35.6	6.1	18 09.8	2.7	59.4
S 12	0 14.3	N 7 06.1	245 00.7	6.1	S18 07.1	2.9	59.4
D 13	15 14.5	05.2	259 25.8	6.1	18 04.2	2.9	59.5
A 14	30 14.7	04.3	273 50.9	6.0	18 01.3	3.1	59.5
Y 15	45 14.9	.. 03.4	288 15.9	6.0	17 58.2	3.2	59.5
16	60 15.1	02.4	302 40.9	6.0	17 55.0	3.3	59.6
17	75 15.3	01.5	317 05.9	6.0	17 51.7	3.4	59.6
18	90 15.5	N 7 00.6	331 30.9	6.0	S17 48.3	3.6	59.6
19	105 15.7	6 59.7	345 55.9	5.9	17 44.7	3.7	59.7
20	120 15.9	58.7	0 20.8	6.0	17 41.0	3.8	59.7
21	135 16.2	.. 57.8	14 45.8	5.9	17 37.2	3.9	59.7
22	150 16.4	56.9	29 10.7	5.9	17 33.3	4.1	59.8
23	165 16.6	56.0	43 35.6	5.9	17 29.2	4.1	59.8
5 00	180 16.8	N 6 55.0	58 00.5	5.8	S17 25.1	4.3	59.8
01	195 17.0	54.1	72 25.3	5.9	17 20.8	4.5	59.9
02	210 17.2	53.2	86 50.2	5.9	17 16.3	4.5	59.9
03	225 17.4	.. 52.3	101 15.1	5.8	17 11.8	4.7	59.9
04	240 17.6	51.3	115 39.9	5.8	17 07.1	4.7	60.0
05	255 17.8	50.4	130 04.7	5.8	17 02.4	4.9	60.0
06	270 18.0	N 6 49.5	144 29.6	5.8	S16 57.5	5.1	60.0
07	285 18.2	48.6	158 54.4	5.8	16 52.4	5.1	60.0
F 08	300 18.4	47.6	173 19.2	5.8	16 47.3	5.3	60.1
R 09	315 18.7	.. 46.7	187 44.0	5.8	16 42.0	5.3	60.1
I 10	330 18.9	45.8	202 08.8	5.8	16 36.7	5.5	60.1
D 11	345 19.1	44.8	216 33.6	5.8	16 31.2	5.7	60.2
A 12	0 19.3	N 6 43.9	230 58.4	5.8	S16 25.5	5.7	60.2
Y 13	15 19.5	43.0	245 23.2	5.8	16 19.8	5.8	60.2
14	30 19.7	42.1	259 48.0	5.8	16 14.0	6.0	60.2
15	45 19.9	.. 41.1	274 12.8	5.8	16 08.0	6.1	60.3
16	60 20.1	40.2	288 37.6	5.8	16 01.9	6.2	60.3
17	75 20.3	39.3	303 02.4	5.8	15 55.7	6.3	60.3
18	90 20.6	N 6 38.4	317 27.2	5.8	S15 49.4	6.4	60.4
19	105 20.8	37.4	331 52.0	5.8	15 43.0	6.6	60.4
20	120 21.0	36.5	346 16.8	5.9	15 36.4	6.6	60.4
21	135 21.2	.. 35.6	0 41.7	5.8	15 29.8	6.8	60.4
22	150 21.4	34.6	15 06.5	5.8	15 23.0	6.9	60.5
23	165 21.6	33.7	29 31.3	5.9	15 16.1	6.9	60.5
6 00	180 21.8	N 6 32.8	43 56.2	5.8	S15 09.2	7.1	60.5
01	195 22.0	31.9	58 21.0	5.9	15 02.1	7.3	60.5
02	210 22.2	30.9	72 45.9	5.8	14 54.8	7.3	60.6
03	225 22.5	.. 30.0	87 10.7	5.9	14 47.5	7.4	60.6
04	240 22.7	29.1	101 35.6	5.9	14 40.1	7.5	60.6
05	255 22.9	28.1	116 00.5	5.9	14 32.6	7.7	60.6
06	270 23.1	N 6 27.2	130 25.4	5.9	S14 24.9	7.7	60.7
07	285 23.3	26.3	144 50.3	6.0	14 17.2	7.8	60.7
S 08	300 23.5	25.3	159 15.3	5.9	14 09.4	8.0	60.7
A 09	315 23.7	.. 24.4	173 40.2	6.0	14 01.4	8.0	60.7
T 10	330 23.9	23.5	188 05.2	5.9	13 53.4	8.2	60.7
U 11	345 24.1	22.5	202 30.1	6.0	13 45.2	8.2	60.8
R 12	0 24.4	N 6 21.6	216 55.1	6.0	S13 37.0	8.4	60.8
D 13	15 24.6	20.7	231 20.1	6.1	13 28.6	8.4	60.8
A 14	30 24.8	19.8	245 45.2	6.0	13 20.2	8.6	60.8
Y 15	45 25.0	.. 18.8	260 10.2	6.1	13 11.6	8.6	60.8
16	60 25.2	17.9	274 35.3	6.1	13 03.0	8.7	60.9
17	75 25.4	17.0	289 00.4	6.1	12 54.3	8.9	60.9
18	90 25.6	N 6 16.0	303 25.5	6.1	S12 45.4	8.9	60.9
19	105 25.8	15.1	317 50.6	6.1	12 36.5	9.0	60.9
20	120 26.1	14.2	332 15.7	6.2	12 27.5	9.1	60.9
21	135 26.3	.. 13.2	346 40.9	6.2	12 18.4	9.2	60.9
22	150 26.5	12.3	1 06.1	6.2	12 09.2	9.3	61.0
23	165 26.7	11.4	15 31.3	6.2	S11 59.9	9.3	61.0
	SD 15.9	d 0.9	SD 16.2		16.4		16.6

Lat.	Twilight Naut.	Twilight Civil	Sunrise	Moonrise 4	5	6	7
°	h m	h m	h m	h m	h m	h m	h m
N 72	////	02 57	04 20	19 29	18 57	18 46	18 38
N 70	01 15	03 20	04 31	18 06	18 18	18 23	18 25
68	02 03	03 37	04 40	17 27	17 51	18 05	18 14
66	02 32	03 51	04 48	16 59	17 30	17 50	18 05
64	02 53	04 02	04 54	16 38	17 13	17 38	17 57
62	03 10	04 12	04 59	16 21	16 59	17 28	17 51
60	03 23	04 20	05 04	16 07	16 48	17 19	17 45
N 58	03 35	04 27	05 08	15 55	16 37	17 12	17 40
56	03 45	04 33	05 12	15 45	16 28	17 05	17 36
54	03 53	04 38	05 15	15 35	16 21	16 59	17 32
52	04 00	04 43	05 18	15 27	16 13	16 53	17 28
50	04 07	04 47	05 21	15 20	16 07	16 48	17 25
45	04 20	04 56	05 26	15 04	15 53	16 37	17 17
N 40	04 31	05 04	05 31	14 51	15 42	16 28	17 11
35	04 39	05 10	05 35	14 40	15 32	16 21	17 06
30	04 46	05 15	05 39	14 30	15 23	16 14	17 01
20	04 57	05 23	05 45	14 13	15 08	16 02	16 53
N 10	05 05	05 29	05 51	13 58	14 55	15 51	16 46
0	05 10	05 35	05 55	13 45	14 43	15 42	16 39
S 10	05 15	05 39	06 00	13 31	14 31	15 32	16 33
20	05 18	05 43	06 05	13 16	14 18	15 21	16 25
30	05 19	05 47	06 11	13 00	14 03	15 09	16 17
35	05 19	05 49	06 14	12 50	13 54	15 03	16 13
40	05 19	05 50	06 17	12 39	13 44	14 55	16 07
45	05 18	05 52	06 21	12 26	13 33	14 45	16 01
S 50	05 17	05 54	06 26	12 10	13 19	14 34	15 54
52	05 16	05 55	06 28	12 02	13 12	14 29	15 50
54	05 15	05 56	06 31	11 54	13 05	14 23	15 46
56	05 13	05 56	06 34	11 45	12 57	14 17	15 42
58	05 12	05 57	06 36	11 34	12 47	14 10	15 37
S 60	05 10	05 58	06 40	11 22	12 37	14 02	15 32

Lat.	Sunset	Twilight Civil	Twilight Naut.	Moonset 4	5	6	7
°	h m	h m	h m	h m	h m	h m	h m
N 72	19 34	20 55	////	20 35	23 10	25 23	01 23
N 70	19 23	20 33	22 31	21 58	23 48	25 45	01 45
68	19 15	20 17	21 49	22 36	24 14	00 14	02 02
66	19 08	20 04	21 21	23 03	24 34	00 34	02 15
64	19 02	19 53	21 01	23 24	24 50	00 50	02 26
62	18 56	19 44	20 45	23 41	25 04	01 04	02 35
60	18 52	19 36	20 32	23 54	25 15	01 15	02 43
N 58	18 48	19 29	20 20	24 06	00 06	01 25	02 50
56	18 44	19 23	20 11	24 17	00 17	01 33	02 56
54	18 41	19 18	20 03	24 26	00 26	01 41	03 02
52	18 38	19 13	19 56	24 34	00 34	01 47	03 07
50	18 36	19 09	19 49	24 41	00 41	01 53	03 11
45	18 30	19 00	19 36	24 56	00 56	02 06	03 21
N 40	18 25	18 53	19 26	00 06	01 09	02 17	03 29
35	18 21	18 47	19 17	00 18	01 20	02 26	03 36
30	18 18	18 42	19 11	00 28	01 29	02 34	03 42
20	18 12	18 34	19 00	00 45	01 45	02 48	03 52
N 10	18 07	18 28	18 53	01 00	01 59	03 00	04 01
0	18 02	18 23	18 47	01 14	02 12	03 11	04 09
S 10	17 57	18 18	18 43	01 28	02 26	03 22	04 17
20	17 52	18 15	18 40	01 43	02 39	03 34	04 26
30	17 47	18 11	18 39	02 01	02 55	03 47	04 36
35	17 44	18 09	18 39	02 10	03 04	03 55	04 42
40	17 41	18 08	18 39	02 22	03 15	04 04	04 48
45	17 37	18 06	18 40	02 35	03 27	04 14	04 56
S 50	17 32	18 04	18 42	02 51	03 42	04 26	05 05
52	17 30	18 04	18 43	02 59	03 49	04 32	05 09
54	17 27	18 03	18 44	03 07	03 56	04 38	05 13
56	17 25	18 02	18 45	03 17	04 05	04 45	05 18
58	17 22	18 01	18 47	03 28	04 14	04 52	05 24
S 60	17 19	18 01	18 49	03 40	04 25	05 01	05 30

Day	SUN Eqn. of Time 00h	SUN Eqn. of Time 12h	SUN Mer. Pass.	MOON Mer. Pass. Upper	MOON Mer. Pass. Lower	Age	Phase
d	m s	m s	h m	h m	h m	d	%
4	00 47	00 57	11 59	19 59	07 29	10	72
5	01 07	01 17	11 59	20 57	08 28	11	82
6	01 27	01 37	11 58	21 55	09 26	12	90

UT	ARIES GHA	VENUS −3.9 GHA	Dec	MARS +0.7 GHA	Dec	JUPITER −1.8 GHA	Dec	SATURN +0.6 GHA	Dec	STARS Name	SHA	Dec
d h	° ′	° ′	° ′	° ′	° ′	° ′	° ′	° ′	° ′		° ′	° ′
7 00	345 59.8	191 56.7	N12 03.1	113 14.8	S20 28.2	212 00.7	N17 48.9	119 24.2	S15 19.5	Acamar	315 17.5	S40 14.6
01	1 02.2	206 56.2	02.0	128 15.5	28.6	227 02.7	48.8	134 26.5	19.6	Achernar	335 25.8	S57 09.5
02	16 04.7	221 55.7	12 00.9	143 16.3	29.0	242 04.6	48.6	149 28.8	19.7	Acrux	173 08.8	S63 10.9
03	31 07.2	236 55.2	11 59.9	158 17.1	. . 29.4	257 06.6	. . 48.5	164 31.0	. . 19.7	Adhara	255 12.0	S28 59.5
04	46 09.6	251 54.7	58.8	173 17.9	29.8	272 08.5	48.4	179 33.3	19.8	Aldebaran	290 48.4	N16 32.2
05	61 12.1	266 54.2	57.8	188 18.7	30.2	287 10.5	48.2	194 35.6	19.8			
06	76 14.6	281 53.7	N11 56.7	203 19.4	S20 30.6	302 12.4	N17 48.1	209 37.9	S15 19.9	Alioth	166 20.5	N55 53.0
07	91 17.0	296 53.1	55.7	218 20.2	31.0	317 14.4	47.9	224 40.2	19.9	Alkaid	152 58.6	N49 14.7
08	106 19.5	311 52.6	54.6	233 21.0	31.4	332 16.3	47.8	239 42.5	20.0	Al Na'ir	27 42.3	S46 53.2
S 09	121 22.0	326 52.1	. . 53.5	248 21.8	. . 31.8	347 18.3	. . 47.7	254 44.8	. . 20.1	Alnilam	275 45.6	S 1 11.6
U 10	136 24.4	341 51.6	52.5	263 22.6	32.2	2 20.2	47.5	269 47.0	20.1	Alphard	217 55.5	S 8 43.3
N 11	151 26.9	356 51.1	51.4	278 23.3	32.6	17 22.2	47.4	284 49.3	20.2			
D 12	166 29.4	11 50.6	N11 50.3	293 24.1	S20 33.0	32 24.1	N17 47.3	299 51.6	S15 20.2	Alphecca	126 10.4	N26 40.3
A 13	181 31.8	26 50.1	49.3	308 24.9	33.4	47 26.1	47.1	314 53.9	20.3	Alpheratz	357 42.2	N29 10.4
Y 14	196 34.3	41 49.6	48.2	323 25.7	33.8	62 28.0	47.0	329 56.2	20.4	Altair	62 07.2	N 8 54.8
15	211 36.7	56 49.1	. . 47.1	338 26.4	. . 34.3	77 30.0	. . 46.9	344 58.5	. . 20.4	Ankaa	353 14.5	S42 13.4
16	226 39.2	71 48.6	46.1	353 27.2	34.7	92 31.9	46.7	0 00.8	20.5	Antares	112 25.2	S26 27.7
17	241 41.7	86 48.1	45.0	8 28.0	35.1	107 33.9	46.6	15 03.0	20.5			
18	256 44.1	101 47.6	N11 43.9	23 28.8	S20 35.5	122 35.9	N17 46.5	30 05.3	S15 20.6	Arcturus	145 55.2	N19 06.6
19	271 46.6	116 47.1	42.9	38 29.5	35.9	137 37.8	46.3	45 07.6	20.6	Atria	107 26.2	S69 03.3
20	286 49.1	131 46.6	41.8	53 30.3	36.3	152 39.8	46.2	60 09.9	20.7	Avior	234 18.1	S59 33.3
21	301 51.5	146 46.1	. . 40.7	68 31.1	. . 36.7	167 41.7	. . 46.1	75 12.2	. . 20.8	Bellatrix	278 31.1	N 6 21.7
22	316 54.0	161 45.6	39.7	83 31.8	37.1	182 43.7	45.9	90 14.5	20.8	Betelgeuse	271 00.5	N 7 24.5
23	331 56.5	176 45.1	38.6	98 32.6	37.5	197 45.6	45.8	105 16.7	20.9			
8 00	346 58.9	191 44.6	N11 37.5	113 33.4	S20 37.9	212 47.6	N17 45.7	120 19.0	S15 20.9	Canopus	263 55.9	S52 42.1
01	2 01.4	206 44.1	36.5	128 34.2	38.3	227 49.5	45.5	135 21.3	21.0	Capella	280 33.2	N46 00.4
02	17 03.9	221 43.6	35.4	143 34.9	38.7	242 51.5	45.4	150 23.6	21.1	Deneb	49 30.5	N45 20.4
03	32 06.3	236 43.1	. . 34.3	158 35.7	. . 39.1	257 53.4	. . 45.3	165 25.9	. . 21.1	Denebola	182 33.1	N14 29.5
04	47 08.8	251 42.6	33.3	173 36.5	39.5	272 55.4	45.1	180 28.2	21.2	Diphda	348 54.8	S17 54.2
05	62 11.2	266 42.1	32.2	188 37.2	39.9	287 57.4	45.0	195 30.4	21.2			
06	77 13.7	281 41.6	N11 31.1	203 38.0	S20 40.3	302 59.3	N17 44.9	210 32.7	S15 21.3	Dubhe	193 51.4	N61 40.3
07	92 16.2	296 41.1	30.0	218 38.8	40.7	318 01.3	44.7	225 35.0	21.3	Elnath	278 11.6	N28 37.0
08	107 18.6	311 40.7	29.0	233 39.6	41.1	333 03.2	44.6	240 37.3	21.4	Eltanin	90 45.6	N51 29.7
M 09	122 21.1	326 40.2	. . 27.9	248 40.3	. . 41.5	348 05.2	. . 44.5	255 39.6	. . 21.5	Enif	33 46.0	N 9 56.8
O 10	137 23.6	341 39.7	26.8	263 41.1	41.9	3 07.1	44.3	270 41.9	21.5	Fomalhaut	15 22.7	S29 32.5
N 11	152 26.0	356 39.2	25.7	278 41.9	42.3	18 09.1	44.2	285 44.1	21.6			
D 12	167 28.5	11 38.7	N11 24.7	293 42.6	S20 42.7	33 11.0	N17 44.0	300 46.4	S15 21.6	Gacrux	172 00.4	S57 11.8
A 13	182 31.0	26 38.2	23.6	308 43.4	43.1	48 13.0	43.9	315 48.7	21.7	Gienah	175 51.7	S17 37.3
Y 14	197 33.4	41 37.7	22.5	323 44.2	43.5	63 15.0	43.8	330 51.0	21.8	Hadar	148 47.0	S60 26.7
15	212 35.9	56 37.2	. . 21.4	338 44.9	. . 43.9	78 16.9	. . 43.6	345 53.3	. . 21.8	Hamal	327 59.5	N23 31.9
16	227 38.3	71 36.7	20.3	353 45.7	44.3	93 18.9	43.5	0 55.6	21.9	Kaus Aust.	83 42.5	S34 22.5
17	242 40.8	86 36.2	19.3	8 46.5	44.7	108 20.8	43.4	15 57.8	21.9			
18	257 43.3	101 35.7	N11 18.2	23 47.2	S20 45.1	123 22.8	N17 43.2	31 00.1	S15 22.0	Kochab	137 20.8	N74 06.1
19	272 45.7	116 35.2	17.1	38 48.0	45.5	138 24.7	43.1	46 02.4	22.1	Markab	13 37.1	N15 17.3
20	287 48.2	131 34.7	16.0	53 48.8	45.9	153 26.7	43.0	61 04.7	22.1	Menkar	314 14.0	N 4 08.8
21	302 50.7	146 34.2	. . 14.9	68 49.5	. . 46.3	168 28.7	. . 42.8	76 07.0	. . 22.2	Menkent	148 06.8	S36 26.5
22	317 53.1	161 33.7	13.9	83 50.3	46.7	183 30.6	42.7	91 09.2	22.2	Miaplacidus	221 40.2	S69 46.6
23	332 55.6	176 33.3	12.8	98 51.0	47.1	198 32.6	42.6	106 11.5	22.3			
9 00	347 58.1	191 32.8	N11 11.7	113 51.8	S20 47.5	213 34.5	N17 42.4	121 13.8	S15 22.4	Mirfak	308 38.9	N49 54.5
01	3 00.5	206 32.3	10.6	128 52.6	47.9	228 36.5	42.3	136 16.1	22.4	Nunki	75 57.1	S26 16.5
02	18 03.0	221 31.8	09.5	143 53.3	48.3	243 38.4	42.2	151 18.4	22.5	Peacock	53 17.5	S56 41.2
03	33 05.5	236 31.3	. . 08.4	158 54.1	. . 48.7	258 40.4	. . 42.0	166 20.6	. . 22.5	Pollux	243 26.9	N27 59.2
04	48 07.9	251 30.8	07.4	173 54.9	49.1	273 42.4	41.9	181 22.9	22.6	Procyon	244 59.0	N 5 11.1
05	63 10.4	266 30.3	06.3	188 55.6	49.5	288 44.3	41.8	196 25.2	22.7			
06	78 12.8	281 29.8	N11 05.2	203 56.4	S20 49.9	303 46.3	N17 41.6	211 27.5	S15 22.7	Rasalhague	96 05.6	N12 33.3
07	93 15.3	296 29.3	04.1	218 57.1	50.3	318 48.2	41.5	226 29.8	22.8	Regulus	207 42.9	N11 53.7
08	108 17.8	311 28.9	03.0	233 57.9	50.7	333 50.2	41.4	241 32.0	22.8	Rigel	281 11.3	S 8 11.1
T 09	123 20.2	326 28.4	. . 01.9	248 58.7	. . 51.1	348 52.1	. . 41.2	256 34.3	. . 22.9	Rigil Kent.	139 50.9	S60 53.8
U 10	138 22.7	341 27.9	11 00.8	263 59.4	51.5	3 54.1	41.1	271 36.6	22.9	Sabik	102 11.5	S15 44.4
E 11	153 25.2	356 27.4	10 59.7	279 00.2	51.9	18 56.1	41.0	286 38.9	23.0			
S 12	168 27.6	11 26.9	N10 58.6	294 00.9	S20 52.3	33 58.0	N17 40.8	301 41.2	S15 23.1	Schedar	349 38.9	N56 37.0
D 13	183 30.1	26 26.4	57.6	309 01.7	52.6	49 00.0	40.7	316 43.4	23.1	Shaula	96 20.7	S37 06.7
A 14	198 32.6	41 25.9	56.5	324 02.4	53.0	64 01.9	40.6	331 45.7	23.2	Sirius	258 33.1	S16 44.2
Y 15	213 35.0	56 25.5	. . 55.4	339 03.2	. . 53.4	79 03.9	. . 40.4	346 48.0	. . 23.2	Spica	158 30.6	S11 14.2
16	228 37.5	71 25.0	54.3	354 04.0	53.8	94 05.9	40.3	1 50.3	23.3	Suhail	222 52.2	S43 29.5
17	243 39.9	86 24.5	53.2	9 04.7	54.2	109 07.8	40.2	16 52.6	23.4			
18	258 42.4	101 24.0	N10 52.1	24 05.5	S20 54.6	124 09.8	N17 40.0	31 54.8	S15 23.4	Vega	80 38.2	N38 48.3
19	273 44.9	116 23.5	51.0	39 06.2	55.0	139 11.7	39.9	46 57.1	23.5	Zuben'ubi	137 04.6	S16 06.0
20	288 47.3	131 23.0	49.9	54 07.0	55.4	154 13.7	39.8	61 59.4	23.5		SHA	Mer. Pass.
21	303 49.8	146 22.6	. . 48.8	69 07.7	. . 55.8	169 15.7	. . 39.6	77 01.7	. . 23.6		° ′	h m
22	318 52.3	161 22.1	47.7	84 08.5	56.2	184 17.6	39.5	92 03.9	23.7	Venus	204 45.7	11 13
23	333 54.7	176 21.6	46.6	99 09.2	56.6	199 19.6	39.4	107 06.2	23.7	Mars	126 34.5	16 25
	h m									Jupiter	225 48.7	9 48
Mer. Pass.	0 51.9	v −0.5	d 1.1	v 0.8	d 0.4	v 2.0	d 0.1	v 2.3	d 0.1	Saturn	133 20.1	15 56

SUN and MOON

UT	SUN GHA	SUN Dec	MOON GHA	v	MOON Dec	d	HP
d h	° ′	° ′	° ′	′	° ′	′	′
7 00	180 26.9	N 6 10.4	29 56.5	6.3	S11 50.6	9.5	61.0
01	195 27.1	09.5	44 21.8	6.3	11 41.1	9.5	61.0
02	210 27.3	08.6	58 47.1	6.3	11 31.6	9.7	61.0
03	225 27.6	.. 07.6	73 12.4	6.3	11 21.9	9.7	61.0
04	240 27.8	06.7	87 37.7	6.3	11 12.2	9.7	61.0
05	255 28.0	05.7	102 03.0	6.4	11 02.5	9.9	61.0
06	270 28.2	N 6 04.8	116 28.4	6.4	S10 52.6	9.9	61.1
07	285 28.4	03.9	130 53.8	6.4	10 42.7	10.1	61.1
S 08	300 28.6	02.9	145 19.2	6.5	10 32.6	10.1	61.1
U 09	315 28.8	.. 02.0	159 44.7	6.5	10 22.5	10.1	61.1
N 10	330 29.1	01.1	174 10.2	6.5	10 12.4	10.3	61.1
D 11	345 29.3	6 00.1	188 35.7	6.5	10 02.1	10.3	61.1
A 12	0 29.5	N 5 59.2	203 01.2	6.5	S 9 51.8	10.4	61.1
Y 13	15 29.7	58.3	217 26.7	6.6	9 41.4	10.4	61.1
14	30 29.9	57.3	231 52.3	6.6	9 31.0	10.5	61.1
15	45 30.1	.. 56.4	246 17.9	6.7	9 20.5	10.6	61.1
16	60 30.3	55.5	260 43.6	6.6	9 09.9	10.7	61.1
17	75 30.6	54.5	275 09.2	6.7	8 59.2	10.7	61.2
18	90 30.8	N 5 53.6	289 34.9	6.8	S 8 48.5	10.7	61.2
19	105 31.0	52.6	304 00.7	6.7	8 37.8	10.9	61.2
20	120 31.2	51.7	318 26.4	6.8	8 26.9	10.9	61.2
21	135 31.4	.. 50.8	332 52.2	6.8	8 16.0	10.9	61.2
22	150 31.6	49.8	347 18.0	6.8	8 05.1	11.0	61.2
23	165 31.8	48.9	1 43.8	6.9	7 54.1	11.1	61.2
8 00	180 32.1	N 5 48.0	16 09.7	6.9	S 7 43.0	11.1	61.2
01	195 32.3	47.0	30 35.6	6.9	7 31.9	11.1	61.2
02	210 32.5	46.1	45 01.5	6.9	7 20.8	11.3	61.2
03	225 32.7	.. 45.1	59 27.4	7.0	7 09.5	11.2	61.2
04	240 32.9	44.2	73 53.4	7.0	6 58.3	11.3	61.2
05	255 33.1	43.3	88 19.4	7.0	6 47.0	11.4	61.2
06	270 33.4	N 5 42.3	102 45.4	7.1	S 6 35.6	11.4	61.2
07	285 33.6	41.4	117 11.5	7.1	6 24.2	11.4	61.2
M 08	300 33.8	40.5	131 37.6	7.1	6 12.8	11.5	61.2
O 09	315 34.0	.. 39.5	146 03.7	7.1	6 01.3	11.5	61.2
N 10	330 34.2	38.6	160 29.8	7.2	5 49.8	11.5	61.2
D 11	345 34.4	37.6	174 56.0	7.2	5 38.3	11.6	61.2
A 12	0 34.7	N 5 36.7	189 22.2	7.2	S 5 26.7	11.7	61.2
Y 13	15 34.9	35.8	203 48.4	7.3	5 15.0	11.6	61.2
14	30 35.1	34.8	218 14.7	7.3	5 03.4	11.7	61.2
15	45 35.3	.. 33.9	232 41.0	7.3	4 51.7	11.7	61.1
16	60 35.5	32.9	247 07.3	7.3	4 40.0	11.8	61.1
17	75 35.7	32.0	261 33.6	7.4	4 28.2	11.7	61.1
18	90 36.0	N 5 31.1	276 00.0	7.4	S 4 16.5	11.8	61.1
19	105 36.2	30.1	290 26.4	7.4	4 04.7	11.9	61.1
20	120 36.4	29.2	304 52.8	7.5	3 52.8	11.8	61.1
21	135 36.6	.. 28.2	319 19.3	7.5	3 41.0	11.9	61.1
22	150 36.8	27.3	333 45.8	7.5	3 29.1	11.8	61.1
23	165 37.0	26.3	348 12.3	7.5	3 17.3	11.9	61.1
9 00	180 37.3	N 5 25.4	2 38.8	7.6	S 3 05.4	11.9	61.1
01	195 37.5	24.5	17 05.4	7.5	2 53.5	12.0	61.1
02	210 37.7	23.5	31 31.9	7.6	2 41.5	11.9	61.0
03	225 37.9	.. 22.6	45 58.5	7.7	2 29.6	12.0	61.0
04	240 38.1	21.6	60 25.2	7.6	2 17.6	11.9	61.0
05	255 38.3	20.7	74 51.8	7.7	2 05.7	12.0	61.0
06	270 38.6	N 5 19.7	89 18.5	7.7	S 1 53.7	12.0	61.0
07	285 38.8	18.8	103 45.2	7.8	1 41.7	12.0	61.0
T 08	300 39.0	17.9	118 12.0	7.7	1 29.7	11.9	61.0
U 09	315 39.2	.. 16.9	132 38.7	7.8	1 17.8	12.0	60.9
E 10	330 39.4	16.0	147 05.5	7.8	1 05.8	12.0	60.9
S 11	345 39.7	15.0	161 32.3	7.9	0 53.8	12.0	60.9
D 12	0 39.9	N 5 14.1	175 59.2	7.8	S 0 41.8	12.0	60.9
A 13	15 40.1	13.1	190 26.0	7.9	0 29.8	11.9	60.9
Y 14	30 40.3	12.2	204 52.9	7.9	0 17.9	12.0	60.9
15	45 40.5	.. 11.3	219 19.8	8.0	S 0 05.9	12.0	60.8
16	60 40.7	10.3	233 46.8	7.9	N 0 06.1	11.9	60.8
17	75 41.0	09.4	248 13.7	8.0	0 18.0	12.0	60.8
18	90 41.2	N 5 08.4	262 40.7	8.0	N 0 30.0	11.9	60.8
19	105 41.4	07.5	277 07.7	8.0	0 41.9	11.9	60.8
20	120 41.6	06.5	291 34.7	8.0	0 53.8	11.9	60.7
21	135 41.8	.. 05.6	306 01.7	8.1	1 05.7	11.9	60.7
22	150 42.1	04.6	320 28.8	8.1	1 17.6	11.9	60.7
23	165 42.3	03.7	334 55.9	8.1	N 1 29.5	11.8	60.7
	SD 15.9	d 0.9	SD 16.7	16.7			16.6

Twilight, Sunrise and Moonrise

Lat.	Naut.	Civil	Sunrise	Moonrise 7	8	9	10
°	h m	h m	h m	h m	h m	h m	h m
N 72	00 33	03 16	04 34	18 38	18 31	18 25	18 19
N 70	01 47	03 35	04 44	18 25	18 26	18 26	18 26
68	02 22	03 50	04 51	18 14	18 21	18 26	18 32
66	02 47	04 02	04 57	18 05	18 17	18 27	18 37
64	03 05	04 12	05 03	17 57	18 13	18 27	18 41
62	03 20	04 20	05 07	17 51	18 10	18 27	18 45
60	03 33	04 28	05 11	17 45	18 07	18 28	18 48
N 58	03 43	04 34	05 14	17 40	18 05	18 28	18 51
56	03 52	04 39	05 18	17 36	18 03	18 28	18 53
54	03 59	04 44	05 20	17 32	18 01	18 28	18 55
52	04 06	04 48	05 23	17 28	17 59	18 28	18 57
50	04 12	04 52	05 25	17 25	17 57	18 29	18 59
45	04 25	05 00	05 30	17 17	17 54	18 29	19 03
N 40	04 34	05 07	05 34	17 11	17 51	18 29	19 07
35	04 42	05 12	05 38	17 05	17 49	18 30	19 10
30	04 48	05 17	05 41	17 01	17 46	18 30	19 13
20	04 58	05 24	05 46	16 53	17 42	18 30	19 17
N 10	05 05	05 29	05 50	16 46	17 39	18 31	19 21
0	05 10	05 34	05 54	16 39	17 36	18 31	19 25
S 10	05 13	05 37	05 58	16 33	17 33	18 32	19 29
20	05 15	05 40	06 03	16 25	17 29	18 32	19 34
30	05 16	05 43	06 07	16 17	17 25	18 33	19 39
35	05 15	05 44	06 10	16 13	17 23	18 33	19 42
40	05 14	05 46	06 13	16 07	17 21	18 33	19 45
45	05 13	05 47	06 16	16 01	17 18	18 34	19 49
S 50	05 10	05 48	06 20	15 54	17 14	18 35	19 53
52	05 09	05 48	06 22	15 50	17 13	18 35	19 55
54	05 08	05 48	06 24	15 46	17 11	18 35	19 58
56	05 06	05 49	06 26	15 42	17 09	18 35	20 00
58	05 04	05 49	06 28	15 37	17 07	18 36	20 03
S 60	05 01	05 49	06 31	15 32	17 04	18 36	20 06

Sunset, Twilight and Moonset

Lat.	Sunset	Civil	Naut.	Moonset 7	8	9	10
°	h m	h m	h m	h m	h m	h m	h m
N 72	19 18	20 35	23 00	01 23	03 31	05 35	07 36
N 70	19 09	20 17	22 01	01 45	03 42	05 38	07 32
68	19 02	20 02	21 28	02 02	03 51	05 41	07 28
66	18 56	19 51	21 05	02 15	03 59	05 43	07 25
64	18 51	19 41	20 47	02 26	04 05	05 45	07 23
62	18 47	19 33	20 32	02 35	04 10	05 46	07 21
60	18 43	19 26	20 20	02 43	04 15	05 48	07 19
N 58	18 40	19 20	20 10	02 50	04 19	05 49	07 17
56	18 37	19 15	20 02	02 56	04 23	05 50	07 16
54	18 34	19 10	19 54	03 02	04 26	05 51	07 14
52	18 31	19 06	19 48	03 07	04 29	05 51	07 13
50	18 29	19 02	19 42	03 11	04 32	05 52	07 12
45	18 25	18 54	19 30	03 21	04 37	05 54	07 10
N 40	18 21	18 48	19 20	03 29	04 42	05 55	07 08
35	18 17	18 43	19 13	03 36	04 46	05 56	07 06
30	18 14	18 38	19 07	03 42	04 50	05 57	07 04
20	18 09	18 31	18 57	03 52	04 56	05 59	07 02
N 10	18 05	18 26	18 51	04 01	05 01	06 01	06 59
0	18 01	18 22	18 46	04 09	05 06	06 02	06 57
S 10	17 57	18 18	18 43	04 17	05 11	06 04	06 55
20	17 53	18 15	18 41	04 26	05 16	06 05	06 52
30	17 49	18 13	18 40	04 36	05 22	06 07	06 50
35	17 46	18 12	18 41	04 42	05 26	06 07	06 48
40	17 43	18 10	18 42	04 48	05 29	06 08	06 46
45	17 40	18 10	18 44	04 56	05 34	06 10	06 44
S 50	17 36	18 09	18 46	05 05	05 39	06 11	06 42
52	17 35	18 08	18 47	05 09	05 41	06 12	06 41
54	17 33	18 08	18 49	05 13	05 44	06 12	06 39
56	17 31	18 08	18 51	05 18	05 47	06 13	06 38
58	17 28	18 08	18 53	05 24	05 50	06 14	06 36
S 60	17 26	18 07	18 56	05 30	05 54	06 15	06 35

SUN and MOON

Day	SUN Eqn. of Time 00h	12h	Mer. Pass.	MOON Mer. Pass. Upper	Lower	Age	Phase
d	m s	m s	h m	h m	h m	d	%
7	01 47	01 57	11 58	22 53	10 24	13	96
8	02 08	02 18	11 58	23 49	11 21	14	99
9	02 29	02 39	11 57	24 44	12 17	15	100

2014 SEPTEMBER 10, 11, 12 (WED., THURS., FRI.)

UT (d h)	ARIES GHA	VENUS −3.9 GHA	VENUS Dec	MARS +0.7 GHA	MARS Dec	JUPITER −1.8 GHA	JUPITER Dec	SATURN +0.6 GHA	SATURN Dec	Name	SHA	Dec
10 00	348 57.2	191 21.1	N10 45.5	114 10.0	S20 57.0	214 21.5	N17 39.2	122 08.5	S15 23.8	Acamar	315 17.5	S40 14.6
01	3 59.7	206 20.6	44.4	129 10.7	57.4	229 23.5	39.1	137 10.8	23.8	Achernar	335 25.8	S57 09.5
02	19 02.1	221 20.1	43.3	144 11.5	57.8	244 25.5	39.0	152 13.1	23.9	Acrux	173 08.8	S63 10.9
03	34 04.6	236 19.7	.. 42.2	159 12.3	.. 58.2	259 27.4	.. 38.8	167 15.3	.. 24.0	Adhara	255 12.0	S28 59.5
04	49 07.1	251 19.2	41.1	174 13.0	58.5	274 29.4	38.7	182 17.6	24.0	Aldebaran	290 48.3	N16 32.2
05	64 09.5	266 18.7	40.0	189 13.8	58.9	289 31.3	38.6	197 19.9	24.1			
06	79 12.0	281 18.2	N10 38.9	204 14.5	S20 59.3	304 33.3	N17 38.4	212 22.2	S15 24.1	Alioth	166 20.5	N55 53.0
W 07	94 14.4	296 17.7	37.8	219 15.3	20 59.7	319 35.3	38.3	227 24.4	24.2	Alkaid	152 58.7	N49 14.7
E 08	109 16.9	311 17.3	36.7	234 16.0	21 00.1	334 37.2	38.1	242 26.7	24.3	Al Na'ir	27 42.3	S46 53.2
D 09	124 19.4	326 16.8	.. 35.6	249 16.8	.. 00.5	349 39.2	.. 38.0	257 29.0	.. 24.3	Alnilam	275 45.5	S 1 11.6
N 10	139 21.8	341 16.3	34.5	264 17.5	00.9	4 41.1	37.9	272 31.3	24.4	Alphard	217 55.5	S 8 43.3
E 11	154 24.3	356 15.8	33.4	279 18.3	01.3	19 43.1	37.7	287 33.5	24.4			
S 12	169 26.8	11 15.3	N10 32.3	294 19.0	S21 01.7	34 45.1	N17 37.6	302 35.8	S15 24.5	Alphecca	126 10.4	N26 40.3
D 13	184 29.2	26 14.9	31.2	309 19.8	02.1	49 47.0	37.5	317 38.1	24.6	Alpheratz	357 42.2	N29 10.4
A 14	199 31.7	41 14.4	30.1	324 20.5	02.4	64 49.0	37.3	332 40.4	24.6	Altair	62 07.2	N 8 54.8
Y 15	214 34.2	56 13.9	.. 29.0	339 21.2	.. 02.8	79 50.9	.. 37.2	347 42.7	.. 24.7	Ankaa	353 14.5	S42 13.4
16	229 36.6	71 13.4	27.9	354 22.0	03.2	94 52.9	37.1	2 44.9	24.7	Antares	112 25.3	S26 27.7
17	244 39.1	86 13.0	26.8	9 22.7	03.6	109 54.9	36.9	17 47.2	24.8			
18	259 41.5	101 12.5	N10 25.7	24 23.5	S21 04.0	124 56.8	N17 36.8	32 49.5	S15 24.9	Arcturus	145 55.2	N19 06.6
19	274 44.0	116 12.0	24.6	39 24.2	04.4	139 58.8	36.7	47 51.8	24.9	Atria	107 26.3	S69 03.3
20	289 46.5	131 11.5	23.5	54 25.0	04.8	155 00.8	36.5	62 54.0	25.0	Avior	234 18.1	S59 33.3
21	304 48.9	146 11.1	.. 22.4	69 25.7	.. 05.2	170 02.7	.. 36.4	77 56.3	.. 25.1	Bellatrix	278 31.1	N 6 21.7
22	319 51.4	161 10.6	21.3	84 26.5	05.5	185 04.7	36.3	92 58.6	25.1	Betelgeuse	271 00.4	N 7 24.5
23	334 53.9	176 10.1	20.2	99 27.2	05.9	200 06.6	36.1	108 00.9	25.2			
11 00	349 56.3	191 09.6	N10 19.1	114 28.0	S21 06.3	215 08.6	N17 36.0	123 03.1	S15 25.2	Canopus	263 55.9	S52 42.1
01	4 58.8	206 09.2	18.0	129 28.7	06.7	230 10.6	35.9	138 05.4	25.3	Capella	280 33.2	N46 00.4
02	20 01.3	221 08.7	16.8	144 29.4	07.1	245 12.5	35.7	153 07.7	25.4	Deneb	49 30.5	N45 20.4
03	35 03.7	236 08.2	.. 15.7	159 30.2	.. 07.5	260 14.5	.. 35.6	168 10.0	.. 25.4	Denebola	182 33.1	N14 29.5
04	50 06.2	251 07.7	14.6	174 30.9	07.9	275 16.5	35.5	183 12.2	25.5	Diphda	348 54.7	S17 54.2
05	65 08.7	266 07.3	13.5	189 31.7	08.2	290 18.4	35.3	198 14.5	25.5			
06	80 11.1	281 06.8	N10 12.4	204 32.4	S21 08.6	305 20.4	N17 35.2	213 16.8	S15 25.6	Dubhe	193 51.4	N61 40.3
T 07	95 13.6	296 06.3	11.3	219 33.2	09.0	320 22.4	35.1	228 19.0	25.7	Elnath	278 11.6	N28 37.0
H 08	110 16.0	311 05.8	10.2	234 33.9	09.4	335 24.3	34.9	243 21.3	25.7	Eltanin	90 45.6	N51 29.7
U 09	125 18.5	326 05.4	.. 09.1	249 34.6	.. 09.8	350 26.3	.. 34.8	258 23.6	.. 25.8	Enif	33 46.0	N 9 56.8
R 10	140 21.0	341 04.9	08.0	264 35.4	10.2	5 28.2	34.7	273 25.9	25.8	Fomalhaut	15 22.7	S29 32.5
S 11	155 23.4	356 04.4	06.8	279 36.1	10.6	20 30.2	34.5	288 28.1	25.9			
D 12	170 25.9	11 04.0	N10 05.7	294 36.9	S21 10.9	35 32.2	N17 34.4	303 30.4	S15 26.0	Gacrux	172 00.4	S57 11.8
A 13	185 28.4	26 03.5	04.6	309 37.6	11.3	50 34.1	34.3	318 32.7	26.0	Gienah	175 51.7	S17 37.3
Y 14	200 30.8	41 03.0	03.5	324 38.3	11.7	65 36.1	34.1	333 35.0	26.1	Hadar	148 47.0	S60 26.7
15	215 33.3	56 02.5	.. 02.4	339 39.1	.. 12.1	80 38.1	.. 34.0	348 37.2	.. 26.1	Hamal	327 59.5	N23 31.9
16	230 35.8	71 02.1	01.3	354 39.8	12.5	95 40.0	33.9	3 39.5	26.2	Kaus Aust.	83 42.6	S34 22.5
17	245 38.2	86 01.6	10 00.1	9 40.6	12.9	110 42.0	33.7	18 41.8	26.2			
18	260 40.7	101 01.1	N 9 59.0	24 41.3	S21 13.2	125 44.0	N17 33.6	33 44.1	S15 26.3	Kochab	137 20.9	N74 06.1
19	275 43.2	116 00.7	57.9	39 42.0	13.6	140 45.9	33.5	48 46.3	26.4	Markab	13 37.1	N15 17.3
20	290 45.6	131 00.2	56.8	54 42.8	14.0	155 47.9	33.3	63 48.6	26.5	Menkar	314 14.0	N 4 08.8
21	305 48.1	145 59.7	.. 55.7	69 43.5	.. 14.4	170 49.9	.. 33.2	78 50.9	.. 26.5	Menkent	148 06.8	S36 26.5
22	320 50.5	160 59.3	54.6	84 44.2	14.8	185 51.8	33.1	93 53.1	26.6	Miaplacidus	221 40.2	S69 46.6
23	335 53.0	175 58.8	53.4	99 45.0	15.1	200 53.8	32.9	108 55.4	26.6			
12 00	350 55.5	190 58.3	N 9 52.3	114 45.7	S21 15.5	215 55.8	N17 32.8	123 57.7	S15 26.7	Mirfak	308 38.8	N49 54.5
01	5 57.9	205 57.9	51.2	129 46.4	15.9	230 57.7	32.7	139 00.0	26.8	Nunki	75 57.1	S26 16.5
02	21 00.4	220 57.4	50.1	144 47.2	16.3	245 59.7	32.5	154 02.2	26.8	Peacock	53 17.5	S56 41.2
03	36 02.9	235 56.9	.. 48.9	159 47.9	.. 16.7	261 01.6	.. 32.4	169 04.5	.. 26.9	Pollux	243 26.9	N27 59.2
04	51 05.3	250 56.5	47.8	174 48.6	17.0	276 03.6	32.3	184 06.8	26.9	Procyon	244 59.0	N 5 11.1
05	66 07.8	265 56.0	46.7	189 49.4	17.4	291 05.6	32.1	199 09.0	27.0			
06	81 10.3	280 55.5	N 9 45.6	204 50.1	S21 17.8	306 07.5	N17 32.0	214 11.3	S15 27.1	Rasalhague	96 05.6	N12 33.3
07	96 12.7	295 55.1	44.5	219 50.8	18.2	321 09.5	31.9	229 13.6	27.1	Regulus	207 42.9	N11 53.7
F 08	111 15.2	310 54.6	43.3	234 51.6	18.6	336 11.5	31.7	244 15.9	27.2	Rigel	281 11.2	S 8 11.1
R 09	126 17.6	325 54.1	.. 42.2	249 52.3	.. 18.9	351 13.4	.. 31.6	259 18.1	.. 27.2	Rigil Kent.	139 50.9	S60 53.8
I 10	141 20.1	340 53.7	41.1	264 53.0	19.3	6 15.4	31.5	274 20.4	27.3	Sabik	102 11.6	S15 44.4
D 11	156 22.6	355 53.2	40.0	279 53.8	19.7	21 17.4	31.3	289 22.7	27.4			
A 12	171 25.0	10 52.7	N 9 38.8	294 54.5	S21 20.1	36 19.3	N17 31.2	304 24.9	S15 27.4	Schedar	349 38.9	N56 37.1
Y 13	186 27.5	25 52.3	37.7	309 55.2	20.5	51 21.3	31.1	319 27.2	27.5	Shaula	96 20.7	S37 06.7
14	201 30.0	40 51.8	36.6	324 56.0	20.8	66 23.3	30.9	334 29.5	27.6	Sirius	258 33.1	S16 44.2
15	216 32.4	55 51.4	.. 35.4	339 56.7	.. 21.2	81 25.3	.. 30.8	349 31.7	.. 27.6	Spica	158 30.6	S11 14.2
16	231 34.9	70 50.9	34.3	354 57.4	21.6	96 27.2	30.7	4 34.0	27.7	Suhail	222 52.1	S43 29.5
17	246 37.4	85 50.4	33.2	9 58.2	22.0	111 29.2	30.5	19 36.3	27.7			
18	261 39.8	100 50.0	N 9 32.1	24 58.9	S21 22.3	126 31.2	N17 30.4	34 38.6	S15 27.8	Vega	80 38.2	N38 48.3
19	276 42.3	115 49.5	30.9	39 59.6	22.7	141 33.1	30.3	49 40.8	27.9	Zuben'ubi	137 04.6	S16 06.0
20	291 44.8	130 49.0	29.8	55 00.3	23.1	156 35.1	30.0	64 43.1	27.9			
21	306 47.2	145 48.6	.. 28.7	70 01.1	.. 23.5	171 37.1	.. 30.0	79 45.4	.. 28.0			
22	321 49.7	160 48.1	27.5	85 01.8	23.8	186 39.0	29.9	94 47.6	28.0			
23	336 52.3	175 47.7	26.4	100 02.5	24.2	201 41.0	29.7	109 49.9	28.1			

	SHA	Mer. Pass.
	° ′	h m
Venus	201 13.3	11 16
Mars	124 31.6	16 21
Jupiter	225 12.3	9 38
Saturn	133 06.8	15 45

	ARIES	VENUS	MARS	JUPITER	SATURN
Mer. Pass.	h m 0 40.1	v −0.5 d 1.1	v 0.7 d 0.4	v 2.0 d 0.1	v 2.3 d 0.1

SUN and MOON

UT (d h)	SUN GHA	SUN Dec	MOON GHA	v	MOON Dec	d	HP
10 00	180 42.5	N 5 02.8	349 23.0	8.1	N 1 41.3	11.9	60.6
01	195 42.7	01.8	3 50.1	8.2	1 53.2	11.8	60.6
02	210 42.9	5 00.9	18 17.3	8.1	2 05.0	11.8	60.6
03	225 43.2	4 59.9	32 44.4	8.2	2 16.8	11.7	60.6
04	240 43.4	59.0	47 11.6	8.2	2 28.5	11.8	60.6
05	255 43.6	58.0	61 38.8	8.3	2 40.3	11.7	60.5
W 06	270 43.8	N 4 57.1	76 06.1	8.2	N 2 52.0	11.7	60.5
07	285 44.0	56.1	90 33.3	8.3	3 03.7	11.6	60.5
E 08	300 44.2	55.2	105 00.6	8.3	3 15.3	11.6	60.4
D 09	315 44.5	.. 54.2	119 27.9	8.3	3 26.9	11.6	60.4
N 10	330 44.7	53.3	133 55.2	8.3	3 38.5	11.6	60.4
E 11	345 44.9	52.3	148 22.5	8.3	3 50.1	11.5	60.4
S 12	0 45.1	N 4 51.4	162 49.8	8.4	N 4 01.6	11.5	60.3
D 13	15 45.3	50.4	177 17.2	8.4	4 13.1	11.4	60.3
A 14	30 45.6	49.5	191 44.6	8.4	4 24.5	11.4	60.3
Y 15	45 45.8	.. 48.6	206 12.0	8.4	4 35.9	11.4	60.3
16	60 46.0	47.6	220 39.4	8.4	4 47.3	11.3	60.2
17	75 46.2	46.7	235 06.8	8.5	4 58.6	11.3	60.2
18	90 46.4	N 4 45.7	249 34.3	8.4	N 5 09.9	11.2	60.2
19	105 46.7	44.8	264 01.7	8.5	5 21.1	11.2	60.1
20	120 46.9	43.8	278 29.2	8.5	5 32.3	11.1	60.1
21	135 47.1	.. 42.9	292 56.7	8.5	5 43.4	11.1	60.1
22	150 47.3	41.9	307 24.2	8.5	5 54.5	11.1	60.0
23	165 47.5	41.0	321 51.7	8.6	6 05.6	10.9	60.0
11 00	180 47.8	N 4 40.0	336 19.3	8.6	N 6 16.5	11.0	60.0
01	195 48.0	39.1	350 46.8	8.6	6 27.5	10.9	59.9
02	210 48.2	38.1	5 14.4	8.6	6 38.4	10.8	59.9
03	225 48.4	.. 37.2	19 42.0	8.6	6 49.2	10.8	59.9
04	240 48.6	36.2	34 09.6	8.6	7 00.0	10.7	59.8
05	255 48.9	35.3	48 37.2	8.6	7 10.7	10.7	59.8
T 06	270 49.1	N 4 34.3	63 04.8	8.7	N 7 21.4	10.6	59.8
H 07	285 49.3	33.4	77 32.5	8.6	7 32.0	10.6	59.7
U 08	300 49.5	32.4	92 00.1	8.7	7 42.6	10.5	59.7
R 09	315 49.7	.. 31.5	106 27.8	8.7	7 53.1	10.4	59.7
S 10	330 50.0	30.5	120 55.5	8.7	8 03.5	10.4	59.6
D 11	345 50.2	29.6	135 23.2	8.7	8 13.9	10.3	59.6
A 12	0 50.4	N 4 28.6	149 50.9	8.8	N 8 24.2	10.2	59.6
Y 13	15 50.6	27.7	164 18.7	8.7	8 34.4	10.2	59.5
14	30 50.9	26.7	178 46.4	8.7	8 44.6	10.1	59.5
15	45 51.1	.. 25.8	193 14.1	8.8	8 54.7	10.0	59.5
16	60 51.3	24.8	207 41.9	8.8	9 04.7	10.0	59.4
17	75 51.5	23.9	222 09.7	8.8	9 14.7	9.9	59.4
18	90 51.7	N 4 22.9	236 37.5	8.8	N 9 24.6	9.9	59.3
19	105 52.0	22.0	251 05.3	8.8	9 34.5	9.7	59.3
20	120 52.2	21.0	265 33.1	8.8	9 44.2	9.7	59.3
21	135 52.4	.. 20.1	280 00.9	8.9	9 53.9	9.7	59.2
22	150 52.6	19.1	294 28.8	8.8	10 03.6	9.5	59.2
23	165 52.8	18.2	308 56.6	8.9	10 13.1	9.5	59.2
12 00	180 53.1	N 4 17.2	323 24.5	8.9	N10 22.6	9.4	59.1
01	195 53.3	16.2	337 52.4	8.9	10 32.0	9.3	59.1
02	210 53.5	15.3	352 20.3	8.9	10 41.3	9.3	59.0
03	225 53.7	.. 14.3	6 48.2	8.9	10 50.6	9.1	59.0
04	240 53.9	13.4	21 16.1	8.9	10 59.7	9.1	59.0
05	255 54.2	12.4	35 44.0	9.0	11 08.8	9.1	58.9
F 06	270 54.4	N 4 11.5	50 12.0	8.9	N11 17.9	8.9	58.9
R 07	285 54.6	10.5	64 39.9	9.0	11 26.8	8.8	58.8
I 08	300 54.8	09.6	79 07.9	9.0	11 35.6	8.8	58.8
D 09	315 55.1	.. 08.6	93 35.9	9.0	11 44.4	8.7	58.8
A 10	330 55.3	07.7	108 03.9	9.0	11 53.1	8.6	58.7
Y 11	345 55.5	06.7	122 31.9	9.0	12 01.7	8.6	58.7
12	0 55.7	N 4 05.8	136 59.9	9.0	N12 10.3	8.4	58.6
13	15 55.9	04.8	151 27.9	9.1	12 18.7	8.4	58.6
14	30 56.2	03.9	165 56.0	9.0	12 27.1	8.3	58.6
15	45 56.4	.. 02.9	180 24.0	9.1	12 35.4	8.2	58.5
16	60 56.6	01.9	194 52.1	9.1	12 43.6	8.1	58.5
17	75 56.8	01.0	209 20.2	9.0	12 51.7	8.0	58.4
18	90 57.0	N 4 00.0	223 48.2	9.1	N12 59.7	7.9	58.4
19	105 57.3	3 59.1	238 16.3	9.2	13 07.6	7.9	58.4
20	120 57.5	58.1	252 44.5	9.1	13 15.5	7.7	58.3
21	135 57.7	.. 57.2	267 12.6	9.1	13 23.2	7.7	58.3
22	150 57.9	56.2	281 40.7	9.2	13 30.9	7.6	58.3
23	165 58.2	55.3	296 08.9	9.1	N13 38.5	7.5	58.2
SD	15.9	d 1.0	SD 16.4		16.2		16.0

Twilight and Moonrise

Lat.	Twilight Naut.	Civil	Sunrise	Moonrise 10	11	12	13
N 72	01 26	03 33	04 48	18 19	18 13	18 06	17 58
N 70	02 11	03 49	04 56	18 26	18 27	18 30	18 35
68	02 40	04 02	05 02	18 32	18 39	18 48	19 01
66	03 01	04 13	05 07	18 37	18 48	19 02	19 21
64	03 17	04 21	05 11	18 41	18 56	19 14	19 38
62	03 30	04 29	05 15	18 45	19 03	19 25	19 51
60	03 41	04 35	05 18	18 48	19 09	19 33	20 02
N 58	03 51	04 41	05 21	18 51	19 14	19 41	20 12
56	03 59	04 45	05 23	18 53	19 19	19 48	20 21
54	04 06	04 50	05 26	18 55	19 24	19 54	20 29
52	04 12	04 53	05 28	18 57	19 27	20 00	20 36
50	04 17	04 57	05 30	18 59	19 31	20 05	20 42
45	04 29	05 04	05 34	19 03	19 39	20 16	20 56
N 40	04 37	05 10	05 37	19 07	19 45	20 25	21 07
35	04 44	05 14	05 40	19 10	19 51	20 33	21 17
30	04 50	05 18	05 42	19 13	19 56	20 40	21 25
20	04 59	05 24	05 47	19 17	20 04	20 52	21 40
N 10	05 05	05 29	05 50	19 21	20 12	21 02	21 53
0	05 09	05 33	05 53	19 25	20 19	21 12	22 05
S 10	05 11	05 36	05 57	19 29	20 26	21 22	22 17
20	05 12	05 38	06 00	19 34	20 34	21 33	22 30
30	05 12	05 40	06 03	19 39	20 43	21 45	22 45
35	05 11	05 40	06 05	19 42	20 48	21 52	22 53
40	05 09	05 41	06 08	19 45	20 54	22 01	23 03
45	05 07	05 41	06 10	19 49	21 01	22 10	23 15
S 50	05 04	05 41	06 13	19 53	21 09	22 22	23 29
52	05 02	05 41	06 15	19 55	21 13	22 27	23 36
54	05 00	05 41	06 16	19 58	21 17	22 33	23 43
56	04 58	05 41	06 18	20 00	21 22	22 40	23 52
58	04 55	05 41	06 20	20 03	21 27	22 47	24 01
S 60	04 52	05 40	06 22	20 06	21 33	22 56	24 12

Twilight and Moonset

Lat.	Sunset	Twilight Civil	Naut.	Moonset 10	11	12	13
N 72	19 02	20 16	22 17	07 36	09 36	11 34	13 32
N 70	18 55	20 01	21 36	07 32	09 23	11 12	12 56
68	18 49	19 48	21 09	07 28	09 13	10 55	12 33
66	18 44	19 38	20 49	07 25	09 05	10 41	12 12
64	18 40	19 30	20 33	07 23	08 59	10 30	11 56
62	18 37	19 23	20 20	07 21	08 53	10 21	11 43
60	18 34	19 16	20 10	07 19	08 48	10 13	11 32
N 58	18 31	19 11	20 01	07 17	08 43	10 06	11 23
56	18 29	19 07	19 53	07 16	08 39	09 59	11 14
54	18 26	19 02	19 46	07 14	08 36	09 54	11 07
52	18 24	18 59	19 40	07 13	08 33	09 49	11 00
50	18 23	18 55	19 35	07 12	08 30	09 44	10 54
45	18 19	18 48	19 24	07 10	08 23	09 34	10 42
N 40	18 16	18 43	19 15	07 08	08 18	09 26	10 31
35	18 13	18 38	19 08	07 06	08 14	09 19	10 22
30	18 11	18 35	19 03	07 04	08 10	09 13	10 14
20	18 07	18 29	18 54	07 02	08 03	09 02	10 00
N 10	18 03	18 24	18 49	06 59	07 57	08 53	09 48
0	18 00	18 21	18 45	06 57	07 51	08 44	09 37
S 10	17 57	18 18	18 42	06 55	07 45	08 36	09 27
20	17 54	18 16	18 41	06 52	07 39	08 27	09 14
30	17 50	18 14	18 43	06 50	07 33	08 16	09 01
35	17 48	18 14	18 43	06 48	07 29	08 10	08 53
40	17 46	18 13	18 45	06 46	07 24	08 03	08 44
45	17 44	18 13	18 47	06 44	07 19	07 55	08 34
S 50	17 41	18 13	18 51	06 42	07 13	07 46	08 21
52	17 39	18 13	18 52	06 41	07 10	07 41	08 15
54	17 38	18 13	18 54	06 39	07 07	07 36	08 09
56	17 36	18 14	18 57	06 38	07 03	07 31	08 02
58	17 35	18 14	19 00	06 36	07 00	07 25	07 54
S 60	17 33	18 14	19 03	06 35	06 55	07 18	07 45

SUN and MOON

Day	SUN Eqn. of Time 00h	12h	Mer. Pass.	MOON Mer. Pass. Upper	Lower	Age	Phase
10	02 50	03 00	11 57	00 44	13 11	16	97
11	03 11	03 21	11 57	01 38	14 05	17	92
12	03 32	03 42	11 56	02 32	14 58	18	84

UT	ARIES GHA	VENUS −3.9 GHA	Dec	MARS +0.7 GHA	Dec	JUPITER −1.8 GHA	Dec	SATURN +0.6 GHA	Dec	STARS Name	SHA	Dec
13 00	351 54.6	190 47.2	N 9 25.3	115 03.2	S21 24.6	216 43.0	N17 29.6	124 52.2	S15 28.2	Acamar	315 17.5	S40 14.6
01	6 57.1	205 46.7	24.1	130 04.0	25.0	231 44.9	29.5	139 54.4	28.2	Achernar	335 25.7	S57 09.6
02	21 59.5	220 46.3	23.0	145 04.7	25.3	246 46.9	29.3	154 56.7	28.3	Acrux	173 08.8	S63 10.9
03	37 02.0	235 45.8	.. 21.9	160 05.4	.. 25.7	261 48.9	.. 29.2	169 59.0	.. 28.4	Adhara	255 12.0	S28 59.5
04	52 04.5	250 45.4	20.7	175 06.1	26.1	276 50.8	29.1	185 01.2	28.4	Aldebaran	290 48.3	N16 32.2
05	67 06.9	265 44.9	19.6	190 06.9	26.5	291 52.8	28.9	200 03.5	28.5			
06	82 09.4	280 44.4	N 9 18.5	205 07.6	S21 26.8	306 54.8	N17 28.8	215 05.8	S15 28.5	Alioth	166 20.5	N55 53.0
S 07	97 11.9	295 44.0	17.3	220 08.3	27.2	321 56.7	28.7	230 08.0	28.6	Alkaid	152 58.7	N49 14.7
A 08	112 14.3	310 43.5	16.2	235 09.0	27.6	336 58.7	28.5	245 10.3	28.7	Al Na'ir	27 42.3	S46 53.2
T 09	127 16.8	325 43.1	.. 15.1	250 09.8	.. 28.0	352 00.7	.. 28.4	260 12.6	.. 28.7	Alnilam	275 45.5	S 1 11.6
U 10	142 19.2	340 42.6	13.9	265 10.5	28.3	7 02.7	28.3	275 14.8	28.8	Alphard	217 55.5	S 8 43.3
R 11	157 21.7	355 42.2	12.8	280 11.2	28.7	22 04.6	28.1	290 17.1	28.9			
D 12	172 24.2	10 41.7	N 9 11.7	295 11.9	S21 29.1	37 06.6	N17 28.0	305 19.4	S15 28.9	Alphecca	126 10.5	N26 40.3
A 13	187 26.6	25 41.2	10.5	310 12.6	29.4	52 08.6	27.9	320 21.6	29.0	Alpheratz	357 42.2	N29 10.4
Y 14	202 29.1	40 40.8	09.4	325 13.4	29.8	67 10.5	27.7	335 23.9	29.0	Altair	62 07.2	N 8 54.8
15	217 31.6	55 40.3	.. 08.2	340 14.1	.. 30.2	82 12.5	.. 27.6	350 26.2	.. 29.1	Ankaa	353 14.5	S42 13.4
16	232 34.0	70 39.9	07.1	355 14.8	30.6	97 14.5	27.5	5 28.4	29.2	Antares	112 25.3	S26 27.7
17	247 36.5	85 39.4	06.0	10 15.5	30.9	112 16.4	27.3	20 30.7	29.2			
18	262 39.0	100 39.0	N 9 04.8	25 16.2	S21 31.3	127 18.4	N17 27.2	35 33.0	S15 29.3	Arcturus	145 55.2	N19 06.6
19	277 41.4	115 38.5	03.7	40 17.0	31.7	142 20.4	27.1	50 35.2	29.4	Atria	107 26.3	S69 03.3
20	292 43.9	130 38.1	02.5	55 17.7	32.0	157 22.4	26.9	65 37.5	29.4	Avior	234 18.0	S59 33.3
21	307 46.4	145 37.6	.. 01.4	70 18.4	.. 32.4	172 24.3	.. 26.8	80 39.8	.. 29.5	Bellatrix	278 31.1	N 6 21.7
22	322 48.8	160 37.2	9 00.3	85 19.1	32.8	187 26.3	26.7	95 42.0	29.5	Betelgeuse	271 00.4	N 7 24.5
23	337 51.3	175 36.7	8 59.1	100 19.8	33.1	202 28.3	26.5	110 44.3	29.6			
14 00	352 53.7	190 36.2	N 8 58.0	115 20.6	S21 33.5	217 30.2	N17 26.4	125 46.6	S15 29.7	Canopus	263 55.9	S52 42.1
01	7 56.2	205 35.8	56.8	130 21.3	33.9	232 32.2	26.3	140 48.8	29.7	Capella	280 33.1	N46 00.4
02	22 58.7	220 35.3	55.7	145 22.0	34.3	247 34.2	26.1	155 51.1	29.8	Deneb	49 30.5	N45 20.4
03	38 01.1	235 34.9	.. 54.5	160 22.7	.. 34.6	262 36.2	.. 26.0	170 53.4	.. 29.9	Denebola	182 33.1	N14 29.5
04	53 03.6	250 34.4	53.4	175 23.4	35.0	277 38.1	25.9	185 55.6	29.9	Diphda	348 54.7	S17 54.2
05	68 06.1	265 34.0	52.3	190 24.1	35.4	292 40.1	25.7	200 57.9	30.0			
06	83 08.5	280 33.5	N 8 51.1	205 24.8	S21 35.7	307 42.1	N17 25.6	216 00.2	S15 30.0	Dubhe	193 51.4	N61 40.3
07	98 11.0	295 33.1	50.0	220 25.6	36.1	322 44.0	25.5	231 02.4	30.1	Elnath	278 11.5	N28 37.0
S 08	113 13.5	310 32.6	48.8	235 26.3	36.5	337 46.0	25.3	246 04.7	30.2	Eltanin	90 45.7	N51 29.7
U 09	128 15.9	325 32.2	.. 47.7	250 27.0	.. 36.8	352 48.0	.. 25.2	261 07.0	.. 30.2	Enif	33 46.0	N 9 56.8
N 10	143 18.4	340 31.7	46.5	265 27.7	37.2	7 50.0	25.1	276 09.2	30.3	Fomalhaut	15 22.7	S29 32.5
D 11	158 20.9	355 31.3	45.4	280 28.4	37.6	22 51.9	24.9	291 11.5	30.4			
A 12	173 23.3	10 30.8	N 8 44.2	295 29.1	S21 37.9	37 53.9	N17 24.8	306 13.8	S15 30.4	Gacrux	172 00.4	S57 11.7
Y 13	188 25.8	25 30.4	43.1	310 29.8	38.3	52 55.9	24.7	321 16.0	30.5	Gienah	175 51.7	S17 37.3
14	203 28.2	40 29.9	41.9	325 30.6	38.7	67 57.9	24.5	336 18.3	30.5	Hadar	148 47.0	S60 26.7
15	218 30.7	55 29.5	.. 40.8	340 31.3	.. 39.0	82 59.8	.. 24.4	351 20.5	.. 30.6	Hamal	327 59.5	N23 31.9
16	233 33.2	70 29.0	39.6	355 32.0	39.4	98 01.8	24.3	6 22.8	30.7	Kaus Aust.	83 42.6	S34 22.5
17	248 35.6	85 28.6	38.5	10 32.7	39.8	113 03.8	24.1	21 25.1	30.7			
18	263 38.1	100 28.1	N 8 37.3	25 33.4	S21 40.1	128 05.8	N17 24.0	36 27.3	S15 30.8	Kochab	137 20.9	N74 06.1
19	278 40.6	115 27.7	36.2	40 34.1	40.5	143 07.7	23.9	51 29.6	30.9	Markab	13 37.1	N15 17.3
20	293 43.0	130 27.2	35.0	55 34.8	40.8	158 09.7	23.8	66 31.9	30.9	Menkar	314 14.0	N 4 08.8
21	308 45.5	145 26.8	.. 33.9	70 35.5	.. 41.2	173 11.7	.. 23.6	81 34.1	.. 31.0	Menkent	148 06.8	S36 26.5
22	323 48.0	160 26.3	32.7	85 36.2	41.6	188 13.6	23.5	96 36.4	31.0	Miaplacidus	221 40.1	S69 46.6
23	338 50.4	175 25.9	31.6	100 36.9	41.9	203 15.6	23.4	111 38.7	31.1			
15 00	353 52.9	190 25.4	N 8 30.4	115 37.7	S21 42.3	218 17.6	N17 23.2	126 40.9	S15 31.2	Mirfak	308 38.8	N49 54.5
01	8 55.3	205 25.0	29.3	130 38.4	42.7	233 19.6	23.1	141 43.2	31.2	Nunki	75 57.1	S26 16.5
02	23 57.8	220 24.6	28.1	145 39.1	43.0	248 21.5	23.0	156 45.4	31.3	Peacock	53 17.5	S56 41.2
03	39 00.3	235 24.1	.. 27.0	160 39.8	.. 43.4	263 23.5	.. 22.8	171 47.7	.. 31.4	Pollux	243 26.9	N27 59.2
04	54 02.7	250 23.7	25.8	175 40.5	43.7	278 25.5	22.7	186 50.0	31.4	Procyon	244 59.0	N 5 11.1
05	69 05.2	265 23.2	24.7	190 41.2	44.1	293 27.5	22.6	201 52.2	31.5			
06	84 07.7	280 22.8	N 8 23.5	205 41.9	S21 44.5	308 29.4	N17 22.4	216 54.5	S15 31.6	Rasalhague	96 05.6	N12 33.3
07	99 10.1	295 22.3	22.3	220 42.6	44.8	323 31.4	22.3	231 56.8	31.6	Regulus	207 42.9	N11 53.7
08	114 12.6	310 21.9	21.2	235 43.3	45.2	338 33.4	22.2	246 59.0	31.7	Rigel	281 11.2	S 8 11.1
M 09	129 15.1	325 21.4	.. 20.0	250 44.0	.. 45.6	353 35.4	.. 22.0	262 01.3	.. 31.7	Rigil Kent.	139 50.9	S60 53.8
O 10	144 17.5	340 21.0	18.9	265 44.7	45.9	8 37.3	21.9	277 03.5	31.8	Sabik	102 11.6	S15 44.3
N 11	159 20.0	355 20.5	17.7	280 45.4	46.3	23 39.3	21.8	292 05.8	31.9			
D 12	174 22.5	10 20.1	N 8 16.6	295 46.1	S21 46.6	38 41.3	N17 21.6	307 08.1	S15 31.9	Schedar	349 38.9	N56 37.1
A 13	189 24.9	25 19.7	15.4	310 46.8	47.0	53 43.3	21.5	322 10.3	32.0	Shaula	96 20.7	S37 06.7
Y 14	204 27.4	40 19.2	14.2	325 47.5	47.3	68 45.3	21.4	337 12.6	32.1	Sirius	258 33.1	S16 44.2
15	219 29.8	55 18.8	.. 13.1	340 48.2	.. 47.7	83 47.2	.. 21.2	352 14.8	.. 32.1	Spica	158 30.6	S11 14.1
16	234 32.3	70 18.3	11.9	355 48.9	48.1	98 49.2	21.1	7 17.1	32.2	Suhail	222 52.1	S43 29.5
17	249 34.8	85 17.9	10.8	10 49.6	48.4	113 51.2	21.0	22 19.4	32.3			
18	264 37.2	100 17.4	N 8 09.6	25 50.3	S21 48.8	128 53.2	N17 20.8	37 21.6	S15 32.3	Vega	80 38.2	N38 48.3
19	279 39.7	115 17.0	08.4	40 51.0	49.1	143 55.1	20.7	52 23.9	32.4	Zuben'ubi	137 04.7	S16 06.0
20	294 42.2	130 16.6	07.3	55 51.7	49.5	158 57.1	20.6	67 26.1	32.4		SHA	Mer.Pass.
21	309 44.6	145 16.1	.. 06.1	70 52.4	.. 49.9	173 59.1	.. 20.4	82 28.4	.. 32.5	Venus	197 42.5	11 18
22	324 47.1	160 15.7	05.0	85 53.1	50.2	189 01.1	20.3	97 30.7	32.6	Mars	122 26.8	16 18
23	339 49.6	175 15.2	03.8	100 53.8	50.6	204 03.0	20.2	112 32.9	32.6	Jupiter	224 36.5	9 29
Mer. Pass.	0 28.3	v −0.5	d 1.1	v 0.7	d 0.4	v 2.0	d 0.1	v 2.3	d 0.1	Saturn	132 52.8	15 35

UT	SUN GHA	SUN Dec	MOON GHA	v	Dec	d	HP
d h	° ′	° ′	° ′	′	° ′	′	′
13 00	180 58.4	N 3 54.3	310 37.0	9.2	N13 46.0	7.4	58.2
01	195 58.6	53.4	325 05.2	9.2	13 53.4	7.3	58.1
02	210 58.8	52.4	339 33.4	9.2	14 00.7	7.2	58.1
03	225 59.0	.. 51.4	354 01.6	9.2	14 07.9	7.1	58.1
04	240 59.3	50.5	8 29.8	9.3	14 15.0	7.1	58.0
05	255 59.5	49.5	22 58.1	9.2	14 22.1	6.9	58.0
06	270 59.7	N 3 48.6	37 26.3	9.3	N14 29.0	6.9	57.9
S 07	285 59.9	47.6	51 54.6	9.3	14 35.9	6.7	57.9
A 08	301 00.2	46.7	66 22.9	9.2	14 42.6	6.7	57.9
T 09	316 00.4	.. 45.7	80 51.1	9.4	14 49.3	6.6	57.8
U 10	331 00.6	44.7	95 19.5	9.3	14 55.9	6.5	57.8
R 11	346 00.8	43.8	109 47.8	9.3	15 02.4	6.4	57.7
D 12	1 01.0	N 3 42.8	124 16.1	9.4	N15 08.8	6.2	57.7
A 13	16 01.3	41.9	138 44.5	9.3	15 15.0	6.2	57.7
Y 14	31 01.5	40.9	153 12.8	9.4	15 21.2	6.1	57.6
15	46 01.7	.. 40.0	167 41.2	9.4	15 27.3	6.1	57.6
16	61 01.9	39.0	182 09.6	9.4	15 33.4	5.9	57.5
17	76 02.2	38.1	196 38.0	9.4	15 39.3	5.8	57.5
18	91 02.4	N 3 37.1	211 06.4	9.5	N15 45.1	5.7	57.5
19	106 02.6	36.1	225 34.9	9.4	15 50.8	5.6	57.4
20	121 02.8	35.2	240 03.3	9.5	15 56.4	5.5	57.4
21	136 03.0	.. 34.2	254 31.8	9.5	16 01.9	5.5	57.3
22	151 03.3	33.3	269 00.3	9.5	16 07.4	5.3	57.3
23	166 03.5	32.3	283 28.8	9.5	16 12.7	5.2	57.3
14 00	181 03.7	N 3 31.3	297 57.3	9.6	N16 17.9	5.2	57.2
01	196 03.9	30.4	312 25.9	9.6	16 23.1	5.0	57.2
02	211 04.2	29.4	326 54.5	9.5	16 28.1	4.9	57.1
03	226 04.4	.. 28.5	341 23.0	9.6	16 33.0	4.9	57.1
04	241 04.6	27.5	355 51.6	9.7	16 37.9	4.7	57.1
05	256 04.8	26.6	10 20.3	9.6	16 42.6	4.7	57.0
06	271 05.1	N 3 25.6	24 48.9	9.7	N16 47.3	4.5	57.0
07	286 05.3	24.6	39 17.6	9.6	16 51.8	4.5	57.0
S 08	301 05.5	23.7	53 46.2	9.7	16 56.3	4.3	56.9
U 09	316 05.7	.. 22.7	68 14.9	9.7	17 00.6	4.3	56.9
N 10	331 05.9	21.8	82 43.6	9.8	17 04.9	4.1	56.8
D 11	346 06.2	20.8	97 12.4	9.7	17 09.0	4.1	56.8
A 12	1 06.4	N 3 19.8	111 41.1	9.8	N17 13.1	3.9	56.8
Y 13	16 06.6	18.9	126 09.9	9.8	17 17.0	3.9	56.7
14	31 06.8	17.9	140 38.7	9.8	17 20.9	3.7	56.7
15	46 07.1	.. 17.0	155 07.5	9.9	17 24.6	3.7	56.7
16	61 07.3	16.0	169 36.4	9.9	17 28.3	3.5	56.6
17	76 07.5	15.0	184 05.3	9.8	17 31.8	3.5	56.6
18	91 07.7	N 3 14.1	198 34.1	10.0	N17 35.3	3.4	56.6
19	106 08.0	13.1	213 03.1	9.9	17 38.7	3.2	56.5
20	121 08.2	12.2	227 32.0	9.9	17 41.9	3.2	56.5
21	136 08.4	.. 11.2	242 00.9	10.0	17 45.1	3.1	56.4
22	151 08.6	10.2	256 29.9	10.0	17 48.2	2.9	56.4
23	166 08.8	09.3	270 58.9	10.1	17 51.1	2.9	56.4
15 00	181 09.1	N 3 08.3	285 28.0	10.0	N17 54.0	2.8	56.3
01	196 09.3	07.4	299 57.0	10.1	17 56.8	2.6	56.3
02	211 09.5	06.4	314 26.1	10.1	17 59.4	2.6	56.3
03	226 09.7	.. 05.4	328 55.2	10.1	18 02.0	2.5	56.2
04	241 10.0	04.5	343 24.3	10.2	18 04.5	2.3	56.2
05	256 10.2	03.5	357 53.5	10.2	18 06.8	2.3	56.2
06	271 10.4	N 3 02.6	12 22.7	10.2	N18 09.1	2.2	56.1
07	286 10.6	01.6	26 51.9	10.2	18 11.3	2.1	56.1
M 08	301 10.9	3 00.6	41 21.1	10.3	18 13.4	2.0	56.1
O 09	316 11.1	2 59.7	55 50.4	10.2	18 15.4	1.8	56.0
N 10	331 11.3	58.7	70 19.6	10.4	18 17.2	1.8	56.0
D 11	346 11.5	57.7	84 49.0	10.3	18 19.0	1.7	56.0
A 12	1 11.7	N 2 56.8	99 18.3	10.4	N18 20.7	1.6	55.9
Y 13	16 12.0	55.8	113 47.7	10.4	18 22.3	1.5	55.9
14	31 12.2	54.9	128 17.1	10.4	18 23.8	1.4	55.9
15	46 12.4	.. 53.9	142 46.5	10.4	18 25.2	1.3	55.8
16	61 12.6	52.9	157 15.9	10.5	18 26.5	1.2	55.8
17	76 12.9	52.0	171 45.4	10.5	18 27.7	1.1	55.8
18	91 13.1	N 2 51.0	186 14.9	10.6	N18 28.8	1.0	55.8
19	106 13.3	50.0	200 44.5	10.6	18 29.8	1.0	55.7
20	121 13.5	49.1	215 14.1	10.6	18 30.8	0.8	55.7
21	136 13.8	.. 48.1	229 43.7	10.6	18 31.6	0.7	55.7
22	151 14.0	47.2	244 13.3	10.7	18 32.3	0.6	55.6
23	166 14.2	46.2	258 43.0	10.6	N18 32.9	0.6	55.6
	SD 15.9	d 1.0	SD 15.7		15.5		15.2

Lat.	Twilight Naut.	Twilight Civil	Sunrise	Moonrise 13	14	15	16
°	h m	h m	h m	h m	h m	h m	h m
N 72	01 58	03 49	05 02	17 58	17 44	☐	☐
N 70	02 32	04 03	05 08	18 35	18 47	19 14	20 06
68	02 56	04 14	05 12	19 01	19 23	19 57	20 49
66	03 14	04 23	05 16	19 21	19 48	20 26	21 18
64	03 28	04 31	05 20	19 38	20 08	20 49	21 40
62	03 40	04 37	05 23	19 51	20 24	21 06	21 58
60	03 50	04 43	05 25	20 02	20 38	21 21	22 12
N 58	03 58	04 47	05 27	20 12	20 49	21 33	22 25
56	04 06	04 51	05 29	20 21	21 00	21 44	22 35
54	04 12	04 55	05 31	20 29	21 09	21 54	22 45
52	04 17	04 58	05 33	20 36	21 17	22 02	22 53
50	04 22	05 01	05 34	20 42	21 24	22 10	23 01
45	04 33	05 08	05 37	20 56	21 39	22 26	23 17
N 40	04 40	05 13	05 40	21 07	21 52	22 40	23 30
35	04 47	05 17	05 42	21 17	22 03	22 51	23 41
30	04 52	05 20	05 44	21 25	22 12	23 01	23 51
20	04 59	05 25	05 47	21 40	22 29	23 18	24 08
N 10	05 04	05 29	05 50	21 53	22 43	23 33	24 23
0	05 08	05 32	05 52	22 05	22 56	23 47	24 37
S 10	05 09	05 34	05 55	22 17	23 10	24 01	00 01
20	05 10	05 35	05 57	22 30	23 24	24 16	00 16
30	05 08	05 36	06 00	22 45	23 41	24 34	00 34
35	05 07	05 36	06 01	22 53	23 51	24 44	00 44
40	05 05	05 36	06 03	23 03	24 02	00 02	00 55
45	05 01	05 35	06 05	23 15	24 15	00 15	01 09
S 50	04 57	05 35	06 07	23 29	24 31	00 31	01 25
52	04 55	05 34	06 08	23 36	24 38	00 38	01 33
54	04 53	05 34	06 09	23 43	24 46	00 46	01 42
56	04 50	05 33	06 10	23 52	24 56	00 56	01 51
58	04 47	05 32	06 11	24 01	00 01	01 06	02 02
S 60	04 43	05 31	06 13	24 12	00 12	01 19	02 15

Lat.	Sunset	Twilight Civil	Twilight Naut.	Moonset 13	14	15	16
°	h m	h m	h m	h m	h m	h m	h m
N 72	18 46	19 58	21 46	13 32	15 36	☐	☐
N 70	18 41	19 45	21 14	12 56	14 33	15 53	16 44
68	18 37	19 34	20 51	12 31	13 58	15 09	16 01
66	18 33	19 26	20 34	12 12	13 33	14 40	15 31
64	18 30	19 18	20 20	11 56	13 13	14 18	15 09
62	18 27	19 12	20 09	11 43	12 57	14 00	14 52
60	18 25	19 07	19 59	11 32	12 44	13 46	14 37
N 58	18 23	19 02	19 51	11 23	12 32	13 33	14 25
56	18 21	18 58	19 44	11 14	12 23	13 23	14 14
54	18 19	18 55	19 38	11 07	12 14	13 13	14 04
52	18 17	18 52	19 32	11 00	12 06	13 05	13 56
50	18 16	18 49	19 27	10 54	11 59	12 57	13 48
45	18 13	18 43	19 18	10 42	11 44	12 41	13 32
N 40	18 11	18 38	19 10	10 31	11 32	12 28	13 19
35	18 09	18 34	19 04	10 22	11 21	12 16	13 07
30	18 07	18 31	18 59	10 14	11 12	12 07	12 57
20	18 04	18 26	18 52	10 00	10 56	11 50	12 40
N 10	18 01	18 22	18 47	09 48	10 43	11 35	12 25
0	17 59	18 20	18 44	09 37	10 30	11 21	12 11
S 10	17 57	18 18	18 42	09 26	10 17	11 07	11 57
20	17 54	18 16	18 42	09 14	10 03	10 52	11 42
30	17 52	18 16	18 43	09 01	09 47	10 35	11 25
35	17 50	18 16	18 45	08 53	09 38	10 25	11 15
40	17 49	18 16	18 47	08 44	09 28	10 14	11 03
45	17 47	18 17	18 51	08 34	09 15	10 01	10 50
S 50	17 45	18 17	18 55	08 21	09 01	09 45	10 33
52	17 44	18 18	18 57	08 15	08 54	09 37	10 26
54	17 43	18 19	19 00	08 08	08 46	09 29	10 17
56	17 42	18 19	19 03	08 02	08 37	09 19	10 07
58	17 41	18 20	19 06	07 54	08 28	09 08	09 56
S 60	17 40	18 21	19 10	07 45	08 17	08 56	09 43

Day	SUN Eqn. of Time 00h	12h	Mer. Pass.	MOON Mer. Pass. Upper	Lower	Age	Phase
d	m s	m s	h m	h m	h m	d	%
13	03 53	04 04	11 56	03 25	15 51	19	76
14	04 14	04 25	11 56	04 17	16 43	20	66
15	04 36	04 47	11 55	05 09	17 34	21	56

UT	ARIES	VENUS −3.9		MARS +0.7		JUPITER −1.9		SATURN +0.6		STARS		
	GHA	GHA	Dec	GHA	Dec	GHA	Dec	GHA	Dec	Name	SHA	Dec
d h	° ′	° ′	° ′	° ′	° ′	° ′	° ′	° ′	° ′		° ′	° ′
16 00	354 52.0	190 14.8 N 8 02.6		115 54.5 S21 50.9		219 05.0 N17 20.0		127 35.2 S15 32.7		Acamar	315 17.5	S40 14.6
01	9 54.5	205 14.4	01.5	130 55.2	51.3	234 07.0	19.9	142 37.5	32.8	Achernar	335 25.7	S57 09.6
02	24 57.0	220 13.9	8 00.3	145 55.9	51.6	249 09.0	19.8	157 39.7	32.8	Acrux	173 08.8	S63 10.9
03	39 59.4	235 13.5	7 59.1	160 56.6 . .	52.0	264 11.0 . .	19.6	172 42.0 . .	32.9	Adhara	255 12.0	S28 59.5
04	55 01.9	250 13.0	58.0	175 57.3	52.3	279 12.9	19.5	187 44.2	33.0	Aldebaran	290 48.3	N16 32.2
05	70 04.3	265 12.6	56.8	190 58.0	52.7	294 14.9	19.4	202 46.5	33.0			
06	85 06.8	280 12.2 N 7 55.6		205 58.7 S21 53.1		309 16.9 N17 19.3		217 48.7 S15 33.1		Alioth	166 20.6	N55 53.0
07	100 09.3	295 11.7	54.5	220 59.4	53.4	324 18.9	19.1	232 51.0	33.1	Alkaid	152 58.7	N49 14.7
T 08	115 11.7	310 11.3	53.3	236 00.1	53.8	339 20.8	19.0	247 53.3	33.2	Al Na'ir	27 42.3	S46 53.2
U 09	130 14.2	325 10.8 . .	52.1	251 00.8 . .	54.1	354 22.8 . .	18.9	262 55.5 . .	33.3	Alnilam	275 45.5	S 1 11.6
E 10	145 16.7	340 10.4	51.0	266 01.5	54.5	9 24.8	18.7	277 57.8	33.3	Alphard	217 55.5	S 8 43.3
S 11	160 19.1	355 10.0	49.8	281 02.2	54.8	24 26.8	18.6	293 00.0	33.4			
D 12	175 21.6	10 09.5 N 7 48.6		296 02.9 S21 55.2		39 28.8 N17 18.5		308 02.3 S15 33.5		Alphecca	126 10.5	N26 40.3
A 13	190 24.1	25 09.1	47.5	311 03.6	55.5	54 30.7	18.3	323 04.6	33.5	Alpheratz	357 42.2	N29 10.4
Y 14	205 26.5	40 08.6	46.3	326 04.3	55.9	69 32.7	18.2	338 06.8	33.6	Altair	62 07.2	N 8 54.8
15	220 29.0	55 08.2 . .	45.1	341 05.0 . .	56.2	84 34.7 . .	18.1	353 09.1 . .	33.7	Ankaa	353 14.5	S42 13.4
16	235 31.5	70 07.8	44.0	356 05.7	56.6	99 36.7	17.9	8 11.3	33.7	Antares	112 25.3	S26 27.7
17	250 33.9	85 07.3	42.8	11 06.4	56.9	114 38.7	17.8	23 13.6	33.8			
18	265 36.4	100 06.9 N 7 41.6		26 07.0 S21 57.3		129 40.6 N17 17.7		38 15.8 S15 33.8		Arcturus	145 55.2	N19 06.6
19	280 38.8	115 06.5	40.5	41 07.7	57.6	144 42.6	17.5	53 18.1	33.9	Atria	107 26.4	S69 03.3
20	295 41.3	130 06.0	39.3	56 08.4	58.0	159 44.6	17.4	68 20.4	34.0	Avior	234 18.0	S59 33.3
21	310 43.8	145 05.6 . .	38.1	71 09.1 . .	58.3	174 46.6 . .	17.3	83 22.6 . .	34.0	Bellatrix	278 31.1	N 6 21.7
22	325 46.2	160 05.2	36.9	86 09.8	58.7	189 48.6	17.1	98 24.9	34.1	Betelgeuse	271 00.4	N 7 24.5
23	340 48.7	175 04.7	35.8	101 10.5	59.1	204 50.5	17.0	113 27.1	34.2			
17 00	355 51.2	190 04.3 N 7 34.6		116 11.2 S21 59.4		219 52.5 N17 16.9		128 29.4 S15 34.2		Canopus	263 55.9	S52 42.1
01	10 53.6	205 03.9	33.4	131 11.9	21 59.8	234 54.5	16.7	143 31.6	34.3	Capella	280 33.1	N46 00.4
02	25 56.1	220 03.4	32.3	146 12.6	22 00.1	249 56.5	16.6	158 33.9	34.4	Deneb	49 30.5	N45 20.4
03	40 58.6	235 03.0 . .	31.1	161 13.3 . .	00.4	264 58.5 . .	16.5	173 36.2 . .	34.4	Denebola	182 33.1	N14 29.5
04	56 01.0	250 02.5	29.9	176 13.9	00.8	280 00.4	16.3	188 38.4	34.5	Diphda	348 54.7	S17 54.2
05	71 03.5	265 02.1	28.7	191 14.6	01.1	295 02.4	16.2	203 40.7	34.6			
06	86 05.9	280 01.7 N 7 27.6		206 15.3 S22 01.5		310 04.4 N17 16.1		218 42.9 S15 34.6		Dubhe	193 51.4	N61 40.2
W 07	101 08.4	295 01.2	26.4	221 16.0	01.8	325 06.4	16.0	233 45.2	34.7	Elnath	278 11.5	N28 37.0
E 08	116 10.9	310 00.8	25.2	236 16.7	02.2	340 08.4	15.8	248 47.4	34.7	Eltanin	90 45.7	N51 29.7
D 09	131 13.3	325 00.4 . .	24.0	251 17.4 . .	02.5	355 10.3 . .	15.7	263 49.7 . .	34.8	Enif	33 46.0	N 9 56.9
N 10	146 15.8	339 59.9	22.9	266 18.1	02.9	10 12.3	15.6	278 52.0	34.9	Fomalhaut	15 22.7	S29 32.5
E 11	161 18.3	354 59.5	21.7	281 18.8	03.2	25 14.3	15.4	293 54.2	34.9			
S 12	176 20.7	9 59.1 N 7 20.5		296 19.4 S22 03.6		40 16.3 N17 15.3		308 56.5 S15 35.0		Gacrux	172 00.4	S57 11.7
D 13	191 23.2	24 58.7	19.3	311 20.1	03.9	55 18.3	15.2	323 58.7	35.1	Gienah	175 51.7	S17 37.3
A 14	206 25.7	39 58.2	18.1	326 20.8	04.3	70 20.3	15.0	339 01.0	35.1	Hadar	148 47.1	S60 26.7
Y 15	221 28.1	54 57.8 . .	17.0	341 21.5 . .	04.6	85 22.2 . .	14.9	354 03.2 . .	35.2	Hamal	327 59.5	N23 31.9
16	236 30.6	69 57.4	15.8	356 22.2	05.0	100 24.2	14.8	9 05.5	35.3	Kaus Aust.	83 42.6	S34 22.5
17	251 33.1	84 56.9	14.6	11 22.9	05.3	115 26.2	14.6	24 07.7	35.3			
18	266 35.5	99 56.5 N 7 13.4		26 23.5 S22 05.7		130 28.2 N17 14.5		39 10.0 S15 35.4		Kochab	137 21.0	N74 06.0
19	281 38.0	114 56.1	12.3	41 24.2	06.0	145 30.2	14.4	54 12.3	35.5	Markab	13 37.1	N15 17.3
20	296 40.4	129 55.6	11.1	56 24.9	06.3	160 32.2	14.2	69 14.5	35.5	Menkar	314 13.9	N 4 08.8
21	311 42.9	144 55.2 . .	09.9	71 25.6 . .	06.7	175 34.1 . .	14.1	84 16.8 . .	35.6	Menkent	148 06.8	S36 26.5
22	326 45.4	159 54.8	08.7	86 26.3	07.0	190 36.1	14.0	99 19.0	35.7	Miaplacidus	221 40.1	S69 46.6
23	341 47.8	174 54.3	07.5	101 27.0	07.4	205 38.1	13.9	114 21.3	35.7			
18 00	356 50.3	189 53.9 N 7 06.4		116 27.6 S22 07.7		220 40.1 N17 13.7		129 23.5 S15 35.8		Mirfak	308 38.8	N49 54.6
01	11 52.8	204 53.5	05.2	131 28.3	08.1	235 42.1	13.6	144 25.8	35.8	Nunki	75 57.1	S26 16.5
02	26 55.2	219 53.1	04.0	146 29.0	08.4	250 44.1	13.5	159 28.0	35.9	Peacock	53 17.6	S56 41.2
03	41 57.7	234 52.6 . .	02.8	161 29.7 . .	08.7	265 46.0 . .	13.3	174 30.3 . .	36.0	Pollux	243 26.9	N27 59.2
04	57 00.2	249 52.2	01.6	176 30.4	09.1	280 48.0	13.2	189 32.5	36.0	Procyon	244 59.0	N 5 11.1
05	72 02.6	264 51.8	7 00.4	191 31.0	09.4	295 50.0	13.1	204 34.8	36.1			
06	87 05.1	279 51.3 N 6 59.3		206 31.7 S22 09.8		310 52.0 N17 12.9		219 37.1 S15 36.2		Rasalhague	96 05.7	N12 33.3
07	102 07.6	294 50.9	58.1	221 32.4	10.1	325 54.0	12.8	234 39.3	36.2	Regulus	207 42.9	N11 53.7
T 08	117 10.0	309 50.5	56.9	236 33.1	10.5	340 56.0	12.7	249 41.6	36.3	Rigel	281 11.2	S 8 11.1
H 09	132 12.5	324 50.1 . .	55.7	251 33.8 . .	10.8	355 58.0 . .	12.5	264 43.8 . .	36.4	Rigil Kent.	139 50.9	S60 53.7
U 10	147 14.9	339 49.6	54.5	266 34.4	11.1	10 59.9	12.4	279 46.1	36.4	Sabik	102 11.6	S15 44.3
R 11	162 17.4	354 49.2	53.3	281 35.1	11.5	26 01.9	12.3	294 48.3	36.5			
S 12	177 19.9	9 48.8 N 6 52.1		296 35.8 S22 11.8		41 03.9 N17 12.1		309 50.6 S15 36.6		Schedar	349 38.9	N56 37.1
D 13	192 22.3	24 48.3	51.0	311 36.5	12.2	56 05.9	12.0	324 52.8	36.6	Shaula	96 20.7	S37 06.7
A 14	207 24.8	39 47.9	49.8	326 37.1	12.5	71 07.9	11.9	339 55.1	36.7	Sirius	258 33.0	S16 44.2
Y 15	222 27.3	54 47.5 . .	48.6	341 37.8 . .	12.8	86 09.9 . .	11.8	354 57.3 . .	36.8	Spica	158 30.6	S11 14.1
16	237 29.7	69 47.1	47.4	356 38.5	13.2	101 11.8	11.6	9 59.6	36.8	Suhail	222 52.1	S43 29.4
17	252 32.2	84 46.6	46.2	11 39.2	13.5	116 13.8	11.5	25 01.8	36.9			
18	267 34.7	99 46.2 N 6 45.0		26 39.8 S22 13.9		131 15.8 N17 11.4		40 04.1 S15 37.0		Vega	80 38.3	N38 48.3
19	282 37.1	114 45.8	43.8	41 40.5	14.2	146 17.8	11.2	55 06.3	37.0	Zuben'ubi	137 04.7	S16 06.0
20	297 39.6	129 45.4	42.7	56 41.2	14.5	161 19.8	11.1	70 08.6	37.1			
21	312 42.0	144 44.9 . .	41.5	71 41.9 . .	14.9	176 21.8 . .	11.0	85 10.8 . .	37.2		SHA	Mer.Pass.
22	327 44.5	159 44.5	40.3	86 42.5	15.2	191 23.8	10.8	100 13.1	37.2	Venus	° ′	h m
23	342 47.0	174 44.1	39.1	101 43.2	15.5	206 25.8	10.7	115 15.3	37.3	Venus	194 13.1	11 20
	h m									Mars	120 20.0	16 15
Mer.Pass. 0 16.5		v −0.4 d 1.2		v 0.7 d 0.3		v 2.0 d 0.1		v 2.3 d 0.1		Jupiter	224 01.4	9 19
										Saturn	132 38.2	15 24

UT	SUN GHA	SUN Dec	MOON GHA	v	MOON Dec	d	HP
d h	° ′	° ′	° ′	′	° ′	′	′
16 00	181 14.4	N 2 45.2	273 12.6	10.8	N18 33.5	0.4	55.6
01	196 14.6	44.3	287 42.4	10.7	18 33.9	0.4	55.5
02	211 14.9	43.3	302 12.1	10.8	18 34.3	0.2	55.5
03	226 15.1	.. 42.3	316 41.9	10.8	18 34.5	0.2	55.5
04	241 15.3	41.4	331 11.7	10.9	18 34.7	0.0	55.5
05	256 15.5	40.4	345 41.6	10.9	18 34.7	0.0	55.4
06	271 15.8	N 2 39.4	0 11.5	10.9	N18 34.7	0.1	55.4
07	286 16.0	38.5	14 41.4	10.9	18 34.6	0.2	55.4
08	301 16.2	37.5	29 11.3	11.0	18 34.4	0.3	55.4
09	316 16.4	.. 36.6	43 41.3	11.0	18 34.1	0.4	55.3
10	331 16.7	35.6	58 11.3	11.1	18 33.7	0.5	55.3
11	346 16.9	34.6	72 41.4	11.1	18 33.2	0.6	55.3
12	1 17.1	N 2 33.7	87 11.5	11.1	N18 32.6	0.7	55.3
13	16 17.3	32.7	101 41.6	11.1	18 31.9	0.7	55.2
14	31 17.5	31.7	116 11.7	11.2	18 31.2	0.9	55.2
15	46 17.8	.. 30.8	130 41.9	11.2	18 30.3	0.9	55.2
16	61 18.0	29.8	145 12.1	11.3	18 29.4	1.1	55.1
17	76 18.2	28.8	159 42.4	11.3	18 28.3	1.1	55.1
18	91 18.4	N 2 27.9	174 12.7	11.3	N18 27.2	1.2	55.1
19	106 18.7	26.9	188 43.0	11.4	18 26.0	1.3	55.1
20	121 18.9	25.9	203 13.4	11.3	18 24.7	1.4	55.1
21	136 19.1	.. 25.0	217 43.7	11.5	18 23.3	1.5	55.0
22	151 19.3	24.0	232 14.2	11.4	18 21.8	1.5	55.0
23	166 19.6	23.1	246 44.6	11.5	18 20.3	1.7	55.0
17 00	181 19.8	N 2 22.1	261 15.1	11.6	N18 18.6	1.7	55.0
01	196 20.0	21.1	275 45.7	11.5	18 16.9	1.9	54.9
02	211 20.2	20.2	290 16.2	11.6	18 15.0	1.9	54.9
03	226 20.4	.. 19.2	304 46.8	11.7	18 13.1	2.0	54.9
04	241 20.7	18.2	319 17.5	11.7	18 11.1	2.1	54.9
05	256 20.9	17.3	333 48.2	11.7	18 09.0	2.2	54.9
06	271 21.1	N 2 16.3	348 18.9	11.7	N18 06.8	2.2	54.8
07	286 21.3	15.3	2 49.6	11.8	18 04.6	2.4	54.8
08	301 21.6	14.4	17 20.4	11.8	18 02.2	2.4	54.8
09	316 21.8	.. 13.4	31 51.2	11.9	17 59.8	2.5	54.8
10	331 22.0	12.4	46 22.1	11.9	17 57.3	2.6	54.7
11	346 22.2	11.5	60 53.0	11.9	17 54.7	2.7	54.7
12	1 22.5	N 2 10.5	75 23.9	12.0	N17 52.0	2.7	54.7
13	16 22.7	09.5	89 54.9	12.0	17 49.3	2.9	54.7
14	31 22.9	08.6	104 25.9	12.0	17 46.4	2.9	54.7
15	46 23.1	.. 07.6	118 56.9	12.1	17 43.5	3.0	54.7
16	61 23.3	06.6	133 28.0	12.1	17 40.5	3.1	54.6
17	76 23.6	05.7	147 59.1	12.2	17 37.4	3.1	54.6
18	91 23.8	N 2 04.7	162 30.3	12.2	N17 34.3	3.3	54.6
19	106 24.0	03.7	177 01.5	12.2	17 31.0	3.3	54.6
20	121 24.2	02.8	191 32.7	12.3	17 27.7	3.4	54.6
21	136 24.5	.. 01.8	206 04.0	12.3	17 24.3	3.5	54.5
22	151 24.7	2 00.8	220 35.3	12.3	17 20.8	3.5	54.5
23	166 24.9	1 59.9	235 06.6	12.4	17 17.3	3.7	54.5
18 00	181 25.1	N 1 58.9	249 38.0	12.4	N17 13.6	3.7	54.5
01	196 25.4	57.9	264 09.4	12.4	17 09.9	3.8	54.5
02	211 25.6	57.0	278 40.8	12.5	17 06.1	3.9	54.5
03	226 25.8	.. 56.0	293 12.3	12.5	17 02.2	3.9	54.5
04	241 26.0	55.0	307 43.8	12.6	16 58.3	4.0	54.4
05	256 26.2	54.1	322 15.4	12.6	16 54.3	4.1	54.4
06	271 26.5	N 1 53.1	336 47.0	12.6	N16 50.2	4.2	54.4
07	286 26.7	52.1	351 18.6	12.7	16 46.0	4.3	54.4
08	301 26.9	51.2	5 50.3	12.7	16 41.7	4.3	54.4
09	316 27.1	.. 50.2	20 22.0	12.7	16 37.4	4.4	54.4
10	331 27.4	49.2	34 53.7	12.8	16 33.0	4.4	54.4
11	346 27.6	48.2	49 25.5	12.8	16 28.6	4.6	54.3
12	1 27.8	N 1 47.3	63 57.3	12.9	N16 24.0	4.6	54.3
13	16 28.0	46.3	78 29.2	12.8	16 19.4	4.7	54.3
14	31 28.2	45.3	93 01.0	13.0	16 14.7	4.7	54.3
15	46 28.5	.. 44.4	107 33.0	12.9	16 10.0	4.8	54.3
16	61 28.7	43.4	122 04.9	13.0	16 05.2	4.9	54.3
17	76 28.9	42.4	136 36.9	13.0	16 00.3	5.0	54.3
18	91 29.1	N 1 41.5	151 08.9	13.1	N15 55.3	5.0	54.3
19	106 29.4	40.5	165 41.0	13.1	15 50.3	5.1	54.3
20	121 29.6	39.5	180 13.1	13.1	15 45.2	5.2	54.2
21	136 29.8	.. 38.6	194 45.2	13.2	15 40.0	5.2	54.2
22	151 30.0	37.6	209 17.4	13.2	15 34.8	5.4	54.2
23	166 30.3	36.6	223 49.6	13.2	N15 29.4	5.3	54.2
	SD 15.9	d 1.0	SD 15.1		14.9		14.8

Tuesday (16), Wednesday (17), Thursday (18)

Moonrise

Lat.	Twilight Naut.	Twilight Civil	Sunrise	Moonrise 16	17	18	19
°	h m	h m	h m	h m	h m	h m	h m
N 72	02 23	04 04	05 16	▭	20 18	22 09	23 51
N 70	02 50	04 16	05 20	20 06	21 21	22 47	24 16
68	03 11	04 26	05 23	20 49	21 57	23 14	24 35
66	03 26	04 33	05 26	21 18	22 22	23 34	24 50
64	03 39	04 40	05 28	21 40	22 41	23 50	25 02
62	03 50	04 45	05 30	21 58	22 57	24 03	00 03
60	03 58	04 50	05 32	22 12	23 10	24 14	00 14
N 58	04 06	04 54	05 34	22 25	23 22	24 24	00 24
56	04 12	04 58	05 35	22 35	23 32	24 32	00 32
54	04 18	05 01	05 36	22 45	23 40	24 40	00 40
52	04 23	05 04	05 38	22 53	23 48	24 46	00 46
50	04 27	05 06	05 39	23 01	23 55	24 53	00 53
45	04 36	05 11	05 41	23 17	24 10	00 10	01 06
N 40	04 44	05 15	05 43	23 30	24 22	00 22	01 16
35	04 49	05 19	05 44	23 41	24 33	00 33	01 26
30	04 54	05 22	05 45	23 51	24 42	00 42	01 34
20	05 00	05 26	05 48	24 08	00 08	00 58	01 47
N 10	05 04	05 29	05 50	24 23	00 23	01 12	02 00
0	05 07	05 31	05 51	24 37	00 37	01 25	02 11
S 10	05 07	05 32	05 53	00 01	00 50	01 37	02 22
20	05 07	05 32	05 54	00 16	01 05	01 51	02 34
30	05 04	05 32	05 56	00 34	01 22	02 07	02 48
35	05 02	05 31	05 57	00 44	01 32	02 16	02 56
40	05 00	05 31	05 58	00 55	01 43	02 26	03 05
45	04 56	05 30	05 59	01 09	01 56	02 39	03 16
S 50	04 51	05 28	06 00	01 25	02 13	02 53	03 28
52	04 48	05 27	06 01	01 33	02 20	03 00	03 34
54	04 45	05 26	06 01	01 42	02 29	03 08	03 41
56	04 42	05 25	06 02	01 51	02 38	03 16	03 48
58	04 38	05 24	06 03	02 02	02 49	03 26	03 56
S 60	04 33	05 22	06 04	02 15	03 01	03 37	04 06

Moonset

Lat.	Sunset	Twilight Civil	Twilight Naut.	Moonset 16	17	18	19
°	h m	h m	h m	h m	h m	h m	h m
N 72	18 31	19 41	21 20	▭	18 13	17 58	17 50
N 70	18 27	19 30	20 54	16 44	17 09	17 20	17 25
68	18 24	19 21	20 35	16 01	16 33	16 53	17 05
66	18 21	19 13	20 19	15 31	16 08	16 32	16 49
64	18 19	19 07	20 07	15 09	15 48	16 16	16 37
62	18 17	19 02	19 57	14 52	15 32	16 02	16 26
60	18 15	18 57	19 49	14 37	15 18	15 50	16 16
N 58	18 14	18 54	19 41	14 25	15 07	15 40	16 08
56	18 13	18 50	19 35	14 14	14 56	15 32	16 01
54	18 12	18 47	19 30	14 04	14 48	15 24	15 54
52	18 10	18 44	19 25	13 56	14 40	15 17	15 48
50	18 10	18 41	19 20	13 48	14 32	15 10	15 43
45	18 07	18 37	19 12	13 32	14 17	14 57	15 32
N 40	18 06	18 33	19 05	13 19	14 04	14 45	15 22
35	18 04	18 30	18 59	13 07	13 53	14 36	15 14
30	18 03	18 27	18 55	12 57	13 44	14 27	15 07
20	18 01	18 23	18 49	12 40	13 28	14 12	14 54
N 10	17 59	18 20	18 45	12 25	13 13	13 59	14 43
0	17 58	18 18	18 42	12 11	13 00	13 47	14 33
S 10	17 56	18 17	18 42	11 57	12 46	13 35	14 22
20	17 55	18 17	18 42	11 42	12 32	13 22	14 11
30	17 53	18 17	18 45	11 25	12 16	13 07	13 59
35	17 53	18 18	18 47	11 15	12 06	12 58	13 51
40	17 52	18 19	18 50	11 03	11 55	12 48	13 43
45	17 50	18 20	18 54	10 49	11 42	12 36	13 33
S 50	17 50	18 22	19 00	10 33	11 26	12 22	13 21
52	17 49	18 23	19 02	10 26	11 19	12 16	13 15
54	17 49	18 24	19 05	10 17	11 10	12 08	13 09
56	17 47	18 25	19 09	10 07	11 01	12 00	13 02
58	17 47	18 26	19 13	09 56	10 51	11 51	12 54
S 60	17 47	18 28	19 17	09 43	10 38	11 40	12 45

SUN / MOON

Day	Eqn. of Time 00h	Eqn. of Time 12h	Mer. Pass.	Mer. Pass. Upper	Mer. Pass. Lower	Age	Phase
d	m s	m s	h m	h m	h m	d	%
16	04 57	05 08	11 55	05 59	18 24	22	46
17	05 19	05 29	11 55	06 48	19 12	23	36
18	05 40	05 51	11 54	07 36	19 59	24	28

UT	ARIES GHA	VENUS −3.9 GHA	Dec	MARS +0.7 GHA	Dec	JUPITER −1.9 GHA	Dec	SATURN +0.6 GHA	Dec	STARS Name	SHA	Dec
19 00	357 49.4	189 43.7	N 6 37.9	116 43.9	S22 15.9	221 27.7	N17 10.6	130 17.6	S15 37.3	Acamar	315 17.4	S40 14.6
01	12 51.9	204 43.2	36.7	131 44.5	16.2	236 29.7	10.4	145 19.8	37.4	Achernar	335 25.7	S57 09.6
02	27 54.4	219 42.8	35.5	146 45.2	16.6	251 31.7	10.3	160 22.1	37.5	Acrux	173 08.9	S63 10.8
03	42 56.8	234 42.4 ..	34.3	161 45.9 ..	16.9	266 33.7 ..	10.2	175 24.3 ..	37.5	Adhara	255 11.9	S28 59.5
04	57 59.3	249 42.0	33.1	176 46.6	17.2	281 35.7	10.1	190 26.6	37.6	Aldebaran	290 48.3	N16 32.2
05	73 01.8	264 41.5	31.9	191 47.2	17.6	296 37.7	09.9	205 28.9	37.7			
06	88 04.2	279 41.1	N 6 30.8	206 47.9	S22 17.9	311 39.7	N17 09.8	220 31.1	S15 37.7	Alioth	166 20.6	N55 52.9
07	103 06.7	294 40.7	29.6	221 48.6	18.2	326 41.7	09.7	235 33.4	37.8	Alkaid	152 58.7	N49 14.6
08	118 09.2	309 40.3	28.4	236 49.2	18.6	341 43.6	09.5	250 35.6	37.9	Al Na'ir	27 42.3	S46 53.3
F 09	133 11.6	324 39.9 ..	27.2	251 49.9 ..	18.9	356 45.6 ..	09.4	265 37.9 ..	37.9	Alnilam	275 45.5	S 1 11.6
R 10	148 14.1	339 39.4	26.0	266 50.6	19.2	11 47.6	09.3	280 40.1	38.0	Alphard	217 55.5	S 8 43.3
I 11	163 16.5	354 39.0	24.8	281 51.2	19.6	26 49.6	09.1	295 42.4	38.1			
D 12	178 19.0	9 38.6	N 6 23.6	296 51.9	S22 19.9	41 51.6	N17 09.0	310 44.6	S15 38.1	Alphecca	126 10.5	N26 40.3
A 13	193 21.5	24 38.2	22.4	311 52.6	20.2	56 53.6	08.9	325 46.9	38.2	Alpheratz	357 42.2	N29 10.4
Y 14	208 23.9	39 37.7	21.2	326 53.2	20.6	71 55.6	08.7	340 49.1	38.3	Altair	62 07.2	N 8 54.8
15	223 26.4	54 37.3 ..	20.0	341 53.9 ..	20.9	86 57.6 ..	08.6	355 51.4 ..	38.3	Ankaa	353 14.5	S42 13.4
16	238 28.9	69 36.9	18.8	356 54.6	21.2	101 59.6	08.5	10 53.6	38.4	Antares	112 25.3	S26 27.7
17	253 31.3	84 36.5	17.6	11 55.2	21.6	117 01.5	08.4	25 55.9	38.5			
18	268 33.8	99 36.1	N 6 16.4	26 55.9	S22 21.9	132 03.5	N17 08.2	40 58.1	S15 38.5	Arcturus	145 55.2	N19 06.6
19	283 36.3	114 35.6	15.2	41 56.6	22.2	147 05.5	08.1	56 00.4	38.6	Atria	107 26.4	S69 03.3
20	298 38.7	129 35.2	14.0	56 57.2	22.6	162 07.5	08.0	71 02.6	38.7	Avior	234 18.0	S59 33.3
21	313 41.2	144 34.8 ..	12.8	71 57.9 ..	22.9	177 09.5 ..	07.8	86 04.8 ..	38.7	Bellatrix	278 31.0	N 6 21.7
22	328 43.7	159 34.4	11.6	86 58.6	23.2	192 11.5	07.7	101 07.1	38.8	Betelgeuse	271 00.4	N 7 24.5
23	343 46.1	174 34.0	10.4	101 59.2	23.5	207 13.5	07.6	116 09.3	38.9			
20 00	358 48.6	189 33.5	N 6 09.3	116 59.9	S22 23.9	222 15.5	N17 07.4	131 11.6	S15 38.9	Canopus	263 55.8	S52 42.1
01	13 51.0	204 33.1	08.1	132 00.6	24.2	237 17.5	07.3	146 13.8	39.0	Capella	280 33.1	N46 00.4
02	28 53.5	219 32.7	06.9	147 01.2	24.5	252 19.5	07.2	161 16.1	39.1	Deneb	49 30.5	N45 20.4
03	43 56.0	234 32.3 ..	05.7	162 01.9 ..	24.9	267 21.4 ..	07.1	176 18.3 ..	39.1	Denebola	182 33.1	N14 29.5
04	58 58.4	249 31.9	04.5	177 02.5	25.2	282 23.4	06.9	191 20.6	39.2	Diphda	348 54.7	S17 54.2
05	74 00.9	264 31.4	03.3	192 03.2	25.5	297 25.4	06.8	206 22.8	39.3			
06	89 03.4	279 31.0	N 6 02.1	207 03.9	S22 25.8	312 27.4	N17 06.7	221 25.1	S15 39.3	Dubhe	193 51.4	N61 40.2
07	104 05.8	294 30.6	6 00.9	222 04.5	26.2	327 29.4	06.5	236 27.3	39.4	Elnath	278 11.5	N28 37.0
S 08	119 08.3	309 30.2	5 59.7	237 05.2	26.5	342 31.4	06.4	251 29.6	39.5	Eltanin	90 45.7	N51 29.7
A 09	134 10.8	324 29.8 ..	58.5	252 05.8 ..	26.8	357 33.4 ..	06.3	266 31.8 ..	39.5	Enif	33 46.0	N 9 56.9
T 10	149 13.2	339 29.4	57.3	267 06.5	27.2	12 35.4	06.1	281 34.1	39.6	Fomalhaut	15 22.7	S29 32.5
U 11	164 15.7	354 28.9	56.1	282 07.2	27.5	27 37.4	06.0	296 36.3	39.6			
R 12	179 18.1	9 28.5	N 5 54.9	297 07.8	S22 27.8	42 39.4	N17 05.9	311 38.6	S15 39.7	Gacrux	172 00.4	S57 11.7
D 13	194 20.6	24 28.1	53.7	312 08.5	28.1	57 41.4	05.7	326 40.8	39.8	Gienah	175 51.7	S17 37.3
A 14	209 23.1	39 27.7	52.5	327 09.1	28.5	72 43.3	05.6	341 43.1	39.8	Hadar	148 47.1	S60 26.6
Y 15	224 25.5	54 27.3 ..	51.3	342 09.8 ..	28.8	87 45.3 ..	05.5	356 45.3 ..	39.9	Hamal	327 59.5	N23 31.9
16	239 28.0	69 26.9	50.1	357 10.5	29.1	102 47.3	05.4	11 47.6	40.0	Kaus Aust.	83 42.6	S34 22.5
17	254 30.5	84 26.4	48.8	12 11.1	29.4	117 49.3	05.2	26 49.8	40.0			
18	269 32.9	99 26.0	N 5 47.6	27 11.8	S22 29.8	132 51.3	N17 05.1	41 52.1	S15 40.1	Kochab	137 21.0	N74 06.0
19	284 35.4	114 25.6	46.4	42 12.4	30.1	147 53.3	05.0	56 54.3	40.2	Markab	13 37.1	N15 17.3
20	299 37.9	129 25.2	45.2	57 13.1	30.4	162 55.3	04.8	71 56.5	40.2	Menkar	314 13.9	N 4 08.9
21	314 40.3	144 24.8 ..	44.0	72 13.7 ..	30.7	177 57.3 ..	04.7	86 58.8 ..	40.3	Menkent	148 06.8	S36 26.5
22	329 42.8	159 24.4	42.8	87 14.4	31.1	192 59.3	04.6	102 01.0	40.4	Miaplacidus	221 40.1	S69 46.6
23	344 45.3	174 23.9	41.6	102 15.1	31.4	208 01.3	04.5	117 03.3	40.4			
21 00	359 47.7	189 23.5	N 5 40.4	117 15.7	S22 31.7	223 03.3	N17 04.3	132 05.5	S15 40.5	Mirfak	308 38.8	N49 54.6
01	14 50.2	204 23.1	39.2	132 16.4	32.0	238 05.3	04.2	147 07.8	40.6	Nunki	75 57.1	S26 16.5
02	29 52.6	219 22.7	38.0	147 17.0	32.4	253 07.3	04.1	162 10.0	40.6	Peacock	53 17.6	S56 41.2
03	44 55.1	234 22.3 ..	36.8	162 17.7 ..	32.7	268 09.3 ..	03.9	177 12.3 ..	40.7	Pollux	243 26.9	N27 59.2
04	59 57.6	249 21.9	35.6	177 18.3	33.0	283 11.3	03.8	192 14.5	40.8	Procyon	244 59.0	N 5 11.1
05	75 00.0	264 21.5	34.4	192 19.0	33.3	298 13.3	03.7	207 16.8	40.8			
06	90 02.5	279 21.0	N 5 33.2	207 19.6	S22 33.6	313 15.2	N17 03.5	222 19.0	S15 40.9	Rasalhague	96 05.7	N12 33.3
07	105 05.0	294 20.6	32.0	222 20.3	34.0	328 17.2	03.4	237 21.3	41.0	Regulus	207 42.9	N11 53.7
08	120 07.4	309 20.2	30.8	237 20.9	34.3	343 19.2	03.3	252 23.5	41.0	Rigel	281 11.2	S 8 11.1
S 09	135 09.9	324 19.8 ..	29.6	252 21.6 ..	34.6	358 21.2 ..	03.2	267 25.7 ..	41.1	Rigil Kent.	139 50.9	S60 53.7
U 10	150 12.4	339 19.4	28.4	267 22.2	34.9	13 23.2	03.0	282 28.0	41.2	Sabik	102 11.6	S15 44.3
N 11	165 14.8	354 19.0	27.2	282 22.9	35.2	28 25.2	02.9	297 30.2	41.2			
D 12	180 17.3	9 18.6	N 5 25.9	297 23.5	S22 35.6	43 27.2	N17 02.8	312 32.5	S15 41.3	Schedar	349 38.9	N56 37.1
A 13	195 19.7	24 18.1	24.7	312 24.2	35.9	58 29.2	02.6	327 34.7	41.4	Shaula	96 20.8	S37 06.7
Y 14	210 22.2	39 17.7	23.5	327 24.8	36.2	73 31.2	02.5	342 37.0	41.4	Sirius	258 33.0	S16 44.2
15	225 24.7	54 17.3 ..	22.3	342 25.5 ..	36.5	88 33.2 ..	02.4	357 39.2 ..	41.5	Spica	158 30.6	S11 14.1
16	240 27.1	69 16.9	21.1	357 26.1	36.8	103 35.2	02.2	12 41.5	41.5	Suhail	222 52.1	S43 29.4
17	255 29.6	84 16.5	19.9	12 26.8	37.1	118 37.2	02.1	27 43.7	41.6			
18	270 32.1	99 16.1	N 5 18.7	27 27.4	S22 37.5	133 39.2	N17 02.0	42 45.9	S15 41.7	Vega	80 38.3	N38 48.3
19	285 34.5	114 15.7	17.5	42 28.1	37.8	148 41.2	01.9	57 48.2	41.8	Zuben'ubi	137 04.7	S16 06.0
20	300 37.0	129 15.3	16.3	57 28.7	38.1	163 43.2	01.7	72 50.4	41.8		SHA	Mer. Pass.
21	315 39.5	144 14.8 ..	15.1	72 29.4 ..	38.4	178 45.2 ..	01.6	87 52.7 ..	41.9		° ′	h m
22	330 41.9	159 14.4	13.8	87 30.0	38.7	193 47.2	01.5	102 54.9	42.0	Venus	190 45.0	11 22
23	345 44.4	174 14.0	12.6	102 30.7	39.0	208 49.2	01.3	117 57.2	42.0	Mars	118 11.3	16 11
Mer. Pass.	h m　0 04.7	v −0.4　d 1.2		v 0.7　d 0.3		v 2.0　d 0.1		v 2.2　d 0.1		Jupiter	223 26.9	9 10
										Saturn	132 23.0	15 13

UT	SUN GHA	SUN Dec	MOON GHA	MOON v	MOON Dec	MOON d	MOON HP
d h	° ′	° ′	° ′	′	° ′	′	′
19 00	181 30.5	N 1 35.7	238 21.8	13.3	N15 24.1	5.5	54.2
01	196 30.7	34.7	252 54.1	13.3	15 18.6	5.5	54.2
02	211 30.9	33.7	267 26.4	13.3	15 13.1	5.5	54.2
03	226 31.1	.. 32.8	281 58.7	13.4	15 07.6	5.7	54.2
04	241 31.4	31.8	296 31.1	13.4	15 01.9	5.7	54.2
05	256 31.6	30.8	311 03.5	13.4	14 56.2	5.7	54.2
06	271 31.8	N 1 29.8	325 35.9	13.5	N14 50.5	5.9	54.2
07	286 32.0	28.9	340 08.4	13.5	14 44.6	5.9	54.1
08	301 32.3	27.9	354 40.9	13.5	14 38.7	5.9	54.1
F 09	316 32.5	.. 26.9	9 13.4	13.6	14 32.8	6.0	54.1
R 10	331 32.7	26.0	23 46.0	13.6	14 26.8	6.1	54.1
I 11	346 32.9	25.0	38 18.6	13.6	14 20.7	6.2	54.1
D 12	1 33.1	N 1 24.0	52 51.2	13.7	N14 14.5	6.2	54.1
A 13	16 33.4	23.1	67 23.9	13.6	14 08.3	6.2	54.1
Y 14	31 33.6	22.1	81 56.5	13.8	14 02.1	6.3	54.1
15	46 33.8	.. 21.1	96 29.3	13.7	13 55.8	6.4	54.1
16	61 34.0	20.1	111 02.0	13.8	13 49.4	6.5	54.1
17	76 34.3	19.2	125 34.8	13.8	13 42.9	6.5	54.1
18	91 34.5	N 1 18.2	140 07.6	13.9	N13 36.4	6.5	54.1
19	106 34.7	17.2	154 40.5	13.8	13 29.9	6.6	54.1
20	121 34.9	16.3	169 13.3	13.9	13 23.3	6.7	54.1
21	136 35.1	.. 15.3	183 46.2	14.0	13 16.6	6.7	54.1
22	151 35.4	14.3	198 19.2	13.9	13 09.9	6.8	54.1
23	166 35.6	13.4	212 52.1	14.0	13 03.1	6.8	54.1
20 00	181 35.8	N 1 12.4	227 25.1	14.0	N12 56.3	6.9	54.1
01	196 36.0	11.4	241 58.1	14.1	12 49.4	7.0	54.0
02	211 36.3	10.4	256 31.2	14.0	12 42.4	7.0	54.0
03	226 36.5	.. 09.5	271 04.2	14.1	12 35.4	7.0	54.0
04	241 36.7	08.5	285 37.3	14.2	12 28.4	7.1	54.0
05	256 36.9	07.5	300 10.5	14.1	12 21.3	7.2	54.0
06	271 37.1	N 1 06.6	314 43.6	14.2	N12 14.1	7.2	54.0
S 07	286 37.4	05.6	329 16.8	14.2	12 06.9	7.2	54.0
A 08	301 37.6	04.6	343 50.0	14.2	11 59.7	7.3	54.0
T 09	316 37.8	.. 03.7	358 23.2	14.3	11 52.4	7.4	54.0
U 10	331 38.0	02.7	12 56.5	14.2	11 45.0	7.4	54.0
R 11	346 38.2	01.7	27 29.7	14.3	11 37.6	7.5	54.0
D 12	1 38.5	N 1 00.7	42 03.0	14.4	N11 30.1	7.5	54.0
A 13	16 38.7	0 59.8	56 36.4	14.3	11 22.6	7.5	54.0
Y 14	31 38.9	58.8	71 09.7	14.4	11 15.1	7.6	54.0
15	46 39.1	.. 57.8	85 43.1	14.4	11 07.5	7.7	54.0
16	61 39.4	56.9	100 16.5	14.4	10 59.8	7.7	54.0
17	76 39.6	55.9	114 49.9	14.4	10 52.1	7.7	54.0
18	91 39.8	N 0 54.9	129 23.3	14.5	N10 44.4	7.8	54.0
19	106 40.0	53.9	143 56.8	14.5	10 36.6	7.9	54.0
20	121 40.2	53.0	158 30.3	14.5	10 28.7	7.8	54.0
21	136 40.5	.. 52.0	173 03.8	14.5	10 20.9	8.0	54.0
22	151 40.7	51.0	187 37.3	14.5	10 12.9	7.9	54.0
23	166 40.9	50.1	202 10.8	14.6	10 05.0	8.0	54.0
21 00	181 41.1	N 0 49.1	216 44.4	14.6	N 9 57.0	8.1	54.0
01	196 41.3	48.1	231 18.0	14.5	9 48.9	8.1	54.0
02	211 41.6	47.1	245 51.5	14.7	9 40.8	8.1	54.0
03	226 41.8	.. 46.2	260 25.2	14.6	9 32.7	8.2	54.0
04	241 42.0	45.2	274 58.8	14.6	9 24.5	8.2	54.0
05	256 42.2	44.2	289 32.4	14.7	9 16.3	8.3	54.1
06	271 42.4	N 0 43.3	304 06.1	14.7	N 9 08.0	8.3	54.1
07	286 42.7	42.3	318 39.8	14.7	8 59.7	8.3	54.1
08	301 42.9	41.3	333 13.5	14.7	8 51.4	8.4	54.1
S 09	316 43.1	.. 40.3	347 47.2	14.7	8 43.0	8.4	54.1
U 10	331 43.3	39.4	2 20.9	14.8	8 34.6	8.4	54.1
N 11	346 43.6	38.4	16 54.7	14.7	8 26.2	8.5	54.1
D 12	1 43.8	N 0 37.4	31 28.4	14.8	N 8 17.7	8.5	54.1
A 13	16 44.0	36.5	46 02.2	14.8	8 09.2	8.6	54.1
Y 14	31 44.2	35.5	60 36.0	14.8	8 00.6	8.6	54.1
15	46 44.4	.. 34.5	75 09.8	14.8	7 52.0	8.6	54.1
16	61 44.7	33.5	89 43.6	14.8	7 43.4	8.7	54.1
17	76 44.9	32.6	104 17.4	14.9	7 34.7	8.7	54.1
18	91 45.1	N 0 31.6	118 51.3	14.8	N 7 26.0	8.7	54.1
19	106 45.3	30.6	133 25.1	14.9	7 17.3	8.7	54.1
20	121 45.5	29.6	147 59.0	14.8	7 08.6	8.8	54.1
21	136 45.8	.. 28.7	162 32.8	14.9	6 59.8	8.8	54.1
22	151 46.0	27.7	177 06.7	14.9	6 51.0	8.9	54.1
23	166 46.2	26.7	191 40.6	14.9	N 6 42.1	8.9	54.1
	SD 16.0	d 1.0	SD 14.7		14.7		14.7

Twilight — Sunrise — Moonrise

Lat.	Naut.	Civil	Sunrise	Moonrise 19	20	21	22
°	h m	h m	h m	h m	h m	h m	h m
N 72	02 44	04 19	05 29	23 51	25 29	01 29	03 05
N 70	03 07	04 29	05 31	24 16	00 16	01 45	03 14
68	03 25	04 37	05 34	24 35	00 35	01 58	03 21
66	03 38	04 43	05 35	24 50	00 50	02 08	03 27
64	03 49	04 49	05 37	25 02	01 02	02 16	03 32
62	03 59	04 53	05 38	00 03	01 12	02 24	03 36
60	04 06	04 57	05 39	00 14	01 21	02 30	03 40
N 58	04 13	05 01	05 40	00 24	01 29	02 35	03 43
56	04 19	05 04	05 41	00 32	01 35	02 40	03 46
54	04 24	05 06	05 42	00 40	01 41	02 45	03 49
52	04 28	05 09	05 42	00 46	01 47	02 49	03 52
50	04 32	05 11	05 43	00 53	01 52	02 52	03 54
45	04 40	05 15	05 44	01 06	02 02	03 00	03 58
N 40	04 47	05 18	05 45	01 16	02 11	03 07	04 02
35	04 51	05 21	05 46	01 26	02 19	03 12	04 06
30	04 55	05 23	05 47	01 34	02 25	03 17	04 09
20	05 01	05 26	05 48	01 47	02 37	03 26	04 14
N 10	05 04	05 28	05 49	02 00	02 47	03 33	04 19
0	05 06	05 30	05 50	02 11	02 56	03 40	04 23
S 10	05 06	05 30	05 51	02 22	03 05	03 47	04 27
20	05 04	05 30	05 52	02 34	03 15	03 54	04 32
30	05 01	05 28	05 52	02 48	03 26	04 03	04 37
35	04 58	05 27	05 53	02 56	03 33	04 07	04 40
40	04 54	05 26	05 53	03 05	03 40	04 13	04 43
45	04 50	05 24	05 53	03 16	03 49	04 19	04 47
S 50	04 44	05 21	05 54	03 28	03 59	04 27	04 52
52	04 41	05 20	05 54	03 34	04 04	04 30	04 54
54	04 37	05 19	05 54	03 41	04 09	04 34	04 56
56	04 33	05 17	05 54	03 48	04 15	04 38	04 59
58	04 29	05 15	05 55	03 56	04 22	04 43	05 02
S 60	04 24	05 13	05 55	04 06	04 29	04 48	05 05

Sunset — Twilight — Moonset

Lat.	Sunset	Civil	Naut.	Moonset 19	20	21	22
°	h m	h m	h m	h m	h m	h m	h m
N 72	18 15	19 24	20 57	17 50	17 44	17 38	17 33
N 70	18 13	19 15	20 35	17 25	17 27	17 27	17 27
68	18 11	19 07	20 19	17 05	17 13	17 19	17 23
66	18 10	19 01	20 06	16 49	17 02	17 12	17 20
64	18 08	18 56	19 55	16 37	16 52	17 05	17 17
62	18 07	18 52	19 46	16 26	16 44	17 00	17 14
60	18 06	18 48	19 38	16 16	16 37	16 55	17 12
N 58	18 05	18 45	19 32	16 08	16 31	16 51	17 09
56	18 05	18 42	19 26	16 01	16 26	16 48	17 08
54	18 04	18 39	19 21	15 54	16 21	16 44	17 06
52	18 03	18 37	19 17	15 48	16 16	16 41	17 04
50	18 03	18 35	19 13	15 43	16 12	16 38	17 03
45	18 02	18 31	19 06	15 32	16 03	16 32	17 00
N 40	18 01	18 28	18 59	15 22	15 56	16 27	16 57
35	18 00	18 25	18 55	15 14	15 49	16 23	16 55
30	17 59	18 23	18 51	15 07	15 44	16 19	16 53
20	17 58	18 20	18 46	14 54	15 34	16 12	16 50
N 10	17 57	18 18	18 43	14 43	15 25	16 06	16 47
0	17 57	18 17	18 41	14 33	15 17	16 01	16 44
S 10	17 56	18 17	18 41	14 22	15 09	15 55	16 41
20	17 56	18 18	18 43	14 11	15 00	15 49	16 38
30	17 55	18 19	18 47	13 59	14 50	15 42	16 34
35	17 55	18 20	18 50	13 51	14 44	15 38	16 32
40	17 55	18 22	18 53	13 43	14 38	15 33	16 30
45	17 54	18 24	18 58	13 33	14 30	15 28	16 27
S 50	17 54	18 26	19 04	13 21	14 21	15 22	16 24
52	17 54	18 28	19 07	13 15	14 16	15 19	16 22
54	17 54	18 29	19 11	13 09	14 12	15 16	16 20
56	17 54	18 31	19 15	13 02	14 06	15 12	16 18
58	17 54	18 33	19 20	12 54	14 00	15 08	16 16
S 60	17 54	18 35	19 25	12 45	13 54	15 03	16 14

SUN and MOON

Day	SUN Eqn. of Time 00h	12h	Mer. Pass.	MOON Mer. Pass. Upper	Lower	Age	Phase
	m s	m s	h m	h m	h m	d	%
19	06 01	06 12	11 54	08 22	20 44	25	19
20	06 23	06 33	11 53	09 07	21 29	26	13
21	06 44	06 55	11 53	09 50	22 12	27	7

UT	ARIES GHA	VENUS −3.9 GHA	Dec	MARS +0.8 GHA	Dec	JUPITER −1.9 GHA	Dec	SATURN +0.6 GHA	Dec	Star Name	SHA	Dec
22 00	0 46.9	189 13.6	N 5 11.4	117 31.3	S22 39.4	223 51.2	N17 01.2	132 59.4	S15 42.1	Acamar	315 17.4	S40 14.6
01	15 49.3	204 13.2	10.2	132 32.0	39.7	238 53.2	01.1	148 01.6	42.2	Achernar	335 25.7	S57 09.6
02	30 51.8	219 12.8	09.0	147 32.6	40.0	253 55.2	01.0	163 03.9	42.2	Acrux	173 08.9	S63 10.8
03	45 54.2	234 12.4	.. 07.8	162 33.2	.. 40.3	268 57.2	.. 00.8	178 06.1	.. 42.3	Adhara	255 11.9	S28 59.4
04	60 56.7	249 12.0	06.6	177 33.9	40.6	283 59.2	00.7	193 08.4	42.4	Aldebaran	290 48.3	N16 32.2
05	75 59.2	264 11.6	05.4	192 34.5	40.9	299 01.2	00.6	208 10.6	42.4			
06	91 01.6	279 11.1	N 5 04.1	207 35.2	S22 41.3	314 03.2	N17 00.4	223 12.9	S15 42.5	Alioth	166 20.6	N55 52.9
07	106 04.1	294 10.7	02.9	222 35.8	41.6	329 05.2	00.3	238 15.1	42.6	Alkaid	152 58.7	N49 14.6
08	121 06.6	309 10.3	01.7	237 36.5	41.9	344 07.2	00.2	253 17.3	42.6	Al Na'ir	27 42.3	S46 53.3
M 09	136 09.0	324 09.9	5 00.5	252 37.1	.. 42.2	359 09.2	17 00.1	268 19.6	.. 42.7	Alnilam	275 45.4	S 1 11.6
O 10	151 11.5	339 09.5	4 59.3	267 37.8	42.5	14 11.2	16 59.9	283 21.8	42.8	Alphard	217 55.5	S 8 43.3
N 11	166 14.0	354 09.1	58.1	282 38.4	42.8	29 13.1	59.8	298 24.1	42.8			
D 12	181 16.4	9 08.7	N 4 56.9	297 39.0	S22 43.1	44 15.1	N16 59.7	313 26.3	S15 42.9	Alphecca	126 10.5	N26 40.3
A 13	196 18.9	24 08.3	55.6	312 39.7	43.4	59 17.1	59.5	328 28.6	43.0	Alpheratz	357 42.2	N29 10.5
Y 14	211 21.4	39 07.9	54.4	327 40.3	43.8	74 19.1	59.4	343 30.8	43.1	Altair	62 07.2	N 8 54.8
15	226 23.8	54 07.5	.. 53.2	342 41.0	.. 44.1	89 21.1	.. 59.3	358 33.0	.. 43.1	Ankaa	353 14.5	S42 13.4
16	241 26.3	69 07.1	52.0	357 41.6	44.4	104 23.1	59.1	13 35.3	43.2	Antares	112 25.3	S26 27.7
17	256 28.7	84 06.6	50.8	12 42.2	44.7	119 25.1	59.0	28 37.5	43.3			
18	271 31.2	99 06.2	N 4 49.6	27 42.9	S22 45.0	134 27.1	N16 58.9	43 39.8	S15 43.3	Arcturus	145 55.2	N19 06.6
19	286 33.7	114 05.8	48.4	42 43.5	45.3	149 29.1	58.8	58 42.0	43.4	Atria	107 26.4	S69 03.3
20	301 36.1	129 05.4	47.1	57 44.2	45.6	164 31.1	58.6	73 44.2	43.5	Avior	234 18.0	S59 33.3
21	316 38.6	144 05.0	.. 45.9	72 44.8	.. 45.9	179 33.1	.. 58.5	88 46.5	.. 43.5	Bellatrix	278 31.0	N 6 21.7
22	331 41.1	159 04.6	44.7	87 45.4	46.2	194 35.1	58.4	103 48.7	43.6	Betelgeuse	271 00.3	N 7 24.5
23	346 43.5	174 04.2	43.5	102 46.1	46.5	209 37.1	58.2	118 51.0	43.7			
23 00	1 46.0	189 03.8	N 4 42.3	117 46.7	S22 46.9	224 39.1	N16 58.1	133 53.2	S15 43.7	Canopus	263 55.8	S52 42.1
01	16 48.5	204 03.4	41.0	132 47.3	47.2	239 41.1	58.0	148 55.4	43.8	Capella	280 33.1	N46 00.4
02	31 50.9	219 03.0	39.8	147 48.0	47.5	254 43.1	57.9	163 57.7	43.9	Deneb	49 30.6	N45 20.4
03	46 53.4	234 02.6	.. 38.6	162 48.6	.. 47.8	269 45.1	.. 57.7	178 59.9	.. 43.9	Denebola	182 33.1	N14 29.5
04	61 55.8	249 02.2	37.4	177 49.3	48.1	284 47.2	57.6	194 02.2	44.0	Diphda	348 54.7	S17 54.2
05	76 58.3	264 01.8	36.2	192 49.9	48.4	299 49.2	57.5	209 04.4	44.1			
06	92 00.8	279 01.3	N 4 35.0	207 50.5	S22 48.7	314 51.2	N16 57.3	224 06.7	S15 44.1	Dubhe	193 51.4	N61 40.2
07	107 03.2	294 00.9	33.7	222 51.2	49.0	329 53.2	57.2	239 08.9	44.2	Elnath	278 11.5	N28 37.0
T 08	122 05.7	309 00.5	32.5	237 51.8	49.3	344 55.2	57.1	254 11.1	44.3	Eltanin	90 45.8	N51 29.7
U 09	137 08.2	324 00.1	.. 31.3	252 52.4	.. 49.6	359 57.2	.. 57.0	269 13.4	.. 44.3	Enif	33 46.0	N 9 56.9
E 10	152 10.6	338 59.7	30.1	267 53.1	49.9	14 59.2	56.8	284 15.6	44.4	Fomalhaut	15 22.7	S29 32.5
S 11	167 13.1	353 59.3	28.9	282 53.7	50.2	30 01.2	56.7	299 17.8	44.5			
D 12	182 15.6	8 58.9	N 4 27.6	297 54.3	S22 50.5	45 03.2	N16 56.6	314 20.1	S15 44.5	Gacrux	172 00.4	S57 11.7
A 13	197 18.0	23 58.5	26.4	312 55.0	50.8	60 05.2	56.4	329 22.3	44.6	Gienah	175 51.7	S17 37.3
Y 14	212 20.5	38 58.1	25.2	327 55.6	51.1	75 07.2	56.3	344 24.6	44.7	Hadar	148 47.1	S60 26.6
15	227 23.0	53 57.7	.. 24.0	342 56.2	.. 51.4	90 09.2	.. 56.2	359 26.8	.. 44.7	Hamal	327 59.5	N23 31.9
16	242 25.4	68 57.3	22.7	357 56.9	51.7	105 11.2	56.1	14 29.0	44.8	Kaus Aust.	83 42.6	S34 22.5
17	257 27.9	83 56.9	21.5	12 57.5	52.0	120 13.2	55.9	29 31.3	44.9			
18	272 30.3	98 56.5	N 4 20.3	27 58.1	S22 52.4	135 15.2	N16 55.8	44 33.5	S15 44.9	Kochab	137 21.1	N74 06.0
19	287 32.8	113 56.1	19.1	42 58.8	52.7	150 17.2	55.7	59 35.8	45.0	Markab	13 37.1	N15 17.3
20	302 35.3	128 55.7	17.9	57 59.4	53.0	165 19.2	55.6	74 38.0	45.1	Menkar	314 13.9	N 4 08.9
21	317 37.7	143 55.3	.. 16.6	73 00.0	.. 53.3	180 21.2	.. 55.4	89 40.2	.. 45.1	Menkent	148 06.8	S36 26.5
22	332 40.2	158 54.9	15.4	88 00.6	53.6	195 23.2	55.3	104 42.5	45.2	Miaplacidus	221 40.0	S69 46.6
23	347 42.7	173 54.5	14.2	103 01.3	53.9	210 25.2	55.2	119 44.7	45.3			
24 00	2 45.1	188 54.1	N 4 13.0	118 01.9	S22 54.2	225 27.2	N16 55.0	134 47.0	S15 45.3	Mirfak	308 38.7	N49 54.6
01	17 47.6	203 53.6	11.7	133 02.5	54.5	240 29.2	54.9	149 49.2	45.4	Nunki	75 57.2	S26 16.5
02	32 50.1	218 53.2	10.5	148 03.2	54.8	255 31.2	54.8	164 51.4	45.5	Peacock	53 17.6	S56 41.2
03	47 52.5	233 52.8	.. 09.3	163 03.8	.. 55.1	270 33.2	.. 54.7	179 53.7	.. 45.6	Pollux	243 26.8	N27 59.2
04	62 55.0	248 52.4	08.1	178 04.4	55.4	285 35.2	54.5	194 55.9	45.6	Procyon	244 59.0	N 5 11.1
05	77 57.4	263 52.0	06.8	193 05.0	55.7	300 37.2	54.4	209 58.1	45.7			
06	92 59.9	278 51.6	N 4 05.6	208 05.7	S22 56.0	315 39.2	N16 54.3	225 00.4	S15 45.8	Rasalhague	96 05.7	N12 33.3
W 07	108 02.4	293 51.2	04.4	223 06.3	56.3	330 41.2	54.1	240 02.6	45.8	Regulus	207 42.9	N11 53.7
E 08	123 04.8	308 50.8	03.2	238 06.9	56.6	345 43.2	54.0	255 04.9	45.9	Rigel	281 11.2	S 8 11.1
D 09	138 07.3	323 50.4	.. 01.9	253 07.5	.. 56.9	0 45.3	.. 53.9	270 07.1	.. 46.0	Rigil Kent.	139 51.0	S60 53.7
N 10	153 09.8	338 50.0	4 00.7	268 08.2	57.2	15 47.3	53.8	285 09.3	46.0	Sabik	102 11.6	S15 44.3
E 11	168 12.2	353 49.6	3 59.5	283 08.8	57.5	30 49.3	53.6	300 11.6	46.1			
S 12	183 14.7	8 49.2	N 3 58.3	298 09.4	S22 57.7	45 51.3	N16 53.5	315 13.8	S15 46.2	Schedar	349 38.9	N56 37.1
D 13	198 17.2	23 48.8	57.0	313 10.0	58.0	60 53.3	53.4	330 16.0	46.2	Shaula	96 20.8	S37 06.7
A 14	213 19.6	38 48.4	55.8	328 10.7	58.3	75 55.3	53.3	345 18.3	46.3	Sirius	258 33.0	S16 44.2
Y 15	228 22.1	53 48.0	.. 54.6	343 11.3	.. 58.6	90 57.3	.. 53.1	0 20.5	.. 46.4	Spica	158 30.6	S11 14.1
16	243 24.6	68 47.6	53.4	358 11.9	58.9	105 59.3	53.0	15 22.7	46.4	Suhail	222 52.1	S43 29.4
17	258 27.0	83 47.2	52.1	13 12.5	59.2	121 01.3	52.9	30 25.0	46.5			
18	273 29.5	98 46.8	N 3 50.9	28 13.2	S22 59.5	136 03.3	N16 52.7	45 27.2	S15 46.6	Vega	80 38.3	N38 48.3
19	288 31.9	113 46.4	49.7	43 13.8	22 59.8	151 05.3	52.6	60 29.5	46.6	Zuben'ubi	137 04.7	S16 06.0
20	303 34.4	128 46.0	48.4	58 14.4	23 00.1	166 07.3	52.5	75 31.7	46.7			
21	318 36.9	143 45.6	.. 47.2	73 15.0	.. 00.4	181 09.3	.. 52.4	90 33.9	.. 46.8			
22	333 39.3	158 45.2	46.0	88 15.7	00.7	196 11.3	52.2	105 36.2	46.8			
23	348 41.8	173 44.8	44.8	103 16.3	01.0	211 13.3	52.1	120 38.4	46.9			

	ARIES	VENUS	MARS	JUPITER	SATURN		SHA	Mer.Pass.
Mer. Pass.	h m 23 49.0	v −0.4 d 1.2	v 0.6 d 0.3	v 2.0 d 0.1	v 2.2 d 0.1	Venus	187 17.8	11 24
						Mars	116 00.7	16 08
						Jupiter	222 53.2	9 00
						Saturn	132 07.2	15 02

UT	SUN GHA	SUN Dec	MOON GHA	v	MOON Dec	d	HP
22 00	181 46.4	N 0 25.8	206 14.5	14.9	N 6 33.2	8.9	54.1
01	196 46.6	24.8	220 48.4	14.9	6 24.3	8.9	54.1
02	211 46.9	23.8	235 22.3	14.9	6 15.4	9.0	54.2
03	226 47.1	.. 22.8	249 56.2	15.0	6 06.4	9.0	54.2
04	241 47.3	21.9	264 30.2	14.9	5 57.4	9.0	54.2
05	256 47.5	20.9	279 04.1	14.9	5 48.4	9.1	54.2
M 06	271 47.7	N 0 19.9	293 38.0	15.0	N 5 39.3	9.0	54.2
O 07	286 48.0	19.0	308 12.0	14.9	5 30.3	9.1	54.2
N 08	301 48.2	18.0	322 45.9	14.9	5 21.2	9.2	54.2
D 09	316 48.4	.. 17.0	337 19.8	15.0	5 12.0	9.1	54.2
A 10	331 48.6	16.0	351 53.8	15.0	5 02.9	9.2	54.2
Y 11	346 48.8	15.1	6 27.8	14.9	4 53.7	9.2	54.2
12	1 49.1	N 0 14.1	21 01.7	15.0	N 4 44.5	9.2	54.2
13	16 49.3	13.1	35 35.7	14.9	4 35.3	9.3	54.2
14	31 49.5	12.1	50 09.6	15.0	4 26.0	9.2	54.3
15	46 49.7	.. 11.2	64 43.6	15.0	4 16.8	9.3	54.3
16	61 49.9	10.2	79 17.6	14.9	4 07.5	9.3	54.3
17	76 50.1	09.2	93 51.5	15.0	3 58.2	9.3	54.3
18	91 50.4	N 0 08.3	108 25.5	14.9	N 3 48.9	9.4	54.3
19	106 50.6	07.3	122 59.4	15.0	3 39.5	9.4	54.3
20	121 50.8	06.3	137 33.4	15.0	3 30.1	9.3	54.3
21	136 51.0	.. 05.3	152 07.4	15.0	3 20.8	9.4	54.3
22	151 51.2	04.4	166 41.3	15.0	3 11.4	9.5	54.3
23	166 51.5	03.4	181 15.3	14.9	3 01.9	9.4	54.3
23 00	181 51.7	N 0 02.4	195 49.2	15.0	N 2 52.5	9.4	54.3
01	196 51.9	01.4	210 23.2	14.9	2 43.1	9.5	54.4
02	211 52.1	N 00.5	224 57.1	14.9	2 33.6	9.5	54.4
03	226 52.3	S 00.5	239 31.0	15.0	2 24.1	9.5	54.4
04	241 52.6	01.5	254 05.0	14.9	2 14.6	9.5	54.4
05	256 52.8	02.5	268 38.9	14.9	2 05.1	9.5	54.4
T 06	271 53.0	S 0 03.4	283 12.8	14.9	N 1 55.6	9.5	54.4
U 07	286 53.2	04.4	297 46.7	14.9	1 46.1	9.6	54.4
E 08	301 53.4	05.4	312 20.6	14.9	1 36.5	9.5	54.4
S 09	316 53.6	.. 06.3	326 54.5	14.9	1 27.0	9.6	54.4
D 10	331 53.9	07.3	341 28.4	14.9	1 17.4	9.6	54.5
A 11	346 54.1	08.3	356 02.3	14.8	1 07.8	9.5	54.5
Y 12	1 54.3	S 0 09.3	10 36.1	14.9	N 0 58.3	9.6	54.5
13	16 54.5	10.2	25 10.0	14.8	0 48.7	9.6	54.5
14	31 54.7	11.2	39 43.8	14.9	0 39.1	9.6	54.5
15	46 55.0	.. 12.2	54 17.7	14.8	0 29.5	9.6	54.5
16	61 55.2	13.2	68 51.5	14.8	0 19.9	9.6	54.5
17	76 55.4	14.1	83 25.3	14.8	0 10.3	9.7	54.5
18	91 55.6	S 0 15.1	97 59.1	14.7	N 0 00.6	9.6	54.6
19	106 55.8	16.1	112 32.8	14.8	S 0 09.0	9.6	54.6
20	121 56.0	17.1	127 06.6	14.8	0 18.6	9.7	54.6
21	136 56.3	.. 18.0	141 40.4	14.7	0 28.3	9.6	54.6
22	151 56.5	19.0	156 14.1	14.7	0 37.9	9.6	54.6
23	166 56.7	20.0	170 47.8	14.7	0 47.5	9.7	54.6
24 00	181 56.9	S 0 20.9	185 21.5	14.7	S 0 57.2	9.6	54.6
01	196 57.1	21.9	199 55.2	14.7	1 06.8	9.6	54.6
02	211 57.4	22.9	214 28.9	14.6	1 16.4	9.7	54.7
03	226 57.6	.. 23.9	229 02.5	14.6	1 26.1	9.6	54.7
04	241 57.8	24.8	243 36.1	14.6	1 35.7	9.7	54.7
05	256 58.0	25.8	258 09.7	14.6	1 45.4	9.6	54.7
W 06	271 58.2	S 0 26.8	272 43.3	14.6	S 1 55.0	9.6	54.7
E 07	286 58.4	27.8	287 16.9	14.6	2 04.6	9.6	54.7
D 08	301 58.7	28.7	301 50.5	14.5	2 14.2	9.7	54.7
N 09	316 58.9	.. 29.7	316 24.0	14.5	2 23.9	9.6	54.8
E 10	331 59.1	30.7	330 57.5	14.5	2 33.5	9.6	54.8
S 11	346 59.3	31.7	345 31.0	14.4	2 43.1	9.6	54.8
D 12	1 59.5	S 0 32.6	0 04.4	14.5	S 2 52.7	9.6	54.8
A 13	16 59.7	33.6	14 37.9	14.4	3 02.3	9.6	54.8
Y 14	32 00.0	34.6	29 11.3	14.4	3 11.9	9.6	54.8
15	47 00.2	.. 35.6	43 44.7	14.3	3 21.5	9.5	54.8
16	62 00.4	36.5	58 18.0	14.4	3 31.0	9.6	54.9
17	77 00.6	37.5	72 51.4	14.3	3 40.6	9.5	54.9
18	92 00.8	S 0 38.5	87 24.7	14.3	S 3 50.1	9.6	54.9
19	107 01.0	39.4	101 58.0	14.2	3 59.7	9.5	54.9
20	122 01.3	40.4	116 31.2	14.3	4 09.2	9.5	54.9
21	137 01.5	.. 41.4	131 04.5	14.2	4 18.7	9.5	54.9
22	152 01.7	42.4	145 37.7	14.1	4 28.2	9.5	55.0
23	167 01.9	43.3	160 10.8	14.2	S 4 37.7	9.5	55.0
SD	16.0	d 1.0	SD 14.8		14.8		14.9

Twilight / Moonrise

Lat.	Naut.	Civil	Sunrise	Moonrise 22	23	24	25
N 72	03 04	04 34	05 42	03 05	04 40	06 15	07 52
N 70	03 23	04 42	05 43	03 14	04 43	06 12	07 43
68	03 38	04 48	05 44	03 21	04 45	06 10	07 36
66	03 50	04 53	05 45	03 27	04 47	06 08	07 30
64	03 59	04 58	05 45	03 32	04 49	06 06	07 25
62	04 08	05 01	05 46	03 36	04 50	06 05	07 20
60	04 14	05 05	05 46	03 40	04 51	06 03	07 16
N 58	04 20	05 07	05 47	03 43	04 52	06 02	07 13
56	04 25	05 10	05 47	03 46	04 53	06 01	07 10
54	04 30	05 12	05 47	03 49	04 54	06 00	07 07
52	04 34	05 14	05 47	03 52	04 55	05 59	07 05
50	04 37	05 15	05 48	03 54	04 56	05 59	07 03
45	04 44	05 19	05 48	03 58	04 57	05 57	06 58
N 40	04 50	05 21	05 48	04 02	04 59	05 56	06 54
35	04 54	05 23	05 49	04 06	05 00	05 55	06 50
30	04 57	05 25	05 49	04 09	05 01	05 54	06 47
20	05 01	05 27	05 49	04 14	05 03	05 52	06 42
N 10	05 04	05 28	05 49	04 19	05 04	05 51	06 38
0	05 04	05 28	05 49	04 23	05 06	05 49	06 33
S 10	05 04	05 28	05 49	04 27	05 07	05 48	06 29
20	05 01	05 27	05 49	04 32	05 09	05 46	06 25
30	04 57	05 25	05 49	04 37	05 11	05 45	06 20
35	04 54	05 23	05 49	04 40	05 12	05 44	06 17
40	04 49	05 21	05 48	04 43	05 13	05 43	06 13
45	04 44	05 18	05 48	04 47	05 15	05 42	06 10
S 50	04 37	05 15	05 47	04 52	05 16	05 40	06 05
52	04 33	05 13	05 47	04 54	05 17	05 40	06 03
54	04 29	05 11	05 47	04 56	05 18	05 39	06 01
56	04 25	05 09	05 46	04 59	05 19	05 38	05 58
58	04 20	05 07	05 46	05 02	05 20	05 37	05 56
S 60	04 14	05 04	05 45	05 05	05 21	05 36	05 53

Sunset / Twilight / Moonset

Lat.	Sunset	Civil	Naut.	Moonset 22	23	24	25
N 72	18 00	19 08	20 37	17 33	17 27	17 22	17 16
N 70	17 59	19 00	20 18	17 27	17 27	17 27	17 27
68	17 59	18 54	20 04	17 23	17 27	17 31	17 36
66	17 58	18 49	19 52	17 20	17 27	17 35	17 43
64	17 58	18 45	19 43	17 17	17 27	17 38	17 49
62	17 58	18 42	19 35	17 14	17 27	17 40	17 55
60	17 57	18 39	19 28	17 12	17 27	17 43	18 00
N 58	17 57	18 36	19 23	17 09	17 27	17 45	18 04
56	17 57	18 34	19 18	17 08	17 27	17 47	18 08
54	17 57	18 32	19 14	17 06	17 27	17 48	18 11
52	17 56	18 30	19 10	17 04	17 27	17 50	18 14
50	17 56	18 28	19 06	17 03	17 27	17 51	18 17
45	17 56	18 25	19 00	17 00	17 27	17 54	18 23
N 40	17 56	18 23	18 54	16 57	17 27	17 57	18 28
35	17 56	18 21	18 50	16 55	17 27	17 59	18 33
30	17 56	18 19	18 47	16 53	17 27	18 01	18 36
20	17 55	18 17	18 43	16 50	17 27	18 04	18 43
N 10	17 56	18 16	18 41	16 47	17 27	18 07	18 49
0	17 56	18 16	18 40	16 44	17 27	18 10	18 55
S 10	17 56	18 17	18 41	16 41	17 27	18 13	19 01
20	17 56	18 18	18 44	16 38	17 27	18 16	19 07
30	17 57	18 21	18 48	16 34	17 26	18 19	19 13
35	17 57	18 22	18 52	16 32	17 26	18 21	19 17
40	17 57	18 25	18 56	16 30	17 26	18 24	19 22
45	17 58	18 27	19 02	16 27	17 26	18 26	19 27
S 50	17 59	18 31	19 09	16 24	17 26	18 29	19 33
52	17 59	18 33	19 13	16 22	17 26	18 31	19 36
54	17 59	18 35	19 17	16 20	17 26	18 32	19 39
56	18 00	18 37	19 21	16 18	17 26	18 34	19 43
58	18 00	18 40	19 27	16 16	17 26	18 36	19 47
S 60	18 01	18 42	19 33	16 14	17 26	18 38	19 51

SUN / MOON

Day	Eqn. of Time 00h	12h	Mer. Pass.	Mer. Pass. Upper	Lower	Age	Phase
d	m s	m s	h m	h m	h m	d	%
22	07 05	07 16	11 53	10 33	22 55	28	3
23	07 26	07 37	11 52	11 16	23 38	29	1
24	07 47	07 58	11 52	12 00	24 22	00	0

UT	ARIES	VENUS −3.9		MARS +0.8		JUPITER −1.9		SATURN +0.6		STARS		
	GHA	GHA	Dec	GHA	Dec	GHA	Dec	GHA	Dec	Name	SHA	Dec
d h	° ′	° ′	° ′	° ′	° ′	° ′	° ′	° ′	° ′		° ′	° ′
25 00	3 44.3	188 44.4 N 3 43.5		118 16.9 S23 01.3		226 15.4 N16 52.0		135 40.6 S15 47.0		Acamar	315 17.4	S40 14.6
01	18 46.7	203 44.0	42.3	133 17.5	01.6	241 17.4	51.8	150 42.9	47.1	Achernar	335 25.7	S57 09.6
02	33 49.2	218 43.6	41.1	148 18.1	01.9	256 19.4	51.7	165 45.1	47.1	Acrux	173 08.9	S63 10.8
03	48 51.7	233 43.2 . .	39.8	163 18.8 . .	02.2	271 21.4 . .	51.6	180 47.3 . .	47.2	Adhara	255 11.9	S28 59.4
04	63 54.1	248 42.8	38.6	178 19.4	02.5	286 23.4	51.5	195 49.6	47.3	Aldebaran	290 48.2	N16 32.2
05	78 56.6	263 42.4	37.4	193 20.0	02.8	301 25.4	51.3	210 51.8	47.3			
06	93 59.0	278 42.0 N 3 36.1		208 20.6 S23 03.0		316 27.4 N16 51.2		225 54.0 S15 47.4		Alioth	166 20.6	N55 52.9
07	109 01.5	293 41.6	34.9	223 21.2	03.3	331 29.4	51.1	240 56.3	47.5	Alkaid	152 58.7	N49 14.6
T 08	124 04.0	308 41.2	33.7	238 21.8	03.6	346 31.4	51.0	255 58.5	47.5	Al Na'ir	27 42.3	S46 53.3
H 09	139 06.4	323 40.8 . .	32.5	253 22.5 . .	03.9	1 33.4 . .	50.8	271 00.8 . .	47.6	Alnilam	275 45.4	S 1 11.6
U 10	154 08.9	338 40.4	31.2	268 23.1	04.2	16 35.4	50.7	286 03.0	47.7	Alphard	217 55.5	S 8 43.3
R 11	169 11.4	353 40.0	30.0	283 23.7	04.5	31 37.4	50.6	301 05.2	47.7			
S 12	184 13.8	8 39.6 N 3 28.8		298 24.3 S23 04.8		46 39.5 N16 50.5		316 07.5 S15 47.8		Alphecca	126 10.5	N26 40.3
D 13	199 16.3	23 39.2	27.5	313 24.9	05.1	61 41.5	50.3	331 09.7	47.9	Alpheratz	357 42.2	N29 10.5
A 14	214 18.8	38 38.8	26.3	328 25.5	05.4	76 43.5	50.2	346 11.9	47.9	Altair	62 07.3	N 8 54.8
Y 15	229 21.2	53 38.4 . .	25.1	343 26.2 . .	05.7	91 45.5 . .	50.1	1 14.2 . .	48.0	Ankaa	353 14.5	S42 13.4
16	244 23.7	68 38.0	23.8	358 26.8	05.9	106 47.5	49.9	16 16.4	48.1	Antares	112 25.3	S26 27.7
17	259 26.2	83 37.6	22.6	13 27.4	06.2	121 49.5	49.8	31 18.6	48.1			
18	274 28.6	98 37.2 N 3 21.4		28 28.0 S23 06.5		136 51.5 N16 49.7		46 20.9 S15 48.2		Arcturus	145 55.2	N19 06.6
19	289 31.1	113 36.8	20.1	43 28.6	06.8	151 53.5	49.6	61 23.1	48.3	Atria	107 26.5	S69 03.3
20	304 33.5	128 36.4	18.9	58 29.2	07.1	166 55.5	49.4	76 25.3	48.4	Avior	234 17.9	S59 33.3
21	319 36.0	143 36.0 . .	17.7	73 29.8 . .	07.4	181 57.6 . .	49.3	91 27.6 . .	48.4	Bellatrix	278 31.0	N 6 21.7
22	334 38.5	158 35.6	16.4	88 30.5	07.7	196 59.6	49.2	106 29.8	48.5	Betelgeuse	271 00.3	N 7 24.5
23	349 40.9	173 35.2	15.2	103 31.1	08.0	212 01.6	49.1	121 32.0	48.6			
26 00	4 43.4	188 34.8 N 3 14.0		118 31.7 S23 08.2		227 03.6 N16 48.9		136 34.3 S15 48.6		Canopus	263 55.8	S52 42.1
01	19 45.9	203 34.4	12.7	133 32.3	08.5	242 05.6	48.8	151 36.5	48.7	Capella	280 33.0	N46 00.4
02	34 48.3	218 34.0	11.5	148 32.9	08.8	257 07.6	48.7	166 38.7	48.8	Deneb	49 30.6	N45 20.4
03	49 50.8	233 33.6 . .	10.3	163 33.5 . .	09.1	272 09.6 . .	48.5	181 41.0 . .	48.8	Denebola	182 33.1	N14 29.5
04	64 53.3	248 33.2	09.0	178 34.1	09.4	287 11.6	48.4	196 43.2	48.9	Diphda	348 54.7	S17 54.2
05	79 55.7	263 32.8	07.8	193 34.7	09.7	302 13.6	48.3	211 45.4	49.0			
06	94 58.2	278 32.4 N 3 06.6		208 35.4 S23 09.9		317 15.7 N16 48.2		226 47.7 S15 49.0		Dubhe	193 51.4	N61 40.2
07	110 00.6	293 32.0	05.3	223 36.0	10.2	332 17.7	48.0	241 49.9	49.1	Elnath	278 11.4	N28 37.0
F 08	125 03.1	308 31.6	04.1	238 36.6	10.5	347 19.7	47.9	256 52.1	49.2	Eltanin	90 45.8	N51 29.7
R 09	140 05.6	323 31.2 . .	02.9	253 37.2 . .	10.8	2 21.7 . .	47.8	271 54.4 . .	49.2	Enif	33 46.0	N 9 56.9
I 10	155 08.0	338 30.8	01.6	268 37.8	11.1	17 23.7	47.7	286 56.6	49.3	Fomalhaut	15 22.7	S29 32.5
11	170 10.5	353 30.4	3 00.4	283 38.4	11.4	32 25.7	47.5	301 58.8	49.4			
D 12	185 13.0	8 30.0 N 2 59.1		298 39.0 S23 11.6		47 27.7 N16 47.4		317 01.0 S15 49.5		Gacrux	172 00.4	S57 11.7
A 13	200 15.4	23 29.6	57.9	313 39.6	11.9	62 29.8	47.3	332 03.3	49.5	Gienah	175 51.7	S17 37.3
Y 14	215 17.9	38 29.2	56.7	328 40.2	12.2	77 31.8	47.2	347 05.5	49.6	Hadar	148 47.1	S60 26.6
15	230 20.4	53 28.8 . .	55.4	343 40.8 . .	12.5	92 33.8 . .	47.0	2 07.7 . .	49.7	Hamal	327 59.4	N23 31.9
16	245 22.8	68 28.4	54.2	358 41.4	12.8	107 35.8	46.9	17 10.0	49.7	Kaus Aust.	83 42.6	S34 22.5
17	260 25.3	83 28.0	53.0	13 42.0	13.0	122 37.8	46.8	32 12.2	49.8			
18	275 27.8	98 27.6 N 2 51.7		28 42.7 S23 13.3		137 39.8 N16 46.7		47 14.4 S15 49.9		Kochab	137 21.1	N74 06.0
19	290 30.2	113 27.2	50.5	43 43.3	13.6	152 41.8	46.5	62 16.7	49.9	Markab	13 37.1	N15 17.3
20	305 32.7	128 26.8	49.3	58 43.9	13.9	167 43.9	46.4	77 18.9	50.0	Menkar	314 13.9	N 4 08.9
21	320 35.1	143 26.5 . .	48.0	73 44.5 . .	14.2	182 45.9 . .	46.3	92 21.1 . .	50.1	Menkent	148 06.8	S36 26.4
22	335 37.6	158 26.1	46.8	88 45.1	14.4	197 47.9	46.1	107 23.4	50.1	Miaplacidus	221 40.0	S69 46.5
23	350 40.1	173 25.7	45.5	103 45.7	14.7	212 49.9	46.0	122 25.6	50.2			
27 00	5 42.5	188 25.3 N 2 44.3		118 46.3 S23 15.0		227 51.9 N16 45.9		137 27.8 S15 50.3		Mirfak	308 38.7	N49 54.6
01	20 45.0	203 24.9	43.1	133 46.9	15.3	242 53.9	45.8	152 30.0	50.4	Nunki	75 57.2	S26 16.5
02	35 47.5	218 24.5	41.8	148 47.5	15.6	257 55.9	45.6	167 32.3	50.4	Peacock	53 17.6	S56 41.2
03	50 49.9	233 24.1 . .	40.6	163 48.1 . .	15.8	272 58.0 . .	45.5	182 34.5 . .	50.5	Pollux	243 26.8	N27 59.2
04	65 52.4	248 23.7	39.3	178 48.7	16.1	288 00.0	45.4	197 36.7	50.6	Procyon	244 58.9	N 5 11.1
05	80 54.9	263 23.3	38.1	193 49.3	16.4	303 02.0	45.3	212 39.0	50.6			
06	95 57.3	278 22.9 N 2 36.9		208 49.9 S23 16.7		318 04.0 N16 45.1		227 41.2 S15 50.7		Rasalhague	96 05.7	N12 33.3
07	110 59.8	293 22.5	35.6	223 50.5	16.9	333 06.0	45.0	242 43.4	50.8	Regulus	207 42.9	N11 53.7
S 08	126 02.3	308 22.1	34.4	238 51.1	17.2	348 08.0	44.9	257 45.7	50.8	Rigel	281 11.1	S 8 11.1
A 09	141 04.7	323 21.7 . .	33.2	253 51.7 . .	17.5	3 10.1 . .	44.8	272 47.9 . .	50.9	Rigil Kent.	139 51.0	S60 53.7
T 10	156 07.2	338 21.3	31.9	268 52.3	17.8	18 12.1	44.6	287 50.1	51.0	Sabik	102 11.6	S15 44.3
U 11	171 09.6	353 20.9	30.7	283 52.9	18.0	33 14.1	44.5	302 52.3	51.0			
R 12	186 12.1	8 20.5 N 2 29.4		298 53.5 S23 18.3		48 16.1 N16 44.4		317 54.6 S15 51.1		Schedar	349 38.9	N56 37.1
D 13	201 14.6	23 20.1	28.2	313 54.1	18.6	63 18.1	44.3	332 56.8	51.2	Shaula	96 20.8	S37 06.7
A 14	216 17.0	38 19.7	27.0	328 54.7	18.9	78 20.1	44.1	347 59.0	51.3	Sirius	258 33.0	S16 44.2
Y 15	231 19.5	53 19.3 . .	25.7	343 55.3 . .	19.1	93 22.2 . .	44.0	3 01.3 . .	51.3	Spica	158 30.6	S11 14.1
16	246 22.0	68 18.9	24.5	358 55.9	19.4	108 24.2	43.9	18 03.5	51.4	Suhail	222 52.1	S43 29.4
17	261 24.4	83 18.5	23.2	13 56.5	19.7	123 26.2	43.8	33 05.7	51.5			
18	276 26.9	98 18.1 N 2 22.0		28 57.1 S23 19.9		138 28.2 N16 43.6		48 08.0 S15 51.5		Vega	80 38.3	N38 48.3
19	291 29.4	113 17.7	20.7	43 57.7	20.2	153 30.2	43.5	63 10.2	51.6	Zuben'ubi	137 04.7	S16 06.0
20	306 31.8	128 17.4	19.5	58 58.3	20.5	168 32.3	43.4	78 12.4	51.7		SHA	Mer.Pass.
21	321 34.3	143 17.0 . .	18.3	73 58.9 . .	20.8	183 34.3 . .	43.3	93 14.6 . .	51.7		° ′	h m
22	336 36.7	158 16.6	17.0	88 59.5	21.0	198 36.3	43.1	108 16.9	51.8	Venus	183 51.4	11 26
23	351 39.2	173 16.2	15.8	104 00.1	21.3	213 38.3	43.0	123 19.1	51.9	Mars	113 48.3	16 05
	h m									Jupiter	222 20.2	8 51
Mer.Pass. 23 37.2		v −0.4	d 1.2	v 0.6	d 0.3	v 2.0	d 0.1	v 2.2	d 0.1	Saturn	131 50.9	14 52

SUN / MOON

UT	SUN GHA	SUN Dec	MOON GHA	v	MOON Dec	d	HP
d h	° ′	° ′	° ′	′	° ′	′	′
25 00	182 02.1	S 0 44.3	174 44.0	14.1	S 4 47.2	9.4	55.0
01	197 02.3	45.3	189 17.1	14.1	4 56.6	9.5	55.0
02	212 02.6	46.3	203 50.2	14.0	5 06.1	9.4	55.0
03	227 02.8	.. 47.2	218 23.2	14.1	5 15.5	9.4	55.0
04	242 03.0	48.2	232 56.3	14.0	5 24.9	9.4	55.0
05	257 03.2	49.2	247 29.3	13.9	5 34.3	9.3	55.1
T 06	272 03.4	S 0 50.2	262 02.2	13.9	S 5 43.6	9.4	55.1
H 07	287 03.6	51.1	276 35.1	13.9	5 53.0	9.3	55.1
U 08	302 03.8	52.1	291 08.0	13.9	6 02.3	9.3	55.1
R 09	317 04.1	.. 53.1	305 40.9	13.8	6 11.6	9.3	55.1
S 10	332 04.3	54.1	320 13.7	13.8	6 20.9	9.2	55.1
D 11	347 04.5	55.0	334 46.5	13.8	6 30.1	9.3	55.2
A 12	2 04.7	S 0 56.0	349 19.3	13.7	S 6 39.4	9.2	55.2
Y 13	17 04.9	57.0	3 52.0	13.7	6 48.6	9.1	55.2
14	32 05.1	58.0	18 24.7	13.6	6 57.7	9.2	55.2
15	47 05.3	.. 58.9	32 57.3	13.6	7 06.9	9.1	55.2
16	62 05.6	0 59.9	47 29.9	13.6	7 16.0	9.1	55.2
17	77 05.8	1 00.9	62 02.5	13.5	7 25.1	9.1	55.3
18	92 06.0	S 1 01.8	76 35.0	13.5	S 7 34.2	9.1	55.3
19	107 06.2	02.8	91 07.5	13.5	7 43.3	9.0	55.3
20	122 06.4	03.8	105 40.0	13.4	7 52.3	9.0	55.3
21	137 06.6	.. 04.8	120 12.4	13.3	8 01.3	8.9	55.3
22	152 06.9	05.7	134 44.7	13.4	8 10.2	8.9	55.4
23	167 07.1	06.7	149 17.1	13.3	8 19.1	8.9	55.4
26 00	182 07.3	S 1 07.7	163 49.4	13.2	S 8 28.0	8.9	55.4
01	197 07.5	08.7	178 21.6	13.2	8 36.9	8.8	55.4
02	212 07.7	09.6	192 53.8	13.2	8 45.7	8.8	55.4
03	227 07.9	.. 10.6	207 26.0	13.1	8 54.5	8.7	55.4
04	242 08.1	11.6	221 58.1	13.1	9 03.2	8.8	55.5
05	257 08.4	12.6	236 30.2	13.1	9 12.0	8.6	55.5
F 06	272 08.6	S 1 13.5	251 02.3	13.0	S 9 20.6	8.7	55.5
R 07	287 08.8	14.5	265 34.3	12.9	9 29.3	8.6	55.5
I 08	302 09.0	15.5	280 06.2	12.9	9 37.9	8.5	55.5
D 09	317 09.2	.. 16.5	294 38.1	12.9	9 46.4	8.6	55.6
A 10	332 09.4	17.4	309 10.0	12.8	9 55.0	8.4	55.6
Y 11	347 09.6	18.4	323 41.8	12.8	10 03.4	8.5	55.6
12	2 09.8	S 1 19.4	338 13.6	12.7	S10 11.9	8.4	55.6
13	17 10.1	20.3	352 45.3	12.7	10 20.3	8.3	55.6
14	32 10.3	21.3	7 17.0	12.6	10 28.6	8.3	55.7
15	47 10.5	.. 22.3	21 48.6	12.6	10 36.9	8.3	55.7
16	62 10.7	23.3	36 20.2	12.5	10 45.2	8.2	55.7
17	77 10.9	24.2	50 51.7	12.5	10 53.4	8.2	55.7
18	92 11.1	S 1 25.2	65 23.2	12.5	S11 01.6	8.1	55.7
19	107 11.3	26.2	79 54.7	12.4	11 09.7	8.1	55.7
20	122 11.5	27.2	94 26.1	12.3	11 17.8	8.0	55.8
21	137 11.8	.. 28.1	108 57.4	12.3	11 25.8	8.0	55.8
22	152 12.0	29.1	123 28.7	12.2	11 33.8	7.9	55.8
23	167 12.2	30.1	137 59.9	12.2	11 41.7	7.9	55.8
27 00	182 12.4	S 1 31.1	152 31.1	12.2	S11 49.6	7.8	55.8
01	197 12.6	32.0	167 02.3	12.1	11 57.4	7.8	55.9
02	212 12.8	33.0	181 33.4	12.0	12 05.2	7.7	55.9
03	227 13.0	.. 34.0	196 04.4	12.0	12 12.9	7.6	55.9
04	242 13.2	34.9	210 35.4	12.0	12 20.5	7.6	55.9
05	257 13.5	35.9	225 06.4	11.9	12 28.1	7.6	55.9
S 06	272 13.7	S 1 36.9	239 37.3	11.8	S12 35.7	7.5	56.0
A 07	287 13.9	37.9	254 08.1	11.8	12 43.2	7.4	56.0
T 08	302 14.1	38.8	268 38.9	11.7	12 50.6	7.4	56.0
U 09	317 14.3	.. 39.8	283 09.6	11.7	12 58.0	7.3	56.0
R 10	332 14.5	40.8	297 40.3	11.6	13 05.3	7.3	56.1
D 11	347 14.7	41.8	312 10.9	11.6	13 12.6	7.2	56.1
A 12	2 14.9	S 1 42.7	326 41.5	11.5	S13 19.8	7.1	56.1
Y 13	17 15.2	43.7	341 12.0	11.5	13 26.9	7.1	56.1
14	32 15.4	44.7	355 42.5	11.4	13 34.0	7.0	56.1
15	47 15.6	.. 45.7	10 12.9	11.4	13 41.0	6.9	56.2
16	62 15.8	46.6	24 43.3	11.3	13 47.9	6.9	56.2
17	77 16.0	47.6	39 13.6	11.3	13 54.8	6.8	56.2
18	92 16.2	S 1 48.6	53 43.9	11.2	S14 01.6	6.7	56.2
19	107 16.4	49.5	68 14.1	11.1	14 08.3	6.7	56.2
20	122 16.6	50.5	82 44.2	11.1	14 15.0	6.6	56.3
21	137 16.8	.. 51.5	97 14.3	11.1	14 21.6	6.6	56.3
22	152 17.0	52.5	111 44.4	11.0	14 28.2	6.4	56.3
23	167 17.3	53.4	126 14.4	10.9	S14 34.6	6.4	56.3
	SD 16.0	d 1.0	SD 15.0		15.2		15.3

Twilight / Sunrise / Moonrise

Lat.	Naut.	Civil	Sunrise	25	26	27	28
°	h m	h m	h m	h m	h m	h m	h m
N 72	03 21	04 48	05 56	07 52	09 33	11 20	13 15
N 70	03 38	04 54	05 55	07 43	09 17	10 53	12 31
68	03 50	04 59	05 55	07 36	09 04	10 33	12 02
66	04 01	05 03	05 54	07 30	08 53	10 18	11 41
64	04 09	05 06	05 54	07 25	08 44	10 05	11 24
62	04 16	05 09	05 54	07 20	08 37	09 54	11 09
60	04 22	05 12	05 53	07 16	08 30	09 45	10 58
N 58	04 27	05 14	05 53	07 13	08 25	09 37	10 47
56	04 32	05 16	05 53	07 10	08 20	09 29	10 38
54	04 36	05 17	05 53	07 07	08 15	09 23	10 30
52	04 39	05 19	05 52	07 05	08 11	09 17	10 23
50	04 42	05 20	05 52	07 03	08 07	09 12	10 17
45	04 48	05 22	05 52	06 58	07 59	09 01	10 03
N 40	04 53	05 24	05 51	06 54	07 53	08 52	09 52
35	04 56	05 26	05 51	06 50	07 47	08 44	09 43
30	04 59	05 27	05 51	06 47	07 42	08 38	09 34
20	05 02	05 28	05 50	06 42	07 33	08 26	09 20
N 10	05 04	05 28	05 49	06 38	07 26	08 16	09 07
0	05 03	05 27	05 48	06 33	07 19	08 06	08 56
S 10	05 02	05 26	05 47	06 29	07 12	07 57	08 44
20	04 59	05 24	05 46	06 25	07 04	07 46	08 32
30	04 53	05 21	05 45	06 20	06 56	07 35	08 17
35	04 49	05 19	05 44	06 17	06 51	07 28	08 09
40	04 44	05 16	05 43	06 13	06 46	07 21	08 00
45	04 38	05 13	05 42	06 10	06 39	07 12	07 49
S 50	04 30	05 08	05 40	06 05	06 32	07 02	07 36
52	04 26	05 06	05 40	06 03	06 28	06 57	07 30
54	04 21	05 04	05 39	06 01	06 25	06 52	07 24
56	04 16	05 01	05 38	05 58	06 20	06 46	07 16
58	04 11	04 58	05 37	05 56	06 16	06 39	07 08
S 60	04 04	04 55	05 36	05 53	06 11	06 32	06 58

Sunset / Twilight / Moonset

Lat.	Sunset	Civil	Naut.	25	26	27	28
°	h m	h m	h m	h m	h m	h m	h m
N 72	17 45	18 52	20 17	17 16	17 10	17 02	16 51
N 70	17 45	18 46	20 02	17 27	17 27	17 30	17 35
68	17 46	18 41	19 49	17 36	17 42	17 51	18 05
66	17 47	18 38	19 39	17 43	17 53	18 07	18 27
64	17 47	18 34	19 31	17 49	18 03	18 21	18 45
62	17 48	18 32	19 24	17 55	18 12	18 32	18 59
60	17 48	18 29	19 19	18 00	18 19	18 42	19 12
N 58	17 48	18 27	19 14	18 04	18 25	18 51	19 22
56	17 49	18 26	19 09	18 08	18 31	18 58	19 32
54	17 49	18 24	19 06	18 11	18 36	19 05	19 40
52	17 49	18 23	19 02	18 14	18 41	19 11	19 47
50	17 50	18 22	19 00	18 17	18 45	19 17	19 54
45	17 50	18 20	18 54	18 23	18 54	19 29	20 08
N 40	17 51	18 18	18 49	18 28	19 02	19 39	20 20
35	17 51	18 17	18 46	18 33	19 08	19 47	20 30
30	17 52	18 16	18 43	18 36	19 14	19 55	20 39
20	17 53	18 15	18 40	18 43	19 24	20 08	20 54
N 10	17 54	18 15	18 39	18 49	19 33	20 19	21 08
0	17 55	18 15	18 39	18 55	19 41	20 30	21 20
S 10	17 56	18 17	18 41	19 01	19 50	20 40	21 33
20	17 57	18 19	18 45	19 07	19 58	20 52	21 46
30	17 58	18 22	18 50	19 13	20 09	21 05	22 01
35	17 59	18 25	18 54	19 17	20 14	21 12	22 10
40	18 00	18 28	18 59	19 22	20 21	21 21	22 21
45	18 02	18 31	19 06	19 27	20 29	21 31	22 32
S 50	18 03	18 36	19 14	19 33	20 38	21 43	22 47
52	18 04	18 38	19 18	19 36	20 43	21 49	22 54
54	18 05	18 40	19 23	19 40	20 47	21 55	23 01
56	18 06	18 43	19 28	19 43	20 53	22 02	23 10
58	18 07	18 46	19 34	19 47	20 59	22 10	23 19
S 60	18 08	18 50	19 41	19 51	21 05	22 19	23 30

SUN / MOON

Day	Eqn. of Time 00h	Eqn. of Time 12h	Mer. Pass.	Mer. Pass. Upper	Mer. Pass. Lower	Age	Phase
d	m s	m s	h m	h m	h m	d	%
25	08 08	08 18	11 52	12 44	00 22	01	1
26	08 29	08 39	11 51	13 30	01 07	02	5
27	08 49	08 59	11 51	14 18	01 54	03	10

UT	ARIES GHA	VENUS −3.9 GHA	Dec	MARS +0.8 GHA	Dec	JUPITER −1.9 GHA	Dec	SATURN +0.6 GHA	Dec	STARS Name	SHA	Dec
d h	° ′	° ′	° ′	° ′	° ′	° ′	° ′	° ′	° ′		° ′	° ′
28 00	6 41.7	188 15.8	N 2 14.5	119 00.7	S23 21.6	228 40.3	N16 42.9	138 21.3	S15 51.9	Acamar	315 17.4	S40 14.6
01	21 44.1	203 15.4	13.3	134 01.3	21.8	243 42.3	42.8	153 23.6	52.0	Achernar	335 25.7	S57 09.6
02	36 46.6	218 15.0	12.1	149 01.9	22.1	258 44.4	42.6	168 25.8	52.1	Acrux	173 08.9	S63 10.8
03	51 49.1	233 14.6	.. 10.8	164 02.5	.. 22.4	273 46.4	.. 42.5	183 28.0	.. 52.2	Adhara	255 11.9	S28 59.4
04	66 51.5	248 14.2	09.6	179 03.1	22.6	288 48.4	42.4	198 30.2	52.2	Aldebaran	290 48.2	N16 32.2
05	81 54.0	263 13.8	08.3	194 03.7	22.9	303 50.4	42.3	213 32.5	52.3			
06	96 56.5	278 13.4	N 2 07.1	209 04.3	S23 23.2	318 52.4	N16 42.1	228 34.7	S15 52.4	Alioth	166 20.6	N55 52.9
07	111 58.9	293 13.0	05.8	224 04.9	23.5	333 54.5	42.0	243 36.9	52.4	Alkaid	152 58.7	N49 14.6
08	127 01.4	308 12.6	04.6	239 05.4	23.7	348 56.5	41.9	258 39.1	52.5	Al Na'ir	27 42.3	S46 53.3
S 09	142 03.9	323 12.2	.. 03.4	254 06.0	.. 24.0	3 58.5	.. 41.8	273 41.4	.. 52.6	Alnilam	275 45.4	S 1 11.6
U 10	157 06.3	338 11.8	02.1	269 06.6	24.3	19 00.5	41.6	288 43.6	52.6	Alphard	217 55.4	S 8 43.3
N 11	172 08.8	353 11.4	2 00.9	284 07.2	24.5	34 02.5	41.5	303 45.8	52.7			
D 12	187 11.2	8 11.0	N 1 59.6	299 07.8	S23 24.8	49 04.6	N16 41.4	318 48.1	S15 52.8	Alphecca	126 10.5	N26 40.3
A 13	202 13.7	23 10.7	58.4	314 08.4	25.0	64 06.6	41.3	333 50.3	52.9	Alpheratz	357 42.2	N29 10.5
Y 14	217 16.2	38 10.3	57.1	329 09.0	25.3	79 08.6	41.1	348 52.5	52.9	Altair	62 07.3	N 8 54.8
15	232 18.6	53 09.9	.. 55.9	344 09.6	.. 25.6	94 10.6	.. 41.0	3 54.7	.. 53.0	Ankaa	353 14.5	S42 13.4
16	247 21.1	68 09.5	54.7	359 10.2	25.8	109 12.7	40.9	18 57.0	53.1	Antares	112 25.3	S26 27.7
17	262 23.6	83 09.1	53.4	14 10.8	26.1	124 14.7	40.8	33 59.2	53.1			
18	277 26.0	98 08.7	N 1 52.2	29 11.4	S23 26.4	139 16.7	N16 40.6	49 01.4	S15 53.2	Arcturus	145 55.3	N19 06.6
19	292 28.5	113 08.3	50.9	44 12.0	26.6	154 18.7	40.5	64 03.6	53.3	Atria	107 26.5	S69 03.3
20	307 31.0	128 07.9	49.7	59 12.5	26.9	169 20.7	40.4	79 05.9	53.3	Avior	234 17.9	S59 33.3
21	322 33.4	143 07.5	.. 48.4	74 13.1	.. 27.2	184 22.8	.. 40.3	94 08.1	.. 53.4	Bellatrix	278 31.0	N 6 21.7
22	337 35.9	158 07.1	47.2	89 13.7	27.4	199 24.8	40.1	109 10.3	53.5	Betelgeuse	271 00.3	N 7 24.5
23	352 38.3	173 06.7	45.9	104 14.3	27.7	214 26.8	40.0	124 12.5	53.6			
29 00	7 40.8	188 06.3	N 1 44.7	119 14.9	S23 27.9	229 28.8	N16 39.9	139 14.8	S15 53.6	Canopus	263 55.7	S52 42.1
01	22 43.3	203 05.9	43.4	134 15.5	28.2	244 30.9	39.8	154 17.0	53.7	Capella	280 33.0	N46 00.4
02	37 45.7	218 05.5	42.2	149 16.1	28.5	259 32.9	39.6	169 19.2	53.8	Deneb	49 30.6	N45 20.4
03	52 48.2	233 05.1	.. 41.0	164 16.7	.. 28.7	274 34.9	.. 39.5	184 21.4	.. 53.8	Denebola	182 33.1	N14 29.5
04	67 50.7	248 04.8	39.7	179 17.2	29.0	289 36.9	39.4	199 23.7	53.9	Diphda	348 54.7	S17 54.2
05	82 53.1	263 04.4	38.5	194 17.8	29.3	304 39.0	39.3	214 25.9	54.0			
06	97 55.6	278 04.0	N 1 37.2	209 18.4	S23 29.5	319 41.0	N16 39.1	229 28.1	S15 54.0	Dubhe	193 51.4	N61 40.2
07	112 58.1	293 03.6	36.0	224 19.0	29.8	334 43.0	39.0	244 30.3	54.1	Elnath	278 11.4	N28 37.0
08	128 00.5	308 03.2	34.7	239 19.6	30.0	349 45.0	38.9	259 32.6	54.2	Eltanin	90 45.8	N51 29.7
M 09	143 03.0	323 02.8	.. 33.5	254 20.2	.. 30.3	4 47.1	.. 38.8	274 34.8	.. 54.3	Enif	33 46.0	N 9 56.9
O 10	158 05.5	338 02.4	32.2	269 20.8	30.5	19 49.1	38.6	289 37.0	54.3	Fomalhaut	15 22.7	S29 32.5
N 11	173 07.9	353 02.0	31.0	284 21.3	30.8	34 51.1	38.5	304 39.2	54.4			
D 12	188 10.4	8 01.6	N 1 29.7	299 21.9	S23 31.1	49 53.1	N16 38.4	319 41.5	S15 54.5	Gacrux	172 00.4	S57 11.7
A 13	203 12.8	23 01.2	28.5	314 22.5	31.3	64 55.1	38.3	334 43.7	54.5	Gienah	175 51.7	S17 37.3
Y 14	218 15.3	38 00.8	27.2	329 23.1	31.6	79 57.2	38.1	349 45.9	54.6	Hadar	148 47.1	S60 26.6
15	233 17.8	53 00.4	.. 26.0	344 23.7	.. 31.8	94 59.2	.. 38.0	4 48.1	.. 54.7	Hamal	327 59.4	N23 31.9
16	248 20.2	68 00.0	24.8	359 24.3	32.1	110 01.2	37.9	19 50.4	54.7	Kaus Aust.	83 42.7	S34 22.5
17	263 22.7	82 59.7	23.5	14 24.9	32.3	125 03.3	37.8	34 52.6	54.8			
18	278 25.2	97 59.3	N 1 22.3	29 25.4	S23 32.6	140 05.3	N16 37.7	49 54.8	S15 54.9	Kochab	137 21.1	N74 06.0
19	293 27.6	112 58.9	21.0	44 26.0	32.9	155 07.3	37.5	64 57.0	55.0	Markab	13 37.1	N15 17.3
20	308 30.1	127 58.5	19.8	59 26.6	33.1	170 09.3	37.4	79 59.3	55.0	Menkar	314 13.9	N 4 08.9
21	323 32.6	142 58.1	.. 18.5	74 27.2	.. 33.4	185 11.4	.. 37.3	95 01.5	.. 55.1	Menkent	148 06.8	S36 26.4
22	338 35.0	157 57.7	17.3	89 27.8	33.6	200 13.4	37.2	110 03.7	55.2	Miaplacidus	221 40.0	S69 46.5
23	353 37.5	172 57.3	16.0	104 28.3	33.9	215 15.4	37.0	125 05.9	55.2			
30 00	8 40.0	187 56.9	N 1 14.8	119 28.9	S23 34.1	230 17.4	N16 36.9	140 08.2	S15 55.3	Mirfak	308 38.7	N49 54.6
01	23 42.4	202 56.5	13.5	134 29.5	34.4	245 19.5	36.8	155 10.4	55.4	Nunki	75 57.2	S26 16.5
02	38 44.9	217 56.1	12.3	149 30.1	34.6	260 21.5	36.7	170 12.6	55.4	Peacock	53 17.6	S56 41.2
03	53 47.3	232 55.7	.. 11.0	164 30.7	.. 34.9	275 23.5	.. 36.5	185 14.8	.. 55.5	Pollux	243 26.8	N27 59.2
04	68 49.8	247 55.3	09.8	179 31.2	35.1	290 25.5	36.4	200 17.0	55.6	Procyon	244 58.9	N 5 11.1
05	83 52.3	262 54.9	08.5	194 31.8	35.3	305 27.6	36.3	215 19.3	55.7			
06	98 54.7	277 54.6	N 1 07.3	209 32.4	S23 35.6	320 29.6	N16 36.2	230 21.5	S15 55.7	Rasalhague	96 05.7	N12 33.3
07	113 57.2	292 54.2	06.0	224 33.0	35.9	335 31.6	36.0	245 23.7	55.8	Regulus	207 42.9	N11 53.7
08	128 59.7	307 53.8	04.8	239 33.6	36.1	350 33.7	35.9	260 25.9	55.9	Rigel	281 11.1	S 8 11.1
T 09	144 02.1	322 53.4	.. 03.5	254 34.1	.. 36.4	5 35.7	.. 35.8	275 28.2	.. 55.9	Rigil Kent.	139 51.0	S60 53.7
U 10	159 04.6	337 53.0	02.3	269 34.7	36.6	20 37.7	35.7	290 30.4	56.0	Sabik	102 11.6	S15 44.3
E 11	174 07.1	352 52.6	1 01.0	284 35.3	36.9	35 39.7	35.6	305 32.6	56.1			
S 12	189 09.5	7 52.2	N 0 59.8	299 35.9	S23 37.1	50 41.8	N16 35.4	320 34.8	S15 56.2	Schedar	349 38.8	N56 37.2
D 13	204 12.0	22 51.8	58.5	314 36.4	37.4	65 43.8	35.3	335 37.1	56.2	Shaula	96 20.8	S37 06.7
A 14	219 14.5	37 51.4	57.3	329 37.0	37.6	80 45.8	35.2	350 39.3	56.3	Sirius	258 33.0	S16 44.2
Y 15	234 16.9	52 51.0	.. 56.0	344 37.6	.. 37.9	95 47.9	.. 35.1	5 41.5	.. 56.4	Spica	158 30.6	S11 14.1
16	249 19.4	67 50.6	54.8	359 38.2	38.1	110 49.9	34.9	20 43.7	56.4	Suhail	222 52.0	S43 29.4
17	264 21.8	82 50.2	53.5	14 38.7	38.4	125 51.9	34.8	35 45.9	56.5			
18	279 24.3	97 49.9	N 0 52.3	29 39.3	S23 38.6	140 54.0	N16 34.7	50 48.2	S15 56.6	Vega	80 38.3	N38 48.3
19	294 26.8	112 49.5	51.0	44 39.9	38.9	155 56.0	34.6	65 50.4	56.6	Zuben'ubi	137 04.7	S16 06.0
20	309 29.2	127 49.1	49.8	59 40.5	39.1	170 58.0	34.4	80 52.6	56.7		SHA	Mer. Pass.
21	324 31.7	142 48.7	.. 48.5	74 41.0	.. 39.4	186 00.0	.. 34.3	95 54.8	.. 56.8		° ′	h m
22	339 34.2	157 48.3	47.3	89 41.6	39.6	201 02.1	34.2	110 57.0	56.9	Venus	180 25.5	11 28
23	354 36.6	172 47.9	46.0	104 42.2	39.9	216 04.1	34.1	125 59.3	56.9	Mars	111 34.1	16 02
	h m									Jupiter	221 48.0	8 41
Mer. Pass.	23 25.4	v −0.4 d 1.2		v 0.6 d 0.3		v 2.0 d 0.1		v 2.2 d 0.1		Saturn	131 34.0	14 41

UT	SUN GHA	SUN Dec	MOON GHA	v	Dec	d	HP
d h	° ′	° ′	° ′	′	° ′	′	′
28 00	182 17.5	S 1 54.4	140 44.3	10.9	S14 41.0	6.4	56.3
01	197 17.7	55.4	155 14.2	10.8	14 47.4	6.2	56.4
02	212 17.9	56.4	169 44.0	10.8	14 53.6	6.2	56.4
03	227 18.1	.. 57.3	184 13.8	10.7	14 59.8	6.1	56.4
04	242 18.3	58.3	198 43.5	10.7	15 05.9	6.1	56.4
05	257 18.5	1 59.3	213 13.2	10.6	15 12.0	5.9	56.5
06	272 18.7	S 2 00.2	227 42.8	10.5	S15 17.9	5.9	56.5
07	287 18.9	01.2	242 12.3	10.5	15 23.8	5.8	56.5
08	302 19.1	02.2	256 41.8	10.5	15 29.6	5.8	56.5
S 09	317 19.4	.. 03.2	271 11.3	10.4	15 35.4	5.6	56.5
U 10	332 19.6	04.1	285 40.7	10.3	15 41.0	5.6	56.6
N 11	347 19.8	05.1	300 10.0	10.3	15 46.6	5.5	56.6
D 12	2 20.0	S 2 06.1	314 39.3	10.2	S15 52.1	5.4	56.6
A 13	17 20.2	07.1	329 08.5	10.2	15 57.5	5.3	56.6
Y 14	32 20.4	08.0	343 37.7	10.1	16 02.8	5.3	56.7
15	47 20.6	.. 09.0	358 06.8	10.1	16 08.1	5.1	56.7
16	62 20.8	10.0	12 35.9	10.0	16 13.2	5.1	56.7
17	77 21.0	10.9	27 04.9	10.0	16 18.3	5.0	56.7
18	92 21.2	S 2 11.9	41 33.9	9.9	S16 23.3	4.9	56.8
19	107 21.4	12.9	56 02.8	9.8	16 28.2	4.9	56.8
20	122 21.7	13.9	70 31.6	9.8	16 33.1	4.7	56.8
21	137 21.9	.. 14.8	85 00.4	9.8	16 37.8	4.7	56.8
22	152 22.1	15.8	99 29.2	9.7	16 42.5	4.5	56.8
23	167 22.3	16.8	113 57.9	9.6	16 47.0	4.5	56.9
29 00	182 22.5	S 2 17.8	128 26.5	9.6	S16 51.5	4.4	56.9
01	197 22.7	18.7	142 55.1	9.5	16 55.9	4.3	56.9
02	212 22.9	19.7	157 23.6	9.5	17 00.2	4.2	56.9
03	227 23.1	.. 20.7	171 52.1	9.5	17 04.4	4.1	57.0
04	242 23.3	21.6	186 20.6	9.4	17 08.5	4.1	57.0
05	257 23.5	22.6	200 49.0	9.3	17 12.6	3.9	57.0
06	272 23.7	S 2 23.6	215 17.3	9.3	S17 16.5	3.8	57.0
07	287 23.9	24.6	229 45.6	9.2	17 20.3	3.8	57.1
08	302 24.1	25.5	244 13.8	9.2	17 24.1	3.6	57.1
M 09	317 24.4	.. 26.5	258 42.0	9.1	17 27.7	3.6	57.1
O 10	332 24.6	27.5	273 10.1	9.1	17 31.3	3.5	57.1
N 11	347 24.8	28.4	287 38.2	9.1	17 34.8	3.3	57.2
D 12	2 25.0	S 2 29.4	302 06.3	8.9	S17 38.1	3.3	57.2
A 13	17 25.2	30.4	316 34.2	9.0	17 41.4	3.2	57.2
Y 14	32 25.4	31.4	331 02.2	8.9	17 44.6	3.0	57.2
15	47 25.6	.. 32.3	345 30.1	8.8	17 47.6	3.0	57.3
16	62 25.8	33.3	359 57.9	8.8	17 50.6	2.9	57.3
17	77 26.0	34.3	14 25.7	8.8	17 53.5	2.8	57.3
18	92 26.2	S 2 35.2	28 53.5	8.7	S17 56.3	2.6	57.3
19	107 26.4	36.2	43 21.2	8.6	17 58.9	2.6	57.4
20	122 26.6	37.2	57 48.8	8.7	18 01.5	2.5	57.4
21	137 26.8	.. 38.2	72 16.5	8.5	18 04.0	2.3	57.4
22	152 27.0	39.1	86 44.0	8.6	18 06.3	2.3	57.4
23	167 27.2	40.1	101 11.6	8.5	18 08.6	2.2	57.5
30 00	182 27.5	S 2 41.1	115 39.1	8.4	S18 10.8	2.0	57.5
01	197 27.7	42.0	130 06.5	8.4	18 12.8	2.0	57.5
02	212 27.9	43.0	144 33.9	8.4	18 14.8	1.8	57.5
03	227 28.1	.. 44.0	159 01.3	8.3	18 16.6	1.8	57.6
04	242 28.3	45.0	173 28.6	8.2	18 18.4	1.6	57.6
05	257 28.5	45.9	187 55.8	8.3	18 20.0	1.5	57.6
06	272 28.7	S 2 46.9	202 23.1	8.2	S18 21.5	1.5	57.6
07	287 28.9	47.9	216 50.3	8.1	18 23.0	1.3	57.7
08	302 29.1	48.8	231 17.4	8.2	18 24.3	1.2	57.7
T 09	317 29.3	.. 49.8	245 44.6	8.0	18 25.5	1.1	57.7
U 10	332 29.5	50.8	260 11.6	8.1	18 26.6	1.0	57.7
E 11	347 29.7	51.7	274 38.7	8.0	18 27.6	0.9	57.8
S 12	2 29.9	S 2 52.7	289 05.7	8.0	S18 28.5	0.7	57.8
D 13	17 30.1	53.7	303 32.7	7.9	18 29.2	0.7	57.8
A 14	32 30.3	54.7	317 59.6	7.9	18 29.9	0.6	57.8
Y 15	47 30.5	.. 55.6	332 26.5	7.9	18 30.5	0.4	57.9
16	62 30.7	56.6	346 53.4	7.8	18 30.9	0.3	57.9
17	77 30.9	57.6	1 20.2	7.8	18 31.2	0.3	57.9
18	92 31.1	S 2 58.5	15 47.0	7.8	S18 31.5	0.1	57.9
19	107 31.3	2 59.5	30 13.8	7.7	18 31.6	0.1	58.0
20	122 31.5	3 00.5	44 40.5	7.7	18 31.6	0.2	58.0
21	137 31.7	.. 01.5	59 07.2	7.7	18 31.4	0.2	58.0
22	152 31.9	02.4	73 33.9	7.6	18 31.2	0.3	58.1
23	167 32.1	03.4	88 00.5	7.7	S18 30.9	0.5	58.1
	SD 16.0	d 1.0	SD 15.4		15.6		15.7

Lat.	Naut.	Civil	Sunrise	Moonrise 28	29	30	1
°	h m	h m	h m	h m	h m	h m	h m
N 72	03 38	05 02	06 09	13 15	15 43	■	■
N 70	03 52	05 06	06 07	12 31	14 06	15 23	16 07
68	04 03	05 10	06 05	12 02	13 26	14 36	15 24
66	04 11	05 13	06 04	11 41	12 59	14 05	14 56
64	04 19	05 15	06 02	11 24	12 38	13 42	14 34
62	04 25	05 17	06 01	11 09	12 21	13 24	14 16
60	04 30	05 19	06 00	10 58	12 07	13 09	14 02
N 58	04 34	05 20	05 59	10 47	11 55	12 56	13 50
56	04 38	05 22	05 59	10 38	11 44	12 45	13 39
54	04 41	05 23	05 58	10 30	11 35	12 36	13 29
52	04 44	05 24	05 57	10 23	11 27	12 27	13 21
50	04 47	05 24	05 57	10 17	11 20	12 19	13 13
45	04 52	05 26	05 55	10 03	11 04	12 03	12 57
N 40	04 56	05 27	05 54	09 52	10 52	11 49	12 44
35	04 58	05 28	05 53	09 43	10 41	11 38	12 32
30	05 00	05 28	05 52	09 34	10 31	11 28	12 22
20	05 03	05 28	05 50	09 20	10 15	11 10	12 05
N 10	05 03	05 28	05 49	09 07	10 01	10 55	11 51
0	05 02	05 26	05 47	08 56	09 47	10 41	11 37
S 10	05 00	05 24	05 45	08 44	09 34	10 27	11 23
20	04 56	05 21	05 43	08 32	09 20	10 12	11 08
30	04 49	05 17	05 41	08 17	09 04	09 55	10 51
35	04 45	05 14	05 40	08 09	08 55	09 45	10 41
40	04 39	05 11	05 38	08 00	08 44	09 34	10 30
45	04 32	05 07	05 36	07 49	08 32	09 21	10 17
S 50	04 23	05 01	05 34	07 36	08 17	09 05	10 01
52	04 18	04 59	05 33	07 30	08 10	08 57	09 53
54	04 13	04 56	05 32	07 24	08 02	08 49	09 45
56	04 08	04 53	05 30	07 16	07 53	08 39	09 35
58	04 01	04 49	05 29	07 08	07 43	08 28	09 24
S 60	03 54	04 45	05 27	06 58	07 32	08 16	09 12

Lat.	Sunset	Civil	Naut.	Moonset 28	29	30	1
°	h m	h m	h m	h m	h m	h m	h m
N 72	17 29	18 36	19 59	16 51	16 12	■	■
N 70	17 32	18 32	19 46	17 35	17 50	18 25	19 38
68	17 34	18 29	19 35	18 05	18 30	19 13	20 21
66	17 35	18 26	19 27	18 27	18 57	19 43	20 48
64	17 37	18 24	19 20	18 45	19 19	20 06	21 10
62	17 38	18 22	19 14	18 59	19 34	20 24	21 27
60	17 39	18 20	19 09	19 12	19 50	20 39	21 42
N 58	17 40	18 19	19 05	19 22	20 02	20 52	21 54
56	17 41	18 18	19 01	19 32	20 13	21 03	22 04
54	17 42	18 17	18 58	19 40	20 22	21 13	22 14
52	17 42	18 16	18 55	19 47	20 30	21 22	22 22
50	17 43	18 15	18 53	19 54	20 38	21 29	22 29
45	17 45	18 14	18 48	20 08	20 54	21 46	22 45
N 40	17 46	18 13	18 44	20 20	21 07	22 00	22 58
35	17 47	18 12	18 42	20 30	21 18	22 11	23 09
30	17 48	18 12	18 40	20 39	21 28	22 21	23 19
20	17 50	18 12	18 38	20 54	21 45	22 39	23 36
N 10	17 52	18 13	18 37	21 08	21 59	22 54	23 50
0	17 54	18 14	18 38	21 20	22 13	23 08	24 04
S 10	17 55	18 16	18 41	21 33	22 27	23 22	24 17
20	17 58	18 20	18 45	21 46	22 41	23 37	24 31
30	18 00	18 24	18 52	22 01	22 58	23 54	24 48
35	18 02	18 27	18 57	22 10	23 08	24 04	00 04
40	18 03	18 30	19 02	22 21	23 19	24 15	00 15
45	18 05	18 35	19 10	22 32	23 32	24 29	00 29
S 50	18 08	18 40	19 19	22 47	23 48	24 45	00 45
52	18 09	18 43	19 24	22 54	23 56	24 53	00 53
54	18 10	18 46	19 29	23 01	24 04	00 04	01 01
56	18 12	18 49	19 35	23 10	24 13	00 13	01 11
58	18 13	18 53	19 41	23 19	24 24	00 24	01 21
S 60	18 15	18 57	19 49	23 30	24 36	00 36	01 34

Day	SUN Eqn. of Time 00ʰ	12ʰ	Mer. Pass.	MOON Mer. Pass. Upper	Lower	Age	Phase
	m s	m s	h m	h m	h m	d	%
28	09 09	09 20	11 51	15 08	02 42	04	17
29	09 30	09 39	11 50	16 00	03 34	05	26
30	09 49	09 59	11 50	16 54	04 27	06	36

UT	ARIES GHA	VENUS −3.9 GHA	Dec	MARS +0.8 GHA	Dec	JUPITER −1.9 GHA	Dec	SATURN +0.6 GHA	Dec	STARS Name	SHA	Dec
1 00	9 39.1	187 47.5	N 0 44.8	119 42.8	S23 40.1	231 06.1	N16 34.0	141 01.5	S15 57.0	Acamar	315 17.4	S40 14.6
01	24 41.6	202 47.1	43.5	134 43.3	40.4	246 08.2	33.8	156 03.7	57.1	Achernar	335 25.6	S57 09.6
02	39 44.0	217 46.7	42.3	149 43.9	40.6	261 10.2	33.7	171 05.9	57.1	Acrux	173 08.8	S63 10.8
03	54 46.5	232 46.3	.. 41.0	164 44.5	.. 40.9	276 12.2	.. 33.6	186 08.2	.. 57.2	Adhara	255 11.9	S28 59.5
04	69 48.9	247 45.9	39.8	179 45.1	41.1	291 14.3	33.5	201 10.4	57.3	Aldebaran	290 48.2	N16 32.2
05	84 51.4	262 45.6	38.5	194 45.6	41.3	306 16.3	33.3	216 12.6	57.4			
06	99 53.9	277 45.2	N 0 37.3	209 46.2	S23 41.6	321 18.3	N16 33.2	231 14.8	S15 57.4	Alioth	166 20.6	N55 52.9
W 07	114 56.3	292 44.8	36.0	224 46.8	41.8	336 20.4	33.1	246 17.0	57.5	Alkaid	152 58.7	N49 14.6
E 08	129 58.8	307 44.4	34.8	239 47.3	42.1	351 22.4	33.0	261 19.3	57.6	Al Na'ir	27 42.3	S46 53.3
D 09	145 01.3	322 44.0	.. 33.5	254 47.9	.. 42.3	6 24.4	.. 32.9	276 21.5	.. 57.6	Alnilam	275 45.4	S 1 11.6
N 10	160 03.7	337 43.6	32.3	269 48.5	42.6	21 26.5	32.7	291 23.7	57.7	Alphard	217 55.4	S 8 43.3
E 11	175 06.2	352 43.2	31.0	284 49.1	42.8	36 28.5	32.6	306 25.9	57.8			
S 12	190 08.7	7 42.8	N 0 29.8	299 49.6	S23 43.0	51 30.5	N16 32.5	321 28.1	S15 57.9	Alphecca	126 10.5	N26 40.3
D 13	205 11.1	22 42.4	28.5	314 50.2	43.3	66 32.6	32.4	336 30.4	57.9	Alpheratz	357 42.2	N29 10.5
A 14	220 13.6	37 42.0	27.3	329 50.8	43.5	81 34.6	32.2	351 32.6	58.0	Altair	62 07.3	N 8 54.8
Y 15	235 16.1	52 41.6	.. 26.0	344 51.3	.. 43.8	96 36.6	.. 32.1	6 34.8	.. 58.1	Ankaa	353 14.5	S42 13.4
16	250 18.5	67 41.2	24.8	359 51.9	44.0	111 38.7	32.0	21 37.0	58.1	Antares	112 25.4	S26 27.7
17	265 21.0	82 40.9	23.5	14 52.5	44.2	126 40.7	31.9	36 39.2	58.2			
18	280 23.4	97 40.5	N 0 22.3	29 53.0	S23 44.5	141 42.7	N16 31.8	51 41.5	S15 58.3	Arcturus	145 55.3	N19 06.6
19	295 25.9	112 40.1	21.0	44 53.6	44.7	156 44.8	31.6	66 43.7	58.3	Atria	107 26.6	S69 03.3
20	310 28.4	127 39.7	19.8	59 54.2	44.9	171 46.8	31.5	81 45.9	58.4	Avior	234 17.9	S59 33.3
21	325 30.8	142 39.3	.. 18.5	74 54.7	.. 45.2	186 48.8	.. 31.4	96 48.1	.. 58.5	Bellatrix	278 31.0	N 6 21.7
22	340 33.3	157 38.9	17.3	89 55.3	45.4	201 50.9	31.3	111 50.3	58.6	Betelgeuse	271 00.3	N 7 24.5
23	355 35.8	172 38.5	16.0	104 55.9	45.7	216 52.9	31.1	126 52.5	58.6			
2 00	10 38.2	187 38.1	N 0 14.8	119 56.4	S23 45.9	231 54.9	N16 31.0	141 54.8	S15 58.7	Canopus	263 55.7	S52 42.1
01	25 40.7	202 37.7	13.5	134 57.0	46.1	246 57.0	30.9	156 57.0	58.8	Capella	280 33.0	N46 00.4
02	40 43.2	217 37.3	12.3	149 57.6	46.4	261 59.0	30.8	171 59.2	58.8	Deneb	49 30.6	N45 20.4
03	55 45.6	232 36.9	.. 11.0	164 58.1	.. 46.6	277 01.0	.. 30.7	187 01.4	.. 58.9	Denebola	182 33.1	N14 29.4
04	70 48.1	247 36.6	09.8	179 58.7	46.8	292 03.1	30.5	202 03.6	59.0	Diphda	348 54.7	S17 54.2
05	85 50.6	262 36.2	08.5	194 59.3	47.1	307 05.1	30.4	217 05.9	59.1			
06	100 53.0	277 35.8	N 0 07.3	209 59.8	S23 47.3	322 07.1	N16 30.3	232 08.1	S15 59.1	Dubhe	193 51.4	N61 40.2
T 07	115 55.5	292 35.4	06.0	225 00.4	47.5	337 09.2	30.2	247 10.3	59.2	Elnath	278 11.4	N28 37.0
H 08	130 57.9	307 35.0	04.8	240 00.9	47.8	352 11.2	30.0	262 12.5	59.3	Eltanin	90 45.8	N51 29.7
U 09	146 00.4	322 34.6	.. 03.5	255 01.5	.. 48.0	7 13.3	.. 29.9	277 14.7	.. 59.3	Enif	33 46.0	N 9 56.9
R 10	161 02.9	337 34.2	02.2	270 02.1	48.2	22 15.3	29.8	292 16.9	59.4	Fomalhaut	15 22.7	S29 32.5
S 11	176 05.3	352 33.8	N 01.0	285 02.6	48.5	37 17.3	29.7	307 19.2	59.5			
D 12	191 07.8	7 33.4	S 0 00.3	300 03.2	S23 48.7	52 19.4	N16 29.6	322 21.4	S15 59.6	Gacrux	172 00.4	S57 11.7
A 13	206 10.3	22 33.0	01.5	315 03.8	48.9	67 21.4	29.4	337 23.6	59.6	Gienah	175 51.7	S17 37.3
Y 14	221 12.7	37 32.6	02.8	330 04.3	49.2	82 23.4	29.3	352 25.8	59.7	Hadar	148 47.1	S60 26.6
15	236 15.2	52 32.3	.. 04.0	345 04.9	.. 49.4	97 25.5	.. 29.2	7 28.0	.. 59.8	Hamal	327 59.4	N23 31.9
16	251 17.7	67 31.9	05.3	0 05.4	49.6	112 27.5	29.1	22 30.3	59.8	Kaus Aust.	83 42.7	S34 22.5
17	266 20.1	82 31.5	06.5	15 06.0	49.9	127 29.6	29.0	37 32.5	15 59.9			
18	281 22.6	97 31.1	S 0 07.8	30 06.6	S23 50.1	142 31.6	N16 28.8	52 34.7	S16 00.0	Kochab	137 21.2	N74 06.0
19	296 25.1	112 30.7	09.0	45 07.1	50.3	157 33.6	28.7	67 36.9	00.1	Markab	13 37.1	N15 17.3
20	311 27.5	127 30.3	10.3	60 07.7	50.6	172 35.7	28.6	82 39.1	00.1	Menkar	314 13.9	N 4 08.9
21	326 30.0	142 29.9	.. 11.5	75 08.2	.. 50.8	187 37.7	.. 28.5	97 41.3	.. 00.2	Menkent	148 06.8	S36 26.4
22	341 32.4	157 29.5	12.8	90 08.8	51.0	202 39.7	28.3	112 43.6	00.3	Miaplacidus	221 39.9	S69 46.5
23	356 34.9	172 29.1	14.0	105 09.4	51.2	217 41.8	28.2	127 45.8	00.3			
3 00	11 37.4	187 28.7	S 0 15.3	120 09.9	S23 51.5	232 43.8	N16 28.1	142 48.0	S16 00.4	Mirfak	308 38.7	N49 54.6
01	26 39.8	202 28.3	16.5	135 10.5	51.7	247 45.9	28.0	157 50.2	00.5	Nunki	75 57.2	S26 16.5
02	41 42.3	217 27.9	17.8	150 11.0	51.9	262 47.9	27.9	172 52.4	00.6	Peacock	53 17.7	S56 41.2
03	56 44.8	232 27.6	.. 19.1	165 11.6	.. 52.2	277 49.9	.. 27.7	187 54.6	.. 00.6	Pollux	243 26.8	N27 59.2
04	71 47.2	247 27.2	20.3	180 12.1	52.4	292 52.0	27.6	202 56.9	00.7	Procyon	244 58.9	N 5 11.1
05	86 49.7	262 26.8	21.6	195 12.7	52.6	307 54.0	27.5	217 59.1	00.8			
06	101 52.2	277 26.4	S 0 22.8	210 13.3	S23 52.8	322 56.1	N16 27.4	233 01.3	S16 00.8	Rasalhague	96 05.7	N12 33.3
07	116 54.6	292 26.0	24.1	225 13.8	53.1	337 58.1	27.3	248 03.5	00.9	Regulus	207 42.8	N11 53.7
F 08	131 57.1	307 25.6	25.3	240 14.4	53.3	353 00.1	27.1	263 05.7	01.0	Rigel	281 11.1	S 8 11.1
R 09	146 59.5	322 25.2	.. 26.6	255 14.9	.. 53.5	8 02.2	.. 27.0	278 07.9	.. 01.1	Rigil Kent.	139 51.0	S60 53.7
I 10	162 02.0	337 24.8	27.8	270 15.5	53.7	23 04.2	26.9	293 10.2	01.1	Sabik	102 11.6	S15 44.3
D 11	177 04.5	352 24.4	29.1	285 16.0	54.0	38 06.3	26.8	308 12.4	01.2			
A 12	192 06.9	7 24.0	S 0 30.3	300 16.6	S23 54.2	53 08.3	N16 26.7	323 14.6	S16 01.3	Schedar	349 38.8	N56 37.2
Y 13	207 09.4	22 23.6	31.6	315 17.1	54.4	68 10.3	26.5	338 16.8	01.3	Shaula	96 20.8	S37 06.7
14	222 11.9	37 23.2	32.8	330 17.7	54.6	83 12.4	26.4	353 19.0	01.4	Sirius	258 32.9	S16 44.2
15	237 14.3	52 22.9	.. 34.1	345 18.3	.. 54.9	98 14.4	.. 26.3	8 21.2	.. 01.5	Spica	158 30.6	S11 14.1
16	252 16.8	67 22.5	35.3	0 18.8	55.1	113 16.5	26.2	23 23.4	01.6	Suhail	222 52.0	S43 29.4
17	267 19.3	82 22.1	36.6	15 19.4	55.3	128 18.5	26.1	38 25.7	01.6			
18	282 21.7	97 21.7	S 0 37.9	30 19.9	S23 55.5	143 20.6	N16 25.9	53 27.9	S16 01.7	Vega	80 38.4	N38 48.3
19	297 24.2	112 21.3	39.1	45 20.5	55.7	158 22.6	25.8	68 30.1	01.8	Zuben'ubi	137 04.7	S16 06.0
20	312 26.7	127 20.9	40.4	60 21.0	56.0	173 24.6	25.7	83 32.3	01.8			
21	327 29.1	142 20.5	.. 41.6	75 21.6	.. 56.2	188 26.7	.. 25.6	98 34.5	.. 01.9			
22	342 31.6	157 20.1	42.9	90 22.1	56.4	203 28.7	25.5	113 36.7	02.0			
23	357 34.0	172 19.7	44.1	105 22.7	56.6	218 30.8	25.3	128 38.9	02.1			

	SHA	Mer. Pass.
Venus	176 59.9	11 30
Mars	109 18.2	16 00
Jupiter	221 16.7	8 31
Saturn	131 16.5	14 30

Mer. Pass.	ARIES	VENUS	MARS	JUPITER	SATURN
h m	23 13.6	v −0.4 d 1.3	v 0.6 d 0.2	v 2.0 d 0.1	v 2.2 d 0.1

UT	SUN GHA	Dec	MOON GHA	v	Dec	d	HP
d h	° ′	° ′	° ′	′	° ′	′	′
1 00	182 32.4	S 3 04.4	102 27.2	7.6	S18 30.4	0.5	58.1
01	197 32.6	05.3	116 53.8	7.5	18 29.9	0.7	58.1
02	212 32.8	06.3	131 20.3	7.6	18 29.2	0.8	58.2
03	227 33.0	.. 07.3	145 46.9	7.5	18 28.4	0.9	58.2
04	242 33.2	08.2	160 13.4	7.5	18 27.5	1.0	58.2
05	257 33.4	09.2	174 39.9	7.4	18 26.5	1.2	58.2
W 06	272 33.6	S 3 10.2	189 06.3	7.5	S18 25.3	1.2	58.3
E 07	287 33.8	11.1	203 32.8	7.4	18 24.1	1.4	58.3
D 08	302 34.0	12.1	217 59.2	7.4	18 22.7	1.4	58.3
N 09	317 34.2	.. 13.1	232 25.6	7.4	18 21.3	1.6	58.3
E 10	332 34.4	14.1	246 52.0	7.3	18 19.7	1.7	58.4
S 11	347 34.6	15.0	261 18.3	7.3	18 18.0	1.9	58.4
D 12	2 34.8	S 3 16.0	275 44.6	7.4	S18 16.1	1.9	58.4
A 13	17 35.0	17.0	290 11.0	7.3	18 14.2	2.0	58.4
Y 14	32 35.2	17.9	304 37.3	7.3	18 12.2	2.2	58.5
15	47 35.4	.. 18.9	319 03.5	7.3	18 10.0	2.3	58.5
16	62 35.6	19.9	333 29.8	7.2	18 07.7	2.4	58.5
17	77 35.8	20.8	347 56.0	7.3	18 05.3	2.5	58.6
18	92 36.0	S 3 21.8	2 22.3	7.2	S18 02.8	2.6	58.6
19	107 36.2	22.8	16 48.5	7.2	18 00.2	2.8	58.6
20	122 36.4	23.7	31 14.7	7.2	17 57.4	2.8	58.6
21	137 36.6	.. 24.7	45 40.9	7.2	17 54.6	3.0	58.7
22	152 36.8	25.7	60 07.1	7.1	17 51.6	3.1	58.7
23	167 37.0	26.7	74 33.2	7.2	17 48.5	3.2	58.7
2 00	182 37.2	S 3 27.6	88 59.4	7.1	S17 45.3	3.3	58.7
01	197 37.4	28.6	103 25.5	7.2	17 42.0	3.4	58.8
02	212 37.6	29.6	117 51.7	7.1	17 38.6	3.5	58.8
03	227 37.8	.. 30.5	132 17.8	7.1	17 35.1	3.7	58.8
04	242 38.0	31.5	146 43.9	7.1	17 31.4	3.7	58.8
05	257 38.2	32.5	161 10.0	7.1	17 27.7	3.9	58.9
T 06	272 38.4	S 3 33.4	175 36.1	7.1	S17 23.8	4.0	58.9
H 07	287 38.6	34.4	190 02.2	7.1	17 19.8	4.1	58.9
U 08	302 38.8	35.4	204 28.3	7.1	17 15.7	4.2	58.9
R 09	317 39.0	.. 36.3	218 54.4	7.1	17 11.5	4.4	59.0
S 10	332 39.2	37.3	233 20.5	7.0	17 07.1	4.4	59.0
D 11	347 39.4	38.3	247 46.5	7.1	17 02.7	4.6	59.0
A 12	2 39.6	S 3 39.2	262 12.6	7.1	S16 58.1	4.6	59.0
Y 13	17 39.8	40.2	276 38.7	7.1	16 53.5	4.8	59.1
14	32 40.0	41.2	291 04.8	7.0	16 48.7	4.9	59.1
15	47 40.2	.. 42.1	305 30.8	7.1	16 43.8	5.0	59.1
16	62 40.4	43.1	319 56.9	7.1	16 38.8	5.1	59.1
17	77 40.6	44.1	334 23.0	7.0	16 33.7	5.2	59.2
18	92 40.8	S 3 45.0	348 49.0	7.1	S16 28.5	5.4	59.2
19	107 41.0	46.0	3 15.1	7.1	16 23.1	5.4	59.2
20	122 41.2	47.0	17 41.2	7.1	16 17.7	5.5	59.2
21	137 41.4	.. 47.9	32 07.3	7.1	16 12.2	5.7	59.3
22	152 41.6	48.9	46 33.4	7.0	16 06.5	5.8	59.3
23	167 41.8	49.9	60 59.4	7.1	16 00.7	5.8	59.3
3 00	182 42.0	S 3 50.8	75 25.5	7.1	S15 54.9	6.0	59.3
01	197 42.1	51.8	89 51.6	7.1	15 48.9	6.1	59.4
02	212 42.3	52.8	104 17.7	7.1	15 42.8	6.2	59.4
03	227 42.5	.. 53.7	118 43.8	7.1	15 36.6	6.3	59.4
04	242 42.7	54.7	133 09.9	7.2	15 30.3	6.4	59.4
05	257 42.9	55.7	147 36.1	7.1	15 23.9	6.5	59.5
F 06	272 43.1	S 3 56.6	162 02.2	7.1	S15 17.4	6.6	59.5
R 07	287 43.3	57.6	176 28.3	7.2	15 10.8	6.7	59.5
I 08	302 43.5	58.6	190 54.5	7.2	15 04.1	6.8	59.5
D 09	317 43.7	3 59.5	205 20.6	7.2	14 57.3	6.9	59.5
A 10	332 43.9	4 00.5	219 46.8	7.2	14 50.4	7.0	59.6
Y 11	347 44.1	01.5	234 13.0	7.1	14 43.4	7.1	59.6
12	2 44.3	S 4 02.4	248 39.1	7.2	S14 36.3	7.2	59.6
13	17 44.5	03.4	263 05.3	7.2	14 29.1	7.3	59.6
14	32 44.7	04.4	277 31.5	7.2	14 21.8	7.4	59.7
15	47 44.9	.. 05.3	291 57.7	7.3	14 14.4	7.5	59.7
16	62 45.1	06.3	306 24.0	7.2	14 06.9	7.6	59.7
17	77 45.3	07.3	320 50.2	7.3	13 59.3	7.7	59.7
18	92 45.5	S 4 08.2	335 16.5	7.2	S13 51.6	7.8	59.7
19	107 45.7	09.2	349 42.7	7.3	13 43.8	7.9	59.8
20	122 45.9	10.1	4 09.0	7.3	13 35.9	7.9	59.8
21	137 46.1	.. 11.1	18 35.3	7.3	13 28.0	8.1	59.8
22	152 46.3	12.1	33 01.6	7.3	13 19.9	8.2	59.8
23	167 46.4	13.0	47 27.9	7.3	S13 11.7	8.2	59.8
	SD 16.0	d 1.0	SD 15.9		16.1		16.2

Twilight / Sunrise / Moonrise

Lat.	Naut.	Civil	Sunrise	Moonrise 1	2	3	4
°	h m	h m	h m	h m	h m	h m	h m
N 72	03 54	05 15	06 23	■■■	17 12	17 00	16 52
N 70	04 05	05 18	06 19	16 07	16 25	16 32	16 35
68	04 14	05 20	06 16	15 24	15 54	16 11	16 21
66	04 22	05 22	06 13	14 56	15 30	15 54	16 10
64	04 28	05 24	06 11	14 34	15 12	15 40	16 01
62	04 33	05 25	06 09	14 16	14 57	15 28	15 53
60	04 37	05 26	06 07	14 02	14 45	15 18	15 45
N 58	04 41	05 27	06 06	13 50	14 34	15 10	15 39
56	04 44	05 28	06 05	13 39	14 24	15 02	15 34
54	04 47	05 28	06 03	13 29	14 16	14 55	15 29
52	04 49	05 29	06 02	13 21	14 08	14 49	15 24
50	04 51	05 29	06 01	13 13	14 01	14 43	15 20
45	04 56	05 30	05 59	12 57	13 47	14 31	15 11
N 40	04 59	05 30	05 57	12 44	13 34	14 21	15 04
35	05 01	05 30	05 55	12 32	13 24	14 12	14 57
30	05 02	05 30	05 54	12 22	13 15	14 05	14 52
20	05 04	05 29	05 51	12 05	12 59	13 52	14 42
N 10	05 03	05 28	05 49	11 51	12 46	13 40	14 33
0	05 01	05 25	05 46	11 37	12 33	13 29	14 25
S 10	04 58	05 23	05 44	11 23	12 20	13 19	14 17
20	04 53	05 19	05 41	11 08	12 07	13 07	14 09
30	04 45	05 13	05 37	10 51	11 51	12 54	13 59
35	04 40	05 09	05 35	10 41	11 42	12 46	13 53
40	04 34	05 06	05 33	10 30	11 31	12 37	13 46
45	04 26	05 01	05 30	10 17	11 19	12 27	13 39
S 50	04 16	04 55	05 27	10 01	11 04	12 15	13 30
52	04 11	04 52	05 26	09 53	10 57	12 09	13 25
54	04 05	04 48	05 24	09 45	10 50	12 03	13 21
56	03 59	04 45	05 22	09 35	10 41	11 56	13 16
58	03 52	04 40	05 20	09 24	10 31	11 47	13 10
S 60	03 43	04 36	05 18	09 12	10 20	11 38	13 03

Sunset / Twilight / Moonset

Lat.	Sunset	Civil	Naut.	Moonset 1	2	3	4
°	h m	h m	h m	h m	h m	h m	h m
N 72	17 14	18 21	19 42	■■■	20 31	22 41	24 45
N 70	17 18	18 18	19 31	19 38	21 18	23 08	25 01
68	17 21	18 16	19 22	20 20	21 48	23 28	25 13
66	17 24	18 15	19 15	20 48	22 11	23 44	25 23
64	17 26	18 13	19 09	21 10	22 28	23 57	25 31
62	17 28	18 12	19 04	21 27	22 43	24 08	00 08
60	17 30	18 11	19 00	21 42	22 55	24 17	00 17
N 58	17 32	18 11	18 56	21 54	23 06	24 25	00 25
56	17 33	18 10	18 53	22 04	23 15	24 32	00 32
54	17 34	18 09	18 50	22 14	23 23	24 39	00 39
52	17 36	18 09	18 48	22 22	23 30	24 44	00 44
50	17 37	18 09	18 46	22 29	23 37	24 50	00 50
45	17 39	18 08	18 42	22 45	23 51	25 01	01 01
N 40	17 41	18 08	18 39	22 58	24 02	00 02	01 10
35	17 43	18 08	18 37	23 09	24 12	00 12	01 18
30	17 44	18 08	18 36	23 19	24 21	00 21	01 24
20	17 47	18 09	18 35	23 36	24 35	00 35	01 36
N 10	17 50	18 11	18 35	23 50	24 48	00 48	01 47
0	17 53	18 13	18 37	24 04	00 04	01 00	01 56
S 10	17 55	18 16	18 41	24 17	00 17	01 12	02 06
20	17 58	18 20	18 46	24 31	00 31	01 24	02 16
30	18 02	18 26	18 54	24 48	00 48	01 39	02 27
35	18 04	18 29	18 59	00 04	00 57	01 47	02 34
40	18 06	18 34	19 06	00 15	01 08	01 56	02 41
45	18 09	18 39	19 14	00 29	01 21	02 07	02 50
S 50	18 12	18 45	19 24	00 45	01 36	02 21	03 00
52	18 14	18 48	19 29	00 53	01 43	02 27	03 05
54	18 16	18 52	19 35	01 01	01 51	02 34	03 10
56	18 18	18 55	19 42	01 11	02 00	02 41	03 16
58	18 20	19 00	19 49	01 21	02 10	02 50	03 22
S 60	18 22	19 05	19 58	01 34	02 21	02 59	03 30

	SUN			MOON			
Day	Eqn. of Time 00h	12h	Mer. Pass.	Mer. Pass. Upper	Lower	Age	Phase
d	m s	m s	h m	h m	h m	d	%
1	10 09	10 19	11 50	17 50	05 22	07	47
2	10 28	10 38	11 49	18 46	06 18	08	58
3	10 47	10 57	11 49	19 43	07 15	09	69

UT	ARIES	VENUS −3.9		MARS +0.8		JUPITER −1.9		SATURN +0.6		STARS		
	GHA	GHA	Dec	GHA	Dec	GHA	Dec	GHA	Dec	Name	SHA	Dec
d h	° ′	° ′	° ′	° ′	° ′	° ′	° ′	° ′	° ′		° ′	° ′
4 00	12 36.5	187 19.3	S 0 45.4	120 23.2	S23 56.8	233 32.8	N16 25.2	143 41.2	S16 02.1	Acamar	315 17.4	S40 14.6
01	27 39.0	202 18.9	46.6	135 23.8	57.1	248 34.9	25.1	158 43.4	02.2	Achernar	335 25.6	S57 09.6
02	42 41.4	217 18.5	47.9	150 24.3	57.3	263 36.9	25.0	173 45.6	02.3	Acrux	173 08.8	S63 10.8
03	57 43.9	232 18.2 . .	49.1	165 24.9 . .	57.5	278 38.9 . .	24.9	188 47.8 . .	02.3	Adhara	255 11.8	S28 59.5
04	72 46.4	247 17.8	50.4	180 25.4	57.7	293 41.0	24.7	203 50.0	02.4	Aldebaran	290 48.2	N16 32.2
05	87 48.8	262 17.4	51.6	195 26.0	57.9	308 43.0	24.6	218 52.2	02.5			
06	102 51.3	277 17.0	S 0 52.9	210 26.5	S23 58.2	323 45.1	N16 24.6	233 54.4	S16 02.6	Alioth	166 20.6	N55 52.9
07	117 53.8	292 16.6	54.2	225 27.1	58.4	338 47.1	24.4	248 56.7	02.6	Alkaid	152 58.7	N49 14.6
S 08	132 56.2	307 16.2	55.4	240 27.6	58.6	353 49.2	24.3	263 58.9	02.7	Al Na'ir	27 42.3	S46 53.3
A 09	147 58.7	322 15.8 . .	56.7	255 28.2 . .	58.8	8 51.2 . .	24.1	279 01.1 . .	02.8	Alnilam	275 45.4	S 1 11.6
T 10	163 01.2	337 15.4	57.9	270 28.7	59.0	23 53.3	24.0	294 03.3	02.8	Alphard	217 55.4	S 8 43.3
U 11	178 03.6	352 15.0	0 59.2	285 29.3	59.2	38 55.3	23.9	309 05.5	02.9			
R 12	193 06.1	7 14.6	S 1 00.4	300 29.8	S23 59.5	53 57.4	N16 23.8	324 07.7	S16 03.0	Alphecca	126 10.5	N26 40.2
D 13	208 08.5	22 14.2	01.7	315 30.4	59.7	68 59.4	23.7	339 09.9	03.1	Alpheratz	357 42.2	N29 10.5
A 14	223 11.0	37 13.8	02.9	330 30.9	23 59.9	84 01.4	23.5	354 12.2	03.1	Altair	62 07.3	N 8 54.8
Y 15	238 13.5	52 13.4 . .	04.2	345 31.5 . .	24 00.1	99 03.5 . .	23.4	9 14.4 . .	03.2	Ankaa	353 14.5	S42 13.5
16	253 15.9	67 13.0	05.4	0 32.0	00.3	114 05.5	23.3	24 16.6	03.3	Antares	112 25.4	S26 27.7
17	268 18.4	82 12.7	06.7	15 32.6	00.5	129 07.6	23.2	39 18.8	03.4			
18	283 20.9	97 12.3	S 1 07.9	30 33.1	S24 00.7	144 09.6	N16 23.1	54 21.0	S16 03.4	Arcturus	145 55.3	N19 06.6
19	298 23.3	112 11.9	09.2	45 33.7	01.0	159 11.7	22.9	69 23.2	03.5	Atria	107 26.6	S69 03.2
20	313 25.8	127 11.5	10.5	60 34.2	01.2	174 13.7	22.8	84 25.4	03.6	Avior	234 17.8	S59 33.2
21	328 28.3	142 11.1 . .	11.7	75 34.7 . .	01.4	189 15.8 . .	22.7	99 27.6 . .	03.6	Bellatrix	278 30.9	N 6 21.7
22	343 30.7	157 10.7	13.0	90 35.3	01.6	204 17.8	22.6	114 29.9	03.7	Betelgeuse	271 00.3	N 7 24.5
23	358 33.2	172 10.3	14.2	105 35.8	01.8	219 19.9	22.5	129 32.1	03.8			
5 00	13 35.6	187 09.9	S 1 15.5	120 36.4	S24 02.0	234 21.9	N16 22.3	144 34.3	S16 03.9	Canopus	263 55.7	S52 42.1
01	28 38.1	202 09.5	16.7	135 36.9	02.2	249 24.0	22.2	159 36.5	03.9	Capella	280 32.9	N46 00.4
02	43 40.6	217 09.1	18.0	150 37.5	02.4	264 26.0	22.1	174 38.7	04.0	Deneb	49 30.6	N45 20.4
03	58 43.0	232 08.7 . .	19.2	165 38.0 . .	02.6	279 28.1 . .	22.0	189 40.9 . .	04.1	Denebola	182 33.1	N14 29.4
04	73 45.5	247 08.3	20.5	180 38.6	02.8	294 30.1	21.9	204 43.1	04.1	Diphda	348 54.7	S17 54.2
05	88 48.0	262 07.9	21.7	195 39.1	03.1	309 32.2	21.7	219 45.3	04.2			
06	103 50.4	277 07.5	S 1 23.0	210 39.6	S24 03.3	324 34.2	N16 21.6	234 47.6	S16 04.3	Dubhe	193 51.3	N61 40.1
07	118 52.9	292 07.2	24.3	225 40.2	03.5	339 36.2	21.5	249 49.8	04.4	Elnath	278 11.4	N28 37.0
08	133 55.4	307 06.8	25.5	240 40.7	03.7	354 38.3	21.4	264 52.0	04.4	Eltanin	90 45.9	N51 29.7
S 09	148 57.8	322 06.4 . .	26.8	255 41.3 . .	03.9	9 40.3 . .	21.3	279 54.2 . .	04.5	Enif	33 46.0	N 9 56.9
U 10	164 00.3	337 06.0	28.0	270 41.8	04.1	24 42.4	21.2	294 56.4	04.6	Fomalhaut	15 22.7	S29 32.5
N 11	179 02.8	352 05.6	29.3	285 42.3	04.3	39 44.4	21.0	309 58.6	04.6			
D 12	194 05.2	7 05.2	S 1 30.5	300 42.9	S24 04.5	54 46.5	N16 20.9	325 00.8	S16 04.7	Gacrux	172 00.4	S57 11.7
A 13	209 07.7	22 04.8	31.8	315 43.4	04.7	69 48.5	20.8	340 03.0	04.8	Gienah	175 51.7	S17 37.3
Y 14	224 10.1	37 04.4	33.0	330 44.0	04.9	84 50.6	20.7	355 05.2	04.9	Hadar	148 47.1	S60 26.6
15	239 12.6	52 04.0 . .	34.3	345 44.5 . .	05.1	99 52.6 . .	20.6	10 07.5 . .	04.9	Hamal	327 59.4	N23 31.9
16	254 15.1	67 03.6	35.5	0 45.1	05.3	114 54.7	20.4	25 09.7	05.0	Kaus Aust.	83 42.7	S34 22.5
17	269 17.5	82 03.2	36.8	15 45.6	05.5	129 56.7	20.3	40 11.9	05.1			
18	284 20.0	97 02.8	S 1 38.0	30 46.1	S24 05.7	144 58.8	N16 20.2	55 14.1	S16 05.2	Kochab	137 21.2	N74 06.0
19	299 22.5	112 02.4	39.3	45 46.7	05.9	160 00.9	20.1	70 16.3	05.2	Markab	13 37.1	N15 17.3
20	314 24.9	127 02.0	40.6	60 47.2	06.1	175 02.9	20.0	85 18.5	05.3	Menkar	314 13.8	N 4 08.9
21	329 27.4	142 01.6 . .	41.8	75 47.7 . .	06.3	190 05.0 . .	19.9	100 20.7 . .	05.4	Menkent	148 06.9	S36 26.4
22	344 29.9	157 01.2	43.1	90 48.3	06.5	205 07.0	19.7	115 22.9	05.4	Miaplacidus	221 39.9	S69 46.5
23	359 32.3	172 00.8	44.3	105 48.8	06.8	220 09.1	19.6	130 25.1	05.5			
6 00	14 34.8	187 00.5	S 1 45.6	120 49.4	S24 07.0	235 11.1	N16 19.5	145 27.4	S16 05.6	Mirfak	308 38.6	N49 54.6
01	29 37.2	202 00.1	46.8	135 49.9	07.2	250 13.2	19.4	160 29.6	05.7	Nunki	75 57.2	S26 16.5
02	44 39.7	216 59.7	48.1	150 50.4	07.4	265 15.2	19.3	175 31.8	05.7	Peacock	53 17.7	S56 41.2
03	59 42.2	231 59.3 . .	49.3	165 51.0 . .	07.6	280 17.3 . .	19.1	190 34.0 . .	05.8	Pollux	243 26.8	N27 59.2
04	74 44.6	246 58.9	50.6	180 51.5	07.8	295 19.3	19.0	205 36.2	05.9	Procyon	244 58.9	N 5 11.1
05	89 47.1	261 58.5	51.8	195 52.0	08.0	310 21.4	18.9	220 38.4	05.9			
06	104 49.6	276 58.1	S 1 53.1	210 52.6	S24 08.2	325 23.4	N16 18.8	235 40.6	S16 06.0	Rasalhague	96 05.7	N12 33.3
07	119 52.0	291 57.7	54.3	225 53.1	08.4	340 25.5	18.7	250 42.8	06.1	Regulus	207 42.8	N11 53.7
08	134 54.5	306 57.3	55.6	240 53.7	08.6	355 27.5	18.6	265 45.0	06.2	Rigel	281 11.1	S 8 11.1
M 09	149 57.0	321 56.9 . .	56.8	255 54.2 . .	08.8	10 29.6 . .	18.4	280 47.2 . .	06.2	Rigil Kent.	139 51.0	S60 53.7
O 10	164 59.4	336 56.5	58.1	270 54.7	09.0	25 31.6	18.3	295 49.5	06.3	Sabik	102 11.7	S15 44.3
N 11	180 01.9	351 56.1	1 59.4	285 55.3	09.1	40 33.7	18.2	310 51.7	06.4			
D 12	195 04.4	6 55.7	S 2 00.6	300 55.8	S24 09.3	55 35.7	N16 18.1	325 53.9	S16 06.5	Schedar	349 38.8	N56 37.2
A 13	210 06.8	21 55.3	01.9	315 56.3	09.5	70 37.8	18.0	340 56.1	06.5	Shaula	96 20.8	S37 06.7
Y 14	225 09.3	36 54.9	03.1	330 56.9	09.7	85 39.9	17.8	355 58.3	06.6	Sirius	258 32.9	S16 44.2
15	240 11.7	51 54.5 . .	04.4	345 57.4 . .	09.9	100 41.9 . .	17.7	11 00.5 . .	06.7	Spica	158 30.6	S11 14.1
16	255 14.2	66 54.1	05.6	0 57.9	10.1	115 44.0	17.6	26 02.7	06.7	Suhail	222 52.0	S43 29.4
17	270 16.7	81 53.7	06.9	15 58.5	10.3	130 46.0	17.5	41 04.9	06.8			
18	285 19.1	96 53.3	S 2 08.1	30 59.0	S24 10.5	145 48.1	N16 17.4	56 07.1	S16 06.9	Vega	80 38.4	N38 48.3
19	300 21.6	111 52.9	09.4	45 59.5	10.7	160 50.1	17.3	71 09.3	07.0	Zuben'ubi	137 04.7	S16 06.0
20	315 24.1	126 52.5	10.6	61 00.1	10.9	175 52.2	17.1	86 11.5	07.0		SHA	Mer. Pass.
21	330 26.5	141 52.1 . .	11.9	76 00.6 . .	11.1	190 54.2 . .	17.0	101 13.8 . .	07.1		° ′	h m
22	345 29.0	156 51.8	13.1	91 01.1	11.3	205 56.3	16.9	116 16.0	07.2	Venus	173 34.3	11 32
23	0 31.5	171 51.4	14.4	106 01.6	11.5	220 58.4	16.8	131 18.2	07.3	Mars	107 00.7	15 57
	h m									Jupiter	220 46.3	8 21
Mer. Pass. 23 01.8		v −0.4	d 1.3	v 0.5	d 0.2	v 2.0	d 0.1	v 2.2	d 0.1	Saturn	130 58.6	14 20

UT	SUN GHA	SUN Dec	MOON GHA	v	MOON Dec	d	HP
d h	° ′	° ′	° ′	′	° ′	′	′
4 00	182 46.6	S 4 14.0	61 54.2	7.4	S13 03.5	8.3	59.9
01	197 46.8	15.0	76 20.6	7.3	12 55.2	8.5	59.9
02	212 47.0	15.9	90 46.9	7.4	12 46.7	8.5	59.9
03	227 47.2	.. 16.9	105 13.3	7.4	12 38.2	8.6	59.9
04	242 47.4	17.9	119 39.7	7.4	12 29.6	8.7	59.9
05	257 47.6	18.8	134 06.1	7.4	12 20.9	8.7	60.0
06	272 47.8	S 4 19.8	148 32.5	7.5	S12 12.2	8.9	60.0
07	287 48.0	20.8	162 59.0	7.4	12 03.3	8.9	60.0
08	302 48.2	21.7	177 25.4	7.5	11 54.4	9.0	60.0
S 09	317 48.4	.. 22.7	191 51.9	7.5	11 45.4	9.1	60.0
A 10	332 48.6	23.6	206 18.4	7.5	11 36.3	9.2	60.1
T 11	347 48.8	24.6	220 44.9	7.5	11 27.1	9.3	60.1
U 12	2 49.0	S 4 25.6	235 11.4	7.5	S11 17.8	9.3	60.1
R 13	17 49.1	26.5	249 37.9	7.6	11 08.5	9.4	60.1
D 14	32 49.3	27.5	264 04.5	7.5	10 59.1	9.5	60.1
A 15	47 49.5	.. 28.5	278 31.0	7.6	10 49.6	9.6	60.1
Y 16	62 49.7	29.4	292 57.6	7.6	10 40.0	9.6	60.2
17	77 49.9	30.4	307 24.2	7.6	10 30.4	9.7	60.2
18	92 50.1	S 4 31.4	321 50.8	7.6	S10 20.7	9.8	60.2
19	107 50.3	32.3	336 17.4	7.7	10 10.9	9.9	60.2
20	122 50.5	33.3	350 44.1	7.7	10 01.0	9.9	60.2
21	137 50.7	.. 34.2	5 10.8	7.6	9 51.1	10.0	60.2
22	152 50.9	35.2	19 37.4	7.7	9 41.1	10.0	60.2
23	167 51.1	36.2	34 04.1	7.8	9 31.1	10.1	60.3
5 00	182 51.2	S 4 37.1	48 30.9	7.7	S 9 21.0	10.2	60.3
01	197 51.4	38.1	62 57.6	7.7	9 10.8	10.3	60.3
02	212 51.6	39.0	77 24.3	7.8	9 00.5	10.3	60.3
03	227 51.8	.. 40.0	91 51.1	7.8	8 50.2	10.4	60.3
04	242 52.0	41.0	106 17.9	7.8	8 39.8	10.4	60.3
05	257 52.2	41.9	120 44.7	7.8	8 29.4	10.5	60.3
06	272 52.4	S 4 42.9	135 11.5	7.8	S 8 18.9	10.5	60.3
07	287 52.6	43.9	149 38.3	7.9	8 08.4	10.6	60.3
08	302 52.8	44.8	164 05.2	7.8	7 57.8	10.7	60.4
S 09	317 53.0	.. 45.8	178 32.0	7.9	7 47.1	10.7	60.4
U 10	332 53.1	46.7	192 58.9	7.9	7 36.4	10.8	60.4
N 11	347 53.3	47.7	207 25.8	7.9	7 25.6	10.8	60.4
D 12	2 53.5	S 4 48.7	221 52.7	8.0	S 7 14.8	10.9	60.4
A 13	17 53.7	49.6	236 19.7	7.9	7 03.9	10.9	60.4
Y 14	32 53.9	50.6	250 46.6	8.0	6 53.0	11.0	60.4
15	47 54.1	.. 51.5	265 13.6	7.9	6 42.0	11.0	60.4
16	62 54.3	52.5	279 40.5	8.0	6 31.0	11.0	60.4
17	77 54.5	53.5	294 07.5	8.0	6 20.0	11.1	60.4
18	92 54.6	S 4 54.4	308 34.5	8.0	S 6 08.9	11.2	60.4
19	107 54.8	55.4	323 01.5	8.1	5 57.7	11.1	60.4
20	122 55.0	56.3	337 28.6	8.0	5 46.6	11.3	60.4
21	137 55.2	.. 57.3	351 55.6	8.1	5 35.3	11.2	60.5
22	152 55.4	58.3	6 22.7	8.1	5 24.1	11.3	60.5
23	167 55.6	4 59.2	20 49.8	8.1	5 12.8	11.3	60.5
6 00	182 55.8	S 5 00.2	35 16.9	8.1	S 5 01.5	11.4	60.5
01	197 56.0	01.1	49 44.0	8.1	4 50.1	11.4	60.5
02	212 56.2	02.1	64 11.1	8.1	4 38.7	11.4	60.5
03	227 56.3	.. 03.1	78 38.2	8.1	4 27.3	11.5	60.5
04	242 56.5	04.0	93 05.3	8.2	4 15.8	11.5	60.5
05	257 56.7	05.0	107 32.5	8.2	4 04.3	11.5	60.5
06	272 56.9	S 5 05.9	121 59.7	8.1	S 3 52.8	11.5	60.5
07	287 57.1	06.9	136 26.8	8.2	3 41.3	11.6	60.5
08	302 57.3	07.9	150 54.0	8.2	3 29.7	11.6	60.5
M 09	317 57.4	.. 08.8	165 21.2	8.2	3 18.1	11.6	60.5
O 10	332 57.6	09.8	179 48.4	8.3	3 06.5	11.6	60.5
N 11	347 57.8	10.7	194 15.7	8.3	2 54.9	11.6	60.5
D 12	2 58.0	S 5 11.7	208 42.9	8.2	S 2 43.3	11.7	60.5
A 13	17 58.2	12.7	223 10.1	8.3	2 31.6	11.7	60.5
Y 14	32 58.4	13.6	237 37.4	8.3	2 19.9	11.7	60.5
15	47 58.5	.. 14.6	252 04.7	8.2	2 08.2	11.7	60.5
16	62 58.7	15.5	266 31.9	8.3	1 56.5	11.7	60.5
17	77 58.9	16.5	280 59.2	8.3	1 44.8	11.7	60.5
18	92 59.1	S 5 17.4	295 26.5	8.3	S 1 33.1	11.8	60.5
19	107 59.3	18.4	309 53.8	8.3	1 21.3	11.7	60.5
20	122 59.5	19.4	324 21.1	8.3	1 09.6	11.8	60.5
21	137 59.6	.. 20.3	338 48.4	8.4	0 57.8	11.7	60.5
22	152 59.8	21.3	353 15.8	8.3	0 46.1	11.8	60.5
23	168 00.0	22.2	7 43.1	8.3	S 0 34.3	11.8	60.5
	SD 16.0	d 1.0	SD 16.4		16.5		16.5

Lat.	Twilight Naut.	Twilight Civil	Sunrise	Moonrise 4	Moonrise 5	Moonrise 6	Moonrise 7
°	h m	h m	h m	h m	h m	h m	h m
N 72	04 08	05 29	06 36	16 52	16 46	16 40	16 34
N 70	04 18	05 30	06 31	16 35	16 37	16 37	16 38
68	04 26	05 31	06 27	16 21	16 29	16 35	16 41
66	04 32	05 32	06 23	16 10	16 23	16 33	16 43
64	04 37	05 32	06 20	16 01	16 17	16 32	16 45
62	04 41	05 33	06 17	15 53	16 13	16 30	16 47
60	04 45	05 33	06 15	15 45	16 08	16 29	16 49
N 58	04 48	05 33	06 13	15 39	16 05	16 28	16 51
56	04 50	05 34	06 11	15 34	16 02	16 27	16 52
54	04 53	05 34	06 09	15 29	15 59	16 26	16 53
52	04 54	05 34	06 07	15 24	15 56	16 25	16 54
50	04 54	05 34	06 06	15 20	15 54	16 25	16 55
45	04 59	05 33	06 03	15 11	15 48	16 23	16 57
N 40	05 02	05 33	06 00	15 04	15 44	16 22	16 59
35	05 03	05 32	05 58	14 57	15 40	16 21	17 01
30	05 04	05 32	05 56	14 52	15 37	16 20	17 02
20	05 04	05 30	05 52	14 42	15 31	16 18	17 05
N 10	05 03	05 27	05 48	14 33	15 25	16 16	17 07
0	05 00	05 24	05 45	14 25	15 21	16 15	17 09
S 10	04 56	05 21	05 42	14 17	15 16	16 14	17 11
20	04 50	05 16	05 38	14 09	15 10	16 12	17 14
30	04 42	05 10	05 34	13 59	15 05	16 11	17 17
35	04 36	05 06	05 31	13 53	15 01	16 10	17 18
40	04 29	05 01	05 28	13 46	14 57	16 09	17 20
45	04 20	04 55	05 25	13 39	14 53	16 07	17 22
S 50	04 09	04 48	05 21	13 30	14 47	16 06	17 25
52	04 03	04 45	05 19	13 25	14 45	16 05	17 26
54	03 57	04 41	05 17	13 21	14 42	16 05	17 27
56	03 50	04 36	05 14	13 16	14 39	16 04	17 28
58	03 42	04 32	05 12	13 10	14 36	16 03	17 30
S 60	03 33	04 26	05 09	13 03	14 32	16 02	17 32

Lat.	Sunset	Twilight Civil	Twilight Naut.	Moonset 4	Moonset 5	Moonset 6	Moonset 7
°	h m	h m	h m	h m	h m	h m	h m
N 72	16 58	18 06	19 25	24 45	00 45	02 47	04 46
N 70	17 04	18 05	19 16	25 01	01 01	02 54	04 46
68	17 09	18 04	19 09	25 13	01 13	02 59	04 45
66	17 12	18 03	19 03	25 23	01 23	03 04	04 45
64	17 16	18 03	18 58	25 31	01 31	03 08	04 45
62	17 18	18 03	18 54	00 08	01 38	03 11	04 44
60	17 21	18 02	18 51	00 17	01 44	03 14	04 44
N 58	17 23	18 02	18 48	00 25	01 50	03 16	04 44
56	17 25	18 02	18 45	00 32	01 54	03 19	04 44
54	17 27	18 02	18 43	00 39	01 59	03 21	04 43
52	17 29	18 02	18 41	00 44	02 03	03 23	04 43
50	17 31	18 02	18 40	00 50	02 06	03 24	04 43
45	17 33	18 03	18 37	01 01	02 14	03 28	04 43
N 40	17 36	18 03	18 35	01 10	02 20	03 31	04 43
35	17 39	18 04	18 33	01 18	02 25	03 34	04 42
30	17 41	18 05	18 32	01 24	02 30	03 36	04 42
20	17 45	18 07	18 32	01 36	02 38	03 40	04 42
N 10	17 48	18 09	18 34	01 47	02 45	03 43	04 41
0	17 52	18 12	18 37	01 56	02 52	03 46	04 41
S 10	17 55	18 16	18 41	02 06	02 58	03 50	04 40
20	17 59	18 21	18 47	02 16	03 05	03 53	04 40
30	18 04	18 28	18 56	02 27	03 13	03 57	04 39
35	18 06	18 32	19 02	02 34	03 17	03 59	04 39
40	18 09	18 37	19 09	02 41	03 22	04 01	04 39
45	18 13	18 43	19 18	02 50	03 28	04 04	04 38
S 50	18 17	18 50	19 30	03 00	03 35	04 07	04 38
52	18 19	18 54	19 35	03 05	03 38	04 09	04 38
54	18 21	18 57	19 41	03 10	03 42	04 10	04 37
56	18 24	19 02	19 49	03 16	03 46	04 12	04 37
58	18 26	19 07	19 57	03 22	03 50	04 14	04 37
S 60	18 29	19 13	20 07	03 30	03 55	04 16	04 36

	SUN			MOON			
Day	Eqn. of Time 00h	Eqn. of Time 12h	Mer. Pass.	Mer. Pass. Upper	Mer. Pass. Lower	Age	Phase
d	m s	m s	h m	h m	h m	d	%
4	11 06	11 15	11 49	20 38	08 11	10	79
5	11 25	11 34	11 48	21 34	09 06	11	88
6	11 43	11 52	11 48	22 28	10 01	12	95

UT	ARIES	VENUS −3.9		MARS +0.8		JUPITER −1.9		SATURN +0.6		STARS		
	GHA	GHA	Dec	GHA	Dec	GHA	Dec	GHA	Dec	Name	SHA	Dec
d h	° ′	° ′	° ′	° ′	° ′	° ′	° ′	° ′	° ′		° ′	° ′
7 00	15 33.9	186 51.0	S 2 15.6	121 02.2	S24 11.7	236 00.4	N16 16.7	146 20.4	S16 07.3	Acamar	315 17.3	S40 14.6
01	30 36.4	201 50.6	16.9	136 02.7	11.9	251 02.5	16.6	161 22.6	07.4	Achernar	335 25.6	S57 09.7
02	45 38.8	216 50.2	18.2	151 03.2	12.1	266 04.5	16.4	176 24.8	07.5	Acrux	173 08.8	S63 10.8
03	60 41.3	231 49.8	. . 19.4	166 03.8	. . 12.3	281 06.6	. . 16.3	191 27.0	. . 07.5	Adhara	255 11.8	S28 59.5
04	75 43.8	246 49.4	20.7	181 04.3	12.4	296 08.6	16.2	206 29.2	07.6	Aldebaran	290 48.2	N16 32.2
05	90 46.2	261 49.0	21.9	196 04.8	12.6	311 10.7	16.1	221 31.4	07.7			
06	105 48.7	276 48.6	S 2 23.2	211 05.4	S24 12.8	326 12.7	N16 16.0	236 33.6	S16 07.8	Alioth	166 20.6	N55 52.8
07	120 51.2	291 48.2	24.4	226 05.9	13.0	341 14.8	15.9	251 35.8	07.8	Alkaid	152 58.7	N49 14.6
08	135 53.6	306 47.8	25.7	241 06.4	13.2	356 16.9	15.7	266 38.0	07.9	Al Na'ir	27 42.4	S46 53.3
09	150 56.1	321 47.4	. . 26.9	256 06.9	. . 13.4	11 18.9	. . 15.6	281 40.2	. . 08.0	Alnilam	275 45.3	S 1 11.6
10	165 58.6	336 47.0	28.2	271 07.5	13.6	26 21.0	15.5	296 42.5	08.1	Alphard	217 55.4	S 8 43.3
11	181 01.0	351 46.6	29.4	286 08.0	13.8	41 23.0	15.4	311 44.7	08.1			
12	196 03.5	6 46.2	S 2 30.7	301 08.5	S24 14.0	56 25.1	N16 15.3	326 46.9	S16 08.2	Alphecca	126 10.6	N26 40.2
13	211 06.0	21 45.8	31.9	316 09.1	14.2	71 27.2	15.2	341 49.1	08.3	Alpheratz	357 42.2	N29 10.5
14	226 08.4	36 45.4	33.2	331 09.6	14.3	86 29.2	15.0	356 51.3	08.3	Altair	62 07.3	N 8 54.8
15	241 10.9	51 45.0	. . 34.4	346 10.1	. . 14.5	101 31.3	. . 14.9	11 53.5	. . 08.4	Ankaa	353 14.5	S42 13.5
16	256 13.3	66 44.6	35.7	1 10.6	14.7	116 33.3	14.8	26 55.7	08.5	Antares	112 25.4	S26 27.7
17	271 15.8	81 44.2	36.9	16 11.2	14.9	131 35.4	14.7	41 57.9	08.6			
18	286 18.3	96 43.8	S 2 38.2	31 11.7	S24 15.1	146 37.5	N16 14.6	57 00.1	S16 08.6	Arcturus	145 55.3	N19 06.6
19	301 20.7	111 43.4	39.4	46 12.2	15.3	161 39.5	14.5	72 02.3	08.7	Atria	107 26.6	S69 03.2
20	316 23.2	126 43.0	40.7	61 12.7	15.5	176 41.6	14.3	87 04.5	08.8	Avior	234 17.8	S59 33.2
21	331 25.7	141 42.6	. . 41.9	76 13.3	. . 15.6	191 43.6	. . 14.2	102 06.7	. . 08.9	Bellatrix	278 30.9	N 6 21.7
22	346 28.1	156 42.2	43.2	91 13.8	15.8	206 45.7	14.1	117 08.9	08.9	Betelgeuse	271 00.2	N 7 24.5
23	1 30.6	171 41.8	44.4	106 14.3	16.0	221 47.8	14.0	132 11.1	09.0			
8 00	16 33.1	186 41.4	S 2 45.7	121 14.8	S24 16.2	236 49.8	N16 13.9	147 13.3	S16 09.1	Canopus	263 55.6	S52 42.1
01	31 35.5	201 41.0	47.0	136 15.4	16.4	251 51.9	13.8	162 15.6	09.1	Capella	280 32.9	N46 00.5
02	46 38.0	216 40.6	48.2	151 15.9	16.6	266 53.9	13.6	177 17.8	09.2	Deneb	49 30.6	N45 20.4
03	61 40.5	231 40.2	. . 49.5	166 16.4	. . 16.7	281 56.0	. . 13.5	192 20.0	. . 09.3	Denebola	182 33.1	N14 29.4
04	76 42.9	246 39.8	50.7	181 16.9	16.9	296 58.1	13.4	207 22.2	09.4	Diphda	348 54.7	S17 54.2
05	91 45.4	261 39.4	52.0	196 17.5	17.1	312 00.1	13.3	222 24.4	09.4			
06	106 47.8	276 39.0	S 2 53.2	211 18.0	S24 17.3	327 02.2	N16 13.2	237 26.6	S16 09.5	Dubhe	193 51.3	N61 40.1
07	121 50.3	291 38.6	54.5	226 18.5	17.5	342 04.2	13.1	252 28.8	09.6	Elnath	278 11.3	N28 37.0
08	136 52.8	306 38.2	55.7	241 19.0	17.6	357 06.3	12.9	267 31.0	09.7	Eltanin	90 45.9	N51 29.7
09	151 55.2	321 37.8	. . 57.0	256 19.6	. . 17.8	12 08.4	. . 12.8	282 33.2	. . 09.7	Enif	33 46.0	N 9 56.9
10	166 57.7	336 37.4	58.2	271 20.1	18.0	27 10.4	12.7	297 35.4	09.8	Fomalhaut	15 22.7	S29 32.5
11	182 00.2	351 37.0	2 59.5	286 20.6	18.2	42 12.5	12.6	312 37.6	09.9			
12	197 02.6	6 36.6	S 3 00.7	301 21.1	S24 18.4	57 14.6	N16 12.5	327 39.8	S16 09.9	Gacrux	172 00.4	S57 11.6
13	212 05.1	21 36.2	02.0	316 21.6	18.5	72 16.6	12.4	342 42.0	10.0	Gienah	175 51.7	S17 37.3
14	227 07.6	36 35.8	03.2	331 22.2	18.7	87 18.7	12.3	357 44.2	10.1	Hadar	148 47.1	S60 26.6
15	242 10.0	51 35.4	. . 04.5	346 22.7	. . 18.9	102 20.7	. . 12.1	12 46.4	. . 10.2	Hamal	327 59.4	N23 31.9
16	257 12.5	66 35.0	05.7	1 23.2	19.1	117 22.8	12.0	27 48.6	10.2	Kaus Aust.	83 42.7	S34 22.5
17	272 14.9	81 34.6	07.0	16 23.7	19.3	132 24.9	11.9	42 50.8	10.3			
18	287 17.4	96 34.2	S 3 08.2	31 24.2	S24 19.4	147 26.9	N16 11.8	57 53.0	S16 10.4	Kochab	137 21.2	N74 05.9
19	302 19.9	111 33.8	09.5	46 24.8	19.6	162 29.0	11.7	72 55.3	10.5	Markab	13 37.1	N15 17.3
20	317 22.3	126 33.4	10.7	61 25.3	19.8	177 31.1	11.6	87 57.5	10.5	Menkar	314 13.8	N 4 08.9
21	332 24.8	141 33.0	. . 12.0	76 25.8	. . 20.0	192 33.1	. . 11.4	102 59.7	. . 10.6	Menkent	148 06.9	S36 26.4
22	347 27.3	156 32.6	13.2	91 26.3	20.1	207 35.2	11.3	118 01.9	10.7	Miaplacidus	221 39.8	S69 46.5
23	2 29.7	171 32.2	14.5	106 26.8	20.3	222 37.3	11.2	133 04.1	10.7			
9 00	17 32.2	186 31.8	S 3 15.7	121 27.3	S24 20.5	237 39.3	N16 11.1	148 06.3	S16 10.8	Mirfak	308 38.6	N49 54.6
01	32 34.7	201 31.4	17.0	136 27.9	20.7	252 41.4	11.0	163 08.5	10.9	Nunki	75 57.2	S26 16.5
02	47 37.1	216 31.0	18.2	151 28.4	20.8	267 43.5	10.9	178 10.7	11.0	Peacock	53 17.7	S56 41.2
03	62 39.6	231 30.6	. . 19.5	166 28.9	. . 21.0	282 45.5	. . 10.8	193 12.9	. . 11.0	Pollux	243 26.7	N27 59.2
04	77 42.1	246 30.2	20.7	181 29.4	21.2	297 47.6	10.6	208 15.1	11.1	Procyon	244 58.9	N 5 11.1
05	92 44.5	261 29.8	22.0	196 29.9	21.3	312 49.7	10.5	223 17.3	11.2			
06	107 47.0	276 29.4	S 3 23.2	211 30.5	S24 21.5	327 51.7	N16 10.4	238 19.5	S16 11.3	Rasalhague	96 05.8	N12 33.3
07	122 49.4	291 29.0	24.5	226 31.0	21.7	342 53.8	10.3	253 21.7	11.3	Regulus	207 42.8	N11 53.7
08	137 51.9	306 28.6	25.7	241 31.5	21.9	357 55.9	10.2	268 23.9	11.4	Rigel	281 11.1	S 8 11.1
09	152 54.4	321 28.2	. . 27.0	256 32.0	. . 22.0	12 57.9	. . 10.1	283 26.1	. . 11.5	Rigil Kent.	139 51.0	S60 53.7
10	167 56.8	336 27.8	28.2	271 32.5	22.2	28 00.0	10.0	298 28.3	11.5	Sabik	102 11.7	S15 44.3
11	182 59.3	351 27.4	29.5	286 33.0	22.4	43 02.1	09.8	313 30.5	11.6			
12	198 01.8	6 27.0	S 3 30.7	301 33.5	S24 22.5	58 04.1	N16 09.7	328 32.7	S16 11.7	Schedar	349 38.8	N56 37.2
13	213 04.2	21 26.6	32.0	316 34.1	22.7	73 06.2	09.6	343 34.9	11.8	Shaula	96 20.9	S37 06.7
14	228 06.7	36 26.2	33.2	331 34.6	22.9	88 08.3	09.5	358 37.1	11.8	Sirius	258 32.9	S16 44.2
15	243 09.2	51 25.7	. . 34.4	346 35.1	. . 23.0	103 10.3	. . 09.4	13 39.3	. . 11.9	Spica	158 30.6	S11 14.1
16	258 11.6	66 25.3	35.7	1 35.6	23.2	118 12.4	09.3	28 41.5	12.0	Suhail	222 52.0	S43 29.4
17	273 14.1	81 24.9	36.9	16 36.1	23.4	133 14.5	09.2	43 43.7	12.1			
18	288 16.5	96 24.5	S 3 38.2	31 36.6	S24 23.5	148 16.5	N16 09.0	58 45.9	S16 12.1	Vega	80 38.4	N38 48.3
19	303 19.0	111 24.1	39.4	46 37.1	23.7	163 18.6	08.9	73 48.1	12.2	Zuben'ubi	137 04.7	S16 06.0
20	318 21.5	126 23.7	40.7	61 37.7	23.9	178 20.7	08.8	88 50.3	12.3		SHA	Mer. Pass.
21	333 23.9	141 23.3	. . 41.9	76 38.2	. . 24.0	193 22.7	. . 08.7	103 52.5	. . 12.4		° ′	h m
22	348 26.4	156 22.9	43.2	91 38.7	24.2	208 24.8	08.6	118 54.7	12.4	Venus	170 08.3	11 34
23	3 28.9	171 22.5	44.4	106 39.2	24.4	223 26.9	08.5	133 56.9	12.5	Mars	104 41.8	15 54
	h m									Jupiter	220 16.8	8 12
Mer. Pass. 22 50.0		v −0.4	d 1.3	v 0.5	d 0.2	v 2.1	d 0.1	v 2.2	d 0.1	Saturn	130 40.3	14 09

SUN and MOON

UT	SUN GHA	SUN Dec	MOON GHA	v	MOON Dec	d	HP
d h	° ′	° ′	° ′	′	° ′	′	′
7 00	183 00.2	S 5 23.2	22 10.4	8.4	S 0 22.5	11.7	60.4
01	198 00.4	24.1	36 37.8	8.4	S 0 10.8	11.8	60.4
02	213 00.6	25.1	51 05.2	8.3	N 0 01.0	11.7	60.4
03	228 00.7 ..	26.1	65 32.5	8.4	0 12.7	11.8	60.4
04	243 00.9	27.0	79 59.9	8.4	0 24.5	11.7	60.4
05	258 01.1	28.0	94 27.3	8.3	0 36.2	11.8	60.4
06	273 01.3	S 5 28.9	108 54.6	8.4	N 0 48.0	11.7	60.4
T 07	288 01.5	29.9	123 22.0	8.4	0 59.7	11.7	60.4
U 08	303 01.7	30.8	137 49.4	8.4	1 11.4	11.8	60.4
E 09	318 01.8 ..	31.8	152 16.8	8.4	1 23.2	11.7	60.4
S 10	333 02.0	32.7	166 44.2	8.4	1 34.9	11.6	60.4
D 11	348 02.2	33.7	181 11.6	8.4	1 46.5	11.7	60.4
A 12	3 02.4	S 5 34.7	195 39.0	8.5	N 1 58.2	11.7	60.3
Y 13	18 02.6	35.6	210 06.5	8.4	2 09.9	11.6	60.3
14	33 02.7	36.6	224 33.9	8.4	2 21.5	11.6	60.3
15	48 02.9 ..	37.5	239 01.3	8.4	2 33.1	11.6	60.3
16	63 03.1	38.5	253 28.7	8.5	2 44.7	11.6	60.3
17	78 03.3	39.4	267 56.2	8.4	2 56.3	11.6	60.3
18	93 03.5	S 5 40.4	282 23.6	8.4	N 3 07.9	11.5	60.3
19	108 03.6	41.3	296 51.0	8.5	3 19.4	11.5	60.2
20	123 03.8	42.3	311 18.5	8.4	3 30.9	11.5	60.2
21	138 04.0 ..	43.2	325 45.9	8.4	3 42.4	11.4	60.2
22	153 04.2	44.2	340 13.3	8.5	3 53.8	11.4	60.2
23	168 04.3	45.2	354 40.8	8.4	4 05.2	11.4	60.2
8 00	183 04.5	S 5 46.1	9 08.2	8.5	N 4 16.6	11.4	60.2
01	198 04.7	47.1	23 35.7	8.4	4 28.0	11.3	60.2
02	213 04.9	48.0	38 03.1	8.5	4 39.3	11.3	60.1
03	228 05.1 ..	49.0	52 30.6	8.4	4 50.6	11.2	60.1
04	243 05.2	49.9	66 58.0	8.5	5 01.8	11.2	60.1
05	258 05.4	50.9	81 25.5	8.4	5 13.0	11.2	60.1
06	273 05.6	S 5 51.8	95 52.9	8.5	N 5 24.2	11.1	60.1
W 07	288 05.8	52.8	110 20.4	8.5	5 35.3	11.1	60.0
E 08	303 05.9	53.7	124 47.9	8.5	5 46.4	11.1	60.0
D 09	318 06.1 ..	54.7	139 15.3	8.5	5 57.5	11.0	60.0
N 10	333 06.3	55.6	153 42.8	8.4	6 08.5	10.9	60.0
E 11	348 06.5	56.6	168 10.2	8.5	6 19.4	10.9	60.0
S 12	3 06.7	S 5 57.5	182 37.7	8.4	N 6 30.3	10.9	59.9
D 13	18 06.8	58.5	197 05.1	8.5	6 41.2	10.8	59.9
A 14	33 07.0	5 59.5	211 32.6	8.4	6 52.0	10.8	59.9
Y 15	48 07.2	6 00.4	226 00.0	8.5	7 02.8	10.7	59.9
16	63 07.4	01.4	240 27.5	8.4	7 13.5	10.6	59.9
17	78 07.5	02.3	254 54.9	8.5	7 24.1	10.6	59.8
18	93 07.7	S 6 03.3	269 22.4	8.5	N 7 34.7	10.6	59.8
19	108 07.9	04.2	283 49.9	8.4	7 45.3	10.5	59.8
20	123 08.1	05.2	298 17.3	8.5	7 55.8	10.4	59.8
21	138 08.2 ..	06.1	312 44.8	8.4	8 06.2	10.4	59.7
22	153 08.4	07.1	327 12.2	8.5	8 16.6	10.3	59.7
23	168 08.6	08.0	341 39.7	8.4	8 26.9	10.3	59.7
9 00	183 08.8	S 6 09.0	356 07.1	8.5	N 8 37.2	10.1	59.7
01	198 09.0	09.9	10 34.6	8.4	8 47.3	10.2	59.6
02	213 09.1	10.9	25 02.0	8.5	8 57.5	10.0	59.6
03	228 09.3 ..	11.8	39 29.5	8.4	9 07.5	10.0	59.6
04	243 09.4	12.8	53 56.9	8.4	9 17.5	10.0	59.6
05	258 09.6	13.7	68 24.3	8.5	9 27.5	9.8	59.5
06	273 09.8	S 6 14.7	82 51.8	8.4	N 9 37.3	9.8	59.5
T 07	288 10.0	15.6	97 19.2	8.5	9 47.1	9.8	59.5
H 08	303 10.1	16.6	111 46.7	8.4	9 56.9	9.6	59.4
U 09	318 10.3 ..	17.5	126 14.1	8.5	10 06.5	9.6	59.4
R 10	333 10.5	18.5	140 41.6	8.4	10 16.1	9.5	59.4
S 11	348 10.7	19.4	155 09.0	8.5	10 25.6	9.5	59.4
D 12	3 10.8	S 6 20.4	169 36.5	8.4	N10 35.1	9.3	59.3
A 13	18 11.0	21.3	184 03.9	8.5	10 44.4	9.3	59.3
Y 14	33 11.2	22.3	198 31.4	8.4	10 53.7	9.3	59.3
15	48 11.3 ..	23.2	212 58.8	8.4	11 03.0	9.1	59.2
16	63 11.5	24.2	227 26.2	8.5	11 12.1	9.1	59.2
17	78 11.7	25.1	241 53.7	8.4	11 21.2	8.9	59.2
18	93 11.8	S 6 26.1	256 21.1	8.5	N11 30.1	8.9	59.1
19	108 12.0	27.0	270 48.6	8.4	11 39.0	8.9	59.1
20	123 12.2	28.0	285 16.0	8.5	11 47.9	8.7	59.1
21	138 12.4 ..	28.9	299 43.5	8.4	11 56.6	8.7	59.1
22	153 12.5	29.8	314 10.9	8.5	12 05.3	8.6	59.0
23	168 12.7	30.8	328 38.4	8.5	N12 13.9	8.5	59.0
	SD 16.0	d 1.0	SD 16.4		16.3		16.2

Moonrise

Lat.	Naut.	Civil	Sunrise	7	8	9	10
°	h m	h m	h m	h m	h m	h m	h m
N 72	04 23	05 42	06 50	16 34	16 28	16 22	16 16
N 70	04 31	05 42	06 43	16 38	16 39	16 41	16 45
68	04 37	05 42	06 37	16 41	16 47	16 55	17 07
66	04 42	05 41	06 33	16 43	16 54	17 07	17 24
64	04 46	05 41	06 29	16 45	17 00	17 17	17 38
62	04 49	05 41	06 25	16 47	17 05	17 25	17 50
60	04 52	05 40	06 22	16 49	17 10	17 33	18 00
N 58	04 54	05 40	06 19	16 51	17 14	17 39	18 09
56	04 56	05 39	06 17	16 52	17 17	17 45	18 17
54	04 58	05 39	06 14	16 53	17 21	17 50	18 24
52	05 00	05 39	06 12	16 54	17 24	17 55	18 30
50	05 01	05 38	06 11	16 55	17 26	17 59	18 36
45	05 03	05 37	06 06	16 57	17 32	18 09	18 48
N 40	05 05	05 36	06 03	16 59	17 37	18 17	18 58
35	05 05	05 35	06 00	17 01	17 41	18 23	19 07
30	05 06	05 33	05 57	17 02	17 45	18 29	19 15
20	05 05	05 31	05 53	17 05	17 52	18 40	19 28
N 10	05 03	05 27	05 48	17 07	17 58	18 49	19 40
0	04 59	05 24	05 44	17 09	18 03	18 57	19 51
S 10	04 54	05 19	05 40	17 11	18 09	19 06	20 02
20	04 47	05 13	05 36	17 14	18 15	19 15	20 14
30	04 38	05 06	05 30	17 17	18 22	19 26	20 28
35	04 31	05 01	05 27	17 18	18 26	19 32	20 36
40	04 24	04 56	05 24	17 20	18 30	19 39	20 45
45	04 14	04 50	05 19	17 22	18 36	19 47	20 56
S 50	04 01	04 41	05 14	17 25	18 42	19 57	21 09
52	03 55	04 37	05 12	17 26	18 45	20 02	21 15
54	03 49	04 33	05 09	17 27	18 48	20 07	21 22
56	03 41	04 28	05 07	17 28	18 52	20 13	21 29
58	03 32	04 23	05 03	17 30	18 56	20 19	21 38
S 60	03 22	04 17	05 00	17 32	19 01	20 27	21 47

Moonset

Lat.	Sunset	Civil	Naut.	7	8	9	10
°	h m	h m	h m	h m	h m	h m	h m
N 72	16 43	17 51	19 09	04 46	06 45	08 45	10 44
N 70	16 50	17 51	19 02	04 46	06 37	08 28	10 16
68	16 57	17 52	18 56	04 45	06 31	08 15	09 56
66	17 01	17 52	18 51	04 45	06 26	08 04	09 39
64	17 05	17 53	18 48	04 45	06 21	07 55	09 26
62	17 09	17 53	18 44	04 44	06 17	07 48	09 15
60	17 12	17 54	18 42	04 44	06 14	07 41	09 05
N 58	17 15	17 54	18 39	04 44	06 11	07 36	08 57
56	17 17	17 55	18 37	04 44	06 08	07 30	08 49
54	17 20	17 55	18 36	04 43	06 06	07 26	08 43
52	17 22	17 56	18 34	04 43	06 03	07 22	08 37
50	17 24	17 56	18 33	04 43	06 01	07 18	08 32
45	17 28	17 57	18 31	04 43	05 57	07 10	08 20
N 40	17 31	17 59	18 30	04 43	05 54	07 03	08 11
35	17 35	18 00	18 29	04 42	05 50	06 58	08 03
30	17 37	18 01	18 29	04 42	05 48	06 53	07 56
20	17 42	18 04	18 30	04 42	05 43	06 44	07 44
N 10	17 47	18 08	18 32	04 41	05 39	06 36	07 33
0	17 51	18 12	18 36	04 41	05 35	06 29	07 23
S 10	17 55	18 16	18 41	04 40	05 31	06 22	07 13
20	18 00	18 22	18 48	04 40	05 27	06 14	07 02
30	18 05	18 30	18 58	04 39	05 22	06 06	06 50
35	18 09	18 34	19 04	04 39	05 19	06 01	06 43
40	18 12	18 40	19 12	04 38	05 16	05 55	06 34
45	18 17	18 47	19 22	04 38	05 13	05 48	06 26
S 50	18 22	18 55	19 35	04 38	05 08	05 40	06 15
52	18 24	18 59	19 41	04 38	05 07	05 37	06 10
54	18 27	19 03	19 48	04 37	05 04	05 33	06 04
56	18 30	19 08	19 56	04 37	05 02	05 29	05 58
58	18 33	19 14	20 05	04 37	04 59	05 24	05 51
S 60	18 37	19 20	20 16	04 36	04 57	05 18	05 43

SUN / MOON

Day	Eqn. of Time 00h	Eqn. of Time 12h	Mer. Pass.	Mer. Pass. Upper	Mer. Pass. Lower	Age	Phase
d	m s	m s	h m	h m	h m	d	%
7	12 00	12 09	11 48	10 55	23 22	13	99
8	12 18	12 26	11 48	11 49	24 16	14	100
9	12 35	12 43	11 47	12 43	00 16	15	99

UT	ARIES	VENUS −4.0		MARS +0.8		JUPITER −1.9		SATURN +0.6		STARS		
	GHA	GHA	Dec	GHA	Dec	GHA	Dec	GHA	Dec	Name	SHA	Dec
d h	° ′	° ′	° ′	° ′	° ′	° ′	° ′	° ′	° ′		° ′	° ′
10 00	18 31.3	186 22.1	S 3 45.7	121 39.7	S24 24.5	238 28.9	N16 08.4	148 59.2	S16 12.6	Acamar	315 17.3	S40 14.7
01	33 33.8	201 21.7	46.9	136 40.2	24.7	253 31.0	08.2	164 01.4	12.6	Achernar	335 25.6	S57 09.7
02	48 36.3	216 21.3	48.2	151 40.7	24.9	268 33.1	08.1	179 03.6	12.7	Acrux	173 08.8	S63 10.7
03	63 38.7	231 20.9 ..	49.4	166 41.2 ..	25.0	283 35.2 ..	08.0	194 05.8 ..	12.8	Adhara	255 11.8	S28 59.5
04	78 41.2	246 20.5	50.7	181 41.7	25.2	298 37.2	07.9	209 08.0	12.9	Aldebaran	290 48.1	N16 32.2
05	93 43.7	261 20.1	51.9	196 42.3	25.4	313 39.3	07.8	224 10.2	12.9			
06	108 46.1	276 19.7	S 3 53.2	211 42.8	S24 25.5	328 41.4	N16 07.7	239 12.4	S16 13.0	Alioth	166 20.6	N55 52.8
07	123 48.6	291 19.3	54.4	226 43.3	25.7	343 43.4	07.6	254 14.6	13.1	Alkaid	152 58.7	N49 14.5
08	138 51.0	306 18.9	55.7	241 43.8	25.8	358 45.5	07.4	269 16.8	13.2	Al Na'ir	27 42.4	S46 53.3
F 09	153 53.5	321 18.4 ..	56.9	256 44.3 ..	26.0	13 47.6 ..	07.3	284 19.0 ..	13.2	Alnilam	275 45.3	S 1 11.6
R 10	168 56.0	336 18.0	58.1	271 44.8	26.2	28 49.7	07.2	299 21.2	13.3	Alphard	217 55.4	S 8 43.3
I 11	183 58.4	351 17.6	3 59.4	286 45.3	26.3	43 51.7	07.1	314 23.4	13.4			
D 12	199 00.9	6 17.2	S 4 00.6	301 45.8	S24 26.5	58 53.8	N16 07.0	329 25.6	S16 13.5	Alphecca	126 10.6	N26 40.2
A 13	214 03.4	21 16.8	01.9	316 46.3	26.6	73 55.9	06.9	344 27.8	13.5	Alpheratz	357 42.2	N29 10.5
Y 14	229 05.8	36 16.4	03.1	331 46.8	26.8	88 57.9	06.8	359 30.0	13.6	Altair	62 07.3	N 8 54.8
15	244 08.3	51 16.0 ..	04.4	346 47.4 ..	27.0	104 00.0 ..	06.7	14 32.2 ..	13.7	Ankaa	353 14.5	S42 13.5
16	259 10.8	66 15.6	05.6	1 47.9	27.1	119 02.1	06.5	29 34.4	13.7	Antares	112 25.4	S26 27.7
17	274 13.2	81 15.2	06.9	16 48.4	27.3	134 04.2	06.4	44 36.6	13.8			
18	289 15.7	96 14.8	S 4 08.1	31 48.9	S24 27.4	149 06.2	N16 06.3	59 38.8	S16 13.9	Arcturus	145 55.3	N19 06.6
19	304 18.2	111 14.4	09.4	46 49.4	27.6	164 08.3	06.2	74 41.0	14.0	Atria	107 26.7	S69 03.2
20	319 20.6	126 14.0	10.6	61 49.9	27.7	179 10.4	06.1	89 43.2	14.0	Avior	234 15.9	S59 33.2
21	334 23.1	141 13.6 ..	11.8	76 50.4 ..	27.9	194 12.5 ..	06.0	104 45.4 ..	14.1	Bellatrix	278 30.9	N 6 21.7
22	349 25.5	156 13.1	13.1	91 50.9	28.1	209 14.5	05.9	119 47.6	14.2	Betelgeuse	271 00.2	N 7 24.5
23	4 28.0	171 12.7	14.3	106 51.4	28.2	224 16.6	05.8	134 49.8	14.3			
11 00	19 30.5	186 12.3	S 4 15.6	121 51.9	S24 28.4	239 18.7	N16 05.6	149 52.0	S16 14.3	Canopus	263 55.6	S52 42.1
01	34 32.9	201 11.9	16.8	136 52.4	28.5	254 20.7	05.5	164 54.2	14.4	Capella	280 32.9	N46 00.5
02	49 35.4	216 11.5	18.1	151 52.9	28.7	269 22.8	05.4	179 56.4	14.5	Deneb	49 30.7	N45 20.4
03	64 37.9	231 11.1 ..	19.3	166 53.4 ..	28.8	284 24.9 ..	05.3	194 58.6 ..	14.6	Denebola	182 33.1	N14 29.4
04	79 40.3	246 10.7	20.6	181 53.9	29.0	299 27.0	05.2	210 00.8	14.6	Diphda	348 54.7	S17 54.2
05	94 42.8	261 10.3	21.8	196 54.4	29.1	314 29.0	05.1	225 03.0	14.7			
06	109 45.3	276 09.9	S 4 23.0	211 54.9	S24 29.3	329 31.1	N16 05.0	240 05.2	S16 14.8	Dubhe	193 51.3	N61 40.1
07	124 47.7	291 09.5	24.3	226 55.4	29.4	344 33.2	04.9	255 07.4	14.8	Elnath	278 11.3	N28 37.0
S 08	139 50.2	306 09.0	25.5	241 55.9	29.6	359 35.3	04.7	270 09.6	14.9	Eltanin	90 45.9	N51 29.7
A 09	154 52.6	321 08.6 ..	26.8	256 56.4 ..	29.8	14 37.4 ..	04.6	285 11.8 ..	15.0	Enif	33 46.0	N 9 56.9
T 10	169 55.1	336 08.2	28.0	271 57.0	29.9	29 39.4	04.5	300 14.0	15.1	Fomalhaut	15 22.7	S29 32.5
U 11	184 57.6	351 07.8	29.3	286 57.5	30.1	44 41.5	04.4	315 16.2	15.1			
R 12	200 00.0	6 07.4	S 4 30.5	301 58.0	S24 30.2	59 43.6	N16 04.3	330 18.4	S16 15.2	Gacrux	172 00.4	S57 11.6
D 13	215 02.5	21 07.0	31.7	316 58.5	30.4	74 45.7	04.2	345 20.6	15.3	Gienah	175 51.7	S17 37.3
A 14	230 05.0	36 06.6	33.0	331 59.0	30.5	89 47.7	04.1	0 22.8	15.4	Hadar	148 47.1	S60 26.6
Y 15	245 07.4	51 06.2 ..	34.2	346 59.5 ..	30.7	104 49.8 ..	04.0	15 25.0 ..	15.4	Hamal	327 59.4	N23 31.9
16	260 09.9	66 05.8	35.5	2 00.0	30.8	119 51.9	03.8	30 27.2	15.5	Kaus Aust.	83 42.7	S34 22.5
17	275 12.4	81 05.3	36.7	17 00.5	30.9	134 54.0	03.7	45 29.4	15.6			
18	290 14.8	96 04.9	S 4 38.0	32 01.0	S24 31.1	149 56.0	N16 03.6	60 31.6	S16 15.7	Kochab	137 21.3	N74 05.9
19	305 17.3	111 04.5	39.2	47 01.5	31.2	164 58.1	03.5	75 33.8	15.7	Markab	13 37.2	N15 17.3
20	320 19.8	126 04.1	40.4	62 02.0	31.4	180 00.2	03.4	90 36.0	15.8	Menkar	314 13.8	N 4 08.9
21	335 22.2	141 03.7 ..	41.7	77 02.5 ..	31.5	195 02.3 ..	03.3	105 38.2 ..	15.9	Menkent	148 06.9	S36 26.4
22	350 24.7	156 03.3	42.9	92 03.0	31.7	210 04.4	03.2	120 40.4	16.0	Miaplacidus	221 39.8	S69 46.5
23	5 27.1	171 02.9	44.2	107 03.5	31.8	225 06.4	03.1	135 42.6	16.0			
12 00	20 29.6	186 02.5	S 4 45.4	122 04.0	S24 32.0	240 08.5	N16 02.9	150 44.8	S16 16.1	Mirfak	308 38.6	N49 54.6
01	35 32.1	201 02.0	46.6	137 04.5	32.1	255 10.6	02.8	165 47.0	16.2	Nunki	75 57.3	S26 16.6
02	50 34.5	216 01.6	47.9	152 05.0	32.3	270 12.7	02.7	180 49.2	16.2	Peacock	53 17.7	S56 41.2
03	65 37.0	231 01.2 ..	49.1	167 05.5 ..	32.4	285 14.8 ..	02.6	195 51.4 ..	16.3	Pollux	243 26.7	N27 59.2
04	80 39.5	246 00.8	50.4	182 06.0	32.6	300 16.8	02.5	210 53.6	16.4	Procyon	244 58.8	N 5 11.1
05	95 41.9	261 00.4	51.6	197 06.5	32.7	315 18.9	02.4	225 55.8	16.5			
06	110 44.4	276 00.0	S 4 52.9	212 07.0	S24 32.9	330 21.0	N16 02.3	240 58.0	S16 16.5	Rasalhague	96 05.8	N12 33.3
07	125 46.9	290 59.6	54.1	227 07.5	33.0	345 23.1	02.2	256 00.2	16.6	Regulus	207 42.8	N11 53.7
08	140 49.3	305 59.1	55.3	242 08.0	33.1	0 25.2	02.1	271 02.4	16.7	Rigel	281 11.0	S 8 11.1
S 09	155 51.8	320 58.7 ..	56.6	257 08.5 ..	33.3	15 27.2 ..	01.9	286 04.6 ..	16.8	Rigil Kent.	139 51.0	S60 53.7
U 10	170 54.3	335 58.3	57.8	272 09.0	33.4	30 29.3	01.8	301 06.8	16.8	Sabik	102 11.7	S15 44.3
N 11	185 56.7	350 57.9	4 59.1	287 09.4	33.6	45 31.4	01.7	316 09.0	16.9			
D 12	200 59.2	5 57.5	S 5 00.3	302 09.9	S24 33.7	60 33.5	N16 01.6	331 11.1	S16 17.0	Schedar	349 38.8	N56 37.2
A 13	216 01.6	20 57.1	01.5	317 10.4	33.8	75 35.6	01.5	346 13.3	17.1	Shaula	96 20.9	S37 06.7
Y 14	231 04.1	35 56.6	02.8	332 10.9	34.0	90 37.6	01.4	1 15.5	17.1	Sirius	258 32.9	S16 44.2
15	246 06.6	50 56.2 ..	04.0	347 11.4 ..	34.1	105 39.7 ..	01.3	16 17.7 ..	17.2	Spica	158 30.6	S11 14.1
16	261 09.0	65 55.8	05.2	2 11.9	34.3	120 41.8	01.2	31 19.9	17.3	Suhail	222 51.9	S43 29.4
17	276 11.5	80 55.4	06.5	17 12.4	34.4	135 43.9	01.1	46 22.1	17.4			
18	291 14.0	95 55.0	S 5 07.7	32 12.9	S24 34.5	150 46.0	N16 00.9	61 24.3	S16 17.4	Vega	80 38.4	N38 48.3
19	306 16.4	110 54.6	09.0	47 13.4	34.7	165 48.0	00.8	76 26.5	17.5	Zuben'ubi	137 04.7	S16 06.0
20	321 18.9	125 54.1	10.2	62 13.9	34.8	180 50.1	00.7	91 28.7	17.6			SHA Mer.Pass.
21	336 21.4	140 53.7 ..	11.4	77 14.4 ..	34.9	195 52.2 ..	00.6	106 30.9 ..	17.6		° ′	h m
22	351 23.8	155 53.3	12.7	92 14.9	35.1	210 54.3	00.5	121 33.1	17.7	Venus	166 41.9	11 35
23	6 26.3	170 52.9	13.9	107 15.4	35.2	225 56.4	00.4	136 35.3	17.8	Mars	102 21.4	15 52
	h m									Jupiter	219 48.2	8 02
Mer. Pass. 22 38.2		v −0.4	d 1.2	v 0.5	d 0.2	v 2.1	d 0.1	v 2.2	d 0.1	Saturn	130 21.5	13 58

UT	SUN GHA	SUN Dec	MOON GHA	v	MOON Dec	d	HP
d h	° ′	° ′	° ′	′	° ′	′	′
10 00	183 12.9	S 6 31.7	343 05.9	8.4	N12 22.4	8.4	59.0
01	198 13.0	32.7	357 33.3	8.5	12 30.8	8.3	58.9
02	213 13.2	33.6	12 00.8	8.4	12 39.1	8.2	58.9
03	228 13.4	.. 34.6	26 28.2	8.5	12 47.3	8.2	58.9
04	243 13.5	35.5	40 55.7	8.5	12 55.5	8.0	58.8
05	258 13.7	36.5	55 23.2	8.5	13 03.5	8.0	58.8
06	273 13.9	S 6 37.4	69 50.7	8.4	N13 11.5	7.9	58.8
07	288 14.0	38.4	84 18.1	8.5	13 19.4	7.8	58.7
08	303 14.2	39.3	98 45.6	8.5	13 27.2	7.7	58.7
F 09	318 14.4	.. 40.3	113 13.1	8.5	13 34.9	7.6	58.7
R 10	333 14.5	41.2	127 40.6	8.5	13 42.5	7.6	58.6
I 11	348 14.7	42.2	142 08.1	8.5	13 50.1	7.4	58.6
D 12	3 14.9	S 6 43.1	156 35.6	8.5	N13 57.5	7.4	58.5
A 13	18 15.0	44.0	171 03.1	8.5	14 04.9	7.2	58.5
Y 14	33 15.2	45.0	185 30.6	8.6	14 12.1	7.2	58.5
15	48 15.4	.. 45.9	199 58.2	8.5	14 19.3	7.0	58.4
16	63 15.5	46.9	214 25.7	8.5	14 26.3	7.0	58.4
17	78 15.7	47.8	228 53.2	8.6	14 33.3	6.9	58.4
18	93 15.9	S 6 48.8	243 20.8	8.5	N14 40.2	6.8	58.3
19	108 16.0	49.7	257 48.3	8.6	14 47.0	6.6	58.3
20	123 16.2	50.7	272 15.9	8.6	14 53.6	6.6	58.3
21	138 16.4	.. 51.6	286 43.5	8.5	15 00.2	6.5	58.2
22	153 16.5	52.5	301 11.0	8.6	15 06.7	6.4	58.2
23	168 16.7	53.5	315 38.6	8.6	15 13.1	6.3	58.2
11 00	183 16.9	S 6 54.4	330 06.2	8.6	N15 19.4	6.2	58.1
01	198 17.0	55.4	344 33.8	8.7	15 25.6	6.1	58.1
02	213 17.2	56.3	359 01.5	8.6	15 31.7	6.0	58.1
03	228 17.4	.. 57.3	13 29.1	8.7	15 37.7	5.9	58.0
04	243 17.5	58.2	27 56.8	8.6	15 43.6	5.8	58.0
05	258 17.7	6 59.1	42 24.4	8.7	15 49.4	5.7	58.0
06	273 17.8	S 7 00.1	56 52.1	8.7	N15 55.1	5.6	57.9
S 07	288 18.0	01.0	71 19.8	8.7	16 00.7	5.5	57.9
A 08	303 18.2	02.0	85 47.5	8.7	16 06.2	5.4	57.8
T 09	318 18.3	.. 02.9	100 15.2	8.7	16 11.6	5.3	57.8
U 10	333 18.5	03.9	114 42.9	8.8	16 16.9	5.2	57.8
R 11	348 18.7	04.8	129 10.7	8.7	16 22.1	5.1	57.7
D 12	3 18.8	S 7 05.7	143 38.4	8.8	N16 27.2	4.9	57.7
A 13	18 19.0	06.7	158 06.2	8.8	16 32.1	4.9	57.7
Y 14	33 19.1	07.6	172 34.0	8.8	16 37.0	4.8	57.6
15	48 19.3	.. 08.6	187 01.8	8.8	16 41.8	4.7	57.6
16	63 19.5	09.5	201 29.6	8.9	16 46.5	4.6	57.6
17	78 19.6	10.4	215 57.5	8.8	16 51.1	4.5	57.5
18	93 19.8	S 7 11.4	230 25.3	8.9	N16 55.6	4.3	57.5
19	108 19.9	12.3	244 53.2	8.9	16 59.9	4.3	57.4
20	123 20.1	13.3	259 21.1	9.0	17 04.2	4.2	57.4
21	138 20.3	.. 14.2	273 49.1	8.9	17 08.4	4.1	57.4
22	153 20.4	15.1	288 17.0	9.0	17 12.5	3.9	57.3
23	168 20.6	16.1	302 45.0	9.0	17 16.4	3.9	57.3
12 00	183 20.7	S 7 17.0	317 13.0	9.0	N17 20.3	3.7	57.3
01	198 20.9	18.0	331 41.0	9.0	17 24.0	3.7	57.2
02	213 21.1	18.9	346 09.0	9.1	17 27.7	3.5	57.2
03	228 21.2	.. 19.8	0 37.1	9.0	17 31.2	3.5	57.2
04	243 21.4	20.8	15 05.1	9.1	17 34.7	3.3	57.1
05	258 21.5	21.7	29 33.2	9.2	17 38.0	3.3	57.1
06	273 21.7	S 7 22.7	44 01.4	9.1	N17 41.3	3.1	57.0
07	288 21.8	23.6	58 29.5	9.2	17 44.4	3.0	57.0
S 08	303 22.0	24.5	72 57.7	9.2	17 47.4	3.0	56.9
U 09	318 22.2	.. 25.5	87 25.9	9.2	17 50.4	2.8	56.9
N 10	333 22.3	26.4	101 54.1	9.3	17 53.2	2.7	56.9
D 11	348 22.5	27.3	116 22.4	9.3	17 55.9	2.6	56.9
A 12	3 22.6	S 7 28.3	130 50.7	9.3	N17 58.5	2.6	56.8
Y 13	18 22.8	29.2	145 19.0	9.4	18 01.1	2.4	56.8
14	33 22.9	30.2	159 47.4	9.3	18 03.5	2.3	56.8
15	48 23.1	.. 31.1	174 15.7	9.4	18 05.8	2.2	56.7
16	63 23.3	32.0	188 44.1	9.5	18 08.0	2.1	56.7
17	78 23.4	33.0	203 12.6	9.5	18 10.1	2.0	56.7
18	93 23.6	S 7 33.9	217 41.1	9.5	N18 12.1	1.9	56.6
19	108 23.7	34.8	232 09.6	9.5	18 14.0	1.8	56.6
20	123 23.9	35.8	246 38.1	9.5	18 15.8	1.7	56.6
21	138 24.0	.. 36.7	261 06.6	9.6	18 17.5	1.6	56.5
22	153 24.2	37.7	275 35.2	9.7	18 19.1	1.5	56.5
23	168 24.3	38.6	290 03.9	9.6	N18 20.6	1.4	56.5
	SD 16.0	d 0.9	SD 16.0		15.7		15.5

Twilight / Sunrise / Moonrise

Lat.	Twilight Naut.	Twilight Civil	Sunrise	Moonrise 10	Moonrise 11	Moonrise 12	Moonrise 13
°	h m	h m	h m	h m	h m	h m	h m
N 72	04 37	05 55	07 04	16 16	16 06	15 30	▭
N 70	04 43	05 54	06 56	16 45	16 54	17 13	17 55
68	04 47	05 52	06 48	17 07	17 24	17 54	18 39
66	04 51	05 51	06 42	17 24	17 47	18 21	19 08
64	04 54	05 49	06 37	17 38	18 06	18 42	19 30
62	04 57	05 48	06 33	17 50	18 21	19 00	19 48
60	04 59	05 47	06 29	18 00	18 33	19 14	20 03
N 58	05 01	05 46	06 26	18 09	18 44	19 26	20 15
56	05 02	05 45	06 23	18 17	18 54	19 37	20 26
54	05 04	05 44	06 20	18 24	19 02	19 46	20 36
52	05 05	05 44	06 17	18 30	19 10	19 54	20 44
50	05 05	05 43	06 15	18 36	19 16	20 02	20 52
45	05 07	05 41	06 10	18 48	19 31	20 18	21 08
N 40	05 08	05 39	06 06	18 58	19 43	20 31	21 21
35	05 08	05 37	06 02	19 07	19 53	20 42	21 33
30	05 07	05 35	05 59	19 15	20 02	20 52	21 43
20	05 06	05 31	05 53	19 28	20 18	21 09	22 00
N 10	05 03	05 27	05 48	19 40	20 32	21 24	22 15
0	04 58	05 23	05 43	19 51	20 45	21 37	22 29
S 10	04 53	05 17	05 38	20 02	20 58	21 51	22 43
20	04 45	05 11	05 33	20 14	21 12	22 06	22 58
30	04 34	05 02	05 27	20 28	21 27	22 23	23 15
35	04 27	04 57	05 23	20 36	21 37	22 33	23 25
40	04 18	04 51	05 19	20 45	21 47	22 44	23 36
45	04 08	04 44	05 14	20 56	22 00	22 58	23 49
S 50	03 54	04 35	05 08	21 09	22 15	23 14	24 06
52	03 48	04 30	05 05	21 15	22 22	23 22	24 13
54	03 40	04 25	05 02	21 22	22 30	23 30	24 22
56	03 32	04 20	04 59	21 29	22 39	23 40	24 32
58	03 22	04 14	04 55	21 38	22 49	23 51	24 42
S 60	03 11	04 07	04 51	21 47	23 01	24 04	00 04

Sunset / Twilight / Moonset

Lat.	Sunset	Twilight Civil	Twilight Naut.	Moonset 10	Moonset 11	Moonset 12	Moonset 13
°	h m	h m	h m	h m	h m	h m	h m
N 72	16 27	17 36	18 54	10 44	12 46	15 13	▭
N 70	16 36	17 38	18 48	10 16	12 00	13 30	14 36
68	16 44	17 40	18 44	09 56	11 29	12 50	13 52
66	16 50	17 41	18 40	09 39	11 07	12 23	13 23
64	16 55	17 43	18 37	09 26	10 49	12 02	13 01
62	16 59	17 44	18 35	09 15	10 35	11 45	12 43
60	17 03	17 45	18 33	09 05	10 22	11 31	12 28
N 58	17 07	17 46	18 31	08 57	10 12	11 19	12 16
56	17 10	17 47	18 30	08 49	10 03	11 08	12 05
54	17 13	17 48	18 29	08 43	09 55	10 59	11 55
52	17 15	17 49	18 28	08 37	09 47	10 51	11 47
50	17 17	17 50	18 27	08 32	09 41	10 44	11 39
45	17 23	17 52	18 26	08 20	09 27	10 28	11 23
N 40	17 27	17 54	18 25	08 11	09 15	10 15	11 10
35	17 31	17 56	18 25	08 03	09 05	10 04	10 58
30	17 34	17 58	18 26	07 56	08 57	09 55	10 48
20	17 40	18 02	18 27	07 44	08 42	09 38	10 31
N 10	17 45	18 06	18 31	07 33	08 29	09 24	10 16
0	17 50	18 11	18 35	07 23	08 17	09 10	10 02
S 10	17 55	18 18	18 41	07 13	08 05	08 57	09 48
20	18 01	18 23	18 49	07 02	07 52	08 42	09 33
30	18 07	18 32	19 00	06 50	07 37	08 26	09 16
35	18 11	18 37	19 07	06 43	07 29	08 16	09 06
40	18 15	18 43	19 16	06 35	07 19	08 05	08 54
45	18 20	18 51	19 27	06 26	07 07	07 52	08 41
S 50	18 27	19 00	19 41	06 15	06 54	07 37	08 25
52	18 29	19 04	19 47	06 10	06 47	07 29	08 17
54	18 33	19 09	19 55	06 04	06 40	07 21	08 08
56	18 36	19 15	20 04	05 58	06 32	07 12	07 59
58	18 40	19 21	20 14	05 51	06 23	07 02	07 48
S 60	18 44	19 29	20 25	05 43	06 13	06 50	07 35

SUN / MOON

Day	Eqn. of Time 00h	Eqn. of Time 12h	Mer. Pass.	Mer. Pass. Upper	Mer. Pass. Lower	Age	Phase
d	m s	m s	h m	h m	h m	d	%
10	12 51	12 59	11 47	01 10	13 37	16	95
11	13 07	13 15	11 47	02 04	14 31	17	88
12	13 23	13 30	11 46	02 57	15 24	18	81

UT	ARIES GHA	VENUS −4.0 GHA	VENUS Dec	MARS +0.9 GHA	MARS Dec	JUPITER −2.0 GHA	JUPITER Dec	SATURN +0.6 GHA	SATURN Dec	STARS Name	SHA	Dec
13 00	21 28.7	185 52.5	S 5 15.1	122 15.9	S24 35.3	240 58.5	N16 00.3	151 37.5	S16 17.9	Acamar	315 17.3	S40 14.7
01	36 31.2	200 52.1	16.4	137 16.4	35.5	256 00.5	00.2	166 39.7	17.9	Achernar	335 25.6	S57 09.7
02	51 33.7	215 51.6	17.6	152 16.9	35.6	271 02.6	00.1	181 41.9	18.0	Acrux	173 08.8	S63 10.7
03	66 36.1	230 51.2	.. 18.9	167 17.4	.. 35.8	286 04.7	16 00.0	196 44.1	.. 18.1	Adhara	255 11.8	S28 59.5
04	81 38.6	245 50.8	20.1	182 17.9	35.9	301 06.8	15 59.8	211 46.3	18.2	Aldebaran	290 48.1	N16 32.2
05	96 41.1	260 50.4	21.3	197 18.4	36.0	316 08.9	59.7	226 48.5	18.2			
M 06	111 43.5	275 50.0	S 5 22.6	212 18.8	S24 36.2	331 11.0	N15 59.6	241 50.7	S16 18.3	Alioth	166 20.6	N55 52.8
O 07	126 46.0	290 49.5	23.8	227 19.3	36.3	346 13.1	59.5	256 52.9	18.4	Alkaid	152 58.7	N49 14.5
N 08	141 48.5	305 49.1	25.0	242 19.8	36.4	1 15.1	59.4	271 55.1	18.5	Al Na'ir	27 42.4	S46 53.3
D 09	156 50.9	320 48.7	.. 26.3	257 20.3	.. 36.6	16 17.2	.. 59.3	286 57.3	.. 18.5	Alnilam	275 45.3	S 1 11.6
A 10	171 53.4	335 48.3	27.5	272 20.8	36.7	31 19.3	59.2	301 59.5	18.6	Alphard	217 55.4	S 8 43.3
Y 11	186 55.9	350 47.9	28.7	287 21.3	36.8	46 21.4	59.1	317 01.7	18.7			
12	201 58.3	5 47.4	S 5 30.0	302 21.8	S24 36.9	61 23.5	N15 59.0	332 03.9	S16 18.8	Alphecca	126 10.6	N26 40.2
13	217 00.8	20 47.0	31.2	317 22.3	37.1	76 25.6	58.9	347 06.1	18.8	Alpheratz	357 42.2	N29 10.5
14	232 03.2	35 46.6	32.5	332 22.8	37.2	91 27.7	58.7	2 08.3	18.9	Altair	62 07.3	N 8 54.8
15	247 05.7	50 46.2	.. 33.7	347 23.3	.. 37.3	106 29.7	.. 58.6	17 10.5	.. 19.0	Ankaa	353 14.5	S42 13.5
16	262 08.2	65 45.8	34.9	2 23.8	37.5	121 31.8	58.5	32 12.7	19.1	Antares	112 25.4	S26 27.7
17	277 10.6	80 45.3	36.2	17 24.2	37.6	136 33.9	58.4	47 14.8	19.1			
18	292 13.1	95 44.9	S 5 37.4	32 24.7	S24 37.7	151 36.0	N15 58.3	62 17.0	S16 19.2	Arcturus	145 55.3	N19 06.5
19	307 15.6	110 44.5	38.6	47 25.2	37.9	166 38.1	58.2	77 19.2	19.3	Atria	107 26.7	S69 03.2
20	322 18.0	125 44.1	39.9	62 25.7	38.0	181 40.2	58.1	92 21.4	19.3	Avior	234 17.7	S59 33.2
21	337 20.5	140 43.6	.. 41.1	77 26.2	.. 38.1	196 42.3	.. 58.0	107 23.6	.. 19.4	Bellatrix	278 30.9	N 6 21.7
22	352 23.0	155 43.2	42.3	92 26.7	38.2	211 44.4	57.9	122 25.8	19.5	Betelgeuse	271 00.2	N 7 24.5
23	7 25.4	170 42.8	43.6	107 27.2	38.4	226 46.4	57.8	137 28.0	19.6			
14 00	22 27.9	185 42.4	S 5 44.8	122 27.7	S24 38.5	241 48.5	N15 57.7	152 30.2	S16 19.6	Canopus	263 55.6	S52 42.1
01	37 30.4	200 42.0	46.0	137 28.1	38.6	256 50.6	57.5	167 32.4	19.7	Capella	280 32.9	N46 00.5
02	52 32.8	215 41.5	47.3	152 28.6	38.7	271 52.7	57.4	182 34.6	19.8	Deneb	49 30.7	N45 20.5
03	67 35.3	230 41.1	.. 48.5	167 29.1	.. 38.9	286 54.8	.. 57.3	197 36.8	.. 19.9	Denebola	182 33.1	N14 29.4
04	82 37.7	245 40.7	49.7	182 29.6	39.0	301 56.9	57.2	212 39.0	19.9	Diphda	348 54.7	S17 54.2
05	97 40.2	260 40.3	50.9	197 30.1	39.1	316 59.0	57.1	227 41.2	20.0			
T 06	112 42.7	275 39.8	S 5 52.2	212 30.6	S24 39.2	332 01.1	N15 57.0	242 43.4	S16 20.1	Dubhe	193 51.3	N61 40.1
U 07	127 45.1	290 39.4	53.4	227 31.1	39.4	347 03.2	56.9	257 45.6	20.2	Elnath	278 11.3	N28 37.0
E 08	142 47.6	305 39.0	54.6	242 31.6	39.5	2 05.2	56.8	272 47.8	20.2	Eltanin	90 45.9	N51 29.7
S 09	157 50.1	320 38.6	.. 55.9	257 32.0	.. 39.6	17 07.3	.. 56.7	287 50.0	.. 20.3	Enif	33 46.1	N 9 56.9
D 10	172 52.5	335 38.1	57.1	272 32.5	39.7	32 09.4	56.6	302 52.2	20.4	Fomalhaut	15 22.7	S29 32.5
A 11	187 55.0	350 37.7	58.3	287 33.0	39.8	47 11.5	56.5	317 54.4	20.5			
Y 12	202 57.5	5 37.3	S 5 59.6	302 33.5	S24 40.0	62 13.6	N15 56.3	332 56.5	S16 20.5	Gacrux	172 00.4	S57 11.6
13	217 59.9	20 36.9	6 00.8	317 34.0	40.1	77 15.7	56.2	347 58.7	20.6	Gienah	175 51.7	S17 37.3
14	233 02.4	35 36.4	02.0	332 34.5	40.2	92 17.8	56.1	3 00.9	20.7	Hadar	148 47.1	S60 26.5
15	248 04.8	50 36.0	.. 03.3	347 35.0	.. 40.3	107 19.9	.. 56.0	18 03.1	.. 20.8	Hamal	327 59.4	N23 32.0
16	263 07.3	65 35.6	04.5	2 35.4	40.4	122 22.0	55.9	33 05.3	20.8	Kaus Aust.	83 42.7	S34 22.5
17	278 09.8	80 35.1	05.7	17 35.9	40.6	137 24.1	55.8	48 07.5	20.9			
18	293 12.2	95 34.7	S 6 06.9	32 36.4	S24 40.7	152 26.2	N15 55.7	63 09.7	S16 21.0	Kochab	137 21.3	N74 05.9
19	308 14.7	110 34.3	08.2	47 36.9	40.8	167 28.2	55.6	78 11.9	21.1	Markab	13 37.2	N15 17.3
20	323 17.2	125 33.9	09.4	62 37.4	40.9	182 30.3	55.5	93 14.1	21.1	Menkar	314 13.8	N 4 08.9
21	338 19.6	140 33.4	.. 10.6	77 37.9	.. 41.0	197 32.4	.. 55.4	108 16.3	.. 21.2	Menkent	148 06.9	S36 26.4
22	353 22.1	155 33.0	11.9	92 38.3	41.2	212 34.5	55.3	123 18.5	21.3	Miaplacidus	221 39.7	S69 46.5
23	8 24.6	170 32.6	13.1	107 38.8	41.3	227 36.6	55.2	138 20.7	21.3			
15 00	23 27.0	185 32.2	S 6 14.3	122 39.3	S24 41.4	242 38.7	N15 55.0	153 22.9	S16 21.4	Mirfak	308 38.6	N49 54.6
01	38 29.5	200 31.7	15.5	137 39.8	41.5	257 40.8	54.9	168 25.1	21.5	Nunki	75 57.3	S26 16.5
02	53 32.0	215 31.3	16.8	152 40.3	41.6	272 42.9	54.8	183 27.3	21.6	Peacock	53 17.8	S56 41.2
03	68 34.4	230 30.9	.. 18.0	167 40.7	.. 41.7	287 45.0	.. 54.7	198 29.5	.. 21.6	Pollux	243 26.7	N27 59.2
04	83 36.9	245 30.4	19.2	182 41.2	41.8	302 47.1	54.6	213 31.6	21.7	Procyon	244 58.8	N 5 11.1
05	98 39.3	260 30.0	20.4	197 41.7	42.0	317 49.2	54.5	228 33.8	21.8			
W 06	113 41.8	275 29.6	S 6 21.7	212 42.2	S24 42.1	332 51.3	N15 54.4	243 36.0	S16 21.9	Rasalhague	96 05.8	N12 33.3
E 07	128 44.3	290 29.1	22.9	227 42.7	42.2	347 53.4	54.3	258 38.2	21.9	Regulus	207 42.8	N11 53.6
D 08	143 46.7	305 28.7	24.1	242 43.1	42.3	2 55.5	54.2	273 40.4	22.0	Rigel	281 11.0	S 8 11.1
N 09	158 49.2	320 28.3	.. 25.4	257 43.6	.. 42.4	17 57.6	.. 54.1	288 42.6	.. 22.1	Rigil Kent.	139 51.0	S60 53.6
E 10	173 51.7	335 27.9	26.6	272 44.1	42.5	32 59.7	54.0	303 44.8	22.2	Sabik	102 11.7	S15 44.3
S 11	188 54.1	350 27.4	27.8	287 44.6	42.6	48 01.8	53.9	318 47.0	22.2			
D 12	203 56.6	5 27.0	S 6 29.0	302 45.1	S24 42.7	63 03.8	N15 53.8	333 49.2	S16 22.3	Schedar	349 38.8	N56 37.2
A 13	218 59.1	20 26.6	30.3	317 45.5	42.9	78 05.9	53.7	348 51.4	22.4	Shaula	96 20.9	S37 06.7
Y 14	234 01.5	35 26.1	31.5	332 46.0	43.0	93 08.0	53.5	3 53.6	22.5	Sirius	258 32.9	S16 44.2
15	249 04.0	50 25.7	.. 32.7	347 46.5	.. 43.1	108 10.1	.. 53.4	18 55.8	.. 22.5	Spica	158 30.6	S11 14.1
16	264 06.5	65 25.3	33.9	2 47.0	43.2	123 12.2	53.3	33 58.0	22.6	Suhail	222 51.9	S43 29.4
17	279 08.9	80 24.8	35.2	17 47.5	43.3	138 14.3	53.2	49 00.1	22.7			
18	294 11.4	95 24.4	S 6 36.4	32 47.9	S24 43.4	153 16.4	N15 53.1	64 02.3	S16 22.8	Vega	80 38.4	N38 48.3
19	309 13.8	110 24.0	37.6	47 48.4	43.5	168 18.5	53.0	79 04.5	22.8	Zuben'ubi	137 04.7	S16 06.0
20	324 16.3	125 23.5	38.8	62 48.9	43.6	183 20.6	52.9	94 06.7	22.9			
21	339 18.8	140 23.1	.. 40.0	77 49.4	.. 43.7	198 22.7	.. 52.8	109 08.9	.. 23.0			
22	354 21.2	155 22.7	41.3	92 49.8	43.8	213 24.8	52.7	124 11.1	23.1			
23	9 23.7	170 22.2	42.5	107 50.3	43.9	228 26.9	52.6	139 13.3	23.1			

		SHA	Mer. Pass.
		° '	h m
Venus		163 02.3	11 38
Mars		99 59.8	15 50
Jupiter		219 20.6	7 52
Saturn		130 02.3	13 48

	ARIES	VENUS	MARS	JUPITER	SATURN
Mer. Pass.	22 26.5	v −0.4 d 1.2	v 0.5 d 0.1	v 2.1 d 0.1	v 2.2 d 0.1

UT	SUN GHA	SUN Dec	MOON GHA	v	Dec	d	HP
13 00	183 24.5	S 7 39.5	304 32.5	9.7	N18 22.0	1.3	56.4
01	198 24.6	40.5	319 01.2	9.8	18 23.3	1.2	56.4
02	213 24.8	41.4	333 30.0	9.7	18 24.5	1.1	56.4
03	228 24.9	.. 42.3	347 58.7	9.8	18 25.6	0.9	56.3
04	243 25.1	43.3	2 27.5	9.9	18 26.5	0.9	56.3
05	258 25.2	44.2	16 56.4	9.8	18 27.4	0.8	56.3
M 06	273 25.4	S 7 45.1	31 25.2	9.9	N18 28.2	0.7	56.2
O 07	288 25.6	46.1	45 54.1	10.0	18 28.9	0.6	56.2
N 08	303 25.7	47.0	60 23.1	10.0	18 29.5	0.5	56.2
D 09	318 25.9	.. 47.9	74 52.1	10.0	18 30.0	0.4	56.1
A 10	333 26.0	48.9	89 21.1	10.0	18 30.4	0.3	56.1
Y 11	348 26.2	49.8	103 50.1	10.1	18 30.7	0.2	56.1
12	3 26.3	S 7 50.7	118 19.2	10.2	N18 30.9	0.1	56.0
13	18 26.5	51.7	132 48.4	10.1	18 31.0	0.0	56.0
14	33 26.6	52.6	147 17.5	10.3	18 31.0	0.1	56.0
15	48 26.8	.. 53.5	161 46.8	10.2	18 30.9	0.2	55.9
16	63 26.9	54.5	176 16.0	10.3	18 30.7	0.3	55.9
17	78 27.1	55.4	190 45.3	10.3	18 30.4	0.4	55.9
18	93 27.2	S 7 56.3	205 14.6	10.4	N18 30.0	0.4	55.8
19	108 27.4	57.3	219 44.0	10.4	18 29.6	0.6	55.8
20	123 27.5	58.2	234 13.4	10.5	18 29.0	0.7	55.8
21	138 27.7	7 59.1	248 42.9	10.5	18 28.3	0.7	55.8
22	153 27.8	8 00.1	263 12.4	10.5	18 27.6	0.9	55.7
23	168 28.0	01.0	277 41.9	10.6	18 26.7	0.9	55.7
14 00	183 28.1	S 8 01.9	292 11.5	10.6	N18 25.8	1.1	55.7
01	198 28.2	02.8	306 41.1	10.7	18 24.7	1.1	55.6
02	213 28.4	03.8	321 10.8	10.7	18 23.6	1.2	55.6
03	228 28.5	.. 04.7	335 40.5	10.7	18 22.4	1.4	55.6
04	243 28.7	05.6	350 10.2	10.8	18 21.0	1.4	55.6
05	258 28.8	06.6	4 40.0	10.9	18 19.6	1.5	55.5
T 06	273 29.0	S 8 07.5	19 09.9	10.9	N18 18.1	1.6	55.5
U 07	288 29.1	08.4	33 39.8	10.9	18 16.5	1.6	55.5
E 08	303 29.3	09.4	48 09.7	11.0	18 14.9	1.8	55.4
S 09	318 29.4	.. 10.3	62 39.7	11.0	18 13.1	1.9	55.4
D 10	333 29.6	11.2	77 09.7	11.0	18 11.2	1.9	55.4
A 11	348 29.7	12.1	91 39.7	11.1	18 09.3	2.1	55.4
Y 12	3 29.9	S 8 13.1	106 09.8	11.2	N18 07.2	2.1	55.3
13	18 30.0	14.0	120 40.0	11.2	18 05.1	2.2	55.3
14	33 30.1	14.9	135 10.2	11.2	18 02.9	2.3	55.3
15	48 30.3	.. 15.9	149 40.4	11.3	18 00.6	2.4	55.3
16	63 30.4	16.8	164 10.7	11.3	17 58.2	2.5	55.2
17	78 30.6	17.7	178 41.0	11.4	17 55.7	2.5	55.2
18	93 30.7	S 8 18.6	193 11.4	11.4	N17 53.2	2.7	55.2
19	108 30.9	19.6	207 41.8	11.5	17 50.5	2.7	55.2
20	123 31.0	20.5	222 12.3	11.5	17 47.8	2.8	55.1
21	138 31.1	.. 21.4	236 42.8	11.5	17 45.0	2.9	55.1
22	153 31.3	22.3	251 13.3	11.6	17 42.1	3.0	55.1
23	168 31.4	23.3	265 43.9	11.7	17 39.1	3.0	55.1
15 00	183 31.6	S 8 24.2	280 14.6	11.7	N17 36.1	3.2	55.0
01	198 31.7	25.1	294 45.3	11.7	17 32.9	3.2	55.0
02	213 31.9	26.1	309 16.0	11.8	17 29.7	3.3	55.0
03	228 32.0	.. 27.0	323 46.8	11.8	17 26.4	3.4	55.0
04	243 32.1	27.9	338 17.6	11.9	17 23.0	3.5	55.0
05	258 32.3	28.8	352 48.5	11.9	17 19.5	3.5	54.9
W 06	273 32.4	S 8 29.8	7 19.4	11.9	N17 16.0	3.6	54.9
E 07	288 32.6	30.7	21 50.3	12.0	17 12.4	3.7	54.9
D 08	303 32.7	31.6	36 21.3	12.1	17 08.7	3.8	54.9
N 09	318 32.8	.. 32.5	50 52.4	12.1	17 04.9	3.9	54.9
E 10	333 33.0	33.5	65 23.5	12.1	17 01.0	3.9	54.8
S 11	348 33.1	34.4	79 54.6	12.2	16 57.1	4.0	54.8
D 12	3 33.3	S 8 35.3	94 25.8	12.3	N16 53.1	4.1	54.8
A 13	18 33.4	36.2	108 57.1	12.2	16 49.0	4.2	54.8
Y 14	33 33.5	37.1	123 28.3	12.4	16 44.8	4.2	54.8
15	48 33.7	.. 38.1	137 59.7	12.3	16 40.6	4.3	54.7
16	63 33.8	39.0	152 31.0	12.4	16 36.3	4.4	54.7
17	78 33.9	39.9	167 02.4	12.5	16 31.9	4.5	54.7
18	93 34.1	S 8 40.8	181 33.9	12.5	N16 27.4	4.5	54.7
19	108 34.2	41.8	196 05.4	12.5	16 22.9	4.6	54.7
20	123 34.4	42.7	210 36.9	12.6	16 18.3	4.7	54.6
21	138 34.5	.. 43.6	225 08.5	12.6	16 13.6	4.8	54.6
22	153 34.6	44.5	239 40.1	12.7	16 08.8	4.8	54.6
23	168 34.8	45.4	254 11.8	12.7	N16 04.0	4.9	54.6
	SD 16.1	d 0.9	SD 15.3		15.1		14.9

Lat.	Naut.	Civil	Sunrise	Moonrise 13	14	15	16
N 72	04 50	06 09	07 19	☐	17 42	19 42	21 27
N 70	04 55	06 05	07 08	17 55	19 03	20 27	21 56
68	04 58	06 02	06 59	18 39	19 42	20 56	22 17
66	05 01	06 00	06 52	19 08	20 09	21 18	22 33
64	05 03	05 58	06 46	19 30	20 29	21 36	22 47
62	05 05	05 56	06 41	19 48	20 46	21 50	22 58
60	05 06	05 54	06 36	20 03	20 59	22 02	23 08
N 58	05 07	05 53	06 32	20 15	21 11	22 12	23 17
56	05 08	05 51	06 29	20 26	21 22	22 21	23 24
54	05 09	05 50	06 26	20 36	21 31	22 29	23 31
52	05 10	05 49	06 23	20 44	21 39	22 36	23 37
50	05 10	05 47	06 20	20 52	21 46	22 43	23 42
45	05 11	05 45	06 14	21 08	22 01	22 57	23 53
N 40	05 11	05 42	06 09	21 21	22 14	23 08	24 03
35	05 10	05 39	06 05	21 33	22 25	23 18	24 11
30	05 09	05 37	06 01	21 43	22 34	23 26	24 18
20	05 07	05 32	05 54	22 00	22 51	23 41	24 31
N 10	05 03	05 27	05 48	22 15	23 05	23 54	24 41
0	04 58	05 22	05 43	22 29	23 18	24 06	00 06
S 10	04 51	05 16	05 37	22 43	23 31	24 18	00 18
20	04 42	05 08	05 31	22 58	23 46	24 30	00 30
30	04 30	04 59	05 23	23 15	24 02	00 02	00 45
35	04 23	04 53	05 19	23 25	24 11	00 11	00 53
40	04 13	04 46	05 14	23 36	24 22	00 22	01 03
45	04 02	04 38	05 08	23 49	24 35	00 35	01 14
S 50	03 47	04 28	05 02	24 06	00 06	00 50	01 28
52	03 40	04 23	04 58	24 13	00 13	00 57	01 34
54	03 32	04 18	04 55	24 22	00 22	01 05	01 41
56	03 23	04 12	04 51	24 32	00 32	01 14	01 49
58	03 12	04 05	04 47	24 42	00 42	01 24	01 57
S 60	02 59	03 57	04 42	00 04	00 55	01 36	02 07

Lat.	Sunset	Civil	Naut.	Moonset 13	14	15	16
N 72	16 12	17 21	18 39	☐	16 33	16 13	16 04
N 70	16 22	17 25	18 35	14 36	15 12	15 28	15 35
68	16 31	17 28	18 32	13 52	14 33	14 58	15 13
66	16 38	17 30	18 29	13 23	14 06	14 35	14 55
64	16 44	17 33	18 27	13 01	13 45	14 18	14 41
62	16 50	17 35	18 26	12 43	13 28	14 03	14 29
60	16 54	17 36	18 24	12 28	13 14	13 51	14 19
N 58	16 59	17 38	18 23	12 16	13 02	13 40	14 10
56	17 02	17 40	18 23	12 05	12 52	13 31	14 02
54	17 05	17 41	18 22	11 55	12 43	13 22	13 55
52	17 08	17 42	18 22	11 47	12 35	13 15	13 49
50	17 11	17 44	18 22	11 39	12 27	13 08	13 43
45	17 17	17 47	18 22	11 23	12 11	12 54	13 31
N 40	17 22	17 49	18 21	11 10	11 58	12 42	13 21
35	17 27	17 52	18 21	10 58	11 47	12 32	13 12
30	17 31	17 55	18 22	10 48	11 38	12 23	13 04
20	17 37	18 00	18 25	10 31	11 21	12 07	12 51
N 10	17 43	18 05	18 29	10 16	11 06	11 54	12 39
0	17 49	18 10	18 34	10 02	10 53	11 41	12 28
S 10	17 55	18 17	18 41	09 48	10 39	11 29	12 17
20	18 02	18 24	18 50	09 33	10 24	11 15	12 05
30	18 09	18 34	19 02	09 16	10 07	10 59	11 51
35	18 14	18 39	19 10	09 06	09 58	10 50	11 43
40	18 19	18 46	19 20	08 54	09 46	10 40	11 34
45	18 24	18 55	19 31	08 41	09 33	10 28	11 24
S 50	18 31	19 05	19 46	08 25	09 17	10 13	11 11
52	18 35	19 10	19 54	08 17	09 09	10 06	11 05
54	18 38	19 16	20 02	08 08	09 01	09 58	10 58
56	18 42	19 22	20 11	07 59	08 51	09 49	10 51
58	18 47	19 29	20 23	07 48	08 41	09 39	10 42
S 60	18 52	19 37	20 36	07 35	08 28	09 28	10 33

Day	SUN Eqn. of Time 00h	12h	Mer. Pass.	MOON Mer. Pass. Upper	Lower	Age	Phase
13	13 38	13 45	11 46	03 50	16 15	19	72
14	13 52	13 59	11 46	04 41	17 05	20	63
15	14 06	14 13	11 46	05 30	17 54	21	53

UT	ARIES	VENUS −4.0		MARS +0.9		JUPITER −2.0		SATURN +0.6		STARS		
	GHA	GHA	Dec	GHA	Dec	GHA	Dec	GHA	Dec	Name	SHA	Dec
d h	° ′	° ′	° ′	° ′	° ′	° ′	° ′	° ′	° ′		° ′	° ′
16 00	24 26.2	185 21.8	S 6 43.7	122 50.8	S24 44.0	243 29.0	N15 52.5	154 15.5	S16 23.2	Acamar	315 17.3	S40 14.7
01	39 28.6	200 21.4	44.9	137 51.3	44.2	258 31.1	52.4	169 17.7	23.3	Achernar	335 25.6	S57 09.7
02	54 31.1	215 20.9	46.2	152 51.8	44.3	273 33.2	52.3	184 19.9	23.4	Acrux	173 08.8	S63 10.7
03	69 33.6	230 20.5	.. 47.4	167 52.2	.. 44.4	288 35.3	.. 52.2	199 22.1	.. 23.4	Adhara	255 11.7	S28 59.5
04	84 36.0	245 20.0	48.6	182 52.7	44.5	303 37.4	52.1	214 24.3	23.5	Aldebaran	290 48.1	N16 32.2
05	99 38.5	260 19.6	49.8	197 53.2	44.6	318 39.5	51.9	229 26.4	23.6			
06	114 41.0	275 19.2	S 6 51.0	212 53.7	S24 44.7	333 41.6	N15 51.8	244 28.6	S16 23.7	Alioth	166 20.6	N55 52.8
T 07	129 43.4	290 18.7	52.3	227 54.1	44.8	348 43.7	51.7	259 30.8	23.7	Alkaid	152 58.7	N49 14.5
H 08	144 45.9	305 18.3	53.5	242 54.6	44.9	3 45.8	51.6	274 33.0	23.8	Al Na'ir	27 42.4	S46 53.3
U 09	159 48.3	320 17.9	.. 54.7	257 55.1	.. 45.0	18 47.9	.. 51.5	289 35.2	.. 23.9	Alnilam	275 45.3	S 1 11.6
R 10	174 50.8	335 17.4	55.9	272 55.6	45.1	33 50.0	51.4	304 37.4	23.9	Alphard	217 55.3	S 8 43.3
S 11	189 53.3	350 17.0	57.1	287 56.0	45.2	48 52.1	51.3	319 39.6	24.0			
D 12	204 55.7	5 16.6	S 6 58.4	302 56.5	S24 45.3	63 54.2	N15 51.2	334 41.8	S16 24.1	Alphecca	126 10.6	N26 40.2
A 13	219 58.2	20 16.1	6 59.6	317 57.0	45.4	78 56.3	51.1	349 44.0	24.2	Alpheratz	357 42.2	N29 10.5
Y 14	235 00.7	35 15.7	7 00.8	332 57.5	45.5	93 58.4	51.0	4 46.2	24.2	Altair	62 07.3	N 8 54.8
15	250 03.1	50 15.2	.. 02.0	347 57.9	.. 45.6	109 00.5	.. 50.9	19 48.4	.. 24.3	Ankaa	353 14.5	S42 13.5
16	265 05.6	65 14.8	03.2	2 58.4	45.7	124 02.6	50.8	34 50.5	24.4	Antares	112 25.4	S26 27.7
17	280 08.1	80 14.4	04.5	17 58.9	45.8	139 04.7	50.7	49 52.7	24.5			
18	295 10.5	95 13.9	S 7 05.7	32 59.3	S24 45.9	154 06.8	N15 50.6	64 54.9	S16 24.5	Arcturus	145 55.3	N19 06.5
19	310 13.0	110 13.5	06.9	47 59.8	46.0	169 08.9	50.5	79 57.1	24.6	Atria	107 26.7	S69 03.2
20	325 15.4	125 13.0	08.1	63 00.3	46.1	184 11.0	50.4	94 59.3	24.7	Avior	234 17.7	S59 33.2
21	340 17.9	140 12.6	.. 09.3	78 00.8	.. 46.2	199 13.1	.. 50.3	110 01.5	.. 24.8	Bellatrix	278 30.9	N 6 21.7
22	355 20.4	155 12.2	10.5	93 01.2	46.3	214 15.2	50.1	125 03.7	24.8	Betelgeuse	271 00.2	N 7 24.5
23	10 22.8	170 11.7	11.8	108 01.7	46.4	229 17.3	50.0	140 05.9	24.9			
17 00	25 25.3	185 11.3	S 7 13.0	123 02.2	S24 46.5	244 19.4	N15 49.9	155 08.1	S16 25.0	Canopus	263 55.6	S52 42.1
01	40 27.8	200 10.8	14.2	138 02.6	46.6	259 21.5	49.8	170 10.3	25.1	Capella	280 32.8	N46 00.5
02	55 30.2	215 10.4	15.4	153 03.1	46.7	274 23.6	49.7	185 12.4	25.1	Deneb	49 30.7	N45 20.5
03	70 32.7	230 10.0	.. 16.6	168 03.6	.. 46.8	289 25.7	.. 49.6	200 14.6	.. 25.2	Denebola	182 33.1	N14 29.4
04	85 35.2	245 09.5	17.8	183 04.1	46.8	304 27.8	49.5	215 16.8	25.3	Diphda	348 54.7	S17 54.2
05	100 37.6	260 09.1	19.0	198 04.5	46.9	319 30.0	49.4	230 19.0	25.4			
06	115 40.1	275 08.6	S 7 20.3	213 05.0	S24 47.0	334 32.1	N15 49.3	245 21.2	S16 25.4	Dubhe	193 51.2	N61 40.1
07	130 42.6	290 08.2	21.5	228 05.5	47.1	349 34.2	49.2	260 23.4	25.5	Elnath	278 11.3	N28 37.0
F 08	145 45.0	305 07.7	22.7	243 05.9	47.2	4 36.3	49.1	275 25.6	25.6	Eltanin	90 46.0	N51 29.7
R 09	160 47.5	320 07.3	.. 23.9	258 06.4	.. 47.3	19 38.4	.. 49.0	290 27.8	.. 25.7	Enif	33 46.1	N 9 56.9
I 10	175 49.9	335 06.9	25.1	273 06.9	47.4	34 40.5	48.9	305 30.0	25.7	Fomalhaut	15 22.8	S29 32.5
D 11	190 52.4	350 06.4	26.3	288 07.3	47.5	49 42.6	48.8	320 32.1	25.8			
A 12	205 54.9	5 06.0	S 7 27.5	303 07.8	S24 47.6	64 44.7	N15 48.7	335 34.3	S16 25.9	Gacrux	172 00.3	S57 11.6
Y 13	220 57.3	20 05.5	28.8	318 08.3	47.7	79 46.8	48.6	350 36.5	26.0	Gienah	175 51.7	S17 37.3
14	235 59.8	35 05.1	30.0	333 08.8	47.8	94 48.9	48.5	5 38.7	26.0	Hadar	148 47.1	S60 26.5
15	251 02.3	50 04.6	.. 31.2	348 09.2	.. 47.9	109 51.0	.. 48.4	20 40.9	.. 26.1	Hamal	327 59.4	N23 32.0
16	266 04.7	65 04.2	32.4	3 09.7	47.9	124 53.1	48.3	35 43.1	26.2	Kaus Aust.	83 42.8	S34 22.5
17	281 07.2	80 03.7	33.6	18 10.2	48.0	139 55.2	48.2	50 45.3	26.3			
18	296 09.7	95 03.3	S 7 34.8	33 10.6	S24 48.1	154 57.3	N15 48.1	65 47.5	S16 26.3	Kochab	137 21.3	N74 05.9
19	311 12.1	110 02.8	36.0	48 11.1	48.2	169 59.4	48.0	80 49.7	26.4	Markab	13 37.2	N15 17.3
20	326 14.6	125 02.4	37.2	63 11.6	48.3	185 01.5	47.8	95 51.8	26.5	Menkar	314 13.8	N 4 08.9
21	341 17.0	140 02.0	.. 38.5	78 12.0	.. 48.4	200 03.6	.. 47.7	110 54.0	.. 26.6	Menkent	148 06.9	S36 26.4
22	356 19.5	155 01.5	39.7	93 12.5	48.5	215 05.8	47.6	125 56.2	26.6	Miaplacidus	221 39.7	S69 46.5
23	11 22.0	170 01.1	40.9	108 13.0	48.6	230 07.9	47.5	140 58.4	26.7			
18 00	26 24.4	185 00.6	S 7 42.1	123 13.4	S24 48.6	245 10.0	N15 47.4	156 00.6	S16 26.8	Mirfak	308 38.5	N49 54.6
01	41 26.9	200 00.2	43.3	138 13.9	48.7	260 12.1	47.3	171 02.8	26.9	Nunki	75 57.3	S26 16.5
02	56 29.4	214 59.7	44.5	153 14.4	48.8	275 14.2	47.2	186 05.0	26.9	Peacock	53 17.8	S56 41.2
03	71 31.8	229 59.3	.. 45.7	168 14.8	.. 48.9	290 16.3	.. 47.1	201 07.2	.. 27.0	Pollux	243 26.7	N27 59.2
04	86 34.3	244 58.8	46.9	183 15.3	49.0	305 18.4	47.0	216 09.4	27.1	Procyon	244 58.8	N 5 11.1
05	101 36.8	259 58.4	48.1	198 15.8	49.1	320 20.5	46.9	231 11.5	27.2			
06	116 39.2	274 57.9	S 7 49.3	213 16.2	S24 49.2	335 22.6	N15 46.8	246 13.7	S16 27.2	Rasalhague	96 05.8	N12 33.3
S 07	131 41.7	289 57.5	50.5	228 16.7	49.2	350 24.7	46.7	261 15.9	27.3	Regulus	207 42.8	N11 53.6
A 08	146 44.2	304 57.0	51.7	243 17.1	49.3	5 26.8	46.6	276 18.1	27.4	Rigel	281 11.0	S 8 11.1
T 09	161 46.6	319 56.6	.. 53.0	258 17.6	.. 49.4	20 29.0	.. 46.5	291 20.3	.. 27.5	Rigil Kent.	139 51.0	S60 53.6
U 10	176 49.1	334 56.1	54.2	273 18.1	49.5	35 31.1	46.4	306 22.5	27.5	Sabik	102 11.7	S15 44.3
R 11	191 51.5	349 55.7	55.4	288 18.5	49.6	50 33.2	46.3	321 24.7	27.6			
D 12	206 54.0	4 55.2	S 7 56.6	303 19.0	S24 49.6	65 35.3	N15 46.2	336 26.9	S16 27.7	Schedar	349 38.8	N56 37.2
A 13	221 56.5	19 54.8	57.8	318 19.5	49.7	80 37.4	46.1	351 29.0	27.7	Shaula	96 20.9	S37 06.7
Y 14	236 58.9	34 54.3	59.0	333 19.9	49.8	95 39.5	46.0	6 31.2	27.8	Sirius	258 32.8	S16 44.2
15	252 01.4	49 53.9	8 00.2	348 20.4	.. 49.9	110 41.6	.. 45.9	21 33.4	.. 27.9	Spica	158 30.6	S11 14.1
16	267 03.9	64 53.4	01.4	3 20.9	50.0	125 43.7	45.8	36 35.6	28.0	Suhail	222 51.9	S43 29.4
17	282 06.3	79 53.0	02.6	18 21.3	50.0	140 45.8	45.7	51 37.8	28.0			
18	297 08.8	94 52.5	S 8 03.8	33 21.8	S24 50.1	155 48.0	N15 45.6	66 40.0	S16 28.1	Vega	80 38.5	N38 48.3
19	312 11.3	109 52.1	05.0	48 22.2	50.2	170 50.1	45.5	81 42.2	28.2	Zuben'ubi	137 04.7	S16 06.0
20	327 13.7	124 51.6	06.2	63 22.7	50.3	185 52.2	45.4	96 44.4	28.3		SHA	Mer. Pass.
21	342 16.2	139 51.1	.. 07.4	78 23.2	.. 50.3	200 54.3	.. 45.3	111 46.5	.. 28.3		° ′	h m
22	357 18.7	154 50.7	08.6	93 23.6	50.4	215 56.4	45.2	126 48.7	28.4	Venus	159 46.0	11 40
23	12 21.1	169 50.2	09.8	108 24.1	50.5	230 58.5	45.1	141 50.9	28.5	Mars	97 36.9	15 47
	h m									Jupiter	218 54.1	7 42
Mer. Pass. 22 14.7		v −0.4	d 1.2	v 0.5	d 0.1	v 2.1	d 0.1	v 2.2	d 0.1	Saturn	129 42.8	13 37

UT	SUN GHA	SUN Dec	MOON GHA	v	MOON Dec	d	HP
d h	° ′	° ′	° ′	′	° ′	′	′
16 00	183 34.9	S 8 46.4	268 43.5	12.8	N15 59.1	4.9	54.6
01	198 35.0	47.3	283 15.3	12.8	15 54.2	5.1	54.6
02	213 35.2	48.2	297 47.1	12.8	15 49.1	5.1	54.5
03	228 35.3	.. 49.1	312 18.9	12.9	15 44.0	5.1	54.5
04	243 35.4	50.1	326 50.8	12.9	15 38.9	5.3	54.5
05	258 35.6	51.0	341 22.7	13.0	15 33.6	5.3	54.5
06	273 35.7	S 8 51.9	355 54.7	13.0	N15 28.3	5.3	54.5
T 07	288 35.9	52.8	10 26.7	13.1	15 23.0	5.5	54.5
H 08	303 36.0	53.7	24 58.8	13.1	15 17.5	5.5	54.5
U 09	318 36.1	.. 54.7	39 30.9	13.1	15 12.0	5.6	54.4
R 10	333 36.3	55.6	54 03.0	13.2	15 06.4	5.6	54.4
S 11	348 36.4	56.5	68 35.2	13.2	15 00.8	5.7	54.4
D 12	3 36.5	S 8 57.4	83 07.4	13.2	N14 55.1	5.7	54.4
A 13	18 36.7	58.3	97 39.6	13.3	14 49.4	5.9	54.4
Y 14	33 36.8	8 59.2	112 11.9	13.4	14 43.5	5.9	54.4
15	48 36.9	9 00.2	126 44.3	13.3	14 37.6	5.9	54.4
16	63 37.0	01.1	141 16.6	13.4	14 31.7	6.0	54.4
17	78 37.2	02.0	155 49.0	13.5	14 25.7	6.1	54.4
18	93 37.3	S 9 02.9	170 21.5	13.5	N14 19.6	6.1	54.3
19	108 37.4	03.8	184 54.0	13.5	14 13.5	6.2	54.3
20	123 37.6	04.7	199 26.5	13.6	14 07.3	6.3	54.3
21	138 37.7	.. 05.7	213 59.1	13.6	14 01.0	6.3	54.3
22	153 37.8	06.6	228 31.7	13.6	13 54.7	6.3	54.3
23	168 38.0	07.5	243 04.3	13.7	13 48.4	6.5	54.3
17 00	183 38.1	S 9 08.4	257 37.0	13.7	N13 41.9	6.4	54.3
01	198 38.2	09.3	272 09.7	13.7	13 35.5	6.6	54.3
02	213 38.4	10.2	286 42.4	13.8	13 28.9	6.6	54.3
03	228 38.5	.. 11.2	301 15.2	13.8	13 22.3	6.6	54.3
04	243 38.6	12.1	315 48.0	13.8	13 15.7	6.7	54.3
05	258 38.7	13.0	330 20.8	13.9	13 09.0	6.8	54.2
06	273 38.9	S 9 13.9	344 53.7	13.9	N13 02.2	6.8	54.2
F 07	288 39.0	14.8	359 26.6	14.0	12 55.4	6.9	54.2
R 08	303 39.1	15.7	13 59.6	14.0	12 48.5	6.9	54.2
I 09	318 39.2	.. 16.6	28 32.6	14.0	12 41.6	7.0	54.2
D 10	333 39.4	17.6	43 05.6	14.0	12 34.6	7.0	54.2
A 11	348 39.5	18.5	57 38.6	14.1	12 27.6	7.1	54.2
Y 12	3 39.6	S 9 19.4	72 11.7	14.1	N12 20.5	7.2	54.2
13	18 39.8	20.3	86 44.8	14.1	12 13.3	7.1	54.2
14	33 39.9	21.2	101 17.9	14.2	12 06.2	7.3	54.2
15	48 40.0	.. 22.1	115 51.1	14.2	11 58.9	7.3	54.2
16	63 40.1	23.0	130 24.3	14.2	11 51.6	7.3	54.2
17	78 40.3	23.9	144 57.5	14.2	11 44.3	7.4	54.2
18	93 40.4	S 9 24.9	159 30.7	14.3	N11 36.9	7.4	54.2
19	108 40.5	25.8	174 04.0	14.3	11 29.5	7.5	54.2
20	123 40.6	26.7	188 37.3	14.3	11 22.0	7.5	54.2
21	138 40.8	.. 27.6	203 10.6	14.4	11 14.5	7.6	54.2
22	153 40.9	28.5	217 44.0	14.4	11 06.9	7.6	54.2
23	168 41.0	29.4	232 17.4	14.4	10 59.3	7.7	54.2
18 00	183 41.1	S 9 30.3	246 50.8	14.4	N10 51.6	7.7	54.2
01	198 41.3	31.2	261 24.2	14.4	10 43.9	7.8	54.2
02	213 41.4	32.1	275 57.6	14.5	10 36.1	7.8	54.2
03	228 41.5	.. 33.1	290 31.1	14.5	10 28.3	7.8	54.2
04	243 41.6	34.0	305 04.6	14.6	10 20.5	7.9	54.2
05	258 41.7	34.9	319 38.2	14.5	10 12.6	8.0	54.2
06	273 41.9	S 9 35.8	334 11.7	14.6	N10 04.6	7.9	54.2
S 07	288 42.0	36.7	348 45.3	14.6	9 56.7	8.0	54.2
A 08	303 42.1	37.6	3 18.9	14.6	9 48.7	8.1	54.2
T 09	318 42.2	.. 38.5	17 52.5	14.6	9 40.6	8.1	54.2
U 10	333 42.3	39.4	32 26.1	14.7	9 32.5	8.1	54.2
R 11	348 42.5	40.3	46 59.8	14.6	9 24.4	8.2	54.2
D 12	3 42.6	S 9 41.2	61 33.4	14.7	N 9 16.2	8.2	54.2
A 13	18 42.7	42.1	76 07.1	14.7	9 08.0	8.3	54.2
Y 14	33 42.8	43.0	90 40.8	14.7	8 59.7	8.3	54.2
15	48 42.9	.. 44.0	105 14.5	14.8	8 51.4	8.3	54.2
16	63 43.1	44.9	119 48.3	14.7	8 43.1	8.4	54.2
17	78 43.2	45.8	134 22.0	14.8	8 34.7	8.4	54.2
18	93 43.3	S 9 46.7	148 55.8	14.8	N 8 26.3	8.5	54.2
19	108 43.4	47.6	163 29.6	14.8	8 17.8	8.5	54.2
20	123 43.5	48.5	178 03.4	14.8	8 09.3	8.5	54.2
21	138 43.7	.. 49.4	192 37.2	14.8	8 00.8	8.5	54.2
22	153 43.8	50.3	207 11.0	14.9	7 52.3	8.6	54.2
23	168 43.9	51.2	221 44.9	14.8	N 7 43.7	8.6	54.2
	SD 16.1	d 0.9	SD 14.8		14.8		14.8

Twilight / Moonrise

Lat.	Naut.	Civil	Sunrise	16	17	18	19
°	h m	h m	h m	h m	h m	h m	h m
N 72	05 03	06 22	07 33	21 27	23 06	24 42	00 42
N 70	05 06	06 17	07 21	21 56	23 25	24 53	00 53
68	05 08	06 13	07 11	22 17	23 39	25 02	01 02
66	05 10	06 09	07 02	22 33	23 51	25 10	01 10
64	05 11	06 06	06 55	22 47	24 01	00 01	01 16
62	05 12	06 04	06 49	22 58	24 09	00 09	01 21
60	05 13	06 01	06 44	23 08	24 17	00 17	01 26
N 58	05 14	05 59	06 39	23 17	24 23	00 23	01 30
56	05 14	05 57	06 35	23 24	24 28	00 28	01 34
54	05 14	05 55	06 31	23 31	24 33	00 33	01 37
52	05 15	05 54	06 28	23 37	24 38	00 38	01 40
50	05 15	05 52	06 25	23 42	24 42	00 42	01 43
45	05 14	05 48	06 18	23 53	24 51	00 51	01 49
N 40	05 14	05 45	06 12	24 03	00 03	00 58	01 54
35	05 12	05 42	06 07	24 11	00 11	01 04	01 58
30	05 11	05 39	06 03	24 18	00 18	01 10	02 02
20	05 07	05 33	05 55	24 31	00 31	01 20	02 08
N 10	05 03	05 27	05 49	24 41	00 41	01 28	02 14
0	04 57	05 21	05 42	00 06	00 51	01 36	02 19
S 10	04 49	05 14	05 35	00 18	01 02	01 44	02 24
20	04 40	05 06	05 28	00 30	01 12	01 52	02 30
30	04 27	04 56	05 22	00 45	01 25	02 01	02 36
35	04 18	04 49	05 15	00 53	01 32	02 07	02 40
40	04 08	04 42	05 10	01 03	01 40	02 13	02 44
45	03 56	04 33	05 03	01 14	01 49	02 20	02 49
S 50	03 40	04 22	04 55	01 28	02 00	02 29	02 55
52	03 32	04 16	04 52	01 34	02 05	02 33	02 57
54	03 23	04 10	04 48	01 41	02 11	02 37	03 00
56	03 13	04 04	04 44	01 49	02 17	02 42	03 04
58	03 01	03 56	04 39	01 57	02 25	02 47	03 07
S 60	02 47	03 47	04 33	02 07	02 33	02 53	03 11

Sunset / Twilight / Moonset

Lat.	Sunset	Civil	Naut.	16	17	18	19
°	h m	h m	h m	h m	h m	h m	h m
N 72	15 56	17 07	18 25	16 04	15 58	15 52	15 47
N 70	16 08	17 12	18 22	15 35	15 38	15 39	15 40
68	16 18	17 16	18 20	15 13	15 22	15 29	15 34
66	16 27	17 20	18 19	14 55	15 10	15 20	15 29
64	16 34	17 23	18 18	14 41	14 59	15 13	15 25
62	16 40	17 26	18 17	14 29	14 50	15 06	15 21
60	16 46	17 28	18 16	14 19	14 42	15 01	15 18
N 58	16 50	17 30	18 16	14 10	14 35	14 56	15 15
56	16 55	17 32	18 15	14 02	14 29	14 52	15 12
54	16 59	17 34	18 15	13 55	14 23	14 48	15 10
52	17 02	17 36	18 15	13 49	14 18	14 44	15 08
50	17 05	17 38	18 15	13 43	14 14	14 41	15 06
45	17 12	17 42	18 16	13 31	14 04	14 34	15 02
N 40	17 18	17 45	18 17	13 21	13 56	14 28	14 58
35	17 23	17 48	18 18	13 12	13 49	14 23	14 55
30	17 27	17 51	18 19	13 04	13 42	14 18	14 53
20	17 35	17 57	18 23	12 51	13 32	14 10	14 48
N 10	17 42	18 03	18 28	12 39	13 22	14 03	14 44
0	17 49	18 10	18 34	12 28	13 13	13 57	14 40
S 10	17 55	18 17	18 42	12 17	13 04	13 50	14 36
20	18 03	18 25	18 51	12 05	12 54	13 43	14 32
30	18 11	18 36	19 05	11 51	12 43	13 35	14 27
35	18 16	18 42	19 13	11 43	12 37	13 30	14 24
40	18 22	18 50	19 23	11 34	12 30	13 25	14 21
45	18 28	18 59	19 36	11 24	12 21	13 19	14 17
S 50	18 36	19 10	19 52	11 11	12 11	13 11	14 13
52	18 40	19 16	20 00	11 05	12 06	13 08	14 11
54	18 44	19 22	20 09	10 58	12 00	13 04	14 08
56	18 49	19 29	20 20	10 51	11 55	13 00	14 06
58	18 54	19 36	20 32	10 42	11 48	12 55	14 03
S 60	18 59	19 45	20 46	10 33	11 40	12 50	14 00

SUN / MOON

Day	Eqn. of Time 00ʰ	12ʰ	Mer. Pass.	Mer. Pass. Upper	Lower	Age	Phase
d	m s	m s	h m	h m	h m	d	%
16	14 19	14 26	11 46	06 17	18 40	22	43
17	14 32	14 38	11 45	07 02	19 24	23	34
18	14 44	14 50	11 45	07 46	20 08	24	26

UT	ARIES GHA	VENUS −4.0 GHA	Dec	MARS +0.9 GHA	Dec	JUPITER −2.0 GHA	Dec	SATURN +0.6 GHA	Dec	STARS Name	SHA	Dec
19 00	27 23.6	184 49.8	S 8 11.0	123 24.5	S24 50.6	246 00.6	N15 45.0	156 53.1	S16 28.6	Acamar	315 17.3	S40 14.7
01	42 26.0	199 49.3	12.2	138 25.0	50.7	261 02.7	44.9	171 55.3	28.6	Achernar	335 25.6	S57 09.7
02	57 28.5	214 48.9	13.4	153 25.5	50.7	276 04.9	44.8	186 57.5	28.7	Acrux	173 08.8	S63 10.7
03	72 31.0	229 48.4 ..	14.6	168 25.9 ..	50.8	291 07.0 ..	44.7	201 59.7 ..	28.8	Adhara	255 11.7	S28 59.5
04	87 33.4	244 48.0	15.8	183 26.4	50.9	306 09.1	44.6	217 01.8	28.8	Aldebaran	290 48.1	N16 32.2
05	102 35.9	259 47.5	17.0	198 26.9	50.9	321 11.2	44.4	232 04.0	28.9			
06	117 38.4	274 47.0	S 8 18.2	213 27.3	S24 51.0	336 13.3	N15 44.3	247 06.2	S16 29.0	Alioth	166 20.5	N55 52.8
07	132 40.8	289 46.6	19.4	228 27.8	51.1	351 15.4	44.2	262 08.4	29.1	Alkaid	152 58.7	N49 14.5
08	147 43.3	304 46.1	20.6	243 28.2	51.2	6 17.5	44.1	277 10.6	29.2	Al Na'ir	27 42.4	S46 53.3
S 09	162 45.8	319 45.7 ..	21.8	258 28.7 ..	51.2	21 19.7 ..	44.0	292 12.8 ..	29.2	Alnilam	275 45.3	S 1 11.6
U 10	177 48.2	334 45.2	23.0	273 29.1	51.3	36 21.8	43.9	307 15.0	29.3	Alphard	217 55.3	S 8 43.3
N 11	192 50.7	349 44.8	24.2	288 29.6	51.4	51 23.9	43.8	322 17.1	29.4			
D 12	207 53.1	4 44.3	S 8 25.4	303 30.1	S24 51.5	66 26.0	N15 43.7	337 19.3	S16 29.5	Alphecca	126 10.6	N26 40.2
A 13	222 55.6	19 43.8	26.6	318 30.5	51.5	81 28.1	43.6	352 21.5	29.5	Alpheratz	357 42.2	N29 10.5
Y 14	237 58.1	34 43.4	27.8	333 31.0	51.6	96 30.2	43.5	7 23.7	29.6	Altair	62 07.4	N 8 54.8
15	253 00.5	49 42.9 ..	29.0	348 31.4 ..	51.7	111 32.4 ..	43.4	22 25.9 ..	29.7	Ankaa	353 14.5	S42 13.5
16	268 03.0	64 42.5	30.2	3 31.9	51.7	126 34.5	43.3	37 28.1	29.8	Antares	112 25.4	S26 27.7
17	283 05.5	79 42.0	31.4	18 32.4	51.8	141 36.6	43.2	52 30.3	29.8			
18	298 07.9	94 41.5	S 8 32.6	33 32.8	S24 51.9	156 38.7	N15 43.1	67 32.4	S16 29.9	Arcturus	145 55.3	N19 06.5
19	313 10.4	109 41.1	33.8	48 33.3	51.9	171 40.8	43.0	82 34.6	30.0	Atria	107 26.7	S69 03.2
20	328 12.9	124 40.6	35.0	63 33.7	52.0	186 42.9	42.9	97 36.8	30.1	Avior	234 17.6	S59 33.2
21	343 15.3	139 40.2 ..	36.2	78 34.2 ..	52.1	201 45.1 ..	42.8	112 39.0 ..	30.1	Bellatrix	278 30.8	N 6 21.7
22	358 17.8	154 39.7	37.4	93 34.6	52.1	216 47.2	42.7	127 41.2	30.2	Betelgeuse	271 00.2	N 7 24.5
23	13 20.3	169 39.2	38.6	108 35.1	52.2	231 49.3	42.6	142 43.4	30.3			
20 00	28 22.7	184 38.8	S 8 39.8	123 35.6	S24 52.3	246 51.4	N15 42.5	157 45.6	S16 30.4	Canopus	263 55.5	S52 42.1
01	43 25.2	199 38.3	41.0	138 36.0	52.3	261 53.5	42.4	172 47.7	30.4	Capella	280 32.8	N46 00.5
02	58 27.6	214 37.8	42.2	153 36.5	52.4	276 55.7	42.3	187 49.9	30.5	Deneb	49 30.7	N45 20.5
03	73 30.1	229 37.4 ..	43.4	168 36.9 ..	52.5	291 57.8 ..	42.2	202 52.1 ..	30.6	Denebola	182 33.0	N14 29.4
04	88 32.6	244 36.9	44.6	183 37.4	52.5	306 59.9	42.1	217 54.3	30.7	Diphda	348 54.7	S17 54.3
05	103 35.0	259 36.5	45.8	198 37.8	52.6	322 02.0	42.0	232 56.5	30.7			
06	118 37.5	274 36.0	S 8 47.0	213 38.3	S24 52.6	337 04.1	N15 41.9	247 58.7	S16 30.8	Dubhe	193 51.2	N61 40.1
07	133 40.0	289 35.5	48.1	228 38.7	52.7	352 06.3	41.8	263 00.9	30.9	Elnath	278 11.2	N28 37.0
08	148 42.4	304 35.1	49.3	243 39.2	52.8	7 08.4	41.7	278 03.0	31.0	Eltanin	90 46.0	N51 29.7
M 09	163 44.9	319 34.6 ..	50.5	258 39.7 ..	52.8	22 10.5 ..	41.6	293 05.2 ..	31.0	Enif	33 46.1	N 9 56.9
O 10	178 47.4	334 34.1	51.7	273 40.1	52.9	37 12.6	41.5	308 07.4	31.1	Fomalhaut	15 22.8	S29 32.6
N 11	193 49.8	349 33.7	52.9	288 40.6	53.0	52 14.7	41.4	323 09.6	31.2			
D 12	208 52.3	4 33.2	S 8 54.1	303 41.0	S24 53.0	67 16.9	N15 41.3	338 11.8	S16 31.3	Gacrux	172 00.3	S57 11.6
A 13	223 54.7	19 32.7	55.3	318 41.5	53.1	82 19.0	41.2	353 14.0	31.3	Gienah	175 51.7	S17 37.3
Y 14	238 57.2	34 32.3	56.5	333 41.9	53.1	97 21.1	41.1	8 16.1	31.4	Hadar	148 47.1	S60 26.5
15	253 59.7	49 31.8 ..	57.7	348 42.4 ..	53.2	112 23.2 ..	41.0	23 18.3 ..	31.5	Hamal	327 59.4	N23 32.0
16	269 02.1	64 31.3	8 58.9	3 42.8	53.2	127 25.4	40.9	38 20.5	31.6	Kaus Aust.	83 42.8	S34 22.5
17	284 04.6	79 30.9	9 00.1	18 43.3	53.3	142 27.5	40.8	53 22.7	31.6			
18	299 07.1	94 30.4	S 9 01.2	33 43.7	S24 53.4	157 29.6	N15 40.7	68 24.9	S16 31.7	Kochab	137 21.4	N74 05.9
19	314 09.5	109 29.9	02.4	48 44.2	53.4	172 31.7	40.6	83 27.1	31.8	Markab	13 37.2	N15 17.3
20	329 12.0	124 29.5	03.6	63 44.6	53.5	187 33.8	40.5	98 29.2	31.9	Menkar	314 13.8	N 4 08.9
21	344 14.5	139 29.0 ..	04.8	78 45.1 ..	53.5	202 36.0 ..	40.4	113 31.4 ..	31.9	Menkent	148 06.9	S36 26.4
22	359 16.9	154 28.5	06.0	93 45.5	53.6	217 38.1	40.3	128 33.6	32.0	Miaplacidus	221 39.6	S69 46.5
23	14 19.4	169 28.0	07.2	108 46.0	53.6	232 40.2	40.2	143 35.8	32.1			
21 00	29 21.9	184 27.6	S 9 08.4	123 46.4	S24 53.7	247 42.3	N15 40.1	158 38.0	S16 32.2	Mirfak	308 38.5	N49 54.7
01	44 24.3	199 27.1	09.6	138 46.9	53.8	262 44.5	40.0	173 40.2	32.2	Nunki	75 57.3	S26 16.5
02	59 26.8	214 26.6	10.7	153 47.3	53.8	277 46.6	39.9	188 42.4	32.3	Peacock	53 17.8	S56 41.3
03	74 29.2	229 26.2 ..	11.9	168 47.8 ..	53.9	292 48.7 ..	39.8	203 44.5 ..	32.4	Pollux	243 26.6	N27 59.2
04	89 31.7	244 25.7	13.1	183 48.3	53.9	307 50.8	39.7	218 46.7	32.5	Procyon	244 58.8	N 5 11.1
05	104 34.2	259 25.2	14.3	198 48.7	54.0	322 53.0	39.6	233 48.9	32.5			
06	119 36.6	274 24.7	S 9 15.5	213 49.2	S24 54.0	337 55.1	N15 39.5	248 51.1	S16 32.6	Rasalhague	96 05.8	N12 33.3
07	134 39.1	289 24.3	16.7	228 49.6	54.1	352 57.2	39.4	263 53.3	32.7	Regulus	207 42.7	N11 53.6
08	149 41.6	304 23.8	17.8	243 50.1	54.1	7 59.3	39.3	278 55.5	32.8	Rigel	281 11.0	S 8 11.1
T 09	164 44.0	319 23.3 ..	19.0	258 50.5 ..	54.2	23 01.5 ..	39.2	293 57.6 ..	32.8	Rigil Kent.	139 51.1	S60 53.6
U 10	179 46.5	334 22.9	20.2	273 51.0	54.2	38 03.6	39.1	308 59.8	32.9	Sabik	102 11.7	S15 44.3
E 11	194 49.0	349 22.4	21.4	288 51.4	54.3	53 05.7	39.0	324 02.0	33.0			
S 12	209 51.4	4 21.9	S 9 22.6	303 51.9	S24 54.3	68 07.8	N15 38.9	339 04.2	S16 33.1	Schedar	349 38.8	N56 37.3
D 13	224 53.9	19 21.4	23.8	318 52.3	54.4	83 10.0	38.8	354 06.4	33.1	Shaula	96 20.9	S37 06.7
A 14	239 56.4	34 21.0	24.9	333 52.7	54.4	98 12.1	38.7	9 08.5	33.2	Sirius	258 32.8	S16 44.2
Y 15	254 58.8	49 20.5 ..	26.1	348 53.2 ..	54.5	113 14.2 ..	38.6	24 10.7 ..	33.3	Spica	158 30.6	S11 14.1
16	270 01.3	64 20.0	27.3	3 53.6	54.5	128 16.4	38.5	39 12.9	33.4	Suhail	222 51.9	S43 29.4
17	285 03.7	79 19.5	28.5	18 54.1	54.6	143 18.5	38.4	54 15.1	33.4			
18	300 06.2	94 19.1	S 9 29.7	33 54.5	S24 54.6	158 20.6	N15 38.3	69 17.3	S16 33.5	Vega	80 38.5	N38 48.3
19	315 08.7	109 18.6	30.8	48 55.0	54.7	173 22.7	38.2	84 19.5	33.6	Zuben'ubi	137 04.7	S16 06.0
20	330 11.1	124 18.1	32.0	63 55.4	54.7	188 24.9	38.1	99 21.6	33.7			
21	345 13.6	139 17.6 ..	33.2	78 55.9 ..	54.7	203 27.0 ..	38.0	114 23.8 ..	33.7		SHA	Mer. Pass.
22	0 16.1	154 17.1	34.4	93 56.3	54.8	218 29.1	38.0	129 26.0	33.8	Venus	156 16.1	11 42
23	15 18.5	169 16.7	35.6	108 56.8	54.8	233 31.3	37.9	144 28.2	33.9	Mars	95 12.8	15 45
										Jupiter	218 28.7	7 32
Mer. Pass. 22 02.9		v −0.5 d 1.2		v 0.5 d 0.1		v 2.1 d 0.1		v 2.2 d 0.1		Saturn	129 22.8	13 27

SUN / MOON

UT (d h)	SUN GHA	SUN Dec	MOON GHA	v	MOON Dec	d	HP
19 00	183 44.0	S 9 52.1	236 18.7	14.9	N 7 35.1	8.7	54.2
01	198 44.1	53.0	250 52.6	14.9	7 26.4	8.7	54.2
02	213 44.2	53.9	265 26.5	14.9	7 17.7	8.7	54.2
03	228 44.4	.. 54.8	280 00.4	14.9	7 09.0	8.7	54.2
04	243 44.5	55.7	294 34.3	14.9	7 00.3	8.8	54.2
05	258 44.6	56.6	309 08.2	14.9	6 51.5	8.8	54.2
06	273 44.7	S 9 57.5	323 42.1	14.9	N 6 42.7	8.9	54.2
07	288 44.8	58.4	338 16.0	14.9	6 33.8	8.9	54.2
08	303 44.9	9 59.3	352 49.9	15.0	6 24.9	8.9	54.2
S 09	318 45.0	10 00.2	7 23.9	14.9	6 16.0	8.9	54.3
U 10	333 45.2	01.1	21 57.8	15.0	6 07.1	9.0	54.3
N 11	348 45.3	02.0	36 31.8	14.9	5 58.1	9.0	54.3
D 12	3 45.4	S10 02.9	51 05.7	15.0	N 5 49.1	9.0	54.3
A 13	18 45.5	03.8	65 39.7	15.0	5 40.1	9.0	54.3
Y 14	33 45.6	04.7	80 13.7	14.9	5 31.1	9.1	54.3
15	48 45.7	.. 05.6	94 47.6	15.0	5 22.0	9.1	54.3
16	63 45.8	06.5	109 21.6	15.0	5 12.9	9.1	54.3
17	78 45.9	07.4	123 55.6	15.0	5 03.8	9.1	54.3
18	93 46.1	S10 08.3	138 29.6	14.9	N 4 54.7	9.2	54.3
19	108 46.2	09.2	153 03.5	15.0	4 45.5	9.2	54.3
20	123 46.3	10.1	167 37.5	15.0	4 36.3	9.2	54.3
21	138 46.4	.. 11.0	182 11.5	15.0	4 27.1	9.2	54.4
22	153 46.5	11.9	196 45.5	14.9	4 17.9	9.3	54.4
23	168 46.6	12.8	211 19.4	15.0	4 08.6	9.3	54.4
20 00	183 46.7	S10 13.7	225 53.4	15.0	N 3 59.3	9.3	54.4
01	198 46.8	14.6	240 27.4	14.9	3 50.0	9.3	54.4
02	213 46.9	15.5	255 01.3	15.0	3 40.7	9.4	54.4
03	228 47.1	.. 16.4	269 35.3	15.0	3 31.4	9.4	54.4
04	243 47.2	17.3	284 09.3	14.9	3 22.0	9.4	54.4
05	258 47.3	18.2	298 43.2	15.0	3 12.6	9.4	54.4
06	273 47.4	S10 19.1	313 17.2	14.9	N 3 03.2	9.4	54.4
07	288 47.5	20.0	327 51.1	14.9	2 53.8	9.4	54.5
08	303 47.6	20.9	342 25.0	15.0	2 44.4	9.5	54.5
M 09	318 47.7	.. 21.8	356 59.0	14.9	2 34.9	9.4	54.5
O 10	333 47.8	22.7	11 32.9	14.9	2 25.5	9.5	54.5
N 11	348 47.9	23.6	26 06.8	14.9	2 16.0	9.5	54.5
D 12	3 48.0	S10 24.5	40 40.7	14.9	N 2 06.5	9.5	54.5
A 13	18 48.1	25.4	55 14.6	14.9	1 57.0	9.5	54.5
Y 14	33 48.2	26.3	69 48.5	14.8	1 47.5	9.6	54.5
15	48 48.3	.. 27.2	84 22.3	14.9	1 37.9	9.5	54.6
16	63 48.4	28.1	98 56.2	14.8	1 28.4	9.6	54.6
17	78 48.6	29.0	113 30.0	14.9	1 18.8	9.5	54.6
18	93 48.7	S10 29.9	128 03.9	14.8	N 1 09.3	9.6	54.6
19	108 48.8	30.8	142 37.7	14.8	0 59.7	9.6	54.6
20	123 48.9	31.7	157 11.5	14.8	0 50.1	9.6	54.6
21	138 49.0	.. 32.5	171 45.3	14.7	0 40.5	9.6	54.6
22	153 49.1	33.4	186 19.0	14.8	0 30.9	9.6	54.7
23	168 49.2	34.3	200 52.8	14.7	0 21.3	9.6	54.7
21 00	183 49.3	S10 35.2	215 26.5	14.8	N 0 11.7	9.7	54.7
01	198 49.4	36.1	230 00.3	14.7	N 0 02.0	9.6	54.7
02	213 49.5	37.0	244 34.0	14.6	S 0 07.6	9.7	54.7
03	228 49.6	.. 37.9	259 07.6	14.7	0 17.3	9.6	54.7
04	243 49.7	38.8	273 41.3	14.7	0 26.9	9.7	54.7
05	258 49.8	39.7	288 15.0	14.6	0 36.5	9.7	54.8
06	273 49.9	S10 40.6	302 48.6	14.6	S 0 46.2	9.7	54.8
07	288 50.0	41.5	317 22.2	14.6	0 55.9	9.6	54.8
08	303 50.1	42.4	331 55.8	14.5	1 05.5	9.6	54.8
T 09	318 50.2	.. 43.2	346 29.3	14.6	1 15.2	9.6	54.8
U 10	333 50.3	44.1	1 02.9	14.5	1 24.8	9.7	54.8
E 11	348 50.4	45.0	15 36.4	14.5	1 34.5	9.7	54.9
S 12	3 50.5	S10 45.9	30 09.9	14.4	S 1 44.2	9.6	54.9
D 13	18 50.6	46.8	44 43.3	14.5	1 53.8	9.7	54.9
A 14	33 50.7	47.7	59 16.8	14.4	2 03.5	9.7	54.9
Y 15	48 50.8	.. 48.6	73 50.2	14.4	2 13.2	9.6	54.9
16	63 50.9	49.5	88 23.6	14.3	2 22.8	9.7	54.9
17	78 51.0	50.4	102 56.9	14.4	2 32.5	9.6	55.0
18	93 51.1	S10 51.2	117 30.3	14.3	S 2 42.1	9.7	55.0
19	108 51.2	52.1	132 03.6	14.3	2 51.8	9.6	55.0
20	123 51.3	53.0	146 36.9	14.2	3 01.4	9.6	55.0
21	138 51.4	.. 53.9	161 10.1	14.2	3 11.0	9.7	55.0
22	153 51.5	54.8	175 43.3	14.2	3 20.7	9.6	55.0
23	168 51.6	55.7	190 16.5	14.2	S 3 30.3	9.6	55.1
SD	16.1	d 0.9	SD 14.8		14.9		15.0

Twilight / Sunrise / Moonrise

Lat.	Naut.	Civil	Sunrise	Moonrise 19	20	21	22
	h m	h m	h m	h m	h m	h m	h m
N 72	05 16	06 35	07 49	00 42	02 17	03 52	05 28
N 70	05 18	06 29	07 34	00 53	02 22	03 51	05 22
68	05 19	06 23	07 22	01 02	02 26	03 50	05 16
66	05 19	06 19	07 13	01 10	02 29	03 50	05 12
64	05 20	06 15	07 04	01 16	02 32	03 49	05 08
62	05 20	06 12	06 57	01 21	02 35	03 49	05 05
60	05 20	06 08	06 51	01 26	02 37	03 49	05 02
N 58	05 20	06 06	06 46	01 30	02 39	03 48	04 59
56	05 20	06 03	06 41	01 34	02 41	03 48	04 57
54	05 20	06 01	06 37	01 37	02 42	03 48	04 55
52	05 19	05 59	06 33	01 40	02 43	03 48	04 53
50	05 19	05 57	06 30	01 43	02 45	03 47	04 51
45	05 18	05 52	06 22	01 49	02 48	03 47	04 48
N 40	05 17	05 48	06 16	01 54	02 50	03 47	04 45
35	05 15	05 44	06 10	01 58	02 52	03 46	04 42
30	05 13	05 41	06 05	02 02	02 54	03 46	04 40
20	05 08	05 34	05 56	02 08	02 57	03 46	04 36
N 10	05 03	05 27	05 49	02 14	03 00	03 46	04 32
0	04 56	05 20	05 41	02 19	03 02	03 45	04 29
S 10	04 48	05 13	05 34	02 24	03 05	03 45	04 26
20	04 37	05 04	05 26	02 30	03 07	03 44	04 23
30	04 23	04 52	05 17	02 36	03 10	03 44	04 19
35	04 14	04 45	05 11	02 40	03 12	03 44	04 17
40	04 03	04 37	05 05	02 44	03 14	03 44	04 14
45	03 50	04 27	04 58	02 49	03 17	03 44	04 11
S 50	03 33	04 15	04 49	02 55	03 19	03 43	04 08
52	03 24	04 09	04 45	02 57	03 21	03 43	04 07
54	03 15	04 03	04 41	03 00	03 22	03 43	04 05
56	03 04	03 56	04 36	03 04	03 24	03 43	04 03
58	02 51	03 47	04 31	03 07	03 25	03 43	04 01
S 60	02 35	03 38	04 24	03 11	03 27	03 43	03 59

Sunset / Twilight / Moonset

Lat.	Sunset	Civil	Naut.	Moonset 19	20	21	22
	h m	h m	h m	h m	h m	h m	h m
N 72	15 39	16 53	18 11	15 47	15 41	15 36	15 30
N 70	15 54	16 59	18 10	15 40	15 39	15 39	15 39
68	16 06	17 05	18 09	15 34	15 38	15 42	15 46
66	16 16	17 09	18 09	15 29	15 36	15 44	15 52
64	16 24	17 13	18 08	15 25	15 35	15 46	15 57
62	16 31	17 17	18 08	15 21	15 34	15 48	16 02
60	16 37	17 20	18 08	15 18	15 33	15 49	16 05
N 58	16 43	17 23	18 08	15 15	15 33	15 50	16 08
56	16 47	17 25	18 08	15 12	15 32	15 51	16 12
54	16 52	17 28	18 09	15 10	15 31	15 53	16 15
52	16 56	17 30	18 09	15 08	15 31	15 53	16 18
50	16 59	17 32	18 10	15 06	15 30	15 54	16 20
45	17 07	17 37	18 11	15 02	15 29	15 56	16 25
N 40	17 13	17 41	18 12	14 58	15 28	15 58	16 29
35	17 19	17 45	18 14	14 55	15 27	15 59	16 32
30	17 24	17 48	18 16	14 53	15 26	16 00	16 36
20	17 33	17 55	18 21	14 48	15 25	16 03	16 41
N 10	17 41	18 02	18 27	14 44	15 24	16 04	16 46
0	17 48	18 09	18 34	14 40	15 23	16 06	16 51
S 10	17 56	18 17	18 42	14 36	15 22	16 08	16 55
20	18 04	18 26	18 53	14 32	15 20	16 10	17 00
30	18 13	18 38	19 07	14 27	15 19	16 12	17 06
35	18 19	18 45	19 16	14 24	15 18	16 13	17 09
40	18 25	18 53	19 27	14 21	15 17	16 14	17 13
45	18 32	19 03	19 41	14 17	15 16	16 16	17 17
S 50	18 41	19 16	19 58	14 13	15 15	16 18	17 22
52	18 45	19 22	20 07	14 11	15 14	16 19	17 25
54	18 50	19 28	20 17	14 08	15 13	16 20	17 27
56	18 55	19 36	20 28	14 06	15 13	16 21	17 30
58	19 01	19 44	20 41	14 03	15 12	16 22	17 33
S 60	19 07	19 54	20 57	14 00	15 11	16 23	17 37

SUN and MOON

Day	SUN Eqn. of Time 00h	12h	Mer. Pass.	MOON Mer. Pass. Upper	Lower	Age	Phase
d	m s	m s	h m	h m	h m	d	%
19	14 56	15 01	11 45	08 27	20 51	25	18
20	15 07	15 12	11 45	09 12	21 34	26	11
21	15 17	15 22	11 45	09 56	22 18	27	6

UT	ARIES GHA	VENUS −4.0 GHA	Dec	MARS +0.9 GHA	Dec	JUPITER −2.0 GHA	Dec	SATURN +0.6 GHA	Dec	STARS Name	SHA	Dec
22 00	30 21.0	184 16.2	S 9 36.7	123 57.2	S24 54.9	248 33.4	N15 37.8	159 30.4	S16 34.0	Acamar	315 17.3	S40 14.7
01	45 23.5	199 15.7	37.9	138 57.7	54.9	263 35.5	37.7	174 32.6	34.0	Achernar	335 25.6	S57 09.7
02	60 25.9	214 15.2	39.1	153 58.1	55.0	278 37.6	37.6	189 34.7	34.1	Acrux	173 08.8	S63 10.7
03	75 28.4	229 14.8	.. 40.3	168 58.6	.. 55.0	293 39.8	.. 37.5	204 36.9	.. 34.2	Adhara	255 11.7	S28 59.5
04	90 30.8	244 14.3	41.4	183 59.0	55.1	308 41.9	37.4	219 39.1	34.3	Aldebaran	290 48.1	N16 32.2
05	105 33.3	259 13.8	42.6	198 59.5	55.1	323 44.0	37.3	234 41.3	34.3			
06	120 35.8	274 13.3	S 9 43.8	213 59.9	S24 55.1	338 46.2	N15 37.2	249 43.5	S16 34.4	Alioth	166 20.5	N55 52.8
W 07	135 38.2	289 12.8	45.0	229 00.4	55.2	353 48.3	37.1	264 45.6	34.5	Alkaid	152 58.7	N49 14.5
E 08	150 40.7	304 12.3	46.1	244 00.8	55.2	8 50.4	37.0	279 47.8	34.6	Al Na'ir	27 42.4	S46 53.4
D 09	165 43.2	319 11.9	.. 47.3	259 01.2	.. 55.3	23 52.6	.. 36.9	294 50.0	.. 34.6	Alnilam	275 45.2	S 1 11.6
N 10	180 45.6	334 11.4	48.5	274 01.7	55.3	38 54.7	36.8	309 52.2	34.7	Alphard	217 55.3	S 8 43.4
E 11	195 48.1	349 10.9	49.7	289 02.1	55.3	53 56.8	36.7	324 54.4	34.8			
S 12	210 50.6	4 10.4	S 9 50.8	304 02.6	S24 55.4	68 59.0	N15 36.6	339 56.6	S16 34.8	Alphecca	126 10.6	N26 40.2
D 13	225 53.0	19 09.9	52.0	319 03.0	55.4	84 01.1	36.5	354 58.7	34.9	Alpheratz	357 42.2	N29 10.5
A 14	240 55.5	34 09.5	53.2	334 03.5	55.5	99 03.2	36.4	10 00.9	35.0	Altair	62 07.4	N 8 54.8
Y 15	255 58.0	49 09.0	.. 54.4	349 03.9	.. 55.5	114 05.4	.. 36.3	25 03.1	.. 35.1	Ankaa	353 14.5	S42 13.5
16	271 00.4	64 08.5	55.5	4 04.4	55.5	129 07.5	36.2	40 05.3	35.1	Antares	112 25.4	S26 27.7
17	286 02.9	79 08.0	56.7	19 04.8	55.6	144 09.6	36.1	55 07.5	35.2			
18	301 05.3	94 07.5	S 9 57.9	34 05.2	S24 55.6	159 11.8	N15 36.0	70 09.6	S16 35.3	Arcturus	145 55.3	N19 06.5
19	316 07.8	109 07.0	9 59.0	49 05.7	55.6	174 13.9	35.9	85 11.8	35.4	Atria	107 26.8	S69 03.2
20	331 10.3	124 06.5	10 00.2	64 06.1	55.7	189 16.0	35.8	100 14.0	35.4	Avior	234 17.6	S59 33.2
21	346 12.7	139 06.1	.. 01.4	79 06.6	.. 55.7	204 18.2	.. 35.7	115 16.2	.. 35.5	Bellatrix	278 30.8	N 6 21.7
22	1 15.2	154 05.6	02.6	94 07.0	55.7	219 20.3	35.6	130 18.4	35.6	Betelgeuse	271 00.1	N 7 24.5
23	16 17.7	169 05.1	03.7	109 07.5	55.8	234 22.4	35.5	145 20.5	35.7			
23 00	31 20.1	184 04.6	S10 04.9	124 07.9	S24 55.8	249 24.6	N15 35.4	160 22.7	S16 35.7	Canopus	263 55.5	S52 42.1
01	46 22.6	199 04.1	06.1	139 08.3	55.8	264 26.7	35.3	175 24.9	35.8	Capella	280 32.8	N46 00.5
02	61 25.1	214 03.6	07.2	154 08.8	55.9	279 28.8	35.2	190 27.1	35.9	Deneb	49 30.7	N45 20.5
03	76 27.5	229 03.1	.. 08.4	169 09.2	.. 55.9	294 31.0	.. 35.1	205 29.3	.. 36.0	Denebola	182 33.0	N14 29.4
04	91 30.0	244 02.6	09.6	184 09.7	55.9	309 33.1	35.0	220 31.5	36.0	Diphda	348 54.7	S17 54.3
05	106 32.4	259 02.2	10.7	199 10.1	56.0	324 35.2	34.9	235 33.6	36.1			
06	121 34.9	274 01.7	S10 11.9	214 10.6	S24 56.0	339 37.4	N15 34.9	250 35.8	S16 36.2	Dubhe	193 51.2	N61 40.0
T 07	136 37.4	289 01.2	13.1	229 11.0	56.0	354 39.5	34.8	265 38.0	36.3	Elnath	278 11.2	N28 37.0
H 08	151 39.8	304 00.7	14.2	244 11.4	56.1	9 41.6	34.7	280 40.2	36.3	Eltanin	90 46.0	N51 29.7
U 09	166 42.3	319 00.2	.. 15.4	259 11.9	.. 56.1	24 43.8	.. 34.6	295 42.4	.. 36.4	Enif	33 46.1	N 9 56.9
R 10	181 44.8	333 59.7	16.6	274 12.3	56.1	39 45.9	34.5	310 44.5	36.5	Fomalhaut	15 22.8	S29 32.6
S 11	196 47.2	348 59.2	17.7	289 12.8	56.2	54 48.1	34.4	325 46.7	36.6			
D 12	211 49.7	3 58.7	S10 18.9	304 13.2	S24 56.2	69 50.2	N15 34.3	340 48.9	S16 36.6	Gacrux	172 00.3	S57 11.6
A 13	226 52.2	18 58.2	20.0	319 13.6	56.2	84 52.3	34.2	355 51.1	36.7	Gienah	175 51.6	S17 37.3
Y 14	241 54.6	33 57.7	21.2	334 14.1	56.2	99 54.5	34.1	10 53.3	36.8	Hadar	148 47.1	S60 26.5
15	256 57.1	48 57.2	.. 22.4	349 14.5	.. 56.3	114 56.6	.. 34.0	25 55.4	.. 36.9	Hamal	327 59.4	N23 32.0
16	271 59.6	63 56.8	23.5	4 15.0	56.3	129 58.7	33.9	40 57.6	36.9	Kaus Aust.	83 42.8	S34 22.5
17	287 02.0	78 56.3	24.7	19 15.4	56.3	145 00.9	33.8	55 59.8	37.0			
18	302 04.5	93 55.8	S10 25.9	34 15.8	S24 56.3	160 03.0	N15 33.7	71 02.0	S16 37.1	Kochab	137 21.4	N74 05.9
19	317 06.9	108 55.3	27.0	49 16.3	56.4	175 05.2	33.6	86 04.2	37.2	Markab	13 37.2	N15 17.3
20	332 09.4	123 54.8	28.2	64 16.7	56.4	190 07.3	33.5	101 06.3	37.2	Menkar	314 13.8	N 4 08.9
21	347 11.9	138 54.3	.. 29.3	79 17.2	.. 56.4	205 09.4	.. 33.4	116 08.5	.. 37.3	Menkent	148 06.9	S36 26.4
22	2 14.3	153 53.8	30.5	94 17.6	56.4	220 11.6	33.3	131 10.7	37.4	Miaplacidus	221 39.6	S69 46.5
23	17 16.8	168 53.3	31.7	109 18.0	56.5	235 13.7	33.2	146 12.9	37.5			
24 00	32 19.3	183 52.8	S10 32.8	124 18.5	S24 56.5	250 15.9	N15 33.1	161 15.1	S16 37.5	Mirfak	308 38.5	N49 54.7
01	47 21.7	198 52.3	34.0	139 18.9	56.5	265 18.0	33.0	176 17.2	37.6	Nunki	75 57.3	S26 16.5
02	62 24.2	213 51.8	35.1	154 19.4	56.5	280 20.1	32.9	191 19.4	37.7	Peacock	53 17.8	S56 41.3
03	77 26.7	228 51.3	.. 36.3	169 19.8	.. 56.6	295 22.3	.. 32.9	206 21.6	.. 37.8	Pollux	243 26.6	N27 59.2
04	92 29.1	243 50.8	37.4	184 20.2	56.6	310 24.4	32.8	221 23.8	37.8	Procyon	244 58.7	N 5 11.1
05	107 31.6	258 50.3	38.6	199 20.7	56.6	325 26.6	32.7	236 25.9	37.9			
06	122 34.0	273 49.8	S10 39.8	214 21.1	S24 56.6	340 28.7	N15 32.6	251 28.1	S16 38.0	Rasalhague	96 05.8	N12 33.3
07	137 36.5	288 49.3	40.9	229 21.5	56.6	355 30.9	32.5	266 30.3	38.1	Regulus	207 42.7	N11 53.6
F 08	152 39.0	303 48.8	42.1	244 22.0	56.7	10 33.0	32.4	281 32.5	38.1	Rigel	281 11.0	S 8 11.1
R 09	167 41.4	318 48.3	.. 43.2	259 22.4	.. 56.7	25 35.1	.. 32.3	296 34.7	.. 38.2	Rigil Kent.	139 51.1	S60 53.6
I 10	182 43.9	333 47.8	44.4	274 22.9	56.7	40 37.3	32.2	311 36.8	38.3	Sabik	102 11.7	S15 44.3
D 11	197 46.4	348 47.3	45.5	289 23.3	56.7	55 39.4	32.1	326 39.0	38.4			
A 12	212 48.8	3 46.8	S10 46.7	304 23.7	S24 56.7	70 41.6	N15 32.0	341 41.2	S16 38.4	Schedar	349 38.8	N56 37.3
Y 13	227 51.3	18 46.3	47.8	319 24.2	56.8	85 43.7	31.9	356 43.4	38.5	Shaula	96 20.9	S37 06.7
14	242 53.8	33 45.8	49.0	334 24.6	56.8	100 45.9	31.8	11 45.6	38.6	Sirius	258 32.8	S16 44.2
15	257 56.2	48 45.3	.. 50.1	349 25.0	.. 56.8	115 48.0	.. 31.7	26 47.7	.. 38.7	Spica	158 30.6	S11 14.1
16	272 58.7	63 44.8	51.3	4 25.5	56.8	130 50.1	31.6	41 49.9	38.7	Suhail	222 51.8	S43 29.4
17	288 01.2	78 44.3	52.4	19 25.9	56.8	145 52.3	31.5	56 52.1	38.8			
18	303 03.6	93 43.8	S10 53.6	34 26.3	S24 56.8	160 54.4	N15 31.4	71 54.3	S16 38.9	Vega	80 38.5	N38 48.3
19	318 06.1	108 43.3	54.7	49 26.8	56.8	175 56.6	31.4	86 56.5	39.0	Zuben'ubi	137 04.7	S16 06.0
20	333 08.5	123 42.8	55.9	64 27.2	56.9	190 58.7	31.3	101 58.6	39.0		SHA	Mer.Pass.
21	348 11.0	138 42.3	.. 57.0	79 27.6	.. 56.9	206 00.9	.. 31.2	117 00.8	.. 39.1		° '	h m
22	3 13.5	153 41.8	58.2	94 28.1	56.9	221 03.0	31.1	132 03.0	39.2	Venus	152 44.5	11 44
23	18 15.9	168 41.3	59.3	109 28.5	56.9	236 05.2	31.0	147 05.2	39.3	Mars	92 47.8	15 43
	h m									Jupiter	218 04.4	7 21
Mer.Pass.	21 51.1	v −0.5	d 1.2	v 0.4	d 0.0	v 2.1	d 0.1	v 2.2	d 0.1	Saturn	129 02.6	13 17

UT	SUN GHA	SUN Dec	MOON GHA	MOON v	MOON Dec	MOON d	MOON HP
d h	° ′	° ′	° ′	′	° ′	′	′
22 00	183 51.7	S10 56.6	204 49.7	14.1	S 3 39.9	9.6	55.1
01	198 51.8	57.4	219 22.8	14.1	3 49.5	9.6	55.1
02	213 51.9	58.3	233 55.9	14.1	3 59.1	9.6	55.1
03	228 52.0	10 59.2	248 29.0	14.0	4 08.7	9.5	55.1
04	243 52.1	11 00.1	263 02.0	14.0	4 18.2	9.6	55.2
05	258 52.2	01.0	277 35.0	13.9	4 27.8	9.5	55.2
06	273 52.2	S11 01.9	292 07.9	14.0	S 4 37.3	9.6	55.2
W 07	288 52.3	02.7	306 40.9	13.8	4 46.9	9.5	55.2
E 08	303 52.4	03.6	321 13.7	13.9	4 56.4	9.5	55.2
D 09	318 52.5	.. 04.5	335 46.6	13.8	5 05.9	9.5	55.3
N 10	333 52.6	05.4	350 19.4	13.8	5 15.4	9.4	55.3
E 11	348 52.7	06.3	4 52.2	13.7	5 24.8	9.5	55.3
S 12	3 52.8	S11 07.2	19 24.9	13.7	S 5 34.3	9.4	55.3
D 13	18 52.9	08.0	33 57.6	13.7	5 43.7	9.4	55.3
A 14	33 53.0	08.9	48 30.3	13.6	5 53.1	9.4	55.3
Y 15	48 53.1	.. 09.8	63 02.9	13.6	6 02.5	9.4	55.4
16	63 53.2	10.7	77 35.5	13.5	6 11.9	9.4	55.4
17	78 53.3	11.6	92 08.0	13.6	6 21.3	9.3	55.4
18	93 53.4	S11 12.4	106 40.6	13.4	S 6 30.6	9.3	55.4
19	108 53.4	13.3	121 13.0	13.4	6 39.9	9.3	55.4
20	123 53.5	14.2	135 45.4	13.4	6 49.2	9.3	55.5
21	138 53.6	.. 15.1	150 17.8	13.4	6 58.5	9.2	55.5
22	153 53.7	16.0	164 50.2	13.2	7 07.7	9.3	55.5
23	168 53.8	16.8	179 22.4	13.3	7 17.0	9.1	55.5
23 00	183 53.9	S11 17.7	193 54.7	13.2	S 7 26.1	9.2	55.5
01	198 54.0	18.6	208 26.9	13.2	7 35.3	9.1	55.6
02	213 54.1	19.5	222 59.1	13.1	7 44.4	9.1	55.6
03	228 54.2	.. 20.4	237 31.2	13.1	7 53.5	9.1	55.6
04	243 54.3	21.2	252 03.3	13.0	8 02.6	9.1	55.6
05	258 54.3	22.1	266 35.3	13.0	8 11.7	9.0	55.6
06	273 54.4	S11 23.0	281 07.3	12.9	S 8 20.7	9.0	55.7
T 07	288 54.5	23.9	295 39.2	12.9	8 29.7	8.9	55.7
H 08	303 54.6	24.7	310 11.1	12.8	8 38.6	8.9	55.7
U 09	318 54.7	.. 25.6	324 42.9	12.8	8 47.5	8.9	55.7
R 10	333 54.8	26.5	339 14.7	12.7	8 56.4	8.9	55.8
S 11	348 54.9	27.4	353 46.4	12.7	9 05.3	8.8	55.8
D 12	3 54.9	S11 28.2	8 18.1	12.7	S 9 14.1	8.8	55.8
A 13	18 55.0	29.1	22 49.8	12.6	9 22.9	8.7	55.8
Y 14	33 55.1	30.0	37 21.4	12.5	9 31.6	8.7	55.8
15	48 55.2	.. 30.9	51 52.9	12.5	9 40.3	8.7	55.9
16	63 55.3	31.7	66 24.4	12.5	9 49.0	8.6	55.9
17	78 55.4	32.6	80 55.9	12.4	S 9 57.6	8.6	55.9
18	93 55.5	S11 33.5					
19	108 55.5	34.4					
20	123 55.6	35.2					
21	138 55.7	.. 36.1					
22	153 55.8	37.0					
23	168 55.9	37.8					
24 00	183 55.9	S11 38.7	182 34.5	12.1	S10 56.7	8.3	56.0
01	198 56.0	39.6	197 05.6	12.0	11 05.0	8.2	56.1
02	213 56.1	40.5	211 36.6	11.9	11 13.2	8.2	56.1
03	228 56.2	.. 41.3	226 07.5	11.8	11 21.4	8.1	56.1
04	243 56.3	42.2	240 38.3	11.9	11 29.5	8.1	56.1
05	258 56.4	43.1	255 09.2	11.7	11 37.6	8.0	56.2
06	273 56.4	S11 43.9	269 39.9	11.7	S11 45.6	7.9	56.2
07	288 56.5	44.8	284 10.6	11.7	11 53.5	7.9	56.2
08	303 56.6	45.7	298 41.3	11.6	12 01.4	7.9	56.2
F 09	318 56.7	.. 46.5	313 11.9	11.5	12 09.3	7.8	56.2
R 10	333 56.8	47.4	327 42.4	11.5	12 17.1	7.8	56.3
I 11	348 56.8	48.3	342 12.9	11.5	12 24.9	7.6	56.3
D 12	3 56.9	S11 49.2	356 43.4	11.3	S12 32.5	7.7	56.3
A 13	18 57.0	50.0	11 13.7	11.4	12 40.2	7.5	56.3
Y 14	33 57.1	50.9	25 44.1	11.2	12 47.7	7.6	56.3
15	48 57.1	.. 51.8	40 14.3	11.2	12 55.3	7.4	56.4
16	63 57.2	52.6	54 44.5	11.2	13 02.7	7.4	56.4
17	78 57.3	53.5	69 14.7	11.1	13 10.1	7.3	56.4
18	93 57.4	S11 54.4	83 44.8	11.0	S13 17.4	7.3	56.4
19	108 57.4	55.2	98 14.8	11.0	13 24.7	7.2	56.4
20	123 57.5	56.1	112 44.8	10.9	13 31.9	7.1	56.5
21	138 57.6	.. 56.9	127 14.8	10.8	13 39.0	7.1	56.5
22	153 57.7	57.8	141 44.6	10.9	13 46.1	7.0	56.5
23	168 57.7	58.7	156 14.5	10.7	S13 53.1	7.0	56.5
	SD 16.1	d 0.9	SD 15.1	15.2			15.3

Lat.	Twilight Naut.	Twilight Civil	Sunrise	Moonrise 22	Moonrise 23	Moonrise 24	Moonrise 25
°	h m	h m	h m	h m	h m	h m	h m
N 72	05 29	06 48	08 04	05 28	07 09	08 55	10 48
N 70	05 29	06 40	07 47	05 22	06 55	08 32	10 12
68	05 29	06 34	07 34	05 16	06 45	08 15	09 46
66	05 28	06 28	07 23	05 12	06 36	08 01	09 26
64	05 28	06 23	07 14	05 08	06 28	07 49	09 10
62	05 28	06 19	07 06	05 05	06 22	07 40	08 57
60	05 27	06 16	06 59	05 02	06 16	07 31	08 46
N 58	05 26	06 12	06 53	04 59	06 11	07 24	08 37
56	05 26	06 09	06 48	04 57	06 07	07 18	08 28
54	05 25	06 06	06 43	04 55	06 03	07 12	08 21
52	05 24	06 04	06 38	04 53	06 00	07 07	08 14
50	05 24	06 01	06 35	04 51	05 56	07 02	08 08
45	05 22	05 56	06 26	04 48	05 49	06 52	07 56
N 40	05 20	05 51	06 19	04 45	05 44	06 44	07 45
35	05 17	05 47	06 13	04 42	05 39	06 37	07 36
30	05 15	05 43	06 07	04 40	05 35	06 31	07 28
20	05 09	05 35	05 58	04 36	05 27	06 20	07 14
N 10	05 03	05 28	05 49	04 32	05 21	06 11	07 03
0	04 55	05 20	05 41	04 29	05 15	06 02	06 51
S 10	04 46	05 11	05 33	04 26	05 09	05 53	06 40
20	04 35	05 01	05 24	04 23	05 02	05 44	06 29
30	04 20	04 49	05 14	04 19	04 55	05 34	06 15
35	04 10	04 42	05 08	04 17	04 51	05 28	06 08
40	03 59	04 33	05 01	04 14	04 46	05 21	05 59
45	03 44	04 22	04 53	04 11	04 41	05 13	05 49
S 50	03 26	04 09	04 43	04 08	04 34	05 03	05 37
52	03 17	04 02	04 39	04 07	04 31	04 59	05 31
54	03 06	03 55	04 34	04 05	04 28	04 54	05 25
56	02 54	03 47	04 29	04 03	04 25	04 49	05 18
58	02 40	03 38	04 23	04 01	04 21	04 43	05 10
S 60	02 23	03 28	04 16	03 59	04 16	04 37	05 01

Lat.	Sunset	Twilight Civil	Twilight Naut.	Moonset 22	Moonset 23	Moonset 24	Moonset 25
°	h m	h m	h m	h m	h m	h m	h m
N 72	15 23	16 39	17 57	15 30	15 24	15 17	15 08
N 70	15 40	16 47	17 58	15 39	15 39	15 41	15 45
68	15 53	16 53	17 58	15 46	15 52	16 00	16 12
66	16 05	16 59	17 59	15 52	16 02	16 14	16 32
64	16 14	17 04	17 59	15 57	16 10	16 27	16 49
62	16 22	17 08	18 00	16 02	16 18	16 37	17 02
60	16 29	17 12	18 00	16 05	16 24	16 46	17 14
N 58	16 35	17 15	18 01	16 09	16 30	16 54	17 24
56	16 40	17 19	18 02	16 12	16 35	17 01	17 33
54	16 45	17 21	18 03	16 15	16 39	17 07	17 40
52	16 49	17 24	18 03	16 17	16 43	17 13	17 47
50	16 53	17 27	18 04	16 20	16 47	17 18	17 54
45	17 02	17 32	18 06	16 25	16 55	17 29	18 07
N 40	17 09	17 37	18 09	16 29	17 02	17 38	18 19
35	17 16	17 41	18 11	16 32	17 08	17 46	18 28
30	17 21	17 45	18 13	16 36	17 13	17 53	18 37
20	17 31	17 53	18 19	16 41	17 22	18 05	18 51
N 10	17 40	18 01	18 26	16 46	17 30	18 15	19 04
0	17 48	18 09	18 33	16 51	17 37	18 25	19 16
S 10	17 56	18 18	18 43	16 55	17 44	18 35	19 28
20	18 05	18 28	18 54	17 00	17 52	18 46	19 41
30	18 15	18 40	19 10	17 06	18 01	18 58	19 56
35	18 21	18 48	19 19	17 09	18 07	19 05	20 04
40	18 28	18 57	19 31	17 13	18 12	19 13	20 14
45	18 36	19 08	19 46	17 17	18 19	19 22	20 25
S 50	18 46	19 21	20 05	17 22	18 28	19 34	20 39
52	18 51	19 28	20 14	17 25	18 32	19 39	20 46
54	18 56	19 35	20 24	17 27	18 36	19 45	20 53
56	19 01	19 43	20 37	17 30	18 40	19 51	21 01
58	19 08	19 52	20 52	17 33	18 46	19 59	21 10
S 60	19 15	20 03	21 09	17 37	18 52	20 07	21 20

A partial eclipse of the Sun occurs on this date. See page 5.

Day	SUN Eqn. of Time 00h	SUN Eqn. of Time 12h	SUN Mer. Pass.	MOON Mer. Pass. Upper	MOON Mer. Pass. Lower	MOON Age	MOON Phase
d	m s	m s	h m	h m	h m	d	%
22	15 27	15 31	11 44	10 40	23 03	28	2	●
23	15 35	15 40	11 44	11 26	23 49	29	0	
24	15 44	15 47	11 44	12 14	24 38	01	0	

UT	ARIES GHA	VENUS −4.0 GHA	Dec	MARS +0.9 GHA	Dec	JUPITER −2.0 GHA	Dec	SATURN +0.6 GHA	Dec	STARS Name	SHA	Dec
25 00	33 18.4	183 40.8	S11 00.5	124 28.9	S24 56.9	251 07.3	N15 30.9	162 07.3	S16 39.3	Acamar	315 17.3	S40 14.7
01	48 20.9	198 40.3	01.6	139 29.4	56.9	266 09.4	30.8	177 09.5	39.4	Achernar	335 25.6	S57 09.7
02	63 23.3	213 39.8	02.8	154 29.8	56.9	281 11.6	30.7	192 11.7	39.5	Acrux	173 08.7	S63 10.7
03	78 25.8	228 39.3	.. 03.9	169 30.3	.. 56.9	296 13.7	.. 30.6	207 13.9	.. 39.6	Adhara	255 11.7	S28 59.5
04	93 28.3	243 38.8	05.1	184 30.7	57.0	311 15.9	30.5	222 16.1	39.6	Aldebaran	290 48.0	N16 32.2
05	108 30.7	258 38.2	06.2	199 31.1	57.0	326 18.0	30.4	237 18.2	39.7			
S 06	123 33.2	273 37.7	S11 07.4	214 31.6	S24 57.0	341 20.2	N15 30.3	252 20.4	S16 39.8	Alioth	166 20.5	N55 52.7
A 07	138 35.7	288 37.2	08.5	229 32.0	57.0	356 22.3	30.2	267 22.6	39.9	Alkaid	152 58.7	N49 14.5
T 08	153 38.1	303 36.7	09.7	244 32.4	57.0	11 24.5	30.1	282 24.8	39.9	Al Na'ir	27 42.4	S46 53.4
U 09	168 40.6	318 36.2	.. 10.8	259 32.9	.. 57.0	26 26.6	.. 30.0	297 26.9	.. 40.0	Alnilam	275 45.2	S 1 11.6
R 10	183 43.0	333 35.7	11.9	274 33.3	57.0	41 28.8	30.0	312 29.1	40.1	Alphard	217 55.3	S 8 43.4
D 11	198 45.5	348 35.2	13.1	289 33.7	57.0	56 30.9	29.9	327 31.3	40.1			
A 12	213 48.0	3 34.7	S11 14.2	304 34.2	S24 57.0	71 33.1	N15 29.8	342 33.5	S16 40.2	Alphecca	126 10.6	N26 40.2
Y 13	228 50.4	18 34.2	15.4	319 34.6	57.0	86 35.2	29.7	357 35.7	40.3	Alpheratz	357 42.2	N29 10.5
14	243 52.9	33 33.7	16.5	334 35.0	57.0	101 37.4	29.6	12 37.8	40.4	Altair	62 07.4	N 8 54.8
15	258 55.4	48 33.2	.. 17.7	349 35.4	.. 57.0	116 39.5	.. 29.5	27 40.0	.. 40.5	Ankaa	353 14.5	S42 13.5
16	273 57.8	63 32.6	18.8	4 35.9	57.0	131 41.7	29.4	42 42.2	40.5	Antares	112 25.4	S26 27.7
17	289 00.3	78 32.1	19.9	19 36.3	57.1	146 43.8	29.3	57 44.4	40.6			
18	304 02.8	93 31.6	S11 21.1	34 36.7	S24 57.1	161 46.0	N15 29.2	72 46.5	S16 40.7	Arcturus	145 55.3	N19 06.5
19	319 05.2	108 31.1	22.2	49 37.2	57.1	176 48.1	29.1	87 48.7	40.8	Atria	107 26.8	S69 03.2
20	334 07.7	123 30.6	23.4	64 37.6	57.1	191 50.3	29.0	102 50.9	40.8	Avior	234 17.6	S59 33.2
21	349 10.1	138 30.1	.. 24.5	79 38.0	.. 57.1	206 52.4	.. 28.9	117 53.1	.. 40.9	Bellatrix	278 30.8	N 6 21.7
22	4 12.6	153 29.6	25.6	94 38.5	57.1	221 54.6	28.9	132 55.2	41.0	Betelgeuse	271 00.1	N 7 24.5
23	19 15.1	168 29.1	26.8	109 38.9	57.1	236 56.7	28.8	147 57.4	41.1			
26 00	34 17.5	183 28.5	S11 27.9	124 39.3	S24 57.1	251 58.9	N15 28.7	162 59.6	S16 41.1	Canopus	263 55.5	S52 42.1
01	49 20.0	198 28.0	29.0	139 39.8	57.1	267 01.0	28.6	178 01.8	41.2	Capella	280 32.7	N46 00.5
02	64 22.5	213 27.5	30.2	154 40.2	57.1	282 03.2	28.5	193 04.0	41.3	Deneb	49 30.8	N45 20.5
03	79 24.9	228 27.0	.. 31.3	169 40.6	.. 57.1	297 05.3	.. 28.4	208 06.1	.. 41.4	Denebola	182 33.0	N14 29.4
04	94 27.4	243 26.5	32.5	184 41.1	57.1	312 07.5	28.3	223 08.3	41.4	Diphda	348 54.7	S17 54.3
05	109 29.9	258 26.0	33.6	199 41.5	57.1	327 09.6	28.2	238 10.5	41.5			
S 06	124 32.3	273 25.4	S11 34.7	214 41.9	S24 57.1	342 11.8	N15 28.1	253 12.7	S16 41.6	Dubhe	193 51.2	N61 40.0
U 07	139 34.8	288 24.9	35.9	229 42.3	57.1	357 13.9	28.0	268 14.8	41.7	Elnath	278 11.2	N28 37.0
N 08	154 37.3	303 24.4	37.0	244 42.8	57.1	12 16.1	27.9	283 17.0	41.7	Eltanin	90 46.0	N51 29.7
D 09	169 39.7	318 23.9	.. 38.1	259 43.2	.. 57.1	27 18.3	.. 27.9	298 19.2	.. 41.8	Enif	33 46.1	N 9 56.9
A 10	184 42.2	333 23.4	39.3	274 43.6	57.1	42 20.4	27.8	313 21.4	41.9	Fomalhaut	15 22.8	S29 32.6
Y 11	199 44.6	348 22.8	40.4	289 44.1	57.1	57 22.6	27.7	328 23.5	42.0			
12	214 47.1	3 22.3	S11 41.5	304 44.5	S24 57.1	72 24.7	N15 27.6	343 25.7	S16 42.0	Gacrux	172 00.3	S57 11.6
13	229 49.6	18 21.8	42.7	319 44.9	57.1	87 26.9	27.5	358 27.9	42.1	Gienah	175 51.6	S17 37.3
14	244 52.0	33 21.3	43.8	334 45.3	57.0	102 29.0	27.4	13 30.1	42.2	Hadar	148 47.1	S60 26.5
15	259 54.5	48 20.8	.. 44.9	349 45.8	.. 57.0	117 31.2	.. 27.3	28 32.2	.. 42.3	Hamal	327 59.3	N23 32.0
16	274 57.0	63 20.2	46.0	4 46.2	57.0	132 33.3	27.2	43 34.4	42.3	Kaus Aust.	83 42.8	S34 22.5
17	289 59.4	78 19.7	47.2	19 46.6	57.0	147 35.5	27.1	58 36.6	42.4			
18	305 01.9	93 19.2	S11 48.3	34 47.1	S24 57.0	162 37.7	N15 27.0	73 38.8	S16 42.5	Kochab	137 21.4	N74 05.8
19	320 04.4	108 18.7	49.4	49 47.5	57.0	177 39.8	26.9	88 41.0	42.6	Markab	13 37.2	N15 17.3
20	335 06.8	123 18.2	50.6	64 47.9	57.0	192 42.0	26.9	103 43.1	42.6	Menkar	314 13.8	N 4 08.8
21	350 09.3	138 17.6	.. 51.7	79 48.3	.. 57.0	207 44.1	.. 26.8	118 45.3	.. 42.7	Menkent	148 06.8	S36 26.4
22	5 11.8	153 17.1	52.8	94 48.8	57.0	222 46.3	26.7	133 47.5	42.8	Miaplacidus	221 39.5	S69 46.5
23	20 14.2	168 16.6	53.9	109 49.2	57.0	237 48.4	26.6	148 49.7	42.9			
27 00	35 16.7	183 16.1	S11 55.1	124 49.6	S24 56.9	252 50.6	N15 26.5	163 51.8	S16 42.9	Mirfak	308 38.5	N49 54.7
01	50 19.1	198 15.5	56.2	139 50.1	57.0	267 52.8	26.4	178 54.0	43.0	Nunki	75 57.3	S26 16.5
02	65 21.6	213 15.0	57.3	154 50.5	57.0	282 54.9	26.3	193 56.2	43.1	Peacock	53 17.9	S56 41.3
03	80 24.1	228 14.5	.. 58.4	169 50.9	.. 56.9	297 57.1	.. 26.2	208 58.4	.. 43.2	Pollux	243 26.6	N27 59.2
04	95 26.5	243 14.0	11 59.6	184 51.3	56.9	312 59.2	26.1	224 00.5	43.2	Procyon	244 58.7	N 5 11.1
05	110 29.0	258 13.4	12 00.7	199 51.8	56.9	328 01.4	26.1	239 02.7	43.3			
M 06	125 31.5	273 12.9	S12 01.8	214 52.2	S24 56.9	343 03.5	N15 26.0	254 04.9	S16 43.4	Rasalhague	96 05.8	N12 33.3
O 07	140 33.9	288 12.4	02.9	229 52.6	56.9	358 05.7	25.9	269 07.1	43.5	Regulus	207 42.7	N11 53.6
N 08	155 36.4	303 11.9	04.1	244 53.0	56.9	13 07.9	25.8	284 09.2	43.5	Rigel	281 10.9	S 8 11.1
D 09	170 38.9	318 11.3	.. 05.2	259 53.5	.. 56.9	28 10.0	.. 25.7	299 11.4	.. 43.6	Rigil Kent.	139 51.1	S60 53.6
A 10	185 41.3	333 10.8	06.3	274 53.9	56.9	43 12.2	25.6	314 13.6	43.7	Sabik	102 11.7	S15 44.3
Y 11	200 43.8	348 10.3	07.4	289 54.3	56.8	58 14.3	25.5	329 15.8	43.8			
12	215 46.3	3 09.7	S12 08.5	304 54.7	S24 56.8	73 16.5	N15 25.4	344 17.9	S16 43.8	Schedar	349 38.8	N56 37.3
13	230 48.7	18 09.2	09.7	319 55.2	56.8	88 18.7	25.3	359 20.1	43.9	Shaula	96 20.9	S37 06.7
14	245 51.2	33 08.7	10.8	334 55.6	56.8	103 20.8	25.3	14 22.3	44.0	Sirius	258 32.8	S16 44.2
15	260 53.6	48 08.1	.. 11.9	349 56.0	.. 56.8	118 23.0	.. 25.2	29 24.5	.. 44.1	Spica	158 30.6	S11 14.1
16	275 56.1	63 07.6	13.0	4 56.4	56.8	133 25.1	25.1	44 26.6	44.1	Suhail	222 51.8	S43 29.4
17	290 58.6	78 07.1	14.1	19 56.9	56.8	148 27.3	25.0	59 28.8	44.2			
18	306 01.0	93 06.5	S12 15.2	34 57.3	S24 56.7	163 29.5	N15 24.9	74 31.0	S16 44.3	Vega	80 38.5	N38 48.3
19	321 03.5	108 06.0	16.4	49 57.7	56.7	178 31.6	24.8	89 33.2	44.4	Zuben'ubi	137 04.7	S16 06.0
20	336 06.0	123 05.5	17.5	64 58.1	56.7	193 33.8	24.7	104 35.3	44.4			
21	351 08.4	138 05.0	.. 18.6	79 58.6	.. 56.7	208 36.0	.. 24.6	119 37.5	.. 44.5			
22	6 10.9	153 04.4	19.7	94 59.0	56.7	223 38.1	24.5	134 39.7	44.6			
23	21 13.4	168 03.9	20.8	109 59.4	56.6	238 40.3	24.5	149 41.9	44.7			

	SHA	Mer. Pass.
Venus	149 11.0	11 47
Mars	90 21.8	15 41
Jupiter	217 41.3	7 11
Saturn	128 42.1	13 06

	ARIES	VENUS	MARS	JUPITER	SATURN
Mer. Pass.	21 39.3	v −0.5 d 1.1	v 0.4 d 0.0	v 2.2 d 0.1	v 2.2 d 0.1

UT	SUN GHA	SUN Dec	MOON GHA	v	MOON Dec	d	HP
d h	° ′	° ′	° ′	′	° ′	′	′
25 00	183 57.8	S11 59.5	170 44.2	10.7	S14 00.1	6.8	56.6
01	198 57.9	12 00.4	185 13.9	10.7	14 06.9	6.8	56.6
02	213 58.0	01.3	199 43.6	10.6	14 13.7	6.8	56.6
03	228 58.0	02.1	214 13.2	10.5	14 20.5	6.6	56.6
04	243 58.1	03.0	228 42.7	10.5	14 27.1	6.6	56.6
05	258 58.2	03.9	243 12.2	10.4	14 33.7	6.5	56.7
06	273 58.3	S12 04.7	257 41.6	10.4	S14 40.2	6.5	56.7
S 07	288 58.3	05.6	272 11.0	10.3	14 46.7	6.4	56.7
A 08	303 58.4	06.4	286 40.3	10.3	14 53.1	6.3	56.7
T 09	318 58.5	07.3	301 09.6	10.2	14 59.4	6.2	56.7
U 10	333 58.6	08.2	315 38.8	10.1	15 05.6	6.1	56.8
R 11	348 58.6	09.0	330 07.9	10.1	15 11.7	6.1	56.8
D 12	3 58.7	S12 09.9	344 37.0	10.1	S15 17.8	6.0	56.8
A 13	18 58.8	10.7	359 06.1	10.0	15 23.8	5.9	56.8
Y 14	33 58.8	11.6	13 35.1	9.9	15 29.7	5.8	56.8
15	48 58.9	12.5	28 04.0	9.9	15 35.5	5.8	56.9
16	63 59.0	13.3	42 32.9	9.8	15 41.3	5.6	56.9
17	78 59.0	14.2	57 01.7	9.8	15 46.9	5.6	56.9
18	93 59.1	S12 15.0	71 30.5	9.7	S15 52.5	5.5	56.9
19	108 59.2	15.9	85 59.2	9.7	15 58.0	5.4	57.0
20	123 59.3	16.8	100 27.9	9.6	16 03.4	5.4	57.0
21	138 59.3	17.6	114 56.5	9.5	16 08.8	5.2	57.0
22	153 59.4	18.5	129 25.0	9.6	16 14.0	5.2	57.0
23	168 59.5	19.3	143 53.6	9.4	16 19.2	5.0	57.0
26 00	183 59.5	S12 20.2	158 22.0	9.4	S16 24.2	5.0	57.1
01	198 59.6	21.0	172 50.4	9.4	16 29.2	4.9	57.1
02	213 59.7	21.9	187 18.8	9.3	16 34.1	4.8	57.1
03	228 59.7	22.7	201 47.1	9.2	16 38.9	4.7	57.1
04	243 59.8	23.6	216 15.3	9.2	16 43.6	4.7	57.1
05	258 59.9	24.5	230 43.5	9.2	16 48.3	4.5	57.2
06	273 59.9	S12 25.3	245 11.7	9.1	S16 52.8	4.4	57.2
S 07	289 00.0	26.2	259 39.8	9.1	16 57.2	4.4	57.2
U 08	304 00.0	27.0	274 07.9	9.0	17 01.6	4.2	57.2
N 09	319 00.1	27.9	288 35.9	8.9	17 05.8	4.2	57.2
D 10	334 00.2	28.7	303 03.8	8.9	17 10.0	4.1	57.3
A 11	349 00.2	29.6	317 31.7	8.9	17 14.1	3.9	57.3
Y 12	4 00.3	S12 30.4	331 59.6	8.8	S17 18.0	3.9	57.3
13	19 00.4	31.3	346 27.4	8.8	17 21.9	3.8	57.3
14	34 00.4	32.1	0 55.2	8.7	17 25.7	3.7	57.3
15	49 00.5	33.0	15 22.9	8.7	17 29.4	3.5	57.4
16	64 00.6	33.8	29 50.6	8.7	17 32.9	3.5	57.4
17	79 00.6	34.7	44 18.3	8.6	17 36.4	3.4	57.4
18	94 00.7	S12 35.5	58 45.9	8.5	S17 39.8	3.3	57.4
19	109 00.7	36.4	73 13.4	8.5	17 43.1	3.2	57.4
20	124 00.8	37.2	87 40.9	8.5	17 46.3	3.0	57.5
21	139 00.9	38.1	102 08.4	8.4	17 49.3	3.0	57.5
22	154 00.9	38.9	116 35.8	8.4	17 52.3	2.9	57.5
23	169 01.0	39.8	131 03.2	8.4	17 55.2	2.8	57.5
27 00	184 01.0	S12 40.6	145 30.6	8.3	S17 58.0	2.6	57.5
01	199 01.1	41.5	159 57.9	8.3	18 00.6	2.6	57.5
02	214 01.2	42.3	174 25.2	8.2	18 03.2	2.4	57.6
03	229 01.2	43.2	188 52.4	8.2	18 05.6	2.4	57.6
04	244 01.3	44.0	203 19.6	8.2	18 08.0	2.2	57.6
05	259 01.3	44.9	217 46.8	8.1	18 10.2	2.2	57.6
06	274 01.4	S12 45.7	232 13.9	8.1	S18 12.4	2.0	57.6
M 07	289 01.4	46.6	246 41.0	8.1	18 14.4	1.9	57.7
O 08	304 01.5	47.4	261 08.1	8.0	18 16.3	1.9	57.7
N 09	319 01.6	48.2	275 35.1	8.0	18 18.2	1.7	57.7
D 10	334 01.6	49.1	290 02.1	8.0	18 19.9	1.6	57.7
A 11	349 01.7	49.9	304 29.1	7.9	18 21.5	1.5	57.7
Y 12	4 01.7	S12 50.8	318 56.0	7.9	S18 23.0	1.4	57.8
13	19 01.8	51.6	333 22.9	7.9	18 24.4	1.2	57.8
14	34 01.8	52.5	347 49.8	7.8	18 25.6	1.2	57.8
15	49 01.9	53.3	2 16.6	7.9	18 26.8	1.1	57.8
16	64 02.0	54.1	16 43.5	7.8	18 27.9	0.9	57.8
17	79 02.0	55.0	31 10.3	7.7	18 28.8	0.8	57.8
18	94 02.1	S12 55.8	45 37.0	7.8	S18 29.6	0.8	57.9
19	109 02.1	56.7	60 03.8	7.7	18 30.4	0.7	57.9
20	124 02.2	57.5	74 30.5	7.7	18 31.0	0.5	57.9
21	139 02.2	58.4	88 57.2	7.7	18 31.5	0.4	57.9
22	154 02.3	12 59.2	103 23.9	7.6	18 31.9	0.3	57.9
23	169 02.3	S13 00.0	117 50.5	7.6	S18 32.2	0.1	58.0
	SD 16.1	d 0.9	SD 15.5		15.6		15.7

Lat.	Twilight Naut.	Twilight Civil	Sunrise	Moonrise 25	26	27	28
°	h m	h m	h m	h m	h m	h m	h m
N 72	05 41	07 02	08 21	10 48	12 58	▬▬	▬▬
N 70	05 40	06 52	08 01	10 12	11 50	13 16	14 10
68	05 39	06 44	07 46	09 46	11 13	12 30	13 25
66	05 37	06 38	07 33	09 26	10 48	11 59	12 55
64	05 36	06 32	07 23	09 10	10 28	11 37	12 33
62	05 35	06 27	07 14	08 57	10 12	11 19	12 15
60	05 34	06 23	07 06	08 46	09 58	11 04	12 00
N 58	05 33	06 19	07 00	08 37	09 47	10 51	11 47
56	05 32	06 15	06 54	08 28	09 37	10 40	11 36
54	05 30	06 12	06 49	08 21	09 28	10 31	11 27
52	05 29	06 09	06 44	08 14	09 20	10 22	11 18
50	05 28	06 06	06 39	08 08	09 13	10 14	11 10
45	05 25	06 00	06 30	07 56	08 58	09 58	10 54
N 40	05 23	05 54	06 22	07 45	08 46	09 45	10 41
35	05 20	05 49	06 15	07 36	08 35	09 33	10 29
30	05 17	05 45	06 09	07 28	08 26	09 23	10 19
20	05 10	05 36	05 59	07 14	08 10	09 06	10 02
N 10	05 03	05 28	05 49	07 03	07 56	08 51	09 47
0	04 55	05 19	05 41	06 51	07 43	08 37	09 33
S 10	04 45	05 10	05 32	06 40	07 31	08 24	09 19
20	04 33	04 59	05 22	06 29	07 17	08 09	09 04
30	04 16	04 46	05 11	06 15	07 01	07 52	08 47
35	04 06	04 38	05 04	06 08	06 52	07 42	08 37
40	03 54	04 28	04 57	05 59	06 42	07 31	08 25
45	03 39	04 17	04 48	05 49	06 30	07 18	08 12
S 50	03 19	04 03	04 38	05 37	06 16	07 02	07 56
52	03 09	03 56	04 33	05 31	06 09	06 54	07 48
54	02 58	03 48	04 27	05 25	06 02	06 46	07 39
56	02 44	03 39	04 21	05 18	05 53	06 37	07 30
58	02 29	03 30	04 15	05 10	05 44	06 26	07 19
S 60	02 09	03 18	04 07	05 01	05 33	06 14	07 06

Lat.	Sunset	Twilight Civil	Twilight Naut.	Moonset 25	26	27	28
°	h m	h m	h m	h m	h m	h m	h m
N 72	15 06	16 25	17 44	15 08	14 48	▬▬	▬▬
N 70	15 25	16 34	17 46	15 45	15 56	16 23	17 25
68	15 41	16 42	17 48	16 12	16 33	17 10	18 10
66	15 53	16 49	17 49	16 32	16 59	17 40	18 39
64	16 04	16 55	17 50	16 49	17 19	18 03	19 02
62	16 13	17 00	17 52	17 02	17 36	18 21	19 19
60	16 20	17 04	17 53	17 14	17 49	18 36	19 34
N 58	16 27	17 08	17 54	17 24	18 01	18 49	19 47
56	16 33	17 12	17 55	17 33	18 11	19 00	19 58
54	16 39	17 15	17 57	17 40	18 21	19 09	20 07
52	16 43	17 18	17 58	17 47	18 29	19 18	20 16
50	16 48	17 21	17 59	17 54	18 36	19 26	20 23
45	16 57	17 27	18 02	18 07	18 51	19 42	20 39
N 40	17 05	17 33	18 05	18 19	19 04	19 56	20 53
35	17 12	17 38	18 08	18 28	19 15	20 07	21 04
30	17 18	17 43	18 11	18 37	19 25	20 17	21 14
20	17 29	17 51	18 17	18 51	19 41	20 35	21 31
N 10	17 38	18 00	18 25	19 04	19 56	20 50	21 46
0	17 47	18 09	18 33	19 16	20 09	21 04	21 59
S 10	17 56	18 18	18 43	19 28	20 22	21 18	22 13
20	18 06	18 29	18 56	19 41	20 37	21 33	22 28
30	18 18	18 43	19 12	19 56	20 53	21 50	22 44
35	18 24	18 51	19 22	20 04	21 03	22 00	22 54
40	18 32	19 00	19 34	20 14	21 14	22 11	23 05
45	18 41	19 12	19 51	20 25	21 27	22 25	23 18
S 50	18 51	19 27	20 11	20 39	21 42	22 41	23 34
52	18 56	19 34	20 21	20 46	21 50	22 49	23 41
54	19 02	19 41	20 32	20 53	21 58	22 57	23 50
56	19 08	19 50	20 46	21 01	22 07	23 07	23 59
58	19 15	20 00	21 02	21 10	22 17	23 18	24 09
S 60	19 23	20 12	21 22	21 20	22 29	23 30	24 21

Day	SUN Eqn. of Time 00h	SUN Eqn. of Time 12h	SUN Mer. Pass.	MOON Mer. Pass. Upper	MOON Mer. Pass. Lower	Age	Phase
d	m s	m s	h m	h m	h m	d	%
25	15 51	15 55	11 44	13 04	00 38	02	3
26	15 58	16 01	11 44	13 56	01 30	03	7
27	16 04	16 07	11 44	14 51	02 23	04	14

UT	ARIES GHA	VENUS −4.0 GHA	Dec	MARS +0.9 GHA	Dec	JUPITER −2.0 GHA	Dec	SATURN +0.5 GHA	Dec	STARS Name	SHA	Dec
28 00	36 15.8	183 03.3	S12 21.9	124 59.8	S24 56.6	253 42.4	N15 24.4	164 44.0	S16 44.7	Acamar	315 17.3	S40 14.7
01	51 18.3	198 02.8	23.0	140 00.3	56.6	268 44.6	24.3	179 46.2	44.8	Achernar	335 25.6	S57 09.8
02	66 20.7	213 02.3	24.2	155 00.7	56.6	283 46.8	24.2	194 48.4	44.9	Acrux	173 08.7	S63 10.7
03	81 23.2	228 01.7 ..	25.3	170 01.1 ..	56.6	298 48.9 ..	24.1	209 50.6 ..	45.0	Adhara	255 11.6	S28 59.5
04	96 25.7	243 01.2	26.4	185 01.5	56.5	313 51.1	24.0	224 52.7	45.0	Aldebaran	290 48.0	N16 32.2
05	111 28.1	258 00.7	27.5	200 02.0	56.5	328 53.3	23.9	239 54.9	45.1			
06	126 30.6	273 00.1	S12 28.6	215 02.4	S24 56.5	343 55.4	N15 23.8	254 57.1	S16 45.2	Alioth	166 20.5	N55 52.7
07	141 33.1	287 59.6	29.7	230 02.8	56.5	358 57.6	23.8	269 59.3	45.3	Alkaid	152 58.7	N49 14.4
T 08	156 35.5	302 59.1	30.8	245 03.2	56.4	13 59.8	23.7	285 01.4	45.3	Al Na'ir	27 42.5	S46 53.4
U 09	171 38.0	317 58.5 ..	31.9	260 03.7 ..	56.4	29 01.9 ..	23.6	300 03.6 ..	45.4	Alnilam	275 45.2	S 1 11.6
E 10	186 40.5	332 58.0	33.0	275 04.1	56.4	44 04.1	23.5	315 05.8	45.5	Alphard	217 55.3	S 8 43.4
S 11	201 42.9	347 57.4	34.1	290 04.5	56.4	59 06.3	23.4	330 08.0	45.6			
D 12	216 45.4	2 56.9	S12 35.3	305 04.9	S24 56.4	74 08.4	N15 23.3	345 10.1	S16 45.6	Alphecca	126 10.6	N26 40.2
A 13	231 47.9	17 56.4	36.4	320 05.3	56.3	89 10.6	23.2	0 12.3	45.7	Alpheratz	357 42.2	N29 10.5
Y 14	246 50.3	32 55.8	37.5	335 05.8	56.3	104 12.8	23.1	15 14.5	45.8	Altair	62 07.4	N 8 54.8
15	261 52.8	47 55.3 ..	38.6	350 06.2 ..	56.3	119 14.9 ..	23.1	30 16.6 ..	45.9	Ankaa	353 14.5	S42 13.6
16	276 55.2	62 54.7	39.7	5 06.6	56.2	134 17.1	23.0	45 18.8	45.9	Antares	112 25.4	S26 27.7
17	291 57.7	77 54.2	40.8	20 07.0	56.2	149 19.3	22.9	60 21.0	46.0			
18	307 00.2	92 53.6	S12 41.9	35 07.5	S24 56.2	164 21.4	N15 22.8	75 23.2	S16 46.1	Arcturus	145 55.3	N19 06.5
19	322 02.6	107 53.1	43.0	50 07.9	56.2	179 23.6	22.7	90 25.3	46.2	Atria	107 26.8	S69 03.2
20	337 05.1	122 52.6	44.1	65 08.3	56.1	194 25.8	22.6	105 27.5	46.2	Avior	234 17.5	S59 33.2
21	352 07.6	137 52.0 ..	45.2	80 08.7 ..	56.1	209 27.9 ..	22.5	120 29.7 ..	46.3	Bellatrix	278 30.8	N 6 21.7
22	7 10.0	152 51.5	46.3	95 09.1	56.1	224 30.1	22.5	135 31.9	46.4	Betelgeuse	271 00.1	N 7 24.5
23	22 12.5	167 50.9	47.4	110 09.6	56.0	239 32.3	22.4	150 34.0	46.5			
29 00	37 15.0	182 50.4	S12 48.5	125 10.0	S24 56.0	254 34.4	N15 22.3	165 36.2	S16 46.5	Canopus	263 55.4	S52 42.1
01	52 17.4	197 49.8	49.6	140 10.4	56.0	269 36.6	22.2	180 38.4	46.6	Capella	280 32.7	N46 00.5
02	67 19.9	212 49.3	50.7	155 10.8	55.9	284 38.8	22.1	195 40.6	46.7	Deneb	49 30.8	N45 20.5
03	82 22.4	227 48.7 ..	51.8	170 11.2 ..	55.9	299 40.9 ..	22.0	210 42.7 ..	46.8	Denebola	182 33.0	N14 29.4
04	97 24.8	242 48.2	52.9	185 11.7	55.9	314 43.1	21.9	225 44.9	46.8	Diphda	348 54.7	S17 54.3
05	112 27.3	257 47.7	54.0	200 12.1	55.8	329 45.3	21.9	240 47.1	46.9			
06	127 29.7	272 47.1	S12 55.1	215 12.5	S24 55.8	344 47.5	N15 21.8	255 49.3	S16 47.0	Dubhe	193 51.1	N61 40.0
W 07	142 32.2	287 46.6	56.2	230 12.9	55.8	359 49.6	21.7	270 51.4	47.1	Elnath	278 11.2	N28 37.0
E 08	157 34.7	302 46.0	57.3	245 13.3	55.7	14 51.8	21.6	285 53.6	47.1	Eltanin	90 46.0	N51 29.7
D 09	172 37.1	317 45.5 ..	58.4	260 13.8 ..	55.7	29 54.0 ..	21.5	300 55.8 ..	47.2	Enif	33 46.1	N 9 56.9
N 10	187 39.6	332 44.9	12 59.5	275 14.2	55.7	44 56.1	21.4	315 57.9	47.3	Fomalhaut	15 22.8	S29 32.6
E 11	202 42.1	347 44.4	13 00.6	290 14.6	55.6	59 58.3	21.3	331 00.1	47.4			
S 12	217 44.5	2 43.8	S13 01.7	305 15.0	S24 55.6	75 00.5	N15 21.3	346 02.3	S16 47.4	Gacrux	172 00.3	S57 11.6
D 13	232 47.0	17 43.3	02.8	320 15.4	55.6	90 02.7	21.2	1 04.5	47.5	Gienah	175 51.6	S17 37.3
A 14	247 49.5	32 42.7	03.9	335 15.9	55.5	105 04.8	21.1	16 06.6	47.6	Hadar	148 47.1	S60 26.5
Y 15	262 51.9	47 42.2 ..	05.0	350 16.3 ..	55.5	120 07.0 ..	21.0	31 08.8 ..	47.7	Hamal	327 59.3	N23 32.0
16	277 54.4	62 41.6	06.0	5 16.7	55.5	135 09.2	20.9	46 11.0	47.7	Kaus Aust.	83 42.8	S34 22.5
17	292 56.9	77 41.1	07.1	20 17.1	55.4	150 11.4	20.8	61 13.2	47.8			
18	307 59.3	92 40.5	S13 08.2	35 17.5	S24 55.4	165 13.5	N15 20.7	76 15.3	S16 47.9	Kochab	137 21.4	N74 05.8
19	323 01.8	107 39.9	09.3	50 18.0	55.3	180 15.7	20.7	91 17.5	48.0	Markab	13 37.2	N15 17.4
20	338 04.2	122 39.4	10.4	65 18.4	55.3	195 17.9	20.6	106 19.7	48.0	Menkar	314 13.8	N 4 08.8
21	353 06.7	137 38.8 ..	11.5	80 18.8 ..	55.3	210 20.0 ..	20.5	121 21.8 ..	48.1	Menkent	148 06.8	S36 26.4
22	8 09.2	152 38.3	12.6	95 19.2	55.2	225 22.2	20.4	136 24.0	48.2	Miaplacidus	221 39.5	S69 46.5
23	23 11.6	167 37.7	13.7	110 19.6	55.2	240 24.4	20.3	151 26.2	48.3			
30 00	38 14.1	182 37.2	S13 14.8	125 20.1	S24 55.1	255 26.6	N15 20.2	166 28.4	S16 48.3	Mirfak	308 38.5	N49 54.7
01	53 16.6	197 36.6	15.9	140 20.5	55.1	270 28.7	20.0	181 30.5	48.4	Nunki	75 57.3	S26 16.5
02	68 19.0	212 36.1	16.9	155 20.9	55.0	285 30.9	20.1	196 32.7	48.5	Peacock	53 17.9	S56 41.3
03	83 21.5	227 35.5 ..	18.0	170 21.3 ..	55.0	300 33.1 ..	20.0	211 34.9 ..	48.6	Pollux	243 26.6	N27 59.2
04	98 24.0	242 34.9	19.1	185 21.7	55.0	315 35.3	19.9	226 37.0	48.6	Procyon	244 58.7	N 5 11.1
05	113 26.4	257 34.4	20.2	200 22.1	54.9	330 37.5	19.8	241 39.2	48.7			
06	128 28.9	272 33.8	S13 21.3	215 22.6	S24 54.9	345 39.6	N15 19.7	256 41.4	S16 48.8	Rasalhague	96 05.8	N12 33.3
07	143 31.3	287 33.3	22.4	230 23.0	54.8	0 41.8	19.6	271 43.6	48.9	Regulus	207 42.7	N11 53.6
T 08	158 33.8	302 32.7	23.4	245 23.4	54.8	15 44.0	19.6	286 45.7	48.9	Rigel	281 10.9	S 8 11.1
H 09	173 36.3	317 32.1 ..	24.5	260 23.8 ..	54.7	30 46.2 ..	19.5	301 47.9 ..	49.0	Rigil Kent.	139 51.0	S60 53.6
U 10	188 38.7	332 31.6	25.6	275 24.2	54.7	45 48.3	19.4	316 50.1	49.1	Sabik	102 11.7	S15 44.3
R 11	203 41.2	347 31.0	26.7	290 24.6	54.6	60 50.5	19.3	331 52.3	49.1			
S 12	218 43.7	2 30.5	S13 27.8	305 25.1	S24 54.6	75 52.7	N15 19.2	346 54.4	S16 49.2	Schedar	349 38.8	N56 37.3
D 13	233 46.1	17 29.9	28.9	320 25.5	54.6	90 54.9	19.1	1 56.6	49.3	Shaula	96 20.9	S37 06.7
A 14	248 48.6	32 29.3	29.9	335 25.9	54.5	105 57.1	19.1	16 58.8	49.4	Sirius	258 32.7	S16 44.2
Y 15	263 51.1	47 28.8 ..	31.0	350 26.3 ..	54.5	120 59.2 ..	19.0	32 00.9 ..	49.4	Spica	158 30.6	S11 14.1
16	278 53.5	62 28.2	32.1	5 26.7	54.4	136 01.4	18.9	47 03.1	49.5	Suhail	222 51.8	S43 29.4
17	293 56.0	77 27.7	33.2	20 27.1	54.4	151 03.6	18.8	62 05.3	49.6			
18	308 58.5	92 27.1	S13 34.2	35 27.6	S24 54.3	166 05.8	N15 18.7	77 07.5	S16 49.7	Vega	80 38.5	N38 48.3
19	324 00.9	107 26.5	35.3	50 28.0	54.3	181 07.9	18.6	92 09.6	49.7	Zuben'ubi	137 04.7	S16 06.0
20	339 03.4	122 26.0	36.4	65 28.4	54.2	196 10.1	18.6	107 11.8	49.8		SHA	Mer. Pass.
21	354 05.8	137 25.4 ..	37.5	80 28.8 ..	54.2	211 12.3 ..	18.5	122 14.0 ..	49.9		° ′	h m
22	9 08.3	152 24.8	38.6	95 29.2	54.1	226 14.5	18.4	137 16.1	50.0	Venus	145 35.4	11 49
23	24 10.8	167 24.3	39.6	110 29.6	54.0	241 16.7	18.3	152 18.3	50.0	Mars	87 55.0	15 39
	h m									Jupiter	217 19.5	7 01
Mer. Pass. 21 27.5	v −0.6	d 1.1		v 0.4	d 0.0	v 2.2	d 0.1	v 2.2	d 0.1	Saturn	128 21.2	12 56

UT	SUN GHA	SUN Dec	MOON GHA	v	MOON Dec	d	HP
28 00	184 02.4	S13 00.9	132 17.1	7.7	S18 32.3	0.1	58.0
01	199 02.4	01.7	146 43.8	7.5	18 32.4	0.1	58.0
02	214 02.5	02.6	161 10.3	7.6	18 32.3	0.2	58.0
03	229 02.5	.. 03.4	175 36.9	7.6	18 32.1	0.2	58.0
04	244 02.6	04.2	190 03.5	7.5	18 32.0	0.4	58.0
05	259 02.6	05.1	204 30.0	7.5	18 31.5	0.6	58.1
06	274 02.7	S13 05.9	218 56.5	7.5	S18 30.9	0.6	58.1
07	289 02.7	06.7	233 23.0	7.5	18 30.3	0.7	58.1
08	304 02.8	07.6	247 49.5	7.5	18 29.6	0.9	58.1
09	319 02.8	.. 08.4	262 16.0	7.5	18 28.7	0.9	58.1
10	334 02.9	09.3	276 42.5	7.4	18 27.8	1.1	58.1
11	349 02.9	10.1	291 08.9	7.5	18 26.7	1.2	58.2
12	4 03.0	S13 10.9	305 35.4	7.4	S18 25.5	1.3	58.2
13	19 03.0	11.8	320 01.8	7.5	18 24.2	1.4	58.2
14	34 03.1	12.6	334 28.3	7.4	18 22.8	1.6	58.2
15	49 03.1	.. 13.4	348 54.7	7.4	18 21.2	1.6	58.2
16	64 03.2	14.3	3 21.1	7.4	18 19.6	1.8	58.3
17	79 03.2	15.1	17 47.5	7.4	18 17.8	1.9	58.3
18	94 03.3	S13 15.9	32 13.9	7.4	S18 15.9	2.0	58.3
19	109 03.3	16.8	46 40.3	7.4	18 13.9	2.1	58.3
20	124 03.3	17.6	61 06.7	7.4	18 11.8	2.2	58.3
21	139 03.4	.. 18.4	75 33.1	7.4	18 09.6	2.3	58.3
22	154 03.4	19.3	89 59.5	7.3	18 07.3	2.4	58.4
23	169 03.5	20.1	104 25.8	7.4	18 04.9	2.6	58.4
29 00	184 03.5	S13 20.9	118 52.2	7.4	S18 02.3	2.7	58.4
01	199 03.6	21.8	133 18.6	7.4	17 59.6	2.8	58.4
02	214 03.6	22.6	147 45.0	7.4	17 56.8	2.8	58.4
03	229 03.7	.. 23.4	162 11.4	7.4	17 54.0	3.1	58.4
04	244 03.7	24.2	176 37.8	7.3	17 50.9	3.1	58.5
05	259 03.7	25.1	191 04.1	7.4	17 47.8	3.2	58.5
06	274 03.8	S13 25.9	205 30.5	7.4	S17 44.6	3.3	58.5
07	289 03.8	26.7	219 56.9	7.4	17 41.3	3.5	58.5
08	304 03.9	27.6	234 23.3	7.5	17 37.8	3.6	58.5
09	319 03.9	.. 28.4	248 49.8	7.4	17 34.2	3.6	58.5
10	334 04.0	29.2	263 16.2	7.4	17 30.6	3.8	58.5
11	349 04.0	30.0	277 42.6	7.4	17 26.8	3.9	58.6
12	4 04.0	S13 30.9	292 09.0	7.5	S17 22.9	4.0	58.6
13	19 04.1	31.7	306 35.5	7.4	17 18.9	4.1	58.6
14	34 04.1	32.5	321 01.9	7.5	17 14.8	4.2	58.6
15	49 04.2	.. 33.3	335 28.4	7.4	17 10.6	4.4	58.6
16	64 04.2	34.2	349 54.8	7.5	17 06.2	4.4	58.6
17	79 04.2	35.0	4 21.3	7.5	17 01.8	4.5	58.7
18	94 04.3	S13 35.8	18 47.8	7.5	S16 57.3	4.7	58.7
19	109 04.3	36.6	33 14.3	7.5	16 52.6	4.8	58.7
20	124 04.3	37.5	47 40.8	7.6	16 47.8	4.8	58.7
21	139 04.4	.. 38.3	62 07.4	7.5	16 43.0	5.0	58.7
22	154 04.4	39.1	76 33.9	7.6	16 38.0	5.1	58.7
23	169 04.5	39.9	91 00.5	7.5	16 32.9	5.1	58.7
30 00	184 04.5	S13 40.8	105 27.0	7.6	S16 27.8	5.3	58.8
01	199 04.5	41.6	119 53.6	7.6	16 22.5	5.4	58.8
02	214 04.6	42.4	134 20.2	7.7	16 17.1	5.5	58.8
03	229 04.6	.. 43.2	148 46.9	7.6	16 11.6	5.6	58.8
04	244 04.6	44.0	163 13.5	7.7	16 06.0	5.7	58.8
05	259 04.7	44.9	177 40.2	7.6	16 00.3	5.8	58.8
06	274 04.7	S13 45.7	192 06.8	7.7	S15 54.5	5.9	58.8
07	289 04.7	46.5	206 33.5	7.7	15 48.6	6.0	58.9
08	304 04.8	47.3	221 00.2	7.8	15 42.6	6.1	58.9
09	319 04.8	.. 48.1	235 27.0	7.7	15 36.5	6.2	58.9
10	334 04.8	49.0	249 53.7	7.8	15 30.3	6.3	58.9
11	349 04.9	49.8	264 20.5	7.8	15 24.0	6.4	58.9
12	4 04.9	S13 50.6	278 47.3	7.8	S15 17.6	6.4	58.9
13	19 04.9	51.4	293 14.1	7.8	15 11.2	6.6	58.9
14	34 05.0	52.2	307 40.9	7.9	15 04.6	6.7	59.0
15	49 05.0	.. 53.1	322 07.8	7.9	14 57.9	6.8	59.0
16	64 05.0	53.9	336 34.7	7.9	14 51.1	6.9	59.0
17	79 05.1	54.7	351 01.6	7.9	14 44.2	6.9	59.0
18	94 05.1	S13 55.5	5 28.5	7.9	S14 37.3	7.1	59.0
19	109 05.1	56.3	19 55.4	8.0	14 30.2	7.1	59.0
20	124 05.2	57.1	34 22.4	8.0	14 23.1	7.3	59.0
21	139 05.2	.. 57.9	48 49.4	8.0	14 15.8	7.3	59.0
22	154 05.2	58.8	63 16.4	8.0	14 08.5	7.4	59.1
23	169 05.2	59.6	77 43.4	8.1	S14 01.1	7.5	59.1
	SD 16.1	d 0.8	SD 15.9	16.0			16.1

Days are labelled along the left margin: **TUESDAY** (28), **WEDNESDAY** (29), **THURSDAY** (30).

Lat.	Twilight Naut.	Civil	Sunrise	Moonrise 28	29	30	31
N 72	05 54	07 15	08 38	▬▬▬	15 32	15 16	15 08
N 70	05 51	07 04	08 15	14 10	14 34	14 43	14 47
68	05 48	06 55	07 58	13 25	13 59	14 19	14 31
66	05 46	06 47	07 44	12 55	13 34	14 00	14 18
64	05 44	06 40	07 32	12 33	13 15	13 45	14 07
62	05 42	06 35	07 23	12 15	12 59	13 32	13 57
60	05 41	06 30	07 14	12 00	12 45	13 21	13 49
N 58	05 39	06 25	07 07	11 47	12 34	13 12	13 42
56	05 37	06 21	07 00	11 36	12 24	13 03	13 36
54	05 36	06 17	06 54	11 27	12 15	12 56	13 30
52	05 34	06 14	06 49	11 18	12 07	12 49	13 25
50	05 33	06 11	06 44	11 10	12 00	12 43	13 21
45	05 29	06 04	06 34	10 54	11 45	12 30	13 11
N 40	05 26	05 58	06 25	10 41	11 32	12 19	13 02
35	05 22	05 52	06 18	10 29	11 21	12 10	12 55
30	05 19	05 47	06 11	10 19	11 12	12 02	12 49
20	05 11	05 37	06 00	10 02	10 56	11 48	12 38
N 10	05 03	05 28	05 50	09 47	10 42	11 36	12 28
0	04 54	05 19	05 40	09 33	10 29	11 24	12 19
S 10	04 44	05 09	05 31	09 19	10 15	11 13	12 10
20	04 30	04 57	05 20	09 04	10 01	11 00	12 00
30	04 13	04 43	05 08	08 47	09 45	10 46	11 49
35	04 02	04 34	05 01	08 37	09 36	10 38	11 42
40	03 49	04 24	04 53	08 25	09 25	10 29	11 35
45	03 33	04 12	04 44	08 12	09 12	10 18	11 27
S 50	03 12	03 56	04 32	07 56	08 57	10 04	11 16
52	03 01	03 49	04 27	07 48	08 50	09 58	11 11
54	02 49	03 41	04 21	07 39	08 42	09 51	11 06
56	02 35	03 32	04 14	07 30	08 33	09 44	11 00
58	02 17	03 21	04 07	07 19	08 23	09 35	10 54
S 60	01 56	03 08	03 59	07 06	08 11	09 25	10 46

Lat.	Sunset	Twilight Civil	Naut.	Moonset 28	29	30	31
N 72	14 48	16 11	17 32	▬▬▬	18 00	20 12	22 14
N 70	15 11	16 22	17 35	17 25	18 58	20 44	22 33
68	15 28	16 31	17 37	18 10	19 32	21 07	22 48
66	15 42	16 39	17 40	18 39	19 56	21 25	23 00
64	15 54	16 46	17 42	19 02	20 15	21 40	23 10
62	16 04	16 52	17 44	19 19	20 31	21 52	23 18
60	16 12	16 57	17 46	19 34	20 44	22 02	23 26
N 58	16 20	17 01	17 48	19 47	20 55	22 11	23 32
56	16 26	17 06	17 49	19 58	21 05	22 19	23 37
54	16 32	17 09	17 51	20 07	21 13	22 26	23 43
52	16 38	17 13	17 52	20 16	21 21	22 32	23 47
50	16 42	17 16	17 54	20 23	21 28	22 38	23 51
45	16 53	17 23	17 58	20 39	21 43	22 50	24 00
N 40	17 01	17 29	18 01	20 53	21 55	23 00	24 07
35	17 09	17 35	18 05	21 04	22 05	23 08	24 14
30	17 16	17 40	18 08	21 14	22 14	23 16	24 19
20	17 27	17 50	18 16	21 31	22 29	23 29	24 29
N 10	17 37	17 59	18 24	21 46	22 43	23 40	24 37
0	17 47	18 08	18 33	21 59	22 55	23 50	24 45
S 10	17 57	18 19	18 44	22 13	23 08	24 01	00 01
20	18 08	18 30	18 57	22 28	23 21	24 12	00 12
30	18 20	18 45	19 15	22 44	23 36	24 24	00 24
35	18 27	18 54	19 26	22 54	23 45	24 31	00 31
40	18 35	19 04	19 39	23 05	23 55	24 40	00 40
45	18 45	19 17	19 56	23 18	24 06	00 06	00 49
S 50	18 56	19 32	20 17	23 34	24 20	00 20	01 00
52	19 02	19 40	20 28	23 41	24 27	00 27	01 06
54	19 08	19 48	20 41	23 50	24 34	00 34	01 11
56	19 14	19 58	20 55	23 59	24 42	00 42	01 18
58	19 22	20 09	21 13	24 09	00 09	00 51	01 25
S 60	19 31	20 21	21 36	24 21	00 21	01 01	01 33

Day	SUN Eqn. of Time 00h	12h	Mer. Pass.	MOON Mer. Pass. Upper	Lower	Age	Phase
d	m s	m s	h m	h m	h m	d	%
28	16 09	16 12	11 44	15 46	03 18	05	22
29	16 14	16 16	11 44	16 42	04 14	06	32
30	16 18	16 20	11 44	17 37	05 10	07	43

UT	ARIES GHA	VENUS −4.0 GHA	Dec	MARS +0.9 GHA	Dec	JUPITER −2.1 GHA	Dec	SATURN +0.5 GHA	Dec	STARS Name	SHA	Dec
d h	° ′	° ′	° ′	° ′	° ′	° ′	° ′	° ′	° ′		° ′	° ′
31 00	39 13.2	182 23.7	S13 40.7	125 30.1	S24 54.0	256 18.9	N15 18.2	167 20.5	S16 50.1	Acamar	315 17.3	S40 14.7
01	54 15.7	197 23.1	41.8	140 30.5	53.9	271 21.0	18.2	182 22.7	50.2	Achernar	335 25.6	S57 09.8
02	69 18.2	212 22.6	42.8	155 30.9	53.9	286 23.2	18.1	197 24.8	50.3	Acrux	173 08.7	S63 10.7
03	84 20.6	227 22.0 . .	43.9	170 31.3 . .	53.8	301 25.4 . .	18.0	212 27.0 . .	50.3	Adhara	255 11.6	S28 59.5
04	99 23.1	242 21.4	45.0	185 31.7	53.8	316 27.6	17.9	227 29.2	50.4	Aldebaran	290 48.0	N16 32.2
05	114 25.6	257 20.9	46.1	200 32.1	53.7	331 29.8	17.8	242 31.3	50.5			
06	129 28.0	272 20.3	S13 47.1	215 32.5	S24 53.7	346 31.9	N15 17.7	257 33.5	S16 50.6	Alioth	166 20.5	N55 52.7
F 07	144 30.5	287 19.7	48.2	230 33.0	53.6	1 34.1	17.7	272 35.7	50.6	Alkaid	152 58.7	N49 14.4
R 08	159 33.0	302 19.1	49.3	245 33.4	53.6	16 36.3	17.6	287 37.9	50.7	Al Na'ir	27 42.5	S46 53.4
I 09	174 35.4	317 18.6 . .	50.3	260 33.8 . .	53.5	31 38.5 . .	17.5	302 40.0 . .	50.8	Alnilam	275 45.2	S 1 11.6
D 10	189 37.9	332 18.0	51.4	275 34.2	53.4	46 40.7	17.4	317 42.2	50.9	Alphard	217 55.2	S 8 43.4
A 11	204 40.3	347 17.4	52.5	290 34.6	53.4	61 42.9	17.3	332 44.4	50.9			
Y 12	219 42.8	2 16.9	S13 53.5	305 35.0	S24 53.3	76 45.0	N15 17.2	347 46.5	S16 51.0	Alphecca	126 10.6	N26 40.2
13	234 45.3	17 16.3	54.6	320 35.4	53.3	91 47.2	17.2	2 48.7	51.1	Alpheratz	357 42.2	N29 10.6
14	249 47.7	32 15.7	55.7	335 35.9	53.2	106 49.4	17.1	17 50.9	51.2	Altair	62 07.4	N 8 54.8
15	264 50.2	47 15.1 . .	56.7	350 36.3 . .	53.2	121 51.6 . .	17.0	32 53.1 . .	51.2	Ankaa	353 14.5	S42 13.6
16	279 52.7	62 14.6	57.8	5 36.7	53.1	136 53.8	16.9	47 55.2	51.3	Antares	112 25.4	S26 27.7
17	294 55.1	77 14.0	58.9	20 37.1	53.0	151 56.0	16.8	62 57.4	51.4			
18	309 57.6	92 13.4	S13 59.9	35 37.5	S24 53.0	166 58.2	N15 16.8	77 59.6	S16 51.5	Arcturus	145 55.3	N19 06.5
19	325 00.1	107 12.8	14 01.0	50 37.9	52.9	182 00.3	16.7	93 01.7	51.5	Atria	107 26.8	S69 03.2
20	340 02.5	122 12.3	02.1	65 38.3	52.8	197 02.5	16.6	108 03.9	51.6	Avior	234 17.5	S59 33.3
21	355 05.0	137 11.7 . .	03.1	80 38.8 . .	52.8	212 04.7 . .	16.5	123 06.1 . .	51.7	Bellatrix	278 30.8	N 6 21.7
22	10 07.5	152 11.1	04.2	95 39.2	52.7	227 06.9	16.4	138 08.2	51.8	Betelgeuse	271 00.1	N 7 24.5
23	25 09.9	167 10.5	05.2	110 39.6	52.7	242 09.1	16.4	153 10.4	51.8			
1 00	40 12.4	182 10.0	S14 06.3	125 40.0	S24 52.6	257 11.3	N15 16.3	168 12.6	S16 51.9	Canopus	263 55.4	S52 42.1
01	55 14.8	197 09.4	07.4	140 40.4	52.5	272 13.5	16.2	183 14.8	52.0	Capella	280 32.7	N46 00.5
02	70 17.3	212 08.8	08.4	155 40.8	52.5	287 15.7	16.1	198 16.9	52.1	Deneb	49 30.8	N45 20.5
03	85 19.8	227 08.2 . .	09.5	170 41.2 . .	52.4	302 17.8 . .	16.0	213 19.1 . .	52.1	Denebola	182 33.0	N14 29.4
04	100 22.2	242 07.6	10.5	185 41.6	52.3	317 20.0	16.0	228 21.3	52.2	Diphda	348 54.7	S17 54.3
05	115 24.7	257 07.1	11.6	200 42.1	52.3	332 22.2	15.9	243 23.4	52.3			
06	130 27.2	272 06.5	S14 12.6	215 42.5	S24 52.2	347 24.4	N15 15.8	258 25.6	S16 52.4	Dubhe	193 51.1	N61 40.0
S 07	145 29.6	287 05.9	13.7	230 42.9	52.1	2 26.6	15.7	273 27.8	52.4	Elnath	278 11.2	N28 37.0
A 08	160 32.1	302 05.3	14.8	245 43.3	52.1	17 28.8	15.6	288 30.0	52.5	Eltanin	90 46.1	N51 29.7
T 09	175 34.6	317 04.7 . .	15.8	260 43.7 . .	52.0	32 31.0 . .	15.6	303 32.1 . .	52.6	Enif	33 46.1	N 9 56.9
U 10	190 37.0	332 04.2	16.9	275 44.1	51.9	47 33.2	15.5	318 34.3	52.7	Fomalhaut	15 22.8	S29 32.6
R 11	205 39.5	347 03.6	17.9	290 44.5	51.9	62 35.4	15.4	333 36.5	52.7			
D 12	220 41.9	2 03.0	S14 19.0	305 44.9	S24 51.8	77 37.5	N15 15.3	348 38.6	S16 52.8	Gacrux	172 00.2	S57 11.6
A 13	235 44.4	17 02.4	20.0	320 45.4	51.7	92 39.7	15.2	3 40.8	52.9	Gienah	175 51.6	S17 37.3
Y 14	250 46.9	32 01.8	21.1	335 45.8	51.7	107 41.9	15.2	18 43.0	53.0	Hadar	148 47.1	S60 26.5
15	265 49.3	47 01.2 . .	22.1	350 46.2 . .	51.6	122 44.1 . .	15.1	33 45.1 . .	53.0	Hamal	327 59.3	N23 32.0
16	280 51.8	62 00.6	23.2	5 46.6	51.5	137 46.3	15.0	48 47.3	53.1	Kaus Aust.	83 42.8	S34 22.5
17	295 54.3	77 00.1	24.2	20 47.0	51.4	152 48.5	14.9	63 49.5	53.2			
18	310 56.7	91 59.5	S14 25.3	35 47.4	S24 51.4	167 50.7	N15 14.8	78 51.6	S16 53.3	Kochab	137 21.4	N74 05.8
19	325 59.2	106 58.9	26.3	50 47.8	51.3	182 52.9	14.8	93 53.8	53.3	Markab	13 37.2	N15 17.4
20	341 01.7	121 58.3	27.4	65 48.2	51.2	197 55.1	14.7	108 56.0	53.4	Menkar	314 13.8	N 4 08.8
21	356 04.1	136 57.7 . .	28.4	80 48.6 . .	51.2	212 57.3 . .	14.6	123 58.2 . .	53.5	Menkent	148 06.8	S36 26.4
22	11 06.6	151 57.1	29.5	95 49.1	51.1	227 59.5	14.5	139 00.3	53.6	Miaplacidus	221 39.4	S69 46.5
23	26 09.1	166 56.5	30.5	110 49.5	51.0	243 01.7	14.4	154 02.5	53.6			
2 00	41 11.5	181 55.9	S14 31.5	125 49.9	S24 50.9	258 03.8	N15 14.4	169 04.7	S16 53.7	Mirfak	308 38.5	N49 54.7
01	56 14.0	196 55.4	32.6	140 50.3	50.9	273 06.0	14.3	184 06.8	53.8	Nunki	75 57.3	S26 16.5
02	71 16.4	211 54.8	33.6	155 50.7	50.8	288 08.2	14.2	199 09.0	53.8	Peacock	53 17.9	S56 41.3
03	86 18.9	226 54.2 . .	34.7	170 51.1 . .	50.7	303 10.4 . .	14.1	214 11.2 . .	53.9	Pollux	243 26.5	N27 59.2
04	101 21.4	241 53.6	35.7	185 51.5	50.6	318 12.6	14.0	229 13.3	54.0	Procyon	244 58.7	N 5 11.1
05	116 23.8	256 53.0	36.8	200 51.9	50.5	333 14.8	14.0	244 15.5	54.1			
06	131 26.3	271 52.4	S14 37.8	215 52.3	S24 50.4	348 17.0	N15 13.9	259 17.7	S16 54.1	Rasalhague	96 05.8	N12 33.3
07	146 28.8	286 51.8	38.8	230 52.8	50.4	3 19.2	13.8	274 19.9	54.2	Regulus	207 42.7	N11 53.6
08	161 31.2	301 51.2	39.9	245 53.2	50.3	18 21.4	13.7	289 22.0	54.3	Rigel	281 10.9	S 8 11.1
S 09	176 33.7	316 50.6 . .	40.9	260 53.6 . .	50.2	33 23.6 . .	13.7	304 24.2 . .	54.4	Rigil Kent.	139 51.0	S60 53.6
U 10	191 36.2	331 50.0	42.0	275 54.0	50.2	48 25.8	13.6	319 26.4	54.4	Sabik	102 11.7	S15 44.3
N 11	206 38.6	346 49.4	43.0	290 54.4	50.1	63 28.0	13.5	334 28.5	54.5			
D 12	221 41.1	1 48.8	S14 44.0	305 54.8	S24 50.0	78 30.2	N15 13.4	349 30.7	S16 54.6	Schedar	349 38.8	N56 37.3
A 13	236 43.5	16 48.2	45.1	320 55.2	49.9	93 32.4	13.3	4 32.9	54.7	Shaula	96 21.0	S37 06.7
Y 14	251 46.0	31 47.6	46.1	335 55.6	49.8	108 34.6	13.3	19 35.0	54.7	Sirius	258 32.7	S16 44.2
15	266 48.5	46 47.0 . .	47.1	350 56.0 . .	49.8	123 36.8 . .	13.2	34 37.2 . .	54.8	Spica	158 30.6	S11 14.1
16	281 50.9	61 46.5	48.2	5 56.4	49.7	138 39.0	13.1	49 39.4	54.9	Suhail	222 51.8	S43 29.4
17	296 53.4	76 45.9	49.2	20 56.9	49.6	153 41.2	13.0	64 41.5	55.0			
18	311 55.9	91 45.3	S14 50.2	35 57.3	S24 49.5	168 43.4	N15 13.0	79 43.7	S16 55.0	Vega	80 38.5	N38 48.3
19	326 58.3	106 44.7	51.3	50 57.7	49.4	183 45.6	12.9	94 45.9	55.1	Zuben'ubi	137 04.7	S16 06.0
20	342 00.8	121 44.1	52.3	65 58.1	49.3	198 47.8	12.8	109 48.1	55.2		SHA	Mer.Pass.
21	357 03.3	136 43.5 . .	53.3	80 58.5 . .	49.3	213 50.0 . .	12.7	124 50.2 . .	55.3		° ′	h m
22	12 05.7	151 42.9	54.4	95 58.9	49.2	228 52.2	12.7	139 52.4	55.3	Venus	141 57.6	11 52
23	27 08.2	166 42.3	55.4	110 59.3	49.1	243 54.4	12.6	154 54.6	55.4	Mars	85 27.6	15 37
	h m									Jupiter	216 58.9	6 50
Mer.Pass. 21 15.7		v −0.6	d 1.1	v 0.4	d 0.1	v 2.2	d 0.1	v 2.2	d 0.1	Saturn	128 00.2	12 45

UT	SUN GHA	SUN Dec	MOON GHA	v	Dec	d	HP
d h	° ′	° ′	° ′	′	° ′	′	′
31 00	184 05.3	S14 00.4	92 10.5	8.1	S13 53.6	7.6	59.1
01	199 05.3	01.2	106 37.6	8.1	13 46.0	7.7	59.1
02	214 05.3	02.0	121 04.7	8.1	13 38.3	7.8	59.1
03	229 05.4 ..	02.8	135 31.8	8.2	13 30.5	7.8	59.1
04	244 05.4	03.6	149 59.0	8.1	13 22.7	8.0	59.1
05	259 05.4	04.4	164 26.1	8.2	13 14.7	8.0	59.1
06	274 05.4	S14 05.3	178 53.3	8.3	S13 06.7	8.1	59.2
07	289 05.5	06.1	193 20.6	8.2	12 58.6	8.2	59.2
F 08	304 05.5	06.9	207 47.8	8.3	12 50.4	8.3	59.2
R 09	319 05.5 ..	07.7	222 15.1	8.3	12 42.1	8.3	59.2
I 10	334 05.5	08.5	236 42.4	8.3	12 33.8	8.4	59.2
D 11	349 05.6	09.3	251 09.7	8.4	12 25.4	8.5	59.2
A 12	4 05.6	S14 10.1	265 37.1	8.3	S12 16.9	8.6	59.2
Y 13	19 05.6	10.9	280 04.4	8.4	12 08.3	8.7	59.2
14	34 05.6	11.7	294 31.8	8.5	11 59.6	8.7	59.3
15	49 05.7 ..	12.5	308 59.3	8.4	11 50.9	8.9	59.3
16	64 05.7	13.3	323 26.7	8.5	11 42.0	8.8	59.3
17	79 05.7	14.1	337 54.2	8.5	11 33.2	9.0	59.3
18	94 05.7	S14 14.9	352 21.7	8.5	S11 24.2	9.0	59.3
19	109 05.8	15.8	6 49.2	8.5	11 15.2	9.1	59.3
20	124 05.8	16.6	21 16.7	8.6	11 06.1	9.2	59.3
21	139 05.8 ..	17.4	35 44.3	8.6	10 56.9	9.3	59.3
22	154 05.8	18.2	50 11.9	8.6	10 47.6	9.3	59.3
23	169 05.8	19.0	64 39.5	8.6	10 38.3	9.4	59.3
1 00	184 05.9	S14 19.8	79 07.1	8.7	S10 28.9	9.4	59.4
01	199 05.9	20.6	93 34.8	8.7	10 19.5	9.5	59.4
02	214 05.9	21.4	108 02.5	8.7	10 10.0	9.6	59.4
03	229 05.9 ..	22.2	122 30.2	8.7	10 00.4	9.7	59.4
04	244 05.9	23.0	136 57.9	8.7	9 50.7	9.7	59.4
05	259 06.0	23.8	151 25.6	8.8	9 41.0	9.7	59.4
06	274 06.0	S14 24.6	165 53.4	8.8	S 9 31.3	9.8	59.4
S 07	289 06.0	25.4	180 21.2	8.8	9 21.5	9.9	59.4
A 08	304 06.0	26.2	194 49.0	8.9	9 11.6	10.0	59.4
T 09	319 06.0 ..	27.0	209 16.9	8.8	9 01.6	10.0	59.4
U 10	334 06.0	27.8	223 44.7	8.9	8 51.6	10.0	59.4
R 11	349 06.1	28.6	238 12.6	8.9	8 41.6	10.1	59.4
D 12	4 06.1	S14 29.4	252 40.5	8.9	S 8 31.5	10.2	59.5
A 13	19 06.1	30.2	267 08.4	8.9	8 21.3	10.2	59.5
Y 14	34 06.1	31.0	281 36.3	9.0	8 11.1	10.3	59.5
15	49 06.1 ..	31.8	296 04.3	9.0	8 00.8	10.3	59.5
16	64 06.1	32.6	310 32.3	9.0	7 50.5	10.4	59.5
17	79 06.2	33.4	325 00.3	9.0	7 40.1	10.4	59.5
18	94 06.2	S14 34.2	339 28.3	9.0	S 7 29.7	10.5	59.5
19	109 06.2	35.0	353 56.3	9.1	7 19.2	10.5	59.5
20	124 06.2	35.8	8 24.4	9.0	7 08.7	10.6	59.5
21	139 06.2 ..	36.6	22 52.4	9.1	6 58.1	10.6	59.5
22	154 06.2	37.4	37 20.5	9.1	6 47.5	10.6	59.5
23	169 06.2	38.1	51 48.6	9.1	6 36.9	10.7	59.5
2 00	184 06.2	S14 38.9	66 16.7	9.2	S 6 26.2	10.7	59.5
01	199 06.3	39.7	80 44.9	9.1	6 15.5	10.8	59.5
02	214 06.3	40.5	95 13.0	9.2	6 04.7	10.8	59.5
03	229 06.3 ..	41.3	109 41.2	9.1	5 53.9	10.9	59.6
04	244 06.3	42.1	124 09.3	9.2	5 43.0	10.8	59.6
05	259 06.3	42.9	138 37.5	9.2	5 32.2	10.9	59.6
06	274 06.3	S14 43.7	153 05.7	9.3	S 5 21.3	11.0	59.6
S 07	289 06.3	44.5	167 34.0	9.2	5 10.3	11.0	59.6
U 08	304 06.3	45.3	182 02.2	9.2	4 59.3	11.0	59.6
N 09	319 06.3 ..	46.1	196 30.4	9.3	4 48.3	11.0	59.6
D 10	334 06.4	46.9	210 58.7	9.3	4 37.3	11.1	59.6
A 11	349 06.4	47.6	225 27.0	9.2	4 26.2	11.1	59.6
Y 12	4 06.4	S14 48.4	239 55.2	9.3	S 4 15.1	11.2	59.6
13	19 06.4	49.2	254 23.5	9.3	4 03.9	11.1	59.6
14	34 06.4	50.0	268 51.8	9.3	3 52.8	11.2	59.6
15	49 06.4 ..	50.8	283 20.1	9.4	3 41.6	11.2	59.6
16	64 06.4	51.6	297 48.5	9.3	3 30.4	11.2	59.6
17	79 06.4	52.4	312 16.8	9.3	3 19.2	11.3	59.6
18	94 06.4	S14 53.2	326 45.1	9.4	S 3 07.9	11.2	59.6
19	109 06.4	53.9	341 13.5	9.3	2 56.7	11.3	59.6
20	124 06.4	54.7	355 41.8	9.4	2 45.4	11.3	59.6
21	139 06.4 ..	55.5	10 10.2	9.3	2 34.1	11.4	59.6
22	154 06.4	56.3	24 38.5	9.4	2 22.7	11.3	59.6
23	169 06.4	57.1	39 06.9	9.4	S 2 11.4	11.3	59.6
	SD 16.1	d 0.8	SD 16.1		16.2		16.2

Lat.	Twilight Naut.	Twilight Civil	Sunrise	Moonrise 31	Moonrise 1	Moonrise 2	Moonrise 3
°	h m	h m	h m	h m	h m	h m	h m
N 72	06 06	07 29	08 56	15 08	15 01	14 55	14 49
N 70	06 02	07 16	08 30	14 47	14 49	14 49	14 50
68	05 58	07 05	08 10	14 31	14 39	14 45	14 50
66	05 55	06 56	07 55	14 18	14 31	14 41	14 51
64	05 52	06 49	07 42	14 07	14 24	14 38	14 52
62	05 50	06 42	07 31	13 57	14 18	14 36	14 52
60	05 47	06 37	07 22	13 49	14 13	14 33	14 53
N 58	05 45	06 32	07 14	13 42	14 08	14 31	14 53
56	05 43	06 27	07 07	13 36	14 04	14 29	14 53
54	05 41	06 23	07 00	13 30	14 00	14 28	14 54
52	05 39	06 19	06 55	13 25	13 57	14 26	14 54
50	05 37	06 15	06 49	13 21	13 54	14 25	14 54
45	05 33	06 08	06 38	13 11	13 47	14 23	14 55
N 40	05 29	06 01	06 29	13 02	13 42	14 19	14 55
35	05 25	05 55	06 21	12 55	13 37	14 17	14 56
30	05 21	05 49	06 14	12 49	13 33	14 15	14 56
20	05 13	05 39	06 01	12 38	13 25	14 11	14 57
N 10	05 04	05 29	05 50	12 28	13 19	14 08	14 57
0	04 54	05 19	05 40	12 19	13 13	14 05	14 58
S 10	04 43	05 08	05 30	12 10	13 06	14 03	14 58
20	04 29	04 56	05 18	12 00	13 00	14 00	14 59
30	04 10	04 40	05 05	11 49	12 52	13 56	15 00
35	03 59	04 31	04 58	11 42	12 48	13 54	15 00
40	03 45	04 20	04 49	11 35	12 43	13 52	15 01
45	03 27	04 07	04 39	11 27	12 37	13 49	15 02
S 50	03 05	03 51	04 27	11 16	12 31	13 46	15 02
52	02 53	03 43	04 21	11 11	12 27	13 45	15 03
54	02 40	03 34	04 15	11 06	12 24	13 43	15 03
56	02 25	03 24	04 08	11 00	12 20	13 42	15 04
58	02 05	03 12	04 00	10 54	12 16	13 40	15 04
S 60	01 41	02 59	03 50	10 46	12 11	13 38	15 05

Lat.	Sunset	Twilight Civil	Twilight Naut.	Moonset 31	Moonset 1	Moonset 2	Moonset 3
°	h m	h m	h m	h m	h m	h m	h m
N 72	14 30	15 57	17 20	22 14	24 12	00 12	02 08
N 70	14 56	16 10	17 24	22 33	24 22	00 22	02 11
68	15 16	16 21	17 28	22 48	24 30	00 30	02 13
66	15 31	16 30	17 31	23 00	24 37	00 37	02 15
64	15 44	16 37	17 34	23 10	24 43	00 43	02 16
62	15 55	16 44	17 36	23 18	24 47	00 47	02 17
60	16 04	16 50	17 39	23 26	24 51	00 51	02 18
N 58	16 13	16 55	17 41	23 32	24 55	00 55	02 19
56	16 20	16 59	17 43	23 37	24 58	00 58	02 20
54	16 26	17 04	17 45	23 43	25 01	01 01	02 21
52	16 32	17 07	17 47	23 47	25 04	01 04	02 22
50	16 37	17 11	17 49	23 51	25 06	01 06	02 22
45	16 48	17 19	17 54	24 00	00 00	01 11	02 24
N 40	16 58	17 26	17 58	24 07	00 07	01 16	02 25
35	17 06	17 32	18 02	24 14	00 14	01 19	02 26
30	17 13	17 38	18 06	24 19	00 19	01 23	02 27
20	17 26	17 48	18 14	24 29	00 29	01 28	02 28
N 10	17 37	17 58	18 23	24 37	00 37	01 33	02 29
0	17 47	18 08	18 33	24 45	00 45	01 38	02 30
S 10	17 58	18 19	18 45	00 01	00 52	01 42	02 31
20	18 09	18 32	18 59	00 12	01 00	01 47	02 33
30	18 22	18 47	19 17	00 24	01 09	01 52	02 34
35	18 30	18 57	19 29	00 31	01 15	01 55	02 35
40	18 39	19 08	19 43	00 40	01 21	01 59	02 35
45	18 49	19 21	20 01	00 49	01 27	02 03	02 36
S 50	19 01	19 38	20 24	01 00	01 36	02 07	02 37
52	19 07	19 46	20 36	01 06	01 39	02 10	02 38
54	19 14	19 55	20 50	01 11	01 44	02 12	02 38
56	19 21	20 05	21 05	01 18	01 48	02 15	02 39
58	19 29	20 17	21 25	01 25	01 53	02 17	02 40
S 60	19 39	20 31	21 51	01 33	01 59	02 21	02 40

Day	SUN Eqn. of Time 00ʰ	SUN Eqn. of Time 12ʰ	SUN Mer. Pass.	MOON Mer. Pass. Upper	MOON Mer. Pass. Lower	Age	Phase
d	m s	m s	h m	h m	h m	d	%
31	16 21	16 22	11 44	18 32	06 05	08	55
1	16 23	16 24	11 44	19 25	06 59	09	66
2	16 25	16 25	11 44	20 18	07 52	10	76

UT	ARIES GHA	VENUS −4.0 GHA	Dec	MARS +0.9 GHA	Dec	JUPITER −2.1 GHA	Dec	SATURN +0.5 GHA	Dec	STARS Name	SHA	Dec
3 00	42 10.7	181 41.7	S14 56.4	125 59.7	S24 49.0	258 56.6	N15 12.5	169 56.7	S16 55.5	Acamar	315 17.3	S40 14.8
01	57 13.1	196 41.1	57.5	141 00.1	48.9	273 58.8	12.4	184 58.9	55.6	Achernar	335 25.6	S57 09.8
02	72 15.6	211 40.5	58.5	156 00.5	48.8	289 01.0	12.3	200 01.1	55.6	Acrux	173 08.7	S63 10.7
03	87 18.0	226 39.9	14 59.5	171 00.9 ..	48.7	304 03.2 ..	12.3	215 03.2 ..	55.7	Adhara	255 11.6	S28 59.5
04	102 20.5	241 39.2	15 00.5	186 01.4	48.7	319 05.4	12.2	230 05.4	55.8	Aldebaran	290 48.0	N16 32.2
05	117 23.0	256 38.6	01.6	201 01.8	48.6	334 07.6	12.1	245 07.6	55.9			
M 06	132 25.4	271 38.0	S15 02.6	216 02.2	S24 48.5	349 09.8	N15 12.0	260 09.7	S16 55.9	Alioth	166 20.5	N55 52.7
O 07	147 27.9	286 37.4	03.6	231 02.6	48.4	4 12.0	12.0	275 11.9	56.0	Alkaid	152 58.7	N49 14.4
N 08	162 30.4	301 36.8	04.6	246 03.0	48.3	19 14.2	11.9	290 14.1	56.1	Al Na'ir	27 42.5	S46 53.4
D 09	177 32.8	316 36.2 ..	05.7	261 03.4 ..	48.2	34 16.4 ..	11.8	305 16.2 ..	56.2	Alnilam	275 45.2	S 1 11.6
A 10	192 35.3	331 35.6	06.7	276 03.8	48.1	49 18.6	11.7	320 18.4	56.2	Alphard	217 55.2	S 8 43.4
Y 11	207 37.8	346 35.0	07.7	291 04.2	48.0	64 20.8	11.7	335 20.6	56.3			
12	222 40.2	1 34.4	S15 08.7	306 04.6	S24 47.9	79 23.0	N15 11.6	350 22.7	S16 56.4	Alphecca	126 10.6	N26 40.1
13	237 42.7	16 33.8	09.7	321 05.0	47.8	94 25.2	11.5	5 24.9	56.5	Alpheratz	357 42.2	N29 10.6
14	252 45.2	31 33.2	10.8	336 05.4	47.7	109 27.4	11.4	20 27.1	56.5	Altair	62 07.4	N 8 54.8
15	267 47.6	46 32.6 ..	11.8	351 05.8 ..	47.7	124 29.6 ..	11.4	35 29.3 ..	56.6	Ankaa	353 14.5	S42 13.6
16	282 50.1	61 32.0	12.8	6 06.3	47.6	139 31.8	11.3	50 31.4	56.7	Antares	112 25.4	S26 27.7
17	297 52.5	76 31.4	13.8	21 06.7	47.5	154 34.0	11.2	65 33.6	56.8			
18	312 55.0	91 30.8	S15 14.8	36 07.1	S24 47.4	169 36.2	N15 11.1	80 35.8	S16 56.8	Arcturus	145 55.2	N19 06.5
19	327 57.5	106 30.1	15.9	51 07.5	47.3	184 38.4	11.1	95 37.9	56.9	Atria	107 26.9	S69 03.1
20	342 59.9	121 29.5	16.9	66 07.9	47.2	199 40.6	11.0	110 40.1	57.0	Avior	234 17.5	S59 33.3
21	358 02.4	136 28.9 ..	17.9	81 08.3 ..	47.1	214 42.8 ..	10.9	125 42.3 ..	57.0	Bellatrix	278 30.7	N 6 21.7
22	13 04.9	151 28.3	18.9	96 08.7	47.0	229 45.0	10.8	140 44.4	57.1	Betelgeuse	271 00.1	N 7 24.4
23	28 07.3	166 27.7	19.9	111 09.1	46.9	244 47.2	10.8	155 46.6	57.2			
4 00	43 09.8	181 27.1	S15 20.9	126 09.5	S24 46.8	259 49.4	N15 10.7	170 48.8	S16 57.3	Canopus	263 55.4	S52 42.1
01	58 12.3	196 26.5	21.9	141 09.9	46.7	274 51.6	10.6	185 50.9	57.3	Capella	280 32.7	N46 00.5
02	73 14.7	211 25.9	23.0	156 10.3	46.6	289 53.8	10.5	200 53.1	57.4	Deneb	49 30.8	N45 20.5
03	88 17.2	226 25.2 ..	24.0	171 10.7 ..	46.5	304 56.1 ..	10.5	215 55.3 ..	57.5	Denebola	182 33.0	N14 29.3
04	103 19.6	241 24.6	25.0	186 11.1	46.4	319 58.3	10.4	230 57.4	57.6	Diphda	348 54.7	S17 54.3
05	118 22.1	256 24.0	26.0	201 11.6	46.3	335 00.5	10.3	245 59.6	57.6			
T 06	133 24.6	271 23.4	S15 27.0	216 12.0	S24 46.2	350 02.7	N15 10.2	261 01.8	S16 57.7	Dubhe	193 51.1	N61 40.0
U 07	148 27.0	286 22.8	28.0	231 12.4	46.1	5 04.9	10.2	276 03.9	57.8	Elnath	278 11.1	N28 37.0
E 08	163 29.5	301 22.2	29.0	246 12.8	46.0	20 07.1	10.1	291 06.1	57.9	Eltanin	90 46.1	N51 29.6
S 09	178 32.0	316 21.5 ..	30.0	261 13.2 ..	45.9	35 09.3 ..	10.0	306 08.3 ..	57.9	Enif	33 46.1	N 9 56.9
D 10	193 34.4	331 20.9	31.0	276 13.6	45.8	50 11.5	09.9	321 10.4	58.0	Fomalhaut	15 22.8	S29 32.6
A 11	208 36.9	346 20.3	32.0	291 14.0	45.7	65 13.7	09.9	336 12.6	58.1			
Y 12	223 39.4	1 19.7	S15 33.0	306 14.4	S24 45.6	80 15.9	N15 09.8	351 14.8	S16 58.2	Gacrux	172 00.2	S57 11.6
13	238 41.8	16 19.1	34.0	321 14.8	45.5	95 18.1	09.7	6 16.9	58.2	Gienah	175 51.6	S17 37.3
14	253 44.3	31 18.5	35.0	336 15.2	45.4	110 20.3	09.6	21 19.1	58.3	Hadar	148 47.1	S60 26.5
15	268 46.8	46 17.8 ..	36.0	351 15.6 ..	45.3	125 22.6 ..	09.6	36 21.3 ..	58.4	Hamal	327 59.3	N23 32.0
16	283 49.2	61 17.2	37.1	6 16.0	45.2	140 24.8	09.5	51 23.4	58.5	Kaus Aust.	83 42.8	S34 22.5
17	298 51.7	76 16.6	38.1	21 16.4	45.1	155 27.0	09.4	66 25.6	58.5			
18	313 54.1	91 16.0	S15 39.1	36 16.8	S24 45.0	170 29.2	N15 09.3	81 27.8	S16 58.6	Kochab	137 21.4	N74 05.8
19	328 56.6	106 15.3	40.1	51 17.2	44.9	185 31.4	09.3	96 29.9	58.7	Markab	13 37.2	N15 17.4
20	343 59.1	121 14.7	41.1	66 17.6	44.8	200 33.6	09.2	111 32.1	58.8	Menkar	314 13.7	N 4 08.8
21	359 01.5	136 14.1 ..	42.1	81 18.1 ..	44.7	215 35.8 ..	09.1	126 34.3 ..	58.8	Menkent	148 06.8	S36 26.4
22	14 04.0	151 13.5	43.1	96 18.5	44.6	230 38.0	09.1	141 36.4	58.9	Miaplacidus	221 39.4	S69 46.5
23	29 06.5	166 12.9	44.0	111 18.9	44.4	245 40.2	09.0	156 38.6	59.0			
5 00	44 08.9	181 12.2	S15 45.0	126 19.3	S24 44.3	260 42.4	N15 08.9	171 40.8	S16 59.0	Mirfak	308 38.5	N49 54.7
01	59 11.4	196 11.6	46.0	141 19.7	44.2	275 44.7	08.8	186 43.0	59.1	Nunki	75 57.4	S26 16.5
02	74 13.9	211 11.0	47.0	156 20.1	44.1	290 46.9	08.8	201 45.1	59.2	Peacock	53 17.9	S56 41.3
03	89 16.3	226 10.4 ..	48.0	171 20.5 ..	44.0	305 49.1 ..	08.7	216 47.3 ..	59.3	Pollux	243 26.5	N27 59.2
04	104 18.8	241 09.7	49.0	186 20.9	43.9	320 51.3	08.6	231 49.5	59.3	Procyon	244 58.7	N 5 11.1
05	119 21.2	256 09.1	50.0	201 21.3	43.8	335 53.5	08.5	246 51.6	59.4			
W 06	134 23.7	271 08.5	S15 51.0	216 21.7	S24 43.7	350 55.7	N15 08.5	261 53.8	S16 59.5	Rasalhague	96 05.9	N12 33.3
E 07	149 26.2	286 07.8	52.0	231 22.1	43.6	5 57.9	08.4	276 56.0	59.6	Regulus	207 42.6	N11 53.6
D 08	164 28.6	301 07.2	53.0	246 22.5	43.5	21 00.2	08.3	291 58.1	59.6	Rigel	281 10.9	S 8 11.1
N 09	179 31.1	316 06.6 ..	54.0	261 22.9 ..	43.3	36 02.4 ..	08.3	307 00.3 ..	59.7	Rigil Kent.	139 51.0	S60 53.6
E 10	194 33.6	331 06.0	55.0	276 23.3	43.2	51 04.6	08.2	322 02.5	59.8	Sabik	102 11.8	S15 44.3
S 11	209 36.0	346 05.3	56.0	291 23.7	43.1	66 06.8	08.1	337 04.6	59.9			
D 12	224 38.5	1 04.7	S15 57.0	306 24.1	S24 43.0	81 09.0	N15 08.0	352 06.8	S16 59.9	Schedar	349 38.8	N56 37.3
A 13	239 41.0	16 04.1	57.9	321 24.5	42.9	96 11.2	08.0	7 09.0	17 00.0	Shaula	96 21.0	S37 06.7
Y 14	254 43.4	31 03.4	58.9	336 24.9	42.8	111 13.4	07.9	22 11.1	00.1	Sirius	258 32.5	S16 44.2
15	269 45.9	46 02.8	15 59.9	351 25.3 ..	42.7	126 15.7 ..	07.8	37 13.3 ..	00.2	Spica	158 30.6	S11 14.1
16	284 48.4	61 02.2	16 00.9	6 25.8	42.5	141 17.9	07.7	52 15.5	00.2	Suhail	222 51.7	S43 29.4
17	299 50.8	76 01.5	01.9	21 26.2	42.4	156 20.1	07.7	67 17.6	00.3			
18	314 53.3	91 00.9	S16 02.9	36 26.6	S24 42.3	171 22.3	N15 07.6	82 19.8	S17 00.4	Vega	80 38.6	N38 48.3
19	329 55.7	106 00.3	03.8	51 27.0	42.2	186 24.5	07.5	97 22.0	00.5	Zuben'ubi	137 04.7	S16 06.0
20	344 58.2	120 59.6	04.8	66 27.4	42.1	201 26.7	07.5	112 24.1	00.5		SHA	Mer. Pass.
21	0 00.7	135 59.0 ..	05.8	81 27.8 ..	42.0	216 29.0 ..	07.4	127 26.3 ..	00.6			h m
22	15 03.1	150 58.4	06.8	96 28.2	41.8	231 31.2	07.3	142 28.5	00.7	Venus	138 17.3	11 55
23	30 05.6	165 57.7	07.8	111 28.6	41.7	246 33.4	07.3	157 30.6	00.8	Mars	82 59.7	15 35
	h m									Jupiter	216 39.6	6 40
Mer. Pass.	21 03.9	v −0.6	d 1.0	v 0.4	d 0.1	v 2.2	d 0.1	v 2.2	d 0.1	Saturn	127 39.0	12 35

SUN / MOON

UT	SUN GHA	SUN Dec	MOON GHA	v	Dec	d	HP
d h	° ′	° ′	° ′	′	° ′	′	′
3 00	184 06.4	S14 57.9	53 35.3	9.4	S 2 00.1	11.4	59.6
01	199 06.5	58.6	68 03.7	9.4	1 48.7	11.4	59.6
02	214 06.5	14 59.4	82 32.1	9.4	1 37.3	11.4	59.6
03	229 06.5	15 00.2	97 00.5	9.4	1 25.9	11.4	59.6
04	244 06.5	01.0	111 28.9	9.4	1 14.5	11.4	59.6
05	259 06.5	01.8	125 57.3	9.4	1 03.1	11.4	59.6
06	274 06.5	S15 02.6	140 25.7	9.4	S 0 51.7	11.4	59.6
07	289 06.5	03.3	154 54.1	9.4	0 40.3	11.4	59.6
08	304 06.5	04.1	169 22.5	9.4	0 28.9	11.4	59.6
09	319 06.5 ..	04.9	183 50.9	9.4	0 17.5	11.4	59.6
10	334 06.5	05.7	198 19.3	9.4	S 0 06.1	11.5	59.6
11	349 06.5	06.5	212 47.7	9.4	N 0 05.4	11.4	59.6
12	4 06.5	S15 07.2	227 16.1	9.4	N 0 16.8	11.4	59.6
13	19 06.5	08.0	241 44.5	9.4	0 28.2	11.4	59.6
14	34 06.5	08.8	256 12.9	9.5	0 39.6	11.4	59.6
15	49 06.5 ..	09.6	270 41.4	9.4	0 51.0	11.5	59.6
16	64 06.5	10.3	285 09.8	9.4	1 02.5	11.4	59.6
17	79 06.5	11.1	299 38.2	9.4	1 13.9	11.4	59.6
18	94 06.5	S15 11.9	314 06.6	9.4	N 1 25.3	11.3	59.6
19	109 06.5	12.7	328 35.0	9.4	1 36.6	11.4	59.6
20	124 06.5	13.5	343 03.4	9.4	1 48.0	11.4	59.6
21	139 06.5 ..	14.2	357 31.8	9.4	1 59.4	11.3	59.6
22	154 06.5	15.0	12 00.2	9.3	2 10.7	11.4	59.5
23	169 06.4	15.8	26 28.5	9.4	2 22.1	11.3	59.5
4 00	184 06.4	S15 16.5	40 56.9	9.4	N 2 33.4	11.3	59.5
01	199 06.4	17.3	55 25.3	9.4	2 44.7	11.3	59.5
02	214 06.4	18.1	69 53.7	9.3	2 56.0	11.2	59.5
03	229 06.4 ..	18.9	84 22.0	9.4	3 07.2	11.3	59.5
04	244 06.4	19.6	98 50.4	9.3	3 18.5	11.2	59.5
05	259 06.4	20.4	113 18.7	9.4	3 29.7	11.2	59.5
06	274 06.4	S15 21.2	127 47.1	9.3	N 3 40.9	11.2	59.5
07	289 06.4	21.9	142 15.4	9.3	3 52.1	11.2	59.5
08	304 06.4	22.7	156 43.7	9.3	4 03.3	11.1	59.5
09	319 06.4 ..	23.5	171 12.0	9.4	4 14.4	11.1	59.5
10	334 06.4	24.3	185 40.4	9.3	4 25.5	11.1	59.5
11	349 06.4	25.0	200 08.7	9.3	4 36.6	11.0	59.4
12	4 06.4	S15 25.8	214 37.0	9.2	N 4 47.6	11.0	59.4
13	19 06.4	26.6	229 05.2	9.3	4 58.6	11.0	59.4
14	34 06.4	27.3	243 33.5	9.3	5 09.6	11.0	59.4
15	49 06.3 ..	28.1	258 01.8	9.2	5 20.6	10.9	59.4
16	64 06.3	28.9	272 30.0	9.3	5 31.5	10.8	59.4
17	79 06.3	29.6	286 58.3	9.2	5 42.3	10.9	59.4
18	94 06.3	S15 30.4	301 26.5	9.2	N 5 53.2	10.8	59.4
19	109 06.3	31.2	315 54.7	9.2	6 04.0	10.7	59.4
20	124 06.3	31.9	330 22.9	9.2	6 14.7	10.8	59.4
21	139 06.3 ..	32.7	344 51.1	9.2	6 25.5	10.6	59.3
22	154 06.3	33.5	359 19.3	9.2	6 36.1	10.7	59.3
23	169 06.3	34.2	13 47.5	9.1	6 46.8	10.6	59.3
5 00	184 06.2	S15 35.0	28 15.6	9.2	N 6 57.4	10.5	59.3
01	199 06.2	35.7	42 43.8	9.1	7 07.9	10.5	59.3
02	214 06.2	36.5	57 11.9	9.1	7 18.4	10.5	59.3
03	229 06.2 ..	37.3	71 40.0	9.1	7 28.9	10.4	59.3
04	244 06.2	38.0	86 08.1	9.1	7 39.3	10.3	59.2
05	259 06.2	38.8	100 36.2	9.1	7 49.6	10.4	59.2
06	274 06.2	S15 39.5	115 04.3	9.1	N 8 00.0	10.2	59.2
07	289 06.1	40.3	129 32.4	9.0	8 10.2	10.2	59.2
08	304 06.1	41.1	144 00.4	9.1	8 20.4	10.2	59.2
09	319 06.1 ..	41.8	158 28.5	9.0	8 30.6	10.1	59.2
10	334 06.1	42.6	172 56.5	9.0	8 40.7	10.0	59.2
11	349 06.1	43.3	187 24.5	9.0	8 50.7	10.0	59.1
12	4 06.1	S15 44.1	201 52.5	9.0	N 9 00.7	9.9	59.1
13	19 06.0	44.9	216 20.5	9.0	9 10.6	9.8	59.1
14	34 06.0	45.6	230 48.5	8.9	9 20.4	9.8	59.1
15	49 06.0 ..	46.4	245 16.4	9.0	9 30.2	9.8	59.1
16	64 06.0	47.1	259 44.4	8.9	9 40.0	9.7	59.1
17	79 06.0	47.9	274 12.3	8.9	9 49.7	9.6	59.0
18	94 06.0	S15 48.6	288 40.2	8.9	N 9 59.3	9.5	59.0
19	109 05.9	49.4	303 08.1	8.9	10 08.8	9.5	59.0
20	124 05.9	50.1	317 36.0	8.9	10 18.3	9.4	59.0
21	139 05.9 ..	50.9	332 03.9	8.9	10 27.7	9.4	59.0
22	154 05.9	51.6	346 31.8	8.8	10 37.1	9.2	58.9
23	169 05.9	52.4	0 59.6	8.8	N10 46.3	9.3	58.9
	SD 16.2	d 0.8	SD 16.2		16.2		16.1

Left column days: MONDAY (3), TUESDAY (4), WEDNESDAY (5)

Twilight / Sunrise / Moonrise

Lat.	Twilight Naut.	Twilight Civil	Sunrise	Moonrise 3	4	5	6
°	h m	h m	h m	h m	h m	h m	h m
N 72	06 18	07 42	09 16	14 49	14 43	14 37	14 31
N 70	06 12	07 28	08 45	14 50	14 50	14 51	14 54
68	06 07	07 16	08 23	14 50	14 56	15 03	15 12
66	06 03	07 06	08 06	14 51	15 01	15 12	15 27
64	06 00	06 57	07 51	14 52	15 05	15 20	15 39
62	05 57	06 50	07 40	14 52	15 09	15 27	15 49
60	05 54	06 44	07 30	14 53	15 12	15 33	15 58
N 58	05 51	06 38	07 21	14 53	15 15	15 39	16 06
56	05 48	06 33	07 13	14 53	15 17	15 43	16 13
54	05 46	06 28	07 06	14 54	15 20	15 48	16 19
52	05 44	06 24	07 00	14 54	15 22	15 52	16 24
50	05 42	06 20	06 54	14 54	15 24	15 55	16 29
45	05 37	06 11	06 42	14 55	15 28	16 03	16 40
N 40	05 32	06 04	06 32	14 55	15 31	16 09	16 49
35	05 27	05 57	06 24	14 56	15 35	16 15	16 57
30	05 23	05 51	06 16	14 56	15 37	16 20	17 04
20	05 14	05 40	06 03	14 57	15 42	16 28	17 16
N 10	05 04	05 29	05 51	14 57	15 46	16 36	17 27
0	04 54	05 17	05 40	14 58	15 50	16 43	17 37
S 10	04 42	05 07	05 29	14 58	15 54	16 50	17 47
20	04 27	04 54	05 17	14 59	15 59	16 58	17 57
30	04 07	04 38	05 03	15 00	16 04	17 07	18 10
35	03 55	04 28	04 55	15 00	16 07	17 12	18 17
40	03 41	04 16	04 46	15 01	16 10	17 18	18 25
45	03 22	04 02	04 35	15 02	16 14	17 25	18 35
S 50	02 58	03 45	04 22	15 02	16 18	17 33	18 46
52	02 46	03 36	04 15	15 03	16 20	17 37	18 52
54	02 31	03 27	04 09	15 03	16 23	17 42	18 58
56	02 14	03 16	04 01	15 04	16 25	17 46	19 04
58	01 53	03 04	03 52	15 04	16 28	17 52	19 12
S 60	01 24	02 49	03 42	15 05	16 32	17 57	19 21

Sunset / Twilight / Moonset

Lat.	Sunset	Twilight Civil	Twilight Naut.	Moonset 3	4	5	6
°	h m	h m	h m	h m	h m	h m	h m
N 72	14 10	15 43	17 08	02 08	04 04	06 00	07 58
N 70	14 41	15 58	17 13	02 11	03 59	05 48	07 36
68	15 03	16 10	17 18	02 13	03 56	05 38	07 19
66	15 20	16 20	17 22	02 15	03 52	05 30	07 06
64	15 35	16 29	17 26	02 16	03 50	05 23	06 54
62	15 47	16 36	17 29	02 17	03 48	05 17	06 45
60	15 57	16 43	17 32	02 18	03 46	05 12	06 37
N 58	16 06	16 48	17 35	02 19	03 44	05 08	06 30
56	16 13	16 53	17 38	02 20	03 42	05 04	06 23
54	16 20	16 58	17 40	02 21	03 41	05 00	06 18
52	16 26	17 02	17 43	02 22	03 40	04 57	06 13
50	16 32	17 06	17 45	02 22	03 38	04 54	06 08
45	16 44	17 15	17 50	02 24	03 36	04 48	05 58
N 40	16 54	17 23	17 55	02 25	03 34	04 42	05 50
35	17 03	17 29	17 59	02 26	03 32	04 38	05 43
30	17 11	17 36	18 04	02 27	03 30	04 34	05 37
20	17 24	17 47	18 13	02 28	03 28	04 27	05 27
N 10	17 36	17 58	18 23	02 29	03 25	04 21	05 17
0	17 47	18 08	18 33	02 30	03 23	04 15	05 09
S 10	17 58	18 20	18 46	02 31	03 20	04 10	05 00
20	18 10	18 34	19 01	02 33	03 18	04 04	04 51
30	18 25	18 50	19 20	02 34	03 15	03 57	04 40
35	18 33	19 00	19 33	02 35	03 13	03 53	04 34
40	18 42	19 12	19 48	02 35	03 12	03 48	04 27
45	18 53	19 26	20 06	02 36	03 09	03 43	04 19
S 50	19 07	19 44	20 31	02 37	03 07	03 37	04 10
52	19 13	19 52	20 43	02 38	03 06	03 34	04 05
54	19 20	20 02	20 58	02 38	03 04	03 31	04 00
56	19 28	20 13	21 15	02 39	03 03	03 28	03 55
58	19 37	20 26	21 38	02 40	03 01	03 24	03 49
S 60	19 47	20 41	22 08	02 40	03 00	03 20	03 42

SUN / MOON

Day	Eqn. of Time 00h	Eqn. of Time 12h	Mer. Pass.	Mer. Pass. Upper	Mer. Pass. Lower	Age	Phase
d	m s	m s	h m	h m	h m	d	%
3	16 26	16 26	11 44	21 10	08 44	11	85
4	16 26	16 25	11 44	22 03	09 36	12	93
5	16 25	16 24	11 44	22 56	10 29	13	97

UT (d h)	ARIES GHA	VENUS −4.0 GHA	VENUS Dec	MARS +0.9 GHA	MARS Dec	JUPITER −2.1 GHA	JUPITER Dec	SATURN +0.5 GHA	SATURN Dec
6 00	45 08.1	180 57.1	S16 08.8	126 29.0	S24 41.6	261 35.6	N15 07.2	172 32.8	S17 00.8
01	60 10.5	195 56.4	09.7	141 29.4	41.5	276 37.8	07.1	187 35.0	00.9
02	75 13.0	210 55.8	10.7	156 29.8	41.4	291 40.1	07.0	202 37.1	01.0
03	90 15.5	225 55.2 ..	11.7	171 30.2 ..	41.2	306 42.3 ..	07.0	217 39.3 ..	01.0
04	105 17.9	240 54.5	12.7	186 30.6	41.1	321 44.5	06.9	232 41.5	01.1
05	120 20.4	255 53.9	13.6	201 31.0	41.0	336 46.7	06.8	247 43.6	01.2
T 06	135 22.9	270 53.2	S16 14.6	216 31.4	S24 40.9	351 48.9	N15 06.8	262 45.8	S17 01.3
H 07	150 25.3	285 52.6	15.6	231 31.8	40.8	6 51.2	06.7	277 47.9	01.3
U 08	165 27.8	300 52.0	16.6	246 32.2	40.6	21 53.4	06.6	292 50.1	01.4
R 09	180 30.2	315 51.3 ..	17.5	261 32.6 ..	40.5	36 55.6 ..	06.5	307 52.3 ..	01.5
S 10	195 32.7	330 50.7	18.5	276 33.0	40.4	51 57.8	06.5	322 54.4	01.6
D 11	210 35.2	345 50.0	19.5	291 33.4	40.3	67 00.0	06.4	337 56.6	01.6
A 12	225 37.6	0 49.4	S16 20.5	306 33.8	S24 40.1	82 02.3	N15 06.3	352 58.8	S17 01.7
Y 13	240 40.1	15 48.7	21.4	321 34.2	40.0	97 04.5	06.3	8 00.9	01.8
14	255 42.6	30 48.1	22.4	336 34.6	39.9	112 06.7	06.2	23 03.1	01.9
15	270 45.0	45 47.5 ..	23.4	351 35.0 ..	39.8	127 08.9 ..	06.1	38 05.3 ..	01.9
16	285 47.5	60 46.8	24.3	6 35.4	39.6	142 11.2	06.1	53 07.4	02.0
17	300 50.0	75 46.2	25.3	21 35.9	39.5	157 13.4	06.0	68 09.6	02.1
18	315 52.4	90 45.5	S16 26.3	36 36.3	S24 39.4	172 15.6	N15 05.9	83 11.8	S17 02.2
19	330 54.9	105 44.9	27.2	51 36.7	39.3	187 17.8	05.8	98 13.9	02.2
20	345 57.3	120 44.2	28.2	66 37.1	39.1	202 20.0	05.8	113 16.1	02.3
21	0 59.8	135 43.6 ..	29.2	81 37.5 ..	39.0	217 22.3 ..	05.7	128 18.3 ..	02.4
22	16 02.3	150 42.9	30.1	96 37.9	38.9	232 24.5	05.6	143 20.4	02.4
23	31 04.7	165 42.3	31.1	111 38.3	38.7	247 26.7	05.6	158 22.6	02.5
7 00	46 07.2	180 41.6	S16 32.0	126 38.7	S24 38.6	262 28.9	N15 05.5	173 24.8	S17 02.6
01	61 09.7	195 41.0	33.0	141 39.1	38.5	277 31.2	05.4	188 26.9	02.7
02	76 12.1	210 40.3	34.0	156 39.5	38.4	292 33.4	05.4	203 29.1	02.7
03	91 14.6	225 39.7 ..	34.9	171 39.9 ..	38.2	307 35.6 ..	05.3	218 31.3 ..	02.8
04	106 17.1	240 39.0	35.9	186 40.3	38.1	322 37.8	05.2	233 33.4	02.9
05	121 19.5	255 38.4	36.8	201 40.7	38.0	337 40.1	05.2	248 35.6	03.0
F 06	136 22.0	270 37.7	S16 37.8	216 41.1	S24 37.8	352 42.3	N15 05.1	263 37.8	S17 03.0
R 07	151 24.5	285 37.1	38.8	231 41.5	37.7	7 44.5	05.0	278 39.9	03.1
I 08	166 26.9	300 36.4	39.7	246 41.9	37.6	22 46.8	05.0	293 42.1	03.2
D 09	181 29.4	315 35.8 ..	40.7	261 42.3 ..	37.4	37 49.0 ..	04.9	308 44.3 ..	03.3
A 10	196 31.8	330 35.1	41.6	276 42.7	37.3	52 51.2	04.8	323 46.4	03.3
Y 11	211 34.3	345 34.5	42.6	291 43.1	37.1	67 53.4	04.7	338 48.6	03.4
12	226 36.8	0 33.8	S16 43.5	306 43.5	S24 37.0	82 55.7	N15 04.7	353 50.8	S17 03.5
13	241 39.2	15 33.1	44.5	321 43.9	36.9	97 57.9	04.6	8 52.9	03.6
14	256 41.7	30 32.5	45.4	336 44.3	36.7	113 00.1	04.5	23 55.1	03.6
15	271 44.2	45 31.8 ..	46.4	351 44.7 ..	36.6	128 02.4 ..	04.5	38 57.3 ..	03.7
16	286 46.6	60 31.2	47.3	6 45.1	36.5	143 04.6	04.4	53 59.4	03.8
17	301 49.1	75 30.5	48.3	21 45.5	36.3	158 06.8	04.3	69 01.6	03.8
18	316 51.6	90 29.8	S16 49.2	36 45.9	S24 36.2	173 09.0	N15 04.2	84 03.7	S17 03.9
19	331 54.0	105 29.2	50.2	51 46.3	36.1	188 11.3	04.2	99 05.9	04.0
20	346 56.5	120 28.5	51.1	66 46.7	35.9	203 13.5	04.1	114 08.1	04.1
21	1 59.0	135 27.9 ..	52.1	81 47.1 ..	35.8	218 15.7 ..	04.1	129 10.2 ..	04.1
22	17 01.4	150 27.2	53.0	96 47.5	35.6	233 18.0	04.0	144 12.4	04.2
23	32 03.9	165 26.5	54.0	111 47.9	35.5	248 20.2	03.9	159 14.6	04.3
8 00	47 06.3	180 25.9	S16 54.9	126 48.3	S24 35.3	263 22.4	N15 03.9	174 16.7	S17 04.4
01	62 08.8	195 25.2	55.8	141 48.7	35.2	278 24.7	03.8	189 18.9	04.4
02	77 11.3	210 24.6	56.8	156 49.1	35.1	293 26.9	03.7	204 21.1	04.5
03	92 13.7	225 23.9 ..	57.7	171 49.5 ..	34.9	308 29.1 ..	03.7	219 23.2 ..	04.6
04	107 16.2	240 23.2	58.7	186 49.9	34.8	323 31.4	03.6	234 25.4	04.7
05	122 18.7	255 22.6	16 59.6	201 50.3	34.6	338 33.6	03.5	249 27.6	04.7
S 06	137 21.1	270 21.9	S17 00.6	216 50.7	S24 34.5	353 35.8	N15 03.5	264 29.7	S17 04.8
A 07	152 23.6	285 21.2	01.5	231 51.2	34.3	8 38.1	03.4	279 31.9	04.9
T 08	167 26.1	300 20.6	02.4	246 51.6	34.2	23 40.3	03.3	294 34.1	05.0
U 09	182 28.5	315 19.9 ..	03.4	261 52.0 ..	34.1	38 42.5 ..	03.3	309 36.2 ..	05.0
R 10	197 31.0	330 19.2	04.3	276 52.4	33.9	53 44.8	03.2	324 38.4	05.1
D 11	212 33.4	345 18.6	05.2	291 52.8	33.8	68 47.0	03.1	339 40.6	05.2
A 12	227 35.9	0 17.9	S17 06.2	306 53.2	S24 33.6	83 49.2	N15 03.1	354 42.7	S17 05.2
Y 13	242 38.4	15 17.2	07.1	321 53.6	33.5	98 51.5	03.0	9 44.9	05.3
14	257 40.8	30 16.6	08.0	336 54.0	33.3	113 53.7	02.9	24 47.0	05.4
15	272 43.3	45 15.9 ..	09.0	351 54.4 ..	33.2	128 55.9 ..	02.9	39 49.2 ..	05.5
16	287 45.8	60 15.2	09.9	6 54.8	33.0	143 58.2	02.8	54 51.4	05.5
17	302 48.2	75 14.5	10.8	21 55.2	32.9	159 00.4	02.8	69 53.5	05.6
18	317 50.7	90 13.9	S17 11.8	36 55.6	S24 32.7	174 02.6	N15 02.7	84 55.7	S17 05.7
19	332 53.2	105 13.2	12.7	51 56.0	32.6	189 04.9	02.6	99 57.9	05.8
20	347 55.6	120 12.5	13.6	66 56.4	32.4	204 07.1	02.6	115 00.0	05.8
21	2 58.1	135 11.9 ..	14.5	81 56.8 ..	32.3	219 09.3 ..	02.5	130 02.2 ..	05.9
22	18 00.6	150 11.2	15.5	96 57.2	32.1	234 11.6	02.5	145 04.4	06.0
23	33 03.0	165 10.5	16.4	111 57.6	32.0	249 13.8	02.4	160 06.5	06.1
Mer. Pass.	h m 20 52.1	v −0.7	d 1.0	v 0.4	d 0.1	v 2.2	d 0.1	v 2.2	d 0.1

STARS

Name	SHA	Dec
Acamar	315 17.2	S40 14.8
Achernar	335 25.6	S57 09.8
Acrux	173 08.6	S63 10.7
Adhara	255 11.6	S28 59.5
Aldebaran	290 48.0	N16 32.2
Alioth	166 20.5	N55 52.7
Alkaid	152 58.7	N49 14.4
Al Na'ir	27 42.5	S46 53.4
Alnilam	275 45.2	S 1 11.7
Alphard	217 55.2	S 8 43.4
Alphecca	126 10.6	N26 40.1
Alpheratz	357 42.2	N29 10.6
Altair	62 07.4	N 8 54.8
Ankaa	353 14.5	S42 13.6
Antares	112 25.4	S26 27.7
Arcturus	145 55.2	N19 06.5
Atria	107 26.9	S69 03.1
Avior	234 17.4	S59 33.3
Bellatrix	278 30.7	N 6 21.7
Betelgeuse	271 00.0	N 7 24.4
Canopus	263 55.4	S52 42.2
Capella	280 32.6	N46 00.5
Deneb	49 30.8	N45 20.5
Denebola	182 33.0	N14 29.3
Diphda	348 54.7	S17 54.3
Dubhe	193 51.0	N61 40.0
Elnath	278 11.1	N28 37.0
Eltanin	90 46.1	N51 29.6
Enif	33 46.1	N 9 56.9
Fomalhaut	15 22.8	S29 32.6
Gacrux	172 00.2	S57 11.5
Gienah	175 51.6	S17 37.3
Hadar	148 47.1	S60 26.4
Hamal	327 59.3	N23 32.0
Kaus Aust.	83 42.8	S34 22.5
Kochab	137 21.4	N74 05.8
Markab	13 37.2	N15 17.4
Menkar	314 13.7	N 4 08.8
Menkent	148 06.8	S36 26.4
Miaplacidus	221 39.3	S69 46.5
Mirfak	308 38.4	N49 54.7
Nunki	75 57.4	S26 16.5
Peacock	53 18.0	S56 41.3
Pollux	243 26.5	N27 59.1
Procyon	244 58.6	N 5 11.1
Rasalhague	96 05.9	N12 33.3
Regulus	207 42.6	N11 53.6
Rigel	281 10.9	S 8 11.2
Rigil Kent.	139 51.0	S60 53.5
Sabik	102 11.8	S15 44.3
Schedar	349 38.9	N56 37.3
Shaula	96 21.0	S37 06.7
Sirius	258 32.7	S16 44.2
Spica	158 30.6	S11 14.2
Suhail	222 51.7	S43 29.4
Vega	80 38.6	N38 48.3
Zuben'ubi	137 04.7	S16 06.0

	SHA	Mer. Pass.
	° ′	h m
Venus	134 34.4	11 58
Mars	80 31.5	15 33
Jupiter	216 21.7	6 29
Saturn	127 17.6	12 25

UT	SUN GHA	Dec	MOON GHA	v	Dec	d	HP
6 THURSDAY							
00	184 05.8	S15 53.1	15 27.4	8.9	N10 55.6	9.1	58.9
01	199 05.8	53.9	29 55.3	8.8	11 04.7	9.1	58.9
02	214 05.8	54.7	44 23.1	8.8	11 13.8	9.0	58.9
03	229 05.8 ..	55.4	58 50.9	8.7	11 22.8	8.9	58.8
04	244 05.7	56.2	73 18.6	8.8	11 31.7	8.8	58.8
05	259 05.7	56.9	87 46.4	8.8	11 40.5	8.8	58.8
06	274 05.7	S15 57.7	102 14.2	8.7	N11 49.3	8.7	58.8
07	289 05.7	58.4	116 41.9	8.8	11 58.0	8.6	58.8
08	304 05.7	59.1	131 09.6	8.8	12 06.6	8.6	58.7
09	319 05.6	15 59.9	145 37.4	8.7	12 15.2	8.4	58.7
10	334 05.6	16 00.6	160 05.1	8.7	12 23.6	8.4	58.7
11	349 05.6	01.4	174 32.8	8.6	12 32.0	8.3	58.7
12	4 05.6	S16 02.1	189 00.4	8.7	N12 40.3	8.2	58.7
13	19 05.5	02.9	203 28.1	8.7	12 48.5	8.2	58.6
14	34 05.5	03.6	217 55.8	8.6	12 56.7	8.0	58.6
15	49 05.5 ..	04.4	232 23.4	8.7	13 04.7	8.0	58.6
16	64 05.4	05.1	246 51.1	8.6	13 12.7	7.9	58.6
17	79 05.4	05.9	261 18.7	8.6	13 20.6	7.8	58.5
18	94 05.4	S16 06.6	275 46.3	8.6	N13 28.4	7.7	58.5
19	109 05.4	07.3	290 13.9	8.6	13 36.1	7.6	58.5
20	124 05.3	08.1	304 41.5	8.6	13 43.7	7.6	58.5
21	139 05.3 ..	08.8	319 09.1	8.6	13 51.3	7.4	58.4
22	154 05.3	09.6	333 36.7	8.6	13 58.7	7.4	58.4
23	169 05.2	10.3	348 04.3	8.5	14 06.1	7.2	58.4
7 FRIDAY							
00	184 05.2	S16 11.1	2 31.8	8.6	N14 13.3	7.2	58.4
01	199 05.2	11.8	16 59.4	8.6	14 20.5	7.1	58.3
02	214 05.2	12.5	31 27.0	8.5	14 27.6	7.0	58.3
03	229 05.1 ..	13.3	45 54.5	8.6	14 34.6	6.9	58.3
04	244 05.1	14.0	60 22.1	8.5	14 41.5	6.8	58.3
05	259 05.1	14.8	74 49.6	8.5	14 48.3	6.8	58.2
06	274 05.0	S16 15.5	89 17.1	8.6	N14 55.1	6.6	58.2
07	289 05.0	16.2	103 44.7	8.5	15 01.7	6.5	58.2
08	304 05.0	17.0	118 12.2	8.5	15 08.2	6.5	58.2
09	319 04.9 ..	17.7	132 39.7	8.5	15 14.7	6.3	58.1
10	334 04.9	18.4	147 07.2	8.8	15 21.0	6.2	58.1
11	349 04.9	19.2	161 34.8	8.5	15 27.2	6.2	58.1
12	4 04.8	S16 19.9	176 02.3	8.5	N15 33.4	6.0	58.0
13	19 04.8	20.6	190 29.8	8.5	15 39.4	6.0	58.0
14	34 04.8	21.4	204 57.3	8.5	15 45.4	5.8	58.0
15	49 04.7 ..	22.1	219 24.8	8.5	15 51.2	5.8	58.0
16	64 04.7	22.8	233 52.3	8.6	15 57.0	5.7	57.9
17	79 04.7	23.6	248 19.9	8.5	16 02.7	5.5	57.9
18	94 04.6	S16 24.3	262 47.4	8.5	N16 08.2	5.5	57.9
19	109 04.6	25.0	277 14.9	8.5	16 13.7	5.3	57.9
20	124 04.5	25.8	291 42.4	8.6	16 19.0	5.3	57.8
21	139 04.5 ..	26.5	306 10.0	8.5	16 24.3	5.1	57.8
22	154 04.5	27.2	320 37.5	8.5	16 29.4	5.1	57.8
23	169 04.4	28.0	335 05.0	8.6	16 34.5	4.9	57.7
8 SATURDAY							
00	184 04.4	S16 28.7	349 32.6	8.5	N16 39.4	4.9	57.7
01	199 04.4	29.4	4 00.1	8.6	16 44.3	4.7	57.7
02	214 04.3	30.2	18 27.7	8.6	16 49.0	4.7	57.7
03	229 04.3 ..	30.9	32 55.3	8.5	16 53.7	4.5	57.6
04	244 04.2	31.6	47 22.8	8.6	16 58.2	4.4	57.6
05	259 04.2	32.3	61 50.4	8.6	17 02.6	4.4	57.6
06	274 04.2	S16 33.1	76 18.0	8.6	N17 07.0	4.2	57.5
07	289 04.1	33.8	90 45.6	8.6	17 11.2	4.1	57.5
08	304 04.1	34.5	105 13.2	8.7	17 15.3	4.0	57.5
09	319 04.0 ..	35.2	119 40.9	8.6	17 19.3	4.0	57.4
10	334 04.0	36.0	134 08.5	8.7	17 23.3	3.8	57.4
11	349 03.9	36.7	148 36.2	8.6	17 27.1	3.7	57.4
12	4 03.9	S16 37.4	163 03.8	8.7	N17 30.8	3.6	57.4
13	19 03.9	38.1	177 31.5	8.7	17 34.4	3.5	57.3
14	34 03.8	38.9	191 59.2	8.7	17 37.9	3.4	57.3
15	49 03.8 ..	39.6	206 26.9	8.8	17 41.3	3.2	57.3
16	64 03.7	40.3	220 54.7	8.8	17 44.5	3.2	57.2
17	79 03.7	41.0	235 22.4	8.8	17 47.7	3.1	57.2
18	94 03.6	S16 41.7	249 50.2	8.8	N17 50.8	3.0	57.2
19	109 03.6	42.5	264 18.0	8.8	17 53.8	2.8	57.1
20	124 03.5	43.2	278 45.8	8.8	17 56.6	2.8	57.1
21	139 03.5 ..	43.9	293 13.6	8.8	17 59.4	2.7	57.1
22	154 03.5	44.6	307 41.4	8.9	18 02.1	2.5	57.1
23	169 03.4	45.3	322 09.3	8.9	N18 04.6	2.4	57.0
	SD 16.2	d 0.7	SD 16.0		15.8		15.6

Lat.	Twilight Naut.	Civil	Sunrise	Moonrise 6	7	8	9
N 72	06 29	07 56	09 37	14 31	14 23	14 08	▭
N 70	06 22	07 39	09 01	14 54	15 00	15 13	15 42
68	06 17	07 26	08 36	15 12	15 26	15 49	16 26
66	06 12	07 15	08 17	15 27	15 46	16 15	16 56
64	06 08	07 06	08 01	15 39	16 03	16 35	17 18
62	06 04	06 58	07 48	15 49	16 16	16 51	17 36
60	06 00	06 51	07 37	15 58	16 28	17 05	17 50
N 58	05 57	06 44	07 28	16 06	16 38	17 17	18 03
56	05 54	06 39	07 19	16 13	16 47	17 27	18 14
54	05 51	06 34	07 12	16 19	16 54	17 36	18 23
52	05 49	06 29	07 05	16 24	17 01	17 44	18 32
50	05 46	06 25	06 59	16 29	17 08	17 51	18 40
45	05 40	06 15	06 46	16 40	17 21	18 07	18 56
N 40	05 35	06 07	06 36	16 49	17 33	18 19	19 09
35	05 30	06 00	06 26	16 57	17 42	18 30	19 21
30	05 25	05 53	06 18	17 04	17 51	18 40	19 31
20	05 15	05 41	06 04	17 16	18 05	18 56	19 48
N 10	05 05	05 30	05 52	17 27	18 18	19 11	20 03
0	04 54	05 19	05 40	17 37	18 30	19 24	20 17
S 10	04 41	05 06	05 28	17 47	18 43	19 38	20 31
20	04 25	04 52	05 16	17 57	18 56	19 52	20 46
30	04 05	04 35	05 01	18 10	19 11	20 09	21 03
35	03 52	04 25	04 52	18 17	19 20	20 19	21 14
40	03 36	04 13	04 42	18 25	19 30	20 30	21 25
45	03 17	03 58	04 31	18 35	19 41	20 43	21 39
S 50	02 51	03 39	04 17	18 46	19 56	20 59	21 55
52	02 38	03 30	04 10	18 52	20 02	21 07	22 03
54	02 23	03 20	04 03	18 58	20 10	21 15	22 12
56	02 04	03 09	03 54	19 04	20 18	21 24	22 21
58	01 40	02 55	03 45	19 12	20 27	21 35	22 33
S 60	01 06	02 39	03 34	19 21	20 38	21 47	22 45

Lat.	Sunset	Twilight Civil	Naut.	Moonset 6	7	8	9
N 72	13 49	15 30	16 57	07 58	09 59	12 06	▭
N 70	14 25	15 47	17 03	07 36	09 22	11 02	12 23
68	14 50	16 00	17 09	07 19	08 57	10 26	11 39
66	15 10	16 11	17 14	07 06	08 37	10 00	11 10
64	15 25	16 21	17 19	06 54	08 22	09 41	10 48
62	15 38	16 29	17 23	06 45	08 09	09 25	10 30
60	15 49	16 36	17 26	06 37	07 58	09 11	10 15
N 58	15 59	16 42	17 29	06 30	07 48	09 00	10 03
56	16 07	16 48	17 33	06 23	07 40	08 50	09 52
54	16 15	16 53	17 35	06 18	07 32	08 41	09 42
52	16 21	16 58	17 38	06 13	07 26	08 33	09 34
50	16 27	17 02	17 41	06 08	07 20	08 26	09 26
45	16 40	17 11	17 46	05 58	07 07	08 11	09 10
N 40	16 51	17 20	17 52	05 50	06 56	07 59	08 57
35	17 00	17 27	17 57	05 43	06 47	07 48	08 45
30	17 09	17 34	18 02	05 37	06 39	07 39	08 36
20	17 23	17 46	18 12	05 27	06 25	07 23	08 18
N 10	17 35	17 57	18 22	05 17	06 14	07 09	08 04
0	17 47	18 09	18 34	05 09	06 02	06 56	07 50
S 10	17 59	18 21	18 47	05 00	05 51	06 43	07 36
20	18 12	18 35	19 03	04 51	05 39	06 29	07 21
30	18 27	18 53	19 23	04 40	05 26	06 14	07 04
35	18 36	19 03	19 36	04 34	05 18	06 04	06 54
40	18 46	19 15	19 52	04 27	05 09	05 54	06 43
45	18 57	19 30	20 12	04 19	04 58	05 42	06 29
S 50	19 12	19 49	20 38	04 10	04 46	05 27	06 13
52	19 18	19 58	20 51	04 05	04 40	05 20	06 05
54	19 26	20 09	21 07	04 00	04 34	05 12	05 57
56	19 34	20 21	21 26	03 55	04 27	05 03	05 47
58	19 44	20 34	21 51	03 49	04 18	04 54	05 36
S 60	19 55	20 51	22 28	03 42	04 09	04 43	05 24

	SUN			MOON			
Day	Eqn. of Time 00h	12h	Mer. Pass.	Mer. Pass. Upper	Lower	Age	Phase
d	m s	m s	h m	h m	h m	d	%
6	16 23	16 22	11 44	23 49	11 23	14	100
7	16 21	16 19	11 44	24 43	12 16	15	100
8	16 18	16 16	11 44	00 43	13 10	16	97

UT	ARIES GHA	VENUS −3.9 GHA	Dec	MARS +0.9 GHA	Dec	JUPITER −2.1 GHA	Dec	SATURN +0.5 GHA	Dec	STARS Name	SHA	Dec
9 00	48 05.5	180 09.8	S17 17.3	126 58.0	S24 31.8	264 16.1	N15 02.3	175 08.7	S17 06.1	Acamar	315 17.2	S40 14.8
01	63 07.9	195 09.2	18.2	141 58.4	31.7	279 18.3	02.2	190 10.9	06.2	Achernar	335 25.6	S57 09.8
02	78 10.4	210 08.5	19.2	156 58.8	31.5	294 20.5	02.2	205 13.0	06.3	Acrux	173 08.6	S63 10.6
03	93 12.9	225 07.8	.. 20.1	171 59.2	.. 31.4	309 22.8	.. 02.1	220 15.2	.. 06.3	Adhara	255 11.6	S28 59.5
04	108 15.3	240 07.1	21.0	186 59.6	31.2	324 25.0	02.0	235 17.3	06.4	Aldebaran	290 48.0	N16 32.2
05	123 17.8	255 06.4	21.9	202 00.0	31.0	339 27.3	02.0	250 19.5	06.5			
06	138 20.3	270 05.8	S17 22.9	217 00.4	S24 30.9	354 29.5	N15 01.9	265 21.7	S17 06.6	Alioth	166 20.4	N55 52.7
07	153 22.7	285 05.1	23.8	232 00.8	30.7	9 31.7	01.8	280 23.8	06.6	Alkaid	152 58.7	N49 14.4
08	168 25.2	300 04.4	24.7	247 01.2	30.6	24 34.0	01.8	295 26.0	06.7	Al Na'ir	27 42.5	S46 53.4
S 09	183 27.7	315 03.7	.. 25.6	262 01.6	.. 30.4	39 36.2	.. 01.7	310 28.2	.. 06.8	Alnilam	275 45.1	S 1 11.7
U 10	198 30.1	330 03.1	26.5	277 02.0	30.3	54 38.5	01.7	325 30.3	06.9	Alphard	217 55.2	S 8 43.4
N 11	213 32.6	345 02.4	27.4	292 02.4	30.1	69 40.7	01.6	340 32.5	06.9			
D 12	228 35.1	0 01.7	S17 28.4	307 02.8	S24 30.0	84 42.9	N15 01.5	355 34.7	S17 07.0	Alphecca	126 10.6	N26 40.1
A 13	243 37.5	15 01.0	29.3	322 03.2	29.8	99 45.2	01.5	10 36.8	07.1	Alpheratz	357 42.2	N29 10.6
Y 14	258 40.0	30 00.3	30.2	337 03.6	29.6	114 47.4	01.4	25 39.0	07.2	Altair	62 07.4	N 8 54.8
15	273 42.4	44 59.6	.. 31.1	352 04.0	.. 29.5	129 49.7	.. 01.3	40 41.2	.. 07.2	Ankaa	353 14.5	S42 13.6
16	288 44.9	59 59.0	32.0	7 04.4	29.3	144 51.9	01.3	55 43.3	07.3	Antares	112 25.4	S26 27.7
17	303 47.4	74 58.3	32.9	22 04.8	29.2	159 54.1	01.2	70 45.5	07.4			
18	318 49.8	89 57.6	S17 33.8	37 05.2	S24 29.0	174 56.4	N15 01.1	85 47.6	S17 07.4	Arcturus	145 55.2	N19 06.5
19	333 52.3	104 56.9	34.7	52 05.6	28.8	189 58.6	01.1	100 49.8	07.5	Atria	107 26.9	S69 03.1
20	348 54.8	119 56.2	35.7	67 06.0	28.7	205 00.9	01.0	115 52.0	07.6	Avior	234 17.4	S59 33.3
21	3 57.2	134 55.5	.. 36.6	82 06.4	.. 28.5	220 03.1	.. 01.0	130 54.1	.. 07.7	Bellatrix	278 30.7	N 6 21.6
22	18 59.7	149 54.8	37.5	97 06.8	28.3	235 05.4	00.9	145 56.3	07.7	Betelgeuse	271 00.0	N 7 24.4
23	34 02.2	164 54.2	38.4	112 07.2	28.2	250 07.6	00.8	160 58.5	07.8			
10 00	49 04.6	179 53.5	S17 39.3	127 07.6	S24 28.0	265 09.9	N15 00.8	176 00.6	S17 07.9	Canopus	263 55.3	S52 42.2
01	64 07.1	194 52.8	40.2	142 08.0	27.9	280 12.1	00.7	191 02.8	08.0	Capella	280 32.6	N46 00.5
02	79 09.6	209 52.1	41.1	157 08.4	27.7	295 14.3	00.6	206 05.0	08.0	Deneb	49 30.9	N45 20.5
03	94 12.0	224 51.4	.. 42.0	172 08.8	.. 27.5	310 16.6	.. 00.6	221 07.1	.. 08.1	Denebola	182 32.9	N14 29.3
04	109 14.5	239 50.7	42.9	187 09.2	27.4	325 18.8	00.5	236 09.3	08.2	Diphda	348 54.7	S17 54.3
05	124 16.9	254 50.0	43.8	202 09.6	27.2	340 21.1	00.5	251 11.4	08.3			
06	139 19.4	269 49.3	S17 44.7	217 10.0	S24 27.0	355 23.3	N15 00.4	266 13.6	S17 08.3	Dubhe	193 51.0	N61 40.0
07	154 21.9	284 48.6	45.6	232 10.4	26.9	10 25.6	00.3	281 15.8	08.4	Elnath	278 11.1	N28 37.0
08	169 24.3	299 48.0	46.5	247 10.8	26.7	25 27.8	00.3	296 17.9	08.5	Eltanin	90 46.1	N51 29.6
M 09	184 26.8	314 47.3	.. 47.4	262 11.2	.. 26.5	40 30.1	.. 00.2	311 20.1	.. 08.5	Enif	33 46.2	N 9 56.9
O 10	199 29.3	329 46.6	48.3	277 11.6	26.4	55 32.3	00.1	326 22.3	08.6	Fomalhaut	15 22.8	S29 32.6
N 11	214 31.7	344 45.9	49.2	292 12.0	26.2	70 34.6	00.1	341 24.4	08.7			
D 12	229 34.2	359 45.2	S17 50.1	307 12.4	S24 26.0	85 36.8	N15 00.0	356 26.6	S17 08.8	Gacrux	172 00.2	S57 11.5
A 13	244 36.7	14 44.5	51.0	322 12.8	25.9	100 39.1	15 00.0	11 28.8	08.8	Gienah	175 51.5	S17 37.3
Y 14	259 39.1	29 43.8	51.9	337 13.2	25.7	115 41.3	14 59.9	26 30.9	08.9	Hadar	148 47.1	S60 26.4
15	274 41.6	44 43.1	.. 52.8	352 13.6	.. 25.5	130 43.6	.. 59.8	41 33.1	.. 09.0	Hamal	327 59.3	N23 32.0
16	289 44.0	59 42.4	53.7	7 14.0	25.3	145 45.8	59.8	56 35.2	09.1	Kaus Aust.	83 42.9	S34 22.5
17	304 46.5	74 41.7	54.6	22 14.4	25.2	160 48.1	59.7	71 37.4	09.1			
18	319 49.0	89 41.0	S17 55.4	37 14.8	S24 25.0	175 50.3	N14 59.7	86 39.6	S17 09.2	Kochab	137 21.4	N74 05.7
19	334 51.4	104 40.3	56.3	52 15.2	24.8	190 52.6	59.6	101 41.7	09.3	Markab	13 37.2	N15 17.4
20	349 53.9	119 39.6	57.2	67 15.6	24.6	205 54.8	59.5	116 43.9	09.3	Menkar	314 13.7	N 4 08.8
21	4 56.4	134 38.9	.. 58.1	82 16.0	.. 24.5	220 57.1	.. 59.5	131 46.1	.. 09.4	Menkent	148 06.8	S36 26.3
22	19 58.8	149 38.2	59.0	97 16.4	24.3	235 59.3	59.4	146 48.2	09.5	Miaplacidus	221 39.3	S69 46.5
23	35 01.3	164 37.5	17 59.9	112 16.8	24.1	251 01.6	59.4	161 50.4	09.6			
11 00	50 03.8	179 36.8	S18 00.8	127 17.2	S24 24.0	266 03.8	N14 59.3	176 52.6	S17 09.6	Mirfak	308 38.4	N49 54.7
01	65 06.2	194 36.1	01.7	142 17.6	23.8	281 06.1	59.2	191 54.7	09.7	Nunki	75 57.4	S26 16.5
02	80 08.7	209 35.4	02.5	157 18.0	23.6	296 08.3	59.2	206 56.9	09.8	Peacock	53 18.0	S56 41.3
03	95 11.2	224 34.7	.. 03.4	172 18.4	.. 23.4	311 10.6	.. 59.1	221 59.0	.. 09.9	Pollux	243 26.5	N27 59.1
04	110 13.6	239 34.0	04.3	187 18.8	23.3	326 12.8	59.1	237 01.2	09.9	Procyon	244 58.6	N 5 11.1
05	125 16.1	254 33.3	05.2	202 19.2	23.1	341 15.1	59.0	252 03.4	10.0			
06	140 18.5	269 32.6	S18 06.1	217 19.6	S24 22.9	356 17.3	N14 58.9	267 05.7	S17 10.1	Rasalhague	96 05.9	N12 33.3
07	155 21.0	284 31.9	07.0	232 20.0	22.7	11 19.6	58.9	282 07.7	10.2	Regulus	207 42.6	N11 53.6
T 08	170 23.5	299 31.2	07.8	247 20.4	22.5	26 21.8	58.8	297 09.9	10.2	Rigel	281 10.9	S 8 11.2
U 09	185 25.9	314 30.5	.. 08.7	262 20.8	.. 22.4	41 24.1	.. 58.8	312 12.0	.. 10.3	Rigil Kent.	139 51.0	S60 53.5
E 10	200 28.4	329 29.8	09.6	277 21.2	22.2	56 26.3	58.7	327 14.2	10.4	Sabik	102 11.8	S15 44.3
S 11	215 30.9	344 29.1	10.5	292 21.6	22.0	71 28.6	58.6	342 16.3	10.4			
D 12	230 33.3	359 28.4	S18 11.3	307 22.0	S24 21.8	86 30.8	N14 58.6	357 18.5	S17 10.5	Schedar	349 38.9	N56 37.3
A 13	245 35.8	14 27.7	12.2	322 22.4	21.6	101 33.1	58.5	12 20.7	10.6	Shaula	96 21.0	S37 06.7
Y 14	260 38.3	29 26.9	13.1	337 22.8	21.5	116 35.4	58.5	27 22.8	10.7	Sirius	258 32.7	S16 44.2
15	275 40.7	44 26.2	.. 14.0	352 23.2	.. 21.3	131 37.6	.. 58.4	42 25.0	.. 10.7	Spica	158 30.5	S11 14.2
16	290 43.2	59 25.5	14.8	7 23.6	21.1	146 39.9	58.3	57 27.2	10.8	Suhail	222 51.7	S43 29.4
17	305 45.7	74 24.8	15.7	22 24.0	20.9	161 42.1	58.3	72 29.3	10.9			
18	320 48.1	89 24.1	S18 16.6	37 24.4	S24 20.7	176 44.4	N14 58.2	87 31.5	S17 11.0	Vega	80 38.6	N38 48.3
19	335 50.6	104 23.4	17.4	52 24.8	20.5	191 46.6	58.2	102 33.7	11.0	Zuben'ubi	137 04.7	S16 06.0
20	350 53.0	119 22.7	18.3	67 25.2	20.4	206 48.9	58.1	117 35.8	11.1		SHA	Mer. Pass.
21	5 55.5	134 22.0	.. 19.2	82 25.6	.. 20.2	221 51.2	.. 58.0	132 38.0	.. 11.2	Venus	130 48.9	12 01
22	20 58.0	149 21.3	20.1	97 26.0	20.0	236 53.4	58.0	147 40.1	11.2	Mars	78 03.0	15 31
23	36 00.4	164 20.5	20.9	112 26.4	19.8	251 55.7	57.9	162 42.3	11.3	Jupiter	216 05.2	6 18
Mer. Pass. 20 40.3		v −0.7	d 0.9	v 0.4	d 0.2	v 2.2	d 0.1	v 2.2	d 0.1	Saturn	126 56.0	12 14

UT	SUN GHA	SUN Dec	MOON GHA	v	MOON Dec	d	HP
d h	° ′	° ′	° ′	′	° ′	′	′
9 00	184 03.4	S16 46.1	336 37.2	8.9	N18 07.0	2.4	57.0
01	199 03.3	46.8	351 05.1	8.9	18 09.4	2.2	57.0
02	214 03.3	47.5	5 33.0	9.0	18 11.6	2.2	56.9
03	229 03.2 · ·	48.2	20 01.0	9.0	18 13.8	2.0	56.9
04	244 03.2	48.9	34 29.0	9.0	18 15.8	1.9	56.9
05	259 03.1	49.6	48 57.0	9.1	18 17.7	1.8	56.8
06	274 03.1	S16 50.4	63 25.1	9.0	N18 19.5	1.7	56.8
07	289 03.0	51.1	77 53.1	9.1	18 21.2	1.6	56.8
08	304 03.0	51.8	92 21.2	9.1	18 22.8	1.5	56.8
S 09	319 02.9 · ·	52.5	106 49.3	9.2	18 24.3	1.4	56.7
U 10	334 02.9	53.2	121 17.5	9.2	18 25.7	1.3	56.7
N 11	349 02.8	53.9	135 45.7	9.2	18 27.0	1.2	56.7
D 12	4 02.8	S16 54.6	150 13.9	9.2	N18 28.2	1.1	56.6
A 13	19 02.7	55.3	164 42.1	9.3	18 29.3	1.0	56.6
Y 14	34 02.7	56.1	179 10.4	9.3	18 30.3	0.9	56.6
15	49 02.6 · ·	56.8	193 38.7	9.4	18 31.2	0.7	56.5
16	64 02.5	57.5	208 07.1	9.3	18 31.9	0.7	56.5
17	79 02.5	58.2	222 35.4	9.4	18 32.6	0.6	56.5
18	94 02.4	S16 58.9	237 03.8	9.5	N18 33.2	0.4	56.5
19	109 02.4	16 59.6	251 32.3	9.5	18 33.6	0.4	56.4
20	124 02.3	17 00.3	266 00.8	9.5	18 34.0	0.3	56.4
21	139 02.3 · ·	01.0	280 29.3	9.5	18 34.3	0.1	56.4
22	154 02.2	01.7	294 57.8	9.6	18 34.4	0.1	56.3
23	169 02.2	02.4	309 26.4	9.7	18 34.5	0.0	56.3
10 00	184 02.1	S17 03.1	323 55.1	9.6	N18 34.5	0.2	56.3
01	199 02.0	03.8	338 23.7	9.7	18 34.3	0.2	56.3
02	214 02.0	04.5	352 52.4	9.8	18 34.1	0.3	56.2
03	229 01.9 · ·	05.3	7 21.2	9.8	18 33.8	0.5	56.2
04	244 01.9	06.0	21 50.0	9.8	18 33.3	0.5	56.2
05	259 01.8	06.7	36 18.8	9.9	18 32.8	0.6	56.1
06	274 01.8	S17 07.4	50 47.7	9.9	N18 32.2	0.8	56.1
07	289 01.7	08.1	65 16.6	9.9	18 31.4	0.8	56.1
08	304 01.6	08.8	79 45.5	10.0	18 30.6	0.9	56.1
M 09	319 01.6 · ·	09.5	94 14.5	10.0	18 29.7	1.0	56.0
O 10	334 01.5	10.2	108 43.5	10.1	18 28.7	1.2	56.0
N 11	349 01.5	10.9	123 12.6	10.1	18 27.5	1.2	56.0
D 12	4 01.4	S17 11.6	137 41.7	10.2	N18 26.3	1.3	55.9
A 13	19 01.3	12.3	152 10.9	10.2	18 25.0	1.4	55.9
Y 14	34 01.3	13.0	166 40.1	10.3	18 23.6	1.5	55.9
15	49 01.2 · ·	13.7	181 09.4	10.3	18 22.1	1.6	55.9
16	64 01.2	14.4	195 38.7	10.3	18 20.5	1.6	55.8
17	79 01.1	15.1	210 08.0	10.4	18 18.9	1.8	55.8
18	94 01.0	S17 15.8	224 37.4	10.5	N18 17.1	1.9	55.8
19	109 01.0	16.5	239 06.9	10.5	18 15.2	2.0	55.7
20	124 00.9	17.2	253 36.4	10.5	18 13.2	2.0	55.7
21	139 00.8 · ·	17.8	268 05.9	10.6	18 11.2	2.2	55.7
22	154 00.8	18.5	282 35.5	10.6	18 09.0	2.2	55.7
23	169 00.7	19.2	297 05.1	10.7	18 06.8	2.3	55.6
11 00	184 00.6	S17 19.9	311 34.8	10.7	N18 04.5	2.4	55.6
01	199 00.6	20.6	326 04.5	10.8	18 02.1	2.5	55.6
02	214 00.5	21.3	340 34.3	10.8	17 59.6	2.6	55.6
03	229 00.4 · ·	22.0	355 04.1	10.9	17 57.0	2.7	55.5
04	244 00.4	22.7	9 34.0	10.9	17 54.3	2.8	55.5
05	259 00.3	23.4	24 03.9	11.0	17 51.5	2.8	55.5
06	274 00.2	S17 24.1	38 33.9	11.0	N17 48.7	3.0	55.5
07	289 00.2	24.8	53 03.9	11.1	17 45.7	3.0	55.4
T 08	304 00.1	25.5	67 34.0	11.1	17 42.7	3.1	55.4
U 09	319 00.0 · ·	26.1	82 04.1	11.1	17 39.6	3.2	55.4
E 10	334 00.0	26.8	96 34.2	11.3	17 36.4	3.3	55.4
S 11	348 59.9	27.5	111 04.5	11.2	17 33.1	3.4	55.3
D 12	3 59.8	S17 28.2	125 34.7	11.4	N17 29.7	3.4	55.3
A 13	18 59.8	28.9	140 05.1	11.3	17 26.3	3.5	55.3
Y 14	33 59.7	29.6	154 35.4	11.4	17 22.8	3.6	55.3
15	48 59.6 · ·	30.3	169 05.8	11.5	17 19.2	3.7	55.2
16	63 59.5	31.0	183 36.3	11.5	17 15.5	3.8	55.2
17	78 59.5	31.6	198 06.8	11.6	17 11.7	3.9	55.2
18	93 59.4	S17 32.3	212 37.4	11.6	N17 07.8	3.9	55.2
19	108 59.3	33.0	227 08.0	11.7	17 03.9	4.0	55.2
20	123 59.3	33.7	241 38.7	11.7	16 59.9	4.1	55.1
21	138 59.2 · ·	34.4	256 09.4	11.8	16 55.8	4.2	55.1
22	153 59.1	35.1	270 40.2	11.8	16 51.6	4.2	55.1
23	168 59.0	35.7	285 11.0	11.9	N16 47.4	4.3	55.1
	SD 16.2	d 0.7	SD 15.4		15.2		15.1

Lat.	Twilight Naut.	Twilight Civil	Sunrise	Moonrise 9	Moonrise 10	Moonrise 11	Moonrise 12
°	h m	h m	h m	h m	h m	h m	h m
N 72	06 41	08 10	10 01	▭	▭	17 03	18 54
N 70	06 33	07 51	09 18	15 42	16 40	18 00	19 29
68	06 26	07 36	08 49	16 26	17 23	18 34	19 54
66	06 20	07 24	08 28	16 56	17 51	18 58	20 13
64	06 15	07 14	08 11	17 18	18 13	19 17	20 28
62	06 11	07 05	07 57	17 36	18 30	19 33	20 41
60	06 06	06 57	07 45	17 50	18 45	19 46	20 52
N 58	06 03	06 51	07 35	18 03	18 57	19 57	21 01
56	05 59	06 44	07 26	18 14	19 08	20 07	21 09
54	05 56	06 39	07 18	18 23	19 17	20 15	21 17
52	05 53	06 34	07 11	18 32	19 25	20 23	21 23
50	05 50	06 29	07 04	18 40	19 33	20 30	21 29
45	05 44	06 19	06 51	18 56	19 49	20 45	21 42
N 40	05 38	06 10	06 39	19 09	20 02	20 57	21 52
35	05 32	06 03	06 29	19 21	20 13	21 07	22 01
30	05 27	05 56	06 21	19 31	20 23	21 16	22 09
20	05 16	05 43	06 06	19 48	20 40	21 31	22 22
N 10	05 06	05 31	05 53	20 03	20 55	21 45	22 34
0	04 54	05 19	05 40	20 17	21 08	21 58	22 45
S 10	04 40	05 06	05 28	20 31	21 22	22 10	22 56
20	04 24	04 51	05 14	20 46	21 37	22 24	23 08
30	04 02	04 33	04 59	21 03	21 54	22 39	23 21
35	03 49	04 24	04 50	21 14	22 03	22 48	23 29
40	03 33	04 09	04 39	21 25	22 15	22 58	23 37
45	03 12	03 54	04 27	21 39	22 28	23 10	23 48
S 50	02 45	03 34	04 12	21 55	22 44	23 25	24 00
52	02 31	03 25	04 05	22 03	22 51	23 32	24 06
54	02 14	03 14	03 57	22 12	23 00	23 39	24 12
56	01 53	03 01	03 48	22 21	23 09	23 48	24 19
58	01 26	02 47	03 38	22 33	23 19	23 57	24 27
S 60	00 43	02 29	03 27	22 45	23 32	24 08	00 08

Lat.	Sunset	Twilight Civil	Twilight Naut.	Moonset 9	Moonset 10	Moonset 11	Moonset 12
°	h m	h m	h m	h m	h m	h m	h m
N 72	13 25	15 16	16 46	▭	▭	14 34	14 22
N 70	14 09	15 35	16 54	12 23	13 13	13 36	13 46
68	14 37	15 50	17 01	11 39	12 30	13 02	13 21
66	14 59	16 03	17 07	11 10	12 01	12 37	13 01
64	15 16	16 13	17 12	10 48	11 40	12 18	12 45
62	15 30	16 22	17 16	10 30	11 22	12 02	12 32
60	15 42	16 30	17 20	10 15	11 08	11 49	12 21
N 58	15 52	16 36	17 24	10 03	10 55	11 37	12 11
56	16 01	16 43	17 28	09 52	10 44	11 27	12 02
54	16 09	16 48	17 31	09 42	10 35	11 19	11 55
52	16 16	16 53	17 34	09 34	10 26	11 11	11 48
50	16 23	16 58	17 37	09 26	10 19	11 04	11 42
45	16 37	17 08	17 43	09 10	10 03	10 48	11 28
N 40	16 48	17 17	17 49	08 57	09 49	10 36	11 17
35	16 58	17 25	17 55	08 45	09 38	10 25	11 08
30	17 07	17 32	18 00	08 36	09 28	10 16	11 00
20	17 22	17 45	18 11	08 18	09 11	10 00	10 45
N 10	17 35	17 57	18 22	08 04	08 56	09 46	10 33
0	17 47	18 09	18 34	07 50	08 42	09 32	10 21
S 10	18 00	18 22	18 48	07 36	08 28	09 19	10 09
20	18 14	18 37	19 05	07 21	08 13	09 05	09 56
30	18 29	18 55	19 26	07 04	07 56	08 48	09 41
35	18 39	19 06	19 40	06 54	07 46	08 39	09 33
40	18 49	19 19	19 56	06 43	07 34	08 28	09 23
45	19 02	19 35	20 17	06 29	07 21	08 15	09 12
S 50	19 17	19 55	20 45	06 13	07 04	07 59	08 58
52	19 24	20 05	20 59	06 05	06 56	07 52	08 51
54	19 32	20 16	21 16	05 57	06 48	07 44	08 44
56	19 41	20 28	21 37	05 47	06 38	07 35	08 36
58	19 51	20 43	22 06	05 36	06 27	07 24	08 27
S 60	20 03	21 01	22 53	05 24	06 14	07 12	08 16

	SUN Eqn. of Time 00h	SUN Eqn. of Time 12h	SUN Mer. Pass.	MOON Mer. Pass. Upper	MOON Mer. Pass. Lower	Age	Phase
Day							
d	m s	m s	h m	h m	h m	d	%
9	16 14	16 11	11 44	01 37	14 03	17	92
10	16 09	16 06	11 44	02 30	14 55	18	86
11	16 03	15 59	11 44	03 20	15 45	19	78

UT	ARIES	VENUS −3.9		MARS +1.0		JUPITER −2.1		SATURN +0.5		STARS		
	GHA	GHA	Dec	GHA	Dec	GHA	Dec	GHA	Dec	Name	SHA	Dec
d h	° ′	° ′	° ′	° ′	° ′	° ′	° ′	° ′	° ′		° ′	° ′
12 00	51 02.9	179 19.8	S18 21.8	127 26.8	S24 19.6	266 57.9	N14 57.9	177 44.5	S17 11.4	Acamar	315 17.2	S40 14.8
01	66 05.4	194 19.1	22.7	142 27.2	19.4	282 00.2	57.8	192 46.6	11.5	Achernar	335 25.6	S57 09.8
02	81 07.8	209 18.4	23.5	157 27.6	19.2	297 02.4	57.8	207 48.8	11.5	Acrux	173 08.6	S63 10.6
03	96 10.3	224 17.7	.. 24.4	172 28.0	.. 19.1	312 04.7	.. 57.7	222 51.0	.. 11.6	Adhara	255 11.5	S28 59.5
04	111 12.8	239 17.0	25.2	187 28.4	18.9	327 07.0	57.6	237 53.1	11.7	Aldebaran	290 47.9	N16 32.2
05	126 15.2	254 16.3	26.1	202 28.8	18.7	342 09.2	57.6	252 55.3	11.8			
06	141 17.7	269 15.5	S18 27.0	217 29.2	S24 18.5	357 11.5	N14 57.5	267 57.4	S17 11.8	Alioth	166 20.4	N55 52.6
W 07	156 20.2	284 14.8	27.8	232 29.6	18.3	12 13.7	57.5	282 59.6	11.9	Alkaid	152 58.7	N49 14.4
E 08	171 22.6	299 14.1	28.7	247 30.0	18.1	27 16.0	57.4	298 01.8	12.0	Al Na'ir	27 42.5	S46 53.4
D 09	186 25.1	314 13.4	.. 29.5	262 30.4	.. 17.9	42 18.3	.. 57.4	313 03.9	.. 12.0	Alnilam	275 45.1	S 1 11.7
N 10	201 27.5	329 12.7	30.4	277 30.8	17.7	57 20.5	57.3	328 06.1	12.1	Alphard	217 55.1	S 8 43.4
E 11	216 30.0	344 11.9	31.3	292 31.2	17.5	72 22.8	57.2	343 08.3	12.2			
S 12	231 32.5	359 11.2	S18 32.1	307 31.6	S24 17.4	87 25.0	N14 57.2	358 10.4	S17 12.3	Alphecca	126 10.6	N26 40.1
D 13	246 34.9	14 10.5	33.0	322 32.0	17.2	102 27.3	57.1	13 12.6	12.3	Alpheratz	357 42.2	N29 10.6
A 14	261 37.4	29 09.8	33.8	337 32.4	17.0	117 29.6	57.1	28 14.7	12.4	Altair	62 07.5	N 8 54.8
Y 15	276 39.9	44 09.1	.. 34.7	352 32.8	.. 16.8	132 31.8	.. 57.0	43 16.9	.. 12.5	Ankaa	353 14.5	S42 13.6
16	291 42.3	59 08.3	35.5	7 33.2	16.6	147 34.1	57.0	58 19.1	12.6	Antares	112 25.4	S26 27.7
17	306 44.8	74 07.6	36.4	22 33.6	16.4	162 36.4	56.9	73 21.2	12.6			
18	321 47.3	89 06.9	S18 37.2	37 34.0	S24 16.2	177 38.6	N14 56.8	88 23.4	S17 12.7	Arcturus	145 55.2	N19 06.4
19	336 49.7	104 06.2	38.1	52 34.4	16.0	192 40.9	56.8	103 25.6	12.8	Atria	107 26.9	S69 03.1
20	351 52.2	119 05.4	38.9	67 34.8	15.8	207 43.1	56.7	118 27.7	12.8	Avior	234 17.4	S59 33.3
21	6 54.6	134 04.7	.. 39.8	82 35.2	.. 15.6	222 45.4	.. 56.7	133 29.9	.. 12.9	Bellatrix	278 30.7	N 6 21.6
22	21 57.1	149 04.0	40.6	97 35.6	15.4	237 47.7	56.6	148 32.0	13.0	Betelgeuse	271 00.0	N 7 24.4
23	36 59.6	164 03.3	41.5	112 36.0	15.2	252 49.9	56.6	163 34.2	13.1			
13 00	52 02.0	179 02.5	S18 42.3	127 36.4	S24 15.0	267 52.2	N14 56.5	178 36.4	S17 13.1	Canopus	263 55.3	S52 42.2
01	67 04.5	194 01.8	43.1	142 36.8	14.8	282 54.5	56.4	193 38.5	13.2	Capella	280 32.6	N46 00.5
02	82 07.0	209 01.1	44.0	157 37.2	14.6	297 56.7	56.4	208 40.7	13.3	Deneb	49 30.9	N45 20.5
03	97 09.4	224 00.4	.. 44.8	172 37.6	.. 14.4	312 59.0	.. 56.3	223 42.9	.. 13.4	Denebola	182 32.9	N14 29.3
04	112 11.9	238 59.6	45.7	187 38.0	14.2	328 01.3	56.3	238 45.0	13.4	Diphda	348 54.7	S17 54.3
05	127 14.4	253 58.9	46.5	202 38.4	14.0	343 03.5	56.2	253 47.2	13.5			
06	142 16.8	268 58.2	S18 47.3	217 38.8	S24 13.8	358 05.8	N14 56.2	268 49.3	S17 13.6	Dubhe	193 51.0	N61 39.9
T 07	157 19.3	283 57.4	48.2	232 39.2	13.6	13 08.1	56.1	283 51.5	13.6	Elnath	278 11.1	N28 37.0
H 08	172 21.8	298 56.7	49.0	247 39.6	13.4	28 10.3	56.1	298 53.7	13.7	Eltanin	90 46.1	N51 29.6
U 09	187 24.2	313 56.0	.. 49.9	262 40.0	.. 13.2	43 12.6	.. 56.0	313 55.8	.. 13.8	Enif	33 46.2	N 9 56.9
R 10	202 26.7	328 55.3	50.7	277 40.4	13.0	58 14.9	55.9	328 58.0	13.9	Fomalhaut	15 22.8	S29 32.6
S 11	217 29.1	343 54.5	51.5	292 40.8	12.8	73 17.1	55.9	344 00.2	13.9			
D 12	232 31.6	358 53.8	S18 52.4	307 41.2	S24 12.6	88 19.4	N14 55.8	359 02.3	S17 14.0	Gacrux	172 00.1	S57 11.5
A 13	247 34.1	13 53.1	53.2	322 41.6	12.4	103 21.7	55.8	14 04.5	14.1	Gienah	175 51.5	S17 37.3
Y 14	262 36.5	28 52.3	54.0	337 42.0	12.2	118 23.9	55.7	29 06.6	14.1	Hadar	148 47.0	S60 26.4
15	277 39.0	43 51.6	.. 54.9	352 42.4	.. 12.0	133 26.2	.. 55.7	44 08.8	.. 14.2	Hamal	327 59.3	N23 32.0
16	292 41.5	58 50.9	55.7	7 42.8	11.8	148 28.5	55.6	59 11.0	14.3	Kaus Aust.	83 42.9	S34 22.5
17	307 43.9	73 50.1	56.5	22 43.2	11.6	163 30.8	55.6	74 13.1	14.4			
18	322 46.4	88 49.4	S18 57.4	37 43.6	S24 11.4	178 33.0	N14 55.5	89 15.3	S17 14.4	Kochab	137 21.4	N74 05.7
19	337 48.9	103 48.6	58.2	52 44.0	11.2	193 35.3	55.5	104 17.5	14.5	Markab	13 37.2	N15 17.4
20	352 51.3	118 47.9	59.0	67 44.4	11.0	208 37.6	55.4	119 19.6	14.6	Menkar	314 13.7	N 4 08.8
21	7 53.8	133 47.2	18 59.8	82 44.8	.. 10.8	223 39.8	.. 55.3	134 21.8	.. 14.7	Menkent	148 06.8	S36 26.3
22	22 56.3	148 46.4	19 00.7	97 45.2	10.6	238 42.1	55.3	149 23.9	14.7	Miaplacidus	221 39.2	S69 46.5
23	37 58.7	163 45.7	01.5	112 45.6	10.4	253 44.4	55.2	164 26.1	14.8			
14 00	53 01.2	178 45.0	S19 02.3	127 46.0	S24 10.2	268 46.6	N14 55.2	179 28.3	S17 14.9	Mirfak	308 38.4	N49 54.7
01	68 03.6	193 44.2	03.1	142 46.4	09.9	283 48.9	55.1	194 30.4	14.9	Nunki	75 57.4	S26 16.5
02	83 06.1	208 43.5	03.9	157 46.8	09.7	298 51.2	55.1	209 32.6	15.0	Peacock	53 18.0	S56 41.3
03	98 08.6	223 42.7	.. 04.8	172 47.2	.. 09.5	313 53.5	.. 55.0	224 34.7	.. 15.1	Pollux	243 26.4	N27 59.1
04	113 11.0	238 42.0	05.6	187 47.6	09.3	328 55.7	55.0	239 36.9	15.2	Procyon	244 58.6	N 5 11.1
05	128 13.5	253 41.2	06.4	202 48.0	09.1	343 58.0	54.9	254 39.1	15.2			
06	143 16.0	268 40.5	S19 07.2	217 48.4	S24 08.9	359 00.3	N14 54.9	269 41.2	S17 15.3	Rasalhague	96 05.9	N12 33.3
07	158 18.4	283 39.8	08.0	232 48.8	08.7	14 02.6	54.8	284 43.4	15.4	Regulus	207 42.6	N11 53.6
08	173 20.9	298 39.0	08.9	247 49.2	08.5	29 04.8	54.8	299 45.6	15.4	Rigel	281 10.8	S 8 11.2
F 09	188 23.4	313 38.3	.. 09.7	262 49.6	.. 08.3	44 07.1	.. 54.7	314 47.7	.. 15.5	Rigil Kent.	139 51.0	S60 53.5
R 10	203 25.8	328 37.5	10.5	277 50.0	08.1	59 09.4	54.7	329 49.9	15.6	Sabik	102 11.8	S15 44.3
I 11	218 28.3	343 36.8	11.3	292 50.4	07.8	74 11.7	54.6	344 52.0	15.7			
D 12	233 30.7	358 36.0	S19 12.1	307 50.8	S24 07.6	89 13.9	N14 54.5	359 54.2	S17 15.7	Schedar	349 38.9	N56 37.4
A 13	248 33.2	13 35.3	12.9	322 51.2	07.4	104 16.2	54.5	14 56.4	15.8	Shaula	96 21.0	S37 06.7
Y 14	263 35.7	28 34.5	13.7	337 51.6	07.2	119 18.5	54.4	29 58.5	15.9	Sirius	258 32.6	S16 44.3
15	278 38.1	43 33.8	.. 14.5	352 52.0	.. 07.0	134 20.8	.. 54.4	45 00.7	.. 16.0	Spica	158 30.5	S11 14.2
16	293 40.6	58 33.0	15.4	7 52.4	06.8	149 23.0	54.3	60 02.9	16.0	Suhail	222 51.6	S43 29.4
17	308 43.1	73 32.3	16.2	22 52.8	06.6	164 25.3	54.3	75 05.0	16.1			
18	323 45.5	88 31.6	S19 17.0	37 53.2	S24 06.3	179 27.6	N14 54.2	90 07.2	S17 16.2	Vega	80 38.6	N38 48.3
19	338 48.0	103 30.8	17.8	52 53.6	06.1	194 29.9	54.2	105 09.3	16.2	Zuben'ubi	137 04.7	S16 06.0
20	353 50.5	118 30.1	18.6	67 54.0	05.9	209 32.1	54.1	120 11.5	16.3		SHA	Mer.Pass.
21	8 52.9	133 29.3	.. 19.4	82 54.4	.. 05.7	224 34.4	.. 54.1	135 13.7	.. 16.4		° ′	h m
22	23 55.4	148 28.5	20.2	97 54.8	05.5	239 36.7	54.0	150 15.8	16.5	Venus	127 00.5	12 04
23	38 57.9	163 27.8	21.0	112 55.2	05.2	254 39.0	54.0	165 18.0	16.5	Mars	75 34.3	15 29
	h m									Jupiter	215 50.2	6 08
Mer. Pass. 20 28.5		v −0.7	d 0.8	v 0.4	d 0.2	v 2.3	d 0.1	v 2.2	d 0.1	Saturn	126 34.3	12 04

UT	SUN GHA	SUN Dec	MOON GHA	v	Dec	d	HP
d h	° ′	° ′	° ′	′	° ′	′	′
12 00	183 59.0	S17 36.4	299 41.9	11.9	N16 43.1	4.4	55.0
01	198 58.9	37.1	314 12.8	12.0	16 38.7	4.5	55.0
02	213 58.8	37.8	328 43.8	12.1	16 34.2	4.6	55.0
03	228 58.7 ..	38.5	343 14.9	12.0	16 29.6	4.6	55.0
04	243 58.7	39.1	357 45.9	12.2	16 25.0	4.7	55.0
05	258 58.6	39.8	12 17.1	12.2	16 20.3	4.7	54.9
W 06	273 58.5	S17 40.5	26 48.3	12.2	N16 15.6	4.9	54.9
E 07	288 58.4	41.2	41 19.5	12.3	16 10.7	4.9	54.9
D 08	303 58.4	41.9	55 50.8	12.3	16 05.8	5.0	54.9
N 09	318 58.3 ..	42.5	70 22.1	12.4	16 00.8	5.0	54.9
E 10	333 58.2	43.2	84 53.5	12.4	15 55.8	5.2	54.8
S 11	348 58.1	43.9	99 24.9	12.5	15 50.6	5.2	54.8
D 12	3 58.0	S17 44.6	113 56.4	12.5	N15 45.4	5.2	54.8
A 13	18 58.0	45.2	128 27.9	12.6	15 40.2	5.4	54.8
Y 14	33 57.9	45.9	142 59.5	12.6	15 34.8	5.4	54.8
15	48 57.8 ..	46.6	157 31.1	12.7	15 29.4	5.4	54.8
16	63 57.7	47.2	172 02.8	12.7	15 24.0	5.6	54.7
17	78 57.6	47.9	186 34.5	12.8	15 18.4	5.6	54.7
18	93 57.6	S17 48.6	201 06.3	12.8	N15 12.8	5.6	54.7
19	108 57.5	49.3	215 38.1	12.9	15 07.2	5.8	54.7
20	123 57.4	49.9	230 10.0	12.9	15 01.4	5.8	54.7
21	138 57.3 ..	50.6	244 41.9	12.9	14 55.6	5.8	54.7
22	153 57.2	51.3	259 13.8	13.0	14 49.8	5.9	54.6
23	168 57.1	51.9	273 45.8	13.1	14 43.9	6.0	54.6
13 00	183 57.1	S17 52.6	288 17.9	13.1	N14 37.9	6.1	54.6
01	198 57.0	53.3	302 50.0	13.1	14 31.8	6.1	54.6
02	213 56.9	53.9	317 22.1	13.2	14 25.7	6.1	54.6
03	228 56.8 ..	54.6	331 54.3	13.3	14 19.6	6.3	54.6
04	243 56.7	55.3	346 26.6	13.3	14 13.3	6.3	54.6
05	258 56.6	55.9	0 58.9	13.3	14 07.0	6.3	54.5
T 06	273 56.6	S17 56.6	15 31.2	13.3	N14 00.7	6.4	54.5
H 07	288 56.5	57.3	30 03.5	13.5	13 54.3	6.5	54.5
U 08	303 56.4	57.9	44 36.0	13.4	13 47.8	6.5	54.5
R 09	318 56.3 ..	58.6	59 08.4	13.5	13 41.3	6.6	54.5
S 10	333 56.2	59.3	73 40.9	13.5	13 34.7	6.6	54.5
D 11	348 56.1	17 59.9	88 13.4	13.6	13 28.1	6.7	54.5
A 12	3 56.0	S18 00.6	102 46.0	13.7	N13 21.4	6.8	54.5
Y 13	18 55.9	01.3	117 18.7	13.6	13 14.6	6.8	54.4
14	33 55.9	01.9	131 51.3	13.7	13 07.8	6.8	54.4
15	48 55.8 ..	02.6	146 24.0	13.8	13 01.0	6.9	54.4
16	63 55.7	03.2	160 56.8	13.7	12 54.1	7.0	54.4
17	78 55.6	03.9	175 29.5	13.9	12 47.1	7.0	54.4
18	93 55.5	S18 04.6	190 02.4	13.8	N12 40.1	7.0	54.4
19	108 55.4	05.2	204 35.2	13.9	12 33.1	7.2	54.4
20	123 55.3	05.9	219 08.1	14.0	12 25.9	7.1	54.4
21	138 55.2 ..	06.5	233 41.1	14.0	12 18.8	7.2	54.4
22	153 55.1	07.2	248 14.1	14.0	12 11.6	7.3	54.4
23	168 55.0	07.8	262 47.1	14.0	12 04.3	7.3	54.3
14 00	183 55.0	S18 08.5	277 20.1	14.1	N11 57.0	7.4	54.3
01	198 54.9	09.1	291 53.2	14.1	11 49.6	7.4	54.3
02	213 54.8	09.8	306 26.3	14.2	11 42.2	7.5	54.3
03	228 54.7 ..	10.5	320 59.5	14.2	11 34.7	7.5	54.3
04	243 54.6	11.1	335 32.7	14.2	11 27.2	7.5	54.3
05	258 54.5	11.8	350 05.9	14.2	11 19.7	7.6	54.3
F 06	273 54.4	S18 12.4	4 39.1	14.3	N11 12.1	7.7	54.3
R 07	288 54.3	13.1	19 12.4	14.3	11 04.4	7.7	54.3
I 08	303 54.2	13.7	33 45.7	14.4	10 56.7	7.7	54.3
D 09	318 54.1 ..	14.4	48 19.1	14.4	10 49.0	7.8	54.3
A 10	333 54.0	15.0	62 52.5	14.4	10 41.2	7.8	54.3
Y 11	348 53.9	15.7	77 25.9	14.4	10 33.4	7.9	54.3
12	3 53.8	S18 16.3	91 59.3	14.5	N10 25.5	7.9	54.3
13	18 53.7	17.0	106 32.8	14.5	10 17.6	7.9	54.3
14	33 53.6	17.6	121 06.3	14.5	10 09.7	8.0	54.3
15	48 53.5 ..	18.3	135 39.8	14.6	10 01.7	8.0	54.2
16	63 53.4	18.9	150 13.4	14.6	9 53.7	8.1	54.2
17	78 53.3	19.5	164 47.0	14.6	9 45.6	8.1	54.2
18	93 53.2	S18 20.2	179 20.6	14.6	N 9 37.5	8.2	54.2
19	108 53.1	20.8	193 54.2	14.7	9 29.3	8.2	54.2
20	123 53.0	21.5	208 27.9	14.7	9 21.2	8.3	54.2
21	138 52.9 ..	22.1	223 01.6	14.7	9 12.9	8.2	54.2
22	153 52.8	22.8	237 35.3	14.7	9 04.7	8.3	54.2
23	168 52.7	23.4	252 09.0	14.8	N 8 56.4	8.4	54.2
	SD 16.2	d 0.7	SD 14.9		14.8		14.8

Twilight / Sunrise / Moonrise

Lat.	Naut.	Civil	Sunrise	Moonrise 12	13	14	15
°	h m	h m	h m	h m	h m	h m	h m
N 72	06 52	08 24	10 32	18 54	20 37	22 14	23 49
N 70	06 42	08 03	09 36	19 29	20 59	22 28	23 57
68	06 35	07 47	09 03	19 54	21 17	22 40	24 03
66	06 28	07 33	08 39	20 13	21 30	22 49	24 08
64	06 22	07 22	08 20	20 28	21 42	22 57	24 12
62	06 17	07 12	08 05	20 41	21 52	23 04	24 16
60	06 13	07 04	07 53	20 52	22 00	23 09	24 19
N 58	06 09	06 57	07 42	21 01	22 07	23 14	24 22
56	06 05	06 50	07 32	21 09	22 14	23 19	24 25
54	06 01	06 44	07 24	21 17	22 19	23 23	24 27
52	05 58	06 39	07 16	21 23	22 24	23 27	24 29
50	05 55	06 34	07 09	21 29	22 29	23 30	24 31
45	05 48	06 23	06 55	21 42	22 39	23 37	24 35
N 40	05 41	06 14	06 43	21 52	22 48	23 43	24 39
35	05 35	06 05	06 32	22 01	22 55	23 48	24 42
30	05 29	05 58	06 23	22 09	23 01	23 53	24 44
20	05 18	05 44	06 08	22 22	23 12	24 01	00 01
N 10	05 06	05 32	05 54	22 34	23 21	24 07	00 07
0	04 54	05 19	05 41	22 45	23 30	24 14	00 14
S 10	04 39	05 05	05 28	22 56	23 39	24 20	00 20
20	04 22	04 50	05 13	23 08	23 48	24 27	00 27
30	04 00	04 31	04 57	23 21	23 59	24 35	00 35
35	03 46	04 20	04 47	23 29	24 05	00 05	00 39
40	03 29	04 06	04 36	23 37	24 12	00 12	00 44
45	03 07	03 50	04 23	23 48	24 21	00 21	00 50
S 50	02 38	03 29	04 08	24 00	00 00	00 30	00 57
52	02 23	03 19	04 00	24 06	00 06	00 35	01 00
54	02 05	03 07	03 52	24 12	00 12	00 40	01 04
56	01 43	02 54	03 42	24 19	00 19	00 45	01 08
58	01 11	02 39	03 32	24 27	00 27	00 51	01 12
S 60	00 06	02 19	03 19	00 08	00 36	00 58	01 17

Sunset / Twilight / Moonset

Lat.	Sunset	Civil	Naut.	Moonset 12	13	14	15
°	h m	h m	h m	h m	h m	h m	h m
N 72	12 56	15 03	16 35	14 22	14 14	14 08	14 02
N 70	13 52	15 24	16 45	13 46	13 51	13 52	13 53
68	14 25	15 41	16 53	13 21	13 32	13 40	13 45
66	14 49	15 54	16 59	13 01	13 17	13 29	13 39
64	15 07	16 06	17 05	12 45	13 05	13 21	13 33
62	15 22	16 15	17 10	12 32	12 55	13 13	13 28
60	15 35	16 24	17 15	12 21	12 46	13 06	13 24
N 58	15 46	16 31	17 19	12 11	12 38	13 01	13 20
56	15 56	16 38	17 23	12 02	12 31	12 56	13 17
54	16 04	16 44	17 27	11 55	12 25	12 51	13 14
52	16 12	16 49	17 30	11 48	12 19	12 47	13 11
50	16 19	16 54	17 33	11 42	12 14	12 43	13 09
45	16 33	17 05	17 40	11 28	12 03	12 35	13 03
N 40	16 46	17 14	17 47	11 17	11 54	12 28	12 59
35	16 56	17 23	17 53	11 08	11 46	12 22	12 55
30	17 05	17 30	17 59	11 00	11 39	12 16	12 51
20	17 21	17 44	18 10	10 45	11 27	12 07	12 45
N 10	17 35	17 57	18 22	10 33	11 17	11 59	12 40
0	17 48	18 10	18 35	10 21	11 07	11 51	12 35
S 10	18 01	18 23	18 49	10 09	10 57	11 44	12 29
20	18 15	18 39	19 07	09 56	10 46	11 35	12 24
30	18 32	18 58	19 29	09 41	10 34	11 26	12 18
35	18 42	19 09	19 43	09 33	10 27	11 21	12 14
40	18 53	19 23	20 00	09 23	10 19	11 14	12 10
45	19 06	19 40	20 22	09 12	10 09	11 07	12 05
S 50	19 22	20 01	20 52	08 58	09 58	10 58	11 59
52	19 29	20 11	21 07	08 51	09 52	10 54	11 57
54	19 38	20 23	21 26	08 44	09 46	10 50	11 54
56	19 47	20 36	21 49	08 36	09 40	10 45	11 50
58	19 58	20 52	22 22	08 27	09 32	10 39	11 47
S 60	20 11	21 12	////	08 16	09 24	10 33	11 43

SUN and MOON

Day	SUN Eqn. of Time 00ʰ	12ʰ	Mer. Pass.	MOON Mer. Pass. Upper	Lower	Age	Phase
d	m s	m s	h m	h m	h m	d	%
12	15 56	15 52	11 44	04 09	16 33	20	70
13	15 48	15 44	11 44	04 56	17 19	21	61
14	15 40	15 35	11 44	05 41	18 03	22	51

2014 NOVEMBER 15, 16, 17 (SAT., SUN., MON.)

UT	ARIES	VENUS −3.9		MARS +1.0		JUPITER −2.2		SATURN +0.5		STARS		
	GHA	GHA	Dec	GHA	Dec	GHA	Dec	GHA	Dec	Name	SHA	Dec
d h	° ′	° ′	° ′	° ′	° ′	° ′	° ′	° ′	° ′		° ′	° ′
15 00	54 00.3	178 27.0	S19 21.8	127 55.6	S24 05.0	269 41.3	N14 53.9	180 20.1	S17 16.6	Acamar	315 17.2	S40 14.8
01	69 02.8	193 26.3	22.6	142 56.0	04.8	284 43.5	53.9	195 22.3	16.7	Achernar	335 25.7	S57 09.8
02	84 05.2	208 25.5	23.4	157 56.3	04.6	299 45.8	53.8	210 24.5	16.7	Acrux	173 08.5	S63 10.6
03	99 07.7	223 24.8 ..	24.2	172 56.7 ..	04.4	314 48.1 ..	53.8	225 26.6 ..	16.8	Adhara	255 11.5	S28 59.5
04	114 10.2	238 24.0	25.0	187 57.1	04.1	329 50.4	53.7	240 28.8	16.9	Aldebaran	290 47.9	N16 32.2
05	129 12.6	253 23.3	25.8	202 57.5	03.9	344 52.7	53.7	255 31.0	17.0			
06	144 15.1	268 22.5	S19 26.6	217 57.9	S24 03.7	359 54.9	N14 53.6	270 33.1	S17 17.0	Alioth	166 20.4	N55 52.6
S 07	159 17.6	283 21.8	27.4	232 58.3	03.5	14 57.2	53.6	285 35.3	17.1	Alkaid	152 58.7	N49 14.3
A 08	174 20.0	298 21.0	28.2	247 58.7	03.3	29 59.5	53.5	300 37.4	17.2	Al Na'ir	27 42.6	S46 53.4
T 09	189 22.5	313 20.3 ..	29.0	262 59.1 ..	03.0	45 01.8 ..	53.5	315 39.6 ..	17.2	Alnilam	275 45.1	S 1 11.7
U 10	204 25.0	328 19.5	29.7	277 59.5	02.8	60 04.1	53.4	330 41.8	17.3	Alphard	217 55.1	S 8 43.4
R 11	219 27.4	343 18.7	30.5	292 59.9	02.6	75 06.3	53.4	345 43.9	17.4			
D 12	234 29.9	358 18.0	S19 31.3	308 00.3	S24 02.4	90 08.6	N14 53.3	0 46.1	S17 17.5	Alphecca	126 10.6	N26 40.1
A 13	249 32.4	13 17.2	32.1	323 00.7	02.1	105 10.9	53.3	15 48.2	17.5	Alpheratz	357 42.2	N29 10.6
Y 14	264 34.8	28 16.5	32.9	338 01.1	01.9	120 13.2	53.2	30 50.4	17.6	Altair	62 07.5	N 8 54.8
15	279 37.3	43 15.7 ..	33.7	353 01.5 ..	01.7	135 15.5 ..	53.2	45 52.6 ..	17.7	Ankaa	353 14.5	S42 13.6
16	294 39.7	58 14.9	34.5	8 01.9	01.5	150 17.8	53.1	60 54.7	17.8	Antares	112 25.4	S26 27.7
17	309 42.2	73 14.2	35.3	23 02.3	01.2	165 20.0	53.1	75 56.9	17.8			
18	324 44.7	88 13.4	S19 36.0	38 02.7	S24 01.0	180 22.3	N14 53.0	90 59.1	S17 17.9	Arcturus	145 55.2	N19 06.4
19	339 47.1	103 12.7	36.8	53 03.1	00.8	195 24.6	53.0	106 01.2	18.0	Atria	107 26.9	S69 03.1
20	354 49.6	118 11.9	37.6	68 03.5	00.5	210 26.9	52.9	121 03.4	18.0	Avior	234 17.3	S59 33.3
21	9 52.1	133 11.1 ..	38.4	83 03.9 ..	00.3	225 29.2 ..	52.9	136 05.5 ..	18.1	Bellatrix	278 30.7	N 6 21.6
22	24 54.5	148 10.4	39.2	98 04.3	24 00.1	240 31.5	52.8	151 07.7	18.2	Betelgeuse	271 00.0	N 7 24.4
23	39 57.0	163 09.6	40.0	113 04.7	23 59.9	255 33.8	52.8	166 09.9	18.3			
16 00	54 59.5	178 08.8	S19 40.7	128 05.1	S23 59.6	270 36.0	N14 52.7	181 12.0	S17 18.3	Canopus	263 55.3	S52 42.2
01	70 01.9	193 08.1	41.5	143 05.5	59.4	285 38.3	52.7	196 14.2	18.4	Capella	280 32.6	N46 00.5
02	85 04.4	208 07.3	42.3	158 05.9	59.2	300 40.6	52.6	211 16.3	18.5	Deneb	49 30.9	N45 20.5
03	100 06.8	223 06.5 ..	43.1	173 06.3 ..	58.9	315 42.9 ..	52.6	226 18.5 ..	18.5	Denebola	182 32.9	N14 29.3
04	115 09.3	238 05.8	43.8	188 06.7	58.7	330 45.2	52.5	241 20.7	18.6	Diphda	348 54.7	S17 54.3
05	130 11.8	253 05.0	44.6	203 07.1	58.5	345 47.5	52.5	256 22.8	18.7			
06	145 14.2	268 04.2	S19 45.4	218 07.5	S23 58.2	0 49.8	N14 52.4	271 25.0	S17 18.8	Dubhe	193 50.9	N61 39.9
07	160 16.7	283 03.5	46.2	233 07.9	58.0	15 52.1	52.4	286 27.2	18.8	Elnath	278 11.1	N28 37.0
S 08	175 19.2	298 02.7	46.9	248 08.3	57.8	30 54.3	52.3	301 29.3	18.9	Eltanin	90 46.2	N51 29.6
U 09	190 21.6	313 01.9 ..	47.7	263 08.7 ..	57.5	45 56.6 ..	52.3	316 31.5 ..	19.0	Enif	33 46.2	N 9 56.9
N 10	205 24.1	328 01.2	48.5	278 09.1	57.3	60 58.9	52.2	331 33.6	19.0	Fomalhaut	15 22.9	S29 32.6
D 11	220 26.6	343 00.4	49.2	293 09.5	57.1	76 01.2	52.2	346 35.8	19.1			
A 12	235 29.0	357 59.6	S19 50.0	308 09.9	S23 56.8	91 03.5	N14 52.1	1 38.0	S17 19.2	Gacrux	172 00.1	S57 11.5
Y 13	250 31.5	12 58.8	50.8	323 10.3	56.6	106 05.8	52.1	16 40.1	19.3	Gienah	175 51.5	S17 37.3
14	265 34.0	27 58.1	51.5	338 10.7	56.4	121 08.1	52.0	31 42.3	19.3	Hadar	148 47.0	S60 26.4
15	280 36.4	42 57.3 ..	52.3	353 11.1 ..	56.1	136 10.4 ..	52.0	46 44.4 ..	19.4	Hamal	327 59.3	N23 32.0
16	295 38.9	57 56.5	53.1	8 11.5	55.9	151 12.7	51.9	61 46.6	19.5	Kaus Aust.	83 42.9	S34 22.5
17	310 41.3	72 55.7	53.8	23 11.9	55.6	166 14.9	51.9	76 48.8	19.5			
18	325 43.8	87 55.0	S19 54.6	38 12.3	S23 55.4	181 17.2	N14 51.9	91 50.9	S17 19.6	Kochab	137 21.4	N74 05.7
19	340 46.3	102 54.2	55.4	53 12.7	55.2	196 19.5	51.8	106 53.1	19.7	Markab	13 37.2	N15 17.4
20	355 48.7	117 53.4	56.1	68 13.1	54.9	211 21.8	51.8	121 55.2	19.8	Menkar	314 13.7	N 4 08.8
21	10 51.2	132 52.6 ..	56.9	83 13.5 ..	54.7	226 24.1 ..	51.7	136 57.4 ..	19.8	Menkent	148 06.8	S36 26.3
22	25 53.7	147 51.9	57.6	98 13.9	54.5	241 26.4	51.7	151 59.6	19.9	Miaplacidus	221 39.2	S69 46.5
23	40 56.1	162 51.1	58.4	113 14.3	54.2	256 28.7	51.6	167 01.7	20.0			
17 00	55 58.6	177 50.3	S19 59.1	128 14.7	S23 54.0	271 31.0	N14 51.6	182 03.9	S17 20.0	Mirfak	308 38.4	N49 54.8
01	71 01.1	192 49.5	19 59.9	143 15.1	53.7	286 33.3	51.5	197 06.1	20.1	Nunki	75 57.4	S26 16.5
02	86 03.5	207 48.8	20 00.6	158 15.5	53.5	301 35.6	51.5	212 08.2	20.2	Peacock	53 18.0	S56 41.3
03	101 06.0	222 48.0 ..	01.4	173 15.9 ..	53.2	316 37.9 ..	51.4	227 10.4 ..	20.3	Pollux	243 26.4	N27 59.1
04	116 08.5	237 47.2	02.2	188 16.3	53.0	331 40.2	51.4	242 12.5	20.3	Procyon	244 58.6	N 5 11.1
05	131 10.9	252 46.4	02.9	203 16.7	52.8	346 42.5	51.3	257 14.7	20.4			
06	146 13.4	267 45.6	S20 03.7	218 17.1	S23 52.5	1 44.8	N14 51.3	272 16.9	S17 20.5	Rasalhague	96 05.9	N12 33.3
07	161 15.8	282 44.9	04.4	233 17.5	52.3	16 47.1	51.2	287 19.0	20.5	Regulus	207 42.6	N11 53.6
08	176 18.3	297 44.1	05.2	248 17.9	52.0	31 49.3	51.2	302 21.2	20.6	Rigel	281 10.8	S 8 11.2
M 09	191 20.8	312 43.3 ..	05.9	263 18.3 ..	51.8	46 51.6 ..	51.2	317 23.3 ..	20.7	Rigil Kent.	139 51.0	S60 53.5
O 10	206 23.2	327 42.5	06.6	278 18.7	51.5	61 53.9	51.1	332 25.5	20.8	Sabik	102 11.8	S15 44.3
N 11	221 25.7	342 41.7	07.4	293 19.1	51.3	76 56.2	51.1	347 27.7	20.8			
D 12	236 28.2	357 40.9	S20 08.1	308 19.5	S23 51.0	91 58.5	N14 51.0	2 29.8	S17 20.9	Schedar	349 38.9	N56 37.4
A 13	251 30.6	12 40.2	08.9	323 19.9	50.8	107 00.8	51.0	17 32.0	21.0	Shaula	96 21.0	S37 06.7
Y 14	266 33.1	27 39.4	09.6	338 20.3	50.5	122 03.1	50.9	32 34.1	21.0	Sirius	258 32.6	S16 44.3
15	281 35.6	42 38.6 ..	10.4	353 20.7 ..	50.2	137 05.4 ..	50.9	47 36.3 ..	21.1	Spica	158 30.5	S11 14.2
16	296 38.0	57 37.8	11.1	8 21.1	50.0	152 07.7	50.8	62 38.5	21.2	Suhail	222 51.6	S43 29.4
17	311 40.5	72 37.0	11.8	23 21.5	49.8	167 10.0	50.8	77 40.6	21.3			
18	326 42.9	87 36.2	S20 12.6	38 21.9	S23 49.5	182 12.3	N14 50.7	92 42.8	S17 21.3	Vega	80 38.6	N38 48.2
19	341 45.4	102 35.4	13.3	53 22.3	49.3	197 14.6	50.7	107 45.0	21.4	Zuben'ubi	137 04.7	S16 06.0
20	356 47.9	117 34.7	14.0	68 22.7	49.0	212 16.9	50.7	122 47.1	21.5			
21	11 50.3	132 33.9 ..	14.8	83 23.1 ..	48.8	227 19.2 ..	50.6	137 49.3 ..	21.5		SHA	Mer. Pass.
22	26 52.8	147 33.1	15.5	98 23.6	48.5	242 21.5	50.6	152 51.4	21.6	Venus	123 09.4	12 08
23	41 55.3	162 32.3	16.3	113 24.0	48.3	257 23.8	50.5	167 53.6	21.7	Mars	73 05.7	15 27
	h m									Jupiter	215 36.6	5 57
Mer. Pass. 20 16.7	v −0.8 d 0.8		v 0.4 d 0.2		v 2.3 d 0.0		v 2.2 d 0.1		Saturn	126 12.6	11 53

UT	SUN GHA	SUN Dec	MOON GHA	v	MOON Dec	d	HP
d h	° ′	° ′	° ′	′	° ′	′	′
15 00	183 52.6	S18 24.1	266 42.8	14.7	N 8 48.0	8.3	54.2
01	198 52.5	24.7	281 16.5	14.8	8 39.7	8.5	54.2
02	213 52.4	25.3	295 50.3	14.9	8 31.2	8.4	54.2
03	228 52.3	.. 26.0	310 24.2	14.8	8 22.8	8.5	54.2
04	243 52.2	26.6	324 58.0	14.9	8 14.3	8.5	54.2
05	258 52.1	27.3	339 31.9	14.8	8 05.8	8.5	54.2
06	273 52.0	S18 27.9	354 05.7	14.9	N 7 57.3	8.6	54.2
S 07	288 51.9	28.5	8 39.6	14.9	7 48.7	8.6	54.2
A 08	303 51.8	29.2	23 13.5	15.0	7 40.1	8.7	54.2
T 09	318 51.7	.. 29.8	37 47.5	14.9	7 31.4	8.6	54.2
U 10	333 51.6	30.4	52 21.4	15.0	7 22.8	8.8	54.2
R 11	348 51.5	31.1	66 55.4	14.9	7 14.0	8.7	54.2
D 12	3 51.4	S18 31.7	81 29.3	15.0	N 7 05.3	8.8	54.2
A 13	18 51.3	32.4	96 03.3	15.0	6 56.5	8.8	54.2
Y 14	33 51.2	33.0	110 37.3	15.0	6 47.7	8.8	54.3
15	48 51.1	.. 33.6	125 11.3	15.1	6 38.9	8.8	54.3
16	63 50.9	34.3	139 45.4	15.0	6 30.1	8.9	54.3
17	78 50.8	34.9	154 19.4	15.1	6 21.2	8.9	54.3
18	93 50.7	S18 35.5	168 53.5	15.0	N 6 12.3	9.0	54.3
19	108 50.6	36.1	183 27.5	15.1	6 03.3	8.9	54.3
20	123 50.5	36.8	198 01.6	15.0	5 54.4	9.0	54.3
21	138 50.4	.. 37.4	212 35.6	15.1	5 45.4	9.0	54.3
22	153 50.3	38.0	227 09.7	15.1	5 36.4	9.1	54.3
23	168 50.2	38.7	241 43.8	15.1	5 27.3	9.1	54.3
16 00	183 50.1	S18 39.3	256 17.9	15.1	N 5 18.2	9.1	54.3
01	198 50.0	39.9	270 52.0	15.1	5 09.1	9.1	54.3
02	213 49.9	40.6	285 26.1	15.1	5 00.0	9.1	54.3
03	228 49.7	.. 41.2	300 00.2	15.2	4 50.9	9.2	54.3
04	243 49.6	41.8	314 34.4	15.1	4 41.7	9.2	54.3
05	258 49.5	42.4	329 08.5	15.1	4 32.5	9.2	54.3
06	273 49.4	S18 43.1	343 42.6	15.1	N 4 23.3	9.2	54.3
S 07	288 49.3	43.7	358 16.7	15.1	4 14.1	9.2	54.4
U 08	303 49.2	44.3	12 50.8	15.2	4 04.9	9.3	54.4
N 09	318 49.1	.. 44.9	27 25.0	15.1	3 55.6	9.3	54.4
D 10	333 49.0	45.5	41 59.1	15.1	3 46.3	9.3	54.4
A 11	348 48.8	46.2	56 33.2	15.1	3 37.0	9.3	54.4
Y 12	3 48.7	S18 46.8	71 07.3	15.1	N 3 27.7	9.4	54.4
13	18 48.6	47.4	85 41.4	15.1	3 18.3	9.3	54.4
14	33 48.5	48.0	100 15.5	15.1	3 09.0	9.4	54.4
15	48 48.4	.. 48.7	114 49.6	15.1	2 59.6	9.4	54.4
16	63 48.3	49.3	129 23.7	15.1	2 50.2	9.4	54.4
17	78 48.1	49.9	143 57.8	15.1	2 40.8	9.4	54.5
18	93 48.0	S18 50.5	158 31.9	15.1	N 2 31.4	9.5	54.5
19	108 47.9	51.1	173 06.0	15.1	2 21.9	9.5	54.5
20	123 47.8	51.7	187 40.1	15.1	2 12.5	9.5	54.5
21	138 47.7	.. 52.4	202 14.2	15.0	2 03.0	9.5	54.5
22	153 47.6	53.0	216 48.2	15.1	1 53.5	9.5	54.5
23	168 47.4	53.6	231 22.3	15.0	1 44.0	9.5	54.5
17 00	183 47.3	S18 54.2	245 56.3	15.0	N 1 34.5	9.5	54.5
01	198 47.2	54.8	260 30.3	15.0	1 25.0	9.6	54.6
02	213 47.0	55.4	275 04.3	15.0	1 15.4	9.5	54.6
03	228 47.0	.. 56.0	289 38.3	15.0	1 05.9	9.6	54.6
04	243 46.8	56.7	304 12.3	15.0	0 56.3	9.5	54.6
05	258 46.7	57.3	318 46.3	14.9	0 46.8	9.6	54.6
06	273 46.6	S18 57.9	333 20.2	15.0	N 0 37.2	9.6	54.6
M 07	288 46.5	58.5	347 54.2	14.9	0 27.6	9.6	54.6
O 08	303 46.3	59.1	2 28.1	14.9	0 18.0	9.6	54.7
N 09	318 46.2	18 59.7	17 02.0	14.9	N 0 08.4	9.6	54.7
D 10	333 46.1	19 00.3	31 35.9	14.8	S 0 01.2	9.6	54.7
A 11	348 46.0	00.9	46 09.7	14.9	0 10.8	9.6	54.7
Y 12	3 45.9	S19 01.5	60 43.6	14.8	S 0 20.4	9.6	54.7
13	18 45.7	02.1	75 17.4	14.8	0 30.0	9.6	54.7
14	33 45.6	02.8	89 51.2	14.8	0 39.6	9.7	54.8
15	48 45.5	.. 03.4	104 25.0	14.8	0 49.3	9.6	54.8
16	63 45.4	04.0	118 58.8	14.7	0 58.9	9.6	54.8
17	78 45.2	04.6	133 32.5	14.7	1 08.5	9.7	54.8
18	93 45.1	S19 05.2	148 06.2	14.7	S 1 18.2	9.6	54.8
19	108 45.0	05.8	162 39.9	14.7	1 27.8	9.7	54.8
20	123 44.9	06.4	177 13.6	14.6	1 37.5	9.6	54.9
21	138 44.7	.. 07.0	191 47.2	14.6	1 47.1	9.7	54.9
22	153 44.6	07.6	206 20.8	14.6	1 56.8	9.6	54.9
23	168 44.5	08.2	220 54.4	14.6	S 2 06.4	9.6	54.9
	SD 16.2	d 0.6	SD 14.8		14.8		14.9

Twilight / Sunrise / Moonrise

Lat.	Twilight Naut.	Twilight Civil	Sunrise	Moonrise 15	16	17	18
°	h m	h m	h m	h m	h m	h m	h m
N 72	07 03	08 38	11 25	23 49	25 23	01 23	02 59
N 70	06 52	08 15	09 55	23 57	25 25	01 25	02 55
68	06 43	07 57	09 17	24 03	00 03	01 26	02 51
66	06 36	07 42	08 50	24 08	00 08	01 28	02 49
64	06 29	07 30	08 30	24 12	00 12	01 29	02 46
62	06 24	07 20	08 14	24 16	00 16	01 30	02 44
60	06 19	07 11	08 00	24 19	00 19	01 30	02 42
N 58	06 14	07 03	07 48	24 22	00 22	01 31	02 41
56	06 10	06 56	07 38	24 25	00 25	01 32	02 40
54	06 06	06 49	07 29	24 27	00 27	01 32	02 38
52	06 02	06 44	07 21	24 29	00 29	01 33	02 37
50	05 59	06 38	07 14	24 31	00 31	01 33	02 36
45	05 51	06 27	06 59	24 35	00 35	01 34	02 34
N 40	05 44	06 17	06 46	24 39	00 39	01 35	02 32
35	05 38	06 08	06 35	24 42	00 42	01 36	02 31
30	05 31	06 00	06 26	24 44	00 44	01 36	02 29
20	05 19	05 46	06 09	00 01	00 49	01 38	02 27
N 10	05 07	05 33	05 55	00 07	00 53	01 39	02 25
0	04 54	05 19	05 41	00 14	00 57	01 39	02 23
S 10	04 39	05 05	05 27	00 20	01 01	01 40	02 21
20	04 21	04 49	05 13	00 27	01 05	01 41	02 19
30	03 58	04 29	04 55	00 35	01 09	01 43	02 17
35	03 43	04 17	04 45	00 39	01 12	01 43	02 15
40	03 26	04 03	04 34	00 44	01 15	01 44	02 14
45	03 03	03 46	04 20	00 50	01 18	01 45	02 12
S 50	02 32	03 24	04 04	00 57	01 22	01 46	02 10
52	02 16	03 14	03 56	01 00	01 24	01 47	02 09
54	01 57	03 02	03 47	01 04	01 26	01 47	02 08
56	01 31	02 47	03 37	01 08	01 28	01 48	02 07
58	00 54	02 31	03 26	01 12	01 31	01 48	02 06
S 60	////	02 10	03 12	01 17	01 34	01 49	02 05

Sunset / Twilight / Moonset

Lat.	Sunset	Twilight Civil	Twilight Naut.	Moonset 15	16	17	18
°	h m	h m	h m	h m	h m	h m	h m
N 72	12 03	14 50	16 26	14 02	13 57	13 51	13 46
N 70	13 33	15 14	16 36	13 53	13 53	13 52	13 52
68	14 12	15 32	16 45	13 45	13 49	13 53	13 57
66	14 38	15 46	16 53	13 39	13 46	13 54	14 01
64	14 59	15 59	16 59	13 33	13 44	13 54	14 05
62	15 15	16 09	17 05	13 28	13 42	13 55	14 08
60	15 29	16 18	17 10	13 24	13 40	13 55	14 11
N 58	15 40	16 26	17 15	13 20	13 38	13 56	14 13
56	15 51	16 33	17 19	13 17	13 37	13 56	14 16
54	16 00	16 39	17 23	13 14	13 35	13 56	14 18
52	16 08	16 45	17 26	13 11	13 34	13 57	14 20
50	16 15	16 51	17 30	13 09	13 33	13 57	14 21
45	16 30	17 02	17 38	13 03	13 31	13 57	14 25
N 40	16 43	17 12	17 45	12 59	13 28	13 58	14 28
35	16 54	17 21	17 52	12 55	13 27	13 58	14 31
30	17 04	17 29	17 58	12 51	13 25	13 59	14 33
20	17 20	17 43	18 10	12 45	13 22	13 59	14 37
N 10	17 35	17 57	18 22	12 40	13 20	14 00	14 41
0	17 48	18 10	18 36	12 35	13 17	14 00	14 44
S 10	18 02	18 24	18 51	12 30	13 15	14 01	14 47
20	18 17	18 41	19 09	12 24	13 12	14 01	14 51
30	18 34	19 01	19 32	12 18	13 09	14 02	14 55
35	18 45	19 13	19 47	12 14	13 08	14 02	14 57
40	18 56	19 27	20 05	12 10	13 06	14 02	15 00
45	19 10	19 44	20 28	12 05	13 04	14 03	15 03
S 50	19 27	20 06	20 59	11 59	13 01	14 03	15 07
52	19 35	20 17	21 15	11 57	13 00	14 03	15 09
54	19 44	20 29	21 35	11 54	12 58	14 04	15 10
56	19 54	20 44	22 01	11 50	12 57	14 04	15 12
58	20 05	21 01	22 42	11 47	12 55	14 04	15 15
S 60	20 19	21 22	////	11 43	12 53	14 05	15 17

SUN / MOON

Day	SUN Eqn. of Time 00h	SUN Eqn. of Time 12h	SUN Mer. Pass.	MOON Mer. Pass. Upper	MOON Mer. Pass. Lower	Age	Phase
d	m s	m s	h m	h m	h m	d	%
15	15 31	15 26	11 45	06 24	18 46	23	42
16	15 21	15 15	11 45	07 07	19 28	24	33
17	15 09	15 04	11 45	07 50	20 11	25	24

UT	ARIES GHA	VENUS −3.9 GHA	Dec	MARS +1.0 GHA	Dec	JUPITER −2.2 GHA	Dec	SATURN +0.5 GHA	Dec	STARS Name	SHA	Dec
d h	° ′	° ′	° ′	° ′	° ′	° ′	° ′	° ′	° ′		° ′	° ′
18 00	56 57.7	177 31.5	S20 17.0	128 24.4	S23 48.0	272 26.1	N14 50.5	182 55.8	S17 21.8	Acamar	315 17.2	S40 14.8
01	72 00.2	192 30.7	17.7	143 24.8	47.8	287 28.4	50.4	197 57.9	21.8	Achernar	335 25.7	S57 09.9
02	87 02.7	207 29.9	18.4	158 25.2	47.5	302 30.7	50.4	213 00.1	21.9	Acrux	173 08.5	S63 10.6
03	102 05.1	222 29.1	.. 19.2	173 25.6	.. 47.3	317 33.0	.. 50.3	228 02.2	.. 22.0	Adhara	255 11.5	S28 59.6
04	117 07.6	237 28.3	19.9	188 26.0	47.0	332 35.3	50.3	243 04.4	22.0	Aldebaran	290 47.9	N16 32.2
05	132 10.1	252 27.5	20.6	203 26.4	46.8	347 37.6	50.3	258 06.6	22.1			
06	147 12.5	267 26.7	S20 21.4	218 26.8	S23 46.5	2 39.9	N14 50.2	273 08.7	S17 22.2	Alioth	166 20.4	N55 52.6
T 07	162 15.0	282 25.9	22.1	233 27.2	46.3	17 42.2	50.2	288 10.9	22.2	Alkaid	152 58.7	N49 14.3
U 08	177 17.4	297 25.2	22.8	248 27.6	46.0	32 44.5	50.1	303 13.0	22.3	Al Na'ir	27 42.6	S46 53.4
E 09	192 19.9	312 24.4	.. 23.5	263 28.0	.. 45.8	47 46.8	.. 50.1	318 15.2	.. 22.4	Alnilam	275 45.1	S 1 11.7
S 10	207 22.4	327 23.6	24.3	278 28.4	45.5	62 49.1	50.0	333 17.4	22.5	Alphard	217 55.1	S 8 43.4
D 11	222 24.8	342 22.8	25.0	293 28.8	45.2	77 51.4	50.0	348 19.5	22.5			
A 12	237 27.3	357 22.0	S20 25.7	308 29.2	S23 45.0	92 53.7	N14 50.0	3 21.7	S17 22.6	Alphecca	126 10.6	N26 40.1
Y 13	252 29.8	12 21.2	26.4	323 29.6	44.7	107 56.0	49.9	18 23.9	22.7	Alpheratz	357 42.3	N29 10.6
14	267 32.2	27 20.4	27.1	338 30.0	44.5	122 58.4	49.9	33 26.0	22.7	Altair	62 07.5	N 8 54.8
15	282 34.7	42 19.6	.. 27.8	353 30.4	.. 44.2	138 00.7	.. 49.8	48 28.2	.. 22.8	Ankaa	353 14.6	S42 13.6
16	297 37.2	57 18.8	28.6	8 30.8	43.9	153 03.0	49.8	63 30.3	22.9	Antares	112 25.4	S26 27.7
17	312 39.6	72 18.0	29.3	23 31.2	43.7	168 05.3	49.7	78 32.5	23.0			
18	327 42.1	87 17.2	S20 30.0	38 31.6	S23 43.4	183 07.6	N14 49.7	93 34.7	S17 23.0	Arcturus	145 55.2	N19 06.4
19	342 44.5	102 16.4	30.7	53 32.0	43.2	198 09.9	49.7	108 36.8	23.1	Atria	107 26.9	S69 03.1
20	357 47.0	117 15.6	31.4	68 32.4	42.9	213 12.2	49.6	123 39.0	23.2	Avior	234 17.3	S59 33.3
21	12 49.5	132 14.8	.. 32.1	83 32.8	.. 42.6	228 14.5	.. 49.6	138 41.1	.. 23.2	Bellatrix	278 30.7	N 6 21.6
22	27 51.9	147 14.0	32.8	98 33.2	42.4	243 16.8	49.5	153 43.3	23.3	Betelgeuse	271 00.0	N 7 24.4
23	42 54.4	162 13.2	33.6	113 33.6	42.1	258 19.1	49.5	168 45.5	23.4			
19 00	57 56.9	177 12.4	S20 34.3	128 34.0	S23 41.9	273 21.4	N14 49.4	183 47.6	S17 23.5	Canopus	263 55.3	S52 42.2
01	72 59.3	192 11.6	35.0	143 34.4	41.6	288 23.7	49.4	198 49.8	23.5	Capella	280 32.6	N46 00.5
02	88 01.8	207 10.8	35.7	158 34.8	41.3	303 26.0	49.4	213 51.9	23.6	Deneb	49 30.9	N45 20.5
03	103 04.3	222 10.0	.. 36.4	173 35.2	.. 41.1	318 28.3	.. 49.3	228 54.1	.. 23.7	Denebola	182 32.9	N14 29.3
04	118 06.7	237 09.2	37.1	188 35.6	40.8	333 30.6	49.3	243 56.3	23.7	Diphda	348 54.7	S17 54.3
05	133 09.2	252 08.4	37.8	203 36.0	40.5	348 33.0	49.2	258 58.4	23.8			
06	148 11.7	267 07.5	S20 38.5	218 36.4	S23 40.3	3 35.3	N14 49.2	274 00.6	S17 23.9	Dubhe	193 50.9	N61 39.9
W 07	163 14.1	282 06.7	39.2	233 36.8	40.0	18 37.6	49.2	289 02.7	24.0	Elnath	278 11.1	N28 37.0
E 08	178 16.6	297 05.9	39.9	248 37.2	39.7	33 39.9	49.1	304 04.9	24.0	Eltanin	90 46.2	N51 29.6
D 09	193 19.0	312 05.1	.. 40.6	263 37.6	.. 39.5	48 42.2	.. 49.1	319 07.1	.. 24.1	Enif	33 46.2	N 9 56.9
N 10	208 21.5	327 04.3	41.3	278 38.0	39.2	63 44.5	49.0	334 09.2	24.2	Fomalhaut	15 22.9	S29 32.6
E 11	223 24.0	342 03.5	42.0	293 38.4	38.9	78 46.8	49.0	349 11.4	24.2			
S 12	238 26.4	357 02.7	S20 42.7	308 38.8	S23 38.7	93 49.1	N14 49.0	4 13.6	S17 24.3	Gacrux	172 00.1	S57 11.5
D 13	253 28.9	12 01.9	43.4	323 39.2	38.4	108 51.4	48.9	19 15.7	24.4	Gienah	175 51.5	S17 37.3
A 14	268 31.4	27 01.1	44.1	338 39.6	38.1	123 53.7	48.9	34 17.9	24.4	Hadar	148 47.0	S60 26.4
Y 15	283 33.8	42 00.3	.. 44.8	353 40.0	.. 37.9	138 56.1	.. 48.8	49 20.0	.. 24.5	Hamal	327 59.3	N23 32.0
16	298 36.3	56 59.5	45.5	8 40.4	37.6	153 58.4	48.8	64 22.2	24.6	Kaus Aust.	83 42.9	S34 22.5
17	313 38.8	71 58.7	46.1	23 40.8	37.3	169 00.7	48.7	79 24.4	24.7			
18	328 41.2	86 57.8	S20 46.8	38 41.2	S23 37.0	184 03.0	N14 48.7	94 26.5	S17 24.8	Kochab	137 21.4	N74 05.7
19	343 43.7	101 57.0	47.5	53 41.6	36.8	199 05.3	48.7	109 28.7	24.8	Markab	13 37.3	N15 17.3
20	358 46.2	116 56.2	48.2	68 42.0	36.5	214 07.6	48.6	124 30.8	24.9	Menkar	314 13.7	N 4 08.8
21	13 48.6	131 55.4	.. 48.9	83 42.4	.. 36.2	229 09.9	.. 48.6	139 33.0	.. 24.9	Menkent	148 06.8	S36 26.3
22	28 51.1	146 54.6	49.6	98 42.8	36.0	244 12.3	48.5	154 35.2	25.0	Miaplacidus	221 39.1	S69 46.5
23	43 53.5	161 53.8	50.3	113 43.2	35.7	259 14.6	48.5	169 37.3	25.1			
20 00	58 56.0	176 53.0	S20 51.0	128 43.6	S23 35.4	274 16.9	N14 48.5	184 39.5	S17 25.2	Mirfak	308 38.4	N49 54.8
01	73 58.5	191 52.1	51.6	143 44.0	35.1	289 19.2	48.4	199 41.6	25.2	Nunki	75 57.4	S26 16.5
02	89 00.9	206 51.3	52.3	158 44.4	34.9	304 21.5	48.4	214 43.8	25.3	Peacock	53 18.1	S56 41.2
03	104 03.4	221 50.5	.. 53.0	173 44.8	.. 34.6	319 23.8	.. 48.4	229 46.0	... 25.4	Pollux	243 26.4	N27 59.1
04	119 05.9	236 49.7	53.7	188 45.2	34.3	334 26.1	48.3	244 48.1	25.4	Procyon	244 58.5	N 5 11.0
05	134 08.3	251 48.9	54.4	203 45.6	34.0	349 28.5	48.3	259 50.3	25.5			
06	149 10.8	266 48.1	S20 55.0	218 46.0	S23 33.7	4 30.8	N14 48.2	274 52.4	S17 25.6	Rasalhague	96 05.9	N12 33.3
T 07	164 13.3	281 47.2	55.7	233 46.4	33.5	19 33.1	48.2	289 54.6	25.6	Regulus	207 42.5	N11 53.5
H 08	179 15.7	296 46.4	56.4	248 46.9	33.2	34 35.4	48.2	304 56.8	25.7	Rigel	281 10.8	S 8 11.2
U 09	194 18.2	311 45.6	.. 57.1	263 47.3	.. 32.9	49 37.7	.. 48.1	319 58.9	.. 25.8	Rigil Kent.	139 51.0	S60 53.5
R 10	209 20.6	326 44.8	57.7	278 47.7	32.6	64 40.0	48.1	335 01.1	25.9	Sabik	102 11.8	S15 44.3
S 11	224 23.1	341 44.0	58.4	293 48.1	32.4	79 42.4	48.0	350 03.3	25.9			
D 12	239 25.6	356 43.1	S20 59.1	308 48.5	S23 32.1	94 44.7	N14 48.0	5 05.4	S17 26.0	Schedar	349 38.9	N56 37.4
A 13	254 28.0	11 42.3	20 59.7	323 48.9	31.8	109 47.0	48.0	20 07.6	26.1	Shaula	96 21.0	S37 06.7
Y 14	269 30.5	26 41.5	21 00.4	338 49.3	31.5	124 49.3	47.9	35 09.7	26.1	Sirius	258 32.6	S16 44.3
15	284 33.0	41 40.7	.. 01.1	353 49.7	.. 31.2	139 51.6	.. 47.9	50 11.9	.. 26.2	Spica	158 30.5	S11 14.2
16	299 35.4	56 39.9	01.8	8 50.1	31.0	154 54.0	47.9	65 14.1	26.3	Suhail	222 51.6	S43 29.4
17	314 37.9	71 39.0	02.4	23 50.5	30.7	169 56.3	47.8	80 16.2	26.3			
18	329 40.4	86 38.2	S21 03.1	38 50.9	S23 30.4	184 58.6	N14 47.8	95 18.4	S17 26.4	Vega	80 38.6	N38 48.2
19	344 42.8	101 37.4	03.7	53 51.3	30.1	200 00.9	47.7	110 20.5	26.5	Zuben'ubi	137 04.7	S16 06.0
20	359 45.3	116 36.6	04.4	68 51.7	29.8	215 03.2	47.7	125 22.7	26.6		SHA	Mer.Pass.
21	14 47.8	131 35.7	.. 05.1	83 52.1	.. 29.5	230 05.6	.. 47.7	140 24.9	.. 26.6		° ′	h m
22	29 50.2	146 34.9	05.7	98 52.5	29.3	245 07.9	47.6	155 27.0	26.7	Venus	119 15.5	12 12
23	44 52.7	161 34.1	06.4	113 52.9	29.0	260 10.2	47.6	170 29.2	26.8	Mars	70 37.1	15 25
	h m									Jupiter	215 24.5	5 46
Mer.Pass. 20 04.9		v −0.8	d 0.7	v 0.4	d 0.3	v 2.3	d 0.0	v 2.2	d 0.1	Saturn	125 50.8	11 43

SUN / MOON

UT	SUN GHA	SUN Dec	MOON GHA	v	MOON Dec	d	HP
d h	° ′	° ′	° ′	′	° ′	′	′
18 00	183 44.3	S19 08.8	235 28.0	14.5	S 2 16.0	9.7	54.9
01	198 44.2	09.4	250 01.5	14.5	2 25.7	9.6	55.0
02	213 44.1	10.0	264 35.0	14.5	2 35.3	9.7	55.0
03	228 44.0	.. 10.6	279 08.5	14.4	2 45.0	9.6	55.0
04	243 43.8	11.2	293 41.9	14.4	2 54.6	9.6	55.0
05	258 43.7	11.8	308 15.3	14.4	3 04.2	9.6	55.0
06	273 43.6	S19 12.4	322 48.7	14.3	S 3 13.8	9.6	55.1
07	288 43.4	13.0	337 22.0	14.3	3 23.4	9.6	55.1
T 08	303 43.3	13.6	351 55.3	14.3	3 33.0	9.7	55.1
U 09	318 43.2	.. 14.2	6 28.6	14.2	3 42.7	9.5	55.1
E 10	333 43.0	14.8	21 01.8	14.2	3 52.2	9.6	55.1
S 11	348 42.9	15.4	35 35.0	14.2	4 01.8	9.6	55.2
D 12	3 42.8	S19 15.9	50 08.2	14.1	S 4 11.4	9.6	55.2
A 13	18 42.6	16.5	64 41.3	14.1	4 21.0	9.5	55.2
Y 14	33 42.5	17.1	79 14.4	14.0	4 30.5	9.6	55.2
15	48 42.4	.. 17.7	93 47.4	14.0	4 40.1	9.5	55.3
16	63 42.2	18.3	108 20.4	14.0	4 49.6	9.5	55.3
17	78 42.1	18.9	122 53.4	13.9	4 59.1	9.5	55.3
18	93 42.0	S19 19.5	137 26.3	13.9	S 5 08.6	9.5	55.3
19	108 41.8	20.1	151 59.2	13.8	5 18.1	9.5	55.3
20	123 41.7	20.7	166 32.0	13.8	5 27.6	9.5	55.4
21	138 41.6	.. 21.3	181 04.8	13.8	5 37.1	9.4	55.4
22	153 41.4	21.8	195 37.6	13.7	5 46.5	9.5	55.4
23	168 41.3	22.4	210 10.3	13.7	5 56.0	9.4	55.4
19 00	183 41.2	S19 23.0	224 43.0	13.6	S 6 05.4	9.4	55.5
01	198 41.0	23.6	239 15.6	13.6	6 14.8	9.3	55.5
02	213 40.9	24.2	253 48.2	13.5	6 24.1	9.4	55.5
03	228 40.7	.. 24.8	268 20.7	13.5	6 33.5	9.3	55.5
04	243 40.6	25.4	282 53.2	13.4	6 42.8	9.3	55.6
05	258 40.5	25.9	297 25.6	13.4	6 52.1	9.3	55.6
06	273 40.3	S19 26.5	311 58.0	13.3	S 7 01.4	9.3	55.6
W 07	288 40.2	27.1	326 30.3	13.3	7 10.7	9.3	55.6
E 08	303 40.0	27.7	341 02.6	13.3	7 20.0	9.2	55.6
D 09	318 39.9	.. 28.3	355 34.9	13.1	7 29.2	9.2	55.7
N 10	333 39.8	28.8	10 07.0	13.2	7 38.4	9.1	55.7
E 11	348 39.6	29.4	24 39.2	13.1	7 47.5	9.2	55.7
S 12	3 39.5	S19 30.0	39 11.3	13.0	S 7 56.7	9.1	55.7
D 13	18 39.3	30.6	53 43.3	13.0	8 05.8	9.1	55.8
A 14	33 39.2	31.2	68 15.3	12.9	8 14.9	9.1	55.8
Y 15	48 39.1	.. 31.7	82 47.2	12.9	8 24.0	9.0	55.8
16	63 38.9	32.3	97 19.1	12.8	8 33.0	9.0	55.9
17	78 38.8	32.9	111 50.9	12.7	8 42.0	8.9	55.9
18	93 38.6	S19 33.5	126 22.6	12.7	S 8 51.0	8.9	55.9
19	108 38.5	34.0	140 54.3	12.7	8 59.9	8.9	55.9
20	123 38.3	34.6	155 26.0	12.6	9 08.8	8.9	56.0
21	138 38.2	.. 35.2	169 57.6	12.5	9 17.7	8.8	56.0
22	153 38.1	35.8	184 29.1	12.5	9 26.5	8.8	56.0
23	168 37.9	36.3	199 00.6	12.4	9 35.3	8.7	56.0
20 00	183 37.8	S19 36.9	213 32.0	12.4	S 9 44.0	8.8	56.1
01	198 37.6	37.5	228 03.4	12.3	9 52.8	8.6	56.1
02	213 37.5	38.0	242 34.7	12.2	10 01.4	8.7	56.1
03	228 37.3	.. 38.6	257 05.9	12.2	10 10.1	8.6	56.1
04	243 37.2	39.2	271 37.1	12.1	10 18.7	8.5	56.2
05	258 37.0	39.8	286 08.2	12.1	10 27.2	8.6	56.2
06	273 36.9	S19 40.3	300 39.3	12.0	S10 35.8	8.4	56.2
07	288 36.7	40.9	315 10.3	11.9	10 44.2	8.5	56.2
T 08	303 36.6	41.5	329 41.2	11.9	10 52.7	8.4	56.3
H 09	318 36.4	.. 42.0	344 12.1	11.8	11 01.1	8.3	56.3
U 10	333 36.3	42.6	358 42.9	11.7	11 09.4	8.3	56.3
R 11	348 36.1	43.2	13 13.6	11.7	11 17.7	8.2	56.4
S 12	3 36.0	S19 43.7	27 44.3	11.7	S11 25.9	8.2	56.4
D 13	18 35.8	44.3	42 15.0	11.5	11 34.1	8.2	56.4
A 14	33 35.7	44.8	56 45.5	11.5	11 42.3	8.1	56.4
Y 15	48 35.5	.. 45.4	71 16.0	11.4	11 50.4	8.0	56.5
16	63 35.4	46.0	85 46.4	11.4	11 58.4	8.0	56.5
17	78 35.2	46.5	100 16.8	11.3	12 06.4	8.0	56.5
18	93 35.1	S19 47.1	114 47.1	11.3	S12 14.4	7.9	56.5
19	108 34.9	47.6	129 17.4	11.1	12 22.3	7.8	56.6
20	123 34.8	48.2	143 47.5	11.1	12 30.1	7.8	56.6
21	138 34.6	.. 48.8	158 17.6	11.1	12 37.9	7.7	56.6
22	153 34.5	49.3	172 47.7	11.0	12 45.6	7.7	56.7
23	168 34.3	49.9	187 17.7	10.9	S12 53.3	7.6	56.7
	SD 16.2	d 0.6	SD 15.0		15.2		15.4

Twilight / Sunrise / Moonrise

Lat.	Twilight Naut.	Twilight Civil	Sunrise	Moonrise 18	Moonrise 19	Moonrise 20	Moonrise 21
°	h m	h m	h m	h m	h m	h m	h m
N 72	07 13	08 53	■	02 59	04 37	06 21	08 13
N 70	07 01	08 27	10 17	02 55	04 27	06 03	07 43
68	06 52	08 07	09 31	02 51	04 18	05 48	07 21
66	06 43	07 51	09 02	02 49	04 12	05 37	07 03
64	06 36	07 38	08 40	02 46	04 06	05 27	06 49
62	06 30	07 27	08 22	02 44	04 01	05 19	06 38
60	06 25	07 17	08 07	02 42	03 56	05 12	06 28
N 58	06 20	07 09	07 55	02 41	03 52	05 05	06 19
56	06 15	07 01	07 44	02 40	03 49	05 00	06 12
54	06 11	06 55	07 35	02 38	03 46	04 55	06 05
52	06 07	06 48	07 26	02 37	03 43	04 50	05 59
50	06 03	06 43	07 19	02 36	03 41	04 46	05 53
45	05 55	06 31	07 03	02 34	03 35	04 38	05 42
N 40	05 47	06 20	06 49	02 32	03 31	04 31	05 32
35	05 40	06 11	06 38	02 31	03 27	04 24	05 24
30	05 34	06 03	06 28	02 29	03 23	04 19	05 16
20	05 21	05 48	06 11	02 27	03 17	04 10	05 04
N 10	05 08	05 34	05 56	02 25	03 12	04 01	04 53
0	04 54	05 20	05 42	02 23	03 07	03 54	04 43
S 10	04 39	05 05	05 27	02 21	03 02	03 46	04 33
20	04 20	04 48	05 12	02 19	02 57	03 38	04 22
30	03 56	04 28	04 54	02 17	02 52	03 29	04 10
35	03 41	04 15	04 44	02 15	02 48	03 24	04 03
40	03 22	04 01	04 32	02 14	02 45	03 18	03 55
45	02 59	03 43	04 17	02 12	02 40	03 11	03 46
S 50	02 26	03 20	04 00	02 10	02 35	03 03	03 35
52	02 09	03 09	03 52	02 09	02 33	02 59	03 29
54	01 48	02 56	03 42	02 08	02 30	02 55	03 24
56	01 20	02 41	03 32	02 07	02 28	02 51	03 18
58	00 32	02 23	03 20	02 06	02 25	02 46	03 11
S 60	////	02 00	03 06	02 05	02 21	02 40	03 03

Sunset / Twilight / Moonset

Lat.	Sunset	Twilight Civil	Twilight Naut.	Moonset 18	Moonset 19	Moonset 20	Moonset 21
°	h m	h m	h m	h m	h m	h m	h m
N 72	■	14 37	16 16	13 46	13 39	13 33	13 24
N 70	13 13	15 03	16 28	13 52	13 52	13 52	13 55
68	13 58	15 23	16 38	13 57	14 02	14 08	14 18
66	14 28	15 39	16 46	14 01	14 10	14 21	14 36
64	14 50	15 52	16 53	14 05	14 17	14 32	14 51
62	15 08	16 03	17 00	14 08	14 23	14 41	15 03
60	15 23	16 13	17 05	14 11	14 28	14 49	15 14
N 58	15 35	16 21	17 10	14 13	14 33	14 55	15 23
56	15 46	16 29	17 15	14 16	14 37	15 02	15 31
54	15 55	16 36	17 19	14 18	14 41	15 07	15 38
52	16 04	16 42	17 23	14 20	14 44	15 12	15 45
50	16 11	16 47	17 27	14 21	14 47	15 17	15 51
45	16 28	17 00	17 36	14 25	14 54	15 26	16 03
N 40	16 41	17 10	17 43	14 28	15 00	15 35	16 14
35	16 52	17 19	17 50	14 31	15 05	15 42	16 23
30	17 02	17 28	17 57	14 33	15 09	15 48	16 30
20	17 19	17 43	18 10	14 37	15 17	15 59	16 44
N 10	17 35	17 57	18 23	14 41	15 23	16 08	16 56
0	17 49	18 11	18 36	14 44	15 29	16 17	17 07
S 10	18 03	18 26	18 52	14 47	15 36	16 26	17 19
20	18 19	18 43	19 11	14 51	15 42	16 35	17 31
30	18 37	19 03	19 35	14 55	15 50	16 46	17 44
35	18 48	19 16	19 50	14 57	15 54	16 53	17 52
40	19 00	19 31	20 09	15 00	15 59	17 00	18 01
45	19 14	19 49	20 33	15 03	16 05	17 08	18 12
S 50	19 32	20 12	21 06	15 07	16 12	17 18	18 25
52	19 40	20 23	21 23	15 09	16 15	17 23	18 31
54	19 50	20 36	21 45	15 10	16 19	17 28	18 38
56	20 00	20 52	22 13	15 12	16 22	17 34	18 45
58	20 12	21 10	23 08	15 15	16 27	17 40	18 54
S 60	20 27	21 33	////	15 17	16 32	17 47	19 03

SUN / MOON

Day	SUN Eqn. of Time 00h	SUN Eqn. of Time 12h	SUN Mer. Pass.	MOON Mer. Pass. Upper	MOON Mer. Pass. Lower	Age	Phase
d	m s	m s	h m	h m	h m	d	%
18	14 58	14 51	11 45	08 33	20 56	26	16
19	14 45	14 38	11 45	09 18	21 41	27	10
20	14 31	14 24	11 46	10 05	22 30	28	5

UT	ARIES GHA	VENUS −3.9 GHA	Dec	MARS +1.0 GHA	Dec	JUPITER −2.2 GHA	Dec	SATURN +0.5 GHA	Dec	STARS Name	SHA	Dec
d h	° ′	° ′	° ′	° ′	° ′	° ′	° ′	° ′	° ′		° ′	° ′
21 00	59 55.1	176 33.3	S21 07.0	128 53.3	S23 28.7	275 12.5	N14 47.6	185 31.3	S17 26.8	Acamar	315 17.2	S40 14.8
01	74 57.6	191 32.4	07.7	143 53.7	28.4	290 14.9	47.5	200 33.5	26.9	Achernar	335 25.7	S57 09.9
02	90 00.1	206 31.6	08.4	158 54.1	28.1	305 17.2	47.5	215 35.7	27.0	Acrux	173 08.5	S63 10.6
03	105 02.5	221 30.8	.. 09.0	173 54.5	.. 27.8	320 19.5	.. 47.4	230 37.8	.. 27.1	Adhara	255 11.5	S28 59.6
04	120 05.0	236 29.9	09.7	188 54.9	27.5	335 21.8	47.4	245 40.0	27.1	Aldebaran	290 47.9	N16 32.2
05	135 07.5	251 29.1	10.3	203 55.3	27.3	350 24.1	47.4	260 42.1	27.2			
06	150 09.9	266 28.3	S21 11.0	218 55.7	S23 27.0	5 26.5	N14 47.3	275 44.3	S17 27.3	Alioth	166 20.4	N55 52.6
07	165 12.4	281 27.5	11.6	233 56.1	26.7	20 28.8	47.3	290 46.5	27.3	Alkaid	152 58.6	N49 14.3
08	180 14.9	296 26.6	12.3	248 56.5	26.4	35 31.1	47.3	305 48.6	27.4	Al Na'ir	27 42.6	S46 53.4
F 09	195 17.3	311 25.8	.. 12.9	263 56.9	.. 26.1	50 33.4	.. 47.2	320 50.8	.. 27.5	Alnilam	275 45.1	S 1 11.7
R 10	210 19.8	326 25.0	13.6	278 57.3	25.8	65 35.8	47.2	335 52.9	27.5	Alphard	217 55.1	S 8 43.4
I 11	225 22.3	341 24.1	14.2	293 57.7	25.5	80 38.1	47.1	350 55.1	27.6			
D 12	240 24.7	356 23.3	S21 14.9	308 58.2	S23 25.2	95 40.4	N14 47.1	5 57.3	S17 27.7	Alphecca	126 10.6	N26 40.1
A 13	255 27.2	11 22.5	15.5	323 58.6	24.9	110 42.8	47.1	20 59.4	27.8	Alpheratz	357 42.3	N29 10.6
Y 14	270 29.6	26 21.6	16.2	338 59.0	24.7	125 45.1	47.0	36 01.6	27.8	Altair	62 07.5	N 8 54.8
15	285 32.1	41 20.8	.. 16.8	353 59.4	.. 24.4	140 47.4	.. 47.0	51 03.7	.. 27.9	Ankaa	353 14.6	S42 13.6
16	300 34.6	56 20.0	17.4	8 59.8	24.1	155 49.7	47.0	66 05.9	28.0	Antares	112 25.4	S26 27.7
17	315 37.0	71 19.1	18.1	24 00.2	23.8	170 52.1	46.9	81 08.1	28.0			
18	330 39.5	86 18.3	S21 18.7	39 00.6	S23 23.5	185 54.4	N14 46.9	96 10.2	S17 28.1	Arcturus	145 55.2	N19 06.4
19	345 42.0	101 17.5	19.4	54 01.0	23.2	200 56.7	46.9	111 12.4	28.2	Atria	107 26.9	S69 03.1
20	0 44.4	116 16.6	20.0	69 01.4	22.9	215 59.0	46.8	126 14.6	28.2	Avior	234 17.2	S59 33.3
21	15 46.9	131 15.8	.. 20.6	84 01.8	.. 22.6	231 01.4	.. 46.8	141 16.7	.. 28.3	Bellatrix	278 30.7	N 6 21.6
22	30 49.4	146 14.9	21.3	99 02.2	22.3	246 03.7	46.8	156 18.9	28.4	Betelgeuse	271 00.0	N 7 24.4
23	45 51.8	161 14.1	21.9	114 02.6	22.0	261 06.0	46.7	171 21.0	28.5			
22 00	60 54.3	176 13.3	S21 22.5	129 03.0	S23 21.7	276 08.4	N14 46.7	186 23.2	S17 28.5	Canopus	263 55.2	S52 42.2
01	75 56.7	191 12.4	23.2	144 03.4	21.4	291 10.7	46.7	201 25.4	28.6	Capella	280 32.5	N46 00.5
02	90 59.2	206 11.6	23.8	159 03.8	21.1	306 13.0	46.6	216 27.5	28.7	Deneb	49 30.9	N45 20.4
03	106 01.7	221 10.8	.. 24.4	174 04.2	.. 20.8	321 15.4	.. 46.6	231 29.7	.. 28.7	Denebola	182 32.9	N14 29.3
04	121 04.1	236 09.9	25.1	189 04.6	20.5	336 17.7	46.6	246 31.8	28.8	Diphda	348 54.7	S17 54.3
05	136 06.6	251 09.1	25.7	204 05.0	20.2	351 20.0	46.5	261 34.0	28.9			
06	151 09.1	266 08.2	S21 26.3	219 05.4	S23 19.9	6 22.3	N14 46.5	276 36.2	S17 28.9	Dubhe	193 50.9	N61 39.9
07	166 11.5	281 07.4	26.9	234 05.8	19.6	21 24.7	46.5	291 38.3	29.0	Elnath	278 11.0	N28 37.0
S 08	181 14.0	296 06.5	27.6	249 06.3	19.3	36 27.0	46.4	306 40.5	29.1	Eltanin	90 46.2	N51 29.6
A 09	196 16.5	311 05.7	.. 28.2	264 06.7	.. 19.0	51 29.3	.. 46.4	321 42.6	.. 29.1	Enif	33 46.2	N 9 56.9
T 10	211 18.9	326 04.9	28.8	279 07.1	18.7	66 31.7	46.4	336 44.8	29.2	Fomalhaut	15 22.9	S29 32.6
U 11	226 21.4	341 04.0	29.4	294 07.5	18.4	81 34.0	46.3	351 47.0	29.3			
R 12	241 23.9	356 03.2	S21 30.1	309 07.9	S23 18.1	96 36.3	N14 46.3	6 49.1	S17 29.4	Gacrux	172 00.1	S57 11.5
D 13	256 26.3	11 02.3	30.7	324 08.3	17.8	111 38.7	46.3	21 51.3	29.4	Gienah	175 51.5	S17 37.3
A 14	271 28.8	26 01.5	31.3	339 08.7	17.5	126 41.0	46.2	36 53.4	29.5	Hadar	148 47.0	S60 26.4
Y 15	286 31.2	41 00.6	.. 31.9	354 09.1	.. 17.2	141 43.3	.. 46.2	51 55.6	.. 29.6	Hamal	327 59.3	N23 32.0
16	301 33.7	55 59.8	32.5	9 09.5	16.9	156 45.7	46.2	66 57.8	29.6	Kaus Aust.	83 42.9	S34 22.5
17	316 36.2	70 58.9	33.1	24 09.9	16.6	171 48.0	46.1	81 59.9	29.7			
18	331 38.6	85 58.1	S21 33.8	39 10.3	S23 16.3	186 50.3	N14 46.1	97 02.1	S17 29.8	Kochab	137 21.4	N74 05.7
19	346 41.1	100 57.3	34.4	54 10.7	16.0	201 52.7	46.1	112 04.2	29.8	Markab	13 37.3	N15 17.3
20	1 43.6	115 56.4	35.0	69 11.1	15.7	216 55.0	46.0	127 06.4	29.9	Menkar	314 13.7	N 4 08.8
21	16 46.0	130 55.6	.. 35.6	84 11.5	.. 15.4	231 57.4	.. 46.0	142 08.6	.. 30.0	Menkent	148 06.7	S36 26.3
22	31 48.5	145 54.7	36.2	99 11.9	15.1	246 59.7	46.0	157 10.7	30.1	Miaplacidus	221 39.1	S69 46.5
23	46 51.0	160 53.9	36.8	114 12.3	14.8	262 02.0	45.9	172 12.9	30.1			
23 00	61 53.4	175 53.0	S21 37.4	129 12.7	S23 14.5	277 04.4	N14 45.9	187 15.1	S17 30.2	Mirfak	308 38.4	N49 54.8
01	76 55.9	190 52.2	38.0	144 13.2	14.2	292 06.7	45.9	202 17.2	30.3	Nunki	75 57.4	S26 16.5
02	91 58.4	205 51.3	38.6	159 13.6	13.9	307 09.0	45.8	217 19.4	30.3	Peacock	53 18.1	S56 41.2
03	107 00.8	220 50.5	.. 39.2	174 14.0	.. 13.6	322 11.4	.. 45.8	232 21.5	.. 30.4	Pollux	243 26.4	N27 59.1
04	122 03.3	235 49.6	39.8	189 14.4	13.3	337 13.7	45.8	247 23.7	30.5	Procyon	244 58.5	N 5 11.0
05	137 05.7	250 48.8	40.4	204 14.8	12.9	352 16.1	45.7	262 25.9	30.5			
06	152 08.2	265 47.9	S21 41.0	219 15.2	S23 12.6	7 18.4	N14 45.7	277 28.0	S17 30.6	Rasalhague	96 05.9	N12 33.3
07	167 10.7	280 47.1	41.6	234 15.6	12.3	22 20.7	45.7	292 30.2	30.7	Regulus	207 42.5	N11 53.5
08	182 13.1	295 46.2	42.2	249 16.0	12.0	37 23.1	45.6	307 32.3	30.7	Rigel	281 10.8	S 8 11.2
S 09	197 15.6	310 45.3	.. 42.8	264 16.4	.. 11.7	52 25.4	.. 45.6	322 34.5	.. 30.8	Rigil Kent.	139 50.9	S60 53.5
U 10	212 18.1	325 44.5	43.4	279 16.8	11.4	67 27.8	45.6	337 36.7	30.9	Sabik	102 11.8	S15 44.3
N 11	227 20.5	340 43.6	44.0	294 17.2	11.1	82 30.1	45.5	352 38.8	31.0			
D 12	242 23.0	355 42.8	S21 44.6	309 17.6	S23 10.8	97 32.4	N14 45.5	7 41.0	S17 31.0	Schedar	349 38.9	N56 37.4
A 13	257 25.5	10 41.9	45.2	324 18.0	10.5	112 34.8	45.5	22 43.1	31.1	Shaula	96 21.0	S37 06.7
Y 14	272 27.9	25 41.1	45.8	339 18.4	10.2	127 37.1	45.5	37 45.3	31.2	Sirius	258 32.6	S16 44.3
15	287 30.4	40 40.2	.. 46.4	354 18.8	.. 09.8	142 39.5	.. 45.4	52 47.5	.. 31.2	Spica	158 30.5	S11 14.2
16	302 32.9	55 39.4	47.0	9 19.3	09.5	157 41.8	45.4	67 49.6	31.3	Suhail	222 51.6	S43 29.4
17	317 35.3	70 38.5	47.6	24 19.7	09.2	172 44.1	45.4	82 51.8	31.4			
18	332 37.8	85 37.6	S21 48.2	39 20.1	S23 08.9	187 46.5	N14 45.3	97 53.9	S17 31.4	Vega	80 38.6	N38 48.2
19	347 40.2	100 36.8	48.8	54 20.5	08.6	202 48.8	45.3	112 56.1	31.5	Zuben'ubi	137 04.7	S16 06.0
20	2 42.7	115 35.9	49.3	69 20.9	08.3	217 51.2	45.3	127 58.3	31.6		SHA	Mer.Pass.
21	17 45.2	130 35.1	.. 49.9	84 21.3	.. 07.9	232 53.5	.. 45.2	143 00.4	.. 31.6		° ′	h m
22	32 47.6	145 34.2	50.5	99 21.7	07.6	247 55.9	45.2	158 02.6	31.7	Venus	115 19.0	12 16
23	47 51.0	160 33.3	51.1	114 22.1	07.3	262 58.2	45.2	173 04.8	31.8	Mars	68 08.7	15 23
Mer.Pass. 19 53.1		v −0.8	d 0.6	v 0.4	d 0.3	v 2.3	d 0.0	v 2.2	d 0.1	Jupiter	215 14.1	5 35
										Saturn	125 28.9	11 33

UT	SUN GHA	SUN Dec	MOON GHA	v	MOON Dec	d	HP
d h	° ′	° ′	° ′	′	° ′	′	′
21 00	183 34.2	S19 50.4	201 47.6	10.8	S13 00.9	7.5	56.7
01	198 34.0	51.0	216 17.4	10.8	13 08.4	7.5	56.7
02	213 33.8	51.5	230 47.2	10.7	13 15.9	7.4	56.8
03	228 33.7	.. 52.1	245 16.9	10.7	13 23.3	7.4	56.8
04	243 33.5	52.7	259 46.6	10.6	13 30.7	7.3	56.8
05	258 33.4	53.2	274 16.2	10.5	13 38.0	7.2	56.8
06	273 33.2	S19 53.8	288 45.7	10.4	S13 45.2	7.2	56.9
07	288 33.1	54.3	303 15.1	10.4	13 52.4	7.1	56.9
08	303 32.9	54.9	317 44.5	10.3	13 59.5	7.0	56.9
F 09	318 32.8	.. 55.4	332 13.8	10.3	14 06.5	7.0	56.9
R 10	333 32.6	56.0	346 43.1	10.1	14 13.5	6.8	57.0
I 11	348 32.4	56.5	1 12.2	10.2	14 20.3	6.9	57.0
D 12	3 32.3	S19 57.1	15 41.4	10.0	S14 27.2	6.7	57.0
A 13	18 32.1	57.6	30 10.4	10.0	14 33.9	6.7	57.1
Y 14	33 32.0	58.2	44 39.4	9.9	14 40.6	6.6	57.1
15	48 31.8	.. 58.7	59 08.3	9.9	14 47.2	6.5	57.1
16	63 31.6	59.3	73 37.2	9.8	14 53.7	6.5	57.1
17	78 31.5	19 59.8	88 06.0	9.7	15 00.2	6.4	57.2
18	93 31.3	S20 00.3	102 34.7	9.6	S15 06.6	6.3	57.2
19	108 31.2	00.9	117 03.3	9.6	15 12.9	6.2	57.2
20	123 31.0	01.4	131 31.9	9.5	15 19.1	6.1	57.2
21	138 30.8	.. 02.0	146 00.4	9.5	15 25.2	6.1	57.3
22	153 30.7	02.5	160 28.9	9.4	15 31.3	6.0	57.3
23	168 30.5	03.1	174 57.3	9.3	15 37.3	5.9	57.3
22 00	183 30.4	S20 03.6	189 25.6	9.3	S15 43.2	5.8	57.3
01	198 30.2	04.1	203 53.9	9.2	15 49.0	5.7	57.4
02	213 30.0	04.7	218 22.1	9.1	15 54.7	5.7	57.4
03	228 29.9	.. 05.2	232 50.2	9.1	16 00.4	5.6	57.4
04	243 29.7	05.8	247 18.3	9.0	16 06.0	5.4	57.4
05	258 29.5	06.3	261 46.3	8.9	16 11.4	5.4	57.5
06	273 29.4	S20 06.8	276 14.2	8.9	S16 16.8	5.3	57.5
S 07	288 29.2	07.4	290 42.1	8.9	16 22.1	5.2	57.5
A 08	303 29.0	07.9	305 10.0	8.7	16 27.3	5.2	57.6
T 09	318 28.9	.. 08.5	319 37.7	8.7	16 32.5	5.0	57.6
U 10	333 28.7	09.0	334 05.4	8.7	16 37.5	4.9	57.6
R 11	348 28.5	09.5	348 33.1	8.5	16 42.4	4.9	57.6
D 12	3 28.4	S20 10.1	3 00.6	8.6	S16 47.3	4.7	57.6
A 13	18 28.2	10.6	17 28.2	8.4	16 52.0	4.7	57.7
Y 14	33 28.0	11.1	31 55.6	8.4	16 56.7	4.6	57.7
15	48 27.9	.. 11.7	46 23.0	8.4	17 01.3	4.4	57.7
16	63 27.7	12.2	60 50.4	8.3	17 05.7	4.4	57.7
17	78 27.5	12.7	75 17.7	8.2	17 10.1	4.3	57.8
18	93 27.4	S20 13.2	89 44.9	8.2	S17 14.4	4.1	57.8
19	108 27.2	13.8	104 12.1	8.1	17 18.5	4.1	57.8
20	123 27.0	14.3	118 39.2	8.1	17 22.6	4.0	57.8
21	138 26.9	.. 14.8	133 06.3	8.0	17 26.6	3.9	57.9
22	153 26.7	15.4	147 33.3	8.0	17 30.5	3.7	57.9
23	168 26.5	15.9	162 00.3	7.9	17 34.2	3.7	57.9
23 00	183 26.4	S20 16.4	176 27.2	7.8	S17 37.9	3.6	57.9
01	198 26.2	16.9	190 54.0	7.8	17 41.5	3.4	58.0
02	213 26.0	17.5	205 20.8	7.8	17 44.9	3.4	58.0
03	228 25.8	.. 18.0	219 47.6	7.7	17 48.3	3.3	58.0
04	243 25.7	18.5	234 14.3	7.7	17 51.6	3.1	58.0
05	258 25.5	19.0	248 41.0	7.6	17 54.7	3.0	58.0
06	273 25.3	S20 19.6	263 07.6	7.6	S17 57.7	3.0	58.1
07	288 25.1	20.1	277 34.2	7.5	18 00.7	2.8	58.1
08	303 25.0	20.6	292 00.7	7.5	18 03.5	2.7	58.1
S 09	318 24.8	.. 21.1	306 27.2	7.4	18 06.2	2.6	58.1
U 10	333 24.6	21.6	320 53.6	7.4	18 08.8	2.5	58.2
N 11	348 24.4	22.2	335 20.0	7.3	18 11.3	2.4	58.2
D 12	3 24.3	S20 22.7	349 46.3	7.3	S18 13.7	2.3	58.2
A 13	18 24.1	23.2	4 12.6	7.3	18 16.0	2.2	58.2
Y 14	33 23.9	23.7	18 38.9	7.2	18 18.2	2.0	58.2
15	48 23.7	.. 24.2	33 05.1	7.2	18 20.2	1.9	58.3
16	63 23.6	24.7	47 31.3	7.2	18 22.1	1.9	58.3
17	78 23.4	25.3	61 57.5	7.1	18 24.0	1.7	58.3
18	93 23.2	S20 25.8	76 23.6	7.1	S18 25.7	1.6	58.3
19	108 23.0	26.3	90 49.7	7.0	18 27.3	1.5	58.3
20	123 22.9	26.8	105 15.7	7.1	18 28.8	1.3	58.4
21	138 22.7	.. 27.3	119 41.8	6.9	18 30.1	1.3	58.4
22	153 22.5	27.8	134 07.7	7.0	18 31.4	1.1	58.4
23	168 22.3	28.3	148 33.7	6.9	S18 32.5	1.1	58.4
	SD 16.2	d 0.5	SD 15.5		15.7		15.9

Twilight / Sunrise / Moonrise

Lat.	Naut.	Civil	Sunrise	21	22	23	24
°	h m	h m	h m	h m	h m	h m	h m
N 72	07 23	09 07	■■■		08 13	10 17	■■■	■■■
N 70	07 10	08 38	10 44	07 43	09 25	11 01	12 11
68	07 00	08 16	09 46	07 21	08 52	10 17	11 23
66	06 51	07 59	09 13	07 03	08 29	09 48	10 52
64	06 43	07 45	08 49	06 49	08 11	09 26	10 29
62	06 36	07 34	08 30	06 38	07 56	09 08	10 10
60	06 30	07 23	08 15	06 28	07 43	08 53	09 55
N 58	06 25	07 14	08 02	06 19	07 32	08 41	09 42
56	06 20	07 07	07 50	06 12	07 23	08 30	09 31
54	06 15	06 59	07 40	06 05	07 14	08 21	09 21
52	06 11	06 53	07 31	05 59	07 07	08 12	09 12
50	06 07	06 47	07 24	05 53	07 00	08 05	09 04
45	05 58	06 34	07 07	05 42	06 46	07 48	08 48
N 40	05 50	06 23	06 53	05 32	06 34	07 35	08 34
35	05 43	06 14	06 41	05 24	06 24	07 24	08 22
30	05 36	06 05	06 31	05 16	06 15	07 14	08 12
20	05 23	05 49	06 13	05 04	06 00	06 57	07 55
N 10	05 09	05 35	05 57	04 53	05 47	06 43	07 40
0	04 55	05 20	05 42	04 43	05 35	06 29	07 26
S 10	04 39	05 05	05 28	04 33	05 23	06 16	07 11
20	04 19	04 48	05 12	04 22	05 10	06 01	06 56
30	03 55	04 27	04 53	04 10	04 55	05 44	06 39
35	03 39	04 14	04 42	04 03	04 46	05 35	06 29
40	03 20	03 58	04 30	03 55	04 37	05 24	06 17
45	02 55	03 40	04 15	03 46	04 25	05 11	06 04
S 50	02 21	03 16	03 56	03 35	04 12	04 55	05 48
52	02 03	03 04	03 48	03 29	04 05	04 48	05 40
54	01 40	02 51	03 38	03 24	03 58	04 40	05 31
56	01 07	02 35	03 27	03 18	03 50	04 31	05 22
58	////	02 15	03 14	03 11	03 41	04 21	05 11
S 60	////	01 51	02 59	03 03	03 31	04 09	04 58

Sunset / Twilight / Moonset

Lat.	Sunset	Civil	Naut.	21	22	23	24
°	h m	h m	h m	h m	h m	h m	h m
N 72	■■■	14 24	16 08	13 24	13 09	■■■	■■■
N 70	12 48	14 53	16 21	13 55	14 02	14 20	15 08
68	13 45	15 15	16 32	14 18	14 35	15 05	15 57
66	14 18	15 32	16 41	14 36	14 59	15 34	16 28
64	14 42	15 46	16 48	14 51	15 18	15 56	16 51
62	15 01	15 58	16 55	15 03	15 33	16 14	17 09
60	15 17	16 08	17 01	15 14	15 46	16 29	17 24
N 58	15 30	16 17	17 07	15 23	15 57	16 42	17 37
56	15 41	16 25	17 12	15 31	16 07	16 53	17 48
54	15 51	16 32	17 16	15 38	16 16	17 02	17 58
52	16 00	16 39	17 21	15 45	16 24	17 11	18 07
50	16 08	16 45	17 25	15 51	16 31	17 18	18 15
45	16 25	16 58	17 34	16 03	16 46	17 35	18 31
N 40	16 39	17 09	17 42	16 14	16 58	17 48	18 45
35	16 51	17 18	17 49	16 23	17 08	18 00	18 56
30	17 01	17 27	17 56	16 30	17 18	18 10	19 06
20	17 19	17 43	18 10	16 44	17 34	18 27	19 24
N 10	17 35	17 57	18 23	16 56	17 47	18 42	19 39
0	17 50	18 12	18 37	17 07	18 00	18 56	19 53
S 10	18 05	18 27	18 54	17 19	18 13	19 10	20 07
20	18 21	18 45	19 13	17 31	18 27	19 25	20 22
30	18 40	19 06	19 38	17 44	18 43	19 42	20 39
35	18 50	19 19	19 54	17 52	18 53	19 52	20 49
40	19 03	19 34	20 13	18 01	19 03	20 03	21 00
45	19 18	19 53	20 38	18 12	19 16	20 17	21 14
S 50	19 37	20 17	21 13	18 25	19 31	20 33	21 30
52	19 45	20 29	21 32	18 31	19 38	20 41	21 37
54	19 55	20 43	21 55	18 39	19 46	20 49	21 46
56	20 06	20 59	22 29	18 45	19 55	20 59	21 55
58	20 19	21 19	////	18 54	20 05	21 10	22 06
S 60	20 34	21 44	////	19 03	20 16	21 22	22 19

SUN / MOON

Day	Eqn. of Time 00h	12h	Mer. Pass.	Mer. Pass. Upper	Lower	Age	Phase
d	m s	m s	h m	h m	h m	d	%
21	14 17	14 09	11 46	10 55	23 21	29	1
22	14 02	13 54	11 46	11 48	24 15	30	0
23	13 46	13 37	11 46	12 43	00 15	01	1

UT	ARIES GHA	VENUS −3.9 GHA	VENUS Dec	MARS +1.0 GHA	MARS Dec	JUPITER −2.2 GHA	JUPITER Dec	SATURN +0.5 GHA	SATURN Dec	Name	SHA	Dec
24 00	62 52.6	175 32.5	S21 51.7	129 22.5	S23 07.0	278 00.6	N14 45.2	188 06.9	S17 31.9	Acamar	315 17.2	S40 14.9
01	77 55.0	190 31.6	52.3	144 22.9	06.7	293 02.9	45.1	203 09.1	31.9	Achernar	335 25.7	S57 09.9
02	92 57.5	205 30.8	52.8	159 23.3	06.4	308 05.2	45.1	218 11.2	32.0	Acrux	173 08.4	S63 10.6
03	108 00.0	220 29.9 ..	53.4	174 23.7 ..	06.0	323 07.6 ..	45.1	233 13.4 ..	32.1	Adhara	255 11.5	S28 59.6
04	123 02.4	235 29.0	54.0	189 24.2	05.7	338 09.9	45.0	248 15.6	32.1	Aldebaran	290 47.9	N16 32.2
05	138 04.9	250 28.2	54.6	204 24.6	05.4	353 12.3	45.0	263 17.7	32.2			
06	153 07.4	265 27.3	S21 55.1	219 25.0	S23 05.1	8 14.6	N14 45.0	278 19.9	S17 32.3	Alioth	166 20.3	N55 52.6
07	168 09.8	280 26.4	55.7	234 25.4	04.8	23 17.0	44.9	293 22.0	32.3	Alkaid	152 58.6	N49 14.3
M 08	183 12.3	295 25.6	56.3	249 25.8	04.4	38 19.3	44.9	308 24.2	32.4	Al Na'ir	27 42.6	S46 53.4
O 09	198 14.7	310 24.7 ..	56.9	264 26.2 ..	04.1	53 21.7 ..	44.9	323 26.4 ..	32.5	Alnilam	275 45.1	S 1 11.7
N 10	213 17.2	325 23.9	57.4	279 26.6	03.8	68 24.0	44.9	338 28.5	32.5	Alphard	217 55.0	S 8 43.4
D 11	228 19.7	340 23.0	58.0	294 27.0	03.5	83 26.4	44.8	353 30.7	32.6			
A 12	243 22.1	355 22.1	S21 58.6	309 27.4	S23 03.2	98 28.7	N14 44.8	8 32.8	S17 32.7	Alphecca	126 10.6	N26 40.0
Y 13	258 24.6	10 21.3	59.1	324 27.8	02.8	113 31.1	44.8	23 35.0	32.8	Alpheratz	357 42.3	N29 10.6
14	273 27.1	25 20.4	21 59.7	339 28.2	02.5	128 33.4	44.7	38 37.2	32.8	Altair	62 07.5	N 8 54.8
15	288 29.5	40 19.5	22 00.3	354 28.6 ..	02.2	143 35.8 ..	44.7	53 39.3 ..	32.9	Ankaa	353 14.6	S42 13.6
16	303 32.0	55 18.7	00.8	9 29.1	01.9	158 38.1	44.7	68 41.5	33.0	Antares	112 25.4	S26 27.7
17	318 34.5	70 17.8	01.4	24 29.5	01.5	173 40.5	44.7	83 43.6	33.0			
18	333 36.9	85 16.9	S22 01.9	39 29.9	S23 01.2	188 42.8	N14 44.6	98 45.8	S17 33.1	Arcturus	145 55.2	N19 06.4
19	348 39.4	100 16.0	02.5	54 30.3	00.9	203 45.2	44.6	113 48.0	33.2	Atria	107 26.9	S69 03.1
20	3 41.8	115 15.2	03.1	69 30.7	00.6	218 47.5	44.6	128 50.1	33.2	Avior	234 17.2	S59 33.3
21	18 44.3	130 14.3 ..	03.6	84 31.1	23 00.2	233 49.9 ..	44.6	143 52.3 ..	33.3	Bellatrix	278 30.6	N 6 21.6
22	33 46.8	145 13.4	04.2	99 31.5	22 59.9	248 52.2	44.5	158 54.5	33.4	Betelgeuse	270 59.9	N 7 24.4
23	48 49.2	160 12.6	04.7	114 31.9	59.5	263 54.6	44.5	173 56.6	33.4			
25 00	63 51.7	175 11.7	S22 05.3	129 32.3	S22 59.3	278 56.9	N14 44.5	188 58.8	S17 33.5	Canopus	263 55.2	S52 42.2
01	78 54.2	190 10.8	05.8	144 32.7	58.9	293 59.3	44.4	204 00.9	33.6	Capella	280 32.5	N46 00.5
02	93 56.6	205 09.9	06.4	159 33.2	58.6	309 01.6	44.4	219 03.1	33.6	Deneb	49 31.0	N45 20.4
03	108 59.1	220 09.1 ..	06.9	174 33.6 ..	58.3	324 04.0 ..	44.4	234 05.3 ..	33.7	Denebola	182 32.8	N14 29.3
04	124 01.6	235 08.2	07.5	189 34.0	57.9	339 06.3	44.4	249 07.4	33.8	Diphda	348 54.7	S17 54.3
05	139 04.0	250 07.3	08.0	204 34.4	57.6	354 08.7	44.3	264 09.6	33.9			
06	154 06.5	265 06.5	S22 08.6	219 34.8	S22 57.3	9 11.0	N14 44.3	279 11.7	S17 33.9	Dubhe	193 50.8	N61 39.9
07	169 09.0	280 05.6	09.1	234 35.2	57.0	24 13.4	44.3	294 13.9	34.0	Elnath	278 11.0	N28 37.0
T 08	184 11.4	295 04.7	09.7	249 35.6	56.6	39 15.7	44.3	309 16.1	34.1	Eltanin	90 46.2	N51 29.6
U 09	199 13.9	310 03.8 ..	10.2	264 36.0 ..	56.3	54 18.1 ..	44.2	324 18.2 ..	34.1	Enif	33 46.2	N 9 56.9
E 10	214 16.3	325 03.0	10.8	279 36.4	56.0	69 20.5	44.2	339 20.4	34.2	Fomalhaut	15 22.9	S29 32.6
S 11	229 18.8	340 02.1	11.3	294 36.8	55.6	84 22.8	44.2	354 22.5	34.3			
D 12	244 21.3	355 01.2	S22 11.9	309 37.3	S22 55.3	99 25.2	N14 44.2	9 24.7	S17 34.3	Gacrux	172 00.0	S57 11.5
A 13	259 23.7	10 00.3	12.4	324 37.7	55.0	114 27.5	44.1	24 26.9	34.4	Gienah	175 51.4	S17 37.3
Y 14	274 26.2	24 59.4	12.9	339 38.1	54.6	129 29.9	44.1	39 29.0	34.5	Hadar	148 46.9	S60 26.4
15	289 28.7	39 58.6 ..	13.5	354 38.5 ..	54.3	144 32.2 ..	44.1	54 31.2 ..	34.5	Hamal	327 59.3	N23 32.0
16	304 31.1	54 57.7	14.0	9 38.9	54.0	159 34.6	44.1	69 33.4	34.6	Kaus Aust.	83 42.9	S34 22.5
17	319 33.6	69 56.8	14.5	24 39.3	53.6	174 37.0	44.0	84 35.5	34.7			
18	334 36.1	84 55.9	S22 15.1	39 39.7	S22 53.3	189 39.3	N14 44.0	99 37.7	S17 34.7	Kochab	137 21.4	N74 05.6
19	349 38.5	99 55.1	15.6	54 40.1	52.9	204 41.7	44.0	114 39.8	34.8	Markab	13 37.3	N15 17.3
20	4 41.0	114 54.2	16.1	69 40.5	52.6	219 44.0	44.0	129 42.0	34.9	Menkar	314 13.7	N 4 08.8
21	19 43.5	129 53.3 ..	16.7	84 41.0 ..	52.3	234 46.4 ..	43.9	144 44.2 ..	35.0	Menkent	148 06.7	S36 26.3
22	34 45.9	144 52.4	17.2	99 41.4	51.9	249 48.8	43.9	159 46.3	35.0	Miaplacidus	221 39.0	S69 46.5
23	49 48.4	159 51.5	17.7	114 41.8	51.6	264 51.1	43.9	174 48.5	35.1			
26 00	64 50.8	174 50.7	S22 18.3	129 42.2	S22 51.3	279 53.5	N14 43.9	189 50.6	S17 35.2	Mirfak	308 38.4	N49 54.8
01	79 53.3	189 49.8	18.8	144 42.6	50.9	294 55.8	43.8	204 52.8	35.2	Nunki	75 57.4	S26 16.5
02	94 55.8	204 48.9	19.3	159 43.0	50.6	309 58.2	43.8	219 55.0	35.3	Peacock	53 18.1	S56 41.2
03	109 58.2	219 48.0 ..	19.8	174 43.4 ..	50.2	325 00.6 ..	43.8	234 57.1 ..	35.4	Pollux	243 26.3	N27 59.1
04	125 00.7	234 47.1	20.4	189 43.8	49.9	340 02.9	43.8	249 59.3	35.4	Procyon	244 58.5	N 5 11.0
05	140 03.2	249 46.2	20.9	204 44.3	49.6	355 05.3	43.7	265 01.5	35.5			
06	155 05.6	264 45.4	S22 21.4	219 44.7	S22 49.2	10 07.6	N14 43.7	280 03.6	S17 35.6	Rasalhague	96 05.9	N12 33.2
W 07	170 08.1	279 44.5	21.9	234 45.1	48.9	25 10.0	43.7	295 05.8	35.6	Regulus	207 42.5	N11 53.5
E 08	185 10.6	294 43.6	22.4	249 45.5	48.5	40 12.4	43.7	310 07.9	35.7	Rigel	281 10.8	S 8 11.2
D 09	200 13.0	309 42.7 ..	23.0	264 45.9 ..	48.2	55 14.7 ..	43.6	325 10.1 ..	35.8	Rigil Kent.	139 50.9	S60 53.5
N 10	215 15.5	324 41.8	23.5	279 46.3	47.9	70 17.1	43.6	340 12.3	35.8	Sabik	102 11.8	S15 44.3
E 11	230 18.0	339 40.9	24.0	294 46.7	47.5	85 19.5	43.6	355 14.4	35.9			
S 12	245 20.4	354 40.0	S22 24.5	309 47.1	S22 47.2	100 21.8	N14 43.6	10 16.6	S17 36.0	Schedar	349 38.9	N56 37.4
D 13	260 22.9	9 39.2	25.0	324 47.6	46.8	115 24.2	43.5	25 18.7	36.0	Shaula	96 21.0	S37 06.7
A 14	275 25.3	24 38.3	25.5	339 48.0	46.5	130 26.5	43.5	40 20.9	36.1	Sirius	258 32.6	S16 44.3
Y 15	290 27.8	39 37.4 ..	26.0	354 48.4 ..	46.1	145 28.9 ..	43.5	55 23.1 ..	36.2	Spica	158 30.5	S11 14.2
16	305 30.3	54 36.5	26.5	9 48.8	45.8	160 31.3	43.5	70 25.2	36.2	Suhail	222 51.5	S43 29.5
17	320 32.7	69 35.6	27.0	24 49.2	45.4	175 33.6	43.5	85 27.4	36.3			
18	335 35.2	84 34.7	S22 27.6	39 49.6	S22 45.1	190 36.0	N14 43.4	100 29.6	S17 36.4	Vega	80 38.7	N38 48.2
19	350 37.7	99 33.8	28.1	54 50.0	44.8	205 38.4	43.4	115 31.7	36.5	Zuben'ubi	137 04.6	S16 06.0
20	5 40.1	114 32.9	28.6	69 50.4	44.4	220 40.7	43.4	130 33.9	36.5			
21	20 42.6	129 32.0 ..	29.1	84 50.9 ..	44.1	235 43.1 ..	43.4	145 36.0 ..	36.6			
22	35 45.1	144 31.2	29.6	99 51.3	43.7	250 45.5	43.3	160 38.2	36.7			
23	50 47.5	159 30.3	30.1	114 51.7	43.4	265 47.8	43.3	175 40.4	36.7			
Mer. Pass. 19 41.3		*v* −0.9	*d* 0.5	*v* 0.4	*d* 0.3	*v* 2.4	*d* 0.0	*v* 2.2	*d* 0.1			

	SHA	Dec
Venus	111 20.0	Mer.Pass. 12 20
Mars	65 40.6	15 21
Jupiter	215 05.2	5 23
Saturn	125 07.1	11 22

UT	SUN GHA	SUN Dec	MOON GHA	v	Dec	d	HP
24 00	183 22.1	S20 28.8	162 59.6	6.9	S18 33.6	0.9	58.4
01	198 22.0	29.4	177 25.5	6.9	18 34.5	0.8	58.5
02	213 21.8	29.9	191 51.4	6.8	18 35.3	0.6	58.5
03	228 21.6	.. 30.4	206 17.2	6.8	18 35.9	0.6	58.5
04	243 21.4	30.9	220 43.0	6.8	18 36.5	0.4	58.5
05	258 21.3	31.4	235 08.8	6.8	18 36.9	0.4	58.5
06	273 21.1	S20 31.9	249 34.6	6.8	S18 37.3	0.2	58.5
07	288 20.9	32.4	264 00.4	6.7	18 37.5	0.2	58.6
08	303 20.7	32.9	278 26.1	6.7	18 37.5	0.0	58.6
M 09	318 20.5	.. 33.4	292 51.8	6.7	18 37.5	0.1	58.6
O 10	333 20.3	33.9	307 17.5	6.6	18 37.4	0.3	58.6
N 11	348 20.2	34.4	321 43.1	6.7	18 37.1	0.4	58.6
D 12	3 20.0	S20 34.9	336 08.8	6.6	S18 36.7	0.5	58.6
A 13	18 19.8	35.4	350 34.4	6.7	18 36.2	0.6	58.7
Y 14	33 19.6	35.9	5 00.1	6.6	18 35.6	0.8	58.7
15	48 19.4	.. 36.4	19 25.7	6.6	18 34.8	0.9	58.7
16	63 19.2	36.9	33 51.3	6.6	18 33.9	0.9	58.7
17	78 19.1	37.4	48 16.9	6.6	18 33.0	1.2	58.7
18	93 18.9	S20 37.9	62 42.5	6.5	S18 31.8	1.2	58.7
19	108 18.7	38.4	77 08.0	6.6	18 30.6	1.3	58.8
20	123 18.5	38.9	91 33.6	6.6	18 29.3	1.5	58.8
21	138 18.3	.. 39.4	105 59.2	6.5	18 27.8	1.6	58.8
22	153 18.1	39.9	120 24.7	6.6	18 26.2	1.7	58.8
23	168 17.9	40.4	134 50.3	6.5	18 24.5	1.8	58.8
25 00	183 17.8	S20 40.9	149 15.8	6.6	S18 22.7	1.9	58.8
01	198 17.6	41.4	163 41.4	6.5	18 20.8	2.1	58.8
02	213 17.4	41.9	178 06.9	6.6	18 18.7	2.2	58.9
03	228 17.2	.. 42.4	192 32.5	6.6	18 16.5	2.3	58.9
04	243 17.0	42.9	206 58.1	6.5	18 14.2	2.4	58.9
05	258 16.8	43.4	221 23.6	6.6	18 11.8	2.5	58.9
06	273 16.6	S20 43.8	235 49.2	6.5	S18 09.3	2.7	58.9
07	288 16.4	44.3	250 14.7	6.6	18 06.6	2.8	58.9
08	303 16.3	44.8	264 40.3	6.6	18 03.8	2.8	58.9
T 09	318 16.1	.. 45.3	279 05.9	6.6	18 01.0	3.1	58.9
U 10	333 15.9	45.8	293 31.5	6.6	17 57.9	3.1	59.0
E 11	348 15.7	46.3	307 57.1	6.6	17 54.8	3.2	59.0
S 12	3 15.5	S20 46.8	322 22.7	6.6	S17 51.6	3.4	59.0
D 13	18 15.3	47.3	336 48.3	6.7	17 48.2	3.4	59.0
A 14	33 15.1	47.7	351 14.0	6.6	17 44.8	3.6	59.0
Y 15	48 14.9	.. 48.2	5 39.6	6.7	17 41.2	3.7	59.0
16	63 14.7	48.7	20 05.3	6.6	17 37.5	3.8	59.0
17	78 14.5	49.2	34 30.9	6.7	17 33.7	4.0	59.0
18	93 14.3	S20 49.7	48 56.6	6.7	S17 29.7	4.0	59.0
19	108 14.1	50.2	63 22.3	6.8	17 25.7	4.2	59.1
20	123 14.0	50.6	77 48.1	6.7	17 21.5	4.2	59.1
21	138 13.8	.. 51.1	92 13.8	6.8	17 17.3	4.4	59.1
22	153 13.6	51.6	106 39.6	6.8	17 12.9	4.5	59.1
23	168 13.4	52.1	121 05.4	6.8	17 08.4	4.6	59.1
26 00	183 13.2	S20 52.6	135 31.2	6.8	S17 03.8	4.7	59.1
01	198 13.0	53.0	149 57.0	6.9	16 59.1	4.8	59.1
02	213 12.8	53.5	164 22.9	6.9	16 54.3	5.0	59.1
03	228 12.6	.. 54.0	178 48.8	6.9	16 49.3	5.0	59.1
04	243 12.4	54.5	193 14.7	6.9	16 44.3	5.1	59.1
05	258 12.2	54.9	207 40.6	7.0	16 39.2	5.3	59.1
06	273 12.0	S20 55.4	222 06.6	7.0	S16 33.9	5.4	59.1
07	288 11.8	55.9	236 32.6	7.0	16 28.5	5.4	59.2
W 08	303 11.6	56.4	250 58.6	7.0	16 23.1	5.6	59.2
E 09	318 11.4	.. 56.8	265 24.6	7.1	16 17.5	5.7	59.2
D 10	333 11.2	57.3	279 50.7	7.1	16 11.8	5.7	59.2
N 11	348 11.0	57.8	294 16.8	7.1	16 06.1	5.9	59.2
E 12	3 10.8	S20 58.3	308 42.9	7.2	S16 00.2	6.0	59.2
S 13	18 10.6	58.7	323 09.1	7.2	15 54.2	6.1	59.2
D 14	33 10.4	59.2	337 35.3	7.2	15 48.1	6.2	59.2
A 15	48 10.2	20 59.7	352 01.5	7.3	15 41.9	6.3	59.2
Y 16	63 10.0	21 00.1	6 27.8	7.3	15 35.6	6.4	59.2
17	78 09.8	00.6	20 54.1	7.3	15 29.2	6.4	59.2
18	93 09.6	S21 01.1	35 20.4	7.3	S15 22.8	6.6	59.2
19	108 09.4	01.5	49 46.7	7.4	15 16.2	6.7	59.2
20	123 09.2	02.0	64 13.1	7.5	15 09.5	6.8	59.2
21	138 09.0	.. 02.5	78 39.6	7.4	15 02.7	6.8	59.2
22	153 08.8	02.9	93 06.0	7.5	14 55.9	7.0	59.2
23	168 08.6	03.4	107 32.5	7.6	S14 48.9	7.1	59.2
	SD 16.2	d 0.5	SD 16.0		16.1		16.1

Lat.	Twilight Naut.	Civil	Sunrise	Moonrise 24	25	26	27
°	h m	h m	h m	h m	h m	h m	h m
N 72	07 33	09 21	■	■	14 09	13 36	13 25
N 70	07 19	08 49	11 29	12 11	12 44	12 56	13 01
68	07 07	08 26	10 02	11 23	12 05	12 29	12 43
66	06 58	08 08	09 25	10 52	11 38	12 08	12 28
64	06 49	07 53	08 58	10 29	11 17	11 51	12 15
62	06 42	07 40	08 38	10 10	11 00	11 37	12 05
60	06 36	07 29	08 22	09 55	10 45	11 25	11 56
N 58	06 30	07 20	08 08	09 42	10 33	11 15	11 48
56	06 25	07 12	07 56	09 31	10 23	11 06	11 41
54	06 20	07 04	07 46	09 21	10 14	10 58	11 34
52	06 15	06 57	07 36	09 12	10 05	10 50	11 29
50	06 11	06 51	07 28	09 04	09 58	10 44	11 24
45	06 02	06 38	07 10	08 48	09 42	10 30	11 12
N 40	05 53	06 26	06 56	08 34	09 29	10 18	11 03
35	05 45	06 16	06 44	08 22	09 18	10 09	10 55
30	05 38	06 07	06 33	08 12	09 08	10 00	10 48
20	05 24	05 51	06 15	07 55	08 51	09 45	10 36
N 10	05 10	05 36	05 59	07 40	08 37	09 32	10 25
0	04 55	05 21	05 43	07 26	08 23	09 20	10 15
S 10	04 39	05 05	05 28	07 11	08 09	09 07	10 05
20	04 19	04 47	05 11	06 56	07 54	08 54	09 55
30	03 53	04 26	04 52	06 39	07 38	08 39	09 43
35	03 37	04 12	04 41	06 29	07 28	08 31	09 35
40	03 17	03 56	04 28	06 17	07 17	08 21	09 27
45	02 52	03 37	04 13	06 04	07 04	08 09	09 18
S 50	02 16	03 12	03 53	05 48	06 48	07 55	09 06
52	01 56	03 00	03 44	05 40	06 40	07 48	09 01
54	01 31	02 46	03 34	05 31	06 32	07 41	08 55
56	00 54	02 29	03 23	05 22	06 23	07 33	08 49
58	////	02 08	03 09	05 11	06 12	07 23	08 41
S 60	////	01 41	02 54	04 58	06 00	07 13	08 33

Lat.	Sunset	Twilight Civil	Naut.	Moonset 24	25	26	27
°	h m	h m	h m	h m	h m	h m	h m
N 72	■	14 12	16 00	■	15 11	17 42	19 48
N 70	12 04	14 44	16 14	15 08	16 35	18 21	20 11
68	13 31	15 07	16 26	15 57	17 14	18 48	20 29
66	14 09	15 26	16 35	16 28	17 41	19 08	20 43
64	14 35	15 41	16 44	16 51	18 01	19 24	20 54
62	14 55	15 53	16 51	17 09	18 18	19 38	21 04
60	15 12	16 04	16 58	17 24	18 32	19 49	21 12
N 58	15 26	16 13	17 03	17 37	18 44	19 59	21 19
56	15 37	16 22	17 09	17 48	18 54	20 08	21 26
54	15 48	16 29	17 14	17 58	19 03	20 15	21 31
52	15 57	16 36	17 18	18 07	19 11	20 22	21 37
50	16 05	16 42	17 22	18 15	19 18	20 28	21 41
45	16 23	16 56	17 32	18 31	19 34	20 41	21 51
N 40	16 37	17 07	17 40	18 45	19 47	20 52	21 59
35	16 50	17 17	17 48	18 56	19 57	21 01	22 07
30	17 01	17 26	17 56	19 06	20 07	21 09	22 13
20	17 19	17 43	18 10	19 24	20 23	21 23	22 23
N 10	17 35	17 58	18 24	19 39	20 37	21 35	22 33
0	17 51	18 13	18 38	19 53	20 50	21 46	22 41
S 10	18 06	18 29	18 55	20 07	21 03	21 58	22 50
20	18 23	18 47	19 15	20 22	21 17	22 10	22 59
30	18 42	19 09	19 41	20 39	21 33	22 23	23 09
35	18 53	19 22	19 57	20 49	21 42	22 31	23 15
40	19 06	19 38	20 17	21 00	21 53	22 40	23 22
45	19 22	19 58	20 43	21 14	22 05	22 50	23 30
S 50	19 41	20 23	21 20	21 30	22 20	23 02	23 39
52	19 50	20 35	21 40	21 37	22 27	23 08	23 44
54	20 01	20 49	22 05	21 46	22 34	23 14	23 48
56	20 12	21 07	22 45	21 55	22 43	23 21	23 53
58	20 26	21 28	////	22 06	22 52	23 29	23 59
S 60	20 42	21 55	////	22 19	23 03	23 38	24 06

	SUN			MOON			
Day	Eqn. of Time 00h	12h	Mer. Pass.	Mer. Pass. Upper	Lower	Age	Phase
d	m s	m s	h m	h m	h m	d	%
24	13 29	13 20	11 47	13 39	01 11	02	5
25	13 11	13 02	11 47	14 36	02 08	03	11
26	12 53	12 44	11 47	15 33	03 05	04	19

UT (d h)	ARIES GHA	VENUS −3.9 GHA	VENUS Dec	MARS +1.0 GHA	MARS Dec	JUPITER −2.2 GHA	JUPITER Dec	SATURN +0.5 GHA	SATURN Dec	Star Name	SHA	Dec
27 00	65 50.0	174 29.4	S22 30.6	129 52.1	S22 43.0	280 50.2	N14 43.3	190 42.5	S17 36.8	Acamar	315 17.2	S40 14.9
01	80 52.5	189 28.5	31.1	144 52.5	42.7	295 52.6	43.3	205 44.7	36.9	Achernar	335 25.7	S57 09.9
02	95 54.9	204 27.6	31.6	159 52.9	42.3	310 54.9	43.3	220 46.8	36.9	Acrux	173 08.4	S63 10.6
03	110 57.4	219 26.7 ..	32.1	174 53.3 ..	42.0	325 57.3 ..	43.2	235 49.0 ..	37.0	Adhara	255 11.4	S28 59.6
04	125 59.8	234 25.8	32.6	189 53.8	41.6	340 59.7	43.2	250 51.2	37.1	Aldebaran	290 47.9	N16 32.2
05	141 02.3	249 24.9	33.1	204 54.2	41.3	356 02.0	43.2	265 53.3	37.1			
06	156 04.8	264 24.0	S22 33.5	219 54.6	S22 40.9	11 04.4	N14 43.2	280 55.5	S17 37.2	Alioth	166 20.3	N55 52.6
07	171 07.2	279 23.1	34.0	234 55.0	40.6	26 06.8	43.1	295 57.7	37.3	Alkaid	152 58.6	N49 14.3
T 08	186 09.7	294 22.2	34.5	249 55.4	40.2	41 09.2	43.1	310 59.8	37.3	Al Na'ir	27 42.6	S46 53.4
H 09	201 12.2	309 21.3 ..	35.0	264 55.8 ..	39.9	56 11.5 ..	43.1	326 02.0 ..	37.4	Alnilam	275 45.0	S 1 11.7
U 10	216 14.6	324 20.4	35.5	279 56.2	39.5	71 13.9	43.1	341 04.1	37.5	Alphard	217 55.0	S 8 43.4
R 11	231 17.1	339 19.5	36.0	294 56.7	39.1	86 16.3	43.1	356 06.3	37.5			
S 12	246 19.6	354 18.6	S22 36.5	309 57.1	S22 38.8	101 18.6	N14 43.0	11 08.5	S17 37.6	Alphecca	126 10.6	N26 40.0
D 13	261 22.0	9 17.7	37.0	324 57.5	38.4	116 21.0	43.0	26 10.6	37.7	Alpheratz	357 42.3	N29 10.6
A 14	276 24.5	24 16.9	37.4	339 57.9	38.1	131 23.4	43.0	41 12.8	37.7	Altair	62 07.5	N 8 54.8
Y 15	291 26.9	39 16.0 ..	37.9	354 58.3 ..	37.7	146 25.8 ..	43.0	56 14.9 ..	37.8	Ankaa	353 14.6	S42 13.7
16	306 29.4	54 15.1	38.4	9 58.7	37.4	161 28.1	43.0	71 17.1	37.9	Antares	112 25.4	S26 27.7
17	321 31.9	69 14.2	38.9	24 59.2	37.0	176 30.5	42.9	86 19.3	37.9			
18	336 34.3	84 13.3	S22 39.4	39 59.6	S22 36.7	191 32.9	N14 42.9	101 21.4	S17 38.0	Arcturus	145 55.2	N19 06.4
19	351 36.8	99 12.4	39.8	55 00.0	36.3	206 35.3	42.9	116 23.6	38.1	Atria	107 26.9	S69 03.0
20	6 39.3	114 11.5	40.3	70 00.4	35.9	221 37.6	42.9	131 25.8	38.1	Avior	234 17.2	S59 33.3
21	21 41.7	129 10.6 ..	40.8	85 00.8 ..	35.6	236 40.0 ..	42.9	146 27.9 ..	38.2	Bellatrix	278 30.6	N 6 21.6
22	36 44.2	144 09.7	41.3	100 01.2	35.2	251 42.4	42.8	161 30.1	38.3	Betelgeuse	270 59.9	N 7 24.4
23	51 46.7	159 08.8	41.7	115 01.7	34.9	266 44.7	42.8	176 32.2	38.4			
28 00	66 49.1	174 07.9	S22 42.2	130 02.1	S22 34.5	281 47.1	N14 42.8	191 34.4	S17 38.4	Canopus	263 55.2	S52 42.3
01	81 51.6	189 07.0	42.7	145 02.5	34.2	296 49.5	42.8	206 36.6	38.5	Capella	280 32.5	N46 00.5
02	96 54.1	204 06.1	43.2	160 02.9	33.8	311 51.9	42.8	221 38.7	38.6	Deneb	49 31.0	N45 20.4
03	111 56.5	219 05.2 ..	43.6	175 03.3 ..	33.4	326 54.3 ..	42.7	236 40.9 ..	38.6	Denebola	182 32.8	N14 29.3
04	126 59.0	234 04.3	44.1	190 03.7	33.1	341 56.6	42.7	251 43.1	38.7	Diphda	348 54.7	S17 54.3
05	142 01.4	249 03.4	44.6	205 04.2	32.7	356 59.0	42.7	266 45.2	38.8			
06	157 03.9	264 02.5	S22 45.0	220 04.6	S22 32.4	12 01.4	N14 42.7	281 47.4	S17 38.8	Dubhe	193 50.8	N61 39.9
07	172 06.4	279 01.5	45.5	235 05.0	32.0	27 03.8	42.7	296 49.5	38.9	Elnath	278 11.0	N28 37.0
F 08	187 08.8	294 00.6	46.0	250 05.4	31.6	42 06.1	42.7	311 51.7	39.0	Eltanin	90 46.2	N51 29.5
R 09	202 11.3	308 59.7 ..	46.4	265 05.8 ..	31.3	57 08.5 ..	42.6	326 53.9 ..	39.0	Enif	33 46.2	N 9 56.9
I 10	217 13.8	323 58.8	46.9	280 06.2	30.9	72 10.9	42.6	341 56.0	39.1	Fomalhaut	15 22.9	S29 32.6
11	232 16.2	338 57.9	47.3	295 06.7	30.5	87 13.3	42.6	356 58.2	39.2			
D 12	247 18.7	353 57.0	S22 47.8	310 07.1	S22 30.2	102 15.7	N14 42.6	12 00.3	S17 39.2	Gacrux	172 00.0	S57 11.5
A 13	262 21.2	8 56.1	48.2	325 07.5	29.8	117 18.0	42.6	27 02.5	39.3	Gienah	175 51.4	S17 37.3
Y 14	277 23.6	23 55.2	48.7	340 07.9	29.4	132 20.4	42.5	42 04.7	39.4	Hadar	148 46.9	S60 26.4
15	292 26.1	38 54.3 ..	49.2	355 08.3 ..	29.1	147 22.8 ..	42.5	57 06.8 ..	39.4	Hamal	327 59.3	N23 32.0
16	307 28.6	53 53.4	49.6	10 08.7	28.7	162 25.2	42.5	72 09.0	39.5	Kaus Aust.	83 42.9	S34 22.5
17	322 31.0	68 52.5	50.1	25 09.2	28.3	177 27.6	42.5	87 11.2	39.6			
18	337 33.5	83 51.6	S22 50.5	40 09.6	S22 28.0	192 29.9	N14 42.5	102 13.3	S17 39.6	Kochab	137 21.4	N74 05.6
19	352 35.9	98 50.7	51.0	55 10.0	27.6	207 32.3	42.5	117 15.5	39.7	Markab	13 37.3	N15 17.3
20	7 38.4	113 49.8	51.4	70 10.4	27.2	222 34.7	42.4	132 17.6	39.8	Menkar	314 13.7	N 4 08.8
21	22 40.9	128 48.9 ..	51.9	85 10.8 ..	26.9	237 37.1 ..	42.4	147 19.8 ..	39.8	Menkent	148 06.7	S36 26.3
22	37 43.3	143 48.0	52.3	100 11.3	26.5	252 39.5	42.4	162 22.0	39.9	Miaplacidus	221 39.0	S69 46.5
23	52 45.8	158 47.0	52.7	115 11.7	26.1	267 41.8	42.4	177 24.1	40.0			
29 00	67 48.3	173 46.1	S22 53.2	130 12.1	S22 25.8	282 44.2	N14 42.4	192 26.3	S17 40.0	Mirfak	308 38.4	N49 54.8
01	82 50.7	188 45.2	53.6	145 12.5	25.4	297 46.6	42.4	207 28.5	40.1	Nunki	75 57.4	S26 16.5
02	97 53.2	203 44.3	54.1	160 12.9	25.0	312 49.0	42.3	222 30.6	40.2	Peacock	53 18.1	S56 41.2
03	112 55.7	218 43.4 ..	54.5	175 13.3 ..	24.7	327 51.4 ..	42.3	237 32.8 ..	40.2	Pollux	243 26.3	N27 59.1
04	127 58.1	233 42.5	55.0	190 13.8	24.3	342 53.8	42.3	252 34.9	40.3	Procyon	244 58.5	N 5 11.0
05	143 00.6	248 41.6	55.4	205 14.2	23.9	357 56.1	42.3	267 37.1	40.4			
06	158 03.0	263 40.7	S22 55.8	220 14.6	S22 23.5	12 58.5	N14 42.3	282 39.3	S17 40.4	Rasalhague	96 05.9	N12 33.2
07	173 05.5	278 39.8	56.3	235 15.0	23.2	28 00.9	42.3	297 41.4	40.5	Regulus	207 42.5	N11 53.5
S 08	188 08.0	293 38.8	56.7	250 15.4	22.8	43 03.3	42.2	312 43.6	40.6	Rigel	281 10.8	S 8 11.2
A 09	203 10.4	308 37.9 ..	57.1	265 15.9 ..	22.4	58 05.7 ..	42.2	327 45.8 ..	40.6	Rigil Kent.	139 50.9	S60 53.5
T 10	218 12.9	323 37.0	57.6	280 16.3	22.1	73 08.1	42.2	342 47.9	40.7	Sabik	102 11.8	S15 44.3
U 11	233 15.4	338 36.1	58.0	295 16.7	21.7	88 10.5	42.2	357 50.1	40.8			
R 12	248 17.8	353 35.2	S22 58.4	310 17.1	S22 21.3	103 12.8	N14 42.2	12 52.2	S17 40.8	Schedar	349 38.9	N56 37.4
D 13	263 20.3	8 34.3	58.9	325 17.5	20.9	118 15.2	42.2	27 54.4	40.9	Shaula	96 21.0	S37 06.7
A 14	278 22.8	23 33.4	59.3	340 18.0	20.6	133 17.6	42.2	42 56.6	41.0	Sirius	258 32.6	S16 44.3
Y 15	293 25.2	38 32.4	22 59.7	355 18.4 ..	20.2	148 20.0 ..	42.1	57 58.7 ..	41.0	Spica	158 30.4	S11 14.2
16	308 27.7	53 31.5	23 00.1	10 18.8	19.8	163 22.4	42.1	73 00.9	41.1	Suhail	222 51.5	S43 29.5
17	323 30.2	68 30.6	00.6	25 19.2	19.4	178 24.8	42.1	88 03.1	41.2			
18	338 32.6	83 29.7	S23 01.0	40 19.7	S22 19.0	193 27.2	N14 42.1	103 05.2	S17 41.2	Vega	80 38.7	N38 48.2
19	353 35.1	98 28.8	01.4	55 20.1	18.7	208 29.6	42.1	118 07.4	41.3	Zuben'ubi	137 04.6	S16 06.0
20	8 37.5	113 27.9	01.8	70 20.5	18.3	223 32.0	42.0	133 09.5	41.4		SHA	Mer. Pass.
21	23 40.0	128 26.9 ..	02.2	85 20.9 ..	17.9	238 34.3 ..	42.0	148 11.7 ..	41.4			
22	38 42.5	143 26.0	02.6	100 21.3	17.5	253 36.7	42.0	163 13.9	41.5	Venus	107 18.7	12 24
23	53 44.9	158 25.1	03.1	115 21.8	17.2	268 39.1	42.0	178 16.0	41.6	Mars	63 12.9	15 19
Mer. Pass. 19 29.5		v −0.9	d 0.5	v 0.4	d 0.4	v 2.4	d 0.0	v 2.2	d 0.1	Jupiter	214 58.0	5 12
										Saturn	124 45.3	11 12

UT	SUN GHA	SUN Dec	MOON GHA	v	MOON Dec	d	HP
d h	° '	° '	° '	'	° '	'	'
27 00	183 08.4	S21 03.8	121 59.1	7.6	S14 41.8	7.1	59.2
01	198 08.2	04.3	136 25.7	7.6	14 34.7	7.3	59.3
02	213 08.0	04.8	150 52.3	7.6	14 27.4	7.3	59.3
03	228 07.8	.. 05.2	165 18.9	7.7	14 20.1	7.4	59.3
04	243 07.6	05.7	179 45.6	7.7	14 12.7	7.5	59.3
05	258 07.4	06.1	194 12.3	7.8	14 05.2	7.6	59.3
06	273 07.2	S21 06.6	208 39.1	7.8	S13 57.6	7.7	59.3
07	288 07.0	07.1	223 05.9	7.8	13 49.9	7.8	59.3
T 08	303 06.8	07.5	237 32.7	7.9	13 42.1	7.8	59.3
H 09	318 06.6	.. 08.0	251 59.6	7.9	13 34.3	8.0	59.3
U 10	333 06.4	08.4	266 26.5	8.0	13 26.3	8.0	59.3
R 11	348 06.2	08.9	280 53.5	8.0	13 18.3	8.1	59.3
S 12	3 06.0	S21 09.3	295 20.5	8.0	S13 10.2	8.2	59.3
D 13	18 05.8	09.8	309 47.5	8.1	13 02.0	8.2	59.3
A 14	33 05.6	10.2	324 14.6	8.1	12 53.8	8.4	59.3
Y 15	48 05.4	.. 10.7	338 41.7	8.1	12 45.4	8.4	59.3
16	63 05.1	11.1	353 08.8	8.2	12 37.0	8.5	59.3
17	78 04.9	11.6	7 36.0	8.3	12 28.5	8.6	59.3
18	93 04.7	S21 12.0	22 03.3	8.2	S12 19.9	8.6	59.3
19	108 04.5	12.5	36 30.5	8.4	12 11.3	8.7	59.3
20	123 04.3	12.9	50 57.9	8.3	12 02.6	8.8	59.3
21	138 04.1	.. 13.4	65 25.2	8.4	11 53.8	8.9	59.3
22	153 03.9	13.8	79 52.6	8.4	11 44.9	8.9	59.3
23	168 03.7	14.3	94 20.0	8.5	11 36.0	9.0	59.3
28 00	183 03.5	S21 14.7	108 47.5	8.5	S11 27.0	9.1	59.3
01	198 03.3	15.2	123 15.0	8.5	11 17.9	9.2	59.3
02	213 03.1	15.6	137 42.5	8.6	11 08.7	9.2	59.3
03	228 02.9	.. 16.1	152 10.1	8.6	10 59.5	9.2	59.3
04	243 02.6	16.5	166 37.7	8.7	10 50.3	9.4	59.3
05	258 02.4	16.9	181 05.4	8.7	10 40.9	9.4	59.3
06	273 02.2	S21 17.4	195 33.1	8.7	S10 31.5	9.4	59.3
07	288 02.0	17.8	210 00.8	8.8	10 22.1	9.6	59.3
08	303 01.8	18.3	224 28.6	8.8	10 12.5	9.6	59.3
F 09	318 01.6	.. 18.7	238 56.4	8.9	10 02.9	9.6	59.3
R 10	333 01.4	19.1	253 24.3	8.9	9 53.3	9.7	59.3
I 11	348 01.2	19.6	267 52.2	8.9	9 43.6	9.8	59.3
D 12	3 00.9	S21 20.0	282 20.1	8.9	S 9 33.8	9.8	59.3
A 13	18 00.7	20.5	296 48.0	9.0	9 24.0	9.9	59.3
Y 14	33 00.5	20.9	311 16.0	9.1	9 14.1	9.9	59.3
15	48 00.3	.. 21.3	325 44.1	9.0	9 04.2	10.0	59.3
16	63 00.1	21.8	340 12.1	9.1	8 54.2	10.0	59.3
17	77 59.9	22.2	354 40.2	9.2	8 44.2	10.1	59.3
18	92 59.7	S21 22.6	9 08.4	9.1	S 8 34.1	10.1	59.3
19	107 59.5	23.1	23 36.5	9.2	8 24.0	10.2	59.3
20	122 59.2	23.5	38 04.7	9.3	8 13.8	10.2	59.3
21	137 59.0	.. 23.9	52 33.0	9.3	8 03.6	10.3	59.3
22	152 58.8	24.3	67 01.3	9.3	7 53.3	10.3	59.2
23	167 58.6	24.8	81 29.6	9.3	7 43.0	10.3	59.2
29 00	182 58.4	S21 25.2	95 57.9	9.4	S 7 32.7	10.4	59.2
01	197 58.2	25.6	110 26.3	9.4	7 22.3	10.5	59.2
02	212 57.9	26.1	124 54.7	9.4	7 11.8	10.5	59.2
03	227 57.7	.. 26.5	139 23.1	9.5	7 01.3	10.5	59.2
04	242 57.5	26.9	153 51.6	9.5	6 50.8	10.6	59.2
05	257 57.3	27.3	168 20.1	9.5	6 40.2	10.5	59.2
06	272 57.1	S21 27.8	182 48.6	9.5	S 6 29.7	10.7	59.2
07	287 56.9	28.2	197 17.1	9.6	6 19.0	10.7	59.2
S 08	302 56.6	28.6	211 45.7	9.6	6 08.3	10.7	59.2
A 09	317 56.4	.. 29.0	226 14.3	9.6	5 57.6	10.7	59.2
T 10	332 56.2	29.5	240 42.9	9.7	5 46.9	10.8	59.2
U 11	347 56.0	29.9	255 11.6	9.7	5 36.1	10.8	59.2
R 12	2 55.8	S21 30.3	269 40.3	9.7	S 5 25.3	10.8	59.2
D 13	17 55.5	30.7	284 09.0	9.7	5 14.5	10.8	59.2
A 14	32 55.3	31.1	298 37.7	9.8	5 03.7	10.9	59.2
Y 15	47 55.1	.. 31.6	313 06.5	9.8	4 52.8	10.9	59.2
16	62 54.9	32.0	327 35.3	9.8	4 41.9	11.0	59.2
17	77 54.7	32.4	342 04.1	9.8	4 30.9	10.9	59.2
18	92 54.4	S21 32.8	356 32.9	9.9	S 4 20.0	11.0	59.2
19	107 54.2	33.2	11 01.8	9.9	4 09.0	11.0	59.2
20	122 54.0	33.6	25 30.7	9.9	3 58.0	11.0	59.2
21	137 53.8	.. 34.0	39 59.6	9.9	3 47.0	11.1	59.1
22	152 53.5	34.5	54 28.5	9.9	3 35.9	11.0	59.1
23	167 53.3	34.9	68 57.4	10.0	S 3 24.9	11.1	59.1
	SD 16.2	d 0.4	SD 16.2		16.2		16.1

Lat.	Twilight Naut.	Twilight Civil	Sunrise	Moonrise 27	Moonrise 28	Moonrise 29	Moonrise 30
°	h m	h m	h m	h m	h m	h m	h m
N 72	07 42	09 36	■■■	13 25	13 18	13 11	13 05
N 70	07 27	09 00	■■■	13 01	13 03	13 04	13 04
68	07 15	08 35	10 18	12 43	12 51	12 58	13 03
66	07 04	08 15	09 36	12 28	12 42	12 52	13 02
64	06 55	08 00	09 07	12 15	12 33	12 48	13 01
62	06 48	07 46	08 46	12 05	12 26	12 44	13 00
60	06 41	07 35	08 28	11 56	12 20	12 41	13 00
N 58	06 35	07 25	08 14	11 48	12 15	12 38	12 59
56	06 29	07 17	08 01	11 41	12 10	12 35	12 59
54	06 24	07 09	07 51	11 34	12 05	12 33	12 59
52	06 19	07 02	07 41	11 29	12 02	12 31	12 58
50	06 15	06 55	07 32	11 24	11 58	12 29	12 58
45	06 05	06 41	07 14	11 12	11 50	12 25	12 57
N 40	05 56	06 29	06 59	11 03	11 44	12 21	12 56
35	05 48	06 19	06 47	10 55	11 38	12 18	12 56
30	05 40	06 10	06 36	10 48	11 33	12 15	12 55
20	05 26	05 53	06 17	10 36	11 24	12 10	12 55
N 10	05 11	05 37	06 00	10 25	11 17	12 06	12 54
0	04 56	05 22	05 44	10 15	11 09	12 02	12 53
S 10	04 39	05 06	05 28	10 05	11 02	11 58	12 53
20	04 19	04 47	05 11	09 55	10 55	11 54	12 52
30	03 52	04 25	04 52	09 43	10 46	11 49	12 52
35	03 36	04 11	04 40	09 35	10 41	11 46	12 51
40	03 15	03 55	04 27	09 27	10 35	11 43	12 51
45	02 49	03 35	04 11	09 18	10 28	11 39	12 50
S 50	02 11	03 09	03 51	09 06	10 20	11 35	12 50
52	01 50	02 56	03 41	09 01	10 17	11 33	12 49
54	01 23	02 41	03 31	08 55	10 13	11 31	12 49
56	00 39	02 24	03 19	08 49	10 08	11 28	12 49
58	////	02 02	03 05	08 41	10 03	11 26	12 48
S 60	////	01 32	02 48	08 33	09 57	11 23	12 48

Lat.	Sunset	Twilight Civil	Twilight Naut.	Moonset 27	Moonset 28	Moonset 29	Moonset 30
°	h m	h m	h m	h m	h m	h m	h m
N 72	■■■	14 00	15 53	19 48	21 48	23 43	25 36
N 70	■■■	14 35	16 08	20 11	22 00	23 48	25 34
68	13 17	15 00	16 21	20 29	22 11	23 52	25 32
66	14 00	15 20	16 31	20 43	22 19	23 55	25 31
64	14 28	15 36	16 40	20 54	22 26	23 58	25 30
62	14 50	15 49	16 48	21 04	22 32	24 01	00 01
60	15 07	16 00	16 55	21 12	22 37	24 03	00 03
N 58	15 22	16 10	17 01	21 19	22 42	24 05	00 05
56	15 34	16 19	17 06	21 26	22 46	24 06	00 06
54	15 45	16 27	17 11	21 31	22 49	24 08	00 08
52	15 54	16 34	17 16	21 37	22 53	24 09	00 09
50	16 03	16 40	17 21	21 41	22 56	24 10	00 10
45	16 21	16 54	17 31	21 51	23 02	24 13	00 13
N 40	16 36	17 06	17 40	21 59	23 07	24 15	00 15
35	16 49	17 17	17 48	22 07	23 12	24 17	00 17
30	17 00	17 26	17 55	22 13	23 16	24 19	00 19
20	17 19	17 43	18 10	22 23	23 23	24 22	00 22
N 10	17 36	17 58	18 24	22 33	23 29	24 24	00 24
0	17 52	18 14	18 40	22 41	23 35	24 27	00 27
S 10	18 07	18 30	18 57	22 50	23 40	24 29	00 29
20	18 25	18 49	19 17	22 59	23 46	24 31	00 31
30	18 45	19 11	19 44	23 09	23 53	24 34	00 34
35	18 56	19 25	20 01	23 15	23 57	24 35	00 35
40	19 10	19 42	20 21	23 22	24 01	00 01	00 37
45	19 26	20 02	20 48	23 30	24 06	00 06	00 39
S 50	19 46	20 28	21 26	23 39	24 12	00 12	00 42
52	19 55	20 41	21 47	23 44	24 14	00 14	00 43
54	20 06	20 56	22 16	23 48	24 17	00 17	00 44
56	20 18	21 14	23 03	23 53	24 21	00 21	00 45
58	20 32	21 36	////	23 59	24 24	00 24	00 47
S 60	20 49	22 07	////	24 06	00 06	00 28	00 48

	SUN			MOON			
Day	Eqn. of Time 00h	Eqn. of Time 12h	Mer. Pass.	Mer. Pass. Upper	Mer. Pass. Lower	Age	Phase
d	m s	m s	h m	h m	h m	d	%
27	12 34	12 24	11 48	16 28	04 01	05	29
28	12 14	12 04	11 48	17 22	04 55	06	40
29	11 54	11 43	11 48	18 14	05 48	07	51

UT	ARIES GHA	VENUS −3.9 GHA	Dec	MARS +1.0 GHA	Dec	JUPITER −2.3 GHA	Dec	SATURN +0.5 GHA	Dec	STARS Name	SHA	Dec
d h	° ′	° ′	° ′	° ′	° ′	° ′	° ′	° ′	° ′		° ′	° ′
30 00	68 47.4	173 24.2	S23 03.5	130 22.2	S22 16.8	283 41.5	N14 42.0	193 18.2	S17 41.6	Acamar	315 17.2	S40 14.9
01	83 49.9	188 23.3	03.9	145 22.6	16.4	298 43.9	42.0	208 20.4	41.7	Achernar	335 25.7	S57 09.9
02	98 52.3	203 22.4	04.3	160 23.0	16.0	313 46.3	42.0	223 22.5	41.8	Acrux	173 08.3	S63 10.6
03	113 54.8	218 21.4 ..	04.7	175 23.4 ..	15.6	328 48.7 ..	42.0	238 24.7 ..	41.8	Adhara	255 11.4	S28 59.6
04	128 57.3	233 20.5	05.1	190 23.9	15.3	343 51.1	42.0	253 26.8	41.9	Aldebaran	290 47.9	N16 32.2
05	143 59.7	248 19.6	05.5	205 24.3	14.9	358 53.5	41.9	268 29.0	42.0			
06	159 02.2	263 18.7	S23 05.9	220 24.7	S22 14.5	13 55.9	N14 41.9	283 31.2	S17 42.0	Alioth	166 20.3	N55 52.5
07	174 04.7	278 17.8	06.4	235 25.1	14.1	28 58.3	41.9	298 33.3	42.1	Alkaid	152 58.6	N49 14.2
08	189 07.1	293 16.8	06.8	250 25.6	13.7	44 00.7	41.9	313 35.5	42.2	Al Na'ir	27 42.7	S46 53.4
S 09	204 09.6	308 15.9 ..	07.2	265 26.0 ..	13.3	59 03.1 ..	41.9	328 37.7 ..	42.2	Alnilam	275 45.0	S 1 11.7
U 10	219 12.0	323 15.0	07.6	280 26.4	13.0	74 05.4	41.9	343 39.8	42.3	Alphard	217 55.0	S 8 43.5
N 11	234 14.5	338 14.1	08.0	295 26.8	12.6	89 07.8	41.9	358 42.0	42.4			
D 12	249 17.0	353 13.2	S23 08.4	310 27.2	S22 12.2	104 10.2	N14 41.8	13 44.2	S17 42.4	Alphecca	126 10.6	N26 40.0
A 13	264 19.4	8 12.2	08.8	325 27.7	11.8	119 12.6	41.8	28 46.3	42.5	Alpheratz	357 42.3	N29 10.6
Y 14	279 21.9	23 11.3	09.2	340 28.1	11.4	134 15.0	41.8	43 48.5	42.6	Altair	62 07.5	N 8 54.8
15	294 24.4	38 10.4 ..	09.6	355 28.5 ..	11.0	149 17.4 ..	41.8	58 50.6 ..	42.6	Ankaa	353 14.6	S42 13.7
16	309 26.8	53 09.5	10.0	10 28.9	10.6	164 19.8	41.8	73 52.8	42.7	Antares	112 25.4	S26 27.7
17	324 29.3	68 08.5	10.4	25 29.4	10.3	179 22.2	41.8	88 55.0	42.8			
18	339 31.8	83 07.6	S23 10.7	40 29.8	S22 09.9	194 24.6	N14 41.8	103 57.1	S17 42.8	Arcturus	145 55.1	N19 06.4
19	354 34.2	98 06.7	11.1	55 30.2	09.5	209 27.0	41.8	118 59.3	42.9	Atria	107 26.9	S69 03.0
20	9 36.7	113 05.8	11.5	70 30.6	09.1	224 29.4	41.7	134 01.5	43.0	Avior	234 17.1	S59 33.3
21	24 39.1	128 04.8 ..	11.9	85 31.1 ..	08.7	239 31.8 ..	41.7	149 03.6 ..	43.0	Bellatrix	278 30.6	N 6 21.6
22	39 41.6	143 03.9	12.3	100 31.5	08.3	254 34.2	41.7	164 05.8	43.1	Betelgeuse	270 59.9	N 7 24.4
23	54 44.1	158 03.0	12.7	115 31.9	07.9	269 36.6	41.7	179 07.9	43.2			
1 00	69 46.5	173 02.1	S23 13.1	130 32.3	S22 07.5	284 39.0	N14 41.7	194 10.1	S17 43.2	Canopus	263 55.2	S52 42.3
01	84 49.0	188 01.1	13.5	145 32.8	07.1	299 41.4	41.7	209 12.3	43.3	Capella	280 32.5	N46 00.5
02	99 51.5	203 00.2	13.8	160 33.2	06.8	314 43.8	41.7	224 14.4	43.4	Deneb	49 31.0	N45 20.4
03	114 53.9	217 59.3 ..	14.2	175 33.6 ..	06.4	329 46.2 ..	41.7	239 16.6 ..	43.4	Denebola	182 32.8	N14 29.2
04	129 56.4	232 58.4	14.6	190 34.0	06.0	344 48.6	41.7	254 18.8	43.5	Diphda	348 54.7	S17 54.3
05	144 58.9	247 57.4	15.0	205 34.5	05.6	359 51.0	41.6	269 20.9	43.6			
06	160 01.3	262 56.5	S23 15.4	220 34.9	S22 05.2	14 53.4	N14 41.6	284 23.1	S17 43.6	Dubhe	193 50.7	N61 39.9
07	175 03.8	277 55.6	15.7	235 35.3	04.8	29 55.8	41.6	299 25.3	43.7	Elnath	278 11.0	N28 37.0
08	190 06.3	292 54.6	16.1	250 35.7	04.4	44 58.2	41.6	314 27.4	43.8	Eltanin	90 46.2	N51 29.5
M 09	205 08.7	307 53.7 ..	16.5	265 36.2 ..	04.0	60 00.6 ..	41.6	329 29.6 ..	43.8	Enif	33 46.2	N 9 56.9
O 10	220 11.2	322 52.8	16.9	280 36.6	03.6	75 03.0	41.6	344 31.7	43.9	Fomalhaut	15 22.9	S29 32.6
N 11	235 13.6	337 51.9	17.2	295 37.0	03.2	90 05.4	41.6	359 33.9	44.0			
D 12	250 16.1	352 50.9	S23 17.6	310 37.4	S22 02.8	105 07.8	N14 41.6	14 36.1	S17 44.0	Gacrux	172 00.0	S57 11.5
A 13	265 18.6	7 50.0	18.0	325 37.9	02.4	120 10.2	41.6	29 38.2	44.1	Gienah	175 51.4	S17 37.4
Y 14	280 21.0	22 49.1	18.4	340 38.3	02.0	135 12.6	41.6	44 40.4	44.2	Hadar	148 46.9	S60 26.4
15	295 23.5	37 48.1 ..	18.7	355 38.7 ..	01.6	150 15.0 ..	41.5	59 42.6 ..	44.2	Hamal	327 59.3	N23 32.0
16	310 26.0	52 47.2	19.1	10 39.1	01.2	165 17.4	41.5	74 44.7	44.3	Kaus Aust.	83 42.9	S34 22.5
17	325 28.4	67 46.3	19.5	25 39.6	00.8	180 19.8	41.5	89 46.9	44.4			
18	340 30.9	82 45.3	S23 19.8	40 40.0	S22 00.5	195 22.2	N14 41.5	104 49.1	S17 44.4	Kochab	137 21.4	N74 05.6
19	355 33.4	97 44.4	20.2	55 40.4	22 00.1	210 24.6	41.5	119 51.2	44.5	Markab	13 37.3	N15 17.3
20	10 35.8	112 43.5	20.5	70 40.8	21 59.7	225 27.0	41.5	134 53.4	44.6	Menkar	314 13.7	N 4 08.8
21	25 38.3	127 42.5 ..	20.9	85 41.3 ..	59.3	240 29.4 ..	41.5	149 55.5 ..	44.6	Menkent	148 06.7	S36 26.3
22	40 40.8	142 41.6	21.3	100 41.7	58.9	255 31.8	41.5	164 57.7	44.7	Miaplacidus	221 38.9	S69 46.5
23	55 43.2	157 40.7	21.6	115 42.1	58.5	270 34.3	41.5	179 59.9	44.8			
2 00	70 45.7	172 39.7	S23 22.0	130 42.6	S21 58.1	285 36.7	N14 41.5	195 02.0	S17 44.8	Mirfak	308 38.4	N49 54.8
01	85 48.1	187 38.8	22.3	145 43.0	57.7	300 39.1	41.4	210 04.2	44.9	Nunki	75 57.4	S26 16.5
02	100 50.6	202 37.9	22.7	160 43.4	57.3	315 41.5	41.4	225 06.4	44.9	Peacock	53 18.1	S56 41.2
03	115 53.1	217 36.9 ..	23.0	175 43.8 ..	56.9	330 43.9 ..	41.4	240 08.5 ..	45.0	Pollux	243 26.3	N27 59.1
04	130 55.5	232 36.0	23.4	190 44.3	56.5	345 46.3	41.4	255 10.7	45.1	Procyon	244 58.5	N 5 11.0
05	145 58.0	247 35.1	23.7	205 44.7	56.1	0 48.7	41.4	270 12.9	45.1			
06	161 00.5	262 34.1	S23 24.1	220 45.1	S21 55.7	15 51.1	N14 41.4	285 15.0	S17 45.2	Rasalhague	96 05.9	N12 33.2
07	176 02.9	277 33.2	24.4	235 45.5	55.2	30 53.5	41.4	300 17.2	45.3	Regulus	207 42.4	N11 53.5
08	191 05.4	292 32.3	24.8	250 46.0	54.8	45 55.9	41.4	315 19.3	45.3	Rigel	281 10.8	S 8 11.2
T 09	206 07.9	307 31.3 ..	25.1	265 46.4 ..	54.4	60 58.3 ..	41.4	330 21.5 ..	45.4	Rigil Kent.	139 50.9	S60 53.5
U 10	221 10.3	322 30.4	25.5	280 46.8	54.0	76 00.7	41.4	345 23.7	45.5	Sabik	102 11.8	S15 44.4
E 11	236 12.8	337 29.5	25.8	295 47.3	53.6	91 03.2	41.4	0 25.8	45.5			
S 12	251 15.2	352 28.5	S23 26.2	310 47.7	S21 53.2	106 05.6	N14 41.4	15 28.0	S17 45.6	Schedar	349 39.0	N56 37.4
D 13	266 17.7	7 27.6	26.5	325 48.1	52.8	121 08.0	41.4	30 30.2	45.7	Shaula	96 21.0	S37 06.7
A 14	281 20.2	22 26.6	26.8	340 48.5	52.4	136 10.4	41.3	45 32.3	45.7	Sirius	258 32.5	S16 44.3
Y 15	296 22.6	37 25.7 ..	27.2	355 49.0 ..	52.0	151 12.8 ..	41.3	60 34.5 ..	45.8	Spica	158 30.4	S11 14.2
16	311 25.1	52 24.8	27.5	10 49.4	51.6	166 15.2	41.3	75 36.7	45.9	Suhail	222 51.5	S43 29.5
17	326 27.6	67 23.8	27.9	25 49.8	51.2	181 17.6	41.3	90 38.8	45.9			
18	341 30.0	82 22.9	S23 28.2	40 50.3	S21 50.8	196 20.0	N14 41.3	105 41.0	S17 46.0	Vega	80 38.7	N38 48.2
19	356 32.5	97 22.0	28.5	55 50.7	50.4	211 22.4	41.3	120 43.2	46.1	Zuben'ubi	137 04.6	S16 06.0
20	11 35.0	112 21.0	28.9	70 51.1	50.0	226 24.9	41.3	135 45.3	46.1		SHA	Mer.Pass.
21	26 37.4	127 20.1 ..	29.2	85 51.6 ..	49.6	241 27.3 ..	41.3	150 47.5 ..	46.2	Venus	103 15.5	12 29
22	41 39.9	142 19.1	29.5	100 52.0	49.2	256 29.7	41.3	165 49.6	46.3	Mars	60 05.8	15 17
23	56 42.4	157 18.2	29.8	115 52.4	48.7	271 32.1	41.3	180 51.8	46.3	Jupiter	214 52.5	5 01
Mer.Pass.	19 17.7	v −0.9 d 0.4		v 0.4 d 0.4		v 2.4 d 0.0		v 2.2 d 0.1		Saturn	124 23.6	11 02

UT	SUN GHA	Dec	MOON GHA	v	Dec	d	HP
d h	° ′	° ′	° ′	′	° ′	′	′
30 00	182 53.1	S21 35.3	83 26.4	10.0	S 3 13.8	11.1	59.1
01	197 52.9	35.7	97 55.4	9.9	3 02.7	11.1	59.1
02	212 52.6	36.1	112 24.3	10.1	2 51.6	11.1	59.1
03	227 52.4	.. 36.5	126 53.4	10.0	2 40.5	11.2	59.1
04	242 52.2	36.9	141 22.4	10.0	2 29.3	11.1	59.1
05	257 52.0	37.3	155 51.4	10.1	2 18.2	11.2	59.1
06	272 51.8	S21 37.7	170 20.5	10.1	S 2 07.0	11.1	59.1
07	287 51.5	38.1	184 49.6	10.1	1 55.9	11.2	59.1
08	302 51.3	38.5	199 18.7	10.1	1 44.7	11.2	59.1
S 09	317 51.1	.. 39.0	213 47.8	10.1	1 33.5	11.2	59.1
U 10	332 50.8	39.4	228 16.9	10.1	1 22.3	11.2	59.1
N 11	347 50.6	39.8	242 46.0	10.2	1 11.1	11.2	59.0
D 12	2 50.4	S21 40.2	257 15.2	10.1	S 0 59.9	11.2	59.0
A 13	17 50.2	40.6	271 44.3	10.2	0 48.7	11.2	59.0
Y 14	32 49.9	41.0	286 13.5	10.2	0 37.5	11.2	59.0
15	47 49.7	.. 41.4	300 42.7	10.2	0 26.3	11.2	59.0
16	62 49.5	41.8	315 11.9	10.2	0 15.1	11.2	59.0
17	77 49.3	42.2	329 41.1	10.2	S 0 03.9	11.2	59.0
18	92 49.0	S21 42.6	344 10.3	10.2	N 0 07.3	11.2	59.0
19	107 48.8	43.0	358 39.5	10.2	0 18.5	11.2	59.0
20	122 48.6	43.4	13 08.7	10.2	0 29.7	11.2	59.0
21	137 48.3	.. 43.8	27 37.9	10.2	0 40.9	11.2	59.0
22	152 48.1	44.2	42 07.1	10.3	0 52.1	11.1	59.0
23	167 47.9	44.6	56 36.4	10.2	1 03.2	11.2	58.9
1 00	182 47.7	S21 44.9	71 05.6	10.3	N 1 14.4	11.2	58.9
01	197 47.4	45.3	85 34.9	10.2	1 25.6	11.1	58.9
02	212 47.2	45.7	100 04.1	10.3	1 36.7	11.1	58.9
03	227 47.0	.. 46.1	114 33.4	10.2	1 47.8	11.2	58.9
04	242 46.7	46.5	129 02.6	10.3	1 59.0	11.1	58.9
05	257 46.5	46.9	143 31.9	10.2	2 10.1	11.1	58.9
06	272 46.3	S21 47.3	158 01.1	10.3	N 2 21.2	11.0	58.9
07	287 46.0	47.7	172 30.4	10.2	2 32.2	11.1	58.9
08	302 45.8	48.1	186 59.6	10.3	2 43.3	11.0	58.9
M 09	317 45.6	.. 48.5	201 28.9	10.2	2 54.3	11.1	58.8
O 10	332 45.3	48.8	215 58.1	10.3	3 05.4	11.0	58.8
N 11	347 45.1	49.2	230 27.4	10.3	3 16.4	10.9	58.8
D 12	2 44.9	S21 49.6	244 56.7	10.2	N 3 27.3	11.0	58.8
A 13	17 44.6	50.0	259 25.9	10.2	3 38.3	10.9	58.8
Y 14	32 44.4	50.4	273 55.1	10.3	3 49.2	10.9	58.8
15	47 44.2	.. 50.8	288 24.4	10.2	4 00.1	10.9	58.8
16	62 43.9	51.2	302 53.6	10.3	4 11.0	10.9	58.8
17	77 43.7	51.5	317 22.9	10.2	4 21.9	10.8	58.8
18	92 43.5	S21 51.9	331 52.1	10.2	N 4 32.7	10.8	58.8
19	107 43.2	52.3	346 21.3	10.2	4 43.5	10.8	58.7
20	122 43.0	52.7	0 50.5	10.2	4 54.3	10.7	58.7
21	137 42.8	.. 53.1	15 19.7	10.2	5 05.0	10.7	58.7
22	152 42.5	53.4	29 48.9	10.2	5 15.7	10.7	58.7
23	167 42.3	53.8	44 18.1	10.2	5 26.4	10.6	58.7
2 00	182 42.1	S21 54.2	58 47.3	10.2	N 5 37.0	10.7	58.7
01	197 41.8	54.6	73 16.5	10.1	5 47.7	10.5	58.7
02	212 41.6	54.9	87 45.6	10.2	5 58.2	10.6	58.7
03	227 41.3	.. 55.3	102 14.8	10.1	6 08.8	10.5	58.6
04	242 41.1	55.7	116 43.9	10.2	6 19.3	10.4	58.6
05	257 40.9	56.1	131 13.1	10.1	6 29.7	10.4	58.6
06	272 40.6	S21 56.4	145 42.2	10.1	N 6 40.1	10.4	58.6
07	287 40.4	56.8	160 11.3	10.1	6 50.5	10.3	58.6
08	302 40.2	57.2	174 40.4	10.1	7 00.8	10.3	58.6
T 09	317 39.9	.. 57.6	189 09.5	10.0	7 11.1	10.3	58.6
U 10	332 39.7	57.9	203 38.5	10.1	7 21.4	10.2	58.6
E 11	347 39.4	58.3	218 07.6	10.1	7 31.6	10.2	58.5
S 12	2 39.2	S21 58.7	232 36.7	10.0	N 7 41.8	10.1	58.5
D 13	17 39.0	59.0	247 05.7	10.0	7 51.9	10.0	58.5
A 14	32 38.7	59.4	261 34.7	10.0	8 01.9	10.0	58.5
Y 15	47 38.5	21 59.8	276 03.7	10.0	8 11.9	10.0	58.5
16	62 38.2	22 00.1	290 32.7	10.0	8 21.9	9.9	58.5
17	77 38.0	00.5	305 01.7	9.9	8 31.8	9.9	58.5
18	92 37.8	S22 00.9	319 30.6	10.0	N 8 41.7	9.8	58.4
19	107 37.5	01.2	333 59.6	9.9	8 51.5	9.8	58.4
20	122 37.3	01.6	348 28.5	9.9	9 01.3	9.7	58.4
21	137 37.0	.. 01.9	2 57.4	9.9	9 11.0	9.6	58.4
22	152 36.8	02.3	17 26.3	9.9	9 20.6	9.6	58.4
23	167 36.6	02.7	31 55.2	9.9	N 9 30.2	9.5	58.4
	SD 16.2	d 0.4	SD 16.1		16.0		15.9

Twilight / Moonrise

Lat.	Naut.	Civil	Sunrise	30	1	2	3
°	h m	h m	h m	h m	h m	h m	h m
N 72	07 51	09 50	■■■	13 05	12 59	12 53	12 47
N 70	07 34	09 10	■■■	13 04	13 04	13 04	13 06
68	07 21	08 43	10 36	13 03	13 08	13 13	13 21
66	07 10	08 23	09 46	13 02	13 11	13 21	13 33
64	07 01	08 06	09 16	13 01	13 14	13 27	13 44
62	06 53	07 52	08 53	13 00	13 16	13 33	13 52
60	06 46	07 40	08 35	13 00	13 18	13 38	14 00
N 58	06 39	07 30	08 19	12 59	13 20	13 42	14 07
56	06 33	07 21	08 07	12 59	13 22	13 46	14 13
54	06 28	07 13	07 55	12 59	13 24	13 50	14 18
52	06 23	07 06	07 45	12 58	13 25	13 53	14 23
50	06 18	06 59	07 36	12 58	13 26	13 56	14 28
45	06 08	06 45	07 18	12 57	13 29	14 02	14 37
N 40	05 59	06 32	07 02	12 56	13 32	14 07	14 45
35	05 50	06 22	06 49	12 56	13 34	14 12	14 52
30	05 43	06 12	06 38	12 55	13 36	14 16	14 58
20	05 28	05 55	06 19	12 55	13 39	14 23	15 09
N 10	05 13	05 39	06 01	12 54	13 42	14 30	15 18
0	04 57	05 23	05 45	12 53	13 44	14 35	15 27
S 10	04 40	05 06	05 29	12 53	13 47	14 41	15 36
20	04 19	04 47	05 12	12 52	13 50	14 48	15 46
30	03 52	04 24	04 51	12 52	13 54	14 55	15 57
35	03 35	04 10	04 39	12 51	13 56	15 00	16 03
40	03 13	03 54	04 26	12 51	13 58	15 04	16 10
45	02 46	03 33	04 09	12 50	14 00	15 10	16 19
S 50	02 07	03 06	03 49	12 50	14 04	15 17	16 29
52	01 45	02 53	03 39	12 49	14 05	15 20	16 34
54	01 15	02 38	03 28	12 49	14 07	15 24	16 39
56	00 18	02 18	03 16	12 49	14 09	15 28	16 45
58	////	01 55	03 01	12 48	14 11	15 32	16 52
S 60	////	01 23	02 44	12 48	14 13	15 37	16 59

Sunset / Twilight / Moonset

Lat.	Sunset	Civil	Naut.	30	1	2	3
°	h m	h m	h m	h m	h m	h m	h m
N 72	■■■	13 48	15 47	25 36	01 36	03 29	05 22
N 70	■■■	14 27	16 03	25 34	01 34	03 19	05 05
68	13 02	14 54	16 16	25 32	01 32	03 12	04 51
66	13 51	15 15	16 27	25 31	01 31	03 06	04 40
64	14 22	15 31	16 36	25 30	01 30	03 01	04 30
62	14 45	15 45	16 45	00 01	01 29	02 56	04 23
60	15 03	15 57	16 52	00 03	01 28	02 52	04 16
N 58	15 18	16 07	16 58	00 05	01 27	02 49	04 10
56	15 31	16 16	17 04	00 06	01 26	02 46	04 04
54	15 42	16 25	17 10	00 08	01 26	02 43	04 00
52	15 52	16 32	17 15	00 09	01 25	02 41	03 55
50	16 01	16 39	17 19	00 10	01 25	02 39	03 51
45	16 20	16 53	17 30	00 13	01 24	02 34	03 43
N 40	16 35	17 05	17 39	00 15	01 23	02 30	03 36
35	16 48	17 16	17 47	00 17	01 22	02 26	03 30
30	17 00	17 26	17 55	00 19	01 21	02 23	03 25
20	17 19	17 43	18 10	00 22	01 20	02 18	03 16
N 10	17 37	17 59	18 25	00 24	01 19	02 13	03 08
0	17 53	18 15	18 41	00 27	01 18	02 09	03 00
S 10	18 09	18 32	18 59	00 29	01 17	02 04	02 53
20	18 27	18 51	19 20	00 31	01 15	02 00	02 45
30	18 47	19 14	19 47	00 34	01 14	01 54	02 36
35	18 59	19 28	20 04	00 35	01 13	01 51	02 30
40	19 13	19 45	20 25	00 37	01 12	01 48	02 24
45	19 29	20 06	20 53	00 39	01 11	01 44	02 18
S 50	19 50	20 32	21 32	00 42	01 10	01 39	02 09
52	20 00	20 46	21 55	00 43	01 10	01 37	02 06
54	20 11	21 02	22 26	00 44	01 09	01 34	02 02
56	20 23	21 21	23 31	00 45	01 08	01 32	01 57
58	20 38	21 44	////	00 47	01 08	01 29	01 52
S 60	20 56	22 18	////	00 48	01 07	01 26	01 46

SUN / MOON

Day	Eqn. of Time 00ʰ	Eqn. of Time 12ʰ	Mer. Pass.	Mer. Pass. Upper	Mer. Pass. Lower	Age	Phase
d	m s	m s	h m	h m	h m	d	%
30	11 33	11 22	11 49	19 06	06 40	08	62
1	11 11	11 00	11 49	19 57	07 31	09	73
2	10 49	10 37	11 49	20 48	08 22	10	82

UT	ARIES	VENUS −3.9		MARS +1.0		JUPITER −2.3		SATURN +0.5		STARS		
	GHA	GHA	Dec	GHA	Dec	GHA	Dec	GHA	Dec	Name	SHA	Dec
d h	° ′	° ′	° ′	° ′	° ′	° ′	° ′	° ′	° ′		° ′	° ′
3 00	71 44.8	172 17.3	S23 30.2	130 52.8	S21 48.3	286 34.5	N14 41.3	195 54.0	S17 46.4	Acamar	315 17.3	S40 14.9
01	86 47.3	187 16.3	30.5	145 53.3	47.9	301 36.9	41.3	210 56.1	46.5	Achernar	335 25.7	S57 09.9
02	101 49.7	202 15.4	30.8	160 53.7	47.5	316 39.3	41.3	225 58.3	46.5	Acrux	173 08.3	S63 10.6
03	116 52.2	217 14.4	. . 31.1	175 54.1	. . 47.1	331 41.8	. . 41.3	241 00.5	. . 46.6	Adhara	255 11.4	S28 59.6
04	131 54.7	232 13.5	31.5	190 54.6	46.7	346 44.2	41.3	256 02.6	46.7	Aldebaran	290 47.9	N16 32.2
05	146 57.1	247 12.6	31.8	205 55.0	46.3	1 46.6	41.2	271 04.8	46.7			
06	161 59.6	262 11.6	S23 32.1	220 55.4	S21 45.9	16 49.0	N14 41.2	286 07.0	S17 46.8	Alioth	166 20.2	N55 52.5
W 07	177 02.1	277 10.7	32.4	235 55.9	45.5	31 51.4	41.2	301 09.1	46.8	Alkaid	152 58.6	N49 14.2
E 08	192 04.5	292 09.7	32.7	250 56.3	45.0	46 53.8	41.2	316 11.3	46.9	Al Na'ir	27 42.7	S46 53.4
D 09	207 07.0	307 08.8	. . 33.1	265 56.7	. . 44.6	61 56.3	. . 41.2	331 13.5	. . 47.0	Alnilam	275 45.0	S 1 11.7
N 10	222 09.5	322 07.8	33.4	280 57.2	44.2	76 58.7	41.2	346 15.6	47.0	Alphard	217 55.0	S 8 43.5
E 11	237 11.9	337 06.9	33.7	295 57.6	43.8	92 01.1	41.2	1 17.8	47.1			
S 12	252 14.4	352 06.0	S23 34.0	310 58.0	S21 43.4	107 03.5	N14 41.2	16 19.9	S17 47.2	Alphecca	126 10.6	N26 40.0
D 13	267 16.9	7 05.0	34.3	325 58.5	43.0	122 05.9	41.2	31 22.1	47.2	Alpheratz	357 42.3	N29 10.6
A 14	282 19.3	22 04.1	34.6	340 58.9	42.6	137 08.3	41.2	46 24.3	47.3	Altair	62 07.5	N 8 54.7
Y 15	297 21.8	37 03.1	. . 34.9	355 59.3	. . 42.1	152 10.8	. . 41.2	61 26.4	. . 47.4	Ankaa	353 14.6	S42 13.7
16	312 24.2	52 02.2	35.2	10 59.7	41.7	167 13.2	41.2	76 28.6	47.4	Antares	112 25.4	S26 27.6
17	327 26.7	67 01.2	35.5	26 00.2	41.3	182 15.6	41.2	91 30.8	47.5			
18	342 29.2	82 00.3	S23 35.8	41 00.6	S21 40.9	197 18.0	N14 41.2	106 32.9	S17 47.6	Arcturus	145 55.1	N19 06.3
19	357 31.6	96 59.3	36.1	56 01.0	40.5	212 20.4	41.2	121 35.1	47.6	Atria	107 26.9	S69 03.0
20	12 34.1	111 58.4	36.5	71 01.5	40.1	227 22.9	41.2	136 37.3	47.7	Avior	234 17.1	S59 33.4
21	27 36.6	126 57.5	. . 36.8	86 01.9	. . 39.6	242 25.3	. . 41.2	151 39.4	. . 47.8	Bellatrix	278 30.6	N 6 21.6
22	42 39.0	141 56.5	37.1	101 02.3	39.2	257 27.7	41.2	166 41.6	47.8	Betelgeuse	270 59.9	N 7 24.4
23	57 41.5	156 55.6	37.4	116 02.8	38.8	272 30.1	41.2	181 43.8	47.9			
4 00	72 44.0	171 54.6	S23 37.6	131 03.2	S21 38.4	287 32.6	N14 41.2	196 45.9	S17 48.0	Canopus	263 55.2	S52 42.3
01	87 46.4	186 53.7	37.9	146 03.6	38.0	302 35.0	41.2	211 48.1	48.0	Capella	280 32.5	N46 00.6
02	102 48.9	201 52.7	38.2	161 04.1	37.5	317 37.4	41.2	226 50.3	48.1	Deneb	49 31.0	N45 20.4
03	117 51.3	216 51.8	. . 38.5	176 04.5	. . 37.1	332 39.8	. . 41.1	241 52.4	. . 48.1	Denebola	182 32.8	N14 29.2
04	132 53.8	231 50.8	38.8	191 04.9	36.7	347 42.2	41.1	256 54.6	48.2	Diphda	348 54.8	S17 54.4
05	147 56.3	246 49.9	39.1	206 05.4	36.3	2 44.7	41.1	271 56.8	48.3			
06	162 58.7	261 48.9	S23 39.4	221 05.8	S21 35.9	17 47.1	N14 41.1	286 58.9	S17 48.3	Dubhe	193 50.7	N61 39.9
T 07	178 01.2	276 48.0	39.7	236 06.3	35.4	32 49.5	41.1	302 01.1	48.4	Elnath	278 11.0	N28 37.0
H 08	193 03.7	291 47.0	40.0	251 06.7	35.0	47 51.9	41.1	317 03.2	48.5	Eltanin	90 46.2	N51 29.5
U 09	208 06.1	306 46.1	. . 40.3	266 07.1	. . 34.6	62 54.4	. . 41.1	332 05.4	. . 48.5	Enif	33 46.2	N 9 56.8
R 10	223 08.6	321 45.1	40.6	281 07.6	34.2	77 56.8	41.1	347 07.6	48.6	Fomalhaut	15 22.9	S29 32.6
S 11	238 11.1	336 44.2	40.8	296 08.0	33.7	92 59.2	41.1	2 09.7	48.7			
D 12	253 13.5	351 43.2	S23 41.1	311 08.4	S21 33.3	108 01.6	N14 41.1	17 11.9	S17 48.7	Gacrux	171 59.9	S57 11.5
A 13	268 16.0	6 42.3	41.4	326 08.9	32.9	123 04.1	41.1	32 14.1	48.8	Gienah	175 51.4	S17 37.4
Y 14	283 18.5	21 41.3	41.7	341 09.3	32.5	138 06.5	41.1	47 16.2	48.9	Hadar	148 46.9	S60 26.4
15	298 20.9	36 40.4	. . 42.0	356 09.7	. . 32.0	153 08.9	. . 41.1	62 18.4	. . 48.9	Hamal	327 59.3	N23 32.0
16	313 23.4	51 39.4	42.2	11 10.2	31.6	168 11.4	41.1	77 20.6	49.0	Kaus Aust.	83 42.9	S34 22.5
17	328 25.8	66 38.5	42.5	26 10.6	31.2	183 13.8	41.1	92 22.7	49.1			
18	343 28.3	81 37.5	S23 42.8	41 11.0	S21 30.8	198 16.2	N14 41.1	107 24.9	S17 49.1	Kochab	137 21.3	N74 05.6
19	358 30.8	96 36.6	43.1	56 11.5	30.3	213 18.6	41.1	122 27.1	49.2	Markab	13 37.3	N15 17.3
20	13 33.2	111 35.6	43.3	71 11.9	29.9	228 21.1	41.1	137 29.2	49.2	Menkar	314 13.7	N 4 08.8
21	28 35.7	126 34.7	. . 43.6	86 12.3	. . 29.5	243 23.5	. . 41.1	152 31.4	. . 49.3	Menkent	148 06.7	S36 26.3
22	43 38.2	141 33.7	43.9	101 12.8	29.0	258 25.9	41.1	167 33.6	49.4	Miaplacidus	221 38.9	S69 46.5
23	58 40.6	156 32.8	44.1	116 13.2	28.6	273 28.4	41.1	182 35.7	49.4			
5 00	73 43.1	171 31.8	S23 44.4	131 13.7	S21 28.2	288 30.8	N14 41.1	197 37.9	S17 49.5	Mirfak	308 38.4	N49 54.8
01	88 45.6	186 30.9	44.7	146 14.1	27.8	303 33.2	41.1	212 40.1	49.6	Nunki	75 57.4	S26 16.5
02	103 48.0	201 29.9	44.9	161 14.5	27.3	318 35.6	41.1	227 42.2	49.6	Peacock	53 18.1	S56 41.2
03	118 50.5	216 29.0	. . 45.2	176 15.0	. . 26.9	333 38.1	. . 41.1	242 44.4	. . 49.7	Pollux	243 26.3	N27 59.1
04	133 53.0	231 28.0	45.5	191 15.4	26.5	348 40.5	41.1	257 46.6	49.8	Procyon	244 58.4	N 5 11.0
05	148 55.4	246 27.1	45.7	206 15.8	26.0	3 42.9	41.1	272 48.7	49.8			
06	163 57.9	261 26.1	S23 46.0	221 16.3	S21 25.6	18 45.4	N14 41.1	287 50.9	S17 49.9	Rasalhague	96 05.9	N12 33.2
07	179 00.3	276 25.1	46.2	236 16.7	25.2	33 47.8	41.1	302 53.1	50.0	Regulus	207 42.4	N11 53.5
08	194 02.8	291 24.2	46.5	251 17.2	24.7	48 50.2	41.1	317 55.2	50.0	Rigel	281 10.8	S 8 11.2
F 09	209 05.3	306 23.2	. . 46.8	266 17.6	. . 24.3	63 52.7	. . 41.1	332 57.4	. . 50.1	Rigil Kent.	139 50.8	S60 53.5
R 10	224 07.7	321 22.3	47.0	281 18.0	23.9	78 55.1	41.1	347 59.6	50.1	Sabik	102 11.8	S15 44.4
I 11	239 10.2	336 21.3	47.3	296 18.5	23.4	93 57.5	41.1	3 01.7	50.2			
D 12	254 12.7	351 20.4	S23 47.5	311 18.9	S21 23.0	109 00.0	N14 41.1	18 03.9	S17 50.3	Schedar	349 39.0	N56 37.4
A 13	269 15.1	6 19.4	47.8	326 19.4	22.6	124 02.4	41.1	33 06.1	50.3	Shaula	96 21.0	S37 06.6
Y 14	284 17.6	21 18.5	48.0	341 19.8	22.1	139 04.8	41.1	48 08.2	50.4	Sirius	258 32.5	S16 44.3
15	299 20.1	36 17.5	. . 48.3	356 20.2	. . 21.7	154 07.3	. . 41.1	63 10.4	. . 50.5	Spica	158 30.4	S11 14.2
16	314 22.5	51 16.6	48.5	11 20.7	21.3	169 09.7	41.1	78 12.5	50.5	Suhail	222 51.4	S43 29.5
17	329 25.0	66 15.6	48.8	26 21.1	20.8	184 12.1	41.1	93 14.7	50.6			
18	344 27.5	81 14.6	S23 49.0	41 21.5	S21 20.4	199 14.6	N14 41.1	108 16.9	S17 50.7	Vega	80 38.7	N38 48.2
19	359 29.9	96 13.7	49.2	56 22.0	19.9	214 17.0	41.1	123 19.0	50.7	Zuben'ubi	137 04.6	S16 06.0
20	14 32.4	111 12.7	49.5	71 22.4	19.5	229 19.4	41.1	138 21.2	50.8		SHA	Mer. Pass.
21	29 34.8	126 11.8	. . 49.7	86 22.9	. . 19.1	244 21.9	. . 41.1	153 23.4	. . 50.8		° ′	h m
22	44 37.3	141 10.8	50.0	101 23.3	18.6	259 24.3	41.1	168 25.5	50.9	Venus	99 10.7	12 33
23	59 39.8	156 09.9	50.2	116 23.7	18.2	274 26.8	41.1	183 27.7	51.0	Mars	58 19.3	15 15
	h m									Jupiter	214 48.6	4 49
Mer. Pass. 19 05.9		v −0.9	d 0.3	v 0.4	d 0.4	v 2.4	d 0.0	v 2.2	d 0.1	Saturn	124 02.0	10 51

UT	SUN GHA	SUN Dec	MOON GHA	v	MOON Dec	d	HP
d h	° ′	° ′	° ′	′	° ′	′	′
3 00	182 36.3	S22 03.0	46 24.1	9.8	N 9 39.7	9.5	58.4
01	197 36.1	03.4	60 52.9	9.8	9 49.2	9.4	58.3
02	212 35.8	03.7	75 21.7	9.9	9 58.6	9.4	58.3
03	227 35.6 ..	04.1	89 50.6	9.7	10 08.0	9.3	58.3
04	242 35.3	04.4	104 19.3	9.8	10 17.3	9.2	58.3
05	257 35.1	04.8	118 48.1	9.8	10 26.5	9.2	58.3
W 06	272 34.8	S22 05.2	133 16.9	9.7	N10 35.7	9.1	58.3
E 07	287 34.6	05.5	147 45.6	9.7	10 44.8	9.0	58.2
D 08	302 34.4	05.9	162 14.3	9.7	10 53.8	9.0	58.2
N 09	317 34.1 ..	06.2	176 43.0	9.7	11 02.8	8.9	58.2
E 10	332 33.9	06.6	191 11.7	9.7	11 11.7	8.9	58.2
S 11	347 33.6	06.9	205 40.4	9.7	11 20.6	8.7	58.2
D 12	2 33.4	S22 07.3	220 09.1	9.6	N11 29.3	8.7	58.2
A 13	17 33.1	07.6	234 37.7	9.6	11 38.0	8.7	58.2
Y 14	32 32.9	08.0	249 06.3	9.6	11 46.7	8.5	58.1
15	47 32.6 ..	08.3	263 34.9	9.6	11 55.2	8.5	58.1
16	62 32.4	08.7	278 03.5	9.5	12 03.7	8.5	58.1
17	77 32.1	09.0	292 32.0	9.6	12 12.2	8.3	58.1
18	92 31.9	S22 09.4	307 00.6	9.5	N12 20.5	8.3	58.1
19	107 31.7	09.7	321 29.1	9.5	12 28.8	8.2	58.1
20	122 31.4	10.1	335 57.6	9.5	12 37.0	8.1	58.0
21	137 31.2 ..	10.4	350 26.1	9.4	12 45.1	8.1	58.0
22	152 30.9	10.7	4 54.5	9.5	12 53.2	7.9	58.0
23	167 30.7	11.1	19 23.0	9.4	13 01.1	7.9	58.0
4 00	182 30.4	S22 11.4	33 51.4	9.4	N13 09.0	7.8	58.0
01	197 30.2	11.8	48 19.8	9.4	13 16.8	7.8	57.9
02	212 29.9	12.1	62 48.2	9.4	13 24.6	7.6	57.9
03	227 29.7 ..	12.4	77 16.6	9.4	13 32.2	7.6	57.9
04	242 29.4	12.8	91 45.0	9.3	13 39.7	7.5	57.9
05	257 29.2	13.1	106 13.3	9.4	13 47.3	7.4	57.9
T 06	272 28.9	S22 13.5	120 41.7	9.3	N13 54.7	7.3	57.9
H 07	287 28.7	13.8	135 10.0	9.3	14 02.0	7.3	57.8
U 08	302 28.4	14.1	149 38.3	9.3	14 09.3	7.1	57.8
R 09	317 28.2 ..	14.5	164 06.6	9.2	14 16.4	7.1	57.8
S 10	332 27.9	14.8	178 34.8	9.3	14 23.5	7.0	57.8
D 11	347 27.7	15.1	193 03.1	9.2	14 30.5	6.9	57.8
A 12	2 27.4	S22 15.5	207 31.3	9.2	N14 37.4	6.8	57.7
Y 13	17 27.2	15.8	221 59.5	9.2	14 44.2	6.7	57.7
14	32 26.9	16.1	236 27.7	9.2	14 50.9	6.7	57.7
15	47 26.7 ..	16.5	250 55.9	9.2	14 57.6	6.5	57.7
16	62 26.4	16.8	265 24.1	9.2	15 04.1	6.5	57.7
17	77 26.1	17.1	279 52.3	9.1	15 10.6	6.4	57.6
18	92 25.9	S22 17.4	294 20.4	9.2	N15 17.0	6.2	57.6
19	107 25.6	17.8	308 48.6	9.1	15 23.2	6.2	57.6
20	122 25.4	18.1	323 16.7	9.1	15 29.4	6.1	57.6
21	137 25.1 ..	18.4	337 44.8	9.1	15 35.5	6.0	57.6
22	152 24.9	18.7	352 12.9	9.1	15 41.5	5.9	57.5
23	167 24.6	19.1	6 41.0	9.1	15 47.4	5.8	57.5
5 00	182 24.4	S22 19.4	21 09.1	9.0	N15 53.2	5.8	57.5
01	197 24.1	19.7	35 37.1	9.1	15 59.0	5.6	57.5
02	212 23.9	20.0	50 05.2	9.0	16 04.6	5.5	57.4
03	227 23.6 ..	20.4	64 33.3	9.0	16 10.1	5.5	57.4
04	242 23.3	20.7	79 01.3	9.1	16 15.6	5.3	57.4
05	257 23.1	21.0	93 29.4	9.0	16 20.9	5.2	57.4
F 06	272 22.8	S22 21.3	107 57.4	9.0	N16 26.1	5.2	57.4
R 07	287 22.6	21.6	122 25.4	9.0	16 31.3	5.0	57.4
I 08	302 22.3	22.0	136 53.4	9.0	16 36.3	5.0	57.3
D 09	317 22.1 ..	22.3	151 21.4	9.0	16 41.3	4.9	57.3
A 10	332 21.8	22.6	165 49.4	9.1	16 46.2	4.7	57.3
Y 11	347 21.6	22.9	180 17.5	9.0	16 50.9	4.7	57.3
12	2 21.3	S22 23.2	194 45.5	9.0	N16 55.6	4.5	57.2
13	17 21.0	23.5	209 13.5	8.9	17 00.1	4.5	57.2
14	32 20.8	23.8	223 41.4	9.0	17 04.6	4.3	57.2
15	47 20.5 ..	24.2	238 09.4	9.0	17 08.9	4.3	57.2
16	62 20.3	24.5	252 37.4	9.0	17 13.2	4.2	57.2
17	77 20.0	24.8	267 05.4	9.0	17 17.4	4.0	57.1
18	92 19.7	S22 25.1	281 33.4	9.0	N17 21.4	4.0	57.1
19	107 19.5	25.4	296 01.4	9.0	17 25.4	3.8	57.1
20	122 19.2	25.7	310 29.4	9.0	17 29.2	3.8	57.1
21	137 19.0 ..	26.0	324 57.4	9.0	17 33.0	3.6	57.0
22	152 18.7	26.3	339 25.4	9.0	17 36.6	3.6	57.0
23	167 18.4	26.6	353 53.4	9.0	N17 40.2	3.4	57.0
	SD 16.3	d 0.3	SD 15.8		15.7		15.6

Lat.	Twilight Naut.	Twilight Civil	Sunrise	Moonrise 3	Moonrise 4	Moonrise 5	Moonrise 6
°	h m	h m	h m	h m	h m	h m	h m
N 72	07 58	10 03	▭	12 47	12 39	12 27	▭
N 70	07 41	09 20	▭	13 06	13 09	13 17	13 37
68	07 27	08 51	10 55	13 21	13 32	13 49	14 18
66	07 16	08 29	09 57	13 33	13 50	14 13	14 47
64	07 06	08 12	09 24	13 44	14 04	14 31	15 09
62	06 58	07 58	09 00	13 52	14 16	14 47	15 26
60	06 50	07 45	08 40	14 00	14 27	14 59	15 40
N 58	06 43	07 35	08 25	14 07	14 36	15 10	15 53
56	06 37	07 25	08 11	14 13	14 44	15 20	16 03
54	06 32	07 17	08 00	14 18	14 51	15 29	16 13
52	06 26	07 10	07 49	14 23	14 57	15 36	16 21
50	06 22	07 03	07 40	14 28	15 03	15 43	16 29
45	06 11	06 48	07 21	14 37	15 16	15 58	16 45
N 40	06 01	06 35	07 05	14 45	15 26	16 10	16 58
35	05 53	06 24	06 52	14 52	15 35	16 21	17 10
30	05 45	06 14	06 40	14 58	15 43	16 30	17 20
20	05 29	05 57	06 20	15 09	15 56	16 46	17 37
N 10	05 14	05 40	06 03	15 18	16 08	17 00	17 52
0	04 58	05 24	05 46	15 27	16 20	17 13	18 06
S 10	04 40	05 07	05 30	15 36	16 31	17 26	18 20
20	04 19	04 48	05 12	15 46	16 43	17 40	18 35
30	03 51	04 24	04 51	15 57	16 57	17 56	18 52
35	03 34	04 10	04 39	16 03	17 05	18 05	19 02
40	03 12	03 53	04 25	16 10	17 14	18 16	19 13
45	02 44	03 32	04 08	16 19	17 25	18 29	19 27
S 50	02 03	03 04	03 47	16 29	17 39	18 44	19 43
52	01 40	02 50	03 37	16 34	17 45	18 51	19 51
54	01 07	02 34	03 26	16 39	17 52	18 59	20 00
56	////	02 15	03 13	16 45	17 59	19 08	20 10
58	////	01 50	02 58	16 52	18 08	19 18	20 21
S 60	////	01 15	02 40	16 59	18 18	19 30	20 33

Lat.	Sunset	Twilight Civil	Twilight Naut.	Moonset 3	Moonset 4	Moonset 5	Moonset 6
°	h m	h m	h m	h m	h m	h m	h m
N 72	▭	13 36	15 41	05 22	07 19	09 21	▭
N 70	▭	14 20	15 58	05 05	06 50	08 32	10 03
68	12 45	14 49	16 12	04 51	06 28	08 01	09 22
66	13 43	15 10	16 24	04 40	06 11	07 38	08 54
64	14 16	15 28	16 34	04 30	05 58	07 20	08 32
62	14 40	15 42	16 42	04 23	05 46	07 05	08 15
60	14 59	15 55	16 50	04 16	05 36	06 52	08 01
N 58	15 15	16 05	16 57	04 10	05 28	06 42	07 48
56	15 29	16 15	17 03	04 04	05 20	06 32	07 38
54	15 40	16 23	17 08	04 00	05 14	06 24	07 28
52	15 51	16 30	17 14	03 55	05 08	06 17	07 20
50	16 00	16 37	17 18	03 51	05 02	06 10	07 13
45	16 19	16 52	17 29	03 43	04 51	05 56	06 57
N 40	16 35	17 05	17 39	03 36	04 41	05 44	06 44
35	16 48	17 16	17 47	03 30	04 33	05 34	06 33
30	17 00	17 26	17 55	03 25	04 26	05 25	06 23
20	17 20	17 44	18 11	03 16	04 13	05 10	06 06
N 10	17 37	18 00	18 26	03 08	04 02	04 57	05 52
0	17 54	18 16	18 42	03 00	03 52	04 45	05 38
S 10	18 11	18 33	19 00	02 53	03 42	04 33	05 24
20	18 28	18 53	19 22	02 45	03 31	04 20	05 10
30	18 49	19 16	19 49	02 36	03 19	04 05	04 53
35	19 02	19 31	20 07	02 30	03 12	03 56	04 43
40	19 16	19 48	20 29	02 24	03 04	03 46	04 32
45	19 33	20 09	20 57	02 18	02 54	03 35	04 19
S 50	19 54	20 37	21 38	02 09	02 43	03 21	04 04
52	20 04	20 51	22 02	02 06	02 38	03 14	03 56
54	20 15	21 07	22 36	02 02	02 32	03 07	03 48
56	20 28	21 27	////	01 57	02 25	02 59	03 39
58	20 44	21 52	////	01 52	02 18	02 50	03 28
S 60	21 02	22 28	////	01 46	02 10	02 39	03 16

	SUN Eqn. of Time 00h	SUN Eqn. of Time 12h	SUN Mer. Pass.	MOON Mer. Pass. Upper	MOON Mer. Pass. Lower	MOON Age	MOON Phase
Day d	m s	m s	h m	h m	h m	d	%
3	10 26	10 14	11 50	21 40	09 14	11	90
4	10 02	09 50	11 50	22 32	10 06	12	95
5	09 38	09 26	11 51	23 25	10 59	13	99

UT (d h)	ARIES GHA	VENUS −3.9 GHA	Dec	MARS +1.0 GHA	Dec	JUPITER −2.3 GHA	Dec	SATURN +0.5 GHA	Dec	STAR Name	SHA	Dec
6 00	74 42.2	171 08.9	S23 50.4	131 24.2	S21 17.8	289 29.2	N14 41.1	198 29.9	S17 51.0	Acamar	315 17.3	S40 14.9
01	89 44.7	186 07.9	50.7	146 24.6	17.3	304 31.6	41.1	213 32.0	51.1	Achernar	335 25.8	S57 09.9
02	104 47.2	201 07.0	50.9	161 25.1	16.9	319 34.1	41.1	228 34.2	51.2	Acrux	173 08.2	S63 10.6
03	119 49.6	216 06.0 ..	51.2	176 25.5 ..	16.4	334 36.5 ..	41.1	243 36.4 ..	51.2	Adhara	255 11.4	S28 59.6
04	134 52.1	231 05.1	51.4	191 25.9	16.0	349 39.0	41.1	258 38.5	51.3	Aldebaran	290 47.9	N16 32.2
05	149 54.6	246 04.1	51.6	206 26.4	15.6	4 41.4	41.1	273 40.7	51.4			
S 06	164 57.0	261 03.2	S23 51.8	221 26.8	S21 15.1	19 43.8	N14 41.1	288 42.9	S17 51.4	Alioth	166 20.2	N55 52.5
A 07	179 59.5	276 02.2	52.1	236 27.3	14.7	34 46.3	41.1	303 45.0	51.5	Alkaid	152 58.5	N49 14.2
T 08	195 01.9	291 01.2	52.3	251 27.7	14.2	49 48.7	41.1	318 47.2	51.6	Al Na'ir	27 42.7	S46 53.4
U 09	210 04.4	306 00.3 ..	52.5	266 28.2 ..	13.8	64 51.2 ..	41.1	333 49.4 ..	51.6	Alnilam	275 45.0	S 1 11.7
R 10	225 06.9	320 59.3	52.7	281 28.6	13.3	79 53.6	41.1	348 51.5	51.7	Alphard	217 55.0	S 8 43.5
D 11	240 09.3	335 58.4	53.0	296 29.0	12.9	94 56.0	41.1	3 53.7	51.7			
A 12	255 11.8	350 57.4	S23 53.2	311 29.5	S21 12.5	109 58.5	N14 41.1	18 55.9	S17 51.8	Alphecca	126 10.5	N26 40.0
Y 13	270 14.3	5 56.4	53.4	326 29.9	12.0	125 00.9	41.1	33 58.0	51.9	Alpheratz	357 42.3	N29 10.6
14	285 16.7	20 55.5	53.6	341 30.4	11.6	140 03.4	41.2	49 00.2	51.9	Altair	62 07.5	N 8 54.7
15	300 19.2	35 54.5 ..	53.9	356 30.8 ..	11.1	155 05.8 ..	41.2	64 02.4 ..	52.0	Ankaa	353 14.6	S42 13.7
16	315 21.7	50 53.6	54.1	11 31.2	10.7	170 08.3	41.2	79 04.5	52.1	Antares	112 25.4	S26 27.6
17	330 24.1	65 52.6	54.3	26 31.7	10.2	185 10.7	41.2	94 06.7	52.1			
18	345 26.6	80 51.6	S23 54.5	41 32.1	S21 09.8	200 13.1	N14 41.2	109 08.9	S17 52.2	Arcturus	145 55.1	N19 06.3
19	0 29.1	95 50.7	54.7	56 32.6	09.3	215 15.6	41.2	124 11.0	52.3	Atria	107 26.8	S69 03.0
20	15 31.5	110 49.7	54.9	71 33.0	08.9	230 18.0	41.2	139 13.2	52.3	Avior	234 17.1	S59 33.4
21	30 34.0	125 48.7 ..	55.1	86 33.5 ..	08.4	245 20.5 ..	41.2	154 15.4 ..	52.4	Bellatrix	278 30.6	N 6 21.6
22	45 36.4	140 47.8	55.3	101 33.9	08.0	260 22.9	41.2	169 17.5	52.4	Betelgeuse	270 59.9	N 7 24.4
23	60 38.9	155 46.8	55.5	116 34.4	07.5	275 25.4	41.2	184 19.7	52.5			
7 00	75 41.4	170 45.9	S23 55.8	131 34.8	S21 07.1	290 27.8	N14 41.2	199 21.9	S17 52.6	Canopus	263 55.2	S52 42.3
01	90 43.8	185 44.9	56.0	146 35.2	06.6	305 30.3	41.2	214 24.0	52.6	Capella	280 32.5	N46 00.6
02	105 46.3	200 43.9	56.2	161 35.7	06.2	320 32.7	41.2	229 26.2	52.7	Deneb	49 31.0	N45 20.4
03	120 48.8	215 43.0 ..	56.4	176 36.1 ..	05.7	335 35.1 ..	41.2	244 28.4 ..	52.8	Denebola	182 32.7	N14 29.2
04	135 51.2	230 42.0	56.6	191 36.6	05.3	350 37.6	41.2	259 30.6	52.8	Diphda	348 54.8	S17 54.4
05	150 53.7	245 41.0	56.8	206 37.0	04.8	5 40.0	41.2	274 32.7	52.9			
S 06	165 56.2	260 40.1	S23 57.0	221 37.5	S21 04.4	20 42.5	N14 41.2	289 34.9	S17 52.9	Dubhe	193 50.6	N61 39.9
U 07	180 58.6	275 39.1	57.2	236 37.9	03.9	35 44.9	41.2	304 37.1	53.0	Elnath	278 11.0	N28 37.0
N 08	196 01.1	290 38.2	57.4	251 38.3	03.5	50 47.4	41.2	319 39.2	53.1	Eltanin	90 46.2	N51 29.5
D 09	211 03.6	305 37.2 ..	57.6	266 38.8 ..	03.0	65 49.8 ..	41.2	334 41.4 ..	53.1	Enif	33 46.2	N 9 56.8
A 10	226 06.0	320 36.2	57.8	281 39.2	02.6	80 52.3	41.2	349 43.6	53.2	Fomalhaut	15 22.9	S29 32.6
Y 11	241 08.5	335 35.3	57.9	296 39.7	02.1	95 54.7	41.2	4 45.7	53.3			
12	256 10.9	350 34.3	S23 58.1	311 40.1	S21 01.7	110 57.2	N14 41.3	19 47.9	S17 53.3	Gacrux	171 59.9	S57 11.5
13	271 13.4	5 33.3	58.3	326 40.6	01.2	125 59.6	41.3	34 50.1	53.4	Gienah	175 51.4	S17 37.4
14	286 15.9	20 32.4	58.5	341 41.0	00.8	141 02.1	41.3	49 52.2	53.5	Hadar	148 46.8	S60 26.4
15	301 18.3	35 31.4 ..	58.7	356 41.5	21 00.3	156 04.5 ..	41.3	64 54.4 ..	53.5	Hamal	327 59.3	N23 32.0
16	316 20.8	50 30.4	58.9	11 41.9	20 59.9	171 07.0	41.3	79 56.6	53.6	Kaus Aust.	83 42.9	S34 22.4
17	331 23.3	65 29.5	59.1	26 42.4	59.4	186 09.4	41.3	94 58.7	53.6			
18	346 25.7	80 28.5	S23 59.3	41 42.8	S20 58.9	201 11.9	N14 41.3	110 00.9	S17 53.7	Kochab	137 21.3	N74 05.6
19	1 28.2	95 27.5	59.4	56 43.3	58.5	216 14.3	41.3	125 03.1	53.8	Markab	13 37.3	N15 17.3
20	16 30.7	110 26.6	59.6	71 43.7	58.0	231 16.8	41.3	140 05.2	53.8	Menkar	314 13.7	N 4 08.8
21	31 33.1	125 25.6	23 59.8	86 44.1 ..	57.6	246 19.2 ..	41.3	155 07.4 ..	53.9	Menkent	148 06.6	S36 26.3
22	46 35.6	140 24.7	24 00.0	101 44.6	57.1	261 21.7	41.3	170 09.6	54.0	Miaplacidus	221 38.8	S69 46.6
23	61 38.1	155 23.7	00.2	116 45.0	56.7	276 24.2	41.3	185 11.7	54.0			
8 00	76 40.5	170 22.7	S24 00.3	131 45.5	S20 56.2	291 26.6	N14 41.3	200 13.9	S17 54.1	Mirfak	308 38.4	N49 54.8
01	91 43.0	185 21.8	00.5	146 45.9	55.7	306 29.1	41.3	215 16.1	54.1	Nunki	75 57.4	S26 16.5
02	106 45.4	200 20.8	00.7	161 46.4	55.3	321 31.5	41.3	230 18.2	54.2	Peacock	53 18.2	S56 41.2
03	121 47.9	215 19.8 ..	00.9	176 46.8 ..	54.8	336 34.0 ..	41.4	245 20.4 ..	54.3	Pollux	243 26.2	N27 59.1
04	136 50.4	230 18.9	01.0	191 47.3	54.4	351 36.4	41.4	260 22.6	54.3	Procyon	244 58.4	N 5 11.0
05	151 52.8	245 17.9	01.2	206 47.7	53.9	6 38.9	41.4	275 24.7	54.4			
M 06	166 55.3	260 16.9	S24 01.4	221 48.2	S20 53.5	21 41.3	N14 41.4	290 26.9	S17 54.5	Rasalhague	96 05.9	N12 33.2
O 07	181 57.8	275 16.0	01.5	236 48.6	53.0	36 43.8	41.4	305 29.1	54.5	Regulus	207 42.4	N11 53.5
N 08	197 00.2	290 15.0	01.7	251 49.1	52.5	51 46.2	41.4	320 31.2	54.6	Rigel	281 10.8	S 8 11.2
D 09	212 02.7	305 14.0 ..	01.9	266 49.5 ..	52.1	66 48.7 ..	41.4	335 33.4 ..	54.6	Rigil Kent.	139 50.8	S60 53.5
A 10	227 05.2	320 13.1	02.0	281 50.0	51.6	81 51.2	41.4	350 35.6	54.7	Sabik	102 11.7	S15 44.4
Y 11	242 07.6	335 12.1	02.2	296 50.4	51.1	96 53.6	41.4	5 37.8	54.8			
12	257 10.1	350 11.1	S24 02.3	311 50.9	S20 50.7	111 56.1	N14 41.4	20 39.9	S17 54.8	Schedar	349 39.0	N56 37.4
13	272 12.6	5 10.1	02.5	326 51.3	50.2	126 58.5	41.4	35 42.1	54.9	Shaula	96 21.0	S37 06.6
14	287 15.0	20 09.2	02.7	341 51.8	49.7	142 01.0	41.4	50 44.3	55.0	Sirius	258 32.5	S16 44.3
15	302 17.5	35 08.2 ..	02.8	356 52.2 ..	49.3	157 03.5 ..	41.4	65 46.4 ..	55.0	Spica	158 30.4	S11 14.2
16	317 19.9	50 07.2	03.0	11 52.7	48.8	172 05.9	41.5	80 48.6	55.1	Suhail	222 51.4	S43 29.5
17	332 22.4	65 06.3	03.1	26 53.1	48.4	187 08.4	41.5	95 50.8	55.1			
18	347 24.9	80 05.3	S24 03.3	41 53.6	S20 47.9	202 10.8	N14 41.5	110 52.9	S17 55.2	Vega	80 38.7	N38 48.2
19	2 27.3	95 04.3	03.4	56 54.0	47.4	217 13.3	41.5	125 55.1	55.3	Zuben'ubi	137 04.6	S16 06.0
20	17 29.8	110 03.4	03.6	71 54.5	47.0	232 15.8	41.5	140 57.3	55.3			
21	32 32.3	125 02.4 ..	03.7	86 54.9 ..	46.5	247 18.2 ..	41.5	155 59.4 ..	55.4		SHA	Mer. Pass.
22	47 34.7	140 01.4	03.9	101 55.4	46.0	262 20.7	41.5	171 01.6	55.5	Venus	95 04.5	12 38
23	62 37.2	155 00.5	04.0	116 55.8	45.6	277 23.1	41.5	186 03.8	55.5	Mars	55 53.4	15 13
Mer. Pass. 18 54.1		v −1.0	d 0.2	v 0.4	d 0.5	v 2.4	d 0.0	v 2.2	d 0.1	Jupiter	214 46.4	4 37
										Saturn	123 40.5	10 41

UT	SUN GHA	SUN Dec	MOON GHA	MOON v	MOON Dec	MOON d	MOON HP
d h	° ′	° ′	° ′	′	° ′	′	′
6 00	182 18.2	S22 26.9	8 21.4	9.0	N17 43.6	3.4	57.0
01	197 17.9	27.2	22 49.4	9.0	17 47.0	3.2	57.0
02	212 17.7	27.5	37 17.4	9.1	17 50.2	3.2	56.9
03	227 17.4 ..	27.8	51 45.5	9.0	17 53.4	3.0	56.9
04	242 17.1	28.1	66 13.5	9.0	17 56.4	2.9	56.9
05	257 16.9	28.4	80 41.5	9.1	17 59.3	2.9	56.9
06	272 16.6	S22 28.8	95 09.6	9.0	N18 02.2	2.7	56.8
07	287 16.4	29.1	109 37.6	9.1	18 04.9	2.6	56.8
S 08	302 16.1	29.4	124 05.7	9.1	18 07.5	2.5	56.8
A 09	317 15.8 ..	29.6	138 33.8	9.1	18 10.0	2.5	56.8
T 10	332 15.6	29.9	153 01.9	9.1	18 12.5	2.3	56.7
U 11	347 15.3	30.2	167 30.0	9.1	18 14.8	2.2	56.7
R 12	2 15.0	S22 30.5	181 58.1	9.1	N18 17.0	2.1	56.7
D 13	17 14.8	30.8	196 26.2	9.2	18 19.1	2.0	56.7
A 14	32 14.5	31.1	210 54.4	9.1	18 21.1	1.9	56.7
Y 15	47 14.3 ..	31.4	225 22.5	9.1	18 23.0	1.8	56.6
16	62 14.0	31.7	239 50.7	9.2	18 24.8	1.7	56.6
17	77 13.7	32.0	254 18.9	9.2	18 26.5	1.6	56.6
18	92 13.5	S22 32.3	268 47.1	9.2	N18 28.1	1.5	56.6
19	107 13.2	32.6	283 15.3	9.3	18 29.6	1.3	56.5
20	122 12.9	32.9	297 43.6	9.2	18 30.9	1.3	56.5
21	137 12.7 ..	33.2	312 11.8	9.3	18 32.2	1.2	56.5
22	152 12.4	33.5	326 40.1	9.3	18 33.4	1.1	56.5
23	167 12.1	33.7	341 08.4	9.4	18 34.5	1.0	56.4
7 00	182 11.9	S22 34.0	355 36.8	9.3	N18 35.5	0.8	56.4
01	197 11.6	34.3	10 05.1	9.4	18 36.3	0.8	56.4
02	212 11.3	34.6	24 33.5	9.4	18 37.1	0.6	56.4
03	227 11.1 ..	34.9	39 01.9	9.4	18 37.7	0.6	56.4
04	242 10.8	35.2	53 30.3	9.5	18 38.3	0.5	56.3
05	257 10.5	35.5	67 58.8	9.4	18 38.8	0.3	56.3
06	272 10.3	S22 35.7	82 27.2	9.6	N18 39.1	0.3	56.3
07	287 10.0	36.0	96 55.8	9.5	18 39.4	0.1	56.3
S 08	302 09.7	36.3	111 24.3	9.5	18 39.5	0.1	56.2
U 09	317 09.5 ..	36.6	125 52.8	9.6	18 39.6	0.1	56.2
N 10	332 09.2	36.9	140 21.4	9.7	18 39.5	0.1	56.2
D 11	347 08.9	37.1	154 50.1	9.6	18 39.4	0.3	56.2
A 12	2 08.7	S22 37.4	169 18.7	9.7	N18 39.1	0.3	56.1
Y 13	17 08.4	37.7	183 47.4	9.7	18 38.8	0.5	56.1
14	32 08.1	38.0	198 16.1	9.8	18 38.3	0.5	56.1
15	47 07.9 ..	38.3	212 44.9	9.7	18 37.8	0.6	56.1
16	62 07.6	38.5	227 13.6	9.9	18 37.2	0.8	56.0
17	77 07.3	38.8	241 42.5	9.8	18 36.4	0.8	56.0
18	92 07.1	S22 39.1	256 11.3	9.9	N18 35.6	1.0	56.0
19	107 06.8	39.3	270 40.2	9.9	18 34.6	1.0	56.0
20	122 06.5	39.6	285 09.1	10.0	18 33.6	1.2	56.0
21	137 06.2 ..	39.9	299 38.1	10.0	18 32.4	1.2	55.9
22	152 06.0	40.2	314 07.1	10.0	18 31.2	1.3	55.9
23	167 05.7	40.4	328 36.1	10.1	18 29.9	1.4	55.9
8 00	182 05.4	S22 40.7	343 05.2	10.1	N18 28.5	1.6	55.9
01	197 05.2	41.0	357 34.3	10.1	18 26.9	1.6	55.8
02	212 04.9	41.2	12 03.4	10.2	18 25.3	1.7	55.8
03	227 04.6 ..	41.5	26 32.6	10.2	18 23.6	1.8	55.8
04	242 04.3	41.8	41 01.8	10.3	18 21.8	1.9	55.8
05	257 04.1	42.0	55 31.1	10.3	18 19.9	2.0	55.7
06	272 03.8	S22 42.3	70 00.4	10.4	N18 17.9	2.1	55.7
07	287 03.5	42.6	84 29.8	10.4	18 15.8	2.2	55.7
M 08	302 03.3	42.8	98 59.2	10.4	18 13.6	2.2	55.7
O 09	317 03.0 ..	43.1	113 28.6	10.5	18 11.4	2.4	55.7
N 10	332 02.7	43.3	127 58.1	10.5	18 09.0	2.5	55.6
D 11	347 02.4	43.6	142 27.6	10.6	18 06.5	2.5	55.6
A 12	2 02.2	S22 43.9	156 57.2	10.6	N18 04.0	2.6	55.6
Y 13	17 01.9	44.1	171 26.8	10.6	18 01.4	2.8	55.6
14	32 01.6	44.4	185 56.4	10.8	17 58.6	2.8	55.5
15	47 01.3 ..	44.6	200 26.2	10.7	17 55.8	2.9	55.5
16	62 01.1	44.9	214 55.9	10.8	17 52.9	3.0	55.5
17	77 00.8	45.1	229 25.7	10.8	17 49.9	3.0	55.5
18	92 00.5	S22 45.4	243 55.5	10.9	N17 46.9	3.2	55.5
19	107 00.2	45.7	258 25.4	11.0	17 43.7	3.3	55.4
20	122 00.0	45.9	272 55.4	10.9	17 40.4	3.3	55.4
21	136 59.7 ..	46.2	287 25.3	11.1	17 37.1	3.4	55.4
22	151 59.4	46.4	301 55.4	11.0	17 33.7	3.5	55.4
23	166 59.1	46.7	316 25.4	11.2	N17 30.2	3.6	55.4
	SD 16.3	d 0.3	SD 15.4		15.3		15.1

Lat.	Twilight Naut.	Twilight Civil	Sunrise	Moonrise 6	Moonrise 7	Moonrise 8	Moonrise 9
°	h m	h m	h m	h m	h m	h m	h m
N 72	08 06	10 17	▬	☐	☐	14 05	16 15
N 70	07 47	09 29	▬	13 37	14 20	15 32	16 59
68	07 33	08 58	11 18	14 18	15 05	16 11	17 29
66	07 21	08 36	10 06	14 47	15 35	16 38	17 50
64	07 11	08 18	09 31	15 09	15 58	16 58	18 08
62	07 02	08 03	09 06	15 26	16 16	17 15	18 22
60	06 54	07 50	08 46	15 40	16 31	17 29	18 34
N 58	06 47	07 39	08 30	15 53	16 43	17 41	18 44
56	06 41	07 29	08 16	16 03	16 54	17 51	18 53
54	06 35	07 21	08 04	16 13	17 04	18 00	19 01
52	06 30	07 13	07 53	16 21	17 12	18 08	19 08
50	06 25	07 06	07 44	16 29	17 20	18 16	19 15
45	06 14	06 51	07 24	16 45	17 36	18 31	19 28
N 40	06 04	06 38	07 08	16 58	17 50	18 44	19 40
35	05 55	06 27	06 55	17 10	18 01	18 55	19 49
30	05 47	06 16	06 43	17 20	18 11	19 04	19 58
20	05 31	05 58	06 22	17 37	18 29	19 21	20 12
N 10	05 16	05 42	06 04	17 52	18 44	19 35	20 25
0	04 59	05 25	05 48	18 06	18 58	19 48	20 37
S 10	04 41	05 08	05 31	18 20	19 12	20 02	20 49
20	04 19	04 48	05 13	18 35	19 27	20 16	21 02
30	03 51	04 24	04 51	18 52	19 44	20 32	21 16
35	03 33	04 10	04 39	19 02	19 54	20 42	21 25
40	03 11	03 52	04 25	19 13	20 06	20 53	21 34
45	02 42	03 31	04 07	19 27	20 19	21 05	21 45
S 50	02 00	03 02	03 46	19 43	20 36	21 21	21 59
52	01 36	02 48	03 36	19 51	20 43	21 28	22 05
54	01 00	02 32	03 24	20 00	20 52	21 36	22 12
56	////	02 11	03 11	20 10	21 02	21 45	22 20
58	////	01 45	02 55	20 21	21 13	21 55	22 28
S 60	////	01 07	02 36	20 33	21 25	22 06	22 38

Lat.	Sunset	Twilight Civil	Twilight Naut.	Moonset 6	Moonset 7	Moonset 8	Moonset 9
°	h m	h m	h m	h m	h m	h m	h m
N 72	▬	13 26	15 37	☐	☐	13 11	12 43
N 70	▬	14 13	15 55	10 03	11 10	11 44	11 58
68	12 25	14 44	16 09	09 22	10 24	11 04	11 28
66	13 36	15 07	16 21	08 54	09 54	10 37	11 06
64	14 12	15 25	16 32	08 32	09 31	10 16	10 48
62	14 37	15 40	16 41	08 15	09 13	09 59	10 34
60	14 57	15 53	16 48	08 01	08 58	09 45	10 21
N 58	15 13	16 04	16 55	07 48	08 46	09 33	10 11
56	15 27	16 13	17 02	07 38	08 35	09 22	10 01
54	15 39	16 22	17 07	07 28	08 25	09 13	09 53
52	15 49	16 30	17 13	07 20	08 17	09 05	09 46
50	15 59	16 37	17 18	07 13	08 09	08 57	09 39
45	16 18	16 52	17 29	06 57	07 52	08 42	09 25
N 40	16 35	17 05	17 39	06 44	07 39	08 28	09 13
35	16 48	17 16	17 48	06 33	07 27	08 17	09 03
30	17 00	17 26	17 56	06 23	07 17	08 08	08 54
20	17 20	17 44	18 12	06 06	07 00	07 51	08 38
N 10	17 38	18 01	18 27	05 52	06 45	07 36	08 25
0	17 55	18 18	18 44	05 38	06 31	07 22	08 12
S 10	18 12	18 35	19 02	05 24	06 17	07 09	07 59
20	18 30	18 55	19 24	05 10	06 01	06 54	07 46
30	18 52	19 19	19 52	04 53	05 44	06 37	07 30
35	19 04	19 34	20 10	04 43	05 34	06 27	07 21
40	19 19	19 51	20 32	04 32	05 22	06 15	07 11
45	19 36	20 13	21 01	04 19	05 09	06 02	06 58
S 50	19 57	20 41	21 44	04 04	04 52	05 46	06 43
52	20 08	20 55	22 09	03 56	04 44	05 38	06 36
54	20 19	21 12	22 45	03 48	04 36	05 30	06 29
56	20 33	21 33	////	03 39	04 26	05 20	06 20
58	20 49	21 59	////	03 28	04 15	05 09	06 10
S 60	21 08	22 39	////	03 16	04 02	04 57	05 59

Day	SUN Eqn. of Time 00h	SUN Eqn. of Time 12h	SUN Mer. Pass.	MOON Mer. Pass. Upper	MOON Mer. Pass. Lower	Age	Phase
d	m s	m s	h m	h m	h m	d	%
6	09 13	09 01	11 51	24 18	11 52	14	100
7	08 48	08 35	11 51	00 18	12 44	15	99
8	08 22	08 09	11 52	01 10	13 35	16	96

UT	ARIES	VENUS −3.9		MARS +1.0		JUPITER −2.3		SATURN +0.5		STARS		
	GHA	GHA	Dec	GHA	Dec	GHA	Dec	GHA	Dec	Name	SHA	Dec
d h	° ′	° ′	° ′	° ′	° ′	° ′	° ′	° ′	° ′		° ′	° ′
9 00	77 39.7	169 59.5	S24 04.2	131 56.3	S20 45.1	292 25.6	N14 41.5	201 05.9	S17 55.6	Acamar	315 17.3	S40 14.9
01	92 42.1	184 58.5	04.3	146 56.7	44.6	307 28.1	41.5	216 08.1	55.6	Achernar	335 25.8	S57 09.9
02	107 44.6	199 57.6	04.5	161 57.2	44.2	322 30.5	41.6	231 10.3	55.7	Acrux	173 08.2	S63 10.6
03	122 47.0	214 56.6	. . 04.6	176 57.6	. . 43.7	337 33.0	. . 41.6	246 12.5	. . 55.8	Adhara	255 11.4	S28 59.7
04	137 49.5	229 55.6	04.7	191 58.1	43.2	352 35.4	41.6	261 14.6	55.8	Aldebaran	290 47.9	N16 32.2
05	152 52.0	244 54.6	04.9	206 58.5	42.7	7 37.9	41.6	276 16.8	55.9			
06	167 54.4	259 53.7	S24 05.0	221 59.0	S20 42.3	22 40.4	N14 41.6	291 19.0	S17 56.0	Alioth	166 20.2	N55 52.5
07	182 56.9	274 52.7	05.1	236 59.4	41.8	37 42.8	41.6	306 21.1	56.0	Alkaid	152 58.5	N49 14.2
08	197 59.4	289 51.7	05.3	251 59.9	41.3	52 45.3	41.6	321 23.3	56.1	Al Na'ir	27 42.7	S46 53.4
T 09	213 01.8	304 50.8	. . 05.4	267 00.3	. . 40.9	67 47.8	. . 41.6	336 25.5	. . 56.1	Alnilam	275 45.0	S 1 11.7
U 10	228 04.3	319 49.8	05.5	282 00.8	40.4	82 50.2	41.6	351 27.6	56.2	Alphard	217 54.9	S 8 43.5
E 11	243 06.8	334 48.8	05.7	297 01.2	39.9	97 52.7	41.6	6 29.8	56.3			
S 12	258 09.2	349 47.9	S24 05.8	312 01.7	S20 39.4	112 55.2	N14 41.7	21 32.0	S17 56.3	Alphecca	126 10.5	N26 40.0
D 13	273 11.7	4 46.9	05.9	327 02.1	39.0	127 57.6	41.7	36 34.1	56.4	Alpheratz	357 42.3	N29 10.6
A 14	288 14.2	19 45.9	06.1	342 02.6	38.5	143 00.1	41.7	51 36.3	56.5	Altair	62 07.5	N 8 54.7
Y 15	303 16.6	34 44.9	. . 06.2	357 03.0	. . 38.0	158 02.6	. . 41.7	66 38.5	. . 56.5	Ankaa	353 14.6	S42 13.7
16	318 19.1	49 44.0	06.3	12 03.5	37.6	173 05.0	41.7	81 40.7	56.6	Antares	112 25.4	S26 27.6
17	333 21.5	64 43.0	06.4	27 04.0	37.1	188 07.5	41.7	96 42.8	56.6			
18	348 24.0	79 42.0	S24 06.6	42 04.4	S20 36.6	203 10.0	N14 41.7	111 45.0	S17 56.7	Arcturus	145 55.1	N19 06.3
19	3 26.5	94 41.1	06.7	57 04.9	36.1	218 12.4	41.7	126 47.2	56.8	Atria	107 26.8	S69 03.0
20	18 28.9	109 40.1	06.8	72 05.3	35.7	233 14.9	41.8	141 49.3	56.8	Avior	234 17.1	S59 33.4
21	33 31.4	124 39.1	. . 06.9	87 05.8	. . 35.2	248 17.4	. . 41.8	156 51.5	. . 56.9	Bellatrix	278 30.6	N 6 21.6
22	48 33.9	139 38.1	07.0	102 06.2	34.7	263 19.8	41.8	171 53.7	57.0	Betelgeuse	270 59.9	N 7 24.4
23	63 36.3	154 37.2	07.2	117 06.7	34.2	278 22.3	41.8	186 55.8	57.0			
10 00	78 38.8	169 36.2	S24 07.3	132 07.1	S20 33.8	293 24.8	N14 41.8	201 58.0	S17 57.1	Canopus	263 55.1	S52 42.3
01	93 41.3	184 35.2	07.4	147 07.6	33.3	308 27.2	41.8	217 00.2	57.1	Capella	280 32.4	N46 00.6
02	108 43.7	199 34.2	07.5	162 08.0	32.8	323 29.7	41.8	232 02.3	57.2	Deneb	49 31.0	N45 20.4
03	123 46.2	214 33.3	. . 07.6	177 08.5	. . 32.3	338 32.2	. . 41.8	247 04.5	. . 57.3	Denebola	182 32.7	N14 29.2
04	138 48.7	229 32.3	07.7	192 09.0	31.8	353 34.7	41.9	262 06.7	57.3	Diphda	348 54.8	S17 54.4
05	153 51.1	244 31.3	07.8	207 09.4	31.4	8 37.1	41.9	277 08.9	57.4			
06	168 53.6	259 30.4	S24 07.9	222 09.9	S20 30.9	23 39.6	N14 41.9	292 11.0	S17 57.4	Dubhe	193 50.6	N61 39.9
07	183 56.0	274 29.4	08.0	237 10.3	30.4	38 42.1	41.9	307 13.2	57.5	Elnath	278 10.9	N28 37.0
W 08	198 58.5	289 28.4	08.1	252 10.8	29.9	53 44.5	41.9	322 15.4	57.6	Eltanin	90 46.2	N51 29.5
E 09	214 01.0	304 27.4	. . 08.2	267 11.2	. . 29.4	68 47.0	. . 41.9	337 17.5	. . 57.6	Enif	33 46.3	N 9 56.8
D 10	229 03.4	319 26.5	08.3	282 11.7	29.0	83 49.5	41.9	352 19.7	57.7	Fomalhaut	15 23.0	S29 32.6
N 11	244 05.9	334 25.5	08.4	297 12.1	28.5	98 52.0	41.9	7 21.9	57.8			
E 12	259 08.4	349 24.5	S24 08.5	312 12.6	S20 28.0	113 54.4	N14 42.0	22 24.0	S17 57.8	Gacrux	171 59.8	S57 11.5
S 13	274 10.8	4 23.5	08.6	327 13.1	27.5	128 56.9	42.0	37 26.2	57.9	Gienah	175 51.3	S17 37.4
D 14	289 13.3	19 22.6	08.7	342 13.5	27.0	143 59.4	42.0	52 28.4	57.9	Hadar	148 46.8	S60 26.4
A 15	304 15.8	34 21.6	. . 08.8	357 14.0	. . 26.6	159 01.9	. . 42.0	67 30.6	. . 58.0	Hamal	327 59.3	N23 32.0
Y 16	319 18.2	49 20.6	08.9	12 14.4	26.1	174 04.3	42.0	82 32.7	58.1	Kaus Aust.	83 42.9	S34 22.4
17	334 20.7	64 19.7	09.0	27 14.9	25.6	189 06.8	42.0	97 34.9	58.1			
18	349 23.2	79 18.7	S24 09.1	42 15.3	S20 25.1	204 09.3	N14 42.0	112 37.1	S17 58.2	Kochab	137 21.3	N74 05.6
19	4 25.6	94 17.7	09.2	57 15.8	24.6	219 11.8	42.1	127 39.2	58.2	Markab	13 37.3	N15 17.3
20	19 28.1	109 16.7	09.3	72 16.3	24.1	234 14.2	42.1	142 41.4	58.3	Menkar	314 13.7	N 4 08.8
21	34 30.5	124 15.8	. . 09.4	87 16.7	. . 23.6	249 16.7	. . 42.1	157 43.6	. . 58.4	Menkent	148 06.6	S36 26.3
22	49 33.0	139 14.8	09.5	102 17.2	23.2	264 19.2	42.1	172 45.8	58.4	Miaplacidus	221 38.8	S69 46.6
23	64 35.5	154 13.8	09.5	117 17.6	22.7	279 21.7	42.1	187 47.9	58.5			
11 00	79 37.9	169 12.8	S24 09.6	132 18.1	S20 22.2	294 24.2	N14 42.1	202 50.1	S17 58.6	Mirfak	308 38.4	N49 54.8
01	94 40.4	184 11.9	09.7	147 18.5	21.7	309 26.6	42.1	217 52.3	58.6	Nunki	75 57.4	S26 16.5
02	109 42.9	199 10.9	09.8	162 19.0	21.2	324 29.1	42.2	232 54.4	58.7	Peacock	53 18.2	S56 41.2
03	124 45.3	214 09.9	. . 09.9	177 19.5	. . 20.7	339 31.6	. . 42.2	247 56.6	. . 58.7	Pollux	243 26.2	N27 59.1
04	139 47.8	229 08.9	09.9	192 19.9	20.2	354 34.1	42.2	262 58.8	58.8	Procyon	244 58.4	N 5 11.0
05	154 50.3	244 08.0	10.0	207 20.4	19.8	9 36.5	42.2	278 00.9	58.9			
06	169 52.7	259 07.0	S24 10.1	222 20.8	S20 19.3	24 39.0	N14 42.2	293 03.1	S17 58.9	Rasalhague	96 05.9	N12 33.2
07	184 55.2	274 06.0	10.2	237 21.3	18.8	39 41.5	42.2	308 05.3	59.0	Regulus	207 42.4	N11 53.5
T 08	199 57.6	289 05.0	10.2	252 21.8	18.3	54 44.0	42.3	323 07.5	59.0	Rigel	281 10.7	S 8 11.2
H 09	215 00.1	304 04.1	. . 10.3	267 22.2	. . 17.8	69 46.5	. . 42.3	338 09.6	. . 59.1	Rigil Kent.	139 50.8	S60 53.4
U 10	230 02.6	319 03.1	10.4	282 22.7	17.3	84 48.9	42.3	353 11.8	59.2	Sabik	102 11.7	S15 44.4
R 11	245 05.0	334 02.1	10.4	297 23.1	16.8	99 51.4	42.3	8 14.0	59.2			
S 12	260 07.5	349 01.1	S24 10.5	312 23.6	S20 16.3	114 53.9	N14 42.3	23 16.1	S17 59.3	Schedar	349 39.0	N56 37.4
D 13	275 10.0	4 00.2	10.6	327 24.1	15.8	129 56.4	42.3	38 18.3	59.4	Shaula	96 21.0	S37 06.6
A 14	290 12.4	18 59.2	10.6	342 24.5	15.3	144 58.9	42.4	53 20.5	59.4	Sirius	258 32.5	S16 44.4
Y 15	305 14.9	33 58.2	. . 10.7	357 25.0	. . 14.9	160 01.4	. . 42.4	68 22.7	. . 59.5	Spica	158 30.4	S11 14.2
16	320 17.4	48 57.2	10.8	12 25.4	14.4	175 03.8	42.4	83 24.8	59.5	Suhail	222 51.4	S43 29.5
17	335 19.8	63 56.3	10.8	27 25.9	13.9	190 06.3	42.4	98 27.0	59.6			
18	350 22.3	78 55.3	S24 10.9	42 26.4	S20 13.4	205 08.8	N14 42.4	113 29.2	S17 59.7	Vega	80 38.7	N38 48.2
19	5 24.8	93 54.3	11.0	57 26.8	12.9	220 11.3	42.4	128 31.3	59.7	Zuben'ubi	137 04.6	S16 06.0
20	20 27.2	108 53.3	11.0	72 27.3	12.4	235 13.8	42.5	143 33.5	59.8		SHA	Mer. Pass.
21	35 29.7	123 52.4	. . 11.1	87 27.8	. . 11.9	250 16.3	. . 42.5	158 35.7	. . 59.8		° ′	h m
22	50 32.1	138 51.4	11.1	102 28.2	11.4	265 18.7	42.5	173 37.9	17 59.9	Venus	90 57.4	12 42
23	65 34.6	153 50.4	11.2	117 28.7	10.9	280 21.2	42.5	188 40.0	S18 00.0	Mars	53 28.3	15 11
	h m									Jupiter	214 46.0	4 26
Mer. Pass. 18 42.3		v −1.0	d 0.1	v 0.5	d 0.5	v 2.5	d 0.0	v 2.2	d 0.1	Saturn	123 19.2	10 31

UT	SUN		MOON					Lat.	Twilight		Sunrise	Moonrise			
									Naut.	Civil		9	10	11	12
	GHA	Dec	GHA	v	Dec	d	HP								
d h	° ′	° ′	° ′	′	° ′	′	′	°	h m	h m	h m	h m	h m	h m	h m
9 00	181 58.9	S22 46.9	330 55.6	11.1	N17 26.6	3.7	55.3	N 72	08 12	10 29	■■■	16 15	18 03	19 43	21 19
01	196 58.6	47.2	345 25.7	11.3	17 22.9	3.7	55.3	N 70	07 53	09 37	■■■	16 59	18 31	20 01	21 30
02	211 58.3	47.4	359 56.0	11.2	17 19.2	3.9	55.3	68	07 38	09 05	■■■	17 29	18 51	20 15	21 39
03	226 58.0 ..	47.7	14 26.2	11.4	17 15.3	3.9	55.3	66	07 25	08 41	10 15	17 50	19 08	20 27	21 46
04	241 57.8	47.9	28 56.6	11.3	17 11.4	4.0	55.2	64	07 15	08 22	09 37	18 08	19 21	20 36	21 52
05	256 57.5	48.2	43 26.9	11.4	17 07.4	4.1	55.2	62	07 06	08 07	09 11	18 22	19 32	20 44	21 57
06	271 57.2	S22 48.4	57 57.3	11.5	N17 03.3	4.2	55.2	60	06 58	07 54	08 51	18 34	19 42	20 51	22 01
07	286 56.9	48.6	72 27.8	11.5	16 59.1	4.2	55.2	N 58	06 51	07 43	08 34	18 44	19 50	20 57	22 05
08	301 56.7	48.9	86 58.3	11.6	16 54.9	4.3	55.2	56	06 44	07 33	08 20	18 53	19 57	21 03	22 09
T 09	316 56.4 ..	49.1	101 28.9	11.6	16 50.6	4.4	55.1	54	06 38	07 24	08 07	19 01	20 04	21 08	22 12
U 10	331 56.1	49.4	115 59.5	11.7	16 46.2	4.5	55.1	52	06 33	07 16	07 57	19 08	20 10	21 12	22 15
E 11	346 55.8	49.6	130 30.2	11.7	16 41.7	4.5	55.1	50	06 28	07 09	07 47	19 15	20 15	21 16	22 17
S 12	1 55.5	S22 49.9	145 00.9	11.8	N16 37.2	4.7	55.1	45	06 16	06 53	07 27	19 28	20 26	21 25	22 23
D 13	16 55.3	50.1	159 31.7	11.8	16 32.5	4.7	55.1	N 40	06 06	06 40	07 11	19 40	20 36	21 32	22 27
A 14	31 55.0	50.3	174 02.5	11.8	16 27.8	4.8	55.1	35	05 57	06 29	06 57	19 49	20 44	21 38	22 31
Y 15	46 54.7 ..	50.6	188 33.3	12.0	16 23.0	4.8	55.0	30	05 49	06 19	06 45	19 58	20 51	21 43	22 35
16	61 54.4	50.8	203 04.3	11.9	16 18.2	4.9	55.0	20	05 33	06 00	06 24	20 12	21 03	21 53	22 41
17	76 54.1	51.0	217 35.2	12.1	16 13.3	5.0	55.0	N 10	05 17	05 43	06 06	20 25	21 14	22 01	22 47
18	91 53.9	S22 51.3	232 06.3	12.0	N16 08.3	5.1	55.0	0	05 00	05 27	05 49	20 37	21 24	22 08	22 52
19	106 53.6	51.5	246 37.3	12.1	16 03.2	5.2	55.0	S 10	04 42	05 09	05 32	20 49	21 34	22 16	22 57
20	121 53.3	51.8	261 08.4	12.2	15 58.0	5.2	54.9	20	04 20	04 49	05 13	21 02	21 44	22 24	23 02
21	136 53.0 ..	52.0	275 39.6	12.2	15 52.8	5.3	54.9	30	03 51	04 25	04 52	21 16	21 56	22 33	23 08
22	151 52.7	52.2	290 10.8	12.3	15 47.5	5.3	54.9	35	03 33	04 10	04 39	21 25	22 03	22 39	23 12
23	166 52.5	52.5	304 42.1	12.3	15 42.2	5.4	54.9	40	03 11	03 52	04 25	21 34	22 11	22 45	23 15
10 00	181 52.2	S22 52.7	319 13.4	12.4	N15 36.8	5.5	54.9	45	02 41	03 30	04 07	21 45	22 20	22 51	23 20
01	196 51.9	52.9	333 44.8	12.4	15 31.3	5.6	54.9	S 50	01 58	03 01	03 45	21 59	22 31	23 00	23 25
02	211 51.6	53.1	348 16.2	12.5	15 25.7	5.6	54.8	52	01 32	02 47	03 35	22 05	22 36	23 04	23 28
03	226 51.3 ..	53.4	2 47.7	12.5	15 20.1	5.7	54.8	54	00 54	02 30	03 23	22 12	22 42	23 08	23 31
04	241 51.1	53.6	17 19.2	12.6	15 14.4	5.8	54.8	56	////	02 09	03 09	22 20	22 48	23 13	23 34
05	256 50.8	53.8	31 50.8	12.6	15 08.6	5.8	54.8	58	////	01 41	02 53	22 28	22 55	23 18	23 37
06	271 50.5	S22 54.1	46 22.4	12.7	N15 02.8	5.9	54.8	S 60	////	00 59	02 34	22 38	23 03	23 24	23 41

W 07	286 50.2	54.3	60 54.1	12.7	14 56.9	6.0	54.8
E 08	301 49.9	54.5	75 25.8	12.8	14 50.9	6.0	54.7
D 09	316 49.7 ..	54.7	89 57.6	12.8	14 44.9	6.1	54.7
N 10	331 49.4	55.0	104 29.4	12.9	14 38.8	6.1	54.7
E 11	346 49.1	55.2	119 01.3	12.9	14 32.7	6.3	54.7

Lat.	Sunset	Twilight		Moonset			
		Civil	Naut.	9	10	11	12
°	h m	h m	h m	h m	h m	h m	h m
N 72	■■■	13 16	15 33	12 43	12 33	12 26	12 20
N 70	■■■	14 08	15 52	11 58	12 04	12 07	12 08
68	■■■	14 40	16 07	11 28	11 43	11 52	11 58
66	13 30	15 04	16 20	11 06	11 26	11 39	11 49
64	14 08	15 23	16 30	10 48	11 12	11 29	11 42
62	14 34	15 38	16 39	10 34	11 00	11 20	11 36
60	14 55	15 51	16 47	10 21	10 50	11 12	11 31
N 58	15 11	16 02	16 55	10 11	10 41	11 05	11 26
56	15 26	16 12	17 01	10 01	10 33	10 59	11 22
54	15 38	16 21	17 07	09 53	10 26	10 54	11 18
52	15 49	16 29	17 13	09 46	10 20	10 49	11 15
50	15 58	16 36	17 18	09 39	10 14	10 45	11 12
45	16 18	16 52	17 29	09 25	10 02	10 35	11 05

1 12	1 48.5	S22 55.4	133 33.2	12.9	N14 26.4	6.2	54.7
13	16 48.5	55.6	148 05.1	13.0	14 20.2	6.4	54.7
14	31 48.2	55.8	162 37.1	13.1	14 13.8	6.4	54.6
15	46 48.0 ..	56.1	177 09.2	13.1	14 07.5	6.5	54.6
16	61 47.7	56.3	191 41.3	13.2	14 01.0	6.5	54.6
17	76 47.4	56.5	206 13.5	13.2	13 54.5	6.6	54.6
18	91 47.1	S22 56.7	220 45.7	13.2	N13 47.9	6.6	54.6
19	106 46.8	56.9	235 17.9	13.3	13 41.3	6.7	54.6
20	121 46.5	57.2	249 50.2	13.3	13 34.6	6.7	54.6
21	136 46.3 ..	57.4	264 22.5	13.4	13 27.9	6.8	54.5
22	151 46.0	57.6	278 54.9	13.4	13 21.1	6.9	54.5
23	166 45.7	57.8	293 27.3	13.5	13 14.2	6.9	54.5

N 40	16 35	17 05	17 39	09 13	09 52	10 27	10 59
35	16 48	17 17	17 48	09 03	09 43	10 20	10 54
30	17 01	17 27	17 57	08 54	09 36	10 14	10 50
20	17 21	17 45	18 13	08 38	09 22	10 04	10 42
N 10	17 39	18 02	18 28	08 25	09 11	09 54	10 36
0	17 56	18 19	18 45	08 12	09 00	09 45	10 29

11 00	181 45.4	S22 58.0	307 59.8	13.5	N13 07.3	6.9	54.5
01	196 45.1	58.2	322 32.3	13.6	13 00.4	7.0	54.5
02	211 44.8	58.4	337 04.9	13.6	12 53.4	7.1	54.5
03	226 44.5 ..	58.6	351 37.5	13.7	12 46.3	7.1	54.5
04	241 44.3	58.8	6 10.2	13.6	12 39.2	7.2	54.5
05	256 44.0	59.1	20 42.8	13.8	12 32.0	7.2	54.4
06	271 43.7	S22 59.3	35 15.6	13.8	N12 24.8	7.2	54.4
07	286 43.4	59.5	49 48.4	13.8	12 17.6	7.4	54.4
T 08	301 43.1	59.7	64 21.2	13.8	12 10.2	7.3	54.4
H 09	316 42.8	22 59.9	78 54.0	13.9	12 02.9	7.4	54.4
U 10	331 42.5	23 00.1	93 26.9	14.0	11 55.5	7.5	54.4
R 11	346 42.3	00.3	107 59.9	14.0	11 48.0	7.5	54.4

S 10	18 14	18 37	19 04	07 59	08 49	09 37	10 23
20	18 32	18 57	19 26	07 46	08 37	09 27	10 16
30	18 54	19 21	19 54	07 30	08 23	09 16	10 08
35	19 07	19 36	20 13	07 21	08 16	09 10	10 04
40	19 21	19 54	20 35	07 11	08 07	09 03	09 59
45	19 39	20 16	21 05	06 58	07 56	08 54	09 53

S 12	1 42.0	S23 00.5	122 32.9	14.0	N11 40.5	7.6	54.4
D 13	16 41.7	00.7	137 05.9	14.1	11 32.9	7.6	54.4
A 14	31 41.4	00.9	151 39.0	14.1	11 25.3	7.6	54.4
Y 15	46 41.1 ..	01.1	166 12.1	14.1	11 17.7	7.7	54.3
16	61 40.8	01.3	180 45.2	14.2	11 10.0	7.7	54.3
17	76 40.5	01.5	195 18.4	14.2	11 02.3	7.8	54.3
18	91 40.2	S23 01.7	209 51.6	14.2	N10 54.5	7.8	54.3
19	106 40.0	01.9	224 24.8	14.3	10 46.7	7.9	54.3
20	121 39.7	02.1	238 58.1	14.3	10 38.8	7.9	54.3
21	136 39.4 ..	02.3	253 31.4	14.4	10 30.9	7.9	54.3
22	151 39.1	02.5	268 04.8	14.4	10 23.0	8.0	54.3
23	166 38.8	02.7	282 38.2	14.4	N10 15.0	8.0	54.3

S 50	20 01	20 45	21 48	06 43	07 43	08 44	09 45
52	20 11	20 59	22 14	06 36	07 37	08 39	09 41
54	20 23	21 17	22 54	06 29	07 31	08 34	09 38
56	20 37	21 38	////	06 20	07 23	08 29	09 34
58	20 53	22 06	////	06 10	07 15	08 22	09 30
S 60	21 13	22 49	////	05 59	07 06	08 15	09 25

	SUN			MOON			
Day	Eqn. of Time		Mer.	Mer. Pass.		Age	Phase
	00ʰ	12ʰ	Pass.	Upper	Lower		
d	m s	m s	h m	h m	h m	d %	
9	07 56	07 43	11 52	02 00	14 25	17 91	
10	07 29	07 16	11 53	02 48	15 12	18 85	
11	07 02	06 48	11 53	03 35	15 57	19 77	

| SD 16.3 | d 0.2 | SD | 15.0 | 14.9 | 14.8 |

UT	ARIES GHA	VENUS −3.9 GHA	Dec	MARS +1.0 GHA	Dec	JUPITER −2.3 GHA	Dec	SATURN +0.5 GHA	Dec	STARS Name	SHA	Dec
12 00	80 37.1	168 49.4	S24 11.2	132 29.1	S20 10.4	295 23.7	N14 42.5	203 42.2	S18 00.0	Acamar	315 17.3	S40 14.9
01	95 39.5	183 48.5	11.3	147 29.6	09.9	310 26.2	42.5	218 44.4	00.1	Achernar	335 25.8	S57 09.9
02	110 42.0	198 47.5	11.3	162 30.1	09.4	325 28.7	42.6	233 46.5	00.1	Acrux	173 08.2	S63 10.6
03	125 44.5	213 46.5 ..	11.4	177 30.5 ..	08.9	340 31.2 ..	42.6	248 48.7 ..	00.2	Adhara	255 11.4	S28 59.7
04	140 46.9	228 45.5	11.4	192 31.0	08.4	355 33.7	42.6	263 50.9	00.3	Aldebaran	290 47.9	N16 32.2
05	155 49.4	243 44.6	11.5	207 31.5	07.9	10 36.2	42.6	278 53.1	00.3			
06	170 51.9	258 43.6	S24 11.5	222 31.9	S20 07.4	25 38.6	N14 42.6	293 55.2	S18 00.4	Alioth	166 20.1	N55 52.5
07	185 54.3	273 42.6	11.6	237 32.4	06.9	40 41.1	42.7	308 57.4	00.4	Alkaid	152 58.5	N49 14.2
08	200 56.8	288 41.6	11.6	252 32.8	06.4	55 43.6	42.7	323 59.6	00.5	Al Na'ir	27 42.7	S46 53.4
F 09	215 59.3	303 40.7 ..	11.6	267 33.3 ..	05.9	70 46.1 ..	42.7	339 01.8 ..	00.6	Alnilam	275 45.0	S 1 11.7
R 10	231 01.7	318 39.7	11.7	282 33.8	05.4	85 48.6	42.7	354 03.9	00.6	Alphard	217 54.9	S 8 43.5
I 11	246 04.2	333 38.7	11.7	297 34.2	04.9	100 51.1	42.7	9 06.1	00.7			
D 12	261 06.6	348 37.7	S24 11.7	312 34.7	S20 04.4	115 53.6	N14 42.8	24 08.3	S18 00.7	Alphecca	126 10.5	N26 40.0
A 13	276 09.1	3 36.8	11.8	327 35.2	03.9	130 56.1	42.8	39 10.4	00.8	Alpheratz	357 42.3	N29 10.6
Y 14	291 11.6	18 35.8	11.8	342 35.6	03.4	145 58.6	42.8	54 12.6	00.9	Altair	62 07.5	N 8 54.7
15	306 14.0	33 34.8 ..	11.9	357 36.1 ..	02.9	161 01.1 ..	42.8	69 14.8 ..	00.9	Ankaa	353 14.7	S42 13.7
16	321 16.5	48 33.8	11.9	12 36.6	02.4	176 03.5	42.8	84 17.0	01.0	Antares	112 25.4	S26 27.6
17	336 19.0	63 32.9	11.9	27 37.0	01.9	191 06.0	42.8	99 19.1	01.1			
18	351 21.4	78 31.9	S24 11.9	42 37.5	S20 01.4	206 08.5	N14 42.9	114 21.3	S18 01.1	Arcturus	145 55.1	N19 06.3
19	6 23.9	93 30.9	12.0	57 37.9	00.9	221 11.0	42.9	129 23.5	01.2	Atria	107 26.8	S69 03.0
20	21 26.4	108 29.9	12.0	72 38.4	20 00.4	236 13.5	42.9	144 25.6	01.2	Avior	234 17.0	S59 33.4
21	36 28.8	123 28.9 ..	12.0	87 38.9	19 59.9	251 16.0 ..	42.9	159 27.8 ..	01.3	Bellatrix	278 30.6	N 6 21.6
22	51 31.3	138 28.0	12.0	102 39.3	59.4	266 18.5	43.0	174 30.0	01.4	Betelgeuse	270 59.9	N 7 24.4
23	66 33.7	153 27.0	12.1	117 39.8	58.9	281 21.0	43.0	189 32.2	01.4			
13 00	81 36.2	168 26.0	S24 12.1	132 40.3	S19 58.4	296 23.5	N14 43.0	204 34.3	S18 01.5	Canopus	263 55.1	S52 42.3
01	96 38.7	183 25.0	12.1	147 40.7	57.9	311 26.0	43.0	219 36.5	01.5	Capella	280 32.4	N46 00.6
02	111 41.1	198 24.1	12.1	162 41.2	57.4	326 28.5	43.0	234 38.7	01.6	Deneb	49 31.1	N45 20.4
03	126 43.6	213 23.1 ..	12.1	177 41.7 ..	56.9	341 31.0 ..	43.1	249 40.9 ..	01.7	Denebola	182 32.7	N14 29.2
04	141 46.1	228 22.1	12.2	192 42.1	56.4	356 33.5	43.1	264 43.0	01.7	Diphda	348 54.8	S17 54.4
05	156 48.5	243 21.1	12.2	207 42.6	55.9	11 36.0	43.1	279 45.2	01.8			
06	171 51.0	258 20.2	S24 12.2	222 43.1	S19 55.4	26 38.4	N14 43.1	294 47.4	S18 01.8	Dubhe	193 50.5	N61 39.8
07	186 53.5	273 19.2	12.2	237 43.5	54.9	41 40.9	43.1	309 49.5	01.9	Elnath	278 10.9	N28 37.0
S 08	201 55.9	288 18.2	12.2	252 44.0	54.4	56 43.4	43.2	324 51.7	02.0	Eltanin	90 46.2	N51 29.5
A 09	216 58.4	303 17.2 ..	12.2	267 44.5 ..	53.9	71 45.9 ..	43.2	339 53.9 ..	02.0	Enif	33 46.3	N 9 56.8
T 10	232 00.9	318 16.3	12.2	282 44.9	53.3	86 48.4	43.2	354 56.1	02.1	Fomalhaut	15 23.0	S29 32.6
U 11	247 03.3	333 15.3	12.2	297 45.4	52.8	101 50.9	43.2	9 58.2	02.1			
R 12	262 05.8	348 14.3	S24 12.2	312 45.9	S19 52.3	116 53.4	N14 43.3	25 00.4	S18 02.2	Gacrux	171 59.8	S57 11.5
D 13	277 08.2	3 13.3	12.2	327 46.4	51.8	131 55.9	43.3	40 02.6	02.3	Gienah	175 51.3	S17 37.4
A 14	292 10.7	18 12.4	12.2	342 46.8	51.3	146 58.4	43.3	55 04.8	02.3	Hadar	148 46.7	S60 26.4
Y 15	307 13.2	33 11.4 ..	12.2	357 47.3 ..	50.8	162 00.9 ..	43.3	70 06.9 ..	02.4	Hamal	327 59.3	N23 32.0
16	322 15.6	48 10.4	12.2	12 47.8	50.3	177 03.4	43.3	85 09.1	02.4	Kaus Aust.	83 42.9	S34 22.4
17	337 18.1	63 09.4	12.2	27 48.2	49.8	192 05.9	43.4	100 11.3	02.5			
18	352 20.6	78 08.4	S24 12.2	42 48.7	S19 49.3	207 08.4	N14 43.4	115 13.5	S18 02.6	Kochab	137 21.2	N74 05.5
19	7 23.0	93 07.5	12.2	57 49.2	48.8	222 10.9	43.4	130 15.6	02.6	Markab	13 37.3	N15 17.3
20	22 25.5	108 06.5	12.2	72 49.6	48.2	237 13.4	43.4	145 17.8	02.7	Menkar	314 13.7	N 4 08.8
21	37 28.0	123 05.5 ..	12.2	87 50.1 ..	47.7	252 15.9 ..	43.4	160 20.0 ..	02.7	Menkent	148 06.6	S36 26.3
22	52 30.4	138 04.5	12.2	102 50.6	47.2	267 18.4	43.5	175 22.2	02.8	Miaplacidus	221 38.7	S69 46.6
23	67 32.9	153 03.6	12.2	117 51.0	46.7	282 20.9	43.5	190 24.3	02.9			
14 00	82 35.4	168 02.6	S24 12.2	132 51.5	S19 46.2	297 23.4	N14 43.5	205 26.5	S18 02.9	Mirfak	308 38.4	N49 54.8
01	97 37.8	183 01.6	12.2	147 52.0	45.7	312 25.9	43.5	220 28.7	03.0	Nunki	75 57.4	S26 16.5
02	112 40.3	198 00.6	12.2	162 52.5	45.2	327 28.4	43.6	235 30.8	03.0	Peacock	53 18.2	S56 41.2
03	127 42.7	212 59.7 ..	12.2	177 52.9 ..	44.7	342 30.9 ..	43.6	250 33.0 ..	03.1	Pollux	243 26.2	N27 59.1
04	142 45.2	227 58.7	12.1	192 53.4	44.1	357 33.4	43.6	265 35.2	03.2	Procyon	244 58.4	N 5 11.0
05	157 47.7	242 57.7	12.1	207 53.9	43.6	12 35.9	43.6	280 37.4	03.2			
06	172 50.1	257 56.7	S24 12.1	222 54.3	S19 43.1	27 38.4	N14 43.7	295 39.5	S18 03.3	Rasalhague	96 05.9	N12 33.2
07	187 52.6	272 55.8	12.1	237 54.8	42.6	42 41.0	43.7	310 41.7	03.3	Regulus	207 42.3	N11 53.5
08	202 55.1	287 54.8	12.1	252 55.3	42.1	57 43.5	43.7	325 43.9	03.4	Rigel	281 10.7	S 8 11.3
S 09	217 57.5	302 53.8 ..	12.0	267 55.7 ..	41.6	72 46.0 ..	43.7	340 46.1 ..	03.4	Rigil Kent.	139 50.7	S60 53.4
U 10	233 00.0	317 52.8	12.0	282 56.2	41.0	87 48.5	43.8	355 48.2	03.5	Sabik	102 11.7	S15 44.4
N 11	248 02.5	332 51.9	12.0	297 56.7	40.5	102 51.0	43.8	10 50.4	03.6			
D 12	263 04.9	347 50.9	S24 12.0	312 57.2	S19 40.0	117 53.5	N14 43.8	25 52.6	S18 03.6	Schedar	349 39.0	N56 37.4
A 13	278 07.4	2 49.9	11.9	327 57.6	39.5	132 56.0	43.8	40 54.8	03.7	Shaula	96 21.0	S37 06.6
Y 14	293 09.8	17 48.9	11.9	342 58.1	39.0	147 58.5	43.8	55 56.9	03.7	Sirius	258 32.5	S16 44.4
15	308 12.3	32 48.0 ..	11.9	357 58.6 ..	38.5	163 01.0 ..	43.9	70 59.1 ..	03.8	Spica	158 30.3	S11 14.2
16	323 14.8	47 47.0	11.9	12 59.1	37.9	178 03.5	43.9	86 01.3	03.9	Suhail	222 51.4	S43 29.5
17	338 17.2	62 46.0	11.8	27 59.5	37.4	193 06.0	43.9	101 03.5	03.9			
18	353 19.7	77 45.0	S24 11.8	43 00.0	S19 36.9	208 08.5	N14 43.9	116 05.6	S18 04.0	Vega	80 38.7	N38 48.1
19	8 22.2	92 44.0	11.8	58 00.5	36.4	223 11.0	44.0	131 07.8	04.0	Zuben'ubi	137 04.6	S16 06.0
20	23 24.6	107 43.1	11.7	73 00.9	35.9	238 13.5	44.0	146 10.0	04.1		SHA	Mer.Pass.
21	38 27.1	122 42.1 ..	11.7	88 01.4 ..	35.3	253 16.0 ..	44.0	161 12.2 ..	04.2		° ′	h m
22	53 29.6	137 41.1	11.6	103 01.9	34.8	268 18.6	44.1	176 14.3	04.2	Venus	86 49.8	12 47
23	68 32.0	152 40.1	11.6	118 02.4	34.3	283 21.1	44.1	191 16.5	04.3	Mars	51 04.1	15 09
	h m									Jupiter	214 47.3	4 14
Mer.Pass. 18 30.5	v −1.0 d 0.0			v 0.5 d 0.5		v 2.5 d 0.0		v 2.2 d 0.1		Saturn	122 58.1	10 20

UT	SUN GHA	Dec	MOON GHA	v	Dec	d	HP
d h	° ′	° ′	° ′	′	° ′	′	′
12 00	181 38.5	S23 02.9	297 11.6	14.5	N10 07.0	8.1	54.3
01	196 38.2	03.1	311 45.1	14.5	9 58.9	8.1	54.3
02	211 37.9	03.3	326 18.6	14.5	9 50.8	8.2	54.3
03	226 37.6 ..	03.4	340 52.1	14.5	9 42.6	8.1	54.3
04	241 37.4	03.6	355 25.6	14.6	9 34.5	8.3	54.3
05	256 37.1	03.8	9 59.2	14.6	9 26.2	8.2	54.2
06	271 36.8	S23 04.0	24 32.8	14.7	N 9 18.0	8.3	54.2
F 07	286 36.5	04.2	39 06.5	14.7	9 09.7	8.3	54.2
R 08	301 36.2	04.4	53 40.2	14.7	9 01.4	8.4	54.2
I 09	316 35.9 ..	04.6	68 13.9	14.7	8 53.0	8.4	54.2
D 10	331 35.6	04.8	82 47.6	14.8	8 44.6	8.4	54.2
A 11	346 35.3	04.9	97 21.4	14.7	8 36.2	8.5	54.2
Y 12	1 35.0	S23 05.1	111 55.1	14.9	N 8 27.7	8.5	54.2
13	16 34.7	05.3	126 29.0	14.8	8 19.2	8.5	54.2
14	31 34.4	05.5	141 02.8	14.9	8 10.7	8.6	54.2
15	46 34.2 ..	05.7	155 36.7	14.8	8 02.1	8.6	54.2
16	61 33.9	05.9	170 10.5	15.0	7 53.5	8.6	54.2
17	76 33.6	06.0	184 44.5	14.9	7 44.9	8.7	54.2
18	91 33.3	S23 06.2	199 18.4	14.9	N 7 36.2	8.7	54.2
19	106 33.0	06.4	213 52.3	15.0	7 27.5	8.7	54.2
20	121 32.7	06.6	228 26.3	15.0	7 18.8	8.7	54.2
21	136 32.4 ..	06.8	243 00.3	15.0	7 10.1	8.8	54.2
22	151 32.1	06.9	257 34.3	15.1	7 01.3	8.8	54.2
23	166 31.8	07.1	272 08.4	15.0	6 52.5	8.8	54.2
13 00	181 31.5	S23 07.3	286 42.4	15.1	N 6 43.7	8.9	54.2
01	196 31.2	07.5	301 16.5	15.1	6 34.8	8.8	54.2
02	211 30.9	07.6	315 50.6	15.1	6 26.0	9.0	54.2
03	226 30.6 ..	07.8	330 24.7	15.2	6 17.0	8.9	54.2
04	241 30.3	08.0	344 58.9	15.1	6 08.1	8.9	54.2
05	256 30.1	08.1	359 33.0	15.2	5 59.2	9.0	54.2
06	271 29.8	S23 08.3	14 07.2	15.1	N 5 50.2	9.0	54.2
S 07	286 29.5	08.5	28 41.3	15.2	5 41.2	9.1	54.2
A 08	301 29.2	08.6	43 15.5	15.2	5 32.1	9.0	54.2
T 09	316 28.9 ..	08.8	57 49.7	15.2	5 23.1	9.1	54.2
U 10	331 28.6	09.0	72 23.9	15.3	5 14.0	9.1	54.2
R 11	346 28.3	09.1	86 58.2	15.2	5 04.9	9.1	54.2
D 12	1 28.0	S23 09.3	101 32.4	15.2	N 4 55.8	9.1	54.2
A 13	16 27.7	09.5	116 06.6	15.3	4 46.7	9.2	54.2
Y 14	31 27.4	09.6	130 40.9	15.2	4 37.5	9.2	54.2
15	46 27.1 ..	09.8	145 15.1	15.3	4 28.3	9.2	54.2
16	61 26.8	10.0	159 49.4	15.3	4 19.1	9.2	54.2
17	76 26.5	10.1	174 23.7	15.3	4 09.9	9.2	54.2
18	91 26.2	S23 10.3	188 58.0	15.3	N 4 00.7	9.3	54.3
19	106 25.9	10.4	203 32.3	15.2	3 51.4	9.2	54.3
20	121 25.6	10.6	218 06.5	15.3	3 42.2	9.3	54.3
21	136 25.3 ..	10.8	232 40.8	15.3	3 32.9	9.3	54.3
22	151 25.0	10.9	247 15.1	15.3	3 23.6	9.3	54.3
23	166 24.7	11.1	261 49.4	15.3	3 14.3	9.4	54.3
14 00	181 24.4	S23 11.2	276 23.7	15.3	N 3 04.9	9.3	54.3
01	196 24.2	11.4	290 58.0	15.4	2 55.6	9.4	54.3
02	211 23.9	11.5	305 32.4	15.3	2 46.2	9.3	54.3
03	226 23.6 ..	11.7	320 06.7	15.3	2 36.9	9.4	54.3
04	241 23.3	11.8	334 41.0	15.3	2 27.5	9.4	54.3
05	256 23.0	12.0	349 15.3	15.3	2 18.1	9.4	54.3
06	271 22.7	S23 12.1	3 49.6	15.2	N 2 08.7	9.5	54.3
07	286 22.4	12.3	18 23.8	15.3	1 59.2	9.4	54.4
S 08	301 22.1	12.4	32 58.1	15.3	1 49.8	9.5	54.4
U 09	316 21.8 ..	12.6	47 32.4	15.3	1 40.3	9.4	54.4
N 10	331 21.5	12.7	62 06.7	15.3	1 30.9	9.5	54.4
D 11	346 21.2	12.9	76 41.0	15.2	1 21.4	9.5	54.4
A 12	1 20.9	S23 13.0	91 15.2	15.3	N 1 11.9	9.4	54.4
Y 13	16 20.6	13.2	105 49.5	15.2	1 02.5	9.5	54.4
14	31 20.3	13.3	120 23.7	15.3	0 53.0	9.5	54.4
15	46 20.0 ..	13.5	134 58.0	15.2	0 43.5	9.5	54.4
16	61 19.7	13.6	149 32.2	15.2	0 34.0	9.6	54.5
17	76 19.4	13.7	164 06.4	15.2	0 24.4	9.5	54.5
18	91 19.1	S23 13.9	178 40.6	15.2	N 0 14.9	9.5	54.5
19	106 18.8	14.0	193 14.8	15.2	N 0 05.4	9.5	54.5
20	121 18.5	14.2	207 49.0	15.1	S 0 04.1	9.6	54.5
21	136 18.2 ..	14.3	222 23.1	15.2	0 13.7	9.5	54.5
22	151 17.9	14.4	236 57.3	15.1	0 23.2	9.6	54.5
23	166 17.6	14.6	251 31.4	15.1	S 0 32.8	9.5	54.5
	SD 16.3	d 0.2	SD 14.8		14.8		14.8

Lat.	Twilight Naut.	Civil	Sunrise	Moonrise 12	13	14	15
°	h m	h m	h m	h m	h m	h m	h m
N 72	08 17	10 40	■■	21 19	22 53	24 27	00 27
N 70	07 58	09 44	■■	21 30	22 58	24 26	00 26
68	07 42	09 10	■■	21 39	23 02	24 25	00 25
66	07 29	08 46	10 23	21 46	23 05	24 24	00 24
64	07 19	08 26	09 43	21 52	23 07	24 23	00 23
62	07 09	08 11	09 16	21 57	23 10	24 23	00 23
60	07 01	07 58	08 55	22 01	23 11	24 22	00 22
N 58	06 54	07 46	08 38	22 05	23 13	24 22	00 22
56	06 47	07 36	08 23	22 09	23 15	24 21	00 21
54	06 41	07 27	08 11	22 12	23 16	24 21	00 21
52	06 35	07 19	08 00	22 15	23 17	24 21	00 21
50	06 30	07 12	07 50	22 17	23 19	24 20	00 20
45	06 19	06 56	07 30	22 23	23 21	24 20	00 20
N 40	06 09	06 43	07 13	22 27	23 23	24 19	00 19
35	05 59	06 31	06 59	22 31	23 25	24 19	00 19
30	05 51	06 21	06 47	22 35	23 27	24 18	00 18
20	05 34	06 02	06 26	22 41	23 29	24 18	00 18
N 10	05 19	05 45	06 08	22 47	23 32	24 17	00 17
0	05 02	05 28	05 50	22 52	23 34	24 16	00 16
S 10	04 43	05 10	05 33	22 57	23 36	24 16	00 16
20	04 21	04 50	05 14	23 02	23 39	24 15	00 15
30	03 52	04 25	04 53	23 08	23 42	24 15	00 15
35	03 34	04 10	04 40	23 12	23 43	24 14	00 14
40	03 11	03 52	04 25	23 15	23 45	24 14	00 14
45	02 41	03 30	04 07	23 20	23 47	24 14	00 14
S 50	01 56	03 01	03 45	23 25	23 50	24 13	00 13
52	01 30	02 46	03 34	23 28	23 51	24 13	00 13
54	00 48	02 28	03 22	23 31	23 52	24 13	00 13
56	////	02 07	03 08	23 34	23 53	24 12	00 12
58	////	01 38	02 52	23 37	23 55	24 12	00 12
S 60	////	00 53	02 32	23 41	23 57	24 12	00 12

Lat.	Sunset	Twilight Civil	Naut.	Moonset 12	13	14	15
°	h m	h m	h m	h m	h m	h m	h m
N 72	■■	13 08	15 31	12 20	12 14	12 09	12 03
N 70	■■	14 04	15 50	12 08	12 08	12 07	12 06
68	■■	14 38	16 06	11 58	12 02	12 06	12 09
66	13 25	15 02	16 19	11 49	11 58	12 06	12 12
64	14 05	15 22	16 29	11 42	11 54	12 04	12 14
62	14 32	15 37	16 39	11 36	11 50	12 03	12 16
60	14 53	15 51	16 47	11 31	11 47	12 03	12 18
N 58	15 11	16 02	16 54	11 26	11 45	12 02	12 19
56	15 25	16 12	17 01	11 22	11 42	12 01	12 20
54	15 37	16 21	17 07	11 18	11 40	12 01	12 22
52	15 48	16 29	17 13	11 15	11 38	12 01	12 23
50	15 58	16 36	17 18	11 12	11 36	12 00	12 24
45	16 19	16 52	17 29	11 05	11 33	11 59	12 26
N 40	16 35	17 06	17 40	10 59	11 29	11 58	12 28
35	16 49	17 17	17 49	10 54	11 27	11 58	12 29
30	17 01	17 28	17 57	10 50	11 24	11 57	12 31
20	17 22	17 46	18 14	10 42	11 20	11 56	12 33
N 10	17 41	18 03	18 30	10 36	11 16	11 55	12 35
0	17 58	18 20	18 40	10 29	11 12	11 54	12 37
S 10	18 15	18 38	19 05	10 23	11 08	11 54	12 39
20	18 34	18 59	19 28	10 16	11 04	11 53	12 41
30	18 56	19 23	19 56	10 08	11 00	11 51	12 44
35	19 09	19 38	20 15	10 04	10 57	11 51	12 45
40	19 24	19 56	20 38	09 59	10 54	11 50	12 46
45	19 41	20 19	21 08	09 53	10 51	11 49	12 48
S 50	20 04	20 48	21 53	09 45	10 47	11 48	12 50
52	20 14	21 03	22 19	09 42	10 45	11 48	12 51
54	20 26	21 20	23 02	09 38	10 43	11 47	12 52
56	20 40	21 42	////	09 34	10 40	11 47	12 54
58	20 57	22 11	////	09 30	10 38	11 46	12 55
S 60	21 17	22 57	////	09 25	10 35	11 45	12 57

Day	SUN Eqn. of Time 00ʰ	12ʰ	Mer. Pass.	MOON Mer. Pass. Upper	Lower	Age	Phase
d	m s	m s	h m	h m	h m	d	%
12	06 35	06 21	11 54	04 19	16 40	20	69
13	06 07	05 53	11 54	05 02	17 23	21	60
14	05 38	05 24	11 55	05 44	18 05	22	50

UT	ARIES	VENUS −3.9		MARS +1.1		JUPITER −2.4		SATURN +0.5		STARS		
	GHA	GHA	Dec	GHA	Dec	GHA	Dec	GHA	Dec	Name	SHA	Dec
d h	° ′	° ′	° ′	° ′	° ′	° ′	° ′	° ′	° ′		° ′	° ′
15 00	83 34.5	167 39.2	S24 11.6	133 02.8	S19 33.8	298 23.6	N14 44.1	206 18.7	S18 04.3	Acamar	315 17.3	S40 14.9
01	98 37.0	182 38.2	11.5	148 03.3	33.3	313 26.1	44.1	221 20.9	04.4	Achernar	335 25.8	S57 10.0
02	113 39.4	197 37.2	11.5	163 03.8	32.7	328 28.6	44.2	236 23.0	04.5	Acrux	173 08.1	S63 10.6
03	128 41.9	212 36.2 ..	11.4	178 04.3 ..	32.2	343 31.1 ..	44.2	251 25.2 ..	04.5	Adhara	255 11.3	S28 59.7
04	143 44.3	227 35.3	11.4	193 04.7	31.7	358 33.6	44.2	266 27.4	04.6	Aldebaran	290 47.9	N16 32.2
05	158 46.8	242 34.3	11.3	208 05.2	31.2	13 36.1	44.2	281 29.6	04.6			
06	173 49.3	257 33.3	S24 11.3	223 05.7	S19 30.6	28 38.6	N14 44.3	296 31.7	S18 04.7	Alioth	166 20.1	N55 52.5
07	188 51.7	272 32.3	11.2	238 06.2	30.1	43 41.2	44.3	311 33.9	04.8	Alkaid	152 58.5	N49 14.2
08	203 54.2	287 31.4	11.2	253 06.6	29.6	58 43.7	44.3	326 36.1	04.8	Al Na'ir	27 42.7	S46 53.4
M 09	218 56.7	302 30.4 ..	11.1	268 07.1 ..	29.1	73 46.2 ..	44.3	341 38.3 ..	04.9	Alnilam	275 45.0	S 1 11.7
O 10	233 59.1	317 29.4	11.1	283 07.6	28.5	88 48.7	44.4	356 40.4	04.9	Alphard	217 54.9	S 8 43.5
N 11	249 01.6	332 28.4	11.0	298 08.1	28.0	103 51.2	44.4	11 42.6	05.0			
D 12	264 04.1	347 27.5	S24 11.0	313 08.5	S19 27.5	118 53.7	N14 44.4	26 44.8	S18 05.0	Alphecca	126 10.5	N26 39.9
A 13	279 06.5	2 26.5	10.9	328 09.0	27.0	133 56.2	44.5	41 47.0	05.1	Alpheratz	357 42.3	N29 10.6
Y 14	294 09.0	17 25.5	10.8	343 09.5	26.4	148 58.7	44.5	56 49.1	05.2	Altair	62 07.5	N 8 54.7
15	309 11.5	32 24.5 ..	10.8	358 10.0 ..	25.9	164 01.3 ..	44.5	71 51.3 ..	05.2	Ankaa	353 14.7	S42 13.7
16	324 13.9	47 23.6	10.7	13 10.4	25.4	179 03.8	44.5	86 53.5	05.3	Antares	112 25.4	S26 27.6
17	339 16.4	62 22.6	10.6	28 10.9	24.9	194 06.3	44.6	101 55.7	05.3			
18	354 18.8	77 21.6	S24 10.6	43 11.4	S19 24.3	209 08.8	N14 44.6	116 57.8	S18 05.4	Arcturus	145 55.1	N19 06.3
19	9 21.3	92 20.6	10.5	58 11.9	23.8	224 11.3	44.6	132 00.0	05.5	Atria	107 26.8	S69 03.0
20	24 23.8	107 19.7	10.5	73 12.4	23.3	239 13.8	44.6	147 02.2	05.5	Avior	234 17.0	S59 33.4
21	39 26.2	122 18.7 ..	10.4	88 12.8 ..	22.7	254 16.4 ..	44.7	162 04.4 ..	05.6	Bellatrix	278 30.6	N 6 21.6
22	54 28.7	137 17.7	10.3	103 13.3	22.2	269 18.9	44.7	177 06.6	05.6	Betelgeuse	270 59.9	N 7 24.4
23	69 31.2	152 16.8	10.2	118 13.8	21.7	284 21.4	44.7	192 08.7	05.7			
16 00	84 33.6	167 15.8	S24 10.2	133 14.3	S19 21.1	299 23.9	N14 44.8	207 10.9	S18 05.7	Canopus	263 55.1	S52 42.4
01	99 36.1	182 14.8	10.1	148 14.7	20.6	314 26.4	44.8	222 13.1	05.8	Capella	280 32.4	N46 00.6
02	114 38.6	197 13.8	10.0	163 15.2	20.1	329 28.9	44.8	237 15.3	05.9	Deneb	49 31.1	N45 20.4
03	129 41.0	212 12.9 ..	09.9	178 15.7 ..	19.6	344 31.5 ..	44.8	252 17.4 ..	05.9	Denebola	182 32.7	N14 29.2
04	144 43.5	227 11.9	09.9	193 16.2	19.0	359 34.0	44.9	267 19.6	06.0	Diphda	348 54.8	S17 54.4
05	159 45.9	242 10.9	09.8	208 16.7	18.5	14 36.5	44.9	282 21.8	06.0			
06	174 48.4	257 09.9	S24 09.7	223 17.1	S19 18.0	29 39.0	N14 44.9	297 24.0	S18 06.1	Dubhe	193 50.5	N61 39.8
07	189 50.9	272 09.0	09.6	238 17.6	17.4	44 41.5	45.0	312 26.1	06.2	Elnath	278 10.9	N28 37.0
T 08	204 53.3	287 08.0	09.5	253 18.1	16.9	59 44.1	45.0	327 28.3	06.2	Eltanin	90 46.2	N51 29.4
U 09	219 55.8	302 07.0 ..	09.5	268 18.6 ..	16.4	74 46.6 ..	45.0	342 30.5 ..	06.3	Enif	33 46.3	N 9 56.8
E 10	234 58.3	317 06.0	09.4	283 19.1	15.8	89 49.1	45.1	357 32.7	06.3	Fomalhaut	15 23.0	S29 32.6
S 11	250 00.7	332 05.1	09.3	298 19.5	15.3	104 51.6	45.1	12 34.8	06.4			
D 12	265 03.2	347 04.1	S24 09.2	313 20.0	S19 14.8	119 54.2	N14 45.1	27 37.0	S18 06.4	Gacrux	171 59.8	S57 11.5
A 13	280 05.7	2 03.1	09.1	328 20.5	14.2	134 56.7	45.1	42 39.2	06.5	Gienah	175 51.3	S17 37.4
Y 14	295 08.1	17 02.1	09.0	343 21.0	13.7	149 59.2	45.2	57 41.4	06.6	Hadar	148 46.7	S60 26.4
15	310 10.6	32 01.2 ..	08.9	358 21.5 ..	13.1	165 01.7 ..	45.2	72 43.6 ..	06.6	Hamal	327 59.3	N23 32.0
16	325 13.1	47 00.2	08.8	13 21.9	12.6	180 04.2	45.2	87 45.7	06.7	Kaus Aust.	83 42.9	S34 22.4
17	340 15.5	61 59.2	08.7	28 22.4	12.1	195 06.8	45.3	102 47.9	06.7			
18	355 18.0	76 58.3	S24 08.6	43 22.9	S19 11.5	210 09.3	N14 45.3	117 50.1	S18 06.8	Kochab	137 21.2	N74 05.5
19	10 20.4	91 57.3	08.5	58 23.4	11.0	225 11.8	45.3	132 52.3	06.9	Markab	13 37.3	N15 17.3
20	25 22.9	106 56.3	08.4	73 23.9	10.5	240 14.3	45.4	147 54.4	06.9	Menkar	314 13.7	N 4 08.8
21	40 25.4	121 55.3 ..	08.3	88 24.3 ..	09.9	255 16.9 ..	45.4	162 56.6 ..	07.0	Menkent	148 06.6	S36 26.3
22	55 27.8	136 54.4	08.2	103 24.8	09.4	270 19.4	45.4	177 58.8	07.0	Miaplacidus	221 38.7	S69 46.6
23	70 30.3	151 53.4	08.1	118 25.3	08.8	285 21.9	45.4	193 01.0	07.1			
17 00	85 32.8	166 52.4	S24 08.0	133 25.8	S19 08.3	300 24.4	N14 45.5	208 03.1	S18 07.1	Mirfak	308 38.4	N49 54.8
01	100 35.2	181 51.5	07.9	148 26.3	07.8	315 27.0	45.5	223 05.3	07.2	Nunki	75 57.4	S26 16.5
02	115 37.7	196 50.5	07.8	163 26.7	07.2	330 29.5	45.5	238 07.5	07.3	Peacock	53 18.2	S56 41.2
03	130 40.2	211 49.5 ..	07.7	178 27.2 ..	06.7	345 32.0 ..	45.6	253 09.7 ..	07.3	Pollux	243 26.2	N27 59.1
04	145 42.6	226 48.5	07.6	193 27.7	06.2	0 34.5	45.6	268 11.9	07.4	Procyon	244 58.4	N 5 11.0
05	160 45.1	241 47.6	07.5	208 28.2	05.6	15 37.1	45.6	283 14.0	07.4			
06	175 47.6	256 46.6	S24 07.4	223 28.7	S19 05.1	30 39.6	N14 45.7	298 16.2	S18 07.5	Rasalhague	96 05.9	N12 33.2
W 07	190 50.0	271 45.6	07.3	238 29.2	04.5	45 42.1	45.7	313 18.4	07.6	Regulus	207 42.3	N11 53.5
E 08	205 52.5	286 44.7	07.2	253 29.6	04.0	60 44.7	45.7	328 20.6	07.6	Rigel	281 10.7	S 8 11.3
D 09	220 54.9	301 43.7 ..	07.0	268 30.1 ..	03.4	75 47.2 ..	45.8	343 22.7 ..	07.7	Rigil Kent.	139 50.7	S60 53.4
N 10	235 57.4	316 42.7	06.9	283 30.6	02.9	90 49.7	45.8	358 24.9	07.7	Sabik	102 11.7	S15 44.4
E 11	250 59.9	331 41.7	06.8	298 31.1	02.4	105 52.2	45.8	13 27.1	07.8			
S 12	266 02.3	346 40.8	S24 06.7	313 31.6	S19 01.8	120 54.8	N14 45.9	28 29.3	S18 07.8	Schedar	349 39.0	N56 37.4
D 13	281 04.8	1 39.8	06.6	328 32.1	01.3	135 57.3	45.9	43 31.5	07.9	Shaula	96 21.0	S37 06.6
A 14	296 07.3	16 38.8	06.4	343 32.5	00.7	150 59.8	45.9	58 33.6	08.0	Sirius	258 32.5	S16 44.4
Y 15	311 09.7	31 37.9 ..	06.3	358 33.0 19	00.2	166 02.4 ..	46.0	73 35.8 ..	08.0	Spica	158 30.3	S11 14.2
16	326 12.2	46 36.9	06.2	13 33.5 18	59.6	181 04.9	46.0	88 38.0	08.1	Suhail	222 51.3	S43 29.5
17	341 14.7	61 35.9	06.1	28 34.0	59.1	196 07.4	46.0	103 40.2	08.1			
18	356 17.1	76 34.9	S24 05.9	43 34.5	S18 58.5	211 10.0	N14 46.1	118 42.4	S18 08.2	Vega	80 38.7	N38 48.1
19	11 19.6	91 34.0	05.8	58 35.0	58.0	226 12.5	46.1	133 44.5	08.2	Zuben'ubi	137 04.5	S16 06.0
20	26 22.0	106 33.0	05.7	73 35.5	57.5	241 15.0	46.1	148 46.7	08.3		SHA	Mer.Pass.
21	41 24.5	121 32.0 ..	05.5	88 35.9 ..	56.9	256 17.6 ..	46.2	163 48.9 ..	08.4		° ′	h m
22	56 27.0	136 31.1	05.4	103 36.4	56.4	271 20.1	46.2	178 51.1	08.4	Venus	82 42.1	12 52
23	71 29.4	151 30.1	05.3	118 36.9	55.8	286 22.6	46.2	193 53.2	08.5	Mars	48 40.6	15 07
	h m									Jupiter	214 50.3	4 02
Mer.Pass. 18 18.7		v −1.0	d 0.1	v 0.5	d 0.5	v 2.5	d 0.0	v 2.2	d 0.1	Saturn	122 37.3	10 10

UT	SUN		MOON					Lat.	Twilight		Sunrise	Moonrise			
	GHA	Dec	GHA	v	Dec	d	HP		Naut.	Civil		15	16	17	18
d h	° '	° '	° '	'	° '	'	'	°	h m	h m	h m	h m	h m	h m	h m
15 00	181 17.3	S23 14.7	266 05.5	15.1	S 0 42.3	9.6	54.6	N 72	08 21	10 49	■■	00 27	02 03	03 43	05 29
01	196 17.0	14.9	280 39.6	15.1	0 51.9	9.5	54.6	N 70	08 01	09 49	■■	00 26	01 56	03 29	05 06
02	211 16.7	15.0	295 13.7	15.0	1 01.4	9.6	54.6	68	07 46	09 14	■■	00 25	01 50	03 17	04 48
03	226 16.4 ..	15.1	309 47.7	15.1	1 11.0	9.5	54.6	66	07 33	08 49	10 29	00 24	01 45	03 08	04 33
04	241 16.1	15.3	324 21.8	15.0	1 20.5	9.6	54.6	64	07 22	08 30	09 47	00 23	01 41	03 00	04 22
05	256 15.8	15.4	338 55.8	15.0	1 30.1	9.5	54.6	62	07 12	08 14	09 19	00 22	01 37	02 54	04 12
06	271 15.5	S23 15.5	353 29.8	14.9	S 1 39.6	9.6	54.7	60	07 04	08 00	08 58	00 22	01 34	02 48	04 03
07	286 15.2	15.6	8 03.7	15.0	1 49.2	9.5	54.7	N 58	06 56	07 49	08 41	00 22	01 32	02 43	03 56
08	301 14.9	15.8	22 37.7	14.9	1 58.7	9.6	54.7	56	06 50	07 39	08 26	00 21	01 29	02 38	03 49
M 09	316 14.6 ..	15.9	37 11.6	14.9	2 08.3	9.5	54.7	54	06 43	07 30	08 13	00 21	01 27	02 34	03 43
O 10	331 14.3	16.0	51 45.5	14.9	2 17.8	9.6	54.7	52	06 38	07 21	08 02	00 21	01 25	02 31	03 38
N 11	346 14.0	16.2	66 19.4	14.8	2 27.4	9.5	54.7	50	06 33	07 14	07 53	00 20	01 23	02 28	03 33
D 12	1 13.7	S23 16.3	80 53.2	14.8	S 2 36.9	9.5	54.8	45	06 21	06 58	07 32	00 20	01 19	02 20	03 23
A 13	16 13.4	16.4	95 27.0	14.8	2 46.4	9.6	54.8	N 40	06 11	06 45	07 15	00 19	01 16	02 15	03 15
Y 14	31 13.1	16.5	110 00.8	14.8	2 56.0	9.5	54.8	35	06 01	06 33	07 01	00 19	01 13	02 10	03 07
15	46 12.8 ..	16.7	124 34.6	14.7	3 05.5	9.5	54.8	30	05 53	06 22	06 49	00 18	01 11	02 05	03 01
16	61 12.5	16.8	139 08.3	14.7	3 15.0	9.5	54.8	20	05 36	06 04	06 28	00 18	01 07	01 57	02 50
17	76 12.2	16.9	153 42.0	14.7	3 24.5	9.6	54.9	N 10	05 20	05 46	06 09	00 17	01 03	01 51	02 41
18	91 11.9	S23 17.0	168 15.7	14.6	S 3 34.1	9.5	54.9	0	05 03	05 29	05 52	00 17	01 00	01 44	02 32
19	106 11.6	17.1	182 49.3	14.6	3 43.6	9.4	54.9	S 10	04 44	05 11	05 34	00 16	00 56	01 38	02 23
20	121 11.3	17.3	197 22.9	14.6	3 53.0	9.5	54.9	20	04 22	04 51	05 15	00 15	00 53	01 32	02 13
21	136 11.0 ..	17.4	211 56.5	14.5	4 02.5	9.5	54.9	30	03 53	04 26	04 53	00 15	00 49	01 24	02 03
22	151 10.7	17.5	226 30.0	14.5	4 12.0	9.5	55.0	35	03 34	04 11	04 41	00 14	00 46	01 20	01 57
23	166 10.4	17.6	241 03.5	14.5	4 21.5	9.4	55.0	40	03 11	03 53	04 26	00 14	00 44	01 15	01 50
16 00	181 10.1	S23 17.7	255 37.0	14.4	S 4 30.9	9.5	55.0	45	02 41	03 30	04 08	00 14	00 41	01 10	01 42
01	196 09.8	17.9	270 10.4	14.4	4 40.4	9.4	55.0	S 50	01 56	03 01	03 45	00 13	00 37	01 03	01 32
02	211 09.5	18.0	284 43.8	14.4	4 49.8	9.4	55.0	52	01 28	02 46	03 34	00 13	00 36	01 00	01 28
03	226 09.2 ..	18.1	299 17.2	14.3	4 59.2	9.4	55.1	54	00 44	02 28	03 22	00 13	00 34	00 57	01 23
04	241 08.9	18.2	313 50.5	14.3	5 08.6	9.4	55.1	56	////	02 06	03 08	00 12	00 32	00 53	01 17
05	256 08.6	18.3	328 23.8	14.2	5 18.0	9.4	55.1	58	////	01 37	02 51	00 12	00 30	00 49	01 11
06	271 08.3	S23 18.4	342 57.0	14.2	S 5 27.4	9.3	55.1	S 60	////	00 48	02 31	00 12	00 27	00 44	01 05
07	286 07.9	18.5	357 30.2	14.1	5 36.7	9.4	55.2								
T 08	301 07.6	18.6	12 03.3	14.1	5 46.1	9.3	55.2	Lat.	Sunset	Twilight		Moonset			
U 09	316 07.3 ..	18.8	26 36.4	14.1	5 55.4	9.3	55.2			Civil	Naut.	15	16	17	18
E 10	331 07.0	18.9	41 09.5	14.0	6 04.7	9.3	55.2								
S 11	346 06.7	19.0	55 42.5	14.0	6 14.0	9.3	55.3	°	h m	h m	h m	h m	h m	h m	h m
D 12	1 06.4	S23 19.1	70 15.5	13.9	S 6 23.3	9.3	55.3	N 72	■■	13 02	15 30	12 03	11 57	11 50	11 43
A 13	16 06.1	19.2	84 48.4	13.9	6 32.6	9.2	55.3	N 70	■■	14 02	15 50	12 06	12 06	12 06	12 07
Y 14	31 05.8	19.3	99 21.3	13.8	6 41.8	9.2	55.3	68	■■	14 37	16 05	12 09	12 13	12 19	12 26
15	46 05.5 ..	19.4	113 54.1	13.8	6 51.0	9.2	55.4	66	13 22	15 02	16 18	12 12	12 20	12 29	12 42
16	61 05.2	19.5	128 26.9	13.7	7 00.2	9.2	55.4	64	14 04	15 21	16 29	12 14	12 25	12 38	12 54
17	76 04.9	19.6	142 59.6	13.7	7 09.4	9.2	55.4	62	14 32	15 37	16 39	12 16	12 30	12 45	13 05
18	91 04.6	S23 19.7	157 32.3	13.6	S 7 18.6	9.1	55.4	60	14 53	15 51	16 47	12 18	12 34	12 52	13 14
19	106 04.3	19.8	172 04.9	13.6	7 27.7	9.1	55.5	N 58	15 10	16 02	16 55	12 19	12 37	12 58	13 22
20	121 04.0	19.9	186 37.5	13.5	7 36.8	9.1	55.5	56	15 25	16 12	17 01	12 20	12 41	13 03	13 29
21	136 03.7 ..	20.0	201 10.0	13.5	7 45.9	9.0	55.5	54	15 38	16 21	17 08	12 22	12 43	13 08	13 36
22	151 03.4	20.1	215 42.5	13.4	7 54.9	9.1	55.5	52	15 49	16 30	17 13	12 23	12 46	13 12	13 41
23	166 03.1	20.2	230 14.9	13.4	8 04.0	9.0	55.6	50	15 58	16 37	17 18	12 24	12 48	13 16	13 47
17 00	181 02.8	S23 20.3	244 47.3	13.3	S 8 13.0	8.9	55.6	45	16 19	16 53	17 30	12 26	12 54	13 24	13 58
01	196 02.5	20.4	259 19.6	13.3	8 21.9	9.0	55.6	N 40	16 36	17 06	17 40	12 28	12 58	13 31	14 07
02	211 02.2	20.5	273 51.9	13.2	8 30.9	8.9	55.6	35	16 50	17 18	17 50	12 29	13 02	13 37	14 15
03	226 01.9 ..	20.6	288 24.1	13.1	8 39.8	8.9	55.7	30	17 02	17 29	17 59	12 31	13 05	13 42	14 22
04	241 01.6	20.7	302 56.2	13.1	8 48.7	8.8	55.7	20	17 23	17 47	18 15	12 33	13 11	13 51	14 34
05	256 01.3	20.8	317 28.3	13.1	8 57.5	8.9	55.7	N 10	17 42	18 05	18 31	12 35	13 16	13 59	14 45
06	271 00.9	S23 20.9	332 00.4	12.9	S 9 06.4	8.8	55.8	0	17 59	18 22	18 48	12 37	13 21	14 07	14 55
W 07	286 00.6	21.0	346 32.3	12.9	9 15.2	8.7	55.8	S 10	18 17	18 40	19 07	12 39	13 26	14 14	15 06
E 08	301 00.3	21.1	1 04.2	12.9	9 23.9	8.8	55.8	20	18 36	19 00	19 30	12 41	13 31	14 22	15 16
D 09	316 00.0 ..	21.1	15 36.1	12.8	9 32.7	8.7	55.9	30	18 58	19 25	19 59	12 44	13 37	14 32	15 29
N 10	330 59.7	21.2	30 07.9	12.7	9 41.4	8.6	55.9	35	19 11	19 40	20 17	12 45	13 40	14 37	15 36
E 11	345 59.4	21.3	44 39.6	12.7	9 50.0	8.6	55.9	40	19 26	19 59	20 40	12 46	13 44	14 43	15 44
S 12	0 59.1	S23 21.4	59 11.3	12.6	S 9 58.6	8.6	55.9	45	19 44	20 21	21 11	12 48	13 48	14 50	15 53
D 13	15 58.8	21.5	73 42.9	12.5	10 07.2	8.6	56.0	S 50	20 06	20 51	21 56	12 50	13 54	14 59	16 05
A 14	30 58.5	21.6	88 14.4	12.5	10 15.8	8.5	56.0	52	20 17	21 06	22 23	12 51	13 56	15 03	16 10
Y 15	45 58.2 ..	21.7	102 45.9	12.4	10 24.3	8.4	56.0	54	20 29	21 24	23 09	12 52	13 59	15 07	16 16
16	60 57.9	21.7	117 17.3	12.4	10 32.7	8.5	56.1	56	20 43	21 46	////	12 54	14 02	15 12	16 23
17	75 57.6	21.8	131 48.7	12.3	10 41.2	8.4	56.1	58	21 00	22 15	////	12 55	14 05	15 17	16 30
18	90 57.3	S23 21.9	146 20.0	12.2	S10 49.6	8.3	56.1	S 60	21 20	23 04	////	12 57	14 09	15 23	16 39
19	105 57.0	22.0	160 51.2	12.1	10 57.9	8.3	56.2								
20	120 56.7	22.1	175 22.3	12.1	11 06.2	8.3	56.2		SUN			MOON			
21	135 56.4 ..	22.2	189 53.4	12.0	11 14.5	8.2	56.2	Day	Eqn. of Time		Mer.	Mer. Pass.		Age	Phase
22	150 56.0	22.2	204 24.4	12.0	11 22.7	8.1	56.2		00ʰ	12ʰ	Pass.	Upper	Lower		
23	165 55.7	22.3	218 55.4	11.9	S11 30.8	8.2	56.3	d	m s	m s	h m	h m	h m	d %	
								15	05 10	04 55	11 55	06 27	18 48	23 41	
								16	04 41	04 26	11 56	07 10	19 33	24 32	
	SD 16.3	d 0.1	SD 14.9		15.1		15.2	17	04 12	03 57	11 56	07 56	20 19	25 23	

UT	ARIES GHA	VENUS −3.9 GHA	Dec	MARS +1.1 GHA	Dec	JUPITER −2.4 GHA	Dec	SATURN +0.5 GHA	Dec	STARS Name	SHA	Dec
18 00	86 31.9	166 29.1	S24 05.1	133 37.4	S18 55.3	301 25.2	N14 46.3	208 55.4	S18 08.5	Acamar	315 17.3	S40 15.0
01	101 34.4	181 28.2	05.0	148 37.9	54.7	316 27.7	46.3	223 57.6	08.6	Achernar	335 25.8	S57 10.0
02	116 36.8	196 27.2	04.9	163 38.4	54.2	331 30.2	46.3	238 59.8	08.6	Acrux	173 08.1	S63 10.6
03	131 39.3	211 26.2 ..	04.7	178 38.9 ..	53.6	346 32.8 ..	46.4	254 02.0 ..	08.7	Adhara	255 11.3	S28 59.7
04	146 41.8	226 25.3	04.6	193 39.3	53.1	1 35.3	46.4	269 04.1	08.8	Aldebaran	290 47.9	N16 32.2
05	161 44.2	241 24.3	04.4	208 39.8	52.5	16 37.8	46.4	284 06.3	08.8			
T 06	176 46.7	256 23.3	S24 04.3	223 40.3	S18 52.0	31 40.4	N14 46.5	299 08.5	S18 08.9	Alioth	166 20.1	N55 52.5
H 07	191 49.2	271 22.3	04.2	238 40.8	51.4	46 42.9	46.5	314 10.7	08.9	Alkaid	152 58.4	N49 14.2
U 08	206 51.6	286 21.4	04.0	253 41.3	50.9	61 45.4	46.5	329 12.9	09.0	Al Na'ir	27 42.7	S46 53.4
R 09	221 54.1	301 20.4 ..	03.9	268 41.8 ..	50.3	76 48.0 ..	46.6	344 15.0 ..	09.0	Alnilam	275 45.0	S 1 11.8
S 10	236 56.5	316 19.4	03.7	283 42.3	49.8	91 50.5	46.6	359 17.2	09.1	Alphard	217 54.9	S 8 43.5
D 11	251 59.0	331 18.5	03.6	298 42.8	49.2	106 53.1	46.6	14 19.4	09.2			
A 12	267 01.5	346 17.5	S24 03.4	313 43.2	S18 48.7	121 55.6	N14 46.7	29 21.6	S18 09.2	Alphecca	126 10.5	N26 39.7
Y 13	282 03.9	1 16.5	03.3	328 43.7	48.1	136 58.1	46.7	44 23.8	09.3	Alpheratz	357 42.3	N29 10.6
14	297 06.4	16 15.6	03.1	343 44.2	47.6	152 00.7	46.7	59 25.9	09.3	Altair	62 07.5	N 8 54.7
15	312 08.9	31 14.6 ..	03.0	358 44.7 ..	47.0	167 03.2 ..	46.8	74 28.1 ..	09.4	Ankaa	353 14.7	S42 13.7
16	327 11.3	46 13.6	02.8	13 45.2	46.5	182 05.8	46.8	89 30.3	09.4	Antares	112 25.3	S26 27.6
17	342 13.8	61 12.7	02.6	28 45.7	45.9	197 08.3	46.9	104 32.5	09.5			
18	357 16.3	76 11.7	S24 02.5	43 46.2	S18 45.4	212 10.8	N14 46.9	119 34.7	S18 09.6	Arcturus	145 55.0	N19 06.3
19	12 18.7	91 10.7	02.3	58 46.7	44.8	227 13.4	46.9	134 36.8	09.6	Atria	107 26.7	S69 03.0
20	27 21.2	106 09.8	02.2	73 47.2	44.3	242 15.9	47.0	149 39.0	09.7	Avior	234 17.0	S59 33.4
21	42 23.7	121 08.8 ..	02.0	88 47.7 ..	43.7	257 18.5 ..	47.0	164 41.2 ..	09.7	Bellatrix	278 30.6	N 6 21.6
22	57 26.1	136 07.8	01.8	103 48.1	43.1	272 21.0	47.0	179 43.4	09.8	Betelgeuse	270 59.8	N 7 24.4
23	72 28.6	151 06.9	01.7	118 48.6	42.6	287 23.5	47.1	194 45.6	09.8			
19 00	87 31.0	166 05.9	S24 01.5	133 49.1	S18 42.0	302 26.1	N14 47.1	209 47.7	S18 09.9	Canopus	263 55.1	S52 42.4
01	102 33.5	181 04.9	01.3	148 49.6	41.5	317 28.6	47.1	224 49.9	10.0	Capella	280 32.4	N46 00.6
02	117 36.0	196 04.0	01.2	163 50.1	40.9	332 31.2	47.2	239 52.1	10.0	Deneb	49 31.1	N45 20.4
03	132 38.4	211 03.0 ..	01.0	178 50.6 ..	40.4	347 33.7 ..	47.2	254 54.3 ..	10.1	Denebola	182 32.6	N14 29.2
04	147 40.9	226 02.0	00.8	193 51.1	39.8	2 36.2	47.3	269 56.5	10.1	Diphda	348 54.8	S17 54.4
05	162 43.4	241 01.1	00.7	208 51.6	39.2	17 38.8	47.3	284 58.6	10.2			
06	177 45.8	256 00.1	S24 00.5	223 52.1	S18 38.7	32 41.3	N14 47.3	300 00.8	S18 10.2	Dubhe	193 50.5	N61 39.8
07	192 48.3	270 59.1	00.3	238 52.6	38.1	47 43.9	47.4	315 03.0	10.3	Elnath	278 10.9	N28 37.0
F 08	207 50.8	285 58.2	00.1	253 53.0	37.6	62 46.4	47.4	330 05.2	10.4	Eltanin	90 46.2	N51 29.4
R 09	222 53.2	300 57.2	24 00.0	268 53.5 ..	37.0	77 49.0 ..	47.4	345 07.4 ..	10.4	Enif	33 46.3	N 9 56.8
I 10	237 55.7	315 56.3	23 59.8	283 54.0	36.5	92 51.5	47.5	0 09.5	10.5	Fomalhaut	15 23.0	S29 32.7
D 11	252 58.1	330 55.3	59.6	298 54.5	35.9	107 54.1	47.5	15 11.7	10.5			
A 12	268 00.6	345 54.3	S23 59.4	313 55.0	S18 35.3	122 56.6	N14 47.6	30 13.9	S18 10.6	Gacrux	171 59.7	S57 11.5
Y 13	283 03.1	0 53.4	59.2	328 55.5	34.8	137 59.2	47.6	45 16.1	10.6	Gienah	175 51.3	S17 37.4
14	298 05.5	15 52.4	59.1	343 56.0	34.2	153 01.7	47.6	60 18.3	10.7	Hadar	148 46.7	S60 26.4
15	313 08.0	30 51.4 ..	58.9	358 56.5 ..	33.7	168 04.2 ..	47.7	75 20.4 ..	10.7	Hamal	327 59.4	N23 32.0
16	328 10.5	45 50.5	58.7	13 57.0	33.1	183 06.8	47.7	90 22.6	10.8	Kaus Aust.	83 42.9	S34 22.4
17	343 12.9	60 49.5	58.5	28 57.5	32.5	198 09.3	47.7	105 24.8	10.9			
18	358 15.4	75 48.5	S23 58.3	43 58.0	S18 32.0	213 11.9	N14 47.8	120 27.0	S18 10.9	Kochab	137 21.2	N74 05.5
19	13 17.9	90 47.6	58.1	58 58.5	31.4	228 14.4	47.8	135 29.2	11.0	Markab	13 37.4	N15 17.3
20	28 20.3	105 46.6	57.9	73 59.0	30.8	243 17.0	47.9	150 31.4	11.0	Menkar	314 13.7	N 4 08.8
21	43 22.8	120 45.7 ..	57.7	88 59.5 ..	30.3	258 19.5 ..	47.9	165 33.5 ..	11.1	Menkent	148 06.5	S36 26.3
22	58 25.3	135 44.7	57.5	104 00.0	29.7	273 22.1	47.9	180 35.7	11.1	Miaplacidus	221 38.6	S69 46.6
23	73 27.7	150 43.7	57.3	119 00.4	29.2	288 24.6	48.0	195 37.9	11.2			
20 00	88 30.2	165 42.8	S23 57.1	134 00.9	S18 28.6	303 27.2	N14 48.0	210 40.1	S18 11.3	Mirfak	308 38.4	N49 54.9
01	103 32.6	180 41.8	56.9	149 01.4	28.0	318 29.7	48.1	225 42.3	11.3	Nunki	75 57.4	S26 16.5
02	118 35.1	195 40.8	56.7	164 01.9	27.5	333 32.3	48.1	240 44.4	11.4	Peacock	53 18.2	S56 41.2
03	133 37.6	210 39.9 ..	56.5	179 02.4 ..	26.9	348 34.8 ..	48.1	255 46.6 ..	11.4	Pollux	243 26.2	N27 59.1
04	148 40.0	225 38.9	56.3	194 02.9	26.3	3 37.4	48.2	270 48.8	11.5	Procyon	244 58.4	N 5 11.0
05	163 42.5	240 38.0	56.1	209 03.4	25.8	18 39.9	48.2	285 51.0	11.5			
06	178 45.0	255 37.0	S23 55.9	224 03.9	S18 25.2	33 42.5	N14 48.3	300 53.2	S18 11.6	Rasalhague	96 05.9	N12 33.2
07	193 47.4	270 36.0	55.7	239 04.4	24.6	48 45.0	48.3	315 55.4	11.6	Regulus	207 42.3	N11 53.5
S 08	208 49.9	285 35.1	55.5	254 04.9	24.1	63 47.6	48.3	330 57.5	11.7	Rigel	281 10.7	S 8 11.3
A 09	223 52.4	300 34.1 ..	55.3	269 05.4 ..	23.5	78 50.1 ..	48.4	345 59.7 ..	11.8	Rigil Kent.	139 50.7	S60 53.4
T 10	238 54.8	315 33.2	55.1	284 05.9	22.9	93 52.7	48.4	1 01.9	11.8	Sabik	102 11.7	S15 44.4
U 11	253 57.3	330 32.2	54.9	299 06.4	22.4	108 55.3	48.5	16 04.1	11.9			
R 12	268 59.8	345 31.2	S23 54.7	314 06.9	S18 21.8	123 57.8	N14 48.5	31 06.3	S18 11.9	Schedar	349 39.1	N56 37.4
D 13	284 02.2	0 30.3	54.5	329 07.4	21.2	139 00.4	48.5	46 08.4	12.0	Shaula	96 20.9	S37 06.6
A 14	299 04.7	15 29.3	54.2	344 07.9	20.7	154 02.9	48.6	61 10.6	12.0	Sirius	258 32.5	S16 44.4
Y 15	314 07.1	30 28.4 ..	54.0	359 08.4 ..	20.1	169 05.5 ..	48.6	76 12.8 ..	12.1	Spica	158 30.3	S11 14.2
16	329 09.6	45 27.4	53.8	14 08.9	19.5	184 08.0	48.7	91 15.0	12.2	Suhail	222 51.3	S43 29.6
17	344 12.1	60 26.5	53.6	29 09.4	19.0	199 10.6	48.7	106 17.2	12.2			
18	359 14.5	75 25.5	S23 53.4	44 09.9	S18 18.4	214 13.1	N14 48.7	121 19.4	S18 12.3	Vega	80 38.7	N38 48.1
19	14 17.0	90 24.5	53.2	59 10.4	17.8	229 15.7	48.8	136 21.5	12.3	Zuben'ubi	137 04.5	S16 06.0
20	29 19.5	105 23.6	52.9	74 10.9	17.3	244 18.2	48.8	151 23.7	12.4		SHA	Mer.Pass.
21	44 21.9	120 22.6 ..	52.7	89 11.4 ..	16.7	259 20.8 ..	48.9	166 25.9 ..	12.4	Venus	78 34.9	12 56
22	59 24.4	135 21.7	52.5	104 11.9	16.1	274 23.4	48.9	181 28.1	12.5	Mars	46 18.1	15 04
23	74 26.9	150 20.7	52.3	119 12.4	15.5	289 25.9	48.9	196 30.3	12.5	Jupiter	214 55.0	3 50
Mer. Pass. 18 07.0		v −1.0 d 0.2		v 0.5 d 0.6		v 2.5 d 0.0		v 2.2 d 0.1		Saturn	122 16.7	9 59

UT	SUN GHA	SUN Dec	MOON GHA	v	Dec	d	HP
d h	° ′	° ′	° ′	′	° ′	′	′
18 00	180 55.4	S23 22.4	233 26.3	11.8	S11 39.0	8.0	56.3
01	195 55.1	22.5	247 57.1	11.7	11 47.0	8.1	56.3
02	210 54.8	22.5	262 27.8	11.7	11 55.1	7.9	56.4
03	225 54.5	.. 22.6	276 58.5	11.6	12 03.0	8.0	56.4
04	240 54.2	22.7	291 29.1	11.5	12 11.0	7.8	56.4
05	255 53.9	22.8	305 59.6	11.5	12 18.8	7.9	56.5
T 06	270 53.6	S23 22.8	320 30.1	11.4	S12 26.7	7.7	56.5
H 07	285 53.3	22.9	335 00.5	11.3	12 34.4	7.7	56.5
U 08	300 53.0	23.0	349 30.8	11.2	12 42.1	7.7	56.6
R 09	315 52.7	.. 23.1	4 01.0	11.2	12 49.8	7.6	56.6
S 10	330 52.4	23.1	18 31.2	11.1	12 57.4	7.6	56.6
D 11	345 52.0	23.2	33 01.3	11.0	13 05.0	7.4	56.7
A 12	0 51.7	S23 23.3	47 31.3	11.0	S13 12.4	7.5	56.7
Y 13	15 51.4	23.3	62 01.3	10.9	13 19.9	7.4	56.7
14	30 51.1	23.4	76 31.2	10.8	13 27.3	7.3	56.8
15	45 50.8	.. 23.5	91 01.0	10.7	13 34.6	7.2	56.8
16	60 50.5	23.5	105 30.7	10.6	13 41.8	7.2	56.8
17	75 50.2	23.6	120 00.3	10.6	13 49.0	7.1	56.9
18	90 49.9	S23 23.7	134 29.9	10.5	S13 56.1	7.1	56.9
19	105 49.6	23.7	148 59.4	10.4	14 03.2	7.0	56.9
20	120 49.3	23.8	163 28.8	10.4	14 10.2	6.9	57.0
21	135 49.0	.. 23.8	177 58.2	10.3	14 17.1	6.9	57.0
22	150 48.7	23.9	192 27.5	10.2	14 24.0	6.8	57.0
23	165 48.3	24.0	206 56.7	10.1	14 30.8	6.7	57.1
19 00	180 48.0	S23 24.0	221 25.8	10.0	S14 37.5	6.7	57.1
01	195 47.7	24.1	235 54.8	10.0	14 44.2	6.5	57.1
02	210 47.4	24.1	250 23.8	9.9	14 50.7	6.5	57.2
03	225 47.1	.. 24.2	264 52.7	9.8	14 57.2	6.5	57.2
04	240 46.8	24.2	279 21.5	9.7	15 03.7	6.3	57.2
05	255 46.5	24.3	293 50.2	9.7	15 10.0	6.3	57.3
F 06	270 46.2	S23 24.4	308 18.9	9.6	S15 16.3	6.2	57.3
R 07	285 45.9	24.4	322 47.5	9.5	15 22.5	6.2	57.3
I 08	300 45.6	24.5	337 16.0	9.4	15 28.7	6.0	57.4
D 09	315 45.3	.. 24.5	351 44.4	9.4	15 34.7	6.0	57.4
A 10	330 44.9	24.6	6 12.8	9.3	15 40.7	5.9	57.4
Y 11	345 44.6	24.6	20 41.1	9.2	15 46.6	5.8	57.5
12	0 44.3	S23 24.7	35 09.3	9.1	S15 52.4	5.8	57.5
13	15 44.0	24.7	49 37.4	9.1	15 58.2	5.6	57.5
14	30 43.7	24.7	64 05.5	9.0	16 03.8	5.6	57.6
15	45 43.4	.. 24.8	78 33.5	8.9	16 09.4	5.4	57.6
16	60 43.1	24.8	93 01.4	8.8	16 14.8	5.4	57.6
17	75 42.8	24.9	107 29.2	8.8	16 20.2	5.3	57.7
18	90 42.5	S23 24.9	121 57.0	8.6	S16 25.5	5.3	57.7
19	105 42.2	25.0	136 24.6	8.6	16 30.8	5.1	57.8
20	120 41.8	25.0	150 52.2	8.6	16 35.9	5.0	57.8
21	135 41.5	.. 25.1	165 19.8	8.4	16 40.9	5.0	57.8
22	150 41.2	25.1	179 47.2	8.4	16 45.9	4.8	57.9
23	165 40.9	25.1	194 14.6	8.3	16 50.7	4.8	57.9
20 00	180 40.6	S23 25.2	208 41.9	8.3	S16 55.5	4.7	57.9
01	195 40.3	25.2	223 09.2	8.2	17 00.2	4.5	58.0
02	210 40.0	25.2	237 36.4	8.1	17 04.7	4.5	58.0
03	225 39.7	.. 25.3	252 03.5	8.0	17 09.2	4.4	58.0
04	240 39.4	25.3	266 30.5	7.9	17 13.6	4.3	58.1
05	255 39.1	25.4	280 57.4	7.9	17 17.9	4.1	58.1
S 06	270 38.7	S23 25.4	295 24.3	7.8	S17 22.0	4.1	58.1
A 07	285 38.4	25.4	309 51.1	7.8	17 26.1	4.0	58.1
T 08	300 38.1	25.5	324 17.9	7.7	17 30.1	3.9	58.2
U 09	315 37.8	.. 25.5	338 44.6	7.6	17 34.0	3.8	58.2
R 10	330 37.5	25.5	353 11.2	7.6	17 37.8	3.6	58.2
D 11	345 37.2	25.5	7 37.8	7.4	17 41.4	3.6	58.3
A 12	0 36.9	S23 25.6	22 04.2	7.5	S17 45.0	3.5	58.3
Y 13	15 36.6	25.6	36 30.7	7.3	17 48.5	3.3	58.3
14	30 36.3	25.6	50 57.0	7.3	17 51.8	3.3	58.4
15	45 36.0	.. 25.7	65 23.3	7.2	17 55.1	3.1	58.4
16	60 35.6	25.7	79 49.5	7.2	17 58.2	3.1	58.4
17	75 35.3	25.7	94 15.7	7.1	18 01.3	2.9	58.5
18	90 35.0	S23 25.7	108 41.8	7.1	S18 04.2	2.8	58.5
19	105 34.7	25.8	123 07.9	7.0	18 07.0	2.7	58.5
20	120 34.4	25.8	137 33.9	6.9	18 09.7	2.6	58.6
21	135 34.1	.. 25.8	151 59.8	6.9	18 12.3	2.5	58.6
22	150 33.8	25.8	166 25.7	6.8	18 14.8	2.4	58.6
23	165 33.5	25.8	180 51.5	6.7	S18 17.2	2.2	58.7
	SD 16.3	d 0.0	SD 15.4		15.7		15.9

Lat.	Twilight Naut.	Civil	Sunrise	Moonrise 18	19	20	21
°	h m	h m	h m	h m	h m	h m	h m
N 72	08 24	10 55	■■	05 29	07 25	09 48	■■
N 70	08 04	09 53	■■	05 06	06 47	08 28	09 57
68	07 48	09 17	■■	04 48	06 20	07 50	09 08
66	07 35	08 52	10 33	04 33	06 00	07 23	08 37
64	07 24	08 33	09 50	04 22	05 44	07 03	08 14
62	07 14	08 16	09 22	04 12	05 30	06 46	07 55
60	07 06	08 03	09 01	04 03	05 19	06 33	07 40
N 58	06 58	07 51	08 43	03 56	05 09	06 21	07 27
56	06 52	07 41	08 28	03 49	05 01	06 11	07 16
54	06 46	07 32	08 16	03 43	04 53	06 02	07 06
52	06 40	07 24	08 05	03 38	04 46	05 54	06 58
50	06 35	07 16	07 55	03 33	04 40	05 46	06 50
45	06 23	07 00	07 34	03 23	04 27	05 31	06 33
N 40	06 12	06 46	07 17	03 15	04 16	05 18	06 20
35	06 03	06 35	07 03	03 07	04 07	05 08	06 08
30	05 54	06 24	06 50	03 01	03 59	04 58	05 58
20	05 38	06 05	06 29	02 50	03 45	04 42	05 41
N 10	05 22	05 48	06 11	02 41	03 33	04 28	05 25
0	05 05	05 31	05 53	02 32	03 22	04 15	05 11
S 10	04 46	05 13	05 36	02 23	03 11	04 02	04 57
20	04 23	04 52	05 17	02 13	02 59	03 48	04 42
30	03 54	04 27	04 55	02 03	02 45	03 32	04 25
35	03 35	04 12	04 42	01 57	02 37	03 23	04 15
40	03 12	03 54	04 27	01 50	02 29	03 13	04 04
45	02 41	03 31	04 09	01 42	02 18	03 01	03 51
S 50	01 56	03 01	03 46	01 32	02 06	02 46	03 34
52	01 28	02 46	03 35	01 28	02 00	02 39	03 27
54	00 41	02 28	03 23	01 23	01 54	02 31	03 18
56	////	02 06	03 09	01 17	01 47	02 23	03 09
58	////	01 36	02 52	01 11	01 39	02 13	02 58
S 60	////	00 46	02 31	01 05	01 30	02 02	02 46

Lat.	Sunset	Twilight Civil	Naut.	Moonset 18	19	20	21
°	h m	h m	h m	h m	h m	h m	h m
N 72	■■	12 59	15 30	11 43	11 32	11 02	■■
N 70	■■	14 01	15 50	12 07	12 11	12 22	12 52
68	■■	14 37	16 06	12 26	12 39	13 01	13 41
66	13 21	15 02	16 19	12 42	13 00	13 28	14 12
64	14 04	15 21	16 30	12 54	13 17	13 49	14 35
62	14 32	15 38	16 40	13 05	13 30	14 06	14 54
60	14 53	15 51	16 48	13 14	13 42	14 20	15 09
N 58	15 11	16 03	16 56	13 22	13 53	14 32	15 22
56	15 26	16 13	17 02	13 29	14 02	14 42	15 33
54	15 38	16 22	17 09	13 36	14 09	14 51	15 43
52	15 49	16 30	17 14	13 41	14 17	15 00	15 52
50	15 59	16 38	17 19	13 47	14 23	15 07	16 00
45	16 20	16 54	17 31	13 58	14 37	15 23	16 17
N 40	16 37	17 08	17 42	14 07	14 48	15 36	16 30
35	16 51	17 19	17 51	14 15	14 58	15 47	16 42
30	17 04	17 30	18 00	14 22	15 07	15 57	16 52
20	17 25	17 49	18 16	14 34	15 22	16 13	17 10
N 10	17 43	18 06	18 33	14 45	15 35	16 28	17 25
0	18 01	18 23	18 50	14 55	15 47	16 42	17 39
S 10	18 18	18 41	19 09	15 05	15 59	16 55	17 53
20	18 37	19 02	19 31	15 16	16 12	17 10	18 08
30	18 59	19 27	20 00	15 29	16 27	17 27	18 26
35	19 12	19 42	20 19	15 36	16 36	17 36	18 36
40	19 28	20 00	20 42	15 44	16 46	17 47	18 47
45	19 46	20 23	21 13	15 53	16 57	18 00	19 01
S 50	20 08	20 53	21 58	16 05	17 11	18 16	19 17
52	20 19	21 08	22 26	16 10	17 18	18 24	19 25
54	20 31	21 26	23 13	16 16	17 25	18 34	19 34
56	20 46	21 48	////	16 23	17 34	18 41	19 43
58	21 02	22 18	////	16 30	17 43	18 52	19 54
S 60	21 23	23 09	////	16 39	17 53	19 04	20 07

Day	SUN Eqn. of Time 00h	12h	Mer. Pass.	MOON Mer. Pass. Upper	Lower	Age	Phase
d	m s	m s	h m	h m	h m	d	%
18	03 42	03 28	11 57	08 43	21 08	26	15
19	03 13	02 58	11 57	09 34	22 01	27	8
20	02 43	02 28	11 58	10 28	22 56	28	3

UT	ARIES GHA	VENUS −3.9 GHA	Dec	MARS +1.1 GHA	Dec	JUPITER −2.4 GHA	Dec	SATURN +0.5 GHA	Dec	STARS Name	SHA	Dec
21 00	89 29.3	165 19.7	S23 52.0	134 12.9	S18 15.0	304 28.5	N14 49.0	211 32.5	S18 12.6	Acamar	315 17.3	S40 15.0
01	104 31.8	180 18.8	51.8	149 13.4	14.4	319 31.0	49.0	226 34.6	12.7	Achernar	335 25.9	S57 10.0
02	119 34.3	195 17.8	51.6	164 13.9	13.8	334 33.6	49.1	241 36.8	12.7	Acrux	173 08.0	S63 10.6
03	134 36.7	210 16.9	.. 51.3	179 14.4	.. 13.3	349 36.2	.. 49.1	256 39.0	.. 12.8	Adhara	255 11.3	S28 59.7
04	149 39.2	225 15.9	51.1	194 14.9	12.7	4 38.7	49.2	271 41.2	12.8	Aldebaran	290 47.8	N16 32.2
05	164 41.6	240 15.0	50.9	209 15.4	12.1	19 41.3	49.2	286 43.4	12.9			
06	179 44.1	255 14.0	S23 50.6	224 15.9	S18 11.5	34 43.8	N14 49.2	301 45.6	S18 12.9	Alioth	166 20.0	N55 52.5
07	194 46.6	270 13.1	50.4	239 16.4	11.0	49 46.4	49.3	316 47.7	13.0	Alkaid	152 58.4	N49 14.1
08	209 49.0	285 12.1	50.2	254 16.9	10.4	64 49.0	49.3	331 49.9	13.0	Al Na'ir	27 42.8	S46 53.4
S 09	224 51.5	300 11.1	.. 49.9	269 17.4	.. 09.8	79 51.5	.. 49.4	346 52.1	.. 13.1	Alnilam	275 45.0	S 1 11.8
U 10	239 54.0	315 10.2	49.7	284 17.9	09.2	94 54.1	49.4	1 54.3	13.2	Alphard	217 54.8	S 8 43.5
N 11	254 56.4	330 09.2	49.4	299 18.4	08.7	109 56.6	49.5	16 56.5	13.2			
D 12	269 58.9	345 08.3	S23 49.2	314 18.9	S18 08.1	124 59.2	N14 49.5	31 58.7	S18 13.3	Alphecca	126 10.5	N26 39.9
A 13	285 01.4	0 07.3	48.9	329 19.4	07.5	140 01.8	49.5	47 00.8	13.3	Alpheratz	357 42.4	N29 10.6
Y 14	300 03.8	15 06.4	48.7	344 19.9	06.9	155 04.3	49.6	62 03.0	13.4	Altair	62 07.5	N 8 54.7
15	315 06.3	30 05.4	.. 48.5	359 20.4	.. 06.4	170 06.9	.. 49.6	77 05.2	.. 13.4	Ankaa	353 14.7	S42 13.7
16	330 08.8	45 04.5	48.2	14 20.9	05.8	185 09.4	49.7	92 07.4	13.5	Antares	112 25.3	S26 27.6
17	345 11.2	60 03.5	48.0	29 21.4	05.2	200 12.0	49.7	107 09.6	13.5			
18	0 13.7	75 02.6	S23 47.7	44 21.9	S18 04.6	215 14.6	N14 49.8	122 11.8	S18 13.6	Arcturus	145 55.0	N19 06.3
19	15 16.1	90 01.6	47.5	59 22.4	04.0	230 17.1	49.8	137 13.9	13.6	Atria	107 26.7	S69 02.9
20	30 18.6	105 00.7	47.2	74 22.9	03.5	245 19.7	49.8	152 16.1	13.7	Avior	234 17.0	S59 33.5
21	45 21.1	119 59.7	.. 46.9	89 23.4	.. 02.9	260 22.3	.. 49.9	167 18.3	.. 13.8	Bellatrix	278 30.6	N 6 21.6
22	60 23.5	134 58.7	46.7	104 23.9	02.3	275 24.8	49.9	182 20.5	13.8	Betelgeuse	270 59.8	N 7 24.4
23	75 26.0	149 57.8	46.4	119 24.4	01.7	290 27.4	50.0	197 22.7	13.9			
22 00	90 28.5	164 56.8	S23 46.2	134 24.9	S18 01.1	305 30.0	N14 50.0	212 24.9	S18 13.9	Canopus	263 55.1	S52 42.4
01	105 30.9	179 55.9	45.9	149 25.4	00.6	320 32.5	50.1	227 27.1	14.0	Capella	280 32.4	N46 00.6
02	120 33.4	194 54.9	45.7	164 25.9	18 00.0	335 35.1	50.1	242 29.2	14.0	Deneb	49 31.1	N45 20.4
03	135 35.9	209 54.0	.. 45.4	179 26.4	17 59.4	350 37.7	.. 50.2	257 31.4	.. 14.1	Denebola	182 32.6	N14 29.2
04	150 38.3	224 53.0	45.1	194 26.9	58.8	5 40.2	50.2	272 33.6	14.1	Diphda	348 54.8	S17 54.4
05	165 40.8	239 52.1	44.9	209 27.4	58.2	20 42.8	50.2	287 35.8	14.2			
06	180 43.3	254 51.1	S23 44.6	224 27.9	S17 57.7	35 45.4	N14 50.3	302 38.0	S18 14.3	Dubhe	193 50.4	N61 39.8
07	195 45.7	269 50.2	44.3	239 28.4	57.1	50 47.9	50.3	317 40.2	14.3	Elnath	278 10.9	N28 37.0
08	210 48.2	284 49.2	44.1	254 28.9	56.5	65 50.5	50.4	332 42.3	14.4	Eltanin	90 46.2	N51 29.4
M 09	225 50.6	299 48.3	.. 43.8	269 29.4	.. 55.9	80 53.1	.. 50.4	347 44.5	.. 14.4	Enif	33 46.3	N 9 56.8
O 10	240 53.1	314 47.3	43.5	284 29.9	55.3	95 55.6	50.5	2 46.7	14.5	Fomalhaut	15 23.0	S29 32.6
N 11	255 55.6	329 46.4	43.3	299 30.4	54.8	110 58.2	50.5	17 48.9	14.5			
D 12	270 58.0	344 45.4	S23 43.0	314 30.9	S17 54.2	126 00.8	N14 50.6	32 51.1	S18 14.6	Gacrux	171 59.7	S57 11.5
A 13	286 00.5	359 44.5	42.7	329 31.4	53.6	141 03.3	50.6	47 53.3	14.6	Gienah	175 51.2	S17 37.4
Y 14	301 03.0	14 43.5	42.4	344 31.9	53.0	156 05.9	50.6	62 55.5	14.7	Hadar	148 46.6	S60 26.4
15	316 05.4	29 42.6	.. 42.1	359 32.4	.. 52.4	171 08.5	.. 50.7	77 57.6	.. 14.7	Hamal	327 59.4	N23 32.0
16	331 07.9	44 41.7	41.9	14 33.0	51.8	186 11.1	50.7	92 59.8	14.8	Kaus Aust.	83 42.9	S34 22.4
17	346 10.4	59 40.7	41.6	29 33.5	51.2	201 13.6	50.8	108 02.0	14.9			
18	1 12.8	74 39.8	S23 41.3	44 34.0	S17 50.7	216 16.2	N14 50.8	123 04.2	S18 14.9	Kochab	137 21.1	N74 05.5
19	16 15.3	89 38.8	41.0	59 34.5	50.1	231 18.8	50.9	138 06.4	15.0	Markab	13 37.4	N15 17.3
20	31 17.7	104 37.9	40.7	74 35.0	49.5	246 21.3	50.9	153 08.6	15.0	Menkar	314 13.7	N 4 08.8
21	46 20.2	119 36.9	.. 40.5	89 35.5	.. 48.9	261 23.9	.. 51.0	168 10.8	.. 15.1	Menkent	148 06.5	S36 26.3
22	61 22.7	134 36.0	40.2	104 36.0	48.3	276 26.5	51.0	183 12.9	15.1	Miaplacidus	221 38.6	S69 46.6
23	76 25.1	149 35.0	39.9	119 36.5	47.7	291 29.1	51.1	198 15.1	15.2			
23 00	91 27.6	164 34.1	S23 39.6	134 37.0	S17 47.1	306 31.6	N14 51.1	213 17.3	S18 15.2	Mirfak	308 38.4	N49 54.9
01	106 30.1	179 33.1	39.3	149 37.5	46.6	321 34.2	51.2	228 19.5	15.3	Nunki	75 57.4	S26 16.5
02	121 32.5	194 32.2	39.0	164 38.0	46.0	336 36.8	51.2	243 21.7	15.3	Peacock	53 18.2	S56 41.2
03	136 35.0	209 31.2	.. 38.7	179 38.5	.. 45.4	351 39.4	.. 51.3	258 23.9	.. 15.4	Pollux	243 26.1	N27 59.1
04	151 37.5	224 30.3	38.4	194 39.0	44.8	6 41.9	51.3	273 26.1	15.5	Procyon	244 58.3	N 5 11.0
05	166 39.9	239 29.4	38.1	209 39.5	44.2	21 44.5	51.3	288 28.3	15.5			
06	181 42.4	254 28.4	S23 37.8	224 40.1	S17 43.6	36 47.1	N14 51.4	303 30.4	S18 15.6	Rasalhague	96 05.8	N12 33.2
07	196 44.9	269 27.5	37.5	239 40.6	43.0	51 49.7	51.4	318 32.6	15.6	Regulus	207 42.3	N11 53.4
08	211 47.3	284 26.5	37.2	254 41.1	42.4	66 52.2	51.5	333 34.8	15.7	Rigel	281 10.7	S 8 11.3
T 09	226 49.8	299 25.6	.. 36.9	269 41.6	.. 41.8	81 54.8	.. 51.5	348 37.0	.. 15.7	Rigil Kent.	139 50.6	S60 53.4
U 10	241 52.2	314 24.6	36.6	284 42.1	41.3	96 57.4	51.6	3 39.2	15.8	Sabik	102 11.7	S15 44.4
E 11	256 54.7	329 23.7	36.3	299 42.6	40.7	112 00.0	51.6	18 41.4	15.8			
S 12	271 57.2	344 22.8	S23 36.0	314 43.1	S17 40.1	127 02.5	N14 51.7	33 43.6	S18 15.9	Schedar	349 39.1	N56 37.4
D 13	286 59.6	359 21.8	35.7	329 43.6	39.5	142 05.1	51.7	48 45.7	15.9	Shaula	96 20.9	S37 06.6
A 14	302 02.1	14 20.9	35.4	344 44.1	38.9	157 07.7	51.8	63 47.9	16.0	Sirius	258 32.4	S16 44.4
Y 15	317 04.6	29 19.9	.. 35.1	359 44.6	.. 38.3	172 10.3	.. 51.8	78 50.1	.. 16.0	Spica	158 30.3	S11 14.3
16	332 07.0	44 19.0	34.8	14 45.1	37.7	187 12.9	51.9	93 52.3	16.1	Suhail	222 51.3	S43 29.6
17	347 09.5	59 18.0	34.5	29 45.7	37.1	202 15.4	51.9	108 54.5	16.2			
18	2 12.0	74 17.1	S23 34.2	44 46.2	S17 36.5	217 18.0	N14 52.0	123 56.7	S18 16.2	Vega	80 38.7	N38 48.1
19	17 14.4	89 16.2	33.9	59 46.7	35.9	232 20.6	52.0	138 58.9	16.3	Zuben'ubi	137 04.5	S16 06.0
20	32 16.9	104 15.2	33.6	74 47.2	35.3	247 23.2	52.1	154 01.1	16.3		SHA	Mer.Pass.
21	47 19.4	119 14.3	.. 33.2	89 47.7	.. 34.7	262 25.8	.. 52.1	169 03.2	.. 16.4		° '	h m
22	62 21.8	134 13.3	32.9	104 48.2	34.1	277 28.3	52.2	184 05.4	16.4	Venus	74 28.4	13 01
23	77 24.3	149 12.4	32.6	119 48.7	33.5	292 30.9	52.2	199 07.6	16.5	Mars	43 56.4	15 02
Mer.Pass.	h m 17 55.2	v −0.9	d 0.3	v 0.5	d 0.6	v 2.6	d 0.0	v 2.2	d 0.1	Jupiter	215 01.5	3 37
										Saturn	121 56.4	9 49

SUN and MOON

UT (d h)	SUN GHA	SUN Dec	MOON GHA	v	Dec	d	HP
21 00	180 33.2	S23 25.9	195 17.2	6.8	S18 19.4	2.1	58.7
01	195 32.8	25.9	209 43.0	6.6	18 21.5	2.1	58.7
02	210 32.5	25.9	224 08.6	6.6	18 23.6	1.9	58.7
03	225 32.2	.. 25.9	238 34.2	6.6	18 25.5	1.8	58.8
04	240 31.9	25.9	252 59.8	6.5	18 27.3	1.7	58.8
05	255 31.6	25.9	267 25.3	6.4	18 29.0	1.5	58.8
06	270 31.3	S23 26.0	281 50.7	6.4	S18 30.5	1.5	58.9
07	285 31.0	26.0	296 16.1	6.4	18 32.0	1.3	58.9
08	300 30.7	26.0	310 41.5	6.3	18 33.3	1.2	58.9
S 09	315 30.3	.. 26.0	325 06.8	6.3	18 34.5	1.1	58.9
U 10	330 30.0	26.0	339 32.1	6.2	18 35.6	0.9	59.0
N 11	345 29.7	26.0	353 57.3	6.2	18 36.5	0.9	59.0
D 12	0 29.4	S23 26.0	8 22.5	6.1	S18 37.4	0.7	59.0
A 13	15 29.1	26.0	22 47.6	6.1	18 38.1	0.6	59.0
Y 14	30 28.8	26.0	37 12.7	6.1	18 38.7	0.5	59.1
15	45 28.5	.. 26.0	51 37.8	6.0	18 39.2	0.3	59.1
16	60 28.2	26.1	66 02.8	6.0	18 39.5	0.3	59.1
17	75 27.9	26.1	80 27.8	6.0	18 39.8	0.1	59.2
18	90 27.5	S23 26.1	94 52.8	5.9	S18 39.9	0.0	59.2
19	105 27.2	26.1	109 17.7	5.9	18 39.9	0.2	59.2
20	120 26.9	26.1	123 42.6	5.9	18 39.7	0.2	59.2
21	135 26.6	.. 26.1	138 07.5	5.8	18 39.5	0.4	59.3
22	150 26.3	26.1	152 32.3	5.8	18 39.1	0.5	59.3
23	165 26.0	26.1	166 57.1	5.8	18 38.6	0.7	59.3
22 00	180 25.7	S23 26.1	181 21.9	5.8	S18 37.9	0.7	59.3
01	195 25.4	26.1	195 46.7	5.7	18 37.2	0.9	59.4
02	210 25.1	26.1	210 11.4	5.7	18 36.3	1.0	59.4
03	225 24.7	.. 26.1	224 36.1	5.7	18 35.3	1.2	59.4
04	240 24.4	26.1	239 00.8	5.7	18 34.1	1.3	59.4
05	255 24.1	26.1	253 25.5	5.6	18 32.8	1.3	59.4
06	270 23.8	S23 26.1	267 50.1	5.7	S18 31.5	1.6	59.5
07	285 23.5	26.0	282 14.8	5.6	18 29.9	1.6	59.5
08	300 23.2	26.0	296 39.4	5.6	18 28.3	1.8	59.5
M 09	315 22.9	.. 26.0	311 04.0	5.6	18 26.5	1.9	59.5
O 10	330 22.6	26.0	325 28.6	5.6	18 24.6	2.0	59.5
N 11	345 22.2	26.0	339 53.2	5.5	18 22.6	2.1	59.6
D 12	0 21.9	S23 26.0	354 17.7	5.6	S18 20.5	2.3	59.6
A 13	15 21.6	26.0	8 42.3	5.6	18 18.2	2.4	59.6
Y 14	30 21.3	26.0	23 06.9	5.5	18 15.8	2.5	59.6
15	45 21.0	.. 26.0	37 31.4	5.6	18 13.3	2.7	59.6
16	60 20.7	26.0	51 56.0	5.5	18 10.6	2.7	59.7
17	75 20.4	25.9	66 20.5	5.6	18 07.9	2.9	59.7
18	90 20.1	S23 25.9	80 45.1	5.6	S18 05.0	3.1	59.7
19	105 19.7	25.9	95 09.6	5.6	18 01.9	3.1	59.7
20	120 19.4	25.9	109 34.2	5.5	17 58.8	3.3	59.7
21	135 19.1	.. 25.9	123 58.7	5.6	17 55.5	3.4	59.7
22	150 18.8	25.9	138 23.3	5.5	17 52.1	3.5	59.8
23	165 18.5	25.8	152 47.8	5.6	17 48.6	3.6	59.8
23 00	180 18.2	S23 25.8	167 12.4	5.6	S17 45.0	3.8	59.8
01	195 17.9	25.8	181 37.0	5.5	17 41.2	3.9	59.8
02	210 17.6	25.8	196 01.5	5.6	17 37.3	4.0	59.8
03	225 17.3	.. 25.8	210 26.1	5.6	17 33.3	4.1	59.8
04	240 16.9	25.7	224 50.7	5.7	17 29.2	4.3	59.9
05	255 16.6	25.7	239 15.4	5.6	17 24.9	4.4	59.9
06	270 16.3	S23 25.7	253 40.0	5.6	S17 20.5	4.4	59.9
07	285 16.0	25.7	268 04.6	5.7	17 16.1	4.6	59.9
08	300 15.7	25.6	282 29.3	5.7	17 11.5	4.6	59.9
T 09	315 15.4	.. 25.6	296 54.0	5.7	17 06.7	4.8	59.9
U 10	330 15.1	25.6	311 18.7	5.7	17 01.9	5.0	59.9
E 11	345 14.8	25.5	325 43.4	5.7	16 56.9	5.1	59.9
S 12	0 14.4	S23 25.5	340 08.1	5.8	S16 51.8	5.2	60.0
D 13	15 14.1	25.5	354 32.9	5.8	16 46.6	5.3	60.0
A 14	30 13.8	25.5	8 57.7	5.8	16 41.3	5.4	60.0
Y 15	45 13.5	.. 25.4	23 22.5	5.8	16 35.9	5.5	60.0
16	60 13.2	25.4	37 47.3	5.9	16 30.4	5.7	60.0
17	75 12.9	25.4	52 12.2	5.9	16 24.7	5.8	60.0
18	90 12.6	S23 25.3	66 37.1	5.9	S16 18.9	5.8	60.0
19	105 12.3	25.3	81 02.0	6.0	16 13.1	6.0	60.0
20	120 12.0	25.2	95 27.0	5.9	16 07.1	6.1	60.0
21	135 11.6	.. 25.2	109 51.9	6.0	16 01.0	6.2	60.0
22	150 11.3	25.2	124 16.9	6.1	15 54.8	6.3	60.0
23	165 11.0	25.1	138 42.0	6.1	S15 48.5	6.5	60.1
SD	16.3	d 0.0	SD 16.1		16.2		16.3

Twilight / Sunrise / Moonrise

Lat.	Naut.	Civil	Sunrise	Moonrise 21	22	23	24
N 72	08 26	10 58	■	■	■	12 01	11 45
N 70	08 06	09 55	■	09 57	10 49	11 08	11 15
68	07 50	09 19	■	09 08	10 03	10 35	10 53
66	07 37	08 54	10 35	08 37	09 33	10 11	10 36
64	07 26	08 34	09 52	08 14	09 11	09 52	10 21
62	07 16	08 18	09 24	07 55	08 53	09 37	10 09
60	07 08	08 05	09 02	07 40	08 38	09 24	09 59
N 58	07 00	07 53	08 45	07 27	08 25	09 12	09 50
56	06 53	07 43	08 30	07 16	08 14	09 02	09 42
54	06 47	07 33	08 17	07 06	08 04	08 54	09 35
52	06 41	07 25	08 06	06 58	07 56	08 46	09 29
50	06 36	07 18	07 56	06 50	07 48	08 39	09 23
45	06 24	07 02	07 36	06 33	07 31	08 24	09 10
N 40	06 14	06 48	07 19	06 20	07 18	08 12	09 00
35	06 05	06 36	07 04	06 08	07 06	08 01	08 51
30	05 56	06 26	06 52	05 58	06 56	07 52	08 43
20	05 39	06 07	06 31	05 41	06 39	07 36	08 30
N 10	05 23	05 49	06 12	05 25	06 24	07 22	08 18
0	05 06	05 32	05 55	05 11	06 10	07 09	08 07
S 10	04 47	05 14	05 37	04 57	05 56	06 56	07 56
20	04 24	04 54	05 18	04 42	05 41	06 42	07 44
30	03 55	04 29	04 56	04 25	05 23	06 26	07 31
35	03 37	04 13	04 43	04 15	05 13	06 16	07 23
40	03 13	03 55	04 28	04 04	05 02	06 06	07 14
45	02 43	03 32	04 10	03 51	04 48	05 53	07 03
S 50	01 57	03 03	03 47	03 34	04 32	05 38	06 50
52	01 29	02 47	03 36	03 27	04 24	05 31	06 44
54	00 42	02 29	03 24	03 18	04 16	05 23	06 38
56	////	02 07	03 10	03 09	04 06	05 14	06 31
58	////	01 37	02 53	02 58	03 55	05 04	06 22
S 60	////	00 46	02 32	02 46	03 42	04 53	06 13

Sunset / Twilight / Moonset

Lat.	Sunset	Civil	Naut.	Moonset 21	22	23	24
N 72	■	12 59	15 31	■	■	14 54	17 11
N 70	■	14 02	15 51	12 52	14 03	15 46	17 40
68	■	14 38	16 07	13 41	14 48	16 19	18 01
66	13 22	15 03	16 20	14 12	15 18	16 42	18 17
64	14 05	15 23	16 31	14 35	15 40	17 01	18 31
62	14 33	15 39	16 41	14 54	15 58	17 16	18 43
60	14 53	15 53	16 49	15 09	16 13	17 28	18 52
N 58	15 12	16 04	16 57	15 22	16 25	17 39	19 01
56	15 27	16 14	17 04	15 33	16 36	17 49	19 08
54	15 40	16 24	17 10	15 43	16 46	17 57	19 15
52	15 52	16 32	17 16	15 52	16 54	18 05	19 20
50	16 01	16 39	17 21	16 00	17 02	18 11	19 26
45	16 22	16 55	17 33	16 17	17 18	18 26	19 37
N 40	16 38	17 09	17 43	16 30	17 31	18 37	19 47
35	16 53	17 21	17 52	16 42	17 43	18 47	19 55
30	17 05	17 31	18 01	16 52	17 52	18 56	20 02
20	17 26	17 50	18 18	17 10	18 09	19 11	20 14
N 10	17 45	18 08	18 34	17 25	18 24	19 24	20 24
0	18 02	18 25	18 51	17 39	18 38	19 37	20 34
S 10	18 20	18 43	19 10	17 53	18 52	19 49	20 44
20	18 39	19 03	19 33	18 08	19 06	20 02	20 54
30	19 01	19 28	20 02	18 26	19 23	20 16	21 06
35	19 14	19 44	20 21	18 36	19 32	20 25	21 13
40	19 29	20 02	20 44	18 47	19 43	20 35	21 20
45	19 47	20 25	21 14	19 01	19 56	20 46	21 29
S 50	20 10	20 54	22 00	19 17	20 12	20 59	21 40
52	20 21	21 10	22 28	19 25	20 19	21 06	21 45
54	20 33	21 28	23 15	19 34	20 27	21 13	21 50
56	20 47	21 50	////	19 43	20 37	21 21	21 56
58	21 04	22 20	////	19 54	20 47	21 29	22 03
S 60	21 25	23 11	////	20 07	20 59	21 39	22 11

SUN and MOON data

Day	SUN Eqn. of Time 00h	12h	Mer. Pass.	MOON Mer. Pass. Upper	Lower	Age	Phase
d	m s	m s	h m	h m	h m	d	%
21	02 13	01 58	11 58	11 25	23 54	29	1
22	01 43	01 28	11 59	12 24	24 53	00	0
23	01 13	00 58	11 59	13 23	00 53	01	3

(Phase: ● new moon)

UT	ARIES	VENUS −3.9		MARS +1.1		JUPITER −2.4		SATURN +0.5		STARS		
	GHA	GHA	Dec	GHA	Dec	GHA	Dec	GHA	Dec	Name	SHA	Dec
d h	° ′	° ′	° ′	° ′	° ′	° ′	° ′	° ′	° ′		° ′	° ′
24 00	92 26.7	164 11.5	S23 32.3	134 49.2	S17 33.0	307 33.5	N14 52.3	214 09.8	S18 16.5	Acamar	315 17.3	S40 15.0
01	107 29.2	179 10.5	32.0	149 49.7	32.4	322 36.1	52.3	229 12.0	16.6	Achernar	335 25.9	S57 10.0
02	122 31.7	194 09.6	31.6	164 50.3	31.8	337 38.7	52.4	244 14.2	16.6	Acrux	173 08.0	S63 10.6
03	137 34.1	209 08.7 . .	31.3	179 50.8 . .	31.2	352 41.2 . .	52.4	259 16.4 . .	16.7	Adhara	255 11.3	S28 59.7
04	152 36.6	224 07.7	31.0	194 51.3	30.6	7 43.8	52.5	274 18.6	16.7	Aldebaran	290 47.8	N16 32.2
05	167 39.1	239 06.8	30.7	209 51.8	30.0	22 46.4	52.5	289 20.8	16.8			
W 06	182 41.5	254 05.8	S23 30.3	224 52.3	S17 29.4	37 49.0	N14 52.6	304 22.9	S18 16.9	Alioth	166 20.0	N55 52.4
E 07	197 44.0	269 04.9	30.0	239 52.8	28.8	52 51.6	52.6	319 25.1	16.9	Alkaid	152 58.4	N49 14.1
D 08	212 46.5	284 04.0	29.7	254 53.3	28.2	67 54.2	52.7	334 27.3	17.0	Al Na'ir	27 42.8	S46 53.4
N 09	227 48.9	299 03.0 . .	29.4	269 53.9 . .	27.6	82 56.7 . .	52.7	349 29.5 . .	17.0	Alnilam	275 45.0	S 1 11.8
E 10	242 51.4	314 02.1	29.0	284 54.4	27.0	97 59.3	52.8	4 31.7	17.1	Alphard	217 54.8	S 8 43.5
S 11	257 53.9	329 01.2	28.7	299 54.9	26.4	113 01.9	52.8	19 33.9	17.1			
D 12	272 56.3	344 00.2	S23 28.4	314 55.4	S17 25.8	128 04.5	N14 52.9	34 36.1	S18 17.2	Alphecca	126 10.4	N26 39.7
A 13	287 58.8	358 59.3	28.0	329 55.9	25.2	143 07.1	52.9	49 38.3	17.2	Alpheratz	357 42.4	N29 10.6
Y 14	303 01.2	13 58.4	27.7	344 56.4	24.6	158 09.7	53.0	64 40.5	17.3	Altair	62 07.5	N 8 54.7
15	318 03.7	28 57.4	27.4	359 56.9 . .	24.0	173 12.3 . .	53.0	79 42.6 . .	17.3	Ankaa	353 14.7	S42 13.7
16	333 06.2	43 56.5	27.0	14 57.4	23.4	188 14.8	53.1	94 44.8	17.4	Antares	112 25.3	S26 27.6
17	348 08.6	58 55.6	26.7	29 58.0	22.8	203 17.4	53.1	109 47.0	17.4			
18	3 11.1	73 54.6	S23 26.3	44 58.5	S17 22.2	218 20.0	N14 53.2	124 49.2	S18 17.5	Arcturus	145 55.0	N19 06.3
19	18 13.6	88 53.7	26.0	59 59.0	21.6	233 22.6	53.2	139 51.4	17.5	Atria	107 26.7	S69 02.9
20	33 16.0	103 52.8	25.6	74 59.5	21.0	248 25.2	53.3	154 53.6	17.6	Avior	234 16.9	S59 33.5
21	48 18.5	118 51.8 . .	25.3	90 00.0 . .	20.4	263 27.8 . .	53.3	169 55.8 . .	17.7	Bellatrix	278 30.5	N 6 21.6
22	63 21.0	133 50.9	25.0	105 00.5	19.8	278 30.4	53.4	184 58.0	17.7	Betelgeuse	270 59.8	N 7 24.4
23	78 23.4	148 50.0	24.6	120 01.1	19.2	293 33.0	53.4	200 00.2	17.8			
25 00	93 25.9	163 49.0	S23 24.3	135 01.6	S17 18.6	308 35.5	N14 53.5	215 02.3	S18 17.8	Canopus	263 55.1	S52 42.4
01	108 28.4	178 48.1	23.9	150 02.1	18.0	323 38.1	53.5	230 04.5	17.9	Capella	280 32.4	N46 00.6
02	123 30.8	193 47.2	23.6	165 02.6	17.4	338 40.7	53.6	245 06.7	17.9	Deneb	49 31.1	N45 20.3
03	138 33.3	208 46.2 . .	23.2	180 03.1	16.8	353 43.3 . .	53.6	260 08.9 . .	18.0	Denebola	182 32.6	N14 29.2
04	153 35.7	223 45.3	22.8	195 03.6	16.2	8 45.9	53.7	275 11.1	18.0	Diphda	348 54.8	S17 54.4
05	168 38.2	238 44.4	22.5	210 04.2	15.6	23 48.5	53.7	290 13.3	18.1			
T 06	183 40.7	253 43.4	S23 22.1	225 04.7	S17 15.0	38 51.1	N14 53.8	305 15.5	S18 18.1	Dubhe	193 50.4	N61 39.8
H 07	198 43.1	268 42.5	21.8	240 05.2	14.4	53 53.7	53.8	320 17.7	18.2	Elnath	278 10.9	N28 37.0
U 08	213 45.6	283 41.6	21.4	255 05.7	13.8	68 56.3	53.9	335 19.9	18.2	Eltanin	90 46.2	N51 29.4
R 09	228 48.1	298 40.7 . .	21.1	270 06.2 . .	13.2	83 58.9 . .	54.0	350 22.1 . .	18.3	Enif	33 46.3	N 9 56.8
S 10	243 50.5	313 39.7	20.7	285 06.7	12.5	99 01.5	54.0	5 24.2	18.3	Fomalhaut	15 23.0	S29 32.6
D 11	258 53.0	328 38.8	20.3	300 07.3	11.9	114 04.1	54.1	20 26.4	18.4			
A 12	273 55.5	343 37.9	S23 20.0	315 07.8	S17 11.3	129 06.6	N14 54.1	35 28.6	S18 18.4	Gacrux	171 59.6	S57 11.5
Y 13	288 57.9	358 37.0	19.6	330 08.3	10.7	144 09.2	54.2	50 30.8	18.5	Gienah	175 51.2	S17 37.4
14	304 00.4	13 36.0	19.2	345 08.8	10.1	159 11.8	54.2	65 33.0	18.6	Hadar	148 46.6	S60 26.4
15	319 02.8	28 35.1 . .	18.9	0 09.3 . .	09.5	174 14.4 . .	54.3	80 35.2 . .	18.6	Hamal	327 59.4	N23 32.0
16	334 05.3	43 34.2	18.5	15 09.9	08.9	189 17.0	54.3	95 37.4	18.7	Kaus Aust.	83 42.8	S34 22.4
17	349 07.8	58 33.2	18.1	30 10.4	08.3	204 19.6	54.4	110 39.6	18.7			
18	4 10.2	73 32.3	S23 17.8	45 10.9	S17 07.7	219 22.2	N14 54.4	125 41.8	S18 18.8	Kochab	137 21.1	N74 05.5
19	19 12.7	88 31.4	17.4	60 11.4	07.1	234 24.8	54.5	140 44.0	18.8	Markab	13 37.4	N15 17.3
20	34 15.2	103 30.5	17.0	75 11.9	06.5	249 27.4	54.5	155 46.2	18.9	Menkar	314 13.7	N 4 08.8
21	49 17.6	118 29.5 . .	16.6	90 12.4 . .	05.9	264 30.0 . .	54.6	170 48.3 . .	18.9	Menkent	148 06.5	S36 26.4
22	64 20.1	133 28.6	16.3	105 13.0	05.3	279 32.6	54.6	185 50.5	19.0	Miaplacidus	221 38.6	S69 46.6
23	79 22.6	148 27.7	15.9	120 13.5	04.7	294 35.2	54.7	200 52.7	19.0			
26 00	94 25.0	163 26.8	S23 15.5	135 14.0	S17 04.0	309 37.8	N14 54.8	215 54.9	S18 19.1	Mirfak	308 38.4	N49 54.9
01	109 27.5	178 25.9	15.1	150 14.5	03.4	324 40.4	54.8	230 57.1	19.1	Nunki	75 57.4	S26 16.5
02	124 30.0	193 24.9	14.8	165 15.1	02.8	339 43.0	54.9	245 59.3	19.2	Peacock	53 18.2	S56 41.2
03	139 32.4	208 24.0 . .	14.4	180 15.6 . .	02.2	354 45.6 . .	54.9	261 01.5 . .	19.2	Pollux	243 26.1	N27 59.1
04	154 34.9	223 23.1	14.0	195 16.1	01.6	9 48.2	55.0	276 03.7	19.3	Procyon	244 58.3	N 5 11.0
05	169 37.3	238 22.2	13.6	210 16.6	01.0	24 50.8	55.0	291 05.9	19.3			
06	184 39.8	253 21.2	S23 13.2	225 17.1	S17 00.4	39 53.4	N14 55.1	306 08.1	S18 19.4	Rasalhague	96 05.8	N12 33.1
07	199 42.3	268 20.3	12.8	240 17.7	16 59.8	54 56.0	55.1	321 10.3	19.4	Regulus	207 42.2	N11 53.4
F 08	214 44.7	283 19.4	12.4	255 18.2	59.2	69 58.6	55.2	336 12.5	19.5	Rigel	281 10.7	S 8 11.3
R 09	229 47.2	298 18.5 . .	12.0	270 18.7 . .	58.5	85 01.2 . .	55.2	351 14.6 . .	19.6	Rigil Kent.	139 50.6	S60 53.4
I 10	244 49.7	313 17.6	11.7	285 19.2	57.9	100 03.8	55.3	6 16.8	19.6	Sabik	102 11.7	S15 44.4
D 11	259 52.1	328 16.6	11.3	300 19.8	57.3	115 06.4	55.4	21 19.0	19.7			
A 12	274 54.6	343 15.7	S23 10.9	315 20.3	S16 56.7	130 09.0	N14 55.4	36 21.2	S18 19.7	Schedar	349 39.1	N56 37.4
Y 13	289 57.1	358 14.8	10.5	330 20.8	56.1	145 11.6	55.5	51 23.4	19.8	Shaula	96 20.9	S37 06.6
14	304 59.5	13 13.9	10.1	345 21.3	55.5	160 14.2	55.5	66 25.6	19.8	Sirius	258 32.4	S16 44.4
15	320 02.0	28 13.0 . .	09.7	0 21.8 . .	54.9	175 16.8 . .	55.6	81 27.8 . .	19.9	Spica	158 30.2	S11 14.3
16	335 04.5	43 12.0	09.3	15 22.4	54.2	190 19.4	55.6	96 30.0	19.9	Suhail	222 51.3	S43 29.6
17	350 06.9	58 11.1	08.9	30 22.9	53.6	205 22.0	55.7	111 32.2	20.0			
18	5 09.4	73 10.2	S23 08.5	45 23.4	S16 53.0	220 24.6	N14 55.8	126 34.4	S18 20.0	Vega	80 38.7	N38 48.1
19	20 11.8	88 09.3	08.1	60 23.9	52.4	235 27.2	55.8	141 36.6	20.1	Zuben'ubi	137 04.5	S16 06.0
20	35 14.3	103 08.4	07.7	75 24.5	51.8	250 29.8	55.9	156 38.8	20.1		SHA	Mer.Pass.
21	50 16.8	118 07.5 . .	07.3	90 25.0 . .	51.2	265 32.4 . .	55.9	171 41.0 . .	20.2		° ′	h m
22	65 19.2	133 06.5	06.9	105 25.5	50.6	280 35.0	56.0	186 43.2	20.2	Venus	70 23.1	13 06
23	80 21.7	148 05.6	06.5	120 26.0	49.9	295 37.6	56.0	201 45.3	20.3	Mars	41 35.7	14 59
	h m									Jupiter	215 09.7	3 25
Mer. Pass. 17 43.4	v −0.9 d 0.4	v 0.5 d 0.6		v 2.6 d 0.1		v 2.2 d 0.1				Saturn	121 36.5	9 38

UT	SUN GHA	SUN Dec	MOON GHA	v	MOON Dec	d	HP
	° ′	° ′	° ′	′	° ′	′	′
24 00	180 10.7	S23 25.1	153 07.1	6.1	S15 42.0	6.5	60.1
01	195 10.4	25.1	167 32.2	6.1	15 35.5	6.6	60.1
02	210 10.1	25.0	181 57.3	6.2	15 28.9	6.7	60.1
03	225 09.8	.. 25.0	196 22.5	6.2	15 22.1	6.8	60.1
04	240 09.5	24.9	210 47.7	6.3	15 15.3	6.9	60.1
05	255 09.1	24.9	225 13.0	6.3	15 08.4	7.1	60.1
06	270 08.8	S23 24.8	239 38.3	6.3	S15 01.3	7.1	60.1
W 07	285 08.5	24.8	254 03.6	6.4	14 54.2	7.3	60.1
E 08	300 08.2	24.7	268 29.0	6.4	14 46.9	7.3	60.1
D 09	315 07.9	.. 24.7	282 54.4	6.4	14 39.6	7.5	60.1
N 10	330 07.6	24.7	297 19.8	6.5	14 32.1	7.5	60.1
E 11	345 07.3	24.6	311 45.3	6.5	14 24.6	7.6	60.1
S 12	0 07.0	S23 24.6	326 10.8	6.6	S14 17.0	7.8	60.1
D 13	15 06.7	24.5	340 36.4	6.6	14 09.2	7.8	60.1
A 14	30 06.3	24.5	355 02.0	6.7	14 01.4	7.9	60.1
Y 15	45 06.0	.. 24.4	9 27.7	6.7	13 53.5	8.0	60.1
16	60 05.7	24.4	23 53.4	6.8	13 45.5	8.1	60.1
17	75 05.4	24.3	38 19.2	6.7	13 37.4	8.2	60.1
18	90 05.1	S23 24.2	52 44.9	6.9	S13 29.2	8.3	60.1
19	105 04.8	24.2	67 10.8	6.9	13 20.9	8.3	60.1
20	120 04.5	24.1	81 36.7	6.9	13 12.6	8.5	60.1
21	135 04.2	.. 24.1	96 02.6	7.0	13 04.1	8.5	60.1
22	150 03.9	24.0	110 28.6	7.0	12 55.6	8.6	60.1
23	165 03.5	24.0	124 54.6	7.1	12 47.0	8.7	60.1
25 00	180 03.2	S23 23.9	139 20.7	7.1	S12 38.3	8.7	60.1
01	195 02.9	23.8	153 46.8	7.2	12 29.6	8.9	60.1
02	210 02.6	23.8	168 13.0	7.2	12 20.7	8.9	60.1
03	225 02.3	.. 23.7	182 39.2	7.2	12 11.8	9.0	60.1
04	240 02.0	23.7	197 05.4	7.3	12 02.8	9.1	60.1
05	255 01.7	23.6	211 31.7	7.4	11 53.7	9.2	60.1
06	270 01.4	S23 23.5	225 58.1	7.4	S11 44.5	9.2	60.1
T 07	285 01.1	23.5	240 24.5	7.5	11 35.3	9.3	60.1
H 08	300 00.7	23.4	254 51.0	7.5	11 26.0	9.4	60.1
U 09	315 00.4	.. 23.3	269 17.5	7.5	11 16.6	9.4	60.1
R 10	330 00.1	23.3	283 44.0	7.6	11 07.2	9.5	60.1
S 11	344 59.8	23.2	298 10.6	7.7	10 57.7	9.6	60.1
D 12	359 59.5	S23 23.1	312 37.3	7.7	S10 48.1	9.6	60.0
A 13	14 59.2	23.1	327 04.0	7.7	10 38.5	9.7	60.0
Y 14	29 58.9	23.0	341 30.7	7.8	10 28.8	9.8	60.0
15	44 58.6	.. 22.9	355 57.5	7.8	10 19.0	9.8	60.0
16	59 58.3	22.8	10 24.3	7.9	10 09.2	9.9	60.0
17	74 58.0	22.8	24 51.2	8.0	9 59.3	9.9	60.0
18	89 57.6	S23 22.7	39 18.2	8.0	S 9 49.4	10.1	60.0
19	104 57.3	22.6	53 45.2	8.0	9 39.3	10.0	60.0
20	119 57.0	22.5	68 12.2	8.1	9 29.3	10.1	60.0
21	134 56.7	.. 22.5	82 39.3	8.1	9 19.2	10.2	60.0
22	149 56.4	22.4	97 06.4	8.2	9 09.0	10.2	60.0
23	164 56.1	22.3	111 33.6	8.2	8 58.8	10.3	60.0
26 00	179 55.8	S23 22.2	126 00.8	8.3	S 8 48.5	10.3	59.9
01	194 55.5	22.2	140 28.1	8.3	8 38.2	10.4	59.9
02	209 55.2	22.1	154 55.4	8.4	8 27.8	10.4	59.9
03	224 54.9	.. 22.0	169 22.8	8.4	8 17.4	10.5	59.9
04	239 54.5	21.9	183 50.2	8.4	8 06.9	10.5	59.9
05	254 54.2	21.8	198 17.6	8.5	7 56.4	10.6	59.9
06	269 53.9	S23 21.7	212 45.1	8.6	S 7 45.8	10.5	59.9
07	284 53.6	21.7	227 12.7	8.6	7 35.3	10.7	59.9
08	299 53.3	21.6	241 40.3	8.6	7 24.6	10.7	59.8
F 09	314 53.0	.. 21.5	256 07.9	8.7	7 13.9	10.7	59.8
R 10	329 52.7	21.4	270 35.6	8.7	7 03.2	10.7	59.8
I 11	344 52.4	21.3	285 03.3	8.8	6 52.5	10.8	59.8
D 12	359 52.1	S23 21.2	299 31.1	8.8	S 6 41.7	10.9	59.8
A 13	14 51.8	21.1	313 58.9	8.9	6 30.8	10.8	59.8
Y 14	29 51.4	21.0	328 26.8	8.9	6 20.0	10.9	59.8
15	44 51.1	.. 21.0	342 54.7	8.9	6 09.1	10.9	59.8
16	59 50.8	20.9	357 22.6	9.0	5 58.2	11.0	59.7
17	74 50.5	20.8	11 50.6	9.0	5 47.2	11.0	59.7
18	89 50.2	S23 20.7	26 18.6	9.1	S 5 36.2	11.0	59.7
19	104 49.9	20.6	40 46.7	9.1	5 25.2	11.0	59.7
20	119 49.6	20.5	55 14.8	9.1	5 14.2	11.1	59.7
21	134 49.3	.. 20.4	69 42.9	9.2	5 03.1	11.1	59.7
22	149 49.0	20.3	84 11.1	9.2	4 52.0	11.1	59.7
23	164 48.7	20.2	98 39.3	9.3	S 4 40.9	11.1	59.6
	SD 16.3	d 0.1	SD 16.4		16.4		16.3

Twilight / Sunrise / Moonrise

Lat.	Naut.	Civil	Sunrise	24	25	26	27
°	h m	h m	h m	h m	h m	h m	h m
N 72	08 27	10 57	▬▬▬	11 45	11 36	11 29	11 23
N 70	08 07	09 55	▬▬▬	11 15	11 18	11 19	11 19
68	07 51	09 20	▬▬▬	10 53	11 04	11 11	11 17
66	07 38	08 55	10 35	10 36	10 52	11 04	11 14
64	07 27	08 35	09 53	10 21	10 42	10 59	11 12
62	07 17	08 19	09 25	10 09	10 34	10 54	11 10
60	07 09	08 06	09 03	09 59	10 27	10 49	11 09
N 58	07 01	07 54	08 46	09 50	10 20	10 45	11 08
56	06 55	07 44	08 31	09 42	10 14	10 42	11 06
54	06 48	07 35	08 18	09 35	10 09	10 39	11 05
52	06 43	07 26	08 07	09 29	10 05	10 36	11 04
50	06 37	07 19	07 58	09 23	10 00	10 33	11 03
45	06 26	07 03	07 37	09 10	09 51	10 28	11 01
N 40	06 15	06 49	07 20	09 00	09 43	10 23	11 00
35	06 06	06 38	07 06	08 51	09 37	10 19	10 58
30	05 57	06 27	06 53	08 43	09 31	10 15	10 57
20	05 41	06 08	06 32	08 30	09 21	10 09	10 55
N 10	05 25	05 51	06 14	08 18	09 12	10 03	10 53
0	05 08	05 34	05 56	08 07	09 04	09 58	10 51
S 10	04 49	05 16	05 39	07 56	08 55	09 53	10 49
20	04 26	04 55	05 20	07 44	08 46	09 47	10 47
30	03 57	04 30	04 58	07 31	08 36	09 41	10 45
35	03 38	04 15	04 45	07 23	08 30	09 38	10 44
40	03 15	03 57	04 30	07 14	08 23	09 33	10 42
45	02 44	03 34	04 12	07 03	08 16	09 29	10 41
S 50	01 59	03 04	03 49	06 50	08 06	09 23	10 39
52	01 31	02 49	03 38	06 44	08 02	09 20	10 38
54	00 45	02 31	03 26	06 38	07 57	09 17	10 37
56	////	02 09	03 12	06 31	07 52	09 14	10 36
58	////	01 39	02 55	06 22	07 46	09 10	10 35
S 60	////	00 49	02 34	06 13	07 39	09 06	10 33

Sunset / Twilight / Moonset

Lat.	Sunset	Civil	Naut.	24	25	26	27
°	h m	h m	h m	h m	h m	h m	h m
N 72	▬▬▬	13 03	15 33	17 11	19 18	21 17	23 12
N 70	▬▬▬	14 05	15 33	17 40	19 34	21 25	23 13
68	▬▬▬	14 40	16 09	18 01	19 47	21 31	23 13
66	13 25	15 05	16 22	18 18	19 57	21 36	23 13
64	14 07	15 25	16 33	18 31	20 06	21 40	23 14
62	14 35	15 41	16 43	18 43	20 13	21 44	23 14
60	14 57	15 54	16 51	18 52	20 20	21 47	23 14
N 58	15 14	16 06	16 59	19 01	20 25	21 50	23 14
56	15 29	16 16	17 06	19 08	20 30	21 53	23 14
54	15 42	16 25	17 12	19 15	20 35	21 55	23 14
52	15 53	16 34	17 17	19 20	20 39	21 57	23 14
50	16 03	16 41	17 23	19 26	20 42	21 59	23 14
45	16 23	16 57	17 34	19 37	20 50	22 03	23 15
N 40	16 40	17 11	17 45	19 47	20 57	22 06	23 15
35	16 54	17 22	17 57	19 55	21 02	22 09	23 15
30	17 07	17 33	18 03	20 02	21 07	22 12	23 15
20	17 28	17 52	18 19	20 14	21 16	22 16	23 15
N 10	17 46	18 09	18 36	20 24	21 23	22 20	23 15
0	18 04	18 26	18 53	20 34	21 30	22 23	23 15
S 10	18 21	18 44	19 11	20 44	21 37	22 27	23 16
20	18 40	19 05	19 34	20 54	21 44	22 31	23 16
30	19 02	19 30	20 03	21 06	21 52	22 35	23 16
35	19 15	19 45	20 22	21 13	21 57	22 37	23 16
40	19 30	20 03	20 45	21 20	22 02	22 40	23 16
45	19 48	20 26	21 15	21 29	22 08	22 43	23 16
S 50	20 11	20 55	22 01	21 40	22 15	22 47	23 16
52	20 22	21 11	22 22	21 45	22 18	22 48	23 16
54	20 34	21 28	23 15	21 50	22 22	22 50	23 16
56	20 48	21 51	////	21 56	22 26	22 52	23 16
58	21 05	22 20	////	22 03	22 31	22 54	23 16
S 60	21 25	22 56	////	22 11	22 36	22 57	23 16

SUN / MOON

Day	Eqn. of Time 00h	Eqn. of Time 12h	Mer. Pass.	Mer. Pass. Upper	Mer. Pass. Lower	Age	Phase
d	m s	m s	h m	h m	h m	d	%
24	00 43	00 28	12 00	14 21	01 52	02	8
25	00 14	00 01	12 00	15 17	02 49	03	16
26	00 16	00 31	12 01	16 11	03 44	04	25

UT	ARIES GHA	VENUS −3.9 GHA	Dec	MARS +1.1 GHA	Dec	JUPITER −2.4 GHA	Dec	SATURN +0.5 GHA	Dec	STARS Name	SHA	Dec
27 00	95 24.2	163 04.7	S23 06.1	135 26.6	S16 49.3	310 40.2	N14 56.1	216 47.5	S18 20.3	Acamar	315 17.3	S40 15.0
01	110 26.6	178 03.8	05.6	150 27.1	48.7	325 42.8	56.1	231 49.7	20.4	Achernar	335 25.9	S57 10.0
02	125 29.1	193 02.9	05.2	165 27.6	48.1	340 45.4	56.2	246 51.9	20.4	Acrux	173 07.9	S63 10.6
03	140 31.6	208 02.0	.. 04.8	180 28.1	.. 47.5	355 48.0	.. 56.3	261 54.1	.. 20.5	Adhara	255 11.3	S28 59.7
04	155 34.0	223 01.1	04.4	195 28.7	46.9	10 50.6	56.3	276 56.3	20.5	Aldebaran	290 47.8	N16 32.2
05	170 36.5	238 00.1	04.0	210 29.2	46.2	25 53.2	56.4	291 58.5	20.6			
06	185 38.9	252 59.2	S23 03.6	225 29.7	S16 45.6	40 55.8	N14 56.4	307 00.7	S18 20.6	Alioth	166 20.0	N55 52.4
S 07	200 41.4	267 58.3	03.2	240 30.3	45.0	55 58.4	56.5	322 02.9	20.7	Alkaid	152 58.3	N49 14.1
A 08	215 43.9	282 57.4	02.7	255 30.8	44.4	71 01.0	56.5	337 05.1	20.7	Al Na'ir	27 42.8	S46 53.4
T 09	230 46.3	297 56.5	.. 02.3	270 31.3	.. 43.8	86 03.6	.. 56.6	352 07.3	.. 20.8	Alnilam	275 45.0	S 1 11.8
U 10	245 48.8	312 55.6	01.9	285 31.8	43.1	101 06.3	56.7	7 09.5	20.8	Alphard	217 54.8	S 8 43.6
R 11	260 51.3	327 54.7	01.5	300 32.4	42.5	116 08.9	56.7	22 11.7	20.9			
D 12	275 53.7	342 53.8	S23 01.1	315 32.9	S16 41.9	131 11.5	N14 56.8	37 13.9	S18 20.9	Alphecca	126 10.4	N26 39.9
A 13	290 56.2	357 52.9	00.6	330 33.4	41.3	146 14.1	56.8	52 16.1	21.0	Alpheratz	357 42.4	N29 10.6
Y 14	305 58.7	12 51.9	23 00.2	345 33.9	40.7	161 16.7	56.9	67 18.3	21.1	Altair	62 07.5	N 8 54.7
15	321 01.1	27 51.0	22 59.8	0 34.5	.. 40.0	176 19.3	.. 57.0	82 20.4	.. 21.1	Ankaa	353 14.7	S42 13.7
16	336 03.6	42 50.1	59.4	15 35.0	39.4	191 21.9	57.0	97 22.6	21.2	Antares	112 25.3	S26 27.7
17	351 06.1	57 49.2	58.9	30 35.5	38.8	206 24.5	57.1	112 24.8	21.2			
18	6 08.5	72 48.3	S22 58.5	45 36.1	S16 38.2	221 27.1	N14 57.1	127 27.0	S18 21.3	Arcturus	145 55.0	N19 06.2
19	21 11.0	87 47.4	58.1	60 36.6	37.6	236 29.7	57.2	142 29.2	21.3	Atria	107 26.6	S69 02.9
20	36 13.4	102 46.5	57.6	75 37.1	36.9	251 32.3	57.2	157 31.4	21.4	Avior	234 16.9	S59 33.5
21	51 15.9	117 45.6	.. 57.2	90 37.6	.. 36.3	266 35.0	.. 57.3	172 33.6	.. 21.4	Bellatrix	278 30.5	N 6 21.6
22	66 18.4	132 44.7	56.8	105 38.2	35.7	281 37.6	57.4	187 35.8	21.5	Betelgeuse	270 59.8	N 7 24.4
23	81 20.8	147 43.8	56.3	120 38.7	35.1	296 40.2	57.4	202 38.0	21.5			
28 00	96 23.3	162 42.9	S22 55.9	135 39.2	S16 34.4	311 42.8	N14 57.5	217 40.2	S18 21.6	Canopus	263 55.1	S52 42.4
01	111 25.8	177 42.0	55.5	150 39.8	33.8	326 45.4	57.5	232 42.4	21.6	Capella	280 32.4	N46 00.6
02	126 28.2	192 41.1	55.0	165 40.3	33.2	341 48.0	57.6	247 44.6	21.7	Deneb	49 31.1	N45 20.3
03	141 30.7	207 40.2	.. 54.6	180 40.8	.. 32.6	356 50.6	.. 57.7	262 46.8	.. 21.7	Denebola	182 32.6	N14 29.2
04	156 33.2	222 39.3	54.1	195 41.4	31.9	11 53.2	57.7	277 49.0	21.8	Diphda	348 54.8	S17 54.4
05	171 35.6	237 38.4	53.7	210 41.9	31.3	26 55.9	57.8	292 51.2	21.8			
06	186 38.1	252 37.4	S22 53.2	225 42.4	S16 30.7	41 58.5	N14 57.8	307 53.4	S18 21.9	Dubhe	193 50.3	N61 39.8
S 07	201 40.6	267 36.5	52.8	240 42.9	30.1	57 01.1	57.9	322 55.6	21.9	Elnath	278 10.9	N28 37.0
U 08	216 43.0	282 35.6	52.4	255 43.5	29.4	72 03.7	58.0	337 57.8	22.0	Eltanin	90 46.2	N51 29.4
N 09	231 45.5	297 34.7	.. 51.9	270 44.0	.. 28.8	87 06.3	.. 58.0	353 00.0	.. 22.0	Enif	33 46.3	N 9 56.8
D 10	246 47.9	312 33.8	51.5	285 44.5	28.2	102 08.9	58.1	8 02.2	22.1	Fomalhaut	15 23.0	S29 32.7
A 11	261 50.4	327 32.9	51.0	300 45.1	27.6	117 11.5	58.1	23 04.4	22.1			
Y 12	276 52.9	342 32.0	S22 50.6	315 45.6	S16 26.9	132 14.2	N14 58.2	38 06.5	S18 22.2	Gacrux	171 59.6	S57 11.5
13	291 55.3	357 31.1	50.1	330 46.1	26.3	147 16.8	58.3	53 08.7	22.2	Gienah	175 51.2	S17 37.4
14	306 57.8	12 30.2	49.7	345 46.7	25.7	162 19.4	58.3	68 10.9	22.3	Hadar	148 46.5	S60 26.4
15	322 00.3	27 29.3	.. 49.2	0 47.2	.. 25.0	177 22.0	.. 58.4	83 13.1	.. 22.3	Hamal	327 59.4	N23 32.0
16	337 02.7	42 28.4	48.7	15 47.7	24.4	192 24.6	58.4	98 15.3	22.4	Kaus Aust.	83 42.8	S34 22.4
17	352 05.2	57 27.5	48.3	30 48.3	23.8	207 27.2	58.5	113 17.5	22.4			
18	7 07.7	72 26.6	S22 47.8	45 48.8	S16 23.2	222 29.9	N14 58.6	128 19.7	S18 22.5	Kochab	137 21.0	N74 05.5
19	22 10.1	87 25.7	47.4	60 49.3	22.5	237 32.5	58.6	143 21.9	22.5	Markab	13 37.4	N15 17.3
20	37 12.6	102 24.8	46.9	75 49.9	21.9	252 35.1	58.7	158 24.1	22.6	Menkar	314 13.7	N 4 08.8
21	52 15.0	117 23.9	.. 46.4	90 50.4	.. 21.3	267 37.7	.. 58.7	173 26.3	.. 22.6	Menkent	148 06.5	S36 26.4
22	67 17.5	132 23.0	46.0	105 50.9	20.6	282 40.3	58.8	188 28.5	22.7	Miaplacidus	221 38.5	S69 46.7
23	82 20.0	147 22.1	45.5	120 51.5	20.0	297 42.9	58.9	203 30.7	22.7			
29 00	97 22.4	162 21.3	S22 45.0	135 52.0	S16 19.4	312 45.6	N14 58.9	218 32.9	S18 22.8	Mirfak	308 38.4	N49 54.9
01	112 24.9	177 20.4	44.6	150 52.5	18.8	327 48.2	59.0	233 35.1	22.8	Nunki	75 57.4	S26 16.5
02	127 27.4	192 19.5	44.1	165 53.1	18.1	342 50.8	59.1	248 37.3	22.9	Peacock	53 18.2	S56 41.2
03	142 29.8	207 18.6	.. 43.6	180 53.6	.. 17.5	357 53.4	.. 59.1	263 39.5	.. 22.9	Pollux	243 26.1	N27 59.1
04	157 32.3	222 17.7	43.2	195 54.1	16.9	12 56.0	59.2	278 41.7	23.0	Procyon	244 58.3	N 5 10.9
05	172 34.8	237 16.8	42.7	210 54.7	16.2	27 58.7	59.2	293 43.9	23.0			
06	187 37.2	252 15.9	S22 42.2	225 55.2	S16 15.6	43 01.3	N14 59.3	308 46.1	S18 23.1	Rasalhague	96 05.8	N12 33.1
M 07	202 39.7	267 15.0	41.7	240 55.7	15.0	58 03.9	59.4	323 48.3	23.1	Regulus	207 42.2	N11 53.4
O 08	217 42.2	282 14.1	41.3	255 56.3	14.3	73 06.5	59.4	338 50.5	23.2	Rigel	281 10.7	S 8 11.3
N 09	232 44.6	297 13.2	.. 40.8	270 56.8	.. 13.7	88 09.2	.. 59.5	353 52.7	.. 23.2	Rigil Kent.	139 50.5	S60 53.4
D 10	247 47.1	312 12.3	40.3	285 57.4	13.1	103 11.8	59.5	8 54.9	23.3	Sabik	102 11.7	S15 44.4
A 11	262 49.5	327 11.4	39.8	300 57.9	12.4	118 14.4	59.6	23 57.1	23.3			
Y 12	277 52.0	342 10.5	S22 39.4	315 58.4	S16 11.8	133 17.0	N14 59.7	38 59.3	S18 23.4	Schedar	349 39.1	N56 37.4
13	292 54.5	357 09.6	38.9	330 59.0	11.2	148 19.6	59.7	54 01.5	23.4	Shaula	96 20.9	S37 06.6
14	307 56.9	12 08.8	38.4	345 59.5	10.5	163 22.3	59.8	69 03.7	23.5	Sirius	258 32.4	S16 44.4
15	322 59.4	27 07.9	.. 37.9	1 00.0	.. 09.9	178 24.9	.. 59.9	84 05.9	.. 23.5	Spica	158 30.2	S11 14.3
16	338 01.9	42 07.0	37.4	16 00.6	09.3	193 27.5	14 59.9	99 08.1	23.6	Suhail	222 51.3	S43 29.6
17	353 04.3	57 06.1	36.9	31 01.1	08.6	208 30.1	15 00.0	114 10.3	23.6			
18	8 06.8	72 05.2	S22 36.4	46 01.7	S16 08.0	223 32.8	N15 00.0	129 12.5	S18 23.7	Vega	80 38.7	N38 48.1
19	23 09.3	87 04.3	36.0	61 02.2	07.4	238 35.4	00.1	144 14.7	23.7	Zuben'ubi	137 04.4	S16 06.1
20	38 11.7	102 03.4	35.5	76 02.7	06.7	253 38.0	00.2	159 16.9	23.8			
21	53 14.2	117 02.5	.. 35.0	91 03.3	.. 06.1	268 40.6	.. 00.2	174 19.1	.. 23.8			
22	68 16.7	132 01.6	34.5	106 03.8	05.4	283 43.3	00.3	189 21.3	23.9			
23	83 19.1	147 00.8	34.0	121 04.3	04.8	298 45.9	00.4	204 23.5	23.9			

	SHA	Mer. Pass.
	° ′	h m
Venus	66 19.6	13 10
Mars	39 15.9	14 57
Jupiter	215 19.5	3 13
Saturn	121 16.9	9 28

	h m				
Mer. Pass.	17 31.6	v −0.9 d 0.5	v 0.5 d 0.6	v 2.6 d 0.1	v 2.2 d 0.1

SUN / MOON

UT	SUN GHA	SUN Dec	MOON GHA	v	Dec	d	HP
d h	° ′	° ′	° ′	′	° ′	′	′
27 00	179 48.4	S23 20.1	113 07.6	9.3	S 4 29.8	11.1	59.6
01	194 48.1	20.0	127 35.9	9.3	4 18.7	11.2	59.6
02	209 47.7	19.9	142 04.2	9.4	4 07.5	11.2	59.6
03	224 47.4	.. 19.8	156 32.6	9.4	3 56.3	11.2	59.6
04	239 47.1	19.7	171 01.0	9.4	3 45.1	11.2	59.6
05	254 46.8	19.6	185 29.4	9.5	3 33.9	11.2	59.6
S 06	269 46.5	S23 19.5	199 57.9	9.5	S 3 22.7	11.3	59.5
A 07	284 46.2	19.4	214 26.4	9.5	3 11.4	11.2	59.5
T 08	299 45.9	19.3	228 54.9	9.6	3 00.2	11.3	59.5
U 09	314 45.6	.. 19.2	243 23.5	9.6	2 48.9	11.2	59.5
R 10	329 45.3	19.1	257 52.1	9.6	2 37.7	11.3	59.5
D 11	344 45.0	19.0	272 20.7	9.7	2 26.4	11.3	59.4
A 12	359 44.7	S23 18.9	286 49.4	9.7	S 2 15.1	11.3	59.4
Y 13	14 44.4	18.8	301 18.1	9.7	2 03.8	11.3	59.4
14	29 44.1	18.6	315 46.8	9.8	1 52.5	11.3	59.4
15	44 43.7	.. 18.5	330 15.6	9.7	1 41.2	11.3	59.4
16	59 43.4	18.4	344 44.3	9.9	1 29.9	11.3	59.4
17	74 43.1	18.3	359 13.2	9.8	1 18.6	11.3	59.3
18	89 42.8	S23 18.2	13 42.0	9.9	S 1 07.3	11.3	59.3
19	104 42.5	18.1	28 10.9	9.8	0 56.0	11.3	59.3
20	119 42.2	18.0	42 39.7	10.0	0 44.7	11.3	59.3
21	134 41.9	.. 17.9	57 08.7	9.9	0 33.4	11.3	59.3
22	149 41.6	17.7	71 37.6	10.0	0 22.1	11.3	59.2
23	164 41.3	17.6	86 06.6	10.0	S 0 10.8	11.3	59.2
28 00	179 41.0	S23 17.5	100 35.6	10.0	N 0 00.5	11.2	59.2
01	194 40.7	17.4	115 04.6	10.0	0 11.7	11.3	59.2
02	209 40.4	17.3	129 33.6	10.0	0 23.0	11.3	59.2
03	224 40.1	.. 17.1	144 02.6	10.1	0 34.3	11.2	59.1
04	239 39.8	17.0	158 31.7	10.1	0 45.5	11.2	59.1
05	254 39.4	16.9	173 00.8	10.1	0 56.7	11.2	59.1
S 06	269 39.1	S23 16.8	187 29.9	10.2	N 1 07.9	11.3	59.1
U 07	284 38.8	16.7	201 59.1	10.1	1 19.2	11.1	59.1
N 08	299 38.5	16.5	216 28.2	10.2	1 30.3	11.2	59.1
D 09	314 38.2	.. 16.4	230 57.4	10.2	1 41.5	11.2	59.0
A 10	329 37.9	16.3	245 26.6	10.2	1 52.7	11.1	59.0
Y 11	344 37.6	16.2	259 55.8	10.2	2 03.8	11.1	59.0
12	359 37.3	S23 16.0	274 25.0	10.2	N 2 14.9	11.1	59.0
13	14 37.0	15.9	288 54.2	10.2	2 26.0	11.1	58.9
14	29 36.7	15.8	303 23.4	10.3	2 37.1	11.0	58.9
15	44 36.4	.. 15.6	317 52.7	10.3	2 48.1	11.1	58.9
16	59 36.1	15.5	332 22.0	10.3	2 59.2	11.0	58.9
17	74 35.8	15.4	346 51.3	10.3	3 10.2	11.0	58.9
18	89 35.5	S23 15.2	1 20.6	10.3	N 3 21.2	10.9	58.8
19	104 35.2	15.1	15 49.9	10.3	3 32.1	10.9	58.8
20	119 34.9	15.0	30 19.2	10.3	3 43.0	10.9	58.8
21	134 34.6	.. 14.8	44 48.5	10.3	3 53.9	10.9	58.8
22	149 34.3	14.7	59 17.8	10.4	4 04.8	10.8	58.8
23	164 34.0	14.6	73 47.2	10.3	4 15.6	10.8	58.7
29 00	179 33.6	S23 14.4	88 16.5	10.4	N 4 26.4	10.8	58.7
01	194 33.3	14.3	102 45.9	10.4	4 37.2	10.8	58.7
02	209 33.0	14.2	117 15.3	10.3	4 48.0	10.7	58.7
03	224 32.7	.. 14.0	131 44.6	10.4	4 58.7	10.6	58.7
04	239 32.4	13.9	146 14.0	10.4	5 09.3	10.7	58.6
05	254 32.1	13.7	160 43.4	10.4	5 20.0	10.6	58.6
M 06	269 31.8	S23 13.6	175 12.8	10.4	N 5 30.6	10.5	58.6
O 07	284 31.5	13.4	189 42.2	10.4	5 41.1	10.5	58.6
N 08	299 31.2	13.3	204 11.6	10.4	5 51.6	10.5	58.5
D 09	314 30.9	.. 13.2	218 41.0	10.4	6 02.1	10.5	58.5
A 10	329 30.6	13.0	233 10.4	10.4	6 12.6	10.4	58.5
Y 11	344 30.3	12.9	247 39.8	10.4	6 23.0	10.3	58.5
12	359 30.0	S23 12.7	262 09.2	10.4	N 6 33.3	10.3	58.5
13	14 29.7	12.6	276 38.6	10.4	6 43.6	10.3	58.4
14	29 29.4	12.4	291 08.0	10.4	6 53.9	10.2	58.4
15	44 29.1	.. 12.3	305 37.4	10.4	7 04.1	10.2	58.4
16	59 28.8	12.1	320 06.8	10.4	7 14.3	10.1	58.4
17	74 28.5	12.0	334 36.2	10.4	7 24.4	10.1	58.4
18	89 28.2	S23 11.8	349 05.6	10.4	N 7 34.5	10.1	58.3
19	104 27.9	11.7	3 35.0	10.4	7 44.6	9.9	58.3
20	119 27.6	11.5	18 04.4	10.4	7 54.5	10.0	58.3
21	134 27.3	.. 11.4	32 33.8	10.4	8 04.5	9.9	58.3
22	149 27.0	11.2	47 03.2	10.4	8 14.4	9.8	58.2
23	164 26.7	11.1	61 32.6	10.3	N 8 24.2	9.8	58.2
	SD 16.3	d 0.1	SD 16.2		16.1		15.9

Twilight / Sunrise / Moonrise

Lat.	Twilight Naut.	Twilight Civil	Sunrise	Moonrise 27	28	29	30
°	h m	h m	h m	h m	h m	h m	h m
N 72	08 26	10 53	■■	11 23	11 17	11 11	11 04
N 70	08 07	09 54	■■	11 19	11 19	11 20	11 20
68	07 51	09 20	■■	11 17	11 21	11 27	11 33
66	07 38	08 55	10 33	11 14	11 23	11 33	11 44
64	07 27	08 35	09 52	11 12	11 25	11 38	11 53
62	07 18	08 19	09 25	11 10	11 26	11 43	12 00
60	07 09	08 06	09 03	11 09	11 28	11 46	12 07
N 58	07 02	07 55	08 46	11 08	11 29	11 50	12 13
56	06 55	07 44	08 32	11 06	11 30	11 53	12 18
54	06 49	07 35	08 19	11 05	11 30	11 56	12 23
52	06 44	07 27	08 08	11 04	11 31	11 58	12 27
50	06 38	07 20	07 58	11 03	11 32	12 01	12 31
45	06 27	07 04	07 38	11 01	11 34	12 06	12 40
N 40	06 16	06 50	07 21	11 00	11 35	12 10	12 47
35	06 07	06 39	07 07	10 58	11 36	12 14	12 53
30	05 58	06 28	06 55	10 57	11 37	12 17	12 58
20	05 42	06 10	06 34	10 55	11 39	12 23	13 08
N 10	05 26	05 52	06 15	10 53	11 41	12 28	13 16
0	05 09	05 35	05 58	10 51	11 42	12 33	13 24
S 10	04 50	05 17	05 40	10 49	11 44	12 38	13 32
20	04 28	04 57	05 21	10 47	11 46	12 43	13 40
30	03 59	04 32	04 59	10 45	11 48	12 49	13 50
35	03 40	04 17	04 47	10 44	11 49	12 53	13 56
40	03 17	03 59	04 32	10 42	11 50	12 57	14 02
45	02 47	03 36	04 14	10 41	11 52	13 01	14 09
S 50	02 02	03 07	03 51	10 39	11 54	13 07	14 19
52	01 34	02 52	03 41	10 38	11 55	13 10	14 23
54	00 50	02 34	03 28	10 37	11 56	13 12	14 27
56	////	02 12	03 14	10 36	11 57	13 16	14 33
58	////	01 43	02 58	10 35	11 58	13 19	14 38
S 60	////	00 54	02 37	10 33	11 59	13 23	14 45

Sunset / Twilight / Moonset

Lat.	Sunset	Twilight Civil	Twilight Naut.	Moonset 27	28	29	30
°	h m	h m	h m	h m	h m	h m	h m
N 72	■■	13 11	15 37	23 12	25 05	01 05	02 57
N 70	■■	14 09	15 56	23 13	24 58	00 58	02 43
68	■■	14 44	16 12	23 13	24 53	00 53	02 31
66	13 30	15 08	16 25	23 13	24 49	00 49	02 22
64	14 11	15 28	16 36	23 14	24 45	00 45	02 14
62	14 38	15 44	16 46	23 14	24 42	00 42	02 08
60	15 00	15 57	16 54	23 14	24 39	00 39	02 02
N 58	15 17	16 09	17 01	23 14	24 36	00 36	01 57
56	15 32	16 19	17 08	23 14	24 34	00 34	01 52
54	15 44	16 28	17 14	23 14	24 32	00 32	01 48
52	15 55	16 36	17 20	23 14	24 30	00 30	01 44
50	16 05	16 43	17 25	23 14	24 29	00 29	01 41
45	16 25	16 59	17 36	23 15	24 25	00 25	01 34
N 40	16 42	17 13	17 47	23 15	24 22	00 22	01 28
35	16 56	17 24	17 56	23 15	24 19	00 19	01 23
30	17 08	17 35	18 05	23 15	24 17	00 17	01 18
20	17 30	17 54	18 21	23 15	24 13	00 13	01 11
N 10	17 48	18 11	18 37	23 15	24 10	00 10	01 04
0	18 05	18 28	18 54	23 16	24 07	00 07	00 57
S 10	18 23	18 46	19 13	23 16	24 03	00 03	00 51
20	18 42	19 06	19 35	23 16	24 00	00 00	00 44
30	19 03	19 31	20 04	23 16	23 56	24 36	00 36
35	19 16	19 46	20 23	23 16	23 54	24 32	00 32
40	19 31	20 04	20 46	23 16	23 51	24 27	00 27
45	19 49	20 26	21 16	23 16	23 48	24 21	00 21
S 50	20 11	20 56	22 01	23 16	23 44	24 14	00 14
52	20 22	21 11	22 28	23 16	23 43	24 11	00 11
54	20 34	21 28	23 12	23 16	23 41	24 07	00 07
56	20 48	21 50	////	23 16	23 39	24 03	00 03
58	21 05	22 19	////	23 16	23 37	23 59	24 24
S 60	21 25	23 07	////	23 16	23 34	23 54	24 16

SUN / MOON

Day	SUN Eqn. of Time 00h	SUN Eqn. of Time 12h	Mer. Pass.	MOON Mer. Pass. Upper	Mer. Pass. Lower	Age	Phase
d	m s	m s	h m	h m	h m	d	%
27	00 46	01 01	12 01	17 03	04 37	05	36
28	01 15	01 30	12 02	17 54	05 29	06	47
29	01 45	01 59	12 02	18 45	06 20	07	58

UT	ARIES	VENUS −3.9		MARS +1.1		JUPITER −2.4		SATURN +0.6		STARS		
	GHA	GHA	Dec	GHA	Dec	GHA	Dec	GHA	Dec	Name	SHA	Dec
d h	° ′	° ′	° ′	° ′	° ′	° ′	° ′	° ′	° ′		° ′	° ′
30 00	98 21.6	161 59.9	S22 33.5	136 04.9	S16 04.2	313 48.5	N15 00.4	219 25.7	S18 24.0	Acamar	315 17.3	S40 15.0
01	113 24.0	176 59.0	33.0	151 05.4	03.5	328 51.1	00.5	234 27.9	24.0	Achernar	335 25.9	S57 10.0
02	128 26.5	191 58.1	32.5	166 06.0	02.9	343 53.8	00.6	249 30.1	24.1	Acrux	173 07.9	S63 10.6
03	143 29.0	206 57.2 ..	32.0	181 06.5 ..	02.3	358 56.4 ..	00.6	264 32.3 ..	24.1	Adhara	255 11.3	S28 59.8
04	158 31.4	221 56.3	31.5	196 07.0	01.6	13 59.0	00.7	279 34.5	24.2	Aldebaran	290 47.8	N16 32.2
05	173 33.9	236 55.4	31.0	211 07.6	01.0	29 01.7	00.8	294 36.7	24.2			
06	188 36.4	251 54.6	S22 30.5	226 08.1	S16 00.3	44 04.3	N15 00.8	309 38.9	S18 24.3	Alioth	166 19.9	N55 52.4
07	203 38.8	266 53.7	30.0	241 08.7	15 59.7	59 06.9	00.9	324 41.1	24.3	Alkaid	152 58.3	N49 14.1
T 08	218 41.3	281 52.8	29.5	256 09.2	59.1	74 09.5	00.9	339 43.3	24.4	Al Na'ir	27 42.8	S46 53.4
U 09	233 43.8	296 51.9 ..	29.0	271 09.7 ..	58.4	89 12.2 ..	01.0	354 45.5 ..	24.4	Alnilam	275 45.0	S 1 11.8
E 10	248 46.2	311 51.0	28.5	286 10.3	57.8	104 14.8	01.1	9 47.7	24.5	Alphard	217 54.8	S 8 43.6
S 11	263 48.7	326 50.2	28.0	301 10.8	57.1	119 17.4	01.1	24 49.9	24.5			
D 12	278 51.1	341 49.3	S22 27.5	316 11.4	S15 56.5	134 20.1	N15 01.2	39 52.1	S18 24.6	Alphecca	126 10.4	N26 39.9
A 13	293 53.6	356 48.4	27.0	331 11.9	55.9	149 22.7	01.3	54 54.3	24.6	Alpheratz	357 42.4	N29 10.6
Y 14	308 56.1	11 47.5	26.5	346 12.5	55.2	164 25.3	01.3	69 56.5	24.7	Altair	62 07.5	N 8 54.7
15	323 58.5	26 46.6 ..	25.9	1 13.0 ..	54.6	179 27.9 ..	01.4	84 58.7 ..	24.7	Ankaa	353 14.7	S42 13.7
16	339 01.0	41 45.8	25.4	16 13.5	53.9	194 30.6	01.5	100 00.9	24.8	Antares	112 25.3	S26 27.7
17	354 03.5	56 44.9	24.9	31 14.1	53.3	209 33.2	01.5	115 03.1	24.8			
18	9 05.9	71 44.0	S22 24.4	46 14.6	S15 52.6	224 35.8	N15 01.6	130 05.3	S18 24.9	Arcturus	145 54.9	N19 06.2
19	24 08.4	86 43.1	23.9	61 15.2	52.0	239 38.5	01.7	145 07.5	24.9	Atria	107 26.6	S69 02.9
20	39 10.9	101 42.2	23.4	76 15.7	51.4	254 41.1	01.7	160 09.7	25.0	Avior	234 16.9	S59 33.5
21	54 13.3	116 41.4 ..	22.8	91 16.2 ..	50.7	269 43.7 ..	01.8	175 11.9 ..	25.0	Bellatrix	278 30.5	N 6 21.6
22	69 15.8	131 40.5	22.3	106 16.8	50.1	284 46.4	01.9	190 14.1	25.1	Betelgeuse	270 59.8	N 7 24.3
23	84 18.3	146 39.6	21.8	121 17.3	49.4	299 49.0	01.9	205 16.3	25.1			
31 00	99 20.7	161 38.7	S22 21.3	136 17.9	S15 48.8	314 51.6	N15 02.0	220 18.5	S18 25.2	Canopus	263 55.1	S52 42.4
01	114 23.2	176 37.9	20.8	151 18.4	48.1	329 54.3	02.1	235 20.7	25.2	Capella	280 32.4	N46 00.6
02	129 25.6	191 37.0	20.2	166 19.0	47.5	344 56.9	02.1	250 22.9	25.3	Deneb	49 31.1	N45 20.3
03	144 28.1	206 36.1 ..	19.7	181 19.5 ..	46.9	359 59.5 ..	02.2	265 25.1 ..	25.3	Denebola	182 32.5	N14 29.1
04	159 30.6	221 35.2	19.2	196 20.1	46.2	15 02.2	02.3	280 27.3	25.4	Diphda	348 54.8	S17 54.4
05	174 33.0	236 34.4	18.6	211 20.6	45.6	30 04.8	02.3	295 29.5	25.4			
06	189 35.5	251 33.5	S22 18.1	226 21.1	S15 44.9	45 07.4	N15 02.4	310 31.7	S18 25.5	Dubhe	193 50.3	N61 39.8
W 07	204 38.0	266 32.6	17.6	241 21.7	44.3	60 10.1	02.5	325 33.9	25.5	Elnath	278 10.9	N28 37.0
E 08	219 40.4	281 31.7	17.1	256 22.2	43.6	75 12.7	02.5	340 36.1	25.6	Eltanin	90 46.2	N51 29.4
D 09	234 42.9	296 30.9 ..	16.5	271 22.8 ..	43.0	90 15.4 ..	02.6	355 38.3 ..	25.6	Enif	33 46.3	N 9 56.8
N 10	249 45.4	311 30.0	16.0	286 23.3	42.3	105 18.0	02.7	10 40.5	25.7	Fomalhaut	15 23.0	S29 32.7
E 11	264 47.8	326 29.1	15.5	301 23.9	41.7	120 20.6	02.7	25 42.7	25.7			
S 12	279 50.3	341 28.3	S22 14.9	316 24.4	S15 41.0	135 23.3	N15 02.8	40 44.9	S18 25.8	Gacrux	171 59.6	S57 11.6
D 13	294 52.8	356 27.4	14.4	331 25.0	40.4	150 25.9	02.9	55 47.1	25.8	Gienah	175 51.2	S17 37.4
A 14	309 55.2	11 26.5	13.8	346 25.5	39.7	165 28.5	02.9	70 49.3	25.9	Hadar	148 46.5	S60 26.4
Y 15	324 57.7	26 25.7 ..	13.3	1 26.1 ..	39.1	180 31.2 ..	03.0	85 51.5 ..	25.9	Hamal	327 59.4	N23 32.0
16	340 00.1	41 24.8	12.8	16 26.6	38.5	195 33.8	03.1	100 53.7	26.0	Kaus Aust.	83 42.8	S34 22.4
17	355 02.6	56 23.9	12.2	31 27.1	37.8	210 36.5	03.1	115 55.9	26.0			
18	10 05.1	71 23.1	S22 11.7	46 27.7	S15 37.2	225 39.1	N15 03.2	130 58.1	S18 26.0	Kochab	137 21.0	N74 05.5
19	25 07.5	86 22.2	11.1	61 28.2	36.5	240 41.7	03.3	146 00.3	26.1	Markab	13 37.4	N15 17.3
20	40 10.0	101 21.3	10.6	76 28.8	35.9	255 44.4	03.3	161 02.5	26.1	Menkar	314 13.7	N 4 08.8
21	55 12.5	116 20.5 ..	10.0	91 29.3 ..	35.2	270 47.0 ..	03.4	176 04.7 ..	26.2	Menkent	148 06.4	S36 26.4
22	70 14.9	131 19.6	09.5	106 29.9	34.6	285 49.7	03.5	191 06.9	26.2	Miaplacidus	221 38.5	S69 46.7
23	85 17.4	146 18.7	08.9	121 30.4	33.9	300 52.3	03.5	206 09.1	26.3			
1 00	100 19.9	161 17.9	S22 08.4	136 31.0	S15 33.3	315 54.9	N15 03.6	221 11.3	S18 26.3	Mirfak	308 38.4	N49 54.9
01	115 22.3	176 17.0	07.8	151 31.5	32.6	330 57.6	03.7	236 13.5	26.4	Nunki	75 57.4	S26 16.5
02	130 24.8	191 16.1	07.3	166 32.1	32.0	346 00.2	03.7	251 15.7	26.4	Peacock	53 18.2	S56 41.1
03	145 27.2	206 15.3 ..	06.7	181 32.6 ..	31.3	1 02.9 ..	03.8	266 17.9 ..	26.5	Pollux	243 26.1	N27 59.1
04	160 29.7	221 14.4	06.2	196 33.2	30.7	16 05.5	03.9	281 20.1	26.5	Procyon	244 58.3	N 5 10.9
05	175 32.2	236 13.5	05.6	211 33.7	30.0	31 08.1	03.9	296 22.3	26.6			
06	190 34.6	251 12.7	S22 05.1	226 34.3	S15 29.4	46 10.8	N15 04.0	311 24.5	S18 26.6	Rasalhague	96 05.8	N12 33.1
07	205 37.1	266 11.8	04.5	241 34.8	28.7	61 13.4	04.1	326 26.7	26.7	Regulus	207 42.2	N11 53.4
T 08	220 39.6	281 11.0	03.9	256 35.4	28.0	76 16.1	04.1	341 28.9	26.7	Rigel	281 10.7	S 8 11.3
H 09	235 42.0	296 10.1 ..	03.4	271 35.9 ..	27.4	91 18.7 ..	04.2	356 31.1 ..	26.8	Rigil Kent.	139 50.5	S60 53.4
U 10	250 44.5	311 09.2	02.8	286 36.5	26.7	106 21.4	04.3	11 33.3	26.8	Sabik	102 11.7	S15 44.4
R 11	265 47.0	326 08.4	02.3	301 37.0	26.1	121 24.0	04.4	26 35.6	26.9			
S 12	280 49.4	341 07.5	S22 01.7	316 37.6	S15 25.4	136 26.6	N15 04.4	41 37.8	S18 26.9	Schedar	349 39.2	N56 37.4
D 13	295 51.9	356 06.7	01.1	331 38.1	24.8	151 29.3	04.5	56 40.0	27.0	Shaula	96 20.9	S37 06.6
A 14	310 54.4	11 05.8	00.6	346 38.7	24.1	166 31.9	04.6	71 42.2	27.0	Sirius	258 32.4	S16 44.4
Y 15	325 56.8	26 04.9	22 00.0	1 39.2 ..	23.5	181 34.6 ..	04.6	86 44.4 ..	27.1	Spica	158 30.2	S11 14.3
16	340 59.3	41 04.1	21 59.4	16 39.8	22.8	196 37.2	04.7	101 46.6	27.1	Suhail	222 51.2	S43 29.6
17	356 01.7	56 03.2	58.9	31 40.3	22.2	211 39.9	04.8	116 48.8	27.2			
18	11 04.2	71 02.4	S21 58.3	46 40.9	S15 21.5	226 42.5	N15 04.8	131 51.0	S18 27.2	Vega	80 38.7	N38 48.0
19	26 06.7	86 01.5	57.7	61 41.4	20.9	241 45.2	04.9	146 53.2	27.3	Zuben'ubi	137 04.4	S16 06.1
20	41 09.1	101 00.7	57.1	76 42.0	20.2	256 47.8	05.0	161 55.4	27.3		SHA	Mer.Pass.
21	56 11.6	115 59.8 ..	56.6	91 42.5 ..	19.5	271 50.5 ..	05.1	176 57.6 ..	27.4		° ′	h m
22	71 14.1	130 59.0	56.0	106 43.1	18.9	286 53.1	05.1	191 59.8	27.4	Venus	62 18.0	13 14
23	86 16.5	145 58.1	55.4	121 43.6	18.2	301 55.8	05.2	207 02.0	27.4	Mars	36 57.2	14 54
	h m									Jupiter	215 30.9	3 00
Mer.Pass. 17 19.8		v −0.9	d 0.5	v 0.5	d 0.6	v 2.6	d 0.1	v 2.2	d 0.0	Saturn	120 57.7	9 17

UT	SUN GHA	SUN Dec	MOON GHA	v	MOON Dec	d	HP
d h	° ′	° ′	° ′	′	° ′	′	′
30 00	179 26.4	S23 10.9	76 01.9	10.4	N 8 34.0	9.7	58.2
01	194 26.1	10.7	90 31.3	10.4	8 43.7	9.7	58.2
02	209 25.8	10.6	105 00.7	10.3	8 53.4	9.6	58.2
03	224 25.5	.. 10.4	119 30.0	10.4	9 03.0	9.5	58.1
04	239 25.2	10.3	133 59.4	10.4	9 12.5	9.5	58.1
05	254 24.9	10.1	148 28.8	10.3	9 22.0	9.5	58.1
06	269 24.6	S23 09.9	162 58.1	10.3	N 9 31.5	9.4	58.1
07	284 24.3	09.8	177 27.4	10.4	9 40.9	9.3	58.1
08	299 24.0	09.6	191 56.8	10.3	9 50.2	9.3	58.0
09	314 23.7	.. 09.4	206 26.1	10.3	9 59.5	9.2	58.0
10	329 23.4	09.3	220 55.4	10.3	10 08.7	9.1	58.0
11	344 23.1	09.1	235 24.7	10.3	10 17.8	9.1	58.0
12	359 22.8	S23 09.0	249 54.0	10.3	N10 26.9	9.0	57.9
13	14 22.5	08.8	264 23.3	10.3	10 35.9	9.0	57.9
14	29 22.2	08.6	278 52.6	10.2	10 44.9	8.9	57.9
15	44 21.9	.. 08.5	293 21.8	10.3	10 53.8	8.8	57.9
16	59 21.6	08.3	307 51.1	10.3	11 02.6	8.7	57.9
17	74 21.3	08.1	322 20.4	10.2	11 11.3	8.7	57.8
18	89 21.0	S23 07.9	336 49.6	10.2	N11 20.0	8.7	57.8
19	104 20.7	07.8	351 18.8	10.2	11 28.7	8.5	57.8
20	119 20.4	07.6	5 48.0	10.2	11 37.2	8.5	57.8
21	134 20.1	.. 07.4	20 17.2	10.2	11 45.7	8.4	57.7
22	149 19.8	07.2	34 46.4	10.2	11 54.1	8.4	57.7
23	164 19.5	07.1	49 15.6	10.2	12 02.5	8.2	57.7
31 00	179 19.2	S23 06.9	63 44.8	10.1	N12 10.7	8.2	57.7
01	194 18.9	06.7	78 13.9	10.2	12 18.9	8.2	57.7
02	209 18.6	06.5	92 43.1	10.1	12 27.1	8.0	57.6
03	224 18.3	.. 06.4	107 12.2	10.2	12 35.1	8.0	57.6
04	239 18.0	06.2	121 41.4	10.1	12 43.1	7.9	57.6
05	254 17.7	06.0	136 10.5	10.1	12 51.0	7.9	57.6
06	269 17.4	S23 05.8	150 39.6	10.1	N12 58.9	7.7	57.6
07	284 17.1	05.6	165 08.7	10.0	13 06.6	7.7	57.5
08	299 16.8	05.5	179 37.7	10.1	13 14.3	7.6	57.5
09	314 16.5	.. 05.3	194 06.8	10.0	13 21.9	7.5	57.5
10	329 16.2	05.1	208 35.8	10.1	13 29.4	7.5	57.5
11	344 15.9	04.9	223 04.9	10.0	13 36.9	7.3	57.4
12	359 15.6	S23 04.7	237 33.9	10.0	N13 44.2	7.3	57.4
13	14 15.3	04.5	252 02.9	10.0	13 51.5	7.2	57.4
14	29 15.0	04.3	266 31.9	10.0	13 58.7	7.2	57.4
15	44 14.7	.. 04.2	281 00.9	10.0	14 05.9	7.0	57.4
16	59 14.4	04.0	295 29.9	9.9	14 12.9	7.0	57.3
17	74 14.1	03.8	309 58.8	10.0	14 19.9	6.9	57.3
18	89 13.8	S23 03.6	324 27.8	9.9	N14 26.8	6.8	57.3
19	104 13.5	03.4	338 56.7	10.0	14 33.6	6.7	57.3
20	119 13.2	03.2	353 25.7	9.9	14 40.3	6.6	57.3
21	134 12.9	.. 03.0	7 54.6	9.9	14 46.9	6.5	57.2
22	149 12.6	02.8	22 23.5	9.9	14 53.4	6.5	57.2
23	164 12.3	02.6	36 52.4	9.9	14 59.9	6.4	57.2
1 00	179 12.0	S23 02.4	51 21.3	9.8	N15 06.3	6.3	57.2
01	194 11.7	02.2	65 50.1	9.9	15 12.6	6.2	57.1
02	209 11.4	02.0	80 19.0	9.8	15 18.8	6.1	57.1
03	224 11.1	.. 01.8	94 47.8	9.9	15 24.9	6.0	57.1
04	239 10.8	01.6	109 16.7	9.8	15 30.9	5.9	57.1
05	254 10.5	01.4	123 45.5	9.8	15 36.8	5.9	57.1
06	269 10.2	S23 01.2	138 14.3	9.8	N15 42.7	5.7	57.0
07	284 10.0	01.0	152 43.1	9.8	15 48.4	5.7	57.0
08	299 09.7	00.8	167 11.9	9.8	15 54.1	5.6	57.0
09	314 09.4	.. 00.6	181 40.7	9.8	15 59.7	5.5	57.0
10	329 09.1	00.4	196 09.5	9.7	16 05.2	5.4	57.0
11	344 08.8	00.2	210 38.2	9.8	16 10.6	5.3	56.9
12	359 08.5	S23 00.0	225 07.0	9.8	N16 15.9	5.2	56.9
13	14 08.2	22 59.8	239 35.8	9.7	16 21.1	5.1	56.9
14	29 07.9	59.6	254 04.5	9.7	16 26.2	5.0	56.9
15	44 07.6	.. 59.4	268 33.2	9.8	16 31.2	5.0	56.9
16	59 07.3	59.2	283 02.0	9.7	16 36.2	4.8	56.8
17	74 07.0	59.0	297 30.7	9.7	16 41.0	4.8	56.8
18	89 06.7	S22 58.8	311 59.4	9.7	N16 45.8	4.6	56.8
19	104 06.4	58.6	326 28.1	9.7	16 50.4	4.6	56.8
20	119 06.1	58.4	340 56.8	9.7	16 55.0	4.4	56.7
21	134 05.8	.. 58.2	355 25.5	9.7	16 59.4	4.4	56.7
22	149 05.5	57.9	9 54.2	9.7	17 03.8	4.3	56.7
23	164 05.3	57.7	24 22.9	9.7	N17 08.1	4.2	56.7
SD	16.3	d 0.2	SD 15.8		15.6		15.5

Twilight / Moonrise

Lat.	Naut.	Civil	Sunrise	Moonrise 30	31	1	2
°	h m	h m	h m	h m	h m	h m	h m
N 72	08 25	10 46	■■■	11 04	10 57	10 48	10 28
N 70	08 06	09 51	■■■	11 20	11 23	11 29	11 42
68	07 50	09 18	■■■	11 33	11 42	11 57	12 20
66	07 38	08 54	10 30	11 44	11 58	12 18	12 46
64	07 27	08 35	09 51	11 53	12 11	12 35	13 07
62	07 18	08 19	09 24	12 00	12 22	12 49	13 23
60	07 09	08 06	09 03	12 07	12 31	13 01	13 37
N 58	07 02	07 54	08 46	12 13	12 39	13 11	13 49
56	06 56	07 44	08 31	12 18	12 47	13 20	14 00
54	06 50	07 36	08 19	12 23	12 53	13 28	14 09
52	06 44	07 28	08 08	12 27	12 59	13 35	14 17
50	06 39	07 21	07 59	12 31	13 04	13 42	14 24
45	06 27	07 04	07 38	12 40	13 16	13 56	14 40
N 40	06 17	06 51	07 22	12 47	13 25	14 07	14 53
35	06 08	06 40	07 08	12 53	13 34	14 17	15 04
30	05 59	06 29	06 56	12 58	13 41	14 26	15 14
20	05 43	06 11	06 35	13 08	13 53	14 41	15 30
N 10	05 27	05 54	06 16	13 16	14 04	14 54	15 45
0	05 11	05 37	05 59	13 24	14 15	15 07	15 58
S 10	04 52	05 19	05 42	13 32	14 25	15 19	16 12
20	04 30	04 59	05 23	13 40	14 37	15 32	16 27
30	04 01	04 34	05 01	13 50	14 49	15 48	16 44
35	03 42	04 19	04 49	13 56	14 57	15 57	16 53
40	03 20	04 01	04 34	14 02	15 06	16 07	17 05
45	02 50	03 39	04 16	14 09	15 16	16 19	17 18
S 50	02 05	03 10	03 54	14 19	15 28	16 33	17 34
52	01 39	02 55	03 43	14 23	15 33	16 40	17 42
54	00 57	02 37	03 31	14 27	15 40	16 48	17 50
56	////	02 16	03 17	14 33	15 47	16 56	18 00
58	////	01 47	03 01	14 38	15 54	17 06	18 10
S 60	////	01 02	02 41	14 45	16 03	17 17	18 23

Twilight / Moonset

Lat.	Sunset	Civil	Naut.	Moonset 30	31	1	2
°	h m	h m	h m	h m	h m	h m	h m
N 72	■■■	13 20	15 41	02 57	04 51	06 47	08 56
N 70	■■■	14 15	16 01	02 43	04 26	06 08	07 42
68	■■■	14 48	16 16	02 31	04 08	05 41	07 05
66	13 36	15 13	16 29	02 22	03 53	05 20	06 39
64	14 16	15 32	16 39	02 14	03 41	05 04	06 19
62	14 43	15 47	16 49	02 08	03 31	04 50	06 02
60	15 03	16 00	16 57	02 02	03 22	04 39	05 49
N 58	15 20	16 12	17 04	01 57	03 15	04 29	05 37
56	15 35	16 22	17 11	01 52	03 08	04 20	05 27
54	15 47	16 31	17 17	01 48	03 02	04 12	05 18
52	15 58	16 39	17 22	01 44	02 57	04 05	05 10
50	16 08	16 46	17 27	01 41	02 52	03 59	05 03
45	16 28	17 02	17 39	01 34	02 41	03 46	04 47
N 40	16 44	17 15	17 49	01 28	02 32	03 35	04 35
35	16 58	17 26	17 58	01 23	02 25	03 26	04 24
30	17 10	17 37	18 07	01 18	02 19	03 18	04 15
20	17 31	17 55	18 23	01 11	02 07	03 03	03 59
N 10	17 50	18 12	18 39	01 04	01 57	02 51	03 45
0	18 07	18 29	18 55	00 57	01 48	02 40	03 31
S 10	18 24	18 47	19 14	00 51	01 39	02 28	03 19
20	18 43	19 07	19 36	00 44	01 29	02 16	03 04
30	19 04	19 32	20 05	00 36	01 18	02 02	02 48
35	19 17	19 47	20 23	00 32	01 12	01 54	02 39
40	19 32	20 05	20 46	00 27	01 04	01 44	02 28
45	19 50	20 27	21 16	00 21	00 56	01 34	02 16
S 50	20 12	20 56	22 00	00 14	00 46	01 21	02 01
52	20 22	21 10	22 26	00 11	00 41	01 15	01 53
54	20 34	21 28	23 07	00 07	00 36	01 08	01 46
56	20 48	21 49	////	00 03	00 30	01 01	01 37
58	21 04	22 17	////	24 24	00 24	00 52	01 27
S 60	21 24	23 01	////	24 16	00 16	00 43	01 15

SUN / MOON

Day	SUN Eqn. of Time 00h	12h	Mer. Pass.	MOON Mer. Pass. Upper	Lower	Age	Phase
d	m s	m s	h m	h m	h m	d	%
30	02 14	02 28	12 02	19 36	07 11	08	69
31	02 43	02 57	12 03	20 27	08 02	09	78
1	03 11	03 25	12 03	21 19	08 53	10	86

EXPLANATION
PRINCIPLE AND ARRANGEMENT

1. *Object.* The object of this Almanac is to provide, in a convenient form, the data required for the practice of astronomical navigation at sea.

2. *Principle.* The main contents of the Almanac consist of data from which the *Greenwich Hour Angle* (GHA) and the *Declination* (Dec) of all the bodies used for navigation can be obtained for any instant of *Universal Time* (UT, specifically UT1, or previously Greenwich Mean Time (GMT)).

The *Local Hour Angle* (LHA) can then be obtained by means of the formula:

$$\text{LHA} = \text{GHA} \; {}^{-\text{ west}}_{+\text{ east}} \; \text{longitude}$$

The remaining data consist of: times of rising and setting of the Sun and Moon, and times of twilight; miscellaneous calendarial and planning data and auxiliary tables, including a list of Standard Times; corrections to be applied to observed altitude.

For the Sun, Moon, and planets the GHA and Dec are tabulated directly for each hour of UT throughout the year. For the stars the *Sidereal Hour Angle* (SHA) is given, and the GHA is obtained from:

$$\text{GHA Star} = \text{GHA Aries} + \text{SHA Star}$$

The SHA and Dec of the stars change slowly and may be regarded as constant over periods of several days. GHA Aries, or the Greenwich Hour Angle of the first point of Aries (the Vernal Equinox), is tabulated for each hour. Permanent tables give the appropriate increments and corrections to the tabulated hourly values of GHA and Dec for the minutes and seconds of UT.

The six-volume series of *Sight Reduction Tables for Marine Navigation* (published in U.S.A. as Pub. No. 229 and in U.K. as N.P. 401) has been designed for the solution of the navigational triangle and is intended for use with *The Nautical Almanac*.

Two alternative procedures for sight reduction are described on pages 277–318. The first requires the use of programmable calculators or computers, while the second uses a set of concise tables that is given on pages 286–317.

The tabular accuracy is $0\!\cdot\!1$ throughout. The time argument on the daily pages of this Almanac is UT1 denoted throughout by UT. This scale may differ from the broadcast time signals (UTC) by an amount which, if ignored, will introduce an error of up to $0\!\cdot\!2$ in longitude determined from astronomical observations. The difference arises because the time argument depends on the variable rate of rotation of the Earth while the broadcast time signals are based on an atomic time-scale. Step adjustments of exactly one second are made to the time signals as required (normally at 24^h on December 31 and June 30) so that the difference between the time signals and UT, as used in this Almanac, may not exceed $0^\text{s}\!\cdot\!9$. Those who require to reduce observations to a precision of better than 1^s must therefore obtain the correction (DUT1) to the time signals from coding in the signal, or from other sources; the required time is given by UT1=UTC+DUT1 to a precision of $0^\text{s}\!\cdot\!1$. Alternatively, the longitude, when determined from astronomical observations, may be corrected by the corresponding amount shown in the following table:

Correction to time signals	Correction to longitude
$-0^\text{s}\!\cdot\!9$ to $-0^\text{s}\!\cdot\!7$	$0\!\cdot\!2$ to east
$-0^\text{s}\!\cdot\!6$ to $-0^\text{s}\!\cdot\!3$	$0\!\cdot\!1$ to east
$-0^\text{s}\!\cdot\!2$ to $+0^\text{s}\!\cdot\!2$	no correction
$+0^\text{s}\!\cdot\!3$ to $+0^\text{s}\!\cdot\!6$	$0\!\cdot\!1$ to west
$+0^\text{s}\!\cdot\!7$ to $+0^\text{s}\!\cdot\!9$	$0\!\cdot\!2$ to west

3. *Lay-out.* The ephemeral data for three days are presented on an opening of two pages: the left-hand page contains the data for the planets and stars; the right-hand page contains the data for the Sun and Moon, together with times of twilight, sunrise, sunset, moonrise and moonset.

The remaining contents are arranged as follows: for ease of reference the altitude-correction tables are given on pages A2, A3, A4, xxxiv and xxxv; calendar, Moon's phases, eclipses, and planet notes (i.e. data of general interest) precede the main tabulations. The Explanation is followed by information on standard times, star charts and list of star positions, sight reduction procedures and concise sight reduction tables, tables of increments and corrections and other auxiliary tables that are frequently used.

MAIN DATA

4. *Daily pages.* The daily pages give the GHA of Aries, the GHA and Dec of the Sun, Moon, and the four navigational planets, for each hour of UT. For the Moon, values of v and d are also tabulated for each hour to facilitate the correction of GHA and Dec to intermediate times; v and d for the Sun and planets change so slowly that they are given, at the foot of the appropriate columns, once only on the page; v is zero for Aries and negligible for the Sun, and is omitted. The SHA and Dec of the 57 selected stars, arranged in alphabetical order of proper name, are also given.

5. *Stars.* The SHA and Dec of 173 stars, including the 57 selected stars, are tabulated for each month on pages 268–273; no interpolation is required and the data can be used in precisely the same way as those for the selected stars on the daily pages. The stars are arranged in order of SHA.

The list of 173 includes all stars down to magnitude 3·0, together with a few fainter ones to fill the larger gaps. The 57 selected stars have been chosen from amongst these on account of brightness and distribution in the sky; they will suffice for the majority of observations.

The 57 selected stars are known by their proper names, but they are also numbered in descending order of SHA. In the list of 173 stars, the constellation names are always given on the left-hand page; on the facing page proper names are given where well-known names exist. Numbers for the selected stars are given in both columns.

An index to the selected stars, containing lists in both alphabetical and numerical order, is given on page xxxiii and is also reprinted on the bookmark.

6. *Increments and corrections.* The tables printed on tinted paper (pages ii–xxxi) at the back of the Almanac provide the increments and corrections for minutes and seconds to be applied to the hourly values of GHA and Dec. They consist of sixty tables, one for each minute, separated into two parts: increments to GHA for Sun and planets, Aries, and Moon for every minute and second; and, for each minute, corrections to be applied to GHA and Dec corresponding to the values of v and d given on the daily pages.

The increments are based on the following adopted hourly rates of increase of the GHA: Sun and planets, 15° precisely; Aries, 15° 02′46; Moon, 14° 19′0. The values of v on the daily pages are the excesses of the actual hourly motions over the adopted values; they are generally positive, except for Venus. The tabulated hourly values of the Sun's GHA have been adjusted to reduce to a minimum the error caused by treating v as negligible. The values of d on the daily pages are the hourly differences of the Dec. For the Moon, the true values of v and d are given for each hour; otherwise mean values are given for the three days on the page.

7. *Method of entry.* The UT of an observation is expressed as a day and hour, followed by a number of minutes and seconds. The tabular values of GHA and Dec, and, where necessary, the corresponding values of v and d, are taken directly from the daily pages for the day and hour of UT; this hour is always *before* the time of observation. SHA and Dec of the selected stars are also taken from the daily pages.

The table of Increments and Corrections for the minute of UT is then selected. For the GHA, the increment for minutes and seconds is taken from the appropriate column opposite the seconds of UT; the v-correction is taken from the second part of the same table opposite the value of v as given on the daily pages. Both increment and v-correction are to be added to the GHA, except for Venus when v is prefixed by a minus sign and the v-correction is to be subtracted. For the Dec there is no increment, but a d-correction is applied in the same way as the v-correction; d is given without sign on the daily pages and the sign of the correction is to be supplied by inspection of the Dec column. In many cases the correction may be applied mentally.

8. *Examples.* (a) Sun and Moon. Required the GHA and Dec of the Sun and Moon on 2014 May 5 at 15^h 47^m 13^s UT.

		SUN			MOON			
		GHA	Dec	d	GHA	v	Dec	d
		° ′	° ′	′	° ′	′	° ′	′
Daily page, May 5^d 15^h		45 49·8	N 16 20·7	0·7	328 50·7	13·3	N 15 17·7	5·9
Increments for	47^m 13^s	11 48·3			11 16·0			
v or d corrections for	47^m		+0·6			+10·5	−4·7	
Sum for	May 5^d 15^h 47^m 13^s	57 38·1	N 16 21·3		340 17·2		N 15 13·0	

(b) Planets. Required the LHA and Dec of (i) Venus on 2014 May 5 at 13^h 15^m 18^s UT in longitude W 120° 24′; (ii) Mars on 2014 May 5 at 13^h 38^m 56^s UT in longitude E 75° 42′.

		VENUS				MARS			
		GHA	v	Dec	d	GHA	v	Dec	d
		° ′	′	° ′	′	° ′	′	° ′	′
Daily page, May 5^d	(13^h)	55 08·5	−0·2	S0 14·4	1·0	228 12·4	2·9	S2 49·8	0·1
Increments (planets)	$(15^m$ $18^s)$	3 49·5				$(38^m$ $56^s)$ 9 44·0			
v or d corrections	(15^m)	−0·1		−0·3		(38^m) +1·9		−0·1	
Sum = GHA and Dec.		58 57·9		S0 14·1		237 58·3		S2 49·7	
Longitude	(west)	−120 24·0				(east) + 75 42·0			
Multiples of 360°		+360							
LHA planet		298 33·9				313 40·3			

(c) Stars. Required the GHA and Dec of (i) *Vega* on 2014 May 5 at 7^h 02^m 18^s UT; (ii) *Spica* on 2014 May 5 at 19^h 43^m 37^s UT.

		Vega		*Spica*	
		GHA	Dec	GHA	Dec
		° ′	° ′	° ′	° ′
Daily page (SHA and Dec)		80 38·3	N 38 47.8	158 30·3	S 11 14.3
Daily page (GHA Aries)	(7^h)	328 04·7		(19^h) 148 34·2	
Increments (Aries)	$(02^m$ $18^s)$	0 34·6		$(43^m$ $37^s)$ 10 56·0	
Sum = GHA star		409 17·6		318 00·5	
Multiples of 360°		−360			
GHA star		49 17·6		318 00·5	

9. *Polaris (Pole Star) tables.* The tables on pages 274–276 provide means by which the latitude can be deduced from an observed altitude of *Polaris*, and they also give its azimuth; their use is explained and illustrated on those pages. They are based on the following formula:

$$\text{Latitude} - H_O = -p\cos h + \tfrac{1}{2}p\sin p \sin^2 h \tan(\text{latitude})$$

where

$$H_O = \text{Apparent altitude (corrected for refraction)}$$
$$p = \text{polar distance of } Polaris = 90° - \text{Dec}$$
$$h = \text{local hour angle of } Polaris = \text{LHA Aries} + \text{SHA}$$

a_0, which is a function of LHA Aries only, is the value of both terms of the above formula calculated for mean values of the SHA (317° 24′) and Dec (N 89° 19′·5) of *Polaris*, for a mean latitude of 50°, and adjusted by the addition of a constant (58′·8).

a_1, which is a function of LHA Aries and latitude, is the excess of the value of the second term over its mean value for latitude 50°, increased by a constant (0′.6) to make it always positive. a_2, which is a function of LHA Aries and date, is the correction to the first term for the variation of *Polaris* from its adopted mean position; it is increased by a constant (0′.6) to make it positive. The sum of the added constants is 1°, so that:

$$\text{Latitude} = \text{Apparent altitude (corrected for refraction)} - 1° + a_0 + a_1 + a_2$$

RISING AND SETTING PHENOMENA

10. *General.* On the right-hand daily pages are given the times of sunrise and sunset, of the beginning and end of civil and nautical twilights, and of moonrise and moonset for a range of latitudes from N 72° to S 60°. These times, which are given to the nearest minute, are strictly the UT of the phenomena on the Greenwich meridian; they are given for every day for moonrise and moonset, but only for the middle day of the three on each page for the solar phenomena.

They are approximately the Local Mean Times (LMT) of the corresponding phenomena on other meridians; they can be formally interpolated if desired. The UT of a phenomenon is obtained from the LMT by:

$$\text{UT} = \text{LMT} \begin{array}{c} + \text{ west} \\ - \text{ east} \end{array} \text{ longitude}$$

in which the longitude must first be converted to time by the table on page i or otherwise.

Interpolation for latitude can be done mentally or with the aid of Table I on page xxxii.

The following symbols are used to indicate the conditions under which, in high latitudes, some of the phenomena do not occur:

    ☐ Sun or Moon remains continuously above the horizon;

    ■ Sun or Moon remains continuously below the horizon;

    //// twilight lasts all night.

Basis of the tabulations. At sunrise and sunset 16′ is allowed for semi-diameter and 34′ for horizontal refraction, so that at the times given the Sun's upper limb is on the visible horizon; all times refer to phenomena as seen from sea level with a clear horizon.

At the times given for the beginning and end of twilight, the Sun's zenith distance is 96° for civil, and 102° for nautical twilight. The degree of illumination at the times given for civil twilight (in good conditions and in the absence of other illumination) is such that the brightest stars are visible and the horizon is clearly defined. At the times given for nautical twilight the horizon is in general not visible, and it is too dark for observation with a marine sextant.

Times corresponding to other depressions of the Sun may be obtained by interpolation or, for depressions of more than 12°, less reliably, by extrapolation; times so obtained will be subject to considerable uncertainty near extreme conditions.

At moonrise and moonset allowance is made for semi-diameter, parallax, and refraction (34′), so that at the times given the Moon's upper limb is on the visible horizon as seen from sea level.

11. *Sunrise, sunset, twilight.* The tabulated times may be regarded, without serious error, as the LMT of the phenomena on any of the three days on the page and in any longitude. Precise times may normally be obtained by interpolating the tabular values for latitude and to the correct day and longitude, the latter being expressed as a fraction of a day by dividing it by 360°, positive for west and negative for east longitudes. In the extreme conditions near ☐, ■ or //// interpolation may not be possible in one direction, but accurate times are of little value in these circumstances.

Examples. Required the UT of (a) the beginning of morning twilights and sunrise on 2014 January 13 for latitude S 48° 55′, longitude E 75° 18′; (b) sunset and the end of evening twilights on 2014 January 15 for latitude N 67° 10′, longitude W 168° 05′.

	(a)	Twilight Nautical	Civil	Sunrise	(b)	Sunset	Twilight Civil	Nautical
From p. 19		d h m	d h m	d h m		d h m	d h m	d h m
LMT for Lat	S 45°	13 03 09	13 03 56	13 04 32	N 66°	15 14 23	15 15 42	15 16 53
Corr. to	S 48° 55′	−30	−20	−16	N 67° 10′	−22	−12	−6
(p. xxxii, Table I)								
Long (p. i)	E 75° 18′	−5 01	−5 01	−5 01	W 168° 05′	+11 12	+11 12	+11 12
UT		12 21 38	12 22 35	12 23 15		16 01 13	16 02 42	16 03 59

The LMT are strictly for January 14 (middle date on page) and 0° longitude; for more precise times it is necessary to interpolate, but rounding errors may accumulate to about 2^m.

(a) to January $13^d - 75°/360° =$ Jan. $12^d\!8$, i.e. $\frac{1}{3}(1\cdot2) = 0\cdot4$ backwards towards the data for the same latitude interpolated similarly from page 17; the corrections are -2^m to nautical twilight, -2^m to civil twilight and -2^m to sunrise.

(b) to January $15^d + 168°/360° =$ Jan. $15^d\!5$, i.e. $\frac{1}{3}(1\cdot5) = 0\cdot5$ forwards towards the data for the same latitude interpolated similarly from page 21; the corrections are $+7^m$ to sunset, $+4^m$ to civil twilight, and $+4^m$ to nautical twilight.

12. *Moonrise, moonset.* Precise times of moonrise and moonset are rarely needed; a glance at the tables will generally give sufficient indication of whether the Moon is available for observation and of the hours of rising and setting. If needed, precise times may be obtained as follows. Interpolate for latitude, using Table I on page xxxii, on the day wanted and also on the preceding day in east longitudes or the following day in west longitudes; take the difference between these times and interpolate for longitude by applying to the time for the day wanted the correction from Table II on page xxxii, so that the resulting time is between the two times used. In extreme conditions near ☐ or ■ interpolation for latitude or longitude may be possible only in one direction; accurate times are of little value in these circumstances.

To facilitate this interpolation the times of moonrise and moonset are given for four days on each page; where no phenomenon occurs during a particular day (as happens once a month) the time of the phenomenon on the following day, increased by 24^h, is given; extra care must be taken when interpolating between two values, when one of those values exceeds 24^h. In practice it suffices to use the daily difference between the times for the nearest tabular latitude, and generally, to enter Table II with the nearest tabular arguments as in the examples below.

Examples. Required the UT of moonrise and moonset in latitude S 47° 10′, longitudes E 124° 00′ and W 78° 31′ on 2014 January 11.

	Longitude E 124° 00′ Moonrise	Moonset	Longitude W 78° 31′ Moonrise	Moonset
	d h m	d h m	d h m	d h m
LMT for Lat. S 45°	11 15 54	11 00 54	11 15 54	11 00 54
Lat correction (p. xxxii, Table I)	+07	−07	+07	−07
Long correction (p. xxxii, Table II)	−20	−13	+11	+09
Correct LMT	11 15 41	11 00 34	11 16 12	11 00 56
Longitude (p. i)	−8 16	−8 16	+5 14	+5 14
UT	11 07 25	10 16 18	11 21 26	11 06 10

ALTITUDE CORRECTION TABLES

13. *General.* In general two corrections are given for application to altitudes observed with a marine sextant; additional corrections are required for Venus and Mars and also for very low altitudes.

Tables of the correction for dip of the horizon, due to height of eye above sea level, are given on pages A2 and xxxiv. Strictly this correction should be applied first and subtracted from the sextant altitude to give apparent altitude, which is the correct argument for the other tables.

Separate tables are given of the second correction for the Sun, for stars and planets (on pages A2 and A3), and for the Moon (on pages xxxiv and xxxv). For the Sun, values are given for both lower and upper limbs, for two periods of the year. The star tables are used for the planets, but additional corrections for parallax (page A2) are required for Venus and Mars. The Moon tables are in two parts: the main correction is a function of apparent altitude only and is tabulated for the lower limb (30′ must be subtracted to obtain the correction for the upper limb); the other, which is given for both lower and upper limbs, depends also on the horizontal parallax, which has to be taken from the daily pages.

An additional correction, given on page A4, is required for the change in the refraction, due to variations of pressure and temperature from the adopted standard conditions; it may generally be ignored for altitudes greater than 10°, except possibly in extreme conditions. The correction tables for the Sun, stars, and planets are in two parts; only those for altitudes greater than 10° are reprinted on the bookmark.

14. *Critical tables.* Some of the altitude correction tables are arranged as critical tables. In these an interval of apparent altitude (or height of eye) corresponds to a single value of the correction; no interpolation is required. At a "critical" entry the upper of the two possible values of the correction is to be taken. For example, in the table of dip, a correction of −4′1 corresponds to all values of the height of eye from 5·3 to 5·5 metres (17·5 to 18·3 feet) inclusive.

15. *Examples.* The following examples illustrate the use of the altitude correction tables; the sextant altitudes given are assumed to be taken on 2014 March 9 with a marine sextant at height 5·4 metres (18 feet), temperature −3°C and pressure 982 mb, the Moon sights being taken at about 10^h UT.

	SUN lower limb		SUN upper limb		MOON lower limb		MOON upper limb		VENUS		*Polaris*	
	°	′	°	′	°	′	°	′	°	′	°	′
Sextant altitude	21	19·7	3	20·2	33	27·6	26	06·7	4	32·6	49	36·5
Dip, height 5·4 metres (18 feet)		−4·1		−4·1		−4·1		−4·1		−4·1		−4·1
Main correction		+13·8		−29·6		+57·4		+60·5		−10·8		−0·8
−30′ for upper limb (Moon)		—		—		—		−30·0		—		—
L, U correction for Moon		—		—		+1·5		+1·7		—		—
Additional correction for Venus		—		—		—		—		+0·3		—
Additional refraction correction		−0·1		−0·6		−0·1		−0·1		−0·5		0·0
Corrected sextant altitude	21	29·3	2	45·9	34	22·3	26	34·7	4	17·5	49	31·6

The main corrections have been taken out with apparent altitude (sextant altitude corrected for index error and dip) as argument, interpolating where possible. These refinements are rarely necessary.

16. *Composition of the Corrections.* The table for the dip of the sea horizon is based on the formula:

Correction for dip $= -1′76\sqrt{\text{(height of eye in metres)}} = -0′97\sqrt{\text{(height of eye in feet)}}$

The correction table for the Sun includes the effects of semi-diameter, parallax and mean refraction.

The correction tables for the stars and planets allow for the effect of mean refraction.

The phase correction for Venus has been incorporated in the tabulations for GHA and Dec, and no correction for phase is required. The additional corrections for Venus and Mars allow for parallax. Alternatively, the correction for parallax may be calculated from $p \cos H$, where p is the parallax and H is the altitude. In 2014 the values for p are:

	Jan. 1	Jan. 9	Jan. 12	Jan. 31	Feb. 16	Mar. 10	Apr. 30	Dec. 31
Venus	0′5	0′6	0′5	0′4	0′3	0′2	0′1	

	Jan. 1	Feb. 9	June 29	Dec. 31
Mars	0′1	0′2	0′1	

The correction table for the Moon includes the effect of semi-diameter, parallax, augmentation and mean refraction.

Mean refraction is calculated for a temperature of 10°C (50°F), a pressure of 1010 mb (29·83 inches), humidity of 80% and wavelength 0·50169 μm.

17. *Bubble sextant observations.*   When observing with a bubble sextant no correction is necessary for dip, semi-diameter, or augmentation. The altitude corrections for the stars and planets on page A2 and on the bookmark should be used for the Sun as well as for the stars and planets; for the Moon it is easiest to take the mean of the corrections for lower and upper limbs and subtract 15′ from the altitude; the correction for dip must not be applied.

AUXILIARY AND PLANNING DATA

18. *Sun and Moon.*   On the daily pages are given: hourly values of the horizontal parallax of the Moon; the semi-diameters and the times of meridian passage of both Sun and Moon over the Greenwich meridian; the equation of time; the age of the Moon, the percent (%) illuminated and a symbol indicating the phase. The times of the phases of the Moon are given in UT on page 4. For the Moon, the semi-diameters for each of the three days are given at the foot of the column; for the Sun a single value is sufficient. Table II on page xxxii may be used for interpolating the time of the Moon's meridian passage for longitude. The equation of time is given daily at 00^h and 12^h UT. The sign is *positive* for unshaded values and *negative* for shaded values. To obtain apparent time add the equation of time to mean time when the sign is *positive*. Subtract the equation of time from mean time when the sign is *negative*. At 12^h UT, when the sign is *positive*, meridian passage of the Sun occurs *before* 12^h UT, otherwise it occurs *after* 12^h UT.

19. *Planets.*   The magnitudes of the planets are given immediately following their names in the headings on the daily pages; also given, for the middle day of the three on the page, are their SHA at 00^h UT and their times of meridian passage.

The planet notes and diagram on pages 8 and 9 provide descriptive information as to the suitability of the planets for observation during the year, and of their positions and movements.

20. *Stars.*   The time of meridian passage of the first point of Aries over the Greenwich meridian is given on the daily pages, for the middle day of the three on the page, to $0^m.1$. The interval between successive meridian passages is $23^h 56^m.1$ (24^h less $3^m.9$) so that times for intermediate days and other meridians can readily be derived. If a precise time is required it may be obtained by finding the UT at which LHA Aries is zero.

The meridian passage of a star occurs when its LHA is zero, that is when LHA Aries + SHA = 360°. An approximate time can be obtained from the planet diagram on page 9.

The star charts on pages 266 and 267 are intended to assist identification. They show the relative positions of the stars in the sky as seen from the Earth and include all 173 stars used in the Almanac, together with a few others to complete the main constellation configurations. The local meridian at any time may be located on the chart by means of its SHA which is 360° − LHA Aries, or west longitude − GHA Aries.

21. *Star globe.*   To set a star globe on which is printed a scale of LHA Aries, first set the globe for latitude and then rotate about the polar axis until the scale under the edge of the meridian circle reads LHA Aries.

To mark the positions of the Sun, Moon, and planets on the star globe, take the difference GHA Aries − GHA body and use this along the LHA Aries scale, in conjunction with the declination, to plot the position. GHA Aries − GHA body is most conveniently found by taking the difference when the GHA of the body is small (less than 15°), which happens once a day.

22. *Calendar.*   On page 4 are given lists of ecclesiastical festivals, and of the principal anniversaries and holidays in the United Kingdom and the United States of America. The calendar on page 5 includes the day of the year as well as the day of the week.

Brief particulars are given, at the foot of page 5, of the solar and lunar eclipses occurring during the year; the times given are in UT. The principal features of the more important solar eclipses are shown on the maps on pages 6 and 7.

23. *Standard times.* The lists on pages 262–265 give the standard times used in most countries. In general no attempt is made to give details of the beginning and end of summer time, since they are liable to frequent changes at short notice. For the latest information consult Admiralty List of Radio Signals Volume 2 (NP 282) corrected by Section VI of the weekly edition of Admiralty Notices to Mariners.

The Date or Calendar Line is an arbitrary line, on either side of which the date differs by one day; when crossing this line on a westerly course, the date must be advanced one day; when crossing it on an easterly course, the date must be put back one day. The line is a modification of the line of the 180th meridian, and is drawn so as to include, as far as possible, islands of any one group, etc., on the same side of the line. It may be traced by starting at the South Pole and joining up to the following positions:

Lat	S 51·0	S 45·0	S 15·0	S 5·0	N 48·0	N 53·0	N 65·5
Long	180·0	W 172·5	W 172·5	180·0	180·0	E 170·0	W 169·0

thence through the middle of the Diomede Islands to Lat N 68°·0, Long W 169°·0, passing east of Ostrov Vrangelya (Wrangel Island) to Lat N 75°·0, Long 180°·0, and thence to the North Pole.

ACCURACY

24. *Main data.* The quantities tabulated in this Almanac are generally correct to the nearest $0\!\!'\!1$; the exception is the Sun's GHA which is deliberately adjusted by up to $0\!\!'\!15$ to reduce the error due to ignoring the v-correction. The GHA and Dec at intermediate times cannot be obtained to this precision, since at least two quantities must be added; moreover, the v- and d-corrections are based on mean values of v and d and are taken from tables for the whole minute only. The largest error that can occur in the GHA or Dec of any body other than the Sun or Moon is less than $0\!\!'\!2$; it may reach $0\!\!'\!25$ for the GHA of the Sun and $0\!\!'\!3$ for that of the Moon.

In practice it may be expected that only one third of the values of GHA and Dec taken out will have errors larger than $0\!\!'\!05$ and less than one tenth will have errors larger than $0\!\!'\!1$.

25. *Altitude corrections.* The errors in the altitude corrections are nominally of the same order as those in GHA and Dec, as they result from the addition of several quantities each correctly rounded off to $0\!\!'\!1$. But the actual values of the dip and of the refraction at low altitudes may, in extreme atmospheric conditions, differ considerably from the mean values used in the tables.

USE OF THIS ALMANAC IN 2015

This Almanac may be used for the Sun and stars in 2015 in the following manner.

For the Sun, take out the GHA and Dec for the same date but for a time $5^h\ 48^m\ 00^s$ *earlier* than the UT of observation; add 87° 00′ to the GHA so obtained. The error, mainly due to planetary perturbations of the Earth, is unlikely to exceed $0\!\!'\!4$.

For the stars, calculate the GHA and Dec for the same date and the same time, but *subtract* $15\!\!'\!1$ from the GHA so found. The error, due to incomplete correction for precession and nutation, is unlikely to exceed $0\!\!'\!4$. If preferred, the same result can be obtained by using a time $5^h\ 48^m\ 00^s$ earlier than the UT of observation (as for the Sun) and adding 86° $59\!\!'\!2$ to the GHA (or adding 87° as for the Sun and subtracting $0\!\!'\!8$, for precession, from the SHA of the star).

The Almanac cannot be so used for the Moon or planets.

LIST I — PLACES FAST ON UTC (mainly those EAST OF GREENWICH)

The times given } *added* to UTC to give Standard Time
below should be } *subtracted* from Standard Time to give UTC.

	h	m		h	m
Admiralty Islands	10		Denmark*†	01	
Afghanistan	04	30	Djibouti	03	
Albania*	01		Egypt, Arab Republic of	02	
Algeria	01		Equatorial Guinea, Republic of	01	
Amirante Islands	04		Eritrea	03	
Andaman Islands	05	30	Estonia*†	02	
Angola	01		Ethiopia	03	
Armenia	04				
Australia			Fiji*	12	
Australian Capital Territory*	10		Finland*†	02	
New South Wales*[1]	10		France*†	01	
Northern Territory	09	30	Gabon	01	
Queensland	10		Georgia	04	
South Australia*	09	30	Germany*†	01	
Tasmania*	10		Gibraltar*	01	
Victoria*	10		Greece*†	02	
Western Australia	08		Guam	10	
Whitsunday Islands	10				
Austria*†	01		Hong Kong	08	
Azerbaijan*	04		Hungary*†	01	
Bahrain	03		India	05	30
Balearic Islands*†	01		Indonesia, Republic of		
Bangladesh	06		Bangka, Billiton, Java, West and		
Belarus	03		Central Kalimantan, Madura, Sumatra	07	
Belgium*†	01		Bali, Flores, South and East		
Benin	01		Kalimantan, Lombok, Sulawesi,		
Bosnia and Herzegovina*	01		Sumba, Sumbawa, West Timor ...	08	
Botswana, Republic of	02		Aru, Irian Jaya, Kai, Moluccas		
Brunei	08		Tanimbar	09	
Bulgaria*†	02		Iran*	03	30
Burma (Myanmar)	06	30	Iraq	03	
Burundi	02		Israel*	02	
			Italy*†	01	
Cambodia	07				
Cameroon Republic	01		Jan Mayen Island*	01	
Caroline Islands[2]	10		Japan	09	
Central African Republic	01		Jordan	03	
Chad	01		Kazakhstan		
Chagos Archipelago & Diego Garcia	06		Western: Aktau, Uralsk, Atyrau ...	05	
Chatham Islands*	12	45	Eastern & Central: Kzyl-Orda, Astana	06	
China, People's Republic of	08		Kenya	03	
Christmas Island, Indian Ocean ...	07		Kerguelen Islands	05	
Cocos (Keeling) Islands	06	30	Kiribati Republic		
Comoro Islands (Comoros)	03		Gilbert Islands	12	
Congo, Democratic Republic			Phoenix Islands[3]	13	
West: Kinshasa, Equateur	01		Line Islands[3]	14	
East: Orientale, Kasai, Kivu, Shaba	02		Korea, North	09	
Congo Republic	01		Korea, South	09	
Corsica*†	01		Kuwait	03	
Crete*†	02		Kyrgyzstan	06	
Croatia*	01				
Cyprus†: Ercan*, Larnaca*	02		Laccadive Islands	05	30
Czech Republic*†	01		Laos	07	
			Latvia*†	02	

---

* Daylight-saving time may be kept in these places.   † For Summer time dates see List II footnotes.

[1] Except Broken Hill Area* which keeps $09^h 30^m$.

[2] Except Pohnpei, Pingelap and Kosrae which keep 11^h and Palau which keeps 09^h.

[3] The Line and Phoenix Is. not part of the Kiribati Republic keep 10^h and 11^h, respectively, slow on UTC.

LIST I — (continued)

	h	m
Lebanon*	02	
Lesotho	02	
Libya	01	
Liechtenstein*	01	
Lithuania*†	02	
Lord Howe Island*	10	30
Luxembourg*†	01	
Macau	08	
Macedonia*, former Yugoslav Republic	01	
Macias Nguema (Fernando Póo) ...	01	
Madagascar, Democratic Republic of	03	
Malawi	02	
Malaysia, Malaya, Sabah, Sarawak ...	08	
Maldives, Republic of The	05	
Malta*†	01	
Mariana Islands	10	
Marshall Islands	12	
Mauritius	04	
Moldova*	02	
Monaco*	01	
Mongolia	08	
Montenegro*	01	
Mozambique	02	
Namibia*	01	
Nauru	12	
Nepal	05	45
Netherlands, The*†	01	
New Caledonia	11	
New Zealand*	12	
Nicobar Islands	05	30
Niger	01	
Nigeria, Republic of	01	
Norfolk Island	11	30
Norway*	01	
Novaya Zemlya	04	
Okinawa	09	
Oman	04	
Pagalu (Annobon Islands)	01	
Pakistan	05	
Palau Islands	09	
Papua New Guinea	10	
Pescadores Islands	08	
Philippine Republic	08	
Poland*†	01	
Qatar	03	
Reunion	04	
Romania*†	02	
Russia [1]		
Kaliningrad	03	
Moscow, St. Petersburg, Volgograd		
Arkhangelsk, Astrakhan, Samara	04	
Ekaterinburg, Ufa, Perm, Novyy Port	06	
Omsk, Novosibirsk, Tomsk	07	
Norilsk, Krasnoyarsk, Dikson	08	

	h	m
Irkutsk, Bratsk, Ulan-Ude	09	
Tiksi, Yakutsk, Chita	10	
Vladivostok, Khabarovsk, Okhotsk		
Sakhalin Island	11	
Petropavlovsk-K., Magadan, Anadyr		
Kuril Islands	12	
Rwanda	02	
Ryukyu Islands	09	
Samoa*	13	
Santa Cruz Islands	11	
Sardinia*†	01	
Saudi Arabia	03	
Schouten Islands	09	
Serbia*	01	
Seychelles	04	
Sicily*†	01	
Singapore	08	
Slovakia*†	01	
Slovenia*†	01	
Socotra	03	
Solomon Islands	11	
Somalia Republic	03	
South Africa, Republic of	02	
Spain*†	01	
Spanish Possessions in North Africa*	01	
Spitsbergen (Svalbard)*	01	
Sri Lanka	05	30
Sudan, Republic of	03	
Swaziland	02	
Sweden*†	01	
Switzerland*	01	
Syria (Syrian Arab Republic)*	02	
Taiwan	08	
Tajikistan	05	
Tanzania	03	
Thailand	07	
Timor-Leste	09	
Tonga	13	
Tunisia	01	
Turkey*	02	
Turkmenistan	05	
Tuvalu	12	
Uganda	03	
Ukraine*	02	
United Arab Emirates	04	
Uzbekistan	05	
Vanuatu, Republic of	11	
Vietnam, Socialist Republic of	07	
Yemen	03	
Zambia, Republic of	02	
Zimbabwe	02	

* Daylight-saving time may be kept in these places.　　† For Summer time dates see List II footnotes.
[1] The boundaries between the zones are irregular; listed are chief towns in each zone.

LIST II — PLACES NORMALLY KEEPING UTC

Ascension Island	Ghana	Irish Republic*†	Morocco*	Sierra Leone
Burkina-Faso	Great Britain†	Ivory Coast	Portugal*†	Togo Republic
Canary Islands*†	Guinea-Bissau	Liberia	Principe	Tristan da Cunha
Channel Islands†	Guinea Republic	Madeira*†	St. Helena	
Faeroes*, The	Iceland	Mali	São Tomé	
Gambia, The	Ireland, Northern†	Mauritania	Senegal	

* Daylight-saving time may be kept in these places.

† Summer time (daylight-saving time), one hour in advance of UTC, will be kept from 2014 March 30^d 01^h to October 26^d 01^h UTC (Ninth Summer Time Directive of the European Union). Ratification by member countries has not been verified.

LIST III — PLACES SLOW ON UTC (WEST OF GREENWICH)

The times given } *subtracted* from UTC to give Standard Time
below should be } *added* to Standard Time to give UTC.

	h	m		h	m
American Samoa	11		Canada (*continued*)		
Argentina	03		Prince Edward Island*	04	
Austral (Tubuai) Islands[1]	10		Quebec, east of long. W. 63°	04	
Azores*†	01		west of long. W. 63°* ...	05	
			Saskatchewan	06	
Bahamas*	05		Yukon*	08	
Barbados	04		Cape Verde Islands	01	
Belize	06		Cayman Islands	05	
Bermuda*	04		Chile*	04	
Bolivia	04		Colombia	05	
Brazil			Cook Islands	10	
Fernando de Noronha I., Trindade I.,			Costa Rica	06	
Oceanic Is.	02		Cuba*	05	
N and NE coastal states, Bahia,			Curaçao Island	04	
Tocantins*, Goiás*, Brasilia*,					
Minas Gerais*, Espirito Santo*,					
S and E coastal states*	03		Dominican Republic	04	
Mato Grosso do Sul*, Mato Grosso*,					
Rondônia, Amazonas, Roraima, Acre	04		Easter Island (I. de Pascua)*	06	
British Antarctic Territory[2,3]	03		Ecuador	05	
			El Salvador	06	
Canada[3]‡					
Alberta*	07		Falkland Islands	03	
British Columbia*	08		Fernando de Noronha Island	02	
Labrador*	04		French Guiana	03	
Manitoba*	06				
New Brunswick*	04		Galápagos Islands	06	
Newfoundland*	03	30	Greenland		
Nunavut*			Danmarkshavn, Mesters Vig	00	
east of long. W. 85°	05		General*	03	
long. W. 85° to W. 102°	06		Scoresby Sound*	01	
west of long. W. 102°	07		Thule*, Pituffik*	04	
Northwest Territories*	07		Grenada	04	
Nova Scotia*	04		Guadeloupe	04	
Ontario, east of long. W. 90°*	05		Guatemala	06	
Ontario, west of long. W. 90°* ...	06		Guyana, Republic of	04	

* Daylight-saving time may be kept in these places.   ‡ Dates for DST are given at the end of List III.
[1] This is the legal standard time, but local mean time is generally used.
[2] Stations may use UTC.
[3] Some areas may keep another time zone.

	h	m
Haiti	05	
Honduras	06	
Jamaica	05	
Johnston Island	10	
Juan Fernandez Islands*	04	
Leeward Islands	04	
Marquesas Islands	09	30
Martinique	04	
Mexico		
General*	06	
Sonora, Sinaloa*, Nayarit*,		
Chihuahua*, Southern District		
of Lower California*	07	
Northern District of Lower California*	08	
Midway Islands	11	
Nicaragua	06	
Niue	11	
Panama, Republic of	05	
Paraguay*	04	
Peru	05	
Pitcairn Island	08	
Puerto Rico	04	
St. Pierre and Miquelon*	03	
Society Islands	10	
South Georgia	02	
Suriname	03	
Trindade Island, South Atlantic ...	02	
Trinidad and Tobago	04	
Tuamotu Archipelago	10	
Tubuai (Austral) Islands	10	
Turks and Caicos Islands*	05	
United States of America ‡		
Alabama	06	
Alaska	09	
Aleutian Islands, east of W. 169° 30′	09	
Aleutian Islands, west of W. 169° 30′	10	
Arizona [1]	07	
Arkansas	06	
California	08	
Colorado	07	
Connecticut	05	
Delaware	05	
District of Columbia	05	
Florida [2]	05	
Georgia	05	
Hawaii [1]	10	

	h	m
United States of America ‡*(continued)*		
Idaho, southern part	07	
northern part	08	
Illinois	06	
Indiana [2]	05	
Iowa	06	
Kansas [2]	06	
Kentucky, eastern part	05	
western part	06	
Louisiana	06	
Maine	05	
Maryland	05	
Massachusetts	05	
Michigan [2]	05	
Minnesota	06	
Mississippi	06	
Missouri	06	
Montana	07	
Nebraska, eastern part	06	
western part	07	
Nevada	08	
New Hampshire	05	
New Jersey	05	
New Mexico	07	
New York	05	
North Carolina	05	
North Dakota, eastern part	06	
western part	07	
Ohio	05	
Oklahoma	06	
Oregon [2]	08	
Pennsylvania	05	
Rhode Island	05	
South Carolina	05	
South Dakota, eastern part	06	
western part	07	
Tennessee, eastern part	05	
western part	06	
Texas [2]	06	
Utah	07	
Vermont	05	
Virginia	05	
Washington D.C.	05	
Washington	08	
West Virginia	05	
Wisconsin	06	
Wyoming	07	
Uruguay*	03	
Venezuela	04	30
Virgin Islands	04	
Windward Islands	04	

* Daylight-saving time may be kept in these places.

‡ Daylight-saving (Summer) time, one hour fast on the time given, is kept during 2014 from March 9 (second Sunday) to November 2 (first Sunday), changing at $02^h 00^m$ local clock time.

[1] Exempt from keeping daylight-saving time, except for a portion of Arizona.

[2] A small portion of the state is in another time zone.

NORTHERN STARS

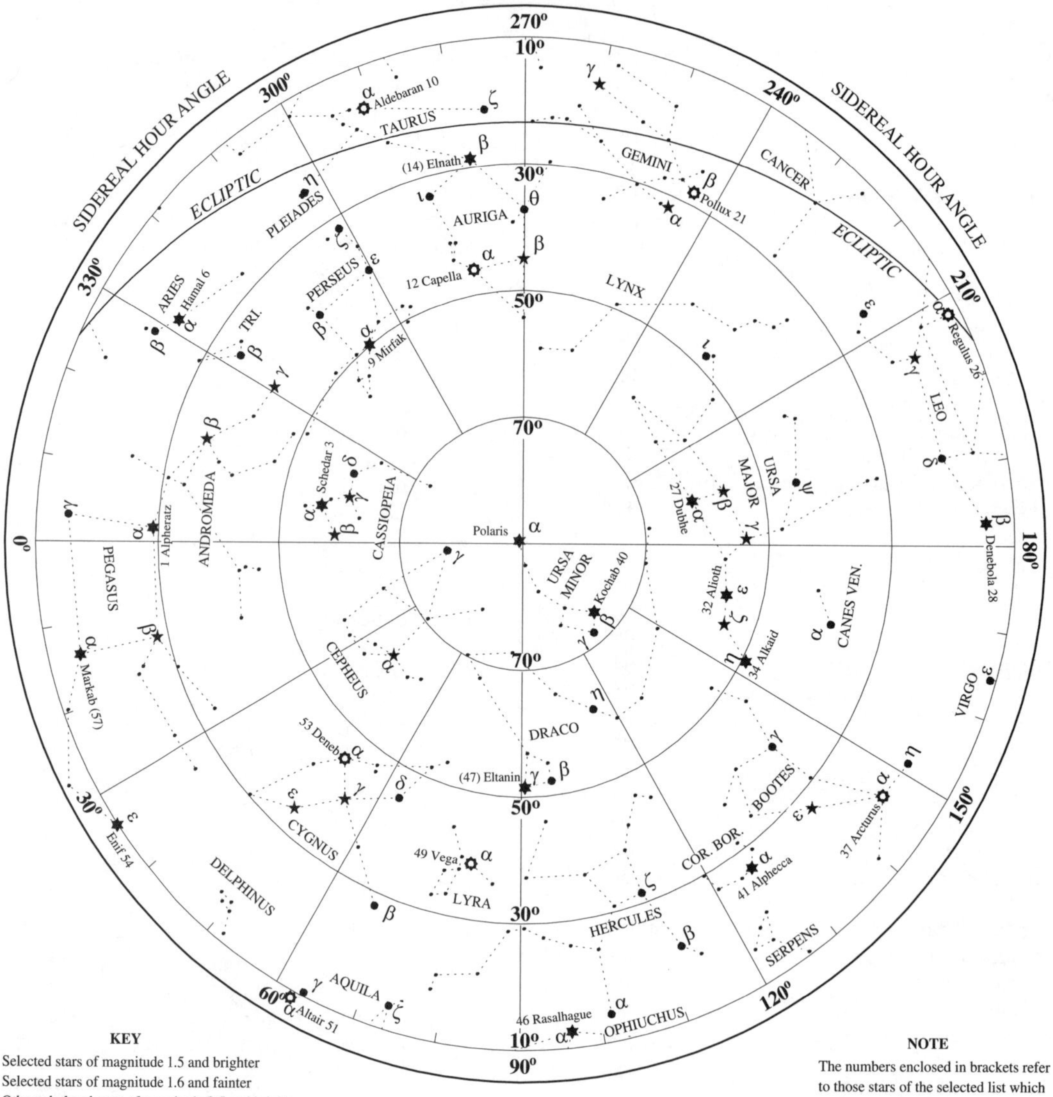

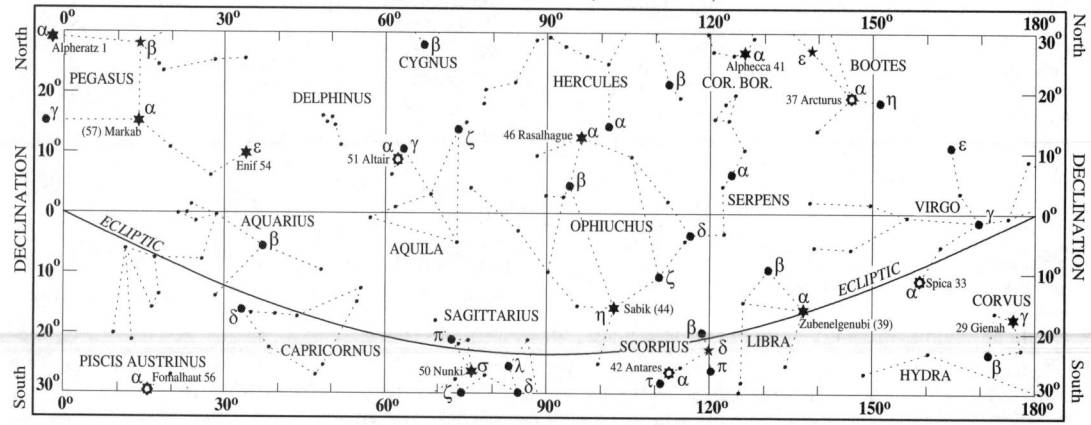

KEY

✿ Selected stars of magnitude 1.5 and brighter
★ Selected stars of magnitude 1.6 and fainter
★ Other tabulated stars of magnitude 2.5 and brighter
● Other tabulated stars of magnitude 2.6 and fainter
· Untabulated stars

NOTE

The numbers enclosed in brackets refer to those stars of the selected list which are not used in Sight Reduction Tables A.P. 3270, N.P. 303.

EQUATORIAL STARS (SHA 0° to 180°)

SIDEREAL HOUR ANGLE

SOUTHERN STARS

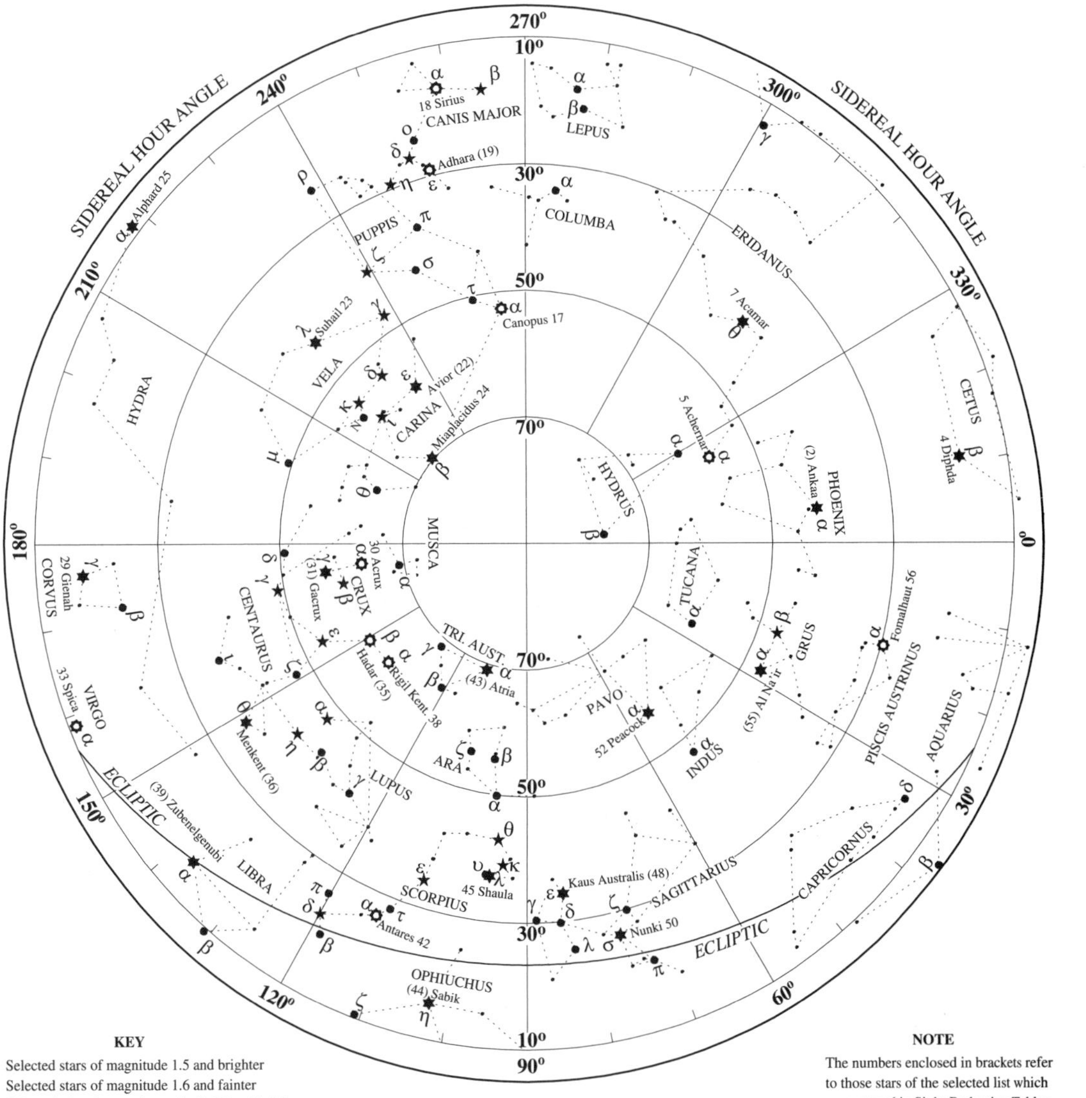

(Circular polar star chart centred on the south celestial pole, showing Sidereal Hour Angle around the circumference and Declination rings at 10°, 30°, 50°, 70°.)

Constellations and stars labelled include: CANIS MAJOR (α, β, 18 Sirius, Adhara (19)), LEPUS (α, β, γ), COLUMBA, ERIDANUS (7 Acamar), CETUS (4 Diphda), PUPPIS (ρ, π, ζ, σ, τ), VELA (λ, Suhail 23, κ), CARINA (δ, ε, Avior (22), Miaplacidus 24, β), Canopus 17, HYDRA, CORVUS (γ, β, 29 Gienah), VIRGO (33 Spica, 29), PHOENIX ((2) Ankaa, α), HYDRUS (α, β), TUCANA, GRUS (α, β, γ), PISCIS AUSTRINUS (α, Fomalhaut 56), AQUARIUS, CENTAURUS (δ, γ, ε, Menkent (36), β, α, γ, Hadar (35), Rigil Kent. 38), CRUX (30 Acrux, (31) Gacrux, β), MUSCA, TRI AUST ((43) Atria), PAVO (α), INDUS (α, β), 52 Peacock, 55 Al Na'ir, LUPUS, ARA (ζ, β, θ), SCORPIUS (π, δ, α, Antares 42, ε, 45 Shaula, υ, κ), LIBRA (α, β, (39) Zubenelgenubi), SAGITTARIUS (γ, δ, ε, ζ, Kaus Australis (48), λ, σ, Nunki 50, π), CAPRICORNUS (δ, β), OPHIUCHUS ((44) Sabik, ζ, η), ECLIPTIC.

SIDEREAL HOUR ANGLE

EQUATORIAL STARS (SHA 180° to 360°)

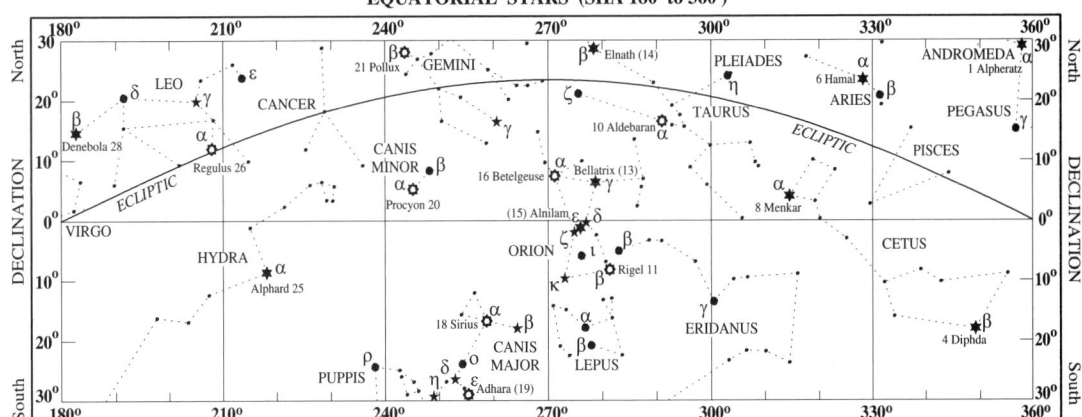

Constellations and stars labelled include: LEO (β, γ, ε, δ, α, Denebola 28, Regulus 26), CANCER, GEMINI (β, 21 Pollux, γ), CANIS MINOR (α, β, Procyon 20), VIRGO, HYDRA (α, Alphard 25), PUPPIS (ρ, η, ε), CANIS MAJOR (18 Sirius, α, β, Adhara (19)), ORION (16 Betelgeuse, Bellatrix (13), γ, (15) Alnilam, ζ, ε, δ, ι, β, Rigel 11, κ), LEPUS (α, β, γ), ζ, Elnath (14), PLEIADES, TAURUS (10 Aldebaran), ARIES (6 Hamal, η, β), ANDROMEDA (1 Alpheratz), PEGASUS (γ), PISCES, CETUS (8 Menkar, α, 4 Diphda, β), ERIDANUS (γ), ECLIPTIC.

SIDEREAL HOUR ANGLE

Mag.	Name and Number		SHA °	JAN.	FEB.	MAR.	APR.	MAY	JUNE	Dec. °	JAN.	FEB.	MAR.	APR.	MAY	JUNE
3·2	γ Cephei		4	60·9	61·5	61·7	61·4	60·8	59·9	N 77	43·0	42·9	42·7	42·6	42·5	42·5
2·5	α Pegasi	57	13	38·1	38·1	38·1	38·0	37·8	37·6	N 15	17·0	16·9	16·9	16·8	16·9	17·0
2·4	β Pegasi		13	53·2	53·2	53·2	53·1	52·9	52·6	N 28	09·7	09·6	09·6	09·5	09·5	09·6
1·2	α Piscis Aust.	56	15	23·8	23·8	23·8	23·7	23·5	23·2	S 29	32·9	32·9	32·8	32·7	32·6	32·5
2·1	β Gruis		19	07·8	07·8	07·8	07·6	07·4	07·0	S 46	48·8	48·7	48·5	48·4	48·3	48·2
2·9	α Tucanæ		25	08·7	08·8	08·7	08·4	08·1	07·7	S 60	11·4	11·3	11·2	11·0	10·9	10·8
1·7	α Gruis	55	27	43·6	43·6	43·5	43·4	43·1	42·8	S 46	53·6	53·5	53·4	53·3	53·2	53·1
2·9	δ Capricorni		33	02·9	02·9	02·8	02·7	02·5	02·2	S 16	03·8	03·7	03·7	03·6	03·6	03·5
2·4	ε Pegasi	54	33	47·0	47·0	46·9	46·7	46·5	46·3	N 9	56·5	56·4	56·4	56·4	56·5	56·6
2·9	β Aquarii		36	55·7	55·6	55·6	55·4	55·2	54·9	S 5	30·5	30·5	30·5	30·4	30·4	30·3
2·4	α Cephei		40	16·7	16·7	16·6	16·2	15·8	15·5	N 62	39·0	38·8	38·7	38·6	38·6	38·7
2·5	ε Cygni		48	18·5	18·5	18·3	18·1	17·9	17·6	N 34	01·6	01·4	01·3	01·3	01·4	01·5
1·3	α Cygni	53	49	31·6	31·6	31·4	31·2	30·9	30·6	N 45	20·0	19·9	19·8	19·7	19·8	19·9
3·1	α Indi		50	22·1	22·0	21·8	21·6	21·2	20·9	S 47	14·5	14·4	14·3	14·2	14·1	14·1
1·9	α Pavonis	52	53	19·2	19·1	18·9	18·5	18·1	17·8	S 56	41·3	41·2	41·0	41·0	40·9	40·9
2·2	γ Cygni		54	19·3	19·2	19·0	18·8	18·5	18·3	N 40	18·3	18·1	18·0	18·0	18·1	18·2
0·8	α Aquilæ	51	62	08·2	08·1	07·9	07·7	07·5	07·3	N 8	54·5	54·4	54·4	54·4	54·5	54·6
2·7	γ Aquilæ		63	16·3	16·2	16·0	15·8	15·6	15·4	N 10	39·0	38·9	38·9	38·9	39·0	39·1
2·9	δ Cygni		63	39·1	39·0	38·8	38·6	38·3	38·1	N 45	10·1	09·9	09·8	09·8	09·9	10·0
3·1	β Cygni		67	10·9	10·8	10·6	10·4	10·2	10·0	N 27	59·5	59·4	59·3	59·3	59·4	59·5
2·9	π Sagittarii		72	21·2	21·1	20·9	20·6	20·4	20·2	S 20	59·9	59·9	59·9	59·9	59·8	59·8
3·0	ζ Aquilæ		73	29·4	29·2	29·0	28·8	28·6	28·5	N 13	53·2	53·1	53·1	53·1	53·2	53·3
2·6	ζ Sagittarii		74	07·6	07·5	07·3	07·0	06·8	06·6	S 29	51·4	51·4	51·4	51·3	51·3	51·3
2·0	σ Sagittarii	50	75	58·2	58·0	57·8	57·6	57·3	57·1	S 26	16·6	16·6	16·5	16·5	16·5	16·5
0·0	α Lyræ	49	80	39·1	38·9	38·7	38·4	38·2	38·1	N 38	47·9	47·8	47·7	47·7	47·8	48·0
2·8	λ Sagittarii		82	47·6	47·4	47·2	47·0	46·8	46·6	S 25	24·6	24·6	24·6	24·6	24·6	24·6
1·9	ε Sagittarii	48	83	43·6	43·4	43·2	42·9	42·7	42·5	S 34	22·5	22·4	22·4	22·4	22·4	22·4
2·7	δ Sagittarii		84	31·8	31·6	31·4	31·1	30·9	30·7	S 29	49·1	49·1	49·1	49·1	49·1	49·1
3·0	γ Sagittarii		88	19·5	19·3	19·1	18·8	18·6	18·4	S 30	25·2	25·2	25·2	25·2	25·2	25·2
2·2	γ Draconis	47	90	46·4	46·2	45·9	45·6	45·4	45·3	N 51	29·3	29·1	29·1	29·1	29·2	29·4
2·8	β Ophiuchi		93	57·6	57·5	57·3	57·1	56·9	56·8	N 4	33·8	33·7	33·7	33·7	33·8	33·9
2·4	κ Scorpii		94	08·3	08·0	07·8	07·5	07·2	07·1	S 39	02·0	01·9	01·9	02·0	02·0	02·0
1·9	θ Scorpii		95	25·2	25·0	24·7	24·4	24·2	24·0	S 43	00·1	00·1	00·1	00·1	00·1	00·2
2·1	α Ophiuchi	46	96	06·4	06·2	06·0	05·8	05·6	05·5	N 12	33·1	33·0	33·0	33·0	33·1	33·2
1·6	λ Scorpii	45	96	21·7	21·5	21·2	20·9	20·7	20·5	S 37	06·6	06·6	06·6	06·6	06·6	06·7
3·0	α Aræ		96	46·3	46·0	45·7	45·3	45·1	44·9	S 49	52·9	52·9	52·9	52·9	53·0	53·0
2·7	υ Scorpii		97	04·3	04·1	03·8	03·6	03·4	03·2	S 37	18·2	18·1	18·2	18·2	18·2	18·2
2·8	β Draconis		97	19·2	18·9	18·6	18·3	18·1	18·0	N 52	17·4	17·3	17·3	17·3	17·4	17·6
2·8	β Aræ		98	23·2	22·8	22·5	22·1	21·8	21·6	S 55	32·3	32·2	32·2	32·2	32·3	32·4
Var.‡	α Herculis		101	10·8	10·6	10·4	10·2	10·1	10·0	N 14	22·5	22·4	22·4	22·4	22·5	22·6
2·4	η Ophiuchi	44	102	12·3	12·1	11·9	11·7	11·5	11·4	S 15	44·4	44·4	44·4	44·4	44·4	44·4
3·1	ζ Aræ		105	03·4	03·0	02·6	02·3	02·0	01·9	S 56	00·4	00·4	00·4	00·4	00·5	00·6
2·3	ε Scorpii		107	14·0	13·7	13·4	13·2	13·0	12·9	S 34	18·9	18·9	18·9	18·9	19·0	19·0
1·9	α Triang. Aust.	43	107	27·8	27·3	26·7	26·2	25·8	25·6	S 69	02·8	02·8	02·8	02·8	02·9	03·1
2·8	ζ Herculis		109	33·0	32·7	32·5	32·3	32·2	32·1	N 31	34·6	34·5	34·5	34·5	34·6	34·8
2·6	ζ Ophiuchi		110	31·1	30·8	30·6	30·4	30·3	30·2	S 10	35·6	35·6	35·7	35·7	35·7	35·6
2·8	τ Scorpii		110	48·7	48·4	48·2	48·0	47·8	47·7	S 28	14·5	14·5	14·5	14·6	14·6	14·6
2·8	β Herculis		112	17·8	17·6	17·3	17·1	17·0	17·0	N 21	27·5	27·4	27·4	27·5	27·6	27·7
1·0	α Scorpii	42	112	26·0	25·7	25·5	25·3	25·1	25·0	S 26	27·6	27·6	27·6	27·7	27·7	27·7
2·7	η Draconis		113	57·8	57·4	57·1	56·7	56·6	56·6	N 61	28·8	28·7	28·7	28·8	28·9	29·1
2·7	δ Ophiuchi		116	13·8	13·6	13·4	13·2	13·1	13·0	S 3	43·7	43·8	43·8	43·8	43·8	43·7
2·6	β Scorpii		118	26·2	25·9	25·7	25·5	25·4	25·3	S 19	50·5	50·5	50·5	50·6	50·6	50·6
2·3	δ Scorpii		119	42·5	42·3	42·0	41·9	41·7	41·6	S 22	39·5	39·6	39·6	39·6	39·7	39·7
2·9	π Scorpii		120	04·4	04·2	04·0	03·8	03·6	03·6	S 26	09·1	09·1	09·2	09·2	09·2	09·2
2·8	β Trianguli Aust.		120	54·1	53·7	53·2	52·9	52·6	52·5	S 63	28·1	28·1	28·1	28·2	28·3	28·5
2·6	α Serpentis		123	45·6	45·4	45·2	45·0	44·9	44·9	N 6	22·9	22·8	22·8	22·8	22·9	23·0
2·8	γ Lupi		125	58·8	58·5	58·2	58·0	57·8	57·8	S 41	12·6	12·6	12·7	12·7	12·8	12·9
2·2	α Coronæ Bor.	41	126	10·9	10·6	10·4	10·2	10·1	10·1	N 26	40·0	39·9	39·9	39·9	40·0	40·2

‡ 2·9 — 3·6

Mag.	Name and Number		SHA °	JULY	AUG.	SEPT.	OCT.	NOV.	DEC.	Declination °	JULY	AUG.	SEPT.	OCT.	NOV.	DEC.
3·2	γ Cephei		4	59·2	58·6	58·4	58·5	58·9	59·6	N 77	42·6	42·7	42·9	43·1	43·3	43·3
2·5	Markab	57	13	37·4	37·2	37·1	37·2	37·2	37·3	N 15	17·1	17·2	17·3	17·3	17·4	17·3
2·4	Scheat		13	52·4	52·2	52·1	52·2	52·3	52·4	N 28	09·7	09·9	10·0	10·1	10·1	10·1
1·2	Fomalhaut	56	15	23·0	22·8	22·7	22·7	22·9	23·0	S 29	32·4	32·4	32·5	32·5	32·6	32·6
2·1	β Gruis		19	06·8	06·6	06·5	06·6	06·7	06·9	S 46	48·2	48·2	48·3	48·4	48·5	48·5
2·9	α Tucanæ		25	07·3	07·1	07·0	07·2	07·4	07·7	S 60	10·9	10·9	11·1	11·2	11·3	11·3
1·7	Al Na'ir	55	27	42·5	42·3	42·3	42·4	42·6	42·7	S 46	53·1	53·1	53·2	53·3	53·4	53·4
2·9	δ Capricorni		33	02·0	01·9	01·9	02·0	02·1	02·2	S 16	03·4	03·4	03·4	03·4	03·5	03·5
2·4	Enif	54	33	46·1	46·0	46·0	46·1	46·2	46·3	N 9	56·7	56·8	56·8	56·9	56·9	56·8
2·9	β Aquarii		36	54·8	54·7	54·7	54·7	54·9	54·9	S 5	30·2	30·1	30·1	30·1	30·1	30·2
2·4	Alderamin		40	15·2	15·1	15·2	15·5	15·8	16·1	N 62	38·9	39·1	39·2	39·3	39·4	39·3
2·5	ε Cygni		48	17·5	17·4	17·5	17·6	17·8	17·9	N 34	01·6	01·8	01·9	02·0	02·0	01·9
1·3	Deneb	53	49	30·5	30·4	30·5	30·7	30·9	31·1	N 45	20·1	20·2	20·4	20·5	20·5	20·4
3·1	α Indi		50	20·7	20·6	20·7	20·9	21·1	21·2	S 47	14·1	14·2	14·3	14·3	14·4	14·3
1·9	Peacock	52	53	17·5	17·5	17·5	17·8	18·0	18·2	S 56	41·0	41·1	41·2	41·2	41·3	41·2
2·2	γ Cygni		54	18·2	18·1	18·2	18·4	18·6	18·7	N 40	18·4	18·5	18·6	18·7	18·7	18·6
0·8	Altair	51	62	07·2	07·1	07·2	07·3	07·5	07·5	N 8	54·7	54·7	54·8	54·8	54·8	54·7
2·7	γ Aquilæ		63	15·3	15·3	15·3	15·5	15·6	15·7	N 10	39·2	39·3	39·3	39·3	39·3	39·2
2·9	δ Cygni		63	38·0	38·0	38·1	38·3	38·5	38·7	N 45	10·2	10·3	10·5	10·5	10·5	10·4
3·1	Albireo		67	09·9	09·9	10·0	10·2	10·3	10·4	N 27	59·7	59·8	59·9	59·9	59·9	59·8
2·9	π Sagittarii		72	20·1	20·1	20·2	20·3	20·5	20·5	S 20	59·8	59·8	59·8	59·8	59·8	59·8
3·0	ζ Aquilæ		73	28·4	28·4	28·5	28·6	28·7	28·8	N 13	53·4	53·5	53·5	53·5	53·5	53·4
2·6	ζ Sagittarii		74	06·5	06·5	06·6	06·7	06·8	06·9	S 29	51·3	51·3	51·4	51·4	51·4	51·3
2·0	Nunki	50	75	57·0	57·0	57·1	57·3	57·4	57·4	S 26	16·5	16·5	16·5	16·5	16·5	16·5
0·0	Vega	49	80	38·0	38·1	38·2	38·4	38·6	38·7	N 38	48·1	48·2	48·3	48·3	48·3	48·1
2·8	λ Sagittarii		82	46·5	46·5	46·6	46·8	46·9	46·9	S 25	24·6	24·6	24·6	24·6	24·6	24·6
1·9	Kaus Australis	48	83	42·4	42·5	42·6	42·7	42·9	42·9	S 34	22·4	22·5	22·5	22·5	22·5	22·4
2·7	δ Sagittarii		84	30·6	30·7	30·8	30·9	31·0	31·1	S 29	49·1	49·1	49·1	49·1	49·1	49·1
3·0	γ Sagittarii		88	18·4	18·4	18·5	18·7	18·8	18·8	S 30	25·2	25·2	25·3	25·3	25·2	25·2
2·2	Eltanin	47	90	45·3	45·4	45·7	45·9	46·1	46·2	N 51	29·5	29·7	29·7	29·7	29·6	29·5
2·8	β Ophiuchi		93	56·7	56·8	56·9	57·0	57·1	57·1	N 4	33·9	34·0	34·0	34·0	34·0	33·9
2·4	κ Scorpii		94	07·0	07·1	07·2	07·4	07·5	07·5	S 39	02·1	02·1	02·1	02·1	02·1	02·0
1·9	θ Scorpii		95	23·9	24·0	24·2	24·4	24·5	24·5	S 43	00·3	00·3	00·3	00·3	00·3	00·2
2·1	Rasalhague	46	96	05·4	05·5	05·6	05·8	05·9	05·9	N 12	33·2	33·3	33·3	33·3	33·3	33·2
1·6	Shaula	45	96	20·5	20·6	20·7	20·9	21·0	21·0	S 37	06·7	06·7	06·7	06·7	06·7	06·6
3·0	α Aræ		96	44·8	44·9	45·1	45·3	45·5	45·4	S 49	53·1	53·2	53·2	53·2	53·1	53·0
2·7	υ Scorpii		97	03·2	03·2	03·4	03·5	03·6	03·6	S 37	18·3	18·3	18·3	18·3	18·3	18·2
2·8	β Draconis		97	18·1	18·2	18·5	18·7	18·9	19·0	N 52	17·8	17·9	17·9	17·9	17·8	17·6
2·8	β Aræ		98	21·6	21·7	21·9	22·2	22·3	22·3	S 55	32·5	32·6	32·6	32·5	32·5	32·4
Var.‡	α Herculis		101	09·9	10·0	10·2	10·3	10·4	10·4	N 14	22·7	22·8	22·8	22·8	22·7	22·6
2·4	Sabik	44	102	11·4	11·4	11·6	11·7	11·8	11·7	S 15	44·4	44·4	44·3	44·3	44·3	44·4
3·1	ζ Aræ		105	01·8	02·0	02·2	02·5	02·6	02·5	S 56	00·7	00·8	00·8	00·7	00·6	00·5
2·3	ε Scorpii		107	12·9	13·0	13·1	13·3	13·3	13·3	S 34	19·1	19·1	19·1	19·0	19·0	19·0
1·9	Atria	43	107	25·7	25·9	26·3	26·7	26·9	26·8	S 69	03·2	03·3	03·3	03·2	03·1	03·0
2·8	ζ Herculis		109	32·1	32·2	32·4	32·6	32·7	32·6	N 31	34·9	35·0	35·0	34·9	34·8	34·7
2·6	ζ Ophiuchi		110	30·2	30·3	30·4	30·5	30·6	30·5	S 10	35·6	35·6	35·6	35·6	35·6	35·6
2·8	τ Scorpii		110	47·7	47·8	47·9	48·1	48·1	48·0	S 28	14·6	14·6	14·6	14·6	14·6	14·6
2·8	β Herculis		112	17·0	17·1	17·2	17·4	17·4	17·4	N 21	27·8	27·8	27·9	27·8	27·7	27·6
1·0	Antares	42	112	25·0	25·1	25·3	25·4	25·4	25·4	S 26	27·7	27·7	27·7	27·7	27·7	27·6
2·7	η Draconis		113	56·7	57·0	57·4	57·7	57·8	57·8	N 61	29·2	29·3	29·3	29·2	29·1	28·9
2·7	δ Ophiuchi		116	13·0	13·1	13·2	13·3	13·4	13·3	S 3	43·7	43·7	43·7	43·7	43·7	43·8
2·6	β Scorpii		118	25·3	25·4	25·6	25·7	25·7	25·6	S 19	50·6	50·6	50·6	50·5	50·5	50·5
2·3	Dschubba		119	41·7	41·8	41·9	42·0	42·0	41·9	S 22	39·7	39·7	39·6	39·6	39·6	39·6
2·9	π Scorpii		120	03·6	03·7	03·8	03·9	03·9	03·8	S 26	09·3	09·3	09·2	09·2	09·2	09·2
2·8	β Trianguli Aust.		120	52·6	52·9	53·2	53·4	53·5	53·3	S 63	28·6	28·6	28·6	28·5	28·4	28·3
2·6	α Serpentis		123	44·9	45·0	45·2	45·3	45·3	45·2	N 6	23·0	23·1	23·1	23·0	23·0	22·9
2·8	γ Lupi		125	57·8	58·0	58·1	58·2	58·3	58·1	S 41	12·9	12·9	12·9	12·8	12·8	12·7
2·2	Alphecca	41	126	10·2	10·3	10·5	10·6	10·6	10·5	N 26	40·2	40·3	40·3	40·2	40·1	40·0

‡ 2·9 — 3·6

Mag.	Name and Number		SHA °	JAN.	FEB.	MAR.	APR.	MAY	JUNE	Declination °	JAN.	FEB.	MAR.	APR.	MAY	JUNE
3·1	γ Ursæ Minoris		129	50·0	49·5	48·9	48·6	48·5	48·7	N 71	46·8	46·7	46·8	46·9	47·1	47·2
2·9	γ Trianguli Aust.		129	56·3	55·7	55·2	54·8	54·6	54·6	S 68	43·5	43·5	43·6	43·7	43·9	44·0
2·6	β Libræ		130	33·5	33·3	33·1	32·9	32·8	32·8	S 9	26·0	26·1	26·1	26·1	26·1	26·1
2·7	β Lupi		135	08·0	07·7	07·4	07·3	07·1	07·1	S 43	11·2	11·2	11·3	11·4	11·5	11·6
2·8	α Libræ	39	137	05·1	04·8	04·6	04·5	04·4	04·4	S 16	05·9	06·0	06·0	06·1	06·1	06·1
2·1	β Ursæ Minoris	40	137	20·6	20·0	19·4	19·1	19·0	19·3	N 74	05·6	05·6	05·6	05·8	05·9	06·1
2·4	ε Bootis		138	36·0	35·8	35·6	35·5	35·4	35·4	N 27	00·8	00·7	00·7	00·8	00·9	01·0
2·3	α Lupi		139	16·8	16·5	16·2	16·0	15·9	15·9	S 47	26·6	26·7	26·8	26·9	27·0	27·1
−0·3	α Centauri	38	139	51·2	50·8	50·5	50·2	50·1	50·2	S 60	53·2	53·3	53·4	53·5	53·7	53·8
2·3	η Centauri		140	53·8	53·5	53·2	53·1	53·0	53·0	S 42	12·9	13·0	13·1	13·2	13·3	13·3
3·0	γ Bootis		141	50·4	50·2	49·9	49·8	49·8	49·8	N 38	14·6	14·6	14·6	14·7	14·8	14·9
0·0	α Bootis	37	145	55·4	55·2	55·0	54·9	54·9	54·9	N 19	06·4	06·4	06·4	06·4	06·5	06·6
2·1	θ Centauri	36	148	07·1	06·8	06·6	06·5	06·4	06·5	S 36	26·1	26·2	26·3	26·4	26·5	26·6
0·6	β Centauri	35	148	47·3	46·9	46·6	46·4	46·3	46·4	S 60	26·1	26·2	26·3	26·5	26·6	26·7
2·6	ζ Centauri		150	53·4	53·1	52·8	52·7	52·7	52·7	S 47	21·2	21·3	21·4	21·5	21·6	21·7
2·7	η Bootis		151	09·6	09·4	09·2	09·1	09·1	09·1	N 18	19·5	19·4	19·4	19·5	19·6	19·6
1·9	η Ursæ Majoris	34	152	58·7	58·4	58·1	58·0	58·0	58·2	N 49	14·3	14·3	14·3	14·5	14·6	14·7
2·3	ε Centauri		154	47·9	47·5	47·3	47·1	47·1	47·2	S 53	32·0	32·1	32·2	32·4	32·5	32·6
1·0	α Virginis	33	158	30·8	30·6	30·4	30·3	30·3	30·4	S 11	14·1	14·2	14·2	14·3	14·3	14·2
2·3	ζ Ursæ Majoris		158	52·7	52·4	52·1	52·1	52·1	52·3	N 54	50·8	50·8	50·9	51·0	51·2	51·3
2·8	ι Centauri		159	38·8	38·6	38·4	38·3	38·3	38·4	S 36	47·0	47·1	47·2	47·4	47·4	47·5
2·8	ε Virginis		164	16·7	16·5	16·3	16·3	16·3	16·3	N 10	52·9	52·8	52·8	52·8	52·9	52·9
2·9	α Canum Venat.		165	49·6	49·4	49·2	49·2	49·2	49·3	N 38	14·3	14·3	14·3	14·4	14·5	14·6
1·8	ε Ursæ Majoris	32	166	20·3	20·0	19·8	19·7	19·8	20·0	N 55	52·7	52·7	52·8	52·9	53·1	53·1
1·3	β Crucis		167	51·2	50·8	50·6	50·6	50·6	50·8	S 59	45·7	45·8	46·0	46·1	46·3	46·3
2·9	γ Virginis		169	24·2	24·0	23·9	23·8	23·8	23·9	S 1	31·7	31·8	31·8	31·8	31·8	31·8
2·2	γ Centauri		169	25·1	24·8	24·6	24·6	24·6	24·7	S 49	02·0	02·2	02·3	02·5	02·6	02·6
2·7	α Muscæ		170	28·7	28·2	28·0	27·9	28·0	28·3	S 69	12·5	12·7	12·8	13·0	13·1	13·2
2·7	β Corvi		171	12·8	12·6	12·4	12·4	12·4	12·5	S 23	28·4	28·5	28·6	28·7	28·8	28·8
1·6	γ Crucis	31	171	60·2	59·8	59·7	59·6	59·7	59·9	S 57	11·3	11·4	11·6	11·8	11·9	11·9
1·3	α Crucis	30	173	08·5	08·1	07·9	07·9	08·0	08·2	S 63	10·4	10·5	10·7	10·9	11·0	11·1
2·6	γ Corvi	29	175	51·7	51·5	51·4	51·4	51·4	51·5	S 17	37·2	37·3	37·4	37·5	37·5	37·5
2·6	δ Centauri		177	43·1	42·8	42·7	42·7	42·8	42·9	S 50	47·9	48·0	48·2	48·3	48·4	48·5
2·4	γ Ursæ Majoris		181	21·3	21·0	20·9	20·9	21·1	21·3	N 53	36·6	36·7	36·8	36·9	37·0	37·1
2·1	β Leonis	28	182	33·1	32·9	32·8	32·8	32·9	33·0	N 14	29·4	29·4	29·4	29·4	29·4	29·5
2·6	δ Leonis		191	16·9	16·7	16·6	16·7	16·8	16·8	N 20	26·5	26·5	26·5	26·6	26·6	26·7
3·0	ψ Ursæ Majoris		192	23·0	22·7	22·7	22·7	22·9	23·0	N 44	25·0	25·0	25·1	25·2	25·3	25·3
1·8	α Ursæ Majoris	27	193	50·9	50·6	50·5	50·6	50·8	51·1	N 61	40·1	40·2	40·3	40·5	40·6	40·6
2·4	β Ursæ Majoris		194	19·4	19·2	19·1	19·2	19·4	19·6	N 56	18·1	18·1	18·2	18·4	18·4	18·5
2·7	μ Velorum		198	08·7	08·5	08·5	08·6	08·8	08·9	S 49	29·6	29·8	30·0	30·1	30·2	30·2
2·8	θ Carinæ		199	07·2	07·0	06·9	07·1	07·4	07·7	S 64	28·0	28·2	28·4	28·5	28·6	28·6
2·3	γ Leonis		204	48·4	48·3	48·3	48·3	48·4	48·5	N 19	45·9	45·9	45·9	46·0	46·0	46·1
1·4	α Leonis	26	207	42·8	42·7	42·7	42·7	42·8	42·9	N 11	53·7	53·6	53·6	53·6	53·7	53·7
3·0	ε Leonis		213	19·9	19·8	19·8	19·9	20·0	20·1	N 23	42·3	42·3	42·3	42·4	42·4	42·4
3·1	N Velorum		217	04·5	04·4	04·4	04·7	04·9	05·1	S 57	05·8	06·0	06·2	06·3	06·3	06·3
2·0	α Hydræ	25	217	55·4	55·3	55·3	55·4	55·5	55·6	S 8	43·4	43·5	43·5	43·6	43·5	43·5
2·5	κ Velorum		219	21·0	20·9	21·0	21·2	21·4	21·7	S 55	04·3	04·5	04·6	04·7	04·8	04·7
2·2	ι Carinæ		220	37·2	37·1	37·2	37·4	37·7	38·0	S 59	20·1	20·3	20·5	20·6	20·6	20·6
1·7	β Carinæ	24	221	38·6	38·5	38·7	39·1	39·5	39·9	S 69	46·5	46·7	46·9	47·0	47·1	47·0
2·2	λ Velorum	23	222	51·7	51·6	51·7	51·8	52·0	52·2	S 43	29·5	29·6	29·8	29·9	29·9	29·8
3·1	ι Ursæ Majoris		224	57·0	56·9	56·9	57·1	57·3	57·4	N 47	58·9	58·9	59·0	59·1	59·1	59·1
2·0	δ Velorum		228	42·8	42·8	43·0	43·2	43·4	43·7	S 54	45·7	45·9	46·1	46·1	46·2	46·1
1·9	ε Carinæ	22	234	17·1	17·1	17·3	17·6	17·9	18·2	S 59	33·4	33·6	33·7	33·8	33·8	33·7
1·8	γ Velorum		237	29·8	29·9	30·0	30·2	30·4	30·6	S 47	22·9	23·0	23·1	23·2	23·2	23·1
2·8	ρ Puppis		237	57·3	57·3	57·4	57·5	57·7	57·8	S 24	20·9	21·0	21·1	21·2	21·1	21·1
2·3	ζ Puppis		238	58·2	58·2	58·3	58·5	58·7	58·8	S 40	02·8	02·9	03·0	03·1	03·1	03·0
1·1	β Geminorum	21	243	26·8	26·8	26·9	27·1	27·2	27·2	N 27	59·3	59·3	59·3	59·3	59·3	59·3
0·4	α Canis Minoris	20	244	58·9	58·9	59·0	59·2	59·3	59·3	N 5	11·1	11·0	11·0	11·0	11·0	11·1

Mag.	Name and Number		SHA							Declination					
				JULY	AUG.	SEPT.	OCT.	NOV.	DEC.		JULY	AUG.	SEPT.	OCT.	NOV.	DEC.
			°	′	′	′	′	′	′	°	′	′	′	′	′	′
3·1	γ Ursæ Minoris		129	49·0	49·5	50·1	50·5	50·6	50·5	N 71	47·3	47·3	47·3	47·1	47·0	46·8
2·9	γ Trianguli Aust.		129	54·8	55·1	55·5	55·8	55·8	55·5	S 68	44·1	44·1	44·1	44·0	43·8	43·7
2·6	β Libræ		130	32·8	32·9	33·1	33·1	33·1	33·0	S 9	26·1	26·0	26·0	26·0	26·0	26·1
2·7	β Lupi		135	07·2	07·4	07·5	07·6	07·6	07·4	S 43	11·6	11·6	11·5	11·5	11·4	11·3
2·8	Zubenelgenubi	39	137	04·4	04·5	04·7	04·7	04·7	04·5	S 16	06·1	06·0	06·0	06·0	06·0	06·0
2·1	Kochab	40	137	19·8	20·4	20·9	21·3	21·4	21·2	N 74	06·1	06·1	06·1	05·9	05·7	05·5
2·4	ε Bootis		138	35·5	35·6	35·8	35·9	35·8	35·7	N 27	01·1	01·1	01·1	01·0	00·9	00·7
2·3	α Lupi		139	16·0	16·2	16·4	16·4	16·4	16·2	S 47	27·1	27·1	27·1	27·0	26·9	26·8
−0·3	Rigil Kent.	38	139	50·4	50·6	50·9	51·0	51·0	50·7	S 60	53·8	53·8	53·8	53·6	53·5	53·4
2·3	η Centauri		140	53·1	53·2	53·4	53·4	53·4	53·2	S 42	13·4	13·4	13·3	13·2	13·1	13·1
3·0	γ Bootis		141	49·9	50·1	50·2	50·3	50·3	50·2	N 38	15·0	15·0	15·0	14·9	14·7	14·5
0·0	Arcturus	37	145	55·0	55·1	55·2	55·3	55·2	55·1	N 19	06·6	06·6	06·6	06·5	06·4	06·3
2·1	Menkent	36	148	06·5	06·7	06·8	06·9	06·8	06·6	S 36	26·6	26·5	26·5	26·4	26·3	26·3
0·6	Hadar	35	148	46·6	46·8	47·0	47·1	47·0	46·7	S 60	26·8	26·8	26·7	26·5	26·4	26·4
2·6	ζ Centauri		150	52·8	53·0	53·2	53·2	53·1	52·9	S 47	21·7	21·7	21·6	21·5	21·4	21·4
2·7	η Bootis		151	09·2	09·3	09·4	09·5	09·4	09·2	N 18	19·7	19·7	19·7	19·6	19·5	19·4
1·9	Alkaid	34	152	58·3	58·5	58·7	58·7	58·7	58·5	N 49	14·8	14·7	14·7	14·5	14·3	14·2
2·3	ε Centauri		154	47·4	47·6	47·7	47·8	47·6	47·4	S 53	32·6	32·6	32·5	32·4	32·3	32·2
1·0	Spica	33	158	30·4	30·5	30·6	30·6	30·5	30·3	S 11	14·2	14·2	14·1	14·1	14·2	14·2
2·3	Mizar		158	52·5	52·7	52·8	52·9	52·8	52·6	N 54	51·3	51·3	51·1	51·0	50·8	50·6
2·8	ι Centauri		159	38·5	38·6	38·7	38·7	38·6	38·4	S 36	47·5	47·4	47·3	47·3	47·2	47·2
2·8	ε Virginis		164	16·4	16·5	16·6	16·6	16·5	16·3	N 10	53·0	53·0	53·0	52·9	52·8	52·7
2·9	Cor Caroli		165	49·5	49·6	49·7	49·7	49·6	49·3	N 38	14·6	14·6	14·5	14·4	14·2	14·1
1·8	Alioth	32	166	20·2	20·4	20·5	20·6	20·4	20·1	N 55	53·2	53·1	53·0	52·8	52·6	52·5
1·3	Mimosa		167	51·0	51·2	51·4	51·4	51·2	50·8	S 59	46·4	46·3	46·2	46·0	45·9	45·9
2·9	γ Virginis		169	24·0	24·1	24·1	24·1	24·0	23·8	S 1	31·7	31·7	31·7	31·7	31·8	31·9
2·2	Muhlifain		169	24·9	25·1	25·2	25·1	25·0	24·7	S 49	02·6	02·5	02·4	02·3	02·2	02·2
2·7	α Muscæ		170	28·7	29·0	29·2	29·2	28·9	28·4	S 69	13·2	13·2	13·0	12·9	12·8	12·7
2·7	β Corvi		171	12·6	12·7	12·7	12·7	12·6	12·3	S 23	28·7	28·7	28·6	28·6	28·6	28·6
1·6	Gacrux	31	171	60·1	60·3	60·4	60·3	60·1	59·8	S 57	11·9	11·9	11·7	11·6	11·5	11·5
1·3	Acrux	30	173	08·4	08·7	08·8	08·8	08·5	08·1	S 63	11·1	11·0	10·9	10·7	10·6	10·6
2·6	Gienah	29	175	51·6	51·7	51·7	51·7	51·5	51·3	S 17	37·4	37·4	37·3	37·3	37·3	37·4
2·6	δ Centauri		177	43·1	43·3	43·3	43·3	43·1	42·7	S 50	48·5	48·4	48·2	48·1	48·1	48·1
2·4	Phecda		181	21·4	21·6	21·6	21·6	21·3	21·0	N 53	37·1	37·0	36·8	36·7	36·5	36·4
2·1	Denebola	28	182	33·0	33·1	33·1	33·1	32·9	32·7	N 14	29·5	29·5	29·5	29·4	29·3	29·2
2·6	δ Leonis		191	16·9	17·0	17·0	16·9	16·7	16·4	N 20	26·7	26·7	26·6	26·5	26·4	26·3
3·0	ψ Ursæ Majoris		192	23·1	23·2	23·2	23·1	22·8	22·5	N 44	25·3	25·2	25·1	25·0	24·8	24·7
1·8	Dubhe	27	193	51·3	51·4	51·4	51·3	50·9	50·5	N 61	40·5	40·4	40·2	40·1	39·9	39·8
2·4	Merak		194	19·8	19·9	19·8	19·7	19·4	19·0	N 56	18·4	18·3	18·2	18·0	17·9	17·8
2·7	μ Velorum		198	09·1	09·2	09·2	09·0	08·7	08·4	S 49	30·1	30·0	29·8	29·7	29·7	29·8
2·8	θ Carinæ		199	07·9	08·1	08·1	07·9	07·5	07·1	S 64	28·6	28·4	28·3	28·2	28·1	28·1
2·3	Algeiba		204	48·6	48·6	48·5	48·4	48·2	47·9	N 19	46·1	46·0	46·0	45·9	45·8	45·7
1·4	Regulus	26	207	43·0	43·0	42·9	42·8	42·6	42·3	N 11	53·7	53·7	53·7	53·6	53·6	53·5
3·0	ε Leonis		213	20·1	20·1	20·0	19·8	19·6	19·4	N 23	42·4	42·4	42·3	42·2	42·1	42·1
3·1	N Velorum		217	05·3	05·3	05·2	05·0	04·6	04·3	S 57	06·2	06·0	05·9	05·8	05·8	05·9
2·0	Alphard	25	217	55·6	55·6	55·5	55·4	55·1	54·9	S 8	43·4	43·4	43·3	43·3	43·4	43·5
2·5	κ Velorum		219	21·8	21·8	21·7	21·5	21·1	20·8	S 55	04·6	04·5	04·3	04·3	04·3	04·4
2·2	ι Carinæ		220	38·1	38·2	38·0	37·8	37·4	37·0	S 59	20·4	20·3	20·1	20·1	20·1	20·2
1·7	Miaplacidus	24	221	40·2	40·3	40·1	39·7	39·2	38·7	S 69	46·9	46·7	46·6	46·5	46·5	46·6
2·2	Suhail	23	222	52·2	52·2	52·1	51·9	51·6	51·4	S 43	29·7	29·6	29·5	29·4	29·4	29·5
3·1	ι Ursæ Majoris		224	57·5	57·4	57·2	57·0	56·7	56·3	N 47	59·0	58·9	58·8	58·7	58·6	58·6
2·0	δ Velorum		228	43·8	43·7	43·6	43·3	43·0	42·7	S 54	46·0	45·8	45·7	45·6	45·6	45·8
1·9	Avior	22	234	18·3	18·2	18·0	17·7	17·3	17·0	S 59	33·6	33·4	33·3	33·2	33·3	33·4
1·8	γ Velorum		237	30·6	30·5	30·4	30·1	29·8	29·6	S 47	23·0	22·8	22·7	22·7	22·7	22·8
2·8	ρ Puppis		237	57·8	57·7	57·5	57·3	57·1	56·9	S 24	21·0	20·8	20·8	20·8	20·8	20·9
2·3	ζ Puppis		238	58·8	58·8	58·6	58·4	58·1	57·9	S 40	02·8	02·7	02·6	02·6	02·6	02·8
1·1	Pollux	21	243	27·2	27·1	26·9	26·7	26·4	26·2	N 27	59·3	59·3	59·2	59·2	59·1	59·1
0·4	Procyon	20	244	59·3	59·2	59·0	58·8	58·6	58·4	N 5	11·1	11·1	11·1	11·1	11·1	11·0

Mag.	Name and Number		SHA							Declination					
			JAN.	FEB.	MAR.	APR.	MAY	JUNE		JAN.	FEB.	MAR.	APR.	MAY	JUNE
		°	′	′	′	′	′	′	°	′	′	′	′	′	′
1·6	α Geminorum	246	07·1	07·0	07·1	07·3	07·4	07·5	N 31	51·2	51·2	51·2	51·3	51·3	51·2
3·3	σ Puppis	247	34·2	34·3	34·4	34·7	34·8	34·9	S 43	20·0	20·2	20·3	20·3	20·3	20·2
2·9	β Canis Minoris	248	00·8	00·8	00·9	01·0	01·1	01·2	N 8	15·4	15·4	15·4	15·4	15·4	15·4
2·4	η Canis Majoris	248	49·7	49·7	49·8	50·0	50·2	50·2	S 29	20·1	20·2	20·3	20·3	20·3	20·2
2·7	π Puppis	250	34·8	34·9	35·0	35·2	35·4	35·5	S 37	07·6	07·7	07·8	07·9	07·8	07·7
1·8	δ Canis Majoris	252	45·0	45·1	45·2	45·4	45·5	45·5	S 26	25·2	25·3	25·4	25·4	25·3	25·2
3·0	o Canis Majoris	254	05·3	05·3	05·5	05·6	05·8	05·8	S 23	51·5	51·6	51·7	51·7	51·6	51·5
1·5	ε Canis Majoris 19	255	11·8	11·8	12·0	12·2	12·3	12·3	S 28	59·7	59·9	59·9	59·9	59·9	59·8
2·9	τ Puppis	257	25·1	25·2	25·4	25·7	25·9	26·0	S 50	38·1	38·3	38·4	38·4	38·3	38·2
−1·5	α Canis Majoris 18	258	33·0	33·0	33·2	33·3	33·4	33·4	S 16	44·4	44·5	44·5	44·5	44·5	44·4
1·9	γ Geminorum	260	21·6	21·7	21·8	21·9	22·0	22·0	N 16	23·0	23·0	23·0	23·0	23·0	23·0
−0·7	α Carinæ 17	263	55·4	55·6	55·8	56·1	56·3	56·4	S 52	42·5	42·6	42·7	42·7	42·6	42·5
2·0	β Canis Majoris	264	09·7	09·8	09·9	10·1	10·2	10·3	S 17	58·1	58·1	58·2	58·2	58·1	58·0
2·6	θ Aurigæ	269	49·2	49·3	49·4	49·6	49·7	49·7	N 37	12·6	12·7	12·7	12·7	12·6	12·6
1·9	β Aurigæ	269	50·9	51·0	51·2	51·4	51·5	51·5	N 44	56·8	56·8	56·8	56·8	56·8	56·7
Var.‡	α Orionis 16	271	00·5	00·6	00·7	00·8	00·9	00·9	N 7	24·3	24·3	24·3	24·3	24·3	24·4
2·1	κ Orionis	272	53·2	53·3	53·4	53·5	53·6	53·6	S 9	40·1	40·2	40·2	40·2	40·2	40·1
1·9	ζ Orionis	274	37·5	37·6	37·7	37·8	37·9	37·9	S 1	56·4	56·4	56·4	56·4	56·4	56·3
2·6	α Columbæ	274	57·2	57·3	57·4	57·6	57·7	57·7	S 34	04·3	04·4	04·4	04·4	04·3	04·2
3·0	ζ Tauri	275	22·2	22·3	22·4	22·5	22·6	22·6	N 21	08·9	08·9	08·9	08·9	08·9	08·8
1·7	ε Orionis 15	275	45·6	45·7	45·8	46·0	46·0	46·0	S 1	11·8	11·9	11·9	11·9	11·8	11·8
2·8	ι Orionis	275	57·7	57·8	57·9	58·1	58·1	58·1	S 5	54·3	54·4	54·4	54·4	54·3	54·2
2·6	α Leporis	276	39·3	39·4	39·5	39·7	39·8	39·7	S 17	49·0	49·1	49·1	49·1	49·0	48·9
2·2	δ Orionis	276	48·7	48·7	48·9	49·0	49·1	49·0	S 0	17·6	17·6	17·6	17·6	17·6	17·5
2·8	β Leporis	277	46·8	46·9	47·1	47·2	47·3	47·3	S 20	45·2	45·3	45·3	45·3	45·2	45·1
1·7	β Tauri 14	278	11·7	11·8	12·0	12·1	12·2	12·1	N 28	37·0	37·0	37·0	37·0	37·0	36·9
1·6	γ Orionis 13	278	31·3	31·3	31·5	31·6	31·7	31·6	N 6	21·5	21·5	21·5	21·5	21·5	21·5
0·1	α Aurigæ 12	280	33·4	33·5	33·7	33·9	34·0	33·9	N 46	00·6	00·7	00·7	00·6	00·6	00·5
0·1	β Orionis 11	281	11·4	11·4	11·6	11·7	11·8	11·7	S 8	11·4	11·4	11·5	11·4	11·4	11·3
2·8	β Eridani	282	51·5	51·5	51·7	51·8	51·9	51·8	S 5	04·3	04·4	04·4	04·4	04·3	04·3
2·7	ι Aurigæ	285	30·8	30·9	31·0	31·2	31·2	31·2	N 33	11·2	11·2	11·2	11·2	11·1	11·1
0·9	α Tauri 10	290	48·6	48·7	48·8	49·0	49·0	48·9	N 16	32·1	32·1	32·1	32·1	32·1	32·1
2·9	ε Persei	300	17·5	17·6	17·8	17·9	17·9	17·8	N 40	03·0	03·0	03·0	03·0	02·9	02·8
3·0	γ Eridani	300	19·4	19·5	19·6	19·7	19·8	19·7	S 13	28·4	28·4	28·4	28·4	28·3	28·2
2·9	ζ Persei	301	14·2	14·4	14·5	14·6	14·6	14·5	N 31	55·5	55·5	55·4	55·4	55·4	55·3
2·9	η Tauri	302	54·7	54·8	55·0	55·1	55·1	55·0	N 24	08·8	08·8	08·8	08·8	08·7	08·8
1·8	α Persei 9	308	39·4	39·6	39·8	39·9	39·9	39·7	N 49	54·7	54·7	54·7	54·6	54·5	54·5
Var.§	β Persei	312	43·2	43·4	43·5	43·6	43·6	43·4	N 41	00·6	00·6	00·6	00·5	00·4	00·4
2·5	α Ceti 8	314	14·5	14·6	14·7	14·8	14·7	14·6	N 4	08·6	08·5	08·5	08·5	08·6	08·6
3·2	θ Eridani 7	315	17·9	18·1	18·2	18·3	18·3	18·2	S 40	15·2	15·3	15·2	15·1	14·9	14·8
2·0	α Ursæ Minoris	317	24·5	37·2	48·6	55·1	53·8	45·8	N 89	19·7	19·7	19·7	19·5	19·4	19·3
3·0	β Trianguli	327	23·9	24·0	24·2	24·2	24·1	23·9	N 35	03·3	03·3	03·2	03·1	03·1	03·1
2·0	α Arietis 6	328	00·2	00·3	00·4	00·4	00·4	00·2	N 23	31·8	31·7	31·7	31·6	31·6	31·7
2·3	γ Andromedæ	328	48·1	48·3	48·4	48·5	48·4	48·1	N 42	24·0	23·9	23·9	23·8	23·7	23·7
2·9	α Hydri	330	11·9	12·1	12·4	12·5	12·4	12·2	S 61	30·4	30·4	30·3	30·1	30·0	29·8
2·6	β Arietis	331	08·5	08·6	08·7	08·7	08·6	08·4	N 20	52·6	52·6	52·5	52·5	52·5	52·5
0·5	α Eridani 5	335	26·5	26·8	26·9	27·0	26·9	26·7	S 57	10·3	10·2	10·1	09·9	09·8	09·6
2·7	δ Cassiopeiæ	338	18·4	18·6	18·8	18·9	18·7	18·3	N 60	18·8	18·7	18·6	18·5	18·4	18·3
2·1	β Andromedæ	342	21·9	22·1	22·1	22·1	22·0	21·8	N 35	41·9	41·8	41·7	41·6	41·6	41·6
Var.‖	γ Cassiopeiæ	345	36·2	36·4	36·6	36·5	36·3	36·0	N 60	47·9	47·8	47·7	47·5	47·4	47·4
2·0	β Ceti 4	348	55·6	55·6	55·7	55·7	55·5	55·3	S 17	54·7	54·7	54·7	54·6	54·5	54·3
2·2	α Cassiopeiæ 3	349	40·1	40·3	40·4	40·3	40·1	39·8	N 56	37·1	37·1	36·9	36·8	36·7	36·7
2·4	α Phœnicis 2	353	15·5	15·6	15·6	15·6	15·4	15·2	S 42	14·0	13·9	13·8	13·7	13·5	13·4
2·8	β Hydri	353	23·8	24·4	24·6	24·6	24·2	23·5	S 77	10·8	10·7	10·5	10·3	10·2	10·0
2·8	γ Pegasi	356	30·5	30·6	30·6	30·6	30·4	30·2	N 15	15·8	15·7	15·7	15·7	15·7	15·8
2·3	β Cassiopeiæ	357	30·8	31·0	31·1	31·0	30·7	30·4	N 59	13·9	13·8	13·7	13·6	13·5	13·5
2·1	α Andromedæ 1	357	43·2	43·2	43·3	43·2	43·0	42·8	N 29	10·2	10·2	10·1	10·0	10·0	10·1

‡ 0·1 — 1·2   § 2·1 — 3·4   ‖ Irregular variable; 2012 mag. 2·1

Mag.	Name and Number		SHA							Declination					
			JULY	AUG.	SEPT.	OCT.	NOV.	DEC.		JULY	AUG.	SEPT.	OCT.	NOV.	DEC.
		°	′	′	′	′	′	′	°	′	′	′	′	′	′
1·6	*Castor*	246	07·4	07·3	07·1	06·9	06·6	06·4	N 31	51·2	51·2	51·1	51·1	51·0	51·0
3·3	σ Puppis	247	34·9	34·8	34·6	34·4	34·1	33·9	S 43	20·0	19·9	19·8	19·8	19·8	20·0
2·9	β Canis Minoris	248	01·1	01·0	00·8	00·6	00·4	00·2	N 8	15·4	15·5	15·5	15·4	15·4	15·3
2·4	η Canis Majoris	248	50·2	50·1	49·9	49·7	49·5	49·3	S 29	20·0	19·9	19·8	19·8	19·9	20·0
2·7	π Puppis	250	35·4	35·3	35·1	34·9	34·6	34·5	S 37	07·6	07·4	07·3	07·3	07·4	07·6
1·8	*Wezen*	252	45·5	45·4	45·2	45·0	44·8	44·6	S 26	25·1	25·0	24·9	24·9	25·0	25·1
3·0	o Canis Majoris	254	05·8	05·6	05·5	05·2	05·0	04·8	S 23	51·4	51·3	51·2	51·2	51·3	51·5
1·5	*Adhara* 19	255	12·3	12·2	12·0	11·8	11·5	11·3	S 28	59·7	59·5	59·5	59·5	59·5	59·7
2·9	τ Puppis	257	26·0	25·8	25·6	25·3	25·0	24·8	S 50	38·0	37·9	37·8	37·8	37·9	38·0
−1·5	*Sirius* 18	258	33·4	33·3	33·1	32·8	32·6	32·5	S 16	44·3	44·2	44·2	44·2	44·3	44·4
1·9	*Alhena*	260	21·9	21·8	21·6	21·4	21·1	21·0	N 16	23·0	23·0	23·0	23·0	23·0	22·9
−0·7	*Canopus* 17	263	56·3	56·2	55·9	55·6	55·3	55·1	S 52	42·3	42·1	42·1	42·1	42·2	42·3
2·0	*Mirzam*	264	10·1	10·0	09·8	09·6	09·3	09·2	S 17	57·9	57·8	57·8	57·8	57·9	58·0
2·6	θ Aurigæ	269	49·5	49·3	49·1	48·8	48·5	48·4	N 37	12·6	12·5	12·5	12·5	12·5	12·6
1·9	*Menkalinan*	269	51·3	51·1	50·8	50·5	50·2	50·0	N 44	56·6	56·6	56·6	56·6	56·6	56·7
Var.‡	*Betelgeuse* 16	270	60·8	60·6	60·4	60·2	60·0	59·9	N 7	24·4	24·5	24·5	24·5	24·4	24·4
2·1	κ Orionis	272	53·5	53·3	53·1	52·9	52·7	52·6	S 9	40·0	39·9	39·9	39·9	40·0	40·1
1·9	*Alnitak*	274	37·8	37·6	37·4	37·2	37·0	36·9	S 1	56·2	56·2	56·1	56·1	56·2	56·3
2·6	*Phact*	274	57·6	57·5	57·2	57·0	56·8	56·7	S 34	04·0	03·9	03·9	03·9	04·0	04·2
3·0	ζ Tauri	275	22·5	22·3	22·0	21·8	21·6	21·5	N 21	08·9	08·9	08·9	08·9	08·9	08·9
1·7	*Alnilam* 15	275	45·9	45·7	45·5	45·3	45·1	45·0	S 1	11·7	11·6	11·6	11·6	11·7	11·7
2·8	ι Orionis	275	58·0	57·8	57·6	57·4	57·2	57·1	S 5	54·2	54·1	54·0	54·1	54·1	54·2
2·6	α Leporis	276	39·6	39·5	39·2	39·0	38·8	38·7	S 17	48·8	48·7	48·7	48·7	48·8	48·9
2·2	δ Orionis	276	48·9	48·7	48·5	48·3	48·1	48·0	S 0	17·4	17·4	17·3	17·4	17·4	17·5
2·8	β Leporis	277	47·2	47·0	46·8	46·6	46·4	46·3	S 20	45·0	44·9	44·8	44·8	44·9	45·0
1·7	*Elnath* 14	278	12·0	11·8	11·5	11·3	11·1	10·9	N 28	36·9	36·9	37·0	37·0	37·0	37·0
1·6	*Bellatrix* 13	278	31·5	31·3	31·1	30·9	30·7	30·6	N 6	21·6	21·7	21·7	21·7	21·6	21·6
0·1	*Capella* 12	280	33·7	33·5	33·1	32·8	32·6	32·4	N 46	00·5	00·4	00·4	00·5	00·5	00·6
0·1	*Rigel* 11	281	11·6	11·4	11·2	11·0	10·8	10·7	S 8	11·2	11·1	11·1	11·1	11·2	11·3
2·8	β Eridani	282	51·7	51·5	51·3	51·1	50·9	50·8	S 5	04·2	04·1	04·1	04·1	04·1	04·2
2·7	ι Aurigæ	285	31·0	30·8	30·5	30·3	30·1	29·9	N 33	11·1	11·1	11·1	11·1	11·2	11·2
0·9	*Aldebaran* 10	290	48·8	48·5	48·3	48·1	47·9	47·9	N 16	32·1	32·2	32·2	32·2	32·2	32·2
2·9	ε Persei	300	17·5	17·3	17·0	16·7	16·6	16·5	N 40	02·8	02·9	02·9	03·0	03·1	03·1
3·0	γ Eridani	300	19·5	19·3	19·1	18·9	18·8	18·7	S 13	28·1	28·0	28·0	28·0	28·1	28·1
2·9	ζ Persei	301	14·3	14·0	13·8	13·6	13·4	13·4	N 31	55·3	55·4	55·4	55·5	55·5	55·6
2·9	*Alcyone*	302	54·8	54·5	54·3	54·1	54·0	53·9	N 24	08·8	08·8	08·9	08·9	09·0	09·0
1·8	*Mirfak* 9	308	39·5	39·1	38·8	38·6	38·4	38·4	N 49	54·4	54·5	54·5	54·6	54·7	54·8
Var.§	*Algol*	312	43·1	42·9	42·6	42·4	42·3	42·2	N 41	00·4	00·5	00·5	00·6	00·7	00·8
2·5	*Menkar* 8	314	14·4	14·2	14·0	13·8	13·7	13·7	N 4	08·7	08·8	08·8	08·9	08·8	08·8
3·2	*Acamar* 7	315	18·0	17·7	17·5	17·3	17·2	17·3	S 40	14·6	14·6	14·6	14·7	14·8	14·9
2·0	*Polaris*	316	93·1	78·4	64·9	55·2	51·1	55·0	N 89	19·2	19·2	19·3	19·5	19·6	19·8
3·0	β Trianguli	327	23·6	23·4	23·2	23·0	23·0	23·0	N 35	03·1	03·2	03·3	03·4	03·5	03·5
2·0	*Hamal* 6	327	59·9	59·7	59·5	59·4	59·3	59·3	N 23	31·7	31·8	31·9	32·0	32·0	32·0
2·3	*Almak*	328	47·9	47·6	47·3	47·2	47·1	47·2	N 42	23·7	23·8	23·9	24·0	24·1	24·2
2·9	α Hydri	330	11·9	11·5	11·1	11·0	11·0	11·2	S 61	29·7	29·7	29·7	29·9	30·0	30·1
2·6	*Sheratan*	331	08·2	07·9	07·7	07·6	07·6	07·6	N 20	52·6	52·7	52·8	52·9	52·9	52·9
0·5	*Achernar* 5	335	26·4	26·0	25·7	25·6	25·6	25·8	S 57	09·5	09·5	09·6	09·7	09·8	10·0
2·7	*Ruchbah*	338	17·9	17·5	17·3	17·1	17·1	17·2	N 60	18·4	18·5	18·6	18·8	18·9	19·0
2·1	*Mirach*	342	21·5	21·2	21·1	21·0	21·0	21·0	N 35	41·7	41·8	41·9	42·0	42·1	42·1
Var.‖	γ Cassiopeiæ	345	35·6	35·2	34·9	34·8	34·9	35·1	N 60	47·5	47·6	47·7	47·9	48·0	48·1
2·0	*Diphda* 4	348	55·1	54·9	54·7	54·7	54·7	54·8	S 17	54·2	54·2	54·2	54·2	54·3	54·4
2·2	*Schedar* 3	349	39·4	39·1	38·9	38·8	38·9	39·0	N 56	36·8	36·9	37·1	37·2	37·4	37·4
2·4	*Ankaa* 2	353	14·9	14·7	14·5	14·5	14·5	14·7	S 42	13·3	13·3	13·4	13·5	13·6	13·7
2·8	β Hydri	353	22·7	22·0	21·6	21·6	21·9	22·5	S 77	10·0	10·0	10·2	10·3	10·5	10·5
2·8	*Algenib*	356	29·9	29·7	29·6	29·6	29·6	29·7	N 15	15·9	16·0	16·1	16·1	16·1	16·1
2·3	*Caph*	357	30·0	29·7	29·5	29·5	29·6	29·8	N 59	13·6	13·7	13·9	14·1	14·2	14·3
2·1	*Alpheratz* 1	357	42·5	42·3	42·2	42·2	42·2	42·3	N 29	10·2	10·3	10·4	10·5	10·6	10·6

‡ 0·1 — 1·2   § 2·1 — 3·4   ‖ Irregular variable; 2012 mag. 2·1

POLARIS (POLE STAR) TABLES, 2014
FOR DETERMINING LATITUDE FROM SEXTANT ALTITUDE AND FOR AZIMUTH

LHA ARIES	0° – 9°	10° – 19°	20° – 29°	30° – 39°	40° – 49°	50° – 59°	60° – 69°	70° – 79°	80° – 89°	90° – 99°	100° – 109°	110° – 119°
°	a_0	a_0	a_0	a_0	a_0	a_0	a_0	a_0	a_0	a_0	a_0	a_0
0	0 29·1	0 24·8	0 21·5	0 19·3	0 18·3	0 18·6	0 20·2	0 22·9	0 26·7	0 31·5	0 37·2	0 43·:
1	28·6	24·4	21·2	19·1	18·3	18·7	20·4	23·2	27·2	32·1	37·8	44·
2	28·2	24·0	20·9	19·0	18·3	18·9	20·6	23·6	27·6	32·6	38·4	44·8
3	27·7	23·7	20·7	18·9	18·3	19·0	20·9	23·9	28·1	33·2	39·0	45·
4	27·3	23·3	20·4	18·8	18·3	19·1	21·1	24·3	28·5	33·7	39·6	46·
5	0 26·8	0 23·0	0 20·2	0 18·7	0 18·3	0 19·3	0 21·4	0 24·7	0 29·0	0 34·3	0 40·3	0 46·8
6	26·4	22·6	20·0	18·6	18·4	19·4	21·7	25·1	29·5	34·8	40·9	47·:
7	26·0	22·3	19·8	18·5	18·4	19·6	22·0	25·5	30·0	35·4	41·5	48·2
8	25·6	22·0	19·6	18·4	18·5	19·8	22·3	25·9	30·5	36·0	42·2	48·
9	25·2	21·7	19·5	18·4	18·6	20·0	22·6	26·3	31·0	36·6	42·8	49·
10	0 24·8	0 21·5	0 19·3	0 18·3	0 18·6	0 20·2	0 22·9	0 26·7	0 31·5	0 37·2	0 43·5	0 50·2

Lat.	a_1	a_1	a_1	a_1	a_1	a_1	a_1	a_1	a_1	a_1	a_1	a_1
°	′	′	′	′	′	′	′	′	′	′	′	′
0	0·5	0·5	0·6	0·6	0·6	0·6	0·6	0·5	0·5	0·4	0·4	0·3
10	·5	·5	·6	·6	·6	·6	·6	·5	·5	·4	·4	·4
20	·5	·6	·6	·6	·6	·6	·6	·5	·5	·5	·4	·4
30	·5	·6	·6	·6	·6	·6	·6	·6	·5	·5	·5	·5
40	0·6	0·6	0·6	0·6	0·6	0·6	0·6	0·6	0·6	0·5	0·5	0·5
45	·6	·6	·6	·6	·6	·6	·6	·6	·6	·6	·6	·6
50	·6	·6	·6	·6	·6	·6	·6	·6	·6	·6	·6	·6
55	·6	·6	·6	·6	·6	·6	·6	·6	·6	·6	·6	·7
60	·6	·6	·6	·6	·6	·6	·6	·6	·7	·7	·7	·7
62	0·7	0·6	0·6	0·6	0·6	0·6	0·6	0·6	0·7	0·7	0·7	0·7
64	·7	·6	·6	·6	·6	·6	·6	·7	·7	·7	·8	·8
66	·7	·7	·6	·6	·6	·6	·6	·7	·7	·8	·8	·8
68	0·7	0·7	0·6	0·6	0·6	0·6	0·6	0·7	0·7	0·8	0·8	0·9

Month	a_2	a_2	a_2	a_2	a_2	a_2	a_2	a_2	a_2	a_2	a_2	a_2
	′	′	′	′	′	′	′	′	′	′	′	′
Jan.	0·8	0·8	0·8	0·8	0·8	0·8	0·8	0·8	0·8	0·7	0·7	0·7
Feb.	·7	·7	·8	·8	·8	·9	·9	·9	·9	·9	·8	·8
Mar.	·5	·6	·7	·7	·8	·8	·9	·9	·9	·9	·9	0·9
Apr.	0·4	0·5	0·5	0·6	0·6	0·7	0·8	0·8	0·9	0·9	0·9	1·0
May	·3	·3	·4	·4	·5	·6	·6	·7	·7	·8	·9	0·9
June	·2	·3	·3	·3	·4	·4	·5	·5	·6	·7	·7	·8
July	0·3	0·3	0·3	0·3	0·3	0·3	0·4	0·4	0·4	0·5	0·6	0·6
Aug.	·4	·4	·3	·3	·3	·3	·3	·3	·3	·4	·4	·5
Sept.	·6	·5	·5	·4	·4	·4	·3	·3	·3	·3	·3	·3
Oct.	0·8	0·7	0·7	0·6	0·5	0·5	0·4	0·4	0·3	0·3	0·3	0·3
Nov.	0·9	0·9	0·8	·8	·7	·7	·6	·5	·4	·4	·3	·3
Dec.	1·0	1·0	1·0	0·9	0·9	0·8	0·7	0·7	0·6	0·5	0·4	0·4

Lat.	AZIMUTH											
°	°	°	°	°	°	°	°	°	°	°	°	°
0	0·4	0·3	0·2	0·1	0·0	359·9	359·7	359·6	359·5	359·5	359·4	359·4
20	0·4	0·3	0·2	0·1	0·0	359·8	359·7	359·6	359·5	359·4	359·4	359·3
40	0·5	0·4	0·3	0·1	0·0	359·8	359·7	359·5	359·4	359·3	359·2	359·2
50	0·6	0·5	0·3	0·1	0·0	359·8	359·6	359·4	359·3	359·2	359·1	359·0
55	0·7	0·6	0·4	0·2	359·9	359·7	359·5	359·4	359·2	359·1	358·9	358·9
60	0·8	0·6	0·4	0·2	359·9	359·7	359·5	359·3	359·1	359·1	358·8	358·7
65	1·0	0·8	0·5	0·2	359·9	359·6	359·4	359·1	358·9	358·7	358·6	358·5

Latitude = Apparent altitude (corrected for refraction) $-1° + a_0 + a_1 + a_2$

The table is entered with LHA Aries to determine the column to be used; each column refers to a range of 10°. a_0 is taken, with mental interpolation, from the upper table with the units of LHA Aries in degrees as argument; a_1, a_2 are taken, without interpolation, from the second and third tables with arguments latitude and month respectively. a_0, a_1, a_2, are always positive. The final table gives the azimuth of *Polaris*.

LHA ARIES	120°–129°	130°–139°	140°–149°	150°–159°	160°–169°	170°–179°	180°–189°	190°–199°	200°–209°	210°–219°	220°–229°	230°–239°
	a_0	a_0	a_0	a_0	a_0	a_0	a_0	a_0	a_0	a_0	a_0	a_0
°	° ′	° ′	° ′	° ′	° ′	° ′	° ′	° ′	° ′	° ′	° ′	° ′
0	0 50·2	0 57·2	1 04·3	1 11·2	1 17·7	1 23·6	1 28·7	1 33·0	1 36·2	1 38·3	1 39·3	1 39·0
1	50·9	58·0	05·0	11·8	18·3	24·1	29·2	33·4	36·5	38·5	39·3	38·9
2	51·6	58·7	05·7	12·5	18·9	24·7	29·7	33·7	36·7	38·6	39·3	38·8
3	52·3	0 59·4	06·4	13·2	19·5	25·2	30·1	34·1	37·0	38·7	39·3	38·6
4	53·0	1 00·1	07·1	13·8	20·1	25·7	30·6	34·4	37·2	38·9	39·3	38·5
5	0 53·7	1 00·8	1 07·8	1 14·5	1 20·7	1 26·3	1 31·0	1 34·8	1 37·4	1 38·9	1 39·3	1 38·4
6	54·4	01·5	08·5	15·1	21·3	26·8	31·4	35·1	37·6	39·0	39·2	38·2
7	55·1	02·2	09·1	15·8	21·9	27·3	31·8	35·4	37·8	39·1	39·2	38·0
8	55·8	02·9	09·8	16·4	22·4	27·8	32·2	35·7	38·0	39·2	39·1	37·9
9	56·5	03·6	10·5	17·0	23·0	28·3	32·6	36·0	38·2	39·2	39·1	37·7
10	0 57·2	1 04·3	1 11·2	1 17·7	1 23·6	1 28·7	1 33·0	1 36·2	1 38·3	1 39·3	1 39·0	1 37·5

Lat.	a_1	a_1	a_1	a_1	a_1	a_1	a_1	a_1	a_1	a_1	a_1	a_1
°	′	′	′	′	′	′	′	′	′	′	′	′
0	0·3	0·3	0·3	0·4	0·4	0·4	0·5	0·5	0·6	0·6	0·6	0·6
10	·4	·4	·4	·4	·4	·5	·5	·5	·6	·6	·6	·6
20	·4	·4	·4	·4	·5	·5	·5	·6	·6	·6	·6	·6
30	·5	·5	·5	·5	·5	·5	·5	·6	·6	·6	·6	·6
40	0·5	0·5	0·5	0·5	0·5	0·6	0·6	0·6	0·6	0·6	0·6	0·6
45	·6	·6	·6	·6	·6	·6	·6	·6	·6	·6	·6	·6
50	·6	·6	·6	·6	·6	·6	·6	·6	·6	·6	·6	·6
55	·7	·7	·7	·6	·6	·6	·6	·6	·6	·6	·6	·6
60	·7	·7	·7	·7	·7	·7	·6	·6	·6	·6	·6	·6
62	0·8	0·8	0·8	0·7	0·7	0·7	0·7	0·6	0·6	0·6	0·6	0·6
64	·8	·8	·8	·8	·7	·7	·7	·6	·6	·6	·6	·6
66	·8	·9	·8	·8	·8	·7	·7	·7	·6	·6	·6	·6
68	0·9	0·9	0·9	0·9	0·8	0·8	0·7	0·7	0·6	0·6	0·6	0·6

Month	a_2	a_2	a_2	a_2	a_2	a_2	a_2	a_2	a_2	a_2	a_2	a_2
	′	′	′	′	′	′	′	′	′	′	′	′
Jan.	0·6	0·6	0·6	0·5	0·5	0·5	0·4	0·4	0·4	0·4	0·4	0·4
Feb.	·8	·7	·7	·7	·6	·6	·5	·5	·4	·4	·4	·3
Mar.	0·9	0·9	0·8	·8	·8	·7	·7	·6	·5	·5	·4	·4
Apr.	1·0	1·0	1·0	0·9	0·9	0·9	0·8	0·7	0·7	0·6	0·6	0·5
May	0·9	1·0	1·0	1·0	1·0	0·9	0·9	·9	·8	·8	·7	·6
June	·8	0·9	0·9	0·9	0·9	1·0	1·0	·9	·9	·9	·8	·8
July	0·7	0·7	0·8	0·8	0·9	0·9	0·9	0·9	0·9	0·9	0·9	0·9
Aug.	·5	·5	·6	·6	·7	·7	·8	·8	·9	·9	·9	·9
Sept.	·4	·4	·4	·5	·5	·6	·6	·7	·7	·8	·8	·8
Oct.	0·3	0·3	0·3	0·3	0·3	0·4	0·4	0·5	0·5	0·6	0·7	0·7
Nov.	·2	·2	·2	·2	·2	·2	·3	·3	·4	·4	·5	·5
Dec.	0·3	0·2	0·2	0·2	0·2	0·1	0·2	0·2	0·2	0·3	0·3	0·4

Lat.	AZIMUTH											
°	°	°	°	°	°	°	°	°	°	°	°	°
0	359·3	359·3	359·3	359·4	359·4	359·5	359·6	359·7	359·8	359·9	0·0	0·1
20	359·3	359·3	359·3	359·3	359·4	359·5	359·6	359·7	359·8	359·9	0·0	0·2
40	359·1	359·1	359·1	359·2	359·3	359·4	359·5	359·6	359·7	359·9	0·0	0·2
50	359·0	359·0	359·0	359·0	359·1	359·2	359·4	359·5	359·7	359·9	0·0	0·2
55	358·8	358·8	358·9	358·9	359·0	359·1	359·3	359·5	359·6	359·8	0·0	0·2
60	358·7	358·7	358·7	358·8	358·9	359·0	359·2	359·4	359·6	359·8	0·1	0·3
65	358·4	358·4	358·4	358·5	358·7	358·8	359·0	359·3	359·5	359·8	0·1	0·3

ILLUSTRATION

In 2014 April 21 at 3h 18m 56s UT in longitude W 37° 14′ the apparent altitude (corrected for refraction), H_O, of Polaris was 49° 31′·6

From the daily pages:	°	′
GHA Aries (23h)	194	56·2
Increment (18m 56s)	4	44·8
Longitude (west)	−37	14
LHA Aries	162	27

	°	′
H_O	49	31·6
a_0 (argument 162° 27′)	1	19·2
a_1 (Lat 50° approx.)		0·6
a_2 (April)		0·9
Sum − 1° = Lat =	49	52·3

POLARIS (POLE STAR) TABLES, 2014
FOR DETERMINING LATITUDE FROM SEXTANT ALTITUDE AND FOR AZIMUTH

LHA ARIES	240° – 249°	250° – 259°	260° – 269°	270° – 279°	280° – 289°	290° – 299°	300° – 309°	310° – 319°	320° – 329°	330° – 339°	340° – 349°	350° – 359
	a_0	a_0	a_0	a_0	a_0	a_0	a_0	a_0	a_0	a_0	a_0	a_0
°	° ′	° ′	° ′	° ′	° ′	° ′	° ′	° ′	° ′	° ′	° ′	° ′
0	I 37·5	I 34·8	I 31·1	I 26·4	I 20·8	I 14·6	I 07·9	I 00·9	0 53·9	0 46·9	0 40·4	0 34·
I	37·3	34·5	30·6	25·8	20·2	14·0	07·2	I 00·2	53·2	46·3	39·8	33·
2	37·0	34·2	30·2	25·3	19·6	13·3	06·5	0 59·5	52·5	45·6	39·1	33·
3	36·8	33·8	29·8	24·8	19·0	12·6	05·8	58·8	51·8	44·9	38·5	32·
4	36·5	33·4	29·3	24·2	18·4	12·0	05·1	58·1	51·1	44·3	37·9	32·
5	I 36·3	I 33·1	I 28·8	I 23·7	I 17·8	I 11·3	I 04·4	0 57·4	0 50·4	0 43·6	0 37·3	0 31·
6	36·0	32·7	28·4	23·1	17·2	10·6	03·7	56·7	49·7	43·0	36·7	31·
7	35·7	32·3	27·9	22·6	16·5	10·0	03·0	56·0	49·0	42·3	36·1	30·
8	35·4	31·9	27·4	22·0	15·9	09·3	02·3	55·3	48·3	41·7	35·5	30·
9	35·1	31·5	26·9	21·4	15·3	08·6	01·6	54·6	47·6	41·0	35·0	29·
10	I 34·8	I 31·1	I 26·4	I 20·8	I 14·6	I 07·9	I 00·9	0 53·9	0 46·9	0 40·4	0 34·4	0 29·

Lat.	a_1	a_1	a_1	a_1	a_1	a_1	a_1	a_1	a_1	a_1	a_1	a_1
°	′	′	′	′	′	′	′	′	′	′	′	′
0	0·6	0·5	0·5	0·4	0·4	0·3	0·3	0·3	0·3	0·4	0·4	0·4
10	·6	·5	·5	·4	·4	·4	·4	·4	·4	·4	·4	·5
20	·6	·5	·5	·5	·4	·4	·4	·4	·4	·4	·5	·5
30	·6	·6	·5	·5	·5	·5	·5	·5	·5	·5	·5	·5
40	0·6	0·6	0·6	0·5	0·5	0·5	0·5	0·5	0·5	0·5	0·5	0·6
45	·6	·6	·6	·6	·6	·6	·6	·6	·6	·6	·6	·6
50	·6	·6	·6	·6	·6	·6	·6	·6	·6	·6	·6	·6
55	·6	·6	·6	·6	·6	·7	·7	·7	·7	·6	·6	·6
60	·6	·6	·7	·7	·7	·7	·7	·7	·7	·7	·7	·7
62	0·6	0·6	0·7	0·7	0·7	0·7	0·8	0·8	0·8	0·7	0·7	0·7
64	·6	·7	·7	·7	·8	·8	·8	·8	·8	·8	·7	·7
66	·6	·7	·7	·8	·8	·8	·8	·9	·8	·8	·8	·7
68	0·6	0·7	0·7	0·8	0·8	0·9	0·9	0·9	0·9	0·9	0·8	0·8

Month	a_2	a_2	a_2	a_2	a_2	a_2	a_2	a_2	a_2	a_2	a_2	a_2
	′	′	′	′	′	′	′	′	′	′	′	′
Jan.	0·4	0·4	0·4	0·5	0·5	0·5	0·6	0·6	0·6	0·7	0·7	0·7
Feb.	·3	·3	·3	·3	·4	·4	·4	·5	·5	·5	·6	·6
Mar.	·3	·3	·3	·3	·3	·3	·3	·3	·4	·4	·4	·5
Apr.	0·4	0·4	0·3	0·3	0·3	0·2	0·2	0·2	0·2	0·3	0·3	0·3
May	·6	·5	·5	·4	·3	·3	·3	·2	·2	·2	·2	·3
June	·7	·7	·6	·5	·5	·4	·4	·3	·3	·3	·3	·2
July	0·8	0·8	0·8	0·7	0·6	0·6	0·5	0·5	0·4	0·4	0·3	0·3
Aug.	·9	·9	·9	·8	·8	·7	·7	·7	·6	·6	·5	·5
Sept.	·9	·9	·9	·9	·9	·9	·8	·8	·8	·7	·7	·6
Oct.	0·8	0·8	0·9	0·9	0·9	0·9	0·9	0·9	0·9	0·9	0·9	0·8
Nov.	·6	·7	·8	·8	·9	·9	1·0	1·0	1·0	1·0	1·0	1·0
Dec.	0·5	0·5	0·6	0·7	0·8	0·8	0·9	1·0	1·0	1·0	1·0	1·1

Lat.	AZIMUTH											
°	°	°	°	°	°	°	°	°	°	°	°	°
0	0·3	0·4	0·5	0·5	0·6	0·6	0·7	0·7	0·7	0·6	0·6	0·5
20	0·3	0·4	0·5	0·6	0·6	0·7	0·7	0·7	0·7	0·7	0·6	0·5
40	0·3	0·5	0·6	0·7	0·8	0·8	0·9	0·9	0·9	0·8	0·7	0·7
50	0·4	0·6	0·7	0·8	0·9	1·0	1·0	1·0	1·0	1·0	0·9	0·8
55	0·4	0·6	0·8	0·9	1·0	1·1	1·2	1·2	1·2	1·1	1·0	0·9
60	0·5	0·7	0·9	1·1	1·2	1·3	1·3	1·3	1·3	1·3	1·2	1·0
65	0·6	0·8	1·1	1·2	1·4	1·5	1·6	1·6	1·6	1·5	1·4	1·2

Latitude = Apparent altitude (corrected for refraction) $-1° + a_0 + a_1 + a_2$

The table is entered with LHA Aries to determine the column to be used; each column refers to a range of 10°. a_0 is taken, with mental interpolation, from the upper table with the units of LHA Aries in degrees as argument; a_1, a_2 are taken, without interpolation, from the second and third tables with arguments latitude and month respectively. a_0, a_1, a_2, are always positive. The final table gives the azimuth of *Polaris*.

SIGHT REDUCTION PROCEDURES

METHODS AND FORMULAE FOR DIRECT COMPUTATION

1. *Introduction.* In this section formulae and methods are provided for *calculating* position at sea from observed altitudes taken with a marine sextant using a computer or programmable calculator.

The method uses analogous concepts and similar terminology as that used in *manual* methods of astro-navigation, where position is found by plotting position lines from their intercept and azimuth on a marine chart.

The algorithms are presented in standard algebra suitable for translating into the programming language of the user's computer. The basic ephemeris data may be taken directly from the main tabular pages of a current version of *The Nautical Almanac*. Formulae are given for calculating altitude and azimuth from the *GHA* and *Dec* of a body, and the estimated position of the observer. Formulae are also given for reducing sextant observations to observed altitudes by applying the corrections for dip, refraction, parallax and semi-diameter.

The intercept and azimuth obtained from each observation determine a position line, and the observer should lie on or close to each position line. The method of least squares is used to calculate the fix by finding the position where the sum of the squares of the distances from the position lines is a minimum. The use of least squares has other advantages. For example it is possible to improve the estimated position at the time of fix by repeating the calculation. It is also possible to include more observations in the solution and to reject doubtful ones.

2. *Notation.*

GHA = Greenwich hour angle. The range of GHA is from $0°$ to $360°$ starting at $0°$ on the Greenwich meridian increasing to the west, back to $360°$ on the Greenwich meridian.

SHA = sidereal hour angle. The range is $0°$ to $360°$.

Dec = declination. The sign convention for declination is north is positive, south is negative. The range is from $-90°$ at the south celestial pole to $+90°$ at the north celestial pole.

$Long$ = longitude. The sign convention is east is positive, west is negative. The range is $-180°$ to $+180°$.

Lat = latitude. The sign convention is north is positive, south is negative. The range is from $-90°$ to $+90°$.

LHA = $GHA + Long$ = local hour angle. The LHA increases to the west from $0°$ on the local meridian to $360°$.

H_C = calculated altitude. Above the horizon is positive, below the horizon is negative. The range is from $-90°$ in the nadir to $+90°$ in the zenith.

H_S = sextant altitude.

H = apparent altitude = sextant altitude corrected for instrumental error and dip.

H_O = observed altitude = apparent altitude corrected for refraction and, in appropriate cases, corrected for parallax and semi-diameter.

Z = Z_n = true azimuth. Z is measured from true north through east, south, west and back to north. The range is from $0°$ to $360°$.

I = sextant index error.

D = dip of horizon.

R = atmospheric refraction.

HP = horizontal parallax of the Sun, Moon, Venus or Mars.
PA = parallax in altitude of the Sun, Moon, Venus or Mars.
SD = semi-diameter of the Sun or Moon.
p = intercept = $H_O - H_C$. Towards is positive, away is negative.
T = course or track, measured as for azimuth from the north.
V = speed in knots.

3. *Entering Basic Data.* When quantities such as *GHA* are entered, which in *The Nautical Almanac* are given in degrees and minutes, convert them to degrees and decimals of a degree by dividing the minutes by 60 and adding to the degrees; for example, if $GHA = 123°$ $45'6$, enter the two numbers 123 and 45·6 into the memory and set $GHA = 123 + 45·6/60 = 123°7600$. Although four decimal places of a degree are shown in the examples, it is assumed that full precision is maintained in the calculations.

When using a computer or programmable calculator, write a subroutine to convert degrees and minutes to degrees and decimals. Scientific calculators usually have a special key for this purpose. For quantities like *Dec* which require a minus sign for southern declination, change the sign from plus to minus after the value has been converted to degrees and decimals, e.g. $Dec = S\,0°\ 12'3 = S\,0°2050 = -0°2050$. Other quantities which require conversion are semi-diameter, horizontal parallax, longitude and latitude.

4. *Interpolation of GHA and Dec* The *GHA* and *Dec* of the Sun, Moon and planets are interpolated to the time of observation by direct calculation as follows: If the universal time is $a^h\ b^m\ c^s$, form the interpolation factor $x = b/60 + c/3600$. Enter the tabular value GHA_0 for the preceding hour (a) and the tabular value GHA_1 for the following hour ($a+1$) then the interpolated value *GHA* is given by

$$GHA = GHA_0 + x(GHA_1 - GHA_0)$$

If the *GHA* passes through 360° between tabular values add 360° to GHA_1 before interpolation. If the interpolated value exceeds 360°, subtract 360° from *GHA*.

Similarly for declination, enter the tabular value Dec_0 for the preceding hour (a) and the tabular value Dec_1 for the following hour ($a+1$), then the interpolated value *Dec* is given by
$$Dec = Dec_0 + x(Dec_1 - Dec_0)$$

5. *Example.* (a) Find the *GHA* and *Dec* of the Sun on 2014 March 6 at $13^h\ 47^m\ 13^s$ UT.

The interpolation factor $\quad x = 47/60 + 13/3600 = 0^h7869$

page 53 $\quad 13^h\ GHA_0 = 12°\ 11'3 = 12°1883$

$\quad 14^h\ GHA_1 = 27°\ 11'5 = 27°1917$

$\quad 13^h7869\ GHA = 12·1883 + 0·7869(27·1917 - 12·1883) = 23°9951$

$\quad 13^h\ Dec_0 = S\,5°\ 34'2 = -5°5700$

$\quad 14^h\ Dec_1 = S\,5°\ 33'2 = -5°5533$

$\quad 13^h7869\ Dec = -5·5700 + 0·7869(-5·5533 + 5·5700) = -5°5569$

GHA Aries is interpolated in the same way as *GHA* of a body. For a star the *SHA* and *Dec* are taken from the tabular page and do not require interpolation, then

$$GHA = GHA\ \text{Aries} + SHA$$

where *GHA* Aries is interpolated to the time of observation.

(b) Find the *GHA* and *Dec* of *Vega* on 2014 March 6 at 13^h 47^m 13^s UT.

The interpolation factor $x = 0\overset{h}{\cdot}7869$ as in the previous example

page 52 13^h *GHA* $\text{Aries}_0 = 359° \; 11\overset{'}{\cdot}2 = 359\overset{\circ}{\cdot}1867$

14^h *GHA* $\text{Aries}_1 = 14° \; 13\overset{'}{\cdot}6 = 374\overset{\circ}{\cdot}2267$ (360° added)

$13^h\cdot7869$ *GHA* Aries $= 359 \cdot 1867 + 0 \cdot 7869(374 \cdot 2267 - 359 \cdot 1867) = 371\overset{\circ}{\cdot}0223$

$SHA = 80° \; 38\overset{'}{\cdot}8 = 80\overset{\circ}{\cdot}6467$

$GHA = GHA \; \text{Aries} + SHA = 91\overset{\circ}{\cdot}6690$ (multiple of 360° removed)

$Dec = N \, 38° \; 47\overset{'}{\cdot}7 = +38\overset{\circ}{\cdot}7950$

6. *The calculated altitude and azimuth.*   The calculated altitude H_C and true azimuth Z are determined from the *GHA* and *Dec* interpolated to the time of observation and from the *Long* and *Lat* estimated at the time of observation as follows:

Step 1.   Calculate the local hour angle

$$LHA = GHA + Long$$

Add or subtract multiples of 360° to set *LHA* in the range 0° to 360°.

Step 2.   Calculate S, C and the altitude H_C from

$$S = \sin Dec$$
$$C = \cos Dec \; \cos LHA$$
$$H_C = \sin^{-1}(S \; \sin Lat + C \; \cos Lat)$$

where $\sin^{-1}$ is the inverse function of sine.

Step 3.   Calculate X and A from

$$X = (S \; \cos Lat - C \; \sin Lat)/\cos H_C$$
$$\text{If} \; X > +1 \quad \text{set} \quad X = +1$$
$$\text{If} \; X < -1 \quad \text{set} \quad X = -1$$
$$A = \cos^{-1} X$$

where $\cos^{-1}$ is the inverse function of cosine.

Step 4.   Determine the azimuth Z

$$\text{If} \; LHA > 180° \quad \text{then} \quad Z = A$$
$$\text{Otherwise} \quad Z = 360° - A$$

7. *Example.*   Find the calculated altitude H_C and azimuth Z when

$$GHA = 53° \quad Dec = S \, 15° \quad Lat = N \, 32° \quad Long = W \, 16°$$

For the calculation

$$GHA = 53\overset{\circ}{\cdot}0000 \quad Dec = -15\overset{\circ}{\cdot}0000 \quad Lat = +32\overset{\circ}{\cdot}0000 \quad Long = -16\overset{\circ}{\cdot}0000$$

Step 1. $LHA = 53 \cdot 0000 - 16 \cdot 0000 = 37 \cdot 0000$

Step 2. $S = -0 \cdot 2588$

$C = +0 \cdot 9659 \times 0 \cdot 7986 = 0 \cdot 7714$

$\sin H_C = -0 \cdot 2588 \times 0 \cdot 5299 + 0 \cdot 7714 \times 0 \cdot 8480 = 0 \cdot 5171$

$H_C = 31\overset{\circ}{\cdot}1346$

Step 3.
$$X = (-0.2588 \times 0.8480 - 0.7714 \times 0.5299)/0.8560 = -0.7340$$
$$A = 137°2239$$

Step 4.   Since $LHA \le 180°$ then $Z = 360° - A = 222°7761$

8. *Reduction from sextant altitude to observed altitude.*   The sextant altitude H_S is corrected for both dip and index error to produce the apparent altitude. The observed altitude H_O is calculated by applying a correction for refraction. For the Sun, Moon, Venus and Mars a correction for parallax is also applied to H, and for the Sun and Moon a further correction for semi-diameter is required. The corrections are calculated as follows:

Step 1.   Calculate dip

$$D = 0°0293\sqrt{h}$$

where h is the height of eye above the horizon in metres.

Step 2.   Calculate apparent altitude

$$H = H_S + I - D$$

where I is the sextant index error.

Step 3.   Calculate refraction (R) at a standard temperature of $10°$ Celsius (C) and pressure of 1010 millibars (mb)

$$R_0 = 0°0167/\tan(H + 7.32/(H + 4.32))$$

If the temperature $T°$ C and pressure P mb are known calculate the refraction from

$$R = f R_0 \qquad \text{where} \qquad f = 0.28P/(T + 273)$$
$$\text{otherwise set} \qquad R = R_0$$

Step 4.   Calculate the parallax in altitude (PA) from the horizontal parallax (HP) and the apparent altitude (H) for the Sun, Moon, Venus and Mars as follows:

$$PA = HP \cos H$$

For the Sun $HP = 0°0024$. This correction is very small and could be ignored.

For the Moon HP is taken for the nearest hour from the main tabular page and converted to degrees.

For Venus and Mars the HP is taken from the critical table at the bottom of page 259 and converted to degrees.

For the navigational stars and the remaining planets, Jupiter and Saturn set $PA = 0$.

If an error of $0'2$ is significant the expression for the parallax in altitude for the Moon should include a small correction OB for the oblateness of the Earth as follows:

$$PA = HP \cos H + OB$$
$$\text{where} \quad OB = -0°0032 \sin^2 Lat \cos H + 0°0032 \sin(2Lat) \cos Z \sin H$$

At mid-latitudes and for altitudes of the Moon below $60°$ a simple approximation to OB is

$$OB = -0°0017 \cos H$$

Step 5.   Calculate the semi-diameter for the Sun and Moon as follows:

Sun: *SD* is taken from the main tabular page and converted to degrees.

Moon: $SD = 0°2724HP$ where *HP* is taken for the nearest hour from the main tabular page and converted to degrees.

Step 6.   Calculate the observed altitude

$$H_O = H - R + PA \pm SD$$

where the plus sign is used if the lower limb of the Sun or Moon was observed and the minus sign if the upper limb was observed.

9. *Example.*   The following example illustrates how to use a calculator to reduce the sextant altitude (H_S) to observed altitude (H_O); the sextant altitudes given are assumed to be taken on 2014 March 9 with a marine sextant, zero index error, at height 5·4 m, temperature $-3°$ C and pressure 982 mb, the Moon sights are assumed to be taken at 10^h UT.

Body limb	Sun lower	Sun upper	Moon lower	Moon upper	Venus −	Polaris −
Sextant altitude: H_S	21·3283	3·3367	33·4600	26·1117	4·5433	49·6083
Step 1. Dip: $D = 0·0293\sqrt{h}$	0·0681	0·0681	0·0681	0·0681	0·0681	0·0681
Step 2. Apparent altitude: $H = H_S + I - D$	21·2602	3·2686	33·3919	26·0436	4·4752	49·5402
Step 3. Refraction: R_0	0·0423	0·2256	0·0251	0·0338	0·1798	0·0142
f	1·0184	1·0184	1·0184	1·0184	1·0184	1·0184
$R = fR_0$	0·0431	0·2298	0·0256	0·0344	0·1831	0·0144
Step 4. Parallax: HP			(54ʹ6) 0·9100	(54ʹ6) 0·9100	(0ʹ3) 0·0050	−
	0·0024	0·0024				
Parallax in altitude: $PA = HP\cos H$	0·0022	0·0024	0·7598	0·8176	0·0050	−
Step 5. Semi-diameter: Sun : $SD = 16·1/60$	0·2683	0·2683	−	−	−	−
Moon : $SD = 0·2724HP$	−	−	0·2479	0·2479	−	−
Step 6. Observed altitude: $H_O = H - R + PA \pm SD$	21·4877	2·7729	34·3740	26·5789	4·2971	49·5258

Note that for the Moon the correction for the oblateness of the Earth of about $-0°0017\cos H$, which equals $-0°0014$ for the lower limb and $-0°0015$ for the upper limb, has been ignored in the above calculation.

10. *Position from intercept and azimuth using a chart.*   An estimate is made of the position at the adopted time of fix. The position at the time of observation is then calculated by dead reckoning from the time of fix. For example if the course (track) *T* and the speed *V* (in knots) of the observer are constant then *Long* and *Lat* at the time of observation are calculated from

$$Long = L_F + t(V/60)\sin T/\cos B_F$$
$$Lat = B_F + t(V/60)\cos T$$

where L_F and B_F are the estimated longitude and latitude at the time of fix and t is the time interval in hours from the time of fix to the time of observation, t is positive if the time of observation is after the time of fix and negative if it was before.

The position line of an observation is plotted on a chart using the intercept

$$p = H_O - H_C$$

and azimuth Z with origin at the calculated position ($Long$, Lat) at the time of observation, where H_C and Z are calculated using the method in section 6, page 279. Starting from this calculated position a line is drawn on the chart along the direction of the azimuth to the body. Convert p to nautical miles by multiplying by 60. The position line is drawn at right angles to the azimuth line, distance p from ($Long$, Lat) towards the body if p is positive and distance p away from the body if p is negative. Provided there are no gross errors the navigator should be somewhere on or near the position line at the time of observation. Two or more position lines are required to determine a fix.

11. *Position from intercept and azimuth by calculation.* The position of the fix may be calculated from two or more sextant observations as follows.

If p_1, Z_1, are the intercept and azimuth of the first observation, p_2, Z_2, of the second observation and so on, form the summations

$$A = \cos^2 Z_1 + \cos^2 Z_2 + \cdots$$
$$B = \cos Z_1 \sin Z_1 + \cos Z_2 \sin Z_2 + \cdots$$
$$C = \sin^2 Z_1 + \sin^2 Z_2 + \cdots$$
$$D = p_1 \cos Z_1 + p_2 \cos Z_2 + \cdots$$
$$E = p_1 \sin Z_1 + p_2 \sin Z_2 + \cdots$$

where the number of terms in each summation is equal to the number of observations.

With $G = AC - B^2$, an improved estimate of the position at the time of fix (L_I, B_I) is given by

$$L_I = L_F + (AE - BD)/(G\cos B_F), \qquad B_I = B_F + (CD - BE)/G$$

Calculate the distance d between the initial estimated position (L_F, B_F) at the time of fix and the improved estimated position (L_I, B_I) in nautical miles from

$$d = 60\sqrt{((L_I - L_F)^2\cos^2 B_F + (B_I - B_F)^2)}$$

If d exceeds about 20 nautical miles set $L_F = L_I$, $B_F = B_I$ and repeat the calculation until d, the distance between the position at the previous estimate and the improved estimate, is less than about 20 nautical miles.

12. *Example of direct computation.* Using the method described above, calculate the position of a ship on 2014 June 28 at $21^h\ 00^m\ 00^s$ UT from the marine sextant observations of the three stars *Regulus* (No. 26) at $20^h\ 39^m\ 23^s$ UT, *Antares* (No. 42) at $20^h\ 45^m\ 47^s$ UT and *Kochab* (No. 40) at $21^h\ 10^m\ 34^s$ UT, where the observed altitudes of the three stars corrected for the effects of refraction, dip and instrumental error, are $32°0620$, $23°4185$ and $47°5156$ respectively. The ship was travelling at a constant speed of 20 knots on a course of 325° during the period of observation, and the position of the ship at the time of fix $21^h\ 00^m\ 00^s$ UT is only known to the nearest whole degree W 15°, N 32°.

Intermediate values for the first iteration are shown in the table. *GHA* Aries was interpolated from the nearest tabular values on page 128. For the first iteration set $L_F = -15°0000$, $B_F = +32°0000$ at the time of fix at 21^h 00^m 00^s UT.

First Iteration

Body No.	Regulus 26	Antares 42	Kochab 40
time of observation	20^h 39^m 23^s	20^h 45^m 47^s	21^h 10^m 34^s
H_O	32·0620	23·4185	47·5156
interpolation factor	0·6564	0·7631	0·1761
GHA Aries	226·7098	228·3143	234·5273
SHA (page 128)	207·7167	112·4167	137·3250
GHA	74·4265	340·7310	11·8523
Dec (page 128)	+11·8950	−26·4617	+74·1017
t	−0·3436	−0·2369	+0·1761
Long	−14·9225	−14·9466	−15·0397
Lat	+31·9062	+31·9353	+32·0481
Z	264·0766	146·8160	1·3022
H_C	32·0389	23·1127	47·9157
p	+0·0231	+0·3058	−0·4001

$$A = 1·7106 \quad B = -0·3327 \quad C = 1·2894 \quad D = -0·6583 \quad E = 0·1353 \quad G = 2·0950$$
$$(A\,E - B\,D)/(G\cos B_F) = +0·0070, \qquad (C\,D - B\,E)/G = -0·3837$$

An improved estimate of the position at the time of fix is

$$L_I = L_F + 0·0070 = -14·9930 \quad \text{and} \quad B_I = B_F - 0·3837 = +31·6163$$

Since the distance between the previous estimated position and the improved estimate $d = 23·0$ nautical miles set $L_F = -14·9930$, and $B_F = +31·6163$ and repeat the calculation. The table shows the intermediate values of the calculation for the second iteration. In each iteration the quantities H_O, *GHA*, *Dec* and *t* do not change.

Second Iteration

Body No.	Regulus 26	Antares 42	Kochab 40
Long	−14·9159	−14·9398	−15·0325
Lat	+31·5225	+31·5516	+31·6644
Z	264·3195	146·7312	1·2897
H_C	32·0721	23·4369	47·5322
p	−0·0100	−0·0183	−0·0166

$$A = 1·7084 \quad B = -0·3377 \quad C = 1·2916 \quad D = -0·0003 \quad E = -0·0004 \quad G = 2·0926$$
$$(A\,E - B\,D)/(G\cos B_F) = -0·0005, \qquad (C\,D - B\,E)/G = -0·0003$$

An improved estimate of the position at the time of fix is

$$L_I = L_F - 0·0005 = -14·9935 \quad \text{and} \quad B_I = B_F - 0·0003 = +31·6160$$

The distance between the previous estimated position and the improved estimated position $d = 0·03$ nautical miles is so small that a third iteration would produce a negligible improvement to the estimate of the position.

USE OF CONCISE SIGHT REDUCTION TABLES

1. *Introduction.*   The concise sight reduction tables given on pages 286 to 317 are intended for use when neither more extensive tables nor electronic computing aids are available. These "NAO sight reduction tables" provide for the reduction of the local hour angle and declination of a celestial object to azimuth and altitude, referred to an assumed position on the Earth, for use in the intercept method of celestial navigation which is now standard practice.

2. *Form of tables.*   Entries in the reduction table are at a fixed interval of one degree for all latitudes and hour angles. A compact arrangement results from division of the navigational triangle into two right spherical triangles, so that the table has to be entered twice. Assumed latitude and local hour angle are the arguments for the first entry. The reduction table responds with the intermediate arguments A, B, and Z_1, where A is used as one of the arguments for the second entry to the table, B has to be incremented by the declination to produce the quantity F, and Z_1 is a component of the azimuth angle. The reduction table is then reentered with A and F and yields H, P, and Z_2 where H is the altitude, P is the complement of the parallactic angle, and Z_2 is the second component of the azimuth angle. It is usually necessary to adjust the tabular altitude for the fractional parts of the intermediate entering arguments to derive computed altitude, and an auxiliary table is provided for the purpose. Rules governing signs of the quantities which must be added or subtracted are given in the instructions and summarized on each tabular page. Azimuth angle is the sum of two components and is converted to true azimuth by familiar rules, repeated at the bottom of the tabular pages.

Tabular altitude and intermediate quantities are given to the nearest minute of arc, although errors of $2'$ in computed altitude may accrue during adjustment for the minutes parts of entering arguments. Components of azimuth angle are stated to $0°1$; for derived true azimuth, only whole degrees are warranted. Since objects near the zenith are difficult to observe with a marine sextant, they should be avoided; altitudes greater than about $80°$ are not suited to reduction by this method.

In many circumstances the accuracy provided by these tables is sufficient. However, to maintain the full accuracy $(0'1)$ of the ephemeral data in the almanac throughout their reduction to altitude and azimuth, more extensive tables or a calculator should be used.

3. *Use of Tables.*

Step 1.   Determine the Greenwich hour angle (GHA) and Declination (Dec) of the body from the almanac. Select an assumed latitude (Lat) of integral degrees nearest to the estimated latitude. Choose an assumed longitude nearest to the estimated longitude such that the local hour angle

$$LHA = GHA \begin{array}{c} - \text{ west} \\ + \text{ east} \end{array} \text{longitude}$$

has integral degrees.

Step 2.   Enter the reduction table with Lat and LHA as arguments. Record the quantities A, B and Z_1. Apply the rules for the sign of B and Z_1: B is minus if $90° < LHA < 270°$: Z_1 has the same sign as B. Set $A° =$ nearest whole degree of A and $A' =$ minutes part of A. This step may be repeated for all reductions before leaving the latitude opening of the table.

Step 3.   Record the declination Dec. Apply the rules for the sign of Dec: Dec is minus if the name of Dec (*i.e.* N or S) is contrary to latitude. Add B and Dec algebraically to produce F. If F is negative, the object is below the horizon (in sight reduction, this can occur when the objects are close to the horizon). Regard F as positive until step 7. Set $F° =$ nearest whole degree of F and $F' =$ minutes part of F.

Step 4. Enter the reduction table a second time with $A°$ and $F°$ as arguments and record H, P, and Z_2. Set $P° = $ nearest whole degree of P and $Z_2° = $ nearest whole degree of Z_2.

Step 5. Enter the auxiliary table with F' and $P°$ as arguments to obtain $corr_1$ to H for F'. Apply the rule for the sign of $corr_1$: $corr_1$ is minus if $F < 90°$ and $F' > 29'$ or if $F > 90°$ and $F' < 30'$, otherwise $corr_1$ is plus.

Step 6. Enter the auxiliary table with A' and $Z_2°$ as arguments to obtain $corr_2$ to H for A'. Apply the rule for the sign of $corr_2$: $corr_2$ is minus if $A' < 30'$, otherwise $corr_2$ is plus.

Step 7. Calculate the computed altitude H_C as the sum of H, $corr_1$ and $corr_2$. Apply the rule for the sign of H_C: H_C is minus if F is negative.

Step 8. Apply the rule for the sign of Z_2: Z_2 is minus if $F > 90°$. If F is negative, replace Z_2 by $180° - Z_2$. Set the azimuth angle Z equal to the algebraic sum of Z_1 and Z_2 and ignore the resulting sign. Obtain the true azimuth Z_n from the rules

$$\begin{array}{llll} \text{For N latitude, if} & LHA > 180° & Z_n = Z \\ \text{if} & LHA < 180° & Z_n = 360° - Z \\ \\ \text{For S latitude, if} & LHA > 180° & Z_n = 180° - Z \\ \text{if} & LHA < 180° & Z_n = 180° + Z \end{array}$$

Observed altitude H_O is compared with H_C to obtain the altitude difference, which, with Z_n, is used to plot the position line.

4. *Example.* (a) Required the altitude and azimuth of *Schedar* on 2014 February 4 at UT 06^h 31^m from the estimated position 5° east, 53° north.

1. Assumed latitude $Lat = $ 53° N
    From the almanac $GHA = $ 221° 46'
    Assumed longitude   5° 14' E
    Local hour angle $LHA = $ 227

2. Reduction table, 1st entry
    $(Lat, LHA) = (53, 227)$ $A = $ 26 07 $A° = 26, A' = 7$
                                 $B = -27$ 12 $Z_1 = -49.4,$ $90° < LHA < 270°$

3. From the almanac $Dec = +56$ 37 Lat and Dec same
    Sum $ = B + Dec$ $F = +29$ 25 $F° = 29, F' = 25$

4. Reduction table, 2nd entry
    $(A°, F°) = (26, 29)$ $H = $ 25 50 $P° = 61$
                                                  $Z_2 = 76.3, Z_2° = 76$

5. Auxiliary table, 1st entry
    $(F', P°) = (25, 61)$ $corr_1 = $ $+22$ $F < 90°, F' < 29'$
    Sum   26 12

6. Auxiliary table, 2nd entry
    $(A', Z_2°) = (7, 76)$ $corr_2 = $ -2 $A' < 30'$

7. Sum $ = $ computed altitude $H_C = +26°$ 10' $F > 0°$

8. Azimuth, first component $Z_1 = -49.4$ same sign as B
           second component $Z_2 = +76.3$ $F < 90°, F > 0°$
    Sum $ = $ azimuth angle $Z = $ 26.9

    True azimuth $Z_n = 027°$ N Lat, $LHA > 180°$

continued on page 318

SIGHT REDUCTION TABLE

B: (−) for 90° < LHA < 270°
Dec:(−) for Lat. contrary name

Z₁: same sign as B
Z₂: (−) for F > 90°

LHA/F	0° A/H	0° B/P	0° Z₁/Z₂	1° A/H	1° B/P	1° Z₁/Z₂	2° A/H	2° B/P	2° Z₁/Z₂	3° A/H	3° B/P	3° Z₁/Z₂	4° A/H	4° B/P	4° Z₁/Z₂	5° A/H	5° B/P	5° Z₁/Z₂	Lat./A	LHA
0 180	0 00	90 00	90·0	0 00	89 00	90·0	0 00	88 00	90·0	0 00	87 00	90·0	0 00	86 00	90·0	0 00	85 00	90·0	180	360
1 179	1 00	90 00	90·0	1 00	89 00	90·0	1 00	88 00	90·0	1 00	87 00	89·9	1 00	86 00	89·9	1 00	85 00	89·9	181	359
2 178	2 00	90 00	90·0	2 00	89 00	90·0	2 00	88 00	89·9	2 00	87 00	89·9	2 00	86 00	89·9	2 00	85 00	89·8	182	358
3 177	3 00	90 00	90·0	3 00	89 00	89·9	3 00	88 00	89·9	3 00	87 00	89·9	3 00	86 00	89·8	2 59	85 00	89·7	183	357
4 176	4 00	90 00	90·0	4 00	89 00	89·9	4 00	88 00	89·9	4 00	87 00	89·9	3 59	85 59	89·8	3 59	84 59	89·7	184	356
5 175	5 00	90 00	90·0	5 00	89 00	89·8	5 00	88 00	89·8	5 00	86 59	89·7	4 59	85 59	89·7	4 59	84 59	89·6	185	355
6 174	6 00	90 00	90·0	6 00	89 00	89·9	6 00	87 59	89·8	6 00	86 59	89·7	5 59	85 59	89·6	5 59	84 58	89·5	186	354
7 173	7 00	90 00	90·0	7 00	89 00	89·9	7 00	87 59	89·8	6 59	86 59	89·6	6 59	85 58	89·5	6 58	84 58	89·4	187	353
8 172	8 00	90 00	90·0	8 00	88 59	89·9	8 00	87 59	89·7	7 59	86 58	89·6	7 59	85 58	89·4	7 58	84 57	89·3	188	352
9 171	9 00	90 00	90·0	9 00	88 59	89·8	9 00	87 59	89·7	8 59	86 58	89·5	8 59	85 57	89·3	8 58	84 56	89·2	189	351
10 170	10 00	90 00	90·0	10 00	88 59	89·8	10 00	87 58	89·6	9 59	86 57	89·5	9 58	85 56	89·2	9 58	84 55	89·1	190	350
11 169	11 00	90 00	90·0	11 00	88 59	89·8	11 00	87 58	89·6	10 59	86 57	89·4	10 58	85 56	89·2	10 57	84 54	89·0	191	349
12 168	12 00	90 00	90·0	12 00	88 59	89·8	12 00	87 57	89·6	11 59	86 56	89·4	11 58	85 55	89·1	11 57	84 53	88·9	192	348
13 167	13 00	90 00	90·0	13 00	88 59	89·8	13 00	87 57	89·5	12 59	86 56	89·3	12 58	85 53	89·0	12 57	84 52	88·8	193	347
14 166	14 00	90 00	90·0	14 00	88 58	89·8	14 00	87 56	89·5	13 59	86 55	89·3	13 58	85 53	88·9	13 57	84 51	88·8	194	346
15 165	15 00	90 00	90·0	15 00	88 58	89·7	14 59	87 56	89·5	14 59	86 54	89·2	14 58	85 52	88·9	14 56	84 49	88·7	195	345
16 164	16 00	90 00	90·0	16 00	88 58	89·7	15 59	87 55	89·4	15 59	86 53	89·1	15 58	85 50	88·8	15 56	84 48	88·6	196	344
17 163	17 00	90 00	90·0	17 00	88 57	89·7	16 59	87 55	89·4	16 59	86 52	89·1	16 57	85 49	88·7	16 56	84 46	88·5	197	343
18 162	18 00	90 00	90·0	18 00	88 57	89·7	17 59	87 54	89·4	17 58	86 51	89·0	17 57	85 48	88·6	17 56	84 45	88·4	198	342
19 161	19 00	90 00	90·0	19 00	88 57	89·7	18 59	87 53	89·3	18 58	86 50	89·0	18 57	85 46	88·5	18 55	84 43	88·3	199	341
20 160	20 00	90 00	90·0	20 00	88 56	89·6	19 59	87 52	89·3	19 58	86 48	88·9	19 57	85 45	88·5	19 55	84 41	88·2	200	340
21 159	21 00	90 00	90·0	21 00	88 56	89·6	20 59	87 52	89·2	20 58	86 47	88·8	20 57	85 43	88·4	20 55	84 39	88·1	201	339
22 158	22 00	90 00	90·0	22 00	88 55	89·6	21 59	87 51	89·2	21 58	86 46	88·8	21 57	85 41	88·3	21 55	84 37	88·0	202	338
23 157	23 00	90 00	90·0	23 00	88 55	89·6	22 59	87 50	89·2	22 58	86 44	88·7	22 56	85 39	88·2	22 54	84 34	87·9	203	337
24 156	24 00	90 00	90·0	24 00	88 54	89·6	23 59	87 49	89·1	23 58	86 43	88·7	23 56	85 37	88·1	23 54	84 32	87·8	204	336
25 155	25 00	90 00	90·0	25 00	88 54	89·5	24 59	87 48	89·1	24 58	86 41	88·6	24 56	85 35	88·1	24 54	84 29	87·7	205	335
26 154	26 00	90 00	90·0	26 00	88 53	89·5	25 59	87 47	89·0	25 58	86 40	88·5	25 56	85 33	88·0	25 54	84 26	87·6	206	334
27 153	27 00	90 00	90·0	27 00	88 53	89·5	26 59	87 45	89·0	26 58	86 38	88·5	26 56	85 31	87·9	26 53	84 24	87·5	207	333
28 152	28 00	90 00	90·0	28 00	88 52	89·5	27 59	87 44	88·9	27 57	86 36	88·4	27 56	85 28	87·8	27 53	84 20	87·3	208	332
29 151	29 00	90 00	90·0	29 00	88 51	89·4	28 59	87 43	88·9	28 57	86 34	88·3	28 55	85 26	87·7	28 53	84 17	87·2	209	331
30 150	30 00	90 00	90·0	30 00	88 51	89·4	29 59	87 41	88·8	29 57	86 32	88·3	29 55	85 23	87·6	29 52	84 14	87·1	210	330
31 149	31 00	90 00	90·0	31 00	88 50	89·4	30 59	87 40	88·8	30 57	86 30	88·2	30 55	85 20	87·5	30 52	84 10	87·0	211	329
32 148	32 00	90 00	90·0	32 00	88 49	89·4	31 59	87 39	88·8	31 57	86 28	88·1	31 55	85 17	87·4	31 52	84 07	86·9	212	328
33 147	33 00	90 00	90·0	33 00	88 48	89·4	32 59	87 37	88·7	32 57	86 25	88·1	32 55	85 14	87·3	32 52	84 03	86·8	213	327
34 146	34 00	90 00	90·0	34 00	88 48	89·3	33 59	87 35	88·7	33 57	86 23	88·0	33 55	85 11	87·2	33 51	83 59	86·6	214	326
35 145	35 00	90 00	90·0	35 00	88 47	89·3	34 59	87 34	88·6	34 57	86 20	87·9	34 54	85 07	87·1	34 51	83 54	86·5	215	325
36 144	36 00	90 00	90·0	36 00	88 46	89·3	35 58	87 32	88·5	35 57	86 18	87·8	35 54	85 04	87·1	35 51	83 50	86·4	216	324
37 143	37 00	90 00	90·0	37 00	88 45	89·2	36 58	87 30	88·5	36 56	86 15	87·7	36 54	85 00	87·0	36 50	83 45	86·2	217	323
38 142	38 00	90 00	90·0	38 00	88 44	89·2	37 58	87 28	88·4	37 56	86 12	87·7	37 53	84 56	86·9	37 50	83 40	86·1	218	322
39 141	39 00	90 00	90·0	39 00	88 43	89·2	38 58	87 26	88·4	38 56	86 09	87·6	38 53	84 52	86·8	38 49	83 35	86·0	219	321
40 140	40 00	90 00	90·0	40 00	88 42	89·2	39 58	87 23	88·3	39 56	86 05	87·5	39 53	84 47	86·7	39 49	83 29	85·8	220	320
41 139	41 00	90 00	90·0	41 00	88 41	89·1	40 58	87 21	88·3	40 56	86 02	87·4	40 53	84 42	86·5	40 49	83 23	85·7	221	319
42 138	42 00	90 00	90·0	42 00	88 39	89·1	41 58	87 19	88·2	41 56	85 58	87·3	41 52	84 37	86·4	41 48	83 17	85·5	222	318
43 137	43 00	90 00	90·0	43 00	88 38	89·1	42 58	87 16	88·1	42 56	85 54	87·2	42 52	84 32	86·3	42 48	83 11	85·4	223	317
44 136	44 00	90 00	90·0	43 59	88 37	89·0	43 58	87 13	88·1	43 55	85 50	87·1	43 52	84 27	86·1	43 47	83 04	85·2	224	316
45 135	45 00	90 00	90·0	44 59	88 35	89·0	44 58	87 10	88·0	44 55	85 46	87·0	44 52	84 21	86·0	44 47	82 57	85·0	225	315

Lat/A	LHA/F	0° A/H	0° B/P	0° Z₁/Z₂	1° A/H	1° B/P	1° Z₁/Z₂	2° A/H	2° B/P	2° Z₁/Z₂	3° A/H	3° B/P	3° Z₁/Z₂	4° A/H	4° B/P	4° Z₁/Z₂	5° A/H	5° B/P	5° Z₁/Z₂	A	LHA
45	135	45 00	90 00	90·0	44 59	88 35	89·0	44 58	87 10	88·0	44 55	85 46	87·0	44 52	84 21	86·0	44 47	82 57	85·0	225	315
46	134	46 00	90 00	90·0	45 59	88 34	89·0	45 58	87 07	87·9	45 55	85 41	86·9	45 51	84 15	85·9	45 46	82 49	84·8	226	314
47	133	47 00	90 00	90·0	46 59	88 32	88·9	46 58	87 04	87·9	46 55	85 36	86·8	46 51	84 09	85·7	46 46	82 41	84·7	227	313
48	132	48 00	90 00	90·0	47 59	88 30	88·9	47 58	87 01	87·8	47 55	85 31	86·7	47 51	84 02	85·6	47 46	82 33	84·5	228	312
49	131	49 00	90 00	90·0	48 59	88 29	88·9	48 58	86 57	87·7	48 55	85 26	86·6	48 50	83 55	85·4	48 45	82 24	84·3	229	311
50	130	50 00	90 00	90·0	49 59	88 27	88·8	49 58	86 53	87·6	49 54	85 20	86·4	49 50	83 47	85·2	49 44	82 15	84·1	230	310
51	129	51 00	90 00	90·0	50 59	88 25	88·8	50 57	86 49	87·5	50 54	85 14	86·3	50 50	83 40	85·1	50 44	82 05	83·9	231	309
52	128	52 00	90 00	90·0	51 59	88 23	88·7	51 57	86 45	87·4	51 54	85 08	86·2	51 49	83 31	84·9	51 43	81 55	83·6	232	308
53	127	53 00	90 00	90·0	52 59	88 20	88·7	52 57	86 41	87·3	52 54	85 01	86·0	52 49	83 22	84·7	52 43	81 44	83·4	233	307
54	126	54 00	90 00	90·0	53 59	88 18	88·6	53 57	86 37	87·2	53 54	84 54	85·9	53 48	83 13	84·5	53 42	81 32	83·2	234	306
55	125	55 00	90 00	90·0	54 59	88 15	88·6	54 57	86 31	87·1	54 53	84 47	85·7	54 48	83 03	84·3	54 41	81 20	82·9	235	305
56	124	56 00	90 00	90·0	55 59	88 13	88·5	55 57	86 26	87·0	55 53	84 39	85·6	55 48	82 52	84·1	55 41	81 06	82·6	236	304
57	123	57 00	90 00	90·0	56 59	88 10	88·5	56 57	86 20	86·9	56 53	84 30	85·4	56 47	82 41	83·9	56 40	80 52	82·4	237	303
58	122	58 00	90 00	90·0	57 59	88 07	88·4	57 57	86 14	86·8	57 52	84 21	85·2	57 47	82 29	83·6	57 39	80 38	82·1	238	302
59	121	59 00	90 00	90·0	58 59	88 04	88·3	58 56	86 07	86·7	58 52	84 11	85·0	58 46	82 16	83·4	58 38	80 22	81·7	239	301
60	120	60 00	90 00	90·0	59 59	88 00	88·3	59 56	86 00	86·5	59 52	84 01	84·8	59 46	82 02	83·1	59 37	80 05	81·4	240	300
61	119	61 00	90 00	90·0	60 59	87 56	88·2	60 56	85 53	86·4	60 51	83 50	84·6	60 45	81 48	82·8	60 37	79 46	81·1	241	299
62	118	62 00	90 00	90·0	61 59	87 52	88·1	61 56	85 45	86·2	61 51	83 38	84·4	61 44	81 32	82·5	61 36	79 27	80·7	242	298
63	117	63 00	90 00	90·0	62 59	87 48	88·0	62 56	85 36	86·1	62 51	83 25	84·1	62 44	81 15	82·2	62 35	79 06	80·3	243	297
64	116	64 00	90 00	90·0	63 59	87 43	88·0	63 56	85 27	85·9	63 50	83 11	83·9	63 43	80 56	81·9	63 33	78 43	79·9	244	296
65	115	65 00	90 00	90·0	64 59	87 38	87·9	64 56	85 17	85·7	64 50	82 56	83·6	64 42	80 36	81·5	64 32	78 18	79·4	245	295
66	114	66 00	90 00	90·0	65 59	87 33	87·8	65 55	85 06	85·5	65 49	82 39	83·3	65 41	80 15	81·1	65 31	77 52	78·9	246	294
67	113	67 00	90 00	90·0	66 59	87 27	87·6	66 55	84 54	85·3	66 49	82 22	83·0	66 40	79 51	80·7	66 29	77 23	78·4	247	293
68	112	68 00	90 00	90·0	67 59	87 20	87·5	67 55	84 40	85·1	67 48	82 02	82·6	67 39	79 26	80·2	67 28	76 51	77·8	248	292
69	111	69 00	90 00	90·0	68 59	87 13	87·4	68 55	84 26	84·8	68 48	81 41	82·2	68 38	78 58	79·7	68 26	76 17	77·2	249	291
70	110	70 00	90 00	90·0	69 59	87 05	87·3	69 54	84 10	84·5	69 47	81 17	81·8	69 37	78 27	79·2	69 25	75 39	76·5	250	290
71	109	71 00	90 00	90·0	70 58	86 56	87·1	70 54	83 53	84·2	70 46	80 51	81·4	70 36	77 53	78·5	70 23	74 58	75·8	251	289
72	108	72 00	90 00	90·0	71 58	86 46	86·9	71 54	83 33	83·9	71 46	80 22	80·8	71 35	77 15	77·7	71 20	74 12	75·0	252	288
73	107	73 00	90 00	90·0	72 58	86 35	86·7	72 53	83 11	83·5	72 45	79 50	80·3	72 33	76 33	77·1	72 18	73 20	74·1	253	287
74	106	74 00	90 00	90·0	73 58	86 23	86·5	73 53	82 47	83·1	73 44	79 14	79·7	73 31	75 46	76·3	73 15	72 23	73·1	254	286
75	105	75 00	90 00	90·0	74 58	86 09	86·3	74 52	82 19	82·6	74 43	78 33	78·9	74 29	74 53	75·4	74 12	71 19	72·0	255	285
76	104	76 00	90 00	90·0	75 58	85 52	86·0	75 52	81 47	82·0	75 41	77 47	78·1	75 27	73 53	74·4	75 09	70 07	70·7	256	284
77	103	77 00	90 00	90·0	76 58	85 34	85·7	76 51	81 11	81·4	76 40	76 53	77·2	76 24	72 44	73·2	76 05	68 45	69·3	257	283
78	102	78 00	90 00	90·0	77 58	85 12	85·3	77 50	80 28	80·7	77 38	75 51	76·2	77 22	71 25	71·8	77 01	67 11	67·7	258	282
79	101	79 00	90 00	90·0	78 57	84 46	84·9	78 49	79 38	79·8	78 36	74 39	74·9	78 18	69 52	70·3	77 56	65 22	65·8	259	281
80	100	80 00	90 00	90·0	79 57	84 14	84·3	79 48	78 38	78·8	79 34	73 12	73·5	79 14	68 04	68·4	78 50	63 16	63·7	260	280
81	99	81 00	90 00	90·0	80 57	83 38	83·7	80 47	77 25	77·6	80 31	71 29	71·7	80 09	65 55	66·2	79 43	60 47	61·2	261	279
82	98	82 00	90 00	90·0	81 56	82 51	82·9	81 45	75 55	76·1	81 28	69 22	69·6	81 04	63 19	63·6	80 34	57 51	58·2	262	278
83	97	83 00	90 00	90·0	82 56	81 51	81·9	82 43	74 01	74·1	82 23	66 44	66·9	81 57	60 09	60·4	81 24	54 20	54·6	263	277
84	96	84 00	90 00	90·0	83 55	80 31	80·6	83 41	71 32	71·6	83 18	63 29	63·5	82 48	56 13	56·4	82 12	50 04	50·3	264	276
85	95	85 00	90 00	90·0	84 54	78 40	78·7	84 37	68 10	68·3	84 10	58 59	59·1	83 36	51 13	51·4	82 56	44 53	45·1	265	275
86	94	86 00	90 00	90·0	85 53	75 57	76·0	85 32	63 24	63·5	85 00	53 05	53·2	84 21	44 56	45·1	83 36	38 34	38·7	266	274
87	93	87 00	90 00	90·0	86 50	71 33	71·6	86 24	56 17	56·3	85 45	44 58	45·0	85 00	36 49	36·9	84 10	30 53	31·0	267	273
88	92	88 00	90 00	90·0	87 46	63 26	63·4	87 10	44 59	45·0	86 24	33 40	33·7	85 32	26 31	26·6	84 37	21 45	21·8	268	272
89	91	89 00	90 00	90·0	88 35	45 00	45·0	87 46	26 33	26·6	86 50	18 25	18·4	85 53	14 01	14·0	84 54	11 17	11·3	269	271
90	90	90 00	90 00	90·0	89 00	00 00	0·0	88 00	00 00	0·0	87 00	00 00	0·0	86 00	00 00	0·0	85 00	00 00	0·0	270	270

N. Lat: for LHA > 180° ... $Z_n = Z$; for LHA < 180° ... $Z_n = 360° - Z$

S. Lat: for LHA > 180° ... $Z_n = 180° - Z$; for LHA < 180° ... $Z_n = 180° + Z$

SIGHT REDUCTION TABLE

B: (−) for 90° < LHA < 270°
Dec:(−) for Lat. contrary name

Z₁: same sign as B
Z₂: (−) for F > 90°

LHA/F	6° A/H	6° B/P	6° Z₁/Z₂	7° A/H	7° B/P	7° Z₁/Z₂	8° A/H	8° B/P	8° Z₁/Z₂	9° A/H	9° B/P	9° Z₁/Z₂	10° A/H	10° B/P	10° Z₁/Z₂	11° A/H	11° B/P	11° Z₁/Z₂	Lat./A	LHA
0 180	0 00	84 00	90·0	0 00	83 00	90·0	0 00	82 00	90·0	0 00	81 00	90·0	0 00	80 00	90·0	0 00	79 00	90·0	180	360
1 179	1 00	84 00	89·9	1 00	83 00	89·9	0 59	82 00	89·9	0 59	81 00	89·9	0 59	80 00	89·8	0 59	79 00	89·8	181	359
2 178	1 59	84 00	89·8	1 59	83 00	89·8	1 59	82 00	89·7	1 59	81 00	89·7	1 58	80 00	89·7	1 58	79 00	89·6	182	358
3 177	2 59	84 00	89·7	2 59	82 59	89·6	2 58	81 59	89·6	2 58	80 59	89·5	2 57	79 59	89·5	2 57	78 59	89·4	183	357
4 176	3 59	83 59	89·6	3 58	82 59	89·5	3 58	81 59	89·4	3 57	80 59	89·4	3 56	79 59	89·3	3 56	78 58	89·2	184	356
5 175	4 58	83 59	89·5	4 58	82 58	89·4	4 57	81 58	89·3	4 56	80 58	89·2	4 55	79 58	89·1	4 54	78 58	89·0	185	355
6 174	5 58	83 58	89·4	5 57	82 58	89·3	5 56	81 57	89·2	5 56	80 57	89·1	5 55	79 57	89·0	5 53	78 56	88·9	186	354
7 173	6 58	83 57	89·3	6 57	82 57	89·1	6 56	81 56	89·0	6 55	80 56	88·9	6 54	79 56	88·8	6 52	78 55	88·7	187	353
8 172	7 57	83 56	89·2	7 56	82 56	89·0	7 55	81 55	88·9	7 54	80 55	88·8	7 53	79 54	88·6	7 51	78 54	88·5	188	352
9 171	8 57	83 56	89·1	8 56	82 55	88·9	8 55	81 54	88·7	8 53	80 53	88·6	8 52	79 53	88·4	8 50	78 52	88·3	189	351
10 170	9 57	83 54	88·9	9 55	82 54	88·8	9 54	81 53	88·6	9 53	80 52	88·4	9 51	79 51	88·2	9 49	78 50	88·1	190	350
11 169	10 56	83 53	88·8	10 55	82 52	88·6	10 53	81 51	88·5	10 52	80 50	88·3	10 50	79 49	88·1	10 48	78 48	87·9	191	349
12 168	11 56	83 52	88·7	11 55	82 51	88·5	11 53	81 49	88·3	11 51	80 48	88·1	11 49	79 47	87·9	11 47	78 46	87·7	192	348
13 167	12 56	83 51	88·6	12 54	82 49	88·4	12 52	81 48	88·2	12 50	80 46	87·9	12 48	79 45	87·7	12 45	78 43	87·5	193	347
14 166	13 55	83 49	88·5	13 54	82 47	88·3	13 52	81 46	88·0	13 49	80 44	87·8	13 47	79 42	87·5	13 44	78 40	87·3	194	346
15 165	14 55	83 47	88·4	14 53	82 45	88·1	14 51	81 43	87·9	14 49	80 41	87·6	14 46	79 39	87·3	14 43	78 37	87·1	195	345
16 164	15 55	83 46	88·3	15 53	82 43	88·0	15 50	81 41	87·7	15 48	80 39	87·4	15 45	79 36	87·1	15 42	78 34	86·9	196	344
17 163	16 54	83 44	88·2	16 52	82 41	87·9	16 50	81 38	87·6	16 47	80 36	87·3	16 44	79 33	87·0	16 41	78 31	86·7	197	343
18 162	17 54	83 42	88·1	17 52	82 39	87·7	17 49	81 36	87·4	17 46	80 33	87·1	17 43	79 30	86·8	17 39	78 27	86·5	198	342
19 161	18 54	83 39	87·9	18 51	82 36	87·6	18 48	81 33	87·3	18 45	80 29	86·9	18 42	79 26	86·6	18 38	78 23	86·2	199	341
20 160	19 53	83 37	87·8	19 51	82 33	87·5	19 48	81 30	87·1	19 45	80 26	86·7	19 41	79 22	86·4	19 37	78 19	86·0	200	340
21 159	20 53	83 35	87·7	20 50	82 30	87·3	20 47	81 26	86·9	20 44	80 22	86·6	20 40	79 18	86·2	20 36	78 14	85·8	201	339
22 158	21 52	83 32	87·6	21 50	82 27	87·2	21 46	81 23	86·8	21 43	80 18	86·4	21 39	79 14	86·0	21 35	78 10	85·6	202	338
23 157	22 52	83 29	87·5	22 49	82 24	87·0	22 46	81 19	86·6	22 42	80 14	86·2	22 38	79 09	85·8	22 33	78 05	85·4	203	337
24 156	23 52	83 26	87·3	23 49	82 21	86·9	23 45	81 15	86·5	23 41	80 10	86·0	23 37	79 05	85·6	23 32	77 59	85·1	204	336
25 155	24 51	83 23	87·2	24 48	82 17	86·7	24 44	81 11	86·3	24 40	80 05	85·8	24 36	78 59	85·4	24 31	77 54	84·9	205	335
26 154	25 51	83 20	87·1	25 48	82 13	86·6	25 44	81 07	86·1	25 39	80 00	85·6	25 35	78 54	85·2	25 29	77 48	84·7	206	334
27 153	26 50	83 16	87·0	26 47	82 09	86·4	26 43	81 02	85·9	26 38	79 55	85·4	26 33	78 48	84·9	26 28	77 42	84·4	207	333
28 152	27 50	83 13	86·8	27 46	82 05	86·3	27 42	80 57	85·8	27 38	79 50	85·2	27 32	78 42	84·7	27 27	77 35	84·2	208	332
29 151	28 50	83 09	86·7	28 46	82 01	86·1	28 41	80 52	85·6	28 37	79 44	85·0	28 31	78 36	84·5	28 25	77 28	84·0	209	331
30 150	29 49	83 05	86·5	29 45	81 56	86·0	29 41	80 47	85·4	29 36	79 38	84·8	29 30	78 29	84·3	29 24	77 21	83·7	210	330
31 149	30 49	83 01	86·4	30 45	81 51	85·8	30 40	80 41	85·2	30 35	79 32	84·6	30 29	78 23	84·0	30 22	77 13	83·5	211	329
32 148	31 48	82 56	86·3	31 44	81 46	85·6	31 39	80 35	85·0	31 34	79 25	84·4	31 27	78 15	83·8	31 21	77 05	83·2	212	328
33 147	32 48	82 51	86·1	32 43	81 40	85·5	32 38	80 29	84·8	32 33	79 18	84·2	32 26	78 08	83·6	32 19	76 57	82·9	213	327
34 146	33 47	82 46	86·0	33 43	81 35	85·3	33 37	80 23	84·6	33 32	79 11	84·0	33 24	78 00	83·3	33 18	76 48	82·7	214	326
35 145	34 47	82 41	85·8	34 42	81 29	85·1	34 37	80 16	84·4	34 30	79 03	83·7	34 23	77 51	83·1	34 16	76 39	82·4	215	325
36 144	35 46	82 36	85·7	35 41	81 22	84·9	35 36	80 09	84·2	35 29	78 55	83·5	35 22	77 42	82·8	35 14	76 29	82·1	216	324
37 143	36 46	82 30	85·5	36 41	81 16	84·8	36 35	80 01	84·0	36 28	78 47	83·3	36 21	77 33	82·5	36 13	76 19	81·8	217	323
38 142	37 45	82 24	85·3	37 40	81 09	84·6	37 34	79 53	83·8	37 27	78 38	83·0	37 19	77 23	82·3	37 11	76 09	81·5	218	322
39 141	38 45	82 18	85·2	38 39	81 01	84·4	38 33	79 45	83·6	38 26	78 29	82·8	38 18	77 13	82·0	38 09	75 58	81·2	219	321
40 140	39 44	82 11	85·0	39 39	80 54	84·2	39 32	79 36	83·3	39 25	78 19	82·5	39 16	77 02	81·7	39 07	75 46	80·9	220	320
41 139	40 44	82 04	84·8	40 38	80 46	84·0	40 31	79 27	83·1	40 23	78 09	82·3	40 15	76 51	81·4	40 05	75 33	80·6	221	319
42 138	41 43	81 57	84·6	41 37	80 37	83·7	41 30	79 17	82·9	41 22	77 58	82·0	41 13	76 39	81·1	41 04	75 21	80·3	222	318
43 137	42 42	81 49	84·4	42 36	80 28	83·5	42 29	79 07	82·6	42 21	77 47	81·7	42 12	76 27	80·8	42 02	75 07	79·9	223	317
44 136	43 42	81 41	84·2	43 35	80 19	83·3	43 28	78 57	82·3	43 19	77 35	81·4	43 10	76 14	80·5	43 00	74 53	79·6	224	316
45 135	44 41	81 33	84·0	44 34	80 09	83·1	44 27	78 46	82·1	44 18	77 22	81·1	44 08	76 00	80·1	43 57	74 38	79·2	225	315

Lat. / A

Lat./A LHA/F	6° A/H	6° B/P	6° Z₁/Z₂	7° A/H	7° B/P	7° Z₁/Z₂	8° A/H	8° B/P	8° Z₁/Z₂	9° A/H	9° B/P	9° Z₁/Z₂	10° A/H	10° B/P	10° Z₁/Z₂	11° A/H	11° B/P	11° Z₁/Z₂	Lat./A LHA	
45	44 41	81 33	84·0	44 34	80 09	83·1	44 27	78 46	82·1	44 18	77 22	81·1	44 08	76 00	80·1	43 57	74 38	79·2	225	315
46	45 41	81 24	83·8	45 34	79 59	82·8	45 26	78 34	81·8	45 16	77 09	80·8	45 06	75 45	79·8	44 55	74 22	78·8	226	314
47	46 40	81 14	83·6	46 33	79 48	82·6	46 24	78 21	81·5	46 15	76 56	80·5	46 04	75 30	79·5	45 53	74 05	78·4	227	313
48	47 39	81 04	83·4	47 32	79 36	82·3	47 23	78 08	81·2	47 13	76 41	80·1	47 03	75 14	79·1	46 51	73 48	78·0	228	312
49	48 38	80 54	83·1	48 31	79 24	82·0	48 22	77 55	80·9	48 12	76 26	79·8	48 01	74 57	78·7	47 48	73 30	77·6	229	311
50	49 38	80 43	82·9	49 30	79 11	81·7	49 20	77 40	80·6	49 10	76 09	79·4	48 58	74 40	78·3	48 46	73 10	77·2	230	310
51	50 37	80 31	82·6	50 29	78 58	81·4	50 19	77 25	80·2	50 08	75 52	79·1	49 56	74 21	77·9	49 43	72 50	76·7	231	309
52	51 36	80 19	82·4	51 27	78 43	81·1	51 18	77 08	79·9	51 06	75 34	78·7	50 54	74 01	77·5	50 40	72 29	76·3	232	308
53	52 35	80 06	82·1	52 26	78 28	80·8	52 16	76 51	79·5	52 04	75 15	78·3	51 52	73 40	77·0	51 37	72 06	75·8	233	307
54	53 34	79 52	81·8	53 25	78 12	80·5	53 14	76 33	79·2	53 02	74 55	77·8	52 49	73 18	76·6	52 35	71 42	75·3	234	306
55	54 33	79 37	81·5	54 24	77 55	80·1	54 13	76 14	78·8	54 00	74 34	77·4	53 47	72 55	76·1	53 31	71 17	74·8	235	305
56	55 32	79 21	81·2	55 22	77 37	79·8	55 11	75 54	78·3	54 58	74 11	76·9	54 44	72 30	75·6	54 28	70 50	74·2	236	304
57	56 31	79 05	80·9	56 21	77 18	79·4	56 09	75 32	77·9	55 56	73 47	76·5	55 41	72 04	75·0	55 25	70 22	73·6	237	303
58	57 30	78 47	80·6	57 18	76 58	79·0	57 07	75 09	77·4	56 53	73 22	75·9	56 38	71 36	74·5	56 21	69 51	73·0	238	302
59	58 29	78 28	80·1	58 16	76 35	78·5	58 05	74 44	77·0	57 51	72 54	75·4	57 35	71 06	73·9	57 17	69 19	72·4	239	301
60	59 28	78 08	79·7	59 14	76 12	78·1	59 03	74 18	76·4	58 48	72 25	74·8	58 32	70 34	73·3	58 13	68 45	71·7	240	300
61	60 26	77 46	79·3	60 12	75 47	77·6	60 01	73 50	75·9	59 45	71 54	74·2	59 28	70 01	72·6	59 09	68 09	71·0	241	299
62	61 25	77 23	78·9	61 12	75 21	77·1	60 58	73 20	75·3	60 42	71 21	73·6	60 24	69 25	71·9	60 05	67 31	70·3	242	298
63	62 23	76 58	78·4	62 10	74 52	76·5	61 56	72 48	74·7	61 39	70 46	72·9	61 20	68 46	71·2	61 00	66 49	69·5	243	297
64	63 22	76 31	77·9	63 08	74 21	76·0	62 53	72 13	74·1	62 35	70 08	72·2	62 16	68 05	70·4	61 55	66 05	68·6	244	296
65	64 20	76 02	77·4	64 06	73 48	75·4	63 50	71 36	73·4	63 32	69 27	71·5	63 12	67 21	69·6	62 50	65 18	67·7	245	295
66	65 18	75 31	76·8	65 03	73 12	74·7	64 47	70 56	72·6	64 28	68 43	70·6	64 07	66 34	68·7	63 44	64 27	66·8	246	294
67	66 16	74 57	76·2	66 01	72 33	74·0	65 43	70 13	71·8	65 23	67 56	69·8	65 02	65 43	67·8	64 38	63 33	65·8	247	293
68	67 14	74 20	75·5	66 58	71 51	73·2	66 40	69 26	71·0	66 19	67 05	68·8	65 56	64 48	66·7	65 32	62 35	64·7	248	292
69	68 12	73 39	74·8	67 55	71 05	72·4	67 36	68 35	70·1	67 14	66 09	67·8	66 50	63 48	65·7	66 25	61 31	63·6	249	291
70	69 09	72 55	74·0	68 51	70 15	71·5	68 31	67 40	69·1	68 09	65 09	66·7	67 44	62 44	64·5	67 17	60 23	62·3	250	290
71	70 07	72 06	73·1	69 48	69 20	70·5	69 27	66 39	68·0	69 03	64 03	65·6	68 37	61 34	63·2	68 09	59 10	61·0	251	289
72	71 03	71 13	72·2	70 44	68 20	69·4	70 21	65 33	66·8	69 57	62 52	64·3	69 29	60 17	61·9	69 00	57 50	59·6	252	288
73	72 00	70 14	71·1	71 39	67 13	68·3	71 16	64 20	65·5	70 50	61 33	62·9	70 21	58 54	60·4	69 50	56 23	58·0	253	287
74	72 56	69 08	70·0	72 34	65 59	67·0	72 09	62 59	64·1	71 42	60 07	61·4	71 12	57 24	58·8	70 40	54 49	56·4	254	286
75	73 52	67 54	68·7	73 29	64 37	65·5	73 03	61 30	62·6	72 34	58 32	59·7	72 02	55 44	57·1	71 28	53 06	54·5	255	285
76	74 48	66 31	67·3	74 23	63 05	64·0	73 55	59 51	60·8	73 24	56 47	57·9	72 51	53 55	55·1	72 16	51 13	52·6	256	284
77	75 42	64 57	65·6	75 16	61 22	62·2	74 46	58 00	58·9	74 14	54 51	55·9	73 39	51 55	53·1	73 02	49 10	50·4	257	283
78	76 36	63 11	63·7	76 08	59 26	60·2	75 37	55 57	56·8	75 02	52 42	53·6	74 26	49 42	50·8	73 47	46 56	48·1	258	282
79	77 29	61 09	61·7	76 59	57 14	57·9	76 26	53 38	54·4	75 49	50 18	51·2	75 11	47 16	48·2	74 30	44 28	45·5	259	281
80	78 21	58 49	59·3	77 49	54 44	55·3	77 13	51 01	51·7	76 35	47 38	48·4	75 55	44 34	45·4	75 11	41 47	42·7	260	280
81	79 12	56 06	56·6	78 37	51 52	52·4	77 59	48 04	48·7	77 18	44 39	45·4	76 35	41 35	42·4	75 49	38 50	39·7	261	279
82	80 01	52 56	53·4	79 23	48 35	49·1	78 42	44 43	45·3	77 59	41 18	41·9	77 13	38 17	39·0	76 26	35 36	36·4	262	278
83	80 47	49 13	49·6	80 07	44 47	45·2	79 23	40 56	41·4	78 37	37 35	38·1	77 49	34 39	35·3	76 59	32 05	32·8	263	277
84	81 31	44 51	45·2	80 47	40 24	40·8	80 01	36 38	37·1	79 12	33 25	33·9	78 21	30 40	31·2	77 29	28 16	28·6	264	276
85	82 12	39 40	39·9	81 24	35 22	35·7	80 34	31 48	32·2	79 43	28 49	29·2	78 50	26 18	26·7	77 56	24 09	24·6	265	275
86	82 48	33 34	33·8	81 57	29 36	29·8	81 04	26 24	26·7	80 09	23 46	24·1	79 14	21 35	21·9	78 18	19 44	20·1	266	274
87	83 18	26 28	26·6	82 23	23 05	23·3	81 28	20 25	20·6	80 31	18 17	18·5	79 34	16 32	16·8	78 36	15 04	15·4	267	273
88	83 41	18 22	18·5	82 43	15 52	16·0	81 45	13 57	14·1	80 47	12 26	12·6	79 48	11 12	11·4	78 49	10 18	10·4	268	272
89	83 55	9 26	9·5	82 56	8 05	8·2	81 56	7 05	7·1	80 57	6 17	6·4	79 57	5 39	5·7	78 57	5 08	5·2	269	271
90	84 00	0 00	0·0	83 00	0 00	0·0	82 00	0 00	0·0	81 00	0 00	0·0	80 00	0 00	0·0	79 00	0 00	0·0	270	270

N. Lat.: for LHA > 180° ... $Z_n = Z$
for LHA < 180° ... $Z_n = 360° - Z$

S. Lat.: for LHA > 180° ... $Z_n = 180° - Z$
for LHA < 180° ... $Z_n = 180° + Z$

SIGHT REDUCTION TABLE

B: (−) for 90° < LHA < 270°
Dec:(−) for Lat. contrary name

Z₁: same sign as B
Z₂: (−) for F > 90°

LHA/F	12° A/H	12° B/P	12° Z₁/Z₂	13° A/H	13° B/P	13° Z₁/Z₂	14° A/H	14° B/P	14° Z₁/Z₂	15° A/H	15° B/P	15° Z₁/Z₂	16° A/H	16° B/P	16° Z₁/Z₂	17° A/H	17° B/P	17° Z₁/Z₂	LHA/A
0 / 180	0 00	78 00	90·0	0 00	77 00	90·0	0 00	76 00	90·0	0 00	75 00	90·0	0 00	74 00	90·0	0 00	73 00	90·0	180 / 360
1 / 179	0 59	78 00	89·8	0 58	77 00	89·8	0 58	76 00	89·8	0 58	75 00	89·7	0 58	74 00	89·7	0 57	73 00	89·7	181 / 359
2 / 178	1 57	78 00	89·6	1 57	77 00	89·5	1 56	76 00	89·5	1 56	74 59	89·5	1 55	73 59	89·4	1 55	72 59	89·4	182 / 358
3 / 177	2 56	77 59	89·4	2 55	76 59	89·3	2 55	75 59	89·3	2 54	74 59	89·2	2 53	73 59	89·2	2 52	72 59	89·1	183 / 357
4 / 176	3 55	77 58	89·2	3 54	76 58	89·1	3 53	75 58	89·0	3 52	74 58	89·0	3 51	73 58	88·9	3 49	72 58	88·8	184 / 356
5 / 175	4 53	77 57	89·0	4 52	76 57	88·9	4 51	75 57	88·8	4 50	74 57	88·7	4 48	73 57	88·6	4 47	72 56	88·5	185 / 355
6 / 174	5 52	77 56	88·7	5 51	76 56	88·6	5 49	75 56	88·5	5 48	74 55	88·4	5 46	73 55	88·3	5 44	72 55	88·2	186 / 354
7 / 173	6 51	77 55	88·5	6 49	76 54	88·4	6 47	75 54	88·3	6 46	74 54	88·2	6 44	73 53	88·1	6 42	72 53	87·9	187 / 353
8 / 172	7 49	77 53	88·3	7 48	76 53	88·2	7 46	75 52	88·1	7 44	74 52	87·9	7 41	73 51	87·8	7 39	72 51	87·6	188 / 352
9 / 171	8 48	77 51	88·1	8 46	76 51	88·0	8 44	75 50	87·8	8 41	74 49	87·7	8 39	73 49	87·5	8 36	72 48	87·3	189 / 351
10 / 170	9 47	77 49	87·9	9 44	76 49	87·7	9 42	75 48	87·6	9 39	74 47	87·4	9 37	73 46	87·2	9 34	72 45	87·0	190 / 350
11 / 169	10 45	77 47	87·7	10 43	76 46	87·5	10 40	75 45	87·3	10 37	74 44	87·1	10 34	73 43	86·9	10 31	72 42	86·7	191 / 349
12 / 168	11 44	77 44	87·5	11 41	76 43	87·3	11 38	75 42	87·1	11 35	74 41	86·9	11 32	73 40	86·6	11 28	72 39	86·4	192 / 348
13 / 167	12 43	77 42	87·3	12 40	76 40	87·0	12 36	75 39	86·8	12 33	74 37	86·6	12 29	73 36	86·4	12 25	72 35	86·1	193 / 347
14 / 166	13 41	77 39	87·0	13 38	76 37	86·8	13 35	75 35	86·6	13 31	74 34	86·3	13 27	73 32	86·1	13 23	72 31	85·8	194 / 346
15 / 165	14 40	77 35	86·8	14 36	76 33	86·6	14 33	75 32	86·3	14 29	74 30	86·0	14 24	73 28	85·8	14 20	72 26	85·5	195 / 345
16 / 164	15 38	77 32	86·6	15 35	76 30	86·3	15 31	75 28	86·0	15 26	74 25	85·8	15 22	73 23	85·5	15 17	72 21	85·2	196 / 344
17 / 163	16 37	77 28	86·4	16 33	76 26	86·1	16 29	75 23	85·8	16 24	74 21	85·5	16 19	73 19	85·2	16 14	72 16	84·9	197 / 343
18 / 162	17 36	77 24	86·1	17 31	76 21	85·8	17 27	75 19	85·5	17 22	74 16	85·2	17 17	73 13	84·9	17 11	72 11	84·6	198 / 342
19 / 161	18 34	77 20	85·9	18 30	76 16	85·6	18 25	75 14	85·2	18 20	74 11	84·9	18 14	73 08	84·6	18 08	72 05	84·3	199 / 341
20 / 160	19 33	77 15	85·7	19 28	76 12	85·3	19 23	75 08	85·0	19 17	74 05	84·6	19 12	73 02	84·3	19 05	71 59	83·9	200 / 340
21 / 159	20 31	77 10	85·4	20 26	76 07	85·1	20 21	75 03	84·7	20 15	73 59	84·3	20 09	72 56	84·0	20 03	71 52	83·6	201 / 339
22 / 158	21 30	77 05	85·2	21 24	76 01	84·8	21 19	74 57	84·4	21 13	73 53	84·0	21 06	72 49	83·6	21 00	71 45	83·3	202 / 338
23 / 157	22 28	77 00	85·0	22 22	75 55	84·5	22 17	74 51	84·1	22 10	73 46	83·7	22 04	72 42	83·3	21 56	71 38	82·9	203 / 337
24 / 156	23 27	76 54	84·7	23 21	75 49	84·3	23 15	74 44	83·9	23 08	73 39	83·4	23 01	72 34	83·0	22 53	71 30	82·6	204 / 336
25 / 155	24 25	76 48	84·5	24 19	75 43	84·0	24 13	74 37	83·6	24 06	73 32	83·1	23 58	72 27	82·7	23 50	71 22	82·2	205 / 335
26 / 154	25 23	76 42	84·2	25 17	75 36	83·7	25 10	74 30	83·3	25 03	73 24	82·8	24 55	72 18	82·3	24 47	71 13	81·9	206 / 334
27 / 153	26 22	76 35	84·0	26 15	75 28	83·5	26 08	74 22	83·0	26 01	73 16	82·5	25 52	72 10	82·0	25 44	71 04	81·5	207 / 333
28 / 152	27 20	76 28	83·7	27 13	75 21	83·2	27 06	74 14	82·7	26 58	73 07	82·2	26 49	72 00	81·7	26 41	70 54	81·2	208 / 332
29 / 151	28 18	76 20	83·4	28 11	75 13	82·9	28 04	74 05	82·4	27 55	72 58	81·8	27 47	71 51	81·3	27 37	70 44	80·8	209 / 331
30 / 150	29 17	76 13	83·2	29 09	75 04	82·6	29 01	73 56	82·0	28 53	72 48	81·5	28 44	71 41	81·0	28 34	70 33	80·4	210 / 330
31 / 149	30 15	76 04	82·9	30 07	74 56	82·3	29 59	73 47	81·7	29 50	72 38	81·2	29 41	71 30	80·6	29 30	70 22	80·0	211 / 329
32 / 148	31 13	75 56	82·6	31 05	74 46	82·0	30 57	73 37	81·4	30 47	72 28	80·8	30 37	71 19	80·2	30 27	70 11	79·6	212 / 328
33 / 147	32 11	75 47	82·3	32 03	74 37	81·7	31 54	73 27	81·1	31 44	72 17	80·5	31 34	71 07	79·9	31 23	69 58	79·2	213 / 327
34 / 146	33 10	75 37	82·0	33 01	74 26	81·4	32 52	73 16	80·7	32 42	72 05	80·1	32 31	70 55	79·5	32 20	69 45	78·8	214 / 326
35 / 145	34 08	75 27	81·7	33 59	74 16	81·0	33 49	73 04	80·4	33 39	71 53	79·7	33 28	70 42	79·1	33 16	69 32	78·4	215 / 325
36 / 144	35 06	75 17	81·4	34 56	74 04	80·7	34 46	72 52	80·0	34 36	71 40	79·4	34 24	70 29	78·7	34 12	69 18	78·0	216 / 324
37 / 143	36 04	75 06	81·1	35 54	73 53	80·4	35 44	72 40	79·7	35 33	71 27	79·0	35 21	70 15	78·3	35 08	69 03	77·6	217 / 323
38 / 142	37 02	74 54	80·8	36 52	73 40	80·0	36 41	72 27	79·3	36 29	71 13	78·6	36 17	70 00	77·8	36 04	68 48	77·1	218 / 322
39 / 141	38 00	74 42	80·4	37 49	73 27	79·7	37 38	72 13	78·9	37 26	70 59	78·2	37 13	69 45	77·4	37 00	68 32	76·7	219 / 321
40 / 140	38 57	74 30	80·1	38 47	73 14	79·3	38 35	71 58	78·6	38 23	70 43	77·8	38 10	69 29	77·0	37 56	68 15	76·3	220 / 320
41 / 139	39 55	74 16	79·8	39 44	72 59	78·9	39 32	71 43	78·2	39 19	70 27	77·3	39 06	69 12	76·5	38 51	67 57	75·8	221 / 319
42 / 138	40 53	74 02	79·4	40 41	72 45	78·5	40 29	71 27	77·7	40 16	70 10	76·9	40 02	68 54	76·1	39 47	67 38	75·3	222 / 318
43 / 137	41 51	73 48	79·0	41 39	72 29	78·2	41 26	71 11	77·3	41 12	69 53	76·4	40 58	68 35	75·6	40 42	67 19	74·7	223 / 317
44 / 136	42 48	73 32	78·6	42 36	72 12	77·7	42 23	70 53	76·9	42 09	69 34	76·0	41 54	68 16	75·1	41 38	66 58	74·2	224 / 316
45 / 135	43 46	73 16	78·3	43 33	71 55	77·3	43 19	70 35	76·4	43 05	69 15	75·5	42 49	67 56	74·6	42 33	66 37	73·7	225 / 315

Lat./A	LHA/F	12° A/H	12° B/P	12° Z_1/Z_2	13° A/H	13° B/P	13° Z_1/Z_2	14° A/H	14° B/P	14° Z_1/Z_2	15° A/H	15° B/P	15° Z_1/Z_2	16° A/H	16° B/P	16° Z_1/Z_2	17° A/H	17° B/P	17° Z_1/Z_2	Lat./A	LHA
45	135	43 46	73 16	78·3	43 33	71 55	77·3	43 19	70 35	76·4	43 05	69 15	75·5	42 49	67 56	74·6	42 33	66 37	73·7	225	315
46	134	44 43	72 59	77·8	44 30	71 37	76·9	44 16	70 15	75·9	44 01	68 54	75·1	43 45	67 35	74·1	43 28	66 15	73·2	226	314
47	133	45 40	72 41	77·4	45 27	71 18	76·4	45 12	69 55	75·5	44 57	68 33	74·5	44 40	67 12	73·5	44 23	65 51	72·6	227	313
48	132	46 38	72 23	77·0	46 24	70 58	76·0	46 09	69 34	75·0	45 53	68 11	74·0	45 35	66 48	73·0	45 17	65 27	72·0	228	312
49	131	47 35	72 03	76·5	47 20	70 37	75·5	47 05	69 11	74·4	46 49	67 47	73·4	46 30	66 23	72·4	46 12	65 01	71·4	229	311
50	130	48 32	71 42	76·1	48 17	70 15	75·0	48 01	68 48	73·9	47 44	67 22	72·9	47 25	65 58	71·8	47 06	64 34	70·8	230	310
51	129	49 29	71 20	75·6	49 13	69 51	74·5	48 57	68 23	73·4	48 39	66 56	72·3	48 20	65 30	71·2	48 00	64 05	70·1	231	309
52	128	50 25	70 57	75·1	50 09	69 27	73·9	49 52	67 57	72·8	49 34	66 29	71·7	49 15	65 02	70·6	48 54	63 35	69·5	232	308
53	127	51 22	70 33	74·6	51 06	69 01	73·4	50 48	67 30	72·2	50 29	66 00	71·0	50 09	64 31	69·9	49 48	63 04	68·8	233	307
54	126	52 19	70 07	74·0	52 02	68 33	72·8	51 43	67 01	71·6	51 24	65 30	70·4	51 03	64 00	69·2	50 41	62 31	68·1	234	306
55	125	53 15	69 40	73·5	52 57	68 04	72·2	52 38	66 30	70·9	52 18	64 58	69·7	51 57	63 26	68·5	51 34	61 56	67·3	235	305
56	124	54 11	69 11	72·9	53 53	67 34	71·6	53 33	65 58	70·3	53 12	64 24	69·0	52 50	62 51	67·8	52 27	61 20	66·6	236	304
57	123	55 07	68 41	72·2	54 48	67 02	70·9	54 28	65 24	69·6	54 06	63 48	68·3	53 43	62 14	67·0	53 19	60 42	65·8	237	303
58	122	56 03	68 09	71·6	55 43	66 28	70·2	55 22	64 48	68·8	55 00	63 11	67·5	54 36	61 35	66·2	54 12	60 01	64·9	238	302
59	121	56 59	67 34	70·9	56 38	65 53	69·5	56 16	64 10	68·1	55 53	62 31	66·7	55 29	60 54	65·4	55 03	59 18	64·1	239	301
60	120	57 54	66 58	70·2	57 33	65 13	68·7	57 10	63 30	67·3	56 46	61 49	65·9	56 21	60 10	64·5	55 55	58 33	63·1	240	300
61	119	58 49	66 20	69·4	58 27	64 32	67·9	58 04	62 47	66·4	57 39	61 04	65·0	57 13	59 24	63·6	56 46	57 46	62·2	241	299
62	118	59 44	65 38	68·6	59 21	63 49	67·1	58 57	62 02	65·5	58 31	60 17	64·0	58 05	58 35	62·6	57 36	56 56	61·2	242	298
63	117	60 38	64 55	67·8	60 15	63 03	66·2	59 50	61 13	64·6	59 23	59 27	63·1	58 55	57 43	61·6	58 26	56 03	60·2	243	297
64	116	61 32	64 08	66·9	61 08	62 14	65·2	60 42	60 22	63·6	60 15	58 34	62·0	59 46	56 49	60·5	59 16	55 06	59·1	244	296
65	115	62 26	63 18	66·0	62 01	61 21	64·2	61 34	59 28	62·6	61 06	57 37	61·0	60 36	55 51	59·4	60 05	54 07	57·9	245	295
66	114	63 20	62 25	65·0	62 53	60 25	63·2	62 26	58 30	61·5	61 56	56 37	59·8	61 25	54 49	58·2	60 53	53 04	56·7	246	294
67	113	64 13	61 27	63·9	63 45	59 25	62·1	63 16	57 27	60·3	62 46	55 34	58·6	62 14	53 44	57·0	61 41	51 57	55·4	247	293
68	112	65 05	60 26	62·8	64 37	58 21	60·9	64 07	56 21	59·1	63 35	54 25	57·4	63 02	52 34	55·7	62 27	50 47	54·1	248	292
69	111	65 57	59 20	61·6	65 27	57 13	59·6	64 56	55 10	57·8	64 23	53 13	56·0	63 49	51 20	54·3	63 14	49 32	52·7	249	291
70	110	66 48	58 08	60·3	66 18	55 59	58·3	65 45	53 55	56·4	65 11	51 55	54·6	64 36	50 01	52·9	63 59	48 12	51·2	250	290
71	109	67 39	56 52	58·9	67 07	54 40	56·8	66 33	52 33	54·9	65 58	50 33	53·1	65 21	48 38	51·3	64 43	46 48	49·7	251	289
72	108	68 29	55 29	57·4	67 55	53 16	55·3	67 20	51 06	53·3	66 44	49 04	51·5	66 06	47 08	49·7	65 26	45 18	48·0	252	288
73	107	69 18	53 59	55·8	68 43	51 42	53·7	68 07	49 33	51·6	67 29	47 30	49·8	66 49	45 33	48·0	66 08	43 43	46·3	253	287
74	106	70 06	52 22	54·1	69 30	50 03	51·9	68 52	47 52	49·8	68 12	45 49	47·9	67 31	43 52	46·1	66 49	42 02	44·4	254	286
75	105	70 53	50 36	52·2	70 15	48 16	50·0	69 36	46 04	47·9	68 55	44 00	46·0	68 12	42 04	44·2	67 29	40 15	42·5	255	285
76	104	71 38	48 42	50·2	70 59	46 20	47·9	70 18	44 08	45·9	69 36	42 05	43·9	68 52	40 09	42·1	68 07	38 21	40·5	256	284
77	103	72 23	46 37	48·0	71 42	44 15	45·7	70 59	42 03	43·7	70 15	40 01	41·7	69 30	38 07	39·9	68 43	36 21	38·3	257	283
78	102	73 06	44 22	45·6	72 23	42 00	43·4	71 38	39 49	41·3	70 53	37 49	39·4	70 06	35 57	37·6	69 18	34 13	36·0	258	282
79	101	73 47	41 55	43·1	73 02	39 34	40·8	72 16	37 26	38·8	71 28	35 27	36·9	70 40	33 38	35·2	69 50	31 58	33·6	259	281
80	100	74 26	39 15	40·3	73 39	36 57	38·1	72 51	34 51	36·1	72 02	32 57	34·3	71 12	31 12	32·6	70 21	29 36	31·1	260	280
81	99	75 02	36 21	37·3	74 14	34 07	35·1	73 24	32 06	33·2	72 34	30 17	31·5	71 42	28 37	29·9	70 50	27 06	28·4	261	279
82	98	75 37	33 13	34·1	74 46	31 05	32·0	73 55	29 10	30·2	73 03	27 27	28·5	72 09	25 53	27·0	71 16	24 29	25·7	262	278
83	97	76 08	29 50	30·6	75 16	27 50	28·6	74 23	26 03	26·9	73 29	24 27	25·4	72 34	23 02	24·0	71 39	21 44	22·8	263	277
84	96	76 36	26 11	26·8	75 42	24 22	25·0	74 48	22 45	23·5	73 52	21 19	22·1	72 56	20 04	20·9	72 00	18 53	19·8	264	276
85	95	77 01	22 18	22·8	76 05	20 41	21·3	75 09	19 16	19·9	74 12	18 01	18·7	73 15	16 54	17·6	72 18	15 55	16·7	265	275
86	94	77 22	18 10	18·6	76 25	16 49	17·3	75 27	15 38	16·1	74 29	14 36	15·1	73 31	13 40	14·2	72 33	12 51	13·5	266	274
87	93	77 38	13 50	14·1	76 40	12 46	13·1	75 41	11 51	12·2	74 43	11 03	11·4	73 44	10 21	10·8	72 45	9 43	10·2	267	273
88	92	77 50	9 19	9·5	76 51	8 36	8·8	75 52	7 58	8·2	74 52	7 25	7·7	73 53	6 56	7·2	72 53	6 31	6·8	268	272
89	91	77 58	4 42	4·8	76 58	4 19	4·4	75 58	4 00	4·1	74 58	3 44	3·9	73 58	3 29	3·6	72 58	3 16	3·4	269	271
90	90	78 00	0 00	0·0	77 00	0 00	0·0	76 00	0 00	0·0	75 00	0 00	0·0	74 00	0 00	0·0	73 00	0 00	0·0	270	270

N. Lat: for LHA > 180° ... Z_n = Z
for LHA < 180° ... Z_n = 360° − Z

S. Lat.: for LHA > 180° ... Z_n = 180° − Z
for LHA < 180° ... Z_n = 180° + Z

LATITUDE / A: 18° – 23°

SIGHT REDUCTION TABLE

B: (−) for 90° < LHA < 270°
Dec:(−) for Lat. contrary name

Z1: same sign as B
Z2: (−) for F > 90°

Lat./A		18°			19°			20°			21°			22°			23°			Lat./A	
LHA/F		A/H	B/P	Z1/Z2	A/H	B/P	Z1/Z2	A/H	B/P	Z1/Z2	A/H	B/P	Z1/Z2	A/H	B/P	Z1/Z2	A/H	B/P	Z1/Z2	LHA	
0	180	0 00	72 00	90·0	0 00	71 00	90·0	0 00	70 00	90·0	0 00	69 00	90·0	0 00	68 00	90·0	0 00	67 00	90·0	180	360
1	179	0 57	72 00	89·7	0 57	71 00	89·7	0 56	70 00	89·6	0 56	69 00	89·6	0 56	68 00	89·6	0 55	67 00	89·6	181	359
2	178	1 54	71 59	89·4	1 53	70 59	89·3	1 53	69 59	89·3	1 52	68 59	89·3	1 51	67 59	89·3	1 50	66 59	89·2	182	358
3	177	2 51	71 59	89·1	2 50	70 59	89·0	2 48	69 59	89·0	2 48	68 59	89·0	2 47	67 58	88·9	2 46	66 58	88·8	183	357
4	176	3 48	71 58	88·8	3 47	70 57	88·7	3 46	69 57	88·6	3 44	68 57	88·6	3 42	67 57	88·6	3 41	66 58	88·4	184	356
5	175	4 45	71 56	88·5	4 44	70 56	88·4	4 42	69 56	88·3	4 40	68 56	88·2	4 38	67 55	88·1	4 36	66 55	88·0	185	355
6	174	5 42	71 54	88·1	5 40	70 54	88·0	5 38	69 54	87·9	5 36	68 54	87·8	5 34	67 53	87·7	5 31	66 53	87·6	186	354
7	173	6 39	71 52	87·8	6 37	70 52	87·7	6 35	69 52	87·6	6 32	68 51	87·5	6 29	67 51	87·4	6 26	66 51	87·3	187	353
8	172	7 36	71 50	87·5	7 34	70 50	87·4	7 31	69 49	87·2	7 28	68 49	87·1	7 22	67 48	87·0	7 22	66 48	86·9	188	352
9	171	8 33	71 47	87·2	8 30	70 47	87·0	8 27	69 46	86·9	8 24	68 46	86·8	8 20	67 45	86·6	8 17	66 45	86·5	189	351
10	170	9 30	71 44	86·9	9 27	70 44	86·7	9 23	69 43	86·5	9 20	68 42	86·4	9 16	67 42	86·2	9 12	66 41	86·1	190	350
11	169	10 27	71 41	86·6	10 24	70 40	86·4	10 20	69 39	86·2	10 16	68 39	86·0	10 11	67 38	85·8	10 07	66 37	85·7	191	349
12	168	11 24	71 37	86·2	11 20	70 36	86·0	11 16	69 35	85·8	11 12	68 34	85·6	11 07	67 33	85·4	11 02	66 32	85·3	192	348
13	167	12 21	71 33	85·9	12 17	70 32	85·7	12 12	69 31	85·5	12 07	68 30	85·3	12 02	67 29	85·1	11 57	66 22	84·8	193	347
14	166	13 18	71 29	85·6	13 13	70 28	85·4	13 08	69 26	85·1	13 03	68 25	84·9	12 58	67 24	84·7	12 52	66 22	84·4	194	346
15	165	14 15	71 24	85·3	14 10	70 23	85·0	14 05	69 21	84·8	13 59	68 20	84·5	13 53	67 18	84·3	13 47	66 17	84·0	195	345
16	164	15 12	71 19	84·9	15 06	70 18	84·7	15 01	69 16	84·4	14 55	68 14	84·1	14 48	67 12	83·9	14 42	66 10	83·6	196	344
17	163	16 09	71 14	84·6	16 03	70 12	84·3	15 57	69 10	84·0	15 50	68 08	83·7	15 44	67 06	83·5	15 37	66 04	83·2	197	343
18	162	17 05	71 08	84·3	16 59	70 06	84·0	16 53	69 03	83·7	16 46	68 01	83·4	16 39	66 59	83·1	16 32	65 57	82·8	198	342
19	161	18 02	71 02	83·9	17 56	69 59	83·6	17 49	68 57	83·3	17 42	67 54	83·0	17 34	66 52	82·7	17 26	65 49	82·3	199	341
20	160	18 59	70 56	83·6	18 52	69 53	83·2	18 45	68 50	82·9	18 37	67 47	82·6	18 29	66 44	82·2	18 21	65 41	81·9	200	340
21	159	19 56	70 49	83·2	19 48	69 45	82·9	19 41	68 42	82·5	19 33	67 39	82·2	19 24	66 36	81·8	19 16	65 33	81·5	201	339
22	158	20 52	70 41	82·9	20 45	69 38	82·5	20 37	68 34	82·1	20 28	67 31	81·8	20 19	66 27	81·4	20 10	65 24	81·0	202	338
23	157	21 49	70 33	82·5	21 41	69 29	82·1	21 32	68 26	81·7	21 24	67 22	81·4	21 14	66 18	81·0	21 05	65 15	80·6	203	337
24	156	22 45	70 25	82·2	22 37	69 21	81·8	22 28	68 17	81·3	22 19	67 12	80·9	22 09	66 09	80·5	21 59	65 05	80·1	204	336
25	155	23 42	70 17	81·8	23 33	69 12	81·4	23 24	68 07	80·9	23 14	67 03	80·5	23 04	65 58	80·1	22 54	64 54	79·7	205	335
26	154	24 38	70 07	81·4	24 29	69 02	81·0	24 20	67 57	80·5	24 09	66 52	80·1	23 59	65 48	79·6	23 48	64 43	79·2	206	334
27	153	25 35	69 58	81·1	25 25	68 52	80·6	25 15	67 47	80·1	25 05	66 42	79·7	24 54	65 36	79·2	24 42	64 32	78·7	207	333
28	152	26 31	69 48	80·7	26 21	68 42	80·2	26 11	67 36	79·7	26 00	66 30	79·2	25 48	65 25	78·7	25 36	64 19	78·3	208	332
29	151	27 27	69 37	80·3	27 17	68 31	79·8	27 06	67 24	79·3	26 55	66 18	78·8	26 43	65 12	78·3	26 30	64 07	77·8	209	331
30	150	28 24	69 26	79·9	28 13	68 19	79·4	28 01	67 12	78·8	27 50	66 06	78·3	27 37	64 59	77·8	27 24	63 53	77·3	210	330
31	149	29 20	69 14	79·5	29 09	68 07	78·9	28 57	67 00	78·4	28 44	65 53	77·8	28 31	64 46	77·3	28 18	63 39	76·8	211	329
32	148	30 16	69 02	79·1	30 04	67 54	78·5	29 52	66 46	77·9	29 39	65 39	77·4	29 26	64 32	76·8	29 12	63 25	76·3	212	328
33	147	31 12	68 49	78·7	31 00	67 41	78·1	30 47	66 32	77·5	30 34	65 24	76·8	30 20	64 17	76·3	30 05	63 09	75·8	213	327
34	146	32 08	68 36	78·2	31 55	67 27	77·6	31 42	66 18	77·0	31 28	65 09	76·3	31 14	64 01	75·8	30 59	62 53	75·2	214	326
35	145	33 04	68 22	77·8	32 51	67 12	77·2	32 37	66 03	76·5	32 23	64 54	75·8	32 08	63 45	75·3	31 52	62 36	74·7	215	325
36	144	33 59	68 07	77·3	33 46	66 57	76·7	33 32	65 47	76·0	33 17	64 37	75·4	33 01	63 28	74·8	32 45	62 19	74·2	216	324
37	143	34 55	67 52	76·9	34 41	66 41	76·2	34 26	65 30	75·5	34 11	64 20	74·9	33 55	63 10	74·2	33 38	62 01	73·6	217	323
38	142	35 50	67 36	76·4	35 36	66 24	75·7	35 21	65 13	75·0	35 05	64 02	74·4	34 48	62 51	73·7	34 31	61 41	73·0	218	322
39	141	36 46	67 19	76·0	36 31	66 06	75·2	36 15	64 54	74·5	35 59	63 43	73·8	35 41	62 32	73·1	35 24	61 21	72·4	219	321
40	140	37 41	67 01	75·5	37 26	65 48	74·7	37 10	64 35	74·0	36 53	63 23	73·3	36 35	62 12	72·6	36 17	61 01	71·8	220	320
41	139	38 36	66 42	75·0	38 20	65 29	74·2	38 04	64 15	73·4	37 46	63 02	72·7	37 28	61 50	72·0	37 09	60 39	71·2	221	319
42	138	39 31	66 23	74·5	39 15	65 08	73·7	38 58	63 54	72·9	38 40	62 41	72·1	38 21	61 28	71·4	38 01	60 16	70·6	222	318
43	137	40 26	66 03	73·9	40 09	64 47	73·1	39 51	63 33	72·3	39 33	62 18	71·5	39 13	61 05	70·7	38 53	59 52	70·0	223	317
44	136	41 21	65 42	73·4	41 03	64 25	72·5	40 45	63 10	71·7	40 26	61 55	70·9	40 06	60 41	70·1	39 45	59 27	69·3	224	316
45	135	42 16	65 19	72·8	41 57	64 02	72·0	41 38	62 46	71·1	41 19	61 30	70·3	40 58	60 15	69·5	40 37	59 01	68·7	225	315

Lat./A	18°			19°			20°			21°			22°			23°			Lat./A
LHA/F	A/H	B/P	Z_1/Z_2	A/H	B/P	Z_1/Z_2	A/H	B/P	Z_1/Z_2	A/H	B/P	Z_1/Z_2	A/H	B/P	Z_1/Z_2	A/H	B/P	Z_1/Z_2	LHA
45	42 16	65 19	72·8	41 57	64 02	72·0	41 38	62 46	71·1	41 19	61 30	70·3	40 58	60 15	69·5	40 37	59 01	68·7	225
46	43 10	64 56	72·3	42 51	63 38	71·4	42 32	62 21	70·5	42 11	61 05	69·6	41 50	59 49	68·8	41 28	58 34	68·0	226
47	44 04	64 32	71·7	43 45	63 13	70·8	43 25	61 55	69·9	43 04	60 38	69·0	42 42	59 21	68·1	42 19	58 06	67·3	227
48	44 58	64 06	71·1	44 38	62 46	70·1	44 18	61 29	69·2	43 56	60 09	68·3	43 33	58 52	67·4	43 10	57 37	66·5	228
49	45 52	63 39	70·4	45 32	62 18	69·5	45 10	60 59	68·5	44 48	59 40	67·6	44 24	58 22	66·7	44 00	57 06	65·8	229
50	46 46	63 11	69·8	46 25	61 49	68·8	46 03	60 29	67·8	45 39	59 09	66·9	45 15	57 51	65·9	44 50	56 34	65·0	230
51	47 39	62 42	69·1	47 17	61 19	68·1	46 55	59 57	67·1	46 31	58 37	66·1	46 06	57 18	65·2	45 40	56 00	64·2	231
52	48 33	62 11	68·4	48 10	60 47	67·4	47 46	59 25	66·4	47 22	58 03	65·4	46 56	56 44	64·4	46 30	55 25	63·4	232
53	49 25	61 38	67·7	49 02	60 13	66·6	48 37	58 51	65·6	48 13	57 28	64·6	47 46	56 07	63·6	47 19	54 48	62·6	233
54	50 18	61 04	67·0	49 54	59 38	65·9	49 29	58 14	64·8	49 03	56 51	63·7	48 36	55 30	62·7	48 08	54 10	61·7	234
55	51 10	60 28	66·2	50 46	59 01	65·1	50 20	57 36	64·0	49 53	56 12	62·9	49 25	54 50	61·9	48 56	53 30	60·8	235
56	52 03	59 50	65·4	51 37	58 23	64·2	51 10	56 56	63·1	50 43	55 32	62·0	50 14	54 09	61·0	49 44	52 48	59·9	236
57	52 54	59 11	64·6	52 28	57 42	63·4	52 00	56 15	62·2	51 32	54 49	61·1	51 02	53 26	60·0	50 32	52 04	59·0	237
58	53 46	58 29	63·7	53 18	56 59	62·5	52 50	55 31	61·3	52 21	54 05	60·2	51 50	52 41	59·1	51 19	51 18	58·0	238
59	54 37	57 45	62·8	54 08	56 14	61·5	53 39	54 45	60·4	53 09	53 18	59·2	52 38	51 53	58·1	52 06	50 30	57·0	239
60	55 27	56 59	61·8	54 58	55 27	60·6	54 28	53 57	59·4	53 57	52 29	58·2	53 25	51 04	57·0	52 52	49 40	55·9	240
61	56 17	56 10	60·9	55 47	54 37	59·6	55 16	53 06	58·3	54 44	51 38	57·1	54 11	50 12	55·9	53 37	48 48	54·8	241
62	57 07	55 19	59·8	56 36	53 45	58·5	56 04	52 13	57·2	55 31	50 44	56·0	54 57	49 17	54·8	54 22	47 53	53·7	242
63	57 56	54 25	58·8	57 24	52 49	57·4	56 51	51 17	56·1	56 17	49 47	54·9	55 42	48 20	53·7	55 06	46 55	52·5	243
64	58 44	53 27	57·6	58 12	51 51	56·3	57 38	50 18	55·0	57 03	48 48	53·7	56 27	47 20	52·5	55 50	45 55	51·3	244
65	59 32	52 27	56·5	58 58	50 50	55·1	58 24	49 16	53·7	57 47	47 45	52·5	57 10	46 17	51·2	56 32	44 52	50·0	245
66	60 19	51 23	55·2	59 45	49 45	53·8	59 09	48 11	52·5	58 32	46 39	51·2	57 53	45 11	49·9	57 14	43 47	48·7	246
67	61 06	50 15	53·9	60 30	48 37	52·5	59 53	47 02	51·1	59 15	45 30	49·9	58 36	44 02	48·6	57 55	42 38	47·4	247
68	61 52	49 04	52·6	61 15	47 25	51·1	60 36	45 50	49·8	59 57	44 18	48·4	59 17	42 50	47·2	58 36	41 26	46·0	248
69	62 37	47 48	51·2	61 58	46 09	49·7	61 19	44 33	48·3	60 39	43 02	47·0	59 57	41 34	45·7	59 15	40 10	44·5	249
70	63 21	46 28	49·7	62 41	44 48	48·2	62 01	43 13	46·8	61 19	41 42	45·4	60 36	40 15	44·2	59 53	38 52	43·0	250
71	64 04	45 03	48·1	63 23	43 24	46·6	62 41	41 49	45·2	61 58	40 18	43·9	61 15	38 52	42·6	60 30	37 29	41·4	251
72	64 45	43 34	46·4	64 04	41 54	44·9	63 21	40 20	43·5	62 37	38 50	42·2	61 52	37 25	40·9	61 06	36 03	39·7	252
73	65 26	41 59	44·7	64 43	40 20	43·2	63 59	38 46	41·8	63 14	37 18	40·5	62 27	35 53	39·2	61 41	34 34	38·0	253
74	66 06	40 19	42·9	65 21	38 41	41·4	64 36	37 08	40·0	63 49	35 41	38·7	63 02	34 18	37·4	62 14	33 00	36·3	254
75	66 44	38 32	40·9	65 58	36 56	39·5	65 11	35 25	38·1	64 23	33 59	36·8	63 35	32 39	35·6	62 46	31 22	34·4	255
76	67 20	36 40	38·9	66 33	35 05	37·4	65 45	33 37	36·1	64 56	32 13	34·8	64 07	30 55	33·6	63 16	29 41	32·5	256
77	67 55	34 42	36·8	67 07	33 09	35·3	66 18	31 43	34·0	65 27	30 22	32·8	64 37	29 06	31·6	63 45	27 55	30·6	257
78	68 29	32 37	34·5	67 39	31 07	33·1	66 48	29 44	31·9	65 57	28 26	30·7	65 05	27 14	29·6	64 13	26 06	28·5	258
79	69 00	30 25	32·2	68 09	29 00	30·8	67 17	27 40	29·6	66 25	26 26	28·5	65 32	25 17	27·4	64 38	24 12	26·4	259
80	69 29	28 07	29·7	68 37	26 46	28·4	67 44	25 30	27·3	66 50	24 20	26·2	65 56	23 15	25·2	65 02	22 15	24·3	260
81	69 57	25 43	27·1	69 03	24 26	25·9	68 09	23 15	24·8	67 14	22 10	23·8	66 19	21 10	22·9	65 23	20 14	22·1	261
82	70 24	23 11	24·5	69 27	22 00	23·3	68 31	20 56	22·3	67 36	19 56	21·4	66 40	19 00	20·6	65 43	18 09	19·8	262
83	70 44	20 34	21·7	69 48	19 29	20·7	68 51	18 31	19·7	67 55	17 37	18·7	66 58	16 47	18·1	66 01	15 59	17·4	263
84	71 03	17 50	18·8	70 07	16 53	17·9	69 09	16 01	17·1	68 12	15 14	16·3	67 14	14 30	15·7	66 16	13 50	15·1	264
85	71 20	15 01	15·8	70 23	14 12	15·0	69 25	13 28	14·3	68 26	12 48	13·7	67 28	12 10	13·1	66 29	11 36	12·6	265
86	71 35	12 07	12·8	70 36	11 27	12·1	69 37	10 51	11·6	68 38	10 18	11·0	67 39	9 48	10·6	66 40	9 20	10·1	266
87	71 46	9 09	9·6	70 46	8 39	9·1	69 47	8 11	8·7	68 48	7 46	8·3	67 48	7 23	8·0	66 49	7 02	7·6	267
88	71 54	6 08	6·4	70 54	5 47	6·1	69 54	5 29	5·8	68 55	5 12	5·6	67 55	4 56	5·3	66 55	4 42	5·1	268
89	71 58	3 04	3·2	70 58	2 54	3·1	69 59	2 45	2·9	68 59	2 36	2·8	67 59	2 28	2·7	66 59	2 21	2·6	269
90	72 00	0 00	0·0	71 00	0 00	0·0	70 00	0 00	0·0	69 00	0 00	0·0	68 00	0 00	0·0	67 00	0 00	0·0	270

N. Lat: for LHA > 180° ... $Z_n = Z$
for LHA < 180° ... $Z_n = 360° - Z$

S. Lat.: for LHA > 180° ... $Z_n = 180° - Z$
for LHA < 180° ... $Z_n = 180° + Z$

SIGHT REDUCTION TABLE

B: (−) for 90° < LHA < 270°
Dec::(−) for Lat. contrary name

Z₁: same sign as B
Z₂: (−) for F > 90°

LHA/F	24° A/H	24° B/P	24° Z₁/Z₂	25° A/H	25° B/P	25° Z₁/Z₂	26° A/H	26° B/P	26° Z₁/Z₂	27° A/H	27° B/P	27° Z₁/Z₂	28° A/H	28° B/P	28° Z₁/Z₂	29° A/H	29° B/P	29° Z₁/Z₂	LHA
0 / 180	0 00	66 00	90·0	0 00	65 00	90·0	0 00	64 00	90·0	0 00	63 00	90·0	0 00	62 00	90·0	0 00	61 00	90·0	180 / 360
1 / 179	0 55	66 00	89·6	0 54	65 00	89·6	0 54	64 00	89·6	0 53	63 00	89·5	0 53	62 00	89·5	0 52	61 00	89·5	181 / 359
2 / 178	1 50	65 59	89·2	1 49	64 59	89·2	1 48	63 59	89·1	1 47	62 59	89·1	1 46	61 59	89·1	1 45	60 59	89·0	182 / 358
3 / 177	2 44	65 58	88·8	2 43	64 58	88·7	2 42	63 58	88·7	2 40	62 58	88·6	2 39	61 58	88·6	2 37	60 58	88·5	183 / 357
4 / 176	3 39	65 57	88·4	3 37	64 57	88·3	3 36	63 57	88·2	3 34	62 57	88·2	3 32	61 57	88·1	3 30	60 56	88·1	184 / 356
5 / 175	4 34	65 55	88·0	4 32	64 55	87·9	4 30	63 55	87·8	4 27	62 55	87·7	4 25	61 55	87·6	4 22	60 54	87·6	185 / 355
6 / 174	5 29	65 53	87·6	5 26	64 53	87·5	5 23	63 53	87·4	5 21	62 52	87·3	5 18	61 52	87·2	5 15	60 52	87·1	186 / 354
7 / 173	6 24	65 50	87·1	6 20	64 50	87·0	6 17	63 50	86·9	6 14	62 50	86·8	6 11	61 49	86·7	6 07	60 49	86·6	187 / 353
8 / 172	7 18	65 47	86·7	7 15	64 47	86·6	7 11	63 47	86·5	7 07	62 46	86·3	7 04	61 46	86·2	6 59	60 46	86·1	188 / 352
9 / 171	8 13	65 44	86·3	8 09	64 44	86·2	8 05	63 43	86·0	8 01	62 43	85·9	7 56	61 42	85·7	7 52	60 42	85·6	189 / 351
10 / 170	9 08	65 40	85·9	9 03	64 40	85·7	8 59	63 39	85·6	8 54	62 39	85·4	8 49	61 38	85·3	8 44	60 38	85·1	190 / 350
11 / 169	10 02	65 36	85·5	9 57	64 35	85·3	9 52	63 35	85·1	9 47	62 34	85·0	9 42	61 33	84·8	9 36	60 33	84·6	191 / 349
12 / 168	10 57	65 32	85·1	10 52	64 31	84·9	10 46	63 30	84·7	10 41	62 29	84·5	10 35	61 28	84·3	10 29	60 28	84·1	192 / 348
13 / 167	11 52	65 27	84·6	11 46	64 26	84·4	11 40	63 25	84·2	11 34	62 24	84·0	11 27	61 23	83·8	11 21	60 22	83·6	193 / 347
14 / 166	12 46	65 21	84·2	12 40	64 20	84·0	12 34	63 19	83·8	12 27	62 18	83·5	12 20	61 17	83·3	12 13	60 16	83·1	194 / 346
15 / 165	13 41	65 15	83·8	13 34	64 14	83·5	13 27	63 13	83·3	13 20	62 11	83·1	13 13	61 10	82·8	13 05	60 09	82·6	195 / 345
16 / 164	14 35	65 09	83·3	14 28	64 07	83·1	14 21	63 06	82·8	14 13	62 04	82·6	14 05	61 03	82·3	13 57	60 02	82·1	196 / 344
17 / 163	15 29	65 02	82·9	15 22	64 00	82·6	15 14	62 59	82·4	15 06	61 57	82·1	14 58	60 56	81·8	14 49	59 54	81·6	197 / 343
18 / 162	16 24	64 55	82·5	16 16	63 53	82·2	16 08	62 51	81·9	15 59	61 49	81·6	15 50	60 47	81·3	15 41	59 46	81·0	198 / 342
19 / 161	17 18	64 47	82·0	17 10	63 45	81·7	17 01	62 43	81·4	16 52	61 41	81·1	16 42	60 39	80·8	16 33	59 37	80·5	199 / 341
20 / 160	18 12	64 39	81·6	18 03	63 36	81·3	17 54	62 34	80·9	17 45	61 32	80·6	17 35	60 30	80·3	17 24	59 28	80·0	200 / 340
21 / 159	19 07	64 30	81·1	18 57	63 28	80·8	18 47	62 25	80·4	18 37	61 23	80·1	18 27	60 20	79·8	18 16	59 18	79·5	201 / 339
22 / 158	20 01	64 21	80·7	19 51	63 18	80·3	19 41	62 15	80·0	19 30	61 13	79·6	19 19	60 10	79·3	19 08	59 08	78·9	202 / 338
23 / 157	20 55	64 11	80·2	20 44	63 08	79·8	20 34	62 05	79·5	20 22	61 02	79·1	20 11	59 59	78·7	19 59	58 57	78·4	203 / 337
24 / 156	21 49	64 01	79·7	21 38	62 58	79·3	21 27	61 54	79·0	21 15	60 51	78·6	21 03	59 48	78·2	20 50	58 45	77·8	204 / 336
25 / 155	22 43	63 50	79·3	22 31	62 46	78·9	22 19	61 43	78·4	22 07	60 39	78·0	21 55	59 36	77·7	21 42	58 33	77·3	205 / 335
26 / 154	23 36	63 39	78·8	23 25	62 35	78·4	23 12	61 31	77·9	22 59	60 27	77·5	22 46	59 24	77·1	22 33	58 20	76·7	206 / 334
27 / 153	24 30	63 27	78·3	24 18	62 22	77·8	24 05	61 18	77·4	23 52	60 14	76·9	23 38	59 10	76·5	23 24	58 07	76·1	207 / 333
28 / 152	25 24	63 14	77·8	25 11	62 10	77·3	24 57	61 05	76·9	24 44	60 01	76·4	24 29	58 57	76·0	24 15	57 53	75·5	208 / 332
29 / 151	26 17	63 01	77·3	26 04	61 56	76·8	25 50	60 51	76·3	25 36	59 47	75·9	25 21	58 42	75·4	25 05	57 38	75·0	209 / 331
30 / 150	27 11	62 48	76·8	26 57	61 42	76·3	26 42	60 37	75·8	26 27	59 32	75·3	26 12	58 27	74·8	25 56	57 23	74·4	210 / 330
31 / 149	28 04	62 33	76·3	27 50	61 27	75·8	27 35	60 22	75·2	27 19	59 16	74·7	27 03	58 11	74·2	26 47	57 07	73·8	211 / 329
32 / 148	28 57	62 18	75·7	28 42	61 12	75·2	28 27	60 06	74·7	28 10	59 00	74·2	27 54	57 54	73·7	27 37	56 50	73·1	212 / 328
33 / 147	29 50	62 02	75·2	29 35	60 56	74·7	29 19	59 49	74·1	29 02	58 43	73·6	28 45	57 38	73·0	28 27	56 32	72·5	213 / 327
34 / 146	30 43	61 46	74·7	30 27	60 39	74·1	30 10	59 32	73·5	29 53	58 26	73·0	29 35	57 20	72·4	29 17	56 14	71·9	214 / 326
35 / 145	31 36	61 28	74·1	31 19	60 21	73·5	31 02	59 14	72·9	30 44	58 08	72·4	30 26	57 01	71·8	30 07	55 55	71·2	215 / 325
36 / 144	32 29	61 10	73·5	32 11	60 02	72·9	31 53	58 55	72·3	31 35	57 48	71·7	31 16	56 41	71·2	30 56	55 35	70·6	216 / 324
37 / 143	33 21	60 52	73·0	33 03	59 43	72·3	32 45	58 35	71·7	32 26	57 28	71·1	32 06	56 21	70·5	31 46	55 14	69·9	217 / 323
38 / 142	34 13	60 32	72·4	33 55	59 23	71·7	33 36	58 15	71·1	33 16	57 07	70·5	32 56	55 59	69·9	32 35	54 53	69·3	218 / 322
39 / 141	35 06	60 11	71·8	34 47	59 02	71·1	34 27	57 53	70·5	34 06	56 45	69·8	33 45	55 37	69·2	33 24	54 30	68·6	219 / 321
40 / 140	35 58	59 50	71·2	35 38	58 40	70·5	35 17	57 31	69·8	34 56	56 22	69·1	34 35	55 14	68·5	34 12	54 07	67·9	220 / 320
41 / 139	36 49	59 28	70·5	36 29	58 17	69·8	36 08	57 08	69·1	35 46	55 59	68·5	35 24	54 50	67·8	35 01	53 42	67·1	221 / 319
42 / 138	37 41	59 04	69·9	37 20	57 54	69·2	36 58	56 43	68·5	36 36	55 34	67·8	36 13	54 25	67·1	35 49	53 17	66·4	222 / 318
43 / 137	38 32	58 40	69·2	38 11	57 29	68·5	37 48	56 18	67·8	37 25	55 08	67·1	37 02	53 59	66·4	36 37	52 50	65·7	223 / 317
44 / 136	39 23	58 15	68·6	39 01	57 03	67·8	38 38	55 52	67·1	38 14	54 41	66·3	37 50	53 32	65·6	37 25	52 23	64·9	224 / 316
45 / 135	40 14	57 48	67·9	39 51	56 36	67·1	39 28	55 24	66·3	39 03	54 13	65·6	38 38	53 04	64·9	38 12	51 54	64·1	225 / 315

Lat./A (F)	A	24° A/H	24° B/P	24° Z1/Z2	25° A/H	25° B/P	25° Z1/Z2	26° A/H	26° B/P	26° Z1/Z2	27° A/H	27° B/P	27° Z1/Z2	28° A/H	28° B/P	28° Z1/Z2	29° A/H	29° B/P	29° Z1/Z2	Lat./A (LHA)
45	135	40 14	57 48	67·9	39 51	56 36	67·1	39 28	55 24	66·3	39 03	54 13	65·6	38 38	53 04	64·9	38 12	51 54	64·1	225
46	134	41 05	57 21	67·2	40 41	56 08	66·4	40 17	54 56	65·6	39 52	53 44	64·8	39 26	52 34	64·1	38 59	51 25	63·3	226
47	133	41 55	56 52	66·4	41 31	55 38	65·6	41 06	54 26	64·8	40 40	53 14	64·0	40 13	52 04	63·3	39 46	50 54	62·5	227
48	132	42 45	56 22	65·7	42 20	55 08	64·9	41 54	53 55	64·0	41 28	52 43	63·2	41 00	51 32	62·5	40 32	50 22	61·7	228
49	131	43 35	55 50	64·9	43 09	54 36	64·1	42 43	53 22	63·2	42 15	52 10	62·4	41 47	50 59	61·6	41 18	49 48	60·9	229
50	130	44 25	55 17	64·1	43 58	54 02	63·3	43 31	52 49	62·4	43 03	51 36	61·6	42 34	50 24	60·8	42 04	49 14	60·0	230
51	129	45 14	54 43	63·3	44 47	53 28	62·4	44 18	52 13	61·6	43 49	51 00	60·7	43 20	49 48	59·9	42 49	48 38	59·1	231
52	128	46 03	54 08	62·5	45 35	52 52	61·6	45 06	51 37	60·7	44 36	50 23	59·8	44 05	49 11	59·0	43 34	48 00	58·2	232
53	127	46 51	53 30	61·6	46 22	52 14	60·7	45 52	50 59	59·8	45 22	49 45	58·9	44 51	48 32	58·1	44 18	47 21	57·2	233
54	126	47 39	52 51	60·8	47 09	51 34	59·8	46 39	50 19	58·9	46 07	49 05	58·0	45 35	47 52	57·1	45 02	46 41	56·3	234
55	125	48 27	52 11	59·8	47 56	50 53	58·9	47 25	49 37	58·0	46 53	48 23	57·0	46 19	47 10	56·2	45 46	45 59	55·3	235
56	124	49 14	51 28	58·9	48 43	50 11	57·9	48 10	48 54	57·0	47 37	47 40	56·1	47 03	46 27	55·2	46 29	45 15	54·3	236
57	123	50 01	50 44	57·9	49 28	49 26	56·9	48 55	48 09	56·0	48 21	46 54	55·0	47 46	45 41	54·1	47 11	44 30	53·3	237
58	122	50 47	49 58	56·9	50 14	48 39	55·9	49 40	47 22	55·0	49 05	46 07	54·0	48 28	44 54	53·1	47 53	43 43	52·3	238
59	121	51 33	49 09	55·9	50 58	47 51	54·9	50 23	46 34	53·9	49 48	45 18	52·9	49 11	44 05	52·0	48 34	42 54	51·1	239
60	120	52 18	48 19	54·8	51 43	47 00	53·8	51 07	45 43	52·8	50 30	44 28	51·8	49 53	43 14	50·9	49 14	42 03	50·0	240
61	119	53 02	47 26	53·7	52 26	46 07	52·7	51 49	44 50	51·7	51 12	43 35	50·7	50 33	42 22	49·7	49 54	41 10	48·8	241
62	118	53 46	46 31	52·6	53 09	45 12	51·5	52 31	43 54	50·5	51 53	42 39	49·5	51 13	41 27	48·6	50 33	40 16	47·6	242
63	117	54 29	45 33	51·4	53 51	44 14	50·3	53 13	42 57	49·3	52 33	41 42	48·3	51 53	40 30	47·3	51 12	39 19	46·4	243
64	116	55 12	44 33	50·2	54 33	43 14	49·1	53 53	41 57	48·1	53 13	40 42	47·1	52 31	39 30	46·1	51 49	38 20	45·2	244
65	115	55 54	43 30	48·9	55 13	42 11	47·8	54 33	40 55	46·8	53 51	39 40	45·8	53 09	38 29	44·8	52 26	37 19	43·9	245
66	114	56 34	42 25	47·6	55 53	41 06	46·5	55 12	39 50	45·4	54 29	38 36	44·5	53 46	37 25	43·5	53 02	36 16	42·6	246
67	113	57 14	41 16	46·2	56 32	39 58	45·1	55 50	38 42	44·1	55 06	37 29	43·1	54 22	36 19	42·1	53 37	35 11	41·2	247
68	112	57 53	40 05	44·8	57 10	38 47	43·7	56 27	37 32	42·7	55 42	36 19	41·7	54 57	35 10	40·7	54 11	34 03	39·8	248
69	111	58 32	38 50	43·3	57 47	37 33	42·2	57 03	36 18	41·2	56 17	35 07	40·2	55 31	33 59	39·3	54 44	32 53	38·4	249
70	110	59 09	37 32	41·8	58 24	36 16	40·7	57 38	35 02	39·7	56 51	33 52	38·7	56 04	32 45	37·8	55 16	31 41	36·9	250
71	109	59 45	36 11	40·2	58 58	34 55	39·2	58 12	33 43	38·1	57 24	32 35	37·2	56 36	31 29	36·3	55 47	30 26	35·4	251
72	108	60 19	34 46	38·6	59 32	33 32	37·6	58 44	32 21	36·5	57 56	31 14	35·6	57 07	30 10	34·7	56 17	29 08	33·8	252
73	107	60 53	33 18	36·9	60 05	32 05	35·9	59 16	30 56	34·9	58 26	29 51	34·0	57 36	28 48	33·1	56 46	27 49	32·2	253
74	106	61 25	31 46	35·2	60 36	30 35	34·2	59 46	29 28	33·2	58 55	28 25	32·3	58 05	27 24	31·4	57 13	26 26	30·6	254
75	105	61 56	30 10	33·4	61 06	29 02	32·4	60 15	27 57	31·4	59 23	26 56	30·5	58 31	25 57	29·7	57 39	25 02	28·9	255
76	104	62 26	28 31	31·5	61 34	27 25	30·5	60 42	26 23	29·6	59 50	25 24	28·8	58 58	24 28	28·0	58 04	23 35	27·2	256
77	103	62 53	26 48	29·6	62 01	25 45	28·6	61 08	24 46	27·8	60 15	23 49	27·0	59 21	22 56	26·2	58 27	22 05	25·5	257
78	102	63 20	25 02	27·6	62 26	24 02	26·7	61 32	23 05	25·9	60 38	22 12	25·1	59 44	21 21	24·4	58 49	20 34	23·7	258
79	101	63 44	23 12	25·5	62 50	22 15	24·7	61 55	21 22	23·9	61 00	20 32	23·2	60 05	19 44	22·5	59 09	19 00	21·8	259
80	100	64 07	21 18	23·4	63 12	20 25	22·6	62 16	19 36	21·9	61 20	18 49	21·2	60 24	18 05	20·6	59 28	17 24	20·0	260
81	99	64 28	19 22	21·3	63 32	18 33	20·5	62 35	17 47	19·9	61 39	17 04	19·2	60 42	16 24	18·6	59 45	15 46	18·1	261
82	98	64 47	17 22	19·1	63 50	16 37	18·4	62 53	15 56	17·8	61 56	15 17	17·2	60 58	14 40	16·7	60 01	14 06	16·2	262
83	97	65 03	15 18	16·8	64 06	14 39	16·2	63 08	14 02	15·6	62 10	13 27	15·1	61 12	12 55	14·7	60 14	12 24	14·2	263
84	96	65 18	13 13	14·5	64 20	12 38	14·0	63 22	12 06	13·5	62 23	11 36	13·0	61 25	11 07	12·6	60 26	10 41	12·2	264
85	95	65 31	11 05	12·1	64 32	10 35	11·7	63 33	10 08	11·3	62 35	9 42	10·9	61 36	9 19	10·6	60 37	8 56	10·2	265
86	94	65 41	8 54	9·8	64 42	8 30	9·4	63 43	8 08	9·1	62 44	7 48	8·8	61 44	7 28	8·5	60 45	7 10	8·2	266
87	93	65 49	6 42	7·3	64 50	6 24	7·1	63 50	6 07	6·8	62 51	5 52	6·6	61 51	5 37	6·4	60 52	5 24	6·2	267
88	92	65 55	4 29	4·9	64 56	4 17	4·7	63 56	4 06	4·6	62 56	3 55	4·4	61 56	3 45	4·3	60 56	3 36	4·1	268
89	91	65 59	2 15	2·5	64 59	2 09	2·4	63 59	2 03	2·3	62 59	1 58	2·2	61 59	1 53	2·1	60 59	1 48	2·1	269
90	90	66 00	0 00	0·0	65 00	0 00	0·0	64 00	0 00	0·0	63 00	0 00	0·0	62 00	0 00	0·0	61 00	0 00	0·0	270

N. Lat: for LHA > 180° ... $Z_n = Z$
for LHA < 180° ... $Z_n = 360° - Z$

S. Lat.: for LHA > 180° ... $Z_n = 180° - Z$
for LHA < 180° ... $Z_n = 180° + Z$

SIGHT REDUCTION TABLE

B: (−) for 90° < LHA < 270°
Dec:(−) for Lat. contrary name

Z₁: same sign as B
Z₂: (−) for F > 90°

Lat./A		30°			31°			32°			33°			34°			35°			Lat./A	
LHA/F	A	A/H	B/P	Z₁/Z₂	A/H	B/P	Z₁/Z₂	A/H	B/P	Z₁/Z₂	A/H	B/P	Z₁/Z₂	A/H	B/P	Z₁/Z₂	A/H	B/P	Z₁/Z₂	A	LHA
0	180	0 00	60 00	90·0	0 00	59 00	90·0	0 00	58 00	90·0	0 00	57 00	90·0	0 00	56 00	90·0	0 00	55 00	90·0	180	360
1	179	0 52	60 00	89·5	0 51	59 00	89·5	0 51	58 00	89·5	0 50	57 00	89·5	0 50	56 00	89·4	0 49	55 00	89·4	181	359
2	178	1 44	59 59	89·0	1 43	58 59	89·0	1 42	57 59	88·9	1 41	56 59	88·9	1 39	55 59	88·9	1 38	54 59	88·9	182	358
3	177	2 36	59 58	88·5	2 34	58 58	88·5	2 33	57 58	88·4	2 31	56 58	88·4	2 29	55 58	88·3	2 27	54 58	88·3	183	357
4	176	3 28	59 56	88·0	3 26	58 56	88·0	3 23	57 56	87·9	3 21	56 56	87·9	3 19	55 56	87·8	3 17	54 56	87·8	184	356
5	175	4 20	59 54	87·5	4 17	58 54	87·4	4 14	57 54	87·3	4 12	56 54	87·3	4 09	55 54	87·2	4 06	54 54	87·1	185	355
6	174	5 12	59 52	87·0	5 08	58 52	86·9	5 05	57 52	86·8	5 02	56 51	86·7	4 58	55 51	86·6	4 55	54 51	86·6	186	354
7	173	6 04	59 49	86·5	6 00	58 49	86·4	5 56	57 48	86·3	5 52	56 48	86·2	5 48	55 48	86·1	5 44	54 48	86·0	187	353
8	172	6 55	59 45	86·0	6 51	58 45	85·9	6 47	57 45	85·7	6 42	56 45	85·6	6 38	55 44	85·5	6 33	54 44	85·4	188	352
9	171	7 47	59 42	85·5	7 42	58 41	85·3	7 37	57 41	85·2	7 32	56 40	85·1	7 27	55 40	84·9	7 22	54 40	84·8	189	351
10	170	8 39	59 37	85·0	8 34	58 37	84·8	8 28	57 36	84·7	8 22	56 36	84·5	8 17	55 36	84·4	8 11	54 35	84·2	190	350
11	169	9 31	59 32	84·4	9 25	58 32	84·3	9 19	57 31	84·1	9 13	56 31	84·0	9 06	55 30	83·8	9 00	54 30	83·6	191	349
12	168	10 22	59 27	83·9	10 16	58 26	83·8	10 09	57 26	83·6	10 03	56 25	83·4	9 56	55 25	83·2	9 48	54 24	83·0	192	348
13	167	11 14	59 21	83·4	11 07	58 20	83·2	11 00	57 20	83·0	10 53	56 19	82·8	10 45	55 18	82·6	10 37	54 18	82·5	193	347
14	166	12 06	59 15	82·9	11 58	58 14	82·7	11 50	57 13	82·5	11 42	56 12	82·3	11 34	55 12	82·1	11 26	54 11	81·9	194	346
15	165	12 57	59 08	82·4	12 49	58 07	82·1	12 41	57 06	81·9	12 32	56 05	81·7	12 23	55 04	81·5	12 14	54 04	81·3	195	345
16	164	13 49	59 01	81·8	13 40	58 00	81·6	13 31	56 58	81·4	13 22	55 57	81·1	13 13	54 57	80·9	13 02	53 56	80·7	196	344
17	163	14 40	58 53	81·3	14 31	57 52	81·1	14 21	56 50	80·8	14 12	55 48	80·5	14 02	54 48	80·3	13 51	53 47	80·1	197	343
18	162	15 31	58 44	80·8	15 22	57 43	80·5	15 12	56 42	80·2	15 01	55 40	80·0	14 51	54 39	79·7	14 40	53 38	79·4	198	342
19	161	16 23	58 35	80·2	16 12	57 34	79·9	16 02	56 32	79·7	15 51	55 31	79·4	15 40	54 30	79·1	15 28	53 29	78·8	199	341
20	160	17 14	58 26	79·7	17 03	57 24	79·4	16 52	56 23	79·1	16 40	55 21	78·8	16 28	54 20	78·5	16 16	53 19	78·2	200	340
21	159	18 05	58 16	79·1	17 53	57 14	78·8	17 42	56 12	78·5	17 29	55 11	78·2	17 17	54 09	77·9	17 04	53 08	77·6	201	339
22	158	18 56	58 05	78·6	18 44	57 03	78·2	18 31	56 01	77·9	18 19	55 00	77·6	18 05	53 59	77·3	17 52	52 56	77·0	202	338
23	157	19 47	57 54	78·0	19 34	56 52	77·7	19 21	55 50	77·3	19 08	54 48	77·0	18 54	53 46	76·6	18 40	52 44	76·3	203	337
24	156	20 37	57 42	77·4	20 24	56 40	77·1	20 11	55 38	76·7	19 57	54 36	76·4	19 42	53 34	76·0	19 28	52 32	75·7	204	336
25	155	21 28	57 30	76·9	21 14	56 27	76·5	21 00	55 25	76·1	20 46	54 23	75·7	20 31	53 21	75·4	20 15	52 19	75·0	205	335
26	154	22 19	57 17	76·3	22 04	56 14	75·9	21 49	55 12	75·5	21 34	54 09	75·1	21 19	53 07	74·7	21 03	52 05	74·4	206	334
27	153	23 09	57 03	75·7	22 54	56 00	75·3	22 39	54 57	74·9	22 23	53 55	74·5	22 07	52 52	74·1	21 50	51 50	73·7	207	333
28	152	23 59	56 49	75·1	23 44	55 46	74·7	23 28	54 43	74·3	23 11	53 40	73·8	22 54	52 37	73·4	22 37	51 35	73·0	208	332
29	151	24 50	56 34	74·5	24 33	55 31	74·1	24 17	54 27	73·6	23 59	53 24	73·2	23 42	52 22	72·8	23 24	51 19	72·4	209	331
30	150	25 40	56 19	73·9	25 23	55 15	73·4	25 05	54 11	73·0	24 48	53 08	72·5	24 29	52 05	72·1	24 11	51 03	71·7	210	330
31	149	26 29	56 02	73·3	26 12	54 59	72·8	25 54	53 54	72·3	25 35	52 52	71·8	25 17	51 48	71·4	24 57	50 45	71·0	211	329
32	148	27 19	55 45	72·6	27 01	54 41	72·2	26 42	53 37	71·7	26 23	52 33	71·2	26 04	51 30	70·7	25 44	50 27	70·3	212	328
33	147	28 09	55 27	72·0	27 50	54 23	71·5	27 31	53 19	71·0	27 11	52 15	70·5	26 50	51 12	70·0	26 30	50 08	69·6	213	327
34	146	28 58	55 09	71·4	28 38	54 04	70·8	28 19	53 00	70·3	27 57	51 56	69·8	27 37	50 52	69·3	27 16	49 49	68·8	214	326
35	145	29 47	54 49	70·7	29 27	53 45	70·2	29 06	52 40	69·6	28 45	51 36	69·1	28 24	50 32	68·6	28 01	49 29	68·1	215	325
36	144	30 36	54 29	70·0	30 15	53 24	69·5	29 54	52 19	68·9	29 32	51 15	68·4	29 10	50 11	67·9	28 47	49 07	67·4	216	324
37	143	31 25	54 08	69·4	31 03	53 03	68·8	30 41	51 58	68·2	30 19	50 53	67·7	29 56	49 49	67·2	29 32	48 45	66·6	217	323
38	142	32 13	53 46	68·7	31 51	52 40	68·1	31 28	51 35	67·5	31 05	50 30	66·9	30 41	49 26	66·4	30 17	48 23	65·9	218	322
39	141	33 02	53 23	68·0	32 39	52 17	67·4	32 15	51 12	66·8	31 51	50 07	66·2	31 27	49 03	65·6	31 02	48 00	65·1	219	321
40	140	33 50	53 00	67·2	33 26	51 53	66·6	33 02	50 48	66·0	32 37	49 43	65·4	32 12	48 38	64·9	31 46	47 34	64·3	220	320
41	139	34 37	52 35	66·5	34 13	51 29	65·9	33 48	50 23	65·3	33 23	49 17	64·7	32 57	48 13	64·1	32 30	47 09	63·5	221	319
42	138	35 25	52 09	65·8	35 00	51 03	65·1	34 34	49 56	64·5	34 08	48 51	63·9	33 42	47 46	63·3	33 14	46 42	62·7	222	318
43	137	36 12	51 43	65·0	35 46	50 36	64·3	35 20	49 29	63·7	34 53	48 24	63·1	34 26	47 19	62·5	33 58	46 15	61·9	223	317
44	136	36 59	51 15	64·2	36 33	50 08	63·6	36 06	49 01	62·9	35 38	47 55	62·3	35 10	46 51	61·6	34 41	45 46	61·0	224	316
45	135	37 46	50 46	63·4	37 19	49 39	62·7	36 51	48 32	62·1	36 22	47 26	61·4	35 53	46 21	60·8	35 24	45 17	60·2	225	315

Lat. / A	30°			31°			32°			33°			34°			35°			Lat. / A
LHA/F	A/H	B/P	Z_1/Z_2	A/H	B/P	Z_1/Z_2	A/H	B/P	Z_1/Z_2	A/H	B/P	Z_1/Z_2	A/H	B/P	Z_1/Z_2	A/H	B/P	Z_1/Z_2	LHA
45	37 46	50 46	63·4	37 19	49 39	62·7	36 51	48 32	62·1	36 22	47 26	61·4	35 53	46 21	60·8	35 24	45 17	60·2	225	315
46	38 32	50 16	62·6	38 04	49 08	61·9	37 36	48 02	61·2	37 06	46 56	60·6	36 37	45 51	59·9	36 06	44 46	59·3	226	314
47	39 18	49 45	61·8	38 49	48 37	61·1	38 20	47 30	60·4	37 50	46 24	59·7	37 19	45 19	59·1	36 48	44 15	58·4	227	313
48	40 04	49 13	61·0	39 34	48 05	60·2	39 04	46 58	59·5	38 33	45 51	58·9	38 02	44 46	58·2	37 30	43 42	57·5	228	312
49	40 49	48 39	60·1	40 19	47 31	59·4	39 48	46 24	58·6	39 16	45 18	57·9	38 44	44 12	57·2	38 11	43 08	56·6	229	311
50	41 34	48 04	59·2	41 03	46 56	58·5	40 31	45 49	57·7	39 59	44 42	57·0	39 26	43 37	56·3	38 52	42 33	55·6	230	310
51	42 18	47 28	58·3	41 46	46 20	57·5	41 14	45 12	56·8	40 41	44 06	56·1	40 07	43 01	55·4	39 32	41 57	54·7	231	309
52	43 02	46 50	57·4	42 29	45 42	56·6	41 56	44 34	55·9	41 22	43 28	55·1	40 47	42 23	54·4	40 12	41 19	53·7	232	308
53	43 46	46 11	56·4	43 12	45 03	55·6	42 38	43 55	54·9	42 03	42 49	54·1	41 28	41 44	53·4	40 52	40 41	52·7	233	307
54	44 29	45 31	55·5	43 54	44 22	54·7	43 19	43 15	53·9	42 44	42 09	53·1	42 07	41 04	52·4	41 30	40 01	51·7	234	306
55	45 11	44 49	54·5	44 36	43 40	53·7	44 00	42 33	52·9	43 24	41 27	52·1	42 46	40 23	51·4	42 09	39 19	50·7	235	305
56	45 53	44 05	53·5	45 17	42 57	52·6	44 40	41 50	51·8	44 03	40 44	51·1	43 25	39 40	50·3	42 46	38 37	49·6	236	304
57	46 35	43 22	52·4	45 58	42 11	51·6	45 20	41 05	50·8	44 42	39 59	50·0	44 03	38 55	49·3	43 24	37 53	48·5	237	303
58	47 16	42 33	51·3	46 38	41 25	50·5	45 59	40 18	49·7	45 20	39 13	48·9	44 40	38 09	48·2	44 00	37 07	47·4	238	302
59	47 56	41 44	50·2	47 17	40 36	49·4	46 38	39 30	48·6	45 58	38 25	47·8	45 17	37 22	47·1	44 36	36 20	46·3	239	301
60	48 35	40 54	49·1	47 56	39 46	48·3	47 16	38 40	47·5	46 35	37 36	46·7	45 53	36 33	45·9	45 11	35 32	45·2	240	300
61	49 14	40 01	47·9	48 34	38 54	47·1	47 53	37 48	46·3	47 11	36 45	45·5	46 29	35 42	44·7	45 46	34 42	44·0	241	299
62	49 53	39 07	46·8	49 11	38 00	45·9	48 29	36 55	45·1	47 46	35 52	44·3	47 03	34 50	43·6	46 19	33 50	42·8	242	298
63	50 30	38 11	45·5	49 48	37 04	44·7	49 05	36 00	43·9	48 21	34 57	43·1	47 37	33 57	42·3	46 53	32 57	41·6	243	297
64	51 07	37 13	44·3	50 23	36 07	43·4	49 40	35 03	42·6	48 55	34 01	41·8	48 10	33 01	41·1	47 25	32 03	40·4	244	296
65	51 43	36 12	43·1	50 58	35 07	42·2	50 14	34 04	41·3	49 28	33 03	40·6	48 43	32 04	39·8	47 56	31 07	39·1	245	295
66	52 18	35 10	41·7	51 33	34 06	40·8	50 47	33 04	40·0	50 01	32 04	39·3	49 14	31 05	38·5	48 27	30 09	37·8	246	294
67	52 52	34 05	40·3	52 06	33 02	39·5	51 19	32 01	38·7	50 32	31 02	37·9	49 44	30 05	37·2	48 56	29 10	36·5	247	293
68	53 25	32 59	38·9	52 38	31 56	38·1	51 50	30 57	37·3	51 02	29 59	36·6	50 14	29 03	35·8	49 25	28 09	35·2	248	292
69	53 57	31 50	37·5	53 09	30 49	36·7	52 21	29 50	35·9	51 32	28 53	35·2	50 43	27 59	34·5	49 53	27 06	33·8	249	291
70	54 28	30 39	36·1	53 39	29 39	35·2	52 50	28 42	34·5	52 00	27 46	33·8	51 10	26 53	33·1	50 20	26 02	32·4	250	290
71	54 58	29 25	34·6	54 08	28 27	33·8	53 18	27 31	33·0	52 28	26 38	32·3	51 37	25 46	31·6	50 46	24 56	31·0	251	289
72	55 27	28 09	33·0	54 37	27 13	32·2	53 46	26 19	31·5	52 54	25 27	30·8	52 03	24 37	30·2	51 10	23 49	29·5	252	288
73	55 55	26 51	31·4	55 03	25 57	30·7	54 12	25 04	30·0	53 19	24 14	29·3	52 27	23 26	28·7	51 34	22 40	28·1	253	287
74	56 21	25 31	29·8	55 29	24 39	29·1	54 36	23 48	28·4	53 43	23 00	27·8	52 50	22 14	27·1	51 57	21 29	26·6	254	286
75	56 46	24 09	28·2	55 53	23 18	27·5	55 00	22 30	26·8	54 06	21 44	26·2	53 12	21 00	25·6	52 18	20 17	25·0	255	285
76	57 10	22 44	26·5	56 16	21 56	25·8	55 22	21 10	25·2	54 28	20 26	24·6	53 33	19 44	24·0	52 38	19 04	23·4	256	284
77	57 33	21 17	24·8	56 38	20 31	24·1	55 43	19 48	23·5	54 48	19 06	23·0	53 53	18 27	22·4	52 57	17 49	21·9	257	283
78	57 54	19 48	23·0	56 59	19 05	22·4	56 03	18 24	21·9	55 07	17 45	21·3	54 11	17 08	20·8	53 15	16 32	20·3	258	282
79	58 13	18 17	21·2	57 17	17 37	20·7	56 21	16 59	20·1	55 25	16 22	19·6	54 28	15 48	19·2	53 31	15 15	18·7	259	281
80	58 32	16 44	19·4	57 35	16 07	18·9	56 38	15 32	18·4	55 41	14 58	17·9	54 44	14 26	17·5	53 47	13 56	17·1	260	280
81	58 48	15 10	17·6	57 51	14 36	17·1	56 53	14 03	16·6	55 56	13 33	16·2	54 58	13 03	15·8	54 00	12 36	15·4	261	279
82	59 03	13 33	15·7	58 05	13 02	15·3	57 07	12 33	14·9	56 09	12 06	14·5	55 11	11 40	14·1	54 13	11 14	13·8	262	278
83	59 16	11 55	13·8	58 18	11 28	13·4	57 19	11 02	13·0	56 21	10 38	12·7	55 22	10 14	12·4	54 24	9 52	12·1	263	277
84	59 28	10 16	11·9	58 29	9 52	11·5	57 30	9 30	11·2	56 31	9 09	10·9	55 32	8 49	10·6	54 33	8 29	10·4	264	276
85	59 37	8 35	9·9	58 38	8 15	9·6	57 39	7 56	9·4	56 40	7 39	9·1	55 41	7 22	8·9	54 41	7 06	8·7	265	275
86	59 46	6 53	8·0	58 46	6 37	7·7	57 47	6 22	7·5	56 47	6 08	7·3	55 48	5 54	7·1	54 48	5 41	7·0	266	274
87	59 52	5 11	6·0	58 52	4 59	5·8	57 52	4 47	5·6	56 53	4 36	5·5	55 53	4 26	5·4	54 53	4 16	5·2	267	273
88	59 56	3 28	4·0	58 57	3 19	3·9	57 57	3 12	3·8	56 57	3 05	3·7	55 57	2 58	3·6	54 57	2 51	3·5	268	272
89	59 59	1 44	2·0	58 59	1 40	1·9	57 59	1 36	1·9	56 59	1 32	1·8	55 59	1 29	1·8	54 59	1 26	1·7	269	271
90	60 00	0 00	0·0	59 00	0 00	0·0	58 00	0 00	0·0	57 00	0 00	0·0	56 00	0 00	0·0	55 00	0 00	0·0	270	270

N. Lat.: for LHA > 180° ... $Z_n = Z$
for LHA < 180° ... $Z_n = 360° - Z$

S. Lat.: for LHA > 180° ... $Z_n = 180° - Z$
for LHA < 180° ... $Z_n = 180° + Z$

SIGHT REDUCTION TABLE

B: (−) for 90° < LHA < 270°
Dec::(−) for Lat. contrary name

Z₁: same sign as B
Z₂:(−) for F > 90°

LHA/F		36° A/H	B/P	Z₁/Z₂	37° A/H	B/P	Z₁/Z₂	38° A/H	B/P	Z₁/Z₂	39° A/H	B/P	Z₁/Z₂	40° A/H	B/P	Z₁/Z₂	41° A/H	B/P	Z₁/Z₂	LHA	
0	180	0 00	54 00	90·0	0 00	53 00	90·0	0 00	52 00	90·0	0 00	51 00	90·0	0 00	50 00	90·0	0 00	49 00	90·0	180	360
1	179	0 49	54 00	89·4	0 48	53 00	89·4	0 47	52 00	89·4	0 47	51 00	89·4	0 46	50 00	89·4	0 45	49 00	89·3	181	359
2	178	1 37	53 59	88·8	1 36	52 59	88·8	1 35	51 59	88·8	1 33	50 59	88·7	1 32	49 59	88·7	1 31	48 59	88·7	182	358
3	177	2 26	53 58	88·2	2 24	52 58	88·2	2 22	51 58	88·2	2 20	50 58	88·1	2 18	49 58	88·1	2 16	48 58	88·0	183	357
4	176	3 14	53 56	87·6	3 12	52 56	87·6	3 09	51 56	87·5	3 06	50 56	87·5	3 04	49 56	87·4	3 01	48 56	87·4	184	356
5	175	4 03	53 54	87·1	3 59	52 54	87·0	3 56	51 54	86·9	3 53	50 54	86·8	3 50	49 54	86·8	3 46	48 54	86·7	185	355
6	174	4 51	53 51	86·5	4 47	52 51	86·4	4 43	51 51	86·3	4 40	50 51	86·2	4 36	49 51	86·1	4 31	48 51	86·1	186	354
7	173	5 39	53 48	85·9	5 35	52 48	85·8	5 31	51 48	85·7	5 26	50 47	85·6	5 21	49 47	85·5	5 17	48 47	85·4	187	353
8	172	6 28	53 44	85·3	6 23	52 44	85·2	6 18	51 44	85·1	6 13	50 44	84·9	6 07	49 43	84·8	6 02	48 43	84·7	188	352
9	171	7 16	53 40	84·7	7 11	52 39	84·6	7 05	51 39	84·4	6 59	50 39	84·3	6 53	49 39	84·2	6 47	48 39	84·1	189	351
10	170	8 05	53 35	84·1	7 58	52 35	83·9	7 52	51 34	83·8	7 45	50 34	83·7	7 39	49 34	83·5	7 32	48 34	83·4	190	350
11	169	8 53	53 30	83·5	8 46	52 29	83·3	8 39	51 29	83·2	8 32	50 29	83·0	8 24	49 29	82·9	8 17	48 28	82·7	191	349
12	168	9 41	53 24	82·9	9 33	52 23	82·7	9 26	51 23	82·5	9 18	50 23	82·4	9 10	49 23	82·2	9 02	48 22	82·1	192	348
13	167	10 29	53 17	82·3	10 21	52 17	82·1	10 13	51 17	81·9	10 04	50 16	81·7	9 55	49 16	81·6	9 46	48 16	81·4	193	347
14	166	11 17	53 10	81·7	11 08	52 10	81·5	10 59	51 10	81·3	10 50	50 09	81·1	10 41	49 09	80·9	10 31	48 09	80·7	194	346
15	165	12 05	53 03	81·0	11 56	52 02	80·8	11 46	51 02	80·6	11 36	50 02	80·4	11 26	49 01	80·2	11 16	48 01	80·0	195	345
16	164	12 53	52 55	80·4	12 43	51 54	80·2	12 33	50 54	80·0	12 22	49 53	79·8	12 11	48 53	79·6	12 00	47 53	79·3	196	344
17	163	13 41	52 46	79·8	13 30	51 46	79·6	13 19	50 45	79·3	13 08	49 45	79·1	12 57	48 44	78·9	12 45	47 44	78·7	197	343
18	162	14 29	52 37	79·2	14 17	51 37	78·9	14 06	50 36	78·7	13 54	49 35	78·4	13 42	48 35	78·2	13 29	47 34	78·0	198	342
19	161	15 16	52 28	78·6	15 04	51 27	78·3	14 52	50 26	78·0	14 39	49 25	77·8	14 27	48 25	77·5	14 13	47 24	77·3	199	341
20	160	16 04	52 17	77·9	15 51	51 16	77·6	15 38	50 16	77·4	15 25	49 15	77·1	15 11	48 14	76·8	14 58	47 14	76·6	200	340
21	159	16 51	52 07	77·3	16 38	51 05	77·0	16 24	50 05	76·7	16 10	49 04	76·4	15 56	48 03	76·1	15 42	47 03	75·9	201	339
22	158	17 39	51 55	76·6	17 24	50 54	76·3	17 10	49 53	76·0	16 56	48 52	75·7	16 41	47 51	75·4	16 25	46 51	75·2	202	338
23	157	18 26	51 43	76·0	18 11	50 42	75·7	17 56	49 41	75·4	17 41	48 40	75·0	17 25	47 39	74·7	17 09	46 38	74·4	203	337
24	156	19 13	51 30	75·3	18 57	50 29	75·0	18 42	49 28	74·7	18 26	48 27	74·3	18 09	47 26	74·0	17 53	46 25	73·7	204	336
25	155	20 00	51 17	74·7	19 44	50 15	74·3	19 27	49 14	74·0	19 10	48 13	73·6	18 53	47 12	73·3	18 36	46 12	73·0	205	335
26	154	20 46	51 03	74·0	20 30	50 01	73·6	20 13	49 00	73·3	19 55	47 59	72·9	19 37	46 58	72·6	19 19	45 57	72·3	206	334
27	153	21 33	50 48	73·3	21 15	49 47	73·0	20 58	48 45	72·6	20 40	47 44	72·2	20 21	46 43	71·9	20 02	45 42	71·5	207	333
28	152	22 19	50 33	72·6	22 01	49 31	72·3	21 43	48 30	71·9	21 24	47 28	71·5	21 05	46 28	71·1	20 45	45 27	70·8	208	332
29	151	23 06	50 17	72·0	22 47	49 15	71·6	22 28	48 14	71·2	22 08	47 12	70·8	21 48	46 11	70·4	21 28	45 11	70·0	209	331
30	150	23 52	50 00	71·3	23 32	48 58	70·8	23 12	47 57	70·4	22 52	46 55	70·0	22 31	45 54	69·6	22 10	44 54	69·3	210	330
31	149	24 37	49 43	70·5	24 17	48 41	70·1	23 57	47 39	69·7	23 36	46 38	69·3	23 14	45 37	68·9	22 52	44 36	68·5	211	329
32	148	25 23	49 25	69·8	25 02	48 23	69·4	24 41	47 21	69·0	24 19	46 19	68·5	23 57	45 18	68·1	23 34	44 17	67·7	212	328
33	147	26 09	49 06	69·1	25 47	48 04	68·7	25 25	47 02	68·2	25 02	46 00	67·8	24 40	44 59	67·3	24 16	43 58	66·9	213	327
34	146	26 54	48 46	68·4	26 32	47 44	67·9	26 09	46 42	67·4	25 45	45 40	67·0	25 22	44 39	66·6	24 58	43 39	66·1	214	326
35	145	27 39	48 26	67·6	27 16	47 23	67·1	26 52	46 21	66·7	26 28	45 20	66·2	26 04	44 19	65·8	25 39	43 18	65·3	215	325
36	144	28 24	48 04	66·9	28 00	47 02	66·4	27 36	46 00	65·9	27 11	44 58	65·4	26 46	43 57	65·0	26 20	42 57	64·5	216	324
37	143	29 08	47 42	66·1	28 44	46 40	65·6	28 19	45 38	65·1	27 53	44 36	64·6	27 27	43 35	64·2	27 01	42 34	63·7	217	323
38	142	29 52	47 19	65·3	29 27	46 17	64·8	29 01	45 15	64·3	28 35	44 13	63·8	28 08	43 12	63·3	27 41	42 12	62·9	218	322
39	141	30 36	46 56	64·5	30 10	45 53	64·0	29 44	44 51	63·5	29 17	43 49	63·0	28 49	42 48	62·5	28 21	41 48	62·0	219	321
40	140	31 20	46 31	63·7	30 53	45 28	63·2	30 26	44 26	62·7	29 58	43 25	62·2	29 30	42 24	61·7	29 01	41 23	61·2	220	320
41	139	32 03	46 05	62·9	31 36	45 03	62·4	31 08	44 01	61·8	30 39	42 59	61·3	30 10	41 58	60·8	29 41	40 58	60·3	221	319
42	138	32 46	45 39	62·1	32 18	44 36	61·5	31 49	43 34	61·0	31 20	42 33	60·5	30 50	41 32	59·9	30 20	40 32	59·4	222	318
43	137	33 29	45 11	61·3	33 00	44 09	60·7	32 30	43 07	60·1	32 00	42 05	59·6	31 30	41 05	59·1	30 59	40 04	58·5	223	317
44	136	34 12	44 43	60·4	33 42	43 41	59·8	33 11	42 38	59·3	32 40	41 37	58·7	32 08	40 36	58·2	31 37	39 36	57·6	224	316
45	135	34 54	44 13	59·6	34 23	43 11	59·0	33 51	42 09	58·4	33 20	41 08	57·8	32 48	40 07	57·3	32 15	39 08	56·7	225	315

Lat./A	LHA/F	36° A/H	36° B/P	36° Z₁/Z₂	37° A/H	37° B/P	37° Z₁/Z₂	38° A/H	38° B/P	38° Z₁/Z₂	39° A/H	39° B/P	39° Z₁/Z₂	40° A/H	40° B/P	40° Z₁/Z₂	41° A/H	41° B/P	41° Z₁/Z₂	Lat./A	LHA
45	135	34 54	44 13	59·6	34 23	43 11	59·0	33 52	42 09	58·4	33 20	41 08	57·8	32 48	40 07	57·3	32 15	39 08	56·7	225	315
46	134	35 35	43 43	58·7	35 04	42 40	58·1	34 32	41 38	57·5	33 59	40 37	56·9	33 26	39 37	56·4	32 53	38 38	55·8	226	314
47	133	36 17	43 11	57·8	35 44	42 09	57·2	35 12	41 07	56·6	34 38	40 06	56·0	34 04	39 06	55·4	33 30	38 07	54·9	227	313
48	132	36 57	42 39	56·9	36 24	41 36	56·2	35 50	40 34	55·7	35 17	39 34	55·1	34 42	38 34	54·5	34 07	37 35	53·9	228	312
49	131	37 38	42 05	55·9	37 04	41 03	55·3	36 30	40 01	54·7	35 55	39 01	54·1	35 19	38 01	53·5	34 43	37 03	53·0	229	311
50	130	38 18	41 30	55·0	37 43	40 28	54·4	37 08	39 27	53·7	36 32	38 27	53·1	35 56	37 27	52·5	35 19	36 29	52·0	230	310
51	129	38 57	40 54	54·0	38 22	39 52	53·4	37 46	38 51	52·8	37 09	37 51	52·1	36 32	36 52	51·6	35 55	35 54	51·0	231	309
52	128	39 36	40 17	53·0	39 00	39 15	52·4	38 23	38 14	51·8	37 46	37 15	51·1	37 08	36 16	50·6	36 30	35 18	50·0	232	308
53	127	40 15	39 38	52·0	39 38	38 37	51·4	39 00	37 36	50·8	38 22	36 37	50·1	37 44	35 39	49·5	37 04	34 42	49·0	233	307
54	126	40 53	38 58	51·0	40 15	37 57	50·4	39 36	36 57	49·7	38 57	35 58	49·1	38 18	35 01	48·5	37 38	34 04	47·9	234	306
55	125	41 30	38 17	50·0	40 52	37 17	49·3	40 12	36 17	48·7	39 32	35 19	48·1	38 52	34 21	47·4	38 11	33 25	46·9	235	305
56	124	42 07	37 35	48·9	41 28	36 35	48·3	40 47	35 36	47·6	40 07	34 38	47·0	39 26	33 41	46·4	38 44	32 45	45·8	236	304
57	123	42 44	36 51	47·9	42 03	35 51	47·1	41 22	34 53	46·5	40 41	33 55	45·9	39 59	32 59	45·3	39 16	32 04	44·7	237	303
58	122	43 19	36 06	46·8	42 38	35 07	46·1	41 56	34 09	45·4	41 14	33 12	44·8	40 31	32 16	44·2	39 48	31 22	43·6	238	302
59	121	43 54	35 20	45·6	43 12	34 21	45·0	42 29	33 24	44·3	41 46	32 27	43·7	41 03	31 32	43·1	40 19	30 39	42·5	239	301
60	120	44 29	34 32	44·5	43 46	33 34	43·8	43 02	32 37	43·2	42 18	31 42	42·5	41 34	30 47	41·9	40 49	29 54	41·3	240	300
61	119	45 02	33 43	43·3	44 18	32 45	42·6	43 34	31 49	42·0	42 49	30 55	41·4	42 04	30 01	40·8	41 18	29 09	40·2	241	299
62	118	45 35	32 52	42·1	44 51	31 55	41·5	44 05	31 00	40·8	43 20	30 06	40·2	42 34	29 14	39·6	41 47	28 22	39·0	242	298
63	117	46 07	32 00	40·9	45 22	31 04	40·3	44 36	30 10	39·6	43 49	29 17	39·0	43 03	28 25	38·4	42 15	27 35	37·8	243	297
64	116	46 39	31 06	39·7	45 52	30 11	39·0	45 06	29 18	38·4	44 18	28 26	37·8	43 31	27 35	37·2	42 43	26 46	36·6	244	296
65	115	47 09	30 11	38·4	46 21	29 17	37·8	45 35	28 25	37·1	44 47	27 34	36·5	43 58	26 44	36·0	43 09	25 56	35·4	245	295
66	114	47 39	29 14	37·1	46 51	28 21	36·5	46 03	27 30	35·9	45 14	26 40	35·3	44 25	25 52	34·7	43 35	25 04	34·2	246	294
67	113	48 08	28 16	35·8	47 19	27 24	35·2	46 30	26 34	34·6	45 40	25 45	34·0	44 50	24 58	33·4	44 00	24 12	32·9	247	293
68	112	48 36	27 17	34·5	47 46	26 26	33·9	46 56	25 37	33·3	46 06	24 50	32·7	45 15	24 03	32·2	44 24	23 19	31·6	248	292
69	111	49 03	26 15	33·1	48 13	25 26	32·5	47 22	24 38	31·9	46 31	23 52	31·4	45 39	23 08	30·8	44 48	22 24	30·3	249	291
70	110	49 29	25 13	31·8	48 38	24 25	31·2	47 46	23 37	30·6	46 55	22 54	30·0	46 03	22 11	29·5	45 10	21 29	29·0	250	290
71	109	49 54	24 08	30·4	49 02	23 22	29·8	48 10	22 37	29·2	47 17	21 54	28·7	46 25	21 12	28·2	45 32	20 32	27·7	251	289
72	108	50 18	23 02	28·9	49 25	22 18	28·4	48 33	21 35	27·8	47 39	20 53	27·3	46 46	20 13	26·8	45 52	19 34	26·3	252	288
73	107	50 41	21 55	27·5	49 48	21 12	26·9	48 54	20 31	26·4	48 00	19 51	25·9	47 06	19 13	25·4	46 12	18 35	25·0	253	287
74	106	51 03	20 47	26·0	50 09	20 06	25·5	49 15	19 26	25·0	48 20	18 48	24·5	47 25	18 11	24·0	46 30	17 36	23·6	254	286
75	105	51 24	19 36	24·5	50 29	18 57	24·0	49 34	18 20	23·5	48 39	17 43	23·1	47 44	17 09	22·6	46 48	16 35	22·2	255	285
76	104	51 43	18 25	23·0	50 48	17 48	22·5	49 52	17 12	22·0	48 57	16 38	21·6	48 01	16 05	21·2	47 05	15 33	20·8	256	284
77	103	52 02	17 12	21·4	51 06	16 37	21·0	50 09	16 04	20·6	49 13	15 31	20·1	48 17	15 00	19·8	47 20	14 31	19·4	257	283
78	102	52 19	15 58	19·9	51 23	15 25	19·5	50 25	14 54	19·0	49 29	14 24	18·7	48 32	13 55	18·3	47 35	13 27	18·0	258	282
79	101	52 35	14 43	18·3	51 37	14 13	17·9	50 40	13 43	17·5	49 43	13 16	17·2	48 46	12 49	16·8	47 48	12 23	16·5	259	281
80	100	52 49	13 27	16·7	51 52	12 59	16·3	50 54	12 32	16·0	49 56	12 06	15·7	48 58	11 42	15·3	48 01	11 18	15·0	260	280
81	99	53 02	12 09	15·1	52 04	11 44	14·7	51 06	11 19	14·4	50 08	10 56	14·1	49 10	10 34	13·8	48 12	10 12	13·6	261	279
82	98	53 14	10 51	13·4	52 16	10 28	13·1	51 18	10 06	12·9	50 19	9 45	12·6	49 20	9 25	12·3	48 22	9 06	12·1	262	278
83	97	53 25	9 31	11·8	52 26	9 11	11·5	51 27	8 52	11·3	50 29	8 34	11·0	49 30	8 16	10·8	48 31	7 59	10·6	263	277
84	96	53 34	8 11	10·1	52 35	7 54	9·9	51 36	7 37	9·7	50 37	7 21	9·5	49 38	7 06	9·3	48 38	6 51	9·1	264	276
85	95	53 42	6 50	8·5	52 43	6 36	8·3	51 43	6 22	8·1	50 44	6 09	7·9	49 44	5 56	7·8	48 45	5 44	7·6	265	275
86	94	53 49	5 29	6·8	52 49	5 17	6·6	51 49	5 06	6·5	50 50	4 55	6·3	49 50	4 45	6·2	48 50	4 35	6·1	266	274
87	93	53 54	4 07	5·1	52 54	3 58	5·0	51 54	3 50	4·9	50 54	3 42	4·8	49 54	3 34	4·7	48 55	3 27	4·6	267	273
88	92	53 57	2 45	3·4	52 57	2 39	3·3	51 57	2 33	3·2	50 57	2 28	3·2	49 57	2 23	3·1	48 58	2 18	3·0	268	272
89	91	53 59	1 23	1·7	52 59	1 20	1·7	51 59	1 17	1·6	50 59	1 14	1·6	49 59	1 11	1·6	48 59	1 09	1·5	269	271
90	90	54 00	0 00	0·0	53 00	0 00	0·0	52 00	0 00	0·0	51 00	0 00	0·0	50 00	0 00	0·0	49 00	0 00	0·0	270	270

N. Lat: for LHA > 180° ... $Z_n = Z$
for LHA < 180° ... $Z_n = 360° − Z$

S. Lat.: for LHA > 180° ... $Z_n = 180° − Z$
for LHA < 180° ... $Z_n = 180° + Z$

SIGHT REDUCTION TABLE

B: (−) for 90° < LHA < 270°
Dec:(−) for Lat. contrary name

Z₁: same sign as B
Z₂: (−) for F > 90°

Lat./A LHA/F	42° A/H	42° B/P	42° Z₁/Z₂	43° A/H	43° B/P	43° Z₁/Z₂	44° A/H	44° B/P	44° Z₁/Z₂	45° A/H	45° B/P	45° Z₁/Z₂	46° A/H	46° B/P	46° Z₁/Z₂	47° A/H	47° B/P	47° Z₁/Z₂	Lat./A LHA
0 / 180	0 00	48 00	90·0	0 00	47 00	90·0	0 00	46 00	90·0	0 00	45 00	90·0	0 00	44 00	90·0	0 00	43 00	90·0	180 / 360
1 / 179	0 45	48 00	89·3	0 44	47 00	89·3	0 43	46 00	89·3	0 42	45 00	89·3	0 42	44 00	89·3	0 41	43 00	89·3	181 / 359
2 / 178	1 29	47 59	88·7	1 28	46 59	88·6	1 26	45 59	88·6	1 25	44 59	88·6	1 23	43 59	88·6	1 22	42 59	88·5	182 / 358
3 / 177	2 14	47 58	88·0	2 12	46 58	88·0	2 09	45 58	87·9	2 07	44 58	87·9	2 05	43 58	87·8	2 03	42 58	87·8	183 / 357
4 / 176	2 58	47 56	87·3	2 55	46 56	87·3	2 53	45 56	87·2	2 50	44 56	87·2	2 47	43 56	87·1	2 44	42 56	87·1	184 / 356
5 / 175	3 43	47 53	86·6	3 39	46 53	86·6	3 36	45 53	86·5	3 32	44 53	86·5	3 28	43 53	86·4	3 24	42 53	86·3	185 / 355
6 / 174	4 27	47 51	86·0	4 23	46 51	85·9	4 19	45 51	85·8	4 14	44 51	85·7	4 10	43 51	85·7	4 05	42 51	85·6	186 / 354
7 / 173	5 12	47 47	85·3	5 07	46 47	85·2	5 02	45 47	85·1	4 57	44 47	85·0	4 51	43 47	85·0	4 46	42 47	84·9	187 / 353
8 / 172	5 56	47 43	84·6	5 51	46 43	84·5	5 45	45 43	84·4	5 39	44 43	84·3	5 33	43 43	84·2	5 27	42 43	84·1	188 / 352
9 / 171	6 41	47 39	84·0	6 34	46 39	83·8	6 28	45 39	83·7	6 21	44 39	83·6	6 14	43 39	83·5	6 07	42 39	83·4	189 / 351
10 / 170	7 25	47 34	83·3	7 18	46 34	83·1	7 11	45 34	83·0	7 03	44 34	82·9	6 56	43 34	82·8	6 48	42 34	82·7	190 / 350
11 / 169	8 09	47 28	82·6	8 01	46 28	82·4	7 53	45 28	82·3	7 45	44 28	82·2	7 37	43 28	82·0	7 29	42 28	81·9	191 / 349
12 / 168	8 53	47 22	81·9	8 45	46 22	81·8	8 36	45 22	81·6	8 27	44 22	81·5	8 18	43 22	81·3	8 09	42 22	81·2	192 / 348
13 / 167	9 37	47 16	81·2	9 28	46 16	81·1	9 19	45 15	80·9	9 09	44 15	80·7	8 59	43 15	80·6	8 49	42 16	80·4	193 / 347
14 / 166	10 21	47 08	80·5	10 11	46 08	80·3	10 01	45 08	80·2	9 51	44 08	80·0	9 40	43 08	79·8	9 30	42 08	79·7	194 / 346
15 / 165	11 05	47 01	79·8	10 55	46 00	79·6	10 44	45 00	79·5	10 33	44 00	79·3	10 21	43 00	79·1	10 10	42 01	78·9	195 / 345
16 / 164	11 49	46 52	79·1	11 38	45 52	78·9	11 26	44 52	78·7	11 14	43 52	78·5	11 02	42 52	78·3	10 50	41 52	78·2	196 / 344
17 / 163	12 33	46 43	78·4	12 21	45 43	78·2	12 08	44 43	78·0	11 56	43 43	77·8	11 43	42 43	77·6	11 30	41 44	77·4	197 / 343
18 / 162	13 17	46 34	77·7	13 04	45 34	77·5	12 51	44 34	77·3	12 37	43 34	77·1	12 24	42 34	76·8	12 10	41 34	76·6	198 / 342
19 / 161	14 00	46 24	77·0	13 46	45 24	76·8	13 33	44 24	76·5	13 19	43 24	76·3	13 04	42 24	76·1	12 50	41 24	75·9	199 / 341
20 / 160	14 43	46 13	76·3	14 29	45 13	76·1	14 15	44 13	75·8	14 00	43 13	75·6	13 45	42 13	75·3	13 29	41 14	75·1	200 / 340
21 / 159	15 27	46 02	75·6	15 12	45 02	75·3	14 56	44 02	75·1	14 41	43 02	74·8	14 25	42 02	74·6	14 09	41 03	74·3	201 / 339
22 / 158	16 10	45 50	74·9	15 54	44 50	74·6	15 38	43 50	74·3	15 22	42 50	74·1	15 05	41 50	73·8	14 48	40 51	73·5	202 / 338
23 / 157	16 53	45 38	74·1	16 36	44 38	73·9	16 19	43 38	73·6	16 02	42 38	73·3	15 45	41 38	73·0	15 27	40 39	72·8	203 / 337
24 / 156	17 36	45 25	73·4	17 18	44 25	73·1	17 01	43 25	72·8	16 43	42 25	72·5	16 25	41 25	72·2	16 06	40 26	72·0	204 / 336
25 / 155	18 19	45 11	72·7	18 00	44 11	72·4	17 42	43 11	72·1	17 23	42 11	71·8	17 04	41 12	71·5	16 45	40 12	71·2	205 / 335
26 / 154	19 01	44 57	71·9	18 42	43 57	71·6	18 23	42 57	71·3	18 03	41 57	71·0	17 44	40 57	70·7	17 24	39 58	70·4	206 / 334
27 / 153	19 43	44 42	71·2	19 24	43 42	70·8	19 04	42 42	70·5	18 43	41 42	70·2	18 23	40 43	69·9	18 02	39 43	69·6	207 / 333
28 / 152	20 25	44 26	70·4	20 05	43 26	70·1	19 44	42 26	69·7	19 23	41 27	69·4	19 02	40 27	69·1	18 40	39 28	68·8	208 / 332
29 / 151	21 07	44 10	69·6	20 46	43 10	69·3	20 25	42 10	68·9	20 03	41 10	68·6	19 41	40 11	68·3	19 18	39 12	67·9	209 / 331
30 / 150	21 49	43 53	68·9	21 27	42 53	68·5	21 05	41 53	68·1	20 42	40 54	67·8	20 19	39 54	67·4	19 56	38 55	67·1	210 / 330
31 / 149	22 30	43 35	68·1	22 08	42 35	67·7	21 45	41 36	67·3	21 21	40 36	67·0	20 58	39 37	66·6	20 34	38 38	66·3	211 / 329
32 / 148	23 11	43 17	67·3	22 48	42 17	66·9	22 24	41 17	66·5	22 00	40 18	66·2	21 36	39 19	65·8	21 11	38 20	65·4	212 / 328
33 / 147	23 53	42 58	66·5	23 28	41 58	66·1	23 04	40 58	65·7	22 39	39 59	65·3	22 14	39 00	65·0	21 48	38 02	64·6	213 / 327
34 / 146	24 33	42 38	65·7	24 08	41 38	65·3	23 43	40 39	64·9	23 17	39 40	64·5	22 51	38 41	64·1	22 25	37 42	63·7	214 / 326
35 / 145	25 14	42 18	64·9	24 47	41 18	64·5	24 22	40 18	64·1	23 56	39 18	63·7	23 29	38 21	63·3	23 02	37 23	62·9	215 / 325
36 / 144	25 54	41 56	64·1	25 28	40 57	63·6	25 01	39 57	63·2	24 34	38 58	62·8	24 06	38 00	62·4	23 38	37 02	62·0	216 / 324
37 / 143	26 34	41 34	63·2	26 07	40 35	62·8	25 39	39 35	62·4	25 11	38 37	61·9	24 43	37 38	61·5	24 14	36 41	61·1	217 / 323
38 / 142	27 14	41 11	62·4	26 46	40 12	61·9	26 17	39 13	61·5	25 48	38 14	61·1	25 19	37 16	60·7	24 50	36 19	60·3	218 / 322
39 / 141	27 53	40 48	61·5	27 24	39 48	61·1	26 55	38 50	60·6	26 25	37 51	60·2	25 55	36 53	59·8	25 25	35 56	59·4	219 / 321
40 / 140	28 32	40 23	60·7	28 02	39 24	60·2	27 32	38 25	59·8	27 02	37 27	59·3	26 31	36 30	58·9	26 00	35 32	58·5	220 / 320
41 / 139	29 11	39 58	59·8	28 40	38 59	59·3	28 10	38 01	58·9	27 38	37 03	58·4	27 07	36 05	58·0	26 35	35 08	57·6	221 / 319
42 / 138	29 49	39 32	58·9	29 18	38 33	58·4	28 46	37 35	58·0	28 14	36 37	57·5	27 42	35 40	57·1	27 09	34 43	56·6	222 / 318
43 / 137	30 27	39 05	58·0	29 55	38 06	57·5	29 23	37 08	57·1	28 50	36 11	56·6	28 17	35 14	56·1	27 43	34 18	55·7	223 / 317
44 / 136	31 05	38 37	57·1	30 32	37 39	56·6	29 59	36 41	56·1	29 25	35 44	55·7	28 51	34 47	55·2	28 17	33 51	54·8	224 / 316
45 / 135	31 42	38 09	56·2	31 08	37 10	55·7	30 34	36 13	55·2	30 00	35 16	54·7	29 25	34 20	54·3	28 50	33 24	53·8	225 / 315

LHA	F	42° A/H	42° B/P	42° Z_1/Z_2	43° A/H	43° B/P	43° Z_1/Z_2	44° A/H	44° B/P	44° Z_1/Z_2	45° A/H	45° B/P	45° Z_1/Z_2	46° A/H	46° B/P	46° Z_1/Z_2	47° A/H	47° B/P	47° Z_1/Z_2	A	LHA
45	135	31 42	38 09	56.2	31 08	37 10	55.7	30 34	36 13	55.2	30 00	35 16	54.7	29 25	34 20	54.3	28 50	33 24	53.8	225	315
46	134	32 19	37 39	55.3	31 45	36 41	54.8	31 10	35 44	54.3	30 34	34 47	53.8	29 59	33 51	53.3	29 23	32 56	52.9	226	314
47	133	32 55	37 08	54.3	32 20	36 11	53.8	31 45	35 14	53.3	31 08	34 18	52.8	30 32	33 22	52.4	29 55	32 27	51.9	227	313
48	132	33 31	36 37	53.4	32 55	35 40	52.9	32 19	34 43	52.3	31 42	33 47	51.9	31 05	32 52	51.4	30 27	31 58	50.9	228	312
49	131	34 07	36 05	52.4	33 30	35 08	51.9	32 53	34 11	51.4	32 15	33 16	50.9	31 37	32 21	50.4	30 59	31 27	49.9	229	311
50	130	34 42	35 31	51.4	34 04	34 35	50.9	33 26	33 39	50.4	32 48	32 44	49.9	32 09	31 50	49.4	31 30	30 56	48.9	230	310
51	129	35 17	34 57	50.4	34 38	34 01	49.9	33 59	33 05	49.4	33 20	32 11	48.9	32 40	31 17	48.4	32 00	30 24	47.9	231	309
52	128	35 51	34 22	49.4	35 12	33 26	48.9	34 32	32 31	48.4	33 52	31 37	47.9	33 11	30 44	47.4	32 30	29 52	46.9	232	308
53	127	36 24	33 45	48.4	35 44	32 50	47.9	35 04	31 56	47.3	34 23	31 02	46.8	33 42	30 10	46.3	33 00	29 18	45.9	233	307
54	126	36 57	33 08	47.4	36 17	32 13	46.8	35 35	31 20	46.3	34 54	30 27	45.8	34 12	29 35	45.3	33 29	28 44	44.8	234	306
55	125	37 30	32 30	46.3	36 48	31 36	45.8	36 06	30 43	45.2	35 24	29 50	44.7	34 41	28 59	44.2	33 58	28 08	43.8	235	305
56	124	38 02	31 51	45.2	37 19	30 57	44.7	36 37	30 04	44.2	35 53	29 13	43.6	35 10	28 22	43.2	34 26	27 32	42.7	236	304
57	123	38 33	31 10	44.1	37 50	30 17	43.6	37 06	29 25	43.1	36 22	28 34	42.6	35 38	27 45	42.1	34 53	26 56	41.6	237	303
58	122	39 04	30 29	43.0	38 20	29 36	42.5	37 36	28 45	42.0	36 51	27 55	41.5	36 06	27 06	41.0	35 20	26 18	40.5	238	302
59	121	39 34	29 46	41.9	38 49	28 55	41.4	38 04	28 04	40.9	37 19	27 15	40.4	36 33	26 27	39.9	35 46	25 39	39.4	239	301
60	120	40 04	29 03	40.8	39 18	28 12	40.2	38 32	27 22	39.7	37 46	26 34	39.2	37 00	25 46	38.8	36 12	25 00	38.3	240	300
61	119	40 32	28 18	39.6	39 46	27 28	39.1	38 59	26 39	38.6	38 12	25 52	38.1	37 25	25 05	37.6	36 37	24 20	37.2	241	299
62	118	41 00	27 32	38.5	40 13	26 43	37.9	39 26	25 56	37.4	38 38	25 09	36.9	37 50	24 23	36.5	37 02	23 39	36.0	242	298
63	117	41 28	26 45	37.3	40 40	25 58	36.8	39 52	25 11	36.3	39 03	24 25	35.8	38 14	23 40	35.3	37 25	22 57	34.9	243	297
64	116	41 54	25 58	36.1	41 06	25 11	35.6	40 17	24 25	35.1	39 28	23 40	34.6	38 38	22 57	34.1	37 48	22 14	33.7	244	296
65	115	42 20	25 09	34.9	41 31	24 23	34.4	40 41	23 38	33.9	39 51	22 55	33.4	39 01	22 12	33.0	38 11	21 31	32.5	245	295
66	114	42 45	24 19	33.6	41 55	23 34	33.1	41 05	22 50	32.7	40 14	22 08	32.2	39 23	21 27	31.8	38 32	20 46	31.3	246	294
67	113	43 10	23 28	32.4	42 19	22 44	31.9	41 28	22 02	31.4	40 37	21 21	31.0	39 45	20 40	30.5	38 53	20 01	30.1	247	293
68	112	43 33	22 35	31.1	42 42	21 53	30.6	41 50	21 12	30.2	40 58	20 32	29.7	40 06	19 53	29.3	39 13	19 15	28.9	248	292
69	111	43 56	21 42	29.8	43 04	21 01	29.4	42 11	20 22	28.9	41 19	19 43	28.5	40 26	19 05	28.1	39 33	18 29	27.7	249	291
70	110	44 18	20 48	28.5	43 25	20 08	28.1	42 32	19 30	27.7	41 38	18 53	27.2	40 45	18 17	26.8	39 51	17 41	26.5	250	290
71	109	44 38	19 53	27.2	43 45	19 15	26.8	42 51	18 38	26.4	41 57	18 02	26.0	41 03	17 27	25.6	40 09	16 53	25.2	251	289
72	108	44 58	18 57	25.9	44 04	18 20	25.5	43 10	17 45	25.1	42 16	17 10	24.7	41 21	16 37	24.3	40 26	16 05	24.0	252	288
73	107	45 17	17 59	24.6	44 23	17 24	24.1	43 28	16 51	23.8	42 33	16 18	23.4	41 38	15 46	23.0	40 42	15 15	22.7	253	287
74	106	45 35	17 01	23.2	44 40	16 28	22.8	43 45	15 56	22.4	42 49	15 25	22.1	41 54	14 54	21.7	40 58	14 25	21.4	254	286
75	105	45 53	16 02	21.8	44 57	15 31	21.4	44 01	15 00	21.1	43 05	14 31	20.8	42 09	14 02	20.4	41 12	13 34	20.1	255	285
76	104	46 09	15 02	20.4	45 12	14 33	20.1	44 16	14 04	19.7	43 19	13 36	19.4	42 23	13 09	19.1	41 26	12 43	18.8	256	284
77	103	46 24	14 02	19.0	45 27	13 34	18.7	44 30	13 07	18.4	43 33	12 41	18.1	42 36	12 15	17.8	41 39	11 51	17.5	257	283
78	102	46 38	13 00	17.6	45 40	12 34	17.3	44 43	12 09	17.0	43 46	11 45	16.7	42 48	11 21	16.5	41 51	10 58	16.2	258	282
79	101	46 51	11 58	16.2	45 53	11 34	15.9	44 55	11 11	15.6	43 57	10 48	15.4	43 00	10 26	15.1	42 02	10 05	14.9	259	281
80	100	47 03	10 55	14.8	46 04	10 33	14.5	45 06	10 12	14.2	44 08	9 51	14.0	43 10	9 31	13.8	42 12	9 12	13.6	260	280
81	99	47 13	9 51	13.3	46 15	9 31	13.1	45 16	9 12	12.8	44 18	8 53	12.6	43 19	8 35	12.4	42 21	8 18	12.2	261	279
82	98	47 23	8 47	11.9	46 24	8 29	11.6	45 26	8 12	11.4	44 27	7 55	11.2	43 28	7 39	11.1	42 29	7 24	10.9	262	278
83	97	47 32	7 42	10.4	46 33	7 27	10.2	45 34	7 11	9.9	44 34	6 57	9.9	43 35	6 43	9.7	42 36	6 29	9.5	263	277
84	96	47 39	6 37	8.9	46 40	6 24	8.8	45 41	6 11	8.6	44 41	5 58	8.5	43 42	5 46	8.3	42 42	5 34	8.2	264	276
85	95	47 46	5 32	7.4	46 46	5 20	7.3	45 46	5 09	7.2	44 47	4 59	7.1	43 47	4 49	6.9	42 48	4 39	6.8	265	275
86	94	47 51	4 26	6.0	46 51	4 17	5.9	45 51	4 08	5.7	44 52	3 59	5.6	43 52	3 51	5.6	42 52	3 43	5.5	266	274
87	93	47 55	3 20	4.5	46 55	3 13	4.4	45 55	3 06	4.3	44 55	3 00	4.2	43 55	2 54	4.2	42 56	2 48	4.1	267	273
88	92	47 58	2 13	3.0	46 58	2 09	2.9	45 58	2 04	2.9	44 58	2 00	2.8	43 58	1 56	2.8	42 58	1 52	2.7	268	272
89	91	47 59	1 07	1.5	46 59	1 04	1.5	45 59	1 02	1.4	44 59	1 00	1.4	43 59	0 58	1.4	43 00	0 56	1.4	269	271
90	90	48 00	0 00	0.0	47 00	0 00	0.0	46 00	0 00	0.0	45 00	0 00	0.0	44 00	0 00	0.0	43 00	0 00	0.0	270	270

N. Lat: for LHA > 180° ... $Z_n = Z$
for LHA < 180° ... $Z_n = 360° - Z$

S. Lat.: for LHA > 180° ... $Z_n = 180° - Z$
for LHA < 180° ... $Z_n = 180° + Z$

SIGHT REDUCTION TABLE

B: (−) for 90° < LHA < 270°
Dec:(−) for Lat. contrary name

Z1: same sign as B
Z2: (−) for F > 90°

LHA/F	Lat./A (LHA/A)	48° A/H	48° B/P	48° Z1/Z2	49° A/H	49° B/P	49° Z1/Z2	50° A/H	50° B/P	50° Z1/Z2	51° A/H	51° B/P	51° Z1/Z2	52° A/H	52° B/P	52° Z1/Z2	53° A/H	53° B/P	53° Z1/Z2	Lat./A (LHA)
0	180	0 00	42 00	90·0	0 00	41 00	90·0	0 00	40 00	90·0	0 00	39 00	90·0	0 00	38 00	90·0	0 00	37 00	90·0	180
1	179	0 40	42 00	89·3	0 39	41 00	89·3	0 39	40 00	89·2	0 38	39 00	89·2	0 37	38 00	89·2	0 36	37 00	89·2	181
2	178	1 20	41 59	88·5	1 19	40 59	88·5	1 17	39 59	88·5	1 16	38 59	88·4	1 14	37 59	88·4	1 12	36 59	88·4	182
3	177	2 00	41 58	87·8	1 58	40 58	87·7	1 56	39 58	87·7	1 53	38 58	87·7	1 51	37 58	87·6	1 48	36 58	87·6	183
4	176	2 41	41 56	87·0	2 37	40 56	87·0	2 34	39 56	86·9	2 31	38 56	86·9	2 28	37 56	86·8	2 24	36 56	86·8	184
5	175	3 21	41 53	86·3	3 17	40 54	86·2	3 13	39 54	86·2	3 09	38 54	86·1	3 05	37 54	86·1	3 00	36 54	86·0	185
6	174	4 01	41 51	85·5	3 56	40 51	85·5	3 51	39 51	85·4	3 46	38 51	85·3	3 41	37 51	85·3	3 36	36 51	85·2	186
7	173	4 41	41 47	84·8	4 35	40 47	84·7	4 30	39 47	84·6	4 24	38 47	84·5	4 18	37 48	84·5	4 12	36 48	84·4	187
8	172	5 21	41 43	84·0	5 14	40 43	83·9	5 08	39 43	83·9	5 01	38 44	83·8	4 55	37 44	83·7	4 48	36 44	83·6	188
9	171	6 01	41 39	83·3	5 53	40 39	83·1	5 46	39 39	83·1	5 39	38 39	83·0	5 32	37 39	82·9	5 24	36 40	82·8	189
10	170	6 40	41 34	82·5	6 32	40 34	82·4	6 25	39 34	82·3	6 16	38 34	82·2	6 08	37 35	82·1	6 00	36 35	82·0	190
11	169	7 20	41 28	81·8	7 11	40 28	81·7	7 03	39 29	81·5	6 54	38 29	81·4	6 45	37 29	81·3	6 36	36 29	81·2	191
12	168	8 00	41 22	81·0	7 50	40 22	80·9	7 41	39 23	80·8	7 31	38 23	80·6	7 21	37 23	80·5	7 11	36 24	80·4	192
13	167	8 39	41 16	80·3	8 29	40 16	80·1	8 19	39 16	80·0	8 08	38 16	79·8	7 58	37 17	79·7	7 47	36 17	79·6	193
14	166	9 19	41 09	79·5	9 08	40 09	79·3	8 57	39 09	79·2	8 45	38 09	79·0	8 34	37 10	78·9	8 22	36 10	78·7	194
15	165	9 58	41 01	78·7	9 47	40 01	78·6	9 35	39 02	78·4	9 22	38 02	78·2	9 10	37 02	78·1	8 58	36 03	77·9	195
16	164	10 38	40 53	78·0	10 25	39 53	77·8	10 12	38 53	77·6	9 59	37 54	77·4	9 46	36 54	77·3	9 33	35 55	77·1	196
17	163	11 17	40 44	77·2	11 04	39 44	77·0	10 50	38 45	76·8	10 36	37 45	76·6	10 22	36 46	76·5	10 08	35 47	76·3	197
18	162	11 56	40 34	76·4	11 42	39 35	76·2	11 27	38 35	76·0	11 13	37 36	75·8	10 58	36 37	75·6	10 43	35 38	75·5	198
19	161	12 35	40 25	75·6	12 20	39 25	75·4	12 05	38 26	75·2	11 49	37 26	75·0	11 34	36 27	74·8	11 18	35 28	74·6	199
20	160	13 14	40 14	74·9	12 58	39 15	74·6	12 42	38 15	74·4	12 26	37 16	74·2	12 09	36 17	74·0	11 53	35 18	73·8	200
21	159	13 52	40 03	74·1	13 36	39 04	73·8	13 19	38 04	73·6	13 02	37 05	73·4	12 45	36 06	73·2	12 27	35 08	73·0	201
22	158	14 31	39 51	73·3	14 14	38 52	73·0	13 56	37 53	72·8	13 38	36 54	72·6	13 20	35 55	72·3	13 02	34 56	72·1	202
23	157	15 09	39 39	72·5	14 51	38 40	72·2	14 33	37 41	72·0	14 14	36 42	71·7	13 55	35 43	71·5	13 36	34 45	71·3	203
24	156	15 48	39 26	71·7	15 29	38 27	71·4	15 09	37 28	71·2	14 50	36 30	70·9	14 30	35 31	70·7	14 10	34 33	70·4	204
25	155	16 26	39 13	70·9	16 06	38 14	70·6	15 46	37 15	70·3	15 25	36 17	70·1	15 05	35 18	69·8	14 44	34 20	69·6	205
26	154	17 03	38 59	70·1	16 43	38 00	69·8	16 22	37 01	69·5	16 01	36 03	69·2	15 39	35 05	69·0	15 18	34 07	68·7	206
27	153	17 41	38 44	69·3	17 20	37 46	69·0	16 58	36 47	68·7	16 36	35 49	68·4	16 14	34 51	68·1	15 51	33 53	67·9	207
28	152	18 19	38 29	68·4	17 56	37 30	68·1	17 34	36 32	67·8	17 11	35 34	67·5	16 48	34 36	67·3	16 25	33 38	67·0	208
29	151	18 56	38 13	67·6	18 33	37 15	67·3	18 09	36 16	67·0	17 46	35 18	66·7	17 22	34 21	66·4	16 58	33 23	66·1	209
30	150	19 33	37 57	66·8	19 09	36 58	66·5	18 45	36 00	66·1	18 20	35 03	65·8	17 56	34 05	65·5	17 31	33 08	65·2	210
31	149	20 10	37 40	66·0	19 45	36 41	65·6	19 20	35 44	65·3	18 55	34 46	65·0	18 29	33 49	64·7	18 03	32 52	64·4	211
32	148	20 46	37 22	65·1	20 21	36 24	64·8	19 55	35 26	64·4	19 29	34 29	64·1	19 02	33 32	63·8	18 36	32 35	63·5	212
33	147	21 22	37 03	64·2	20 56	36 06	63·9	20 30	35 08	63·6	20 03	34 11	63·2	19 35	33 14	62·9	19 08	32 18	62·6	213
34	146	21 58	36 44	63·4	21 31	35 47	63·0	21 04	34 49	62·7	20 36	33 53	62·3	20 08	32 56	62·0	19 40	32 00	61·7	214
35	145	22 34	36 25	62·5	22 06	35 27	62·1	21 38	34 30	61·8	21 10	33 33	61·4	20 41	32 37	61·1	20 12	31 41	60·8	215
36	144	23 10	36 04	61·6	22 41	35 07	61·3	22 12	34 10	60·9	21 43	33 14	60·5	21 13	32 18	60·2	20 43	31 22	59·9	216
37	143	23 45	35 43	60·8	23 15	34 46	60·4	22 45	33 50	60·0	22 15	32 53	59·6	21 45	31 58	59·3	21 14	31 02	59·0	217
38	142	24 20	35 21	59·9	23 49	34 25	59·5	23 19	33 28	59·1	22 48	32 33	58·7	22 16	31 37	58·4	21 45	30 42	58·0	218
39	141	24 54	34 59	59·0	24 23	34 02	58·6	23 52	33 07	58·2	23 20	32 11	57·8	22 48	31 16	57·5	22 15	30 21	57·1	219
40	140	25 28	34 36	58·1	24 57	33 40	57·7	24 24	32 44	57·3	23 52	31 49	56·9	23 19	30 54	56·5	22 45	30 00	56·2	220
41	139	26 02	34 12	57·1	25 30	33 16	56·7	24 57	32 21	56·3	24 23	31 26	56·0	23 49	30 32	55·6	23 15	29 38	55·2	221
42	138	26 36	33 47	56·2	26 02	32 52	55·8	25 28	31 57	55·4	24 54	31 02	55·0	24 20	30 08	54·6	23 45	29 15	54·3	222
43	137	27 09	33 22	55·3	26 35	32 27	54·9	26 00	31 32	54·5	25 25	30 38	54·1	24 50	29 45	53·7	24 14	28 52	53·3	223
44	136	27 42	32 56	54·3	27 07	32 01	53·9	26 31	31 07	53·5	25 55	30 13	53·1	25 19	29 20	52·7	24 43	28 28	52·4	224
45	135	28 14	32 29	53·4	27 38	31 35	53·0	27 02	30 41	52·5	26 26	29 48	52·1	25 48	28 55	51·8	25 11	28 03	51·4	225

Lat./A LHA/F	48° A/H	48° B/P	48° Z₁/Z₂	49° A/H	49° B/P	49° Z₁/Z₂	50° A/H	50° B/P	50° Z₁/Z₂	51° A/H	51° B/P	51° Z₁/Z₂	52° A/H	52° B/P	52° Z₁/Z₂	53° A/H	53° B/P	53° Z₁/Z₂	Lat./A LHA
45 / 135	28 14	32 29	53·4	27 38	31 35	53·0	27 02	30 41	52·5	26 25	29 48	52·1	25 48	28 55	51·8	25 11	28 03	51·4	225 / 315
46 / 134	28 46	32 01	52·4	28 10	31 08	52·0	27 32	30 14	51·6	26 55	29 22	51·2	26 17	28 29	50·8	25 39	27 38	50·4	226 / 314
47 / 133	29 18	31 33	51·4	28 41	30 40	51·0	28 02	29 47	50·6	27 24	28 57	50·2	26 46	28 02	49·8	26 07	27 12	49·4	227 / 313
48 / 132	29 49	31 04	50·5	29 11	30 11	50·0	28 32	29 19	49·6	27 53	28 27	49·2	27 14	27 36	48·8	26 34	26 46	48·4	228 / 312
49 / 131	30 20	30 34	49·5	29 41	29 42	49·0	29 01	28 50	48·6	28 21	27 59	48·2	27 41	27 08	47·8	27 01	26 18	47·4	229 / 311
50 / 130	30 50	30 04	48·5	30 10	29 12	48·0	29 30	28 20	47·6	28 49	27 30	47·2	28 08	26 40	46·8	27 27	25 51	46·4	230 / 310
51 / 129	31 20	29 32	47·5	30 39	28 41	47·0	29 58	27 50	46·6	29 17	27 00	46·2	28 35	26 11	45·8	27 53	25 22	45·4	231 / 309
52 / 128	31 49	29 00	46·4	31 07	28 09	46·0	30 26	27 19	45·6	29 44	26 30	45·2	29 01	25 41	44·8	28 19	24 53	44·4	232 / 308
53 / 127	32 18	28 27	45·4	31 36	27 37	45·0	30 53	26 48	44·5	30 10	25 59	44·1	29 27	25 11	43·7	28 44	24 24	43·3	233 / 307
54 / 126	32 46	27 53	44·4	32 03	27 04	43·9	31 20	26 15	43·5	30 36	25 27	43·1	29 52	24 40	42·7	29 08	23 53	42·3	234 / 306
55 / 125	33 14	27 19	43·3	32 30	26 30	42·9	31 46	25 42	42·4	31 02	24 55	42·0	30 17	24 08	41·6	29 32	23 23	41·2	235 / 305
56 / 124	33 42	26 44	42·2	32 57	25 55	41·8	32 12	25 08	41·4	31 27	24 22	41·0	30 41	23 36	40·6	29 56	22 51	40·2	236 / 304
57 / 123	34 08	26 07	41·1	33 23	25 20	40·7	32 37	24 34	40·3	31 51	23 48	39·9	31 05	23 03	39·5	30 19	22 19	39·1	237 / 303
58 / 122	34 34	25 30	40·1	33 48	24 44	39·6	33 02	23 58	39·2	32 15	23 14	38·8	31 28	22 29	38·4	30 41	21 46	38·0	238 / 302
59 / 121	35 00	24 53	39·0	34 13	24 07	38·5	33 26	23 22	38·1	32 39	22 38	37·7	31 51	21 55	37·3	31 03	21 13	37·0	239 / 301
60 / 120	35 25	24 14	37·8	34 37	23 30	37·4	33 50	22 46	37·0	33 02	22 03	36·6	32 13	21 20	36·2	31 25	20 39	35·9	240 / 300
61 / 119	35 49	23 35	36·7	35 01	22 51	36·3	34 12	22 08	35·9	33 24	21 26	35·5	32 35	20 45	35·1	31 46	20 04	34·8	241 / 299
62 / 118	36 13	22 55	35·6	35 24	22 12	35·2	34 35	21 30	34·8	33 45	20 49	34·4	32 56	20 09	34·0	32 06	19 29	33·7	242 / 298
63 / 117	36 36	22 14	34·4	35 46	21 32	34·0	34 56	20 51	33·6	34 06	20 11	33·3	33 16	19 32	32·9	32 26	18 53	32·5	243 / 297
64 / 116	36 58	21 32	33·3	36 08	20 52	32·9	35 17	20 12	32·5	34 27	19 33	32·1	33 36	18 54	31·8	32 45	18 17	31·4	244 / 296
65 / 115	37 20	20 50	32·1	36 29	20 10	31·7	35 38	19 32	31·3	34 47	18 54	31·0	33 55	18 16	30·6	33 03	17 40	30·1	245 / 295
66 / 114	37 41	20 07	30·9	36 49	19 28	30·5	35 58	18 51	30·2	35 06	18 14	29·8	34 13	17 38	29·5	33 21	17 02	29·1	246 / 294
67 / 113	38 01	19 23	29·7	37 09	18 46	29·4	36 17	18 09	29·0	35 24	17 33	28·6	34 31	16 59	28·3	33 38	16 24	28·0	247 / 293
68 / 112	38 21	18 38	28·5	37 28	18 02	28·2	36 35	17 27	27·8	35 42	16 53	27·5	34 48	16 19	27·1	33 55	15 46	26·8	248 / 292
69 / 111	38 40	17 53	27·3	37 46	17 18	27·0	36 53	16 44	26·6	35 59	16 11	26·3	35 05	15 38	26·0	34 11	15 07	25·7	249 / 291
70 / 110	38 58	17 07	26·1	38 04	16 33	25·7	37 10	16 01	25·4	36 15	15 29	25·1	35 21	14 58	24·8	34 26	14 27	24·5	250 / 290
71 / 109	39 15	16 20	24·9	38 20	15 48	24·5	37 26	15 17	24·2	36 31	14 46	23·9	35 36	14 16	23·6	34 41	13 47	23·3	251 / 289
72 / 108	39 31	15 33	23·6	38 36	15 02	23·3	37 41	14 32	23·0	36 46	14 03	22·7	35 50	13 34	22·4	34 55	13 07	22·1	252 / 288
73 / 107	39 47	14 45	22·4	38 51	14 16	22·1	37 56	13 47	21·8	37 00	13 19	21·5	36 04	12 52	21·2	35 08	12 25	20·9	253 / 287
74 / 106	40 02	13 56	21·1	39 06	13 28	20·8	38 10	13 01	20·5	37 13	12 35	20·3	36 17	12 09	20·0	35 21	11 44	19·8	254 / 286
75 / 105	40 16	13 07	19·8	39 19	12 41	19·5	38 23	12 15	19·3	37 26	11 50	19·0	36 29	11 26	18·8	35 33	11 02	18·5	255 / 285
76 / 104	40 29	12 17	18·5	39 32	11 53	18·3	38 35	11 28	18·0	37 38	11 05	17·8	36 41	10 42	17·6	35 44	10 20	17·3	256 / 284
77 / 103	40 41	11 27	17·3	39 44	11 04	17·0	38 47	10 41	16·8	37 49	10 19	16·5	36 52	9 58	16·3	35 54	9 37	16·1	257 / 283
78 / 102	40 53	10 36	16·0	39 55	10 15	15·7	38 57	9 54	15·5	38 00	9 33	15·3	37 02	9 14	15·1	36 04	8 54	14·9	258 / 282
79 / 101	41 04	9 45	14·7	40 05	9 25	14·4	39 07	9 06	14·2	38 09	8 47	14·0	37 11	8 29	13·9	36 13	8 11	13·7	259 / 281
80 / 100	41 13	8 53	13·3	40 15	8 35	13·2	39 16	8 17	13·0	38 18	8 00	12·8	37 19	7 44	12·6	36 21	7 27	12·5	260 / 280
81 / 99	41 22	8 01	12·0	40 23	7 45	11·9	39 25	7 29	11·7	38 26	7 13	11·5	37 27	6 58	11·4	36 28	6 43	11·2	261 / 279
82 / 98	41 30	7 09	10·7	40 31	6 54	10·5	39 32	6 40	10·4	38 33	6 26	10·3	37 34	6 12	10·1	36 35	5 59	10·0	262 / 278
83 / 97	41 37	6 16	9·4	40 38	6 03	9·2	39 39	5 50	9·1	38 40	5 38	9·0	37 40	5 26	8·9	36 41	5 15	8·7	263 / 277
84 / 96	41 43	5 23	8·1	40 44	5 12	7·9	39 44	5 01	7·8	38 45	4 50	7·7	37 45	4 40	7·6	36 46	4 30	7·5	264 / 276
85 / 95	41 48	4 29	6·7	40 49	4 20	6·6	39 49	4 11	6·5	38 49	4 02	6·4	37 50	3 54	6·3	36 50	3 45	6·3	265 / 275
86 / 94	41 52	3 36	5·4	40 53	3 28	5·3	39 53	3 21	5·2	38 53	3 14	5·1	37 53	3 07	5·1	36 54	3 01	5·0	266 / 274
87 / 93	41 56	2 42	4·0	40 56	2 36	4·0	39 56	2 31	3·9	38 56	2 26	3·9	37 56	2 20	3·8	36 56	2 16	3·8	267 / 273
88 / 92	41 58	1 48	2·7	40 58	1 44	2·6	39 58	1 41	2·6	38 58	1 37	2·5	37 58	1 34	2·5	36 58	1 30	2·5	268 / 272
89 / 91	42 00	0 54	1·3	41 00	0 52	1·3	40 00	0 50	1·3	39 00	0 49	1·3	38 00	0 47	1·3	37 00	0 45	1·3	269 / 271
90 / 90	42 00	0 00	0·0	41 00	0 00	0·0	40 00	0 00	0·0	39 00	0 00	0·0	38 00	0 00	0·0	37 00	0 00	0·0	270 / 270

N. Lat.: for LHA > 180° ... $Z_n = Z$
for LHA < 180° ... $Z_n = 360° - Z$

S. Lat.: for LHA > 180° ... $Z_n = 180° - Z$
for LHA < 180° ... $Z_n = 180° + Z$

B: (−) for 90° < LHA < 270°
Dec:(−) for Lat. contrary name

Z₁: same sign as B
Z₂: (−) for F > 90°

SIGHT REDUCTION TABLE

LHA/F	F	54° A/H	54° B/P	54° Z₁/Z₂	55° A/H	55° B/P	55° Z₁/Z₂	56° A/H	56° B/P	56° Z₁/Z₂	57° A/H	57° B/P	57° Z₁/Z₂	58° A/H	58° B/P	58° Z₁/Z₂	59° A/H	59° B/P	59° Z₁/Z₂	LHA	LHA°
0	180	0 00	36 00	90·0	0 00	35 00	90·0	0 00	34 00	90·0	0 00	33 00	90·0	0 00	32 00	90·0	0 00	31 00	90·0	180	360
1	179	0 35	36 00	89·2	0 34	35 00	89·2	0 34	34 00	89·2	0 33	33 00	89·2	0 32	32 00	89·2	0 31	31 00	89·1	181	359
2	178	1 11	35 59	88·4	1 09	34 59	88·4	1 07	33 59	88·3	1 05	32 59	88·3	1 04	31 58	88·3	1 02	30 59	88·3	182	358
3	177	1 46	35 58	87·6	1 43	34 58	87·5	1 41	33 58	87·5	1 38	32 58	87·5	1 35	31 58	87·5	1 33	30 58	87·4	183	357
4	176	2 21	35 56	86·8	2 18	34 56	86·7	2 14	33 56	86·7	2 11	32 56	86·6	2 07	31 56	86·6	2 04	30 56	86·6	184	356
5	175	2 56	35 54	86·0	2 52	34 54	85·9	2 48	33 54	85·9	2 43	32 54	85·8	2 39	31 54	85·8	2 34	30 54	85·7	185	355
6	174	3 31	35 51	85·1	3 26	34 51	85·1	3 21	33 51	85·0	3 16	32 51	85·0	3 11	31 52	84·9	3 05	30 52	84·9	186	354
7	173	4 06	35 48	84·3	4 00	34 48	84·3	3 54	33 48	84·2	3 48	32 48	84·1	3 42	31 48	84·1	3 36	30 49	84·0	187	353
8	172	4 42	35 44	83·5	4 35	34 44	83·4	4 28	33 44	83·4	4 21	32 45	83·3	4 14	31 45	83·2	4 07	30 45	83·1	188	352
9	171	5 17	35 40	82·7	5 09	34 40	82·6	5 01	33 40	82·5	4 53	32 41	82·4	4 45	31 41	82·3	4 37	30 41	82·3	189	351
10	170	5 51	35 35	81·9	5 43	34 35	81·8	5 34	33 36	81·7	5 26	32 36	81·6	5 17	31 36	81·5	5 08	30 37	81·4	190	350
11	169	6 26	35 30	81·1	6 17	34 30	81·0	6 08	33 31	80·8	5 58	32 31	80·7	5 48	31 31	80·6	5 38	30 32	80·5	191	349
12	168	7 01	35 24	80·2	6 51	34 24	80·1	6 41	33 25	80·0	6 30	32 25	79·9	6 20	31 26	79·8	6 09	30 27	79·7	192	348
13	167	7 36	35 18	79·4	7 25	34 18	79·3	7 14	33 19	79·2	7 02	32 19	79·0	6 51	31 20	78·9	6 39	30 21	78·8	193	347
14	166	8 11	35 11	78·6	7 59	34 12	78·5	7 46	33 12	78·3	7 34	32 13	78·2	7 23	31 14	78·1	7 09	30 15	77·9	194	346
15	165	8 45	35 04	77·8	8 32	34 04	77·6	8 19	33 05	77·5	8 06	32 06	77·3	7 53	31 07	77·2	7 40	30 08	77·1	195	345
16	164	9 19	34 56	76·9	9 06	33 57	76·8	8 52	32 58	76·6	8 38	31 58	76·5	8 24	31 00	76·3	8 10	30 01	76·2	196	344
17	163	9 54	34 47	76·1	9 39	33 48	75·9	9 25	32 49	75·8	9 10	31 50	75·6	8 55	30 52	75·5	8 40	29 53	75·3	197	343
18	162	10 28	34 39	75·3	10 13	33 40	75·1	9 57	32 41	74·9	9 41	31 42	74·8	9 25	30 43	74·6	9 09	29 45	74·4	198	342
19	161	11 02	34 29	74·4	10 46	33 30	74·2	10 29	32 32	74·1	10 13	31 33	73·9	9 56	30 31	73·7	9 39	29 36	73·6	199	341
20	160	11 36	34 19	73·6	11 19	33 21	73·4	11 02	32 22	73·2	10 44	31 24	73·0	10 27	30 25	72·8	10 09	29 27	72·7	200	340
21	159	12 10	34 09	72·7	11 52	33 10	72·5	11 34	32 12	72·3	11 15	31 14	72·2	10 57	30 15	72·0	10 38	29 17	71·8	201	339
22	158	12 43	33 58	71·9	12 24	33 00	71·7	12 06	32 01	71·5	11 46	31 03	71·3	11 27	30 05	71·1	11 07	29 07	70·9	202	338
23	157	13 17	33 46	71·0	12 57	32 48	70·8	12 37	31 50	70·6	12 17	30 52	70·4	11 57	29 54	70·2	11 37	28 57	70·0	203	337
24	156	13 50	33 34	70·2	13 29	32 36	70·0	13 09	31 38	69·7	12 48	30 41	69·5	12 27	29 43	69·4	12 06	28 46	69·1	204	336
25	155	14 23	33 22	69·3	14 02	32 24	69·1	13 40	31 26	68·9	13 18	30 29	68·6	12 56	29 31	68·4	12 34	28 34	68·2	205	335
26	154	14 56	33 09	68·5	14 34	32 11	68·2	14 11	31 14	68·0	13 49	30 16	67·8	13 26	29 19	67·5	13 03	28 22	67·3	206	334
27	153	15 29	32 55	67·6	15 06	31 58	67·3	14 42	31 00	67·1	14 19	30 03	66·9	13 55	29 06	66·6	13 31	28 10	66·4	207	333
28	152	16 01	32 41	66·7	15 37	31 44	66·5	15 13	30 47	66·2	14 49	29 50	66·0	14 24	28 53	65·7	14 00	27 57	65·5	208	332
29	151	16 33	32 26	65·8	16 09	31 29	65·6	15 44	30 32	65·3	15 19	29 36	65·1	14 53	28 39	64·8	14 28	27 43	64·6	209	331
30	150	17 05	32 11	65·0	16 40	31 14	64·7	16 14	30 17	64·4	15 48	29 21	64·2	15 22	28 25	63·9	14 55	27 29	63·7	210	330
31	149	17 37	31 55	64·1	17 11	30 58	63·8	16 44	30 02	63·5	16 17	29 06	63·3	15 50	28 10	63·0	15 23	27 15	62·7	211	329
32	148	18 09	31 38	63·2	17 42	30 42	62·9	17 14	29 46	62·6	16 47	28 51	62·3	16 19	27 55	62·1	15 50	27 00	61·8	212	328
33	147	18 40	31 21	62·3	18 12	30 25	62·0	17 44	29 30	61·7	17 15	28 34	61·4	16 47	27 39	61·2	16 17	26 45	60·9	213	327
34	146	19 11	31 04	61·4	18 42	30 08	61·1	18 13	29 13	60·8	17 44	28 18	60·5	17 14	27 23	60·2	16 44	26 29	60·0	214	326
35	145	19 42	30 46	60·5	19 12	29 50	60·2	18 42	28 55	59·9	18 12	28 01	59·6	17 42	27 06	59·3	17 11	26 12	59·0	215	325
36	144	20 13	30 27	59·6	19 42	29 32	59·2	19 11	28 37	58·9	18 40	27 43	58·6	18 09	26 49	58·4	17 37	25 55	58·1	216	324
37	143	20 43	30 07	58·7	20 12	29 13	58·3	19 40	28 19	58·0	19 08	27 25	57·7	18 36	26 31	57·4	18 03	25 38	57·1	217	323
38	142	21 13	29 48	57·7	20 41	28 53	57·4	20 08	27 59	57·1	19 35	27 06	56·8	19 02	26 13	56·5	18 29	25 20	56·2	218	322
39	141	21 43	29 27	56·8	21 10	28 33	56·4	20 36	27 40	56·2	20 03	26 47	55·8	19 29	25 54	55·5	18 55	25 02	55·2	219	321
40	140	22 12	29 06	55·8	21 38	28 13	55·5	21 04	27 20	55·2	20 30	26 27	54·9	19 55	25 35	54·6	19 20	24 43	54·3	220	320
41	139	22 41	28 44	54·9	22 06	27 51	54·5	21 31	26 59	54·3	20 56	26 07	53·9	20 21	25 15	53·6	19 45	24 24	53·3	221	319
42	138	23 10	28 22	53·9	22 34	27 29	53·6	21 58	26 37	53·3	21 22	25 46	52·9	20 46	24 55	52·6	20 10	24 04	52·3	222	318
43	137	23 38	27 59	53·0	23 02	27 07	52·6	22 25	26 15	52·6	21 48	25 24	52·0	21 11	24 34	51·7	20 34	23 43	51·4	223	317
44	136	24 06	27 36	52·0	23 29	26 44	51·7	22 51	25 53	51·7	22 14	25 02	51·0	21 36	24 12	50·7	20 58	23 23	50·4	224	316
45	135	24 34	27 11	51·0	23 55	26 20	50·7	23 17	25 30	50·7	22 39	24 40	50·0	22 00	23 50	49·7	21 21	23 01	49·4	225	315

Lat. / A		54°			55°			56°			57°			58°			59°			Lat. / A	
	LHA/F	A/H	B/P	Z_1/Z_2	A/H	B/P	Z_1/Z_2	A/H	B/P	Z_1/Z_2	A/H	B/P	Z_1/Z_2	A/H	B/P	Z_1/Z_2	A/H	B/P	Z_1/Z_2	LHA	
45	135	24 34	27 11	51·0	23 56	26 20	50·7	23 17	25 30	50·3	22 39	24 40	50·0	22 00	23 50	49·7	21 21	23 01	49·4	225	315
46	134	25 01	26 47	50·0	24 24	25 56	49·7	23 43	25 06	49·4	23 04	24 17	49·0	22 25	23 28	48·7	21 45	22 39	48·4	226	314
47	133	25 28	26 22	49·1	24 48	25 32	48·7	24 08	24 42	48·4	23 28	23 53	48·0	22 48	23 05	47·7	22 08	22 17	47·4	227	313
48	132	25 54	25 56	48·1	25 14	25 06	47·7	24 33	24 17	47·4	23 53	23 29	47·0	23 11	22 41	46·7	22 30	21 54	46·4	228	312
49	131	26 20	25 29	47·1	25 39	24 40	46·7	24 58	23 52	46·4	24 16	23 05	46·0	23 34	22 17	45·7	22 52	21 31	45·4	229	311
50	130	26 46	25 02	46·0	26 04	24 14	45·7	25 22	23 26	45·3	24 40	22 39	45·0	23 57	21 53	44·7	23 14	21 07	44·4	230	310
51	129	27 11	24 34	45·0	26 28	23 47	44·7	25 45	23 00	44·3	25 02	22 14	44·0	24 19	21 28	43·7	23 36	20 43	43·4	231	309
52	128	27 36	24 06	44·0	26 52	23 19	43·6	26 09	22 33	43·3	25 25	21 48	43·0	24 41	21 03	42·7	23 57	20 18	42·3	232	308
53	127	28 00	23 37	43·0	27 16	22 51	42·6	26 32	22 06	42·3	25 47	21 21	41·9	25 02	20 37	41·6	24 17	19 53	41·3	233	307
54	126	28 24	23 07	41·9	27 40	22 22	41·6	26 54	21 38	41·2	26 09	20 54	40·9	25 23	20 10	40·6	24 37	19 27	40·3	234	306
55	125	28 47	22 37	40·9	28 01	21 53	40·5	27 16	21 09	40·2	26 30	20 26	39·9	25 44	19 43	39·5	24 57	19 01	39·2	235	305
56	124	29 10	22 07	39·8	28 24	21 23	39·5	27 37	20 40	39·1	26 50	19 57	38·8	26 04	19 16	38·5	25 17	18 34	38·2	236	304
57	123	29 32	21 35	38·8	28 45	20 52	38·4	27 58	20 10	38·1	27 11	19 29	37·8	26 23	18 48	37·4	25 35	18 07	37·1	237	303
58	122	29 54	21 03	37·7	29 06	20 21	37·3	28 19	19 40	37·0	27 31	18 59	36·7	26 42	18 19	36·4	25 54	17 40	36·1	238	302
59	121	30 15	20 31	36·6	29 27	19 50	36·3	28 38	19 09	35·9	27 50	18 30	35·6	27 01	17 50	35·3	26 12	17 12	35·0	239	301
60	120	30 36	19 58	35·5	29 47	19 18	35·2	28 58	18 38	34·9	28 09	17 59	34·5	27 19	17 21	34·2	26 29	16 43	34·0	240	300
61	119	30 56	19 24	34·4	30 07	18 45	34·1	29 17	18 06	33·8	28 27	17 29	33·5	27 37	16 51	33·2	26 46	16 14	32·9	241	299
62	118	31 16	18 50	33·3	30 26	18 12	33·0	29 35	17 34	32·7	28 45	16 57	32·4	27 54	16 21	32·1	27 03	15 45	31·8	242	298
63	117	31 35	18 15	32·2	30 44	17 38	31·9	29 53	17 02	31·6	29 02	16 26	31·3	28 10	15 50	31·0	27 19	15 15	30·7	243	297
64	116	31 53	17 40	31·1	31 02	17 04	30·8	30 10	16 28	30·5	29 19	15 53	30·2	28 26	15 19	29·9	27 35	14 45	29·6	244	296
65	115	32 11	17 04	30·0	31 19	16 29	29·7	30 27	15 55	29·4	29 35	15 21	29·1	28 42	14 48	28·8	27 50	14 15	28·5	245	295
66	114	32 29	16 28	28·8	31 36	15 54	28·5	30 43	15 20	28·2	29 50	14 48	28·0	28 57	14 16	27·7	28 04	13 44	27·4	246	294
67	113	32 45	15 51	27·7	31 52	15 18	27·4	30 59	14 46	27·1	30 05	14 14	26·8	29 12	13 43	26·6	28 18	13 13	26·3	247	293
68	112	33 01	15 14	26·5	32 08	14 42	26·3	31 14	14 11	26·0	30 20	13 40	25·7	29 26	13 10	25·5	28 31	12 41	25·2	248	292
69	111	33 17	14 36	25·4	32 23	14 05	25·1	31 28	13 35	24·8	30 34	13 06	24·6	29 39	12 37	24·4	28 44	12 09	24·1	249	291
70	110	33 32	13 57	24·2	32 37	13 28	24·0	31 42	12 59	23·7	30 47	12 31	23·5	29 52	12 04	23·2	28 57	11 37	23·0	250	290
71	109	33 46	13 18	23·1	32 51	12 51	22·8	31 55	12 23	22·6	31 00	11 56	22·3	30 04	11 30	22·1	29 09	11 04	21·9	251	289
72	108	33 59	12 39	21·9	33 04	12 13	21·6	32 08	11 46	21·4	31 12	11 21	21·2	30 16	10 56	21·0	29 20	10 31	20·8	252	288
73	107	34 12	12 00	20·7	33 16	11 34	20·5	32 20	11 09	20·2	31 23	10 45	20·0	30 27	10 21	19·8	29 30	9 58	19·6	253	287
74	106	34 24	11 19	19·5	33 28	10 55	19·3	32 31	10 32	19·1	31 34	10 09	18·9	30 37	9 46	18·7	29 41	9 24	18·5	254	286
75	105	34 36	10 39	18·3	33 39	10 16	18·1	32 42	9 54	17·9	31 44	9 32	17·7	30 47	9 11	17·5	29 50	8 50	17·4	255	285
76	104	34 46	9 58	17·1	33 49	9 37	16·9	32 52	9 16	16·7	31 54	8 56	16·6	30 57	8 36	16·4	29 59	8 16	16·2	256	284
77	103	34 56	9 17	15·9	33 59	8 57	15·7	33 01	8 38	15·6	32 03	8 19	15·4	31 05	8 00	15·2	30 07	7 42	15·1	257	283
78	102	35 06	8 35	14·7	34 08	8 17	14·5	33 10	7 59	14·4	32 11	7 41	14·2	31 13	7 24	14·1	30 15	7 07	13·9	258	282
79	101	35 14	7 54	13·5	34 16	7 37	13·3	33 18	7 20	13·2	32 19	7 04	13·0	31 21	6 48	12·9	30 22	6 32	12·8	259	281
80	100	35 22	7 11	12·3	34 24	6 56	12·1	33 25	6 41	12·0	32 26	6 26	11·9	31 27	6 12	11·7	30 29	5 57	11·6	260	280
81	99	35 29	6 29	11·1	34 30	6 15	10·9	33 32	6 01	10·8	32 33	5 48	10·7	31 34	5 35	10·6	30 35	5 22	10·5	261	279
82	98	35 36	5 46	9·9	34 37	5 34	9·7	33 37	5 22	9·6	32 38	5 10	9·5	31 39	4 58	9·4	30 40	4 47	9·3	262	278
83	97	35 41	5 04	8·6	34 42	4 53	8·5	33 43	4 42	8·4	32 43	4 32	8·3	31 44	4 21	8·2	30 45	4 11	8·2	263	277
84	96	35 46	4 21	7·4	34 47	4 11	7·3	33 47	4 02	7·2	32 48	3 53	7·1	31 48	3 44	7·1	30 49	3 36	7·0	264	276
85	95	35 51	3 37	6·2	34 51	3 30	6·1	33 51	3 22	6·0	32 52	3 14	5·9	31 52	3 07	5·9	30 52	3 00	5·8	265	275
86	94	35 54	2 54	4·9	34 54	2 48	4·9	33 54	2 42	4·8	32 55	2 36	4·8	31 55	2 30	4·7	30 55	2 24	4·7	266	274
87	93	35 57	2 11	3·7	34 57	2 06	3·7	33 57	2 01	3·6	32 57	1 57	3·6	31 57	1 52	3·5	30 57	1 48	3·5	267	273
88	92	35 58	1 27	2·5	34 59	1 24	2·4	33 59	1 21	2·4	32 59	1 18	2·4	31 59	1 15	2·4	30 59	1 12	2·3	268	272
89	91	36 00	0 44	1·2	35 00	0 42	1·2	34 00	0 40	1·2	33 00	0 39	1·2	32 00	0 37	1·2	31 00	0 36	1·2	269	271
90	90	36 00	0 00	0·0	35 00	0 00	0·0	34 00	0 00	0·0	33 00	0 00	0·0	32 00	0 00	0·0	31 00	0 00	0·0	270	270

N. Lat.: for LHA > 180°... $Z_n = Z$
for LHA < 180°... $Z_n = 360° - Z$

S. Lat.: for LHA > 180°... $Z_n = 180° - Z$
for LHA < 180°... $Z_n = 180° + Z$

SIGHT REDUCTION TABLE

B: (−) for 90° < LHA < 270°
Dec:(−) for Lat. contrary name

Z₁: same sign as B
Z₂: (−) for F > 90°

LHA/F	60° A/H	60° B/P	60° Z_1/Z_2	61° A/H	61° B/P	61° Z_1/Z_2	62° A/H	62° B/P	62° Z_1/Z_2	63° A/H	63° B/P	63° Z_1/Z_2	64° A/H	64° B/P	64° Z_1/Z_2	65° A/H	65° B/P	65° Z_1/Z_2	LHA
0	0 00	30 00	90·0	0 00	29 00	90·0	0 00	28 00	90·0	0 00	27 00	90·0	0 00	26 00	90·0	0 00	25 00	90·0	180
1	0 30	30 00	89·1	0 29	29 00	89·1	0 28	28 00	89·1	0 27	27 00	89·1	0 26	26 00	89·1	0 25	25 00	89·1	181
2	1 00	29 59	88·3	0 58	28 58	88·3	0 56	27 59	88·2	0 54	26 59	88·2	0 53	25 58	88·2	0 51	24 59	88·2	182
3	1 30	29 58	87·4	1 27	28 58	87·4	1 24	27 58	87·4	1 22	26 58	87·3	1 19	25 58	87·3	1 16	24 58	87·3	183
4	2 00	29 56	86·5	1 56	28 56	86·5	1 53	27 57	86·5	1 49	26 57	86·4	1 45	25 57	86·4	1 41	24 57	86·4	184
5	2 30	29 54	85·7	2 25	28 54	85·6	2 21	27 55	85·6	2 16	26 55	85·5	2 11	25 55	85·5	2 07	24 55	85·5	185
6	3 00	29 52	84·8	2 54	28 52	84·7	2 49	27 52	84·7	2 43	26 52	84·6	2 38	25 53	84·6	2 32	24 53	84·6	186
7	3 30	29 49	83·9	3 23	28 49	83·9	3 17	27 49	83·8	3 10	26 50	83·8	3 04	25 50	83·7	2 57	24 50	83·7	187
8	3 59	29 45	83·1	3 52	28 46	83·0	3 45	27 46	82·9	3 37	26 46	82·9	3 30	25 47	82·8	3 22	24 47	82·7	188
9	4 29	29 42	82·2	4 21	28 42	82·1	4 13	27 42	82·0	4 04	26 43	82·0	3 56	25 43	81·9	3 47	24 44	81·8	189
10	4 59	29 37	81·3	4 50	28 38	81·2	4 41	27 38	81·1	4 31	26 39	81·1	4 22	25 39	81·0	4 13	24 40	80·9	190
11	5 28	29 33	80·4	5 18	28 33	80·4	5 08	27 34	80·3	4 58	26 34	80·2	4 48	25 35	80·1	4 38	24 36	80·0	191
12	5 58	29 27	79·6	5 47	28 28	79·5	5 36	27 29	79·4	5 25	26 29	79·3	5 14	25 30	79·2	5 02	24 31	79·1	192
13	6 27	29 22	78·7	6 16	28 22	78·6	6 04	27 23	78·5	5 52	26 24	78·4	5 40	25 25	78·3	5 27	24 26	78·2	193
14	6 57	29 15	77·8	6 44	28 16	77·7	6 31	27 17	77·6	6 18	26 18	77·5	6 05	25 20	77·4	5 52	24 21	77·3	194
15	7 26	29 09	76·9	7 13	28 10	76·8	6 59	27 11	76·7	6 45	26 12	76·6	6 31	25 14	76·5	6 17	24 15	76·4	195
16	7 55	29 02	76·1	7 41	28 03	75·9	7 26	27 04	75·8	7 11	26 06	75·7	6 56	25 07	75·5	6 41	24 09	75·4	196
17	8 24	28 54	75·2	8 09	27 56	75·0	7 53	26 57	74·9	7 38	25 59	74·8	7 22	25 00	74·6	7 06	24 02	74·5	197
18	8 53	28 46	74·3	8 37	27 48	74·1	8 20	26 50	74·0	8 04	25 51	73·9	7 47	24 53	73·7	7 30	23 55	73·6	198
19	9 22	28 38	73·4	9 05	27 40	73·2	8 48	26 41	73·1	8 30	25 43	72·9	8 12	24 45	72·8	7 55	23 48	72·7	199
20	9 51	28 29	72·5	9 33	27 31	72·3	9 14	26 33	72·2	8 56	25 35	72·0	8 37	24 37	71·9	8 19	23 40	71·7	200
21	10 19	28 19	71·6	10 00	27 22	71·4	9 41	26 24	71·3	9 22	25 26	71·1	9 02	24 29	71·0	8 43	23 32	70·8	201
22	10 48	28 10	70·7	10 28	27 12	70·5	10 08	26 15	70·4	9 48	25 17	70·2	9 27	24 20	70·0	9 07	23 23	69·9	202
23	11 16	27 59	69·8	10 55	27 02	69·6	10 34	26 05	69·5	10 13	25 08	69·3	9 52	24 11	69·1	9 30	23 14	69·0	203
24	11 44	27 49	68·9	11 22	26 51	68·7	11 00	25 54	68·5	10 38	24 58	68·4	10 16	24 01	68·2	9 54	23 04	68·0	204
25	12 12	27 37	68·0	11 49	26 40	67·8	11 27	25 44	67·6	11 04	24 47	67·4	10 41	23 51	67·3	10 17	22 55	67·1	205
26	12 40	27 26	67·1	12 16	26 29	66·9	11 53	25 33	66·7	11 29	24 36	66·5	11 05	23 40	66·3	10 41	22 44	66·2	206
27	13 07	27 13	66·2	12 43	26 17	66·0	12 18	25 21	65·8	11 54	24 25	65·6	11 29	23 29	65·4	11 04	22 34	65·2	207
28	13 35	27 01	65·3	13 09	26 05	65·1	12 44	25 09	64·9	12 18	24 13	64·7	11 53	23 18	64·5	11 27	22 23	64·3	208
29	14 02	26 48	64·4	13 36	25 52	64·1	13 09	24 56	63·9	12 43	24 01	63·7	12 16	23 06	63·5	11 49	22 11	63·3	209
30	14 29	26 34	63·4	14 02	25 39	63·2	13 35	24 43	63·0	13 07	23 49	62·8	12 40	22 54	62·6	12 12	21 59	62·4	210
31	14 55	26 20	62·5	14 28	25 25	62·3	14 00	24 30	62·1	13 31	23 36	61·8	13 03	22 41	61·6	12 34	21 47	61·4	211
32	15 22	26 05	61·6	14 53	25 11	61·3	14 24	24 16	61·1	13 55	23 22	60·9	13 26	22 28	60·7	12 56	21 35	60·5	212
33	15 48	25 50	60·6	15 19	24 56	60·4	14 49	24 02	60·2	14 19	23 08	59·9	13 49	22 15	59·7	13 18	21 22	59·5	213
34	16 14	25 35	59·7	15 44	24 41	59·5	15 13	23 47	59·2	14 42	22 54	59·0	14 11	22 01	58·8	13 40	21 08	58·6	214
35	16 40	25 19	58·8	16 09	24 25	58·5	15 37	23 32	58·3	15 06	22 39	58·0	14 34	21 47	57·8	14 02	20 54	57·6	215
36	17 05	25 02	57·8	16 33	24 09	57·6	16 01	23 17	57·3	15 29	22 24	57·1	14 56	21 32	56·9	14 23	20 40	56·6	216
37	17 31	24 45	56·9	16 58	23 53	56·6	16 25	23 00	56·4	15 51	22 09	56·1	15 18	21 17	55·9	14 44	20 26	55·7	217
38	17 56	24 28	55·9	17 22	23 36	55·7	16 48	22 44	55·4	16 14	21 53	55·2	15 39	21 01	54·9	15 05	20 11	54·7	218
39	18 20	24 10	55·0	17 46	23 18	54·7	17 11	22 27	54·4	16 36	21 36	54·2	16 01	20 46	54·0	15 25	19 55	53·7	219
40	18 45	23 52	54·0	18 09	23 00	53·7	17 34	22 10	53·5	16 58	21 19	53·2	16 22	20 29	53·0	15 46	19 39	52·7	220
41	19 09	23 33	53·0	18 33	22 42	52·8	17 56	21 52	52·5	17 20	21 02	52·2	16 43	20 13	52·0	16 06	19 23	51·8	221
42	19 33	23 13	52·1	18 56	22 23	51·8	18 19	21 34	51·5	17 41	20 44	51·3	17 03	19 55	51·0	16 26	19 07	50·8	222
43	19 56	22 54	51·1	19 18	22 04	50·8	18 40	21 15	50·5	18 02	20 26	50·3	17 24	19 38	50·0	16 45	18 50	49·8	223
44	20 19	22 33	50·1	19 41	21 44	49·8	19 02	20 56	49·5	18 23	20 08	49·3	17 44	19 20	49·0	17 04	18 33	48·8	224
45	20 42	22 12	49·1	20 03	21 24	48·8	19 23	20 36	48·6	18 43	19 49	48·3	18 03	19 02	48·1	17 23	18 15	47·8	225

B: (−) for 90° < LHA < 270° for Lat. contrary name

Z₂: (−) for F > 90°

Lat. / A — LHA/F (left) ; Lat. / A — LHA (right)

Lat. / A	LHA/F	60°			61°			62°			63°			64°			65°			Lat. / A	LHA
		A/H	B/P	Z_1/Z_2	A/H	B/P	Z_1/Z_2	A/H	B/P	Z_1/Z_2	A/H	B/P	Z_1/Z_2	A/H	B/P	Z_1/Z_2	A/H	B/P	Z_1/Z_2		
45	135	20 42	22 12	49·1	20 03	21 24	48·8	19 23	20 36	48·6	18 43	19 49	48·3	18 03	19 02	48·1	17 23	18 15	47·8	225	315
46	134	21 05	21 51	48·1	20 25	21 04	47·8	19 44	20 16	47·6	19 04	19 29	47·3	18 23	18 43	47·1	17 42	17 57	46·8	226	314
47	133	21 27	21 30	47·1	20 46	20 43	46·8	20 05	19 56	46·6	19 24	19 10	46·3	18 42	18 24	46·1	18 00	17 39	45·8	227	313
48	132	21 49	21 07	46·1	21 07	20 21	45·8	20 25	19 35	45·6	19 43	18 50	45·3	19 01	18 04	45·1	18 18	17 20	44·8	228	312
49	131	22 10	20 45	45·1	21 28	19 59	44·8	20 45	19 14	44·6	20 02	18 29	44·3	19 19	17 45	44·0	18 36	17 01	43·8	229	311
50	130	22 31	20 22	44·1	21 48	19 37	43·8	21 05	18 52	43·5	20 21	18 08	43·3	19 37	17 24	43·0	18 53	16 41	42·8	230	310
51	129	22 52	19 58	43·1	22 08	19 14	42·8	21 24	18 30	42·5	20 40	17 47	42·3	19 55	17 04	42·0	19 10	16 21	41·8	231	309
52	128	23 12	19 34	42·1	22 28	18 51	41·8	21 43	18 08	41·5	20 58	17 25	41·2	20 13	16 43	41·0	19 27	16 01	40·8	232	308
53	127	23 32	19 10	41·0	22 47	18 27	40·7	22 01	17 45	40·5	21 15	17 03	40·2	20 30	16 21	40·0	19 44	15 41	39·7	233	307
54	126	23 52	18 45	40·0	23 06	18 03	39·7	22 19	17 21	39·4	21 33	16 40	39·2	20 46	16 00	39·0	20 00	15 20	38·7	234	306
55	125	24 11	18 19	39·0	23 24	17 38	38·7	22 37	16 58	38·4	21 50	16 17	38·2	21 03	15 38	37·9	20 15	14 58	37·7	235	305
56	124	24 29	17 54	37·9	23 42	17 13	37·6	22 54	16 34	37·4	22 07	15 54	37·1	21 19	15 15	36·9	20 31	14 37	36·7	236	304
57	123	24 48	17 27	36·9	23 59	16 48	36·6	23 11	16 09	36·3	22 23	15 31	36·1	21 34	14 53	35·8	20 46	14 15	35·6	237	303
58	122	25 05	17 01	35·8	24 17	16 22	35·5	23 28	15 44	35·3	22 39	15 07	35·0	21 49	14 29	34·8	21 00	13 53	34·6	238	302
59	121	25 23	16 34	34·8	24 33	15 56	34·5	23 44	15 19	34·2	22 54	14 42	34·0	22 04	14 06	33·8	21 14	13 30	33·5	239	301
60	120	25 40	16 06	33·7	24 50	15 29	33·4	23 59	14 53	33·2	23 09	14 18	32·9	22 19	13 42	32·7	21 28	13 07	32·5	240	300
61	119	25 56	15 38	32·6	25 05	15 03	32·4	24 15	14 27	32·1	23 24	13 53	31·9	22 33	13 18	31·7	21 42	12 44	31·5	241	299
62	118	26 12	15 10	31·5	25 21	14 35	31·3	24 29	14 01	31·1	23 38	13 27	30·8	22 46	12 54	30·6	21 55	12 21	30·4	242	298
63	117	26 27	14 41	30·5	25 36	14 08	30·2	24 44	13 34	30·0	23 52	13 01	29·8	22 59	12 29	29·5	22 07	11 57	29·3	243	297
64	116	26 42	14 12	29·4	25 50	13 39	29·1	24 57	13 07	28·9	24 05	12 35	28·7	23 12	12 04	28·5	22 19	11 33	28·3	244	296
65	115	26 57	13 43	28·3	26 04	13 11	28·1	25 11	12 40	27·8	24 18	12 09	27·6	23 24	11 39	27·4	22 31	11 09	27·2	245	295
66	114	27 11	13 13	27·2	26 17	12 42	27·0	25 24	12 12	26·8	24 30	11 43	26·6	23 36	11 13	26·4	22 43	10 44	26·2	246	294
67	113	27 24	12 43	26·1	26 30	12 13	25·9	25 36	11 44	25·7	24 42	11 16	25·5	23 48	10 47	25·3	22 54	10 20	25·1	247	293
68	112	27 37	12 12	25·0	26 43	11 44	24·8	25 48	11 16	24·6	24 54	10 48	24·4	23 59	10 21	24·2	23 04	9 55	24·0	248	292
69	111	27 50	11 41	23·9	26 55	11 14	23·7	26 00	10 47	23·5	25 05	10 21	23·3	24 09	9 55	23·1	23 14	9 29	23·0	249	291
70	110	28 01	11 10	22·8	27 06	10 44	22·6	26 11	10 18	22·4	25 15	9 53	22·2	24 20	9 29	22·0	23 24	9 04	21·9	250	290
71	109	28 13	10 39	21·7	27 17	10 14	21·5	26 21	9 49	21·3	25 25	9 25	21·1	24 29	9 01	21·0	23 33	8 38	20·8	251	289
72	108	28 24	10 07	20·6	27 27	9 43	20·4	26 31	9 20	20·2	25 35	8 57	20·0	24 38	8 34	19·9	23 42	8 12	19·7	252	288
73	107	28 34	09 35	19·4	27 37	9 12	19·3	26 41	8 50	19·1	25 44	8 28	18·9	24 47	8 07	18·8	23 50	7 46	18·6	253	287
74	106	28 44	09 03	18·3	27 47	8 41	18·2	26 50	8 20	18·0	25 52	8 00	17·8	24 55	7 39	17·7	23 58	7 19	17·6	254	286
75	105	28 53	8 30	17·2	27 55	8 10	17·0	26 58	7 50	16·9	26 01	7 31	16·7	25 03	7 12	16·6	24 06	6 53	16·5	255	285
76	104	29 01	7 57	16·1	28 04	7 38	15·9	27 06	7 20	15·8	26 08	7 02	15·6	25 10	6 44	15·5	24 13	6 26	15·4	256	284
77	103	29 09	7 24	14·9	28 11	7 06	14·8	27 13	6 49	14·7	26 15	6 32	14·5	25 17	6 16	14·4	24 19	5 59	14·3	257	283
78	102	29 17	6 51	13·8	28 18	6 34	13·7	27 20	6 19	13·5	26 22	6 03	13·4	25 23	5 47	13·3	24 25	5 32	13·2	258	282
79	101	29 24	6 17	12·7	28 25	6 02	12·5	27 27	5 48	12·4	26 28	5 33	12·3	25 29	5 19	12·2	24 31	5 05	12·1	259	281
80	100	29 30	5 44	11·5	28 31	5 30	11·4	27 32	5 17	11·3	26 33	5 03	11·2	25 35	4 50	11·1	24 36	4 38	11·0	260	280
81	99	29 36	5 10	10·4	28 37	4 57	10·3	27 38	4 45	10·2	26 38	4 33	10·1	25 39	4 22	10·0	24 40	4 10	9·9	261	279
82	98	29 41	4 36	9·2	28 41	4 25	9·1	27 42	4 14	9·0	26 43	4 03	9·0	25 44	3 53	8·9	24 44	3 43	8·8	262	278
83	97	29 45	4 01	8·1	28 46	3 52	8·0	27 46	3 42	7·9	26 47	3 33	7·8	25 48	3 24	7·8	24 48	3 15	7·7	263	277
84	96	29 49	3 27	6·9	28 50	3 19	6·9	27 50	3 11	6·8	26 50	3 03	6·7	25 51	2 55	6·7	24 51	2 47	6·6	264	276
85	95	29 52	2 53	5·8	28 53	2 46	5·7	27 53	2 39	5·7	26 53	2 33	5·6	25 54	2 26	5·6	24 54	2 20	5·5	265	275
86	94	29 55	2 18	4·6	28 55	2 13	4·6	27 56	2 07	4·5	26 56	2 02	4·5	25 56	1 57	4·4	24 56	1 52	4·4	266	274
87	93	29 57	1 44	3·5	28 57	1 40	3·4	27 57	1 36	3·4	26 58	1 32	3·4	25 58	1 28	3·3	24 58	1 24	3·3	267	273
88	92	29 59	1 09	2·3	28 59	1 06	2·3	27 59	1 04	2·3	26 59	1 01	2·2	25 59	0 59	2·2	24 59	0 56	2·2	268	272
89	91	30 00	0 35	1·2	29 00	0 33	1·1	28 00	0 32	1·1	27 00	0 31	1·1	26 00	0 29	1·1	25 00	0 28	1·1	269	271
90	90	30 00	0 00	0·0	29 00	0 00	0·0	28 00	0 00	0·0	27 00	0 00	0·0	26 00	0 00	0·0	25 00	0 00	0·0	270	270

N. Lat: for LHA > 180° ... $Z_n = Z$
for LHA < 180° ... $Z_n = 360° - Z$

S. Lat.: for LHA > 180° ... $Z_n = 180° - Z$
for LHA < 180° ... $Z_n = 180° + Z$

SIGHT REDUCTION TABLE

B: (−) for 90° < LHA < 270°
Dec:(−) for Lat. contrary name

Z_1: same sign as B
Z_2: (−) for F > 90°

LHA/F	66° A/H	B/P	Z_1/Z_2	67° A/H	B/P	Z_1/Z_2	68° A/H	B/P	Z_1/Z_2	69° A/H	B/P	Z_1/Z_2	70° A/H	B/P	Z_1/Z_2	71° A/H	B/P	Z_1/Z_2	LHA/A	LHA
0	0 00	24 00	90·0	0 00	23 00	90·0	0 00	22 00	90·0	0 00	21 00	90·0	0 00	20 00	90·0	0 00	19 00	90·0	180	180
1	0 24	24 00	89·1	0 23	23 00	89·1	0 22	22 00	89·1	0 22	21 00	89·1	0 21	20 00	89·1	0 20	19 00	89·1	179	181
2	0 49	23 59	88·2	0 47	22 59	88·2	0 45	21 59	88·1	0 43	20 59	88·1	0 41	19 59	88·1	0 39	18 59	88·1	178	182
3	1 13	23 58	87·3	1 10	22 58	87·2	1 07	21 58	87·2	1 04	20 58	87·2	1 02	19 58	87·2	0 59	18 58	87·2	177	183
4	1 38	23 57	86·3	1 34	22 57	86·3	1 30	21 57	86·3	1 26	20 57	86·3	1 22	19 57	86·2	1 18	18 57	86·2	176	184
5	2 02	23 55	85·4	1 57	22 55	85·4	1 52	21 55	85·4	1 47	20 56	85·3	1 42	19 56	85·3	1 38	18 56	85·3	175	185
6	2 26	23 53	84·5	2 20	22 53	84·5	2 15	21 53	84·4	2 09	20 54	84·4	2 03	19 54	84·4	1 57	18 54	84·3	174	186
7	2 50	23 50	83·6	2 44	22 51	83·6	2 37	21 51	83·5	2 30	20 51	83·5	2 23	19 52	83·4	2 16	18 52	83·4	173	187
8	3 15	23 48	82·7	3 07	22 48	82·6	2 59	21 48	82·6	2 52	20 49	82·5	2 44	19 49	82·5	2 36	18 50	82·4	172	188
9	3 39	23 44	81·8	3 30	22 45	81·7	3 22	21 45	81·6	3 13	20 46	81·6	3 04	19 46	81·5	2 55	18 47	81·5	171	189
10	4 03	23 41	80·8	3 53	22 41	80·8	3 44	21 42	80·7	3 34	20 42	80·7	3 24	19 43	80·6	3 14	18 44	80·5	170	190
11	4 27	23 36	79·9	4 17	22 37	79·9	4 06	21 38	79·8	3 55	20 39	79·7	3 45	19 40	79·6	3 34	18 41	79·6	169	191
12	4 51	23 32	79·0	4 40	22 33	78·9	4 28	21 34	78·9	4 16	20 35	78·8	4 05	19 36	78·7	3 53	18 37	78·6	168	192
13	5 15	23 27	78·1	5 03	22 28	78·0	4 50	21 29	78·0	4 37	20 31	77·8	4 25	19 32	77·8	4 12	18 33	77·7	167	193
14	5 39	23 22	77·2	5 25	22 23	77·1	5 12	21 24	77·0	4 58	20 26	76·9	4 45	19 27	76·8	4 31	18 28	76·7	166	194
15	6 03	23 16	76·2	5 48	22 18	76·1	5 34	21 19	76·0	5 19	20 21	76·0	5 05	19 22	75·9	4 50	18 24	75·8	165	195
16	6 26	23 10	75·3	6 11	22 13	75·2	5 56	21 13	75·1	5 40	20 15	75·0	5 25	19 17	74·9	5 09	18 19	74·8	164	196
17	6 50	23 04	74·4	6 34	22 06	74·3	6 17	21 08	74·2	6 01	20 09	74·1	5 44	19 11	74·0	5 28	18 14	73·9	163	197
18	7 13	22 57	73·5	6 56	21 59	73·3	6 39	21 01	73·2	6 22	20 03	73·1	6 04	19 06	73·0	5 46	18 08	72·9	162	198
19	7 37	22 50	72·5	7 19	21 52	72·4	7 00	20 54	72·3	6 42	19 57	72·2	6 24	18 59	72·1	6 05	18 02	72·0	161	199
20	8 00	22 42	71·6	7 41	21 45	71·5	7 22	20 47	71·4	7 02	19 50	71·2	6 43	18 53	71·1	6 24	17 56	71·0	160	200
21	8 23	22 34	70·7	8 03	21 37	70·5	7 43	20 40	70·4	7 23	19 43	70·3	7 02	18 46	70·2	6 42	17 49	70·1	159	201
22	8 46	22 26	69·7	8 25	21 29	69·6	8 04	20 32	69·5	7 43	19 35	69·3	7 22	18 39	69·2	7 00	17 42	69·1	158	202
23	9 09	22 17	68·8	8 47	21 21	68·7	8 25	20 24	68·5	8 03	19 28	68·4	7 41	18 31	68·3	7 19	17 35	68·1	157	203
24	9 31	22 08	67·9	9 09	21 12	67·7	8 46	20 16	67·6	8 23	19 19	67·4	8 00	18 24	67·3	7 37	17 28	67·2	156	204
25	9 54	21 58	66·9	9 30	21 03	66·8	9 07	20 07	66·6	8 43	19 11	66·5	8 19	18 15	66·3	7 55	17 20	66·2	155	205
26	10 16	21 49	66·0	9 52	20 53	65·8	9 27	19 57	65·7	9 02	19 02	65·5	8 37	18 07	65·4	8 12	17 12	65·2	154	206
27	10 38	21 38	65·0	10 13	20 43	64·9	9 48	19 48	64·7	9 22	18 53	64·6	8 56	17 58	64·4	8 30	17 03	64·3	153	207
28	11 00	21 28	64·1	10 34	20 33	63·9	10 08	19 38	63·8	9 41	18 43	63·6	9 14	17 49	63·5	8 48	16 55	63·3	152	208
29	11 22	21 17	63·1	10 55	20 22	63·0	10 28	19 28	62·8	10 00	18 34	62·6	9 33	17 39	62·5	9 05	16 46	62·3	151	209
30	11 44	21 05	62·2	11 16	20 11	62·0	10 48	19 17	61·8	10 19	18 23	61·7	9 51	17 30	61·5	9 22	16 36	61·4	150	210
31	12 06	20 53	61·2	11 37	20 00	61·1	11 07	19 06	60·9	10 38	18 13	60·7	10 09	17 20	60·5	9 39	16 27	60·4	149	211
32	12 27	20 41	60·3	11 57	19 48	60·1	11 27	18 55	59·9	10 57	18 02	59·7	10 27	17 09	59·6	9 56	16 17	59·4	148	212
33	12 48	20 29	59·3	12 17	19 36	59·1	11 46	18 43	58·9	11 15	17 51	58·8	10 44	16 58	58·6	10 13	16 06	58·4	147	213
34	13 09	20 16	58·4	12 37	19 23	58·2	12 06	18 31	58·0	11 34	17 39	57·8	11 02	16 47	57·6	10 29	15 56	57·5	146	214
35	13 29	20 02	57·4	12 57	19 10	57·2	12 24	18 19	57·0	11 52	17 27	56·8	11 19	16 36	56·7	10 46	15 45	56·5	145	215
36	13 50	19 49	56·4	13 17	18 57	56·2	12 43	18 06	56·0	12 10	17 15	55·9	11 36	16 24	55·7	11 02	15 34	55·5	144	216
37	14 10	19 34	55·5	13 36	18 44	55·3	13 02	17 53	55·1	12 27	17 03	54·9	11 53	16 12	54·7	11 18	15 23	54·5	143	217
38	14 30	19 20	54·5	13 55	18 30	54·3	13 20	17 40	54·1	12 45	16 50	53·9	12 09	16 00	53·7	11 34	15 11	53·5	142	218
39	14 50	19 05	53·5	14 14	18 15	53·3	13 38	17 26	53·1	13 02	16 37	52·9	12 26	15 48	52·7	11 49	14 59	52·6	141	219
40	15 09	18 50	52·5	14 33	18 01	52·3	13 56	17 12	52·1	13 19	16 23	51·9	12 42	15 35	51·7	12 05	14 47	51·6	140	220
41	15 29	18 34	51·5	14 51	17 46	51·3	14 14	16 57	51·1	13 36	16 09	50·9	12 58	15 22	50·8	12 20	14 34	50·6	139	221
42	15 48	18 18	50·6	15 09	17 30	50·3	14 31	16 43	50·1	13 52	15 55	49·9	13 14	15 08	49·8	12 35	14 21	49·6	138	222
43	16 06	18 02	49·6	15 27	17 15	49·4	14 48	16 28	49·2	14 09	15 41	49·0	13 29	14 54	48·8	12 50	14 08	48·6	137	223
44	16 25	17 46	48·6	15 45	16 59	48·4	15 05	16 12	48·2	14 25	15 26	48·0	13 45	14 40	47·8	13 04	13 55	47·6	136	224
45	16 43	17 29	47·6	16 02	16 42	47·4	15 22	15 57	47·2	14 41	15 11	47·0	14 00	14 26	46·8	13 19	13 41	46·6	135	225

Lat. / A

Lat. / A	LHA/F	66° A/H	66° B/P	66° Z_1/Z_2	67° A/H	67° B/P	67° Z_1/Z_2	68° A/H	68° B/P	68° Z_1/Z_2	69° A/H	69° B/P	69° Z_1/Z_2	70° A/H	70° B/P	70° Z_1/Z_2	71° A/H	71° B/P	71° Z_1/Z_2	Lat. / A	LHA
45	135	16 43	17 29	47·6	16 02	16 42	47·4	15 22	15 57	47·2	14 41	15 11	47·0	14 00	14 26	46·8	13 19	13 41	46·6	45	225
46	134	17 01	17 11	46·6	16 19	16 26	46·4	15 38	15 41	46·2	14 56	14 56	46·0	14 15	14 11	45·8	13 33	13 27	45·6	46	226
47	133	17 18	16 53	45·6	16 36	16 09	45·4	15 54	15 24	45·2	15 12	14 40	45·0	14 29	13 56	44·8	13 46	13 13	44·6	47	227
48	132	17 36	16 35	44·6	16 53	15 51	44·4	16 10	15 08	44·2	15 27	14 24	44·0	14 43	13 41	43·8	14 00	12 58	43·6	48	228
49	131	17 53	16 17	43·6	17 09	15 34	43·4	16 25	14 51	43·2	15 42	14 08	43·0	14 58	13 26	42·8	14 13	12 44	42·6	49	229
50	130	18 09	15 58	42·6	17 25	15 16	42·4	16 41	14 33	42·1	15 56	13 52	41·9	15 11	13 10	41·8	14 27	12 29	41·6	50	230
51	129	18 26	15 39	41·6	17 41	14 57	41·3	16 56	14 16	41·1	16 10	13 35	40·9	15 25	12 54	40·8	14 39	12 14	40·6	51	231
52	128	18 42	15 20	40·5	17 56	14 39	40·3	17 10	13 58	40·1	16 24	13 18	39·9	15 38	12 38	39·7	14 52	11 58	39·6	52	232
53	127	18 57	15 00	39·5	18 11	14 20	39·3	17 24	13 40	39·1	16 38	13 00	38·9	15 51	12 21	38·7	15 04	11 42	38·6	53	233
54	126	19 13	14 40	38·5	18 26	14 01	38·3	17 39	13 22	38·1	16 51	12 43	37·9	16 04	12 05	37·7	15 16	11 26	37·5	54	234
55	125	19 28	14 20	37·5	18 40	13 41	37·3	17 52	13 03	37·1	17 04	12 25	36·9	16 16	11 48	36·7	15 28	11 10	36·5	55	235
56	124	19 42	13 59	36·4	18 54	13 21	36·2	18 06	12 44	36·0	17 17	12 07	35·8	16 28	11 30	35·7	15 40	10 54	35·5	56	236
57	123	19 57	13 38	35·4	19 08	13 01	35·2	18 19	12 25	35·0	17 29	11 49	34·8	16 40	11 13	34·6	15 51	10 37	34·5	57	237
58	122	20 11	13 17	34·4	19 21	12 41	34·2	18 31	12 05	34·0	17 42	11 30	33·8	16 52	10 55	33·6	16 02	10 20	33·5	58	238
59	121	20 24	12 55	33·3	19 34	12 20	33·1	18 44	11 45	33·1	17 53	11 11	32·8	17 03	10 37	32·6	16 12	10 03	32·4	59	239
60	120	20 37	12 33	32·3	19 47	11 59	32·1	18 56	11 25	32·1	18 05	10 52	31·7	17 14	10 19	31·6	16 23	9 46	31·4	60	240
61	119	20 50	12 11	31·2	19 59	11 38	31·1	19 08	11 05	31·1	18 16	10 33	30·7	17 24	10 00	30·5	16 33	9 29	30·4	61	241
62	118	21 03	11 48	30·2	20 11	11 16	30·0	19 19	10 44	30·0	18 27	10 13	29·7	17 35	9 42	29·5	16 42	9 11	29·4	62	242
63	117	21 15	11 26	29·2	20 22	10 54	29·0	19 30	10 24	29·0	18 37	9 53	28·6	17 45	9 23	28·5	16 52	8 53	28·3	63	243
64	116	21 27	11 03	28·1	20 34	10 32	27·9	19 41	10 03	27·9	18 47	9 33	27·6	17 54	9 04	27·4	17 01	8 35	27·3	64	244
65	115	21 38	10 39	27·0	20 44	10 10	26·9	19 51	9 41	26·9	18 57	9 13	26·5	18 03	8 45	26·4	17 10	8 17	26·3	65	245
66	114	21 49	10 16	26·0	20 55	9 48	25·8	20 01	9 20	25·8	19 07	8 52	25·5	18 12	8 25	25·4	17 18	7 58	25·2	66	246
67	113	21 59	9 52	24·9	21 05	9 25	24·8	20 10	8 58	24·7	19 16	8 32	24·5	18 21	8 06	24·3	17 26	7 40	24·2	67	247
68	112	22 09	9 28	23·9	21 14	9 02	23·7	20 19	8 36	23·7	19 24	8 11	23·4	18 29	7 46	23·3	17 34	7 21	23·1	68	248
69	111	22 19	9 04	22·8	21 24	8 39	22·6	20 28	8 14	22·6	19 33	7 50	22·4	18 37	7 26	22·2	17 42	7 02	22·1	69	249
70	110	22 28	8 39	21·7	21 32	8 16	21·6	20 37	7 52	21·6	19 41	7 29	21·3	18 45	7 06	21·2	17 49	6 43	21·1	70	250
71	109	22 37	8 15	20·7	21 41	7 52	20·5	20 45	7 30	20·5	19 48	7 07	20·2	18 52	6 45	20·1	17 56	6 24	20·0	71	251
72	108	22 45	7 50	19·6	21 49	7 28	19·4	20 52	7 07	19·4	19 56	6 46	19·2	18 59	6 25	19·1	18 02	6 04	19·0	72	252
73	107	22 53	7 25	18·5	21 56	7 04	18·4	21 00	6 44	18·4	20 03	6 24	18·1	19 05	6 04	18·0	18 08	5 45	17·9	73	253
74	106	23 01	7 00	17·4	22 04	6 40	17·3	21 06	6 21	17·3	20 09	6 02	17·1	19 12	5 44	17·0	18 14	5 25	16·9	74	254
75	105	23 08	6 34	16·3	22 10	6 16	16·2	21 13	5 58	16·2	20 15	5 40	16·0	19 17	5 23	15·9	18 20	5 06	15·8	75	255
76	104	23 15	6 09	15·3	22 17	5 52	15·2	21 19	5 35	15·2	20 21	5 18	15·0	19 23	5 02	14·9	18 25	4 46	14·8	76	256
77	103	23 21	5 43	14·2	22 23	5 27	14·1	21 24	5 12	14·1	20 26	4 56	13·9	19 28	4 41	13·8	18 30	4 26	13·7	77	257
78	102	23 27	5 17	13·1	22 28	5 03	13·0	21 30	4 48	13·0	20 31	4 34	12·8	19 33	4 20	12·7	18 34	4 06	12·7	78	258
79	101	23 32	4 51	12·0	22 33	4 38	11·9	21 35	4 24	11·9	20 36	4 11	11·8	19 37	3 58	11·7	18 38	3 46	11·6	79	259
80	100	23 37	4 25	10·9	22 38	4 13	10·8	21 39	4 01	10·8	20 40	3 49	10·7	19 41	3 37	10·6	18 42	3 25	10·6	80	260
81	99	23 41	3 59	9·8	22 42	3 48	9·8	21 43	3 37	9·8	20 44	3 26	9·6	19 45	3 16	9·6	18 45	3 05	9·5	81	261
82	98	23 45	3 33	8·7	22 46	3 23	8·7	21 46	3 13	8·7	20 47	3 03	8·6	19 48	2 54	8·5	18 48	2 45	8·5	82	262
83	97	23 49	3 06	7·7	22 49	2 58	7·6	21 50	2 49	7·6	20 50	2 41	7·5	19 51	2 32	7·4	18 51	2 24	7·4	83	263
84	96	23 52	2 40	6·6	22 52	2 32	6·5	21 52	2 25	6·5	20 53	2 18	6·4	19 53	2 11	6·4	18 54	2 04	6·3	84	264
85	95	23 54	2 13	5·5	22 54	2 07	5·4	21 55	2 01	5·4	20 55	1 55	5·4	19 55	1 49	5·3	18 55	1 43	5·3	85	265
86	94	23 56	1 47	4·4	22 56	1 42	4·3	21 57	1 37	4·3	20 57	1 32	4·3	19 57	1 27	4·3	18 57	1 23	4·2	86	266
87	93	23 58	1 20	3·3	22 58	1 16	3·3	21 58	1 13	3·3	20 58	1 09	3·2	19 58	1 05	3·2	18 58	1 02	3·2	87	267
88	92	23 59	0 53	2·2	22 59	0 51	2·2	21 59	0 48	2·2	20 59	0 46	2·1	19 59	0 44	2·1	18 59	0 41	2·1	88	268
89	91	24 00	0 27	1·1	23 00	0 25	1·1	22 00	0 24	1·1	21 00	0 23	1·1	20 00	0 22	1·1	19 00	0 21	1·1	89	269
90	90	24 00	0 00	0·0	23 00	0 00	0·0	22 00	0 00	0·0	21 00	0 00	0·0	20 00	0 00	0·0	19 00	0 00	0·0	90	270

N. Lat.: for LHA > 180° ... $Z_n = Z$
for LHA < 180° ... $Z_n = 360° − Z$

S. Lat.: for LHA > 180° ... $Z_n = 180° − Z$
for LHA < 180° ... $Z_n = 180° + Z$

SIGHT REDUCTION TABLE

B: (−) for 90° < LHA < 270°
Dec:(−) for Lat. contrary name

Z₁: same sign as B
Z₂: (−) for F > 90°

Lat./A LHA/F	72° A/H	72° B/P	72° Z_1/Z_2	73° A/H	73° B/P	73° Z_1/Z_2	74° A/H	74° B/P	74° Z_1/Z_2	75° A/H	75° B/P	75° Z_1/Z_2	76° A/H	76° B/P	76° Z_1/Z_2	77° A/H	77° B/P	77° Z_1/Z_2	Lat./A LHA
0	0 00	18 00	90·0	0 00	17 00	90·0	0 00	16 00	90·0	0 00	15 00	90·0	0 00	14 00	90·0	0 00	13 00	90·0	180
1	0 19	18 00	89·0	0 18	17 00	89·0	0 17	16 00	89·0	0 16	15 00	89·0	0 15	14 00	89·0	0 13	13 00	89·0	181
2	0 37	17 59	88·1	0 35	16 59	88·1	0 33	15 59	88·1	0 31	14 59	88·1	0 29	14 00	88·1	0 27	13 00	88·1	182
3	0 56	17 59	87·1	0 53	16 59	87·1	0 50	15 59	87·1	0 47	14 59	87·1	0 44	13 59	87·1	0 40	12 59	87·1	183
4	1 14	17 58	86·2	1 10	16 58	86·2	1 06	15 58	86·2	1 02	14 58	86·1	0 58	13 58	86·1	0 54	12 58	86·1	184
5	1 33	17 56	85·2	1 28	16 56	85·2	1 23	15 57	85·2	1 18	14 57	85·2	1 12	13 57	85·1	1 07	12 57	85·1	185
6	1 51	17 54	84·3	1 45	16 55	84·3	1 39	15 55	84·2	1 33	14 55	84·2	1 27	13 56	84·2	1 21	12 56	84·2	186
7	2 09	17 52	83·3	2 03	16 53	83·3	1 56	15 53	83·3	1 48	14 54	83·2	1 41	13 54	83·2	1 34	12 54	83·2	187
8	2 28	17 50	82·4	2 20	16 51	82·3	2 12	15 51	82·3	2 04	14 52	82·3	1 56	13 52	82·2	1 48	12 53	82·2	188
9	2 46	17 48	81·4	2 37	16 48	81·4	2 28	15 49	81·4	2 19	14 49	81·3	2 10	13 50	81·3	2 01	12 51	81·3	189
10	3 05	17 45	80·5	2 55	16 45	80·4	2 45	15 46	80·4	2 35	14 47	80·3	2 24	13 48	80·3	2 14	12 49	80·3	190
11	3 23	17 41	79·5	3 12	16 42	79·5	3 01	15 43	79·4	2 50	14 44	79·4	2 39	13 45	79·3	2 28	12 46	79·3	191
12	3 41	17 38	78·6	3 29	16 39	78·5	3 17	15 40	78·5	3 05	14 41	78·4	2 53	13 42	78·4	2 41	12 44	78·3	192
13	3 59	17 34	77·6	3 46	16 35	77·5	3 33	15 37	77·5	3 20	14 38	77·4	3 07	13 39	77·4	2 54	12 41	77·3	193
14	4 17	17 30	76·7	4 03	16 31	76·6	3 49	15 33	76·5	3 35	14 34	76·5	3 21	13 36	76·4	3 07	12 38	76·3	194
15	4 35	17 25	75·7	4 20	16 27	75·6	4 05	15 29	75·6	3 50	14 31	75·5	3 35	13 32	75·4	3 20	12 34	75·4	195
16	4 53	17 21	74·7	4 37	16 23	74·7	4 21	15 25	74·6	4 05	14 27	74·5	3 49	13 29	74·5	3 33	12 31	74·4	196
17	5 11	17 16	73·8	4 54	16 18	73·7	4 37	15 20	73·6	4 20	14 22	73·5	4 03	13 25	73·5	3 46	12 27	73·4	197
18	5 29	17 10	72·8	5 11	16 13	72·7	4 53	15 15	72·7	4 35	14 18	72·6	4 17	13 20	72·5	3 59	12 23	72·4	198
19	5 46	17 05	71·9	5 28	16 07	71·8	5 09	15 10	71·7	4 50	14 13	71·6	4 31	13 16	71·5	4 12	12 19	71·4	199
20	6 04	16 59	70·9	5 44	16 02	70·8	5 25	15 05	70·7	5 05	14 08	70·6	4 45	13 11	70·5	4 25	12 14	70·5	200
21	6 21	16 52	69·9	6 01	15 56	69·8	5 40	14 59	69·7	5 19	14 03	69·7	4 58	13 06	69·6	4 37	12 10	69·5	201
22	6 39	16 46	69·0	6 17	15 50	68·9	5 56	14 53	68·8	5 34	13 57	68·7	5 12	13 01	68·6	4 50	12 05	68·5	202
23	6 56	16 39	68·0	6 34	15 43	67·9	6 11	14 47	67·8	5 48	13 51	67·7	5 25	12 56	67·6	5 03	12 00	67·5	203
24	7 13	16 32	67·1	6 50	15 36	67·1	6 26	14 41	66·9	6 03	13 45	66·7	5 39	12 50	66·6	5 15	11 55	66·5	204
25	7 30	16 25	66·1	7 06	15 29	66·0	6 41	14 34	65·9	6 17	13 39	65·8	5 52	12 44	65·6	5 27	11 49	65·6	205
26	7 47	16 17	65·1	7 22	15 22	65·0	6 56	14 27	64·9	6 31	13 32	64·8	6 05	12 38	64·6	5 40	11 43	64·6	206
27	8 04	16 09	64·1	7 38	15 14	64·0	7 11	14 20	63·9	6 45	13 26	63·8	6 18	12 32	63·7	5 52	11 37	63·6	207
28	8 20	16 00	63·2	7 53	15 06	63·0	7 26	14 12	62·9	6 59	13 19	62·8	6 31	12 25	62·7	6 04	11 31	62·6	208
29	8 37	15 52	62·2	8 09	14 58	62·1	7 41	14 05	61·9	7 13	13 11	61·8	6 44	12 18	61·7	6 16	11 25	61·6	209
30	8 53	15 43	61·2	8 24	14 50	61·1	7 55	13 57	61·0	7 26	13 04	60·9	6 57	12 11	60·7	6 27	11 18	60·6	210
31	9 09	15 34	60·3	8 40	14 41	60·1	8 10	13 49	59·9	7 40	12 56	59·9	7 09	12 04	59·8	6 39	11 12	59·7	211
32	9 25	15 24	59·3	8 55	14 32	59·1	8 24	13 40	59·0	7 53	12 48	58·9	7 22	11 56	58·8	6 51	11 05	58·7	212
33	9 41	15 15	58·3	9 10	14 23	58·2	8 38	13 31	58·0	8 06	12 40	58·0	7 34	11 49	57·8	7 02	10 57	57·7	213
34	9 57	15 05	57·3	9 25	14 13	57·2	8 52	13 22	57·0	8 19	12 31	56·9	7 46	11 41	56·8	7 14	10 50	56·7	214
35	10 13	14 54	56·3	9 39	14 04	56·2	9 06	13 13	56·1	8 32	12 23	55·9	7 59	11 33	55·8	7 25	10 43	55·7	215
36	10 28	14 44	55·4	9 54	13 54	55·2	9 19	13 04	55·1	8 45	12 14	54·9	8 11	11 24	54·8	7 36	10 35	54·7	216
37	10 43	14 33	54·4	10 08	13 43	54·2	9 33	12 54	54·1	8 58	12 05	53·9	8 22	11 16	53·8	7 47	10 27	53·7	217
38	10 58	14 22	53·4	10 22	13 33	53·2	9 46	12 44	53·1	9 10	11 55	53·0	8 34	11 07	52·8	7 58	10 19	52·7	218
39	11 13	14 11	52·4	10 36	13 22	52·2	9 59	12 34	52·1	9 22	11 46	52·0	8 45	10 58	51·8	8 08	10 10	51·7	219
40	11 27	13 59	51·4	10 50	13 11	51·3	10 12	12 23	51·1	9 35	11 36	51·0	8 57	10 49	50·8	8 19	10 02	50·7	220
41	11 42	13 47	50·4	11 04	13 00	50·3	10 25	12 13	50·1	9 47	11 26	50·0	9 08	10 39	49·9	8 29	9 53	49·7	221
42	11 56	13 34	49·4	11 17	12 48	49·3	10 38	12 02	49·1	9 58	11 16	49·0	9 19	10 30	48·9	8 39	9 44	48·7	222
43	12 10	13 22	48·4	11 30	12 36	48·3	10 50	11 51	48·1	10 10	11 05	48·0	9 30	10 20	47·9	8 49	9 35	47·7	223
44	12 24	13 09	47·4	11 43	12 24	47·3	11 02	11 39	47·3	10 21	10 55	47·0	9 40	10 10	46·9	8 59	9 26	46·7	224
45	12 37	12 56	46·4	11 56	12 12	46·3	11 14	11 28	46·1	10 33	10 44	46·0	9 51	10 00	45·9	9 09	9 16	45·7	225

Lat. / A

LHA/F	F	A/H	B/P	Z_1/Z_2	A/H	B/P	Z_1/Z_2	A/H	B/P	Z_1/Z_2	A/H	B/P	Z_1/Z_2	A/H	B/P	Z_1/Z_2	A/H	B/P	Z_1/Z_2	LHA	LHA
45	135	12 37	12 56	46.4	11 56	12 12	46.3	11 14	11 28	46.1	10 33	10 44	46.0	9 51	10 00	45.9	9 09	9 16	45.7	225	315
46	134	12 51	12 43	45.4	12 08	11 59	45.3	11 26	11 16	45.1	10 44	10 33	45.0	10 01	9 50	44.9	9 19	9 07	44.7	226	314
47	133	13 04	12 30	44.4	12 21	11 47	44.3	11 38	11 04	44.1	10 55	10 21	44.0	10 11	9 39	43.9	9 28	8 57	43.7	227	313
48	132	13 17	12 16	43.4	12 33	11 34	43.3	11 49	10 52	43.1	11 05	10 10	43.0	10 21	9 28	42.9	9 37	8 47	42.7	228	312
49	131	13 29	12 02	42.4	12 45	11 21	42.3	12 00	10 39	42.1	11 16	9 58	42.0	10 31	9 17	41.9	9 46	8 37	41.7	229	311
50	130	13 42	11 48	41.4	12 57	11 07	41.3	12 11	10 27	41.1	11 26	9 46	41.0	10 41	9 06	40.9	9 55	8 26	40.7	230	310
51	129	13 54	11 33	40.4	13 08	10 53	40.3	12 22	10 14	40.1	11 36	9 34	40.0	10 50	8 55	39.8	10 04	8 16	39.7	231	309
52	128	14 06	11 19	39.4	13 19	10 40	39.2	12 33	10 01	39.1	11 46	9 22	39.0	10 59	8 44	38.8	10 13	8 05	38.7	232	308
53	127	14 17	11 04	38.4	13 30	10 26	38.2	12 43	9 47	38.1	11 56	9 10	38.0	11 08	8 32	37.8	10 21	7 55	37.7	233	307
54	126	14 29	10 49	37.4	13 41	10 11	37.2	12 53	9 34	37.1	12 05	8 57	36.9	11 17	8 20	36.8	10 29	7 44	36.7	234	306
55	125	14 40	10 33	36.4	13 51	9 57	36.2	13 03	9 20	36.1	12 14	8 44	35.9	11 26	8 08	35.8	10 37	7 33	35.7	235	305
56	124	14 51	10 18	35.3	14 02	9 42	35.2	13 13	9 07	35.1	12 23	8 31	34.9	11 34	7 56	34.8	10 45	7 21	34.7	236	304
57	123	15 01	10 02	34.3	14 12	9 27	34.2	13 22	8 53	34.0	12 32	8 18	33.9	11 42	7 44	33.8	10 52	7 10	33.7	237	303
58	122	15 12	9 46	33.3	14 21	9 12	33.2	13 31	8 38	33.0	12 41	8 05	32.9	11 50	7 32	32.8	11 00	6 58	32.7	238	302
59	121	15 22	9 30	32.3	14 31	8 57	32.1	13 40	8 24	32.0	12 49	7 51	31.9	11 58	7 19	31.8	11 07	6 47	31.7	239	301
60	120	15 31	9 14	31.3	14 40	8 41	31.1	13 49	8 10	31.0	12 57	7 38	30.9	12 06	7 06	30.8	11 14	6 35	30.6	240	300
61	119	15 41	8 57	30.2	14 49	8 26	30.1	13 57	7 55	30.0	13 05	7 24	29.8	12 13	6 54	29.7	11 21	6 23	29.6	241	299
62	118	15 50	8 40	29.2	14 58	8 10	29.1	14 05	7 40	28.9	13 13	7 10	28.8	12 20	6 41	28.7	11 27	6 11	28.6	242	298
63	117	15 59	8 23	28.2	15 06	7 54	28.0	14 13	7 25	27.9	13 20	6 56	27.8	12 27	6 27	27.7	11 34	5 59	27.6	243	297
64	116	16 08	8 06	27.2	15 14	7 38	27.0	14 21	7 10	26.9	13 27	6 42	26.8	12 34	6 14	26.7	11 40	5 47	26.6	244	296
65	115	16 16	7 49	26.1	15 22	7 22	26.0	14 28	6 55	25.9	13 34	6 28	25.8	12 40	6 01	25.7	11 46	5 34	25.6	245	295
66	114	16 24	7 32	25.1	15 29	7 05	25.0	14 35	6 39	24.9	13 41	6 13	24.7	12 46	5 47	24.6	11 52	5 22	24.5	246	294
67	113	16 32	7 14	24.1	15 37	6 49	23.9	14 42	6 24	23.8	13 47	5 59	23.7	12 52	5 34	23.6	11 57	5 09	23.5	247	293
68	112	16 39	6 56	23.0	15 44	6 32	22.9	14 48	6 08	22.8	13 53	5 44	22.7	12 58	5 20	22.6	12 02	4 57	22.5	248	292
69	111	16 46	6 38	22.0	15 50	6 15	21.9	14 55	5 52	21.8	13 59	5 29	21.7	13 03	5 06	21.6	12 07	4 44	21.5	249	291
70	110	16 53	6 20	20.9	15 57	5 58	20.8	15 01	5 36	20.7	14 05	5 14	20.6	13 08	4 52	20.6	12 12	4 31	20.5	250	290
71	109	16 59	6 02	19.9	16 03	5 41	19.8	15 06	5 20	19.7	14 10	4 59	19.6	13 13	4 38	19.5	12 17	4 18	19.5	251	289
72	108	17 05	5 44	18.9	16 09	5 24	18.8	15 12	5 04	18.7	14 15	4 44	18.6	13 18	4 24	18.5	12 21	4 05	18.4	252	288
73	107	17 11	5 26	17.8	16 14	5 06	17.7	15 17	4 48	17.6	14 20	4 29	17.6	13 23	4 10	17.5	12 25	3 52	17.4	253	287
74	106	17 17	5 07	16.8	16 19	4 49	16.7	15 22	4 31	16.6	14 24	4 13	16.5	13 27	3 56	16.5	12 29	3 38	16.4	254	286
75	105	17 22	4 48	15.7	16 24	4 31	15.7	15 26	4 15	15.6	14 29	3 58	15.5	13 31	3 42	15.4	12 33	3 25	15.4	255	285
76	104	17 27	4 30	14.7	16 29	4 14	14.6	15 31	3 58	14.5	14 33	3 43	14.5	13 35	3 27	14.4	12 36	3 12	14.3	256	284
77	103	17 31	4 11	13.6	16 33	3 56	13.6	15 35	3 41	13.5	14 37	3 27	13.5	13 38	3 13	13.4	12 40	2 58	13.3	257	283
78	102	17 36	3 52	12.6	16 37	3 38	12.5	15 38	3 25	12.5	14 40	3 11	12.4	13 41	2 58	12.4	12 43	2 45	12.3	258	282
79	101	17 39	3 33	11.6	16 41	3 20	11.5	15 42	3 08	11.4	14 43	2 56	11.4	13 44	2 43	11.3	12 45	2 31	11.3	259	281
80	100	17 43	3 14	10.5	16 44	3 02	10.4	15 45	2 51	10.4	14 46	2 40	10.3	13 47	2 29	10.3	12 48	2 18	10.3	260	280
81	99	17 46	2 55	9.5	16 47	2 44	9.4	15 48	2 34	9.4	14 49	2 24	9.3	13 49	2 14	9.3	12 50	2 04	9.2	261	279
82	98	17 49	2 35	8.4	16 50	2 26	8.4	15 50	2 17	8.3	14 51	2 08	8.3	13 52	1 59	8.2	12 52	1 50	8.2	262	278
83	97	17 52	2 16	7.4	16 52	2 08	7.3	15 53	2 00	7.3	14 53	1 52	7.2	13 54	1 44	7.2	12 54	1 37	7.2	263	277
84	96	17 54	1 57	6.3	16 54	1 50	6.3	15 55	1 43	6.2	14 55	1 36	6.2	13 55	1 30	6.2	12 56	1 23	6.2	264	276
85	95	17 56	1 37	5.3	16 56	1 32	5.2	15 56	1 26	5.2	14 56	1 20	5.2	13 57	1 15	5.2	12 57	1 09	5.1	265	275
86	94	17 57	1 18	4.2	16 57	1 13	4.2	15 58	1 09	4.2	14 58	1 04	4.1	13 58	1 00	4.1	12 58	0 55	4.1	266	274
87	93	17 58	0 58	3.2	16 59	0 55	3.1	15 59	0 52	3.1	14 59	0 48	3.1	13 59	0 45	3.1	12 59	0 42	3.1	267	273
88	92	17 59	0 39	2.1	16 59	0 37	2.1	15 59	0 34	2.1	14 59	0 32	2.1	13 59	0 30	2.1	13 00	0 28	2.1	268	272
89	91	17 59	0 19	1.1	17 00	0 18	1.1	16 00	0 17	1.0	15 00	0 16	1.0	14 00	0 15	1.0	13 00	0 14	1.0	269	271
90	90	18 00	0 00	0.0	17 00	0 00	0.0	16 00	0 00	0.0	15 00	0 00	0.0	14 00	0 00	0.0	13 00	0 00	0.0	270	270

N. Lat: for LHA > 180° ... $Z_n = Z$

for LHA < 180° ... $Z_n = 360° - Z$

for LHA > 180° ... $Z_n = Z$

for LHA < 180° ... $Z_n = 360° - Z$

S. Lat: for LHA > 180° ... $Z_n = 180° - Z$

for LHA < 180° ... $Z_n = 180° + Z$

SIGHT REDUCTION TABLE

B: (−) for 90° < LHA < 270°
Dec:(−) for Lat. contrary name

Z₁: same sign as B
Z₂: (−) for F > 90°

LHA/F	78° A/H	78° B/P	78° Z₁/Z₂	79° A/H	79° B/P	79° Z₁/Z₂	80° A/H	80° B/P	80° Z₁/Z₂	81° A/H	81° B/P	81° Z₁/Z₂	82° A/H	82° B/P	82° Z₁/Z₂	83° A/H	83° B/P	83° Z₁/Z₂	Lat./A	LHA
0 180	0 00	12 00	90·0	0 00	11 00	90·0	0 00	10 00	90·0	0 00	9 00	90·0	0 00	8 00	90·0	0 00	7 00	90·0	180	360
1 179	0 12	12 00	89·0	0 11	11 00	89·0	0 10	10 00	89·0	0 09	9 00	89·0	0 08	8 00	89·0	0 07	7 00	89·0	181	359
2 178	0 25	12 00	88·0	0 23	11 00	88·0	0 21	10 00	88·0	0 19	9 00	88·0	0 17	8 00	88·0	0 15	6 59	88·0	182	358
3 177	0 37	11 59	87·1	0 34	10 59	87·1	0 31	9 59	87·0	0 28	8 59	87·0	0 25	7 59	87·0	0 22	6 59	87·0	183	357
4 176	0 50	11 58	86·1	0 46	10 58	86·1	0 42	9 59	86·1	0 38	8 59	86·0	0 33	7 59	86·0	0 29	6 59	86·0	184	356
5 175	1 02	11 57	85·1	0 57	10 58	85·1	0 52	9 58	85·1	0 47	8 58	85·1	0 42	7 58	85·0	0 37	6 58	85·0	185	355
6 174	1 15	11 56	84·1	1 09	10 56	84·1	1 02	9 57	84·1	0 56	8 57	84·1	0 50	7 57	84·1	0 44	6 58	84·1	186	354
7 173	1 27	11 55	83·1	1 20	10 55	83·1	1 13	9 56	83·1	1 06	8 56	83·1	0 58	7 56	83·1	0 51	6 57	83·1	187	353
8 172	1 39	11 53	82·2	1 31	10 54	82·1	1 23	9 54	82·1	1 15	8 55	82·1	1 07	7 55	82·1	0 58	6 56	82·1	188	352
9 171	1 52	11 51	81·2	1 43	10 52	81·2	1 33	9 53	81·1	1 24	8 53	81·1	1 15	7 54	81·1	1 06	6 55	81·1	189	351
10 170	2 04	11 49	80·2	1 54	10 50	80·2	1 44	9 51	80·1	1 33	8 52	80·1	1 23	7 53	80·1	1 13	6 54	80·1	190	350
11 169	2 16	11 47	79·2	2 05	10 48	79·2	1 54	9 49	79·1	1 43	8 50	79·1	1 31	7 51	79·1	1 20	6 52	79·1	191	349
12 168	2 29	11 45	78·3	2 16	10 46	78·2	2 04	9 47	78·2	1 52	8 48	78·1	1 39	7 50	78·1	1 27	6 51	78·1	192	348
13 167	2 41	11 42	77·3	2 28	10 43	77·2	2 14	9 45	77·2	2 01	8 46	77·2	1 48	7 48	77·1	1 34	6 49	77·1	193	347
14 166	2 53	11 39	76·3	2 39	10 41	76·2	2 24	9 43	76·2	2 10	8 44	76·2	1 56	7 46	76·1	1 41	6 48	76·1	194	346
15 165	3 05	11 36	75·3	2 50	10 38	75·3	2 35	9 40	75·2	2 19	8 42	75·2	2 04	7 44	75·1	1 48	6 46	75·1	195	345
16 164	3 17	11 33	74·3	3 01	10 35	74·3	2 45	9 37	74·2	2 28	8 39	74·2	2 12	7 42	74·1	1 56	6 44	74·1	196	344
17 163	3 29	11 29	73·4	3 12	10 32	73·3	2 55	9 34	73·2	2 37	8 37	73·2	2 20	7 39	73·2	2 03	6 42	73·1	197	343
18 162	3 41	11 26	72·4	3 23	10 28	72·3	3 05	9 31	72·3	2 46	8 34	72·2	2 28	7 37	72·2	2 09	6 40	72·1	198	342
19 161	3 53	11 22	71·4	3 34	10 25	71·3	3 14	9 28	71·3	2 55	8 31	71·2	2 36	7 34	71·2	2 16	6 37	71·1	199	341
20 160	4 05	11 18	70·4	3 45	10 21	70·3	3 24	9 24	70·3	3 04	8 28	70·2	2 44	7 31	70·2	2 23	6 35	70·1	200	340
21 159	4 16	11 13	69·4	3 55	10 17	69·4	3 34	9 21	69·3	3 13	8 25	69·2	2 52	7 28	69·2	2 30	6 32	69·1	201	339
22 158	4 28	11 09	68·4	4 06	10 13	68·4	3 44	9 17	68·3	3 22	8 21	68·2	2 59	7 25	68·2	2 37	6 30	68·1	202	338
23 157	4 40	11 04	67·5	4 17	10 09	67·4	3 53	9 13	67·3	3 30	8 18	67·3	3 07	7 22	67·2	2 44	6 27	67·2	203	337
24 156	4 51	10 59	66·5	4 27	10 04	66·4	4 03	9 09	66·3	3 39	8 14	66·3	3 15	7 19	66·2	2 50	6 24	66·2	204	336
25 155	5 02	10 54	65·5	4 38	9 59	65·4	4 13	9 05	65·3	3 47	8 10	65·3	3 22	7 16	65·2	2 57	6 21	65·2	205	335
26 154	5 14	10 49	64·5	4 48	9 55	64·4	4 22	9 00	64·3	3 56	8 06	64·3	3 30	7 12	64·2	3 04	6 18	64·2	206	334
27 153	5 25	10 43	63·5	4 58	9 50	63·4	4 31	8 56	63·4	4 04	8 02	63·3	3 37	7 08	63·2	3 10	6 15	63·2	207	333
28 152	5 36	10 38	62·5	5 08	9 44	62·4	4 41	8 51	62·4	4 13	7 58	62·3	3 45	7 04	62·2	3 17	6 11	62·2	208	332
29 151	5 47	10 32	61·5	5 18	9 39	61·4	4 50	8 46	61·4	4 21	7 53	61·3	3 52	7 00	61·2	3 23	6 08	61·2	209	331
30 150	5 58	10 26	60·5	5 28	9 33	60·5	4 59	8 41	60·4	4 29	7 49	60·3	3 59	6 56	60·2	3 30	6 04	60·2	210	330
31 149	6 09	10 20	59·6	5 38	9 28	59·5	5 08	8 36	59·4	4 37	7 44	59·3	4 07	6 52	59·3	3 36	6 00	59·2	211	329
32 148	6 20	10 13	58·6	5 48	9 22	58·5	5 17	8 30	58·4	4 45	7 39	58·3	4 14	6 48	58·3	3 42	5 57	58·2	212	328
33 147	6 30	10 06	57·6	5 58	9 16	57·5	5 26	8 25	57·4	4 53	7 34	57·3	4 21	6 43	57·3	3 48	5 53	57·2	213	327
34 146	6 41	10 00	56·6	6 08	9 09	56·5	5 34	8 19	56·4	5 01	7 29	56·3	4 28	6 39	56·3	3 54	5 49	56·2	214	326
35 145	6 51	9 53	55·6	6 17	9 03	55·5	5 43	8 13	55·4	5 09	7 24	55·3	4 35	6 34	55·3	4 00	5 45	55·2	215	325
36 144	7 01	9 45	54·6	6 26	8 56	54·5	5 51	8 07	54·4	5 17	7 18	54·3	4 42	6 29	54·3	4 06	5 40	54·2	216	324
37 143	7 11	9 38	53·6	6 36	8 49	53·5	6 00	8 01	53·4	5 24	7 13	53·3	4 48	6 24	53·3	4 12	5 36	53·2	217	323
38 142	7 21	9 31	52·6	6 45	8 43	52·5	6 08	7 55	52·4	5 32	7 07	52·3	4 55	6 19	52·3	4 18	5 32	52·2	218	322
39 141	7 31	9 23	51·6	6 54	8 35	51·5	6 16	7 48	51·4	5 39	7 01	51·3	5 01	6 14	51·3	4 24	5 27	51·2	219	321
40 140	7 41	9 15	50·6	7 03	8 28	50·5	6 25	7 42	50·4	5 46	6 55	50·3	5 08	6 09	50·3	4 30	5 22	50·2	220	320
41 139	7 50	9 07	49·6	7 11	8 21	49·5	6 32	7 35	49·4	5 53	6 49	49·4	5 14	6 03	49·3	4 35	5 18	49·2	221	319
42 138	8 00	8 59	48·6	7 20	8 13	48·5	6 40	7 28	48·4	6 01	6 43	48·4	5 21	5 58	48·3	4 41	5 13	48·2	222	318
43 137	8 09	8 50	47·6	7 29	8 05	47·5	6 48	7 21	47·4	6 07	6 36	47·4	5 27	5 52	47·3	4 46	5 08	47·2	223	317
44 136	8 18	8 42	46·6	7 37	7 58	46·5	6 56	7 14	46·4	6 14	6 30	46·4	5 33	5 46	46·3	4 51	5 03	46·2	224	316
45 135	8 27	8 33	45·6	7 45	7 50	45·5	7 03	7 06	45·4	6 21	6 23	45·4	5 39	5 41	45·3	4 57	4 58	45·2	225	315

Lat. / A	LHA/F	78° A/H	78° B/P	78° Z₁/Z₂	79° A/H	79° B/P	79° Z₁/Z₂	80° A/H	80° B/P	80° Z₁/Z₂	81° A/H	81° B/P	81° Z₁/Z₂	82° A/H	82° B/P	82° Z₁/Z₂	83° A/H	83° B/P	83° Z₁/Z₂	Lat. / A	LHA
45	135	8 27	8 33	45·6	7 45	7 50	45·5	7 03	7 06	45·4	6 21	6 23	45·4	5 39	5 41	45·3	4 57	4 58	45·2	315	225
46	134	8 36	8 24	44·6	7 53	7 41	44·5	7 11	6 59	44·4	6 28	6 17	44·4	5 45	5 35	44·3	5 02	4 53	44·2	314	226
47	133	8 45	8 15	43·6	8 01	7 33	43·5	7 18	6 51	43·4	6 34	6 10	43·4	5 51	5 28	43·3	5 07	4 47	43·2	313	227
48	132	8 53	8 06	42·6	8 09	7 25	42·5	7 25	6 44	42·4	6 41	6 03	42·4	5 56	5 22	42·3	5 12	4 42	42·2	312	228
49	131	9 02	7 56	41·6	8 17	7 16	41·5	7 32	6 36	41·4	6 47	5 56	41·4	6 02	5 16	41·3	5 17	4 36	41·2	311	229
50	130	9 10	7 47	40·6	8 24	7 07	40·5	7 39	6 28	40·4	6 53	5 49	40·3	6 07	5 10	40·3	5 21	4 31	40·2	310	230
51	129	9 18	7 37	39·6	8 32	6 58	39·5	7 45	6 20	39·4	6 59	5 42	39·3	6 13	5 03	39·3	5 26	4 25	39·2	309	231
52	128	9 26	7 27	38·6	8 39	6 49	38·5	7 52	6 12	38·4	7 05	5 34	38·3	6 18	4 57	38·3	5 31	4 19	38·2	308	232
53	127	9 33	7 17	37·6	8 46	6 40	37·5	7 58	6 03	37·4	7 11	5 27	37·3	6 23	4 50	37·3	5 35	4 14	37·2	307	233
54	126	9 41	7 07	36·6	8 53	6 31	36·5	8 05	5 55	36·4	7 16	5 19	36·3	6 28	4 43	36·3	5 39	4 08	36·2	306	234
55	125	9 48	6 57	35·6	9 00	6 22	35·5	8 11	5 47	35·4	7 22	5 11	35·3	6 33	4 37	35·3	5 44	4 02	35·2	305	235
56	124	9 56	6 47	34·6	9 06	6 12	34·5	8 17	5 38	34·4	7 27	5 04	34·3	6 38	4 30	34·3	5 48	3 56	34·2	304	236
57	123	10 03	6 36	33·6	9 13	6 03	33·5	8 22	5 29	33·4	7 32	4 56	33·3	6 42	4 23	33·3	5 52	3 50	33·2	303	237
58	122	10 09	6 26	32·6	9 19	5 53	32·5	8 28	5 20	32·4	7 37	4 48	32·3	6 47	4 16	32·3	5 56	3 43	32·2	302	238
59	121	10 16	6 15	31·6	9 25	5 43	31·5	8 34	5 11	31·4	7 42	4 40	31·3	6 51	4 08	31·2	6 00	3 37	31·2	301	239
60	120	10 22	6 04	30·6	9 31	5 33	30·5	8 39	5 02	30·4	7 47	4 32	30·3	6 55	4 01	30·2	6 04	3 31	30·2	300	240
61	119	10 29	5 53	29·5	9 36	5 23	29·5	8 44	4 53	29·4	7 52	4 23	29·3	6 59	3 54	29·2	6 07	3 24	29·2	299	241
62	118	10 35	5 42	28·5	9 42	5 13	28·4	8 49	4 44	28·4	7 56	4 15	28·3	7 04	3 46	28·2	6 11	3 18	28·2	298	242
63	117	10 41	5 31	27·5	9 47	5 03	27·4	8 54	4 35	27·4	8 01	4 07	27·3	7 07	3 39	27·2	6 14	3 11	27·2	297	243
64	116	10 46	5 19	26·5	9 52	4 52	26·4	8 59	4 25	26·4	8 05	3 58	26·3	7 11	3 32	26·2	6 17	3 05	26·2	296	244
65	115	10 52	5 08	25·5	9 57	4 42	25·4	9 03	4 16	25·4	8 09	3 50	25·3	7 15	3 24	25·2	6 20	2 58	25·2	295	245
66	114	10 57	4 56	24·5	10 02	4 31	24·4	9 08	4 06	24·4	8 13	3 41	24·3	7 18	3 16	24·2	6 24	2 52	24·2	294	246
67	113	11 02	4 45	23·5	10 07	4 21	23·4	9 12	3 56	23·3	8 17	3 32	23·3	7 22	3 09	23·2	6 26	2 45	23·2	293	247
68	112	11 07	4 33	22·4	10 11	4 10	22·4	9 16	3 47	22·3	8 20	3 24	22·2	7 25	3 01	22·2	6 29	2 38	22·1	292	248
69	111	11 12	4 21	21·4	10 16	3 59	21·4	9 20	3 37	21·4	8 24	3 15	21·2	7 28	2 53	21·2	6 32	2 31	21·1	291	249
70	110	11 16	4 09	20·4	10 20	3 48	20·3	9 23	3 27	20·3	8 27	3 06	20·2	7 31	2 45	20·2	6 35	2 24	20·1	290	250
71	109	11 20	3 58	19·4	10 24	3 37	19·3	9 27	3 17	19·3	8 30	2 57	19·2	7 34	2 37	19·2	6 37	2 17	19·1	289	251
72	108	11 24	3 45	18·4	10 27	3 26	18·3	9 30	3 07	18·3	8 33	2 48	18·2	7 36	2 29	18·2	6 39	2 10	18·1	288	252
73	107	11 28	3 33	17·4	10 31	3 15	17·3	9 34	2 57	17·3	8 36	2 39	17·2	7 39	2 21	17·2	6 42	2 03	17·1	287	253
74	106	11 32	3 21	16·3	10 34	3 04	16·3	9 37	2 47	16·2	8 39	2 30	16·1	7 41	2 13	16·1	6 44	1 56	16·1	286	254
75	105	11 35	3 09	15·3	10 37	2 53	15·3	9 39	2 37	15·2	8 41	2 21	15·2	7 44	2 05	15·1	6 46	1 49	15·1	285	255
76	104	11 38	2 57	14·3	10 40	2 42	14·3	9 42	2 27	14·2	8 44	2 12	14·2	7 46	1 57	14·1	6 47	1 42	14·1	284	256
77	103	11 41	2 44	13·3	10 43	2 30	13·3	9 44	2 16	13·2	8 46	2 02	13·2	7 48	1 49	13·1	6 49	1 35	13·1	283	257
78	102	11 44	2 32	12·3	10 45	2 19	12·2	9 47	2 06	12·2	8 48	1 53	12·1	7 49	1 40	12·1	6 51	1 28	12·1	282	258
79	101	11 47	2 19	11·2	10 48	2 07	11·2	9 49	1 56	11·2	8 50	1 44	11·1	7 51	1 32	11·1	6 52	1 21	11·1	281	259
80	100	11 49	2 07	10·2	10 50	1 56	10·2	9 51	1 45	10·2	8 52	1 35	10·1	7 53	1 24	10·1	6 54	1 13	10·1	280	260
81	99	11 51	1 54	9·2	10 52	1 45	9·2	9 53	1 35	9·1	8 53	1 25	9·1	7 54	1 16	9·1	6 55	1 06	9·1	279	261
82	98	11 53	1 42	8·2	10 53	1 33	8·1	9 54	1 24	8·1	8 55	1 16	8·1	7 55	1 07	8·1	6 56	0 59	8·1	278	262
83	97	11 55	1 29	7·2	10 55	1 21	7·1	9 55	1 14	7·1	8 56	1 06	7·1	7 56	0 59	7·1	6 57	0 51	7·1	277	263
84	96	11 56	1 16	6·1	10 56	1 10	6·1	9 57	1 03	6·1	8 57	0 57	6·1	7 57	0 50	6·0	6 58	0 44	6·0	276	264
85	95	11 57	1 04	5·1	10 57	0 58	5·1	9 58	0 53	5·1	8 58	0 47	5·1	7 58	0 42	5·0	6 58	0 37	5·0	275	265
86	94	11 58	0 51	4·1	10 58	0 47	4·1	9 59	0 42	4·0	8 59	0 38	4·0	7 59	0 34	4·0	6 59	0 29	4·0	274	266
87	93	11 59	0 38	3·1	10 59	0 35	3·1	9 59	0 32	3·0	8 59	0 28	3·0	7 59	0 25	3·0	6 59	0 22	3·0	273	267
88	92	12 00	0 26	2·0	11 00	0 23	2·0	10 00	0 21	2·0	9 00	0 19	2·0	8 00	0 17	2·0	7 00	0 15	2·0	272	268
89	91	12 00	0 13	1·0	11 00	0 12	1·0	10 00	0 11	1·0	9 00	0 10	1·0	8 00	0 08	1·0	7 00	0 07	1·0	271	269
90	90	12 00	0 00	0·0	11 00	0 00	0·0	10 00	0 00	0·0	9 00	0 00	0·0	8 00	0 00	0·0	7 00	0 00	0·0	270	270

N. Lat: for LHA > 180° ... Zₙ = Z
      for LHA < 180° ... Zₙ = 360° − Z

S. Lat: for LHA > 180° ... Zₙ = 180° − Z
      for LHA < 180° ... Zₙ = 180° + Z

SIGHT REDUCTION TABLE

B: (−) for 90° < LHA < 270°
Dec:(−) for Lat. contrary name

Z₁: same sign as B
Z₂: (−) for F > 90°

LHA/F	84° A/H	84° B/P	84° Z₁/Z₂	85° A/H	85° B/P	85° Z₁/Z₂	86° A/H	86° B/P	86° Z₁/Z₂	87° A/H	87° B/P	87° Z₁/Z₂	88° A/H	88° B/P	88° Z₁/Z₂	89° A/H	89° B/P	89° Z₁/Z₂	LHA
0 180	0 00	6 00	90.0	0 00	5 00	90.0	0 00	4 00	90.0	0 00	3 00	90.0	0 00	2 00	90.0	0 00	1 00	90.0	180 360
1 179	0 06	6 00	89.0	0 05	5 00	89.0	0 04	4 00	89.0	0 03	3 00	89.0	0 02	2 00	89.0	0 01	1 00	89.0	181 359
2 178	0 13	6 00	88.0	0 10	5 00	88.0	0 08	4 00	88.0	0 06	3 00	88.0	0 04	2 00	88.0	0 02	1 00	88.0	182 358
3 177	0 19	6 00	87.0	0 16	5 00	87.0	0 13	4 00	87.0	0 09	3 00	87.0	0 06	2 00	87.0	0 03	1 00	87.0	183 357
4 176	0 25	5 59	86.0	0 21	4 59	86.0	0 17	3 59	86.0	0 13	3 00	86.0	0 08	2 00	86.0	0 04	1 00	86.0	184 356
5 175	0 31	5 59	85.0	0 26	4 59	85.0	0 21	3 59	85.0	0 16	2 59	85.0	0 10	2 00	85.0	0 05	1 00	85.0	185 355
6 174	0 38	5 58	84.0	0 31	4 58	84.0	0 25	3 59	84.0	0 19	2 59	84.0	0 13	1 59	84.0	0 06	1 00	84.0	186 354
7 173	0 44	5 57	83.0	0 37	4 58	83.0	0 29	3 58	83.0	0 22	2 59	83.0	0 15	1 59	83.0	0 07	1 00	83.0	187 353
8 172	0 50	5 57	82.0	0 42	4 57	82.0	0 33	3 58	82.0	0 25	2 58	82.0	0 17	1 59	82.0	0 08	0 59	82.0	188 352
9 171	0 56	5 56	81.0	0 47	4 56	81.0	0 38	3 57	81.0	0 28	2 58	81.0	0 19	1 59	81.0	0 09	0 59	81.0	189 351
10 170	1 02	5 55	80.1	0 52	4 55	80.0	0 42	3 56	80.0	0 31	2 57	80.0	0 21	1 58	80.0	0 10	0 59	80.0	190 350
11 169	1 09	5 53	79.1	0 57	4 55	79.0	0 46	3 56	79.0	0 34	2 57	79.0	0 23	1 58	79.0	0 11	0 59	79.0	191 349
12 168	1 15	5 52	78.1	1 02	4 53	78.0	0 50	3 55	78.0	0 37	2 56	78.0	0 25	1 57	78.0	0 12	0 59	78.0	192 348
13 167	1 21	5 51	77.1	1 07	4 52	77.0	0 54	3 54	77.0	0 40	2 55	77.0	0 27	1 57	77.0	0 13	0 58	77.0	193 347
14 166	1 27	5 49	76.1	1 12	4 51	76.1	0 58	3 53	76.0	0 44	2 55	76.0	0 29	1 56	76.0	0 15	0 58	76.0	194 346
15 165	1 33	5 48	75.1	1 18	4 50	75.1	1 02	3 52	75.0	0 47	2 54	75.0	0 31	1 56	75.0	0 16	0 58	75.0	195 345
16 164	1 39	5 46	74.1	1 23	4 48	74.1	1 06	3 51	74.0	0 50	2 53	74.0	0 33	1 55	74.0	0 17	0 58	74.0	196 344
17 163	1 45	5 44	73.1	1 28	4 47	73.1	1 10	3 50	73.0	0 53	2 52	73.0	0 35	1 55	73.0	0 18	0 57	73.0	197 343
18 162	1 51	5 42	72.1	1 33	4 45	72.1	1 14	3 48	72.0	0 56	2 51	72.0	0 37	1 54	72.0	0 19	0 57	72.0	198 342
19 161	1 57	5 41	71.1	1 38	4 44	71.1	1 18	3 47	71.0	0 59	2 50	71.0	0 39	1 53	71.0	0 20	0 57	71.0	199 341
20 160	2 03	5 38	70.1	1 42	4 42	70.1	1 22	3 46	70.1	1 02	2 49	70.0	0 41	1 53	70.0	0 21	0 56	70.0	200 340
21 159	2 09	5 36	69.1	1 47	4 40	69.1	1 26	3 44	69.1	1 04	2 48	69.0	0 43	1 52	69.0	0 22	0 56	69.0	201 339
22 158	2 15	5 34	68.1	1 52	4 38	68.1	1 30	3 43	68.1	1 07	2 47	68.0	0 45	1 51	68.0	0 22	0 56	68.0	202 338
23 157	2 20	5 32	67.1	1 57	4 36	67.1	1 34	3 41	67.1	1 10	2 46	67.0	0 47	1 50	67.0	0 23	0 55	67.0	203 337
24 156	2 26	5 29	66.1	2 02	4 34	66.1	1 38	3 39	66.1	1 13	2 44	66.0	0 49	1 50	66.0	0 24	0 55	66.0	204 336
25 155	2 32	5 26	65.1	2 07	4 32	65.1	1 41	3 38	65.1	1 16	2 43	65.0	0 51	1 49	65.0	0 25	0 54	65.0	205 335
26 154	2 38	5 24	64.1	2 11	4 30	64.1	1 45	3 36	64.1	1 19	2 42	64.0	0 53	1 48	64.0	0 26	0 54	64.0	206 334
27 153	2 43	5 21	63.1	2 16	4 27	63.1	1 49	3 34	63.1	1 22	2 40	63.0	0 54	1 47	63.0	0 27	0 53	63.0	207 333
28 152	2 49	5 18	62.1	2 21	4 25	62.1	1 53	3 32	62.1	1 24	2 39	62.0	0 56	1 46	62.0	0 28	0 53	62.0	208 332
29 151	2 54	5 15	61.1	2 25	4 23	61.1	1 56	3 30	61.1	1 27	2 37	61.0	0 58	1 45	61.0	0 29	0 52	61.0	209 331
30 150	3 00	5 12	60.1	2 30	4 20	60.1	2 00	3 28	60.1	1 30	2 36	60.0	1 00	1 44	60.0	0 30	0 52	60.0	210 330
31 149	3 05	5 09	59.1	2 34	4 17	59.1	2 04	3 26	59.1	1 33	2 34	59.0	1 02	1 43	59.0	0 31	0 51	59.0	211 329
32 148	3 11	5 06	58.1	2 39	4 15	58.1	2 07	3 24	58.1	1 35	2 33	58.0	1 04	1 42	58.0	0 32	0 51	58.0	212 328
33 147	3 16	5 02	57.1	2 43	4 12	57.1	2 11	3 21	57.1	1 38	2 31	57.0	1 05	1 41	57.0	0 33	0 50	57.0	213 327
34 146	3 21	4 59	56.1	2 48	4 09	56.1	2 14	3 19	56.1	1 41	2 29	56.0	1 07	1 39	56.0	0 34	0 50	56.0	214 326
35 145	3 26	4 55	55.1	2 52	4 06	55.1	2 18	3 17	55.1	1 43	2 27	55.0	1 09	1 38	55.0	0 34	0 49	55.0	215 325
36 144	3 31	4 52	54.1	2 56	4 03	54.1	2 21	3 14	54.1	1 46	2 26	54.0	1 11	1 37	54.0	0 35	0 49	54.0	216 324
37 143	3 36	4 48	53.2	3 00	4 00	53.1	2 24	3 12	53.1	1 48	2 24	53.0	1 12	1 36	53.0	0 36	0 48	53.0	217 323
38 142	3 41	4 44	52.2	3 05	3 57	52.1	2 28	3 09	52.1	1 51	2 22	52.0	1 14	1 35	52.0	0 37	0 47	52.0	218 322
39 141	3 46	4 40	51.2	3 09	3 53	51.1	2 31	3 07	51.1	1 53	2 20	51.0	1 16	1 33	51.0	0 38	0 47	51.0	219 321
40 140	3 51	4 36	50.2	3 13	3 50	50.1	2 34	3 04	50.1	1 56	2 18	50.0	1 17	1 32	50.0	0 39	0 46	50.0	220 320
41 139	3 56	4 32	49.2	3 17	3 47	49.1	2 37	3 01	49.1	1 58	2 16	49.0	1 19	1 31	49.0	0 39	0 45	49.0	221 319
42 138	4 01	4 28	48.2	3 21	3 43	48.1	2 41	2 58	48.1	2 00	2 14	48.0	1 20	1 29	48.0	0 40	0 45	48.0	222 318
43 137	4 05	4 24	47.2	3 24	3 40	47.1	2 44	2 56	47.1	2 03	2 12	47.0	1 22	1 28	47.0	0 41	0 44	47.0	223 317
44 136	4 10	4 19	46.2	3 28	3 36	46.1	2 47	2 53	46.1	2 05	2 10	46.0	1 23	1 26	46.0	0 42	0 43	46.0	224 316
45 135	4 14	4 15	45.2	3 32	3 32	45.1	2 50	2 50	45.1	2 07	2 07	45.0	1 25	1 25	45.0	0 42	0 42	45.0	225 315

Lat/A	LHA/F	A/H	B/P	Z1/Z2	A/H	B/P	Z1/Z2	A/H	B/P	Z1/Z2	A/H	B/P	Z1/Z2	A/H	B/P	Z1/Z2	A/H	B/P	Z1/Z2	LHA
45	135	4 14	4 15	45·2	3 32	3 32	45·1	2 50	2 50	45·1	2 07	2 07	45·0	1 25	1 25	45·0	0 42	0 42	45·0	225
46	134	4 19	4 11	44·2	3 36	3 29	44·1	2 53	2 47	44·1	2 09	2 05	44·0	1 26	1 23	44·0	0 43	0 41	44·0	226
47	133	4 23	4 06	43·2	3 39	3 25	43·1	2 55	2 44	43·1	2 12	2 03	43·0	1 28	1 22	43·0	0 44	0 40	43·0	227
48	132	4 27	4 01	42·2	3 43	3 21	42·1	2 58	2 41	42·1	2 14	2 01	42·0	1 29	1 20	42·0	0 45	0 40	42·0	228
49	131	4 31	3 57	41·2	3 46	3 17	41·1	3 01	2 38	41·1	2 16	1 58	41·0	1 31	1 19	41·0	0 45	0 39	41·0	229
50	130	4 36	3 52	40·2	3 50	3 13	40·1	3 04	2 34	40·1	2 18	1 56	40·0	1 32	1 17	40·0	0 46	0 39	40·0	230
51	129	4 40	3 47	39·2	3 53	3 09	39·1	3 06	2 31	39·1	2 20	1 53	39·0	1 33	1 16	39·0	0 47	0 38	39·0	231
52	128	4 43	3 42	38·2	3 56	3 05	38·1	3 09	2 28	38·1	2 22	1 51	38·0	1 35	1 14	38·0	0 47	0 37	38·0	232
53	127	4 47	3 37	37·2	3 59	3 01	37·1	3 12	2 25	37·1	2 24	1 48	37·0	1 36	1 12	37·0	0 48	0 36	37·0	233
54	126	4 51	3 32	36·1	4 03	2 57	36·1	3 14	2 21	36·1	2 26	1 46	36·0	1 37	1 11	36·0	0 49	0 35	36·0	234
55	125	4 55	3 27	35·1	4 06	2 52	35·1	3 17	2 18	35·1	2 27	1 43	35·0	1 38	1 09	35·0	0 49	0 34	35·0	235
56	124	4 58	3 22	34·1	4 09	2 48	34·1	3 19	2 14	34·1	2 29	1 41	34·0	1 39	1 07	34·0	0 50	0 34	34·0	236
57	123	5 02	3 17	33·1	4 12	2 44	33·1	3 21	2 11	33·1	2 31	1 38	33·0	1 41	1 05	33·0	0 50	0 33	33·0	237
58	122	5 05	3 11	32·1	4 14	2 39	32·1	3 23	2 07	32·1	2 33	1 35	32·0	1 42	1 04	32·0	0 51	0 32	32·0	238
59	121	5 08	3 06	31·1	4 17	2 35	31·1	3 26	2 04	31·1	2 34	1 33	31·0	1 43	1 02	31·0	0 51	0 31	31·0	239
60	120	5 12	3 00	30·1	4 20	2 30	30·1	3 28	2 00	30·1	2 36	1 30	30·0	1 44	1 00	30·0	0 52	0 30	30·0	240
61	119	5 15	2 55	29·1	4 22	2 26	29·1	3 30	1 56	29·1	2 37	1 27	29·0	1 45	0 58	29·0	0 52	0 29	29·0	241
62	118	5 18	2 49	28·1	4 25	2 21	28·1	3 32	1 53	28·1	2 39	1 25	28·0	1 46	0 56	28·0	0 53	0 28	28·0	242
63	117	5 21	2 44	27·1	4 27	2 16	27·1	3 34	1 49	27·1	2 40	1 22	27·0	1 47	0 54	27·0	0 53	0 27	27·0	243
64	116	5 23	2 38	26·1	4 30	2 12	26·1	3 36	1 45	26·1	2 42	1 19	26·0	1 48	0 53	26·0	0 54	0 26	26·0	244
65	115	5 26	2 33	25·1	4 32	2 07	25·1	3 37	1 42	25·1	2 43	1 16	25·0	1 49	0 51	25·0	0 54	0 25	25·0	245
66	114	5 29	2 27	24·1	4 34	2 02	24·1	3 39	1 38	24·1	2 44	1 13	24·0	1 50	0 49	24·0	0 55	0 24	24·0	246
67	113	5 31	2 21	23·1	4 36	1 57	23·1	3 41	1 34	23·1	2 46	1 10	23·0	1 50	0 47	23·0	0 55	0 23	23·0	247
68	112	5 34	2 15	22·1	4 38	1 53	22·1	3 42	1 30	22·0	2 47	1 07	22·0	1 51	0 45	22·0	0 56	0 22	22·0	248
69	111	5 36	2 09	21·1	4 40	1 48	21·1	3 44	1 26	21·0	2 48	1 05	21·0	1 52	0 43	21·0	0 56	0 22	21·0	249
70	110	5 38	2 04	20·1	4 42	1 43	20·1	3 46	1 22	20·0	2 49	1 02	20·0	1 53	0 41	20·0	0 56	0 21	20·0	250
71	109	5 40	1 58	19·1	4 44	1 38	19·1	3 47	1 18	19·0	2 50	0 59	19·0	1 53	0 39	19·0	0 57	0 20	19·0	251
72	108	5 42	1 52	18·1	4 45	1 33	18·1	3 48	1 14	18·0	2 51	0 56	18·0	1 54	0 37	18·0	0 57	0 19	18·0	252
73	107	5 44	1 46	17·1	4 47	1 28	17·1	3 49	1 10	17·0	2 52	0 53	17·0	1 55	0 35	17·0	0 57	0 18	17·0	253
74	106	5 46	1 40	16·1	4 48	1 23	16·1	3 51	1 06	16·0	2 53	0 50	16·0	1 55	0 33	16·0	0 58	0 17	16·0	254
75	105	5 48	1 33	15·1	4 50	1 18	15·1	3 52	1 02	15·0	2 54	0 47	15·0	1 56	0 31	15·0	0 58	0 16	15·0	255
76	104	5 49	1 27	14·1	4 51	1 13	14·1	3 53	0 58	14·0	2 55	0 44	14·0	1 56	0 29	14·0	0 58	0 15	14·0	256
77	103	5 51	1 21	13·1	4 52	1 08	13·0	3 54	0 54	13·0	2 56	0 41	13·0	1 57	0 27	13·0	0 58	0 13	13·0	257
78	102	5 52	1 15	12·1	4 53	1 03	12·0	3 55	0 50	12·0	2 56	0 37	12·0	1 57	0 25	12·0	0 59	0 12	12·0	258
79	101	5 53	1 09	11·1	4 54	0 57	11·0	3 56	0 46	11·0	2 57	0 34	11·0	1 58	0 23	11·0	0 59	0 11	11·0	259
80	100	5 55	1 03	10·1	4 55	0 52	10·0	3 56	0 42	10·0	2 57	0 31	10·0	1 58	0 21	10·0	0 59	0 10	10·0	260
81	99	5 56	0 57	9·0	4 56	0 47	9·0	3 57	0 38	9·0	2 58	0 28	9·0	1 59	0 19	9·0	0 59	0 09	9·0	261
82	98	5 56	0 50	8·0	4 57	0 42	8·0	3 58	0 33	8·0	2 58	0 25	8·0	1 59	0 17	8·0	0 59	0 08	8·0	262
83	97	5 57	0 44	7·0	4 58	0 37	7·0	3 58	0 29	7·0	2 59	0 22	7·0	1 59	0 15	7·0	1 00	0 07	7·0	263
84	96	5 58	0 38	6·0	4 58	0 31	6·0	3 59	0 25	6·0	2 59	0 19	6·0	2 00	0 13	6·0	1 00	0 06	6·0	264
85	95	5 58	0 31	5·0	4 59	0 26	5·0	3 59	0 21	5·0	2 59	0 16	5·0	2 00	0 10	5·0	1 00	0 05	5·0	265
86	94	5 59	0 25	4·0	4 59	0 21	4·0	3 59	0 17	4·0	3 00	0 13	4·0	2 00	0 08	4·0	1 00	0 04	4·0	266
87	93	6 00	0 19	3·0	5 00	0 16	3·0	4 00	0 13	3·0	3 00	0 09	3·0	2 00	0 06	3·0	1 00	0 03	3·0	267
88	92	6 00	0 13	2·0	5 00	0 10	2·0	4 00	0 08	2·0	3 00	0 06	2·0	2 00	0 04	2·0	1 00	0 02	2·0	268
89	91	6 00	0 06	1·0	5 00	0 05	1·0	4 00	0 04	1·0	3 00	0 03	1·0	2 00	0 02	1·0	1 00	0 01	1·0	269
90	90	6 00	0 00	0·0	5 00	0 00	0·0	4 00	0 00	0·0	3 00	0 00	0·0	2 00	0 00	0·0	1 00	0 00	0·0	270

N. Lat: for LHA > 180° ... $Z_n = Z$
for LHA < 180° ... $Z_n = 360° - Z$

S. Lat: for LHA > 180° ... $Z_n = 180° - Z$
for LHA < 180° ... $Z_n = 180° + Z$

AUXILIARY TABLE

Sign of $corr_1$ for F′. *Reverse* sign if $F > 90°$. ↓

Sign for $corr_2$ for A′. ↓

F′ +/−	1 59	2 58	3 57	4 56	5 55	6 54	7 53	8 52	9 51	10 50	11 49	12 48	13 47	14 46	15 45	16 44	17 43	18 42	19 41	20 40	21 39	22 38	23 37	24 36	25 35	26 34	27 33	28 32	29 31	□ 30	−/+ A′
P°	′	′	′	′	′	′	′	′	′	′	′	′	′	′	′	′	′	′	′	′	′	′	′	′	′	′	′	′	′	′	Z°_2
1	0	0	0	0	0	0	0	0	0	0	0	0	0	0	0	0	0	0	0	0	0	0	0	0	0	0	0	0	1	1	89
2	0	0	0	0	0	0	0	0	0	0	0	0	0	0	1	1	1	1	1	1	1	1	1	1	1	1	1	1	1	1	88
3	0	0	0	0	0	0	0	0	0	1	1	1	1	1	1	1	1	1	1	1	1	1	1	1	1	1	1	1	2	2	87
4	0	0	0	0	0	0	0	1	1	1	1	1	1	1	1	1	1	1	1	1	1	2	2	2	2	2	2	2	2	2	86
5	0	0	0	0	0	1	1	1	1	1	1	1	1	1	1	1	1	2	2	2	2	2	2	2	2	2	2	2	3	3	85
6	0	0	0	0	1	1	1	1	1	1	1	1	1	1	2	2	2	2	2	2	2	2	2	3	3	3	3	3	3	3	84
7	0	0	0	0	1	1	1	1	1	1	1	1	2	2	2	2	2	2	2	2	3	3	3	3	3	3	3	3	4	4	83
8	0	0	0	1	1	1	1	1	1	1	2	2	2	2	2	2	2	3	3	3	3	3	3	3	3	4	4	4	4	4	82
9	0	0	0	1	1	1	1	1	1	2	2	2	2	2	2	3	3	3	3	3	3	3	4	4	4	4	4	4	5	5	81
10	0	0	1	1	1	1	1	1	2	2	2	2	2	2	3	3	3	3	3	3	4	4	4	4	4	5	5	5	5	5	80
11	0	0	1	1	1	1	1	2	2	2	2	2	2	3	3	3	3	3	4	4	4	4	4	5	5	5	5	5	6	6	79
12	0	0	1	1	1	1	1	2	2	2	2	2	3	3	3	3	4	4	4	4	4	5	5	5	5	5	6	6	6	6	78
13	0	0	1	1	1	1	2	2	2	2	2	3	3	3	3	4	4	4	4	4	5	5	5	5	6	6	6	6	7	7	77
14	0	0	1	1	1	1	2	2	2	2	3	3	3	3	4	4	4	4	5	5	5	5	6	6	6	6	7	7	7	7	76
15	0	1	1	1	1	2	2	2	2	3	3	3	3	4	4	4	4	5	5	5	5	6	6	6	6	7	7	7	8	8	75
16	0	1	1	1	1	2	2	2	2	3	3	3	4	4	4	4	5	5	5	6	6	6	6	7	7	7	7	8	8	8	74
17	0	1	1	1	1	2	2	2	3	3	3	4	4	4	4	5	5	5	6	6	6	6	7	7	7	8	8	8	8	9	73
18	0	1	1	1	2	2	2	2	3	3	3	4	4	4	5	5	5	6	6	6	6	7	7	7	8	8	8	9	9	9	72
19	0	1	1	1	2	2	2	3	3	3	4	4	4	5	5	5	6	6	6	7	7	7	7	8	8	8	9	9	9	10	71
20	0	1	1	1	2	2	2	3	3	3	4	4	4	5	5	5	6	6	6	7	7	8	8	8	9	9	9	10	10	10	70
21	0	1	1	1	2	2	3	3	3	4	4	4	5	5	5	6	6	6	7	7	8	8	8	9	9	9	10	10	10	11	69
22	0	1	1	1	2	2	3	3	3	4	4	4	5	5	6	6	6	7	7	7	8	8	9	9	9	10	10	10	11	11	68
23	0	1	1	2	2	2	3	3	4	4	4	5	5	5	6	6	7	7	7	8	8	9	9	9	10	10	11	11	11	12	67
24	0	1	1	2	2	2	3	3	4	4	4	5	5	6	6	7	7	7	8	8	9	9	9	10	10	11	11	11	12	12	66
25	0	1	1	2	2	3	3	3	4	4	5	5	5	6	6	7	7	8	8	8	9	9	10	10	11	11	11	12	12	13	65
26	0	1	1	2	2	3	3	4	4	4	5	5	6	6	7	7	7	8	8	9	9	10	10	11	11	11	12	12	13	13	64
27	0	1	1	2	2	3	3	4	4	5	5	5	6	6	7	7	8	8	9	9	10	10	10	11	11	12	12	13	13	14	63
28	0	1	1	2	2	3	3	4	4	5	5	6	6	7	7	8	8	8	9	9	10	10	11	11	12	12	13	13	14	14	62
29	0	1	1	2	2	3	3	4	4	5	5	6	6	7	7	8	8	9	9	10	10	11	11	12	12	13	13	14	14	15	61
30	0	1	1	2	2	3	3	4	4	5	5	6	6	7	7	8	8	9	9	10	10	11	11	12	12	13	13	14	14	15	60
31	1	1	2	2	3	3	4	4	5	5	6	6	7	7	8	8	9	9	10	10	11	11	12	12	13	13	14	14	15	15	59
32	1	1	2	2	3	3	4	4	5	5	6	6	7	7	8	8	9	10	10	11	11	12	12	13	13	14	14	15	15	16	58
33	1	1	2	2	3	3	4	4	5	5	6	7	7	8	8	9	9	10	10	11	11	12	13	13	14	14	15	15	16	16	57
34	1	1	2	2	3	3	4	4	5	6	6	7	7	8	8	9	10	10	11	11	12	12	13	13	14	15	15	16	16	17	56
35	1	1	2	2	3	3	4	5	5	6	6	7	7	8	9	9	10	10	11	11	12	13	13	14	14	15	15	16	17	17	55
36	1	1	2	2	3	4	4	5	5	6	6	7	8	8	9	9	10	11	11	12	12	13	14	14	15	15	16	16	17	18	54
37	1	1	2	2	3	4	4	5	5	6	7	7	8	8	9	10	10	11	11	12	13	13	14	14	15	16	16	17	17	18	53
38	1	1	2	2	3	4	4	5	6	6	7	7	8	9	9	10	10	11	12	12	13	14	14	15	15	16	17	17	18	18	52
39	1	1	2	3	3	4	4	5	6	6	7	8	8	9	9	10	11	11	12	13	13	14	14	15	16	16	17	18	18	19	51
40	1	1	2	3	3	4	4	5	6	6	7	8	8	9	10	10	11	12	12	13	13	14	15	15	16	17	17	18	19	19	50

Top-left argument: **−A' / +** , **Z₂°**
Bottom-left argument: **F' +/−** , **P°**

Right-side note: For Z₂ < 10°, use 10°
Bottom note: For P > 80°, use 80°

P°	30/30	29/31	28/32	27/33	26/34	25/35	24/36	23/37	22/38	21/39	20/40	19/41	18/42	17/43	16/44	15/45	14/46	13/47	12/48	11/49	10/50	9/51	8/52	7/53	6/54	5/55	4/56	3/57	2/58	1/59	Z₂°
41	~	~	18	~	~	16	~	~	14	~	~	~	~	~	10	~	~	~	~	~	~	~	~	~	~	~	~	~	~	~	49
42	20	19	19	18	17	17	16	15	15	14	13	12	12	11	11	10	9	9	8	7	7	6	5	5	4	3	3	2	1	1	48
43	20	19	19	18	17	17	16	15	15	14	13	13	12	11	11	10	9	9	8	7	7	6	5	5	4	3	3	2	1	1	47
44	21	20	19	18	18	17	16	16	15	15	14	13	12	12	11	10	10	9	8	8	7	6	5	5	4	3	3	2	1	1	46
45	21	20	20	19	18	18	17	16	16	15	14	13	13	12	11	11	10	9	8	8	7	6	6	5	4	3	3	2	1	1	45
46	22	21	20	19	18	18	17	17	16	15	14	14	13	12	12	11	10	9	9	8	7	6	6	5	4	4	3	2	1	1	44
47	22	21	20	19	19	18	18	17	16	15	15	14	13	12	12	11	10	10	9	8	7	7	6	5	4	4	3	2	1	1	43
48	23	22	21	20	19	19	18	17	16	16	15	14	13	13	12	11	11	10	9	8	8	7	6	6	4	4	3	2	1	1	42
49	23	22	21	20	19	19	18	18	17	16	15	14	13	13	12	11	11	10	9	8	8	7	6	6	5	4	3	2	2	1	41
50	23	22	21	21	20	19	18	18	17	16	15	15	14	13	12	11	11	10	9	8	8	7	6	6	5	4	3	2	2	1	40
51	24	23	22	21	20	19	19	18	17	16	16	15	14	13	12	12	11	11	9	9	8	7	6	6	5	4	3	2	2	1	39
52	24	23	22	21	20	20	19	18	17	17	16	15	14	13	13	12	11	11	10	9	8	7	6	6	5	4	3	2	2	1	38
53	24	23	22	22	21	20	19	18	18	17	16	15	14	14	13	12	12	11	10	9	8	7	6	6	5	4	3	3	2	1	37
54	25	24	23	22	21	20	19	19	18	17	16	15	15	14	13	12	12	11	10	9	8	7	6	6	5	4	3	3	2	1	36
55	25	24	23	22	21	20	20	19	18	17	16	16	15	14	13	12	12	11	10	9	8	7	7	6	5	4	3	3	2	1	35
56	25	24	23	23	22	21	20	19	18	17	17	16	15	14	13	12	12	11	10	9	8	7	7	6	5	4	3	3	2	1	34
57	25	25	24	23	22	21	20	19	19	18	17	16	15	15	13	13	12	12	11	9	8	8	7	6	5	4	4	3	2	1	33
58	26	25	24	23	22	21	20	20	19	18	17	16	15	15	14	13	12	12	11	9	8	8	7	6	5	4	4	3	2	1	32
59	26	25	24	23	23	22	21	20	19	18	17	16	16	15	14	13	13	12	11	9	9	8	7	6	5	4	4	3	2	1	31
60	26	25	24	23	23	22	21	20	19	18	17	16	16	15	14	13	13	12	11	10	9	8	7	6	5	5	4	3	2	1	30
61	26	26	24	24	23	22	21	20	19	18	17	17	16	15	14	13	13	12	11	10	9	8	7	6	5	5	4	3	2	1	29
62	27	26	25	24	23	22	21	20	19	19	18	17	16	16	14	13	13	12	11	10	9	8	7	6	5	5	4	3	2	1	28
63	27	26	25	24	23	22	21	20	20	19	18	17	16	16	14	13	13	12	11	10	9	8	7	6	6	5	4	3	2	1	27
64	27	26	25	24	24	23	22	21	20	19	18	17	16	16	14	13	13	12	11	10	9	8	7	7	6	5	4	3	2	1	26
65	27	26	25	24	24	23	22	21	20	19	18	17	16	16	15	14	14	12	11	10	9	8	8	7	6	5	4	3	2	1	25
66	27	27	26	25	24	23	22	21	20	19	18	17	16	16	15	14	13	12	11	10	9	8	8	7	6	5	4	3	2	1	24
67	28	27	26	25	24	23	22	21	20	19	18	17	17	16	15	14	13	12	11	10	9	8	8	7	6	5	4	3	2	1	23
68	28	27	26	25	24	23	22	21	20	19	19	18	17	16	15	14	13	12	11	10	9	8	8	7	6	5	4	3	2	1	22
69	28	27	26	25	25	23	22	22	21	20	19	18	17	16	15	14	14	13	12	10	9	8	8	7	6	5	4	3	2	1	21
70	28	27	26	25	25	24	23	22	21	20	19	18	17	16	15	14	14	13	12	10	9	8	8	7	6	5	4	3	2	1	20
71	28	28	26	26	25	24	23	22	21	20	19	18	17	16	15	14	14	13	12	11	9	9	8	7	6	5	4	3	2	1	19
72	29	28	27	26	25	24	23	22	21	20	19	19	17	17	16	15	14	13	12	11	10	9	8	7	6	5	4	3	2	1	18
73	29	28	27	26	25	24	23	22	21	20	20	19	18	17	16	15	14	13	12	11	10	9	8	7	6	5	4	3	2	1	17
74	29	28	27	26	25	24	23	22	21	20	20	19	18	17	16	15	14	13	12	11	10	9	8	7	6	5	4	3	2	1	16
75	29	28	27	26	25	24	23	22	22	21	20	19	18	17	16	15	14	13	12	11	10	9	8	7	6	5	4	3	2	1	15
76	29	28	27	26	25	24	23	22	22	21	20	19	18	17	16	15	14	13	12	11	10	9	8	7	6	5	4	3	2	1	14
77	29	29	27	26	25	24	23	22	22	21	20	19	18	17	16	15	14	13	12	11	10	9	8	7	6	5	4	3	2	1	13
78	29	29	27	26	26	25	23	23	22	21	20	19	18	17	16	15	14	13	12	11	10	9	8	7	6	5	4	3	2	1	12
79	30	29	28	27	26	25	24	23	23	21	20	19	18	17	16	15	14	13	12	11	10	9	8	7	6	5	4	3	2	1	11
80	30	29	28	27	26	25	24	23	23	21	20	19	18	17	16	15	14	13	12	11	10	9	8	7	6	5	4	3	2	1	10

For Z₂ < 10°, use 10°

For P > 80°, use 80°

USE OF CONCISE SIGHT REDUCTION TABLES (continued)

4. *Example.* (b) Required the altitude and azimuth of *Vega* on 2014 July 29 at UT
04^h 50^m from the estimated position 152° west, 15° south.

1. Assumed latitude $\quad\quad\quad$ *Lat* = $\quad$ 15° S
    From the almanac $\quad\quad\quad$ *GHA* = $\quad$ 99° 54′
    Assumed longitude $\quad\quad\quad\quad\quad$ 151° 54′ W
    Local hour angle $\quad\quad\quad$ *LHA* = 308

2. Reduction table, 1st entry
    (*Lat, LHA*) = (15, 308) $\quad\quad$ *A* = $\quad$ 49 $\;$ 34 $\quad$ $A° = 50, A' = 34$
    $\quad\quad\quad\quad\quad\quad\quad\quad\quad\quad$ *B* = +66 $\;$ 29 $\quad$ $Z_1 = +71{\cdot}7,$ $\quad\quad\quad\quad\quad$ $LHA > 270°$
3. From the almanac $\quad\quad\quad$ *Dec* = −38 $\;$ 48 $\quad\quad\quad\quad\quad\quad\quad\quad$ *Lat* and *Dec* contrary
    Sum = *B* + *Dec* $\quad\quad\quad$ *F* = +27 $\;$ 41 $\quad$ $F° = 28, F' = 41$

4. Reduction table, 2nd entry
    (*A°, F°*) = (50, 28) $\quad\quad\quad$ *H* = $\quad$ 17 $\;$ 34 $\quad$ $P° = 37$
    $\quad\quad\quad\quad\quad\quad\quad\quad\quad\quad\quad\quad\quad\quad\quad$ $Z_2 = 67{\cdot}8, Z_2° = 68$

5. Auxiliary table, 1st entry
    (*F′, P°*) = (41, 37) $\quad\quad$ $corr_1 =$ $\quad\quad$ −11 $\quad\quad\quad\quad\quad\quad$ $F < 90°, F' > 29'$
    Sum $\quad\quad\quad\quad\quad\quad\quad\quad\quad\quad\quad\quad$ 17 $\;$ 23
6. Auxiliary table, 2nd entry
    (*A′, Z₂°*) = (34, 68) $\quad\quad$ $corr_2 =$ $\quad\quad$ +10 $\quad\quad\quad\quad\quad\quad\quad\quad$ $A' > 30'$
7. Sum = computed altitude $\quad$ *Hc* = +17° $\;$ 33′ $\quad\quad\quad\quad\quad\quad\quad\quad$ $F > 0°$

8. Azimuth, first component $\quad\quad$ $Z_1 = +71{\cdot}7$ $\quad\quad\quad\quad\quad\quad$ same sign as *B*
    $\quad\quad\quad\quad$ second component $\quad$ $Z_2 = +67{\cdot}8$ $\quad\quad\quad\quad\quad\quad$ $F < 90°, F > 0°$
    Sum = azimuth angle $\quad\quad\quad$ $Z = $ 139·5

    True azimuth $\quad\quad\quad\quad\quad\quad$ $Z_n = $ 040° $\quad\quad\quad\quad\quad\quad$ S *Lat*, *LHA* > 180°

5. *Form for use with the Concise Sight Reduction Tables.* The form on the following
page lays out the procedure explained on pages 284-285. Each step is shown, with notes
and rules to ensure accuracy, rather than speed, throughout the calculation. The form is
mainly intended for the calculation of star positions. It therefore includes the formation
of the Greenwich hour of Aries (*GHA* Aries), and thus the Greenwich hour angle of the
star (*GHA*) from its tabular sidereal hour angle (*SHA*). These calculations, included in
step 1 of the form, can easily be replaced by the interpolation of *GHA* and *Dec* for the
Sun, Moon or planets.

The form may be freely copied, however, acknowledgement of the source is requested.

Date & UT of observation		Body	Estimated Latitude & Longitude	
	h m s		° ' ° '	

Step	Calculate Altitude & Azimuth		Summary of Rules & Notes
Assumed latitude	$Lat =$ °		Nearest estimated latitude, integral number of degrees.
Assumed longitude	$Long =$ ° '		Choose $Long$ so that LHA has integral number of degrees.
1. From the almanac:	$Dec =$ ° '		Record the Dec for use in Step 3.
GHA Aries h	$=$ ° '		Needed if using SHA. Tabular value.
Increment m s	$=$ ° '		for minutes and seconds of time.
SHA	$SHA =$ ° '		
$GHA = GHA\ Aries + SHA$	$GHA =$ ° '		Remove multiples of 360°.
Assumed longitude	$Long =$ ° '		West longitudes are negative.
$LHA = GHA + Long$	$LHA =$ °		Remove multiples of 360°.
2. Reduction table, 1st entry			
$(Lat, LHA) = ($ °, °$)$	$A =$ ° '	$A° =$ °	nearest whole degree of A.
record A, B and Z_1.		$A' =$ '	minutes part of A.
	$B =$ ° '		B is minus if $90° < LHA < 270°$.
		$Z_1 =$ °	Z_1 has the same sign as B.
3. From step 1	$Dec =$ ° '		Dec is minus if contrary to Lat.
$F = B + Dec$	$F =$ ° '		Regard F as positive until step 7.
		$F° =$ °	nearest whole degree of F.
		$F' =$ '	minutes part of F.
4. Reduction table, 2nd entry			
$(A°, F°) = ($ °, °$)$	$H =$ ° '	$P° =$ °	nearest whole degree of P.
record H, P and Z_2.		$Z_2 =$ °	
5. Auxiliary table, 1st entry			
$(F', P°) = ($ ', °$)$	$corr_1 =$ '		$corr_1$ is minus if $F < 90°$ & $F' > 29'$,
record $corr_1$			or if $F > 90°$ & $F' < 30'$.
6. Auxiliary table, 2nd entry			$Z_2°$ nearest whole degree of Z_2.
$(A', Z_2°) = ($ ', °$)$	$corr_2 =$ '		$corr_2$ is minus if $A' < 30'$.
record $corr_2$			
7. Calculated altitude $=$	$H_C =$ ° '		H_C is minus if F is negative, and
$H_C = H + corr_1 + corr_2$			object is below the horizon.
8. Azimuth, 1st component	$Z_1 =$ °		Z_1 has the same sign as B.
2nd component	$Z_2 =$ °		Z_2 is minus if $F > 90°$. If F is negative, $Z_2 = 180° - Z_2$
$Z = Z_1 + Z_2$	$Z =$ °		Ignore the sign of Z.
		N Lat:	If $LHA > 180°$, $Z_n = Z$, or if $LHA < 180°$, $Z_n = 360° - Z$,
		S Lat:	If $LHA > 180°$, $Z_n = 180° - Z$, or if $LHA < 180°$, $Z_n = 180° + Z$.
True azimuth	$Z_n =$ °		©HMNAO

For use with *The Nautical Almanac's* Concise Sight Reduction Tables pages 284-318.

CONVERSION OF ARC TO TIME

0°–59°		60°–119°		120°–179°		180°–239°		240°–299°		300°–359°			0′00	0′25	0′50	0′75
°	h m	°	h m	°	h m	°	h m	°	h m	°	h m	′	m s	m s	m s	m s
0	0 00	60	4 00	120	8 00	180	12 00	240	16 00	300	20 00	0	0 00	0 01	0 02	0 03
1	0 04	61	4 04	121	8 04	181	12 04	241	16 04	301	20 04	1	0 04	0 05	0 06	0 07
2	0 08	62	4 08	122	8 08	182	12 08	242	16 08	302	20 08	2	0 08	0 09	0 10	0 11
3	0 12	63	4 12	123	8 12	183	12 12	243	16 12	303	20 12	3	0 12	0 13	0 14	0 15
4	0 16	64	4 16	124	8 16	184	12 16	244	16 16	304	20 16	4	0 16	0 17	0 18	0 19
5	0 20	65	4 20	125	8 20	185	12 20	245	16 20	305	20 20	5	0 20	0 21	0 22	0 23
6	0 24	66	4 24	126	8 24	186	12 24	246	16 24	306	20 24	6	0 24	0 25	0 26	0 27
7	0 28	67	4 28	127	8 28	187	12 28	247	16 28	307	20 28	7	0 28	0 29	0 30	0 31
8	0 32	68	4 32	128	8 32	188	12 32	248	16 32	308	20 32	8	0 32	0 33	0 34	0 35
9	0 36	69	4 36	129	8 36	189	12 36	249	16 36	309	20 36	9	0 36	0 37	0 38	0 39
10	0 40	70	4 40	130	8 40	190	12 40	250	16 40	310	20 40	10	0 40	0 41	0 42	0 43
11	0 44	71	4 44	131	8 44	191	12 44	251	16 44	311	20 44	11	0 44	0 45	0 46	0 47
12	0 48	72	4 48	132	8 48	192	12 48	252	16 48	312	20 48	12	0 48	0 49	0 50	0 51
13	0 52	73	4 52	133	8 52	193	12 52	253	16 52	313	20 52	13	0 52	0 53	0 54	0 55
14	0 56	74	4 56	134	8 56	194	12 56	254	16 56	314	20 56	14	0 56	0 57	0 58	0 59
15	1 00	75	5 00	135	9 00	195	13 00	255	17 00	315	21 00	15	1 00	1 01	1 02	1 03
16	1 04	76	5 04	136	9 04	196	13 04	256	17 04	316	21 04	16	1 04	1 05	1 06	1 07
17	1 08	77	5 08	137	9 08	197	13 08	257	17 08	317	21 08	17	1 08	1 09	1 10	1 11
18	1 12	78	5 12	138	9 12	198	13 12	258	17 12	318	21 12	18	1 12	1 13	1 14	1 15
19	1 16	79	5 16	139	9 16	199	13 16	259	17 16	319	21 16	19	1 16	1 17	1 18	1 19
20	1 20	80	5 20	140	9 20	200	13 20	260	17 20	320	21 20	20	1 20	1 21	1 22	1 23
21	1 24	81	5 24	141	9 24	201	13 24	261	17 24	321	21 24	21	1 24	1 25	1 26	1 27
22	1 28	82	5 28	142	9 28	202	13 28	262	17 28	322	21 28	22	1 28	1 29	1 30	1 31
23	1 32	83	5 32	143	9 32	203	13 32	263	17 32	323	21 32	23	1 32	1 33	1 34	1 35
24	1 36	84	5 36	144	9 36	204	13 36	264	17 36	324	21 36	24	1 36	1 37	1 38	1 39
25	1 40	85	5 40	145	9 40	205	13 40	265	17 40	325	21 40	25	1 40	1 41	1 42	1 43
26	1 44	86	5 44	146	9 44	206	13 44	266	17 44	326	21 44	26	1 44	1 45	1 46	1 47
27	1 48	87	5 48	147	9 48	207	13 48	267	17 48	327	21 48	27	1 48	1 49	1 50	1 51
28	1 52	88	5 52	148	9 52	208	13 52	268	17 52	328	21 52	28	1 52	1 53	1 54	1 55
29	1 56	89	5 56	149	9 56	209	13 56	269	17 56	329	21 56	29	1 56	1 57	1 58	1 59
30	2 00	90	6 00	150	10 00	210	14 00	270	18 00	330	22 00	30	2 00	2 01	2 02	2 03
31	2 04	91	6 04	151	10 04	211	14 04	271	18 04	331	22 04	31	2 04	2 05	2 06	2 07
32	2 08	92	6 08	152	10 08	212	14 08	272	18 08	332	22 08	32	2 08	2 09	2 10	2 11
33	2 12	93	6 12	153	10 12	213	14 12	273	18 12	333	22 12	33	2 12	2 13	2 14	2 15
34	2 16	94	6 16	154	10 16	214	14 16	274	18 16	334	22 16	34	2 16	2 17	2 18	2 19
35	2 20	95	6 20	155	10 20	215	14 20	275	18 20	335	22 20	35	2 20	2 21	2 22	2 23
36	2 24	96	6 24	156	10 24	216	14 24	276	18 24	336	22 24	36	2 24	2 25	2 26	2 27
37	2 28	97	6 28	157	10 28	217	14 28	277	18 28	337	22 28	37	2 28	2 29	2 30	2 31
38	2 32	98	6 32	158	10 32	218	14 32	278	18 32	338	22 32	38	2 32	2 33	2 34	2 35
39	2 36	99	6 36	159	10 36	219	14 36	279	18 36	339	22 36	39	2 36	2 37	2 38	2 39
40	2 40	100	6 40	160	10 40	220	14 40	280	18 40	340	22 40	40	2 40	2 41	2 42	2 43
41	2 44	101	6 44	161	10 44	221	14 44	281	18 44	341	22 44	41	2 44	2 45	2 46	2 47
42	2 48	102	6 48	162	10 48	222	14 48	282	18 48	342	22 48	42	2 48	2 49	2 50	2 51
43	2 52	103	6 52	163	10 52	223	14 52	283	18 52	343	22 52	43	2 52	2 53	2 54	2 55
44	2 56	104	6 56	164	10 56	224	14 56	284	18 56	344	22 56	44	2 56	2 57	2 58	2 59
45	3 00	105	7 00	165	11 00	225	15 00	285	19 00	345	23 00	45	3 00	3 01	3 02	3 03
46	3 04	106	7 04	166	11 04	226	15 04	286	19 04	346	23 04	46	3 04	3 05	3 06	3 07
47	3 08	107	7 08	167	11 08	227	15 08	287	19 08	347	23 08	47	3 08	3 09	3 10	3 11
48	3 12	108	7 12	168	11 12	228	15 12	288	19 12	348	23 12	48	3 12	3 13	3 14	3 15
49	3 16	109	7 16	169	11 16	229	15 16	289	19 16	349	23 16	49	3 16	3 17	3 18	3 19
50	3 20	110	7 20	170	11 20	230	15 20	290	19 20	350	23 20	50	3 20	3 21	3 22	3 23
51	3 24	111	7 24	171	11 24	231	15 24	291	19 24	351	23 24	51	3 24	3 25	3 26	3 27
52	3 28	112	7 28	172	11 28	232	15 28	292	19 28	352	23 28	52	3 28	3 29	3 30	3 31
53	3 32	113	7 32	173	11 32	233	15 32	293	19 32	353	23 32	53	3 32	3 33	3 34	3 35
54	3 36	114	7 36	174	11 36	234	15 36	294	19 36	354	23 36	54	3 36	3 37	3 38	3 39
55	3 40	115	7 40	175	11 40	235	15 40	295	19 40	355	23 40	55	3 40	3 41	3 42	3 43
56	3 44	116	7 44	176	11 44	236	15 44	296	19 44	356	23 44	56	3 44	3 45	3 46	3 47
57	3 48	117	7 48	177	11 48	237	15 48	297	19 48	357	23 48	57	3 48	3 49	3 50	3 51
58	3 52	118	7 52	178	11 52	238	15 52	298	19 52	358	23 52	58	3 52	3 53	3 54	3 55
59	3 56	119	7 56	179	11 56	239	15 56	299	19 56	359	23 56	59	3 56	3 57	3 58	3 59

The above table is for converting expressions in arc to their equivalent in time; its main use in this Almanac is for the conversion of longitude for application to LMT (*added* if *west*, *subtracted* if *east*) to give UT or vice versa, particularly in the case of sunrise, sunset, etc.

i

0ᵐ

s	SUN PLANETS	ARIES	MOON	v or d	Corrⁿ	v or d	Corrⁿ	v or d	Corrⁿ
00	0 00·0	0 00·0	0 00·0	0·0	0·0	6·0	0·1	12·0	0·1
01	0 00·3	0 00·3	0 00·2	0·1	0·0	6·1	0·1	12·1	0·1
02	0 00·5	0 00·5	0 00·5	0·2	0·0	6·2	0·1	12·2	0·1
03	0 00·8	0 00·8	0 00·7	0·3	0·0	6·3	0·1	12·3	0·1
04	0 01·0	0 01·0	0 01·0	0·4	0·0	6·4	0·1	12·4	0·1
05	0 01·3	0 01·3	0 01·2	0·5	0·0	6·5	0·1	12·5	0·1
06	0 01·5	0 01·5	0 01·4	0·6	0·0	6·6	0·1	12·6	0·1
07	0 01·8	0 01·8	0 01·7	0·7	0·0	6·7	0·1	12·7	0·1
08	0 02·0	0 02·0	0 01·9	0·8	0·0	6·8	0·1	12·8	0·1
09	0 02·3	0 02·3	0 02·1	0·9	0·0	6·9	0·1	12·9	0·1
10	0 02·5	0 02·5	0 02·4	1·0	0·0	7·0	0·1	13·0	0·1
11	0 02·8	0 02·8	0 02·6	1·1	0·0	7·1	0·1	13·1	0·1
12	0 03·0	0 03·0	0 02·9	1·2	0·0	7·2	0·1	13·2	0·1
13	0 03·3	0 03·3	0 03·1	1·3	0·0	7·3	0·1	13·3	0·1
14	0 03·5	0 03·5	0 03·3	1·4	0·0	7·4	0·1	13·4	0·1
15	0 03·8	0 03·8	0 03·6	1·5	0·0	7·5	0·1	13·5	0·1
16	0 04·0	0 04·0	0 03·8	1·6	0·0	7·6	0·1	13·6	0·1
17	0 04·3	0 04·3	0 04·1	1·7	0·0	7·7	0·1	13·7	0·1
18	0 04·5	0 04·5	0 04·3	1·8	0·0	7·8	0·1	13·8	0·1
19	0 04·8	0 04·8	0 04·5	1·9	0·0	7·9	0·1	13·9	0·1
20	0 05·0	0 05·0	0 04·8	2·0	0·0	8·0	0·1	14·0	0·1
21	0 05·3	0 05·3	0 05·0	2·1	0·0	8·1	0·1	14·1	0·1
22	0 05·5	0 05·5	0 05·2	2·2	0·0	8·2	0·1	14·2	0·1
23	0 05·8	0 05·8	0 05·5	2·3	0·0	8·3	0·1	14·3	0·1
24	0 06·0	0 06·0	0 05·7	2·4	0·0	8·4	0·1	14·4	0·1
25	0 06·3	0 06·3	0 06·0	2·5	0·0	8·5	0·1	14·5	0·1
26	0 06·5	0 06·5	0 06·2	2·6	0·0	8·6	0·1	14·6	0·1
27	0 06·8	0 06·8	0 06·4	2·7	0·0	8·7	0·1	14·7	0·1
28	0 07·0	0 07·0	0 06·7	2·8	0·0	8·8	0·1	14·8	0·1
29	0 07·3	0 07·3	0 06·9	2·9	0·0	8·9	0·1	14·9	0·1
30	0 07·5	0 07·5	0 07·2	3·0	0·0	9·0	0·1	15·0	0·1
31	0 07·8	0 07·8	0 07·4	3·1	0·0	9·1	0·1	15·1	0·1
32	0 08·0	0 08·0	0 07·6	3·2	0·0	9·2	0·1	15·2	0·1
33	0 08·3	0 08·3	0 07·9	3·3	0·0	9·3	0·1	15·3	0·1
34	0 08·5	0 08·5	0 08·1	3·4	0·0	9·4	0·1	15·4	0·1
35	0 08·8	0 08·8	0 08·4	3·5	0·0	9·5	0·1	15·5	0·1
36	0 09·0	0 09·0	0 08·6	3·6	0·0	9·6	0·1	15·6	0·1
37	0 09·3	0 09·3	0 08·8	3·7	0·0	9·7	0·1	15·7	0·1
38	0 09·5	0 09·5	0 09·1	3·8	0·0	9·8	0·1	15·8	0·1
39	0 09·8	0 09·8	0 09·3	3·9	0·0	9·9	0·1	15·9	0·1
40	0 10·0	0 10·0	0 09·5	4·0	0·0	10·0	0·1	16·0	0·1
41	0 10·3	0 10·3	0 09·8	4·1	0·0	10·1	0·1	16·1	0·1
42	0 10·5	0 10·5	0 10·0	4·2	0·0	10·2	0·1	16·2	0·1
43	0 10·8	0 10·8	0 10·3	4·3	0·0	10·3	0·1	16·3	0·1
44	0 11·0	0 11·0	0 10·5	4·4	0·0	10·4	0·1	16·4	0·1
45	0 11·3	0 11·3	0 10·7	4·5	0·0	10·5	0·1	16·5	0·1
46	0 11·5	0 11·5	0 11·0	4·6	0·0	10·6	0·1	16·6	0·1
47	0 11·8	0 11·8	0 11·2	4·7	0·0	10·7	0·1	16·7	0·1
48	0 12·0	0 12·0	0 11·5	4·8	0·0	10·8	0·1	16·8	0·1
49	0 12·3	0 12·3	0 11·7	4·9	0·0	10·9	0·1	16·9	0·1
50	0 12·5	0 12·5	0 11·9	5·0	0·0	11·0	0·1	17·0	0·1
51	0 12·8	0 12·8	0 12·2	5·1	0·0	11·1	0·1	17·1	0·1
52	0 13·0	0 13·0	0 12·4	5·2	0·0	11·2	0·1	17·2	0·1
53	0 13·3	0 13·3	0 12·6	5·3	0·0	11·3	0·1	17·3	0·1
54	0 13·5	0 13·5	0 12·9	5·4	0·0	11·4	0·1	17·4	0·1
55	0 13·8	0 13·8	0 13·1	5·5	0·0	11·5	0·1	17·5	0·1
56	0 14·0	0 14·0	0 13·4	5·6	0·0	11·6	0·1	17·6	0·1
57	0 14·3	0 14·3	0 13·6	5·7	0·0	11·7	0·1	17·7	0·1
58	0 14·5	0 14·5	0 13·8	5·8	0·0	11·8	0·1	17·8	0·1
59	0 14·8	0 14·8	0 14·1	5·9	0·0	11·9	0·1	17·9	0·1
60	0 15·0	0 15·0	0 14·3	6·0	0·1	12·0	0·1	18·0	0·2

1ᵐ

s	SUN PLANETS	ARIES	MOON	v or d	Corrⁿ	v or d	Corrⁿ	v or d	Corrⁿ
00	0 15·0	0 15·0	0 14·3	0·0	0·0	6·0	0·2	12·0	0·3
01	0 15·3	0 15·3	0 14·6	0·1	0·0	6·1	0·2	12·1	0·3
02	0 15·5	0 15·5	0 14·8	0·2	0·0	6·2	0·2	12·2	0·3
03	0 15·8	0 15·8	0 15·0	0·3	0·0	6·3	0·2	12·3	0·3
04	0 16·0	0 16·0	0 15·3	0·4	0·0	6·4	0·2	12·4	0·3
05	0 16·3	0 16·3	0 15·5	0·5	0·0	6·5	0·2	12·5	0·3
06	0 16·5	0 16·5	0 15·7	0·6	0·0	6·6	0·2	12·6	0·3
07	0 16·8	0 16·8	0 16·0	0·7	0·0	6·7	0·2	12·7	0·3
08	0 17·0	0 17·0	0 16·2	0·8	0·0	6·8	0·2	12·8	0·3
09	0 17·3	0 17·3	0 16·5	0·9	0·0	6·9	0·2	12·9	0·3
10	0 17·5	0 17·5	0 16·7	1·0	0·0	7·0	0·2	13·0	0·3
11	0 17·8	0 17·8	0 16·9	1·1	0·0	7·1	0·2	13·1	0·3
12	0 18·0	0 18·0	0 17·2	1·2	0·0	7·2	0·2	13·2	0·3
13	0 18·3	0 18·3	0 17·4	1·3	0·0	7·3	0·2	13·3	0·3
14	0 18·5	0 18·6	0 17·7	1·4	0·0	7·4	0·2	13·4	0·3
15	0 18·8	0 18·8	0 17·9	1·5	0·0	7·5	0·2	13·5	0·3
16	0 19·0	0 19·1	0 18·1	1·6	0·0	7·6	0·2	13·6	0·3
17	0 19·3	0 19·3	0 18·4	1·7	0·0	7·7	0·2	13·7	0·3
18	0 19·5	0 19·6	0 18·6	1·8	0·0	7·8	0·2	13·8	0·3
19	0 19·8	0 19·8	0 18·9	1·9	0·0	7·9	0·2	13·9	0·3
20	0 20·0	0 20·1	0 19·1	2·0	0·1	8·0	0·2	14·0	0·4
21	0 20·3	0 20·3	0 19·3	2·1	0·1	8·1	0·2	14·1	0·4
22	0 20·5	0 20·6	0 19·6	2·2	0·1	8·2	0·2	14·2	0·4
23	0 20·8	0 20·8	0 19·8	2·3	0·1	8·3	0·2	14·3	0·4
24	0 21·0	0 21·1	0 20·0	2·4	0·1	8·4	0·2	14·4	0·4
25	0 21·3	0 21·3	0 20·3	2·5	0·1	8·5	0·2	14·5	0·4
26	0 21·5	0 21·6	0 20·5	2·6	0·1	8·6	0·2	14·6	0·4
27	0 21·8	0 21·8	0 20·8	2·7	0·1	8·7	0·2	14·7	0·4
28	0 22·0	0 22·1	0 21·0	2·8	0·1	8·8	0·2	14·8	0·4
29	0 22·3	0 22·3	0 21·2	2·9	0·1	8·9	0·2	14·9	0·4
30	0 22·5	0 22·6	0 21·5	3·0	0·1	9·0	0·2	15·0	0·4
31	0 22·8	0 22·8	0 21·7	3·1	0·1	9·1	0·2	15·1	0·4
32	0 23·0	0 23·1	0 22·0	3·2	0·1	9·2	0·2	15·2	0·4
33	0 23·3	0 23·3	0 22·2	3·3	0·1	9·3	0·2	15·3	0·4
34	0 23·5	0 23·6	0 22·4	3·4	0·1	9·4	0·2	15·4	0·4
35	0 23·8	0 23·8	0 22·7	3·5	0·1	9·5	0·2	15·5	0·4
36	0 24·0	0 24·1	0 22·9	3·6	0·1	9·6	0·2	15·6	0·4
37	0 24·3	0 24·3	0 23·1	3·7	0·1	9·7	0·2	15·7	0·4
38	0 24·5	0 24·6	0 23·4	3·8	0·1	9·8	0·2	15·8	0·4
39	0 24·8	0 24·8	0 23·6	3·9	0·1	9·9	0·2	15·9	0·4
40	0 25·0	0 25·1	0 23·9	4·0	0·1	10·0	0·3	16·0	0·4
41	0 25·3	0 25·3	0 24·1	4·1	0·1	10·1	0·3	16·1	0·4
42	0 25·5	0 25·6	0 24·3	4·2	0·1	10·2	0·3	16·2	0·4
43	0 25·8	0 25·8	0 24·6	4·3	0·1	10·3	0·3	16·3	0·4
44	0 26·0	0 26·1	0 24·8	4·4	0·1	10·4	0·3	16·4	0·4
45	0 26·3	0 26·3	0 25·1	4·5	0·1	10·5	0·3	16·5	0·4
46	0 26·5	0 26·6	0 25·3	4·6	0·1	10·6	0·3	16·6	0·4
47	0 26·8	0 26·8	0 25·5	4·7	0·1	10·7	0·3	16·7	0·4
48	0 27·0	0 27·1	0 25·8	4·8	0·1	10·8	0·3	16·8	0·4
49	0 27·3	0 27·3	0 26·0	4·9	0·1	10·9	0·3	16·9	0·4
50	0 27·5	0 27·6	0 26·2	5·0	0·1	11·0	0·3	17·0	0·4
51	0 27·8	0 27·8	0 26·5	5·1	0·1	11·1	0·3	17·1	0·4
52	0 28·0	0 28·1	0 26·7	5·2	0·1	11·2	0·3	17·2	0·4
53	0 28·3	0 28·3	0 27·0	5·3	0·1	11·3	0·3	17·3	0·4
54	0 28·5	0 28·6	0 27·2	5·4	0·1	11·4	0·3	17·4	0·4
55	0 28·8	0 28·8	0 27·4	5·5	0·1	11·5	0·3	17·5	0·4
56	0 29·0	0 29·1	0 27·7	5·6	0·1	11·6	0·3	17·6	0·4
57	0 29·3	0 29·3	0 27·9	5·7	0·1	11·7	0·3	17·7	0·4
58	0 29·5	0 29·6	0 28·2	5·8	0·1	11·8	0·3	17·8	0·4
59	0 29·8	0 29·8	0 28·4	5·9	0·1	11·9	0·3	17·9	0·4
60	0 30·0	0 30·1	0 28·6	6·0	0·2	12·0	0·3	18·0	0·5

ii

2 m/s	SUN PLANETS	ARIES	MOON	v or Corrn d		v or Corrn d		v or Corrn d	
s	° ′	° ′	° ′	′	′	′	′	′	′
00	0 30·0	0 30·1	0 28·6	0·0	0·0	6·0	0·3	12·0	0·5
01	0 30·3	0 30·3	0 28·9	0·1	0·0	6·1	0·3	12·1	0·5
02	0 30·5	0 30·6	0 29·1	0·2	0·0	6·2	0·3	12·2	0·5
03	0 30·8	0 30·8	0 29·3	0·3	0·0	6·3	0·3	12·3	0·5
04	0 31·0	0 31·1	0 29·6	0·4	0·0	6·4	0·3	12·4	0·5
05	0 31·3	0 31·3	0 29·8	0·5	0·0	6·5	0·3	12·5	0·5
06	0 31·5	0 31·6	0 30·1	0·6	0·0	6·6	0·3	12·6	0·5
07	0 31·8	0 31·8	0 30·3	0·7	0·0	6·7	0·3	12·7	0·5
08	0 32·0	0 32·1	0 30·5	0·8	0·0	6·8	0·3	12·8	0·5
09	0 32·3	0 32·3	0 30·8	0·9	0·0	6·9	0·3	12·9	0·5
10	0 32·5	0 32·6	0 31·0	1·0	0·0	7·0	0·3	13·0	0·5
11	0 32·8	0 32·8	0 31·3	1·1	0·0	7·1	0·3	13·1	0·5
12	0 33·0	0 33·1	0 31·5	1·2	0·1	7·2	0·3	13·2	0·6
13	0 33·3	0 33·3	0 31·7	1·3	0·1	7·3	0·3	13·3	0·6
14	0 33·5	0 33·6	0 32·0	1·4	0·1	7·4	0·3	13·4	0·6
15	0 33·8	0 33·8	0 32·2	1·5	0·1	7·5	0·3	13·5	0·6
16	0 34·0	0 34·1	0 32·5	1·6	0·1	7·6	0·3	13·6	0·6
17	0 34·3	0 34·3	0 32·7	1·7	0·1	7·7	0·3	13·7	0·6
18	0 34·5	0 34·6	0 32·9	1·8	0·1	7·8	0·3	13·8	0·6
19	0 34·8	0 34·8	0 33·2	1·9	0·1	7·9	0·3	13·9	0·6
20	0 35·0	0 35·1	0 33·4	2·0	0·1	8·0	0·3	14·0	0·6
21	0 35·3	0 35·3	0 33·6	2·1	0·1	8·1	0·3	14·1	0·6
22	0 35·5	0 35·6	0 33·9	2·2	0·1	8·2	0·3	14·2	0·6
23	0 35·8	0 35·8	0 34·1	2·3	0·1	8·3	0·3	14·3	0·6
24	0 36·0	0 36·1	0 34·4	2·4	0·1	8·4	0·4	14·4	0·6
25	0 36·3	0 36·3	0 34·6	2·5	0·1	8·5	0·4	14·5	0·6
26	0 36·5	0 36·6	0 34·8	2·6	0·1	8·6	0·4	14·6	0·6
27	0 36·8	0 36·9	0 35·1	2·7	0·1	8·7	0·4	14·7	0·6
28	0 37·0	0 37·1	0 35·3	2·8	0·1	8·8	0·4	14·8	0·6
29	0 37·3	0 37·4	0 35·6	2·9	0·1	8·9	0·4	14·9	0·6
30	0 37·5	0 37·6	0 35·8	3·0	0·1	9·0	0·4	15·0	0·6
31	0 37·8	0 37·9	0 36·0	3·1	0·1	9·1	0·4	15·1	0·6
32	0 38·0	0 38·1	0 36·3	3·2	0·1	9·2	0·4	15·2	0·6
33	0 38·3	0 38·4	0 36·5	3·3	0·1	9·3	0·4	15·3	0·6
34	0 38·5	0 38·6	0 36·7	3·4	0·1	9·4	0·4	15·4	0·6
35	0 38·8	0 38·9	0 37·0	3·5	0·1	9·5	0·4	15·5	0·6
36	0 39·0	0 39·1	0 37·2	3·6	0·2	9·6	0·4	15·6	0·7
37	0 39·3	0 39·4	0 37·5	3·7	0·2	9·7	0·4	15·7	0·7
38	0 39·5	0 39·6	0 37·7	3·8	0·2	9·8	0·4	15·8	0·7
39	0 39·8	0 39·9	0 37·9	3·9	0·2	9·9	0·4	15·9	0·7
40	0 40·0	0 40·1	0 38·2	4·0	0·2	10·0	0·4	16·0	0·7
41	0 40·3	0 40·4	0 38·4	4·1	0·2	10·1	0·4	16·1	0·7
42	0 40·5	0 40·6	0 38·7	4·2	0·2	10·2	0·4	16·2	0·7
43	0 40·8	0 40·9	0 38·9	4·3	0·2	10·3	0·4	16·3	0·7
44	0 41·0	0 41·1	0 39·1	4·4	0·2	10·4	0·4	16·4	0·7
45	0 41·3	0 41·4	0 39·4	4·5	0·2	10·5	0·4	16·5	0·7
46	0 41·5	0 41·6	0 39·6	4·6	0·2	10·6	0·4	16·6	0·7
47	0 41·8	0 41·9	0 39·8	4·7	0·2	10·7	0·4	16·7	0·7
48	0 42·0	0 42·1	0 40·1	4·8	0·2	10·8	0·5	16·8	0·7
49	0 42·3	0 42·4	0 40·3	4·9	0·2	10·9	0·5	16·9	0·7
50	0 42·5	0 42·6	0 40·6	5·0	0·2	11·0	0·5	17·0	0·7
51	0 42·8	0 42·9	0 40·8	5·1	0·2	11·1	0·5	17·1	0·7
52	0 43·0	0 43·1	0 41·0	5·2	0·2	11·2	0·5	17·2	0·7
53	0 43·3	0 43·4	0 41·3	5·3	0·2	11·3	0·5	17·3	0·7
54	0 43·5	0 43·6	0 41·5	5·4	0·2	11·4	0·5	17·4	0·7
55	0 43·8	0 43·9	0 41·8	5·5	0·2	11·5	0·5	17·5	0·7
56	0 44·0	0 44·1	0 42·0	5·6	0·2	11·6	0·5	17·6	0·7
57	0 44·3	0 44·4	0 42·2	5·7	0·2	11·7	0·5	17·7	0·7
58	0 44·5	0 44·6	0 42·5	5·8	0·2	11·8	0·5	17·8	0·7
59	0 44·8	0 44·9	0 42·7	5·9	0·2	11·9	0·5	17·9	0·7
60	0 45·0	0 45·1	0 43·0	6·0	0·3	12·0	0·5	18·0	0·8

3 m/s	SUN PLANETS	ARIES	MOON	v or Corrn d		v or Corrn d		v or Corrn d	
s	° ′	° ′	° ′	′	′	′	′	′	′
00	0 45·0	0 45·1	0 43·0	0·0	0·0	6·0	0·4	12·0	0·7
01	0 45·3	0 45·4	0 43·2	0·1	0·0	6·1	0·4	12·1	0·7
02	0 45·5	0 45·6	0 43·4	0·2	0·0	6·2	0·4	12·2	0·7
03	0 45·8	0 45·9	0 43·7	0·3	0·0	6·3	0·4	12·3	0·7
04	0 46·0	0 46·1	0 43·9	0·4	0·0	6·4	0·4	12·4	0·7
05	0 46·3	0 46·4	0 44·1	0·5	0·0	6·5	0·4	12·5	0·7
06	0 46·5	0 46·6	0 44·4	0·6	0·0	6·6	0·4	12·6	0·7
07	0 46·8	0 46·9	0 44·6	0·7	0·0	6·7	0·4	12·7	0·7
08	0 47·0	0 47·1	0 44·9	0·8	0·0	6·8	0·4	12·8	0·7
09	0 47·3	0 47·4	0 45·1	0·9	0·1	6·9	0·4	12·9	0·8
10	0 47·5	0 47·6	0 45·3	1·0	0·1	7·0	0·4	13·0	0·8
11	0 47·8	0 47·9	0 45·6	1·1	0·1	7·1	0·4	13·1	0·8
12	0 48·0	0 48·1	0 45·8	1·2	0·1	7·2	0·4	13·2	0·8
13	0 48·3	0 48·4	0 46·1	1·3	0·1	7·3	0·4	13·3	0·8
14	0 48·5	0 48·6	0 46·3	1·4	0·1	7·4	0·4	13·4	0·8
15	0 48·8	0 48·9	0 46·5	1·5	0·1	7·5	0·4	13·5	0·8
16	0 49·0	0 49·1	0 46·8	1·6	0·1	7·6	0·4	13·6	0·8
17	0 49·3	0 49·4	0 47·0	1·7	0·1	7·7	0·4	13·7	0·8
18	0 49·5	0 49·6	0 47·2	1·8	0·1	7·8	0·5	13·8	0·8
19	0 49·8	0 49·9	0 47·5	1·9	0·1	7·9	0·5	13·9	0·8
20	0 50·0	0 50·1	0 47·7	2·0	0·1	8·0	0·5	14·0	0·8
21	0 50·3	0 50·4	0 48·0	2·1	0·1	8·1	0·5	14·1	0·8
22	0 50·5	0 50·6	0 48·2	2·2	0·1	8·2	0·5	14·2	0·8
23	0 50·8	0 50·9	0 48·4	2·3	0·1	8·3	0·5	14·3	0·8
24	0 51·0	0 51·1	0 48·7	2·4	0·1	8·4	0·5	14·4	0·8
25	0 51·3	0 51·4	0 48·9	2·5	0·1	8·5	0·5	14·5	0·8
26	0 51·5	0 51·6	0 49·2	2·6	0·2	8·6	0·5	14·6	0·9
27	0 51·8	0 51·9	0 49·4	2·7	0·2	8·7	0·5	14·7	0·9
28	0 52·0	0 52·1	0 49·6	2·8	0·2	8·8	0·5	14·8	0·9
29	0 52·3	0 52·4	0 49·9	2·9	0·2	8·9	0·5	14·9	0·9
30	0 52·5	0 52·6	0 50·1	3·0	0·2	9·0	0·5	15·0	0·9
31	0 52·8	0 52·9	0 50·3	3·1	0·2	9·1	0·5	15·1	0·9
32	0 53·0	0 53·1	0 50·6	3·2	0·2	9·2	0·5	15·2	0·9
33	0 53·3	0 53·4	0 50·8	3·3	0·2	9·3	0·5	15·3	0·9
34	0 53·5	0 53·6	0 51·1	3·4	0·2	9·4	0·5	15·4	0·9
35	0 53·8	0 53·9	0 51·3	3·5	0·2	9·5	0·6	15·5	0·9
36	0 54·0	0 54·1	0 51·5	3·6	0·2	9·6	0·6	15·6	0·9
37	0 54·3	0 54·4	0 51·8	3·7	0·2	9·7	0·6	15·7	0·9
38	0 54·5	0 54·6	0 52·0	3·8	0·2	9·8	0·6	15·8	0·9
39	0 54·8	0 54·9	0 52·3	3·9	0·2	9·9	0·6	15·9	0·9
40	0 55·0	0 55·2	0 52·5	4·0	0·2	10·0	0·6	16·0	0·9
41	0 55·3	0 55·4	0 52·7	4·1	0·2	10·1	0·6	16·1	0·9
42	0 55·5	0 55·7	0 53·0	4·2	0·2	10·2	0·6	16·2	0·9
43	0 55·8	0 55·9	0 53·2	4·3	0·3	10·3	0·6	16·3	1·0
44	0 56·0	0 56·2	0 53·4	4·4	0·3	10·4	0·6	16·4	1·0
45	0 56·3	0 56·4	0 53·7	4·5	0·3	10·5	0·6	16·5	1·0
46	0 56·5	0 56·7	0 53·9	4·6	0·3	10·6	0·6	16·6	1·0
47	0 56·8	0 56·9	0 54·2	4·7	0·3	10·7	0·6	16·7	1·0
48	0 57·0	0 57·2	0 54·4	4·8	0·3	10·8	0·6	16·8	1·0
49	0 57·3	0 57·4	0 54·6	4·9	0·3	10·9	0·6	16·9	1·0
50	0 57·5	0 57·7	0 54·9	5·0	0·3	11·0	0·6	17·0	1·0
51	0 57·8	0 57·9	0 55·1	5·1	0·3	11·1	0·6	17·1	1·0
52	0 58·0	0 58·2	0 55·4	5·2	0·3	11·2	0·7	17·2	1·0
53	0 58·3	0 58·4	0 55·6	5·3	0·3	11·3	0·7	17·3	1·0
54	0 58·5	0 58·7	0 55·8	5·4	0·3	11·4	0·7	17·4	1·0
55	0 58·8	0 58·9	0 56·1	5·5	0·3	11·5	0·7	17·5	1·0
56	0 59·0	0 59·2	0 56·3	5·6	0·3	11·6	0·7	17·6	1·0
57	0 59·3	0 59·4	0 56·6	5·7	0·3	11·7	0·7	17·7	1·0
58	0 59·5	0 59·7	0 56·8	5·8	0·3	11·8	0·7	17·8	1·0
59	0 59·8	0 59·9	0 57·0	5·9	0·3	11·9	0·7	17·9	1·0
60	1 00·0	1 00·2	0 57·3	6·0	0·4	12·0	0·7	18·0	1·1

^{m} 4	SUN PLANETS	ARIES	MOON	v or Corr^n d		v or Corr^n d		v or Corr^n d	
s	° ′	° ′	° ′	′	′	′	′	′	′
00	1 00·0	1 00·2	0 57·3	0·0	0·0	6·0	0·5	12·0	0·9
01	1 00·3	1 00·4	0 57·5	0·1	0·0	6·1	0·5	12·1	0·9
02	1 00·5	1 00·7	0 57·7	0·2	0·0	6·2	0·5	12·2	0·9
03	1 00·8	1 00·9	0 58·0	0·3	0·0	6·3	0·5	12·3	0·9
04	1 01·0	1 01·2	0 58·2	0·4	0·0	6·4	0·5	12·4	0·9
05	1 01·3	1 01·4	0 58·5	0·5	0·0	6·5	0·5	12·5	0·9
06	1 01·5	1 01·7	0 58·7	0·6	0·0	6·6	0·5	12·6	0·9
07	1 01·8	1 01·9	0 58·9	0·7	0·1	6·7	0·5	12·7	1·0
08	1 02·0	1 02·2	0 59·2	0·8	0·1	6·8	0·5	12·8	1·0
09	1 02·3	1 02·4	0 59·4	0·9	0·1	6·9	0·5	12·9	1·0
10	1 02·5	1 02·7	0 59·7	1·0	0·1	7·0	0·5	13·0	1·0
11	1 02·8	1 02·9	0 59·9	1·1	0·1	7·1	0·5	13·1	1·0
12	1 03·0	1 03·2	1 00·1	1·2	0·1	7·2	0·5	13·2	1·0
13	1 03·3	1 03·4	1 00·4	1·3	0·1	7·3	0·5	13·3	1·0
14	1 03·5	1 03·7	1 00·6	1·4	0·1	7·4	0·6	13·4	1·0
15	1 03·8	1 03·9	1 00·8	1·5	0·1	7·5	0·6	13·5	1·0
16	1 04·0	1 04·2	1 01·1	1·6	0·1	7·6	0·6	13·6	1·0
17	1 04·3	1 04·4	1 01·3	1·7	0·1	7·7	0·6	13·7	1·0
18	1 04·5	1 04·7	1 01·6	1·8	0·1	7·8	0·6	13·8	1·0
19	1 04·8	1 04·9	1 01·8	1·9	0·1	7·9	0·6	13·9	1·0
20	1 05·0	1 05·2	1 02·0	2·0	0·2	8·0	0·6	14·0	1·1
21	1 05·3	1 05·4	1 02·3	2·1	0·2	8·1	0·6	14·1	1·1
22	1 05·5	1 05·7	1 02·5	2·2	0·2	8·2	0·6	14·2	1·1
23	1 05·8	1 05·9	1 02·8	2·3	0·2	8·3	0·6	14·3	1·1
24	1 06·0	1 06·2	1 03·0	2·4	0·2	8·4	0·6	14·4	1·1
25	1 06·3	1 06·4	1 03·2	2·5	0·2	8·5	0·6	14·5	1·1
26	1 06·5	1 06·7	1 03·5	2·6	0·2	8·6	0·6	14·6	1·1
27	1 06·8	1 06·9	1 03·7	2·7	0·2	8·7	0·7	14·7	1·1
28	1 07·0	1 07·2	1 03·9	2·8	0·2	8·8	0·7	14·8	1·1
29	1 07·3	1 07·4	1 04·2	2·9	0·2	8·9	0·7	14·9	1·1
30	1 07·5	1 07·7	1 04·4	3·0	0·2	9·0	0·7	15·0	1·1
31	1 07·8	1 07·9	1 04·7	3·1	0·2	9·1	0·7	15·1	1·1
32	1 08·0	1 08·2	1 04·9	3·2	0·2	9·2	0·7	15·2	1·1
33	1 08·3	1 08·4	1 05·1	3·3	0·2	9·3	0·7	15·3	1·1
34	1 08·5	1 08·7	1 05·4	3·4	0·3	9·4	0·7	15·4	1·2
35	1 08·8	1 08·9	1 05·6	3·5	0·3	9·5	0·7	15·5	1·2
36	1 09·0	1 09·2	1 05·9	3·6	0·3	9·6	0·7	15·6	1·2
37	1 09·3	1 09·4	1 06·1	3·7	0·3	9·7	0·7	15·7	1·2
38	1 09·5	1 09·7	1 06·3	3·8	0·3	9·8	0·7	15·8	1·2
39	1 09·8	1 09·9	1 06·6	3·9	0·3	9·9	0·7	15·9	1·2
40	1 10·0	1 10·2	1 06·8	4·0	0·3	10·0	0·8	16·0	1·2
41	1 10·3	1 10·4	1 07·0	4·1	0·3	10·1	0·8	16·1	1·2
42	1 10·5	1 10·7	1 07·3	4·2	0·3	10·2	0·8	16·2	1·2
43	1 10·8	1 10·9	1 07·5	4·3	0·3	10·3	0·8	16·3	1·2
44	1 11·0	1 11·2	1 07·8	4·4	0·3	10·4	0·8	16·4	1·2
45	1 11·3	1 11·4	1 08·0	4·5	0·3	10·5	0·8	16·5	1·2
46	1 11·5	1 11·7	1 08·2	4·6	0·3	10·6	0·8	16·6	1·2
47	1 11·8	1 11·9	1 08·5	4·7	0·4	10·7	0·8	16·7	1·3
48	1 12·0	1 12·2	1 08·7	4·8	0·4	10·8	0·8	16·8	1·3
49	1 12·3	1 12·4	1 09·0	4·9	0·4	10·9	0·8	16·9	1·3
50	1 12·5	1 12·7	1 09·2	5·0	0·4	11·0	0·8	17·0	1·3
51	1 12·8	1 12·9	1 09·4	5·1	0·4	11·1	0·8	17·1	1·3
52	1 13·0	1 13·2	1 09·7	5·2	0·4	11·2	0·8	17·2	1·3
53	1 13·3	1 13·5	1 09·9	5·3	0·4	11·3	0·8	17·3	1·3
54	1 13·5	1 13·7	1 10·2	5·4	0·4	11·4	0·9	17·4	1·3
55	1 13·8	1 14·0	1 10·4	5·5	0·4	11·5	0·9	17·5	1·3
56	1 14·0	1 14·2	1 10·6	5·6	0·4	11·6	0·9	17·6	1·3
57	1 14·3	1 14·5	1 10·9	5·7	0·4	11·7	0·9	17·7	1·3
58	1 14·5	1 14·7	1 11·1	5·8	0·4	11·8	0·9	17·8	1·3
59	1 14·8	1 15·0	1 11·3	5·9	0·4	11·9	0·9	17·9	1·3
60	1 15·0	1 15·2	1 11·6	6·0	0·5	12·0	0·9	18·0	1·4

^{m} 5	SUN PLANETS	ARIES	MOON	v or Corr^n d		v or Corr^n d		v or Corr^n d	
s	° ′	° ′	° ′	′	′	′	′	′	′
00	1 15·0	1 15·2	1 11·6	0·0	0·0	6·0	0·6	12·0	1·1
01	1 15·3	1 15·5	1 11·8	0·1	0·0	6·1	0·6	12·1	1·1
02	1 15·5	1 15·7	1 12·1	0·2	0·0	6·2	0·6	12·2	1·1
03	1 15·8	1 16·0	1 12·3	0·3	0·0	6·3	0·6	12·3	1·1
04	1 16·0	1 16·2	1 12·5	0·4	0·0	6·4	0·6	12·4	1·1
05	1 16·3	1 16·5	1 12·8	0·5	0·0	6·5	0·6	12·5	1·1
06	1 16·5	1 16·7	1 13·0	0·6	0·1	6·6	0·6	12·6	1·2
07	1 16·8	1 17·0	1 13·3	0·7	0·1	6·7	0·6	12·7	1·2
08	1 17·0	1 17·2	1 13·5	0·8	0·1	6·8	0·6	12·8	1·2
09	1 17·3	1 17·5	1 13·7	0·9	0·1	6·9	0·6	12·9	1·2
10	1 17·5	1 17·7	1 14·0	1·0	0·1	7·0	0·6	13·0	1·2
11	1 17·8	1 18·0	1 14·2	1·1	0·1	7·1	0·7	13·1	1·2
12	1 18·0	1 18·2	1 14·4	1·2	0·1	7·2	0·7	13·2	1·2
13	1 18·3	1 18·5	1 14·7	1·3	0·1	7·3	0·7	13·3	1·2
14	1 18·5	1 18·7	1 14·9	1·4	0·1	7·4	0·7	13·4	1·2
15	1 18·8	1 19·0	1 15·2	1·5	0·1	7·5	0·7	13·5	1·2
16	1 19·0	1 19·2	1 15·4	1·6	0·1	7·6	0·7	13·6	1·2
17	1 19·3	1 19·5	1 15·6	1·7	0·2	7·7	0·7	13·7	1·3
18	1 19·5	1 19·7	1 15·9	1·8	0·2	7·8	0·7	13·8	1·3
19	1 19·8	1 20·0	1 16·1	1·9	0·2	7·9	0·7	13·9	1·3
20	1 20·0	1 20·2	1 16·4	2·0	0·2	8·0	0·7	14·0	1·3
21	1 20·3	1 20·5	1 16·6	2·1	0·2	8·1	0·7	14·1	1·3
22	1 20·5	1 20·7	1 16·8	2·2	0·2	8·2	0·8	14·2	1·3
23	1 20·8	1 21·0	1 17·1	2·3	0·2	8·3	0·8	14·3	1·3
24	1 21·0	1 21·2	1 17·3	2·4	0·2	8·4	0·8	14·4	1·3
25	1 21·3	1 21·5	1 17·5	2·5	0·2	8·5	0·8	14·5	1·3
26	1 21·5	1 21·7	1 17·8	2·6	0·2	8·6	0·8	14·6	1·3
27	1 21·8	1 22·0	1 18·0	2·7	0·2	8·7	0·8	14·7	1·3
28	1 22·0	1 22·2	1 18·3	2·8	0·3	8·8	0·8	14·8	1·4
29	1 22·3	1 22·5	1 18·5	2·9	0·3	8·9	0·8	14·9	1·4
30	1 22·5	1 22·7	1 18·7	3·0	0·3	9·0	0·8	15·0	1·4
31	1 22·8	1 23·0	1 19·0	3·1	0·3	9·1	0·8	15·1	1·4
32	1 23·0	1 23·2	1 19·2	3·2	0·3	9·2	0·8	15·2	1·4
33	1 23·3	1 23·5	1 19·5	3·3	0·3	9·3	0·9	15·3	1·4
34	1 23·5	1 23·7	1 19·7	3·4	0·3	9·4	0·9	15·4	1·4
35	1 23·8	1 24·0	1 19·9	3·5	0·3	9·5	0·9	15·5	1·4
36	1 24·0	1 24·2	1 20·2	3·6	0·3	9·6	0·9	15·6	1·4
37	1 24·3	1 24·5	1 20·4	3·7	0·3	9·7	0·9	15·7	1·4
38	1 24·5	1 24·7	1 20·7	3·8	0·3	9·8	0·9	15·8	1·4
39	1 24·8	1 25·0	1 20·9	3·9	0·4	9·9	0·9	15·9	1·5
40	1 25·0	1 25·2	1 21·1	4·0	0·4	10·0	0·9	16·0	1·5
41	1 25·3	1 25·5	1 21·4	4·1	0·4	10·1	0·9	16·1	1·5
42	1 25·5	1 25·7	1 21·6	4·2	0·4	10·2	0·9	16·2	1·5
43	1 25·8	1 26·0	1 21·8	4·3	0·4	10·3	0·9	16·3	1·5
44	1 26·0	1 26·2	1 22·1	4·4	0·4	10·4	1·0	16·4	1·5
45	1 26·3	1 26·5	1 22·3	4·5	0·4	10·5	1·0	16·5	1·5
46	1 26·5	1 26·7	1 22·6	4·6	0·4	10·6	1·0	16·6	1·5
47	1 26·8	1 27·0	1 22·8	4·7	0·4	10·7	1·0	16·7	1·5
48	1 27·0	1 27·2	1 23·0	4·8	0·4	10·8	1·0	16·8	1·5
49	1 27·3	1 27·5	1 23·3	4·9	0·4	10·9	1·0	16·9	1·5
50	1 27·5	1 27·7	1 23·5	5·0	0·5	11·0	1·0	17·0	1·6
51	1 27·8	1 28·0	1 23·8	5·1	0·5	11·1	1·0	17·1	1·6
52	1 28·0	1 28·2	1 24·0	5·2	0·5	11·2	1·0	17·2	1·6
53	1 28·3	1 28·5	1 24·2	5·3	0·5	11·3	1·0	17·3	1·6
54	1 28·5	1 28·7	1 24·5	5·4	0·5	11·4	1·0	17·4	1·6
55	1 28·8	1 29·0	1 24·7	5·5	0·5	11·5	1·1	17·5	1·6
56	1 29·0	1 29·2	1 24·9	5·6	0·5	11·6	1·1	17·6	1·6
57	1 29·3	1 29·5	1 25·2	5·7	0·5	11·7	1·1	17·7	1·6
58	1 29·5	1 29·7	1 25·4	5·8	0·5	11·8	1·1	17·8	1·6
59	1 29·8	1 30·0	1 25·7	5·9	0·5	11·9	1·1	17·9	1·6
60	1 30·0	1 30·2	1 25·9	6·0	0·6	12·0	1·1	18·0	1·7

iv

6ᵐ

m 6	SUN PLANETS	ARIES	MOON	v or d	Corrⁿ	v or d	Corrⁿ	v or d	Corrⁿ
s	° ′	° ′	° ′	′	′	′	′	′	′
00	1 30·0	1 30·2	1 25·9	0·0	0·0	6·0	0·7	12·0	1·3
01	1 30·3	1 30·5	1 26·1	0·1	0·0	6·1	0·7	12·1	1·3
02	1 30·5	1 30·7	1 26·4	0·2	0·0	6·2	0·7	12·2	1·3
03	1 30·8	1 31·0	1 26·6	0·3	0·0	6·3	0·7	12·3	1·3
04	1 31·0	1 31·2	1 26·9	0·4	0·0	6·4	0·7	12·4	1·3
05	1 31·3	1 31·5	1 27·1	0·5	0·1	6·5	0·7	12·5	1·4
06	1 31·5	1 31·8	1 27·3	0·6	0·1	6·6	0·7	12·6	1·4
07	1 31·8	1 32·0	1 27·6	0·7	0·1	6·7	0·7	12·7	1·4
08	1 32·0	1 32·3	1 27·8	0·8	0·1	6·8	0·7	12·8	1·4
09	1 32·3	1 32·5	1 28·0	0·9	0·1	6·9	0·7	12·9	1·4
10	1 32·5	1 32·8	1 28·3	1·0	0·1	7·0	0·8	13·0	1·4
11	1 32·8	1 33·0	1 28·5	1·1	0·1	7·1	0·8	13·1	1·4
12	1 33·0	1 33·3	1 28·8	1·2	0·1	7·2	0·8	13·2	1·4
13	1 33·3	1 33·5	1 29·0	1·3	0·1	7·3	0·8	13·3	1·4
14	1 33·5	1 33·8	1 29·2	1·4	0·2	7·4	0·8	13·4	1·5
15	1 33·8	1 34·0	1 29·5	1·5	0·2	7·5	0·8	13·5	1·5
16	1 34·0	1 34·3	1 29·7	1·6	0·2	7·6	0·8	13·6	1·5
17	1 34·3	1 34·5	1 30·0	1·7	0·2	7·7	0·8	13·7	1·5
18	1 34·5	1 34·8	1 30·2	1·8	0·2	7·8	0·8	13·8	1·5
19	1 34·8	1 35·0	1 30·4	1·9	0·2	7·9	0·9	13·9	1·5
20	1 35·0	1 35·3	1 30·7	2·0	0·2	8·0	0·9	14·0	1·5
21	1 35·3	1 35·5	1 30·9	2·1	0·2	8·1	0·9	14·1	1·5
22	1 35·5	1 35·8	1 31·1	2·2	0·2	8·2	0·9	14·2	1·5
23	1 35·8	1 36·0	1 31·4	2·3	0·2	8·3	0·9	14·3	1·5
24	1 36·0	1 36·3	1 31·6	2·4	0·3	8·4	0·9	14·4	1·6
25	1 36·3	1 36·5	1 31·9	2·5	0·3	8·5	0·9	14·5	1·6
26	1 36·5	1 36·8	1 32·1	2·6	0·3	8·6	0·9	14·6	1·6
27	1 36·8	1 37·0	1 32·3	2·7	0·3	8·7	0·9	14·7	1·6
28	1 37·0	1 37·3	1 32·6	2·8	0·3	8·8	1·0	14·8	1·6
29	1 37·3	1 37·5	1 32·8	2·9	0·3	8·9	1·0	14·9	1·6
30	1 37·5	1 37·8	1 33·1	3·0	0·3	9·0	1·0	15·0	1·6
31	1 37·8	1 38·0	1 33·3	3·1	0·3	9·1	1·0	15·1	1·6
32	1 38·0	1 38·3	1 33·5	3·2	0·3	9·2	1·0	15·2	1·6
33	1 38·3	1 38·5	1 33·8	3·3	0·4	9·3	1·0	15·3	1·7
34	1 38·5	1 38·8	1 34·0	3·4	0·4	9·4	1·0	15·4	1·7
35	1 38·8	1 39·0	1 34·3	3·5	0·4	9·5	1·0	15·5	1·7
36	1 39·0	1 39·3	1 34·5	3·6	0·4	9·6	1·0	15·6	1·7
37	1 39·3	1 39·5	1 34·7	3·7	0·4	9·7	1·1	15·7	1·7
38	1 39·5	1 39·8	1 35·0	3·8	0·4	9·8	1·1	15·8	1·7
39	1 39·8	1 40·0	1 35·2	3·9	0·4	9·9	1·1	15·9	1·7
40	1 40·0	1 40·3	1 35·4	4·0	0·4	10·0	1·1	16·0	1·7
41	1 40·3	1 40·5	1 35·7	4·1	0·4	10·1	1·1	16·1	1·7
42	1 40·5	1 40·8	1 35·9	4·2	0·5	10·2	1·1	16·2	1·8
43	1 40·8	1 41·0	1 36·2	4·3	0·5	10·3	1·1	16·3	1·8
44	1 41·0	1 41·3	1 36·4	4·4	0·5	10·4	1·1	16·4	1·8
45	1 41·3	1 41·5	1 36·6	4·5	0·5	10·5	1·1	16·5	1·8
46	1 41·5	1 41·8	1 36·9	4·6	0·5	10·6	1·1	16·6	1·8
47	1 41·8	1 42·0	1 37·1	4·7	0·5	10·7	1·2	16·7	1·8
48	1 42·0	1 42·3	1 37·4	4·8	0·5	10·8	1·2	16·8	1·8
49	1 42·3	1 42·5	1 37·6	4·9	0·5	10·9	1·2	16·9	1·8
50	1 42·5	1 42·8	1 37·8	5·0	0·5	11·0	1·2	17·0	1·8
51	1 42·8	1 43·0	1 38·1	5·1	0·6	11·1	1·2	17·1	1·9
52	1 43·0	1 43·3	1 38·3	5·2	0·6	11·2	1·2	17·2	1·9
53	1 43·3	1 43·5	1 38·5	5·3	0·6	11·3	1·2	17·3	1·9
54	1 43·5	1 43·8	1 38·8	5·4	0·6	11·4	1·2	17·4	1·9
55	1 43·8	1 44·0	1 39·0	5·5	0·6	11·5	1·2	17·5	1·9
56	1 44·0	1 44·3	1 39·3	5·6	0·6	11·6	1·3	17·6	1·9
57	1 44·3	1 44·5	1 39·5	5·7	0·6	11·7	1·3	17·7	1·9
58	1 44·5	1 44·8	1 39·7	5·8	0·6	11·8	1·3	17·8	1·9
59	1 44·8	1 45·0	1 40·0	5·9	0·6	11·9	1·3	17·9	1·9
60	1 45·0	1 45·3	1 40·2	6·0	0·7	12·0	1·3	18·0	2·0

7ᵐ

m 7	SUN PLANETS	ARIES	MOON	v or d	Corrⁿ	v or d	Corrⁿ	v or d	Corrⁿ
s	° ′	° ′	° ′	′	′	′	′	′	′
00	1 45·0	1 45·3	1 40·2	0·0	0·0	6·0	0·8	12·0	1·5
01	1 45·3	1 45·5	1 40·5	0·1	0·0	6·1	0·8	12·1	1·5
02	1 45·5	1 45·8	1 40·7	0·2	0·0	6·2	0·8	12·2	1·5
03	1 45·8	1 46·0	1 40·9	0·3	0·0	6·3	0·8	12·3	1·5
04	1 46·0	1 46·3	1 41·2	0·4	0·1	6·4	0·8	12·4	1·6
05	1 46·3	1 46·5	1 41·4	0·5	0·1	6·5	0·8	12·5	1·6
06	1 46·5	1 46·8	1 41·6	0·6	0·1	6·6	0·8	12·6	1·6
07	1 46·8	1 47·0	1 41·9	0·7	0·1	6·7	0·8	12·7	1·6
08	1 47·0	1 47·3	1 42·1	0·8	0·1	6·8	0·9	12·8	1·6
09	1 47·3	1 47·5	1 42·4	0·9	0·1	6·9	0·9	12·9	1·6
10	1 47·5	1 47·8	1 42·6	1·0	0·1	7·0	0·9	13·0	1·6
11	1 47·8	1 48·0	1 42·8	1·1	0·1	7·1	0·9	13·1	1·6
12	1 48·0	1 48·3	1 43·1	1·2	0·2	7·2	0·9	13·2	1·7
13	1 48·3	1 48·5	1 43·3	1·3	0·2	7·3	0·9	13·3	1·7
14	1 48·5	1 48·8	1 43·6	1·4	0·2	7·4	0·9	13·4	1·7
15	1 48·8	1 49·0	1 43·8	1·5	0·2	7·5	0·9	13·5	1·7
16	1 49·0	1 49·3	1 44·0	1·6	0·2	7·6	1·0	13·6	1·7
17	1 49·3	1 49·5	1 44·3	1·7	0·2	7·7	1·0	13·7	1·7
18	1 49·5	1 49·8	1 44·5	1·8	0·2	7·8	1·0	13·8	1·7
19	1 49·8	1 50·1	1 44·8	1·9	0·2	7·9	1·0	13·9	1·7
20	1 50·0	1 50·3	1 45·0	2·0	0·3	8·0	1·0	14·0	1·8
21	1 50·3	1 50·6	1 45·2	2·1	0·3	8·1	1·0	14·1	1·8
22	1 50·5	1 50·8	1 45·5	2·2	0·3	8·2	1·0	14·2	1·8
23	1 50·8	1 51·1	1 45·7	2·3	0·3	8·3	1·0	14·3	1·8
24	1 51·0	1 51·3	1 45·9	2·4	0·3	8·4	1·1	14·4	1·8
25	1 51·3	1 51·6	1 46·2	2·5	0·3	8·5	1·1	14·5	1·8
26	1 51·5	1 51·8	1 46·4	2·6	0·3	8·6	1·1	14·6	1·8
27	1 51·8	1 52·1	1 46·7	2·7	0·3	8·7	1·1	14·7	1·8
28	1 52·0	1 52·3	1 46·9	2·8	0·4	8·8	1·1	14·8	1·9
29	1 52·3	1 52·6	1 47·1	2·9	0·4	8·9	1·1	14·9	1·9
30	1 52·5	1 52·8	1 47·4	3·0	0·4	9·0	1·1	15·0	1·9
31	1 52·8	1 53·1	1 47·6	3·1	0·4	9·1	1·1	15·1	1·9
32	1 53·0	1 53·3	1 47·9	3·2	0·4	9·2	1·2	15·2	1·9
33	1 53·3	1 53·6	1 48·1	3·3	0·4	9·3	1·2	15·3	1·9
34	1 53·5	1 53·8	1 48·3	3·4	0·4	9·4	1·2	15·4	1·9
35	1 53·8	1 54·1	1 48·6	3·5	0·4	9·5	1·2	15·5	1·9
36	1 54·0	1 54·3	1 48·8	3·6	0·5	9·6	1·2	15·6	2·0
37	1 54·3	1 54·6	1 49·0	3·7	0·5	9·7	1·2	15·7	2·0
38	1 54·5	1 54·8	1 49·3	3·8	0·5	9·8	1·2	15·8	2·0
39	1 54·8	1 55·1	1 49·5	3·9	0·5	9·9	1·2	15·9	2·0
40	1 55·0	1 55·3	1 49·8	4·0	0·5	10·0	1·3	16·0	2·0
41	1 55·3	1 55·6	1 50·0	4·1	0·5	10·1	1·3	16·1	2·0
42	1 55·5	1 55·8	1 50·2	4·2	0·5	10·2	1·3	16·2	2·0
43	1 55·8	1 56·1	1 50·5	4·3	0·5	10·3	1·3	16·3	2·0
44	1 56·0	1 56·3	1 50·7	4·4	0·6	10·4	1·3	16·4	2·1
45	1 56·3	1 56·6	1 51·0	4·5	0·6	10·5	1·3	16·5	2·1
46	1 56·5	1 56·8	1 51·2	4·6	0·6	10·6	1·3	16·6	2·1
47	1 56·8	1 57·1	1 51·4	4·7	0·6	10·7	1·3	16·7	2·1
48	1 57·0	1 57·3	1 51·7	4·8	0·6	10·8	1·4	16·8	2·1
49	1 57·3	1 57·6	1 51·9	4·9	0·6	10·9	1·4	16·9	2·1
50	1 57·5	1 57·8	1 52·1	5·0	0·6	11·0	1·4	17·0	2·1
51	1 57·8	1 58·1	1 52·4	5·1	0·6	11·1	1·4	17·1	2·1
52	1 58·0	1 58·3	1 52·6	5·2	0·7	11·2	1·4	17·2	2·2
53	1 58·3	1 58·6	1 52·9	5·3	0·7	11·3	1·4	17·3	2·2
54	1 58·5	1 58·8	1 53·1	5·4	0·7	11·4	1·4	17·4	2·2
55	1 58·8	1 59·1	1 53·3	5·5	0·7	11·5	1·4	17·5	2·2
56	1 59·0	1 59·3	1 53·6	5·6	0·7	11·6	1·5	17·6	2·2
57	1 59·3	1 59·6	1 53·8	5·7	0·7	11·7	1·5	17·7	2·2
58	1 59·5	1 59·8	1 54·1	5·8	0·7	11·8	1·5	17·8	2·2
59	1 59·8	2 00·1	1 54·3	5·9	0·7	11·9	1·5	17·9	2·2
60	2 00·0	2 00·3	1 54·5	6·0	0·8	12·0	1·5	18·0	2·3

8 m/s	SUN PLANETS	ARIES	MOON	v or d	Corrn	v or d	Corrn	v or d	Corrn
s	° ′	° ′	° ′	′	′	′	′	′	′
00	2 00·0	2 00·3	1 54·5	0·0	0·0	6·0	0·9	12·0	1·7
01	2 00·3	2 00·6	1 54·8	0·1	0·0	6·1	0·9	12·1	1·7
02	2 00·5	2 00·8	1 55·0	0·2	0·0	6·2	0·9	12·2	1·7
03	2 00·8	2 01·1	1 55·2	0·3	0·0	6·3	0·9	12·3	1·7
04	2 01·0	2 01·3	1 55·5	0·4	0·1	6·4	0·9	12·4	1·8
05	2 01·3	2 01·6	1 55·7	0·5	0·1	6·5	0·9	12·5	1·8
06	2 01·5	2 01·8	1 56·0	0·6	0·1	6·6	0·9	12·6	1·8
07	2 01·8	2 02·1	1 56·2	0·7	0·1	6·7	0·9	12·7	1·8
08	2 02·0	2 02·3	1 56·4	0·8	0·1	6·8	1·0	12·8	1·8
09	2 02·3	2 02·6	1 56·7	0·9	0·1	6·9	1·0	12·9	1·8
10	2 02·5	2 02·8	1 56·9	1·0	0·1	7·0	1·0	13·0	1·8
11	2 02·8	2 03·1	1 57·2	1·1	0·2	7·1	1·0	13·1	1·9
12	2 03·0	2 03·3	1 57·4	1·2	0·2	7·2	1·0	13·2	1·9
13	2 03·3	2 03·6	1 57·6	1·3	0·2	7·3	1·0	13·3	1·9
14	2 03·5	2 03·8	1 57·9	1·4	0·2	7·4	1·0	13·4	1·9
15	2 03·8	2 04·1	1 58·1	1·5	0·2	7·5	1·1	13·5	1·9
16	2 04·0	2 04·3	1 58·4	1·6	0·2	7·6	1·1	13·6	1·9
17	2 04·3	2 04·6	1 58·6	1·7	0·2	7·7	1·1	13·7	1·9
18	2 04·5	2 04·8	1 58·8	1·8	0·3	7·8	1·1	13·8	2·0
19	2 04·8	2 05·1	1 59·1	1·9	0·3	7·9	1·1	13·9	2·0
20	2 05·0	2 05·3	1 59·3	2·0	0·3	8·0	1·1	14·0	2·0
21	2 05·3	2 05·6	1 59·5	2·1	0·3	8·1	1·1	14·1	2·0
22	2 05·5	2 05·8	1 59·8	2·2	0·3	8·2	1·2	14·2	2·0
23	2 05·8	2 06·1	2 00·0	2·3	0·3	8·3	1·2	14·3	2·0
24	2 06·0	2 06·3	2 00·3	2·4	0·3	8·4	1·2	14·4	2·0
25	2 06·3	2 06·6	2 00·5	2·5	0·4	8·5	1·2	14·5	2·1
26	2 06·5	2 06·8	2 00·7	2·6	0·4	8·6	1·2	14·6	2·1
27	2 06·8	2 07·1	2 01·0	2·7	0·4	8·7	1·2	14·7	2·1
28	2 07·0	2 07·3	2 01·2	2·8	0·4	8·8	1·2	14·8	2·1
29	2 07·3	2 07·6	2 01·5	2·9	0·4	8·9	1·3	14·9	2·1
30	2 07·5	2 07·8	2 01·7	3·0	0·4	9·0	1·3	15·0	2·1
31	2 07·8	2 08·1	2 01·9	3·1	0·4	9·1	1·3	15·1	2·1
32	2 08·0	2 08·4	2 02·2	3·2	0·5	9·2	1·3	15·2	2·2
33	2 08·3	2 08·6	2 02·4	3·3	0·5	9·3	1·3	15·3	2·2
34	2 08·5	2 08·9	2 02·6	3·4	0·5	9·4	1·3	15·4	2·2
35	2 08·8	2 09·1	2 02·9	3·5	0·5	9·5	1·3	15·5	2·2
36	2 09·0	2 09·4	2 03·1	3·6	0·5	9·6	1·4	15·6	2·2
37	2 09·3	2 09·6	2 03·4	3·7	0·5	9·7	1·4	15·7	2·2
38	2 09·5	2 09·9	2 03·6	3·8	0·5	9·8	1·4	15·8	2·2
39	2 09·8	2 10·1	2 03·8	3·9	0·6	9·9	1·4	15·9	2·3
40	2 10·0	2 10·4	2 04·1	4·0	0·6	10·0	1·4	16·0	2·3
41	2 10·3	2 10·6	2 04·3	4·1	0·6	10·1	1·4	16·1	2·3
42	2 10·5	2 10·9	2 04·6	4·2	0·6	10·2	1·4	16·2	2·3
43	2 10·8	2 11·1	2 04·8	4·3	0·6	10·3	1·5	16·3	2·3
44	2 11·0	2 11·4	2 05·0	4·4	0·6	10·4	1·5	16·4	2·3
45	2 11·3	2 11·6	2 05·3	4·5	0·6	10·5	1·5	16·5	2·3
46	2 11·5	2 11·9	2 05·5	4·6	0·7	10·6	1·5	16·6	2·4
47	2 11·8	2 12·1	2 05·7	4·7	0·7	10·7	1·5	16·7	2·4
48	2 12·0	2 12·4	2 06·0	4·8	0·7	10·8	1·5	16·8	2·4
49	2 12·3	2 12·6	2 06·2	4·9	0·7	10·9	1·5	16·9	2·4
50	2 12·5	2 12·9	2 06·5	5·0	0·7	11·0	1·6	17·0	2·4
51	2 12·8	2 13·1	2 06·7	5·1	0·7	11·1	1·6	17·1	2·4
52	2 13·0	2 13·4	2 06·9	5·2	0·7	11·2	1·6	17·2	2·4
53	2 13·3	2 13·6	2 07·2	5·3	0·8	11·3	1·6	17·3	2·5
54	2 13·5	2 13·9	2 07·4	5·4	0·8	11·4	1·6	17·4	2·5
55	2 13·8	2 14·1	2 07·7	5·5	0·8	11·5	1·6	17·5	2·5
56	2 14·0	2 14·4	2 07·9	5·6	0·8	11·6	1·6	17·6	2·5
57	2 14·3	2 14·6	2 08·1	5·7	0·8	11·7	1·7	17·7	2·5
58	2 14·5	2 14·9	2 08·4	5·8	0·8	11·8	1·7	17·8	2·5
59	2 14·8	2 15·1	2 08·6	5·9	0·8	11·9	1·7	17·9	2·5
60	2 15·0	2 15·4	2 08·9	6·0	0·9	12·0	1·7	18·0	2·6

9 m/s	SUN PLANETS	ARIES	MOON	v or d	Corrn	v or d	Corrn	v or d	Corrn
s	° ′	° ′	° ′	′	′	′	′	′	′
00	2 15·0	2 15·4	2 08·9	0·0	0·0	6·0	1·0	12·0	1·9
01	2 15·3	2 15·6	2 09·1	0·1	0·0	6·1	1·0	12·1	1·9
02	2 15·5	2 15·9	2 09·3	0·2	0·0	6·2	1·0	12·2	1·9
03	2 15·8	2 16·1	2 09·6	0·3	0·0	6·3	1·0	12·3	1·9
04	2 16·0	2 16·4	2 09·8	0·4	0·1	6·4	1·0	12·4	2·0
05	2 16·3	2 16·6	2 10·0	0·5	0·1	6·5	1·0	12·5	2·0
06	2 16·5	2 16·9	2 10·3	0·6	0·1	6·6	1·0	12·6	2·0
07	2 16·8	2 17·1	2 10·5	0·7	0·1	6·7	1·1	12·7	2·0
08	2 17·0	2 17·4	2 10·8	0·8	0·1	6·8	1·1	12·8	2·0
09	2 17·3	2 17·6	2 11·0	0·9	0·1	6·9	1·1	12·9	2·0
10	2 17·5	2 17·9	2 11·2	1·0	0·2	7·0	1·1	13·0	2·1
11	2 17·8	2 18·1	2 11·5	1·1	0·2	7·1	1·1	13·1	2·1
12	2 18·0	2 18·4	2 11·7	1·2	0·2	7·2	1·1	13·2	2·1
13	2 18·3	2 18·6	2 12·0	1·3	0·2	7·3	1·2	13·3	2·1
14	2 18·5	2 18·9	2 12·2	1·4	0·2	7·4	1·2	13·4	2·1
15	2 18·8	2 19·1	2 12·4	1·5	0·2	7·5	1·2	13·5	2·1
16	2 19·0	2 19·4	2 12·7	1·6	0·3	7·6	1·2	13·6	2·2
17	2 19·3	2 19·6	2 12·9	1·7	0·3	7·7	1·2	13·7	2·2
18	2 19·5	2 19·9	2 13·1	1·8	0·3	7·8	1·2	13·8	2·2
19	2 19·8	2 20·1	2 13·4	1·9	0·3	7·9	1·3	13·9	2·2
20	2 20·0	2 20·4	2 13·6	2·0	0·3	8·0	1·3	14·0	2·2
21	2 20·3	2 20·6	2 13·9	2·1	0·3	8·1	1·3	14·1	2·2
22	2 20·5	2 20·9	2 14·1	2·2	0·3	8·2	1·3	14·2	2·2
23	2 20·8	2 21·1	2 14·3	2·3	0·4	8·3	1·3	14·3	2·3
24	2 21·0	2 21·4	2 14·6	2·4	0·4	8·4	1·3	14·4	2·3
25	2 21·3	2 21·6	2 14·8	2·5	0·4	8·5	1·3	14·5	2·3
26	2 21·5	2 21·9	2 15·1	2·6	0·4	8·6	1·4	14·6	2·3
27	2 21·8	2 22·1	2 15·3	2·7	0·4	8·7	1·4	14·7	2·3
28	2 22·0	2 22·4	2 15·5	2·8	0·4	8·8	1·4	14·8	2·3
29	2 22·3	2 22·6	2 15·8	2·9	0·5	8·9	1·4	14·9	2·4
30	2 22·5	2 22·9	2 16·0	3·0	0·5	9·0	1·4	15·0	2·4
31	2 22·8	2 23·1	2 16·2	3·1	0·5	9·1	1·4	15·1	2·4
32	2 23·0	2 23·4	2 16·5	3·2	0·5	9·2	1·5	15·2	2·4
33	2 23·3	2 23·6	2 16·7	3·3	0·5	9·3	1·5	15·3	2·4
34	2 23·5	2 23·9	2 17·0	3·4	0·5	9·4	1·5	15·4	2·4
35	2 23·8	2 24·1	2 17·2	3·5	0·6	9·5	1·5	15·5	2·5
36	2 24·0	2 24·4	2 17·4	3·6	0·6	9·6	1·5	15·6	2·5
37	2 24·3	2 24·6	2 17·7	3·7	0·6	9·7	1·5	15·7	2·5
38	2 24·5	2 24·9	2 17·9	3·8	0·6	9·8	1·6	15·8	2·5
39	2 24·8	2 25·1	2 18·2	3·9	0·6	9·9	1·6	15·9	2·5
40	2 25·0	2 25·4	2 18·4	4·0	0·6	10·0	1·6	16·0	2·5
41	2 25·3	2 25·6	2 18·6	4·1	0·6	10·1	1·6	16·1	2·5
42	2 25·5	2 25·9	2 18·9	4·2	0·7	10·2	1·6	16·2	2·6
43	2 25·8	2 26·1	2 19·1	4·3	0·7	10·3	1·6	16·3	2·6
44	2 26·0	2 26·4	2 19·3	4·4	0·7	10·4	1·6	16·4	2·6
45	2 26·3	2 26·7	2 19·6	4·5	0·7	10·5	1·7	16·5	2·6
46	2 26·5	2 26·9	2 19·8	4·6	0·7	10·6	1·7	16·6	2·6
47	2 26·8	2 27·2	2 20·1	4·7	0·7	10·7	1·7	16·7	2·6
48	2 27·0	2 27·4	2 20·3	4·8	0·8	10·8	1·7	16·8	2·7
49	2 27·3	2 27·7	2 20·5	4·9	0·8	10·9	1·7	16·9	2·7
50	2 27·5	2 27·9	2 20·8	5·0	0·8	11·0	1·7	17·0	2·7
51	2 27·8	2 28·2	2 21·0	5·1	0·8	11·1	1·8	17·1	2·7
52	2 28·0	2 28·4	2 21·3	5·2	0·8	11·2	1·8	17·2	2·7
53	2 28·3	2 28·7	2 21·5	5·3	0·8	11·3	1·8	17·3	2·7
54	2 28·5	2 28·9	2 21·7	5·4	0·9	11·4	1·8	17·4	2·8
55	2 28·8	2 29·2	2 22·0	5·5	0·9	11·5	1·8	17·5	2·8
56	2 29·0	2 29·4	2 22·2	5·6	0·9	11·6	1·8	17·6	2·8
57	2 29·3	2 29·7	2 22·5	5·7	0·9	11·7	1·9	17·7	2·8
58	2 29·5	2 29·9	2 22·7	5·8	0·9	11·8	1·9	17·8	2·8
59	2 29·8	2 30·2	2 22·9	5·9	0·9	11·9	1·9	17·9	2·8
60	2 30·0	2 30·4	2 23·2	6·0	1·0	12·0	1·9	18·0	2·9

10 m	SUN PLANETS	ARIES	MOON	v or Corrⁿ d		v or Corrⁿ d		v or Corrⁿ d	
s	° ′	° ′	° ′	′	′	′	′	′	′
00	2 30·0	2 30·4	2 23·2	0·0	0·0	6·0	1·1	12·0	2·1
01	2 30·3	2 30·7	2 23·4	0·1	0·0	6·1	1·1	12·1	2·1
02	2 30·5	2 30·9	2 23·6	0·2	0·0	6·2	1·1	12·2	2·1
03	2 30·8	2 31·2	2 23·9	0·3	0·1	6·3	1·1	12·3	2·2
04	2 31·0	2 31·4	2 24·1	0·4	0·1	6·4	1·1	12·4	2·2
05	2 31·3	2 31·7	2 24·4	0·5	0·1	6·5	1·1	12·5	2·2
06	2 31·5	2 31·9	2 24·6	0·6	0·1	6·6	1·2	12·6	2·2
07	2 31·8	2 32·2	2 24·8	0·7	0·1	6·7	1·2	12·7	2·2
08	2 32·0	2 32·4	2 25·1	0·8	0·1	6·8	1·2	12·8	2·2
09	2 32·3	2 32·7	2 25·3	0·9	0·2	6·9	1·2	12·9	2·3
10	2 32·5	2 32·9	2 25·6	1·0	0·2	7·0	1·2	13·0	2·3
11	2 32·8	2 33·2	2 25·8	1·1	0·2	7·1	1·2	13·1	2·3
12	2 33·0	2 33·4	2 26·0	1·2	0·2	7·2	1·3	13·2	2·3
13	2 33·3	2 33·7	2 26·3	1·3	0·2	7·3	1·3	13·3	2·3
14	2 33·5	2 33·9	2 26·5	1·4	0·2	7·4	1·3	13·4	2·3
15	2 33·8	2 34·2	2 26·7	1·5	0·3	7·5	1·3	13·5	2·4
16	2 34·0	2 34·4	2 27·0	1·6	0·3	7·6	1·3	13·6	2·4
17	2 34·3	2 34·7	2 27·2	1·7	0·3	7·7	1·3	13·7	2·4
18	2 34·5	2 34·9	2 27·5	1·8	0·3	7·8	1·4	13·8	2·4
19	2 34·8	2 35·2	2 27·7	1·9	0·3	7·9	1·4	13·9	2·4
20	2 35·0	2 35·4	2 27·9	2·0	0·4	8·0	1·4	14·0	2·5
21	2 35·3	2 35·7	2 28·2	2·1	0·4	8·1	1·4	14·1	2·5
22	2 35·5	2 35·9	2 28·4	2·2	0·4	8·2	1·4	14·2	2·5
23	2 35·8	2 36·2	2 28·7	2·3	0·4	8·3	1·5	14·3	2·5
24	2 36·0	2 36·4	2 28·9	2·4	0·4	8·4	1·5	14·4	2·5
25	2 36·3	2 36·7	2 29·1	2·5	0·4	8·5	1·5	14·5	2·5
26	2 36·5	2 36·9	2 29·4	2·6	0·5	8·6	1·5	14·6	2·6
27	2 36·8	2 37·2	2 29·6	2·7	0·5	8·7	1·5	14·7	2·6
28	2 37·0	2 37·4	2 29·8	2·8	0·5	8·8	1·5	14·8	2·6
29	2 37·3	2 37·7	2 30·1	2·9	0·5	8·9	1·6	14·9	2·6
30	2 37·5	2 37·9	2 30·3	3·0	0·5	9·0	1·6	15·0	2·6
31	2 37·8	2 38·2	2 30·6	3·1	0·5	9·1	1·6	15·1	2·6
32	2 38·0	2 38·4	2 30·8	3·2	0·6	9·2	1·6	15·2	2·7
33	2 38·3	2 38·7	2 31·0	3·3	0·6	9·3	1·6	15·3	2·7
34	2 38·5	2 38·9	2 31·3	3·4	0·6	9·4	1·6	15·4	2·7
35	2 38·8	2 39·2	2 31·5	3·5	0·6	9·5	1·7	15·5	2·7
36	2 39·0	2 39·4	2 31·8	3·6	0·6	9·6	1·7	15·6	2·7
37	2 39·3	2 39·7	2 32·0	3·7	0·6	9·7	1·7	15·7	2·7
38	2 39·5	2 39·9	2 32·2	3·8	0·7	9·8	1·7	15·8	2·8
39	2 39·8	2 40·2	2 32·5	3·9	0·7	9·9	1·7	15·9	2·8
40	2 40·0	2 40·4	2 32·7	4·0	0·7	10·0	1·8	16·0	2·8
41	2 40·3	2 40·7	2 32·9	4·1	0·7	10·1	1·8	16·1	2·8
42	2 40·5	2 40·9	2 33·2	4·2	0·7	10·2	1·8	16·2	2·8
43	2 40·8	2 41·2	2 33·4	4·3	0·8	10·3	1·8	16·3	2·9
44	2 41·0	2 41·4	2 33·7	4·4	0·8	10·4	1·8	16·4	2·9
45	2 41·3	2 41·7	2 33·9	4·5	0·8	10·5	1·8	16·5	2·9
46	2 41·5	2 41·9	2 34·1	4·6	0·8	10·6	1·9	16·6	2·9
47	2 41·8	2 42·2	2 34·4	4·7	0·8	10·7	1·9	16·7	2·9
48	2 42·0	2 42·4	2 34·6	4·8	0·8	10·8	1·9	16·8	2·9
49	2 42·3	2 42·7	2 34·9	4·9	0·9	10·9	1·9	16·9	3·0
50	2 42·5	2 42·9	2 35·1	5·0	0·9	11·0	1·9	17·0	3·0
51	2 42·8	2 43·2	2 35·3	5·1	0·9	11·1	1·9	17·1	3·0
52	2 43·0	2 43·4	2 35·6	5·2	0·9	11·2	2·0	17·2	3·0
53	2 43·3	2 43·7	2 35·8	5·3	0·9	11·3	2·0	17·3	3·0
54	2 43·5	2 43·9	2 36·1	5·4	0·9	11·4	2·0	17·4	3·0
55	2 43·8	2 44·2	2 36·3	5·5	1·0	11·5	2·0	17·5	3·1
56	2 44·0	2 44·4	2 36·5	5·6	1·0	11·6	2·0	17·6	3·1
57	2 44·3	2 44·7	2 36·8	5·7	1·0	11·7	2·0	17·7	3·1
58	2 44·5	2 45·0	2 37·0	5·8	1·0	11·8	2·1	17·8	3·1
59	2 44·8	2 45·2	2 37·2	5·9	1·0	11·9	2·1	17·9	3·1
60	2 45·0	2 45·5	2 37·5	6·0	1·1	12·0	2·1	18·0	3·2

11 m	SUN PLANETS	ARIES	MOON	v or Corrⁿ d		v or Corrⁿ d		v or Corrⁿ d	
s	° ′	° ′	° ′	′	′	′	′	′	′
00	2 45·0	2 45·5	2 37·5	0·0	0·0	6·0	1·2	12·0	2·3
01	2 45·3	2 45·7	2 37·7	0·1	0·0	6·1	1·2	12·1	2·3
02	2 45·5	2 46·0	2 38·0	0·2	0·0	6·2	1·2	12·2	2·3
03	2 45·8	2 46·2	2 38·2	0·3	0·1	6·3	1·2	12·3	2·4
04	2 46·0	2 46·5	2 38·4	0·4	0·1	6·4	1·2	12·4	2·4
05	2 46·3	2 46·7	2 38·7	0·5	0·1	6·5	1·2	12·5	2·4
06	2 46·5	2 47·0	2 38·9	0·6	0·1	6·6	1·3	12·6	2·4
07	2 46·8	2 47·2	2 39·2	0·7	0·1	6·7	1·3	12·7	2·4
08	2 47·0	2 47·5	2 39·4	0·8	0·2	6·8	1·3	12·8	2·5
09	2 47·3	2 47·7	2 39·6	0·9	0·2	6·9	1·3	12·9	2·5
10	2 47·5	2 48·0	2 39·9	1·0	0·2	7·0	1·3	13·0	2·5
11	2 47·8	2 48·2	2 40·1	1·1	0·2	7·1	1·4	13·1	2·5
12	2 48·0	2 48·5	2 40·3	1·2	0·2	7·2	1·4	13·2	2·5
13	2 48·3	2 48·7	2 40·6	1·3	0·2	7·3	1·4	13·3	2·5
14	2 48·5	2 49·0	2 40·8	1·4	0·3	7·4	1·4	13·4	2·6
15	2 48·8	2 49·2	2 41·1	1·5	0·3	7·5	1·4	13·5	2·6
16	2 49·0	2 49·5	2 41·3	1·6	0·3	7·6	1·5	13·6	2·6
17	2 49·3	2 49·7	2 41·5	1·7	0·3	7·7	1·5	13·7	2·6
18	2 49·5	2 50·0	2 41·8	1·8	0·3	7·8	1·5	13·8	2·6
19	2 49·8	2 50·2	2 42·0	1·9	0·4	7·9	1·5	13·9	2·7
20	2 50·0	2 50·5	2 42·3	2·0	0·4	8·0	1·5	14·0	2·7
21	2 50·3	2 50·7	2 42·5	2·1	0·4	8·1	1·6	14·1	2·7
22	2 50·5	2 51·0	2 42·7	2·2	0·4	8·2	1·6	14·2	2·7
23	2 50·8	2 51·2	2 43·0	2·3	0·4	8·3	1·6	14·3	2·7
24	2 51·0	2 51·5	2 43·2	2·4	0·5	8·4	1·6	14·4	2·8
25	2 51·3	2 51·7	2 43·4	2·5	0·5	8·5	1·6	14·5	2·8
26	2 51·5	2 52·0	2 43·7	2·6	0·5	8·6	1·6	14·6	2·8
27	2 51·8	2 52·2	2 43·9	2·7	0·5	8·7	1·7	14·7	2·8
28	2 52·0	2 52·5	2 44·2	2·8	0·5	8·8	1·7	14·8	2·8
29	2 52·3	2 52·7	2 44·4	2·9	0·6	8·9	1·7	14·9	2·9
30	2 52·5	2 53·0	2 44·6	3·0	0·6	9·0	1·7	15·0	2·9
31	2 52·8	2 53·2	2 44·9	3·1	0·6	9·1	1·7	15·1	2·9
32	2 53·0	2 53·5	2 45·1	3·2	0·6	9·2	1·8	15·2	2·9
33	2 53·3	2 53·7	2 45·4	3·3	0·6	9·3	1·8	15·3	2·9
34	2 53·5	2 54·0	2 45·6	3·4	0·7	9·4	1·8	15·4	3·0
35	2 53·8	2 54·2	2 45·8	3·5	0·7	9·5	1·8	15·5	3·0
36	2 54·0	2 54·5	2 46·1	3·6	0·7	9·6	1·8	15·6	3·0
37	2 54·3	2 54·7	2 46·3	3·7	0·7	9·7	1·9	15·7	3·0
38	2 54·5	2 55·0	2 46·6	3·8	0·7	9·8	1·9	15·8	3·0
39	2 54·8	2 55·2	2 46·8	3·9	0·7	9·9	1·9	15·9	3·0
40	2 55·0	2 55·5	2 47·0	4·0	0·8	10·0	1·9	16·0	3·1
41	2 55·3	2 55·7	2 47·3	4·1	0·8	10·1	1·9	16·1	3·1
42	2 55·5	2 56·0	2 47·5	4·2	0·8	10·2	2·0	16·2	3·1
43	2 55·8	2 56·2	2 47·7	4·3	0·8	10·3	2·0	16·3	3·1
44	2 56·0	2 56·5	2 48·0	4·4	0·8	10·4	2·0	16·4	3·1
45	2 56·3	2 56·7	2 48·2	4·5	0·9	10·5	2·0	16·5	3·2
46	2 56·5	2 57·0	2 48·5	4·6	0·9	10·6	2·0	16·6	3·2
47	2 56·8	2 57·2	2 48·7	4·7	0·9	10·7	2·1	16·7	3·2
48	2 57·0	2 57·5	2 48·9	4·8	0·9	10·8	2·1	16·8	3·2
49	2 57·3	2 57·7	2 49·2	4·9	0·9	10·9	2·1	16·9	3·2
50	2 57·5	2 58·0	2 49·4	5·0	1·0	11·0	2·1	17·0	3·3
51	2 57·8	2 58·2	2 49·7	5·1	1·0	11·1	2·1	17·1	3·3
52	2 58·0	2 58·5	2 49·9	5·2	1·0	11·2	2·1	17·2	3·3
53	2 58·3	2 58·7	2 50·1	5·3	1·0	11·3	2·2	17·3	3·3
54	2 58·5	2 59·0	2 50·4	5·4	1·0	11·4	2·2	17·4	3·3
55	2 58·8	2 59·2	2 50·6	5·5	1·1	11·5	2·2	17·5	3·4
56	2 59·0	2 59·5	2 50·8	5·6	1·1	11·6	2·2	17·6	3·4
57	2 59·3	2 59·7	2 51·1	5·7	1·1	11·7	2·2	17·7	3·4
58	2 59·5	3 00·0	2 51·3	5·8	1·1	11·8	2·3	17·8	3·4
59	2 59·8	3 00·2	2 51·6	5·9	1·1	11·9	2·3	17·9	3·4
60	3 00·0	3 00·5	2 51·8	6·0	1·2	12·0	2·3	18·0	3·5

12ᵐ

m 12 s	SUN PLANETS ° ′	ARIES ° ′	MOON ° ′	v or d ′	Corrⁿ ′	v or d ′	Corrⁿ ′	v or d ′	Corrⁿ ′
00	3 00·0	3 00·5	2 51·8	0·0	0·0	6·0	1·3	12·0	2·5
01	3 00·3	3 00·7	2 52·0	0·1	0·0	6·1	1·3	12·1	2·5
02	3 00·5	3 01·0	2 52·3	0·2	0·0	6·2	1·3	12·2	2·5
03	3 00·8	3 01·2	2 52·5	0·3	0·1	6·3	1·3	12·3	2·6
04	3 01·0	3 01·5	2 52·8	0·4	0·1	6·4	1·3	12·4	2·6
05	3 01·3	3 01·7	2 53·0	0·5	0·1	6·5	1·4	12·5	2·6
06	3 01·5	3 02·0	2 53·2	0·6	0·1	6·6	1·4	12·6	2·6
07	3 01·8	3 02·2	2 53·5	0·7	0·1	6·7	1·4	12·7	2·6
08	3 02·0	3 02·5	2 53·7	0·8	0·2	6·8	1·4	12·8	2·7
09	3 02·3	3 02·7	2 53·9	0·9	0·2	6·9	1·4	12·9	2·7
10	3 02·5	3 03·0	2 54·2	1·0	0·2	7·0	1·5	13·0	2·7
11	3 02·8	3 03·3	2 54·4	1·1	0·2	7·1	1·5	13·1	2·7
12	3 03·0	3 03·5	2 54·7	1·2	0·3	7·2	1·5	13·2	2·8
13	3 03·3	3 03·8	2 54·9	1·3	0·3	7·3	1·5	13·3	2·8
14	3 03·5	3 04·0	2 55·1	1·4	0·3	7·4	1·5	13·4	2·8
15	3 03·8	3 04·3	2 55·4	1·5	0·3	7·5	1·6	13·5	2·8
16	3 04·0	3 04·5	2 55·6	1·6	0·3	7·6	1·6	13·6	2·8
17	3 04·3	3 04·8	2 55·9	1·7	0·4	7·7	1·6	13·7	2·9
18	3 04·5	3 05·0	2 56·1	1·8	0·4	7·8	1·6	13·8	2·9
19	3 04·8	3 05·3	2 56·3	1·9	0·4	7·9	1·6	13·9	2·9
20	3 05·0	3 05·5	2 56·6	2·0	0·4	8·0	1·7	14·0	2·9
21	3 05·3	3 05·8	2 56·8	2·1	0·4	8·1	1·7	14·1	2·9
22	3 05·5	3 06·0	2 57·0	2·2	0·5	8·2	1·7	14·2	3·0
23	3 05·8	3 06·3	2 57·3	2·3	0·5	8·3	1·7	14·3	3·0
24	3 06·0	3 06·5	2 57·5	2·4	0·5	8·4	1·8	14·4	3·0
25	3 06·3	3 06·8	2 57·8	2·5	0·5	8·5	1·8	14·5	3·0
26	3 06·5	3 07·0	2 58·0	2·6	0·5	8·6	1·8	14·6	3·0
27	3 06·8	3 07·3	2 58·2	2·7	0·6	8·7	1·8	14·7	3·1
28	3 07·0	3 07·5	2 58·5	2·8	0·6	8·8	1·8	14·8	3·1
29	3 07·3	3 07·8	2 58·7	2·9	0·6	8·9	1·9	14·9	3·1
30	3 07·5	3 08·0	2 59·0	3·0	0·6	9·0	1·9	15·0	3·1
31	3 07·8	3 08·3	2 59·2	3·1	0·6	9·1	1·9	15·1	3·1
32	3 08·0	3 08·5	2 59·4	3·2	0·7	9·2	1·9	15·2	3·2
33	3 08·3	3 08·8	2 59·7	3·3	0·7	9·3	1·9	15·3	3·2
34	3 08·5	3 09·0	2 59·9	3·4	0·7	9·4	2·0	15·4	3·2
35	3 08·8	3 09·3	3 00·2	3·5	0·7	9·5	2·0	15·5	3·2
36	3 09·0	3 09·5	3 00·4	3·6	0·8	9·6	2·0	15·6	3·3
37	3 09·3	3 09·8	3 00·6	3·7	0·8	9·7	2·0	15·7	3·3
38	3 09·5	3 10·0	3 00·9	3·8	0·8	9·8	2·0	15·8	3·3
39	3 09·8	3 10·3	3 01·1	3·9	0·8	9·9	2·1	15·9	3·3
40	3 10·0	3 10·5	3 01·3	4·0	0·8	10·0	2·1	16·0	3·3
41	3 10·3	3 10·8	3 01·6	4·1	0·9	10·1	2·1	16·1	3·4
42	3 10·5	3 11·0	3 01·8	4·2	0·9	10·2	2·1	16·2	3·4
43	3 10·8	3 11·3	3 02·1	4·3	0·9	10·3	2·1	16·3	3·4
44	3 11·0	3 11·5	3 02·3	4·4	0·9	10·4	2·2	16·4	3·4
45	3 11·3	3 11·8	3 02·5	4·5	0·9	10·5	2·2	16·5	3·4
46	3 11·5	3 12·0	3 02·8	4·6	1·0	10·6	2·2	16·6	3·5
47	3 11·8	3 12·3	3 03·0	4·7	1·0	10·7	2·2	16·7	3·5
48	3 12·0	3 12·5	3 03·3	4·8	1·0	10·8	2·3	16·8	3·5
49	3 12·3	3 12·8	3 03·5	4·9	1·0	10·9	2·3	16·9	3·5
50	3 12·5	3 13·0	3 03·7	5·0	1·0	11·0	2·3	17·0	3·5
51	3 12·8	3 13·3	3 04·0	5·1	1·1	11·1	2·3	17·1	3·6
52	3 13·0	3 13·5	3 04·2	5·2	1·1	11·2	2·3	17·2	3·6
53	3 13·3	3 13·8	3 04·4	5·3	1·1	11·3	2·4	17·3	3·6
54	3 13·5	3 14·0	3 04·7	5·4	1·1	11·4	2·4	17·4	3·6
55	3 13·8	3 14·3	3 04·9	5·5	1·1	11·5	2·4	17·5	3·6
56	3 14·0	3 14·5	3 05·2	5·6	1·2	11·6	2·4	17·6	3·7
57	3 14·3	3 14·8	3 05·4	5·7	1·2	11·7	2·4	17·7	3·7
58	3 14·5	3 15·0	3 05·6	5·8	1·2	11·8	2·5	17·8	3·7
59	3 14·8	3 15·3	3 05·9	5·9	1·2	11·9	2·5	17·9	3·7
60	3 15·0	3 15·5	3 06·1	6·0	1·3	12·0	2·5	18·0	3·8

13ᵐ

m 13 s	SUN PLANETS ° ′	ARIES ° ′	MOON ° ′	v or d ′	Corrⁿ ′	v or d ′	Corrⁿ ′	v or d ′	Corrⁿ ′
00	3 15·0	3 15·5	3 06·1	0·0	0·0	6·0	1·4	12·0	2·7
01	3 15·3	3 15·8	3 06·4	0·1	0·0	6·1	1·4	12·1	2·7
02	3 15·5	3 16·0	3 06·6	0·2	0·0	6·2	1·4	12·2	2·7
03	3 15·8	3 16·3	3 06·8	0·3	0·1	6·3	1·4	12·3	2·8
04	3 16·0	3 16·5	3 07·1	0·4	0·1	6·4	1·4	12·4	2·8
05	3 16·3	3 16·8	3 07·3	0·5	0·1	6·5	1·5	12·5	2·8
06	3 16·5	3 17·0	3 07·5	0·6	0·1	6·6	1·5	12·6	2·8
07	3 16·8	3 17·3	3 07·8	0·7	0·2	6·7	1·5	12·7	2·9
08	3 17·0	3 17·5	3 08·0	0·8	0·2	6·8	1·5	12·8	2·9
09	3 17·3	3 17·8	3 08·3	0·9	0·2	6·9	1·6	12·9	2·9
10	3 17·5	3 18·0	3 08·5	1·0	0·2	7·0	1·6	13·0	2·9
11	3 17·8	3 18·3	3 08·7	1·1	0·2	7·1	1·6	13·1	2·9
12	3 18·0	3 18·5	3 09·0	1·2	0·3	7·2	1·6	13·2	3·0
13	3 18·3	3 18·8	3 09·2	1·3	0·3	7·3	1·6	13·3	3·0
14	3 18·5	3 19·0	3 09·5	1·4	0·3	7·4	1·7	13·4	3·0
15	3 18·8	3 19·3	3 09·7	1·5	0·3	7·5	1·7	13·5	3·0
16	3 19·0	3 19·5	3 09·9	1·6	0·4	7·6	1·7	13·6	3·1
17	3 19·3	3 19·8	3 10·2	1·7	0·4	7·7	1·7	13·7	3·1
18	3 19·5	3 20·0	3 10·4	1·8	0·4	7·8	1·8	13·8	3·1
19	3 19·8	3 20·3	3 10·7	1·9	0·4	7·9	1·8	13·9	3·1
20	3 20·0	3 20·5	3 10·9	2·0	0·5	8·0	1·8	14·0	3·2
21	3 20·3	3 20·8	3 11·1	2·1	0·5	8·1	1·8	14·1	3·2
22	3 20·5	3 21·0	3 11·4	2·2	0·5	8·2	1·8	14·2	3·2
23	3 20·8	3 21·3	3 11·6	2·3	0·5	8·3	1·9	14·3	3·2
24	3 21·0	3 21·6	3 11·8	2·4	0·5	8·4	1·9	14·4	3·2
25	3 21·3	3 21·8	3 12·1	2·5	0·6	8·5	1·9	14·5	3·3
26	3 21·5	3 22·1	3 12·3	2·6	0·6	8·6	1·9	14·6	3·3
27	3 21·8	3 22·3	3 12·6	2·7	0·6	8·7	2·0	14·7	3·3
28	3 22·0	3 22·6	3 12·8	2·8	0·6	8·8	2·0	14·8	3·3
29	3 22·3	3 22·8	3 13·0	2·9	0·7	8·9	2·0	14·9	3·4
30	3 22·5	3 23·1	3 13·3	3·0	0·7	9·0	2·0	15·0	3·4
31	3 22·8	3 23·3	3 13·5	3·1	0·7	9·1	2·0	15·1	3·4
32	3 23·0	3 23·6	3 13·8	3·2	0·7	9·2	2·1	15·2	3·4
33	3 23·3	3 23·8	3 14·0	3·3	0·7	9·3	2·1	15·3	3·4
34	3 23·5	3 24·1	3 14·2	3·4	0·8	9·4	2·1	15·4	3·5
35	3 23·8	3 24·3	3 14·5	3·5	0·8	9·5	2·1	15·5	3·5
36	3 24·0	3 24·6	3 14·7	3·6	0·8	9·6	2·2	15·6	3·5
37	3 24·3	3 24·8	3 14·9	3·7	0·8	9·7	2·2	15·7	3·5
38	3 24·5	3 25·1	3 15·2	3·8	0·9	9·8	2·2	15·8	3·6
39	3 24·8	3 25·3	3 15·4	3·9	0·9	9·9	2·2	15·9	3·6
40	3 25·0	3 25·6	3 15·7	4·0	0·9	10·0	2·3	16·0	3·6
41	3 25·3	3 25·8	3 15·9	4·1	0·9	10·1	2·3	16·1	3·6
42	3 25·5	3 26·1	3 16·1	4·2	0·9	10·2	2·3	16·2	3·6
43	3 25·8	3 26·3	3 16·4	4·3	1·0	10·3	2·3	16·3	3·7
44	3 26·0	3 26·6	3 16·6	4·4	1·0	10·4	2·3	16·4	3·7
45	3 26·3	3 26·8	3 16·9	4·5	1·0	10·5	2·4	16·5	3·7
46	3 26·5	3 27·1	3 17·1	4·6	1·0	10·6	2·4	16·6	3·7
47	3 26·8	3 27·3	3 17·3	4·7	1·1	10·7	2·4	16·7	3·8
48	3 27·0	3 27·6	3 17·6	4·8	1·1	10·8	2·4	16·8	3·8
49	3 27·3	3 27·8	3 17·8	4·9	1·1	10·9	2·5	16·9	3·8
50	3 27·5	3 28·1	3 18·0	5·0	1·1	11·0	2·5	17·0	3·8
51	3 27·8	3 28·3	3 18·3	5·1	1·1	11·1	2·5	17·1	3·8
52	3 28·0	3 28·6	3 18·5	5·2	1·2	11·2	2·5	17·2	3·9
53	3 28·3	3 28·8	3 18·8	5·3	1·2	11·3	2·5	17·3	3·9
54	3 28·5	3 29·1	3 19·0	5·4	1·2	11·4	2·6	17·4	3·9
55	3 28·8	3 29·3	3 19·2	5·5	1·2	11·5	2·6	17·5	3·9
56	3 29·0	3 29·6	3 19·5	5·6	1·3	11·6	2·6	17·6	4·0
57	3 29·3	3 29·8	3 19·7	5·7	1·3	11·7	2·6	17·7	4·0
58	3 29·5	3 30·1	3 20·0	5·8	1·3	11·8	2·7	17·8	4·0
59	3 29·8	3 30·3	3 20·2	5·9	1·3	11·9	2·7	17·9	4·0
60	3 30·0	3 30·6	3 20·4	6·0	1·4	12·0	2·7	18·0	4·1

14^m	SUN PLANETS	ARIES	MOON	v or d	Corrⁿ	v or d	Corrⁿ	v or d	Corrⁿ
s	° ′	° ′	° ′	′	′	′	′	′	′
00	3 30·0	3 30·6	3 20·4	0·0	0·0	6·0	1·5	12·0	2·9
01	3 30·3	3 30·8	3 20·7	0·1	0·0	6·1	1·5	12·1	2·9
02	3 30·5	3 31·1	3 20·9	0·2	0·0	6·2	1·5	12·2	2·9
03	3 30·8	3 31·3	3 21·1	0·3	0·1	6·3	1·5	12·3	3·0
04	3 31·0	3 31·6	3 21·4	0·4	0·1	6·4	1·5	12·4	3·0
05	3 31·3	3 31·8	3 21·6	0·5	0·1	6·5	1·6	12·5	3·0
06	3 31·5	3 32·1	3 21·9	0·6	0·1	6·6	1·6	12·6	3·0
07	3 31·8	3 32·3	3 22·1	0·7	0·2	6·7	1·6	12·7	3·1
08	3 32·0	3 32·6	3 22·3	0·8	0·2	6·8	1·6	12·8	3·1
09	3 32·3	3 32·8	3 22·6	0·9	0·2	6·9	1·7	12·9	3·1
10	3 32·5	3 33·1	3 22·8	1·0	0·2	7·0	1·7	13·0	3·1
11	3 32·8	3 33·3	3 23·1	1·1	0·3	7·1	1·7	13·1	3·2
12	3 33·0	3 33·6	3 23·3	1·2	0·3	7·2	1·7	13·2	3·2
13	3 33·3	3 33·8	3 23·5	1·3	0·3	7·3	1·8	13·3	3·2
14	3 33·5	3 34·1	3 23·8	1·4	0·3	7·4	1·8	13·4	3·2
15	3 33·8	3 34·3	3 24·0	1·5	0·4	7·5	1·8	13·5	3·3
16	3 34·0	3 34·6	3 24·3	1·6	0·4	7·6	1·8	13·6	3·3
17	3 34·3	3 34·8	3 24·5	1·7	0·4	7·7	1·9	13·7	3·3
18	3 34·5	3 35·1	3 24·7	1·8	0·4	7·8	1·9	13·8	3·3
19	3 34·8	3 35·3	3 25·0	1·9	0·5	7·9	1·9	13·9	3·4
20	3 35·0	3 35·6	3 25·2	2·0	0·5	8·0	1·9	14·0	3·4
21	3 35·3	3 35·8	3 25·4	2·1	0·5	8·1	2·0	14·1	3·4
22	3 35·5	3 36·1	3 25·7	2·2	0·5	8·2	2·0	14·2	3·4
23	3 35·8	3 36·3	3 25·9	2·3	0·6	8·3	2·0	14·3	3·5
24	3 36·0	3 36·6	3 26·2	2·4	0·6	8·4	2·0	14·4	3·5
25	3 36·3	3 36·8	3 26·4	2·5	0·6	8·5	2·1	14·5	3·5
26	3 36·5	3 37·1	3 26·6	2·6	0·6	8·6	2·1	14·6	3·5
27	3 36·8	3 37·3	3 26·9	2·7	0·7	8·7	2·1	14·7	3·6
28	3 37·0	3 37·6	3 27·1	2·8	0·7	8·8	2·1	14·8	3·6
29	3 37·3	3 37·8	3 27·4	2·9	0·7	8·9	2·2	14·9	3·6
30	3 37·5	3 38·1	3 27·6	3·0	0·7	9·0	2·2	15·0	3·6
31	3 37·8	3 38·3	3 27·8	3·1	0·7	9·1	2·2	15·1	3·6
32	3 38·0	3 38·6	3 28·1	3·2	0·8	9·2	2·2	15·2	3·7
33	3 38·3	3 38·8	3 28·3	3·3	0·8	9·3	2·2	15·3	3·7
34	3 38·5	3 39·1	3 28·5	3·4	0·8	9·4	2·3	15·4	3·7
35	3 38·8	3 39·3	3 28·8	3·5	0·8	9·5	2·3	15·5	3·7
36	3 39·0	3 39·6	3 29·0	3·6	0·9	9·6	2·3	15·6	3·8
37	3 39·3	3 39·9	3 29·3	3·7	0·9	9·7	2·3	15·7	3·8
38	3 39·5	3 40·1	3 29·5	3·8	0·9	9·8	2·4	15·8	3·8
39	3 39·8	3 40·4	3 29·7	3·9	0·9	9·9	2·4	15·9	3·8
40	3 40·0	3 40·6	3 30·0	4·0	1·0	10·0	2·4	16·0	3·9
41	3 40·3	3 40·9	3 30·2	4·1	1·0	10·1	2·4	16·1	3·9
42	3 40·5	3 41·1	3 30·5	4·2	1·0	10·2	2·5	16·2	3·9
43	3 40·8	3 41·4	3 30·7	4·3	1·0	10·3	2·5	16·3	3·9
44	3 41·0	3 41·6	3 30·9	4·4	1·1	10·4	2·5	16·4	4·0
45	3 41·3	3 41·9	3 31·2	4·5	1·1	10·5	2·5	16·5	4·0
46	3 41·5	3 42·1	3 31·4	4·6	1·1	10·6	2·6	16·6	4·0
47	3 41·8	3 42·4	3 31·6	4·7	1·1	10·7	2·6	16·7	4·0
48	3 42·0	3 42·6	3 31·9	4·8	1·2	10·8	2·6	16·8	4·1
49	3 42·3	3 42·9	3 32·1	4·9	1·2	10·9	2·6	16·9	4·1
50	3 42·5	3 43·1	3 32·4	5·0	1·2	11·0	2·7	17·0	4·1
51	3 42·8	3 43·4	3 32·6	5·1	1·2	11·1	2·7	17·1	4·1
52	3 43·0	3 43·6	3 32·8	5·2	1·3	11·2	2·7	17·2	4·2
53	3 43·3	3 43·9	3 33·1	5·3	1·3	11·3	2·7	17·3	4·2
54	3 43·5	3 44·1	3 33·3	5·4	1·3	11·4	2·8	17·4	4·2
55	3 43·8	3 44·4	3 33·6	5·5	1·3	11·5	2·8	17·5	4·2
56	3 44·0	3 44·6	3 33·8	5·6	1·4	11·6	2·8	17·6	4·3
57	3 44·3	3 44·9	3 34·0	5·7	1·4	11·7	2·8	17·7	4·3
58	3 44·5	3 45·1	3 34·3	5·8	1·4	11·8	2·9	17·8	4·3
59	3 44·8	3 45·4	3 34·5	5·9	1·4	11·9	2·9	17·9	4·3
60	3 45·0	3 45·6	3 34·8	6·0	1·5	12·0	2·9	18·0	4·4

15^m	SUN PLANETS	ARIES	MOON	v or d	Corrⁿ	v or d	Corrⁿ	v or d	Corrⁿ
s	° ′	° ′	° ′	′	′	′	′	′	′
00	3 45·0	3 45·6	3 34·8	0·0	0·0	6·0	1·6	12·0	3·1
01	3 45·3	3 45·9	3 35·0	0·1	0·0	6·1	1·6	12·1	3·1
02	3 45·5	3 46·1	3 35·2	0·2	0·1	6·2	1·6	12·2	3·2
03	3 45·8	3 46·4	3 35·5	0·3	0·1	6·3	1·6	12·3	3·2
04	3 46·0	3 46·6	3 35·7	0·4	0·1	6·4	1·7	12·4	3·2
05	3 46·3	3 46·9	3 35·9	0·5	0·1	6·5	1·7	12·5	3·2
06	3 46·5	3 47·1	3 36·2	0·6	0·2	6·6	1·7	12·6	3·3
07	3 46·8	3 47·4	3 36·4	0·7	0·2	6·7	1·7	12·7	3·3
08	3 47·0	3 47·6	3 36·7	0·8	0·2	6·8	1·8	12·8	3·3
09	3 47·3	3 47·9	3 36·9	0·9	0·2	6·9	1·8	12·9	3·3
10	3 47·5	3 48·1	3 37·1	1·0	0·3	7·0	1·8	13·0	3·4
11	3 47·8	3 48·4	3 37·4	1·1	0·3	7·1	1·8	13·1	3·4
12	3 48·0	3 48·6	3 37·6	1·2	0·3	7·2	1·9	13·2	3·4
13	3 48·3	3 48·9	3 37·9	1·3	0·3	7·3	1·9	13·3	3·4
14	3 48·5	3 49·1	3 38·1	1·4	0·4	7·4	1·9	13·4	3·5
15	3 48·8	3 49·4	3 38·3	1·5	0·4	7·5	1·9	13·5	3·5
16	3 49·0	3 49·6	3 38·6	1·6	0·4	7·6	2·0	13·6	3·5
17	3 49·3	3 49·9	3 38·8	1·7	0·4	7·7	2·0	13·7	3·5
18	3 49·5	3 50·1	3 39·0	1·8	0·5	7·8	2·0	13·8	3·6
19	3 49·8	3 50·4	3 39·3	1·9	0·5	7·9	2·0	13·9	3·6
20	3 50·0	3 50·6	3 39·5	2·0	0·5	8·0	2·1	14·0	3·6
21	3 50·3	3 50·9	3 39·8	2·1	0·5	8·1	2·1	14·1	3·6
22	3 50·5	3 51·1	3 40·0	2·2	0·6	8·2	2·1	14·2	3·7
23	3 50·8	3 51·4	3 40·2	2·3	0·6	8·3	2·1	14·3	3·7
24	3 51·0	3 51·6	3 40·5	2·4	0·6	8·4	2·2	14·4	3·7
25	3 51·3	3 51·9	3 40·7	2·5	0·6	8·5	2·2	14·5	3·7
26	3 51·5	3 52·1	3 41·0	2·6	0·7	8·6	2·2	14·6	3·8
27	3 51·8	3 52·4	3 41·2	2·7	0·7	8·7	2·2	14·7	3·8
28	3 52·0	3 52·6	3 41·4	2·8	0·7	8·8	2·3	14·8	3·8
29	3 52·3	3 52·9	3 41·7	2·9	0·7	8·9	2·3	14·9	3·8
30	3 52·5	3 53·1	3 41·9	3·0	0·8	9·0	2·3	15·0	3·9
31	3 52·8	3 53·4	3 42·1	3·1	0·8	9·1	2·4	15·1	3·9
32	3 53·0	3 53·6	3 42·4	3·2	0·8	9·2	2·4	15·2	3·9
33	3 53·3	3 53·9	3 42·6	3·3	0·9	9·3	2·4	15·3	4·0
34	3 53·5	3 54·1	3 42·9	3·4	0·9	9·4	2·4	15·4	4·0
35	3 53·8	3 54·4	3 43·1	3·5	0·9	9·5	2·5	15·5	4·0
36	3 54·0	3 54·6	3 43·3	3·6	0·9	9·6	2·5	15·6	4·0
37	3 54·3	3 54·9	3 43·6	3·7	1·0	9·7	2·5	15·7	4·1
38	3 54·5	3 55·1	3 43·8	3·8	1·0	9·8	2·5	15·8	4·1
39	3 54·8	3 55·4	3 44·1	3·9	1·0	9·9	2·6	15·9	4·1
40	3 55·0	3 55·6	3 44·3	4·0	1·0	10·0	2·6	16·0	4·1
41	3 55·3	3 55·9	3 44·5	4·1	1·1	10·1	2·6	16·1	4·2
42	3 55·5	3 56·1	3 44·8	4·2	1·1	10·2	2·6	16·2	4·2
43	3 55·8	3 56·4	3 45·0	4·3	1·1	10·3	2·7	16·3	4·2
44	3 56·0	3 56·6	3 45·2	4·4	1·1	10·4	2·7	16·4	4·2
45	3 56·3	3 56·9	3 45·5	4·5	1·2	10·5	2·7	16·5	4·3
46	3 56·5	3 57·1	3 45·7	4·6	1·2	10·6	2·7	16·6	4·3
47	3 56·8	3 57·4	3 46·0	4·7	1·2	10·7	2·8	16·7	4·3
48	3 57·0	3 57·6	3 46·2	4·8	1·2	10·8	2·8	16·8	4·3
49	3 57·3	3 57·9	3 46·4	4·9	1·3	10·9	2·8	16·9	4·4
50	3 57·5	3 58·2	3 46·7	5·0	1·3	11·0	2·8	17·0	4·4
51	3 57·8	3 58·4	3 46·9	5·1	1·3	11·1	2·9	17·1	4·4
52	3 58·0	3 58·7	3 47·2	5·2	1·3	11·2	2·9	17·2	4·4
53	3 58·3	3 58·9	3 47·4	5·3	1·4	11·3	2·9	17·3	4·5
54	3 58·5	3 59·2	3 47·6	5·4	1·4	11·4	2·9	17·4	4·5
55	3 58·8	3 59·4	3 47·9	5·5	1·4	11·5	3·0	17·5	4·5
56	3 59·0	3 59·7	3 48·1	5·6	1·4	11·6	3·0	17·6	4·5
57	3 59·3	3 59·9	3 48·4	5·7	1·5	11·7	3·0	17·7	4·6
58	3 59·5	4 00·2	3 48·6	5·8	1·5	11·8	3·0	17·8	4·6
59	3 59·8	4 00·4	3 48·8	5·9	1·5	11·9	3·1	17·9	4·6
60	4 00·0	4 00·7	3 49·1	6·0	1·6	12·0	3·1	18·0	4·7

ix

16 m	SUN PLANETS	ARIES	MOON	v or Corrⁿ d		v or Corrⁿ d		v or Corrⁿ d	
s	° ′	° ′	° ′	′	′	′	′	′	′
00	4 00·0	4 00·7	3 49·1	0·0	0·0	6·0	1·7	12·0	3·3
01	4 00·3	4 00·9	3 49·3	0·1	0·0	6·1	1·7	12·1	3·3
02	4 00·5	4 01·2	3 49·5	0·2	0·1	6·2	1·7	12·2	3·4
03	4 00·8	4 01·4	3 49·8	0·3	0·1	6·3	1·7	12·3	3·4
04	4 01·0	4 01·7	3 50·0	0·4	0·1	6·4	1·8	12·4	3·4
05	4 01·3	4 01·9	3 50·3	0·5	0·1	6·5	1·8	12·5	3·4
06	4 01·5	4 02·2	3 50·5	0·6	0·2	6·6	1·8	12·6	3·5
07	4 01·8	4 02·4	3 50·7	0·7	0·2	6·7	1·8	12·7	3·5
08	4 02·0	4 02·7	3 51·0	0·8	0·2	6·8	1·9	12·8	3·5
09	4 02·3	4 02·9	3 51·2	0·9	0·2	6·9	1·9	12·9	3·5
10	4 02·5	4 03·2	3 51·5	1·0	0·3	7·0	1·9	13·0	3·6
11	4 02·8	4 03·4	3 51·7	1·1	0·3	7·1	2·0	13·1	3·6
12	4 03·0	4 03·7	3 51·9	1·2	0·3	7·2	2·0	13·2	3·6
13	4 03·3	4 03·9	3 52·2	1·3	0·4	7·3	2·0	13·3	3·7
14	4 03·5	4 04·2	3 52·4	1·4	0·4	7·4	2·0	13·4	3·7
15	4 03·8	4 04·4	3 52·6	1·5	0·4	7·5	2·1	13·5	3·7
16	4 04·0	4 04·7	3 52·9	1·6	0·4	7·6	2·1	13·6	3·7
17	4 04·3	4 04·9	3 53·1	1·7	0·5	7·7	2·1	13·7	3·8
18	4 04·5	4 05·2	3 53·4	1·8	0·5	7·8	2·1	13·8	3·8
19	4 04·8	4 05·4	3 53·6	1·9	0·5	7·9	2·2	13·9	3·8
20	4 05·0	4 05·7	3 53·8	2·0	0·6	8·0	2·2	14·0	3·9
21	4 05·3	4 05·9	3 54·1	2·1	0·6	8·1	2·2	14·1	3·9
22	4 05·5	4 06·2	3 54·3	2·2	0·6	8·2	2·3	14·2	3·9
23	4 05·8	4 06·4	3 54·6	2·3	0·6	8·3	2·3	14·3	3·9
24	4 06·0	4 06·7	3 54·8	2·4	0·7	8·4	2·3	14·4	4·0
25	4 06·3	4 06·9	3 55·0	2·5	0·7	8·5	2·3	14·5	4·0
26	4 06·5	4 07·2	3 55·3	2·6	0·7	8·6	2·4	14·6	4·0
27	4 06·8	4 07·4	3 55·5	2·7	0·7	8·7	2·4	14·7	4·0
28	4 07·0	4 07·7	3 55·7	2·8	0·8	8·8	2·4	14·8	4·1
29	4 07·3	4 07·9	3 56·0	2·9	0·8	8·9	2·4	14·9	4·1
30	4 07·5	4 08·2	3 56·2	3·0	0·8	9·0	2·5	15·0	4·1
31	4 07·8	4 08·4	3 56·5	3·1	0·9	9·1	2·5	15·1	4·2
32	4 08·0	4 08·7	3 56·7	3·2	0·9	9·2	2·5	15·2	4·2
33	4 08·3	4 08·9	3 56·9	3·3	0·9	9·3	2·6	15·3	4·2
34	4 08·5	4 09·2	3 57·2	3·4	0·9	9·4	2·6	15·4	4·2
35	4 08·8	4 09·4	3 57·4	3·5	1·0	9·5	2·6	15·5	4·3
36	4 09·0	4 09·7	3 57·7	3·6	1·0	9·6	2·6	15·6	4·3
37	4 09·3	4 09·9	3 57·9	3·7	1·0	9·7	2·7	15·7	4·3
38	4 09·5	4 10·2	3 58·1	3·8	1·0	9·8	2·7	15·8	4·3
39	4 09·8	4 10·4	3 58·4	3·9	1·1	9·9	2·7	15·9	4·4
40	4 10·0	4 10·7	3 58·6	4·0	1·1	10·0	2·8	16·0	4·4
41	4 10·3	4 10·9	3 58·8	4·1	1·1	10·1	2·8	16·1	4·4
42	4 10·5	4 11·2	3 59·1	4·2	1·2	10·2	2·8	16·2	4·5
43	4 10·8	4 11·4	3 59·3	4·3	1·2	10·3	2·8	16·3	4·5
44	4 11·0	4 11·7	3 59·6	4·4	1·2	10·4	2·9	16·4	4·5
45	4 11·3	4 11·9	3 59·8	4·5	1·2	10·5	2·9	16·5	4·5
46	4 11·5	4 12·2	4 00·0	4·6	1·3	10·6	2·9	16·6	4·6
47	4 11·8	4 12·4	4 00·3	4·7	1·3	10·7	2·9	16·7	4·6
48	4 12·0	4 12·7	4 00·5	4·8	1·3	10·8	3·0	16·8	4·6
49	4 12·3	4 12·9	4 00·8	4·9	1·3	10·9	3·0	16·9	4·6
50	4 12·5	4 13·2	4 01·0	5·0	1·4	11·0	3·0	17·0	4·7
51	4 12·8	4 13·4	4 01·2	5·1	1·4	11·1	3·1	17·1	4·7
52	4 13·0	4 13·7	4 01·5	5·2	1·4	11·2	3·1	17·2	4·7
53	4 13·3	4 13·9	4 01·7	5·3	1·5	11·3	3·1	17·3	4·8
54	4 13·5	4 14·2	4 02·0	5·4	1·5	11·4	3·1	17·4	4·8
55	4 13·8	4 14·4	4 02·2	5·5	1·5	11·5	3·2	17·5	4·8
56	4 14·0	4 14·7	4 02·4	5·6	1·5	11·6	3·2	17·6	4·8
57	4 14·3	4 14·9	4 02·7	5·7	1·6	11·7	3·2	17·7	4·9
58	4 14·5	4 15·2	4 02·9	5·8	1·6	11·8	3·2	17·8	4·9
59	4 14·8	4 15·4	4 03·1	5·9	1·6	11·9	3·3	17·9	4·9
60	4 15·0	4 15·7	4 03·4	6·0	1·7	12·0	3·3	18·0	5·0

17 m	SUN PLANETS	ARIES	MOON	v or Corrⁿ d		v or Corrⁿ d		v or Corrⁿ d	
s	° ′	° ′	° ′	′	′	′	′	′	′
00	4 15·0	4 15·7	4 03·4	0·0	0·0	6·0	1·8	12·0	3·5
01	4 15·3	4 15·9	4 03·6	0·1	0·0	6·1	1·8	12·1	3·5
02	4 15·5	4 16·2	4 03·9	0·2	0·1	6·2	1·8	12·2	3·6
03	4 15·8	4 16·5	4 04·1	0·3	0·1	6·3	1·8	12·3	3·6
04	4 16·0	4 16·7	4 04·3	0·4	0·1	6·4	1·9	12·4	3·6
05	4 16·3	4 17·0	4 04·6	0·5	0·1	6·5	1·9	12·5	3·6
06	4 16·5	4 17·2	4 04·8	0·6	0·2	6·6	1·9	12·6	3·7
07	4 16·8	4 17·5	4 05·1	0·7	0·2	6·7	2·0	12·7	3·7
08	4 17·0	4 17·7	4 05·3	0·8	0·2	6·8	2·0	12·8	3·7
09	4 17·3	4 18·0	4 05·5	0·9	0·3	6·9	2·0	12·9	3·8
10	4 17·5	4 18·2	4 05·8	1·0	0·3	7·0	2·0	13·0	3·8
11	4 17·8	4 18·5	4 06·0	1·1	0·3	7·1	2·1	13·1	3·8
12	4 18·0	4 18·7	4 06·2	1·2	0·4	7·2	2·1	13·2	3·9
13	4 18·3	4 19·0	4 06·5	1·3	0·4	7·3	2·1	13·3	3·9
14	4 18·5	4 19·2	4 06·7	1·4	0·4	7·4	2·2	13·4	3·9
15	4 18·8	4 19·5	4 07·0	1·5	0·4	7·5	2·2	13·5	3·9
16	4 19·0	4 19·7	4 07·2	1·6	0·5	7·6	2·2	13·6	4·0
17	4 19·3	4 20·0	4 07·4	1·7	0·5	7·7	2·2	13·7	4·0
18	4 19·5	4 20·2	4 07·7	1·8	0·5	7·8	2·3	13·8	4·0
19	4 19·8	4 20·5	4 07·9	1·9	0·6	7·9	2·3	13·9	4·1
20	4 20·0	4 20·7	4 08·2	2·0	0·6	8·0	2·3	14·0	4·1
21	4 20·3	4 21·0	4 08·4	2·1	0·6	8·1	2·4	14·1	4·1
22	4 20·5	4 21·2	4 08·6	2·2	0·6	8·2	2·4	14·2	4·1
23	4 20·8	4 21·5	4 08·9	2·3	0·7	8·3	2·4	14·3	4·2
24	4 21·0	4 21·7	4 09·1	2·4	0·7	8·4	2·5	14·4	4·2
25	4 21·3	4 22·0	4 09·3	2·5	0·7	8·5	2·5	14·5	4·2
26	4 21·5	4 22·2	4 09·6	2·6	0·8	8·6	2·5	14·6	4·3
27	4 21·8	4 22·5	4 09·8	2·7	0·8	8·7	2·5	14·7	4·3
28	4 22·0	4 22·7	4 10·1	2·8	0·8	8·8	2·6	14·8	4·3
29	4 22·3	4 23·0	4 10·3	2·9	0·8	8·9	2·6	14·9	4·3
30	4 22·5	4 23·2	4 10·5	3·0	0·9	9·0	2·6	15·0	4·4
31	4 22·8	4 23·5	4 10·8	3·1	0·9	9·1	2·7	15·1	4·4
32	4 23·0	4 23·7	4 11·0	3·2	0·9	9·2	2·7	15·2	4·4
33	4 23·3	4 24·0	4 11·3	3·3	1·0	9·3	2·7	15·3	4·5
34	4 23·5	4 24·2	4 11·5	3·4	1·0	9·4	2·7	15·4	4·5
35	4 23·8	4 24·5	4 11·7	3·5	1·0	9·5	2·8	15·5	4·5
36	4 24·0	4 24·7	4 12·0	3·6	1·1	9·6	2·8	15·6	4·6
37	4 24·3	4 25·0	4 12·2	3·7	1·1	9·7	2·8	15·7	4·6
38	4 24·5	4 25·2	4 12·5	3·8	1·1	9·8	2·9	15·8	4·6
39	4 24·8	4 25·5	4 12·7	3·9	1·1	9·9	2·9	15·9	4·6
40	4 25·0	4 25·7	4 12·9	4·0	1·2	10·0	2·9	16·0	4·7
41	4 25·3	4 26·0	4 13·2	4·1	1·2	10·1	2·9	16·1	4·7
42	4 25·5	4 26·2	4 13·4	4·2	1·2	10·2	3·0	16·2	4·7
43	4 25·8	4 26·5	4 13·6	4·3	1·3	10·3	3·0	16·3	4·8
44	4 26·0	4 26·7	4 13·9	4·4	1·3	10·4	3·0	16·4	4·8
45	4 26·3	4 27·0	4 14·1	4·5	1·3	10·5	3·1	16·5	4·8
46	4 26·5	4 27·2	4 14·4	4·6	1·3	10·6	3·1	16·6	4·8
47	4 26·8	4 27·5	4 14·6	4·7	1·4	10·7	3·1	16·7	4·9
48	4 27·0	4 27·7	4 14·8	4·8	1·4	10·8	3·2	16·8	4·9
49	4 27·3	4 28·0	4 15·1	4·9	1·4	10·9	3·2	16·9	4·9
50	4 27·5	4 28·2	4 15·3	5·0	1·5	11·0	3·2	17·0	5·0
51	4 27·8	4 28·5	4 15·6	5·1	1·5	11·1	3·2	17·1	5·0
52	4 28·0	4 28·7	4 15·8	5·2	1·5	11·2	3·3	17·2	5·0
53	4 28·3	4 29·0	4 16·0	5·3	1·5	11·3	3·3	17·3	5·0
54	4 28·5	4 29·2	4 16·3	5·4	1·6	11·4	3·3	17·4	5·1
55	4 28·8	4 29·5	4 16·5	5·5	1·6	11·5	3·4	17·5	5·1
56	4 29·0	4 29·7	4 16·7	5·6	1·6	11·6	3·4	17·6	5·1
57	4 29·3	4 30·0	4 17·0	5·7	1·7	11·7	3·4	17·7	5·2
58	4 29·5	4 30·2	4 17·2	5·8	1·7	11·8	3·4	17·8	5·2
59	4 29·8	4 30·5	4 17·5	5·9	1·7	11·9	3·5	17·9	5·2
60	4 30·0	4 30·7	4 17·7	6·0	1·8	12·0	3·5	18·0	5·3

x

18ᵐ

m 18 s	SUN PLANETS	ARIES	MOON	v or d	Corrⁿ	v or d	Corrⁿ	v or d	Corrⁿ
00	4 30·0	4 30·7	4 17·7	0·0	0·0	6·0	1·9	12·0	3·7
01	4 30·3	4 31·0	4 17·9	0·1	0·0	6·1	1·9	12·1	3·7
02	4 30·5	4 31·2	4 18·2	0·2	0·1	6·2	1·9	12·2	3·8
03	4 30·8	4 31·5	4 18·4	0·3	0·1	6·3	1·9	12·3	3·8
04	4 31·0	4 31·7	4 18·7	0·4	0·1	6·4	2·0	12·4	3·8
05	4 31·3	4 32·0	4 18·9	0·5	0·2	6·5	2·0	12·5	3·9
06	4 31·5	4 32·2	4 19·1	0·6	0·2	6·6	2·0	12·6	3·9
07	4 31·8	4 32·5	4 19·4	0·7	0·2	6·7	2·1	12·7	3·9
08	4 32·0	4 32·7	4 19·6	0·8	0·2	6·8	2·1	12·8	3·9
09	4 32·3	4 33·0	4 19·8	0·9	0·3	6·9	2·1	12·9	4·0
10	4 32·5	4 33·2	4 20·1	1·0	0·3	7·0	2·2	13·0	4·0
11	4 32·8	4 33·5	4 20·3	1·1	0·3	7·1	2·2	13·1	4·0
12	4 33·0	4 33·7	4 20·6	1·2	0·4	7·2	2·2	13·2	4·1
13	4 33·3	4 34·0	4 20·8	1·3	0·4	7·3	2·3	13·3	4·1
14	4 33·5	4 34·2	4 21·0	1·4	0·4	7·4	2·3	13·4	4·1
15	4 33·8	4 34·5	4 21·3	1·5	0·5	7·5	2·3	13·5	4·2
16	4 34·0	4 34·8	4 21·5	1·6	0·5	7·6	2·3	13·6	4·2
17	4 34·3	4 35·0	4 21·8	1·7	0·5	7·7	2·4	13·7	4·2
18	4 34·5	4 35·3	4 22·0	1·8	0·6	7·8	2·4	13·8	4·3
19	4 34·8	4 35·5	4 22·2	1·9	0·6	7·9	2·4	13·9	4·3
20	4 35·0	4 35·8	4 22·5	2·0	0·6	8·0	2·5	14·0	4·3
21	4 35·3	4 36·0	4 22·7	2·1	0·6	8·1	2·5	14·1	4·3
22	4 35·5	4 36·3	4 22·9	2·2	0·7	8·2	2·5	14·2	4·4
23	4 35·8	4 36·5	4 23·2	2·3	0·7	8·3	2·6	14·3	4·4
24	4 36·0	4 36·8	4 23·4	2·4	0·7	8·4	2·6	14·4	4·4
25	4 36·3	4 37·0	4 23·7	2·5	0·8	8·5	2·6	14·5	4·5
26	4 36·5	4 37·3	4 23·9	2·6	0·8	8·6	2·7	14·6	4·5
27	4 36·8	4 37·5	4 24·1	2·7	0·8	8·7	2·7	14·7	4·5
28	4 37·0	4 37·8	4 24·4	2·8	0·9	8·8	2·7	14·8	4·6
29	4 37·3	4 38·0	4 24·6	2·9	0·9	8·9	2·7	14·9	4·6
30	4 37·5	4 38·3	4 24·9	3·0	0·9	9·0	2·8	15·0	4·6
31	4 37·8	4 38·5	4 25·1	3·1	1·0	9·1	2·8	15·1	4·7
32	4 38·0	4 38·8	4 25·3	3·2	1·0	9·2	2·8	15·2	4·7
33	4 38·3	4 39·0	4 25·6	3·3	1·0	9·3	2·9	15·3	4·7
34	4 38·5	4 39·3	4 25·8	3·4	1·0	9·4	2·9	15·4	4·7
35	4 38·8	4 39·5	4 26·1	3·5	1·1	9·5	2·9	15·5	4·8
36	4 39·0	4 39·8	4 26·3	3·6	1·1	9·6	3·0	15·6	4·8
37	4 39·3	4 40·0	4 26·5	3·7	1·1	9·7	3·0	15·7	4·8
38	4 39·5	4 40·3	4 26·8	3·8	1·2	9·8	3·0	15·8	4·9
39	4 39·8	4 40·5	4 27·0	3·9	1·2	9·9	3·1	15·9	4·9
40	4 40·0	4 40·8	4 27·2	4·0	1·2	10·0	3·1	16·0	4·9
41	4 40·3	4 41·0	4 27·5	4·1	1·3	10·1	3·1	16·1	5·0
42	4 40·5	4 41·3	4 27·7	4·2	1·3	10·2	3·1	16·2	5·0
43	4 40·8	4 41·5	4 28·0	4·3	1·3	10·3	3·2	16·3	5·0
44	4 41·0	4 41·8	4 28·2	4·4	1·4	10·4	3·2	16·4	5·1
45	4 41·3	4 42·0	4 28·4	4·5	1·4	10·5	3·2	16·5	5·1
46	4 41·5	4 42·3	4 28·7	4·6	1·4	10·6	3·3	16·6	5·1
47	4 41·8	4 42·5	4 28·9	4·7	1·4	10·7	3·3	16·7	5·1
48	4 42·0	4 42·8	4 29·2	4·8	1·5	10·8	3·3	16·8	5·2
49	4 42·3	4 43·0	4 29·4	4·9	1·5	10·9	3·4	16·9	5·2
50	4 42·5	4 43·3	4 29·6	5·0	1·5	11·0	3·4	17·0	5·2
51	4 42·8	4 43·5	4 29·9	5·1	1·6	11·1	3·4	17·1	5·3
52	4 43·0	4 43·8	4 30·1	5·2	1·6	11·2	3·5	17·2	5·3
53	4 43·3	4 44·0	4 30·3	5·3	1·6	11·3	3·5	17·3	5·3
54	4 43·5	4 44·3	4 30·6	5·4	1·7	11·4	3·5	17·4	5·4
55	4 43·8	4 44·5	4 30·8	5·5	1·7	11·5	3·5	17·5	5·4
56	4 44·0	4 44·8	4 31·1	5·6	1·7	11·6	3·6	17·6	5·4
57	4 44·3	4 45·0	4 31·3	5·7	1·8	11·7	3·6	17·7	5·5
58	4 44·5	4 45·3	4 31·5	5·8	1·8	11·8	3·6	17·8	5·5
59	4 44·8	4 45·5	4 31·8	5·9	1·8	11·9	3·7	17·9	5·5
60	4 45·0	4 45·8	4 32·0	6·0	1·9	12·0	3·7	18·0	5·6

19ᵐ

m 19 s	SUN PLANETS	ARIES	MOON	v or d	Corrⁿ	v or d	Corrⁿ	v or d	Corrⁿ
00	4 45·0	4 45·8	4 32·0	0·0	0·0	6·0	2·0	12·0	3·9
01	4 45·3	4 46·0	4 32·3	0·1	0·0	6·1	2·0	12·1	3·9
02	4 45·5	4 46·3	4 32·5	0·2	0·1	6·2	2·0	12·2	4·0
03	4 45·8	4 46·5	4 32·7	0·3	0·1	6·3	2·0	12·3	4·0
04	4 46·0	4 46·8	4 33·0	0·4	0·1	6·4	2·1	12·4	4·0
05	4 46·3	4 47·0	4 33·2	0·5	0·2	6·5	2·1	12·5	4·1
06	4 46·5	4 47·3	4 33·4	0·6	0·2	6·6	2·1	12·6	4·1
07	4 46·8	4 47·5	4 33·7	0·7	0·2	6·7	2·2	12·7	4·1
08	4 47·0	4 47·8	4 33·9	0·8	0·3	6·8	2·2	12·8	4·2
09	4 47·3	4 48·0	4 34·2	0·9	0·3	6·9	2·2	12·9	4·2
10	4 47·5	4 48·3	4 34·4	1·0	0·3	7·0	2·3	13·0	4·2
11	4 47·8	4 48·5	4 34·6	1·1	0·4	7·1	2·3	13·1	4·3
12	4 48·0	4 48·8	4 34·9	1·2	0·4	7·2	2·3	13·2	4·3
13	4 48·3	4 49·0	4 35·1	1·3	0·4	7·3	2·4	13·3	4·3
14	4 48·5	4 49·3	4 35·4	1·4	0·5	7·4	2·4	13·4	4·4
15	4 48·8	4 49·5	4 35·6	1·5	0·5	7·5	2·4	13·5	4·4
16	4 49·0	4 49·8	4 35·8	1·6	0·5	7·6	2·5	13·6	4·4
17	4 49·3	4 50·0	4 36·1	1·7	0·6	7·7	2·5	13·7	4·5
18	4 49·5	4 50·3	4 36·3	1·8	0·6	7·8	2·5	13·8	4·5
19	4 49·8	4 50·5	4 36·6	1·9	0·6	7·9	2·6	13·9	4·5
20	4 50·0	4 50·8	4 36·8	2·0	0·7	8·0	2·6	14·0	4·6
21	4 50·3	4 51·0	4 37·0	2·1	0·7	8·1	2·6	14·1	4·6
22	4 50·5	4 51·3	4 37·3	2·2	0·7	8·2	2·7	14·2	4·6
23	4 50·8	4 51·5	4 37·5	2·3	0·7	8·3	2·7	14·3	4·6
24	4 51·0	4 51·8	4 37·7	2·4	0·8	8·4	2·7	14·4	4·7
25	4 51·3	4 52·0	4 38·0	2·5	0·8	8·5	2·8	14·5	4·7
26	4 51·5	4 52·3	4 38·2	2·6	0·8	8·6	2·8	14·6	4·7
27	4 51·8	4 52·5	4 38·5	2·7	0·9	8·7	2·8	14·7	4·8
28	4 52·0	4 52·8	4 38·7	2·8	0·9	8·8	2·9	14·8	4·8
29	4 52·3	4 53·1	4 38·9	2·9	0·9	8·9	2·9	14·9	4·8
30	4 52·5	4 53·3	4 39·2	3·0	1·0	9·0	2·9	15·0	4·9
31	4 52·8	4 53·6	4 39·4	3·1	1·0	9·1	3·0	15·1	4·9
32	4 53·0	4 53·8	4 39·7	3·2	1·0	9·2	3·0	15·2	4·9
33	4 53·3	4 54·1	4 39·9	3·3	1·1	9·3	3·0	15·3	5·0
34	4 53·5	4 54·3	4 40·1	3·4	1·1	9·4	3·1	15·4	5·0
35	4 53·8	4 54·6	4 40·4	3·5	1·1	9·5	3·1	15·5	5·0
36	4 54·0	4 54·8	4 40·6	3·6	1·2	9·6	3·1	15·6	5·1
37	4 54·3	4 55·1	4 40·8	3·7	1·2	9·7	3·2	15·7	5·1
38	4 54·5	4 55·3	4 41·1	3·8	1·2	9·8	3·2	15·8	5·1
39	4 54·8	4 55·6	4 41·3	3·9	1·3	9·9	3·2	15·9	5·2
40	4 55·0	4 55·8	4 41·6	4·0	1·3	10·0	3·3	16·0	5·2
41	4 55·3	4 56·1	4 41·8	4·1	1·3	10·1	3·3	16·1	5·2
42	4 55·5	4 56·3	4 42·0	4·2	1·4	10·2	3·3	16·2	5·3
43	4 55·8	4 56·6	4 42·3	4·3	1·4	10·3	3·3	16·3	5·3
44	4 56·0	4 56·8	4 42·5	4·4	1·4	10·4	3·4	16·4	5·3
45	4 56·3	4 57·1	4 42·8	4·5	1·5	10·5	3·4	16·5	5·4
46	4 56·5	4 57·3	4 43·0	4·6	1·5	10·6	3·4	16·6	5·4
47	4 56·8	4 57·6	4 43·2	4·7	1·5	10·7	3·5	16·7	5·4
48	4 57·0	4 57·8	4 43·5	4·8	1·6	10·8	3·5	16·8	5·5
49	4 57·3	4 58·1	4 43·7	4·9	1·6	10·9	3·5	16·9	5·5
50	4 57·5	4 58·3	4 43·9	5·0	1·6	11·0	3·6	17·0	5·5
51	4 57·8	4 58·6	4 44·2	5·1	1·7	11·1	3·6	17·1	5·6
52	4 58·0	4 58·8	4 44·4	5·2	1·7	11·2	3·6	17·2	5·6
53	4 58·3	4 59·1	4 44·7	5·3	1·7	11·3	3·7	17·3	5·6
54	4 58·5	4 59·3	4 44·9	5·4	1·8	11·4	3·7	17·4	5·7
55	4 58·8	4 59·6	4 45·1	5·5	1·8	11·5	3·7	17·5	5·7
56	4 59·0	4 59·8	4 45·4	5·6	1·8	11·6	3·8	17·6	5·7
57	4 59·3	5 00·1	4 45·6	5·7	1·9	11·7	3·8	17·7	5·8
58	4 59·5	5 00·3	4 45·9	5·8	1·9	11·8	3·8	17·8	5·8
59	4 59·8	5 00·6	4 46·1	5·9	1·9	11·9	3·9	17·9	5·8
60	5 00·0	5 00·8	4 46·3	6·0	2·0	12·0	3·9	18·0	5·9

20ᵐ

m 20 s	SUN PLANETS ° ′	ARIES ° ′	MOON ° ′	v or d ′	Corrⁿ ′	v or d ′	Corrⁿ ′	v or d ′	Corrⁿ ′
00	5 00·0	5 00·8	4 46·3	0·0	0·0	6·0	2·1	12·0	4·1
01	5 00·3	5 01·1	4 46·6	0·1	0·0	6·1	2·1	12·1	4·1
02	5 00·5	5 01·3	4 46·8	0·2	0·1	6·2	2·1	12·2	4·2
03	5 00·8	5 01·6	4 47·0	0·3	0·1	6·3	2·2	12·3	4·2
04	5 01·0	5 01·8	4 47·3	0·4	0·1	6·4	2·2	12·4	4·2
05	5 01·3	5 02·1	4 47·5	0·5	0·2	6·5	2·2	12·5	4·3
06	5 01·5	5 02·3	4 47·8	0·6	0·2	6·6	2·3	12·6	4·3
07	5 01·8	5 02·6	4 48·0	0·7	0·2	6·7	2·3	12·7	4·3
08	5 02·0	5 02·8	4 48·2	0·8	0·3	6·8	2·3	12·8	4·4
09	5 02·3	5 03·1	4 48·5	0·9	0·3	6·9	2·4	12·9	4·4
10	5 02·5	5 03·3	4 48·7	1·0	0·3	7·0	2·4	13·0	4·4
11	5 02·8	5 03·6	4 49·0	1·1	0·4	7·1	2·4	13·1	4·5
12	5 03·0	5 03·8	4 49·2	1·2	0·4	7·2	2·5	13·2	4·5
13	5 03·3	5 04·1	4 49·4	1·3	0·4	7·3	2·5	13·3	4·5
14	5 03·5	5 04·3	4 49·7	1·4	0·5	7·4	2·5	13·4	4·6
15	5 03·8	5 04·6	4 49·9	1·5	0·5	7·5	2·6	13·5	4·6
16	5 04·0	5 04·8	4 50·2	1·6	0·5	7·6	2·6	13·6	4·6
17	5 04·3	5 05·1	4 50·4	1·7	0·6	7·7	2·6	13·7	4·7
18	5 04·5	5 05·3	4 50·6	1·8	0·6	7·8	2·7	13·8	4·7
19	5 04·8	5 05·6	4 50·9	1·9	0·6	7·9	2·7	13·9	4·7
20	5 05·0	5 05·8	4 51·1	2·0	0·7	8·0	2·7	14·0	4·8
21	5 05·3	5 06·1	4 51·3	2·1	0·7	8·1	2·8	14·1	4·8
22	5 05·5	5 06·3	4 51·6	2·2	0·8	8·2	2·8	14·2	4·9
23	5 05·8	5 06·6	4 51·8	2·3	0·8	8·3	2·8	14·3	4·9
24	5 06·0	5 06·8	4 52·1	2·4	0·8	8·4	2·9	14·4	4·9
25	5 06·3	5 07·1	4 52·3	2·5	0·9	8·5	2·9	14·5	5·0
26	5 06·5	5 07·3	4 52·5	2·6	0·9	8·6	2·9	14·6	5·0
27	5 06·8	5 07·6	4 52·8	2·7	0·9	8·7	3·0	14·7	5·0
28	5 07·0	5 07·8	4 53·0	2·8	1·0	8·8	3·0	14·8	5·1
29	5 07·3	5 08·1	4 53·3	2·9	1·0	8·9	3·0	14·9	5·1
30	5 07·5	5 08·3	4 53·5	3·0	1·0	9·0	3·1	15·0	5·1
31	5 07·8	5 08·6	4 53·7	3·1	1·1	9·1	3·1	15·1	5·2
32	5 08·0	5 08·8	4 54·0	3·2	1·1	9·2	3·1	15·2	5·2
33	5 08·3	5 09·1	4 54·2	3·3	1·1	9·3	3·2	15·3	5·2
34	5 08·5	5 09·3	4 54·4	3·4	1·2	9·4	3·2	15·4	5·3
35	5 08·8	5 09·6	4 54·7	3·5	1·2	9·5	3·2	15·5	5·3
36	5 09·0	5 09·8	4 54·9	3·6	1·2	9·6	3·3	15·6	5·3
37	5 09·3	5 10·1	4 55·2	3·7	1·3	9·7	3·3	15·7	5·4
38	5 09·5	5 10·3	4 55·4	3·8	1·3	9·8	3·3	15·8	5·4
39	5 09·8	5 10·6	4 55·6	3·9	1·3	9·9	3·4	15·9	5·4
40	5 10·0	5 10·8	4 55·9	4·0	1·4	10·0	3·4	16·0	5·5
41	5 10·3	5 11·1	4 56·1	4·1	1·4	10·1	3·5	16·1	5·5
42	5 10·5	5 11·4	4 56·4	4·2	1·4	10·2	3·5	16·2	5·5
43	5 10·8	5 11·6	4 56·6	4·3	1·5	10·3	3·5	16·3	5·6
44	5 11·0	5 11·9	4 56·8	4·4	1·5	10·4	3·6	16·4	5·6
45	5 11·3	5 12·1	4 57·1	4·5	1·5	10·5	3·6	16·5	5·6
46	5 11·5	5 12·4	4 57·3	4·6	1·6	10·6	3·6	16·6	5·7
47	5 11·8	5 12·6	4 57·5	4·7	1·6	10·7	3·7	16·7	5·7
48	5 12·0	5 12·9	4 57·8	4·8	1·6	10·8	3·7	16·8	5·7
49	5 12·3	5 13·1	4 58·0	4·9	1·7	10·9	3·7	16·9	5·8
50	5 12·5	5 13·4	4 58·3	5·0	1·7	11·0	3·8	17·0	5·8
51	5 12·8	5 13·6	4 58·5	5·1	1·7	11·1	3·8	17·1	5·8
52	5 13·0	5 13·9	4 58·7	5·2	1·8	11·2	3·8	17·2	5·9
53	5 13·3	5 14·1	4 59·0	5·3	1·8	11·3	3·9	17·3	5·9
54	5 13·5	5 14·4	4 59·2	5·4	1·8	11·4	3·9	17·4	5·9
55	5 13·8	5 14·6	4 59·5	5·5	1·9	11·5	3·9	17·5	6·0
56	5 14·0	5 14·9	4 59·7	5·6	1·9	11·6	4·0	17·6	6·0
57	5 14·3	5 15·1	4 59·9	5·7	1·9	11·7	4·0	17·7	6·0
58	5 14·5	5 15·4	5 00·2	5·8	2·0	11·8	4·0	17·8	6·1
59	5 14·8	5 15·6	5 00·4	5·9	2·0	11·9	4·1	17·9	6·1
60	5 15·0	5 15·9	5 00·7	6·0	2·1	12·0	4·1	18·0	6·2

21ᵐ

m 21 s	SUN PLANETS ° ′	ARIES ° ′	MOON ° ′	v or d ′	Corrⁿ ′	v or d ′	Corrⁿ ′	v or d ′	Corrⁿ ′
00	5 15·0	5 15·9	5 00·7	0·0	0·0	6·0	2·2	12·0	4·3
01	5 15·3	5 16·1	5 01·0	0·1	0·0	6·1	2·2	12·1	4·3
02	5 15·5	5 16·4	5 01·1	0·2	0·1	6·2	2·2	12·2	4·4
03	5 15·8	5 16·6	5 01·4	0·3	0·1	6·3	2·3	12·3	4·4
04	5 16·0	5 16·9	5 01·6	0·4	0·1	6·4	2·3	12·4	4·4
05	5 16·3	5 17·1	5 01·8	0·5	0·2	6·5	2·3	12·5	4·5
06	5 16·5	5 17·4	5 02·1	0·6	0·2	6·6	2·4	12·6	4·5
07	5 16·8	5 17·6	5 02·3	0·7	0·3	6·7	2·4	12·7	4·6
08	5 17·0	5 17·9	5 02·6	0·8	0·3	6·8	2·4	12·8	4·6
09	5 17·3	5 18·1	5 02·8	0·9	0·3	6·9	2·5	12·9	4·6
10	5 17·5	5 18·4	5 03·0	1·0	0·4	7·0	2·5	13·0	4·7
11	5 17·8	5 18·6	5 03·3	1·1	0·4	7·1	2·5	13·1	4·7
12	5 18·0	5 18·9	5 03·5	1·2	0·4	7·2	2·6	13·2	4·7
13	5 18·3	5 19·1	5 03·8	1·3	0·5	7·3	2·6	13·3	4·8
14	5 18·5	5 19·4	5 04·0	1·4	0·5	7·4	2·7	13·4	4·8
15	5 18·8	5 19·6	5 04·2	1·5	0·5	7·5	2·7	13·5	4·8
16	5 19·0	5 19·9	5 04·5	1·6	0·6	7·6	2·7	13·6	4·9
17	5 19·3	5 20·1	5 04·7	1·7	0·6	7·7	2·8	13·7	4·9
18	5 19·5	5 20·4	5 04·9	1·8	0·6	7·8	2·8	13·8	4·9
19	5 19·8	5 20·6	5 05·2	1·9	0·7	7·9	2·8	13·9	5·0
20	5 20·0	5 20·9	5 05·4	2·0	0·7	8·0	2·9	14·0	5·0
21	5 20·3	5 21·1	5 05·7	2·1	0·8	8·1	2·9	14·1	5·1
22	5 20·5	5 21·4	5 05·9	2·2	0·8	8·2	2·9	14·2	5·1
23	5 20·8	5 21·6	5 06·1	2·3	0·8	8·3	3·0	14·3	5·1
24	5 21·0	5 21·9	5 06·4	2·4	0·9	8·4	3·0	14·4	5·2
25	5 21·3	5 22·1	5 06·6	2·5	0·9	8·5	3·0	14·5	5·2
26	5 21·5	5 22·4	5 06·9	2·6	0·9	8·6	3·1	14·6	5·2
27	5 21·8	5 22·6	5 07·1	2·7	1·0	8·7	3·1	14·7	5·3
28	5 22·0	5 22·9	5 07·3	2·8	1·0	8·8	3·2	14·8	5·3
29	5 22·3	5 23·1	5 07·6	2·9	1·0	8·9	3·2	14·9	5·3
30	5 22·5	5 23·4	5 07·8	3·0	1·1	9·0	3·2	15·0	5·4
31	5 22·8	5 23·6	5 08·0	3·1	1·1	9·1	3·3	15·1	5·4
32	5 23·0	5 23·9	5 08·3	3·2	1·1	9·2	3·3	15·2	5·4
33	5 23·3	5 24·1	5 08·5	3·3	1·2	9·3	3·3	15·3	5·5
34	5 23·5	5 24·4	5 08·8	3·4	1·2	9·4	3·4	15·4	5·5
35	5 23·8	5 24·6	5 09·0	3·5	1·3	9·5	3·4	15·5	5·6
36	5 24·0	5 24·9	5 09·2	3·6	1·3	9·6	3·4	15·6	5·6
37	5 24·3	5 25·1	5 09·5	3·7	1·3	9·7	3·5	15·7	5·6
38	5 24·5	5 25·4	5 09·7	3·8	1·4	9·8	3·5	15·8	5·7
39	5 24·8	5 25·6	5 10·0	3·9	1·4	9·9	3·5	15·9	5·7
40	5 25·0	5 25·9	5 10·2	4·0	1·4	10·0	3·6	16·0	5·7
41	5 25·3	5 26·1	5 10·4	4·1	1·5	10·1	3·6	16·1	5·8
42	5 25·5	5 26·4	5 10·7	4·2	1·5	10·2	3·7	16·2	5·8
43	5 25·8	5 26·6	5 10·9	4·3	1·5	10·3	3·7	16·3	5·8
44	5 26·0	5 26·9	5 11·1	4·4	1·6	10·4	3·7	16·4	5·9
45	5 26·3	5 27·1	5 11·4	4·5	1·6	10·5	3·8	16·5	5·9
46	5 26·5	5 27·4	5 11·6	4·6	1·6	10·6	3·8	16·6	5·9
47	5 26·8	5 27·6	5 11·9	4·7	1·7	10·7	3·8	16·7	6·0
48	5 27·0	5 27·9	5 12·1	4·8	1·7	10·8	3·9	16·8	6·0
49	5 27·3	5 28·1	5 12·3	4·9	1·8	10·9	3·9	16·9	6·1
50	5 27·5	5 28·4	5 12·6	5·0	1·8	11·0	3·9	17·0	6·1
51	5 27·8	5 28·6	5 12·8	5·1	1·8	11·1	4·0	17·1	6·1
52	5 28·0	5 28·9	5 13·1	5·2	1·9	11·2	4·0	17·2	6·2
53	5 28·3	5 29·1	5 13·3	5·3	1·9	11·3	4·0	17·3	6·2
54	5 28·5	5 29·4	5 13·5	5·4	1·9	11·4	4·1	17·4	6·2
55	5 28·8	5 29·7	5 13·8	5·5	2·0	11·5	4·1	17·5	6·3
56	5 29·0	5 29·9	5 14·0	5·6	2·0	11·6	4·2	17·6	6·3
57	5 29·3	5 30·2	5 14·3	5·7	2·0	11·7	4·2	17·7	6·3
58	5 29·5	5 30·4	5 14·5	5·8	2·1	11·8	4·2	17·8	6·4
59	5 29·8	5 30·7	5 14·7	5·9	2·1	11·9	4·3	17·9	6·4
60	5 30·0	5 30·9	5 15·0	6·0	2·2	12·0	4·3	18·0	6·5

xii

22ᵐ

m 22 s	SUN PLANETS	ARIES	MOON	v or d	Corrⁿ	v or d	Corrⁿ	v or d	Corrⁿ
	° ′	° ′	° ′	′	′	′	′	′	′
00	5 30·0	5 30·9	5 15·0	0·0	0·0	6·0	2·3	12·0	4·5
01	5 30·3	5 31·2	5 15·2	0·1	0·0	6·1	2·3	12·1	4·5
02	5 30·5	5 31·4	5 15·4	0·2	0·1	6·2	2·3	12·2	4·6
03	5 30·8	5 31·7	5 15·7	0·3	0·1	6·3	2·4	12·3	4·6
04	5 31·0	5 31·9	5 15·9	0·4	0·2	6·4	2·4	12·4	4·7
05	5 31·3	5 32·2	5 16·2	0·5	0·2	6·5	2·4	12·5	4·7
06	5 31·5	5 32·4	5 16·4	0·6	0·2	6·6	2·5	12·6	4·7
07	5 31·8	5 32·7	5 16·6	0·7	0·3	6·7	2·5	12·7	4·8
08	5 32·0	5 32·9	5 16·9	0·8	0·3	6·8	2·6	12·8	4·8
09	5 32·3	5 33·2	5 17·1	0·9	0·3	6·9	2·6	12·9	4·8
10	5 32·5	5 33·4	5 17·4	1·0	0·4	7·0	2·6	13·0	4·9
11	5 32·8	5 33·7	5 17·6	1·1	0·4	7·1	2·7	13·1	4·9
12	5 33·0	5 33·9	5 17·8	1·2	0·5	7·2	2·7	13·2	5·0
13	5 33·3	5 34·2	5 18·1	1·3	0·5	7·3	2·7	13·3	5·0
14	5 33·5	5 34·4	5 18·3	1·4	0·5	7·4	2·8	13·4	5·0
15	5 33·8	5 34·7	5 18·5	1·5	0·6	7·5	2·8	13·5	5·1
16	5 34·0	5 34·9	5 18·8	1·6	0·6	7·6	2·9	13·6	5·1
17	5 34·3	5 35·2	5 19·0	1·7	0·6	7·7	2·9	13·7	5·1
18	5 34·5	5 35·4	5 19·3	1·8	0·7	7·8	2·9	13·8	5·2
19	5 34·8	5 35·7	5 19·5	1·9	0·7	7·9	3·0	13·9	5·2
20	5 35·0	5 35·9	5 19·7	2·0	0·8	8·0	3·0	14·0	5·3
21	5 35·3	5 36·2	5 20·0	2·1	0·8	8·1	3·0	14·1	5·3
22	5 35·5	5 36·4	5 20·2	2·2	0·8	8·2	3·1	14·2	5·3
23	5 35·8	5 36·7	5 20·5	2·3	0·9	8·3	3·1	14·3	5·4
24	5 36·0	5 36·9	5 20·7	2·4	0·9	8·4	3·2	14·4	5·4
25	5 36·3	5 37·2	5 20·9	2·5	0·9	8·5	3·2	14·5	5·4
26	5 36·5	5 37·4	5 21·2	2·6	1·0	8·6	3·2	14·6	5·5
27	5 36·8	5 37·7	5 21·4	2·7	1·0	8·7	3·3	14·7	5·5
28	5 37·0	5 37·9	5 21·6	2·8	1·0	8·8	3·3	14·8	5·6
29	5 37·3	5 38·2	5 21·9	2·9	1·1	8·9	3·3	14·9	5·6
30	5 37·5	5 38·4	5 22·1	3·0	1·1	9·0	3·4	15·0	5·6
31	5 37·8	5 38·7	5 22·4	3·1	1·2	9·1	3·4	15·1	5·7
32	5 38·0	5 38·9	5 22·6	3·2	1·2	9·2	3·5	15·2	5·7
33	5 38·3	5 39·2	5 22·8	3·3	1·2	9·3	3·5	15·3	5·7
34	5 38·5	5 39·4	5 23·1	3·4	1·3	9·4	3·5	15·4	5·8
35	5 38·8	5 39·7	5 23·3	3·5	1·3	9·5	3·6	15·5	5·8
36	5 39·0	5 39·9	5 23·6	3·6	1·4	9·6	3·6	15·6	5·9
37	5 39·3	5 40·2	5 23·8	3·7	1·4	9·7	3·6	15·7	5·9
38	5 39·5	5 40·4	5 24·0	3·8	1·4	9·8	3·7	15·8	5·9
39	5 39·8	5 40·7	5 24·3	3·9	1·5	9·9	3·7	15·9	6·0
40	5 40·0	5 40·9	5 24·5	4·0	1·5	10·0	3·8	16·0	6·0
41	5 40·3	5 41·2	5 24·7	4·1	1·5	10·1	3·8	16·1	6·0
42	5 40·5	5 41·4	5 25·0	4·2	1·6	10·2	3·8	16·2	6·1
43	5 40·8	5 41·7	5 25·2	4·3	1·6	10·3	3·9	16·3	6·1
44	5 41·0	5 41·9	5 25·5	4·4	1·7	10·4	3·9	16·4	6·1
45	5 41·3	5 42·2	5 25·7	4·5	1·7	10·5	3·9	16·5	6·2
46	5 41·5	5 42·4	5 25·9	4·6	1·7	10·6	4·0	16·6	6·2
47	5 41·8	5 42·7	5 26·2	4·7	1·8	10·7	4·0	16·7	6·3
48	5 42·0	5 42·9	5 26·4	4·8	1·8	10·8	4·1	16·8	6·3
49	5 42·3	5 43·2	5 26·7	4·9	1·8	10·9	4·1	16·9	6·3
50	5 42·5	5 43·4	5 26·9	5·0	1·9	11·0	4·1	17·0	6·4
51	5 42·8	5 43·7	5 27·1	5·1	1·9	11·1	4·2	17·1	6·4
52	5 43·0	5 43·9	5 27·4	5·2	2·0	11·2	4·2	17·2	6·5
53	5 43·3	5 44·2	5 27·6	5·3	2·0	11·3	4·2	17·3	6·5
54	5 43·5	5 44·4	5 27·9	5·4	2·0	11·4	4·3	17·4	6·5
55	5 43·8	5 44·7	5 28·1	5·5	2·1	11·5	4·3	17·5	6·6
56	5 44·0	5 44·9	5 28·3	5·6	2·1	11·6	4·4	17·6	6·6
57	5 44·3	5 45·2	5 28·6	5·7	2·1	11·7	4·4	17·7	6·6
58	5 44·5	5 45·4	5 28·8	5·8	2·2	11·8	4·4	17·8	6·7
59	5 44·8	5 45·7	5 29·0	5·9	2·2	11·9	4·5	17·9	6·7
60	5 45·0	5 45·9	5 29·3	6·0	2·3	12·0	4·5	18·0	6·8

23ᵐ

m 23 s	SUN PLANETS	ARIES	MOON	v or d	Corrⁿ	v or d	Corrⁿ	v or d	Corrⁿ
	° ′	° ′	° ′	′	′	′	′	′	′
00	5 45·0	5 45·9	5 29·3	0·0	0·0	6·0	2·4	12·0	4·7
01	5 45·3	5 46·2	5 29·5	0·1	0·0	6·1	2·4	12·1	4·7
02	5 45·5	5 46·4	5 29·8	0·2	0·1	6·2	2·4	12·2	4·8
03	5 45·8	5 46·7	5 30·0	0·3	0·1	6·3	2·5	12·3	4·8
04	5 46·0	5 46·9	5 30·2	0·4	0·2	6·4	2·5	12·4	4·9
05	5 46·3	5 47·2	5 30·5	0·5	0·2	6·5	2·5	12·5	4·9
06	5 46·5	5 47·4	5 30·7	0·6	0·2	6·6	2·6	12·6	4·9
07	5 46·8	5 47·7	5 31·0	0·7	0·3	6·7	2·6	12·7	5·0
08	5 47·0	5 48·0	5 31·2	0·8	0·3	6·8	2·7	12·8	5·0
09	5 47·3	5 48·2	5 31·4	0·9	0·4	6·9	2·7	12·9	5·1
10	5 47·5	5 48·5	5 31·7	1·0	0·4	7·0	2·7	13·0	5·1
11	5 47·8	5 48·7	5 31·9	1·1	0·4	7·1	2·8	13·1	5·1
12	5 48·0	5 49·0	5 32·1	1·2	0·5	7·2	2·8	13·2	5·2
13	5 48·3	5 49·2	5 32·4	1·3	0·5	7·3	2·9	13·3	5·2
14	5 48·5	5 49·5	5 32·6	1·4	0·5	7·4	2·9	13·4	5·2
15	5 48·8	5 49·7	5 32·9	1·5	0·6	7·5	2·9	13·5	5·3
16	5 49·0	5 50·0	5 33·1	1·6	0·6	7·6	3·0	13·6	5·3
17	5 49·3	5 50·2	5 33·3	1·7	0·7	7·7	3·0	13·7	5·4
18	5 49·5	5 50·5	5 33·6	1·8	0·7	7·8	3·1	13·8	5·4
19	5 49·8	5 50·7	5 33·8	1·9	0·7	7·9	3·1	13·9	5·4
20	5 50·0	5 51·0	5 34·1	2·0	0·8	8·0	3·1	14·0	5·5
21	5 50·3	5 51·2	5 34·3	2·1	0·8	8·1	3·2	14·1	5·5
22	5 50·5	5 51·5	5 34·5	2·2	0·9	8·2	3·2	14·2	5·6
23	5 50·8	5 51·7	5 34·8	2·3	0·9	8·3	3·3	14·3	5·6
24	5 51·0	5 52·0	5 35·0	2·4	0·9	8·4	3·3	14·4	5·6
25	5 51·3	5 52·2	5 35·2	2·5	1·0	8·5	3·3	14·5	5·7
26	5 51·5	5 52·5	5 35·5	2·6	1·0	8·6	3·4	14·6	5·7
27	5 51·8	5 52·7	5 35·7	2·7	1·1	8·7	3·4	14·7	5·8
28	5 52·0	5 53·0	5 36·0	2·8	1·1	8·8	3·4	14·8	5·8
29	5 52·3	5 53·2	5 36·2	2·9	1·1	8·9	3·5	14·9	5·8
30	5 52·5	5 53·5	5 36·4	3·0	1·2	9·0	3·5	15·0	5·9
31	5 52·8	5 53·7	5 36·7	3·1	1·2	9·1	3·6	15·1	5·9
32	5 53·0	5 54·0	5 36·9	3·2	1·3	9·2	3·6	15·2	6·0
33	5 53·3	5 54·2	5 37·2	3·3	1·3	9·3	3·6	15·3	6·0
34	5 53·5	5 54·5	5 37·4	3·4	1·3	9·4	3·7	15·4	6·0
35	5 53·8	5 54·7	5 37·6	3·5	1·4	9·5	3·7	15·5	6·1
36	5 54·0	5 55·0	5 37·9	3·6	1·4	9·6	3·8	15·6	6·1
37	5 54·3	5 55·2	5 38·1	3·7	1·4	9·7	3·8	15·7	6·1
38	5 54·5	5 55·5	5 38·4	3·8	1·5	9·8	3·8	15·8	6·2
39	5 54·8	5 55·7	5 38·6	3·9	1·5	9·9	3·9	15·9	6·2
40	5 55·0	5 56·0	5 38·8	4·0	1·6	10·0	3·9	16·0	6·3
41	5 55·3	5 56·2	5 39·1	4·1	1·6	10·1	4·0	16·1	6·3
42	5 55·5	5 56·5	5 39·3	4·2	1·6	10·2	4·0	16·2	6·3
43	5 55·8	5 56·7	5 39·5	4·3	1·7	10·3	4·0	16·3	6·4
44	5 56·0	5 57·0	5 39·8	4·4	1·7	10·4	4·1	16·4	6·4
45	5 56·3	5 57·2	5 40·0	4·5	1·8	10·5	4·1	16·5	6·5
46	5 56·5	5 57·5	5 40·3	4·6	1·8	10·6	4·2	16·6	6·5
47	5 56·8	5 57·7	5 40·5	4·7	1·8	10·7	4·2	16·7	6·5
48	5 57·0	5 58·0	5 40·7	4·8	1·9	10·8	4·2	16·8	6·6
49	5 57·3	5 58·2	5 41·0	4·9	1·9	10·9	4·3	16·9	6·6
50	5 57·5	5 58·5	5 41·2	5·0	2·0	11·0	4·3	17·0	6·7
51	5 57·8	5 58·7	5 41·5	5·1	2·0	11·1	4·3	17·1	6·7
52	5 58·0	5 59·0	5 41·7	5·2	2·0	11·2	4·4	17·2	6·7
53	5 58·3	5 59·2	5 41·9	5·3	2·1	11·3	4·4	17·3	6·8
54	5 58·5	5 59·5	5 42·2	5·4	2·1	11·4	4·5	17·4	6·8
55	5 58·8	5 59·7	5 42·4	5·5	2·2	11·5	4·5	17·5	6·9
56	5 59·0	6 00·0	5 42·6	5·6	2·2	11·6	4·5	17·6	6·9
57	5 59·3	6 00·2	5 42·9	5·7	2·2	11·7	4·6	17·7	6·9
58	5 59·5	6 00·5	5 43·1	5·8	2·3	11·8	4·6	17·8	7·0
59	5 59·8	6 00·7	5 43·4	5·9	2·3	11·9	4·7	17·9	7·0
60	6 00·0	6 01·0	5 43·6	6·0	2·4	12·0	4·7	18·0	7·1

24 m	SUN PLANETS	ARIES	MOON	v or Corrⁿ d	v or Corrⁿ d	v or Corrⁿ d
s	° ′	° ′	° ′	′ ′	′ ′	′ ′
00	6 00·0	6 01·0	5 43·6	0·0 0·0	6·0 2·5	12·0 4·9
01	6 00·3	6 01·2	5 43·8	0·1 0·0	6·1 2·5	12·1 4·9
02	6 00·5	6 01·5	5 44·1	0·2 0·1	6·2 2·5	12·2 5·0
03	6 00·8	6 01·7	5 44·3	0·3 0·1	6·3 2·6	12·3 5·0
04	6 01·0	6 02·0	5 44·6	0·4 0·2	6·4 2·6	12·4 5·1
05	6 01·3	6 02·2	5 44·8	0·5 0·2	6·5 2·7	12·5 5·1
06	6 01·5	6 02·5	5 45·0	0·6 0·2	6·6 2·7	12·6 5·1
07	6 01·8	6 02·7	5 45·3	0·7 0·3	6·7 2·7	12·7 5·2
08	6 02·0	6 03·0	5 45·5	0·8 0·3	6·8 2·8	12·8 5·2
09	6 02·3	6 03·2	5 45·7	0·9 0·4	6·9 2·8	12·9 5·3
10	6 02·5	6 03·5	5 46·0	1·0 0·4	7·0 2·9	13·0 5·3
11	6 02·8	6 03·7	5 46·2	1·1 0·4	7·1 2·9	13·1 5·3
12	6 03·0	6 04·0	5 46·5	1·2 0·5	7·2 2·9	13·2 5·4
13	6 03·3	6 04·2	5 46·7	1·3 0·5	7·3 3·0	13·3 5·4
14	6 03·5	6 04·5	5 46·9	1·4 0·6	7·4 3·0	13·4 5·5
15	6 03·8	6 04·7	5 47·2	1·5 0·6	7·5 3·1	13·5 5·5
16	6 04·0	6 05·0	5 47·4	1·6 0·7	7·6 3·1	13·6 5·6
17	6 04·3	6 05·2	5 47·7	1·7 0·7	7·7 3·1	13·7 5·6
18	6 04·5	6 05·5	5 47·9	1·8 0·7	7·8 3·2	13·8 5·6
19	6 04·8	6 05·7	5 48·1	1·9 0·8	7·9 3·2	13·9 5·7
20	6 05·0	6 06·0	5 48·4	2·0 0·8	8·0 3·3	14·0 5·7
21	6 05·3	6 06·3	5 48·6	2·1 0·9	8·1 3·3	14·1 5·8
22	6 05·5	6 06·5	5 48·8	2·2 0·9	8·2 3·3	14·2 5·8
23	6 05·8	6 06·8	5 49·1	2·3 0·9	8·3 3·4	14·3 5·8
24	6 06·0	6 07·0	5 49·3	2·4 1·0	8·4 3·4	14·4 5·9
25	6 06·3	6 07·3	5 49·6	2·5 1·0	8·5 3·5	14·5 5·9
26	6 06·5	6 07·5	5 49·8	2·6 1·1	8·6 3·5	14·6 6·0
27	6 06·8	6 07·8	5 50·0	2·7 1·1	8·7 3·6	14·7 6·0
28	6 07·0	6 08·0	5 50·3	2·8 1·1	8·8 3·6	14·8 6·0
29	6 07·3	6 08·3	5 50·5	2·9 1·2	8·9 3·6	14·9 6·1
30	6 07·5	6 08·5	5 50·8	3·0 1·2	9·0 3·7	15·0 6·1
31	6 07·8	6 08·8	5 51·0	3·1 1·3	9·1 3·7	15·1 6·2
32	6 08·0	6 09·0	5 51·2	3·2 1·3	9·2 3·8	15·2 6·2
33	6 08·3	6 09·3	5 51·5	3·3 1·3	9·3 3·8	15·3 6·2
34	6 08·5	6 09·5	5 51·7	3·4 1·4	9·4 3·8	15·4 6·3
35	6 08·8	6 09·8	5 52·0	3·5 1·4	9·5 3·9	15·5 6·3
36	6 09·0	6 10·0	5 52·2	3·6 1·5	9·6 3·9	15·6 6·4
37	6 09·3	6 10·3	5 52·4	3·7 1·5	9·7 4·0	15·7 6·4
38	6 09·5	6 10·5	5 52·7	3·8 1·6	9·8 4·0	15·8 6·5
39	6 09·8	6 10·8	5 52·9	3·9 1·6	9·9 4·0	15·9 6·5
40	6 10·0	6 11·0	5 53·1	4·0 1·6	10·0 4·1	16·0 6·5
41	6 10·3	6 11·3	5 53·4	4·1 1·7	10·1 4·1	16·1 6·6
42	6 10·5	6 11·5	5 53·6	4·2 1·7	10·2 4·2	16·2 6·6
43	6 10·8	6 11·8	5 53·9	4·3 1·8	10·3 4·2	16·3 6·7
44	6 11·0	6 12·0	5 54·1	4·4 1·8	10·4 4·2	16·4 6·7
45	6 11·3	6 12·3	5 54·3	4·5 1·8	10·5 4·3	16·5 6·7
46	6 11·5	6 12·5	5 54·6	4·6 1·9	10·6 4·3	16·6 6·8
47	6 11·8	6 12·8	5 54·8	4·7 1·9	10·7 4·4	16·7 6·8
48	6 12·0	6 13·0	5 55·1	4·8 2·0	10·8 4·4	16·8 6·9
49	6 12·3	6 13·3	5 55·3	4·9 2·0	10·9 4·5	16·9 6·9
50	6 12·5	6 13·5	5 55·5	5·0 2·0	11·0 4·5	17·0 6·9
51	6 12·8	6 13·8	5 55·8	5·1 2·1	11·1 4·5	17·1 7·0
52	6 13·0	6 14·0	5 56·0	5·2 2·1	11·2 4·6	17·2 7·0
53	6 13·3	6 14·3	5 56·2	5·3 2·2	11·3 4·6	17·3 7·1
54	6 13·5	6 14·5	5 56·5	5·4 2·2	11·4 4·7	17·4 7·1
55	6 13·8	6 14·8	5 56·7	5·5 2·2	11·5 4·7	17·5 7·1
56	6 14·0	6 15·0	5 57·0	5·6 2·3	11·6 4·7	17·6 7·2
57	6 14·3	6 15·3	5 57·2	5·7 2·3	11·7 4·8	17·7 7·2
58	6 14·5	6 15·5	5 57·4	5·8 2·4	11·8 4·8	17·8 7·3
59	6 14·8	6 15·8	5 57·7	5·9 2·4	11·9 4·9	17·9 7·3
60	6 15·0	6 16·0	5 57·9	6·0 2·5	12·0 4·9	18·0 7·4

25 m	SUN PLANETS	ARIES	MOON	v or Corrⁿ d	v or Corrⁿ d	v or Corrⁿ d
s	° ′	° ′	° ′	′ ′	′ ′	′ ′
00	6 15·0	6 16·0	5 57·9	0·0 0·0	6·0 2·6	12·0 5·1
01	6 15·3	6 16·3	5 58·2	0·1 0·0	6·1 2·6	12·1 5·1
02	6 15·5	6 16·5	5 58·4	0·2 0·1	6·2 2·6	12·2 5·2
03	6 15·8	6 16·8	5 58·6	0·3 0·1	6·3 2·7	12·3 5·2
04	6 16·0	6 17·0	5 58·9	0·4 0·2	6·4 2·7	12·4 5·3
05	6 16·3	6 17·3	5 59·1	0·5 0·2	6·5 2·8	12·5 5·3
06	6 16·5	6 17·5	5 59·3	0·6 0·3	6·6 2·8	12·6 5·4
07	6 16·8	6 17·8	5 59·6	0·7 0·3	6·7 2·8	12·7 5·4
08	6 17·0	6 18·0	5 59·8	0·8 0·3	6·8 2·9	12·8 5·4
09	6 17·3	6 18·3	6 00·1	0·9 0·4	6·9 2·9	12·9 5·5
10	6 17·5	6 18·5	6 00·3	1·0 0·4	7·0 3·0	13·0 5·5
11	6 17·8	6 18·8	6 00·5	1·1 0·5	7·1 3·0	13·1 5·6
12	6 18·0	6 19·0	6 00·8	1·2 0·5	7·2 3·1	13·2 5·6
13	6 18·3	6 19·3	6 01·0	1·3 0·6	7·3 3·1	13·3 5·7
14	6 18·5	6 19·5	6 01·3	1·4 0·6	7·4 3·1	13·4 5·7
15	6 18·8	6 19·8	6 01·5	1·5 0·6	7·5 3·2	13·5 5·7
16	6 19·0	6 20·0	6 01·7	1·6 0·7	7·6 3·2	13·6 5·8
17	6 19·3	6 20·3	6 02·0	1·7 0·7	7·7 3·3	13·7 5·8
18	6 19·5	6 20·5	6 02·2	1·8 0·8	7·8 3·3	13·8 5·9
19	6 19·8	6 20·8	6 02·5	1·9 0·8	7·9 3·4	13·9 5·9
20	6 20·0	6 21·0	6 02·7	2·0 0·9	8·0 3·4	14·0 6·0
21	6 20·3	6 21·3	6 02·9	2·1 0·9	8·1 3·4	14·1 6·0
22	6 20·5	6 21·5	6 03·2	2·2 0·9	8·2 3·5	14·2 6·0
23	6 20·8	6 21·8	6 03·4	2·3 1·0	8·3 3·5	14·3 6·1
24	6 21·0	6 22·0	6 03·6	2·4 1·0	8·4 3·6	14·4 6·1
25	6 21·3	6 22·3	6 03·9	2·5 1·1	8·5 3·6	14·5 6·2
26	6 21·5	6 22·5	6 04·1	2·6 1·1	8·6 3·7	14·6 6·2
27	6 21·8	6 22·8	6 04·4	2·7 1·1	8·7 3·7	14·7 6·2
28	6 22·0	6 23·0	6 04·6	2·8 1·2	8·8 3·7	14·8 6·3
29	6 22·3	6 23·3	6 04·8	2·9 1·2	8·9 3·8	14·9 6·3
30	6 22·5	6 23·5	6 05·1	3·0 1·3	9·0 3·8	15·0 6·4
31	6 22·8	6 23·8	6 05·3	3·1 1·3	9·1 3·9	15·1 6·4
32	6 23·0	6 24·0	6 05·6	3·2 1·4	9·2 3·9	15·2 6·5
33	6 23·3	6 24·3	6 05·8	3·3 1·4	9·3 4·0	15·3 6·5
34	6 23·5	6 24·5	6 06·0	3·4 1·4	9·4 4·0	15·4 6·5
35	6 23·8	6 24·8	6 06·3	3·5 1·5	9·5 4·0	15·5 6·6
36	6 24·0	6 25·1	6 06·5	3·6 1·5	9·6 4·1	15·6 6·6
37	6 24·3	6 25·3	6 06·7	3·7 1·6	9·7 4·1	15·7 6·7
38	6 24·5	6 25·6	6 07·0	3·8 1·6	9·8 4·2	15·8 6·7
39	6 24·8	6 25·8	6 07·2	3·9 1·7	9·9 4·2	15·9 6·8
40	6 25·0	6 26·1	6 07·5	4·0 1·7	10·0 4·3	16·0 6·8
41	6 25·3	6 26·3	6 07·7	4·1 1·7	10·1 4·3	16·1 6·8
42	6 25·5	6 26·6	6 07·9	4·2 1·8	10·2 4·3	16·2 6·9
43	6 25·8	6 26·8	6 08·2	4·3 1·8	10·3 4·4	16·3 6·9
44	6 26·0	6 27·1	6 08·4	4·4 1·9	10·4 4·4	16·4 7·0
45	6 26·3	6 27·3	6 08·7	4·5 1·9	10·5 4·5	16·5 7·0
46	6 26·5	6 27·6	6 08·9	4·6 2·0	10·6 4·5	16·6 7·1
47	6 26·8	6 27·8	6 09·1	4·7 2·0	10·7 4·5	16·7 7·1
48	6 27·0	6 28·1	6 09·4	4·8 2·0	10·8 4·6	16·8 7·1
49	6 27·3	6 28·3	6 09·6	4·9 2·1	10·9 4·6	16·9 7·2
50	6 27·5	6 28·6	6 09·8	5·0 2·1	11·0 4·7	17·0 7·2
51	6 27·8	6 28·8	6 10·1	5·1 2·2	11·1 4·7	17·1 7·3
52	6 28·0	6 29·1	6 10·3	5·2 2·2	11·2 4·8	17·2 7·3
53	6 28·3	6 29·3	6 10·6	5·3 2·3	11·3 4·8	17·3 7·4
54	6 28·5	6 29·6	6 10·8	5·4 2·3	11·4 4·8	17·4 7·4
55	6 28·8	6 29·8	6 11·0	5·5 2·3	11·5 4·9	17·5 7·4
56	6 29·0	6 30·1	6 11·3	5·6 2·4	11·6 4·9	17·6 7·5
57	6 29·3	6 30·3	6 11·5	5·7 2·4	11·7 5·0	17·7 7·5
58	6 29·5	6 30·6	6 11·8	5·8 2·5	11·8 5·0	17·8 7·6
59	6 29·8	6 30·8	6 12·0	5·9 2·5	11·9 5·1	17·9 7·6
60	6 30·0	6 31·1	6 12·2	6·0 2·6	12·0 5·1	18·0 7·7

26 m	SUN PLANETS	ARIES	MOON	v or Corrn d	v or Corrn d	v or Corrn d
s	° ′	° ′	° ′	′ ′	′ ′	′ ′
00	6 30·0	6 31·1	6 12·2	0·0 0·0	6·0 2·7	12·0 5·3
01	6 30·3	6 31·3	6 12·5	0·1 0·0	6·1 2·7	12·1 5·3
02	6 30·5	6 31·6	6 12·7	0·2 0·1	6·2 2·7	12·2 5·4
03	6 30·8	6 31·8	6 12·9	0·3 0·1	6·3 2·8	12·3 5·4
04	6 31·0	6 32·1	6 13·2	0·4 0·2	6·4 2·8	12·4 5·5
05	6 31·3	6 32·3	6 13·4	0·5 0·2	6·5 2·9	12·5 5·5
06	6 31·5	6 32·6	6 13·7	0·6 0·3	6·6 2·9	12·6 5·6
07	6 31·8	6 32·8	6 13·9	0·7 0·3	6·7 3·0	12·7 5·6
08	6 32·0	6 33·1	6 14·1	0·8 0·4	6·8 3·0	12·8 5·7
09	6 32·3	6 33·3	6 14·4	0·9 0·4	6·9 3·0	12·9 5·7
10	6 32·5	6 33·6	6 14·6	1·0 0·4	7·0 3·1	13·0 5·7
11	6 32·8	6 33·8	6 14·9	1·1 0·5	7·1 3·1	13·1 5·8
12	6 33·0	6 34·1	6 15·1	1·2 0·5	7·2 3·2	13·2 5·8
13	6 33·3	6 34·3	6 15·3	1·3 0·6	7·3 3·2	13·3 5·9
14	6 33·5	6 34·6	6 15·6	1·4 0·6	7·4 3·3	13·4 5·9
15	6 33·8	6 34·8	6 15·8	1·5 0·7	7·5 3·3	13·5 6·0
16	6 34·0	6 35·1	6 16·1	1·6 0·7	7·6 3·4	13·6 6·0
17	6 34·3	6 35·3	6 16·3	1·7 0·8	7·7 3·4	13·7 6·1
18	6 34·5	6 35·6	6 16·5	1·8 0·8	7·8 3·4	13·8 6·1
19	6 34·8	6 35·8	6 16·8	1·9 0·8	7·9 3·5	13·9 6·1
20	6 35·0	6 36·1	6 17·0	2·0 0·9	8·0 3·5	14·0 6·2
21	6 35·3	6 36·3	6 17·2	2·1 0·9	8·1 3·6	14·1 6·2
22	6 35·5	6 36·6	6 17·5	2·2 1·0	8·2 3·6	14·2 6·3
23	6 35·8	6 36·8	6 17·7	2·3 1·0	8·3 3·7	14·3 6·3
24	6 36·0	6 37·1	6 18·0	2·4 1·1	8·4 3·7	14·4 6·4
25	6 36·3	6 37·3	6 18·2	2·5 1·1	8·5 3·8	14·5 6·4
26	6 36·5	6 37·6	6 18·4	2·6 1·1	8·6 3·8	14·6 6·4
27	6 36·8	6 37·8	6 18·7	2·7 1·2	8·7 3·8	14·7 6·5
28	6 37·0	6 38·1	6 18·9	2·8 1·2	8·8 3·9	14·8 6·5
29	6 37·3	6 38·3	6 19·2	2·9 1·3	8·9 3·9	14·9 6·6
30	6 37·5	6 38·6	6 19·4	3·0 1·3	9·0 4·0	15·0 6·6
31	6 37·8	6 38·8	6 19·6	3·1 1·4	9·1 4·0	15·1 6·7
32	6 38·0	6 39·1	6 19·9	3·2 1·4	9·2 4·1	15·2 6·7
33	6 38·3	6 39·3	6 20·1	3·3 1·5	9·3 4·1	15·3 6·8
34	6 38·5	6 39·6	6 20·3	3·4 1·5	9·4 4·2	15·4 6·8
35	6 38·8	6 39·8	6 20·6	3·5 1·5	9·5 4·2	15·5 6·8
36	6 39·0	6 40·1	6 20·8	3·6 1·6	9·6 4·2	15·6 6·9
37	6 39·3	6 40·3	6 21·1	3·7 1·6	9·7 4·3	15·7 6·9
38	6 39·5	6 40·6	6 21·3	3·8 1·7	9·8 4·3	15·8 7·0
39	6 39·8	6 40·8	6 21·5	3·9 1·7	9·9 4·4	15·9 7·0
40	6 40·0	6 41·1	6 21·8	4·0 1·8	10·0 4·4	16·0 7·1
41	6 40·3	6 41·3	6 22·0	4·1 1·8	10·1 4·5	16·1 7·1
42	6 40·5	6 41·6	6 22·3	4·2 1·9	10·2 4·5	16·2 7·2
43	6 40·8	6 41·8	6 22·5	4·3 1·9	10·3 4·5	16·3 7·2
44	6 41·0	6 42·1	6 22·7	4·4 1·9	10·4 4·6	16·4 7·2
45	6 41·3	6 42·3	6 23·0	4·5 2·0	10·5 4·6	16·5 7·3
46	6 41·5	6 42·6	6 23·2	4·6 2·0	10·6 4·7	16·6 7·3
47	6 41·8	6 42·8	6 23·4	4·7 2·1	10·7 4·7	16·7 7·4
48	6 42·0	6 43·1	6 23·7	4·8 2·1	10·8 4·8	16·8 7·4
49	6 42·3	6 43·4	6 23·9	4·9 2·2	10·9 4·8	16·9 7·5
50	6 42·5	6 43·6	6 24·2	5·0 2·2	11·0 4·9	17·0 7·5
51	6 42·8	6 43·9	6 24·4	5·1 2·3	11·1 4·9	17·1 7·6
52	6 43·0	6 44·1	6 24·6	5·2 2·3	11·2 4·9	17·2 7·6
53	6 43·3	6 44·4	6 24·9	5·3 2·3	11·3 5·0	17·3 7·6
54	6 43·5	6 44·6	6 25·1	5·4 2·4	11·4 5·0	17·4 7·7
55	6 43·8	6 44·9	6 25·4	5·5 2·4	11·5 5·1	17·5 7·7
56	6 44·0	6 45·1	6 25·6	5·6 2·5	11·6 5·1	17·6 7·8
57	6 44·3	6 45·4	6 25·8	5·7 2·5	11·7 5·2	17·7 7·8
58	6 44·5	6 45·6	6 26·1	5·8 2·6	11·8 5·2	17·8 7·9
59	6 44·8	6 45·9	6 26·3	5·9 2·6	11·9 5·3	17·9 7·9
60	6 45·0	6 46·1	6 26·6	6·0 2·7	12·0 5·3	18·0 8·0

27 m	SUN PLANETS	ARIES	MOON	v or Corrn d	v or Corrn d	v or Corrn d
s	° ′	° ′	° ′	′ ′	′ ′	′ ′
00	6 45·0	6 46·1	6 26·6	0·0 0·0	6·0 2·8	12·0 5·5
01	6 45·3	6 46·4	6 26·8	0·1 0·0	6·1 2·8	12·1 5·5
02	6 45·5	6 46·6	6 27·0	0·2 0·1	6·2 2·8	12·2 5·6
03	6 45·8	6 46·9	6 27·3	0·3 0·1	6·3 2·9	12·3 5·6
04	6 46·0	6 47·1	6 27·5	0·4 0·2	6·4 2·9	12·4 5·7
05	6 46·3	6 47·4	6 27·7	0·5 0·2	6·5 3·0	12·5 5·7
06	6 46·5	6 47·6	6 28·0	0·6 0·3	6·6 3·0	12·6 5·8
07	6 46·8	6 47·9	6 28·2	0·7 0·3	6·7 3·1	12·7 5·8
08	6 47·0	6 48·1	6 28·5	0·8 0·4	6·8 3·1	12·8 5·9
09	6 47·3	6 48·4	6 28·7	0·9 0·4	6·9 3·2	12·9 5·9
10	6 47·5	6 48·6	6 28·9	1·0 0·5	7·0 3·2	13·0 6·0
11	6 47·8	6 48·9	6 29·2	1·1 0·5	7·1 3·3	13·1 6·0
12	6 48·0	6 49·1	6 29·4	1·2 0·6	7·2 3·3	13·2 6·1
13	6 48·3	6 49·4	6 29·7	1·3 0·6	7·3 3·3	13·3 6·1
14	6 48·5	6 49·6	6 29·9	1·4 0·6	7·4 3·4	13·4 6·1
15	6 48·8	6 49·9	6 30·1	1·5 0·7	7·5 3·4	13·5 6·2
16	6 49·0	6 50·1	6 30·4	1·6 0·7	7·6 3·5	13·6 6·2
17	6 49·3	6 50·4	6 30·6	1·7 0·8	7·7 3·5	13·7 6·3
18	6 49·5	6 50·6	6 30·8	1·8 0·8	7·8 3·6	13·8 6·3
19	6 49·8	6 50·9	6 31·1	1·9 0·9	7·9 3·6	13·9 6·4
20	6 50·0	6 51·1	6 31·3	2·0 0·9	8·0 3·7	14·0 6·4
21	6 50·3	6 51·4	6 31·6	2·1 1·0	8·1 3·7	14·1 6·5
22	6 50·5	6 51·6	6 31·8	2·2 1·0	8·2 3·8	14·2 6·5
23	6 50·8	6 51·9	6 32·0	2·3 1·1	8·3 3·8	14·3 6·6
24	6 51·0	6 52·1	6 32·3	2·4 1·1	8·4 3·9	14·4 6·6
25	6 51·3	6 52·4	6 32·5	2·5 1·1	8·5 3·9	14·5 6·6
26	6 51·5	6 52·6	6 32·8	2·6 1·2	8·6 3·9	14·6 6·7
27	6 51·8	6 52·9	6 33·0	2·7 1·2	8·7 4·0	14·7 6·7
28	6 52·0	6 53·1	6 33·2	2·8 1·3	8·8 4·0	14·8 6·8
29	6 52·3	6 53·4	6 33·5	2·9 1·3	8·9 4·1	14·9 6·8
30	6 52·5	6 53·6	6 33·7	3·0 1·4	9·0 4·1	15·0 6·9
31	6 52·8	6 53·9	6 33·9	3·1 1·4	9·1 4·2	15·1 6·9
32	6 53·0	6 54·1	6 34·2	3·2 1·5	9·2 4·2	15·2 7·0
33	6 53·3	6 54·4	6 34·4	3·3 1·5	9·3 4·3	15·3 7·0
34	6 53·5	6 54·6	6 34·7	3·4 1·6	9·4 4·3	15·4 7·1
35	6 53·8	6 54·9	6 34·9	3·5 1·6	9·5 4·4	15·5 7·1
36	6 54·0	6 55·1	6 35·1	3·6 1·7	9·6 4·4	15·6 7·2
37	6 54·3	6 55·4	6 35·4	3·7 1·7	9·7 4·4	15·7 7·2
38	6 54·5	6 55·6	6 35·6	3·8 1·7	9·8 4·5	15·8 7·2
39	6 54·8	6 55·9	6 35·9	3·9 1·8	9·9 4·5	15·9 7·3
40	6 55·0	6 56·1	6 36·1	4·0 1·8	10·0 4·6	16·0 7·3
41	6 55·3	6 56·4	6 36·3	4·1 1·9	10·1 4·6	16·1 7·4
42	6 55·5	6 56·6	6 36·6	4·2 1·9	10·2 4·7	16·2 7·4
43	6 55·8	6 56·9	6 36·8	4·3 2·0	10·3 4·7	16·3 7·5
44	6 56·0	6 57·1	6 37·0	4·4 2·0	10·4 4·8	16·4 7·5
45	6 56·3	6 57·4	6 37·3	4·5 2·1	10·5 4·8	16·5 7·6
46	6 56·5	6 57·6	6 37·5	4·6 2·1	10·6 4·9	16·6 7·6
47	6 56·8	6 57·9	6 37·8	4·7 2·2	10·7 4·9	16·7 7·7
48	6 57·0	6 58·1	6 38·0	4·8 2·2	10·8 5·0	16·8 7·7
49	6 57·3	6 58·4	6 38·2	4·9 2·2	10·9 5·0	16·9 7·7
50	6 57·5	6 58·6	6 38·5	5·0 2·3	11·0 5·0	17·0 7·8
51	6 57·8	6 58·9	6 38·7	5·1 2·3	11·1 5·1	17·1 7·8
52	6 58·0	6 59·1	6 39·0	5·2 2·4	11·2 5·1	17·2 7·9
53	6 58·3	6 59·4	6 39·2	5·3 2·4	11·3 5·2	17·3 7·9
54	6 58·5	6 59·6	6 39·4	5·4 2·5	11·4 5·2	17·4 8·0
55	6 58·8	6 59·9	6 39·7	5·5 2·5	11·5 5·3	17·5 8·0
56	6 59·0	7 00·1	6 39·9	5·6 2·6	11·6 5·3	17·6 8·1
57	6 59·3	7 00·4	6 40·2	5·7 2·6	11·7 5·4	17·7 8·1
58	6 59·5	7 00·6	6 40·4	5·8 2·7	11·8 5·4	17·8 8·2
59	6 59·8	7 00·9	6 40·6	5·9 2·7	11·9 5·5	17·9 8·2
60	7 00·0	7 01·1	6 40·9	6·0 2·8	12·0 5·5	18·0 8·3

28ᵐ

m 28	SUN PLANETS	ARIES	MOON	v or Corrⁿ d	v or Corrⁿ d	v or Corrⁿ d
s	° ′	° ′	° ′	′ ′	′ ′	′ ′
00	7 00·0	7 01·1	6 40·9	0·0 0·0	6·0 2·9	12·0 5·7
01	7 00·3	7 01·4	6 41·1	0·1 0·0	6·1 2·9	12·1 5·7
02	7 00·5	7 01·7	6 41·3	0·2 0·1	6·2 2·9	12·2 5·8
03	7 00·8	7 01·9	6 41·6	0·3 0·1	6·3 3·0	12·3 5·8
04	7 01·0	7 02·2	6 41·8	0·4 0·2	6·4 3·0	12·4 5·9
05	7 01·3	7 02·4	6 42·1	0·5 0·2	6·5 3·1	12·5 5·9
06	7 01·5	7 02·7	6 42·3	0·6 0·3	6·6 3·1	12·6 6·0
07	7 01·8	7 02·9	6 42·5	0·7 0·3	6·7 3·2	12·7 6·0
08	7 02·0	7 03·2	6 42·8	0·8 0·4	6·8 3·2	12·8 6·1
09	7 02·3	7 03·4	6 43·0	0·9 0·4	6·9 3·3	12·9 6·1
10	7 02·5	7 03·7	6 43·3	1·0 0·5	7·0 3·3	13·0 6·2
11	7 02·8	7 03·9	6 43·5	1·1 0·5	7·1 3·4	13·1 6·2
12	7 03·0	7 04·2	6 43·7	1·2 0·6	7·2 3·4	13·2 6·3
13	7 03·3	7 04·4	6 44·0	1·3 0·6	7·3 3·5	13·3 6·3
14	7 03·5	7 04·7	6 44·2	1·4 0·7	7·4 3·5	13·4 6·4
15	7 03·8	7 04·9	6 44·4	1·5 0·7	7·5 3·6	13·5 6·4
16	7 04·0	7 05·2	6 44·7	1·6 0·8	7·6 3·6	13·6 6·5
17	7 04·3	7 05·4	6 44·9	1·7 0·8	7·7 3·7	13·7 6·5
18	7 04·5	7 05·7	6 45·2	1·8 0·9	7·8 3·7	13·8 6·6
19	7 04·8	7 05·9	6 45·4	1·9 0·9	7·9 3·8	13·9 6·6
20	7 05·0	7 06·2	6 45·6	2·0 1·0	8·0 3·8	14·0 6·7
21	7 05·3	7 06·4	6 45·9	2·1 1·0	8·1 3·8	14·1 6·7
22	7 05·5	7 06·7	6 46·1	2·2 1·0	8·2 3·9	14·2 6·7
23	7 05·8	7 06·9	6 46·4	2·3 1·1	8·3 3·9	14·3 6·8
24	7 06·0	7 07·2	6 46·6	2·4 1·1	8·4 4·0	14·4 6·8
25	7 06·3	7 07·4	6 46·8	2·5 1·2	8·5 4·0	14·5 6·9
26	7 06·5	7 07·7	6 47·1	2·6 1·2	8·6 4·1	14·6 6·9
27	7 06·8	7 07·9	6 47·3	2·7 1·3	8·7 4·1	14·7 7·0
28	7 07·0	7 08·2	6 47·5	2·8 1·3	8·8 4·2	14·8 7·0
29	7 07·3	7 08·4	6 47·8	2·9 1·4	8·9 4·2	14·9 7·1
30	7 07·5	7 08·7	6 48·0	3·0 1·4	9·0 4·3	15·0 7·1
31	7 07·8	7 08·9	6 48·3	3·1 1·5	9·1 4·3	15·1 7·2
32	7 08·0	7 09·2	6 48·5	3·2 1·5	9·2 4·4	15·2 7·2
33	7 08·3	7 09·4	6 48·7	3·3 1·6	9·3 4·4	15·3 7·3
34	7 08·5	7 09·7	6 49·0	3·4 1·6	9·4 4·5	15·4 7·3
35	7 08·8	7 09·9	6 49·2	3·5 1·7	9·5 4·5	15·5 7·4
36	7 09·0	7 10·2	6 49·5	3·6 1·7	9·6 4·6	15·6 7·4
37	7 09·3	7 10·4	6 49·7	3·7 1·8	9·7 4·6	15·7 7·5
38	7 09·5	7 10·7	6 49·9	3·8 1·8	9·8 4·7	15·8 7·5
39	7 09·8	7 10·9	6 50·2	3·9 1·9	9·9 4·7	15·9 7·6
40	7 10·0	7 11·2	6 50·4	4·0 1·9	10·0 4·8	16·0 7·6
41	7 10·3	7 11·4	6 50·6	4·1 1·9	10·1 4·8	16·1 7·6
42	7 10·5	7 11·7	6 50·9	4·2 2·0	10·2 4·8	16·2 7·7
43	7 10·8	7 11·9	6 51·1	4·3 2·0	10·3 4·9	16·3 7·7
44	7 11·0	7 12·2	6 51·4	4·4 2·1	10·4 4·9	16·4 7·8
45	7 11·3	7 12·4	6 51·6	4·5 2·1	10·5 5·0	16·5 7·8
46	7 11·5	7 12·7	6 51·8	4·6 2·2	10·6 5·0	16·6 7·9
47	7 11·8	7 12·9	6 52·1	4·7 2·2	10·7 5·1	16·7 7·9
48	7 12·0	7 13·2	6 52·3	4·8 2·3	10·8 5·1	16·8 8·0
49	7 12·3	7 13·4	6 52·6	4·9 2·3	10·9 5·2	16·9 8·0
50	7 12·5	7 13·7	6 52·8	5·0 2·4	11·0 5·2	17·0 8·1
51	7 12·8	7 13·9	6 53·0	5·1 2·4	11·1 5·3	17·1 8·1
52	7 13·0	7 14·2	6 53·3	5·2 2·5	11·2 5·3	17·2 8·2
53	7 13·3	7 14·4	6 53·5	5·3 2·5	11·3 5·4	17·3 8·2
54	7 13·5	7 14·7	6 53·8	5·4 2·6	11·4 5·4	17·4 8·3
55	7 13·8	7 14·9	6 54·0	5·5 2·6	11·5 5·5	17·5 8·3
56	7 14·0	7 15·2	6 54·2	5·6 2·7	11·6 5·5	17·6 8·4
57	7 14·3	7 15·4	6 54·5	5·7 2·7	11·7 5·6	17·7 8·4
58	7 14·5	7 15·7	6 54·7	5·8 2·8	11·8 5·6	17·8 8·5
59	7 14·8	7 15·9	6 54·9	5·9 2·8	11·9 5·7	17·9 8·5
60	7 15·0	7 16·2	6 55·2	6·0 2·9	12·0 5·7	18·0 8·6

29ᵐ

m 29	SUN PLANETS	ARIES	MOON	v or Corrⁿ d	v or Corrⁿ d	v or Corrⁿ d
s	° ′	° ′	° ′	′ ′	′ ′	′ ′
00	7 15·0	7 16·2	6 55·2	0·0 0·0	6·0 3·0	12·0 5·9
01	7 15·3	7 16·4	6 55·4	0·1 0·0	6·1 3·0	12·1 5·9
02	7 15·5	7 16·7	6 55·7	0·2 0·1	6·2 3·0	12·2 6·0
03	7 15·8	7 16·9	6 55·9	0·3 0·1	6·3 3·1	12·3 6·0
04	7 16·0	7 17·2	6 56·1	0·4 0·2	6·4 3·1	12·4 6·1
05	7 16·3	7 17·4	6 56·4	0·5 0·2	6·5 3·2	12·5 6·1
06	7 16·5	7 17·7	6 56·6	0·6 0·3	6·6 3·2	12·6 6·2
07	7 16·8	7 17·9	6 56·9	0·7 0·3	6·7 3·3	12·7 6·2
08	7 17·0	7 18·2	6 57·1	0·8 0·4	6·8 3·3	12·8 6·3
09	7 17·3	7 18·4	6 57·3	0·9 0·4	6·9 3·4	12·9 6·3
10	7 17·5	7 18·7	6 57·6	1·0 0·5	7·0 3·4	13·0 6·4
11	7 17·8	7 18·9	6 57·8	1·1 0·5	7·1 3·5	13·1 6·4
12	7 18·0	7 19·2	6 58·0	1·2 0·6	7·2 3·5	13·2 6·5
13	7 18·3	7 19·4	6 58·3	1·3 0·6	7·3 3·6	13·3 6·5
14	7 18·5	7 19·7	6 58·5	1·4 0·7	7·4 3·6	13·4 6·6
15	7 18·8	7 20·0	6 58·8	1·5 0·7	7·5 3·7	13·5 6·6
16	7 19·0	7 20·2	6 59·0	1·6 0·8	7·6 3·7	13·6 6·7
17	7 19·3	7 20·5	6 59·2	1·7 0·8	7·7 3·8	13·7 6·7
18	7 19·5	7 20·7	6 59·5	1·8 0·9	7·8 3·8	13·8 6·8
19	7 19·8	7 21·0	6 59·7	1·9 0·9	7·9 3·9	13·9 6·8
20	7 20·0	7 21·2	7 00·0	2·0 1·0	8·0 3·9	14·0 6·9
21	7 20·3	7 21·5	7 00·2	2·1 1·0	8·1 4·0	14·1 6·9
22	7 20·5	7 21·7	7 00·4	2·2 1·1	8·2 4·0	14·2 7·0
23	7 20·8	7 22·0	7 00·7	2·3 1·1	8·3 4·1	14·3 7·0
24	7 21·0	7 22·2	7 00·9	2·4 1·2	8·4 4·1	14·4 7·1
25	7 21·3	7 22·5	7 01·1	2·5 1·2	8·5 4·2	14·5 7·1
26	7 21·5	7 22·7	7 01·4	2·6 1·3	8·6 4·2	14·6 7·2
27	7 21·8	7 23·0	7 01·6	2·7 1·3	8·7 4·3	14·7 7·2
28	7 22·0	7 23·2	7 01·9	2·8 1·4	8·8 4·3	14·8 7·3
29	7 22·3	7 23·5	7 02·1	2·9 1·4	8·9 4·4	14·9 7·3
30	7 22·5	7 23·7	7 02·3	3·0 1·5	9·0 4·4	15·0 7·4
31	7 22·8	7 24·0	7 02·6	3·1 1·5	9·1 4·5	15·1 7·4
32	7 23·0	7 24·2	7 02·8	3·2 1·6	9·2 4·5	15·2 7·5
33	7 23·3	7 24·5	7 03·1	3·3 1·6	9·3 4·6	15·3 7·5
34	7 23·5	7 24·7	7 03·3	3·4 1·7	9·4 4·6	15·4 7·6
35	7 23·8	7 25·0	7 03·5	3·5 1·7	9·5 4·7	15·5 7·6
36	7 24·0	7 25·2	7 03·8	3·6 1·8	9·6 4·7	15·6 7·7
37	7 24·3	7 25·5	7 04·0	3·7 1·8	9·7 4·8	15·7 7·7
38	7 24·5	7 25·7	7 04·3	3·8 1·9	9·8 4·8	15·8 7·8
39	7 24·8	7 26·0	7 04·5	3·9 1·9	9·9 4·9	15·9 7·8
40	7 25·0	7 26·2	7 04·7	4·0 2·0	10·0 4·9	16·0 7·9
41	7 25·3	7 26·5	7 05·0	4·1 2·0	10·1 5·0	16·1 7·9
42	7 25·5	7 26·7	7 05·2	4·2 2·1	10·2 5·0	16·2 8·0
43	7 25·8	7 27·0	7 05·4	4·3 2·1	10·3 5·1	16·3 8·0
44	7 26·0	7 27·2	7 05·7	4·4 2·2	10·4 5·1	16·4 8·1
45	7 26·3	7 27·5	7 05·9	4·5 2·2	10·5 5·2	16·5 8·1
46	7 26·5	7 27·7	7 06·2	4·6 2·3	10·6 5·2	16·6 8·2
47	7 26·8	7 28·0	7 06·4	4·7 2·3	10·7 5·3	16·7 8·2
48	7 27·0	7 28·2	7 06·6	4·8 2·4	10·8 5·3	16·8 8·3
49	7 27·3	7 28·5	7 06·9	4·9 2·4	10·9 5·4	16·9 8·3
50	7 27·5	7 28·7	7 07·1	5·0 2·5	11·0 5·4	17·0 8·4
51	7 27·8	7 29·0	7 07·4	5·1 2·5	11·1 5·5	17·1 8·4
52	7 28·0	7 29·2	7 07·6	5·2 2·6	11·2 5·5	17·2 8·5
53	7 28·3	7 29·5	7 07·8	5·3 2·6	11·3 5·6	17·3 8·5
54	7 28·5	7 29·7	7 08·1	5·4 2·7	11·4 5·6	17·4 8·6
55	7 28·8	7 30·0	7 08·3	5·5 2·7	11·5 5·7	17·5 8·6
56	7 29·0	7 30·2	7 08·5	5·6 2·8	11·6 5·7	17·6 8·7
57	7 29·3	7 30·5	7 08·8	5·7 2·8	11·7 5·8	17·7 8·7
58	7 29·5	7 30·7	7 09·0	5·8 2·9	11·8 5·8	17·8 8·8
59	7 29·8	7 31·0	7 09·3	5·9 2·9	11·9 5·9	17·9 8·8
60	7 30·0	7 31·2	7 09·5	6·0 3·0	12·0 5·9	18·0 8·9

30ᵐ

30	SUN PLANETS	ARIES	MOON	v or Corrⁿ d	v or Corrⁿ d	v or Corrⁿ d
s	° ′	° ′	° ′	′ ′	′ ′	′ ′
00	7 30·0	7 31·2	7 09·5	0·0 0·0	6·0 3·1	12·0 6·1
01	7 30·3	7 31·5	7 09·7	0·1 0·1	6·1 3·1	12·1 6·2
02	7 30·5	7 31·7	7 10·0	0·2 0·1	6·2 3·2	12·2 6·2
03	7 30·8	7 32·0	7 10·2	0·3 0·2	6·3 3·2	12·3 6·3
04	7 31·0	7 32·2	7 10·5	0·4 0·2	6·4 3·3	12·4 6·3
05	7 31·3	7 32·5	7 10·7	0·5 0·3	6·5 3·3	12·5 6·4
06	7 31·5	7 32·7	7 10·9	0·6 0·3	6·6 3·4	12·6 6·4
07	7 31·8	7 33·0	7 11·2	0·7 0·4	6·7 3·4	12·7 6·5
08	7 32·0	7 33·2	7 11·4	0·8 0·4	6·8 3·5	12·8 6·5
09	7 32·3	7 33·5	7 11·6	0·9 0·5	6·9 3·5	12·9 6·6
10	7 32·5	7 33·7	7 11·9	1·0 0·5	7·0 3·6	13·0 6·6
11	7 32·8	7 34·0	7 12·1	1·1 0·6	7·1 3·6	13·1 6·7
12	7 33·0	7 34·2	7 12·4	1·2 0·6	7·2 3·7	13·2 6·7
13	7 33·3	7 34·5	7 12·6	1·3 0·7	7·3 3·7	13·3 6·8
14	7 33·5	7 34·7	7 12·8	1·4 0·7	7·4 3·8	13·4 6·8
15	7 33·8	7 35·0	7 13·1	1·5 0·8	7·5 3·8	13·5 6·9
16	7 34·0	7 35·2	7 13·3	1·6 0·8	7·6 3·9	13·6 6·9
17	7 34·3	7 35·5	7 13·6	1·7 0·9	7·7 3·9	13·7 7·0
18	7 34·5	7 35·7	7 13·8	1·8 0·9	7·8 4·0	13·8 7·0
19	7 34·8	7 36·0	7 14·0	1·9 1·0	7·9 4·0	13·9 7·1
20	7 35·0	7 36·2	7 14·3	2·0 1·0	8·0 4·1	14·0 7·1
21	7 35·3	7 36·5	7 14·5	2·1 1·1	8·1 4·1	14·1 7·2
22	7 35·5	7 36·7	7 14·7	2·2 1·1	8·2 4·2	14·2 7·2
23	7 35·8	7 37·0	7 15·0	2·3 1·2	8·3 4·2	14·3 7·3
24	7 36·0	7 37·2	7 15·2	2·4 1·2	8·4 4·3	14·4 7·3
25	7 36·3	7 37·5	7 15·5	2·5 1·3	8·5 4·3	14·5 7·4
26	7 36·5	7 37·7	7 15·7	2·6 1·3	8·6 4·4	14·6 7·4
27	7 36·8	7 38·0	7 15·9	2·7 1·4	8·7 4·4	14·7 7·5
28	7 37·0	7 38·3	7 16·2	2·8 1·4	8·8 4·5	14·8 7·5
29	7 37·3	7 38·5	7 16·4	2·9 1·5	8·9 4·5	14·9 7·6
30	7 37·5	7 38·8	7 16·7	3·0 1·5	9·0 4·6	15·0 7·6
31	7 37·8	7 39·0	7 16·9	3·1 1·6	9·1 4·6	15·1 7·7
32	7 38·0	7 39·3	7 17·1	3·2 1·6	9·2 4·7	15·2 7·7
33	7 38·3	7 39·5	7 17·4	3·3 1·7	9·3 4·7	15·3 7·8
34	7 38·5	7 39·8	7 17·6	3·4 1·7	9·4 4·8	15·4 7·8
35	7 38·8	7 40·0	7 17·9	3·5 1·8	9·5 4·8	15·5 7·9
36	7 39·0	7 40·3	7 18·1	3·6 1·8	9·6 4·9	15·6 7·9
37	7 39·3	7 40·5	7 18·3	3·7 1·9	9·7 4·9	15·7 8·0
38	7 39·5	7 40·8	7 18·6	3·8 1·9	9·8 5·0	15·8 8·0
39	7 39·8	7 41·0	7 18·8	3·9 2·0	9·9 5·0	15·9 8·1
40	7 40·0	7 41·3	7 19·0	4·0 2·0	10·0 5·1	16·0 8·1
41	7 40·3	7 41·5	7 19·3	4·1 2·1	10·1 5·1	16·1 8·2
42	7 40·5	7 41·8	7 19·5	4·2 2·1	10·2 5·2	16·2 8·2
43	7 40·8	7 42·0	7 19·8	4·3 2·2	10·3 5·2	16·3 8·3
44	7 41·0	7 42·3	7 20·0	4·4 2·2	10·4 5·3	16·4 8·3
45	7 41·3	7 42·5	7 20·2	4·5 2·3	10·5 5·3	16·5 8·4
46	7 41·5	7 42·8	7 20·5	4·6 2·3	10·6 5·4	16·6 8·4
47	7 41·8	7 43·0	7 20·7	4·7 2·4	10·7 5·4	16·7 8·5
48	7 42·0	7 43·3	7 21·0	4·8 2·4	10·8 5·5	16·8 8·5
49	7 42·3	7 43·5	7 21·2	4·9 2·5	10·9 5·5	16·9 8·6
50	7 42·5	7 43·8	7 21·4	5·0 2·5	11·0 5·6	17·0 8·6
51	7 42·8	7 44·0	7 21·7	5·1 2·6	11·1 5·6	17·1 8·7
52	7 43·0	7 44·3	7 21·9	5·2 2·6	11·2 5·7	17·2 8·7
53	7 43·3	7 44·5	7 22·1	5·3 2·7	11·3 5·7	17·3 8·8
54	7 43·5	7 44·8	7 22·4	5·4 2·7	11·4 5·8	17·4 8·8
55	7 43·8	7 45·0	7 22·6	5·5 2·8	11·5 5·8	17·5 8·9
56	7 44·0	7 45·3	7 22·9	5·6 2·8	11·6 5·9	17·6 8·9
57	7 44·3	7 45·5	7 23·1	5·7 2·9	11·7 5·9	17·7 9·0
58	7 44·5	7 45·8	7 23·3	5·8 2·9	11·8 6·0	17·8 9·0
59	7 44·8	7 46·0	7 23·6	5·9 3·0	11·9 6·0	17·9 9·1
60	7 45·0	7 46·3	7 23·8	6·0 3·1	12·0 6·1	18·0 9·2

31ᵐ

31	SUN PLANETS	ARIES	MOON	v or Corrⁿ d	v or Corrⁿ d	v or Corrⁿ d
s	° ′	° ′	° ′	′ ′	′ ′	′ ′
00	7 45·0	7 46·3	7 23·8	0·0 0·0	6·0 3·2	12·0 6·3
01	7 45·3	7 46·5	7 24·1	0·1 0·1	6·1 3·2	12·1 6·4
02	7 45·5	7 46·8	7 24·3	0·2 0·1	6·2 3·3	12·2 6·4
03	7 45·8	7 47·0	7 24·5	0·3 0·2	6·3 3·3	12·3 6·5
04	7 46·0	7 47·3	7 24·8	0·4 0·2	6·4 3·4	12·4 6·5
05	7 46·3	7 47·5	7 25·0	0·5 0·3	6·5 3·4	12·5 6·6
06	7 46·5	7 47·8	7 25·2	0·6 0·3	6·6 3·5	12·6 6·6
07	7 46·8	7 48·0	7 25·5	0·7 0·4	6·7 3·5	12·7 6·7
08	7 47·0	7 48·3	7 25·7	0·8 0·4	6·8 3·6	12·8 6·7
09	7 47·3	7 48·5	7 26·0	0·9 0·5	6·9 3·6	12·9 6·8
10	7 47·5	7 48·8	7 26·2	1·0 0·5	7·0 3·7	13·0 6·8
11	7 47·8	7 49·0	7 26·4	1·1 0·6	7·1 3·7	13·1 6·9
12	7 48·0	7 49·3	7 26·7	1·2 0·6	7·2 3·8	13·2 6·9
13	7 48·3	7 49·5	7 26·9	1·3 0·7	7·3 3·8	13·3 7·0
14	7 48·5	7 49·8	7 27·2	1·4 0·7	7·4 3·9	13·4 7·0
15	7 48·8	7 50·0	7 27·4	1·5 0·8	7·5 3·9	13·5 7·1
16	7 49·0	7 50·3	7 27·6	1·6 0·8	7·6 4·0	13·6 7·1
17	7 49·3	7 50·5	7 27·9	1·7 0·9	7·7 4·0	13·7 7·2
18	7 49·5	7 50·8	7 28·1	1·8 0·9	7·8 4·1	13·8 7·2
19	7 49·8	7 51·0	7 28·4	1·9 1·0	7·9 4·1	13·9 7·3
20	7 50·0	7 51·3	7 28·6	2·0 1·1	8·0 4·2	14·0 7·4
21	7 50·3	7 51·5	7 28·8	2·1 1·1	8·1 4·3	14·1 7·4
22	7 50·5	7 51·8	7 29·1	2·2 1·2	8·2 4·3	14·2 7·5
23	7 50·8	7 52·0	7 29·3	2·3 1·2	8·3 4·4	14·3 7·5
24	7 51·0	7 52·3	7 29·5	2·4 1·3	8·4 4·4	14·4 7·6
25	7 51·3	7 52·5	7 29·8	2·5 1·3	8·5 4·5	14·5 7·6
26	7 51·5	7 52·8	7 30·0	2·6 1·4	8·6 4·5	14·6 7·7
27	7 51·8	7 53·0	7 30·3	2·7 1·4	8·7 4·6	14·7 7·7
28	7 52·0	7 53·3	7 30·5	2·8 1·5	8·8 4·6	14·8 7·8
29	7 52·3	7 53·5	7 30·7	2·9 1·5	8·9 4·7	14·9 7·8
30	7 52·5	7 53·8	7 31·0	3·0 1·6	9·0 4·7	15·0 7·9
31	7 52·8	7 54·0	7 31·2	3·1 1·6	9·1 4·8	15·1 7·9
32	7 53·0	7 54·3	7 31·5	3·2 1·7	9·2 4·8	15·2 8·0
33	7 53·3	7 54·5	7 31·7	3·3 1·7	9·3 4·9	15·3 8·0
34	7 53·5	7 54·8	7 31·9	3·4 1·8	9·4 4·9	15·4 8·1
35	7 53·8	7 55·0	7 32·2	3·5 1·8	9·5 5·0	15·5 8·1
36	7 54·0	7 55·3	7 32·4	3·6 1·9	9·6 5·0	15·6 8·2
37	7 54·3	7 55·5	7 32·6	3·7 1·9	9·7 5·1	15·7 8·2
38	7 54·5	7 55·8	7 32·9	3·8 2·0	9·8 5·1	15·8 8·3
39	7 54·8	7 56·0	7 33·1	3·9 2·0	9·9 5·2	15·9 8·3
40	7 55·0	7 56·3	7 33·4	4·0 2·1	10·0 5·3	16·0 8·4
41	7 55·3	7 56·6	7 33·6	4·1 2·2	10·1 5·3	16·1 8·5
42	7 55·5	7 56·8	7 33·8	4·2 2·2	10·2 5·4	16·2 8·5
43	7 55·8	7 57·1	7 34·1	4·3 2·3	10·3 5·4	16·3 8·6
44	7 56·0	7 57·3	7 34·3	4·4 2·3	10·4 5·5	16·4 8·6
45	7 56·3	7 57·6	7 34·6	4·5 2·4	10·5 5·5	16·5 8·7
46	7 56·5	7 57·8	7 34·8	4·6 2·4	10·6 5·6	16·6 8·7
47	7 56·8	7 58·1	7 35·0	4·7 2·5	10·7 5·6	16·7 8·8
48	7 57·0	7 58·3	7 35·3	4·8 2·5	10·8 5·7	16·8 8·8
49	7 57·3	7 58·6	7 35·5	4·9 2·6	10·9 5·7	16·9 8·9
50	7 57·5	7 58·8	7 35·7	5·0 2·6	11·0 5·8	17·0 8·9
51	7 57·8	7 59·1	7 36·0	5·1 2·7	11·1 5·8	17·1 9·0
52	7 58·0	7 59·3	7 36·2	5·2 2·7	11·2 5·9	17·2 9·0
53	7 58·3	7 59·6	7 36·5	5·3 2·8	11·3 5·9	17·3 9·1
54	7 58·5	7 59·8	7 36·7	5·4 2·8	11·4 6·0	17·4 9·1
55	7 58·8	8 00·1	7 36·9	5·5 2·9	11·5 6·0	17·5 9·2
56	7 59·0	8 00·3	7 37·2	5·6 2·9	11·6 6·1	17·6 9·2
57	7 59·3	8 00·6	7 37·4	5·7 3·0	11·7 6·1	17·7 9·3
58	7 59·5	8 00·8	7 37·7	5·8 3·0	11·8 6·2	17·8 9·3
59	7 59·8	8 01·1	7 37·9	5·9 3·1	11·9 6·2	17·9 9·4
60	8 00·0	8 01·3	7 38·1	6·0 3·2	12·0 6·3	18·0 9·5

32 s	SUN PLANETS	ARIES	MOON	v or d Corrⁿ	v or d Corrⁿ	v or d Corrⁿ	33 s	SUN PLANETS	ARIES	MOON	v or d Corrⁿ	v or d Corrⁿ	v or d Corrⁿ
00	8 00·0	8 01·3	7 38·1	0·0 0·0	6·0 3·3	12·0 6·5	00	8 15·0	8 16·4	7 52·5	0·0 0·0	6·0 3·4	12·0 6·7
01	8 00·3	8 01·6	7 38·4	0·1 0·1	6·1 3·3	12·1 6·6	01	8 15·3	8 16·6	7 52·7	0·1 0·1	6·1 3·4	12·1 6·8
02	8 00·5	8 01·8	7 38·6	0·2 0·1	6·2 3·4	12·2 6·6	02	8 15·5	8 16·9	7 52·9	0·2 0·1	6·2 3·5	12·2 6·8
03	8 00·8	8 02·1	7 38·8	0·3 0·2	6·3 3·4	12·3 6·7	03	8 15·8	8 17·1	7 53·2	0·3 0·2	6·3 3·5	12·3 6·9
04	8 01·0	8 02·3	7 39·1	0·4 0·2	6·4 3·5	12·4 6·7	04	8 16·0	8 17·4	7 53·4	0·4 0·2	6·4 3·6	12·4 6·9
05	8 01·3	8 02·6	7 39·3	0·5 0·3	6·5 3·5	12·5 6·8	05	8 16·3	8 17·6	7 53·6	0·5 0·3	6·5 3·6	12·5 7·0
06	8 01·5	8 02·8	7 39·6	0·6 0·3	6·6 3·6	12·6 6·8	06	8 16·5	8 17·9	7 53·9	0·6 0·3	6·6 3·7	12·6 7·0
07	8 01·8	8 03·1	7 39·8	0·7 0·4	6·7 3·6	12·7 6·9	07	8 16·8	8 18·1	7 54·1	0·7 0·4	6·7 3·7	12·7 7·1
08	8 02·0	8 03·3	7 40·0	0·8 0·4	6·8 3·7	12·8 6·9	08	8 17·0	8 18·4	7 54·4	0·8 0·4	6·8 3·8	12·8 7·1
09	8 02·3	8 03·6	7 40·3	0·9 0·5	6·9 3·7	12·9 7·0	09	8 17·3	8 18·6	7 54·6	0·9 0·5	6·9 3·9	12·9 7·2
10	8 02·5	8 03·8	7 40·5	1·0 0·5	7·0 3·8	13·0 7·0	10	8 17·5	8 18·9	7 54·8	1·0 0·6	7·0 3·9	13·0 7·3
11	8 02·8	8 04·1	7 40·8	1·1 0·6	7·1 3·8	13·1 7·1	11	8 17·8	8 19·1	7 55·1	1·1 0·6	7·1 4·0	13·1 7·3
12	8 03·0	8 04·3	7 41·0	1·2 0·7	7·2 3·9	13·2 7·2	12	8 18·0	8 19·4	7 55·3	1·2 0·7	7·2 4·0	13·2 7·4
13	8 03·3	8 04·6	7 41·2	1·3 0·7	7·3 4·0	13·3 7·2	13	8 18·3	8 19·6	7 55·6	1·3 0·7	7·3 4·1	13·3 7·4
14	8 03·5	8 04·8	7 41·5	1·4 0·8	7·4 4·0	13·4 7·3	14	8 18·5	8 19·9	7 55·8	1·4 0·8	7·4 4·1	13·4 7·5
15	8 03·8	8 05·1	7 41·7	1·5 0·8	7·5 4·1	13·5 7·3	15	8 18·8	8 20·1	7 56·0	1·5 0·8	7·5 4·2	13·5 7·5
16	8 04·0	8 05·3	7 42·0	1·6 0·9	7·6 4·1	13·6 7·4	16	8 19·0	8 20·4	7 56·3	1·6 0·9	7·6 4·2	13·6 7·6
17	8 04·3	8 05·6	7 42·2	1·7 0·9	7·7 4·2	13·7 7·4	17	8 19·3	8 20·6	7 56·5	1·7 0·9	7·7 4·3	13·7 7·6
18	8 04·5	8 05·8	7 42·4	1·8 1·0	7·8 4·2	13·8 7·5	18	8 19·5	8 20·9	7 56·7	1·8 1·0	7·8 4·4	13·8 7·7
19	8 04·8	8 06·1	7 42·7	1·9 1·0	7·9 4·3	13·9 7·5	19	8 19·8	8 21·1	7 57·0	1·9 1·1	7·9 4·4	13·9 7·8
20	8 05·0	8 06·3	7 42·9	2·0 1·1	8·0 4·3	14·0 7·6	20	8 20·0	8 21·4	7 57·2	2·0 1·1	8·0 4·5	14·0 7·8
21	8 05·3	8 06·6	7 43·1	2·1 1·1	8·1 4·4	14·1 7·6	21	8 20·3	8 21·6	7 57·5	2·1 1·2	8·1 4·5	14·1 7·9
22	8 05·5	8 06·8	7 43·4	2·2 1·2	8·2 4·4	14·2 7·7	22	8 20·5	8 21·9	7 57·7	2·2 1·2	8·2 4·6	14·2 7·9
23	8 05·8	8 07·1	7 43·6	2·3 1·2	8·3 4·5	14·3 7·7	23	8 20·8	8 22·1	7 57·9	2·3 1·3	8·3 4·6	14·3 8·0
24	8 06·0	8 07·3	7 43·9	2·4 1·3	8·4 4·6	14·4 7·8	24	8 21·0	8 22·4	7 58·2	2·4 1·3	8·4 4·7	14·4 8·0
25	8 06·3	8 07·6	7 44·1	2·5 1·4	8·5 4·6	14·5 7·9	25	8 21·3	8 22·6	7 58·4	2·5 1·4	8·5 4·7	14·5 8·1
26	8 06·5	8 07·8	7 44·3	2·6 1·4	8·6 4·7	14·6 7·9	26	8 21·5	8 22·9	7 58·7	2·6 1·5	8·6 4·8	14·6 8·2
27	8 06·8	8 08·1	7 44·6	2·7 1·5	8·7 4·7	14·7 8·0	27	8 21·8	8 23·1	7 58·9	2·7 1·5	8·7 4·9	14·7 8·2
28	8 07·0	8 08·3	7 44·8	2·8 1·5	8·8 4·8	14·8 8·0	28	8 22·0	8 23·4	7 59·1	2·8 1·6	8·8 4·9	14·8 8·3
29	8 07·3	8 08·6	7 45·1	2·9 1·6	8·9 4·8	14·9 8·1	29	8 22·3	8 23·6	7 59·4	2·9 1·6	8·9 5·0	14·9 8·3
30	8 07·5	8 08·8	7 45·3	3·0 1·6	9·0 4·9	15·0 8·1	30	8 22·5	8 23·9	7 59·6	3·0 1·7	9·0 5·0	15·0 8·4
31	8 07·8	8 09·1	7 45·5	3·1 1·7	9·1 4·9	15·1 8·2	31	8 22·8	8 24·1	7 59·8	3·1 1·7	9·1 5·1	15·1 8·4
32	8 08·0	8 09·3	7 45·8	3·2 1·7	9·2 5·0	15·2 8·2	32	8 23·0	8 24·4	8 00·1	3·2 1·8	9·2 5·1	15·2 8·5
33	8 08·3	8 09·6	7 46·0	3·3 1·8	9·3 5·0	15·3 8·3	33	8 23·3	8 24·6	8 00·3	3·3 1·8	9·3 5·2	15·3 8·5
34	8 08·5	8 09·8	7 46·2	3·4 1·8	9·4 5·1	15·4 8·3	34	8 23·5	8 24·9	8 00·6	3·4 1·9	9·4 5·2	15·4 8·6
35	8 08·8	8 10·1	7 46·5	3·5 1·9	9·5 5·1	15·5 8·4	35	8 23·8	8 25·1	8 00·8	3·5 2·0	9·5 5·3	15·5 8·7
36	8 09·0	8 10·3	7 46·7	3·6 2·0	9·6 5·2	15·6 8·5	36	8 24·0	8 25·4	8 01·0	3·6 2·0	9·6 5·4	15·6 8·7
37	8 09·3	8 10·6	7 47·0	3·7 2·0	9·7 5·3	15·7 8·5	37	8 24·3	8 25·6	8 01·3	3·7 2·1	9·7 5·4	15·7 8·8
38	8 09·5	8 10·8	7 47·2	3·8 2·1	9·8 5·3	15·8 8·6	38	8 24·5	8 25·9	8 01·5	3·8 2·1	9·8 5·5	15·8 8·8
39	8 09·8	8 11·1	7 47·4	3·9 2·1	9·9 5·4	15·9 8·6	39	8 24·8	8 26·1	8 01·8	3·9 2·2	9·9 5·5	15·9 8·9
40	8 10·0	8 11·3	7 47·7	4·0 2·2	10·0 5·4	16·0 8·7	40	8 25·0	8 26·4	8 02·0	4·0 2·2	10·0 5·6	16·0 8·9
41	8 10·3	8 11·6	7 47·9	4·1 2·2	10·1 5·5	16·1 8·7	41	8 25·3	8 26·6	8 02·2	4·1 2·3	10·1 5·6	16·1 9·0
42	8 10·5	8 11·8	7 48·2	4·2 2·3	10·2 5·5	16·2 8·8	42	8 25·5	8 26·9	8 02·5	4·2 2·3	10·2 5·7	16·2 9·0
43	8 10·8	8 12·1	7 48·4	4·3 2·3	10·3 5·6	16·3 8·8	43	8 25·8	8 27·1	8 02·7	4·3 2·4	10·3 5·8	16·3 9·1
44	8 11·0	8 12·3	7 48·6	4·4 2·4	10·4 5·6	16·4 8·9	44	8 26·0	8 27·4	8 02·9	4·4 2·5	10·4 5·8	16·4 9·2
45	8 11·3	8 12·6	7 48·9	4·5 2·4	10·5 5·7	16·5 8·9	45	8 26·3	8 27·6	8 03·2	4·5 2·5	10·5 5·9	16·5 9·2
46	8 11·5	8 12·8	7 49·1	4·6 2·5	10·6 5·7	16·6 9·0	46	8 26·5	8 27·9	8 03·4	4·6 2·6	10·6 5·9	16·6 9·3
47	8 11·8	8 13·1	7 49·3	4·7 2·5	10·7 5·8	16·7 9·0	47	8 26·8	8 28·1	8 03·7	4·7 2·6	10·7 6·0	16·7 9·3
48	8 12·0	8 13·3	7 49·6	4·8 2·6	10·8 5·9	16·8 9·1	48	8 27·0	8 28·4	8 03·9	4·8 2·7	10·8 6·0	16·8 9·4
49	8 12·3	8 13·6	7 49·8	4·9 2·7	10·9 5·9	16·9 9·2	49	8 27·3	8 28·6	8 04·1	4·9 2·7	10·9 6·1	16·9 9·4
50	8 12·5	8 13·8	7 50·1	5·0 2·7	11·0 6·0	17·0 9·2	50	8 27·5	8 28·9	8 04·4	5·0 2·8	11·0 6·1	17·0 9·5
51	8 12·8	8 14·1	7 50·3	5·1 2·8	11·1 6·0	17·1 9·3	51	8 27·8	8 29·1	8 04·6	5·1 2·8	11·1 6·2	17·1 9·5
52	8 13·0	8 14·3	7 50·5	5·2 2·8	11·2 6·1	17·2 9·3	52	8 28·0	8 29·4	8 04·9	5·2 2·9	11·2 6·3	17·2 9·6
53	8 13·3	8 14·6	7 50·8	5·3 2·9	11·3 6·1	17·3 9·4	53	8 28·3	8 29·6	8 05·1	5·3 3·0	11·3 6·3	17·3 9·7
54	8 13·5	8 14·9	7 51·0	5·4 2·9	11·4 6·2	17·4 9·4	54	8 28·5	8 29·9	8 05·3	5·4 3·0	11·4 6·4	17·4 9·7
55	8 13·8	8 15·1	7 51·3	5·5 3·0	11·5 6·2	17·5 9·5	55	8 28·8	8 30·1	8 05·6	5·5 3·1	11·5 6·4	17·5 9·8
56	8 14·0	8 15·4	7 51·5	5·6 3·0	11·6 6·3	17·6 9·5	56	8 29·0	8 30·4	8 05·8	5·6 3·1	11·6 6·5	17·6 9·8
57	8 14·3	8 15·6	7 51·7	5·7 3·1	11·7 6·3	17·7 9·6	57	8 29·3	8 30·6	8 06·1	5·7 3·2	11·7 6·5	17·7 9·9
58	8 14·5	8 15·9	7 52·0	5·8 3·1	11·8 6·4	17·8 9·6	58	8 29·5	8 30·9	8 06·3	5·8 3·2	11·8 6·6	17·8 9·9
59	8 14·8	8 16·1	7 52·2	5·9 3·2	11·9 6·4	17·9 9·7	59	8 29·8	8 31·1	8 06·5	5·9 3·3	11·9 6·6	17·9 10·0
60	8 15·0	8 16·4	7 52·5	6·0 3·3	12·0 6·5	18·0 9·8	60	8 30·0	8 31·4	8 06·8	6·0 3·4	12·0 6·7	18·0 10·1

34^m

34	SUN PLANETS	ARIES	MOON	v or Corr^n d	v or Corr^n d	v or Corr^n d
s	° ′	° ′	° ′	′ ′	′ ′	′ ′
00	8 30·0	8 31·4	8 06·8	0·0 0·0	6·0 3·5	12·0 6·9
01	8 30·3	8 31·6	8 07·0	0·1 0·1	6·1 3·5	12·1 7·0
02	8 30·5	8 31·9	8 07·2	0·2 0·1	6·2 3·6	12·2 7·0
03	8 30·8	8 32·1	8 07·5	0·3 0·2	6·3 3·6	12·3 7·1
04	8 31·0	8 32·4	8 07·7	0·4 0·2	6·4 3·7	12·4 7·1
05	8 31·3	8 32·6	8 08·0	0·5 0·3	6·5 3·7	12·5 7·2
06	8 31·5	8 32·9	8 08·2	0·6 0·3	6·6 3·8	12·6 7·2
07	8 31·8	8 33·2	8 08·4	0·7 0·4	6·7 3·9	12·7 7·3
08	8 32·0	8 33·4	8 08·7	0·8 0·5	6·8 3·9	12·8 7·4
09	8 32·3	8 33·7	8 08·9	0·9 0·5	6·9 4·0	12·9 7·4
10	8 32·5	8 33·9	8 09·2	1·0 0·6	7·0 4·0	13·0 7·5
11	8 32·8	8 34·2	8 09·4	1·1 0·6	7·1 4·1	13·1 7·5
12	8 33·0	8 34·4	8 09·6	1·2 0·7	7·2 4·1	13·2 7·6
13	8 33·3	8 34·7	8 09·9	1·3 0·7	7·3 4·2	13·3 7·6
14	8 33·5	8 34·9	8 10·1	1·4 0·8	7·4 4·3	13·4 7·7
15	8 33·8	8 35·2	8 10·3	1·5 0·9	7·5 4·3	13·5 7·8
16	8 34·0	8 35·4	8 10·6	1·6 0·9	7·6 4·4	13·6 7·8
17	8 34·3	8 35·7	8 10·8	1·7 1·0	7·7 4·4	13·7 7·9
18	8 34·5	8 35·9	8 11·1	1·8 1·0	7·8 4·5	13·8 7·9
19	8 34·8	8 36·2	8 11·3	1·9 1·1	7·9 4·5	13·9 8·0
20	8 35·0	8 36·4	8 11·5	2·0 1·2	8·0 4·6	14·0 8·1
21	8 35·3	8 36·7	8 11·8	2·1 1·2	8·1 4·7	14·1 8·1
22	8 35·5	8 36·9	8 12·0	2·2 1·3	8·2 4·7	14·2 8·2
23	8 35·8	8 37·2	8 12·3	2·3 1·3	8·3 4·8	14·3 8·2
24	8 36·0	8 37·4	8 12·5	2·4 1·4	8·4 4·8	14·4 8·3
25	8 36·3	8 37·7	8 12·7	2·5 1·4	8·5 4·9	14·5 8·3
26	8 36·5	8 37·9	8 13·0	2·6 1·5	8·6 4·9	14·6 8·4
27	8 36·8	8 38·2	8 13·2	2·7 1·6	8·7 5·0	14·7 8·5
28	8 37·0	8 38·4	8 13·4	2·8 1·6	8·8 5·1	14·8 8·5
29	8 37·3	8 38·7	8 13·7	2·9 1·7	8·9 5·1	14·9 8·6
30	8 37·5	8 38·9	8 13·9	3·0 1·7	9·0 5·2	15·0 8·6
31	8 37·8	8 39·2	8 14·2	3·1 1·8	9·1 5·2	15·1 8·7
32	8 38·0	8 39·4	8 14·4	3·2 1·8	9·2 5·3	15·2 8·7
33	8 38·3	8 39·7	8 14·6	3·3 1·9	9·3 5·3	15·3 8·8
34	8 38·5	8 39·9	8 14·9	3·4 2·0	9·4 5·4	15·4 8·9
35	8 38·8	8 40·2	8 15·1	3·5 2·0	9·5 5·5	15·5 8·9
36	8 39·0	8 40·4	8 15·4	3·6 2·1	9·6 5·5	15·6 9·0
37	8 39·3	8 40·7	8 15·6	3·7 2·1	9·7 5·6	15·7 9·0
38	8 39·5	8 40·9	8 15·8	3·8 2·2	9·8 5·6	15·8 9·1
39	8 39·8	8 41·2	8 16·1	3·9 2·2	9·9 5·7	15·9 9·1
40	8 40·0	8 41·4	8 16·3	4·0 2·3	10·0 5·8	16·0 9·2
41	8 40·3	8 41·7	8 16·5	4·1 2·4	10·1 5·8	16·1 9·3
42	8 40·5	8 41·9	8 16·8	4·2 2·4	10·2 5·9	16·2 9·3
43	8 40·8	8 42·2	8 17·0	4·3 2·5	10·3 5·9	16·3 9·4
44	8 41·0	8 42·4	8 17·3	4·4 2·5	10·4 6·0	16·4 9·4
45	8 41·3	8 42·7	8 17·5	4·5 2·6	10·5 6·0	16·5 9·5
46	8 41·5	8 42·9	8 17·7	4·6 2·6	10·6 6·1	16·6 9·5
47	8 41·8	8 43·2	8 18·0	4·7 2·7	10·7 6·2	16·7 9·6
48	8 42·0	8 43·4	8 18·2	4·8 2·8	10·8 6·2	16·8 9·7
49	8 42·3	8 43·7	8 18·5	4·9 2·8	10·9 6·3	16·9 9·7
50	8 42·5	8 43·9	8 18·7	5·0 2·9	11·0 6·3	17·0 9·8
51	8 42·8	8 44·2	8 18·9	5·1 2·9	11·1 6·4	17·1 9·8
52	8 43·0	8 44·4	8 19·2	5·2 3·0	11·2 6·4	17·2 9·9
53	8 43·3	8 44·7	8 19·4	5·3 3·0	11·3 6·5	17·3 9·9
54	8 43·5	8 44·9	8 19·7	5·4 3·1	11·4 6·6	17·4 10·0
55	8 43·8	8 45·2	8 19·9	5·5 3·2	11·5 6·6	17·5 10·1
56	8 44·0	8 45·4	8 20·1	5·6 3·2	11·6 6·7	17·6 10·1
57	8 44·3	8 45·7	8 20·4	5·7 3·3	11·7 6·7	17·7 10·2
58	8 44·5	8 45·9	8 20·6	5·8 3·3	11·8 6·8	17·8 10·2
59	8 44·8	8 46·2	8 20·8	5·9 3·4	11·9 6·8	17·9 10·3
60	8 45·0	8 46·4	8 21·1	6·0 3·5	12·0 6·9	18·0 10·4

35^m

35	SUN PLANETS	ARIES	MOON	v or Corr^n d	v or Corr^n d	v or Corr^n d
s	° ′	° ′	° ′	′ ′	′ ′	′ ′
00	8 45·0	8 46·4	8 21·1	0·0 0·0	6·0 3·6	12·0 7·1
01	8 45·3	8 46·7	8 21·3	0·1 0·1	6·1 3·6	12·1 7·2
02	8 45·5	8 46·9	8 21·6	0·2 0·1	6·2 3·7	12·2 7·2
03	8 45·8	8 47·2	8 21·8	0·3 0·2	6·3 3·7	12·3 7·3
04	8 46·0	8 47·4	8 22·0	0·4 0·2	6·4 3·8	12·4 7·3
05	8 46·3	8 47·7	8 22·3	0·5 0·3	6·5 3·8	12·5 7·4
06	8 46·5	8 47·9	8 22·5	0·6 0·4	6·6 3·9	12·6 7·5
07	8 46·8	8 48·2	8 22·8	0·7 0·4	6·7 4·0	12·7 7·5
08	8 47·0	8 48·4	8 23·0	0·8 0·5	6·8 4·0	12·8 7·6
09	8 47·3	8 48·7	8 23·2	0·9 0·5	6·9 4·1	12·9 7·6
10	8 47·5	8 48·9	8 23·5	1·0 0·6	7·0 4·1	13·0 7·7
11	8 47·8	8 49·2	8 23·7	1·1 0·7	7·1 4·2	13·1 7·8
12	8 48·0	8 49·4	8 23·9	1·2 0·7	7·2 4·3	13·2 7·8
13	8 48·3	8 49·7	8 24·2	1·3 0·8	7·3 4·3	13·3 7·9
14	8 48·5	8 49·9	8 24·4	1·4 0·8	7·4 4·4	13·4 7·9
15	8 48·8	8 50·2	8 24·7	1·5 0·9	7·5 4·4	13·5 8·0
16	8 49·0	8 50·4	8 24·9	1·6 0·9	7·6 4·5	13·6 8·0
17	8 49·3	8 50·7	8 25·1	1·7 1·0	7·7 4·6	13·7 8·1
18	8 49·5	8 50·9	8 25·4	1·8 1·1	7·8 4·6	13·8 8·2
19	8 49·8	8 51·2	8 25·6	1·9 1·1	7·9 4·7	13·9 8·2
20	8 50·0	8 51·5	8 25·9	2·0 1·2	8·0 4·7	14·0 8·3
21	8 50·3	8 51·7	8 26·1	2·1 1·2	8·1 4·8	14·1 8·3
22	8 50·5	8 52·0	8 26·3	2·2 1·3	8·2 4·9	14·2 8·4
23	8 50·8	8 52·2	8 26·6	2·3 1·4	8·3 4·9	14·3 8·5
24	8 51·0	8 52·5	8 26·8	2·4 1·4	8·4 5·0	14·4 8·5
25	8 51·3	8 52·7	8 27·0	2·5 1·5	8·5 5·0	14·5 8·6
26	8 51·5	8 53·0	8 27·3	2·6 1·5	8·6 5·1	14·6 8·6
27	8 51·8	8 53·2	8 27·5	2·7 1·6	8·7 5·1	14·7 8·7
28	8 52·0	8 53·5	8 27·8	2·8 1·7	8·8 5·2	14·8 8·8
29	8 52·3	8 53·7	8 28·0	2·9 1·7	8·9 5·3	14·9 8·8
30	8 52·5	8 54·0	8 28·2	3·0 1·8	9·0 5·3	15·0 8·9
31	8 52·8	8 54·2	8 28·5	3·1 1·8	9·1 5·4	15·1 8·9
32	8 53·0	8 54·5	8 28·7	3·2 1·9	9·2 5·4	15·2 9·0
33	8 53·3	8 54·7	8 29·0	3·3 2·0	9·3 5·5	15·3 9·1
34	8 53·5	8 55·0	8 29·2	3·4 2·0	9·4 5·6	15·4 9·1
35	8 53·8	8 55·2	8 29·4	3·5 2·1	9·5 5·6	15·5 9·2
36	8 54·0	8 55·5	8 29·7	3·6 2·1	9·6 5·7	15·6 9·2
37	8 54·3	8 55·7	8 29·9	3·7 2·2	9·7 5·7	15·7 9·3
38	8 54·5	8 56·0	8 30·2	3·8 2·2	9·8 5·8	15·8 9·3
39	8 54·8	8 56·2	8 30·4	3·9 2·3	9·9 5·9	15·9 9·4
40	8 55·0	8 56·5	8 30·6	4·0 2·4	10·0 5·9	16·0 9·5
41	8 55·3	8 56·7	8 30·9	4·1 2·4	10·1 6·0	16·1 9·5
42	8 55·5	8 57·0	8 31·1	4·2 2·5	10·2 6·0	16·2 9·6
43	8 55·8	8 57·2	8 31·3	4·3 2·5	10·3 6·1	16·3 9·6
44	8 56·0	8 57·5	8 31·6	4·4 2·6	10·4 6·2	16·4 9·7
45	8 56·3	8 57·7	8 31·8	4·5 2·7	10·5 6·2	16·5 9·8
46	8 56·5	8 58·0	8 32·1	4·6 2·7	10·6 6·3	16·6 9·8
47	8 56·8	8 58·2	8 32·3	4·7 2·8	10·7 6·3	16·7 9·9
48	8 57·0	8 58·5	8 32·5	4·8 2·8	10·8 6·4	16·8 9·9
49	8 57·3	8 58·7	8 32·8	4·9 2·9	10·9 6·4	16·9 10·0
50	8 57·5	8 59·0	8 33·0	5·0 3·0	11·0 6·5	17·0 10·1
51	8 57·8	8 59·2	8 33·3	5·1 3·0	11·1 6·6	17·1 10·1
52	8 58·0	8 59·5	8 33·5	5·2 3·1	11·2 6·6	17·2 10·2
53	8 58·3	8 59·7	8 33·7	5·3 3·1	11·3 6·7	17·3 10·2
54	8 58·5	9 00·0	8 34·0	5·4 3·2	11·4 6·7	17·4 10·3
55	8 58·8	9 00·2	8 34·2	5·5 3·3	11·5 6·8	17·5 10·4
56	8 59·0	9 00·5	8 34·4	5·6 3·3	11·6 6·9	17·6 10·4
57	8 59·3	9 00·7	8 34·7	5·7 3·4	11·7 6·9	17·7 10·5
58	8 59·5	9 01·0	8 34·9	5·8 3·4	11·8 7·0	17·8 10·6
59	8 59·8	9 01·2	8 35·2	5·9 3·5	11·9 7·0	17·9 10·6
60	9 00·0	9 01·5	8 35·4	6·0 3·6	12·0 7·1	18·0 10·7

36	SUN PLANETS	ARIES	MOON	v or Corrⁿ d		v or Corrⁿ d		v or Corrⁿ d	
s	° ′	° ′	° ′	′	′	′	′	′	′
00	9 00·0	9 01·5	8 35·4	0·0	0·0	6·0	3·7	12·0	7·3
01	9 00·3	9 01·7	8 35·6	0·1	0·1	6·1	3·7	12·1	7·4
02	9 00·5	9 02·0	8 35·9	0·2	0·1	6·2	3·8	12·2	7·4
03	9 00·8	9 02·2	8 36·1	0·3	0·2	6·3	3·8	12·3	7·5
04	9 01·0	9 02·5	8 36·4	0·4	0·2	6·4	3·9	12·4	7·5
05	9 01·3	9 02·7	8 36·6	0·5	0·3	6·5	4·0	12·5	7·6
06	9 01·5	9 03·0	8 36·8	0·6	0·4	6·6	4·0	12·6	7·7
07	9 01·8	9 03·2	8 37·1	0·7	0·4	6·7	4·1	12·7	7·7
08	9 02·0	9 03·5	8 37·3	0·8	0·5	6·8	4·1	12·8	7·8
09	9 02·3	9 03·7	8 37·5	0·9	0·5	6·9	4·2	12·9	7·8
10	9 02·5	9 04·0	8 37·8	1·0	0·6	7·0	4·3	13·0	7·9
11	9 02·8	9 04·2	8 38·0	1·1	0·7	7·1	4·3	13·1	8·0
12	9 03·0	9 04·5	8 38·3	1·2	0·7	7·2	4·4	13·2	8·0
13	9 03·3	9 04·7	8 38·5	1·3	0·8	7·3	4·4	13·3	8·1
14	9 03·5	9 05·0	8 38·7	1·4	0·9	7·4	4·5	13·4	8·2
15	9 03·8	9 05·2	8 39·0	1·5	0·9	7·5	4·6	13·5	8·2
16	9 04·0	9 05·5	8 39·2	1·6	1·0	7·6	4·6	13·6	8·3
17	9 04·3	9 05·7	8 39·5	1·7	1·0	7·7	4·7	13·7	8·3
18	9 04·5	9 06·0	8 39·7	1·8	1·1	7·8	4·7	13·8	8·4
19	9 04·8	9 06·2	8 39·9	1·9	1·2	7·9	4·8	13·9	8·5
20	9 05·0	9 06·5	8 40·2	2·0	1·2	8·0	4·9	14·0	8·5
21	9 05·3	9 06·7	8 40·4	2·1	1·3	8·1	4·9	14·1	8·6
22	9 05·5	9 07·0	8 40·6	2·2	1·3	8·2	5·0	14·2	8·6
23	9 05·8	9 07·2	8 40·9	2·3	1·4	8·3	5·0	14·3	8·7
24	9 06·0	9 07·5	8 41·1	2·4	1·5	8·4	5·1	14·4	8·8
25	9 06·3	9 07·7	8 41·4	2·5	1·5	8·5	5·2	14·5	8·8
26	9 06·5	9 08·0	8 41·6	2·6	1·6	8·6	5·2	14·6	8·9
27	9 06·8	9 08·2	8 41·8	2·7	1·6	8·7	5·3	14·7	8·9
28	9 07·0	9 08·5	8 42·1	2·8	1·7	8·8	5·4	14·8	9·0
29	9 07·3	9 08·7	8 42·3	2·9	1·8	8·9	5·4	14·9	9·1
30	9 07·5	9 09·0	8 42·6	3·0	1·8	9·0	5·5	15·0	9·1
31	9 07·8	9 09·2	8 42·8	3·1	1·9	9·1	5·5	15·1	9·2
32	9 08·0	9 09·5	8 43·0	3·2	1·9	9·2	5·6	15·2	9·2
33	9 08·3	9 09·8	8 43·3	3·3	2·0	9·3	5·7	15·3	9·3
34	9 08·5	9 10·0	8 43·5	3·4	2·1	9·4	5·7	15·4	9·4
35	9 08·8	9 10·3	8 43·8	3·5	2·1	9·5	5·8	15·5	9·4
36	9 09·0	9 10·5	8 44·0	3·6	2·2	9·6	5·8	15·6	9·5
37	9 09·3	9 10·8	8 44·2	3·7	2·3	9·7	5·9	15·7	9·6
38	9 09·5	9 11·0	8 44·5	3·8	2·3	9·8	6·0	15·8	9·6
39	9 09·8	9 11·3	8 44·7	3·9	2·4	9·9	6·0	15·9	9·7
40	9 10·0	9 11·5	8 44·9	4·0	2·4	10·0	6·1	16·0	9·7
41	9 10·3	9 11·8	8 45·2	4·1	2·5	10·1	6·1	16·1	9·8
42	9 10·5	9 12·0	8 45·4	4·2	2·6	10·2	6·2	16·2	9·9
43	9 10·8	9 12·3	8 45·7	4·3	2·6	10·3	6·3	16·3	9·9
44	9 11·0	9 12·5	8 45·9	4·4	2·7	10·4	6·3	16·4	10·0
45	9 11·3	9 12·8	8 46·1	4·5	2·7	10·5	6·4	16·5	10·0
46	9 11·5	9 13·0	8 46·4	4·6	2·8	10·6	6·4	16·6	10·1
47	9 11·8	9 13·3	8 46·6	4·7	2·9	10·7	6·5	16·7	10·2
48	9 12·0	9 13·5	8 46·9	4·8	2·9	10·8	6·6	16·8	10·2
49	9 12·3	9 13·8	8 47·1	4·9	3·0	10·9	6·6	16·9	10·3
50	9 12·5	9 14·0	8 47·3	5·0	3·0	11·0	6·7	17·0	10·3
51	9 12·8	9 14·3	8 47·6	5·1	3·1	11·1	6·8	17·1	10·4
52	9 13·0	9 14·5	8 47·8	5·2	3·2	11·2	6·8	17·2	10·5
53	9 13·3	9 14·8	8 48·0	5·3	3·2	11·3	6·9	17·3	10·5
54	9 13·5	9 15·0	8 48·3	5·4	3·3	11·4	6·9	17·4	10·6
55	9 13·8	9 15·3	8 48·5	5·5	3·3	11·5	7·0	17·5	10·6
56	9 14·0	9 15·5	8 48·8	5·6	3·4	11·6	7·1	17·6	10·7
57	9 14·3	9 15·8	8 49·0	5·7	3·5	11·7	7·1	17·7	10·8
58	9 14·5	9 16·0	8 49·2	5·8	3·5	11·8	7·2	17·8	10·8
59	9 14·8	9 16·3	8 49·5	5·9	3·6	11·9	7·2	17·9	10·9
60	9 15·0	9 16·5	8 49·7	6·0	3·7	12·0	7·3	18·0	11·0

37	SUN PLANETS	ARIES	MOON	v or Corrⁿ d		v or Corrⁿ d		v or Corrⁿ d	
s	° ′	° ′	° ′	′	′	′	′	′	′
00	9 15·0	9 16·5	8 49·7	0·0	0·0	6·0	3·8	12·0	7·5
01	9 15·3	9 16·8	8 50·0	0·1	0·1	6·1	3·8	12·1	7·6
02	9 15·5	9 17·0	8 50·2	0·2	0·1	6·2	3·9	12·2	7·6
03	9 15·8	9 17·3	8 50·4	0·3	0·2	6·3	3·9	12·3	7·7
04	9 16·0	9 17·5	8 50·7	0·4	0·3	6·4	4·0	12·4	7·8
05	9 16·3	9 17·8	8 50·9	0·5	0·3	6·5	4·1	12·5	7·8
06	9 16·5	9 18·0	8 51·1	0·6	0·4	6·6	4·1	12·6	7·9
07	9 16·8	9 18·3	8 51·4	0·7	0·4	6·7	4·2	12·7	7·9
08	9 17·0	9 18·5	8 51·6	0·8	0·5	6·8	4·3	12·8	8·0
09	9 17·3	9 18·8	8 51·9	0·9	0·6	6·9	4·3	12·9	8·1
10	9 17·5	9 19·0	8 52·1	1·0	0·6	7·0	4·4	13·0	8·1
11	9 17·8	9 19·3	8 52·3	1·1	0·7	7·1	4·4	13·1	8·2
12	9 18·0	9 19·5	8 52·6	1·2	0·8	7·2	4·5	13·2	8·3
13	9 18·3	9 19·8	8 52·8	1·3	0·8	7·3	4·6	13·3	8·3
14	9 18·5	9 20·0	8 53·1	1·4	0·9	7·4	4·6	13·4	8·4
15	9 18·8	9 20·3	8 53·3	1·5	0·9	7·5	4·7	13·5	8·4
16	9 19·0	9 20·5	8 53·5	1·6	1·0	7·6	4·8	13·6	8·5
17	9 19·3	9 20·8	8 53·8	1·7	1·1	7·7	4·8	13·7	8·6
18	9 19·5	9 21·0	8 54·0	1·8	1·1	7·8	4·9	13·8	8·6
19	9 19·8	9 21·3	8 54·3	1·9	1·2	7·9	4·9	13·9	8·7
20	9 20·0	9 21·5	8 54·5	2·0	1·3	8·0	5·0	14·0	8·8
21	9 20·3	9 21·8	8 54·7	2·1	1·3	8·1	5·1	14·1	8·8
22	9 20·5	9 22·0	8 55·0	2·2	1·4	8·2	5·1	14·2	8·9
23	9 20·8	9 22·3	8 55·2	2·3	1·4	8·3	5·2	14·3	8·9
24	9 21·0	9 22·5	8 55·4	2·4	1·5	8·4	5·3	14·4	9·0
25	9 21·3	9 22·8	8 55·7	2·5	1·6	8·5	5·3	14·5	9·1
26	9 21·5	9 23·0	8 55·9	2·6	1·6	8·6	5·4	14·6	9·1
27	9 21·8	9 23·3	8 56·2	2·7	1·7	8·7	5·4	14·7	9·2
28	9 22·0	9 23·5	8 56·4	2·8	1·8	8·8	5·5	14·8	9·3
29	9 22·3	9 23·8	8 56·6	2·9	1·8	8·9	5·6	14·9	9·3
30	9 22·5	9 24·0	8 56·9	3·0	1·9	9·0	5·6	15·0	9·4
31	9 22·8	9 24·3	8 57·1	3·1	1·9	9·1	5·7	15·1	9·4
32	9 23·0	9 24·5	8 57·4	3·2	2·0	9·2	5·8	15·2	9·5
33	9 23·3	9 24·8	8 57·6	3·3	2·1	9·3	5·8	15·3	9·6
34	9 23·5	9 25·0	8 57·8	3·4	2·1	9·4	5·9	15·4	9·6
35	9 23·8	9 25·3	8 58·1	3·5	2·2	9·5	5·9	15·5	9·7
36	9 24·0	9 25·5	8 58·3	3·6	2·3	9·6	6·0	15·6	9·8
37	9 24·3	9 25·8	8 58·5	3·7	2·3	9·7	6·1	15·7	9·8
38	9 24·5	9 26·0	8 58·8	3·8	2·4	9·8	6·1	15·8	9·9
39	9 24·8	9 26·3	8 59·0	3·9	2·4	9·9	6·2	15·9	9·9
40	9 25·0	9 26·5	8 59·3	4·0	2·5	10·0	6·3	16·0	10·0
41	9 25·3	9 26·8	8 59·5	4·1	2·6	10·1	6·3	16·1	10·1
42	9 25·5	9 27·0	8 59·7	4·2	2·6	10·2	6·4	16·2	10·1
43	9 25·8	9 27·3	9 00·0	4·3	2·7	10·3	6·4	16·3	10·2
44	9 26·0	9 27·5	9 00·2	4·4	2·8	10·4	6·5	16·4	10·3
45	9 26·3	9 27·8	9 00·5	4·5	2·8	10·5	6·6	16·5	10·3
46	9 26·5	9 28·1	9 00·7	4·6	2·9	10·6	6·6	16·6	10·4
47	9 26·8	9 28·3	9 00·9	4·7	2·9	10·7	6·7	16·7	10·4
48	9 27·0	9 28·6	9 01·2	4·8	3·0	10·8	6·8	16·8	10·5
49	9 27·3	9 28·8	9 01·4	4·9	3·1	10·9	6·8	16·9	10·6
50	9 27·5	9 29·1	9 01·6	5·0	3·1	11·0	6·9	17·0	10·6
51	9 27·8	9 29·3	9 01·9	5·1	3·2	11·1	6·9	17·1	10·7
52	9 28·0	9 29·6	9 02·1	5·2	3·3	11·2	7·0	17·2	10·8
53	9 28·3	9 29·8	9 02·4	5·3	3·3	11·3	7·1	17·3	10·8
54	9 28·5	9 30·1	9 02·6	5·4	3·4	11·4	7·1	17·4	10·9
55	9 28·8	9 30·3	9 02·8	5·5	3·4	11·5	7·2	17·5	10·9
56	9 29·0	9 30·6	9 03·1	5·6	3·5	11·6	7·3	17·6	11·0
57	9 29·3	9 30·8	9 03·3	5·7	3·6	11·7	7·3	17·7	11·1
58	9 29·5	9 31·1	9 03·6	5·8	3·6	11·8	7·4	17·8	11·1
59	9 29·8	9 31·3	9 03·8	5·9	3·7	11·9	7·4	17·9	11·2
60	9 30·0	9 31·6	9 04·0	6·0	3·8	12·0	7·5	18·0	11·3

xx

38ᵐ

38	SUN PLANETS	ARIES	MOON	v or d Corrⁿ	v or d Corrⁿ	v or d Corrⁿ
s	° ′	° ′	° ′	′ ′	′ ′	′ ′
00	9 30·0	9 31·6	9 04·0	0·0 0·0	6·0 3·9	12·0 7·7
01	9 30·3	9 31·8	9 04·3	0·1 0·1	6·1 3·9	12·1 7·8
02	9 30·5	9 32·1	9 04·5	0·2 0·1	6·2 4·0	12·2 7·8
03	9 30·8	9 32·3	9 04·7	0·3 0·2	6·3 4·0	12·3 7·9
04	9 31·0	9 32·6	9 05·0	0·4 0·3	6·4 4·1	12·4 8·0
05	9 31·3	9 32·8	9 05·2	0·5 0·3	6·5 4·2	12·5 8·0
06	9 31·5	9 33·1	9 05·5	0·6 0·4	6·6 4·2	12·6 8·1
07	9 31·8	9 33·3	9 05·7	0·7 0·4	6·7 4·3	12·7 8·1
08	9 32·0	9 33·6	9 05·9	0·8 0·5	6·8 4·4	12·8 8·2
09	9 32·3	9 33·8	9 06·2	0·9 0·6	6·9 4·4	12·9 8·3
10	9 32·5	9 34·1	9 06·4	1·0 0·6	7·0 4·5	13·0 8·3
11	9 32·8	9 34·3	9 06·7	1·1 0·7	7·1 4·6	13·1 8·4
12	9 33·0	9 34·6	9 06·9	1·2 0·8	7·2 4·6	13·2 8·5
13	9 33·3	9 34·8	9 07·1	1·3 0·8	7·3 4·7	13·3 8·5
14	9 33·5	9 35·1	9 07·4	1·4 0·9	7·4 4·7	13·4 8·6
15	9 33·8	9 35·3	9 07·6	1·5 1·0	7·5 4·8	13·5 8·7
16	9 34·0	9 35·6	9 07·9	1·6 1·0	7·6 4·9	13·6 8·7
17	9 34·3	9 35·8	9 08·1	1·7 1·1	7·7 4·9	13·7 8·8
18	9 34·5	9 36·1	9 08·3	1·8 1·2	7·8 5·0	13·8 8·9
19	9 34·8	9 36·3	9 08·6	1·9 1·2	7·9 5·1	13·9 8·9
20	9 35·0	9 36·6	9 08·8	2·0 1·3	8·0 5·1	14·0 9·0
21	9 35·3	9 36·8	9 09·0	2·1 1·3	8·1 5·2	14·1 9·0
22	9 35·5	9 37·1	9 09·3	2·2 1·4	8·2 5·3	14·2 9·1
23	9 35·8	9 37·3	9 09·5	2·3 1·5	8·3 5·3	14·3 9·2
24	9 36·0	9 37·6	9 09·8	2·4 1·5	8·4 5·4	14·4 9·2
25	9 36·3	9 37·8	9 10·0	2·5 1·6	8·5 5·5	14·5 9·3
26	9 36·5	9 38·1	9 10·2	2·6 1·7	8·6 5·5	14·6 9·4
27	9 36·8	9 38·3	9 10·5	2·7 1·7	8·7 5·6	14·7 9·4
28	9 37·0	9 38·6	9 10·7	2·8 1·8	8·8 5·6	14·8 9·5
29	9 37·3	9 38·8	9 11·0	2·9 1·9	8·9 5·7	14·9 9·6
30	9 37·5	9 39·1	9 11·2	3·0 1·9	9·0 5·8	15·0 9·6
31	9 37·8	9 39·3	9 11·4	3·1 2·0	9·1 5·8	15·1 9·7
32	9 38·0	9 39·6	9 11·7	3·2 2·1	9·2 5·9	15·2 9·8
33	9 38·3	9 39·8	9 11·9	3·3 2·1	9·3 6·0	15·3 9·8
34	9 38·5	9 40·1	9 12·1	3·4 2·2	9·4 6·0	15·4 9·9
35	9 38·8	9 40·3	9 12·4	3·5 2·2	9·5 6·1	15·5 9·9
36	9 39·0	9 40·6	9 12·6	3·6 2·3	9·6 6·2	15·6 10·0
37	9 39·3	9 40·8	9 12·9	3·7 2·4	9·7 6·2	15·7 10·1
38	9 39·5	9 41·1	9 13·1	3·8 2·4	9·8 6·3	15·8 10·1
39	9 39·8	9 41·3	9 13·3	3·9 2·5	9·9 6·4	15·9 10·2
40	9 40·0	9 41·6	9 13·6	4·0 2·6	10·0 6·4	16·0 10·3
41	9 40·3	9 41·8	9 13·8	4·1 2·6	10·1 6·5	16·1 10·3
42	9 40·5	9 42·1	9 14·1	4·2 2·7	10·2 6·5	16·2 10·4
43	9 40·8	9 42·3	9 14·3	4·3 2·8	10·3 6·6	16·3 10·5
44	9 41·0	9 42·6	9 14·5	4·4 2·8	10·4 6·7	16·4 10·5
45	9 41·3	9 42·8	9 14·8	4·5 2·9	10·5 6·7	16·5 10·6
46	9 41·5	9 43·1	9 15·0	4·6 3·0	10·6 6·8	16·6 10·7
47	9 41·8	9 43·3	9 15·2	4·7 3·0	10·7 6·9	16·7 10·7
48	9 42·0	9 43·6	9 15·5	4·8 3·1	10·8 6·9	16·8 10·8
49	9 42·3	9 43·8	9 15·7	4·9 3·1	10·9 7·0	16·9 10·8
50	9 42·5	9 44·1	9 16·0	5·0 3·2	11·0 7·1	17·0 10·9
51	9 42·8	9 44·3	9 16·2	5·1 3·3	11·1 7·1	17·1 11·0
52	9 43·0	9 44·6	9 16·4	5·2 3·3	11·2 7·2	17·2 11·0
53	9 43·3	9 44·8	9 16·7	5·3 3·4	11·3 7·3	17·3 11·1
54	9 43·5	9 45·1	9 16·9	5·4 3·5	11·4 7·3	17·4 11·2
55	9 43·8	9 45·3	9 17·2	5·5 3·5	11·5 7·4	17·5 11·2
56	9 44·0	9 45·6	9 17·4	5·6 3·6	11·6 7·4	17·6 11·3
57	9 44·3	9 45·8	9 17·6	5·7 3·7	11·7 7·5	17·7 11·4
58	9 44·5	9 46·1	9 17·9	5·8 3·7	11·8 7·6	17·8 11·4
59	9 44·8	9 46·4	9 18·1	5·9 3·8	11·9 7·6	17·9 11·5
60	9 45·0	9 46·6	9 18·4	6·0 3·9	12·0 7·7	18·0 11·6

39ᵐ

39	SUN PLANETS	ARIES	MOON	v or d Corrⁿ	v or d Corrⁿ	v or d Corrⁿ
s	° ′	° ′	° ′	′ ′	′ ′	′ ′
00	9 45·0	9 46·6	9 18·4	0·0 0·0	6·0 4·0	12·0 7·9
01	9 45·3	9 46·9	9 18·6	0·1 0·1	6·1 4·0	12·1 8·0
02	9 45·5	9 47·1	9 18·8	0·2 0·1	6·2 4·1	12·2 8·0
03	9 45·8	9 47·4	9 19·1	0·3 0·2	6·3 4·1	12·3 8·1
04	9 46·0	9 47·6	9 19·3	0·4 0·3	6·4 4·2	12·4 8·2
05	9 46·3	9 47·9	9 19·5	0·5 0·3	6·5 4·3	12·5 8·2
06	9 46·5	9 48·1	9 19·8	0·6 0·4	6·6 4·3	12·6 8·3
07	9 46·8	9 48·4	9 20·0	0·7 0·5	6·7 4·4	12·7 8·4
08	9 47·0	9 48·6	9 20·3	0·8 0·6	6·8 4·5	12·8 8·4
09	9 47·3	9 48·9	9 20·5	0·9 0·6	6·9 4·5	12·9 8·5
10	9 47·5	9 49·1	9 20·7	1·0 0·7	7·0 4·6	13·0 8·6
11	9 47·8	9 49·4	9 21·0	1·1 0·7	7·1 4·7	13·1 8·6
12	9 48·0	9 49·6	9 21·2	1·2 0·8	7·2 4·7	13·2 8·7
13	9 48·3	9 49·9	9 21·5	1·3 0·9	7·3 4·8	13·3 8·8
14	9 48·5	9 50·1	9 21·7	1·4 0·9	7·4 4·9	13·4 8·8
15	9 48·8	9 50·4	9 21·9	1·5 1·0	7·5 4·9	13·5 8·9
16	9 49·0	9 50·6	9 22·2	1·6 1·1	7·6 5·0	13·6 9·0
17	9 49·3	9 50·9	9 22·4	1·7 1·1	7·7 5·1	13·7 9·0
18	9 49·5	9 51·1	9 22·6	1·8 1·2	7·8 5·1	13·8 9·1
19	9 49·8	9 51·4	9 22·9	1·9 1·3	7·9 5·2	13·9 9·2
20	9 50·0	9 51·6	9 23·1	2·0 1·3	8·0 5·3	14·0 9·2
21	9 50·3	9 51·9	9 23·4	2·1 1·4	8·1 5·3	14·1 9·3
22	9 50·5	9 52·1	9 23·6	2·2 1·5	8·2 5·4	14·2 9·3
23	9 50·8	9 52·4	9 23·8	2·3 1·5	8·3 5·5	14·3 9·4
24	9 51·0	9 52·6	9 24·1	2·4 1·6	8·4 5·5	14·4 9·5
25	9 51·3	9 52·9	9 24·3	2·5 1·6	8·5 5·6	14·5 9·5
26	9 51·5	9 53·1	9 24·6	2·6 1·7	8·6 5·7	14·6 9·6
27	9 51·8	9 53·4	9 24·8	2·7 1·8	8·7 5·7	14·7 9·7
28	9 52·0	9 53·6	9 25·0	2·8 1·8	8·8 5·8	14·8 9·7
29	9 52·3	9 53·9	9 25·3	2·9 1·9	8·9 5·9	14·9 9·8
30	9 52·5	9 54·1	9 25·5	3·0 2·0	9·0 5·9	15·0 9·9
31	9 52·8	9 54·4	9 25·7	3·1 2·0	9·1 6·0	15·1 9·9
32	9 53·0	9 54·6	9 26·0	3·2 2·1	9·2 6·1	15·2 10·0
33	9 53·3	9 54·9	9 26·2	3·3 2·2	9·3 6·1	15·3 10·1
34	9 53·5	9 55·1	9 26·5	3·4 2·2	9·4 6·2	15·4 10·1
35	9 53·8	9 55·4	9 26·7	3·5 2·3	9·5 6·3	15·5 10·2
36	9 54·0	9 55·6	9 26·9	3·6 2·4	9·6 6·3	15·6 10·3
37	9 54·3	9 55·9	9 27·2	3·7 2·4	9·7 6·4	15·7 10·3
38	9 54·5	9 56·1	9 27·4	3·8 2·5	9·8 6·5	15·8 10·4
39	9 54·8	9 56·4	9 27·7	3·9 2·6	9·9 6·5	15·9 10·5
40	9 55·0	9 56·6	9 27·9	4·0 2·6	10·0 6·6	16·0 10·5
41	9 55·3	9 56·9	9 28·1	4·1 2·7	10·1 6·6	16·1 10·6
42	9 55·5	9 57·1	9 28·4	4·2 2·8	10·2 6·7	16·2 10·7
43	9 55·8	9 57·4	9 28·6	4·3 2·8	10·3 6·8	16·3 10·7
44	9 56·0	9 57·6	9 28·8	4·4 2·9	10·4 6·8	16·4 10·8
45	9 56·3	9 57·9	9 29·1	4·5 3·0	10·5 6·9	16·5 10·9
46	9 56·5	9 58·1	9 29·3	4·6 3·0	10·6 7·0	16·6 10·9
47	9 56·8	9 58·4	9 29·6	4·7 3·1	10·7 7·0	16·7 11·0
48	9 57·0	9 58·6	9 29·8	4·8 3·2	10·8 7·1	16·8 11·1
49	9 57·3	9 58·9	9 30·0	4·9 3·2	10·9 7·2	16·9 11·1
50	9 57·5	9 59·1	9 30·3	5·0 3·3	11·0 7·2	17·0 11·2
51	9 57·8	9 59·4	9 30·5	5·1 3·4	11·1 7·3	17·1 11·3
52	9 58·0	9 59·6	9 30·8	5·2 3·4	11·2 7·4	17·2 11·3
53	9 58·3	9 59·9	9 31·0	5·3 3·5	11·3 7·4	17·3 11·4
54	9 58·5	10 00·1	9 31·2	5·4 3·6	11·4 7·5	17·4 11·5
55	9 58·8	10 00·4	9 31·5	5·5 3·6	11·5 7·6	17·5 11·5
56	9 59·0	10 00·6	9 31·7	5·6 3·7	11·6 7·6	17·6 11·6
57	9 59·3	10 00·9	9 32·0	5·7 3·8	11·7 7·7	17·7 11·7
58	9 59·5	10 01·1	9 32·2	5·8 3·8	11·8 7·8	17·8 11·7
59	9 59·8	10 01·4	9 32·4	5·9 3·9	11·9 7·8	17·9 11·8
60	10 00·0	10 01·6	9 32·7	6·0 4·0	12·0 7·9	18·0 11·9

40ᵐ	SUN PLANETS	ARIES	MOON	v or d / Corrⁿ		v or d / Corrⁿ		v or d / Corrⁿ	
s	° ′	° ′	° ′	′	′	′	′	′	′
00	10 00·0	10 01·6	9 32·7	0·0	0·0	6·0	4·1	12·0	8·1
01	10 00·3	10 01·9	9 32·9	0·1	0·1	6·1	4·1	12·1	8·2
02	10 00·5	10 02·1	9 33·1	0·2	0·1	6·2	4·2	12·2	8·2
03	10 00·8	10 02·4	9 33·4	0·3	0·2	6·3	4·3	12·3	8·3
04	10 01·0	10 02·6	9 33·6	0·4	0·3	6·4	4·3	12·4	8·4
05	10 01·3	10 02·9	9 33·9	0·5	0·3	6·5	4·4	12·5	8·4
06	10 01·5	10 03·1	9 34·1	0·6	0·4	6·6	4·5	12·6	8·5
07	10 01·8	10 03·4	9 34·3	0·7	0·5	6·7	4·5	12·7	8·6
08	10 02·0	10 03·6	9 34·6	0·8	0·5	6·8	4·6	12·8	8·6
09	10 02·3	10 03·9	9 34·8	0·9	0·6	6·9	4·7	12·9	8·7
10	10 02·5	10 04·1	9 35·1	1·0	0·7	7·0	4·7	13·0	8·8
11	10 02·8	10 04·4	9 35·3	1·1	0·7	7·1	4·8	13·1	8·8
12	10 03·0	10 04·7	9 35·5	1·2	0·8	7·2	4·9	13·2	8·9
13	10 03·3	10 04·9	9 35·8	1·3	0·9	7·3	4·9	13·3	9·0
14	10 03·5	10 05·2	9 36·0	1·4	0·9	7·4	5·0	13·4	9·0
15	10 03·8	10 05·4	9 36·2	1·5	1·0	7·5	5·1	13·5	9·1
16	10 04·0	10 05·7	9 36·5	1·6	1·1	7·6	5·1	13·6	9·2
17	10 04·3	10 05·9	9 36·7	1·7	1·1	7·7	5·2	13·7	9·2
18	10 04·5	10 06·2	9 37·0	1·8	1·2	7·8	5·3	13·8	9·3
19	10 04·8	10 06·4	9 37·2	1·9	1·3	7·9	5·3	13·9	9·4
20	10 05·0	10 06·7	9 37·4	2·0	1·4	8·0	5·4	14·0	9·5
21	10 05·3	10 06·9	9 37·7	2·1	1·4	8·1	5·5	14·1	9·5
22	10 05·5	10 07·2	9 37·9	2·2	1·5	8·2	5·5	14·2	9·6
23	10 05·8	10 07·4	9 38·2	2·3	1·6	8·3	5·6	14·3	9·7
24	10 06·0	10 07·7	9 38·4	2·4	1·6	8·4	5·7	14·4	9·7
25	10 06·3	10 07·9	9 38·6	2·5	1·7	8·5	5·7	14·5	9·8
26	10 06·5	10 08·2	9 38·9	2·6	1·8	8·6	5·8	14·6	9·9
27	10 06·8	10 08·4	9 39·1	2·7	1·8	8·7	5·9	14·7	9·9
28	10 07·0	10 08·7	9 39·3	2·8	1·9	8·8	5·9	14·8	10·0
29	10 07·3	10 08·9	9 39·6	2·9	2·0	8·9	6·0	14·9	10·1
30	10 07·5	10 09·2	9 39·8	3·0	2·0	9·0	6·1	15·0	10·1
31	10 07·8	10 09·4	9 40·1	3·1	2·1	9·1	6·1	15·1	10·2
32	10 08·0	10 09·7	9 40·3	3·2	2·2	9·2	6·2	15·2	10·3
33	10 08·3	10 09·9	9 40·5	3·3	2·2	9·3	6·3	15·3	10·3
34	10 08·5	10 10·2	9 40·8	3·4	2·3	9·4	6·3	15·4	10·4
35	10 08·8	10 10·4	9 41·0	3·5	2·4	9·5	6·4	15·5	10·5
36	10 09·0	10 10·7	9 41·3	3·6	2·4	9·6	6·5	15·6	10·5
37	10 09·3	10 10·9	9 41·5	3·7	2·5	9·7	6·5	15·7	10·6
38	10 09·5	10 11·2	9 41·7	3·8	2·6	9·8	6·6	15·8	10·7
39	10 09·8	10 11·4	9 42·0	3·9	2·6	9·9	6·7	15·9	10·7
40	10 10·0	10 11·7	9 42·2	4·0	2·7	10·0	6·8	16·0	10·8
41	10 10·3	10 11·9	9 42·4	4·1	2·8	10·1	6·8	16·1	10·9
42	10 10·5	10 12·2	9 42·7	4·2	2·8	10·2	6·9	16·2	10·9
43	10 10·8	10 12·4	9 42·9	4·3	2·9	10·3	7·0	16·3	11·0
44	10 11·0	10 12·7	9 43·2	4·4	3·0	10·4	7·0	16·4	11·1
45	10 11·3	10 12·9	9 43·4	4·5	3·0	10·5	7·1	16·5	11·1
46	10 11·5	10 13·2	9 43·6	4·6	3·1	10·6	7·2	16·6	11·2
47	10 11·8	10 13·4	9 43·9	4·7	3·2	10·7	7·2	16·7	11·3
48	10 12·0	10 13·7	9 44·1	4·8	3·2	10·8	7·3	16·8	11·3
49	10 12·3	10 13·9	9 44·4	4·9	3·3	10·9	7·4	16·9	11·4
50	10 12·5	10 14·2	9 44·6	5·0	3·4	11·0	7·4	17·0	11·5
51	10 12·8	10 14·4	9 44·8	5·1	3·4	11·1	7·5	17·1	11·5
52	10 13·0	10 14·7	9 45·1	5·2	3·5	11·2	7·6	17·2	11·6
53	10 13·3	10 14·9	9 45·3	5·3	3·6	11·3	7·6	17·3	11·7
54	10 13·5	10 15·2	9 45·6	5·4	3·6	11·4	7·7	17·4	11·7
55	10 13·8	10 15·4	9 45·8	5·5	3·7	11·5	7·8	17·5	11·8
56	10 14·0	10 15·7	9 46·0	5·6	3·8	11·6	7·8	17·6	11·9
57	10 14·3	10 15·9	9 46·3	5·7	3·8	11·7	7·9	17·7	11·9
58	10 14·5	10 16·2	9 46·5	5·8	3·9	11·8	8·0	17·8	12·0
59	10 14·8	10 16·4	9 46·7	5·9	4·0	11·9	8·0	17·9	12·1
60	10 15·0	10 16·7	9 47·0	6·0	4·1	12·0	8·1	18·0	12·2

41ᵐ	SUN PLANETS	ARIES	MOON	v or d / Corrⁿ		v or d / Corrⁿ		v or d / Corrⁿ	
s	° ′	° ′	° ′	′	′	′	′	′	′
00	10 15·0	10 16·7	9 47·0	0·0	0·0	6·0	4·2	12·0	8·3
01	10 15·3	10 16·9	9 47·2	0·1	0·1	6·1	4·2	12·1	8·4
02	10 15·5	10 17·2	9 47·5	0·2	0·1	6·2	4·3	12·2	8·4
03	10 15·8	10 17·4	9 47·7	0·3	0·2	6·3	4·4	12·3	8·5
04	10 16·0	10 17·7	9 47·9	0·4	0·3	6·4	4·4	12·4	8·6
05	10 16·3	10 17·9	9 48·2	0·5	0·3	6·5	4·5	12·5	8·6
06	10 16·5	10 18·2	9 48·4	0·6	0·4	6·6	4·6	12·6	8·7
07	10 16·8	10 18·4	9 48·7	0·7	0·5	6·7	4·6	12·7	8·8
08	10 17·0	10 18·7	9 48·9	0·8	0·6	6·8	4·7	12·8	8·9
09	10 17·3	10 18·9	9 49·1	0·9	0·6	6·9	4·8	12·9	8·9
10	10 17·5	10 19·2	9 49·4	1·0	0·7	7·0	4·8	13·0	9·0
11	10 17·8	10 19·4	9 49·6	1·1	0·8	7·1	4·9	13·1	9·1
12	10 18·0	10 19·7	9 49·8	1·2	0·8	7·2	5·0	13·2	9·1
13	10 18·3	10 19·9	9 50·1	1·3	0·9	7·3	5·0	13·3	9·2
14	10 18·5	10 20·2	9 50·3	1·4	1·0	7·4	5·1	13·4	9·3
15	10 18·8	10 20·4	9 50·6	1·5	1·0	7·5	5·2	13·5	9·3
16	10 19·0	10 20·7	9 50·8	1·6	1·1	7·6	5·3	13·6	9·4
17	10 19·3	10 20·9	9 51·0	1·7	1·2	7·7	5·3	13·7	9·5
18	10 19·5	10 21·2	9 51·3	1·8	1·2	7·8	5·4	13·8	9·5
19	10 19·8	10 21·4	9 51·5	1·9	1·3	7·9	5·5	13·9	9·6
20	10 20·0	10 21·7	9 51·8	2·0	1·4	8·0	5·5	14·0	9·7
21	10 20·3	10 21·9	9 52·0	2·1	1·5	8·1	5·6	14·1	9·8
22	10 20·5	10 22·2	9 52·2	2·2	1·5	8·2	5·7	14·2	9·8
23	10 20·8	10 22·4	9 52·5	2·3	1·6	8·3	5·7	14·3	9·9
24	10 21·0	10 22·7	9 52·7	2·4	1·7	8·4	5·8	14·4	10·0
25	10 21·3	10 23·0	9 52·9	2·5	1·7	8·5	5·9	14·5	10·0
26	10 21·5	10 23·2	9 53·2	2·6	1·8	8·6	5·9	14·6	10·1
27	10 21·8	10 23·5	9 53·4	2·7	1·9	8·7	6·0	14·7	10·2
28	10 22·0	10 23·7	9 53·7	2·8	1·9	8·8	6·1	14·8	10·2
29	10 22·3	10 24·0	9 53·9	2·9	2·0	8·9	6·2	14·9	10·3
30	10 22·5	10 24·2	9 54·1	3·0	2·1	9·0	6·2	15·0	10·4
31	10 22·8	10 24·5	9 54·4	3·1	2·1	9·1	6·3	15·1	10·4
32	10 23·0	10 24·7	9 54·6	3·2	2·2	9·2	6·4	15·2	10·5
33	10 23·3	10 25·0	9 54·9	3·3	2·3	9·3	6·4	15·3	10·6
34	10 23·5	10 25·2	9 55·1	3·4	2·4	9·4	6·5	15·4	10·7
35	10 23·8	10 25·5	9 55·3	3·5	2·4	9·5	6·6	15·5	10·7
36	10 24·0	10 25·7	9 55·6	3·6	2·5	9·6	6·6	15·6	10·8
37	10 24·3	10 26·0	9 55·8	3·7	2·6	9·7	6·7	15·7	10·9
38	10 24·5	10 26·2	9 56·1	3·8	2·6	9·8	6·8	15·8	10·9
39	10 24·8	10 26·5	9 56·3	3·9	2·7	9·9	6·8	15·9	11·0
40	10 25·0	10 26·7	9 56·5	4·0	2·8	10·0	6·9	16·0	11·1
41	10 25·3	10 27·0	9 56·8	4·1	2·8	10·1	7·0	16·1	11·1
42	10 25·5	10 27·2	9 57·0	4·2	2·9	10·2	7·1	16·2	11·2
43	10 25·8	10 27·5	9 57·2	4·3	3·0	10·3	7·1	16·3	11·3
44	10 26·0	10 27·7	9 57·5	4·4	3·0	10·4	7·2	16·4	11·3
45	10 26·3	10 28·0	9 57·7	4·5	3·1	10·5	7·3	16·5	11·4
46	10 26·5	10 28·2	9 58·0	4·6	3·2	10·6	7·3	16·6	11·5
47	10 26·8	10 28·5	9 58·2	4·7	3·3	10·7	7·4	16·7	11·6
48	10 27·0	10 28·7	9 58·4	4·8	3·3	10·8	7·5	16·8	11·6
49	10 27·3	10 29·0	9 58·7	4·9	3·4	10·9	7·5	16·9	11·7
50	10 27·5	10 29·2	9 58·9	5·0	3·5	11·0	7·6	17·0	11·8
51	10 27·8	10 29·5	9 59·2	5·1	3·5	11·1	7·7	17·1	11·8
52	10 28·0	10 29·7	9 59·4	5·2	3·6	11·2	7·7	17·2	11·9
53	10 28·3	10 30·0	9 59·6	5·3	3·7	11·3	7·8	17·3	12·0
54	10 28·5	10 30·2	9 59·9	5·4	3·7	11·4	7·9	17·4	12·0
55	10 28·8	10 30·5	10 00·1	5·5	3·8	11·5	8·0	17·5	12·1
56	10 29·0	10 30·7	10 00·3	5·6	3·9	11·6	8·0	17·6	12·2
57	10 29·3	10 31·0	10 00·6	5·7	3·9	11·7	8·1	17·7	12·2
58	10 29·5	10 31·2	10 00·8	5·8	4·0	11·8	8·2	17·8	12·3
59	10 29·8	10 31·5	10 01·1	5·9	4·1	11·9	8·2	17·9	12·4
60	10 30·0	10 31·7	10 01·3	6·0	4·2	12·0	8·3	18·0	12·5

42 ᵐ s	SUN PLANETS	ARIES	MOON	v or Corrⁿ d	v or Corrⁿ d	v or Corrⁿ d
	° ′	° ′	° ′	′ ′	′ ′	′ ′
00	10 30·0	10 31·7	10 01·3	0·0 0·0	6·0 4·3	12·0 8·5
01	10 30·3	10 32·0	10 01·5	0·1 0·1	6·1 4·3	12·1 8·6
02	10 30·5	10 32·2	10 01·8	0·2 0·1	6·2 4·4	12·2 8·6
03	10 30·8	10 32·5	10 02·0	0·3 0·2	6·3 4·5	12·3 8·7
04	10 31·0	10 32·7	10 02·3	0·4 0·3	6·4 4·5	12·4 8·8
05	10 31·3	10 33·0	10 02·5	0·5 0·4	6·5 4·6	12·5 8·9
06	10 31·5	10 33·2	10 02·7	0·6 0·4	6·6 4·7	12·6 8·9
07	10 31·8	10 33·5	10 03·0	0·7 0·5	6·7 4·7	12·7 9·0
08	10 32·0	10 33·7	10 03·2	0·8 0·6	6·8 4·8	12·8 9·1
09	10 32·3	10 34·0	10 03·4	0·9 0·6	6·9 4·9	12·9 9·1
10	10 32·5	10 34·2	10 03·7	1·0 0·7	7·0 5·0	13·0 9·2
11	10 32·8	10 34·5	10 03·9	1·1 0·8	7·1 5·0	13·1 9·3
12	10 33·0	10 34·7	10 04·2	1·2 0·9	7·2 5·1	13·2 9·4
13	10 33·3	10 35·0	10 04·4	1·3 0·9	7·3 5·2	13·3 9·4
14	10 33·5	10 35·2	10 04·6	1·4 1·0	7·4 5·2	13·4 9·5
15	10 33·8	10 35·5	10 04·9	1·5 1·1	7·5 5·3	13·5 9·6
16	10 34·0	10 35·7	10 05·1	1·6 1·1	7·6 5·4	13·6 9·6
17	10 34·3	10 36·0	10 05·4	1·7 1·2	7·7 5·5	13·7 9·7
18	10 34·5	10 36·2	10 05·6	1·8 1·3	7·8 5·5	13·8 9·8
19	10 34·8	10 36·5	10 05·8	1·9 1·3	7·9 5·6	13·9 9·8
20	10 35·0	10 36·7	10 06·1	2·0 1·4	8·0 5·7	14·0 9·9
21	10 35·3	10 37·0	10 06·3	2·1 1·5	8·1 5·7	14·1 10·0
22	10 35·5	10 37·2	10 06·5	2·2 1·6	8·2 5·8	14·2 10·1
23	10 35·8	10 37·5	10 06·8	2·3 1·6	8·3 5·9	14·3 10·1
24	10 36·0	10 37·7	10 07·0	2·4 1·7	8·4 6·0	14·4 10·2
25	10 36·3	10 38·0	10 07·3	2·5 1·8	8·5 6·0	14·5 10·3
26	10 36·5	10 38·2	10 07·5	2·6 1·8	8·6 6·1	14·6 10·3
27	10 36·8	10 38·5	10 07·7	2·7 1·9	8·7 6·2	14·7 10·4
28	10 37·0	10 38·7	10 08·0	2·8 2·0	8·8 6·2	14·8 10·5
29	10 37·3	10 39·0	10 08·2	2·9 2·1	8·9 6·3	14·9 10·6
30	10 37·5	10 39·2	10 08·5	3·0 2·1	9·0 6·4	15·0 10·6
31	10 37·8	10 39·5	10 08·7	3·1 2·2	9·1 6·4	15·1 10·7
32	10 38·0	10 39·7	10 08·9	3·2 2·3	9·2 6·5	15·2 10·8
33	10 38·3	10 40·0	10 09·2	3·3 2·3	9·3 6·6	15·3 10·8
34	10 38·5	10 40·2	10 09·4	3·4 2·4	9·4 6·7	15·4 10·9
35	10 38·8	10 40·5	10 09·7	3·5 2·5	9·5 6·7	15·5 11·0
36	10 39·0	10 40·7	10 09·9	3·6 2·6	9·6 6·8	15·6 11·1
37	10 39·3	10 41·0	10 10·1	3·7 2·6	9·7 6·9	15·7 11·1
38	10 39·5	10 41·3	10 10·4	3·8 2·7	9·8 6·9	15·8 11·2
39	10 39·8	10 41·5	10 10·6	3·9 2·8	9·9 7·0	15·9 11·3
40	10 40·0	10 41·8	10 10·8	4·0 2·8	10·0 7·1	16·0 11·3
41	10 40·3	10 42·0	10 11·1	4·1 2·9	10·1 7·2	16·1 11·4
42	10 40·5	10 42·3	10 11·3	4·2 3·0	10·2 7·2	16·2 11·5
43	10 40·8	10 42·5	10 11·6	4·3 3·0	10·3 7·3	16·3 11·5
44	10 41·0	10 42·8	10 11·8	4·4 3·1	10·4 7·4	16·4 11·6
45	10 41·3	10 43·0	10 12·0	4·5 3·2	10·5 7·4	16·5 11·7
46	10 41·5	10 43·3	10 12·3	4·6 3·3	10·6 7·5	16·6 11·8
47	10 41·8	10 43·5	10 12·5	4·7 3·3	10·7 7·6	16·7 11·8
48	10 42·0	10 43·8	10 12·8	4·8 3·4	10·8 7·7	16·8 11·9
49	10 42·3	10 44·0	10 13·0	4·9 3·5	10·9 7·7	16·9 12·0
50	10 42·5	10 44·3	10 13·2	5·0 3·5	11·0 7·8	17·0 12·0
51	10 42·8	10 44·5	10 13·5	5·1 3·6	11·1 7·9	17·1 12·1
52	10 43·0	10 44·8	10 13·7	5·2 3·7	11·2 7·9	17·2 12·2
53	10 43·3	10 45·0	10 13·9	5·3 3·8	11·3 8·0	17·3 12·3
54	10 43·5	10 45·3	10 14·2	5·4 3·8	11·4 8·1	17·4 12·3
55	10 43·8	10 45·5	10 14·4	5·5 3·9	11·5 8·1	17·5 12·4
56	10 44·0	10 45·8	10 14·7	5·6 4·0	11·6 8·2	17·6 12·5
57	10 44·3	10 46·0	10 14·9	5·7 4·0	11·7 8·3	17·7 12·5
58	10 44·5	10 46·3	10 15·1	5·8 4·1	11·8 8·4	17·8 12·6
59	10 44·8	10 46·5	10 15·4	5·9 4·2	11·9 8·4	17·9 12·7
60	10 45·0	10 46·8	10 15·6	6·0 4·3	12·0 8·5	18·0 12·8

43 ᵐ s	SUN PLANETS	ARIES	MOON	v or Corrⁿ d	v or Corrⁿ d	v or Corrⁿ d
	° ′	° ′	° ′	′ ′	′ ′	′ ′
00	10 45·0	10 46·8	10 15·6	0·0 0·0	6·0 4·4	12·0 8·7
01	10 45·3	10 47·0	10 15·9	0·1 0·1	6·1 4·4	12·1 8·8
02	10 45·5	10 47·3	10 16·1	0·2 0·1	6·2 4·5	12·2 8·8
03	10 45·8	10 47·5	10 16·3	0·3 0·2	6·3 4·6	12·3 8·9
04	10 46·0	10 47·8	10 16·6	0·4 0·3	6·4 4·6	12·4 9·0
05	10 46·3	10 48·0	10 16·8	0·5 0·4	6·5 4·7	12·5 9·1
06	10 46·5	10 48·3	10 17·0	0·6 0·4	6·6 4·8	12·6 9·1
07	10 46·8	10 48·5	10 17·3	0·7 0·5	6·7 4·9	12·7 9·2
08	10 47·0	10 48·8	10 17·5	0·8 0·6	6·8 4·9	12·8 9·3
09	10 47·3	10 49·0	10 17·8	0·9 0·7	6·9 5·0	12·9 9·3
10	10 47·5	10 49·3	10 18·0	1·0 0·7	7·0 5·1	13·0 9·4
11	10 47·8	10 49·5	10 18·2	1·1 0·8	7·1 5·1	13·1 9·5
12	10 48·0	10 49·8	10 18·5	1·2 0·9	7·2 5·2	13·2 9·6
13	10 48·3	10 50·0	10 18·7	1·3 0·9	7·3 5·3	13·3 9·6
14	10 48·5	10 50·3	10 19·0	1·4 1·0	7·4 5·4	13·4 9·7
15	10 48·8	10 50·5	10 19·2	1·5 1·1	7·5 5·4	13·5 9·8
16	10 49·0	10 50·8	10 19·4	1·6 1·2	7·6 5·5	13·6 9·9
17	10 49·3	10 51·0	10 19·7	1·7 1·2	7·7 5·6	13·7 9·9
18	10 49·5	10 51·3	10 19·9	1·8 1·3	7·8 5·7	13·8 10·0
19	10 49·8	10 51·5	10 20·2	1·9 1·4	7·9 5·7	13·9 10·1
20	10 50·0	10 51·8	10 20·4	2·0 1·5	8·0 5·8	14·0 10·2
21	10 50·3	10 52·0	10 20·6	2·1 1·5	8·1 5·9	14·1 10·2
22	10 50·5	10 52·3	10 20·9	2·2 1·6	8·2 5·9	14·2 10·3
23	10 50·8	10 52·5	10 21·1	2·3 1·7	8·3 6·0	14·3 10·4
24	10 51·0	10 52·8	10 21·3	2·4 1·7	8·4 6·1	14·4 10·4
25	10 51·3	10 53·0	10 21·6	2·5 1·8	8·5 6·2	14·5 10·5
26	10 51·5	10 53·3	10 21·8	2·6 1·9	8·6 6·2	14·6 10·6
27	10 51·8	10 53·5	10 22·1	2·7 2·0	8·7 6·3	14·7 10·7
28	10 52·0	10 53·8	10 22·3	2·8 2·0	8·8 6·4	14·8 10·7
29	10 52·3	10 54·0	10 22·5	2·9 2·1	8·9 6·5	14·9 10·8
30	10 52·5	10 54·3	10 22·8	3·0 2·2	9·0 6·5	15·0 10·9
31	10 52·8	10 54·5	10 23·0	3·1 2·2	9·1 6·6	15·1 10·9
32	10 53·0	10 54·8	10 23·3	3·2 2·3	9·2 6·7	15·2 11·0
33	10 53·3	10 55·0	10 23·5	3·3 2·4	9·3 6·7	15·3 11·1
34	10 53·5	10 55·3	10 23·7	3·4 2·5	9·4 6·8	15·4 11·2
35	10 53·8	10 55·5	10 24·0	3·5 2·5	9·5 6·9	15·5 11·2
36	10 54·0	10 55·8	10 24·2	3·6 2·6	9·6 7·0	15·6 11·3
37	10 54·3	10 56·0	10 24·4	3·7 2·7	9·7 7·0	15·7 11·4
38	10 54·5	10 56·3	10 24·7	3·8 2·8	9·8 7·1	15·8 11·5
39	10 54·8	10 56·5	10 24·9	3·9 2·8	9·9 7·2	15·9 11·5
40	10 55·0	10 56·8	10 25·2	4·0 2·9	10·0 7·3	16·0 11·6
41	10 55·3	10 57·0	10 25·4	4·1 3·0	10·1 7·3	16·1 11·7
42	10 55·5	10 57·3	10 25·6	4·2 3·0	10·2 7·4	16·2 11·7
43	10 55·8	10 57·5	10 25·9	4·3 3·1	10·3 7·5	16·3 11·8
44	10 56·0	10 57·8	10 26·1	4·4 3·2	10·4 7·5	16·4 11·9
45	10 56·3	10 58·0	10 26·4	4·5 3·3	10·5 7·6	16·5 12·0
46	10 56·5	10 58·3	10 26·6	4·6 3·3	10·6 7·7	16·6 12·0
47	10 56·8	10 58·5	10 26·8	4·7 3·4	10·7 7·8	16·7 12·1
48	10 57·0	10 58·8	10 27·1	4·8 3·5	10·8 7·8	16·8 12·2
49	10 57·3	10 59·0	10 27·3	4·9 3·6	10·9 7·9	16·9 12·3
50	10 57·5	10 59·3	10 27·5	5·0 3·6	11·0 8·0	17·0 12·3
51	10 57·8	10 59·6	10 27·8	5·1 3·7	11·1 8·0	17·1 12·4
52	10 58·0	10 59·8	10 28·0	5·2 3·8	11·2 8·1	17·2 12·5
53	10 58·3	11 00·1	10 28·3	5·3 3·8	11·3 8·2	17·3 12·5
54	10 58·5	11 00·3	10 28·5	5·4 3·9	11·4 8·3	17·4 12·6
55	10 58·8	11 00·6	10 28·7	5·5 4·0	11·5 8·3	17·5 12·7
56	10 59·0	11 00·8	10 29·0	5·6 4·1	11·6 8·4	17·6 12·8
57	10 59·3	11 01·1	10 29·2	5·7 4·1	11·7 8·5	17·7 12·8
58	10 59·5	11 01·3	10 29·5	5·8 4·2	11·8 8·6	17·8 12·9
59	10 59·8	11 01·6	10 29·7	5·9 4·3	11·9 8·6	17·9 13·0
60	11 00·0	11 01·8	10 29·9	6·0 4·4	12·0 8·7	18·0 13·1

44ᵐ	SUN PLANETS	ARIES	MOON	v or d Corrⁿ		v or d Corrⁿ		v or d Corrⁿ	
s	° ′	° ′	° ′	′	′	′	′	′	′
00	11 00·0	11 01·8	10 29·9	0·0	0·0	6·0	4·5	12·0	8·9
01	11 00·3	11 02·1	10 30·2	0·1	0·1	6·1	4·5	12·1	9·0
02	11 00·5	11 02·3	10 30·4	0·2	0·1	6·2	4·6	12·2	9·0
03	11 00·8	11 02·6	10 30·6	0·3	0·2	6·3	4·7	12·3	9·1
04	11 01·0	11 02·8	10 30·9	0·4	0·3	6·4	4·7	12·4	9·2
05	11 01·3	11 03·1	10 31·1	0·5	0·4	6·5	4·8	12·5	9·3
06	11 01·5	11 03·3	10 31·4	0·6	0·4	6·6	4·9	12·6	9·3
07	11 01·8	11 03·6	10 31·6	0·7	0·5	6·7	5·0	12·7	9·4
08	11 02·0	11 03·8	10 31·8	0·8	0·6	6·8	5·0	12·8	9·5
09	11 02·3	11 04·1	10 32·1	0·9	0·7	6·9	5·1	12·9	9·6
10	11 02·5	11 04·3	10 32·3	1·0	0·7	7·0	5·2	13·0	9·6
11	11 02·8	11 04·6	10 32·6	1·1	0·8	7·1	5·3	13·1	9·7
12	11 03·0	11 04·8	10 32·8	1·2	0·9	7·2	5·3	13·2	9·8
13	11 03·3	11 05·1	10 33·0	1·3	1·0	7·3	5·4	13·3	9·9
14	11 03·5	11 05·3	10 33·3	1·4	1·0	7·4	5·5	13·4	9·9
15	11 03·8	11 05·6	10 33·5	1·5	1·1	7·5	5·6	13·5	10·0
16	11 04·0	11 05·8	10 33·8	1·6	1·2	7·6	5·6	13·6	10·1
17	11 04·3	11 06·1	10 34·0	1·7	1·3	7·7	5·7	13·7	10·2
18	11 04·5	11 06·3	10 34·2	1·8	1·3	7·8	5·8	13·8	10·2
19	11 04·8	11 06·6	10 34·5	1·9	1·4	7·9	5·9	13·9	10·3
20	11 05·0	11 06·8	10 34·7	2·0	1·5	8·0	5·9	14·0	10·4
21	11 05·3	11 07·1	10 34·9	2·1	1·6	8·1	6·0	14·1	10·5
22	11 05·5	11 07·3	10 35·2	2·2	1·6	8·2	6·1	14·2	10·5
23	11 05·8	11 07·6	10 35·4	2·3	1·7	8·3	6·2	14·3	10·6
24	11 06·0	11 07·8	10 35·7	2·4	1·8	8·4	6·2	14·4	10·7
25	11 06·3	11 08·1	10 35·9	2·5	1·9	8·5	6·3	14·5	10·8
26	11 06·5	11 08·3	10 36·1	2·6	1·9	8·6	6·4	14·6	10·8
27	11 06·8	11 08·6	10 36·4	2·7	2·0	8·7	6·5	14·7	10·9
28	11 07·0	11 08·8	10 36·6	2·8	2·1	8·8	6·5	14·8	11·0
29	11 07·3	11 09·1	10 36·9	2·9	2·2	8·9	6·6	14·9	11·1
30	11 07·5	11 09·3	10 37·1	3·0	2·2	9·0	6·7	15·0	11·1
31	11 07·8	11 09·6	10 37·3	3·1	2·3	9·1	6·7	15·1	11·2
32	11 08·0	11 09·8	10 37·6	3·2	2·4	9·2	6·8	15·2	11·3
33	11 08·3	11 10·1	10 37·8	3·3	2·4	9·3	6·9	15·3	11·3
34	11 08·5	11 10·3	10 38·0	3·4	2·5	9·4	7·0	15·4	11·4
35	11 08·8	11 10·6	10 38·3	3·5	2·6	9·5	7·0	15·5	11·5
36	11 09·0	11 10·8	10 38·5	3·6	2·7	9·6	7·1	15·6	11·6
37	11 09·3	11 11·1	10 38·8	3·7	2·7	9·7	7·2	15·7	11·6
38	11 09·5	11 11·3	10 39·0	3·8	2·8	9·8	7·3	15·8	11·7
39	11 09·8	11 11·6	10 39·2	3·9	2·9	9·9	7·3	15·9	11·8
40	11 10·0	11 11·8	10 39·5	4·0	3·0	10·0	7·4	16·0	11·9
41	11 10·3	11 12·1	10 39·7	4·1	3·0	10·1	7·5	16·1	11·9
42	11 10·5	11 12·3	10 40·0	4·2	3·1	10·2	7·6	16·2	12·0
43	11 10·8	11 12·6	10 40·2	4·3	3·2	10·3	7·6	16·3	12·1
44	11 11·0	11 12·8	10 40·4	4·4	3·3	10·4	7·7	16·4	12·2
45	11 11·3	11 13·1	10 40·7	4·5	3·3	10·5	7·8	16·5	12·2
46	11 11·5	11 13·3	10 40·9	4·6	3·4	10·6	7·9	16·6	12·3
47	11 11·8	11 13·6	10 41·1	4·7	3·5	10·7	7·9	16·7	12·4
48	11 12·0	11 13·8	10 41·4	4·8	3·6	10·8	8·0	16·8	12·5
49	11 12·3	11 14·1	10 41·6	4·9	3·6	10·9	8·1	16·9	12·5
50	11 12·5	11 14·3	10 41·9	5·0	3·7	11·0	8·2	17·0	12·6
51	11 12·8	11 14·6	10 42·1	5·1	3·8	11·1	8·2	17·1	12·7
52	11 13·0	11 14·8	10 42·3	5·2	3·9	11·2	8·3	17·2	12·8
53	11 13·3	11 15·1	10 42·6	5·3	3·9	11·3	8·4	17·3	12·8
54	11 13·5	11 15·3	10 42·8	5·4	4·0	11·4	8·5	17·4	12·9
55	11 13·8	11 15·6	10 43·1	5·5	4·1	11·5	8·5	17·5	13·0
56	11 14·0	11 15·8	10 43·3	5·6	4·2	11·6	8·6	17·6	13·1
57	11 14·3	11 16·1	10 43·5	5·7	4·2	11·7	8·7	17·7	13·1
58	11 14·5	11 16·3	10 43·8	5·8	4·3	11·8	8·8	17·8	13·2
59	11 14·8	11 16·6	10 44·0	5·9	4·4	11·9	8·8	17·9	13·3
60	11 15·0	11 16·8	10 44·3	6·0	4·5	12·0	8·9	18·0	13·4

45ᵐ	SUN PLANETS	ARIES	MOON	v or d Corrⁿ		v or d Corrⁿ		v or d Corrⁿ	
s	° ′	° ′	° ′	′	′	′	′	′	′
00	11 15·0	11 16·8	10 44·3	0·0	0·0	6·0	4·6	12·0	9·1
01	11 15·3	11 17·1	10 44·5	0·1	0·1	6·1	4·6	12·1	9·2
02	11 15·5	11 17·3	10 44·7	0·2	0·2	6·2	4·7	12·2	9·3
03	11 15·8	11 17·6	10 45·0	0·3	0·2	6·3	4·8	12·3	9·3
04	11 16·0	11 17·9	10 45·2	0·4	0·3	6·4	4·9	12·4	9·4
05	11 16·3	11 18·1	10 45·4	0·5	0·4	6·5	4·9	12·5	9·5
06	11 16·5	11 18·4	10 45·7	0·6	0·5	6·6	5·0	12·6	9·6
07	11 16·8	11 18·6	10 45·9	0·7	0·5	6·7	5·1	12·7	9·6
08	11 17·0	11 18·9	10 46·2	0·8	0·6	6·8	5·2	12·8	9·7
09	11 17·3	11 19·1	10 46·4	0·9	0·7	6·9	5·2	12·9	9·8
10	11 17·5	11 19·4	10 46·6	1·0	0·8	7·0	5·3	13·0	9·9
11	11 17·8	11 19·6	10 46·9	1·1	0·8	7·1	5·4	13·1	9·9
12	11 18·0	11 19·9	10 47·1	1·2	0·9	7·2	5·5	13·2	10·0
13	11 18·3	11 20·1	10 47·4	1·3	1·0	7·3	5·5	13·3	10·1
14	11 18·5	11 20·4	10 47·6	1·4	1·1	7·4	5·6	13·4	10·2
15	11 18·8	11 20·6	10 47·8	1·5	1·1	7·5	5·7	13·5	10·2
16	11 19·0	11 20·9	10 48·1	1·6	1·2	7·6	5·8	13·6	10·3
17	11 19·3	11 21·1	10 48·3	1·7	1·3	7·7	5·8	13·7	10·4
18	11 19·5	11 21·4	10 48·5	1·8	1·4	7·8	5·9	13·8	10·5
19	11 19·8	11 21·6	10 48·8	1·9	1·4	7·9	6·0	13·9	10·5
20	11 20·0	11 21·9	10 49·0	2·0	1·5	8·0	6·1	14·0	10·6
21	11 20·3	11 22·1	10 49·3	2·1	1·6	8·1	6·1	14·1	10·7
22	11 20·5	11 22·4	10 49·5	2·2	1·7	8·2	6·2	14·2	10·8
23	11 20·8	11 22·6	10 49·7	2·3	1·7	8·3	6·3	14·3	10·8
24	11 21·0	11 22·9	10 50·0	2·4	1·8	8·4	6·4	14·4	10·9
25	11 21·3	11 23·1	10 50·2	2·5	1·9	8·5	6·4	14·5	11·0
26	11 21·5	11 23·4	10 50·5	2·6	2·0	8·6	6·5	14·6	11·1
27	11 21·8	11 23·6	10 50·7	2·7	2·0	8·7	6·6	14·7	11·1
28	11 22·0	11 23·9	10 50·9	2·8	2·1	8·8	6·7	14·8	11·2
29	11 22·3	11 24·1	10 51·2	2·9	2·2	8·9	6·7	14·9	11·3
30	11 22·5	11 24·4	10 51·4	3·0	2·3	9·0	6·8	15·0	11·4
31	11 22·8	11 24·6	10 51·6	3·1	2·4	9·1	6·9	15·1	11·5
32	11 23·0	11 24·9	10 51·9	3·2	2·4	9·2	7·0	15·2	11·5
33	11 23·3	11 25·1	10 52·1	3·3	2·5	9·3	7·1	15·3	11·6
34	11 23·5	11 25·4	10 52·4	3·4	2·6	9·4	7·1	15·4	11·7
35	11 23·8	11 25·6	10 52·6	3·5	2·7	9·5	7·2	15·5	11·8
36	11 24·0	11 25·9	10 52·8	3·6	2·7	9·6	7·3	15·6	11·8
37	11 24·3	11 26·1	10 53·1	3·7	2·8	9·7	7·4	15·7	11·9
38	11 24·5	11 26·4	10 53·3	3·8	2·9	9·8	7·4	15·8	12·0
39	11 24·8	11 26·6	10 53·6	3·9	3·0	9·9	7·5	15·9	12·1
40	11 25·0	11 26·9	10 53·8	4·0	3·0	10·0	7·6	16·0	12·1
41	11 25·3	11 27·1	10 54·0	4·1	3·1	10·1	7·7	16·1	12·2
42	11 25·5	11 27·4	10 54·3	4·2	3·2	10·2	7·7	16·2	12·3
43	11 25·8	11 27·6	10 54·5	4·3	3·3	10·3	7·8	16·3	12·4
44	11 26·0	11 27·9	10 54·7	4·4	3·3	10·4	7·9	16·4	12·4
45	11 26·3	11 28·1	10 55·0	4·5	3·4	10·5	8·0	16·5	12·5
46	11 26·5	11 28·4	10 55·2	4·6	3·5	10·6	8·0	16·6	12·6
47	11 26·8	11 28·6	10 55·5	4·7	3·6	10·7	8·1	16·7	12·7
48	11 27·0	11 28·9	10 55·7	4·8	3·6	10·8	8·2	16·8	12·7
49	11 27·3	11 29·1	10 55·9	4·9	3·7	10·9	8·3	16·9	12·8
50	11 27·5	11 29·4	10 56·2	5·0	3·8	11·0	8·3	17·0	12·9
51	11 27·8	11 29·6	10 56·4	5·1	3·9	11·1	8·4	17·1	13·0
52	11 28·0	11 29·9	10 56·7	5·2	3·9	11·2	8·5	17·2	13·0
53	11 28·3	11 30·1	10 56·9	5·3	4·0	11·3	8·6	17·3	13·1
54	11 28·5	11 30·4	10 57·1	5·4	4·1	11·4	8·6	17·4	13·2
55	11 28·8	11 30·6	10 57·4	5·5	4·2	11·5	8·7	17·5	13·3
56	11 29·0	11 30·9	10 57·6	5·6	4·2	11·6	8·8	17·6	13·3
57	11 29·3	11 31·1	10 57·9	5·7	4·3	11·7	8·9	17·7	13·4
58	11 29·5	11 31·4	10 58·1	5·8	4·4	11·8	9·0	17·8	13·5
59	11 29·8	11 31·6	10 58·3	5·9	4·5	11·9	9·0	17·9	13·6
60	11 30·0	11 31·9	10 58·6	6·0	4·6	12·0	9·1	18·0	13·7

46ᵐ

46ᵐ s	SUN PLANETS	ARIES	MOON	v or d / Corrⁿ	v or d / Corrⁿ	v or d / Corrⁿ
00	11 30·0	11 31·9	10 58·6	0·0 0·0	6·0 4·7	12·0 9·3
01	11 30·3	11 32·1	10 58·8	0·1 0·1	6·1 4·7	12·1 9·4
02	11 30·5	11 32·4	10 59·0	0·2 0·2	6·2 4·8	12·2 9·5
03	11 30·8	11 32·6	10 59·3	0·3 0·2	6·3 4·9	12·3 9·5
04	11 31·0	11 32·9	10 59·5	0·4 0·3	6·4 5·0	12·4 9·6
05	11 31·3	11 33·1	10 59·8	0·5 0·4	6·5 5·0	12·5 9·7
06	11 31·5	11 33·4	11 00·0	0·6 0·5	6·6 5·1	12·6 9·8
07	11 31·8	11 33·6	11 00·2	0·7 0·5	6·7 5·2	12·7 9·8
08	11 32·0	11 33·9	11 00·5	0·8 0·6	6·8 5·3	12·8 9·9
09	11 32·3	11 34·1	11 00·7	0·9 0·7	6·9 5·3	12·9 10·0
10	11 32·5	11 34·4	11 01·0	1·0 0·8	7·0 5·4	13·0 10·1
11	11 32·8	11 34·6	11 01·2	1·1 0·9	7·1 5·5	13·1 10·2
12	11 33·0	11 34·9	11 01·4	1·2 0·9	7·2 5·6	13·2 10·2
13	11 33·3	11 35·1	11 01·7	1·3 1·0	7·3 5·7	13·3 10·3
14	11 33·5	11 35·4	11 01·9	1·4 1·1	7·4 5·7	13·4 10·4
15	11 33·8	11 35·6	11 02·1	1·5 1·2	7·5 5·8	13·5 10·5
16	11 34·0	11 35·9	11 02·4	1·6 1·2	7·6 5·9	13·6 10·5
17	11 34·3	11 36·2	11 02·6	1·7 1·3	7·7 6·0	13·7 10·6
18	11 34·5	11 36·4	11 02·9	1·8 1·4	7·8 6·0	13·8 10·7
19	11 34·8	11 36·7	11 03·1	1·9 1·5	7·9 6·1	13·9 10·8
20	11 35·0	11 36·9	11 03·3	2·0 1·6	8·0 6·2	14·0 10·9
21	11 35·3	11 37·2	11 03·6	2·1 1·6	8·1 6·3	14·1 10·9
22	11 35·5	11 37·4	11 03·8	2·2 1·7	8·2 6·4	14·2 11·0
23	11 35·8	11 37·7	11 04·1	2·3 1·8	8·3 6·4	14·3 11·1
24	11 36·0	11 37·9	11 04·3	2·4 1·9	8·4 6·5	14·4 11·2
25	11 36·3	11 38·2	11 04·5	2·5 1·9	8·5 6·6	14·5 11·2
26	11 36·5	11 38·4	11 04·8	2·6 2·0	8·6 6·7	14·6 11·3
27	11 36·8	11 38·7	11 05·0	2·7 2·1	8·7 6·7	14·7 11·4
28	11 37·0	11 38·9	11 05·2	2·8 2·2	8·8 6·8	14·8 11·5
29	11 37·3	11 39·2	11 05·5	2·9 2·2	8·9 6·9	14·9 11·5
30	11 37·5	11 39·4	11 05·7	3·0 2·3	9·0 7·0	15·0 11·6
31	11 37·8	11 39·7	11 06·0	3·1 2·4	9·1 7·1	15·1 11·7
32	11 38·0	11 39·9	11 06·2	3·2 2·5	9·2 7·1	15·2 11·8
33	11 38·3	11 40·2	11 06·4	3·3 2·6	9·3 7·2	15·3 11·9
34	11 38·5	11 40·4	11 06·7	3·4 2·6	9·4 7·3	15·4 11·9
35	11 38·8	11 40·7	11 06·9	3·5 2·7	9·5 7·4	15·5 12·0
36	11 39·0	11 40·9	11 07·2	3·6 2·8	9·6 7·4	15·6 12·1
37	11 39·3	11 41·2	11 07·4	3·7 2·9	9·7 7·5	15·7 12·2
38	11 39·5	11 41·4	11 07·6	3·8 2·9	9·8 7·6	15·8 12·2
39	11 39·8	11 41·7	11 07·9	3·9 3·0	9·9 7·7	15·9 12·3
40	11 40·0	11 41·9	11 08·1	4·0 3·1	10·0 7·8	16·0 12·4
41	11 40·3	11 42·2	11 08·3	4·1 3·2	10·1 7·8	16·1 12·5
42	11 40·5	11 42·4	11 08·6	4·2 3·3	10·2 7·9	16·2 12·6
43	11 40·8	11 42·7	11 08·8	4·3 3·3	10·3 8·0	16·3 12·6
44	11 41·0	11 42·9	11 09·1	4·4 3·4	10·4 8·1	16·4 12·7
45	11 41·3	11 43·2	11 09·3	4·5 3·5	10·5 8·1	16·5 12·8
46	11 41·5	11 43·4	11 09·5	4·6 3·6	10·6 8·2	16·6 12·9
47	11 41·8	11 43·7	11 09·8	4·7 3·6	10·7 8·3	16·7 12·9
48	11 42·0	11 43·9	11 10·0	4·8 3·7	10·8 8·4	16·8 13·0
49	11 42·3	11 44·2	11 10·3	4·9 3·8	10·9 8·4	16·9 13·1
50	11 42·5	11 44·4	11 10·5	5·0 3·9	11·0 8·5	17·0 13·2
51	11 42·8	11 44·7	11 10·7	5·1 4·0	11·1 8·6	17·1 13·3
52	11 43·0	11 44·9	11 11·0	5·2 4·0	11·2 8·7	17·2 13·3
53	11 43·3	11 45·2	11 11·2	5·3 4·1	11·3 8·8	17·3 13·4
54	11 43·5	11 45·4	11 11·5	5·4 4·2	11·4 8·8	17·4 13·5
55	11 43·8	11 45·7	11 11·7	5·5 4·3	11·5 8·9	17·5 13·6
56	11 44·0	11 45·9	11 11·9	5·6 4·3	11·6 9·0	17·6 13·6
57	11 44·3	11 46·2	11 12·2	5·7 4·4	11·7 9·1	17·7 13·7
58	11 44·5	11 46·4	11 12·4	5·8 4·5	11·8 9·1	17·8 13·8
59	11 44·8	11 46·7	11 12·6	5·9 4·6	11·9 9·2	17·9 13·9
60	11 45·0	11 46·9	11 12·9	6·0 4·7	12·0 9·3	18·0 14·0

47ᵐ

47ᵐ s	SUN PLANETS	ARIES	MOON	v or d / Corrⁿ	v or d / Corrⁿ	v or d / Corrⁿ
00	11 45·0	11 46·9	11 12·9	0·0 0·0	6·0 4·8	12·0 9·5
01	11 45·3	11 47·2	11 13·1	0·1 0·1	6·1 4·8	12·1 9·6
02	11 45·5	11 47·4	11 13·4	0·2 0·2	6·2 4·9	12·2 9·7
03	11 45·8	11 47·7	11 13·6	0·3 0·2	6·3 5·0	12·3 9·7
04	11 46·0	11 47·9	11 13·8	0·4 0·3	6·4 5·1	12·4 9·8
05	11 46·3	11 48·2	11 14·1	0·5 0·4	6·5 5·1	12·5 9·9
06	11 46·5	11 48·4	11 14·3	0·6 0·5	6·6 5·2	12·6 10·0
07	11 46·8	11 48·7	11 14·6	0·7 0·6	6·7 5·3	12·7 10·1
08	11 47·0	11 48·9	11 14·8	0·8 0·6	6·8 5·4	12·8 10·1
09	11 47·3	11 49·2	11 15·0	0·9 0·7	6·9 5·5	12·9 10·2
10	11 47·5	11 49·4	11 15·3	1·0 0·8	7·0 5·5	13·0 10·3
11	11 47·8	11 49·7	11 15·5	1·1 0·9	7·1 5·6	13·1 10·4
12	11 48·0	11 49·9	11 15·7	1·2 1·0	7·2 5·7	13·2 10·5
13	11 48·3	11 50·2	11 16·0	1·3 1·0	7·3 5·8	13·3 10·5
14	11 48·5	11 50·4	11 16·2	1·4 1·1	7·4 5·9	13·4 10·6
15	11 48·8	11 50·7	11 16·5	1·5 1·2	7·5 5·9	13·5 10·7
16	11 49·0	11 50·9	11 16·7	1·6 1·3	7·6 6·0	13·6 10·8
17	11 49·3	11 51·2	11 16·9	1·7 1·3	7·7 6·1	13·7 10·8
18	11 49·5	11 51·4	11 17·2	1·8 1·4	7·8 6·2	13·8 10·9
19	11 49·8	11 51·7	11 17·4	1·9 1·5	7·9 6·3	13·9 11·0
20	11 50·0	11 51·9	11 17·7	2·0 1·6	8·0 6·3	14·0 11·1
21	11 50·3	11 52·2	11 17·9	2·1 1·7	8·1 6·4	14·1 11·2
22	11 50·5	11 52·4	11 18·1	2·2 1·7	8·2 6·5	14·2 11·2
23	11 50·8	11 52·7	11 18·4	2·3 1·8	8·3 6·6	14·3 11·3
24	11 51·0	11 52·9	11 18·6	2·4 1·9	8·4 6·7	14·4 11·4
25	11 51·3	11 53·2	11 18·8	2·5 2·0	8·5 6·7	14·5 11·5
26	11 51·5	11 53·4	11 19·1	2·6 2·1	8·6 6·8	14·6 11·6
27	11 51·8	11 53·7	11 19·3	2·7 2·1	8·7 6·9	14·7 11·6
28	11 52·0	11 53·9	11 19·6	2·8 2·2	8·8 7·0	14·8 11·7
29	11 52·3	11 54·2	11 19·8	2·9 2·3	8·9 7·0	14·9 11·8
30	11 52·5	11 54·5	11 20·0	3·0 2·4	9·0 7·1	15·0 11·9
31	11 52·8	11 54·7	11 20·3	3·1 2·5	9·1 7·2	15·1 12·0
32	11 53·0	11 55·0	11 20·5	3·2 2·5	9·2 7·3	15·2 12·0
33	11 53·3	11 55·2	11 20·8	3·3 2·6	9·3 7·4	15·3 12·1
34	11 53·5	11 55·5	11 21·0	3·4 2·7	9·4 7·4	15·4 12·2
35	11 53·8	11 55·7	11 21·2	3·5 2·8	9·5 7·5	15·5 12·3
36	11 54·0	11 56·0	11 21·5	3·6 2·9	9·6 7·6	15·6 12·4
37	11 54·3	11 56·2	11 21·7	3·7 2·9	9·7 7·7	15·7 12·4
38	11 54·5	11 56·5	11 22·0	3·8 3·0	9·8 7·8	15·8 12·5
39	11 54·8	11 56·7	11 22·2	3·9 3·1	9·9 7·8	15·9 12·6
40	11 55·0	11 57·0	11 22·4	4·0 3·2	10·0 7·9	16·0 12·7
41	11 55·3	11 57·2	11 22·7	4·1 3·2	10·1 8·0	16·1 12·7
42	11 55·5	11 57·5	11 22·9	4·2 3·3	10·2 8·1	16·2 12·8
43	11 55·8	11 57·7	11 23·1	4·3 3·4	10·3 8·2	16·3 12·9
44	11 56·0	11 58·0	11 23·4	4·4 3·5	10·4 8·2	16·4 13·0
45	11 56·3	11 58·2	11 23·6	4·5 3·6	10·5 8·3	16·5 13·1
46	11 56·5	11 58·5	11 23·9	4·6 3·6	10·6 8·4	16·6 13·1
47	11 56·8	11 58·7	11 24·1	4·7 3·7	10·7 8·5	16·7 13·2
48	11 57·0	11 59·0	11 24·3	4·8 3·8	10·8 8·6	16·8 13·3
49	11 57·3	11 59·2	11 24·6	4·9 3·9	10·9 8·6	16·9 13·4
50	11 57·5	11 59·5	11 24·8	5·0 4·0	11·0 8·7	17·0 13·5
51	11 57·8	11 59·7	11 25·1	5·1 4·0	11·1 8·8	17·1 13·5
52	11 58·0	12 00·0	11 25·3	5·2 4·1	11·2 8·9	17·2 13·6
53	11 58·3	12 00·2	11 25·5	5·3 4·2	11·3 8·9	17·3 13·7
54	11 58·5	12 00·5	11 25·8	5·4 4·3	11·4 9·0	17·4 13·8
55	11 58·8	12 00·7	11 26·0	5·5 4·4	11·5 9·1	17·5 13·9
56	11 59·0	12 01·0	11 26·2	5·6 4·4	11·6 9·2	17·6 13·9
57	11 59·3	12 01·2	11 26·5	5·7 4·5	11·7 9·3	17·7 14·0
58	11 59·5	12 01·5	11 26·7	5·8 4·6	11·8 9·3	17·8 14·1
59	11 59·8	12 01·7	11 27·0	5·9 4·7	11·9 9·4	17·9 14·2
60	12 00·0	12 02·0	11 27·2	6·0 4·8	12·0 9·5	18·0 14·3

48ᵐ

48 s	SUN PLANETS	ARIES	MOON	v or Corrⁿ d	v or Corrⁿ d	v or Corrⁿ d
00	12 00·0	12 02·0	11 27·2	0·0 0·0	6·0 4·9	12·0 9·7
01	12 00·3	12 02·2	11 27·4	0·1 0·1	6·1 4·9	12·1 9·8
02	12 00·5	12 02·5	11 27·7	0·2 0·2	6·2 5·0	12·2 9·9
03	12 00·8	12 02·7	11 27·9	0·3 0·2	6·3 5·1	12·3 9·9
04	12 01·0	12 03·0	11 28·2	0·4 0·3	6·4 5·2	12·4 10·0
05	12 01·3	12 03·2	11 28·4	0·5 0·4	6·5 5·3	12·5 10·1
06	12 01·5	12 03·5	11 28·6	0·6 0·5	6·6 5·3	12·6 10·2
07	12 01·8	12 03·7	11 28·9	0·7 0·6	6·7 5·4	12·7 10·3
08	12 02·0	12 04·0	11 29·1	0·8 0·6	6·8 5·5	12·8 10·3
09	12 02·3	12 04·2	11 29·3	0·9 0·7	6·9 5·6	12·9 10·4
10	12 02·5	12 04·5	11 29·6	1·0 0·8	7·0 5·7	13·0 10·5
11	12 02·8	12 04·7	11 29·8	1·1 0·9	7·1 5·7	13·1 10·6
12	12 03·0	12 05·0	11 30·1	1·2 1·0	7·2 5·8	13·2 10·7
13	12 03·3	12 05·2	11 30·3	1·3 1·1	7·3 5·9	13·3 10·8
14	12 03·5	12 05·5	11 30·5	1·4 1·1	7·4 6·0	13·4 10·8
15	12 03·8	12 05·7	11 30·8	1·5 1·2	7·5 6·1	13·5 10·9
16	12 04·0	12 06·0	11 31·0	1·6 1·3	7·6 6·1	13·6 11·0
17	12 04·3	12 06·2	11 31·3	1·7 1·4	7·7 6·2	13·7 11·1
18	12 04·5	12 06·5	11 31·5	1·8 1·5	7·8 6·3	13·8 11·2
19	12 04·8	12 06·7	11 31·7	1·9 1·5	7·9 6·4	13·9 11·2
20	12 05·0	12 07·0	11 32·0	2·0 1·6	8·0 6·5	14·0 11·3
21	12 05·3	12 07·2	11 32·2	2·1 1·7	8·1 6·5	14·1 11·4
22	12 05·5	12 07·5	11 32·4	2·2 1·8	8·2 6·6	14·2 11·5
23	12 05·8	12 07·7	11 32·7	2·3 1·9	8·3 6·7	14·3 11·6
24	12 06·0	12 08·0	11 32·9	2·4 1·9	8·4 6·8	14·4 11·6
25	12 06·3	12 08·2	11 33·2	2·5 2·0	8·5 6·9	14·5 11·7
26	12 06·5	12 08·5	11 33·4	2·6 2·1	8·6 7·0	14·6 11·8
27	12 06·8	12 08·7	11 33·6	2·7 2·2	8·7 7·0	14·7 11·9
28	12 07·0	12 09·0	11 33·9	2·8 2·3	8·8 7·1	14·8 12·0
29	12 07·3	12 09·2	11 34·1	2·9 2·3	8·9 7·2	14·9 12·0
30	12 07·5	12 09·5	11 34·4	3·0 2·4	9·0 7·3	15·0 12·1
31	12 07·8	12 09·7	11 34·6	3·1 2·5	9·1 7·4	15·1 12·2
32	12 08·0	12 10·0	11 34·8	3·2 2·6	9·2 7·4	15·2 12·3
33	12 08·3	12 10·2	11 35·1	3·3 2·7	9·3 7·5	15·3 12·4
34	12 08·5	12 10·5	11 35·3	3·4 2·7	9·4 7·6	15·4 12·4
35	12 08·8	12 10·7	11 35·6	3·5 2·8	9·5 7·7	15·5 12·5
36	12 09·0	12 11·0	11 35·8	3·6 2·9	9·6 7·8	15·6 12·6
37	12 09·3	12 11·2	11 36·0	3·7 3·0	9·7 7·8	15·7 12·7
38	12 09·5	12 11·5	11 36·3	3·8 3·1	9·8 7·9	15·8 12·8
39	12 09·8	12 11·7	11 36·5	3·9 3·2	9·9 8·0	15·9 12·9
40	12 10·0	12 12·0	11 36·7	4·0 3·2	10·0 8·1	16·0 12·9
41	12 10·3	12 12·2	11 37·0	4·1 3·3	10·1 8·2	16·1 13·0
42	12 10·5	12 12·5	11 37·2	4·2 3·4	10·2 8·2	16·2 13·1
43	12 10·8	12 12·8	11 37·5	4·3 3·5	10·3 8·3	16·3 13·2
44	12 11·0	12 13·0	11 37·7	4·4 3·6	10·4 8·4	16·4 13·3
45	12 11·3	12 13·3	11 37·9	4·5 3·6	10·5 8·5	16·5 13·3
46	12 11·5	12 13·5	11 38·2	4·6 3·7	10·6 8·6	16·6 13·4
47	12 11·8	12 13·8	11 38·4	4·7 3·8	10·7 8·6	16·7 13·5
48	12 12·0	12 14·0	11 38·7	4·8 3·9	10·8 8·7	16·8 13·6
49	12 12·3	12 14·3	11 38·9	4·9 4·0	10·9 8·8	16·9 13·7
50	12 12·5	12 14·5	11 39·1	5·0 4·0	11·0 8·9	17·0 13·7
51	12 12·8	12 14·8	11 39·4	5·1 4·1	11·1 9·0	17·1 13·8
52	12 13·0	12 15·0	11 39·6	5·2 4·2	11·2 9·1	17·2 13·9
53	12 13·3	12 15·3	11 39·8	5·3 4·3	11·3 9·1	17·3 14·0
54	12 13·5	12 15·5	11 40·1	5·4 4·4	11·4 9·2	17·4 14·1
55	12 13·8	12 15·8	11 40·3	5·5 4·4	11·5 9·3	17·5 14·1
56	12 14·0	12 16·0	11 40·6	5·6 4·5	11·6 9·4	17·6 14·2
57	12 14·3	12 16·3	11 40·8	5·7 4·6	11·7 9·5	17·7 14·3
58	12 14·5	12 16·5	11 41·0	5·8 4·7	11·8 9·5	17·8 14·4
59	12 14·8	12 16·8	11 41·3	5·9 4·8	11·9 9·6	17·9 14·5
60	12 15·0	12 17·0	11 41·5	6·0 4·9	12·0 9·7	18·0 14·6

49ᵐ

49 s	SUN PLANETS	ARIES	MOON	v or Corrⁿ d	v or Corrⁿ d	v or Corrⁿ d
00	12 15·0	12 17·0	11 41·5	0·0 0·0	6·0 5·0	12·0 9·9
01	12 15·3	12 17·3	11 41·8	0·1 0·1	6·1 5·0	12·1 10·0
02	12 15·5	12 17·5	11 42·0	0·2 0·2	6·2 5·1	12·2 10·1
03	12 15·8	12 17·8	11 42·2	0·3 0·2	6·3 5·2	12·3 10·1
04	12 16·0	12 18·0	11 42·5	0·4 0·3	6·4 5·3	12·4 10·2
05	12 16·3	12 18·3	11 42·7	0·5 0·4	6·5 5·4	12·5 10·3
06	12 16·5	12 18·5	11 42·9	0·6 0·5	6·6 5·4	12·6 10·4
07	12 16·8	12 18·8	11 43·2	0·7 0·6	6·7 5·5	12·7 10·5
08	12 17·0	12 19·0	11 43·4	0·8 0·7	6·8 5·6	12·8 10·6
09	12 17·3	12 19·3	11 43·7	0·9 0·7	6·9 5·7	12·9 10·6
10	12 17·5	12 19·5	11 43·9	1·0 0·8	7·0 5·8	13·0 10·7
11	12 17·8	12 19·8	11 44·1	1·1 0·9	7·1 5·9	13·1 10·8
12	12 18·0	12 20·0	11 44·4	1·2 1·0	7·2 5·9	13·2 10·9
13	12 18·3	12 20·3	11 44·6	1·3 1·1	7·3 6·0	13·3 11·0
14	12 18·5	12 20·5	11 44·9	1·4 1·2	7·4 6·1	13·4 11·1
15	12 18·8	12 20·8	11 45·1	1·5 1·2	7·5 6·2	13·5 11·1
16	12 19·0	12 21·0	11 45·3	1·6 1·3	7·6 6·3	13·6 11·2
17	12 19·3	12 21·3	11 45·6	1·7 1·4	7·7 6·4	13·7 11·3
18	12 19·5	12 21·5	11 45·8	1·8 1·5	7·8 6·4	13·8 11·4
19	12 19·8	12 21·8	11 46·1	1·9 1·6	7·9 6·5	13·9 11·5
20	12 20·0	12 22·0	11 46·3	2·0 1·7	8·0 6·6	14·0 11·6
21	12 20·3	12 22·3	11 46·5	2·1 1·7	8·1 6·7	14·1 11·6
22	12 20·5	12 22·5	11 46·8	2·2 1·8	8·2 6·8	14·2 11·7
23	12 20·8	12 22·8	11 47·0	2·3 1·9	8·3 6·8	14·3 11·8
24	12 21·0	12 23·0	11 47·2	2·4 2·0	8·4 6·9	14·4 11·9
25	12 21·3	12 23·3	11 47·5	2·5 2·1	8·5 7·0	14·5 12·0
26	12 21·5	12 23·5	11 47·7	2·6 2·1	8·6 7·1	14·6 12·0
27	12 21·8	12 23·8	11 48·0	2·7 2·2	8·7 7·2	14·7 12·1
28	12 22·0	12 24·0	11 48·2	2·8 2·3	8·8 7·3	14·8 12·2
29	12 22·3	12 24·3	11 48·4	2·9 2·4	8·9 7·3	14·9 12·3
30	12 22·5	12 24·5	11 48·7	3·0 2·5	9·0 7·4	15·0 12·4
31	12 22·8	12 24·8	11 48·9	3·1 2·6	9·1 7·5	15·1 12·5
32	12 23·0	12 25·0	11 49·2	3·2 2·6	9·2 7·6	15·2 12·5
33	12 23·3	12 25·3	11 49·4	3·3 2·7	9·3 7·7	15·3 12·6
34	12 23·5	12 25·5	11 49·6	3·4 2·8	9·4 7·8	15·4 12·7
35	12 23·8	12 25·8	11 49·9	3·5 2·9	9·5 7·8	15·5 12·8
36	12 24·0	12 26·0	11 50·1	3·6 3·0	9·6 7·9	15·6 12·9
37	12 24·3	12 26·3	11 50·3	3·7 3·1	9·7 8·0	15·7 13·0
38	12 24·5	12 26·5	11 50·6	3·8 3·1	9·8 8·1	15·8 13·0
39	12 24·8	12 26·8	11 50·8	3·9 3·2	9·9 8·2	15·9 13·1
40	12 25·0	12 27·0	11 51·1	4·0 3·3	10·0 8·3	16·0 13·2
41	12 25·3	12 27·3	11 51·3	4·1 3·4	10·1 8·3	16·1 13·3
42	12 25·5	12 27·5	11 51·5	4·2 3·5	10·2 8·4	16·2 13·4
43	12 25·8	12 27·8	11 51·8	4·3 3·5	10·3 8·5	16·3 13·4
44	12 26·0	12 28·0	11 52·0	4·4 3·6	10·4 8·6	16·4 13·5
45	12 26·3	12 28·3	11 52·3	4·5 3·7	10·5 8·7	16·5 13·6
46	12 26·5	12 28·5	11 52·5	4·6 3·8	10·6 8·7	16·6 13·7
47	12 26·8	12 28·8	11 52·7	4·7 3·9	10·7 8·8	16·7 13·8
48	12 27·0	12 29·0	11 53·0	4·8 4·0	10·8 8·9	16·8 13·9
49	12 27·3	12 29·3	11 53·2	4·9 4·0	10·9 9·0	16·9 13·9
50	12 27·5	12 29·5	11 53·4	5·0 4·1	11·0 9·1	17·0 14·0
51	12 27·8	12 29·8	11 53·7	5·1 4·2	11·1 9·2	17·1 14·1
52	12 28·0	12 30·0	11 53·9	5·2 4·3	11·2 9·2	17·2 14·2
53	12 28·3	12 30·3	11 54·2	5·3 4·4	11·3 9·3	17·3 14·3
54	12 28·5	12 30·5	11 54·4	5·4 4·5	11·4 9·4	17·4 14·4
55	12 28·8	12 30·8	11 54·6	5·5 4·5	11·5 9·5	17·5 14·4
56	12 29·0	12 31·1	11 54·9	5·6 4·6	11·6 9·6	17·6 14·5
57	12 29·3	12 31·3	11 55·1	5·7 4·7	11·7 9·6	17·7 14·6
58	12 29·5	12 31·6	11 55·4	5·8 4·8	11·8 9·7	17·8 14·7
59	12 29·8	12 31·8	11 55·6	5·9 4·9	11·9 9·8	17·9 14·8
60	12 30·0	12 32·1	11 55·8	6·0 5·0	12·0 9·9	18·0 14·9

50ᵐ

50	SUN PLANETS	ARIES	MOON	v or d Corrⁿ	v or d Corrⁿ	v or d Corrⁿ
s	° ′	° ′	° ′	′ ′	′ ′	′ ′
00	12 30·0	12 32·1	11 55·8	0·0 0·0	6·0 5·1	12·0 10·1
01	12 30·3	12 32·3	11 56·1	0·1 0·1	6·1 5·1	12·1 10·2
02	12 30·5	12 32·6	11 56·3	0·2 0·2	6·2 5·2	12·2 10·3
03	12 30·8	12 32·8	11 56·5	0·3 0·3	6·3 5·3	12·3 10·4
04	12 31·0	12 33·1	11 56·8	0·4 0·3	6·4 5·4	12·4 10·4
05	12 31·3	12 33·3	11 57·0	0·5 0·4	6·5 5·5	12·5 10·5
06	12 31·5	12 33·6	11 57·3	0·6 0·5	6·6 5·6	12·6 10·6
07	12 31·8	12 33·8	11 57·6	0·7 0·6	6·7 5·6	12·7 10·7
08	12 32·0	12 34·1	11 57·7	0·8 0·7	6·8 5·7	12·8 10·8
09	12 32·3	12 34·3	11 58·0	0·9 0·8	6·9 5·8	12·9 10·9
10	12 32·5	12 34·6	11 58·2	1·0 0·8	7·0 5·9	13·0 10·9
11	12 32·8	12 34·8	11 58·5	1·1 0·9	7·1 6·0	13·1 11·0
12	12 33·0	12 35·1	11 58·7	1·2 1·0	7·2 6·1	13·2 11·1
13	12 33·3	12 35·3	11 58·9	1·3 1·1	7·3 6·1	13·3 11·2
14	12 33·5	12 35·6	11 59·2	1·4 1·2	7·4 6·2	13·4 11·3
15	12 33·8	12 35·8	11 59·4	1·5 1·3	7·5 6·3	13·5 11·4
16	12 34·0	12 36·1	11 59·7	1·6 1·3	7·6 6·4	13·6 11·4
17	12 34·3	12 36·3	11 59·9	1·7 1·4	7·7 6·5	13·7 11·5
18	12 34·5	12 36·6	12 00·1	1·8 1·5	7·8 6·6	13·8 11·6
19	12 34·8	12 36·8	12 00·4	1·9 1·6	7·9 6·6	13·9 11·7
20	12 35·0	12 37·1	12 00·6	2·0 1·7	8·0 6·7	14·0 11·8
21	12 35·3	12 37·3	12 00·8	2·1 1·8	8·1 6·8	14·1 11·9
22	12 35·5	12 37·6	12 01·1	2·2 1·9	8·2 6·9	14·2 12·0
23	12 35·8	12 37·8	12 01·3	2·3 1·9	8·3 7·0	14·3 12·0
24	12 36·0	12 38·1	12 01·6	2·4 2·0	8·4 7·1	14·4 12·1
25	12 36·3	12 38·3	12 01·8	2·5 2·1	8·5 7·2	14·5 12·2
26	12 36·5	12 38·6	12 02·0	2·6 2·2	8·6 7·2	14·6 12·3
27	12 36·8	12 38·8	12 02·3	2·7 2·3	8·7 7·3	14·7 12·4
28	12 37·0	12 39·1	12 02·5	2·8 2·4	8·8 7·4	14·8 12·5
29	12 37·3	12 39·3	12 02·8	2·9 2·4	8·9 7·5	14·9 12·5
30	12 37·5	12 39·6	12 03·0	3·0 2·5	9·0 7·6	15·0 12·6
31	12 37·8	12 39·8	12 03·2	3·1 2·6	9·1 7·7	15·1 12·7
32	12 38·0	12 40·1	12 03·5	3·2 2·7	9·2 7·7	15·2 12·8
33	12 38·3	12 40·3	12 03·7	3·3 2·8	9·3 7·8	15·3 12·9
34	12 38·5	12 40·6	12 03·9	3·4 2·9	9·4 7·9	15·4 13·0
35	12 38·8	12 40·8	12 04·2	3·5 2·9	9·5 8·0	15·5 13·0
36	12 39·0	12 41·1	12 04·4	3·6 3·0	9·6 8·1	15·6 13·1
37	12 39·3	12 41·3	12 04·7	3·7 3·1	9·7 8·2	15·7 13·2
38	12 39·5	12 41·6	12 04·9	3·8 3·2	9·8 8·2	15·8 13·3
39	12 39·8	12 41·8	12 05·1	3·9 3·3	9·9 8·3	15·9 13·4
40	12 40·0	12 42·1	12 05·4	4·0 3·4	10·0 8·4	16·0 13·5
41	12 40·3	12 42·3	12 05·6	4·1 3·5	10·1 8·5	16·1 13·6
42	12 40·5	12 42·6	12 05·9	4·2 3·5	10·2 8·6	16·2 13·6
43	12 40·8	12 42·8	12 06·1	4·3 3·6	10·3 8·7	16·3 13·7
44	12 41·0	12 43·1	12 06·3	4·4 3·7	10·4 8·8	16·4 13·8
45	12 41·3	12 43·3	12 06·6	4·5 3·8	10·5 8·8	16·5 13·9
46	12 41·5	12 43·6	12 06·8	4·6 3·9	10·6 8·9	16·6 14·0
47	12 41·8	12 43·8	12 07·0	4·7 4·0	10·7 9·0	16·7 14·1
48	12 42·0	12 44·1	12 07·3	4·8 4·0	10·8 9·1	16·8 14·1
49	12 42·3	12 44·3	12 07·5	4·9 4·1	10·9 9·2	16·9 14·2
50	12 42·5	12 44·6	12 07·8	5·0 4·2	11·0 9·3	17·0 14·3
51	12 42·8	12 44·8	12 08·0	5·1 4·3	11·1 9·3	17·1 14·4
52	12 43·0	12 45·1	12 08·2	5·2 4·4	11·2 9·4	17·2 14·5
53	12 43·3	12 45·3	12 08·5	5·3 4·5	11·3 9·5	17·3 14·6
54	12 43·5	12 45·6	12 08·7	5·4 4·5	11·4 9·6	17·4 14·6
55	12 43·8	12 45·8	12 09·0	5·5 4·6	11·5 9·7	17·5 14·7
56	12 44·0	12 46·1	12 09·2	5·6 4·7	11·6 9·8	17·6 14·8
57	12 44·3	12 46·3	12 09·4	5·7 4·8	11·7 9·8	17·7 14·9
58	12 44·5	12 46·6	12 09·7	5·8 4·9	11·8 9·9	17·8 15·0
59	12 44·8	12 46·8	12 09·9	5·9 5·0	11·9 10·0	17·9 15·1
60	12 45·0	12 47·1	12 10·2	6·0 5·1	12·0 10·1	18·0 15·2

51ᵐ

51	SUN PLANETS	ARIES	MOON	v or d Corrⁿ	v or d Corrⁿ	v or d Corrⁿ
s	° ′	° ′	° ′	′ ′	′ ′	′ ′
00	12 45·0	12 47·1	12 10·2	0·0 0·0	6·0 5·2	12·0 10·3
01	12 45·3	12 47·3	12 10·4	0·1 0·1	6·1 5·2	12·1 10·4
02	12 45·5	12 47·6	12 10·6	0·2 0·2	6·2 5·3	12·2 10·5
03	12 45·8	12 47·8	12 10·9	0·3 0·3	6·3 5·4	12·3 10·6
04	12 46·0	12 48·1	12 11·1	0·4 0·3	6·4 5·5	12·4 10·6
05	12 46·3	12 48·3	12 11·3	0·5 0·4	6·5 5·6	12·5 10·7
06	12 46·5	12 48·6	12 11·6	0·6 0·5	6·6 5·7	12·6 10·8
07	12 46·8	12 48·8	12 11·8	0·7 0·6	6·7 5·8	12·7 10·9
08	12 47·0	12 49·1	12 12·1	0·8 0·7	6·8 5·8	12·8 11·0
09	12 47·3	12 49·4	12 12·3	0·9 0·8	6·9 5·9	12·9 11·1
10	12 47·5	12 49·6	12 12·5	1·0 0·9	7·0 6·0	13·0 11·2
11	12 47·8	12 49·9	12 12·8	1·1 0·9	7·1 6·1	13·1 11·2
12	12 48·0	12 50·1	12 13·0	1·2 1·0	7·2 6·2	13·2 11·3
13	12 48·3	12 50·4	12 13·3	1·3 1·1	7·3 6·3	13·3 11·4
14	12 48·5	12 50·6	12 13·5	1·4 1·2	7·4 6·4	13·4 11·5
15	12 48·8	12 50·9	12 13·7	1·5 1·3	7·5 6·4	13·5 11·6
16	12 49·0	12 51·1	12 14·0	1·6 1·4	7·6 6·5	13·6 11·7
17	12 49·3	12 51·4	12 14·2	1·7 1·5	7·7 6·6	13·7 11·8
18	12 49·5	12 51·6	12 14·4	1·8 1·5	7·8 6·7	13·8 11·8
19	12 49·8	12 51·9	12 14·7	1·9 1·6	7·9 6·8	13·9 11·9
20	12 50·0	12 52·1	12 14·9	2·0 1·7	8·0 6·9	14·0 12·0
21	12 50·3	12 52·4	12 15·2	2·1 1·8	8·1 7·0	14·1 12·1
22	12 50·5	12 52·6	12 15·4	2·2 1·9	8·2 7·0	14·2 12·2
23	12 50·8	12 52·9	12 15·6	2·3 2·0	8·3 7·1	14·3 12·3
24	12 51·0	12 53·1	12 15·9	2·4 2·1	8·4 7·2	14·4 12·4
25	12 51·3	12 53·4	12 16·1	2·5 2·1	8·5 7·3	14·5 12·4
26	12 51·5	12 53·6	12 16·4	2·6 2·2	8·6 7·4	14·6 12·5
27	12 51·8	12 53·9	12 16·6	2·7 2·3	8·7 7·5	14·7 12·6
28	12 52·0	12 54·1	12 16·8	2·8 2·4	8·8 7·5	14·8 12·7
29	12 52·3	12 54·4	12 17·1	2·9 2·5	8·9 7·6	14·9 12·8
30	12 52·5	12 54·6	12 17·3	3·0 2·6	9·0 7·7	15·0 12·9
31	12 52·8	12 54·9	12 17·5	3·1 2·7	9·1 7·8	15·1 13·0
32	12 53·0	12 55·1	12 17·8	3·2 2·7	9·2 7·9	15·2 13·0
33	12 53·3	12 55·4	12 18·0	3·3 2·8	9·3 8·0	15·3 13·1
34	12 53·5	12 55·6	12 18·3	3·4 2·9	9·4 8·1	15·4 13·2
35	12 53·8	12 55·9	12 18·5	3·5 3·0	9·5 8·2	15·5 13·3
36	12 54·0	12 56·1	12 18·7	3·6 3·1	9·6 8·2	15·6 13·4
37	12 54·3	12 56·4	12 19·0	3·7 3·2	9·7 8·3	15·7 13·5
38	12 54·5	12 56·6	12 19·2	3·8 3·3	9·8 8·4	15·8 13·6
39	12 54·8	12 56·9	12 19·5	3·9 3·3	9·9 8·5	15·9 13·6
40	12 55·0	12 57·1	12 19·7	4·0 3·4	10·0 8·6	16·0 13·7
41	12 55·3	12 57·4	12 19·9	4·1 3·5	10·1 8·7	16·1 13·8
42	12 55·5	12 57·6	12 20·2	4·2 3·6	10·2 8·8	16·2 13·9
43	12 55·8	12 57·9	12 20·4	4·3 3·7	10·3 8·8	16·3 14·0
44	12 56·0	12 58·1	12 20·6	4·4 3·8	10·4 8·9	16·4 14·1
45	12 56·3	12 58·4	12 20·9	4·5 3·9	10·5 9·0	16·5 14·2
46	12 56·5	12 58·6	12 21·1	4·6 3·9	10·6 9·1	16·6 14·2
47	12 56·8	12 58·9	12 21·4	4·7 4·0	10·7 9·2	16·7 14·3
48	12 57·0	12 59·1	12 21·6	4·8 4·1	10·8 9·3	16·8 14·4
49	12 57·3	12 59·4	12 21·8	4·9 4·2	10·9 9·4	16·9 14·5
50	12 57·5	12 59·6	12 22·1	5·0 4·3	11·0 9·4	17·0 14·6
51	12 57·8	12 59·9	12 22·3	5·1 4·4	11·1 9·5	17·1 14·7
52	12 58·0	13 00·1	12 22·6	5·2 4·5	11·2 9·6	17·2 14·8
53	12 58·3	13 00·4	12 22·8	5·3 4·5	11·3 9·7	17·3 14·8
54	12 58·5	13 00·6	12 23·0	5·4 4·6	11·4 9·8	17·4 14·9
55	12 58·8	13 00·9	12 23·3	5·5 4·7	11·5 9·9	17·5 15·0
56	12 59·0	13 01·1	12 23·5	5·6 4·8	11·6 10·0	17·6 15·1
57	12 59·3	13 01·4	12 23·8	5·7 4·9	11·7 10·0	17·7 15·2
58	12 59·5	13 01·6	12 24·0	5·8 5·0	11·8 10·1	17·8 15·3
59	12 59·8	13 01·9	12 24·2	5·9 5·1	11·9 10·2	17·9 15·4
60	13 00·0	13 02·1	12 24·5	6·0 5·2	12·0 10·3	18·0 15·5

52ᵐ	SUN PLANETS	ARIES	MOON	v or Corrⁿ d		v or Corrⁿ d		v or Corrⁿ d	
s	° ′	° ′	° ′	′	′	′	′	′	′
00	13 00·0	13 02·1	12 24·5	0·0	0·0	6·0	5·3	12·0	10·5
01	13 00·3	13 02·4	12 24·7	0·1	0·1	6·1	5·3	12·1	10·6
02	13 00·5	13 02·6	12 24·9	0·2	0·2	6·2	5·4	12·2	10·7
03	13 00·8	13 02·9	12 25·2	0·3	0·3	6·3	5·5	12·3	10·8
04	13 01·0	13 03·1	12 25·4	0·4	0·4	6·4	5·6	12·4	10·9
05	13 01·3	13 03·4	12 25·7	0·5	0·4	6·5	5·7	12·5	10·9
06	13 01·5	13 03·6	12 25·9	0·6	0·5	6·6	5·8	12·6	11·0
07	13 01·8	13 03·9	12 26·1	0·7	0·6	6·7	5·9	12·7	11·1
08	13 02·0	13 04·1	12 26·4	0·8	0·7	6·8	6·0	12·8	11·2
09	13 02·3	13 04·4	12 26·6	0·9	0·8	6·9	6·0	12·9	11·3
10	13 02·5	13 04·6	12 26·9	1·0	0·9	7·0	6·1	13·0	11·4
11	13 02·8	13 04·9	12 27·1	1·1	1·0	7·1	6·2	13·1	11·5
12	13 03·0	13 05·1	12 27·3	1·2	1·1	7·2	6·3	13·2	11·6
13	13 03·3	13 05·4	12 27·6	1·3	1·1	7·3	6·4	13·3	11·6
14	13 03·5	13 05·6	12 27·8	1·4	1·2	7·4	6·5	13·4	11·7
15	13 03·8	13 05·9	12 28·0	1·5	1·3	7·5	6·6	13·5	11·8
16	13 04·0	13 06·1	12 28·3	1·6	1·4	7·6	6·7	13·6	11·9
17	13 04·3	13 06·4	12 28·5	1·7	1·5	7·7	6·7	13·7	12·0
18	13 04·5	13 06·6	12 28·8	1·8	1·6	7·8	6·8	13·8	12·1
19	13 04·8	13 06·9	12 29·0	1·9	1·7	7·9	6·9	13·9	12·2
20	13 05·0	13 07·1	12 29·2	2·0	1·8	8·0	7·0	14·0	12·3
21	13 05·3	13 07·4	12 29·5	2·1	1·8	8·1	7·1	14·1	12·3
22	13 05·5	13 07·7	12 29·7	2·2	1·9	8·2	7·2	14·2	12·4
23	13 05·8	13 07·9	12 30·0	2·3	2·0	8·3	7·3	14·3	12·5
24	13 06·0	13 08·2	12 30·2	2·4	2·1	8·4	7·4	14·4	12·6
25	13 06·3	13 08·4	12 30·4	2·5	2·2	8·5	7·4	14·5	12·7
26	13 06·5	13 08·7	12 30·7	2·6	2·3	8·6	7·5	14·6	12·8
27	13 06·8	13 08·9	12 30·9	2·7	2·4	8·7	7·6	14·7	12·9
28	13 07·0	13 09·2	12 31·1	2·8	2·5	8·8	7·7	14·8	13·0
29	13 07·3	13 09·4	12 31·4	2·9	2·5	8·9	7·8	14·9	13·0
30	13 07·5	13 09·7	12 31·6	3·0	2·6	9·0	7·9	15·0	13·1
31	13 07·8	13 09·9	12 31·9	3·1	2·7	9·1	8·0	15·1	13·2
32	13 08·0	13 10·2	12 32·1	3·2	2·8	9·2	8·0	15·2	13·3
33	13 08·3	13 10·4	12 32·3	3·3	2·9	9·3	8·1	15·3	13·4
34	13 08·5	13 10·7	12 32·6	3·4	3·0	9·4	8·2	15·4	13·5
35	13 08·8	13 10·9	12 32·8	3·5	3·1	9·5	8·3	15·5	13·6
36	13 09·0	13 11·2	12 33·1	3·6	3·2	9·6	8·4	15·6	13·7
37	13 09·3	13 11·4	12 33·3	3·7	3·2	9·7	8·5	15·7	13·7
38	13 09·5	13 11·7	12 33·5	3·8	3·3	9·8	8·6	15·8	13·8
39	13 09·8	13 11·9	12 33·8	3·9	3·4	9·9	8·7	15·9	13·9
40	13 10·0	13 12·2	12 34·0	4·0	3·5	10·0	8·8	16·0	14·0
41	13 10·3	13 12·4	12 34·2	4·1	3·6	10·1	8·8	16·1	14·1
42	13 10·5	13 12·7	12 34·5	4·2	3·7	10·2	8·9	16·2	14·2
43	13 10·8	13 12·9	12 34·7	4·3	3·8	10·3	9·0	16·3	14·3
44	13 11·0	13 13·2	12 35·0	4·4	3·9	10·4	9·1	16·4	14·3
45	13 11·3	13 13·4	12 35·2	4·5	3·9	10·5	9·2	16·5	14·4
46	13 11·5	13 13·7	12 35·4	4·6	4·0	10·6	9·3	16·6	14·5
47	13 11·8	13 13·9	12 35·7	4·7	4·1	10·7	9·4	16·7	14·6
48	13 12·0	13 14·2	12 35·9	4·8	4·2	10·8	9·5	16·8	14·7
49	13 12·3	13 14·4	12 36·2	4·9	4·3	10·9	9·5	16·9	14·8
50	13 12·5	13 14·7	12 36·4	5·0	4·4	11·0	9·6	17·0	14·9
51	13 12·8	13 14·9	12 36·6	5·1	4·5	11·1	9·7	17·1	15·0
52	13 13·0	13 15·2	12 36·9	5·2	4·6	11·2	9·8	17·2	15·1
53	13 13·3	13 15·4	12 37·1	5·3	4·6	11·3	9·9	17·3	15·1
54	13 13·5	13 15·7	12 37·4	5·4	4·7	11·4	10·0	17·4	15·2
55	13 13·8	13 15·9	12 37·6	5·5	4·8	11·5	10·1	17·5	15·3
56	13 14·0	13 16·2	12 37·8	5·6	4·9	11·6	10·2	17·6	15·4
57	13 14·3	13 16·4	12 38·1	5·7	5·0	11·7	10·2	17·7	15·5
58	13 14·5	13 16·7	12 38·3	5·8	5·1	11·8	10·3	17·8	15·6
59	13 14·8	13 16·9	12 38·5	5·9	5·2	11·9	10·4	17·9	15·7
60	13 15·0	13 17·2	12 38·8	6·0	5·3	12·0	10·5	18·0	15·8

53ᵐ	SUN PLANETS	ARIES	MOON	v or Corrⁿ d		v or Corrⁿ d		v or Corrⁿ d	
s	° ′	° ′	° ′	′	′	′	′	′	′
00	13 15·0	13 17·2	12 38·8	0·0	0·0	6·0	5·4	12·0	10·7
01	13 15·3	13 17·4	12 39·0	0·1	0·1	6·1	5·4	12·1	10·8
02	13 15·5	13 17·7	12 39·3	0·2	0·2	6·2	5·5	12·2	10·9
03	13 15·8	13 17·9	12 39·5	0·3	0·3	6·3	5·6	12·3	11·0
04	13 16·0	13 18·2	12 39·7	0·4	0·4	6·4	5·7	12·4	11·1
05	13 16·3	13 18·4	12 40·0	0·5	0·4	6·5	5·8	12·5	11·1
06	13 16·5	13 18·7	12 40·2	0·6	0·5	6·6	5·9	12·6	11·2
07	13 16·8	13 18·9	12 40·5	0·7	0·6	6·7	6·0	12·7	11·3
08	13 17·0	13 19·2	12 40·7	0·8	0·7	6·8	6·1	12·8	11·4
09	13 17·3	13 19·4	12 40·9	0·9	0·8	6·9	6·2	12·9	11·5
10	13 17·5	13 19·7	12 41·2	1·0	0·9	7·0	6·2	13·0	11·6
11	13 17·8	13 19·9	12 41·4	1·1	1·0	7·1	6·3	13·1	11·7
12	13 18·0	13 20·2	12 41·6	1·2	1·1	7·2	6·4	13·2	11·8
13	13 18·3	13 20·4	12 41·9	1·3	1·2	7·3	6·5	13·3	11·9
14	13 18·5	13 20·7	12 42·1	1·4	1·2	7·4	6·6	13·4	11·9
15	13 18·8	13 20·9	12 42·4	1·5	1·3	7·5	6·7	13·5	12·0
16	13 19·0	13 21·2	12 42·6	1·6	1·4	7·6	6·8	13·6	12·1
17	13 19·3	13 21·4	12 42·8	1·7	1·5	7·7	6·9	13·7	12·2
18	13 19·5	13 21·7	12 43·1	1·8	1·6	7·8	7·0	13·8	12·3
19	13 19·8	13 21·9	12 43·3	1·9	1·7	7·9	7·0	13·9	12·4
20	13 20·0	13 22·2	12 43·6	2·0	1·8	8·0	7·1	14·0	12·5
21	13 20·3	13 22·4	12 43·8	2·1	1·9	8·1	7·2	14·1	12·6
22	13 20·5	13 22·7	12 44·0	2·2	2·0	8·2	7·3	14·2	12·7
23	13 20·8	13 22·9	12 44·3	2·3	2·1	8·3	7·4	14·3	12·8
24	13 21·0	13 23·2	12 44·5	2·4	2·1	8·4	7·5	14·4	12·8
25	13 21·3	13 23·4	12 44·7	2·5	2·2	8·5	7·6	14·5	12·9
26	13 21·5	13 23·7	12 45·0	2·6	2·3	8·6	7·7	14·6	13·0
27	13 21·8	13 23·9	12 45·2	2·7	2·4	8·7	7·8	14·7	13·1
28	13 22·0	13 24·2	12 45·5	2·8	2·5	8·8	7·8	14·8	13·2
29	13 22·3	13 24·4	12 45·7	2·9	2·6	8·9	7·9	14·9	13·3
30	13 22·5	13 24·7	12 45·9	3·0	2·7	9·0	8·0	15·0	13·4
31	13 22·8	13 24·9	12 46·2	3·1	2·8	9·1	8·1	15·1	13·5
32	13 23·0	13 25·2	12 46·4	3·2	2·9	9·2	8·2	15·2	13·6
33	13 23·3	13 25·4	12 46·7	3·3	2·9	9·3	8·3	15·3	13·6
34	13 23·5	13 25·7	12 46·9	3·4	3·0	9·4	8·4	15·4	13·7
35	13 23·8	13 26·0	12 47·1	3·5	3·1	9·5	8·5	15·5	13·8
36	13 24·0	13 26·2	12 47·4	3·6	3·2	9·6	8·6	15·6	13·9
37	13 24·3	13 26·5	12 47·6	3·7	3·3	9·7	8·6	15·7	14·0
38	13 24·5	13 26·7	12 47·9	3·8	3·4	9·8	8·7	15·8	14·1
39	13 24·8	13 27·0	12 48·1	3·9	3·5	9·9	8·8	15·9	14·2
40	13 25·0	13 27·2	12 48·3	4·0	3·6	10·0	8·9	16·0	14·3
41	13 25·3	13 27·5	12 48·6	4·1	3·7	10·1	9·0	16·1	14·4
42	13 25·5	13 27·7	12 48·8	4·2	3·7	10·2	9·1	16·2	14·4
43	13 25·8	13 28·0	12 49·0	4·3	3·8	10·3	9·2	16·3	14·5
44	13 26·0	13 28·2	12 49·3	4·4	3·9	10·4	9·3	16·4	14·6
45	13 26·3	13 28·5	12 49·5	4·5	4·0	10·5	9·4	16·5	14·7
46	13 26·5	13 28·7	12 49·8	4·6	4·1	10·6	9·5	16·6	14·8
47	13 26·8	13 29·0	12 50·0	4·7	4·2	10·7	9·5	16·7	14·9
48	13 27·0	13 29·2	12 50·2	4·8	4·3	10·8	9·6	16·8	15·0
49	13 27·3	13 29·5	12 50·5	4·9	4·4	10·9	9·7	16·9	15·1
50	13 27·5	13 29·7	12 50·7	5·0	4·5	11·0	9·8	17·0	15·2
51	13 27·8	13 30·0	12 51·0	5·1	4·5	11·1	9·9	17·1	15·2
52	13 28·0	13 30·2	12 51·2	5·2	4·6	11·2	10·0	17·2	15·3
53	13 28·3	13 30·5	12 51·4	5·3	4·7	11·3	10·1	17·3	15·4
54	13 28·5	13 30·7	12 51·7	5·4	4·8	11·4	10·2	17·4	15·5
55	13 28·8	13 31·0	12 51·9	5·5	4·9	11·5	10·3	17·5	15·6
56	13 29·0	13 31·2	12 52·1	5·6	5·0	11·6	10·3	17·6	15·7
57	13 29·3	13 31·5	12 52·4	5·7	5·1	11·7	10·4	17·7	15·8
58	13 29·5	13 31·7	12 52·6	5·8	5·2	11·8	10·5	17·8	15·9
59	13 29·8	13 32·0	12 52·9	5·9	5·3	11·9	10·6	17·9	16·0
60	13 30·0	13 32·2	12 53·1	6·0	5·4	12·0	10·7	18·0	16·1

xxviii

54ᵐ

m 54 / s	SUN PLANETS	ARIES	MOON	v or d	Corrⁿ	v or d	Corrⁿ	v or d	Corrⁿ
00	13 30·0	13 32·2	12 53·1	0·0	0·0	6·0	5·5	12·0	10·9
01	13 30·3	13 32·5	12 53·3	0·1	0·1	6·1	5·5	12·1	11·0
02	13 30·5	13 32·7	12 53·6	0·2	0·2	6·2	5·6	12·2	11·1
03	13 30·8	13 33·0	12 53·8	0·3	0·3	6·3	5·7	12·3	11·2
04	13 31·0	13 33·2	12 54·1	0·4	0·4	6·4	5·8	12·4	11·3
05	13 31·3	13 33·5	12 54·3	0·5	0·5	6·5	5·9	12·5	11·4
06	13 31·5	13 33·7	12 54·5	0·6	0·5	6·6	6·0	12·6	11·4
07	13 31·8	13 34·0	12 54·8	0·7	0·6	6·7	6·1	12·7	11·5
08	13 32·0	13 34·2	12 55·0	0·8	0·7	6·8	6·2	12·8	11·6
09	13 32·3	13 34·5	12 55·2	0·9	0·8	6·9	6·3	12·9	11·7
10	13 32·5	13 34·7	12 55·5	1·0	0·9	7·0	6·4	13·0	11·8
11	13 32·8	13 35·0	12 55·7	1·1	1·0	7·1	6·4	13·1	11·9
12	13 33·0	13 35·2	12 56·0	1·2	1·1	7·2	6·5	13·2	12·0
13	13 33·3	13 35·5	12 56·2	1·3	1·2	7·3	6·6	13·3	12·1
14	13 33·5	13 35·7	12 56·4	1·4	1·3	7·4	6·7	13·4	12·2
15	13 33·8	13 36·0	12 56·7	1·5	1·4	7·5	6·8	13·5	12·3
16	13 34·0	13 36·2	12 56·9	1·6	1·5	7·6	6·9	13·6	12·4
17	13 34·3	13 36·5	12 57·2	1·7	1·5	7·7	7·0	13·7	12·4
18	13 34·5	13 36·7	12 57·4	1·8	1·6	7·8	7·1	13·8	12·5
19	13 34·8	13 37·0	12 57·6	1·9	1·7	7·9	7·2	13·9	12·6
20	13 35·0	13 37·2	12 57·9	2·0	1·8	8·0	7·3	14·0	12·7
21	13 35·3	13 37·5	12 58·1	2·1	1·9	8·1	7·4	14·1	12·8
22	13 35·5	13 37·7	12 58·3	2·2	2·0	8·2	7·4	14·2	12·9
23	13 35·8	13 38·0	12 58·6	2·3	2·1	8·3	7·5	14·3	13·0
24	13 36·0	13 38·2	12 58·8	2·4	2·2	8·4	7·6	14·4	13·1
25	13 36·3	13 38·5	12 59·1	2·5	2·3	8·5	7·7	14·5	13·2
26	13 36·5	13 38·7	12 59·3	2·6	2·4	8·6	7·8	14·6	13·3
27	13 36·8	13 39·0	12 59·5	2·7	2·5	8·7	7·9	14·7	13·4
28	13 37·0	13 39·2	12 59·8	2·8	2·5	8·8	8·0	14·8	13·4
29	13 37·3	13 39·5	13 00·0	2·9	2·6	8·9	8·1	14·9	13·5
30	13 37·5	13 39·7	13 00·3	3·0	2·7	9·0	8·2	15·0	13·6
31	13 37·8	13 40·0	13 00·5	3·1	2·8	9·1	8·3	15·1	13·7
32	13 38·0	13 40·2	13 00·7	3·2	2·9	9·2	8·4	15·2	13·8
33	13 38·3	13 40·5	13 01·0	3·3	3·0	9·3	8·4	15·3	13·9
34	13 38·5	13 40·7	13 01·2	3·4	3·1	9·4	8·5	15·4	14·0
35	13 38·8	13 41·0	13 01·5	3·5	3·2	9·5	8·6	15·5	14·1
36	13 39·0	13 41·2	13 01·7	3·6	3·3	9·6	8·7	15·6	14·2
37	13 39·3	13 41·5	13 01·9	3·7	3·4	9·7	8·8	15·7	14·3
38	13 39·5	13 41·7	13 02·2	3·8	3·5	9·8	8·9	15·8	14·4
39	13 39·8	13 42·0	13 02·4	3·9	3·5	9·9	9·0	15·9	14·4
40	13 40·0	13 42·2	13 02·6	4·0	3·6	10·0	9·1	16·0	14·5
41	13 40·3	13 42·5	13 02·9	4·1	3·7	10·1	9·2	16·1	14·6
42	13 40·5	13 42·7	13 03·1	4·2	3·8	10·2	9·3	16·2	14·7
43	13 40·8	13 43·0	13 03·4	4·3	3·9	10·3	9·4	16·3	14·8
44	13 41·0	13 43·2	13 03·6	4·4	4·0	10·4	9·4	16·4	14·9
45	13 41·3	13 43·5	13 03·8	4·5	4·1	10·5	9·5	16·5	15·0
46	13 41·5	13 43·7	13 04·1	4·6	4·2	10·6	9·6	16·6	15·1
47	13 41·8	13 44·0	13 04·3	4·7	4·3	10·7	9·7	16·7	15·2
48	13 42·0	13 44·3	13 04·6	4·8	4·4	10·8	9·8	16·8	15·3
49	13 42·3	13 44·5	13 04·8	4·9	4·5	10·9	9·9	16·9	15·4
50	13 42·5	13 44·8	13 05·0	5·0	4·5	11·0	10·0	17·0	15·4
51	13 42·8	13 45·0	13 05·3	5·1	4·6	11·1	10·1	17·1	15·5
52	13 43·0	13 45·3	13 05·5	5·2	4·7	11·2	10·2	17·2	15·6
53	13 43·3	13 45·5	13 05·7	5·3	4·8	11·3	10·3	17·3	15·7
54	13 43·5	13 45·8	13 06·0	5·4	4·9	11·4	10·4	17·4	15·8
55	13 43·8	13 46·0	13 06·2	5·5	5·0	11·5	10·4	17·5	15·9
56	13 44·0	13 46·3	13 06·5	5·6	5·1	11·6	10·5	17·6	16·0
57	13 44·3	13 46·5	13 06·7	5·7	5·2	11·7	10·6	17·7	16·1
58	13 44·5	13 46·8	13 06·9	5·8	5·3	11·8	10·7	17·8	16·2
59	13 44·8	13 47·0	13 07·2	5·9	5·4	11·9	10·8	17·9	16·3
60	13 45·0	13 47·3	13 07·4	6·0	5·5	12·0	10·9	18·0	16·4

55ᵐ

m 55 / s	SUN PLANETS	ARIES	MOON	v or d	Corrⁿ	v or d	Corrⁿ	v or d	Corrⁿ
00	13 45·0	13 47·3	13 07·4	0·0	0·0	6·0	5·6	12·0	11·1
01	13 45·3	13 47·5	13 07·7	0·1	0·1	6·1	5·6	12·1	11·2
02	13 45·5	13 47·8	13 07·9	0·2	0·2	6·2	5·7	12·2	11·3
03	13 45·8	13 48·0	13 08·1	0·3	0·3	6·3	5·8	12·3	11·4
04	13 46·0	13 48·3	13 08·4	0·4	0·4	6·4	5·9	12·4	11·5
05	13 46·3	13 48·5	13 08·6	0·5	0·5	6·5	6·0	12·5	11·6
06	13 46·5	13 48·8	13 08·8	0·6	0·6	6·6	6·1	12·6	11·7
07	13 46·8	13 49·0	13 09·1	0·7	0·6	6·7	6·2	12·7	11·7
08	13 47·0	13 49·3	13 09·3	0·8	0·7	6·8	6·3	12·8	11·8
09	13 47·3	13 49·5	13 09·6	0·9	0·8	6·9	6·4	12·9	11·9
10	13 47·5	13 49·8	13 09·8	1·0	0·9	7·0	6·5	13·0	12·0
11	13 47·8	13 50·0	13 10·0	1·1	1·0	7·1	6·6	13·1	12·1
12	13 48·0	13 50·3	13 10·3	1·2	1·1	7·2	6·7	13·2	12·2
13	13 48·3	13 50·5	13 10·5	1·3	1·2	7·3	6·8	13·3	12·3
14	13 48·5	13 50·8	13 10·8	1·4	1·3	7·4	6·8	13·4	12·4
15	13 48·8	13 51·0	13 11·0	1·5	1·4	7·5	6·9	13·5	12·5
16	13 49·0	13 51·3	13 11·2	1·6	1·5	7·6	7·0	13·6	12·6
17	13 49·3	13 51·5	13 11·5	1·7	1·6	7·7	7·1	13·7	12·7
18	13 49·5	13 51·8	13 11·7	1·8	1·7	7·8	7·2	13·8	12·8
19	13 49·8	13 52·0	13 12·0	1·9	1·8	7·9	7·3	13·9	12·9
20	13 50·0	13 52·3	13 12·2	2·0	1·9	8·0	7·4	14·0	13·0
21	13 50·3	13 52·5	13 12·4	2·1	1·9	8·1	7·5	14·1	13·0
22	13 50·5	13 52·8	13 12·7	2·2	2·0	8·2	7·6	14·2	13·1
23	13 50·8	13 53·0	13 12·9	2·3	2·1	8·3	7·7	14·3	13·2
24	13 51·0	13 53·3	13 13·1	2·4	2·2	8·4	7·8	14·4	13·3
25	13 51·3	13 53·5	13 13·4	2·5	2·3	8·5	7·9	14·5	13·4
26	13 51·5	13 53·8	13 13·6	2·6	2·4	8·6	8·0	14·6	13·5
27	13 51·8	13 54·0	13 13·9	2·7	2·5	8·7	8·0	14·7	13·6
28	13 52·0	13 54·3	13 14·1	2·8	2·6	8·8	8·1	14·8	13·7
29	13 52·3	13 54·5	13 14·3	2·9	2·7	8·9	8·2	14·9	13·8
30	13 52·5	13 54·8	13 14·6	3·0	2·8	9·0	8·3	15·0	13·9
31	13 52·8	13 55·0	13 14·8	3·1	2·9	9·1	8·4	15·1	14·0
32	13 53·0	13 55·3	13 15·1	3·2	3·0	9·2	8·5	15·2	14·1
33	13 53·3	13 55·5	13 15·3	3·3	3·1	9·3	8·6	15·3	14·2
34	13 53·5	13 55·8	13 15·5	3·4	3·1	9·4	8·7	15·4	14·2
35	13 53·8	13 56·0	13 15·8	3·5	3·2	9·5	8·8	15·5	14·3
36	13 54·0	13 56·3	13 16·0	3·6	3·3	9·6	8·9	15·6	14·4
37	13 54·3	13 56·5	13 16·2	3·7	3·4	9·7	9·0	15·7	14·5
38	13 54·5	13 56·8	13 16·5	3·8	3·5	9·8	9·1	15·8	14·6
39	13 54·8	13 57·0	13 16·7	3·9	3·6	9·9	9·2	15·9	14·7
40	13 55·0	13 57·3	13 17·0	4·0	3·7	10·0	9·3	16·0	14·8
41	13 55·3	13 57·5	13 17·2	4·1	3·8	10·1	9·3	16·1	14·9
42	13 55·5	13 57·8	13 17·4	4·2	3·9	10·2	9·4	16·2	15·0
43	13 55·8	13 58·0	13 17·7	4·3	4·0	10·3	9·5	16·3	15·1
44	13 56·0	13 58·3	13 17·9	4·4	4·1	10·4	9·6	16·4	15·2
45	13 56·3	13 58·5	13 18·2	4·5	4·2	10·5	9·7	16·5	15·3
46	13 56·5	13 58·8	13 18·4	4·6	4·3	10·6	9·8	16·6	15·4
47	13 56·8	13 59·0	13 18·6	4·7	4·3	10·7	9·9	16·7	15·4
48	13 57·0	13 59·3	13 18·9	4·8	4·4	10·8	10·0	16·8	15·5
49	13 57·3	13 59·5	13 19·1	4·9	4·5	10·9	10·1	16·9	15·6
50	13 57·5	13 59·8	13 19·3	5·0	4·6	11·0	10·2	17·0	15·7
51	13 57·8	14 00·0	13 19·6	5·1	4·7	11·1	10·3	17·1	15·8
52	13 58·0	14 00·3	13 19·8	5·2	4·8	11·2	10·4	17·2	15·9
53	13 58·3	14 00·5	13 20·1	5·3	4·9	11·3	10·5	17·3	16·0
54	13 58·5	14 00·8	13 20·3	5·4	5·0	11·4	10·5	17·4	16·1
55	13 58·8	14 01·0	13 20·5	5·5	5·1	11·5	10·6	17·5	16·2
56	13 59·0	14 01·3	13 20·8	5·6	5·2	11·6	10·7	17·6	16·3
57	13 59·3	14 01·5	13 21·0	5·7	5·3	11·7	10·8	17·7	16·4
58	13 59·5	14 01·8	13 21·3	5·8	5·4	11·8	10·9	17·8	16·5
59	13 59·8	14 02·0	13 21·5	5·9	5·5	11·9	11·0	17·9	16·6
60	14 00·0	14 02·3	13 21·7	6·0	5·6	12·0	11·1	18·0	16·7

56ᵐ	SUN PLANETS	ARIES	MOON	v or Corrⁿ d	v or Corrⁿ d	v or Corrⁿ d
s	° ′	° ′	° ′	′ ′	′ ′	′ ′
00	14 00·0	14 02·3	13 21·7	0·0 0·0	6·0 5·7	12·0 11·3
01	14 00·3	14 02·6	13 22·0	0·1 0·1	6·1 5·7	12·1 11·4
02	14 00·5	14 02·8	13 22·2	0·2 0·2	6·2 5·8	12·2 11·5
03	14 00·8	14 03·1	13 22·4	0·3 0·3	6·3 5·9	12·3 11·6
04	14 01·0	14 03·3	13 22·7	0·4 0·4	6·4 6·0	12·4 11·7
05	14 01·3	14 03·6	13 22·9	0·5 0·5	6·5 6·1	12·5 11·8
06	14 01·5	14 03·8	13 23·2	0·6 0·6	6·6 6·2	12·6 11·9
07	14 01·8	14 04·1	13 23·4	0·7 0·7	6·7 6·3	12·7 12·0
08	14 02·0	14 04·3	13 23·6	0·8 0·8	6·8 6·4	12·8 12·1
09	14 02·3	14 04·6	13 23·9	0·9 0·8	6·9 6·5	12·9 12·1
10	14 02·5	14 04·8	13 24·1	1·0 0·9	7·0 6·6	13·0 12·2
11	14 02·8	14 05·1	13 24·4	1·1 1·0	7·1 6·7	13·1 12·3
12	14 03·0	14 05·3	13 24·6	1·2 1·1	7·2 6·8	13·2 12·4
13	14 03·3	14 05·6	13 24·8	1·3 1·2	7·3 6·9	13·3 12·5
14	14 03·5	14 05·8	13 25·1	1·4 1·3	7·4 7·0	13·4 12·6
15	14 03·8	14 06·1	13 25·3	1·5 1·4	7·5 7·1	13·5 12·7
16	14 04·0	14 06·3	13 25·6	1·6 1·5	7·6 7·2	13·6 12·8
17	14 04·3	14 06·6	13 25·8	1·7 1·6	7·7 7·3	13·7 12·9
18	14 04·5	14 06·8	13 26·0	1·8 1·7	7·8 7·3	13·8 13·0
19	14 04·8	14 07·1	13 26·3	1·9 1·8	7·9 7·4	13·9 13·1
20	14 05·0	14 07·3	13 26·5	2·0 1·9	8·0 7·5	14·0 13·2
21	14 05·3	14 07·6	13 26·7	2·1 2·0	8·1 7·6	14·1 13·3
22	14 05·5	14 07·8	13 27·0	2·2 2·1	8·2 7·7	14·2 13·4
23	14 05·8	14 08·1	13 27·2	2·3 2·2	8·3 7·8	14·3 13·5
24	14 06·0	14 08·3	13 27·5	2·4 2·3	8·4 7·9	14·4 13·6
25	14 06·3	14 08·6	13 27·7	2·5 2·4	8·5 8·0	14·5 13·7
26	14 06·5	14 08·8	13 27·9	2·6 2·4	8·6 8·1	14·6 13·7
27	14 06·8	14 09·1	13 28·2	2·7 2·5	8·7 8·2	14·7 13·8
28	14 07·0	14 09·3	13 28·4	2·8 2·6	8·8 8·3	14·8 13·9
29	14 07·3	14 09·6	13 28·7	2·9 2·7	8·9 8·4	14·9 14·0
30	14 07·5	14 09·8	13 28·9	3·0 2·8	9·0 8·5	15·0 14·1
31	14 07·8	14 10·1	13 29·1	3·1 2·9	9·1 8·6	15·1 14·2
32	14 08·0	14 10·3	13 29·4	3·2 3·0	9·2 8·7	15·2 14·3
33	14 08·3	14 10·6	13 29·6	3·3 3·1	9·3 8·8	15·3 14·4
34	14 08·5	14 10·8	13 29·8	3·4 3·2	9·4 8·9	15·4 14·5
35	14 08·8	14 11·1	13 30·1	3·5 3·3	9·5 8·9	15·5 14·6
36	14 09·0	14 11·3	13 30·3	3·6 3·4	9·6 9·0	15·6 14·7
37	14 09·3	14 11·6	13 30·6	3·7 3·5	9·7 9·1	15·7 14·8
38	14 09·5	14 11·8	13 30·8	3·8 3·6	9·8 9·2	15·8 14·9
39	14 09·8	14 12·1	13 31·0	3·9 3·7	9·9 9·3	15·9 15·0
40	14 10·0	14 12·3	13 31·3	4·0 3·8	10·0 9·4	16·0 15·1
41	14 10·3	14 12·6	13 31·5	4·1 3·9	10·1 9·5	16·1 15·2
42	14 10·5	14 12·8	13 31·8	4·2 4·0	10·2 9·6	16·2 15·3
43	14 10·8	14 13·1	13 32·0	4·3 4·0	10·3 9·7	16·3 15·3
44	14 11·0	14 13·3	13 32·2	4·4 4·1	10·4 9·8	16·4 15·4
45	14 11·3	14 13·6	13 32·5	4·5 4·2	10·5 9·9	16·5 15·5
46	14 11·5	14 13·8	13 32·7	4·6 4·3	10·6 10·0	16·6 15·6
47	14 11·8	14 14·1	13 32·9	4·7 4·4	10·7 10·1	16·7 15·7
48	14 12·0	14 14·3	13 33·2	4·8 4·5	10·8 10·2	16·8 15·8
49	14 12·3	14 14·6	13 33·4	4·9 4·6	10·9 10·3	16·9 15·9
50	14 12·5	14 14·8	13 33·7	5·0 4·7	11·0 10·4	17·0 16·0
51	14 12·8	14 15·1	13 33·9	5·1 4·8	11·1 10·5	17·1 16·1
52	14 13·0	14 15·3	13 34·1	5·2 4·9	11·2 10·5	17·2 16·2
53	14 13·3	14 15·6	13 34·4	5·3 5·0	11·3 10·6	17·3 16·3
54	14 13·5	14 15·8	13 34·6	5·4 5·1	11·4 10·7	17·4 16·4
55	14 13·8	14 16·1	13 34·9	5·5 5·2	11·5 10·8	17·5 16·5
56	14 14·0	14 16·3	13 35·1	5·6 5·3	11·6 10·9	17·6 16·6
57	14 14·3	14 16·6	13 35·3	5·7 5·4	11·7 11·0	17·7 16·7
58	14 14·5	14 16·8	13 35·5	5·8 5·5	11·8 11·1	17·8 16·8
59	14 14·8	14 17·1	13 35·8	5·9 5·6	11·9 11·2	17·9 16·9
60	14 15·0	14 17·3	13 36·1	6·0 5·7	12·0 11·3	18·0 17·0

57ᵐ	SUN PLANETS	ARIES	MOON	v or Corrⁿ d	v or Corrⁿ d	v or Corrⁿ d
s	° ′	° ′	° ′	′ ′	′ ′	′ ′
00	14 15·0	14 17·3	13 36·1	0·0 0·0	6·0 5·8	12·0 11·5
01	14 15·3	14 17·6	13 36·3	0·1 0·1	6·1 5·8	12·1 11·6
02	14 15·5	14 17·8	13 36·5	0·2 0·2	6·2 5·9	12·2 11·7
03	14 15·8	14 18·1	13 36·8	0·3 0·3	6·3 6·0	12·3 11·8
04	14 16·0	14 18·3	13 37·0	0·4 0·4	6·4 6·1	12·4 11·9
05	14 16·3	14 18·6	13 37·2	0·5 0·5	6·5 6·2	12·5 12·0
06	14 16·5	14 18·8	13 37·5	0·6 0·6	6·6 6·3	12·6 12·1
07	14 16·8	14 19·1	13 37·7	0·7 0·7	6·7 6·4	12·7 12·2
08	14 17·0	14 19·3	13 38·0	0·8 0·8	6·8 6·5	12·8 12·3
09	14 17·3	14 19·6	13 38·2	0·9 0·9	6·9 6·6	12·9 12·4
10	14 17·5	14 19·8	13 38·4	1·0 1·0	7·0 6·7	13·0 12·5
11	14 17·8	14 20·1	13 38·7	1·1 1·1	7·1 6·8	13·1 12·6
12	14 18·0	14 20·3	13 38·9	1·2 1·2	7·2 6·9	13·2 12·7
13	14 18·3	14 20·6	13 39·2	1·3 1·2	7·3 7·0	13·3 12·7
14	14 18·5	14 20·9	13 39·4	1·4 1·3	7·4 7·1	13·4 12·8
15	14 18·8	14 21·1	13 39·6	1·5 1·4	7·5 7·2	13·5 12·9
16	14 19·0	14 21·4	13 39·9	1·6 1·5	7·6 7·3	13·6 13·0
17	14 19·3	14 21·6	13 40·1	1·7 1·6	7·7 7·4	13·7 13·1
18	14 19·5	14 21·9	13 40·3	1·8 1·7	7·8 7·5	13·8 13·2
19	14 19·8	14 22·1	13 40·6	1·9 1·8	7·9 7·6	13·9 13·3
20	14 20·0	14 22·4	13 40·8	2·0 1·9	8·0 7·7	14·0 13·4
21	14 20·3	14 22·6	13 41·1	2·1 2·0	8·1 7·8	14·1 13·5
22	14 20·5	14 22·9	13 41·3	2·2 2·1	8·2 7·9	14·2 13·6
23	14 20·8	14 23·1	13 41·5	2·3 2·2	8·3 8·0	14·3 13·7
24	14 21·0	14 23·4	13 41·8	2·4 2·3	8·4 8·1	14·4 13·8
25	14 21·3	14 23·6	13 42·0	2·5 2·4	8·5 8·1	14·5 13·9
26	14 21·5	14 23·9	13 42·3	2·6 2·5	8·6 8·2	14·6 14·0
27	14 21·8	14 24·1	13 42·5	2·7 2·6	8·7 8·3	14·7 14·1
28	14 22·0	14 24·4	13 42·7	2·8 2·7	8·8 8·4	14·8 14·2
29	14 22·3	14 24·6	13 43·0	2·9 2·8	8·9 8·5	14·9 14·3
30	14 22·5	14 24·9	13 43·2	3·0 2·9	9·0 8·6	15·0 14·4
31	14 22·8	14 25·1	13 43·4	3·1 3·0	9·1 8·7	15·1 14·5
32	14 23·0	14 25·4	13 43·7	3·2 3·1	9·2 8·8	15·2 14·6
33	14 23·3	14 25·6	13 43·9	3·3 3·2	9·3 8·9	15·3 14·7
34	14 23·5	14 25·9	13 44·2	3·4 3·3	9·4 9·0	15·4 14·8
35	14 23·8	14 26·1	13 44·4	3·5 3·4	9·5 9·1	15·5 14·9
36	14 24·0	14 26·4	13 44·6	3·6 3·5	9·6 9·2	15·6 15·0
37	14 24·3	14 26·6	13 44·9	3·7 3·5	9·7 9·3	15·7 15·0
38	14 24·5	14 26·9	13 45·1	3·8 3·6	9·8 9·4	15·8 15·1
39	14 24·8	14 27·1	13 45·4	3·9 3·7	9·9 9·5	15·9 15·2
40	14 25·0	14 27·4	13 45·6	4·0 3·8	10·0 9·6	16·0 15·3
41	14 25·3	14 27·6	13 45·8	4·1 3·9	10·1 9·7	16·1 15·4
42	14 25·5	14 27·9	13 46·1	4·2 4·0	10·2 9·8	16·2 15·5
43	14 25·8	14 28·1	13 46·3	4·3 4·1	10·3 9·9	16·3 15·6
44	14 26·0	14 28·4	13 46·5	4·4 4·2	10·4 10·0	16·4 15·7
45	14 26·3	14 28·6	13 46·8	4·5 4·3	10·5 10·1	16·5 15·8
46	14 26·5	14 28·9	13 47·0	4·6 4·4	10·6 10·2	16·6 15·9
47	14 26·8	14 29·1	13 47·3	4·7 4·5	10·7 10·3	16·7 16·0
48	14 27·0	14 29·4	13 47·5	4·8 4·6	10·8 10·4	16·8 16·1
49	14 27·3	14 29·6	13 47·7	4·9 4·7	10·9 10·4	16·9 16·2
50	14 27·5	14 29·9	13 48·0	5·0 4·8	11·0 10·5	17·0 16·3
51	14 27·8	14 30·1	13 48·2	5·1 4·9	11·1 10·6	17·1 16·4
52	14 28·0	14 30·4	13 48·5	5·2 5·0	11·2 10·7	17·2 16·5
53	14 28·3	14 30·6	13 48·7	5·3 5·1	11·3 10·8	17·3 16·6
54	14 28·5	14 30·9	13 48·9	5·4 5·2	11·4 10·9	17·4 16·7
55	14 28·8	14 31·1	13 49·2	5·5 5·3	11·5 11·0	17·5 16·8
56	14 29·0	14 31·4	13 49·4	5·6 5·4	11·6 11·1	17·6 16·9
57	14 29·3	14 31·6	13 49·7	5·7 5·5	11·7 11·2	17·7 17·0
58	14 29·5	14 31·9	13 49·9	5·8 5·6	11·8 11·3	17·8 17·1
59	14 29·8	14 32·1	13 50·1	5·9 5·7	11·9 11·4	17·9 17·2
60	14 30·0	14 32·4	13 50·4	6·0 5·8	12·0 11·5	18·0 17·3

58	SUN PLANETS	ARIES	MOON	v or Corrⁿ d	v or Corrⁿ d	v or Corrⁿ d
s	° ′	° ′	° ′	′ ′	′ ′	′ ′
00	14 30·0	14 32·4	13 50·4	0·0 0·0	6·0 5·9	12·0 11·7
01	14 30·3	14 32·6	13 50·6	0·1 0·1	6·1 5·9	12·1 11·8
02	14 30·5	14 32·9	13 50·8	0·2 0·2	6·2 6·0	12·2 11·9
03	14 30·8	14 33·1	13 51·1	0·3 0·3	6·3 6·1	12·3 12·0
04	14 31·0	14 33·4	13 51·3	0·4 0·4	6·4 6·2	12·4 12·1
05	14 31·3	14 33·6	13 51·6	0·5 0·5	6·5 6·3	12·5 12·2
06	14 31·5	14 33·9	13 51·8	0·6 0·6	6·6 6·4	12·6 12·3
07	14 31·8	14 34·1	13 52·0	0·7 0·7	6·7 6·5	12·7 12·4
08	14 32·0	14 34·4	13 52·3	0·8 0·8	6·8 6·6	12·8 12·5
09	14 32·3	14 34·6	13 52·5	0·9 0·9	6·9 6·7	12·9 12·6
10	14 32·5	14 34·9	13 52·8	1·0 1·0	7·0 6·8	13·0 12·7
11	14 32·8	14 35·1	13 53·0	1·1 1·1	7·1 6·9	13·1 12·8
12	14 33·0	14 35·4	13 53·2	1·2 1·2	7·2 7·0	13·2 12·9
13	14 33·3	14 35·6	13 53·5	1·3 1·3	7·3 7·1	13·3 13·0
14	14 33·5	14 35·9	13 53·7	1·4 1·4	7·4 7·2	13·4 13·1
15	14 33·8	14 36·1	13 53·9	1·5 1·5	7·5 7·3	13·5 13·2
16	14 34·0	14 36·4	13 54·2	1·6 1·6	7·6 7·4	13·6 13·3
17	14 34·3	14 36·6	13 54·4	1·7 1·7	7·7 7·5	13·7 13·4
18	14 34·5	14 36·9	13 54·7	1·8 1·8	7·8 7·6	13·8 13·5
19	14 34·8	14 37·1	13 54·9	1·9 1·9	7·9 7·7	13·9 13·6
20	14 35·0	14 37·4	13 55·1	2·0 2·0	8·0 7·8	14·0 13·7
21	14 35·3	14 37·6	13 55·4	2·1 2·0	8·1 7·9	14·1 13·7
22	14 35·5	14 37·9	13 55·6	2·2 2·1	8·2 8·0	14·2 13·9
23	14 35·8	14 38·1	13 55·9	2·3 2·2	8·3 8·1	14·3 13·9
24	14 36·0	14 38·4	13 56·1	2·4 2·3	8·4 8·2	14·4 14·0
25	14 36·3	14 38·6	13 56·3	2·5 2·4	8·5 8·3	14·5 14·1
26	14 36·5	14 38·9	13 56·6	2·6 2·5	8·6 8·4	14·6 14·2
27	14 36·8	14 39·2	13 56·8	2·7 2·6	8·7 8·5	14·7 14·3
28	14 37·0	14 39·4	13 57·0	2·8 2·7	8·8 8·6	14·8 14·4
29	14 37·3	14 39·7	13 57·3	2·9 2·8	8·9 8·7	14·9 14·5
30	14 37·5	14 39·9	13 57·5	3·0 2·9	9·0 8·8	15·0 14·6
31	14 37·8	14 40·2	13 57·8	3·1 3·0	9·1 8·9	15·1 14·7
32	14 38·0	14 40·4	13 58·0	3·2 3·1	9·2 9·0	15·2 14·8
33	14 38·3	14 40·7	13 58·2	3·3 3·2	9·3 9·1	15·3 14·9
34	14 38·5	14 40·9	13 58·5	3·4 3·3	9·4 9·2	15·4 15·0
35	14 38·8	14 41·2	13 58·7	3·5 3·4	9·5 9·3	15·5 15·1
36	14 39·0	14 41·4	13 59·0	3·6 3·5	9·6 9·4	15·6 15·2
37	14 39·3	14 41·7	13 59·2	3·7 3·6	9·7 9·5	15·7 15·3
38	14 39·5	14 41·9	13 59·4	3·8 3·7	9·8 9·6	15·8 15·4
39	14 39·8	14 42·2	13 59·7	3·9 3·8	9·9 9·7	15·9 15·5
40	14 40·0	14 42·4	13 59·9	4·0 3·9	10·0 9·8	16·0 15·6
41	14 40·3	14 42·7	14 00·1	4·1 4·0	10·1 9·8	16·1 15·7
42	14 40·5	14 42·9	14 00·4	4·2 4·1	10·2 9·9	16·2 15·8
43	14 40·8	14 43·2	14 00·6	4·3 4·2	10·3 10·0	16·3 15·9
44	14 41·0	14 43·4	14 00·9	4·4 4·3	10·4 10·1	16·4 16·0
45	14 41·3	14 43·7	14 01·1	4·5 4·4	10·5 10·2	16·5 16·1
46	14 41·5	14 43·9	14 01·3	4·6 4·5	10·6 10·3	16·6 16·2
47	14 41·8	14 44·2	14 01·6	4·7 4·6	10·7 10·4	16·7 16·3
48	14 42·0	14 44·4	14 01·8	4·8 4·7	10·8 10·5	16·8 16·4
49	14 42·3	14 44·7	14 02·1	4·9 4·8	10·9 10·6	16·9 16·5
50	14 42·5	14 44·9	14 02·3	5·0 4·9	11·0 10·7	17·0 16·6
51	14 42·8	14 45·2	14 02·5	5·1 5·0	11·1 10·8	17·1 16·7
52	14 43·0	14 45·4	14 02·8	5·2 5·1	11·2 10·9	17·2 16·8
53	14 43·3	14 45·7	14 03·0	5·3 5·2	11·3 11·0	17·3 16·9
54	14 43·5	14 45·9	14 03·3	5·4 5·3	11·4 11·1	17·4 17·0
55	14 43·8	14 46·2	14 03·5	5·5 5·4	11·5 11·2	17·5 17·1
56	14 44·0	14 46·4	14 03·7	5·6 5·5	11·6 11·3	17·6 17·2
57	14 44·3	14 46·7	14 04·0	5·7 5·6	11·7 11·4	17·7 17·3
58	14 44·5	14 46·9	14 04·2	5·8 5·7	11·8 11·5	17·8 17·4
59	14 44·8	14 47·2	14 04·4	5·9 5·8	11·9 11·6	17·9 17·5
60	14 45·0	14 47·4	14 04·7	6·0 5·9	12·0 11·7	18·0 17·6

59	SUN PLANETS	ARIES	MOON	v or Corrⁿ d	v or Corrⁿ d	v or Corrⁿ d
s	° ′	° ′	° ′	′ ′	′ ′	′ ′
00	14 45·0	14 47·4	14 04·7	0·0 0·0	6·0 6·0	12·0 11·9
01	14 45·3	14 47·7	14 04·9	0·1 0·1	6·1 6·0	12·1 12·0
02	14 45·5	14 47·9	14 05·2	0·2 0·2	6·2 6·1	12·2 12·1
03	14 45·8	14 48·2	14 05·4	0·3 0·3	6·3 6·2	12·3 12·2
04	14 46·0	14 48·4	14 05·6	0·4 0·4	6·4 6·3	12·4 12·3
05	14 46·3	14 48·7	14 05·9	0·5 0·5	6·5 6·4	12·5 12·4
06	14 46·5	14 48·9	14 06·1	0·6 0·6	6·6 6·5	12·6 12·5
07	14 46·8	14 49·2	14 06·4	0·7 0·7	6·7 6·6	12·7 12·6
08	14 47·0	14 49·4	14 06·6	0·8 0·8	6·8 6·7	12·8 12·7
09	14 47·3	14 49·7	14 06·8	0·9 0·9	6·9 6·8	12·9 12·8
10	14 47·5	14 49·9	14 07·1	1·0 1·0	7·0 6·9	13·0 12·9
11	14 47·8	14 50·2	14 07·3	1·1 1·1	7·1 7·0	13·1 13·0
12	14 48·0	14 50·4	14 07·5	1·2 1·2	7·2 7·1	13·2 13·1
13	14 48·3	14 50·7	14 07·8	1·3 1·3	7·3 7·2	13·3 13·2
14	14 48·5	14 50·9	14 08·0	1·4 1·4	7·4 7·3	13·4 13·3
15	14 48·8	14 51·2	14 08·3	1·5 1·5	7·5 7·4	13·5 13·4
16	14 49·0	14 51·4	14 08·5	1·6 1·6	7·6 7·5	13·6 13·5
17	14 49·3	14 51·7	14 08·7	1·7 1·7	7·7 7·6	13·7 13·6
18	14 49·5	14 51·9	14 09·0	1·8 1·8	7·8 7·7	13·8 13·7
19	14 49·8	14 52·2	14 09·2	1·9 1·9	7·9 7·8	13·9 13·8
20	14 50·0	14 52·4	14 09·5	2·0 2·0	8·0 7·9	14·0 13·9
21	14 50·3	14 52·7	14 09·7	2·1 2·1	8·1 8·0	14·1 14·0
22	14 50·5	14 52·9	14 09·9	2·2 2·2	8·2 8·1	14·2 14·1
23	14 50·8	14 53·2	14 10·2	2·3 2·3	8·3 8·2	14·3 14·2
24	14 51·0	14 53·4	14 10·4	2·4 2·4	8·4 8·3	14·4 14·3
25	14 51·3	14 53·7	14 10·6	2·5 2·5	8·5 8·4	14·5 14·4
26	14 51·5	14 53·9	14 10·9	2·6 2·6	8·6 8·5	14·6 14·5
27	14 51·8	14 54·2	14 11·1	2·7 2·7	8·7 8·6	14·7 14·6
28	14 52·0	14 54·4	14 11·4	2·8 2·8	8·8 8·7	14·8 14·7
29	14 52·3	14 54·7	14 11·6	2·9 2·9	8·9 8·8	14·9 14·8
30	14 52·5	14 54·9	14 11·8	3·0 3·0	9·0 8·9	15·0 14·9
31	14 52·8	14 55·2	14 12·1	3·1 3·1	9·1 9·0	15·1 15·0
32	14 53·0	14 55·4	14 12·3	3·2 3·2	9·2 9·1	15·2 15·1
33	14 53·3	14 55·7	14 12·6	3·3 3·3	9·3 9·2	15·3 15·2
34	14 53·5	14 55·9	14 12·8	3·4 3·4	9·4 9·3	15·4 15·3
35	14 53·8	14 56·2	14 13·0	3·5 3·5	9·5 9·4	15·5 15·4
36	14 54·0	14 56·4	14 13·3	3·6 3·6	9·6 9·5	15·6 15·5
37	14 54·3	14 56·7	14 13·5	3·7 3·7	9·7 9·6	15·7 15·6
38	14 54·5	14 56·9	14 13·8	3·8 3·8	9·8 9·7	15·8 15·7
39	14 54·8	14 57·2	14 14·0	3·9 3·9	9·9 9·8	15·9 15·8
40	14 55·0	14 57·5	14 14·2	4·0 4·0	10·0 9·9	16·0 15·9
41	14 55·3	14 57·7	14 14·5	4·1 4·1	10·1 10·0	16·1 16·0
42	14 55·5	14 58·0	14 14·7	4·2 4·2	10·2 10·1	16·2 16·1
43	14 55·8	14 58·2	14 14·9	4·3 4·3	10·3 10·2	16·3 16·2
44	14 56·0	14 58·5	14 15·2	4·4 4·4	10·4 10·3	16·4 16·3
45	14 56·3	14 58·7	14 15·4	4·5 4·5	10·5 10·4	16·5 16·4
46	14 56·5	14 59·0	14 15·7	4·6 4·6	10·6 10·5	16·6 16·5
47	14 56·8	14 59·2	14 15·9	4·7 4·7	10·7 10·6	16·7 16·6
48	14 57·0	14 59·5	14 16·1	4·8 4·8	10·8 10·7	16·8 16·7
49	14 57·3	14 59·7	14 16·4	4·9 4·9	10·9 10·8	16·9 16·8
50	14 57·5	15 00·0	14 16·6	5·0 5·0	11·0 10·9	17·0 16·9
51	14 57·8	15 00·2	14 16·9	5·1 5·1	11·1 11·0	17·1 17·0
52	14 58·0	15 00·5	14 17·1	5·2 5·2	11·2 11·1	17·2 17·1
53	14 58·3	15 00·7	14 17·3	5·3 5·3	11·3 11·2	17·3 17·2
54	14 58·5	15 01·0	14 17·6	5·4 5·4	11·4 11·3	17·4 17·3
55	14 58·8	15 01·2	14 17·8	5·5 5·5	11·5 11·4	17·5 17·4
56	14 59·0	15 01·5	14 18·0	5·6 5·6	11·6 11·5	17·6 17·5
57	14 59·3	15 01·7	14 18·3	5·7 5·7	11·7 11·6	17·7 17·6
58	14 59·5	15 02·0	14 18·5	5·8 5·8	11·8 11·7	17·8 17·7
59	14 59·8	15 02·2	14 18·8	5·9 5·9	11·9 11·8	17·9 17·8
60	15 00·0	15 02·5	14 19·0	6·0 6·0	12·0 11·9	18·0 17·9

TABLES FOR INTERPOLATING SUNRISE, MOONRISE, ETC.

TABLE I—FOR LATITUDE

Tabular Interval 10°	5°	2°	5^m	10^m	15^m	20^m	25^m	30^m	35^m	40^m	45^m	50^m	55^m	60^m	1^{h}05^m	1^{h}10^m	1^{h}15^m	1^{h}20^m
0 30	0 15	0 06	0	0	1	1	1	1	1	2	2	2	2	2	0 02	0 02	0 02	0 02
1 00	0 30	0 12	0	1	1	2	2	3	3	3	4	4	4	5	05	05	05	05
1 30	0 45	0 18	1	1	2	3	3	4	4	5	5	6	7	7	07	07	07	07
2 00	1 00	0 24	1	2	3	4	5	5	6	7	7	8	9	10	10	10	10	10
2 30	1 15	0 30	1	2	4	5	6	7	8	9	9	10	11	12	12	13	13	13
3 00	1 30	0 36	1	3	4	6	7	8	9	10	11	12	13	14	0 15	0 15	0 16	0 16
3 30	1 45	0 42	2	3	5	7	8	10	11	12	13	14	16	17	18	18	19	19
4 00	2 00	0 48	2	4	6	8	9	11	13	14	15	16	18	19	20	21	22	22
4 30	2 15	0 54	2	4	7	9	11	13	15	16	18	19	21	22	23	24	25	26
5 00	2 30	1 00	2	5	7	10	12	14	16	18	20	22	23	25	26	27	28	29
5 30	2 45	1 06	3	5	8	11	13	16	18	20	22	24	26	28	0 29	0 30	0 31	0 32
6 00	3 00	1 12	3	6	9	12	14	17	20	22	24	26	29	31	32	33	34	36
6 30	3 15	1 18	3	6	10	13	16	19	22	24	26	29	31	34	36	37	38	40
7 00	3 30	1 24	3	7	10	14	17	20	23	26	29	31	34	37	39	41	42	44
7 30	3 45	1 30	4	7	11	15	18	22	25	28	31	34	37	40	43	44	46	48
8 00	4 00	1 36	4	8	12	16	20	23	27	30	34	37	41	44	0 47	0 48	0 51	0 53
8 30	4 15	1 42	4	8	13	17	21	25	29	33	36	40	44	48	0 51	0 53	0 56	0 58
9 00	4 30	1 48	4	9	13	18	22	27	31	35	39	43	47	52	0 55	0 58	1 01	1 04
9 30	4 45	1 54	5	9	14	19	24	28	33	38	42	47	51	56	1 00	1 04	1 08	1 12
10 00	5 00	2 00	5	10	15	20	25	30	35	40	45	50	55	60	1 05	1 10	1 15	1 20

Table I is for interpolating the LMT of sunrise, twilight, moonrise, etc., for latitude. It is to be entered, in the appropriate column on the left, with the difference between true latitude and the nearest tabular latitude which is *less* than the true latitude; and with the argument at the top which is the nearest value of the difference between the times for the tabular latitude and the next higher one; the correction so obtained is applied to the time for the tabular latitude; the sign of the correction can be seen by inspection. It is to be noted that the interpolation is not linear, so that when using this table it is essential to take out the tabular phenomenon for the latitude *less* than the true latitude.

TABLE II—FOR LONGITUDE

Long. East or West	Difference between the times for given date and preceding date (for east longitude) or for given date and following date (for west longitude)																	
	10^m	20^m	30^m	40^m	50^m	60^m	1^h+ 10^m	20^m	30^m	1^h+ 40^m	50^m	60^m	2^{h}10^m	2^{h}20^m	2^{h}30^m	2^{h}40^m	2^{h}50^m	3^{h}00^m
0	0	0	0	0	0	0	0	0	0	0	0	0	0 00	0 00	0 00	0 00	0 00	0 00
10	0	1	1	1	1	2	2	2	2	3	3	3	04	04	04	04	05	05
20	1	1	2	2	3	3	4	4	5	6	6	7	07	08	08	09	09	10
30	1	2	2	3	4	5	6	7	7	8	9	10	11	12	12	13	14	15
40	1	2	3	4	6	7	8	9	10	11	12	13	14	16	17	18	19	20
50	1	3	4	6	7	8	10	11	12	14	15	17	0 18	0 19	0 21	0 22	0 24	0 25
60	2	3	5	7	8	10	12	13	15	17	18	20	22	23	25	27	28	30
70	2	4	6	8	10	12	14	16	17	19	21	23	25	27	29	31	33	35
80	2	4	7	9	11	13	16	18	20	22	24	27	29	31	33	36	38	40
90	2	5	7	10	12	15	17	20	22	25	27	30	32	35	37	40	42	45
100	3	6	8	11	14	17	19	22	25	28	31	33	0 36	0 39	0 42	0 44	0 47	0 50
110	3	6	9	12	15	18	21	24	27	31	34	37	40	43	46	49	0 52	0 55
120	3	7	10	13	17	20	23	27	30	33	37	40	43	47	50	53	0 57	1 00
130	4	7	11	14	18	22	25	29	32	36	40	43	47	51	54	0 58	1 01	1 05
140	4	8	12	16	19	23	27	31	35	39	43	47	51	54	0 58	1 02	1 06	1 10
150	4	8	13	17	21	25	29	33	38	42	46	50	0 54	0 58	1 03	1 07	1 11	1 15
160	4	9	13	18	22	27	31	36	40	44	49	53	0 58	1 02	1 07	1 11	1 16	1 20
170	5	9	14	19	24	28	33	38	42	47	52	57	1 01	1 06	1 11	1 16	1 20	1 25
180	5	10	15	20	25	30	35	40	45	50	55	60	1 05	1 10	1 15	1 20	1 25	1 30

Table II is for interpolating the LMT of moonrise, moonset and the Moon's meridian passage for longitude. It is entered with longitude and with the difference between the times for the given date and for the preceding date (in east longitudes) or following date (in west longitudes). The correction is normally *added* for west longitudes and *subtracted* for east longitudes, but if, as occasionally happens, the times become earlier each day instead of later, the signs of the corrections must be reversed.

INDEX TO SELECTED STARS, 2014

Name	No	Mag	SHA	Dec		No	Name	Mag	SHA	Dec
Acamar	7	3·2	315	S 40		1	Alpheratz	2·1	358	N 29
Achernar	5	0·5	335	S 57		2	Ankaa	2·4	353	S 42
Acrux	30	1·3	173	S 63		3	Schedar	2·2	350	N 57
Adhara	19	1·5	255	S 29		4	Diphda	2·0	349	S 18
Aldebaran	10	0·9	291	N 17		5	Achernar	0·5	335	S 57
Alioth	32	1·8	166	N 56		6	Hamal	2·0	328	N 24
Alkaid	34	1·9	153	N 49		7	Acamar	3·2	315	S 40
Al Na'ir	55	1·7	28	S 47		8	Menkar	2·5	314	N 4
Alnilam	15	1·7	276	S 1		9	Mirfak	1·8	309	N 50
Alphard	25	2·0	218	S 9		10	Aldebaran	0·9	291	N 17
Alphecca	41	2·2	126	N 27		11	Rigel	0·1	281	S 8
Alpheratz	1	2·1	358	N 29		12	Capella	0·1	281	N 46
Altair	51	0·8	62	N 9		13	Bellatrix	1·6	279	N 6
Ankaa	2	2·4	353	S 42		14	Elnath	1·7	278	N 29
Antares	42	1·0	112	S 26		15	Alnilam	1·7	276	S 1
Arcturus	37	0·0	146	N 19		16	Betelgeuse	Var.*	271	N 7
Atria	43	1·9	107	S 69		17	Canopus	−0·7	264	S 53
Avior	22	1·9	234	S 60		18	Sirius	−1·5	259	S 17
Bellatrix	13	1·6	279	N 6		19	Adhara	1·5	255	S 29
Betelgeuse	16	Var.*	271	N 7		20	Procyon	0·4	245	N 5
Canopus	17	−0·7	264	S 53		21	Pollux	1·1	243	N 28
Capella	12	0·1	281	N 46		22	Avior	1·9	234	S 60
Deneb	53	1·3	50	N 45		23	Suhail	2·2	223	S 43
Denebola	28	2·1	183	N 14		24	Miaplacidus	1·7	222	S 70
Diphda	4	2·0	349	S 18		25	Alphard	2·0	218	S 9
Dubhe	27	1·8	194	N 62		26	Regulus	1·4	208	N 12
Elnath	14	1·7	278	N 29		27	Dubhe	1·8	194	N 62
Eltanin	47	2·2	91	N 51		28	Denebola	2·1	183	N 14
Enif	54	2·4	34	N 10		29	Gienah	2·6	176	S 18
Fomalhaut	56	1·2	15	S 30		30	Acrux	1·3	173	S 63
Gacrux	31	1·6	172	S 57		31	Gacrux	1·6	172	S 57
Gienah	29	2·6	176	S 18		32	Alioth	1·8	166	N 56
Hadar	35	0·6	149	S 60		33	Spica	1·0	159	S 11
Hamal	6	2·0	328	N 24		34	Alkaid	1·9	153	N 49
Kaus Australis	48	1·9	84	S 34		35	Hadar	0·6	149	S 60
Kochab	40	2·1	137	N 74		36	Menkent	2·1	148	S 36
Markab	57	2·5	14	N 15		37	Arcturus	0·0	146	N 19
Menkar	8	2·5	314	N 4		38	Rigil Kentaurus	−0·3	140	S 61
Menkent	36	2·1	148	S 36		39	Zubenelgenubi	2·8	137	S 16
Miaplacidus	24	1·7	222	S 70		40	Kochab	2·1	137	N 74
Mirfak	9	1·8	309	N 50		41	Alphecca	2·2	126	N 27
Nunki	50	2·0	76	S 26		42	Antares	1·0	112	S 26
Peacock	52	1·9	53	S 57		43	Atria	1·9	107	S 69
Pollux	21	1·1	243	N 28		44	Sabik	2·4	102	S 16
Procyon	20	0·4	245	N 5		45	Shaula	1·6	96	S 37
Rasalhague	46	2·1	96	N 13		46	Rasalhague	2·1	96	N 13
Regulus	26	1·4	208	N 12		47	Eltanin	2·2	91	N 51
Rigel	11	0·1	281	S 8		48	Kaus Australis	1·9	84	S 34
Rigil Kentaurus	38	−0·3	140	S 61		49	Vega	0·0	81	N 39
Sabik	44	2·4	102	S 16		50	Nunki	2·0	76	S 26
Schedar	3	2·2	350	N 57		51	Altair	0·8	62	N 9
Shaula	45	1·6	96	S 37		52	Peacock	1·9	53	S 57
Sirius	18	−1·5	259	S 17		53	Deneb	1·3	50	N 45
Spica	33	1·0	159	S 11		54	Enif	2·4	34	N 10
Suhail	23	2·2	223	S 43		55	Al Na'ir	1·7	28	S 47
Vega	49	0·0	81	N 39		56	Fomalhaut	1·2	15	S 30
Zubenelgenubi	39	2·8	137	S 16		57	Markab	2·5	14	N 15

*0·1 — 1·2

xxxiii

ALTITUDE CORRECTION TABLES 0°–35°— MOON

App. Alt.	0°–4° Corrn	5°–9° Corrn	10°–14° Corrn	15°–19° Corrn	20°–24° Corrn	25°–29° Corrn	30°–34° Corrn	App. Alt.
00	0° 34.5	5° 58.2	10° 62.1	15° 62.8	20° 62.2	25° 60.8	30° 58.9	00
10	36.5	58.5	62.2	62.8	62.2	60.8	58.8	10
20	38.3	58.7	62.2	62.8	62.1	60.7	58.8	20
30	40.0	58.9	62.3	62.8	62.1	60.7	58.7	30
40	41.5	59.1	62.3	62.8	62.0	60.6	58.6	40
50	42.9	59.3	62.4	62.7	62.0	60.6	58.5	50
00	1° 44.2	6° 59.5	11° 62.4	16° 62.7	21° 62.0	26° 60.5	31° 58.5	00
10	45.4	59.7	62.4	62.7	61.9	60.4	58.4	10
20	46.5	59.9	62.5	62.7	61.9	60.4	58.3	20
30	47.5	60.0	62.5	62.7	61.9	60.3	58.2	30
40	48.4	60.2	62.5	62.7	61.8	60.3	58.2	40
50	49.3	60.3	62.6	62.7	61.8	60.2	58.1	50
00	2° 50.1	7° 60.5	12° 62.6	17° 62.7	22° 61.7	27° 60.1	32° 58.0	00
10	50.8	60.6	62.6	62.6	61.7	60.1	57.9	10
20	51.5	60.7	62.6	62.6	61.6	60.0	57.8	20
30	52.2	60.9	62.7	62.6	61.6	59.9	57.8	30
40	52.8	61.0	62.7	62.6	61.6	59.9	57.7	40
50	53.4	61.1	62.7	62.6	61.5	59.8	57.6	50
00	3° 53.9	8° 61.2	13° 62.7	18° 62.5	23° 61.5	28° 59.7	33° 57.5	00
10	54.4	61.3	62.7	62.5	61.4	59.7	57.4	10
20	54.9	61.4	62.7	62.5	61.4	59.6	57.4	20
30	55.3	61.5	62.8	62.5	61.3	59.5	57.3	30
40	55.7	61.6	62.8	62.4	61.3	59.5	57.2	40
50	56.1	61.6	62.8	62.4	61.2	59.4	57.1	50
00	4° 56.4	9° 61.7	14° 62.8	19° 62.4	24° 61.2	29° 59.3	34° 57.0	00
10	56.8	61.8	62.8	62.4	61.1	59.3	56.9	10
20	57.1	61.9	62.8	62.3	61.1	59.2	56.9	20
30	57.4	61.9	62.8	62.3	61.0	59.1	56.8	30
40	57.7	62.0	62.8	62.3	61.0	59.1	56.7	40
50	58.0	62.1	62.8	62.2	60.9	59.0	56.6	50

HP	L U	L U	L U	L U	L U	L U	L U	HP
54.0	0.3 0.9	0.3 0.9	0.4 1.0	0.5 1.1	0.6 1.2	0.7 1.3	0.9 1.5	54.0
54.3	0.7 1.1	0.7 1.2	0.8 1.2	0.8 1.3	0.9 1.4	1.1 1.5	1.2 1.7	54.3
54.6	1.1 1.4	1.1 1.4	1.1 1.4	1.2 1.5	1.3 1.6	1.4 1.7	1.5 1.8	54.6
54.9	1.4 1.6	1.5 1.6	1.5 1.6	1.6 1.7	1.6 1.8	1.8 1.9	1.9 2.0	54.9
55.2	1.8 1.8	1.8 1.8	1.9 1.8	1.9 1.9	2.0 2.0	2.1 2.1	2.2 2.2	55.2
55.5	2.2 2.0	2.2 2.0	2.3 2.1	2.3 2.1	2.4 2.2	2.4 2.3	2.5 2.4	55.5
55.8	2.6 2.2	2.6 2.2	2.6 2.3	2.7 2.3	2.7 2.4	2.8 2.4	2.9 2.5	55.8
56.1	3.0 2.4	3.0 2.5	3.0 2.5	3.0 2.5	3.1 2.6	3.1 2.6	3.2 2.7	56.1
56.4	3.3 2.7	3.4 2.7	3.4 2.7	3.4 2.7	3.4 2.8	3.5 2.8	3.5 2.9	56.4
56.7	3.7 2.9	3.7 2.9	3.8 2.9	3.8 2.9	3.8 3.0	3.8 3.0	3.9 3.0	56.7
57.0	4.1 3.1	4.1 3.1	4.1 3.1	4.1 3.1	4.2 3.2	4.2 3.2	4.2 3.2	57.0
57.3	4.5 3.3	4.5 3.3	4.5 3.3	4.5 3.3	4.5 3.3	4.5 3.4	4.6 3.4	57.3
57.6	4.9 3.5	4.9 3.5	4.9 3.5	4.9 3.5	4.9 3.5	4.9 3.5	4.9 3.6	57.6
57.9	5.3 3.8	5.3 3.8	5.2 3.8	5.2 3.7	5.2 3.7	5.2 3.7	5.2 3.7	57.9
58.2	5.6 4.0	5.6 4.0	5.6 4.0	5.6 4.0	5.6 3.9	5.6 3.9	5.6 3.9	58.2
58.5	6.0 4.2	6.0 4.2	6.0 4.2	6.0 4.2	6.0 4.1	5.9 4.1	5.9 4.1	58.5
58.8	6.4 4.4	6.4 4.4	6.4 4.4	6.3 4.4	6.3 4.3	6.3 4.3	6.2 4.2	58.8
59.1	6.8 4.6	6.8 4.6	6.8 4.6	6.7 4.6	6.7 4.5	6.6 4.5	6.6 4.4	59.1
59.4	7.2 4.8	7.1 4.8	7.1 4.8	7.1 4.8	7.0 4.7	7.0 4.7	6.9 4.6	59.4
59.7	7.5 5.1	7.5 5.0	7.5 5.0	7.5 5.0	7.4 4.9	7.3 4.8	7.2 4.8	59.7
60.0	7.9 5.3	7.9 5.3	7.9 5.2	7.8 5.2	7.8 5.1	7.7 5.0	7.6 4.9	60.0
60.3	8.3 5.5	8.3 5.5	8.2 5.4	8.2 5.4	8.1 5.3	8.0 5.2	7.9 5.1	60.3
60.6	8.7 5.7	8.7 5.7	8.6 5.7	8.6 5.6	8.5 5.5	8.4 5.4	8.2 5.3	60.6
60.9	9.1 5.9	9.0 5.9	9.0 5.9	8.9 5.8	8.8 5.7	8.7 5.6	8.6 5.4	60.9
61.2	9.5 6.2	9.4 6.1	9.4 6.1	9.3 6.0	9.2 5.9	9.1 5.8	8.9 5.6	61.2
61.5	9.8 6.4	9.8 6.3	9.7 6.3	9.7 6.2	9.5 6.1	9.4 5.9	9.2 5.8	61.5

DIP

Ht. of Eye (m)	Corrn	Ht. of Eye (ft)	Ht. of Eye (m)	Corrn	Ht. of Eye (ft)
2.4	−2.8	8.0	9.5	−5.5	31.5
2.6	−2.9	8.6	9.9	−5.6	32.7
2.8	−3.0	9.2	10.3	−5.7	33.9
3.0	−3.1	9.8	10.6	−5.8	35.1
3.2	−3.2	10.5	11.0	−5.9	36.3
3.4	−3.3	11.2	11.4	−6.0	37.6
3.6	−3.4	11.9	11.8	−6.1	38.9
3.8	−3.5	12.6	12.2	−6.2	40.1
4.0	−3.6	13.3	12.6	−6.3	41.5
4.3	−3.7	14.1	13.0	−6.4	42.8
4.5	−3.8	14.9	13.4	−6.5	44.2
4.7	−3.9	15.7	13.8	−6.6	45.5
5.0	−4.0	16.5	14.2	−6.7	46.9
5.2	−4.1	17.4	14.7	−6.8	48.4
5.5	−4.2	18.3	15.1	−6.9	49.8
5.8	−4.3	19.1	15.5	−7.0	51.3
6.1	−4.4	20.1	16.0	−7.1	52.8
6.3	−4.5	21.0	16.5	−7.2	54.3
6.6	−4.6	22.0	16.9	−7.3	55.8
6.9	−4.7	22.9	17.4	−7.4	57.4
7.2	−4.8	23.9	17.9	−7.5	58.9
7.5	−4.9	24.9	18.4	−7.6	60.5
7.9	−5.0	26.0	18.8	−7.7	62.1
8.2	−5.1	27.1	19.3	−7.8	63.8
8.5	−5.2	28.1	19.8	−7.9	65.4
8.8	−5.3	29.2	20.4	−8.0	67.1
9.2	−5.4	30.4	20.9	−8.1	68.8
9.5		31.5	21.4		70.5

MOON CORRECTION TABLE

The correction is in two parts; the first correction is taken from the upper part of the table with argument apparent altitude, and the second from the lower part, with argument HP, in the same column as that from which the first correction was taken. Separate corrections are given in the lower part for lower (L) and upper(U) limbs. All corrections are to be **added** to apparent altitude, *but 30′ is to be subtracted from the altitude of the upper limb.*

For corrections for pressure and temperature see page A4.

For bubble sextant observations ignore dip, take the mean of upper and lower limb corrections and subtract 15′ from the altitude.

App. Alt. = Apparent altitude = Sextant altitude corrected for index error and dip.

ALTITUDE CORRECTION TABLES 35°–90°— MOON

App. Alt.	35°–39° Corrn	40°–44° Corrn	45°–49° Corrn	50°–54° Corrn	55°–59° Corrn	60°–64° Corrn	65°–69° Corrn	70°–74° Corrn	75°–79° Corrn	80°–84° Corrn	85°–89° Corrn	App. Alt.
00	35 56.5	40 53.7	45 50.5	50 46.9	55 43.1	60 38.9	65 34.6	70 30.0	75 25.3	80 20.5	85 15.6	00
10	56.4	53.6	50.4	46.8	42.9	38.8	34.4	29.9	25.2	20.4	15.5	10
20	56.3	53.5	50.2	46.7	42.8	38.7	34.3	29.7	25.0	20.2	15.3	20
30	56.2	53.4	50.1	46.5	42.7	38.5	34.1	29.6	24.9	20.0	15.1	30
40	56.2	53.3	50.0	46.4	42.5	38.4	34.0	29.4	24.7	19.9	15.0	40
50	56.1	53.2	49.9	46.3	42.4	38.2	33.8	29.3	24.5	19.7	14.8	50
00	36 56.0	41 53.1	46 49.8	51 46.2	56 42.3	61 38.1	66 33.7	71 29.1	76 24.4	81 19.6	86 14.6	00
10	55.9	53.0	49.7	46.0	42.1	37.9	33.5	29.0	24.2	19.4	14.5	10
20	55.8	52.9	49.5	45.9	42.0	37.8	33.4	28.8	24.1	19.2	14.3	20
30	55.7	52.8	49.4	45.8	41.9	37.7	33.2	28.7	23.9	19.1	14.2	30
40	55.6	52.6	49.3	45.7	41.7	37.5	33.1	28.5	23.8	18.9	14.0	40
50	55.5	52.5	49.2	45.5	41.6	37.4	32.9	28.3	23.6	18.7	13.8	50
00	37 55.4	42 52.4	47 49.1	52 45.4	57 41.4	62 37.2	67 32.8	72 28.2	77 23.4	82 18.6	87 13.7	00
10	55.3	52.3	49.0	45.3	41.3	37.1	32.6	28.0	23.3	18.4	13.5	10
20	55.2	52.2	48.8	45.2	41.2	36.9	32.5	27.9	23.1	18.2	13.3	20
30	55.1	52.1	48.7	45.0	41.0	36.8	32.3	27.7	22.9	18.1	13.2	30
40	55.0	52.0	48.6	44.9	40.9	36.6	32.2	27.6	22.8	17.9	13.0	40
50	55.0	51.9	48.5	44.8	40.8	36.5	32.0	27.4	22.6	17.8	12.8	50
00	38 54.9	43 51.8	48 48.4	53 44.6	58 40.6	63 36.4	68 31.9	73 27.2	78 22.5	83 17.6	88 12.7	00
10	54.8	51.7	48.3	44.5	40.5	36.2	31.7	27.1	22.3	17.4	12.5	10
20	54.7	51.6	48.1	44.4	40.3	36.1	31.6	26.9	22.1	17.3	12.3	20
30	54.6	51.5	48.0	44.2	40.2	35.9	31.4	26.8	22.0	17.1	12.2	30
40	54.5	51.4	47.9	44.1	40.1	35.8	31.3	26.6	21.8	16.9	12.0	40
50	54.4	51.2	47.8	44.0	39.9	35.6	31.1	26.5	21.7	16.8	11.8	50
00	39 54.3	44 51.1	49 47.7	54 43.9	59 39.8	64 35.5	69 31.0	74 26.3	79 21.5	84 16.6	89 11.7	00
10	54.2	51.0	47.5	43.7	39.6	35.3	30.8	26.1	21.3	16.4	11.5	10
20	54.1	50.9	47.4	43.6	39.5	35.2	30.7	26.0	21.2	16.3	11.4	20
30	54.0	50.8	47.3	43.5	39.4	35.0	30.5	25.8	21.0	16.1	11.2	30
40	53.9	50.7	47.2	43.3	39.2	34.9	30.4	25.7	20.9	16.0	11.0	40
50	53.8	50.6	47.0	43.2	39.1	34.7	30.2	25.5	20.7	15.8	10.9	50

HP	L	U	L	U	L	U	L	U	L	U	L	U	L	U	L	U	L	U	L	U	L	U	HP
54.0	1.1	1.7	1.3	1.9	1.5	2.1	1.7	2.4	2.0	2.6	2.3	2.9	2.6	3.2	2.9	3.5	3.2	3.8	3.5	4.1	3.8	4.5	54.0
54.3	1.4	1.8	1.6	2.0	1.8	2.2	2.0	2.5	2.2	2.7	2.5	3.0	2.8	3.2	3.1	3.5	3.3	3.8	3.6	4.1	3.9	4.4	54.3
54.6	1.7	2.0	1.9	2.2	2.1	2.4	2.3	2.6	2.5	2.8	2.7	3.0	3.0	3.3	3.2	3.5	3.5	3.8	3.8	4.0	4.0	4.3	54.6
54.9	2.0	2.2	2.2	2.3	2.3	2.5	2.5	2.7	2.7	2.9	2.9	3.1	3.2	3.3	3.4	3.5	3.6	3.8	3.9	4.0	4.1	4.3	54.9
55.2	2.3	2.3	2.5	2.4	2.6	2.6	2.8	2.8	3.0	2.9	3.2	3.1	3.4	3.3	3.6	3.5	3.8	3.7	4.0	4.0	4.2	4.2	55.2
55.5	2.7	2.5	2.8	2.6	2.9	2.7	3.1	2.9	3.2	3.0	3.4	3.2	3.6	3.4	3.7	3.5	3.9	3.7	4.1	3.9	4.3	4.1	55.5
55.8	3.0	2.6	3.1	2.7	3.2	2.8	3.3	3.0	3.5	3.1	3.6	3.3	3.8	3.4	3.9	3.6	4.1	3.7	4.2	3.9	4.4	4.0	55.8
56.1	3.3	2.8	3.4	2.9	3.5	3.0	3.6	3.1	3.7	3.2	3.8	3.3	4.0	3.4	4.1	3.6	4.2	3.7	4.4	3.8	4.5	4.0	56.1
56.4	3.6	2.9	3.7	3.0	3.8	3.1	3.9	3.2	3.9	3.3	4.0	3.4	4.1	3.5	4.3	3.6	4.4	3.7	4.5	3.8	4.6	3.9	56.4
56.7	3.9	3.1	4.0	3.1	4.1	3.2	4.1	3.3	4.2	3.3	4.3	3.4	4.3	3.5	4.4	3.6	4.5	3.7	4.6	3.8	4.7	3.8	56.7
57.0	4.3	3.2	4.3	3.3	4.3	3.3	4.4	3.4	4.4	3.4	4.5	3.5	4.5	3.5	4.6	3.6	4.7	3.6	4.7	3.7	4.8	3.8	57.0
57.3	4.6	3.4	4.6	3.4	4.6	3.4	4.6	3.5	4.7	3.5	4.7	3.5	4.7	3.6	4.8	3.6	4.8	3.6	4.8	3.7	4.9	3.7	57.3
57.6	4.9	3.6	4.9	3.6	4.9	3.6	4.9	3.6	4.9	3.6	4.9	3.6	4.9	3.6	4.9	3.6	5.0	3.6	5.0	3.6	5.0	3.6	57.6
57.9	5.2	3.7	5.2	3.7	5.2	3.7	5.2	3.7	5.2	3.7	5.1	3.6	5.1	3.6	5.1	3.6	5.1	3.6	5.1	3.6	5.1	3.6	57.9
58.2	5.5	3.9	5.5	3.8	5.5	3.8	5.4	3.8	5.4	3.7	5.4	3.7	5.3	3.7	5.3	3.6	5.2	3.6	5.2	3.5	5.2	3.5	58.2
58.5	5.9	4.0	5.8	4.0	5.8	3.9	5.7	3.9	5.6	3.8	5.6	3.8	5.5	3.7	5.5	3.6	5.4	3.6	5.3	3.5	5.3	3.4	58.5
58.8	6.2	4.2	6.1	4.1	6.0	4.1	6.0	4.0	5.9	3.9	5.8	3.8	5.7	3.7	5.6	3.6	5.5	3.5	5.4	3.5	5.3	3.4	58.8
59.1	6.5	4.3	6.4	4.3	6.3	4.2	6.2	4.1	6.1	4.0	6.0	3.9	5.9	3.8	5.8	3.6	5.7	3.5	5.6	3.4	5.4	3.3	59.1
59.4	6.8	4.5	6.7	4.4	6.6	4.3	6.5	4.2	6.4	4.1	6.2	3.9	6.1	3.8	6.0	3.7	5.8	3.5	5.7	3.4	5.5	3.2	59.4
59.7	7.1	4.7	7.0	4.5	6.9	4.4	6.8	4.3	6.6	4.1	6.5	4.0	6.3	3.8	6.1	3.7	6.0	3.5	5.8	3.3	5.6	3.2	59.7
60.0	7.5	4.8	7.3	4.7	7.2	4.5	7.0	4.4	6.9	4.2	6.7	4.0	6.5	3.9	6.3	3.7	6.1	3.5	5.9	3.3	5.7	3.1	60.0
60.3	7.8	5.0	7.6	4.8	7.5	4.7	7.3	4.5	7.1	4.3	6.9	4.1	6.7	3.9	6.5	3.7	6.3	3.5	6.0	3.2	5.8	3.0	60.3
60.6	8.1	5.1	7.9	5.0	7.7	4.8	7.6	4.6	7.3	4.4	7.1	4.2	6.9	3.9	6.7	3.7	6.4	3.4	6.2	3.2	5.9	2.9	60.6
60.9	8.4	5.3	8.2	5.1	8.0	4.9	7.8	4.7	7.6	4.5	7.3	4.2	7.1	4.0	6.8	3.7	6.6	3.4	6.3	3.2	6.0	2.9	60.9
61.2	8.7	5.4	8.5	5.2	8.3	5.0	8.1	4.8	7.8	4.5	7.6	4.3	7.3	4.0	7.0	3.7	6.7	3.4	6.4	3.1	6.1	2.8	61.2
61.5	9.1	5.6	8.8	5.4	8.6	5.1	8.3	4.9	8.1	4.6	7.8	4.3	7.5	4.0	7.2	3.7	6.9	3.4	6.5	3.1	6.2	2.7	61.5

CONVERSION OF ARC TO TIME

-59° h m	60°-119° °	h m	120°-179° °	h m	180°-239° °	h m	240°-299° °	h m	300°-359° °	h m	'	0'.00 m s	0'.25 m s	0'.50 m s	0'.75 m s
0 00	60	4 00	120	8 00	180	12 00	240	16 00	300	20 00	0	0 00	0 01	0 02	0 03
0 04	61	4 04	121	8 04	181	12 04	241	16 04	301	20 04	1	0 04	0 05	0 06	0 07
0 08	62	4 08	122	8 08	182	12 08	242	16 08	302	20 08	2	0 08	0 09	0 10	0 11
0 12	63	4 12	123	8 12	183	12 12	243	16 12	303	20 12	3	0 12	0 13	0 14	0 15
0 16	64	4 16	124	8 16	184	12 16	244	16 16	304	20 16	4	0 16	0 17	0 18	0 19
0 20	65	4 20	125	8 20	185	12 20	245	16 20	305	20 20	5	0 20	0 21	0 22	0 23
0 24	66	4 24	126	8 24	186	12 24	246	16 24	306	20 24	6	0 24	0 25	0 26	0 27
0 28	67	4 28	127	8 28	187	12 28	247	16 28	307	20 28	7	0 28	0 29	0 30	0 31
0 32	68	4 32	128	8 32	188	12 32	248	16 32	308	20 32	8	0 32	0 33	0 34	0 35
0 36	69	4 36	129	8 36	189	12 36	249	16 36	309	20 36	9	0 36	0 37	0 38	0 39
0 40	70	4 40	130	8 40	190	12 40	250	16 40	310	20 40	10	0 40	0 41	0 42	0 43
0 44	71	4 44	131	8 44	191	12 44	251	16 44	311	20 44	11	0 44	0 45	0 46	0 47
0 48	72	4 48	132	8 48	192	12 48	252	16 48	312	20 48	12	0 48	0 49	0 50	0 51
0 52	73	4 52	133	8 52	193	12 52	253	16 52	313	20 52	13	0 52	0 53	0 54	0 55
0 56	74	4 56	134	8 56	194	12 56	254	16 56	314	20 56	14	0 56	0 57	0 58	0 59
1 00	75	5 00	135	9 00	195	13 00	255	17 00	315	21 00	15	1 00	1 01	1 02	1 03
1 04	76	5 04	136	9 04	196	13 04	256	17 04	316	21 04	16	1 04	1 05	1 06	1 07
1 08	77	5 08	137	9 08	197	13 08	257	17 08	317	21 08	17	1 08	1 09	1 10	1 11
1 12	78	5 12	138	9 12	198	13 12	258	17 12	318	21 12	18	1 12	1 13	1 14	1 15
1 16	79	5 16	139	9 16	199	13 16	259	17 16	319	21 16	19	1 16	1 17	1 18	1 19
1 20	80	5 20	140	9 20	200	13 20	260	17 20	320	21 20	20	1 20	1 21	1 22	1 23
1 24	81	5 24	141	9 24	201	13 24	261	17 24	321	21 24	21	1 24	1 25	1 26	1 27
1 28	82	5 28	142	9 28	202	13 28	262	17 28	322	21 28	22	1 28	1 29	1 30	1 31
1 32	83	5 32	143	9 32	203	13 32	263	17 32	323	21 32	23	1 32	1 33	1 34	1 35
1 36	84	5 36	144	9 36	204	13 36	264	17 36	324	21 36	24	1 36	1 37	1 38	1 39
1 40	85	5 40	145	9 40	205	13 40	265	17 40	325	21 40	25	1 40	1 41	1 42	1 43
1 44	86	5 44	146	9 44	206	13 44	266	17 44	326	21 44	26	1 44	1 45	1 46	1 47
1 48	87	5 48	147	9 48	207	13 48	267	17 48	327	21 48	27	1 48	1 49	1 50	1 51
1 52	88	5 52	148	9 52	208	13 52	268	17 52	328	21 52	28	1 52	1 53	1 54	1 55
1 56	89	5 56	149	9 56	209	13 56	269	17 56	329	21 56	29	1 56	1 57	1 58	1 59
2 00	90	6 00	150	10 00	210	14 00	270	18 00	330	22 00	30	2 00	2 01	2 02	2 03
2 04	91	6 04	151	10 04	211	14 04	271	18 04	331	22 04	31	2 04	2 05	2 06	2 07
2 08	92	6 08	152	10 08	212	14 08	272	18 08	332	22 08	32	2 08	2 09	2 10	2 11
2 12	93	6 12	153	10 12	213	14 12	273	18 12	333	22 12	33	2 12	2 13	2 14	2 15
2 16	94	6 16	154	10 16	214	14 16	274	18 16	334	22 16	34	2 16	2 17	2 18	2 19
2 20	95	6 20	155	10 20	215	14 20	275	18 20	335	22 20	35	2 20	2 21	2 22	2 23
2 24	96	6 24	156	10 24	216	14 24	276	18 24	336	22 24	36	2 24	2 25	2 26	2 27
2 28	97	6 28	157	10 28	217	14 28	277	18 28	337	22 28	37	2 28	2 29	2 30	2 31
2 32	98	6 32	158	10 32	218	14 32	278	18 32	338	22 32	38	2 32	2 33	2 34	2 35
2 36	99	6 36	159	10 36	219	14 36	279	18 36	339	22 36	39	2 36	2 37	2 38	2 39
2 40	100	6 40	160	10 40	220	14 40	280	18 40	340	22 40	40	2 40	2 41	2 42	2 43
2 44	101	6 44	161	10 44	221	14 44	281	18 44	341	22 44	41	2 44	2 45	2 46	2 47
2 48	102	6 48	162	10 48	222	14 48	282	18 48	342	22 48	42	2 48	2 49	2 50	2 51
2 52	103	6 52	163	10 52	223	14 52	283	18 52	343	22 52	43	2 52	2 53	2 54	2 55
2 56	104	6 56	164	10 56	224	14 56	284	18 56	344	22 56	44	2 56	2 57	2 58	2 59
3 00	105	7 00	165	11 00	225	15 00	285	19 00	345	23 00	45	3 00	3 01	3 02	3 03
3 04	106	7 04	166	11 04	226	15 04	286	19 04	346	23 04	46	3 04	3 05	3 06	3 07
3 08	107	7 08	167	11 08	227	15 08	287	19 08	347	23 08	47	3 08	3 09	3 10	3 11
3 12	108	7 12	168	11 12	228	15 12	288	19 12	348	23 12	48	3 12	3 13	3 14	3 15
3 16	109	7 16	169	11 16	229	15 16	289	19 16	349	23 16	49	3 16	3 17	3 18	3 19
3 20	110	7 20	170	11 20	230	15 20	290	19 20	350	23 20	50	3 20	3 21	3 22	3 23
3 24	111	7 24	171	11 24	231	15 24	291	19 24	351	23 24	51	3 24	3 25	3 26	3 27
3 28	112	7 28	172	11 28	232	15 28	292	19 28	352	23 28	52	3 28	3 29	3 30	3 31
3 32	113	7 32	173	11 32	233	15 32	293	19 32	353	23 32	53	3 32	3 33	3 34	3 35
3 36	114	7 36	174	11 36	234	15 36	294	19 36	354	23 36	54	3 36	3 37	3 38	3 39
3 40	115	7 40	175	11 40	235	15 40	295	19 40	355	23 40	55	3 40	3 41	3 42	3 43
3 44	116	7 44	176	11 44	236	15 44	296	19 44	356	23 44	56	3 44	3 45	3 46	3 47
3 48	117	7 48	177	11 48	237	15 48	297	19 48	357	23 48	57	3 48	3 49	3 50	3 51
3 52	118	7 52	178	11 52	238	15 52	298	19 52	358	23 52	58	3 52	3 53	3 54	3 55
3 56	119	7 56	179	11 56	239	15 56	299	19 56	359	23 56	59	3 56	3 57	3 58	3 59

The above table is for converting expressions in arc to their equivalent in time; its main use in this Almanac is for the conversion of longitude for application to LMT (*added* if *west*, *subtracted* if *east*) to give UT or vice versa, particularly in case of sunrise, sunset, etc.

i

NAO CONCISE SIGHT REDUCTION FORM

Date & UT of observation				Body	Estimated Latitude & Longitu
	h	m	s		° ′ °

Step	Calculate Altitude & Azimuth	Summary of Rules & Notes
Assumed latitude	$Lat =$ °	Nearest estimated latitude, integral number of degrees.
Assumed longitude	$Long =$ ° ′	Choose $Long$ so that LHA has integral number of degrees.
1. From the almanac:	$Dec =$ ° ′	Record the Dec for use in Step 3.
GHA Aries ^{h}	$=$ ° ′	Needed if using SHA. Tabular val
Increment ^{m} ^{s}	$=$ ° ′	for minutes and seconds of time.
SHA	$SHA =$ ° ′	
$GHA = GHA\ Aries + SHA$	$GHA =$ ° ′	Remove multiples of 360°.
Assumed longitude	$Long =$ ° ′	West longitudes are negative.
$LHA = GHA + Long$	$LHA =$ °	Remove multiples of 360°.
2. Reduction table, 1st entry $(Lat, LHA) = ($ °, °$)$ record A, B and Z_1.	$A =$ ° ′ $\quad A° =$ °	nearest whole degree of A.
	$A' =$ ′	minutes part of A.
	$B =$ ° ′	B is minus if $90° < LHA < 270°$.
	$Z_1 =$ °	Z_1 has the same sign as B.
3. From step 1	$Dec =$ ° ′	Dec is minus if contrary to Lat.
$F = B + Dec$	$F =$ ° ′	Regard F as positive until step 7.
	$F° =$ °	nearest whole degree of F.
	$F' =$ ′	minutes part of F.
4. Reduction table, 2nd entry $(A°, F°) = ($ °, °$)$ record H, P and Z_2.	$H =$ ° ′ $\quad P° =$ °	nearest whole degree of P.
	$Z_2 =$ °	
5. Auxiliary table, 1st entry $(F', P°) = ($ ′, °$)$ record $corr_1$	$corr_1 =$ ′	$corr_1$ is minus if $F < 90°$ & $F' > 2$ or if $F > 90°$ & $F' < 3$
6. Auxiliary table, 2nd entry $(A', Z_2°) = ($ ′, °$)$ record $corr_2$	$corr_2 =$ ′	$Z_2°$ nearest whole degree of Z_2. $corr_2$ is minus if $A' < 30'$.
7. Calculated altitude $=$ $Hc = H + corr_1 + corr_2$	$Hc =$ ° ′	Hc is minus if F is negative, and object is below the horizon.
8. Azimuth, 1st component	$Z_1 =$ °	Z_1 has the same sign as B.
2nd component	$Z_2 =$ °	Z_2 is minus if $F > 90°$.
$Z = Z_1 + Z_2$	$Z =$ °	If F is negative, $Z_2 = 180° - Z_2$ Ignore the sign of Z.
		N Lat: If $LHA > 180°$, $Z_n = Z$, or if $LHA < 180°$, $Z_n = 360° - Z$,
True azimuth	$Z_n =$ °	S Lat: If $LHA > 180°$, $Z_n = 180° - Z$, or if $LHA < 180°$, $Z_n = 180° + Z$.

©HMNA

For use with *The Nautical Almanac's* Concise Sight Reduction Tables pages 284-318.

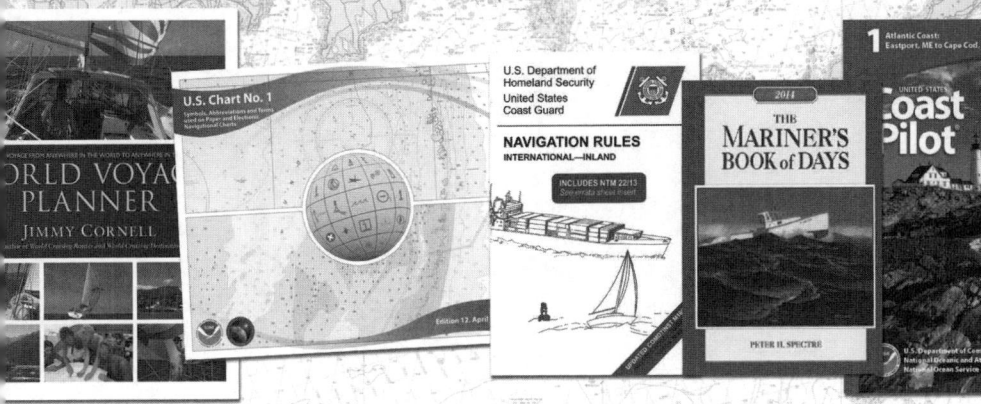
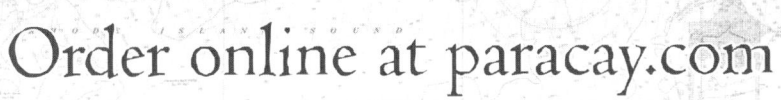

Celestial Navigation
at your fingertips

Complete package for celestial navigation on your iPad, iPhone, iPod Touch
Android device. Performs celestial sight reductions, calculates fixes, prese
them visually, manages sights on multiple trips and assists in sight plann
Includes Almanac of the Sun, Moon, planets and stars for the ye
1980-2099. All this for less than the price of the Nautical Almanac for a sir
year!

navimatics.com

Islamorada

NAVIGATIONAL SUPPLIES & SERVICE | TELS: (507)228-4348 / 228-6069

Business Office: Bldg 808 Balboa Road, (former Canal Zone), Republic of Panama

Business Hours: 0800 - 1700 hours (Local) or 1300 - 2200 hours (UTC). Fax: 507-228-1234

...a is the appointed Admiralty chart agent in the Republic of Panama, and the largest nautical bookstore in Latin America. Located in Balboa, and on the Panama ... Islamorada is ideally positioned to provide products and services to ships in transit through the Isthmus, as well as to other countries throughout the region.

Charts | Paper Charts | Nautical Publications | Maritime Software | Instruments | Flags & Pennants | IMO Signs

...al Books

...on, Seamanship

... Salvage

...sign & Naval Architecture

... & Leisure

...Engineering

...Vork

...ks

... Business, Maritime Law

...ations

...s & Sight Reduction Tables

...ll Signs, Ship Stations, ... Stations, MMS

... Guides - Atlas, Guide to Port Entry

...olas, Marpol, STCW95
...ange of Stock)

Plotting Instrument

Binoculars & Magnifying Glasses

Sextants

Weather Instruments

Clocks & Chronometers

Global Positioning Systems (GPS)

Iridium Satellite Telephones

Brands

C. Plath

B. Cooke & Sons

Blundell Harley

ACR

Admiralty

Oceangrafix

Maui Jim

Reactor Watches

Davis Instruments

and more.

Software For:

Electronic Chart Viewers and ECDIS Software/Hardware

Interactive Diesel Engine Training

Tide Tables & Tidal Current Tables

Electronic Charts

Port Guides

Vessel Traffic Services

Superyacht operations

Fleet Tracking

Nautical Surveys

Because of our strategic location, we are able to provide fast delivery of charts and other important products to ships calling on ports throughout Latin America and the Caribbean Basin.

ADMIRALTY
INTERNATIONAL CHART AGENT

IMO PUBLISHING
AUTHORIZED DISTRIBUTOR

OceanGrafix
Accurate Charts. Confident Boating.
PC PC MARITIME

Seamanship INTERNATIONAL

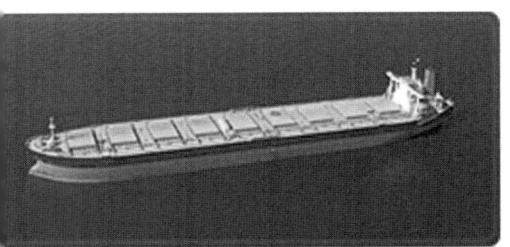

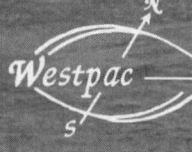